Brill's Encyclopedia of Hinduism

HANDBOOK OF ORIENTAL STUDIES
HANDBUCH DER ORIENTALISTIK

SECTION TWO
INDIA

edited by

J. Bronkhorst
A. Malinar

VOLUME 22/4

Brill's Encyclopedia of Hinduism

Volume IV:
Historical Perspectives
Poets, Teachers, and Saints
Relation to other Religions and Traditions
Hinduism and Contemporary Issues

Edited by
Knut A. Jacobsen
(*Editor-in-Chief*)

Associate Editors
Helene Basu
Angelika Malinar
Vasudha Narayanan

TUTA SUB AEGIDE PALLAS · 1683 ·

BRILL

LEIDEN • BOSTON
2012

Library of Congress Cataloging-in-Publication Data

Brill's encyclopedia of Hinduism / edited by Knut A. Jacobsen (editor-in-chief); associate editors, Helene Basu, Angelika Malinar, Vasudha Narayanan.
p. cm. — (Handbook of oriental studies. Section three, India, ISSN 0169-9377; v. 22/4)
ISBN 978-90-04-17895-3 (hardback : alk. paper)
1. Hinduism—Encyclopedias. I. Jacobsen, Knut A., 1956- II. Basu, Helene. III. Malinar, Angelika. IV. Narayanan, Vasudha.
BL1105.B75 2009
294.503—dc22

2009023320

ISSN 0169-9377
ISBN 978 90 04 17895 3

PRINTED BY DRUKKERIJ WILCO B.V. - AMERSFOORT, THE NETHERLANDS

Table of Contents, Volume IV

Also available online – www.brill.com

Preface

This is the fourth of the five volumes of *Brill's Encyclopedia of Hinduism*. The goal of the *Encyclopedia* is to present the latest scholarship on all aspects of the Hindu religious traditions. The *Encyclopedia* makes available in-depth critical scholarship, and the depth and breadth of information provided in this work are unmatched by any reference work on Hinduism. I hope it will appeal to a wide range of readers. At the foundation of the *Encyclopedia* is a fascination with a phenomenon that we as humans share, and in the examination of this phenomenon, the emphasis is on critical knowledge. Hinduism as a religious tradition functions on a number of different levels, from the most complex architecture, philosophy, and linguistic activity to the performance of short ritual acts: a woman connecting for a brief moment to a statue of the god Gaṇeśa in a wayside shrine on her way to work, a Hindu holy man performing his morning rituals in the Himalaya, a young boy learning to recite Sanskrit ritual texts at a school for priest education in South India, a dance performance in a temple, an astrologer giving advice to a client, the tying of a short thread to a tree by a pilgrim at a Hindu sacred place, a meeting of the organizational committee of a Hindu temple anywhere in the world, a philosophical discussion at an assembly of learned persons in Benares, artisans making stone sculptures for temples, Vedic sacred formulas and texts recited daily, and manuscripts of Hinduism being preserved in facilities and libraries worldwide. In these and many other ways, the Hindu traditions are performed by hundreds of millions of people every day. The goal of the *Encyclopedia* is to present the Hindu traditions as they take place on all these levels. Hinduism, it is often observed, has no common church and no common creed, and it is not based on a holy book or a single founder. That may be so, but Hinduism has many organizations, many creeds, many sacred texts, and founders of a number of organizations and knowledge traditions. The vision of this work is to approach the mosaic and network of Hindu traditions in all their multiplicity, and as both historical and contemporary institutions from different angles and in a variety of contexts, and to document a number of connections and networks.

For many scholars whose work is dedicated to understanding the history, structure, and pluralism of Hindu traditions, Hinduism is definitely the world's most exciting religion. This enthusiasm for the subject is displayed in the articles of the *Encyclopedia*. The articles are clear, comprehensive, interesting and exciting, and they do justice to the Hindu traditions both in the context of ancient civilizations and as global living traditions.

I am thankful to the many authors who shared their great knowledge of the Hindu traditions and contributed the articles to volume IV of the *Encyclopedia*. They represent the best of scholarship on Hinduism in Indology, religious studies, history, anthropology, sociology, art history, and other academic disciplines.

Knut A. Jacobsen

List of Contributors

Bailey, Greg, is reader in Sanskrit at La Trobe University, Australia, and author and editor of 11 books and many articles in journals and edited volumes on early Hindu mythology, the *Mahābhārata*, and the Purāṇas. These include *The Mythology of Brahmā* (1983), *Materials for the Study of Ancient Indian Ideologies* (1985), *The Gaṇeśa Purāṇa* (2 vols., 1995 and 2008), *The Sociology of Early Buddhism* (2003, with I. Mabbett), and *Love Lyrics by Amaru, Bhartṛhari and Bilhana* (2005, with R. Gombrich).

Barz, Richard K., after teaching various courses in Indian studies in universities in the United States, Denmark, and Australia, has recently retired as senior lecturer in Hindi and Urdu at the Australian National University in Canberra. He has written articles and coedited books on Vallabha and related subjects in devotional Hinduism, linguistics, and Hindi and Urdu language and literature in India and Mauritius. He is the author of *The Bhakti Sect of Vallabhācārya* (1976 and 1992). A collection of articles on the Gaṅgā River, which he coedited with A. Doron and B. Nelson, is currently in press.

Beck, Guy L., is lecturer in Hinduism, Asian religions, and religion and music at Tulane University in New Orleans. He is the author of *Sonic Theology: Hinduism and Sacred Sound* (1993) and *Sonic Liturgy: Ritual and Music in Hindu Tradition* (2012). His other works include the edited volumes *Alternative Krishnas: Regional and Vernacular Variations on a Hindu Deity* (2005), *Sacred Sound: Experiencing Music in World Religions* (2006), and *Vaishnava Temple Music in Vrindaban: The Radhavallabha Songbook* (2011), a book and archive of devotional music. Guy L. Beck is a trained vocalist in Hindustani classical music and has been awarded an AIIS (American Institute of Indian Studies) Performing Arts Fellowship and a United States Fulbright-Nehru Senior Research Fellowship. As a visiting fellow at the Oxford Centre for Hindu Studies, he delivered the 2001 Michaelmas Lectures on Hinduism and Music and was a participant in the 2011 Eranos Conference in Switzerland on Love and the Musical Arts.

Begrich, Roger, teaches at the Department of Social and Cultural Anthropology at the University of Zurich, Switzerland. He is a legal, political, and medical anthropologist and works with Ādivāsīs in the central Indian state of Jharhand. He specializes in the anthropology of the contemporary Indian State, drug and alcohol research, in critical indigenous theory, as well as in theories of subjectivity, sovereignty, and law. He is completing his Ph.D. dissertion on indigeneity and alcohol in Jharkhand at the Department of Anthropology at the Johns Hopkins University in Baltimore, USA.

Brackett, Jeffrey M., is associate professor of religious studies at Ball State University (Muncie, Indiana), where he teaches in the Department of Philosophy and Religious Studies. He writes about devotional Hindu traditions in Maharashtra, India, and about pedagogy. Select publications include "Hanumān Jayantī in Maharashtra" in *Studying Hinduism in Practice*, edited by H.P. Rodrigues (2011); "Sending Students into the Field" in *Teaching Undergraduate Research in Religious Studies*, edited by B. McNary-Zak and R. Todd Peters (2011); "The Upwardly Mobile Monkey-God: Village and Urban Mārutīs in Maharashtra" in *Speaking Truth to Power: Religion, Caste, and the Subaltern Question in India*, edited by M. Bhagavan and A. Feldhaus (2008); and (with V. Dev) "Hanuman at the Center of Maharashtrian Village Life: A Translation of Vyankatesh Madgulkar's Marathi Story, 'Temple,'" *Journal of Vaishnava Studies* (2004).

Bronkhorst, Johannes, did his Indological studies in India, where he obtained his first doctorate (1979). He did a second doctorate in Leiden (1980) and was appointed professor of Sanskrit and Indian studies at the University of Lausanne in 1987, where he taught until 2011. He has been editor of Brill's Indological Library and of the Handbook of Oriental Studies since 1991. Some of his recent books are

Greater Magadha: Studies in the Culture of Early India (2007), *Buddhism in the Shadow of Brahmanism* (2011), and *Language and Reality: On an Episode in Indian Thought* (2011). J. Bronkhorst has been concentrating so far on the history of Indian thought in the broadest sense but has in recent years been trying to get a clearer picture of the circumstances in which these forms of thought could develop.

Brown, C. Mackenzie, is professor of South Asian Religions and Religion and Science at Trinity University, San Antonio, Texas. In the early part of his career, he focused on puranic texts dealing with the Great Goddess but for the last ten years has concentrated on religion and science, especially within the Hindu traditions. He is author of *Hindu Perspectives on Evolution: Darwin, Dharma, and Design* (2012). Recent articles include "Hindu and Christian Creationism: 'Transposed Passages' in the Geological Book of Life," *Zygon* (2002), "The Conflict between Religion and Science in Light of the Patterns of Religious Belief Among Scientists," *Zygon* (2003), "The Western Roots of Avataric Evolutionism in Colonial India," *Zygon* (2007), "Colonial and Post-Colonial Elaborations of Avataric Evolutionism," *Zygon* (2007), "The Design Argument in Classical Hindu Thought," *International Journal of Hindu Studies* (2008), "Hindu Responses to Darwinism: Assimilation and Rejection in a Colonial and Post-Colonial Context," *Science and Education* (2010), "Vivekananda and the Scientific Legitimation of Advaita Vedānta," in *Handbook on Religion and the Authority of Science*, edited by J.R. Lewis and O. Hammer, (2011), and "Origins: The Hindu Case," in *The Routledge Companion Reader to Religion and Science*, edited by J. Haag *et al.* (2012).

Burger, Maya, is professor of Indian studies and the history of religions at the University of Lausanne. Her main focus is on premodern and modern Indian religious traditions and Hindi literature. She is interested in the "connected" histories of India and Europe, reflecting on the circulation of cultural transfers, for instance in the history of *yoga*. Most recently she has published two edited volumes – *India in Translation: A Plurality of Voices* (2010) and *Religions in Play: Games, Rituals and Virtual Worlds* (2012).

Caracchi, Pinuccia, is professor of Hindi language and literature at the University of Turin, where she has been working since 1985 in the Department of Oriental Studies. Her main research field is medieval Hindi literature, focusing on the *sant*s and the *Rāmcaritmānas*, but her publications include also essays on different aspects of Hinduism. Her main books are *Vita di Rāmānanda: Il Rāmāndajanmotsava dell'Agastya-saṃhitā* (1989), *Grammatica hindī* (1992; [6]2007), *Rāmānanda e lo yoga dei sant* (1999), *Racconti hindī del Novecento* (2004), a translation of *Sevā-mārg* of Premcand with an essay on *sevā* in Hindi tradition (2008), and *Ad antiche fonti: Voci dell'Induismo attraverso il tempo*, in collaboration with S. Piano (2012). Among her articles are "Who Was a Hindu for Kabīr? Was Kabīr a Hindu?" in *Feeding the Self, Feeling the Way* (2005) and "La *kathā* nel tempo e nell'eternità: note in margine a *Rāmcaritmānas I, 33.2–34*" in *Tīrthayātra: Essays in Honour of Stefano Piano* (2010; coedited). She is scientific director for the Indological section of *Kervan: International Journal of Afro-Asiatic Studies* (*www.kervan.unito.it/*).

Carrin, Marine, anthropologist, is director of research with the Centre National de la Recherche Scientifique at the LISST, Centre d'Anthropologie, Universite de Toulouse–II Le Mirail. She is the author of *La Fleur et l'Os: Symbolisme et rituel chez les Santal* (1986) and *Enfants de la Deesse: Pretrise et devotion feminine au Bengal* (1997) as well as a large number of articles, and she has edited *Managing Distress: Therapeutic Cults in South Asia* (1999). She has published with C. Jaffrelot *Tribus et Basses castes Resistance et Autonomie dans la Societe Indienne* (2002). She has recently published with H. Tambs-Lyche *An Encounter of Peripheries Santals, Missionaries, and Their Changing Worlds, 1867–1900* (2008) and a collective book, *People of the Jangal: Reformulating Identities and Adaptations in Crisis* (2008). She is finalizing a book on Santal ritual discourse and has recently published a dozen articles on the Bhuta cults in South Kanara, India. She is currently teaching at Centre d'Anthropologie in Toulouse.

Chapple, Christopher Key, is Doshi Professor of Indic and Comparative Theology at Loyola Marymount University in Los Angeles. He has published over a dozen books, including *Karma and Creativ-*

ity (1986), *Nonviolence to Animals, Earth, and Self in Asian Traditions* (1993), *Reconciling Yogas: Haribhadra's Array of Views on Yoga* (2003), and *Yoga and the Luminous* (2008) and several edited volumes on religion and ecology, including *Ecological Prospects* (1994), *Hinduism and Ecology* (2000), *Jainism and Ecology* (2002), and *Yoga and Ecology* (2009). He is the editor of *Worldviews: Global Religions, Culture, and Ecology* (Brill) and serves on the advisory boards for the Ahimsa Center (Cal Polytechnic University, Pomona), the Green Yoga Association, the Dharma Association of North America, and the Forum on Religion and Ecology (Yale).

Coward, Harold, is professor of history and founding director of the Centre for Studies in Religion and Society at the University of Victoria in Canada. He is author and editor of many books and numerous articles in journals and edited volumes on various aspects of Hinduism in South Asia and in Canada. He is author of *Bhartrhari* (1976), *Sphota Theory of Language* (1980), *Hindu Ethics: Purity, Abortion and Euthanasia* (with Julius Lipner and Katherine Young [1989]), *The Philosophy of the Grammarians* (with K. Kunjunni Raja [1990]), *Derrida and Indian Philosophy* (1990), *Yoga and Psychology: Language, Memory and Mysticism* (2002), and *Human Rights and The Hindu Tradition* (2005). Other recent publications include the edited volumes *The South Asian Religious Diaspora in Britain, Canada and the United States* (2000) and *Indian Critiques of Gandhi* (2004). He is a fellow of the Royal Society of Canada.

Davis, Donald R., is associate professor of South Asian religions at the University of Wisconsin-Madison. He is the author of *The Boundaries of Hindu Law: Tradition, Custom, and Politics in Late Medieval Kerala* (2004) and *The Spirit of Hindu Law* (2010). He also coedited *Hinduism and Law: An Introduction* (2010).

Dundas, Paul, is reader in Sanskrit in the Asian Studies subject group of the School of Literatures, Languages and Cultures, University of Edinburgh. The main area of his research and publication is Jain history and sectarianism. He is the author of *The Jains* (^{2}2002) and *History, Scripture and Controversy in a Medieval Jain Sectarian Tradition* (2007).

Findly, Ellison B., is professor of religion and Asian studies at Trinity College, Hartford, Connecticut, and author and editor of several books and numerous articles on aspects of Hinduism, Buddhism, Islam, and Shamanism in South and Southeast Asia. She is the author of *From the Courts of India: Indian Miniatures From the Worcester Art Museum* (1981), *Nur Jahan: Empress of Mughal India (1611–1627)* (1993; Indian edition 2001); *Dåna: Giving and Getting in Pali Buddhism* (2003), *Plant Lives: Borderline Beings in Indian Traditions* (2008), and *Spirits in the Loom: Religion and Design in Lao-Tai Textiles* (2013). Other publications include the edited volumes *Indian Textiles and Trade* (an issue of *Asian Art and Culture*), Sackler Gallery, Washington DC (1996) and *Women's Buddhism, Buddhism's Women* (2000) and the coedited volumes *The Islamic Impact* (1984) and *Women, Religion and Social Change* (1985; Vietnamese translation 2011). Upcoming publications include a book and a film titled *Tending the Spirits: Shamanic Experience in Northern Laos.*

Forsthoefel, Thomas, Ph.D., is professor and chair of religious studies at Mercyhurst University in Erie, Pennsylvania. He has published numerous articles on Indian philosophy and religion in journals such as *Philosophy East and West, Journal of Ecumenical Studies, International Journal of Hindu Studies, Journal of Vaishnava Studies*, and *Horizons.* He has written or edited four books: *Knowing beyond Knowledge*, a study of the cognitive dimension of religious experience in classical and modern Advaita; *Gurus in America*, an edited volume that considers the social and philosophical negotiations in late 20th-century development of Hindu spiritual leadership in America; *Soulsong: Seeking Holiness, Coming Home*, a cross-cultural exploration of holiness and human flourishing; and *The Dalai Lama: Essential Writings*, an edited volume, with substantive introduction, of the philosophical, ethical, and meditation teachings of the Dalai Lama.

Friedlander, Peter G., is senior lecturer in Hindi and Buddhist studies at La Trobe University, Melbourne, and he researches in the areas of South Asian religious traditions, Hindi literature, Buddhism, and South Asian news media. He is the author (with W. Callawaert) of *The Life and Works of Raidas* (1992), *A Descriptive Catalogue of the Hindi Manuscripts in the Library of the Wellcome Institute for the History of Medicine* (1996), and (with H. Aveling) *The Songs of Daya Bai* (2005). Other recent publications include Learning Languages as Expressions of Cultures," *Electronic Journal of Foreign Language Teaching* (2011), "Before Translation?" in *Translation in Asia* (2011), "Tagore, Kabir and Underhill," *Seminar* (2011), "The Body and World in Buddhism," in *Medicine, Religion, and the Body* (2010), "Dhammapada Traditions and Translations," *Journal of Religious History* (2009), and "Buddhism and Politics" in *Routledge Handbook of Religion and Politics* (2009).

Gispert-Sauch, George, is professor emeritus in the Faculty of Theology of the Vidyajyoti College of Theology in Delhi. A member of the Society of Jesus born in Spain in 1930, he was assigned to work in India in 1949 and has since then studied and written on Indian subjects, especially the historical and theological contacts between Hinduism and Christianity. He holds an M.A. in Sanskrit and Pali by the University of Bombay and a Doctorate in Theology from the Catholic University of Paris (Institut Catholique). He began teaching theology at St. Mary's Theological College in Kurseong, Darjeeling, in 1967. This college was transferred to Delhi in 1972 under the new name of Vidyajyoti College of Theology. He has authored *Bliss in the Upanishads* (1977), *Christianity in India: Two Thousand Years of Faith* (2004, in cooperation with Leonard Fernando), and *Gems from India* (2006) and edited or coedited several volumes. He has contributed many articles in dictionaries and journals, especially in the monthly *Vidyajyoti Journal of Theological Reflection*, of which he is the secretary.

Glucklich, Ariel, is professor of theology at Georgetown University, where he teaches Hinduism. He is the author of several books and journal articles touching on Hinduism and religion in general. His work includes *The Sense of Adharma* (1994) and *The Strides of Vishnu* (2007). He has spent time in Banaras researching street practitioners of magic and folk medicine (*ojhas*) and published *The End of Magic* (1997). His interests also include the psychology of religion, and he has authored a number of works in that field, including *Sacred Pain* (2001) and *Dying for Heaven* (2009).

Golovkova, Anna, has received her M.A. in Middle Eastern and Asian languages and cultures at Columbia University and an M.St. in oriental studies at Oxford University. She is currently a Ph.D. student at Cornell University. Her research focuses on the early Tantras and commentaries of the cult of Tripurasundarī (Śrīvidyā).

Gottschalk, Peter, is a professor of religion at Wesleyan University. His research and teaching concentrate on the confluence of religious cultures in South Asia, with a particular focus on Muslims and Hindus in rural India. Among other works, he has written *Religion, Science, and Empire: Classifying Hindus and Muslims in British India* (2002) and *Beyond Hindu and Muslim: Multiple Indentity in Narratives from Village India* (2000; Indian ed. 2001), coedited *Engaging South Asian Religions: Boundaries, Appropriations, and Resistance* (2011), and codesigned the interactive Web site "A Virtual Village" (virtuavillage.wesleyan.edu). His forthcoming book is entitled *UnAmerican Religion: A History of Discrimination from Colonial Heresy to Modern Islamophobia.*

Gupta, Ravi M., is associate professor of religious studies at the College of William and Mary. He is the author of *The Caitanya Vaiṣṇava Vedānta of Jīva Gosvāmī: When Knowledge Meets Devotion* (2007) and coeditor of *The Bhāgavata Purāṇa: Sacred Text and Living Tradition* (2012). He is currently working on an abridged translation of the *Bhāgavatapurāṇa* as well as an edited volume on Caitanya Vaiṣṇava philosophy. His research interests lie in the intersection of Vedānta philosophy, puranic commentary, and North Indian *bhakti* traditions, about which he has published many articles in journals and edited volumes.

Hawley, John Stratton (more informally, Jack), is professor of religion at Barnard College, Columbia University. He has written or edited 16 books; three more are forthcoming. These largely concern Hinduism and the *bhakti* traditions of North India, as in *Three Bhakti Voices: Mirabai, Surdas, and Kabir in Their Time and Ours* (2005) and *The Memory of Love: Surdas Sings to Krishna* (2009). The edited volumes range more widely – for instance, *Saints and Virtues, Fundamentalism and Gender* and (with K. Patton) *Holy Tears: Weeping in the Religious Imagination.* Jack Hawley has served as director of Columbia University's South Asia Institute and has received multiple awards from the National Endowment for the Humanities, the Smithsonian, and the American Institute of Indian Studies. He has been a Guggenheim Fellow.

Hopkins, Steven P., received his Ph.D. from Harvard University in the comparative study of religion in 1995 and is currently professor of religion in the Department of Religion at Swarthmore College in Pennsylvania. The recipient of fellowships from the Fulbright Foundation, the American Institute of Indian Studies, and the National Endowment for the Humanities as well as the 2010 South Asia Council of the Association for Asian Studies A.K. Ramanujan Book Prize for Translation, Hopkins' major field is South Indian Vaiṣṇavism with special attention to the work of medieval South Indian saint-poet and philosopher Veṅkaṭanātha, though he teaches various comparative courses in the areas of religion and literature, including a seminar on William Blake. In addition to *Singing the Body of God: The Hymns of Vedāntadeśika in Their South Indian Tradition* (2002) and *An Ornament for Jewels: Love Poems for the Lord of Gods by Vedāntadeśika* (2007), Hopkins has coedited a book with John B. Carman entitled *Tracing Common Themes: Comparative Courses in the Study of Religion* (1990) and is author of several articles on Veṅkaṭanātha in the history of South Indian devotional literatures, including more comparative studies such as "Extravagant Beholding: Love, Ideal Bodies, and Particularity" in *History of Religions* (2007) and "'I Walk Weeping in Pangs of a Mother's Torment for Her Children': Women's Laments in the Poetry and Prophecies of William Blake" in *Journal of Religious Ethics* (2009). He is currently at work on a book tentatively entitled *The Flight of Love* – a study of time, love, and landscape in Sanskrit Sandeśakāvyas (messenger poems) in medieval South Asia – along with a comparative book on love, ideal bodies, and particularity and a book-length study of women's laments in religious literatures.

Horstmann, Monika (Monika Boehm-Tettelbach), retired as head of the Department of Modern South Asian Languages and Literatures, South Asia Institute, Heidelberg University, Germany. Her research focuses on North Indian literatures and religious movements from the early modern period and on the interface between religion and politics. She is the author of several books and edited volumes, among these the monograph *In Favour of Govinddevjī* (1999) and the edited volumes *Images of Kabīr* (2002) and *Bhakti in Current Research, 2001–2003* (2006). Recent and forthcoming books include *Der Zusammenhang der Welt* (2009) and *Jaipur 1778: The Making of a King* (forthcoming).

Jackson, William J., is professor emeritus at Indiana University-Purdue University at Indianapolis (IUPUI), where he taught in the Department of Religious Studies for 25 years. He served as the first Lake Scholar at the Lake Family Institute on Faith and Giving, Philanthropic Studies Center, IUPUI, 2005–2008, and published *The Wisdom of Generosity: A Reader in American Philanthropy* (2008). He has published several books about South Indian religious culture, including *Tyāgarāja: Life and Lyrics, Songs of Three Great South Indian Saints*, and *Vijayanagara Visions.* He also wrote *Vijayanagara Voices* (2005) and *Tyāgarāja and the Renewal of Tradition* (1994). He is also the author of *Heaven's Fractal Net: Retrieving Lost Visions in the Humanities* (2008), about the symbolic meanings of fractal-like geometrical patterns found in the world's cultures. He is currently working on a book exploring the "cultural DNA of America," deep stories, symbols, emblems, values, and aspirations formative and influential in American life.

Jacobsen, Knut A., is professor in the history of religions at the University of Bergen and author and editor of many books and numerous articles in journals and edited volumes on various aspects on religions in South Asia and in the South Asian diasporas. He is the author of *Prakṛti in Sāṃkhya-Yoga:*

Material Principle: Religious Experience, Ethical Implications (1999; Indian edition 2002), *Kapila: Founder of Sāṃkhya and Avatāra of Viṣṇu* (2008), and *Pilgrimage in the Hindu Tradition: Salvific Space* (2013). Other recent publications include the edited volumes *South Asians in the Diaspora: Histories and Religious Traditions* (2004), *Theory and Practice of Yoga: Essays in Honour of Gerald James Larson* (2005), *South Asian Religions on Display: Religious Processions in South Asia and in the Diaspora* (2008), *South Asian Christian Diaspora: Invisible Diaspora in Europe and North America* (2008), *Modern Indian Culture and Society* (2009), *Sikhs in Europe: Migration, Identities and Representations* (2011), *Sikhs Across Borders: Transnational Practices among European Sikhs* (2012), and *Yoga Powers: Extraordinary Capacities Attained through Meditation and Concentration* (2012).

Keune, Jon, is a postdoctoral fellow in the Centre for Modern Indian Studies at Georg-August-Universität Göttingen in Germany. He received his Ph.D. from Columbia University, where his dissertation investigated the cultural memories of the 16th-century Marathi saint-poet Eknāth in terms of caste and social critique. He is the author of "The Varkari Tradition and Their Pilgrimages in Maharashtra" in *Introducing Hinduism* (ed. Pratap Penumala, forthcoming 2012), a Marathi article on the academic study of religion in India published in the journal *Pratiṣṭhān* (2010), "Gathering the Bhaktas in Marathi" in the *Journal of Vaishnava Studies* (2007), and "The Inter- and Intra-religious Conversions of Nehemiah Nilakantha Goreh" in the *Journal of Hindu-Christian Studies* (2004).

Knutson, Jesse Ross, is assistant professor in the Department of Asian Languages and Civilizations at Seoul National University. His scholarly interests are Sanskrit language and literature and the historical role of literary art in ancient and early medieval South Asia, on which he has published numerous articles, including "History beyond the Reality Principle: Literary and Political Territories in Sena Period Bengal" (2012), "The Vernacular Cosmopolitan: Jayadeva's Gitagovinda" (2011), and "The Political Poetic of the Sena Court" (2010). He is completing a monograph on the literary salon of the Sena court of 12th/13th-century Bengal and its afterlife in early Middle Bengali poetry entitled *Into the Crepuscule of Sanskrit Court Poetry.*

Kotani, Hiroyuki, was formerly professor in early modern and modern history of India at the Tokyo Metropolitan University and is presently member of Science Council of Japan and professor emeritus at Tokyo Metropolitan University. He is the author of *Western India in Historical Transition: Seventeenth to Early Twentieth Centuries* (2002) and many other books written in Japanese, including *Marx and Asia: A Criticism of Asiatic Mode of Production* (1979) and *Medieval Society of India: Villages, Castes and Landlords* (1989).

Kulke, Hermann, is retired professor of Asian History, Kiel University. He did his Ph.D. in Indology in Freiburg on the temple city of Chidambaram in 1976 and his *Habilitation* in Indian History on Gajapati kingship of Orissa at the South Asia Institute at Heildelberg University in 1975. He was co-founder of the first and coordinator of the second Orissa Research Project of the German Research Council. His fields of specialization are early and early medieval history of India and Southeast Asia, early state formation, Indian Ocean Studies, and historiography. Major publications include *Cidambaramahatmya* (1971); *The Devaraja Cult* (1978); *The Cult of Jagannath and the Regional Tradition of Orissa* (co-editors A. Eschmann & G.C. Tripathi; 1978); *Jagannatha-Kult und Gajapati-Konigtum* (1979); *Hinduism Reconsidered* (co-editor G.-D. Sontheimer; 1989); *Kings and Cults: State Formation and Legitimation in India and Southeast Asia* (1993); *The State in India 1000–1700* (1995); *Jagannath Revisited* (co-editor B. Schnepel; 2002); *Indische Geschichte bis 1750* (2005); *Nagapattinam to Suvarnadwipa: Reflections on the Chola Naval Expeditions to Southeast Asia* (2010); *A History of India* (co-author D. Rothermund; ^{5}2010).

Kumar, P. Pratap, is professor of Hinduism and comparative religions in the School of Religion and Theology at the University of KwaZulu Natal, South Africa. In addition to several scholarly essays and articles, his publications include *The Goddess Lakṣmī: The Divine Consort in South Indian Vaiṣṇava Tradition* (1997), *Hindus in South Africa: Their Traditions and Beliefs* (2000), *Methods and Theories in* *the Study of Religions: Perspectives from the Study of Hinduism and other Indian Religions* (2004), and *Religious Pluralism and the Diaspora* (2006). He is the president of the Association for the Study of Religion in Southern Africa. He was also one of the editors of the Numen Book Series of the International Association for the History of Religions, published by Brill.

Larson, Gerald James, is professor emeritus in religious studies at the University of California-Santa Barbara and Tagore Professor Emeritus of Indian Cultures and Civilization at Indiana University, Bloomington. Dr. Larson is the author or editor of some 12 books and well over 100 scholarly articles on cross-cultural philosophy of religion, history of religions, classical Sanskrit, and South Asian history and culture. His recent books include *India's Agony over Religion* (1995; repr. 1997), *Changing Myths and Images* (2000), and *Religion and Personal Law in Secular India: A Call to Judgment* (2002). His most recent publication is volume XII of the *Encyclopedia of Indian Philosophies*, coedited with the late Ram Shankar Bhattacharya, entitled *Yoga: India's Philosophy of Meditation* (2008). Also, a collection of essays has been published in his honor, *Theory and Practice of Yoga: Essays in Honour of Gerald James Larson*, edited by K.A. Jacobsen (2005; repr. 2008). During his career at University of California-Santa Barbara, he received the Distinguished Teaching Award from the Academic Senate (1989). His Web site is www.geraldjameslarson.com.

Lawrence, David Peter, obtained his Ph.D. from the University of Chicago and has taught at universities in Hong Kong, Canada, and the United States. Presently, he is associate professor in the Department of Philosophy and Religion at the University of North Dakota. He specializes in nondual Kashmiri Śaivism and related areas of Hindu and Buddhist philosophy and religion and is more broadly concerned with the use of philosophy as a mode of cross-cultural dialogue. His publications include *Rediscovering God with Transcendental Argument: A Contemporary Interpretation of Monistic Kashmiri Śaiva Philosophy* (1999) and *The Teachings of the Odd-Eyed One: A Study and Translation of the Virūpākṣapañcāśikā with the Commentary of Vidyācakravartin* (2008). During academic year 2011–2012, Dr. Lawrence was recipient of a Fulbright-Nehru Senior Research Fellowship for work in India toward completion of a new annotated translation and study of Abhinavagupta's *Īśvarapratyabhijñāvimarśinī*.

Lipner, Julius, is professor of Hinduism and the comparative study of religion in the divinity faculty at the University of Cambridge. He has authored or edited 12 books, has published numerous articles in scholarly journals and edited works, and has also lectured widely around the world. His books, two of which have won major international awards, include *The Face of Truth: A Study of Meaning and Metaphysics in the Vedāntic Theology of Rāmānuja* (1986), *Brahmabandhab Upadhyay: The Life and Thought of a Revolutionary* (1999), *Anandamaṭh or The Sacred Brotherhood* (2005), and the second edition of *Hindus: Their Religious Beliefs and Practices* (substantially revised and enlarged, 2010). He is a fellow of the British Academy.

Little, Layne R., is lecturer in the Department of Religious Studies and the Department of South Asian Studies at the University of California at Berkeley. In addition to articles published on the Tamil *siddha*s and on medieval Tamil literary history, he is coauthor of Oxford University Press' *Invitation to World Religions*.

Lochtefeld, James G., is professor of religion and director of Asian studies at Carthage College in Wisconsin. The unifying thread running throughout his research is the interrelationship among texts, tradition, and modern religious life, particularly as manifested in Hindu pilgrimage sites. He is the author of *God's Gateway: Identity and Meaning in a Hindu Pilgrimage Place* (2010), in which he examines Sanskrit texts, archival documents, and its current identity as a vibrant, modern city to construct a comprehensive picture of the North Indian pilgrimage city of Hardwar. Other published articles have examined the Hindu pilgrimage tradition, the history and development of the *kumbhamelā*, and the rise of Hindu nationalism. His current research examines the effects of tourism promotion on Himalayan pilgrimage sites and the connection between Sikh pilgrimage sites and Sikh identity.

Lutgendorf, Philip, is professor of Hindi and modern Indian studies and has taught in the University of Iowa's Department of Asian Languages and Literature since 1985. He regularly offers Hindi-language classes as well as courses on written and oral narrative traditions of South Asia, including Indian film. His book on the performance of the epic *Rāmāyaṇa*, *The Life of a Text* (1991), won the A.K. Coomaraswamy Prize of the Association for Asian Studies. He received a Guggenheim Fellowship in 2002–2003 for his research on the popular Hindu "monkey-god" Hanuman, which has appeared as *Hanuman's Tale: The Messages of a Divine Monkey* (2007). His interests include epic performance traditions, folklore and popular culture, and mass media. He maintains a Web site devoted to Indian popular cinema, also known as Bollywood (www.uiowa.edu/~incinema).

Lutjeharms, Rembert, is a research fellow and librarian at the Oxford Centre for Hindu Studies. The main subject of his research is the early history of the Caitanya Vaiṣṇava tradition and the 16th-century Bengali Vaiṣṇava poet Kavikarṇapūra, who was the subject of his Ph.D. dissertation submitted to the University of Oxford ("Splendour of Speech: The Theology of Kavikarṇapūra's Poetics," 2010). He is also an editor of the *Journal of Hindu Studies*.

Martin, Nancy M., is associate professor of religious studies at Chapman University and life member of Clare Hall, Cambridge University. Her publications include articles on Hindu devotional literature, practice, and performance and on gender and religion. Her soon-to-be-published monograph on Mīrabāī spans the range from early manuscript traditions to nationalist, Rajput, and low-caste appropriations of the saint to women spiritual leaders today called by her name. Dr. Martin's current projects include *The Renunciant Rani and the Weaver of Protest*, a comparative study of Mīrabāī and Kabīr in Rajasthani folk traditions and a documentary examining interreligious harmony and conflict in contemporary India. Her publications also include a series of coedited volumes on comparative religious ethics: *The Meaning of Life in the World Religions*, *Love, Sex and Gender in the World Religions*, *Ethics in the World Religions*, and *Human Rights and Responsibilities in the World Religions*.

McDaniel, June, is a professor in the Department of Religious Studies at the College of Charleston in South Carolina. Her field is history of religions, and her research has focused on Bengali *bhakti*, *tantra*, and folk religion as well as Bengali understandings of religious and mystical experience. She has published three books: *The Madness of the Saints: Ecstatic Religion in Bengal* (1989), *Making Virtuous Daughters and Wives: An Introduction to Women's Brata Rituals in Bengali Folk Religion* (2003), and *Offering Flowers, Feeding Skulls: Popular Goddess Worship in West Bengal* (2004). She has also published numerous articles and papers. Her most recent research has been on the development and adaptation of Hinduism in Indonesia.

Michael, R. Blake, is Swan-Collins-Allen Professor of World Religions and Christian Mission and chairperson of the Department of Religion at Ohio Wesleyan University. He previously served there, for two decades, as associate dean of academic affairs and has also served as adjunct professor of world religions at the Methodist Theological School in Ohio. He is author of *The Origins of Vīraśaiva Sects* (1992) as well as of numerous chapters and articles on the Liṅgāyata or Vīraśaiva tradition. These include "Work as Worship in Vīraśaiva Tradition," "'*Liṅga*' as Lord Supreme in the *Vacana*-s of Basava," "Women of the *Śūnyasaṃpādane*," and "Foundation Myths of the Two Denominations of Vīraśaivism."

Mokashi-Punekar, Rohini, is professor at the Department of Humanities and Social Sciences, Indian Institute of Technology Guwahati. Besides several papers in books and journals, she is the author of *On the Threshold: Songs of Chokhamela* (2005), *Untouchable Saints: An Indian Phenomenon* (2005), coedited with Eleanor Zelliot, and *Vikram Seth: An Introduction* (2009). She is currently engaged in translating medieval Vārkarī poetry from Marathi, an anthology of which will be published by Penguin in their Black Classics series.

Narayana Rao, Velcheru, taught Telugu and Indian literatures for 38 years at University of Wisconsin-Madison. He also taught at the University of Chicago and is currently visiting distinguished professor of South Asian Studies at Emory. He has written more than 15 books, many of them in collaboration with David Shulman and Sanjay Subrahmanyam. *Textures of Time: Writing History in South India*, in collaboration with David Shulman and Sanjay Subrahmanyam (2003), *Girls for Sale, Kanyasulkam: A Play form Colonial India* (2007), and *How Úrvashi Was Won*, a translation of Kalidasa's *Vikramorvaśīya*, in collaboration with David Shulman (2009), are among his recent works.

Narayanan, Vasudha, is distinguished professor in the Department of Religion at the University of Florida and a past president of the American Academy of Religion. She was educated at the Universities of Madras and Bombay, and at Harvard University. She is the author or editor of seven books and over a hundred articles, chapters in books, and encyclopedia entries. Her books include *The Life of Hinduism* (2007, with J. Stratton Hawley), *Hinduism* (2004, 2009), *The Vernacular Veda: Revelation, Recitation, and Ritual* (1994), *The Way and the Goal: Expressions of Devotion in the Early Śrīvaiṣṇava Tradition* (1987), and *The Tamil Veda: Piḷḷaṉ's Interpretation of the Tiruvāymoḻi*. Her research has been supported by several organizations, including the Centre for Khmer Studies, the American Council of Learned Societies, National Endowment for the Humanities (1987, 1989–1990, and 1998–1999), the John Simon Guggenheim Foundation, the American Institute of Indian Studies/Smithsonian, and the Social Science Research Council. She is currently working on research into Hindu traditions in Cambodia.

Nelson, Lance E., is professor of theology and religious studies at the University of San Diego. He received his Ph.D. in religious studies from McMaster University. Dr. Nelson's research focuses on medieval Hindu theology, particularly Advaita Vedānta, and his writings on aspects of South Asian religious and philosophical thought have appeared in books, reference works, and scholarly journals in the United States and India. He edited *Purifying the Earthly Body of God: Religion and Ecology in Hindu India* (1998).

Nesbitt, Eleanor, is professor emerita in religions and education at the University of Warwick. She is the author of many publications on religious transmission and socialization in the Christian, Hindu, and Sikh communities in the United Kingdom. Her books include *Sikhism: A Very Short Introduction* (2005), *Intercultural Education: Ethnographic and Religious Approaches* (2004), *Interfaith Pilgrims* (2003), and *The Religious Lives of Sikh Children: A Coventry Based Study* (2000). With Gopinder Kaur, she published *Guru Nanak* (1999) and with Robert Jackson, *Hindu Children in Britain* (1993).

Novetzke, Christian Lee, is an associate professor in the South Asia Program, the Comparative Religion Program, and the International Studies Program at the University of Washington's Jackson School of International Studies. Professor Novetzke researches and writes about religion, history, and culture in South Asia, as well as theoretical issues in the study of religion in general and its intersection with historiography. He works with Marathi and Hindi materials, including textual, ethnographic, and visual/filmic sources. Professor Novetzke specializes in the study of Maharashtra from the 2nd millennium CE to the present. His recent book *Religion and Public Memory* (2008) won the American Academy of Religion's award "Best First Book in the History of Religions" in 2009. The book has been published in India under the title *History, Bhakti, and Public Memory* (2008).

Odin, Jaishree K., is professor of interdisciplinary studies at the University of Hawai'i. She has worked extensively on medieval Kashmiri literature. She is the author of two books on the Kashmiri Śaiva poet Lalla: *To the Other Shore: Lalla's Life and Poetry* (1999) and *Mystical Verses of Lalla* (2007). A book chapter on this topic was published in *The Valley of Kashmir: The Making and Unmaking of a Composite Culture* (2008). Other essays have appeared in *Manushi* and *La Revue de l'Inde*.

Parpola, Asko, is professor emeritus of Indology at the University of Helsinki, Finland. His main research targets have been Sāmavedic texts and traditions (with field work in Kerala and Tamil Nadu),

Indus civilization with its script and religion, and linguistics and archaeology in India and Eurasia. Among his books are *The Śrautasūtras of Lāṭyāyana and Drāhyayaṇa and Their Commentaries* (2 vols., 1968–1969), *The Literature and Study of the Jaiminīya Sāmaveda* (1973), *The Sky Garment* (1985), and *Deciphering the Indus Script* (1994, repr. 2000, 2009). He has edited *Corpus of Indus Seals and Inscriptions* (so far 3 vols.; 1987 with J.P. Joshi, 1991 with S.G.M. Shah, and 2010 with B.M. Pande & P. Koskikallio), *South Asian Religion and Society* (1986 with B. Smidt Hansen), *South Asian Archaeology 1993* (2 vols., 1994 with P. Koskikallio), *Changing Patterns of Family and Kinship in South Asia* (1998, with S. Tenhunen), and *Early Contacts between Uralic and Indo-European* (2001, with C. Carpelan & P. Koskikallio).

Pechilis, Karen, is National Endowment for the Humanities Distinguished Professor of Humanities, professor of Asian and comparative religions, and chair of the Religious Studies Program in the College of Liberal Arts at Drew University. For four years (2004–2008), she was director of the interdisciplinary Humanities Program, and thus she is an experienced teacher of both Asian and Western humanities courses. She brings the history of religions methodology to her research specializations of devotional Hinduism and women in religion. She has published the monographs *Interpreting Devotion: The Poetry and Legacy of a Female Bhakti Saint of India* (2011) and *The Embodiment of Bhakti* (1999, as Karen Pechilis Prentiss). She edited and contributed the introduction and an essay to *The Graceful Guru: Hindu Female Gurus in India and the United States* (2004). She is coediting *South Asian Religions: Tradition and Today* (2012; with Selva J. Raj) and *Refiguring the Body: Embodiment in South Asian Religions* (forthcoming; with Barbara Holdrege). She is currently on the editorial boards of the *Journal of Feminist Studies in Religion* and the *International Journal of Hindu Studies.*

Proferes, Theodore N., is senior lecturer in ancient Indian religions at the School of Oriental and African Studies in London. He has written articles on the historical development of the Vedic liturgy, ancient Indian ritual practice, and the process of formation of the Vedic canon. His first book, *Vedic Ideals of Sovereignty and the Poetics of Power*, examines the intersection of political and religious ideology from the Ṛgvedic hymns to the early Upaniṣads.

Quack, Johannes, studied religious studies, philosophy, and anthropology at the universities of Bayreuth, Edinburgh, and Heidelberg. He worked as a lecturer in the departments of religious studies and anthropology at the universities of Heidelberg, Luzern, Münster, and Tübingen. J. Quack was a postdoctoral researcher at the Cluster of Excellence "Asia and Europe in a Global Context" at Heidelberg University and visiting scholar at the Division of Social and Transcultural Psychiatry and the Department of Social Studies of Medicine at McGill University. Currently he is head of an Emmy Noether research group on the Diversity of Non-Religion at the University of Frankfurt. He published the monograph *Disenchanting India: Organized Rationalism and Criticism of Religion in India* (2012) and coedited the books *Religion und Kritik in der Moderne* and (2012) *The Problem of Ritual Efficacy* (2010).

Randeria, Shalini, is professor in and chair of Department of Social Anthropology and Sociology at the Graduate Institute of International and Development Studies, Geneva. She is visiting professor at the Social Science Research Centre, Berlin (WZB) and a member of the Senate of the German Research Council. She has been president of the European Association of Social Anthropologists (EASA) and a fellow of the Institute of Advanced Studies, Berlin and has held the Max Weber Professorship for Sociology at the University of Munich. She has published widely on the anthropology of globalization, law, the state, and social movements. Her empirical research on India also addresses issues of postcoloniality and multiple modernities. Among her publications are the edited volumes *Border Crossings. Grenzverschiebungen und Grenzüberschreitungen in einer globalisierten Welt* (2012), *Jenseits des Eurozentrismus. Postkoloniale Perspektiven in den Geschichts- und Kulturwissenschaften* (22012), *Vom Imperialismus zum Empire. Nicht-westliche Perspektiven auf Globalisierung* (2009), *Konfigurationen der Moderne. Diskurse zu Indien* (2004), *Worlds on the Move: Globalisation, Migration and Cultural Security* (2004).

Rothgery, Eric J., is assistant professor of religion at Roanoke College. He teaches courses in South Asian religions, specializing in mystical, healing, and ritual traditions shared by Hindus and Muslims. He is currently working to turn his dissertation "Generating and Mediating Religious Identities: Islamic Healing Rituals Shared by Hindus and Muslims in the *Dargāh*s of Hyderabad, India" (University of Iowa, 2008) into a book.

Saha, Shandip, is assistant professor of religious studies at Athabasca University in Canada. His research focuses on religion and politics in Medieval India, religion and immigration in Canada, and globalized forms of Hinduism. His current research on the history of the Vaiṣṇava *bhakti* community known as the Puṣṭimārga has been published in the *Bulletin of the School of African and Oriental Studies* (2006), *South Asia Review* (2007), *The International Journal of Hindu Studies* (2007), and in the forthcoming volumes *Religious Interactions in Mughal India* and *Introducing Hinduism*. His research on globalization and immigration has been published in *Religion, Globalization, and Culture* (2007) and in the forthcoming volume *Growing Up Canadian: Hindus, Muslims, and Buddhists.*

Scheifinger, Heinz, is lecturer in sociology-anthropology at Universiti Brunei Darussalam. He has conducted extensive research that investigates the complex relationship between the Internet and Hinduism. Of particular interest have been the ways in which the medium is shaping contemporary Hinduism. H. Scheifinger's publications include "Hinduism and Cyberspace," *Religion* (2008), "The Jagannath Temple and Online Darshan," *Journal of Contemporary Religion* (2009), "*Om*-line Hinduism: World Wide Gods on the Web," *Australian Religion Studies Review* (2010), "Hinduism and Hyper-Reality" in *Handbook of Hyper-real Religions* (2012), and "Hindu Worship Online and Offline" in *Digital Religion: Understanding Religious Practice in New Media Worlds* (2012).

Schouten, Jan Peter, is a minister of the Protestant Church in the Netherlands, presently attached to the Grote Kerk in Naarden. He studied theology and sociology at the Free University in Amsterdam. He obtained his doctor's degree cum laude at Utrecht University, with a thesis about Vīraśaivism. His monographs include *Revolution of the Mystics: On the Social Aspects of Vīraśaivism* (1991; Indian edition 1995; Kannada translation 2000), *Goddelijke vergezichten: Mystiek uit India voor westerse lezers* (1995), and *Jesus as Guru: The Image of Christ among Hindus and Christians in India* (2008; Indian edition 2012). He also published many articles in journals and edited volumes about *bhakti*, interreligious dialogue, and the Hindu diaspora in Europe.

Sheridan, Daniel P., Ph.D., is professor of theology at Saint Joseph's College of Maine. Formerly, he was vice president for academic affairs at Saint Joseph's College and before that associate provost at Loyola University in New Orleans. Dr. Sheridan is a historian of religion with an expertise in Hindu theology and has written extensively on the *Bhāgavatapurāṇa* and on Madhva's Dvaita Vedānta. He is the author of two books involving Hindu thought: *The Advaitic Theism of the Bhāgavata Purāṇa* (1986) and *Loving God: Kṛṣṇa and Christ: A Christian Commentary on the Nārada Sūtras* (2008).

Shukla-Bhatt, Neelima, is assistant professor in the South Asia Studies program at Wellesley College in Wellesley, Massachusetts, with a teaching focus on religion and the cultures of South Asia. Her work includes articles on devotional poetry of India, Hindu women's religious life, and religion and media in South Asia: "Govinda's Glory: Krishna-*Lila* in the Songs of Narasinha Mehta" (2007), "Performance as Translation, Mira in Gujarat" (2007), "A Reflection on the Challenges to Hindu Women in the Twenty-first Century" (2009), "Media of Miracles, Miracle of Media: Clairvoyants and Commercials on South Asian Television in the Diaspora" (2008), and "Celebrating Materiality: Garbo and the Goddess in Gujarat" (forthcoming). Her book coauthored with Surendra Bhana – *A Fire Blazed in the Ocean: Gandhi and the Poetics of Satyagraha in South Africa, 1909–1911* (2011) – explores poetry of the first *satyāgraha* led by Gandhi. Her book on Narasiṃha Mehtā – *Moving Songs, Circulating Stories: The Saint-poet Narasinha Mehta of Gujarat* – is forthcoming.

Singh, Upinder, is professor in the Department of History, University of Delhi. Her research publications range over various aspects of ancient Indian social, economic, religious, and intellectual history; the history of archaeology; and the modern histories of ancient sites and monuments. She is the author of *Kings, Brāhmaṇas, and Temples in Orissa: An Epigraphic Study (AD 300–1147)* (1994), *The Discovery of Ancient India: Early Archaeologists and the Beginnings of Archaeology* (2004), *Ancient Delhi* ([1999] 2006), and *A History of Ancient and Early Medieval India: From the Stone Age to the 12th Century* (2008). Her edited volumes are *Delhi: Ancient History* (2006), *Ancient India: New Research* (coedited with Nayanjot Lahiri [2009]), and *Rethinking Early Medieval India* (2011).

Sinha, Vineeta, is associate professor at the Department of Sociology and head of the South Asian Studies Programme at the National University of Singapore. Her areas of research include the following: material religion, religion–state encounters, religion and commodification, and diaspora Hinduism. Apart from publishing numerous articles and chapters on these subjects, she is the author of *A New God in the Diaspora? Muneeswaran Worship in Contemporary Singapore* (2005), *Religion and Commodification: Merchandizing Diasporic Hinduism* (2010), and *Religion-State Encounters in Hindu Domains: From the Straits Settlements to Singapore* (2011). She is also the editor of the *Asian Journal of Social Science.*

Speziale, Fabrizio, holds a CNRS (Centre national de la recherche scientifique) chair in Iranian studies at the University Sorbonne Nouvelle – Paris 3. He is a specialist in Indo-Persian studies and has published numerous articles on the Persianate and Muslim scientific and religious cultures of South Asia. He is the author of *Soufisme, religion et médecine en Islam indien* (2010). Other recent publications include the edited and coedited volumes *Il Trattato aureo sulla medicina attribuito a l'imām ʿAlī al-Riḍā* (2009), *Muslim Cultures in the Indo-Iranian World during the Early-Modern and Modern Periods* (2010), *La congiunzione dei due oceani* (2011), and *Hospitals in Iran and India, 1500–1950s* (2012).

Stausberg, Michael, is professor of religion at the University of Bergen, Norway, and a member of the Norwegian Academy of Science and Letters. He has published on a wide variety of subjects such as definitions of magic, religion and modern tourism, research methods in the study of religion, theories of religion, the history of the study of religions, and theories of rituals. For Zoroastrianism, in addition to numerous articles and a book on the perception of Zarathustra in early modern Europe, Michael Stausberg is the author of a standard handbook in three volumes (*Die Religion Zarathushtras* [2002–2004]) and the editor of *Zoroastrian Rituals in Context* (2004). He is currently coediting the *Wiley-Blackwell Companion to Zoroastrianism* (2013).

Urban, Hugh B., is professor of religious studies and South Asian studies at Ohio State University. He is primarily interested in Hindu tantric traditions of northeast India, but he has also written widely on the influence of South Asian traditions on new religions in the United States and Europe. He is the author of seven books, including *Tantra: Sex, Secrecy, Politics and Power in the Study of Religion* (2003), *The Economics of Ecstasy: Tantra, Secrecy and Power in Colonial Bengal* (2001), and *The Power of Tantra: Religion, Sexuality and the Politics of South Asian Studies* (2010). He is currently working on a new project on the controversial *guru* Osho (also known as Bhagwan Shree Rajneesh) entitled *Zorba the Buddha: Globalization, Late Capitalism and Postmodern Spirituality in the Osho Movement.*

Valpey, Kenneth, is a permanent research fellow at the Oxford Centre for Hindu Studies (Oxford University) and has also been a regular visiting scholar at the Chinese University of Hong Kong in the Department of Cultural and Religious Studies, where he has been appointed to the Professorship in Indian Religions. In addition to his book *Attending Kṛṣṇa's Image: Caitanya Vaiṣṇava Murti-sevā as Devotional Truth* (2005), he has published articles on Hindu and Gauḍīya Vaiṣṇava thought and practice in the *Journal of Vaishnava Studies*, the *Journal of Hindu Studies*, and the *Beide Journal of Philosophy* (University of Peking). The chapter "Art and Visual Hermeneutics" in *Continuum Companion to Hinduism* has been published in 2011, and, in collaboration with Ravi M. Gupta, two volumes on the *Bhāgavatapurāṇa* are forthcoming. Since 1978 he is a regular visitor to Navadvip, West Bengal – a major center of Gauḍīya Vaiṣṇava tradition.

Vanita, Ruth, professor at the University of Montana and former reader at Delhi University, India, was founding coeditor of *Manushi*, India's first nationwide feminist journal, from 1978 to 1990. She is the author of several books, including *Sappho and the Virgin Mary: Same-Sex Love and the English Literary Imagination* (1996), *Love's Rite: Same-Sex Marriage in India and the West* (2005), *Gandhi's Tiger and Sita's Smile: Essays on Gender, Culture and Sexuality* (2005), and *A Play of Light: Selected Poems* (1994). With Saleem Kidwai, she edited *Same-Sex Love in India: Readings from Literature and History* (2000). She has translated numerous works of fiction and poetry from Hindi to English and has also published widely on Shakespeare. Her most recent book, *Gender, Sex and the City: Urdu Rekhti Poetry 1780–1870*, appeared in 2012.

Verghese, Anila, is principal of Sophia College for Women, Mumbai, India. She has been doing research on Vijayanagara City and the Vijayanagara Empire since 1985. She is the author of *Religious Traditions at Vijayanagara: As Revealed through Its Monuments* (1995), *Archaeology, Art and Religion: New Perspectives on Vijayanagara* (2000), *Hampi: Monumental Legacy* (2001), and coauthor of *Sculpture at Vijayanagara: Iconography and Style* (1998). She is coeditor of *South India under Vijayanagara: Art and Archaeology* (2011). She has also published over 50 scholarly articles and has lectured extensively on the religious traditions, art, and architecture of Vijayanagara.

Viswanath, Rupa, is professor of Indian religions and director at the Center for Modern Indian Studies, University of Göttingen. She has also held positions at the University of Pennsylvania and Cambridge University, where she remains a Fellow of Lucy Cavendish College. Her research and writing primarily address the practices of secular regimes, histories of slavery in colonial South Asia, the political economy and politics of caste, the politics of conversion, and the practices of postcolonial citizenship. Her first book, *The Pariah Problem: Religion, Welfare and Caste in Modern India*, is forthcoming from Columbia University Press. Her current research examines how the concept of a democratic "people" emerged in the vernacular in late colonial and postcolonial South India and the kinds of reconfiguration this required of religious subjects and of concepts of "society" and of "the political."

Williamson, Lola, is assistant professor of religious studies and director of peace studies at Millsaps College in Jackson, Mississippi. Articles and contributions to edited books and encyclopedias focus on the transmission of Hinduism to the United States through immigration as well as through *yoga* and meditation movements. She is the author of *Transcendent in America: Hindu-Inspired Meditation Movements as New Religion* (2010) and coeditor of *Homegrown Gurus: From Hinduism in America to American Hinduism* (forthcoming).

Wujastyk, Dagmar, is a postdoctoral research fellow at the URPP (University Research Priority Program) Asia and Europe at the University of Zurich, Switzerland. Her current research project – "When the Vaidya Met the Doctor: Medical Exchanges in 16th-19th-century India and the Re-imagining of a Great Medical Tradition" – aims to discover and document the intellectual forces that so dramatically changed the representation of Āyurveda in 16th- to 19th-century indigenous South Asian medical literature after the practice of European medicine became widespread in South Asia. Dr. Wujastyk is the author of *Well-Mannered Medicine: Medical Ethics and Etiquette in Classical Ayurveda* (2012) and coeditor of *Modern and Global Ayurveda: Pluralism and Paradigms* (2008).

Zelliot, Eleanor, Laird Bell Professor of History emerita, Carleton College, 1969–1997, is a specialist on the social history of India. She received a Distinguished Service Award from the American Association of Asian Studies. She has edited or written five books on the movement among untouchables in India led by Dr. B.R. Ambedkar, on saint-poets of the medieval period, and on current Hinduism: *Dr. Babasaheb Ambedkar and the Untouchable Movement* (2004), *Untouchable Saints: An Indian Phenomenon* (2005), *The Experience of Hinduism: Essays on Religion in Maharashtra* (1999), *From Untouchable to Dalit: Essays on the Ambedkar Movement* (2005), and *An Anthology of Dalit Literature (Poems)* (1992). She has also written over 80 articles, including "Gandhi and Ambedkar: A Study in Leadership" and "Bibliography on Untouchability" in *The Untouchables in Contemporary India*, "The Medieval Bhakti Movement in History: An Essay on the Literature in English" in *Hinduism: New Essays in the History of Religions*, and "Dalit: New Cultural Context of an Old Marathi Word."

Notes for Users

Organization. The *Encyclopedia of Hinduism* contains in-depth, critical research articles that are thematically organized, rather than short, alphabetically organized dictionary entries containing only information that would be easily retrieved from the internet. The organization of articles within each theme is alphabetical. Many local gods and goddesses, festivals, castes, sacred places, saints, organizations, and so on are not given separate entries, but information about them is nevertheless found in a number of articles. The index, to be included in volume V, will be comprehensive for all volumes and will serve as the alphabetical tool of the *Encyclopedia.*

Common terms and concepts. Some terms – such as those for certain bodies of Hindu sacred texts such as Śruti ("Revealed Texts"), Smṛti ("Texts Committed to Memory": texts based on revelation but composed by humans), Āgama ("Scripture": texts considered revelation by certain Hindu traditions), and those for the three major divisions of the Hindu traditions, Vaiṣṇava (traditions related to the worship of the god Viṣṇu and his embodiments), Śaiva (traditions related to the worship of the god Śiva and his entourage), and Śākta (traditions related to the worship of the Goddess, Śakti, and goddesses identified with her) – are used and referred to in a number of articles and are explained and treated in articles (for Śruti and Smṛti, see articles in section *Sacred Texts and Languages* [vol. II]; for Vaiṣṇava, Śaiva, and Śākta, articles in section *Religious Traditions* [vol. III]), in addition to being index words and searchable through the index.

Hinduism includes many gods and goddesses, but many Hindus and many Hindu textual traditions also insist that behind the multiplicity of gods there is in reality only one God, or that all the goddesses similarly are manifestations of one and the same great Goddess. To cope with this plurality of conceptions of the divine, the generic term God is used when speaking of the one God of whom it is believed that all distinct gods or goddesses are but forms, and the term Goddess is used when speaking of the one Goddess, of whom all distinct goddesses are believed to be manifestations. The Devī refers to the Goddess, while *devī* refers to one of the many goddesses, *devī*s.

Bodies of literatures (Vedas, Purāṇas, etc.) are printed in roman, but separate publications are italicized.

References. Cross-references (symbol: →) to other articles indicate that the subject is dealt with there or that supplementary information is available in those articles. Sometimes the article to which reference is made is shortened (e.g. → *tīrtha* instead of → *tīrtha* and *tīrthayātrā*). To identify the articles in volumes IV and V referred to by the cross-references, the sections of volumes IV and V listed at the end of volume III can be consulted.

Transliteration. *Brill's Encyclopedia of Hinduism* recognizes the diversity and plurality of Hinduism and the terminology that can be applied to it, but for the purposes of the publication, we have for the most part used one spelling style for each term, while avoiding unnecessary Sanskritization and allowing for some local spellings. We have tried to keep diacritics to a minimum: if diacritics were applied to all words derived from Indian languages, then even the word Hindu would be spelled Hindū; adhering to such a strict linguistic practice would serve little purpose. Diacritics are used for a number of terms and concepts from Sanskrit and other Indian languages, for gods, goddesses, texts, schools, and for personal names, but not for most persons and organizations from 19th and 20th centuries who have become part of English-language discourse (e.g. Mahatma Gandhi and not Mahātmā Gāndhī, Jawaharlal Nehru and not Javāharlāl Nehrū, Vivekananda and not Vivekānanda, Bhaktivedanta and not Bhaktivedānta, Ramnamis and not Rāmnāmīs). We do not use diacritics on many Anglicized words derived from Sanskrit or other Indian languages such as brahmanic(al), upanisadic(al), puranic(al), agamic(al) and shastric(al). To emphasize the *Encyclopedia*'s contemporary character, we do not use diacritics on place names, states, regions, languages, scripts, eras, periods, dynasties, kingdoms, and empires (e.g. Maharashtra and not Mahārāṣṭra, Varanasi and not Vārāṇasī, Allahabad and not Allāhābād, Kushanas and not Kuṣāṇas), except mythical and literary place names. We have used diacritics for rivers such as Gaṅgā and Yamunā to emphasize their feminine gender. Literary periods have diacritics (e.g. Caṅkam period). For transliteration from Sanskrit, we have used the scheme issued by the Transliteration Committee of the Geneva Oriental Congress (September 1894), which is the standard for academic works (now called International Alphabet of Sanskrit Transliteration [IAST]). For Chinese transliteration, the Pinyin transliteration system is used. We have allowed for some traditional spellings such as Sri Chand instead of Sri Cand, which would be unrecognizable to the Sikhs. For caste names and months, we have allowed for different local spellings. A member of the caste (*varṇa/jāti*) spelled in Sanskrit Brāhmaṇa is spelled here Brahman for the sake of full-text search, the collective body of texts is spelled Brāhmaṇas, the god is Brahmā, while the transcendent absolute is spelled *brahman* (lowercase and italics). The four *varṇa*s are capitalized, not italicized (e.g. Kṣatriya); *jāti*s (castes) are capitalized and not italicized and have mostly been printed without the required diacritics. Brāhmaṇa is sometimes used for the Brahman caste when the *caturvarṇa* (four class) system is referred to. Months have been written in many languages and in many ways (e.g. Kartik, Karttik, Kārttik, Kārttika [Oct–Nov]) but are accompanied by the Gregorian-calendar equivalents in brackets. For Tamil transliteration, one of the common schemes is used, in which the palatal s is usually rendered as c, and the alveolars as ṉ, ṟ, ḻ.

Pronunciation. Hindu religious traditions, textual as well as oral, are followed, observed, and performed in a number of different languages, mostly South Asian, and even Sanskrit words are pronounced differently in the different regions of India. Nevertheless, some readers might find the following guide for pronunciation of Sanskrit words useful: vowels are pronounced as they are written and pronounced in Latin, Italian, and German. A line above a vowel means length. Consonants correspond, with a few exceptions, to English consonants. Aspirate consonants should be pronounced with an aspiration immediately followed (examples: gh pronounced as in doghouse, th as in hothouse), while unaspirated stops should be pronounced without any aspiration; the dentals (ṭ, ṭh, ḍ, ḍh, and ṇ) should be pronounced with the tip of the tongue touching the teeth, and c and ch are pronounced tsj; ṅ is pronounced like ng in singer, and ñ is pronounced nj; ś is pronounced with the tongue in the same position as in ya; and ṣ is like English sh. Tamil is economical in its use of consonants, and unlike in Sanskrit the same letter may be pronounced in several ways. The letter transliterated as k, for instance, may be pronounced as k, g, or h, depending on the position of the letter and also the geographic origin of the speaker.

Sources. Primary sources are listed in the prelims section of each volume, secondary sources at the end of each article. The * denotes a manuscript. The (*) means that besides print edition(s) also manuscript(s) were consulted.

Authorship. The articles are signed with the name of the author. The author's academic affiliation and additional biographical information are given in the List of Contributors.

Forthcoming articles. One article intended for volume II, two articles intended for volume III, and eight articles intended for volume IV will appear as appendices in volume V. "Śaiva Āgamas" will appear in the section *Sacred Texts*, "Devadāsīs/Courtesans" and "Slavery" will appear in the section *Society*, "Rajasthan Kingdoms" will appear in the section *Historical Perspectives*, "Hinduism and Dravidian Identity" and "Hinduism and Judaism" will appear in the section *Relation to Other Religions and Traditions*, "Feminism," "Globalization," "Nationalism," "Politics and Media," and "Secularism" will appear in the sections *Hinduism and Contemporary Issues*.

KNUT A. JACOBSEN

Primary Sources

Abhidānacintāmaṇi	*Hemacandra's Abhidānacintāmaṇi: Ein systematisch angeordnetes synonymisches Lexikon,* trans. O. Böthlingk & C. Rieu, St. Petersburg, 1847.
Abhidharmakośa	*L'Abhidharmakośa de Vasubandhu: Traduction et annotations*, trans. L. de la Vallée Poussin, Brussels, 1923–1931, repr. 1971.
	Abhidharmakośa of Vasubandhu, Chapter I: Dhātunirdeśa, ed. Y. Ejima, Tokyo, 1989.
Abhidharmakośa(bhāṣya)	*Abhidharmakośa(bhāṣya) of Vasubandhu*, ed. P. Pradhan, Patna, ^{2}1975.
Abhidharmakośavyākhyā	*Abhidharmakośavyākhyā of Yaśomitra*, vol. I, ed. D. Shastri, Varanasi, ^{2}1981.
Abhijñānaśākuntala	*Abhijñānaśākuntala by Kālidāsa with Vaikhānasaśrīnivāsācārya [= Tirumalācārya Śrīnivāsācārya]'s Vyākhyā and Rāghavabhaṭṭa's Dyotanikā*, 1954.
Ādeśapadavyākhyā	**Ādeśapadavyākhyā*, ms. 1285(B) at the Maharaja Mansingh Pustak Prakash, Jodhpur, n.d.
Advaitasiddhi	*Advaitasiddhi of Madhusudana Sarasvati*, ed. K. Bhattacharya, Delhi, 1992.
Āgamaḍambara	*Much Ado about Religion by Bhaṭṭa Jayanta*, ed. C. Deszö, New York, 2005.
Āgamaprāmāṇya	*Āgamaprāmāṇya of Yāmunācārya*, ed. M. Narasimhachary, Baroda, 1976.
	Yāmuna's Āgamaprāmāṇyam or Treatise on the Validity of Pāñcarātra: Sanskrit Text and English Translation, J.A.B. van Buitenen, Madras, 1971.
Agnipurāṇa	*Agnipurāṇa of Maharṣi Vedavyāsa*, ed. U. Baladeva Upādhyāya, Vārāṇasi, 1966.
	The Agni Purana, N. Gangadharan, Delhi, 1985.
Ahirbudhnyasaṃhitā	*Ahirbudhnya-Saṃhitā of the Pāñcarātrāgama*, 2 vols., ed. by M.D. Ramanujacharya under the Supervision of F. Otto Schrader, rev. by V. Krishnamacharya, ALS 4, Madras, 1916, ^{2}1986 (first repr.).
	Pāñcarātra Saṃhitās and Early Vaiṣṇava Theology with a Translation and Critical Notes from Chapters on Theology in the Ahirbudhnya Saṃhitā, M. Matsubara, Delhi, 1994.
Aikkiyaviyal	*Śrīmaṟaiñāṉacampantanāyaṉar aruḷicceyta caivac ciṟu nūlkaḷ (mutaṟpakuti*), ed. T.C. Mīṉāṭciccuntaram Piḷḷai, Thiruvavaduthurai, 1954.
Ā'īn-i Akbarī	*'Allāmī, Abū'l-Fażl: The Ā'īn-i-Akbar*, trans. and ed. H. Blochmann & S.L. Goomer, Delhi, 1871, 1965.
	Ā'īn-i Akbarī, Abū al-Fażl, 3 vols., trans. H. Blochmann, D.C. Phillott, H.S. Jarrett & J. Sarkar, Calcutta, 1929–1948.
Aitareyabrāhmaṇa	*Aitareya Brāhmaṇa*, ed. T. Aufrecht, Bonn, 1897.
	The Aitareya and Kauṣītaki Brāhmaṇas of the Rigveda, trans. A.B. Keith, HOS 25, Delhi, 1971.
	Aitareyabrāhmaṇa with the Commentary of Bhaṭṭa Bhāskara Miśra, ed. A.M. Sastri & L. Srinivasacharya, Delhi, repr. 1985.

Aitareyāraṇyaka	*Aitareyāraṇyaka*, ed. A.B. Keith, Delhi, repr. 1995.
Ajitāgama	*Ajitāgama*, 3 vols., ed. N.R. Bhatt, PIFI 24, Pondicherry, crit. ed. 1964, 1967, 1991.
Alakhbānī	*Alakhbānī or Rushdnāmā of Shaikh Abd-ul-Quddus Gangohi*, ed. S.A.A. Rizvi & S. Zaidi, Aligarh, 1971.
Al-Qawl al-jamīl	*Al-Qawl al-jamīl*, Šāh Walī Allāh, Delhi, n.d.
Amanaskayoga	"Amanaskayoga," ed. J. Birch, BA thesis, University of Sydney, 2006. *Amanaskayoga*, ed. R.L. Shrivastav, Gorakhpur, 1980.
Amarakośa	*Amarakośa with Unpublished South Indian Commentaries*, crit. ed. A.A. Ramnathan, Adyar, 1971.
Amaraughaprabodha	"Amaraughaprabodha," ed. K. Mallik, in: *idem, The Siddha Siddhānta Paddhati and Other Works of Nāth Yogis*, Poona, 1954.
Amaraughaśāsana	*Amaraughaśāsana of Gorakṣanātha*, ed. P. Mukund Rām Śāstrī, KSTS 20, Srinagar, 1918.
Amṛtānubhava	*Amṛtānubhava*, B.P. Bahirat, Bombay, 1963. *Amrutanubhav (= The Nectar of Divine Experience)*, Madhava, Pune, 1981. *Jñāndev's Anubhavamrut: The Immortal Experience of Being*, D. Chitre, New Delhi, 1996.
Amṛtasiddhi	**Amṛtasiddhi*, mss. 1242 and 1243 at the Maharaja Mansingh Pustak Prakash, Jodhpur, n.d.
Aṅguttaranikāya	*Aṅguttaranikāya*, ed. R. Morris & E. Hardy, London, 1888–1900.
Anteṣṭividhi	"The Anteṣṭividhi: A Manual on the Last Rite of the Lakulīśa Pāśupatas," D. Acharya, *JA* 298/1, 2010, 129–152.
Anurāg Sāgar	*The Ocean of Love: The Anurag Sagar of Kabir*, ed. and trans. A. Singh Ji, New Hampshire, 1982.
Aparokṣānubhūti	*Aparokṣānubhūti or Self-realization or Rājayoga of Śaṅkarācārya*, ed. and trans. J.L. Gupta "Chaitanya", Delhi, 2004 (Hind., Eng.) *Rāja-Yoga: Being a Translation of the Vākyasudha or Dṛgdṛśyaviveka of Bhāratitīrtha [Part I] and the Aparokṣānubhūti of Śrī Śankarāchārya [Part II]: With Introduction and Notes*, trans. M.N. Dvivedi, Ahmedabad, 1890.
Āpastambadharmasūtra	*Dharmasūtras: The Law Codes of Āpastamba, Gautama, Baudhāyana and Vasiṣtha*, trans. P. Olivelle, Dehli, 1999.
Āpastambaśrautasūtra	*The Śrauta Sūtra of Āpastamba*, 3 vols., ed. R. Garbe, Calcutta, 1882–1902, repr. Delhi, 1990. *Das Śrautasūtra des Āpastamba*, trans. W. Caland, Göttingen, 1921. *Āpastamba-Śrauta-Sūtra*, ed. G.U. Thite, Delhi 2004.
Āṟāyirappaṭi	*Bhagavad Viṣayam*, 10 vols., ed. S. Kirusnasvami Ayyankar, Madras, 1924–1930.
Arthaśāstra	*The Kauṭilīya Arthaśāstra*, 3 vols., ed. and trans. R.P. Kangle, R.P., Bombay, ^{2}1969.
Āryabhaṭīya	*Āryabhaṭīya of Āryabhaṭa: Critically Edited With Introduction, English Translation, Notes, Comments, and Indexes*, ed. K.S. Shukla, New Delhi, 1976. *The Āryabhaṭīya of Āryabhaṭa: An Ancient Indian Work on Mathematics and Astronomy*, W.G. Clark, Chicago, 1930.
Āryāsaptaśatī	*Āryāsaptaśatī: With the Commentary of Ananta by Govardhana*, ed. Pandit Durgaprasad, Kasinath Pandurang Parab & Vasudev Laxman Sastri Pansikar, Delhi, 1988. *Āryāsaptaśatī o Gauḍavaṅga: Sanskrit Text with Bengali Translation and Commentary*, ed. and trans. Śrī Jāhnavī Kumār Chakrabarty, Calcutta, 1972.
Aṣṭādaśabhedanirṇaya	*Aṣṭādaśabhedanirṇaya: Explication des dix-huit différences (entre les deux branches de l'École de Rāmānuja) de Śrī Vātsya Raṅganātha. Édition critique, Traduction et Notes*, S. Siauve, Pondicherry, 1978.

Aṣṭādhyāyī
Aṣṭādhyāyī: Pâṇini's Grammatik. Herausgegeben, übersetzt, erläutert und mit verschiedenen Indices versehen von Otto Böhtlingk, Delhi, 1998.
Kātyāyana's First Vārttika on Pāṇini's Aṣṭādhyāyī, Mahābhāṣya of Patañjali, ed. F. Kielhorn, vol. 1/2, Pune, ^{3}1962.

Atharvapariśiṣṭa
"The Pāśupata Observance (*Atharvapariśiṣṭa* 40)," P. Bisschop, & A. Griffiths, *IIJ* 46/4, 2003, 315–348.

Atharvaveda
Atharvaveda, ed. V. Bandhu, Hoshiarpur, 1960–1962.

Atharvavedasaṃhitā
Atharvaveda Saṃhitā, trans. W.D. Whitney, 2 vols., Cambridge MA, 1905; ed. R. Roth & W.D. Whitney, 2 vols., Berlin, 1924.
Atharvaveda-Saṃhitā, W.D. Whitney, Delhi, 1996.
Atharva-Veda Saṃhitā: Text with English Translation, Śloka Index and Names of Ṛṣis and Devatās. W.D. Whitney, 2 vols., Delhi, 1987.

Ātmabodha
Self-Knowledge (Atmabodha), trans. Swami Nikhilananda, New York, 1946.

Avadhūtagītā
Avadhūtagītā, ed. P. Thomi, RTÜ 4, Wichtrach, 1996.

Bālakrishnanāṭakamu
Bālakrishnanāṭakamu by T. Veṅgamāmba, ed. K.J. Krishnamurti, Tirupati, 2007.

Basavapurāṇa
Basavapurāṇa [of Bhimakavi], ed. R.C. Hiremath, Dharwar, 1971. (Kan.)
Basava Purāṇamu [of Pālkurike Sōmanātha], Madras, 1966. (Tel.)
"The Basava-Purāṇa of the Lingaits," trans. G. Würth, *JBombayBRAS* 8/24, 1865, 65–97.

Baudhāyanadharmasūtra
Dharmasūtras: The Law Codes of Āpastamba, Gautama, Baudhāyana and Vasiṣṭha, trans. P. Olivelle, Dehli, 1999.
The Baudhayana-Dharmasutra, ed. with Govinda's *Vivaraṇa* commentary by Umesa Chandra Pandeya, KSS 104, Varanasi, 1972.

Baudhāyanaśrautasūtra
The Baudhāyana Śrauta Sūtra, vol. II, ed. by W. Caland, Calcutta, 1907.
The Baudhāyana Śrautasūtra, crit. ed. and trans. C.G. Kashikar, New Delhi, 2003.

Bhagavadgītā
Bhagavad Gītā with Eleven Commentaries, ed. and trans. S.G.S. Sadhale, Delhi, 2000.
Bhagavadgītā, trans. B. Miller, New York, 1986.
Die Bhagavadgītā, trans. R. Garbe, Leipzig, 1905.
The Kashmir Recension of the Bhagavadgītā, ed. F.O. Schrader, Stuttgart, 1930.
The Bhagavadgītā, with the Sanatsujatīya and the Anugītā, ed. and trans. K.T. Telang, Oxford, 1882.
Śrīmad Bhagavadgītā-rahasya or Karma-Yoga-Śāstra: Including an External Examination of the Gītā, the Original Sanskrit Stanzas, Their English Translation, Commentaries on the Stanzas, and a Comparison of Eastern and Western Doctrines etc., 2 vols., trans. B.S. Sukthankar, ed. B.G. Tilak, Poona, 1935.
The Bhagavad-Gītā with a Commentary Based on the Original Sources, ed. and trans. R. Zaehner, Oxford, 1969.
Śrīmadbhagavadgītā (with Rāmānuja's Commentary), ed. V.G. Apte, ĀSS 92, 1923.

Bhagavaī
Viyāhapannatti (Bhagavaī): The Fifth Anga of the Jaina Canon, J. Deleu, LSJRS 10, Delhi, 1970, repr. 1996.
Bhagavaī Viāhapaṇṇattī, ed. Muni Nathamal, Anga Suttāni 2, Ladnun, V.S. 2031.
Viyāhapaṇṇattisuttaṁ, ed. Bechardas J. Doshi & Amritlal Mohanlal Bhojak, 3 vols., Jaina-Āgama-Series 4, Bombay, 1974–1982.

Bhāgavatapurāṇa
Śrīmadbhāgavata Śrīdharī Ṭīkā, Varanasi, 1962.
Bhāgavata Purāṇa of Kṛṣṇa Dvaipāyana Vyāsa with Sanskrit Commentary Bhāvārthabodhinī of Śrīdharasvāmin, ed. J.L. Shastri, Delhi, 1983.

Srimad-Bhāgavatam with Notes from a Dozen Commentaries, trans. N. Raghunathan, 2 vols., Madras, 1976.

Srimad Bhagavata: The Holy Book of God, trans. S. Tapasyananda, 4 vols., Madras, 1980–1992.

Srimad-Bhāgavata-Mahāpurāṇa with Sanskrit Text and English Translation, trans. C.L. Goswami, 2 Vols, Gorakhpur, 1971, ^{2}1982.

The Bhāgavata-Purāṇa, 4 vols., trans. and annotated by G.V. Tagare, Delhi, 1992.

Śrīmadbhāgavata: dvādaśa skandha sampūrṇa, Śaṅkaradeva, Dibrugarh, 1989.

Śrīmad Bhāgavata Mahāpurāṇam, with the Sanskrit commentaries of Śrīdhara Svāmin's Bhāvārthadīpikā, Śrī Vaṃśīdhara's Bhāvārthadīpikāprakāśa, Śrī Rādhāramaṇadāsa Gosāmin's Dīpinī, Śrīmad Vīrarāghava's Bhāgavatacandrikā, Śrīmad Vijayadhvajatīrtha's Padaratnāvalī, Śrīmad Jīva Gosvāmin's Kramasaṃdarbha, Śrīmad Viśvanātha Cakravartin's Sārārthadarśinī, Śrīmad Śukadeva's Siddhāntapradīpa, Śrīmad Vallabhācarya's Subodhinī, Śrī Puruṣottamacaraṇa Gosvāmin's Subodhinīprakāśaḥ, Śrī Giridharalāla's Bālaprabodhinī, ed. Kṛṣṇaśaṅkara Śāstrī, Ahmedabad, 1965.

Bhāgavatasandarbha — *Bhāgavatasandarbha (with the Gopālatoṣaṇī Commentary of Śyāmdās)*, 6 vols., Jīva Gosvāmī, Hindi trans., Śyāmdās, Vrindavan, 1984–1999.

Bhaktalīlāmṛt — "Bhaktalīlāmṛt [of Bhīmasvāmī Śirgāvkar]," in: *Rāmdās āṇi Rāmdāsī: Bhāg Dusrā*, Dhule, 1906, 1–170.

Bhaktalīlāmṛta — *Life of Eknath: Śrī Eknath charitra, Translated from the Bhaktalīlāmṛta*, ed. J.E. Abbott *et al.*, Poona 1928, 1981.

Life of Tukaram: Translation from Mahipati's Bhaktalilamrita Chapters 25 to 40, ed. J.E. Abbott *et al.*, Poona, 1930, 1980.

Nectar from Indian Saints, ed. J.E. Abbott *et al.*, Poona, 1935.

Bhaktamāla — *Bhakta-māla, Gosvāmī Śrī Nābhājī kṛta Śrī-bhakta-māla, Śrī Priyādāsajī praṇīta ṭīkā-kavitta*, ed. S.B. Rupakala, Lucknow, 1977.

Bhaktamāl, Priyādāsjī praṇit ṭīkā-kavitta, Sītārāmśaraṇ Bhagavānprasād Rūpkalā viracit Bhaktisudhāsvad tilak sahit, Nābhādās, Lucknow, 1903, 1914, ^{6}1977.

Rāghavdās kṛt bhaktmāl, ed. A. Nāhṭā, Jodhpur, 1965 (Hind.).

Nābhādās: Śrī Bhaktamāl, ed. Rupkala (Rūpkalā = S. Bhagavānprasād), Lucknow, 1961.

Bhaktavijaya — *Stories of Indian Saints: A Translation of Mahipati's Marathi Bhaktavijaya*, ed. J.E. Abbott *et al.*, Poona 1933, 1982.

Bhaktirasāmṛtasindhu — *The Bhaktirasāmṛtasindhu of Rūpa Gosvāmin*, ed. and trans. D.L. Haberman, Delhi, 2003.

Bhaktirasāmṛtasindhu by Rūpa Gosvāmī, ed. Haridāsa Dāsa, Navadvipa, 1961.

Bhaktiratnākāra — *Bhaktiratnākāra of Narahari Cakravartī [Ghanaśyāma Dāsa]*, ed. by Rāmanārāyaṇa Vidyāratna, Murshidabad, 3rd ed. Bengali San 1332 (= 1926).

Bhaktiratnākara — *Bhaktiratnākara of Narahari Cakravartī Ṭhākura*, Kolkata, 1987.

Bhaktiratnākara, Śaṅkaradeva, Patiala, 1982.

Narahari Cakravartī, Bhaktiratnākara, ed. Nandalāl Vidyāsāgara, Calcutta, 1960.

Bhaktiratnāvalī — *Bhakti Ratnāvalī*, Mādhavadeva, New Delhi, 2009.

Bhārgavatantra — *Bhargava Tantram (A Pancaratragama Text)*, ed. by Raghava Prasad Chaudhary, KSV 8, Allahabad, 1981.

Bhāṣāpariccheda — *Bhāṣāpariccheda with Siddhānta-muktavālī by Viśvanātha-nyāya-pañcānana*, trans. by Swami Madhvananda, Kolkata, 2004.

Bhāṣāvaṃśāvalī	*Bhāṣāvaṃśāvalī*, ed. N. Pauḍela & D. Laṃsāla, 2 vols., Vikram 2020, 2033.
Bījagaṇita	"Bījagaṇitaof Bhāskara," ed. T. Hayashi, *SCIAMVS* 10, 2009, 3–302.
Bījak	*Kabīr bījak*, ed. S. Singh, Allahabad, 1972 (Hind.).
	The Bijak of Kabir, trans. L. Hess & S. Singh, Delhi, 1983, 2001.
Brahmāṇḍapurāṇa	*Brahmāṇḍapurāṇa*, trans. G.V. Tagare, Delhi, 1983.
	The Brahmāṇḍa-Mahāpurāṇam, ed. K.V. Sarma, Varanasi, 1983.
	Brahmāṇḍa Purāṇa, ed. J.L. Shastri, Delhi, 1973.
Brahmapurāṇa	*Sanskrit Text and Indices of the Brahmapurāṇa*, ed. P. Schreiner & R. Söhnen, Wiesbaden, 1986.
Brahmasamhitā	*Brahma-Samhitā with Commentary by Shri Shrila Jeeva Goswāmi* by Jīva Gosvāmī; ET: *Bhakti Siddhānta Saraswati*, ed. Bhakti Vilās Tirtha, Madras, 1973.
Brahmasiddhi	*Brahmasiddhi of Maṇḍana Miśra*, ed. S.K. Sastri, Madras, 1937.
Brāhmasphuṭasiddhānta	*Brāhmasphuṭasiddhānta*, ed. S. Dvivedī, Benares, 1901–1902.
Brahmasūtra	*Le Vedanta: Etude sur les Brahma-sutra et leurs cinq commentaires*, V.S. Ghate, Paris, 1918; ET: *The Vedānta: A Study of the Brahma-sūtras with the Bhāṣyas of Śaṃkara, Rāmānuja, Nimbārka, Madhva, and Vallabha*, Poona, 1981.
	The Brahmasutrabhashya of Srikanthacharya with the commentary Sivarkamanidipika by Appayadikshita edited with Sutrarthacandrika, 2 vols., ed. R. Halasyanatha Sastri, New Delhi, 1986.
Brahmasūtrabhāṣya	*Bhagavadgītā with Śaṅkara's Bhāṣya*, ed. N. Vilinatha, Madras, 1971.
	Brahma Sutra Bhashya, ed. Panchamukhi, Delhi, 1994.
	Brahmasūtraśāṃkarabhāṣyam, ed. J.L. Shastri, Delhi, 1980.
	Brahmasūtraśāṅkarabhāṣya, ed. with three subcommentaries by Pt. A. Shastri & V.L. Shastri Pansikar, Varanasi, 2000.
	Śrīmad-dvaipāyana-praṇīta-brahmasūtrāṇi. Ānandagiri-kṛta-ṭīkā-saṃvalita-śāṃkara-bhāṣya-sametāni, ed. Nārāyaṇa Śāstrī Ekasaṃbekare, ĀSS 21/1–2, 1890–1891.
	The Sacred Books of the East, vols. XXXIV, XXXVIII: The Vedānta Sūtras of Bādarāyaṇa: With the Commentary by Śaṅkara, trans. G. Thibaut, Oxford, 1890, 1896.
Brahmasūtragovindabhāṣya	*Brahma-sūtra-govinda-bhāṣyam of Baladeva Vidyābhūṣaṇa*, ed. with Hindi trans. by Rāsavihāri Dāsa and Narasiṃha Dāsa, Mathura, Vikram 2011 (= 1955).
Brahmayāmala	**Brahmayāmala*, ms. 3–370 at the National Archives Kathmandu (= unpublished transcription and partial edition by S. Hatley & C. Kiss based on manuscript 3–370 [palm-leaf] of the National Archives, Kathmandu [Nepal-German Manuscript Preservation Project, reel n. A 42–46]), Kathmandu, dated 1052 CE.
Bṛhadāraṇyakopaniṣadbhāṣya	*Śhrimat Sureswarácharya-viracitaṃ Bṛihadáraṇyakopanishadbhásh yavártikam with its Commentary by Śrímat Ánandajnyána*, ed. Pandit Kasínátha Śasrtrí Ágáśe, ĀSS 16/1–3, Puṇyākhyapattana (= Pune), 1892–1894.
Bṛhadbhāgavatāmṛta	*Śrī Bṛhad Bhāgavatāmṛta of Śrīla Sanātana Gosvāmī*, G. Dasa (Dāsa), vol. I, Los Angeles, 2002.
Bṛhajjātaka	*The Bṛihajjâtakam of Varâha Mihira*, trans. S. Vijnanananda, New Delhi, [1]1912, 1979.
Bṛhaspatismṛti	*Bṛhaspatismṛti (Reconstructed)*, ed. K.V. Rangaswami Aiyangar, GaOS 85, Baroda, 1941.
Bṛhatkhecarīprakāśa	**Bṛhatkhecarīprakāśa*, ms. 14575 at the Scindia Oriental Research Institute Library, Ujjain, n.d.
Bṛhatsaṃhitā	*Bṛhatsaṃhitā*, vols. I–II, ed. with the commentary of Bhaṭṭotpala by A.V. Tripāṭhī, SBG 97, Varanasi, 1968.

	Varāhamihira's Bṛhat Saṃhitā [then follows] Bṛhatsaṃhitā [in Nāgarī] With English Translation, Exhaustive Notes and Literary Comments, 2 parts, by Prof. M. Ramakrishna Bhat, Delhi, 1981–1982.
Bṛhatstotraratnākara	*Bṛhat-stotra-ratnākaraḥ I and II*, ed. R.N. Ācārya, Varanasi, 1983.
Caitanyabhāgavata	*Caitanyabhāgavata* of Vṛndāvana Dasa, Mayapur, 1997.
Caitanyacandrāmṛta	*Caitanya Candrāmṛtam* of Prabodhānanda, trans. Sarvabhāvana Dāsādhikarī, Vrindavan, 2004.
Caitanyacaritāmṛta	*The Caitanya Caritāmṛta of Kṛṣṇdāsa Kavirāja: A Translation and Commentary*, trans. E.C. Dimock Jr., ed. T.K. Stewart, Cambridge MA, HOS 56, 2000.
	Murāri Gupta, Kṛṣnacaitanyacaritāmṛta, ed. Swami B.V. Bhāgavata, Vrindavan, 2006.
	Śrī Caitanya-Caritāmṛta of Kṛṣṇadāsa Kavirāja Gosvāmī with Original Bengali Text, ed. and trans. Kṛṣṇadāsa Kavirāja & A.C. Bhaktivedanta Swami Prabhupāda, Los Angeles, 1975, [2]1996, 2002.
	Caitanyacaritāmṛta by Kṛṣṇadāsa Kavirāja, ed. Bhakti Kevala Auḍulomi, Calcutta, 1957.
Cāṇakyarājanīti	*Cāṇakya-Rāja-Nīti*, trans. L. Sternbach, Madras, 1963.
Candraśekhar	*Candraśekhar kāhinī bā candranāth māhātmya*, Caṭṭagrām, n.d.
Candrāvalokana	**Candrāvalokana*, ms. D 4345 at the Government Oriental Manuscripts Library, Chennai, n.d.
Caṅkaṟpanirākaraṇam	*Meykaṇṭacāttiraṅkal*, publ. Department of Saivasiddhanta, University of Mandras, Chennai, 1988.
	Śrīmaṟaiṉāṉacampantanāyaṉar aruḷicceyta caivac ciṟu nūlkaḷ (mutaṟpakuti), ed. T.C. Mīṉāṭcicuntaram Piḷḷai, Thiruvavaduthurai, 1954.
Carakasaṃhitā	*Carakasaṃhitā of Agniveśa, with the Āyurveda-Dīpikā Commentary of Cakrapāṇidatta*, ed. J. Trikamji, New Delhi, [5]1992.
	The Caraka Saṃhitā, 6 vols., Translations in Hindi, Gujarati and English by the Shree Gulabkunverba Ayurvedic Society, Jamnagar, 1949.
Caryāgītikoṣa	*Caryāgītikoṣa: With a Modern Bengali Translation and Facsimile of the Manuscript*, ed. Nilaratan Sen, Calcutta, 2001.
Caurāsī Baiṭhak Caritra	*Chaurasi Baithak: Eightyfour Seats of Shri Vallabhacharya*, Shyam Das, Baroda, 1985.
Caurāsīpad	*The Caurāsī Pad of Śrī Hit Harivaṃś*, C.S.J. White, Honolulu, 1977; repr. "'The Love of Rādhā': A Translation of the Caurāsī Pad of Śrī Hit Harivaṃś with Commentary," *JVS* 7/1, 1998, 101–180.
	The Eighty-four Hymns of Hita Harivaṃśa: An Edition of the Caurāsī Pada, R. Snell, Delhi, 1991.
Cencunāṭakamu	*Cencunāṭakamu*, ed. K.J. Krishnamurti, Tirupati, 2007.
Chāndogyopaniṣad	*The Early Upaniṣads: Annotated Text and Translation*, ed. P. Olivelle, New York, 1998.
Chāndogyopaniṣadbhāṣya	*The Chha'ndogya Upanishad with the Commentary of Sankara A'cha'rya and the Gloss of A'nanda Giri*, ed. E. Röer, Calcutta, 1850.
Cintyāgama	**Cintyāgama*, paper transcript (T.13) at the French Institute of Pondicherry, n.d.
Civanāṉaittiyār	*Civanāṉacittiyār cupakkam civākkirayōkikaḷ uraiyuṭaṉ* (with Śivāgrayogī's commentary), publ. Thiruvavaduthurai Adheenam, Thiruvavaduthurai, 1965.
Civanāṉapōtam	*Civanāṉaptamum vārttikameṉṉum poḻippuraiyum civanāṉacuvāmika ceyta tirāviṭamāpāṭiyam eṉṉum Civanāṉapōtamāpāṭiyamum*, ed. Swaminathapanditar, 1906.
	Meykaṇṭacāttiraṅkal, publ. Department of Saivasiddhanta, University of Mandras, Chennai, 1988.

Civappirakācam — *Civappirakācam by Umāpati with the Commentary by Maturaiccivappirakācar*, ed. P. Ramanatha Pillai, Tirunelveli, 1975.
Meykaṇṭacāttiraṅkal, publ. Department of Saivasiddhanta, University of Mandras, Chennai, 1988.

Dabistān-i maḏāhib — *The Dabistan or School of Manners*, D. Shea & A. Troyer, New York, [1]1843, 1901.
Dabistān-i maḏāhib, Mīr Ḏu'l-Fiqār Ardistānī Mawbadšāh; ET: D. Shea & A. Troyer, *Hinduism during the Mughal India of the 17th Century*, Patna, 1998.

Dādūjanmalīlā — *The Hindī Biography of Dādū Dayāl (Janmalīlā)*, ed. and trans. W.M. Callewaert, Delhi, 1988.

Dādūvāṇī — *Śrī Dādūdayāljī kī vāṇī: With Hindi Translation and Commentary*, ed. Svāmī Nārāyaṇdās, Jaipur, n.d. (c. 1969) (Hind.).
Śrī Dādūdayāljī kī vāṇī saṭīk, ed. Maṅgaldās Svāmī, Jaipur, n.d. (c. 1951) (Hind.).

Dānakelikaumudī — *Dānakelikaumudī* by Rūpa Gosvāmī, ed. Purīdāsa Mahāśaya, Vrindavan, 1947.

Dānasāgara — *Ballālasena, Dānasāgara*, ed. B. Bhattacharya, Calcutta, 1956.

Dasam Granth — *Sri Dasam Granth Sahib Text and Translation*, ed. J. Singh & D. Singh, 1999.

Daśaprakaraṇāni — *Daśaprakaraṇāni*, 4 vols., ed. P.P Lakṣmīnārāyaṇopādhyāya, Bangalore, 1971.

Daśavidhahetunirūpaṇa — *[Vaikhānasasmārtasūtra]= Vaikhānasagṛhyasūtra [with Vaikhānasadharmasūtra and -pravarasūtra]*, with Śrīnivāsa-makhin [=-Dīkṣita]'s *Tātparyacintāmaṇi* commentary and his *Daśavidhahetunirūpaṇa*, and extracts from Nṛsiṃhāgnicit Vājapeyin [= Nṛsiṃha Vājapeyin]'s commentary, ed. R. Pārthasārathi Bhaṭṭācārya, Śaka 1889 (= 1967 CE).

Dattātreyayogaśāstra — *Dattātreyayogaśāstra*, ed. B. Avasthi, Delhi, 1982.
**Dattātreyayogaśāstra*, mss. 1936 and 1937 at the Maharaja Mansingh Pustak Prakash, Jodhpur, n.d.
**Dattātreyayogaśāstra*, ms. 4107 at the Oriental Institute Baroda, Vadodara, n.d.
**Dattātreyayogaśāstra*, ms. 6/4–399 at the Prajna Pathashala Mandal, Mumbai, n.d.
**Dattātreyayogaśāstra*, mss. 4369, R5579, and 5585 at the Government Oriental Manuscripts Library, Chennai, n.d.

Devībhāgavatapurāṇa — Devībhāgavatapurāṇa Vijnananda, Swami, trans. Sri Mad Devī Bhāgavata Purāṇa, n.d.

Devīgītā — *The Devī Gītā, The Song of the Goddess: A Translation, Annotation, and Commentary*, trans. C.M. Brown, Albany, 1998
The Song of the Goddess, the Devi Gita: Spiritual Counsel of the Great Goddess, trans. C.M. Brown, Albany, 2002.

Devīkalottarāgama — **Devīkalottarāgama*, paper transcript (T.89) at the French Institute of Pondicherry, n.d.

Devīmāhātmya — *Devī Māhātmyam*, trans. S. Jagadiswarananda, Madras, 1953.

Devīnāmavilāsa — *The Devīnāmavilāsa of Sāhib Kaul*, ed. M. Kaul, Delhi, 1942, 1989.

Dhammasaṅgaṇi — *Dhammasaṅgaṇi*, ed. E. Müller, London, 1885.

Dharmottarapradīpa — *Dharmottarapradīpa*, ed. D. Malvania, TSWS 2, Patna, [2]1971.

Dhūrtākhyāna — *Haribhadra: Ballade des coquins*, ed. J.-P. Osier & N. Balbir, Paris, 2004.

Dhvanyāloka — *The Dhvanyāloka of Ānandavardhana with the Locana of Abhinavagupta*, ed. with introduction by D.H.H. Ingalls, trans. by D.H.H. Ingalls *et al.*, Cambridge MA, 1990.
Dhvanyāloka of Ānandavardhana with the Locana of Abhinavagupta, 3 vols., ed. R. Tripāṭhi, Delhi, 1975–1981.

Dhvanyālokalocana — *The Dhvanyāloka of Ānandavardhana with the Locana of Abhinavagupta*, ed. with introduction by D.H.H. Ingalls, trans. by D.H.H. Ingalls *et al.*, Cambridge MA, 1990.

Dīghanikāya — *Dīghanikāya*, ed. T.W. Rhys Davids & J.E. Carpenter, London, 1890–1911.

Digvijaya — *Sankara -Dig-Vijaya: The Traditional Life of Sri Sankaracharya, by Madhava-Vidyaranya*, trans. T. Swami, Madras, n.d.

Dīkṣātattvaprakāśa — *Dīkṣātattvaprakāśa, Paṇḍita Śrī Dulāreprasāda Śāstriṇā saṃgṛhītaḥ*, Calcutta, 1924, [2]1966.

Divyasūricarita — *The Divya Suri Caritam by Garudavahana Pandita*, Bombay, 1798.

Dvādaśastotra — *Dvādaśastotra of Śrī Madhvācārya*, Madras, 1975.

Dvipadabhāgavatamu — *Dvipadabhāgavatamu* by T. Veṅgamāmba, books 1 & 2, ed. Gopikrishna, Hyderabad, 2009.

Epigraphia Indica — *Epigraphia Indica*, 42 vols., Delhi, 1892–1978.

Gadyarāja — *Gadyarāja: A Fourteenth Century Marathi Version of the Kṛṣṇa Legend*, trans. I.M.P. Raeside, Bombay, 1989.

Gadyatraya — *Rāmānujagranthamālā*, ed. P.B. Annangaracariar, Kanci, 1974.

Gaṇakārikā — *Gaṇakārikā, with the Ratnaṭīkā of Bhāsarvajña*, ed., C.D. Dalal, GaOS 15, Baroda, 1920, repr. 1966.

Gaṇeśagītā — *Gaṇeśagītā: A Study, Translation with Notes and a Condensed Rendering of the Commentary of Nīlakaṇṭha*, ed. and trans. K. Yoroi, The Hague, 1968.

Gaṇeśapurāṇa — *The Gaṇeśa Purāṇa*, trans. G. Bailey, vols. I–II, Wiesbaden, 1995, 2008.

Gaṇeśatāpanīyopaniṣad — "Die Gaṇeśatāpanīya-Upaniṣad, Teil 1: Text und Übersetzung, Teil 2: Anmerkungen, " (unpubl.) diss., Marburg University, 1965.

Gārgīyajyotiṣa — *The Yuga Purāṇa: Critically Edited, With an English Translation and a Detailed Introduction*, ed. and trans. J.E. Mitchener, Calcutta, 1986.

Garuḍapurāṇa — *The Garuḍapurāṇa (Sāroddhāra)*, trans. E. Wood & S.V. Subrahmanyam, Allahabad, 1911.
Garuḍapurāṇam, ed. R. Bhattacarya, Varanasi, 1964.

Gāthā (Eknāth) — *Śrīeknāthmahārāj Yāñcyā Abhaṅgācī Gāthā*, ed. T.H. Āvaṭe, Poona, 1908.
Eknāthsvāmīkṛt Abhaṅgācī Gāthā, publ. Induprakāś, Mumbai, 1906.
Śrīeknāth Mahārājāñcyā Abhaṅgāñcī Gāthā, ed. T. Tātyā, Mumbai, 1903.
Eknāthī Gāthā, ed. R.Ś. Gondhaḷekar, Poona, 1893.

Gautamadharmasūtra — *Dharmasūtras: The Law Codes of Āpastamba, Gautama, Baudhāyana and Vasiṣṭha*, trans. P. Olivelle, Dehli, 2.

Gheraṇḍasaṃhitā — *Das Indische Yoga-Lehrbuch Gheraṇḍa-Saṃhitā. Aus dem Sanskrit Übersetzt, Kommentiert und mit Abbildungen Herausgegeben*, ed. and trans. P. Thomi, Wichtrach, [2]2006.
Gheraṇḍasaṃhitā, ed. J. Mallinson, New York, 2004.

Gītābhāṣya — *Rāmānuja on the Bhagavadgītā: A Condensed Rendering of His Gītābhāṣya with Copious Notes and Introduction*, ed. and trans. J.A.B. van Buitenen, The Hague, 1951.
Rāmānujagranthamālā, ed. P.B. Annangaracariar, Kanci, 1974.

Gītagovinda — *Jayadeva's Gitagovinda: Love Song of the Dark Lord*, B. Stoler-Miller, Delhi, 1984.
Gītagovindakāvyam: With Kāntamiśra's Padabhāvārthacandrikā, ed. Candraśekhara Hota, Allahabad, 1997.
Le Gītagovinda de Jayadeva: Texte, Concordance, et Index, H. Quellet, Hildesheim, 1978.
Gītagovindakāvyam: With the Sañjivanī of Vanamālibhaṭṭa, Padadyotanikā of Nārāyaṇa Paṇḍita, and Jayantī of Kṛṣṇa, Jayadeva, Hyderabad, 1969.
Gītagovinda: With King Mānāṅka's Commentary, ed. V.M. Kulkarni, Ahmedabad, 1965.
Gītagovinda, ed. Harekṛṣṇa Mukhopadhyāya, Calcutta, 1957.

Gītagovindakāvyam: With the Raskapriyā of Kumbhakarṇa and the Rasamañjarī of Śaṅkaramiśra, ed. Mangesh Ramkrishna Telang & Vasudev Laxman Panshikar, Bombay, 1899.

Gītārthasaṃgraha — *Gītārthasaṅgraha of Abhinavagupta: Translation with an Introductory Study*, ed. and trans. A. Sharma, Leiden, 1983.
Abhinavagupta's Commentary on the Bhagavad Gītā: Gītārtha Saṃgraha, trans. B. Marjanovic, Varanasi, 2002.
Śrīmad Bhagavad Gītā With Commentary by Mahāmāheshvara Rājānaka Abhinava Gupta, ed. L.R. Brahamachārī, Srinagar, 1933.

Gobhilagṛhyasūtra — *Gobhilagṛhyasūtra*, ed. F. Knauer, Dorpat, 1884.

Gopālacampū — *Gopālacampū*, Jīva Gosvāmī, ed. Purīdās, Dhaka, 1947.

Gopālarājavaṃśāvalī — *Gopālarājavaṃśāvalī*, ed. and trans. D. Vajrācārya & Kamal P. Malla, Wiesbaden, 1985.

Gorakhbāṇī — *Gorakhbāṇī*, ed. P.D. Badathval, Allahabad, 1960.

Gorakṣasaṃhitā — *Gorakṣasaṃhitā*, ed. J.S. Pandeya, SBG 111, Varanasi, 1976.

Gorakṣaśataka — **Gorakṣaśataka*, ms. R 7874 at the Government Oriental Manuscripts Library, Chennai, n.d..

Gorakṣasiddhāntasaṃgraha — *Gorakṣasiddhāntasaṃgraha*, ed. J.S. Pandeya, SBG 110, Varanasi, 1973.

Gorakṣavijaya — *Gorakṣavijaya of Vidyāpati*, ed. H. Mishra, Patna, 1984.

Gosāīṃ Carit — *Gosāīṃ-carit*, K. Gupta, 1964.

Govindalīlāmṛta — *Govindalīlāmṛta* by Kṛṣṇadāsa Kavirajā, ed. Haridāsa Śāstrī, Vrindavan, 1981.

Guṇamālā — *Guṇamālā*, Śaṅkaradeva, Jorhat, 1975.

Gurū Granth Sāhib — *(Śrī) Gurū Granth Sāhib with Complete Index*, 2 parts, W.M. Callewaert, Delhi, 1996.

Haribhaktivilāsa — *Gopālabhaṭṭa Gosvāmī: Śrī Śrī Haribhaktivilāsaḥ*, Dacca, 1946.
Haribhaktivilāsa of Gopāla Bhaṭṭa, ed. by Haridāsa Śāstri, Vrindavan, 1986.

Haripaṭh — *L'Invocation: Le Haripath de Dnyandev*, C. Vaudeville, Paris, 1969.

Harivaṃśa — *The Harivaṃśa: Being the Khila or Supplement to the Mahābhārata, for the First Time Critically Edited*, ed. P.L. Vaidya, 2 vols., Poona, 1969–1971.

Haṭha(yoga)pradīpikā — *Haṭhapradīpikā of Svātmārāma (10 chapters): With Yogaprakāśikā Commentary by Bālakṛṣṇa*, ed. M.L. Gharote & P. Devnath, Lonavla, 2001.
Haṭhapradīpikā of Svātmārāma, ed. S. Digambarji & P. Jhā, Lonavla, 1970.

Haṭhapradīpikā Siddhāntamuktāvalī — **Haṭhapradīpikā Siddhāntamuktāvalī*, ms. 6756 at Maharaja Mansingh Pustak Prakash, Jodhpur, n.d.

Haṭhapradīpikājyotsnā — *Haṭhapradīpikājyotsnā of Brahmānanda*, ed. S. Maheśānand, B. Śarmā, J. Sahāy & R. Bodhe, Lonavla, 2002.

Haṭharatnāvalī — *Haṭharatnāvalī*, ed. M.L. Gharote, P. Devnath & V.K. Jha, Lonavla, 2002.

Hīr Vāris Śāh — *The Adventures of Hir and Ranjha*, Waris Shah, London, 1973.

Hitacaritra — *Hita-Caritra* by Uttamdās, Nagari Pracarini Sabha, Mayasankar Yajnik collection, MS 4822, 1760.

Īśānaśivagurudevapaddhati — *Īśānaśivagurudevapraṇītā*, ed. T. Ganapati Sastri, 4 vols., New Delhi, 1990.

Iṣṭasiddhi — *Iṣṭasiddhi of Vimuktātman*, ed. M. Hiriyanna, Baroda, 1933.

Īśvarapratyabhijñākārikā — *The Īśvarapratyabhijñākārikā of Utpaladeva with the Author's Vṛtti*, ed. F. Torella, Delhi, 2002.

Īśvarapratyabhijñākārikāvṛtti — *The Īśvarapratyabhijñākārikā of Utpaladeva with the Author's Vṛtti*, ed. F. Torella, Delhi, 2002.

The Siddhitrayī and the Īśvarapratyabhijākārikāvṛtti, ed. M.K. Shastri, Srinagar, 1921.

Īśvarapratyabhijñāvimarśinī — *Bhāskarī: A Commentary on the Īśvarapratyabhijñāvimarśinī of Ācārya Abhinavagupta* (Abhinavagupta's text with Bhāskarī commentary), 3 vols., ed. and trans. K.A. Subramania Iyer and K.C. Pandey, Delhi, 1986.

Īśvarapratyabhijñāvivṛtivimarśinī — *The Īśvarapratyabhijñāvivṛtivimarśinī by Abhinavagupta*, 3 vols., ed. by M.K. Shastri, Delhi, 1987.

Īśvarasaṃhitā — *Īśvarasaṃhitā Anantācāryais saṃśodhitā*, Śāstramuktāvaḷī 45, Kanchipuram, 1923.

Jaiminīyabrāhmaṇa — *Jaiminīya Brāhmaṇa of the Sāmaveda Critically Edited*, ed. R. Vira & L. Chandra, Delhi, 1954.

Jātaka — *The Jātaka or Stories of the Buddha's Former Births*, vol. III, ed. E.B. Cowell, trans. H.T. Francis & R.A. Neil, London, 1957.

Jayākhyasaṃhitā — *Jayākhyasaṃhitā of Pāñcarātra Āgama, Critically Edited with Introduction in Sanskrit, Indices, etc.*, ed. Embar Krishnamacharya, GaOS 54, Baroda, 1967.

Jñānāmṛtasārasaṃhitā — *The Nárada Pancha Rátra in the Original Sanscrit*, ed. by K.M. Banerjea, BI.NS. 17, 25, 34, 75, Calcutta, 1865.

Jnānāvaraṇabhāṣya — *Śivajnānabodha with with the Commentary Called Jnānāvaraṇabhāṣya by Veḷḷiyampalavāṇamuṇivar*, ed. T. Ganesan, forthcoming.

Jñāneśvarī — *(Śrī)-Jñāneśvarī of Jñānadeva*, ed. G.S. Naṇadīkar, 5 vols., Mumbai, 2001.

The Jñāneśvarī, trans. R.S. Lokapur, Belgaum, 1995.

Jnaneshwar's Gita: A Rendering of the Jnaneshwari, trans. S. Kripananda, Albany, 1989.

Sri Jnanadeva's Bhāvārtha Dīpikā: Otherwise Known as Jnāneshwari, R.K. Bhagwat, Madras, 1979.

Śrījñāneśvarī, V.K. Rajwade, Mumbai, 1977.

Jnāneshvari (Bhāvārthadipikā), V.G. Pradhan & H.M. Lambert, London, 1967.

Kabīr Granthāvalī — *Kabīr Granthāvalī*, Pārasanātha Tivārī, Ilāhābād, 1989; Prayāga, 1961.

Kabīr Granthāvali by Śyāmasundaradāsa, Prayāga, 1928; Kāśī, 1951.

Kabīr Vāṇī — *Kabīr Vāṇī*, Charlotte Vaudeville, Institut français d'Indologie, Pondichéry, 1982.

Kadaḷiya karpura — *Kadaḷiya karpura*, H. T[h]ipperudra Swamy, Mysore, ^{7}1986; ET: *Soul unto the Sublime*, Hubli, 1982.

Kalātattvakośa — *Kalātattvakośa*, vol. V: *Form/Shape (ākāra/ākṛti)*, ed. R.C. Sharma, New Delhi, 2002.

Kālikāpurāṇa — *Kālikāpurāṇa*, trans. B. Shastri, Delhi, 1991.

Kalyāṇ Tīrthāṅk — *Kalyāṇ Tīrthāṅk*, Gorakhpur, 1957 (Hind.).

Kāmasūtra — *The Kama sutra of Vatsyayana*, trans. R. Burton, New York, 1964.

Kāmasūtra — *The Complete Kāma Sutra*, trans. A. Danielou, Rochester, 1994.

Kāmikāgama — *Kāmikāgama*, vol. I: *Pūrvabhāga*, vol. II: *Uttarabhāga*, publ. South Indian Archakar Association, Chennai, 1975, 1988.

Kaṇādasūtravivṛti — *Vaiśeṣikadarśanam*, ed. N. Shiromani, Calcutta, 1886.

Kanhāvat — *Kanhāvat of Malik Muhammad Jāyasī*, ed. P.L. Gupta, Varanasi, 1981.

Kāśyapasaṃhitā — *Kāśyapasaṃhitā of Vṛddhajīvaka*, ed. J. Trikamji & S. Sharma, NSS 1, Kathmandu, (microfiche) 1938.

Kāṭhaka. Die Saṃhitā der Kaṭha-Śākhā, ed. L. von Schroeder, 3 vols., Leipzig, 1900–1910, repr. ed. K.L. Janert, Wiesbaden, 1970.

Kathāsaritsāgara — *The Ocean of Stories* being C.H. Tawneys translation of Somadeva's *Kathā Sarit Sāgara*, ed. N.M. Penzer, 10 vols., Boston, 1924ff.

Kāṭhakasaṃhitā	*Kāṭhaka: Die Saṃhitā der Kaṭha-Śākhā*, 3 vols., ed. L. von Schröder, Leizig, 1900–1910, repr. 1979.
Kaṭhopaniṣad	*Kaṭhopaniṣad No. 3 in Daśopanishads, with the Commentary of Sri Upanishad-Brahma-Yogin*, ed. C. Kunhan Raja, vol. I, Madras, 1935.
Kātyāyanaśrautasūtra	*Kātyāyana-Śrautasūtra: Text with English Translation and Notes*, ed. G.U. Thite, Delhi, 2006.
	Kātyāyana Śrauta Sūtra, ed. and trans. H.G. Ranade, Poona, 1978.
Kaulajñānanirṇaya	"Kaulajñānanirṇaya,", ed. P.C. Bagchi, in: *idem*, *Kaulajñānanirṇaya and Some Minor Texts of the School of Matsyendranātha*, CSS 3, Calcutta, 1934.
Kauśikasūtra	*Altindisches Zauberritual: Probe einer Uebersetzung der wichtigsten Theile des Kauśika Sūtra*, W. Caland, Amsterdam, 1900.
Kauṣītakibrāhmaṇa	*Kauṣītaki Brāhmaṇa: Text*, ed. S. Sarma, VOHD suppl. 9/1, Wiesbaden, 1968.
	The Aitareya and Kauṣītaki Brāhmaṇas of the Rigveda, trans. A.B. Keith, HOS 25, Delhi, 1971.
Kauṣītakyupaniṣad	"Kauṣītaki Upaniṣad," ed. A. Frenz, *IIJ* 11, 1968–1969, 79–129.
Kavitāvalī	*Tulsī Dās: Kavitāvalī*, F.R. Allchin, 1964.
Kāvyanirṇaya	*Bhikhārīdās: Kāvyanirṇaya*, ed. Ved Prakash (Ved Prakāś), Delhi, 2006.
	Bhikhārīdās: Kāvyanirṇaya, ed. J. Caturvedi (Caturvedī), Mathura, 1959.
Khaḍgamālāstotra	*Śrīvidyā Khaḍgamālā*, ed. S.S. Shastri, Madras, 1954.
Khecarīvidyā	*The Khecarīvidyā of Ādinātha: A Critical Edition and Annotated Translation of an Early Text of Haṭhayoga*, ed. J. Mallinson, London, 2007.
Kiraṇāgama	*Bhatta Ramakantha's Commentary on the Kiranatantra, vol. I, chs. 1–6*, ed. D. Goodall, crit. ed., PIFI 86/1, Pondicherry, 1998.
	Kiraṇāgama, ed. T.R. Panchapagesa Sivacharya & K.M. Subrahmanya Sastri, Devakottai, 1932.
Kiraṇatantra	*Bhaṭṭa Rāmakaṇṭha's Commentary on the Kiraṇatantra*, vol. I: *chapters 1–6*, ed. D. Goodall, Pondicherry, 1998.
Kiraṇāvalī	*Kiraṇāvalī*, ed. J.S. Jetly, GaOS 154, Baroda, 1971.
Kiraṇāvalīprakāśa	*Kiraṇāvālī*, appendix (617–706), ed. N.C. Vedantatirtha, BI 200/4, Calcutta, 1956.
Kiraṇāvalīṭīkā	*Kiraṇāvālī*, appendix (617–706), ed. N.C. Vedantatirtha, BI 200/4, Calcutta, 1956.
Kīrtanaghoṣa	*Kīrttana-ghoṣa āru Nāma-ghoṣa*, Śaṅkaradeva, Guwahati, 1962.
Kīrtanalu	*The Complete Kritis of Sri Thyagaraja: Compiled by Maddali Venkata Subbayya, Telugu Script with English Transliteration and Translation*, M.V. Subbayya, Hyderabad, 2008.
	Tyagaraja Keertanalu, K.V. Shastri, 1975.
Kitāb taḥqīq mā li'l-Hind	*Kitāb taḥqīq mā li'l-Hind*, A.R. al-Bīrūnī; ET: E.C. Sachau, *Albērūnī's India*, London, 1910.
Kriyādhikāra	*Kriyādhikāra,* ed. by R.B. Pārthasārathi Bhaṭṭācārya, Tirupati, 1953.
Kriyāsaṃgrahapañjikā	*Kuladatta's Kriyāsaṃgrahapañjikā*, ed. T. Tanemura, Groningen, 2004.
Kṛtyakalpataru	*Kṛtyakalpataru by Bhaṭṭa Lakṣmīdhara*, ed. K.V.R. Aiyyangar, 11 vols., GaOS 92, 98, 100–102, 106, 110–112, 119, 123, Baroda, 1941–1953.
Kṛṣṇasandarbha	*Kṛṣṇasandarbha and Its Critical Study* by Jīva Gosvāmī, ed., Chinmayi Chatterjee, Calcutta, 1986.
Kumārasaṃbhava	*Kālidāsa's Kumārasaṃbhava*, trans. M.R. Kale, cantos I–VIII, 1981, repr. 1986.
Kūrmapurāṇa	*The Kūrma Purāṇa with English Translation*, trans. A. Bhattacharya, S. Mukherji, V.K. Varma & G.S. Rai, ed. A.S. Gupta, Varanasi, 1972.
	Kūrmapurāṇa, ed. A.S. Gupta, Varanasi, 1972.
Laghubhāgavatāmṛta	*Laghubhāgavatāmṛta* by Rūpa Gosvāmī, ed. Bhakti Prajnan Yati, Mayapura, 1995.

Lakṣmītantra	*Lakṣmī Tantra: A Pāñcarātra Text*, trans. S. Gupta, 1972, repr. 2003, 2007.
Lakṣmīviśiṣṭādvaitabhāṣya	*Lakṣmīviśiṣṭādvaitabhāṣya by Śrīnivāsa Dīkṣita, with Sundararāja's Nigamacūḍādarpaṇa commentary*, ed. Addaṅkitirumalai Śrīnivāsa-tātācārya, 1896.
Lalitāsahasranāma	*Lalitāsahasranāma (Taken from Brahmāṇḍapurāṇa), Containing "Saubhagyabhāskara" Sanskrit Commentary of Bhāskararāya, with Hindi Commentary by Shri Bharat Bhushan*, Vrajajivan Prachyabharati Granthamala 43, Delhi, 2009.
Lallā-Vākyāni	*Mystical Verses of Lallā*, J. Kak, Delhi, 2007. *Lallā-Vākyāni: Or The Wise Sayings of Lal Ded*, ed. and trans. G. Grierson & L.D. Barnett, London, 1920.
Laṅkāvatārasūtra	*Laṅkāvatārasūtra*, ed. P.L. Vaidya, BST 3, Darbhanga, 1963.
Līlāvatī	*Līlāvatī*, 2 vols., ed. V.G. Āpaṭe, Pune, 1937.
Liṅgadhāraṇacandrikā	*Lingadhāranachandrikā of Nandikeshwara*, ed. and trans. M.R. Sakhara, Belgaum, n.d. (c. 1942).
	Liṅgadhāraṇacandrikā [of Nandikeśvara], Kāśī, 1905. (Skt.)
Liṅgapurāṇa	*Liṅgapurāṇa of Sage Kṛṣṇa Dvaipāyana Vyāsa, with Sanskrit commentary Śivatoṣiṇī of Gaṇeśa Nātu*, ed. J.L. Shastri, 1985.
Mādhavamahotsava	*Mādhavamahotsava* by Jīva Gosvāmī, Bengali trans. Haridās Dās, Nabadwip, 1942.
Mādhuryakadambinī	*Mādhurya-kadambinī of Viśvanātha Cakravartī*, version 3 (based on three editions), on: www.granthamandira.com (accessed January, 2011).
Mahābhāgavatapurāṇa	*Mahābhāgavatapurāṇa: An Ancient Treatise on Śakti Cult*, ed. P. Kumar, Delhi, 1983.
Mahābhārata	*The Mahābhārata for the First Time Critically Edited*, ed. V.S. Sukthankar, S.K. Belvalkar, F.D. Edgerton *et al.*, 19 vols., Poona, 1927–1966.
	Mahabharata of Krishna-Dwaipayana Vyasa, trans. and ed. K.M. Ganguli, 4 vols., 1883–1896, repr. 2004.
	The Mahābhārata: Book 11. The Book of the Women; Book 12. The Book of Peace. Part One, trans. J. Fitzgerald, Chicago, 2004.
	The Mahābhārata, trans. K.M. Ganguli, New Delhi, 2004.
	The Mahābhārata, vol. II/2: *The Book of the Assembly Hall*; vol. III: *The Book of the Forest*, trans. J.A.B. van Buitenen, Chicago, 1975.
	Das Mahābhārata und seine Theile, 4 vols., ed. A. Holtzmann, Kiel, 1892–1895.
Mahābhāṣya	*Kātyāyana's First Vārttika on Pāṇini's Aṣṭādhyāyī, Mahābhāṣya of Patañjali*, ed. F. Kielhorn, vol. I/2, Pune, ^{3}1962.
	The Vyâkaranamahâbhâshya of Patanjali, ed. F. Kielhorn, 3 vols., Bombay, 1880–1885.
Mahādēviyakkanapurāṇa	*Cannabasavāṅkana Mahādēviyakkana purāṇa*, ed. B.N. Chandraiah, Mysore, 1968.
Mahānuśāsana	*Mathamnay Setu or Mahanushasanam*, P. Mishra, Dwarka, 2001.
Mahārthmañjarī	*Mahārthmañjarī of Maheśvarānanda with the Autocommentary Parimala*, ed. V. Dvivedi, Varanasi, 1972.
Mahāvaṃśa	*Mahāvamsa: The Great Chronicle of Ceylon*, trans. W. Geiger, London, 1912.
Maḫzan al-ʿulūm	*Maḫzan al-ʿulūm*, Vraja Mohana, n.l., 1867.
Maitrāyaṇisaṃhitā	*Maitrāyaṇisaṃhitā: Die Saṃhitā der Maitrāyaṇīya-Śākhā*, ed. L. von Schroeder, 4 vols., Wiesbaden, 1970, 1881–1886.
Maitrāyaṇīyopaniṣad	*The Maitrāyaṇīya Upaniṣad: A Critical Essay, with Text, Translation and Commentary*, ed. and trans. J.A.B. van Buitenen, The Hague, 1962.
	Maitrāyaṇyupaniṣad, in: V.P. Limaye and R.D. Vadekar, eds., *Eighteen Principal Upaniṣads*, vol. I, Poona, 1958, 325–357.

Majjhimanikāya	*Majjhimanikāya*, ed. V. Trenckner & R. Chalmers, London, 1888–1899.
Majmaʿ al-baḥrayn	*Majmaʿ al-baḥrayn*, M. Dārā Šikōh; ET: ed. M. al-Ḥaqq, *Majmaʿ-ul-Baḥrain or the Mingling of the Two Oceans*, Calcutta, 1998.
Mālinīślokavārttika	*Abhinavagupta's Philosophy of Revelation: Mālinīślokavārttika 1, 1–399*, J. Hanneder, Groningen, 1998.
Mālinīvijayavārttika	*Śrī Mālinīvijaya Vārttikam*, ed. M.K., Srinagar, 1921.
Mālinīvijayottaratantra	*The Yoga of the Mālinīvijayottaratantra: Chapters 1–4, 7, 11–17*, S. Vasudeva, Pondicherry, 2004.
	Śrī Mālinīvijayottara Tantram, ed. M.K. Shastri, Delhi, 1984.
Manthānabhairavatantra	*Manthānabhairavatantram Kumārikākhaṇḍaḥ: The Section Concerning the Virgin Goddess of the Tantra of the Churning Bhairava*, 14 vols., ed. and trans. M. Dyczkowski, 2009.
Mantramahodadhi	*Mantramahodadhiḥsaṭīkaḥ*, Bombay, 1910, rev. ed. 1962, repr. 1983.
Manuśāstravivaraṇa	*Bhāruci's Commentary on the Manusmṛti (The Manu-Śāstra-Vivaraṇa, Books 6–12)*, 2 vols., ed. J.D.M. Derrett, Wiesbaden, 1975.
Manusmṛti	*Manu's Code of Law: A Critical Edition and Translation of the Mānava-Dharmaśāstra*, ed. and trans. P. Olivelle, New York, 2005.
	Manusmṛti with the Sanskrit Commentary Manvarthamuktāvalī of Kullūka Bhaṭṭa, ed. J.L. Shastri, Delhi, 1983.
	Manu-Smṛti with the Manubhāṣya of Medhātithi, 2 vols., ed. and trans. G. Jha, 2 vols., Calcutta, 1932–1939.
	Manusmṛti: The Laws of Manu, transl. by W. Doninger with B.K. Smith, New Delhi, 1991.
	Manusmṛti, vols. I–VI, ed. with the commentaries of Medhātithi, Sarvajñanārāyaṇa, Kullūka, Rāghavānanda, Nandana, Rāmacandra, Maṇirāma, Govindarāja, & Bhāruci by J.H. Dave, Bombay, 1972–1984.
	The Laws of Manu, trans. G. Bühler, *Sacred Books of the East*, vol. XXV, Oxford, 1886.
	Manava-Dharma-Sastra or the Institutes of Manu, ed. G.C. Haughton, London, 1825.
Manvarthamuktāvalī	*Manusmṛti with the Sanskrit Commentary Manvarthamuktāvalī of Kullūka Bhaṭṭa*, ed. J.L. Shastri, Delhi, 1983.
Māpāṭiyam	*Civanāṉaptamum vārttikameṉṉum poḻippuraiyum civanāṉacuvāmika ceyta tirāviṭamāpāṭiyam eṉṉum Civanāṉapōtamāpāṭiyamum*, ed. Swaminathapanditar, 1906.
Mārkaṇḍeyapurāṇa	*The Márcaṇḍeya Puráṇa*, ed. K.M. Banerjea, Calcutta, 1862, repr. 1980.
	Mārkaṇḍeya Purāṇa, transl. F.E. Pargiter, Calcutta, 1904.
	Mārkaṇḍeya Purāṇa, Delhi, 1983.
	Mārkaṇḍeyapurāṇa, ed. K.M. Banerjea, Calcutta, 1862.
Mārkaṇḍeyasaṃhitā	*Mārkaṇḍeya Saṃhitā*, Tirupati, 1984.
Mataṅgapārameśvaratantra	*Mataṅgapārameśvaratantra: Kriyāpāda, Caryāpāda and Yogapāda, with the Commentary of Bhaṭṭa Rāmakaṇṭha up to Kriyāpāda 11:12b.*, ed. N.R. Bhatt, PIFI 65, Pondicherry, 1982.
Matsyapurāṇa	*Matsyapurāṇa*, ĀSS 54, Poona, 1907.
Mayamata	*Mayamatam: Treatise of Housing, Architecture and Iconography*, ed. B. Dagens, 2 vols., New Delhi, 1994.
	Traité sanskrit d'architecture, vol. I: *Première Partie: Ch. I à XXV, Edition Critique, Traduction et Notes*, vol. II : *Deuxième Partie: Ch. XXVI–XXXVI et Index-glossaire général, Edition Critique, Traduction et Notes*, by Bruno Dagens, PIFI 40/1–2, Pondichéry, 1970–1976.
Meymmoḻiccaritai	*Iḷaṅkārikkuṭi meymoḻittēvar aruḷiya Meymmoḻiccaritai*, ed. M. Caṇmukam Piḷḷai, Chennai, 1977.

Mīmāṃsābhāṣya — *Śrīmajjaiminipraṇīte Mīmāṃsādarśane Ādita Ārabhya Dvitīyādhyāyaprathamapādāntaḥ [...] Śrīkumārilabhaṭṭviracitatantravārtikāsahitaśābarabhāṣyasametaś ca*, ed. Subbā Śāstrin & Vināyaka Gaṇeśa Āpaṭe [= Āpṭe], ĀSS 97, Pune, 1929.

Mīmāṃsāślokavārttika — *The Mimāṃsāślokavārtika with the Commentary Kāśikā of Sucaritamiśra*, ed. K. Sāmbaśiva Śāstrī, TSS 90, 99, 150, Trivandrum, 1926, 1929, 1943.

(Mīmāṃsā)ślokavārttika, trans. G. Jha, Calcutta, 1907.

A Hindu Critique of Buddhist Epistemology: Kumārila on Perception: The "Determination of Perception" Chapter of Kumārilabhaṭṭa's Ślokavārttika, Translation and Commentary, trans. J. Taber, London, 2005.

Mīmāṃsāsūtrabhāṣyanibandhana — *Der Organizsmus des urheberlosen Veda. Ein Studie der Niyoga-Lehre Prabhākaras mit ausgewählten übersetzungen der Bṛhatī*, K. Yoshimizu, Vienna, 1997.

Miragāvatī — "Miragāvatī of Kutubana: Avadhī Text with Critical Notes," ed. D.F. Plukker, diss., Universiteit van Amsterdam, 1981.

Mṛgendrāgama — *Śrīmṛgendram kāmikopāgamam vidyāyogapādadvayamilitam śrībhaṭṭanārāyaṇakaṇṭh aviracitayā vṛttyā tadvyākhyayāghoraśivācāryaviracaitay ādīpikayā cālaṃkṛtam* (with the commentary *Vṛtti* by Nārāyaṇakaṇṭha and subcommentary *Dīpikā* by Aghoraśivācārya).

Mṛgendrāgamavṛtti — *Śrīmṛgendram kāmikopāgamam vidyāyogapādadvayamilitam śrībhaṭṭanārāyaṇakaṇṭh aviracitayā vṛttyā tadvyākhyayāghoraśivācāryaviracaitayā dīpikayā cālaṃkṛtam* (with the commentary *Vṛtti* by Nārāyaṇakaṇṭha and subcommentary *Dīpikā* by Aghoraśivācārya).

Muhūrtadīpika — *Vidyāmādhavīyam*, vol. I, ed. with Viṣṇu's *Muhūrtadīpika* commentary by R.S. Sastry, Mysore, 1998.

Mūlamadhyamakakārikā — *Mūlamadhyamakakārikās (Mādhyamikasūtras) de Nagarjuna avec la Prasannapadā de Candrakīrti*, ed. L. de la Vallée Poussin, St. Petersburg, 1903.

Muttiniccayam — *Muttiniccayam* (*Muttiniccayamūlamum vel̲l̲iyampalavāṉamuṉi variyar̲r̲iyaruḷiya cir̲r̲uraiyum. nāṉa campanta tēcikacuvāmika*), publ. Progressive Accukkūṭam, Chennai, 1934.

Nācciyār Tirumoḻi — *The Secret Garland: Antal's Tiruppavai and Nacciyar Tirumoli*, trans. A. Venkatesan, New York, 2010.

Naiṣadhacarita — *Naiṣadhacarita of Śrīharṣa*, K.K. Handiqui, Poona, 1956.

Naiṣadhīyacarita — *Naiṣadhīyacarita: With the Commentary of Nārāyaṇa* by Śrīharṣa, ed. Śivadattaśarmā, Lucknow, 1988.

Nāmaghoṣa — *Nāma Ghoṣa*, Mādhavadeva, Jorhat, 1975.

Nālāyira Divya Prabandham — *Nālāyirattivviyappirapantam*, ed. K.V. Rettiyar, Madras, 1981.

Sri Tivyappirapantam, 4 vols., Madras, 1956.

Nalayira Divya Prabandham, http://www.ramanuja.org/sv/prabandham/index.html.

Nāṉāmirtam — *Vākīcamuṉivar aruḷicceyta nāṉāmirtam mūlamum paḻaiya uraiyum* (= *Nāṉāmirtam*), ed. Turaicāmi Piḷḷai, Chidambaram, 1987.

Nāradasmṛti — *The Nāradasmṛti*, 2 vols., ed. and trans. R.W. Lariviere, Philadelphia, 1989.

Nareśvaraparīkṣā — *Nareśvaraparīkṣā with the Commentary Prakāśa by Rāmakaṇṭha*, ed. M.K. Shastri, KSTS 45, Srinagar, 1926.

Nāṭyaśāstra — *Nāṭyaśāstra of Bharatamuni with the Commentary Abhinavabharati*, GaOS 36, Baroda, [2]1956.

Nāṭyaśāstra ascribed to Bharata-Muni (A Treatise on Ancient Indian Dramaturgy and Histrionics), 2 vols., trans. M. Ghosh, CSS 118, Varanasi, 1967, repr. 2007.

	The Nāṭyaśāstra, trans. M. Ghosh, Calcutta, 1961.
	The Nāṭyaśāstra: English Translation with Critical Notes, trans. A. Rangacharya, New Delhi, 1996.
	Nāṭyaśāstra of Bharatamuni with the Commentary Abhinavabhāratī by Abhinavaguptāchārya, 4 vols., ed. Dr. R.S. Nagar and K.L. Joshi. Delhi, 1981–1984.
Navanādhacharitra	*Navanādhacharitra of Gauraṇa*, ed. K. Ramakrishnaiya, MUTS 7, Madras, 1937.
Navyanyāyabhāṣāpradīpa	*Navyanyāya-bhāṣāpradīpaḥ*, ed. M. Nyayaratna, Calcutta, 1973.
Nemināthapurāṇa	*The Epic of Nemi (Neminātha-purāṇa) of Karṇapārya*, S. Anacker, Shravanabelagola, 2002.
Netratantra	*Netratantram (Mṛtyuñjaya Bhattārakaḥ) with the Commentary Udyota of Kṣemarājācārya*, ed. V. Dvivedi, Delhi, 1985.
	Netratantra with Commentary (Uddyota) by Kṣemarāja, ed. M.K. Shastri, KSTS 46, Srinagar, 1926.
Netratantroddyota	*Netratantra with Commentary (Uddyota) by Kṣemarāja*, ed. M.K. Shastri, KSTS 46, Srinagar, 1926.
Nigamacūḍādarpaṇa	*Lakṣmīviśiṣṭādvaitabhāṣya by Śrīnivāsa Dīkṣita, with Sundararāja's Nigamacūḍādarpaṇa commentary*, ed. Addaṅkitirumalai Śrīnivāsatātācārya, 1896.
Niśvāsatattvasaṃhitā	**Niśvāsatattvasaṃhitā*, ms. 1–227 at the National Archives Kathmandu, Kathmandu, n.d.
Nītisāra	*The Nītisāra by Kāmandaki*, ed. and trans. R. Mitra, Calcutta, 1861.
Nityāṣoḍaśikārṇava	*(Vāmakeśvaratantrāntargataḥ) nityāṣoḍaśikārṇavaḥ. Śrībhāskararāyonnītasetubandhākhyavyākhyāsahitaḥ*, ed. K.V. Abhyaṃkar, Pune, 1973.
Nityotsava	*Nityotsava of Umānandanātha (Supplement to Paraśurāma-kalpa-sūtra)*, ed. A. Mahadeva Sastri, rev. and enlarged by Trivikrama Tirtha, Baroda, 1977.
Nṛsimhaśatakamu	*Nṛsimhaśatakamu* by T. Veṅgamāmba, ed. K.J. Krishnamurti, Tirupati, 2007.
Nyāyakandalī	*Padārthadharmasaṅgraha*, ed. V.S. Dvivedin, VZS 4, Varanasi, 1895.
Nyāyakandalīpañjikā	*Nyāyakandalīpañjikā*, ed. J.S. Jetly & V.G. Parikh, GaOS 174, Baroda, 1991.
Nyāyakumudacandra	*Nyāyakumudacandra of Śrimat Prabhācandrācārya*, ed. M. Jain, Bombay, 1938.
Nyāyakusumāñjali	*Nyāyakusumāñjali: Edited with Hindi Translation*, D. Jha, Varanasi, 1973.
Nyāyalīlāvatī	*Nyāyalīlāvatī*, ed. H. Shastri & D. Shastri, CSS 64, Varanasi, 1927–1934.
Nyāyamañjarī	*Nyāyamañjarī*, ed. Pt. Surya Narayan Shukla, Banaras, 1936.
Nyāyamañjarīgranthibhaṅga	*Nyāyamañjarīgranthibhaṅga of Cakradhara*, ed. N.J. Shah, Ahmedabad, 1972.
Nyāyasāra	*Nyāyasāra*, ed. V.S. Abhyankar, Pune, 1922.
Nyayasūtra	*Nyayasūtras: Nyāyadarśana: Text with Vātsyāyana's Bhāṣya*, ed. by A. Thakur, Darbhanga, 1967.
	Gautama's Nyāyasūtras (with Vātsyāyana-Bhāṣya) Translated into English, trans. G. Jha, Poona, 1939.
	Nyāyadarśanam, ed. by Tarkatirthas, 1936–1944.
	Die Nyāyasūtra's, ed. W. Ruben, Leipzig, 1928.
Nyāyavārttika	*Nyāyavārttika*, ed. A. Thakur, NCG 2, New Delhi, 1997.
Nyāyavārttikatātparyaṭīkā	*Nyāyavārttikatātparyaṭīkā*, ed. A. Thakur, NCG 3, New Delhi, 1996.
Padārthadharmasaṃgraha	*Praśastapādabhāṣya (Padārthadharmasaṅgraha) with Commentary Nyāyakandalī of Śrīdharabhaṭṭa*, ed. D.J. Sharman, Varanasi, 1963.
	Padārthadharmasaṅgraha, ed. V.S. Dvivedin, VZS 4, Varanasi, 1895.

Padārthasaṃgrahaṭīkā	*Padārthasaṅgrahaṭīkā*, ed. G. Kaviraj & D. Shastri, CSS 61, Varanasi, 1930.
Padāvalī	*The Hindi Padāvalī of Nāmdev*, ed. W.M. Callewaert & M. Lath, Delhi, 1989.
Padmapurāṇa	*Padma Purāṇa*, ĀSS 131, Poona, 1893. *Padmamahāpurāṇa*, Delhi, 1895, repr. 1984.
Pādmasaṃhitā	*Padma Samhita*, crit. ed. by Seetha Padmanabhan and R.N. Sampath (part 1), Seetha Padmanabhan and V. Varadachari (part 2), PPPS 3, 4, Madras, 1974, 1982.
Padmāvatī	*The Padumāwati of Malik Muḥammad Jaisi*, ed. G.A.Grierson & S. Dvivedi, Calcutta, 1911.
Paitāmahasiddhānta	"The Paitāmahasiddhānta of the Viṣṇudharmottarapurāṇa," ed. D. Pingree, *Brahmavidyā* 31/32, 1967/1968, 472–510.
Pampāmāhātmya	"Pampāmāhātmya," in: V. Filliozat, *Kālāmukha and Pāśupata Temples in Dharwar*, app. 2, 4, Chennai, 2000.
Pañcapādikā	*Pañcapādikā of Śri Padmapādācārya and Pañcapādikāvivaraṇa of Śrī Prakāśātman*, ed. S. Shastri, S., & S.R.K. Shastri, Madras, 1958.
Pañcapādikāvivaraṇa	*Pañcapādikā of Śri Padmapādācārya and Pañcapādikāvivaraṇa of Śrī Prakāśātman*, ed. S. Shastri, S., & S.R.K. Shastri, Madras, 1958.
Pañcaprakriyā	*Pañcaprakriyā of Sarvajñātman*, ed. T.R. Chintamani, Madras, 1946.
Pāñcarātrarakṣā	*Śrī Pāñcarātra Rakṣā of Śrī Vedānta Deśika*, crit. ed. with Notes and Variant Readings by M. Duraiswami Aiyangar and T. Venugopalacharya with an Introduction in English by G. Srinivasa Murti, ALS 36, Madras, 1942.
Pañcārthabhāṣya	"Pañcārthabhāṣya on Pāśupatasūtra 1.37–39: Recovered from a Newly Identified Manuscript," P. Bisschop, *JIPh* 33/5–6, 2005, 529–551. *Pāśupatasūtra with Kauṇḍinya's Pañcārthabhāṣya*, ed. A. Sastri, TSS 143, Trivandrum, 1940.
Pañcasiddhāntikā	*The Pañcasiddhāntikā of Varāhamihira*, part 1–2, ed. and trans. D. Pingree; comm. O. Neugebauer & D. Pingree, HFS 6/1, Copenhagen, 1970.
Pañcāvaraṇastava	*The Pañcāvaraṇastava of Aghoraśivācārya: A Twelfth-Century South Indian Prescription for the Visualisation of Sadāśiva and His Retinue*, ed. D. Goodall *et al.*, Pondicherry, 2005.
Parabrahmotthāpanasthala	"Jain Arguments against Vedānta Monistic Theism: A Translation of the *Parabrahmotthāpanasthala* of Bhuvanasundarasūri," F. van den Bossche, *JIPh* 25/4, 1997, 337–374.
Parākhyatantra	*The Parākhyatantra: A Scripture of the Śaiva Siddhānta*, ed. D. Goodall, Pondicherry, 2004.
Paramārthasāra	*Introduction to Tantric Philosophy: The Paramārthasāra of Abhinavagupta with the Commentary of Yogarāja*, ed. L. Bansat-Boudon & K. Tripathi, London, 2010. *Paramārthasāra of Abhinavagupta with the Commentary of Yogaraja*, publ. Kashmir Research Department, KSTS 7, Srinagar, 1916.
Paramasaṃhitā	*Paramasaṃhitā [of the Pāñcharātra]*, ed. and trans. into English with an introduction by S. Krishnaswami Aiyangar, GaOS 86, Baroda, 1940.
Pārameśvarasaṃhitā	*Pārameśvarasaṃhitā Govindācāryaiḥ saṃskṛtā, anekavidhādarśādibhiḥ saṃyojitā ca*, Srirangam, 1953.
Paramōpatecam	*Śrīmaṟaiṉāṉacampantaṉāyaṉar aruḷicceyta caivac ciṟu nūlkaḷ (mutaṟpakuti)*, ed. T.C. Mīṉāṭcicuntaram Piḷḷai, Thiruvavaduthurai, 1954.
Parātriṃśikātattvavivaraṇa	*Il commento di Abhinavagupta alla Parātriṃśikā (Parātriṃśikātattvavi varaṇam): Traduzione e testo by Abhinavagupta*, ed. R. Gnoli, Rome, 1985.
Parātriśikālaghuvṛtti	*Parātriśikālaghuvṛtti and Parātriśikāvivṛtti*, ed. by J. Zadoo Shastri, Srinagar, 1947.

Parātrīśikāvivaraṇa — *A Trident of Wisdom: Translation of Parātrīśikā-Vivaraṇa*, trans. J. Singh, Albany, 1989.

Paripāṭal — *Paripāṭal*, ed. and Fr. transl. by F. Gros, 1968.

Pāśupatasūtra — *Pāśupatasūtra with Kauṇḍinya's Pañcārthabhāṣya*, ed. A. Sastri, TSS 143, Trivandrum, 1940.
"The Sūtrapāṭha of the Pāśupatasūtra," P. Bisschop, *IIJ* 49/1–2, 2006, 1–21.

Paticupācappaṉuvah — *Śrīmaṟaiṉāṉacampantanāyaṉar aruḷicceyta caivac ciṟu nūlkaḷ (mutaṟpakuti)*, ed. T.C. Mīṉāṭcicuntaram Piḷḷai, Thiruvavaduthurai, 1954.

Pātravidhi — "The Pātravidhi: A Lakulīśa Pāśupata Manual on Purification and Use of the Initiate's Pot," D. Acharya, in: C. Watanabe, M. Desmarais & Y. Honda, eds., *Saṃskṛtasādhutā: Studies in honour of Professor Ashok Aklujkar*, New Delhi, 2011, 1–28.

Pauṣkarāgama — *Pauṣkarasaṃhitā (jnānapādaḥ) śrīmadumāpatiśivācāryaviracitabhāṣyopetā*, ed. P. Ramasastri, Chidambaram, 1925.

Pauṣkarasaṃhitā — *Śrīpāñcarātrāgame Ratnatrayāntargatā Śrīpauṣkarasaṃhitā/Sree Poushkara Samhita, One of the Three Gems in Pancharatra*, ed. His Holiness Sree Yatiraja Sampathkumara Ramanuja Muni of Melkote, Bangalore, 1934.

Pavanadūta — *Pavanadūtam* by Dhoyī (Dhoyika), ed. Chintaharan Chakravarti, Calcutta, 1926. "Pavanadūtam: With an Appendix on the Sena Kings," in: Monmohan Chakravarti, ed., *Journal and Proceedings of the Asiatic Society of Bengal, New Series* 1, 1905, 41–71.

Picumata — see *Brahmayāmala*

Prabhuliṅgalīle — Basawanal, S.S., ed., *Cāmarasa kṛta Prabhuliṅgalīle*, Dharwar, 1971.

Prahlāda Bhakti Vijayam — *Tyāgarāja's Prahlāda Bhakti Vijayam*, P. Sambamoorthy, 1965.

Pramāṇavārttikabhāṣya — *Pramāṇavārttikabhāṣyam or Vārtikālaṅkāraḥ of Prajñākaragupta*, ed. R. Sāṅkṛtyāyana, Patna, 1953.

Pramāṇavārttikavṛttiṭīkā — *Pramāṇavārttikavṛttiṭīkā of KarṇakagominI*, ed. R. Sāṅkṛtyāyana, Allahabad, 1944.

Pramāṇaviniścaya — *Dharmakīrti's Pramāṇaviniścaya: Chapters 1 and 2*, ed. E. Steinkellner, Vienna, 2007.

Pratimānāṭaka — *Pratimānāṭaka of Bhāsa: Edited with Introd., Translation, Critical and Explanatory Notes and Appendices*,by Shivaram Mahadeo Paranjape, Poona, 1927.

Praśnatantra — *Tājikanīlakaṇṭhī* (including *Praśnatantra*), ed. with Viśvanātha's commentary, Hind. trans. and commentary by Kedāradatta Jośī, Delhi, 2008.

Pratyabhijñāhṛdaya — *Pratyabhijñāhṛdayam: The Secret of Self-Recognition*, ed. J. Singh, Delhi, 1980.

Prāyaścittavidhi — "The Prāyaścittavidhi: A Manual on Atonement of the Lakulīśa Pāśupatas," D. Acharya, *JIS*, forthcoming.

Rādhākṛṣṇagaṇoddeśadīpikā — *Rādhākṛṣṇagaṇoddeśadīpikā* by Rūpa Gosvāmī, ed. Medinīndralāla Mitra, Calcutta, n.d.

Ragales — *Mahākavi Hampeya Hariharadevakṛta Nūtana Purātanara Ragalegalu*, ed. M.S. Sunkapura, Dharwar, 1976.

Raghuvaṃśa — *The Raghuvaṃśa of Kālidāsa, with the Commentary of Mallinātha*, ed. G.R. Nandargikar, Delhi, ^{4}1971.

Rahasyatrayasāra — *Srimad Rahasyatrayasiira of Srf Vedantadesika*, trans. M.R. Rajagopala Ayyangar, Kumbakonam, 1956.

Rājamārtaṇḍa — *Yogasūtras of Patañjali with Bhojavṛtti called Rājamārtaṇḍa (in English Translation)*, J.R. Ballantyne & G.S. Deva, ed. with introduction by A.C. Sastri, Delhi, 1990.

Rājataraṅgiṇī	*Rājataraṅgiṇī of Jonarāja* by Jonaraja, trans. J.C. Dutt, Delhi, 1986.
Rājayogāmṛtasāramu	*Rājayogāmṛtasāramu*, ed. K.J. Krishnamurti, Tirupati, 2007.
Rāmabhadradīkṣita	*The Patañjali-charita*, KM 51, Bombay, 1985.
Rāmānandajanmotsava	*Rāmānandajanmotsava, Paṇḍit-Rāmnārāyaṇadāsajī kṛta bhāṣāṭīkayā'laṅkṛtā*, Raṇahar Pustakālaya, Dakor, 1906.
Rāmavijaya	*Rāmavijaya: śabārtha ślokārtha o baragīta sahita*, Śaṅkaradeva, Darbhanga, 1989.
Rāmāyaṇa	*The Vālmīki Rāmāyaṇa: Critical Edition*, ed. G.H. Bhatt & U.P. Shah, 7 vols., Baroda, 1960–1975.
	The Ramayana of Valmeelti in the original Sungscrit with a Prose Translation and Explanatory Notes, 5 vols., ed. W. Carey & J. Marshman, Serampore, 1806–1810, repr. 1823.
	The Rāmāyaṇa of Vālmīki: An Epic of Ancient India, vol. I: *Bālakāṇḍa*, ed. R. P. Goldman, annotation by R.P. Goldman & S.J. Sutherland, Princeton, 1984.
	The Rāmāyaṇa of Vālmīki: An Epic of Ancient India, vol. II: *Ayodhyākāṇḍa*, trans. S.I. Pollock, ed. R.P. Goldman, Princeton, 1986.
	The Rāmāyaṇa of Vālmīki: An Epic of Ancient India, vol. III: *Araṇyakāṇḍa*, trans. S.I. Pollock, ed. R.P. Goldman, Princeton, 1991.
	The Rāmāyaṇa of Vālmīki: An Epic of Ancient India, vol. IV: *Kiṣkindhākāṇḍa*, trans. R. Lefeber, ed. R.P. Goldman, Princeton, 1994.
	The Rāmāyaṇa of Vālmīki: An Epic of Ancient India, vol. V: *Sundarakāṇḍa*, ed. R.P. Goldman & S.J. Sutherland, Princeton, 1996.
	The Rāmāyaṇa of Vālmīki: An Epic of Ancient India, vol. VI: *Yuddhakāṇḍa*, ed. R.P. Goldman & S.J. Sutherland, Princeton, 2009.
	The Rāmāyaṇa of Vālmīki, trans. H.P. Shastri, 3 vols., London, 1952–1959, rev. ed. 1962.
	Ramayana id es carmen epicum de Ramae rebus gestis poetae antiquissimi Valmicis opus. 3 vols., ed. and trans. A.W. von Schlegel, Bonn, 1829–1838.
	The Yuddhakāṇḍa: The Sixth Book of the Vālmīki-Rāmāyaṇa: The National Epic of India, ed. P.L. Vaidya, Baroda, 1971.
Rāmcaritamānas	*Tulsīdās, Rāmcaritamānas*, ed. S.N. Chaube, Kashi, 1947.
	The Rāmāyaṇa of Tulsi Dās, trans. F.S. Growse, Cawnpore, 1891, rev. ed. Delhi, 1978.
	Tulsi Ramayan in English Verse, S.D. Gupta, New Delhi, 2010.
	Tulasidasa's Shriramacharitamanasa, R.C. Prasad, 1988.
	The Gospel of Love: An English Rendering of Tulasi's Shri Rama Charita Manasa, C.L. Dhody, 1987.
	The Ramayana of Tulsidas, A.G. Atkins, 2 vols., 1966.
	The Holy Lake of the Acts of Rāma, W.D.P. Hill, London, 1952.
	Śrī Rāmacharitamānasa: Or the Mānasa Lake Brimming over with Exploits of Śrī Rāma, C. Goswami, 1949.
Rasagaṅgādhara	*The Rasagaṅgādhara: With the Commentary of Nāgeśa Bhaṭṭa by Jagannātha*, ed. Paṇḍit Durgāprasād & Kāśināth Parab, Bombay, 1888.
Rasasāra	*Rasasāra*, ed. G. Jha & G. Kaviraj, PWSBTS 5, Varanasi, 1922.
Rashasyatrayasāram	*Śrīmadrashasyatrayasāram: With the Commentary Sāravistaram of Abhinava Tēcika Vīrārākavācāryiar*, Veṅkaṭanātha (Vedāntadeśika), 2 vols., Madras, 1980.
Ratnaṭīkā	*Gaṇakārikā, with the Ratnaṭīkā of Bhāsarvajña*, ed., C.D. Dalal, GaOS 15, Baroda, 1920, repr. 1966.
Ratnatraya	*Aṣṭaprakaraṇamtattvaprakāśatattvasaṅgrahatattvatrayanirṇayaratnatrayabhogakārikānādakārikāmokṣakārikāparamokṣanirāsakārikākhyasiddhānta-*

	śaivīyāṣṭagranthānām saṭī kānām samāhāraḥ, ed. V. Dviveda, Varanasi, 1988.
Rauravāgama	*Rauravāgama*, 3 vols., ed. N.R. Bhatt, PIFI 18, Pondicherry, crit. ed. 1961, 1985 (repr. 1972), 1988.
Record of Buddhistic Kingdoms	*A Record of Buddhistic Kingdoms Being an Account by the Chinese Monk Fa-Hein of Travels in India and Ceylon (AD 399–414) in Search of the Buddhist Books of Discipline*, trans. J. Legge, ^{1}1986, 1991.
Ṛgveda	*Ṛgveda-Saṁhitā: The Sacred Hymns of the Brāhmans Together with the Commentary of Sāyanāchārya*, ed. F.M. Müller, vols. 1–5, Varanasi, ^{1}1890.
	Der Rig-Veda, aus dem Sanskrit ins Deutsche, trans. K.F. Geldner, 3 vols., Cambridge MA, 1951.
	Rig Veda: A Metrically Restored Text With an Introduction and Notes, ed. B.A. van Nooten & G.B. Holland, HOS 50, Cambridge MA, 1994.
	Ṛg Veda, trans. W. Doniger, New York, 1981.
	Die Hymnen des Ṛigveda, T. Aufrecht, 2 vols., Bonn, 1887.
Śābdabodhamīmāṃsā	*Śābdabodhamīmāṃsā: An Inquiry into Indian Theories of Verbal Cognition*, ed. N.S.R. Tatacharya, New Delhi, 2005–2008.
Sabhālakṣaṇa Mattu Prasaṅga Pīṭhike	*Yakṣagāna Sabhālakṣaṇa Mattu Prasaṅga Pīṭhike (Vaṃśāvaḷi Sahitavāgi)*, Udupi, 1967.
Ṣaḍdarśanasamuccaya	*Ṣaḍdarśanasamuccaya of Haribhadra*, ed. L. Suali, Calcutta, 1905; ET in: D. Chattopadhyaya & M.K. Gangopadhyaya, *Cārvāka/Lokāyata: An Anthology of Source Materials and Some Recent Studies*, Delhi, 1990, 257–297.
	Ṣaḍdarśanasamuccaya (of Rājaśekhara), ed. Haragovindadas & Becardas, ŚYJG 17, Varanasi, ^{2}1913.
Ṣaddarśanasamuccaya Laghuvṛtti	*Tarkarahasyadīpikā*, Appendix I, ed. M. Jain, JMGSG 36, New Delhi, ^{2}1981.
Sādhanadīpikā	*Sādhanadīpikā* by Rādhākṛṣṇa Gosvāmī, ed. Haridāsa Śāstrī, Vrindavan, n.d.
Saduktikarṇāmṛta	*Saduktikarṇāmṛta* by Śrīdharadāsa, ed. Sureś Chandra Banerji, Calcutta, 1965.
Śaivāgamādimāhātmyasaṃgraha	*Śaivāgamādimāhātmyasaṃgraha of Jnānaprakāśa*, ed. T. Ganesan, forthcoming.
Śāktānandataraṅgiṇī	*Brahmanandagiri's Sakatanandtarangini: Text with Hindi Translation*, ed. R.K. Rai, Varanasi, 1993.
Śāktopaniṣads	*The Śākta Upaniṣads*, tarns. A.G. Krishna Warrrier, Madras, 1967.
Samāj Śṛṅkhalā	*Samāj-Śriṅkhalā*, ed. Govinda Saran Sastri, Vrindaban, 1988 (Hind.).
Saṃbandhavārtika	*The Saṃbandha-Vārtika of Sureśvarācārya*, ed. and trans. T.M.P. Mahadevan, Madras, 1972.
Sāṃkhyakārikā	"Sāṃkhyakārikā: Sanskrit and English," in: G.J. Larson, *Classical Sāṃkhya: An Interpretation of Its History and Meaning*, Delhi, 1979, 235–277.
	The Sāṅkhyakārikā of Īśvara Kṛṣṇa, trans. S.S.S. Sastri, Madras, repr. 1973.
	"Sāṃkhyakārikā," in: R.C. Pandeya, ed., *Yuktidīpikā: An Ancient Commentary on the Sāṃkhya-Kārikā of Īśvarakṛṣṇa*, Delhi, 1967, app. 1.
Sāṃkhyasāra	*Sāṃkhyasāra: Text and Translation with Notes by Dr. Shiv Kumar*, ed. and trans. S. Kumar, Delhi, 1988.

Sāṃkhyasūtra — *The Sāṃkhya Aphorisms of Kapila*, trans. and ed. I. . Ballantyne, Delhi, repr. 1984.

Saṃyuttanikāya — *Saṃyuttanikāya*, ed. L. Feer, 1884–1898.

Saṃkṣepaśārīraka — *Saṃkṣepaśārīrakam*, ed. H.N. Apte, Poona, 1918.

Saṃskāravidhi — "The Saṃskāravidhi: A Manual on the Transformatory Rite of the Lakulīśa-Pāśupatas," D. Acharya, in: D. Goodall & A. Padoux, eds., *Tantric Studies in Memory of Hélène Brunner*, CI 106, Pondicherry, 2007.

Śaṅkaradevamādhavadevar Jīvanacaritra — *Śaṅkaradeva-Mādhavadevar Jīvana-caritra*, D. Ṭhākura, Tezpur, 1900.

Śaṅkaravijaya — *Śaṅkaravijaya*, ed. J. Tarkapanchánana, Calcutta, 1868.

Sant Guṇ Sāgar — *Śrī sant guṇ sāgar, by Mādhavdās, ed. and comm.*, ed. S. Śāstrī, Bhairana, VS 2056 (= 1999–2000) (Hind.).

Santavijaya — *Rāmdās: Translation of Mahipatī's Santavijaya*, J.E. Abbott, Poona, 1932.
Mahārāṣṭrakavisantamālā, n. 8, Rāmdās, Mahipatīkṛta Santavijāyance, n.d.; ET: *The Poet-Saints of Mahārāshtra, No. 8, Rāmdās, Translation of Mahipatī's Santavijaya*, J.E. Abbott, 1932.

Saptapdārthī — *Saptapdārthī: Edited with Introduction, Translation, and Notes*, D. Gurumurti, Madras, 1943.

Saptatiratnamālikā — "Saptatiratnamālikā," in: *Guruparamparā Prabhāvam of Śrī Brahmatantrasvatantra Swāmi*, S. Aṇṇaṉ, Śrī Prativādi Bhayaṅkara, Madras, 1968, 53–67.

Śāradātilaka — *Śāradātilakam of Śrī Lakśmaṇadeśikendra* [*sic*] *with Padārthādarśa Commentary by Śrīmad Rāghava Bhaṭṭa*, ed. M. Jha Bakshi. Varanasi, [3]1986.

Śārṅgadharapaddhati — *Śārṅgadharapaddhati*, ed. P. Peterson, Bombay, 1888.

Sarvadarśanasaṃgraha — *Sarvadarśanasaṃgraha of Mādhavācārya: Sanskrit Text, English Translation, Notes and Appendix*, transl. by E.B. Cowell & A.E. Gough, ed. by K.L. Joshi, Delhi, 1986.
Sarvadarśanasaṃgraha of Sāyaṇa-Mādhava: Edited with an Original Commentary in Sanskrit, ed. V.S. Abhyankar, Poona, 1924, [2]1978.

Sarvajnanottarāgama — **Sarvajnanottarāgama*, paper transcript (T.334) at the French Institute of Pondicherry, n.d.

Sarvamūlagrantha — *Sarvamūlagranthāḥ*, ed. Prabhanjanacharya, Bangalore, 1999.
Sarvamūlagranthāḥ, ed. B. Govindācārya, 5 vols. Bangalore,, 1969–1974.

Sarvāṅgī — *The Sarvāṅgī of Gopāldās*, ed. W.M. Callewaert, Delhi, 1993.

Sarvānukramaṇī — *Kātyāyana's Sarvānukramaṇī of the Rigveda, with Extracts from Shadgurusishya's Commentary Entitled Vedārthadīpikā*, ed. A.A. Macdonell, Oxford, 1886.

Sarvasamvādinī — *Sarvasamvādinī with Commentary Cūrṇikā by Jīva Gosvāmī* by Jīva Gosvāmī, ed. Purīdās, Vrindavan, 1953.

Śatakatrayādisubhāṣitasaṃgraha — *Śatakatrayādi-subhāṣitasaṃgraha: The Epigrams Attributed to Bhartṛhari*, ed. D.D. Kosambi, Bombay, 1948.

Śatapathabrāhmaṇa — *The Çatapatha Brāhmaṇa in the Mādhyandina-Çākhā with Extracts from the Commentaries of Sāyaṇa, Harisvāmin and Dvivedaganga*, ed. A. Weber, CSS 96, Varanasi, 1855, repr. 1964.
Śatapathabrāhmaṇa, ed. C. Shastri, P. Shastri & R. Dikshita, Varanasi, [3]1998.
Śatapatha Brāhmaṇa: Śrīmadvājasaneyimādhyandinaśatapathabrāhmaṇam (with Sāyaṇa's Commentary and the Commentary by Śrī Hari Svāmī), ed. by "Several Learned Persons," n.d.
Śatapathabrahmaṇa, trans. by J. Eggeling, Part 1–4, Motilal Banarasidass, Delhi, 1963.

Śataratnasaṃgraha — *Śataratnasaṃ grahaḥ saṭīkaḥ umāpatiśivācāryasaṃgṛhītaḥ pancānana śāstrisampāditaḥ* (= *Śataratnasaṃgraha*), ed. P. Sastri, Calcutta, 1944.

Ṣaṭsāhasrasaṃhitā — *The Ṣaṭsāhasrasaṃhitā Chapters 1–5*, ed. and trans. J.A. Schoterman, Leiden, 1982.

Ṣaṭsthalasiddhānta	*Sri Siddalingeshwara Shatsthala Siddanta*, G.S. Bale, Edison, 1997.
Sāttvatasaṃhitā	*The Sāttvata Saṃhitā with Comment[a]ry by Alaśiṅga Bhaṭṭa*, Foreword by Dr. Gaurinath Shastri, ed. Vajra Vallabha Dwivedi, LRTP 6, Varanasi, 1982.
Śaunakīyācaturādhyāyikā	*Śaunakīyā Caturādhyāyikā: A Prātiśākhya of the Śaunakīya Atharvaveda*, ed. M.M. Deshpande, Cambridge UK, 1997.
Saundaryalaharī	*Saundarya-Laharī of Śrī Śaṃkarācārya: With Commentaries Saubhāgyavardhanī of Kaivalyāśrama, Lakṣmīdharā of Lakṣmīdharācārya, Aruṇāmodinī of Kāmeśvarasūrin, English Translation and Notes*, by R. Anantakṛṣṇa Śāstrī and K.R. Gāru, Prayogas illustrated with Yantras, Madras, 1957.
	Saundarya-Lahari of Sri Samkara-Bhagavatpada, ed. S. Sastri & S. Ayengar, Madras, 1937.
	Saundaryalaharī of Śaṅkarācārya with the Lakṣmīdhara Commentary, ed. S. Malaviya, Vrajajivan Prachyabharati Granthamala 101, Delhi, 2009.
	Saundarya-Laharī of Sri Sankaracārya, Tapasyananda, Chennai, 1987.
	The Saundaryalahari: Or Flood of Beauty Traditionally Ascribed to Śaṅkarācārya, ed. and trans. W.N. Brown, HOS 43, Cambridge, 1958.
Sekaśubhodaya	*Sekaśubhodaya of Halayudha Miśra*, ed. S. Sen, BIS, 286, Calcutta, 1963.
Siddhāntaleśasaṃgraha	*Appayya Dīkṣita: Siddhāntaleśasaṃgraha*, ed. and trans. S.S. Suryanarayana Shastri, Madras, 1937.
Siddhāntamuktavālī	*Bhāṣāpariccheda with Siddhānta-muktavālī by Viśvanātha-nyāyapañcānana,* trans. by Swami Madhvananda, Kolkata, 2004.
Siddhāntapaṭal	*Siddhānta Paṭal* by Rāmānanda, Śrī Durgā Pustak Bhaṇḍār, Allahabad, n.d.
Siddhāntasārāvali	*Siddhāntasārāvali of Trilocanaśiva* (with the commentary of Anantaśambhu), publ. in: *BGOMLM* 17–20, Chennai.
Siddhasiddhāntapaddhati	*Siddhasiddhāntapaddhati of Gorakṣanātha*, ed. M.L. Gharote & G.K. Pai, Lonavla, 2005.
Siddhasiddhāntasaṃgraha	*Siddhasiddhāntasaṃgraha*, ed. G.N. Kaviraja, PWSBT13, Benares City, 1925.
Siddhitrayī	*The Siddhitrayī and the Īśvarapratyabhijākārikāvṛtti,* ed. M.K. Shastri, Srinagar, 1921.
Siddhitrayi	*Sri Yamunacharya's Siddhi Trayi*, ed. R. Ramanujachari & K. Srinivasacharya, Madras, 1972.
Śivadṛṣṭi	*The Śivadṛṣṭi of Śrīsomānandanātha with the Vṛtti by Utpaladeva*, ed. M.K. Shastri, Pune, 1934.
Śivajnānabodha	*Śivajnānabodha with with the Commentary Called Jnānāvaraṇabhāṣya by Veḷḷiyampalavāṇamuṉivar*, ed. T. Ganesan, forthcoming.
	Śivajnānabodhaḥ: Śivajnānabodha with the Laghuṭīkā of Śivāgrayogī, ed. T. Ganesan, Chennai, crit. ed. 2003.
	Śivajnānabodhavṛttiḥ jnānaprakāśāyāryeṇa viracitā, ed. Muttukkumaracuvami, Jaffna, Kali year 5029.
	Śivajnānabodha with the commentary called Vṛtti by Sadāśivaśivācārya, publ. in: *BGOMLM* 16/1, Chennai, 1963.
	Śivajnānabodhaḥ śrīmacchivāgrabhāṣyopetaḥ, ed. D. Tampiran & K. Sastri, Kumbakonam, n.d.
Śivajnānabodhavṛtti	*Śivajnānabodhavṛttiḥ jnānaprakāśāyāryeṇa viracitā*, ed. Muttukkumaracuvami, Jaffna, Kali year 5029.
	Śivajnānabodha with the commentary called Vṛtti by Sadāśivaśivācārya, publ. in: *BGOMLM* 16/1, Chennai, 1963.
Śivajnānabodhopanyāsa	*Śivajnānabodhopanyāsaḥ*: *A Commentary on the Śivajnānabodha by Nigamajnānadeśika*, ed. T. Ganesan, New Delhi, crit. ed. 2009.

Śivamahimnastava — *Śivamahimnastava of Puṣpadanta*, ed. Narayanapatisarma, Varanasi, 21983.

Śivapurāṇa — *Śivamahāpurāṇam*, parts I and II, ed. K. Kṛṣṇadāsa & K. Puṣpendra, 1986.
The Śivamahāpurāṇam, vol. I, Delhi, 1986.
Śiva-Purāṇa, parts I–IV, 1969–1970, repr. 1982–1987.

Śivasaṃhitā — *Śivasaṃhitā*, ed. J. Mallinson, New York, 2007.

Śivasūtra — *The Aphorisms of Śiva: The Śiva Sūtra with Bhāskara's Commentary, the Vārttika*, trans. M.S.G. Dyczkowski, Albany, 1992.
Śivasūtras: The Yoga of Supreme Identity; Text of the Sūtras and the Commentary Vimarśinī of Kṣemarāja, ed. and trans. J. Singh, Delhi, 1979.

Śivasūtravārttika — *The Aphorisms of Śiva: The Śiva Sūtra with Bhāskara's Commentary, the Vārttika*, trans. M.S.G. Dyczkowski, Albany, 1992.

Śivasūtravimarśinī — *Śivasūtras: The Yoga of Supreme Identity; Text of the Sūtras and the Commentary Vimarśinī of Kṣemarāja*, ed. and trans. J. Singh, Delhi, 1979.

Skandapurāṇa — *The Skandamahāpurāṇa*, ed. K. Śrīkṛṣṇadāsa, Delhi, 1867, repr. 1986.
Skandamahāpurāṇam, ed. K. Kṣemarāja & N. Siṃha, 1986–1987.
The Skandapurāṇa, Volume 1, Adhyāyas 1–25: Critically Edited with Prolegomena and English Synopsis, ed. R. Adriaensen, H.T. Bakker & H. Isaacson, Groningen, 1998.
Studies in the Skandapurāṇa, vol. III: *Harānandalaharī: Volume in Honour of Professor Minoru Hara on his Seventieth Birthday*, ed. R. Tsuchida & A. Wezler, Reinbek, 2000.

Ṣoḍaśagrantha — *The Grace of Lord Krishna: The Sixteen Verse-Treatises (Ṣoḍaśagranthāḥ) of Vallabhacharya*, trans. J.D. Redington, Delhi, 2000.

Somaśambhupaddhati — *Somaśambhupaddhati*, 4 vols., ed. and trans. H. Brunner-Lachaux, Pondicherry, 1963–1998.

Spandakārikā — *The Stanzas of Vibration: The Spandakārikā with Four Commentaries*, M.S.G. Dyczkowski, Albany, 1992.
Spanda-Kārikās: The Divine Creative Pulsation (With Kṣemarāja's Nirṇaya), ed. J. Singh, Delhi, 1980.

Śrāmaṇyaphalasūtra — *Das Śrāmaṇyaphala-Sūtra. Synoptische Übersetzung und Glossar der chinesischen Fassungen verglichen mit dem Sanskrit und Pāli*, K. Meisig, FBI 19, Wiesbaden, 1987.

Śrautakośa — *Śrautakośa (Encyclopaedia of Vedic Sacrificial Ritual Comprising the Two Complementary Sections, Namely the Sanskrit Section and the English Section)*, ed. R.N. Dandekar & C.K. Kashikar, Poona, 1958–1994.

Śrī Bayālīs Līlā — *Śrī Bayālīs-Līlā by Śrī Hita Dhruvadās Jī Maharāj*, ed. L. Goswami, Vrindaban, Vikram 2028 (= 1962).

Śrībhāṣya — *Śrī Bhāṣya of Rāmānujācārya*, ed. V.S. Abhyankar, Bombay, 1914.
The Vedānta-Sūtras with the Commentary of Rāmānuja, trans. G. Thibaut, Oxford, 1904.
Rāmānujagranthamālā, ed. P.B. Annangaracariar, Kanci, 1974.

Śrīkaṇṭhabhāṣya — The *Brahmasutrabhashya of Srikanthacharya with the commentary Sivarkamanidipika by Appayadikshita edited with Sutrarthacandrika*, 2 vols., ed. R. Halasyanatha Sastri, New Delhi, 1986.

Śrīkārabhāṣya — *Śrīkāra Bhāṣya*, 2 vols., ed. C. Hayavadana Rao, Bangalore, 1936. (Skt.)
Śrīkara Bhāṣyaṃ [of Śrīpati Paṇḍita], Mysore, 1954. (Skt.)

Śrīkhaṇḍyākhyān — *Śrīsant Eknāth Mahārāj yāñce Ovibaddha Caritra (of Keśavsvāmī)*, ed. P.E. Pānse, Nagpur, 1980.
"Eknāth-caritra [of Keśavsvāmī]," in: *Śrīeknāth Mahārājāñcyā Abhaṅgāñcī Gāthā*, ed. T. Tātyā, Mumbai, 1903, 1–124.

Śrīkṛṣṇakīrttana — *Śrīkṛṣṇakīrttana* by Baḍu Caṇḍīdāsa, ed. Basanta Rañjan Rāy Bidbadballabh, Kolkata, 1974.
Śrīkṛṣṇakīrttana: With a Modern Bengali Translation and Facsimile of the Manuscript Śrīkṛṣṇakīrttan by Baḍu Caṇḍīdāsa, ed. Nilaratan Sen, 2 vols., Kolkata, 1974.

Śrīmadbhaga vadarcāprakaraṇa — *Śrīmadbhagavadarcāprakaraṇa by Nṛsiṃha Vājapeyayājin [=Vājapeyin]*, ed. D. Raṃgācārya, 1936.

Śrīmukundamālā — *Śrīmukundamāla* [sic], ed. K.R. Pisharoti, Annamalainagar, 1933.

Śrīpraśnasaṃhitā — *Śrīpraśna Samhitā* [*sic*], ed. S. Padmanabhan with the Foreword of Dr. V. Raghavan, KSV 12, Tirupati, 1969.

Śrīrādhārasasudhānidhi — *Śrī Rādhā Rasa Sudhā-Nidhi of Śrī Hita Harivaṃś*, ed. S.K.S. Ali, Vrindaban, 1977.

Śrīrādhārasasudhānidhistotra — *Śrī Rādhā-Sudhā-Nidhi-Stotram*, ed. L. Goswami, Bombay, 1991.
Śrī Rādhā-Sudhā-Nidhi of Śrī Hit Harivaṃś, ed. S.K.S. Ali, Vrindavan, 1977.

Śrītēcikastōtramālā — *Śrītēcikastōtramālā* by Veṅkaṭanātha (Vedāntadeśika), ed. Śrī Rāmatēcikācāryar Svāmi, Madras, 1982.

Śrīvacanabhūṣaṇa(m) — *Śrīvacanabhūṣaṇa of Pillai Lokācārya: Edition with English Translation,* R. Lester, Madras, 1979.
Srimatvaravaramunintrakrantamalai, ed. P.B. Annangaracariya, Kanci, 1966.

Śrīvallabhadigvijaya — *Śrīvallabhadigvijayam or Śrīyadunāthadigvijaya*, Yadunātha, Baroda, 1985.

Stotrasamuccaya — *Stotrasamuccaya: A Collection of Rare and Unpublished Stotras [I]*, ed. K.P. Aithal, ALS 99, Madras, 1969.

Subhāṣitatriśatī — *Subhāṣitatriśatī*, ed. D.D. Kosambi, Bombay, 1957.

Subhāṣitratnakoṣa — *Subhāṣitratnakoṣa* by Vidyākara, ed. D.D. Kosambi & V.V. Gokhale, Cambridge MA, 1957.

Sumadhvavijaya — *Sumadhvavijayaḥ*, ed. B. Prabhanjanacharya, Bangalore, 1989, [2]1996.
Nārāyaṇa Paṇḍitācārya's Sumadhva Vijaya, D.R.V. Rau, Visakhapatnam, 1982.

Sundarabāhustāva — *Stotramālā*, ed. P.B. Annangaracariyar, Kanci, 1974, 15–42.

Śūnyasaṃpādane — *Śūnyasampādane*, 5 vols., ed. S.C. Nandimath, L.M.A. Menezes, R.C. Hiremath & M.S.Sunkapur, Dharwar, 1965–1972 (Kan.).
Śūnyasaṃpādane [of Gūḷūra Siddhavīraṇāryaru], Bijapur, 1930. (Kan.)

Sūrsāgar — *Sampūrṇ Sūrsāgar (Śrīkṛṣṇa Līlātmak)* by Sūrdās, ed. K.L. Gupta, 5 vols., Allahabad, 2005.
Sūrsāgar by Sūrdās, ed. M. Gupta, Agra, 1979.
Sūrsāgar by Sūrdās, ed. Jagannāthdās "Ratnākar" *et al.*, 2 vols., Varanasi, 1972, 1976.

Sūryasiddhānta — "Translation of the Sūrya-Siddhānta, a Textbook of Hindu Astronomy, with Notes and an Appendix," ed. E. Burgess, JAOS 6, 1858–1860, 141–498.

Suśrutasaṃhitā — *Suśrutasaṃhitā of Suśruta, with the Nibandhasaṅgraha Commentary of Śrī Ḍalhaṇāchārya and the Nyāyacandrikā Pañjikā of Gayadāsāchārya on Nidānasthāna*, ed. J. Trikamji & N. Ram, JaiAS 34. Varanasi, [7]2002.
Suśruta Saṃhitā: Text with English Translation, a Full and Comprehensive Introduction, Additional Text, Different Readings, Notes, Comparative Views, Index, Glossary and Plates, ed. L. Dwivedi, 3 vols., Varanasi, 1998.

Sūyagaḍa *Studien zum Sūyagaḍa. Die Jainas und die anderen Weltanschauungen vor der Zeitenwende*, W.B. Bollée, SSIUH 24, Wiesbaden, 1977.

Svacchandatantra "The Svacchandatantram: History and Structure of a Śaiva Scripture," 2 vols., W.J. Arraj, diss., University of Chicago, 1988.

The Svacchanda Tantra with Commentary "Udyota" by Kṣemarājācārya, ed. V. Dvivedi, Delhi, 1985.

Svacchandatantra with the Commentary of Kṣemarāja, ed. M.K. Shastrī, KSTS 31, 38, 44, 48, 51, 53, 56, Bombay, 1921–1935.

Svacchandatantroddyota *Svacchandatantra with the Commentary of Kṣemarāja*, ed. M.K. Shastrī, KSTS 31, 38, 44, 48, 51, 53, 56, Bombay, 1921–1935.

Svāyambhuvasūtrasaṃgraha *Svāyambhuvasūtrasaṃgrahaḥ vidyāpādaḥ sadyojyotiṣk tatīkāsahitaḥ* (The Taṇtra of Svayambhū with the Commentary of Sadyojyoti), ed. and trans. P.-S. Filliozat, New Delhi, 1994.

Śvetāśvataropaniṣad "Die Śvetāśvataropaniṣad: Einleitung - Edition und Übersetzung von Adhyāya I," ed. T. Oberlies, *WZKS* 39, 1995, 61–102.

Syādvādaratnākara *Syādvādaratnākara of Vādidevasūri*, ed. L. Motilāla, Pune, 1926–1927.

Taḏkira-yi ġawṯiyya *Taḏkira-yi ġawṯiyya*, Gul Hasan Qalandar Qadiri, Delhi, 1918.

Taittirīyabrāhmaṇa *The Taittirīya Brāhmaṇa of the Black Yajur Veda, with the Commentary of Sāyaṇācarya*, ed. R. Mitra, vol. III, Calcutta, 1870.

The Taittirīya Brāhmaṇa with the Commentary of Bhaṭṭa Bhāskara Miśra, ed. A.M. Sastri, A. Mahadeva, R. Shama Sastry & L. Srinivasacharya, Delhi, 1911–1921, repr. 1985.

Taittirīya-Brāhmaṇa, ed. P. Kumar, vols. I–III, Delhi, 1998.

Taittirīya-Brāhmaṇa: Searchable Non-accented Transliterated Text, ed. S. Sarma, Chennai, 2005, http://www.sanskritweb.net/yajurveda/tb-find.pdf.

Taittirīyabrāhmaṇam. E. Mahādevaśāstriṇāsampāditā, Delhi, repr. 1985.

The Taittirīyabrāhmaṇa of the Black Yajur Veda, ed. R. Mitra, Osnabrück, 1855.

Taittirīyasaṃhitā *Taittirīyasaṃhitā*, ed. A. Weber, 2 vols., IS 11–13, Leipzig, 1871–1872, repr. 1973.

Taittirīya-Saṃhitā, vol. I/2, ed. N.S. Sonatakke & T.N. Dharmadhikari, Poona, 1972.

The Veda of the Black Yajus School Entitled Taittiriya Sanhita: Translated from the Original Sanskrit Prose and Verse by Arthur Berriedale Keith, HOS 18, Delhi, repr. n.d.

Taittirīyopaniṣad *Taittirīyopaniṣad*, trans. by Swāmī Śarvānanda, Mylapore, 1965.

Taittirīyopaniṣad with Śaṃkarabhāṣyam, ed. V.S. Islampurkar, Poona, 1929.

Taittirīyopaniṣadbhāṣya *Taittirīyopaniṣad with Śaṃkarabhāṣyam*, ed. V.S. Islampurkar, Poona, 1929.

Tājikabhūṣaṇa *Tājikabhūṣaṇa*, ed. with Hindi trans. by Sītārāma Śāstrī, Mumbai, 2008.

Tājikanīlakaṇṭhī *Tājikanīlakaṇṭhī* (including *Praśnatantra*), ed. with Viśvanātha's commentary, Hind. trans. and commentary by Kedāradatta Jośī, Delhi, 2008.

Tantrāloka *La lumiere sur le Tantras: Chapitres 1 a 5 du Tantrāloka*, ed. and trans. L. Silburn & A. Padoux, Paris, 1998.

The Tantrāloka of Abhinavagupta with the Commentary of Jayaratha, 8 vols., ed. and trans. M.K. Shastri, Delhi, 1987.

The Tantrāloka of Abhinava Gupta with Commentary by Rājānaka Jayaratha, ed. M.K. Shastri, 12 vols., Allahabad, 1918–1938.

Tantrālokaviveka *The Tantrāloka of Abhinavagupta with the Commentary of Jayaratha*, 8 vols., ed. and trans. M.K. Shastri, Delhi, 1987.

Tantrasāra — *The Tantrasāra of Abhinavagupta*, ed. by M.R. Shastri, Delhi, repr. 1982.

Tantravārttika — *Śrīmajjaiminipraṇīte Mīmāṃsādarśane Ādita Ārabhya Dvitīyādhyāyaprathamapādāntaḥ* [...] *Śrīkumārilabhaṭṭviracitatantravārtikāsahitaśābarabhāṣyasametaś ca*, ed. Subbā Śāstrin & Vināyaka Gaṇeśa Āpaṭe [= Āpṭe], ĀSS 97, Pune, 1929.
Kumārila Bhaṭṭa's Tantravārttika (A Commentary on Śabara's Bhāṣya on the Pūrvamīmāṃṣā Sūtras of Jaimini), trans. G. Jha, 2 vols., Delhi, 1998.

Tāntrikābhidhānakośa — *Tāntrikābhidhānakośa: A Dictionary of Technical Terms from Hindu Tantric Literature,* (vol. I & II: ed. H. Brunner, G. Oberhammer & A. Padoux) vol. III: ed. D. Goodall, M. Rastelli, Vienna, forthcoming.

Tarkabhāṣā — *The Tarkabhāṣā of Keśavamiśra: Edited with an Introduction, Translation into English and Notes (Explanatory and Critical)*, ed. A.B. Gajendragadkar & R.D. Karmarkar, Pune, 1991.

Tarkarahasyadīpikā — *Tarkarahasyadīpikā*, ed. M. Jain, JMGSG 36, New Delhi, ^{2}1981.

Tarkasaṃgraha — *Tarkasaṅgraha with Dīpikā,* ed. and trans. Y.S. Athalye, BSS 55, Pune, 1974.

Tātparyacintāmaṇi — *[Vaikhānasasmārtasūtra]= Vaikhānasagṛhyasūtra [with Vaikhānasadharmasūtra and -pravarasūtra]*, with Śrīnivāsa-makhin [=-Dīkṣita]'s *Tātparyacintāmaṇi* commentary and his *Daśavidhahetunirūpaṇa*, and extracts from Nṛsiṃhāgnicit Vājapeyin [= Nṛsiṃha Vājapeyin]'s commentary, ed. R. Pārthasārathi Bhaṭṭācārya, Śaka 1889 (= 1967 CE).

Tattuvaviḷakkam — *Tattuvaviḷakkam of Campantacaranalayacuvamikal* (title page missing; to be found at the French Institute of Pondicherry).

Tattvabindu — *Tattvabindu by Vācaspatimiśra with Tattvavibhāvanā by Ṛṣiputra Parameśvara*, ed. V. Rāmaswami Sastri, Madras, 1936.

Tattvacintāmaṇi — *Pūrṇānanda's Śrītattvacintāmaṇi: Critically Edited from Original Manuscripts (Chapters I–XVIII) with an original commentary by Bhuvanmohan Sankhyatirtha and (Chapters XIX–XXVI) with Notes*, ed. C. Bhattacharya, Introduction by P. Bagchi, Delhi, repr. 1994.
Tattvacintāmaṇi, ed. N.S. Ramanuja Tatacharya, Tirupati, 1972–1999

Tattvakaumudī — *Tattvakaumudī: Vācaspati Miśra's Commentary on the Sāṃkhya-Kārikās*, trans. G. Jha, Poona, 1965.

Tattvapradīpikā — *Tattvapradīpikā*, ed. Yogindrananda, Benares, 1974.

Tattvaprakāśa — *Aṣṭaprakaraṇam tattvaprakāśatattvasaṅgrahatattvatrayanirṇayaratnatrayabhogakārikānādakārikāmokṣakārikāparamokṣanirāsakārikākhyasiddhānta śaivīyāṣṭagranthānām saṭī kānām samāhāraḥ*, ed. V. Dviveda,Varanasi, 1988.

Tattvaprakāśavṛtti — *Aṣṭaprakaraṇam tattvaprakāśatattvasaṅgrahatattvatrayanirṇayaratnatrayabhogakārikānādakārikāmokṣakārikāparamokṣanirāsakārikākhyasiddhānta śaivīyāṣṭagranthānām saṭī kānām samāhāraḥ*, ed. V. Dviveda,Varanasi, 1988.

Tattvasamāsasūtra — *Tattvasamāsasūtra with the Commentary of Bhāvāganeśa*, ed. R.S. Bhattacharya, Banaras, n.d.

Tattvasaṃgraha — *Tattvasaṅgraha of Śāntarakṣita with the Commentary of Kamalaśīla*, ed. E. Krishnamacharya, Baroda, 1926.

Tattvasandarbha — *Tattvasandarbha* by Jīva Gosvāmī; ET: *Gopiparāṇadhana Dāsa*, Los Angeles, forthcoming.

Tattvavaiśāradī — *The Yoga-System of Patañjali Or the Ancient Hindu Doctrine of Concentration of Mind Embracing The Mnemonic Rules Called Yoga-Sūtras of Patañjali and The Comment, called Yoga-bhāṣya, attributed to Veda-Vyāsa and the Explanation, called Tattva-Vaiśāradī, of Vāchaspati-Miśra translated form the original Sanskrit by James Haughten Woods, 1914*, Delhi, 1988.

Tattvavibhāvanā	*Tattvabindu by Vācaspatimiśra with Tattvavibhāvanā by Ṛṣiputra Parameśvara*, ed. V. Rāmaswami Sastri, Madras, 1936.
Tattvavinirṇaya	*Srimad-Viṣṇu-Tattva-Vinirṇaya of Śrī Madhvācārya*, S.S. Raghavachar, Mangalore, 1959.
Tattvopaplavasiṃha	*Jayarāśi Bhaṭṭa's Tattvopaplavasiṃha (An Introduction, Sanskrit Text, English Translation and Notes)*, E.A. Solomon, Delhi, 2010.
Tēvāram	*Tēvāram*, 2 vols., ed. T.V. Gopal Iyer, PIFI 68/1–2, Pondichery, crit. ed. 1984, 1985.
Theragāthā	*The Elders' Verses I: Theragāthā*, trans. K.R. Norman, London, 1969.
	The Thera- and Therī-gāthā: Stanzas Ascribed to the Elders of the Buddhist Order of Recluses, ed. H. Oldenberg & R. Pischel, London, 1966.
Tīrthacintāmaṇi	*Tīrthacintāmaṇi of Vācaspati Miśra*, ed. K. Smrititīrtha, BI 195, Calcutta, 1912.
Tīrthakamalākara	*Tīrthakamalākara, i.e. Laghutristhalīsetu, by Kamalākara Bhaṭṭa*, Benares, 1953.
Tīrthenduśekhara	*Tīrthenduśekhara by Nāgeśabhaṭṭa*, ed. S.N. Sukla, PWSBTS 66, Benares, 1936.
Tirukkuṟaḷ	*Tirukkuṟaḷ*, W.H. Drew, J. Lazarus & F.W. Ellis, New Delhi, 1886, repr. 1989.
	The "Sacred Kurraḷ" of Tiruvaḷḷuva-Nāyanār, G.U. Pope, London, 1886.
Tiruneṟiviḷakkam	*Tiruneṟiviḷakkam*, publ. in: *Cittāntam*, malar 32, itaḻ 10, n.d.
Tiruppāvai	*Āṇṭāḷ: Antalarulicceyta Tiruppāvai*, Madras, 1976.
	The Poems of Āṇṭāḷ: Tiruppāvai and Nācchiyar Tirumoḻi, trans. P.S. Sunderam, Bombay, 1987.
	Consider our Vow: An English Translation of Tiruppāvai and Tiruvempāvai, trans. N. Cutler, Madurai, 1979.
	The Secret Garland: Antal›s Tiruppavai and Nacciyar Tirumoli, trans. A. Venkatesan, New York, 2010.
Tiruvāymoḻi	*Poems of Āṇṭāḷ: Tiruppāvai and Nācchiyar Tirumoḻi*, trans. P.S. Sunderam, Bombay, 1987.
	Tiruvāymoḻi, 10 vols., ed. P.B. Annangaraciyar, Kanci, 1949–1963.
	Tiruvāymoḻi English Glossary, 2 vols., Satyamurti Ayyangar, Bombay, 1981.
Tiruvempāvai	*Consider our Vow: An English Translation of Tiruppāvai and Tiruvempāvai*, trans. N. Cutler, Madurai, 1979.
Tristhālisetu	*Tristhālisetu by Narayana Bhaṭṭa*, ed. G.Ś. Gokhale, ĀSS, Poone, 1915.
Tristhalīsetusārasaṃgraha	*Tristhalīsetusārasaṃgraha by Bhaṭṭoj Dikṣita*, ed. S.N. Sukla, PWSSTS 65, Benares, 1936.
Uḍutaḍiya Akkamahādēviya ragaḷe	*Hariharana Uḍutaḍiya Akkamahādēviya ragaḷe*, ed. T.S. Shama Rao, Mysore, ²2011.
Uṇmaiviḷakkkam	*Uṇmaiviḷakkkam*, publ. The Department of Saivasiddhanta, University of Madras, Chennai, 1988.
Upadeśasāhasrī	*Upadeśasāhasrī: A Thousand Teachings*, trans. S. Jagananda, Madras, 1941, ⁵1973.
	A Thousand Teachings: The Upadeśasāhasrī of Śaṅkara, ed. S. Mayeda, Albany, 1992.
Uttamabrahmavidyāsāra	*Uttamabrahmavidyāsāra*, ed. U.C. Śrīnivāsa Bhaṭṭācārya, B. Vīrarāghavācārya & U. Vēṃkaṭanarasiṃhācārya, 1921.
Vacanas (Akkamahādēvi)	*Mahādēviyakkagaḷa Vacanagaḷu*, Dharwar, 1973. (Kan.)
	Vacanas of Akkamahādēvi [Mahādēviyakka], trans. A. Menezes & S.M. Angadi, Dharwar, 1973.
	Songs for Śiva: Vacanas of Akka Mahadevi, V. Chaitanya, Walnut Creek, 2005.

	Akkana vacanagaḷu, ed. S. Basavaraju, Mysore, ^{3}1977.
	At the Lord's Feet: An English Translation of Selected Vachanas of Akka Mahadevi (A Woman Saint of Karnataka) and Some Mahādēviyakkana vacanagaḷu, ed. R.C. Hiremath, Dharwad, ^{2}1973.
Vacanas (Allama Prabhu)	*Allama Prabhudēvara Vacanagaḷu*, Dharwar, 1976. (Kan.).
Vacanas (Basava)	*Basavaṇṇavara Vacanagaḷu*, ed. R.C. Hiremath, Dharwar, 1968. (Kan.)
	Vachanas of Basavaṇṇa, ed. H. Deveerappa, trans. L.M.A. Menezes & S.M. Angadi, Sirigere, 1967.
Vādaratnāvalī	*The Jewel-Necklace of Argument: Vādaratnāvalī of Viṣṇudāsācārya*, trans. E. Gerow, New Haven, 1990.
Vaikhānasagṛhyasūtra	*[Vaikhānasasmārtasūtra]= Vaikhānasagṛhyasūtra [with Vaikhānasadharmasūtra and -pravarasūtra]*, with Śrīnivāsa-makhin [=-Dīkṣita]'s *Tātparyacintāmaṇi* commentary and his *Daśavidhahetunirūpaṇa*, and extracts from Nṛsiṃhāgnicit Vājapeyin [= Nṛsiṃha Vājapeyin]'s commentary, ed. R. Pārthasārathi Bhaṭṭācārya, Śaka 1889 (= 1967 CE).
Vaikhānasasmārtasūtra	*Vaikhānasasmārtasūtram*, ed. W. Caland, Calcutta, 1927; trans. W. Caland, Calcutta, 1929.
Vaikhānasaśrautasūtra	*Vaikhānasaśrautasūtra*, ed. W. Caland, 1941.
Vaiśeṣikasūtra	*The Vaiśeṣika Sûtras of Kaṇâda With the Commentary of Śaṅkara Miśra and Extracts From the Gloss of Jayanârâyaṇa*, trans. N. Sinha, Allahabad, 1911.
	Vaiśeṣikasūtras, trans. N. Sinha, New York, 1974.
	Vaiśeṣikasūtra of Kaṇāda with the Commentary of Candrānanda, ed. Jambuvijayaji, GaOS 136, Baroda, 1961.
Vaiśeṣikasūtravārttika	*Vaiśeṣikasūtravārttika/Kaṇādasūtravārttika* called *Tarkasāgara* ("*Kaṇādasūtranibandha*"), ed. A. Thakur, MKG 21, Darbhanga, 1985.
Vaiśeṣikasūtravṛtti	*Vaiśeṣikasūtra of Kaṇāda with the Commentary of Candrānanda*, ed. Jambuvijayaji, GaOS 136, Baroda, 1961.
Vaiśeṣikasūtravyākhyā	*Vaiśeṣikasūtravyākhyā*, ed. A. Thakur, MGP 1, Darbhanga, 1957.
Vaiśeṣikasūtropaskāra	*Vaiśeṣikasūtropaskāra*, ed. N. Mishra, KSS 195, Varanasi, ^{2}1969.
Vaiṣṇavamatābjabhāskara	*Śrīvaiṣṇavamatābjabhāskara, Svāmī Rāmeśvarānandācārya praṇita Prabhā-kiraṇa sahitaḥ*, Rāmānandācarya, Porbandar, 1980.
Vājasaneyimādhyandinaśuklayajurvedasaṃhitā	*Vājasaneyi-Mādhyandina-Śukla-Yajurveda-Saṃhitā, with the Mantra-Bhāṣya of Uvaṭa, the Vedadīpa-Bhāṣya of Mahīdhara, Appendices, an Alphabetical List of Mantras and a Short Introduction*, ed. P.J. Shastri, Delhi, 1971.
Vākyasudha	*Rāja-Yoga: Being a Translation of the Vākyasudha or Dṛgdṛśyaviveka of Bhāratitīrtha [Part I] and the Aparokṣānubhūti of Śrī Śankarāchārya [Part II]: With Introduction and Notes*, trans. M.N. Dvivedi, Ahmedabad, 1890.
Vāmakeśvarīmata	*NityāṣoḍaśikārṇavaḥŚivānandakṛtarjuvimarśinī-vidyānandakṛtārtharatnāvalī-bhāskararāyakṛtasetubandhākhyaṭīkātrayasahita-bhāṣābhāṣyavibhūṣitaḥ*, ed. S.N. Khaṇḍelavāla, Caukhamba Surabharati Granthamala 509, Varanasi, 2011.
	The Vāmakeśvarīmatam with the Commentary of Rājānaka Jayaratha, ed. M.K. Shastri, Kashmir Series of Texts and Studies 66, Srinagar, 1945.
Vāmanapurāṇa	*The Vāmanapurāṇa, with English Translation*, ed. A.S. Gupta, Varanasi, 1968.
Varadarājapañcāśat	*Varadarājapañcāśat: With Sanskrit Commentary by Karūr Śrīnivāsācārya*, P.-S. Filliozat, Bombay, 1990.
Varadarājastāva	*Stotramālā*, ed. P.B. Annangaracariyar, Kanci, 1974, 15–42.
Vārāṅ Bhāī Gurdās	*Vārāṅ Bhāī Gurdās*, ed. J. Singh, Patiala, 1998.

Vārttika — *Kātyāyana's First Vārttika on Pāṇini's Aṣṭādhyāyī, Mahābhāṣya of Patañjali*, ed. F. Kielhorn, vol. 1/2, Pune, ^{3}1962.

Vāsishṭarāmāyaṇamu — *Vāsishṭarāmāyaṇamu* by T. Veṅgamāmba, ed. K.J. Krishnamurti, Tirupati, 2007.

Vasiṣṭhadharmasūtra — *Dharmasūtras: The Law Codes of Āpastamba, Gautama, Baudhāyana and Vasiṣṭha*, trans. P. Olivelle, Dehli, 1999.

Vāsiṣṭhamahārāmāyaṇatātparyaprakāśa — *The Yogavāsiṣṭha of Vālmīki: With the Commentary Vāsiṣṭhamahārāmāyaṇatātparya Prakāsha*, 2 vols., Delhi, repr. 1981.

Vasiṣṭhasaṃhitā — *Vasiṣṭhasaṃhitā (Yogakāṇḍa)*, ed. S. Maheshananda, B.R. Sharma, G.S. Sahay & R.K. Bodhe, Lonavla, rev. ed. 2005.

Vātsyāyanabhāṣya — *Gautama's Nyāyasūtras (with Vātsyāyana-Bhāṣya) Translated into English*, trans. G. Jha, Poona, 1939.
Nyayasūtras: Nyāyadarśana: Text with Vātsyāyana's Bhāṣya, ed. A. Thakur, Darbhanga, 1967.

Vāyupurāṇa — *Mahāmuniśrīmadvyāsapraṇītaṃ Vāyupurāṇam. etat pustakam ānandāśramasthapaṇḍitaiḥ sapāṭhāntaranirdeśaṃ saṃśodhitam. tac ca Hari Nārāyaṇa Āpaṭe ity anena (...) prakāśitam*, Poona, 1905.
Vāyupurāṇa, ed. K. Krishnadas, Bombay 1895, repr. 1983.
Śrīmad-Vāyu-Mahāpurāṇam Śrīmad-Vāyu-Mahāpurāṇam, Bombay, 1933.
The Vāyu Purāṇa, trans. G.V. Tagare, 2 vols., Delhi, 1987–1988.

Vedāntakaustubha — *Vedāntapārijātasaurabha of Nimbārka and Vedāntakaustubha of Śrīnivāsa (Commentaries on the Brahma-sūtras)*, vol. I–II., ed. R. Bose, Calcutta, 1940–1941.

Vedāntaparibhāṣa — *Dharmarājādhvārīndra: Vedāntaparibhāṣa*, ed. and trans. S.S. Suryanarayana Shastri, Madras, 1942.

Vedāntapārijātasaurabha — *Vedāntapārijātasaurabha of Nimbārka and Vedāntakaustubha of Śrīnivāsa (Commentaries on the Brahma-sūtras)*, vol. I–II., ed. R. Bose, Calcutta, 1940–1941.

Vedāntasāra — *Sadānandayogīndra: Vedāntasāraḥ with Rāmatīrtha's Vidvanmanorañjanī*, ed. Brahmacārī Medhācaitanya, Calcutta, 1993.

Vedāntasūtra — *The Vedāntasūtras with Commentary of Rāmānuja*, ed. and trans. G. Thibaut, SBE 48, Oxford, 1904.
The Vedānta Sūtras of Badarāyaṇa with the Commentary by Śaṅkarācārya, trans. G. Thibaut, Delhi, 1992.
Vedāntasūtras with the Commentary of Śrī Madhvācharya, trans. S.S. Rao, Tirupati, 1936.

Vedārthasaṃgraha — *Introduction to the Vedārthasaṃgraha of Sri Rāmānujacharya*, S.S. Raghavachar, Mangalore, 1973
Rāmānuja's Vedārthasaṃgraha, ed. J.A.B. van Buitenen, Poona, 1956.
Rāmānujagranthamālā, ed. P.B. Annangaracariar, Kanci, 1974.
Vedārthasaṃgraha of Śrī Rāmānujācārya, S.S. Raghavachar, Mysore, 1956.

Vīdēvdād — *Vīdēvdād 10–12: Critical Edition, Translation and Commentary of the Avestan and Pahlavi Texts*, M.Á. Andrés-Toledo, Salamanca, 2009.

Vidhavavivāha — *Vidhavavivāha*, Ishwar Chandra Vidyasagar, Calcutta, 1856; ET: trans. B. Hatcher, *Hindu Widow Marriage*, New York, 2011.

Vidyāmādhavīya — *Vidyāmādhavīyam,* vol. I, ed. with Viṣṇu's *Muhūrtadīpika* commentary by R.S. Sastry, Mysore, 1998.

Vijñānabhairava — *Vijñānabhairava or Divine Consciousness: A Treasury of 112 Types of Yoga*, ed. J. Singh, Delhi, 1979.

Vikramacarita — *Vikrama's Adventures or The Thirty-two Tales of the Throne: A Collection of Stories about King Vikrama, as Told by the Thirty-two-Statuettes*

	That Supported His Throne, trans. F. Edgerton, 2 vols., Cambridge MA, 1926, repr. Delhi, 1993. (= *Vikramacarita*)
Vimānārcanākalpa	*Vimānārcanākalpa*, ed. Raghunāthacakravārtin & S. Mādhavācārya, Madras, 1926.
Vinayapatrikā	*Tulsī Dās: The Petition to Rām*, F.R. Allchin, 1966.
Vinayapiṭaka	*Vinaya-Piṭaka: The Book of Discipline*, vol. I: *Suttavibhaṅga*, trans. I.B. Horner, London, 1938.
Vīramitrodaya	*Vīramitrodaya of Mitra Miśra*, ed. P. Śarmā *et al.*, 21 vols., CSS 30, Benares, 1913–1936.
	Vīramitrodaya: Paribhāṣā-Prakāśa, ed. Mitramiśra, Benares, 1896.
Virūpākṣapañcāśikā	"Virūpākṣapañcāśikā (With Vidyācakravartin's Vivṛti)," in: G. Kaviraj, ed., *Tantrasaṁgraha (Part 1)*, Varanasi, 1970, 1–22.
	The Teachings of the Odd-Eyed One: A Study and Translation of the Virūpākṣapañcāśikā with the Commentary of Vidyācakravartin, D.P. Lawrence, Albany, 2008.
Viṣṇudharmasūtra	*Viṣṇudharmāḥ: Precepts for the Worship of Viṣṇu*, part 1: *Adhyāyas 1–43*, part 2: *Adhyāyas 44–81*, part 3: *Adhyāyas 82–105*, ed. R. Grünendahl, Wiesbaden, 1983.
Viṣṇudharmottarapurāṇa	*Viṣṇudharmottara-purāṇa: Third Kaṇḍa Critically Edited with Introduction, Notes, etc. (Vol. 1: Text, Critical Notes, etc.)*, by Priyabala Shah, GaOS 130, Baroda, 1958.
	The Viṣṇudharmottarapurāṇam, Delhi, 1985.
Viṣṇupārijātamu	*Viṣṇupārijātamu* by T. Veṅgamāmba, ed. U. Lakshmikantamma, Hyderabad, 1965.
Viṣṇupurāṇa	*The Viṣṇumahāpurāṇam*, Delhi, 1910, repr. 1985.
	Śrīviṣṇupurāṇa, trans. Ś. Gupta, Gorakhpur, 1990.
	Viṣṇu Purāṇa with Śrīdharasvāmin's Commentary and Śrīkālipadatarkācārya's Gloss, SaS 1, Calcutta, 1965
	The Vishnu Purana, trans. H.H. Wilson, Calcutta, 1972.
Viṣṇusahasranāma	*Sri Visnusahasranama*, trans. S. Sathyamurthi Ayyangar, Bangalore, 1996.
	Sri Vishnu Sahasranama with the Bhashya of Sri Parasara Bhattar, ed. A.S. Raghavan, Madras, 1983.
Viṣṇusaṃhitā	*The Viṣṇu Saṃhitā*, ed. by M.M. Gaṇapati Sāstrī, With an Elaborate Introduction by N.P. Unni, TSS 85, Delhi, rev. ed. 1991.
Viṣṇusmṛti	*The Law Code of Viṣṇu: A Critical Edition and Annotated Translation of the Vaiṣṇava-Dharmaśāstra*, ed. and trans. P. Olivelle, HOS 73, Cambridge MA, 2009.
Viṣṇutattvavinirṇaya	*Śrīmad-Viṣṇu-Tattva-Vinirṇaya of Śrī Madhvācārya*, ed. S.S. Raghavachar, Mangalore, 1959.
Vivekacūḍamaṇi	*Vivekachudamani of Sri Sankaracharya*, Swami Madhvananda, Mayavati, [5]1952.
Vivekamārtaṇḍa	*Das Gorakṣaśataka* (= *Vivekamārtaṇḍa*), ed. F. Nowotny, Cologne, 1976.
	**Vivekamārtaṇḍa of Gorakṣadeva*, ms. 4110 at the Oriental Institute Baroda, Vadodara, n.d.
Vyāsabhāṣya	*Yoga Philosophy of Patañjali Containing his Yoga Aphorisms with the Commentary of Vyāsa in the Original Sanskrit, and Annotations Thereon with Copious Hints on the Practice of Yoga by Swāmi Hariharānanda Āraṇya*, Calcutta, 1981.
Vyāsavāṇī	*Vyāsa-Vāṇī: Harirām Vyāsa*, ed. S.R. Goswami, Mathura, 1973.
Vyavahāramayūkha	*The Vyavahára Mayúkha, in Original, with an English Translation*, ed. and trans. V.N. Mandlik, Bombay, 1880.

Vyomavatī see *Padārthasaṃgrahaṭīkā*

Yajñādhikāra *Yajñādhikāra*, Eguvarpalayam, 1931.

Yajurvedasaṃhitā *Yajurveda Saṃhitā: Sanskrit Text with English Translation*, trans. R.T.H. Griffith, Delhi, 1899, repr. 1997.

Yantracintāmaṇi *Yantracintāmaṇiḥ of Dāmodara*, crit. ed. by H.-G. Türstig, Stuttgart 1988.

Yatidharmaprakāśa *Vāsudevāśrama Yatidharmaprakāśa: A Treatise on World Renunciation*, vol. II, ed. P. Olivelle, Leiden, 1977.

Yatidharmasummucaya *Rules and Regulations of Brahmanical Asceticism: Yatidharma-summucaya of Yādava Prakāśa*, ed. and trans. P. Olivelle, Albany, 1995.

Yavanajātaka *The Yavanajātaka of Sphujidhvaja*, ed., trans., and comm. D. Pingree, Cambridge MA, 1978.

The Yavanajātaka of Sphujidhvaja, ed. with annotated ET by D. Pingree, Cambridge USA, 1978.

Yogabīja *Yogabīja*, ed. R.L. Śrīvāstav, Gorakhpur, 1982.

Yogapradīpakā *Jogpradīpakā of Jayatarāma*, ed. M.L. Gharote, Jodhpur, 1999.

Yogaprakāśikā *Haṭhapradīpikā of Svātmārāma (10 chapters): With Yogaprakāśikā Commentary by Bālakṛṣṇa*, ed. M.L. Gharote & P. Devnath, Lonavla, 2002.

Yogasārasaṃgraha *Yogasārasaṅgraha*, trans. G.N. Jha, ed. A. Kumar, Delhi, 1995.

Yogasūtra *Yoga Philosophy of Patañjali Containing his Yoga Aphorisms with the Commentary of Vyāsa in the Original Sanskrit, and Annotations Thereon with Copious Hints on the Practice of Yoga by Swāmi Hariharānanda Āraṇya*, Calcutta, 1981.

The Yoga-Sūtras of Patañjali: Sanskrit Text and English Translation Together with an Introduction and an Appendix, and Notes on Each Sūtra Based upon Several Authentic Commentaries – All in English, trans. M.N. Dvivedi, Madras, 1890.

The Yoga Philosophy: Being the Text of Patanjali, with Bhoja Raja's Commentary, with their translations in English by Dr. Ballantyne and Govind Shastri Deva, an Introduction by Col. Olcott and an Appendix, T. Tatya, 21885.

Yogasūtravṛtti *The Yoga Philosophy: Being the Text of Patanjali, with Bhoja Raja's Commentary, with their translations in English by Dr. Ballantyne and Govind Shastri Deva, an Introduction by Col. Olcott and an Appendix*, T. Tatya, 21885.

Yogavāsiṣṭha *The Yoga-Vāsiṣṭha-Mahārāmāyaṇa of Vālmiki: Translated From the Original Sanskrit*, trans. V.-L. Mitra, 4 vols., Delhi, repr. 1978.

The Yogavāsiṣṭha of Vālmīki: With the Commentary Vāsiṣṭhamahārāmāyaṇatātparya Prakāsha, 2 vols., Delhi, repr. 1981.

Yogavāsiṣṭha *Muntaḫab-i Jūg-bāsasht (Selections from the Yoga-vāsiṣṭha)*, ed. F. Mujtabā'ī, Tehran, 2006.

Yoginīhṛdaya *Yoginīhṛdayam Amṛtānandayogikṛtadīpikayā Bhāṣānuvādena ca Sahitam*, ed. V. Dviveda, Delhi, 2011.

Le Coeur de la Yoginī: Yoginīhṛdaya avec le commentaire Dīpikā d'Amṛtānanda, A. Padoux, PICI 63, Paris, 1994.

Yoginīhṛdayam with Commentaries Dipikā of Amṛtānanda and Setubandha of Bhāskararāya, G. Kaviraja, Varanasi, 1979.

Yuktidīpikā *Yuktidīpikā*, ed. A. Wezler & S. Motegi, ANIS 44, Stuttgart, 1998.

Yuktidīpikā, trans. S. Kumar & D.N. Bhargava, Delhi, 1990.

Primary Source Abbreviations

AbhiBhā.	*Abhinavabhārati*
AbhK.	*Abhidharmakośa*
AbhKBh.	*Abhidharmakośabhāṣya*
AbhKVyā.	*Abhidharmakośavyākhyā*
ĀdHṛ.	*Ādityahṛdaya*
ĀG.	*Ādigranth*
AgP.	*Agnipurāṇa*
AhirSa.	*Ahirbudhnyasaṃhitā*
AitĀ.	*Aitereyāraṇyaka*
AitBr.	*Aitareyabrāhmaṇa*
AjiĀg.	*Ajitāgama*
ĀK.	*Ānandakanda*
AK.	*Amarakośa*
AmPrab.	*Amaraughaprabodha*
AN.	*Aṅguttaranikāya*
AṇuBh.	*Aṇubhāṣya*
Anuvyā.	*Anuvyākhyāna*
ĀpDhS.	*Āpastambadharmasūtra*
ĀpGS.	*Āpastambagṛhyasūtra*
ĀpŚS.	*Āpastambaśrautasūtra*
ĀpSulS.	*Āpastambaśulbasūtra*
Āry.	*Āryabhaṭīya*
ArŚ.	*Arthaśāstra*
AṣṭA.	*Aṣṭādhyāyī*
AṟTiVa.	*Aṟputattiruvantāti*
AṣṭHṛSa.	*Aṣṭāṅgahṛdayasaṃhitā*
AṣṭSa.Sū.	*Aṣṭaṅgahṛdayasaṃhitā.Sūtrasthāna*
ĀśvGS.	*Āśvalāyanagṛhyasūtra*
ĀtBo.	*Ātmabodha*
ĀtTatVi.	*Ātmatattvaviveka*
AV.	*Atharvaveda*
AVP.	*Atharvaveda: Paippalāda recension*
AVŚ.	*Atharvaveda: Śaunakīya recension*
AvvKu.	*Avvaikkuṟaḷ*
ĀyDīp.	*Āyurvedadīpikā*
Balarām.	*Balarāmāyaṇa*
BĀU.	*Bṛhadāraṇyakopaniṣad*
BĀUBh.	*Bṛhadāraṇyakopaniṣadbhāṣya*
BauDhS.	*Baudhāyanadharmasūtra*
BhāgP.	*Bhāgavatapurāṇa*
BhārT.	*Bhārgavatantra*
BhaVai.	*Bhagavaī*
BheSa.	*Bhelasaṃhitā*
BhG.	*Bhagavadgītā*
BhKal.	*Bhāmākalāpamu*
BhMā.	*Bhaktamāl*

BhPr.	*Bhāvaprakāśa*
BhRaĀk.	*Bhaktiratnākara*
BhRaAm.	*Bhaktirasāmṛtasindhu*
BhRaĀv.	*Bhaktiratnāvalī*
BHSD	*Buddhist Hybrid Sanskrit Grammar and Dictionary*
BhVa.	*Bhaktivardhinī*
BīG.	*Bījagaṇita*
BISM	*Bhārat Itihāsa Saṁśodhak Mandal*
BrāṇḍaP.	*Brahmāṇḍapurāṇa*
BṛBh.	*Bṛhadbhāṣya*
BṛDhP.	*Bṛhaddharmapurāṇa*
BṛhBhAm.	*Bṛhadbhāgavatāmṛta*
BṛhSa.	*Bṛhatsaṃhitā*
BrP.	*Brahmapurāṇa*
BrS.	*Brahmasūtra*
BrSBh.	*Brahmasūtrabhāṣya*
BrSi.	*Brāhmasphuṭasiddhānta*
BṛSm.	*Bṛhaspatismṛti*
BṛŚṛPad.	*Bṛhatśṛṅgadharapaddhati*
BrY.	*Brahmayāmala*
BuCar.	*Buddhacarita*
CaiBh.	*Caitanyabhāgavata*
CaiC.	*Caitanyacaritāmṛta*
CaiCan.	*Caitanyacandrāmṛta*
CarSa.	*Carakasaṃhitā*
CarSa.Ci	*Caraka.Samhitā.Cikitsāsthāna*
CarSa.Ni.	*Carakasaṃhita.Nidanasthāna*
CarSa.Śā.	*Carakasaṃhitā.Śārirasthāna*
CarSa.Sū.	*Carakasaṃhita.Sūtrasthāna*
CarSa.Vi.	*Carakasaṃhitā.Vimānasthāna*
CaŚat.	*Caṇḍīśataka*
ChāU.	*Chāndogyopaniṣad*
ChāUBh.	*Chāndogyopaniṣadbhāṣya*
Cilapp.	*Cilappatikāram*
CiMā.	*Ciṟiyamātal*
CiÑāCi.	*Civañāṉacittiyār*
CiÑāPō.	*Civañāṉapōtam*
CiPira.	*Civappirakācam*
CNāṭ.	*Ceñcu Nāṭakamu*
CūS.	*Cūladukkhakkhandhasutta*
CuVa.	*Cullavagga*
DāJLī.	*Dādūjanmalīla*
Daś.	*Daśakumāracarita*
DaśŚl.	*Daśaślokī*
DaU.	*Dattātreyopaniṣad*
DāVā.	*Dādūvāṇī*
DYŚa.	*Dattātreyayogaśāstra*
DBhāgP.	*Devībhāgavatapurāṇa*
DePañc.	*Devanāyakapañcāśat*
DhPra.	*Dharmottarapradīpa*
DhS.	*Dhammasaṅgaṇi*
DhvaĀl.	*Dhvanyāloka*
DN.	*Dīghanikāya*

DM.	*Devīmāhātmya*
EI	*Epigrahia Indica*
GaṇK.	*Gaṇakārikā*
GaP.	*Garuḍapurāṇa*
GāT.	*Gāyatrītantra*
GauDhS.	*Gautamadharmasūtra*
GauDī.	*Gauragaṇoddeśadīpikā*
GītaGov.	*Gītāgovinda*
GobhGS.	*Gobhilagṛhyasūtra*
GoŚat.	*Gorakṣaśataka*
GovLī.	*Govindalīlāmṛta*
GTātp.	*Gītātātparya*
HanBā.	*Hanumānbāhuk*
HarC.	*Harṣacarita*
HirGS.	*Hiraṇyakeśīgṛhyasūtra*
HRat.	*Haṭharatnāvalī*
HV.	*Harivaṃśa*
H(Y)P.	*Haṭhayogapradīpikā*
HYPṬ.	*Haṭhayogapradīpikāṭīkā*
ĪśPraK.	*Īśvarapratyabhijñākārikā*
ĪśPraKVṛ.	*Īśvarapratyabhijñākārikāvṛtti*
ĪśPraVim.	*Īśvarapratyabhijñāvimarśinī*
ĪśSa.	*Īśvarasaṃhitā*
ĪśŚai.	*Īśānaśaivagurudevapaddhati*
ĪśU.	*Īśopaniṣad*
JaiBr.	*Jaiminīyabrāhmaṇa*
JaiUBr.	*Jaiminīyopaniṣadbrāhmaṇa*
JaySa.	*Jayākhyasaṃhitā*
JñāSa.	*Jñānāmṛtasārasaṃhitā*
JyoVe.Ṛg	*Jyotiṣavedāṅga.Ṛgveda* recension
KaĀv.	*Kavitāvalī*
KaG.	*Kabīr Granthāvalī*
KālŚat.	*Kālahastīśvara Śatakamu*
KāmĀg.	*Kāmikāgama*
KāmS.	*Kāmasūtra*
KaṇC.	*Kaṇṇinuṉ Ciṟuttampu*
KāP.	*Kālikāpurāṇa*
KaPa.	*Kabīr Parcāī*
KarBh.	*Karṇabhāra*
KarSto.	*Karpūrādistotra*
Kāś.	*Kāśikāvṛtti*
KāśSa.In.	*Kāśyapasaṃhitā.Indriyasthāna*
KāśSa.Ka.	*Kāśyapasaṃhitā.Kalpasthāna*
KāṭhGS.	*Kāthakagṛhyasūtra*
KāṭhSa.	*Kāṭhakasaṃhitā*
KaṭhU.	*Kaṭhopaniṣad*
KaṭhUBh.	*Kaṭhopaniṣadbhāṣya*
KātŚS.	*Kātyāyanaśrautasūtra*
KauṣU.	*Kauṣītakopaniṣad*
KāvĀd.	*Kāvyādarśa*
KāvAl.	*Kāvyālaṃkāra*
KāVil.	*Kāmakalāvilāsa*
KāvMī.	*Kāvyamīmāṃsā*
KCaic	*Kṛṣṇacaitanyacaritāmṛta*

KīGh.	*Kīrtanaghoṣa*
KeU.	*Kenopaniṣad*
KhVid.	*Khecarīvidyā*
KirĀg.	*Kiraṇāgama*
KirĀv.	*Kiraṇāvalī*
KirĀvṬī.	*Kiraṇāvalīṭīkā*
KirT.	*Kiraṇatantra*
KoS	*Koshur Samachar*
KrDī.	*Kramadīpikā*
KSS.	*Kathāsaritsāgara*
KumSambh.	*Kumārasambhava*
KūP.	*Kūrmapurāṇa*
KuT.	*Kulārṇavatantra*
LakṣT.	*Lakṣmītantra*
LaS.	*Laṅkāvatārasūtra*
LBhAm.	*Laghubhāgavatāmṛta*
LDC.	*Liṅgadhāraṇacandrikā*
Līlāv.	*Līlāvatī*
LiP.	*Liṅgapurāṇa*
LS	*Lokmat Sahitya*
MaBh.	*Mahābhāṣya*
MaBh.P.	*Mahābhāṣya.Paspaśāhnika*
MaiSa.	*Maitrāyaṇīsaṃhitā*
MaitriU.	*Maitryupaniṣad*
MaiU.	*Maitrāyaṇīyopaniṣad*
MāKad.	*Mādhuryakadambinī*
MālA.	*Mālavikāgnimitra*
MaMañ.	*Mahārthamañjarī*
MaNāU.	*Mahānārayaṇopaniṣad*
MāṇḍU.	*Māṇḍukyopaniṣad*
ManuBh.	*Manubhāṣya*
MārP.	*Mārkaṇḍeyapurāṇa*
MārSa.	*Mārkaṇḍeyasaṃhitā*
MāŚlVā.	*Mālinīślokavārttika*
MaSm.	*Manusmṛti*
MaSta.	*Mahimnaḥstava*
MatĀg.	*Mataṅgapārameśvarāgama*
MatKāñ.	*Maturaikkāñci*
MatP.	*Matsyapurāṇa*
MatSa.	*Matsyendrasaṃhitā*
MaVā.	*Mahāvāṇī*
MāViT.	*Mālinīvijayottaratantra*
MāViVā.	*Mālinīvijayavārttika*
MBh.	*Mahābhārata*
MBhāgP.	*Mahābhāgavatapurāṇa*
MBhPa.	*Mahābhāratatātparyanirṇaya*
MCT.	*Mahācīnatantra*
Megh.	*Meghadhūta*
Mitā.	*Mitākṣarā*
MīmS.	*Mīmāṃsāsūtra*
MīmSBh.	*Mīmāṃsāstrabhāṣya*
MIS.	*Marāṭhyāñcyā Itihāsācīṃ Sādhaneṃ*
MkP.	*Mārkaṇḍeyapurāṇa*

MLaSto.	*Mahālakṣmīstotra*
MMU.	*Mantramahodadhi*
MN.	*Majjhimanikāya*
MoMud.	*Mohamudgara*
MNirT.	*Mahānirvāṇatantra*
MṛgĀg.	*Mṛgendrāgama*
MSBh.	*Mīmāṃsāsūtrabhāṣya*
MŚlVāKā.	*Mīmāṃsāślokavārttikakāśikā*
MtP.	*Matsyapurāṇa*
MuDī.	*Muhūrtadīpikā*
MuMā.	*Mukundamālā*
MuTiVa.	*Mutal Tiruvantāti*
MūTiVa.	*Mūṉṟam Tiruvantāti*
MuU.	*Muṇḍakopaniṣad*
MuUBh.	*Muṇḍakopaniṣadbhāṣya*
NācTiMo.	*Nācciyār Tirumoḻi*
NāGh.	*Nāmaghoṣa*
NarParī.	*Nareśvaraparīkṣā*
NarParīPr.	*Nareśvaraparīkṣāprakāśa*
NāSm.	*Nāradasmṛti*
NāTiVa	*Nāṉmukaṉ Tiruvantāti*
NāṭŚā.	*Nāṭyaśāstra*
NB	*Nav Bhārat*
NeT.	*Netratantra*
NiLak.	*Nirodhalakṣaṇa*
Nir.	*Nirukta* (of Yāska)
NīSā.	*Nītisāra*
NīŚat.	*Nītiśataka*
NiŚe.	*Nighaṇṭuśeṣa*
NPP	*Nāgarī Pracāriṇī Patrikā*
NyāBh.	*Nyāyabhāṣya*
NyāK.	*Nyāyakandalī*
NyāKPañj.	*Nyāyakandalīpañjikā*
NyāMañ.	*Nyāyamañjarī*
NyāVā.	*Nyāyavārttika*
NyāS.	*Nyāyasūtra*
NyāSVār.	*Nyāyasutravārttika*
NyāVārTṬī.	*Nyāyavārttikatātparyaṭīkā*
NyāSVṛ.	*Nyāyasūtravṛtti*
PaDhSaṅg.	*Padārthadharmasaṅgraha*
PādSa.	*Pādmasaṃhitā*
PañBh.	*Pañcārthabhāṣya*
PāñRa.	*Pāñcarātrarakṣā*
ParĀg.	*Parākhyāgama*
ParSa.	*Paramasaṃhitā*
PārSa.	*Pārameśvarasaṃhitā*
PāS.	*Pāśupatasūtra*
PaSaṅgṬī.	*Padārthasaṅgrahaṭīkā*
PaTr.	*Parātrīśikā*
PaTrV.	*Parātrīśikāvivaraṇa*
PauṣĀg.	*Pauṣkarāgama*
PauṣSa.	*Pauṣkarasaṃhitā*
PāVi.	*Pātravidhi*

PdP.	*Padmapurāṇa*
PdSa.	*Pādmasaṃhitā*
PED	*Pali-English Dictionary*
PerTiMo.	*Periyatirumoḻi*
PeTiMo.	*Perumāl Tirumoḻi*
PrCU.	*Prabodhacandrodaya*
PrMā.	*Praśnamārga*
PrT.	*Praśnatantra*
PrU.	*Praśnopaniṣad*
PST.	*Prapañcasāratantra*
Puṟ.	*Puṟanāṉūṟu*
RaĀv.	*Ratnāvalī*
RaGa.	*Rasagaṅgādhara*
RaghV.	*Raghuvaṃśa*
RaiVā.	*Raidāsvāṇī*
RājSā.	*Rājayoga Sāramu*
Rām.	*Rāmāyaṇa*
RaMañ.	*Rasamañjarī*
RāmRSto.	*Rāmarakṣāstotra*
RaSā.	*Rasasāra*
RasAr.	*Rasārṇava*
RasCu.	*Rasendracūḍāmaṇi*
RasHṛT.	*Rasahṛdayatantra*
RasRaSam.	*Rasaratnasamuccaya*
RaṬī.	*Ratnaṭīkā*
RaTr.	*Ratnatraya*
RaĀv.	*Ratnāvalī*
RCM.	*Rāmcaritmānas*
RūSi.	*Rūpasiddhi*
ṚV.	*Ṛgveda*
RVKh.	*Ṛgvedakhila*
SadKar.	*Saduktikarṇāmṛta*
SaṃgBh.	*Saṃgrahabhāṣya*
SāṃK.	*Sāṃkhyakārikā*
SaṃNir.	*Saṃnyāsanirṇaya*
SāṃS.	*Sāṃkhysūtra*
SāṃSā.	*Sāṃkhyasāra*
SaṃsVi.	*Saṃskāravidhi*
SāṃTKau.	*Sāṃkhyatattvakaumudī*
SaṅgRaĀk.	*Saṅgītaratnākara*
ŚāṅkhGS.	*Śāṅkhāyaṇagṛhyasūtra*
SāPā.	*Sāmantapāsādikā*
SāPañc.	*Sāmbapañcāśikā*
Sar.	*Saroddhāra*
SarĀg.	*Sarvajñānottarāgama*
SarMūGr.	*Sarvamūlagrantha*
SātSa.	*Sātvatasaṃhitā*
ŚatSaṃg.	*Śataratnasaṃgraha*
ŚatTr.	*Śatakatraya*
SauLa.	*Saundaryalaharī*
ŚāV.	*Śāktavijñāna*
ŚBr.	*Śatapathabrāhmaṇa*
ŚBrK.	*Śatapathabrāhmaṇa: Kāṇvīya recension*

ŚBrM.	*Śatapathabrāhmaṇa: Mādhyandina recension*
ṢDSam.	*Ṣaḍdarśanasamuccaya*
ṢDSam.LVṛ.	*Ṣaddarśanasamuccaya.Laghuvṛtti*
SidPad.	*Siddhasiddhāntapaddhati*
ŚiDṛ.	*Śivadṛṣṭi*
ŚiDṛVṛ.	*Śivadṛṣṭivṛtti*
SidTr.	*Siddhitrayī*
ŚiJñ.	*Śivajñānabodha*
ŚiJñUpany.	*Śivajñānabodhopanyāsa*
ŚiJñV.	*Śivajñānabodhavṛtti*
SiMĀv.	*Siddhāntamuktāvalī*
SiRa.	*Siddhāntarahasya*
ŚiS.	*Śivasūtra*
ŚiStoĀv.	*Śivastotrāvalī*
ŚiSV.	*Śivasūtravimarśinī*
SmSth.	*Smṛtisthaḷ*
SN.	*Saṃyuttanikāya*
SPā.	*Sūtrapāṭha*
SpK.	*Spandakārikā*
SpN.	*Spandanirṇaya*
ŚrīBh.	*Śrībhāṣya*
ŚrīGuR.	*Śrīguṇaratnakośa*
ŚrīKaBh.	*Śrīkaṇṭhabhāṣya*
ŚrīKīr.	*Śrīkṛṣṇakīrtana*
ŚrīPrSa.	*Śrīpraśnasaṃhitā*
ŚrīRā.	*Śrīrādhārasasudhānidhi*
ŚṛṅPr.	*Śṛṅgāraprakāśa*
ŚṛṅŚat.	*Śṛṅgāraśataka*
ŚSaṃp	*Śūnyasaṃpādane*
ŚTT.	*Śāradātilakatantra*
SuMVij.	*Sumadhvavijaya*
SūŚat.	*Sūryaśataka*
SuśrSa.	*Suśrutasaṃhitā*
SuśrSa.Ci.	*Suśrutasaṃhitā. Cikitsāsthāna*
SuśrSa.Sū.	*Suśrutasaṃhitā. Sūtrasthāna*
SvaT.	*Svacchandatantra*
ŚvetU.	*Śvetāśvataropaniṣad*
TĀ.	*Tantrāloka*
TāBhū.	*Tājikabhūṣaṇa*
TaiBr.	*Taittirīyabrāhmaṇa*
TaiSa.	*Taittīriyasaṃhitā*
TaiU.	*Taittirīyopaniṣad*
TarRahDī.	*Tarkarahasyadīpikā*
TātDī.	*Tātparyadīpikā*
TatPr.	*Tattvaprakāśa*
TatSaṃkh.	*Tattvasaṃkhyāna*
TatVai.	*Tattvavaiśāradī*
TatVi.	*Tattvaviveka*
TĀVi.	*Tantrālokaviveka*
TiCaVi.	*Tiruccantaviruttam*
TiMā.	*Tirumalāi*
TiMu.	*Tirumuṟai*
TiMuP.	*Tirumuṟaikaṇṭapurāṇam*

TiMuPa.	*Tirumurukāṟṟuppaṭai*
TiNeVi.	*Tiruneṟiviḷakkam*
TiVāy.	*Tiruvāymoḻi*
TiViP.	*Tiruviḷaiyāṭaṟpurāṇam*
TiVir.	*Tiruviruttam*
TNŚat.	*Tarigoṇḍa Nṛsimhaśatakamu*
TSā.	*Tantrasāra*
TVā.	*Tantravārttika*
Ullekh.	*Ullekhanī*
UpāKh.	*Upādhikhaṇḍana*
UttJh.	*Uttarajjhayaṇa/Uttarajhāyā*
VādŚS.	*Vādhulaśrautasūtra*
VāgAl.	*Vāgbhaṭālaṃkāra*
VaiDhS.	*Vaikhānasadharmasūtra*
VaiS.	*Vaiśeṣikasūtra*
VaiŚat.	*Vairāgyaśataka*
VaiSmS.	*Vaikhānasasmārtasūtra*
VaiSUp.	*Vaiśeṣikasūtropaskāra*
VaiSVṛ.	*Vaiśeṣikasūtravṛtti*
VājPrāt.	*Vājasaneyiprātiśākhya*
VājSa.	*Vājasaneyisaṃhitā*
VākPad.	*Vākyapadīya*
VāMa.	*Vāmakeśvarīmata*
VāmP.	*Vāmanapurāṇa*
VaP.	*Varāhapurāṇa*
VarPad.	*Varuṇapaddhati*
Vārtt.	*Vārttikā*
VasDhS.	*Vasiṣṭhadharmasūtra*
VAT.	*Vidyārṇavatantra*
VedKau.	*Vedāntakaustubha*
VedPāSau.	*Vedāntapārijātasaurabha*
VedSaṃg.	*Vedārthasaṃgraha*
ViCū.	*Vivekacūḍāmaṇi*
ViDhP.	*Viṣṇudharmottarapurāṇa*
VijBhai.	*Vijñānabhairava*
ViM.	*Vivekamārtaṇḍa*
VinP.	*Vinayapiṭaka*
VinPa.	*Vinaypatrikā*
ViPā.	*Viṣṇu Pārijatamu*
ViPā.	*Villipāratam*
ViSa.	*Viṣṇusaṃhitā*
ViSah.	*Viṣṇusahasranāma*
ViSm.	*Viṣṇusmṛti*
ViTatVinir.	*Viṣṇutattva(vi)nirṇaya*
ViyPa.	*Viyāhapannatti*
VyāBh.	*Vyāsabhāṣya*
YCu.	*Yakoppu Cuṇṇam*
YHṛ.	*Yoginīhṛdaya*
YugŚa.	*Yugalaśataka*
YS.	*Yogasūtra*
YSBhV.	*Yogasūtrabhāṣyavivaraṇa*
YukDī.	*Yuktidīpikā*

Journals and Series

AA	*Arts Asiatiques*
AAAG	*Annals of the Association of American Geographers*
AAE	*Arabian Archaeology and Epigraphy*
AaM	*Anthropology and Medicine*
AARAS	American Academy of Religion Academy Series
AASF-B/H	Annales Academiae Scientiarum Fennicae B/Humaniora
ABORI	*Annals of the Bhandarkar Oriental Research Institute*
ABS	*American Behavioral Scientist*
AcA	*Acta Asiatica*
ACK	*Amar Chitra Kathā*
AE	*American Ethnologist*
AÉPHÉ	*Annuaire de L'École Pratique des Hautes Études*
AES	*Archives Européennes de Sociologie*
AER	*American Economic Review*
AFS	*Asian Folklore Studies*
AGSK	Abhandlungen der Geistes- und Sozialwissenschaftlichen Klasse
AHES	*Archive for History of Exact Sciences*
AI (BASI).NS	*Ancient India (Bulletin of the Archaeological Survey of India). New Series*
AIP	*Archiv für Indische Philosophie*
AJP	*American Journal of Philology*
AJS	*American Journal of Sociology*
AJSS	*Asian Journal of Social Science*
AKAWB	*Abhandlungen der Königlichen Akademie der Wissenschaften in Berlin*
AKM	Abhandlungen für die Kunde des Morgenlandes
AL	*Annali Lateranensi*
ALB	*Adyar Library Bulletin*
ALS	Adyar Library Series
AM	*Asian Music*
AmAn	*American Anthropologist*
AmAn.NS.	*American Anthropologist.NS*
AMTM	*Asian Medicine – Tradition and Modernity*
ANIS	Alt- und Neu-Indische Studien
AnM	*Anthropology and Medicine*
Ansoc	*Anneé sociologique*
Ansoc. NS	*Anneé sociologique. Nouveau Style*
AO	*Acta Orientalia*
AOR	*Annals of Oriental Research*
AOSS	American Oriental Society Series
AP	*Antiquorum Philosophia*
APa	*Ancient Pakistan*
APh	*Asian Philosophy*
APQ	*American Philosophical Quarterly*
AR	*Asiatick Researches*
ARA	*Annual Review of Anthropology*
AR/BR	*Archiv für Religionswissenschaft/Beiträge zur Religionswissenschaft*

ArsO	*Ars Orientalis*
ARSR	*Australian Religion Studies Review*
ArtA	*Artibus Asiae*
AS	*American Scientist*
ASt	*Asian Studies*
ASB	*Archives of Sexual Behavior*
AS/ÉA	*Asiatische Studien/Études Asiatiques*
AsE	*Asian Ethnology*
ASMS	Asiatic Society Monograph Series
ASR	*Asian Studies Review*
ĀSS	Ānandāśrama Sanskrit Series
ASSR	*Archives de sciences sociales des religions*
ASu	*Asian Survey*
AT	*Anthropology Today*
ATJ	*Asian Theatre Journal*
ATR	*Annals of Tourism Research*
BAI	*Bulletin of the Asia Institute*
BASI	*Bulletin of the Anthropological Survey of India*
BDCRI	*Bulletin of the Deccan College Research Institute*
BDIMB	*Boletim Do Instituto Menezes Bragança*
BEFEO	*Bulletin de l'École Française d'Éxtrême Orient*
BÉHÉ.Sr	*Bibliothèque de l'École des Hautes Études, Sciences religieuses*
BEI	*Bulletin d'Études Indiennes*
BEPB	*Bulletin des Études Portuaises et Bresiliennes*
BF	Baghdader Forschungen
BGOMLM	*Bulletin of the Government Oriental Manuscripts Library Madras*
BI	Bibliotheca Indica
BIL	Brill's Indological Library
BIS	*Berliner Indologische Studien*
BIS	Bibliotheca Indica Series
BJ	*Basava Journal*
BJP	*British Journal of Psychiatry*
BKGA	Beiträge zur Kultur und Geistesgeschichte Asiens
BKI	*Bijdragen tot de Taal-, Land- en Volkenkunde van Nederlandsch-Indië*
BKSSL	Beiträge zur Kenntnis südasiatischer Sprachen und Literaturen
BMJ	*British Medical Journal*
BollS	Bollingen Series
BOS	Bhandarkar Oriental Series
BOS.NS	Bonner Orientalistische Studien. Neue Serie
BPP	*Bengal Past and Present*
BRSS	Berkeley Religious Studies Series
BPWM	*Bulletin of the Prince of Wales Museum*
BSOAS	*Bulletin of the School of Oriental and African Studies*
BSOS	*Bulletin of Oriental Studies*
BSPS	Bombay Sanskrit and Prakrit Series
BSS	Bombay Sanskrit Series
BST	Buddhist Sanskrit Texts
BTF	*Bangalore Theological Forum*
BV	Bharatiya Vidya
BWHO	*Bulletin of the World Health Organization*
CA	*Cultural Anthropology*
CAJ	*Central Asiatic Journal*
CAS	*Contributions to Asian Studies*

CaSA	Cahiers de la Société Asiatique
CC	*Cultural Critique*
CCP	*Commonwealth and Comparative Politics*
CD	*Current Dialogues*
CERO.NI	Collectio Editionum Rariorum Orientalum. Noviter Impressarium
CES	Collection Emile Senart
CGIP	*Computer Graphics and Image Processing*
CI	Collection Indologie
CII	*Corpus Inscriptionum Iranicarum*
CII	*Corpus Inscriptiorum Indicanum*
CIS	*Contributions to Indian Sociology*
CIS.NS	*Contributions to Indian Sociology. New Series*
CMAJ	*Canadian Medical Association Journal*
CMEW	*Comparative Medicine East and West*
CMP	*Culture, Medicine and Psychiatry*
CO	*Christian Orient*
CONJ	*Canadian Oncological Nursing Journal*
CP	*Comprehensive Psychiatry*
CPh	*Classical Philology*
CrAS	*Critical Asian Studies*
CrC	*Cross Currents*
CrIS	*Cracow Indological Studies*
CSA	*Contemporary South Asia*
CSAS	Cambridge South Asian Studies
CSS	Chowkhamba Sanskrit Series
CSSA	Cambridge Studies in Social Anthropology
CSSAAME	*Comparative Studies of South Asia, Africa and the Middle East*
CSSH	*Comparative Studies in Society and History*
CuA	*Current Anthropology*
DC	*Dance Chronicle*
DCMS	Deccan College Monograph Series
DEP	*Development Economics Papers*
DGR	Diederichs Gelbe Reihe
DJAAAS	*Daedalus: Journal of the American Academy of Arts and Sciences*
DRdM	Die Religionen der Menschheit
DRJ	*Dance Research Journal*
DRT	Disputationes Rheno-Trajectinae
DS	*Deccan Studies*
DUMOPS	Duke University Monographs and Occasional Papers Series
EA	*Eastern Anthropologist*
EaA	*Education about Asia*
EBHR	*European Bulletin of Himalayan Research*
EcW	*Economic Weekly*
EDCC	*Economic Development and Cultural Change*
EE	*Environmental Ethics*
ÉFEO.ÉT	École française d'Extrême-Orient, Études thématiques
EFEO.R	L'École Française d'Extrême-Orient: Réimpressions
EH	*Ethnohistory*
EI	*Epighraphia Indica*
EIP	*Encyclopedia of Indian Philosophies*
EJCN	*European Journal of Cardiovascular Nursing*
EJS	*European Journal of Sociology*
EJVS	*Electronic Journal of Vedic Studies*

EoI	*Encyclopedia of India*
EM	*Ethnomusicology*
EPW	*Economic and Political Weekly*
ERC	*Ethnic Racial Studies*
ERE	*Encyclopaedia of Religion and Ethics*
ÉVP	Études védiques et pāṇinéennes
EW	*East and West*
FBI	Freiburger Beiträge zur Indologie
FCS/SAS	Foreign and Comparative Studies/South Asian Series
FEQ	*The Far Eastern Quarterly*
FiR	*Fieldwork in Religion*
FiU	*Folklore in Use*
FSSACS	French Studies in South Asian Culture and Society
GaOS	Gaekwad Oriental Series
GGA	*Göttingische Gelehrte Anzeigen*
GGI	Gods and Goddesses in India
GH	*Gender and History*
GIAPA	Grundriss der Indo-Arischen Philologie und Altertumskunde
GJKSV	*Ganganatha Jha Kendriya Sanskrit Vidyapeetha*
GOS	Groningen Oriental Studies
GR	Geographica Religionum
GS	*Gender and Society*
GS	Glasenapp Stiftung
HA	*Historische Anthropologie*
HdO	Handbuch der Orientalistiek
HFS	Historisk-filosofiske Skrifter
HeR	*Hedgehog Review*
HIL	History of Indian Literature
HiR	*Historical Research*
HLDW	*Hindi: Language, Discourse, Writing*
HLJ	*Hastings Law Journal*
HOS	Harvard Oriental Series
HOS.OM	Harvard Oriental Series, Opera Minora
HR	*History of Religions*
HRQ	*Human Rights Quarterly*
HSPCIC	History of Science, Philosophy and Culture in Indian Civilization
HT	*Hinduism Today*
HTM	*Hinduism Today Magazine*
HTR	*Harvard Theological Review*
HWJ	*History Workshop Journal*
IA	*Indian Antiquary*
IAn	*Indian Anthropologist*
IAQR	*The Imperial and Asiatic Quarterly Review*
IAR	Indian Archaeology in Retrospect
IAs	*Internationales Asienforum*
IB	*India and Beyond*
IBK/JIBS	*Indogaku Bukkyōgaku Kenkyū/ Journal of Indian and Buddhist Studies*
IC	*Indian Culture*
ICQ	*India International Quarterly*
IEPh	*Internet Encyclopedia of Philosophy*
IESHR	*Indian Economic and Social History Review*
IHQ	*Indian Historical Quarterly*
IHR	*The Indian Historical Review*

IICQ	*India International Centre Quarterly*
IIJ	*Indo-Iranian Journal*
IJAHD	*International Journal of Aging and Human Development*
IJCP	*International Journal of Cultural Property*
IJGS	*Indian Journal of Gender Studies*
IJGT	*International Journal of Group Tensions*
IJHS	*International Journal of Hindu Studies*
IJHSc	*Indian Journal of History of Science*
IJHSp	*International Journal of the History of Sport*
IJLC	*International Journal of Law in Context*
IJP	*Indian Journal of Psychiatry*
IJPN	*International Journal of Palliative Nursing*
IJPS	*International Journal of Punjab Studies*
IJSP	*International Journal of Social Psychiatry*
IJTS	*International Journal of Tantric Studies*
ILS	*Illustrated London News*
IM	*Immigrants and Minorities*
IPA	*Indian Philosophical Annual*
IPC	*Indian Philosophy and Culture*
IOCPS	Institute of Oriental Culture Special Series
IrA	*Iranica Antiqua*
IS	Indische Studien
IS	*Iranian Studies*
ISPP	*Indian Studies Past and Present*
IT	Indica et Tibetica
IT	*Indologica Taurinensia*
JA	*Journal Asiatique*
JAAR	*Journal of the American Academy of Religion*
JAAS	*Journal of Asian and African Studies*
JAC.E	Jahrbuch für Antike und Christentum. Ergänzungsband
JAF	*Journal of American Folklore*
JAH	*Journal of African History*
JaiAS	Jaikrishnadas Ayurveda Series
JAOS	*Journal of the American Oriental Society*
JAR	*Journal of Anthropological Research*
JAS	*Journal of Asian Studies*
JASB	*Journal of the Anthropological Society of Bombay*
JAsSB	*Journal of the Asiatic Society of Bombay*
JASo	*Journal of the Asiatic Society*
JAsSM	*Journal of the Asiatic Society of Mumbai*
JBombayBRAS	*Journal of the Bombay Branch of the Royal Asiatic Society*
JBORS	*Journal of the Bihar and Orissa Research Society*
JCMC	*Journal of Computer-Mediated Communication*
JCR	*Journal of Contemporary Religion*
JCS	*Journal of Church and State*
JDH	*Journal of Design History*
JDL	*Journal of the Department of Letters*
JDS	*Journal of Developing Societies*
JEAS	*Journal of the European Ayurvedic Society*
JES	*Journal of Ecumenical Studies*
JESHO	*Journal of the Economic and Social History of the Orient*
JFSR	*Journal of Feminist Studies in Religion*
JGJRI	*Journal of the Ganganath Jha Research Institute*

JHCS	*Journal of Hindu-Christian Studies*
JHI	*Journal of the History of Ideas*
JHS	*Journal of the History of Sexuality*
JHSt	*Journal of Hindu Studies*
JIABS	*Journal of the International Association of Buddhist Studies*
JIAS	*Journal of the Indian Anthropological Society*
JIBS	*Journal of Indian and Buddhist Studies*
JICPR	*Journal of the Indian Council for Philosophy Research*
JIESMS	Journal of Indo-European Studies Monograph Series
JIF	*Journal of Indian Folkloristics*
JIFMC	*Journal of the International Folk Music Council*
JIH	*Journal of Indian History*
JIPh	*Journal of Indian Philosophy*
JIS	*Journal of Indological Studies*
JISOA	*Journal of the Indian Society of Oriental Art*
JJ	*Jain Journal*
JKS	*Journal of Kerala Studies*
JKUH	*Journal of the Karnatak University: Humanities*
JLM	*Journal of Law and Medicine*
JLS	*Journal of Lesbian Studies*
JMadrasU	*Journal of Madras University*
JMGSG	Jñānapīṭha Mūrtidevī Granthamālā Sanskrit Grantha
JMSUB	*Journal of the Maharaja Sayajirao University of Baroda*
JMU	*Journal of the Mysore University*
JNRC	*Journal of the Nepal Research Centre*
JOI	*Journal of the Oriental Institute*
JOR	*Journal of Oriental Research*
JP	*Journal of Pain*
JPC	*Journal of Pastoral Care*
JPHS	*Journal of the Pakistan Historical Society*
JPS	*Journal of Punjab Studies*
JPTS	*Journal of the Pali Text Society*
JRAI	*Journal of the Royal Anthropological Institute*
JRAI.NS	*Journal of the Royal Anthropological Institute. New Series*
JRAS	*Journal of the Royal Asiatic Society*
JRASBeng	*Journal of the Royal Asiatic Society Bengal*
JRASGBI	*Journal of the Royal Asiatic Society of Great Britain and Ireland*
JRE	*Journal of Religion in Europe*
JRH	*Journal of Religious History*
JS	*Journal for Semitics*
JSAL	*Journal of South Asian Literature*
JSR	*Journal of Social Research*
JSR	*Journal of Social Research*
JSAH	*Journal of the Society of Architectural Historians*
JSAI	*Jerusalem Studies in Arabic and Islam*
JSAS	*Journal of Southeast Asian Studies*
JSS	*Journal of Social Sciences*
JUB	*Journal of the University of Bombay*
JUH	*Journal of Urban History*
JVS	*Journal of Vaishnava Studies*
JWH	*Journal of World History*
KM	Kāvyamālā

KPAWPHKS	Königlich Preussischen Akademie der Wissenschaften, Philologisch-historische Klasse, Sitzungsberichte
KS	*Kannada Studies*
KSAS	Key Studies in Asian Studies
KSEW	Kleine Schriften Ernst Windisch
KSHJ	Kleine Schriften Hermann Jacobi
KSHO	Kleine Schriften Hermann Oldenberg
KSMW	Kleine Schriften von Michael Witzel
KSPH	Kleine Schriften Paul Hacker
KSPT	Kleine Schriften Paul Thieme
KSS	Kashi Sanskrit Series
KSTS	Kashmir Series of Texts and Studies
KSV	Kendriya Sanskrit Vidyapeetha
KZ	*Zeitschrift für vergleichende Sprachforschung auf dem Gebiet der indogermanischen Sprachen, begründet von A. Kuhn*
LAHPOP	Linguistics, Archaeology and the Human Past: Occasional Paper
LCPh	*Les Cahiers de Philosophie*
LNAI	Lecture Notes in Artificial Intelligence
LHR	*Law and History Review*
LRTP	Library Rare Texts Publications
LSJRS	Lala Sundarlal Jain Research Series
LT	*Literature and Theology*
Man.NS	*Man. New Style*
MAQ	*Medical Anthropology Quarterly*
MAS	*Modern Asian Studies*
MASI	Memoirs of the Archaeological Survey of India
Mcb	*Mélanges chinois et bouddhiques*
MD	*Modern Drama*
MeA	Münchner ethnologische Abhandlungen
MedA	*Medical Anthropology*
MGP	Mithilāvidyāpīṭha Granthamālā Prācīnācāryagranthāvālī
MGSI	*Memoir of the Geological Society of India*
MHJ	*Medieval History Journal*
MHSI	Monumenta Historica Societatis Iesu
MiI	*Man in India*
MIS	Mithila Institute Series
MIO	*Methodological Innovations Online*
MJLS	*Madras Journal of Literature and Science*
MKAW.AL	Mededeelingen der Koninklijke Akademie van Wetenschappen, Afdeeling Letterkunde
MKG	Mahārājādhirāja Kāmeśvarasiṃha Granthamālā
ML	*Medical Law*
MQ	*Mystics Quarterly*
MR	Machikaneyama Ronso
MRDTB	*Memoirs of the Research department of Toyo Bunko*
MSC	Manuscripts in the Schøyen Collection
MSFOu	Mémoires de la Société Finno-Ougrienne
MSS	*Münchener Studien zur Sprachwissenschaft*
MTSR	*Method and Theory in the Study of Religion*
MUTS	Madras University Telegu Series
NAWG.PHK	*Nachrichten der Akademie der Wissenschaften in Göttingen. Philologish-historische Klasse*
NC	*The Nineteenth Century*
NCG	Nyāyacaturgranthikā

NCTRA	*Numazu College of Technology Research Annual*
NGJI	*National Geographical Journal of India*
NH	*Natural History*
NNGMCP	*Newsletter of the Nepalese German Manuscript Cataloguing Project*
NR	*Nova Religio*
NRT	*Nouvelle revue théologique*
NSS	Nepal Sanskrit Series
NZJAS	*New Zealand Journal of Asian Studies*
ÖAWPHKD	Österreichische Akademie der Wissenschaften, Philosophisch-Historische Klasse, Denkschriften
ÖAWPHKS	Österreichische Akademie der Wissenschaften, Philosophisch-historische Klasse, Sitzungsberichte
ÖAWVKSKS	Österreichische Akademie der Wissenschaften, Veröffentlichungen der Kommission für Sprachen und Kulturen Südasiens
OHJRI	*Online – Heidelberg Journal of Religions on the Internet*
OLA	Orientalia Lovaniensia Analecta
OLP	*Orientalia Lovaniensia Periodica*
OS	*Orientalia Suecana*
OTF.NS	Oriental Translation Fund, New Series
PAPS	*Proceedings of the American Philosophical Society*
PB	*Prabuddha Bharata*
PCR	*Perspectives in Clinical Research*
PICI	Publications de l'institut de civilisation indienne
PDR	*Population and Development Review*
PÉFEO	Publications de l'École française d'Extrême-Orient
PEW	*Philosophy East and West*
PIEA	Philosophia Indica: Einsichten-Ansichten
PIFI	Publications de l'Institut Français d'Indologie
PiH	Perspectives in History
PDNRL	Publications of the De Nobili Research Library
PO	*Poona Orientalist*
POS	Poona Oriental Series
PP	*Past and Present*
PPPS	Pāñcarātra Parisodhanā Pariṣad Series
PR	*Paragrana*
PRPT	Purāṇa Research Publications Tübingen
PSM	Poet-Saints of Maharashtra
PSPSH	Poznan Studies in the Philosophy of the Sciences and the Humanities
PV	*Pacific Viewpoint*
PWSBTS	Princess of Wales Saraswati Bhavana Texts and Studies
PWSBTS.RS	Princess of Wales Saraswati Bhavana Texts and Studies. Reprint Series
QJSA	*Quarterly Journal of Studies on Alcohol*
RAI.NS	*Royal Anthropological Institute. New Style*
RBN	*Religieuze Bewegingen in Nederland*
RC	*Religion Compass*
ResAA	*Res: Anthropology and Aesthetics*
RG	*Religion and Gender*
RGG	*Religion in Geschichte und Gegenwart*
RHR	*Revue de l'Histoire des Religions*
RL	*Roopa Lekha*
RO	Rocznik Orientalistyczny
RPP	*Religion Past and Present*
RS	Religionswissenschaftliche Studien

RSA	*Religions of South Asia*
RSR	*Religious Studies Review*
RSS	*Rivista di studi Sudasiatici*
RTÜ	Reihe Texte und Übersetzungen
RWA	Reihe Wort und Antwort
SA	*South Asia*
SACS	*South Asian Cultural Studies*
SAR	*South Asia Research*
SARel	*South Asian Religions*
SAS	*South Asian Studies*
SaS	Sanātanaśāstram Series
SATR	Studies in Asian Thought and Religion
SB	*Sociological Bulletin*
SBE	Sacred Books of the East
SBG	Sarasvatī Bhavana Granthamālā
SchAS	Schweizer Asiatische Studien
SCI	Studies of Classical India
SdR	Symbolik der Religionen
SES	*Senri Ethnological Studies*
SF	*Sikh Formations*
SFS	*Studies in Formative Spirituality*
SGDOS	Sri Garib Dass Oriental Series
SGKAS	Schriften zur Geschichte und Kultur des Alten Orients
SGM	*Scottish Geographical Magazine*
SHR	Studies in the History of Religions
SI	*Studia Indolognicze*
SIASMS	Scandinavian Institute of Asian Studies Monograph Series
SiH	*Studies in History*
SII	*Studien zur Indologie und Iranistik*
SII.M	Studien zur Indologie und Iranistik, Monographie
SiR/SR	*Studies in Religion/Science Religieuses*
SITES.NS	*SITES: A Journal of Social Anthropology and Cultural Studies, New Series*
SIUH	Studia Indologica Universitatis Halensis
SJLS	*Singapore Journal of Legal Studies*
SJoA	*Soutwestern Journal of Anthropology*
SN	*Sangeet Natak*
SO	ScriptOralia
SoAn	*Social Analysis*
SoAr	*Sovietskaya Arkheologiya*
SoC	*Senses of Cinema*
SocA	*Social Anthropology*
SoF	*Social Forces*
SOR	Serie Orientale Roma
SoS	*Social Scientist*
SP	*Social Problems*
SP	Sanmati Publication
SPBMS	Studia Philologica Buddhica Monograph Series
SPHKKAW	*Sitzungsberichte der philosophisch-historischen Klasse der kaiserlichen Akademie der Wissenschaften*
SPP	Sino-Platonic Papers
SR	*Social Research*
SS	*Social Scientist*
SRAA	*Silk Road Art and Archaeology*

SRV	*Sri Ramanuja Vani*
SSIUH	Schriftenreihe des Südasien-Instituts der Universität Heidelberg
SSM	*Social Science and Medicine*
SSPS	Sanskrit Sahitya Parishad Series
ST	*Social Text*
StA	*Studia Asiatica*
StII	*Studien zur Indologie und Iranistik*
StM	*Studia Missionalia*
StO	*Studia Orientalia*
StOR	Studies in Oriental Religions
StR/SR	*Studies in Religion/Sciences religieuses*
STT	*Stud Tribes Tribals*
SuA	*Suomen Antropologi*
ŚYJG	Śrīyaśovijayajainagranthamālā
TAB	*The Art Bulletin*
TBM	*The Burlington Magazine*
TC	*Tamil Civilization*
TDR	*The Drama Review*
TG	*Tourism Geographies*
TKVNM	*Tijdschrift van de Koninklijke Vereniging voor Nederlandse Muziekgeschiedenis*
TMS	*The Midwest Sociologist*
TP	*Textual Practice*
TPa	*T'oung Pao*
TPS	*Transactions of the Philological Society*
TS	*Tantric Studies*
TSAM	*Traditional South Asian Medicine*
TSS	Trivandrum Sanskrit Series
TSSR	*Trends in Social Science Research*
TSWS	Tibetan Sanskrit Works Series
UCeylonR	*University of Ceylon Review*
ULR	*Utrecht Law Review*
VBA	*Visva-Bharati Annals*
VIJ	*Vishveshvaranand Indological Journal*
VKNAW.AL.NR	Verhandelingen der Koninklijke Nederlandse Akademie van Wetenschappen, Afdeling Letterkunde, Nieuwe Reeks
VR	*Visible Religion*
VS	*Victorian Studies*
VZS	Vizianagaram Sanskrit Series
WA	*World Archaeology*
WECR	*Worldviews: Environment, Culture, Religion*
WM	*Waste Management*
WSIQ	*Women's Studies International Quarterly*
WSTB	Wiener Studien zur Tibetologie und Buddhismuskunde
WZKM	*Wiener Zeitschrift für die Kunde des Morgenlandes*
WZKMUL	*Wissenschaftliche Zeitschrift der Karl-Marx-* Universität Leipzig
WZKSAIP	*Wiener Zeitschrift für die Kunde Südasiens und Archiv für Indische Philosophie*
YJ	*Yoga Journal*
ZAA.S	Zeitschrift für Anglistik und Amerikanistik, Studies
ZDMG.S	*Zeitschrift der Deutschen Morgenländischen Gesellschaft. Supplementband*
ZE	*Zeitschrift für Ethnologie*
ZMR	*Zeitschrift für Missionswissenschaft und Religionswissenschaft*
ZRG	*Zeitschrift für Religions- und Geisteswissenschaft*
ZS	Zentralasiatische Studien
ZVR	*Zeitschrift für vergleichende Rechtswissenschaft*

General Abbreviations

app.	appendix
approx.	approximately
Arab.	Arabic
Avest.	Avestan
Ass.	Assamese
b.	born
Bal.	Balinese
BCE	before the Common Era
bot.	botanical
c.	circa
CE	Common Era
cent./cents.	century/centuries
comm.	commentary
crit. ed.	critical edition
ch./chs.	chapter/chapters
cit.	cited by
d.	died
dir.	director
diss.	dissertation
ed./eds.	editor, edited by/editors
ET	English translation
et al.	and others
etym.	etymology
f./ff.	following page/following pages
fem.	feminine
fig.	figure
fl.	*floruit*
FS	*Festschrift*
Ger.	German
Germ.	Germanic
Grk.	Greek
Guj.	Gujarati
h.	here
Hind.	Hindi
incl.	including
Intro.	Introductory section
Iran.	Iranian
Ital.	Italian
Kan.	Kannara
Kash.	Kashmiri
km/km^2	kilometer/kilometer squared
Lat.	Latin
lit.	literally
m	meter
Mah.Pr.	Maharashtri Prakrit
masc.	masculine

Mal.	Malayam
Mar.	Marathi
ms./mss.	manuscript/manuscripts
n.d.	no date
n.l.	no location
n/nn	note/notes
NGO	nongovernmental organization
no./nos.	number/numbers
nom.	nominative
p./pp.	page/pages
Pal.	Pali
Pt.	Paṇḍit
Pers.	Persian
pl.	plate
pl.	plural
Port.	Portuguese
prod.	producer
publ.	published by/publisher
Punj.	Punjabi
r.	reigned
recon.	reconstructed
repr.	reprint
rev. ed.	revised edition
Rs.	Rupee
sing.	singular
Skt.	Sanskrit
śl.	*śloka*
Śmt.	Śrīmatī (Mrs.)
spec.	special
st.	stanza
Sum.	Sumerian
suppl.	supplement
s.v.	*sub voce*
Tam.	Tamil
Tel.	Telegu
Tib.	Tibetan
Toch.	Tocharian
trans.	translator, translated by, translation
unpubl.	unpublished
v/vv.	verse/verses
Ved.	Vedic
vol./vols.	volume/volumes
WHO	World Health Organization

Historical Perspectives

Indus Civilization (–1750 BCE)

The Indus (or Mature Harappan) civilization flourished 2600–1900 BCE. It was the most extensive urban culture of its time with an area of 800,000 km^2, one thousand settlements, and one million people. Its discovery was announced by J. Marshall in 1924 on the basis of excavations started a couple of years earlier at two large sites, Harappa in the Punjab and Mohenjo-daro in Sind. A lot of archaeological research has been done since, and there are good descriptions of the data recovered (select literature in bibliography). Due to limited source material and difficulties in its interpretation, some fundamental aspects have remained poorly understood. After an overview of the Indus civilization and its evolution, the present article deals with the contentious problems of Harappan language, religion, and script, which are of particular interest for the history of Hinduism. Space allows only an outline of select parts of my synthetic reconstruction and the evidence on which it is based (detailed references and further material can be found in my publications cited in the bibliography, especially Parpola, 1994). Readers interested in differing opinions can consult an archaeologist's surveys of the manifold attempts to understand the Indus script (Possehl, 1996) and the Harappan religion (Possehl, 2007).

Rise and Fall of the Indus Civilization

The Indus civilization results from a long cultural evolution that can be followed in unbroken succession from Neolithic times to the Early Iron Age at Mehrgarh and the neighboring sites Nausharo, Sibri, and Pirak near the Bolan Pass, which links Baluchistan with the plains of Sind.

From 7000 to 4300 BCE, some 35 small Neolithic villages with mud-brick houses are known from the highland valleys of western Pakistan. Hunting gave way to raising locally domesticated humped cattle, sheep, and goats. Wheat and barley were cultivated, reaped using sickles with microlithic blades, and stored in communal granaries. Pottery was handmade, and terracotta figurines of human females and bulls reflect fertility cults. People were buried with ornaments whose seashells, lapis lazuli, and turquoise are evidence of long-distance trade.

In the Chalcolithic stage 4300–3200 BCE, settlements grew in number and size. Dams and irrigation canals were built, especially for growing cotton. Copper metallurgy developed, and the bow drill was used in lapidary workshops. Pottery became wheel-thrown and beautifully painted, their motifs evidencing contacts with southern Turkmenistan and northern Iran. In Baluchistan, the early Togau Ware was succeeded by the Kechi Beg Ware 3800 BCE, when villages started spreading eastward to the Indus plains and beyond, to Cholistan drained by the Ghaggar-Hakra River, the chief domain of the Hakra Ware, and southward to Gujarat.

The Early Harappan cultural phase that flourished from 3200 to 2600 BCE had four regional varieties: Damb Sadaat in the Quetta Valley and in southern Afghanistan (Mundigak); Nal and Kulli in southern Baluchistan and Amri in southern Sind, spreading to Kutch (Kachchh) and northern Gujarat as well; Sothi-Siswal in the eastern plains of the Punjab, Haryana, and Uttar Pradesh; and Kot Diji in most of the Indus Valley.

Yearly floods, sometimes catastrophic, make the Indus Valley a challenging environment. Settlements had to be above the floodplain, which required artificial foundations. Wide fields and fertile silt enabled large-scale agriculture. A ploughed field excavated at Kalibangan has the same crisscross pattern that prevails in the region today. Communal granaries were replaced by large storage jars in house units. Potter's marks at many sites also suggest private ownership, and stamp seals bearing geometrical motifs point to development in administration. Towns with walls and grid-pattern streets were constructed, and advances were made in all crafts. Mastery of air reduction in burning enabled making high-quality luxury ceramics. Terracotta models of bullock carts attest to improved transport, which led to considerable cultural uniformity.

Similarities in pottery, seals, figurines, ornaments, and so on attest to caravan trade with southern Turkmenistan and with the Iranian

Plateau, including Shahr-i Sokhta in Seistan and Tepe Yahya in Kerman, where Proto-Elamite accounting tablets have been discovered. Proto-Elamite bevel-rimmed vessels have been found at Mir-i Qalat in Pakistani Makran. Contact with the Proto-Elamite culture (3200–2600 BCE) may have given the idea of logo-syllabic writing, but the Indus script was in any case created independently.

A transition phase from 2600 to 2500 BCE turned the Early Harappan culture into the Mature Harappan culture alias Indus civilization. Many constituent elements were already present, but the scale and sophistication of their use rose to a higher level. Distinctive components include the fully developed Indus script; stamp seals carved with writing and/or animal and other iconographic motifs; highly standardized weights and measures, polished stone cubes reflecting binary and decimal systems; large-scale use of burnt brick with a standardized size in the ratio 1:2:4 most effective for bonding; metallurgy with copper, alloyed to bronze (mostly with tin), lead, silver, gold, and electrum; highly developed lapidary art with sophisticated micro-drilling of very long beads of hard carnelian and chemical staining of decorative patterns; two growing seasons in agriculture (barley, wheat, oats, lenses, beans, mustard, jujube, and linen during winter; millets, cotton, sesamum, melons, jute, hemp, grapes, and dates in summer during the monsoon); and adoption of water traffic, which enabled moving large and heavy loads long distances and even sea trade with Mesopotamia. Analysis of the provenience of minerals has revealed the extent of the Harappan interaction sphere, networks, and trade routes (Law, 2011).

Exactly where the Mature Harappan culture came into being is uncertain. Its dynamic expansion displaced Early Harappan cultures with violence, for large-scale burning took place at Nausharo, Amri, Kot Diji, and Gumla. Scarcity of bronze weapons has been interpreted as indicating absence of warfare, but Harappan art does depict spearmen and archers. Herodotus (7.65) tells that Indian soldiers in the Persian army of 479 BCE "carried bows of cane, and arrows also of cane," and the Sumerian text *Enki and the World Order* speaks of Meluhhan reeds, which "heroes work as weapons in battle-fields."

Mature Harappan society was so well organized that it could complete enormous building projects, such as the preplanned city of Mohenjo-daro. Its acropolis stands on a 12-meter-high artificial mud-brick platform of 20 ha; just this foundation required ten thousand labor years. The main street of the residential lower city was 7.6 m wide and ran north-south. Many houses were two-storied, with spacious rooms built around a courtyard. Side-lane entrances protected from the dust and crowd of the streets. Mohenjo-daro excelled all other ancient cities in water engineering: its estimated 700 deep, brick-lined wells (75 of them exposed) were ingeniously constructed with tapering bricks that have prevented them from collapsing for four thousand years. The houses usually had waterproof bathing platforms and privies, and wastewater went out through pipes and chutes through walls to the regularly maintained network of covered street drains.

The acropolis or "citadel" presumably was Mohenjo-daro's cultic and administrative center. Its large "public" buildings include an "assembly hall" divided into five aisles by four rows of five

Fig. 1: American-Pakistani HARP excavations at Harappa in 2000. One of the circular platforms near the so-called "granary", suspected (but not yet confirmed) to have connection with indigo dyeing and textile industry (J.M. Kenoyer, personal communication; photo by Asko Parpola).

Fig. 2: Dholavira, Kutch (Kachchh), the largest of several water reservoirs, 73.4 m long, 29.3 m wide and 10.6 m deep, provided with flights of 30 steps in three corners. Excavations continued in 2008 (photo by Asko Parpola).

brick pillars each; a "granary" or "warehouse" with an assumed ventilation system (27 separate blocks of brickwork beneath a lost wooden floor); a "great bath" having a 7-by-13-meter pool watertight with bitumen, a 2-meter-high corbelled outlet, verandas, a well, and ranges of rooms; and, across the street from the great bath, "college of priests."

The acropolis of Mohenjo-daro has somewhat different counterparts at Allahdino, Banawali, Chanhu-daro, Dholavira, Harappa, Kalibangan, Kot Diji, Lothal, Nausharo, Rakhigarhi, Surkotada, and Sutkagen-dor; some of them are clearly defensive, but the main purpose seems to have been political, impressing people with their monumentality (Eltsov, 2008). While bricks were used in the Indus Valley, which lacks stones, the 100-hectare site Dholavira in Kutch was stone-built and provided several large water tanks.

The Indus civilization does not have such magnificent palaces and temples as Mesopotamia and Egypt, but potential palaces and temples have been identified. From the "palace" of Mohenjo-daro's DK-G Block 1 come two seals interpreted below as having belonged to high priests of important deities. HR-B Block 2 is a single building measuring 40 by 80 m with 136 rooms and courtyards. Its monumental entrance gate, constructed with ring-stone posts, is similar to the gates leading to the acropolis of Dholavira. Next to Block 2 is the "little bath," a pool surrounded by rooms with bathing platforms and a well (Vidale, 2010). HR-A House I, a small but monumental "temple," had two symmetrical stairways leading to a courtyard with a central ring of brickwork, comparable to the protective enclosures of sacred trees on Indus tablets.

Harappan cities were ahead of their western counterparts in civic amenities, such as wells and drains, and social equality. It has therefore been suggested that the Harappans were governed by councils rather than single leaders. Yet their glyptic art includes several Mesopotamian motifs related to royalty. The Indus leaders had a strong authority that undoubtedly had an ideological foundation. Priests played a vital role in the administration of ancient Mesopotamia and historical South Asia.

Fig. 3: Dholavira, Kutch (Kachchh), the north gate to the acropolis. From the floor of its western side chamber comes the most monumental Indus inscription known so far, a three-meter-long (now decayed) wooden signboard, inlaid with stone mosaics forming ten script signs each 37 cm high, possibly containing a royal title (see Parpola, 1994, 108, 113; photo by Asko Parpola).

Up to the Gulf, sea trade with the ancient Near East was wholly in Harappan hands, for the only object of clearly western Asiatic origin in the Greater Indus Valley is a "Dilmun-type" seal from Lothal, the Harappan port town (with a warehouse and dockyard) in Gujarat. Jewelry from the royal graves of Ur (2500 BCE) include typically Harappan long, barrel-shaped carnelian beads and beads stained with the motif of concentric circles. Some 20 Indus seals have been found in Mesopotamia; of the datable ones, nine have been attributed to the Akkadian period (2334–2154 BCE) and two to the Isin and Larsa dynasties (2000–1800 BCE).

Indus people had trading posts on the Makran coast (Sutkagen-dor), in Oman (from where they imported copper), along the Gulf, and in Mesopotamia. Harappan cube weights and more than a hundred "Gulf-type" round stamp seals, many of them with Indus script and a Harappan-style bison on the obverse and a Harappan-style boss on the reverse, come from the islands of Failaka and Bahrain. Dated 2100–2000 BCE, these "Gulf-type" seals were the models for the round "Dilmun-type" stamp seals (uninscribed and with motifs influenced by Mesopotamian glyptics) that replaced them (Laursen, 2010).

Sumerians and Akkadians had been sailing up to the copper-producing Oman since 3000 BCE. Cuneiform texts speak of three foreign countries involved in sea trade: Dilmun, Magan, and Meluhha. King Sargon the Great (2334–2279 BCE) reverses the normal order, placing the most distant Meluhha first, when he boasts in one of his inscriptions, "Ships from Meluhha, ships from Magan, [and] ships from Dilmun he [i.e. Sargon] made lay anchor at the harbor of Akkad." There is consensus that Dilmun denotes the islands of Failaka and Bahrain and the adjacent east coast of Arabia, Magan stands for the Oman Peninsula and the opposite coast of Iran, and Meluhha designates Greater Indus Valley. Goods imported from Meluhha include lapis lazuli (the Harappan colony of Shortughai is near the lapis mines in Afghanistan), carnelian, ivory, fowls (native to

India and domesticated by Harappans), *haya*-birds (peacocks) screaming in palaces, and "sea-wood" (hard-wooded mangrove).

Some Indus seals from western Asia are typically Harappan square stamp seals; their inscriptions, too, agree with South Asian Indus texts, which have uniform sign sequences. Some other seals have common Indus signs in quite dissimilar sequences. Apparently these Harappan trade agents were bilingual and had local names, some adopting also the local cylinder type of seal. The Meluhhan language was not understood in Mesopotamia, for one Akkadian cylinder seal belonged to "Su-ilishu, interpreter of the Meluhhan language."

Forty-four cuneiform texts mention Meluhha as a village in southern Mesopotamia or as a proper name of some people residing there – others have purely Sumerian names. This Meluhha village was also called Guabba: originally on the coast, it was close to the city of Girsu (Lagash), where 4,272 women and 1,800 children from Guabba worked as weavers (Vermaak, 2008). Guabba's association with textile industry strengthens the assumption that cotton was among the principal Harappan trade items.

Between 2000 and 1900 BCE, the Indus civilization came to an end in the Indus Valley, although it lingered some centuries longer in Gujarat and Maharashtra (Daimabad). Multiple causes are assumed for its gradual deterioration and the eventual collapse of urban life, which made the Indus script and seals superfluous. Stagnant water of irrigation canals may have dissolved ground salts and made fields uncultivable. Thick layers of silt in Mohenjo-daro attest to catastrophic floods, and people lying unburied in streets died of malaria. The climate is supposed to have become drier, and the Indus and Ghaggar-Hakra Rivers changed their courses.

Harappans did not disappear, but their culture started changing. There is clear continuity into the posturban Jhukar culture in Sind and the Cemetery H culture in the Punjab and Cholistan. Early and Mature Harappan cultural heritage likewise continues in the Ochre Colored Pottery (OCP) culture (with Copper Hoards) of the Doab and upper Gangetic Valley, and in the various Chalcolithic cultures of Gujarat, Rajasthan, Madhya Pradesh, and Maharashtra.

The traditional Harappan burial mode was inhumation with grave goods in separate graveyards. In Cemetery-H of Harappa, where the new cremation burial prevails, funerary urns are painted with peacocks, which, within their bodies, take horizontal human beings to the stars. This tells something of Harappan ideas of the afterlife.

One important factor of change was the influx of new people from Central Asia. They brought to the Greater Indus Valley the domesticated horse, donkey, and camel and the Indo-Aryan language. These immigrants came from the Bactria and Margiana Archaeological Complex (BMAC). An early wave came to Baluchistan (Sibri), Sind (Chanhudaro), and Rajasthan (Gilund) in circa 1900 BCE. Another wave came to Swat (Gandhāra Grave culture) in circa 1600 BCE. Composers of the oldest rgvedic hymns (the "Family Books"; see → Vedas) probably came with King Divodāsa and his (grand?)son Sudās from Seistan through eastern Afghanistan to the Punjab in the 14th century BCE. The strongholds of inimical Dāsas, broken open with Indra's help, were not Harappan cities, but fortified manors inherited from the BMAC in circa 1500 BCE by Proto-Śaka–speaking Iranians of the Yaz-1 culture, who had come riding from the steppes of southeastern Europe (Parpola, 2002; 2005a; 2005b; 2009b; forthcoming a).

The BMAC (2400–1500 BCE) formed in southern Turkmenistan and northern Afghanistan under cultural influences from Mesopotamia, Elam, and southwestern Turkmenistan. Its people originally spoke a language known only from the many loanwords it left in Indo-Aryan and Iranian languages (Lubotsky, 2001). From 2000 BCE onward, the BMAC was infiltrated by Proto-Indo-Aryan speakers, who came from the Sintashta culture of the southern Urals and its successors, the Andronovo cultures of Kazakhstan. The horse-drawn chariot created in the Sintashta culture was soon after 2000 BCE introduced to the BMAC and to northern Iran, Anatolia, and Syria, where Proto-Indo-Aryan–speaking princes ruled the Mitanni Kingdom from 1500 to 1300 BCE. The Sintashta culture goes back to the Yamnaya (Pit Grave) culture of the Pontic-Caspian steppes (3300–2500 BCE) and this to the Late Tripolye culture (4100–3400 BCE), where Late Proto-Indo-European speakers invented the ox-drawn wagon and cart (Mallory, 1989; Anthony, 2007; Parpola, 2008).

Harappan Language

The problem of Harappan language must be viewed in the light of these posturban developments. Indo-Iranian languages, nowadays spoken by three-quarters of South Asia's population, and in the Indus Valley since the 2nd millennium BCE, do not qualify as the language of the Indus script and the majority of the Harappan people, whose culture was rather different from that of the rgvedic hymns. The domesticated horse was important in the cultures of early Indo-Iranian speakers, and there is no unambiguous evidence for Equus caballus in South Asia before 2000 BCE. The ambiguous evidence comes from the wild ass, the only native equid (Parpola & Janhunen, 2011).

While various minority languages and dialects are likely to have been spoken in the Greater Indus Valley, there was only one written Harappan language. This can be seen from the uniformity of sign sequences in South Asian Indus inscriptions, while Indus seals found in the Near East have both Indus-like and totally different sign sequences. If the written language belonged to a vanished language family not known from other sources, the Indus script can never be deciphered. As the Harappan population numbered around one million, and their cultural spread was wide, survival of related languages is likely, and the Harappan language can be expected to have left traces in the extensive vedic literature.

Increasing numbers of loanwords and even structural borrowings from Dravidian have been identified with certainty from the *Ṛgveda* and other vedic texts composed in northwest India between 1200 and 500 BCE, before any intensive contact between North and South India. Moreover, one heavily Iranianized Dravidian language, Brahui, is still spoken in Baluchistan and Sind. Until 1750 CE, when Baluchi took over, Brahui was the prestige language of Baluchistan, cradle of the Indus civilization.

Speakers of Dravidian languages constitute one-quarter of South Asia's population, being the largest linguistic group after Indo-Aryan. Tamil has records since the 2nd century BCE and an extensive and original ancient literature. Most of the 26 languages are spoken in central and southern India. The first Neolithic and Chalcolithic cultures of these regions, earlier thinly populated by Mesolithic hunter-gatherers, resulted from the spread of livestock from the Early Harappan cultures via Gujarat and Rajasthan. Southernmost India was settled when mounted Megalithic cultures with Black-and-Red Ware started spreading southward from Gujarat, Rajasthan, and Madhya Pradesh in 800 BCE. The carriers of these Early Iron Age cultures probably substantiated the linguistic Aryanization of Gujarat and Maharashtra (which have a sizeable Dravidian substratum vocabulary) but were linguistically Dravidianized farther south.

Speakers of Munda languages constitute one percent of South Asia's population. They are mainly spoken in eastern India, the westernmost Korku in central India being an isolated offshoot. The Munda languages belong to the Austro-Asiatic language family, and their linguistic relatives are in Southeast Asia.

The remaining linguistic groups are even smaller minorities. There are no linguistic traces farther south of the isolate Burushaski spoken in northernmost Pakistan. Burushaski must have come from the north after the Himalayan group of Tibeto-Burman languages, which were probably spoken in the Northern Neolithic of the Swat Valley and Kashmir, since this culture has links with China. Northern Neolithic had some contact with the Kot Diji culture, which continued to occupy northernmost Indus Valley even in Mature Harappan times.

Historical evidence thus strongly suggests that the Harappans mainly spoke Proto-Dravidian. This is endorsed by the Indus script and religious evidence.

Harappan Religion

Art motifs (ably analyzed by Franke-Vogt, 1991) and architectural remains are among the main sources for Harappan religion. For their successful interpretation we can resort to comparison with related and better-known religions, especially those of later South Asia and the ancient Near East, with which the Indus civilization was in contact. Even regularities valid for all or most agriculturally based riverine and urban cultures can be useful for reconstructing Harappan religion. Thus predicting floods and fixing seasonal farming operations and associated festivals necessitated solar-time reckoning. This directed priestly attention to heavenly phenomena, and astronomy/astrology became an important part of religion.

It is reasonable to expect that historical South Asia has preserved Harappan traditions. Late Harappan people outnumbered Indo-Aryan-speaking immigrants. Fusion of these principal population groups continued for many centuries with mixed marriages and growing bilingualism. Newcomers' need to deal with the majority population gave local leaders and priests a chance to act as middlemen and obtain important positions in the emerging new social order.

Our sources result from the ensuing syncretism, which requires acculturation analysis (Parpola, 2004). A comparison with local flora and fauna helps in identifying native components. To sift apart the contributions of the different waves of Indo-Aryan–speaking immigrants, we have to know their religious background. This approach is utilized below. In acculturation analysis, one needs to look also outside South Asia. Components of vedic and other Indian religions not paralleled in Iranian and/or other Indo-European traditions may have their roots in the Indus civilization. Thus the *nakṣatra* calendar (see → astrology), first hinted at in the late marriage hymn of the *Ṛgveda* (10.95) and not attested in the Iranian tradition, almost certainly comes from the Harappans, who needed solar time reckoning.

Religious continuity from the Indus civilization to later times has often been seriously doubted. I recently noted (Parpola, 2011a, 25–30) a case where present-day Gujarati tribes seem to have preserved a Harappan religious tradition virtually unchanged for four thousand years. Many Indus sacrificial tablets and some seals bear crocodile images. A Mature Harappan potsherd from Amri in Sind shows two crocodiles that have no hind legs; instead, a bar projecting out in 90° angle from the back part of the body links it with the border of the image. An explanation of this puzzling scene is supplied by the unique crocodile cult of some 50 tribal villages in southern Gujarat, documented by E. Fischer and H. Shah (1971). Four- or eight-faceted images of crocodiles, normally a couple, are made of wood and installed on wooden posts. The installation ceremony celebrates their wedding, and the images are worshipped by smearing them with red vermilion paste and with offerings of chicken or goats and milk or alcohol, afterward consumed by the participants. The male crocodile can be substituted with a *liṅga*-like post or the couple with a single crocodile having a head at either end. This crocodile cult is both communal and individual: people ask the crocodile gods for cows to give milk and calves and for good crops, offspring, or help against illness and sorcery, making a vow to install and worship the god if the boon is granted.

The Neolithic villages of Baluchistan have clay figurines of human females and bulls as their principal surviving religious objects. The female figurines undoubtedly portray the earth goddess, who, after seeds have been sown into her womb, generates plants and nurtures people like a mother gives birth to children and takes care of them. In many archaic religions, the thundering and raining sky was conceived as a roaring bull, whose semen fertilizes his spouse the earth. The bull also relates to the other main source of food, animal husbandry.

Early Harappan religion is reflected in the motifs of painted pottery. The following continue in the Indus civilization and are clearly important: water buffalo, fish, fish scale, fig tree (*pīpal* or *banyan*), and intersecting circles. Shift of cultural focus from piedmont to floodplains increased the importance of water in general and of rivers with their animals. Especially noteworthy is the prominence of water buffalo, from Sind (Kot Diji) to the

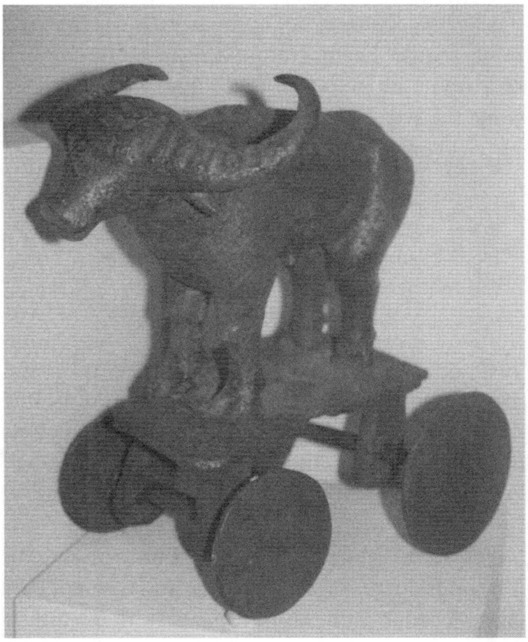

Fig. 4: Daimabad, Maharashtra, the southernmost Indus site. Water buffalo 31 cm high and 25 cm long, standing on a platform attached to four solid wheels. One of four bronze sculptures weighing together over 60 kg, found in a hoard in 1974 and ascribed to the Late Harappan or Chalcolithic period (photo by Asko Parpola).

upper Indus Valley (Rahman Dheri, Burzahom). Water buffalo belongs to river fauna, as it must bathe daily. With the single exception of tiger, wild buffalo is the most dangerous beast of South Asia.

Terracotta figurines of human females and a variety of male animals continue earlier fertility cults in Early and Mature Harappan periods. Male human figurines make their first appearance in Early Harappan Mehrgarh VII. They are usually turbaned and sometimes have a child in arms. Numerous similar male figures accompany a goddess seated on a throne in a unique clay model of a cultic boat (Vidale, 2011). Of the human figurines excavated at Harappa, 1,143 were identified as female (some holding infants) and 407 as male. Most of the 500 human and animal figurines recorded at Mohenjo-daro came from "terminal rooms" of the houses, having a single entrance, thus comparable to later South Asian → *pūjā* rooms (Ardeleanu-Jansen, 1992). Incidentally, the term *pūjā* probably comes from the Proto-Dravidian root *pūcu-*, used for "smearing" sacred objects and persons with red vermilion or yellow turmeric paste (Charpentier, 1927); vermilion was applied to the parting of hair in Harappan female figurines (Kenoyer, 1998, 44, 186).

Life in Indian villages has not changed much since Early Harappan times until very recently, and Indian folk religion is particularly conservative.

> Every village has its own special guardian mother, called *Mātā* or *Ambā*. Generally there is also a male deity, who protects like the female from all adverse and demoniacal influences. But the mother is the favorite object of adoration. (Monier-Williams, 1891, 222)

Such a *grāmadevatā* (village deity) personifies the village and its soil, out of which the local potter makes her cult images. She is not only prayed to for blessings like children, health, and animals, but also feared, for she can bring about terrible calamity like a pestilence, if neglected or angered.

Early and Mature Harappan cultures are the ultimate sources of the Neolithic and Chalcolithic cultures that formed in central and southern India. It is therefore quite significant that a special form of goddess cult matching indications of what Harappan religion may have been like is preserved on village level all over Dravidian-speaking South India. Village goddesses have been worshipped there with water-buffalo sacrifices associated with a subordinate male deity, called buffalo king (Tel. Pōtu Rāju), represented by a wooden post, stone pillar, or *pīpal* tree. The power of the goddesses is limited to the village, their temples being on its borders and center. To bless the village and to cleanse it of evil, the buffalo victim or its severed head is taken in a procession around the village and then discarded beyond its limits along with the temporary clay images of the goddess (Biardeau, 2004). In Tamil Nadu, the yearly *māriyammaṉ* festival celebrates the marriage of the goddess Māriyammaṉ and the sacrificed buffalo. The low-caste bridegroom had tricked into marriage the high-caste goddess, who on discovering the fraud killed the culprit and transformed him into a tree (Beck, 1981).

M. Biardeau rightly distinguishes the village-level goddess cult of South India from the goddess cult of princely houses, which alone is found in North India. The royal goddess cult, sometimes involving the sacrifice of hundreds of buffalos, is associated with military expeditions. Warfare traditionally started around the autumnal equinox, when the rains stop (the "bull of heaven" dying!) and roads become passable. The *navarātri* festival culminating in the *vijayadaśamī* celebrates the victory of the virginal, lion- or tiger-riding goddess → Durgā over the buffalo-demon (Mahiṣāsura). On his death, this formidable enemy and wooer is turned into a devoted servant of the goddess.

The earliest literary sources of this military goddess cult are the original *Skandapurāṇa* (68.10–23) of 500–700 CE and the *Devīmāhātmya* of 750–800 CE (Yokochi, 2005). Mahiṣāsuramardinī ("Slayer of the Buffalo-Demon") images are earlier, from Kushana times; the invading Kushanas are thought to have introduced Durgā's cult to India (Stietencron, 1983). The Kushanas in turn adopted the cult of goddess Nanaya or Nana upon their arrival in Afghanistan in circa 150 BCE. Still worshipped there as "Bibi Nani," Nanaya is a variant of the Mesopotamian goddess Inanna-Ištar, who came to Afghanistan circa 2000 BCE, being depicted there on BMAC seals in Mesopotamian dress and flanked by lions (Potts, 2001). Her cult was inherited by the Proto-Śaka–speaking successors of the BMAC circa 1500 BCE: the Dāsa chief Śambara and his "autumnal" fortresses encountered by rgvedic Aryans circa 1300 BCE are connected with the tantric god Śambara and the *navarātri* with its *śabarotsava* (Parpola, 2002; forthcoming a).

M. Biardeau (2004) derives the post of the buffalo-king from the similarly shaped vedic sacrificial pole (*yūpa*) and the buffalo sacrifice from the royal horse sacrifice (*aśvamedha*; see → *yajña*) of the Veda. In my view, the *aśvamedha* largely goes back to Harappan buffalo sacrifice. Spearing of water buffalo is represented on several Harappan objects. This Harappan tradition survived in the Indus Valley until at least 1200 BCE. Rgvedic religion focused on praising Indra with hymns and offering him *soma* drink, but several hymns mention hundreds of water buffalos offered to increase Indra's warring strength (*ṚV.* 5.29.7–8; 6.17.11; 8.12.8, 77.10). This shows that at an early stage of acculturation, this impressive local cult associated with warring was at least witnessed if not adopted by some rgvedic people.

After the *Ṛgveda*, water buffalo sacrifice totally disappears from vedic literature, excepting its inclusion in the *aśvamedha* catalogue of manifold subsidiary animal victims (*MaiSa.* 3.14.10; *varuṇāya mahiṣān*). Here, the water buffalo is sacred to Varuṇa, the rival of Indra as the divine king. In Hinduism, the buffalo is associated with Mahiṣāsura (who has Varuṇa's lordly title *asura*) and with → Yama, the god of death, who, like Varuṇa, is the righteous king (Dharmarāja). The central deities of the earlier wave of Indo-Aryan speakers are the Aśvin twins connected with the horse-drawn chariot and their doubles, the dual kings Mitra and Varuṇa (Parpola, 2005a; 2005b). The horse and the chariot race of the *vājapeya* (see → yajña) are their contributions in the "agonistic pre-classical rituals" of the Veda (Heesterman, 1962; 1967). It seems that at first Varuṇa was identified with the head of the Harappan pantheon and his buffalo, but later, buffalo sacrifice was totally banned from vedic culture, and horse substituted for it in royal rituals. Later even the violent and sexual acts of "preclassical" rituals were purged out by substituting them with verbal and other symbols. Outside the vedic realm, the Harappan tradition continued, eventually developing into Śaiva-Śākta Tantrism.

The earth goddess personified by a lion is, in a veiled manner, attested in vedic texts of circa 700 BCE as the bride and killer of the buffalo. Goddess Vāc is equated with the earth and addressed as *aṣāḍhā* (invincible; *ŚBr.* 7.4.2.32–39) and as *simhī* (lioness) and *mahiṣī* (female buffalo), as securing victory over the demons (*ŚBr.* 3.5.1–2; Parpola, 1999). The *aśvamedha* culminates in the sacred marriage of the chief victim with the chief queen, who personifies the earth. The queen's title *mahiṣī* suggests that her royal husband, represented by the victim, was *mahiṣa*, the great beast, water-buffalo bull, and that the victim originally was water buffalo. A seal from Chanhu-daro supplies a Harappan counterpart to this "sacred marriage": a bison bull with exposed penis is about to mount a prostrate human female with legs apart and vulva visible (Parpola, 1985, 103).

J. Marshall (1931, 52–55) gave the name "Proto-Śiva" to an impressive male deity depicted on a seal from Mohenjo-daro. Most of his arguments have been rejected (Franke-Vogt, 1991, 79–82). The "*yoga* posture," characteristic of seated Harappan deities, seems to come from Proto-Elamite art (Parpola, 1984). "Proto-Śiva" wears buffalo's horns and should therefore rather be called "Proto-Mahiṣa" (Hiltebeitel, 1978), but as Mahiṣāsura is sometimes identified with → Śiva, the traditional label may be kept. "Proto-Śiva" is ithyphallic and surrounded by four male beasts noted for strength and virility: elephant, rhinoceros, tiger, and water buffalo. He probably has four rather than three faces, looking into all directions like the Hindu god → Brahmā, successor to the vedic creator-god Prajāpati.

Prajāpati first created the goddess Vāc out of himself and then wanted to pair with his own daughter. She escaped his incestuous advances by becoming the female of one animal species after another, Prajāpati becoming the corresponding male. They thus created all the different animals. In the *Devīmāhātmya*, Mahiṣa similarly becomes one ferocious male animal after another, to be killed by Durgā as a human warrior (Parpola, 1992).

These myths make all male animals manifestations of one Prajāpati/Mahiṣa. This may explain the animals of the "Proto-Śiva" seal, and the Harappan seals depicting composite beasts whose various body parts belong to two or more species. The most elaborate one has zebu's horns, human face, elephant's tusks and trunk, wild goat's neck and front legs, "unicorn" bull's body, tiger's hind legs, and a snake for a tail. In the *aśvamedha*, various animals are tied to the different body parts of the horse (*ŚBr.* 13.2.2). Most of the real male animals on Indus seals are wild, yet a manger is usually placed in front of them. This may indicate that, as in the *aśvamedha* and South Indian buffalo sacrifices, the victim was consecrated one year ahead of the sacrifice, and could then wander at will as divine, "fed and tended by one and all"

(Biardeau, 2004, 87–88). In the *aśvamedha*, there are wild victims, but they are freed (*ŚBr.* 13.2.4).

The *Kālikāpurāṇa* grades the victims pleasing the Goddess from the most valuable (man, buffalo, *śarabha* [markhor goat], lion, tiger, and rhinoceros) to the cheapest (fish). Vedic *aśvamedha* and *puruṣamedha* have similar long lists of subsidiary victims (*VājSa.* 30). Vedic human sacrifice is considered theoretical, but the *Vādhūlaśrautasūtra* (11.21) mentions as the carver of the sacrificed horse a virginal (*asiktaretas*) youth (*kumāra*) who was garlanded and lamented as if he was to die, because in former times, he himself was cut up. A human victim is mentioned in the *Ṛgveda* (10.90.6–16) as the primeval man (*puruṣa*) out of whose severed limbs the world came into being (Parpola, 2007). Sacrifice of a human warrior is implied by the Mahiṣāsura myth. In ancient South India, heroes even cut their own head to secure the goddess' favor and victory to their king (Vogel, 1930–1932). In *Jātaka* 353, a king wanting to conquer Takṣaśilā is advised by his chaplain to sacrifice one thousand captive princes to a *banyan* tree housing a deity to gain victory. A seal from Mohenjo-daro shows a kneeling worshipper with hands raised in prayer in front of a banyan and its deity; on a *balipīṭha* (bench for sacrificial offerings) is a severed head of a warrior, recognizable from his chignon. The seven women at the bottom of the seal can be identified as the *saptamātṛkās* (seven mothers), worshipped as aspects of the Goddess.

The Harappans also had a tiger-riding goddess of war, who wore markhor's horns topped by an acacia branch. On a cylinder seal from Kalibangan, she holds by hand two warriors who are spearing each other. Mesopotamian influence is visible in the seal type and in the warriors' chignon hair, worn by princely warriors in the Near East around 2400 BCE. I turn to Near Eastern religions to shed more light on her cult (Parpola, forthcoming b).

In Anatolia, in circa 7000 BCE, the earth goddess was sculpted as a woman sitting on a lion-throne and giving birth; bulls were sacrificed to her. In the 1st millennium BCE, the mystic cult of her successor, the Anatolian goddess Cybele, included taurobolium, pouring sin-cleansing blood of the sacrificed bull on the worshipper. Cybele's lions guarded city gates, and city walls crowned her mountain-head.

The principal Mesopotamian goddess Inanna-Ištar had the lion and planet Venus as her symbols. As the evening star, she presided over sexual love and prostitutes. As the star of morning, the time of attacks, she was a bloodthirsty warrior, standing by her princely favorites. Fertility of vegetation, animals, and humans was believed to depend on the union of Inanna and her lover Dumuzi, a young shepherd. In their sacred marriage, celebrated on the new year's day, Dumuzi was identified with the king, but the marriage was enacted by priestly personnel, while people participated in processions, dance, music, and banquets. When Inanna tried to conquer the underworld ruled by her sister, she could not return without Dumuzi becoming her replacement. Dumuzi's death was ritually lamented, but he was allowed to return for six months every year.

Proto-Elamite art of 3100–2700 BCE represents the lion and the bull as adversaries. On one seal, an enormous bull masters two small lions, and a giant lion dominates two small bulls. Next to the lion is a pictogram similar to Sumerian KI, "earth." In Proto-Elamite art, the lion is often female and thus represents a goddess. All this agrees with the Sumerian myth, where *ki*, "earth," was the female counterpart of *an*, "heaven"; their union produced many plants. The symmetrically balanced victories and defeats of the lion and the bull, comparable to the alternation of day and night, suggest that these two are personifications of opposite and complementary cosmic forces.

In early Sumerian art of 3400–3100 BCE, the king hunts lions and wild bulls. He is a match for these mightiest of beasts, kings of animals. The Proto-Elamite fight between the lion and the bull developed in Mesopotamia into the "contest" scene, where a human hero kills a bull, and a bull-man kills a lion. This is the dominant motif of royal seals since 2600 BCE. The six-locked hero replacing the lion apparently represents the king, for in Mesopotamian poems, King Gilgamesh kills sky-god An's "bull of heaven" (Sum. GU_4-AN-NA).

During the 60-year-long rule of Sargon the Great, the wild aurochs bull of the "contest" scene was suddenly replaced with the water buffalo, an animal not earlier present in Mesopotamia. In other Sargonic seals, water buffalo is connected with the Sumerian water-god Enki. Meluhhan ships supposedly brought buffalos as royal gifts to Sargon. In the Harappan images of buffalo spearing, the spearman places one foot on the beast's head. From Sargon's times onward, this pose signifies victory in Mesopotamian glyptics. The

Sumerian motif of the king holding back two lions with bare hands, in use from 3400 to 2500 BCE, was adopted into Indus seals. The Harappans replaced lions with tigers but retained the hero's Mesopotamian hair style (six locks or chignon).

The lion and the bull had astral counterparts in the zodiacal signs Leo and Taurus, called in Sumerian ^{mul}UR.GU.LA (lion; Alpha Leonis being the "royal star," *šarru* [= Regulus]) and ^{mul}GU$_4$-AN-NA (bull of heaven). Sumerian sculptures of a reclining bull, covered with inlaid trefoils and quatrefoils, date from 3100–2900 and 2100–1900 BCE. These "bulls of heaven" compare with the cow-shaped Egyptian "lady of heaven" covered with trefoils. The trefoil resembles the Sumerian pictogram (triangle of three stars) MUL "constellation." A fragmentary bull sculpture from Mohenjo-daro is covered with red-colored trefoils and figures-of-eight.

Near Eastern gods and divine kings had festive cloths with golden stars and rosettes sewn on them, called "sky garment" (Sum. AN.MA). A Syrian deity is described in the 5th century CE as "clad in a patterned robe like the sky" and "called Starclad, since by night starry mantles illuminate the sky" (Nonnus, *Dionysiaca* 40.367–369, 408–416). The dress of the priest-king statue from Mohenjo-daro wears "sky garment" decorated with trefoils, figures of eight, and dots in circle, originally filled with red paste. This Harappan dress seems to have passed on to the vedic royal consecration. The king was invested with the *tārpya* garment belonging to the divine king Varuṇa, who is associated with the waters and the night sky. The *tārpya* garment had images of sacrificial fireplaces (*dhiṣṇya*) sewn onto it. In the → *Mahābhārata* (3.43), the stars are pious ancient sages standing on their fireplaces (*dhiṣṇya*) in the sky (Parpola, 1985).

The Indus Script

Some five thousand texts in the enigmatic Indus script survive on seals, seal impressions, small tablets, and potsherds. But multilingual texts (the usual key to unknown scripts) are lacking, the script is not related to any other known script, all texts are very short, and there is hardly any historical information about the Indus people. These obstacles are not the only reason why so many attempts have failed to solve the problem: in addition come false methods and assumptions. Yet the case is not totally hopeless. Successful decipherments of other scripts and the history of writing give methodological guidance. They underline the importance of several preparatory tasks, such as collection of all available material (*CISI*, vols. I–III/1), establishing the direction of writing (in Indus texts normally from right to left, reversed in seal stamps), reliable readings of the texts and a list of distinct signs and their variants, compilation of statistics and concordances (Mahadevan, 1977), and identifying which kind of writing system is involved.

When the Indus script was created circa 2600 BCE, all existing scripts were of the logo-syllabic type. In addition to its age, the number of distinct signs (around 400) and the "word" length (from one to four signs) support this typological classification of the Indus script. Syllabic and alphabetic scripts developed later (c. 2300 and c. 1600 BCE, respectively), through simplification of logo-syllabic scripts that had been used for many centuries, and they had essentially fewer graphemes (around 100 and fewer than 50 respectively) and greater "word" lengths.

In early logo-syllabic scripts, most signs were originally pictures denoting the objects or ideas that they depicted. Abstract concepts such as "life" were expressed by means of the rebus or picture-puzzle principle based on punning: any given sign could stand not only for the word (Gk. *logos*, word) that named the thing depicted, but also for its phonetic shape, its syllable(s). Thus in Archaic Sumerian script, the arrow-shaped sign stands for Sumerian *ti* (arrow) and for *ti* (life) and *ti* (rib).

For Sumerian speakers, these were not just three different words pronounced alike; their phonetic identity revealed an otherwise hidden connection among the concepts involved. A Sumerian myth tells how goddess Nin-ti, mistress of *life*, healed the *rib* of sick water-god Enki. Homophonies are language specific: in the Hebrew version – the creation of Eve (Mother of All *Living*) out of Adam's *rib* – the myth has lost its original punning motivation as the key words are not alike. Successful study of the Indus script may reveal similar wordplay behind Indian myths and rituals of Harappan origin whose meaning has become blurred with post-Harappan language shifts.

Without extensive translations, a complete decipherment of an unknown logo-syllabic script is not possible, but a limited decipherment of some signs is feasible. If the outward shape of a sign is pictorially explicit and can be understood, then it yields the sign's pictorial meaning. Contextual clues may allow conclusions about what a given sign was actually purported to mean in a specific text, its hypothetical intended semantic meaning. If both the pictorial and the intended meaning of a sign can be determined, and they coincide, then this strengthens the assumed shared meaning but yields no phonetic reading. If the pictorial and intended meanings differ, then the intended meaning may result from the sign's use as a rebus in phonetic meaning. Then one can look for two homophonous words (whose linguistic reconstructions fulfill critical requirements) that match the pictorial and intended meanings in the assumed Indus language reconstructable from known related languages.

Cross-checking becomes possible if two signs following each other in a recurring sequence (or two components of a composite sign) can both be interpreted and yield compound words that have actually existing counterparts in languages assumed to be related with the Indus language. As in crossword puzzles, accumulation of cross-checks increases the credibility of proposed interpretations. Equally important control is their cultural fit and explanatory power.

Small bifacial tablets usually have on one side the sign looking like U (variant V), preceded or not by one, two, three, or four vertical strokes representing numbers one to four (U may be repeated instead: UUU = "three U"). An exceptional tablet has a longer text beginning with "four U," while next to it, a kneeling human being extends a U-shaped object toward a sacred tree. This suggests that U depicts a vessel of offerings. A kneeling worshipper is occasionally attached to the U-sign in the sequence one/two/three/four + U. The interpretation is supported by a tablet showing an anthropomorphic deity seated on a throne and flanked by kneeling worshippers, one holding the offering vessel, the other with hands raised in adoration. The intended semantic meaning agrees with the pictorial meaning of U, "pot in profile." We need not know what it was called in the Indus language to understand the meaning of the sign.

The same applies to the "fish" sign when it is added after "four U" in three tablets and between "four" and "U" in one tablet. These sequences may mean "four pots fish" and "four fish pots." Naturalistic fish are painted on Early and Mature Harappan pots, and the hypothesis of Harappan fish offerings to sacred trees agrees with the offering of fish, meat, and strong drinks (in pots) to fertility spirits on festive days in early historical India (*Jātaka* 113). Sacred trees, the favorite abodes of these → *yakṣa*s and *yakṣī*s, were made to grow and bear fruit by pouring at their roots "fish-water" (water with pieces of fish in it; *AgP.* 247.28). In ancient Mesopotamia as well, "fish were an important item of food, not for men only, but also for the gods" (van Buren, 1948, 102–103).

But a sign is not fully deciphered as long as its ancient pronunciation has not been recovered. The function of an inscribed artifact provides another kind of contextual clue to the general meaning of its text. Most Indus texts are seals. Ancient seal impressions have been preserved on clay tags, which have traces of cloth, strings, and other packing material on the reverse, indicating that Harappan seals were used in economic transactions. Almost a hundred such clay tags with seal impressions have survived in the burnt-down warehouse of the harbor town Lothal in Gujarat. Some bear more than one seal stamp, attesting to Harappan bureaucratic procedures. One tag stamped with an Indus seal comes from Mesopotamia, where seals were used in like manner. Indus seal inscriptions may therefore chiefly contain proper names or titles of the seal owners, as do ancient Near Eastern seal inscriptions.

The fish sign, both plain and modified with various diacritic additions, occurs very frequently on Indus seals. But fish is never mentioned in Mesopotamian seal inscriptions, although economic texts there often speak of fish. This suggests that the fish signs denote something other than fish on Indus seals. The usual word for fish in Dravidian languages is *mīn*. Its Proto-Dravidian reconstruction agrees with *mīn* (star). In the cuneiform script, every divine name is marked as such by a prefixed sign depicting a star but meaning "god." This classificatory sign occurs in seal inscriptions very frequently, because personal names usually had divine names as their components. In Mesopotamia, astronomy played an important role, and all principal gods had particular stars or planets as their symbols. The Harappans needed a star calendar and adopted Mesopotamian art motifs with astral symbolism. In Hinduism, too, stars and planets are worshipped and have Hindu divinities as their "overlords." Vedic Gṛhyasūtras further prescribe that children should be given secret star names. The fish signs may therefore stand for Proto-Dravidian star names, used as symbols for gods and as component parts of human proper names.

The Dravidian linguistic association between fish and star seems to be reflected on Harappan painted pottery from Amri: starlike dots in circle surrounded by rays occur inside and outside naturally depicted fish. In the Near East, the star symbol, placed next to the god's head, distinguished divinities even in pictorial representations. A seal from Mohenjo-daro depicts a squatting Indus deity in this fashion, with a star on either side of the head. Early Harappan pottery has star symbols similar to the cuneiform star sign, but in the Indus script, such a sign does not occur. This is understandable for reasons of economy, fully in agreement with the principles of early writing and the rebus principle: *mīn* means both fish and star, and the same sign can be used in both meanings. Indeed, both words seem to be derived from the verbal root *min*,"to glitter," *mīn* originally denoting "a glittering object," whether in the water or in the sky. At least Tamils have conceived stars as fish swimming in a heavenly ocean or river. This may explain why "fish" was chosen as the "pictorial meaning" of the sign instead of "star." Fish is an important motif of Early Harappan painted pottery, and the water-god seems to have headed the Indus pantheon. His symbol, therefore, became the marker of divinity, just as in Mesopotamia the star, thought to have originally been a symbol for just the sky-god An, was transferred from this chief god to all deities: in the Sumerian script, the star pictogram means both sky (*an*) and god (*dingir*).

On a tablet from Mohenjo-daro, a seated anthropomorphic god with a horned crown is flanked on either side by a crocodile and a fish, identical in shape with the fish sign. On a cylinder seal made in Mesopotamia by a Harappan craftsman, the same god is depicted with a pair of water buffalos under his throne, flanked on either side by a fish and a hooded and horned snake, and wearing a crown of buffalo horns topped by banyan leaves. Mesopotamian glyptics represent the water-god Enki with rivers issuing from both sides of his body and with fish swimming in these rivers. Enki is praised as a phallic god, who fecundates the soil with his semen – either flood or rain water.

In Hinduism, Varuṇa is the lord of waters, which is his title also in the Veda. Varuṇa's mount is either water monster *makara* or fish (Tam. *mīṉūrti*). Love-god Kāma likewise rides on *makara* and bears fish in his flag. Fish, with its phallic shape and phenomenal reproduction rate, symbolizes fertility and is used as an aphrodisiac in South Asia. As the principal aquatic animal, fish is offered to water in the *aśvamedha* (*MaiSa.* 3.14.2). The importance of the water cult in the Indus civilization is reflected in the public and private bathrooms of Mohenjo-daro as well as its wells and drainage systems. Mohenjo-daro may have had even *ghāṭ* -like bathing places; the word *ghāṭ* in any case has a Dravidian etymology (*kaṭṭay*, "dam," "embankment," "bank of river" and *kaṭa-*, "to cross over") and supports the old derivation of related Hindu traditions from the Indus civilization (Parpola, 2003).

Numerals are written with groups of vertical strokes as in many ancient scripts, this being confirmed by their mutual interchangeability before specific signs, including the plain fish. The sequence "6" + "fish" yields the Old Tamil name of the Pleiades, *aṟu-mīṉ*, literally six stars. The sequence "3" + "fish" corresponds to *mu-m-mīṉ*, three stars, the Old Tamil name of the *mṛgaśīrṣa* constellation. The sequence "7" + "fish" equals the Old Tamil name of Ursa Major (Big Dipper), *eḻu-mīṉ*. This sequence forms the entire inscription in one large seal from Harappa; it can be compared to large dedicatory seals presented to divinities in Mesopotamia. Vedic texts identify the stars of Ursa Major with the ancient seven sages (*saptarṣayaḥ*). These mythical ancestors of priestly clans and their wives, Arundhatī and the Pleiades, play an important role in central Hindu myths that appear to be of Harappan origin: the birth of Rudra-Skanda, the vedic-Hindu counterpart of Tamil → Murukaṉ (whose Old Tamil names Muruku and Vēḷ seem to occur in Indus texts), and the origins of the phallic *liṅga* cult and the *nakṣatra* calendar (Parpola, 1994; 2009a). The seven sages moreover have a counterpart in the seven sages of the Mesopotamian religion, represented as half fish, half men: both groups are said to have survived the Flood, a myth primarily at home in a riverine civilization.

Even nonnumeral attributes of the fish signs can be systematically interpreted from the same premises. One looks like a roof placed over the fish sign. Proto-Dravidian *mēy-mīn* (roof-fish) is nearly homophonous with *may-mīn* (black star). The latter compound is attested in Old Tamil as the name of the planet Saturn. Saturn is mostly rather dim, and, in Sanskrit texts, too, it is associated with the color black (see → *navagrahas*). As a slow planet, Saturn in Buddhist and Jain iconography rides the proverbially slow turtle. The pictogram could thus symbolize Saturn not only phonetically but also as a picture of his vehicle, the turtle, an aquatic animal (fish) covered with a shell (roof).

Another diacritic is drawn directly or obliquely across the body of the fish sign, halving it. Dividing a fish into two equal parts is a motif in Indian folklore. Proto-Dravidian *pacu* (to halve, divide in two) is homophonous with *pacu* (green, fresh, and cool). The resulting compound *pacu-mīn* is attested in the meaning green fish, and *paccai*, literally greenness, is a Tamil name for the planet Mercury.

A scene on an extraordinary seal from a "palace" in Mohenjo-daro was interpreted above: the goddess inside a *banyan* tree receives the offering of a warrior's severed head, while her kneeling high priest raises hands in supplication. The last two signs of the accompanying inscription are the same as the last two signs of the "Proto-Śiva" seal found in the same palace. The last sign is pictorially clear: a human being drawn in stick fashion. It probably stands for Proto-Dravidian *āḷ*/*āṇ* (man, servant), which matches the Mesopotamian priestly titles "man/servant of god NN." The penultimate sign resembles Early Harappan pictures of bull's head; this most frequently occurring Indus sign may be read *ā*/*ān* ([male or female] cow) and could here represent the genitive suffix *-ā*. The foregoing sign in the "Proto-Śiva" seal is the plain fish, symbol of the water-god. In the fig-deity seal, it is fish with a dot in the stomach. The dot probably is the red dot put on the forehead, especially at marriage and by married women and by men at goddess worship. In Dravidian South India, it is called *poṭṭu* (which also means "drop," like Skt. *bindu*). The compound *boṭu-mīn* (from *poṭṭu-mīn*) in Central Dravidian Pengo means "a kind of fish," which the cognates identify as *rohita* fish. Sanskrit *rohita* means "red" and "carp" (Cyprinus/Labeo rohita). In Karnataka, the married couple catches a carp and uses its red scales to make each other a forehead mark. *Rohiṇī*, the feminine form of *rohita* (red), is the Sanskrit name of the red star Aldebaran, which rose together with the sun at vernal equinox in 3054 BCE, in Early Harappan times. The Pleiades had this position in 2240 BCE, but there are indications that *rohiṇī* was the original new-year star of the *nakṣatra* calendar. The Gṛhyasūtras and Old Tamil texts mention *rohiṇī* as the star most auspicious for marriage. Rohiṇī as the faithful wife of the moon is a model for a Hindu wife. The *Atharvaveda* (*AVŚ*. 13.1.22), however, makes Rohiṇī the mate of the rising sun, Rohita, and a goddess of war. Sanskrit *rohiṇī* also denotes a marriageable young virgin who has just attained menstruation. The red *rohiṇī* star, therefore, may have been imagined to be a drop of menstrual blood, a suitable symbol for the goddess.

A recurring sequence of Indus signs is "fig tree" + "fish." The pictorial meaning "fig tree" comes from a similar three-branched-fig motif of Early, Mature, and Late Harappan painted pottery. "Fig" + "fish" has a counterpart in the Old Tamil compound *vaṭa-mīṉ*. Tamil *vaṭam* (*banyan* tree) and its cognates in other Dravidian languages have not been included in the *Dravidian Etymological Dictionary* (Burrow & Emeneau, 1984), being considered loans from Sanskrit *vaṭa* (*banyan*). The Sanskrit word, however, is first attested in the epics and has a very good etymology in Proto-Dravidian *vaṭam* (rope, cord). Ropelike air roots characterize *banyan*, which is called in Tamil also *vaṭa-maram* (rope tree). The homophony with Proto-Dravidian *vaṭa* (north) explains the puranic ascription of the *banyan* to the northern direction as its symbolic tree. The sequence "fig tree" + "fish" thus yields the compound *vaṭa-mīn* (north star), which in Old Tamil is the name of the tiny star Alcor in Ursa Major.

The seven stars of Ursa Major are the seven sages, and Alcor is Arundhatī, the faithful wife of the sage Vasiṣṭha. She was not seduced by Agni/Śiva like the other wives, and therefore she was allowed to remain with her husband; the others were divorced and form the separate six-star constellation Pleiades. Alcor is shown to the bride in a marriage ceremony as a model to be emulated. Originally *vaṭa-mīn* probably denoted the nearby pole star, also shown to the bride. In 4000–1900 BCE, the pole star was Thuban, close to Ursa Major and Vasiṣṭha's star Mizar. As the immobile center of the rotating heavens, the pole star is called in Sanskrit *dhruva* (immobile, firm). The bridegroom addresses the pole star with a long *mantra* originally belonging to the royal consecration, *varuṇasava* (Varuṇa's sacrifice), saying among other things: "I know thee as the nave of the universe; may I become the nave of this country" (*nabhyaṃ tvā sarvasya veda, nabhyam aham asya janapadasya bhūyāsam; HirGS*. 1.23.1). Varuṇa is the divine king, and the pole star is a symbol of royalty like the mighty *banyan* tree, the tree belonging to Varuṇa (*nyagrodho vāruṇo vṛkṣaḥ; GobhGS.* 4.7.24; Parpola, 1994, 245–246).

In the Purāṇas (*ViP.* 2.9; *MtP.* 127.122–124), it is asked, why do the stars and planets not fall down from the sky? The reply is that these heavenly bodies are bound to the pole star with invisible "ropes of wind." These "ropes" seem to refer to the air roots of the cosmic *banyan* tree, which King Varuṇa according to the *Ṛgveda* (1.24.10) holds up in the sky. Such a conception follows naturally from the Dravidian name *vaṭa-mīn* (north star = *banyan* star = rope star).

Bibliography

Agrawal, D.P., *The Indus Civilization: An Interdisciplinary Perspective*, New Delhi, 2007.

Agrawal, D.P., *The Archaeology of India*, SIASMS 46, London, 1982.

Anthony, D.W., *The Horse, the Wheel, and Language: How Bronze-Age Riders from the Eurasian Steppes Shaped the Modern World*, Princeton, 2007.

Ardeleanu-Jansen, A., "New Evidence on the Distribution of Artifacts: An Approach towards a Qualitative-Quantitative Assessment of the Terracotta Figurines of Mohenjo-daro," in: C. Jarrige, ed., *South Asian Archaeology 1989*, Madison, 1992, 5–14.

Beck, B., "The Goddess and the Demon: A Local South Indian Festival and Its Wider Context," in: M. Biardeau, ed., *Autour de la Déesse hindoue*, Puruṣārtha 5, Paris, 1981, 83–136.

Biardeau, M., *Stories about Posts: Vedic Variations around the Hindu Goddess*, Chicago, 2004.

Buren, E.D. van, "Fish Offerings in Ancient Mesopotamia," *Iraq* 10/2, 1948, 101–121.

Burrow, T., & M.B. Emeneau, *A Dravidian Etymological Dictionary*, Oxford, rev. ed. 1984.

Charpentier, J., "The Meaning and Etymology of *pūjā*," *IA* 65, 1927, 93–99, 130–136.

CISI (= *Corpus of Indus Seals and Inscriptions*), vols. I, II, III/1, AASF-B/H 239, 240, 359, Helsinki, 1987–2010.

Daniels, P.T., & W. Bright, eds., *The World's Writing Systems*, New York, 1996.

Eltsov, P.A., *From Harappa to Hastinapura: A Study of the Earliest South Asian City and Civilization*, Leiden, 2008.

Fischer, E., & H. Shah, *Mogra Dev, Tribal Crocodile Gods: Wooden Crocodile Images of Chodhri, Gamit and Vasava Tribes, South Gujarat (India)*, Ahmedabad, 1971.

Franke-Vogt, U.,"Der Golfhandel im späten 3. und frühen 2. Jt. v. Chr.," in: K. Bartl, R. Bernbeck & M. Heinz, eds., *Zwischen Euphrat und Indus*, Hildesheim, 1995a, 114–133.

Franke-Vogt, U., "Zwischen Evolution und Revolution. Die Entstehung der Induskultur," in: K. Bartl, R. Bernbeck & M. Heinz, eds., *Zwischen Euphrat und Indus*, Hildesheim, 1995b, 100–113.

Franke-Vogt, U., *Die Glyptik aus Mohenjo-Daro*, vols. I–II, BF 13, Mainz, 1991.

Hart, G.L., *The Poems of Ancient Tamil: Their Milieu and Their Sanskrit Counterparts*, Berkeley, 1975.

Heesterman, J.C., "The Case of the Severed Head," *WZKS* 11, 1967, 22–43.

Heesterman, J.C., "*Vrātya* and Sacrifice," *IIJ* 6, 1962, 1–37.

Hiltebeitel, A., "The Indus Valley 'Proto-Śiva,' Reexamined through Reflections on the Goddess, the Buffalo, and the Symbolism of *vāhanas*," *Anthropos* 73, 1978, 767–797.

Jansen, M., M. Mulloy & G. Urban, eds., *Forgotten Cities on the Indus*, Mainz, 1991.

Jansen, M., *Die Indus-Zivilisation. Wiederentdeckung einer frühen Hochkultur*, Cologne, 1986.

Jarrige, C., *et al.*, eds., *Mehrgarh Field Reports 1974–1985: From Neolithic Times to the Indus Civilization*, Karachi, 1995.

Jarrige, J.-F., G. Quivron & C. Jarrige, *Nindowari, Pakistan: La culture de Kulli*, Paris, 2011.

Kenoyer, J.M., *Ancient Cities of the Indus Valley Civilization*, Karachi, 1998.

Krishnamurti, B., *The Dravidian Languages*, Cambridge UK, 2003.

Laursen, S.T., "The Westward Transmission of Indus Valley Sealing Technology: Origin and Development of the 'Gulf Type' Seal and Other Administrative Technologies in Early Dilmun, c. 2100–2000 BC," *AAE* 21, 2010, 96–134.

Law, R.W., *Inter-regional Interaction and Urbanism in the Ancient Indus Valley: A Geologic Provenience Study of Harappa's Rock and Mineral Assemblage*, LAHPOP 11, Kyoto, 2011.

Les cités oubliées de l'Indus: Archéologie du Pakistan, publ. Musée Guimet, Paris, 1988.

Lubotsky, A., "The Indo-Iranian Substratum," in: C. Carpelan, A. Parpola & P. Koskikallio, eds., *Early Contacts between Uralic and Indo-European: Linguistic and Archaeological Considerations*, MSFOu 242, Helsinki, 2001, 301–317.

Mackay, E.J.H., *Chanhu-daro Excavations*, 1935–36, AOS 20, New Haven, 1943.

Mackay, E.J.H., *Further Excavations at Mohenjo-daro*, vols. I–II, Delhi, 1937–1938.

Mahadevan, I., *The Indus Script: Texts, Concordance and Tables*, MASI 77, New Delhi, 1977.

Mallory, J.P., *In Search of the Indo-Europeans: Language, Archaeology and Myth*, London, 1989.

Marshall, J., ed., *Mohenjo-Daro and the Indus Civilization*, 3 vols., London, 1931.

Marshall, J., "First Light on a Long-Forgotten Civilization," *ILN* Sep 20, 1924, 528–532, 548.

Monier-Williams, M., *Brāhmanism and Hinduism: Or, Religious Life in India*, London, [4]1891.

Nonnus, *Dionysiaca*, 3 vols., London, 1956–1963.

Osada, T., & H. Endo, eds., *Linguistics, Archaeology and the Human Past: Occasional Paper* 12, Kyoto, 2011; repr. *Current Studies on the Indus Civilization*, vol. IX, New Delhi, 2012.

Parpola, A., "The Dāsas of the Ṛgveda as Proto-Sakas of the Yaz I – related Cultures: With a Revised Model for the Protohistory of Indo-Iranian Speakers," in: M.E. Huld, K. Jones-Bley & D. Miller, eds., *Archaeology and Language: Indo-European Studies Presented to James P. Mallory*, JIESMS 60, Washington DC, forthcoming a.

Parpola, A., "Motifs of Early Iranian, Mesopotamian and Harappan Art (and Script), Reflecting Contacts and Ideology," in: T. Osada & M. Witzel, eds., *Cultural Relations between the Indus and the Iranian Plateau during the Third Millennium* BCE, HOS.OM 7, Cambridge MA, forthcoming b.

Parpola, A., "Crocodile in the Indus Civilization and Later South Asian Traditions," in: T. Osada & H. Endo, eds., *Linguistics, Archaeology and the Human Past: Occasional Paper* 12, Kyoto, 2011a, 1–58; repr. in: T. Osada & H. Endo, eds., *Current Studies on Indus Civilization*, vol. IX, New Delhi, 2012, 1–58.

Parpola, A., "The Harappan Unicorn in Eurasian and South Asian Perspectives," in: T. Osada & H. Endo, eds., *Linguistics, Archaeology and the Human Past: Occasional Paper* 12, Kyoto, 2011b, 125–188; repr. in: T. Osada & H. Endo, eds., *Current Studies on Indus Civilization*, vol. IX, New Delhi, 2012, 125–188.

Parpola, A., "'Hind leg' + 'fish': Towards Further Understanding of the Indus Script," *Scripta* 1, 2009a, 37–76.

Parpola, A., "The Face Urns of Gandhāra and the Nāsatya Cult," in: M. Willis, ed., *Migration, Trade, and Peoples*, vol. III: *European Association of South Asian Archaeologists: Proceedings of the Eighteenth Congress, London, 2005*, London, 2009b, 149–162.

Parpola, A., "Proto-Indo-European Speakers of the Late Tripolye Culture as the Inventors of Wheeled Vehicles: Linguistic and Archaeological Considerations of the PIE Homeland Problem," in: K. Jones-Bley *et al.*, eds., *Proceedings of the Nineteenth Annual UCLA Indo-European Conference, November 2–3, 2007*, JIESMS 54, Washington DC, 2008, 1–59.

Parpola, A., "Human Sacrifice in India in Vedic Times and Before," in: J.N. Bremmer, ed., *The Strange World of Human Sacrifice*, Leuven, 2007, 157–177.

Parpola, A., "Gandhāra Graves and the Gharma Pot, the Nāsatyas and the Nose: In Pursuit of the Chariot Twins," *APa* 16, 2005a, 73–107.

Parpola, A., "The Nāsatyas, the Chariot and Proto-Aryan Religion," *JIS* 16–17, 2005b, 1–63.

Parpola, A., "From Archaeology to a Stratigraphy of Vedic Syncretism," in: A. Griffiths & J.E.M. Houben, eds., *The Vedas: Texts, Language and Ritual*, GOS 20, Groningen, 2004, 479–515.

Parpola, A., "Sacred Bathing Place and Transcendence," in: O. Qvarnström, ed., *Jainism and Early Buddhism: Essays in Honor of Padmanabh S. Jaini*, Fremont, 2003, 523–574.

Parpola, A., "Pre-Proto-Iranians of Afghanistan as initiators of Śākta Tantrism: On the Scythian/Saka Affiliation of the Dāsas, Nuristanis and Magadhans," *IrA* 37, 2000, 233–324.

Parpola, A., "Vāc as a Goddess of Victory in the Veda and Her Relation to Durgā," *Zinbun* 34/2, 1999, 101–143.

Parpola, A., "Sāvitrī and Resurrection," in: A. Parpola & S. Tenhunen, eds., *Changing Patterns of Family and Kinship in South Asia*, StOr 84, Helsinki, 1998, 167–312.

Parpola, A., *Deciphering the Indus Script*, Cambridge UK, 1994.

Parpola, A., "Metamorphoses of Mahiṣa Asura and Prajāpati," in: A.W. van den Hoek *et al.*, eds., *Ritual, State and History in South Asia: Essays in Honour of J.C. Heesterman*, Leiden, 1992, 275–308.

Parpola, A., *The Sky Garment: A Study of the Harappan Religion and Its Relation to the Mesopotamian and Later Indian Religions*, StOr 57, Helsinki, 1985.

Parpola, A., "New Correspondences between Harappan and Near Eastern Glyptic Art," in: B. Allchin, ed., *South Asian Archaeology 1981*, Cambridge UK, 1984, 176–195.

Parpola, A., & J. Janhunen, "On the Asiatic Wild Asses and Their Vernacular Names," in: T. Osada & H. Endo, eds., *Linguistics, Archaeology and the Human Past: Occasional Paper* 12, Kyoto, 2011, 59–124; repr. in: T. Osada & H. Endo, eds., *Current Studies on Indus Civilization*, vol. IX, New Delhi, 2012, 59–124.

Possehl, G.L., "The Indus Civilization," in: J.R. Hinnells, ed., *Handbook of Ancient Religions*, Cambridge UK, 2007, 418–489.

Possehl, G.L., *The Indus Civilization: A Contemporary Perspective*, Walnut Creek, 2002.

Possehl, G.L., *Indus Age: The Beginnings*, Philadelphia, 1999.

Possehl, G.L., *Indus Age: The Writing System*, Philadelphia, 1996.

Potts, D.T., "Nana in Bactria," *SRAA* 7, 2001, 23–35.

Robinson, A., *The Story of Writing*, London, 1995.

Settar, S., & R. Korisettar, eds., *Protohistory: Archaeology of the Harappan Civilization*, IAR 2, New Delhi, 2002.

Stietencron, H. von, "Die Göttin Durgā Mahiṣāsuramardinī. Mythos, Darstellung und geschichtliche Rolle bei der Hinduisierung Indiens," *VR* 2, 1983, 118–166.

Van Buren, E.D., "Fish Offerings in Ancient Mesopotamia," *Iraq* 10/2, 1948, 101–121.

Vats, M.S., *Excavations at Harappā*, 2 vols., Delhi, 1940.

Vermaak, P.S., "Guabba, the Meluhhan Village in Mesopotamia," *JS* 17/2, 2008, 454–471.

Vidale, M., *The Lady of the Spiked Throne: The Power of a Lost Ritual*, Trieste, 2011.

Vidale, M., "Aspects of Palace Life at Mohenjo-Daro," *SAS* 26/1, 2010, 59–76.

Vogel, J.P., "The Head-Offering to the Goddess in Pallava Sculpture," *BSOAS* 6, 1930–1932, 539–543.

Wright, R.P., *The Ancient Indus: Urbanism, Economy, and Society*, New York, 2010.

Yokochi, Y., "The Rise of the Warrior Goddess in Ancient India: A Study of the Myth Cycle of Kauśikī-Vindhyavāsinī in the Skandapurāṇa," diss., Groningen University, 2005.

Asko Parpola

Vedic Period (1750–400 BCE)

"Vedic period" refers to the epoch during which the corpus of liturgies, ritual commentaries, and speculative texts known as the → Vedas was composed and then defined as a religious canon. More loosely, the application of the expression may be extended back in time to include the formative phase of vedic culture on the grounds that no cultural product springs, fully formed, into existence, and the earliest extant vedic texts must have had precursors that are not preserved. The common stock of myths, legends, rituals (→ *yajña*s), and even turns of phrase found in the earliest vedic hymns points back in time and suggests a process of development that preceded the production of those compositions incorporated into the earliest portions of the vedic canon. While this extension of the term is reasonable and conceptually useful, it also lacks any certain limit.

The earliest external point of reference for the existence of a cultural and linguistic complex resembling that reflected in the earliest vedic texts is found not in the South Asian subcontinent but in the Middle East. It is attested in Hittite sources datable to the 14th century BCE that the Mitanni Kingdom in northern Syria was ruled by a military elite speaking a dialect of Old Indic (i.e. Sanskrit), which is closely related to the dialect of Sanskrit in which the Vedas are composed. Furthermore, the Mitanni leaders swore alliances in the name of deities that were important within the vedic pantheon and provided expert horse trainers whose Old Indic technical terminology was preserved even in Hittite manuals (Thieme, 1960; Mayrhofer, 1966; 1974; see also → vedic gods). It is therefore reasonable to conclude that the distinctive religious, linguistic, and military culture represented in the earliest parts of the Veda was fully developed by the mid-1300s BCE. This date agrees well with the relative chronologies that have been proposed for the early vedic period on the basis of linguistic and intertextual evidence, both within Sanskrit textual traditions and in relation to the *Avesta*; thus it is probably approximately correct to say that the vedic period, strictly defined, begins in the 14th or 15th century BCE and, more loosely defined, in the 18th. The uncertainty regarding the precise absolute chronology of the vedic texts makes it hazardous to correlate them with other evidence, such as that of archaeology (for an illustration of how difficult it can be to extrapolated historical information from the vedic texts, see Hock, 2005). Nevertheless, such correlations, particularly with ceramic cultures, have been made and will be discussed here in relation to the political, social, religious, and economic patterns as they emerge from the evidence of the vedic texts.

What we refer to as "the vedic canon" is defined by the Sanskrit exegetical tradition as Śruti, roughly "revelation," and terminates with the early → Upaniṣads. From this perspective, the end of the vedic period can be said to correspond to the final composition and redaction of the upanishadic texts. (However, it is important to note that the Śrautasūtras, though not classified as Śruti, are an integral part of the vedic ritual tradition, and most of them should be included as sources for any investigation of the vedic period [Brucker, 1980].) The calendric date given to the end of the vedic period depends on our reckoning of the chronology of the early Upaniṣads. Generally, this chronology is estimated in relation to the dating of the life of the Buddha, whose philosophy of no-self is generally considered to be a reaction against the upanishadic notion of → *ātman*. However, since the opposite argument that the Upaniṣads are products of influence from Buddhism has also been made (Bronkhorst, 2007), and since the date of the Buddha is itself a contested issue, no firm conclusion can be drawn regarding the absolute date of the closure of the vedic canon. A reasonable estimate is 500–400 BCE.

It is important to remember that, by defining the period in question in relation to a specific textual corpus, we run the risk of skewing history by presenting it in the light shed on it by only one community of agents. It is certain that, in addition to the bearers of the vedic texts, other communities thrived within the South Asian subcontinent during this period, interacting with them and influencing them. The values, practices, and institutions with which the vedic texts are primarily concerned reflect the cultural identity of only one group and are presented from the perspective of only one class within this group – the priests. All of what we know about other communities from this period must be extrapolated from the vedic texts or gleaned from archaeological remains, which are neither plentiful nor easily interpreted.

The Migrations of the *Ārya*/*Airiia* and the Post-urban Harappan Phase

Although the names of many different (and sometimes warring) tribes are known, all of them refer to themselves as *ārya* (Aryan); by so doing, they testify to a single cultural identity that is regularly affirmed through common rituals and through the demonization of other communities who do not share *ārya* practices and who probably speak different languages. The designation "*ārya*" is one of several indications that the vedic Indians were culturally related to communities settled in ancient Iran and Afghanistan. Speaking a dialect closely related to vedic Sanskrit, they called themselves *ārya* (Avest. *airiia*), and their religion held many ritual and mythological features in common with vedic religion. On the basis of these shared characteristics, the conclusion is drawn that the two cultural and linguistic groups stemmed from a common source community, referred to by scholars as Indo-Iranians, while the marked differences between them, especially as regards certain inversions of ritual and myth, demonstrate that by the time of the earliest textual evidence – the *Ṛgveda* and the *Avesta* – the communities had diverged, though contact between speakers of Indic dialects and speakers of Iranian dialects would have, no doubt, persisted in border areas.

While some have argued that the Sanskrit language and vedic culture were indigenous to the subcontinent, the linguistic evidence points to an introduction of these cultural features from regions in the northwest that were earlier inhabited by Indo-Iranians (on the linguistic evidence, see Burrow, 1973; Harmatta, 1981; 1992; Hock, 1999; Mallory [1989] is still useful for an overview of the archaeological issues [see also Mallory, 2002]; compare with Bryant, 2001; on the Indo-Iranians and the archaeological backdrop, see also Lamberg-Karlovsky, 2005). Given the appearance of the Old Indic-speaking Mitanni elite in western Asia, it is likely that the distinctive character of this cultural and linguistic community developed before they descended into the subcontinent through the northwest mountain passes, infiltrating the core area of Harappan (→ Indus Valley) culture.

As is well known, the height of Harappan civilization was characterized by a highly developed urban culture that was shared among many sites in the Harappan cultural sphere. However, its latest phase, beginning sometime at the start of the 2nd millennium, is marked by a process of de-urbanization (Allchin, 1995; Lal, 1997). This entailed not only a reduction in the size of settlements and the absence of monumental architecture but also the loss of writing and of urban craft specialization. The development of regional cultural variants in the post-urban phase is a sign of deteriorating central control, as is the decreased volume of long-distance trade (Chakrabarti, 1998). It is unlikely that there was a single cause of the demise of Harappan urbanism and the fragmentation of its cultural forms into several localized complexes. Climatic changes and tectonic shifts, with the attendant effects on river systems, as well as the incomplete integration of hunting-gathering populations in the eastern regions of the Harappan area, have been cited as possible contributing factors to the general breakdown of the urbanized civilization (Allchin, 1995; Chakrabarti, 1998).

There is no evidence to support the outdated view that the demise of the Harappan civilization was due to large-scale invasions. Nevertheless, signs of the introduction of a hitherto unknown culture have been identified, with some researchers interpreting hearths discovered at Kalibangan as a possible "indication of the presence of Indo-Aryan speakers already during the Harappan urban phase" (Allchin, 1995, 48). More plausibly, the Cemetery H culture, named after a find at Harappa but found more widely across the → Punjab and Haryana, reveals a change of funerary practice from grave burial to cremation, which is suggestive of practices recorded in the *Ṛgveda*. The duration of the Cemetery H culture is uncertain, though it seems to overlap with the estimated date of the early rgvedic period (Parpola, 2002; see also Allchin, 1995). To the northwest of the Indus Plains, the Gandhara Grave culture represents the archaeological attestation of another intrusive cultural complex that included inhumation and, for the first time in the region, the domesticated horse. As the *Ṛgveda* knows both of inhumation and of cremation, it is possible that both the Gandhara Grave culture and the Cemetery H culture contributed to the practices reflected in the rgvedic hymns. The appearance of the horse is crucial, because it was unknown to the Harappans and well known to the peoples mentioned in the *Ṛgveda* (Parpola, 2002; see also Allchin, 1995). The Cemetery H culture and the Gandhara Grave culture have been associated either with different waves of Indo-Aryan elements (Parpola, 2002) or with different stages of early Indo-Aryan cultural formation (Allchin, 1995) leading up to the period of rgvedic hymn composition. Although it is not possible to establish conclusively that either complex is a forerunner of the vedic culture or peoples, the time frame fits well with the other evidence.

A good deal of discussion has been given to the question of how the Indo-Aryan language was introduced into the subcontinent. The outdated model of a massive invasion of a new population, the outright imposition of their language on the existing inhabitants of the region, and the wholesale destruction of the preceding Bronze Age civilization of the Indus has given way to more nuanced theories (Shaffer, 1984). Beginning from the premise that the Indo-Aryan language and culture were introduced into the subcontinent, some have asked whether this necessarily involves the introduction of a new population, arguing that languages, as well as other cultural productions, may be adopted by new users without a shift of population, and that such a shift is not, in any case, attestable (Schaffer, 1986; Schaffer & Lichtenstein, 1995). Others have pointed out that racial identity, cultural identity, and linguistic identity are by no means necessarily coterminous, and the dynamics of language change must be considered within a more comprehensive model of social change (Deshpande, 1995; Erdosy, 1995).

On the basis of what is known at this point, a plausible scenario might be the following: the deurbanization of the Harappan civilization was the result of a gradual system collapse, whereby its economy and administrative structures eroded. This undermined the foundations of the highly urbanized major centers, such as Harappa and Mohenjo-daro, and shifted the population to smaller, less organized rural settlements. In the wake of the resulting power vacuum, small, migratory groups of pastoralists began to drift in from areas to the northwest, where pressures on resources had led to reduced possibilities for the grazing of cattle. Interactions between the newcomers and existing populations developed, some symbiotic and some parasitic. Continuing over a long period of time, this process gradually led to the transformation of economies and cultures in the region, as pastoralists and settled rural communities interacted with one another and sometimes merged, creating new cultural identities and facilitating language change as bilingualism gradually ceded place to a common means for communication and the assertion of group identity. Under certain circumstances, older populations would have preserved their status and sovereignty while adopting linguistic and cultural practices of the newcomers, while under other circumstances, local populations may well have been subjugated, contributing to the development of increasingly stratified societies. It would be a long time before this process had worked itself out and an entirely new civilization stabilized itself across the northern part of the subcontinent in the middle vedic period.

The Rgvedic Period: Clans, Chieftains, and Migratory Pastoralism (c. 1500–1200 BCE)

Regardless of what may have happened prior to the creation of the *ārya*s' first extant self-portrayals contained in the hymns of the *Ṛgveda*, when we first learn of them directly, they inhabit the northwestern regions of the South Asian subcontinent, in the vicinity of the Indus River system, which they call the *saptasindhu*s (*sapta sindavaḥ*; the seven rivers), and the greater Punjab. References are made to the rivers of eastern Afghanistan in the west and to the → Yamunā (and, in one late passage, even the → Gaṅgā) in the east, while the Himalayas in the north and the Indian Ocean in the south are both known but are not significant settlement areas. The vedic peoples themselves do not have permanent settlements, but they make frequent assaults on enemies protected by fortified enclosures (*pur*), the precise nature of which is difficult to define on the basis of the texts but which clearly serve the function of forts (Stuhrmann, 2008; see also Rau, 1976), and it has been suggested that they may be related to fortified villages discovered in ancient Bactria and Margiana (Parpola, 1988; 1997).

The political and economic circumstance described in the text is one in which many small tribes or tribal federations compete with one another for cattle and pasture land. Several dozen or so such tribes are mentioned by name, the most important being the Pūru, the Bharata, and the closely related Yadu and Turvaśa (Oldenberg, 1881; Witzel, 1995b). The political history of the period would have been characterized by shifting alliances and temporary tribal coalitions. Something of this can be glimpsed in the highly mythologized renderings of events presented in the hymns. For example, the Bharatas, under the leadership of Divodāsa, are depicted as shattering the mountain fortresses of the powerful Śambara and at the same time subjugating the Yadu and Turvaśa tribes (*ṚV.* 9.61.1–2). While Śambara is everywhere in the *Ṛgveda* referred to as an enemy of the Bharatas and was certainly not considered a member of the *ārya* cultural sphere, the Yadu and Turvaśa are, in other passages, presented as allies of the Bharata and as frequent sponsors of the *soma* rite (Witzel, 1995b). A generation or two later, however, we find the Yadu and Turvaśa allied with the Pūrus against the Bharata tribe, led now by Divodāsa's son or grandson, Sudās (*ṚV.* 7.18).

Each tribe would have been led by a chieftain (*rājan*) responsible for leading the tribe on military campaigns and for securing divine assistance by employing priests to perform necessary rituals (Gonda, 1966; Santucci, 1976; Scharfe, 1992). It has been argued that the main ritual of the *Ṛgveda*, the *soma* rite (see → *yajña*), was instrumental to the process of choosing and legitimating this tribal leader (Oberlies, 1998).

The early vedic tribes were composed of clans in a segmentary system according to which smaller social units coalesce in a larger, centralized organization in order to face common outside threats such as war or natural disaster. Notions of real or imagined kinship would have played a role here, as the members of the clans would have perceived themselves to be bound in extensive networks of lineage on which they could rely in times of trouble (Scharfe, 1985; 1989; Oberlies, 1998). Central to the affirmation of group identity was the symbolism of fire, which represented the sovereignty residing in each clan group and which could be passed into a communal tribal fire to represent the formation of alliances between clans (Proferes, 2007). It is stated explicitly in the early vedic texts that the clans (*viś*) select the chieftain who will lead them, probably from among a number of competing clan lords (*viśpati*; Zimmer, 1985). The assembly of clan leaders convened by the chieftain was called a *sabhā* and constituted the main political forum.

The vedic economy was based mainly on the rearing of cattle and sheep, supplemented by small-scale land cultivation. The settlement pattern of the vedic groups was divided into alternating seasons of fixed habitation (*kṣema*) and migratory mobilization (*yoga*), depending on the availability of resources (Oberlies, 1998). Provided pasture land was sufficient and there was no pressure from other groups, the vedic groups would have peacefully raised their cattle and livestock and cultivated barley, dispersed in numerous and sometimes far-flung clan settlements. When resources became scarce, or when more-powerful competing groups drove them from their settlement areas, the clans would come together, hitching up wagons and chariots and pressing forth with their animals in search of new land and resources. This often involved raids on the land and herds of other groups and amounted to military mobilization. Shares of the booty obtained in this way were ritually distributed to the clan lords by the tribal chieftain, and the chieftain, in turn, was due tribute.

The contrast between the two modes of living of peaceful settlement and migratory military mobilization are reflected in the system of ethics reflected in the rgvedic religion. On the one hand, great emphasis is placed on strength and valor in battle, and there is a constant concern that the gods provide them with both sufficient numbers of warriors and direct assistance in the confrontations with their enemies. The emphasis on warrior ethics can be seen most clearly in the figure of the god Indra, whose glorious victories in war were regularly praised in ritual and who was summoned before a battle to fight on the side of his worshippers. The ethics of peacetime, on the other hand, emphasized the stable organization of civil society and is represented by the *ādityas*, particularly Varuṇa, Mitra, and Aryaman (see → vedic gods), who oversaw and enforced oaths, alliances, and marriage vows and thus regulated interclan and interpersonal relations as well as proper personal conduct and the just distribution of the shares of a community's resources (Oberlies, 1998).

Within the clans, society was organized by household or family, each led by a *pater familias* (*gṛhapati*) with legal control over and responsibility for the members of his household. Class stratification was limited, though it is clear that the priestly lineages responsible for the production of ritual poetry and the performance of the great rites already stood somewhat apart from others, as the training of ritual experts required specialization. The priest-poets responsible for the liturgical poetry recited in the rites were, to some degree at least, itinerant, serving different chieftains, from whom they received gifts (*dakṣiṇā*) of cattle, precious metal ornaments, and even women in return for their contributions to the ritual performances (Patel, 1929).

In the early vedic period, ethnic identity was based on common language and ritual practice, as well as on real or imagined kinship structures tracing descent from a common ancestor, such as Manu. There is, in this period, no discernible link between communal identity and territorial sovereignty, and tribes and clans moved from one territory to another. As settlements were only semipermanent, location was marked by rivers.

Although the political relationships among the various *ārya* polities were complex and, presumably, mediated by customary law even on the occasion of conflict, relations with non-*ārya* groups are represented as existing outside all lawful structures and were defined virtually exclusively by military aggression. The mentality of "us versus them" governs the way in which the rgvedic poets speak of any community who does not observe vedic ritual practices, speak the Vedic language, or worship the vedic gods, and non-*ārya* are represented as figures of evil and homologized with forces of cosmic chaos bent on the destruction of *ārya* livelihood (Oberlies, 1998). The composers of the rgvedic hymns identify the non-*ārya* primarily by their failure to press *soma* in ritual or possess proper speech, and little, if any, evidence is available to support obvious difference in phenotype (Hock, 2002; 2005).

Despite their negative representation in the early vedic texts, there can be little doubt that non-*ārya* peoples interacted with the vedic groups in peaceful ways as well and contributed positively to the gradual transformation of both the *ārya* society and the *ārya* economy. Some scholars see linguistic evidence of interactions with speakers of Dravidian and/or Munda languages as increasingly apparent in the vedic textual corpus in the form of loan words and phonology (Kuiper, 1991; Deshpande, 1995).

The Period of the Late *Ṛgveda* and the *Atharvaveda, Sāmaveda,* and *Yajurveda Mantras*: Ascendancy of the Kuru Kingdom (c. 1200–1000 BCE)

Significant transformations of the vedic social, political, and ritual organizations, as well as of the vedic economy, begin to become apparent in the latest hymns of the *Ṛgveda* and can be traced in the *mantra* portions of the other vedic collections (*Atharvaveda, Yajurveda*, and *Sāmaveda*). These changes coincide with a gradual eastern expansion of the vedic groups from the western Punjab to the eastern Punjab, Haryana, and eventually into the land between the Yamunā and the Gaṅgā Rivers. It was during this period that vedic civilization developed the institutional structures that would become so influential in the subcontinent over the course of the next 500 years. At the root of the changes taking place during this period lies the consolidation of political power. The dozens of small, migratory tribes mentioned throughout the *Ṛgveda* receive scant mention in the later Vedic texts, which instead portray polities with emerging state structures, increasing territorial identification, and increased class differentiation within society.

According to available evidence, the first of such consolidated tribal states was that of the Kuru (Witzel, 1997a). The Kuru tribe is first mentioned in two passages of related hymns in the very latest part of the rgvedic collection (*ṚV.* 10.32.4; 10.33.9), where we learn that a man named Kuruśravaṇa ("Fame of the Kurus") has been chosen as *rājan*, a word that in this period came to mean king rather than chieftain. From the fact that Kuruśravaṇa is stated to belong to the line of the Pūru king Trasadasyu, it is clear that the Kurus incorporated older rgvedic tribes including, no doubt, the Bharata (Oldenberg, 1881). In the *Ṛgvedakhila*, a slightly later appendage to the *Ṛgveda*, we find lauded the rich kingdom of the Kuru king Parikṣit, father of Janamejaya, who is himself remembered in the *Śathapathabrāhmaṇa* and, later, in the → *Mahābhārata*. The domain of the Kuru kings was centered in an area slightly farther to the east, not far from modern Delhi, and became known in the Sanskrit tradition as Kurukṣetra ("Field of the Kurus") admired ever after as the classical center of vedic orthodoxy. The identification of the Kuru confederation with a particular geographical location indicates that the transition to territorial states had begun.

In an attempt to promote political unity, the Kurus undertook to redesign the religious and political culture of the vedic groups, centralizing and standardizing many important institutions. Given the nature of the evidence available to us, this is most evident in the organization of the vedic ritual institutions. The priestly clans that had hitherto been responsible for the production of the liturgical poetry so crucial to the grand vedic ceremonies for worshipping the gods were divested of this responsibility, and custodianship of the liturgies was invested in priestly offices, which later bifurcated into the various vedic branches (*śakhā*), or schools (Proferes, 2003b). Careful records of the priestly lineages were maintained, of course, but they served only as pedigrees to qualify individuals for a newly recognized social class, the Brāhmaṇas (Brahmans), whose members were the only ones eligible to officiate at the sacred rites.

Furthermore, whereas the old rgvedic priestly clans were primarily occupied with preserving the best liturgies produced within their own lineages and composing new ones, a new liturgical structure was developed that incorporated the works of the important lineages of the past but left almost no room for the production of new material. The only exception was the liturgy for the new rite of the *agnicayana* (see → *yajña*), developed under Kuru sponsorship as a more grand and elaborate display than the older rgvedic rites (Proferes, 2003a) and one that involves the use of brick, the building block of permanent settlements. Though we are still far from the establishment of major permanent habitation centers, and the old pattern of *yoga* and *kṣema* was still being practiced, it is significant that the technology used in the construction of permanent structures was being adopted by the vedic ritualists as a status marker.

The reformation, elaboration, and consolidation of the ritual system was part of a sustained attempt to project power and influence through culture. This process is sometimes referred to generally as "Sanskritization," meaning the spread not only of the Sanskrit language across northern India but also of the cultural forms and practices characteristic of *ārya* civilization. This process was facilitated by non-*ārya* elites wishing to adapt to and adopt features of the dynamic and powerful polities developing on their borders, while populations merging with or subsumed by the eastward expansion of vedic groups would equally have been part of the process.

Older patterns of social and economic practice were gradually adapted to the changing environment. Whereas, in the rgvedic period, clans that were joined together through formal vow (*vrata*) engaged in cattle raids and the search for new pastureland together, in a slightly later period, the vedic tribes saw the *vrātya*s – not early ascetics or *yogin*s but rather younger sons impoverished by primogeniture – heading off together to neighboring lands to accumulate wealth through extortion or confiscation (Falk, 1986).

Changes to the old social structure can be discerned in the changes of the meaning of certain important socio-descriptive terms. Most notably, the term *viś*, "clan," which in the *Ṛgveda* referred to a migratory settlement group structured in accord with the principles of segmentary kinship, can be used, in the plural, as a synonym for the subjects (*prajā*, lit. offspring) of a king (Rau, 1957) and designates the third estate, or caste, of the classical *varṇa* system first enunciated in the *Puruṣasūkta* (*ṚV*. 10.90). There, the *viś* are set in contrast to the priests and those eligible to rule (*kṣatriya*) as members of a lower *ārya* class responsible for animal husbandry and agriculture and, later, mercantile trade. It is often said in slightly later texts that the Brahmans and the Kṣatriyas work together to exploit the Viś, whereas in earlier texts, the clans called by this appellation played an important role in acclaiming the king. Thus it is apparent that, as time passed, the older clan structures gradually broke down and were supplemented and replaced by class stratification (see Thapar, 1984).

Such changes affected the character of vedic kingship. The simple unction ceremonies found in *mantra* texts like the *Atharvaveda* are transformed into elaborate ritual performances designed to display the increased wealth and status of the ever-more-powerful king (Witzel, 1997; Proferes, 2007), and it has even been argued that the complex architecture of the classical royal consecration rite retains features of more primitive phases in the development of vedic kingship (Kulke, 1992). Another shift that was likely to have been underway at this time was toward the strengthening of dynastic kingship. Tribal chieftains, particularly those from influential clans, might often have been able to arrange for a continuation of rule in the hands of an offspring or fellow clansman. Nevertheless, because the acclamation of the clans depended on the qualities of the individual and the belief that he was best suited to lead the multiclan tribes, an individual from another clan could always be chosen. The early theory of vedic sovereignty thus invests any leader with only temporary rule, understanding that it must be renewed in order to continue. At the same time, however, dynastic ascension is also known from early texts and was clearly practiced by the Kuru, whose king Parikṣit was followed by his son, Janamejaya.

The political landscape must not have developed uniformly, however. The existence of oligarchic ethnic polities (*janapada*) alongside kingdoms in later periods suggests that the principles of clan sovereignty continued well into the subsequent period. Such polities, known to us from the Buddhist texts, consisted of a clan or a confederation of clans and were led by assemblies (*saṃgha*) consisting of the family leaders or the clan leaders. Such polities appear to have eschewed the developing administrative regimentation of the kingdoms and the divisions of social class involved with them, though menial labor was carried out by members outside the kin group and thus of inferior status, yet belonging within the individual households of clan families. It appears, too, that these *gaṇasaṃgha* polities were not inclined to patronize the Brahmans, and their religious culture was likely markedly different from that of the kingdoms. All of this suggests the possibility of the parallel development of the political culture of these polities from the earliest vedic period. It is also conceivable that *jāti* organization represents a reflex of earlier clan organization.

The eastward expansions of the *ārya* groups involved the increasing adoption of rice cultivation, and it is significant that the liturgical reformation promoted by the Kurus incorporated the ritual use of rice for the first time. It may be that the introduction of iron into the subcontinent during this period facilitated the clearing of land by means of iron chopping tools, increasing the amount of arable land, which would, in turn, support an increase in population.

In sum, the period of the latest parts of the *Ṛgveda* and the *mantra*s of the other vedic Saṃhitās is a watershed during which classical vedic culture was created, defined, and disseminated. At the same time, many aspects of the preclassical (i.e. the rgvedic period) culture were lost or intentionally discarded in the interest of new power structures, social organizations, and cultural forms.

The Period of Brāhmaṇa Exegetical Prose (c. 1100–600 BCE)

The earliest extant examples of Brāhmaṇa exegetical prose (see → Vedas and Brāhmaṇas), such as that contained in the *Maitrāyaṇīsaṃhitā* and the *Kaṭhasaṃhitā*, continue to refer primarily to the Kuru and were composed in the heartland of classical vedic culture, Kurukṣetra (Witzel, 1997b; 1989). Slightly later, Saṃhitā prose texts such as the *Taittirīyasaṃhitā* speak of the Pañcālas as well as of the Kuru-Pañcālas; thus it is evident that, in time, the Kuru tribe became closely related to another tribal confederation inhabiting the land to the southeast in the Gaṅgā–Yamunā Doab in modern-day → Uttar Pradesh.

Gradually, vedic culture spread eastward, through the Gaṅgā basin, into areas already occupied by the peoples of Kosala and Videha. According to the *Jaiminīyabrāhmaṇa* and the *Śathapathabrāhmaṇa*, the orthodox Brahmans from farther west looked down on the way in which the peoples of these regions pronounced Sanskrit, which suggests strong dialect differences between the prestige area and the eastern periphery. The latter text refers to a difference in funerary practice, with the easterners building funerary mounds that have been seen as precursors to the Buddhist *stūpa* (Bronkhorst, 2007). These examples suggest marked differences in certain important areas of cultural practice. This would be in keeping with the view that vedic culture was introduced into these regions from the west, with the east retaining its own character. The most likely scenario is that the royal elites of certain eastern peoples viewed their northwestern neighbors as bearers of a prestige culture and thus sought to assert their own status by adopting aspects of it. The apocryphal legend of the Videha leader Videgha Māthava and his house priest Gotama Rāhūgaṇa moving eastward with Agni Vaiśvānara, the fire god symbolizing both the vedic ritual and the rule of the vedic kings, suggests that the leaders of the eastern polities took pains to derive their own lineage and practice from the vedic heartlands farther to the west. Similarly, western Brahmans from Kurukṣetra are commonly depicted at the court of eastern kings such as Janaka of Videha. It is known from the Buddhist texts of the Pali canon that not all Indo-Aryan–speaking polities in the east practiced Brahmanical culture as it had been defined in by the Kuru-Pañcālas (Thapar, 2002).

It is illustrative that the meaning of the word *grāma* can be seen to develop within the vedic texts; originally it referred to a mobile wagon train by means of which vedic groups moved from place to place, setting up secure temporary settlements as they did so by circling their vehicles and raising temporary sheds; the leader of the *grāma* (*grāmaṇī*) was equivalent to a clan lord (see Thapar, 1984). Only in relatively late middle vedic texts does the word *grāma* take on the meaning of village, that is, a small permanent settlement, its standard meaning in later Sanskrit usage (Rau, 1997). It has been argued that the acquisition of control of such permanent settlements by Kṣatriyas striving for status through territorial consolidation marks an early stage of state development (Kulke, 1991).

The cultural complex associated with Painted Grey Ware overlaps chronologically and geographically with the vedic texts of the middle vedic period, covering the Punjab, Haryana, and Uttar Pradesh in the period from approximately 1000 to approximately 400 BCE (Tripathi, 1976; Parpola, 2002). This corresponds very well with the estimated time frame of the spread of vedic culture from Kurukṣetra southeastward, and the suggestion has been made that the emergence of Painted Grey Ware was associated with the consolidation of power by the Kuru tribe and the eastward dissemination of its culture (Parpola, 2002). The co-occurrence of iron for the first time in some Painted Grey Ware sites would thus be in accord with the fact that iron is first mentioned in texts associated with the emerging prominence of the Kuru. In addition, the consistency of the style over such a long period suggests a relatively stable political and cultural environment such as that suggested by the burgeoning middle vedic polities.

It is often said that, over the course of its formative period, the vedic religion was transformed from an externally focused regiment of ritual practice aimed at securing prosperity in this world and a bright place in the next to a body of esoteric doctrines leading to a gnosis that, once internalized, achieves the higher goal of spiritual liberation. The elements of this gnosis – → *karman*, rebirth (→ *saṃsāra*), and spiritual → liberation – have long been considered by some to have been introduced into Brahmanical vedic religion from the outside. The fact that these doctrines are depicted, in certain Upaniṣads, as being taught to Brahmans by kings, has been considered by some to reflect a historical fact, leading to the view that the ideas were innovations of the Kṣatriya class that were adopted by Brahmans and integrated into the late vedic religion reflected in the Upaniṣads. Others have considered these ideas to grow orthogenetically from within the vedic priestly tradition through a natural process of reflection on the external elements of sacrifice and their implication, combined with a process of internalization and ethicization over time (Tull, 1989). Recently, the discussion has been enlivened by J. Bronkhorst's (2007) proposal that the distinctive features of late vedic religion are the result of the influence of the pre-*ārya* culture of "greater Magadha," the regions east of where the Gaṅgā and the Yamunā Rivers merge and home of the religious doctrines of Buddhism, Jainism, and the → Ājīvikas. According to this view, the appearance of the new religious ideas of *karman* and rebirth were introduced into the vedic textual corpus under the influence of the religious culture of the eastern populations. This thesis has the great merit of trying to take into account the influence of the established cultures on the vedic tradition as it was being adopted across the subcontinent, an influence that has been effaced in the historical record due to the paucity of evidence. Without ascribing to the details of the thesis as J. Bronkhorst has presented it (particularly its relative chronologies), it is reasonable and important to acknowledge that vedic culture was progressively shaped by its interactions with the peoples who adopted it and adapted it within the context of their own religious and political cultures.

Conclusion

Though the details have, in large degree, been lost to time, the broad trajectory of the vedic period is reflected in the extant sources with relative clarity. From a clan-based society organized politically around petty chieftainships and relying on pastoralism and small-scale agriculture, there gradually emerged highly stratified societies organized into territorially identified state polities with increasingly diversified economies and developed trade; some of these developed into dynastic kingships, while others preserved the sovereignty of clan leaders through the institutionalized assemblies. In the course of these developments, the contributions of the pre-*ārya* populations would have exerted a persistent influence on a conservative but ever-adapting vedic culture.

Two pivotal moments can be discerned in the history of the vedic religious tradition, and these must also reflect changes affecting other aspects of society at the time. The first is the reformation of the ritual tradition at the end of the rgvedic period, when the liturgies of various priestly families were consolidated and a unitary ritual system developed. Accompanying this was a full-scale reorganization of the ritual institutions, resulting in the end of lineage-based control over ritual and the establishment of an ecumenical liturgical system based on priestly offices and the training institutions associated with them. Such reform was motivated, it appears, by political interests, as the first kings of the Kuru dynasty sought to unify the religious institutions in support of their assertion of a unified political authority.

The second major change to the vedic religious tradition may be seen in the increasing emphasis on esoteric knowledge in the later Kuru-Pañcāla and eastern texts, particularly the *Śatapathabrāhmaṇa* and the Upaniṣads. Alongside the performance of ritual, quasi-agonistic forums of debate over the inner sense of religious matters became a characteristic feature of the culture; this change, too, was closely associated with political interests and the specific requirements of the kings of the period. Rooted in the ritual *brahmodya*s, the display of esoteric knowledge in the presence of the king trumps even the performance of the grand vedic rituals, winning renown for learned Brahmans and glory for the sovereign who offers them patronage.

The closure of the revealed Veda canon (Śruti) marks the end of the vedic period as it has here been defined. Such a closure marks a fundamental shift in the perspective that the tradition has of itself, as it divorces the mundane, historical present from the eternal sacred past, of which the textual corpus is the sole talisman.

Bibliography

Allchin, F.R., *The Archaeology of Early Historic South Asia: The Emergence of Cities and States*, Cambridge UK, 1995.

Bronkhorst, J., *Greater Magadha: Studies in the Culture of Early India*, Leiden, 2007.

Brucker, E., *Die spätvedische Kulturepoche nach den Quellen der Śrauta-, Gṛhya-, und Dharmasūtras. Der Siedlungsraum*, Wiesbaden, 1980.

Bryant, E., *The Quest for the Origins of Vedic Culture*, Delhi, 2000.

Burrow, T., "The Proto-Indoaryans," *JRAS* 2, 1973, 123–140.

Chakrabarti, D.K., *The Archaeology of Ancient Indian Cities*, Delhi, 1998.

Deshpande, M., "Vedic Aryans, Non-Vedic Aryans, and Non-Aryans: Judging the Linguistic Evidence of the Veda," in: G. Erdosy, ed., *The Indo Aryans of Ancient South Asia: Language, Material Culture and Ethnicity*, Berlin, 1995, 67–84.

Deshpande, M., & P. Hook, eds., *Aryan and Non-Aryan in India*, Ann Arbor, 1979.

Erdosy, G., "Language, Material Culture and Ethnicity: Theoretical Perspectives," in: G. Erdosy, ed., *The Indo Aryans of Ancient South Asia: Language, Material Culture and Ethnicity*, Berlin, 1995, 1–31.

Erdosy, G., *Urbanisation in Early Historic India*, Oxford, 1988.

Falk, H., *Bruderschaft und Würfelspiel*, Freiburg, 1986.

Gonda, J., *Ancient Indian Kingship from the Religious Point of View*, Leiden, 1966.

Gonda, J., " 'Gifts' and 'Giving' in the Ṛgveda," *VIJ* 2, 1964, 9–30.

Harmatta, J., "The Emergence of the Indo-Iranians: The Indo-Iranian Languages," in: A.H. Dani & V.M. Masson, eds., *History of Civilizations of Central Asia*, Paris, 1992, 357–378.

Harmatta, J., "Proto-Iranians and Proto-Indians in Central Asia in the 2nd Millennium BC," in: B.A. Litvinsky *et al.*, eds., *Ethnic Problems in the History of Central Asia in the Early Period*, Moscow, 1981, 75–83.

Hock, H.H., "Philology and the Historical Interpretation of the Vedic Texts," in: E.F. Bryant & L.L. Patton, eds., *The Indo-Aryan Controversy: Evidence and Inference in Indian History*, London, 2005, 282–308.

Hock, H.H., "Wem gehört die Vergangenheit? Früh- und Vorgeschichte und indische Selbswahrnehmung. 'Arier' und 'Draviden,' " in: M. Bergunder & R.P. Das, eds., *Konstruktionen der Vergangenheit als Grundlage für Selbst- and Fremdwahrnehmungen Südasiens*, Halle, 2002, 232–250.

Hock, H.H., "Out of India? The Linguistic Evidence," in: J. Bronkhorst, ed., *Aryan and Non-Aryan in South Asia*, Cambridge MA, 1999, 1–18.

Kuiper, F.B.J., *Aryans in the Rigveda*, Amsterdam, 1991.

Kulke, H., "The Rājasūya: A Paradigm of Early State Formation?" in: A.W. van den Hoek, D.H.A. Kolff & M.S. Oort, eds., *Ritual, State and History in South Asia: Essays in Honour of J.C. Heesterman*, Leiden, 1992, 188–198.

Kulke, H., "Grāmakāma – 'das Verlangen nach einem Dorf.' Überlegungen zum Beginn frühstaatlicher Entwicklung im vedischen Indien," *Saeculum* 42, 1991, 111–128.

Lal, B.B., *The Earliest Civilization of South Asia: Rise, Maturity and Decline*, New Delhi, 1997.

Lamberg-Karlovsky, C.C., "Archaeology and Language: The Case of the Bronze Age Indo-Iranians," in: E.F. Bryant & L.L. Patton, eds., *The Indo-Aryan Controversy: Evidence and Inference in Indian History*, London, 2005, 142–177.

Mallory, J.P., "Archaeological Models and Asian Indo-Europeans," in: N. Sims-Williams, ed., *Indo-Iranian Languages and Peoples*, Oxford, 2002.

Mallory, J.P., *In Search of the Indo-Europeans: Language, Archaeology and Myth*, London, 1989.

Mayrhoffer, M., *Die Arier im Vorderen Orient – ein Mythos?* ÖAWPHKS 294/3, Vienna, 1974.

Mayrhoffer, M., *Die Indo-Arier im Alten Vorderasien*, Wiesbaden, 1966.

Oberlies, T., *Die Religion des Rgveda*, vol. I: *Das Religiöse System des Rgveda*, Vienna, 1998.

Oldenberg, H., *Buddha, sein Leben, seine Lehre*, Berlin, 1881.

Parpola, A., "From the Dialects of Old Indo-Aryan to Proto-Indo-Aryan and Proto-Iranian," in: N. Sims-Williams, ed., *Indo-Iranian Languages and Peoples*, Oxford, 2002, 43–102.

Parpola, A., "The Dāsas and the Coming of the Aryans," in: M. Witzel, ed., *Inside the Texts, Beyond the Texts: New Approaches to the Study of the Vedas*, Cambridge MA, 1997, 193 -202.

Parpola, A., "The Coming of the Aryans to Iran and India and the Cultural and Ethnic Identity of the Dāsas," *StOr* 64, 1988, 195–302.

Patel, M., "Die *Danastuti's* des *Rigveda*," diss., University of Marburg, 1929.

Proferes, T.N., *Vedic Ideals of Sovereignty and the Poetics of Power*, New Haven, 2007.

Proferes, T.N., "Kuru Kings, Tura Kāvaṣeya, and the *-tvāya* Gerund," *BSOAS* 66/2, 2003a, 210–219.

Proferes, T.N., "Remarks on the Transition from Rgvedic Composition to Śrauta Compilation," *IIJ* 46, 2003b, 1–21.

Rau, W., "The Earliest Literary Evidence for Permanent Vedic Settlements," in: M. Witzel, ed., *Inside the Texts, Beyond the Texts: New Approaches to the Study of the Vedas*, Cambridge MA, 1997, 203–206.

Rau, W., *The Meaning of Pur in Vedic Literature*, Munich, 1976.

Rau, W., *Staat und Gesellschaft im alten Indien nach den Brāhmaṇa-Texten dargestellt*, Wiesbaden, 1957.

Santucci, J.A., "Aspects of the Nature and Functions of Vedic Kingship," in: A.L. Basham, ed., *Kingship in Asia and Early America*, Mexico City, 1976, 83–113.

Scharfe, H., "Sacred Kingship, Warlords and Nobility," in: A.W. van den Hoek, D.H.A. Kolff & M.S. Oort, eds., *Ritual, State and History in South Asia: Essays in Honour of J.C. Heesterman*, Leiden, 1992, 309–322.

Scharfe, H., *The State in Indian Tradition*, Leiden, 1989.

Scharfe, H., "The Vedic Word for 'King,'" *JAOS* 105/3, 1985, 543–548.

Shaffer, J.G., "Cultural Development in the Eastern Punjab," in: J.R. Lukacs, ed., *Studies in the Archaeology of India and Pakistan*, New York, 1986, 77–90.

Shaffer, J.G., "The Indo-Aryan Invasions: Cultural Myth and Archaeological Reality," in: J.L. Lukacs, ed., *The Peoples of South Asia*, New York, 1984, 74–90.

Shaffer, J.G., & D.A. Lichtenstein, "The Concepts of 'Cultural Tradition' and 'Palaeoethnicity' in South Asian Archaeology," in: G. Erdosy, ed., *The Indo-Aryans of Ancient South Asia: Language, Material Culture and Ethnicity*, Berlin, 1995, 126–154.

Stuhrmann, R., "Rgvedisch *pur-*," *EJVS* 15/1, 2008.

Thapar, R., *Early India: From the Origins to AD 1300*, London, 2002.

Thapar, R., *From Lineage to State: Social Formations in the Mid-first Millenium B.C. in the Ganga Valley*, Bombay, 1984.

Thieme, P., "The 'Aryan' Gods of the Mitanni Treaties," *JAOS* 80/4, 1960, 301–317.

Tripathi, V., *The Painted Grey Ware: An Iron Age Culture of Northern India*, Delhi, 1976.

Tull, H., *The Vedic Origins of Karma*, New York, 1989.

Witzel, M., "Early Sanskritization: Origins and Development of the Kuru State," in: B. Kölver, ed., *Recht, Staat und Verwaltung im klassischen Indien/The State, the Law and Administration in Classical India*, Munich, 1997a, 27–52.

Witzel, M., "The Development of the Vedic Canon and Its Schools: The Social and Political Milieu," in: M. Witzel, ed., *Inside the Texts, Beyond the Texts: New Approaches to the Study of the Vedas*, Cambridge MA, 1997b, 257–345.

Witzel, M., "Early Indian History: Linguistic and Textual Parameters," in: G. Erdosy, ed., *The Indo-Aryans of Ancient South Asia*, Berlin, 1995a, 85–125.

Witzel, M., "Rgvedic History: Poets, Chieftains and Polities," in: G. Erdosy, ed., *The Indo-Aryans of Ancient South Asia*, Berlin, 1995b, 307–354.

Witzel, M., "Tracing the Vedic Dialects," in: C. Caillat, ed., *Dialectes dans les littératures indo-aryennes*, Paris, 1989, 97–264.

Zimmer, S., "*Viśām pati-* und *Viśpati-*," *MSS* 44, 1985, 291–304.

THEODORE PROFERES

Historical Perspectives:

Between 400 BCE and 600 CE

The religious tradition that, with the benefit of hindsight, can be referred to as Hinduism has throughout its history been marked by exceptional diversity and plurality in thought and practice. Different forms of theism and → atheism, and sectarianism and nonsectarianism, have coexisted, and several distinct but interrelated sects can be identified within the overarching Hindu tradition. The religious domain intersected with the social, and this is reflected in the Sanskrit word → *dharma*, which has much broader connotations than the English "religion." The main focus of this essay is the early history of puranic Hinduism (a set of beliefs and practices that are reflected most vividly in Sanskrit texts known as the → Purāṇas) within the larger historical context.

Ancient Indian religious traditions cannot be understood in isolation; they have to be seen as interacting parts of a larger religious landscape. Devotional trends that marked puranic Hinduism also emerged in Buddhism and Jainism, albeit revolving around *buddhas*, *bodhisattvas*, and *tīrthaṅkaras*. There was also an overlap in conceptual vocabulary, ethics, and symbols (see Hinduism and Buddhism). The ideas of → *karman* (the connections between actions and their consequences across successive lives) and salvation (*mokṣa*; see → liberation) consisting of a release from → *saṃsāra* (the cycle of birth and death) were present in Hinduism, Buddhism, and Jainism, although there were significant differences in how they were understood. There also existed a range of religious ideas and practices that lay outside the frame of the major religious traditions. During the early part of the period under review, religious identities must have been quite fluid, and interactions among religious traditions and sects were marked by dialogue, debate, and competition for followers and patronage.

In order to reconstruct the history of Hinduism and the intersection between religious precept and practice, in addition to analyzing texts, it is essential to examine the evidence from archaeology (see Bacus & Lahiri, 2004). This is so because the textual sources represent normative perspectives of male religious elites. They often give the impression of pan-Indian processes, highlight dominant traditions, and mask regional and local complexities and diversities. There is also the problem of the uncertain chronology of many texts, and the debate regarding the date of the Buddha has important implications for dating them and the historical developments that they reflect. Inscriptions, coins, sculptures, and structural and artifactual remains from archaeological sites are associated with their own interpretative problems, but they do provide a more firm chronological anchoring. These indicate that although parts of some of the major Purāṇas were composed in the 4th–5th centuries CE, the trends that they reflect developed over many centuries before that.

The Sanskrit epics (the → *Mahābhārata* and → *Rāmāyaṇa*), and even more so the Purāṇas, indicate a transition from vedic religion based on sacrifice (→ *yajña*) toward one centered on devotion to the gods. Although the word → *bhakti* (from the root *bhaj-*, "to share," "to participate" – in this context, in the divine) is often used to characterize this devotion, this word has many nuances, and the relationship between deity and devotee assumed different forms and expression. While theism is emphasized in the epics and Purāṇas, the theistic ideas include polytheism (the worship of many deities) and monolatry (the worship of a supreme deity without denying the existence of other deities). These coexisted with a range of monistic and nontheistic ideas and notions of piety and were embedded in a variegated but partially shared cosmological, mythological, and philosophical matrix.

Some of the gods who emerged as major foci of worship in puranic Hinduism are known from the older vedic tradition. Vedic sacrifice retained an importance, especially in the political sphere, and the → Veda itself was accorded a position of prestige and authority. However, in spite of such links and elements of continuity, there were also significant changes. While the historical contexts of these religious processes can be identified (see Singh, 2008, 320–545), their roots were multilinear and complex. The changes seem to have partly originated in the milieu of the vedic texts but even more so in older, nonvedic substrata of popular, local, folk, and tribal religions. Certain aspects of the new developments have been traced archaeologically to protohistoric times and to chalcolithic (especially Harappan; see → Indus civilization) and early Iron Age cultures; and there are more direct connections with the ancient cults of → *yakṣa*s and *yakṣī*s (deities associated with water, fertility, trees, and the forest), *nāga*s and *nāgī*s (serpent deities associated with water and fertility; see → sacred animals), and fertility goddesses.

The evolution of Hinduism should be seen as the cumulative outcome of a complex series of cultural encounters between Brahmanical and non-Brahmanical traditions that occurred in different places at different points in time. These cannot be adequately understood in terms of the problematic categories of Aryan and non-Aryan, and these categories will therefore be avoided in this discussion. The concepts of Sanskritization and Brahmanization have sometimes been used to refer to the Brahmanical appropriation and refashioning of non-Brahmanical traditions, but the term "Hinduization" seems more appropriate. This is because although Brahmans played an important role in these processes, and although the Brahmanical elements occupied a position of dominance, the interactions between Brahmanical and non-Brahmanical traditions were reciprocal, even if asymmetrically so. Further, the Brahmanical tradition (never fixed or monolithic) was itself remolded in the course of these interactions, and the result was a new, evolving, and changing religious synthesis that can be called Hinduism.

It should be emphasized that although religious assimilation is an important feature of Hinduization, its underlying historical processes were often based on tension, conflict, and violence and included social and political subordination and marginalization. For instance, the forest (which covered vast areas in the subcontinent) was an area of rich economic potential and therefore had to be subjugated and controlled by ancient states, but the forest tribes presented a perennial challenge to their political authority. This tension between the state and the forest underlay the incorporation of tribal deities into Hindu pantheons.

Although they were not a homogeneous group and all of them were not priests, Brahmans were the leading agents of Hinduization, and the proliferation of Brahman settlements through royal land grants was closely connected with developments in the religious sphere (Singh, 2009). Political processes such as state formation and imperial expansion also played a key role, as did the enduring relationship between kings and certain sections of the Brahman community. Later vedic texts and early Buddhist literature refer to royal grants of land to Brahmans, and the references increase thereafter. The geographical extension of Brahmanical influence into eastern and southern India is connected with Brahman migrations, although it is likely that there was also a certain amount of absorption of local priesthoods into Brahman ranks. Brahmans, Brahman settlements, and Brahman landowners became important nodes of interaction between Brahmanical and tribal/regional/local traditions and were important parts of the social and religious interactions reflected in the Purāṇas.

The early historic period in North India dates from around the 6th century BCE, a time of exceptional philosophical and religious ferment, associated especially with the Buddha and Mahāvīra and with the beginning of the institutionalization of the Buddhist and Jaina monastic orders (some scholars assign 5th–4th cents. BCE to the Buddha and these developments). The early historic period is also associated with state formation, urbanization, and an acceleration of craft production and trade – trends that continued into the subsequent centuries. For the purpose of discussing the early history of puranic Hinduism, the period under review can be subdivided into three phases – circa 400–200 BCE, circa 200 BCE–300 CE, and circa 300–600 CE. Since the composition of many of the major texts extended across these chronological divisions, there is considerable overlap in the developments that are discussed below.

Prelude and Beginnings, circa 400–200 BCE

In the 4th century BCE, the Maurya Empire (c. 324/321–187 BCE) was built on the foundations of the imperialism of earlier Magadhan dynasties. This was a virtually all-India empire, but the control of the center over various areas must have varied considerably. Although the Harappan civilization (c. 2600–1900 BCE) is the oldest literate culture in the subcontinent, the inscriptions of the Maurya king Aśoka are among the oldest specimens of deciphered writing in South Asia.

Among the Sanskrit brahmanical (see → Vedas and Brāhmaṇas) texts whose composition falls broadly within circa 400–200 BCE are the Vedāṅga (lit. "limbs of the Veda"). These include the Kalpasūtras (aphorisms on ritual), which are further subdivided into the Śrautasūtras (which deal with vedic sacrifices), Gṛhyasūtras (which deal mainly with domestic rituals and rites of passage), and Dharmasūtras (which deal with *dharma*). It is difficult to assign specific dates or provenance to these texts. P.V. Kane (1997, xi) places the main Śrautasūtras and some of the Gṛhyasūtras between circa 800 BCE and 400 BCE. He also dates the Dharmasūtras of Āpastamba, Gautama, Baudhāyana, and Vasiṣṭha and the Gṛhyasūtras such as those of Pāraskara and Baudhāyana to between c. 600 BCE and 300 BCE. However, P. Olivelle (2000, 10) places the composition of the Dharmasūtras of Āpastamba, Gautama, and Baudhāyana between the beginning of the 3rd century BCE and the mid-2nd century BCE and that of Vasiṣṭha thereafter.

The word *dharma* is derived from the root *dhṛ-*, "to maintain," "to support," or "to sustain," and refers to the laws that govern the universe and human society. The importance of this concept in religious, social, and political discourse is not confined to the Hindu tradition. Along with → *artha* (material gain) and → *kāma* (sensual pleasure), *dharma* forms part of a triad of *puruṣārtha*s (goals of human existence), to which *mokṣa* (liberation from the cycle of rebirth) was also sometimes added. Within the Brahmanical tradition, *dharma* became a special subject of inquiry, whose results were embodied in texts known as → Dharmaśāstra (see Kane, 1997; Lingat, 1973), of which the Dharmasūtras were the earliest. These texts reflect a significant attempt of a section of the Brahman intelligentsia to codify social and religious norms.

Dharmaśāstra texts are normative and represent the ideas and ideology of the Brahman *dharma* experts. Because the norms that they laid down were considered obligatory by their composers, *dharma* also means duty. The basic framework of duties was provided by the four *varṇa*s (hereditary social classes) and → *āśrama*s (life stages), as well as gender, marital status, and age. The four *varṇa*s, which are first mentioned in later vedic texts, were the Brāhmaṇas (Brahmans; associated with knowledge and performing sacrifices), Kṣatriyas (warriors and rulers), Vaiśyas (agriculturists, herders, and traders), and Śūdras (who were supposed to serve the higher *varṇa*s). The four *āśrama*s, which are mentioned from the time of the Dharmasūtras onward, were applicable only to males of the first three *varṇa*s; they comprise *brahmacarya* (the stage of celibate studenthood), *gṛhastha* (the householder stage), *vānaprastha* (partial renunciation), and *saṃnyāsa* (complete renunciation). Originally conceptualized as four alternative paths that could be chosen by an individual, the *āśrama* scheme assumed its classical form of four sequential life stages at about the turn of the millennium (Olivelle, 1993). *Varṇa* and *āśrama* should be understood as two important, enduring cornerstones in the Brahmanical conceptualization of the normative social order rather than as a description of actual social structure or practice. Social identity and interaction in ancient India were based on the intersection of various elements such as gender, lineage, family, class, and caste (*jāti*); social organization varied significantly across regions and underwent considerable change over time. Dharmaśāstra texts laid down prescriptions on a variety of subjects including etiquette, food consumption, marriage, relationships within the household, sexual practices, rites of passage, property and inheritance, sins and expiation, penances, offerings to the ancestors, civil and criminal law (it is not clear to what extent these texts were actually used in legal cases), and the duties of the king.

The Dharmaśastra tradition recognized three sources of *dharma*: Śruti (the Veda), Smṛti (the remembered tradition, which includes the Vedāṅgas, Purāṇas, epics, Dharmaśāstra, and Nītiśāstra or works on polity), and *sadācāra*/*śiṣṭācāra* (the conduct of the wise and learned, generally understood as custom). The recognition of custom as a valid source of *dharma*; the mention of the *dharma*s of different *deśa*s (countries; see → regions and regional traditions), *jāti*s (castes), and *kula*s (families); and the idea of *āpaddharma* (justified departures from *dharma* norms in times of acute distress or emergency) indicate that the *dharma* experts acknowledged variations in social and religious practice. Differences of opinion on certain issues among these experts show that *dharma* was the subject of lively debate among the Brahman intelligentsia.

Inscribed on natural rock and pillars in far-flung areas of the subcontinent, the inscriptions of the Maurya emperor Aśoka (mostly in the Prakrit language and the Brahmi script, with the use of the Kharosthi script, Greek, and Aramaic in the northwest) make a distinction between two levels of the religious domain. On the one hand, there were various sects, referred to as *pāsaṇḍa*s, among which there seems to have been a certain amount of tension and discord, which Aśoka was keen to reduce. On the other hand, there is *dhamma* (the Prakrit form of *dharma*), propagated with great passion by the emperor, which stood for the good, explained as a set of ethical norms that cut across sectarian divides, although it had a Buddhist tinge. These ethical norms included virtues such as truthfulness, compassion, liberality, non-injury to all living beings, and proper conduct *vis-à-vis* close social associates. They were connected with a belief in rebirth, heaven, and merit (*puṇñya*) and demerit (*apuṇñya, pāpa*) – ideas that seem to have been embedded in the larger religious and cultural landscape. Aśoka's edicts frequently mention Brahmans and Śramaṇas (renunciants), and life-cycle rituals (→ *saṃskāra*s), some of which the emperor criticizes as being useless. It is not clear whether these rituals had associations with any specific religious sect. Regarding specific religious denominations, Aśoka's inscriptions refer to the Buddhist *sangha*, as well as to the Nirgranthas (Jainas) and → Ājīvikas, but there is nothing that is suggestive of specifically Hindu sects or religious practices.

Hints of Hindu sectarianism come from Greek accounts, especially that of Megasthenes (see Roller, 2012). Often considered the ambassador of the Hellenistic king Seleukos Nikator to the court of the Maurya king Candragupta Maurya, Megasthenes actually seems to have been an associate of Sibyrtius, the Macedonian satrap of Arachosia (Bosworth, 1996). His *Indika* is a lost work, but later writings such as those of Diodoros, Strabo, Arrian, and Pliny contain epitomes (paraphrases) from it. These give a few glimmers of evidence regarding Indian religious history, not all of which were based on Megasthenes, and which have to be evaluated in the context of the larger Greek ethnographic tradition. The Greeks noticed in India the worship of certain deities who reminded them of their own gods Heracles and Dionysos and therefore gave these Hindu gods the corresponding Greek names. The Indian Dionysos has been identified with various deities such as → Śiva, → Kṛṣṇa, → Rāma, Sūrya (see → *navagraha*s), Soma (see → *navagraha*s), Skanda (see → Murukaṉ), and Balarāma; as an amalgam of several gods; and as Manu (the mythical progenitor of humans), the *holī* festival, a king, or a cultural hero of the Muṇḍas. The Indian Heracles has been variously identified with Kṛṣṇa, Śiva, a proto-Śiva, Balarāma, a *yakṣa*, or as an amalgam of several Indian gods (Karttunen, 1989, 211–219). However, the strongest identification of Dionysos seems to be with Śiva, and the most likely connection of Heracles is with Kṛṣṇa.

The *Arthaśāstra* of Kauṭilya cannot be used as a source specifically for the Maurya Empire, because although the origins of this political treatise may lie in the Maurya period, additions and changes extended into the early centuries of the Common Era. Further, since it is a normative work, it cannot be understood as descriptive of any specific state or society. However, its vocabulary, including its religious vocabulary, could not have been entirely invented, and some of its statements seem to reflect broad trends that were evolving between circa 300 BCE and 200 CE. The text (Kangle, 1969) reveals a complex and variegated religious landscape, peopled by Brahmans learned in the Vedas, renunciants, Buddhist monks and nuns, and members of the Ājīvika sect. In contrast to the Aśokan inscriptions, in the *Arthaśāstra*, the term *pāsaṇḍa* has negative connotations and probably refers to non-Brahmanical sects. The religious practices mentioned by Kauṭilya include sacrifice, temple worship, the performance of life-cycle rituals and → *vrata*s (vows), and visiting and bathing in places of pilgrimage (→ *tīrtha*s). Magic, black magic, sorcery, charms, and → *mantra*s (incantations) are also mentioned, as are the worship of mountains, rivers (including the → Gaṅgā), snakes, and trees, as well as a belief in evil spirits. Kauṭilya refers to the tutelary deities of the city and the king and mentions the worship of various gods, including Indra (see → vedic gods), → Yama, and Varuṇa. A rite in honor of Rudra is mentioned (*ArŚ.* 14.1.34), and there is reference to a devotee of the god Saṃkarṣaṇa, who is associated with an intoxicating beverage (*ArŚ.* 13.3.54). Agricultural rites, such as *mantra*s recited on the occasion of the first sowing of seeds, include salutations to Prajāpati, Kāśyapa, and Devī Sītā (*ArŚ.* 2.24.27).

Kauṭilya refers to the worship of images of deities (*daivatapratimā*) in temples (*devagṛha, devakula,* and *devāyatana*) and uses the terms *pūjana*/→ *pūjā* in conjunction with the gods. He recommends that shrines of Aparājita, Apratihata, Jayanta, and Vaijayanta and those of Śiva, Vaiśravaṇa, the Aśvins, Śrī (→ Śrī Lakṣmī), and Madirā should be built in the center of the city. The city gates should be presided over by → Brahmā, Indra, Yama, and

Senāpati, and there is also mention of temples of the deities of the quarters outside the city (*ArŚ.* 2.4.17–20). The references to *devapatha* (the god's path; *ArŚ.* 2.3.13) and *devaratha* (the god's chariot; *ArŚ.* 2.33.5) suggest → processions of images of the gods, and there is mention of → festivals in honor of deities (*ArŚ.* 12.5.1). The institutionalization of temples is suggested by references to their property (*devadravya; ArŚ.* 1.18.9; 2.1.27), and there is mention of disputes related to penance groves, temples, sacrificial grounds, and holy places (*ArŚ.* 3.9.23). The text refers to the *devatādhayakṣa*, apparently an officer in charge of temples (*ArŚ.* 2.6.2), but this may be seen as part of Kauṭilya's model of all-pervasive state control in a model state.

Apart from the *Arthaśāstra*, certain *sūtra*s (4.3.95–97) in the *Aṣṭādhyāyī* – the circa 4th-century BCE grammatical work of Pāṇini (see → language and linguistics) – are relevant for the early history of Hinduism. *Aṣṭādhyāyī* 4.3.97 reads *vāsudevārjunābhyām vun*, indicating the use of the *vun* suffix in the context of word affixes that denote *bhakti*. On the basis of Patañjali's commentary on this *sūtra*, it has been suggested that in Pāṇini's time, Vāsudeva and Arjuna were considered to be more than Kṣatriyas – that is, they were considered gods. However, this is far from certain, as the word *bhakti* in this text does not necessarily mean devotional worship; it can have other connotations such as to like, to belong to, or to be loyal to.

The Formative Stage, circa 200 BCE–300 CE

Situated between two empires – the Maurya and the Gupta – the period from circa 200 BCE to circa 300 CE was marked by a subcontinental acceleration of state formation and urbanism, including in the Deccan and the far south. The invasions of the Indo-Greeks, Scytho-Parthians, and Kushanas from the northwest led to the inflow of new cultural influences. There was an intensification of trade within the subcontinent and between its regions and the Mediterranean lands, east Asia, and Southeast Asia. Although the process of puranic composition began in the later part of this period, the evidence from archaeology and sculpture suggests the existence of certain elements of puranic Hinduism before the composition and compilation of the puranic corpus was complete.

An important feature of religious practice in puranic Hinduism was devotion (*bhakti*) to the gods, expressed through *pūjā* – the ritual worship of deities who were believed to be resident in consecrated images – in domestic and/or temple contexts. New forms of worship were accompanied by new religious ideas, pantheons, and mythologies, and new kinds of pious activities were valorized. Sacred spaces came to be more clearly demarcated, developed, and institutionalized through the building of shrines in brick and stone, and their sources of patronage can often be identified through donative inscriptions. All this must have been accompanied by a gradual elaboration of temple liturgy and priesthoods. As the composition of key textual sources stretched beyond 300 CE, the religious trends that emerged in the period of circa 200 BCE–300 CE should be understood as having reached maturity during circa 300–600 CE, and they are therefore discussed both in this and in the subsequent section.

A.K. Coomaraswamy (1971, 36) explains the emergence of *bhakti* from the older *yakṣa*, *nāga*, and goddess cults. The sculptural evidence from Mathura (Mathura district, → Uttar Pradesh) confirms this hypothesis: the popularity of these cults between the 2nd century BCE and the 1st century CE is evident from stone sculptures, including colossal images of *yakṣa*s, *yakṣī*s, and *nāga*s. Further, remains of a stone *nāga* temple (apsidal temple number 2) have been found at nearby Sonkh. But from the 2nd century CE onward, deities of the Hindu pantheons – especially Śiva, Viṣṇu, Sūrya, → Durgā, and Lakṣmī – replaced the older deities in stone sculpture, although they continued to be represented in terracotta art (Singh, 2004). The displacement and marginalization of the older deities by those belonging to the Hindu pantheons occurred in other parts of the subcontinent too.

Puranic Hinduism should not be seen as a monolithic edifice. There was neither canon nor an institutionalized priesthood, and the texts that embody important religious ideas display not only common threads but also a certain amount of diversity in ideas and practice. The "puranic process" consisted of a complex series of reciprocal cultural encounters between Brahmanism and local/regional/tribal traditions (see Chakrabarti, 2001; Nath, 2001). As far as the idea of god is concerned, along with the emergence of sects that reflected monolatry, polytheistic tendencies remained important. In the ethical domain, *dharma* continued to be an important issue of exploration and exposition. The *yajña* of the earlier age (which had been strongly critiqued by Buddhism and Jainism) coexisted with newer elements such as *pūjā*, vows, → gift giving, and pilgrimage, which became increasingly important. Although the householder was considered central to the social fabric, the renunciatory tradition was of enduring importance in the larger religious landscape. In fact, the Hindu tradition recognized two paths, that of *pravṛtti* and that of *nivṛtti* (Bailey, 1985). The path of *pravṛtti* was a world-affirming one, where the goals were happiness and success in this world and the attainment of a favorable rebirth, including heaven, in the next. The *nivṛtti* path had a negative perspective on worldly life and sought liberation (*mokṣa, mukti*) from the cycle of birth and death. The tension between these two paths was only partially resolved with the incorporation of *saṃnyāsa* into the *āśrama* scheme.

It is difficult to demarcate the religious from the philosophical domain. Religious traditions and sects (see → *sampradāya*) had implicit or explicit (and sometimes overlapping) metaphysics, epistemology, and ethics. Many philosophical schools had a soteriological element, and their philosophical vocabulary, especially that of → Sāṃkhya, → Vedānta, and → Yoga, permeated the religious sphere. While the origins of the schools that later came to be considered the six classical systems of philosophical thought (*darśana*s) may lie in earlier times, certain important texts were written during the period of circa 200 BCE–300 CE – Jaimini's *Mīmāṃsāsūtra*, Bādarāyaṇa's *Brahmasūtra*, the *Yogasūtra, Vaiśeṣikasūtra*, and *Nyāyasūtra*. The *Sāṃkhyakārikā* may belong to the 4th–5th centuries, but Sāṃkhya philosophy is much older (see Larson, 1979). The absorption and recasting of a variety of philosophical concepts are evident in texts such as the → *Bhagavadgītā* (see below). They are also evident in the centrality and reworking of the concepts of → *prakṛti*, → *śakti*, and → *māyā* in the cosmogony and cosmology of the Great Goddess tradition (Pintchman, 1994). However, an evaluation of the precise nature of the influence of philosophical thought on early Hinduism requires a reevaluation of the history and ideas of the ancient philosophical schools. A.J. Nicholson (2011) has argued that the lines between Sāṃkhya and Yoga were initially blurred; that early Sāṃkhya, which had a major impact on the → Upaniṣads, epics, and the Purāṇas, was not an atheistic philosophy; and that atheism of some form or other was present in Vaiśeṣika, Mīmāṃsā, and later Sāṃkhya. Further investigations into ancient Indian intellectual history would help explicate the web of relationships between the philosophical and religious domains.

The Dharmaśāstra texts of this period include the *Mānavadharmaśāstra* (often referred to as the *Manusmṛti*) and *Yājñavalkyasmṛti*. P.V. Kane (1941, xi) dates the former to circa 200 BCE–200 CE and the latter to circa 100–300 CE; P. Olivelle (2005, 25) places the composition of the *Mānavadharmaśāstra* in the 2nd–3rd centuries CE. These texts carry forward from the Dharmasūtras the discussion of the duties of the *varṇa*s and *āśrama*s and other topics related to *dharma*, but the *Mānavadharmaśāstra* contains more elaborate disquisitions on statecraft and law and indicates a coopting of issues that were until then considered the domain of Arthaśastra (the study of political economy). P. Olivelle (2005, 39–41, 46–47) suggests that this text was written by a group of Brahmans who were keen to reassert Brahman privilege, define the ideal Brahman and ideal king, and reestablish the Brahman–Kṣatriya alliance.

The religious trends of the time are more clearly reflected in the *Rāmāyaṇa* and *Mahābhārata*, both written in Sanskrit. Often considered religious epics, in the traditional reckoning, the *Mahābhārata* is Itihāsa (history) and the *Rāmāyaṇa* the *Ādikāvya* (the first Kāvya or literary creation). Both evolved over a long period of time and contain many chronological layers, and their period of composition is the subject of debate. Originally heroic tales with many layers of religious accretions, these works have had enormous cultural impact in India and beyond, especially in Southeast Asia, an impact not confined to the Hindu world or to ancient times. The epics existed in various forms – as oral narratives, as written texts in different languages, and in artistic and performative traditions. Their narrative structure and the multiplicity in their forms of transmission made them powerful media for disseminating social and religious norms and values at the popular level.

The *Mahābhārata*, traditionally ascribed to Vyāsa and said to consist of a hundred thousand verses, is clearly not the work of a single author. Its composition can be placed roughly between circa 400 BCE and 400 CE, although J. Kirste Kirste (1900) and A. Hiltebeitel (2001, 18–20) have suggested a shorter time frame, between the mid-2nd century BCE and the turn of the Common Era. The central narrative of the work, arranged in 18 *parvans* (books), unfolds in the Indo-Gangetic divide and the upper Gaṅgā Valley. It revolves around a power struggle between two sets of cousins – the five Pāṇḍavas versus the hundred Kaurava brothers – and a terrible 18-day war that they fought along with their allies on the battlefield of Kurukṣetra. But the epic itself boasts of its encyclopedic nature, and there is much in it that has a tenuous connection (if that) with the main plot. J.L. Fitzgerald (2004, 53–54) describes the *Mahābhārata* as the first canonical library of Hinduism and argues that the text represents a concerted attempt of the Brahmans to reassert their position in the face of challenges presented by new doctrines, especially Buddhism and Jainism, that had attracted royal patronage.

The philosophical–religious landscape of the *Mahābhārata* is varied (Sutton, 2000) and includes older elements such as vedic sacrifice and newer ones such as *bhakti*, vows, and pilgrimage. The text contains a variety of soteriologies, ethical codes, and ritual ideas. Its discussions on *dharma* and renunciation reveal tensions, conflicts, and moral dilemmas as well as an attempt to weld several disparate elements together. This is especially manifest in the *Bhagavadgītā* (which is part of the epic), where, on the eve of the great war, Arjuna has to decide whether it is moral to kill his kinsmen. The *Bhagavadgītā* contains different ideas of theism – an impersonal cosmic god who is the creator, preserver, and destroyer of the world and a god who is more immediate and is worthy of *bhakti*. According to A. Malinar (2007, 237–38), the text reflects cosmological monotheism, a special type of monotheism which is quite different from that of the Islamic and Judeo-Christian traditions – → Kṛṣṇa is one among many divine beings, but is presented as the highest and only god of liberation and creation, and as partially present in different aspects of the cosmos. Although the term *avatāra* does not occur in the *Bhagavadgītā*, the germs of the idea of Viṣṇu's *avatāra*s (the god's "descents," often translated as reincarnations), elaborated on in the Purāṇas, are present. Apart from Kṛṣṇa, the *Mahābhārata* mentions many other deities including Viṣṇu, Nārāyaṇa, Śiva, Brahmā, and Durgā; however, there are very few references to the worship of images of gods in temples.

The stages in the composition of the *Rāmāyaṇa*, traditionally ascribed to Vālmīki, can be placed between circa 500 BCE and 300 CE (see Brockington, 1984), although R. Goldman (1984, 23) suggests that the epic was probably composed between circa 750 and 500 BCE. This long poem, consisting of about twenty thousand verses arranged in seven *kāṇḍa*s or books, is "arguably one of the three or four most important and widely influential texts ever written" (Goldman & Sutherland Goldman, 2004, 75). It tells the story of Rāma, prince of the kingdom of Kośala (located in the middle Gaṅgā Valley); his banishment to the forest due to his stepmother's plot; the abduction of his wife Sītā (see → Draupadī and Sītā) by Rāvaṇa, the king of Laṅkā; his victory over Rāvaṇa; and his return to his capital Ayodhyā along with his beloved Sītā. Like the *Mahābhārata*, the *Rāmāyaṇa* too has a rich and variegated religious landscape (see Brockington, 1984, 194–225), blending the old with the new. The central characters, especially Rāma and Sītā, are represented as ideal archetypes, worthy of emulation in the way they discharge their *dharma*, especially their familial duties. But Rāma was no ordinary mortal – by the time the epic assumed its final form, he was identified with the god Viṣṇu, worthy not only of admiration and emulation but also of *bhakti*.

The Purāṇas are the other major category of texts that vividly reveal the ongoing religious processes and syntheses (see Hazra, 1940; Rocher, 1986) and reflect a powerful attempt of their Brahman composers to revitalize, recast, and propagate Brahmanical religious and social norms. It is difficult to ascertain the geographical context of these works. Tradition ascribes the composition of the Purāṇas to Vyāsa and speaks of 18 Mahāpurāṇas (Major Purāṇas) and 18 Upapurāṇas (Minor Purāṇas), although the actual number of texts is greater. The conventional list of the 18 Mahāpurāṇas consists of the following: *Brahmapurāṇa*, *Padmapurāṇa*, *Viṣṇupurāṇa*, *Śivapurāṇa*, *Bhāgavatapurāṇa*, *Nāradapurāṇa*, *Mārkaṇḍeyapurāṇa*, *Agnipurāṇa*, *Bhaviṣyapurāṇa*, *Brahmavaivartapurāṇa*, *Liṅgapurāṇa*, *Varāhapurāṇa*, *Skandapurāṇa*, *Vāmanapurāṇa*, *Kūrmapurāṇa*, *Matsyapurāṇa*, *Garuḍapurāṇa*, and *Brahmāṇḍapurāṇa*. R.C. Hazra (1940, 175–189) and other scholars have suggested a chronology for certain sections of the Purāṇas, but these texts are extremely difficult to date. Some parts may belong to circa 200–500 CE, but these mingle with later additions. Certain Purāṇas, such as the *Bhāgavatapurāṇa* (usually dated between the 8th and the 10th cent.) and the *Skandapurāṇa*, seem to be later.

Tradition associates the Purāṇas with five subjects (*pañcalakṣaṇas*), namely *sarga* (the creation of the universe), *pratisarga* (its re-creation after dissolution), *vaṃsa* (genealogies of the gods and other beings), the *manvantaras* (periods of time associated with the various Manus), and *vaṃśānucarita* (accounts of kings). However, as a matter of fact, all Purāṇas do not necessarily deal with all five topics, and they actually deal with many others. The epic–puranic tradition connected itself with the vedic tradition – the *Mahābhārata* and the Purāṇas claim to be the fifth Veda – but reflects a religiosity that is quite different. Apart from cosmogonies and royal genealogies, the Purāṇas are a rich storehouse of religious mythology as well as ideas on a variety of issues including the duties of the *varṇas*, *āśramas*, and women. They also discuss the consecration (*pratiṣṭhā*) and worship of images of deities in temples. Like the epics, puranic material circulated in various forms, including didactic narration (Kathās), and had enormous influence in molding social and religious norms and practices at the popular level.

The epics, and more so the Purāṇas, valorize and give detailed classifications and descriptions of various kinds of pious activities and emphasize their efficacy through the narration of mythological stories. These pious activities include *vratas* (vows) – acts of devotion, austerity, or abstention performed for specified periods, usually for attaining specific objectives such as wealth, health, longevity, the birth of a son, expiation for a sin, heaven, or liberation from the cycle of rebirth (see Kane, 1958, 1–462). Pilgrimage, too, is lauded in the Purāṇas, and the detailed descriptions of *tīrthas* (sacred places), which have great purificatory potential and where communion with the gods is facilitated, indicate the steady expansion of pilgrimage networks. Several major Hindu pilgrimage centers (such as Gaya in eastern India) were considered sacred by Buddhists and Jainas too. *Dāna* (making ritual gifts), especially to worthy Brahmans, is described in the Purāṇas as having the potential of yielding great merit (*puñya*), and these texts introduced a new series of gifts called the *mahādānas* (great gifts). Charitable activities were considered part of a type of *dharma* called *pūrta* (lit. that which is filled), as opposed to *iṣṭadharma* (the *dharma* of sacrifice). *Pūrtadharma* included constructing wells, tanks, and temples; maintaining public gardens; offering gifts; and distributing food to the needy. Such pious activities could be performed by all people regardless of their gender, class, or caste, including by women and Śūdras.

The king–Brahman relationship and royal grants to Brahmans were key elements in the religious processes of this and later periods (see also → priests). Although literary references to such grants go back to earlier times, the earliest epigraphic evidence for this phenomenon belongs to the 1st-century BCE Deccan: the Nanaghat inscription of the Satavahana queen Nāgaṃnikā refers to villages as part of the sacrificial fee offered to priests in the context of the performance of certain Śrauta (vedic) sacrifices by her husband Sātakarṇi (I). The 2nd-century CE Nasik inscription of Uṣavadāta, son-in-law of the Shaka Kshatrapa ruler Nahapāṇa, describes the donor as having given 16 villages to the gods and Brahmans. (In addition to gifting land to Brahmans, these rulers made grants to Buddhist monks.) As mentioned earlier, the Brahmans were not a homogenous group. They included Śrauta Brahmans, who were associated with the vedic tradition, and → Smārta Brahmans, who were participants and agents in the new emerging religious synthesis of puranic Hinduism. Of course, this was not necessarily a strict division, and it is quite likely that Brahmans who were described in inscriptions as vedic scholars also had a role to play in popularizing puranic religion.

The worship of the gods Viṣṇu and Śiva and the goddess Durgā becomes evident in this period, and we see the beginnings of an elaboration of their mythologies and the formation of pantheons. Puranic tradition somewhat artificially divides the Purāṇas according to → *guṇas* (qualities) of *rajas, sattva*, and *tamas* (associated respectively with energy and activity, purity and lightness, and darkness and heaviness) and deity (Brahmā, Viṣṇu, and Śiva). Certain Purāṇas reflect a sectarianism that is best described as monolatry. For instance, the *Viṣṇupurāṇa* extols the greatness of Viṣṇu, while the *Śivapurāṇa* and *Liṅgapurāṇa* highlight the greatness of Śiva. However, the description of a supreme god is accompanied by an acknowledgment of the existence of a multitude of other gods. Further, the relationship among the various gods did not necessarily take a hierarchical form. Within the Purāṇas, the idea of a supreme god coexisted with the idea of a complementarity of the gods arising out of a division of labor among them. This is evident in the triad of the gods Brahmā, Viṣṇu, and Śiva, associated respectively with the creation, preservation, and destruction of the world. The Purāṇas also contain the idea that the various gods were manifestations of one divine being.

Early Vaiṣṇava Elements

The term "Vaiṣṇavism" is usually used to collectively refer to several distinct cults (especially those of Nārāyaṇa, Vāsudeva-Kṛṣṇa, and the goddesses Śrī and Lakṣmī), which at some point in time came to be associated with the god Viṣṇu (see Jaiswal, 1980, 32–115). The primacy of Viṣṇu in this set of deities seems to have been a relatively late phenomenon, and even after these associations were established, many of the worshippers of the various deities who came to be incorporated into the Vaiṣṇava fold considered their gods as independent and not in any way subordinate to Viṣṇu.

One of the important concepts in Vaiṣṇavism was the idea of the *avatāra*s (from *ava* + *tṛ-*, "to descend"), according to which Viṣṇu descends to the earth in different forms at different points in time in order to destroy evil and protect *dharma*. It was connected with the idea of cyclical time in which there were a series of *mahāyuga*s (great ages), each consisting of four *yuga*s (ages) – *kṛtayuga, tretāyuga, dvāparayuga*, and *kaliyuga* – which were marked by a systematic decline in *dharma* (see → cosmic cycles). Each *mahāyuga* ended with the dissolution of the world and was followed by its re-creation. Early expressions of the idea of the *avatāra*s can be traced to the *Rāmāyaṇa* and *Mahābhārata*, but it is elaborated on in the Purāṇas.

The *Mahābhārata* contains many more references to Nārāyaṇa than to Viṣṇu, and the term "Vaiṣṇava" as a worshipper of Viṣṇu occurs rarely in the text (though it is mentioned frequently in the Purāṇas). Nārāyaṇa (who is also mentioned in later vedic texts) is described as a great god associated with asceticism, *yoga*, and sacrifice. According to S. Jaiswal (1980, 37–39), the epithet Bhāgavata ("One Who Belongs to Bhagavān," that is, a devotee of the great lord), which later came to be an epithet of worshippers of Vāsudeva-Kṛṣṇa, originally referred to devotees of Nārāyaṇa (see → Bhāgavatas). Although the *Mahābhārata* identifies Viṣṇu with Nārāyaṇa, the latter's prominence indicates Nārāyaṇa's greater importance at the time when the epic was composed.

As already mentioned, one of the earliest possible allusions to the veneration of Vāsudeva-Kṛṣṇa (Kṛṣṇa, son of Vāsudeva) is Pāṇini's explanation of the word "Vāsudevaka" as one whose object of *bhakti* is Vāsudeva, although the word *bhakti* here can be interpreted in different ways. The term that came to be often used for a devotee of this god was Bhāgavata (worshipper of the lord). The Vāsudeva-Kṛṣṇa of the *Mahābhārata, Bhagavadgītā*, and the Purāṇas is an extremely complex character. The first detailed story of his life is found in the *Harivaṃśa*, an appendix to the *Mahābhārata*, but the legends that came to be associated with him seem to be drawn from several milieux. While the cult of Vāsudeva-Kṛṣṇa had its origins in the Mathura area, the pastoral elements associated with his childhood as well as the erotic stories concerning him and the *gopī*s (cowherd girls) that are elaborated on in texts such as the *Harivaṃśa, Viṣṇupurāṇa, Brahmapurāṇa*, and *Bhāgavatapurāṇa* may have been drawn from legends prevalent among the Ābhīra tribe, which may have entered the subcontinent in the 1st century BCE. F. Hardy points out that although the historicity of Kṛṣṇa remains a matter of speculation among scholars, the religious tradition itself views him as "a god who had entered human history"; this belief in his historicity remained an important element in his theology and created a tension between Kṛṣṇa as a historical figure and as an eternal god (Hardy, 1983, 18–19, 23).

Within the *Mahābhārata*, special importance attaches to the *Bhagavadgītā* (Song of the Lord), which weaves together many philosophical elements. The *Bhagavadgītā*'s idea of *karmayoga* emphasizes the importance of following *dharma*, the eternal nature of the → *ātman* (self), and the renunciation of the fruits of actions, not of actions themselves. These ideas are tied to *bhakti*, and Kṛṣṇa emerges as an all-powerful god who descends to the earth from time to time and has the ability to lead his *bhakta*s (devotees) to liberation from the cycle of rebirth. In this text, the term *bhakti* has a variety of meanings including to be loyal or devoted to, or to concentrate one's mind on the god. F. Hardy distinguishes between the intellectual *bhakti* of the *Bhagavadgītā* and the emotional Kṛṣṇa *bhakti* of the *Bhāgavatapurāṇa* and Tamil → Āḻvār poetry (Hardy, 1983, 26–27).

An important source of the Kṛṣṇa legends was the veneration of heroes of the Vṛṣṇi clan of the Mathura area. According to Arrian (*Indika* 8.4–5; 1st–2nd cents. CE), Heracles was honored mostly by the Sourasenoi (Shurasenas) in their great cities of Methora (Mathura) and Kleisobora (Kṛṣṇapura?), through whose land flowed the river Jomanes (Yamunā; Roller, 2012, 24–25). An inscription dating to the late 1st century BCE/early 1st century CE from the Mathura area refers to a *toraṇa* (gateway) and *vedikā* (railing) that were part of a *mahāsthāna* (big temple) of Vāsudeva. Initially, Vāsudeva-Kṛṣṇa was one of five brothers venerated as *pañcavīra*s (five heroes) by the Vṛṣṇis; the others were Baladeva/Balarāma, Pradyumna, Sāmba, and Aniruddha. The prevalence of the worship of these heroes is indicated by the Mora inscription belonging to the reign of King Śoḍāsa (late 1st cent. BCE/early 1st cent. CE), which refers to the setting up of images of the *pañcavīra*s. The Mathura area has also yielded several "kinship triads" – sculptural reliefs representing Vāsudeva-Kṛṣṇa, his brother Baladeva, and his sister Ekānaṃśā.

It is clear that the worship of Vāsudeva-Kṛṣṇa was not confined to the Mathura area. A late 2nd-century BCE Prakrit inscription on a stone pillar at Besnagar (in Vidisha district, Madhya Pradesh) records the setting up of a *garuḍadhvaja* (a pillar surmounted by the figure of Garuḍa, the bird that was the vehicle of Viṣṇu; see → *vāhana*s) of Vāsudeva, the god of gods (*devadeva*; Sircar, 1942, 88–89). The person responsible for this was Heliodora (Heliodorus), a Bhāgavata, son of Diya (Dion) of Takkhasilā (Takṣaśilā). Heliodora is further described as the *yonadūta* (Greek ambassador) of the great king Aṃtalikita (Antialkidas) to the king Kāsīputra Bhāgabhadra in the latter's 14th regnal year. Traces of the foundations of a shrine have been found in the vicinity of the pillar – it was a simple, apsidal structure with a brick plinth, and its superstructure was probably made of wood, mud, and thatch.

That the worship of Kṛṣṇa and Balarāma was also prevalent in the northwest is indicated by six silver drachms of the 2nd-century BCE Indo-Greek king Agathokles found at Ai Khanoum in north Afghanistan (Filliozat, 1973). These bear a representation of Balarāma (holding a miniature plow in his left hand and a pestle in his right) on the obverse and Vāsudeva-Kṛṣṇa (holding a large *cakra* and what may be a conch shell) on the reverse (Guillaume, 1991, 81–116). The deities wear what appear to be Greek helmets, scabbards, and boots. A pair of figures carved on rock at Chilas in Kashmir seems to be holding a plow and disc, and Kharosthi inscriptions found in the area confirm its identification with Balarāma and Kṛṣṇa.

Further evidence comes from Rajasthan. A 1st-century BCE inscription from Ghosundi (Chittorgarh district) tells of a stone enclosure for a place of worship (*pūjāśilāprākāra*) known as Nārāyaṇavāṭaka, dedicated to Saṃkarśaṇa and Balarāma. The donor Sarvatāta, described as a Bhāgavata and as one who had performed the *aśvamedha* sacrifice (see → *yajña*), seems to have been a local ruler of the area (Sircar, 1942, 90–91). Ghosundi is not far from Nagari – the site of the ancient city of Mādhyamikā – and remains of a rectangular stone enclosure found there at a place called Hathibada may represent the temple alluded to in the inscription.

The epics and Purāṇas consider the goddess Śrī Lakṣmī to be the consort of Viṣṇu. Śrī and Lakṣmī originally seem to have been two separate goddesses – Śrī (her name means prosperity or well-being) may have been a fertility goddess, while Lakṣmī (lit. token, sign, or mark) may have been a deity connected with luck and prosperity (Jaiswal, 1980, 92–93). Gajalakṣmī (the goddess Lakṣmī flanked by two elephants pouring water over her from their upraised trunks) appears on several coins of this period. An early representation of Gajalakṣmī has been found on a broken terracotta plaque at Atranjikhera (in Etah district, Uttar Pradesh) in a circa 200–50 BCE context. The plaque was found within the precincts of an apsidal structure with a circumambulatory path, which may have been a temple dedicated to this goddess. Another early carving of Lakṣmī has been found at pre-Kushana levels at Sonkh near Mathura. Representations of the Gajalakṣmī type frequently occur at Buddhist sites such as Sanchi and Bharhut in central India, where they are usually interpreted as representations of the Buddha's mother Māyā.

Early Śaiva Elements

The origins of the worship of a deity who is in some ways similar to the puranic Śiva may lie in protohistoric times, and there are close resemblances between the fierce Rudra of the *Ṛgveda* and the Śiva of the Purāṇas. The *Śvetāśvataropaniṣad* describes Rudra-Śiva as ruler of all the worlds, creator and protector of all beings, and the highest

→ *brahman*, who dwells in all beings and encompasses the universe; through knowing him, people attain immortality (Bhandarkar, 1965, 106–111). The Sibae tribe, mentioned in Greek accounts of Alexander's invasion, may have been worshippers of Śiva. Patañjali's commentary on *Aṣṭādhyāyī* 5.2.76 describes the Śiva *bhāgavata*s (in this case, worshippers of the lord Śiva) as wearing animal hides and wielding an iron lance as an emblem of the deity.

Phallic worship seems to have had very ancient roots in nonvedic fertility cults, but between circa 200 BCE and 300 CE, the connection between Śiva and the → *liṅga* (the god's phallic emblem) came to be established and is reflected both in literary and in archaeological sources. The *liṅga* was often associated with the → *yoni*, which represented the female generative organ. The explicit connection between Śiva and the *liṅga* is represented in the *mukhaliṅga*s (phallic emblems with the face of the god engraved on them) and *vigrahaliṅga*s (phallic emblems with the entire figure of the god engraved on them) that are found from this period onward. An example of the latter is the 2nd-/1st-century BCE *vigrahaliṅga* from Gudimallam (in Chittoor district, Andhra Pradesh). Anthropomorphic images of Śiva are also found at various sites, and Śaiva emblems (such as the *liṅga*, trident, and his vehicle, the bull) occur frequently on coins of this period.

Several Purāṇas elaborate on Śiva's greatness, his mythology, and his worship. However, certain Śaiva sects existed on the margins of the vedic–puranic tradition and even outside it (Lorenzen, 1972; Sanderson, 1988). A distinction can also be made between a worshipper of Śiva (expressed, for instance, in epithets such as Māheśvara) and a person initiated into one of the Śaiva sects, which had their specific sets of theology, rituals, and practices (Sanderson, 1988, 660). The → Pāśupata sect, with its ascetic associations, was one of the earliest of these sects, and it will be discussed, along with others, further on.

Goddess Worship

The social implications of the worship of the divine feminine in patriarchal societies are an important but complex issue (see Hiltebeitel & Erndle, 2000). The worship of goddesses, many of them related with fertility, had prehistoric roots. The Vedas refer to several goddesses, but they are overshadowed by the gods. These earlier manifestations of goddess worship have to be distinguished from the puranic phenomenon of the cult of a supreme Goddess (see → Mahādevī). As is the case with Vaiṣṇavism, which brought together many different deities and their cults and worshippers, the Purāṇas also connected various goddesses whose worship was prevalent in different parts of the subcontinent and presented the idea that all these goddesses were different manifestations of a single Great Goddess (known by names such as Devī, Śakti, and Durgā) – a supreme deity representing the primordial female principle and power (*śakti*) that underlies the universe. This idea is the basis of the Śakti or Śākta cult, which really comes to the fore in the post-300 CE period but whose roots can be traced to the preceding centuries.

The names of some of the goddesses who later came to be considered different aspects of the Great Goddess are mentioned in late vedic texts (Banerjea, 1966, 112–121), but the idea of the worship of a Great Goddess occurs in a more developed form in the *Mahābhārata*, in its supplement the *Harivaṃśa*, and in the Purāṇas. The two *Durgāstotra*s in praise of the Goddess in the *Virāṭaparvan* and in the *Bhīṣmaparvan* of the *Mahābhārata* and the *Āryāstava* in the *Harivaṃśa* reflect Śākta ideas. The *Āryāstava* addresses the Goddess by various names such as Āryā, Nārāyaṇī, Tribhuvaneśvarī, Śrī, Kātyāyanī, Kauśikī, Aparṇā, and Nagnaśabarī. It associates her with the mountains, caves, rivers, and forests; it describes her as fond of meat, wine, and sacrifice; and it lauds her as a protectress who pervades the universe. Her association with the mountains and the forests and the reference to her being worshipped by tribes such as the Śabaras, Barbaras, and Pulindas point to the strong tribal element in the Śakti cult.

One of the most popular forms of the Goddess was Mahiṣāsuramardinī, slayer of the buffalo-demon Mahiṣa (see → Durgā). Early Mahiṣāsuramardinī images have been found in and around Mathura. At nearby Sonkh, in apsidal temple number 1, excavators identified some nine structural phases that were dated to the 1st and 2nd centuries CE (Hartel, 1993, 64–67, 245). Many plaques with representations of Mahiṣāsuramardinī were found in and near this shrine, and a sandstone plaque depicting a *matṛkā* (one of the "mothers," discussed below) found there may have been the central image in the temple.

The Religious Milieu of Early Historic South India

In South India, the roots of the later *bhakti* tradition (which dates from the 6th or 7th cent. onward) can be traced to the period of composition of the poems of early classical Tamil literature, often referred to as Caṅkam literature (see → Tamil texts). This corpus includes six of the eight anthologies of poems in the super-anthology known as the *Eṭṭutokai*; nine of the ten songs of another super-anthology, the *Pattuppāṭṭu*; and the earliest parts of the Tamil grammar called the *Tolkāppiyam*. The poetry of the anthologies can be divided into *akam* and *puṟam*, love poetry and heroic poetry, respectively. The contents of the Caṅkam corpus are generally dated between circa 300 BCE and 300 CE, although K.V. Zvelebil (1974, 9) narrows the dates down to circa 100 BCE–250 CE (their compilation occurred much later). The evidence from these texts can be correlated with that from Tamil-Brahmi inscriptions and megalithic sites. These sources reflect a transition to the early historic phase in the far south marked by the emergence of cities and a polity consisting of many tribal chieftaincies and the kingdoms of the Cholas, Ceras, and Pandiyas.

The religious and social milieu of Caṅkam literature reveals some awareness of northern elements, but it possessed its own unique characteristics. The category of the supernatural or divine is reflected in terms such as *kaṭavuḷ* and *aṇaṅku*. There is also the idea of a personalized representative of the divine in the form of specific deities and the idea that this divinity can be encountered in earthly reality (Hardy, 1983, 136, 141). The most important god is → Murukaṉ, a deity who wields a lance with a leaf-shaped end and who is associated with the poetic landscape (*tiṇai*) of the mountains called *kuṟiñci*. He is connected with hunting, war, and protection and is worshipped with offerings of garlands, music, and dance. There are also references to the *vēlaṉ* (shaman) being possessed by Murukaṉ and curing those afflicted with disease.

Brahmans were important agents of the transmission of the northern (or more specifically the epic–puranic) religious traditions to South India, and the Caṅkam poems refer to their presence in the courts of kings and chieftains and their performance of sacrifices. Many of them may have been northern migrants, but some must have been local men.

The northern gods Kṛṣṇa and Śiva were known to the Tamil poets but were molded into the Tamil cultural landscape. Kṛṣṇa was known as Māyōṉ ("One with Dark Complexion"; a literal Tamil translation of "Kṛṣṇa"), but references to him are few (see Hardy, 1983, 151–160). A song in the *Pattupāṭṭu* (*Maturaikkāñci* 590–599) mentions Māyōṉ as one who wore the beautiful garland and who defeated many demons; *Puṟanāṉūṟu* 57 describes him as worthy of praise. Viṣṇu/Kṛṣṇa/Nārāyaṇa elements occur in other poems in references to a deity whose chest is marked with Śrī, who reclines on a serpent couch, who is associated with a bird banner, and who wields a discus. The Tamil poets were also familiar with Vāliyōṉ (Balarāma), and his fair body is contrasted with his brother's dark one. According to F. Hardy (1983, 155–156), the worship of Māyōṉ was closely associated with the royal court of Kanchipuram and even more so with the Pandiya dynasty of Madurai, although he emphasizes that the religious landscape of this kingdom was very variegated.

As for Śiva (Hart, 1975, 25, 56–57), *Puṟanāṉūṟu* 6 refers to a king circumambulating a temple of the three-eyed god (Śiva) who is worshipped by sages, while *Aiñkuṟunūṟu* 181 associates the three-eyed god with the four Vedas. *Puṟanāṉūṟu* 56 refers to the god as a destroyer and mentions his matted hair, mace, and flag in the form of a bull. *Puṟanāṉūṟu* 55 refers to his giving the gods victory over the three-walled cities, although some of the specific details are different from the northern versions of the story. Kārttikeya (the older son of Śiva in puranic mythology) was also worshipped in South India, under the name Subrahmaṇya, and the popular god Murukaṉ eventually came to be identified with him. It may be noted that remains of an ancient Śiva temple, which may belong to the 2nd century BCE, have been found at Gudimallam in Andhra Pradesh, along with a *vigrahaliṅga* (Sarma, 1994).

Other northern gods mentioned in the Caṅkam poems include Indra (who is referred to either by this name or as Neṭiyōn) and Lakṣmī or Śrī, known by the Tamil name Tiru or Tirumakaḷ. G.L. Hart (1975, 63) has pointed out that the terms used for the indigenous Tamil gods (*kaṭavuḷ* and *aṇaṅku*) are not used for the northern gods. Instead, the latter are referred to as *celvaṉ* (which means "wealthy one"). Indra (Tam. Intiraṉ) is the only god who retains his Sanskrit name, while Śiva is referred to only by means of epithets.

The element of devotional worship that was to become so strong in South Indian Hindu *bhakti* of later centuries can be traced to certain poems of the Caṅkam corpus (Zvelebil, 1974, 88–94). These include references to Cevvēḷ-Murukaṉ and Māyōṉ-Tirumāl in the late classical text the *Paripāṭal* (c. 350–500 CE) and the hymn to Murukaṉ called the *Tirumurukāṟṟupaṭai* (The Guide to Lord Muruku) in the *Pattupāṭṭu*. In both cases, there is a compression of elements of the god's mythology in his epithets, allusion to his love toward humans, and mention of his specific abodes. It has been further suggested by K.V. Zvelebil that the Pāṭān heroic poems, which are associated with praising the king patron and asking him for gifts, and which have an intensely intimate and personal tone, were the precursors of the later Tamil *bhakti* hymns addressed to Viṣṇu and Śiva.

Caṅkam literature contains one allusion to characters and events connected with the *Mahābhārata* and two to those of the *Rāmāyaṇa*, indicating that the northern epic stories were known in South India (Hart, 1975, 61–62).

The Variegated Religious Landscape

The variegated religious landscape and the attempts of political elites to link themselves with its elements are evident from archaeology, inscriptions, and coins. Kushana coins depict several deities belonging to the Hindu, Buddhist, Hellenistic, and west Asian traditions. A vivid example of the variegated religious landscape comes from Nagarjunakonda (in Guntur district, Andhra Pradesh) – the site of Vijayapuri, capital of the Ikshvaku dynasty (c. 225–325 CE). Here, in addition to many Buddhist *stūpa*s and monasteries, there were also several Hindu temples (usually of brick and stone and in one case wood), marked by considerable variety in architecture (Soundararajan, 2006, 200–245). These included temples dedicated to Viṣṇu, Śiva, Kārttikeya, and Kārttikeya's consort Devasenā; a temple that seems to have been dedicated to both Viṣṇu and Śiva; and a large temple complex dedicated to Sarvadeva (referring either to Śiva or to all the gods). At the same time, in several inscriptions, Ikshvaku kings proclaimed their performance of grand vedic sacrifices such as the *aśvamedha, vājapeya,* and *agniṣṭoma* (see → *yajña*). In fact, archaeologists have identified the site of the performance of an *aśvamedha* sacrifice (replete with a tank, a tortoise-shaped altar, and a horse skeleton on a platform) in the center of the citadel.

This should make it apparent that although devotional worship of the gods in temple contexts was coming to the fore, sacrifice continued to be part of the religious landscape and was especially important for the legitimation of political power in the ideology of kingship. Like the Ikshvakus, kings of other dynasties such as the Satavahanas also claimed in their inscriptions to have performed various vedic sacrifices. *Yūpa*s (sacrificial posts) are represented on coins of the Arjunayanas and Yaudheyas. That the performance of *yajña*s was not confined to political elites is indicated by two stone *yūpa*s found at Isapur in Mathura, one of which has an inscription (dated to the 24th regnal year of the Kushana king Vasiṣka) recording the performance of a 12-night *sattra* (a type of sacrifice) by a Brahman named Droṇāla.

Material evidence of the performance of sacrifices includes a circa 2nd-century BCE brick altar in the shape of a hawk, associated with human and animal bones, found during excavations outside the eastern gate of Kausambi (in Allahabad district, Uttar Pradesh). According to G.R. Sharma (1960, 26), these altars represent *agnicayana* fire altars for a *puruṣamedha* (human sacrifice), but this interpretation has been questioned (Bakker, 2008–2009). Three hawk-shaped brick altars were discovered at Jagatgram (near Kalsi in Uttaranchal), and 3rd-century CE inscriptions found there mention the performance of several *aśvamedha*s by a ruler named Śīlavarman. Less dramatic, but no less important, are the fire pits discovered at various sites, including in Mathura. Those excavated at Sanghol (Ludhiana district, Punjab) yielded botanical material, whose analysis indicated that various types of plants, grain, fruits, and wood had been offered into the fire.

Puranic Hinduism, circa 300–600 CE

Between circa 300 and 600 CE, the political history of the subcontinent was dominated by the Gupta dynasty in the North and the Vakataka dynasty in the Deccan. In the far south, a period of disturbance attributed to a people called the Kalabhras eventually made way for the establishment and consolidation of Pallava rule. Some historians view the Gupta age as having witnessed the beginnings of a feudal order, but others have critiqued the very idea of Indian feudalism. This period is noted for its fine aesthetic production in the spheres of literature and sculpture, which contributed in large measure to the idea of its being considered a "classical age" from the cultural point of view. Rather than viewing circa 300–600 CE as a period of a Brahmanical revival, it is better to see it as having witnessed a further development of puranic Hinduism. Wars and imperial expansion of the kind that are vividly described in the Allahabad pillar inscription of the Gupta emperor Samudragupta were an important part of the historical underpinnings of this religious process.

Compared to the earlier period, there is more abundant dateable material evidence in the form of temple remains and sculptures, especially from central India. The basic structure of the Hindu temple was established during circa 300–600 CE (see Huntington, 1985, 187–196, 206–219), and stone sculpture reveals the existence of iconographic conventions executed with fine aesthetic conception and skill. Remains of structural temples include the Viṣṇu temple at Tigawa, the Śiva temples at Bhumara and Khoh, and the so-called Pārvatī Temple (probably originally dedicated to Śiva) at Nachna Kuthara (all in Madhya Pradesh); the Viṣṇu temple at Deogarh and a brick and terracotta temple at Bhitargaon (in Uttar Pradesh); and temple ruins at Dah Parbatia (in Assam). Recently, remains of four Gupta-period temples were discovered during excavations at Lathiya (Ghazipur district, Uttar Pradesh; Mani *et al.*, 2011). The earlier temples of this period usually had a small square *garbhagṛha* (sanctum), small portico, flat roof, and ornamentation on the doorways. Those of the 5th/6th centuries were more elaborate in plan; they were built on a raised plinth, had a *śikhara* (spire), and had relief sculptures on the outer walls. There are cave shrines at Udayagiri (Vidisha district, Madhya Pradesh), and the deities represented on the walls of cave 6 provide the earliest extant example of a unified Hindu iconographic program (Huntington, 1985, 189–190). Stone sculptures of deities have been found at various sites, and two nearly human-sized terracotta sculptures of the river goddesses Gaṅgā and → Yamunā found at Ahichchhatra (in Bareilly district, Uttar Pradesh) once probably flanked a temple entrance. Along with a further development of sects focusing on the worship of Viṣṇu, Śiva, and Śakti, there was a continuation of the idea of the interrelatedness of deities. The latter is reflected, for instance, in the idea of Harihara, who is part Viṣṇu and part Śiva. The patronage extended by urban elites to various religious traditions and sects can be traced through donative inscriptions.

As mentioned earlier, the composition of the epics and the Purāṇas extended into this period. The *Nāradasmṛti* is an important Dharmaśāstra work of the time. The efflorescence in many branches of literature and learning extended to philosophy and is represented by a rich commentarial tradition that systematized and amplified the thought of various philosophical schools. Important texts include Vātsyāyana's *Nyāyasūtrabhāṣya* and Uddyotakara's *Nyāyavārttikā*, Praśastapāda's commentary on the *Vaiśeṣikasūtra*, Īśvarakṛṣṇa's *Sāṃkhyakārikā*, and Vyāsa's commentary on the *Yogasūtra*.

One of the important aspects of the evolving process of puranic synthesis was a significant increase in the practice of royal land grants, which can be interpreted as a royal strategy aimed at building social alliances in order to consolidate political power in a cultural context in which *dāna* (ritual giving), especially to Brahmans, was considered a particularly meritorious pious activity. Villages gifted to Brahmans were known as *brahmadeya*s, *agrahāra*s, or *śāsana*s. During these and subsequent centuries, most of the inscriptions recording land grants specified certain exemptions and privileges that were bestowed on the recipients. The imperial Guptas made comparatively few grants, but the Vakatakas and the subordinates of the Guptas made many more. That this practice was not restricted to North India is indicated by 3rd- to 4th-century land grants made by the Pallavas. In fact, from the 5th/6th centuries onward, grants to Brahmans became a regular feature of royal policy among dynasties all over the subcontinent. Brahmans competed successfully for patronage with Vaiṣṇava and Śaiva temples and with Buddhist and Jaina monasteries. (Temples were to become major recipients of royal patronage from about the 10th cent. onward.) The proliferation of Brahman settlements, where Brahmans formed a dominant land-owning group, had a major impact on agrarian relations. These settlements also increased the influence of Brahmans as cultural mediators at the village level and became important loci of the intersection of the Brahmanical tradition with local and tribal

Fig. 1: The Viṣṇu temple at Deogarh (photo ©Aditya Arya, used by courtesy).

traditions. Some of these settlements became renowned centers of Brahmanical learning.

Apart from syncretic and assimilative tendencies, the religious landscape of this period was also marked by doctrinal debates and competition for patronage. By this time, the great religious traditions had successfully subordinated and marginalized the *yakṣa* and *nāga* cults. The inclusion of the Buddha in some lists of Viṣṇu's *avatāras* in the Purāṇas is sometimes seen as an example of syncretism, but it seems to be more an instance of absorption and marginalization, because the function of the Buddha *avatāra* was to delude the wicked, and he never appears as the central object of worship in Vaiṣṇava temples.

This period also saw the emergence of → Tantra, which came to have a strong impact on all Indian religions (Gupta *et al.*, 1979; Bhattacharyya, 1982; Padoux, 1987). Tantra consisted of a set of doctrines and practices taught by preceptors to select initiates toward the goal of attaining supernatural powers and liberation, and it included the worship of fearsome deities, yogic practices, and sexual rites. The relationship of Tantra with the vedic and epic–puranic traditions was ambiguous. The → Pāñcarātra was an important early Tantric sect among the Vaiṣṇavas, while the → Kāpālikas, Kālāmukhas, and Nāths (see → Nāth Sampradāya) were the major Śaiva sects. Śāktism, too, was greatly influenced by Tantra.

The Vaiṣṇava Tradition

Between circa 300 and circa 600 CE, the Vaiṣṇava pantheon became more consolidated with the absorption of the cults of Nārāyaṇa, Vāsudeva-Kṛṣṇa, Saṃkarṣaṇa-Balarāma, and Śrī Lakṣmī. At the same time, these deities also remained the focus of independent worship. The term *bhāgavata* occurs frequently in inscriptions, while the term "Vaiṣṇava" is still infrequent (although it occurs often in the Purāṇas). Vaiṣṇava elements are prominent in Gupta sources – several kings of this dynasty have the title *paramabhāgavata* (great devotee of the lord), the Garuḍa was their symbol, and Gajalakṣmī is depicted on certain Gupta coins.

The idea of Viṣṇu's *avatāras* became more developed and prominent. The number of *avatāras* eventually came to be reckoned as ten, and they were associated with the different *yugas*. They included animal, animal-human, and human forms, but the names vary in different texts. One of the frequently occurring lists consists of Matsya (fish), Kūrma (tortoise), Varāha (boar), and Narasiṃha (man-lion) in the *kṛtayuga*; Vāmana (dwarf) and Paraśurāma (son of Jamadagni) in the *tretāyuga*; Rāma (son of Daśaratha) at the cusp of the *tretāyuga* and *dvāparayuga*; Kṛṣṇa at the cusp of the *dvāparayuga and kaliyuga*; and Buddha and Kalki in the *kaliyuga*. Apart from its devotional elements, Vaiṣṇavism also came to be associated with → *ahiṃsā* (noninjury), asceticism (→ *tapas*), and *yoga*.

Fig. 2: Viṣṇu reclining on the serpent Śeṣa at Deogarh (photo ©Aditya Arya, used by courtesy).

The *Nārāyaṇīyaparvan* of the *Mahābhārata* refers to *caturvyūha* and *pañcakāla* – concepts that were associated with the Vaiṣṇava Pāñcarātra sect (see Matsubara, 1994; Schreiner, 1997). *Caturvyūha* is the idea of the four emanations of Viṣṇu, with Vāsudeva representing the supreme reality, Saṃkarṣaṇa representing matter (*prakṛti*), Pradyumna representing cosmic mind (*manas*), and Aniruddha representing cosmic self-consciousness (*ahaṃkāra*). The *pañcakālas* comprise five acts of worship – *abhigamana* (approaching the temple with the mind focused on the deity), *upādāna* (collecting material for worship), *ijyā* (worship), *svādhyāya* (studying the texts), and the performance of *yoga*.

At Udayagiri (in Madhya Pradesh), cave 5 has a large relief composition depicting Varāha in his Nṛvarāha form (with a man's body and a boar's head) lifting the earth out of the ocean with his tusks, an exquisite artistic rendering of a famous puranic story. A large free-standing sculpture of Nṛvarāha has been found at Eran (Madhya Pradesh), which has also yielded a pillar with a double-sided Garuḍa capital. The Viṣṇu temple at Deogarh (known as the Daśāvatāra Temple) has relief sculptures of Viṣṇu resting on the serpent Śeṣa, Gaṇeśa (→ Gaṇapati/Gaṇeśa), the ascetic saints Nara and Nārāyaṇa, the river goddesses Gaṅgā and Yamunā, and the Kṛṣṇa, Nṛsiṃha, and Vāmana *avatāras*. Stone sculptures of this period include a Harihara from Madhya Pradesh and Kṛṣṇa lifting Mount Govardhana from Varanasi (Varanasi district, Uttar Pradesh). The Mehrauli iron pillar in Delhi, with its inscription recording the setting up of a standard of Viṣṇu, was in all likelihood originally surmounted by a *garuḍa* figure. The four Gupta-period temples discovered at Lathiya (in Uttar Pradesh) were associated with a sandstone pillar surmounted by an inverted lotus and eight broken lions. The sectarian affiliations of the temples are not certain, but a Garuḍa capital found in the vicinity suggests the Vaiṣṇava affiliation of at least one of them.

Fig. 3: A Gajalakṣmī of unknown provenance (photo ©Archaeological Survey of India, used by courtesy).

The Śaiva Tradition

The Purāṇas describe the many different aspects and attributes of Śiva, the fierce god who combined within himself the seemingly contradictory elements of asceticism and eroticism (O'Flaherty, 1973). Textual and archaeological evidence from this period indicates the emergence of a Śaiva pantheon, which included the god's consort → Pārvatī, their sons Kārttikeya and Gaṇeśa, and the river goddess Gaṅgā. Śaivism was closely associated with the cult of the Goddess, and both were strongly influenced by Tantra.

The worship of Śiva within a temple context is indicated by the temple remains at Bhumara and Khoh in Madhya Pradesh. An inscription in cave 7 at Udayagiri refers to the gift of the cave, described as a temple of Śambhu (Śiva), by Vīrasena, a minister of King Candragupta II. The Maitraka rulers of Valabhi (in Gujarat) describe themselves as *paramamāheśvara* (supreme worshipper of Maheśvara, i.e. Śiva). An inscription from Mathura dated to the year 61 of the Gupta era refers to the setting up of two *śivaliṅgas* in a teachers' shrine (*gurvāyatana*) in honor of his teacher and teacher's teacher by a person named Uditācārya, and it addresses the worshippers of Maheśvara. At Elephanta, off the coast of Mumbai in western India, cave 1, dated to the mid-6th century, has a shrine preceded by a large pillared hall, the most striking feature of which is a magnificent relief carving of Maheśvara with three visible faces.

Later Śaiva tradition distinguishes two streams or paths – the older, Atimārga (outer path), which was open to ascetics, and where the goal was salvation, and the Mantramārga (path of the *mantras*), which was open to ascetics as well as householders, and which aimed not only at salvation but also at acquiring supernatural powers (*siddhis*) and experiencing pleasures (*bhoga*) in other worlds (Sanderson, 1988). The Pāśupata, with strong ascetic associations, seems to be the oldest of the Śaiva sects and is mentioned in the *Mahābhārata* (Lorenzen, 1972, 173–192). Its philosophical basis included the concepts of the individual soul (*paśu*), god (*pati*), and worldly fetters (*pāśa*). The goal of the aspirant was liberation, which could be attained through the grace of Śiva. The putative founder of the sect was Lakulīśa (or Nakulīśa), literally "The Lord Who Wields the Club." (Some scholars consider the Lākulas – followers of Lakulīśa – as a branch or a further development of the Pāśupata sect.) According to tradition, Lakulīśa was an incarnation of Śiva born in a Brahman family of Lāṭa or Bhṛgukaccha. It is possible that the legends grew around a circa 2nd-century historical figure. Lakulīśa is represented in the early temples of Orissa in eastern India and in cave 1 at Elephanta in western India, and the Pāśupata sect also seems to have had a following in the Mathura area. From the 7th century onward, textual references, inscriptions, and temple sculptures indicate the existence of Pāśupata ascetics and temples in many other parts of the subcontinent, as well as in Southeast Asia. The Kālāmukhas, who were influential in the Karnataka area between the 11th and the 13th centuries, seem to have taken over Pāśupata doctrines and practices (Lorenzen, 1972, 183).

The → Kāpālika sect (Lorenzen, 1972, 13–14, 53, 83–85) may have originated in South India or in the Deccan, and early references to it occur in the *Gāthāsaptaśatī* and the *Lalitavistara*. The latter talks of men who shave their heads, wear red clothes, smear their bodies with ash, and carry a triple staff, pot, skull, and *khaṭvāṅga* (a club or staff with a skull at the top). The references to this sect increase between the 5th and the 7th centuries, and it seems to have declined by about the 14th century. The Kāpālikas had strong ascetic leanings and were connected with a vow or penance known as the *mahāvrata* (great vow), whose aim was communion with Śiva. The sect also had *bhakti* elements, the object of devotion usually being Śiva in his fierce → Bhairava form. Sacrifice was one of the ways to propitiate the god, and several texts associate the Kāpālikas with animal and human sacrifice.

Fig. 4: A *mukhaliṅga* from Khoh (photo ©Aditya Arya, used by courtesy).

The Sākta Tradition

As mentioned above, the epics and Purāṇas drew together various goddesses and represented them as different forms of a single Great Goddess. According to N.N. Bhattacharya (1974, 73), the independent worship of this Great Goddess is really a feature of circa 300–600 CE. During this period, Śāktism came to be closely connected with Śaivism and with Tantra. In Tantra (Pintchman, 1994, 110–111), the absolute is considered as having a female and male aspect, although its essence is considered singular at the highest level. The male aspect of God can act only through his *śakti* (energy), represented in the form of a Great Goddess. In Śākta Tantra, this Goddess is usually accorded greater importance than the male aspect of godhead.

The greatness of the Goddess is elaborated on in several Purāṇas. Especially important is the *Devīmāhātmya*, which is part of the

Mārkaṇḍeyapurāṇa and is dated to the 6th/7th century CE. The *Devīmāhātmya* is a devotional text that gives an account of the Great Goddess, connecting her with elements of the vedic and the later theistic traditions and integrating myths drawn from different sources. The text identifies the Goddess as an ultimate reality that is transcendent, internal, and immanent (Coburn, 1984, 303–305). It narrates certain episodes in which the gods, tormented by demons, beseeched the Goddess for help, and she came to their rescue. The most celebrated of these episodes is one in which she was born from the combined anger and energy of all the gods and killed Mahiṣa, the buffalo-demon, after a fierce battle. Images of Mahiṣāsuramardinī are carved in stone reliefs at Udayagiri and Bhumara in central India.

The pacific aspects of the Great Goddess are reflected in her → Sarasvatī and Lakṣmī forms, and her maternal aspect in her *mātṛkā* forms. The *mātṛkās* are generally listed as seven (on occasion as nine): Brahmāṇī, Māheśvarī, Kaumārī, Vaiṣṇavī, Vārāhī, Indrāṇī, and Yamī/Cāmuṇḍā (the *Mārkaṇḍeyapurāṇa* substitutes the last two with Nārasiṃhī and Aindrī). They are described as the *śaktis* (powers) of seven gods, who emerged from their bodies and helped the Goddess kill the demon Niśumbha. The *Nārāyaṇīstuti* of the *Devīmāhātmya* concludes by listing the various forms that the Goddess will assume in future ages, announcing that whenever demons trouble the world, she will appear to destroy them. There are clear resonances here of the *avatāra* doctrine.

The epic–puranic tradition gave Durgā a variety of family connections. For instance, the *Harivaṃśa* describes her as the sister of Indra and Viṣṇu; elsewhere, she is described as Ekānaṃśā or Bhadrā, the sister of Vāsudeva-Kṛṣṇa. In places in the *Mahābhārata*, she is referred to as the wife of Nārāyaṇa or of Śiva. Eventually, her closest association was with Śiva, as his consort Pārvatī or Umā, and representations of the divine couple came to be carved on many temple walls.

The close connection between Śaivism and Śāktism is evident in the explanation of the sacred places associated with the Goddess known as the *śaktipīṭhas* (see Sircar, 1948). The kernel of the story, narrated in the *Mahābhārata* and in several Purāṇas, tells of a sacrifice performed by Dakṣa, to which he did not invite his daughter Satī and her husband Śiva; Satī felt insulted and died of grief. Later texts such as the *Devībhāgavata* and *Kālikāpurāṇa* carried this story forward, narrating that Satī's body was carried away by her grief-stricken husband Śiva, and that the places where the various parts of her body (dismembered due to divine intervention) fell became the *śaktipīṭhas*.

The Cultic Worship of Other Deities

As mentioned above, although Viṣṇu, Śiva, and Śakti/Devī emerged as three major foci of cultic worship between circa 300 and circa 600 CE, they were not the only ones. Several Purāṇas describe the origin of the worship of Sūrya and mention priests and festivals associated with him (Banerjea, 1966, 133–146). The *Sūryahṛdaya* hymn in the *Kūrmapurāṇa* praises him as the greatest god, who includes all other gods within him. The *Bhaviṣyapurāṇa* refers to the Magas, who seem to have been priests of Iranian descent who worshipped the fire and the sun. Inscriptional evidence testifies to the patronage of temples dedicated to the sun god, especially in central India, during the 5th and 6th centuries. The Mandasor inscription of the time of Kumāragupta I and Bandhuvarman records the building and renovation of a Sūrya temple in Daśapura by a guild of silk weavers. The Indore copper plate belonging to the reign of Skandagupta records a grant made by one Devaviṣṇu for the maintenance of a lamp in a Sūrya temple. A Gwalior inscription dated to the reign of the Hun ruler Mihirakula records the building of a temple dedicated to this deity. Inscriptions of the Shalankayana dynasty of the Andhra region refer to their worship of Citrarathasvāmin (Sūrya), apart from Vāsudeva-Kṛṣṇa.

The earliest representations of the god Kārttikeya occur on punch-marked coins of earlier centuries that indicate that he was an object of popular worship well before he was absorbed into the family of Śiva as his older son. The Bilsad stone pillar inscription (early 5th cent.) records the building of a gateway with a flight of steps, the establishment of a *sattra* (in this context, a charitable feeding house), and the erection of the column on which the inscription was inscribed at a temple of Mahāsena (Kārttikeya) by a person named Dhruvaśarman. The Gupta emperor Kumāragupta I used the peacock (the vehicle of Kārttikeya) as his symbol, and there is a relief carving of Kārttikeya in cave 3 at Udayagiri. Kings of the Kadamba dynasty of western India were devotees of this god, and his worship was also popular in South India, where he was known as Subrahmaṇya.

Gaṇeśa or Gaṇapati, the elephant-headed younger son of Śiva, was associated with bestowing success and removing obstacles from the path of his devotees. Texts describe him as the leader of the *gaṇa*s – the unruly followers of Rudra-Śiva – and as having the mouse as his vehicle.

Brahmā, one of the triad of gods mentioned in the Purāṇas, is eulogized in the *Brahmapurāṇa* and is represented in temple sculpture (for instance, at Bhumara), but there are no extant temples of this period dedicated to him.

Religious Developments in South India

The *Cilappatikāram* and *Maṇimēkalai* are the two great Tamil epics; the former belongs to the 5th century CE, while the latter is a little later (Zvelebil, 1974, 132). Although the *Cilappatikāram* has a strong Jaina tinge, its religious landscape is very diverse. It refers to vedic rituals, the *rājasūya* (a sacrifice connected with royal consecration), temple worship, and various deities including Indra, Śiva, Viṣṇu, Durgā, and Murukaṉ. Kaṇṇaki, the heroine of the *Cilappatikāram*, was regarded as an incarnation of the goddess Pattiṉi, and the reference to the construction of a Pattiṉi shrine by the Cera king Cenkuṭṭuvaṉ reflects an attempt to legitimize the antiquity of a central Pattiṉi temple that existed at Vanchi at the time when the epic was written. In later times, this goddess was Hinduized and assimilated into the → Kālī cult.

Compared to the Caṅkam poems, there are many more references to Māyōṉ (Kṛṣṇa) in the *Cilappatikāram*, and he is associated with the pastoral landscape (*mullai*). Canto 17 describes how at Maturai, the cowherd women performed a dance called the *kuravai*, re-creating an episode in the life of the god in which he fought seven bulls and married the women who tended them, including one named Piṉṉai. In the course of the song and dance, there is mention of various incidents connected with Kṛṣṇa's life. The episodes mentioned in the canto not only indicate familiarity with details of Kṛṣṇa's life amid the cowherds of Vrindavan but also include some elements that are unknown in the northern tradition.

Although the beginning and early development of South Indian *bhakti* can be traced to the milieu of late classical Tamil literature, there is a qualitative change from the 6th/7th century onward, when the Āḻvār and → Nāyaṉār saints expressed through their songs their devotion toward Viṣṇu and Śiva, respectively (see Ramanujan, 1973; 1981; Dehejia, 1988). According to tradition, there were 12 Āḻvār and 63 Nāyaṉār saints. Their devotionalism – intimate, intense, and ecstatic – was expressed in the Tamil language, was deeply rooted in Tamil culture and centered on the institution of the temple. While a significant proportion of saints were Brahmans, some of them came from less exalted social backgrounds, and a few were women. The *bhakti* movement expanded the social access to sacred space and created communities of *bhakta*s within which social hierarchies could be transcended to some extent.

The Religious Affiliations of Political Elites

The continuing political importance of *yajña* is indicated by the fact that several kings who ruled between circa 300 and 600 CE claimed in their inscriptions to have performed Śrauta sacrifices. The Vakataka ruler Pravarasena announced his performance of four *aśvamedha*s and of the *agniṣṭoma, aptoryama, ukthya, ṣoḍaśin, bṛhaspatisava,* and *vājapeya* sacrifices. The remains of a stellate-plan *liṅga* temple have been found at Mansar (Nagpur district, Maharashtra), which seems to represent the site of Pravarapura, the capital of the Vakataka king Pravarasena II. One of the dramatic discoveries there, on a hawk-shaped brick sacrificial altar (*śyenaciti*), was a colossal lime effigy of a man with a smashed head, which may represent the remains of an ancient construction sacrifice (Bakker, 2008–2009).

Epic–puranic elements entered the epigraphic *praśasti*s (eulogies), and kings increasingly proclaimed their sectarian affiliations in inscriptions and on coins and seals. Several kings of the Gupta dynasty proclaimed themselves Bhāgavatas, while the Vakataka rulers variously described themselves as worshippers of Śiva and Viṣṇu. The motifs on Gupta coins include the *aśvamedha* horse, Viṣṇu, the peacock (Kārttikeya's vehicle), and various goddesses, including Lakṣmī. A free-standing larger-than-life sandstone sculpture of a horse found at Khairigarh and presently in the Lucknow Museum (Uttar Pradesh) may possibly be connected with an *aśvamedha* sacrifice conducted by Samudragupta. Seals found at Bhita (Allahabad district, Uttar Pradesh) have sectarian emblems such as the *liṅga*, trident, bull, conch, wheel, and Gajalakṣmī. Along with announcing their sectarian affiliations through titles such as Paramabhāgavata and Paramamāheśvara, ruling elites often extended patronage to a variety of religious sects. While this is usually interpreted as evidence of the "tolerance" of the Indian religious tradition, it is better understood as a pragmatic religious policy pursued by rulers in a pluralistic religious context where religious traditions were not necessarily seen as antagonistic and where religious identities and boundaries were not necessarily defined or perceived in exclusive terms.

Hinduism outside India

In the course of the 1st millennium CE, Hindu and Buddhist influences from India traveled to island and mainland Southeast Asia, parallel to the process of state formation in those regions (Casparis & Mabbett, 1992). The process of cultural transmission is the subject of debate, but in addition to interactions through trade networks, Brahman migrations must have played an important role. In the historiography of Southeast Asia, the old "Indianization" framework has long been abandoned and has been replaced by an analysis of the "localization" of Indian (and other, including Chinese) influences as they mingled with autochthonous elements (Wolters, 1982).

The evidence of early Brahmanical influence in Southeast Asia includes several Sanskrit inscriptions. The late 4th-century stone *yūpa* inscriptions from Kutai (in east Kalimantan) mention a ruler named Mūlavarman who performed sacrifices and made generous gifts to Brahmans. A 5th-century inscription found near Bagor in West Java refers to a ruler named Pūrṇavarman as a devotee of Viṣṇu, and a pair of footprints (a symbol of the god Viṣṇu) carved on the stone is described as that of the king. In → Cambodia, Śaivism and the *liṅga* cult were closely linked with kingship. Early Vaiṣṇava influence is discernible in a 6th-century inscription of Queen Kulaprabhāvatī, which refers to her establishing a hermitage and reservoir for Brahmans and mentions Viṣṇu and the serpent Śeṣa. In central Vietnam, where Śaivism mingled with older local cults of earth gods, the structural remains and inscriptions from the site of Mỹ So'n offer evidence of a royal Śaiva cult. In south Vietnam, etched images on gold plaques discovered during excavations at the sites of Go Thap and Da Noi indicate the spread of the worship of a wide range of Hindu deities to this region by the mid-1st millennium, their representations rendered according to local artistic idiom (Lien, 2011).

There is thus considerable evidence of Hindu – and Buddhist – influences mingling with indigenous traditions in Southeast Asia from the 4th century CE onward, and these influences became stronger in the subsequent period. However, what we actually see is a complex process of foreign elements "retreating into local statements" (Wolters, 1982, 56–68), and it should be emphasized that the history of Southeast Asia cannot simply be reduced to a study of foreign influences. As is the case with the Hinduization process as it traversed the culturally diverse regions of the Indian subcontinent, Hindu influences in Southeast Asia mingled with indigenous cultures. The result was a series of religious and cultural syntheses that were unique and quite different from what is seen in the Indian subcontinent.

Bibliography

Bacus, E.A., & N. Lahiri, eds., *World Archaeology*, vol. XXXVI/3: *The Archaeology of Hinduism*, 2004.

Bailey, G.M., *Materials for the Study of Ancient Indian ideologies: Pravṛtti and Nivṛtti*, Torino, 1985.

Bakker, H., "Puruṣamedha, Mansarapuruṣa, Vāstupuruṣa: The Images of Man in the Sacrificial Context," *JIS* 20 & 21, 2008–2009, 1–23.

Banerjea, J.N., *Paurāṇic and Tāntric Religion (Early Phase)*, Calcutta, 1966.

Bhandarkar, R.G., *Vaiṣṇavism, Śaivism and Minor Religious Systems*, Varanasi, 1965.

Bhattacharyya, N.N., *History of the Śākta Religion*, New Delhi, 1974.

Bhattacharyya, N.N., *History of the Tantric Religion: A Historical, Ritualistic and Philosophical Study*, New Delhi, 1982, 1992.

Bosworth, A.B., "The Historical Setting of Megasthenes' Indica," *CPh* 91/2, 1996, 113–127.

Brockington, J.L., *Righteous Rāma: The Evolution of an Epic*, Delhi, 1984.

Chakrabarti, K., *Religious Process: The Purāṇas and the Making of a Regional Tradition*, New Delhi, 2001.

Coburn, T.B., *Devī-Māhātmya: The Crystallization of the Goddess Tradition*, Delhi, 1984.

Coomaraswamy, A., *Yakshas*, New Delhi, 1971, 1980.

Casparis, J.G. de, & I.W. Mabbett, "Religion and Popular Beliefs of Southeast Asia before c. 1500," in: N. Tarling, ed., *The Cambridge History of Southeast Asia*, vol I: *From Early Times to c. 1500*, Cambridge UK, 1992, 1999, 276–339.

Dehejia, V., *Slaves of the Lord: The Path of the Tamil Saints*, Delhi, 1988.

Filliozat, J., "Representations de Vāsudeva et Saṃkarṣṇa au siècle IIe avant J.C.," *AA* 26, 1973, 113–123.

Fitzgerald, J.L., "Mahabhārata," in: S. Mittal & G. Thursby, eds., *The Hindu World*, New York, 2004, 2005, 52–75.

Goldman, R.P., trans., *The Rāmāyaṇa of Vālmīki: An Epic of Ancient India*, Delhi, 1984, 2007.

Goldman, R.P., & S.J. Sutherland Goldman, "Rāmāyaṇa," in: S. Mittal & G. Thursby, eds., *The Hindu World*, New York, 2004, 2005, 75–96.

Guillaume, O., ed., *Graeco-Bactrian and Indian Coins from Afghanistan*, FSSACS 5, Delhi, 1991.

Gupta, S., D.J. Hoens & T. Goudriaan, *Hindu Tantrism*, Leiden, 1979.

Hardy, F., *Viraha-bhakti: The Early History of Kṛṣṇa Devotion in South India*, Delhi, 1983.

Hart III, G.L., *The Poems of Ancient Tamil: Their Milieu and Their Sanskrit Counterparts*, Berkeley, 1975.

Hartel, H., *Excavations at Sonkh: 2500 Years of a Town in Mathura District*, Berlin, 1993.

Hazra, R.C., *Studies in the Purāṇic Records on Hindu Rites and Customs*, Delhi, 1940, 1975.

Hiltebeitel, A., *Rethinking the Mahābhārata: A Reader's Guide to the Education of the Dharma King*, Chicago, 2001.

Hiltebeitel, A., & K.M. Erndl, eds., *Is the Goddess a Feminist? The Politics of South Asian Goddesses*, New York, 2000.

Huntington, S., *The Art of Ancient India: Buddhist, Hindu, Jain*, New York, 1985, 1993.

Jaiswal, S., *The Origin and Development of Vaiṣṇavism: Vaiṣṇavism from 200 BC to AD 500*, New Delhi, 1980, 1981.

Kane, P.V., *History of Dharmaśāstra (Ancient and Mediaeval Religious and Civil Law)*, Poona, vol. II/1, 1941, [3]1997, vol. V/1, 1958, [3]1994.

Kangle, R.P., *The Kauṭilīya Arthaśāstra*, vol. I, Delhi, 1969, 1992.

Karttunen, K., *India in Early Greek Literature*, Helsinki, 1989.

Kirste Kirste, J., "Zur Mahābhāratafrage," *WZKM* 14, 1900, 214–224.

Larson, G.J., *Classical Sāṃkhya: An Interpretation of Its History and Meaning*, Delhi, rev. ed. [2]1979.

Lien, Le Thi, "Hindu Deities in Southern Vietnam," in: P.-Y. Manguin, A. Mani & G. Wade, eds., *Early Interactions between South and Southeast Asia: Reflections on Cross-cultural Exchange*, Singapore, 2011, 407–431.

Lingat, R., *The Classical Law of India*, New Delhi, 1973.

Lorenzen, D.N., *The Kāpālikas and Kālāmukhas: Two Lost Śaivite Sects*, Delhi, 1972.

Malinar, A., *The Bhagavadgītā: Doctrines and Contexts*, Cambridge, 2007.

Mani, B.R., I.D. Dwivedi, S.K. Manjul & A. Manjul, "Excavations at Lathiya (Ghazipur District, Uttar Pradesh: 2009–10)," *AI (BASI).NS* 1, 2011, 213–232.

Matsubara, M., *Pāñcarātra Saṃhitās & Early Vaiṣṇava Theology: With a Translation and Critical Notes from Chapters on Theology in the Ahirbudhnya Saṃhitā*, Delhi, 1994.

Nath, V., *Purāṇas and Acculturation: A Historico-Anthropological Perspective*, New Delhi, 2001.

Nicholson, A.J., *Unifying Hinduism: Philosophy and Identity in Indian Intellectual History*, Ranikhet, 2011.

O'Flaherty, W.D., *Asceticism and Eroticism in the Mythology of Śiva*, London, 1973.

Olivelle, P., trans., *Manu's Code of Law: A Critical Edition and Translation of the Mānava-Dharmaśāstra*, New Delhi, 2005, 2006.

Olivelle, P., ed., *The Law Codes of Āpastamba, Gautama, Baudhāyana, and Vasiṣṭha*, Delhi, 2000, 2003.

Olivelle, P., *The Āśrama System: History and Hermeneutics of a Religious Institution*, New York, 1993.

Padoux, A., "'Tantrism' and 'Hindu Tantrism,'" in: M. Eliade, ed., *The Encyclopaedia of Religion*, vol. XIV, New York, 1987, 272–280.

Pintchman, T., *The Rise of the Goddess in the Hindu Tradition*, Albany, 1994.

Ramanujan, A.K., *Hymns for the Drowning: Poems for Viṣṇu by Nammāḻvār*, New Delhi, 1981, 1993.

Ramanujan, A.K., *Speaking of Śiva*, Harmondsworth, 1973.

Rocher, L., *The Purāṇas*, HIL 2, Wiesbaden, 1986.

Roller, D.W., "Megasthenes (715)," in: I. Worthington, ed., *Brill's New Jacoby*, Leiden, 2012, http://referenceworks.brillonline.com/entries/brill-s-new-jacoby/megasthenes-715-a715.

Sanderson, A., "Saivism and the Tantric Tradition," in: S. Sutherland, L. Houlden, P. Clarke & F. Hardy, *The World's Religions*, London, 1988, 660–704.

Sarma, I.K., *Parashuramesvara Temple at Gudimallam*, Nagpur, 1994.

Schreiner, P., ed., *Studien zum Nārāyaṇīya/Studies in the Nārāyaṇīya*, Wiesbaden, 1997.

Sharma, G.R., *The Excavations at Kauśāmbī (1957–59)*, Allahabad, 1960.

Singh, U., "Brāhmaṇa Settlements in Ancient and Early Medieval India," in: B.D. Chattopadhyaya, ed., *History of Science, Philosophy and Culture in Indian Civilization*, vol. II/5: *A Social History of Early India*, Delhi, 2009, 159–175.

Singh, U., *A History of Ancient and Early Medieval India from the Stone Age to the 12th Century*, Delhi, 2008.

Singh, U., "Cults and Shrines in Early Historical Mathura (c. 200 BC–AD 200)," *WA* 36/3, 2004, 378–398.

Sircar, D.C., ed., *The Śākta Pīṭhas*, Delhi, 1948, 1973.

Sircar, D.C., *Select Inscriptions Bearing on Indian History and Civilization*, vol. I, Calcutta, 1942, [2]1965.

Soundararajan, K.V., ed., *Nagarjunakonda (1954–60)*, vol II: *The Historical Period : Memoirs of the Archaeological Survey of India No. 75*, New Delhi, 2006.

Sutton, N., *Religious Doctrines in the Mahābhārata*, Delhi, 2000.

Wolters, O.W., *History, Culture, and Region in Southeast Asian Perspectives*, Singapore, 1982.

Zvelebil, K.V., *Tamil Literature*, HIL X/1 Wiesbaden, 1974.

Upinder Singh

Hindu Medieval Regional Kingdoms (600–1526 CE)

Periodization of Medieval India

Since the beginning of modern Indian historiography, periodization was a matter of controversial debates (Thapar, 2000, 3–20; Kulke, 2005, 97–105; Sahu, 2006). Inspired by the classical European threefold classification of ancient, medieval, and modern history, J. Mill distinguished in 1818 in *The History of British India* among the three epochs of Hindu, Muhammedan, and British India. But he did not merely divide the history of India into three epochs; he segregated it ultimately into three separate cultures (Thapar, 2000, 158). J. Mill's colonial representation of Indian history became the "hegemonic textbook" (Mukhia, 1999) of 19th-century British India, as it served as a teleological justification of → British rule as the culmination of Indian history. Even after hundred years, V.A. Smith's *Oxford History of India* (1919), the first genuinely scholarly British history of India, adopted (though in a slightly modified way) J. Mills' periodization by its major chapters "Ancient and Hindu India," "India in the Muslim Period," and "India in the British Period." In view of the subject of this article, it is revealing that the *Oxford History of India* devotes more or less exactly the same scope to Alexander's India campaign and the short period of Indo-Greek rulers in northwest India as to the important medieval Hindu kingdoms. R. Thapar's appraisal that J. Mill's "theory was to become axiomatic to the periodization of Indian history and is still with us, though sometimes in disguised form" (Thapar, 2000, 52), is valid also for the Indian History Congress, founded in 1935. During its annual conferences, India's history is still divided into the three sections: ancient, medieval, and modern history. As in V.A. Smith's *Oxford History of India*, medieval is synonymous with "India in the Muslim Period" and thus confined to the period of the Delhi Sultanate and the → Mughal Empire from circa 1200 to 1750. The long period of seven centuries, from the fall of the Gupta Empire in the 6th century CE to the establishment of the Delhi Sultanate in early 13th century, is still assigned to ancient India, scantily defined as post-Gupta period. As South India was conquered by the Delhi Sultanate temporarily only in the early 14th century, "ancient history" continues there even a century longer. Established at the height of Indian Independence movement, the idea behind this classification of the Indian History Congress was, in contrast to the colonial *divide et impera* policy, to allow Indian Muslims their due share in Indian history, an idea that was, however, increasingly critizised by Hindu-nationalist historians. It is therefore not astonishing that the 11 volumes of the great national *History and Culture of the Indian People*, conceived and edited by R.C. Majumdar, the doyen of Hindu-national historians, has no "medieval volume" (see also Gottlob, 2002).

However, these debates were only skirmishes in comparison to the heated disputes that flared up since the publication of R.S. Sharma's *Indian Feudalism: c. 300–1200* in 1965 and the emergence of a disputatious Marxist "School of Indian Feudalism" in the 1970s (Sahu, 2006; Kulke, 1984; Kulke, 1995, 6–18). Its aim was to establish, against Marx's concept of oriental despotism and the asiatic mode of production, "the unfortunate thesis that Marx had once propounded" (Habib, 1974, 38) – the existence of an Indian feudalism – thus allowing India to participate in Marx's progressive modes of production that Marx had denied to India and Asian countries. I shall shortly come back to a few details of the concept of Indian feudalism. What matters in the context of the periodization of medieval India is the fact that it was R.S. Sharma's concept of medieval Indian feudalism that rescued medieval India from its exclusive identification with "Muslim India" and the seven centuries of a seemingly irrelevant "post-Gupta" period from its encapsulation in ancient India.

Another major outcome of the heated debates on the controversial existence of feudalism in medieval India, in the long term perhaps even its most important gain, is that the hitherto quite neglected "dark age" between the "golden age" of the Guptas and the foundation of the Delhi Sultanate was suddenly in the limelight of Indian historiography. Like the Kurukṣetra of the → *Mahābhārata*, it became the arena of an unconciliatory historiographical struggle of two kindred clans of Indian historians (Chattopadhyaya, 1983; Jha, 2000, *Introduction*; Sharma, 1995; Sahu, 2006; Kulke, 1982). Whereas hitherto the "dark age" had been illuminated only sporadically by regional and primarily dynastic histories (e.g. Altekar, 1934; Majumdar, 1943; Sastri, 1955; Derret, 1957), it now became an issue of nationwide interest and conflicts, as, for example, in the heated textbook controversies. It rose like a phoenix from the ashes as the new *avatāra* "early medieval India." In her recently published *Rethinking Early Medieval India*, U. Singh puts Sharma's impact in the right words:

> His *Indian Feudalism* (1965) was a radical intervention... At one sweep, the older histories of early medieval India with their dynastic frameworks and mournful view of the advent of Muslim rule appeared superficial. The focus was firmly shifted away from political narrative to political processes and agrarian change. The historiography of early medieval India would never be the same again. (Singh, 2011, 5)

The conceptual founding father of early medieval India is clearly B.D. Chattopadhyaya. Having delivered his seminal presidential address at the Indian Congress in 1983 (Chattopadhyaya, 1983), he published in 1994 *The Making of Early Medieval India*. Its title is significant in two senses. It not only depicts social, economic, and political processes that lead to the emergence of medieval India, but also identifies him as the "maker" of early medieval India as a new paradigm of Indian historiography.

But the existence of early medieval India as a distinct epoch with its peculiar social, political, and cultural identities should also anticipate the existence of "late medieval India," encompassing not only post-13th-century Muslim states. After all, the age of the Delhi Sultanate (1206–1526) is also distinguished by the still existing powerful regional Hindu kingdoms, for instance, the Gajapati kingdom of → Orissa, → Vijayanagara, and several kingdoms in → Rajasthan, whose political culture was increasingly influenced by their powerful Muslim contemporaries. However, "late medieval India" has until now only rarely entered textbooks of Indian history (e.g. Kulke & Rothermund, 1986) and has not yet been conceptualized as "early medieval India." To complicate the matter even more, S. Subrahmanyam has come forward with strong arguments to disassociate Mughal India from medieval and assign it to "early modern India" (Subrahmanyam, 1997; see also Kulke, 1982). As most prominent proponents of a new school of Mughal historians, they are thus directly competing with the Aligarh Muslim University, which is considered to be the center of research on Muslim history in India. Its journal, entitled *Medieval India: Researches in India, 1200–1750*, published by I. Habib, stands paradigmatically for its innumerable outstanding publications on "Muslim India" and particulary Mughal India, based primarily on Indo-Persian sources. Thus, paradoxically, India still seems to have two separate though overlapping medieval epochs, the Hindu "early medieval" and the Muslim "medieval." Here, too, one might still detect the legacy of J. Mill's periodization.

The Medieval Hindu State: Issues and Debates

The Concept of Indian Feudalism

In the same decades of the last century, when the periodisation of India's "early medieval" was not only controversially debated but also newly defined, the nature of the early medieval Indian state, too, became an issue of equally controversial discourses that generated three competing but well-established concepts: the feudal state, the segmentary state, and the processual integrative state (Singh, 2011; Kulke, 1995). They were preceded by the above-mentioned regional and dynastic histories of A.S. Altekar, R.C. Majumdar, and K.A.N. Sastri, whose writings

> may be characterized with the advantage of hindsight as traditional or conventional. They were marked by a meticulous concern for accuracy and obsessive avoidance of systematic generalization and evaluation. They usually presented a descriptive account of government and administration... and went on to create the picture of centralized, unitarian imperial states, with numerous and powerful bureaucracies. (Sahu, 2006, 67)

According to R.S. Sharma, the early emergence of feudalism can be traced back in India to the 3rd and 4th centuries CE, which were distinguished by the decline of pan-Asian trade and urban economy and by the paucity of coinage. The major cause of the emergence of economic and social (and consequently political) feudal structures was the ever-increasing number of land grants to Brahmans, religious institutions, and, albeit relatively less often, local officials. This created a class of land-owning intermediaries who were not cultivators, yet eternally furnished with innumerable immunities similar to those in the European medieval period (Bhattacharya, 1985) and with royal prerogatives – for example, the right to levy taxes and pass laws. The transfer of these rights to the landlords and the increasing attachment of the village population to the soil cultivated by them resulted in their gradual bondage and serfdom. Politically this development led increasingly to the decentralization, fragmentation, and weakening of royal power, caused "by the widespread practice of granting big and small territories to vassals and officials who entrenched themselves territorially and ended up as independent potentates" (Sharma, 1965, 159). According to the Indian feudalism theory, early medieval state formation had thus a decisively negative character, as the many small kingdoms are supposed to have emerged in a protracted process of fragmentation "from above" at the cost of former lager political entities.

As expected, the criticism flooded in and led not only to heated debates the following decades but also to the heyday of attention to the Indian feudalism, when three presidential addresses were devoted to it at the Indian History Congresses in 1979 and 1980 (D.N. Jha, B.N.S. Yadava, and H. Mukhia) – a fascinating story that cannot be repeated here in detail (see, e.g., Kulke, 1984; 1995, 6–18). D.C. Sircar, the then-doyen of ancient Indian history, subsumed the critique of his "conservative" colleagues already at a symposium at Calcutta University, where R.S. Sharma presented his feudalism concept for the first time. In the short article "Landlordism Confused with Feudalism," D.C. Sircar declared that feudalism "is a misnomer in the early Indian context" (Sircar, 1966, 62). Severer was the critique of concerned scholars like H. Mukhia, B.N.S. Yadava, and B.D. Chattopadhyaya. H. Mukhia questions several essentials in the concept of Indian feudalism – for example, that serfdom was a dominant feature of medieval India. And he rightly points out that "it is a moot point whether such complex social structures [like feudalism] can be established through administrative and legal procedures" (Mukhia, 1980, 113). B.D. Chattopadhyaya too questioned the

> rather one-track argument, wholly centred around a particular value attached to the evidence of land grants in the structure in pre-Gupta and Gupta times. In fact, in no state system, however centralized, can there be a single focus or level of power, and the specificity of differential distribution of power in early medieval polity may be an issue more complex than has hitherto been assumed. (Chattopadhyaya, 1983, 207)

Similar criticism of "one-track arguments" of the early writings on Indian feudalism had the desired effect. Thus even D.N. Jha, next to R.S. Sharma the most prolific proponent of the concept, had pointed out already in his 1979 presidential address that

> the explanation of feudal development only in terms of foreign trade, whose decline to a large extent depended on factors external to the Indian situation... has recently led to a rethinking on the part of the exponents of the Indian feudal model from the vantage point of internal social contradictions. (quoted in Kulke, 1995, 13)

The search for and the analysis of possible cases of social crisis became increasingly a major agenda of the "Feudalism School," a topic that was overdue in any case. However, the outcome of this (re)search was rather meager, as it is more or less confined to the so-called crisis of the *kaliyuga* (see → cosmic cycles), about which few articles were published, for instance, by R.S. Sharma and B.N.S. Yadava (see Jha, 2000). The evils of the *kaliyuga* are frequently referred to in the 1st millennium CE in the *Mahābhārata*, → Purāṇas, and inscriptions. However, it is doubtful whether these references, primarily to upheavals of the → caste system and rituals allegedly endangering the social position of the Brahmans, reflected actual social unrest or an ideological crisis of mostly Brahmanical authors (Sahu, 1997, 2006). But the *kaliyuga* crisis became a much-needed argument to explain the rise of feudalism by sharp class antagonism instead of an externally caused economic crisis. R.S. Sharma therefore concluded an anthology of his articles *Early Medieval Indian Society: A Study in Feudalisation* with the clear statement that "the social crisis of the Kali age paved the way for the beginning of the early medieval period" (Sharma, 2001, 283). External factors are no longer mentioned, a conclusion that would have been unthinkable in his early works on Indian feudalism.

By paying closer attention to religion and ideology, the Indian feudalism concept witnessed an important improvement during the 1980s and 1990s. In his 1980 presidential address "The Problems of the Emergence of Feudal Relations in Early India," B.N.S. Yadava had already instigated a search for evidence of the subjugation of the peasants by landlords through non-economic coercion. B.D. Chattopadhyaya, too, criticized in his influential presidential address the neglect of religion in the feudalism concept.

> From the perspective of the interdependence between temporal power and sacred authority, it becomes understandable that assignments such as *brahmadeyas* and *devadāna* were not an administrative but a socio-religious necessity for the temporal power. (Chattopadhyaya, 1983, 211)

In this context B.D. Chattopadhyaya refers also to K. Veluthat's article on "Royalty and Divinity" (Veluthat, 1979) and H. Kulke's "Royal Temple Policy" (Kulke, 1978; see also Kulke, 1982). The increasing influence of new religio-ideological studies is well documented in D.N. Jha's *The Feudal Order: State, Society and Ideology in Medieval India*, the most comprehensive anthology of "feudalism articles" (Jha, 2000). Out of its 16 articles, 6 constitute the third part, *Feudal Ideology*, its first chapter being significantly *Bhakti Movement in South India* by M.G.S. Narayanan and K. Veluthat. To remark in passing, not a single article in the first chapter, *Transition to Feudalism*, refers to the previously important external factors; however, two refer to the *kaliyuga* by R.S. Sharma and B.N.S. Yadava.

The Segmentary State

> In the context of South India, it was not Sharma but Burton Stein who shook things up. Stein's *Peasant State and Society in Medieval South India* was published in 1980, but Stein had put forward a searing critique of the traditional historiography well before that. It was a hard-hitting but convincing critique, designed to pave the way for a definite shift in the way in which the South Indian state and society had been theorized. (Singh, 2011, 8)

The segmentary state became, next only to Indian feudalism, the most important but also most controversial theory of the early medieval Indian state (Kulke, 1995, 18–31). However, it has also rightly been pointed out that "Stein's segmentary state hypothesis did not find much support among Indian historians" (Singh, 2011, 39n30). B. Stein "reconsidered" his concept several times and modified it considerably (Stein, 1991). Whereas R.S. Sharma's concept of Indian feudalism was originally primarily based on and derived from the early medieval states of North India and stepwise extended spatially by other authors to South India (e.g. Veluthat, 1993; Nandi, 2000; Karashima, 2001), B. Stein's concept of the segmentary state pertains only to South India. Its focus is the Chola Empire, which was then expanded chronologically to the Vijayanagara Empire in his volume of the *New Cambridge History of India* (1989).

The segmentary state concept is derived from A. Southall's anthropological study of the Alur society in eastern Africa (Southall, 1956), which Stein summarized as follows: "In a segmentary state sovereignty is dual. It consists of actual political sovereignty, or control, and what Southall terms 'ritual hegemony' or 'ritual sovereignty'" (Stein, 1980, 274). Accordingly, B. Stein, too, distinguishes between *ritual* sovereignty as a loose and custodial hegemony exercised by the king at the top of the pyramidal segmentary structure, on the one hand, and *political* sovereignty, consisting of the direct rule or control exercised by local authorities and little kings in their immediate localities, on the other (Stein, 1980, 274). B. Stein regards the several hundreds of autonomous and highly developed nuclear areas (Tam. *nāṭus*) in the river basins as seats of actual political power and as the central element of the South Indian Chola state, which therefore "may be best described as a multi-centred system." In their central dynastic core area, the Cholas exercised an uncontested monopoly of authority and power, based on a fairly well-developed administration that, however, faded off gradually into mere ritual sovereignty in its intermediate zones and periphery. The ritual sovereignty of the Cholas was based on the royal → Śiva cult as "the overarching ideological element which makes these units segments of a whole." The thousands of copper-plate and stone inscriptions of the Cholas, which conventional historians conceive as manifestations of actual political control, had as a primary function the distribution of the standardized message of their great kingship to all places of the realm. They have to be taken as evidence of ritual sovereignty rather than actual political control, a difference that, according to B. Stein, is fundamental. The persons who were distributing the royal message were involved in the ritual sovereignty that converted a congeries of local political systems into a segmentary state. In 1985 B. Stein even went a step further when he argued that "the Chola state existed as a state only as the hundreds of the *nādus* of its realm recognized the overlordship, the ritual sovereignty, of Chola kings" (Stein, 1985a, 394).

On the one hand, B. Stein's theory was praised as an appropriate "alternative model to the unitary state model" (Spencer, 1983, 7) and as "an immensely powerful deconstructive tool" against conventional models (Dirks, 1987, 403). On the other hand, B. Stein has been strongly criticized by historians of South India for drastically diminishing the administrative control and power of the Chola state even during its "imperial phase" in the 11th century (Kulke, 1982, 1995). Thus, for instance, Y. Subbarayalu asserts in his rejoinder to B. Stein that in the century from the middle of Rājarāja I's reign, around 1000 CE, through to the reign of Kulōttuṅka I in early 12th century, there was a clear disappearance of chiefly troops, and that "inscriptions are bewilderingly silent about the chiefs who were, it seems, replaced by [Chola] officials" (Subbarayalu, 1982, 270). K.R. Hall, too, detects during this period "a move toward centralization" (Hall, 1980, 196) and J. Heitzman points out that "more 'segmentary' or 'feudal' political organizations succumbed to royal dominance" (Heitzman, 1995). Even D. Shulman, who admits "that there is no doubt that this model is far more accurate than the older 'imperial' one developed by Nilakanta [i.e. K.A.N.] Sastri and his school," also rightly points out that "the Chola state is incomparably more complex, more loaded with inherent stresses and conflicts, than Alur society" (Shulman, 1985, 19f.).

In 1983 B.D. Chattopadhyaya took up the issue in the broader context of early medieval India. He criticized the idea that the concept of ritual sovereignty defines the state as a "ritual space" or "state *sans* politics," relegating different foci of power to the periphery instead of analyzing their transformation into vital components of the political structure of an "integrative polity" (Chattopadhyaya, 1983). Very recently N. Karashima again summarized his strong critique:

> I also criticized it by pointing out that Stein's theory was nothing but a new version of the old theory of the stagnation of the Oriental Society, based on unchanging village communities, with the village of the old theory having been replaced by the segment (*nadu*). There are many points to be criticized in his theory, but the crucial point is his categorical denial of centralization or even the efforts made towards it by the Chola kings of the middle period [11th and early 12th centuries]. (Karashima, 2009, 3)

The sometimes heated debates particularly with proponents of Indian feudalism are well documented in the belligerent essays of B. Stein and R.S. Sharma in defense of their models (Stein, 1985a, 1991 [1995]; Sharma, 1995).

The other questionable thesis of B. Stein's segmentary state concept, its sharp distinction between "ritual sovereignty" and "actual political control," became a matter of controversial but fruitful debates of this author and B. Stein (Kulke, 2010; see also Singh, 2011, 9f.). Already shortly after the publication of B. Stein's *Peasant State and Society*, I admitted the heuristic value of this distinction that has hitherto been completely neglected by conventional historians (Kulke, 1982). But as in further publications too, I questioned its strict application to early medieval Hindu kingdoms, particularly to the powerful empires of the Cholas and to Vijayanagara, and interpreted instead the so-called ritual sovereignty as "ritual policy" and successful means to enhance, validate, and legitimatize "actual political control" (Kulke, 1995; 2005; 2010). However, it has also been pointed out (Kulke, 2010, 612–619) that B. Stein, too, seems to have already been aware of the political implication of "ritual sovereignty" when he wrote,

> What Rajaraja and his successors perfected was a conception of dharmic incorporation which did two things: *it strengthened Chola authority and it provided locality chiefs with stronger ritual or symbolic bases for their own local rule.* (Stein, 1982, 339; italics added by author)

In 1989 he even admitted, "I am now convinced that in India the proposition is incorrect, that [instead] *lordship for Hindus always and necessarily combined ritual and political authority*" (Stein, 1989, 160; italics added by author). As his thoroughly revised article of 1995 was his last statement on the segmentary state before his death in the next year, we are kept in the dark as to whether B. Stein would have modified his concept accordingly.

The Processual Integrative State

The third concept depicts the early medieval state in India as a "processual integrative state." Whereas the theories of Indian feudalism and the segmentary state in South India are applying already existing specified models of the premodern state to India and attempt to define the early medieval Indian state accordingly, the processual integrative model views the premodern Indian state as a permanently changing polity. "Processual," because it defines the early medieval state as an outcome of constant changes, contestation, and realignment. Its main epistemological interest is therefore to detect processes that caused and generated the emergence, consolidation, extension, and decline of these polities. "Integrative," because a major precondition of the success (or failure) of these processes is their capacity to integrate various sociopolitical and cultural facets of local, subregional, and regional elements. In its essence this model depicts processes of state formation rather than "the state." A more appropriate designation therefore could also be "processual integrative mode of state formation."

As for the prehistory of this model, there can be no doubt that its protagonists have been and are still strongly influenced by the concepts of Indian feudalism and the segmentary state, respectively, by their constructive disputes with these theories (Chattopadhyaya, 1983; 1994, *Introduction*; Kulke, 1982; 2006; Sahu, 2003; 2006). But despite the critical inspirations they received from these concepts (in this context see, e.g., Stein, 1969, and Kulke, 1978, 126ff.), it was the intellectual unease with the inaptness of these ultimately static concepts to explain emic processes of state formation and social development as well as their regional differences that resulted in the stepwise development of alternative explanations or models, looking at the state not as a static entity. It was, as B.P. Sahu points out, instead "dynamic, multilayered, poly-centred, and expanding or shrinking regularly" (Sahu , 2003).

An important impetus for this body of research was provided by B.D. Chattopadhyaya's abovementioned Presidential Address in 1983 on the political processes and state structures in early medieval India. In later years many valuable contributions followed, some of which he brought together in the above-mentioned publication *The Making of Early Medieval India* (Chattopadhyaya, 1994; see particularly the *Introduction*, 1–37). Among other things, he points to three characteristic processes of the early medieval "integrative polity":

1. the expansion of state society through the process of local state formation;

2. peasantization of tribes and caste formation; and

3. cult appropriation and integration (Chattopadhyaya, 1994, 16, 160).

Whereas Chattopadhyaya emphasizes particularly horizontal integrative processes that emanate from emerging centres of political power, I highlight vertical processes by distinguishing three phases of integration and territorial expansion at different phases of early medieval state formation. They begin with the founding of local chiefdoms and move ahead, through a gradual territorial and administrative setting up of early kingdoms, to finally expand into a regional kingdom – and, though rarely, even to an "imperial kingdom" (Kulke, 1978, 1993, 1997, 2006). All these different phases of state formation require and, to a large extend, depend on distinct strategies of integration that vary from region to region and from the different stages of state formation. They range from the integration of socio-economically or militarily important tribes into the caste system or the recognition of a tribal goddess (*ṭhakuraṇī*) as tutelary deity (*kuladevatā*) by an early king to the recognition of powerful regional deity as state deity (*rāṣṭradevatā*) by an "imperial king." The important contiguous question of various modes of "ritual integration" has already been indicated above in the context of the debate "ritual sovereignty" versus "ritual policy."

In his above mentioned Presidential Address the concept of legitimation has recently been taken up again as another important aspect of integrative state formation by B.P. Sahu.

> Legitimation was necessary for communities experiencing local state formation as well as in complex state societies. Legitimation of power and the shaping of dominant ideology were, as they usually are, complex processes. They were continuously changing, dynamic and absorptive as against the generally assumed simple reflective and mechanical constructions. This was in consonance with the rich cultural mosaic and change intrinsic to early Indian societies. (Sahu, 2003; for a discussion see also Kulke, 1993, and Mabbett, 1985)

Legitimation through an intended ritual policy is an effective means of integration – or, vice versa, integration, as a most essential prerequisite of state formation, is based on legitimation.

Finally, the concept of "little kingdoms" has to be mentioned at least shortly as the most recent conceptual "acquisition" of the integrative state model. The term "little kingdom" was coined by B. Cohn in the early 1960s in his study of 18th-century Benares (Cohn, 1962) and applied to the south Indian princely state of Pudukkottai (Dirks, 1987). It became an important conceptual tool of the study of early and late medieval state formation in Orissa in the 1990s by G. Berkemer (1993) and B. Schnepel (1997) in the "jungle kingdom" of Jeypore in Orissa. In this context S. Sinha's seminal study on "Rajputization" of tribal leaders in Chhotanagpur in the 16th to 18th centuries has to be mentioned (Sinha, 1962). The "little kingdom" was the topic of a panel of a conference at Heidelberg, which was published by G. Berkemer and M. Frenz under the meaningful title *Sharing Sovereignty: The Little Kingdom in South Asia* (Berkemer & Frenz, 2003). "For the sake of model-building," G. Berkemer points out more recently,

> one can begin with a very simple observation: there can be no great king without little kings who are sovereign rulers within their own kingdoms. The ideological base we must be looking for is the need of a ruler to gain the status of universal king by his dominion over lesser kings. This idea of kingship contrasts with dynastic ideas of kingship where the focus is on the royal charisma exclusively transmitted within one family, or ideas of royal power vested in a military elite. Such historical situations lead to less complex models. The little kingdom model does not exclude such ideas, but considers them of lesser structural importance. (Berkemer, forthcoming)

Or, to put it also in a simple way, the essence or *raison d'être* of the little kingdom and its concept is the fact that a "great king" requires "little kings," as the little king requires the great king and his integration into the royal court for the legitimation and validation of his raised position in his own local society. As a consequence of this awareness, local and subregional identities came to the fore of the concept of medieval state formation. Thus, whereas the first Orissa Research Project in the 1970s studied coastal Orissa with its Brahmans, Gajapatis, Puri, and its Jagannātha cult (Eschmann, 1978), the second Orissa Research Project focused more recently on Orissa's mountainous hinterland and concluded with a final report *Centres Out There? Facets of Subregional Identities in Orissa* (Kulke & Berkemer, 2011).

The integrative model, too, has generated conflicting responses.

> It has had both admirers and critics as well. Regional studies by a host of younger historians on Orissa, Andhra, Rajasthan [Sinha Kapur, 2002; Teuscher, 2002] Gujarat and Tamil Nadu in the later part of the 1980s and 90s adopted and endorsed the integrative framework. Among the criticisms there are broadly three kinds of reservations: first, that the economic dimensions need to be addressed, secondly that it is essentially a narrative of regionalism, and finally that one does not get very much about the structural features of the state apparatus. (Sahu, 2006)

In her reader on early medieval India, U. Singh concludes that "of the three frameworks of early medieval India, Kulke and Chattopadhya's model brings out the relationship between the socio-political, religious, and cultural domains most successfully" (Singh, 2011, 11). But she also raises several issues. Thus my "discussion of religion tends to be state-centric," and my focus on legitimation should not allow us to forget that land grants effected transfer of land rights, and therefore it is necessary to examine their impact on agrarian relations in detail (Singh, 2011, 12).

The Regional Kingdoms of Early Medieval India: An Overview

Harṣa and the Emergence of the Early Medieval Regional Centers in the 7th Century

Until about 500 CE, the history of the vast South Asian subcontinent was dominated by North India as the → Indus Valley civilization, and (with the exception of the central Indian Satavahanas) the great empires of ancient India from the times of the Mauryas to the Guptas originated from North India. In contrast to "ancient India," the Middle Ages were characterized by the pan-Indian process of the emergence of regional centers of power in various parts of the subcontinent, by far the most far-reaching and lasting event of the post-Gupta period. It became apparent for the first time during Harṣa's reign (606–647 CE; Devahuti, 1970).

Unlike during the 5th century, when the Gupta Empire was at its peak without serious opponents, Harṣa's empire was surrounded by powerful adversaries. To the east, Śāśāṅka, the first significant ruler of → Bengal, defied Harṣa until his death (c. 621; Majumdar, 1971). It was the year 630 that proved to be a turning point in the history of India. In the attempt to emulate Samudragupta and to expand his domains up to central India, Harṣa's army was defeated by Pulakeśin II, the Chalukya king of Badami (Vātāpi) in western central India (Ramesh, 1984; see also → Karnataka). Xuanzang, the Chinese Buddhist monk who travelled extensively in India from 630 to 643, euphemistically reports the defeat of his royal patron, stating that Harṣa had not yet been able to defeat the Chalukyas. But Pulakeśin, playing on Harṣa's name, boasted in an inscription that he had robbed Harṣa of joy (i.e. *harṣa*) when he routed his troop of elephants. His victory over the "lord of the entire north" (*sakalottarapatheśvara*), which Pulakeśin proudly announced in this inscription, ended till the early 14th century, when the *sulṭāns* of Delhi marched ahead toward central and South India, all attempts of North Indian rulers to spread their power permanently across the Vindhya Mountains and the Narmadā River toward the South. North India had lost its hegemony in South Asia (Kulke, 2010, 72–94).

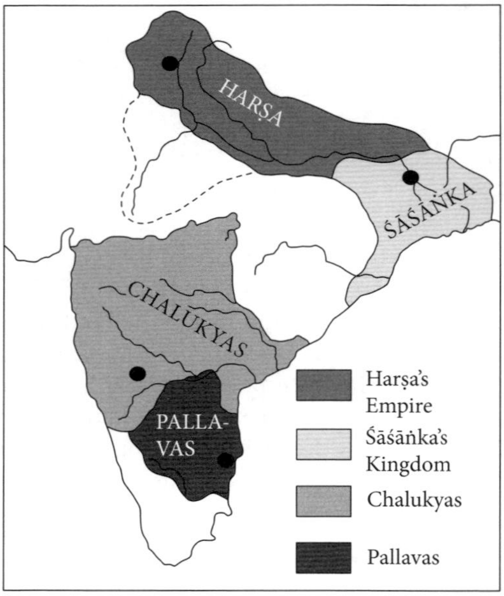

Map 1: Regional kingdoms in the early 7th century CE.
© Hermann Kulke

However, Pulakeśin (609–642) and his central Indian dynasty were in no way the only "lords of the south." The Chalukyas were embroiled in a bitter struggle with the Pallava dynasty from Kanchipuram in present-day Tamil Nadu. In his early years, Pulakeśin was victorious, conquering Kanchipuram and defeating the Pallavas in alliance with their tributaries in the farther south, the Cholas and Pandyas. However, in Pulakeśin's later years, the Pallavas regained their leading position in the south under the King Narasimmavarmaṉ (Skt. Narasiṃhavarman; 630–638), who defeated and killed Pulakeśin as he fought to defend his capital city Badami in 642. For 12 years, the Chalukyas of Badami seem to have disappeared until Pulakeśin's son Vikramāditya I sacked Kanchipuram in revenge of the Pallava assault and restored the fortune of the Chalukyas.

These wars among Harṣa in North India, Śāśāṅka in eastern India, Pulakeśin in western central India, and the Pallavas in the southeast, the four regional power centers – which determined the course of Indian history from the early medieval period onward – became evident for the first time in the early 7th century. Central, eastern, and southern India emerge as "equal partners" in Indian history. The dominance of the north made way for a balance of powers between regional kingdoms of early medieval India.

The Configuration of the Early Medieval Regional Centers

The history of early medieval India seems to be the history of the constant rise and fall of great regional kingdoms and endless wars between them and a multitude of little kingdoms. But the contours of this apparently perplexing picture become intelligible once we consider the paradigm shift in the early medieval period. For seven centuries, the historical process was defined by an astonishing continuity of autonomous state formation *within* the foci of regional power. This process was characterized less by fragmentation, as pointed out likewise by conventional historians and adherents of the concept of Indian feudalism, but rather by the intensification of polygenous regional processes of state formation. However, on the pan-Indian level, they were interlinked by a multitude of religious, cultural, social, and – to a lesser degree – political ties. The astonishing continuity within the regional foci of power of early medieval India effected an unexpected balance of power. It was likewise based on the strength of these regional kingdoms to defend themselves against neighboring kingdoms, and on their weakness and inability to transform short-lived military successes into permanent annexation of areas often several hundred kilometers away. These regional foci of power will be shortly introduced before delineating transregional warfare as the shady side of their balance of power.

The North

When Harṣa selected the holy city of Kanauj as the capital of his fast-growing empire, the center of North Indian power was shifted westward from Patna (ancient Pāṭaliputra), the center of both the Maurya and the Gupta Empires, to the center of the Gaṅgā-Yamunā Doab ("Land of Two Rivers"), which remained with Agra and Delhi the core region of North India right up to the present day (Ray, 1973). A century after Harṣa's death, Kanauj became once more the capital of a great conqueror, Yaśovarman. His realm was soon destroyed by an even greater conqueror, Lalitāditya of → Kashmir (c. 724–760), whose far-flung empire also collapsed after his death. Already in 783 it was conquered by King Vatsarāja of the Gurjara-Pratiharas, but it remained, as will be shown soon, the contested and coveted "imperial center" of North

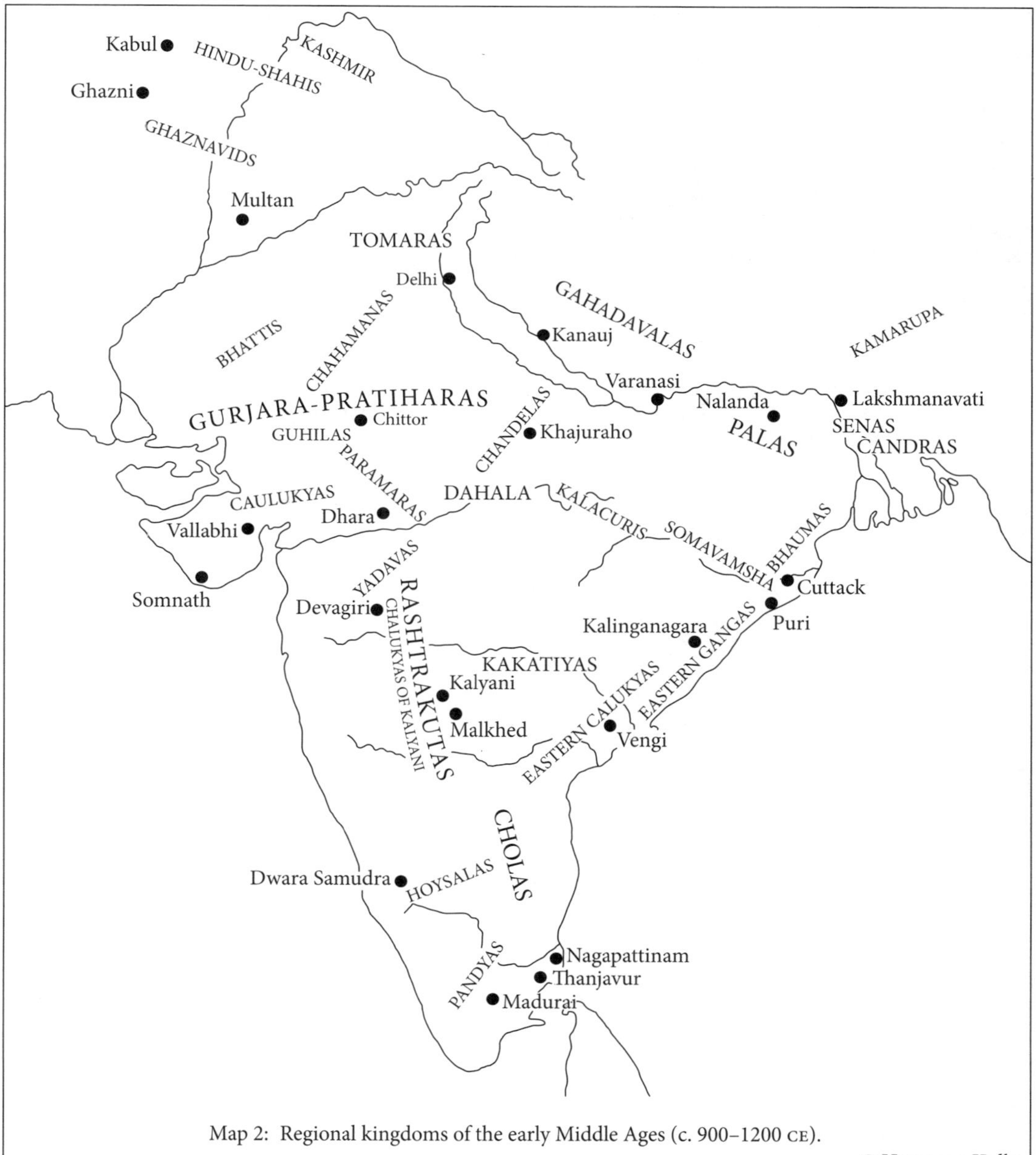

Map 2: Regional kingdoms of the early Middle Ages (c. 900–1200 CE).

India until the 10th century. Since the rise of the Gurjara-Pratiharas as the first important Rajput dynasty, North Indian history was dominated throughout the Middle Ages by various Rajput dynasties (D.R. Sharma, 1966; for the early Rajput history, see Chattopdhyaya, 1976). Rajputs were for centuries a bulwark against early Arab invasions of North India. They also challenged again and again, though with alternating success, even the Delhi Sultanate. From the early 9th to mid-10th century, the "imperial" Gurjara-Pratiharas of Kanauj were the supreme power of North India, though temporally contested by the east Indian Palas and the central Indian Rashtrakutas

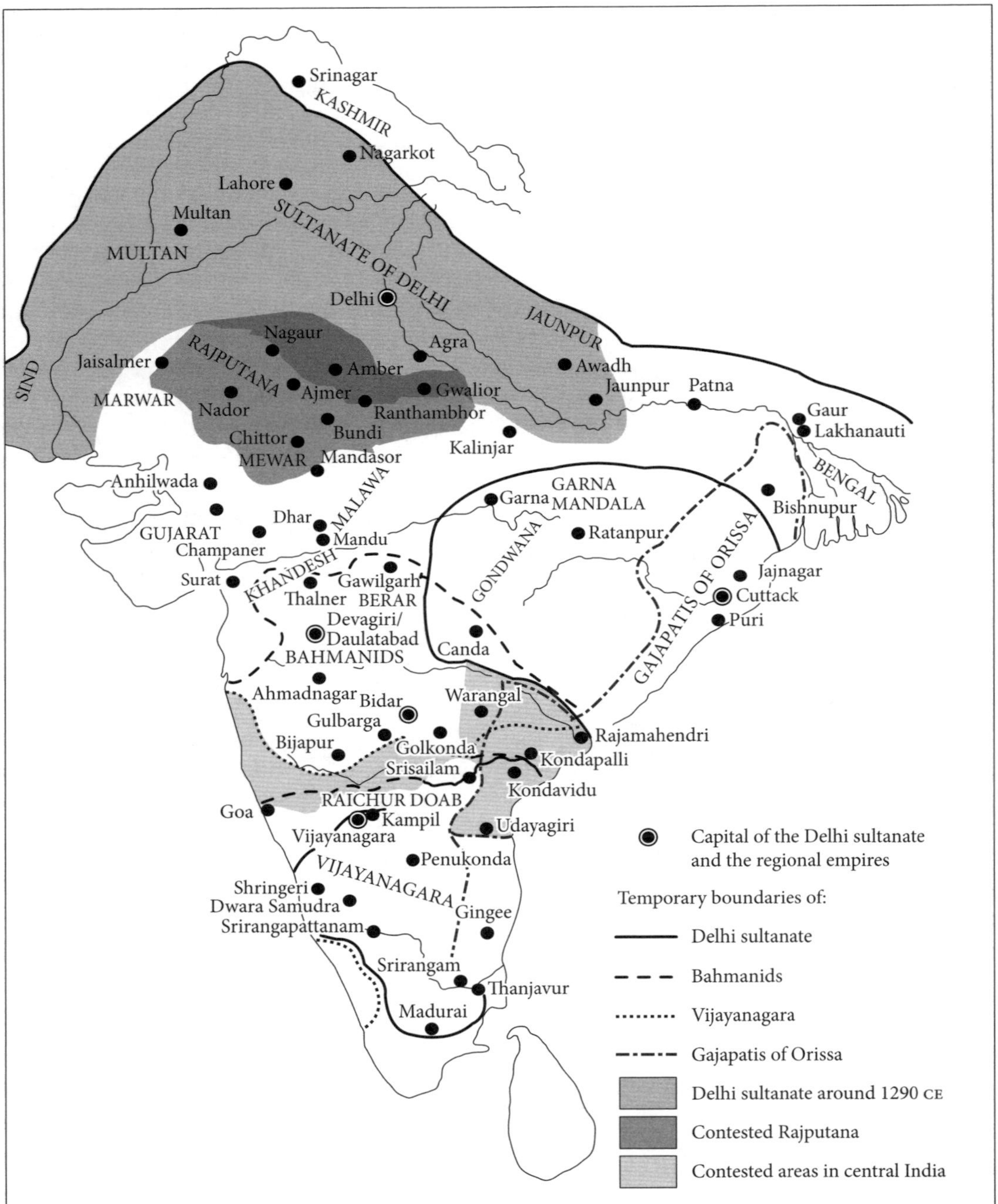

Map 3: Delhi Sultanate and regional empires of the late Middle Ages (c. 1200–1526 CE).

(Mishra, 1938; Puri, 1999). After having reached the peak of their power in the second half of the 10th century, several tributary Rajput dynasties regained their independence. Most important among them were the Chandela of Bundelkhand and the Chahamanas (also known as Chauhans) of Delhi. As one of the very few Hindu dynasties of this age, the Chandelas were able to repel in 1023 Maḥmūd of Ghazni in one of his devastating invasions of North India. Soon after their victory they built the world-famous temples at their capital Khajuraho. The Chahamanas became famous in later centuries as the embodiment of Rajput ideals, as their last king, Pṛthivīrāja, lost his life as leader of the Rajput troops in the fateful second battle of Tarain in 1192. Out of the resistance against the Delhi Sultanate emerged in the 14th century a "third generation" of powerful dynasties, like the Guhila/Shishodiyas of Chittor/Udaipur in Mewar, the Rathors of Jodhpur in Marwar, and the Kachwahas of Amber/Jaipur, which survived the later Delhi Sultanate and the Mughals, and whose castles and palaces are now among the main tourist attractions in India.

The Northeast

The shift of the center of political power from Patna to Kanauj enabled the rulers of eastern India to rise to prominence. Śāśāṅka had made a beginning, but he died without nameable successors. It was only under the Pala dynasty that northeastern India again became an important regional center (Majumdar, 1971; Morrison, 1970; Bhattacharya, 1985; Bagchi, 1993). Founded by Gopāla (c. 770–821), they controlled large parts of Bihar and Bengal. In the 9th century, under Gopāla and Dharmapāla they represented India's northeast very well in the above-mentioned imperial struggle for Kanauj with the Gurjara-Pratihara and the Rashtrakutas. They were famous as India's last Buddhist dynasty; under their rule the great monastery of Nalanda became a veritable Asian Buddhist university, and their art had a deep impact on Buddhist art in Southeast Asia, particularly in Java and it great Borobudur. The Palas were succeeded in 1120 by the Sena dynasty, which was ousted by in the early 13th century by the expanding Delhi Sultanate. Even under Islamic rule, Bengal retained a great amount of independence as a sultanate in its own right until it became a province of the Mughal Empire.

The Central Deccan

The early medieval period began in the important western region of the central Deccan with the rise of the Chalukyas of Badami starting in the 6th century (Ramesh, 1984). As already mentioned, their important position in Indian history arises from their historical deed to have stopped once and for all North Indian medieval kingdoms from extending their realm to central and South India. Moreover, after having defeated Harṣa, Pulakeśin conquered the fertile Kṛṣṇā-Godāvarī delta in → Andhra Pradesh, where he installed his brother Viṣṇuvardhana at Vengi. He became the ancestor of the future Eastern Chalukyas, which became, with often changing alliances, an important buffer state among the more powerful kingdoms of Orissa, central India, and → Tamil Nadu until it was integrated into the Chola Empire in late 11th century.

However, the greatness in Indian history and culture of the Chalukyas of Badami is based particularly upon the fame of their seminal contributions to the development of early medieval art and architecture in central and South India. Already Aihole, their first capital in the 5th century, has rightly been called the cradle of central Indian Hindu rock cut-caves and temples, a development that culminated in the marvelous caves of Badami (dated 578) and the UNESCO heritage temples of Pattadakal of the 7th and early 8th centuries. Chalukya temple architecture and the iconography of their sculptures directly influenced art and architecture of the Pallavas at Kanchipuram and Mahabalipuram as well as of the Rashtrakutas at Ellora. Its world-famous Kailāsanātha Temple, after all, the world's largest rock-cut temple, was a replica of the Virūpākṣa Temple at Pattadakal. The chiseling of about 400,000 tons of stone began shortly after Dantidurga (735–756), the founder of the Rashtrakuta dynasty of Malkhed (Mānyakheṭa), had defeated the last Chalukya king in 753.

In succession to the Chalukyas of Badami, the Rashtrakutas of Malkhed towered above their predecessors and emerged in the 8th century as the most powerful rulers of the Deccan – and, as will be shown soon, eclipsed temporarily under Kṛṣṇa III (939–968) all other contemporary regional powers and became the hub of political power for the whole of India when it briefly dominated vast parts of India from Rameshwaram opposite Sri Lanka up to Kanauj (Altekar, 1967). But already in 973 they were ousted by Taila of the

Chalukyas of Kalyani, who claimed to be related to the Chalukyas of Badami. In the mid-12th century, they were ousted by the Yadava dynasty, which established its capital at Devagiri. With its still most impressive hill fortress, starting in 1327 it became for few years the capital of the Delhi Sultanate under Muḥammad bin Tuġluq, who changed its name to Daulatabad. Only few years later, in 1347, during the rapid disintegration of the Delhi Sultanate, Bahman Šāh founded the Bahmani Sultanate, whose centers at Gulbarga and Bidar were close to those of the Rashtrakutas of Malkhed and the Chalukyas of Kalyani. Already a year earlier, in 1346, Vijayanagar had been established at the southern rim of the Deccan, not far from the Badami of the early Chalukyas, as the capital of the last great Hindu empire of South India and parts of central India.

The South

In the "far south," in the three major river valleys of Tamil Nadu, the dynastic nuclear areas of the Pallavas, Cholas, and Pandyas remained perennial centers of political power. The nuclear area of the Pallavas was Tondaimandalam with its capital at Kanchipuram in the hinterland of present-day Chennai (Madras). They were the premier power of the south from the late 6th to the 9th century CE. The Pallavas are famous for their creation of an innovative Dravidian style of temple architecture, best known from the marvelous temples in their capital, Kanchipuram, and in particular from the port town Mamallapuram (Mahabalipuram) with its shore temple (see fig. 1) The Pallava architecture deeply influenced art and architecture of the emerging "Indianized" states of Southeast Asia. When their power declined, the ancient Cholas emerged once more under Āditya I or Ātitta Cōḻaṉ (871–907) and ruled the south until the middle of the 13th century from Thanjavur (Tanjore) in Cholamandalam or Coromandel (see below). After a protracted period of decline, the Cholas were ousted in 1279 by Kulacēkaraṉ of the Pandya dynasty of Madurai in their ancient nuclear area farther to the south. Although they became for a short time the supreme power of the south, they did not rise to an imperial level like their great antagonists, the Cholas. Already in 1309–1311, they succumbed to the inroad of Malik Kāfūr, the general of the Delhi Sultanate. It was Vijayanagara that followed in the Cholas' footsteps.

Peripheral Areas

In addition to these major foci of regional power in medieval India, there existed several important

Fig.1: Shore temple, Mamallapuram, early 8th century (photo by Hermann Kulke).

intermediate regions and political centers that occasionally interfered in the struggles of the great regional powers. One of them was the mountainous region of southern Karnataka, where the Western Ganga dynasty had ruled since the 5th century. In the early 13th century, the Hoysala dynasty of this region played an important role as allies of the last Chola rulers (Derrett, 1957). Farther to the west, at the narrow coastal strip of the Malabar coast in present-day → Kerala, prosperous dynasties and kingdoms existed like the Kulaśekhara dynasty of Mahodayapuram (late 8th century to 1102). They were in constant wars of defense against their imperial neighbors like the Rashtrakutas in the north and the Cholas in the east, who were eager to tap Malabar's lucrative maritime trade. Another seemingly peripheral area was Orissa, with several successively ruling dynasties (see below). In the northwest there is the once-flourishing kingdom of Kashmir, whose history is well known from the Kalhaṇa's *Rājataraṅgiṇī*, a 12th-century chronicle of Kashmir, India's most famous premodern historical writing. Kashmir rose to prominence in the 8th century, when Lalitāditya conquered large parts of North India. It became a center of Buddhist learning and Śaiva philosophy and created the famous temple of the sun-god at Martand in the 6th century, which exhibits interesting details of late Roman architecture. In 1349 it was conquered by Šāh Mīr, who became the first Muslim ruler of Kashmir. In the northeast, → Assam (Kāmārūpa) remained fairly isolated and independent throughout this period.

Interregional Conflicts and Warfare

Confusing history of India from about 600 to 1200, with its dozens of regional kingdoms and often rather short-lived dynasties, falls into a pattern. The major political processes occurred mostly within four to five coexisting foci of powerful regional kingdoms, each of which was dominated by its premier dynasty. None, however, of them was able to control its powerful neighbors for any length of time. On the one hand, due to this balance of power, there was a great deal of political stability within these great regions, which fostered the evolution of distinct regional cultures. But, on the other hand, this balance of power was also a challenge to ambitious rulers and gave rise to frequent confrontation and sometimes even multiple interregional clashes as another characteristic of medieval Indian history. This unfortunate feature of India's Middle Ages will be exemplified by the situation in late 8th century to the end of 9th century, when the confrontations were particularly intense.

The Gurjara-Pratiharas in the north, the Palas in the east, and the Rashtrakutas on the Deccan Plateau emerged as powerful dynasties almost at the same time. Vatsarāja, the founder of the Gurjara-Pratihara dynasty, conquered large parts of Rajasthan and of northwestern India around 783. At the same time, the early Palas, Gopāla and particularly his powerful successor Dharmapāla (c. 770–821), extended their sway from Bengal westward. A clash was then inevitable. Vatsarāja defeated the Pala king near Allahabad. In the meantime the Rashtrakutas had consolidated their hold on the Deccan and were looking northward. The third Rashtrakuta king, Dhruva (c. 770–793), invaded the Gangetic Plains with a large army and defeated both Vatsarāja and Dharmapāla. After Dhruva's death, when Rashtrakuta power was eclipsed for some time, Dharmapāla took his chance and captured Kanauj. There he held court where countless kings "bowed down before him with trembling crowns and showered their praise upon him," as it is proclaimed in one of his inscriptions.

But soon Vatsarāja's son, Nāgabhaṭa, restored the glory of the Gurjara-Pratiharas, recaptured Kanauj, and then proceeded to vanquish Dharmapāla. This victory made the new Rashtrakuta king, Govinda III, very jealous. He pounced upon Nāgabhaṭa, who had to flee to the desert of Rajasthan while Dharmapāla quickly annexed Kanauj once more. In the following generation of rulers, Dharmapāla's son Devapāla (c. 821–860) was the most prominent. He could extend his sway, as the contemporary Gurjara-Pratiharas and Rashtrakutas were weak rulers. But in the 9th century, the Gurjara-Pratihara kings, Bhoja (836–885) and Mahendrapāla (885–910), proved to be more powerful than their contemporaries of the other two dynasties, whom they defeated several times. Kanauj then emerged again as the main focus of power in India.

Toward the end of the 9th century, the Rashtrakutas gained strength once more under Indra III and under the great Kṛṣṇa III (939–968), whose power made an impact on all major regions of India. Whereas the Rashtrakutas had so far mostly intervened in the affairs of the north, Kṛṣṇa III turned to the south and vanquished the newly emerging Cholas, who had only recently defeated the Pallavas. In an inscription of 959 that Kṛṣṇa III left proudly in Tondaimandalam, he stated,

> With the intention of conquering the South (*dakṣiṇa-dig*) he uprooted the Chola dynasty and bestowed the lands of their realm on his own relatives. The mighty overlords of the Mandalas, like the Cheras and Pandyas and others as well as the ruler of Simhala [Sri Lanka] he reduced to the status of tributaries (*kara-dā*). He established a column of victory at Rameshvaram. (*EI* IV, 1896, 278)

This inscription seems to document an exception to the above-mentioned rule that the victorious kings of one region were unable to replace rulers of another conquered region and to extend their administrative control over it. Kṛṣṇa III obviously tried to do just that, and there seems to be the beginnings of a new centralized interregional empire. But if the distant ruler wished to retain his hold on another region, he had to be prepared for frequent intervention, and this was costly and diminished the resources of his own region, which would in turn become vulnerable to intervention by third parties or to subversion from within. The latter happened to the mighty Rashtrakuta Empire. Only six years after the death of Kṛṣṇa III, Taila, the governor of a large province of the empire, usurped the throne of the Rashtrakutas. In 982, the grandson of Kṛṣṇa III, who had tried in vain to recapture the throne, ended his life by fasting himself to death. Taila, who claimed to be an offspring of the early dynasty of the Chalukyas of Badami, had risen to prominence in the service of Kṛṣṇa III, who had entrusted him with the defense of the north of the empire while he himself was devoting all his energy to the subjection of the Cholas.

When the Chalukyas of Kalyani gained control over central India, the political situation in two of the other major regions had drastically changed. By the end of the 10th century, the mighty Gurjara-Pratiharas were almost forgotten. After fighting against many enemies, among them the Arabs of Sind, their power had dwindled. ʿAlī al-Masʿūdī, a traveler from Baghdad who visited Kanauj in the early 10th century, reported that the Pratiharas maintained four large armies of about 700,000 to 900,000 men each. One army was specifically assigned the task of fighting against the Muslim ruler of Multan in the Indus Valley, and another one had to deal with the Rashtrakutas, whom ʿAlī al-Masʿūdī regarded as the natural enemies of the Pratiharas. The maintenance of such large armies with their thousands of horses, camels, and elephants must have placed a heavy burden on the people. When their power dwindled, the Gurjara-Pratiharas still managed to retain their capital, Kanauj, but most of their territory was usurped by former tributary princes, particularly by the Rajputs. The decline of political unity in North India was hastened by the annual invasions of Maḥmūd of Ghazni in the period from 1001 to 1027. He looted all regions from Gujarat to Varanasi (Benares) and destabilized the whole political system. North India did not recover from this onslaught until it was finally conquered by the Turks from Afghanistan in the late 12th century.

Regional State Formation: Two Case Studies

Orissa

In the following, a few aspects of the development of early medieval states from early local state formation to imperial kingdoms will be depicted exemplarily by Orissa and the Cholas in Tamil Nadu. As already mentioned, Orissa provides an excellent example of the three-tier development of processual integrative state formation from local chieftaincies to little subregional kingdoms and finally to powerful regional kingdoms (Kulke, 1978; 1979; 1986; Panda, 1990; 1995). In the 4th and 3rd centuries BCE, Orissa had already been a province of the North Indian empires under the Nandas and Mauryas, and in the 1st century BCE, it had even generated a major kingdom under Khāravela for one generation. But these polities were either imposed from above or dynastically imported from the neighboring region Dakshina Koshala. It was only several centuries after the decline of Khāravela's short-lived realm that incipient indigenous state formation occurred with the emergence of strong chieftaincies and early little kingdoms. Whereas the early "imported developments" had taken place in Orissa's coastal region, the new, locally emerging processes of early state formation had their origin in its periphery and the

Map 4: Territorial development of Orissa (c. 600–1400 CE).

mountainous hinterland, which was populated by tribals who still make up nearly half of its contemporary population.

As in many other regions in post-Gupta central and South India, this development was initiated by local chieftains. They began to strengthen and validate the consolidation of their local power and translocal authority with the help and advice of invited Brahmans and by agrarian extension, enhancement of trade, and stepwise integration of their still purely tribal hinterland and their deities into their "royal pantheon." The incipient activities of tribal chieftains are scarcely known, as they are only rarely documented in inscriptions produced by the next generation of the already slightly "Hinduized" early kingdoms. Thus, for instance, we know of a king in a predominantly tribal area near Sonpur in western Orissa who is praised around 500 CE as a "devotee of the feet of [the goddess] Stambheśvarī (*stambheśvarīpādabhakta*)." In the 6th to 8th centuries, Stambheśvarī ("The Lady of the [Wooden] Pillar") was the tutelary deity of the Sulki dynasty in the Dhenkanal area and in the following centuries of the Bhanja dynasty of Boudh. In these areas in the hinterland of central Orissa, the originally purely tribal goddess Stambheśvarī is still worshipped in villages (Eschmann, 1978, 79–98; Kulke, 1979, 120).

The rise of a tribal chief around 400 CE is still discernible in the revealing legend of origin of the Shailobhbava dynasty in southern Orissa in several 7th-century inscriptions. Pulindasena, a ruler in Kalinga, was tired of ruling his realm, and, therefore, he prayed to Śiva to install a new young ruler instead. The god granted him this wish. A rock split open (*śilaśakalodbhedī*), and out of it stepped a young man whom Pulindasena called Śailodbhava ("Born from the Rock") and who became the founder of a new dynasty (Kulke, 1979; Banpur inscription, late 7th cent. [*EI* XXIX, 32ff.]). This legend and the names of the two kings clearly point to their tribal origin. The Pulindas were a tribe that had already been known to Aśoka, and Pulindasena must have been a war chieftain (*sena*) of that tribe. Their successors, the Shailodbhavas, descended from their mountainous homeland and settled in the fertile Rishikulya Valley. But several generations passed before a member of that dynasty could celebrate a great vedic horse sacrifice (*aśvamedha* [see → *yajña*]) with the help of his Brahmanical priests and establish in circa 600 the Shailodbhavas as the first fully Hinduized dynasty in southern and temporarily also in coastal central Orissa.

The further political development of Orissa is characterized by a constant territorial expansion of the regional kingdom, which increasingly incorporated several nuclear areas. This process was not only an "expansion from within" but also one of "addition from without." The expansion of emerging early kingdoms was often caused by emerging forces at the periphery and their quest for the control of the highly developed and prosperous rice-growing nuclear region at the center, rather than by a centrifugal expansion emerging from these centers. Early medieval state formation in Orissa therefore owed its dynamics to a large extent to a sequence of conquests of the royal center by mighty neighbors who then added their own nuclear areas to the expanding kingdom. In 736 the Shailodbhavas were dislodged in this way by the Bhaumakaras, who united their nuclear area north of the Mahānadī delta with the Shailodbhava area in southern Orissa. The Bhaumakaras are famous as the last Buddhist rulers in coastal eastern India and their edificial contributions to Orissa's "Golden Triangle" of Buddhist monasteries at Ratnagiri, Udayagiri, and Lalitagiri in the Cuttack district. In the 10th century, the Somavamshi kings Yayāti I and Yayāti II of western Orissa conquered coastal Orissa and added their own nuclear areas to the already existing regional kingdom, centered around the fertile Mahānadī delta in coastal Orissa. They came from Dakshina Koshala on the upper Mahānadī and had slowly worked their way downstream, conquering in due course also the small but important nuclear area of Khinjali Mandala of the Bhanja rulers of Boudh. The new regional kingdom now comprised five nuclear areas, three at the coast and two in the hinterland. Under the Somavamsha, their capital Bhubaneswar became one of India's most impressive centers of Hindu architecture, with the great Liṅgarāja Temple at its center.

In 1112, Anantavarman Choḍagaṅgadeva of the Eastern Ganga dynasty of Kalinganagara in southern Orissa (in present-day northern Andhra Pradesh) defeated the last Somavamshi (Mukhunda Rao, 1991). By uniting his own homeland Kalinga with the already well-established kingdom of the Somavamshis and by beginning the construction of the monumental Jagannātha Temple at Puri (see fig. 2), Choḍagaṅgadeva laid literarily the foundation stone of the emerging "imperial regional kingdom" of Orissa (Panda, 1990). The construction of the Jagannātha Temple was not an expression of the above-mentioned "ritual sovereignty." Outdoing with it the Liṅgarāja Temple of the Somavamshis as the thus far greatest temple of eastern India and competing directly in its height with the Peruvaṭaiyār Kōyil (more commonly known as Bṛhadīśvara or Rājarājeśvara Temple) built by Rājarāja I in Thanjavur, India's hitherto greatest temple at the capital of his dynastic hereditary enemies, the Cholas, it was an explicit act of ritual policy. And as it was dedicated to Jagannātha, a "wooden deity" (*dārudevatā*) of formerly tribal origin, it was also an act of imperial integrative policy, comparable with the above-mentioned worship of Stambheśvarī by earlier Hinduized kings in the tribal hinterland (Eschmann, 1978).

Choḍagaṅgadeva's successors continued and even outmatched his ritual policy. In 1230 King Anaṅgabhīma dedicated his empire to Jagannātha and claimed to rule as his son (*putra*) and vassal (Ori. *rāuta*) under his order (*ādeśa*; Kulke, 1979, 49–70; 1981). And Anaṅgabhīma's son and successor, Narasiṃha I (1238–1264), constructed not only India's greatest temple, but also the world-famous sun temple at Konark. He was also one of the few Indian rulers who not only man-

Fig. 2: Jagannātha Temple, Puri, drawing by an unknown Indian artist, 1822 (© Victoria & Albert Museum, London, used by courtesy).

aged to defend themselves against the superior military force of Muslim armies but also launched offensives against them in Bengal. This might have been a reason why Orissa has been spared Muslim aggressions in following centuries, except a short incursion of Fīrūz Šāh in 1361, which, however, had no lasting consequences. The Gangas continued to rule more or less peacefully without greater incidents until 1434, when their last ruler, Bhānudeva IV, was ousted in 1434 in a *coup d'état* by Kapilendra, the powerful military leader (*nāyaka*) of Telugu-speaking south Orissa (Mukherjee, 1953).

Kapilendra founded the short-lived but powerful Suryavamsha, which also became known as the Gajapati dynasty. Initially still facing the opposition of supporters of the overthrown Gangas, he threatened them in several inscriptions with the wrath of Lord Jagannātha and the confiscation of their goods. In the following years, the "Orissan Empire" reached its zenith when its armies advanced successfully as far as Bengal and in the south well beyond Chennai into the region of Tiruchirappalli. For a short while, Orissa was the mightiest Hindu kingdom. Under Kapilendra's son Puruṣottama (1467–1497), Orissa suffered grave setbacks in the south at the hands of Vijayanagara and the central Indian Bahmani Sultanate. But due to his legendary romance with the princess of Kanchipuram/Vijayanagara and the inauguration of the royal ritual sweeping of the divine cars, still the climax of Puri's great annual *rathayātrā*, he is venerated as the greatest Gajapati. He was succeeded by his son Pratāparudra, during whose reign → Caitanya lived in Puri for nearly 20 years. But under his long rule until 1540, Orissa again suffered several hard blows that were a prelude to its downfall in 1568. The cause is to be sought in the almost simultaneous appearance of three powerful foes: in the north the recuperation of the sultanate of Bengal, in the west the new central Indian sultanate of Golconda, and in the south the empire of Vijayanagara, whose most powerful ruler, Kṛṣṇadēvarāya, embarked upon systematic wars of conquest in south Orissa in 1512. There were also intrigues and betrayals at the court of the Gajapati king. After a brief period of grace under its last king, Mukundadeva, Orissa fell to the treason of several high-ranking officers and to a surprise attack of the *sulṭān* of Bengal in 1568, whose troops occupied Orissa until 1590/1592, when they were defeated by Akbar's Rajput general Mansiṅgh and Orissa became a province of the Mughal Empire.

The Chola Empire

The Cholas along with the Pandyas were well known to Aśoka in the 3rd century BCE and to the classical European authors in the following centuries and exhibited remarkable indication of early urbanization and state formation in the Caṅkam period of the early centuries of the Common Era (see → Tamil texts). Starting in the late 4th century, they came increasingly under the influence of the Pallavas as the first early Hindu kingdom of Tamil Nadu and finally became a tributary state of them around 600 CE.

The rise of the Cholas as successor of the Pallavas as dominant power of Tamil Nadu in the 9th century was achieved in a now-familiar way (Sastri, 1955). They served as loyal tributary princes under the Pallavas and reasserted their independence when Pallava power declined due to the constant confrontation with the mighty Rashtrakutas. While the Pallavas were busy in the north, the Cholas defended the Pallava realm against the southern Pandyas until the Cholas under Āditya took their chance and challenged his Pallava overlord on the battlefield around 897. The encounter took the famous heroic form of a duel in front of the two armies. Āditya I or Ātitta Cōḻaṉ and finally his son Parāntaka (907–955) integrated the northern nuclear area of the Pallavas into their centrally located homeland around Thanjavur and began to extend their realm into the southern nuclear area of the Pandyas. However, as already mentioned, in 949 Parāntaka was defeated by the Rashtrakutas king Kṛṣṇa III, who repelled the Cholas as tributaries to their original nuclear area in the Kāvērī Valley for several decades.

The subsequent rise of the Cholas to imperial power was unique in early medieval Indian history (Subbarayalu, 1982; Heitzman, 1995; Karashima, 2001). Toward the end of the 10th century, Uttama Cōḻaṉ and finally his son Rājarāja I (988–1014) and grandson Rājendra I or Irācēntira Cōḻaṉ (1014–1047) restored and enhanced the Chola power with a hitherto unknown vengeance by the successful formation of a central administration previously unknown in South India and by extending their territorial boundaries far beyond their original "homeland." Rājarāja vanquished the Pandyas and the Ceras in Kerala, conquered → Sri Lanka, and sacked its venerable old capital, Anuradhapura. At the end of his reign, he even captured the distant Maldives Islands.

His son Rājendra I continued this aggressive policy with equal vigor. He conquered Vengi, the capital of the Eastern Chalukyas, captured the capital of the Chalukyas of Kalyani, and sent his fleet again to the Maldives and Sri Lanka in 1017. In the years 1022 to 1025, he seems to have carried out a master plan of truly imperial expansion that aimed at the control of the flourishing Indian trade. After having completed the plan of his father to conquer southern and central India and having finally subdued South India's offshore islands, he undertook two campaigns, previously unknown in South Indian history. In the year 1022/1023, his troops advanced on the eastern coast up to the Gaṅgā, subduing the rulers of Andhra and the Somavamsha ruler of Orissa, as well as Mahipāla, the Pala king of Bengal. Rājendra returned with holy water from the Gaṅgā, with which he consecrated a "liquid pillar of victory" in a huge tank near his new capital, named Gangaikondacholapuram ("The City of the Cōḻa Who Conquered the Gaṅgā").

Only three years later, he sent a mighty fleet to Sumatra and Malaya, where his army defeated the mighty Srivijaya Empire and all its tributary princes (Sastri, 1955, 209–220; Spencer, 1983; Kulke, 2009). Recent research has clearly shown that it was a deliberate imperial policy of the Cholas to enhance its control of the lucrative Indian Ocean trade between South Asia and China. In recent decades this trade had increased considerably by the rise of the Fatimid caliphate in Egypt and the powerful Tang dynasty of China in the late 10th century as well as by the expansion of the Angkor Empire to the Malay Peninsula. But obviously the trade of the famous South Indian merchant guilds (Abraham, 1988; Karashima, 2009) had been obstructed by a similar policy followed by the maritime kingdom of Srivijaya, which controlled the Malacca and Sunda straits through which eastern trade had to pass. Obviously in order to avoid this confrontation, a large number of missions had been exchanged during these years between those states that were involved in the eastern Indian Ocean trade. The Cholas for the first time sent two missions to China and received two each from Srivijaya and Angkor. The king of Srivijaya in 1005 had even

Fig. 3: Rājarājeśvara Temple, Thanjavur, early 11th century (photo by Hermann Kulke).

constructed a monastery in Nagapattinam, the major harbor of the Cholas. For its maintenance, Rājarāja donated the revenue of a neighboring village, and this was renewed by Rājendra in 1017. Therefore, why Rājendra attacked Srivijaya is unknown. But doubtless it was the expression of imperial policy.

The monumental temple architecture of the "imperial Cholas" – and the royal rituals – was as impressive as their territorial expansion (Heitzman, 1977). The Bṛhadīśvara or Rājarājeśvara Temple in Thanjavur was completed in the year 1010 (see fig. 3). With a temple tower measuring 61 meters, it was twice as high as any in India. A few decades later, Rājendra also consecrated a slightly smaller but proportionally more balanced temple in his new capital city in Gangaikondacholapuram. In the core area of the empire, their successors built other great temples in the 11th century. Each was endowed with generous ownership titles to land spread across the empire. Money grants made to the temples by eminent individuals in the empire were invested in irrigation programs in neighboring villages as credit with fixed rates of interest, with the result that the revenues and tax collections from these villages correspondingly also increased. Thus the fertile central region in the lower reaches of the Kāvērī River came under an added network of ritual and economic levies. This was geared toward the imperial temples and the Chola rulers, whose names were often linked to that of the temple god (for instance, Rājarājeśvara at Thanjavur), and who were also present everywhere in the great sculptures on the outer walls of the temple in divine and royal form (Spencer, 1969; Karashima, 1999). Rājarāja was thus known not only as the founder of the Chola Empire, but also as the creator of a monumental temple architecture unknown in India up until his time. Within a few decades, its influence spread to distant parts of India as an increasing number of monumental temple complexes began to be built in the capital cities of other regional kingdoms. Particularly impressive is the series of great temples in Orissa with the Liṅgarāja Temple in Bhubaneswar, built around 1060, the Jagannātha Temple in Puri, whose construction began around 1135, and the sun temple in Konark, the biggest known temple in India, built in about 1250 (Kulke, 1978).

Bibliography

Ali, D., *Courtly Culture and Political Life in Early Medieval India*, Cambridge UK, 2004.

Altekar, A.S., *The Rāṣṭrakūṭas and Their Times*, Pune, 1934, rev. ed. 1967.

Appadurai, A., "Kings, Sects and Temples in South India, 1350–1700 A.D.," in: B. Stein, ed., *South Indian Temples: An Analytical Reconsideration*, Delhi, 1978, 47–74.

Bagchi, J., *The History and Culture of the Palas of Bengal and Bihar*, Delhi, 1993.

Berkemer, G., "Little Kingdom," in: H. Kulke, ed., *The State in India 1000–1700*, Delhi, rev. ed., forthcoming.

Berkemer, G., *Little Kingdoms in Kalinga. Ideologie, Legitimation und Politik regionaler Eliten*, Stuttgart, 1993.

Berkemer, G., & M. Frenz, eds., *Sharing Sovereignty: The Little Kingdom in South Asia*, Berlin, 2003.

Bhatia, P., *The Paramāras (c. 800–1305 A.D.): A Study in the Political and Cultural History of Their Kingdoms*, Delhi, 1970.

Bhattacharya, S., *Landschenkungen und staatliche Entwicklung im frühmittelalterlichen Bengalen (5. bis 13. Jh. n. Chr.)*, Wiesbaden, 1985.

Chakrabarti, K., *Religious Process: The Purāṇas and the Making of a Regional Tradition*, Delhi, 2001.

Champakalakshmi, R., *Trade, Ideology and Urbanization: South India 300 B.C. to A.D. 1300*, Delhi, 1996.

Champakalakshmi, R., "Peasant State and Society in Medieval South India: A Review Article," *IESHR* 18, 1981, 411–426.

Chattopadhyaya, B.D., "Space, History and Cultural Process: Some Ideas on the Ingredients of Subregional Identity," in: H. Kulke & G. Berkemer, eds., *Centres Out There? Facets of Subregional Identities in Orissa*, Delhi, 2011, 21–38.

Chattopadhyaya, B.D., "Festival as Rituals: An Exploration into the Convergence of Rituals and the State," in: A. Michaels *et al.*, eds., *Ritual Dynamics and the Science of Ritual*, vol. III/4: H. Kulke & U. Skoda, eds., *State and Ritual in India*, Wiesbaden, 2010, 627–646.

Chattopadhyaya, B.D., *Representing the Other: Sanskrit Sources and the Muslims (Eighth to Fourteenth Century)*, Delhi, 1998.

Chattopadhyaya, B.D., "Autonomous Spaces and the Authority of the State: The Contradiction and Its Resolution in Theory and Practice in Early India," in: B. Kölver, ed., *Recht, Staat und Verwaltung im klassischen Indien (The State, the Law, and Administration in Classical India)*, Munich, 1997, 1–14.

Chattopadhyaya, B.D., "State and Economy in North India: Fourth Century to Twelfth Century," in: R.Thapar, ed., *Recent Perspectives of Early Indian History*, Bombay, 1995, 309–346.

Chattopadhyaya, B.D., *The Making of Early Medieval India*, Delhi, 1994.

Chattopadhyaya, B.D., "Political Process and the Structure of Polity in Early Medieval India," presidential address at the Indian History Congress, ancient India section, 44th session, Burdwan, 1983; repr. in H. Kulke, ed., *The State in India 1000–1700*, Delhi, 11995, 195–232.

Chattopadhyaya, B.D., "Origin of the Rajputs: The Political, Economic and Social Processes in Early Medieval Rajasthan," *IHR* 3, 1976, 59–82; repr. *The Making of Early Medieval India*, Delhi, 1994.

Cohn, B., "Political Systems in Eighteenth-Century India: The Benares Region," *JAOS* 82, 1962, 312–320; repr. in: *idem, An Anthropologist among the Historians and Other Esssays*, Delhi, 1987, 1–18.

Derrett, J.D.M., *The Hoysalas: A Medieval Indian Royal Family*, Madras, 1957.

Devahuti, D., *Harsha: A Political Study*, Delhi, 1970.

Dirks, N.B., *The Hollow Crown: Ethnohistory of an Indian Kingdom*, Cambridge UK, 1987.

Eschmann, A., H. Kulke & G.C. Tripathi, eds., *The Cult of Jagannath and the Regional Tradition of Orissa*, Delhi, 1978.

Gopal, B.R., *The Rashtrakutas of Malkhed: Studies in Their History and Culture*, Mysore, 1994.

Gottlob, M., *Historisches Denken im modernen Südasien*, Frankfurt, 2002.

Grewal, J.S., ed., *The State and Society in Medieval India*, Delhi, 2005.

Gurukkal, R., *Social Formations in Early South India*, New Delhi, 2010.

Gurukkal, R., "Temples as Sites of Social and Religious Interaction," in: B.D. Chattopadhyaya, ed., *History of Science, Philosophy and Culture in Indian Civilization*, vol. II/5: *A Social History of Early India*, Delhi, 2009, 199–212.

Habib, I., "Problems of Marxist Historical Analysis," in: *Science and Human Progress: Essays in Honour of the Late Prof. D.D. Kosambi*, publ. Kosambi Committee, Bombay, 1974, 34–47.

Hall, K.R., *Trade and Statecraft in the Age of Cōḻas*, Delhi, 1980.

Heitzman, J., *Gifts of Power: Lordship in an Early Indian State*, Delhi, 1997.

Heitzman, J., "State Formation in South India, 850–1280," in: H. Kulke, ed., *The State in India 1000–1700*, Delhi, 11995, 162–194. See above.

Jha, D.N., ed., *The Feudal Order: State Society and Ideology in Early Medieval India*, New Delhi, 2000.

Karashima, N., "South Indian Merchant Guilds in the Indian Ocean and Southeast Asia," in: N. Karashima, *South Indian Society in Transition: Ancient to Medieval*, Delhi, 2009, 199–223; repr. in H. Kulke, ed., *Nagapattinam to Suvarnadwipa: Reflections on the Chola Naval Expeditions to Southeast Asia*, Singapore, 2009, 135–157.

Karashima, N., *History and Society in South India*, Delhi, 2001.

Karashima, N., ed., *Kingship in Indian History*, Delhi, 1999.

Kulke, H., & G. Berkemer, eds., *Centres Out There? Facets of Subregional Identities in Orissa*, Delhi, 2011.

Kulke, H., "Ritual Sovereignty and Ritual Policy: Some Historiographic Reflections," in: A. Michaels *et al.*, eds., *Ritual Dynamics and the Science of Ritual*, vol. III/4: H. Kulke & U. Skoda, eds., *State and Ritual in India*, Wiesbaden, 2010, 603–626.

Kulke, H., "The Naval Expeditions of the Cholas in the Context of Asian History," in: H. Kulke, ed., *Nagapattinam to Suvarnadwipa: Reflections on the Chola Naval Expeditions to Southeast Asia*, Singapore, 2009, 1–20.

Kulke, H., "The Integrative Model of State Formation in Early Medieval India: Some Historiographical Remarks," in: M. Kimura & M. Tanabe, eds., *The State in India: Past and Present*, Delhi, 2006, 59–82.

Kulke, H., *Indische Geschichte bis 1750 (Oldenbourg Grundriss der Geschichte* 34), Munich, 2005; rev. ET: *History of Pre-colonial India: Issues and Debates*, Delhi, forthcoming.

Kulke, H., "The Early and the Imperial Kingdom: A Processural Model of Integrative State Formation in Early Medieval India," in: H. Kulke, ed., *The State in India 1000–1700*, Delhi, 1995, 233–262; repr. in: H. Kulke, *Kings and Cults: State Formation and Legitimation in India and Southeast Asia*, Delhi, 1997, 233–263; and repr. in U. Singh, ed., *Rethinking Early Medieval India: A Reader*, Delhi, 2011, 91–120.

Kulke, H., ed., *The State in India 1000–1700*, Delhi, 1995.

Kulke, H., "Fragmentation and Segmentation versus Integration? Reflections on the Concepts of Indian Feudalism and the Segmentary State in Indian History," *SiH* 4, 1982a, 93–113.

Kulke, H., "Gibt es ein indisches Mittelalter? Versuch einer eurasiatischen Geschichtsbetrachtung," *Saeculum* 33, 1982b, 221–239; rev. ET: "Periodization of pre-Modern Historical Processes in India and Europe: Some Reflections," *IHR* 19, 1996, 21–36.

Kulke, H., "King Anaṅgabhīma III, the Veritable Founder of the Gajapati Kingship and of the Jagannātha Trinity at Puri," *JRAS* 113/1, 1981, 26–39.

Kulke, H., *Jagannatha-Kult und Gajapati-Königtum. Ein Beitrag zur Geschichte religiöser Legitimation hinduistischer Herrscher*, Wiesbaden, 1979.

Kulke, H., "Royal Temple Policy and the Structure of Medieval Hindu Kingdoms," in: A. Eschmann, H. Kulke & G.C. Tripathi, eds., *The Cult of Jagannath and the Regional Tradition of Orissa*, Delhi, 1978, 125–138.

Kulke, H., & D. Rothermund, *A History of India*, London, [5]2010.

Mabbett, L.W., "A Survey of the Background to the Variety of Political Traditions in South-east Asia", "Introduction: The Comparative Study of Traditional Asian Political Institutions," in: *idem*, ed., *Patterns of Kingship and Authority in Traditional Asia*, London, 1985.

Majumdar, R.C., ed., *The Age of Imperial Kanauj*, Bombay, 1955.

Majumdar, R.C., ed., *The History of Bengal*, vol. I: *Hindu Period*, Patna, 1943, repr. 1971.

Minakshi, C., *Administration and Social Life under the Pallavas*, Madras, 1938.

Mishra, U.B., *The Gurjara-Pratihāras*, Delhi, 1968.

Morrison, B.M., *Political Centers and Cultural Regions in Early Bengal*, Tucson, 1970.

Mukherjee, P., *History of the Gajapati Kings of Orissa and Their Successors*, Calcutta, 1953.

Mukhia, H., ed., *The Feudalism Debate*, Delhi, 1999.

Mukhia, H., "Was There Feudalism in Indian History," presidential address at the Indian History Congress, 41st session, Bombay, 1980; repr. in H. Kulke, ed., *The State in India 1000–1700*, Delhi, 1995, 86–133.

Mukunda Rao, N., *Kalinga under the Eastern Gangas (ca. 900 A.D. to ca. 1200 A.D.)*, Delhi, 1991.

Nandi, R.N., *State Formation, Agrarian Growth and Social Change in Feudal South India, c. AD 600–1200*, Delhi, 2000.

Nandi, R.N., *Religious Institutions and Cults in the Deccan, c. A.D. 600–1000*, Delhi, 1973.

Panda, S.K., *Herrschaft und Verwaltung im östlichen Indien unter den späten Gangas (ca. 1038–1434)*, Stuttgart, 1986; ET: *The State and Statecraft in Medieval Orissa under the Later Eastern Gangas (1038–1434)*, Calcutta, 1995.

Panda, S.K., "From Kingdom to Empire: A Study of Medieval State Formation under the Eastern Gangas, A.D. 1038–1434," *IHR* 17, 1990, 48–59.

Panda, S.K., "The Krishna Godavari Delta: A Bone of Contention between the Gajapatis of Orissa and the Rayas of Vijayanagara," in: A.L. Dallapiccola, ed., *Vijayanagara – City and Empire: New Currents of Research*, vol. II, Wiesbaden, 1985, 88–96.

Puri, P.N., *The History of the Gurjara-Pratihāra*, Delhi, 1999.

Ramesh, K.V., *Chalukyas of Vātāpi*, Delhi, 1984.

Ray, H.C., *The Dynastic History of Northern India: Early and Medieval Period*, 2 vols., Calcutta, 1931–1936, repr. Delhi, 1973.

Sahu, B.P., "Recent Perspectives of the State and Debates in Early Indian History," in: H. Kulke & B.P. Sahu, eds., *Integrative Processes and the State in Early India*, Delhi, forthcoming a.

Sahu, B.P., *The Changing Gaze: Regions and the Constructions of Early India*, Delhi, forthcoming b.

Sahu, B.P., "Early Medieval Indian Polity, Indian Feudalism and Alternative Histories," paper presented at the *Symposium on History and History Writing in India*, Dec 28–30, Indian History Congress, Kannur, 2006a.

Sahu, B.P., "Ways of Seeing: History and Historiography of the State in Early India," in: M. Brandtner & S.K. Panda, eds., *Interrogating History: Essays for Hermann Kulke*, Delhi, 2006b, 63–82.

Sahu, B.P., "Legitimation, Ideology and State in Early India," presidential address at the Indian History Congress, ancient India section, 64th session, Mysore, 2003.

Sahu, B.P., "The Early State in Orissa: From the Perspective of Changing Form of Patronage and Legitimation," in: B. Pati, B.P. Sahu & T. Venkatasubramiam, eds., *Negotiating India's Past: Essays in Memory of Partha Sarathi Gupta*, New Delhi, 2002, 29–51.

Sahu, B.P., "Conception of the Kali Age in Early India: A Regional Perspective," *TSSR* 4, 1997, 26–36.

Sastri, K.A.N., *A History of South India from Prehistoric Times to the Fall of Vijayanagara*, Madras, 1955a.

Sastri, K.A.N., *The Cōḻas*, Madras, rev. ed. [2]1955b.

Schnepel, B., *Die Dschungelkönige. Ethnohistorische Aspekte von Politik und Ritual in Südorissa/Indien*, Stuttgart, 1997; ET: *The Jungle Kings: Ethnohistorical Aspects of Politics and Ritual in Orissa*, Delhi, 2002.

Sharma, D.R., *Rajasthan through the Ages*, vol. I: *From the Earliest Times to 1316 A.D.*, Bikaner, 1966.
Sharma, R.S., *Early Medieval Indian Society: A Study in Feudalisation*, Delhi, 2001.
Sharma, R.S., "How Feudal Was Indian Feudalism," in: H. Kulke, ed., *The State in India 1000–1700*, Delhi, 1995, 48–95.
Sharma, R.S., "The Problem of Transition from Ancient to Medieval in Indian History," *IHR* 1, 1974, 1–10.
Sharma, R.S., *Indian Feudalism: C. 300–1200*, Calcutta, 1965.
Shulman, D., *The King and the Clown in South Indian Myth and Poetry*, Princeton, 1985.
Singh, U., ed., *Rethinking Early Medieval India: A Reader*, Delhi, 2011.
Singh, U., *A History of Ancient and Early Medieval India from the Stone Age to the 12th Century*, Delhi, 2008.
Singh, U., *Kings Brāhmaṇas and Temples in Orissa: An Epigraphic Study (300–1147 A.D.)*, Delhi, 1994.
Sinha Kapur, N., *State Formation in Rajasthan: Mewar during the Seventh – Fifteenth Centuries*, Delhi, 2002.
Sircar, D.C., "Landlordism Confused with Feudalism," in: D.C. Sircar, ed., *Land System and Feudalism in Ancient India*, Calcutta, 1966, 57–61.
Smith, V.A., *The Oxford History of India*, Oxford, 1919.
Southall, A., *Alur Society*, Cambridge UK, 1956.
Spencer, G.W., *The Politics of Expansion: The Chola Conquest of Sri Lanka and Srivijaya*, Madras, 1983.
Spencer, G.W., "Religious Networks and Royal Influence in Eleventh Century South India," *JESHO* 12/1, 1969, 42–56.
Stein, B., "The Segmentary State: Interim Reflections," *Puruṣārtha* 13, 1991, 217–288; repr. in H. Kulke, ed., *The State in India 1000–1700*, Delhi, 1995, 134–161.
Stein, B., "State Formation and Economy Reconsidered," *MAS* 19, 1985, 387–413.
Stein, B., *Peasant State and Society in Medieval South India*, Delhi, 1980.
Subbarayalu, Y., *South India under the Cholas*, Delhi, 2012.
Subbarayalu, Y., "The Chola State," *SiH* 4, 1982, 265–306.
Subrahmanyam, S., "Connected Histories: Notes towards a Reconfiguration of Early Modern Eurasian," *MAS* 31, 1997, 735–762.
Teuscher, U., *Königtum in Rajasthan. Legitimation in Mewar des 7. bis 15. Jahrhunderts*, Berlin, 2002.
Thapar, R., *Early India from the Origins to AD 1300*, London, 2002.
Thapar, R., *Cultural Pasts: Essays in Early Indian History*, Delhi, 2000.
Veluthat, K., "Ideology and Legitimation: Early Medieval South India," in: D.N. Jha & E. Vanina, eds., *Mind over Matter: Essays on Mentalities in Medieval India*, Delhi, 2009a, 3–14.
Veluthat, K., *The Early Medieval In South India*, Delhi, 2009b.
Veluthat, K., "The Temple and the State: Religion and Politics in Early Medieval South India," in: R. Champakalakshmi, K. Veluthat & T.R Venugopalan, eds., *State and Society in Pre-modern South India*, Thrissur, 2002, 96–110.
Veluthat, K., *Political Structure of Early Medieval South India: 600–1300 A.D.*, Delhi, 1993.
Veluthat, K., "Royalty and Divinity: Legitimation of Monarchical Power in the South," *Proceedings of the Indian History Congress, 39th session*, Hyderabad, 1979, 231–239.
Venkatasubrahmanian, T.K., "Chiefdom to State: Reflections on the Kaveri Delta Social Formations," Presidential Address at the Indian History Congress, ancient India section, 57th session, Madras, 1996.
Yadava, B.N.S., *Society and Culture in Northern India in the Twelfth Century*, Allahabad, 1973.

Hermann Kulke

Vijayanagara (1336–1646)

The Vijayanagara Empire had arisen out of the chaotic conditions in peninsular India in the first half of the 14th century CE when the earlier Hindu kingdoms of South India and the Deccan had been swept away by the invasions of the Delhi sultans. However, the control of the latter over this region lasted very briefly. Successful revolts against Muḥammad bin Tuġluq, the Delhi sultan, resulted in the emergence of the Vijayanagara Empire around the year 1336 and of the Bahmani Sultanate in 1347. The Vijayanagara Empire lasted for approximately three centuries under four dynasties: Sangama (1336–1485), Saluva (1485–1505), Tuluva (1505–1565), and Aravidu (1565–1646). The greatest of the Vijayanagara monarchs was Kṛṣṇadēvarāya of the Tuluva line, who ruled from 1509 to 1529.

The capital of the first three dynasties was the city of Vijayanagara, situated on the southern bank of the Tuṅgabhadrā River, a tributary of the Kṛṣṇā. From Vijayanagara city they ruled over a fairly large territory, comprising a substantial part of the modern South Indian states of Karnataka and Andhra Pradesh, and almost the whole of Tamil Nadu. In January 1565, at the Battle of Talikota, the Vijayanagara forces suffered a severe military defeat at the hands of a confederacy of the Deccan Sultanates that had arisen on the ruins of the Bahmani state by the early 16th century. Vijayanagara city was sacked and ruined following

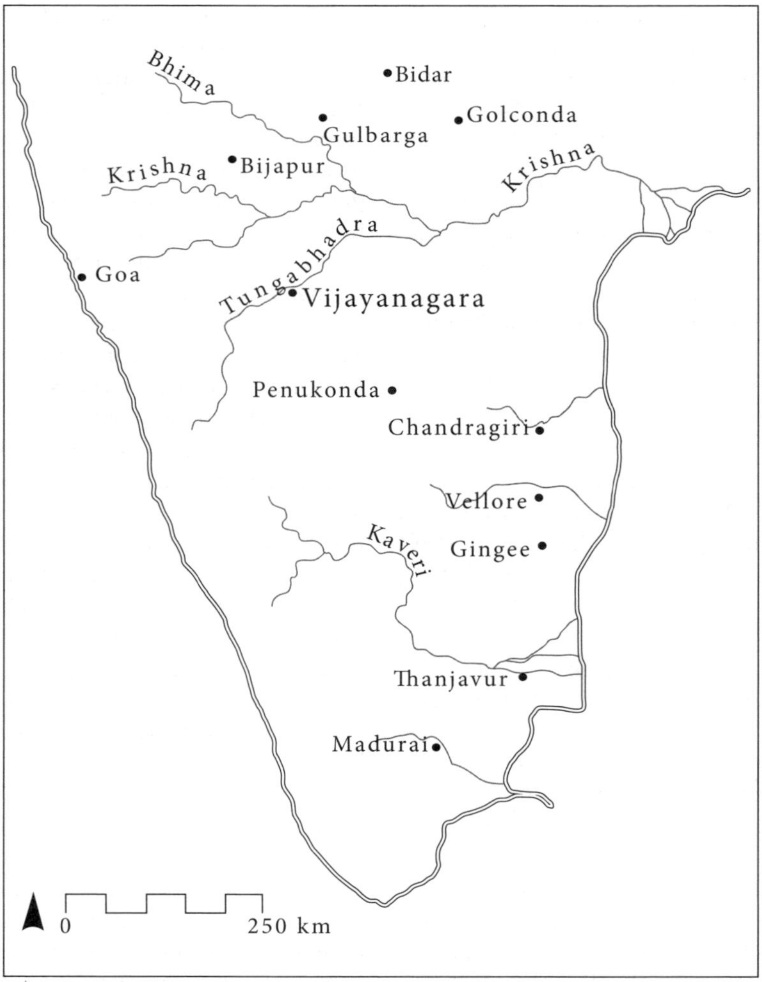

Fig. 1: Map of Peninsular India (by the Vijayanagara Research Project and with the kind permission of its directors, Dr. John M. Fritz and Dr. George Michell).

this debacle at Talikota. Faced with increasing military threat from the Deccan Sultanates, especially Bijapur and Golconda, the Aravidus not only abandoned Vijayanagara city, but also kept moving their capital farther south, first to Penukonda, then to Chandragiri, and finally to Vellore.

In medieval Indian history, Vijayanagara stands out as a "Hindu" polity at a time when the majority of the states in India were ruled by Muslim monarchs. Many historians writing about the nature of the Vijayanagara Empire emphasize that it was a Hindu empire not only promoting Hinduism but also acting as a bulwark against the southward expansion of Islam. This traditional notion regarding the essence of the Vijayanagara state has been challenged by others who claim that "this kind of interpretation stems from a modern nationalist sentiment and an only slightly older indologism" (Stein, 1983, 73). Yet, though the Hindu nature of the Vijayanagara state should not be overstressed, it must be accepted that it did create conditions for the promotion of Hindu culture and institutions, and it succeeded in limiting the expansion of Muslim political power in the Deccan and southern India for over two centuries. At the same time, it must also be mentioned that while actively supporting and encouraging Hinduism and Hindu religious establishments, the Vijayanagara rulers also extended protection and, in some instances, even patronage to persons and institutions of other religious groups, for example, the Jains and Muslims, within their capital and empire.

The centuries just prior to the establishment of the Vijayanagara Empire were marked by intense Hindu religious activity in South India. From the 5th to the 9th century CE, the → Āḻvārs and → Nāyaṉārs of → Tamil Nadu had preached a religion of devotion, rooted in the local language, with focus on → Viṣṇu and → Śiva, respectively. A similar revivalist movement was the 12th-century Vīraśaiva (→ Liṅgāyats) reform spearheaded by the saint → Basava in → Karnataka. Besides these devotional poet-saints who popularized Hinduism by preaching devotion to Śiva or Viṣṇu, between the 8th and 13th centuries CE, South India produced philosopher-saints such as → Śankara, → Rāmānuja, and → Madhva, whose vedantic schools of thought are respectively known as Advaita, Viśiṣṭādvaita, and Dvaita (see → Vedānta). The writings in Sanskrit of these saints and their followers had given Hinduism a sound philosophical base. The Hindu revival in South India that had preceded the founding of the Vijayanagara Empire in the 14th century had led to the virtual disappearance of Buddhism from this region and the relegation of Jainism to a status of the religion of a small, though influential, minority. This Hindu revival was taken forward in South India between the 14th and 16th centuries due to the active encouragement and patronage of the Vijayanagara state.

The support and encouragement extended to Hinduism and its religious men and institutions by the Vijayanagara court and elite are testified to by numerous inscriptions and literary sources. Under the patronage of the early Vijayanagara sovereigns, notably Bukka I (r. 1356–1377), a syndicate of scholars undertook the prodigious task of commenting upon the Saṃhitās of all the four → Vedas and many of the Brāhmaṇas and Āraṇyakas (Nilakanta Sastri, 1958, 331), and a codification of the Hindu philosophical systems was effected in the *Sarvadarśanasaṃgraha*. In order to promote Hindu religious studies, lands in villages and sometimes even whole villages were gifted to individual Brahman scholars or to groups of Brahmans. Also, gifts to ascetics and sectarian leaders by monarchs and other elites were common. For example, Kṛṣṇadēvarāya granted a number of villages to the Madhva saint Vyāsarāya (Verghese, 1995, 3). Endowments were also made to *maṭha*s or monasteries (see also → religious endowments).

The Vijayanagara rulers encouraged pilgrimages within their own empire, possibly to integrate the different language zones within the realm. Besides, visits to the North Indian sacred sites had become increasingly difficult due to the rule over northern India by Muslim rulers. The important pilgrimage centers within the realm included the following: Virupaksapura, Chidambaram, Kalahasti, Tirumala-Tirupati, Kanchipuram, Srisailam, Thiruvannamalai, Harihara, Ahobalam, Srirangam, Jambukeshvaram, Kumbhakonam, Gokarna, and Rameshvaram.

Inscriptions scattered throughout South India bear witness to the benefactions to temples by the Vijayanagara state. The rulers and their subordinates built hundreds of new temples, repaired or made extensive additions to several old ones, settled disputes between temple servants and votaries of rival sects, and endowed temples richly with lands, money, taxes due to the state, and jewels for daily worship or for new festivals that were instituted. Besides state support, temples also enjoyed wide patronage from private donors such as rich individuals, sectarian leaders, professional guilds, and communal groups (Verghese, 1995, 3).

The celebration of public rituals was an important royal function. For it was believed that flourishing festivals would strengthen → *dharma*, establish the presence of divine powers in the kingdom, and stimulate the cosmic flow of → gifts and fertility. During this period the most important royal festival was undoubtedly the nine-day *mahānavamī* celebration, which ended in the tenth day of *daśaharā* or *vijayadaśamī* (Verghese, 1995, 3–4). Domingo Paes, a Portuguese visitor to the court of Kṛṣṇadēvarāya, has left a detailed and vivid account of this festival (Sewell, 1984, 269–274). A careful perusal of his account makes clear that this festival, although basically religious in character, had political, economic, social, and military significance. The focus of the ceremonies was upon the reigning king and the revitalization of his realm. So important was the *mahānavamī* ritual that following the break-up of the Vijayanagara Empire, the court celebration of this festival was adopted by Vijayanagara's successor states, such as Mysore (Verghese, 1995, 4, 105–106). Another important festival celebrated by king and commoner alike was *vasantotsava*, the spring festival, celebrated in the month of *caitra* (Mar–Apr). While the *mahānavamī* pageantry was a dazzling, yet solemn, religious spectacle with the king at the center as a dignified ritualist, *vasantotsava* was a boisterous celebration in which the king, the royal ladies, and the commoners engaged in the free-for-all play with colored water and the enjoyment of dance, music, and drama (Verghese, 1995, 107; Verghese, 2000, 222–238).

The Vijayanagara monarchs of the Sangama dynasty were Śaiva in affiliation, while the rulers of the Saluva, Tuluva, and Aravidu dynasties were Vaiṣṇavas. However, whatever their personal sectarian affiliation, on the whole the rulers extended their support and patronage to all the Hindu sects and temples. The Hindu sects that were important during the Vijayanagara period included the → Smārtas, as well as various groups of Śaivas and Vaiṣṇavas.

The Smārtas are the followers of the Advaita philosophy of Śaṅkarācārya. They worship the five principal deities of Hinduism – Śiva, Viṣṇu, Devī (see → Mahādevī), Sūrya (see → *navagrahas*), and Gaṇeśa (→ Gaṇapati/Gaṇeśa), together known as the *pañcāyatana* – but they give preference to Śiva. The two important *maṭhas*, namely Sringeri in Karnataka and Kanchipuram in Tamil Nadu, besides a number of others, propagated the Smārta religious system and the Advaita philosophy during the Vijayanagara period. The rulers of Vijayanagara, especially the early Sangamas, maintained a close link with the Sringeri *maṭha*, and royal inscriptions from 1346 onward reveal this link (Verghese, 1995, 4). Indeed, the rise to importance of Sringeri dates from this period, for of the pontiffs of this *maṭha*, there is clear historical evidence only from Śrī Vidyātīrtha, who headed the *maṭha* at the time of the foundation of Vijayanagara, onward. So great was the association between the Sringeri *maṭha* and the Vijayanagara polity that one of the popular foundation myths of Vijayanagara city and empire assigns a pivotal role to Śrī Vidyāraṇya, who headed the *maṭha* from 1375 to 1386, to their establishment along with the Sangama brothers, Harihara I and Bukka I. However, this story is based on late texts and spurious records; epigraphical evidence demonstrates that Vidyāraṇya became highly influential only from the period of the reign of the third Sangama ruler, Harihara II (1377–1404; Verghese, 1995, 111).

Prior to the Vijayanagara period, the → Pāśupata sect and its offshoots, the → Kāpālika and the Kālamukha, were important Śaiva sects. But the Pāśupatas and the Kāpālikas appear to have lost their influence by the time of the origin of Vijayanagara. The Kālamukhas were very popular in South India between the 9th and the 14th centuries. They were so called because of the black streak worn across the forehead (Briggs, 1938, 223). A number of Kālamukha *gurus* were associated with the early Sangama rulers (Verghese, 1995, 112). However, after the 15th century, we do not hear anymore about the Kālamukhas; they appear to have been absorbed into the reformist Vīraśaiva sect. This is indicated by the fact that many of the former Kālamukha temples and *maṭhas* were henceforth controlled by Vīraśaivas. Even more significant, perhaps, is the fact that few Vīraśaivas are found in areas not formerly dominated by the Kālamukhas (Lorenzen, 1972, 170).

Another school of Śaivism that flourished in the Deccan during this period was the → Nāth Sampradāya. The followers of this sect are known as Nāth *yogīs*, or → Kānphaṭās. They are votaries of Śiva and Śakti (see → Mahādevī), with a strong bias toward the Śākta tradition. The 15th-century Telugu work *Navanāthacaritramu* by Gauranna mentions members of this sect in Andhra. Srisailam was an important center of this sect, and it was also popular in coastal Karnataka during this period (Verghese, 1995, 5). The Italian traveler Pietro Della Valle, who passed through Mangalore in 1623 CE, gives a detailed account of a Nāth monastery at Kadiri (Grey, 1892, vol. II, 345–352). In many Vijayanagara period monuments, both within the capital city as well as elsewhere in the empire, we come across sculptural representations of the Nāth *yogīs* or *siddhas* (Verghese, 2001, 179–187; Shaw, 2011, 236–248), which indicates the presence and activities of votaries of this sect.

Another important Śaiva school was that of the Tamil → Śaiva Siddhānta. It is based on the Vedas, the 28 → Śaiva Āgamas and their Upāgamas, and the mystical poems of the Śaiva saints of Tamil Nadu, namely, the 63 Nāyaṉārs. Perhaps, the most influential Śaiva sect during this period was the Vīraśaiva sect. Vīraśaivas are also known as Liṅgāyats on account of the → *liṅga* that the followers of this sect wear on their person. Besides the Vedas, the Śaiva Āgamas, and the → Purāṇas, the Vīraśaivas also accept the authority of the 63 Nāyaṉārs and the 770 later Vīraśaiva saints. It is believed that the later Sangama rulers belonged to this sect. Some Vīraśaivas rose high in state service in the mid-15th century (Verghese, 1995, 5, 112).

There were a number of important Śiva temples and pilgrimage sites in the Vijayanagara Empire. The principal deity of Vijayanagara city, the site that is now known as Hampi, was a local deity called Virūpākṣa, a form of Śiva. The Virūpākṣa cult and temple had already gained prominence at the site by the 12th century CE. However, it was only with the establishment of the Vijayanagara Kingdom and its capital at Hampi that the Virūpākṣa cult gained immense popularity; the temple assumed the proportions of one of the great temples of southern India and a major center of pilgrimage. The foundation stories of the capital city and empire reveal that the selection of this site as their capital by the founders of the Vijayanagara polity was not accidental, for besides the strategic importance of this spot, its links with Virūpākṣa was a prime reason for the choice. The founders, sons of a chieftain named Saṅgama, adopted Virūpākṣa as their family deity, and this tradition was continued by the entire Sangama dynasty. Their dynasty, capital, and empire were placed under the special protection of god Virūpākṣa. Even though the personal and family deities of the monarchs of the Saluva, Tuluva, and Aravidu dynasties were Vaiṣṇava deities, they retained Virūpākṣa as the patron deity of the empire for as long as Hampi-Vijayanagara remained the capital and even for a couple of decades after the shift of the capital in 1565 (Verghese, 1995, 17–19; Verghese, 2000, 97).

The first Vijayanagara monarch adopted "Śrī Virūpākṣa" as his sign manual, and this was continued by the subsequent Sangama rulers and even by the Saluvas, Tuluvas, and first two Aravidu rulers. Many inscriptions of Vijayanagara rulers end with this sign manual, which takes the place of the signature of the respective ruler. Besides kings, very occasionally members of the royal family or others closely associated with it also used the sign manual of "Śrī Virūpākṣa" (Verghese, 2000, 98). Prior to the establishment of the Vijayanagara Empire, the temple of Virūpākṣa at Hampi was a fairly small shrine. During the Vijayanagara period, the Virūpākṣa cult and temple reached the peak of favor and popularity from the mid-14th century to the early 16th century, that is, from the foundation of the state until the end of the reign of Kṛṣṇadēvarāya. As a result, the temple was greatly expanded with the addition of pillared halls and galleries, subshrines, towering gateways, two enclosure walls, and a long chariot street in front (Verghese 2000, 99). Numerous benefactions were also made to the Virūpākṣa temple of gifts of land, jewelry, and money by kings, members of the royal family, and private donors (Verghese, 2000, 100–102).

An interesting Vijayanagara practice was that of often recording grants made by kings and even others in the presence of a deity; evidently the god was invoked as a witness. A careful perusal of all such grants registered at Vijayanagara city during the entire period that it served as the capital highlights the importance of Virūpākṣa, since the overwhelming majority were those made in his presence. The only other deity before whom a sizeable number of donations were recorded was god Viṭṭhala, whose temple in Vijayanagara city was the most important Vaiṣṇava one; but these grants made in the presence of Viṭṭhala number only about one-third those registered in the presence of Virūpākṣa. A study of inscriptions recording grants made in the presence of these two divinities reveals an interesting shift. While under the Sangamas practically all such grants were made with Virūpākṣa as witness, in the Tuluva period, a change is evident, with gradually more being registered in the presence of Viṭṭhala (Verghese, 2000, 103–104). The outstanding importance of Virūpākṣa during the Vijayanagara

Fig. 2: Virūpākṣa Temple at Hampi-Vijayanagara, seen from its chariot street (photo by Anila Verghese).

period resulted in two more temples to this deity being set up within the capital city and a number being founded elsewhere in the empire (Verghese, 2000, 104–107).

There were a number of other important Śaiva deities and temples within the Vijayanagara territory, which received extensive patronage during these centuries and which emerged or continued as major pilgrimage centers. One of the greatest Śaiva temples within the Vijayanagara Empire was the one at Srisailam in the Andhra zone enshrining the Mallikārjuna *liṅga*. This is considered to be one of the twelve *jyotirliṅga*s (see → *liṅga*) and hence a very important pilgrimage spot. In this temple there are inscriptions that record the benefactions of a number of Vijayanagara monarchs as well as grants made by chiefs and others during this period. Just as the importance of the Virūpākṣa Temple of Hampi resulted in the setting up of temples to him in other parts of the empire, similarly Śiva as Mallikārjuna came to be enshrined in temples within the capital city and elsewhere (Verghese, 1995, 26–27). Besides the *jyotirliṅga*s, in South India the elemental *liṅga*s of earth, fire, water, and so on are also revered, and the sites associated with these were significant pilgrimage centers. Among these, three appear to have received patronage from Vijayanagara royalty, particularly Kṛṣṇadēvarāya, namely Kalahasti in the Andhra zone and Thiruvannamalai and Chidambaram in the Tamil area. Kalahasti is not far from the great Vaiṣṇava pilgrimage center of Tirumala-Tirupati, which Kṛṣṇadēvarāya visited seven times during his reign. On many of his visits to Tirumala-Tirupati, the king also visited Kalahasti and made rich donations to this temple, including the construction of a great *gopura* (gateway of a South Indian temple) in 1517 (Verghese, 2011, 115–127). The king also visited the Aruṇācalēcuvar Temple at Thiruvannamalai during the course of his great tour of pilgrimage of his southern territories that he embarked on in 1516–1517, and he is credited with building a *gopura* there and making other additions to the temple including that of a thousand-pillar hall (*Annual Report on South Indian Epigraphy*, 1902, no. 574). Chidambaram, which had been a major Śaiva center during the Chola period, continued to be fairly important during the Vijayanagara period as well. In Chidambaram, Kṛṣṇadēvarāya is believed to have constructed the northern *gopura* of the temple (*Annual Report on South Indian Epigraphy*, 1913, no. 371).

Virūpākṣa, Mallikārjuna, Kālahastīśvara, and Aruṇācalēcuvar are worshipped only in the aniconic form of the *liṅga*. There are other minor Śaiva deities, worshipped in the iconic form, who were also popular during the Vijayanagara period, among which mention must be made of Vīrabhadra and Nandi; the popularity of both was largely due to the wide prevalence of Vīraśaivism, for both these divinities were venerated by members of this sect. Vīrabhadra is one of the *saṃhāra*, or destructive, aspects of Śiva. The myth of the origin of Vīrabhadra provides a clue to his popularity with the Vīraśaivas. He was especially created by Śiva to destroy the *yajña* of Dakṣa and to wreak havoc on the sacrificial place (see → Pārvatī). Therefore, the Vīraśaivas, who reject vedic traditions, have a special affinity to him. The most important Vīrabhadra temple in the Vijayanagara Empire was the temple at Lepakshi in Andhra, which was greatly expanded in the 16th century by the brothers Virūpaṇṇa and Vīraṇṇa, important chieftains during the reign of the Tuluva king Acyutarāya (1529–1542). The king also made grants to this temple (Verghese, 1995, 23–24). The cult of Nandi or Nandikeśvara, Śiva's vehicle and a great Śaiva devotee, was of importance for the Vīraśaivas because Basava, the founder of this sect, is considered to be an incarnation of Nandi. Besides all these Śaiva deities, of course, Gaṇeśa was also a popular divinity in those days as in other periods.

In pre-Vijayanagara times, Vaiṣṇavism had received a great boost in South India due to the work of two great *ācārya*s or teachers (→ *gurus* and *ācārya*s), Rāmānuja and Madhva in the 11th–12th and 13th-early 14th centuries, respectively. Rāmānujācārya followed in the tradition of the Āḻvārs, whose devotional songs in Tamil in praise of Viṣṇu had been compiled into the *Nālāyira Tivya Pirapantam* (*Nālāyira Divya Prabandam*). The Āḻvārs were followed by a line of teachers, of whom the greatest was Rāmānuja. According to his system, Viṣṇu is the supreme deity, accompanied by → Śrī Lakṣmī, who represents divine → grace. That is why this religious movement is known as → Śrīvaiṣṇavism. It won many followers in Tamil Nadu and also in Karnataka. In the early 14th century, Śrīvaiṣṇavism split into two subsects, the Vaṭakalai or the northern school and the Teṉkalai or southern school. Among the main differences between the two is that the Vaṭakalais favor the Sanskrit philosophical literature, while the Teṉkalais give more importance to the Tamil *Nālāyira Tivya Pirapantam*. Also, according to the Vaṭakalais, for the attainment of salvation (see → liberation), individual effort is the first step, while for the Teṉkalais, only surrender to the lord is necessary. Madhva preached the philosophy of Dvaita in Karnataka and a religion of devotion to Viṣṇu. The → Kṛṣṇa *maṭha* at Udupi where Madhvācārya set up a temple of Śrī → Kṛṣṇa is the historical and spiritual center of the Madhva sect. Madhva is believed to have set up eight *maṭhas* in Udupi for the conduct of worship in this temple. It is, however, three other *maṭhas* founded by some of his closest disciples and their successors that had a wider influence in South India, namely the Vyāsarāya Maṭha, the Rāghavendra Maṭha, and the Uttarādi Maṭha (see also → Mādhva Sampradāya). Both Śrīvaiṣṇavism and Mādhvaism had a wide following during the Vijayanagara period (Verghese, 1995, 6, 113).

Mādhva and Śrīvaiṣṇava ascetics and teachers were active in Vijayanagara city and empire. A number of Mādhva monks had come into the area in and around Hampi even before the founding of the Vijayanagara state. Many continued to be active here during the empire period, the most famous of all being Vyāsarāya, who was very influential during the reigns of the founder of the Saluva line as well as those of Kṛṣṇadēvarāya and Acyutarāya (Verghese, 1995, 113–114). A special place of honor belongs to the *bhakta* poet-saints known as Haridāsas (see → Smārtas), many of whom were disciples of Mādhva ascetics. Since the Haridāsas were particularly devoted to Viṭṭhala, and with Hampi-Vijayanagara becoming a major center of the Viṭṭhala cult, Vijayanagara city was frequented by them. Vyāsarāya greatly popularized the Haridāsa movement, and some of the greatest of the Haridāsas, including Purandaradāsa and Kanakadāsa, were his disciples. While the Mādhvas were active in Vijayanagara city and empire from the 14th century onward, the Śrīvaiṣṇavas gained ground mainly under the Saluvas, Tuluvas, and Aravidus. A number of Śrīvaiṣṇava *guru*s became influential at court. Some of the illustrious Śrīvaiṣṇava families during this time were the Tātācāryas, the Tāḷḷapāka family of poet-saints, and the Kandāḍai and Bhaṭṭar families (Verghese, 1995, 113–114).

Although the Śrīvaiṣṇavas worship all the forms of Viṣṇu and his incarnations, the most important deities and temple sites for them are the following: Raṅganātha of Srirangam, Śrīnivāsa (or Veṅkaṭeśa or Tiruveṅkalanātha; see → Veṅkaṭeśvara) of Tirumala-Tirupati, and Varadarāja of Kanchipuram. All these, particularly the temple at Tirumala-Tirupati, enjoyed tremendous patronage during the Vijayanagara times, especially under the second, third, and fourth dynasties.

The pilgrimage site of Tirumala-Tirupati figures in the earliest Tamil secular literature of the Caṅkam age (see → Tamil texts) and also in the poems of the Āḻvārs. After a long history as a sacred pilgrimage place, the temple at Tirumala-Tirupati rose to the status of a great temple in the Vijayanagara period. The Sangamas were Śaivas and hence less interested in this Viṣṇu temple. In the mid-15th century, the temple attracted the attention of the Saluva family, whose base was in this area. Sāḷuva Narasiṃha was an important patron while still only a military commander, and when he became king, full imperial patronage was extended to this temple by him, and this continued under the Tuluvas and the Aravidu rulers as well. Due to extensive patronage, in the 16th century, it emerged as the greatest temple in South India. Of the 1250 inscriptions from Tirumala-Tirupati that have been published, a disproportionately large number of inscriptions belong to the Vijayanagara period (Sastry, 1930, 2–3). Fewer than 150 are of the pre-Vijayanagara period. The maximum are of the reign periods of Kṛṣṇadēvarāya, namely 221, and of Acyutarāya, namely 251. Kṛṣṇadēvarāya made seven visits to the temple, often with his two queens, and on each occasion he made lavish donations. Acyutarāya even had himself crowned king in this temple. The statues of Kṛṣṇadēvarāya with his two queens and of Acyutarāya with his consort, all facing the sanctum sanctorum, are prominently placed just inside the main *gopura* of the temple (Verghese, 1995, 69–74). So great was the popularity of Tiruveṅkalanātha of Tirumala-Tirupati that in Vijayanagara city and its environs, at least eight temples and shrines were set up for him, the greatest of which was the Tiruveṅkalanātha Temple built in 1534 CE by Salakarāja Tirumala, the brother-in-law and prime minister of Acyutarāya, in a suburb named Achyutarayapura (*South Indian Inscriptions*, IX/2, no. 564).

Of the three great Śrīvaiṣṇava temples, the one at Srirangam dedicated to Raṅganātha, a reclining form of Viṣṇu, is undoubtedly the most sacred. This spiritual center of immense sanctity was sacked in the early 14th-century invasions of the Delhi Sultanate armies into southern India, and worship in it was temporarily halted. The reconsecration of the temple and the restoration of worship in it occurred due to Vijayanagara state patronage during the 14th century. Even though the Tirumala-Tirupati Temple received more donations during the 16th century, the Raṅganātha Temple consistently continued to receive extensive

Fig. 3: Aerial view of the Tiruveṅkalanātha Temple of 1534 CE at Hampi-Vijayanagara (photograph by Anna L. Dallapiccola, used by courtesy).

benefactions from both state and private donors right through the Vijayanagara period. The popularity of the cult of Raṅganātha is evident from the fact that there are a number of temples dedicated to this deity in Hampi-Vijayanagara as well (Verghese, 1995, 75–77).

The Varadarājasvāmi Temple at Kanchipuram, the third great Śrīvaiṣṇava pilgrimage center, did flourish during the Vijayanagara period. However, it did not enjoy the same level of patronage, from either state or private donors, as did those at Tirumala-Tirupati and Srirangam. During this period, the maximum benefactions were received by it from Kṛṣṇadēvarāya and Acyutarāya. There is no evidence of any temple of this divinity at the site of Hampi-Vijayanagara (Verghese 1995, 77–78).

The Mādhvas in particular and the Śrīvaiṣṇavas, though to a lesser extent, are great devotees of Kṛṣṇa. Mādhvas worship Kṛṣṇa as a baby boy; Viṭṭhala is considered to be a form of Kṛṣṇa (Verghese, 1995, 54). Yet, Kṛṣṇa worship, though extant in the Vijayanagara Empire, did not assume the status of a major cult. In 1515 Kṛṣṇadēvarāya installed in the capital city a *mūrti* of Bālakṛṣṇa ("Boy Kṛṣṇa") in a grandiose temple that he built within a suburb named Krishnapura (*South Indian Inscriptions*, IV, nos. 254, 255). Though the main center of Viṭṭhala worship is Pandharpur in → Maharashtra, Viṭṭhala was a popular deity in South India, particularly Karnataka, even before the founding of the Vijayanagara Empire. The most important center of Viṭṭhala worship within the empire was the great Viṭṭhala Temple in the capital city, which in the mid-16th century, especially the two and a half decades before the sack and destruction of the city in 1565 CE, received such extensive patronage that it emerged as the major religious center in Vijayanagara city, eclipsing in popularity and grandeur even the Virūpākṣa Temple (Verghese 1995, 63–65). The Kṛṣṇa and Viṭṭhala temples in Vijayanagara city, though there was Mādhva activity in them, appear to have been served by Śrīvaiṣṇava *pujārī*s (Verghese, 1995, 58–59, 65–66).

Besides the abovementioned great temples and cults, there were also many others. For example, Harihara, the syncretic deity who is half Viṣṇu and half Śiva, had his own following, with two kings of Vijayanagara bearing this name. The main center of Harihara worship in South India is the Harihareśvara Temple at Harihara in the Chitradurga district of Karnataka. This temple, which was in existence before the foundation of the Vijayanagara polity, continued to be highly popular during this period also. Folk and minor deities were also worshipped. For example, throughout South India the village deities are usually folk goddesses, and this tradition continued during the Vijayanagara times as well. → Hanumān, whose birthplace was believed to be very close to Hampi, was a very popular divinity in the capital city. Great veneration was also accorded to women who became → *satī*s and to men who died in a heroic manner. Therefore, numerous *satī* stones and hero stones are found in the capital city and elsewhere in the empire.

This brief survey demonstrates the vibrancy of Hinduism in the Vijayanagara period. Under the protection and patronage of the Vijayanagara polity, Hindu religion and religious institutions undoubtedly flourished.

Bibliography

Annual Reports on South Indian Epigraphy, publ. The Archaeological Survey of India, Madras, 1887ff.

Briggs, G.W., *Gorakhnath and the Kanphata Yogis*, Calcutta, 1938.

Grey, E., ed., *The Travels of Pietro Della Valle in India*, 2 vols., London, 1892.

Lorenzen, D.N., *The Kāpālikas and Kālāmukhas: Two Lost Śaivite Sects*, New Delhi, 1972.

Nilakanta Sastri, K.A., *A History of South India: From Prehistoric Times to the fall of Vijayanagar*, Bombay, [2]1958.

Sastry, S.S., *Report on the Inscriptions of the Devasthanam Collection with Illustrations*, Madras, 1930.

Sewell, R., *A Forgotten Empire*, Delhi, repr. 1984.

Shaw, R., "Shaivite Ascetic Iconography: Important Associations between Srisailam, Hampi-Vijayanagara and Sringeri," in: A. Verghese & A.L. Dallapiccola, eds., *South India under Vijayanagara: Art and Archaeology*, New Delhi, 2011, 236–248.

South Indian Inscriptions, publ. The Archaeological Survey of India, 23 vols., Madras, 1890–1979.

Stein, Burton, "Vijayanagara and the Transition to Patrimonial System," in: A.L. Dallapiccola, ed., *Vijayanagara – City and Empire: New Currents of Research*, Stuttgart, vol. I, 1983, 73–87.

Verghese, A., "Krsnadevaraya's Grants and Constructional Activities Related to His Kalinga War (A.D.1513–1517)," *JAsSM* 83, 2011, 115–127.

Verghese, A., "A Rare Depiction of Nine *Yogis* in the Somesvara Temple, Ulsoor," *JAsSB* 75, 2001, 179–187.

Verghese, A., *Archaeology, Art and Religion: New Perspectives on Vijayanagara*, New Delhi, 2000.

Verghese, A., *Religious Traditions at Vijayanagara: As Revealed through the Monuments*, Delhi, 1995.

Anila Verghese

Mughal Empire (1526–1759)

The origins of the Mughal Empire date back to 1526, when the Timurid ruler of central Asia – Bābūr – invaded North India in the final years of the Delhi Sultanate, which ruled over North India between 1206 and 1526. Bābūr ruled from 1526 to 1530, and after his death, the fight for the control of North India was continued by his son, Humāyūn. Humāyūn ruled over North India between 1530 and 1538, when he was overthrown by the Afghan ruler Šīr Šāh Sūrī (r. 1540–1545). Afghan rule over North India continued until 1555, at which point Humāyūn managed to regain control of North India, only to then die the following year from injuries sustained in a fall. The territories over which Humāyūn ruled fell to the hands of his son Akbar (r. 1556–1605), who was 14 years old at the time of his ascension to his father's throne. Akbar ruled with the aid of his regent Bairam Ḫān until 1560, at which point Akbar began to assume the reins of power himself. During his reign, Akbar took over the fortress cities of Agra, Delhi, Lahore, and Jaunpur; conquered the Hindu Rājpūt kingdoms in Rajasthan; and occupied the Punjab, Gujarat, and Bengal as well.

When his reign as emperor ended, Akbar left his successors a sprawling empire that stretched from Kabul to Kashmir, from the Punjab to Gujarat, and from Bengal to Assam. He also bequeathed to them a highly centralized structure of governance that endured for the existence of the empire. This included a bureaucratic structure manned by both Hindus and Muslims – a standardized system of revenue collection and land assessment that would provide the foundation for a prosperous economy and the use of Persian as the official language of governance across the land. Akbar and his forefathers were Turks of the Timurid dynasty, but in India, this Turkish-speaking elite of Central Asia were known as Mughals or Mongols. Thus, the empire that Akbar established in North India came to be known as the Mughal Empire.

Jahāngīr (r. 1605–1627), whose reign was marked by two rebellions led by his sons, succeeded Akbar in 1605. The first rebellion, carried out by Prince Ḫusraw (1587–1622), was defeated and was followed later by another rebellion by his second son, Ḫurram, in 1622. Ḫurram was defeated, was exiled to the Deccan, and returned to Agra after his father's death in 1627. Ḫurram became Šāh Jahān (1627–1658), the great Mughal patron of the arts who commissioned the now famous Taj Mahal. Šāh Jahān's sons, Dārā Šikōh (1615–1658) and Awrangzēb (Aurangzeb), began fighting for the throne when Šāh Jahān fell ill in 1657. One year later, Awrangzēb (r. 1658–1707) won the succession battle, and, after imprisoning his father, he began his long reign as the last great emperor of the Mughal Empire. Awrangzēb's attempts to expand his empire into the Deccan by trying to quell the territorial expansion efforts of the Hindu chiefs known as the → Marathas triggered what came to be known as Deccan Wars. The Deccan campaigns began to place serious economic stress on the empire and, in turn, helped cause the Afghan Rebellions between 1667 and 1675, the Jāṭ Rebellion of 1669, and the Satnāmī Rebellion of 1672. When Awrangzēb died in 1707, his attempts to expand Mughal territories in the Deccan ultimately failed, and the empire began to slowly decline after years of economic and political turmoil.

Awrangzēb's son, Bahādur Šāh I (r. 1707–1712), managed to quell the many crises that plagued the empire, but after his death, the empire became embroiled in succession battles and power struggles. After Bahādur Šāh's death in 1712, the empire witnessed a series of four short-lived reigns between 1712 and 1719 before the 29-year rule of Muḥammad Šāh (r. 1719–1748). Muḥammad Šāh, however, no longer ruled over a united empire. The empire had disintegrated into smaller successor states, Delhi was sacked by the Afghan Nādir Šāh in 1739, and other portions of the empire fell into the hands of the British. The more the British continued to expand across North India, the more Mughal territories were reduced, until in 1759, Emperor Šāh ʿĀlam II (r. 1759–1806) was forced to accept British suzerainty. The last two Mughal emperors who followed Šāh ʿĀlam II – Akbar Šāh II (r. 1806–1837) and Bahādūr Šāh II (r. 1837–1858) – were reduced to being titular rulers under British protection. When, in 1857, Bahādūr Šāh II was deposed by the British and exiled to Burma for his participation in the 1857 Sepoy Rebellion against the British, the Mughal Empire ceased to exist.

The Creation and Administration of the Mughal State

Mughal political authority was based in large part on the divine right to rule. Akbar's chief ideologue, Abū al-Fażl ʿAllāmī (1551–1602), traced the lineage of the ruling emperors back to Adam in order to underline that they belonged to all of humanity and that the divine wisdom the emperors had received from God through Adam was to be used in the interests of the state (Richards, 1998, 143–150). Mughal rule, then, was based on the concept of paterfamilias. The empire was like a large family, and the emperor was a divine fatherlike figure who used his power and wisdom as absolute ruler for the prosperity and well-being of those under his care (Mukhia, 2004, 51–52). This emphasis on good governance and social stability meant that the Mughals were not interested in decimating their enemies and reducing them to a state of servitude. There was no doubt that the wars fought against their opponents were brutal and could bring about widespread destruction, but once territories were won, Mughal royal ideology stressed that the emperor was to show mercy on his opponents by encompassing them and making them active participants within the larger imperial political structure. This was, in part, achieved through the practice of cementing marriage alliances with members of the Hindu Rājpūt kingdoms (see → Rajasthan kingdoms). Once the Rājpūts accepted Mughal suzerainty by marrying one of their daughters to the emperor, they were invited to join the Mughal nobility and were allowed to remain as the titular heads of their lands so they could maintain their religious and social customs. The effect of this practice was threefold. Firstly, the composition of the Mughal nobility came to reflect the ethnic diversity of the empire, with Hindus taking their place among the elite of Mughal society along with those of Central Asian and Iranian descent. Secondly, the marriage alliances reinforced the image of the emperor as a benevolent and compassionate figure willing to shelter even the conquered underneath his wing. Thirdly, it enabled the emperor to form a vast kinship structure that could help maintain his empire.

The Structure of the Mughal State

The resulting structure that encompassed not only the Mughal nobility but also the entire governing structure of the empire came to be known as the *manṣabdārī* system. Those who held administrative and military posts in the Mughal Empire were assigned a particular numerical rank (*manṣab*) personally by the emperor that ranged from 10 to 5,000, with a ranking of 500 being necessary to be considered a member of the Mughal nobility. Lower-ranking *manṣab* holders (*manṣabdār*s) may have occupied administrative positions as scribes or accountants and were paid in cash directly from the imperial treasury. Noblemen (*amīr*s) tended to hold the higher-ranking military and bureaucratic positions such as governorships in the *manṣabdārī* system and were expected to maintain a military entourage that was for the use not only of the individual nobleman but also of the emperor when he needed it. Noblemen were quite frequently posted by the emperor in different parts of the empire in order to maintain imperial authority and, consequently, they were given *jāgīr*s. *Jāgīr*s could only be held by noblemen and referred to lands assigned to members of the nobility as a form of salary. The *jāgīr* could consist of a single village or groups of villages over which the nobleman in his capacity as a landowner (*jāgīrdār*) could collect revenue. A portion of the revenue went to the imperial government in Delhi, while the rest was kept by the individual nobleman as a salary and to maintain his household and military entourage.

*Jāgīr*s, however, were never meant to be personal fiefdoms. The imperial government was all too aware of the possibility that a *jāgīr* could become the power base around which opposition to the emperor could coalesce. Consequently, noblemen could not have any military or administrative control over their *jāgīr*s nor would the emperor give them a permanent posting in a particular region. Noblemen, instead, were regularly shifted by the emperor to various postings across the empire in order to prevent the creation of regional powerbases that could threaten the emperor's authority. The *manṣabdār*s, then, were largely the creation of the emperor. Their fate in the Mughal administrative system was purely dependent on the emperor, who could elevate or devalue their *manṣab* ranking or circumvent the power of *jāgīrdār*s by using the imperial government to control their movements by frequent re-postings throughout the empire (Shivram, 2008, 56–78).

The *manṣabdārī* system was a highly ordered administrative system that revolved around the ruling emperor and carried out his authority using a lexicon of standardized imperial terminology. All government business was carried out in Persian, and property rights, criminal law, and even currency became standardized throughout the empire. The imperial government consisted of a chief administrator (*dīwān*) who was responsible for the supervision of all government postings as well as all matters related to finance ranging from revenue collection to audits and budgetary reviews. The *mīr baḫšī*, who was ranked directly below the *dīwān*, was responsible for supervising the assignations of rankings, and he also served as chief intelligence officer for the emperor throughout the empire. Below the *mīr baḫšī* was the chief ecclesiastical officer (*ṣadr*), whose principal role was the administration of religious charities and to advise the emperor on which religious communities should be deemed eligible as tax-exempt charities.

The administration at the central level was then replicated at the level of the provinces (*ṣūbaḥ*) into which the empire was divided. Each province was run by a governor (*nāẓim*) who was directly answerable to the emperor himself, while the provincial *dīwān*s, *baḫšī*s, and *ṣadr*s answered directly to their imperial counterparts. The provinces were divided into *sarkār*s or districts whose law and order were maintained by the *faujdār*, while in the *pargana*s or subdistricts, there were judges (*qāżī*s) and two officials known as the *qānūngo* and *čaudarī* who dealt with tax assessments and revenue collection. These two individuals were appointed by the governor but answered directly to the emperor himself (Habib, 2009, 77–86; Streusand, 2011, 264–272).

The Mughal Economy

The Mughal Empire was agrarian in nature, and it was the revenue generated from this agrarian economy that helped sustain the empire's material well-being. With the greatest population concentration in the Mughal Empire centered on the fertile Gangetic Plain, a substantial agrarian surplus was ensured for the empire with the help of the monsoon rains and imperial investment in infrastructure in the form of dams, canals, and other forms of irrigation. This surplus included wheat, rice, barley, tobacco, cotton, and hemp, which then formed the basis for a manufacturing sector that produced goods for overseas trading that included cotton textiles, silk products, refined sugars, alcohol, and opium. Thus, the revenue demands placed on the peasantry and artisanal sections of Mughal society were quite high. These groups sold their goods at the market for cash, but it is estimated that close to one-third of their revenue was extracted for taxation and distributed to appointed recipients at the provincial and *pargana* level before the remainder was sent to the imperial treasury (Streusand, 2011, 273–279).

The empire, although being agrarian in nature, was connected to both overland and overseas trade routes. Overland routes crisscrossed the entire Mughal Empire and connected Delhi and Agra to important urban centers in western and eastern India and other major centers in northern and central India such as Varanasi and Burhanpur. The diversity of this trade was managed by a specialized group of traders named Banjaras who managed the overland transport of goods by using large convoys of bullock carts that could number into the thousands, while the overseas routes were managed by the Baniyas or the Hindu and Jain mercantile communities that were centered in the coastal towns of Surat and Ahmedabad in Gujarat. The Baniyas were given great latitude by the Mughals because their trade with Europeans ensured that the empire became a major center of international trade. This, in turn, helped the imperial government to achieve a type of economic integration into international markets that paralleled the attempts at political integration that the Mughals were hoping to achieve domestically. Thus, the Baniyas came to amass such great wealth that they ventured into the world of high finance by becoming bankers (*ṣarrāf*s) and brokers who could use their financial power as leverage in dealing with European traders (Moosvi, 2005, 141–145). The 17th-century Baniya of Surat, Vīrjī Vorā, for example, had amassed a huge fortune through his trade ventures and would take advantage of the chronic cash shortage faced by English and Dutch traders in India to charge them extremely high interest loans. Vorā would then manipulate the disbursement of these loans to further his business interests. Thus, for example, when the British refused to transport goods belonging to Vorā and his fellow merchants to the Persian Gulf, Vorā immediately asked the British for the immediate repayment of a 30,000-rupee debt. The British, unable to pay the debt, capitulated instead to Vorā's demands to transport their goods (Mehta, 1991, 55–58).

Religion and State in the Mughal Empire

The success of the Mughal Empire, therefore, was built on the successful integration of diverse political and economic interests into a single governing structure managed by a highly complex imperial bureaucracy. How did the state, however, endeavor to manage the vast religious diversity of North India? During the Sultanate period, the group of Muslim scholars and jurists known collectively as *ʿulamā* had firmly established themselves in North India with the help of state religious patronage, and their influence in Muslim society was rivaled only by the presence of the Islamic mystics known as Sufis. A large section of the population was attracted to Sufi masters (*šayḫs*) not only for their religious knowledge but also because they were seen as miracle workers whose blessings were to be sought in times of difficulties. This type of charisma extended well beyond the *šayḫ*'s death. The divine power of the deceased *šayḫ* was said to remain within his tomb (*dargāh*) and was transferred to his descendants, who continued the practice of spiritual instruction through the formation of orders (*silsila*s; Siddiqui, 1989). During the sultanate period, the support of Sufi orders, such as the Čištīs, Firdawsīs, Qādirīs, Naqšbandīs, and Suhrawardīs, was seen as essential to legitimizing a ruler's power (Grewal, 2006, 324–329; Schimmel, 2004, 121–124). The role of the Sufis in North Indian society, however, was not without controversy. The Delhi-based Čištiyya order, for example, was known for its contentious relationship with the Delhi sultans and had raised the ire of the *ʿulamā* for its introduction of ecstatic singing as a means of inducing spiritual ecstasy.

The Sufis, however, were not the only community that ran into conflict with sections of the Muslim community in western India. Two communities that established themselves in India during the sultanate period – the Ismāʿīlī branch of Šīʿa Islam and the orthodox Sunni sect known as the Mahdawīs – both encountered opposition to their bases in western India because, in addition to the Prophet Muḥammad, they accepted their own religious heads as sources of authority. In the case of the Mahdawīs, they viewed their leader Muḥammad Kāẓimī (1443–1505) as a type of messianic figure who would establish a new age of righteousness on earth. The presence of the Ismāʿīlīs and the Mahdawīs would later set the stage for the Rawšānīs. The founder of the Rawšānīs – Bāyāzīd Anṣārī (1525–1572) – proclaimed that he possessed mystical powers and exhorted his followers among Afghan tribesmen to take up arms against anyone who opposed his religious authority, including the Mughals. The movement proved to be unsuccessful. Bāyāzīd and his successor Jalāl al-Dīn were both killed by the Mughals (Ahmad, 2006, 303–309).

The Islamic presence in North India had a profound impact on the region's religious landscape. The fall of Hindu kingdoms to the rulers of the Sultanate resulted in a decline of state patronage for Brahmanical learning in major pilgrimage centers clustered around the Gangetic Plain (Chandra, 2003a, 295–299). The resulting void in religious leadership within Hindu society came to be filled by non-Brahmanical castes. In pilgrimage centers, like Varanasi, for example, state patronage of Hindu religious and educational institutions was replaced at the local level by wealthy Vaiśya or mercantile communities, while other forms of religious leadership in North India came from the → Sants, whose sharp critique of Brahmanical Hinduism was voiced by their lower-caste membership of weavers, cobblers, tailors, and goldsmiths.

The → Punjab, in contrast, had developed its own unique religious culture because of its isolation from the Gangetic Plain. This culture was an amalgam of religious influences ranging from the esoteric practices of Nāth *yogī*s (see → Nāth Sampradāya) to elements of Vaiṣṇava and Śākta practices. This culture became even more complex with the added presence of Sufis and members of the *ʿulamā* who had accompanied Muslim rulers as they entered North India through the Punjab (Grewal, 1997, 9–27). It was out of this milieu that emerged a member of the Punjabi mercantile community by the name of Nānak (1469–1539) who, in the so-called *Bāburvāṇī* sections of the *Gurū Granth Sāhib*, describes with graphic and moving intensity the death and devastation left in the aftermath of Bābūr's invasion of the Punjab. Nānak, however, chose not to uphold the norms of Brahmanical Hinduism and instead placed his faith in the chanting of the name of the divine. Those who followed Nānak were known as Nānakpanthīs and would later become known as Sikhs (see also → Hinduism and Sikhism). The Mughals thus inherited an extremely complex religious landscape from their Sultanate predecessors. Both Hinduism and Islam were characterized by a great internal diversity, and in the midst of these communities were smaller religious groups that included Nānakpanthīs as well as Jains, Jews, Zoroastrians, and Christians who had all established their own places of worship within the empire.

The empire's movement toward religious inclusion, however, was a slow process. Both Bābūr and Humāyūn continued the Sultanate practice of supporting the *ʿulamā* and the Sufis, as did Akbar in the early part of his reign. The *ʿulamā* at court had full control over the distribution of religious endowments, and attempts were made by Akbar to ally the state with the Čištiyya order through pilgrimages to the shrine of Muʿin al-Dīn Čištī (1141–1230) at Ajmer and the construction of a mausoleum for the much-revered Šayẖ Salīm Čištī (1478–1572) within the precincts of Akbar's capital at Fatehpur Sikri (Chandra, 2006, 166–169). The organization of religious debates that began in 1575 at Fatehpur Sikri among Christians, Muslims, and Hindus, however, represented an important turning point in both the emperor's relationship with the *ʿulamā* and the overall shaping of Mughal religious policy. The debates, in part, were meant to symbolically reinforce the idea that the emperor transcended all the religious divisions within his empire and possessed the wisdom to pass final judgment on who won the religious debates taking place before him. The debates, however, were also an indication of Akbar's increasing disenchantment with the Islamic religious establishment. Akbar had found the performance of Muslim scholars at the Fatehpur Sikri debates to be rather wanting, and as he increasingly took a deep intellectual interest in the religious beliefs of non-Muslim communities, the rift between the emperor and Muslim orthodoxy became increasingly large (Chandra, 2006, 169–172).

This rift was further exacerbated by matters of politics. There was opposition from orthodox circles over Akbar's decision to reward his Hindu noblemen for their loyalty to the empire by revoking the pilgrimage tax and poll tax (*jizya*) on Hindus in the period between 1563 and 1564. There were also struggles between the *ʿulamā* and the emperor over issues of religious authority. When the court *ʿulamā* ordered the execution of a prominent Brahman from Mathura for theft and blasphemy against Akbar's expressed wishes for a much more lenient sentence of imprisonment, Akbar responded by issuing a decree in 1573 giving him the power to override the decisions of the *ʿulamā* for the greater benefit of the empire. The *ʿulamā* found themselves further marginalized after Akbar instituted universal religious tolerance (*ṣulḥ-i-kul*) as a state policy in 1581 and then concentrated the power to distribute religious endowments in the hands of the imperial administration (Chandra, 2006, 172–175). Religious communities looking for tax exemptions as charitable institutions made their requests for imperial patronage to the provincial ecclesiastical officer, who then forwarded requests to Delhi, where imperial authorities would decide if petitioners were worthy of imperial largesse. It seems, however, that communities were never entitled to direct financial assistance from imperial coffers to finance the construction and maintenance of their religious institutions. They were, instead, entitled to tax-exempt tracts of land from the state on which to build their religious institutions, which were then usually financed by private patrons. In return for their status as charitable institutions, all that religious communities were required to do was to express their loyalty to the emperor by praying for the continual welfare of the Mughal state (Rashid, 1961).

Religious patronage thus became a simultaneous expression of both tolerance and political authority. The permission given by Akbar to Rājpūt nobles to build temples on tax-free lands given by the state to Vaiṣṇava devotional (→ *bhakti*) communities in Vrindavan and Mathura was, at one level, an expression of cultural engagement with the local populace who wrote and performed devotional poetry and plays in the Hindi vernacular known as Brajbhasha (Busch, 2010, 274–275). It was, however, also a means of maintaining the emperor's political authority by using the magnificent temple complexes built on state-owned land as visual reminders of the emperor's benevolent authority (Asher, 1992b).

Jahāngīr, too, would follow in his father's footsteps. During his first regnal year, Jahāngīr bestowed alms to needy Muslim holy men and journeyed to the Hindu pilgrimage site of

Haridwar, where he made generous donations to ascetics who spent their time in isolation practicing → *yoga*. He became the patron of two important religious figures, of whom the first was the Qādirī Sufi master Miyān Mīr of Lahore, and the second was the Vaiṣṇava ascetic of Ujjain named Jadrūp. Jadrūp's knowledge of philosophy had so impressed Jahāngīr that the emperor made multiple visits to the ascetic and dismissed his brother-in-law, Ḥākim Beg, from imperial service for harassing Jadrūp when the ascetic moved to Mathura (Chandra, 2006, 252–253). At the same time, however, Jahāngīr still exhibited his father's concern for using religious patronage as a means of ensuring political stability. Jahāngīr wrote in his memoirs about the need to build religious and secular buildings in order to bring economic and political stability to the empire's hinterlands (Rogers & Beveridge, 1978, 7–8), and his patronage of the Bengali → Gauḍīya Vaiṣṇava community of Vrindavan between 1612 and 1619 was a clear continuation of the Mughal policy of making religious communities active participants in the Mughal imperium (Mukherjee, 1988). Religious communities, by pledging their allegiance to the emperor, became what Jahāngīr called the empire's "armies of prayer" (Rogers & Beveridge, 1978, 11).

If Jahāngīr continued to follow Akbar's policy of inclusionary politics, why would his son Šāh Jahān declare the empire to be an Islamic state and enforce a ban on the construction of temples, churches, and synagogues during his reign? Šāh Jahān may have been bowing to pressure from members of the Muslim religious establishment who felt marginalized during the reigns of Akbar and Jahāngīr. He may also have wanted to atone for committing fratricide in his quest for the Mughal throne. The measures, however, seemed to be cosmetic, for Šāh Jahān did not ultimately abandon the precedents set by his father and grandfather. Šāh Jahān continued to extend Mughal patronage to the devotional communities of Vrindavan and Mathura and eventually gave control of the Govind Devjī Temple in Vrindavan directly to the Amber family of Rājpūts, who were the temple's long-standing patrons (Mukherjee, 1988, 287–289). In 1634, Šāh Jahān went to the lengths of issuing a royal edict repealing a local ordinance banning the ringing of the temple bell at the Madan Mohan Temple in Vrindavan on the grounds that it obstructed Hindus from performing their religious duties. Furthermore, in 1639, he gave permission to a Jain merchant named Śāntidās to build a new Jain temple in Gujarat (Chandra, 2006, 255). When, in 1654, Awrangzēb heard of the new temple, he used his position as state governor to convert the temple into a mosque, until he was stopped by none other than Šāh Jahān himself.

Awrangzēb's attempt to convert Śāntidās' temple into a mosque was not surprising. He was known for his deep religious piety, his observance of Islamic law (*šarīʿa*), and his sober lifestyle, which he then brought to the royal court upon his ascension to the throne. Artists and musicians were dismissed from their positions at court, the celebration of Hindu festivals was discontinued, and elements of court rituals were modified, such as the practice of weighing the emperor against his weight in gold. Muslim religious scholars came to enjoy greater patronage and were commissioned by Awrangzēb to produce a digest of legal rulings based on the Ḥanafī school of Islamic law, which was later called the *Fatāwā-yi ʿĀlamgīrī*. Efforts were also made to rule according to *šarīʿa* by posting officials across the empire to enforce bans on drinking, gambling, drug use, and prostitution. Šāh Jahān's ban on the construction of non-Muslim shrines was retained, and, in 1679, the *jizya* was reimposed on Hindus by the emperor.

The extent to which these measures represented a movement toward transforming the Mughal state into a type of theocracy is somewhat debatable. The number of Hindu noblemen in Awrangzēb's service exceeded the number in the employ of any of his predecessors (Ali, 2001, 22–26), and the ban on the construction of new temples did not necessarily lead to a decline in state patronage for Hindu communities. Islamic law still permitted the renewal of preexisting land grants to non-Muslim communities, as long as they pledged their loyalty to the emperor. Consequently, Awrangzēb could still continue to enjoy the support of the *ʿulamā* without having to alienate the Hindu nobles in his service. Awrangzēb continued to renew land grants to Hindu ascetics in the Punjab because of his interest in their practice of alchemy (→ *rasāyana*), and he agreed, in 1703, to subsidize the religious activities of the Gauḍīya Vaiṣṇavas in Vrindavan (Chandra, 2006, 279; Goswamy, 1967, 120–124). He also, in 1659, issued an edict that protected Brahmans in the city of Varanasi from harassment by making it clear to his local officials that the Brahmans merited state protection so that they could continue to pray undisturbed for the continuance of the empire (Eaton, 2004, 56).

The pragmatic approach that shaped Awrangzēb's attitude toward construction of temples could also be seen in the case of the *jizya*. The reimposition of the *jizya* did not occur shortly after Awrangzēb's ascension to the throne but 22 years into his reign, as a response to the political and financial crisis caused by the prolonged Deccan campaigns. The reinstatement of the *jizya* was used to finance the costly campaigns in the Deccan, and it was another example of Awrangzēb's ongoing efforts to maintain the support of the court *ʿulamā*. When the court's chief religious judge refused to crown Awrangzēb on the grounds that he committed fratricide and unlawfully imprisoned his ailing father in order to gain the Mughal throne, Awrangzēb took two measures. Firstly, he had the judge replaced, and, secondly, he began to take measures that would secure *ʿulamā* support such as increasing their political influence at court and enforcing Islamic law. The reintroduction of the *jizya* represented the culmination of Awrangzēb's efforts to maintain *ʿulamā* support for his regime. *ʿUlamā* support for the Deccan campaigns was waning, and the *jizya* was used by Awrangzēb as a means to rally orthodox support for his military efforts (Chandra, 2003b, 318–321; 2006, 280–283).

The instances in which the collection of the *jizya* was used as an opportunity to harass Hindus could be interpreted as an effort to use the *jizya* as an instrument to impose Islam on Hindus, but the efforts were not sanctioned by the state. These instances occurred at the local level, and both tax collectors and local religious judges used the collection of the *jizya* to extort money from Hindus or to engage in their own localized form of religious politics. The protests and strikes launched by Hindu merchants against the *jizya* demonstrated, for a certain segment of Awrangzēb's Muslim nobles, how the reimposition of the *jizya* was politically inexpedient and indicative of the excessive power that the *ʿulamā* was beginning to have over the state (Chandra, 2003b, 320–324).

The popularity of the *jizya* began to increasingly wane at court after the death of Awrangzēb. The tax seems to have never been collected during the reign of his successor, Bahādur Šāh I (r. 1707–1712), and serious efforts to collect it were made by his successor Farruḫ Siyār (r. 1713–1719) only toward the later part of his reign, in 1717, as a means of replenishing the imperial treasury. When Farruḫ Siyār was deposed in 1719, merchants staged strikes to thwart efforts to collect the *jizya* and were supported by the governors of the Punjab and Awadh as well as by Rājpūt rulers who argued that the *jizya* was not only economically regressive but also a form of unfair punishment to Hindus who historically were always loyal to the empire. The *jizya* from that point onward was simply abandoned as a part of official Mughal governing policy (Chandra, 2003c, 350–353).

The history of the *jizya* is indicative of how certain constraints made it difficult for the Mughal state to impose Islam on the majority of its subjects. For many Mughal noblemen of Muslim descent, the blurring between politics and religion meant the deterioration of good governance, while Hindu nobles were aware that forced conversion would alienate the Hindu population on whom the political well-being of the empire depended. During the reign of Akbar, calls for the conversion of Hindus by individuals like the courtier ʿAbd al-Qādir Badāʾūnī (1540–1615) were summarily ignored by the emperor, while Jahāngīr had Aḥmad Sirhindī (1561–1624), a Sufi Naqšbandī, imprisoned for a year because the *šayḫ* repeatedly called for the slaughter of cows as well as the economic and political discrimination of Hindus (Friedmann, 1971, 69–75). Šāh Jahān would follow the precedent set by his predecessors even after declaring the empire to be an Islamic state. When the followers of Aḥmad Sirhindī and the Islamic scholar ʿAbd al-Ḥaqq wrote letters to the emperor calling for the strict implementation of the *šarīʿa*, the humiliation of Hindus, and the revival of the *jizya*, their requests were all rejected by Šāh Jahān (Chandra, 2006, 256). The only request that was honored was the ban on the construction of new temples, but, as was noted above, this was never fully enforced.

If the state was not used as an instrument of enforcing Islam, then how does one explain the instances of conversion within the empire? Akbar came to regret his attempts of forcible conversion in the early part of his reign, and Jahāngīr, upon his ascension to the throne, explicitly ordered his nobles not to engage in attempts to convert the local populace to Islam. In some cases, conversion was the product of genuine intellectual interest. A Brahman charged with helping with the Persian translation of the *Atharvaveda* at Akbar's court converted to Islam after he came to the conclusion that Islam was theologically superior to Hinduism. Another Hindu at Akbar's court who was studying Persian converted to Islam after his teacher extolled to him the virtues of the Prophet Muḥammad. In some cases, the conversions seemed to be purely for practical purposes. Rulers may have converted to Islam in order to gain imperial support during succession crises or to evade legal action from the state. Thus, one finds the example of an accountant (*munšī*) from Rajasthan who sought protection with Mughal officials by converting to Islam in order to evade being charged with the murder of a prominent Hindu nobleman in Awrangzēb's court. Similarly, one finds a Hindu ruler from central India named Kiśan Siṅgh, who, in a bid to overthrow his father, converted to Islam in order to gain military support from Awrangzēb, only to later slaughter Awrangzēb's Muslim officers, after the sudden poisoning of his father no longer necessitated imperial military assistance (Mukhia, 2004, 30–34).

In most cases, however, conversions occurred the most in the hinterlands of the empire, far from the reach of the state and the influence of Brahmanical orthodoxy. The agents of conversion in these instances were not the state but the members of Sufi orders who undertook colonization efforts in hinterland areas like Bengal. In Kashmir, in contrast, the predominance of Islam was largely due to the efforts of Sufis who won over the local populace through the debates they held with local Hindu religious leaders. In other words, conversion was a gradual process accomplished through acculturation and not through the efforts of the Mughal State (Malik, 2008, 182–187).

Since conversion was not a particular concern of Mughal rulers, instances of temple desecration during the Mughal regime need to be seen primarily as political acts and not as expressions of religious zeal. The Mughals were aware that temples were important symbols of royal sovereignty for Hindu rulers, and, consequently, temples could become sites around which political opposition could coalesce. Noblemen who were given political postings as governors or army commanders were prevented from developing local power bases by being routinely shifted from one geographical location to another. If, however, a Hindu officer was found guilty of political insubordination or open rebellion, the Mughals would seek to teach the individual a lesson by desecrating a religious shrine. Thus, for example, the reason why a temple was desecrated by Jahāngīr in 1613 in Rajasthan was because the temple was owned by a relation of the Rājpūt ruler Amar Siṅgh, who openly defied Mughal authority. In a similar vein, Šāh Jahān had ordered the destruction of a major Hindu temple in the kingdom of Orchha because the temple's chief patron was Jujhar Siṅgh, who was openly rebelling against the emperor. The destruction of the Keśav Dev Temple of Mathura and the Viśvanāth Temple of Varanasi by Awrangzēb were motivated by similar reasons to those of his predecessors. The destruction of the Viśvanāth Temple in 1669 was a form of political retaliation against Jai Siṅgh of Amber for his aid of the Marathas, while the 1670 desecration of the Keśav Dev Temple took place because the railing of the temple had been constructed by his brother and rival to the Mughal throne, Dārā Šikōh (Eaton, 2004, 60–62). In the case of temples destroyed by Awrangzēb in Thatta, Multan, and Varanasi, Awrangzēb's reason was to prevent the spread of what was reported as teachings that were considered potentially subversive to the empire. The nature of the teachings is unknown, but it was clear that for Awrangzēb, these sites were viewed as being a potential political threat to his regime that needed to be contained (Eaton, 2004, 62–63).

The goal of Mughal religious policy, then, was not to enforce Islam but to effectively manage the religiously diverse nature of the empire for the benefit of the state. The inhabitants of the empire did not identify themselves as belonging to a single religious community bound together by core religious characteristics but as being part of a religiously pluralistic society. Hindus and Muslims expressed their religious identities in terms of their sectarian affiliations such as being Vaiṣṇavas, Śaivas, or Śāktas or as members of a particular Sufi order or branch of Šīʿa Islam like the Ismāʿīlīs. When they articulated the differences among one another, it seemed to be rarely in terms of theology. Muslims were designated by Hindus as → *mleccha*s and *yāvana*s, which were terms derived from Sanskrit for foreign invaders, regardless of religious affiliation, and for any group of people, indigenous or otherwise, who fell outside the caste system. Hindus, however, were viewed as the residents of Hindustan because of their proximity to the Indus River. They were, to a certain extent, also viewed in religious terms by their Muslim counterparts because of their belief in reincarnation and their worship of gods and goddesses (Ali, 2006, 109–118).

The Mughals clearly understood the religious diversity of their empire and attempted to manage it through the use of patronage. Mughal patronage may have been, at one level, a genuine expression of religious piety and cultural engagement, but it was always linked to the larger concern of political stability. Patronage helped contribute to this stability by assimilating religious communities into the larger framework of the state and using them as instruments or symbols of political authority. This approach to religious politics, in turn, generated a type of "competitive spirituality" in which members of religious communities lived neither in harmony nor in acrimony together during the Mughal period. They learned to accommodate one another in North Indian society while at the same time competing against one another for both popular and state support (Alam, 1989).

It is difficult then to argue that various rebellions and conflicts that occurred during the reign of Awrangzēb were a direct response to the emperor's religious conservatism. The wars in the Deccan were caused by the territorial ambitions of both the Mughals and the Marathas, while the tensions between Awrangzēb and the influential Rājpūt kingdoms of Mewar and Marwar were due to the emperor's intervention in the internal political affairs of the two kingdoms. Similarly, the conflict between the Sikhs and Awrangzēb was not rooted in differences over religion but in a battle for political and social influence among the peasantry in the Punjab countryside. It was, however, not difficult for these type of conflicts to take on a religious tinge. Just as Awrangzēb reimposed the *jizya* to win popular religious support for his regime, the Maratha chief Śivajī and Rājpūt rulers like Rāj Siṅgh of Mewar consciously cultivated images as ideal Hindu rulers in order to consolidate their regional power bases. This use of religion, however, did not translate into any sort of alliance based on either shared political or shared religious convictions. The Marathas, on the contrary, began to invade Rajasthan and eventually sacked the wealthy Vaiṣṇava temple of Nathdwara at the beginning of the 19th century (Saha, 2004, 195–197).

The Decline of the Mughal State

What caused the decline of the Mughal Empire, if it was not religion? In order to answer this question, it is important to understand that the Mughal state was not as centralized and authoritarian as it may seem on first glance. The assignation of *manṣab*s by the emperor, the limits placed on the movements of *jāgīrdār*s, the use of patronage to buy popular religious support, and the complex means of ensuring political accountability within the Mughal government were all attempts to centralize all political and social authority in the hands of the state. The Mughals, however, still had to enter into power-sharing agreements at the local level to ensure the well-being of the empire. The Mughals entered into various credit arrangements with the Baniyas in order to ensure the financial solvency of the imperial administration, and it was recognized that the extraction of revenue from the local peasantry could not be done without entering into power-sharing agreements with the local landowning aristocracy known as *zamīndār*s. These individuals agreed to collect imperial revenues directly from the peasants on the condition that they would be able to keep ten percent of what they collected before forwarding the remainder to the imperial administration. By co-opting the *zamīndār*s into the Mughal administration as revenue collectors, one is left with the impression that the Mughals were able to extend their rule into the rural countryside; but this was something of an illusion. *Zamīndār*s could easily refuse to collect taxes if they were unhappy with the tax assessment set by the imperial administration, and they could demand that the assessment be renegotiated either peacefully or under the threat of military force by mobilizing the armed contingents of peasants who protected *zamīndārī* estates.

The Mughal emperor, then, did not hold absolute authority over every level of Indian society. The Mughal governmental structure, on the contrary, was based on a complex set of power relationships. The imperial government used political patronage and honors to control the imperial nobility and bureaucracy, while the provincial bureaucracy aided the imperial administration in ensuring control over the body of *jāgīrdār*s to which provincial and imperial bureaucrats themselves belonged. The imperial government, meanwhile, tried to exert control over the local aristocracy, only to find that their power was stymied by the *zamīndār*s' ability to use their direct relationship with the peasantry and their status as revenue collectors as a form of political leverage. It was the slow unraveling of these relationships that accounts for the beginning of the regime's demise under the reign of Awrangzēb. The Afghan, Jāṭ, and Satnāmī rebellions were all manifestations of peasant and *zamīndārī* discontent over the encroachment of the Mughals into their political autonomy. In a similar vein, the conflict between the Sikhs and the Mughals started when the local peasantry turned to the heads (*gurūs*) of the Sikh community to voice their discontent with the imperial administration (Habib, 2009, 82–83). In the case of the Deccan, the long and costly wars waged against the Marathas and the independent kingdoms of Golconda and Bijapur resulted in a widening gap between the demand for *manṣabdār* assignments and the generation of the revenue necessary to meet those demands. The pressure put on *zamīndār*s and peasants alike caused widespread revolts, and governors and nobles both came to establish independent power bases in the provinces because it became increasingly evident that, as the *jāgīrdārī* crisis worsened, they could no longer rely on imperial patronage for upward social mobility (Chandra, 1998, 352–360). In other words, what seemed to occur during the reign of Awrangzēb was that the empire reached the limits of its expansion, the structure of imperial governance began to fail, and an irreversible process of decline began.

Mughal Court Life

At the peak of its power, the Mughal Empire became famed for its political and economic strength and for the opulent lifestyle led by the emperor and the members of the Mughal political elite. At the royal court, this relationship between the emperor and his nobles was expressed through a highly complex set of rituals designed to ensure the loyalty of the nobility to the ruling sovereign. Akbar, drawing on Abū al-Fażl's declaration that only those with spiritual insight could view a divine ray of light that emanated from the eyebrows of the emperor, attempted to bind the higher-ranking members of the nobility through the formation of an elite brotherhood that required initiates to pledge their willingness to sacrifice their life, religion, honor, and wealth in the service of the emperor and follow a set of rituals that involved the worship of fire and the sun. This new brotherhood – known as the Dīn-i-Ilahī – drew on Hindu, Sufi, and Zoroastrian religious practices, but it did not last long. It did, however, represent an early stage in the development of court rituals that were designed to define the relationship between the emperor and his subjects. One of these important rituals was modeled along the lines of how Hindus would have a glimpse (*darśan*) of a deity in a temple. In the Mughal context, this practice was known as *jharoka darśan* and involved the emperor giving his first public audience of the day from a balcony (*jharoka*) so that his subjects at court could pay their obeisances to him. The second of these rituals was influenced by the Hindu coronation ceremony (*rājyābhiṣeka*), which established the emperor as a universal man who embodied all the elements of the earth. This ritual constituted of weighing the emperor on his birthday and distributing his weight in various commodities that included gold, silk, perfumes, coppers, grains, vegetables, and salts.

Court ritual, however, would eventually evolve into elaborate rules of etiquette that needed to be followed closely when in the presence of the emperor. Noblemen would have to enter the court barefoot in the same way in which one would enter a temple or a mosque, and they were required to speak in hushed tones in order to preserve the atmosphere of sanctity that was to be created before the entry of the emperor. Drums were to announce the presence of the emperor, for whom his symbols of sovereignty – his throne, a parasol, yak tail whisks, and various standards – were readied for his use upon his arrival at court. Noblemen were expected to greet him with the performance of the *kurniš*, which was a gesture of submission and humility made to the emperor by placing one's right hand on his forehead and bending the head downward (Shivram, 2009, 18–20). A variant of the *kurniš* was the *taslīm*, which required the individual to place his or her hand on the ground and raise it to the top of his or head while slowly standing up. If the nobleman had received a gift from the emperor, he was required to perform the *taslīm* three times in front of the emperor upon receipt of the gift. This practice gradually evolved, and by the time of Awrangzēb's reign, the number of *taslīm*s became increasingly elaborate and was a means of defining rank. Everyone in the court performed three *taslīms* to the emperor except for the royal princes, who had to perform only two, and if one received a gift in Awrangzēb's court, one had to perform four *taslīms* before and after receiving the honor (Mukhia, 2004, 90–94).

The bestowal of gifts and titles was an almost routine occurrence at the royal court. When noblemen attended the royal court, their physical proximity to the emperor was predetermined to reflect their individual *manṣab* rankings and the degree of access that they had to the emperor himself (Shivram, 2009, 23–24). The receipt of an honor at the hands of the emperor, then, was considered to be of great importance for noblemen hoping to rise through the ranks of the nobility. The most obvious sign of favor was the increase of one's *manṣab* ranking, for it indicated that the nobleman was an extension of the emperor's power. The receipt of clothing from the emperor was also considered to be symbolic not only of how noblemen had earned the favor of the emperor but also of how they believed they were sharing in the glory and effulgence of their emperor (Mukhia, 2004, 163–165; Shivram, 2009, 23). Thus, the bestowal of robes or headgear that had been touched by the emperor was seen as a definite sign of favor by the emperor, as were royal visits to noblemen's households or even the smallest amount of eye contact with the emperor (Shivram, 2009, 24–31).

There were restrictions on what could be worn by noblemen. Akbar and Jahāngīr, for example, decreed that certain types of cloths with special embroideries and certain types of loincloths could not be worn by anyone but the emperor, and by the time of Šāh Jahān and Awrangzēb, the bright, festive colors worn by noblemen when attending court were gradually discouraged or banned in order to match the more somber and conservative lifestyle that both led during their lifetimes. Restrictions, however, did not extend only to clothes. The recitation of Friday prayers in the name of anyone but the emperor, the issuing of coins, calling for an assembly of fellow noblemen, the meting out of capital punishment, hunting lions, riding alongside the emperor, or using certain types of umbrellas were considered to be royal prerogatives.

Any attempt, then, to engage in such activities was considered to be a challenge to royal sovereignty for which there was no excuse. There was a large body of material known as Aḫlāq literature that dealt specifically with etiquette both within and outside the realm of the court, and, consequently, any infractions of these rules resulted in punishments that ranged from the revoking of one's *manṣab* rankings to public humiliation and imprisonment. Thus, in the case of Laškar Ḫān, one of Akbar's senior bureaucrats who held the position of *mīr baḫšī*, his rudeness to the emperor resulted in being tied to the tail of a horse and being paraded in public before finally being imprisoned (Mukhia, 2004, 98). In the case of the royal family, punishments could be equally if not more harsh. When Awrangzēb, for example, heard that his son Muʿaẓẓam sat on a raised platform while holding court in Kabul, Awrangzēb issued an order for Muʿazzam to be publically pulled off the platform, which was then destroyed (Mukhia, 2004, 87–88). In the case of Jahāngīr's son Ḫusraw, the punishment was much more severe. Ḫusraw was blinded on the orders of his father for starting a rebellion and was eventually put to death by his brother and future emperor Šāh Jahān. One, however, would have thought that Jahāngīr may have been somewhat merciful toward Ḫusraw. Jahāngīr, after all, himself had led a failed rebellion against his father, Akbar, with whom he was reconciled due largely to the efforts of his paternal grandmother, Ḥamīda Begum (1527–1604).

Mughal Women

Whether the influence of Ḥamīda Begum was indicative of the type of influence held by all women at the Mughal court is difficult to assess, given that scholarly work on the Mughal women and the nature of the royal household is still in its infancy. The emperor was married to multiple women, who could be of either royal or common birth, and, in addition, kept a large number of concubines, who held the lowest status within the royal household. The royal household, moreover, consisted of the emperor's children and both his close and his distant female relatives such as his mother, aunts, and cousins. The women of the royal household were all given monthly incomes and gifts according to their status, and they were attended on by armed women and eunuchs whose proximity to their mistresses was determined by their level of trustworthiness and reliability. This entire complex of individuals who made up the royal household was called the *ḥarām*, which was an Islamic term denoting a place of sanctity and indicated that the space allotted to the members of the royal household was a type of sacred space that complemented the sanctity associated with the royal court. Thus, it was not surprising that the royal household headed by the emperor was called the divine household (*ahl al-bayt*), which was a term commonly used to refer to the household of the Prophet Muḥammad (Lal, 2007, 51–54).

Women who were members of the imperial *ḥarām* enjoyed a particularly high and exalted status within Mughal court life. The senior female relatives of the household were all held in the highest esteem and given suitable honorable honorifics and titles to reflect the moral and physical perfection that women of the imperial household were required to maintain. During the reign of Akbar, for example, Ḥamīda Begum was given the title of Maryam-Makānī, which equated her with the Virgin Mary, while Akbar's stepmother, Ḥajjī Begum, and his foster mother, Māham Anaga (d. 1562), were given titles that referred to them as paragons of chastity. Princesses were given names like Jahān Ārā ("Adornment of the World") or Gulbadan ("One Who Has the Body of a Rose") to emphasize their physical perfection and chastity. The practice of seclusion was thus justified on the grounds that it was imperative to protect the moral and physical perfection of the imperial women, and veiling was necessary to protect their modesty and, by extension, the sanctity of the entire empire (Lal, 2007, 55–56).

The status of women in the *ḥarām* was, then, somewhat paradoxical. Their spiritual and moral perfection elevated them to such a level that it ended up restricting their sphere of influence to the realm of the *ḥarām* instead of broadening their influence in the public sphere. Thus, in public records and chronicles, the activities of women went unrecorded and unnoticed to the point that they were even omitted from royal birth announcements. No mention was made of Ḥamīda Begum in the accounts of Akbar's birth, and when Akbar's long-standing desire to have a male heir was fulfilled and celebrated with great pomp and circumstance, no mention was ever made of Jahāngīr's mother in either the royal birth announcement or the congratulatory notes sent to the emperor by other noblemen. Akbar had repeatedly prayed to the Sufi saint Šayḫ Salīm Čištī for a son, and it was the saint to whom Jahāngīr's birth was ultimately attributed (Lal, 2007, 56–58).

This, however, did not mean that the women of the *ḥarām* spent their time in idle pursuits and servicing the physical needs of their husbands. Stories about debauchery and illicit affairs in the *ḥarām* made for good gossip both in royal circles and at the local bazaar, but they hardly represented the reality of life in the *ḥarām*. Inside the *ḥarām*, women were educated and had access to their close family members and confidants as well as astrologers, poets, dancers, and midwives. They frequently made excursions outside the confines of the palace wall and travelled with the emperor if the royal court needed to be shifted to a different geographical location during military campaigns or during the course of the emperor's travels. Indeed, the most comprehensive account of Humāyūn's reign – the *Humāyūn-nāma* – was written not by a male courtier but by Humāyūn's sister, Gulbadan Begum (1523–1603).

Noblewomen were equally involved in the internal affairs of the royal court. Just as the emperor listened to the petitions of the needy from his throne, the women in the imperial *ḥarām* also had the authority to do the same, including issuing decrees in their names for the donation of charitable funds or for the construction of mosques and schools. Thus, for example, one sees throughout Mughal history how queens and other high-ranking noblewomen used this authority to become patrons of the arts and literature. Akbar's mother, Ḥamīda Begum, issued a number of decrees for the construction of mosques, rest homes, and wells, while Māham Anaga was responsible for the founding of a college and a mosque in Delhi. Šāh Jahān's wife, Mumtāz Maḥal, was known for providing pensions to impoverished scholars and their families, and Mumtāz's daughter Jahān Ārā (1614–1681) was widely known for religious piety and her biography of the Sufi saint Muʿin al-Dīn Čištī (Schimmel, 2004, 150–155).

In a similar vein, women of the royal household could use their authority to influence the course of court politics. The most obvious example of this was Jahāngīr's wife Nūr Jahān. Nūr Jahān, who came from a politically powerful family whose members were high-ranking members of Jahāngīr's administration, was the daughter of Jahāngīr's finance minister, who became independently wealthy upon the demise of her father. Nūr Jahān used her power to have coins struck in her name, engaged in trade negotiations and the importation of luxury items from Europe, and accumulated large amounts of money from both the collection of custom duties and the accumulation of many landholdings. Nūr Jahān then used her wealth to become a patron of the arts who was known for her elaborate construction of mausoleums, palaces, and gardens as well as the patron of charities that catered to the needs of the poor and orphaned (Schimmel, 2004, 149–150).

Arts and Literature

The style of architecture in which the garden, palaces, and other large monuments commissioned by Nūr Jahān and other members of the Mughal elite were built was a visual expression of the creative interaction between Iranian artists who had migrated to the Mughal court in the mid-15th century and the Hindu artists who had joined the Mughal court as it expanded across North India. Mughal architecture thus combined the staple features of Persian architecture — such as elaborate arches and quadrilateral gardens (*čār bāġs*) with typical features of Indian architecture such as balconies known as *jharokās*, small pavilions with cobbled domes (*chatrīs*), and domed pavilions known as *banglas* - to provide an architectural style that was at once aesthetically pleasing and a powerful visual statement of Mughal political ideology (Mitter, 2001, 107–109). This is best represented in the architecture of Fatehpur Sikri, which served as the capital of the empire between 1571 and 1585 during the reign of Akbar. Influenced by Abū al-Fażl's use of solar imagery and the Hindu notion of the sovereign as world conqueror, the audience hall at Fatehpur was constructed using Hindu architectural devices such as elaborate pillars to symbolize the emperor's function as *axis mundi* and the *chatrīs* over the royal throne in order protect subjects from the emperor's radiance (Mitter, 2001, 111–115). Similarly, Akbar's authority over both the realm of the secular and the realm of the sacred was symbolized by the construction of the *ibādat-ḫāna*, where the emperor sat on a throne in an elevated balcony and passed judgment on the religious debates that were held in front of him. A similar architectural strategy would later be employed by Šāh Jahān with the construction of his capital city, Shahjahanabad, in what is now old Delhi. The massive congregational mosque was modeled on the mosque at Fatehpur Sikri and was built to underline not only the emperor's support of Islam but also his authority over both the sacred and the secular. This was accomplished by the inclusion of Persian inscriptions praising the emperor within the walls of the mosque (Asher, 1992a, 202–203).

Mughal painting styles, too, would be used in the service of royal ideology. The royal ateliers represented the cosmopolitan nature of Mughal culture, with both Indian and Iranian artists working together to produce the manuscripts and illustrations for Persian literary texts, official court chronicles, and even both manuscripts of the two Hindu religious epics, the *Mahābhārata* and the *Rāmāyaṇa*. Mughal art, however, would take on a new dimension with Mughal exposure to European art in the form of the illustrated *Royal Polyglot Bible*, which was brought to the Mughal court by missionaries hoping to convert Akbar to Christianity (Beach, 1992, 54–55). Symbols of divinity and royalty found in the Polyglot Bible, such as the lamb, the lion, and the halo, or more specific figures, such as Jesus and the Virgin Mary, were adapted by Mughal artists to help buttress aspects of royal ideology. Jahāngīr, for example, took the title of "Light of the Faith" (Nūr-al-Dīn) and would underline this visually through a portrait that depicts the deceased Šayḫ Salīm Čištī legitimizing Jahāngīr's right to rule by handing him a globe. Šāh Jahān – whose name means "Emperor of the World" – would also employ a similar visual strategy by depicting himself standing on a globe with both a lion and a lamb coexisting peacefully at his feet to symbolize the just nature of his rule (Asher, 2004, 179–183). Even Awrangzēb, who was known for his orthodox observance of Islam, did not abandon the visual strategy of his predecessors. Portraits of the emperor juxtaposed his image as a devout, orthodox Muslim with symbols of Mughal suzerainty, including the halo to depict the emperor as a saintly ruler concerned with the good of the empire.

The manuscripts in which these images were found were, of course, written in Persian. Persian was made the official language of the Mughal Empire; it was held in great esteem as a vehicle for literary expression and became even more so with the influx of intellectuals from Iran into the Mughal court. Official court histories such as the *Akbar-nāma* and the *Šāhjahān-nāma* praising the ruling emperor and his family were written in Persian (Moosvi, 2009), and so were the travelogues of individuals like ʿAbd al-Karīm Kašmīrī and Ānand Rām Muḫliṣ; they provided valuable details about Mughal society and life that would otherwise be omitted from court histories

(Alam, 2010). In addition, Hindu texts like the *Rāmāyaṇa* and the *Yogavāsiṣṭha* were translated into Persian for consumption within and outside the royal court (Cole, 2002, 22–23). The continued patronage of Persian by the Mughal emperors would help to encourage the development of Persian poetry in the 16th and 17th centuries by Persian-speaking Iranian immigrants as well as from poets born in India. These poets initially confined themselves to the long-standing literary conventions associated with Persian poetry found in the Arab world, but their experimentation with both Persian and Indian literary forms gave rise to a more florid and abstract style of poetry that was framed as a new form of poetic discourse known as Tāzagu'i. The most important representative of this style was the poet Bedil (1814–1873), whose abstract poetry won accolades both within and outside India as well as great criticism from those who felt that he had abandoned the simplicity of traditional Persian poetry (Alam, 1998, 335–342).

The preeminence of Persian at the Mughal court, however, did not mean the displacement of the various Hindi vernaculars – collectively called Hindavi by Indo-Persian poets – spoken in Mughal India. Hindavi, on the contrary, continued to shape the culture of Mughal India in very substantial ways. Regional forms of Hindi such as Rajasthani, Bhojpuri, and Avadhi were used by the Sant devotional communities of the Mughal period, whose representatives such as → Dādū Dayāl and Mālūkdās continued the Sant social critique of Hindu and Muslim religious orthodoxy. In the Awadh region, which comprised the cities of Lucknow, Jaunpur, and Varanasi, the regional language of Avadhi was long used by Sufi poets like Jāyasī (1477–1522) and Mīr Sayyid Manjhan for their romances (Premākhyan). In the 16th century, Avadhi was later used by the poet → Tulsīdās (1532–1623) for what would become his spectacularly popular retelling of the *Rāmāyaṇa* known as the *Rāmcaritmānas*. Meanwhile, in the area around the political centers of Delhi and Agra, devotional poetry to → Kṛṣṇa was written in Brajbhasha by the Vaiṣṇava communities of Mathura and Vrindavan, who, as noted above, were the recipients of Mughal patronage (McGregor, 1984, 46–117). Mughal emperors eventually became patrons of Brajbhasha poets, who used their skills to develop a new form of courtly poetry known as Rītī Kāvya (Busch, 2010, 276–306).

The impact of Hindavi in Mughal India would also be felt, as North India's Hindavi-speaking population interacted with the empire's Persian speakers. The interaction between these two languages produced Urdu, which, although linguistically similar to Hindavi, contained a heavy proportion of Persian and Arabic words and was written in the same script as both languages. Given the dominance of Persian at the Mughal court, Urdu would only flourish as a literary language after the empire began to decline in power and dissolve into smaller, independent states that would eventually fall under British rule. Two schools of Urdu poetry began to coalesce around the Mughal court in Delhi and in Lucknow, which became the capital of Awadh after it had established itself as an independent state in 1772. The rivalry between the Lucknow and Delhi schools of Urdu poetry would help in popularizing the short lyrical poem known as the Ġazal and the Urdu adaptation of the Persian elegaic form known as the Qaṣīda. The Qaṣīda was associated primarily with the poet Saudā (1713–1781), who lived during the reign of Muḥammad Šāh, while the foremost exponents of the Ġazal were Urdu literature's most famous poets, the Delhi-based Mīr Taqī Mīr (1723–1810) and Mirzā Asad Allāh H̬ān Ġālib (1797–1869), who lived during the reign of the last Mughal emperor, Bahādūr Šāh II (Schimmel, 2004, 256–261). Bahādūr Šāh II himself was well known for his Ġazal corpus, and it is the following verses from his poetry that perhaps best describe the bleak state of the Mughal Empire in its final period of decline as well as a certain sense of yearning for the golden age of Mughal rule, when even Europeans had to bend to the economic and political power of the Mughal emperors:

> I am the light of no one's eye
> The balm of no one's heart –
> I am no use to anyone
> A handful of dust, that's all. (Schimmel, 2004, 260–261)

Bibliography

Ahmad, I., "Ism'ailis, Mahdawis, and Raushanyas," in: J.S. Grewal, ed., *Religious Movements and Institutions in Medieval India*, New Delhi, 2006, 296–317.

Alam, M., & S. Subrahmanyam, *Indo-Persian Travels in the Age of Discoveries 1400–1800*, Cambridge MA, 2010.

Alam, M., "The Pursuit of Persian: Language in Mughal Politics," *MAS* 32/2, 1998, 317–349.
Alam, M., "Competition and Co-existence: Indo-Islamic Interaction in Medieval North India," *Itinerario* 13/1, 1989, 37–60.
Ali, M.A., *Mughal India: Studies in Polity, Ideas, Society, and Culture*, New Delhi, 2006.
Ali, M.A., *The Mughal Nobility under Aurangzeb*, New Delhi, rev. ed. 2001.
Asher, C.B., "A Ray from the Sun: Mughal Ideology and Visual Construction," in: M.T. Kapstein, ed., *The Presence of Light: Divine Radiance and Religious Experience*, Chicago, 2004, 161–194.
Asher, C.B., *Architecture of Mughal India*, Cambridge UK, 1992a.
Asher, C.B., "The Architecture of Raja Man Singh: A Study in Mughal Sub-imperial Patronage," in: B. Stoller Miller, ed., *The Powers of Art: Patronage in Indian Culture*, New Delhi, 1992b, 183–201.
Beach, M.C., *Mughal and Rajput Painting*, Cambridge UK, 1992.
Busch, A., "Hidden in Plain View: Brajbhasha Poets at the Mughal Court," *MAS* 44/2, 2010, 267–309.
Chandra, S., *Medieval India from Sultanat to the Mughals*, vol. II: *Mughal Empire (1526–1748)*, New Delhi, rev. ed. 2006.
Chandra, S., "The Historical Background to the Rise of the Bhakti Movement in Northern India," in: S. Chandra, ed., *Essays on Medieval Indian History*, New Delhi, 2003a, 285–304.
Chandra, S., "*Jizyah* and the State in India during the Seventeenth Century," in: S. Chandra, ed., *Essays on Medieval Indian History*, New Delhi, 2003b, 305–324.
Chandra, S., "*Jizyah* in the Post-Aurangzeb Period," in: S. Chandra, ed., *Essays on Medieval Indian History*, New Delhi, 2003c, 346–353.
Chandra, S., "Review of the Crisis of the Jagirdari System," in: M. Alam & S. Subrahmanyam, eds., *The Mughal State, 1526–1750*, New Delhi, 1998, 347–360.
Cole, J.I., "Iranian Culture and South Asia, 1500–1900," in: N.R. Keddie & R. Matthee, eds., *Iran and the Surrounding World: Interactions in Culture and World Politics*, Seattle, 2002, 15–35.
Eaton, R., *Temple Desecration and Muslim States in Medieval India*, Gurgaon, 2004.
Friedmann, Y., *Shaykh Ahmad Sirhindi: An Outline of His Thought and a Study of His Image in the Eyes of Posterity*, Montreal, 1971.
Goswamy, B.N., & J.S. Grewal, *The Mughals and the Jogis of Jakhbar: Some madad-i-ma'ash and Other Documents*, Simla, 1967.
Grewal, J.S., "Sūfism in Medieval India," in: J.S. Grewal, ed., *Religious Movements and Institutions in Medieval India*, New Delhi, 2006, 318–352.
Grewal, J.S., *The Sikhs of the Punjab*, New Delhi, 1997.
Habib, I., "The Mughal Empire," in J.S. Grewal, ed., *The State and Society in Medieval India*, New Delhi, 2009, 77–86.
Lal, R., "Hierarchies of Age and Gender in the Mughal Construction of Domesticity and Empire," in: M.R. Greer, W.D. Mignolo & M. Quilligan, eds., *Rereading the Black Legend: The Discourses of Religious and Racial Difference in the Renaissance Empires*, Chicago, 2007, 48–67.
Lal, R., *Domesticity and Power in the Early Mughal World*, Cambridge UK, 2005.
Malik, J., *Islam in South Asia: A Short History*, Leiden, 2008.
McGregor, R.S., *Hindi Literature from Its Beginnings to the Nineteenth Century*, Wiesbaden, 1984.
Mehta, M., *Indian Merchants and Entrepreneurs in Historical Perspective with Special Reference to Shroffs of Gujarat: 17th to 19th Centuries*, Delhi, 1991.
Mitter, P., *Indian Art*, Oxford, 2001.
Moosvi, S., "Medieval Indo-Persian Historiography," in: B. Ray, ed., *Different Types of History*, New Delhi, 2009, 59–69.
Moosvi, S., "Merchants in Medieval India," in: J.S. Grewal, ed., *The State and Society in Medieval India*, Delhi, 2005.
Mukherjee, T., & I. Habib "The Evidence of the Sale-Deeds of Vrindaban and Aritha," in: *Proceedings of the Indian History Congress 50th Session*, 1989, 236–255.
Mukherjee, T., & I. Habib. "The Mughal Administration and the Temples of Vrindavan during the Reigns of Jahangir and Shah Jahan," in: *Proceedings of the Indian History Congress 49th Session*, 1988, 287–300.
Mukherjee, T., & I. Habib, "Akbar and the Temples of Mathura and Its Environs," in: *Proceedings of the Indian History Congress 48th Session*, 1987, 234–250.
Mukhia, H., *The Mughals of India*, Oxford, 2004.
Rashid, S.A., "*Madad-i-Ma'ash* Grants under the Mughals," *JPHS* 9, 1961, 98–108.
Raychaudhuri, T., "The State and the Economy: The Mughal in Empire," in: T. Raychaudhuri & I. Habib, eds., *The Cambridge Economic History of India*, vol. I: *c. 1200–c. 1750*, Cambridge UK, 1982, 172–193.
Rogers, A., & H. Beveridge, *Tuzuk-i Jahangiri or the Memoirs of Jahangir*, New Delhi, 1978.
Richards, J.F., "The Formulation of Imperial Authority under Akbar and Jahangir," in: M. Alam & S. Subrahmanyam, eds., *The Mughal State, 1526–1750*, New Delhi, 1998, 126–168.
Saha, S., *Creating a Community of Grace: A History of the Puṣṭi Mārga in Northern and Western India (1493–1905)*, University of Ottawa, 2004.
Schimmel, A., *The Empire of the Great Mughals*, London, 2004.
Shivram, B., *Jagirdars in the Mughal Empire during the Reign of Akbar*, New Delhi, 2008.
Shivram, B., "The Authority of the *Padshah* in Sixteenth-Century Mughal India," *SACS* 2/2, 2009, 11–38.
Siddiqui, I.H., "The Eary Chishti Dargahs," in: C. Troll, ed., *Muslim Shrines in India: Their Character, History, and Significance*, New Delhi, 1989, 1–23.
Streusand, D., *Islamic Gunpowder Empires: Ottomans, Safavids, and Mughals*, Boulder, 2011.

Shandip Saha

Maratha (1674–1818)

The term "Maratha" has a wide range of meaning. In its widest sense, it denotes the people of → Maharashtra in general who speak the Marathi language, but, in its narrowest sense, it denotes the warrior class of Maharashtra in the medieval age, popularly known as 96 families of the Maratha. In this article, the term "Maratha" will be used in its widest sense.

Maratha Kingdom: Mystery of Śivājī's *Hindavī Svarājya*

In the first half of the 14th century, Maharashtra began to be ruled by Muslim powers, beginning with the Tughluqs and Bahmanis (1347–1527). In 1490, the Nizam Shahi rulers of Ahmednagar and Adil Shahi rulers of Bijapur became independent of the Bahmanis. The Bhonsle family, in which Śivājī (1627 or 1630–1680), the founder of the Maratha Kingdom, was born, first served the Nizam Shahi and then the Adil Shahi. Around 1645, Śivājī began to struggle to carve out an independent state from the Adil Shahi, making the hilly region of the Western Ghats his base. From the 1660s, the → Mughals, instead of the Adil Shahi, loomed large in Maharashtra under Aurangzeb (r. 1658–1707), with whom Śivājī was initially compelled to negotiate. In the 1670s, however, Śivājī consolidated his foothold, and finally in 1674, he was enthroned as the first king of the Maratha Kingdom at Raigad. The driving force for the Maratha independence was the Maratha local chiefs such as the Jedhes, Deshmukh of Bhor, and other Deshmukhs of the Balamaval region in the Western Ghats. A Deshmukh (Mar. *deśmukh*) was, in nature, the hereditary headman of the local community, as will be discussed below, but these Deshmukhs rose to prominence in the local society to form the local lord class, leading a band of around five hundred to one thousand followers. Śivājī rallied them under his banner for establishing an independent kingdom.

One of the controversial problems regarding the Maratha Kingdom is whether Śivājī had an aspiration to establish a "Hindu Empire," resisting the invading "Muslim powers."

V.D. Savarkar, the proponent of *hindutva* ideology, claimed that "it was the Hindavi Swarajya, the Hindu Empire – that was the great ideal which had fired the imagination and goaded the actions of Shivaji while he was but in his teens" (Savarkar, 1989, 57), basing this on a letter of Śivājī, the original of which, he indicated, V.K. Rajvade – the compiler of the *Marāṭhyāñcyā Itihāsācīṃ Sādhaneṃ* – possessed. This is actually the letter of Śivājī dated Apr 17, 1645, addressed to Dādājī Naras Prabhu, Deshpande (Mar. *deśpāṇḍe*, registrar) of Rohira Khor (*MIS.*, vol. XV, no. 268). G.S. Sardesai translated part of the same letter as follows:

> The (Adilshahi) Shah is entirely misinformed. Neither you nor I have turned disloyal. Please see me with that letter (of censure from Shah) immediately. You have no reason to feel distressed. Raireshvar, the divine master of your valley, inspire you and me alike and gives us success. He gives us power enough to establish Hindawi-Swarajya. (Sardesai, 1946, 100)

In his publication *New History of the Marathas*, vol. I (1946), G.S. Sardesai apparently translated this part from the *Marāṭhyāñcyā Itihāsācīṃ Sādhaneṃ* (vol. XV, no. 268), but the date of this letter given by him is not correct. Further, he changed the name of god from Rohireśvar in the original Marathi letter to Raireśvar, but his explanation for this in the footnote (Sardesai, 1946, 100) is not convincing. In his earlier publication *Marāṭhī Riyāsat*, vol. I (2 1988, 150), G.S. Sardesai quoted the relevant part of the original letter from the *Marāṭhyāñcyā Itihāsācīṃ Sādhaneṃ* without any change.

The problem is the term *hindavī svarājya* used in this letter of Śivājī. There is no doubt that this letter is authentic, as it has been reproduced in *Marāṭhyāñcyā Itihāsācīṃ Sādhaneṃ* by V.K. Rajvade. Then, the problem in point is why Śivājī used the term *hindavī svarājya* only in this letter addressed to an obscure Deshpande in the very early stage of his struggle for independence. He never used this term again in his later career. If he had a strong aspiration to establish a "Hindu Empire" as claimed by V.D. Savarkar, he must have used the term *hindavī svarājya*, at least, in the coronation oath in 1674. But he did not do so. The term *hindavī svarājya* used by Śivājī only once in his youth is, therefore, somewhat mysterious and problematic.

Struggles against Tāmramukhī (Mughals)

In 1680, Śivājī demised and was succeeded by his elder son, Sambhājī. Sambhājī continued to fight wars with the Mughals under Aurangzeb, but in 1689 he was captured and cruelly executed. Raigad, the capital fort of the Maratha Kingdom, was stormed by the Mughals, and Śāhū, the son of Sambhājī, was taken captive in the Mughal camp. Rājārām, the half brother of Sambhājī, fled from Raigad to the south and was enthroned as the third king of the Maratha Kingdom. Being physically week, Rājārām himself was not a brave warrior as his father was, but he did share a strong will to resist the Mughals.

Rājārām sent many letters of appeal to the Maratha people like Maratha local chiefs (mainly Deshmukhs) in Maharashtra from his base in Jinji (today Gingee) in the far south of India. In these letters of appeal, Rājārām called the Mughals, especially Aurangzeb, Tāmramukhī or simply Tāmra (lit. a copper-faced one), indicating a red-faced monkey or man. Rājārām appealed for the Maratha people to defend *mahārāṣṭra dharma* ("the spirit of Maharashtrians"; this term is attributed to the Maratha saint → Rāmdās; see Ranade, 1961, 64), by struggling against Tāmramukhīs, the monkeylike, strange-looking Mughals. In a letter addressed to Nāgojī Māne, Deshmukh of Mhaswad, for example, Rājārām wrote:

> You had once sided with *tāmra*, but the *rājya* of *svāmī* (king) is the *rājya* of god, there must not be the molestation of *tāmra* in this *rājya* and *mahārāṣṭradharma* should be defended.... With this intention in mind, you wholeheartedly served the *svāmī*. (trans. by author; *Selections from the Government Records in the Alienation Office Poona, Sanads & Letters*, 1913, ch. V, no. 9, see also ch. V, no. 11; *MIS.*, vol. XV, no. 288)

Again, in his letter addressed to Bājī Jedhe, Deshmukh of Bhor, Rājārām wrote, "This *rājya* is *mahārāṣṭra rājya*, for which you endured hardships" (*MIS.*, vol. XV, no. 282). It means that the self-identity of Rājārām and Maratha people was more physical and regional/ethnic, as Maharashtrians not like Tāmramukhīs, than religious as Hindus against Muslims. It is thus irrelevant to find a religious war in the struggle between the Mughals and the Marathas in this period.

Peśvāī: Maratha Kingdom under Peshvas

Rājārām died in 1700, leaving his wife, Tārābāī, as the regent. She took over her husband's will and commanded the Maratha forces herself to fight against the Mughals. In 1707, Aurangzeb, now old and tired of war with the Marathas for more than 25 years, demised in Aurangabad, and Śāhū, the son of Sambhājī in Mughal custody, left the Mughal camp to return to Maharashtra. He was crowned in 1708 as the fourth king of the Maratha Kingdom after a severe contention with Tārābāī.

Having been in Mughal custody for more than 15 years, Śāhū (r. 1708–1749) could not consolidate his foothold in Maharashtra. He appointed Bāḷājī Viśvanāth, a Brahman from Konkan, as Peshva (Mar. *peśvā*, prime minister) in 1714. Bāḷājī Viśvanāth led the Maratha forces to the north and reached Delhi, the seat of the Mughals, in 1719 for the first time in Maratha history. In 1720, however, Bāḷājī Viśvanāth died, and his son Bājīrāv succeeded to the office of Peshva. Bājīrāv Peśvā left Pune in 1736 for the expedition to the north and attacked Delhi in 1737. At the same time, Bājīrāv Peśvā gradually wrested the real power from Śāhū, who became practically confined in Satara. Bājīrāv Peśvā died in 1740, and his son Baḷājī Bājīrāv succeeded to the office of Peshva. Śāhū finally transferred all the power to Baḷājī Bājīrāv Peśvā at his death in 1749.

Thus began the Peśvāī (the rule of Peshvas), and Pune, the seat of the Peshvas, became the capital city of the Maratha Kingdom. Under Peśvāī of Bājīrāv and Baḷājī Bājīrāv, the Maratha Kingdom rose to the zenith of its power, overwhelming the Mughals almost all across India.

In January 1761, however, the huge Maratha army that advanced northward to Delhi was completely defeated by the Afghan forces commanded by Aḥmad Shāh Durrānī in Panipat to the north of Delhi. Baḷājī Bājīrāv Peśvā, shocked by the death of his eldest son in Panipat, died in June 1761 and was succeeded by his second son, Mādhavrāv.

In spite of the setback caused by the defeat in Panipat, the Maratha forces soon regained power. This time, however, a new class of Maratha chiefs rose to prominence. The most outstanding among them were the Shindes of Gwalior, Holkars of Indor, Bhonsles of Nagpur, and Gaikwads of Baroda, all of whom did not belong to traditional Maratha chief families like

Deshmukhs. With Peshva at its center, these Maratha chiefs formed a loose alliance, which the British of the East India Company called the Maratha Confederacy, though there was no Marathi term that corresponded to this.

Vatan System: Structure of Local Society

The local society in the Maratha Kingdom was composed of the twofold regional communities, that is, the village community and the local community that was made up of about 50 villages and generally corresponded to the local administration division (district) of the state variously designated as *pargaṇā*, *tālukā*, and *taraf*.

The key term for understanding the structure and social dynamism of the local society is *vatan*, which denoted every hereditary office in the local society with the remuneration or perquisites accrued from it. The regular members of the village community and local community had their respective *vatan*s so that they were designated as *vatandār* (holder of the *vatan*).

The village community consisted of various *vatandār*s on the village level. The village headman was Patil, whose *vatan* was called *pāṭīlkī*, and village accountant Kulkarni with the *vatan* called *kuḷkarṇīpaṇ*. The peasants, who were regular members of the village community, were designated as *vatandār* Kunbi, in contrast with tenants-at-will called *sukhvastī* or *upārī*, who mostly cultivated the land belonging to the village community (Fukazawa, 1991, 151–154; Kotani, 2002, 24–25). The artisan and service castes such as Sutar (carpenter), Lohar (iron-smith), Kumbhar (potter), Joshi (priest), Parit (washerman), and Nhavi (barber), and some members of untouchable castes, like the Mahar, Mang, and Chambhar, had their respective *vatan*s so that they were *vatandār*s. They were also designated as *balutedār, balute* meaning the tax-free land and/or perquisites provided to them by the village community as a whole (Fukazawa, 1991, ch. 8; Kulkarni, 1996, 66–74). There was a popular saying, "*sāṭhīpraja va bārābalute*" (families of 60 peasants and 12 sorts of *balutedār*s), which meant all members of the village community (*Śiva Caritra Sāhitya*, I, no. 22; VIII, no. 70; Kotani, 2002, 24, 35). This ratio of peasants and artisan/service castes must have constituted the ideal type of village community for the people of Maharashtra in this period.

The local community, however, was composed of about 50 villages. Of the local community, Deshmukh was the headman and Deshpande the writer/registrar. Deshmukh and Deshpande were *vatandār*s who held *deśmukhī vatan* and *deśpāṇḍepāṇ vatan*, respectively. Castes like the Sutar, Lohar, Kumbhar, Nhavi, Parit, and others formed the primary group of each caste within the extent of the local community, in which there existed a *mhetar* (headman) of each caste. The office of the *mhetar* (headman) was also a *vatan*.

Thus the structure of the local society in the Maratha Kingdom can be characterized as the Vatan system (Kotani, 2002, chs. 1–5). The Vatan system, however, was not a flat communal structure that did not include the unequal or exploitative relationships. Deshmukh was actually the local lord who appropriated a considerable portion of the social resources produced in the local society. Patil was the master of his village who had the right to take various shares from almost all members of the village.

In spite of this, Patil and Deshmukh continued to function as the headman of the village community and local community, respectively. The village community and local community often held the community meeting called *pañcāyat* or *sabhā* to work out solutions to disputes as well as to confirm hereditary rights like *vatan*. In one case, for example, a quarrel occurred in a village in *taraf* Ale, *prānt* (province) Junnar, regarding the *vaḍīlpaṇ* (seniority right) of the *pāṭīlkī vatan* between two sons from the different wives of the former Patil (1780–1781). The villagers (*pāṇḍharī*) met together in the village-community meeting (*pañcāyat*) and decided that the son of the first wife should have the *vaḍīlpaṇ* (*Selections from Satara Rajas' and Peshwas' Diaries*, vol. VIII, no. 864). When a dispute at the local-community level arose, the local-community meeting was convened. As an example, in a dispute regarding the village boundary between a village and three neighboring villages, the local-community meeting (*pañcāyatgot*) of *subhā* (province) Payaghat and Balaghat (in the Nizam's territories) was convened and decided that the Patil of the village should walk around the boundary alleged to be right by him, placing a cowhide on his head as an ordeal (*divya*). The Patil succeeded in the ordeal, and the boundary was settled as alleged by him, but he had to be purified (*śuddha*) of the sin of wearing the cowhide (1744–1745; *Selections from Satara Rajas' and Peshwas' Diaries*, vol. I, no. 280; Gune, 1953, 100–101).

The local society in the Maratha Kingdom, thus, contained within itself two contradictory sets of social relationships between the *vatandārs*, namely, that of the communal-horizontal relationships and that of the exploitative-vertical relationships.

Development of Market Economy

As the market economy steadily developed in the 17th and 18th centuries, however, various new *vatans* began to be introduced in the village community. The most popular among them were the *vatans* of Teli (oilman), Vani (merchant), and Tamboli (*pānsupārī* [betel leaf roll] seller). As an example, a Tamboli asked the Patil of a village in *tālukā* Karepathar, *prānt* Pune, to bestow him the Tamboli *vatan* of the village. Complying with his request, the Patil gave him the Tamboli *vatan* with a plot of land in the village residence area (*pāṇḍharī*) on which to erect a shop, under the condition of payment of a fixed tax (1783; Oturkar, no. 71). In this case, the Tamboli became a *vatandār* of the village but not a *balutedār*. The Tamboli sold *pān* (betel leaf) and *pānsupārī* prepared by him in his shop to the villagers. In the same manner, the *vatandār* Teli of a village pressed oil and sold it in his shop to the villagers. These *vatandārs* were, so to say, the secondary *vatandārs* who were commodity producers/sellers without being provided *balute* by the village as a whole in contrast with such primary *vatandārs* (*balutedārs*) as Sutar, Lohar, Kumbhar, Nhavi, Parit, Joshi, and so on.

Thus, as the market economy developed, the village came to accept more and more secondary *vatandārs* who resided in the village and opened their shops to sell respective commodities.

As another result of the development of the market economy, some *vatans*, especially lucrative *vatans* like those of Deshmukh and Patil, became the transferable and saleable properties or commodities. In one case, the Patil of a village in *parganā* Karde, *sarkār* Junnar, sold a half share of his *vatan* for Rs. 7,751, as he had deeply fallen into debt by reason of the trouble involving his *vatan* (1730–1731; *Selections from Satara Rajas' and Peshwas' Diaries*, vol. I, no. 289). In yet another case, the Patil of a village in *taraf* Patas, *prānt* Pune, sold a half share of his *vatan* for Rs. 701, having been struck by a severe famine to be reduced to "an absolute want of every kind of sustenance" (1799; Elphinstone, 1872, app. 1–5). When such *vatans* were offered for sale, even kings were eager to buy them. In one case, for example, Śivājī bought the *pāṭīlkī vatan* of a village in *tālukā* Nirthadi, *prānt* Pune, and granted it to his daughter. After her death, Rājārām, the third king, bestowed it on his daughter (1696; *Selections from the Peshwa Dafter*, vol. XXXI, no. 67).

Thus, the development of market economy caused various changes in the local society and made the Vatan system an increasingly complicated societal fabric.

Maratha Government and Local Society

The Maratha government utilized the village community and local community as part of the local administration system of the state, as its bureaucratic apparatus on the local-society level was not sufficiently well organized to be able to maintain the authority of state as well as societal order in the local society. Thus, the extent of the local community generally corresponded to the local administration division (district). Accordingly, Deshmukh and Deshpande functioned as the hereditary district officers, while Patil and Kulkarni functioned as the hereditary village officers.

In the Maratha Kingdom, the land tax was levied on the village as a whole. When the autumnal harvest time came near, the district officials visited all the villages in the district to inspect the yield of the year and settled the land tax of each village with Patil. Patil had the obligation to pay the entire land tax levied on the village as a whole. There were even cases in which the Patil who failed to pay the land tax of the village was arrested and thrown in jail (e.g. in 1748–1749; *Selections from Satara Rajas' and Peshwas' Diaries*, vol. III, no. 413). When a village was devastated by foreign armed forces like the Mughals or struck by natural calamities like famine or epidemics, the Patil of the village asked the government for remission of the land tax.

Deshmukh and Deshpande represented the interests of the local community with regard, for example, to the yearly settlement of land tax of the villages in the district. In one case, the Deshmukh and Deshpande of *tālukā* Avasari, *prānt* Junnar, presented themselves to the district office to request remission of the land tax of a village in the district under the following circumstances: this village had been plundered to devastation by the Mughals, so that four years' remission of the land tax had been granted by the Maratha government. In the first two years, the village could have paid the remitted land tax, but in the third year, *kharīf* (autumnal harvest) was completely destroyed by the failure of monsoon, and *rabī* (spring harvest) could not even be seeded. On this ground, the Deshmukh and Deshpande requested the further remission of the land tax of the third and fourth years (*Selections from the Peshwa Dafter*, vol. XXXIX, no. 59).

As the reward for their quasi-official duties, Deshmukh and Deshpande were granted tax-free villages and/or lands in the district, while Patil and Kulkarni were granted tax-free lands in the village. From these villages and lands, they could collect the money and allowance in kind equivalent to the land tax and other taxes levied on them by the Maratha government.

Thus, the total social resources produced in the local society were divided into the following three parts: the first part to the direct producers (peasants) to maintain their livelihood, the second part to the *vatandār*s other than the *vatandār* Kunbis to sustain the Vatan system as the very basis of the society and the state, and the third part to the state as taxes to keep the state apparatus in motion. Most probably, the ratio of division into these three parts would be one-third of the total social resources to each part, that is to say, one-third to the direct producers (peasants), one-third to the *vatandār*s for the maintenance of the Vatan system, and the remaining one-third to the state.

Brahmanical Rituals: *Yajña*, *Śānti*, and *Prāyaścitta*

In the Maratha Kingdom, various Brahmanical rituals were performed, of which the most conspicuous were → *yajña*, *śānti*, and *prāyaścitta*.

Yajña was the typical Brahmanical ritual performed by a *yajamāna* (patron) to gain personal merit, employing Brahmans and defraying the expenditure for it. *Yajña* with animal sacrifice was named *paśu bandha* (Kane, 2 1974, 1109–1132). In the Maratha Kingdom, though *brahmahatyā* and *gohatyā* (Brahman killing and cow killing) were assumed to be two of the most serious *doṣas* (sin, crime), *yajña* involving the sacrifice of even cows was performed under the auspices of the Peshva government. In one such case, a Brahman decided to perform *yajña* in a village in *pargaṇā* Nevasa on the river Godāvarī. The Peshva government issued an order to the district official to provide him with the necessary materials and labor forces required for *yajña* (*Selections from Satara Rajas' and Peshwas' Diaries*, vol. II, no. 331). The materials designated in the order included a vast number of bricks to prepare the *vedi* (altar) and *kuṇḍa* (sacrificial fireplace), timbers for erecting *maṇḍapa* (sacrificial pavilion), *samidh* (sacrificial sticks), and so on. Many Gavandis (bricklayers) and Sutars (carpenters) were called to the ritual place to burn and lay bricks and erect the *maṇḍapa*, respectively. Many Kumbhars (potters) were also called together to prepare the earthenware necessary for the ritual at the spot, especially various types of water jars. Two provisions of the order prescribed as follows:

(1) *gāī savatsa* (cows with calves) should be bought by Rs. 600 to give to him, and
(2) *gāī 7 sar 2 vṛṣabha 5 paśu yajñā*s (2 cows and 5 bullocks, in all 7 animals for *yajña*) should be given to him.

(There must be some confusion in this provision of the source. G.C. Vad, the compiler of the source book, interpreted this part to mean "7 cows with calves, 2 bullocks, 5 animals for sacrifice." But this interpretation seems not to be convincing, as the cows with calves were most probably meant for *godāna* [donation of a milk cow], not for sacrifice.) Yet in another case of *yajña* performed by a Brahman in the Kushatarpana village on the right bank of the Godāvarī, he was provided with, among others, 4 *yūpa*s (*Selections from Satara Rajas' and Peshwas' Diaries*, vol. V, no. 238). *Yūpa* was a pillar to which a sacrificial animal was bound. Thus, in this *yajña*, at least four animals were sacrificed, though it is not clear whether cows were included among them.

Śānti was the propitiatory ritual performed on the occasions when *adbhuta* (extraordinary phenomena) like an eclipse, a thunderbolt, an earthquake, or an epidemic occurred (Kane, vol. V, 2 1977, 719–814). In one case, a *duṣṭa graha* (bad star) appeared on the zodiac in Narayangad fort so that the Peshva government ordered the Havaldar of the fort to summon Brahmans and make them perform *śānti*, defraying Rs. 10 to 15 (*Selections from Satara Rajas' and Peshwas' Diaries*, vol. II, no. 319). In Mahuli fort, the flagpole bearing a new flag for the *dasarā* festival was struck by a *vīj* (thunderbolt) and split into two parts. The cause of this *adbhuta* was attributed to the anger of Śani (Saturn; see → *navagrahas*), and a hundred thousand *japas* (repeating prayers in an undertone) were chanted to Śani by summoned Brahmans (*Selections from Satara Rajas' and Peshwas' Diaries*, vol. II, no. 312). Yet in another case, *dukhaṇeṃ* (disease) spread in Visapur fort, and 100–120 persons were taken ill, of whom 25 eventually died (*Selections from Satara Rajas' and Peshwas' Diaries*, vol. II, no. 326). The Havaldar of the fort asked the Peshva government for permission to perform *adbhuta śānti*, to which the government gave the sanction (for further details of *śānti*, see Kotani, 2002, 232–233).

Prāyaścitta, the purification ceremony of *doṣa* (sin, crime), must be the most popularly and widely performed Brahmanical ritual in the Maratha Kingdom, as *doṣa* in precolonial Maharashtra included a much wider range of offensive or faulty acts than sins and crimes in the modern senses. It was the commonplace procedure that a man who committed a serious *doṣa* like murder was made to undergo *prāyaścitta* after suffering the state punishment such as imprisonment (e.g. *Selections from Satara Rajas' and Peshwas' Diaries*, vol. VIII, no. 892). In addition to ordinary *doṣas* like this, there were various *doṣas* characteristic of the Hindu culture, a typical example of which was *gohatyā* (cow killing). In one case, a Kunbi (peasant) of a village in *tālukā* Khedebare unintentionally killed his cow while milking her. Having committed the serious *doṣa* of cow killing, he was seized with the fear that he would be made to fall into *naraka* (hell) if he did not undergo *prāyaścitta* to purify himself of his *doṣa* of cow killing. Thus, he presented himself to the government office in Pune and asked to be punished. Accordingly, the Peshva government ordered the Patil of his village to send him to a holy place on the river Kṛṣṇā and ask Brahmans there to perform *prāyaścitta* on him (Oturkar, no. 191; Kotani, 2002, 197–198). There were even *doṣas* applicable only to Brahmans. Typical of such *doṣas* was eating meat (*māsabhakṣaṇa*) and drinking liquor (*surāpāna*). For example, a Brahman who was the Kulkarni of a village in *tālukā* Khed, *sarkār* Junnar, began to live with a dancing girl and took to drinking liquor and eating meat. His *doṣa* was assumed to be transmitted to his relatives through *saṃsarga* (social intercourse) so that the Peshva government ordered them to undergo *prāyaścitta* (*Selections from the Peshwa Dafter*, vol. XLIII, no. 29; for further details of *prāyaścitta*, see Kotani, 2002, ch. 10).

Thus, the Brahmanical culture or value permeated down to the local society through various Brahmanical rituals, especially *prāyaścitta*.

Devī Worship: *Śānti* as Village Ritual

In spite of the infiltration of the Brahmanical culture, the local society still maintained its own culture notably exemplified by Devī worship (see → Mahādevī). The typical ritual of Devī worship was *śānti*, but *śānti* performed in the local society was quite different in nature from the state ritual of *śānti* performed by Brahmans as referred to above. *Śānti* in the local society was the village ritual in which all the members of the village took part. The conspicuous feature of *śānti* as the village ritual was the animal sacrifice to appease the anger of Devī indicated, for example, by an epidemic. Thus, in the village ritual of *śānti*, the *vatandār* Mahar and Mang (see above) played the key role of sacrificing the animal and shedding the blood on Devī in the figure of an idol made of clay by *vatandār* Kumbhar.

In the villages, even without the occurrence of extraordinary phenomena like epidemics, *śānti* was performed as, so to speak, a yearly event on such festive occasions as *dasarā*. In one such *śānti*, a buffalo decorated with turmeric and garlands was made to walk around the village boundary, following the *vatandār* Mahar and Mang, who held a pot of *peḍhā* (sweetmeat; the *peḍhās* must be thrown over the village boundary by them to entice evil spirits haunting the village outside the village boundary; see Whitehead, 1916, 46–53). Meanwhile, the *vatandār* Sutar prepared a *ratha* (float), in which an idol of Devī made of clay by the *vatandār* Kumbhar was put. The villagers drew around the *ratha* throughout the village and eventually came to the *maṇḍapa* erected for *śānti*, in which the idol of Devī was installed. After walking around the village boundary, the buffalo came before the *maṇḍapa*, where the *vatandār* Mahar and Mang cut off the head of the buffalo. All the villagers, old and young, came to the *maṇḍapa* to worship the idol of Devī. On the fourth day, the ritual was completed, and the idol was brought to the village boundary and thrown out of the village (*MIS.*, vol. XXI, no. 215; Kotani, 2002, 127–128, 233–234). Thus, *śānti* in the local society was quite different in nature from the Brahmanical *śānti*. It means that the local society continued to maintain its own culture even under the strong influence of the Brahmanical culture.

Downfall of Maratha Kingdom (Peshva Government)

In 1772 Mādhavrāv Peśvā died after a lengthy bout with an illness. His younger brother, Nārāyaṇrāv, succeeded to the office of Peshva, but he was assassinated the following year. Raghunāthrāv, Nārāyaṇrāv's uncle, who was suspected of being involved in the assassination, became the Peshva. In 1774, however, a posthumous son of Nārāyaṇrāv was born to be named Mādhavrāv Nārāyaṇ and was appointed to the office of Peshva, replacing Raghunāthrāv. Nānā Phaḍnīs, the regent of the infant Peshva, came to hold the real power of the Peshva government. In 1775, Raghunāthrāv asked the help of the army of the British East India Company to confront the Peshva government. This war, popularly called the First Anglo-Maratha War, continued until 1782. In 1795, Mādhavrāv Nārāyaṇ Peśvā, having long been depressed under the regency of Nānā Phaḍnīs, committed suicide, and Bājīrāv II, the son of Raghunāthrāv, succeeded him as Peshva. In 1800, Nānā Phaḍnīs died, leaving Bājīrāv II in serious trouble with leading Maratha chiefs like the Holkars and Gaikwads. In 1802, Yaśvantrāv Holkar attacked Pune, and Bājīrāv II escaped to Bombay to ask for help from the army of the East India Company. In 1803, he retuned to Pune with the army of the East India Company, against which the Shindes, Bhonsles, Holkars, and some other Maratha chiefs began to fight (the Second Anglo-Maratha War). All the Maratha chiefs, however, signed peace treaties with the East India Company by 1805 to become the so-called native states (the final breakdown of the Maratha Confederacy). In 1817, Bājīrāv II, long under the patronage of the East India Company, suddenly attacked the army of the East India Company stationed in the suburbs of Pune but was defeated in 1818 (the Third Anglo-Maratha War). It brought about the downfall of the Maratha Kingdom (Peshva government) and the beginning of British colonial rule in western India.

Bibliography

Elphinstone, M., *Report on the Territories conquered from the Paishwa*, Bombay, ²1872.

Fukazawa, H., *The Medieval Deccan: Peasants, Social System and States, Sixteenth to Eighteenth Centuries*, New Delhi, 1991.

Gune, V.T., *The Judicial System of the Marathas*, Poona, 1953.

Kane, P.V., *History of Dharmaśāstra*, vol. II, Poona, ²1974; vol. V, Puna, ²1977.

Kotani, H., *Western India in Historical Transition: Seventeenth to Early Twentieth Centuries*, New Delhi, 2002.

Kulkarni, A.R., *Medieval Maharashtra*, New Delhi, 1996.

Marāṭhyāñcyā Itihāsācīṃ Sādhaneṃ, ed. V.K. Rajvade, 22 vols., Poona, 1898–1919.

Oturkar, R.V., ed., *Peśve Kālīn Sāmājik va Ārthik Patravyavahār*, Pune, 1950.

Ranade, M.G., *Rise of the Maratha Power*, New Delhi, 1961.

Sardesai, G.S., *Marāṭhī Riyāsat*, vol. I, Mumbai, ¹1902, ²1988.

Sardesai, G.S., *New History of the Marathas*, vol. I, Bombay, 1946.

Savarkar, V.D., *Hindutva: Who is a Hindu*, New Delhi, ¹1923, ⁶1989.

Selections from the Government Records in the Alienation Office Poona, Sanads & Letters, ed. G.C. Vad, Bombay, 1913.

Selections from the Peshwa Dafter, ed. G.S. Sardesai, 45 vols., Bombay, 1930–1934.

Selections from Satara Rajas' and Peshwas' Diaries, ed. G.C. Vad, 9 vols., Poona, 1905–1911.

Śiva Caritra Sāhitya, publ. Bharat Itihas Samshodak Mandal, 13 vols., Pune, 1926–1965.

Whitehead, H., *The Village Gods in South India*, Oxford, 1916.

H. KOTANI

British Rule (1757–1947)

Probably for most Hindus, the era of British imperialist rule brought little more significant change than the preceding era. Living in villages seldom visited by government officials and perhaps enjoying improved communications while suffering the consequences of increased land assessments, during much of this period the majority of Indians experienced the same degree of social, cultural, and religious change as their ancestors did under the rule of the → Mughals and other indigenous states. However, the dynamics at play in South Asia's cities and the changes wrought by both Britons and Indians in this era set in motion forces that would irrevocably alter the subcontinent's human landscape for most of its inhabitants within two generations of India's and → Pakistan's Independence in 1947. While only a minority of South Asia's 300 million citizens knew it at that time, new or renewed notions of Hindu reform, Hindu → nationalism, and Hindu identity emerged in the period of British rule as mass communications, representative government, and vote-bank politics coalesced in cities and their immediately adjacent rural areas. The rapid transportation and communication systems developed under the aegis of European imperialism helped transmit these changes not only across the subcontinent but also throughout the Hindu diaspora, which had been globalized by British labor and trade policies among its colonies and territories.

Defining an era of history on the basis of foreign political rule can be misleading, since it might suggest that changes during it resulted solely from outside influence. During the era of British imperialist rule, important changes occurred among Hindu forms of practice, belief, sensibility, and self-identity that had little to nothing to do with the British presence. While avoiding this pitfall, one must not dismiss the impact of the British state and its accompanying cultural hegemony. These were uniform neither in their extent nor in their causes. Nor did these occur without at least some Indian engagement. However powerful British governance and however persuasive European cultures, many Hindus (like many Muslims, Sikhs, and Jains) participated willingly in their engagement with the West, even as many others resisted. Most South Asians experienced a minimum of direct interaction with Britons, living in rural areas far removed from opportunities of routine contact and lines of cultural transmission. Others inhabited Indian princely states, which may have been more or less under British supervision, but involved fewer Britons in the everyday affairs of its residents than territories under the government of India.

"Hinduism"

Perhaps no issue better illustrates the contentious perspectives on this period than the history of the term "Hinduism." Some have argued that Hindus used equivalent, indigenous terms before the British arrival, others that Hindus coined the name in the context of dialogue with the British, and yet others that Britons were the first to adapt the term. While the earliest documented use of the word "Hinduism" belongs to the Scottish missionary Charles Grant in 1787, it remains uncertain whether he coined the term or just made the first recorded use of it (Oddie, 2006, 71). Whatever the case, by the 19th century, an entity by that name was posited and identified by many Indians and Westerners as a religion.

Coterminous with Indians' postulation of Hinduism was their adaptation of the concept of religion. Although Sanskritist A. Nicholson has demonstrated a self-consciousness among some premodern Indians of being Hindu based on the beliefs and practices stemming from → Vedānta philosophical traditions referred to as *astika* (Nicholson, 2010, 196–201), this identity did not conform fully with the notions of religion imposed by Western administrators and scholars. Moreover, while the Islamic concept of *dīn* approximates the broadest notion of the European idea of religion, the more specific ideal of an institutionalized system of beliefs and morality – derived from central texts that are controlled by particular specialists – that is distinct from political, economic, and scientific realms owes it presence in South Asia to Western contact. Despite these origins, the term underwent changes and added dimensions as a result of social interactions with and intellectual contributions by Indians as well as by other peoples colonized and imperially subjugated by Europeans. In the end, then, the concepts associated with religion during the era of British imperial rule may have had their deepest roots in Europe, but their fruition relied on exposure to many non-European soils.

Hindus increasingly sought to describe their practices and beliefs as a singular religion – sometimes called Hinduism and other times called *sanātanadharma* (the eternal religion; see → *dharma*) – in order to claim the mantle of religion for themselves. This reflected a growing desire among Hindus to be associated with a religion, an impulse influenced by their efforts to resist Christian proselytization, to claim government benefits accorded to members of identifiable religions, to create a constituency as part of their democratic political ambitions, and to enjoy the recognition of their practices and beliefs as a religion in the increasingly universalized language of world religion. Even if recent research is correct in its suggestion that an indigenous formulation of Hindu traditions understood them in a manner more in accord with modern notions of religion than earlier scholarship has admitted, the British state helped to irrevocably alter Hindu self-understandings by administratively introducing a new categorical paradigm.

While largely restricted to South Asia, the entity called "Hinduism" eventually became popularly understood both there and in the West to be one of a select number of "world religions," a category for religions assumed to be based on certain expected prerequisites: a "canon" of "sacred books," established moral codes, a male authoritative hierarchy, and specific required practices, often performed in dedicated buildings found in communities across a vast geographic range. In European eyes, Hinduism had graduated from the geographically constrained status of "ethnic religion" or "national religion" to join the ranks of "world religions" in the pantheon of religious scholarship that coalesced between the 17th and 20th centuries. As a world religion, Hinduism could be accorded a status akin to that of Christianity, Islam, Judaism, and Buddhism (though no universal consensus existed regarding the complete list of world religions; Masuzawa, 2005, 205). Early modern Advaita Vedāntists may have compared their practices and beliefs with Muslims, Buddhists, and Jains and dismissed them as *nāstikas* (deniers; Nicholson, 2010, 200). However, they were not compelled by a commitment to an abstract, universal notion of religion to qualify and classify all religions as European Christians hastened to do. Indeed, over time, Europeans felt compelled toward a global classification of religions, even those that posed no immediate ideological or proselytizing threat to Christianity (or secularism). In many ways, these new categories of religious differentiation replaced those of medieval Western Christianity, which commonly divided the world into pagans (or heathens), Jews, Christians, and Saracens (Muslims). The Roman Catholic Church understood these categories of people to correlate with a teleological salvation history, in which humanity benefited from increasingly truer forms of religion, except for the instance of Muslims, who represented either a heretical schism or a satanic plot among haplessly duped Christians. Even when less hierarchical views of the various world religions prevailed, European and Indian audiences tended to view those included in this category as more developed than those classified as folk religions, tribal religions, and native religions. These terms often implied a developmental limitation based on a progressive teleology that for some supplanted – even as it borrowed from – Western Christian teleologies.

The Nature of British Imperial Rule

While throughout its 200-year history the British state hesitated to change many of the apparatuses of revenue collection, political surveillance, and information gathering deployed by the Mughal state, it made significant changes that often had profound effects on the ground, especially in the long run.

The history of the British state divides into two periods: Company Raj (1757–1858) and Crown Rule (1858–1947). Although founded in 1600, the East India Company did not become an effective trade presence until close to the 18th century. Once established, this presence relied on a series of factories (fortified warehouses) in which goods, merchants, and their protective forces could be housed. In 1756, a dispute with Bengal's Mughal-appointed *nawāb* (ruler) led to his occupation of the Calcutta (now Kolkata) factory and a subsequent counterattack by the East India Company's army. The Bengal governor's defeat at Plassey and a subsequent, more substantial company victory at Buxar (now Baksar) in 1764 led eventually to the Mughal recognition of the company as provincial tax collector. No mundane task, revenue collection brought not only a new, lucrative, revenue stream for the East India Company but also a need to understand more about Bengal's people in order to, first, maximize their profit and, second, after an initial period of particularly rapacious behavior, execute their perceived responsibilities of government.

The East India Company's early attempts to learn about the natural and human landscapes of Bengal (and, increasingly, other provinces) relied both on broad, state-sponsored surveys and on narrow, individual-initiated studies by some of their employees. From the start, East India Company officials tended to view religion as an inherent quality of all Indians. While trying to determine what groups made up the unfamiliar populations of South Asia, Britons distinguished them according to religious identity: Hindu, Muslim, Sikh, Jain, Christian, and so on. Although many of the subcontinent's inhabitants may have associated themselves with such identities, not all did, and few did all the time. Nor did the inhabitants presume that identifying with one group inherently meant excluding themselves from others; self-descriptions mixing identities presumed by Britons to be exclusively Hindu or Muslim were not uncommon. Such unexpected declarations tended to figure in official reports only as examples of aberrations that had to be excised in order to fit the classificatory schema common to the increasingly dense official record and the widening range of published books. If Indians primarily identified themselves by religion, and religions were primarily defined by beliefs, then the presumption followed that religions with mutually exclusive belief systems irreconcilably divided the subcontinent. In other words, Britons and other Europeans anticipated that divergent convictions regarding the plurality of divinity, the veneration of images, and the consumption of meat must create insurmountable communal divisions that fractured society like so many geological fault lines. Meanwhile, the rationalists among them viewed Indian thought as inherently religious and, hence, nonrational. Hence, the Western study of philosophy often excluded Indian systematic thought as something other than rational, which, as R. King has demonstrated, tended to be labeled as mystical (King, 1999, 28–34).

The allowance of British missionaries in 1813 helped re-inscribe this impression in Western minds. While the company initially prohibited missionary activity in its territories for fear of disturbing its trade, the rising English evangelical

Fig. 1: Anglican Cathedral Church of the Resurrection (built 1887), Lahore, Pakistan (photo by Peter Gottschalk).

movement successfully overcame this opposition through political pressure. European missionaries had already worked in South India long before this. Men like the Catholic Roberto de Nobili (1577–1656) and the Protestant Bartholomaeus Ziegenbalg (1683–1719) generated a significant amount of material, although members of the two wings of European Christianity seldom read each other's accounts. In their efforts to create and distribute vernacular Bibles, British missionaries accelerated existing European efforts – both missionary and secular – to translate Indian languages. Baptist missionary William Carey (1761–1834) – one of the first Britons in this effort – worked with Mritunjaya and other Bengali → *paṇḍits* to produce six complete translations of the Bible, seven written grammars of various Indian languages, and dictionaries in Sanskrit, Bengali, and Marathi (Porter, 1996, 190–191). Significantly, this work allowed Carey to make inroads into the company's college at Fort William in Calcutta, which gave him access to the *paṇḍits* there as well as entrance to the Asiatic Society (Oddie, 2006, 108). Meanwhile, their effort to understand those whom they sought to convert led the missionaries to a close observation of local practices, which lent their resulting reports substantial authority among the broad European audiences who sought more information about "exotic" India.

By the mid-19th century, the East India Company controlled directly or indirectly most of the subcontinent through political maneuvering and military conquest. However, a series of rebellions that began among disgruntled sepoys (*sipāhī*, soldiers) in 1857 spread across much of North India, eventually involving a variety of disaffected groups. Called "the Mutiny" by Britons and "the First War of Independence" by nationalists, the violence was as ferocious as it was unexpected, and it created what historian C.A. Bayly describes as an especially acute "information panic" (Bayly, 1996, 316). Ending the East India Company's rule and taking direct control of its most valuable territory in 1858, the British Crown government set about understanding as much as it could afford about the entire subcontinent and all its residents, launching a variety of expensive projects. These included the Archaeological Survey of India (1871), the Census of India (1872), and the Ethnographic Survey of India (1901). Breaking the pattern set by the Mughals, these organizations provided information not only for the exclusive use of the state but also for the education of both a European and Indian public. Throughout most of these projects, religious identification remained the most salient category of differentiation and comparison. Significantly, in the post-1857 period, an Indian public slowly coalesced that increasingly sought British representations and European-originated forms of knowledge to complement their own understandings of their natural and social environment. They gradually appropriated British conceptualizations of indigenous social categories, even as they contributed to those conceptualizations.

While Europeans may have lent the impetus for the collection and canonization of a select body of "sacred Hindu scriptures," many Hindus – particularly Brahmans near European centers like Madras (now Chennai) and Calcutta – contributed by proffering their choices of texts for Western review and translation. Europeans had long before identified Brahmans as the Hindu elite whose control of sacred and genealogical books seemed to signify their role as indigenous-knowledge authorities. The earliest European missionaries and amateur enthusiasts had employed Brahmans to engage Hindu texts that promised insight into religion, society, history, and myth. Even while some (though certainly not all) Europeans dismissed Brahmans as pious frauds and their books as fantastic exaggerations, they continued to rely on them to provide material for Western analysis and judgment. In no small way, Hindu interlocutors such as these helped engender what anthropologist V. Das has described as the "semitification of Hinduism." The East India Company's initial endeavor to establish a Hindu legal system as part of their new responsibility for governance demonstrated this dynamic. "Eleven of the most respectable pandits of Bengal" as chosen by the first governor-general, Warren Hastings, acceded to his request to determine which components of the Śāstras should be assembled into a code for British judges – who now adjudicated legal cases – to use. A Bengali Muslim translated their selected Sanskrit passages into Persian, which a Briton then rendered into English (Cohn, 1996, 66–67). Many other Indians participated in the Western knowledge systems introduced to and developed in South Asia. Although often unacknowledged, Indians served as essential interlocutors, translators, and analysts in European projects. Some participated for want of employment, and others because it offered an avenue of advancement in the British bureaucracy.

Pandit Ram Gharib Chaube (late 1850s–1914) represents one of the most famous instances of this collaboration. The long-time companion of Indian civil servant William Crooke, he helped Crooke in both his official and unofficial pursuits to record and analyze instances of folk narrative and practices (Naithani, 2002, xxiii–xlvii).

As the Raj succeeded in establishing ever-larger numbers of Western model schools, universities, museums, exhibitions, zoos, and botanical gardens, increasing numbers of Indians were compelled by their own zeal to involve themselves in Western efforts to understand the human and natural landscape of South Asia. Their faith in European-originated sciences stemmed from the promise it appeared to present of offering new insights into their country's historical past, anthropological present, and sociological future. In doing so, these Indians helped contribute to the effort to construct a "syndicated Hinduism," which historian R. Thapar describes as an endeavor to incorporate almost all practices and beliefs not belonging to Muslims, Jains, Sikhs, Christians, or tribals into a singular religion (Thapar, 1997). People such as travel writer Bholanauth Chunder, archaeologist K.N. Dikshit, and anthropologist B.S. Guha enthusiastically participated in the coalescing genres and disciplines that originated in Europe but took shape in no small manner in various imperial and colonial contexts. Overwhelmingly, the Hindus who made these contributions were men, since the few women who were afforded the education that would allow them proactively to participate in these knowledge projects would unlikely have been allowed by their families to engage – as necessary to the position – in public and private concourse with European men. Many women, however, served as interlocutors. The inestimable number of women approached by and providing information to ethnographers, mapmakers, census takers, and other data gatherers went largely unnamed in the notes and publications of the knowledge brokers.

Yet other Indians, however, distrusted European representations in whole or part, with some engaging in protracted rebuttals in the widening public discourse provided by public debates, print newspapers, and published pamphlets and books. For instance, in his 1917 travelogue *Rambles in Bihar*, which celebrated his home state, Ramgopal Singh Chowdhari applauded villagers who resisted officials as they attempted to remove local artifacts in the name of archaeology. Many leaders of social reform and religious revival movements – such as → Dayananda Saraswati, → Vivekananda, and Mohandas → Gandhi – took public exception to the portrayals of Hindu practices and beliefs by European officials, missionaries, and civilians.

Perhaps the single greatest subject of new scholarly endeavor involved the search for the origins of Indians, of their religions, of their texts, and of their social structures. Europeans tended to dismiss the empirical veracity of the origin narratives that many Hindus embraced from the → Vedas, Dharmasūtras (see → Dharmaśāstra), and various written family traditions in favor of the results of the crystallizing disciplines of historiography, linguistics, ethnology, and archaeology. Many Europeans deployed these forms of knowledge in their home countries, too, to dispute and supplant earlier narrative forms that they dismissed as folklore and myth. Dependent on an empirical, rationalist approach to data, the new disciplines often viewed previous Indian origin accounts as misleading at best and fictive at worst. Instead of accepting them as authoritative in what they described, the practitioners of the new disciplines often viewed them as survivals of less-advanced forms of thinking that offered kernels of truth buried beneath centuries, if not millennia, of fictive accretions. Historians, therefore, sought to determine the beginnings of Hinduism using the Vedas, which they viewed as a historical production that necessarily needed critical analysis in order to tease out the few pertinent hints of its invention. Company servant and one of the first self-styled orientalists, Sir William Jones (1746–1794) learned Sanskrit and Persian from *paṇḍit*s and *munšī*s (tutors) in pursuit of his legal duties. He used linguistic analysis of both to advance an argument regarding the common origins of these and many European languages, which supposedly spread through the expansions of an original "Indo-European" people. His work demonstrates how some of this scholarship, far from affirming an alien Asian other, promoted historical – if not cognitive – links between Indians and Europeans.

The research of Sir William and other members of the Asiatic Society of Bengal that he helped found in 1784 (and which barred Indians from membership until 1829) preceded the rush to epistemic specialization that characterized the 19th century and the many disciplines that then took shape. Literally in line with the themes of uncovering and unearthing by which European-

Fig. 2: Beginning in 1904, the Archaeological Survey of India sought to uncover and partly restore the Mundeśvarī *mandir* (built c. 7th cent. BCE) in Bihar, India (photo by Peter Gottschalk).

originated disciplines understood their task, one new discipline – archaeology – sought clues to Indian origins in the ground. By the mid-19th century, Indians and Britons cooperated in the Archaeological Survey of India to "bring to light" the subcontinent's ancient past. In another example, racial studies impelled ethnology in the latter part of the century to substantiate linguistic theories regarding an invasion by Sanskrit-speaking Indo-Europeans (Aryans) who purportedly displaced indigenous Dravidians. The perception that these disciplines corroborated each others' findings and abided by the scientific method helped instantiate faith in science (what might be termed "scientism"). This posited a singular, corporate science, with Europeans as its key authorities. Growing numbers of Indians participated in this science, many preferring it to the forms of knowledge that it threatened to displace in whole and part.

Another dimension of this effort to determine origins involved the definitions of Hindu and Indian. Europeans tended to view Hindus as original to South Asia and Muslims as invaders. Combined with the essentialization of Indians according to religion, this meant that India was inherently Hindu (with Jain, Buddhist, and Sikh traditions viewed as so many religious spinoffs), while Muslims – even contemporary ones – remained culturally alien. This is where the various complex dimensions of diverse knowledge projects – some promoted by the British state, others practiced unofficially by state servants, and yet others pursued by nonofficials, European and Indian – intersected in a transformative dynamic. Defined as essentially Indian while categorically delineated from Muslims by European-modeled histories, censuses, ethnographies, and excavations, Hindus increasingly viewed themselves as historically and culturally distinct from Muslims. Meanwhile, the nascent electoral politics allowed by the British motivated some to cultivate self-aware Hindu constituencies by playing on pro-Hindu, if not anti-Muslim and anti-Christian, themes.

The evidence of the import of this complex dynamic readily appeared in the elections for the legislative assemblies near the end of British rule. Slowly acceding to demands for evidence of progress toward self-rule, the British government allowed the first steps of representative government, allotting reserved seats for different religious groups in proportion to their percentage of the overall population. The resulting electoral efforts politicized religious identification. Groups such as the Hindu Mahasabha wrangled with government officials over who counted as a Hindu, trying to appropriate Jains, Sikhs, and → Ādivāsīs (or tribals) into the category, even as representatives of these communities often argued for their autonomy. Meanwhile, even the secular Indian National Congress under Mohandas Gandhi's leadership deployed Hindu-themed icons and emblems (such as Bhārat Mātā, "Mother India") in their bid to typify themselves as quintessentially Indian. Some Muslim party members, like Muhammad Ali Jinnah, who despaired for the place of Muslims in a Hindu-defined India, eventually joined the Muslim League. Ultimately, many (though not all) of these Muslims opted for Pakistan as a Muslim-majority homeland. In other words, the new politics of democratic representation encouraged Indians more than ever to appropriate the religious terms of their self-identification that the British state had helped essentialize.

Meanwhile, the British government – during both Company Raj and Crown Rule – often relied on and involved themselves in Hindu practices and institutions more intimately than the occasional, ethnocentrically dismissive language of Britons toward Hindus might suggest. Particularly when they displaced indigenous rulers, the British found themselves having to adapt to Indic forms of political theatre and patronage and, so, unexpectedly assumed roles of protector and patron of rituals and temples (as well as mosques, shrines, and *gurudvārās*). Nevertheless, the British seldom undertook exactly the same patterns of interaction as the Indian sovereigns who preceded them. For instance, Britons increasingly attempted to regulate temple operations through a centralized bureaucracy, despite the fact that, earlier, temples often had enjoyed a general autonomy in their operations. Moreover, the British government gradually sought to mediate religious disputes through a judiciary process, replacing earlier expectations that the ruler directly intervened as arbitrator (Appadurai, 1981, 105–106, 110). An increasingly vocal opposition at home sought to compel the British government in India (which they variously considered Christian or secular) to divorce itself from entanglements in which it seemingly supported alien religions.

The ambiguous relationship of British rule to indigenous religiosity can perhaps be best demonstrated by the Britons' relationship with warrior ascetics, who – far from the stereotypes of nonviolent if not effete Hindu men – could pose both an important military resource and a worrisome internal threat to the state. Britons as quickly patronized various groups of warrior ascetics, such as the *nāgās* (see → *akhāṛās*), in the effort to establish their Indian empire as suppressed them in the effort to secure it (Pinch, 2006, 10, 84–86, 256). In an example of less intentional involvement in Hindu affairs, the efforts made by the British government to determine, stabilize, and reify the borders of native states while establishing their religious identity led in at least one instance to the establishment of a "Hindu state" that understood its religious identity in far more absolute ways than previous ones. Replacing the more fluid systems of territorial definition, ritual exchange, and cross-religious patronage, the Dogra rulers, when they first assumed control of Kashmir in the mid-19th century, felt spurred by British government proclamations to establish a concrete border around their territories, control the Hindu temples within their domain, and legitimate their rule relative to the Hindu minority, not the Muslim majority. Soon thereafter, changes in British expectations required the Dogras to protect all their subjects according to rights that corresponded to their subjects' supposed religious identities. This prompted their subjects to express discontent in terms of their rights as defined by their assumed religious identities (Rai, 2004, 111–129). Overall, therefore, British efforts to insert themselves into the variegated and intricate complexities of South Asian sociopolitical life inevitably meant involvements in religious contexts that made many Britons, especially evangelicals, deeply uneasy.

"Reform," "Revival," and "Tradition"

Hindu traditions have always been dynamic and pluralistic, as the development between the 8th and 13th centuries of the multiple major schools of Vedānta alone demonstrates. However, European Orientalism often had portrayed South Asia as long defunct of change and innovation, at least since the dominion of Muslim states beginning in the 12th century (which, in turn, relied on the common European stereotype of a brutish, oppressive Islam suffocating an effeminate, docile Hinduism). With this as a premise, each modern proponent and movement of change in Hindu thought and practice tended to be viewed as responding to the European presence, either by assimilating Western secular or Western Christian ideals, or by reacting defensively against the same. Once again, an accurate portrayal of these developments must neither overestimate nor underestimate the importance of British rule and missionary activity in Hindu lives. Nevertheless, the responses of these reformers and revivalists often relied on a claim of Hindu universality that imagined all of the various literary, philosophical, and devotional traditions as part of a singular Hinduism or *sanātanadharma*.

The missionary presence on the subcontinent was never uniform. Portuguese and French missionaries predated the first permanent British presence by two hundred years, while the first British missionaries had to work out of the Dutch settlement in Serampore due to the East India Company's objection to their presence. However, an English government directive in 1813 forced the East India Company to open the door to missionary efforts throughout British-controlled territories. These endeavors tended to concentrate in urban centers that offered the densest population of opportunity. However, some missionaries sought to focus on, or at least complement their urban efforts with, rural tours. Such, for example, were the efforts of William Bowley, an Anglo-Indian based in Chunar outside Benares (Varanasi) who exercised his "perambulations" into the countryside surrounding his home church. Nevertheless, most of India's villages never had frequent contact with missionaries. Those that did often responded negatively to the aggressive denigrations that some of the proselytizers practiced on them.

In their publications, conferences, and museums, missionaries often charged that Hinduism emasculated its male devotees, oppressed its female members, and practiced ignorant idolatry and barbaric sacrifices. Frequently, British authors and illustrators promoted portrayals of Hindus practicing → *satī*, thuggee (ritual murder by robber-devotees posing as travellers), and suicide under the wheels of the Jagannāth festival chariot (see → Orissa), even a half century or more after these practices effectively had been halted. Britons tended to show particular concern in the 19th century for the "woman question," which gravitated toward issues not only of *satī* but also of polygyny, child marriage, widow remarriage, and female education. Even Europeans who embraced Hindu traditions, such as → Theosophical Society founder Madame Blavatsky (1831–1891) and member Annie Besant (1847–1933), criticized current conditions for women as degradations of more ideal past conditions. Government focus on such issues never disappeared during the Raj, as evidenced by the 1947 Devadasi Act, which forbade the practice of dedicating girls to temple service – a tradition that Britons long had equated with forced prostitution (Forbes, 1999, 12, 53, 185). Not coincidentally, these Western concerns for the "woman question" culminated in tempo with Victorian-age concerns regarding the safety and welfare of women in Britain. Repeatedly, British moral concerns for India either found parallels among similar concerns for Britons at home or served to reinforce the propriety of Anglo-Saxon norms.

As historian G. Oddie has described, Christian missionaries – both British and Indian – tended to take three views of Hindus and other religious communities. In the first, only Christianity represented a true religion; all other traditions were debasements or falsities at best and satanic dupes at worst. In the second, Christians considered other religious traditions as containing some truths, which would come into fulfillment through contact with the superior and ultimate Christian truth. In the last, far less common, perspective, all religious traditions had the capacity of containing Christ's truth and thus were equally valid. The many memoirs and travelogues that missionaries penned demonstrate that attitudes often varied even within the mind of a single missionary. While their training in Britain or India may have imparted a more rigid approach toward Hindu and other traditions than other Britons held, some missionaries found themselves as often moved by the sincerity that they saw in a particular devotee's faith in a deity as repelled by the practices that they observed in a temple. In his widely read memoir, Reginald Heber, archbishop of Calcutta (and, thus, in charge of the Anglican Church on the subcontinent), recounted one such moment when he visited William Bowley's outpost at Chunar. While condemning what he saw in some of Benares' nearby temples, Heber described his awe at the venerations made by local Hindus to "the Almighty" at an imageless shrine within the fortification (Heber, 1873, 272). Despite such instances of empathy, many if not most missionary public admonishments and published accounts set Hindus, Muslims, and other non-Christians on the defensive.

Once again, the disparities in cultural and political power between Europeans and Indians contributed to circumstances in which the latter often incorporated the former's descriptions into their self-understandings. Although Hindus always far outnumbered Christians in British India, their relative power of representation diminished when European missionaries employed the first printing presses on the subcontinent. Missionary translations and analyses of Hindu religious literature often introduced perspectives that Hindus themselves recapitulated. For instance, it was not uncommon for English-speaking Hindus to use the term *idol* to describe a *mūrti*, despite the negative associations with which Europeans had imbued the word. The broadsheets, pamphlets, and books prodigiously published by missionaries found their way into many Hindu hands across India. Hindus soon responded in kind.

Within this context, some Hindus viewed the rise in prominence of the Bengali Brahman → Rammohun Roy (1772–1833) and the Brahmo Samaj (Society of Brahman) that he founded in 1828 as a capitulation to Christian – specifically Protestant – → critiques of Hinduism and theology of Christ. With its propagation of a monotheism that eschewed image worship and polytheism and its condemnation of casteism, the Brahmo Samaj drew criticism from some Hindus who believed it had surrendered to the missionaries. While Christian thought certainly had its influence on Rammohun, so did Islam and rationalism. However, one of his earliest publications, *Brahmunical Magazine*, sought to counter missionary criticisms and misrepresentations. He ultimately broke even with the Unitarians, whose Trinitarian theology he considered to be redolent of the polytheism he abjured in all religions (Pennington, 2005, 145–146).

The Calcutta intellectuals who initially made up the Brahmo Samaj represented a privileged class of Bengalis later known as *bhadralok* (respectable people): those whose families had succeeded in adapting to the new, British-defined order following the Mughal decline. They accommodated themselves not only to the new regime's economic realities but also to the cultural hegemony slowly solidifying around British centers of power and education. Despite these accommodations and Rammohun's initial attraction to the Western-originated Unitarian Church, the *bhadralok* involved in the Brahmo Samaj challenged Christian missionaries, especially under the leadership of Rammohun's successor, Debendranath Tagore (1817–1905; the poet Rabindranath → Tagore's father). Part of their response was a valorization of women's roles in vedic times, during which the glorified earlier civilization purportedly allowed women high status and free mobility in society, before a decline led to the current situation, which they – like many British commentators – disparaged. In 1866, the issue of women's education split the Brahmo Samaj, and a splinter group led by → Keshub Chandra Sen (1838–1884) worked with Mary Carpenter to establish a normal school in league with the government (Forbes, 1999, 15–16, 41, 43).

A half century later, Dayananda Saraswati (1824–1883) founded the Arya Samaj (Society of the Honorable) as yet another attempt to alter existing Hindu traditions. A Brahman *saṃnyāsī* who had travelled across northern India, from his native Gujarat to Bengal, Dayananda gradually determined that Hindus needed to shed postvedic traditions as accretions to the central truth of the four Vedas. In his view, India's current subservience to European rule could be traced to the decline of the vedic religion following the social decimations depicted in the → *Mahābhārata*. He proposed abandoning the Brāhmaṇas, → Upaniṣads, Itihāsas, and → Purāṇas as foreign to the original Aryan religion. To this end, caste became irrelevant, as everyone's duty derived equally from the injunctions to perform vedic sacrifices and engage in vedic learning. Like the Brahmo Samaj before it, the Arya Samaj emphasized social reform as a central plank of the movement, which included various women's issues such as dowry, polygyny, and female education. However, unlike the Brahmos, the Aryas occasionally took a highly strident line against both Christians and Muslims, as they sought a broad resistance to proselytization. Hence, the Arya Samaj later offered *śuddhi* (purificatory reconversion) to Christian and Muslim converts. In another contestation with Muslims, Dayananda advocated for the use of Sanskrit, Hindi, and the Devanagari script just when imperial officials had reaffirmed the use of Urdu in government education and bureaucracy. Meanwhile, new Arya Samaj converts occasionally and emphatically denounced their previous traditions: some publicly destroyed the images of their earlier worship in bazaars. This prompted traditionalists to protest, at times violently (Jones, 1989, 32, 34, 36, 40, 70, 202; Forbes, 1999, 20).

These traditionalists – upholders of a Brahmanic-defined orthodoxy (or, perhaps, orthopraxy) – were often described as *sanātanī*s, both for their defense of *sanātanadharma* and for their organization into societies that included the term in their names. Although *dharmasabhā*s (organizations created by Brahmans to define and maintain certain moral norms) had existed previously, those founded from the 1930s onward tended to represent *sanātanī* responses to challenges posed by missionaries, reformers, revivalists, and legislators. In their efforts to preserve tradition, they used British models of organization and parliamentary procedure, while codifying doctrines and/or practices in new ways. *Sanātanī*s tended to emphasize the authority of both Śruti and Smṛti literature at a time when many of the reform and revival movements sought a more streamlined canon. They particularly defended the applicability of the Dharmaśāstras both in civil and in religious law and for reaffirming *varṇāśramadharma* (the division of duties among the four *varṇa*s during the four stages of life; Dalmia, 1997, 1–3, 7–8).

By the end of the century, another – though less aggressive – movement arose under the initiative of Swami Vivekananda (1863–1902). Born Narendranath Datta, this member of the Calcutta *bhadralok* took tutelage under → Ramakrishna (1836–1886), a Bengali tantric *bhakta* dedicated to → Kālī. Ordained as his master's successor, Narendranath became leader of the remaining disciples. Renaming himself Vivekananda, the *saṃnyāsī* traveled to the World Parliament of Religion in Chicago, in part to raise funds. As a result of his address at the 1893 event, Vivekananda found himself commanding a large Western audience, many of whom embraced his portrayal of Hinduism as an Eastern, spiritual counterbalance to the West's materialism. Diverging from Ramakrishna's views, Vivekananda sidestepped Kālī → *bhakti* and sought to popularize a reformulation of Advaita Vedānta that he termed "practical Vedānta." As the name suggests, Vivekananda's approach intended to emphasize → *sevā* (service) and social support, and his efforts culminated in 1895, when he founded the Vedanta Society in New York. Two years later, he sought to implement the neo-Vedānta model in India by establishing the monastic → Ramakrishna Mission in Calcutta.

Vivekananda's successful use of the World Parliament of Religion as a platform for addressing Americans and Europeans demonstrated that despite the unbalanced powers of representation, at times Hindus could navigate institutions of Western hegemony and project their own portrayals of their traditions. The fact that the parliament coincided with the international Columbian Exposition was of no small consequence. For almost a century, the imperial powers had used similar occasions – such as the Great Exhibition at the Crystal Palace of 1851 and the Paris Exhibition of 1867 – to present to other Europeans the supposed characteristics of their dominated and colonized subjects, including their religions. Indeed, the Columbian Exposition even included the East India Building, which incorporated an Indian-themed bazaar into an Indo-Muslim–style structure designed by an American architect.

Vivekananda's success in reorienting so much of Hindu thought in the direction of his practical Vedānta with its emphasis on *sevā* is apparent in its influence on Mohandas Karamchand Gandhi (1869–1948). Raised in a Bania-caste family that provided viziers for a Gujarati court, Gandhi's initial religious predispositions derived from his family's Vaiṣṇava devotion and his mother's Jain austerities. Over the arc of his development as a young law student in London through his initial law career and political interests in South Africa to his return to India as a nationalist leader, Gandhi engaged a variety of religious thought. This included the ministrations of Protestant missionaries, the writings of Europeans like Leo Tolstoy and John Ruskin, and the *bhakti* of the → *Bhagavadgītā* (first encountered in English translation). But the title of Gandhi's autobiography, *The Story of My Experiments with Truth* (1927–1929), demonstrates how the imperative of experience as the only authentic avenue to truth – which featured so centrally in Vivekananda's teaching – had become a major theme in Gandhi's perspectives.

Gandhi's popularity earned him the title *mahātmā* (great-souled man), which reflected how much of his social and political vision was inflected through Hindu thinking and practice. One of the first components of his strategy for social change was → *ahiṃsā* (nonviolence), which derived perhaps more from Jain traditions than from Hindu ones. Later, Gandhi developed the strategy of *satyāgraha* (firmness in truth) as a means to assert Indian self-determination through stern self-control and strident action. A variety of Western and Indian authors and texts served as his influences, including Tolstoy, the Gospels, and the *Bhagavadgītā*. Throughout his career as an activist, Gandhi used vows and fasting to communicate his agenda and press his goals, while inveighing his followers to commit to *sevā* for community and nation. Meanwhile, in a bid to project a personal image of nonattachment, he recast his social position in 1906 as that of a *brahmacarya* (someone committed to chastity and asceticism), despite his current responsibilities as a householder to his wife and children. Gandhi explicitly disconnected his decision from the Śastras, emphasizing the influence of experience instead and demonstrating once again the influence on him of Vivekananda's vedantic vision (Gandhi, 1993, 208, 318–319). Vivekananda's and Gandhi's success in not only promoting Advaita Vedānta but also projecting it as essential to Hinduism found further popular reinforcement – both in and out of India – in Sarvepalli→ Radhakrishnan (1888–1975), who wrote a number of books extolling Vedānta as a touchstone for all forms of Hinduism. His later election to independent India's presidency cemented his public prominence both domestically and internationally (King, 1999, 135–136).

These various movements, and others that disagreed with them, engaged in a sometimes tense set of interchanges and debates over the century. Pamphlets and other publications expounded their individual positions and addressed those of their competitors and detractors. Also, *śāstrārth*s (debates) became popular venues for proponents of various sides to engage one another in front of a public (Jones, 1989, 70). While especially learned representatives of various schools of *darśana* (philosophy) had debated with one another from the positions of their diverse perspectives, the various reform, revival, and *sanātanī* movements often played out in public venues through addresses, debates, and publications. As Indians gradually established regional and national political stages for democratic self-governance, the contestation regarding who was truly Hindu and what made up proper Hinduism heated the newly crystallized public sphere.

Nationalism

While the notion of Āryāvarta ("Land of the Aryans") had existed centuries earlier, the view of all Indians as composing a corporation of citizens who, combined, created an autonomous and sovereign nation derived from Western concepts still under development when Britons first arrived in South Asia. The nascent urges both of self-rule and of democracy quickened nationalist impulses among India's educated elite, who, in the early 20th century, set about fashioning a mass nationalist movement. The majority of South Asia's inhabitants may have self-identified as residents of their families, villages, cities, regions, linguistic areas, and/or provinces, but not as Indians. Moreover, the meaning of the label *Indian* was anything but self-evident. Were children born on the subcontinent to British parents Indian? Indeed, until the mid-19th century, the term "Anglo-Indian" was reserved specifically for this group, until coalescing racist sentiment shifted the term to individuals with both a British and an Indian parent, liberating full-blooded Anglos from the hyphenated Indian identity. Henceforth, children of Britons – whether born in South Asia or the United Kingdom – would be known simply as British. Probably both as a result of pre-British Hindu rhetoric that portrayed Muslims as → *mleccha*s (Skt., barbarian) and *yāvana*s (Skt., Greek), and due to European scholarship that portrayed contemporary Muslims as foreign, some Hindus asserted that despite a millennium and a century and a half of Muslim presence in South Asia, Muslims were not Indian. Revisiting the language of origins discussed above, many European authors considered Indians as essentially Hindu and, thus, Muslims as essentially Turkic, Persian, and Arab. This rehearsed centuries-old, European Islamophobic stereotypes of Muslims as invaders who force conversion, a stereotype that originated with the successful 7th-century Arab Muslim conquest and conversion of Christians in the lands of the southern Mediterranean. However, such views were far from universal among Hindus.

The support of the Indian National Congress for the Khilafat movement reflected the effort of its Hindu-majority leadership to emphasize exactly this point. As the victorious Allies pondered at the end of the First World War what to do with the caliph of the now defunct Ottoman Empire, Gandhi and other Congress leaders seized the opportunity to make common cause

Fig. 3: Main gate, Banaras Hindu University (founded 1916), Varanasi, India (photo by Peter Gottschalk).

with more Indian Muslims by joining their efforts to preserve the caliphate. However, the perfunctory dissolution of the caliphate by the new, secular Turkish government forestalled the gesture. Despite this effort, the Indian National Congress progressively alienated increasing numbers of Muslims with its use of Hindu-themed language, icons, and metaphors. Although not promoting a Hindu nationalism *per se*, the efforts of Gandhi, Jawaharlal Nehru, and other Congress leaders to create a constituency focused on what they perceived to be the themes likely to rally the most Indians often relied on Hindu cultural symbols. In other words, in order to express and popularize an Indian identity using terms and images familiar to most South Asians and unconnected to Britons, the Congress drew upon many Hindu themes and issues, suggesting that Indianness meant Hinduness. So, for instance, the party's use of an anthropomorphized image of India to focus patriotism led, in 1938, to Gandhi inaugurating the Bhārat Mātā Mandir (Mother India Temple) in Varanasi. A large marble relief map in the center of the North Indian–style temple seemingly transposed devotion to the *devī* and devotion to nation. While equating patriotism with image veneration distressed some Muslims, a far greater disturbance stirred in response to the 1922 Cow Protection Act. Aimed squarely at the Muslim butchers who prepared beef, the Congress-proposed act threatened many Muslim livelihoods and dinners. This, in addition to Congress' unwillingness to reserve seats for Muslims in Hindu-majority provincial councils, provoked many party Muslims to resign and join the Muslim League, which eventually proposed halving any future independent nation into a Muslim-majority Pakistan and a Hindu-majority India.

If the Indian National Congress promoted a Hindu nationalism by default, the Hindu Mahasabha did so with intent. Established in 1915 not as a political party but as an organizational effort (*saṅgathan*) within the Indian National Congress, the Mahasabha was meant to solidify what its members viewed as a disordered, though singular, Hindu community. In doing so, the Mahasabha drew support from both the Arya Samaj and *sanātanī* organizations. Among its leaders were Madan Mohan Malaviya (1861–1946) and Lala Lajpat Rai (1865–1928), whose differences manifested the variety of perspectives in the early Mahasabha. Malaviya promoted the popular notion of "Hindi, Hindu, Hindustan" that sought to collapse seemingly disparate linguistic, religious, and territorial identities into an essentialized Indian identity. He founded the Hindi-instruction Banaras Hindu University in 1916, following Sayyid Ahmad Khan's establishment of the Urdu-language Anglo-Mohammedan Oriental College in Aligarh in 1875. Malaviya served twice as president to the Indian National Congress and three times to the Mahasabha. In contrast with Malaviya's approach, Lajpat Rai – another Congress member – expressed a more inclusive view that emphasized a pluralism of constituencies in an independent India. By the 1920s, the Hindu Mahasabha emerged as a force outside the Congress and a movement that shared many goals with the aggressive Arya Samaj, including *śuddhi* (reconversion) campaigns (Hansen, 1999, 76–77, 92). In 1935, the Congress Party excluded the Mahasabha from its ranks due to the organization's communalism. Thirteen years later, a splinter group conspired successfully to assassinate Mohandas Gandhi in retribution for his efforts to compensate Pakistan for losses suffered during Partition (Jaffrelot, 1996, 33, 86–87).

The Rashtriya Swayamsevak Sangh (RSS; National Volunteer Organization) represented a more aggressive outgrowth of the Hindu Mahasabha. Its organizers fashioned the RSS as an organization devoted to national *sevā* in the form of a force trained to martially defend an inherently Hindu India from its Muslim, Christian, and other projected foes. Keshav Baliram Hedgewar (1889–1940) declared the Sangh's establishment in 1925 with the stated intent of fostering physical and intellectual training using a paramilitary model. Under his impetus in Nagpur, Central Provinces, the Sangh's iconic uniform of khaki shirts and pants became standard. The Sangh borrowed various traditions in its efforts to prepare Hindu males for national service. These included physical-training regimes from → *akhāṛā*s (wrestling clubs), where wrestlers drew on yogic and devotional practices in their muscular exercises. The need for Hindu physical self-protection appeared to them justified by the British strength of arms, by the Islamophobic history of Muslim invasion and chauvinism that many European scholars promoted, and by the Muslim League's contemporary Direct Action campaigns that sought to provoke British and congressional support for an independent Muslim homeland through violence against Hindus. Lal Krishna Advani (1927–), future president of the RSS affiliate, the Bharatiya Janata Party, later reflected on his decision to join the organization in 1942. Voicing a distrust in the Congress' ability to achieve independence, Advani explained,

> Much more was needed and the RSS approach used to be that unless we first build up, form a nucleus of people willing to sacrifice their life for the country India would not become independent. (Jaffrelot, 1996, 72)

The organization criticized Congress' ultimate acquiescence to the Muslim League's demand for Pakistan. When former member Nathuram Godse assassinated Gandhi the year after Independence, Prime Minister Nehru – who feared both the Sangh's armed power and its virulent communalism – moved the Congress government to ban the organization, at a time when it was led by Madhav Sadashiv Golwalkar.

Vinayak Damodar Savarkar (1883–1966) provided perhaps the most important articulation of the ideology behind the Hindu Mahasabha, the RSS, and other Hindu nationalist groups in the late Raj period. Eponymous with his most influential work's title, the notion of *hindutva* (Hinduness) served as the lynchpin of his thought. A Citpāvan Brahman from Maharasthra, Savarkar produced his manifesto in 1923 while incarcerated for violent nationalist activities (Zavos, 2000, 177). In his book, he decisively identified being Hindu with a nationalist allegiance to the land.

> We have found that the first important essential qualification of a Hindu is that to him the land that extends from Sindhu to Sindhu is the Fatherland (Pitribhu) the Motherland (Matribhu) the land of his patriarchs and forefathers [*sic.*]. (Savarkar, 2003, 110)

Notably, he also viewed the Hindhu *dharma* as encompassing all the "sects and systems" generated from the soil of the land, thus encompassing "Vaidik and Non-Vaidik" (i.e. both those derived and those not derived from the Vedas) without prejudice. In contrast, Muslims and Christians, according to Savarkar, view Arabia and Palestine as their holy lands (Savarkar, 2003, 110–113).

If Savarkar provided the ideology for Hindu nationalism, then the novel *Ānandamaṭh* (Monastery of Peace) offered a stirring historical myth to help propel it. Written in 1882 by the Bengali Brahman Bankim Chandra Chatterjee (1838–1894), the novel offered a fictive account of what became termed the Sannyasi Rebellion – a series of skirmishes between the British and armed monks between the 1760s and 1800 (Pinch,

1996, 24). The book portrayed the *saṃnyāsīs* as patriots fighting Muslim soldiers employed by the East India Company, repeating the theme of Muslim oppression of Hindus found in many of Bankim Chandra's works. While the novel had its own influential career, the song *Bande Mātaram* (Reverence to the Mother) that it included took on a life of its own. Deifying the motherland, Bankim Chandra's song became even more popular an expression of Hindu nationalism when the Bengali poet, novelist, and playwright Rabindranath Tagore later put it to music. After Independence, the government accepted it as the national song of India.

The Politics of Being Hindu

As campaigns for democratic governance gathered momentum at the end of the 19th century, questions naturally arose regarding both how the government should be configured and how democratic representation could be secured. Various socially or economically disadvantaged groups, such as Muslims and lower-status *jāti*s, sought guarantees that their voices would not be drowned by higher-status and more privileged upper-caste Hindus. Concerns were also voiced in terms of representation in education and government employment. The Government of India Act of 1935 established special electoral representation to → castes and tribes that the government included in special lists, or schedules. In doing so, the government created meta-categories of so-called "depressed" groups, namely Scheduled Castes, Scheduled Tribes, and Other Backward Classes (Bayly, 1999, 274). These reinforced the importance of caste (and religious) identities already present in pre-British India and reaffirmed by various private and state-sponsored knowledge projects, from the Asiatic Society of Bengal through the Census of India to the Ethnographic Survey of India.

The notion of "scheduled castes" firmly demonstrated the power of the administrative bureaucracy to shape realities on the ground, even as various *jāti* organizations sought to define their own positions. In order to determine which *jāti*s merited reserved seats in government employ, in democratic elections, and in universities, the central government established a schedule. In essence, this simple act of listing fossilized the ranking of dozens of *jāti*s relative to "nonscheduled castes." Recognizing the potential benefits, many *jāti* groups campaigned to be included on the schedule. Meanwhile, other *jāti*s sought to improve their position in the ranking of ritual purity and social acceptance. Some organizations renamed their groups, so Camars (traditionally leather workers) became Mocis, at the same time as Muslim *jāti*s such as Julaha (associated with weaving) became Ansaris (a name earlier connected with the residents of Medina who hosted the first Islamic society). Meanwhile, in 1934 the Gwalas, Koeries, and Kurmis joined to forge the Triveni Sangh caste association in an effort to protect themselves against upper-caste political maneuvering (Pandey, 1990, 84, 204). These endeavors demonstrated well how castes were hardly the permanently wrought and unchangeably inflexible social structure that many Westerners had represented. Indeed, early British surveyors remarked on efforts of various *jāti*s to claim higher status than popularly accorded to them, some with more success than others (Pinch, 1996, 81–84).

These efforts at *jāti* status improvement also demonstrate the power of the British system that linked knowledge projects to bureaucratic control. Although the Mughal and other pre-British indigenous states occasionally counted the male members of particular castes in some towns or regions, none made as systematic and totalistic an attempt as the British government would. The first all-India census was attempted in 1872, and – for the first time – a subcontinental government sought to count every single inhabitant under its direct rule (and many under indirect rule). Manifesting the British fixation on religion and caste as the essential qualities of Indian society, during each decadal census, every householder had to declare the religious and caste identity of each member of his or her household (among other data), and the enumerators recorded these on a paper slip. Although this liberal recording method was unconstrained by British preconceptions, the tabulators who took the slips and sorted them relied on classificatory pigeonholes. These could not accept every identity offered to enumerators, since only a certain number of holes could practically be accommodated. Hence an enumerator's slip for a person who declared himself or herself a "Muslim Brahman" had to be placed into either "Muslim" or "Brahman," and not into both. Such category-defying self-identifications were not wholly uncommon. Moreover, the effort to publish the tabulated outcomes of the census often meant that only the most populated *jāti*s found their way onto the multiple spreadsheets composing the census reports and enjoyed the social and political prominence that accompanied this. These reports reflected another departure from pre-British states, since the British government did not jealously guard this information for itself as a form of state intelligence, as would have been common with the Mughals and others. Instead, it distributed much of this information through mass publications purposively dispatched to universities, libraries, and newspapers – in India and abroad – for dissemination among a gradually more literate public. This compelled *jāti* groups to seek strength in numbers in order to obtain more political credibility and public notice, which in turn motivated them to standardize a *jāti* identity so that their population could be counted as such and appear as large as possible. As with religion, so with *jāti*, the British did not *create* this form of South Asian identity, but they created the bureaucratic and political systems that motivated Indians to embrace a more reified form of these identities than had existed before.

Meanwhile, other forces helped remold *jāti* identity. Propelled in part by the need to identify religiously, nominally Hindu princely states increasingly relied on models of dharmic kingdoms and pious rule for their legitimation and projected more concrete *jāti* categories in their efforts to establish a royally led, moral society. Meanwhile, many of the social and economic upheavals triggered by the British order prompted some disrupted groups to assert both the superiority of their *jāti* and the inferiority of others in their effort to create a more concrete hierarchy. It was just another logical step to conclude, as Britons so often did, that *jāti* served as a critical component of national society, especially for those nationalists who imagined Hindus as both a distinct nation and a distinct race. These views reified group identities and the relations among groups in accord with pan-Indian expectations of *jāti* – which included anticipated types of work and degrees of purity – thus obfuscating both local dynamics and social variability. As a consequence, subsequent efforts at "uplift" among *jāti*s presumed to be "depressed castes" thus served to reinscribe assumptions of pan-Indian social place and ritual status. While nationalist campaigns attempting to instill a corporate sense of duty made it incumbent on more privileged *jāti*s to participate in improving the lot of "backward" ones, they equally held the latter groups responsible for eschewing their own purportedly unhealthy and/or polluting behavior. In sum, social, state, and religious interests among both Britons and Indians combined to significantly sharpen *jāti* consciousness among Hindus, and other groups, while the published accounts of government knowledge projects helped inscribe these more deeply in the minds of an increasingly literate public (Bayly, 1999, 106, 116–117; 2001, 368, 372–373).

Responding in indeterminate parts to both British and Indian critiques of *jāti*, various Hindu reformers and revivalists proposed changes. These were far more variegated than they were successful. Some portrayed *jāti* in its present form as incompatible with the alternative forms of Hinduism that they proposed. For instance, Rammohun Roy promoted the abandonment of the inhumane discriminations that he considered inherent in the *jāti* system. In contrast, the Arya Samaj under Dayananda Saraswati sought to redistribute *varṇa* membership according to individuals' demonstrated commitment to vedic learning and sacrifice, which were previously the reserve of Brahmans. He proposed a *varṇa vyavasthā* (*varṇa* arrangement) that restructured society based on individual merit. He portrayed the *varṇa*s not as fixed, family-inherited identities but as individually earned identities. There should be Brahmans, Dayananda argued, but they could be drawn from any section of society so long as they commanded the Sanksrit learning necessary to promote a truly vedic society. For those non-Brahmans already educated in the manner that the Arya Samaj leader envisioned, this offered an enticing vision. However, later generations of Arya Samajis recognized the improbable nature of this plan (Jones 1989, 32–33, 204–205).

Despite these efforts at change, some Hindu nationalists argued that *jāti* represented a critical – if sometimes misunderstood – component of the Hindu nation. These argued that *jāti* derived from the vedic system of four *varṇa*s, a Hindu-derived social ordering that, in its ancient foundation, served to unite previously divided clans and races. Vivekananda shared a similar perspective (Bayly, 1999, 102–103). For him, *jāti* provided a malleable, necessary system by which Hindus could express their individualism and maintain their civilization. In fact, he viewed caste as a universal social phenomenon and *jāti* as only the Hindu form. In Vivekananda's mind, because barriers erected around *jāti* had led to India's decline, *jāti* must be allowed to operate in a manner that does not constrict the ability of the individual to pursue spiritual development by exercising her or his *jāti* mobility (Basu, 2002, 104–111). In contrast, Vinayak Damodar Savarkar proposed a *hindutva* vision based on *rāṣṭra – jāti – saṃskṛti* (nation–race–culture), in which the combined *jāti*s have preserved the singular blood of the Hindu race. This perspective emphasized the importance of horizontal stratification as a means of simultaneously unifying Hindus and maintaining their social order (Zavos, 2000, 180–181).

Savarkar's notion of Hindus representing a distinct race protected from impurities reworked an older European notion about them. The promise that India held for European research relied in part on a view that the country's society was an ancient form fossilized in time. As the race science of ethnology took shape in the mid-19th century – sharpening hazier concepts of race with the biological progressivism then gaining currency – many Europeans considered the subcontinent an excellent laboratory for racial studies with individual *jāti*s as the specimen. The strict endogamy that these scholars presumed the castes practiced was expected to severely stratify not only Hindu societies but also their bloodlines. Simultaneously, British government servants exercised an increasingly distant social interaction with Indians, which before the turn of the 18th century had often been quite convivial. The intermarriage between British men and Indian women that once occurred with some frequency became, with the acceleration of racial consciousness, increasingly unacceptable for reasons of miscegenation. This divorce was mirrored in European scholarship, as language and race – once considered to be reflective of each other in India – became disconnected, for philologists who often relied on native speakers had their authority challenged by ethnologists and other practitioners of race science who often worked at a remove from the general population. Nevertheless, many Europeans and Indians considered some connections to have remained between language and race, as suggested in period narratives that depicted Aryans and non-Aryans as distinct peoples speaking in different tongues and occasionally combating each other. Meanwhile, the term "nation" also diverged from its once synonymous relation with race as it took on more democratic political meanings toward the end of the 19th century (Trautmann, 1997, 191, 193, 197).

The tensions between the two most influential *jāti* activists of the 20th century reflected both how deeply embedded the issues of *jāti* were in Indian communities and how divergent Hindu perspectives on those issues could be. Coincidentally, the 1924 *satyāgraha* at Vaikom in Travancore state not only represented Mohandas Gandhi's first public action in support of low castes but also prompted the first public reflection on Gandhi's efforts by fellow Congress member Bhimrao Ramji → Ambedkar (1891–1956). On the one hand, Mohandas Gandhi promoted an uplift program for the group of low castes referred to as *avarṇa* (without *varṇa*) and "Untouchable" (→ Dalit). This involved inveighing caste Hindus to voluntarily cease discriminating against Dalits – whom he referred to as Harijans (children of god) – by allowing them into all temples, by opening access to all roads, and by not delegating to them alone the most demeaning forms of labor. On the other hand, Ambedkar made strident efforts to secure legal protections for "depressed" classes, motivated by his own experiences of belonging to the Dalit Mahar community from Maharasthra. Although still conciliatory at the time of the Vaikom *satyāgraha*, Ambedkar would become convinced that neither Gandhi nor Hinduism offered any avenue for the changes he sought. Indeed, he strongly protested even the nomenclature of Harijan, which he considered patronizing (Zelliot, 2008).

Ambedkar's frustration with caste Hindus, Gandhi, and the Indian National Congress Party grew steadily. His rejection of Hindu orthodoxy led him to publicly burn a copy of the *Manusmṛti* in 1927. By 1931, Ambedkar openly broke with Gandhi over the Congress leader's unwillingness to support separate electorates for "depressed" classes in provincial legislative assemblies, and in 1935 he declared his intent to leave Hinduism (Zelliot, 2008). In some ways, Ambedkar's mixture of Hindu critique, social reform, and ultimate conversion echoed the earlier life of Pandita Ramabai (1858–1922). A Brahman child widow who publicly converted to Christianity, Ramabai set about addressing Hindu women's issues, particularly through education and a home for widows. She found a ready audience of support during a tour of the United States, which had been primed by the publication of her book *High Caste Hindu Woman* in 1887.

The culminating energy of Ambedkar's attacks on Congress led him to write *What Congress and Gandhi Have Done to the Untouchables*, with a pointed jab at Gandhi wrapped in a reference to his *jāti*:

> To sum up, the Brahmin enslaves the mind and the Bania enslaves the body. Between them, they divide the spoils which belong to the governing classes. (Ambedkar, 1979, 217)

Despite this vehemence, Ambedkar and Congress enjoyed a rapprochement in 1946, which opened the way for Ambedkar to serve as the chairman for the Indian constitution's drafting committee. Nevertheless, his criticism of casteism remained, and in 1956 he led hundreds of thousands of others in converting to Buddhism (Rodrigues, 2002, 15–17, 148).

Diaspora

While South Asian traders plying the Arabian Sea, the Bay of Bengal, and the Indian Ocean had established various Indian communities outside the subcontinent in the period before British rule, the efficiencies, effectiveness, and decreased expense associated with modern forms of transportation and communication combined with the newly globalized capital, industrial, business, and labor markets created a new context for emigration. The system of indentured labor was especially responsible for drawing South Asians from across the subcontinent to British territories in Fiji, Mauritius, Southeast Asia, sub-Saharan Africa, and the Caribbean. Indians represented 85% of all the indentured immigrants within the British Empire, with more than 1,250,000 taking work outside of South Asia. In many instances, quotas ensured that at least one female was included for every three men (Northrup, 1999, 89, 96). Meanwhile, Indian merchants and professionals also made their way to jobs abroad, with some settling there permanently. In a relatively understudied dynamic, Hindus established communities abroad that often involved reformulated relationships with other Indian religious groups such as Muslims, while establishing new ones with communities indigenous to their new homes.

To take one example, Hindus in Natal province in southern Africa created new fusions with Muslim Indian immigrants, while also forging an increasingly defined Indian identity. Mohandas Gandhi offers the most famous example of the political mobilization of Hindus and Muslims as Indians. During the better part of two decades (1893–1914), Gandhi found employment in → South Africa as a barrister, after encountering obstacles in the courts of his native Kathiawad in Gujarat. He served the primarily Muslim community of Gujarat traders who had taken residence there. The racist and religious denigrations that he suffered at the hands of white South African officials spurred him toward the Indian identity politics that he would perfect as a leader in the Indian National Congress. However, indentured labor made up the majority of South Asian emigration to South Africa. Between 1860 and 1911, 152,184 immigrants arrived there, mostly male and overwhelmingly Hindu. A little more than half of the laborers remained in South Africa on completion of their contractual five years of service. Many of these Hindu laborers contributed to nominally Muslim commemorations such as *muharram*. By the end of the century, a group of Western-educated Hindus joined Hindu reformers in denouncing these collaborations. Arya Samaj missionaries from India had the most success in attempting to alter Hindu practices, but this still made little change, at least until the formation of the South African Maha Sabha in 1912 (Vahed, 2002, 77–79, 82, 90–92).

In another example, Indian indentured laborers replaced African and African-heritage slave labor in → Trinidad beginning in the mid-19th century, after the 1834 abolition of slavery. Like South Africa, Trinidad played host to immigrants who decided against returning to the subcontinent. Already socially marginalized because of their position in the indentured labor system, Hindus were further alienated by the unwelcoming white response to their particular types of dress, food, and religious practices. The shared sense of being *jahājis* (immigrants) in a foreign colonial context helped cement a sense of solidarity among subordinated caste identities and, eventually, led to a stronger Indian national identity. Meanwhile, the combination of a relative shortage of women and their success as wage earners meant that they could reconfigure gender relationships relative to the preexisting patriarchal norms (Kannabiran, 1998, 53–55).

Bibliography

Ambedkar, B.R., *B.R. Dr. Babasaheb Ambedkar: Writings and Speeches*, vol. IX, Bombay, 1979.

Appadurai, A., *Worship and Conflict under Colonial Rule: A South Indian Case*, Cambridge UK, 1981.

Basu, S., *Religious Revivalism as Nationalist Discourse: Swami Vivekananda and New Hinduism in Nineteenth-Century Bengal*, New Delhi, 2002.

Bayly, C.A., *Empire and Information: Intelligence Gathering and Social Communication in India, 1780–1870*, Cambridge UK, 1996.

Bayly, S., *Caste, Society and Politics in India from the Eighteenth Century to the Modern Age*, Cambridge UK, 2001.

Bayly, S., "Hindu Modernisers and the 'Public' Arena: Indigenous Critiques of Caste in Colonial India," in: W. Radice, *Swami Vivekananda and the Modernisation of Hinduism*, New Delhi, 1999, 93–137.

Cohn, B.S., *Colonialism and Its Forms of Knowledge: The British in India*, Princeton, 1996.

Dalmia, V., *The Nationalization of Hindu Traditions: Bhāratendu Hariśchandra and Nineteenth-Century Banaras*, Delhi, 1997.

Forbes, G. *The New Cambridge History of India*, vol. IV/2: *Women in Modern India*, Cambridge UK, 1999.

Gandhi, M., *An Autobiography: The Story of My Experiments with Truth*, Boston, 1993.

Gottschalk, P., *Religion, Science, and Empire: Classifying Hinduism and Islam in British India*, New York, 2012.

Hansen, T.B., *The Saffron Wave: Democracy and Hindu Nationalism in Modern India*, Princeton, 1999.

Heber, R., *Narrative of a Journey through the Upper Provinces of India, from Calcutta to Bombay, 1824–1825 (with Notes upon Ceylon): An Account of a Journey to Madras and the Southern Provinces, 1826; and Letters Written in India*, vol. I, London, 1873.

Jaffrelot, C., *The Hindu Nationalist Movement in India*, New York, 1996.

Jones, K., *Arya Dharm: Hindu Consciousness in 19th-Century Punjab*, New Delhi, 1989.

Kannabiran, K., "Mapping Migration, Gender, Culture and Politics in the Indian Diaspora: Commemorating Indian Arrival in Trinidad," *EPW* 33/44, 1998, 53–57.

King, R., *Orientalism and Religion: Postcolonial Theory, India and "The Mystic East"*, London, 1999.

M., *The Gospel of Ramakrishna*, New York, 1947.

Masuzawa, T., *The Invention of World Religions*, Chicago, 2005.

Mill, J., *The History of British India*, London, 1817.

Naithani, S., "Introduction," in: W. Crooke & R.G. Chaube, *Folktales from Northern India*, Denver, 2002, xxiii–xlvii.

Nicholson, A.J., *Unifying Hinduism: Philosophy and Identity in Indian Intellectual History*, New York, 2010.

Northrup, D., "Migration from Africa, Asia, and the South Pacific," in: A. Porter, ed., *The Oxford History of the British Empire*, vol.III: *The Nineteenth Century*, New York, 1999, 88–100.

Oddie, G.A., *Imagined Hinduism: British Protestant Missionary Constructions of Hinduism, 1793–1900*, New Delhi, 2006.

Pandey, G., *The Construction of Communalism in Colonial North India*, Delhi, 1990.

Pennington, B., *Was Hinduism Invented? Britons, Indians, and the Colonial Construction of Religion*, New York, 2005.

Pinch, W., *Warrior Ascetics and Indian Empires*, Cambridge UK, 2006.

Pinch, W., *Peasants and Monks in British India*, Berkeley, 1996.

Porter, A., *Religion versus Empire? British Protestant Missionaries and Overseas Expansion, 1700–1914*, New York, 2004.

Porter, A., "Empires of the Mind," in: P.J. Marshall, *Cambridge Illustrated History of the British Empire*, Cambridge UK, 1996, 185–223.

Rai, M., *Hindu Rulers, Muslim Subjects: Islam, Rights, and the History of Kashmir*, Delhi, 2004.

Rodrigues, V., ed., *The Essential Writings of B.R. Ambedkar*, New Delhi, 2002.

Savarkar, V.D., *Hindutva*, New Delhi, 2003.

Thapar, R., "Syndicated Hinduism," in: G.-D. Sontheimer & H. Kulke, *Hinduism Reconsidered*, New Delhi, 1997, 54–81.

Tod, J., *Annals and Antiquities of Rajasthan: Or the Central and Western Rajput States of India*, 2 vols., New Delhi, 1829, repr. 2002.

Trautmann, T.R., *Aryans and British India*, Berkeley, 1997.

Vahed, G., "Constructions of Community and Identity among Indians in Colonial Natal, 1860–1910: The Role of the *Muharram* Festival," *JAH* 42, 2002, 77–93.

Zavos, J., *The Emergence of Hindu Nationalism in India*, New Delhi, 2000.

Zelliot, E., "Gandhi and Ambedkar: A Study in Leadership," in: I. Banerjee-Dube, *Caste in History*, New Delhi, 2008, 197–209.

Peter Gottschalk

Independent India (1947–)

R. Guha, in *India After Gandhi: The History of the World's Largest Democracy*, offers the following observation about Hindu religion:

> It is possible to view the Hindu faith as a river with many branches, tributaries that feed into the mainstream and distributaries that leave it. But perhaps this image is mistaken, for in many respects there is no main river at all. This is a religion that was decentralized like no other. (Guha, 2007, 578)

If such is the case regarding Hindu traditions before Independence, the situation has become even more complex since Independence in 1947. Modern India – with its 28 states (each having a distinctive linguistic-cultural identity), 600,000 villages, 4,599 distinct communities, 325 languages in 12 separate language families, and 24 different scripts as described in the People of India project of the Anthropological Survey of India (Larson, 1995, 11) – gives a new dimension to the meaning of the word "pluralism." Moreover, since the expression "Hindu religion" and the abstract noun "Hinduism" are both used to describe the religious identity of some 80.5% of this massive conglomeration of around 1.2 billion people (*Census of India*, 2011), it is small wonder that R. Frykenberg has commented in exasperation that the use of the term "Hinduism" in the singular has led most discussions of religion in modern India into "trackless deserts of nonsense" (Frykenberg, 1991, 31–33). Be that as it may, little is to be gained from dwelling on the impossibility of the task at hand except to point out that the present essay seeks only to provide a rough overview of a highly complex subject area. It is to be hoped, however, that even this rough overview may be heuristically instructive in highlighting some of the curious textures and shapes that one encounters as one tries to characterize the dense complexities of Hinduism in post-Independence India since 1947. In attempting this rough overview, seven divisions and/or categories appear to be important by way of determining the range and texture of post-Independence Hinduism:

1. Partition Hinduism – that is, the tragic creation narrative of Independence India, in which a legacy of cataclysmic violence defines the basic identity of the two new nation-states that emerged: India and → Pakistan .

2. "Neo-Hindu" Hinduism – a tripartite set of post-Independence discourses, namely (a) the Gandhian-Nehruvian civil ideology of the secular state, (b) the *hindutva* ideology that tends to identify Hindu and/or Hinduism with Indic culture *tout ensemble* (see → nationalism), and (c) the set of Hindu international missionary movements founded by revered *guru* figures or spiritual teachers with various centers in India and throughout the world.

3. Folk Hinduism, or the set of archaic spiritualities, including local demons and spirits, magico-religious practices, shamanistic traditions, and so forth, that are as widely present in India since Independence as they have been for millennia in the South Asian region.

4. Literate Hinduism, which encompasses the Vedic, Sanskritic, and vernacular traditions of the law books or prescribed codes of conduct (→ Dharmaśāstras), the great epics (→ *Mahābhārata* and → *Rāmāyaṇa*), the → Purāṇas, the → Tantras, the various → *bhakti* theologies (Vaiṣṇava, Śaiva, and Śākta), and the technical philosophies (→ Vedānta, → Nyāya and Navyanyāya, the various → Yogas, and so forth); all of these traditions continue to be maintained in post-Independence India and together can be referred to as behavioral ritual obligations of group rank and stations in life or simply the rules pertaining to → caste and stage of life (*varṇāśramadharma*).

5. Monastic Hinduism, including the → Daśanāmī orders and the various other *sampradāya*s or religious orders in independent India.

6. Pilgrimage Hinduism, including not only the important pilgrimage sites (→ *tīrtha*s) throughout the South Asian region but also the great *melā*s or → festivals that bring massive gatherings of pilgrims together periodically.

7. Finally, diaspora Hinduism – the sizable populations of expatriate Hindus throughout the world struggling to adapt, reshape, and preserve elements of the Hindu heritage in their new national environments. Let me comment on each of these divisions or categories.

Partition Hinduism

Whatever else one might wish to say about Hindu traditions in post-Independence India, in many ways, the most important observation is the basic paradigm shift in religious sensibility among many Hindus since Independence. The achievement of independence, while on one level a celebratory occasion of joy and hope, was on its darker underside a profoundly negative event replete with some of the worst violence in the entire history of the subcontinent, which involved the displacement of huge populations, the loss of property, separation of families, and a legacy of suspicion and hostility that continues to the present day. Partition was not only an ambivalent political event but also a profound and ambivalent religious event in which masses of Hindus (and Muslims) recognized, many for the first time, that Hindu religious sensibilities could not coexist with Muslim sensibilities in a modern, democratic polity. → Gandhi 's argument that Partition was a "patent untruth" (Larson, 1995, 189) was proved wrong, and the Gandhian nonviolent, non-cooperation ideology (*satyāgraha*), while having been effective as a dissidence strategy against the British Raj, was finally found to be unworkable "on the ground" for any of the other players in the unfolding drama of Partition, namely J. Nehru, V. Patel, Jinnah, and, finally, even Lord Mountbatten and the British authorities. J. Nehru's "tryst with destiny" (McArthur, 1992, 234–37) was revealed as largely a secular Neo-Hindu destiny that could only be realized by surgically cutting off the far northwest and large portions of the northeast (to become West Pakistan and East Pakistan, now → Bangladesh). Moreover, shortly after Partition, the conundrum of Kashmir would become the exception that would prove the rule. That is, a predominantly Muslim population, under the leadership of a Hindu *mahārāja*, would accede to largely Hindu India thereby creating an anomaly within both India and Pakistan, with Hindus claiming that a majority Muslim state would legitimate the "secular" credentials of the emerging nation-state of India and with Muslims in Pakistan claiming that Kashmir must find its ultimate destiny within the Islamic Republic of Pakistan. The conflict over Kashmir is perhaps the most salient symbol of the religious significance of Partition. It is an open sore on the body of independent India that will never heal until a new status for Kashmir is properly renegotiated by India, Pakistan, and the people of the Kashmir region.

What makes Partition an important religious event is the stark antithesis of religious sensibilities between Hindus and Muslims, sensibilities that encompass ideology (and theology), historical understanding, basic values, social organization, and law. Islamic religion, on analogy or in continuity with the older Jewish and Christian religions that arose in the Mediterranean region of Late Antiquity, focuses on an abstract belief system centering on one God (Allāh), a master text (the *Qurʾān*), a master historical narrative (a "*Heilsgeschichte*"), a master community (the Dar al-Islam), a specific sacred space (Mecca), and an all-encompassing sacred as well as personal law (*šarīʿa*). Hindu religion, in contrast, on analogy or in continuity with other "*dharma*" traditions such as Buddhism and Jainism that stretch back to the 1st millennium BCE, is dramatically different in almost every respect. Instead of one transcendent deity, there is a polymorphic set of disparate deities or no deity at all. Instead of a single master historical narrative or *Heilsgeschichte*, there is wide-ranging multi-narrativity. Instead of a single authoritative text, there is pervasive multitextuality, both written and oral. Instead of an abstract set of beliefs or credo (orthodoxy), there is the absence of any sort of cognitive regulation but various traditions, instead, of orthopraxis that differs from one birth group (*jāti*) to another and from one stage of life to another. And in place of a cohesive believing community, some sort of Dar al-Islam, there are pluralistic sets of mini communities, to some degree normatively hierarchical in an official idiom of *varṇa* or "caste" but in reality a splintered texture of birth groups (*jāti*) that vary from region to region on the subcontinent.

This is not to say that Partition was only a religious event, nor is it to say that even though Hindu and Muslim religious sensibilities are the antithesis of each other, there were not some important commonalities as well, especially on a popular, everyday level. Politically, both Hindus and Muslims disliked and distrusted what they considered to be the "divide and rule" tactics of the British Raj. They were both largely unpersuaded by the proselytizing of the missionaries, who flooded into the subcontinent in significant numbers after gaining permission to enter the country through the Charter Act of 1813. They both detested the arrogance and racism of the Raj. Perhaps most of all, they were weary of the mindless hypocrisy of the British Raj that espoused the Enlightenment principles of freedom, self-determination, and democracy, while carefully postponing the full implementation of the same principles almost up until the last day of the British presence on the subcontinent. Even when the time for full implementation finally arrived, there was a mad rush for the exit, without adequate preparation or safeguards, which became undoubtedly an important causal factor for the terrible violence that ensued. Both Hindus and Muslims suffered terribly because of the British penchant for all too often operating in a "fit of absent-mindedness," to use Lord Palmerston's famous quip regarding the British Raj as a whole (Larson, 1995, 49).

Likewise, even though their religious sensibilities differed markedly, there were also commonalities between Hindus and Muslims on other cultural (nonreligious) levels, which included – in addition to their joint dislike of the political dominance of the Raj – the cuisines of India; the classical → music traditions of India; pilgrimage traditions in and around the subcontinent; the painting, sculpture, and architecture traditions; linguistic interactions in both the various vernaculars (Hindi, Urdu, etc.) and the classical languages (Sanskrit and Arabic); patterns of everyday interaction in terms of trade, marketing, and local public education; and, perhaps most obviously, the great fondness among all citizens for Bollywood cinema, television programs, popular magazines, and newspapers. These commonalities frequently cross religious boundaries and make up the complex and dense civil society of modern "secular" India (see also → secularism). In addition, there are the significant influence and use of the English language and the legacy of British culture and institutional structures in general in independent India. English, along with Hindi, is one of the two official languages of communication. With regard to this latter point, however, it is important to note that there is no majority language in modern India since Independence. Hindi and English are designated as official languages for governmental communications and publications, but Hindi is spoken by less than half (about 40%) of the population and English by only 3% to 5%.

When using the expression "Partition Hinduism," therefore, the point is to recognize that Hinduism in post-Independence India has a number of new features that taken together suggest a significantly different religion from the one that was practiced on the subcontinent before. The most salient of these new features include (a) the recognition that Hinduism itself has now emerged as a distinct cultural phenomenon functioning in a modern democratic polity that requires its practitioners to take account of all sorts of minority religious traditions (Christian, Jewish, Muslim, Buddhist, Jain, Sikh, Parsi, etc.) as well as socially deprived and underdeveloped minority communities (→ Dalits, tribals, and Other Backward Classes [OBC]); (b) the recognition that the largest minority religious tradition could not be plausibly accommodated within the new independent polity and had to be surgically detached and constituted as a separate modern polity, namely, the sizable pre-Partition Muslim populations primarily in the northwest and northeast of the subcontinent (to become Pakistan and eventually Bangladesh); and, most importantly, (c) the recognition of the need for a new civil discourse that would unite the various regional versions of Hindu belief and practice (both elite and popular) into an all-India ideology that could bring together the vast Hindu majority and the various (religious and social) minority communities.

This latter feature – that is, the need for new all-India ideologies – has generated a profoundly important debate that continues in India up until today and will continue to unfold in the subcontinental region for many years to come.

"Neo-Hindu" Hinduism

That debate has to do with what I have called elsewhere the Neo-Hindu "hybrid discourse of modernity" (Larson, 1995, 178–226). By the expression "neo-Hindu" is meant a general framework of discourse or mind-set, undoubtedly Hindu in inspiration but characterized by a number of distinctive features that clearly separate the manner in which the notion of Hinduism is understood in comparison with older usage. By the expression "hybrid discourse of modernity" is meant the manner in which the language of modernity has a unique inflection in contemporary India.

Like Partition Hinduism, the Neo-Hindu hybrid discourse of modernity is an important dimension of what the term "Hinduism" has come to mean in post-Independence India. These new (neo) features include the following:

- promulgation of a self-conscious national (all-India) awareness over and above regional differences;
- commitment to the reform of outdated religious practices;
- rejection of the inequities of the traditional caste system;
- emancipation of women;
- improvement of social conditions for the poor, including positive discrimination or affirmative-action programs for Dalits (untouchables), tribals, and Other Backward Classes;
- economic progress of the entire nation;
- attitude of appreciation for all religions;
- use of modern educational methods; and, finally,
- use of English (in addition to the regional vernaculars) and modern means of communication (newspapers, pamphlets, tracts, films, television, public broadcasting, etc.).

Within this general Neo-Hindu framework, there are three distinct and sometimes contending interpretations of Neo-Hindu, namely, (a) the Gandhian-Nehruvian civil ideology of India as a secular state, with an institutional base largely in the Indian National Congress; (b) the *hindutva* (lit. Hindu-ness) religious ideology of India as primarily a civilization-based cultural identity, with an institutional base largely in what has come to be called the Sangh Parivar (Family of [Hindu] Associations), including the conservative Bharatiya Janata Party (BJP; Indian People's Party), the Vishwa Hindu Parishad (VHP; World Council of Hindus), the Rashtriya Swayamsevak Sangh (RSS; National Assembly of Volunteers), and some other, smaller regional associations; and (c) a set of Neo-Hindu international missionary movements, founded by various Indian *gurus* or spiritual virtuosos who profess one or another type of meditation or → *yoga* together with a belief in the unity of all religions. The institutional base of these movements is not only in India but also throughout the world among Indian diaspora communities as well as among people of diverse nationalities – for example, the → Ramakrishna Math and Mission, the Integral Yoga movement of → Aurobindo, the International Society for Krishna Consciousness (→ ISKCON), the Siddha Yoga movement of Swami → Muktananda and Gurumayi, the Spiritual Regeneration Movement or Transcendental Meditation (TM) of → Maharishi Mahesh Yogi, the → Sathya Sai Baba Movement in Andhra Pradesh, and many others (see below for details).

These varieties of Neo-Hindu religious orientation all have their roots in 19th- and 20th-century pre-Independence movements in India but have emerged since 1947 as salient manifestations of post-Independence Neo-Hinduism. At first glance, it might seem odd to include the Gandhian-Nehruvian civil ideology of the secular state as a Neo-Hindu religious ideology, but there appear to be good reasons for doing so. To be sure, Gandhi's passionate commitment to nonviolent noncooperation (*satyāgraha*) was much more than a political strategy. It was also a profound religious vision that tapped into some of the oldest themes of asceticism and renunciation in the Hindu tradition, and Gandhi himself embodied those themes in his own lifestyle. J. Nehru, to the contrary, was an agnostic, and while he was devoted to Gandhi as a friend and mentor, he had little patience with the religious proclivities of Gandhi. Nehru wanted a modern industrial society fashioned from the "commanding heights" (Larson, 1995, 199) in the manner of many of the ideas of Fabian socialism (Larson, 1995, 194), with a clear separation between religion and the new state of India. Nevertheless, the Gandhian Hindu religiosity hovered over the Indian nationalist movement and convinced many – for example, Sayyid Ahmed Khan, Muhammad Iqbal, Muhammad Ali Jinnah, and other important figures in the founding of Pakistan – that, finally, the secular state that Gandhi and Nehru wanted was, in the final analysis, a Neo-Hindu state. W.N. Brown has put it in the following way:

> though Gandhi abhorred Hindu-Muslim communalism and partition, he nevertheless contributed to them. He could not in his time have become the political leader of the majority group in India, fortified by mass support, without being religious, he could not be religious without being Hindu. He could not be Hindu without being suspect to the Muslim community. (Brown, 1963, 104)

The Gandhian-Nehruvian nation-state became a Neo-Hindu secular state, an interesting coalition of forward or high-caste Hindu elites that together with Scheduled Castes, Schedules Tribes, Other Backward Classes, and the Muslim minorities that remained in India after Partition operated as a powerful coalition to rule India for the first half century of its Independence.

In an interview for the magazine *India Today*, V.P. Singh, prime minister of India in 1989–1990, made the same observation in a slightly more caustic manner.

> (V.P. Singh talking) What has been established in the past half a century is the upper caste Hindu raj, depriving the backwards and the minorities...
> Q: *But aren't we a secular nation?*
> A: That's just gloss. But in various forms the political system has reacted against the upper caste Hindu raj... The reaction arises because they [the backward groups] are not party to the operations of power...
> Q: *Is the structure not delivering what Gandhi and Nehru wanted?*
> A: An iniquitous social structure has produced an iniquitous power structure. (*India Today*, Oct 31, 1992; cited in Larson, 1995, 178)

What V.P. Singh is noticing in these comments is that the so-called secular state of modern India, or the Gandhian-Nehruvian civil ideology of the secular state, is an "upper caste Hindu raj," or, in other words, a Neo-Hindu ideology. S. → Radhakrishnan makes the point in a more judicious manner as follows:

> It may appear somewhat strange that our government should be a secular one while our culture is rooted in spiritual values. Secularism here does not mean irreligion or atheism or even stress on material comforts. It proclaims that it lays stress on the universality of spiritual values, which may be attained in a variety of ways... This is the meaning of a secular conception of the state though it is not generally understood. (Smith, 1963, 147)

The Sangh Parivar, unlike the Gandian-Nehruvian ideology of the secular state, is quite explicit in its recognition that the nation-state of India is very much a Hindu state. Instead of cloaking its discourse in the progressive modern jargon of "secularism," "pluralism," and "modernity," however, it proclaims that the terms "Hindu" and "Hinduism" are much more than narrow religious notions. They refer to a distinctive civilization that includes all of the indigenous religious traditions of the subcontinent – Hindu (Śaiva, Vaiṣṇava, Śākta, Tantra, etc.), Buddhist, Jain, Sikh, and various tribal spiritualities – hence the expression *hindutva* (Hindu-ness), first introduced by V.D. Savarkar, as a way of characterizing Hindu culture as a total civilization. Only Islam and Christian traditions are excluded from the general sense of Hindu civilization, since their origins lie outside the subcontinental region. Islam and Christianity claim to be universal spiritualities, but they need to recognize that they occupy only a secondary place as minorities within the "motherland" of the larger Hindu civilization. They are certainly welcome in India, but they must recognize their proper place within the larger, encompassing Neo-Hindu context.

Followers of the Sangh Parivar criticize the Gandhian-Nehruvian ideology of the secular state as a form of what they call "pseudo secularism" insofar as the Gandhian-Nehruvian "secularists" continually back away from supporting a uniform civil code for India, refuse to challenge the "special status" of Kashmir, and are much too concerned with always giving the minorities what they want in order to maintain their elitist, so-called secular Hindu Raj. The followers of the Gandhian-Nehruvian ideology frequently respond with their own counter-criticism, claiming that the Sangh Parivar is a "communal" set of narrow, right-wing groups that tend toward "fascist"-like behavior.

Both critiques are on occasion true enough but, unfortunately, often descend into little more than mutual name calling. What is closer to the truth is that the Gandhian-Nehruvian Neo-Hindu secular state is a liberal interpretation of the basic Neo-Hindu ideology, whereas the Sangh Parivar is a conservative interpretation of that very same basic ideology. If, as one commentator has put it, the Gandhian-Nehruvian secular state is "Hindu Chauvinism with a Liberal Mask" (Embree, 1987, 74), then one could reasonably suggest that the Sangh Parivar is "Hindu Chauvinism with a Conservative Mask."

Both interpretations grow out of the nationalist freedom struggle in the 20th century, the former associated primarily with the Gandhian nonviolent non-cooperation (*satyāgraha*) political movement from 1915 onward, with its base in the Indian National Congress, and the latter with the founding of the conservative Hindu party – the Mahāsabhā (Great Assembly) – in 1914, followed by the publication of V.D. Savarkar's *Hindutva* tract in 1923, and issuing further in the founding of the Rashtriya Swayamsevak Sangh in 1925 by K.B. Hedgewar, who led the Rashtriya Swayamsevak Sangh and the growing Sangh Parivar groups from 1940 to 1973, when he was succeeded by M.S. Golwakar. The current leader of the Rashtriya Swayamsevak Sangh is Mohan Madhukar Bhagwat.

For the first 50 years of Independence (the late 1940s through the late 1990s), the dominant interpretation of the Neo-Hindu ideology was the Gandhian-Nehruvian version under the leadership primarily of Nehru and his daughter, Indira Gandhi. Since the mid-1990s (with the prime ministership of Atal Bihari Vajpayee in 1996 and again from 1999 until 2004), the Gandhian-Nehruvian ideology has been receding in favor of the Sangh Parivar orientation. From the middle of the first decade of the 21st century, the Indian National Congress (in league with various minor parties) has reasserted itself, but overall it appears to be the case that both Neo-Hindu ideologies are equal contenders with respect to the future direction of the Neo-Hindu Indian nation-state.

The third interpretation of Neo-Hindu religious thought has to do with Neo-Hindu international missionary movements. Like the other two types of interpretation of the basic category of Neo-Hindu, the missionary movements derive their inspiration from pre-Independence sources in India from the 19th century and the first half of the 20th century. As early as 1828, a reformist group was formed in Bengal – the Brahmo Sabha (The Society of God; later renamed → Brahmo Samaj) – by → Rammohun Roy (1772–1833), a Bengali Brahman who was influenced by Christian ideas regarding one God but who decided to remain a Hindu, having reached the conclusion that vedic and upanishadic ideas were equal or even superior to Christian notions. Some years later (in 1867), a similar reformist Hindu group – known as the Prarthana Sabha (Prayer Society) – was formed in Bombay by Keshub Chandra Sen (1838–1884), again not only under strong Christian influence but also suggesting that Hindu thought was equal or superior to Christian thought. A few years later, yet another group was formed in the Punjab region by Dayananda Saraswati (1827–1883) known as the → Arya Samaj (Aryan Society), a more militant conservative group, openly hostile to both Christian and Islamic missionizing, and arguing for a reconversion to Hindu religion by Christian and Islamic converts through a "purification" ritual. The founders of these three reformist movements planted the seeds for reversing the missionizing impulse of the Christian and Islamic traditions and proclaiming, instead, the superiority of vedic and upanishadic religiosity, although these three movements never developed much of an international constituency.

Two movements that truly can be said to be international missionary movements, however, are, first, the Ramakrishna Mission and Math, inspired by the famed spiritual saint Shri → Ramakrishna (birth name Gadadhar Chatterjee; 1836–1886), a simple Bengali Brahman priest, together with his most famous disciple, Swami → Vivekananda (birth name Narendranath Datta; 1862–1902), and, second, the Integral Yoga movement, founded by philosopher and holy man Shri Aurobindo (birth name Aurobindo Ghose; 1872–1950).

The Ramakrishna Math or monastic movement was organized in 1887, when Swami Vivekananda and some other disciples of Shri Ramakrishna took monastic vows. Ramakrishna himself had spent his entire adult life as a priest in a temple devoted to the goddess → Kālī in the district of Dakshineshwar, near Calcutta. He had had a number of extraordinary mystical experiences over the years and had attracted a small group of followers, one of whom was Narendranath Datta, later to be given the spiritual name Swami Vivekananda. After Ramakrishna's death, Vivekananda made a pilgrimage around India and determined, finally, to propagate the message of his *guru*. Vivekananda developed and taught a simplified version of monistic Vedānta philosophy and a synthesized version of the varieties of *yoga* taught in the → *Bhagavadgītā*, and he combined those ideas with a program for social action and social reform for modern India and a program for missionizing outside of India. He attended the World Parliament of Religions in 1893 in Chicago as a representative of Hinduism, and his considerable oratorical skills made a deep impression on the popular press and on certain liberal religious intellectual circles. He traveled widely in the United States and converted a number of Americans. In 1897, after his return to India, he established the Ramakrishna Mission in India along with a series of Vedanta Societies in the → United States, Europe, and Latin America. The headquarters of the movement was located at Belur Math, in the Howrah district, near Calcutta. Since India's Independence in 1947, the movement has gradually grown in India and around the world. In the United States, there are missionary Vedanta Societies in California, Georgia, Illinois, Massachusetts, New York, Oregon,

Washington, and Washington DC. There are Vedanta Centers as well in Argentina, Canada, France, Japan, and Singapore. It is fair to say that the Ramakrishna Mission and its various Vedanta Societies represent a well-known "face" of Neo-Hindu international missionary work in the world today.

A similar Neo-Hindu international missionary movement is the one founded by the philosopher and holy man mentioned above, Aurobindo Ghose. Aurobindo was educated in England and on his return to India joined the nationalist movement in the early 20th century. At first he was a militant extremist, advocating violence in the freedom struggle against the British. During a period of imprisonment for his radical activities in 1909, however, he underwent a deep conversion experience, and instead of pursuing his political radicalism, he retired to Pondicherry (Puducherry) in South India. He established an *āśram* or monastic-like community there in order to practice and propagate what he called "Integral Yoga," an interesting combination or synthesis of various types of *yoga* together with an evolutionary philosophy that seeks to focus on developing the notion of an emerging supermind, somewhat comparable to the evolutionary ideas of the French Jesuit thinker T. de Chardin. In 1920, a French woman, Mirra Alfassa (whose later married name became Mira Richard), was profoundly impressed by Aurobindo's integral *yoga* and decided to live permanently in the *āśram*. She came to be known as the "Mother." With Aurobindo she developed the Integral Yoga *āśram* in Pondicherry. Aurobindo died in 1950, and Mira Richard as the "Mother" continued to lead the movement until her own death in 1973. She was instrumental in the founding of an experimental city, Auroville, a utopian community experiment in international living, located a few kilometers north of the Aurobindo *āśram*. Since the Independence of India in 1947, the Aurobindo Neo-Hindu international missionary movement has established Study Centers throughout India and many other Study Centers around the world – some 15 throughout the United States, one in Canada (Quebec), and a number of others in western Europe.

Many more recent examples of Neo-Hindu international missionary movements have appeared in the 20th century, especially in the turbulent cultural period of the 1960s, when two parallel social transformations were occurring: on the one hand, radical student political movements in the United States, western Europe, Japan, India, and elsewhere, involving mass attempts to change the political landscape, and, on the other hand, spiritual renewal groups of a Neo-Hindu sort that represented innovative alternatives to conventional religious institutions that were clearly being rejected.

There are numerous such Neo-Hindu missionary groups, but, as mentioned earlier, four are especially well known in as well as outside of India and may be considered typical of these sorts of groups.

1. The International Society for Krishna Consciousness (ISKCON) was founded in New York in 1966 by A.C. Bhaktivedanta Prabhupad (birth name Abhay Charan De; 1896–1977). He was a Bengali businessman who became a → Gauḍīya Vaiṣṇava monk in 1959 and felt called to carry the message of devotional Vaiṣṇavism to the West. ISKCON is also known as the Hare Krishna Movement. The focus of the movement is on emotional devotion to → Kṛṣṇa. The movement retains a strong base in India in Vrindavan, in the Mathura district of Uttar Pradesh in North India – the sacred grove in which Kṛṣṇa danced with young maiden devotees and a beloved pilgrimage destination in contemporary India.

2. The Siddha Yoga Movement, established as a legal foundation (SYDA; Siddha Yoga Dham of America) in the United States in 1978 by Swami (Baba) Muktananda (birth name Krishna; 1908–1982), is another widely known Neo-Hindu missionary movement. Its headquarters is in an *āśram* at Ganeshpuri, in the state of Maharashtra. The movement has also maintained a major *āśram* in South Fallsburg, New York. The movement is a blend of classical and tantric *yoga* practices, focusing on → *śakti* (power or divine energy). Followers believe that power can descend suddenly onto a devotee by the mere presence or touch of the *guru*. This belief follows some old Śaiva traditions from the region of Kashmir. After the death of Swami Muktananda in 1982, leadership of the movement was taken over by Gurumayi Chidvilasananda.

3. The Spiritual Regeneration Movement or Transcendental Meditation (TM) is yet another Neo-Hindu missionary movement, which was established in the late 1950s in the United States and Europe by Maharishi Mahesh Yogi (birth name Mahesh Prasad Varma; 1917–2008). In

1960 it came to be known as the International Meditation Society (IMS) and eventually the Students International Meditation Society (SIMS). The international headquarters was relocated to Switzerland and ultimately (in 1990) to the Netherlands. Maharishi Mahesh Yogi taught a simple technique of sound meditation. The devotee is given a sacred *mantra* or sound and then told to meditate for half an hour or one hour every day. The idea is to bring about a relaxed state of mind and to purify one's awareness.

4. Finally, mention may be made of Sathya Sai Baba (birth name Satya Narayan; 1926–2011), Indian holy man and healer from Puttaparthi in the state of Andhra Pradesh. When he was 14, he had a vision in which he was revealed as being a reincarnation of an older holy man, the → Shirdi Sai Baba, who had lived in Maharashtra and who had died in 1918. Sathya Sai Baba was considered to be a great healer, capable of producing ashes in his hand at will as well as of other miracles, especially miracles of healing. He had several million followers in India and reportedly as many as ten million followers internationally, including a sizable number of Americans.

Whereas the Gandhian-Nehruvian Neo-Hindu civil ideology of the secular state and the Sangh Parivar Neo-Hindu ideology of *hindutva* are both clearly religious-*cum*-political interpretations of post-Independence Hinduism, this third set of Neo-Hindu spiritualities is interestingly different albeit still clearly Neo-Hindu in inspiration. The common features of these post-Independence Neo-Hindu missionary movements include the following (Larson, 1995, 139):

1. devotion to a deified *guru* or teacher,
2. total obedience to the will of the *guru*,
3. the practice of one or another type of *yoga* or disciplined meditation,
4. the claim that all religions are basically true,
5. the claim that one's ethnic identity is not essential in order to be a follower,
6. and, finally, the tendency to deemphasize secular political involvement of any kind.

Folk Hinduism

Thus far the focus has been on attitudes and beliefs of Hinduism that are distinctly different from attitudes and beliefs of Hinduism in the pre-Independence period. The expression "Neo-Hindu" has been one useful way of characterizing this unique paradigm shift in religious understanding that pertains to what has happened both as a result of Partition and with the accompanying ideological (and/or theological) Neo-Hindu interpretations. Now it is important to locate what has been said so far in the broader framework of Hindu spirituality in the subcontinental region since Independence.

The anthropologist A. Bharati, some years back, offered a useful heuristic overview of Hindu traditions in terms of three separate categories: "village Hinduism," literate or scripture-based "Sanskrit, Vedic Hinduism," and, finally, "renaissance Hinduism" or what has been called thus far Neo-Hindu Hinduism (1981, 9ff., 11ff.). A. Bharati has also suggested (again as a rough characterization in the absence of precise demographic data) that approximately two-thirds of practicing Hindus are Vaiṣṇava (followers of Viṣṇu or one of his incarnations, mainly Kṛṣṇa or → Rāma), and one-third are Śaiva (followers of → Śiva) or Śākta (devotees of the Great Goddess [→ Mahādevī]).

If these divisions are reasonably plausible, given the provisional figures of the census of 2011, then altogether there are about 970 million Hindus in present-day India (80.5% of the total population of 1,210,193,422 and counting). This total figure for Hindus is somewhat suspect, since it includes the Scheduled Castes (Dalits or "downtrodden," formerly referred to as untouchables) and Scheduled Tribes, which make up nearly 25% (more precisely 23.5%) of the total population (or approx. 300 million people) and some of whom are unhappy with the label "Hindu" because of long-standing discrimination.

In any case, leaving aside the admittedly interesting political issue of how Hindu and non-Hindu groups might characterize themselves, of the 970 million Hindus in the official 80.5% of the census of 2011, probably only 5% to 10% could plausibly be included within the "renaissance Hinduism" grouping (that is, the Neo-Hindu population) – in other words, no more than perhaps 97 to 100 million people. These are largely the highly educated urban elites of post-Independence India.

A. Bharati's second grouping, "Sanskrit, Vedic Hinduism" – that is, literate, scripture-based believing Hindus, whom A. Bharati estimated at 13% to 15% but who, with the increased economic prosperity in recent years, have probably grown to as high as 20% to 25% of the population – would include as many as 250 million to 300 million people. This grouping comprises the educated, literate new middle class, again largely urban but including smaller population areas around the subcontinent as well. To some degree, this large grouping would be deeply influenced by Neo-Hindu ideas (especially by the *hindutva* ideology of the Sangh Parivar), but in many respects, they would hold to a premodern traditional Hinduism as well. Many professional religious people (monks, holy men, holy women, and *yogī*s) would be included in this grouping.

A. Bharati's third grouping, or what he calls "village Hinduism," would be the nonurban Hinduism characteristic of the 600 thousand villages scattered throughout India, with a rather massive population of roughly 500 to 600 million – as many as half, in other words, of the total Hindu population and including Scheduled Castes, Scheduled Tribes, and Other Backward Classes. This third grouping has benefitted considerably from the positive discrimination (affirmative action) policies of the government of India and has made important strides in education and social development generally. These improvements have occurred especially since improved economic policies have been put in place under the prime ministership of Narasimha Rao in 1995, whose economic minister at the time of the economic takeoff was Manmohan Singh, the current prime minister of India since 2004.

Overall, then, even with this cursory overview of the levels of Hindu spirituality in post-Independence India, the complexity of what is meant by the term "Hinduism" becomes increasingly clear. Sociologist S.C. Dube has put the matter in the following way:

> Hinduism, such as it is, is a loosely structured federation of faiths rather than a faith. Hindu civilization represents a pattern of stabilized pluralism with well-developed linkages and patterns of interdependence between its insoluble segments that enjoy varying degrees of autonomy and identity. Birth and minimal cognitive participation are enough to identify one as belonging to the Hindu faith. (Dube & Basilov, 1983, 1)

The label "folk Hinduism" for what A. Bharati has called "village Hinduism" is meant to identify not so much the social-anthropological context of what A. Bharati calls "village" Hinduism but, rather, the distinctive spirituality of this dimension of Hindu practice. B. and R. Allchin's description of this sort of spirituality is nicely encapsulated in the following observation:

> Throughout the length and breadth of India there are found today, at the folk level, rites and festivals which are intimately associated with the changing seasons, the sowing and harvesting of crops and the breeding of cattle and other livestock. There is also a whole pantheon of local gods and goddesses some of whom remain unassimilated while others have been absorbed at different levels into the sanskritized hierarchy of gods of the "great" or classical Indian tradition. There can be no doubt that a very large part of this modern folk religion is extremely ancient and contains traits which originated during the earliest periods of stock raising and agricultural settlement. (Allchin, 1982, 99)

Remembering that this level of Hindu practice occurs in almost every corner of the subcontinent by as many as several hundred million adherents in present-day India, an interesting paradox or conundrum emerges. To write about Hinduism in post-Independence India is in an important sense to write about prehistoric, archaic India as well, since the oldest folk religiosity is as present today on the subcontinent as it was before the beginning of recorded history. W. Faulkner's famous line comes to mind as being particularly significant in understanding this aspect of Hindu spirituality: "The past is never dead. It's not even past" (1951, 92). The tradition's own characterization of itself – namely, Hinduism as the *sanātanadharma* (eternal law or unchanging tradition[s] of conduct) – is more than a little diagnostic in this regard. In other words, in our scholarly efforts to focus on modern historical distinctions, sometimes it may be useful to remember that as many as half of the adherents of what we are studying neither believe in nor value our modern historical distinctions! There is a mind-set of unchanging continuity with India's archaic folk traditions that is still prevalent among millions of Hindus in post-Independence India.

Literate Hinduism

There is no need to comment in detail on the parameters of what is called literate, scripture-based, or simply classical Hindu spirituality, since this multivolume encyclopedia of Hinduism addresses all of these matters in great detail. What is pertinent for at least some brief comments under this heading, however, is the manner in which the notion of caste has shifted in significance in post-Independence India. The English term "caste" derives from the Latin *castus* (pure or chaste) and then from the Portuguese *casta* (pure breed); it was first used by the Portuguese in the 16th century to describe the peculiar social groupings that they noticed among the people of India.

In classical Sanskrit, there are two terms for the notion of caste, *varṇa* and *jāti*, and the difference between the two terms is diagnostic for understanding the shifts in the interpretation of the meaning of caste in the modern and post-Independence period. The term *varṇa*, meaning color or form in Sanskrit, is the official "Brahmanical" or normative notion for caste in Indian intellectual history, and it refers to the well-known hierarchical ordering of four social groupings: priests, rulers, merchants/traders, and servants. The hierarchy is determined or defined largely on the basis of ritual purity or obligation, which in turn is based on a combination of factors involving heredity, endogamy, occupation, and commensality. Caste in this sense is profoundly linked to what it is to be a Hindu, and it is this religious view of caste that is presupposed in the elite literature (sacred and popular) of India, including the → Vedas and → Upaniṣads, the law books, the epics, the → Purāṇas, and so forth. Those who are completely impure or polluted in this ritual sense fall outside the system and are sometimes referred to as very low or outcast (Caṇḍāla) or not to be touched (*aspṛśya*), from which the modern terms "untouchable" and the official government of India designation "Scheduled Caste" are derived. These groups are impure or polluted due to the polluting tasks that they have been assigned to perform – handling the dead (both animal and human), cleaning latrines, removing refuse, and so forth. More recently, the term for the "not to be touched" is "Dalit," meaning downtrodden or oppressed.

The system as a whole is an ideal construct and is often referred to as the system of behavioral ritual obligations of group rank and stages in life or simply the rules pertaining to caste and stage of life (*varṇāśramadharma*), an expression that itself is often taken as synonymous with the term "Hindu." It is difficult to know if this normative construct with its apparent rigidity and obviously discriminative intent was in fact ever of any great importance in actual social life throughout the history of the subcontinent, although it certainly appears to have been the case in what has been called the "Brahmin imaginary" – that is, the elite Brahmanical ideology/theology widely prevalent in the sacerdotal literature (Doniger, 2009, 29). In any case, during much of the period of British hegemony on the subcontinent, this basically normative and religious interpretation in terms of *varṇa* was emphasized (and frequently overemphasized). As has been noted by many researchers, the British census itself proved to be a mechanism not only for maintaining but also for inflating the salience of this older hieratic and religious significance of caste.

The other term for caste – *jāti*, which means in Sanskrit birth group, genus, kind, or subcaste – is an empirical "on-the-ground" understanding of caste and refers to the thousands of social groups in the various regions of the subcontinent that are interrelated in terms of kinship, occupation, social interaction, and ritual obligations. These *jāti*s are, to be sure, likewise hierarchical and involve ritual obligations of one kind or another, but they represent overall a much more fluid and changing social reality. The hierarchies vary from region to region or even village to village, and the hierarchical interactions appear to change over time. Such a view of caste is likely a more accurate reflection of actual social reality than the "official" *varṇa* system of the "Brahmin imaginary." One can see the difficulties to some extent already in the elite religious literature (e.g. law books such as the *Mānavadharmaśāstra*), wherein the compilers struggle mightily to weave many of the empirical *jāti* or subcaste groups into one of the "official" four normative groups. Even a casual reading, however, reveals that the attempted conflations are hopeless compromises.

This process of caste mobility has been studied extensively in recent research, beginning already with the groundbreaking work of M.N. Srinivas (1969) and his theory of Sanskritization, whereby lower-ranking groups in a particular area begin to imitate the values of higher-ranking groups and thereby improve their social status within a given geographical area. The theory holds that Sanskritization can be considered a first step toward a kind of secularization – that is, attempts by social groups to begin a process of separating ritual purity from social status and power by using strategies of religious mimesis as a device for changing their social status.

When such strategies for social change are combined with Neo-Hindu calls for caste reform, one begins to see a direct attack on the older hierarchical religious system of *varṇāśramadharma* as a religious construct of what it means to be a Hindu. A process of de-sacralization – or, if you will, de-religionization – begins to appear, which in many ways becomes India's theory of secularization. Whereas secularization is usually understood as the separation of religious institutions such as a church from the institutions of the state, in India, where there is an absence of religious institutions such as a church, the admittedly odd functional equivalent becomes something like the sacerdotal caste system. When separated from their religious roots, castes begin to function as independent social groups with specific interests. This is exactly what started to happen already in the 19th and early 20th centuries and became even more prominent in post-Independence India. Traditional castes often become "caste associations." As a recent study put it,

> "caste spirit" took the form of "caste associations," organizations that aimed to define the unity and promote the social and political interests of their respective castes as defined in the census. Caste associations made ample use of new publishing technologies to create and disseminate caste directories, caste histories, and other kinds of informational pamphlets that aided the construction of these identities across a wider region. As a result of these kinds of efforts... caste increasingly became a basis for collective identity at a regional and even national level. These organizations effectively transformed what had previously been a fairly localized phenomenon... into political and social units operating in relation to the nation as a whole, crafting new histories and identities, lobbying for their group interests and forming political parties... Caste was becoming the language of political organization. (Mines, 2009, 42–43)

Secularization of the caste system has been a fundamental component of the development of the democratic polity of the Indian nation-state since Independence. Political parties and their platforms; positive discrimination policies (affirmative action programs); human rights campaigns; the system of "reservations" (especially designated seats) for Dalits, tribals, or Other Backward Classes in education, legislative bodies, and government jobs; and much more are all based on the secularization of caste. In every region of the modern Indian nation-state (the Hindi heartland, West Bengal, Kerala, Tamil Nadu, Jammu and Kashmir, etc.), the democratic politics of post-Independence India is unintelligible apart from the continuing significance of caste.

One final observation should be made. The secularization of caste also relates to the issue of a uniform civil code for India. Shortly after Independence, B.R. → Ambedkar, India's distinguished first law minister (and also a Dalit), led the political struggle to establish for the first time a uniform civil code for all the people of the new state (Larson, 2001, 1–11). He argued that the de-sacralization of caste now made it possible for groups that had maintained their personal community law on the grounds of religious legitimation to move in the direction of a uniform civil code regardless of religious identity.

B.R. Ambedkar had also been arguing earlier (in the 1930s) that the time had come for abolishing caste in India or at least providing separate voting status for untouchables, who were now recognized as an independent minority group. Regarding this latter issue, Gandhi vigorously opposed B.R. Ambedkar and argued instead for the older religious view of caste. Gandhi was against the secularization of caste and wanted to restore the "Brahmin imaginary" of caste as a harmonious system of reciprocal obligation with untouchables to be thought of as "Children of God" (Harijans) who are humble servants of the nation. Gandhi, of course, also said many times that caste has nothing to do with religion, but most observers, and especially Muslims, recognized that Gandhi's reformed vision of caste was very much a Neo-Hindu vision and had a great deal to do with religion. In 1932 Gandhi undertook a "fast unto death" to stop the establishment of a separate voting status for untouchables. He was successful in thwarting separate voting status, but ultimately his paternalistic view of untouchables or Harijans was not accepted. Quite to the contrary, the secularization of caste continued to move even more rapidly into the language of political organization (Larson, 1995, 187).

Returning to the issue of a uniform civil code just after Independence, B.R. Ambedkar introduced the Hindu Code Bill in 1948 as a first step toward the development of a uniform civil code. There was a great deal of opposition in parliament, and the bill was set aside unpassed in 1951. This defeat for B.R. Ambedkar triggered his resignation as law minister as well as his conversion to Buddhism. However, in the mid-1950s, the Hindu Code Bill was reintroduced piecemeal, resulting in the passage of the Hindu Marriage Act (1955), the Hindu Succession Act (1956), the Hindu Minority and Guardianship Act (1956), and the Hindu Adoptions and Maintenance Act (1956; Larson, 2001, 5–6). Unfortunately, a uniform civil code for all the people of India has not yet been achieved, and over these intervening years, sentiments regarding the need for a uniform civil code have dramatically shifted. As I have written in "Secularism in Indian Law,"

> For many years, especially during Nehru's leadership, a uniform civil code was favored as a tool to develop India as a secular state. In recent years, this has been reversed. At the beginning of the twenty-first century, those who want a more Hindu-oriented India favor a uniform civil code as a way of eliminating the personal law of the Muslim community, but this is hardly a realistic endeavor. Secularists, by contrast, are now learning that maintaining the system of personal laws is a way of preserving minority rights and maintaining a culture-specific secular cultural pluralism. (Larson, 2009, www.oxford-legalhistory.com/entry?entry=+77.e717)

Monastic Hinduism

It suffices to say under this heading that monastic traditions in post-Independence India are alive and thriving. Estimates for the number of "professional religious," or monastics, in India range anywhere from 8 million to 15 million (Klostermaier, 1989, 329). The precise number is nearly impossible to determine, because many independent holy men (→ *sādhus*) or *yogīs* are itinerant ascetics and are only loosely related to an established order. The most well-known religious order is the Daśanāmī ("Ten-Named"; nonsectarian but predominantly Śaiva and Śākta in orientation), established, according to tradition, by the great Indian thinker and religious reformer → Śaṅkara (c. 700 CE), whose philosophy of Advaita Vedānta (monist or nondualist Vedānta) is to a large degree the basic intellectual orientation for the various orders. The Daśanāmī order has a fourfold institutional structure (based on different geographical regions) located at

1. the Śriṅgeri Maṭh (monastery) in the state of Karnataka (the south);
2. the Govardhan Maṭh in Puri in the state of Orissa (the east);
3. the Śārada Maṭh in Dwarka in the state of Gujarat (the west); and
4. the Jyotir Maṭh in Badrinath in the state of Uttar Pradesh (the north).

In the first center are the Bhāratī, Purī, and Sarasvatī orders. In the second center are the Āraṇya and Vāna orders. In the third are the Tīrtha and Āśrama orders, and in the fourth are the Giri, Pārvata, and Sāgara orders. The leaders of each of these centers are considered to be in a direct *guruparamparā* (*guru* lineage) with the great Śaṅkara.

Also, there are four Vaiṣṇava *sampradāyas*:

1. the Rāmānuja Sampradāya (see → Śrīvaiṣṇavism), sometimes called the Śrī or Lakṣmī tradition, based on the philosophy of Viśiṣṭādvaita (the nondualism of modified → *brahman*) of → Rāmānuja (c. 1017–1137) – a form of Vedānta philosophy that has a strong theistic component, in contrast with the pure monistic thought of Śaṅkara;
2. the → Mādhva Sampradāya, a dualist tradition of Vedānta (Dvaita), founded by Madhva (c. 1197–1276);
3. the → Nimbārka Sampradāya, a dualist-*cum*-nondualist interpretation of Vedānta (Bhedābheda), founded by Nimbārka (c. 12th cent.); and
4. the → Vallabha Sampradāya, a purified nondualist tradition (Śuddhādvaita) but "purified" in the sense that the highest form of nondualism is Lord Kṛṣṇa himself, founded by → Vallabha (c. 16th cent).

These Vaiṣṇava traditions are for the most part to be found in South India, but there are northern Vaiṣṇava monastic traditions in the Hindi heartland as well. There are the → Rāmānandī *vairāgīs* (renouncers) in locations such as Varanasi, Ayodhya, and elsewhere, who are said to have been founded, according to tradition, by a certain → Rāmānanda, an ascetic from the Śrīvaiṣṇava tradition who worked in the 14th or 15th century in the northern city of Varanasi. Also, there is the untouchable community known as Ramnamis, located primarily in and around Chhattisgarh in central India (see → Madhya

Pradesh and Chhatisgarh). In addition to the Rāmānandīs and the Ramnamis, there are numerous Śaiva monastic lineages – for example, the Śaiva *nāga* ascetics, naked ascetics whose bodies are smeared with ashes and who usually belong to militant or martial-art groups known as → *ākhāṛas* (lit. wrestling arena or training center). These militant groups can be traced back many centuries (some even to the time of the great Śaṅkara) and were originally formed for purposes of defense and protection. Likewise, there are the Śaiva Nāth *yogīs* or Gorakhnāthīs (see → Nāth Sampradāya), the → Aghorīs, the Udāsīs (see → *sādhus*), and so forth (Hartsuiker, 1993, 30–59; Bedi & Bedi, 1991, 49–96).

There is no institutional central authority for these monastic traditions in Hinduism. Even the *śaṅkarācāryas* (the heads of each of the four Daśanāmi Maṭhs) have no jurisdiction beyond the confines of their own monastery. Authority rests, rather, with the charismatic power of the particular *guru* or holy person, and followers or devotees receive blessings simply by taking *darśana* (the simple act of direct seeing; see → *pūjā* and darśan) of the *sādhu* or *guru*. Religious authority, both spiritual and institutional, is widely diffused throughout the countless millions of practicing Hindus in post-Independence India, ranging from the authority of the magician or shaman in countless ongoing folk rituals throughout the subcontinent, on the one hand, to the sophisticated instructions of the most highly accomplished spiritual virtuoso and scholar, on the other.

Pilgrimage Hinduism

A fascinating component of Hinduism in post-Independence India is the widespread practice of pilgrimage. Religious journeys to sacred places (*tīrthayātrā*) have been common in India for centuries for purposes of fulfilling vows, seeing holy temples and shrines, making a particular wish such as for the birth of a child, overcoming disease, doing penance, or offering thanksgiving for blessings. The practice is not noticed in the older vedic and upanishadic literature, but it becomes prominent in epic and puranic texts in the last few centuries before the Common Era and the first centuries of the Common Era and thereafter. The first clear textual references to pilgrimage are found in Buddhist and Jain sources, and it could well be the case that Hindus borrowed the practice from the Buddhists and Jains.

There are hundreds of pilgrimage sites in and around the subcontinent, and they have continued to be prominent in post-Independence India. Some pilgrimage sites have an all-India importance or scope, and seven main locations (*saptamahātīrthas*) are usually mentioned in this regard: Allahabad (or Prayag), Ayodhya, Mathura, and Varanasi in Uttar Pradesh, and Haridwar in Uttarakhand; Dwarka in Gujarat; and Ujjain in Madhya Pradesh. Many other pilgrimage sites are only regional or specifically sectarian locations. In some lists, Nasik (Maharashtra) appears in place of one of the above-mentioned seven (Bharati, 1970, 94–100).

Pilgrimage in India is not simply a matter of journeying to a specific place. It has, usually, a threefold referent. The first are the specific location, time, and place for a given festival or gathering (*melā*), which may be said to be the external social (*ādhibhautika*) context of the pilgrimage. The second referent is the internal spiritual journey of the pilgrim, which is in India the symbolic devotional and/or yogic (*ādhyātmika*) journey through the body and mind. The third, and to some degree the most important, referent is the celestial, cosmic, or astrological journey (*ādhidaivika*).

The best example of this threefold referent is the massive *kumbhamelā* pilgrimage that occurs in 12-year cycles and involves four of the principal pilgrimage sites – Allahabad, Nasik, Ujjain, and Haridwar. The sites were chosen on the basis of an old story of a cosmic struggle for a pot of celestial nectar that resulted in four drops being spilled that landed on each of the four sacred sites. The 12-year cycle or "full" *kumbhamelā* traces the movement of the planet Jupiter as it traverses the signs of the zodiac. The half *kumbhamelā* is when Jupiter is directly opposite Aquarius, the sixth year of the cycle. The most important sacred gathering is the one at Allahabad every 12th year, when millions of Hindus (with estimates in recent years of up to 30 million and more) gather to take their sacred bath at prescribed astrological moments. Allahabad or Prayāga is especially sacred because it marks the confluence of three great rivers (*trivenī*) – the → Gaṅgā, the → Yamunā, and the legendary Sarasvatī. The time for the holy gathering is when the royal planet, Jupiter (Graharāja ["King among Planets"], sometimes called Bṛhaspati), enters the asterism Aquarius (*kumbha* or waterpot) of the zodiac (hence the name *kumbhamelā*) around Jan 20. The specific sacred bathing moments are based on the actual appearance on the horizon of the main planet (Jupiter) and two minor planets. The most recent *kumbhamelā* was held in 2001, and the next one to occur, auspiciously enough, will be at about the same time as the publication of this volume of *Brill's Encyclopedia of Hinduism*, January–February 2013. The seven special bathing times in 2013 will be on Jan 27 and Feb 6, 10, 15, 17, 18, and 25.

Diaspora Hinduism

In the mid-1990s, estimates of the number of Hindus outside of India were roughly between 40 and 50 million, and the ten largest populations of Hindus outside of India were and are in Nepal, Bangladesh, Indonesia, the Gulf states, Sri Lanka, Pakistan, Malaysia, the United States, South Africa, and Mauritius. Countries with more than a hundred thousand Asian Indians include the United Kingdom, Bhutan, Myanmar, Trinidad, Fiji, Guyana, Singapore, Kenya, Canada, and Surinam. Altogether there are approximately 32 countries in the world with Asian Indian populations of more than one thousand (Vertovec, 2000, 14; Rukmani, 2001). It must be emphasized that these numbers are only rough estimates. Accurate and precise statistics are impossible to find.

In the United States, people from India are found in all 50 states. According to the US census of 2000, there were over two million "Asian Indians" – people from India or people of Asian Indian descent – living in the United States. That number has increased considerably since 2000, but since not all Asian Indians are Hindu, a reasonable estimate would be that roughly 80% of Asian Indians are Hindu. An estimate of more than two million Hindus is, thus, probably reasonable for the present time. The largest concentrations of Asian Indians are in the states of New York and California and in such urban areas as New York City, Chicago, Los Angeles, Houston, Philadelphia, and the San Francisco Bay area. Hindus residing in the United States are for the most part highly educated and prosperous and have become prominent in such areas as medicine, law, engineering, aerospace, business, and the arts. The high education levels and overall prosperity of Asian Indians in the United States are not typical of other Asian diaspora populations around the world, however, since US immigration policies are considerably more restrictive than those of most other countries in the world. There are, therefore, important differences in the Hindu diasporas around the world, and it is difficult and unfair to generalize about the diasporas overall.

One thoughtful typology regarding the Hindu diasporas was put forth some years back in S. Vertovec's book *The Hindu Diaspora: Comparative Patterns* (2000, 162–163). S. Vertovec identifies, first, what he calls a "trend for caste, sectarian and linguistic/regional traditions and communities to remain more or less intact," and he cites Great Britain and East Africa as Hindu diasporas that have pursued this trend. Second, he identifies a trend that presents "a kind of universal Hinduism," a "unitary" Hinduism in diaspora that is, oddly enough, a "transnational nationalism," which is the sort of universal, unitary Hinduism embodied by the Vishwa Hindu Parishad and its *hindutva* universalism. All varieties of Hinduism are welcome into such a religious nationalism, but there is a stress on a substantive unitary core. Third, he identifies a trend toward what he calls an "ecumenical" Hinduism, which recognizes the great variety of Hinduisms and combines and brings together the varieties side by side in temples, community centers, and other Hindu organizations. Distinctions of community, region, and caste are allowed to interact freely. The "ecumenical" mind-set has been typical of the Hindu diaspora in the United States. In Europe and elsewhere, the first two types are perhaps more prevalent.

A somewhat different typology was proposed many years ago by the distinguished historian P. Spear, who was attempting to identify the types of behavioral responses that appeared among the people of India with the coming of the British. His typology is to some degree still relevant for understanding the contemporary Hindu diasporas (1958, 177–191). He identifies five types of distinctive responses:

1. a "military" or openly hostile response or taking up arms against the intruders;
2. a "reactionary" response or the attempt to reconstitute the older political order, for example, the North Indian Rebellion (formerly called "The Mutiny") in 1857–1858;

3. a "westernizing" response or assimilating to the new values;

4. an "orthodox" response or maintenance of the older religion with appropriate reform; and

5. the "solution of synthesis" or an effort to adapt to the newcomers in which innovation and assimilation gradually occur together with an ongoing agenda of preserving the unique values of the many traditions of Hinduism (and those of other religious traditions, too).

P. Spear goes on to argue that the first four responses all eventually failed. In skirmish after skirmish, the "military" or hostile and aggressive responses were defeated. Likewise, the "reactionary" attempt to reconstitute the old political order proved to be a disaster. The "westernizing" response led to confusion and disorientation for generations of Indian intellectuals. Only the "solution of synthesis" was able to prevail in the work of such figures as Rammohun Roy, Sayyid Ahmed Khan, Swami Vivekananda, V.D. Savarkar, Muhammad Iqbal, R. Tagore, M.K. Gandhi, Muhammad Ali Jinnah, and J. Nehru. All pursed the "solution of synthesis" in their own unique ways, sometimes generating intense conflict with others and at other times accomplishing incredibly important goals for the future. P. Spear concludes that such a willingness to attain a synthesis that is neither fearful of the new nor dismissive of the old is "the ideological secret of modern India" (Spear, 1958, 187).

The Hindus of post-Independence India together with the Hindu diasporas throughout the world would do well to remember this ideological secret as they struggle to shape the Hinduisms of the future.

Bibliography

Allchin, B. & R., *The Rise of Civilization in India and Pakistan*, Cambridge UK, 1982.

Bedi, R., & R. Bedi, *Sadhus: The Holy Men of India*, New Delhi, 1991.

Bharati, A., *Hindu Views and Ways and the Hindu-Muslim Interface*, New Delhi, 1981.

Bharati, A., "Pilgrimage Sites and Indian Civilization," in: J.W. Elder, ed., *Chapters in Indian Civilization*, vol. I, Dubuque, 1970, 83–126.

Brown, W.N., *The United States, India and Pakistan*, Cambridge MA, 1963. *Census of India*, www.censusindia.gov.in/2011-prov-results.

Doniger, W., *The Hindus: An Alternative History*, New York, 2009.

Dube, S.C., "Harmonizing Dimension in Hindu Civilization Processes," in: S.C. Dube & V.N. Basilov, eds., *Secularization in Multi-religious Societies*, New Delhi, 1983, 1.

Embree, A., "Religion and Politics," in: M.M. Bouton, ed., *India Briefing, 1987*, Delhi, 1987, 74.

Faulkner, W., *Requiem for a Nun*, New York, 1951.

Frykenberg, R., "The Emergence of Modern 'Hinduism' as a Concept and as an Institution: A Reappraisal with Special Reference to South India," in: G.D. Sontheimer & H. Kulke, eds., *Hinduism Reconsidered*, Delhi, 1991, 31–33.

Guha, R., *India after Gandhi: The History of the World's Largest Democracy*, New York, 2007.

Hartsuiker, D., *Sādhus: India's Mystic Holy Men*, Rochester, 1993.

Klostermaier, K.K., *A Survey of Hinduism*, Albany, 1989.

Larson, G.J., "Secularism in Indian Law," in: S.N. Katz, ed., *The Oxford International Encyclopedia of Legal History*, 2009, www.oxfordlegalhistory.com/entry?entry=+277.e717.

Larson, G.J., ed., *Religion and Personal Law in Secular India: A Call to Judgment*, Bloomington, 2001.

Larson, G.J., *India's Agony over Religion*, Albany, 1995.

McArthur, B., ed., *Penguin Book of Twentieth Century Speeches*, London, 1992.

Mines, D.P., *Caste in India*, KIAS 4, Ann Arbor, 2009.

Rukmani, T.S., ed., *Hindu Diaspora: Global Perspectives*, Delhi, 2001.

Smith, D.E., *India as a Secular State*, Princeton, 1963.

Spear, P., *India, Pakistan and the West*, London, 1958.

Srinivas, M.N., *Social Change in Modern India*, Berkeley, 1969.

Vertovec, S., *The Hindu Diaspora: Comparative Patterns*, London, 2000.

Gerald J. Larson

Poets, Teachers, and Saints

Abhinavagupta

Abhinavagupta (c. 960–1020 CE) is widely renowned as the most authoritative and influential proponent of nondual → Kashmiri Śaivism, and probably even Hindu → Tantra in general. While certain innovations often credited to him in the areas of Pratyabhijñā nondual Śaiva philosophy and Sanskrit poetics should properly be ascribed to predecessors, nevertheless his brilliance, erudition, and profundity in these areas are unsurpassed. Moreover, Abhinavagupta integrated his work on these subjects with his own central project of developing a philosophical hermeneutics of tantric religion on the basis of the Pratyabhijñā philosophy. As such, Abhinavagupta laid the groundwork for a broadly coherent "meta-" system of nondual Kashmiri Śaivism, more encompassing in scope than its various constituents. Dialectically bridging a vast range of transgressive and orthoprax, theoretical, aesthetic, symbolic, ritual, ethical, and soteriological themes, Abhinava's works were exemplary for much of nondual Śaiva as well as other traditions of Hindu Tantra throughout South Asia.

Life

Abhinavagupta provides information about himself in the conclusions of his *Tantrāloka* (37.33–85; see Shastri & Shastri, 1987, vol. VIII, 3693–3718) and *Parātrīśikāvivaraṇa* (see Singh, 1989, 103–106, 270–272), as well as in brief comments scattered throughout his writings. Another resource is the eulogy, *Gurunāthaparāmarśa*, by a contemporary of his, Madhurāja (Raghavan, 1981, 1–16). Most recent scholars accept the following basic facts about his life (see Pandey, 1963, 3–26; Rastogi, 1987, 19–55; Sanderson, 1987; Dupuche, 2003, 3–7; Baumer, 2011, 7–10):

Abhinavagupta was a Brahman, descended from an 8th-century scholar named Atrigupta. The Kashmiri king Lalitāditya had brought Atrigupta from Kanauj to Pravarapura, present-day Srinagar, after he conquered Kanauj. Abhinava asserts that his father, Narasiṃhagupta, and mother, Vimalā, conceived him in a Kaula sexual ritual, and he accordingly views his parents as having respectively embodied → Śiva and his integral consort, Śakti. Abhinavagupta ascribes great significance to his having thus been born from a *yoginī* (*yoginībhū*), and the sage is still regarded by Kashmiri *paṇḍits* as having been an incarnation of Bhairava. Abhinavagupta's mother died when he was two, and his father raised him. He believed that the early death of his mother was an important motivating factor in his religious advancement. He had a brother, Manoratha, and a sister, Ambā.

The sage's first teacher in Sanskrit grammar was his father. When studying literature and poetics, he became possessed by great devotion to the god Śiva and forever renounced a householder's life. Though Abhinavagupta never married, he intimates that he did have personal experience in Kaula sexual rituals. Abhinavagupta is supposed to have studied with a great many academic as well as spiritual teachers, from nondual Kashmiri Śaiva as well as rival traditions, including Buddhism and Jainism (for lists of Abhinavagupta's teachers, see Pandey, 1963, 12; Rastogi, 1987, 54–55).

Abhinavagupta considered two of his teachers to have had the greatest impact on him. One of these was Lakṣmanagupta, a student of Utpaladeva. Lakṣmanagupta taught Abhinava the Pratyabhijñā philosophy, which became central to his own intellectual work. Abhinavagupta ascribes paramount importance to his teacher Śambhunātha, whom he may have met in Jālandhara, and who initiated him into Kaula texts and practices. Also important to Abhinavagupta was Śambhunātha's consort and "messenger" (*dūtī*), Bhagavatī. Abhinava is supposed to have achieved his liberative realization through the Kaula practices taught by Śambhunātha.

Kashmiri legend has it that Abhinavagupta did not die but rather entered into a cave known as Bhairava cave along with 1,200 disciples and was never seen again. Regardless of whether any part of that is true, Abhinavagupta is alleged to have had a large number of disciples. One of these was his brother Manoratha. His most famous student was his cousin Kṣemarāja, who further developed his teacher's philosophical hermeneutics in lengthy commentaries on tantric scriptures and Śāstras and a simplified manual of nondual Śaiva doctrine and practice in the light of that hermeneutics, the *Pratyabhijñāhṛdaya* (Heart of Recognition; see Singh, 1980).

Major Works

The vast corpus of Abhinavagupta's surviving writings may usefully be divided into four classes:

(1) commentaries on Pratyabhijñā philosophy;
(2) his own Pratyabhijñā-grounded philosophical hermeneutics of tantric symbolism and practice;
(3) commentaries on poetics-aesthetics; and
(4) some devotional hymns.

We may consider each of these in order.

While rooted particularly in the tradition known as Trika ("Triadism," named for its advertence to triads of cosmological principles and modes of practice), the Pratyabhijñā became the most authoritative philosophical theology for several other traditions of nondual Śaivism and Hindu Tantra. Utpaladeva (c. 900–950 CE) composed the foundational works of the Pratyabhijñā system on the basis of initiatives of his teacher Somānanda (c. 900–950 CE; see Shastri, 1934; Nemec, 2011). These foundational works comprise the *Īśvarapratyabhijñākārikā*, the autocommentaries *Vṛtti* (2002) and the now fragmentary *Vivṛti* (Torella, 1988; 2007a; 2007b; 2007c; 2007d), and the *Siddhitrayī* (Three Proofs; see Shastri, 1921a).

Abhinavagupta expounded and advanced the Pratyabhijñā in meticulous and erudite commentaries, the *Īśvarapratyabhijñāvimarśinī* (see Subramania Iyer & Pandey, 1986), on Utpaladeva's *Kārikā*, and the *Īśvarapratyabhijñāvivṛtivimarśinī* (see Shastri, 1987), on the largely missing *Vivṛti*. There has been some controversy about how much credit should be ascribed to Abhinavagupta in the development of the Pratyabhijñā system. As noted above, there is presently available only the shorter of Utpaladeva's autocommentaries, which is mostly concerned with clarifying the basic meaning of the verses. We have only fragments of Utpaladeva's longer *Vivṛti*. While the fragments are quite informative, it is still often impossible to distinguish arguments of Abhinavagupta that had direct precedent in Utpaladeva from those that either build upon or depart from that scholar's teachings. It does seem likely that many of the Pratyabhijñā theories often ascribed to Abhinavagupta were actually originated by Utpaladeva. At present we may say only that Abhinavagupta's commentaries are highly illuminating, while they also have the quality of original thought.

While Abhinavagupta's Pratyabhijñā commentaries are of great importance, this thinker's paramount significance in the history of Tantra was his utilization of the Pratyabhijñā theories and categories to formulate a nondual Śaiva philosophical hermeneutics of tradition (Āgama). His important works in this genre include his *magnum opus, Tantrāloka* (see Shastri & Shastri, 1987; Silburn & Padoux, 1998), the summary of that text in the *Tantrasāra* (see Shastri, 1982; see also Sanderson, 2005), the *Parātrīśikāvivaraṇa* (see Singh, 1989; see also Baumer, 2011), and the *Mālinīvijayavārttikam* (see Shastri, 1921b; see Hanneder, 1998). Also to be included here are Abhinavagupta's Śaiva commentary on the *Bhagavadgītā*, the *Gītārthasaṃgraha* (see Brahamachari, 1933; Marjanovic, 2002), and other short digests of Śaiva beliefs and practices, such as the *Paramārthasāra* (see Bansat-Boudon & Tripathi, 2010) – a reworking of the Vaiṣṇava Ādiśeṣa's text of the same name – and the *Bodhapañcadaśikā* (see Hughes, 1994, 21–34).

In these writings, Abhinava utilized ideas from the Pratyabhijñā philosophy to interpret and organize, in a coherent nondualist rubric, the diverse aspects of Trika symbolism, doctrine, and practice. In that nondualism, Abhinavagupta accords the highest credence to the Trika scripture, *Mālinīvijayottaratantra* (which in some respects actually may be interpreted as dualistic; see Sanderson, 1992). Under the rubric of the philosophically rationalized Trika, Abhinava synthesized an enormous range of symbolism and practice from Kaula, Krama, and Spanda Tantra, as well as other Hindu and Buddhist philosophical and religious traditions.

Abhinavagupta is also renowned for his works on Sanskrit poetry and drama. While he mentions aesthetic ideas throughout his writings, his major works on this subject are two voluminous commentaries, the *Abhinavabhāratī* on Bharata's *Nāṭyaśāstra* (see Nagar & Joshi, 1981–1984) and the *Dhvanyālokalocana* on Ānandavardhana's *Dhvanyāloka* (see Tripathi, 1975–1981; Ingalls, Masson & Patwardhan, 1990). Abhinavagupta's interpretation of aesthetic experience as homologous to and practically approaching the nondual Śaiva spiritual realization, as conceived in terms of his hermeneutics, was a paradigmatic resource for conceptions of the relation of aesthetic and religious experience throughout South Asian history.

Abhinavagupta additionally wrote a large number of devotional hymns (Stotras), expressing his religious devotion in terms of various themes of tantric symbolism and practice. These include the *Bhairavastotra*, *Devīstotra*, *Śivaśaktistotra*, *Kramastotra*, and the *Dehasthadevatācakrastotra* (for a translation of a selection of the Stotras, see Silburn, 1970).

This article will not enter into the controversy about the chronology of these different groupings of Abhinavagupta's writings (for further treatment of Abhinavagupta's writings including lost works, see Pandey, 1963; Raghavan, 1981; Rastogi, 1987, 55–63). However, it should be noted that, besides Abhinava's use of Pratyabhijñā categories in tantric symbolic-ritual and aesthetic works, throughout his texts he makes numerous other cross-references and allusions among various theories. Thus the scholar may be said to have laid the groundwork for a much broader, largely coherent system encompassing all the subjects of his writings.

Besides his accomplishments in the individual areas, much of Abhinavagupta's genius and enduring influence lies in his creation of this comprehensive system. This synthesis was read backward into the normative interpretation of its constituent traditions and largely defines what is now called "Kashmir Śaivism." Historians such as A. Sanderson and D.J. White have rightly drawn attention to Abhinavagupta's pivotal role in the medieval Brahmanic, philosophical, and aesthetic "domesticization" of transgressive elements of tantric traditions, and the "overcoding" of these traditions into ever more encompassing systems. Certainly Abhinavagupta did in these ways contribute greatly to the transformation of the meanings of tantric symbols, doctrines, and practices. However, the transformation in question should not be conceived in a blanket manner as distortion. Abhinava's aims were quite different from those of contemporary historiography. He primarily justified his views on philosophical and theological grounds, and they should accordingly be evaluated chiefly in those terms (Lawrence, 2008b, 8–10).

The following sections will overview some of the main teachings presented by Abhinavagupta in his various writings, noting, when possible, ideas that he held in common with his predecessors, and what seem to be some of his distinctive formulations.

Religious and Philosophical Project of the Pratyabhijñā System

Abhinavagupta and Utpaladeva conceive the Pratyabhijñā system simultaneously as a philosophical apologetics, structured according to → Nyāya categories for publicly assessable discourse, and an internalized tantric ritual that may potentially lead "all humanity" to the soteriological recognition (*pratyabhijñā*) "I am Śiva." Nondual Śaiva ritual practices generally endeavor to recapitulate the central myth of Śiva's emanation and control of the world through Śakti. These practices range from Kaula sexual rituals in which the male and female partners become Śiva and Śakti (Dupuche, 2003; White, 2003; Silburn, 1988; Chalier-Visuvalingam, 2012), through internalized contemplations of → *mantra*s (Alper, 1989; Muller-Ortega, 1992) and → *maṇḍala*s (Sanderson, 1986), and philosophical and theosophical speculations. The Pratyabhijñā thinkers likewise describe the modus operandi of the system according to the same ritual pattern, as the "revealing of Śakti" (*śaktyāviṣkaraṇa*). One endeavors to recognize identity with Śiva by the realization of one's possession of his integral consort and power, through whom he emanates and controls the universe.

Abhinavagupta additionally frames Śakti as the reason of a classic Nyāya "inference for the sake of others" (*parārthānumāna*). According to the scholastic logic, the reason identifies a quality in the inferential subject, that is, "I," known to be invariably concomitant with the predicate "Śiva." Thus I am Śiva because I have his quality, Śakti, the capacity of emanating and controlling the universe (Lawrence, 1999, 35–65).

In technical philosophical discussions, Śakti is often divided into special modalities that designate Śiva's emanatory power as operative in the respective spheres of explanation. The most encompassing of these are the knowledge and action *śakti*s (*jñānaśakti* and *kriyāśakti*), invoked in the fields roughly corresponding to epistemology and metaphysics/ontology.

Idealistic Epistemology of Recognition

The Pratyabhijñā philosophy describes the realization conveyed as the recognition "I am Śiva" in order to address problems of epistemology that had been formulated by the Buddhist epistemology and logic school of Dignāga and Dharmakīrti. According to this school, there are no grounds in the momentary and discrete perceptual data (*svalakṣana*), for the recognitions of any enduring entities as identified by linguistic or conceptual interpretation (*savikalpaka jñāna*). In debates over several centuries, the Buddhist philosophers had propounded arguments attacking on these bases many concepts that seemed commonsensical and were religiously significant to the various Hindu philosophical schools – such as ideas of external objects, ordinary and ritual action, an enduring self, god, and revelation (Lawrence, 1999, 67–84).

The Pratyabhijñā philosophers' response to the problematic posed by the Buddhists revolutionized earlier Hindu approaches and may be characterized as a form of transcendental argumentation. Abhinavagupta and Utpaladeva interpret the central nondual Śaiva myth of Śiva's emanation and control of the universe through Śakti as itself an act of self-recognition (*ahampratyavamarśa*, *pratyabhijñā*). Furthermore, the thinkers equate Śiva's self-recognition (Śakti) with the principle of supreme speech (*parāvāk*) – the essence of *mantras* – which they derive from the linguistic philosopher → Bhartṛhari; they thereby appropriate that theorist's explanation of creation as linguistic in nature. Thus the nondual Śaiva philosophers ascribe to recognition-speech a primordial status and affirm it to constitute the very facts that the Buddhists say preclude it. In effect, the Pratyabhijñā system endeavors to lead the student to participate in the recognition "I am Śiva" by demonstrating that all experiences and their contents are expressions of the recognition that "I am Śiva."

Utpaladeva and Abhinavagupta's epistemology of perceptual cognition may be divided into arguments centered around two sets of terms: (1) *prakāśa* and (2) *vimarśa* with cognates such as *pratyavamarśa* and *parāmarśa*.

Among the backgrounds to the concept of *prakāśa* are the upanishadic-vedantin notion of self-luminosity (*svaprakāśatva*) and the related Yogācāra Buddhist notion of self-consciousness (*svasaṃvedana*); it is an "illumination" or "bare subjective awareness" that validates each cognition, so that one knows that one knows. The thrust of the arguments about *prakāśa* is idealistic. The Śaivas contend that, as no object is known without validating awareness, this awareness actually constitutes all objects as its real but inseparable contents. This all leads not to solipsism as usually understood in the West, but a conception of a universal awareness. All sentient and insentient beings are essentially one awareness.

Vimarśa and its cognates have the significance of apprehension or judgment with a recognitive structure, as applying prepossessed linguistic interpretation to present items of experience, and may be glossed as "recognitive apprehension." Abhinavagupta and Utpaladeva's arguments centering on these terms develop earlier considerations of Bhartṛhari on the linguistic nature of experience. The philosophers refute the Buddhist contention that recognition is a contingent reaction to direct experience by claiming that it is integral or transcendental to all experience. We build upon a subtle, innate form of recognitive-linguistic apprehension in learning conventional language. A recognitive ordering of our most basic experiences also accounts for our ability to remember them, as well as our capacity to perform rapid behaviors.

The two phases of argument operate together. The idealistic *prakāśa* arguments make the recognition shown by the *vimarśa* arguments to be integral to all epistemic processes, constitutive of them and their objects. Moreover, the recognition generating all things belongs to one subject and must be its self-recognition. As it is through the monistic subject's self-recognition that all phenomena are created, the Pratyabhijñā thinkers have ostensibly demonstrated their cosmogonic myth of Śiva's emanation through Śakti in terms of self-recognition. The student, by coming to see this self-recognition as the inner reality of all that is experienced, is led to full participation in it. Because the recognition of an objective "this" (or "this is yellow") is a recognition of myself, therefore I am Śiva.

Abhinavagupta and Utpaladeva apply the same approach to the explanation of other topics of epistemology, from memory to conceptual processes such as inference and negation (Lawrence, 1999, 85–132).

Conceptions of Identity and Egoity

Utpaladeva and Abhinavagupta in their Pratyabhijñā works, and Abhinavagupta in his writings on tantric symbolism and ritual, as well as aesthetics, articulate what may be described as a philosophical psychology of identity. The Kashmiri Śaiva philosophers describe the empowered Śiva identity recognized by the practitioner as a higher sense of "I" (*aham*) or, more abstractly, "I-hood" (*ahambhāva*), which also came to be called "perfect I-hood" (*pūrṇāhaṃtā*). Sometimes Abhinavagupta dialectically qualifies this conception in relation to a more apophatic statement of the status of the supreme lord; for example, he sometimes suggests that what he calls *anuttara* (the unsurpassed) is above the perfect I-hood. On other occasions, Abhinavagupta, like Utpaladeva, treats the higher I-hood as another schema of the ultimate. While it had precursors, M. Hulin and M. Dyczkowski have rightly observed the historical innovativeness of this Kashmir Śaiva conception of "egoity" and its great influence on later tantric traditions (Hulin, 1978; Dyczkowski, 1992).

Contrary to earlier Hindu and Buddhist thought, the Pratyabhijñā system and Pratyabhijñā-inspired Tantra do not advocate the surrender of ordinary egoistic identity, referred to by such terms as "I-concept" (*ahaṃkāra*), "pride" or "self-conception" (*abhimāna*), "I-amness" (*asmitā*), and "I-hood" (*ahaṃtā*). For this mode of thinking, the human ego is an immanent expression of god's identity that must be universalized and transfigured into its essential nature as perfect I-hood. Abhinavagupta further elaborates that integral to the perfect egoity of god is a state of satiety he variously describes as "rest in the self" (*svātmaviśrānti*), "self-enjoyment" (*svātmopabhoga*), and "self-relishing" (*svātmacamatkara, svaviṣayāsvāda*). Through practices ranging from the Kaula sexual ritual through aesthetic appreciation and philosophical and theosophical contemplations, ordinary selfish pleasures are transfigured into that divine satiety (Lawrence, 2008b).

Linguistic Speculations

On the basis of the equation of Śakti/self-recognition with supreme speech, Utpaladeva and Abhinavagupta use Bhartṛharian and Pratyabhijñā metaphysics to explain linguistically the mythico-ritual drama of the self's/Śiva's creation and control of the world through Śakti. Following Bhartṛhari's Vyākaraṇa school, they interpret being or existence (*sattā*), the generic referent of language, as action (*kriyā*). This view itself originated in Brahmanic interpretations of the Veda as expressing injunctions for sacrifice. The Kashmiri Śaivas further agree with much of vedic exegetics in conceiving the action that is being as both narrative and recapitulatory ritual action.

The Pratyabhijñā philosophers further utilize theories of Sanskrit syntax to explain Śiva's action. The relevant considerations pertain to how verbs articulating action relate to declined nouns indicating the concomitants of action (*kārakas*) – in English, roughly, the agent, object, instrument, purpose, source, and location. I have previously compared Sanskrit speculations on this subject to K. Burke's notion of a "grammar of motives" and characterized the distinctive Śaiva approach to it as a "mythico-ritual syntax of omnipotence" (Lawrence, 1998; 1999, 133–154).

E. Gerow and I have separately argued that there is a tendency in many traditions of Hindu and Buddhist philosophy to denigrate the role of the agent (*kartṛkāraka*) in the syntactic nexus (Gerow, 1982; Lawrence, 1998). This tendency seems to reflect not only the agent's bondage to → *karma* in rebirth for Hindus and Buddhists – as emphasized by E. Gerow – but also its subordination to the order of objective ritual behavior – pertaining to sacrifice, caste, life cycle, and so on, in orthodox Brahmanic norms.

Utpaladeva and Abhinavagupta develop a syntax of omnipotence by taking up and radicalizing earlier understandings of the positive albeit delimited role of the agent, particularly from the Vyākaraṇa, and Nyāya and → Vaiśeṣika traditions. According to the Śaivas, all causal processes and things constituting the universe are synthesized and impelled by the agency of Śiva/the self in his cosmic acts. The self is *svatantra* (autonomous) rather than *paratantra* (heteronomous), like all other things. The Śaivas ultimately reduce the entire action of existence to agency. As Abhinavagupta explains, "Being is the agency of the act of becoming, that is, the freedom characteristic of an agent regarding all actions" (see Subramania Iyer & Pandey, 1986, vol. I, 258–259).

This theory of omnificent syntactic agency is ritually axiomatic as well as mythical. Utpaladeva describes the method of the Pratyabhijñā philosophy, in a manner homologous to the epistemology of recognition, as leading to salvation through the contemplation of one's status as the agent of the universe (see Subramania Iyer & Pandey, 1986, vol. II, 309). Abhinavagupta likewise, in his explanation of the preliminary ceremonies of the tantric ritual, identifies various components of the ritual – such as the location, ritual implements, and objects of sacrifice, for example, flowers and oblations – with the Sanskrit grammatical cases. He explains that the aspirant's goal in the ritual action is identification with Śiva as agent of all the cases (see Shastri & Shastri, 1987, vol. VI, 2516–2520; Shastri, 1982, 135ff.; Lawrence, 1998).

Abhinavagupta supplements this philosophy of action with his own theorization on the semantics and syntax of grammatical persons, gender, number, and verbal tenses. To briefly recount his approach to the first of these, the grammatical persons are the familiar triad – he/she/it/they (called in Skt. the "first person" and in English the "third person"), you (Skt. "middle person," Eng. "second person"), and I/we (Skt. "final person," Eng. "first person").

Abhinava acknowledges, like contemporary theorists such as C.S. Peirce and É. Benveniste, that in ordinary discourse the three persons are defined by their mutual distinctions and are arbitrary in their reference. However, he also ranks them hierarchically. He affirms the privilege of I/we as indicating the enunciator of discourse, over the addressee you and the non-interlocutory he/she/it, on the basis of their degrees of extension. That is, you can include he/she/it/they, and I/we can include you as well as he/she/it/they.

According to Abhinavagupta, the ranking of the three persons reflects the structure of emanation in a Trika Śaiva cosmological triad. That is, I as the enunciator of discourse corresponds to the omnipotent self as Śiva, as the whole universe is ultimately my supreme speech. The addressee, you, is identified with Śakti according to the model of Śiva's self-revelatory dialogues with Śakti in the tantric scriptures. The non-interlocutory he/she/it represents the unenlightened human (*nara*) reduced to the condition of inert objects. The self's foundational agency-cum-act of speech, with, as, and through Śakti constitutes all limited circumstances of discourse, including all interlocutors and objects.

Abhinava again prescribes a contemplation of return in which all forms of he/she/it are personalized as absorbed into you, Śakti. And I as cosmic discursive agent realize you to be my integral power and consort. The philosopher indicates in both his Pratyabhijñā and aesthetic writings that the same contemplative agenda should inform the hermeneutic reception of philosophy as well as poetry and drama. That is, I should identify with both what is stated in the philosophy and the universalized representations of the emotions of literary characters (see Nagar & Joshi, 1981, vol. I, 277–279; Lawrence, 2008a).

Abhinavagupta engages in a variety of further philosophical and "theosophical" speculations on the linguistic aspects of first-person egoity. He thus formulates a kind of theosophical contemplation of the nature of perfect I-hood as encompassing all speech and referents, in terms of an occult etymology of the word *aham* (I) itself. He asserts that the word *aham* is derived from a grammatical procedure of abbreviation (*pratyāhāra*) as encompassing all the phonemes from the first, *a*, to the last, *ha*. Combined with the final graphemic *bindu, ṃ* – the sounds of *aham* correspond to the entire cosmic cycle of emission and reabsorption. This explanation also justifies the choice of *aham* as a favorite Kashmir Śaiva *mantra*.

Abhinavagupta develops an overlapping scheme that prescribes contemplations on the tantric self as possessing six "courses" (*adhvan*s) of the emanation of supreme speech, also designated collectively as the sixfold course. The six courses are analyzed into two triads according to the root bifurcation of supreme speech into expressive speech (*vācaka*) and the referents of that speech (*vācya*). The triad of expressive speech comprises, in descending order, the increasingly concrete phonemes (*varṇa*), *mantra*s, and words (*pada*). The three corresponding courses of referents are cosmic segments (*kalā*), cosmic principles (*tattva*), and cosmic realms (*bhuvana*). This scheme is utilized as a map of the cosmic-linguistic totality. The student contemplates all the courses as emanating from his or her own I-hood (Padoux, 1990, 330–371).

Universalization of the Body and Reflected Identity

Abhinavagupta follows nondual Kashmir Śaiva and other tantric traditions in equating the body of the realized being with Śakti in all her cosmic transformations (Flood, 1993; 2006). This equation of the cosmic emanation through Śakti with the body is explained linguistically on the basis of the Śaiva appropriations of Bhartṛhari's linguistic idealism, as well as → Mīmāṃsā conceptions of the eternal cosmic status of *mantras* and their constituent phonemes. Abhinavagupta, in his accounts of "phonematic emanation," thus correlates various aspects of cosmic embodiment with idealized speech sounds (Padoux, 1990).

Abhinavagupta enjoins a number of tantric practices to realize the higher form of embodiment. Among these are the divinizing projection of mantric syllables (*nyāsa*) on the body and ritual implements, and the purification of the body's constituent elements (*bhūtaśuddhi*), performed as preliminaries to worship. He also prescribes a variety of practices to awaken Śakti as Kuṇḍalinī, symbolized in the form of a serpent, dormant in the energy center (*cakra*) at the base of the spine. As she ascends through higher energy centers, she divinizes the subtle physiology of the human body (Silburn, 1988). In the sexual ritual, the male and female partners physically become Śiva and Śakti and realize their primordial unity in their very genitalia and sexual fluids (Dupuche, 2003; White, 2003; Silburn, 1988; Chalier-Visuvalingam, 2012).

Another important bodily symbol for Abhinavagupta is the heart (*hṛdaya*). Abhinava variously identifies the heart with Śiva or the essence of Śiva, Śakti, *mantra*, and the entire universe as one's cosmic embodiment. Contemplations, *mantras*, and other ritual practices focusing on the realization of the heart provide another path for the liberative self-realization (Muller-Ortega, 1992).

Closely related to the transformation of embodiment is Abhinavagupta's advancement of theory and practices focused on the model of the reflection (*pratibimba*). Building upon earlier Śaiva and other South Asian religious and philosophical ideas, Abhinava interprets the entire process of emanation through Śakti/speech/self-recognition as the reflection of one's true identity. He explains various modes of practice, including contemplations of the phonemic symbolism of *mantras*, the sexual ritual, aesthetic experience, and the Pratyabhijñā philosophy itself, as means for identification with Śiva through the realization that everything is one's reflection. In Abhinava's account, the *mantra aham* (I) itself is reflected as *mahā* (great; Lawrence, 2005).

Classification of Means Types (*Upāyas*)

In his *Tantrāloka* and *Tantrasāra*, Abhinavagupta propounds a typology of religious practices into four "means types" (*upāyas*). Abhinava's classification is built upon an earlier analysis of three types of mystical submersion (*samāveśa*) in his favored scripture, the *Mālinīvijayottaratantra* (Shastri, 1984, 9; Shastri & Shastri, 1987, vol. I, 167–170; vol. II, 203). Abhinavagupta says that he learned the classification of means types specifically from his teacher, Śambhunātha (Dyczkowski, 1987, 171).

Abhinavagupta defines the first means type on the basis of its being above the scheme of means proper; he calls this the "nonmeans" (*anupāya*), referring to the direct experience of ultimate reality with little or no effort. The highest level of practice is realizing that one is already self-realized as Śiva.

Abhinava frames the three means proper as operating on the three levels of the Trika tradition's cosmic triads. In descending order, these are the means of Śambhu (also known as Śiva, *śāmbhava upāya*), the means of Śakti (*śākta upāya*), and the individual means (*āṇava upāya*) – named after the triad of Śiva, Śakti, and human (*nara*, *aṇu*). These types are similarly correlated with the homologous triads of goddesses supreme (Parā), supreme-nonsupreme or intermediate (Parāparā), and nonsupreme or lower (Aparā); the conditions of unity (*abheda*), unity-and-diversity (*bhedābheda*), and diversity (*bheda*); and the will *śakti* (*icchāśakti*), cognition *śakti* (*jñānaśakti*), and action *śakti* (*kriyāśakti*).

As should be evident from some of the terms just given, the means descend from the most unitive and intuitive non-means and means of Śambhu to the most concrete practices of the individual means. The intermediate means of Śakti focuses more on mental practices involving the pursuit of the pure wisdom (*śuddhavidyā*) of one's status as Śakti possessor, through good reasoning (*sattarka*) and the purification of conceptualization (*vikalpasaṃskāra*). Here are included Krama tantric contemplations of one's possession of *maṇḍalas* of Śaktis as Kālīs (Rastogi, 1967; 1979). The indications are also that Abhinavagupta places the Pratyabhijñā philosophy proper within this means type (Lawrence, 1999, 57–65; Rastogi, 1967, 388).

Aesthetics

Abhinavagupta in his voluminous *Abhinavabhāratī* and *Dhvanyālokalocana*, and in brief discussions scattered throughout his other writings, again produced perhaps the most exemplary and influential formulations of poetics in South Asian history. As with other aspects of his thought, Abhinavagupta did not create his aesthetics from nothing but developed his ideas by refining those of others in his commentaries (see Nagar & Joshi, 1981–1984; Tripathi, 1975–1981; Ingalls, Masson & Patwardhan, 1990). Abhinavagupta's approach to the homologies between aesthetic and religious experience may be further linked to the broader nondual Śaiva agenda of the approach to the divine Śiva self through the immanent activity of his Śakti (Pandey, 1972; Larson, 1974).

Abhinava brilliantly advances traditions of poetics-aesthetics founded in Bharata's *Nāṭyaśāstra* in interpreting the generation of the various aesthetic sentiments (→ *rasa*s) from the depicted emotions and other psychological expressions of dramatic actors, the functions of → music and → dance, and so on.

Ānandavardhana theory of the suggestion (*dhvani*) of aesthetic sentiments (*rasa*) by the formal structures of literature was itself an elaboration of Bhartṛhari's semantics of manifestation (*sphoṭa*) and intuition (*pratibhā*). Abhinavagupta in turn situates Ānandavardhana's theory within the Pratyabhijñā system's reformulation of Bhartṛhari, in its conceptions of Śiva's Śakti as his supreme speech (*parāvāk*), self-recognition (*ahampratyavamarśa*), and intuition (*pratibhā*).

Abhinavagupta was also deeply influenced by the theory of the universalization (*sādhāraṇīkaraṇa*) of emotions in the aesthetic sentiments developed by Ānandavardhana's critic, Bhaṭṭanāyaka. Abhinava affirms linkages between the theory of universalization and the Spanda tradition's program of contemplatively absorbing particular expressions of Śakti as cosmic pulsation (*viśeṣaspanda*) into Śakti as universal cosmic pulsation (*sāmānyaspanda*). Likewise, he invokes the Pratyabhijñā rationalizations of Śakti as self-recognition in his frequent explanation of processes of recognitive synthesis (*anusaṃdhāna*) and apperception (*anuvyavasāya*) in synthesizing the expressions of emotions by literary characters (Kuanpoonpol, 1991).

Abhinavagupta also explains the experience of *rasa*s analogously to *śaktyāviṣkaraṇa* in philosophy and tantric sex, as a comprehension of emotions in their perfection or completeness (*pūrṇatā*) and an absorption into the self (*ātmaviśrānti*; see Shastri & Shastri, 1987, vol. II, 177–179). Abhinavagupta affirms that a mutual reflection (*pratibimba*) of identity occurs among the participants in tantric rites as well as the audience of singing and dancing (see Shastri & Shastri, 1987, vol. VII, 3264–3266). His reconceptualization of universalization within a reception theory, in terms of a reduction to first person experience, was noted above.

Mention may further be made of Abhinavagupta's theorization on the peaceful aesthetic sentiment (*śāntarasa*) as the telos of the aesthetic experience (Masson and Patwardhan, 1969). Although it is not clear how close Abhinava believed aesthetic experience could take one to → liberation, it is clear that he situates or overcodes key features of his aesthetics within basic structures of nondual Śaiva symbolism, doctrine, and practice.

Ethics

Belying representations of monistic "mysticism" and Hindu Tantra as amoral or immoral (Kripal, 2002; Samuel, 1993, 242–243), Abhinava, like Utpaladeva and other nondual Kashmiri Śaivas, affirms strong concerns for the well-being of others. In his *Tantrāloka*, Abhinavagupta explains that those (such as himself) who have destroyed all taints of worldly existence and are perfect in their identification with Śiva are occupied only with the benefit of humanity (see Shastri & Shastri, 1987, vol. II, 342–343). Abhinavagupta emphasizes that the Pratyabhijñā philosophy as initiated by Utpaladeva is motivated by compassion for all who are afflicted by birth and death, without restrictions based on caste or anything else (see Subramania Iyer & Pandey, 1986, vol. I, 29–32).

In his *Tantrāloka*, Abhinava expounds a series of practical rules (*samaya*) for Śaiva initiates, many of which bear upon ethics. For example, one should overcome personal qualities such as arrogance, passion, and envy and refrain from doing or saying anything that is untrue or injurious to others. One should also endeavor to stop those who are bent on harming others. One should venerate the → *guru*, the *guru*'s family, and women and pursue the well-being of all living beings (see Shastri & Shastri, 1987, vol. VI, 2398–2724;

on the Śaiva ethics, see Lawrence, 2008b, 53–55; Ratie, 2009).

Approach to Diversity

At the time of the development of nondual Śaiva traditions, Kashmir was characterized by a remarkable ferment of cultural, religious, and philosophical diversity. Abhinavagupta develops suggestions of Utpaladeva to formulate a quite remarkable theory of epistemic divergence that may still be relevant to the heightened problematics now associated with globalization. According to this theory, perceptual and inferential claims are contingent upon traditions (*prasiddhi, āgama*). Traditions likewise are diversified according to the various purposes and eligibilities of their adherents in different places and times. Cognitive claims are also affected by the emotional proclivities (*ruci*) of those who make them.

Abhinavagupta propounds a criteriology for assessing cognitive claims that eschews considerations of correspondence with an interdependent reality in favor of coherentism and pragmatism. Each claim must be tested as to noncontradiction or coherence (*abādha* or *sthairya*) in the realization of practical values (*arthakriyā*).

Abhinava ranks cognitive claims according to their comparative "completeness" or "perfection" (*pūrṇatva*). He explains subordinated claims not as simply wrong but rather "imperfect" or "incomplete cognition" (*apūrṇakhyāti*). For him, competing traditions all have some truth because their followers do achieve their goals, that is, various worldly objectives and sorts of spiritual liberation. However, the Śaiva liberation is perfect and includes the fruits of all other traditions. From this point of view, the Śaiva applications of the inference for the sake of others reveal facts once grasped only partially to be constituted in Śiva's self-recognition or supreme speech. Nevertheless, Abhinavagupta acknowledges that other traditions will inevitably view themselves as superior, thereby providing his tradition with a procedural openness and amenability to new intellectual engagements (Lawrence, 2000; Lawrence, forthcoming).

Bibliography

Bansat-Boudon, L., & K. Tripathi, *Introduction to Tantric Philosophy: The Paramārthasāra of Abhinavagupta with the Commentary of Yogarāja*, London, 2010.

Baumer, B., *Abhinavagupta's Hermeneutics of the Absolute: Anuttaraprakriyā*, Delhi, 2011.

Brahamachari (Brahamachārī), L.R., ed., *Śrīmad Bhagavad Gītā With Commentary by Mahāmāheshvara Rājānaka Abhinava Gupta*, Srinagar, 1933.

Chalier-Visuvalingam, E., "Union and Unity in Hindu Tantrism," 2012, www.infinityfoundation.com/mandala/i_es/i_es_visuv_e_unity.htm.

Dupuche, J.R, trans., *Abhinavagupta: The Kula Ritual, as Elaborated in Chapter 29 of the Tantrāloka*, Delhi, 2003.

Dyczkowski, M.S.G., "Self Awareness, Own Being, Egoity," in: Vasugupta, *et al.*, *The Stanzas of Vibration: The Spandakārikā with Four Commentaries*, Albany, 1992, 37–48.

Dyczkowski, M.S.G., *The Doctrine of Vibration: An Analysis of the Doctrines and Practices of Kashmir Shaivism*, Albany, 1987.

Flood, G., *The Tantric Body: The Secret Tradition of Hindu Religion*, London, 2006.

Flood, G., *Body and Cosmology in Kashmir Śaivism*, San Francisco, 1993.

Gerow, E., "What is Karma (Kiṃ Karmeti): An Exercise in Philosophical Semantics," *IT* 10, 1982, 87–116.

Hanneder, J., *Abhinavagupta's Philosophy of Revelation: Mālinīślokavārttika 1, 1–399*, Groningen, 1998.

Hughes, J., ed., *Self Realization in Kashmir Shaivism*, Albany, 1994.

Hulin, M., *Le principe de l'ego dans le pensee indienne classique: La notion d'Ahamkara*, Paris, 1978.

Ingalls, D.H.H., J.M. Masson & M.V. Patwardhan, *The "Dhvanyāloka" of Ānandavardhana with the "Locana" of Abhinavagupta*, Cambridge MA, 1990.

Kripal, J.J., "Debating the Mystical as the Ethical: An Indological Map," in: G. William Barnard & J.J. Kripal, eds., *Crossing Boundaries: Essays on the Ethical Status of Mysticism*, New York, 2002, 15–69.

Kuanpoonpol, P., "Pratibhā: The Concept of Intuition in the Philosophy of Abhinavagupta," diss., Harvard University, 1991.

Larson, G.J., "The Sources for Śakti in Abhinavagupta's Kāsmīr Śaivism: A Linguistic and Aesthetic Category," *PEW* 24, 1974, 41–56.

Lawrence, D.P., "The Plurality and Contingency of Knowledge, and Its Rectification According to the Pratyabhijñā," in: N. Rastogi & M. Rastogi, eds., *Perspectives on Abhinavagupta*, Delhi, forthcoming.

Lawrence, D.P., "Abhinavagupta's Philosophical Hermeneutics of Grammatical Persons," *JHS* 1, 2008a, 11–25.

Lawrence, D.P., *The Teachings of the Odd-Eyed One: A Study and Translation of the Virūpākṣapañcāśikā with the Commentary of Vidyācakravartin*, Albany, 2008b.

Lawrence, D.P., "Kashmiri Śaiva Philosophy," *IEPh*, 2005a.

Lawrence, D.P., "Remarks on Abhinavagupta's Use of the Analogy of Reflection," *JIP* 33, 2005b, 583–599.

Lawrence, D.P., "Zu Abhinavaguptas Offenbarungstheorie," *Polylog* 5, 2000, 6–18.

Lawrence, D.P., *Rediscovering God with Transcendental Argument: A Contemporary Interpretation of Monistic Kashmiri Śaiva Philosophy*, Albany, 1999.

Lawrence, D.P., "The Mythico-Ritual Syntax of Omnipotence," *PE W* 48, 1998, 592–622.

Marjanovic, B., *Abhinavagupta's Commentary on the Bhagavad Gītā: Gītārtha Saṃgraha*, Varanasi, 2002.

Masson, J.L., & M.V. Patwardhan, *Śāntarasa and Abhinavagupta's Philosophy of Aesthetics*, Pune, 1969.

Muller-Ortega, P.E., "Tantric Meditation: Vocalic Beginnings," in: T. Goudriaan, ed., *Ritual and Speculation in Early Tantrism: Studies in Honor of Andre Padoux*, Albany, 1992, 227–245.

Muller-Ortega, P.E., *The Triadic Heart of Śiva: Kaula Tantricism of Abhinavagupta in the Non-dual Śaivism of Kashmir*, Albany, 1989.

Nagar, R.S., & K.L. Joshi, eds., *Nāṭyaśāstra of Bharatamuni with the Commentary Abhinavabhāratī by Abhinavaguptāchārya*, 4 vols., Delhi, 1981–1984.

Nemec, J., *The Ubiquitous Śiva: Somānanda's Śivadṛṣṭi and His Tantric Interlocutors*, Oxford, 2011.

Padoux, A., *Vāc: The Concept of the Word in Selected Hindu Tantras*, Albany, 1990.

Pandey, K.C., *Comparative Aesthetics*, 2 vols., Varanasi, 1972.

Pandey, K.C., *Abhinavagupta: An Historical and Philosophical Study*, Varanasi, 1963.

Raghavan, V., *Abhinavagupta and His Works*, Varanasi, 1981.

Rastogi, N., *Introduction to the Tantrāloka: A Study in Structure*, Delhi, 1987.

Rastogi, N., *The Krama Tantricism of Kashmir: Historical and General Sources*, vol. I, Delhi, 1979.

Rastogi, N., "The Philosophy of Krama Monism of Kashmir: An Analytical Study," 2 vols., diss., Lucknow University, 1967.

Ratie, I., *Le soi et l'autre: Identite, difference et alterite dans la philosophe de la pratyabhijñā*, Leiden, 2011.

Ratie, I., "Remarks on Compassion and Altruism in the Pratyabhijñā Philosophy," *JIP* 37, 2009, 349–366.

Samuel, G., *Civilized Shamans: Buddhism in Tibetan Societies*, Washington DC, 1993.

Sanderson, A., "The Śaiva Exegesis in Kashmir," in: D. Goodall & A. Padoux, eds., *Melanges tantrique a la memoire d'Helene Brunner*, Pondichery, 2007, 231–442.

Sanderson, A., "A Commentary on the Opening Verses of the Tantrasāra of Abhinavagupta," in: S. Das & E. Furlinger, eds., *Sāmarasya: Studies in Indian Arts, Philosophy, and Interreligious Dialogue, in Honor of Bettina Baumer*, Delhi, 2005, 89–148.

Sanderson, A., "Meaning in Tantric Ritual," in: A.-M. Blondeau & K. Schipper, eds., *Essais sur le rituel, III*, Louvain, 1995, 15–95.

Sanderson, A., "The Doctrine of the Mālinīvijayottaratantra," in: T. Goudriaan, ed., *Ritual and Speculation in Early Tantrism: Studies in Honor of Andre Padoux*, Albany, 1992, 281–312.

Sanderson, A., "Śaivism and the Tantric Traditions," in: S. Sutherland *et al.*, eds., *The World's Religions*, London, 1988, 660–704.

Sanderson, A., "Abhinavagupta," in: M. Eliade, ed., *The Encyclopedia of Religion*, vol. I, New York, 1987, 8–9.

Sanderson, A., "Maṇḍala and Āgamic Identity in the Trika of Kashmir," in: A. Padoux, ed., *Mantras et diagrammes rituels dans l'hindouisme*, Paris, 1986, 169–214.

Sanderson, A., "Purity and Power among the Brahmans of Kashmir," in: M. Carrithers, S. Collins & S. Lukes, eds., *The Category of the Person: Anthropology, Philosophy, History*, Cambridge UK, 1985, 190–216.

Sastri, M.R., ed., *The Tantrasāra of Abhinavagupta*, Delhi, 1982.

Shastri, M.K., ed., *The Īśvarapratyabhijñāvivṛtivimarśinī by Abhinavagupta*, 3 vols., 1987.

Shastri, M.K., ed., *Śrī Mālinīvijayottara Tantram*, Delhi, 1984.

Shastri, M.K., ed., *The Śivadṛṣṭi of Srisomānandanātha with the Vritti by Utpaladeva*, Pune, 1934.

Shastri, M.K., ed., *The Siddhitrayī and the Īśvarapratyabhijñākārikāvṛtti*, Srinagar, 1921a.

Shastri, M.K., ed., *Śrī Mālinīvijaya Vārttikam*, Srinagar, 1921b.

Shastri, M.K., & M.R. Shastri, eds., *The Tantrāloka of Abhinavagupta with the Commentary of Jayaratha*, 8 vols., Delhi, 1987.

Silburn, L., *Kuṇḍalinī: The Energy of the Depths; A Comprehensive Study Based on the Scriptures of Nondualistic Kashmir Śaivism*, Albany, 1988.

Silburn, L., *Hymnes de Abhinavagupta*, Paris, 1970.

Silburn, L., & A. Padoux, *La Lumiere sur le tantras: Chapitres 1 a 5 du Tantrāloka*, Paris, 1998.

Singh, J.S., ed., *A Trident of Wisdom: Translation of Parātrīśikā-Vivaraṇa*, Albany, 1989.

Singh, J.S., ed., *Pratyabhijñāhṛdayam: The Secret of Self-Recognition*, Delhi, 1980.

Subramania Iyer, K.A., & K.C. Pandey, eds., *Bhāskarī: A Commentary on the Īśvarapratyabhijñāvimarśinī of Ācārya Abhinavagupta (Abhinavagupta's Text with Bhāskarī Commentary)*, 3 vols., Delhi, 1986.

Torrella, R., "Studies in Utpaladeva's Īśvarapratyabhijñāvivṛti, Part I: Apoha and Anupalabdhi in a Śaiva Garb," in: K. Preisendanz, ed., *Expanding and Merging Horizons: Contributions to South Asian and Cross-cultural Studies in Commemoration of Wilhelm Halbfass*, Vienna, 2007a, 473–490.

Torella, R., "Studies in Utpaladeva's Īśvarapratyabhijñāvivṛti, Part II: What is Memory," in: K, Klaus & J.-U. Hartmann, eds., *Indica et Tibetica. Festschrift für Michael Hahn zum 65. Geburtstag*, Vienna, 2007b, 539–563.

Torella, R., "Studies in Utpaladeva's Īśvarapratyabhijñāvivṛti, Part III: Can a Cognition Become the Object of Another Cognition?" in: D. Goodall & A. Padoux, eds., *Melanges tantrique a la memoire d'Helene Brunner*, Pondichery, 2007c, 475–484.

Torella, R., "Studies in Utpaladeva's Īśvarapratyabhijñā-vivṛti, Part IV: Light of the Subject – Light of the Object," in: B. Kellner *et al.*, eds., *Pramāṇakīrtiḥ: Papers Dedicated to Ernst Steinkellner on the Occasion of His 70th Birthday*, Vienna, 2007d, 925–939.
Torella, R., ed., *The Īśvarapratyabhijñākārikā of Utpaladeva with the Author's Vṛtti*, Delhi, 2002.
Torrella, R., "A Fragment of Utpaladeva's Īśvara-pratyabhijñā-vivṛti: Edition and Translation," *EW* 38, 1988, 137–174.
Tripathi (Tripāṭhi), R., ed., *Dhvanyāloka of Ānandavardhana with the Locana of Abhinavagupta*, 3 vols., Delhi, 1975–1981.
White, D.G., *Kiss of the Yoginī: "Tantric Sex" in Its South Asian Contexts*, Chicago, 2003.

David P. Lawrence

Akkamahādēvi

Akkamahādēvi (or Mahādēviyakka) is one of the foremost poet-saints of the Vīraśaiva (→ Liṅgāyat) tradition. She lived in the second half of the 12th century ce. When she was still a young woman, she joined the community of Vīraśaiva devotees, which was founded by → Basava in Kalyana circa 1160. Unlike most of Basava's companions, she had a strong tendency toward asceticism. Finally, she left the Kalyana community and set out on a solitary journey to the holy hill of Srisailam. There she attained the ultimate mystical experience of complete union with the godhead.

Akkamahādēvi is famous because of the exceptional beauty and intensity of her poetry. Devotional poems constituted an important vehicle for religious experience in Vīraśaivism as in all → *bhakti* movements. But, especially in the Vīraśaiva community at Kalyana, poetry played a major role in the exchange of ideas among the devotees. Basava had institutionalized the religious discussion in his Anubhava Maṇṭapa (Hall of Spiritual Experience). This was the meeting place of the devotees, where they exchanged their insights, mostly expressed in small poems. The central idea of the Vīraśaiva movement was the possibility for all devotees to make a personal contribution to the development of the religious tradition. Therefore, not the conventional Sanskrit literature was authoritative but poetical texts, composed by the devotees in the vernacular language, Kannada. These small poems in free verse were called Vacanas. Many devotees, men and women alike, contributed to the Vacana literature. A huge number of Vacanas has been preserved. Almost 1,400 poems are attributed to the originator of the movement, Basava, and even more to his successor, Cannabasava. Akkamahādēvi, with her 340 *Vacana*s, is not the most prolific poet. However, the superb quality of her verses makes her definitely one of the most important *vacanakāra*s (authors of Vacanas). Among the Vīraśaiva devotees, she had a distinct position as an accomplished mystic and an honored member of the community, in spite of her young age. Soon after she entered the community at Kalyana, it became customary to address her as "Akka," which is the Kannada word for an elder sister.

Fig. 1. Devotional print of Akkamahādēvi.

Life

Although the hagiographical literature about Akkamahādēvi is heavily colored by pious fantasy, it is not impossible to reconstruct the historical substratum of her life history. Especially her own *Vacana*s constitute a valuable source of her spiritual achievements in the context of the crucial occurrences in her life.

In contemporary sources, she is designated as Uḍutaḍiya Mahādēviyakka. Therefore, we can be sure that she hailed from a place called Uḍutaḍi. Probably this is the modern village of Uduthadi near Shikaripur in Shimoga district. It must be remarked, however, that at least two other villages in Karnataka claim to be ancient Uḍutaḍi. A great crisis occurred in Akkamahādēvi's youth. The local chieftain, King Kauśika, according to later hagiographies, was impressed by her beauty and wanted to marry her. Young Akkamahādēvi, however, had a strong inclination toward spirituality and mystics. She was a devotee of → Śiva; she worshipped the godhead in his form as Mallikārjuna. Married life did not attract her, and the local ruler, who was a Jaina, was the least suitable bridegroom, in her view. Nevertheless, she consented to the marriage, because she could not resist the pressure that the chieftain exerted on her and her family. As could be expected, the marriage proved to be a disaster. Akkamahādēvi suffered immensely under the tension between the expectations of family life and her strong desire to be absorbed in devotion to the godhead. The two relationships could not be combined. Several of her *Vacana*s testify to this unbearable inner conflict.

> Inside my husband, outside my lover,
> I cannot handle them both!
> Everyday life and supreme quest,
> I cannot handle both!
> Oh Lovely Lord of the Jasmines,
> a pear and an apple
> cannot be held in one hand.
> (trans. by author; Hiremath, 1973, 60; Basavaraju, 1977, 92; Ramanujan, 1973, 127; Mahesh, 1977, 134; Schouten, 1991, 167–168; Chaitanya, 2005, 48)

It is obvious that Akkamahādēvi could not continue her life as a wedded woman for long. The rift was inevitable. At a certain moment, she threw off her clothes and left her husband's house as a wandering ascetic, naked.

Her journey brought her to Kalyana, where she took refuge with the Vīraśaiva community. Her naked appearance caused quite a commotion, and she was not accepted right away by the devotees. In the Vīraśaiva community, wandering ascetics were definitely revered, as they were in all Śaiva circles. However, a young woman dressed "in air" (*digambara*) raised questions and dispute. In due course, though, Akkamahādēvi was accepted because of her sincere devotion. Her stay in the Vīraśaiva community proved to be fruitful. Much of her poetry was composed in this period, and several *Vacana*s testify to her gratitude toward Basava and the other devotees for their inspiration and guidance. Nevertheless, she remained to some extent an outsider among the devotees in Kalyana. Basava had emphasized that practicing spirituality could be combined with normal family life, also for women. Many of the female devotees were attracted by this new, even revolutionary, ideal. Akkamahādēvi's radical asceticism was not in line with the main orientation of her sisters in the Kalyana fellowship. Therefore, it is not surprising that Akkamahādēvi did not remain in Kalyana for the rest of her life. After some time, she left the community and pursued her personal quest. She resumed wandering and undertook a pilgrimage to Srisailam, where the temple of her favorite god, Mallikārjuna, was located. There she lived for some time in the famous plantain grove near the sanctuary and experienced a complete union with her divine lover. Tradition has it that she passed away in her early twenties.

Poetry

The poetical heritage of Akkamahādēvi consists of 430 *Vacana*s and some small collections of other poetry. In the latter category, the best-known work is *Yōgāṅgatrividhi*, a compilation of 67 verses in *tripadi* meter. However, the *Vacana*s are the poems for which Akkamahādēvi has become famous. Even in her own time, she was regarded as the very best Vacana poet, and it is quite remarkable that such an honor has been bestowed on a woman! Cannabasava, who succeeded Basava as leader of the Vīraśaiva community, wrote the following: "Ten poems of the Chief (Basava) are equal to only one of Akka Mahādēvi" (Hiremath, 1971, 251).

Vacanas are poems in free-verse form. Usually they are short and pithy, which makes it easy to memorize them. The poems are not in Sanskrit but in Kannada, the vernacular language of the region where Vīraśaivism arose. In quite a number of instances, however, single Sanskrit words or sentences are included, which usually puts some emphasis on a certain concept or reasoning. The *vacanakāra*s did not employ stylistic devices such as rhyme or meter. But the Vacanas are characterized by a rhythm, brought about by a deliberate choice of words, in which repetition, parallelism, and wordplay are striking. Some poets used this poetic medium in the first place for the propagation of their insights and produced, as a result, rather dry, moralizing verses. However, this is certainly not so in the case of Akkamahādēvi. She is generally considered to be "the most poetic of the Vīraśaivas" (Brooks, 2002, 21). Her verses are vivid and charming, with remarkable imagery and a highly creative use of the Kannada language.

In their last lines, Vacanas contain always the name of a certain deity, one of the numerous manifestations of Śiva. Normally, this divine name is in the vocative, and, consequently, the poem is addressed to the godhead as a prayer or an emotional outpouring. Every poet has his or her own favorite deity. The name of this personal god functions as a kind of devotional signature in his or her Vacanas. Such an identification mark, which reveals the authorship of a Vacana, is called *aṅkita* or *mudrike*. Akkamahādēvi always used Cannamallikārjuna as an *aṅkita* in her poems. It could be translated as "The Lovely Lord of the Jasmines." Mallikārjuna is the deity who is worshipped in the temple on the holy hill of Srisailam. The hill is an extraordinary sacred place, because it is one of the 12 *jyotirliṅga* shrines where Śiva is believed to have appeared as a huge column of light. Throughout her lifetime, Akkamahādēvi felt attracted to this sacred place. Mallikārjuna has always been her favorite deity, whom she regarded as her divine husband. It is obvious that her spiritual quest had to find its culminating point at Srisailam. And it is not at all surprising that her devotional poems are addressed to the godhead of Srisailam, the lord of the jasmines.

Akkamahādēvi's poetry is *bhakti* literature. Her verses are meant to express a loving devotion toward a personal god. In her case, this deity is Śiva, in his special form of Mallikārjuna. The aspect of love, so typical of *bhakti* spirituality, is strongly emphasized. The Vīraśaiva poetry is a continuation of the verses of the Tamil Śiva devotees of former centuries, the → Nāyaṉārs and Māṇikkavācakar. Akkamahādēvi in particular resembles in many respects the old Śaiva devotional literature of the southernmost part of India.

Akkamahādēvi's poems deal with a number of spiritual themes. In the first place, we find many verses that express a deep-felt longing for → liberation and unity with the lord. These verses are not specifically Vīraśaiva; they could have been written in many other devotional movements as well. Sometimes, these verses even have an otherworldly orientation, which is hardly in line with the ideals of Basava's spiritual community in Kalyana. Rather than social values such as community spirit and dignity of labor, outright asceticism and repudiation of worldly life are highlighted. We find a good example of this type of poetry in Akkamahādēvi's most famous *Vacana*:

As the silkworm
  that spins its cocoon
  by its own passion
  and gets inwrapped
  in its own thread,
  and dies, –
  likewise I am burning up with desire
  for all that comes to my mind.
Break this greed of my mind,
  and show me the way out to you,
  Lovely Lord of the Jasmines.

(trans. by author; Hiremath, 1973, 13; Basavaraju, 1977, 59; Menezes & Angadi, 1973, 85; Ramanujan, 1973, 41, 46–47, 116; Patil, 1975, 12; Mahesh, 1977, 123; Seshagiri Rao, 1981, 5; Ananthanarayana, 1988, 48; Schouten, 1991, 116–117; Schouten, 1995, 125–126; Chaitanya, 2005, 61)

The poem presents a striking image of the manner in which human beings can be entangled in worldly desires. The instinct of the silkworm urges it to fabricate the threads, which will eventually become the cause of its death as a worm. It gets wrapped up more and more in its own activity, and it does not find a way to extricate itself. In a similar way, Akkamahādēvi considers her own inner urge to be the root of her misery, leading finally to spiritual death. Inevitable is the process in which the human mind gradually gets caught up in suffocating desire, unless the lord will cut through this cocoon. Apparently, liberation cannot be achieved by human efforts; it can only be given by a divine power. In a typical *bhakti* attitude, Akkamahādēvi begs the lord of the jasmines to grant her the liberation in which she will be joined with him. The way out of entanglement is the way to conjunction with god. This poem, in which the necessity of divine intervention is emphasized, contains an interesting wordplay. Among the Kannada words, there is one Sanskrit term. It is the word *sneha* in the first line, which is translated here as "passion." It means both the sticky secretion that the silkworm uses in order to produce its threads and passion or attachment to mundane life. Thus, Akkamahādēvi expresses in one eye-catching word the metaphor that is worked out in the imagery of the complete poem.

A second theme in Akkamahādēvi's poetry is the devotion to god in the form of a love relationship. It is remarkable that she used in this respect both the image of marital union and that of adultery. The latter simile is applied when her verses give a picture of the tension between her married life with Kauśika and her longing for union with the lord of the jasmines. Being absorbed in devotion next to family life is regarded as a kind of extramarital relation: "Inside my husband, outside my lover." However, most poems in this category express the happiness that Akkamahādēvi experiences in the relationship with the god who is to her the real husband. One of the clearly erotic verses in her oeuvre may illustrate this point.

Blissful is the bed, –
his looks are my jewels, his embrace my clothing,
his kisses are my food, his sweet words my stimulant.
Yes, passion is my perfume.
The union with the Lovely Lord of the Jasmines
is really supreme pleasure.
(trans. by author; Hiremath, 1973, 113; Basavaraju, 1977, 111; Menezes & Angadi, 1973, 27; Mahesh, 1977, 122; Seshagiri Rao, 1981, 35; Chaitanya, 2005, 118)

This mode of devotion is called *satipatibhakti*, devotion as the love of a woman for her husband. The mystical union with the deity is described in a figurative language that is derived from experience with marital happiness. Love life supplies the images by which spiritual achievements can be brought into sight. Akkamahādēvi regards the lord of the jasmines as her real husband. Just as intimacy and lovemaking with a human lover give happiness, so the bond with the divine husband brings about the highest enjoyment. Akkamahādēvi is not the only *bhakti* poet who employed this special type of spiritual language. Particularly women mystics had a preference for this kind of devotion. There are examples from *bhakti* poetry from several ages and in several languages; 16th-century → Mīrābāī from Rajasthan is certainly the most famous one. However, erotic imagery in *bhakti* poetry is certainly not limited to the verses of female poets. Some male devotees, too, composed verses in this style, which is all the more remarkable since they had to assume a female role in this imagery. A good example from Akkamahādēvi's circle is Basava, the leader of the Vīraśaiva community, who wrote a few poems that express *satipatibhakti*. Akkamahādēvi was with her verses in good company. But it remains remarkable that she, who was so inclined toward an ascetic attitude toward life, also wrote quite a number of explicit erotic verses.

In the third place, we find in Akkamahādēvi's poetical oeuvre a number of verses that emphasize a particular aspect of devotion that is related to love. It is called *viraha*, the experience of separation. When the beloved is absent, only then is the intensity of love felt in the strongest way. The painful experience of being abandoned makes the devotee realize his or her urgent need for union with the godhead. The verses in the *viraha* mode express this urgency, and, consequently, they are characterized by intense sorrow and longing. Akkamahādēvi was one of the first to write poems of this kind. Three centuries later, the genre became rather popular due to the poetry of particularly → Kabīr and Mīrābāī. One of the finest poems by Akkamahādēvi in this style is the following:

Like a captured elephant,
away from the herd,
remembers his mountains,
so I remember.
Like an encaged parrot
in its captivity
remembers its mate,
so I remember.
Oh you, Lovely Lord of the Jasmines,
show me your loveliness,
saying: "Come here, my child!"
(trans. by author; Hiremath, 1973, 15; Basavaraju, 1977, 182–183; Menezes & Angadi, 1973, 15; Ramanujan, 1973, 136; Mahesh, 1977, 133; Seshagiri Rao, 1981, 57; Schouten, 1995, 133; Chaitanya, 2005, 64)

Two animals of completely different background are depicted: the big, wild elephant from the forest and the small, tame bird in its cage in the house. But both share the same sentiment. Alone and out of place, they yearn for being again among their own kind. Likewise, the poetess is longing for reunion with the lord of the jasmines.

So far, categories of poetry were discussed that are not specifically Vīraśaiva. Longing for liberation and mystical union are general *bhakti* subjects that could be found in all devotional movements. However, Akkamahādēvi belonged to the Vīraśaiva community. Thus, as a fourth category in this survey, I include the Vacanas that are characteristic of the spirituality of this tradition.

The most conspicuous symbol of Vīraśaivism is the *iṣṭaliṅga*, the small object of worship that is worn round the neck by the followers of the movement; hence they are often called Liṅgāyats, → *liṅga* wearers. Quite a number of Akkamahādēvi's *Vacana*s deal with the practice of *liṅga* worship, for instance the following poem:

When, risen from your resting place,
oh *śivaliṅga*, you have come on my hand,
gleaning and glowing,
shining in your splendor, sparkling,
my body and mind are fainting
while my eyes are fixed on the *liṅga*.
I am delighted with Śiva's bliss
and joining in the pure devotion of the saints,
without shame, I unite myself with you,
Lovely Lord of the Jasmines.
(trans. by author; Hiremath, 1973, 116; Basavaraju, 1977, 150–151; Menezes & Angadi, 1973, 1; Mahesh, 1977, 114; Chaitanya, 2005, 107)

The *iṣṭaliṅga* is placed on the flat of the hand and then worshipped. However, this is not only an act of adoration but also a method of meditation. By gazing at the *liṅga* on the outstretched hand, the Vīraśaivas attain their spiritual experiences. They regard the *liṅga* as more than a symbol: it embodies the presence of Śiva. Akkamahādēvi appears to have been well aware of this significance of the *iṣṭaliṅga*. She describes in her *Vacana* a mystical sensation that is typically Vīraśaiva.

Finally, there is a fifth category of poems. After all, personal spirituality and *liṅga* meditation are only one aspect of Vīraśaivism. The movement of Basava and his followers emphasized the importance of shared devotion and community life. These aspects can be found as well in the *Vacana*s of Akkamahādēvi. Notwithstanding the fact that she was inclined to put her personal spiritual quest first, she demonstrated a definite allegiance to the community of devotees at Kalyana. In several poems, she expresses her allegiance to Basava and the other leading persons of the community. For Akkamahādēvi, too, Kalyana is an inspiring place. In the following *Vacana*, she compares Basava's settlement even with Śiva's heavenly abode.

It is right to say
that Kalyana is Kailāsa:
Kalyana from the inside
and Kalyana from the outside!
Who can grasp this quality?
Oh Lord, I notice already
the movements of your true devotees.
I long to see your devotee Basava.
Hear, oh Lovely Lord of the Jasmines! (trans. by author; Hiremath, 1973, 88; Basavaraju, 1977, 142; Menezes & Angadi, 1973, 142; Mahesh, 1977, 104)

Hagiographical Literature

The life of Akkamahādēvi was a source of inspiration for several writers in the subsequent centuries. The first one to devote a poetical work to her was Harihara (also called Harīśvara). This famous Kannada poet, who was a Vīraśaiva himself, wrote his *Uḍutaḍiya Akkamahādēviya ragaḷe* probably in the first decades of the 13th century. It is a fairly long composition, consisting of seven cantos, alternately in verse and in prose. The *ragaḷe* form of poetry was Harihara's specialty; it is a composition in which the lines can have different numbers of syllables but rhyme at the end and mostly also at the beginning. Two hundred years later, in the first half of the 15th century, another work appeared in which the life story of Akkamahādēvi was included. It was the influential *Prabhuliṅgalīle*, a hagiography about the mystic Allama Prabhu, who was in that time considered to have been the real leader of the 12th-century Vīraśaiva community at Kalyana – and not Basava. This long poetical work was written by a Brahman poet named Cāmarasa. He read the extensive book at the court of Vijayanagara king Prauḍhadēvarāya II (1424–1446).

In the same century, a work was written that would become one of the most authoritative scriptures of the Vīraśaivas. The *Śūnyasaṃpādane* (The Attainment of the Void) is a most remarkable composition. Basically, it is a kind of anthology of *Vacana*s of Basava and other poets from the initial period of the Vīraśaiva tradition. These 12th-century poems are placed in a narrative framework. Thereby, the book pretends to be a report of the discussions that took place in the Anubhava Maṇṭapa around the year 1165. Each chapter of it is devoted to one of the saints, and chapter 16 tells of the arrival of Akkamahādēvi at Kalyana. There are four versions of the book, the first dating back to 1420 and the final recension edited by Gūḷūra Siddhavīraṇārya in the first decade of the 16th century.

Finally, a comprehensive hagiography devoted to Akkamahādēvi was written in the 16th century. Its title is *Mahādēviyakkana purāṇa*, and it was composed by Cannabasavāṅka circa 1550. This long poetical work consists of 1606 stanzas, mainly in *ṣaṭpadi* form (a verse form consisting of six lines per stanza of which the third and sixth are longer than the other four).

Although all hagiographical authors extol the mystical achievements of Akkamahādēvi, it appears that it is not easy to write a eulogy about this unconventional woman saint. Her behavior is in some respects quite offensive, and the biographers take great pains to make the deviances in her life presentable. In the first place, her rift with Kauśika is problematical, because a saintly woman should not offer resistance against her husband. The usual solution, already found in Harihara's poem, is to emphasize that the husband was to blame for this conflict. Legend has it that young Akkamahādēvi consented to the marriage under some strict conditions, to which Kauśika agreed. She would be able to continue her worship of Śiva, she would be permitted to have contact with the devotees, and she would have the freedom to serve her →*guru*. Besides, violations of these terms of marriage could not be forgiven more than three times. As could be expected, in due course, Kauśika had broken the conditions thrice, and Akkamahādēvi was fully entitled to leave the palace and to go on her way. Later authors had an even more radical solution in order to defend Akkamahādēvi against the reproach of marital insubordination. While Harihara still took it for granted that she was actually married to Kauśika, Cāmarasa denied that the marriage was performed. In his representation, Akkamahādēvi went so far as to demand from the king that he convert to Śaivism before marrying her. Of course, he refused to change religion, which saved her from married life.

The second offensive trait in Akkamahādēvi's behavior is her roaming about in the nude. A vow of nudity was not unusual for male ascetics, but in the case of women, nakedness was regarded as highly inappropriate. In all hagiographies, it is confirmed that Akkamahādēvi was naked when she left the palace and made her solitary journey. However, the usual representation is that she covered her body with her long hair, which makes her appearance at least to some extent less scandalous. But more ingenious is the account of the *Śūnyasaṃpādane*. In it, it is told that Akkamahādēvi was not an ordinary human being but an incarnation of a heavenly nymph, a *rudrakannike*. Such a celestial figure is, of course, not bound to earthly conventions and can permit herself to be "dressed in air" (*digambara*).

Nevertheless, the place of such a female ascetic in society remains problematic. Did Akkamahādēvi really join the Vīraśaiva community of Basava in Kalyana? Harihara omitted this whole period of Akkamahādēvi's life. However, in both the *Prabhuliṅgalīle* and the *Śūnyasaṃpādane*, the arrival of the wandering female saint at Kalyana is an important episode. The author of the *Śūnyasaṃpādane*, in particular, emphasized that Akkamahādēvi was not admitted to the community without inquiry. Allama Prabhu subjected her to a severe interrogation before she was acknowledged as a true mystic. And even then, she did not stay among the devotees, but, on the directions of Allama Prabhu, she set out for Srisailam. In the eyes of the hagiographers, Akkamahādēvi could not have been a devotee in a community, but she had to make her solitary quest.

Akkamahādēvi in Modern Time

Among the Vīraśaiva saints, Akkamahādēvi is still one of the most popular characters. To be sure, she is considered to be the most important female mystic in this tradition. Her spiritual attitude, characterized by a combination of *liṅga* worship and bridal mysticism, deserves particular attention.

During the 20th century, a number of anthologies of Akkamahādēvi's *Vacana*s have been published. As in the case of Āṇṭāḷ and Mīrābāī, the poetry of Akkamahādēvi exerts a special attraction on female devotees. It is not a coincidence that several editions of her *Vacana*s are dedicated to women (Menezes & Angadi, 1973; Patil, 1975; Mahesh, 1977). Moreover, quite a few popular books and booklets about her life and work appeared in Kannada. In 1962, a novel about Akkamahādēvi, written by H. Thipperudra Swamy, was published under the title *Kadaḷiya karpura* and offered a refreshing depiction of her life and her spiritual quest (Schouten, 1995, 143–150).

Various places connected with Akkamahādēvi's life have become pilgrim's destinations. In Uduthadi (Shimoga district), where she probably was born, a large statue of her was erected.

Additionally, an image of the saint is worshipped in the local temple. Pilgrims come also to Basavakalyan (Bidar district), which was the center of the Vīraśaiva movement in the 12th century, where Akkamahādēvi stayed for some time. Srisailam, where she attained enlightenment and passed away, has always been a sacred place that has attracted many pilgrims. Nowadays, visitors can see a bronze statue of Akkamahādēvi in the sanctuary. It is also possible to make a boat tour to a cave at the riverside, a few kilometers from the temple, called Akkamahādēvi Cave. This would be the place where the saint meditated and worshipped the *liṅga*.

However, the importance of Akkamahādēvi is based first and foremost on her excellent poetry. The *Vacanas* of this saint constitute a rare example of both literary beauty and mystical experience.

Bibliography

Ananthanarayana, S., *Thus Sang the Veerashaiva Mystics*, vol. III: *Akkamahadevi*, Hubli, 1988.

Basavaraju, S., ed., *Akkana vacanagaḷu*, Mysore, [3]1977.

Basawanal, S.S., ed., *Cāmarasa kṛta Prabhuliṅgalīle*, Dharwar, 1971.

Bhoosnurmath, S.S., & A. Menezes, eds., *Śūnyasaṃpādane*, vol. IV, Dharwar, 1970.

Brooks, T., "In Search of Śiva: Mahādēviyakka's Vīraśaivism," *APh* 12/1, 2002, 21–34.

Chaitanya, V., *Songs for Śiva: Vacanas of Akka Mahadevi*, Walnut Creek, 2005.

Chandraiah, B.N., ed., *Cannabasavāṅkana Mahādēviyakkana purāṇa*, Mysore, 1968.

Chekki, D.A., *The Philosophy and Ethics of the Vīraśaiva Community*, Lewiston, 2003.

Hiremath, R.C., ed., *Mahādēviyakkana vacanagaḷu*, Dharwad, [2]1973.

Hiremath, R.C., ed., *Ṣaṭsthalacakravarti Cannabasavaṇṇanavara vacanagaḷu*, Dharwar, [2]1971.

Kinsley, D., "Devotion as an Alternative to Marriage in the Lives of Some Hindu Women Devotees," in: J. Lele, ed., *Tradition and Modernity in Bhakti Movements*, Leiden, 1981, 83–93.

Mahesh, *La bhakti yoga de Akkamaha Devi: Shiva Yoga*, Paris, 1977.

Menezes, A., & S.M. Angadi, *Vacanas of Akkamahādēvi*, Dharwar, 1973.

Michael, R.B., "Women of the Śūnyasaṃpādane: Housewives and Saints in Vīraśaivism," *JAOS* 103/2, 1983, 361–368.

Mudaliar, C.Y., "Religious Experiences of Hindu Women: A Study of Akka Mahadevi," *MQ* 17/3, 1991, 137–146.

Patil, B.A., *Akka Mahadevi the Divine Cuckoo: English Rendering of Akka's 50 Vacanas*, Gulbarga, 1975.

Puranik, S., *Mahādēvi*, Dharwad, 1986.

Ramanujan, A.K., "The Kannada *Vacanas* of Mahādēviyakka: Love as Metaphor," in: E.C. Dimock Jr., ed., *The Literatures of India: An Introduction*, Chicago, [2]1978, 165–170.

Ramanujan, A.K., *Speaking of Śiva*, Harmondsworth, 1973.

Ramaswamy, V., *Walking Naked: Women, Society, Spirituality in South India*, Shimla, 1997.

Sasnur, H.T., "Akka Mahadevi," in: G.S. Halappa, ed., *Studies in Education and Culture: In Honour of Shri D.C. Pavate*, Bangalore, 1959, 373–379.

Schouten, J.P., "The Unconventional Woman Saint: Images of Akka Mahādēvi," in: R. Kloppenborg & W.J. Hanegraaff, eds., *Female Stereotypes in Religious Traditions*, Leiden, 1995, 123–150.

Schouten, J.P., *Revolution of the Mystics: On the Social Aspects of Vīraśaivism*, Kampen, 1991, repr. Delhi, 1995.

Seshagiri Rao, D., *At the Lord's Feet: An English Translation of Selected Vachanas of Akka Mahadevi (A Woman Saint of Karnataka) and Some Miscellanea*, Bangalore, 1981.

Shama Rao, T.S., ed., *Hariharana Uḍutaḍiya Akkamahādēviya ragaḷe*, Mysore, [2]2011.

Shintri, S., *Akka Mahadevi*, Sirigere, 1983.

Shintri, S., "A Mystic's Message: An Interpretation of Akkamahadevi's Life," *JKUH* 20, 1976, 61–67.

Sreekantaiya, T.N., "Akka Mahādēvī," in: S. Ghanananda & J. Stewart-Wallace, eds., *Women Saints, East and West*, Hollywood, 1979, 30–40.

Thipperudra Swamy, H., *The Vīraśaiva Saints: A Study*, Mysore, 1968.

T[h]ipperudra Swamy, H., *Kadaḷiya karpura*, Mysore, [7]1986; ET: *Soul unto the Sublime*, Hubli, 1982.

JAN PETER SCHOUTEN

Āḻvārs

The word "Āḻvārs" is traditionally derived from the Tamil root *aḻ-*, "to be deep," and the title Āḻvār was given to 11 men and 1 woman who are said to have been immersed deep in the love of → Viṣṇu. Though traditional dating in the → Śrīvaiṣṇava community places them as having lived several thousand years ago, the 12 Āḻvārs, Poykai, Pūtam, Pēy, Tirumaḻicai, Kulacēkarāḻvār, Toṇṭaraṭippoṭiyālvār, Tiruppāṉāḻvār, Periyāḻvār, Āṇṭāl, Tirumaṅkai, Nammāḻvār, and Maturakavi, probably lived between the 8th and the late 9th or early 10th century CE. Many of them traveled from temple to temple singing in praise of Viṣṇu. The 24 poems of the Āḻvārs, as we have them now, are called the *Nālāyira Tivya Pirapantam* (The Sacred Collect of Four Thousand Verses; Skt. *Nālāyira Divya Prabandham*, popularly known as the *Divya Prabandham*).

The Śrīvaiṣṇava community of South India, which crystallized around the 11th century CE, reveres and worships the Āḻvārs in home and temple rituals. Our knowledge of the Āḻvārs is derived primarily through the literature and rituals of this community. Temple inscriptions after the 12th or 13th century mention works and their introduction into temple liturgies. Images of the Āḻvārs are found in Śrīvaiṣṇava temples all around the world.

The poems are socially significant. First, they were composed in the → Tamil language, rather than Sanskrit; second, the poets were of many castes; and finally, there is one woman, Āṇṭāl, in the group of Āḻvārs. The Tamil language in which the poems are composed is celebrated by the poets. For the first time within Hinduism, devotion was expressed in a mother tongue, a "language...continuous with the language of one's earliest childhood and family, one's local folk and folklore" (Ramanujan, 1981, 132). Unlike Sanskrit, it was a spoken language, associated with powerful emotions. Some of the Āḻvārs were Brahmans; others came from the other castes. Tiruppāṉāḻvār was said to be a *pañcamam* (lit. of the fifth [caste]) or an "outcaste." Āṇṭāl, a woman, is considered to be one of the most important of the poets. According to received tradition, she was disdainful of the idea of marrying a human being and practiced votive rituals to marry Viṣṇu or → Kṛṣṇa himself. The Āḻvārs and their poems therefore are at the center of the Śrīvaiṣṇava worldview in which devotees consider faith to be more important than caste or gender, and the Tamil language to be a delightful medium through which they could express their emotions.

The *Divya Prabandham*, especially the poems called *Tiruvāymoḻi*, composed by the 9th-century poet Nammāḻvār ("Our Āḻvār"), also known as Caṭakōpaṉ, and the *Tiruppāvai* of Āṇṭāl, has been of seminal importance in the piety and liturgy of the Śrīvaiṣṇava community and also extraordinarily significant in the history of Hindu literature. These are the first "vernacular" works within the Hindu consciousness to be considered as "revealed"; they are also the first works in a local language to be introduced as part of domestic and temple liturgy among the many Hindu traditions. Unlike the Sanskrit → Vedas, which could only be recited by male members of the upper castes, the *Divya Prabandham* has been recited by men and women of all castes of Śrīvaiṣṇava society. The songs have been historically significant as a key part of the Tamil devotional literature that influenced the religious patterns in medieval northern India. The force of rhythmic and lyrical vernacular poetry composed by people from various castes, the retelling of familiar narratives in the local language, the glorification of the temples in the local landscape – all these factors contributed to the popularization of → *bhakti*. The devotion voiced in the *Tiruvāymoḻi* and the *Divya Prabandham* was transmitted through the *Bhāgavatapurāṇa* and the teacher → Rāmānanda (c. 14th–15th cents. CE), as well as through Sanskrit hymns and oral tradition, and it appeared in different forms in the teachings of → Caitanya, → Vallabha, → Sūrdās, → Kabīr, and Gurū Nānak.

The later *bhakti* poems in northern India are different in many ways from those of the Āḻvārs; but there are also significant differences among the various Āḻvārs. Within the Śrīvaiṣṇava tradition, in most of the secondary literature, as well as this essay, the Āḻvār poetry is seen collectively and as a corpus. There are, however, both explicit and subtle differences between the poems and their composers. Each poet has an individual personality and takes on different roles in the poems; the love of Periyāḻvār for Kṛṣṇa, for instance, is different from the roles taken on by Tirumaṅkai in addressing various incarnations of Viṣṇu. In other words, while scholars from diverse backgrounds treat the Āḻvār corpus as just that – a *body* of literature – there is considerable difference in style and content among the various works. Every Āḻvār, every poem, is distinctive; there are differences in the masks they wear, the personae they assume, the literary conventions they favor, the places they love, the narrative frames they live in, the focus and passion of their poems.

The songs of the Āḻvārs are recited and performed in domestic, temple, and public spaces. Theologians have commented upon them since the 12th century, and Śrīvaiṣṇavas discuss them extensively on Internet sites today. With the simultaneous assertion that the *Divya Prabandham* was equivalent to the Vedas and with the performative traditions the *bhakti* songs received a good hearing and high visibility.

The Poems of the Āḻvārs

The poems are not arranged in the chronological order of their composition but are divided into four sections, each containing about a thousand verses.

The works are usually printed in the following order:

Author	Work
First Thousand	
1. Periyāḻvār	*Tiruppallāṇṭu*
2. Periyāḻvār	*Periyāḻvār Tirumoḻi*
3. Āṇṭāl	*Tiruppāvai*
4. Āṇṭāl	*Nācciyār Tirumoḻi*
5. Kulacēkarāḻvār	*Perumāḷ Tirumoḻi*
6. Tirumaḻicai	*Tiruccantaviruttam*
7. Toṇṭaraṭippoṭiyālvār	*Tirumālai*
8. Toṇṭaraṭippoṭiyālvār	*Tirupaḷḷiyeḻucci*
9. Tiruppāṉāḻvār	*Amalaṉātippirāṉ*
10. Maturaikavi	*Kaṇṇinuṉ Ciṟuttāmpu*
Second Thousand	
11. Tirumaṅkai	*Periyatirumoḻi*
12. Tirumaṅkai	*Tirukkuṟuntāṇṭakam*
13. Tirumaṅkai	*Tiruneṭuntāṇṭakam*
Third Thousand	
14. Poykai	*Mutal Tiruvantāti*
15. Pūtam	*Iraṇṭām Tiruvantāti*
16. Pēy	*Mūṉṟām Tiruvantāti*
17. Tirumaḻicai	*Nāṉmukaṉ Tiruvantāti*
18. Nammāḻvār	*Tiruviruttam*
19. Nammāḻvār	*Tiruvāciriyam*
20. Nammāḻvār	*Periyatiruvantāti*
21. Tirumaṅkai	*Tiruveḻukūṟṟirukkai*
22. Tirumaṅkai	*Ciṟiyatirumaṭal*
23. Tirumaṅkai	*Periyatirumaṭal*
Fourth Thousand	
24. Nammāḻvār	*Tiruvāymoḻi*

There are some variations to this order in printed form of the works of the Āḻvārs, and the third and fourth thousand are occasionally interchanged. The *Rāmānuja Nūṟṟantāti*, a poem composed by Tiruvaraṅkattu Amutanār (c. 11th cent.) in praise of his teacher, → Rāmānuja, is always added to the poems of the Āḻvārs. Sometimes, works exalting either the Āḻvārs or their works, like the *Caṭakōparantāti* (a poem in praise of Nammāḻvār, attributed to the Tamil poet Kampaṉ [c. 12th cent.?]) and *Tiruvāymoḻi Nūṟṟantāti* (composed by Maṇavāḷamāmuṉi, a noted Śrīvaiṣṇava teacher in the 14th–15th cents., in honor of Nammāḻvār's poem, the *Tiruvāymoḻi*), are appended to this corpus.

Biographies of the Āḻvārs

There are very few historical allusions in the poetry of the Āḻvārs themselves, except for rare references to a king, and certainly not enough to give any details of their lives. While the written commentarial tradition on the poetry of the Āḻvārs began with Rāmānuja's cousin Tirukkurukaippirāṉ Piḷḷāṉ writing a commentary on the *Tiruvāymoḻi* in the late 11th century, and anecdotes about the Āḻvārs' lives are found in this and later commentaries, the first detailed written hagiographical texts are probably as late as the 12th or 13th century CE.

There are about five famous biographies of the Āḻvārs and the early teachers (Tam. *ācāriyas*; Skt. *ācāryas*) written between the late 12th and late 14th/early 15th centuries. There are two works called *Guruparamparāprabhāvam* (The Splendor of the Succession of Teachers) in Manipravala (lit. "Gems and Corals," an allusion to the combination of Tamil and Sanskrit). The earlier one (followed largely by the Teṉkalai Śrīvaiṣṇavas) was probably composed around the 13th century by Piṉpaḻaḻakiya Perumāḷ Jīyar, and the later one, which is shorter, was probably composed around the 15th century. The Sanskrit work *Divyasūricarita*

(The Narrative of the Divine Beings; c. 12th–15th cents.) composed by Garuḍa Vāhana Paṇḍita also recounts the life stories of the Āḻvārs. In the 15th century (or possibly a little later), there also appeared a biography of all the Āḻvārs in Tamil verse; the *Āḻvārkaḷ Vaipavam* was written by Vaṭivaḻakiya Nampi Tācar and contained not only the life stories of the Āḻvārs, but also a summary of their poems. The *Periyatirumuṭi Aṭaivu* was possibly composed in the 16th century and is almost like a short "who's who" entry on each Āḻvār and *ācārya*, giving astrological details of their birth; the names of their works, their teachers, and their main students; and a short laudatory verse.

Written narratives contain accounts of miraculous births of the Āḻvārs, and their devotional activities, which are sometimes seen as exemplary. In addition, many of them portray the Āḻvārs not as ordinary human beings, but as incarnations (→ *avatāra*) of the divine weapons or attributes of Viṣṇu, such as the conch, discus, mace, and so on. Āṇṭāl is portrayed variously as the incarnation of either → Bhūdevī (the earth goddess) or Nīḷādevī, a consort of Viṣṇu worshipped only by the Śrīvaiṣṇava community.

The biographies also portray the Āḻvārs as coming from diverse castes and different economic classes. Some speak of themselves as chieftains (Kulacēkarāḻvār), and the woman poet Āṇṭāl connects herself with her "foster" father, Periyāḻvār. Most of them are known by multiple names; some are given names, while others are titles and epithets given by the community. Names such as Periyāḻvār ("The Big Āḻvār") or Nammāḻvār ("Our Āḻvār") are popular titles/names endowed by the Śrīvaiṣṇava community, but the poets refer to themselves as Viṣṇucitta ("He Whose Consciousness Is Viṣṇu") and Caṭakōpaṉ, respectively. Āṇṭāl ("She Who Rules") is also an honorific title, and she calls herself Kōtai ("Wreath of Flowers"). Others are known in the community by the legendary place of birth (Poykai, "Lake") or as being possessed by the intense fervor of their devotion (Pūtam or Pēy, "Ghost," or "Supernatural Spirit").

The first three Āḻvārs are frequently grouped together, and their poems also bear a striking resemblance to one another. Tirumaṅkai is said to have been a local chieftain who became a Vaiṣṇava under the influence of the woman he loved. In order to feed a thousand Vaiṣṇavas every day, as per the wishes of his beloved, the narratives say he resorted to highway robbery, until he had a divine encounter with Viṣṇu and Lakṣmī (→ Śrī Lakṣmī) and became a devotee. Although there is no direct mention of these details in his poems, Tirumaṅkai does express regrets about his earlier lifestyle in his poem:

> I desired the pleasures
> of women with beautiful breasts,
> women with delicate foreheads, wide shoulders,
> and smiles radiant like the glowing moon;
> and now,
> knowing the error of my ways,
> ignorant and unable
> to end the misery of repeated births,
> I think and fret.
> Ashamed of my copulation with young women,
> I have come and reached your sacred feet,
> My Lord at Naimicāraṇiyam [i.e. Naimiṣāraṇya, Nimsar]. (*PerTiMo.* 1.6.1)
>
> Without any feeling and with cruel mind,
> with actions filled with rage,
> Wandering with packs of dogs,
> rejoicing in sport,
> I ran and roamed, destroying several lives.
> The world of the god of death
> has to be refashioned
> to fit my crimes.
> O supreme one! O you on the sea of milk!
> Searching, I have come and reached your sacred feet,
> My Lord at Naimicāraṇiyam. (*PerTiMo.* 1.6.6).

After the 11th century CE, Śrīvaiṣṇava literature considers Caṭakōpaṉ (9th cent.) or Nammāḻvār to be a paradigmatic devotee and his poem, the *Tiruvāymoḻi*, as the equivalent of the Sanskrit *Sāmaveda*. Āṇṭāl, the woman poet, is also venerated with great enthusiasm. Āṇṭāl composed two poems in which she particularly voices her love for Viṣṇu-Nārāyaṇa, whom she frequently sees in his manifestation as Kṛṣṇa. In the *Tiruppāvai*, she imagines herself to be a cowherd girl waking up her friends and then going on to wake up Kṛṣṇa, whom she calls → Rāma, Māl, and other various names of Viṣṇu.

While images of the Āḻvārs are found in large Śrīvaiṣṇava temples in South India, an icon of Āṇṭāl is usually found in almost all Śrīvaiṣṇava temples in India and abroad. Her icon is found in the Śrīvaiṣṇava holy places in South India including Srirangam, Kanchipuram, and Sriperumbudur, as well as Pittsburgh, Atlanta, Toronto,

Orlando, Chicago, Malibu, Miami, and Rochester. Her shrine is frequently on Viṣṇu's left side, symmetrical with that of Śrī Lakṣmī, whose shrine is on Viṣṇu's right-hand side. The iconographic placing conveys the impression that she is a manifestation of Bhūdevī, the earth goddess, who, along with Lakṣmī, is depicted as Viṣṇu's consort in South Indian temples. In many of the American temples, she is simply identified as Bhūdevī, so people from other parts of India may have some understanding of who she is. Āṇṭāḷ, however, does not speak of herself as a goddess, and this identification seems to have come several centuries after her time. Most South Indian men and women identify Āṇṭāḷ as a woman poet who was passionately in love with god. Śrīvaiṣṇava hagiographies are consistent in saying that she refused to get married, and instead longed for union with Viṣṇu – a wish that was apparently fulfilled, according to these biographical accounts.

The Revealed Nature of the Poems

Like many of the other Hindu traditions, the Śrīvaiṣṇava tradition accepts the Sanskrit Vedas, the epics → *Rāmāyaṇa* and → *Mahābhārata*, and the → Purāṇas as scripture. In addition to these, they also hold that the poems of the Āḻvārs are "revealed," and on par with the Vedas. Śrīvaiṣṇava texts portray the songs of the Āḻvārs as being revealed in two ways: initially as revealed by Viṣṇu through the 12 Āḻvārs and later, after they were apparently forgotten by human beings, revealed by Nammāḻvār to Nātamuṉi (Skt. Nāthamuni), the first Śrīvaiṣṇava *ācārya* (Narayanan, 1994, 36–38).

Śrīvaiṣṇava hagiography states that Nātamuṉi instituted the recitation of the Āḻvār poems in temples and in homes, alongside the Vedas, and even today, during worship, the Śrīvaiṣṇavas switch from Tamil to Sanskrit frequently. Selections from the *Divya Prabandham* are chanted at weddings, funerals, ancestral rites, and daily worship at home. The idea that these verses are equivalent to the Veda is reinforced through Śrīvaiṣṇava literature and ritual.

While all the works of the *Divya Prabandham* are considered to be sacred and the term "Veda" is applied to them collectively, the *Tiruppāvai* of Āṇṭāḷ and the *Tiruvāymoḻi* of Nammāḻvār are of particular importance. The *Tiruvāymoḻi* is referred to as *the* Veda or *the* Upaniṣad more often than any other work. Just as the Āḻvārs do not refer to themselves as divine, they do not compare their works to the Vedas. Chronologically, the earliest statement to this effect comes from Maturakavi, the disciple of Nammāḻvār. Maturakavi is the only Āḻvār who wrote exclusively in praise of his human teacher and not Viṣṇu. In his brief poem *Kaṇṇinuṇ Ciṟuttāmpu* (The Short Knotted String), he says,

> He [i.e. Nammāḻvār] proclaimed the meaning of the secret [*maṟai*, i.e. Vedas] that are so difficult to understand.
>
> He sang the inner meaning of the Vētam in such a way that they became firmly established in my mind. (*KaṇC.* 8, 9)

The basis for regarding the *Tiruvāymoḻi* as a revealed text comes from the work itself. Nammāḻvār claims that Viṣṇu-Nārāyaṇa sings about himself using the poet as an instrument.

> What can I say of the Lord
> who lifted me up for all time,
> and made me himself, everyday?
> My radiant one, the first one,

Fig. 1: Line drawing of Āṇṭāḷ.

My Lord, sings of himself,
through me, in sweet Tamil. (*TiVāy.* 7.9.1)

The Śrīvaiṣṇava tradition acknowledges the twofold nature of its heritage and the equivalence of the revelations in Sanskrit and Tamil by calling its theology Ubhaya Vedānta ("Dual Vedānta"). This is expressed in a number of ways including the adoption of a situational language known as Manipravala, which is a mixture of Sanskrit and Tamil. The language becomes the medium through which the teachers gave their oral commentaries on the *Divya Prabandham* and the language in which the commentaries were also recorded.

Theology in the Poems of the Āḻvārs

The Supremacy of Viṣṇu-Nārāyaṇa

Viṣṇu, who is more frequently called Nārāyaṇa or Nāraṇaṉ by the Āḻvārs, is the supreme deity, and → Brahmā, → Śiva, and all celestial and human beings are seen to be his devotees. The Āḻvārs speak of Śiva and Brahmā worshipping Viṣṇu's feet (*TiVāy.* 7.6.2) and in other verses speak of Viṣṇu dwelling within the two gods. Even the actions of redemption usually associated with Śiva are attributed to Viṣṇu; he is said to dwell in and control Śiva and Brahmā and thus is responsible for their salvific acts:

Beyond the range of the divine ones' intelligence,
He, the first one of the skies and everything thereon,
Cause of the creator, most supreme one, ate them all!
He indwells; as Araṉ [i.e. Śiva] and as Ayaṉ [i.e. Brahmā],
He burnt the triple cities, enlightened the immortals,
destroys and then creates the worlds.
(*TiVāy.* 1.1.8)

The verse says that according to the Āḻvārs, Viṣṇu, being the inner soul of Śiva, destroyed the three cities and gave life to Mārkaṇḍeya; as Brahmā, he enunciates the Vedas and enlightens the immortal ones. He protects, creates, and destroys; he *is* Brahmā and Śiva (*TiVāy.* 8.4.9). This conviction of Viṣṇu being the only supreme deity makes them condemn other religious

Fig. 2: Fresco of Nammāḻvār near the ceiling of a shrine within the Srirangam temple complex (photo by Vasudha Narayanan).

positions. Tirumaṅkai refers to Buddhists and Jains as "ignorant" (*PerTiMo.* 9.8.9); Toṇṭaraṭippoṭiyālvār asserts that those who know the sacred books would not stoop so low as to hear Buddhist or Jaina doctrines that teach "false *dharma*" (*TiMā.* 7).

The Āḻvārs do not address any verses to Viṣṇu's consorts directly, and it is important to note this, especially because of Śrī's increased importance in later Śrīvaiṣṇava theology. However, the three consorts of Viṣṇu – Tiru (Śrī or Lakṣmī), Pārmakaḷ (the lady of the earth; Bhū in Sanskrit writings) and Nappiṉṉai, who is unique to Tamil literature – are mentioned frequently. Tiru seems to be the primary consort. Viṣṇu is addressed as Tirumāl and as one who has Malarmakaḷ ("Lady of the Lotus"; an epithet of Śrī) on his chest. Tiru's grace is sometimes mentioned in addition to Viṣṇu's grace. However, there is no direct poem addressed to her, nor is she seen to personify grace. The closest that we get to the notion of Tiru embodying mercy is in a verse of Periyāḻvār, where he says,

> *Even* if the Lady of the Lotus complains about his servant, [My Lord] will exclaim "My servant would not do thus; but even if he did, why, he did well!" (*PerTiMo.* 4.9.2).

The Paradox of Divine Nature

The Āḻvār poetry depicts Viṣṇu as transcendent and immanent; as having a divine, auspicious form and being formless; as encompassing all paradoxes and yet as close as the nearest temple; and as supreme and accessible, ruling from heaven and also as abiding on earth.

The all-pervasive nature of Viṣṇu is mentioned several times by the Āḻvārs. He is in everything, and everything is in him; he is diffused through the universe like "life in a body," and yet he is also the supreme being who contains everything by swallowing the entire universe:

> Becoming all things
> Spread on open space, fire,
>   wind, water and earth,
> He is diffused through them all.
> Hidden, he pervades,
>   like life in a body.
> The radiant scripture [*curuti*, i.e. Śruti] speaks
>   of the divine one who ate all this.
>   (*TiVāy.* 1.1.7)

Viṣṇu is seen as a personal deity with a handsome form, holding aloft his weapons, and Nammāḻvār compares the glory of the divine body to molten gold, and his eyes, feet, and arms to the lotus blossoms (*TiVāy.* 2.5.2, 3). Tiruppāṇāḻvār's only poem in the canon, which is called *Amalaṉātippirāṉ* (The Pure Primordial Lord), is a detailed description of Viṣṇu enshrined in Srirangam. The poem starts (vss. 1–11) with the divine feet and proceeds to the head, describing every part of Viṣṇu's body. And yet, several Āḻvār verses say that this deity also transcends all thought and is formless. Consider the following poem of Nammāḻvār:

> If you say he exists, he does,
>   his forms are these forms,
> If you say he does not,
>   his formlessness
>   is of these non-forms.
>
> If he has the qualities
>   of existence and nonexistence,
>   he is in two states,
>   he who pervades without end. (*TiVāy.* 1.1.9)

The use of paradox is significant in the poetry of the Āḻvārs. Viṣṇu is said to also be and transcend all paradoxes, and yet he is portrayed as close as the nearest temple:

> Being virtue and sin, union and separation
> Being all of these,
> Being memory and
>   forgetfulness
> Being existence and nonexistence,
> Being none of these,
> The Lord resides
>   in Tiruviṇṇakar ["Sacred Celestial City,"]
>   that is surrounded by lofty mansions.
> See the sweet grace of Kaṇṇaṉ [i.e. Kṛṣṇa],
> Is this false? (*TiVāy.* 6.3.4)

In general, the Āḻvārs, along with Sanskrit literature, tend to describe Viṣṇu as the "purest of the pure" (*pavitrānāṃ pavitram*; introduction to the *Viṣṇusahasranāma*). However, Nammāḻvār describes him as having both a form of brilliance and a form of filth, as being straightforward and crooked (*TiVāy.* 6.3.7). The Āḻvārs simply express the paradoxes and do not try to reconcile them; it is in the commentaries on the Āḻvār poetry that are recorded after the late 11th century that the Śrīvaiṣṇava theologians try to reconcile paradoxes and bring the theological statements in harmony with other accepted religious literature such as the Upaniṣads, epics, and the Purāṇas.

Besides these theological paradoxes, the Āḻvār poetry has hundreds of contrasting word pictures in the verses, drawing freely from Sanskrit puranic and epic narratives as well as from local Tamil traditions. This wordplay is a popular literary strategy in Āḻvār literature and one that has delighted generations of devotees. Viṣṇu is said to have killed a bird but ride on another, the eagle Garuḍa (*TiCaVi.* 19); as Kṛṣṇa, he subdued the snake Kāliya and in his supreme form is said to recline on the serpent Ananta in the ocean of milk (*PerTiMo.* 3.5.11); he destroyed the elephant Kuvalayāpīṭam and yet came to the rescue of the elephant Gajendra (*TiCaVi.* 40; *PerTiMo.* 4.2.5; 5.1.8; *CiMā.* 35-36); as Kṛṣṇa, he sucked the life out Pūtanā's breasts but was nourished by the breast of his foster mother Yaśodā (*PerTiMo.* 2.2.8; *MūTiVa.* 74; *TiCaVi.* 36); as Kṛṣṇa, Viṣṇu stood *under* the mountain Govardhana lifting it, and in his iconic incarnation (*arcāvatāra*), he stands on *top* of the mountain Veṅkaṭa. Most important, according to Nammāḻvār, as the man-lion Narasiṃha, Viṣṇu's claws tore the chest of the demon Hiraṇya, but this very deity abides in the heart of the poet (*TiVāy.* 9.4.7). These verses contrast two different aspects of one image or symbol and the paradoxes are relished by Śrīvaiṣṇava audiences.

The Manifestations and the Salvific Acts of Viṣṇu

Many of the Āḻvār poems are addressed to Viṣṇu enshrined in the temple – a deity known by a local name – and to his many descents or *avatāras*. The Āḻvārs are very familiar with the mythology of the Purāṇas and the epics and also seem to have access to other traditions (possibly oral) from which they know several stories. The Āḻvārs' devotion is primarily expressed through this sustained and repeated remembrance and recollections of the salvific actions and deeds of Viṣṇu.

According to the Āḻvārs, the incarnations of Viṣṇu-Nārāyaṇa, as well as his perceived full presence in his "worshippable" form in the temple, proclaim his ability and desire to save all beings and to destroy the evil that exists in the forms of demons. Thus, the Āḻvār poems clearly indicate that the promise of salvation is offered and divine grace is seen when Viṣṇu destroys the demons Madhu and Kaiṭabha and rescues the Vedas, or kills the evil Kaṃsa, or rushes to the help of the stricken elephant king Gajendra, answers the call of Draupadī who is being stripped of her garments and modesty, or initiates any one of the many actions that have potential salvific value. Such recollections of past deeds of Viṣṇu provide the existential context for the Āḻvārs' desire to see him in a temple, to sing the glory of his name, to bow before, worship, and serve him – and in the repeated plea for, or in the recognition of his grace. The same Viṣṇu, who as Rāma destroyed Laṅkā, will destroy the Āḻvār's sins (*TiVāy.* 3.6.2). The frequent allusions to myth are not a unique feature of the Āḻvār poetry. Talking of the well-known Tamil Śaiva poet Māṇikkavācakar, G. Yocum notes,

> When Māṇikkavācakar refers to various aspects of Śiva's character, he frequently does so by alluding to one or another of the pan-Indian myths about the god. Although the poet's use of such myths is extensive, it is also selective.... When Māṇikkavācakar cites one of the widely acknowledged incidents in Śiva's biography, he does so because it correlates closely with his personal experience of the deity. There is no idle retelling of the myths in this text. These myths are referred to because they illuminated some aspect of the god's character which Māṇikkavācakar knows first hand. (Yocum, 1982, 138)

The Āḻvārs mention the various incarnations of Viṣṇu frequently, but the lists are different. Tirumaṅkai mentions the descents as a fish, tortoise, boar, man-lion, dwarf (Vāmana), man with an axe (Paraśurāma), Rāma, swan, and Kṛṣṇa (*PerTiMo.* 1.4.1–10), but in an earlier set of verses lists the set of ten incarnations that in later generations becomes the "official" one: the fish, tortoise, boar, man-lion, dwarf, Paraśurāma, Rāma, Balarāma, Kṛṣṇa, and Kalki, (*PerTiMo.* 8.8.1–10). Periyāḻvār refers to these ten incarnations (*PerTiMo.* 4.9.9), but in addition to these, the Āḻvārs also speak about Viṣṇu's *avatāra* as a *haṃsa* (variously translated as a goose or a swan) in connection with the dissolution of the worlds (*PeTiMo.* 9.2.10; 9.4.2; 10.9.1; 11.4.9) and as a horse-headed person (Hayagrīva; *PeTiMo.* 4.5.6; 5.3.2; 7.8.2; *TiVāy.* 2.8.5).

The reasons for the *avatāras* is stated in many instances: Viṣṇu-Nārāyaṇa descends for the welfare of the "fourteen worlds" (*TiCaVi.* 79). As Kṛṣṇa, to "relieve the burden of this earth, he was born in northern Maturai" (*TiVāy.* 9.1.10); he also comes to "remove the sorrow of the earth-maiden and give her life" (*PeTiMo.* 8.8.9).

Periyāḻvār states that he was born as "the son of Vāsudeva to remove the suffering of the gods in heaven" (*PerTiMo.* 1.2.16).

Of the various incarnations of Viṣṇu, Rāma and Kṛṣṇa figure most prominently in the Āḻvār poems. The Āḻvārs praise all the *avatāras*, but only Rāma and Kṛṣṇa are addressed directly in a "mythic situation" – that is, addressed by the Āḻvār assuming the persona of a character in the puranic story and speaking in the voice of that mythic character. However, exclusive *bhakti* to Rāma or Kṛṣṇa is not found in the Āḻvār poems, and in this respect the works are very different from the devotional poetry of Sūrdās or Tulsīdās in northern India. The focus of the Āḻvārs devotion is the deity enshrined in local temples, and this local deity is identified as Viṣṇu and all his manifestations.

While the Āḻvārs do refer to Kṛṣṇa hundreds of times, it would not be correct to call this "Kṛṣṇa *bhakti*," or call the devotionalism of the Āḻvārs "Kṛṣṇaism." Periyāḻvār, whose songs in the first part of the poem *Periyāḻvār Tirumoḻi* depict an intense love for Kṛṣṇa, also speaks in the voice of Hanumān, Rāma's messenger to Sītā. Kulacēkarāḻvār, who talks in the guise of Kausalyā (Rāma's mother in the epic) and Daśaratha (Rāma's father) in his *Perumāḷ Tirumoḻi* (8.1–11; 9.1–11), also assumes the voice of Devakī, the biological mother of Kṛṣṇa, who missed his childhood entirely (*PeTiMo.* 7.1–10). This Āḻvār also identifies himself as a cowherd girl complaining of Kṛṣṇa's lies (*PeTiMo.* 6.1–10); and both Rāma and Kṛṣṇa are seen as identical with the deity in the temples.

Kṛṣṇa is mentioned in early Tamil literature that was composed between the 1st and 5th centuries CE (Ate, 2011, 75-78; Hardy, 2001), but the figure of Rāma, while known, does not seem to be very important (Champakalakshmi,1981, 44-45; 117-118; Murugesan, 1982, 254) In South India, the Āḻvār poetry is among the earliest literature that attests to the popularity of Rāma. R. Champakalakshmi, discussing the evolving importance of Rāma in South India, notes that

> inscriptional evidence…comes only from a record of about the seventh-eighth centuries A.D.…as the earliest sculptural representations belong to about the first half of the tenth century A.D However, Rama occupies a place of great honour in the hymns of the…Alvars of the seventh-ninth centuries A.D (Champakalakshmi, 1981, 117)

Given the paucity of references to the *Rāmāyaṇa* in earlier classical Tamil poetry, the Āḻvārs' awareness of the story as well as the in-depth knowledge of the various incidents is striking in itself. Even more important is the fact that they seem to have had access to another tradition, possibly oral tradition from which they drew their stories. We also see, for the first time in Tamil literature, poets actually participating in the story of Rāma, by identifying themselves as and then talking in the guise of various characters in the epic. Rāma is also the only character in Āḻvār poetry to whom the poets sing from the view point of another male; Kulacēkarāḻvār puts himself in the place of Daśaratha grieving over the departure of Rāma, and Tirumaṅkai actually identifies himself with the defeated demons of Laṅkā seeking Rāma's protection and then sings through their voices. Rāma is not excluded from the "parental" or erotic sentiments expressed by the Āḻvārs, and this is to be noted because it is usually Kṛṣṇa who is the focus of erotic and maternal emotions in later North Indian poetry.

Tamil Conventions in the Āḻvār Poetry

The Āḻvār poetry reflects a uniquely Tamil milieu. Viṣṇu is called Māl, a Tamil word that means "The Wondrous One," and this is the name that is used very often. Many characters and stories are also uniquely Tamil – Kṛṣṇa's consort is not Rādhā as in the north, but Nappiṉṉai, who is his cousin. In South India, cross-cousin marriages are common (see kinship), and Nappiṉṉai is portrayed as Kṛṣṇa's maternal uncle's daughter, a relationship that is considered to be traditionally appropriate for marriages in the Tamil country. In dozens of verses in Āḻvār poems, we hear that in order to wed Nappiṉṉai, Kṛṣṇa tamed seven bulls in a public tournament. The taming of the bulls is again unique to these parts and is still practiced in Tamil Nadu during the month of January.

The Āḻvārs' songs owe a lot to earlier Caṅkam literature and flow naturally from the earlier Tamil literature. And yet, the poets are also conscious of Sanskrit literature; indeed, their *bhakti* is as much contextualized in the epics and puranic lore as it is in Tamil conventions. The poetry is, as is much else in the Hindu traditions, simultaneously a local matter as well as an expression of selective

Sanskrit traditions, some of which are shared with people from other regions or communities. The stories the Āḻvārs narrate or refer to, as well as the Vedas and the Vedāṅgas they extol, are part of the Sanskrit literature. However, the nature of the *bhakti* they express, the landscape they laud, is very South Indian, very Tamil, very local. The personae and voices they assume come from both Sanskrit and Tamil literatures.

Prominent in the Tamil heritage is the use of the five forms of landscapes seen in Caṅkam poetry in situations of love. These are adapted in the devotional poetry of the Āḻvārs. Another important feature in the Āḻvār poetry is that the devotion is addressed to the local Viṣṇu, with a local name, enshrined in the local Tamil landscape, in dozens of villages. The third is the articulation of Tamil love traditions like "riding the *maṭal*" (see below). And finally, among the many literary conventions we see in Tamil poetry, we can choose one important feature – the kinds of roles assumed by the Āḻvārs. Most of these are stylized characters from Caṅkam poetry, and others are from the stories of Rāma and Kṛṣṇa. Specifically, one can see that there is a literary conceit wherein the Āḻvār sometimes speaks of himself or herself in the third person at moments of perceived "union" with the deity.

Aintiṇai: The Five Landscapes in Tamil Poetry

The Āḻvār poetry displays full knowledge of the earlier Tamil views on landscape aesthetics and literature and they are aware that specific sceneries signify specific emotions for the poet. The early Tamil Caṅkam poetry (composed around the first centuries of the Common Era) spoke of five landscapes and corelated them to five moods or situations one could encounter in matters of love. Thus, a poem set on the seashore indicated that there a lover was pining for her beloved, the mountainous terrain suggested a rapturous union, and so on. The passionate poems of the Āḻvārs are set not just in the lush Tamil countryside with its banana trees, coconut groves, and mango plantations, but also in this stylized, aesthetic, literary, and emotional interior landscape with crashing waves, stormy clouds, and mountain winds signifying moments of ecstatic union with and anguished separation from the lover.

The five landscapes are signified by five symbols of flora – either flowers or trees in the Tamil milieu. The landscapes are the following:

(1) *kuṟiñci*, named after a flower that blooms on a mountain side once in 12 years. Reference to this situation indicated the secretive meeting of lovers, which may take place during the day or night;

(2) *neytal*, named after a water flower. This situation in love is depicted by the seashore and signifies separation from the beloved;

(3) *pālai*, a tree sometimes seen in deserts, signifying wasteland and elopement;

(4) *mullai* (one variety of the jasmine flower), which indicates forests or meadows. This situation in love frequently describes separation, but one in which the woman is more or less sure about the return of her beloved; and

(5) *marutam*, a red flower, indicating farming lands, sometimes river tracts. This scene indicates a jealous wife, angry with her husband who may have visited courtesans.

While the love of heroes and heroines in Caṅkam poetry is located in these landscapes, and many of the Āḻvārs express their love in this symbolic world rich in meaning to the audience, there is no evidence of these conceits in later North Indian devotional poetry. One simply does not find the stylized landscapes, and the repertoire of "role playing" is more limited than that in the South.

Āṇṭāl and other Āḻvārs refer to Vrindavan, Ayodhya, and a handful of places in North India as sacred, but the places that they most lovingly describe are all in South India. Specifically, the Tamil terrain is praised using conventions grounded in Tamil literature.

Viṣṇu *bhakti*: Grounded in the Tamil Terrain

The Āḻvārs sang about temples in several cities, towns, forests, and mountains. After the poems were collected and redacted by Nātamuṉi, the first Śrīvaiṣṇava *ācārya* (c. 10th cent. CE), the community began to celebrate the 108 places that the Āḻvārs glorified in their hymns. Śrīvaiṣṇava hagiography speaks about all the poems being revealed to Nātamuṉi and the poems, in all, contain references to a 108 places. There is no historical information to indicate how the poems were redacted and anthologized. However, the 108 sacred places include 106 places in India – most of them in the south – and two that are not in this world. The last two are Vaikuṇṭha, or the heavenly permanent abode of Viṣṇu, and the ocean of milk. The glorification of these places focused on the temples that housed Viṣṇu and became focal points of the pilgrimage. It is these temples that the Āḻvārs praised; it is in these temples that the Āḻvārs songs came to be sung and the Āḻvārs came to be revered (see also → *tīrtha* and *tīrthayātrā*).

Kṛṣṇa in Tamil poetry is frequently called Kaṇṇaṉ ("The Dear One"), and he sports as much on the banks of the Yamunā as he does in the Tamil landscape. Rāma lives in Ayodhya and in the local temple in Tamil Nadu. Although there are several verses in which the Āḻvārs speak to Rāma or Kṛṣṇa, their poems are addressed to Viṣṇu – to be specific, Viṣṇu in a local village or town, who has a local name. Unlike some North Indian poets who focused to a considerable extent on either Rāma or Kṛṣṇa, in the south, the Āḻvārs composed primarily to Viṣṇu, especially in his enshrined form in the local temple. This form, called *arcāvatāra* in Śrīvaiṣṇava theology, is considered to be an actual incarnation of Viṣṇu, equivalent in status to Viṣṇu's *avatāra*s as Rāma or Kṛṣṇa. The local icon is considered to be absolutely, completely Viṣṇu – the same Viṣṇu who incarnated himself as the fish, the tortoise, as Rāma or Kṛṣṇa. The Āḻvārs moved seamlessly between Viṣṇu and his descents, identifying one with the other. In the following poem, Kulacēkarāḻvār identifies Rāma with the deity enshrined in Tillai Chitrakutam, more popularly known as Chidambaram:

> In the beautiful city of Ayōtti [i.e. Ayodhya], encircled by towers,
> A flame that lit up all the worlds appeared in the solar race,
> and gave life to all the heavens.
> This warrior, with dazzling eyes,
> Rāma, dark as a cloud, the first one, my only Lord
> is in Tirucittirakūṭam [i.e. Chitrakut], the city of Tillai [i.e. Chidambaram].
> When is the day
> when my eyes behold him
> and rejoice? (*PerTiMo.* 10.1)

The most popular of the 108 sacred places is Srirangam, near the modern city of Tirucchirapalli. All the Āḻvārs (except Maturakavi) sang in praise of the lord in this temple. The most verses on any subject are addressed to this deity. Some references are very specific; Toṇṭaraṭippoṭiyālvār talks specifically of Viṣṇu reclining with his back to the north and facing Laṅkā in the south, an unusual axis for the *arcā* (*TiMā.* 19). In verse 4 of his *Tirupaḷḷiyeḻucci* (Awakening the Lord from Bed; a genre of panegyric addressed to the king to wake him in the morning), Toṇṭaraṭippoṭiyālvār refers to the lord of Srirangam as "the king of Ayodhyā" and as "the bull among celestials, who with his bow ruined the entire clan of demons at Laṅkā," thus identifying him with Rāma. Indeed, 247 verses are written in praise of Srirangam and the manifestation of Viṣṇu in that temple, and the sacred hill Vēṅkaṭam (popularly known today as Tirumala-Tirupati) is the focus of 202 songs. Every place had its local legends and a story that explained the presence of the deity there.

The Āḻvārs describe the beauty of the sacred place, praise its prosperity, and also say that the place itself has salvific power. The sins (*viṉai*s) of one who goes to Anantapuram (today Thiruvananthapuram) will vanish (*TiVāy.* 10.2.2), and just saying the name Tirumāliruñcōlai ("The Grove Where the Lord Abides") is enough for the lord to fill the heart of the poet (*TiVāy.* 10.8.1). It is the local deity whose beauty entrances the Āḻvār; it is to this deity that they send messages of love; it is this deity whom they address as a lover and with whom they seek union. While Kṛṣṇa and, to a lesser extent, Rāma are the focus of a devotion that is simultaneously erotic and submissive, an overwhelming number of songs, where the Āḻvār assumes the role of the "heroine," are addressed to Viṣṇu enshrined in a temple.

The lord in a temple is also seen to be the same god who is within the *bhakta*'s heart. Tirumaḻicai identifies the holy places of pilgrimage near Kanchipuram but identifies what he sees outside with the divinity he claims to have found within himself:

> The days are gone when I saw,
> at Ūrakam, the standing Lord.
> At Pāṭakam I beheld my father sitting,
> and at Veḥka he reclined.
> I was not born then; and when I was born
> I never did forget
> that he stands, abides, and reclines
> within my heart. (Ūrakam, Pāṭakam, and
> Veḥka are shrines/temples in or near
> Kanchipuram; *TiCaVi.* 64)

Rāma Stories Unique to the Tamil Āḻvār Tradition

The Āḻvārs speak about stories connected to Rāma and Kṛṣṇa not found in Sanskrit literature (Ate, 2011, 373-392; Narayanan, 1987, 26–30). When Hanumān is sent as a messenger to Sītā, he gives proof to show he is an authentic envoy of Rāma, also in Vālmīki's *Rāmāyaṇa*. In the *Periyāḻvār*

Tirumoḻi, the Āḻvār talks in the voice of Hanumān, who narrates several stories to Sītā to prove that he was sent by Rāma. Hanumān mentions many incidents, and one is not found in Vālmīki's *Rāmāyaṇa*. He relates that one night, in an intimate moment, Sītā tied Rāma with a garland of jasmine flowers – presumably indicating that no one other than those two would know about an incident from their personal lives. Hanumān, by narrating this, hopes to instill confidence in Sītā and have her believe in the veracity of narrator.

There are other stories connected to Rāma that are unique to the Āḻvārs. In one of them, Tirumaḻicai says that he does not even have the faith of the squirrel that tried to help Rāma build the bridge to Laṅkā and recounts some details (*TiMā*. 27). Tirumaṅkai refers to a story in which Rāma, pleased with Hanumān, says he would like to sit and eat with him (*PerTiMo*. 5.8.2). A longer, more complete incident is the focus of the poetry by some Āḻvārs. As reconstructed from the Āḻvār verses, Rāvaṇa comes in disguise to seek a boon from Brahmā; Viṣṇu in the form of a baby appears on Brahmā's lap and tries to signal and warn Brahmā that it is Rāvaṇa who stands in front of him by pointing to his ten toes. The ten toes were to indicate the ten heads of Rāvaṇa; Viṣṇu was trying to warn Brahmā against giving rash boons to Rāvaṇa, but the Āḻvār references do not make clear whether Brahmā heeded the advice (*NaTiVa*. 44; *MūTiVa*. 77–78)

The origins of these stories are not known. They are not in any of the Sanskrit epics or early Purāṇas, and one has to assume the existence of other works that are not available now or an oral Tamil tradition in South India from where the Āḻvārs draw these incidents. These are complete incidents and different from poetic imagination and rhetoric, of which we do find a considerable amount, in the Āḻvār poetry.

Tamil Conventions of Love: Riding the *Maṭal*

Several Tamil treatises composed in the 1st millennium CE contain information on grammatical rules, social conventions, psychological states and moods of human beings, and a variety of other subjects. One such convention is called "riding the *maṭal*." *Maṭal* literally translates as "riding the palmyra horse" and refers to both the ritual by which a male threatened to embark on this act as well as a poem in which such acts were contemplated. This was an act of desperation and only undertaken by a man when he felt that his love for a woman was unrequited. The action, which involved making a mock horse from the sharp blades of a palmyra tree and then riding it in public, was considered to be shameful and disgraceful.

The earliest literature that mentions the *maṭal* is classical Caṅkam love poetry. In Āḻvār poetry, one sees male devotional poets who talk in a woman's voice in their compositions proclaiming their love for Viṣṇu. They feel that their love is unrequited and threaten to indulge in this act of riding the *maṭal*. In the early Tamil literature, ordinarily, the heroine, the village leaders, and families of the young man and woman would all be convinced of a man's passion if he threatened to do this act, and they hastily facilitate his union with his beloved. The Tamil work *Kaḷaviyal Eṉṟa Iṟaiyaṉār Akapporuḷ*, an 8th-century text on love with a commentary by Nakkīraṉār, elucidates the variation and nuances of the conventions of lovers "riding the *maṭal*" (Buck & Paramasivam, 2001).

Nammāḻvār and Tirumaṅkai, two male poets, incorporate many of the love situations described in the secular Tamil Caṅkam literature into their devotional poems. Specifically, Nammāḻvār and Tirumaṅkai sing of their passion for Viṣṇu, and when their love does not seem to be reciprocated, they threaten to "ride the palmyra horse." Tirumaṅkai threatens to do this in two poems: the *Periyatirumaṭal* (The Sacred Long *Maṭal*) and the *Ciṟiyatirumaṭal* (The Sacred Short *Maṭal*). In all these poems, the male poet assumes the role of the lovelorn girl and speaks of Viṣṇu as "her" beloved.

Nammāḻvār, in a girl's voice, says "she" will ride the *maṭal* to show the extremity of "her" passion for Viṣṇu:

Lifting my modesty, stealing my heart
  the Lord of the divine ones reaches the high heavens.
My friend, this I swear:
I shall shock all the earth,
I shall do weird deeds
  and like a wild woman
  ride the palmyra stem like a horse.
With no sense of shame, I shall ride
  the palmyra stem through every street in town
  and women from all the lands will cheer me on
And I shall demand from the Lord
  a cool blossom from the *tuḻāi* [i.e. *tulsī*] plant
  and adorn my head with it. (*TiVāy*. 5.3.9–10)

The poem makes it clear that Nammāḻvār, a male poet, is speaking in the voice of a woman and that "her" actions are considered to be shameful. She is challenging Viṣṇu to respond to what Tamil literature considers to be the desperate cry of a lover. While the milieu and ritual context resemble that of the classical Caṅkam poetry, some important shifts have taken place. The speaker is a male, experiencing the emotions of a woman and speaking in "her" voice, and the hero is not a local lad but is the ultimate male (Puruṣottama, i.e. Viṣṇu). These shifts are also seen in Tirumaṅkai's poetry. This persona of a young girl in love is only one of the roles assumed by Tirumaṅkai, Nammāḻvār, Kulacēkarāḻvār, Periyāḻvār, and Āṇṭāl.

Role Playing in Āḻvār Poetry

Five of the twelve Āḻvārs periodically assume the role of various characters from Tamil or Sanskrit literature and express their love through the words of these personae. The Caṅkam literature has many characters who are recognized easily by the Tamil audience; specifically, in the *akam* (love) poetry, we hear the voices of a woman in love, a man in love, and the friend, the mother, and the foster mother (the woman who had been the wet nurse) of the woman in love. Some of the Āḻvārs speak in these voices, although it is seldom that they assume the role of a male figure. In addition to these persona(e), they also assume roles made familiar to us in 16th and 17th centuries by North Indian poets – the roles of Yaśodā and the cowherd girls who express different kinds of love to Kṛṣṇa.

The Voice of a Young Woman Seeking Her Beloved

A popular literary strategy in many genres of literature in India, the poet – whether male or female – speaks in the voice of a young woman who is in love with the deity. Such poems are popular in the performing arts and are centerpieces of classical Indian dances in South India. The Āḻvārs identify themselves as either a young girl seen in Caṅkam poetry or as a cowherd girl who is in love with Kṛṣṇa. This poem of Nammāḻvār is typical of this genre:

You're unfair, Kaṇṇā, you're unfair!
When you make love and embrace my full breasts,
a tidal wave of pleasure, unchecked by our union,
rises to the firmament, and soars beyond,
making my wits drown in the flood.
And then it recedes like a dream.
My passion permeates my inner life
and throbs in every cell of my body
my soul cannot bear this burden.
If I am to be separated from you,
every time you go to graze the cows,
I die. (*TiVāy.* 10.3.2)

Āṇṭāl, too, imagines herself to be a cowherd girl and at the end of one of her poems asks her friends if they have seen Kṛṣṇa. They reply that they have seen him in Viruntāvaṉam (i.e Vrindavan). In her concluding poems, one can almost hear her sigh of happiness that Kṛṣṇa has been seen:

A prankster
who knows no *tarumam* [i.e. *dharma*]
He whose eyebrows arch
like the bow Cāraṅkam [i.e. Sāraṅga]
in his hand
handsome one
without equal
have you seen him?

He whose form is dark
whose face glows bright
like the sun that fans
on the peaks
of the rising hills
We have seen him
here, in Viruntāvaṉam. (*NaTiMo.* 14.6)

The intimacy of the poet and the poetic irony are visible in these Tamil poems. Āṇṭāl, who from all accounts is familiar with the Sanskrit literature, describes Kṛṣṇa as one who knows no *dharma*; and yet in this poem she explicitly chides with the familiar intimacy seen only in the vernacular poems that he knows no *dharma*. The audience for the poem would understand that this Kṛṣṇa is the very person who asserts in the *Bhagavadgītā* that he comes into being age after age to establish *dharma*.

Bhakti from the Viewpoint of a Mother

Rāma and more frequently Kṛṣṇa are seen as babies and toddlers, and the *Divya Prabandham* has several poems celebrating the childhood of these *avatāras*. In later literature, this mode of *bhakti* is called *vātsalyabhāva*; in Tamil, this genre of poems is called Piḷḷaitamiḻ (Tamil [verses in praise] of Children). Tamil poets have excelled in their compositions addressed to the supreme being in the form of a child. The deities who inspired these verses were Murukaṉ and Viṣṇu (as Rāma and more popularly as Kṛṣṇa), and the goddess Mīnākṣī (Tam. Mīnāṭci) of Maturai. It is also seen in Tamil Islamic poems in later centuries (Richman, 1997). From the early songs of Periyāḻvār and other poets, later students of Tamil formulated several categories to describe the various types of verses. Not all of them are found in the works of the Āḻvārs.

One of the stages noted in the genre of Piḷḷaitamiḻ is one where a mother sings a lullaby to the child. Kulacēkarāḻvār, assuming the voice of Rāma's mother, Kausalyā, sings a lullaby for her son. All Tamil lullabies, such as this one, end with the formulaic words *tālelo.*

The other day,
As a baby on the banyan leaf,
You swallowed the worlds.
You killed Vāli [i.e. Vālin]
  and gave the kingdom to his brother;
O dark gem of Kaṇappuram [i.e. Kannapuram]
  where the waves wash gems to the shore;
O ruler of the city called Āli! [i.e. Thiruvali]
O you who abide in Ayōtti [i.e. Ayodhya]!
Tā le lo! (*PerTiMo.* 8.7)

Kulacēkarāḻvār, Periyāḻvār, and Tirumaṅkai sing lullabies to the baby Kṛṣṇa. The *Periyāḻvār Tirumoḻi* contains the most extensive and detailed expressions of Piḷḷaitamiḻ. In about two hundred verses, the poet, who identifies himself as Yaśodā, the foster mother of the child, enjoys the childhood of Kṛṣṇa. Many of these songs are still sung in Tamil households. The themes of the poems include the festivities at the birth of the baby, singing of the lullaby, showing the moon, the swaying movement of the child (which is likened to a tender plant), teaching him to clap his hands, his halting footsteps, asking him to drink his milk, playing hide and seek, bathing him, piercing his ears, combing his hair, adorning his head with flowers, and giving him protective amulets.

The "maternal" poems are addressed to both Rāma and Kṛṣṇa, but there are many more written to Kṛṣṇa than to Rāma. The poems also differ in texture. In singing to Rāma, his dignity and valor are stressed; in singing to Kṛṣṇa, the Āḻvārs rejoice in and chide him for his childhood mischief, and they tease him while simultaneously being awestruck at this human manifestation of that which is formless.

Voices of Male Figures Addressed to Rāma

In addition to these traditionally popular voices, some Āḻvārs speak in unusual voices – Tirumaṅkai, for instance, speaks in the voice of the defeated demons (*rākṣasas*) in the battle of Laṅkā, and Kulacēkarāḻvār speaks in the voice of Daśaratha, who is grief stricken at the departure of Rāma. This poetry is also based on the concept of *viraha* or separation from one's beloved, but the *viraha* here is that from the viewpoint of the father, not the mother or lover, which are more popular.

Without hearing him call me "Father" with
  pride and with love,
Without clasping his chest adorned with gems
  to mine,
Without embracing him, without smoothing
  his forehead,
Without seeing his graceful gait, majestic like
  the elephant,
Without seeing his face [glowing] like the lotus
  flower,
I, wretched one,
  having lost my son, my Lord,
Still live. (*PeTiMo.* 9.6)

The Āḻvārs speak of many incidents in the *Rāmāyaṇa* that are not mentioned by Vālmīki. Some of the verses in which the Āḻvār expresses surrender to Viṣṇu are also different than what we may expect. Rather than speak in the voice of a character close to Kṛṣṇa or Rāma, Tirumaṅkai speaks in the voice of the defeated *rākṣasas* of Laṅkā:

Our Irāvaṇaṉ [i.e. Rāvaṇa],
King with long red-gold hair,
  carried away a goddess called Cītai [i.e. Sītā].
Look, he held her captive
  in that fragrant grove.
This was his undoing.
Kumpaṉ [i.e. Kumbha], and now Nikumpaṉ
  [i.e. Nikumbha]
have fallen in war.
Death comes in the form of a man,
Do not slay us with your bow,
We fear,
We beat our drums, we dance our surrender.
  (*PerTiMo.* 10.2.5)

Instead of speaking words of grief at separation from the viewpoint of a cowherd girl or words of surrender, which could have been spoken possibly by Hanumān or even the demon Vibhīṣaṇa, that is, people who are very close to Kṛṣṇa or Rāma. Tirumaṅkai in this poem expresses his surrender in a most unusual way. The context seems to be located in the Tamil traditions of war – it was assumed that when an enemy surrendered to a king, the king should protect the life of the person who had sought him as refuge even if his own life was threatened in the process.

The Āḻvār poems, especially those in which they assume the voice of other characters, are themes for classical *bharatanāṭyam* dances in South India.

Āḻvār Poetry in the Performing Arts

A defining moment in textual devotion comes when the Tamil songs of the Āḻvārs were anthologized by Nātamuṉi and set to music. Hagiographies narrate how the entire *Divya Prabandham*, which had been hitherto forgotten, was revealed to Nātamuṉi while he was in a meditative trance.

The *Guruparamparāprabhāvam* says that Nātamuṉi was very knowledgeable in music. He was, apparently, asked to be a referee in a music competition between two courtesans. One of them was adept at *human* music, and the other had mastered *divine* music. A local king had apparently ruled in favor of the "human" music, and the other dancer, piqued, had taken her case to the people. Nātamuṉi, who was entranced by the intricacies of her rhythm and singing techniques, explained the superiority of her music to the king and brought her recognition.

Nātamuṉi then set the *Divya Prabandham* to the form of divine music practiced by the courtesan, choreographed the songs, and taught it to his two nephews (see Ayyankar, 1975, 121–122) These songs were performed first in the Viṣṇu temple in Kāṭṭumaṉṉār Kōyil (near the town of Chidambaram) and then in other temples.

Nammāḻvār had clearly envisaged the *Tiruvāymoḻi* as being sung and danced in praise of Viṣṇu:

O you who want to break
  the hold of deeds
  and stop them from coming close,
Worship the feet of the Lord,
  singing and dancing these ten [verses]
  from the thousand Tamil songs
  sung by Caṭakōpaṉ who hails from Kurukūr
    [i.e. Alwarthirunagari]
  a city with lofty mansions. (*TiVāy*. 9.10.11)

The descendants of Nātamuṉi who continued the service of singing and dancing in the temples came to be called *araiyar*s (from the root *arai-*, "to declaim"). The modes of singing that existed in those days are no longer in existence; except for the *araiyar* tradition, which claims continuity, there is no other form of singing that is said to reach back over the centuries. The enactment of particular verses of Nammāḻvār or myths that are alluded to in the *Tiruvāymoḻi* during the annual festival of recitation in *mārkaḻi* (Dec–Jan) is called *araiyar cēvai* (service by the *araiyar*). The *araiyar* tradition is closer to recitation than to classical South Indian music today (though they use cymbals to beat time), but it has traditionally been called "singing."

The performative traditions have continued, although the forms of music and interpretations have changed considerably over the centuries. Although Āḻvār poetry has always been recited and sung in domestic and temple spaces as well as in street procession since the late 20th century, the hymns have enjoyed an overwhelming popularity in the "secular" stage as well. Ariyakudi Ramanuja Iyengar (1890–1967) popularized the singing of Āṇṭāl's *Tiruppāvai* in 30 different *rāga*s between 1950 and 1960. Along with these new interpretations in Carnatic music came the dances in the style that has been called *bharatanāṭyam* since the 1930s. Vyjayanthimala (later Vyjayanthimala Bali), a famous movie actress and a well-known classical dancer, choreographed the verses of Āṇṭāl and danced the 30 verses. In the 1980s various *bhajan* groups in Chennai focused on retuning and singing the hymns of the Āḻvārs. Television channels, radio stations, classical music concerts, and dance programs in South India all feature songs of the Āḻvārs, and they continue to be popular in South Indian arts performed in temple, domestic, and public spaces in global Hindu arenas.

(All translations are by the author, unless otherwise stated.)

Bibliography

Ate, L., *Yaśodā's Songs to Her Playful Son, Kṛṣṇa: Periyāḻvār's 9th Century Tamil Tirumoḻi*, Woodland Hills, 2011.

Ayyankar, S.K., ed., *Āṟāyirappaṭi Guruparamparāprabhāvam*, Tiruchirappalli, 1975.

Buck, D.C., & K. Paramasivam, *The Study of Stolen Love*, New York, 2001.

Carman, J., & V. Narayanan, *The Tamil Veda: Piḷḷāṉ's Interpretation of the Tiruvāymoḻi*, Chicago, 1989.

Champakalakshmi, R., *Vaiṣṇava Iconography in the Tamil Country*, New Delhi, 1981.

Clooney, F., "Nammāḻvār's Glorious Tiruvallavāḻ: An Exploration in the Methods and Goals of Śrīvaiṣṇava Commentary," *JAOS* 111, 1991, 260–276.

Clooney, F.,"I Created Land and Sea: A Tamil Case of God-Consciousness and Its Śrīvaiṣṇava Interpretation," *Numen* 35, 1988, 138–159.

Edholm, E.A., & C. Suneson, "The Seven Bulls and Kṛṣṇa's Marriage to Nīḷa/NappiNNai in Sanskrit and Tamil Literature," *Temenos* 8, 1972, 29–53.

Hardy, F., *Viraha-bhakti: The Early History of Kṛṣṇa Devotion in South India*, Delhi, 2001.

Hudson, D., "Piṉṉai, Krishna's Cowherd Wife," in: J.S. Hawley & D. Wulff, eds., *The Divine Consort: Rādhā and the Goddesses of India*, Berkeley, 1982, 238–261.

Hudson, D., "Bathing in Krishna," *HTR* 78, 1980, 539–566.

Murugesan, M., *Sangam Age*, Madras, 1982.

Narayanan, V., "'With the Earth as a Lamp and the Sun as the Flame': Lighting Devotion in South India," *IJHS* 11/3, 2008, 227–253.

Narayanan, V., "Weaving Garlands of Tamil Poems," in: E. Bryant, ed., *An Anthology of Krishna-Resources*, New York, 2007, 187–204.

Narayanan, V., "The Life and Lyrics of Tiruppan Alvar," in: E. Zelliot & R. Mokashi-Punekar, eds., *Untouchable Saints: An Indian Phenomenon*, New Delhi, 2005, 55–82.

Narayanan, V., "Gender in a Devotional Universe," in: G. Flood, ed., *The Blackwell Companion to Hinduism*, London, 2003a, 569–587.

Narayanan, V., "Two Processions: Andal's Wedding and Nammalvar's Moksha," *JVS* 12/1, 2003b.

Narayanan, V., "The *Ramayana* in the Theology and Experience of the Srivaisnava Community," *JVS* 2/4, 1994a, 55–90.

Narayanan, V., *The Vernacular Veda: Revelation, Recitation, and Ritual*, Columbia, 1994b.

Narayanan, V., "The Sacred Utterance of the Silent Seer: Speech and Sight in the Revelation of the Tamil Veda," *JVS* 2/1, 1993, 79–112.

Narayanan, V., "Oral and Written Comments on the Tiruvāymoḻi," in: J. Timm, ed., *Text in Context: Traditional Hermeneutics in South Asia*, Albany, 1992, 85–107.

Narayanan, V., *The Way and the Goal: Expressions of Devotion in the Early Śrīvaiṣṇava Tradition*, Washington DC, 1987.

Ramanujan, A.K., *Hymns for the Drowning: Poems for Viṣṇu by Nammāḻvār*, Princeton, 1981.

Richman, P., *Extraordinary Child: Poems from a South Indian Devotional Genre*, Honolulu, 1997.

Varadachari, K.C., *Alvars of South India*, Bombay, 1970.

Venkatesan, A., *The Secret Garland: Āṇṭāḷ's Tiruppāvai and Nācciyār Tirumoḻi*, New York, 2010.

Venkatesan, A., "Double the Pleasure: Reading Nammalvar's *Tiruviruttam*," in: M. Kannan & J. Clare, eds., *Passages: The Relationships between Tamil and Sanskrit in South India*, Pondicherry, 2009.

Venkatesan, A., "A Woman's Kind of Love: Female Longing in the Alvar Poetry," *JHCS* 20, 2007a, 16–24.

Venkatesan, A., "Why Abandon a Lovely Rabbit to Chase after a Crow: The Talaivi in the Maṭal Poems of Tirumaṅkayāḻvār," in: *Tropes, Territories and Competing Realities*, Toronto, 2007b.

Yocum, G., *Hymns to the Dancing Śiva: A Study of Māṇikkavācakar's Tiruvācakam*, New Delhi, 1982.

VASUDHA NARAYANAN

Avvaiyār

Avvaiyār (also known as Avvai and Auvaiyār) is revered as a poet, moral philosopher, saint, folkloric heroine, and an embodiment of Tamil culture and identity. Over the centuries, a number of literary works, diverse in both style and content, and spanning several centuries, have been ascribed to her. Therefore it is not surprising that her depiction in mythic narratives, folklore, and popular culture are equally complex.

In 1708 the Lutheran missionary Bartholomaus Ziegenbalg (1682–1719), who was stationed in Tranquebar (now Tharangambadi), Tamil Nadu, translated the moral maxims attributed to Avvaiyār into German and published it as the *Malabarische Moralia*, granting her the distinction of being among the first Tamil writers whose work was translated into a European language. No doubt, Ziegenbalg was motivated by the growing interest in proverbs and folklore in 18th-century Europe. This preoccupation with folklore was echoed in 19th-century Tamil Nadu and was instrumental in ensuring that Avvaiyār occupied a significant place in the reimagining of Tamil cultural identity in the late 19th and early 20th centuries.

In spite of having had a global audience for so long, Avvaiyār remains an enigmatic figure. Her elusive identity is rooted in her very name, an epithet that simply means "Old Woman." So it is no wonder that we can identify no fewer than three authors who share this *nom de plume*, and who have composed works in a range of genres across a period that extends from the 1st century CE to the 14th century CE, and even later.

The earliest Avvaiyār is believed to have been a Tamil classical poet who was active during the Caṅkam period (1–3 cents. CE; see → Tamil texts). From the poems attributed to her, we can deduce from the internal evidence of her poems that she hailed from a class of wandering minstrels or *pāṇar*s. Female *pāṇar*s were called *pāṭiṉi* or *pāṭṭiyār*, an appellation that can be easily confused with *pātti*, "grandmother." Perhaps this led to her initially being characterized as the "Old Woman" (Zvelebil, 1975, 170n27).

Life as a *pāṭṭiyār* was difficult, as *pāṇar*s were near the bottom of the social hierarchy. As a woman, she must have faced added difficulties securing adequate patronage, and she often mentions her impoverished condition in her poetry. Her perpetual wandering in search of royal benefactors also occasionally lent an air of melancholy to her compositions, which were typically more celebratory and robust:

> My legs are aching, paining
> Fast have I walked
>   and a weary distance journeyed...
> What place shall I call my own?
> A wanderer like me. (Rajagopalachari, 1971, 143)

Verses such as this give insight into the inner life of the *pāṇar*s as they roamed from court to court composing praise poems for kings and chieftains while in search of royal gifts and support, and Avvaiyār's own wandering is said to have taken her as far northwest as the Mysore region.

What we know of the Caṅkam period Avvaiyār can be gleaned from the scant evidence of her poems. A total of 59 poems ascribed to her appear in the four earliest works of the Caṅkam anthologies (Thompson, 1948, 399). While nearly half of these poems deal with *akam* ("the interior"; love), 33 of her compositions are included in the *Puṟanāṉūṟu*, a Caṅkam anthology of four hundred poems concerned with war, ethics, and public life. The content of her many *puṟam* ("the exterior"; kings and war) poems celebrate the valor and virtue of her royal patrons, but distinguish themselves by also seeking to establish virtues such as generosity and hospitality as part of the Tamil cultural norm:

> Whether town or forest
> Whether lowland or hill,
> In whatever way people are good
> The earth is good.
> Long may it prosper. (*Puṟ.* 187; trans. Annamalai & Schiffman, 1968, 14)

The internal evidence of her poems also reveals that Avvaiyār served in the Takatur court during the reign of Atikamāṉ Neṭumāṉ Añci (c. 1st–2nd cents. CE), "whose lands are thought to have been in Mysore round about Kolar" (Thompson, 1948, 401). In the *Puṟanāṉūṟu*, Auvaiyār mentions the medicinal myrobalan fruit (Tam. *nelli*; Skt. *amalā*; bot. Emblica officinalis) presented to her by her patron, King Neṭumāṉ Añci. As this fruit has widely been venerated in South India for its properties of conferring longevity, this passage is often invoked to explain why works ascribed to Avvaiyār appear over a span of several centuries.

> King in the line of Atiyaṉs!
> You who pour out the toddy that makes men roar!
> You whose powerful hand with its sliding bracelets
> triumphs and brandishes an infallible sword that brings you victory,
> cutting your enemies down on the field!
> Añci of the golden garland, rich in murderous battle!
> May you live as long as he lives on whose head the crescent moon glows,
> whose neck is as dark blue as sapphires!
> O greatness!
> Without considering how difficult it is to obtain the sweet fruit of the myrobalan plant with its tiny leaves,
> which has to be plucked from a crevice on the summit of an ancient mountain hard to climb,
> you kept silence in your heart about its powers,
> and so that you might rescue me from death,
> you gave me that fruit! (*Puṟ*. 91; trans. Hart, 1999, 65)

As noted above, in spite of the royal support she received, her poverty was also legendary, even alluded to in the poem cited above. An apocryphal tale is told of a time when a dancing girl named Cilampi gave the great poet Kampaṉ – author of the Tamil → *Rāmāyaṇa*, the *Irāmāvatāram* – five hundred gold coins to compose a poem about her. But for such a poetic luminary, he felt this pathetic sum only warranted a simple two-line couplet. Poor Cilampi was very disappointed. Seeing how distraught she was, Avvaiyār extended those two lines into a magnificent stanza and asked only for a meager cup of rice gruel (*kūḻ*) as payment. This is how she came to be known by the epithet Kūḻukkuppāti ("She Who Sang for Gruel"; Ramaswami, 1992, 145).

The second Avvaiyār – an author of the 9th–10th centuries – is most widely known, her enduring appeal cemented in the easy and accessible collections of proverbs and ethical maxims attributed to her. These works include the famous *Ātticūṭi, Mūturai, Nalvaḻi*, and the *Koṉṟaivēntaṉ*. Because most of these compositions proffer a straightforward and commonsense wisdom, memorization of these didactic maxims was a mainstay in the beginning years of formal education for Tamil children in the *tiṇṇai* or verandah schools before 1800, and they were carried over into the modern Tamil curriculum. Avvaiyār's sayings were understood as having a moral–pedagogic function, teaching children about not only virtue, but also how to embody it (Raman, 2010, 44). While some of Avvaiyār's maxims in the *Ātticūṭi* and *Koṉṟaivēntaṉ* are direct and simple – "Respect Learning" or "Desire to Act Virtuously" – others are more profound and invite deeper reflection. Among these, one was featured by NASA in its Cosmic Question Exhibit, which began touring museums throughout the United States in February 2003:

> What we have learned
> Is like a handful of earth;
> What we have yet to learn
> Is like the whole world.

The third Avvaiyār probably lived sometime between the 12th and 14th centuries. Her compositions of this period are linked in style and content to the songs and writings of the Tamil *cittar*s, an antinomian band of *yogī*-alchemists (for *cittar*s, see → Tamil Nadu). Such works employ apophatic language to stake out a blending of → Tantra with a nondual (Advaita → Vedānta) philosophical position. Of the several works attributed to this third Avvaiyār, the *Vināyakarakaval*, a short hymn to Vināyakaṉ (i.e. → Gaṇapati/Gaṇeśa) in the *akaval* meter, is very well known and despite its esoteric content is often memorized and recited by Tamil devotees.

> He has concentrated my mind,
> Clarified my intellect, and said,
> "Light & Darkness
> share a common place."
> He presses me down
> into the grace giving ecstasy.
> In my ear he renders limitless bliss. (Little, 2012)

The *Avvaikkuṟaḷ* (Avvai's Couplets) is another of Avvaiyār's important *cittar*-style works. It comprises 310 couplets on yogic cosmology and philosophy, and an ideological continuity can be easily discerned between the *Vināyakarakaval* and the *Avvaikkuṟaḷ*. Stylistically, however, the *Avvaikkuṟaḷ* differs quite significantly from the *Vināyakarakaval*, perhaps gesturing toward another Avvaiyār who might have been active at the same time. A couple of samples from the *Avvaikkuṟaḷ* will suffice to indicate the points of continuity and departure between these two works:

Except by the body, there can be no realization at all.
It is a state that is mediated by the body.

When the stainless outlook is attained by the mind,
The body reveals god. (*AvvKu.* 15, 16; trans. by author)

Though the lives of these many Avvaiyārs are spread over the space of more than a millennium, in Tamil memory they have been conflated into a single figure. This Avvaiyār of popular imagination has come to embody Tamil culture itself. But beyond her role as a benevolent matriarch, she is also understood to be an enlightened ascetic and adept *yoginī*. In contemporary Tamil imagination, Avvaiyār looms large as the archetypal wise old woman. Grey haired, dressed in white, and bent upon her staff, she is imagined to have lived for centuries, and she wanders in and out of Tamil folktales. Sometimes deified in folk memory, Avvaiyār is said to be forever seated in the crescent moon spooling out an endless thread of white cotton from her spinning wheel (Kandaswamy, 2004, 127).

Auvaiyār is also worshipped in a more formal context as the embodiment of Tamil culture and identity. The Tamil Nadu government sponsors an annual festival at her most famous shrine in Thulasiyappattinam village (near Vedaranyam, Nagappattinam district) during the month of *paṅkuṉi* (Mar–Apr). Here, Avvaiyār is worshipped as the female counterpart to Tiruvaḷḷuvar, the author of the famous *Tirukkuṟaḷ*, who in several Tamil myths is regarded as her brother. During the annual festival, contributions to Tamil culture are celebrated as scholars present lectures on Avvaiyār at her shrine within the Aruḷmiku Viśvanāthasvāmi Tirukkōvil complex.

While it is Avvaiyār's folkloric persona that unites these various literary figures, tropes of other South Indian female saints are also echoed in the mythic tales associated her, particularly in her rejection of marriage and domesticity. In one famous story, as the young Avvaiyār approached marriageable age, she is said to have rejected domestic bliss. Instead, she prayed to Gaṇeśa to transform her youthful form into that of a crone, a wish that was promptly granted. In this aspect, her hagiography echoes that of the famous 6th-century Tamil Śaiva poet, Kāraikkālammaiyār.

In another well-known story, Avvaiyār becomes a symbol for the inevitable false pride that fame ushers in, a pride that ought to be quickly squelched. As Avvaiyār had gained great renown during her own lifetime as a wise wandering poet, she was full of self-importance. So a mischievous boy played a trick that reminded her of the limits of her insight. One day, as she was wandering through the forest, she noticed a hunter boy seated on the bough of a *jampunāval* tree (rose apple; bot. Syzygium jambos). Hungry, she asked the boy if he might pick her a *jampu* fruit. He asked her if she wanted a hot *jampu* or a cold *jampu*. Perplexed, she flippantly replied, "Give me a hot fruit." The boy shook the bough, and several *jampu* fruits fell down onto the sandy ground below. She picked one up and began to blow the dirt off so she could eat it. Flashing a wry smile, the boy asked her if the *jampu* was too hot to eat. Thinking, "What a clever trick!" she suddenly realized it was the god → Murukaṉ in disguise. Having thus "cooled" her pride, he appeared before her in his true form and blessed her. Her shrine in Thulasiyappattinam is said to mark the site of this encounter.

The 1953 film *Avvaiyar*, starring K.B. Sundarambal (1908–1980), has done much to anchor popular constructions of Avvaiyār (see also → Tamil cinema). The opening song of the film is a lullaby to the adopted infant Avvaiyār and situates her place and function within the wider narrative.

Hush! Sweet baby, hush.
Hush heiress to the Tamil race.
A gift of the penance of yore!
The world is blessed to have you.
A treasure I came across,
O Queen of Art,
as a fragrant breeze was blowing,
and we were bathing in the river.
To Tamil Nadu you chose to come
Ah! My Queen of Speech!
To glorify Tamil to the world,
you came to a *pāṇaṉ's* house.
Sweet little parrot of mine,
you sleep, my gift divine.

But even with a sweet lullaby that invokes her destiny to embody Tamil, the baby cries and reaches out, only placated when she is allowed to embrace a nearby icon of Gaṇeśa. One of the ladies in attendance then exclaims in surprise that since the child has such wisdom, she should be called "Avvai."

Clearly, this Tamil film subsumes her role as a literary figure into that of a religious one, by emphasizing her place in countless sacred narratives. Oftentimes, the film insinuates her into scenes that she traditionally had not occupied, with a special emphasis placed on her relationship with Murukaṉ, the quintessentially Tamil deity. Along with tales such as the "hot fruit" story recounted above, the film also includes an adaption of the myth of Murukaṉ and Gaṇeśa's race around the world to win the "fruit of wisdom" (*jñānapaḻam*). This well-known tale relates how the trickster sage Nārada gave → Śiva and Umā a magical fruit that conferred supreme knowledge. Both their sons, Murukaṉ and Gaṇeśa, clamored to eat the sweet fruit. Since supreme knowledge cannot be divided, their divine parents proposed a race around the world to see who might win the fruit. While Murukaṉ quickly flew off on his peacock, Gaṇeśa won by a clever ruse of his own: he circumambulated Śiva and Umā (who embody all the world) and was awarded the fruit. When Murukaṉ returned, he was distraught at Gaṇeśa's victory. Abandoning the world, he ran away to become *a yogī*. It is then that Avvaiyār arrived to comfort him, singing, "*paḻam nī appā!*" (you are the fruit, my lad!), asserting that he, who is the very embodiment of knowledge, need not seek it outside of himself. This, of course, provides a folk etymology for the famous hilltop shrine of Palani (*paḻam* + *nī*), one of the six most important pilgrimage sites of Murukaṉ in Tamil country.

The earliest version of the race between Gaṇeśa and Murukaṉ appears in the *Śivapurāṇa* (2.4.19.4–66; 2.4.20.1–37), and it differs fundamentally from the account given in the 1953 film. In the *Śivapurāṇa* the sibling gods race to win brides, and the defeated Skanda (Murukaṉ) flees to Mount Krauñca to live eternally as a bachelor. However, the *Paḻaṉittalapurāṇam* (13.27–73), composed in 1628 by Pālasuprahmaṇiyar Kavirāyar, introduces the motif of the fruit of knowledge, but makes no mention of Avvaiyār. Instead, it concludes with Śiva himself offering the words that placate Murukaṉ and that bestow a name of Palani upon his hilltop abode:

> ... Śiva became lonesome for his son, so he went there with Umā. She said to Murukaṉ. "Come back to us dear son, and drink milk from my breasts," and Śiva said, "You who are eternally a child and yet a man, is a pomegranate a fruit? *You* are the fruit (*paḻa'nī*)!" Murukaṉ bowed to his father, and Śiva agreed to his wish that they dwell together at that place, which has ever since been known as Paḻaṉi. (Shulman, 1980, 84–85)

Thus, without a textual precedent, it is possible that the 1953 Tamil film about Avvaiyār introduced her into this famous myth, a presence that became so common that the 1965 Tamil film *Tiruviḷaiyāṭal*, about the marvelous deeds of Śiva, opens with the confrontation about the fruit of knowledge and Avvaiyār's (played ably once again by K.P. Sundarambal) attempts to soothe the offended Murukaṉ.

From the available evidence, it appears that most of the stories associated with Avvaiyār are apocryphal oral tales culled together in the last two to three centuries. Nevertheless, there is one early textual source that must have contributed to galvanizing the formation of her folkloric persona. The *Kapilarakaval*, dating back to at least the first half of the 10th century (Kandaswamy, 2004, 125), builds a fantastic family of literary saints, making Vaḷḷuvar, Atikamāṉ, Kapilar, and Avvaiyār siblings (along with three other sisters). In this text, these four great Tamil poets were the offspring of a sagely Brahman father and a mother of the low Pulaiya caste. In his introduction to the *Kapilarakaval*, G.U. Pope (1820–1909) characterizes it as a "wild and utterly incredible tradition" (Zvelebil, 1975, 124n80). But oddly the *Jñāṉāmirutam*, a 12th-century → Śaiva Siddhānta work, also makes reference to a similar pair of star-crossed lovers who sire a family of seven children all destined for literary greatness. Here the children go unnamed, but one commentator lists the siblings in accordance with those found in the *Kapilarakaval*.

The filial link between Avvaiyār and Vaḷḷuvar brought her to the forefront of missionary and colonial discussions on Tamil literary and cultural history in the 19th century. From the several versions of the story circulating in the 19th century, S. Blackburn constructs the following composite version:

> A Brahmin, named Bhagavan, travelled on pilgrimage when he stopped in a choultry to rest and met a Paraiyar woman, named Adi. Because she, a low-caste woman, approached him, he beat her with a metal ladle and cut her head. Having driven her away, Bhagavan continued on to Benares, where he performed certain rituals and then he returned home on the same route. Adi had grown into a beautiful

woman and seeing her but not recognizing her, the Brahmin fell madly in love with her. Their marriage was soon arranged, but as the bridegroom poured fragrant oil on his bride's head he noticed the healed wound and asked if she were the woman he had attacked. When she said yes, he fled, and she followed.

Eventually finding him, she asked that he accept her as his wife and he agreed on one condition: that they abandon whatever children she might bear. She accepted this, and during their travelling, seven children were born: four girls and three boys.

The first girl was Auvaiyar, the legendary author of ethical writings [and nearly as famous as Vaḷḷuvar]; the second girl became the Tamil goddess Mariamma; the third became the goddess Bhadra-kali and the forth the Tamil goddess Valliyamma [later wed to Murukaṉ]. The first-born son became a poet patronized by a Chera king; the second was Kapilar [another popular poet and author of the *Kapilarakaval*]; the third and final son, the youngest of seven children, was Valluvar. (Blackburn, 2000, 460)

S. Blackburn's in-depth study of the Vaḷḷuvar legend notes how the interpretation of Vaḷḷuvar's mixed-caste origins at this time yielded increasingly elaborate discussion and speculation on Tamil literary history and culture. For instance, the missionary Charles Gover in an 1871 work read the mixed-caste marriage and the couple's seven children, of whom Avvaiyār was the oldest and Vaḷḷuvar was the youngest, as encapsulating Tamil literary history:

> Unlike his European predecessors, who used the legend to understand past history, Gover presented the Valluvar legend as evidence of a moral trajectory in Tamil literary history which informed the present; later tellings… simply followed suit. (Blackburn, 2000, 459)

More recent narrative traditions continue to invoke and expand on Avvaiyār's role as the wise matriarch of Tamil culture, in printed works such as *Auvaiyār Vāḻvum Vākkum* (Veluppillai, 2002) or in theatrical performances. Increasingly, Avvaiyār has become a popular subject for modern female empowerment and has been featured in many *bharatanāṭyam* → dance dramas, such as Kala Pradarshini's 2011 production, *Penmai Chudar* (Light of Womanhood), which offered a review of various female cultural luminaries including Avvaiyār, and Narthaki Nataraj's performance as Avvaiyār in *Sutta Pazham* (Hot Fruit), premiering in Chennai in December 2011 at the Natyadarsan conference on "Mad and Divine Women."

Bibliography

Annamalai, E., & H. Schiffman, "Twelve Caṅkam Poems," *Mahfil* 4/3, 1968, 13–20.

Blackburn, S., "Corruption and Redemption: The Legend of Valluvar and Tamil Literary History," *MAS* 34/2, 2000, 449–482.

Cevalkuḷam Acca Pulavar A.S. Kurucāmi, *Auvaiyāriṉ Aṟanūlkaḷ*, Chennai, 2010 (Tam.).

Ceṭṭiyār, T.T., *Avvaiyāriṉ Viṉāyakar Akavalum Kuṇṭaliṉi Yōkamum*, Chennai, 2009 (Tam.).

"Cosmic Question Exhibit," http://www.nasa.gov/audience/foreducators/informal/features/F_Cosmic_Questions_prt.htm (accessed Aug 2012).

Hart, G.L., *The Four Hundred Songs of War and Wisdom*, New York, 1999.

Kandaswamy, S.N., *The Yoga of Siddha Avvai*, Quebec, 2004.

Little, L.R., "Vināyakarakavaḷ," http://www.alchemywebsite.com/vinayaga.html (accessed August 2012).

Little, L.R. *Avaiyar's Vinayagar Agaval*, http://www.alchemywebsite.com/vinayaga.html, 1995.

Rajagopalachari, C., *Auvaiyār: A Great Tamil Poetess*, Bombay, 1971.

Raman, B., "Disciplining the Senses, Schooling the Mind: Inhabiting Virtue in the Tamil Tinnai Schools," in: A. Pandian & D. Ali, eds., *Ethical Life in South Asia*, Bloomington, 2010, 43–60.

Ramaswamy, V., "Rebels–Conformists? Women Saints in Medieval South India," *Anthropos* 87, 1/3, 1992, 133–146.

Shulman, D., *Tamil Temple Myths: Sacrifice and Divine Marriage in the South Indian Śaiva Tradition*, Princeton, 1980.

Thompson, M.S.H., "The Avvai of the Caṅkam Anthologies," *BSOAS* 12/2, London, 1948, 399–402.

Veluppillai, N.M., *Auvaiyār Vāḻvum Vākkum*, Chennai, 2002 (Tam.).

Zvelebil, K., *Tamil Literature*, Leiden, 1975.

LAYNE R. LITTLE

Basava

Basava (or Basavēśvara or Basavaṇṇa) is the purported founder of the → Liṅgāyat (or Vīraśaiva) religious movement. His most likely dates are 1105–1167 CE, though some argue for 1134–1196 CE. As with most founders, there are both traditional versions of his life and challenges to the very claim that he, rather than a group of mystical teachers (*ācāryas*), founded the movement. Those traditional views, even if verified in broad scope, are challenged in their details by historical and epigraphical evidence. Certainly his person, both traditional and historical, has played an important role for Liṅgāyats both as exemplar of proper piety and as model of thoroughly modern devotion. Beneath those perspectives has consistently run the energetic devotion and popular appeal of his religious verses (*vacanas*), which reflect a vital devotion to Lord → Śiva, a sincerely reformatory social and political consciousness, and a popular, if sometimes whimsical, poetic beauty.

Basava through His *Vacanas*

Collections and editions of Basava's *vacanas* began to appear shortly after his death and flourish today in contemporary devotional and didactic books, pamphlets, audio recordings, movies, Web sites, and even comic books. Basava's *vacanas* reflect several themes:

- a simple and sincere individual piety;
- a persistent social conscience marked by a generous empathy for the lowly and socially despised, including women;
- an insistence on personal and social morality as the mark of a truly devoted person;
- a secularized devotionalism expressed in mundane activity and occupation;
- an impatience with the forms and rituals of established religion;
- a disdain for the undeserved privileges of a hereditary priestly group – the Brahmans; and, overarching it all,
- an ardent, almost fanatical, devotion to the one true lord and singular god worthy of adoration – that is, Lord Śiva.

Basava's Sincere Simplicity

The sincerity of Basava's devotion is reflected in the ways he invoked the tenderest human emotions as a pathway to the lord's presence. Touchingly in a celebrated *vacana*, Basava utilized the image of a mother's quick and reflexive protection of her child as analogy for the lord's immediacy in the life of the devotee.

> As a mother runs
> close behind her child
> with his hand on a cobra
> or a fire, the lord of the meeting rivers
> stays with me every step of the way
> and looks after me. (*Vacana* 1146; trans. Ramanujan, 1973, 71)

Again the tenderness of the image and the totality of the loving, protecting response make a profound devotional point in the simplest and most direct of ways.

Basava's Social Conscience

The intimacy and tenderness of these images leads to another of Basava's characteristics – his concern for the socially low and oppressed. He was particularly concerned with the innate human predilection for wealth and status. For example, in one story, a thief had broken into his home and was stealing some jewelry when apprehended by Basava's wife. She latched onto the thief's arm and would not let go. Basava, however, instructed her that such attachment to wealth was unbecoming a devotee, bade her release the poor fellow, and warned that this event might well be a spiritual test staged by Śiva himself.

> ...If into my unworthy house a thief come by stealth
> It may be none other than the lord himself
> Our Lord of the Meeting Rivers (*Vacana* 1133; trans. by author)

The preference for piety over wealth runs throughout Basava's poetic corpus. However, it is important not to perceive Basava as essentially a revolutionary economic reformer. His concern was that persons of all castes and ranks were to be measured, not by the size of their purses, nor the lineage of their births, but by the depth of their devotion. Certainly caste birth was not the primary determinant of spiritual worth (see Yaravintelimath, 1987).

Vyāsa was a fisher's son;
Durvāsa was a cobbler's;
And Maṇḍōdari was the daughter of a frog! ...
Don't look to caste; for caste was cast by the past...
Look to our Lord Kūḍala Saṅgama's charge:
"The only one well-born is the one to Śiva sworn." (*Vacana* 588; trans. by author)

Similarly Liṅgāyats strove to remove most of the gender restrictions of Brahmanical Hinduism (see Yaravintelimath, 2006), as they insisted on the full participation of women in the devotional life of spiritual attainment. For example, Basava praised Mahādēviyakka (or → Akkamahādevi) in the presence of the assembled *śaraṇa*s (saintly devotees) at Kalyana.

Ye saints! See the body of a woman;
See the form unsoiled!
Forgetting her self in chaste piety, she is utterly unspoiled!
Her body rests comfortably upon her now,
firm in her sacred vow.
That's our Mahādēviyakka, O Kūḍala Saṅgamadēvā! (*Vacana* 1285; *ŚSaṃp.* 16.48; trans. by author)

Overlooking the physical form of the devotee, in this case the comely form of a young nude, Basava called the *śaraṇa*s' attention to the depth of her piety and the resoluteness of her devotion. Caste as well as gender distinctions, in Basava's *vacana*s, were replaced by ardent devotion and simple worship of Lord Śiva.

In a slightly edgier tone, Basava chided those incorrigibly possessed by the spirit of wealth.

But those possessed by the love of wealth
Never whisper a prayer until that very moment
When the motivator named Poverty grabs them!
O Lord Kūḍala Saṅgamadēvā. (*Vacana* 132; trans. by author)

In this *vacana* as in others, Basava clearly was less interested in questions of distribution of wealth than in cultivation of devotion and piety. The order of society needed inversion as an impetus for conversion, but not solely for reasons of economic reform.

Basava's Moral Conscience

The appeal of Basava's religious movement was to a broad spectrum of society. Many sought help with practical matters of how to live a mundane life with integrity and compassion. For those, Basava provided simple guidance and reinforcement of achievable moral virtues.

Don't steal, don't kill, and don't lie.
Don't be angry and don't be scornful;
Don't glorify yourself and don't find fault in others.
This is your inner goodness and your outer holiness;
This is the path to our Lord Kūḍala Saṅgama! (*Vacana* 235; trans. by author)

This *vacana* reflects the practical, everyday morality expected from a socially diverse group without resorting to sophisticated philosophizing. Another *vacana* emphasizes positive characteristics by praising the virtue of compassion.

What kind of religion can be
Without compassion demonstrated?
Compassion always needs to be
Towards all beings animated;
Compassion is the root
Of all religious truth:
Saṅgama cares naught
For faith not thus wrought. (*Vacana* 247; trans. by author)

The straightforward simplicity of Basava and his movement demanded simple, everyday morality – eschewing of vices and enhancing of virtues. Complex it was not; though compelling it could be.

Basava's Ethic of Secular Work as Devotion

Basava's disdain for the abusive privilege of the Brahman class was clear; but there was also, in his musings, a more constructive response to caste ascriptions of occupation. He came to value honest work in a worldly occupation – not as a distraction from devotion but as a form of devotional enhancement, a form of prayerful worship in mundane activity.

Show me the feet of an ardent devotee,
though he be a farmer,
who takes delight in serving his guests
with the wages of his labor...
For, his body is clean
and pure is his mind;

his conduct is spotless;
his speech divine...
I have faith abundant in such a man.
O Lord of the Meeting Rivers. (*VacŚāSā*. 1.2.18; cited by Sadasivaiah, 1967, 51; trans. by author)

It is precisely this celebration of mundane occupation performed in devotion to the lord that has often gained attention for Basava's movement in Western sociological scholarship (Michael, 1982, 1990). Perhaps the most famous and most succinct statement of the principle is identification of worldly work with heaven itself as it appears in another of Basava's somewhat whimsical poems.

When the devotee snores, he's chanting a prayer;
When he sits awake, that's the holy watch night;
Where the devotee walks, that's a holy site;
When the devotee works, that is heaven itself [*kāyakavē kailāsa*]!
O Lord of the Meeting Rivers. (*Vacana* 872; trans. by author)

Thus Basava not only contemns the empty ritualism and hypocritical purity of the traditional caste system and its Brahman elite but also positively evaluates mundane occupations even by "unclean" castes when that work emanates from a heart purely devoted to the lord.

Basava's Antiritualism

The most distinctive and creative aspects of Basava's *vacana*s are reserved for his disdain of religion as usual. He openly, repeatedly, and sometimes humorously mocked the rituals of Brahmanical Hindu practice, which he saw as empty forms devoid of devotional ardor. Comparing the bowing, the hand folding, and the recitations of Brahmanical ritual to ordinary objects of experience, Basava longed for an inner ardor, a pious passion, from those who followed his path of devotion to Lord Śiva.

See-saw watermills bow their heads.
So what?
Do they get to be devotees to the Master?
The tongs join hands.
So what?
Can they be humble in service to the Lord?
Parrots recite.
So what?
Can they read the Lord?
How can the slaves of the Bodiless God,
Desire [Kāma],
know the way
our Lord's Men move
or the stance of their standing?
(*Vacana* 125; trans. Ramanujan, 1973, 76)

The whimsy of the images is testimony to Basava's creativity; but the point of the poem cannot be mistaken. Empty ritual based on formal motions is no substitute for true worship based on pure devotion. With a similar humor and a bit more pathos, Basava empathized with a lamb marked for the sacrificial offering.

The lamb vowed for celebrations
ate leaves used for the decorations.
Not suspecting the coming kill,
only its belly, it sought to fill.
Born that day, he'd die that day.
But tell me:
Did the slayers live?
O Kūḍala Saṅgama Dēvā. (*Vacana* 129; trans. by author)

The humor of the lamb eating the sacred decorations on the altar reflects Basava's insistence on inner devotional piety rather than external ritual performance; but his disdain for the insincerity and hypocrisy of the ritual specialists – in this case animal sacrificers – is not always tempered by similar humor. His disdain for Brahmans was undisguised.

Basava's Anti-Brahmanism

Tradition says that Basava was born to pious Brahman parents but revolted at the ceremonialism they attempted to instill in him. Specifically, he is said, in his eighth year, to have refused investiture (*upanayana*) with the sacred thread (see → *yajñopavīta*). Thereafter, his attacks on Brahmanical ritualism and caste privilege were frequent and fervent. For example, he mocked those who performed the fire ritual to the fire god but showed no respect when threatened by a house fire.

Where they worship fire, in a Brahman's house,
they'll offer fine things, (honey) and butter,
when the fire breaks out, they'll be quick to douse,
with street dust and water from the gutter.
Then they'll yell the name
Kūḍala to blame. (*Vacana* 584; trans. by

author)

For Basava, Brahmans were hypocritical functionaries who only performed their rituals in order to receive emolument but with no true sense of devotion. He further attacked Brahmans for exploiting their literacy to read empty and meaningless words in formal but foolish ceremony.

> ... What, then, the usefulness of caste?
> If you're a blacksmith, you heat;
> if you're a washerman, you beat;
> if you're a weaver, you throw woofs;
> if you're a Brahman, you read books!
> Is anyone saved just by words they hear?
> O Kūḍala Saṅgama, Dear,
> But truly well-born is he,
> who knows true divinity! (*Vacana* 589; trans. by author)

Again Basava's words reflect his rejection of caste privilege and his insistence that whatever duty one performs can be a holy one if done with true devotion to the lord. The lowest place in the caste hierarchy, he thought, should be reserved for those who reap its privileges without evidencing true devotion. Those, in his view, were the Brahmans.

In one of his *vacana*s, he cited a popular saying that well summarized this perspective:

> The Brahmin is an ass,
> toting the Vedas as his load. (*Vacana* 586; trans. by author)

Basava's Ardent Śaivism

It should come as no surprise that Basava and his followers demonstrated an intense devotion to Lord Śiva. After all, their very name Vīraśaiva means "ardent Śaiva" or "heroic Śaiva." What bears special note, however, is that this ardent Śaivism was not only a devotional intensification but also an explicit rejection of other forms of divinity and of other "Hindu" sects. This exclusivist particularism appears in several of Basava's *vacana*s, but his position is best summarized in one of them where he cautioned that worshipping other gods is like inviting a cur into one's home – a cur that then bites the master and brings the collapse of that home.

> ... Housed in the inner shrine
> Of the world's lord, they say
> That other gods there be:
> O Kūḍala Saṅgama Lord,
> It is like a thievish dog
> You have brought home and tamed, and now
> Barks at his master! (*Vacana* 564; trans. Menezes & Angadi, 1967, 183)

In this *vacana*, Basava left little doubt about the exclusive nature of his and his followers' devotion to Lord Śiva alone; clearly he was promoting not simply ardent but exclusive devotion to Lord Śiva. Elsewhere, employing somewhat more whimsical images, he again made the point.

> God, gods; there are so many gods,
> there's no place to put down a foot.
> The only god is our God, Lord Kūḍala Saṅgama
> Dēvā! (*Vacana* 561; trans. by author)

Gently, firmly, humorously, but uncompromisingly, Basava urged devotion to the one god – Śiva in his manifestation as Lord Kūḍala Saṅgama.

Throughout the corpus of Basava's poesy, the themes that define and distinguish the Liṅgāyat movement throughout its history emerge with clarity and force. Undergirded by a deep devotional piety, Liṅgāyat tradition follows Basava in his spurning of elaborate ritualism, of hieratic elitism, and of hereditary classism. In turn, his musings and his example inspire a vital morality, an intense social equality, and a secularized sense of holy work. Not surprisingly, these characteristics of the *vacana*s find origin, justification, and perpetuation based on the traditional life story of Basava.

Basava's Biography

Basava in the *Basavapurāṇa*

The personality and teachings of Basava, the author of these *vacana*s, have their roots in his life story. In his 13th-century Telugu language composition, the *Basavapurāṇamu*, Pālkurike Somanātha relates those pious traditions (see *Basavapurāṇamu*, 1952; Brown, 1840, 273–290; Narayana Rao, 1990, 41–266; Würth, 1865, 66–97).

In the *Basavapurāṇa*, Basava's birth and life are divinely initiated. Informed of the dearth of true devotion on earth, Lord Śiva dispatches his alter ego Nandi. Entering the womb of the pious Brahman lady Mādalāmbā, performing yogic feats there, and taking birth as Basava, he is immediately invested with *liṅga mantra* during a visitation by Kūḍalasaṅgama Śiva. In his eighth year, while being prepared by his father Mādirāja for Brahmanical initiation, Basava rebels, refuses the investiture, and contemns his father's formalism with the words

> How can you speak of brahminism and devotion in the same breath!
> Brahminism is a completely separate teaching.
> It has a different god and different mantra...
> The tradition and the path are both different. (Narayana Rao, 1990, 57)

Then, accompanied by his sister, Nāgamma, Basava leaves home and goes to Kappaḍi Kūḍala Saṅgama, at the confluence of the Kṛṣṇā and Malaprabhā Rivers. There his sincere devotion to Saṅgamēśvara Śiva attracts the attention of his maternal uncle Baladēva, advisor to King Bijjaḷa of Kalyana. Baladēva weds his daughter, Gaṅgādēvi, to Basava and invites his son-in-law to take a position, purportedly commander in chief but probably treasurer, in the king's administration.

At Kalyana, Basava establishes a haven, the Anubhava Maṇṭapa, and a hostel, the Mahāmane, for the growing contingent of non-Brahmanical devotees of Lord Śiva. His own nephew Cennabasava, the renowned mystic Allama Prabhu, the accomplished *yogī* Siddharāmayya, and a host of other Śaiva devotees (*śaraṇa*s) accept his hospitality. Numerous miracles attest to Basava's piety, as when all sorts of mundane objects – an eggplant, a cup, even goat droppings – are transformed into → *liṅga*s for the worship of the lord.

The *Basavapurāṇa* continues with a series of miraculous events and parables. For example, Basava gives all the king's treasury to the *śaraṇa*s and is accused of embezzlement, but opens the coffers to reveal that they are still miraculously brim full. Basava gives his wife's saree to a needy *śaraṇa*, but miraculously, *à la* → Draupadī, the saree's length multiplies, and his wife remains clothed. And, with typical whimsy, a devotee seeing Śiva Naṭarāja in his frantic dance surmises that he must have rheumatism, makes offerings to seek a cure for him, and therefrom receives divine blessing. A number of other stories follow, all of which stress Basava's role in helping the *śaraṇa*s affirm that devotion confers extraordinary powers but that pride is a dangerous thing. Even Basava himself is briefly chided for the pride he takes in his *vacana* compositions.

Some of the characters in these stories also figure prominently in the *Śūnyasaṃpādane* – for example, Maḍivāḷa Mācayya and Mōḷigeya Mārayya; others are of figures rather obscure elsewhere in Vīraśaiva tradition. Most are reflective of themes found elsewhere in Śaiva literature – specifically among the sixty-three → Nāyaṉārs.

In *Basavapurāṇa*, the Vīraśaiva *śaraṇa*s constantly conflict with followers of other religious paths. Ekānta Rāmayya is particularly vigilant against Buddhists and Jains, besting them in debate and in miracles. He destroys all Jaina temples and wins the utter capitulation of the Jains to Śiva's superiority. The story of Ṣōḍḍaladeva Bācayya patently demonstrates the particularist bent of Basava's movement. As keeper of King Bijjaḷa's granaries, Ṣōḍḍaladeva closes them to all non-Śaivas – all Jains, Vaiṣṇavas, Advaitas, and so on. In a countermove, the king builds a Vaiṣṇava temple and orders all to worship there. Ṣōḍḍaladeva refuses, challenges Bijjaḷa to a debate, and successfully argues sole devotion to Śiva against all cultic pretenders – Viṣṇu, Brahmā, Veda, Nārāyaṇa, Agni, Vāyu, Sūrya, Candra, Kāma, and so on.

The final struggle depicted in *Basavapurāṇa* is the triumph of the Vīraśaiva *śaraṇa*s over the Brahmans at Kalyana. When Brahmans complain to the king about the increase of untouchables around Kalyana, Basava has an untouchable borne upon a palanquin right into the king's very court. When a low-caste maidservant is accidently brushed by a Brahman's touch, she must take a purificatory bath to remove that taint. And, again somewhat whimsically, a low-caste *śaraṇa* teaches his dog to howl in perfect imitation of Brahmans chanting the Veda.

The climax of these conflicts comes when Basava's father-in-law, *à la* Dakṣa, celebrates a ritual feast and feeds the Brahman guests before feeding Basava and the *śaraṇa*s. In order to atone the affront, the father-in-law agrees to slay a traitor on Basava's behest should the occasion arise, which, of course, it does in short order. King Bijjaḷa has two of the *śaraṇa*s blinded for a caste offense; Basava calls due his father-in-law's promise, the king is assassinated, and Basava and his band flee Kalyana and take refuge in meditating on the *liṅga* at Kūḍala Saṅgama.

There, Basava seeks ultimate union with Kūḍala Saṅgama Śiva, pleading, "You are supreme bliss! You are the ecstatic being! Let my mind, words, body, actions, and consciousness rest in you. For I have done everything that you have commanded me to do." Then in rapt meditation, Basava became absorbed by the *liṅga* itself, and "flowers rained upon the earth... And while victory cries rang out, the devotees danced" (Narayana Rao, 1990, 265).

Throughout these episodes, one theme must not be overlooked – the violent nature of some of the encounters. While later Vīraśaivism may have evolved into a relatively peaceful and largely agrarian tradition, the *śaraṇa*s of the *Basavapurāṇa* certainly deserved the appellation *vīra* (heroic, mighty, powerful, strong, robust, brave, warlike). For example, Maḍivāḷa Mācayya killed a man who accidently touched his load of recently laundered clothing, and he also killed the king's elephant sent against him. Kinnara Brahmayya killed a man in a dispute over a sheep. Ḍohara Kakkayya killed a Brahman singer for reciting Vaiṣṇava rather than Śaiva stories. And, of course, at Basava's instigation, his father-in-law assassinated King Bijjaḷa. Living at the royal capital and intensely dedicated to ardent worship of Śiva alone, they were constantly engaged in intrigue and were not reluctant to use violence to protect their ardently Śaiva band (Narayana Rao, 1990, 131–134, 173, 243, 264).

The image of Basava presented in puranic works accords well with the content of his poetic compositions. Though a bit more dramatic and perhaps a bit more chauvinistic than the *vacana* image, these accounts reflect a sincere, compassionate reformist, dedicated to defending both devotion to and devotees of his lord, Śiva.

Basava in Inscriptions

Basavapurāṇa provides a portrait of Basava's life that informs, by precept and example, the religious life of the devotional community (see Desai, 1968, 163). But as history, such material is suspect, not the least because of its supernatural components. Yet two Jain Purāṇas – the *Bijjaḷarāyacarite* and *Bijjaḷarāyapurāṇa* – serve to confirm the general patterns of Basava's life and activities. Of course, by portraying Basava as a vile and manipulative menace to their version of true piety, they give a very different interpretation of his motives and effects (Desai, 1968, 128). The Jain sources still reflect a great deal of literary license and probably date from a period later than the Vīraśaiva texts themselves; but they generally affirm the *Basavapurāṇa*'s account of events. Unfortunately, firmer evidence – epigraphical evidence – is hard to interpret, sometimes difficult to date in itself, and, in this case, rather sparse.

There are no known contemporaneous inscriptions that mention Basava and link him with Bijjaḷa or Kalyana. But over a half dozen epigraphs datable to the 13th century do refer to a Basava in connection with the northern Karnataka region. One, of 1251 CE, refers to Karasthaḷa Basavideva. "Karasthaḷa" could be a place name (near Hampi) but could also refer to the Liṅgāyat practice of meditating upon the personalized *liṅga* (*iṣṭaliṅga*) in the palm of the hand (*karasthaḷa*). It is further utilized as a proper name for one order of Vīraśaiva ascetics (*jaṅgama*s). The famous Arjunwad Inscription of 1260 CE not only refers to Saṅgana Basava but also praises devotion (*bhakti*) to *jaṅgama* and to *liṅga* – both crucial components of Vīraśaiva piety (Desai, 1968, 3, 132–133, plates 22, 23). Two inscriptions of about 1262 CE reference Saṅgana Basava, associate him with worship of *jaṅgama* and *liṅga*, and explicitly portray him as a manifestation of Nandi, son of Saṅgamēśvara. In two further inscriptions of about 1280 CE, Saṅgana Basavayya and Basavarāja are mentioned among the names of other Śaiva devotees (Desai, 1968, 133–134). Several more inscriptions from the 14th century refer to Saṅgamanātha Basavarājadēva, Basavēśvara, Basavarasa, Kāśyapa Basavarasa, and so forth; but, besides being even later, these also exhibit genealogical confusions that bring their relevance into question (Desai, 1968, 134–147).

Hence it is the Arjunwad Inscription that provides the best, though imperfect, evidence for Basava's existence and activities. Though written a century after Basava's purported activities, it contains reference to Saṅgana Basava, a genealogy traceable through his family, and many details consistent with the record of *Basavapurāṇa*. Members of his lineage are praised for their ardent devotion to Śiva, their consistent worship of *jaṅgama* and *liṅga*, and their beneficence toward like-minded devotees. The inscription concludes with veneration to Saṅgamēśvara and with praise for Basavēśvara as the inspiration for the benefaction of the Arjunēśvar Temple at Arjunwad (Desai, 1968, 367–374).

At the end of the day, the epigraphical record establishes the existence of some figure called Basava whose time and place are consistent with the claims of the textual tradition. Much beyond that cannot be determined with certainty.

Basava in Contemporary Piety

The image of Basava in the traditional textual and legendary materials emphasizes his pious and miraculous nature. The scant epigraphic evidence associates him with other pious devotees known from the same textual sources but does little to provide a full view of his life. Finally, what may be most important about Basava is his image among contemporary Liṅgāyats, where he has taken on an increasingly prominent role as a religious and social reformer in the modern mold. His social egalitarianism, antiritualism, antihierarchism, vernacularism, secular asceticism, and devotional individualism all seem the hallmarks of the thoroughly modern man. Hence hundreds of books and pamphlets on his life, scholarly researches and translations of his corpus, fulsome governmental commemorations of him, a society for studying his life and works, and even a journal issued in his name attest to this contemporary fascination for a Basava who seems uniquely relevant after eight and a half centuries.

Examples of some of those biographies range from P.B. Desai's (1968) thorough exposition of the literary and epigraphic sources to *Amar Chitra Katha*'s renderings and cinema productions such as *Kranti Yogi Basavanna*. Publications of his works enjoy a similar vigor, for example those from Karnataka University, Dharwar, and translations such as that edited from the Oriental Research Institute, Mysore. Similarly publication of the traditional literature about him includes critical editions of *Basavapurāṇa* (1971) as well as excellent translations of some of that material (e.g. Narayana Rao, 1990).

But this revival of interest in Basava can perhaps best be seen in the tendency of some contemporary organizations to place a distance between what they like to call Liṅgāyatism, or sometimes Basav(a)ism, and what they refer to somewhat derogatorily as Vīraśaivism (for more detail on this phenomenon, see → Liṅgāyats). Prominent in this vein would be the movement founded by Swami Lingananda and carried forward by Mate Mahadevi at the Vishwa Kalyana Mission near Bangalore and its retreat center at Kappadi Kudala Sangama (i.e. Kudalasangama; Mahādēvi, 1973). The Sadharus, followers of Shivamurthy Swamiji of Sirigere, are a somewhat more moderate version of the same phenomenon. They publish translations of Basava's *vacana*s, run schools in which Basava's teaching forms the basis for moral and spiritual culture, and so on. One of their projects is, in fact, the Basavaism Center in Chitradurga. Both of these organizations emphasize Basava, the religious and social reformer, over and against the more traditional ritualism, hierarchism, and latent caste-ism of the broader Vīraśaiva movement.

A more intellectual version of this revival of interest in Basava can be seen in the Basava Samithi organization, headquartered in the modern city of Bangalore. Dedicated to the study and propagation of Basava's ideals, this organization holds conferences, workshops, and lectures dedicated to the heritage of Basava, the reformer. They also publish the *Basava Journal*, whose contents will invariably include articles on humanism in Basava (*BJ* 9/1), Basava and Gandhi (*BJ* 11/2), Basava's anticaste-ism (*BJ* 9/2; 9/3), Basava's rationalistic *Weltanschauung* (*BJ* 9/3; 12/3), Basava on women's rights (*BJ* 8/4; 9/1), Basava against superstition (*BJ* 6/3), Basava the Luther of India (*BJ* 7/3), Basava and Marx (*BJ* 11/4), Basava and democracy (*BJ* 12/1), and so forth.

It is this rationalist, egalitarian, socially reformatory image of Basava that fuels the contemporary resurgence of interest in the Liṅgāyat tradition despite the inevitable pressures for secularization and modernization of South Indian society. Basava was, has been, and remains an image of Liṅgāyat faith in face of potent political and economic forces whether in the worship and teaching centers of Karnataka or in the spiritual lives and devotional activities of Liṅgāyats in global diaspora.

Conclusion

The figure of Basava has been an inspiration to the religious devotion and social conscience of Liṅgāyats for over eight centuries. The content of his poetic devotional compositions, the legendary feats of social reform and religious reformation, the ever-changing vitality he brought to religious life, and the sometimes gentle whimsy with which he flavored his poems and parables continue to inspire the spiritual lives of Liṅgāyats in the present day as they have since the 12th century (see Wodeyar, 1967; Zvelebil, 1984).

Perhaps that influence is best summarized in one of his most celebrated *vacana*s, wherein

Basava humbly asked to have himself fashioned into a lute so that his heart might play forth songs of praise to his beloved Lord Śiva.

> From my head, make the bout;
> From my body, make the neck;
> From my nerves, make the strings;
> And from my fingers, make the pick;
> Press upon my heart, Lord
> and play thy thirty two licks;
> O Kūḍala Saṅgama Lord! (*Vacana* 498; trans. by author)

Bibliography

Brown, C.P., "Account of the Basava Puran," *MJLS* 12, 1840, 271–291.

Desai, P.B., *Basavēśvara and His Times*, Dharwar, 1968.

Mahādēvi, *Revolution in Kalyana*, Dharwar, 1973.

Michael, R.B., "Laicization of the Ascetic Ideal," in: A.B. Creel & V. Narayanan, eds., *Monastic Life in the Christian and Hindu Tradition*, Lewiston, 1990, 405–441.

Michael, R.B., "Women of the *Śūnyasaṃpādane*," *JAOS* 103/2, 1983, 361–368.

Michael, R.B., "Work as Worship in Vīraśaiva Tradition," *JAAR* 50/4, 1982, 101–115.

Narayana Rao, V., *Śiva's Warriors: The Basava Purāṇa of Pālkurike Somanātha*, Princeton, 1990.

Palekar, S.A., *Basaveshwara's Politics and Philosophy*, New Delhi, 2006.

Ramanujan, A.K., *Speaking of Śiva*, Baltimore, 1973.

Sadasivaiah, H.M., *A Comparative Study of Two Vīraśaiva Monasteries*, Mysore 1967.

Wodeyar, S.S., *et al.*, eds., *Śrī Basavēśvara: Commemoration Volume*, Bangalore, 1967.

Würth, G., trans., ed., "The Basava Purana of the Lingaits [of Pālkurike Sōmanāth]," *JBombayBRAS* 8/24, 1865–1866, 65–97.

Yaravintelimath, C.R., *Vacanas of Women Saints*, Bangalore, 2006.

Yaravintelimath, C.R., *The Caste Eradication Vacanas of Śri Basaveswara*, Dharwar, 1987.

Zvelebil, K.V., *The Lord of the Meeting Rivers*, New Delhi, 1984.

R. Blake Michael

Bhartṛhari

Of the two famous figures named Bhartṛhari in early historical India, more is known about the religious tendencies of the grammarian, author of the *Vākyapadīya* (see also → language and linguistics), than of the poet. This entry is about the poet and describes and analyzes what can be gleaned about (his) religion from the collection called *Śatakatraya* (Triad of the Hundreds), made up of the *Nītiśataka* (Hundred on Conduct), the *Śṛṅgāraśataka* (Hundred on Sensuality), and the *Vairāgyaśataka* (Hundred on Disenchantmant). Bhartṛhari has been translated, though not studied, more than any other Sanskrit poet, and from the point of view of reception, his poetry has remained a fundamental component in the Sanskrit canon and continues to evoke a response from both a literary and religious perspective among educated Hindus today. The collection of poems reveals a profound knowledge of the Sanskrit tradition as it had evolved up until the time when he lived, perhaps the 4th–5th centuries CE, and this understanding of the tradition contains a strong critical element because it deliberately undermines received Brahmanical knowledge associated with particular modes of living. Consequently, a reading of his poetry is demanding because of the assumed knowledge, against which his critical flourishes are made. But his popularity is equally a consequence of a reader's attraction to the deep sense of resignation about the fractured tone of existence seeping through so many of his poems.

Bhartṛhari remains important not just because of his concentration on some fundamental themes – conduct, sensuality, and disenchantment – of early Indian culture, but also because he focuses on stereotypes whose validity his poems constantly undercut. This being the case, he invites modern readers to question why these particular stereotypes were chosen for critique and whether there was a historical basis for his choice. Was he dealing with fundamental lifestyle possibilities of his time, or was he demonstrating how fossilized some of these really were? D.D. Kosambi in his always insightful studies on the poet and his poetry wants to relate these stereotypes to the legendary biography associated with the poet's life, but he equally points out that these themes (he does not use the word "stereotype") remained popular given the number of commentaries on the poems and the occurrence of individual poems in so many anthologies.

One way to undertake a study of the religious themes in the collection of poems is to list all references to deities, religious practices, and technical terms used elsewhere in religious texts; allusions to well-known myths; and anything else contributing to a full demarcation of his religious world. It will not, of course, provide us with a full view of religion in India of this time, because Bhartṛhari was neither an ethnographer nor a cataloguer of popular beliefs and practices. Instead we are given a view of one man's understanding of traditional and widely known religio-philosophical beliefs/practices and of their broader significance in the cultural context of his time as he creates it.

The same exercise could be undertaken for Manu, Gautama, Vyāsa, or any other prominent name attributed to a particular text or lauded as a teacher within a text. Yet in the case of Bhartṛhari, other factors are to be taken into consideration. He is a poet famed as taking a skeptical view of the culture in which he is embedded, yet of which at the same time he functions as a highly effective critic. Almost like a Nāgārjuna, he wants to deconstruct all the prominent cultural and religious positions he has inherited. And these are many because his knowledge of both Sanskrit literature and daily life must have been considerable. As such his poetry provides a unique insight into a received vision of Hindu culture and the possibilities of dissent arising out of this.

Previous Scholarship

It is something of a paradox to find that though Bhartṛhari's poems have been translated more than two hundred times into European languages, there exists no complete study of the poems. All of the translations contain brief introductions, and several articles have been written on different aspects of his poetry, mainly by D.D. Kosambi (1941, 1945–1946), the great editor of several different recensions (1948, 1957) of the poems, and by the author of this entry. Most introductions provide a summary of the main themes of the poems and attempt to contextualize them in a broader Kāvya context, with the addition of some speculations about the poet's life, where the fragments of biographical information become interpretative clues to the contents of the poems themselves. Only one article is exclusively devoted to Bhartṛhari's religion and that is by J. Filliozat (1954), who focuses primarily on the first verse of the *Nītiśataka* and specifically on the compound *cinmātrā* or "mind only," which is an adjective of the absolute and reduces the world to a psychic representation. It may connect Bhartṛhari with some ideas underlying the *Vākyapādiya* (also authored by a Bhartṛhari) and explains why the Chinese pilgrim Yijing regarded him as a Buddhist.

A. Passi (1989, 241–243), in the afterword to an excellent Italian translation of Bhartṛhari's poems, lists four possible elements pertaining to religion:

1. mention of Śruti (revealed teachings), more so than of the → Veda themselves;
2. the mention of the → Purāṇas in poem 191 (see also Kosambi, 1948);
3. technical terms associated with → Vedānta; and
4. an allusion to → Tantra in 149 (see also Kosambi, 1948).

The latter two have also been focused upon briefly by earlier scholars, but A. Passi still expresses considerable reservation about what these references can tell us:

> But very little appears on the surface in all this which allows a more precise characterization of the poet's beliefs; smoky and elusive as historical evidence, the religious elements are presented functioning as the frames in which occur the general themes of the work. (Passi, 1989, 243)

D.D. Kosambi published several editions of the *Śatakatraya*. His inspiring 1948 edition of the poems contains two hundred poems common to all recensions, as well as his 1957 edition of the southern recension, which I have used for this article (unless otherwise indicated), containing slightly more than three hundred poems. He rightly argued (Kosambi, 2009a, 561–562) that in the name Bhartṛhari we are dealing with a tradition of poems, which while originally forming a nucleus was later collected into an anthology by means of additions made long after Bhartṛhari's death. Unlike some earlier scholars, he doubts that he was a Vedāntin and is confident he was not a king – as is sometimes suggested in later texts – who renounced the world because of disenchantment with the world (see also Passi, 1989, 232). From D.D. Kosambi's perspective the poems suggest he was a hungry poet familiar with the splendor of kings' courts and was resigned to his own inauspicious lot (Kosambi, 2009a, 556–566).

Sources

Bhartṛhari's only known work is a collection of poems given the title, perhaps by later anthologists, of *Śatakatraya*. Scholars are unanimous about the unlikelihood of ever being able to come definitively to a final date for when the nucleus of the initial collection of poems was composed. Yet their popularity has remained until the present day, meaning that they have held a relevance throughout the last fifteen hundred years, evidenced by the number of commentaries on them and the huge number of manuscripts.

In later anthologies the poems are considered *subhāṣitas* or "well-polished sayings" that could be extracted from their poetic context and used for other literary purposes. Moreover, the thematic and compositional consistency of the two hundred poems in the 1948 edition, and arguably the three hundred of the southern recension, suggests a strong commonality among them, justifying their status of being regarded as standing among the earliest part of the Bhartṛhari corpus. The individual poems are entirely self-contained, though later commentators such as the important Rāmacandrabudhendra (perhaps 16th cent. CE) group them into thematically related groups within the individual sections of three. Though dominated by the three thematic frames, individual poems sometimes are placed in different *Śatakas* according to the edition, so that it is often difficult to use immediate context and narrative sequentiality as interpretative possibilities.

The imagery and content found in the poems is not new. It is found in literature even up to six hundred years prior to it, if we accept a date of the 4th–5th centuries CE. But this would not have been a concern to an educated audience who knew these sources and maintained a sufficient knowledge of Sanskrit – only a language of the literate elite in Bhartṛhari's time – and expected that great poets would rework traditional material (Passi, 1989, 228). A direct expression of the traditional nature of the contents of these poems is the extensive use of technical terms often found elsewhere in texts like the → *Mahābhārata*, the

Purāṇas, the → Upaniṣads, and early Buddhist literature. Whether this forms a concentrated vocabulary is a moot point. *Tṛṣṇā* or thirst/craving is one instance and occurs in a series of poems found in the *Vairāgyaśataka*. To this can be added various words for mind (*citta/cetanā/cetas/manas*), old age (*jarā/jīrṇa*), happiness and unhappiness (*sukha/duḥkha*), mistaken knowledge (*mūḍha/moha/vibhrama*), ontologically negative forms of existence (→ *saṃsāra/bhava*), and motivating causes for human life situations, such as fate (*vidhi*) and → *karman*. It is of course possible that these could simply be general shared terms across a number of texts all reflecting the mainstreaming of the philosophical axioms associated with Buddhism and upanishadic thought. The use of technical terms in poetry is necessarily different from their use in philosophical or shastric texts, such that the poetry may well be leaning towards an implied critique of their universal acceptance. In all cases their use in the *Śatakatraya* must be anchored in the more general critique of culture in which the poet is engaged (Bailey, 1994).

While there are allusions to myths in the poems, there is no mention of, or even allusion to, the epics in his poems, texts whose massive presence inspired much Kāvya from Aśvaghoṣa onwards. It is inconceivable that he did not know them, but his concern with → kingship, such a vital component of both epics, is a strongly pragmatic one, focused on the survival of the kings' adviser and the poet in the environment of the court, not a theoretical one as in the *Mahābhārata*.

The Limits of His Worldview

In reading Bhartṛhari's poetry, both Western and Indian readers have real difficulty in locating one particular vantage point from which the poems as a whole can be interpreted. Leaving aside whether this is a naive mode of reading, it seems the refusal to countenance a holistic and architectonic interpretative frame is a deliberate strategy designed to adopt multiple reading frames, where one can potentially undercut the other. This is most evident in the intentionality of the *Śṛṅgāraśataka* and the *Vairāgyaśataka*, where the underlying ethos of each stands in contrast to the other, as it does elsewhere in early Indian thought. This is a strategy of presentation that may be reflected in the very widespread use of the prefix *vi-* in the poems, a prefix often denoting difference and separation. It occurs in each of the *Śatakas* and totals more than all other prefixes combined. A. Passi (1989, 234) argues that there is no single point of view emerging from any of the verses, nor any attempts to eliminate the apparent contradictions between the dominant themes implied in the headings of the individual *Śatakas*. Yet the sense of resignation to worldly frustrations and the absence of an underlying absolute truth may be taken as a unified position in its own right.

Given the interpretative interconnectedness of the *Śṛṅgāraśataka* and the *Vairāgyaśataka*, might it be expected that the underlying tone – albeit critical – of those poems defines the boundaries of his religious/cultural world? What is surprising is that if this is so, guidance to these boundaries is explicitly given in the *Nītiśataka* and the *Śṛṅgāraśataka*. They are represented as possibilities for lifestyles, and the following verse is the most elliptically iconic of the representation of these possibilities (see Bailey, 1994, 5):

kusumastabakasyeva dvayī vṛttir manasvinas
mūrdhni vā sarvalokasya śīryate vana eva vā

As for a flower cluster
So for a reflective man two lifestyles are possible:
To be at the head of all people
Or just to wither in the forest. (*NīŚat.* 25)

Thus presented in behavioral terms is the royal and the ascetic lifestyle, where the king is a model of all men who do not adopt the ascetic's position. Translated into sensuous images with an implied metaphysical undertone, it is expressed in these terms:

yadāsīd ajñānaṃ smaratimirasaṃskārajanitaṃ
tadā dṛṣṭaṃ nārīmayam idam aśeṣaṃ jagad api
idānīm asmākaṃ paṭutaravivekāñjanajuṣāṃ
samībhūtā dṛṣṭis tribhuvanam api brahma manute

When the influence of passion's darkness
Engendered ignorance in me,
Then this entire world
Appeared only to consist of woman.
Now I delight in the ointment
Of discrimination most keen,
And my vision has become impartial.
Even the triple-world is Brahma, I conclude. (*ŚṛṅŚat.* 69)

Lifestyle limits represented by sensuality and discriminating knowledge point directly to the didactic and poetic intent of the *Śṛṅgāraśataka* and the

Vairāgyaśataka and offer considerably more specialization than is found in verse 25 above, which embraces kingship as well. For Bhartṛhari, as for Indian thought in general, the question is one *of continuity between* the two limits, with the accompanying implication that the one must necessarily cancel out the other, but never fade into the other. Ascetic practice negates sensuality, except where it is mediated within a devotional context, a possibility to which the poet alludes in a series of seven poems (*VaiŚat.* 83–90) of unabashed Śaiva devotionalism.

The complication in the *Śatakatraya* is the *Nītiśataka* as it focuses on conduct in general and the judgment thereof, but it coalesces with the other two in raising the questions of lifestyle paths and their function as evaluative guidelines for behavior. It can be read as providing the broader context in which what is questioned in the other two *Śataka*s is presented. Each of the three can easily be interpreted as dealing, respectively, with → *artha*, → *kāma*, → *dharma*. And *mokṣa* or → liberation from rebirth as a fourth, because it is implied everywhere in the *Vairāgyaśataka*. But that would be too limiting, as these categorical frames are reflected right across the three *Śataka*s, seemingly fulfilling Bhartṛhari's agenda of questioning the three lifestyle options, while accepting them with resignation in any case. But for this questioning to be successful, and because of his extensive use of traditional literary and religious material, it was necessary for him to use both mythological and more didactic (shastric) imagery.

A further element in the *Nītiśataka*, one that also frames the other two *Śataka*s, is the theme of evaluation of greatness/nobility and smallness/roguishness. Words for judging and measuring are used repeatedly, as are similes and known metaphors, such as those involving comparisons with grass as a measure of worthlessness, and the use of the adjective *mahat* (great) as a descriptor of character. Exemplary are verses 58, 64, and 73. But it is not so much appearance (Aklujkar, 2000, 13) as what one does that is the mark of a person. This theme then becomes mediated into an exploration of fate and *karman* as a causal motivation of human status and behavior. It suggests that the surface thrust of the *Nītiśataka* is to define the conduct of kings and courtiers/poets/advisers and to allude to the abstract values lying behind these. As such it takes up subjects studied extensively in the epics, where the differences between fate and causal factors are never satisfactorily resolved.

Religious Imagery

Classifying the extent and bearing of the references to ritual, asceticism, and devotion (including mythology) in the poems can provide an insight into the religious inclinations underlying them, whether these were of the poet himself or the tradition in which the poems were collected. Care must be exercised, however, because in the name *Vairāgyaśataka* the reader is already presented with a prejudgment of the poet's emphasis on the ascetic lifestyle and the motives for adopting it as social practice.

Ritual

References to ritual performance seem minimal, though this gap is likely a reflection of the poet/tradition's own predilections, not an accurate assessment of ritual activity in the religious life of the time. Given the centrality of ritual in so much of Hindu/Buddhist religious life, one might have expected it to be given a considerable profile in the poems. Certainly Bhartṛhari is aware of Brahmans performing vedic rituals, but this is an awareness in passing and little more. Lifestyle practices are confined to ascetic behavior and the blustering of the puffed-up → *paṇḍit* (*ŚṛṅŚat.* 72), but to little more.

Arguably only five poems refer to the vedic ritual (→ *yajña*) and none to → *pūjā*, the only reference (*NīŚat.* 16) being to a verbal variant of this where it means "[knowledge is] honored" not "ritual performance." In the *Nītiśataka* (46) a sacrificial priest is mentioned as being burnt by the sacrificial fire, and in the *Vairāgyaśataka* (3) there is a possible allusion to tantric ritual in which → *mantra*s are said to be applied in a cemetery; the *Vairāgyaśataka* (23) refers to the smoke of fire in vedic sacrifices; and in the *Vairāgyaśataka* (44) a flurry of rituals is mentioned in conjunction with the recitation of the Purāṇas and the Śāstras. These sparse references simply confirm the low profile given to ritual in Bhartṛhari's poetry, yet paradoxically this absence may register an underlying importance as their casual mention indicates their likely ubiquitous presence in everyday life.

Mythology

As expected of a poet of the 4th/5th century CE, Bhartṛhari displays an extensive knowledge of Hindu mythology, primarily as this must have been originally transmitted through the two epics and the early puranic tradition. But this knowledge is evidenced through allusions and specific references rather than through tellings of complete myths, the practice of which would violate Sanskrit poetics. It can be assumed that those to whom his poems were directed were highly competent in their own knowledge of these myths and that the mere mention of the name of a deity would have been sufficient to evoke the whole mythic narrative in the hearer's mind. In this respect, he would have been tapping into knowledge extant in the Hindu community at many levels. At the very least, Bhartṛhari knows the outline of puranic mythology in terms of the cosmogonic functions of the *trimūrti* of → Brahmā, → Viṣṇu, and → Śiva and of the roles of other gods such as → Yama. The latter god and Kāma play a conspicuous role in his poems because of the centrality of the theme of sensuality (→ *kāma*) in the *Śṛṅgāraśataka* and of death in the *Vairāgyaśataka*.

It is not possible to conclude on the basis of the poems whether he believed in the gods. Poetry is elliptical and strongly reflective, Bhartṛhari's especially so, and does not allow a response to such questions as that. He does, however, show a tendency to elevate Śiva above other gods, this being especially the case (but not exclusively) in the *Vairāgyaśataka*. But this elevation is in relation to other characters in the poems, and it cannot necessarily be tied back into Bhartṛhari's own beliefs even if it is highly suggestive.

The following table lists explicit mention of gods and other mythological characters:

Name	Reference	Number
Śiva (Maheśvara, Hara, Bhava)	*NīŚat.* 1, 10, 51, 88, 92 *ŚṛṅŚat.* 1, 32, 64 *VaiŚat.* 1, 6, 15, 17, 30, 45, 60, 68, 83–90	24
Viṣṇu	*NīŚat.* 67, 81, 92 *ŚṛṅŚat.* 1 *VaiŚat.* 84	5
Bṛhaspati	*NīŚat.* 81	1
Indra	*NīŚat.* 28, 40, 81 *ŚṛṅŚat.* 10 *VaiŚat.* 40	5 (by implication)
Brahmā	*NīŚat.* 3, 7, 14, 40, 68, 86 92 *ŚṛṅŚat.* 1, 75; VŚ 29, 40, 97	12 (*NīŚat.* 7, 14 [= Vidhātṛ], 40 [= Dhātṛ], 86 [= Vidhi])
Sūrya	*NīŚat.* 92	1
Lakṣmī	*VaiŚat.* 93	1
Kāma	*ŚṛṅŚat.* 11, 13, 15, 19, 20, 26, 29, 30, 64, 73, 76, 79 *VaiŚat.* 1, 17	14 (*ŚṛṅŚat.* 13 [by implication])
Śeṣa	*NīŚat.* 27	1
Pṛthu	*NīŚat.* 37	1
Viśvāmitra	*ŚṛṅŚat.* 80	1
Parāśara	*ŚṛṅŚat.* 80	1
Yama	*ŚṛṅŚat.* 98 *VaiŚat.* 50	2 (in the sense of death)

On the basis of a statistical count, Śiva emerges first, with Kāma and Brahmā coming second and third, respectively. Viṣṇu and Indra tie at fourth. The relatively high occurrence of Kāma is consistent with the principal theme of the *Śṛṅgāraśataka*, where Kāma as a symbol of love must play a significant role. Brahmā appears mainly in the *Nītiśataka* and especially in verses dealing with fate (40, 86), and is depicted in some as being a figure of ignorance and bluster (3, 7). In no sense is there any hint that he is an object of worship or veneration, as is often the case with Śiva. Instead, he is always seemingly an object of ridicule. Nor does Viṣṇu appear as an object of veneration, although there are certainly references to devotional attitudes, and → *bhakti* (to Śiva [*NīŚat.* 51; *VaiŚat.* 68]) is mentioned several times.

One explanation for the many references to Śiva, Brahmā, and Kāma, which constitute 51 out of the total of 70 references, is the influence of an important set of myths of the Śaiva cycle as a subtext. In its fuller form, this mythic narrative involves Śiva's contrasting erotic and ascetic personas as they emerge constantly across his mythology, the ascetic and antisensuous aspect being expressed in his destruction of Kāma, the embodiment of *śṛṅgāra*, and his famous decapitation of Brahmā when the latter is leering at → Pārvatī. Although Brahmā is mentioned in the poems primarily in conjunction with fate, aspects of creation, and misused knowledge, the relatively greater number of references to him, Kāma, and Śiva must have resonated easily with a traditional audience and have inspired reminiscence of the complete Śaiva myth cycle where they play well-known roles.

Devotion

A concentration of seven consecutive verses in the southern recension of the *Vairāgyaśataka* further confirms the significance of Śiva elsewhere in the broader collection. In each of them, Śiva is mentioned, usually under a different name. These verses are important not just because of their allusion to aspects of Śiva's mythology, including iconic appearance and some theological aspects, but also because they may tell us something of Bhartṛhari's personal beliefs. Obviously they suggest he was a Śaiva, although, except for his implied conflict with Kāma, we are not given extensive allusions to specific aspects of his mythology.

Although all of these occur in the *Vairāgyaśataka*, the collection ostensibly dealing with asceticism as worldview and practice, there is a very strong devotional tinge about them even where their anchoring within a conspicuous ascetic context initially justifies their inclusion in the *Vairāgyaśataka*. In verse 83 it is said that in the face of approaching death, the only refuge (*anyā gatiḥ*) is devotion at Śiva's feet. The next verse (84) is more theologically inclined, contrasting Viṣṇu and Śiva as inner and outer in respect of their relation to the world/individual soul. It is partially reminiscent of the theological differences explored in texts like the *Kūrmapurāṇa*, but there and elsewhere the poet can see no intellectual conflict in the apparent difference between the two. Yet, the final words in the poem are fundamental: "Even so, I am devoted to the god whose crest is the young moon." So too is verse 85 explicitly devotional, but within the framework of asceticism, often so strongly associated with Śiva:

> ...Oppressed by the experiences of transient existence,
> Crying out loudly "Śiva! Śiva! Śiva!"
> When will we reach that state
> Filled with so many inner tears?

The act of crying out to Śiva by repetition of his name is definitely reminiscent of the kind of → *kīrtana* that remains such a prominent devotional practice to the present day. It is also noteworthy that the resulting experience is a highly emotional one, quite in contrast with Śiva's frequently publicized and ascetically motivated withdrawal from the emotions. Yet verse 86 is equally emotional for the devotee and reverts to a form of devotion seen already in 83, because in 86 there is equally a claim for refuge at Śiva's feet:

> ...In the auspicious forest
> We will spend the nights,
> Filled with a full autumnal moon's rays,
> Our sole refuge – contemplation of Hara's feet.

Like the other poems of this group, this one too evokes lush images of the forest and sharply distinguishes the attitude of *vairāgya* – defining the subjects' disaffection from transitory existence (*bhava/saṃsāra*) – from the highly emotional plea to Śiva to help them out of *saṃsāra*. Verse 87 takes all of the relevant images: asceticism, a sacred place, and acts of devotion, such as performance of bodily obeisance (*añjali*) and the recitation of Śiva's names. The next verse is not dissimilar but introduces a common theme of this poet, the oppression of poets by kings. But the word for misery/pain used here is *duḥkha*, a technical term in both early Buddhist and some Hindu texts. If there is a difference between this and the previous poems, it lies in the concentration of words for devotional actions. In both verses 89 and 90, the subject has already achieved the ascetic status, but something seems still to be lacking, and it is devotion to Śiva that removes this lack. Of these two poems, 89 fits best the poet's generally skeptical tone because in spite of his adoption of the ascetic lifestyle, both physically and mentally, *karman* still has not been eradicated.

In sum, this series of poems stands out from the rest in the *Vairāgyaśataka* in evoking a very strong devotional sense among ascetics who are elsewhere treated with the poet's traditional skepticism. Any questioning tone is substantially lacking here, and the typical appeal of the devotee to the favor of the *bhakti* god is what comes into play. One prominent stream of asceticism flowing out of the Upaniṣads and from early Buddhism eschewed any kind of devotional emotionalism, but in these poems, it is so highly profiled in conjunction with ascetic practices, yet the allusions to such practices and accompanying (un-)emotional states are not suggestive of a completeness. Only devotion brings completeness.

These verses are found near the end of the *Vairāgyaśataka* and hence the *Śatakatraya* itself, and their positioning may be significant. The final ten verses all extol the peacefulness of the ascetic life without any hint of qualification or reservation. Yogic → meditation and the contemplative lifestyle in an isolated region provide the perfect balm for the kind of world weariness so often exuding from Bhartṛhari's poems. It cannot be certain whether this means pure meditative asceticism is the next stage beyond the devotional behavior recommended in verses 83–90, because the ascetic practices mentioned in these seven verses are not dissimilar to those found in verses 90–100.

Asceticism

Though asceticism (→ *tapas*) and devotional impulses seemingly effect a conclusion to the *Śatakatraya* if it is read sequentially, a critique of ascetic behavior, on the one hand, and the inability of people to sustain ascetic practices, on the other hand, are mounted in the initial poems of the *Vairāgyaśataka*. The poems in this *Śataka* reflect a highly realistic view of the ascetic lifestyle and work effectively to undermine the idealistic vision of this given in so many other texts. Whether Bhartṛhari saw himself as an ascetic or considered poets as living ascetic lives is a moot point, even if it has been woven into his constructed biography in later Sanskrit literature. And in some poems, there is always the impression of a conflict between living life to the full, captive to the senses and the frustration of not having done so when the ascetic life is being practiced, thus continuing the practice of sounding a warning against any wholesale acceptance of a particular lifestyle to the exclusion of others.

Many of the poems reiterate the fundamental axioms of the ascetic's worldview: the shallowness and transience of existence (*VaiŚat.* 11, 20, 34–36, 39, 49, 51, 72, 79), the dominance of time and old age (*VaiŚat.* 43, 38, 41–44, 47, 73–75, 85–86), the ubiquity of death and pain (*VaiŚat.* 30, 32, 33, 37, 49), the entrapment of the mind by the senses (*VaiŚat.* 11–13, 15, 28, 54, 63, 81), false knowledge about the true nature of existence and infatuation with it (*VaiŚat.* 10, 17, 18, 20, 43), the ubiquity of craving (*VaiŚat.* 2–4, 7–8, 29, 53), and achievement of the highest bliss/repose (*VaiŚat.* 10, 14, 40, 53, 63, 90, 95, 100). This is standard fare for all texts previous to the *Śatakatraya* that treat asceticism, and it provides a background – again conveying the sense of transmitted traditional knowledge – for Bhartṛhari's own, more contentious reflections on asceticism.

A poem like the following conveys the high point of acceptance of asceticism as an optimum lifestyle:

> His huge bed is the earth
> His long arm a broad pillow,
> The sky for a canopy,
> The pleasant wind a fan,
> The autumn moon his lamp,
> His delight, attachment to the woman called indifference.
> Easily sleeps the tranquil ascetic,
> Like the prosperous king. (*VaiŚat.* 94; 190; trans. by author)

And yet the strongly idealistic images beautifully sketched here are always counterbalanced by reservations made in poems such as this one:

> Tasteless food begged but once a day,
> As a bed the earth, company just one's own body.
> Clothes, a patchwork of one hundred withered rags.

Damn! Even so, sense objects do not give up.
(*VaiŚat.* 15; trans. by author)

Conclusion

Bhartṛhari was very highly educated in Sanskrit literature and skillfully reworks the fundamental axioms that had contributed to Hinduism becoming a distinctive religio-social system in the early centuries of the Common Era. Always though there emerges from the poems a sense of frustration with dependence on any absolutes as a lifestyle foundation and a weariness arising from this frustration. This is never translated into a sharp asceticism and rejection of the world of the senses found in early Buddhist literature and the 12th book, the *Śāntiparvan*, of the *Mahābhārata*. Rather, Bhartṛhari's asceticism, even where it is tempered by devotion to Śiva, is described in highly sensuous terms, such that it becomes another form of entrapment, just like the image of the woman so powerfully depicted in the *Śṛṅgāraśataka*.

Bibliography

Aklujkar, A., "Love or Leave? Bhartṛhari's (?) Dilemma," in: V.H. Bhayayani, ed., *Anusandhana*, vol. XVII, Ahmedabad, 2000, 2–31.

Bailey, G., *Bhartṛhari's Critique of Culture*, Melbourne, 1994.

Filliozat, J., "A propos de la religion de Bhartṛhari," in: *Silver Jubilee Volume of the Zinbun-Kagaku-Kenkyushyo*, Kyoto, 1954: 116–120; ET: in: J. Filliozat, ed., *Religion, Philosophy, Yoga: A Selection of Articles*, Delhi, 1991, 41–46.

Kosambi, D.D., "On the Authorship of the Śatakatrayī," in: B. Chattopadhyaya, ed., *The Oxford India Kosambi: Combined Methods in Indology and Other Writings*, New Delhi, 2009a, 555–567.

Kosambi, D.D., "The Quality of Renunciation in Bhartṛhari's Poetry," in: B. Chattopadhyaya, ed., *The Oxford India Kosambi: Combined Methods in Indology and Other Writings*, New Delhi, 2009b, 703–720.

Kosambi, D.D., ed., *Subhāṣitatriśatī*, Bombay, 1957.

Kosambi, D.D., ed., *Śatakatrayādi-subhāṣitasaṃgraha: The Epigrams Attributed to Bhartṛhari*, Bombay, 1948.

Passi, A., *Bhaṛthari: Sulla saggezza mondana, sull'amore e sulla rinuncia*, Milan, 1989 (It.).

GREG BAILEY

Caitanya

Caitanya, generally referred to by his followers as Śrī Caitanya Mahāprabhu or Śrī Kṛṣṇa Caitanya Mahāprabhu (1486–1533), holds a position of particular prominence in and well beyond → Bengal as the founding inspiration, preceptor, and divinity of the → Gauḍīya Vaiṣṇavas, who are for this reason also referred to as Caitanya Vaiṣṇavas. It is to the person of Caitanya that divinity was attributed by followers from early on; and according to the accounts of his several early biographers, Caitanya's identity as → Kṛṣṇa was at times made explicit by Caitanya himself through words, actions, and manifestations of form. In simultaneous counterpoint with the notion of Caitanya's divinity was his ever-present "mood" (*bhāva*) as *bhakta* of Kṛṣṇa and particularly as Kṛṣṇa's eternal devotee-consort → Rādhā, and arguably it is out of this tension of identities that a rich tradition concerning his life course and legacy was elaborated through theological reflection, poetry, music, drama, worship practices, and eventually film. As recent scholarship has shown, in the development of Caitanya's "biographical image" (Reynolds & Capps, cited in Stewart, 2010, 7n4), the available early sources on Caitanya's life and teachings invariably reflect the devotional perceptions and presuppositions of those sources' authors and their communities (Stewart, 2010, 9–16); still, arguably considerable historical substance is discernible or inferable in these sources – beyond the particular intentions of the individual authors – such that the richness in detail and extent of these accounts provide considerable material for building a picture of his life with reasonably clear delineations and for gaining a vivid sense of the theological convictions that he lived by and taught his followers.

There are seven prominent early biographies of Caitanya that are extant in complete form (Dimock, 1999, 83–99). The earliest of these, the Sanskrit *Kṛṣṇacaitanyacaritāmṛta* of Murāri Gupta, was apparently written during Caitanya's life, and hence it served to guide later biographers. Next is the longest of the seven works, Vṛndāvanadāsa's Bengali *Caitanyabhāgavata*. There are two Sanskrit compositions by Kavikarṇapūra – *Kṛṣṇacaitanyacaritāmṛtamahākāvya* and *Caitanyacandrodayanāṭaka*, the latter in the form of an allegorical drama. Jayānanda's *Caitanyamaṅgala* and Locanadāsa's work of the same name are also extant. The last of the seven works to be composed was the *Caitanyacaritāmṛta* of Kṛṣṇadāsa Kavirāja, probably completed by 1615. It is this work that has enjoyed preeminence within the Gauḍīya Vaiṣṇava community, and, while taking some of the others into account, it is largely on the basis of this work that I will here sketch the main contours of this picture of Caitanya's life, followed by a look at three significant episodes therein. After considering Caitanya as teacher, I will then outline ways in which he became an object of worship in early and contemporary times.

Early Years: Tradition and Transformation

Although both the *Caitanyabhāgavata* and the *Caitanyacaritāmṛta* are composed in three parts, suggesting early, middle, and late periods, the chronology of Caitanya's life lends itself to a fairly symmetrical division of two equal periods that we may designate as "early years" and "later years," and both of these periods may be further conveniently partitioned into two phases.

All seven of Caitanya's early biographers were concerned with portraying Caitanya's birth as cosmically and religiously purposeful, noting the significance of the temporal and geographical location of this event. Born in Nabadvip (in present-day West Bengal) on the full-moon day of *phālguna* (Feb–Mar) in 1486, the child's birth was deemed by biographers to be a divine advent, signaled by the fact that it was the occasion of a lunar eclipse – a time when the local populace would take precautions against inauspiciousness by calling out the divine name Hari while standing partially submerged in a branch of the → Gaṅgā River that flows through Nabadvip. Further, we are informed, the fact that the divine name was being recited at the time of his birth was a telling indicator of the child's future mission, namely, to propagate recitation of divine names (*harināma saṃkīrtana*; see → *kīrtan* and *bhajan*) as the principal devotionally salvific religious practice for the present cosmic age, *kaliyuga* (see → cosmic cycles).

Jagannātha Miśra and his wife, Śacī, who named their newborn second son Viśvambhara and nicknamed him Nimāi, were Brahmans by caste. Jagannātha Miśra had migrated from the Sylhet district of present-day Bangladesh and, it has been argued, previously from Jajpur in Orissa to Sylhet (Das, 1989). Readers are given to understand that the boy's parents – acting as pious adherents of Hindu ritual life – found their perfection and real purpose in their doting attention to this charming, mischievous, and precocious son, in the pained absence of his elder brother Viśvarūpa, who at a young age left home as a renunciant, never to be heard of again. The picture of these early years is elaborated in the biographies with several episodes showing Viśvambhara as an extraordinary child, indicative of his identity as Kṛṣṇa and reminiscent of Kṛṣṇa's childhood exploits.

While Nimāi was still a student, his father died, and as the only son at home, he was obliged to marry and support his wife and mother through teaching and scholarship. Soon after marrying, he ventured to eastern Bengal (present-day Bangladesh) to seek fortune as a scholar in order to maintain his household; but on returning home some months later, he found that his wife, Lakṣmīpriyā, had died from the intensity of suffering her husband's long absence (*CaiBh.* 1.14). On the behest of his mother, he subsequently married Viṣṇupriyā, the daughter of a local → *paṇḍit*, Sanātana Miśra (Kapoor, 1977, 20).

Early biographers portray Viśvambhara (Nimāi) in his youth as a prominent figure in the local culture of Brahmanical learning, an upcoming *paṇḍit* who showed particular promise in Sanskrit grammar. It was as a young householder that Caitanya – at this time often referred to as Nimāi Paṇḍit – is said to have debated on Sanskrit prosody with a renowned preceptor of the → Nimbārka school of Vaiṣṇavism, Keśava Bhaṭṭa. The occasion is seen as a demonstration of Caitanya's superhuman erudition, which, however, he would soon thereafter be moved to abandon.

Marking the beginning of the second, though relatively short, portion of Caitanya's early life, in 1508 or 1509, he departed Nabadvip with a few of his students on a pilgrimage to Gaya, ostensibly to perform obsequies (*śrāddha*) for his father. There he met the Vaiṣṇava ascetic Īśvara Purī and received from him initiation into the utterance of a → *mantra* for the worship of Kṛṣṇa. By all reports, the effects of this meeting and a subsequent vision of Kṛṣṇa were life transforming, so that on his return to Nabadvip Caitanya showed no other interest than to hear and speak about his beloved Lord Kṛṣṇa with rapturous intensity. This condition of apparent madness made the normal pursuit of his scholarly profession and household duties impossible, precipitating his turn toward the celebratory and proselytizing activities of Kṛṣṇa → *bhakti* that would become the trademark of the communities comprising his followers – the practice of congregational singing and dancing in praise of Kṛṣṇa known as *saṃkīrtana*.

Later Years: Peregrination and Divine Rapture

In a further and more radical move away from the life of a Brahman *paṇḍit*-householder, in 1509 or 1510 – within a year or so of his meeting with Īśvara Purī and at the relatively young age of 23 or 24 (Eidlitz, 1968, 522; Kapoor, 1977, 24) – Nimāi Paṇḍit took formal vows of renunciation (*saṃnyāsa*), receiving the name Kṛṣṇa Caitanya from his *saṃnyāsaguru*, Keśava Bhāratī. Apparently it was not until soon after taking these vows that Caitanya consulted with his mother, who, in hopes of at least hearing occasional news of her son, prevailed upon him to live out his life of separation from family in Puri, a relatively nearby destination of considerable pilgrimage traffic from Bengal. Except for two extensive journeys – one to southern India (1510–1512) and one to Vrindavan via Bengal (1514–1516) – Caitanya seems to have remained in Puri until his demise in 1533.

Accounts of the early biographers concerning Caitanya's post-*saṃnyāsa* travels (constituting the first portion of the later years) tend to highlight three related types of activity, namely, meeting and winning over (by argument, charisma, or both) persons whose philosophical or theological positions were more or less opposed to those of Caitanya, methodically instructing the tenets of Kṛṣṇa *bhakti* to persons thus converted or persons who had become his followers from early on, and inspiring masses of people to participate in joyful *saṃkīrtana*. Regarding Caitanya's winning of arguments, clearly a pattern is meant to be seen with respect to discursive encounters in his pre-*saṃnyāsa* days, such as the meetings with Keśava Bhaṭṭa. A discernible wider Indian premodern hagiographical pattern is also relevant, namely, that of the religious "conqueror of all directions" (*digvijaya*), whereby a traveling saint encounters and either converts or puts to flight a variety of opponents, one after another, whether by debate or by some form of divine intervention (Smith, 2000, 135–158). In the case of Caitanya, a narrow specification of this pattern emerges in the emphasis on his defeat and conversion of Vedāntins of the nondualist (*advaitavāda* or *māyāvāda*) persuasion (see → Vedānta). Also within the period of Caitanya's post-*saṃnyāsa* travels was his two-month visit to Vrindavan, possibly in 1515, followed by his meeting with and instructing two key followers, Sanātana Gosvāmī and → Rūpa Gosvāmī. In Kṛṣṇadāsa's *Caitanyacaritāmṛta* account (2.17–18), Caitanya's sojourn in Vrindavan serves as a clear confirmation of his identity as Kṛṣṇa, as he is shown to constantly lose himself in remembrance of this identity as prompted by the familiar sights of Kṛṣṇa's home.

Descriptions of Caitanya's final 18 years while residing in Puri focus on his increasing absorption in devotional feelings that identified him with the rapturous moods of intense longing said to have been exhibited by Kṛṣṇa's consorts, headed by Rādhā, during and after Kṛṣṇa's childhood and youth in Vrindavan. However, set within this dominant theme are several episodes in which Caitanya has a striking variety of exchanges with different followers (e.g. Raghunātha Dāsa, Haridāsa, and Jagadānanda Paṇḍit), suggesting a concern by his biographers to record as much detail as possible in the life of this person, whom they perceived as divine (O'Connell, 1993).

No single definitive account of Caitanya's passing away is known or accepted, nor is there agreement on the year, estimations of which range from 1528 to 1534 (Majumdar, 1969, 247–248). Some of the early biographers only hint at the subject, while others offer miraculous or nonmiraculous accounts. In all cases, the sense of divine intentionality that coheres in the accounts of Caitanya's birth does so here as well: fulfilling his own purpose, Caitanya descended to the world, exhibited divine acts (*līlā*s, in his case characterized by the spirit of service to the divine), and returned to his atemporal realm having accomplished his mission of bringing Kṛṣṇa *bhakti* in its fullest expression to the world.

Three Key Episodes in Caitanya's Life

Short summaries of three selected episodes – one from the second portion of Caitanya's early life (in Nabadvip) and two from the first portion of his later life (in Puri) – will serve to highlight important features of Caitanya's life and teachings.

Confrontation in Nabadvip: Meeting the *Kājī*

In the first few months of Caitanya's newfound devotion upon returning to Nabadvip from Gaya, he and his followers kept their nocturnal *saṃkīrtana* celebrations behind closed doors – usually at the house of Caitanya's senior Brahman friend, Śrīvāsa. In his *Caitanyabhāgavata* (2.23), Vṛndāvanadāsa indicates that tensions grew as persons excluded from these gatherings due to not being Kṛṣṇa *bhakta*s became inimical. Yet there were also pious citizens who would come by day bringing respectful offerings for Caitanya and would be kindly received and offered instruction. It is in this context that the *Caitanyabhāgavata* (2.23.76) represents Caitanya exhorting his guests to chant the names of god contained in the *mahāmantra* (great invocation) consisting of three names in vocative case:

hare kṛṣṇa hare kṛṣṇa kṛṣṇa kṛṣṇa hare hare
hare rāma hare rāma rāma rāma hare hare.

As increasing numbers of Nabadvip residents followed Caitanya's advice and took up this practice in their homes, and as their enthusiastic singing, dancing, and playing of accompanying instruments spilled out into the streets, they were soon confronted by the local Muslim magistrate, the *kājī*. Encouraged by those Hindus who had become inimical to Caitanya and his followers, the *kājī* and his men harassed and beat the devotees, threatening them with further punishment and forced conversion to Islam should they persist with their public *saṃkīrtana* activities. We are told that upon hearing of this, Caitanya became enraged, ordering his close comrade Nityānanda to gather the Vaiṣṇavas for a protest march performing *saṃkīrtana* while bearing torches. "Millions" of people are said to have eagerly gathered in response to the call; indeed, writes Vṛndāvanadāsa, this momentous devotional parade became an event of cosmic proportions, as even the various disguised celestial divinities joined in.

The *Caitanyabhāgavata* and *Caitanyacaritāmṛta* give divergent accounts of the ensuing meeting with the *kājī*. According to the former text, following Caitanya's orders, the people of Nabadvip proceeded to ransack his property, stopping short of burning his house down, although Caitanya initially had commanded them to do so. Then, with the "spirit of the heretics broken," Caitanya resumed joyful *saṃkīrtana*, certain that there will be no more trouble from the officials (*CaiBh.* 2.23.392–427).

The *Caitanyacaritāmṛta* account (1.17), explicitly referring to the *Caitanyabhāgavata*'s version, acknowledges its general contours, including mention of the damage done to the *kājī*'s house and garden. However, the *Caitanyacaritāmṛta* version includes an extended dialogue between Caitanya and the *kājī* in which the latter shows submissive acceptance of and even devotion to Caitanya and his mission. In the course of the discussion, Caitanya challenged the Muslim administrator regarding Islamic practices of cow killing and the status of Islamic Śāstras (scriptures), and, we are told, the *kājī* readily conceded all Caitanya's assertions on the subject. Caitanya then broached the topic of public *saṃkīrtana*, at which the *kājī* confessed having in the previous night received a visitation from → Viṣṇu in the form of the man-lion → *avatāra*, Nṛsiṃha: following the *kājī*'s aggressive attack and prohibition, Nṛsiṃha had warned him that any further persecution of the Vaiṣṇavas would result in his immediate death.

Both versions of this episode highlight Caitanya's power to inspire and mobilize masses of people to celebrate *saṃkīrtana*, and both indicate that Caitanya responded with quick resolve and righteous anger at the news of opposition. The *Caitanyabhāgavata* portrays Caitanya as simultaneously fierce and jubilant, while the *Caitanyacaritāmṛta* adds an image of gentle, thoughtful firmness of conviction along with a talent for charming persuasion. Present-day Caitanyaite Vaiṣṇavas celebrate this event as a major turning point in the collective life of the tradition; as such it is remembered as a moment of unparalleled popularity of Caitanya and his message.

Winning Recognition in Puri: Meeting Vāsudeva Sarvabhauma Bhaṭṭācārya

Soon after accepting *saṃnyāsa* vows and receiving his mother's order to settle in Puri, Caitanya arrived there with a few companions and immediately entered the town's grand temple of Jagannātha. In the *Caitanyabhāgavata* (3.2) and *Caitanyacaritāmṛta* (2.6) accounts, he immediately fainted as he lunged forward to embrace the sacred image. While unconscious, he was carried, by command of the respected scholar Vāsudeva Sarvabhauma Bhaṭṭācārya, to the latter's home, where, according to *Caitanyabhāgavata*, he returned to external consciousness after nine hours.

The *Caitanyabhāgavata* and *Caitanyacaritāmṛta* accounts diverge on the nature of the subsequent encounter between Caitanya and Sarvabhauma, though arguably their underlying message is the same. In the *Caitanyabhāgavata*, Sarvabhauma exhibits the attitude and understanding of a Kṛṣṇa *bhakta* who is concerned for Caitanya's spiritual well-being in his newly adopted renounced order, warning him that *saṃnyāsa* is an easy trap for increasing one's pride. In this account, Caitanya induces Sarvabhauma to instruct him in the meaning of a particular verse of the *Bhāgavatapurāṇa* (1.7.10), one that celebrates *bhakti* as a superior attitude to the self-satisfaction (*ātmārāma*) of sages lacking *bhakti*. Sarvabhauma obliges with admirable erudition, only to be humbled by Caitanya's more extensive and devotionally insightful exegesis of the same verse. Caitanya then exhibits to Sarvabhauma his divine identity in the forms of Kṛṣṇa, → Rāma, and the renunciant Caitanya – all combined, with six arms – whom Sarvabhauma then joyfully hastens to worship (*CaiBh.* 3.3).

The *Caitanyacaritāmṛta* account is structured essentially as an elaboration of the *Caitanyabhāgavata* account, whereby readers are made privy to the conclusion of a discourse on Vedānta in which Sarvabhauma is portrayed as an adherent of → Śaṅkara's nondualist school. In Kṛṣṇadāsa's account, Sarvabhauma ends his seven-day-long vedantic exegesis with an invitation for Caitanya to expound his own understanding of the text, and Caitanya proceeds to refute and best his teacher (whereby his arguments reflect and, some would argue, are likely drawn by Kṛṣṇadāsa, from the works of → Jīva Gosvāmī, Caitanya's later prominent philosophical exponent; Dimock, 1999, 416–418n195).

What is clearly conveyed in both accounts is that Caitanya comes to be seen by a widely renowned scholar to be of divine identity; in Puri, Caitanya was henceforth treated with deference that well exceeded what would be shown an ordinary *saṃnyāsī*. That Sarvabhauma had been profoundly transformed due to his interaction with Caitanya is highlighted in a conversation reported in the *Caitanyacaritāmṛta* (2.6.233–252; Dimock, 1999, 421–422) between Caitanya and Sarvabhauma, wherein the latter displays a fierce aversion to *mukti* – the nondualist vedantic aspiration for → liberation – as constituting a "punishment" for trying to avoid one's position as eternal subordinate to the supreme lord.

Ecstatic Dancing in Jagannātha's *rathayātrā*

An episode recounted in both the *Caitanyacaritāmṛta* (2.13) and the *Caitanyacandrodayanāṭaka* (act 10; but not mentioned in *Caitanyabhāgavata*) is Jagannātha's annual chariot festival (*rathayātrā*) in Puri, → Orissa, in which Caitanya and his followers took active part by performing exuberant *saṃkīrtana*. Here attention is particularly given to Caitanya's display of intense devotional emotions in a public context. In the *Caitanyacaritāmṛta* account, prior to the commencement of the chariot procession, Caitanya organized his followers into four groups of *saṃkīrtana* singers and dancers, each of whom Kṛṣṇadāsa named; three additional groups, with members from three different towns in Bengal, are also mentioned. As the → procession with the huge chariots of the temple images Jagannātha, Subhadrā, and Baladeva were drawn from their temple to the Guṇḍicā Temple some three kilometers distant, Caitanya joined his *saṃkīrtana* performers, exhibiting extreme bodily transformations identified as physical eruptions of devotional ecstasy (*sāttvikabhāvas*), including tears shooting from his eyes, froth oozing from his mouth, teeth chattering, and even blood appearing from his skin (*CaiC.* 2.13.77–80, 96–106; Dimock, 1999, 522–524). Kṛṣṇadāsa also writes that Caitanya manifested himself simultaneously in all seven groups (thus showing a power associated with Kṛṣṇa in his similar acts of replication in the *rāsa* dance; *CaiC.* 2.13.51–53; Dimock, 1999, 520–521). Kavikarṇapūra (who may have witnessed the event as a child) emphasizes the intensity of Caitanya's devotional emotions that he spontaneously exhibited when he was prompted by various moods suggested in the songs sung by his close companion Svarūpa Damodara. Kṛṣṇadāsa elaborates on this theme while also articulating the special "internal" meaning of this display: Caitanya, rapt in the identity of Rādhā, was reenacting how she and her cowherdess friends are (according to tradition) to have induced Kṛṣṇa to return to Vrndavan from Kurukshetra, after long absence. That this special meaning was known to only a few of Caitanya's followers is also a point of emphasis in the *Caitanyacaritāmṛta* (2.13.127–128). Noteworthy is also this text's attention to the king, Pratāparudra (1497–1540), whose devotion to Caitanya the *Caitanyacaritāmṛta* takes pains to illustrate (*CaiC.* 2.13.172–180; 2.14.3–20; Dimock, 1999, 531–532, 534–535).

Caitanya's Teachings

The only work that is widely accepted (as having been written by Caitanya both in the tradition and by scholars) is a collection of eight Sanskrit stanzas that came to be known as the *Śikṣāṣṭaka*. Each of these takes the form of praise and devotional reflection rather than injunction, though as suggested by their inclusion and elaboration in the final chapter of *Caitanyacaritāmṛta* (3.20), they are taken by the tradition as Caitanya's essential theological instruction. Of these eight stanzas, four (1–3, 6) deal explicitly with the practice and results of uttering divine names (*harināmajapa* and *saṃkīrtana*), while the remaining four are expressions of eternal relationality between individual selves and Kṛṣṇa, devotional surrender to Kṛṣṇa, and the devotional sense of longing in absence (*virahabhakti*) that was exemplified in Caitanya's life. Translations of the first and eighth of these stanzas are included here:

> That which polishes the mirror of the mind, which extinguishes the forest-fire of the heat of worldly life, which spreads the radiance of the moonlight of auspiciousness, which is the soul of the bride of knowledge, which expands the ocean of joy, which on the first day of waxing gives nectar of the full moon, bathing the souls of all, that Kṛṣṇa-*nāma-saṃkīrtana* conquers all with its excellence. (*CaiC.* 3.20. *śloka* 3; trans. Dimock, 1999, 993)
>
> He may crush my breasts in embracing me, a slave to his feet, he may destroy my heart by not appearing to me, he may be a libertine wherever he wants, but still he is the lord of my heart, and there is no other. (*CaiC.* 3.20. *śloka* 10; trans. Dimock, 1999, 995)

The detailed instructions imparted by Caitanya to his learned followers Sanātana Gosvāmī and Rūpa Gosvāmī – as described in the

Caitanyacaritāmṛta – have raised modern scholarly doubt as to whether these were actually spoken by the master, not least since Kṛṣṇadāsa's text, while placing the teachings on Caitanya's lips, quotes anachronistically from these followers' own writings (De, 1986, 103–104). It has been further suggested that Caitanya's "whole mode of life was against his being a thinker" (Kennedy, 1925, 88), hence that he could not have articulated the complex theological doctrines attributed to him. However, in my view, such suspicions are unnecessarily conjectural, especially in light of three considerations. First, it is widely accepted that Caitanya exhibited intellectual astuteness in his youth, and although he is said to have dramatically abandoned learning for devotion after his visit to Gaya, there is no reason to suppose that he lost his intellectual faculties in the process; second, arguably he was able to attract such learned followers as Sanātana Gosvāmī and Rūpa Gosvāmī because of his intellectual as much as his devotional persuasive powers; and third, there is ample account during the later years of his life that his experiences of devotional ecstasies did not keep him from holding reasoned discussions, nor from carrying on daily routines of a strictly observant Brahmanical *saṃnyāsī*. Uncontested is the fact that Caitanya taught, by example and precept, Kṛṣṇa *bhakti* – devotional surrender to Kṛṣṇa as Bhagavān, the supreme being – as the best occupation for human beings aiming for what he deemed the highest goal, beyond liberation, namely, all-consuming love (*prema*) for Kṛṣṇa as the all-attractive divine eternal reciprocator of love. In this capacity, Caitanya is regarded today as the foundational preceptor of Gauḍīya Vaiṣṇava theology and practice.

Conceptions of Caitanya's Divinity and Practices of His Worship

All early biographers, as well as later biographers who followed the earlier accounts, represented Caitanya as a divine being. The earliest accounts described miraculous powers and events, leading to the notion that Caitanya was an *avatāra* of Viṣṇu; others considered him to be Svayam Bhagavān – the original supreme lord, identified as Kṛṣṇa – while Locanadāsa (author of *Caitanyamaṅgala*) considered him to be a divinity in his own right (Stewart, 2010, 101). In his work *Bṛhadbhāgavatāmṛta*, Sanātana Gosvāmī, the seniormost of the Vrindavan preceptor-followers of Caitanya – the "six *gosvāmī*s" – represents Caitanya as the *bhaktarūpa* (devotee form) of Kṛṣṇa:

> Realizing that the ecstasy of His beloved devotees is even sweeter than His own, out of greed [*lobha*] the Lord descended to this world in the form of His own devotee. Dressed as a renunciant, golden in effulgence, He bears the name Śrī Kṛṣṇa Caitanya. All glories to that Lord Hari, who has appeared as the son of Mother Śacī! (*BṛhBhAm.* 1.1.3; trans. Dasa, 2002, 12)

Kṛṣṇadāsa's *Caitanyacaritāmṛta* consolidated various theories of Caitanya's identity that had circulated up to his time, rejecting almost none yet unfolding a detailed comprehension of Caitanya as the combined form of Kṛṣṇa and Rādhā. This last conceptualization, which to the present day enjoys acceptance among most of Caitanya's followers, appears to have been aimed against what was considered by its author (Kṛṣṇadāsa) a heretical theory, namely, that Caitanya, like Kṛṣṇa, evoked erotic attraction in his immediate followers – a mood that came to be known as *gauranāgarabhāva* (Stewart, 2010, chs. 2–4, 139–142). Another marginal theory about Caitanya's divinity is that of some Vaiṣṇava → Sahajiyās who have regarded Caitanya as a practitioner of *sahajasādhanā* (involving tantric ritual sexual practices), as an exemplar for and preceptor of their view that Kṛṣṇa and Rādhā are embodied in *all* human beings – male and female, respectively (Gupta, 1976, 115; see O'Connell, 2003 for a refutation of this view, based on examination of important early Caitanya followers).

What virtually all early biographers held in common in their regard for Caitanya was their amazement at his extraordinary physical appearance. They agree that he was exceptionally tall, with long arms "extending to the knees," and possessing a "golden" complexion (hence he was referred to as Gaurāṅga ("Having Golden Limbs") and as Gaurasundara ("Whose Beauty Is That of Gold"). Caitanya's golden complexion in particular came to be understood as an indicator of his identity with (golden-complexioned) Rādhā (Stewart, 2010, 124–125).

What came to be the orthodox view of Caitanya's identity – that Caitanya was none other than the original divinity Kṛṣṇa in the mood and complexion of Rādhā appearing in a later age and in a different locality – soon led to the articulation of further implications of divine continuity. Since Kṛṣṇa had been present in Vrindavan with his many associates, these same associates must have appeared again as associates of Caitanya; these were to be named and identified with their Vṛndāvana personas, especially by Kavikarṇapūra in his *Gauragaṇoddeśadīpikā* (Little Light on the Identification of Gaura's Associates, 1576). Moreover, taking the sense of continuity a step further, certain devotees of Caitanya would be identified as embodiments of Caitanya himself: in the generation after Caitanya, Śrīnivāsa would be seen as such (Stewart, 2010, 305, 320–324), and more recently, among others, one Prabhu Jagadbandhu (d. 1921) has been regarded as a "combined form" of Caitanya and his associate Nityānanda (Kapoor, 1995, 93–94).

Along with and soon after contemporaries' identification of Caitanya as a divinity, they and later followers took up acts and practices of his worship. The early biographies describe occasions when Caitanya outwardly exhibited what were understood to be characteristics and actions showing his identity as an *avatāra* (or multiple *avatāras*) of Viṣṇu or of Kṛṣṇa. Appearing with the four arms of Viṣṇu or with six arms (signifying a composite form of Kṛṣṇa, Rāma, and Caitanya), or exhibiting the mood (*bhāva*) of various Viṣṇu *avatāras* compelled those present at the time to offer obeisance and prayerful praises (e.g. as described in *Caitanyabhāgavata* 2.10, during Caitanya's "grand revelation" [*mahāmahāprakāśa*] in the house of his friend Śrīvāsa).

Aside from narrative biographical writings, an extensive eulogistic literature, including pastimes (*līlā*) songs, developed around the figure of Caitanya, especially Bengali song series (*padāvalīs*) consisting of *gauralīlā padas* (songs describing Gaura's, i.e. Caitanya's, divine activities). Among these, the descriptions of his activities in Nabadvip are the most prominent (Chatterjee, 1983, 216–217; see also Wulff, 1995). A less extensive body of Sanskrit poetry eulogizing Caitanya also exists. Vāsudeva Sarvabhauma (mentioned above) is credited with composing one hundred verses praising Caitanya, two of which are quoted in *Caitanyacandrodayanāṭaka* (6.74–75) and *Caitanyacaritāmṛta* (2.6. *śloka* 20–21; Dimock, 1999, 420). Rūpa Gosvāmī, a principal direct follower of Caitanya residing in Vrindavan, composed three Sanskrit eight-verse (*aṣṭaka*) prayers in praise of Caitanya, set as the opening stanzas of his work *Stavamālā*; and Rūpa's close associate Raghunātha Dāsa composed both an eight-verse and a twelve-verse Caitanya eulogy. Also notable for its rhetorical flourish is Prabodhānanda Sarasvatī's *Caitanyacandrāmṛta* (The Nectar of Moon-like Caitanya), consisting of 143 four-line Sanskrit stanzas.

Formalized and routinized worship of Caitanya took shape with the establishment of his image (*mūrti*) in shrines and temples, mainly in Bengal and Bangladesh but also in Orissa, Assam, and Manipur. One wooden image of Caitanya presently worshipped in Nabadvip as Dhāmeśvara was, according to oral tradition, bestowed by Caitanya himself on his wife Viṣṇupriyā upon his taking *saṃnyāsa* vows. According to another tradition, the first physical (wooden) images of Caitanya together with his close associate Nityānanda were carved by their follower Gauridāsa, a resident of Ambika Kalna (near Nabadvip), under the direct guidance of Caitanya and Nityānanda during their final visit to his home (*BhRaĀk.* 7.346–387). And several temples in Orissa have images of Caitanya claimed to date from his time (Das, 1989). The worship of Caitanya in such temple images has since then proliferated widely, particularly through missionizing activities of recent and current preceptors of the tradition, notably, in the 20th century, of → Bhaktisiddhanta Saraswati and his disciple A.C. → Bhaktivedanta Prabhupada and their respective missions, the Gaudiya Math and the International Society for Krishna Consciousness (→ ISKCON).

Eventually, written formal prescriptions for the ritual worship of Caitanya appeared: one example, the *Bhakticandrikā* ascribed to one Lokānanda Ācārya, claims to contain the direct instruction of Caitanya's associate Narahari Sārkara – a manual on worship of Caitanya and initiation into a Caitanya *mantra* (De, 1986, 447n1). More recent manuals prescribe elaborate visualizations and meditations: Caitanya and specified associates are mapped onto symmetrical graphic arrangements (*maṇḍalas*), and sequences of Caitanya's daily activities are outlined to facilitate practitioners' pursuit of devotional moods (*rāgānugabhaktisādhana*) in relation to Caitanya (McDaniel, 1993).

Regarding calendrical observances, the beginning of public celebration of Caitanya's birthday was marked by a large festival that was held at the birthplace of Narottamadās at Kheturi, in present-day Bangladesh, several decades after Caitanya's passing (*BhRaĀk.* ch. 10). Caitanya's advent is now observed widely as *gaurapūrṇimā*, coinciding with *phālguna* (Feb–Mar) full-moon day, when also many regions of India celebrate *holī*. A stanza by Prabodhānanda Sarasvatī in his *Caitanyacandrāmṛta* suggests both the joyful spirit of remembrance of Caitanya generated in this celebration, as a reenactment of the festivity said to have been embodied in him, and the simultaneous sense of longing for Caitanya's presence experienced by his followers as they remember places associated with his life:

> In this world are still present the most glorious and fortunate township of Gauḍa (Nabadvip), the shores along the ocean (at Puri), the sovereign of Śrī Puruṣottama, Madhupati (Jagannātha), and his divine names. Hari! Hari! Alas! Nowhere, however, can be seen a festival of love like the one you held, o Caitanya! O reservoir of grace! Will I ever again witness your divine opulence? (*CaiCan.* 140)

Bibliography

Chatterjee, A.N., *Śrīkṛṣṇa Caitanya: A Historical Study on Gauḍīya Vaiṣṇavism*, New Delhi, 1983.

Das, F.M., "Foot-Prints of Śrī Chaitanya Mahāprabhu in Jajpur," in: H.C. Das, ed., *Śrī Chaitanya in the Religious Life of India*, Calcutta, 1989.

Dasa (Dāsa), G., *Śrī Bṛhad Bhāgavatāmṛta of Śrīla Sanātana Gosvāmī*, vol. I, Los Angeles, 2002.

De, S.K., Early History of Vaisnava Faith and Movement in Bengal, Calcutta, 1986.

Dimock Jr., E.C., *Caitanya Caritāmṛta of Kṛṣṇadāsa Kavirāja: A Translation and Commentary*, Cambridge MA, 1999.

Dimock Jr., E.C., "Religious Biography in India: The 'Nectar of the Acts' of Caitanya," in: F.E. Reynolds & D. Capps, eds., *The Biographical Process: Studies in the History and Psychology of Religion*, The Hague, 1976, 109–120.

Eidlitz, W., *Krsna-Caitanya. Sein Leben und Seine Lehre*, Stockholm, 1968.

Gupta, S.D., *Obscure Religious Cults*, Calcutta, 1976.

Kapoor, O.B.L., *The Saints of Bengal*, Caracas, 1995.

Kapoor, O.B.L., *The Philosophy and Religion of Śrī Caitanya*, New Delhi, 1977.

Kennedy, M.T., The Chaitanya Movement, Calcutta, 1925.

Majumdar, A.K., *Caitanya – His Life and Doctrines: A Study in Vaiṣṇavism*, Bombay, 1969.

McDaniel, J., "Dancing in the Hidden Vṛndāvana: The Ritual Service of Caitanya," *JVS* 1/3, 1993, 72–82.

O'Connell, J.T., "Historicity in the Biographies of Caitanya," *JVS* 1/2, 1993, 102–132.

O'Connell, J.T., "Chaitanya's Associates Were Not Sahajiyās," in: P. Sarkar, ed., *Shraddhalekhamala: Sukumar Sen Centennial Volume*, Kolkata, 2003, 404–436.

Smith, W.L., *Patterns in North Indian Hagiography*, Stockholm, 2000.

Stewart, T.K., *The Final Word: The Caitanya Caritāmṛta and the Grammar of Religious Tradition*, Oxford, 2010.

Wulff, D., "The Play of Emotion: Līlākīrtan in Bengal," in: W.S. Sax, ed., *The Gods at Play: Līlā in South Asia*, New York, 1995, 99–114.

Kenneth Valpey

Cokhāmeḷā

Literary and hagiographical accounts accept that Cokhāmeḷā was born in the second half of the 13th century CE, probably around the time → Jñāndev was born, and that he died in 1338 in Mangalwedha, a small town quite close to Pandharpur, → Maharashtra (Ranade, 1961). The central features of Cokhāmeḷā's identity as remembered through countless retellings are his untouchable Mahar caste and his profound devotion to Viṭṭhal – two seemingly irreconcilable aspects twinned together in this figure. These are reflected in his *abhanga*s, over three hundred in number, and in the corpus of stories that make up received accounts of Cokhāmeḷā's life. While a large number of Cokhāmeḷā's *abhanga*s express his devotion, there exist several poems that question the social order that sees him as defiled and unfit to enter the Viṭṭhal Temple in Pandharpur. As common to traditions of the → Vārkarī Sampradāy, both the *abhanga*s and the narrations of biography are circulated through modes of performance and written accounts. The contours of Cokhāmeḷā's sacred life may be formed by pooling together biographical strands in songs attributed to him as well as in the songs attributed to contemporary poet-saints of the 14th century, mainly → Nāmdev and Janābāī. His family – his wife Soyrābāī, his son Karmameḷā, his sister Nirmalā, and his brother-in-law Bankā Mahar, all poets in their own right – speak about Cokhāmeḷā's → *bhakti* and his deprivation. In the 18th century, the preeminent Brahman Vārkarī hagiographer Mahīpati weaves into his story about Cokhāmeḷā in the *Bhaktavijaya* all these threads and creates through this process another powerfully evocative narration of the Mahar saint's life and works (Abbott, 1982).

Sacred Biography and Poems

A folk song attributed to Nāmdev narrates the birth of Cokhāmeḷā and is cited by S.B. Kadam in the introduction to his volume of Cokhāmeḷā's collected poems (Kadam, 1998). The poem contains in its last lines the *mudrikā* ("signature") of Nāmdev – Cokhāmeḷā's *guru* and friend – though it does not figure in any of the collected works of Nāmdev. There was once a devout village headman, the Patil, – so runs the story – who entrusted a Mahar couple with the task of carrying a basket of ripening mangos to Pandharpur. This couple, as it turns out, would soon become Cokhāmeḷā's parents. Hoisting the heavy basket on to their shoulders, the couple trudged along the road. As they neared Pandharpur, they were accosted by an aged and hungry Brahman who begged for some food. Overcome by pity, the wife chose a mango and laid it in the Brahman's palms. The Brahman tasted it and, finding it sour, handed it back to her. She tucked the tasted mango in the folds of her saree. When the couple reached Pandharpur and the fruit was counted and found one short, the wife took the tasted mango out only to find that it had turned into a lovely baby – Cokhāmeḷā. The aged Brahman, it was discovered, was none other than the lord of Pandharpur, Viṭṭhal. Though there is a Brahman involved in Cokhāmeḷā's birth, as in that of most saints from the lower castes, there is no attempt in this case to Brahmanize Cokhāmeḷā's origins. His parents were Mahar and are seen to have been engaged in regular Mahar duties – acting as messengers and load bearers for the village Patil. "*Cokhā*" in Marathi means to suck and to taste: here it is Viṭṭhal himself who partakes of a fruit, and the partly eaten fruit turns into Cokhāmeḷā. Divine love marks Cokhāmeḷā, even as his caste position stigmatizes him within society, and this conflict between perception and putative reality is the rubric through and around which the stories about his life are structured.

The legends surrounding Cokhāmeḷā's death also picture him amid his caste community, performing such tasks that were generally assigned to Mahars. It is again Nāmdev's *abhanga* that narrates the following story. Cokhāmeḷā was enlisted by the new Muslim ruler (after the eclipse of the Yadava Kingdom in Maharashtra) to build the walls of a fort at Mangalwedha, along with several members of his community. A portion of the wall collapsed on the laborers while they were building it, burying several Mahars at work, including Cokhāmeḷā. Pāṇḍurang (i.e. Viṭṭhal) himself, claims Nāmdev in his *abhanga*, instructed him to bring Cokhāmeḷā's body to Pandharpur, telling him to get those bones that called out "Viṭṭhal, Viṭṭhal." Cokhāmeḷā's *samādhi* (memorial), believed to be the one consecrated by Nāmdev, can be seen today near the foot of the steps leading to the great door of the Pāṇḍurang Temple, where he was wont to stand. In death, as in life, Cokhāmeḷā's customary place is on the threshold of the temple (Mokashi-Punekar, 2005).

Mahīpati's poems dramatize stories about how Cokhāmeḷā could never enter the temple to worship his beloved god. In his narration of Cokhāmeḷā's life, Mahīpati underscores the central paradox of the Mahar devotee's situation: his marginality in the caste hierarchy, as seen in the Brahman priests' scorn for his devotion and Viṭṭhal's special love for him, the social order notwithstanding. One day, according to Mahīpati, Cokhāmeḷā stood in worship outside the door as was his practice. It was late in the evening, and the priests had locked the doors and gone away. The lord of Pandharpur himself came to Cokhāmeḷā standing outside and, taking him by hand, "lovingly led him into the innermost shrine" (Abbott, 1982, 379). A Brahman priest overheard Cokhāmeḷā talking to Viṭṭhal and thought that the duties of Brahmans would cease if a Mahar could touch the sacred image with all its ornaments and garments. The priest banished Cokhāmeḷā to the other bank of the Chandrabhāgā (i.e. Bhimā) River, lest the errant Viṭṭhal keep bringing him back into the temple. Cokhāmeḷā went to the other bank and worshipped Pāṇḍurang from afar, and he built there a pillar of lights (which, incidentally, stood in place until a few decades ago, as photographs reveal [Kadam, 1969]). Viṭṭhal, however, could not be kept away and came to dine with him there. One day Cokhāmeḷā's wife Soyrābāī accidentally spilled some curds on the god while serving them food. A Brahman priest passing by was enraged to hear Cokhāmeḷā scolding Soyrābāī for the accident and slapped him across his face. But when the priest went into the temple, he found that the cheek of the god was swollen, and his garments had curd spilled on them. And so the Brahman repented and took Cokhāmeḷā by the hand into the temple again (Abbott, 1982).

The story summarized above ends on a happier note. Cokhāmeḷā's own *abhanga*s do not speak of any such change of heart on the part of the Brahmans, reflecting, as they do, a social structure that is antithetical to his spiritual aspirations. While a large number of *abhanga*s reflect stock Vārkarī themes, there is still a significant number of Cokhāmeḷā's poems that question and register a protest against unrelenting structures of society. The poems do not repose hope in divine intervention. They express instead a poignant sadness that indicates personal experience; this voice from the past is a sure guide to the authenticity of the poet-saint's historical presence, seen for instance in the following *abhanga*:

My father and begetter of the world,
  how are you not moved?
  why the weight of this world
  on my shoulders?
  why are you and I
  severed like this?
Our joy and sorrow in this:
  birth, age and death.
Why
  do you look on
  with such fond pride?
Overcome, Chokha stands
  at the great door
  hands folded for Vitthoba. (Mokashi-Punekar, 2002, 8)

There is yet another story narrated by Nāmdev that is partially reflected in one of Cokhāmeḷā's *abhanga*s, an instance of how myth and poetry weave into each other in *bhakti* traditions. It begins, as in the story told above, with Viṭṭhal leading Cokhāmeḷā into his inner shrine in the temple, where the god placed his *tulsī* (holy basil) garland around the neck of his favorite devotee. It was discovered in the morning on the next day that the gold necklace on Viṭṭhal's image had been stolen, and the obvious suspect was the untouchable Mahar saint. Search parties found Cokhāmeḷā on the sands of the Chandrabhāgā, oblivious to the fact that the *tulsī* necklace around his neck was really gold. It was decided that Cokhāmeḷā must be punished; he was tied to bullocks and was about to be dragged to death when Viṭṭhal himself held the cattle by their horns and so saved his devotee. Cokhāmeḷā's poem dramatizes the scene without, however, the satisfactory ending in the story:

They thrash me, Vithu,
  now don't walk so slow.
The pandits whip,
  some crime,
  don't know what:
How did Vithoba's necklace come round your
  throat,
  they curse and strike
  and say I polluted you.
Do not send the cur at your door away,
  giver of everything.
You,

Chakrapani,
  yours is the deed.
With folded hands
Chokha begs
I revealed our secret,
  don't turn away. (Mokashi-Punekar, 2002, 6)

Not all *abhangas* express pathos. In the following poem, Cokhāmeḷā reflects philosophically with an existential angst on the nature of defilement:

Five elements compound the body impure;
  all things mix, thrive in the world.
Then who is pure and who impure?
The body is rooted in impurity.
From the beginning to the end,
  endless impurities heap themselves.
Who is it can be made pure?
Says Chokha, I am struck with wonder,
  can there be any such beyond pollution?
  (Mokashi-Punekar, 2002, 57)

An interesting example of how language reflects caste positions is the following *abhanga*, where Cokhāmeḷā makes use of the traditional greeting *johār*, a term of address for the upper caste. This laconic and terse verse underscores the bitter reality of caste inequity in an ironic fashion:

Johar, mai-baap, johar.
I am the mahar of your mahars.
I am come,
  starved
  for your leavings.
The servant of your servants
  waits with hope.
I have brought, says Chokha,
  my bowl
  for your leavings. (Mokashi-Punekar, 2002, 68)

The poem in which anger and despair are the most visible is the following one, where Cokhāmeḷā seems to realize, in an instant of epiphany, the defiled nature of the universe. When all existence is touched at its very origin with pollution, how can gods or scriptures, which are but mental constructs of the same defiled body, be anything but defiled?

Vedas and the shastras
  polluted; puranas inauspicious
  impure; the body, the soul
  contaminated; the manifest
Being is the same.
Brahma polluted, Vishnu too;
Shankar is impure, inauspicious.
Birth impure, dying is impure:
  says Chokha,
  pollution stretches
  without beginning
  and end. (Mokashi-Punekar, 2002, 60)

Such anger, however, is rarely seen in Cokhāmeḷā's *abhangas*, which generally express protest with a degree of philosophical calm and piety, accepting fate and the karmic cycle (Zelliot, 1995). We must turn to his son Karmameḷā for a voice that articulates a more radical note of dissent.

Karmameḷā and Baṅkā Mahar

Śrīsakaḷasantgāthā (The Collected Poems of All Saint-Poets) lists 27 *abhangas* attributed to Karmameḷā, Cokhāmeḷā's often angry son. These poems express a sense of rebellion that is quite absent from those of his father, whose life seems to have been lived out within the set of prescribed rules of → *dharma*, even as his verse condemned caste in the strongest terms. There exist *abhangas* attributed to Nāmdev; Soyrābāī and Nirmalā, Cokhāmeḷā's wife and sister, respectively; and Baṅkā, Nirmalā's husband – these narrate the many developing threads of the story of Karmameḷā's miraculous birth (Zelliot, 2005a). In deft and rather realistic strokes, these poems describe the somewhat grouchy husband Cokhāmeḷā, who escaped the mess of childbirth and went to his sister Nirmalā in another village, and of Viṭṭhal himself, who came in the guise of Nirmalā to assist Soyrābāī in her labor. One of Karmameḷā's *abhangas* refers to this miracle and questions Viṭṭhal with characteristic urgency and bitterness.

How, Narayana, do you forget?
My father is your ward; you
  bathed me as an infant: why is
  everything so hard now?
Take care, your reputation is at stake:
  your good name has to survive.
Says Chokha's Karmamela,
Please god, you must never forget me. (Mokashi-Punekar, 2005, 146)

This voice is youthful and hotheaded, and Karmameḷā has no reservations in advising Viṭṭhal to take care, for Viṭṭhal's reputation is at stake as the creator of an unjust society. Some of Karmameḷā's poems reflect angst and describe a god who is powerless to change the social structure, a god at the mercy of human beings. In the following poem that makes use of irony as a literary device, Karmameḷā seems to exonerate Viṭṭhal of the cruelty of the world, for a merciful god could not have created this awful place.

> From now onwards, Hari,
> don't reproach me. You look after
> your interests and I'll manage
> mine. What is the point
> of blaming you for our destiny?
> My heart is my witness:
> I won't waste more words.
> Says Karmamela, you should know,
> Narayana,
> both our hearts. (Mokashi-Punekar, 2005, 147)

Karmameḷā, perhaps being the youngest, is the most rebellious among the five members of this remarkable 14th-century untouchable family who all speak of injustices in the caste hierarchy. His uncle Baṅkā Mahar's poems reveal profound devotion to Viṭṭhal and to other members of the family, in particular Cokhāmeḷā, whom he acknowledges as his *guru* in a number of poems. It is accepted that Baṅkā and Soyrābāī were brother and sister and married to another brother–sister pair of – Cokhā and Nirmalā (Mokashi-Punekar, 2005). This is a closely knit family bonded together by ties of blood and devotion. Baṅkā has around 39 *abhanga*s attributed to him in *Śrīsakaḷasantgāthā*, and many of these sing of his beloved *guru* Cokhāmeḷā. While Viṭṭhal is often infused with maternal qualities and referred to as Viṭhāī ("Mother Viṭṭhal") in *abhanga*s by several Vārkarī poet-saints, it is unusual to see a feminine identity given to a male *guru*, as in the following poem:

> Mother Dnyaneshwar [i.e. Jñāndev] is the king of wisdom:
> he engulfed Kechar in a flood of mercy.
> Kechar came to shelter at Dnyaneshwar's feet and graced Namdev.
> With his hand on Chokha's head, Namdev taught him these syllables: Vi th th la.
> Chokha is my guru mother,
> says Banka.
> I prostrate myself at his feet. (Mokashi-Punekar, 2005, 144)

A poem sequence of 11 *abhanga*s narrates the miraculous conception of Karmameḷā. Baṅkā describes in broad and realistic strokes the story of his sad and childless sister Soyrābāī, who was visited by Viṭṭhal himself in the guise of a poor old Brahman begging for food. Caught between the fear of transgressing caste norms and a pity for his plight, she gave him some rice and curd. The Brahman told her that she could ask him for whatever she wanted, but, of course, she did not do so. Viṭṭhal gave her some *prasād* and told her that she would soon have a baby. When he got back home, Cokhāmeḷā told her that she had behaved improperly, and, once the time of birth came, he went away to his sister's house, as described above. Baṅkā does not, however, narrate the birth story but only says that Hari came to Cokhāmeḷā's house and stayed there happily ever after.

Baṅkā's deft delineation of Cokhāmeḷā's role fits into the accepted notion of *bhakta*s sacrificing worldly attachments in the cause of their devotion. In his *abhanga* about Gorā the potter, Baṅkā does not refer to the horrifying story of the potter trampling his son to death while mixing the clay, even as he is engrossed in meditating on the name. Instead, he tells a more tender tale of how Gorā is helped by Viṭṭhal in his daily labor – a description characteristic of the *abhanga*s of the Vārkarī poets, who are more often than not householder saints and members of productive castes. Many of these *abhanga*s picture Viṭṭhal as a loving companion who runs around and helps his beloved devotee saints burdened by menial chores that their castes impose. Baṅkā describes Viṭṭhal helping Gorā in his daily tasks thus:

> Look at this miracle:
> Hari has turned a potter in Gora's yard.
> His eagle that flies over the three worlds
> is now a donkey; and his glory is kept aside.
> Filling the gunny sacks with clay,
> he heaves them in, helped by Rukhmai.
> Banka wonders at the silence of the Vedas
> on Hari's love for his devotees. (Mokashi-Punekar, 2005, 145)

The last two lines are tongue in cheek and a powerful indictment of Brahmanical texts that fail, unlike *bhakti* literary traditions, to engage with the shared experience and connections of love. It is these loving ties that form the substance of Baṅkā's *abhanga*s.

Soyrābāī and Nirmalā

Cokhāmeḷā's wife, Soyrābāī, very unusually for someone of her gender and caste, also wrote poetry alluding to her low social position and poverty, referring to herself as Cokhā's Mahari in her compositions. Though she wrote a sizable number of poems (62 in number are attributed to Soyrābāī in *Śrīsakaḷasantgāthā*), not too many studies are available either on her or on Nirmalā – Cokhāmeḷā's sister – though together they appear to be a very rare instance of women poet-saints from an untouchable caste writing in a medieval *bhakti* tradition. Two *abhangas* by Soyrābāī are, however, well known in mainstream popular Marathi devotional music. One of them, which has been rendered by the acclaimed Hindustani classical vocal maestro Bhimsen Joshi, is translated below:

> Sing this joyous Name lovingly, chant a prayer to Vithoba.
> This worldly life will be happy if you chant the Name again and again.
> Lust and anger become helpless; look! Desires and longings flee.
> Say Hari Hari lovingly, says Chokha's Mahari. (Zelliot, 2005b, 158)

A couplet from another of Soyrābāī's *abhangas* has been used as an invocation by V.L. Bhave in the first edition of his *Maharashtra Saraswat*, a history on Marathi literature:

> I'll place a leaf before you and I will serve you family food.
> O God, it's not fit for you, but imagine it sweet and accept it.

These lines express Soyrābāī's acknowledgment of her low status and her humility. Some of her other poems speak about the restrictions imposed by the Brahmans on her and Cokhāmeḷā. Like her more famous husband, she also depicts poignant images of waiting on the threshold and an understanding that caste norms are unjust social constructions that have little to do with actual pollution:

> Not a creature in the world has a place of origin anywhere other than in gore.
> This is the glory of God; defilement exists within.
> The body is polluted from within. Be sure of it, says the Mahari of Chokha. (Zelliot, 2005b, 159)

Just as Baṅkā Mahar expresses devotion to Cokhāmeḷā, several *abhangas* of Soyrābāī refer to Nirmalā, Cokhāmeḷā's sister, with loving affection. Nirmalā only speaks of her brother Cokhāmeḷā in the 24 *abhangas* attributed to her in *Śrīsakaḷasantgāthā*; in fact, her *mudrikā* in the *abhangas* is "Cokhā's sister." A majority of Nirmalā's poems dwells on the sorrows that life entails and the relentless fashion in which worldliness imposes itself on spiritual aspirations.

> Ocean of mercy, listen to my prayer.
> Let me lay my head at your feet.
> There are many ways, but I do not know them.
> I can only embrace your feet with all my strength.
> My body, my mind, my thoughts are restless.
> What can I do? I have no strength to quiet my mind.
> I cannot free myself from *sansar*;
> it embraces me, it takes you far from me.
> Nirmala says, what shall I do?
> You have left me far behind. (Zelliot, 2005b, 163)

Janābāī, one of the two well-known female poets of the Vārkarī tradition (the other being Kānhopātrā), narrates her workaday world in great detail, describing her unending household chores in which only Viṭṭhal is ever her help and companion. Neither Soyrābāī nor Nirmalā, however, describes their everyday domestic realities, in the same fashion in which Cokhāmeḷā does not describe the tasks that he is otherwise supposed to have performed according to poems attributed to saint-poets such as Janābāī and Nāmdev. The five members of Cokhāmeḷā's family speak of the restrictions imposed on them as Mahars and the disabilities that they face in the performance and fulfillment of their religious or spiritual desires. They articulate in no uncertain terms their resistance to social constructions that exclude them; however, there is a silence in their poetry on what constituted a Mahar's life in terms of caste division of labor in the premodern period. To understand this and to situate Cokhāmeḷā's poetry, we need always to read Cokhāmeḷā in the context of the other poet-saints' *abhangas* about him and see these in the context of the hagiographic stories in circulation through the centuries, which the above sections have attempted to do.

Cokhāmeḷā in Marathi Film and Drama

There exist four representations of Cokhāmeḷā in mainstream Marathi drama and film, and each of these may be perceived to be mediated by the ideology of the playwright or director. *Sangit Uhshap* was a musical play written by Savarkar and performed after the Censor Board changed the ending of the play to a happy one in 1927 (Sapkal, 2005). Though the play presents Cokhāmeḷā's life in the context of upper-caste hegemony, it nevertheless shows its main protagonist telling his son Karmameḷā not to denigrate either the Brahmans or Hinduism. In fact, it is Cokhāmeḷā who is made to declare to the Muslim king the superiority of Hinduism over other religions and his total unwillingness to convert, despite his hardships in the face of → untouchability. The play culminates in Cokhāmeḷā's *darśan* of Viṭṭhal and his subsequent delivery through divine intervention, therefore quite completely eliding the idea of social justice in the here and now. The play is quite clearly a vehicle for Sarvarkar's interpretation of Hinduism and his propaganda of it as a superior religion, which fits into the larger political ideology of this writer. In contrast, *Yugayatra* by M.B. Chitnis – a close associate of → Ambedkar – presents Cokhāmeḷā in the context of his life as a laboring Mahar who is debarred from the Viṭṭhal Temple. Though the protagonist is shown to accept his karmic fate with resignation, he is also depicted as a representative of the oppressed laboring castes exploited by the upper caste in the village. Cokhāmeḷā's caste identity is submerged into the larger identity of oppressed working classes ideologically forged in the play.

Sant Cokhamela, released along with several other realistic films about Vārkarī saints in the 1930s and 1940s, was directed by D.K. Kale and is the first cinematic depiction of the Mahar saint's life. While the film tape is not readily available, there exists a published screenplay of the film, which focuses on the well-known incidents in Cokhāmeḷā's life, representing him as a devout Mahar, hemmed in by caste restrictions (Sapkal, 2005). A major departure from the plays is the dominance that the film gives to the legendary character of Anant Bhaṭ, supposed to be Cokhāmeḷā's Brahman scribe, who is pictured in this film as a staunch supporter of the Mahar devotee. The copy of a later film, titled *Johar May-bap or Sant Chokha Mela* (1950), can be watched today, since it was rereleased in 1981 with the title *Hi Wat Pandharichi*. While this is a moving film, representing Cokhāmeḷā as a toiling, bonded laborer doing all kinds of odd jobs, it does not sufficiently focus on Cokhāmeḷā's caste identity and contents itself with showing him as a moral and righteous devotee.

All four representations of Cokhāmeḷā discussed above do justice only to some aspects of his hagiography and may thus be rather partial and mediated accounts of the life and poetry of this significant *bhakti* figure and are indicative to a large extent of the times in which they were produced and the ideologies of their authors.

Cokhāmeḷā and Dalit Movement and Literature

The figure of Cokhāmeḷā and those of his family members, their poetry, and the stories woven around them constitute a living fund of memory and literature for the Vārkarīs and indeed for the people in the Marathi-speaking region. It is intriguing, however, to see what relationship the → Dalit movement has had, in its modern political, social, and literary manifestations, with the living memory of this resistance. The word "*dalit*" was chosen by the Mahar community leaders in the 1960s to indicate a people whose culture and history had been "ground down" and "broken and crushed to pieces." Critical analyses of the Dalit movement in its early and later phases engage with its beginnings in the late 19th century as an offshoot of the non-Brahman movement under the leadership of Jotirao Phule (also known as → Jyotiba Phule; Zelliot, 1992) and its development into radical protest under B.R. Ambedkar in the 1930s–1950s, that is, the nationalist and post-Independence years.

The early phase of the Dalit movement in Maharashtra can be traced from the 1880s in the interventions made by the Anarya Dosh Pariharak Mandal. The president of this organization for the Dalits was a Mahar – Gopal Baba Valangkar – former cadre of the British army and a close associate of Phule (Constable, 1997). He drew up a petition addressed to the Bombay government in 1894, drawing attention to the plight of the untouchables and requesting the authorities to readmit Mahars into the British Army. The petition included a verse most likely penned by Pandit Kondiram, who described the degraded conditions of the Mahars around the turn of the century. His earthy Marathi using naturalistic description looks forward to the vigor and deliberate coarseness of language used by the modern Dalit writers.

In 1888, the Anarya Dosh Pariharak Mandal published a *Vinanti Patra* attacking Brahmanical conceptions about the origins of *varṇāśrāma* and affirmed egalitarian *bhakti* as true Dalit identity that emphasized an alternative Hindu culture and community. This Hindu devotional identity was drawn as much from the Vārkarī *bhakti* tradition of Cokhāmeḷā and Tukārām as from the influence of Christian missionary writings on *bhakti* (Constable, 1997). Throughout the 1890s, the Anarya Dosh Pariharak Mandal wrote petitions and addressed audiences using → *kīrtans* and examples from Hindu scriptures to bring its message to the untouchable castes in Maharashtra, emphasizing devotion and calling on them to awaken to the exploitation of the upper castes. The figure of Cokhāmeḷā was an enabling and significant aspect of Dalit identity in this early phase, which continued well into the first couple of decades of the 20th century. Many new initiatives started by the movement carried the name of Cokhāmeḷā: a night school in Pune, a hostel in Nagpur, and a reform society in Vidharbha were all named after the Mahar poet-saint. One of the most well-known Mahar leaders of these decades was Kisan Fagu Bansode, who made pilgrimages to Pandharpur to collect Cokhameḷā's *abhangas* and wrote a play on his life. One of his poems reads as follows:

> Why do you endure curses?
> Cokha went into the temple resolutely,
> Why do you, ashamed, stay far off?
> You are the descendants of Cokha.
> Why do your fear to enter the temple?
> Brace yourself like a wrestler, come,
> Together let us conquer pollution. (Zelliot, 1992, 11)

The emergence of Ambedkar during the national movement and his involvement in the cause of the untouchables from the 1920s marked a slow waning of the significance of Cokhāmeḷā as a figure of emulation for the Mahars. Though Cokhāmeḷā and his family questioned caste, this protest was contained by their *bhakti*, and their lives were circumscribed within caste hierarchy. This could not satisfy Ambedkar, a lawyer educated in American and European universities and a modernist in his approach, who sought political means in his passionate struggle to ensure equal constitutional and social status for the Dalits. Even in the early years when he initiated *satyāgraha* (nonviolent resistance) for temple entry and encouraged untouchables to adopt Brahmanical practices, Cokhāmeḷā's piety did not hold much appeal to him. His first newspaper carried an *abhanga* by Tukārām under its title, and he occasionally quoted from Jñāndev (Zelliot, 1992); however, he repudiated untouchables who adopted caste names such as Cokhāmeḷā; the term Harijan, too, was equally repugnant to him, for he saw in both a submission to Brahmanical dominance and patronization (Zelliot, 1992). Cokhāmeḷā's devotion could not serve as an inspiration for the militant and uncompromising mood of protest that took shape from the 1930s onward. Only a permanent severance from Hinduism would satisfy the radical nature of untouchable resistance in Maharashtra by 1956, when millions of untouchables converted to Buddhism following the example of their leader Ambedkar. Though this was a religious conversion, it was a profoundly political statement – a declaration of a permanent exit from an ancient religion that had offered only condemnation for the most powerless within its folds.

Dalit literature in the last few decades reflects this profound change in "cosmology": it is modern in politics and modernist in its aesthetics. The first Dalit literature conference was held in Maharashtra in 1959; though at the time there were very few Dalit writers, predominant among those present were the newly converted Buddhists. By the 1970s, the Dalit Panthers (inspired by the Black Panthers of North America) were already being recognized for their raw and powerful writing that underwrote protest and affirmed cultural and literary independence from Brahmanical norms. Mainstream Marathi literature focused on emotional and intellectual/metaphysical aspects; this protest literature focused with urgency and passion on the deprivations and degradations of the body and material want (Jaaware, 2001). The depictions of suffering in these works are a trenchant critique of upper-caste social norms. This modernist literature is unable to accommodate or forge connections with a medieval literature from which Cokhāmeḷā's gentler voice of protest can be heard.

Bibliography

Abbott, J.E., *et al.*, *Stories of Indian Saints: A Translation of Mahipati's Marathi Bhaktavijaya*, Pune, 1933, ²1982.

Bhave, V.L., *Maharashtra Saraswat*, Bombay, 1898, ²1963.

Constable, P., "Early Dalit Literature and Culture in Late Nineteenth- and Early Twentieth-Century Western India," *MAS* 31/2, 1997, 317–338.

Deleury, G.A., *The Cult of Vithoba*, Pune, 1960.

Glushkova, I., "Norms and Values in the Varkari Tradition," in: M. Kosambi, ed., *Intersections: Socio-cultural Trends in Maharashtra*, New Delhi, 2000, 47–58.

Jaaware, A., "Eating, and Eating with, the Dalit: A Re-consideration Touching upon Marathi Poetry," in: K. Satchidanandan, ed., *Indian Poetry: Modernism and After*, New Delhi, 2001, 262–293.

Kadam, S.B., *Shri Sant Chokhamela: Charitra ani Abhang*, Mumbai, 1969, [2]1998.

Karve, I., "On the Road: A Maharashtrian Pilgrimage," in: E. Zelliot & M. Berntsen, eds., *The Experience of Hinduism: Essays in Religion in Maharashtra*, Albany, 1988, 143–173.

Kulkarni, A.R., "The Mahar Watan: A Historical Perspective," in: M. Kosambi, ed., *Intersections: Socio-cultural Trends in Maharashtra*, New Delhi, 2000, 121–140.

Mokashi-Punekar, R., "Banka Mahar and Karmamela," in: E. Zelliot & R. Mokashi-Punekar, eds., *Untouchable Saints: An Indian Phenomenon*, New Delhi, 2005, 143–155.

Mokashi-Punekar, R., *On the Threshold: Songs of Chokhamela*, New Delhi, 2002, [2]2005.

Nagaraj, D.R., *The Flaming Feet: A Study of the Dalit Movement in India*, Bangalore, 1993, repr. 2010.

Nemade, B., "The Revolt of the Underprivileged: Style in the Expression of the Warkari Movement in Maharashtra," in: J. Lele, ed., *Tradition and Modernity in Bhakti Movements*, Leiden, 1982, 113–123.

Novetzke, C.L., *Religion and Public Memory*, New York, 2008.

O'Hanlon, R., *Caste, Conflict and Ideology: Mahatma Jotirao Phule and Low Caste Protest in Nineteenth Century Western India*, Cambridge UK, 1985, [2]2002.

Pollock, S., "The Cosmopolitan Vernacular," *JAS* 57/1, 1998, 6–39.

Ranade, R.D., *Pathway to God in Marathi Literature*, Bombay, 1961.

Sapkal, A., "Representations of Chokhamela in Marathi Film and Drama," in: E. Zelliot & R. Mokashi-Punekar, eds., *Untouchable Saints: An Indian Phenomenon*, New Delhi, 2005, 179–184.

Vaudeville, C., "Cokhāmeḷā: An Untouchable Saint of Maharashtra," in: V. Dalmia, ed., *Myths, Saints and Legends in Medieval India*, Delhi, 1996, 221–240.

Zelliot, E., "The Story of Karmamela's Birth," in: E. Zelliot & R. Mokashi-Punekar, eds., *Untouchable Saints: An Indian Phenomenon*, New Delhi, 2005a, 149–158.

Zelliot, E., "Soyrabai and Nirmala," in: E. Zelliot & R. Mokashi-Punekar, eds., *Untouchable Saints: An Indian Phenomenon*, New Delhi, 2005b, 157–168.

Zelliot, E., "Chokhamela: Piety and Protest," in: D.N. Lorenzen, ed., *Bhakti Religion in North India: Community Identity and Political Action*, Albany, 1995, 212–220.

Zelliot, E., *From Untouchable to Dalit: Essays on the Ambedkar Movement*, New Delhi, 1992.

Rohini Mokashi-Punekar

Dādū Dayāl

Dādū Dayāl (1545?–1603) was a religious teacher and poet in the → Sant tradition who lived in → Rajasthan and gave rise to a sect named the Dādūpanth ("Path of Dādū"). Dādū is the respectful endearing Rajasthani term for "grandfather" rather than a variant of the Muslim name Dāʿūd. *Dayāl(u)* ("Compassionate"), sometimes also *Dīndayāl(u)* ("Compassionate with the Afflicted"), is an epithet attached to his name. Both epithets were used by Dādū himself for God and were hence applied by his followers to the master himself.

Life

On Dādū's life, the only near-contemporary sources are the hagiographies *Dādūjanmalīlā* and *Bhaktmāl* written by his disciples Jangopāl, at an unknown time soon after Dādū's death (see Callewaert, 1988), and Rāghavdās, composed in 1660 (see Nāhṭā, 1965), respectively, whereas his compositions started being collected during his lifetime. A third hagiography – named *Sant guṇ sāgar* and composed by Mādhavdās, a follower of Dādū living in Guler in the Kangra district of Himachal Pradesh – was written allegedly between 1593 and 1603, that is, during the lifetime of Dādū. No ancient manuscripts of this are available, but in its printed version (Śāstrī, VS 2056), it is anachronistic in reporting events that took place after its alleged completion. Though inauthentic, it may have been written to have an edge on the Sikhs who were in power in Guler from the early 19th century. Jangopāl, from a trader caste well represented in Dādū's following, wrote from the perspective of an eyewitness of the formation of the sect's nucleus as it was gravitating around the master and his successors in Naraina (Jaipur district), the last residence of Dādū. Rāghavdās, who has a *nāgā* pedigree (see → *sādhus*; see → *akhāṛās*), differs from Jangopāl. Firstly, he created the taxonomy of disciples, purportedly numbering 52 main disciples and another 100, who were less closely related to the master. Mādhavdās, too, enumerates those 52 plus 100 disciples, but he was hardly preceding Rāghavdās. Secondly, and related to that strategy,

Fig. 1: A Dādūpanthī *nāgā*. Wall painting, Udaipur *jamāt*, Shekhavati, Rajasthan (photo by Monika Horstmann).

Rāghavdās placed the Dādūpanth within the range of the wider Hindu sectarian organization. This can be seen as a reaction to the then fairly recent formation of the → Daśanāmī *saṃnyāsī* military organization of *nāgā*s and related to the rise of a corresponding Vaiṣṇava and Dādūpanthī military organization, which is a replica of that of the *saṃnyāsī nāgā*s.

Dādū was born in a caste of cotton carders (Piñjārā, Dhuniyā). The traditional date of his birth (the eighth day of the bright half of the lunar month of *phālguna* [Feb–Mar]) is conspicuous for coinciding with one prominent day of the spring festival (*holī*). One major strand in the development of Dādū's hagiography, noticeable from half a century after his death in the recrafting of Jangopāl's text, reflects an attempt to replace his artisan origin with a Brahmanical genealogy. According to Jangopāl, Dādū's birthplace was Ahmedabad in Gujarat. Here, some groups of Hindu cotton carders had turned Muslim in the 9th century (Massignon, 1922, 66) but retained their social and religious traditions. Ahmedabad is not mentioned in other early sources on Dādu's life, and neither he nor his following sought to relate to Ahmedabad. According to Jangopāl, in 1573 Dādū settled in Sambhar, where his first son, Garībdās, was born in 1575. There is thus a gap of about a decade in the information about him between his alleged departure from Ahmedabad and his arrival in Rajasthan. Dādū had another son, Maskīndās, and two daughters, Havā and Bāī, Bāī being a household name rather than a proper name. While Jangopāl records these four as Dādū's children, engendered without sexual contact with his wife, Rāghavdās lists them as the first four of Dādū's disciples (Nāhṭā, 1965, v. 361), which shows how Dādū was projected progressively as a *sādhu*. All his children at some point became involved in the management of the emerging Dādūpanth. In about 1579, Dādū moved to Amber (Amer), the residence of the Kachvaha king Bhagavantdās (r. 1573–1589). The hagiography reports that in 1585 he was received by Emperor Akbar at Fatehpur Sikri on the recommendation of King Bhagavantdās, whose daughter had been married in the previous year to Akbar's son Salīm (later on, Emperor Jahāngīr). Though this is not attested outside Dādūpanthī sources, it is not easy to dismiss as spurious that Dādū was presented to Akbar. This event of great significance for Dādū may have been a very minor affair for the imperial court. In Amber, Dādū resided close to the royal residence, under the watchful eyes of the court. Had he or his followers fraudulently boasted of that meeting, which also implicated the king, this might have had dire consequences, including his expulsion from Amber. However, he continued living there until 1593. If the meeting is a legend created after Dādū's death, the patronage extended by Emperor Jahāngīr to Dādū's son and successor Garībdās would lack an obvious cause. From Amber, Dādū retired for a year and a half to the lonely place of Karaṛālā (today Kalyanpur) and took up a more or less peripatetic life. Finally, in 1602 he moved to Naraina, where he had been given land by a Kachvaha noble. He died on May 8, 1603 (eighth day, dark half of the lunar month of *jyeṣṭha* [May–Jun]). According to his wish, his body was taken to the hill site of Bhairana, where it was disposed of in the wilderness. Dādū thereby posthumously enacted the myth of → Kabīr 's funeral, which is said to have been conducted in neither the Muslim nor the Hindu fashion, as well as his commitment to altruism even toward scavenger animals. The five places mentioned – Sambhar, Amber, Kalyanpur, Bhairana, and Naraina – figure as the holy sites of the Dādūpanth, determine its sacred geography, and, in the order mentioned, govern the sect's annual festive cycle. Dādū's Rajasthan was home to Hindu, Jain, and Islamic traditions. Here, the Sant tradition related closely to Nāth *yoga* (see → Nāth Sampradāya) and Nizārī Ismā'īlī traditions. The Sants challenged the orthodox, be they Hindu or Muslim. Dādū's hagiography reports that while he lived in Sambhar, he clashed with orthodoxy (*DāJLī.* 3). His teachings need to be seen against the backdrop of all the traditions mentioned and with an understanding that when he emphasized his "middle way" among the traditions, he indicated that he was not rejecting them, but rather by going beyond them restored their pristine intent. Like most Indian traditions, the Sants emphasize the → *guru* who imparts spiritual knowledge to his or her disciple, whereas Dādū is denied to have had a human *guru*. Rather, he is reported to have had twice in his life the vision of a mystical *guru*, first as an 11-year-old and then once again at the age of 18. By claiming that he had been granted mystic revelation, hagiography certainly authenticated his authority. The hagiographical accounts name that *guru* "Old Bābā (*bābā būḍhāu*)" (*DāJLī.* 1.7), a designation common enough. W.G. Orr (1947, 54) proposed to identify him with Shaykh Buḍḍhan, a Qādirīya

Sufi, and another current hypothesis is that Dādū was a Nizārī Ismāʿīlī from Gujarat and as such related to the worshippers of Rāmdev Pīr, a hero-saint whose Nizārī connection has been established and whose followers inhabit the catchment area of the Dādūpanth (Khan, 1997, 257; see also → Gujarat). Dādū is himself quite articulate about what he experienced, and that personal account is given pride of place in the *Dādūvāṇī*, which was canonized soon after his death. In the first distich of the *Dādūvāṇī*, which follows the benedictory stanzas of reverence to the supreme being and the saints, Dādū says that the divine *guru* revealed himself to him mystically (here using the typical Sufi expression *gaib māṃhiṃ*, "invisibly, in hidden"):

> *dādū gaiba māṁhi milyā, pāyā hama parasāda, masataki mere kara dharyā, daṣyā agama agādha.*
>
> Mystically he met with me: I received his grace, he placed his hand on my head; an initiation inaccessible and unfathomable. (*DāVā.* 1.3; trans. by author)

Though Dādū was married and had a family, the image of him as a *sādhu* started emerging about half a century after his death. Only since 1693, however, when Jaitrām (d. 1732) became *mahant* (abbot) of Naraina, has the incumbent on the seat of Dādū always been a *sādhu*, notwithstanding a preference of the *sādhu* over the householder ideal perceivable from the very beginning. Dādū, in accordance with the general understanding of the Sants, considered worldly life an obstacle for the experience of the supreme, and accordingly he was perceived as a religious figure detached from involvement in a family. This view concurred with the misogyny of *sādhus*, who see the endless cycle of birth and death as hinging on luring female power. Nonetheless, the lineage of leaders of the earliest Dādūpanth as it was in power in Naraina was confined to Dādū's family – his own son, Garībdās, became his father's successor, and Dādū's other children, too, exercised authority in the growing community.

Work

The *Dādūvāṇī* (Words of Dādū), also called *Anbhaivāṇī* (Words of Experience), consists of distichs (*sākhīs*) and songs (*pads*). Their language is Western Hindi with Rajasthani features and admixtures of other regional languages. In certain portions of the work, Persian vocabulary, mainly as Sufis used it, is densely represented. This linguistic state reflects the various traditions of the region as they were transmitted orally, in popular verses and by religious singers. The collection of Dādū's sayings began during his lifetime. The earliest known manuscript dates from 1614, but it awaits collation with other ancient manuscripts, which start from 1636. The utterances of Dādū were, as uniformly attested by at least two of Dādū's own disciples as well as by Rāghavdās (Horstmann, 2006), recorded by his amanuensis Mohandās Daftarī. He also assigned the compositions to the appropriate chapters in the *Dādūvāṇī* and edited them in 37 chapters of distichs and 27 chapters of songs, one chapter for each musical mode (*rāg*). The final editing of the compilation was made by Mohandās Daftarī, reportedly in cooperation with Dādū's disciples Rajjab and Jagjīvandās, themselves distinguished authors (for views on Rajjab's contribution, see Siṃhal, 2010). In a clearly spurious part, Mādhavdās' hagiography claims that the *Dādūvāṇī* was installed as an object of veneration on the eighth day of the bright half of *āṣāḍha* (Jun–Jul), that is, a month after Dādū's death in Bhairana (*DāVā.* 25.1). As Mādhavdās is said to have resided in Guler, this may point to rivalry with the Sikhs, whose *Ādigranth* (or *Gurū Granth Sāhib*) was installed in the Harimandir of Rāmdāspur (the future Amritsar) on Aug 16, 1604. The earliest-known complete versions of the *Dādūvāṇī* are in the format of the so-called *Pañcvāṇī* (The Words of the Five), often supplemented by other material. This pentad consists of the oeuvres of five authors arranged in the following sequence: (1) Dādū, (2) Kabīr, (3) → Nāmdev, (4) Raidās (→ Ravidās), and (5) Hardās. Hardās is the only one among these with whom neither a sect nor a particular community identifies, although Dādūpanthīs of the first two generations still speak of followers of his. He may have been a renunciant in the → Rāmānandī tradition, for his devotion to → Rām Raghupati – whom he worshipped in both a *saguṇa* and *nirguṇa* fashion (see → *nirguṇa* and *saguṇa*), finding perfection in the veneration of the name of Rām – points to that tradition (Siṃhal, 2007, 32–34). The pentad of authors reflects the spiritual family in which Dādū ranks chronologically last, but, for Dādū's community, supreme. The 37 chapters of distichs of the *Dādūvāṇī* have thematic captions that reflect the homiletic topics they served (Horstmann, 2009; Horstmann, forthcoming). The 27 chapters of songs are concluded by the five *ārtīs* of Dādū. These are litanies of praise serving a liturgical purpose that are chanted and not sung, though they are incorporated in the chapter of *rāg dhanāsarī*. Whereas the canonized sequence of the *Pañcvāṇī* has existed from the beginning of the Dādūpanthī literary tradition, the transmission of the oeuvres constituent thereof exhibits variants, both in the number of compositions and to some extent in the assignment of songs to musical modes.

Teaching

Homiletic discourses or instruction given by Dādū have not been recorded, but such activities of his are mentioned by Jangopāl (Horstmann, 2006, 174–175). Dādū's *sākhīs* may have had their original function in such instruction, and his *pads* also had a place therein. Religious discourse was built around such compositions, his own as well as those of other authors, as well as the anonymous oral tradition. They form the nucleus of his teaching, the essence of which is recorded in the second benedictory *sākhī* of Dadū's oeuvre:

> The supreme being, immanent and transcendent, is my God Nirañjana,
> Without form, pure – Dādū makes reverence to him. (*DāVā 1.2*)

The supreme being is identical with the human soul. It is called by names of god such as Rām and Hari, but also *satguru* (true *guru*), who may have human shape but is essentially the supreme. If he or she is able to turn his or her mind away from the world, a human being may experience the identity of his or her soul with the supreme. That revelation is the fruit of → *bhakti*, which is bestowed upon humans by divine → grace and hence cannot be mediated by rituals. As there is only one true being inherent in all creatures, all humans are entitled to *bhakti*. Whereas grace is spontaneous and cannot be managed by a person, the community of devotees (*satsaṅg*) prepares the individual devotee for *bhakti*. It is in the gathering of the like-minded that the devotee learns to discipline and disentangle his or her mind from the world. *Bhakti* needs to be cultivated both individually and in community with fellow devotees. If the devotee attains *bhakti* and realizes his or her true being beyond time and change, his or her migration in the → *saṃsāra* comes to an end, and the devotee merges with the supreme. Whereas a human being is able to experience unity with the supreme, that irreversible merging takes place upon death.

While he conceived of himself as standing in the tradition of the Sants, Dādū was particularly attached to Kabīr, whom he often quotes. He denied being either Hindu or Muslim but preached a "middle way" among all creeds, leading to an interior realization of the unqualified supreme. Accordingly, he rejected iconic worship and discouraged exterior forms of religion, such as orthodox (*varṇāśrama*) rituals, pilgrimage, and austerities (→ *tapas*), as well as religious signs applied on the body and the wearing of a religious habit, both of which are common markers of religious identity. The rejection of all these, of a metaphysical justification of social stratification, and of the superiority of the orthodox mores of the religious establishment led to clashes with the representatives of that establishment, as his hagiographers emphasize. In so doing, they use Sant hagiographical stock motifs and tropes. Several considerations should warn against taking them at their face value as well as against the image of Dādū as the subaltern, holding steadfastly and triumphantly out against the dominant orthodoxy. The Sant religion was by Dādū's time hardly perceived as a scandalous novelty, for his region had for a long time seen religious countercurrents against the orthodox establishment, particularly vigorous among which were the earlier Sant and Ismāʿīlī traditons. Dādū's religious message thus ran in a rather familiar groove.

Like other Sants, Dādū also relied on the concepts of Nāth *yoga*. They run through his oeuvre, and there is one particularly long composition of his (*Kāyābelī* [The Creeper of the Body]) that delineates the yogic process. There is every reason to believe that both Dādū and many of his following practiced Nāth *yoga*. This is attested by texts, paintings, and also the meditation caves used by the Dādūpanthīs in the fashion of the Nāth *yogīs*.

The Dādūpanth

For the current *sādhu* and *sādhvī* constituency, no exact numbers are available, but the monastic constituency has been shrinking continuously, whereas the householder followers of Dādū are becoming increasingly articulate. Currently the

Fig. 2: A Dādūpanthī nun in the courtyard of her *maṭh* in Idva, Nagaur district, Rajasthan (photo by Monika Horstmann).

sādhus may not exceed 150, inclusive of a few *sādhvīs*. The rapid decline in their numbers can be gauged from comparative figures: 15,000 *nāgās* alone in 1875 against 5,499 of them in 1929; an estimate of 3,000 to 4,000 *sādhus* attending the functions of the 400th anniversary of Dādū in 1945.

The earliest followers of Dādū belonged to a wide range of castes and comprised Hindus and Muslims, renouncers and householders. The patronage of him and his followers must have been lavish, as is evidenced by the local communities that formed in his name during his lifetime and the multitude of manuscripts produced right from the formative stage of the sect.

After Dādū's death, the organization of what was an emergent sect was still fluid. The current designation, Dādūpanth, is first encountered in Rāghavdās' *Bhaktmāl* (v. 361). Rāghavdās made an express effort to place the *panth* of Dādū within the range of the influential, established sects of his time. These were the four orthodox Vaiṣṇava sects (the → Gauḍīya, → Vallabha, Rāmānandī, and → Nimbārka Sampradāyas) and the Daśanāmī *saṃnyāsīs*. He juxtaposes the former with the four founders of *nirguṇa sampradāyas*, namely Nānak, Kabīr, Dādū, and the first Nirañjanī *mahant* Jagannāth (the Nirañjanīs are a Sant sect known for their remarkable literature and the way in which they mediate orthodox and heterodox religion, and should not be confused with the Daśanāmī Nirañjanīs). The number of 52 disciples of Dādū echoes the 52 *maṛhīs* (i.e. subdivisions of *akhāṛās*) of the Daśanāmī *saṃnyāsīs* and, derived from these, groups of Vaiṣṇava *bairāgīs*, according to the *Bhaktmāl* (vv. 341–342). Whereas the Vaiṣṇava teachers are like the four *vyūhas* of Viṣṇu, according to Rāghavdās and in agreement with a prevalent sectarian discourse, the *nirguṇī mahants* are legitimated by Nirañjana, the innate supreme, himself. This goes to show that half a century after Dādū's death, the Dādūpanth had attained shape, but that neither organizational issues nor the legitimation of the *nirguṇa* teachers was beyond debate. Dādū himself may have been content with gathering around himself followers who held the Sant "middle course." Garībdās, his celibate son, was recognized by Dādū's followers at Naraina and other places, if not by all lineages. Jangopāl (*DāJLī.* 16.16; Callewaert, 1988) describes how the forehead mark of succession was applied to Garībdās, and he thereby, in an express juridical act forestalling oppositional claims, installed himself on Dādū's seat at Naraina. In this way, the lineage of Naraina, where Dādū had spent the last months before his death and which was thereby especially privileged, was started. The succession at Naraina was for three generations vested in Dādū's family. After Garībdās' death (1637), the succession was contested. Garībdās had chosen one Kevalrām as his successor, but Kevalrām was deposed after four years by Maskīndās, Garībdās' younger brother. From Kevalrām issued the Garībdāsot lineage of the Dādūpanth. In Naraina, Kevalrām is acknowledged by a cenotaph built slightly apart from the cenotaphs of the other leaders of the Dādūpanth. Dādū's two daughters are regarded by Rāghavdās in his *Bhaktmāl* (v. 361) as two of his 52 disciples, and Sundardās the Younger (see below), in eight verses not preserved in all manuscripts (see Śarmā, 1933, 168–171, app. "kha"), intimates that for some time they were jointly managing the affairs of Naraina, but despite their acclaimed efficiency ceded their position to Maskīndās. Upon his death in 1648, followed by another bout of conflict over succession, he was succeeded by a son of his, Fakīrdās. When Fakīrdās died in 1793, the Naraina community was in disarray. Not a few of the lineages of Dādū's disciples, who had spread far and wide, were by that time estranged to the seat of Naraina. Patronage during that period of almost a century may have favored local lineages of *sādhus* from one's own community rather than being vested in a central sectarian authority. Rāghavdās listed Dādū's second-generation disciples. Some of these, however, while in their writings paying reverence to their *guru*, who was a disciple of Dādū, do not mention Dādū at all. This speaks against a stable constitution of the followers of Dādū during the first two generations. Whereas a large, though numerically not fixed, number of disciples gravitated around Dādū, as is also articulated by first-generation disciples in their works, the second generation of disciples did not necessarily identify themselves as members of a Dādūpanth. It also needs to be borne in mind that Sant sects could be quite porous and not necessarily exclusivist. In 1693 and in the fourth generation after Dādū, Jaitrām – a celibate Brahman – was made abbot of Naraina. In the first decades of the 18th century, eventually, the Kachvaha ruler Savāī Jaisingh made it a binding rule that the leader (*svāmī*) of the Dādūpanth must be a celibate Brahman. While this had been observed since, the current abbot, Gopāldās (since 2001), is a Jāṭ. The Jāṭs are spread over wide regions of North India. Originally they were a militant peasant community and founded several states. Many of them prosperous and politically influential, they are strongly represented in Rajasthan and Haryana. Under Jaitrām, the modern Dādūpanthī organization was created, with a clear prerogative accorded to the abbot of Naraina as the head of the sect. The designation Dādūpanth became almost a synonym of the monastic constituency. The prerogative of Naraina was underpinned by a set of rules to which the various monastic branches were made to agree. Calling for regular confirmation, it has hence been executed and in courtly ostentation brought to the attention of the public mainly during the annual *melā*s of the sect. The *svāmī* of Naraina, by the current terminology called the *ācārya*, with the Dādūpanthīs by monastic lineage attached to that place, came to form the *khālsā* (Arab. *khāliṣa*, "crown-land," a Mughal revenue term), reminding one of the Sikh terminology (see → Hinduism and Sikhism). Despite that organizational umbrella, the branches, with regard to varying lifestyles and involvement in worldly affairs, have retained their characteristic profiles. Though the abbot of Naraina confirms the succession in the various monastic lineages, he does not adjudicate their affairs, nor has he a right to their property.

Barring the *nāgā*s, the formerly practiced ideal lifestyle of Dādūpanthīs was that of peripatetic *sādhus* who were nonetheless anchored in a *maṭh*, a monastery. This might range from a modest shrine with one or two rooms attached to a spacious temple complex, possessing and managing agricultural land. Of special importance used to be the kitchen, which was always prepared to feed visitors, an institution called *sadāvrat*. Whereas these monasteries are, except for a resident *mahant* and some staff, almost empty throughout the major part of the year, they may draw huge crowds for sectarian festivals. In regions of Marwar, where there are still monasteries forming centers of a local web of lay followers, the relationship is maintained by the daily begging tours to the villages of these followers (Thiel-Horstmann, 1986). The sect comprises four monastic branches, all of which have been reduced now to small numbers:

(1) *Virakta*s (renouncers), monks and nuns living a peripatetic life, either solitary or in a group gathered around a (*mahā*)*maṇḍaleśvar* (now no

longer a function, but only a title), a leader within a certain catchment area of the monastic constituency. *Virakta*s are expected to give homiletic instruction to the community that hosts them for shorter or longer stays. Homiletic requirements have given rise to a spate of literature serving as tools for preaching (Horstmann, 2009; Horstmann, forthcoming).

(2) *Uttarādhā*s ("northerners"), initiated by Dādū's disciple Bābā Banvārīdās, who migrated to the north, where his branch spread from its epicenter in Ratia, in the Hissar district of Haryana. A generally wealthy constituency, it is distinguished by the fact that it also comprises *gharbārī sādhu*s, who follow a worldly profession and live in their own houses. Also specific to that northern branch and located in the region of Narnaul are married *sādhu*s. Political circumstances caused the migration of *uttarādhā*s back to southern areas, so that they also spread in Rajasthan, Madhya Pradesh, and other parts of northern and central India. The patronage of that wealthy group is especially manifest in the temple of Naraina, built by a wealthy *uttarādhā* physician in 1827.

(3) *Nāgā*s, who trace their origin to Sundardās the Elder (as distinguished from Sundardās the Younger, the poet-scholar), allegedly a contemporary of Dādū and a scion of the royal house of Bikaner, as was first reported by Rāghavdās. Himself an elusive figure, Sundardās' companion or disciple Prahlāddās of Ghatra traced his own line from him. Prahlāddās' disciple was Hāpojī, a son of the royal house of the Kachvahas of Amber from a servant mother. Rāghavdās belongs to the *nāgā* generation after Hāpojī. Sundardās the Elder is not mentioned by Jangopāl in his hagiography. This indicates that from an early period on there were *nāgā*s attached to Dādū, though not organizationally related to him in a direct line and distant in lifestyle from other disciples. *Nāgā*s are fighting *sādhu*s, and it was this function that brought about the ascendancy of the Dādūpanthī *nāgā*s. Rāghavdās, however, reports no fighting activities, but rather depicts a brotherhood cultivating Rajput ideals and courtly culture, mainly expressed in literary pursuits (Hastings, 2002). The *nāgā*s did not recognize the authority of the seat of Naraina. This was only redressed under Jaitrām by the introduction of procedures borrowed from the Rajput courts. According to these, the rank of the leaders of the other *sādhu*s was ceremonially balanced against that of the *nāgā*s and became expressed in the precedence and sitting order during the sectarian feasts and gatherings. As a military organization with a somewhat loose attachment to the Vaiṣṇava *nāgā*s, the Dādūpanthī *nāgā*s were institutionalized in 1755. Those Vaiṣṇava *nāgā*s were not only Rāmānandīs but also others from the group of the four *sampradāya*s named above, including the → Rādhāvallaba Sampradāya. In the same year, the Dādūpanthī *nāgā*s promptly caused a schism by disregarding the reforms of Jaitrām and trying in vain to install their own candidate on the seat of Naraina. The *nāgā*s gained ascendancy in the period of the decline of the Mughal Empire and the emergence of new regional powers. In the process, the *nāgā*s, serving the Kachvaha kings of Jaipur, established a link with that court. After Jaipur had become a British protectorate in 1818, the *nāgā*s were deployed to discipline rebellious tributaries of the Jaipur court and employed in the tax collection and other administrative duties. The various military units, *jamāt*s (regiments) and *thāmbhā*s (settlements, cantonments) as subunits of these, organized on the numerical model of the Vaiṣṇava *nāgā*s (*bairāgī*s) and, ultimately, the *saṃnyāsī nāgā*s, were strategically located in outposts of the Jaipur state. The *nāgā* batallion of Jaipur State was disbanded as late as 1938. The courtly allure of the *nāgā* leaders and the wealth accruing from their militant exploits translated into a remarkable literary and cultural production, as is shown by the great number of manuscripts written or commissioned by them and the musical, artistic, and architectural tradition that they cultivated.

(4) *Tapasvī*s (ascetics) or *khākī* (ash smeared) *virakta*s, who have absorbed the ideal of the lone ascetic that is commonly found in both the Vaiṣṇava and the *Daśanāmī saṃnyāsī* tradition. They keep a sacred fire (*dhūnī*), the ashes of which they smear on their body. The consumption of cannabis to enhance religious vision is popular among them. At the feasts and functions of the Dādūpanth, they neither mingle with others nor share in the communal meals, but stay in their own camp.

While there are no forehead or body marks (→ *tilak*s) distinctive of Dādūpanthīs, the lifestyles of the various groups and their monastic garbs differ.

In the process of the decrease in the *sādhu* constituency of the sect, lay followers have pronounced and enacted their claim of genuine trustees of the religion and ethics of Dādū. This is also expressed by the formation of a Dādūpanthī lay movement, inspired and organized by former *nāgā*s. Laicized *sādhu*s have also entertained claims on the property of their former monastic lineages, which is the cause of ongoing conflicts. Three trends are being clearly articulated, also by the present abbot of Naraina: (1) Dādū's path runs beyond the established creeds; (2) Dādū was not primarily interested in founding a monastic order, which was rather the consequence of his particular Sant attitude toward the world; (3) with the *sādhu* constituency dying out, the lay followers have to be empowered by education to carry on the legacy of Dādū.

Ritual

Dādū rejected iconic representations of the divine, and the respective ritual as well as exterior signs of religious affiliation or renunciation, such as body marks, religious emblems, and a monastic habit. A nucleus of a specific Dādūpanthī religious practice, however, formed already during his lifetime. It consisted of *bhajan* (see → *kīrtan* and *bhajan*), homilies, and communal meals. The *ārtī* formed the liturgical nucleus; the liturgy as it is known now was perhaps agreed upon in the late 17th century. The object of worship became the *Dādūvāṇi*, kept in the shrine of a temple or in a special niche in a private home. The *Dādūvāṇī* of the Naraina Temple is also taken out in processions. Correspondingly, modern processions of lay Dādūpanthīs also feature the *Dādūvāṇī*. From about the late 17th century, responding to organizational issues and the perceived erosion of Dādūpanthī ideals, treatises defining monastic rules and the ethos of Dādūpanthī monks started appearing, not a few of these building on an earlier Vaiṣṇava format of the genre (Thiel-Horstmann, 1991b). The non-iconic thrust of Dādū's doctrine came to be amalgamated with various local forms of religious expression, of which an especially powerful one is the cult of the cenotaphs, where the dead *guru*s are remembered and worshipped by the devotees. The dead *guru*s and saints are represented either by inscribed slabs with a bas-relief of their feet (see fig. 3) or, occasionally and quite recently, by statues representing the live *guru*. A picture of Dādū is often found in the shrine next to his *Dādūvāṇī*. The most commonly represented motifs are Dādū's encounter with his mystical *guru*, his interview with Akbar, or a portrait of him that is of 20th-century origin. Even the full-sized statues of *guru*s may receive

Fig. 3: Worship at the cenotaph of Jaitrām at the site of the cenotaphs of the *mahant*s of Naraina (photo by Monika Horstmann).

the veneration of the devotees similarly to the images of temple deities. Such worship by the lay followers is not discouraged by the *mahants*, but they do not perform it themselves. Room is thereby provided for the agency of the followers patronizing a particular place. The power to work miracles of healing, granting fertility, and alleviating physical and psychological ailments is attributed to *gurus*, living or dead, and also serves as a motive for the worship of their cenotaphs, perhaps the most notable case being that of the cenotaph of Abbot Jaitrām in Naraina. Sant worship is often grafted on those popular cults. The worship at the cenotaphs thus bears similarity to that of the graves of Muslim saints. A variant of the caves, which both Sants and Nāth *yogīs* used for meditation, are the chambers in the basements of cenotaphs serving a similar purpose.

The annual festival of the Dādūpanth starts in Amber and culminates, accompanied by a religious fair of several days, in Naraina, on the birthday of Dādū as it was fixed in hagiography. It represents a process corresponding to that of the *holī* festival in the form in which it was celebrated in princely Rajasthan. Like *holī*, the festival process starts with the first preparations on *vasantpañcamī* (fifth day of the bright half of the lunar month of *māgha* [Jan–Feb]) and culminates on the eighth bright day of *phālguna* (Feb–Mar), Dādū's birthday. This is the *phāg* day, when the spring festival was formerly celebrated with pomp at the courts of Rajasthan and concluded by the actual *holī* festival on the full-moon day of *phālguna*. During those several weeks, pilgrimages are made to the five sacred places related to stages of Dādū's life. The pilgrimage circuit thus circumscribes the historical core of the realm of Dādū. The second specifically Dādūpanthī festival commemorates Dādū's death on the eighth day of the dark half of the month of *jyeṣṭha* (May–Jun).

Bibliography

Callewaert, W.M., ed., *The Hindī Biography of Dādū Dayāl (Janmalīlā)*, Delhi, 1988.

Caturvedī, P., ed., *Dādūdayāl granthāvalī*, Varanasi, VS 2023 (= CE 1966–1967; Hind.).

Hastings, J.M., "Poets, Sants, and Warriors: The Dadu Panth, Religious Change and Identity Formation in Jaipur State, circa 1562–1860 CE," diss., University of Wisconsin–Madison, 2002.

Horstmann, M., "The Example in Dādūpanthī Homiletics," in: F. Orsini, ed., *Tellings, Not Texts: Singing, Story-Tellings and Performance*, forthcoming.

Horstmann, M., "Texts and How to Practise Them," in: G. Colas & G. Gerschheimer, eds., *Écrire et transmettre en Inde classique*, ÉFEO.ÉT 23, Paris, 2009, 27–42.

Horstmann, M., "An Indian Sacred Journey," in: J. Gengnagel, M. Horstmann & G. Schwedler, eds., *Prozessionen, Wallfahrten, Aufmärsche. Bewegung zwischen Religion und Politik in Europa und Asien seit dem Mittelalter*, Cologne, 2008, 336–360.

Horstmann, M., "Dādūpanthī Anthologies of the Eighteenth and Nineteenth Centuries," in: M. Horstmann, ed., *Bhakti in Current Research, 2001–2003*, New Delhi, 2006, 163–177.

Horstmann, M., ed., "Dādū: Pad," in: W.M. Callewaert & B. Op de Beeck, *Nirguṇ bhakti sāgar: Devotional Hindī Literature*, 2 vols., New Delhi, 1991, 201–279.

Khan, D.-S., *Conversions and Shifting Identities: Ramdev Pir and the Ismailis in Rajasthan*, New Delhi, 1997.

Maṅgaldās Svāmī, ed., *Śrī Dādūdayāljī kī vāṇī saṭīk*, Jaipur, n.d. (c. 1951; Hind.).

Massignon, L., *Essai sur l'origine du lexique technique de la mystique musulmane*, Paris, 1922.

Nāhṭā, A., ed., *Rāghavdās kṛt bhaktmāl*, Jodhpur, 1965 (Hind.).

Orr, W.G., *A Sixteenth-Century Indian Mystic: Dadu and His Followers*, London, 1947.

Śarmā, H., ed., *Sundar-granthāvalī*, Kolkata, VS 1993 (= CE 1936–1937; Hind.).

Śāstrī, S., ed., *Śrī sant guṇ sāgar [by Mādhavdās]*, Bhairana, VS 2056 (= CE 1999–2000; Hind.).

Siṃhal, B.K., ed., *Hardās-granthāvalī*, Delhi, 2007 (Hind.).

Siṃhal, B.K., *Rajjab kī sarbaṃgī*, Raigarh, 2010 (Hind.).

Svāmī Nārāyaṇdās, ed., *Śrī Dādūdayāljī kī vāṇī*, Jaipur, n.d. (c. 1969; Hind.).

Thiel-Horstmann, M., *Dādū: Lieder*, Stuttgart, 1991a.

Thiel-Horstmann, M., "Treatises on Dadupanthi Monastic Discipline," in: C. Singh & N. Vashishtha, eds., *Pathways to Literature, Art and Archaeology: Pt. Gopal Narayan Bahura Felicitation Volume*, vol. I, Jaipur, 1991b, 95–113.

Thiel-Horstmann, M., "Dādūpanthī Sermons," in: M. Thiel-Horstmann & R.K. Barz, eds., *Living Texts from India*, Wiesbaden, 1989, 141–183.

Thiel-Horstmann, M., *Symbiotic Antinomy: The Social Organisation of a North Indian Sect*, Canberra, 1986.

Monika Horstmann

Eknāth

Eknāth (also spelled Ekanātha) was a saint-poet who lived in the ancient town of Paithan, in west-central India (the modern state of → Maharashtra), during the 16th century. He is revered as one of the four main figures (with → Jñāndev, → Nāmdev, and → Tukārām) whose religious poetry makes up the textual core of the major Marathi → *bhakti* tradition – the → Vārkarī Sampradāy. According to tradition, Eknāth was an only child born in a Brahman family, but he was raised by his grandparents since his parents died shortly after his birth. He spent much of his youth as a disciple of a syncretic *guru*, Janārdana, who worked for a local Muslim ruler in the fort town of Daulatabad (near modern Aurangabad). After graduating from Janārdana's tutelage, Eknāth undertook a long pilgrimage through northern India and then returned to Paithan, married, and settled into a life of reading, observing devotional rituals, performing → *kīrtan*s, and composing religious poetry. Eknāth was the most prolific of the Marathi saint-poets, composing a diverse corpus mainly in Marathi, including a scholarly commentary on the 11th book (*skandha*) of the *Bhāgavatapurāṇa*, an edition of Jñāndev's *Jñāneśvarī*, several short philosophical treatises, a large collection of poems called his *Gāthā*, and a Marathi rendering of the → *Rāmāyaṇa*, which was left incomplete at his death. In hagiographies, Eknāth is consistently portrayed as a model devotee (and according to some, an → *avatār*) of Viṭṭhal, whose nondualistic perspective made him compassionate especially toward untouchables, despite strong condemnation from his fellow Brahmans. The theme of Eknāth transgressing caste boundaries was amplified in 20th-century Marathi plays and films, which tended to portray Eknāth as a gentle but insistent critic of caste. Among contemporary Vārkarīs, Eknāth is remembered less as a social critic than as a great teacher whose lessons of nondualism and devotion (*bhakti*) extended to all regardless of caste and gender, and as the ideal example of how one can integrate spiritual aspirations into everyday life as a married householder.

Biography

The exact dates of Eknāth's birth and death are not known with certainty, but epigraphic and literary evidence indicates that he probably died in 1599 and may have been born in 1533 (this position was first argued by Pangarkar, 1910). An alternative, traditional view holds that Eknāth lived between 1540 and 1609. Little is known about Eknāth's ancestors aside from a hagiographical story about his great-grandfather Bhānudās, who returned the statue of Viṭṭhal to Pandharpur (see → Vārkarī Sampradāy) from the capital of the ruler who had removed it (traditionally but inconclusively identified as King Kṛṣṇadevarāya and the city of Vijayanagar). Evidence suggests that several generations before Eknāth was born, his ancestors migrated to Paithan from the village of Mhaisal, which lies on what is now the Karnataka-Maharashtra border. Although Eknāth's life occurred mostly within the realm of the Nizam Shah Sultanate (or Ahmadnagar Sultanate), neither his own writings nor hagiographies about him mention Muslim rulers or administrators in detail. Eknāth and his family are unequivocally remembered as Deshastha Brahmans, but their traditional occupations are unknown. Hagiographies depict Bhānudās as a cloth merchant, while Eknāth's writings and hagiographies contain Persian financial terminology that implies that Eknāth may have worked for a time as a scribe or accountant (*kulkarṇi*). Eknāth also may have inherited rights to land and income that supported him materially throughout his life. Stories about him never mention him working for money or experiencing financial hardship.

Most hagiographies claim that Eknāth's parents died shortly after he was born (because of inauspicious stars, according to some of his writings), so he was raised and educated by his loving grandparents. At the age of 12, Eknāth departed from Paithan and became the disciple of a married householder and apparent *yogī* named Janārdana. The most commonly known hagiography claims that Janārdana was the fort commander (*killedār*) of Daulatabad; another source says he was a weapon-bearing administrative officer (*mutsaddi*) in Ahmadnagar who was later transferred to Daulatabad. All sources agree that Janārdana was employed and appreciated by the local Muslim ruler (perhaps Burhan Nizam Shah I, r. 1510–1553). Little is remembered about Janārdana except that he regularly practiced some form of yogic meditation and was an ardent devotee of the god Dattātreya. According to the hagiographies, Eknāth was a devoted disciple who enthusiastically served Janārdana, excelling in his Sanskrit and Marathi studies and advancing quickly in his practice of meditation. Impressed with Eknāth's progress, Janārdana is said to have introduced Eknāth personally to the god Dattātreya, whom Janārdana regularly met. (Dattātreya in these stories about Eknāth is not explicitly linked to the formal Dattātreya tradition that began in the 15th cent., as described in the *Gurucaritra*, although some later interpreters try to make this connection.) In the hagiographical descriptions of this meeting, Dattātreya appears dressed as a Muslim mendicant (*malaṅg*) who shares a meal with Janārdana – an image that contributed to a modern dispute about this man's true identity. Some scholars argued that Eknāth's grand- *guru* was a Ṣūfī, but this figure may have been a syncretic holy man who defied easy categorization (see Deák, 2005).

After Eknāth met Dattātreya and received Janārdana's final blessing, he is said to have gone on a long pilgrimage to holy sites in northern India. His pilgrimage concluded when Janārdana commanded him to return to Paithan, get married, and raise a family. Eknāth obediently complied, and he is said to have dwelled in Paithan for the entirety of his adult life, aside from a few stories about trips to Varanasi and Pandharpur. According to one story, some religious authorities in Varanasi heard that Eknāth was composing a commentary on the *Bhāgavatapurāṇa* in Marathi, and they were so outraged that they summoned Eknāth from Paithan to appear before them. Eknāth's humility, the quality of his writing, and a miraculous event that saved his manuscript from being destroyed in a river ultimately converted the Brahmans, and they set Eknāth and his text atop an elephant and paraded him throughout the city. Questions of this story's historicity aside, the colophons of two compositions by Eknāth state that they were completed in Varanasi (the *Rukmiṇī Svayaṁvara* in 1571 and the *Eknāthī Bhāgavat* in 1573).

Eknāth and his wife Girijā had two daughters, named Gaṅgā and Godā, and a son named Hari. According to hagiographies, Hari was very intelligent but socially and religiously conservative. He disapproved of Eknāth using Marathi for religious compositions and eating food cooked by non-Brahmans. In protest, Hari moved to Varanasi to pursue his career as a Sanskrit → *paṇḍit*. Through Eknāth's patient efforts and a miraculous event, Hari was eventually persuaded to return to Paithan and adopt Eknāth's more liberal ways. One of Eknāth's daughters had a son, Mukteśvar, who became the first great Marathi scholar-poet or *paṇḍitkavi* (whose ornate and intellectual style differed from that of the more accessible, popular *santkavi*s or saint-poets). Mukteśvar appears to have composed the first extant hagiographical story about Eknāth (see below).

According to tradition, Eknāth instituted an annual memorial celebration of his *guru* Janārdana's death, on the sixth day of the second or dark half of the month of *phālgun* (Feb–Mar). After Eknāth's death, this celebration came to honor him as well, since the date is remembered also for being the day on which Eknāth was born, met Dattātreya, received his *guru*'s final blessing, and died. Popularly called *eknāth ṣaṣṭhī*, this date is celebrated especially in Paithan with a large four-day festival (see below).

In addition to the chronologically ordered stories about Eknāth (his birth, discipleship, marriage, and death), hagiographical sources narrate a large number of what could be called "independent episodes" that do not connect to one another or fit a particular sequence. These include stories about Eknāth attracting great audiences to his *kīrtan* performances, going on pilgrimage to Pandharpur (see → Vārkarī Sampradāy), having a dream that led him to renovate the tomb of the saint Jñāndev and edit the *Jñāneśvarī*, and miraculously imbuing a mentally impaired disciple with the ability to complete his *Rāmāyaṇa* rendering after he died. In another well-known story, Eknāth prepares a feast for Brahmans on the occasion of his ancestors' annual death memorial (*śrāddha*) but ends up serving the food to a group of hungry untouchables (or → Brahmā, → Viṣṇu, and → Śiva disguised as Muslim mendicants, in another version) before the Brahmans arrive. When the Brahmans then refuse to eat a second batch of food prepared for them, Eknāth's deceased ancestors miraculously appear and consume it themselves. Some stories depict deities (→ Kṛṣṇa, Dattātreya, Viṣṇu, Viṭṭhal, and the → Gaṅgā personified as a woman) being so impressed by Eknāth's reputation that they secretly come to see or serve him.

Many independent episodes follow a pattern – Eknāth's actions outrage his fellow Brahmans, they attempt to publicly humiliate him, Eknāth humbly endures their antagonism, and he is ultimately vindicated by a wondrous occurrence. This happens in a few cases in which Eknāth's use of Marathi is at issue, such as in Varanasi. More frequently, the Brahmans are outraged by Eknāth's free and respectful interactions with untouchables. In one popular story, Eknāth picks up a crying Mahār (untouchable) boy standing lost and forgotten on scorching sand of a riverbank. Another story depicts Eknāth allowing a starving untouchable thief who had escaped from prison to live with him until his strength returned, which makes such an impression on the man that he renounces thievery. In the most controversial story, Eknāth accepts an invitation from an untouchable couple to eat a meal at their home. Marathi audiences and authors apparently found this story of commensality challenging; the hagiographers tried in various ways to narratively dampen the radicalness of Eknāth's act while maintaining the integrity of his promise to eat with the couple.

The circumstances that led to Eknāth's death are unknown, but he is remembered to have taken *jalasamādhi* (ritual suicide by self-drowning that is considered auspicious) in 1599 by entering the Godāvarī River, which flows around Paithan. His followers established a stone memorial on the riverbank; this developed into one of the two Eknāth-related temples in Paithan – the Eknāth Samādhi Mandir. The other temple, the Gāvātle Mandir ("In-Town Temple"), is said to be where Eknāth lived and worshipped. Families of his descendants continue to reside around this structure. It is primarily these descendants who have institutionalized Eknāth's memory; he was not followed by a prominent lineage of disciples.

Hagiographical Sources

Fragmentary information about Eknāth's life is found in the colophons of some of his compositions, but the main sources of information are hagiographical compositions that appeared in the two centuries after his death: three texts solely about Eknāth and two further texts that compile his stories with those of other Marathi and North

Fig. 1: Eknāth Samādhi Mandir in Paithan (photo by Jon Keune).

Indian poet-saints. The earliest text is the influential and oft-repeated *Śrīkhaṇḍyākhyān* (Tale of Śrīkhaṇḍyā; sometimes called the *Eknāthcaritra* [Story of Eknāth]), and it is attributed to Eknāth's famous grandson Mukteśvar, who lived around the first half of the 17th century. The longest edition of this Marathi text is only 94 verses (see Ok, 1906, 275–281). It is composed in the *ovī* style and occasionally embellished with *śleṣa* (phrases crafted to have two meanings). The text narrates how the god Kṛṣṇa was so impressed by Eknāth's reputation that he disguised himself as a poor Brahman and worked clandestinely in Eknāth's home as a servant named Śrīkhaṇḍyā (after the sandalwood or *śrīkhaṇḍa* that he ground daily for Eknāth's devotional use). The *Śrīkaṇḍyākhyān* says nothing about the rest of Eknāth's life

The *Pratiṣṭhāncaritra* (Story of Pratiṣṭhān, the traditional name of the town Paithan) may be the earliest attempt to narrate the life of Eknāth in its entirety. The text contains no date, but by correlating pieces of information that the obscure author reveals about himself in the text with the genealogical data of the family that possessed the manuscript (who claimed to be descendants of Eknāth), it seems that the *Pratiṣṭhāncaritra* may have been composed as early as 1700. The *Pratiṣṭhāncaritra* circulated little if at all, remaining virtually unknown to the general public until it was published in 1948. Marathi scholars have regarded the text as an early, alternative hagiography of Eknāth, even though the details about it and its author's background are unclear. The *Pratiṣṭhāncaritra* is 1,029 *ovī* verses long, and it narrates events that span Eknāth's life and death. The *Pratiṣṭhāncaritra* places relatively little emphasis on wondrous events and Eknāth's ability to work miracles, focusing instead on the extremeness and single-mindedness of Eknāth's *guru* devotion. It depicts scenes in which Eknāth gleefully cleans his *guru*'s toilet by hand, and Eknāth hides in order to consume the contents of his *guru*'s spittoon that his *guru* had ordered him to throw away – examples of Eknāth's conviction that everything associated with his *guru* is blessed. In the *Pratiṣṭhāncaritra*, Eknāth remembers Janārdana fervently throughout his life, integrating devotion to him into a nondual vision of the world. In multiple places in the text, Eknāth is said to have perceived his *guru*'s presence within people in general (*janījanārdana*), which impelled Eknāth to serve others as he would serve his *guru*, regardless of caste. Although his behavior disregards caste, Eknāth is never depicted as explicitly condemning it in the *Pratiṣṭhāncaritra* or any other hagiography.

The *Eknāthcaritra* of Keśavsvāmī, composed in 1760, was the most influential hagiography of Eknāth, and its renditions of many stories have now become standard. Comprising over 2,600 *ovī* verses, the *Eknāthcaritra* is also much longer than the earlier two hagiographies. Keśavsvāmī's stories circulated widely, partially due to the fact that they, to a large extent, were repeated (without crediting Keśavsvāmī) by the most prominent Vārkarī hagiographer Mahīpati in his *Bhaktalīlāmṛt* (Essence of the Saints' Divine Play). Little is known about Keśavsvāmī except that he belonged to the spiritual descendants of Eknāth in Paithan and perhaps to his blood lineage as well. Unlike the *Pratiṣṭhāncaritra*, the *Eknāthcaritra* takes little interest in extreme acts of devotion or the idea that Eknāth perceives his *guru* in other people. Instead, Keśavsvāmī views Eknāth as an *avatār* (of Viṣṇu, Kṛṣṇa, or Viṭṭhal, in different passages) who came to uplift the world and the lowly. These major differences between the two texts and many significant discrepancies in their renditions of particular stories (such as whether Eknāth ran off to find his *guru* without telling anyone, or he was sent to Janārdana by his grandfather) imply that each text was written with little or no knowledge of the other. Keśavsvāmī is the first written source of several popular stories, such as Eknāth picking up the untouchable boy from hot sand and eating a meal at an untouchable couple's home. The latter story became essential for depictions of Eknāth in Marathi theatre and film (see below). In Keśavsvāmī's rendition, Eknāth promises to eat at the untouchables' home, but when the mealtime actually arrives, two images of Eknāth are seen simultaneously – one at the untouchables' home and the other sitting at Eknāth's home. Unlike later authors who repeated this story, Keśavsvāmī offers no explanation for why two images appeared.

Stories about Eknāth are also found in several collective hagiographies, or compilations of stories about many saints in one volume. The earliest extant example of this is Mahīpati's famous *Bhaktavijay* (Victory of the Devotees, composed in 1762), which contained a small number of stories about Eknāth. Mahīpati's sources for these stories are unclear, since they differ significantly from the three hagiographical texts mentioned above (on Mahīpati, see Keune, 2007). For example, in the *Bhaktavijay*, Eknāth is raised by his parents, who continue living until he is an adult. Mahīpati's *Bhaktalīlāmṛt*, completed in 1774, largely repeated Keśavsvāmī's stories about Eknāth. Mahīpati's renditions were also translated by the American Congregationalist missionary, scholar, and philanthropist J.E. Abbott and thereby became the main source of information about Eknāth that was available to non-Marathi audiences (Abbott, 1927; 1935). In the *Bhaktalīlāmṛt*, Mahīpati repeats Keśavsvāmī's stories, sometimes almost verbatim, but he adapted some stories in notable ways as well. For example, when two images of Eknāth appear in order to eat at the untouchables' home and stay in his own home, Mahīpati takes care to explain that Eknāth actually remained at home while the god Viṭṭhal took on the form of Eknāth and ate with the untouchables. Mahīpati thus ensures that this episode is understood as a miraculous event rather than a radical social deed of transgressing caste boundaries.

In 1797, Bhīmasvāmī Śirgāvkar also composed a collective hagiography called the *Bhaktalīlāmṛt* that contained strikingly different stories about Eknāth (some with a notably anti-Muslim orientation that none of the other hagiographies had). These stories are not widely known and may be the result of Bhīmasvāmī's own creativity. Other Marathi authors composed occasional poetry and praise songs about Eknāth as well, but they are too numerous and diverse to list here (see Keune, 2011). The main theme expressed in them is Eknāth's greatness and divinity; only a small minority of the texts mentions Eknāth's social relations.

Compositions

The corpus of texts attributed to Eknāth is massive and diverse, making him the most prolific and arguably the most multifaceted of the Marathi poet-saints. The remarkable variety of literary registers of these compositions – philosophical investigations, commentaries on Sanskrit texts, Marathi renderings of classic Sanskrit stories, sets of verses about deities and saints, earthy but allegorical dramatic poems, and slightly risqué songs of *gopī*s – prompted some Marathi scholars to refer to Eknāth as Lokśikṣak ("Teacher of the People"), since he tailored his compositions carefully to appeal to diverse audiences. The great majority of the songs are in Marathi, but a small number are in Hindi, and some include words and phrases from other languages (Kannada, Telugu, Persian, Urdu, and Dakhani) that were undoubtedly spoken around him.

Eknāth's Marathi commentary on the 11th book (*skandha*) of the *Bhāgavatapurāṇa*, known as the *Eknāthī Bhāgavat*, is considered his *magnum opus* and takes its place alongside the *Jñāneśvarī* and Tukārām's collection of poetry (his *Gāthā*) as the most foundational texts of the Vārkarī Sampradāy. Eknāth's choice of the 11th *skandha* over the 10th *skandha* (the mythological source of much erotic Kṛṣṇaite poetry in North Indian languages) reflects a key difference between the Vārkarī Sampradāy and its *bhakti* cousins to the north. Rather than view longing and desire between Kṛṣṇa and → Rādhā as a model for the devotee's relationship to god, Eknāth lifts up the non-erotic friendship between Kṛṣṇa and his devoted companion Uddhav. Comprising around 18 thousand *ovī*s and full of pedagogical metaphors, the *Eknāthī Bhāgavat* closely follows its Sanskrit forebear, in which Kṛṣṇa teaches Uddhav and comforts him at the news that the Yādava clan (to which Uddhav and Kṛṣṇa belong) will be destroyed. Eknāth highlights the importance of devotion to one's *guru*, and at several points he vociferously defends his choice to compose in Marathi (for English translations of excerpts see Abbott, 1927; Skyhawk, 1990).

The other long composition by Eknāth is his *Bhāvārtha Rāmāyaṇa* (Essential *Rāmāyaṇa*), a Marathi rendering of the great Sanskrit epic that mainly follows the Vālmīki edition but incorporates other Sanskrit versions as well. Eknāth completed the first five books (*kāṇḍa*s) and 44 chapters of the final book – some 25 thousand *ovī*s – before he died. According to tradition, Eknāth wondrously endowed a dull disciple named Gāvbā with the ability to render the remainder of the *Rāmāyaṇa* into Marathi. Other Marathi authors composed conclusions to the *Bhāvārtha Rāmāyaṇa* as well. Eknāth's interpretation is highly metaphorical, consistently drawing spiritual lessons from the events that occur. Some modern Marathi scholars have insisted that this text is Eknāth's veiled critique of Muslim rule during his time (for example, Eknāth depicts the *rākṣasa* demons as having beards; Joshi, 2004; Tulpule, 1991). As this interpretation diverges greatly from the tenor of Eknāth's other works, however, it may reveal more about the modern interpreters than about Eknāth.

A number of short compositions are regularly and reliably ascribed to Eknāth. His *Catuḥślokī Bhāgavat* was chronologically his first composition, commenting on the *Bhāgavatapurāṇa* 2.9.32–35 to emphasize the importance of *bhakti* and service, in slightly over one thousand *ovīs*. The beginning of the text describes how Eknāth composed it at the command of his *guru* while on a pilgrimage. His *Rukmiṇīsvayaṃvar* renders the story of Rukmiṇī's selection of Kṛṣṇa as her husband and subsequent wedding (from the tenth *skandha* of the *Bhāgavatapurāṇa*) into 1,700 Marathi verses. Because of its focus on Rukmiṇī's behavior toward Kṛṣṇa, it has been viewed traditionally as something of a textbook for Maharashtrian brides-to-be. Far more manuscripts of *Rukmiṇīsvayaṃvar* exist than of any other text by Eknāth, due to the popular belief that copying it by hand could auspiciously bring an eligible daughter a good husband. Several philosophical works discuss aspects of vedantic thought and *bhakti*: the 670-verse *Hastāmalak* (named after a supposed disciple of → Śaṅkara), the 450-verse *Śukāṣṭaka* (The Eight Verses of Śuka), the 500-verse *Svātmasukh* (Joy of the Self), the 154-verse *Ānandalahari* (Wave of Bliss), and the 221-verse *Ānandānubhav* (Experience of Bliss). These are the most well known of Eknāth's short treatises. Other, more obscure texts have been attributed to Eknāth as well, but modern Marathi scholars have presented strong arguments that they probably were composed by a slightly later author who was named Eknāth (see "Eknāth of Bīḍ" in: Khanolkar, 1977).

Several thousand short poems that are attributed to Eknāth have been compiled and published in a *Gāthā* or formal collection of his poetry (as were the *Gāthās* of the other major Marathi poet-saints). Although *kīrtan* performers and Vārkarī leaders traditionally maintained their own collections of Eknāth's poems over the centuries, efforts to create an exhaustive collection are relatively recent. The four earliest editions of Eknāth's *Gāthā* were published between 1896 and 1906, but none of the editors revealed their sources or methods in any detail. Thus it is impossible to discern how "critical" these collections are, and no thorough attempts have yet been made to assess the possibility that some poems may have been inserted later under his name. Such questions of authorship are not primary for the Vārkarī tradition, however, and the poems contained in the largest *Gāthā* edition (Avate, 1908) are regarded by most Vārkarīs to be Eknāth's own work.

Editors arranged the *Gāthā*'s roughly four thousand poems under various themes and topics – a classification system was largely but not completely consistent among various editions. Nearly a quarter of the collection comprises praise songs to various deities: Viṭṭhal, Śiva, Harihara, Kṛṣṇa, and the power of → Rām's and Hari's names. A large number extol the virtues of religious practices, such as listening to *kīrtan* performance, making the pilgrimage to Pandharpur, repeating the name of god, and revering one's *guru* and the saints. The *Gāthā* contains a large cycle of poetry about Kṛṣṇa's life, including songs that are based on games played by the cowherds and cowgirls, as well as a number of small but quite popular songs called *gauḷaṇs* that express the *gopīs*' longing for Kṛṣṇa. Notably, many of the poems describe episodes in the lives of other Vārkarī saints, which would make Eknāth one of the earliest sources of hagiography and information about some of these figures, if these poems were indeed composed by Eknāth. Saints included are Jñāndev and his three siblings, as well as Nāmdev, Gorā Kumbhār, Sāvatā Māḷī, and → Cokhāmeḷā. Of all the songs in the *Gāthā*, the ones for which Eknāth is most famous are approximately three hundred metaphorical drama-poems called *bhārūḍs* (see Crow, 1988). Eknāth's *bhārūḍs* take many forms, such as a character (acrobat, snake charmer, fortune teller, sweeper), festival event or game, animal, dialogue between two speakers (such as a Hindu and a Muslim; see Zelliot, 1982), or official letters to rulers. Each depicts a common, mundane aspect of the world that carries a spiritual message. The final verse of a *bhārūḍ* sometimes unlocks the spiritual meaning clearly, but it is also up to the performer (who usually enacts the given *bhārūḍ* somehow, such as dressing like a character) to ensure that the audience understands properly. Many of the characters depicted in Eknāth's *bhārūḍs* are socially marginal, and over 30 of the compositions are specifically about untouchables (Mahārs, specifically). That Eknāth has these characters teach his audiences (and in some *bhārūḍs*, Brahman interlocutors) spiritual lessons has provoked some scholars to wonder about the social context of these remarkable compositions (see Zelliot, 1980; 1987).

Finally, mention must also be made of widespread (and not ungrounded) belief that Eknāth critically edited Jñāndev's classic Marathi rendering of the *Bhagavadgītā*, commonly known as the *Jñāneśvarī*. Nearly all manuscripts of the *Jñāneśvarī* conclude with an obviously appended colophon testifying to Eknāth's efforts to "repurify" (*pratiśuddha*) this text in 1584 from a confusing array of alternate readings and errors that are said to have accrued in the nearly three centuries between Jñāndev and Eknāth (see → Jñāndev).

Legacies

As for material legacy, archival records show that the two temples related to Eknāth in Paithan and the immediate families of Eknāth's descendants enjoyed a modest degree of patronage from various local rulers (both Hindu and Muslim) over the centuries for the upkeep and development of institutions related to Eknāth's memory. Some descendants still live in the town and manage the two temples, which remain quite active and are the foci of pilgrimage activities during the celebration of *eknāth ṣaṣṭhī* (as described earlier). In recent years, attendance of the four-day celebration has easily exceeded a hundred thousand visitors, many of whom undertake walking pilgrimages to Paithan and stay there in makeshift tents on the Godāvarī riverbank. For the annual pilgrimage (*vārī*) in the month of *āṣāḍh* (Jun–Jul), stylized silver replicas of Eknāth's sandals (*pādukā*s) are taken out of the Gāvātle Mandir and carried on a silver-plated *pālkhī* or palanquin that is usually placed in a wagon and pulled for long stretches by bullocks. Pilgrims from around Paithan join descendants of Eknāth to undertake the 250 km journey from Paithan to Pandharpur over the course of 18 days, stopping frequently along the way to allow villagers a chance to touch the sandals, offer a small donation, and provide the pilgrims with food, water, snacks, and shelter (see Keune, forthcoming).

As for the legacies of Eknāth's texts, the *Eknāthī Bhāgavat* and *Bhāvārtha Rāmāyaṇa* continue to

Fig. 2: Palanquin with Eknāth's sandals is set down during a break while on pilgrimage to Pandharpur. To the left of palanquin, Vārkarī women carry *tulsī* plants on their head (a common practice for women pilgrims on *vārī*). To the right stand a *copdār* (mace-bearer) and man playing a traditional instrument (called *vīṇā* in Marathi) to accompany pilgrims singing *bhajans* (photo by Jon Keune).

be read occasionally for the public by groups of devotees in the practice of *pārāyaṇ* – a scheduled, serial reading of passages over many days until the entire text is finished. In some villages, a *pārāyaṇ* of the *Bhāvārtha Rāmāyaṇa* can involve groups of villagers donning burlap cloth over their feet, bodies, and heads, and making an impromptu pilgrimage into the countryside, to commemorate Rāmā's banishment to the forest. Passages from the *Eknāthī Bhāgavat* and Eknāth's *Gāthā* are regularly used in *kīrtan*s, in which the main performer will read the passage aloud, lead the audience in singing *bhajan*s, and then comment on the passage's meaning and relevance. Some of Eknāth's *bhārūḍ*s continue to be performed as well, sometimes during Vārkarī events and on pilgrimage, but also as parts of urban cultural events that showcase Maharashtrian folk culture. *bhārūḍ*s have also been popular to produce on video compact discs, which are sold in music shops for the sake of entertainment and devotion.

The legacy of Eknāth's memory in 20th-century Maharashtra is complex. An influential line of historical understanding perceived Eknāth's importance as working to overcome caste divisions and unite Hindu Marathi speakers in the 16th century, thereby preparing the ground for the Maratha king Śivājī to defeat local Muslim rulers and establish self-rule in the region (Ranade, 1900; Kulkarni, 1968). Following this train of thought, some interpreters of Eknāth and the larger Vārkarī tradition took on a decidedly nationalist orientation. At the same time, Vārkarīs themselves continued to revere Eknāth mainly as an innovative integrator of religious traditions (Dattātreya and Vārkarī devotion), a model of a spiritually adept householder, and an enlightened teacher who sought to bring his message of liberation to everyone regardless of caste or learning (Pangarkar, 1910; Ranade, 1933; Phatak, 1963).

Marathi film and theater productions about Eknāth in the 20th century tended to focus on his interaction with untouchables. Keshav Sitaram Thackeray's play *Kharā Brāmhaṇ* (True Brahman) in 1933 controversially portrayed Eknāth working for greater social inclusion for untouchables, because he held anti-Brahman and pro-*hindutva* sentiments. The Prabhat Film Company's black and white feature *Dharmātmā* (dir. V. Shantaram, 1935) took some creative liberties with the story of Eknāth eating at the untouchable couples' home, crafting it into a gentle but insistent critique of discrimination against untouchables. The film ran afoul with the Bombay Board of Censors on the grounds that it offended political and religious sensibilities, and it was released to the public only after the studio carried out some notable (and occasionally awkward) revisions (see Skyhawk, 2005; Keune, 2011). *Dharmātmā* introduced Marathi audiences to a delightful, young untouchable girl named Jāī, whom Eknāth treated as a daughter in the film. This character was so persuasive and memorable that some people in later generations came to remember her as an essential historical figure in Eknāth's life, although she was actually created for the film. Between 1964 and 1974, a popular play, *Bhāva Toci Dev* (Devotion Itself Is God), toured around and performed in rural Maharashtrian venues some 1,500 times. The focus of this music-filled comedy was Eknāth's compassionate and respectful relationship with untouchable characters, and the main source of humor was the efforts of bumbling, arrogant Brahmans who sought to condemn him. It should be kept in mind, however, that while Marathi producers were remembering Eknāth as a compassionate friend of untouchables on the stage and screen, organized movements of untouchables on the ground were led by men like Bhimrao → Ambedkar to abandon the Vārkarī tradition altogether. Thus relatively few → Dalits in 21st-century Maharashtra find Eknāth worth remembering at all, much less as a critic of caste.

Bibliography

Abbott, J.E. *et al.*, *Nectar from Indian Saints*, Poona, 1935.

Abbott, J.E. *et al.*, *The Life of Eknāth*, Poona, 1927.

Avate (Āvaṭe), T.H., ed., *Śrīeknāthmahārāj Yāñcyā Abhaṅgācī Gāthā*, Poona, 1908.

Crow, R.W., "The *Bhāruḍ*s of the Marāṭhī Sant Eknāth," diss., University of Pennsylvania, 1988.

Deák, D., "Maharashtra Saints and the Sufi Tradition: Eknath, Chand Bodhle and the Datta Sampradaya," *DS* 3/2, 2005, 22–47.

Joshi (Jośī), P.N., *Prācīn Marāṭhī Vāṅmāyācā Itihās*, Puṇe, 2004 (Mar.).

Keune, J., "The Varkaris in Western India," in: P. Penumala, ed., *Introducing Hinduism*, London, forthcoming.

Keune, J., "Eknāth Remembered and Reformed: Bhakti, Brahmans, and Untouchables in Marathi Historiography," diss., Columbia University, 2011.

Keune, J., "Gathering the Bhaktas in Marāṭhī," *JVS* 15/2, 2007, 169–187.

Khanolkar (Khānolkar), G.D., ed., *Marāṭhī Vāṅmaykoś (Khaṇḍa Pahilā)*, Mumbai, 1977 (Mar.).
Ok, D.K., *Mahārāṣṭra-Kavivarya-Mukteśvarkṛt Sphuṭa-kāvyeṁ*, Mumbai, 1906 (Mar.).
Pangarkar (Pāṅgārkar), L.R., *Eknāth Caritra*, Poona, 1910 (Mar.).
Phatak (Phāṭak), N.R., *Śrī Eknāth: Vāṅmay āṇi Kārya*, Mumbai, 1950 (Mar.).
Ranade, M.G., *Rise of the Maratha Power*, Delhi, 1900.
Ranade, R.D., *Mysticism in Maharashtra*, Delhi, 1933.
Skyhawk, H., "The Social Expression of the Unity with the Divine: The Saint's Conduct as a Component of Hindu Ethics," in: A. Malik *et al.*, eds., *In the Company of Gods*, Delhi, 2005, 211–222.
Skyhawk, H., *Bhakti und Bhakta. Untersuchungen zum Heilsbegriff und zur Religiösen Umwelt des Śrī Sant Ekanāth*, Stuttgart, 1990.
Tulpule, S.G., "Eknāth's Treatment of the Rāmāyaṇa as a Socio-Political Metaphor," in: M. Thiel-Horstmann, ed., *Rāmāyaṇa and Rāmāyaṇas*, Wiesbaden, 1991, 139–152.
Zelliot, E., "Eknath's Bharude: The Sant as a Link between Cultures," in: K. Schomer, & W.H. McLeod, eds., *The Sants*, Delhi, 1987, 91–110.
Zelliot, E., "A Medieval Encounter between Hindu and Muslim – Eknath's *Hindu-Turk Samvad*," in: F.W. Clothey, ed., *Images of Man*, Madras, 1982, 171–195.
Zelliot, E., "Chokhamela and Eknath: Two 'Bhakti' Modes of Legitimacy for Modern Change," *JAAS* 15/1–2, 1980, 136–156.

Jon Keune

Gārgī

Gārgī Vācaknavī is a woman philosopher from the early upanishadic era who participated in a tournament held at the court of King Janaka of Videha (see → Bihar). Her story is known from an account in the *Bṛhadāraṇyakopaniṣad* (see → Upaniṣads), which is one of very few to highlight the lives of gifted women thinkers in ancient India. These stories undermine a traditional vision of women as silent and invisible bystanders to male dominance of vedic intellectual life. Gārgī's performance at the philosophical tournament raises serious questions about the social intentions of the Upaniṣad, the inclinations of the subject of interrogation and eventual winner of the contest (Yājñavalkya), and the literary and philosophic motivations of the composers who attribute to Gārgī not only the most spirited personality of all the characters present but also the most heterodox of philosophic styles.

Gārgī and the Vedic Context

Gārgī's appearance in the *Bṛhadāraṇyakopaniṣad* occurs as two important changes in ancient Indian life emerge: a dramatic reversal of early opportunities for women interested in education, and a development of the traditional vedic ritual into a variety of more satisfying religious options, including that of the Upaniṣads. Although the history of women in India at this time reflects an increasingly inflexible social structure that, over the centuries, comes to undermine whatever status women may have as independent participants in civic and intellectual affairs, the vedic period represents an era of relative advantage and possibility for women.

A woman has some opportunities in this early period because she is a necessary partner to her husband in both the → domestic ritual and the solemn ritual (see → *yajña*). As *ardhāṅginī*, the wife is half of the whole ritual unit based in the husband, and, in that the sacrificer must be married, no sacrifice can be performed without her. The gods, for example, will not accept a sacrifice offered by a bachelor, and a husband needs his wife to accompany him in the symbolic ascent to heaven during worship (*ṚV.* 1.72.5; *TaiBr.* 3.7.5; *ŚBrM.* 5.2.1.8–10; *MaSm.* 9.45; Kane, vol. II, 1974, 256–259; Jamison, 1996, 10, 30). A woman is expected to participate in not only in the sacred rites of the home and in the solemn ritual in public with her husband, but also in some ritual moments where she might perform ritual tasks herself. Although technically, neither the wife nor the husband can perform Śrauta tasks alone, some Gṛhyasūtras (manuals of domestic rites of passage) allow the wife, for example, to make daily offerings into the domestic fire (Jamison, 1996, 36). The autonomous connection of women to ritual practice reaches back to the *Ṛgveda*, for the priestess Viśvavārā (*ṚV.* 5.28.1) and the poetess Apālā (*ṚV.* 8.91) are each associated with preparation of the solemn rites. A wife's responsibility to her husband as a philosophical guide is an important part of her coparticipation with him in religious affairs. In this, she is called a *sahadharmiṇī*, one who not only shares in the duties of her husband, but also can be an intellectual companion to her husband in issues of the mind.

To be a *sahadharmiṇī* presupposes an education for the wife, who can marry, some early sources say, only after concluding a specified period of study. This may account for the coeducational nature of the early forest universities and most certainly means that parents may have a responsibility for educating their daughters and beginning such an education with the traditional ritual of the *upanayana* (ritual of initiation into the period of study; Raja, 1950, 106–111; Sengupta, 1974, 45, 80–81, 128–130; Kane, vol. II, 1974, 294–295). The differences between boys and girls during studenthood are that girls are not to grow matted hair, wear deerskin or bark garments, go out beyond their homes to beg their daily food, or be taught by anyone except a near male relative. Vedic education for girls appears to be serious and rigorous, at least in the early period, for the *Ṛgveda* notes a number of female sages (→ *ṛṣi*) – Viśvavārā, Apālā, and Ghoṣa, for example – and later literature honors three women scholars in the *ṛṣitarpaṇa* (water presented to visionary poets as libation; besides Gārgī, Vaḍavā Prātītheyī and Sulabhā Maitreyī; *ĀśvGS.* 3.4.4), a list of the sages to whose memory a daily tribute of respect should be paid.

This early emphasis upon education means that women can become ascetics (*brahmacariṇī*; see also → female ascetics) or live in single-sex hostels and study freely. Among female students, there are, generally, two classes, both of whom learn vedic hymns and prayers and study the manuals for the performance of the sacraments: the *sadyovadhū*, who studies until becoming a wife at the age of 15 or 16, and the *brahmavādinī*, a discourser on → *brahman*, who studies for a lifetime. It is the *brahmavādinī* who memorizes liturgical materials and carries on specialized studies in Pūrvamīmāṃsā (see → Mīmāṃsā), by which adepts discuss the diverse philosophical problems of the vedic sacrifice. The Pūrvamīmāṃsā is perhaps the intellectual challenge of the day, and the literature suggests that its female students are among those who speak out at the popular assembly (*vidatha*). Moreover, the appearance of these names for women teachers – *upādhyāyānī* and *ācāryā* – suggests that teaching is a profession open to women, as evidenced in the experience of Paṭācārā, a well-known early female teacher of Buddhist nuns. With teaching, a woman can become economically self-reliant and, trained in a wide range of subjects (grammar, poetry, literature, theology, and philosophy), can attract a broad range of students, male as well as female (Sengupta, 1974, 69; Kane, vol. II, 1974, 366).

Gradually, however, the position of women declines, and by the time of the → Dharmaśāstras, women are more or less excluded from formal education. The ceremony of marriage, for instance, comes to be recognized as taking the place of the *upanayana* for women, for whom, according to Manu, meaning now is found in service to their husbands rather than in that to their "spiritual fathers" and in care of the domestic fire rather than in that of the sacred fire. The role of the wife as *sahadharmiṇī* is supplanted by that of the wife as *pativratā*, whereby a woman loses herself in the personality of her husband and will, as asceticism becomes more prominent, retire to the forest with him (*MaSm.* 2.67; 5.147–149; Kane, vol. II, 1974, 918; vol. III, 1993, 536).

Many developments contribute to this general decline, and especially to the exclusion of women from public, institutional aspects of religion. With a lowered marriage age increasingly in vogue, there is little time left for the study of an ever-more cumbersome tradition. Furthermore, with the growing emphasis on sacrifices to the ancestors that males normally perform, sons come to be much preferred over daughters. Consequently, young women increasingly focus their attention on producing a sufficient number of male sacrificers. Male children are also more desirable economically and socially, for they not only can provide the life-long labor needed to support an extended family but also do not have to be equipped with lavish dowries. A young woman's real → *dharma*, then, comes to be that of mothering male children by one of her own caste (*MaSm.* 9.8–9, 32–34). To legitimize this new low status of women, legislators finally declared that women are impotent (*nirindriya*) and equivalent to falsehood (*anṛta*) itself (*MaSm.* 9.18).

The second major change of this time is the expansion of religious options beyond the traditional vedic ritual to new spiritual alternatives. According to the old system, the cosmos is "homologically" created through complex procedures on the ritual ground, and man is virtuous only if he masters the intricate techniques of the ritual. Seen as increasingly ineffective, however, this system gives way to others, the most important of which is that of the Upaniṣads, the heir to the → Vedas. The *Bṛhadāraṇyakopaniṣad*, as the oldest of these secret doctrinal texts, reflects a society no longer concerned with the safety of its borders or the stability of its economic system, but rather one able to support both leisure-time activities, such as philosophical tournaments, and leisure-time classes and institutions.

Since the period – at least in its earlier centuries – acknowledges the intellectual prowess of women, it would follow that the upanishadic movement is even more beneficial to them. As the family unit's hold over the traditional spiritual life of the individual breaks down, women can take advantage of an opportunity for participation in the new intellectual life of the culture. In actual fact, however, women appear primarily in the first Upaniṣad, the *Bṛhadāraṇyakopaniṣad*, for when the Dharmaśāstras finally take account of these new developments, their compilers see women as even more necessary to the maintenance of the family unit as men retreat into the forest.

Gārgī at the Tournament

The tournament at Janaka's court in Videha occurs just as this precipitous decline in the intellectual life of women, and the shift in religious life from ritualism to contemplation, emerge. King Janaka has offered a prize of one thousand cows plus ten thousand gold coins to whichever of the

Brahmans present can demonstrate knowledge of the supreme *brahman*. The teacher Yājñavalkya immediately appropriates the cows by asking his student, Sāmaśravas, to drive them home. The other Brahmans become angry and put questions to Yājñavalkya to find out if he is in fact the greatest of the Brahmans. What follows (*BĀU*. 3.1.1–9.28) is perhaps the most significant example of the dialectical mode of argumentation we have from the period, in which the contributions made by Yājñavalkya in response to the nine sets of questions posed to him move philosophic inquiry out of its liturgical context. In the interrogation that ensues, Gārgī is the first participant to be challenged and the only participant to speak not once but twice (Black, 2007, 150), and she distinguishes herself as the most eminent of the philosophers present.

Aśvala, the *hotṛ* (→ priest) of Janaka (*BĀU*. 3.1.2–10), opens the questions with sacrificial analogies. Although Yājñavalkya shows that he is well versed in the symbolic correspondences between parts of the sacrifice and nature, the *Bṛhadāraṇyakopaniṣad* will lead from this point on to show that ritualism is outdated. Jāratkārava Ārtabhāga (*BĀU*. 3.2.1–13) begins the second round of questioning with a series on the essences of the senses, and, as he proceeds to his final question about what survives death, he is able to elicit from Yājñavalkya the doctrine of man's return to nature according to his just desserts: man's body, he suggests, will return to the elements according to the principle of sympathetic analogy. What survives, however, is → *karman*, but this new doctrine (that one "becomes" good by a good deed and evil by an evil one) is so innovative and controversial that it cannot be discussed in public, and Yājñavalkya leads Ārtabhāga from the room in order to finish the discussion in private.

Bhujyu Lāhyāyani (*BĀU*. 3.3.1–2) puts forth a third set of questions and, being interested in psychic research, elicits from Yājñavalkya a description of the divine worlds where the great men of old have gone. He is followed by Uṣasta Cākrāyaṇa (*BĀU*. 3.4.1–2), who at last begins the posing of serious philosophical problems. Uṣasta is concerned with the soul (→ *ātman*) that is within everything, and Yājñavalkya's response points to a personal self in all things, a hearer of sound and a seer of sight that the person himself can neither hear nor see. Kahola Kauṣītakeya (*BĀU*. 3.1) continues Uṣasta's questions and discovers from Yājñavalkya that the only personal response to knowledge of the *ātman* is the naive life of a child, that of the *muni*, the silent sage, who lives transcending opposites and is a spiritual achiever simply by being what he is.

Gārgī Vācaknavī is the sixth questioner (*BĀU*. 3.6.1), and, using the ancient ritual imagery of the warp and the woof (e.g. the weaving of the rgvedic sacrifice), she moves Yājñavalkya back toward a first principle in a series of infinitely regressive questions in the form (Black, 2007, 155) "on what is water woven, on air; on what is air woven." Telling her that she is questioning too much about the deity (*devatā*) who cannot be overly questioned, he tells her to stop asking questions or her head will fall off. Upon this rebuke, Gārgī falls silent (*upararāma*).

As the seventh questioner and as Yājñavalkya's superior and, some say, Gārgī's defender (Black, 2007, 84–85), Uddālaka Āruṇi (*BĀU*. 3.7.1–23) takes up Gārgī's imagery of the woven thread. He elicits from Yājñavalkya the innovative doctrine of *antaryāmi*, the inner controller, an immortal principle immanent in all objects in the universe, and yet separate from and unknown to them.

Not put off by Yājñavalkya's rebuke, however, Gārgī (*BĀU*. 3.8.1–12) enters the debate a second time, as the eighth participant, and questions him about that on which the universe is strung and threaded, that is, on the nature of the first principle called in verse eight the "imperishable" (*akṣara*) – the differences between the terms "inner controller" and "imperishable" are discussed in → Śaṅkara's commentary, the *Bṛhadāraṇyakopaniṣadbhāṣya*. When Yājñavalkya tells her "ether," she repeats her question, and Yājñavalkya then describes the principle in question the only way he can, with a long series of negatives (the *via negativa*): not coarse, not fine; not short, not long; and so on. *Brahman* is, as before, neither a substance nor possessed of attributes or referents (Radhakrishan, 169, 232).

Vidagdha Śākalya (*BĀU*. 3.9.1–26) is the ninth and last questioner and takes Yājñavalkya detail by detail through the resting places of the various gods and spirits. Finally, following a method similar to Gārgī's regressive questioning, Vidagdha elicits from Yājñavalkya a sophisticated version of the earlier series of negatives, the famous doctrine of *neti neti* (not this, not this). When asked himself, however, about the nature of this upanishadic entity known merely by *neti neti*, Vidagdha, a persistent and overconfident critic, cannot respond, and the curse that has been so lightly bandied about among the participants in the tournament – "if you do not know, your head will fall off" – is finally cast upon him, and robbers carry off his bones (see Black, 2007, 80–88).

Gārgī's Achievement and Contributions

The tragic conclusion to the tournament does not, however, hide the achievements of the participants, especially the philosophic structures elicited from Yājñavalkya. From his remarks at Janaka's court, the foundation for the development of→ Vedānta is laid, and any further concern with the ideology of ritual is seriously undermined. In assessing the performance of the interrogators themselves, however, it is Gārgī whose contributions and style are judged by many to be the most important.

M.D. Paradkar suggests that, because Gārgī is considered to be the most astute of all the participants, she is allowed to have a second chance to confront Yājñavalkya – a skilled philosopher who finds her a worthy opponent. Gārgī, M.D. Paradkar notes, is considered the spokesperson in the tournament, brings the subtlest philosophical questions before Yājñavalkya, and launches them with coolness and confidence, showing that she is a debater of the very highest rank. Moreover, her fame is grounded in her foreswearing the world of wealth and material pleasures for the difficult world of knowledge, and, in that, she sets a high standard (Paradkar, 26.1–4, 30). Her philosophical method for pursuing the origins of things by using a series of infinite regressions is frustrating for him and may suggest a weakness in his position. Other scholars recognize her high achievement as well. P.V. Kane and P.S. Sastri point out Gārgī's great thirst for knowledge and active quest for a foundational consciousness (Kane, vol. II, 1974, 366; Sastri, 1954, 171). And B. Black (2007, 134) notes Gārgī's superior knowledge over that of several of the Brahmans – knowledge argued by a woman but recognized only when reiterated by a male Brahman.

Any evaluation of the consensus that Gārgī is the wisest and most articulate of the interrogators, however, must take account of the negative assessments as well. F. Edgerton claims that the text itself reveals no evidence that she is regarded as especially bold in her questions (Edgerton, 1965, 135). And for some, Gārgī seems disconcerted at the great skill of her adversary and in need of using her womanly modesty to refrain from any further questioning. Others charge that she is rude to torment Yājñavalkya in the way she does, with question after question, as this pursuit via infinite regress recapitulates the excessive curiosity women are known to have in philosophical discussions. That is, in insisting on asking more questions, Gārgī is being typically womanly in speaking over and over again.

In assessing Gārgī within the *Bṛhadāraṇyakopaniṣad* account of the tournament, three themes emerge. First, many scholars take the text at face value and understand Gārgī as the wisest and most eloquent of the disputants, whose spirited and courageous personality gets her into trouble with her philosophic adversary. Second, others understand the text as a literary narrative, designed not only for the transmission of knowledge, but also for amusement and pleasure. And, third, still others consider the text as testing, or rebuking, certain heterodox philosophic ideas that carry danger in the upanishadic context. Consonant with the derogatory assessments of Gārgī, what better way to introduce such off-beat elements than through the character of a woman?

In the first approach, compilers of the *Bṛhadāraṇyakopaniṣad* would be seen as supporters of the intellectual life for women. In addition to this extended account of Gārgī, the *Bṛhadāraṇyakopaniṣad* has an extraordinary dialogue between Yājñavalkya and one of his two wives, Maitreyī (*BĀU*. 4.5.1–15), in which this *brahmavādinī* renounces her share of Yājñavalkya's property and, because of her searching questions, is judged capable of receiving her husband's esoteric teachings. This passage, moreover, casts Yājñavalkya as an early champion of women's economic rights: against the background of an ongoing debate about whether a sonless "widow" should inherit her husband's wealth, he, about to undergo a "spiritual death," hopes to divide all his property between his two wives.

In the second approach, the characterization of Gārgī is viewed with conscious literary and dramatic intent to introduce, for example, certain narrative elements such as suspense and levity. More specifically, structural elements in the Upaniṣads, such as dialogue, are seen to give theatrical effect and to highlight the artistic and philosophic value of the story form. The dialogue structure in the *Bṛhadāraṇyakopaniṣad*, then, has the advantage not only of rendering the event vivid and immediate, but also of portraying the vices and virtues of personalities in action. One of the dominant themes in drama is of woman as the companion of man, of the heroine as dependent upon her relation to the hero for her own characterization – that is, of the woman as *ardhāṅginī*, a necessary half for the wholeness of the unit. The relationship between Gārgī and Yājñavalkya, though not one of marriage, is certainly one of intimate collegiality, and, while Gārgī no doubt makes her mark only in relation to Yājñavalkya, he is just as dependent upon her and her pointed questioning for the verbalization of his doctrine. Gārgī is not only Yājñavalkya's most acerbic opponent and therefore his most useful dialectical ally, but also, surprisingly, his greatest admirer and enthusiast. It is up to her to legitimize the contest by calling it a *brahmodya* (a debate about *brahman; BĀU.*3.8.1, 12), and she is the main one to recognize Yājñavalkya's clear intellectual preeminence and eventual victory. The *ardhāṅginī* model, then, seems most fitting here, with Gārgī cast as Yājñavalkya's "*sahadharmiṇī*," who – though she may thwart, contrast, disrupt, and distract – uniquely enables Yājñavalkya to play off her to advance the discussion.

The third approach is of a conscious philosophic characterization of Gārgī's style. Like the other interrogators, she is interested in the nature of the first principle. She pursues her quest, however, with a method whose questions ultimately cannot be answered. In the infinite regression method, each new question responds to the answer of the previous question, of the sort, "what must there be for X to be, Y; what must there be for Y to be, etc.?" Traditionally, the process of the infinite regress is to show how the aspirant can come to realize his or her own self as fully present and undeviating and to reveal the self to be both immanent and transcendent, beyond all attributes, and "uncaused." If this kind of sequence of questions could, as appears possible on the surface, lead to the self as the first principle, then Yājñavalkya's rebuke is uncalled for. This is not the case, however, for Gārgī's fault (according to tradition) is in disregarding the proper method of inquiry into the nature of the absolute, a process accessed only through the → transmission of knowledge from a teacher or a text.

Gārgī's transgression is not that she does not understand the ineffable nature of the absolute but that she attempts to get to this knowledge through unorthodox means; she asks a series of straightforward questions using the relationships she observes in the world. Thus Śaṅkara describes Gārgī's inquiry as one based on inference taken from evidence of the orderliness of the world – with his point being that she should find knowledge of the transcendent only through scripture and not logic (Radhakrishnan, 1969, 223), or as E. Roer notes, Gārgī should refrain from asking improper questions as they cannot be answered by argument, only by the Śāstras (Roer, 1931, 280).

Gārgī's method of inquiry in this first answer is foreign to that of the vedic tradition upon which the Upaniṣads rest. When the poets of the *Ṛgveda* and *Atharvaveda* (see → Vedas) become more advanced philosophers and begin to ask abstract questions about a first principle, the type of question raised is mostly journalistic – for example, "Who does such and such a cosmic deed?" and "How is the division into specific phenomena made?" – all questions that can be given a specific answer and do not, in and of themselves, lead to a new question. Likewise in the brahmanic period, all speculation about a first principle is specific in nature: "What reward will I get if I do this in the ritual?" or, "What is the natural correlate of this liturgical element?" In this way, philosophical questions prior to the upanishadic period are (1) understood as answerable and (2) answerable only with doctrine from within the system.

While epistemology is taken more seriously in the upanishadic period, Gārgī's type of inquiry, the *regressus ad infinitum*, conforms to a type of logical reasoning found not only in the Upaniṣads but also in an experientially based form, for example, in early Buddhist Suttas (Skt. Sūtras). In the Upaniṣads, this regressive questioning might lead, it is believed, to a first principle that is not bound by a causal system, but in Buddhist dialogue, where everything is understood to have a precondition: "What must there be for X to exist?" can never be answered with "nothing." If hidden in Yājñavalkya's rebuke is a confrontation between accepted and nonaccepted modes of interrogation, between questions that could lead back to a belief in an uncaused principle and those same questions revealing that the answers to all such questions are conditioned, then Gārgī must be seen as treading on dangerous and potentially heretical ground. The rebuke to be silent could be a reminder that there is a first principle, that it is ineffable, and that no amount of questioning will give one knowledge of it. Or, the rebuke to silence may suggest that the *regressus ad infinitum* takes the questioner out of upanishadic territory and into the heterodox territory of, say, early Buddhism, where all experience is understood to be caused and conditioned, that is, where there is recognition that there can be no proof for (or against) the notion of a first cause. Or, from the point of view of the Gārgī portrayed in the Upaniṣad, the silence following the rebuke may simply be more of a courtesy than acquiescence.

Gārgī's second interchange with Yājñavalkya (*BĀU.* 3.8) takes place after his abrupt rebuke and her silence, when he is again the gracious and well-mannered philosophic master. While Gārgī appears back on safer ground with more traditional material up for discussion, what she is able to do is still significant as, under her questioning, she elicits some basic and critical principles. The first results from her pressing him about the support of the visible world, and especially about what supports ether. According to Śaṅkara, Yājñavalkya is here faced with a serious problem. If he does not explain the principle, he will lay himself open to the charge of what in logic is called "noncomprehension"; if he does try to explain it, however, he will be guilty of what is called a "contradiction," an attempt to explain what cannot be explained (Radhakrishnan, 1969, 232). It appears as well that Gārgī herself may think the question unanswerable but that she presses Yājñavalkya to provide an image for the futility of language in this regard. And that image is the doctrine of *via negative*, implicit in his long series of what *brahman* is not (*BĀU.* 3.8.8) and expressed in his subsequent answer to Uddālaka as *neti neti* (not this, not this; *BĀU.* 3.9.26). This doctrine is at the heart of Yājñavalkya's thought, and it is to Gārgī's great credit that at her moment in the debate, Yājñavalkya reveals it.

The second doctrine elicited by Gārgī is the immanence of "an imperishable" (*akṣara*), which is known, Yājñavalkya tells Gārgī, because of the order present in the world around us. And this order in the world suggests that there is a design as well; "the imperishable" being in control of the movements of the seasons and the rivers, for example (*BĀU.* 3.8.9), implies that the world is as "he" willed it. Using language already found in his answer to Uṣasta (*BĀU.*3.4.2), Yājñavalkya describes the "imperishable" as the seer of seeing, the hearer of hearing, the thinker of thinking, and the knower of knowing, who "himself" is unseen, unheard, unthought of, and unknown.

Gārgī, then, is portrayed as not only accepting doctrines but also telling the others they cannot defeat Yājñavalkya in arguments. Her silence at this point, then, seals the discussion and may well reflect the upanishadic compilers' desire to characterize Gārgī as a good and dutiful "half" of the dialectic whole she forms with Yājñavalkya.

The *Bṛhadāraṇyakopaniṣad* here, then, hints at two themes in early Buddhism: the series of infinite regress that the Buddha attends to when debating the Brahmans, and the inability of language to approach any truths beyond the empirical, which is reflected in a teacher's silence. Both are in the "philosophic air" of the time, and in the Upaniṣad both are associated with Gārgī. Certainly Janaka's tournament brings forth other new material – Ārtabhāga and *karman*, Kahoḍa and the *muni*, and Uddālaka and the *antaryāmi* – but it is critical that further assessments of Gārgī and the details of the tournament take into account the great philosophic and religious creativity of other traditions of the period that may bear on the issues raised here.

Any assessment of Gārgī, then, must consider some larger issues of the text. First, there are definite feminist tendencies in sections of the *Bṛhadāraṇyakopaniṣad* that render it unique among the Upaniṣads of its period and that establish the clear possibility that Gārgī is faithfully rendered as a remarkable female philosopher at the fore of her field. (That the *Bṛhadāraṇyakopaniṣad* may have exaggerated her achievements is hardly likely given what is probably the conservative context in which the text is compiled; see also → feminism) In a second, contrasting view, she is characterized as a typical female: on the one hand, she introduces suspense and comic relief by thwarting, disrupting, and even sidetracking the discussion, and, on the other hand, she is the necessary partner, the "other half," to Yājñavalkya's dialectical search for truth, without whom the truth cannot be found. In either case, her character is a tool used by textual composers to confirm traditional views about women in a decidedly untraditional format. Third, the *Bṛhadāraṇyakopaniṣad*, and the whole upanishadic movement, gain immensely from any renunciation of heterodoxy; if there is such a concern, Gārgī's character may have been used to illustrate the results of philosophical confusion, the foibles of persistent "Buddhistic" questioning, and the desirability of acquiescence to a new tradition and to its central system of *guruśiṣya* (teacher-student realtionship) etiquette. In spite of any such "uses" of the Gārgī character, it would be hard to deny the overall significance of Gargi as perceived by the Indian tradition: an affirmation of women as productive colleagues in the ongoing search for truth.

Bibliography

Aufrecht, T., *Die Hymnen des Ṛigveda*, 2 vols., Bonn, 1887.

Black, B., *The Character of the Self in Ancient India: Priests, Kings and Women in the Early Upaniṣads*, Albany, 2007.

Edgerton, F., *The Beginnings of Indian Philosophy*, Cambridge MA, 1965.

Findly, E.B., "Gārgī at the King's Court: Women and Philosophic Innovation in Ancient India," in: E.B. Findly & Y.Y. Haddad, *Women, Religion, and Social Change*, Albany, 1985, 37–58.

Haughton, G.C., ed., *Manava-Dharma-Sastra or The Institutes of Manu*, London, 1825.

Jamison, S.W., *Sacrificed Wife / Sacrificer's Wife*, New York, 1996.

Kane, P.V., *History of Dharmaśāstra*, vol. II/1–3, Poona, ^{2}1974, ^{3}1993.

Mitra, R., *The Taittirīyabrāhmaṇa of the Black Yajur Veda*, Osnabruck, 1855.

Paradkar, M.D., *Contributions of Women to Ancient and Medieval Sanskrit Literature*, BV 26/1–4, New Delhi.

Radhakrishnan, S., ed., *The Principal Upaniṣads*, London, 3 1969.

Raja, C.K., *Some Aspects of Education in Ancient India*, Adyar, 1950.

Roer, E., *The Twelve Principal Upaniṣads: With Notes from the Commentaries of Śaṅkarācārya*, Adyar, 1931.

Sastri, P.S., "Two Women Thinkers of the Upanishadic Age," *PB*, 1954, 171.

Sengupta, P., *The Story of Women of India*, New Delhi, 1974.

Weber, A., *The Śatapathabrāhmaṇa in Mādhyadina-Śākhā*, Berlin, 1855.

Ellison B. Findly

Hit Harivaṃś

Hit Harivaṃś (1502–1552 CE) was a Vaiṣṇava poet and saint associated with Vrindavan and the medieval → *bhakti* movement in North India. Hit Harivaṃś – together with → Caitanya and the six *gosvāmīs* of the → Gauḍīya Sampradāya, → Vallabha and the *aṣṭachāp* poets, Śrī Bhaṭṭa and Harivyāsadevācārya of the → Nimbārka Sampradāya, and Svāmī Haridās of the → Haridāsī Sampradāya – are recognized by historians as pioneers in establishing Vrindavan as a major pilgrimage destination and center of the *bhakti* tradition. Vrindavan is believed to be the geographical location of the childhood activities of the incarnation of → Kṛṣṇa who was born, according to pious tradition, in roughly 3000 BCE in the nearby town of Mathura. Also native to the Mathura region, Hit Harivaṃś is noteworthy for composing exceptional devotional poetry in both Brajbhasha and Sanskrit, elevating the theological status of → Rādhā to the level of supreme being; establishing the worship of the deity of Rādhāvallabha ("Dearest of Rādhā," i.e. Kṛṣṇa); founding the Vaiṣṇava lineage known as the → Rādhāvallabha Sampradāya, which has remained independent of the orthodox schools of Vaiṣṇavism; and inaugurating the temple music genre known as *samaj gāyan* (see → *kīrtan*), a devotional form of *dhrupad* singing that has remained a core element in the Rādhāvallabha → *sevā* or worship tradition for nearly five hundred years. Hit Harivaṃś was also linked to Svāmī Haridās and the Rādhāvallabha poet Harirām Vyās, who were referred to as the *haritrayī* ("three Haris"). This article outlines previous scholarship on Hit Harivaṃś, including his literary works *Caurāsipad* and *Śrīrādhāsudhānidhi*, and then briefly describes the theology and religious practices associated with his community known as the Rādhāvallabha Sampradāya.

The most comprehensive introduction to the religious, social, political, and geographic context of Hit Harivaṃś, including a study of the important Braj religious leaders and traditions, is A.W. Entwistle's *Braj: Centre of Krishna Pilgrimage* (1987). Scholars and practitioners both within and outside the Rādhāvallabha Sampradāya have contributed toward the publication of critical editions, commentaries, and in some cases English translations of important literature. Among Indian scholars within the tradition, the names of L.C. Goswami and S.K.S. Ali are well known. L.C. Goswami and S.K.S. Ali have edited and commented on the writings of Hit Harivaṃś in Hindi. Most of the writings and manuscripts attributed to members of the Rādhāvallabha Sampradāya, with dates, were tabulated by S.K.S. Ali in *Śrī Hita Rādhāvallabhīya Sahityā Ratnāvali* (1950). V. Snatak (1957) was the first Indian academic outside the tradition to give serious attention to Hit Harivaṃś and the Rādhāvallabha Sampradāya. C.S.J. White (1977) and R. Snell (1991) are the first Western scholars, studying under V. Snatak and L.C. Goswami, respectively, to create full-length studies in English. Prior to these, Hit Harivaṃś and his tradition had been all but ignored in Western scholarship, as most orientalist writings mentioned him only in passing or in footnotes. The most extensive coverage in the 19th century was by F.S. Growse, in *Mathurā: A District Memoir* (1883), where he surveyed "The Rādhā Vallabhīs" (199–216), including the earliest translation of verses 1–25 of Harivaṃś' Sanskrit work *Śrīrādhāsudhānidhi* (203–208), and verses 1–12 of his Brajbhasha work *Caurāsipad* (208–215). Some biographical details are also given (199–202).

Biography

The reconstruction of an accurate biography of Hit Harivaṃś, as with many medieval religious figures in India, entails many problems with dating and source materials. According to R. Snell (1991, 5), "It is not possible… to present an authoritative biography of the bhakta [Hit Harivaṃś] to whom the CP [*Caurāsipad*] is ascribed." Besides the normal embellishments found in Vaiṣṇava hagiographies, one firm obstacle is the lack of access to temple archives:

> Vaiṣṇava hagiographies cannot be regarded as objective historical statements, and the temple records of the Rādhāvallabha Sampradāya tradition, which would no doubt yield much genealogical information, have so far remained inaccessible to outside researchers. (Snell, 1991, 5)

In addition, many of the known aspects are problematic:

> Barely a single aspect of Harivaṃśa's life as related by any one source – save perhaps his devotion to Rādhā – remains uncontested by some contradictory statement elsewhere; and yet the roots of these inconsistencies are not inaccessible to research and may often be traced to confused interpretations of extant texts. (Snell, 1991, 5)

Through the years, secondary sources have relied on the few primary sources that have been available and so generally do not present new material. The earliest references are not biographical but salutations in texts written by contemporaries like Prabodhānanda Sarasvati. As outlined by R. Snell (1991, 27–28), the primary sources are mentioned below.

The 16th Century

Prabodhānanda Sarasvati refers to Hit Harivaṃś as "luminary of the Vyās dynasty" in the texts of *Śrihitaharivaṃśacandrāṣṭaka* and *Vṛndāvanamahimāmṛta*. Harivaṃś' son Kṛṣṇadās refers to Harivaṃś as Vaiyāsiki ("Son of Vyāsa") in his *Karṇānanda* of 1578.

The 17th Century

Harirām Vyās (16th–17th cents.) praises Harivaṃś in his poems and connects his name with Svāmī Haridās. Dhruvadās (c. 1593–1641 CE) eulogizes Harivaṃś and his sons in his *Bhaktanāmāvali*. Dāmodaradās in his *Sevakvāṇī* attaches the prefix Hita ("Well," "Good") to the name of Harivaṃś and provides information about his parents and details of his birth. A clear sectarian theology is established by the time of this text, wherein Hit Harivaṃś is described as an incarnation of → Viṣṇu in the *kaliyuga* (see → cosmic cycles) for the protection of → *dharma* during the ascendency of Muslim rule. Nābhādās' *Bhaktamālā* outlines the teachings of Harivaṃś in regard to *bhakti*.

The 18th Century

Uttamdās recounts the details of Harivaṃś' birth, life, marriages, and offspring, along with major dates, in his *Hitacaritra* (1760 CE). Bhagavat Mudita's *Rasikānanyamālā* recounts the lives of many of Harivaṃś' disciples.

There are additional references to Hit Harivaṃś outside the tradition – for example, in the Vallabhite hagiographic anthology known as the *Caurāsi Vaiṣṇavana kī Vartā* and in the Bengali *Bhaktamālā* of Kṛṣṇadās Bābā (c. 1762 CE), which briefly mentions Harivaṃś and that he was a disciple of Gopāla Bhaṭṭa of the Caitanya Sampradāya. Some additional biographical details appear in C.S.J. White (1977, 26–28), as orally reported to him by Baba Jiwan Goswami in February 1969, in Vrindavan. This account emphasizes the fact that among all the other Vaiṣṇava *ācāryas* who came to Vrindavan, including Vallabha, Nimbārka, and the Caitanya *gosvāmī*s, Hit Harivaṃś was the only one born in the Mathura district, or the Braj area.

The narrative of the life of Hit Harivaṃś that is most widely accepted within the tradition is that of the 18th-century follower Uttamdās in his work *Hitacaritra*, reproduced here in full as translated and presented in R. Snell:

> Harivaṃśa's home was in the town of Devana (Deoband, Saharanpur District, U.P), in a family of Gauḍa brahmins – Yajurvedīs of the *mādhyaṃdinī* branch, members of the Kaśyapa *gotra*. His father, Vyāsa Miśra, was a wealthy and renowned astrologer whose fame had reached the king. Vyāsa Miśra was summoned to court, where he was given great wealth and received the king's favor in full measure. After some time at court, he returned home laden with wealth, yet unhappy because of his childlessness. Soon, Kṛṣṇa appeared to Vyāsa's ascetic brother Nṛsiṃhāśrama in a dream and announced his intention of becoming incarnate as the joint form of Hari and *vaṃśa* (= *vaṃsī*, flute). Vyāsa's wife Tārā Rānī was soon with child; Vyāsa was overjoyed, and resumed his position at court. On Monday, the 11th day of the bright half of the month of Vaiśākha, in the year v.s. 1559 (A.D. 1502), in the village of Bāda near Gokula, Harivaṃśa became manifest as the crown-jewel or *rasika*s; he was to be a refuter of *karma* and *jñāna* and a proponent of the way of *prema bhakti*. The joy of his birth was like the joy of Kṛṣṇa's birth described by śuka [in *Bhāgavatapurāṇa*]. At an early age Harivaṃśa thrilled to hear the name of Rādhā; his childhood acts were beyond description. At the age of seven his *yajñopavīta* ceremony was performed, and later he became married to a girl named Rukminī. He began to teach *bhakti* in such a way that each person's devotion to a particular form of the deity increased. Rādhā appeared to Harivaṃśa in a dream and told him that the *yugalamantra* was written on the topmost leaf of a peepul tree near his door, and that he was to make it known in the

world. Rādhā further ordered him to look in the well in his father's garden, where he would find a two-armed image (of Kṛṣṇa) in the flute-holding pose. Harivaṃśa followed these commands, and established the image in a temple in Devana which he then served for some time. On the death of his father Vyāsa Miśra, Harivaṃśa was summoned to court in his father's place; but he refused the summons, rejecting the worldly status which the royal post entailed. He fathered three sons and a daughter, all of whom married; they were all initiated by him as his disciples. On receiving a further command from Rādhā, Harivaṃśa left home and set out for Vrindaban, leaving his family behind. Again Rādhā appeared to him in a dream and told him that in the village of Caḍathāvali (understood as Charthawal, near Muzaffarnagar, U.P.) he would encounter a wealthy brahmin who would offer Harivaṃśa his two daughters in marriage; Harivaṃśa was to accept them, counting them as colleagues in the devotional life. He was also to take from the brahmin a second image of Kṛṣṇa, which he was to take to Vrindaban and worship there. Accordingly, Harivaṃśa went on with his two new brides Kṛṣṇadāsī and Manoharī to Vrindaban, where he was delighted by the transcendental beauty of the natural surroundings. He went to a high spot by the bank of the Yamunā, where there was a throng of Braj people who were thrilled to realize that he had come to live there. They put a bow and arrow in his hands, and offered him as much land as he could cover in a bow-shot; he fired the arrow, which flew 'from the old building'... as far as Cīraghāṭa. He built a beautiful temple and consecrated the image of Rādhāvallabha there on the 13th day of the bright half of the month of Kārttika, v.s. 1592 (A.D. 1535). He established the service of the deity with seven food-offerings (*bhoga*) through the eight periods of the day (*yāma*), according to the season. He rejected all orthodox precepts and prohibitions in favour of pure devotion, and renounced fast-days because they denied him the consumption of *prasāda*. He ignored the ten rites of passage (*saṃskāra*) and defeated ceremonialists, Śaivas, Śāktas and the followers of other doctrines; many people came for his *darśana*, and so populated Vrindāban. (Snell, 1991, 19–21)

Some areas of dispute, however, have arisen with regard to this account. The birth date and year in Uttamdās is refuted by some later writers like G.P. Sharma and given as 1473 CE instead of 1502 CE. While V. Snatak supports the findings of Uttamdās, as did orientalist G. Grierson, R. Snell suggests that the positing of the earlier date by G.P. Sharma was intended to gain sectarian advantage by having Hit Harivaṃś precede the birth of Vallabha (1479 CE) and Caitanya (1486 CE). A core problem is that, according to R. Snell (1991, 31), "None of Harivaṃśa's own works, and few other texts regarded as contemporary to his floruit, are dated." Yet all sources agree on the birthplace of Harivaṃś in Bad, with the original family home in Deoband.

A.W. Entwistle connects Hit Harivaṃś with other geographic locations in his account:

> Legend has it that he [Hit Harivaṃś] first settled on a patch of high ground beside the Yamuna. Some local people offered him as much land as he could cover with an arrow. He managed to shoot it as far as Chir Ghat, where he founded a *rās maṇḍal*. The patch of high ground is said to be the place where the temple of Radhavallabh now stands; between the two is the garden called Seva Kunj, where he first installed Radhavallabh for worship in 1534. He is believed to have spent the rest of his life in Vrindaban and to have frequented the pond called Man Sarovar on the opposite bank of the Yamuna. The only other places outside Vrindaban where he is commemorated are a *baiṭhak* [seat] beside the Radhavallabh temple on the bank of Radhakund and Vyas Bhavan, an ashram run by ascetic followers at Bad, his place of birth. (Entwistle, 1987, 155)

An issue of continuing debate is the original sectarian affiliation or inspiration behind Hit Harivaṃś. While various writers have posited → Madhva, Vallabha, Nimbārka, and Caitanya affiliations, R. Snell (1991, 35–37) dispelled these claims as fallacious and reinforced the traditional view that Harivaṃś developed his own unique form of *bhakti*. The strongest claim has been that of Caitanya Vaiṣṇavas, who insisted that Harivaṃś was a disciple of their own Gopāla Bhaṭṭa Gosvāmī. This is shown, however, to be a notion that appears only in later Bengali sources like *Bhaktamālā* of Kṛṣṇadās Bābā (c. 1762 CE) and *Premavilāsa* of Nityānanda.

Another pressing controversy involves the authorship of the Sanskrit text known as the *Śrīrādhāsudhānidhi* attributed to Harivaṃś. The Caitanya tradition asserts that this text is the product of their own Prabodhānanda Sarasvati, who wrote several Sanskrit works in a similar style. However, R. Snell (1991, 43–46) demonstrated that this issue, while not absolutely resolved as yet, leans more solidly with Rādhāvallabhites, as several manuscripts held at the Vrindavan Research Institute reveal erasures and replacement of phrases by members of the Caitanya tradition. In addition, the 16 commentaries on this text within the Rādhāvallabha tradition contrast with the lack of the same among Caitanyaites. However, further research at the relevant archives needs to be undertaken in order to finally settle this question. J.K. Brzezinski (1998) has presented the case from the Caitanya perspective.

Literary Works

Hit Harivaṃś' principal work in Brajbhasha is the *Caurāsipad*, 84 verses covering the topics of *nikuñjavihāra* (the intimate love pastimes of Rādhā and Kṛṣṇa taking place in eternal time), the *rāsalīlā* or round dance, Rādhā's *māna* or pride, and descriptions of the spring and autumn scenery of Vrindavan. Besides the *Caurāsipad*, there is a Sanskrit work glorifying Rādhā, *Śrīrādhāsudhānidhi* (The Treasury of Rādhā's Nectar), a short text in Brajbhasha called *Sphuṭvāṇī*, and a prayer in Sanskrit to the goddess → Yamunā.

In his translation of the poems of the *Caurāsipad*, C.S.J. White (1977) provided an introductory section on the religious beliefs and ritual traditions of the Rādhāvallabha Sampradāya, drawing mostly on the earlier Hindi scholarship of V. Snatak. C.S.J. White (1996) had also translated the *Sphuṭvāṇī* as well as two letters to a disciple named Śrī Viṭṭhaldās, called *Śrī Mukh Pātrī*. In R. Snell's critical edition (1991) of the *Caurāsipad*, there is the original Braj script and English translation accompanied by many useful details regarding the various manuscripts and conventions associated with spelling, grammar, and vocabulary.

Due to the erotic nature of Harivaṃś' poems, Indian natives are reluctant to have them translated and discussed by outsiders, with the attendant risk of misconception as mere sexual imagery associated with human relationships. The published translations of R. Snell (1991) are the most sensitive to these issues. Yet the unique "spiritual aesthetic" of Brajbhasha Vaiṣṇava poetry tends to make it unlikely that its naive beauty can be transferred by endeavoring for similar effects in English. Below is an example of four lines from a poem by Hit Harivaṃś with translation by R. Snell.

nayau neha nava raṃga nayau rasa
navala syāma bṛṣabhāna kisorī
nava pītāmbara, navala cūnarī
naī – naī būndana, bhījata gorī

New is the love, novel the merriment and new the delight
of young Śyāma [Kṛṣṇa] and Vṛṣabhānu's daughter [Rādhā];
new is his yellow garment and new her many-coloured sari,
and with ever new raindrops is the fair one drenched. (*CauPad.* 54; trans. Snell, 1991, 231–232)

The *Śrīrādhāsudhānidhi* is a Sanskrit text of 270 verses that describe Rādhā's supreme status within the Hindu tradition. Consulting the translation of L.C. Goswami (1991, 1, 50, 62, 109), we find that devotion to Rādhā is eulogized as "the secret of the Upanishads" (*ŚrīRā.* 204), "the quintessence of all human attainments (*artha* [wealth], *dharma* [religiosity], *kāma* [sense pleasure] and *moksha* [liberation])" (*ŚrīRā.* 2), and that which surpasses all other religious acts, including communion with Kṛṣṇa:

> If anyhow we get the sole privilege to serve Śrī Rādhā... What have we to do then with religions [*dharma*], multitude of Gods, Brahma, Shiva and even the efforts to meet Shri Shyam Sundar (Kṛṣṇa)? (*ŚrīRā.* 115)

Kṛṣṇa even chants the name of Rādhā – which contains wisdom that is beyond the → Vedas – as his favorite → *mantra*:

> May the Supreme Knowledge – Beyond the scope of the Vedas – in the form of two letters – Rā and Dhā, dawn upon my mind! This name – Rādhā is incessantly muttered by Hari (Śrī Kṛṣṇa) with tearful eyes, and He is extremely charmed by the rapture of love. (*ŚrīRā.* 15)

There are precedents for the subordination of Kṛṣṇa to Rādhā in the *Gītagovinda* (12th cent. CE) by → Jayadeva, where Kṛṣṇa is portrayed as subordinate to Rādhā in a particular verse (10.9) in which he submits to Rādhā by having her place her feet on his head. Hit Harivaṃś, however, extended this notion by elevating Rādhā to the level of supreme being.

Theology

Hit Harivaṃś was widely recognized for his distinctive role of placing Rādhā in the supreme position. The name "Rādhāvallabha" refers to Kṛṣṇa as "the dearest of Rādhā." Contrary to most Vaiṣṇava traditions that venerated Kṛṣṇa as supreme, Hit Harivaṃś placed Rādhā as the principal figure in the theological hierarchy, with Kṛṣṇa always at her side as the most intimate servant or husband of God, in this case Rādhā. As discerned by C.S.J. White (1977, 35), "Hari Vaṃś is closely allied to the Vaiṣṇava schools that have Kṛṣṇa as the chief deity – the difference being that Hari Vaṃś extols Rādhā above Kṛṣṇa." R. Snell (1991, 329) has shown in his research that, while there are verses describing Kṛṣṇa alone, "the protracted thematic sequence *Caurāsi-Pad* 37–42 introduces themes in which Kṛṣṇa is dependent on Rādhā and suffering in her absence."

While there is little to resemble a theological treatise or a formal declaration in these matters, the religious perspective of Hit Harivaṃś is articulated in various places in his works. On the basis of these references, C.S.J. White has provided a concise summary:

> Rādhā is the very ground of being. She is eternal power and the giver of bliss in the universe. Being absolute she is without form and qualities, and yet her devotees are her companions (*sakhi* or *sahacari*) who adore her while she is amorously sporting with Kṛṣṇa. It is through Rādhā's physical manifestations and the grasp of her psychological character that a devotee at length finds the route to her eternal aspect. The love-play and the granting of all wishes and desires for the devotees are merely aids to that discovery. Rādhā is without equal in the universe for beauty, and her power constantly defeats the god of love, Kāmadeva [compare Cupid]...Simply put, she is the goddess of love to Kṛṣṇa. (White, 1977, 28–29)

While most Braj Vaiṣṇava groups venerate Rādhā in some fashion, it was due to the influence of Hit Harivaṃś and his strong emphasis on Rādhā that several other Vaiṣṇava *sampradāya*s that had originally revered mainly Kṛṣṇa, or the divine couple Rādhā and Kṛṣṇa, elevated Rādhā in their theology (see Rosenstein, 1998).

As a result of its own unique theological perspective, the Rādhāvallabha Sampradāya was distanced from orthodox Vaiṣṇava schools as established by → Rāmānuja, Madhva, Nimbārka, and Viṣnusvāmī:

> The Rādhāvallabha Sampradāya does not claim affiliation to the "classical" Vaiṣṇava *Catuh-Sampradāya* [four *sampradāyas*], nor does it specifically profess any one of the major philosophical positions of classical Hinduism. Its claim to autonomy as a sampradāya in its own right rests on its following a particular mode or style of *bhakti*, and in the maintaining of distinct lines of authority descending from Hita Harivaṃśa himself. (Snell, 1991, 3)

Since the Rādhāvallabha scriptural canon was devoted to creating a new theological understanding of Rādhā and Kṛṣṇa, the tradition did not build on → Vedānta, → Mīmāṃsā, or → Yoga philosophies, as did other Vaiṣṇava sects. Moreover, the Rādhāvallabha Sampradāya avoided the practice of traditional Hindu *dharma* and Vaiṣṇava rituals: "The use of Vedic ritual and the observance of certain generally accepted Vaiṣṇava practices, such as the Ekādaśi Vrata, are spurned as irrelevancies" (Snell, 1991, 5). The Rādhāvallabha tradition lauds the householder stage of life as ideal and does not endorse renunciation of world and family, as do other Vaiṣṇava groups.

In Hit Harivaṃś' perspective, Rādhā and Kṛṣṇa are eternally married and constantly engage in love play. Absorption in these conjugal activities by the Rādhāvallabha devotee is sustained through a kind of spiritual voyeurism through the eyes of a spectator *sakhī* or handmaiden to the couple. And while the descriptions of Rādhā and Kṛṣṇa's love play may appear erotic to the outsider, the insider's approach is nonliteral and intended to attain the realization of intense spiritual love. This experience of *śṛṅgārarasa* (conjugal love; see → *rasa*) in the form of Rādhā and Kṛṣṇa's eternal pastime was believed to transcend all other known experiences of *bhakti*. Salvation for the devotees consists of permanent mystical participation in that divine love, attained not through solitary renunciation or private devotions but by joining in the temple *sevā*, or worship services, and participating in the musical sessions of *samāj gāyan*, which are believed to reenact the divine pastimes in a kind of "sonic liturgy," as if they were happening at that particular moment.

Sevā

The liturgical system of temple service or schedule of worship is called *sevā*. The Rādhāvallabha *sevā* comprises daily worship routines as well as seasonal festivals distributed over an annual liturgical calendar. As originally directed by Hit Harivaṃś, the Rādhāvallabha temple priests maintain a strict regimen of daily worship, which rotates around the waking, bathing, feeding, dressing, and retiring the deity – a statue of Kṛṣṇa playing the flute. Rādhā is represented only symbolically, by a small tablet with her name inscribed, indicating her inconceivable status. There are seven daily services during eight periods of the day (*aṣṭayama*) in the Rādhāvallabha temple (for the services, see → Rādhāvallabha Sampradāya). According to the record, "He [Hit Harivaṃś] established the service of the deity with seven food offerings (*bhog*) through the eight periods of the day (*yama*), according to the season" (White, 1977, 31). The festivals are structured around a solar and lunar calendar, with some dates varying from year to year due to lunar calculations. All of these occasions entail the singing of songs known as *samāj gāyan* that are linked to the temple *sevā* in accordance with specific pastimes of Rādhā and Kṛṣṇa.

The Rādhāvallabha liturgical hymnal is the *Śrī Rādhāvallabhajī kā Varṣotsava* (1978–1980) in three volumes, originally published in four volumes as *Śriṅgārarasasāgara* (1956–1962). A second edition of two volumes of the later version was published in 1994 (vol. II) and 1996 (vol. III). Besides numerous poems of saints in the Rādhāvallabha and other traditions, most of the *Caurāsipad* (84 songs) of Hit Harivaṃś is contained in this collection, the largest anthology of Brajbhasha devotional poems. Most of the songs in the three volumes of the hymnal are organized according to the seasons and holidays that are celebrated in the main temple. The liturgical year begins at the start of volume I with songs of the season of *vasant* (spring), followed by *holī*. Then volume II covers the rainy season and *jhūlan* (swing ceremony) in the summer, with volume III and the autumn *rāsalīlā* and *kārttika* (Oct–Nov) songs, as well as evening lullabies.

As evident through analysis, the Brajbhasha poems of Harivaṃś were written as songs and composed for the purpose of offering them in liturgical worship. Moreover, the songs are believed to have been divinely inspired and function as vehicles for religious experiences. In the edition of the *Caurāsipad* published by the Rādhāvallabha Sampradāya headquarters in Vrindavan, there are various *rāgas* or classical melodic patterns mentioned alongside the songs, according to the number of occurrences: *sāraṅg* (16), *gaurī* (9), *kānharau* (9), *vilāval* (7), *dev gandhār* (7), *dhanāsri* (7), *kalyāṇ* (6), *vibhās* (6), *malār* (5), *kedār* (4), *toḍī* (4), *āsāvarī* (2), and *basant* (2). The present performance tradition is mostly faithful to these indications, yet there are qualifying circumstances that led to many of the *rāgas* being modified with a different character from their classical counterparts. Nonetheless, numerous kinds of devotional music in northern India can be stylistically traced back to the poets and musicians of the Braj area, including Hit Harivaṃś, the *aṣṭachāp* poets, and Svāmī Haridās.

The first Western attempt to analyze Hit Harivaṃś' poems in musical performance is an article by R. Snell (1983, which reappears in R. Snell 1991). Including some transcriptions, he discusses the metrical structure of eight poems of the *Caurāsipad* and how these structures were manifest in performance in terms of their rhythms. Regarding comparative scholarship of Braj musical traditions, the work of S. Thielemann is indicative of empathetic understanding and sincere engagement. In her two-volume *Musical Traditions of Vaiṣṇava Temples in Vraja: A Comparative Study of Samāja and the Dhrupad Tradition of North Indian Classical Music* (2001), many songs from five major Vaiṣṇava *sampradāyas* of Braj are presented and analyzed utilizing both Indian and Western musical notations: Caitanya Sampradāya, Rādhāvallabha Sampradāya, Nimbārka Sampradāya, Haridāsī Sampradāya, and Vallabha Sampradāya. The section on Rādhāvallabha temple music (vol. I, 143–215) includes analyses of six songs in performance: three from the *Caurāsipad* and one from the *Sphuṭvāṇī* by Hit Harivaṃś, one by Ramarāya Prabhu, and one by their most prolific poet, Cācā Vṛindābandās. The intention of S. Thielemann is to compare different renderings of the same poem in order to demonstrate that various interpretations exist. The first monograph devoted solely to the liturgical music of the Rādhāvallabha Sampradāya is *Vaiṣṇava Temple Music in Vrindaban: The Rādhāvallabha Sampradāya Songbook* (2011), compiled and edited by G.L. Beck, which contains the Braj text, Roman transliteration, and English translation of 108 songs with accompanying notes and recorded samples on 18 compact discs.

The main temple of Rādhāvallabha established by Hit Harivaṃś houses the longest-continuing tradition of *samāj gāyan*, with performances twice daily. Throughout the liturgical year, a select group of trained musicians and *bhakta*s perform the devotional poems of Hit Harivaṃś. Several other temples and shrines in Vrindaban support *samāj gāyan* as well. Compared with more visible and popular temples in the area, however, the Rādhāvallabha worship and music are conducted largely in secluded enclaves, relished only by accomplished devotees who understand and appreciate the aesthetic feelings and devotional nuances of the literature and music. Yet on special festivals like *holī* in the spring, the main temple is overcrowded, and giant syringes of colored water are squirted on pilgrims by priests from the altar. On the November feast of *annakūṭ*, the entire altar area is covered with sumptuous food offerings.

Hit Harivaṃś is gradually being recognized within India as one of the outstanding Hindi (Brajbhasha) poets of the medieval period. His style is chaste and sophisticated yet pervaded by an elevated devotional quality that draws on classical Sanskrit vocabulary and earlier Apabhramsha verse. Lesser known is the traditional style of rendering his poems musically (*samāj gāyan*), which, if more widely disseminated and appreciated, would be claimed as one of the priceless treasures of *bhakti* expression.

Bibliography

Ali, S.K.S., ed., *Śrī Rādhā-Sudhā-Nidhi of Śrī Hit Harivaṃś*, Vrindavan, 1977 (Hind.).

Ali, S.K.S., *Śrī Hita Rādhāvallabhīya Sahityā Ratnāvali*, Bombay, 1950 (Hind.).

Ali, S.K.S., "Vrindāban kī Samāj Sangīt Paramparā," in: S.K.S. Ali, ed., *Hitvāṇī*, Vrindavan, n.d., 29–32, 137–144 (Hind.).

Beck, G.L., *Sonic Liturgy: Ritual and Music in Hindu Tradition*, Columbia, 2012.

Beck, G.L., *Vaiṣṇava Temple Music in Vrindāban: The Rādhāvallabha Sampradāya Songbook*, Kirksville, 2011.

Beck, G.L., ed., *Alternative Krishnas: Regional and Vernacular Variations on a Hindu Deity*, Albany, 2005a.

Beck, G.L., "Krishna as Loving Husband of God: The Alternative Krishnology of the Rādhāvallabha Sampradāya," in: G.L. Beck, ed., *Alternative Krishnas: Regional and Vernacular Variations on a Hindu Deity*, Albany, 2005b, 65–90.

Beck, G.L., "Samāj-Gāyan for Rādhā and Krishna: Devotional Music in the Rādhāvallabha Sampradāya," *JVS* 7/1, 1998, 85–100.

Brzezinski, J.K., "Prabodhānanda, Hit Harivaṃśa and the Rādhā-rasa-sudhā-nidhi," *JVS* 7/1, 1998, 19–61.

Entwistle, A.W., *Braj: Centre of Krishna Pilgrimage*, Groningen, 1987.

Growse, F.S., *Mathurā: A District Memoir*, Allahabad, 2 1883.

Goswami (Gosvāmī), L.C., trans., *Śrī-Rādhā-Sudhā-Nidhi-Stotram*, Bombay, 1991 (Hind.).

Goswami (Gosvāmī), L.C., ed., *Śrī Rādhāvallabhajī kā Varṣotsava*, vols. I–III, Vrindavan, 1978–1980 (Hind.).

Goswami (Gosvāmī), L.C., *Śrī Hita Harivaṃś Gosvāmī: Sampradāy aur Sahityā*, Vrindavan, 1957 (Hind.).

Goswami (Gosvāmī), S., *Kṛṣṇa Bhakti Kāvya men Sakhī Bhāv*, Varanasi, 1966 (Hind.).

Goswami (Gosvāmī), S.R., ed., *Vyāsavāṇī: Harirām Vyās*, Mathura, 1973 (Hind.).

Khandelwal, J., *Braj Jīvan aur unkā Kavittā Sahityā*, Vrindavan, 1992 (Hind.).

Mital, P., *Braj ke Dharm Sampradāyon kā Itihās*, Delhi, 1968 (Hind.).

Pauwels, H.R.M., *In Praise of Holy Men: Hagiographic Poems by and about Harirām Vyās*, Groningen, 2002.

Pauwels, H.R.M., *Kṛṣṇa's Round Dance Reconsidered: Harirām Vyās's Hindi Rās-pañcādhyāyī*, Surrey, 1996.

Rosenstein, L., "The Rādhāvallabha Sampradāya and the Haridāsī Sampradāyas: A Comparison," *JVS* 7/1, 1998, 5–18.

Sharma, G.P., *Śrī Hita Caritra*, Calcutta, 1919.

Snatak (Snātak), V., *Rādhāvallabha Sampradāy Siddhānt aur Sahityā*, Delhi, 1957, repr. 1968 (Hind.).

Snell, R., "The Nikuñj as Sacred Space in the Poetry of the Rādhāvallabhī Tradition," *JVS* 7/1, 1998, 63–84.

Snell, R., *The Eighty-four Hymns of Hita Harivaṃśa: An Edition of the Caurāsī Pada*, Delhi, 1991.

Snell, R., "Metrical Forms in Braj Bhāṣā Verse: The Caurāsī Pada in Performance," in: M. Theil-Horstmann, ed., *Bhakti in Current Research 1979–1982*, Berlin, 1983, 353–383.

Theil-Horstmann, M., ed., *Bhakti in Current Research 1979–1982*, Berlin, 1983.

Thielemann, S., *Musical Traditions of Vaiṣṇava Temples in Vraja: A Comparative Study of Samāja and the Dhrupad Tradition of North Indian Classical Music*, New Delhi, 2001.

White, C.S.J., "Śrī Rādhā and the Rādhāvallabha Sampradāy," *JVS* 10/1, 2001, 91–113.

White, C.S.J., *The Caurāsī Pad of Śrī Hit Harivaṃś*, Honolulu, 1977; repr. "'The Love of Rādhā': A Translation of the Caurāsī Pad of Śrī Hit Harivaṃś with Commentary," *JVS* 7/1, 1998, 101–180.

White, C.S.J., "The Remaining Hindi Works of Śrī Hit Harivaṃś," *JVS* 4/4, 1996, 87–104.

Guy L. Beck

Jayadeva

Jayadeva is a uniquely celebrated Sanskrit poet of 12th/13th-century → Bengal and the hallmark of medieval creativity in the language. His song-poem *Gītagovinda* has been so celebrated, especially in the eastern zone of the subcontinent, as to spawn a multitude of claims about his Maithili, Oriya, or Assamese origins. All of the available evidence points, however, to his service at the court of Lakṣmaṇasena of Bengal (1178–1205). He was a member of a vibrant literary salon that included the poets Dhoyī, Govardhana, Śaraṇa, and Umāpatidhara, as well as the Sena kings themselves; thus the poet's genius and originality must be seen not simply as the literary effervescence of one man but rather as that of a socially and historically constituted moment. Yet Jayadeva and his work are by far the most widely known and circulated of Sena-period cultural products. The work is as unique as the poet's status in tradition. In what follows, I first explore the history of this peculiar status as a route to the history and historicity of the work itself.

Jayadeva In and Out of Tradition: Who Is Jayadeva? Who Was Jayadeva?

It should give us a slight pause that two of Sanskrit literature's most famous detractors – unified in their condemnation from across a vast historical and ideological gulf – A.B. Keith and D.D. Kosambi, respectively, both wrote of the *Gītagovinda* with unqualified enthusiasm:

> Jayadeva's work is a masterpiece and it surpasses in its completeness of effect any other Indian poem. It has all the perfection of the miniature word-pictures which are so common in Sanskrit poetry, with the beauty which arises as Aristotle asserts from magnitude and arrangement. (Keith, 1928, 194)

> Jayadeva, an author trained in music as well as the Brahmin's craft... who wandered far to gain real insight into the minds of his people. His life and art were one; he had romantically wooed and wedded a beautiful wife; they continued to travel, he singing verses of his own while she danced. This was not on the same level as the ordinary country jongleur, for in their performance they exemplified the sublime love of Rādhā and Kṛṣṇa, a theme Jayadeva developed in his *Gītagovinda* for Lakṣmaṇasena's court. But in his country songs he used a more popular idiom... A festival is still annually celebrated at Jayadeva's birthplace Kenduli, not in memory of his *Gītagovinda* but because he introduced a new and joyous life with faith in a personal god who is close to rich and poor. (Kosambi, 1957, 54)

Appreciation for the work seems to have been contagious, yet virtually every modern scholar to study the *Gītagovinda* has called it something different in terms of its genre category. A.B. Keith and several other scholars identified it with the Bengali Yātrā (Keith, 1928, 194). V. Raghavan suggested it be identified with a type called the Citrarāgakāvya (1963, 549). A.A. Macdonell said it represented a "transitional stage between pure lyric and pure drama" (1965, 290). H. Tieken most recently identified it as a combination of two forms enumerated in the *Nāṭyaśāstra*, the Lāsya and the Catuṣpadā (2001, 194). I think it is fair to call these results inconclusive, and they testify to its formal exceptionality.

In earlier times, the marvel that was Jayadeva's poem did not go unquestioned; the remarks in the *Rasagaṅgādhara* of the last great classicist of the tradition, Jagannātha Paṇḍitarāja (c. late 17th cent.), offer testimony.

> Jayadeva and others, in the *Gītagovinda* and other works, have broken with this condition [of propriety] accepted by all connoisseurs, just as if they were wild rutting elephants. Thus it is inappropriate for someone of the present, following their example, to compose descriptions in this manner... The explicit depiction, including all its attendant external signs, of the erotic love of gods being consummated, just as if it were that of humans, is improper. (Pandit Durgaprasad & Kashinath Parab, 1888, 52)

Here, it is hard to decide whether Jagannātha Paṇḍitarāja objects more to the poem's form or to its content. On the one hand, the problem seems to be what the poem is about: the erotic love of gods. On the other hand, the critic targets a mode of description: "explicit depiction, including all... attendant external signs" (*sphūṭīkṛta sakalānubhāvavarṇanam*). The poem's impropriety is clearly comprehensive in Jagannātha Paṇḍitarāja's mind, implicating the structure as well as the spirit of the work.

Who is Jayadeva? Who was Jayadeva? Let us answer these questions by first asking another one: who was Jagannātha Paṇḍitarāja? S. Pollock has provided some useful inroads here.

> [T]here are intimations in his poetry of a new interaction between Sanskrit and vernacular-language writing. Some of his poetry... is probably indebted to earlier texts in Old Hindi; one poem in the *Bhāminīvilāsa* is almost certainly derived from a text of Bihārilāl, a celebrated poet of the previous generation. What such parallels above all indicate, unfortunately, is how very little information we have, even for a period as relatively late as the end of the seventeenth century, about the real interactions between cosmopolitan and vernacular courtly poets. Little is known about their familiarity with each others' works; about what it signified (to them or their audiences) to adapt vernacular verse into Sanskrit, or Sanskrit verse into the vernacular. (Pollock, 2001, 17)

Granted that our information is less than we would like it to be, answers to some of these crucial questions are at least suggested by Jagannātha Paṇḍitarāja's reaction to Jayadeva. If Jayadeva, by introducing peculiar meters and other characteristic vernacular features such as rhyme, refrain, and brevity, had rendered the Sanskrit vernacular during the first era of the literary vernacular's ascendance (early 2nd mill. CE), Jagannātha Paṇḍitarāja, by introducing Persian and vernacular themes and conventions into classical Sanskrit forms, did just the reverse: making the vernacular Sanskrit, during a period when the process begun in Jayadeva's time had completed itself, when literary life had come to be dominated by the vernaculars, and Sanskrit was nearing its last days as an organic literary force. The tables were turned by Jagannātha Paṇḍitarāja's time, but the two poets had comparable roles to play in the working out of a single dialectical process of Sanskrit-vernacular negotiation.

What did it mean to adapt the vernacular into Sanskrit or Sanskrit into the vernacular? Clearly, the latter was profoundly unacceptable to Jagannātha Paṇḍitarāja, while there was a discernible role for the former. What this type of process meant for others, slightly less invested in the classical cosmopolitan mode, is, however, a longer story, as a few significant examples will serve to make clear.

The oversight is a telling one in B. Stein's (posthumous) *History of India* (1998, 123): "In the twelfth century, bhakti hymns were composed in Bengali by the saint Jayadev". The confusion as to Jayadeva's language, baffling at first, alludes to a long tradition of seeing him as a vernacular poet-saint. The earliest textual incarnation of this tradition is the early 17th-century Brajbhasha hagiography *Bhaktamālā*, by Nābhādās of Galta, where the author of the *Gītagovinda* is depicted as a saint and mystic, the stuff of legends and miracles, alongside other canonical vernacular poet-saints. (Kosambi's biographical panegyric [1957], quoted above, is indebted to this text.) It is as if Jayadeva had a separate career as a vernacular poet, without actually having written anything in the vernacular. Verses in a short Sanskritic form of New Indo-Aryan are ascribed to a "Jaidev" in the Sikh holy book, the *Gurū Granth Sāhib*, alongside true vernacular poet-saints such as → Sūrdās and → Ravidās (see Singh, 2003). The → *nirguṇa bhakti* (devotion to god without form) verses in the *Gurū Granth Sāhib* have nothing in common with Jayadeva's oeuvre, but nonetheless scholars have tended to mechanically assume the correctness of the attribution (e.g. Keith, 1928; Chatterji, 1973; Kosambi, 1957; and, more recently, Singh, 2003). Through these sorts of appropriations, the notion of Jayadeva as a vernacular saint was crystallized, but the origin of the tradition most probably lies in the land where the poet's career first took off.

The popular understanding of Jayadeva today still bears the weight of the → Gauḍīya Vaiṣṇava movement's appropriation of his work. The most fascinating aspect of this school, which first started to thrive in Bengal during the first half of the 16th century, is its theologization of aesthetics or aestheticization of theology, first formulated by one of the saint → Caitanya's chief disciples, → Rūpa Gosvāmī. In the work of this poet and theologian-philosopher, the language of Sanskrit poetics was brought to bear on the religious experience of devotion to → Kṛṣṇa. An erotic attachment to Kṛṣṇa was even celebrated as the supreme state of religious observance. Literary works depicting the erotized aspect of the deity became scripture, and the Gauḍīya Vaiṣṇavas were the first ones to quote extensively from the *Gītagovinda* in their theoretical writings. One legacy of these mystics' great appreciation for the *Gītagovinda* is that the poem has become indissociable from them in the modern imagination, as witnessed by, for instance, B.C. Chattopadhyaya's reference to a Jayadeva song in his novel *Ānandamaṭh* (The Abbey of Bliss) as "the sweet *stotra* composed by the *gosvāmī*," as well as the widespread manner of casually referring to the poet as "Jayadeva *gosvāmī*" in contemporary articles and editions of the *Gītagovinda* in Bengal (Chattopadhyaya, 1882; Jayadeva is referred to as "Jayadeva *gosvāmī*" both in the introduction to Mukhopadhyay's edition, published in 1957, and in a 1999 article by Chakrabarti).

Sanskrit and vernacular (Bengali) coexisted comfortably in the literary works of the Gauḍīya Vaiṣṇavas. There was extensive poetic production in both languages, but the theoretical writing was all done in Sanskrit. The Gauḍīya Vaiṣṇava movement represents the most forceful attempt ever to situate → *bhakti*, originally and predominantly a vernacular phenomenon, within the terms of Sanskrit theoretical orthodoxy, and Jagannātha objected very strongly in writing to this as well. Jagannātha holds that *bhakti* only merits the status of a *bhāva* (subordinate feeling) and not *rasa*; also emphasizing that one cannot just go on inventing new *rasa*s in disregard of the original nine-fold scheme. He begins by pointing out that *bhakti* is obviously incompatible with the aesthetic emotion of *śāntarasa* ("quietude"), what is otherwise perhaps the most directly spiritual of *rasa* experiences. Jagannātha Paṇḍitarāja's parallel condemnations indicate what is in fact a parallel trajectory in the *Gītagovinda* and Gauḍīya Vaiṣṇavaism. Both had adapted *bhakti*/vernacular elements to unfamiliar Sanskrit genres.

Thus the anachronism of calling Jayadeva a *gosvāmī* parallels the anachronism of calling him a vernacular poet. In fact, we have very little of anything that seems like vernacular poetry from Bengal at the time of the Sena dynasty. Not only did Jayadeva not write in Bengali during the 12th and 13th centuries, but also virtually no one else did that we know of. So why has he been thought of as a vernacular poet? Clearly, it is because he played such a crucial role in the original Sanskrit appropriation of the vernacular that he became inseparable from the vernacular and the popular, even though he was in so many ways a fundamentally classical poet. He could not quite fit into the classical tradition and so was assigned an alternate identity by posterity, straddling the realm of the vernacular and vernacular religiosity.

This was not, however, the only possible outcome. An early commentary on the *Gītagovinda*, Śaṅkaramiśra's *Rasamañjarī*, offers an aggressive interpretation of the oft-quoted third verse, in which Jayadeva praises himself and the other poets of the Sena salon:

> Umāpatidhara makes words blossom and Jayadeva alone knows the perfection of verbal arrangement. Śaraṇa deserves praise for his deftness in abstruse compositions. Govardhana has no rival for his crafting of true subjects of supreme erotic sentiment. Dhoyī, who commits speech to memory on once hearing it, is king of poets. (Telang & Laxman, 1899, 9)

Śaṅkaramiśra assigns the poet an exceptional status of an altogether different sort. He refuses to entertain the comparison between the poet and his contemporaries, which the verse articulates, and reinterprets all the praises for Jayadeva's fellow poets into aspersions. The following passage is amusing:

> A minister of Lakṣmaṇasena named Umāpatidhara "makes speech blossom," that is, he proliferates it. Thus Umāpatidhara's speech is devoid of sweetness, devoid of pleasant features of word and meaning.
>
> A poet named Śaraṇa is "notable," that is, praiseworthy "in the speedy composition of abstruse poetry." And thus the work of the poet Śaraṇa, too, is fraught with the defects of hidden meaning and so forth, and devoid of the pleasant features of clarity and so on.
>
> For his fashioning the best examples of literature "in which the erotic sentiment is supreme"... for his weaving it into poetry, "no one competes with master Govardhana." Here, with the phrase "erotic," the sense is that he is only competent with respect to poetic works in which the erotic sentiment is dominant. When it comes to the depiction of other sentiments, he, too, is verily inadequate... His "mastery" is with reference to the study of random subjects, useless for the composition of good poetry. Thus "master" [*ācārya*] is said sarcastically. And thus the sense is that he is not a good poet and does not have the heart of a good poet.
>
> Dhoyī... is a master of sounds [*śrutidhara*, "memorizing discourse on first hearing it," generally meaning wise, learned, and intelligent],

> which is to say that he understands composition merely as an object of listening. The sense is that he only grasps the utterance in terms of its pronunciation.
>
> "Only Jayadeva knows the refinement of verbal arrangement," the quintessence of composing works endowed with tropes and pleasant verbal features. Thus there is no satisfaction in hearing others' poems as there is in hearing Jayadeva's poem. The sense is that only this one is to be listened to. (Telang & Laxman, 1899, 9–10)

Here, there is nothing of the miraculous, simply a miraculously good poet. Likewise, the peculiar Sanskrit Sufi tale from medieval Bengal, the *Sekaśubhodayā*, recognizes Jayadeva to have been a court poet. It tells, in simple Sanskrit with the occasional Bengali verse interspersed, the story of the arrival in Lakṣmaṇasena's kingdom of a Sufi saint who proceeds to establish his absolute authority through magical acts and general charisma. Jayadeva, Govardhana, Umāpatidhara, and so on are all characters in this narrative, which S. Sen (1963) dated to the second half of the 16th century, but here again, Jayadeva is a court poet, not a saintly ascetic.

A sentimentalized religious view of the poet has nonetheless become current today as witnessed by many recent cultural products. Examples include the *Amar Chitra Katha* comic *Jayadeva* (on *Amar Chitra Katha*, see Chandra, 2008) and more recently the Bengali series *Jayadeb-Padmābatī* (first aired on Nov 13, 2005), which aired on ETV Bangla in India. Jayadeva's virtually unknown political poetry, with its occasional gore and brutality, has been edited out of our image of this author for centuries. Countless verses by Jayadeva from the Sena anthology *Saduktikarṇā mṛta* delight in orgiastic evocations of bloodshed typical of the courtly tradition, as for example in the following stunning poem:

> Clusters of waves of arrows shoot forth and crash into hosts of rutting elephants;
> they tumble down and seem like islands in the ocean of the blood of his enemies.
> Ghoul-ladies lay atop them after sex with their lovers and drink blood-wine from shared goblets,
> using pairs of the nostrils of elephant trunks as straws. (*SadKar.* 1564)

Jayadeva has himself been edited out of the history of courtly Kāvya to some extent.

To find out how Jayadeva may have himself participated in this process, we can begin by asking some questions about form. How do the poem's structure and form condition its peculiar status? How was the *Gītagovinda* classical and unclassical, vernacular and unvernacular? How did it enshrine something of a vernacular *bhakti* style yet also retain a relationship to high classicism?

Form

It takes no more than a glance at the *Gītagovinda* to reveal that it is utterly unlike any work of Sanskrit literature that preceded it, from the most purely formal point of view. Each of the 12 chapters (*sargas*) of the poem contains between one and four songs (adding up to a total of about 24 and constituting the overwhelming bulk of the text), whose metrics and aesthetics are decidedly vernacular in their resonance. Yet, the meters correspond to nothing exactly anywhere else in Sanskrit, Prakrit, or vernacular poetry. (S. Sandahl-Forgue [1977] scanned all the meters, noting that one of them corresponds to the Bengali *payar*. Inquiry into the *Gītagovinda* meters has otherwise pretty much met a dead end.) Several features, however, give the verses a distinctly vernacular character. The meters are for the most part very short, and they feature invariable end rhyme. Unvarying end rhyme has a life in South Asia, just as it does in European languages. Rhyme had some minor appearance from time to time in Sanskrit poetry, but it never formed the ultimate principle for meter and style, while it was central to vernacular poetics from the beginning. In Europe, distribution of the importance of rhyme across the classical-vernacular divide is basically equivalent (Beare, 1957, ch. 25). It seems that rhyme started to gain some minor importance in medieval Latin verse, yet this was still on a scale that dwarfed the Sanskrit tradition (Jayadeva was one of the few authors ever to compose in unvarying end rhyme).

The meters of the *Gītagovinda*'s songs are also not quantitative in the classical way (based on fixed alternations of heavy and light syllables). Rather, they use a stress accent, like vernacular verse in South Asia, as well as Europe, employing the alternative principle of *mātrā* or *mora*, "syllabic instant," in which heavy and light syllables still count but only in terms of their overall quantity. Long and short syllables occur haphazardly, instead of falling into the grandly patterned order of the classical. Again, the meters are not exactly those used in any vernacular language (or anywhere else, for that matter).

It might not be all that unintuitive how the fragrance of the vernacular could be more readily drawn into Sanskrit through an inexact imitation. Writing Sanskrit in a vernacular meter, through too close identification of dissimilar entities, could have paradoxically drawn attention to the inescapable difference of Sanskrit. Bringing in the feel and fragrance of the vernacular through the use of peculiar metrical experimentations could paradoxically allow Sanskrit to invoke the vernacular in a more compelling fashion.

A comparison may help show what is meant by "the feel of the vernacular." I will examine a verse from the last book of Baḍu Caṇḍīdās' early–middle Bengali *Śrīkṛṣṇakīrtana*, alongside a stanza from one of the *Gītagovinda*'s songs. This is a verse in Caṇḍīdās' Bengali:

> *āyiśo la baḍāyi rākhaho parāṇ*
> *sahiteṃ nāroṃmanamathabāṇ.*

> Come Baḍāyi, save my life!
> I cannot endure the arrows of the heart-churning love god. (*ŚrīKīr.* 10.7.1)

This is a verse in Jayadeva's Sanskrit:

> *tyajati na pāṇitalena kapolam*
> *bālaśaśinam iva sāyam alolam.*

> Her hand does not forsake her cheek,
> which looks like the young crescent moon motionless in the evening sky. (*GītaGov.* 4.2.6)

A lilting stress accent is shared by the two verses. Rich alliteration is likewise evident, as is the end rhyme shared by both verses. The *Gītagovinda*'s similarity to the vernacular is immediately evident; so is the fact that it is not exactly the vernacular. E. Gerow painstakingly analyzed the prosody of Jayadeva's meters and demonstrated that they are not as free as vernacular meters. He drew attention to an element of "fixity," that is, a preference for certain sequences of syllables (Gerow, 1989, 552). His conclusion, however, that the *Gītagovinda* does not hence evoke the vernacular is myopic. The fixity that he discovered is rather one of the key elements of the poem's inexactitude in vernacular imitation, a crucial part of what makes the vernacular evocation compelling and haunting.

The songs transcend Sanskrit. They abound in figures of sound (*śabdālaṅkāras*; e.g. alliterations), such that they can be appreciated independently of their comprehension. Many can be easily understood by someone who knows virtually no Sanskrit. There is effectively one set of relationships among the words, one syntactical structure that needs to be grasped, and then the rest becomes clear by analogy, if the vocabulary is more or less familiar. As is the case today, some of the names of Kṛṣṇa/Viṣṇu and some Sanskrit vocabulary would have been well within the grasp of someone who was completely illiterate or unlearned in eastern India/Bengal about eight hundred years ago. S. Kaviraj (2003, 512) has mentioned the possibility of reading some of Jayadeva's verses as Bengali, especially where locative singular endings, repetitively layered in the songs, overlap between the two languages.

Yet the songs' transcendence of Sanskrit is also in a sense negated. The stylistic and metrical departure of the songs is embedded in the classical tradition by the poem's architecture: the songs never stand alone in the poem; they are invariably encircled by Sanskrit verses in a multitude of elaborate classical-quantitative meters. At the end of each song, just before the verse in classical meter, however, a formal feature appears that decidedly demarcates the vernacular territory from the classical one. Each song ends with a *bhaṇita* (signature) verse of a type that any reader of North Indian *bhakti* poetry will find familiar. The convention of the signatory verse clearly has its origin in vernacular genres, the oldest of them presumably from the South, and it was something very new to Sanskrit at this time. It was never destined to hold much importance in the history of Sanskrit poetry, while for the vernacular, especially *bhakti* poetry, it was integral.

While we may be able to locate prototypical *bhaṇita* verses in vernacular works earlier than the *Gītagovinda* – the archaic Bengali Caryāgīti (or Caryāpada) poems include them – certain other features that cannot but strike the modern Bengali or Maithili reader as quintessentially vernacular can only be attested in the wake of the *Gītagovinda*. The word *padāvali*, "arrangement of words," in the poem's second verse, as an adjective for Jayadeva's poetry, has, for example, come to denote a specific vernacular genre of *bhakti* lyric in medieval Maithili, Bengali, Brajbuli, and so on, and Jayadeva's *padāvalī*s are often mentioned side by side with those of the vernacular poets Vidyāpati and Caṇḍīdās. It is to be assumed, then, that the *Gītagovinda* was both constituted by early vernacular poetry, some of which may not have come down to us, and constitutive of its emergent idioms.

Yet the elements of contradiction in Jayadeva's poem also go beyond the horizontal categories of cosmopolitan and vernacular, attaining to something more vertical. As D.D. Kosambi's remarks implied, however ecstatically (quoted above), and as I have also alluded, the poem is in part a genuinely popular work, even if it is also an elite, courtly product. As noted, the songs can be understood and appreciated without knowledge of Sanskrit, and the *Gītagovinda* has historically proven itself popular, spawning adaptations in popular dance and painting for centuries. Central to this elite–popular negotiation is the poem's peculiar religiosity. → Stotras suffused with some kind of *bhakti* had of course already been composed in Sanskrit, but it was something else to taint high Kāvya like Jayadeva did (or Śāstra like the Gauḍīyas did). Sanskrit Kāvya was, in a sense, a very secular phenomenon. In it, mythology and religion were subordinated to fundamentally aestheticopolitical imperatives by the early medieval period, and the effusive religiosity that creeps forth from time to time in the *Gītagovinda* is somewhat out of tune with the grand tradition of courtly literature. This brings us to questions of content. How does the poem contain and at once exceed the ethos of courtly Kāvya?

Content

The theme of Kṛṣṇa as cowherd-libertine had prior to the *Gītagovinda* received scant attention in Sanskrit's highest literary register. Its earliest-known textual elaboration is found in the Sanskrit → Purāṇas, where Kāvya's signature eroticism is not usually evident. The courtly Kāvya mode of love tends to be characterized by an absence–presence dialectic. The two modes of love, *vipralambhaśṛṇgāra* (love in absence or separation) and *sambhogaśṛṇgāra* (love in union or enjoyment), specified by the poeticians, continually haunt each other, with fantasy threatening to overtake reality in a kind of "hallucinatory wishful psychosis," as S. Freud might have put it (1917 [1915], 3042). The love story of Kṛṣṇa and → Rādhā, with its mutual fixation and anguish – incidentally a very obscure if not totally unknown tale prior to the *Gītagovinda* – serves to present the bucolic romping Kṛṣṇa in these psychological and aesthetic terms.

If, on the level of form, the *Gītagovinda* had made cosmopolitan Kāvya vernacular, on the level of content, a rustic theme (with a likely folk origin) was made cosmopolitan and urbane. In this sense, the trajectories of form and content are equal and opposite: on the level of form, courtly Kāvya becomes its other, while on the level of content, Kāvya's other becomes courtly. The inverse departures of form and content balance each other in a sort of cultural double negative. This serves to acknowledge the precise force of each term that the poem manipulates, while also throwing these terms up in the air. I can call this the mutual negotiation of form and content, a process whereby a special – perhaps it would also be correct to say abstract or mystical – perspective is created in terms of which to experience and understand the poem. Partly through this mechanism, the *Gītagovinda* came to acquire a peculiar and exceptional status.

This brings us to questions of context. If the poem's departures of form and content are mutually implicatory and mutually constitutive, and if the poem's religious ethos is likewise implicated in this complex cultural operation, then in what kind of time and space were such gestures meaningful? How does the *Gītagovinda* relate to its courtly context and the works of other Sena poets? How does it relate to Jayadeva's other works?

Context

Many of the martial verses by Jayadeva in the royal anthology *Saduktikarṇāmṛta* would seem to preempt his later image as a world-renouncing mystic (see above). Yet, there are also many poems ascribed to him in the *Saduktikarṇāmṛta* that have tender, amorous themes. Although only a few of them are also found in the *Gītagovinda*, many others are strongly reminiscent of that poem's often delicate eroticism. Many of the verses attributed to the Sena kings in the anthology are erotic as well, and there also seems to be a broader stylistic convergence. For this reason, it would be unsurprising to learn that Jayadeva had been a tutor to the kings, perhaps alongside the other poets. Lakṣmaṇasena and his grandson Keśavasena both echo explicitly in one of their poems part of the final quarter of the first verse of the *Gītagovinda*. The verses were certainly composed as part of a *samasyāpūraṇa* (a game in which contestants are obliged to compose a poem with a pregiven ending).

> *rādhāmā dhavayor jayanti*
> *yamunākū le rahaḥkelayaḥ*. (Jayadeva; *GītaGov.* 1.1)

> *rādhāmādhavayor jayanti*
> *valitasmerā lasā dṛṣṭayaḥ*. (Lakṣmaṇasena; *SadKar.* 272)

> *rādhāmādhavayor jayanti*
> *madhurasmerā lasā dṛṣṭayaḥ*. (Keśavasena; *SadKar.* 270)

The *Gītagovinda* presents other definite indications of its immediate social context. It concludes with the following phrase:

> *bhrūkṣepalakṣmīlavakrīte dāsa ivopasevitapadāmbhoje kutaḥ saṃbhramaḥ*

> Why are you agitated about this man bowing at your lotus-feet like a slave purchased with a mere droplet of your darting eyebrow's majesty? (*GītaGov.* 11.22)

A verse by Govardhana, echoing the phrasing and the sentiment, ends with the following words:

> *kṣīrodacañcaladṛgañcalapātamātraiḥ krī te jane ka iva saṃbhramasaṃnirodhaḥ*

> When the mere pulsing of your eyes' edges, trembling like the sea of milk, has purchased this man as your slave, why do you check your excitement? (*SadKar.* 513)

It is evident that the writers of this court were in conversation, hearing or reading one another's works and composing in a manner that registered this. The immediate horizon for the poets' productions was the Sena salon; their intertextuality and mutual resonance present them as a cohesive group, a first horizon of transmission.

There were other kinds of circulations, equally material but more mysterious. The 13th-century Sena anthology *Saduktikarṇāmṛta* is especially rich in the attention it gives to local Bengal poets and includes the works of the Sena kings themselves, alongside their highly original professional court poets Jayadeva, Govardhana, Dhoyī, and so on. The only other place (besides Rūpa Gosvāmī's 16th-cent. *Padyāvalī*) where we find verses of the Sena kings, along with a few verses ascribed to Jayadeva and Govardhana (which are found neither in their respective works nor in the *Saduktikarṇāmṛta*), is the anthology from the Cahamana court of Hammīra (c. early 14th-cent. Rajasthan), the *Śārṅgadharapaddhati*. Why or how this happened I am not sure, but it may demonstrate some early direct contact with the Sena court. This contact is hardly unlikely: if the early medieval polity was newly local, this period likewise witnessed the networking of localities, what amounted to a qualitatively new species of *trans*-locality. Later Rajput kings would also become among the most accomplished commentators on Jayadeva's *Gītagovinda*: Rājā Mānāṅka and Rāṇa Kumbha.

Bibliography

Allen, W.H., & W. Beare, *Latin Verse and European Song*, London, 1957.

Callewaert, W.M., ed., *Śrī Gurū Granth Sāhib*, Delhi, 1996.

Chandra, N., *The Classic Popular: Amar Chitra Katha 1967–2007*, Delhi, 2008.

Chatterji, S.K., *Jayadeva*, Delhi, 1973.

Chatterji, S.K., *The Origin and Development of the Bengali Language*, Calcutta, 1926.

Chattopadhyaya, B., *The Making of Early Medieval India*, Delhi, 1994.

Chattopadhyaya, B.C., *Ānandamaṭh*, Kolkata, 2003.

Chowdury, A.M., *Dynastic History of Bengal, c. 750–1200 A.D.*, Dacca, 1967.

De, S.K., *Bengal's Contribution to Sanskrit Literature and Studies in Bengal Vaiṣṇavism*, Calcutta, 1960.

De, S.K., *Early History of Vaiṣṇava Faith and Movement in Bengal*, Calcutta, 1942.

Freud, S., "Mourning and Melancholia," in: J. Strachey, trans., *The Standard Edition of the Complete Psychological Works of Sigmund Freud*, vol. XIV, London, 1917 (1915), 3040–3052.

Gerow, E., "Jayadeva's Poetics and the Classical Style," *JAOS* 109/4, 1989, 533–544.

Kaviraj, S., "The Two Histories of Literary Culture in Bengal," in: S. Pollock, ed., *Literary Cultures in History: Reconstructions from South Asia*, Berkeley, 2003, 503–566.

Keith, A.B., *A History of Sanskrit Literature*, London, 1928, repr. 1961, 1993.

Knutson, J., "History beyond the Reality Principle: Literary and Political Territories in Sena Period Bengal," *CSSAAME*, forthcoming.

Knutson, J., "The Vernacular Cosmopolitan: Jayadeva's *Gītagovinda*," in: Y. Bronner, W. Cox & L. McCrea, eds., *South Asian Texts in History: Critical Engagements with Sheldon Pollock*, Ann Arbor, 2011, 125–149.

Knutson, J., "The Political Poetic of the Sena Court," *JAS* 69/2, 2010, 371–401.

Kosambi, D.D., "An Introduction to the *Subhāṣitaratnakoṣa* (1957)," in: B. Chattopadhyaya, ed., *Combined Methods in Indology and Other Writings*, Delhi, 2002, 721–752.

MacDonell, A.A., *A History of Sanskrit Literature*, Delhi, 1965.
Moretti, F., *Signs Taken for Wonders: Essays in the Sociology of Literary Forms*, London, 1983.
Pai, A., & A.C. Katha, *Jayadev*, Bombay, 1980.
Pandit Durgaprasad & Kashinath Parab, eds., *The Rasagaṅgādhara of Jagannātha Paṇḍit: With the Commentary of Nāgeśa Bhaṭṭa*, Bombay, 1888.
Pollock, S., *The Language of the Gods in the World of Men: Sanskrit, Culture, and Power in Premodern India*, New Delhi, 2007.
Pollock, S., ed., *Literary Cultures in History: Reconstructions from South Asia*, Berkeley, 2003.
Pollock, S., "The Death of Sanskrit," *CSSH* 43/2, 2001, 392–426.
Pollock, S., "Cosmopolitan and Vernacular in History," *Public Culture* 12/3, 2000, 591–625.
Pollock, S., "India in the Vernacular Millennium: Literary Culture and Polity, 1000–1500," *Daedalus* 127, 1998a, 41–74.
Pollock, S., "The Cosmopolitan Vernacular," *JAS* 57/1, 1998b, 6–37.
Pollock, S., "The Sanskrit Cosmopolis, 300–1300: Transculturation, Vernacularization, and the Question of Ideology," in: J.E.M. Houben, ed., *The Ideology and Status of Sanskrit: Contributions to the History of the Sanskrit Language*, Leiden, 1996, 197–249.
Raghavan, V., *Bhoja's Śṛṅgāra Prakāsā*, Madras, 1963; repr. *Bhoja's Śṛṅgāra Prakāsā*, Oxford, 1998.
Sandahl-Forgue, S., *Le Gītagovinda de Jayadeva: Tradition et Innovation dans le Kāvya*, Stockholm, 1977.
Singh, P., *The Bhagats of the Guru Granth Sahib: Sikh Self-definition and the Bhagat Bani*, Delhi, 2003.
Telang, M.R., & V.D. Laxman, eds., *Gītagovindakāvyam: With the Raskapriyā of Kumbhakarṇa and the Rasamañjarī of Śaṅkaramiśra*, Bombay, 1899.
Tieken, H., *Kāvya in South India: Old Tamil Caṅkam Poetry*, Groningen, 2001.
Trump, E., trans., *Ādi Granth*, London, 1877.

Jesse Knutson

Jīva Gosvāmī

The Caitanya Vaiṣṇava tradition, also known as → Gauḍīya Vaiṣṇavism due to its Bengali origins, was founded in the early 16th century by Śrī Kṛṣṇa → Caitanya (1486–1534). Caitanya brought a wave of → Kṛṣṇa devotion to eastern India, particularly the regions of → Bengal and → Orissa. Although he left little by way of written work, the movement he inspired produced a wide array of poetical, philosophical, and ritual literature dedicated to Kṛṣṇa. Much of the school's early literature was composed by the six *gosvāmī*s (ascetic adepts) of Vrindavan, namely, Rūpa (→ Rūpa Gosvāmī), Sanātana, Raghunāthadāsa, Raghunāthabhaṭṭa, Gopalabhaṭṭa, and Jīva. Rūpa and Sanātana were given a mandate by Caitanya to systematize and expound his teaching, and the others were sent at different times to join them. They wrote exclusively in Sanskrit, despite the increasing use of vernacular languages for writing during their time.

Of the six *gosvāmī*s of Vrindavan, the youngest and most prolific was Jīva Gosvāmī (c. 1517–1608), the nephew of Rūpa and Sanātana. To the community of Vaiṣṇavas who consider themselves followers of Caitanya, Jīva Gosvāmī has epitomized – from his own time to the present day – the highest ideal of devotional erudition used in the service of Kṛṣṇa. Indeed, teachers and scholars of Caitanya Vaiṣṇavism have used superlatives freely in describing his accomplishments. S.K. De calls Jīva Gosvamī "the highest court of appeal in doctrinal matters so long as he lived" (De, 1986, 150); M.T. Kennedy, "probably the greatest theologian of the Brindaban group" (Kennedy, 1925, 137); S.M. Elkman, "an unusually versatile and prolific writer" (Elkman, 1986, 23); A.C. → Bhaktivedanta Prabhupada, "the greatest scholar of Śrīmad Bhāgavatam" (Prabhupāda, 1987, 2.9.32); and J. Chakravarti, "one of the greatest of philosophers that India ever produced" (Chakravarti, 1975, 59).

Fig. 1: Painting of Jīva Gosvāmī.

Life

Other than Kṛṣṇadāsa Kavirāja, the author of *Caitanyacaritāmṛta*, none of Caitanya's biographers mentions Jīva, for he had no direct role to play in Caitanya's life. Nevertheless, information can be gleaned from later Bengali works and inferred from what we know of Jīva's uncles, Rūpa and Sanātana, who were close associates of Caitanya.

Jīva's father, Vallabha Mallik, was the youngest of the three brothers and, like Rūpa and Sanātana, was employed in the service of the Bengal government. Vallabha, along with his brothers Rūpa and Sanātana, met Caitanya in Ramakeli, West Bengal, and there Vallabha received from Caitanya the name Anupama. He was present in Prayag in the year 1516, when Caitanya instructed Rūpa in the theology of *bhakti*. Upon returning to Bengal, however, Anupama passed away unexpectedly. The latest possible year for Jīva's birth, therefore, is 1517.

According to the *Bhaktiratnākara* of Narahari Cakravartī, as a boy Jīva was intellectually precocious and exceptionally devoted to the worship of Kṛṣṇa. After completing his primary studies, Jīva traveled to Navadvīpa (today Nabadwip), where he met Nityānanda, who encouraged him to join his uncles in Vrindavan and lead a life of renunciation. The *Caitanyacaritāmṛta* describes their meeting as follows:

> Jīva Gosvāmin went from Gauḍa [Bengal] to Mathurā, having begged leave from Nityānanda Prabhu. Prabhu in love held his feet on his head, and embraced him because of his relationship with Rūpa and Sanātana. He gave his command, "Go quickly to Vṛndāvana; Prabhu [Caitanya] has given that place to your family." So receiving this order he came, and reaped the fruits of the command. Writing many *śāstra*s, he preached *bhakti* for a long time. (Dimock, 1999, 3.4.223–226)

Before settling in Vrindavan, Jīva spent some time in Kāśī (Benares), where he continued his studies in Sanskrit grammar and philosophy. The exact duration or content of his studies are not known, although Jīva's writings display fluency in the texts and doctrines of the six *darśana*s (orthodox schools of Indian philosophy) as well as the various schools of Vedānta. The *Bhaktiratnākara* mentions Madhusūdana Vācaspati as his teacher, although there is difference of opinion on Vācaspati's identity. S.K. De claims that he was none other than the famous Advaitin Madhusūdana Sarasvati (De, 1986, 111), while N.C. Jana argues more convincingly that Sarasvati would have been too young then to become Jīva's teacher (Jana, 1970, 151). In any case, Jīva was present in Vrindavan by 1541, the year *Bhaktirasāmṛtasindhu* was completed, since he helped Rūpa edit the book. He was loved by the other *gosvāmī*s as a trusted student and colleague, and at least three of them (Sanātana, Rūpa, and Raghunāthadāsa) left their assets to him. Jīva passed away in Vrindavan after 1608, the year in which he reconfirmed his will.

While Jīva Gosvāmī's reputation derives largely from his versatile and vigorous pen, his importance for the early Caitanya movement was not limited to his literary output. Almost from the time he arrived in Vrindavan to assist his uncles, Jīva was involved in securing the future of the fledgling movement, in terms of both its physical and theological assets. His name is recorded in several legal documents relating to land for the *gosvāmī*s' temples. The most significant of these is an edict dated 1568, wherein the Mughal emperor Akbar gives official recognition to the custodians of the Madanamohana Temple and the Govindadeva Temple at the behest of the Rajput king, Toḍarmal, who in turn made his request on behalf of Jīva Gosvāmī (Brzezinski, 2007, 56). It seems that Rūpa Gosvāmī had already passed away by this time, leaving legal responsibility for the temples in the hands of Jīva.

Jīva also worked to maintain the theological unity and vitality of Caitanya's movement. R. Chakrabarty notes that differences of opinion arose within the Bengali Vaiṣṇava community after Caitanya's departure due to the lack of any "comprehensive theological and ritualistic structure" (Chakrabarty, 1985, 207). Jīva worked to provide this structure, not only by writing theological treatises such as the *Bhāgavatasandarbha*, but also by training the next generation of Caitanya Vaiṣṇavas, most notably Śrīnivāsa, Narottama, and Śyāmānanda. Through them, he sent the *gosvāmī* literature to Bengal and Orissa around 1570 and guided the development of the movement in those regions. A 17th-century work called *Karṇānanda*, for example, mentions a letter sent by Jīva in response to a query from Narottama and other Bengali devotees. There, Jīva clarifies a matter of devotional practice (*sādhanā*), by stating that the regulated physical practice of → *bhakti* should continue even when the devotee is performing more esoteric, meditative practice – a view that became standard in later tradition (Delmonico, 1999, 97). J. Brzezinski writes,

> Jīva Gosvāmi… evidently had a strong hold on both the emerging and established leaders of the post-Caitanya Vaiṣṇava movement in Bengal, as is evident through numerous visits made by not only the above-mentioned trio and their disciples, but by other important figures. Most prominent amongst these was, no doubt, Jāhnavā Devī [the wife of Nityānanda], who went to Vṛndāvana with a large group of disciples at least twice. On both occasions, although treated with great deference by Jīva, she received instructions from him. (Brzezinski, 2007, 58–59)

Conscious of his responsibilities until the very end, Jīva left a will detailing how the Gosvāmī temples, libraries, and other assets should be managed and perpetuated in his absence. The manuscript, signed by Kṛṣṇadāsa Kavirāja and other noteworthy Caitanya Vaiṣṇavas of the time, is the earliest extant document of its kind in India (see Mukherjee & Wright, 1979).

Works

Kṛṣṇadāsa Kavirāja estimates the size of Jīva Gosvāmī's writings as 400,000 verses (*CaiC.* 3.4.222) and especially praises two works – *Bhāgavatasandarbha* and *Gopālacampū*. Jīva's student Kṛṣṇadāsa Adhikārī provides a list of 25 works by his teacher, which J. Brzezinski has classified into four types: treatises on theology and philosophy, commentaries on other works, manuals on grammar and poetics, and poetic compositions (Brzezinski, 2007, 63). The most well-known works in each category are the *Bhāgavatasandarbha*, the *Durgamasaṅgamanī* commentary on Rūpa Gosvāmī's *Bhaktirasāmṛtasindhu*, the *Harināmāmṛtavyākaraṇa*, and the *Gopālacampū*, respectively. Depending on the nature of the work, Jīva draws on a range of upanishadic, puranic, commentarial, or technical literature in his writing. His immediate sources are his uncles, Rūpa and Sanātana, and nearly every work draws from or builds upon a related work by them. Jīva offers obeisance to them at the beginning of most of his books. He also draws frequently from Śrīdhara Svāmī's commentary on the *Bhāgavatapurāṇa*, → Rāmānuja 's *Śrībhāṣya*, and the writings of → Madhva (for specific examples see Gupta, 2007, 63–91).

Kṛṣṇadāsa Adhikārī's list, reorganized using the above categories, is provided here along with a short description of each work, largely drawn from J. Brzezinski (2007). N.C. Jana (1970) and S.K. De (1986) provide more extensive studies of these works.

Theology and Philosophy

1. *Bhāgavatasandarbha* in six parts, constituting a comprehensive exposition of Caitanya Vaiṣṇava philosophy. Jīva also wrote a supplement to the *Bhāgavatasandarbha* called the *Sarvasaṃvādinī*, which discusses epistemological issues of *pramāṇa* (sources of valid knowledge) and argues for the divinity of Caitanya, among other themes.

2. *Rādhākṛṣṇārcanadīpikā* justifies the worship of → Rādhā along with Kṛṣṇa. This work draws heavily from the *Kṛṣṇasandarbha* and Jīva refers to it in his commentary on the *Brahmasaṃhitā*.

Fig. 2: Painting of the six *gosvāmīs*.

Commentaries

3. *Durgamasaṅgamanī*, a major commentary on the *Bhaktirasāmṛtasindhu* of Rūpa Gosvāmī.

4. *Locanarocanī*, a commentary on the *Ujjvalanīlamaṇi* of Rūpa Gosvāmī.

5. *Kramasandarbha*, a running commentary on the *Bhāgavatapurāṇa*. Many of Jīva's comments consist of material from the *Bhāgavatasandarbha*, which is placed in its appropriate location within the *Bhāgavatapurāṇa*.

6. *Digdarśinī*, a commentary on the *Brahmasaṃhitā*, a → Pāncarātra text discovered by Caitanya during his tour of South India.

7. *Sukhabodhinī*, a commentary on the *Gopālatāpanīyopaniṣad*, a Vaiṣṇava Upaniṣad held in high regard by followers of Caitanya. The *Sukhabodhinī* is drawn largely from Prabhodānanda Sarasvatī's commentary on the same.

8. *Gāyatrīvyākhyā*, a short commentary on several verses from the *Agnipurāṇa* that explain the *gāyatrīmantra*.

9. A commentary on the *Yogasārastava*, a poem praising Kṛṣṇa found in the *Padmapurāṇa*.

10. *Laghuvaiṣṇavatoṣaṇī*, an abridged version of Sanātana Gosvāmī's *Vaiṣṇavatoṣaṇī* commentary on the tenth book of the *Bhāgavatapurāṇa*.

Manuals on Grammar and Poetics

11. *Harināmāmṛtavyākaraṇa*, a Sanskrit grammar based on Pāṇini's system, where every grammatical term is replaced by a name of Kṛṣṇa. Each rule of grammar thus becomes a string of Kṛṣṇa's names and gains a second, theological meaning.

12. *Dhātusaṅgraha*, a collection of verbal roots in Sanskrit, included within the *Harinamāmṛtavyākaraṇa*.

13. *Bhaktirasāmṛtaśeṣa*, a manual of Sanskrit poetics, based closely on the *Sāhityadarpaṇa* of Vīśvanātha Kavirāja. As the *Harināmāmṛtavyākaraṇa* does for Sanskrit grammar, this work

provides a Kṛṣṇa-ized version of *alaṃkāra* (Sanskrit poetics). The example verses are often drawn from *Gopālacampū*.

14. *Bhāvārthasūcakacampū*, a manual delineating the characteristics of Campū literature (see below).

Poetry

15. *Gopālacampū*, Jīva Gosvāmī's literary *magnum opus*, narrating Kṛṣna's life in prose and poetry.

16. *Mādhavamahotsava* portrays Rādhā's coronation as queen of Vrindavan, written according to the conventions of a Mahākāvya (classical poetry).

17. *Kṛṣṇapādapadmacihna*, a description of markings found on Kṛṣṇa's feet, derived from the *Padmapurāṇa*.

18. *Rādhikāpādapadmacihna*, a description of markings found on Rādhā's feet.

19. *Gopālavirudāvalī*, a short work consisting of *viruda*s – laudatory poems composed solely of names. This is one of the earliest examples of the Virudāvalī genre, and it follows the structure of Rūpa Gosvāmī's *Govindavirudāvalī* (Brzezinski, 1996, 124).

20. *Saṃkalpakalpadruma*, a description of Kṛṣṇa's activities during the eight periods of the day and night. This was probably Jīva's last composition.

Theological and Philosophical Contributions

Laying a secure philosophical foundation for devotional practice is a task common to all schools of Vaiṣṇavism, and the materials for such an enterprise usually come from the realm of → Vedānta philosophy. Nearly every theistic school since the time of → Śaṅkara, the famous 8th-century nondualist teacher, has engaged with the vedantic tradition, usually by writing a commentary on the *Brahmasūtra*.

Despite its foundational role in Hindu theistic traditions, Vedānta found itself on uncertain ground during the 15th and 16th centuries, due largely to the rise of influential devotional movements across North India. Some of these movements established their influence by deliberately setting themselves apart from the vedantic pursuits of earlier Vaiṣṇava schools. They saw the emphasis on Vedānta as the hallmark of knowledge-oriented systems, in contrast to their own exclusive absorption in devotion (*bhakti*).

The Caitanya tradition of Bengal, however, attempted to create a theological system that held these tensions in balance – to engage in vedantic discourse and at the same time practice an ecstatic form of devotion to Kṛṣṇa. A key architect of this balance was Jīva Gosvamī, who offered a systematic and comprehensive exposition of Caitanya Vaiṣṇava philosophy in his six-part work, *Bhāgavatasandarbha*. Here, Jīva pushes at the boundaries of Vedānta in several ways:

Purāṇa to Vedānta

The *Bhāgavatapurāṇa* lies at the very heart of Caitanya Vaiṣṇavism, and Caitanya regarded the Purāṇa as the perfect and natural commentary on the *Brahmasūtra*. The *Bhāgavata* is indeed replete with vedantic themes, and because it enjoys undisputed preeminence among followers of Caitanya, it provided an excellent bridge for the community to enter the realm of Vedānta (Gupta, 2007, 25). In the *Bhāgavatasandarbha*, Jīva provides a commentary on the first five aphorisms of the *Brahmasūtra*, which is likely the first Purāṇa-based commentary on the *Brahmasūtra*. Particularly interesting is his use of Śrīdhara Svāmī, the author of the *Bhāvārthadīpikā* commentary on the *Bhāgavatapurāṇa* (Gupta, 2007, 65).

Syncretic Sources

Jīva not only blurs boundaries of genre in his work, but also intentionally crosses lines of difference between earlier vedantic teachers. Jīva employs terminology, concepts, and themes from Śaṅkara, Rāmānuja, and Madhva, the founders of the three most prominent schools of Vedānta, and when he sees that a particular argument has already been made well elsewhere, he simply directs the reader accordingly. He often brings these diverse thinkers into dialogue, even on issues of traditional disagreement.

Vedānta to *Preman*

For followers of Caitanya, the goal of all philosophy and practice is to cultivate unmotivated, spontaneous love (*preman*) for Kṛṣṇa. The traditional Hindu aims of religion, wealth, pleasure, and even → liberation are rejected in favor of a fifth and final goal, namely, *preman*. Any endeavor that does not ultimately lead to this end is considered useless. Thus, the traditional purpose of vedantic study is transformed, for now its main function is not to provide liberation from the cycle of rebirth. Instead, through the study of Vedānta, one gains an acceptable, scriptural foundation for the experience of pure love.

Unity in Difference

Jīva Gosvāmī was the first to expound in writing the Caitanya Vaiṣṇava doctrine of *acintyabhedābheda*, the view that the relationship between god and his energies (the world and living entities) is *bhedābheda*, simultaneously different and nondifferent. Like most Vedāntins, Caitanya Vaiṣṇavas hold that all reality emanates from a single source. And yet, this intimate unity between the world and god must be pried apart, lest the vagaries of the temporal world impinge upon his blissful perfection. Both oneness and difference are equally reasonable, supported by scripture, and necessary; therefore, both must be held together. This is inconceivable to the human mind, and so the relation of *bhedābheda* is called *acintya* (inconceivable). The term *acintyabhedābheda* is not widely used as the official name of Caitanyite Vedānta in the early literature of the school, although both the elements (*acintya* and *bhedābheda*) are ubiquitously discussed and frequently juxtaposed. The clearest statement of nomenclature is found in the *Sarvasaṃvādinī*, where Jīva Gosvāmī lists the names of different teachers and their schools of Vedānta and then concludes by saying, "but my view is *acintyabhedābheda*" (Gupta, 2007, 46).

Confluence of Traditions

Jīva Gosvāmī was situated on the cusp between a solid and time-tested heritage of Sanskrit vedantic exegesis and a fresh yet powerful tide of devotion to Kṛṣṇa, much of which was being expressed in vernacular languages. His writing crosses what one might today call "disciplinary boundaries," for he brought into dialogue four major streams of classical Hinduism: the various systems of Vedānta, the ecstatic *bhakti* movements, the puranic commentarial tradition, and the aesthetic theory of Sanskrit poetics. With training in, and commitments to, all of these traditions, Jīva Gosvāmī was able to tie them together with considerable ingenuity and yet still produce a distinctly Caitanya Vaiṣṇava system of theology.

The *Bhāgavatasandarbha*

The word *sandarbha* literally means "weaving" or "arranging"; the *Bhāgavatasandarbha* is a thematic arrangement of the *Bhāgavatapurāṇa*, woven with the intention of systematically and comprehensively expounding Caitanya Vaiṣṇava doctrine and practice. The text is complete in six volumes, called *Tattvasandarbha, Bhagavatsandarbha, Paramātmasandarbha, Kṛṣṇasandarbha, Bhaktisandarbha*, and *Prītisandarbha*.

The first three *Sandarbhas* are especially rich in philosophical content; in *Tattvasandarbha* Jiva discusses the sources of valid knowledge (*pramāṇa*), argues for the preeminence of the *Bhāgavatapurāṇa*, and delineates his own methodology and sources. The *Bhāgavatsandarbha* and *Paramātmasandarbha* discuss the nature of the personal godhead (Bhagavān), the world (→ *prakṛti* / → *māyā*), and living entities (*jīvas*). These three *Sandarbhas* address questions of ontology in a relatively nonsectarian way, using methods of reasoning and proof texts that would be acceptable to an audience much broader than the followers of Caitanya. Only when major issues regarding the status of the world, the personal nature of divinity, and the individuality of the *jīvas* have been settled does Jīva Gosvāmī go on (in the *Kṛṣṇasandarbha*) to identify that divinity with Kṛṣṇa, in the way that Caitanya Vaiṣṇavas know him: son of Nanda, lord of the cows, and beloved of Śrī Rādhā. This kind of less sectarian approach is a hallmark of vedantic writing, which requires awareness of a universe of discourse broader than one's own community. It also makes apparent Jīva's intention in the *Sandarbhas* to address (and convince) an audience beyond Caitanya Vaiṣṇavas. E. Lott notes, for example, that there is a "striking difference in style" between Rāmānuja's devotional writings and his vedantic ones, where there is "a remarkable avoidance of strictly sectarian material" (Lott, 1980, 4).

In *Bhaktisandarbha* and *Prītisandarbha*, Jīva Gosvāmī borrows from two works by Rūpa Gosvāmī on the aesthetics of devotion – the *Bhaktirasāmṛtasindhu* and the *Ujjvalanīlamaṇi*. The content of *Bhaktisandarbha* corresponds roughly to the first part (of four) of *Bhaktirasāmṛtasindhu*, while *Prītisandarbha* deals with the subject matter of the remaining three parts as well as the *Ujjvalanīlamaṇi*. Despite the overlap

Fig. 3: The Rādhā Dāmodara Temple in Jaipur (photo by Ravi M. Gupta).

in content, Jīva adds his distinctive approach and emphases in the *Sandarbhas*. For example, Jīva gives greater attention to the exoteric aspects of devotion; while Rūpa devotes only one part of the *Bhaktirasāmṛtasindhu* to regulated practice (*sādhanā*), Jīva dedicates his largest *Sandarbha* to its exposition. Even when Jīva deals with more esoteric aspects of → *rasa*, he often intersperses his discussion with philosophical considerations that may have been of less concern to Rūpa Gosvāmī.

The *Bhāgavatasandarbha* was probably one of Jīva's early works. He refers to or quotes from it in a number of his other writings, including the *Rādhākṛṣṇārcanādīpikā, Kramasandarbha, Durgamasaṅgamiṇī*, the *Digdarśinī* commentary on the *Brahmasaṁhitā*, and the *Gopālacampū*. J. Brzezinski estimates the *Bhāgavatasandarbha* 's composition to have been between 1555 and 1561 (Brzezinski, 2007, 55–56). The former year is the date of *Mādhavamahotsava*, an early work, and the latter is the year in which Devakīnandana Dāsa wrote the *Vaiṣṇavavandanā*, wherein he praises Jīva Gosvāmī as a great scholar and devotee. Since Jīva's reputation was clearly established by this time, it is likely that he had already written his philosophical *magnum opus*, the *Bhāgavatasandarbha*.

Literary and Poetic Contributions

The *Bhāgavatapurāṇa* holds pride of place in the Caitanya Vaiṣṇava tradition as the fount of both philosophical thought and aesthetic expression. And so, like his philosophical writing, Jīva Gosvāmī's literary work shows a similar focus on the Purāṇa. He frequently selects narratives from the tenth book of the *Bhāgavatapurāṇa*, which tells Kṛṣṇa's life story, and elaborates or reorganizes them in order to elicit a stronger experience of *rasa* in the learned reader.

Jīva's writing displays the characteristics of an author who is well versed in the conventions of medieval Sanskrit poetics, as exemplified in the compositions of Subandhu and Bāṇa. Jīva also demonstrates extraordinary fluency in Sanskrit meters. The ninth chapter of the *Mādhavamahotsava*, for example, employs not fewer than 47 different meters, some of which cannot be identified using any extant manual of Sanskrit poetry (De, 1986, 470). The *Gopālacampū*, his final composition, employs 38 different meters (Brzezinski, 1996, 109). Alliteration, puns, elaborate metaphors, and verses with dual meanings are commonplace in these works.

Gopālacampū

The *Gopālacampū*, written near the end of Jīva's career, represents a signal contribution to the corpus of Caitanya Vaiṣṇava literature and to Sanskrit literature in general. The *Gopālacampū* is the largest and most elaborate work of the Campū genre – a mixed composition of prose and poetry. The Campū style affords a unique medium to blend theological reflection and poetic narrative, and Jīva's work offers both. Jīva wrote the *Gopālacampū* to elaborate on themes found in the *Kṛṣṇasandarbha*, the fourth part of the *Bhāgavatasandarbha*, which discusses Kṛṣṇa's ontological position and activities. Nevertheless, his primary concern in the *Gopālacampū* is aesthetic – he aims to elicit and intensify the experience of *rasa* found in the *Bhāgavatapurāṇa*'s description of Kṛṣṇa's *līlā*. To this end, Jīva reorganizes, elaborates, and even adds new narratives to the *Bhāgavatapurāṇa*'s account (Brzezinski, 1996, 108). The resequencing of events in Kṛṣṇa's life follows the *Vaiṣṇavatoṣaṇī*, Sanātana Gosvāmī's commentary on the tenth book of the *Bhāgavatapurāṇa*. The most significant additions to the narrative occur near the end of the *Bhāgavatapurāṇa*'s account: in the *Gopālacampū*, Kṛṣna returns to Vraja after his long absence, marries Rādhā and the *gopī*s, and finally ascends with them to his eternal, nonmaterial abode of Goloka. Jīva provides an argument for the existence and supremacy of Kṛṣṇa's abode, Goloka.

The *Gopālacampū* consists of two parts, dated by the author himself to 1589 and 1594, respectively, and each part is further subdivided into three smaller *campū*s (Brzezinski, 1992, 61). The first part tells of Kṛṣṇa's childhood in Vraja, including the killing of Putanā, stealing of butter, subduing of Kāliya, lifting of Mount Govardhana, and the *rasa* dance. The second part tells of Kṛṣṇa's departure from Vraja and subsequent activities, including the killing of Kaṃsa, Nanda's return to Vraja without Kṛṣṇa, Uddhava's visit to Vraja, the marriages of Kṛṣṇa and Balarāma, Kṛṣṇa's meeting with the residents of Vraja at Kurukṣetra, Kṛṣṇa's return to Vraja, Rādhā and Kṛṣṇa's wedding, and the return to Goloka.

The marriage of Rādhā and Kṛṣṇa, as depicted in *Gopālacampū* and other works by Jīva, has led to some theological disagreement within the tradition. Most Caitanya Vaiṣṇava teachers have held the view that Rādhā and Kṛṣṇa's relationship is extramarital (*parakīya*). The inappropriateness and risk involved in such a relationship adds to the intensity and sweetness of Rādhā and the *gopī*s' relationship with Kṛṣṇa. This flavor of relationship is not available in Dvārakā, for example, where Kṛṣṇa's queens have a married (*svakīya*) and socially acceptable relationship with their husband.

Despite the fact that Jīva argues for the *svakīya* interpretation, he leaves much doubt about his own view on the matter by including an enigmatic verse in his *Locanarocanī* (found in all manuscripts), suggesting that he espoused the *svakīya* doctrine on someone else's request, but his own view was the opposite. Rādhākṛṣṇadāsa, the head priest of the Govindadeva Temple in the mid-17th century, suggests in his *Sādhanadīpikā* that the "other" whom Jīva wanted to please was a dear disciple named Gopāladāsa, whom Jīva mentions by name at the end of his *Harināmāmṛtavyākaraṇa* (Delmonico, 1999, 96). Furthermore, in his *Karṇānanda*, Yadunandana records an exchange of letters between Jīva and devotees in Bengal (Rāmacandra Kavirāja, Govindadāsa, and Narottamadāsa), in which the latter request Jīva to clarify which doctrine he accepted. Again, Jīva's reply is enigmatic; he says simply that his view is the same as that of his student, Śrīnivasācārya. According to Yadunandana, Śrīnivāsa supported the doctrine of *parakīya* (Delmonico, 1999, 95). Later tradition has sought to honor Jīva's *svakīya* statements by pointing out that the ontological relationship between Rādhā and Kṛṣṇa is *svakīya* – Rādhā is Kṛṣṇa's internal energy and therefore belongs to him alone – although the two take on an extramarital relationship in order to intensify their love.

Influence on Later Tradition

The significant role that Jīva Gosvāmī played in shaping the institutional structure, theological foundation, and devotional practice of the Caitanya tradition should be apparent from the preceding material. It is nevertheless worth mentioning some of the more tangible ways in which Jīva Gosvāmī has influenced later tradition, up to the present day:

1. Kṛṣṇadāsa Kavirāja relied on the *gosvāmī*s' writings as source material, and so Jīva's influence is palpable in the *Caitanyacaritāmṛta*, which came to be regarded by the tradition as the authoritative biography of Caitanya.
2. The *Tattvasandarbha* received commentaries by Baladeva Vidyābhuṣaṇa, a central figure in 18th-century Caitanya Vaiṣṇavism, and Radhamohana, his contemporary (see Elkman, 1986, 51–55). Jīva's works continue to be translated, commented upon, and used as proof texts by the tradition today. Some examples are the publications of Haridas Das in Nabadwip, Puridas and Shyamdas in Vrindavan, Bhaktisiddhanta Saraswati and C. Chatterjee in Kolkata, and Gopiparanadhana Dasa in Govardhan.
3. Jīva Gosvāmī's temple to Rādhā Dāmodara in Vrindavan and its counterpart in Jaipur (where the original icons are now located) are much smaller than the temples to Govindadeva, but they nevertheless play an important role in the worship life of contemporary Caitanya Vaiṣṇavas. A.C. Bhaktivedanta Swami Prabhupada, founder of → ISKCON, spent several years as a renunciant at the Rādha Dāmodara Temple in Vrindavan, making it a place of pilgrimage for his followers.
4. The library of the Rādhā-Dāmodara Temple in Vrindavan contains some of the oldest surviving manuscripts of Caitanyite literature, including some from the collection of Raghunāthadāsa Gosvāmī, who bequeathed his personal library to Jīva. The Rādha-Dāmodara Temple manuscripts are now housed at the Vrindavan Research Institute.

Bibliography

Brahmachari, M., *Vaiṣṇava Vedānta (The Philosophy of Śrī Jīva Gosvāmī)*, Calcutta, 1974.

Broo, M., "Jīva Gosvāmin and the Extent of the Vedic Paradigm," *JVS* 15/1, 2006, 5–29.

Brzezinski, J., "Jīva Goswami: Biography and Bibliography," *JVS* 15/2, 2007, 51–80.

Brzezinski, J., "Verse and Prose Poetry in the Goplālacampū," *JVS* 4/4, 1996, 105–138.

Brzezinski, J., "Goloka Vṛndāvana: A Translation of Jīva Gosvāmī's Gopāla-campū (Chapter One)," *JVS* 1/1, 1992, 61–98.

Chakrabarty, R., *Vaiṣṇavism in Bengal 1486–1900*, Calcutta, 1985.

Chakravarti, J., *Bengal Vaisnavism and Sri Chaitanya*, Calcutta, 1975.

Chatterjee Sastri, A., *Jiva Gosvamin*, Calcutta, 1996.

Dasgupta, S.N., *A History of Indian Philosophy*, 5 vols., London, 1949.

De, S.K., *Early History of the Vaiṣṇava Faith and Movement in Bengal from Sanskrit and Bengali Sources*, Calcutta, 1986.

Delmonico, N., "Trouble in Paradise: A Seventeenth Century Conflict in the Caitanya Vaiṣṇava Tradition," *JVS* 8/1, 1999, 91–101.

Dimock, E.C. Jr., *Caitanya Caritāmṛta of Kṛṣṇadāsa Kavirāja: A Translation and Commentary*, HOS 56, Cambridge MA, 1999.

Elkman, S.M., *Jīva Gosvāmin's Tattvasandarbha: A Study on the Philosophical and Sectarian Development of the Gauḍīya Vaiṣṇava Movement*, Delhi, 1986.

Gupta, R.M., "On Conceiving the Inconceivable: Jīva Gosvāmī's Presentation of Acintya-bhedābheda," *JVS* 16/2, 2008, 103–117.

Gupta, R.M., *The Caitanya Vaiṣṇava Vedānta of Jīva Gosvāmī: When Knowledge Meets Devotion*, London, 2007.

Gupta, R.M., "Making Space for Vedānta: Canon and Commentary in Caitanya Vaiṣṇavism," *IJHS* 10/1, 2006, 75–90.

Jana, N.C., *Vṛndābaner Chay Gosvāmī*, Calcutta, 1970.

Kapoor, O.B.L., *The Gosvāmīs of Vṛndāvana*, Caracas, 1995.

Kapoor, O.B.L., *The Philosophy and Religion of Sri Caitanya: The Philosophical Background of the Hare Krishna Movement*, New Delhi, 1977.

Kennedy, M.T., *The Caitanya Movement: A Study of Vaishnavism in Bengal*, Calcutta, 1925.

Lott, E., *Vedāntic Approaches to God*, London, 1980.

Morales, F.G., "*Bhāgavata-Śabda Pramāṇa*: The Epistemology of Jīva Gosvāmin in the Context of Vaidika Philosophy," diss., University of Wisconsin–Madison, 2002.

Mukherjee, T., & J.C., Wright, "An Early Testamentary Document in Sanskrit," *BSOAS* 42/2, 1979.

Prabhupada, A.C. Bhaktivedanta Swami, *Śrīmad Bhāgavatam*, 18 vols., Los Angeles, 1987.

"Radhadamodarji Thikana Mandir – Jaipur," www.radhadamodarji.com.

"Radha Damodar Mandir – Vrindavan," www.radhadamodarmandir.com.

Ravi M. Gupta

Jñāndev

Jñāndev or Jñāneśvar (also Dnyaneshwar, Dnyandeo, Jnanadeva, and Gnyaneshwar) is remembered as a poet-saint who was born in Alandi (or possibly Apegav, east of Paithan on the Godāvarī River), in what is today → Maharashtra, sometime in the third quarter of the 13th century CE. Born to a Deshastha Brahman family, he is said to have mastered Sanskrit and much of its philosophical literature as a child. He is remembered as one of the first masters of Marathi as a literary language, having composed at least four distinctive works (see below). His most famous text is a Marathi rendering of the famous Sanskrit poetic-philosophical work the → *Bhagavadgītā*. This Marathi text is popularly and eponymously called the *Jñāneśvarī*, after one of Jñāndev's common appellations, Jñāneśvar ("Lord of Knowledge"). The *Jñāneśvarī* is often regarded as the first masterpiece of the Marathi language and Jñāndev as the progenitor of Marathi as a literary medium. Jñāndev is also one of the first figures of the Vārkarī religious community, the → Vārkarī Sampradāy, along with → Nāmdev, primarily, and several other figures including Jñāndev's own siblings: the brothers Nivṛtti and Sopān and Jñāndev's younger sister, Muktā – all of whom are revered as saints. Jñāndev is also remembered to have been a master *yogī* of the Nāth lineage (as were his siblings, Nāmdev, and many other Vārkarī figures; see → Nāth Sampradāya). Together with Nāmdev (to whom the first biography of Jñāndev is attributed), Jñāndev is said to have travelled throughout India, but, unlike Nāmdev, hardly any record exists of Jñāndev north of the Marathi-speaking regions. He is said to have voluntarily entombed himself at the age of 21 in Alandi (20 km north of modern Pune). A large temple that houses his *samādhi* or tomb prominently stands in Alandi to commemorate this event, and the town has become a hub of Vārkarī education and pilgrimage activity. Vārkarī followers of Jñāndev bring a palanquin (*pālkhī*) bearing symbols of him (such as stylized replicas of his sandals or *pādukā*s) from Alandi to Pandharpur in the month of *āṣāḍha* (Jun–Jul) on the pilgrimage known as the *vārī*. In contemporary Marathi contexts, the *Jñāneśvarī* is read in a vibrant tradition called *pravacana*, in which a passage is recited and discussed by a learned person and then by a gathered audience in the process of self-development or *svadhyāya*.

Biography

Jñāndev's commonly cited lifespan is from 1275 to 1296 CE, and most hagiographical accounts place his birth and entombment in the town of Alandi, in what is today western Maharashtra. He is remembered to have been born to Deshastha Brahman parents named Viṭṭhal and Rukmiṇī (after the presiding deity of Pandharpur and his consort) and to have been their second son along with Jñāndev's older brother Nivṛtti, his younger brother Sopān, and his younger sister Muktā. The key source for Jñāndev's biography is a series of three song collections attributed to Nāmdev, a fellow saint and contemporary of Jñāndev. These three song collections are the *Ādī* (Beginning), the *Tīrthāvaḷī* (Travelogue), and the *Samādhi* (The Entombment). The most well-known narrations of Jñāndev's life, particularly as depicted in Mahīpati's influential collective hagiography *Bhaktavijay* (Victory of the *Bhakta*s; 18th cent.), are drawn from these three texts.

The *Ādī* tells a series of stories about Jñāndev's early life that is well known and revered in Maharashtra. It recalls that Jñāndev's father, Viṭṭhal, though married to Rukmiṇī, took a vow of *sannyāsa* (renunciation) and rejected his Brahmanical and familial duties in order to live in Benares as a Śaiva renunciant and *yogī*. In Benares, he received word that Rukmiṇī was pregnant, and so he returned home to care for the child. However, because he had taken a vow to renounce his worldly life and duties, he was rejected from the Brahman community of Alandi. Despite this caste exclusion, Viṭṭhal's children learned Sanskrit and mastered Sanskrit learning at a very young age. In addition, they became adepts in the yogic tradition of the Śaiva Nāths, like their father. After the birth of his fourth child, the daughter Muktā, Viṭṭhal and Rukmiṇī resolved to find a way for their children to be restored to the Brahman caste and therefore traveled to Paithan, a center of Brahmanical orthodoxy. In Paithan, a council of Brahmans called the four children before them to be judged. They ridiculed Jñāndev and his family, and, as a test, they told Jñāndev to recite the Vedas. Instead of doing so himself, he "caused" (by yogic power or by prayer to Viṭṭhal) a nearby water buffalo to recite the Vedas instead. This miracle showed the council that Viṭṭhal and Rukmiṇī's children were untainted by their father's caste transgression. This is the extent of the story told within the *Ādī* attributed to Nāmdev. However, popular memory and many other retellings continue by adding a story about the fate of Jñāndev's parents. Although they were impressed with Jñāndev and his siblings, the council did not absolve Jñāndev's parents, who were instructed to commit ritual suicide by drowning themselves in a river (*jalasamādhi*). Viṭṭhal and Rukmiṇī complied, thus leaving their children to grow up as orphans.

It is some time after leaving Paithan, but before the events of the next song collection, the *Tīrthāvaḷī*, that Jñāndev is said to have composed his Marathi rendering of the Sanskrit *Bhagavadgītā*. According to popular and traditional memory, Jñāndev was only 15 to 19 years old when he composed this massive work.

The *Tīrthāvaḷī* (Travelogue) narrates the next key portion of Jñāndev's biography. The *Tīrthāvaḷī* records that Jñāndev heard of the great *bhakti* of Nāmdev in Pandharpur, and he felt compelled to meet this acclaimed saint. Jñāndev also wanted to convert Nāmdev to a nondualistic (*advaita*) philosophical position and to convince him of the virtues of *yoga* and of the worship of god in a way that transcends qualities (→ *nirguṇa*). Upon meeting Nāmdev in Pandharpur, Jñāndev requested that the god Viṭṭhal allow Nāmdev to take leave of his worship in Pandharpur and travel around India with Jñāndev to visit sacred sites. This story is primarily a tale about Nāmdev and Viṭṭhal and not a central feature of Jñāndev's biography, although it emphasizes the vital connection between Nāmdev and Jñāndev as the dual progenitors of the Vārkarī tradition, its pilgrimage, and its literary and performative practices. (For more on the travels of Jñāndev and Nāmdev, see → Nāmdev.)

The *Samādhī* is the last of the narrative triptych attributed to Nāmdev about Jñāndev's life, and it records one of the most important stories about Jñāndev. At the age of 21 (or perhaps 25), Jñāndev is said to have accomplished all his worldly aims: he had mastered *yoga* as taught by the Nāth tradition, he had formed a deep friendship with Nāmdev and brought his family into the "family of saints" (*sant parivar*) that surrounded Nāmdev in Pandharpur, and he had composed several works on his various beliefs and practices, most prominently the *Jñāneśvarī*. Having fulfilled these worldly goals, Jñāndev resolved to "take *samādhi*" by voluntarily entombing himself in Alandi, a practice not uncommon for religious adepts of South Asia among Hindus, Muslims, Buddhists, and Jains. The Sanskrit term *samādhi* means "concentration" or "concerted effort," but in this case, it more specifically connotes a kind of final act of great concentrated effort to conclude one's worldly life, as well as the very place in which this final act is undertaken, a tomblike structure still available for viewing in Alandi today. A third meaning of *samādhi* indicates a text, like an elegy, that recounts such an act and place, such as Nāmdev's *Samādhi* about Jñāndev's final act. There are also *samādhi* compositions for several other Marathi saints who were contemporaries of Nāmdev.

The *Samādhi* recalls that Jñāndev resolved to enter a tomb and thereby conclude his brief life. The text portrays many poignant debates that he had with his friends and family, who both admired his decision and wept at the thought of losing him. His friends – especially Nāmdev and the *sant parivar* of Pandharpur – gathered in Alandi and spent an entire night singing songs about him and singing praises of Viṭṭhal. Even Viṭṭhal himself came from Pandharpur to see the event. A long procession escorted Jñāndev to his tomb, where he then bid farewell to his friends and family. He entered the small structure and sat in meditation as his family and friends sealed the tomb from the outside. In Marathi – Jñāndev's state then, as now – is called *sanjīvan samādhi*, which can mean "taking *samādhi* while alive," but more aptly indicates the belief that Jñāndev continues to live, by a thin thread of breath, within the tomb in Alandi, resting in the deepest yogic meditative state. This understanding of *sanjīvan samādhi* is demonstrated in a story about the 16th-century poet-saint → Eknāth, who is said to have visited Jñāndev's tomb, opened the door, and encountered Jñāndev alive inside.

Legacy

Jñāndev's legacy endured in many ways beyond his lifetime. In terms of the literary history of Marathi, Jñāndev is remembered as having been the progenitor of Marathi as a literary language via his composition of the *Jñāneśvarī*, although he may not have been the very first figure to have composed in Marathi (scholars have debated whether Mukundarāj's *Vivekasindhū* and some → Mahānubhav literature may have preceded Jñāndev's work but with less fame). Nonetheless, Jñāndev is often considered to have brought the language to its literary apex and provided Marathi with its first fulsome philosophical text. Jñāndev is remembered by some as a Brahman who opposed caste-based discrimination, having brought the Sanskrit *Bhagavadgītā* into a vernacular linguistic realm for the purpose of making it accessible to non-Brahmans and women, and also through his associations with low-caste figures, especially Nāmdev. In general, however, Jñāndev's compositions do not issue a strong criticism of caste hierarchy or explicitly promote social change. Because of his acclaimed journey to Pandharpur to visit Viṭṭhal and Nāmdev, Jñāndev has been identified by some as the first pilgrim or Vārkarī to undertake the pilgrimage to Pandharpur that is at the heart of the Vārkarī tradition. In keeping with this memory as the first famous Vārkarī, the retinue of pilgrims around Jñāndev's palanquin (*pālkhī*) has taken a central role in the *vārī* pilgrimage in the 20th and 21st centuries. When the Jñāndev *pālkhī* (one of the two largest in the whole pilgrimage) arrives at the outskirts of Pandharpur each year, the Nāmdev *pālkhī* comes out to meet it, and then the Jñāndev *pālkhī* is usually the first one to proceed into Pandharpur. Jñāndev is often referred to as Māulī ("Mother") – a gender-bending designation that indicates his role in birthing the Vārkarī tradition and nurturing the pilgrims in their spiritual lives. This use of a female term for Jñāndev parallels the dual-gendered naming of the Vārkarī's deity at Pandharpur (see → Vārkarī Sampradāy), who is regularly called Father Viṭṭhal (Viṭhobā) and sometimes Mother Viṭṭhal (Viṭhāī).

In the modern period, four films have been produced about the life of Jñāndev. The most famous, *Sant Dnyaneshwar*, was made in 1940 by V.G. Damle ands. Fattelal for Prabhat Film Studios. It is one of the most beloved of the "saint" films of Marathi cinema, along with the film *Sant Tukaram*, made in 1938. Alandi, the town in Maharashtra most closely associated with Jñāndev, maintains and has expanded the site that is said to have been the tomb entered by Jñāndev in 1296 CE. A vibrant devotional culture surrounds the site of the *samādhi* there, and the *pālkhī* that makes the pilgrimage to Pandharpur in Jñāndev's name originates from Alandi. It is not accidental that this town has become one of the major educational and training centers for young Vārkarī boys who aspire to become *kīrtaṅkar*s (performers of → *kīrtan*) and leaders within the tradition. Today, across Marathi-speaking areas of India and worldwide, people meet to recite sections of the *Jñāneśvarī* in the context of a *pravacana*, a lecture based on a selection from the text, expounded by a learned individual for a community of believers. This is one of the chief ways in which the *Jñāneśvarī* remains a living text today. In addition, the contemporary Swadhyay Pariwar or Swadhyay Movement, founded by Pandurang (Shastri) Athavale in Mumbai in 1942, uses the *Jñāneśvarī* and the *Bhagavadgītā* as core texts for its *pravacana*s. The memory of Jñāndev and the *Jñāneśvarī* are also revered in some groups within the modern Siddha Yoga tradition.

Compositions

Four texts are regularly attributed to Jñāndev – a Marathi rendering of the *Bhagavadgītā* that is known most commonly as the *Jñāneśvarī*, a collection of his short devotional poetry (*Gāthā*), the esoteric *Anubhavāmṛt* (The Nectar of Experience), and a stylized letter to a *yogī* called the *Cāṅgdevpāsaṣṭī* (The Sixty-five [Verses to] Cāṅgdev). These four compositions are strikingly diverse and in some ways inconsistent with one another (for example, in their use of different signature tags or *mūdrikā*s), which has prompted some scholars to question the traditional view that all of them were authored by a single 13th-century figure (see Kiehnle, 1997, for a summary of the positions on authorship, especially in relation to the *Gāthā*). Popular opinion and the Vārkarī tradition, however, strongly insist that all of these were composed by Jñāndev himself. Short compositions with more dubitable claims to authorship by Jñāndev abound as well, testifying to the immense popularity and attractive power of Jñāndev's name through the centuries.

Jñāneśvarī (or *Bhāvārthadīpikā*, *Jñāndevī*)

Jñāndev's Marathi rendering of the *Bhagavadgītā* is notably the first treatment of this Sanskrit text in a vernacular language. Jñāndev does not provide a name for this composition within the text itself, and thus it has been referred to in multiple ways. The eponymous title *Jñāneśvarī* appears in songs about Jñāndev that are attributed to Nāmdev (13th cent.) and Eknāth (16th cent.). Less frequently, this text is called the *Bhāvārthadīpikā* (Lamp of Essential Meaning), after a reference to it in a song attributed to the poetess Janābāī (13th–14th cents.). Still other songs attributed to Nāmdev and Eknāth refer to the text as the *Jñāndevī*, although this title did not come into wide usage. In modern Marathi, the name *Jñāneśvarī* is undoubtedly the most common.

In the conclusion of the *Jnāneśvarī*, Jñāndev mentions completing the text in a town on the bank of the Godāvarī River now called Nevāse (60 km north of Ahmadnagar) during the rule of the king Rāmacandra (usually identified as the Seuṇa Yādava king Rāmadeva, r. 1271–1309 CE). Many manuscripts of the *Jñāneśvarī* also conclude with a colophon that specifies that the text was completed in the year 1290 CE. This colophon also refers to the text as a "commentary" (*ṭīkā*) that was composed by Jñāneśvar and written down by a scribe named Saccidānanda. This appearance of the name Jñāneśvar here is surprising, however, since in the rest of the text, only the name Jñāndev ever appears. Although some scholars (Bhave & Tulpule, 1982) have suggested that the colophon with the 1290 date might be a later emendation to the text, the date of composition roughly around the turn of the 13th century has never been intensively called into question.

Despite this perhaps appended reference to the text as a *ṭīkā*, the *Jñāneśvarī* is not a commentary in the classic Sanskrit sense, with glosses of difficult words, discussions of unclear passages, or references to previous commentators. Instead, it is a creative retelling of the *Bhagavadgītā*'s narrative and philosophical lessons in Marathi – something that the text does without referring explicitly to the original Sanskrit verses that it closely follows. The *Jñāneśvarī* is divided into the same 18 chapters as the *Bhagavadgītā*, but it is more than 12 times longer – around nine thousand verses (some manuscripts have nearly ten thousand and others slightly fewer than nine thousand). Jñāndev spreads his attention unevenly across the text, giving some chapters of the *Bhagavadgītā* (chs. 13 and 15 on the nature of consciousness and yogic techniques) much more intensive consideration than others (chs. 1–4, which establish the narrative). The *Jñāneśvarī* is composed in the flexible Marathi *ovī* style, which became one of the most popular poetic forms throughout the history of Marathi literature. An *ovī* consists of four feet (*caraṇs*), each of which varies in length between 5 and 15 syllables, with the fourth foot tending to be shorter than the first three. In Jñāndev's *ovī*s (unlike some later variations), the final syllables of the first three feet are identical or very similar, whereas the final syllable of the fourth foot is completely different. This pattern of final syllables is what characterizes Jñāndev's *ovī*s more than any adherence to a strict meter or rhythm. Although he did not invent the *ovī*, Jñāndev is commonly regarded as the master of this form.

Although popular opinion routinely associates Jñāndev's philosophy with → Śaṅkara's Advaita Vedānta (see → Vedānta), the *Jñāneśvarī* is not obviously indebted to Śaṅkara's commentary on the *Bhagavadgītā*. Similarly, comparisons with the commentaries of → Abhinavagupta and → Rāmānuja reveal no evident relationship in terms of either philosophical terms or analogical illustrations employed. Throughout the *Jñāneśvarī*, Jñāndev consistently praises his *guru* and brother Nivṛtti (Nivṛttināth), and in the conclusion, he offers a chain of transmission through which he claims to have received his teaching: Śiva, Matsyendranāth, Gorakṣanāth (Gorakhnāth), Gahiṇīnāth, Nivṛttināth, and Jñāndev. Some Marathi scholars (Bhave & Tulpule, 1982, 33–34) have noted the existence of a manuscript called the *Gorakṣagītā* that claims to be Gahiṇīnāth's transcription of Gorakhnāth's teachings on the *Bhagavadgītā*, but there is no solid evidence that this text actually dates to the 13th century or that it precedes the *Jñāneśvarī*. Maharashtrian scholars have attempted to present Jñāndev's philosophy *vis-à-vis* different classical Indian thinkers, but none of these interpretations has become standard (see Bahiraṭ, 1984). Although a thorough, systematic explication of Jñāndev's philosophy in the *Jñāneśvarī* is not forthcoming, it is clear that Jñāndev incorporates a nondual perspective, a strong emphasis on → *bhakti*, and a keen interest in *kuṇḍalinīyoga* (see → Yoga) ideas and techniques. It thus makes more sense to understand Jñāndev's distinct philosophy as synthesizing several streams of thought rather than inheriting a single, well-defined tradition.

More than for any of its philosophical positions, the *Jñāneśvarī* is known for its extensive and poetic use of creative, natural analogies to illustrate → Kṛṣṇa's teachings and for its informal, sometimes even personal and humorous style (e.g. Jñāndev often reminds himself not to get carried away with providing illustrations). A short passage in the *Jñāneśvarī*'s conclusion (Lokapur, 1995, 18.1772–1780) has become popular as a benedictory prayer at Vārkarī events and among many Marathi speakers. This poetic, nine-verse passage is referred to as the *Pasāyadān* (Skt. *prasādadāna*, "giving of blessing or grace"), in which Jñāndev invokes god to turn the ways of the wicked to good ends and to foster the well-being of all.

Some noteworthy patterns in the *Jnāneśvarī* distinguish it from the *Bhagavadgītā*. In Jñāndev's rendering, *bhakti* is not only taught by Kṛṣṇa but also consistently and overtly exemplified by the relationship between Arjuna and Kṛṣṇa. Arjuna regularly conveys his intense devotion to Kṛṣṇa and treats him reverentially as a deity, and Kṛṣṇa responds, saying that Arjuna's devotion is so overpoweringly endearing that Kṛṣṇa cannot but reveal to him all of his secret knowledge. In one especially poignant scene, Jñāndev depicts Kṛṣṇa recoiling slightly at the prospect of teaching Arjuna about nondual reality, since enlightening Arjuna in this way (to realize his ultimate identity with Kṛṣṇa) might end up depriving Kṛṣṇa of a dear friend and conversation partner (*Jñāneśvarī* 6.113–119 [ed. Lokapur, 1995, 266–267]). In passages such as these, the *Jñāneśvarī* demonstrates the common Vārkarī insistence on holding together seemingly contradictory ideas of nonduality and *bhakti*. It is also likely that the Kṛṣṇa of the *Bhāgavatapurāṇa* in his full devotional glory had influenced Jñāndev's perception of the more stoic Kṛṣṇa in the *Bhagavadgītā*.

Jñāndev consistently praises and invokes his *guru* Nivṛtti, highlighting the necessity of a *guru* for obtaining a proper understanding of both *bhakti* and reality. In parts of the *Jñāneśvarī*, Jñāndev refers to his *guru* as a sort of conversation partner, sometimes stating that Nivṛtti steps in to remind him to stay focused on interpreting the *Bhagavadgītā* and not get lost in narrative tangents. As is well known among Marathi speakers, Jñāndev highlights the utility and appropriateness of composing in Marathi. To describe the language of his work, he frequently uses the word *marhāṭe*, which in some cases means "clear" or "straightforward" and in other cases names the Marathi language itself. In his conclusion, Jñāndev explains that he deliberately chose to compose in Marathi *ovīs*, so that the message of the *Bhagavadgītā* would be attractive to all listeners, and even children would be able to understand it (*Jñāneśvarī* 18.1720–1721 [ed. Lokapur, 1995, 1672]). In this way, the *Jñāneśvarī* initiates a tradition among some Marathi *bhakti* poet-saints (picked up especially by Eknāth) to use Marathi in order to make the knowledge of classic Sanskrit religious texts accessible to everyone regardless of gender, intelligence, and caste.

The most famous text in all of Marathi literature, the *Jñāneśvarī* unsurprisingly has a vast and complex manuscript history. A demonstration of its early popularity is seen in the additional five-verse colophon found in many manuscripts, testifying to an important editorial intervention by Eknāth. This colophon states that in 1584, Eknāth "repurified" (*pratiśuddha kelī*) the text that had become corrupted and inconsistent over time through repetition. Some hagiographical accounts of Eknāth's life mention his editorial work on the *Jñāneśvarī* in the context of a set of wondrous stories about Eknāth renovating Jñāndev's tomb in Alandi. Over the centuries, the archaic language of the *Jñāneśvarī* clearly created problems of interpretation among some audiences, resulting in a sizable number of texts in the 17th and 18th centuries that explained difficult Old Marathi words in a more contemporary idiom. In 1903, the prominent Marathi historian V.K. Rajwade announced that he had discovered a manuscript of the *Jñāneśvarī* that predated the version edited by Eknāth (who, Rajwade claimed, apparently did not have access to the most authentic manuscripts) and therefore more closely reflected Jñāndev's own 13th-century syntax. V.K. Rajwade edited and published this manuscript in 1909, which was adopted (in a slightly altered form) in 1960 by the government of Maharashtra in its official publication of the *Jñāneśvarī*. Known for his Brahman chauvinism, V.K. Rajwade also used this manuscript of the *Jñāneśvarī* to argue for a very close relationship between Sanskrit and Marathi grammar, which he claimed was evidence of a linguistic golden age of pure Marathi. Leaders of the Vārkarī tradition at the time rejected V.K. Rajwade's edition of the *Jnāneśvarī*, which so enraged V.K. Rajwade that he tossed his precious, old manuscript into a river, effectively destroying it (see Wakankar, 2010).

An alternative edition of the *Jñāneśvarī* that used manuscripts with the Eknāth colophon was published in 1910 by one of the main *guru* lineages in Alandi, the Sakhre Sampraday, whose founder, Nana Maharaj Sakhre, claimed to have had a personal revelation (*sākṣātkār*) of Jñāndev himself, thereby acquiring a unique authority to speak about the *Jñāneśvarī*. The Sakhre edition and its extensive commentary in modern Marathi has been reprinted and revised many times, and it remains the standard edition of the *Jñāneśvarī* in use by members of the Vārkarī tradition. An English translation of the Sakhre edition (Bhagwat, 1979) has been published, and V.K. Rajwade's edition has been translated into English twice: first by an international team sponsored by UNESCO (Lambert & Pradhan, 1967) and later in an annotated, interlinear format that highlights the possible Kannada background of Jñāndev's language (Lokapur, 1995). The English of the Lambert and Pradhan edition was later revised (not retranslated) as well (Kripananda, 1989).

Anubhavāmṛt (or *Amṛtānubhav*)

This composition has received much less scholarly attention and is not commonly recited by Vārkarīs, although it is commonly assumed that Jñāndev composed it soon after finishing his *Jñāneśvarī*. Little background about the *Anubhavāmṛt* is known, although it is sometimes said that the text derives from a lesson that Jñāndev received from his *guru* and brother Nivṛtti. In contrast to his approach in the *Jñāneśvarī*, in his *Anubhavāmṛt*, Jñāndev shows little concern for making his teaching accessible to a wide audience. Subsequently, several commentaries on it were composed in Marathi and Sanskrit to clarify its meaning. Because of the text's esoteric subject and language, it has remained primarily a philosopher's text.

Comprising around eight hundred Marathi *ovīs*, the *Anubhavāmṛt* begins with a five-verse invocation in Sanskrit to Jñāndev's *guru* Nivṛtti, to the coupled Śiva- *jīva* and Śiva-Śakti, and then to → Śiva alone. The text proceeds through many terse, abstract demonstrations of the illusory nature of dualisms that belie the nondual essence of reality. One important 20th-century interpreter of the *Anubhavāmṛt* insists that this text ought to be read as a Marathi explication of what is basically → Kashmir Śaiva philosophy (particularly Vasugupta's *Spandakārikā* and *Śivasūtra*), which Jñāndev may have encountered in some form through the Maharashtrian Nāth tradition into which he had been initiated (see Chitre, 1996).

Cāṅgdevpāsaṣṭī

As its name implies, this text comprises of 65 verses (*ovīs*) written about a man named Cāṅgdev. Although scholars debated for some time whether the *Cāṅgdevpāsaṣṭī* was composed by the same author as the *Jñāneśvarī* and *Anubhavāmṛt*, arguments for how themes from both of the earlier texts are present in the *Cāṅgdevpāsaṣṭī* have proven generally persuasive, and this text is widely accepted as Jñāndev's own (see Bhave & Tulpule, 1982, 721). Nothing about the figure of Cāṅgdev is known aside from what is stated in this text and in the hagiographical stories that accrued around it. The 18th-century *Bhaktavijay* of Mahīpati depicts Cāṅgdev as an accomplished but arrogant *yogī* who, through his practice of *yoga*, had acquired the power to fly and defy death for 1,500 years. Cāṅgdev is also said to have ridden a fearsome tiger as a mount and carried a snake as a whip, which is one of the popular images in the iconography of Jñāndev. The premise for the composition of this text is that Cāṅgdev had heard of Jñāndev's fame and attempted to contact him, but he could not think of what he should write to be respectful yet maintain his ego. Jñāndev heard of this and interpreted it as indicative of Cāṅgdev's long but hollow life, and so he wrote a letter to Cāṅgdev in order to convey a philosophical lesson that Cāṅgdev's *yoga* practice had not yet provided. Although the hagiographical stories about Cāṅgdev tend to depict his encounter with Jñāndev as a triumph of wisdom and *bhakti* over the egoism of yogic power, the poetic text of the *Cāṅgdevpāsaṣṭī* pertains more limitedly to the exposition of nondual philosophy. Of the four major compositions attributed to Jñāndev, the *Cāṅgdevpāsaṣṭī* has received the least attention from scholars and popular readers.

Gāthā

Near the end of the 19th century, Marathi literary scholars and devotees began to compile and publish the short and occasional songs (*abhaṅgas*) of the saint-poets that were scattered among the working notebooks (*bāḍas*) of Vārkarī *kīrtan* performers. The first of these collections (*gāthā*) of poetry attributed to Jñāndev appeared in 1891, and several different editions of the *Jñāndev Gāthā* have been published since then, all with slightly different sets of poems. C. Kiehnle's research on these compositions documented 1,250 different songs, of which 1,100 had been printed (Kiehnle, 1992, 126). The collection that is considered standard by followers of the Vārkarī tradition (the *Sakalasantagāthā* [Collection of Poetry of All the Saints]) contains around nine hundred poems. The wide variety of topics, stylistic differences, and multiple authorial signature tags (*mūdrikās*) contained among these songs has led most scholars to believe that the songs were composed by multiple authors, reflecting Jñāndev's outstanding reputation and the multiple traditions (especially the Vārkarīs and the Nāths) that revere him as a spiritual leader. The most common of the signature tags in the *Jñāndev Gāthā* are *jñāndev mhaṇe* (Jñāndev says) and *bāparakhumādevīvara* ([Our] Father, the husband of the goddess Rakhumāī/Rukmiṇī [i.e. Viṭṭhal]). The *Gāthā* songs deal with many topics: praising the glory of the Vārkarīs' sacred town Pandharpur, stories of Kṛṣṇa's childhood, allegorical dramatizations to teach spiritual messages, short homilies (*upadeś*) about spiritual virtues, and stylized conversations between Jñāndev and his *guru*. C. Kiehnle has dealt extensively with a set of relatively little-known songs attributed to Jñāndev that deal with *yoga* and tantric topics (see Kiehnle, 1997). The most famous and popular of Jñāndev's songs is the *Haripāṭh* (Recitation of [the Name of] God) – a 27-verse *abhaṅga* that is regularly recited at Vārkarī *kīrtans*, during pilgrimage, and at other events (see Vaudeville, 1969).

Bibliography

Abbott, J.E., & N.R. Godbole, *Stories of Indian Saints: A Translation of Mahipati's Marathi Bhaktavijaya*, Delhi, 1982.

Bahirat, B.P., *The Philosophy of Jñānadeva: As Gleaned from the Amṛtānubhava*, Delhi, 1984.

Bahirat, B.P., *Amṛtānubhava*, Bombay, 1963.

Baviskar, M., *Changdeopasasti: The Mystic Letter to Sri Changdeo*, Pune, 1981.

Bhagwat, R.K., *Sri Jnanadeva's Bhāvārtha Dīpikā: Otherwise Known as Jnāneshwari*, Madras, 1979.

Bhave, V.L., &s.G. Tuḷpule, *Mahārāṣṭra Sārasvat*, Mumbai, 6 1982.

Chitre, D., *Jñāndev's Anubhavamrut: The Immortal Experience of Being*, New Delhi, 1996.

Edwards, J.F., *Dnyāneshwar: The Out-Caste Brāhmin*, Poona, 1941.

Kiehnle, C., *Jñāndev Studies I–III*, Stuttgart, 1997.

Kiehnle, C. "Authorship and Redactorship of the Jñāndev *Gāthā*," in: R. McGregor, ed., *Devotional Literature in South Asia: Current Research 1985–1988*, Cambridge UK, 1992, 126–137.

Kripananda, *Jnāneshwar's Gītā: A Rendering of the Jnāneśhwarī*, Albany, 1989.

Lokapur, R.S., *The Jñāneśwarī: Text as Adopted by V.K. Rajwade*, Belgaum, 1995.

Madhava, *Amrutanubhav = The Nectar of Divine Experience*, Pune, 1981.

Pradhan, V.G., & H.M. Lambert, *Jnāneshvari (Bhāvārthadipikā)*, London, 1967.

Rajwade, V.K., *Śrījñāneśvarī*, Mumbai, 1977.

Ranade, R.D., *Jnaneshwar: The Guru's Guru*, Albany, 1994.

Ranade, R.D., *Pathway to God in Marathi Literature*, Bombay, 1961.

Shete, V.T., & R.C. Dhere, *Śrījñāneśvara Vividha Darśana: Naū Abhyāsakāñce Jñānadevavishayaka Vivecaka Lekha*, Pune, 1975.

Tulpule,s.G., *Classical Marāṭhī Literature: From the Beginning to A.D. 1818*, Wiesbaden, 1979.

Vaudeville, C., *L'Invocation: Le Haripath de Dnyandev*, Paris, 1969.

Wakankar, M., "System and History in Rajwade's 'Grammar' for the *Dnyaneswari* (1909)," in: M. Wakankar, ed., *Subalternity and Religion: The Prehistory of Dalit Empowerment in South Asia*, New York, 2010, 93–124.

Christian Novetzke & Jon Keune

Kabīr

In the 15th–16th centuries, there lived in Benares a poet-singer known as Kabīr (?–1518), weaver by trade and rebel in religious matters, who bequeathed to posterity a living tradition of singing his "truth" about worldly and divine questions and proposing a new, direct practice to experience extraworldly dimensions. For the last five hundred years, his poem-songs have enjoyed tremendous acclaim, locally and internationally, and are a source of inspiration and imitation. For many adherents to his views, he is a spiritual master (*guru*) and founder of a recognized community (*panth*); his poems have multiplied over centuries to become a living oral and written tradition under the name of Kabīr. However, Kabīr as a historical personality has to be seen against the religious background of his time and place. Tradition has preserved (and at the same time created) a number of details about his biography and person. Yet, whatever is known comes from the sources that constitute that very tradition. The dates of available manuscripts and the differences of language, style, and message that can be observed in them (even though they cannot be unambiguously dated and localized) demand that the historical Kabīr be methodologically distinguished from the image created by his followers and identified with the nondocumented historical Kabīr. At the present state of research, his message (and to a hypothetical degree, the historical Kabīr) can only be sketched as a profile of elements that, taken globally and comprehensively, add up to what characterizes the literary and religious figure Kabīr. If preference is given in this essay to the reconstruction as closely as possible of a historical Kabīr, this is neither to deny nor to underestimate the importance of Kabīr as a living tradition (on this debate, see Agrawal, 2010).

Kabīr's Time: Sants, *Bhakta*s, and Wandering Ascetics of Various Faiths

The 15th and 16th centuries were in North India a period during which religious movements expressed themselves in local languages to assert their own, often critical and anti-institutional, views of life and religion. Another source of new thoughts continued to be the increasing presence of Islam on the subcontinent. With the end of the dynasty of the Lodi and the battle of Panipat (1526), Bābūr – the central Asian conqueror – established the → Mughal dynasty, which reigned over India for the next three hundred years as the last empire before the British. This period corresponds to the time during which Kabīr's poem-songs started to be written down. During the rule of invading dynasties, the relations between locals and foreigners led not only to tension but also to mutual stimulation and exchange. This is particularly true for religious matters, especially among the communities who were not related to Brahmanical traditions and who tried to convey, in their own languages, their proper spiritual paths or to reassess their value, if they were from lower social backgrounds.

Important vectors for change and transmission were the itinerant religious specialists, mostly the ascetics, be they Muslim (*faqīr*) or Hindu (→ *sādhu, vairāgī, yogī*). The figure of Kabīr blurs theologically constructed boundaries; until today he has been seen as a Muslim by many Muslims and as a Hindu by many Hindus. Kabīr certainly shares ideas and practices with Sufis (which testifies to a field of interactions), such as an abstract way to qualify the divine *aparampāra/warā ʾal-warāʾ* (beyond the beyond/behind the behind); notions expressing the total dependence on or surrender to the divine, *prapatti/tawakkul*; or, on the level of practice, the ways to communicate, *japa/ḏikr* (recitation; see also Lawrence, 1987, 369).

However, the Sufis express themselves in a Persian/Arabic idiom, whereas Kabīr's background is Hindi/Sanskrit. His vocabulary – such as *cakra, bindu*, and *manas* – inscribes him into a Sanskritic environment and associates him with the worldviews that correlate with such terms (e.g with the Haṭha → Yoga tradition). He shares with the Vaiṣṇava the love for the name or the many names of the divine and the intense love for or the belief in divine → grace (*anugraha*). Kabīr is steeped in local and folk traditions (e.g. *viraha*, the pain experienced when separated from the beloved, and the many allusions to rural life and local images). His language, references, and metaphors confirm that Kabīr participated in any and all surrounding idioms. "→ Sant" is a title or appellation for holy men of this period who shared enough common traits to make them distinct from others (Schomer & McLeod, 1987); yet it is a movement for which a high degree of permeability among various religious strands (today classified by categories such as Vaiṣṇavism, Buddhism, Sufism, Nāthism [see → Nāth Sampradāya]), Sikhism is typical. The Sants, also known as *nirguṇī* poets, claim that religious experience belongs to all and can be expressed in one's own local language; experience prevails over institutionalized forms: it is an inner, revealed experience of a nonqualified (→ *nirguṇa*) extraworldly entity or absolute beyond word.

Kabīr's Life in Sources and Traditions

Whereas the various proposed dates of Kabīr's birth are a disputed matter, most scholars agree that he died in 1518. Sources of information are scarce. In the early poems attributed to him, there is almost no information in this respect. He is quoted two times in the *Ā'īn-i Akbarī* (1598) – a chronic of Akbar's reign – by Abū al-Fażl ʿAllāmī, referring specifically to his spiritual perspective (Vaudeville, 1974; Mitchell, 1999). Otherwise, most of the information regarding his life derives from later hagiographical sources. Separating facts from legends in hagiographical literature is a provisional approach to finding the historical Kabīr; however, for the time being, it is the only option.

There is no unanimity about the following questions: Did Kabīr have a master, and if yes, was it → Rāmānanda (for a discussion on the figure of Rāmānanda, see Agrawal, 2009) or Šayḫ Taqī? Was he Muslim or was he of Brahmanical origin and found as a baby to be raised by a Muslim woman? Most probably he was a weaver (Julāhā) who lived a family life with two children in Benares/Kāśī. Though he belonged to a Muslim community, Kabīr positioned himself outside any religious affiliation other than the companionship of the Sants and *bhagat*s – that is, of devotees of a deity addressed as *bhagavān*/*bhagat* and venerated with an attitude of → *bhakti*. He is depicted as publicly singing poems to awaken in people their "religious" awareness – that is, awareness of their own dependence on the divine source and force in a world seen as fragile, painful, and transient. He was outspoken, if not provocative, and he often ridiculed Brahmans and *mullā*s along with their institutions. Characteristic of this intellectual position is a search for something new and in opposition to older traditions, privileging an apophatic approach to the divine (i.e. talking of the divine in negation). This is formally corroborated by the fact that 1 out of 18 verses in the *Kabīr Granthāvalī* contains a negation (stated by Callewaert, 2000b, 111). P. Agrawal (2010) insists on portraying Kabīr as an individualistic thinker, important among the merchant societies of his time, which contributed to the spread of his knowledge.

Legends explain what the Indian traditions deemed worthy to retain about his life; hence they show primarily how *they* wanted to see Kabīr. The most important hagiographies are the *Kabīr Parcāī* of Anantdās, the *Bhaktamāla* of Nābhādās, and the *Bhaktamāl* of Raghavadās. Sufi stories are later and may be found in Persian sources, such as the *Ḫazīna al-āṣafiyya* (A Treasury of the Pure Ones; 1864–1865) and the *Taḏkira-yi awliyā'-i Hind* (A Remembrance of the Friends of God of India; late 19th cent.).

In spite of their legendary character, early narratives about the life of Kabīr, such as the *Kabīr Parcaī* of Anantdās, are a rich source of information. On the one hand, they do contain factual information (habits, descriptions, and dates) that can be compared with and confirmed by other historical sources, and, on the other hand, they contain material that can be used to understand how a figure like Kabīr was perceived and integrated in the more general picture of religious backgrounds of the time. Anantdās produced his work around 1600, hence it illustrates the reception history of Kabīr at an early stage (see Callewaert, 2000a; Lorenzen, 1992; Mitchell, 1999). How did Anantdās, a member of the → Rāmānandī tradition, depict Kabīr for the generations to come? Three examples may illustrate how the narrator captures Kabīr's religious position and frames it in a way acceptable to his own beliefs.

The first example shows Kabīr as a highly advanced spiritual personality. He was often put on trial by Brahmans and *qāžī*s (upholders of Islamic law) who wished to destroy his power and influence; in the sections 10–12 of the *Kabīr Parcaī*, Hari (another name of → Viṣṇu) himself, with the help of an *apsarā* (Skt. *apsaras*, a celestial female seducer [see → *gandharva*s and *apsarases*]), tests the firmness of Kabīr's faith. The *apsarā*, however, has to report to Hari that no bewitchment had hold on Kabīr, however hard she tried:

> If the sun were to rise in the west, if the mountain were to tremble, if fire were to become cold, if the polar star were to move to the south, even then Kabīr wouldn't lose his wisdom. (*KaPa.* 11.2; trans. Lorenzen, 1992, 121)

This steadfastness, described in a traditional manner known to the audience, is rewarded with the full vision of Hari in his most divine form, who invites Kabīr to make his demands. Again, in what is clearly a topos of the true *bhakta*, the latter declines all wishes, being satisfied by the divine vision.

The second example illustrates Kabīr's supposed encounter with the Muslim emperor Sikander Lodī. Brahmans and *mullās* take advantage of his visit to Benares to denounce Kabīr's bad behavior – namely, his not taking into account religious differences and hierarchies. The furious Sikander Lodī proceeds to test Kabīr, the weaver, who has renounced his tradition and opted for the admiration of → Rām alone. Yet, Kabīr's power is such that no trial succeeds (drowning, trampling by elephant, etc.), and Sikander finally falls at his feet in admiration.

> I see Ram in all living beings. Without bhakti to Hari, no work can prosper. I recognized the guru and Gobinda through devotion. That is why Sikander could do nothing to me. (*KaPa.* 9.15; trans. Lorenzen, 1992, 115)

Kabīr's *bhakti* is shown as a weapon stronger than that of the Muslim emperor.

The last example of a traditional account depicts the quarrel between Muslims and Hindus at the time of Kabīr's death. Both religious groups wished to receive the dead body of Kabīr, either to burry or to burn it, in accordance with their respective beliefs and rites. In this case, Anantdās is in accordance with what we know from Kabīr's verses, as his narration ridicules the greed and the attachment to the body of the two groups. Under the heap of flowers brought by his followers (Hindu and Muslim) to honor and cover the dead Kabīr, no body was left to be disputed.

> When Kabīr became an immortal, he did not abandon his body. Kabīr left this world taking his body with him. The devotees were astonished. When they saw the flowers [were all that remained], they went home. (*KaPa.* 13.5; trans. Lorenzen, 1992, 126)

Among the many miracles and powers ascribed to Kabīr, this last event underlines Kabīr's non-affiliation with any canonized tradition.

The numerous and well-known legends confirm how admired and respected Kabīr was, not only among the *bhagat*s but also across a wider audience. Already by the late 16th century, there were so many songs attributed to him that it is doubtful that they all stem from him. This implies that there was a wide enough audience and group of followers who liked his poems and identified with them to such a degree that they could compose in this fashion and in his name.

The Kabīr texts display many incongruities in the eyes of posterity: he is a Muslim yet a Hindu; he is a *vairāgī* yet a householder; and he lives in and for the absolute yet speaks of Hari, Raḥīm, Rām, and Govind. This probably simply confirms the fact that behind Kabīr's poem-songs, there are many authors at work, or that Kabīr changed his ideas during his lifetime or did not mind taking perspectives that appear contradictory, from today's standpoint.

Singing and Composing: From Performance to Written Collections

Kabīr has never *written* anything but composed and rendered his poem-songs orally, most probably accompanied by music, much in the style of the oral traditions that exist up to the present. As is often the case with teachers of his time, Kabīr's words were written down *after* his time and have grown over the centuries into large collections of manuscripts.

Before being written down, these popular poem-songs traveled with the religious and commercial itinerants and during this process incorporated local elements from the regions through which they passed, be it on the level of language or of content. The poem-songs were also imitated by singers who must have found this style attractive. The oral tradition is likely to have been broader than what has been written down. The question of authenticity remains a preoccupation for scholars (see e.g. Hawley, 1988, on authorship). Various scholars have shown that most of the songs that are appreciated today by Kabīr lovers are not found in the older manuscripts. The extremes go from attributing just a few lines to Kabīr to accepting all that comes under his name.

The most important collections are the following:

1. the *Bījak*, which has three different recensions, associated with different branches of the → Kabīrpanth (earliest manuscript dated 1805);
2. the Punjab collection or *Ādigranth/Gurū Granth Sāhib* collection, as part of the holy script of the Sikh religion (1604) containing 243 *sākhīs* and 221 *padas* attributed to Kabīr (see below); and
3. the so-called Western or Rajasthani recension, collected from the *Pañcvāṇī* (Songs of the Five) of the Dādūpanth (see → Dādū Dayāl), also known as the *Kabīr Granthāvalī*, containing 403 *padas*, 59 *aṅgas*, and some *ramainīs* (see below).

(For a discussion on the differences among the three collections, see Hess, 1987; Callewaert, 2000b.) The better-known editions identified as *Kabīr Granthāvalī* are by Shyamasundardasa (1928), P. Tivari (crit. ed.; 1961), and by C. Vaudeville (1982).

The Millenium Kabīr Vāṇī of W. Callewaert (2000b) contains 593 *padas* from manuscripts dated between 1570 and 1681 (including details about the manuscripts and their dates and concordances). W. Callewaert's edition is based on the earliest-known manuscripts, hence the constituted text comes closest to the period of Kabīr. The earliest documents are from 1570, and the entire collection testifies to what was deemed important in the name of Kabīr by the late 17th century. This collection does not contain the most famous Kabīr songs of today.

To call Kabīr's compositions "poem-songs" means to say that they are composed and sung in rhymes, with *pada* and *dohā* as their most frequent forms. In a *dohā*, each verse is composed of two rhyming lines of equal length. The *dohā* are called *sākhī* (or in the *Gurū Granth Sāhib, saloku*) – "witness" – and more often than not have a didactic purpose. The *padas* are short and composed quite loosely in a metrical system but mostly set to a musical melody, *rāga*, with a refrain, the *ṭek* (in the *Gurū Granth Sāhib* called *rahāu*). *Padas* express ideas and convey convictions in a simple manner, close to the folk-song tradition.

Both styles – *dohā* and *padas* – were also used by → Sahajiyās and Jains for their propagation of doctrines (Vaudeville, 1974, 54). Certain poems are called *sabds* (*sabads* or *śabda*) and *ramainīs*. *Śabda* is the name for *padas* in the *Bījak* collection, whereas *ramainīs* are satirical or didactic poems in the *caupāī* meter (quatrain of two identical lines). All types of verses can be rendered in the context of musical and prayer gatherings, such as → *kīrtan* and → *bhajan* singing.

Kabīr (and Sant poets in general) uses common language in the conviction that religious and social ideas should be understood by all. However, sometimes Kabīr's style can be highly allusive, complex (if not obscure), and riddled with metaphorical expressions. Some poems use a cryptic language for which a contextualized background is necessary, for example those containing Nāth *yoga* references. The *Bījak* contains poems using the so-called inverted language (*ulaṭī bhāṣā*) operating on a nondiscursive or nonrational level. These poems act as awakeners by puzzling the listeners, who are denied their habitual mode of understanding the world.

Whereas in the *Bījak* and in the *Gurū Granth Sāhib* the poems are not thematically classified, the Rajasthani recension (e.g. the *Sarvāṅgī*, a compilations of verses made in the Dādūpanth) orders them in chapters by subject: *Guru kau Aṅga* (Chapter on the *Guru*), *Viraha kau Aṅga* (Chapter on Separation), and so on. Another mode of classification is by *rāga*, as for example in the *Gurū Granth Sāhib*.

Each *dohā* and *pada* contains the "signature" found at the end of the poem and known as *bhaṇitā* or *mudrikā* (stamp). This serves to identify the author and is a general practice in northern and central India from the 15th century onward. Many an author must have put the name of a famous poet in their composition in order to show affiliation with the tradition.

Kabīr's language is mostly characterized as the idiom of the *sādhus* (traveling ascetics) known as *saddhukkaṛī bhāṣā*. It shows linguistic influences from Punjabi, Rajashtani, Avadhi, Braj, and Khari Boli, which again speaks of the traveling of the poems and the local compositions of imitators of Kabīr's style.

Traits, Elements, and Perspectives in Kabīr's Compositions

What then did Kabīr tell his contemporaries that impressed them to the point that they started imitating his words and views?

Given the peculiarities of the sources and of the tradition, the only way (even though subjective and hypothetical) to come to know Kabīr is through a content analysis of the texts attributed to him. The emphasis on a profile deduced from opinions, doctrines, stylistic peculiarities, and patterns of thought and expression allows us to create the image of Kabīr as a distinct literary figure.

Such a profile cannot but be provisional, and new manuscript evidence would entail that it changes. A separate profile could be made according to regional, linguistic, and chronological criteria. In order to present here a comprehensive picture of Kabīr, the three main collections are consulted. The following passages have been selected as representative of Kabīr's ideas and style. Providing the full context of the quotes would require an extensive literary presentation, which is not possible in this essay.

(1) Kabīr often resorts to the vocative, especially in the *Bījak*, in order to draw attention. His wish to attract people also indicates his aim to teach. Hence a fundamental element of his profile is that he *had* an audience and *wanted* to have one.

"Oh Saint, as an awakened one, don't fall asleep" (*Bījak, śabda* 2). This quote also addresses those who follow the path of spiritual awakening and asks them not to be satisfied (fall asleep) with whatever achievement they made on the path. Kabīr's popularity is assured because he knows how to speak to the people and uses idiomatic expressions referring to the daily life and images known to the folk. Kabīr was a poet but not in the sense of a classical poet (*kavi*). More spontaneous, his rhymes are meant to be heard or sung and remembered.

(2) Feelings are often in the foreground when he conveys convictions, though there is no systematized treatise on theology or philosophy. Singing and reciting are the modes of transmission, public and oral, yet any religious endeavor is in vain if not done on the basis of an inner realization. Kabīr is not a poet who describes nature but a spiritual master who teaches what and how to believe. The singing of the holy name (*nāma*) is useless, even if it is a joyful praise, if the reality it stands for has not been realized – the devotee would still be among the ordinary people, caught up in the cycle of death and birth.

> Singing padas delights the heart, reciting sākhīs is a joy, but if you know not the Reality [behind] the Name, Yama's noose will fall on your neck! (*KaG.2.* 33.5; trans. Vaudeville, 1974, 309)

(3) Kabīr lived in a world in which he did not find much happiness, and he turned inward to gain peace. His spiritual experience was deeply inspired by his love for Rām, a name used to designate his unqualified god/absolute (other names include Hari, Govind, and Nirañjan). His Rām is sometimes simply described as the *karatā*, the doer, who is perfect. Sometimes he rather saw him as having neither face nor forehead, nor form of any kind; he is more subtle than the fragrance of flowers. Yet he is seen as indispensable to life:

> No happiness, neither at day nor at night, not even in dream, Kabīr says, separated from Rām, no happiness, neither in light nor in shadow. (*KaG.2.* 3.4)

(4) Kabīr had a personal relation with this Rām. Though often employing yogic language and referring to Tantra-inspired methods of inner transformation, Kabīr was first of all a *bhakta*, in the sense that he believed in Rām and counted and depended on his love and favor/grace.

> I was drowning but was saved [when] the wave of the master rose [i.e. his grace]; when I saw the boat falling into pieces, I jumped outside. (*KaG.2.* 1.10)

> Kabīr, what good deed can you do, if Rām comes not to your help? (*KaG.2.* 8.3; Vaudeville, 1974, 195)

(5) Kabīr was a religious critic. He did not like Brahmans and *mullās* or any form of institutionalized religion symbolized by buildings and rites. He was also not lenient with *yogīs* and *sādhus*, or for that matter with hypocrites who saw religion as only a matter of outside insignias, and he was opposed to religion entailing hierarchical social structures or language exclusivity. Sacrificing animals in the name of religion or venerating statues was not what he understood as a spiritual path:

> Killing living beings, they make pūjā to stones, they have no knowledge. (*Bījak, śabda* 4)

In the same vein, he mocks those attributing Brahmanhood to birth rather than to qualification earned by meditation and inner realization:

> In the womb, no clan, no caste, the entire creation comes from Brahman's seed… if a brāhmiṇī has given you birth as a brāhmaṇ,

then why did you not come another way… says Kabīr, the one who meditates [the] brahman, this one is named brāhmaṇ among us. (*ĀG.* 324.7)

(6) For Kabīr, religious matters are based on an inner revelation or experience (*anubhāva*). Better than the term "religion," the terms "spirituality" or "mystic" describe his search of an intense experience of the divine. The inner experience is central to his songs and a recurrent element of his sayings. It often stands in contrast to later appropriations that framed his sayings in a more institutionalized manner. For Kabīr, only few have realized what they preach, yet as long as this is not achieved, their preaching is meaningless.

> I've seen many Muslim masters and saints, they study the holy book; they teach [many] remedies to the disciples, [but] what about this same knowledge inside them? (*Bījak, śabda* 4)

(7) The spiritual path is very difficult and meant for courageous followers who are ready to give up ordinary attractions:

> Such one cannot be found who burns down his own house, Who knocks down the five Fellows [e.g. the senses] and remains absorbed in Rām. (*KaG.2.* 5.1; trans. Vaudeville, 1974, 187)

> Kabīr, the lane is narrow and the Mind a nimble Thief: absorb yourself in Hari's praise, let nothing else enter your mind. (*KaG.2.* 29.10; trans. Vaudeville, 1974, 292)

The road of spiritual realization is difficult because it demands the control of the senses and the mind. In the quoted verses, the second line ends with a eulogy to the total absorption in Hari or Rām, which is the sole means of assuring control over the senses and the mind.

(8) Humans need to be guided in life, but the true master is the one revealed inside oneself, as the *sadguru*, the real master. Without form, the true master appears to his beloved revealed in *śabda* – the word beyond word, the revealed word. When the arrow (the word as sharp as an arrow) hits the devotee, he is changed forever:

> The true master is a real hero, who sent śabda like an arrow, the moment he succeeded, I fell to the ground, deeply wounded inside. (*KaG.2.* 1.9)

(9) To be separated from the divine means utter suffering, which is expressed with the concept of *viraha* (separation). *Viraha* is as sharp as the bite of a snake; the pain is intolerable, and the only remedy for it lies with the divine itself. Comparing this experience to the suffering of a woman who waits for her husband or lover to come back is a well-known idiom. Many lines express the deep longing of the abandoned lover or wife (the soul?) waiting to unite with the beloved (god, the divine?):

> The abandoned one stands on the road, running she asks the traveller, say a word from my beloved, when will he come and meet. (*KaG.2.* 3.5)

(10) On the level of practice, in order to remain in or with the absolute, Kabīr favors the recitation of the name of the divine (*japa*) as well as the audition of the *śabda*, the word revealed inside the *bhakta*.

> Saying continuously you, to me I do not remain, having sacrificed in rounds, [I] became sacrifice, wherever I look, there is you. (*KaG.2.* 2.9)

> My spirit memorizes Rām, my spirit is only Rām, now that my spirit became Rām, before whom should I bow my head. (*KaG.2.* 2.8)

> In the three worlds, tilak [mark on the forehead, alluding here to meditation] on Rām is the essence, the simple Kabīr, has given his forehead and his beauty has become without end. (*KaG.2.* 2.3)

Sumiraṇa (*smaraṇa*), the constant remembrance of the divine or living in the rhythm of the divine, is another central part of Kabīr's spiritual practice. Related to this keeping in memory, breathing in rhythm also participates in the capacity to make life identical to Rām *japa*. This intense practice may have given Kabīr the aura to function as a model for his audience.

(11) To provoke or awaken his audience from wasting their lives in blind beliefs and customs, Kabīr used a riddled language, not as a coded language that only insiders would understand but as a nonrational statement to indicate the limits of our understanding of the world:

> He runs without two feet everywhere, without eyes he sees the world… The singer never and nowhere sings, the mute sings day and night. (*Bījak, śabda* 2)

(12) Kabīr can be very provocative, which is shown here by his desire to die in Maghar. He cherished a city that had a very bad reputation

(Maghar) and despised a city as cherished by Hindus as Kāśī, especially at the time of death. This point illustrates Kabīr's opposition to Hindu or Muslim superstitions.

> I spoilt my whole life [in] the city of Śiva, at time of death, awaken, I come to Magahar. (*ĀG.* 326.15)

(13) For the one who experienced inwardly the divine, the world has no impact.

> He gave [me] a lamp of oil, a never ending light, the bargaining is done, I will not return to the market. (*KaG.2.* 1.15)

That he will not return to the market may well mean that he steps out of the cycle of lives, alluding, on the one hand, to his belief in → *karma* and → *saṃsāra* and, on the other, to the belief in → *jīvanmukti* (liberation in life).

The sketchy profile outlined by these quotes does not have the freshness and flavor of their oral and sung version. Kabīr has been admired and has been a source of inspiration for many. Even if such a profile includes traits common to a period and its religious movements as a whole, it is exceptional and unique enough to support the assumption of the existence of a real person who incorporated most of it. Kabīr was not only a poet-singer for unprivileged lower castes (as contemporary subaltern studies would have it, though I do agree that he and his Sant friends allow us insight into yet unknown, local, and popular faiths) but also a fresh inspiration for society at large, as is testified by the widespread appropriation of his thoughts and words. His views, protests, and simple "truths voicing" radiate far beyond any particular class. Hence Kabīr is central for the understanding of the composite nature of religious traditions of his time. His work functions as a true mirror for Sant traditions with all their local varieties, shared experiences, and stands as a landmark of innovative spiritualities.

(Unless stated otherwise, translations are by the author.)

Bibliography

Agrawal, P., "In Search of Ramanand: The Guru of Kabir and Others," in: I. Banerjee-Dube & S. Dube, eds., *From Ancient to Modern: Religion, Power, and Community in India*, New Delhi, 2009, 135–170.

Agrawal, P., *Akath Kahānī Prem kī: Kabīr kī Kavitā aur Unkā Samay*, New Delhi, 2010 (Hind.).

Callewaert, W., *The Hagiographies of Anantadās: The Bhakti Poets of North India*, Richmond, 2000a.

Callewaert, W., *The Millenium Kabīr Vāṇī*, New Delhi, 2000b.

Callewaert, W., *Śrī Guru Granth Sāhib: With Complete Index*, 2 vols., Delhi, 1996.

Hawley, J.S., *Three Bhakti Voices: Mirabai, Surdas, and Kabir in Their Times and Ours*, New Delhi, 2005.

Hawley, J.S., "Author and Authority in the Bhakti Poetry of North India," *JAS* 47/2, 1988, 269–290.

Hess, L., & S. Singh, *The Bijak of Kabir*, Delhi, 1983, [2]2002.

Hess, L., "Three Kabir Collections: A Comparative Study," in: K. Schomer & W.H. MacLeod, eds., *The Sants: Studies in the Devotional Tradition of India*, Berkeley, 1987, 111–141.

Horstmann, M., ed., *Images of Kabīr*, Delhi, 2002.

Lawrence, B., "The Sant Movement and North Indian Sufis," in: K. Schomer & W.H. McLeod, eds., *The Sants: Studies in the Devotional Tradition of India*, Berkeley, 1987, 359–373.

Lorenzen, D.N., *Kabir Legends and Antanta-das's Kabir Parachai*, Delhi, 1992.

Mitchell, S., *Traditional Biographies of Kabīr*, Ann Arbor, 1999.

Rupakala, S.B., *Nābhādās, Śrī Bhaktamāl*, Lucknow, 1969 (Hind.).

Schomer, K., & W.H. McLeod, eds., *The Sants: Studies in the Devotional Tradition of India*, Berkeley, 1987.

Shyamasundaradasa (Śyāmasundaradāsa), ed., *Kabīr Granthāvali*, Prayag, 1928, repr. 1951 (Hind.).

Singh, S., ed., *Kabīr bījak*, Allahabad, 1972 (Hind.).

Tivari (Tivārī), P., ed., *Kabīr Granthāvalī*, Allahabad, 1989, repr. 1961 (Hind.).

Vaudeville, C., *Kabīr*, Oxford, 1974; repr. *A Weaver Named Kabir*, Delhi, 1993.

Vaudeville, C., ed., *Kabīr Vāṇī: Recension occidentale*, Pondicherry, 1982 (Hind.).

Vaudeville, C., *Au cabaret de l'amour*, Paris, 1959.

Westcott, G.H., *Kabir and the Kabir Panth*, Calcutta, 1907.

Maya Burger

Lallā

Lallā (also known as Lalleśvarī or Lal Ded) is a 14th-century Śaiva mystic poet from → Kashmir. Even though Lallā is an integral part of Kashmiri language and culture, no reference to her exists in the medieval Sanskrit literature. Jonarāja's *Rājataraṅgiṇī*, a chronicle of the period when Lallā lived, does not mention her at all. The reason for this neglect could be that the medieval chronicles primarily focused on kings and the political intrigues surrounding them. Lallā, however, lived in the countryside, and it was the common people who treasured her verses. Lallā is thus more a part of the Kashmiri folk imagination than the elite Brahmanical tradition.

Fig. 1: "Lallā" (an intaglio print by Joseph Singer, 2006).

Life and Legends

We have only orally transmitted legends about Lallā's life, as she was a part of the daily repertoire in most Kashmiri households for centuries. She was born into a Brahman family somewhere between 1317 and 1320 in Pandrenthan, Kashmir (Kaul, 1973). She was most probably educated at home as was the custom in those days, especially in Brahman families. She was given in marriage to Nica Bhaṭ of Pampore at a young age. Legends speak about her mother-in-law as a tyrant who filled her married life with suffering. She would serve her a thin layer of rice on top of a small round stone to make it seem she was being served a large portion. Lallā would quietly eat whatever she was served without protest. Some legends describe her marriage as not being consummated, while others say she was a disobliging wife.

According to one legend, Lallā walked to a nearby river in Zinypor village before dawn every day to fetch a pitcher of water as was the custom in those days. But instead of directly filling the pitcher from a nearby river and returning home, she would cross the river to visit the shrine of Naṭa Keśava → Bhairava. Suspecting her of infidelity, her husband quietly followed her one day on her morning ritual. He found her sitting alone by the riverbank in deep contemplation. Enraged at this diversion, he went home. As she returned with the pitcher of water on her head, he confronted her angrily and smashed the pitcher with a stick. Even though the pitcher broke, according to the legend, the water stayed miraculously intact on her head. Lallā calmly went inside the house and poured the water into smaller vessels until all were full. She took the leftover water and threw it outside, where a pond was formed. Later on, the pond was named Lalla Trag (Lallā's Pond; Koul, 1921, 321). The incident marks the time of her renunciation when she left her home and became a wandering ascetic.

Lallā's Verses: The Text

Lallā's compositions, originally uttered in old Kashmiri, come to us in a form that is fairly modern, except for occasional archaic expressions with obscure or unknown meaning. Each verse, consisting of four lines, usually stands as an independent unit, though there are a few in a question – answer format – one verse stating the question and the next the answer. In 1920 Sir G. Grierson and L.D. Barnett put together the first scholarly collection of verses in the West, which was based on two manuscripts written in the Sharada alphabet of Kashmir, a 60-verse collection translated into Sanskrit by Rājānaka Bhāskara about two hundred years earlier, and an oral recension from an old Brahman named Dharmadās Darveś, who recited these verses as part of his family tradition. Since it has not been possible to date the two manuscripts on which the Grierson collection is partly based, it has yet to be determined for how long the transmission of Lallā's poetry was exclusively oral.

As is common with any oral tradition, it is hard to imagine that her verses come to us without any change. The additions, deletions, and re-inscriptions were probably minimal because of a very strong oral tradition in medieval Kashmir where some Brahman families specialized in the rote memorization of oral or written texts passed on from the teacher to disciples, or within the family from one generation to another. G. Grierson and L.D. Barnett note that the "respect for the authoress and the metrical form of the songs have preserved a great many archaic forms of expression" (Grierson & Barnett, 1920, 7). For this reason, the Grierson collection of 109 verses is regarded as the most authentic of Lallā's verses. In the 1930s, A. Koul published 75 additional verses in the *Indian Antiquary*. Later collections have primarily relied on these two sources.

Lallā is truly an integral part of Kashmiri language, literature, and culture and has been honored as the first modern Kashmiri poet. The linguistic and philological importance of Lallā's compositions in the history of Kashmiri language is attributed to the fact that her verses represent "a significant landmark in the linguistic transition from old to modern Kashmiri" (Kaul, 1973, 61). Some scholars have even written that her verses have made the Kashmiri language suitable for philosophical thought, as all such writing during her time was in Sanskrit, the language in which only the elite were proficient. In order to convey highly esoteric ideas to common people, Lallā introduced terms and concepts originally absent from the Kashmiri language. The richness of her language, the turn of phrases, and the metaphors she uses have become standard expressions in modern Kashmiri.

Inner Journey

A tapestry of Lallā's inner journey can be created by closely reading her verses that record her experiences. Most of her verses contain vivid metaphors without resorting to any explanation, and it is left to the reader to make connections and suggestively experience their import. The verses can be divided into three groups – the first group deals with the beginning of her spiritual quest, the second group represents her experiences with sustained introspective contemplation, and in the third group of verses, she turns her attention outward as she takes on the role of a teacher in order to teach others about the nature of limited knowledge and the means to overcome it.

In the initial stages of her journey, Lallā depicts the worldly life as a river that she needs to cross in order to reach the other shore. She has yet to prepare herself physically and mentally for the journey. She compares her weak will to an "untwisted rope" that is not strong enough to pull the "boat" she is riding. Her novice self is like "a shop without a lock in the midst of the marketplace" and as such an easy target for worldly desires that can rob her of her aspiration to move forward on her path. In a verse, she describes her body as a "cauldron" full of sensory impressions that tie her to the world. In yet another verse, she compares her body to a house and her sense organs to its doors and windows that must be kept shut in order for her to stay focused on her practice. Her scattered attention is like the "water oozing from unbaked clay saucers" and her restless mind like a horse galloping away from one thought to another. She must discipline her "mindhorse" in order to move forward on her quest. In a verse, she says,

I gently lament for you.
O Mind, you are in love with illusion.
Not a shadow of this worldly splendor will
accompany you.
Oh, why do you forget your real nature? (Kak,
2007, v. 5)

Lallā seems to have some awareness of the social construction of gender. She says she came to the world with the hope to realize her full potential. However, the ginner and the carder of society reduce her to a miserable state and turn her into utility-full fine yarn to be hung on the weaver's loom. Thus, she says,

I, Lallā, set out hoping to bloom
like a cotton flower.
The ginner and the carder gave me hard blows.
After the spinner spun me into fine yarn,
I was stretched on the loom/in the weaver's
shop.

When the washerman dashed me
on a slab of stone,
rubbing me with much soap and washing soda
and the tailor cut me into bits with scissors,
I, Lallā, attained supreme bliss. (Kak, 2007, vv. 13–14)

In the above verses, the first is a reflection on the society's role in shaping her identity, and the second refers to her own agency that enables her to work toward her emancipation. Lallā compares this shift to the woven material passing from the weaver's loom into the hands of the washerman, who washes it thoroughly, and the tailor, who cuts it into bits. Both the washerman and tailor symbolically represent different aspects of her higher self that guide her as she frees herself from the social conditioning. Lallā the daughter, Lallā the daughter-in-law, and Lallā the wife are torn into shreds as she forges a new identity that is not confined to socially prescribed modes of behavior.

The path that Lallā chooses for herself is not easy to follow. She has to constantly remind herself of the transitory nature of worldly existence in order to stay steadfast on her path. She exercises rigorous self-discipline and renounces all sensory pleasures as she turns inward. In a world bustling with activity all around her, Lallā strives to be detached.

As a wandering ascetic who rejects all social conventions, she is frequently subject to ridicule and abuse. Lallā develops a thick skin for insults and abuses that are hurled at her, and she learns not to lose her equanimity. Thus, she says,

I endured verbal abuse and slander.
Scandals broke out
about my past and present.
I am Lallā
and my yearning never stopped.
When I achieved my goal,
nothing affected me. (Kak, 2007, v. 20)

A story about Lallā relates how street urchins would sometimes hurl insults at her. Once a kindhearted shopkeeper, a cloth merchant, scolds them for their behavior and sends them away. Lallā calmly asks the shopkeeper to take a long piece of cloth, cut it into two equal parts, and weigh the parts separately. Then she drapes one piece on her left shoulder and the second piece on her right shoulder and goes on her way. As soon as someone calls her a bad name, she ties a knot in the piece on one shoulder, and when someone is respectful toward her she ties a knot in the piece on her other shoulder. In the evening she brings back the two pieces of cloth to the shopkeeper and asks him to weigh them separately once again – both weigh exactly as they had before. She thus demonstrates to the shopkeeper that she is unaffected by either respect shown to her or insults thrown at her just as the two pieces of cloth weigh the same irrespective of the number of good or bad knots tied into them (Koul, 1921, 306).

Relationship with the Śaiva Tradition

Lallā's verses reveal her deep knowledge of the esoteric practices of → Kashmir Śaivism. She was initiated into Śaiva → *yoga* at a young age by Siddha Śrī Kaṇṭh, and through her sincere practice, it is said, she soon surpassed even her teacher. Since the esoteric Śaiva teachings were imparted only to a select few during her time, Lallā is the first woman we know of who openly spoke about these practices to common people.

We cannot forget that her verses were addressed to common people in the countryside. For this reason, Lallā used metaphors and similes from everyday life that were directly accessible to the common people. Her verses also reflect her awareness of the mixed audience that she was addressing. Accordingly, some of her verses speak about the need for devotion to → Śiva, and then there are others that describe Śiva as the transcendental reality that permeates the physical reality, and yet others focus on the need to do away entirely with the duality of all kinds in order to find a totally new space for the actualizing self, which is beyond thought constructs.

The Kashmiri Śaivas describe the ultimate reality as pure consciousness that is the fundamental ground of both the subjective as well as the objective reality. → Liberation means to realize one's own nature (*svasvabhāva*) as pure consciousness. The *Śivasūtra* point out that the individual consciousness is imprisoned in the world that is created out of thought constructs. The self gets attached to the material reality, which is dependent on the world of sense objects. Becoming attached, it is affected by states of pleasure and pain, which create impressions that further bind the self to a world that appears divided and separate. The first step toward realizing self-knowledge involves getting rid of the ego consciousness or "I-ness" and opening up to the Śiva consciousness. This stage is reflected in Lallā's verses, which focus on the purification of her thoughts and actions as she slowly cultivates an attitude of detachment and turns within. She is filled with intense yearning and love for the object of her quest. She "suffers the fire of love" as she awakens the Śiva within her. She conveys the experience of "awakening her darling" by using vivid images of "grinding" the heart in the "mortar of love," and "burning" and "roasting" it, and "tasting" it herself.

> I ground my heart in the mortar of love.
> Evil thoughts left me
> and I became calm.
> I burned and roasted it
> and tasted it myself.
> How do I know
> if this practice will let me live or die?
> (Kak, 2007, v. 18)

The love experienced with so much intensity is not the egoistical or narcissistic love but rather the love for the boundless reality within her. In the fire of this love, Lallā forges her mind and body. She has momentary glimpses of the bliss of communion with Śiva. This experience prepares her for more advanced stages of her practice. In a verse, she says,

> When I was attached to the self,
> you remained hidden from me.
> Time passed as I searched for you.
> When I saw you within –
> you and I were united
> in ecstasy.
> (Kak, 2007, v. 32)

She describes Śiva or the higher self as the substratum of the phenomenal reality and compares it to salt dissolved in water. Just as it is not possible to see the dissolved salt, so it is impossible, from a limited perspective, to experience the higher self as the basis of reality. As the water evaporates, it leaves behind the salt; similarly, contemplation on the self when worldly desires and preoccupations are renounced leads to the realization of the higher self. In order to clarify the relationship of the higher self to the self, Lallā uses the metaphor of water and its two other forms as they appear in nature: ice and snow. As the clouds in the sky dispel, and the sun reveals its face, both ice and snow melt and turn into water, even though ice and snow both have their own unique properties as well as modes of existence. In other words, when the individual consciousness realizes its oneness with the higher self, the subject–object duality is erased, and the higher self, which is the quintessential nature of both, is revealed in its fullness.

> Cold changes water into ice or snow.
> Discernment shows the three different states
> are not really different.
> When the sun of consciousness shines,
> the plurality is dissolved into oneness.
> The universe appears throughout permeated
> with Śiva. (Kak, 2007, v. 63)

In yet another verse, Lallā captures the continuity between the self and the higher self in the image of Śiva in the form of a net subtly permeating the entire phenomenal world. People might differ on the basis of gender, caste, or religious creed, but all are permeated with the higher self or Śiva consciousness, which is like the bright sun that shines equally everywhere.

In a few verses, Lallā makes reference to a specific practice in the → Kashmir Śaiva tradition that revolves around controlling the *prāṇaśakti* (vital breath). This method of meditation involves watching the inhalation (*apāna*) and exhalation (*prāṇa*) along with the cessation of all thoughts. The *Vijñānabhairava* gives innumerable techniques for this purpose. And one of them is *haṃsā*, which involves meditation on the middle space between the in-breath and out-breath (Kak, 2007, v. 22). Fixing one's attention on the space between two thoughts is yet another extension of this practice. Through constant absorption in *haṃsā*, Lallā experiences the higher self or Śiva as the essential nature of both the outer world of diversity and the inner world of the contemplating higher self. Regarding this practice, Lallā says,

> The region of the navel is naturally ablaze.
> The breath moves up the throat
> to the *brahmarandhra*
> from which the river flows.
> For this reason, *Huh* (inhaled breath) is cold
> and *Hah* (exhaled breath) is hot.
>
> I took the reins of the mind horse.
> Through practice, I learned breath control.
> Then only the orb of the moon melted
> and dripped down into my body –
> nothingness merged with nothingness. (Kak, 2007, vv. 26, 29)

Lallā describes the process of realizing the highest state in terms of crossing six forests or six paths and seizing the seventh. The reference in the above verses is to breathing practices that involve the ascent of the vital breath through the psychic centers of the body. The "six forests" refer to the six energy centers along the spine – *mūlādhāra, svādhisthāna, manipura, anāhata, viśuddhā, ājñā.* The seventh center, the *brahmarandhra,* on the crown of the head symbolizes the transcendental reality or the "abode of light." In advanced stages of the practice, the activation of the seventh psychic center through the ascent of the vital breath stimulates the release of nurturing energy (symbolized by the melting of the moon) that flows down the body.

> I became absorbed in
> the sacred syllable Oṃ.
> I burned myself like coal.
> Leaving behind six paths,
> I seized the seventh –
> And then, I, Lallā, reached
> the abode of light. (Kak, 2007, v. 28)

Transgressing the distinctions between the inside and the outside or the subject and the object opens an entirely new space that refuses to be contained in any dualistic conceptual framework. Elaborating further on this new space, Lallā says,

> Speech or mind and
> manifest or transcendent
> have no existence there.
> Yogic silence has no place there.
> Śiva and Śakti don't live there.
> Seek whatever is left –
> that is my advice. (Kak, 2007, v. 95)

The most profound of Lallā's verses, then, convey the experience that is beyond any anthropomorphic representation. As it is impossible to describe that which is beyond any intellectual categories or linguistic descriptions, she speaks about this final state in terms of nothingness coming in touch with nothingness.

> The sun sets,
> the moon shines.
> The moon vanishes,
> consciousness remains.
> Consciousness disappears,
> nothingness remains –
> the physical, spiritual, and metaphysical
> merge into nothingness. (Kak, 2007, v. 31)

The sun illuminates the world of objects – the setting of the sun then represents an introspective state when the individual withdraws attention from the objective sphere and rests in the subjective sphere, which in this verse is compared to the shining of the moon. As the attention is withdrawn further, only consciousness remains, which too is surpassed in more advanced stages of practice when the self-consciousness merges with the absolute consciousness, and this state is beyond description. Lallā does not specify actual techniques in her verses but uses instead metaphors or analogies to convey her experiences. The current that runs through her verses reflects her belief that enlightened perspective can be realized through one's own striving, even as notions of grace and ignorance are an important part of her thought. As she progresses on her path, Lallā eventually reaches an advanced state when she experiences the world as an expression of the highest reality.

Teachings

After Lallā renounces her home, she spends the rest of her life as a wandering ascetic. She, however, retains a partial bond with the community as a social critic and teacher. She teaches people not to follow blindly what is written in religious scriptures. Reading scriptures can be beneficial in the beginning, but those who engage in mindless recitation of prayers, chanting of → *mantra*s, or turning of rosary beads are chasing illusions. Similarly, renunciation in itself without disciplining the mind and the body does not lead to self-realization. In a verse, Lallā says,

> Some renounce their home
> and some their hermitage.
> All is futile
> if the mind is not under control.
> Meditate on your breath
> day and night,
> and stay wherever you are. (Kak, 2007, v. 98)

Also, objects of ritual worship – for example, *kuśa* grass, sesame seeds, lamps, or water – are unnecessary, as is making animal offerings to idols. While commenting on the goat sacrifice done in those days to appease gods and goddesses, Lallā says that it is foolish to give offerings of living creatures to dead stones, as goats live on grass and water, and their wool covers our bodies and keeps us warm. She urges people to develop compassion for all sentient beings and transform from within in order to make progress on the spiritual path. The real practice, according to Lallā, is deliberate self-introspection accompanied by the disciplining of one's ego. Also important is to transform one's character through renouncing negative traits and engaging in good deeds performed with detachment.

Kill your mortal enemies –
  lust, anger, and desire.
Otherwise they would kill you
  with their arrows.
Calm them with self restraint
  and good thoughts.
Recognize their nature and their power. (Kak, 2007, v. 134)

Since the attention constantly slips out of the five senses, Lallā emphasizes the need to control one's mind. Furthermore, it is important to cultivate moderation in eating and drinking, as it is conducive to introspection. Lallā does not approve of starving the body through fasting or austerities or even performing religious ceremonies. The real religious practice is to engage in good deeds that are performed in the spirit of detachment.

Don't torture your body
  with thirst and starvation.
When the body is exhausted,
  take care of it.
Cursed be your fasts
  and religious ceremonies.
Be good to others –
  that is the real religious practice. (Kak, 2007, v. 118)

As a wandering ascetic, Lallā relied on food offered to her by others who belonged to a community other than her own. She critiqued the social practices of her time when the upper-caste Hindus did not consider the food cooked by Muslims or Hindus of lower castes as clean enough to be consumed.

I renounced
  falsehood, deceit, and hypocrisy.
I told my mind to follow this teaching.
Only One I found in everyone –
What is wrong with eating with anyone? (Kak, 2007, v. 121)

Lallā preaches tolerance toward religious practices other than one's own, as she believes all people, irrespective of their caste, religion, or gender, are equal. Her emphasis on religious tolerance is in agreement with the monist Śaiva philosophy, which is open to other religious perspectives. She refrains from identifying herself with any sect or religion. The Śiva consciousness, she says, is beyond artificial divisions. People might call this state Śiva, Keśava, Mahavīra, or Buddha, but these are just different names assigned to the same reality. Thus, Lallā says,

The world is full of differences.
If you are tolerant,
  you will be happy.
If you renounce anger, hate, and animosity,
  you will see Śiva's face. (Kak, 2007, v. 146)

The single message that emerges from many of her verses is the need for transformation of one's character through renouncing negative traits like anger, hate, animosity, greed, and hypocrisy, among others, and adopting noble traits like compassion, selflessness, and love for the other irrespective of caste or creed. In a verse, Lallā says,

Śiva is omnipresent.
Don't differentiate between
Hindus and Muslims.
If you are wise,
  you will recognize your true Self –
  that is your real acquaintance with the lord.
  (Kak, 2007, v. 83)

Lallā elaborates on the above concept by referring to the earth as the source of stones that serve different functions. Some stones end up in the grinding stone (a tool for grinding wheat that nourishes the body), and others adorn temple altars as idols. Still others are used for building pavements for people to tread upon. Though serving different culturally specific purposes, all stones come from the same earth. Similarly, individuals might differ on the basis of their religious beliefs, but they are permeated with the same divine consciousness. Lallā thus brings people's attention to the need for personal morality anchored in honesty, selflessness, and compassion rather than on rules of conduct based on religious bigotry.

Relationship with the Rišī Sufi Tradition

Lallā's critique of social and religious practices of her time, and perhaps early references to her in the Persian hagiographic documents and chronicles, have led a few scholars to conclude that she either adopted Sufi mysticism or was influenced by it, or she brought about its synthesis with Hinduism (Temple, 1924; Hasan, 1959; Bazaz, 1959; Bamzai, 1962; Sufi, 1974). Recent scholars have refuted such claims based on the study of either the Persian sources or the content of verses, or both (Rafiqi, 1972; Kaul, 1973; Odin, 1999). Even though Lallā's verses point beyond doubt that she was a serious Śaiva practitioner, the missionary outlook of the Sufis could have shaped her concern for the people in her community, as legends speak of Sufi and Hindu mystics gathering together frequently to exchange ideas and experiences.

A legend describes Lallā's first encounter with the 14th-century Muslim mystic Nūr al-Dīn Rišī (also known as Šayẖ Nūr al-Dīn or Nūnd Rišī, 1378–1439), the founder of the medieval Rišī Sufi movement of Kashmir. When Nūr al-Dīn was born, according to the legend, he refused to accept his mother's milk. On the third day, Lallā visited their home and took him into her arms and said, "You were not ashamed to be born, then why be ashamed of drinking?" (Koul, 1921, 309). This legend has been interpreted as Lallā acknowledging Nūr al-Dīn as her spiritual heir. She could not have been his direct teacher, as the date of her death is somewhere around the late 1370s or even the early 1380s, when Nūr al-Dīn must have been a young child. It is clear, however, that he held her in great esteem and that she was a source of inspiration for him. In one of his verses, Nūr al-Dīn says,

> That Lallā of Padmanpura
> She drank nectar by mouthfuls
> She saw Śiva everywhere
> O, Lord, bestow such a boon on me. (Saqi, 1985, 148; trans. by author)

In folk memory and hagiographical accounts, the same or similar verses are attributed to both Lallā and Nūr al-Dīn. J.L. Kaul's study of Persian sources reveals that 35 verses in various Lallā collections are also part of various *Nūr-nāmā* and *Rišī-nāma*, the biographies of Nūr al-Dīn. The mixing up of some of the verses, however, is only present in later biographies of the mystic (Kaul, 1973, 40). Since we have no concrete evidence to show whether the Lallā manuscripts or copies of manuscripts – the basis of the Grierson collection – were written before or after the earliest *Nur-nāmā* recorded two hundred years after Nūr al-Dīn's death, one cannot ascertain the true originator of the handful of verses that have been attributed to both of them.

Over the centuries, Lallā's verses were sung by village minstrels and later became a part of Kashmiri classical music (*ṣūfīānā kalām*), as they were now used as sacred invocations to open the assembly of Sufis (Majlis-i ʿārifīn). Even later Sufi poets reference Lallā's verses. Lallā and Nūr al-Dīn are closely linked to the narrative of religious syncretism and communal harmony (*kašmīriyat*) in Kashmir. Both are equally revered by Hindus and Muslims, as they practiced what they preached, and they taught the masses in the vernacular language.

Conclusion

Lallā's poetry occupies an important place in women's literary history, not only in India but also in the world. She was a woman with faith in her vision as she pursued her path in the face of many obstacles. The path she took, however, was very much determined by the discursive as well as social formations of the patriarchal Kashmiri society. Even within the constraints, Lallā contributed in the only way she could by serving as a beacon of light to oppressed people. She urged them to have courage to seek self-knowledge in order to free themselves from bonds of ignorance. She compared the path of wisdom to a kitchen garden, which must be nurtured with self-restraint, tranquility, and good deeds performed with detachment. Lallā has continued to inspire people for centuries to model their lives on a vision of reality that has potential for creating a good society based on equality, mutual respect, and caring.

Bibliography

Bamzai, P.N.K., *A History of Kashmir*, Delhi, 1962.
Bazaz, P.N., *Daughters of the Vitasta*, New Delhi, 1959.
Grierson, G., & L.D. Barnett, eds., *Lallā-Vākyāni: Or The Wise Sayings of Lal Ded*, London, 1920.
Hasan, M., *Kashmir under the Sultans*, Calcutta, 1959.
Kachru, B., *Kashmiri Literature*, Wiesbaden, 1981.
Kak, J., *Mystical Verses of Lallā*, Delhi, 2007.
Kaul, J.L., *Lal Ded*, New Delhi, 1973.
"Lalded," *KoS* 9/1, 1971, 1–58.
Kotru, N.K., *Lal Ded: Her Life and Sayings*, Srinagar, 1989.
Koul, A., "'Life Sketch of Laleshwari' and 'Lallā-Vākyāni'," *IA* 50, 1921, 309–312; 59, 1930, 108–130; 60, 1931, 191–193; 61, 1932, 13–16; 62, 1933, 108–111.
Lakshman Joo, S., *Kashmir Shaivism: The Secret Supreme*, New York, 1988.
Mishra, K., *Kashmir Śaivism: The Central Philosophy of Tantrism*, Cambridge MA, 1993.
Odin, J.K., *To the Other Shore: Lalla's Life and Poetry*, New Delhi, 1999.

Pandit, B.N., *History of Kashmir Saivism*, Srinagar, 1990.
Parimoo, B.N., *The Ascent of Self*, Delhi, [2]1987.
Rafiqi, A.Q., *Sufism in Kashmir: Fourteenth to the Sixteenth Century*, Srinagar, 1972, rev. ed. 2003.
Ray, S.C., *Early History and Culture in Kashmir*, Delhi, 1969.
Saqi, M.L., ed., *Kulliyāt-i-Shaikh u'l-ʿālam*, Srinagar, 1985.
Sufi, G.M.D., *Kashir: A History of Kashmir*, New Delhi, 1974.
Temple, R.C., *The Religion and Teachings of Lallā*, New Delhi, 1924.

Jaishree K. Odin

Madhva

Madhva (1238–1317 CE) was the founder of the theological, philosophical, and commentarial school of Dvaita Vedānta, also known as Tattvavāda (lit. teaching of reality). His teaching is a major decisive point of departure in the long-running vedantic debate between theism and monism. Of the three major forms of Vedānta, Madhva's Dvaita Vedānta (dualistic Vedānta) was the third to be founded, after the Advaita Vedānta (nondualistic Vedānta) of → Śaṅkara (650–700? CE) and the Viśiṣṭādvaita Vedānta (qualified nondualistic Vedānta) of → Rāmānuja (1056–1137 CE; for the different schools, see → Vedānta). On theological, philosophical, and textual grounds, Madhva develops the theistic protest against the nontheistic nondualism or monism of the Advaita Vedānta of Śaṅkara much further than Rāmānuja had done in the 12th century. For Śaṅkara, the authoritative texts of the Vedānta that taught difference have only practical and heuristic import. In his interpretation, they are subordinated to the nondifference texts. For him, the difference texts lead by indirection to the real teaching of the → Upaniṣads – that there is no difference or no dualism among → *brahman*, individual selves (*jīva*s), and the other features of the world of appearance. The reason for the appearance of difference was the operation of → *māya*, the force of illusion. For Madhva, these very same texts about difference teach the true and primary import of the Upaniṣads. These texts are not to be subordinated to the nondifference texts. Madhva thus initiated a sharp polemic against what he asserted was the demonic teaching and interpretation of Śaṅkara, who he claimed was a disguised Buddhist. Instead, for Madhva, *brahman* is God, understood and identified by name as → Viṣṇu. Viṣṇu is the primary personal and divine reality who is metaphysically different, theologically transcendent, and eternally independent from the *jīva* – the individual self – on the one hand, and also different from the plurality of the other beings of the universe, on the other. This is the overall import of the authoritative scriptural texts:

> Therefore, as non-difference is contracted by all the sources of knowledge, it is not the purport of the scriptures. On the contrary, the highest meaning of all the scriptures is the preeminence of Viṣṇu over every other entity. (*ViTatVi.* 1.98)

Thus, the fundamental teaching of the vedantic texts, correctly and authoritatively interpreted by Madhva, was a monotheism that proposed the eternal metaphysical difference between God as independent and everything else as eternally dependent on God.

Although often neglected by contemporary historians of Hindu thought, and by Hindu philosophers, Madhva and the school of theologians, philosophers, and commentators who followed him – like Jayatīrtha (c. 1335–1385 CE) and Vyāsatīrtha (1460–1539 CE) – represent perhaps the finest dialectic thinkers within the philosophical traditions of Hinduism. Contrary to the contemporary preeminence of Śaṅkara and of his version of Advaita Vedānta as India's putative best and representative form of philosophical and theological thought, in the judgment of the great historian of Indian philosophys. Dasgupta,

> There is a general belief amongst many that the monism of Śaṅkara presents the final phase of Indian thought... But the readers of the present volume who will be introduced to the philosophy of Jaya-tīrtha and particularly of Vyāsa-tīrtha will realize the strength and uncompromising impressiveness of the dualistic position. (Dasgupta, vol. IV, 1949, viii)

The Life of Madhva

The traditional biographies of medieval Hinduism are often dismissed as lacking historical value. This is not the case with Madhva, whose life may be known with considerable historical accuracy. In fact, Madhva's earliest biography has had considerable historical significance in its own right. It may well be that the hagiography, or sacred biography, of Madhva, even though he lived perhaps five hundred years after Śaṅkara, was written before the received sacred biographies of Śaṅkara. According to Sheridan,

> Notice should be taken of the reversal of the order of the sacred life stories and biographies, Madhva and then Śaṅkara. Although Śaṅkara lived in the seventh century and Madhva in the thirteenth and fourteenth, Madhva's sacred biography was composed within a decade of his death while the numerous extant sacred

> biographies of Śaṅkara were composed no earlier than the fourteenth and fifteenth centuries. (Sheridan, 2007, 125)

Ironically, the actual life of Madhva as reported by his contemporaries may have heavily impacted the received narrative and understanding of the life of Śaṅkara.

Very soon after the death of Madhva in 1318 CE, the *Sumadhvavijaya*, the *Aṇumadhvavijaya*, the *Madhvavijayabhāvaprakāśika*, and the *Maṇimañjari* of Nārāyaṇa Paṇḍitācārya were composed. These are sacred biographies in verse based on the sacred memories of Madhva, narrated and composed by a contemporary of Madhva who had known him personally. For example, Nārāyaṇa Paṇḍitācārya's father, Trivikrama, had been an early convert of Madhva. The writings of these two – along with the internal evidence from Madhva's own writings, especially from the colophons of his works, and also from the traditions of the eight Mādhva *maṭhas* established by Madhva – are the primary sources for the sacred biography of Madhva. This biography has substantial historical content, but it is nonetheless a sacred biography because it has the theological purpose of presenting Madhva as the authoritative interpreter of Vedānta and its scriptural texts. Nārāyaṇa Paṇḍitācārya wrote from a theological perspective that must be acknowledged before reviewing the life of Madhva. Five themes run throughout the works of Nārāyaṇa Paṇḍitācārya.

1. Viṣṇu is the named identity of the sole transcendent and independent God;
2. Vyāsa, the compiler of the → Vedas, the Upaniṣads, the → Purāṇas, and the *Brahmasūtra*, was the → *avatāra* of Viṣṇu;
3. Madhva himself was the *avatāra* of Vāyu, the son of Viṣṇu;
4. The purpose of Madhva's appearance had been to undo the commentarial evil committed by Śaṅkara, who was the evil *avatāra* of the demon Maṇimat killed by Bhīma in the → *Mahābhārata* and who was a disguised follower of the Buddha;
5. Madhva depended for his interpretation of the Vedānta texts on his own *guru*, who was Vyāsa, the *avatāra* of Viṣṇu.

Therefore Madhva taught with the authority of God himself, who had explicated the scriptures to Madhva. And therefore Madhva with this authority corrected the mistaken interpretations of the scriptures by the demonic Śaṅkara, which lacked any authority.

Madhva was born in 1238 CE to Śivaḷḷi Brahman parents in the village of Pajaka, near Udupi in Tulunadu, about 65 km north of Mangalore in → Karnataka. Udupi is about 50 km from Sringeri, the home of one of the Advaita *maṭhas*, supposedly founded by Śaṅkara himself. Karnataka was a melting pot of Jains, Vīraśaivas (→ Liṅgāyats), Advaitins, and Viśiṣṭādvaitins. Madhva's birth name was Vāsudeva. From the age of seven, he precociously studied the full range of the Vedas and Śāstras. He would eventually cite more than 240 works in his writings. He was initiated as a *saṃnyāsin* in the Tīrtha order by his Advaita *guru* Acyutaprekṣa at the age of 16. His renunciation name was Pūrṇaprajña ("The One Whose Knowledge Is Full"). Thus under this *guru*, Madhva studied the Advaita classics, starting with the *Iṣṭasiddhi* of the Advaitin Vimuktātman (fl. 950 CE). He was immediately dissatisfied with the Advaita interpretation of the Vedānta texts and saw that it was mistaken. The troubled teacher-to-student relationship between Acyutaprekṣa and Madhva was quickly inverted when Madhva pointed out 32 errors in Vimuktātman's first sentence of the *Iṣṭasiddhi*. Nonetheless, Madhva was appointed the head of the *maṭha* of Acyutaprekṣa with the name of Ānandatīrtha ("The Teacher of Bliss"). The name of Madhva ("Sweet") by which he is usually known is thought to be the equivalent of Ānandatīrtha. It also, for esoteric reasons, suggests that Madhva was the *avatāra* of Vāyu and that he interpreted the scriptures with authority. Thus, on another occasion, Madhva was asked about a variant reading in the *Bhāgavatapurāṇa*, "How do you know what was not read by you in this birth?" Madhva answered, "All this I knew in my former births" (*SuMVij*. 4.53).

Accompanied by Acyutaprekṣa, Madhva undertook an extensive tour of South India for two or three years (1256–1258 CE). He visited Trivandrum, Kanyakumari, Srirangam, and Rameshwaram. He learned about the other forms that opposition to Śaṅkara's interpretation of the *Brahmasūtra* had taken. Thus he met and debated with followers of Rāmānuja. Unconvinced and regarding their views as incomplete, he resolved to establish a new *siddhānta*, established doctrine. His opponents challenged him to compose a Bhāṣya or commentary since the public exposition of the meaning of the *Brahmasūtra* was inappropriate by one who had not yet composed a Bhāṣya. First, however, on his return to Udupi, Madhva began to compose a commentary on the → *Bhagavadgītā* according to his dualist theology of God's independent relationship with dependent individual selves and with the dependent world.

With Acyutaprekṣa's blessing, Madhva then made a pilgrimage north to Badarīkāśrama (today Badrinath), the remote Himalayan *āśrama* of Vyāsa, the *avatāra* of Viṣṇu, the supreme God. On reaching Badarī, Madhva recited his completed *Gītābhāṣya* in front of the image of Nārāyaṇa. It repeatedly stated, "Let it be spoken" (*SuMVij.* 6.41). Vyāsa then bid Madhva to go farther to Uttara Badarī, Vyāsa's own hermitage. Many Brahmans and → *ṛṣis* were there. Madhva saw the *badarī* tree on which hung the Purāṇas and the *Mahābhārata*. Madhva prostrated before Vyāsa, who sat under the tree. Viṣṇu, in the form of his *avatāra* as Vyāsa, then embraced Madhva, who was the *avatāra* of Vāyu, the son of Viṣṇu. Madhva therefore heard the true import of the scriptures imparted by his true *guru* Vyāsa, who was the very authoritative compiler of the eternal scriptures themselves and the *avatāra* of God himself. Madhva was told,

> The interpretation of the heart of the *sūtras*, dear to the truthful, is obstructed by others who, according to their own desires, spoil the natural meaning of the Śruti and Smṛti, which having been corrupted, is set aside. Undo this evil done by the wicked ones, lead the people back to the auspicious path. O learned one, make an unhesitating interpretation of the *sūtras* and by grace link the Śruti and the Smṛti. (*SuMVij.* 8.45–46; trans. by author)

From then on, Vyāsa indwelled Madhva's mind so that Madhva henceforth spoke the words that Vyāsa had taught him. Madhva then taught from a mind in which Vyāsa dwelled. At Badarīkāśrama, he dictated the now authoritative *Brahmasūtrabhāṣya*.

> He composed the interpretation that teaches the countless true qualities of Vāsudeva, which is very dear to the heart of the divine Vyāsa and which is free from all defects on the path and gives devotion and knowledge and eternal welfare. (*SuMVij.* 9.8; trans. by author)

Madhva returned to Udupi via Bihar and Bengal, recruiting such key disciples as Padmanābhatīrtha and Naraharitīrtha. Finally, Acyutaprekṣa himself accepted that Madhva's criticism of Advaita was valid, and that with the publication of commentaries on the *Bhagavadgītā* and on the *Brahmasūtra*, Madhva has indeed established a new *siddhānta*.

Madhva later visited Badarī on a second northern tour (c. 1280–1290 CE). Vyāsa then gave him the *vyāsapuṣṭi* stones indwelled by Nārāyaṇa and his consort Lakṣmī (→ Śrī Lakṣmī). Madhva was commissioned to write a commentary on the *Mahābhārata*, in which Madhva himself had been a character in his *avatāra* Bhīma. Thus Madhva visited Hastināpura and then Kāśī. At Kāśī, he debated the ever-present Advaitins, what he called the Māyāvādins ("followers of illusory power"). One of them responded, "This interpretation is associated with authority. It cannot be refuted by our widespread Māyāvāda. It is not without the support of reasoning" (*SuMVij.* 10.48). Madhva then reached Kurukṣetra, where he found the mace that belonged to Bhīma, his previous incarnation as a warrior.

On his return to Udupi, Madhva laid permanent foundations for his community of Dvaitins. He installed an image of → Kṛṣṇa from Dwarka that had been found offshore in the mud. He introduced a significant change and innovation in the vedic sacrifices (→ *yajña*) by replacing animals with flour-made substitutes. He again encountered the Advaitins Padmatīrtha and Puṇḍarika Pūrī, who futilely challenged the authority of his interpretations. They lament,

> Is this Madhva indeed Vedavyāsa? Is he the appearance of the Veda? Is this body with the gentle smile divine? We have seen him and his compassionate voice cut the root of the teaching of *māyā*... the time of the destruction of our teaching by him is like the water of the end of the world at the time of the destruction of the world. (*SuMVij.* 12.12; trans. by author)

Madhva's reply was to expound the *Ṛgveda* in accord with his Dvaitin interpretation. Frustrated in debate, the Advaitin Padmatīrtha stole Madhva's extensive library of texts and commentaries. Through the intervention of a local king – one Jayasiṃha – the volumes of the library were returned to Śaṅkarācārya, who was Nārāyaṇa Paṇḍitācārya's uncle and Madhva's librarian. The king himself came to meet Madhva at the Viṣṇumaṅgala Temple. Together they heard the *Bhāgavatapurāṇa* recited by one of Madhva's disciples, Hṛṣikeśatīrtha. Hṛṣikeśatīrtha was later commissioned to collect all 37 of Madhva's writings into the *Sarvamūlagrantha* (Collection of All the Fundamentals). A palm-leaf copy of this is extant and is the basis for the contemporary edition by B. Govindacharya. It seems that one of the organizing principles behind Nārāyaṇa Paṇḍitācārya's *Sumadhvavijaya* was the chronological sequence of Madhva's writings, all of which are mentioned directly or indirectly in the poem.

At another public recitation of the *Bhāgavatapurāṇa*, Madhva met Trivikrama, an Advaitin householder and the father of Nārāyaṇa Paṇḍitācārya. Trivikrama studied Madhva's *Brahmasūtrabhāṣya* and then heard Madhva's public exposition. In the argument that followed, Madhva refuted the various forms of → Sāṃkhya, → Mīmāṃsā, → Vaiśeṣika, Indian logic, and of Buddhist thought. The debate between Madhva and Trivikrama went on for 15 days. Finally, Trivikrama surrendered, "May the permanent service of the dust of your lotus-like feet be given to me" (*SuMVij.* 15.70). In reply, Madhva ordered Trivikrama to compose the *Tattvapradīpa* (Lamp of Reality), the earliest commentary on Madhva's *Brahmasūtrabhāṣya*, which was thus composed during Madhva's lifetime.

Before his death, Madhva founded in Udupi eight *maṭhas*, which still exist today. Nārāyaṇa Paṇḍitācārya, without mentioning the disappearance or death of Madhva (1317 CE), concludes this telling of the sacred life story with the praise of Madhva by the gods who claim Madhva as their *guru*,

> Praise to the lord of every being, you came for the prosperity of those who saluted you. Praise to Lord Hanumān, dear to Rāma, who has the quality of *guru*. Praise to the mighty Bhīma, beloved of Bhagavān Kṛṣṇa. Praise to Lord Madhva. (*SuMVij.* 16.57; trans. by author)

According to the *Aṇumadhvacarita*, attributed to Hṛṣikeśatīrtha, Madhva disappeared from view on the ninth day of the bright half of the lunar month of *māgha* (Jan–Feb) 1318 CE.

Madhva as Commentator

Overall, Madhva perceived his own written work as an authoritative commentary on a divine compilation of, and commentary on, the scriptures by Vyāsa himself. Vyāsa was Madhva's *guru* who taught him how to read the scriptures. Therefore, Madhva was first and foremost an authoritative commentator. Only in this context should he then be considered a theologian or a philosopher. In his own self-understanding as found in the colophons of his written works, Madhva was taught the authoritative interpretation by Vyāsa, also known as Bādarāyaṇa. This is not a later imputation. The *Brahmasūtra* of Bādarāyaṇa (5th cent. BCE) were a synthetic and rational attempt to understand and coordinate the conflicting senses of the vedic scriptures, which together constitute a scriptural revelation for Vedānta. Its 564 *sūtra*s or aphorisms refer to, and organize, the most significant passages of the Upaniṣads. A translation of the first 11 aphorisms, according to Madhva's understanding and interpretation, states that *brahman*, the supreme reality, originator, maintainer, and destroyer of the universe, can be known by means of an exegetical concordance of the passages of scripture; it very much summarizes Madhva's teaching:

> (1) Now, then, is the inquiry into *brahman*. (2) From whence are the world's states of creation, maintenance, and dissolution – that is *brahman*. (3) Revelation is the source of the knowledge of the *brahman*. (4) That knowledge is derived from a concordance of the texts of scripture. (5) The *brahman* is not inexpressible, as it is an object of knowledge. (6) Can the object of our inquiry really be the individual self? No, because, in referring to it, revelation uses the word "self" [*ātman*]. (7) Revelation also declares that one committed to it attains liberation. (8) Neither does revelation declare it undesirable. (9) Besides, the individual self enters into that self. (10) The teaching is uniform in this regard. (11) And so the revelation proclaims the *brahman* [the knowable, the supreme]. (*BrS.* 1.1–11; trans. by author)

Difference and the Inner Witness

In order to establish the "concordance of the texts of the scriptures," Madhva discovered in the *Brahmasūtra* an architectonic model of scriptural exegesis or interpretation profoundly dissimilar from the interpretative models of his vedantic predecessors Śaṅkara and Rāmānuja. He puts the Archimedean postulate of metaphysical dualistic difference in place of the monistic nondifference of Śaṅkara and of the difference-in-identity of Rāmānuja. This Archimedean point of metaphysical difference allows Madhva to reduce the apparently conflicting meanings of different scriptural passages to a consistent, coherent, and logical theological teaching.

> Revelation [in some places] proclaims the lord endowed with perfections like omniscience to be different from the individual self. Subordinate to this is revelation [in other places] in so far as it proclaims identity. The "identity" scripture can have no authority in so far as it discords with its suzerain "difference" scripture. In scriptural texts declaring independence, excellence, the identity of place and thought and similarity [between God and individual self] – in such texts, affirmations of identity are literally true. Such texts, according to occasion, allow for a breadth of interpretation. But the "difference scripture" is tolerant of no such breadth. How then can it fail to have the greater force? (modified from Pereira, 1976, 128)

Madhva justifies his teaching of metaphysical difference, otherwise known through everyone's ordinary experience of the world, by proposing the *a priori* existence of the unerring agent and judge of validity the *sākṣin* – the inner witness, or apperceiver, of real difference. The concept of the *sākṣin* is a distinctive and unique feature of Madhva's thought and is an underappreciated but significant contribution to Indian philosophy. The inner witness is the foundation of Madhva's realistic epistemology and thus the rational keystone for his exegesis of scripture and for his entire theological system. The inner witness is fundamentally the terminal irreducible core of the reflective and reflexive consciousness, experience, and awareness that an individual human knowing being possesses when it knows that it knows. It provides the guarantee of validity for all experiential knowledge as transitive, that is, as knowledge of something else. The inner witness grounds the absolute certainty and the validity of the knowledge that the realities that exist are distinct and separate, that is, different. The inner witness is self-luminous and self-validating. It grounds the salvific import of revelation.

What the inner witness knows as different cannot be sublated by a greater form of knowledge as in Śaṅkara's nondualism, where difference does not ultimately exist. Experiential knowledge of an object that is free from sublation is possible. As Madhva in his *Anuvyākhyāna* states, "Without recognizing the *sākṣin*, there is no knowledge of any kind. Whatever then is known on the evidence of *sākṣin* must be accepted as real and true" (*Anuvyā.* 1.4.100–101; modified from Sharma, 1963, 45).

Knowledge has to be confirmed, and so has the knowledge of the confirmation to be confirmed in turn. In order to avoid an infinite regress, Madhva proposes the existence of the transcendental intuitive inner witness, which is the final guarantor of the validity of knowledge. This inner witness is revealed to us by an examination of the three forms of valid knowledge – experience, inference, and revelation. For each of these to be a valid knowledge, metaphysical difference must exist, or otherwise the validity of each form of knowledge could not be explained. It would also be impossible to accept the teaching of revelation about → liberation. For Madhva, without the existence of the inner witness to perceive difference, no judgments of validity could be made, and thus it could not be determined from the interpretation of scripture that liberation is possible. "Nevertheless, accepting the truth of Madhvācārya's system necessitates accepting the unquestionable validity of *sākṣī*" (Sarma, 2003, 30). With the teaching of difference based on the inner witness, Madhva can present a coherent epistemology of realism. Without the teaching of the inner witness, as in the *māyāvāda* of Śaṅkara's Advaita, Madhva maintains that the result on rational grounds would be incoherent and internally contradictory. Without the teaching about the *sākṣin*, the interpretation of the vedic texts is incomprehensible.

The Independent Reality and Dependent Realities

Madhva's ontology may be summarized by his statement that "There are two orders of reality – the independent and the dependent" (Sharma, 1963, 25). Ordinary experience directly contacts the fact of the diversity of what appears as external reality. Indeed, what appears in experience may occasionally be discovered to be only an illusionary appearance when the evidence of its existence is contradicted. But when the evidence is not contradicted, then it appears as real, and it is real. In order to be consistent, Śaṅkara cannot teach that all appearance is illusory. More important than the distinction between appearance and reality, played off each other, is the distinction between independent reality and dependent realities brought into a real relation of dependent difference. The independent reality is God, the → Iśvara or Lord, who brings order to the many dependent realities. This relationship of distinction is not one of superimposition of the many on the one, but instead one of metaphysical dependence of the many on the one independent reality. The many do not disappear into the realm of the illusory. The teaching of the Upaniṣads does not support the deduction of the falsity of the many. Knowledge of the one independent reality leads to knowledge of the many dependent realities. Each reality is unique and has its own nature, which means that each reality is different from the others. Knowledge of this is liberating, since whoever realizes that a person is always born dependent on the eternal God is released from *saṃsāra*. Dependent realities, whether eternal or noneternal, are dependent on God's will and governed by it.

Madhva claims that the universe of all that is not God – independent reality – is ruled by five differences. In his *Viṣṇutattvavinirṇaya*, he says,

> The universe has five differences: there is the difference between the *jīva* and the lord. There is the difference between the lord and non-sentient material realities. There is the difference between the individual *jīvas*. There is a difference between *jīvas* and non-sentient material realities. There is the difference between one non-sentient material reality and another. The difference between these five is real. (*ViTatVi.* 1.340; trans. by author)

These five differences are fundamental to Madhva's vision of what is real. They are the reason why reality is dual and not nondual. They are not illusory and are sublatable to a more real unity. These five differences clearly differentiate Dvaita Vedānta from the opposing schools of Vedānta.

The Individual Selves

According to Madhva's *Viṣṇutattvavinirṇaya*,

> As stated in the *Parama Śrutu*, "He who suffers and enjoys, who bound [in *saṁsāra*] and [obtains] *mokṣa*, liberation [from it and] who knows [himself] as 'I am,' he is the *jīva*," enduring self. (*ViTatVi.* 1.290; trans. Sarma 2003, 76)

The individual self is uniquely separate and real. Consciousness is its distinguishing feature. Except when plagued by bondage, the individual self is fundamentally blissful. The individual self is connected with the body and the sense organs, which can cause it suffering. Yet the individual self is eternal, enduring, until liberation, through the many lives of *saṃsāra*. For Madhva, there are three categories of individual selves: (1) those who are eternally free from immersion in *saṃsāra*, (2) those who have achieved liberation from *saṃsāra*, and (3) those who are immersed in the bondage of *saṃsāra*. There are two forms of these latter – those who may be liberated and those who are eternally not eligible for liberation from *saṃsāra*.

Individual selves, like God, have free will. If they are immersed in the bondage of *saṃsāra* and are eligible for liberation, then they have their own responsibility for their state of existence. Madhva teaches the classical Hindu view of → *karman*. Thus the individual self through its own actions is immersed in *saṃsāra*. The real cause of bondage is ignorance of the independent and transcendent God, and knowledge of God's real nature qualifies one for liberation. In the end, liberation depends on God's free act of revelation. Madhva teaches a form of the path of *bhakti* or devotion to God. Actions performed on this path without any concern for their results undo the bondage of the individual self and qualifies one for the final gift of God, which is liberation. This → grace of God, coordinated with the actions of the individual self, provides a beatific vision of God's own blissful nature.

Brahman as God

For Madhva, *brahman* is the sole independent reality because he is the sole self-dependent reality. Therefore, *brahman* is eternally independent of the world and of individual selves, which are eternally dependent on *brahman*. However, *brahman* is not the world's material cause. The world is not a modification of *brahman*.

> The Supreme Being's transcendence is not expressed by means of analogy of being, but by making Viṣṇu a "*tattva sui generis*," with certain specific attributes... Transcendence, in the final analysis is not the total otherness in being, the otherness in existence itself, but the fact of being

> the greatest in a hierarchy of existents. (Puthiadam, 1985, 321)

As the inner controller of all individual selves, *brahman* is also immanent but in the sense of the copresence of one and another. The ultimate and independent reality is *saguṇa*, *brahman* with qualities. *Brahman* as God is the supreme personal being who is the ultimate object of the loving devotion of human persons. They desire a loving relationship with the God who listens to and answers prayers and comforts the afflicted. God has all the qualities that are not negative, such as existence, joy, consciousness, and so on. The form of *brahman* taught by Śaṅkara is *nirguṇa*, without qualities. Such a *brahman* is impersonal and cannot function as the supreme personal reality of God and as the object of the love of human persons.

God, for Madhva, is Viṣṇu, who creates, maintains, and destroys the world in its cycles. Viṣṇu is eminently knowable and filled with joy. Human persons depend on God for the ordering of all their activities, knowledge, and existence. The supreme personal being, independent and transcendent, has a will that causes the cyclic changes in the world of creation, maintenance, and destruction. Through all of the cycles, though, the five differences remain real. Individual selves are thus coexistent and coeternal with God. Madhva does not teach anything like the Jewish, Christian, of Muslim view of a creator God. Such a God creates the world and everything in it out of nothing, not out of God's own being or out of something else. Madhva's view of God is the closest among the Hindu views to Western monotheism, but it is clearly different on the point of creation out of nothing. All reality, independent and dependent, is the coexistence and coeternality of the independent God and the dependent individual selves and the dependent world. Madhva

> breaks away from the spell of Advaita and chalks a line of thought in which the One and the Many are considered real and true, Madhva does not want to devalue the Many because of the infinity and Truth of the One. (Puthidam, 1985, 323)

Madhva's Major Works

Madhva was a very prolific author and commentator. He produced 37 written works, which were collected during his lifetime into the *Sarvamūlagrantha* (Compendium of All the Fundamentals). The works can be divided into four groups.

The first group deals with theistic commentaries on the threefold basic texts of Vedānta: two commentaries on the *Bhagavadgītā*, four commentaries and treatises on the *Brahmasūtra*, and the commentaries on ten Upaniṣads. Madhva's most basic work is the *Brahmasūtrabhāṣya* in which most of the significant points of his theological and philosophical system can be found. Its style is straightforward and expository. Characteristic of Madhva, it is filled with citations from a wide range of vedantic and Vaiṣṇava literature. Unusual among the founders of vedantic systems, Madhva wrote three more commentaries on the *Brahmasūtra*. The *Anuvyākhyāna*, composed late in his life, is also an important work commenting on the *Brahmasūtra*, but it also supplements and comments on Madhva's own *Brahmasūtrabhāṣya*. In B.N.K. Sharma's view,

> It is a work in which Madhva has put forth his best efforts at interpretation and criticism. It is undoubtedly a classic in the fullest sense of the term. It is his *magnum opus*. It has logic, dialectic fire, unity, eloquence and a certain stately music of words. (Sharma, 1981, 122)

It is important as Madhva's best and most detailed refutation of the teaching and interpretations of Śaṅkara and his school.

The second group of works is the *daśaprakaraṇa*, the ten treatises on philosophical themes. In this group, the *Viṣṇutattvavinirṇaya* (The Complete Ascertainment of the Nature of Viṣṇu) stands out. In it, Madhva establishes that Viṣṇu is the primary import of the teaching of the Vedas and the vedantic texts. Since the Vedas are without author, Madhva treats their self-validity. Then he establishes his teaching about the ineradicable difference between God and all other reality. The third group of Madhva's works is the *purāṇaprasthāna*, commentaries on *Mahābhārata*, which includes a treatment of the → *Rāmāyaṇa*, and on the *Bhāgavatapurāṇa*, both of which are the earliest extant commentaries on these important religious texts of Vaiṣṇavism. He also wrote a theistic commentary on the *Ṛgveda*, the *Ṛgbhāṣya*. Madhva's fourth group are his minor treatises on religious practices and his poetic texts – for example, the *Kṛṣṇāmṛtamahārṇava*, 242 verses in praise of Kṛṣṇa, and the *Dvādaśastotra*, a beautiful Stotra that has been compared to Jayadeva's *Gītagovinda*.

Conclusion

Madhva's philosophical and theological teaching, rooted in an authoritative interpretation of the vedic and vedantic texts, is one of Hinduism's greatest achievements. Negatively, the Dvaita Vedānta of Madhva may be defined as a dialectical critique of Śaṅkara's nondualism. Debate, dialectic, and argument are an integral part of its divine mission from Viṣṇu. For if Śaṅkara had perpetuated the Buddhist Nāgārjuna's use of the dialectic,

> the criticism dissolvent of metaphysics, Madhva may be said to have perfected the dialectic of the dialectic, the criticism dissolvent of the criticism, and reconstitutive of metaphysical thought. (Pereira, 1976, 124)

Madhva says the following in his *Anuvyākhyāna*:

> Therefore, devotees who cherish the Lord, whose understanding [is] pure, [and] who understand the scriptural authorities, they would always [strive to] destroy the darkness [of ignorance]. (*Anuvyā*. 2.2.8; trans. Sarma, 2003, 97)

Certainly, in the 14th century, the Dvaitin arguments with the Advaitins may be seen to have prevailed. In any case, the Advaita school, after its encounter with Madhva in the 14th century, rethought its argumentation and took a decidedly devotional turn toward *bhakti*.

Positively, Madhva taught with the authority of one who had Vyāsa as his *guru*. His interpretations are more direct and less convoluted than those of other schools of Vedānta. Alone among the many schools of Hinduism, he taught, in accord with the scriptures, the eternal damnation of certain kinds of individual selves. He moved the practice of his community away from animal sacrifice. He taught that members of all castes, even the lowest ones, could under certain conditions study the scriptural texts. The inquiry into the nature of *brahman*, that is, of God identified as Viṣṇu, is the goal of all individual selves who are eligible for liberation. For this inquiry, Madhva provided both an authoritative interpretation and the rigorous dialectic of philosophical reason.

Bibliography

Dasgupta, S., *A History of Indian Philosophy*, vol. IV, Cambridge UK, 1949, repr. 1975.

Pereira, J., *Hindu Theology: A Reader*, Garden City, 1976.

Puthiadam, I., *Viṣṇu the Ever Free: A Study of the Mādhva Concept of God*, Madurai, 1985.

Sarma, D., "Madhvācārya and Vyāsatīrtha," *JVS* 15/2, 2007, 145–168.

Sarma, D., *An Introduction to Mādhva Vedānta*, Burlington, 2003.

Sharma, B.N.K., *Philosophy of Śrī Madhvācārya*, Delhi, 1986a.

Sharma, B.N.K., *The Brahmasūtras and Their Principal Commentaries: Critical Exposition*, Bombay, 1986b.

Sharma, B.N.K., *History of the Dvaita School of Vedānta and Its Literature*, Delhi, 1981.

Sharma, B.N.K., *Madhva's Teaching in His Own Words*, Bombay, 1963.

Sheridan, D.P., "The Dueling Biographies of Madhva and Śaṅkara," *JVS* 15/2, 2007, 123–144.

Sheridan, D.P., "Vyāsa as Madhva's Guru: Biographical Context for a Vedāntic Commentator," in: J. Timm, ed., *Texts in Context: Traditional Hermeneutics in South Asia*, Albany, 1992, 109–125.

Siauve, S., *La Doctrine de Madhva*, Pondicherry, 1968.

Daniel P. Sheridan

Mīrābāī

Mīrābāī (born c. 1500 CE), a royal Rājpūt woman and a devotee of → Kṛṣṇa, is one of the most well-loved saints of devotional Hinduism (→ *bhakti*). The story of her life has captured people's imagination across class, caste, language, religion, culture, geography, and time. At once the tale of a religious exemplar, an impassioned romance, and a heroic saga of struggle and triumph against adversity, her life has been retold and performed in multiple genres. The devotional songs (*bhajans*; see → *kīrtan and bhajan*) that she is said to have composed are equally popular and widely known, articulating not only her love and longing for her divine beloved but also her defiance of social norms and renunciation of worldly values. Indeed, her story and songs have become a vehicle for many others to speak of their own diverse experiences, values, and dreams and to come to terms with and shape individual, communal, and national identities.

Fig. 1: Mīrābāī in Merta (photo Nancy M. Martin).

The Life of Mīrābāī

As a beloved saint, Mīrābāī (also known as Mīrā, Meera, and Meerabai) belongs more to the realm of hagiography and popular memory than to history, and indeed traditional historical sources yield little information about her (Hawley, 2005, 89–98). Indian scholars have uncovered a wealth of references to her in North Indian hagiographic literature, beginning in the latter half of the 16th century (Brajaratnadas, 1948; Prabhat, 1999; Shekhavat, 1974; Martin, 1995, 32–114). Nābhādās gives us the first real details of her life in his *Bhaktamāl* (c. 1600), with fuller renderings emerging in Priyādās' *Bhaktirasabodhinī* (1712 CE) and the *Premambodh* (1693 CE). Nābhādās describes her as a woman without fear or shame who abandoned the constraints of family tradition to sing of her lord in a very public way (Rupkala, 1969, 713–723; Hawley, 2004, 123). "Wicked ones" tried to poison her because of her actions, but she was completely unharmed. For Nābhādās she was "like a *gopī*... in this degenerate age" – willing to risk it all in her overpowering love for her irresistible lord, even as the cowherding women (*gopīs*) of his adoptive community in Braj were, at the time of his original incarnation, disregarding all social restrictions and propriety in their desire to be with Kṛṣṇa (whom Mīrābāī characteristically calls Giridhar, "The Mountain Lifter," in a reference to his childhood raising of Mount Govardhan to protect this cowherding community from the torrential rains of Indra's ire; Martin, 1995, 44). Nābhādās' compact lines invoke rather than detail her story, suggesting that she was already well known to his listeners.

A century later, Priyādās wrote his commentary on Nābhādās' work, recounting full-blown life stories of the saints therein (Rupkala, 1969, 717–722; Hawley, 2004, 123–127; Martin, 1995, 45–66). He tells of Mīrā being born in Merta (a principality within the kingdom of Marwar in western Rajasthan) and of her childhood devotion. Her marriage is arranged to a *rāṇā* (a title specific to the ruler in the kingdom of Mewar in southern Rajasthan), but though she goes through the wedding ritual, she remains absorbed in her lord. Arriving at her marital home, she immediately angers her mother-in-law by refusing to worship their family goddess and thus to bring blessings to her newly married husband.

The enraged *rāṇā* (here seemingly her father-in-law) banishes her to a separate palace, but to her, this is no punishment – she can worship as she pleases in the company of fellow devotees and holy men (→ *sādhus*). Her sister-in-law tries to dissuade her from such associations, to no avail. With neither isolation nor persuasion having any effect, the *rāṇā* sends her poison, but drinking it, she only looks more radiant. His attempt to catch her in a compromising situation also fails. When his spy reports her laughing and talking as if to a lover in her chambers, he bursts in, sword in hand, but she is alone before her image of Kṛṣṇa.

In other tellings, Mīrā's persecutor may be her husband, brother-in-law, or father, but it is always a male family member. Additional assassination attempts are also reported: she is sent a poisonous snake in a basket said to contain a diamond necklace, garland for Kṛṣṇa, or → *śālagrām* (a special black stone used in lieu of an image in Vaiṣṇava worship) and scorpions in a bag said to contain jeweled toe-rings. But in her hands, each miraculously becomes these promised items. A bed of nails concealed beneath flowers becomes only soft petals beneath her weight, and a ravenous lion meant to devour her lies quietly before her when she worships him as Narasiṃh (the man-lion incarnation of → Viṣṇu). Of her childhood, it is said that when she saw a wedding procession, she asked her mother who her groom would be and then took to heart her mother's seemingly playful response that she was betrothed to Kṛṣṇa. She is also said to have circled her image of Kṛṣṇa during the wedding ceremony; alternately, Kṛṣṇa is reported to have come to marry her himself the evening before (Macauliffe, 1903).

Priyādās continues his tale, recounting a series of episodes between Mīrābāī and three men outside her marital and natal families – a lustful *sādhu*, the → Gauḍīya Vaiṣṇava *guru* → Jīva Gosvāmī, and the → Mughal emperor Akbar. The *sādhu* tells Mīrā that Kṛṣṇa has ordered her to surrender her body to his lust. She consents but sets up a beautifully decorated bed in the midst of the devotees, saying that if indeed Kṛṣṇa ordered this act, then there should be no shame in its public performance. The *sādhu*'s lust evaporates, and instead he becomes her disciple. On a pilgrimage to Vrindavan, the holy city of Kṛṣṇa's childhood and adolescence, she meets the famed Jīva Gosvāmī, who breaks his vow not to be in the presence of women to do so. Subsequent tellers recount this episode as a test of sorts, with him first refusing to meet her and doing so only after she reminds him that all human souls are female in relation to the decidedly male Kṛṣṇa. Hearing of her beauty, the emperor Akbar also comes to hear Mīrā sing, with his court musician Tan Sēn. Subsequent tellers add that they came disguised as *sādhus* and offered Mīrā the gift of a jeweled necklace for Kṛṣṇa, and some describe this encounter as the principal cause for Mīrā's persecution – her discourse with this Muslim ruler and enemy of Mewar constituted a dishonoring of her Rājpūt in-laws (Behari, 2008, 13–16). Priyādās' tale concludes with her going to dwell in Dwarka – another very famous Vaiṣṇava pilgrimage site, where the mature Kṛṣṇa established his kingdom. Finally the *rāṇā* has a change of heart and sends Brahman priests to bring Mīrā back home. She asks to take leave of Kṛṣṇa in the temple before departing and then merges with his image, no more to be seen, as the tale comes to a close.

In the story that Priyādās tells, Mīrā's life reflects standard elements found in the life stories of other saints, particularly other women saints (Ramanujan, 1982; Sangari, 2006, 230; Martin, 1995, 52–66). In the Gauḍīya Sampradāya to which Priyādās belongs, the relationship between devotee and Kṛṣṇa is epitomized by the relationship between the *gopī*s and Kṛṣṇa, articulated in the language of erotic love, and the story that he tells has a further logic that emerges from this understanding. Kṛṣṇa's reciprocal love for Mīrā stands in dramatic contrast to the murderous rage of the controlling *rāṇā*. Each of her encounters with other men outside the family reflects further dimensions of women *bhakta*s' experience – the lustful *sādhu*'s seeing her only as an object for his desire, Jīva Gosvāmī's initial rejection of her because of an aversion to women arising from male projection of desire onto women, and the chaste patronage of Akbar, which also affirms devotion to god as transcending the divide between Hindu and Muslim.

The tale that Priyādās tells profoundly affects many subsequent tellings, but it is by no means the only story being told about Mīrābāī even in his time. A quite different story emerges in the *Premambodh* (Ocean of Love), composed in 1693 CE for performance in the court of the tenth Sikh *gurū*, Gobind Singh, in the Punjab region (Hawley & Mann, 2008; forthcoming). Here Mīrābāī is the disciple of the untouchable Cāmar saint Raidās (or → Ravidās, a saint recognized by the Sikhs as sharing their *gurū*s' insight). She is married to a prince named Giridhari, whom she does not realize is actually the god incarnate, but she refuses to consummate the marriage unless he, too, is a devotee (though she is portrayed as very much wanting to do so). Yet he refuses to recite the name of → Rām (a generic term for god appropriate to the Sikh conception of the divine as *nirguṇ* or beyond form). When he learns that he has done so in his sleep and thus spoken the word that should ideally be his last, he immediately goes into a meditative trance and dies. Mīrābāī realizes then that he truly was god. She is beside herself with grief, and only Kṛṣṇa's return releases her. They are at last joined in the ocean of love for one night before he vanishes. She goes on in subsequent scenes to become a renowned religious teacher, to overcome a lustful *sādhu* (whose inner desire here becomes an external disease healed by Mīrā), and to incur the wrath of her father for her actions, though her parents are ultimately won over by Kṛṣṇa's appearance listening to their daughter sing.

The story told is quite differently from that of Priyādās, but it also seems to assume knowledge of similar portrayals, for much of its humor lies in shattering expectations of how Mīrābāī should behave. Further, the story reflects Sikh theology and values rather than Gauḍīya Vaiṣṇava ones, and it records an alternate and still popular strand of tradition that has Mīrā as Raidās' disciple. The story of Mīrābāī that the Maharashtrian → Vārkarī hagiographer Mahīpati told some half a century later similarly transposes Mīrābāī's story into a Vārkarī milieu, with the conflict arising between Mīrābāī and her parents in this tradition, in which the love of god for the devotee is modeled on parental love (Abott & Godbole, 1988, vol. II, 66–77). Mahīpati clearly knows of but rejects Priyādās' portrayal of Mīrā, drawing on other circulating traditions and situating her in his own devotional milieu, even as Priyādās reflects aspects of Gauḍīya Vaiṣṇava devotion in his tale and the author of the *Premambodh* Sikh traditions and concerns.

There is no original version of Mīrābāī's story of which all others are variants, but rather there are a number of fascinating "tellings," each revealing as much about the tellers and their audiences, communities, and times as about the saint herself (Ramanujan, 1991, 24–25). The narrative and the song traditions that grow up around her are thus constituted by an abundance of circulating traditions that allow for continuing experience, engagement, and expansion (Hawley & Mann, forthcoming; Shukla-Bhatt, 2007, 274). The "historical" biography of Mīrābāī emerging at the end of the 19th century, no less than these hagiographic tales, partakes of this same quality of participatory engagement. Nationalist writers and Rājpūt historians, too, would bring their own values and agendas to their search for the historical Mīrā and would draw on and react to these circulating traditions in the shaping of their tellings of her life. For nationalists she became an exemplar of strong, heroic Indian women, and her pan-Indian fame led Rājpūts in Rajasthan also to seek to reclaim her as one of their own (Martin, 2000b).

Mīrā's ostensive biography was first published in 1898 by esteemed historian Munshi Deviprasad; in it, Mīrā is portrayed as a proper and devoted Rājpūt wife who turns seriously to devotion only after the death of her husband, father-in-law, and father, and who is persecuted only by a despicable brother-in-law, Vikramājīt (Deviprasad, 1954). Gone is the rebellious woman of Nābhādās, replaced by a woman who turns to devotion and renunciation in response to sorrow and the realization of the transitoriness of earthly happiness – a socially appropriate vocation for a widow. This tale is propagated as the historical truth about Mīrā, taught in Hindi literature classes and immortalized in the *Amar Chitra Katha* comic book series (Chandrakant, 1972; Hawley, 2005, 139–164). Yet the evidence for its particular details is very slender at best.

The historicity of this biography hinges on a single reference in a mid-17th-century text, *Naiṇsī rī Khyāt*, in which the author notes of Bhojrāj, son of Rāṇā Sāṅgā of Mewar, that "people say" that Mīrābāī Rāṭhor was married to him (see Sakariya, 1960, 21; Hawley, 2005, 90). Not only is this a kind of hearsay report quite different from other parts of this text recounting the history of the Rājpūts of Marwar, but the earliest available copy of the text is also dated 1842 CE, making it possible that this reference may not have been in the original and instead could have been inserted centuries later (Taft, 2002, 165–168; 2009, 329). Even so, the known year of Bhojrāj's marriage – 1516 CE – is used by historians to determine the year of Mīrā's birth and her family lineage and to describe her subsequent life based on the wider records available about the Meṛtīya Rāṭhors and ruling Sisodiya Rājpūts of Mewar. For the basic events in her life, these historians must rely on earlier hagiographers, and they and other nationalist writers seem to have conformed Mīrā's life story to the pattern of other Indian heroines popular in the 19th century (Martin, 2000b). This family of tellings, too, has the same perspectival quality as those of Priyādās, Mahīpati, and the *Premambodh* – offering us a particular conception of Mīrā but by no means the singularly "true" one, beside which all others should be judged in error. Nevertheless, the tales told by nationalists and Rājpūt historians have been interwoven and widely disseminated as the truth about the saint (Goetz, 1966; Behari, 2008).

P. Mukta has claimed that, in earlier centuries, the Rājpūts explicitly sought to erase the memory of Mīrā because she so dishonored her natal and marital families (Mukta, 1994, 69–71, 178–181). Though the evidence to support this assertion is insufficient to definitively prove outright suppression, the silence of historical documents suggests at the very least indifference, until her national popularity made reclaiming her expedient. In this reclamation, these Rājpūt historians portrayed her unequivocally as a good Rājpūt wife and claimed the authority of history for their telling, explicitly seeking to eliminate other possible stories of Mīrābāī. What might those other tales have been? Even Rājpūt women interviewed by L. Harlan in the 1980s told a different story, claiming that Mīrābāī was indeed a source of shame to the Rājpūts and that she wrongly refused her earthly husband. For them her exceptional behavior becomes acceptable only in her death, proving the prior marriage that she had claimed to Kṛṣṇa and making her an ideal wife (*pativratā*) of her lord, thereby reinforcing rather than breaking this norm (Harlan, 1992, 205–222).

In rural → Rajasthan, Mīrā's story is also performed in folk dramas (*khyāls*) as a romance, with her love for a socially inappropriate, albeit divine, lover contrasting starkly with the gender norms and expectations that ensure social cohesion and stability (Martin, 1995, 324–337). An epic-song tradition called *Mīrā Janma Patrī* (Mīrā's Horoscope), sung among lower-caste communities, recounts the tale of a royal woman seeking to follow her spiritual calling but forced to marry against her will, suspected of sorcery because of her devotional practice, and ultimately cast out by her husband when he learns that she is the disciple of the leatherworker Raidās (Mukta, 1994, 112–114, 233–234; Martin, 1999). Rājpūt historians and nationalists seemingly wanted to eliminate any challenge from Mīrā's story through their own reformulation of her tale as history, but in the wider and unbounded circulating traditions around her, her actions and character remain problematic and potentially disruptive. Mīrā's story can always be and is told again and again in other ways and filled with alternate meanings.

New contexts and narrative genres continue to expand these tellings as people continue to identify with Mīrābāī and her story in a multitude of ways. Some 18 movies have been made of Mīrā's life starting in the silent era, television series have been broadcast in 1993 and 2009, and a host of novels have been written about her, in tacit recognition of the essential engagement of imagination in all such tellings (Martin, 2010; Rajadhyaksha & Willemen, 1999). Of the films, M.S. Subbhulakshmi's starring role in E. Duncan's *Meera* (Tam. 1945; Hind. 1947) is of particular note (though Gulzar's 1979 film may have had more lasting influence due to its availability and repeated broadcast; Pauwels, 2010). At that crucial time, Mīrā was lifted up as a unifying pan-Indian heroine representing the best of Indian culture and religion, particularly in the face of the violence of Partition, and M.S. Subbhulakshmi, as Mīrā, became an ambassador for the nation via film-festival showings and concert performances abroad (de Groot, 2006). The 1993 television series, *Meerabai* (dir. Ved Rahi), came out in the wake of the destruction of the Bābrī Masjid and carries a strong condemnation of the destructiveness of internecine violence. Mīrābāī's story in these various written, oral, and visual tellings becomes a vehicle for addressing crucial issues and concerns, and all these diverse tellings add to the flow of circulating narrative traditions of Mīrābāī, influencing one another and future tellings in an intertextual abundance that has been a hallmark of Mīrā's story seemingly from its inception.

The Songs of Mīrābāī

Mīrābāī is known for her devotional songs (*bhajans*) as much as for her story, and they, too, partake of the same quality of participation and abundance, with the 16th-century individual woman joined by a chorus of other singers across the centuries, composing and performing in her name. In perhaps the most famous song attributed to her, Mīrā proclaims that hers is Giridhar Gopāl ("Mountain-Lifting Cowherd") – there is no other in all the three worlds. In another, she claims to have purchased him in the market for the cost of her life, a price that the world considers dear but she considers cheap. Elsewhere she speaks of being sold into his hands and of being his servant in life after life, serving without pay. She sings of tying bells to her ankles and dancing away even as others criticize her and try to hurt her and laughing as she knowingly drinks the *rāṇā*'s poison. And she speaks in impassioned words of her love and longing for her divine beloved – suffering terribly in his absence yet unable to turn away, longing to meet him and ecstatic at his coming.

Drawing on the imagery of Kṛṣṇa's youthful incarnation in Braj and tropes of classical and folk love lyrics as her identity and that of the *gopīs* merge, Mīrābāī sings of the coming of the rainy season – a time for lovers to be together that makes separation all the more unbearable – and of sleepless nights and losing mind, body, and sense in her longing, of staring down the road watching endlessly for Kṛṣṇa to come and of preparing a bed and sweets for his enjoyment, of anticipated and joyous meetings and of marrying him in a dream, of playing *holī* with even the sky filling with color, and of being addicted to his name, her heart wounded by the arrow of love. Her eyes betray her, captivated as she is at first glance, and she describes his appearance in exquisite detail – peacock crown, jeweled garland, and yellow silk at his waist, his flute Muralī in his hands as he dances and his eyes enticing her with sidelong glances. She asks for his protection, reminding him of all those devotees whom he has helped in the past, and she complains of his seeming indifference, calling him a *jogī* (*yogī*) or renouncer who is attached to no one and warning others about falling in love with such a one. At other times, she also speaks of and to the *rāṇā*, renouncing the things of his world – traditional wedding ornaments and the luxuries of her palace life – to embrace the life of the simplest devotee. The trappings of wealth and privilege mean nothing to her, and the *rāṇā* ultimately has no power over her, because she does not want anything that he can offer. She will follow her heart and will not be deterred, her own destiny many lifetimes in the making. In all the songs attributed to her, her character and life story give additional layers of meaning, because it is Mīrābāī who is said to sing them.

Hundreds of songs have been attributed to Mīrābāī. Even as it is not possible to isolate the "historical Mīrā," it is also not possible to determine Mīrābāī's actual words. Extensive manuscript studies have yielded only a limited number of songs recorded in the 17th century (Hawley, 2005, 98–116). The earliest song appears in a 1604 CE recension of the Sikh *Ādigranth*, though it was later removed from the finalized version (Callewaert, 1991). Because neither Mīrā nor her songs were ever formally adopted by any devotional *sampradāy*, nor did any *panth* develop around her as it did for other saints like → Kabīr and Raidās, there are not the same kinds of early clearly datable collections of her works that would allow for even an early core of songs to be identified. Those songs that we have are scattered through collections among those of other saints in manuscripts that may have originated as the notebooks of itinerant singers but later developed into a scribal tradition.

In the 20th century, the work of collecting and publishing songs of Mīrā has been undertaken by scholars, with the largest collection including 1,312 songs (Swarup, 1957). Among these works, P. Caturvedi's collection of 202 poems drawn from unspecified manuscripts, first published in 1932 and in its 18th edition as of 1989, is perhaps the most widely disseminated, having also been translated into English in full by A.J. Alston in 1980 (Caturvedi, 1989; Alston, 1980). In 1949, L.P. Sukul published a set of 102 poems that he claimed to be from manuscripts dating back to Mīrā's time and recorded by her maidservant, but other scholars have raised serious reservations about the language of the poems, the story of the preservation of the manuscripts, and the lack of similar dedicated manuscripts of this type for other saints at this early date (Sukul, 1949a; 1949b; Hawley, 2005, 100–103; Callewaert, 1991, 206–207). Further, all copies of the manuscripts that L.P. Sukul allegedly used mysteriously disappeared, and it now appears that, paralleling the earlier claims of Rājpūt historians, this publication may have been an attempt to present a limited set of very popular songs of Mīrābāī, with claims of certain authorship, and in so doing to establish an academically legitimized canon of Mīrā songs for Hindi literature, a canon that also sought to delegitimize songs that ran counter to nationalist and Rājpūt historians' portrayals of Mīrā (Hawley, 2005, 102). Still despite the doubts raised about L.P. Sukul's claims and perhaps in appreciation of the clear editorial agenda, this set of admittedly popular poems continues to be reproduced in Hindi academic literature as representative of Mīrā's authentic works.

However, other concerns and themes appear in songs sung elsewhere in Mīrābāī's name, particularly by low-caste communities, in the all-night singing sessions called *jāgaraṇ*s that are the principle mode of religious practice in rural India. Here there are songs that clearly address the *rāṇā* and reject his world and his power, that reject the ideology of a wife's salvation coming through serving her husband as her god, and that challenge practices of arranged and exogamous marriage, the treatment of widows, the glorification of → *satī*, and female infanticide as well as caste-based oppression (Mukta, 1994; Bhatnagar *et al.*, 2005, 169–233; Martin, 2000a). Mīrā stands in solidarity with the poor and all those who have suffered at the hands of a "*rāṇā*" of any kind in her renunciation of the privileges of her caste and class to live as they do and in her suffering from the same prejudices and violence, particularly because of her association with Raidās. Hers is a voice that speaks of dignity and of embracing a more egalitarian value system where worth is not determined by material possessions, birth status, or social hierarchies but is built on the foundation that all are beloved of god and have received a precious human birth and on shared spiritual practice and ever-deepening devotion.

In her groundbreaking work on Mīrābāī among such communities in Rajasthan and Saurashtra (Gujarat), P. Mukta argues further that Mīrā belonged first and foremost to people in these lower artisan classes who carried her memory and kept her voice alive across the centuries, her songs articulating their longing and suffering as well as their aspirations and alternate vision of the world (1994). This "imagined community of Mīrābāī" would be betrayed by the Rājpūts and nationalists like → Gandhi who then sought to usurp her. Drawing on material from *jāgaraṇ*s in Madhya Pradesh and Uttar Pradesh as well as Gujarat, R. Bhatnagar *et al.* also identify "codes" within such songs that are readily recognizable by and reflect the perspectives and protest of not only low-caste communities but also women more broadly, including Rājpūt women (2005, 175–178). Clearly Mīrā's songs are very popular among low-caste communities, yet her popularity also crosses over the boundaries of gender, caste and class, and culture and language. Many have found their voice in hers – a voice not restrained by social and religious norms but rather one that articulates not only struggle, unbearable longing, and suffering but also courage, fearlessness, passion, and joy, calling others, too, to a life of dignity and fulfillment.

Mīrābāī as a Model

Devotees across the centuries have seen Mīrā as the embodiment of devotion itself, as *bhakti* incarnate, and she is lauded and celebrated as such. Yet she has also been controversial, never fully adopted by any *bhakti sampradāy* (teaching lineage) or *panth* (path). For those of → *nirguṇ* persuasion like the Sikhs, it might be argued that she is too *saguṇa* in her devotion to Kṛṣṇa. For the followers of the Puṣṭimārg (or → Vallabha Sampradāya), she never acknowledged their founder → Vallabha as a divine incarnation or as her *guru*, and so she is rejected not once but three times in the 17th-century *Caurāsī Vaiṣṇavan kī Vārtā* (Hawley, 2005, 95–98). This also might be reason enough for other *sampradāy*s to keep her at a distance. Some have drawn her in by associating her with their practices and *guru*s, like Priyādās and Mahīpati did, but she is never fully incorporated into any *sampradāy*. It is her behavior as a woman that appears most problematic, for in the vast majority of tellings, she just does not behave as more ordinary women are expected to do, her actions challenging the existing structures of dominance and her words speaking resistance as readily as religious renunciation.

Still the power of her independent character and her single-minded dedication is admired, and so people seek to channel and control this exemplary potential for their own ends. To do so, her tale is sometimes told in an exceptionalist way – her miraculous and heroic life is contrasted with the lives of other more ordinary women, so that she becomes the exception that proves the rule. She is portrayed as married not to the *rāṇā* but to Kṛṣṇa, so that really she is upholding *pativratā* ideals in relation to her divine husband. Alternatively she is made into a good wife after all, only turning to devotion after her husband's death as a widow and only leaving her marital home on the advice of the illustrious male saint → Tulsīdās. In telling her story in this way, the radical nature of her renunciation is diffused, her unrestrained actions violating gender and caste norms are transformed into willing compliance always under the direction of men, and the violence of her persecution is reduced to the arbitrary acts of an aberrant individual. Yet her story, like the saint herself, cannot be ultimately restrained, and these key elements of challenge resurface in many tellings and songs. Still, feminist writers like K. Sangari have found Mīrā's emancipatory potential wanting, because poetry attributed to her employs images of subordination, transposing these relations to the human–divine relation but not fundamentally questioning them, whether it be marital relations or that of slave or servant to master or king (Sangari, 2006). Ambivalence continues to attend Mīrā for those with both conservative and liberative social agendas, even as they recognize her powerful appeal.

Yet Mīrā has in fact been a transformative model for a number of women and also men. Even within nationalist circles, Rabindranath → Tagore invoked Mīrā in his 1914 story "Letter from a Wife" as his heroine steps away from her abusive marital home and husband into a new life of her own (1914). Gandhi, too, drew heavily on Mīrābāī to inspire women to stand up against their husbands in the name of truth and even to leave them, though he also reinforced normative behavior for women in characterizing her as the embodiment of *satyāgraha* and lauding her patient and loving endurance of the *rāṇā*'s torments and her renunciation of physical desires (Kishwar & Vanita, 1989, 86–87; Mukta, 1994, 182–200). Across the 20th century, Mīrā's example has paved the way for individual women to live lives outside normative gender expectations, as artists, spiritual adepts, and activists. For example, Mahadevi Varma (a leading figure in the Chayavad romantic movement in Hindi poetry in the 1920s and 1930s) found acceptance for her impassioned poetry and her choice of a single lifestyle dedicated to literature and Gandhian activism, in large part through people's identification of her with Mīrā (Schomer, 1983). Other women have chosen to join orders of renouncers and draw on Mīrā as precedent for and validation of their choices (de Napoli, 2010, 301). Select Vaiṣṇava women have identified even more deeply with Mīrā as they moved into independent positions of spiritual leadership (Martin, 1996). Though they often faced initial opposition, both these individual women and their larger communities took Mīrābāī's example as a way to come to terms with their life choices. Indeed, social-activist scholar M. Kishwar suggests that Mīrā's example ultimately paves the way in Indian society for acceptance of and respect for women who demonstrate a similar dedication of their lives to some greater cause beyond traditional family life, religious or otherwise (2001, 30). In more ordinary and less comprehensive ways, also, Mīrā continues to inspire people around the world, especially women, not only to find their own voices and to articulate their pain and longing but also to celebrate an impassioned life and to follow their heart's desire, as they too identify with her in myriad ways, are transformed by this encounter, and make their own contributions to the circulating traditions of story and song that surround her (Martin, 2010).

Bibliography

Abbott, J.E., & N.R. Godbole, trans., *Stories of the Saints: Translation of Mahipati's Marathi Bhaktavijaya*, Delhi, 1933, repr. 1988.

Alston, A.J., *The Devotional Poems of Mira Bai*, Delhi, 1980.

Behari, B., *The Story of Mira Bai*, Gorakhpur, 1935, repr. 2008.

Bhatnagar, R., R. Dube & R. Dube, *Female Infanticide in India: A Feminist Cultural History*, Albany, 2005.

Brajaratnadas (Brajaratnadās), *Mīrā Mādhurī*, Varanasi, 1948, [2]1956, [3]1970 (Hind.).

Callewaert, W.M., "The 'Earliest' Song of Mīrā," *OLP* 22, 1991, 201-214.

Caturvedi (Caturvedī), P., *Mīrābāī kī Padāvalī*, Allahabad, 1932, [18]1989 (Hind.).

Chandrakant, K., "Mirabai," *ACK* 535/36, Bombay, 1972.

Deviprasad (Devīprasād), M., *Mīrābāī kā Jīvan Charitra*, Calcutta, 1954 (Hind.).

Goetz, H., *Mirabai: Her Life and Times*, Bombay, 1966.

Groot, R. de, "The Reception in the Netherlands of an Indian Singing Saint: Meerabai in Film, in Translation and in Concert," *TKVNM* 56/1, 2006, 25–65.

Harlan, L., *Religion and Rajput Women: The Ethic of Protection in Contemporary Narratives*, Berkeley, 1992.

Hawley, J.S., *Three Bhakti Voices: Mirabai, Surdas and Kabir in Their Times and Ours*, New York, 2005.

Hawley, J.S., & M. Juergensmeyer, *Songs of the Saints of India*, Delhi, rev. ed. 2004.

Hawley, J.S., & G.S. Mann, "Mirabai in the Court of Guru Gobind Singh," in: A. Busch & T. de Bruijn, eds., *People in Motion, Ideas in Motion: Culture and Circulation in Pre-modern South Asia*, Leiden, forthcoming.

Hawley, J.S., & G.S. Mann, "Mirabai in the *Pothi Prem Ambodh*," *JPS* 15/1–2, 2008, 199–226.

Kishwar, M., "Traditional Female Moral Exemplars in India," *EaA* 6/3, 2001, 22–31.

Kishwar, M., & R. Vanita, "Poison to Nectar: The Life and Work of Mirabai," *Manushi* 50–52, 1989, 74–93.

Macauliffe, M.A., "The Legend of Mīrā Bāī, the Rajput Poetess," *IA* 32, 1903, 329–335.

Martin, N.M., "Mirabai Comes to America: The Translation and Transformation of a Saint," *JHSt* 3, 2010, 12–35.

Martin, N.M., "Mirabai and Kabir in Rajasthani Folk Traditions: Meghwal and Manganiyar Repertoires," in: M. Offredi, ed., *The Banyon Tree: Essays on Early Literature in New Indo-Aryan Languages*, Delhi, 2000a, 391–418.

Martin, N.M., "Mirabai in the Academy and the Politics of Identity," in: M. Bose, ed., *Faces of the Feminine from Ancient, Medieval and Modern India*, New York, 2000b, 162–182.

Martin, N.M., "*Mira Janma Patri* and Other Tales of Resistance and Appropriation," in: R. Joshi & N.K. Singhi, eds., *Religion, Ritual, and Royalty*, Jaipur, 1999, 227–261.

Martin, N.M., "Mirabai: Inscribed in Text, Embodied in Life," in: S. Rosen, ed., *Vaiṣṇavī: Women and the Worship of Krishna*, Delhi, 1996, 7-46.

Martin, N.M., "Dyed in the Color of Her Lord: Multiple Representations in the Mirabai Tradition," diss., Graduate Theological Union, 1995.

Mukta, P., *Upholding the Common Life: The Community of Mirabai*, New Delhi, 1994.

Napoli, A.D. de, "'Crossing over the Ocean of Existence': Performing 'Mysticism' and Exerting Power by Female Sādhus in Rajasthan," *JHSt* 3, 2010, 298–336.

Pauwels, H.R.M., "Who Is Afraid of Mirabai? Gulzar's Antidote to Mira's Poison," in: D. Dimitrova, ed., *Religion in Literature and Film in South Asia*, New York, 2010, 45–67.

Prabhat, C.L., *Mīrā Jīvan aur Kāvya*, 2 vols., Jodhpur, 1999 (Hind.).

Rajadhyaksha, A., & P. Willemen, *Encyclopedia of Indian Cinema*, London, rev. ed. 1999.

Ramanujan, A.K., "Three Hundred Rāmāyaṇas: Five Examples and Three Thoughts on Translation," in: P. Richman, ed., *Many Rāmāyaṇas: The Diversity of a Narrative Tradition in South Asia*, Berkeley, 1991, 22–49.

Ramanujan, A.K., "On Women Saints," in: J.S. Hawley & D.M. Wulff, eds., *The Divine Consort: Rādhā and the Goddesses of India*, Boston, 1982, 316–324.

Rupkala (Rūpkalā), S.B.P., *Śrī Bhaktamāl of Nābhādās: With the Bhaktirasabodhinī commentary of Priyādās*, Lucknow, 1969 (Hind.).

Sakariya, B., ed., *Muṅhatā Naiṇsī rī Khyāt*, vol. I, Jodhpur, 1960 (Hind.).

Sangari, K., "Mirabai: The Female Voice and Oral Compositions," in: J.S. Grewal, ed., *History of Science, Philosophy and Culture in Indian Civilization*, vol. VII/2: *Religious Movements and Institutions in India*, Delhi, 2006, 228–260.

Schomer, K., *Mahadevi Varma and the Chhayavad Age of Modern Hindi Poetry*, Berkeley, 1983.

Shekhavat (Śekhāvat), K.S., *Mīrābāī kā Jivanvṛtta evam Kāvya*, Jodhpur, 1974 (Hind.).

Shukla-Bhatt, N., "Performance as Translation: Mīrā in Gujarat," *IJHS* 11/3, 2007, 273–298.

Sukul, L.P., "Padāvalī Paricay," in: S.N. Sarma *et al.*, eds., *Mīrā Smṛti Granth*, Calcutta, 1949a.

Sukul, L.P., "Mīrā Padāvalī," in: S.N. Sarma *et al.*, eds., *Mīrā Smṛti Granth*, Calcutta, 1949b.

Swarup (Svarūp), Swami A., *Mīrā Sudhā Sindhu*, Bhilwara, 1957 (Hind.).

Taft, F., "Six Incarnations of Mirabai," in: V. Joshi & S. Singh, eds., *Culture, Polity, and Economy*, Jaipur, 2009, 163–172.

Taft, F., "The Elusive Historical Mira: A Note," in: L.A. Babb, V. Joshi & M.W. Meister, eds., *Multiple Histories: Culture and Society in the Study of Rajasthan*, Jaipur, 2002, 313–335.

Tagore, R., "A Letter from a Wife," in: K. Bardhan, trans., *Of Women, Outcastes, Peasants and Rebels: A Selection of Bengali Short Stories*, Berkeley, 1990, 96–109.

Films

Meera, dir. S.S. Gulzar, 1979 (Hind.).

Meera, dir. E. Duncan, 1945 (Tam.), 1947 (Hind.).

NANCY M. MARTIN

Nāmdev

Nāmdev (also, Nāmadeva, Nāmdeo, Bhagat Nāmdev, Nāma) was born around 1270 CE in the area of modern-day Maharashtra and possibly in the vicinity of Narsi Bamani in the Hingoli district. He is commonly thought to have died in 1350, though the place and time of his death vary according to the religious and cultural groups that remember him. He is recalled in Marathi sources to have been born within a relatively low caste of tailors (Śiṃpī) and in North Indian sources to have been born to a family of calico printers (Chīpī). He lived a life devoted to singing songs to various manifestations of Indic divinities, including Viṭṭhal (see → Maharashtra), → Kṛṣṇa, → Rām, and → Śiva, and as such he is remembered as a → Sant and a *bhakta*. He is one of the first figures of the genre of → *bhakti* religious expression in central, western, and northern India, and his legacy has spread throughout the areas of modern-day Maharashtra, Gujarat, Rajasthan, northern India, and Punjab. He is revered in several religious lineages, including those of the → Vārkarīs, the Dādūpanthīs (see → Dādū Dayāl), the → Kābirpanthīs, and among Sikhs, where he is one of the key *bhagat*s (devotees) of the *Gurū Granth Sāhib*. Nāmdev is remembered in all these contexts for traveling throughout India during his lifetime, and hence spreading his voice to these various religious-literary traditions. Memorials to Nāmdev, often marking places he supposedly visited in his lifetime, are spread throughout these regions, particularly in Maharashtra and Punjab. As a result of this great diversity, there is no uniform biography of Nāmdev, no agreed-upon corpus of songs attributed to him, and no single tradition that recognizes Nāmdev as their primary spiritual intercessor (as there is for → Kābir or for the Sikh *gurū*s, for example). Indeed, the songs attributed to Nāmdev span a host of languages – Marathi, Brajbhasha, Hindi, Gujarati, Rajasthani, and Punjabi. The plasticity and high degree of flexibility associated with the legacy of Nāmdev have all contributed to the ability of many traditions over many time periods to invoke his name and his remembrance, and hence a vibrant, eight-centuries-long living tradition surrounds the many manifestations of Nāmdev's remembrance in South Asia.

Biography

The earliest sources for a record of Nāmdev's life are songs or *abhaṅg*s attributed to Nāmdev himself. One of the peculiarities of this figure is his position as both the first biographer of the Vārkarī tradition in Marathi and one of the first autobiographers composing in Marathi. The key texts that convey autobiographical information about Nāmdev are actually biographies of → Jñāndev attributed to Nāmdev. These include the *Ādi* or "Beginning" about Jñāndev's early life, the *Tīrthavalī* or "Travelogue" about a pilgrimage undertaken by Nāmdev and Jñāndev throughout India, and the *Samādhi* about Jñāndev's self-entombment at the age of 21. In addition, several biographers relayed his life story. In Marathi, the chief biographer is Mahīpati in the 18th century, though we receive information on Nāmdev's life from songs attributed to other Sants, such as Janābāī. In North Indian and other sources, biographical songs and full hagiographies regarding Nāmdev are attributed to many figures such as → Narasiṃha Mehtā (15th cent.), Harirām Vyās (16th cent.; see → Haridāsī Sampradāya), Anantdās (16th cent.), Nābhādās (17th cent.), Priyadās (18th cent.), and Rāghavadās (18th cent.). In addition, Nāmdev is mentioned in songs attributed to Kābir (15th cent.), Raidās (16th cent.; → Ravidās), Dhana (17th cent.), and in the *Prem Ambodh Pothī* of the 17th century. In the modern period, these premodern sources became the foundation for many hagiographical and scholarly treatments as well, especially in Marathi and Hindi.

These many sources offer various and differing accounts of Nāmdev's life that cannot be captured easily. In general, Nāmdev is remembered to have been born in the area of India today called Maharashtra, possibly in the town of Narsi Bamani and possibly in Pandharpur, sometime in the late 13th century or early 14th century – the generally accepted dates of life for Nāmdev are 1270–1350, though many scholars vociferously challenge these dates, opting for a later life span. He is said to have been born to a low-caste family of tailors (Śiṃpī), though in North India he is often considered a member of a calico-printer caste (Chīpī).

However, the metaphor of tailoring is present throughout Nāmdev's biographical legacy from Maharashtra to northern India, and so he is generally remembered to have been a tailor. His caste is sometimes considered Śūdra, and many poems attributed to Nāmdev and others reinforce this low-caste status; however, other followers of Nāmdev and fellow Śiṃpī/Chīpī caste members have argued that the caste is actually Kṣatriya and not Śūdra.

In any case, Nāmdev's Maharashtrian origins are not in dispute. Popular hagiography indicates that Nāmdev's father, Dāmāśet, and his mother, Gonāī, taught Nāmdev the trade of the tailor. Though Nāmdev had siblings, at some point Dāmāśet and Gonāī brought into their home an orphan (in some retellings) named Janābāī; in other stories, Janābāī was adopted into the home of Nāmdev as an adult. She is sometimes called Nāmdev's "maidservant," but her function as a fellow "saint-poet" and hagiographer is far more complex, and she served as Nāmdev's first biographer, as well as a biographer of other saints, and a composer in her own right. In addition to Janābāī, around Nāmdev several more saints gathered, indeed, an entire "family of saints" (*sant parivār*), including many figures, such as his own family, and his wife Rājāī. The family extended, for example, to Jñāndev, who is probably the chief saint associated with Nāmdev. In addition we find such figures as Gorā Kumbhar (Gorā the Potter); a gardener named Sāvatā; Naraharī, a goldsmith; the barber, Senā; Kanhopatra, a dancing girl; and perhaps most poignantly, → Cokhāmeḷā, an "untouchable," whose songs detailing his suffering of caste social violence remain today very important testaments. This family of saints assembled at the onset of the Marathi Vārkarī tradition is a crucial social mode that prefigures the way in which all subsequent Marathi Vārkarī saints will be intertwined in a genealogy of sainthood for centuries. For example, → Eknāth, in the 16th century, is said to have dreamed of Jñāndev and through this dream reconnected to Jñāndev by discovering the site of his entombment or *samādhi* in Alandi, as well as discovering his famous text, the *Jñāneśvarī*, and restoring the text to its "original form"; similarly, → Tukārām, in the 17th century, is said to have dreamed of Nāmdev and taken on as his life's work the completion of Nāmdev's vow to compose thousands of songs to god. In this way, the collection of saints that surrounds Nāmdev becomes archetypical of the transhistorical family of saints that will form the core Vārkarī tradition in Maharashtra.

Another undisputed aspect of Nāmdev's biography is, at least in his early life, his deep devotion to the Hindu deity Viṭṭhal, the chief focus of devotion for Vārkarīs. Nāmdev's relationship to Viṭṭhal is described in metaphorical terms as either that of a child to a parent (*vatsalya*) or a friend to a friend (*sākhya*). Nāmdev is situated in Pandharpur in his early life as a great devotee (*bhakta*) of Viṭṭhal who spends his days composing songs (*abhaṅgs*) in rich praise of Viṭṭhal, in the genre of *saguṇa bhakti* (see → *nirguṇa* and *saguṇa*), and performing those songs for others in an art form Nāmdev is said to have innovated in Marathi, called → *kīrtan*. Indeed, so great is Nāmdev's devotion that Jñāndev comes from Alandi to meet this famous *bhakta* and experience the power of his devotion through observing a *kīrtan*. Other traditions that revere Nāmdev – such as those of North India and Punjab – also recall the power of Nāmdev's public performance of *kīrtan*. One ubiquitous story throughout Nāmdev's pan-Indian remembrance recalls how Nāmdev was performing a *kīrtan* before a Śaiva temple but was compelled by a group of Brahmans who officiated at the temple to move his performance behind the temple, so worshippers would not be defiled by his presence and the presence of his ragtag ensemble as they entered the temple. Nāmdev obliged, and as he restarted his *kīrtan* behind the temple, the temple itself turned to face him.

Nāmdev's relationship with Jñāndev deserves special mention. These two figures are largely attributed the inauguration of Vārkarī religious practice – including textual forms (*ovī*, *abhaṅg*, etc.), performance arts (*pravacana* [discourse or speech] and *kīrtan*), and the twice-annual pilgrimage to Pandharpur. The latter event, now synonymous with Vārkarī practice (though perhaps originating in earnest in the 17th cent., not the 13th cent.), revolves around the relationship between Nāmdev and Jñāndev detailed in the text mentioned above, the *Tīrthavalī* or "Travelogue." In this text, a story is told of how Jñāndev came to Pandharpur to meet the great *bhakta* Nāmdev but harbored as well a desire to convert Nāmdev from what Jñāndev considered a simplistic, unphilosophical *saguṇa* devotion to the "image" of god. In order to do this, Jñāndev asked Viṭṭhal for permission to take Nāmdev on a journey to pilgrimage places throughout India – both Śaiva and Vaiṣṇava. From the narrative of the *Tīrthavalī* (reproduced in Mahīpati's *Bhaktavijay*), it seems that Jñāndev believed that separating Nāmdev from Viṭṭhal and showing Nāmdev that Pandharpur was just another pilgrimage place, like so many others, would help Nāmdev see Jñāndev's philosophical *nirguṇa* or "formless" nondualism as the correct vision of religious experience, a position Jñāndev held as a Nāth *yogī* (see → Nāth Sampradāya). However, the effect of this separation is to further reinforce Nāmdev's attachment to the specific figure of Viṭṭhal – indeed, the narrative tells us of Viṭṭhal's own heartache at being separated from Nāmdev. The text provides a long-running debate on *nirguṇa* and *saguṇa* in the particular form of a dialogue about dualism (*dvaita*) and nondualism (*advaita*) that Nāmdev and Jñāndev carry out in the midst of their travels. The denouement of the debate comes when the two saints encounter a village suffering a drought, and the saints themselves are seeking water. They find a well, but it is too deep, and they cannot draw water from the bottom. Jñāndev sees an opportunity to prove the superiority of his *yoga* and the self-reliance of *saguṇa advaita* philosophy. Through *yoga*, he makes himself very small and flies down the side of the well. He returns with a full bucket of water, just enough for himself and for Nāmdev. But instead of drinking the water, Nāmdev begins to pray and call out to Viṭṭhal for help. Viṭṭhal hears the distress of his beloved devotee, and suddenly the well gushes over with water, providing nourishment not only for Jñāndev and Nāmdev, but also for the entire village. Jñāndev learns his lesson and admits that Nāmdev's *bhakti* has its merits. They return to Pandharpur, and thereafter Jñāndev vows to come to Pandharpur every year to see Nāmdev and Viṭṭhal. It is this vow made by Jñāndev to visit Nāmdev and Viṭṭhal that is the origin of the Vārkarī pilgrimage, called the *vārī*, or at least its origin in collective memory. It is remembered when, by tradition, the Nāmdev *pālkhī* (palanquin) is brought out from the Nāmdev Mandir in Pandharpur just as pilgrims are arriving from all over Maharashtra. The Nāmdev *pālkhī* is carried just outside of Pandharpur, where it greets the *pālkhī* of Jñāndev from Alandi and walks with that *pālkhī* and its contingent into Pandharpur to meet Viṭṭhal. Despite the vital nature of this connection between Nāmdev and Jñāndev, it is interesting to note, here, that no compositions exist attributed to Jñāndev that mention Nāmdev, even while Nāmdev is attributed almost all the essential biographical information we have about Jñāndev.

This story of Nāmdev and Jñāndev's philosophical debates belies the more complex nature of Nāmdev's Marathi and pan-Indian religio-philosophical orientation, which transcends a *nirguṇa/saguṇa* or dual/nondual divide. Indeed, Nāmdev's object of devotion is Viṭṭhal, but Viṭṭhal's representation is neither Śaiva nor Vaiṣṇava exclusively. Viṭṭhal is an amalgamation represented through the complex imagery that captures the deity's features, characterists drawn both from Kṛṣṇaite and Śaiva sources. In addition, the Vārkarī saints themselves have complex devotional lineages or *paramparās*, mixing devout Vaiṣṇava practices with initiation into Nāth *yogī* lineages, as Jñāndev and Eknāth, as well as Nāmdev, abundantly. Nāmdev, too, enters a Śaiva Nāth lineage according to tradition when he takes the Nāth *yogī* Visobhā Khecara as his *guru*. This aspect of Nāmdev's religious sentiment – as a figure at the nexus of Śaiva and Vaiṣṇava, *yogī* and *bhakta, saguṇa* and *nirguṇa*, dual and nondual – is central to his remembrance outside of Maharashtra as well, particularly in northern India among the Kābirpanthīs, Dādūpanthīs, and especially the Sikhs.

Nāmdev's hagiography, both in Marathi and in North Indian sources, accommodates this shift or nuance in his religious sentiment through yet another story of his pan-Indian peregrinations. Popular memory recalls that Nāmdev would undertake a second, much longer, sojourn to northern India that would take up the bulk of his life. Nāmdev would be compelled to undertake this journey as a response to the heartache he felt at the self-entombment of his dear friend, Jñāndev, combined with his initiation into Nāth Śaivism and consequently his interest in expanding his religious learning outside of the Marathi-speaking regions. A textual record of this second journey may exist, also under the title *Tīrthavalī*, which is also the oldest textual record of any Nāmdev composition (attributed to 1581 CE in a colophon).

Whatever the details or historical veracity of this journey, it is clear that North Indians remember Nāmdev as their own. His memorials (*smṛtisthaḷa*s) and temples (*mandir*s) dot the landscape of modern-day Gujarat, Rajasthan, Uttar Pradesh, Himachal Pradesh, and Punjab, and in all these places various religious groups – such as the Dādūpanthīs, Kābirpanthīs, and Sikhs – remember Nāmdev, integrate his songs into their literary-spiritual canons, and depict him within the genealogies of their religions. Of all these locations for the memory of Nāmdev, it is in Sikhism especially that we find Nāmdev ensconced in a primary position. In this context, he is one of the oldest *bhagat*s of the *Gurū Granth Sāhib*, and he is highly revered by Sikhs as a foundational inspiration to Gurū Nānak along with other key *bhagats*. Yet even in this context, where Nāmdev's songs in the *Gurū Granth Sāhib* tend toward the *nirguṇa* variety, we still hear that his personal deity is "Bitthula," a reference to Viṭṭhal, and that he was a Marathi speaker, a fact that is conveyed in the rather unconventional language of Nāmdev's songs preserved in the Sikh textual tradition. As a Sikh *bhagat* and Sant in North India, Nāmdev's legacy takes on familiar shapes, especially within Sikhism, as, for example, when Nāmdev is threatened by a Muslim sultan to be executed via elephant trampling while in northern India, unless he embraces Islam. When Nāmdev refuses, the enraged elephant, rather than trampling Nāmdev, bows at his feet. Many other stories tell of Nāmdev facing the possibility of martyrdom, only to be saved by Viṭṭhal, and many of these stories, likely originating in northern India, were later adopted in the 18th century by Marathi hagiographers, thus completing the circle Nāmdev's legacy forms between Maharashtra and northern India.

This circle is perhaps not entirely complete, as a debate has continued over centuries regarding Nāmdev's final resting place. As with many figures and religions (Hindu, Buddhism, Islamic, Christian, Sikh), the final resting place of a vital religious figure is an important historical point, for around such places are often built memorials, temples, and pilgrimage practices, which in turn are often endowed with funds and the faith of centuries of followers. Nāmdev's legacy is no exception. There are several places in northern India that claim to be the place where Nāmdev left this world, but of them all, two receive the most patronage. For Vārkarīs, this place is Pandharpur, to which they believe Nāmdev returned after his long, difficult time traveling and living in northern India, only to come to breathe his last breath on the steps of the Viṭṭhal's temple. For Sikhs and many other North Indian admirers of Nāmdev, they believe this final resting place is Ghuman in Punjab, where Nāmdev is richly remembered as having died surrounded by his devoted North Indian companions.

It is not until the advent of modern cinema that this paradox receives resolution. The 1991 film *Sant Namdev*, directed by Yeshwant Pethkar, concludes by depicting Nāmdev resting upon a cot in Ghuman, tended to by his devotees. He asks them to fetch water for him, and in that moment Viṭṭhal appears to him in a vision and beckons him back to Pandharpur. When Nāmdev's devotees return with water, they find their teacher missing, without a trace, and conclude (rightly it seems) that god has taken him bodily beyond this earth. However, the film continues and shows Nāmdev materializing in Pandharpur, moments from death, weak, and lying upon the steps to Viṭṭhal's temple, unable to gather the strength to climb all the way into the temple's chamber. And so Viṭṭhal comes to him and holds him as he dies, and his body dematerializes. Thus, Nāmdev's death occurs in both places, and in neither – as he, like Kābir, dissolves into the rich religious memory he has left behind.

This "afterlife" for Nāmdev's legacy has taken many forms. One form is the conspicuous "copying" of Nāmdev – both his *nom de plume*, "Nāma," and the style and content of his compositions – by various other "Nāmdevs" from the 16th to 18th century. Naturally the compositions of these other Nāmdevs are conflated with the compositions of an "original" Nāmdev of the 14th century, yet this conflation seems to have been intentional. The tradition of writing in the idiom, and even in the name, of a previous and famous composer is a long-held practice in South Asia (and perhaps elsewhere, as with Shakespeare). While this poses a substantial and important conundrum for modern philology, the existence of these many "Nāmas" was intentional, the construction of a self-referential genealogy of like-minded thinkers and composers spread out over several centuries. The first of these other "Nāmas" was likely a figure named Viṣṇudās Nāma of the 16th century, possibly associated with Eknāth. We know that this figure is distinct from the Nāmdev of the 14th century because of other works composed by him with his name containing his colophon with dates in the 16th century. However, some Marathi scholars believe it is this 16th-century Nāmdev who composed the hagiographies of Jñāndev that also tell of the life of Nāmdev – the *Tīrthavalī* and the *Samādhi*. Indeed, some have argued that it is this latter Nāmdev, of the 16th century, who traveled throughout India. In any case, yet more Nāmas emerged over the centuries, for example, Nāma Yaśvant of the late 16th century and Śiṃpī Nāma of the 18th century. Like Viṣṇudās Nāma, these latter two figures composed songs in the vein and with the subject matter of Nāmdev songs, yet they also composed materials that clearly indicate a different subject and author, as well as a different time period. Rather than see these other "Nāmas" as conflating their work with the original Nāmdev's compositions, we should view this practice as both commonplace and intentional in the construction of a lasting genealogy – built on honor and reputation – based on compositions attributed to the Nāmdev of the 13th century.

In the colonial and postcolonial periods, Nāmdev has been marshaled as a figure of national integration due in large part to his pan-Indian appeal, particularly across geographical expanses and among various Hindu groups and Sikhs. A chair of Nāmdev studies exists in Pune University, and the Nāmdev Mandir is a vital entity in the religious culture of Pandharpur. Nāmdev's remembrance is vibrantly present today in India, especially in Maharashtra, northern India, and Punjab, where many organizations, temple foundations, memorial sites, and groups of devotees – particular members of the Śiṃpī and Chīpī castes – remember Nāmdev with great reverence. Nāmdev has, in particular, been the common thread that has brought many Sikh devotees from Ghuman to Pandharpur and many Maharashtrian devotees from Pandharpur to Ghuman. Indeed, eight centuries after Nāmdev's purported life, he continues his travels in such cultural forms across central, western, and northern India.

Sources

There are many sources for the life, compositions, and legacy of Nāmdev, as well as multiple scholarly examinations, which can be found in Marathi, Hindi, and Punjabi primarily, but also in English. There are no translations of Nāmdev's compositions, as a collection, in English or any other non-Indian language, but rather they exist here and there in various studies. For Hindi songs in English, see particularly the work of W. Callewaert and M. Lath (1989) and within translations of the *Gurū Granth Sāhib*. For Marathi materials in English, see C.L. Novetzke (2008).

Manuscript Sources

Manuscripts containing songs attributed to Nāmdev are to be found throughout India, especially in Maharashtra, Rajasthan, and Punjab. In Maharashtra, the oldest manuscript containing Nāmdev compositions bears the date 1581 CE and is a Marathi recounting of Nāmdev's solo journey throughout India, called the *Tīrthavalī*, but it is a version much different from the one commonly reprinted in collections of Nāmdev songs and commonly referenced in discussions of Nāmdev (and reinvented by Mahīpati in the *Bhaktavijay*). This is one of the few manuscripts in the Marathi collection that is dedicated entirely to Nāmdev and in this case entirely to a single composition. The latter version of the *Tīrthavalī* is dated to 1731 CE and appears in a massive manuscript containing a collection of songs from many Maharashtrian figures, including Tukārām (17th cent.), Jñāndev, and Eknāth, as well as a broad collection of songs attributed to Nāmdev (as well as the other "Nāmas" such as Viṣṇudās Nāma). A third manuscript found by the government of India during their preparation of the *Śrī Nāmdev Gāthā* in the 1960s records a massive manuscript from Dhule attributed the date 1636 CE. These are the largest and oldest collections of Nāmdev songs in Marathi, though throughout Maharashtra, as well as areas of Gujarat, Karnataka, Tamil Nadu, Andhra Pradesh, and elsewhere, manuscripts exist that contain Nāmdev materials in both Marathi and Hindi. In almost all cases, these materials are contained in *bāḍa*s (notebooks) carried by *kīrtan* performers for at least the last four centuries. In most cases, these *bāḍa*s are organized by "author" or "saint" rather than by melody or *rāg*, and sometimes they are organized by theme, perhaps reflecting their use in common thematic subjects for *kīrtan*s.

In Rajasthan in particular, and intersecting with the materials of the Dādūpanth, the Kābirpanth, and the Nāth tradition, many manuscripts contain songs attributed to Nāmdev. The earliest of these is dated to 1636 in the Dādūpanth collection of manuscripts, though it is likely a copy, suggesting that the Dādūpanth manuscript tradition is perhaps as old as the Marathi tradition. The Dādūpanth manuscripts are organized by *rāg* (melody) and by "author," usually situating Nāmdev amid a regular host of associated *bhaktas*, including Dādū, Kābir, Raidās, and Haridās. In the Nāth tradition, manuscripts have surfaced containing Nāmdev compositions that date back to as far as 1669.

In Punjab, the compilation and preservation of the *Gurū Granth Sāhib* records 61 songs attributed to Nāmdev, organized according to *rāg* and "author," as is the North Indian tradition. These songs are present in the *Ādigranth* of 1604 as well as the *Gurū Granth Sāhib*'s final form in 1704. In the Fatehpur manuscript of 1582, 11 songs are attributed to Nāmdev.

Printed Collections

There are many Marathi collections of Nāmdev songs. The oldest is a lithograph of the story of Jñāndev's entombment or *samādhi* attributed to Nāmdev, published in 1849 by R.S. Gondhalekar. In 1892, R.S. Gondhalekar also published a collection of Nāmdev songs, followed by a collection two years later compiled by T. "Tatya" Gharat. Many others have followed from then until now, including three new collections from 2000 to 2010. However, of all these publications in Marathi, two merit distinction. The first is a volume dedicated to Nāmdev, and to his companions and family members, as part of the large collection of songs attributed to the Vārkarī saints called the *Sakaḷa Santa Gāthā* (The Collection of [Songs] of All the [Vārkarī] Saints). This compilation contains over 2,400 songs attributed to Nāmdev and was edited first by T.H. Avate, originally published in 1908, and has been subsequently reprinted over the last hundred years. This is the largest collection of Nāmdev songs in Marathi with the aim of providing access to all songs attributed to Nāmdev. In other words, this is not a critically edited edition but a compilation of all known "Nāmdev" songs, and thus it contains no editorial or philological apparatus, such as notes about sources or variance. It is considered by Vārkarīs to be the chief source of the songs of the Vārkarī saints – second only to private manuscript collections.

The second collection of Nāmdev's songs that merits distinction is the government of Maharashtra's edition, published in 1970. From 1960 to 1970, an editorial committee composed of Marathi textual scholars and historians worked on behalf of the state government of Maharashtra (formed, itself, in 1960) to create the first critically edited compilation of songs attributed to Nāmdev, called the *Śrī Nāmdev Gāthā*. This collection contains 2,337 songs. Given the difference between the number of songs in the unedited *Sakaḷa Santa Gāthā* and the edited *Śrī Nāmdev Gāthā*, it should be clear that the editors of the *Śrī Nāmdev Gāthā* did not choose to eliminate songs because they were not attested in manuscripts collected by the committee. Instead, where available, the editors note manuscript representations of songs and variations but do not eliminate "nonattested" songs. Thus the government edition of Nāmdev's songs – commissioned as it was as a service to the new linguistic state of Maharashtra and its citizenry – was meant to combine philological method with political means.

In Hindi the first printed collection of Nāmdev's songs was edited by B. Mishra and R. Maurya in 1964, the *Sant Nāmdev kī Hindī Padāvalī*. This is a critical edition of Nāmdev's songs utilizing manuscripts from Patiala, Banaras, Ghuman, Pandharpur, and Pune. Of course, any printed edition of the *Gurū Granth Sāhib* also serves as a compendium for Nāmdev's Hindi materials, and any English translation will also contain an English rendering of those Nāmdev songs within the *Gurū Granth Sāhib*. The most recent and the most authoritative edition of Nāmdev's Hindi songs to date is the work of W. Callewaert and M. Lath, *The Hindī Padāvalī of Nāmdev* (1989). This outstanding work of philological investigation also presents selected English translations of songs and an exhaustive review of materials available for the study of Nāmdev's legacy, in particular for details regarding his pan-Indian hagiography.

Cinematic Sources

Aside from manuscripts and printed editions, another "primary" medium for accessing Nāmdev's legacy are the films made about him or that feature him as a chief character. In the 20th century, at least five films have been made about the life of Nāmdev, in Marathi and Hindi. The first film, a silent film, *Sant Namdev*, was made by the pioneer of Indian cinema D.G. Phalke in 1921 and is perhaps the first film about any "saint" of India of any kind. In 1937 B. Apte directed the film *Namace Mahima* (Nāmdev's Glory). Both films have subsequently been lost in the public record. In 1940 Nāmdev was an important character in – and an unacknowledged first source for – the biography of Jñāndev depicted in the film *Sant Dnyaneshwar*. In 1949 K. Talpade directed *Sant Namdev* in Marathi, and this quickly became the standard celluloid retelling of Nāmdev's life. In 1955 D.K. Films produced *Patitapavan* (The Savior of the Sinner), a Hindi film on the life of Nāmdev that accentuated a well-known (though unverifiable) story that Nāmdev had been a robber in his youth; the film was protested vociferously by Nāmdev followers in northern India and Maharashtra and was withdrawn from circulation in 1956. In 1991 Y. Pethkar produced a film, also called *Sant Namdev*, with dialogue in Marathi, Hindi, Gujarati, and Punjabi, that sought to engage Nāmdev's entire life story in India, a project that brought together Nāmdev's Maharashtrian legacy with his North Indian and Punjabi legacy.

Bibliography

Adkar, S.K., *Hindī Nirguṇa-kāvya kā Prārambha aur Nāmdev kī Hindī Kavitā*, Allahabad, 1972 (Hind.).

Avate, T.H., *Sakaḷa Santa Gāthā*, Pune, 1908 (Mar.).

Babar, S., *et al.*, *Śrī Nāmdev Gāthā*, Bombay, 1970 (Mar.).

Bhagat Ram, B., *Śrī Svāmī Nāmdev*, Ghuman, 1936 (Mar.).

Callewaert, W., *The Sarvāṅgī of the Dādūpanthī Rajab*, Leuven, 1978.

Callewaert, W., & M. Lath, *The Hindī Padāvalī of Nāmdev*, Leuven, 1989.

Caturvedi, P., *Uttara Bhārat kī Sant Paramparā*, Prayag, 1951 (Hind.).

Deleury, G.A., *The Cult of Vithoba*, Pune, 1960.

Gharat, T., *Nāmdevāṁcyā āṇi Tyāṁcyā Kuṭuṁbātīla va Samakālīnasādhūṁcyā Abhaṅgāṁcī Gāthā*, Bombay, 1894 (Mar.).

Gondhalekar, R.S., ed., *Nāmdevācī Gāthā*, Pune, 1892.

Gondhalekar, R.S., ed., *Nāmadevakṛta Jnānadevācyā Samādhice Abhaṅga*, Pune, 1849 (Mar.).

Inamdar, H.V., *Nāmā Mhaṇe*, Pune, 1999 (Mar.).

Irlekar, S., *Nāmdevakṛta Jñāneśvar Caritra*, Pune, 1995 (Mar.).

Joshi, S.P., *Panjābāṁtīl Nāmdev*, Bombay, 1940 (Mar.).

Kamat, A., & R.C. Dhere, *Eka Vijay Yātra*, Pune, 1970 (Mar.).

Karandikar, M., *Nāmdev*, New Delhi, 1970.

Kavitkar, G.V., R.M. Bongale, R.C. Dhere, A. Kamat, & V.M. Bachal., eds., *Caṃdramā Jo Alāṃchana*, Pune, 1980 (Mar.).

Kavitkar, G.V., D. Kir, H. Inamdar, N. Relekar, & N. Mirajkar, eds., *Śrī Nāmdev: Caritra, Kāvya āṇi Kārya*, Bombay, 1970 (Mar.).

Koratkar, K.R.. "Nāmdevācī Narsī," *BISM* 7, 1926, 1–4 (Mar.).

Kulkarni, S.R., *Sāhitya Setu*, Mumbai, 1998 (Mar.).

Kulkarni, S.B., "Sant Nāmdevāṃcī Assal Vaṃśāvaḷī," *LS* 9, 1995, 2 (Mar.).

Kulkarni, S.B., "Punjābātīl Nāmdev: Viṣṇudās Nāmā," *NB (Jan–Mar)*, 1993a, 44–57 (Mar.).

Kulkarni, S.B., "Santa Nāmdevāce Eka Āparanparik Pracinā Caritra," *Yugavāṇī* 47, 1993b, 52–68 (Mar.).

Kulkarni, S.B., "Sant Nāmdevgāthyātīl Cār Nāmdev," *Yugavāṇī* 46, 1992a, 6–10 (Mar.).

Kulkarni, S.B., "Smṛtisthalātīl Nāmdev," *Yugavāṇī* 46, 1992b, 23–25 (Mar.).

Lorenzen, D., *Praises to a Formless God: Nirguni Texts from North India*, Albany, 1996.

Machwe, P., *Namdev: Life and Philosophy*, Patiala, 1968.

Mishra, B., & R.N. Maurya, *Sant Nāmdev kī Hindī Padāvalī*, Poona, 1964 (Hind.).

Nath, J., *Nāmdev the Saint-Poet*, New Delhi, 1983.

Novetzke, C.L., *Religion and Public Memory: A Cultural History of Saint Nāmdev in India*, New York, 2008a.

Novetzke, C.L., "The Making of a Marathi Humanist," in: A. Feldhaus & M. Bhagavan, eds., *Claiming Power from Below: Dalits and the Subaltern Question in South Asia*, Delhi, 2008b, 30–46.

Novetzke, C.L., "The Theographic and the Historiographic in an Indian Sacred Life Story," *SF* 3/2, 2007, 169–184.

Novetzke, C.L., "A Family Affair," in: G. Beck, ed., *Alternative Krishnas*, Albany, 2005, 113–138.

Novetzke, C.L., "Divining an Author: The Idea of Authorship in an Indian Religious Tradition," *HR* 42/3, 2003, 213–242.

Pataskar, P.N., *Śrī Santa Śiromaṇi Bālbhakta Śrī Nāmdev Mahārāj He Daroḍekhor Hote Kāy?*, Pune, 1935 (Mar.).

Puranadas, *Janam Sākhī Śrī Svāmī Nāmdevjī kī*, 1888 (Hind.).

Relekar, N.N., H. Inamdar, & N. Mirajkar, eds., *Śrī Nāmdev Darśan*, Kolhapur, 1970 (Mar.).

Singh, M., *Bhakta Śiromaṇi Nāmdev kī Nāyī Jīvanī, Nāyī Padāvālī*, Ambala, 1949 (Hind.).

Singh, N., *Bhagat Nāmdev in the Guru Grantha*, Patiala, 1981.

Vaudeville, C., *Myths, Saints and Legends in Medieval India*, Delhi, 1996.

Christian Lee Novetzke

Narasiṃha Mehtā

Narasiṃha Mehtā (also known as Narasinha Mehtā; c. 1414–1481 CE) is the most popular devotional poet of Gujarat in western India. He is known for his exquisite *pads* (lyrics) of → *bhakti* (devotion) in Gujarati, the language of → Gujarat. He is also widely honored in India as an ardent devotee of → Kṛṣṇa and a saint with deep sympathies for the marginalized of his society.

Narasiṃha is a major figure among the Hindu poet-saints whose songs and sacred biographies in vernacular languages have circulated for centuries through performance in all layers of society and have definitively shaped the religious and cultural histories of their regions. These songs and narratives contributed significantly to the spread of devotional faith in medieval North India (from the 14th to the 17th cent.), a phenomenon often termed the "*bhakti* movement." The songs of some poet-saints also form important parts of the literary history of their regions and continue to be performed today in both devotional and nonreligious contexts as their cherished cultural heritage. Narasiṃha Mehtā is such a poet-saint of Gujarat.

Devotional songs attributed to Narasiṃha have been sung in Gujarat and neighboring Rajasthan for five centuries. Hagiographic narratives about him have circulated more broadly in North India since the early 17th century. Since the mid-20th century, his song defining a religious person in terms of compassion and moral integrity has circulated internationally as Mahatma → Gandhi's favorite hymn. In contemporary times, many songs attributed to him are also performed in secular contexts such as cultural shows in Gujarat and among the diaspora Gujarati speakers. The songs and hagiography of Narasiṃha also circulate widely through popular media such as compact discs, film, television, and now YouTube. They form a vibrant current of *bhakti* in North India and a cherished part of the cultural heritage of Gujarat.

Life

Dates and Historical Context

Scant information of historical accuracy is available about Narasiṃha Mehtā's life, as is common among poet-saints of medieval India. His traditional biography has circulated mainly through oral traditions and through hagiographic texts composed in different parts of North India since the 17th century. Even though Narasiṃha's historicity has not been questioned in Gujarat, the dates of his life were a matter of extensive debates in Gujarati scholarship in the early 20th century.

One school suggested 16th-century dates for Narasiṃha, arguing that his lyrics reflect an influence of the literature of the → Gauḍīya Vaiṣṇava sect of Kṛṣṇa devotion founded by → Caitanya Mahāprabhu (16th cent.). Another school argued for 15th-century dates, stressing that Narasiṃha's lyrics do not reflect the influence of sects devoted exclusively to Kṛṣṇa but draw on myths as contained in Sanskrit → Purāṇas and poetry. The latter school based its argument largely on the recurrent allusions to the poets of two Sanskrit classics of Kṛṣṇa devotion – *Bhāgavatapurāṇa* (c. 9th cent.) and the *Gītagovinda* (12th cent.) – in Narasiṃha's lyrics and the absence of references to the Gauḍīya Vaiṣṇava tradition (Shastri, 2005, 27–89). The 15th-century dates of birth and death – circa 1414–1481 – are now generally accepted. These dates place Narasiṃha in the early phase of Kṛṣṇa *bhakti* poetry in regional languages of North India that is based on myths about Kṛṣṇa's childhood and adolescence among the cowherds of idyllic Vraja (Braj), as contained in the *Bhāgavatapurāṇa*. Narasiṃha precedes the well-known Hindi poets of Kṛṣṇa *bhakti* → Sūrdās and → Mīrābāī (a female poet of Rajasthan), both of whom belonged to the 16th century. But he follows the early poet-saints of the → Vārkarī Sampradāy of → Maharashtra, such as → Nāmdev (c. 14th cent. CE), with whom he shares many aspects of his *bhakti*.

Along with the dates, there is general agreement among scholars that Narasiṃha Mehtā lived most of his life in Junagadh in the Saurashtra Peninsula of Gujarat and that he belonged to the high-caste Brahman community of Nāgars, who worship → Śiva as their chief deity while also venerating other Hindu deities. These details place Narasiṃha in a context in which many religious currents coexisted. Junagadh is situated in the foothills of Mount Girnar, an important center for Buddhist, Hindu, and Jain religions since ancient times. In the 15th century, temples dedicated to Jain *tīrthaṅkaras* (realized souls) and Hindu deities such as the Great Goddess (→ Mahādevī), Śiva, and Kṛṣṇa were found in the city of Junagadh and on Mount Girnar. The Hindu population of the region largely followed religious practices in which worship of a number of deities had a place. The allusions to different religious currents in Narasiṃha's songs and hagiography are relatable to this religious milieu.

Politically, it was a period of instability in Junagadh. The Hindu Chudasama rulers of Junagadh were subservient to the sultans of Gujarat, who were Muslims. During Narasiṃha's lifetime, Junagadh was annexed to the Gujarat Sultanate. Muslim saints and teachers had also begun to settle in the area. But no references to Islam or to the political turmoil are found in Narasiṃha's songs or hagiography, indicating that the shift in political power did not disturb their circulation as popular devotional forms.

Traditional Biography

In contrast to the absence of historical documentation, a large number of traditional sources for Narasiṃha's biography are found. An early reference to Narasiṃha is found in the famous hagiographic compendium in Hindi, the *Bhaktamāl*, written around 1600 CE by Nābhādās possibly in northern Rajasthan, many hundred kilometers away from Narasiṃha's city Junagadh. Here, Narasiṃha is praised for spreading devotion in a region in which the ritual-oriented religion dominated; but no biographical information is given.

From the mid-17th century, several Ākhyāns (long narrative poems meant for public performance) about him are available in Gujarati. A fuller biography of Narasiṃha begins to emerge from these poems. A long poem in Rajasthani – *Narsī jī ro Māhero* (The Ceremonial Gift of Narasiṃha) – is popularly attributed to the woman poet Mīrābāī. Beyond western India, two major hagiographic compendia written in the 18th century – Priyadās' commentary on *Bhaktamāl*, *Bhaktirasabodhinī* (c. 1712 CE), composed in Vrindavan in North India, and Mahīpati's Marathi *Bhaktavijaya* (1768), written in southern Maharashtra – also include Narasiṃha's sacred biography. While the focus in each of these texts from different parts of India shifts slightly according to the religious perspective of the narrator, they all extol Narasiṃha as an exemplary devotee who stood firm in his faith against all odds. Within Gujarat, Ākhyāns such as *Narasaiṃ Mehtā nu Ākhyān* and popular songs from the 18th century onward also portray him as a proponent of equality in devotion, associating closely with low-caste devotees and being persecuted by the religious and political elite of his society for it. The broad outlines of Narasiṃha's biography as emerging from the premodern sources are as follows.

Narasiṃha was born in a small town, Talaja, in the Saurashtra Peninsula in Gujarat in the community of Nāgar Brahmans. He lost his parents at a young age and lived with his elder brother and sister-in-law in Junagadh. When he came of age, he spent most of his time in the company of holy men traveling through the city and did not make a proper living. The family had him married to Maṇekbāī, expecting him to become responsible. But he did not change. On being bitterly taunted by his sister-in-law, Narasiṃha left home and, wandering aimlessly, reached a deserted Śiva temple. Here, he meditated on the deity for seven days. At last, Śiva appeared before him and offered to grant him any wish. Narasiṃha asked for whatever was dear to Śiva himself. Śiva revealed his own fondness for watching the *rāslīlā* (Kṛṣṇa's circular dance with the cowherd women [*gopīs*]; see → *līlā*). He then transported Narasiṃha to the realm where Kṛṣṇa dances eternally with the *gopīs*. Kṛṣṇa rewarded Narasiṃha with the gift of devotional singing and promised to be forever at his beck and call.

Doubly blessed by both Śiva and Kṛṣṇa, Narasiṃha returned to the earth and began his vocation of singing *bhajans* (devotional songs; see → *kīrtan* and *bhajan*) in the city of Junagadh. He wandered, dancing ecstatically on the streets of the city in the company of devotees, including women and mendicants. He also accepted invitations to sing from the untouchables, whom the upper-caste Hindus consider too polluted to touch. His popularity grew among the masses, but he remained poor. Because of his poverty and unorthodox ways, he was ridiculed and severely persecuted by his community and the powerful of his society. On the occasions of his son's wedding and his daughter's pregnancy ceremony, when he was expected to give customary gifts, his community members ridiculed him for his lack of wealth and instigated his relatives to ask for expensive things. On another occasion, they misguided a group of pilgrims to obtain a promissory note from Narasiṃha to be cashed in the pilgrimage center Dwarka, telling them that although he appeared poor, the poet was in reality a rich man.

They instigated the king of Junagadh, Māṇḍalik, who challenged the saint to prove the truthfulness of his devotion by getting from Kṛṣṇa the garland that had been put on the divine image in a temple. They also threw Narasiṃha out of the community for his association with the untouchables. In all incidents of testing, Narasiṃha remained absorbed in his devotional singing with unshaken faith. Every time, Kṛṣṇa rescued his devotee at the critical moment, often appearing on the scene disguised as a merchant and declaring that he was Narasiṃha's servant.

Narasiṃha's traditional biography follows a common pattern in hagiographic narratives of medieval North India in stressing the power of *bhakti* through his moral victory in all incidents of persecution by the orthodox and the powerful. But several aspects of sacred biography mark him as a poet-saint with distinctive *bhakti* sensitivity and reflect the specific cultural context of the development of his hagiography. They also enhance the appeal of his songs for their performers and challenge the dominant social norms of the culture. Narasiṃha's initiation into Kṛṣṇa devotion through Śiva's grace, for example, reflects a Hindu milieu in which exclusive *bhakti* to a single deity was not a norm. C. Vaudeville suggests that this aspect of Narasiṃha's biography reflects a gradual shift from synthesis of *bhakti* of Śiva and → Viṣṇu, as found in the songs of early saints of Maharashtra, to a focus on Viṣṇu, especially in his incarnation as Kṛṣṇa, in the later *bhakti* poetry of North India (1987b, 226–228). Narasiṃha's persecution because of his voluntary poverty and Kṛṣṇa's appearance on the scene as a wealthy merchant who himself honors the poet-saint challenge the emphasis on wealth in the mercantile culture of Gujarat. The poet-saint's association with low-caste and untouchable devotees despite his own high-caste status reinforces the messages about the meaninglessness of caste in his songs. Narasiṃha's caste is especially important in defining his distinctive *bhakti* sensitivity, because many poet-saints of the medieval period who articulated protest against caste hierarchies themselves belonged to low-caste backgrounds. For Narasiṃha the stakes were higher.

Poetry

As with the biographical details, no authoritative compilation of Narasiṃha's poetic works from the period of his accepted dates is found. The earliest extant manuscript containing Narasiṃha's lyrics is dated Vikram Saṃvat 1668 (= 1611 CE). It contains only 15 lyrics, focusing on the theme of love between Kṛṣṇa and the *gopīs*, the cowherd women of Braj. Later manuscripts contain a larger number of lyrics and other poetic works on varied themes. These include poems on subjects related to Kṛṣṇa such as his childhood pranks and amorous encounters including the *rāslīlā*, mystical poems glorifying the all-pervading divine, lyrics of moral teachings, and autobiographical and long narrative poems. The autobiographical poems narrate episodes of his son's wedding, his daughter's pregnancy, the promissory note, and the garland episode. Other long poems include *Sudāmācarit* (Life of Sudāmā), based on the narrative about Kṛṣṇa's friendship with Sudāmā, and *Cāturī*, based on the love story of Kṛṣṇa and → Rādhā as presented in the *Gītagovinda*. The corpus found at the end of the 19th century contained more than a thousand poems integrating many currents of *bhakti*. The growth of the corpus of poems as found in manuscripts has led some Gujarati scholars to raise questions about the authenticity of poetic works found in later manuscripts (e.g. Kothari, 1994, 27). However, most others maintain that because of the predominantly oral nature of poems' transmission, manuscript dates do not provide an accurate basis for determining authenticity or lack thereof.

While the corpus of Narasiṃha's poems is large, his wide popularity as a *bhakti* poet rests on the lyrics that have circulated through musical performance. The long narrative poems as well as a large number of lyrics with explicit eroticism have literary significance, but they are not found in musical performance. Narasiṃha's popular lyrics fall broadly into two categories:

(1) lyrics based on myths about Kṛṣṇa's life among the cowherds of Vraj, including his amorous adventures with the *gopīs*, and (2) lyrics of contemplation on the all-pervading divine and of moral reflection. Those in the first group fall within the current of devotion termed *saguṇa bhakti* (see → *nirguṇa* and *saguṇa*) or devotion to the divine with form and attributes, with which well-known Hindi poets → Tulsīdās, Sūrdās, and Mīrābāī are associated. Those in the second category are more fluid and share features with lyrics of poets like → Kabīr who are known as proponents of *nirguṇa bhakti* or devotion to the all-pervading and ineffable divine without form and attributes.

The coexistence of the two categories in the same corpus sometimes provides grounds for questions of authenticity (Kothari, 1999, 380–387). Yet the two categories have been found to be compatible by the performers and fit the description of lay piety in medieval India, as discussed by C. Vaudeville (1987a, 21–40), in which different currents of *bhakti* were synthesized. In this too, Narasiṃha's corpus parallels poems of Vārkarī saints in whose songs such synthesis is found. Lyrics in both categories are sung in popular tunes, which are credited to Narasiṃha, who is known for his musical acumen. Especially popular are his morning hymns (*Prabhātiyāṃ*) sung at daybreak, which have also attracted scholarly attention (Mallison, 1986).

Narasiṃha's lyrics about Kṛṣṇa's life in Vraja draw extensively on the *Bhāgavatapurāṇa* and the *Gītagovinda*. But they often present the themes with interpretations that highlight a specific aspect of the story. In the lyrics of this type, a major focus is on the power of love. Kṛṣṇa's divine status and grace are highlighted in some lines. But so is his relationship of love with Vraja residents, which makes his divine sporting (*līlā*) on the earth meaningful. The poems in this category, expressing *bhakti* in a relational context, are generally in the form of dramatic dialogue or monologue. They can be further divided into two subcategories: (1) poems about Kṛṣṇa's childhood among the cowherds and (2) lyrics about the love between him and the *gopī*s.

Even though small in number, the lyrics about Kṛṣṇa's childhood place Narasiṃha among the earliest poets in the vernacular languages of North India to write on the themes (such as the stealing of butter) later famously explored in the songs of Sūrdās (Bryant, 1978). Other early regional Kṛṣṇa *bhakti* poets, such as Vidyāpati of Mithilā (c. 14th cent.) and Caṇḍīdās of Bengal (c. 15th cent.), have focused mainly on *gopī* themes. The portrayal of Kṛṣṇa's bond of love with low-caste cowherds is also used by Narasiṃha to point to the meaninglessness of caste hierarchies, as in the following lines:

Look, Narahari [i.e. Kṛṣṇa] dances daily
in the courtyard of a cowherd.
The one who is reluctant to enter Brahma's [i.e. Brahmā's] dream
is bound here to affection.

How beautiful Hari looks
with his anklets ringing sweetly!
Blessed are the cowherds.
What [can be gained] from being of high caste?
(Jesalpura, 1981, 133)

Another song draws on the narrative about Kṛṣṇa's love for butter and integrates it with the myth of the churning of the cosmic ocean, the *Kṣīrodamathana*, to highlight the power of love between him and his foster mother, Yaśodā. The celestial figures who played central roles in the churning of the milky ocean to get nine jewels (Mount Meru, who played the churning pole; serpent Vāsuki was the churning rope; etc.) are terrified when Kṛṣṇa offers to help Yaśodā in churning the curds. A small pot in a cowherd's home acquires cosmic significance with the power of love between a human mother and a divine child. The celestials – → Brahmā and Indra – urge Kṛṣṇa not to churn. A cowherd woman exclaims that she has the treasures that the celestials had sought.

Yaśodā woke up early to churn the curds;
the holder of the Sarang bow [i.e. Kṛṣṇa] woke
to give her a helping hand.

"Mother Yaśodā, let me churn your curds, please.
I will not break your pot, do not worry please."

"I certainly will break," Mount Meru shuddered,
"if he makes me the churning pole."
"What will happen to me?" Vāsuki panicked,
"It will take my life to be the churning cord."

Brahmā, Indra, and others clasped his feet:
"Lord of Gokul, drop the cord, please!"
Yaśodā said, "I have all nine treasures with me."
She had Narsaīyā's [i.e. Narasiṃha's] Lord, the lover of devotees. (Jesalpura, 1981, 139)

Narasiṃha's songs with the theme of Kṛṣṇa's romantic adventures are mostly in the voice of a *gopī*, as is common in Kṛṣṇa *bhakti* poetry of North India. Yet several of them, such as the following, are remarkable in the way in which they express a *gopī*'s confidence as a devotee and suggest that gender hierarchy – as propounded by the male religious elite, who are masters of rituals and ascetic practices – is baseless.

What was my good merit that I was born a woman?
Śri Hari [i.e. Kṛṣṇa] pleads with me with such meekness.
The one whom they call eternal, whom no one knows,
that beloved of Kamalā [i.e. Viṣṇu], embraces me.

The one whom you cannot find in vast sacrifices,
whom you cannot see in meditation,
whom you cannot reach through painful rites,
him you may see with a loving glance. (Jesalpura, 1981, 361)

An important way in which Narasiṃha's corpus differs from those of other major Kṛṣṇa *bhakti* poets is that it contains a very small number of poems about the *gopīs*' pain of separation after Kṛṣṇa leaves Vraja. Of the two states of love in the *gopīs*' *bhakti* portrayed in the *Bhāgavatapurāṇa* – union and separation – the latter is generally treated as a higher form of devotion and has been extensively explored by poets. Narasiṃha's corpus mainly contains poems of union. If presented, separation is short-lived and ends in union. In focusing on union as a more permanent state of loving devotion, Narasiṃha's corpus remains closer to the *Gītagovinda*, which depicts a temporary separation between Kṛṣṇa and his favorite *gopī* Rādhā but ends in their blissful union.

Among the most popular of Narasiṃha's songs are his morning hymns of mystical contemplation, which are held as some of the finest lyrics in the Gujarati language, expressing profound thought in accessible and elegant diction. These hymns express a sense of wonder at the all-pervading divine beyond human comprehension, referenced sometimes by Kṛṣṇa's names, other times as Śiva, and still other times as → *brahman* (the ultimate in → Vedānta). Many of them end with a suggestion that even in its cosmic glory, the divine is accessible to a loving heart.

In the entire universe, it is only you Śri Hari
appearing in endless different forms.

You are the divine in a body.
You are the inner substance of light.
Becoming the word in the Void,
You reside in the Vedas.

You are the seed in the tree; you are the tree in the seed;
I see the veils so close.
Narasaĩyo says: He is what my heart is searching.
Let me love. He will manifest himself with love. (Jesalpura, 1981, 383)

Other popular songs of Narasiṃha are on the nature of *bhakti* and spiritual quest. While some stress love as the core of *bhakti*, others emphasize inner search for the self and reject external markers of religiousness, including consciousness about caste, as "gimmicks to fill the belly" (Jesalpura, 1981, 386). A few songs convey moral teachings about detachment and love for fellow beings as fundamental to spiritual advancement. One of them is Gandhi's favorite hymn, *Vaiṣṇavajana*, which identifies compassion as the first mark of religiousness: "Call only that one a Vaishnava who understands other's pain" (Jesalpura, 1981, 382). This song, F. Mallison shows, has strong parallels with ethical teachings of Jainism, a religion widely prevalent in Gujarat (2000, 295–296).

Narasiṃha's songs of spiritual reflection and moral teachings share many thematic and stylistic features with *nirguṇa bhakti* poetry. The lyrics glorifying the all-pervading divine use paradoxical language to allude to the ineffable. The songs of moral teaching often address the listener directly and use sharply critical language – features associated with Kabīr's poems (Hess & Singh, 1986, 135–161). Yet they do not share the negative view of the phenomenal world often expressed by poets of *nirguṇa bhakti*, who refer to it as a trap and aspire to escape the cycles of birth (→ *saṃsāra*). To the contrary, in Narasiṃha's view, people of Hari

do not seek liberation
they ask for endless rebirths,
forever to serve, forever to sing. (Jesalpura, 1981, 359)

His songs recommend seeing the world as eternal sporting ground of the divine, which can be enjoyed with a proper religious perspective.

While Narasiṃha's songs convey important themes from pan-Indian currents of *bhakti* poetry, to a great extent their appeal to their performers derives from their integration of regional elements. In the Kṛṣṇa *līlā* songs, the depiction of Braj often reflects Gujarat's natural landscape and cultural traditions. In the songs of reflection, expressions drawn from sacred Sanskrit texts are interwoven with colloquial Gujarati idioms, making them accessible for the masses. The tunes of the songs also integrate pan-Indian melodic structures and rhythms with those of regional folk music.

With their focus on love as the essence of spirituality, their dismissal of caste and gender hierarchies as meaningless, their stress on inner search, their reference to the world as a playground of the divine, their accessibility, and their appealing tunes, Narasiṃha's songs have remained popular in performance for centuries. Even though Narasiṃha is not given a place in the core hagiographic texts of Vaiṣṇava sects such as the Puṣṭimārg (or → Vallabha Sampradāya) of → Vallabha and the → Swaminarayanas, which have a stronghold in Gujarat, his songs are often sung by the members of the sects in informal gatherings. Some of his songs are found even in compilations of devotional songs circulating in Ismāʿīlī Muslim communities of Gujarat (Asani, 1992). They have exerted great influence on subsequent religious poetry in Gujarat – Hindu and non-Hindu.

Narasiṃha as a Cultural Icon

Since the mid-19th century, Narasiṃha Mehtā has been a major focus in scholarly works on Gujarat's culture. In the works of nationalist scholars from the British colonial period, who compiled anthologies of premodern poetry and wrote the literary history of Gujarat, Narasiṃha was recognized as the pivotal figure of Gujarati poetry and given the title of Ādikavi ("First Poet") of the language. His lyrics became part of school and college curricula and began to be performed in nonreligious contexts such as cultural shows. The wide popularity of his songs also led to their regular airing on the radio and to the production of numerous audio records, which are sold even among non-Hindus. Biographies of Narasiṃha also have continued to be written. In the 20th century, biographical works written by two major figures in Gujarati literature – K.M. Munshi (1887–1971) and P. Patel (1912–1989) – were published. Narasiṃha's hagiography has been retold in five films since the early 1930s in Gujarati, Hindi, and Rajasthani. Since the early 1990s, two television series in Gujarati have also been made. Video clips of Narasiṃha's biography now circulate on the Internet through Web sites such as YouTube. The modern channels of transmission have contributed greatly to establishing Narasiṃha as a cultural icon of Gujarat. Gujarati speakers of diverse religious backgrounds in India and in the diaspora associate him with their cultural identity.

Narasiṃha and Gandhi

Narasiṃha Mehtā was a favorite devotional poet of Gandhi, a Gujarati himself. Gandhi was especially drawn to Narasiṃha's songs of spiritual and moral reflection and referred to them recurrently in his writings. He integrated the singing of *Vaiṣṇavajana* in all important public events of his life and equated it with the → *Bhagavadgītā* in its ability to offer moral inspiration to him.

Gandhi also highlighted Narasiṃha's association with the untouchables in his efforts to remove the practice of → untouchability from Hindu society (1999, vol. XVI, 137–141; vol. XXVI, 236). He adopted the term Harijan ("Person of God") to refer to the untouchables from a song that is believed to have been sung by the saint when ridiculed by his community for his disregard for caste distinctions (Gandhi, 1999, vol. LIII, 166; vol. LX, 27–29).

Gandhi's engagement with Narasiṃha's songs and narratives played a pivotal role in bringing to attention their moral relevance in the public sphere beyond traditional religion. It has greatly influenced public discourses. *Vaiṣṇavajana* is heard across the globe during events related to humanitarian and peace-building work, and it is a marker of Indian identity in the diaspora (Shukla-Bhatt, forthcoming). Gujarati scholarship and popular media underscore the egalitarian implications of Narasiṃha's biography. A successful bilingual film, *Narsi Bhagat/Narsi Mehtā* (1940), and a 27-episode Gujarati television series, *Narasaiyo* (1991), which reached all levels of society, greatly stress social equality as an aspect of the poet-saint's *bhakti*. The series also suggests that Narasiṃha provides a model for religious harmony in his integration of reverence for Śiva with Kṛṣṇa *bhakti*.

Conclusion

As a beloved poet-saint of Gujarat, Narasiṃha Mehtā is a major figure in the history of the spread of *bhakti* in North India. Even though little historical information is available about Narasiṃha, his image as an exemplary devotee of Kṛṣṇa with ecumenical *bhakti* sensitivity, with broad human sympathies, and with profound spiritual insight has been firmly established in the public memory through performances of songs and hagiographic narratives associated with him. This image, which can be seen as culturally shaped, is both authentic and authoritative for the performers and listeners of songs and narratives. It distinctively represents their *bhakti* understanding and aspirations. Narasiṃha's significance derives also from the moral inspiration that his hagiography and songs provided to a person of Gandhi's stature, who harnessed their popularity for constructive purposes in public life. The popularity of these songs and narratives as cultural forms beyond the Hindu fold has facilitated their circulation in modern media and provides a platform for diverse communities to meet. Narasiṃha Mehtā represents the vitality of a popular current of Hindu *bhakti* to serve as a religious and cultural source of enduring significance.

Bibliography

Abbott, J.E., & N. Godbole, trans., *Stories of Indian Saints: An English Translation of Mahipati's Marathi Bhaktavijaya*, vols. I–II, Delhi, 1988.

Asani, A., *The Harvard Collection of Ismaili Literature in Indic Languages: A Descriptive Catalog and Finding Aid*, Boston, 1992.

Bhagat, N., "Twenty-five Lyrics, Narasinh Mehta," in: K. Ayyappa Paniker, ed., *Medieval Indian Literature: An Anthology*, vol. II, New Delhi, 1999, 89–101.

Bhayani, H.C., *Prācin-Madhykālīna Kṛṣṇa-Kāvya ane Narasinh Svādhyaya*, Ahmedabad, 1986 (Guj.).

Bryant, K., *Poems to the Child-God: Structures and Strategies in the Poetry of Sūrdās*, Berkeley, 1978.

Carman, J., "Bhakti," in: L. Jones, ed., *Encyclopedia of Religion*, vol. II, Detroit, 22005, 856–860.

Chaudhari, R., ed., *Narasiṃha Mehtā Āswād ane Swādhyāya*, Mumbai, 1983 (Guj.).

Dave, I., *Ādikavi nī Ārṣvaṇī, Narasinha Mehta nī Tattvadarṣī Kavitā*, Rajkot, 1973 (Guj.).

Desai, I.S., ed., *Narasiṃha Mehtā krut Kāvyasangraha*, Mumbai, 1913 (Guj.).

Dholakia, D., *Narasiṃhacaritravimarṣa*, Bhuj, 1992 (Guj.).

Dhruv, K.H., ed., *Narasaī Mehtānū Ākhyān*, Ahmedabad, 2000 (Guj.).

Gandhi, M.K., *The Collected Works of Mahatma Gandhi*, 98 vols. (electronic book), New Delhi, 1999.

Hawley, J.S., ed., *Saints and Virtues*, Berkeley, 1987.

Hess, L., & S. Singh, trans., *The Bījak of Kabir*, Delhi, 1986.

Jesalpura, S., ed., *Narasiṃha Mehtānī Kavya Krutio*, Ahmedabad, 1981 (Guj.).

Joshi, U., "Narasiṃha Mehtā," in: U. Joshi, A. Raval & Y. Shukla, eds., *Gujarātī Sāhitya no Itihās*, vol. II, Ahmedabad, 2005, 104–197 (Guj.).

Kelkar, S., "Translation of Narsinh Mehtā's Poems into English: With a Critical Introduction," 2007, http://sachinketkar.webs.com/apps/documents/.

Kothari, J., "Narasinha Mehtanā Pado – Kartutva no Koyado," *Uddeś* 9/10, 12, 1999, 380–387, 445–454; *Uddeś* 10/2, 1999, 49–58 (Guj.).

Kothari, J., *Narasinha Mehta*, Delhi, 1994.

Mallison, F., "The Definition of a Vaiṣṇava according to Medieval Gujarātī Devotional Poetry," in: M.K. Gautam & G.H. Schokker, eds., *Bhakti in Current Research: 1982-85*, Lucknow, 2000, 291–300.

Mallison, F., *Au point du Jour: Le Prabhātiyāṃ de Narasiṃha Mahetā, poete et saint vishnouite du Gujarat*, Paris, 1986.

Mehta, R.L., & A.V. Dave, eds., *Narasiṃha Mehtā Adhyayan Granth*, 1983 (Guj.).

Mukta, P., *Upholding the Common Life: The Community of Mirabai*, Delhi, 1997.

Munshi, K.M., *Gujarat and Its Literature: From Early Times to 1852*, Bombay, 1967.

Munshi, K.M., *Narasaīyo Bhakta Harino*, Ahmedabad, 1933 (Guj.).

Narayanan, V., *The Vernacular Veda: Revelation, Recitation, and Ritual*, Columbia, 1994.

Novetzke, C., *Religion and Public Memory: A Cultural History of Saint Namdev in India*, New York, 2008.

Patel, P., *Param Vaiṣṇava Narasinh Mehtā*, Ahmedabad, 2009 (Guj.).

Rupakala, S.B., ed., *Śrī Bhaktamāl, Sri Priyadas-ji Ṭīkā, Bhaktisudhāsvād*, Lucknow, 1964 (Hind.).

Schomer, K., & W.H. McLeod, *The Sants: Studies in a Devotional Tradition of India*, Berkeley, 1987.

Shastri, K.K., *Narasiṃha Mehto, Ek Adhyayan*, Ahmedabad, 2005 (Guj.).

Shastri, K.K., & S. Jesalpura, eds., *Premānand nī Kāvyakrutio*, Ahmedabad, 1998 (Guj.).

Shukla-Bhatt, N., *Moving Songs, Circulating Stories: The Saint-Poet Narasiṃha Mehta of Gujarat*, forthcoming.

Shukla-Bhatt, N., "Govinda's Glory: Kṛṣṇa-*līlā* in Songs of Narasiṃha Mehta," in: E. Bryant, ed., *Kṛṣṇa : A Sourcebook*, New York, 2007, 255–284.

Tripathi, G.M., *The Classical Poets of Gujarat and Their Influence on Society and Morals*, Bombay, 1958.

Trivedi, J.N., ed., *Narsījī ro Māhero*, Jodhpur, 1972 (Raj.).

Vaudeville, C., "*Sant Mat*: Santism as the Universal Path to Sanctity," in: K. Schomer & W.H. McLeod, eds., *The Sants: Studies in a Devotional Tradition of India*, Berkeley, 1987a, 21–40.

Vaudeville, C., "The Shaiva-Vaishnava Synthesis in Maharashtrian Santism," in: K. Schomer & W.H. McLeod, eds., *The Sants: Studies in a Devotional Tradition of India*, Berkeley, 1987b, 215–228.

Neelima Shukla-Bhatt

Nāyaṉārs

Nāyaṉār literally means “leader” (its plural form is Nāyaṉmār) and is a title or epithet for the 63 canonized saints of Tamil Śaivism, with its concomitant philosophical system, → Śaiva Siddhānta. Though not formally canonized as saints until the middle part of 12th century, most of the Nāyaṉmār lived between the 6th and 11th centuries. Among these 63 saints, some were poets who composed devotional songs to → Śiva (Tam. Civaṉ), and some were important family figures linked to these aforementioned poet-saints, but the majority can be seen as models of the ideal devotee, illustrating the social and communal diversity of the Tamil Śaiva community. The most important of the Nāyaṉmār are the three early male poets, Appar, Campantar, and Cuntarar, whom the tradition regards as the *camāya ācāriya* or “founders of the faith.” All three were historical figures, whose compositions known as the *Tēvāram* compose the most important part of the Tamil Śaiva devotional canon. But before exploring the lives and songs of these saints, it is fitting to survey the textual sources that represent them.

Tirumuṟai

The sacred works of the Nāyaṉmār poet-saints were incorporated in the 12-volume *Tirumuṟai* (Sacred Tradition or Sacred Text), the official Tamil Śaiva Siddhānta canon. The job of compiling the *Tirumuṟai* began in the late 11th or early 12th century, when Nampi Āṇṭār Nampi (11th cent. CE?), a Śaiva Brahman, arranged the first 11 books (Dehejia, 2002, 18). The *Tirumuṟai* achieved its final form in the mid-12th century with the addition of the 12th and final book, the *Periyapurāṇam* (The Great Story), also known as the *Tiruttoṇṭarpurāṇam* (The Ancient Story of the Holy Servants). This work, authored by Cēkkiḻār, an official in the court of the Chola king Kultōttuṅka II (r. 1133–1150 CE), closed the Tamil Śaiva canon with its authoritative account of the lives of the 63 Nāyaṉmār.

Although the term *nāyaṉār* is now used to refer to the group of Śaiva saints, even in the *Periyapurāṇam*, it was only Śiva who was referred to as such. The terms *nāyaṉār* and *nāyaṉmār* do not enter into usage to refer to this special group of exemplary individuals until nearly a century after the *Periyapurāṇam* was composed. The earliest known reference appears in an inscription mentioning the three most important of these saints (the “*mūvar*”) in an inscription made in the year 1256 during the reign of Rajendra Cola III (Monius, 2004, 113). While the *Periyapurāṇam* is an essential part of any discussion on the Nāyaṉmār, it owed much to works that preceded, inspired, and informed it. These include the compositions that comprise the first 11 books of the *Tirumuṟai.*

The first seven books of the *Tirumuṟai* are collectively called the *Tēvāram* (The Garland of God) and are solely dedicated to the compositions of a group of three Nāyaṉmār, Appar, Campantar, and Cuntarar, saints who are collectively called the *mūvar* (the three). In the *Tirumuṟai*, Campantar's works comprise books 1–3, and Appar's make up volumes 4–6, while Cuntarar's compositions form volume 7. Indeed, it is Cuntarar's short *Tiruttoṇṭattokai* (Collection of the Sacred Servants), which concludes the seventh book of the *Tirumuṟai*, that is the earliest account of Śiva's most esteemed and exemplary devotees. In this work, Cuntarar calls himself the servant of the servants of Śiva, asserting a key value of Tamil Śaiva devotionalism, and one articulated repeatedly in the narratives about the Nāyaṉmār: that of the primacy of the Śaiva devotional community, and one's submission to exemplary devotion.

Tirumuṟaikaṇṭapurāṇam

As Appar, Campantar, and Cuntarar traveled the Tamil regions, they mapped a sacred Śaiva geography through song. Some of these hymns endured in the living memory of Śaiva devotees throughout the early medieval period, but legend has it that the vast bulk of them were forgotten and were only recovered miraculously in the late 11th century CE. The 14th-century Tamil work attributed to the Śaiva theologian Umāpati Civācāriyar, the *Tirumuṟaikaṇṭapurāṇam* recounts the story of the rediscovery of the ancient *Tēvāram* hymns, a recovery that was the foundation for the formation of the *Tirumuṟai* canon.

Though composed several centuries after the lives of the *mūvar*, the *Tirumuṟaikaṇṭapurāṇam* is essential in understanding the Nāyaṉmār. Not only does it map how Śaiva Siddhānta tradition remembers the formation of its literary, liturgical, and religious canon, but it also enacts, in a self-reflexive way, the emergent roles these saints are understood to have had within temple worship. As we shall soon see, the recovery of the Tamil Śaiva canon begins with the intervention of the iconic forms of the saints that were in worship. It is an odd juxtaposition, to be sure, where the iconic body of the deified saint precedes his own (soon to be reconstituted) textual voice.

The *Tirumuṟaikaṇṭapurāṇam* begins with a lamentation of loss. The Chola king Apayakulacēkaraṉ weeps upon hearing a few songs of the *mūvar* and is incredulous that the hymns are disorganized and sung in a haphazard way and without any real organization. The very moment the king expresses his grief at the state of these songs, a boy – Nampi Āṇṭār Nampi – is born to a family of Śaiva temple priests in Naraiyur. As befitting a miracle-child, Nampi is trained in the → Vedas, Āgamas (→ Śaiva Āgamas), and priest craft directly by Gaṇeśa (→ Gaṇapati/Gaṇeśa) himself – a divine feat that soon reaches the ears of the king (vv. 4, 5). The king tests the boy's divine connection, and miracles abound. So the king entrusts Nampi with the sacred task: "to make known throughout the land the sacred hymns of the three great saints" (*TiMuP.* 9; Prentiss, 2001, 30).

Entrusted with the monumental task, the young boy prays to Gaṇeśa and is granted a riddle in response:

> Behind [the image of] the Lord of the Dark Throat who dances in the hall in the place where the manuscripts are kept; his beautiful lotus like hand marks the spot. (*TiMuP.* 12; Prentiss, 2001, 31)

Realizing immediately that he is being directed to Chidambaram, Nampi informs Apayakulacēkaraṉ that there is a great storehouse of *mūvar*'s hymns hidden in the temple. When the king and Nampi arrive, the king announces to the gathered group of priests and devotees that the lost hymns must have been previously locked away in a hidden temple vault. In response, the devotees suggest a way to gain access to the secret chamber:

> If the *mūvar* who preserve (*vaitta*) Tamil come here, the room will spontaneously unlock,' the king himself held a festival for the Lord of the Hall (*ampalam*) who is truth and virtue and processed [images of] the *mūvar* who sang Tamil around the beautiful streets toward the right side of the temple of the leader of the gods. Bringing them inside to the location of the Tamil [compositions] that melt the mind completely, the king declared that [the *mūvar*] had arrived. (*TiMuP.* 19; Prentiss, 2001, 34)

This brief but significant moment in the *Tirumuṟaikaṇṭapurāṇam* reveals that although the bulk of the *Tēvāram* poems might have been lost, the memory of the poets themselves was very much alive. Already informally canonized, the three poets had been memorialized in worship, and in this narrative of loss and recovery, the *mūvar's* processional icons enlivened by their spirit are essential to recovering their own lost texts (Gros, 2009, 235).

> The arrival of the blessed *mūvar* at the western side of the hall (*ampalam*) of the Lord of the Dance [proved that] the unbroken seal [on the chamber] matched their henna-dyed palms, and, to the surprise of those who looked on, the door flew open. It was immediately apparent that small white ants covered the pages of the hymns of great knowledge (*ñāna*), like the five senses that conceal the innate wisdom of people who rely on them, and the king felt grieved. (*TiMuP.* 20; Prentiss, 2001, 34)

Even as the *Tirumuṟaikaṇṭapurāṇam* exaggerates the loss – tens of thousands of verses lost to white ants – the text nonetheless speaks poignantly to the fragility of textual transmission and the reality that haunts even the most dedicated of manuscript conservators. The gathered devotees proceed to make a thorough accounting of this loss, mourning their irreversible destruction. What remained of the *mūvars*' poems was then organized with great care, and verses 28–33 of the *Tirumuṟaikaṇṭapurāṇam* details the organization of the extant hymns into specific volumes arranged by content, and the standardization of their formal recitation.

> Since there were seven crores of [known] *mantras*, in that manner the king arranged the *Tirumuṟais* as seven [books]. Similarly, the [known] *mantras* possessed eleven [types of] relationships; thus, the king [sought to] complete a total number of eleven muṟais [texts] from [the collection of seven] plus four [*muṟais* 8–11, with the writing of the eleventh described in the next verse].
>
> Then, after Nampi had understood by grace the order of [the servants to the Lord accord-

ing to Cuntarar's list, the] Tiruttoṇṭattokai, and after he had received grace in the form of information from the elephant-faced Lord on the good service performed by each of these leaders (*Nāyaṉmārar* [*sic*]), he composed [their life stories] in the pleasing *antāti* meter.

When he had composed in sweet Tamil [the stories of] the sixty-three who are famous for receiving grace (*tīr āruḷ cēr*), along with the nine holy groups [of servants], he set out for (Tiru) Erukkattampuliyar, which is famous among people for its greatness, so that the collection would become widely known.

The Lord said, "Once upon a time I blessed with the knowledge of music a lady who belongs to a proper lineage of musicians (*pāṇaṉār*) who play the melodious *yāḻ* [an ancient stringed instrument]." After Nampi summoned her and learned about the good music that [emerges from] the *paṇ* [ancient melody] as a mode of sacred sound (*curuti* [Skt. *śruti*]), he felt satisfied [that her knowledge was accurate and complete].

The king heard a voice from the heavens saying, "Bring that lady before the Lord of the Dance in the hall [and ask her to] order the songs according to their *paṇ*. If you do this, it will be as good as [if I myself] set the *muṟai* to music." (*TiMuP*. 28–33; Prentiss, 2001, 37, 38)

Nampi composed his own hymn, the *Tiruttoṇṭartiruvantāti*, to formally enumerate the saints mentioned in Cuntarar's earlier work. As a final step to institutionalize the *Tēvāram* songs and to ensure their survival into posterity, each of the *mūvars*' compositions was set to a specific melodic scale known as *paṇ*. While the ancient *paṇ*s had also been lost along with the three poets' compositions, a sole woman, the last living keeper of the singing tradition, enabled its recovery. Nonetheless, the *Tirumuṟaikaṇṭapurāṇam* fails to mention the name of this woman, a nameless female virtuoso who set all the hymns to music and essentially imbued the hymns with the aesthetic power to endure.

Although inscriptional evidence informs us that recitation of the Tamil songs as part of temple worship goes back to the mid-9th century, it was the melodic fixing of these hymns, backed by the power of the Chola court, legitimated through the *Tirumuṟaikaṇṭapurāṇam* and embodied in the figure of the *ōtuvār* (reciter/singer), that firmly established the *Tēvāram*'s liturgical place within temple rites.

Tiruttoṇṭattokai and *Tiruttoṇṭartiruvantāti*

While the *Periyapurāṇam* is the primary canonical hagiography of Śaiva Siddhānta, there were previous listings of the saints who become the Nāyaṉmār. Among the earliest as noted above is Cuntarar's hymn, *Tiruttoṇṭattokai* (Collection of the Sacred Servants). This first enumeration of Śaiva saints, which permanently fixed their ordering, may be dated roughly to the early 9th century. Despite being a fairly truncated collection of praise poems, Cuntarar's work induced a shift from oral folkloric Śaiva tradition and clearly set up the conditions for the process of formal canonization later initiated by Nampi Āṇṭār Nampi under the direction of Apayakulacēkaraṉ. Indeed, in his *Tiruttoṇṭartiruvantāti* (Sacred *Antāti* Verses on the Sacred Servants), Nampi embroidered Cuntarar's brief praise of the 63 exemplary devotees with hagiographic details, and for his efforts, the *Tiruvantāti* was included in the 11th book of the *Tirumuṟai*. Ultimately, Cēkkiḻār's definitive 12th-century *Periyapurāṇam* synthesized materials about the lives of the 63 saints from a variety of sources: Cuntarar's *Tiruttoṇṭattokai* and Nampi's *Tiruttoṇṭartiruvantāti*, passing autobiographical references in *Tēvāram* poems of the *mūvar* hymns and more comprehensive, contemporaneous oral narrative traditions. (For examples of references to the Nāyaṉmār in *Tēvāram* hymns, including a translation of the *Tiruttoṇṭattokai*, see Peterson, 1989, 323–336.) In examining this most elaborate and final formulation of Tamil Śaiva hagiography, exemplified in the *Periyapurāṇam*, it is clear that the three cornerstones of this work are the lives of the *mūvar*.

Lives and Poetry of the *Mūvar*

Mūvar means "the three" and was an epithet coined to refer collectively to Appar, Campantar, and Cuntarar, to mark the unique contribution in the formation, development, and spread of the institutions of Śaiva → *bhakti* in the Tamil-speaking South. Not only do the *mūvar*s' songs make up more than half of the *Tirumuṟai*, but they are also further distinguished by being the first seven books of the canon, and by being assigned the distinctive, collective title, "*Tēvāram*." In addition, they are foremost among those few select works of the *Tirumuṟai* that serve a liturgical function in temple rites when cited by the *ōtuvār*. These liturgical works are collectively called the *Pañcapurāṇam* (The Five Ancients) and include *Tēvāram, Tiruvācakam, Tiruvicaippā, Tiruppallāṇṭu*, and the *Periyapurāṇam* itself.

The significance of these saints cannot be overestimated, and in the hagiographical tradition, these Nāyaṉmār have swept cadres of family members and significant associates into the domain of Śaiva sainthood simply by virtue of association. Not only do the *mūvars*' works dominate the Śaiva canon but their hagiographies also make up the lion's share of the *Periyapurāṇam* as well. Beyond even this, it is Cuntarar himself who first delineated the *Tiruttoṇṭar* (The Sacred Servants). This fact likely inspired Nampi and Cēkkiḻār to present the stories of the 63 saints with Cuntarar's hagiography as their respective works' framing chapters. Thus, "Cuntarar's pre-history in Kailasa, Śiva's abode," and "his final ascent to Śiva's world" (Peterson, 1994, 197) form the framing device encapsulating the lives of the remaining 62 Śaiva saints.

Appar, Campantar, and Cuntarar clearly embodied the ideal devotee in Śaiva Siddhanta, owing to the emotive resonance of their devotion and the relentlessness of their sectarian zeal. Theirs was a spiritual obstinacy that was perpetually demonstrated, even when confronting their most intimate human frailties. The very establishment of Śaiva sainthood emerges from their enduring renown – as it is reasonable to infer from the account given in *Tirumuṟaikaṇṭapurāṇam* that the formal institutional worship of Saiva saints must have begun with the veneration these three wandering poets.

Tirunāvukkaracar or Appar

Tirunāvukkaracar, or Appar as he is popularly known, is thought to have lived roughly between 570 and 670 CE and was a contemporary of the younger Campantar. He contributed 313 hymns to the *Tēvāram*, which constitute books 4–6 of the *Tirumuṟai*.

The *Periyapurāṇam*'s account of Appar's life (*PerP.* 1283–1694) speaks directly to the tensions between the competing traditions of Jainism and Śaivism. Appar's story reveals the important alliances among poets, the agricultural classes, and kings in establishing the hegemony of Śaivism in Tamil country.

Appar's given name was Maruḷnīkkiyār. He was born to a Vēḷāḷar (agricultarist) family in the town of Thiruvamur. His family was Śaiva, but in his youth he converted to Jainism. After taking monastic vows, he rose through the ranks and eventually became the head of the monastic order that was situated in Patalipputtira (Pāṭaliputra, now Patna). But one day, he began suffering from terrible stomach pains, to the extent that he would swoon in agony. None of the incantations of his brother monks brought him a sliver of relief but instead exacerbated his condition. His sister, Tilakavatiyār, came to him and pleaded with him to appeal to Lord Śiva for comfort and relief. In utter desperation he accepted sacred ash offered to Śiva and smeared it over his body. She then led him into the temple of the lord at Athihai Virattanam, where he poured out his heart in song and was instantly healed. A divine voice was heard echoing through the temple, and the lord himself bestowed the name Tirunāvukkaracar ("King of Speech") upon him.

The Jains were furious that their own leader had turned away from them and taken up the Śaiva path. They complained to the Pallava king that his conversion would deliver a great blow to the Jain faith and demanded that Appar be punished. Mahendravarman Pallava, himself an ardent Jain, ordered Tirunāvukkaracar's immediate arrest. Under the guidance of the Jains, the king locked him in a blazing lime kiln, fed him poisoned milk rice, had him trampled by an elephant, and finally, in utter frustration, lashed him to large stones and had him flung into the sea. But time and again, by the power of his heartfelt songs, he emerged unscathed. In the end, Varuṇaṉ himself – god of the oceans – carried him away to safety. Soon after, King Mahendravarman sought him out and, falling at Tirunāvukkaracar's feet, begged his forgiveness. Then, forsaking Jainism once and for all, the king took refuge in the Śaiva path.

Tirunāvukkaracar lived for more than 80 years and spent his life wandering from temple to temple praising Śiva with his songs and serving his fellow devotees in the humblest of ways. Iconographically he is depicted carrying a hoe, which he would use to cut the grass that grew between the paving stones of the temples he visited, embodying the ideal of humble service to Śiva and his devotees. Appar's agricultural affiliations are also indicated reflected in his poetry, in which he often turns to metaphors of cultivation to speak of the care and nurture that service to Śiva entails. Appar's poetry is also marked by the autobiographical, particularly in his lamentations of what he perceives as his misguided time as a Jain. In fact, his sets of ten verses (*patikams*) generally conclude with some kind of reference to this time of his life.

A shaven monk, I stood by the words
of the base, ignorant Jains.
I was a hypocrite, running away
and bolting the door
at the sight of lotus-eyed young women.
A miserable sinner
who did not know the Lord of Arur
who saved my soul and possessed me,
I was one who starves to death,
begging for food in a deserted town.
(*TiMu.* 4.5.8; Peterson, 1989, 292)

Appar travelled with the child saint Campantar for a time. It is Campantar who is credited with addressing the older man as Appar ("Father"), an epithet that would persist, and enabling in characterizing him as the wise old father figure of Tamil Śaivism.

Tiruñānacampantar or Campantar

Tiruñānacampantar ("Kin to Divine Wisdom"), or simply Campantar, was a contemporary of the poet Appar, and the internal evidence from his poems suggests that he lived between approximately 665 and 681 CE. He contributed 383 hymns to the *Tēvāram*, which constitute the opening three volumes of the *Tirumurai*. Unlike Appar, who left the fold of Śaivism to return to it anew and with renewed committment, Campantar's story (*PerP.* 1899–3154) suggests that love for Śiva is native to one's being and is nurtured to full bloom through loving service and a zealous evangelism. It is noteworthy that his compositions appear first in the canon. Like Appar, Campantar too traveled widely, singing Śiva's sacred places into being, and forging significant alliances with royal patrons.

In the *Periyapurāṇam*, Campantar is depicted as a child prodigy who at the age of three had a transformative experience that immediately propelled him to sainthood. He was born in Cirkali to a devout Brahman family. One day, when left behind by his father beside the temple tank, the young boy began to cry of thirst. The goddess → Pārvatī appeared before him and offered the child a golden cup filled with her own divine milk. When his father returned, he saw the child happily playing with an empty gold cup, and saw his mouth still wet with milk dripping down his chin. When asked where he had gotten the cup of milk, the boy laughed and, pointing upward to an image of the goddess Pārvatī that adorned the temple tower, composed his first poem, which is as follows:

He wears a woman's earring on one ear;
riding on his bull,
crowned with the pure white crescent moon,
his body smeared with ash from the burning-ground,
he is the thief who stole my heart.
He is the Lord who lives in fine Piramapuram,
where he once blesses with grace
Brahma of the lotus seat
who worshipped him. (*TiMu.* 1.1.1;
Peterson, 1989, 270, 271)

Even as a child, Campantar is credited with having made four great pilgrimages across → Tamil Nadu to visit the many temple abodes of Śiva. He was typically accompanied by a grand retinue of fellow devotees and would spontaneously compose a hymn at each site he visited. Tirunīlakaṇṭayāḻpāṇar a *pāṇar* musician (later to be canonized among the Nāyaṉmār), always accompanied Campantar, setting the young boy's hymns to music. Likely, Campantar's followers assisted in recoding his extemporaneous songs in writing as they accompanied him on these numerous pilgrimages (Peterson, 1989, 20).

Campantar also met up with Tirunāvukkaracar, with whom he shared a deep affection and, like the elderly saint he befriended, is said to have performed many miracles. But among all of his sacred adventures, he is best remembered for his conversion of the Pandiya king of Madurai, and his wresting control of that region from the Jains. In some regards, this narrative echoes events from Tirunāvukkaracar's own hagiography as it revolves around theological contests of healing that inspire conversion, the emphasis of which may be to counter the medicinal skills that the Jains were renowned for.

The Pandiya king of Madurai, Kūṉ Pāṇṭiyaṉ ("Hunchback Pāṇṭiya"), was a Jain, but his wife, Maṅkaiyarkkaraci, and his chief minister, Kulacciṟaiyār, were devout Śaivas. When the queen and minister heard of Campantar's visit to

Madurai, they were delighted and welcomed him with gifts. As the boy drew near the city, auspicious signs filled the land, dispelling the darkness that had hung over the Pandiyan people because of the evil influences of the Jains. In the *Periyapurāṇam*, the Jains are described as shameless, and Campantar as a lamp of wisdom:

> The shameless Jains had spread their religion like a pall of darkness and ignominy over the land. Now to chase away the gloom, a lamp of wisdom was to shine forth, filling all the worlds with its radiance and renewing the fortunes of the Śaivite path. This was the fruit of penances performed by the people of the Tamil land ruled by the Pāṇṭiya kings, who rode to their conquests on bull elephants. (*PerP*. 2548; McGlashan, 2006, 223)

The Jains, threatened by Campantar's arrival, immediately raced to inform the king that the young boy and his band of followers had arrived to defeat them in debate. They confided with the king that they, not wanting to use direct violence, would employ their magic incantations to set fire to the monastery in which Campantar was staying, thus driving away Campantar and his cohorts. The king approved their scheme, but when the Jain monks' strongest spells had no effect on the monastery that housed the holy child, they began to fret that soon they would lose the king's royal favor. So, abandoning their magic, they took up torches and set the monastery alight with their own hands.

When the Śaiva devotees quickly doused the flames and informed Campantar of the events, he immediately discerned that the Jains were behind the wicked deed. He cursed the king to bear the heat of their evil actions for not maintaining justice in his kingdom. By the power of Campantar's holy song, the fire that had threatened the monastery now assailed the king in the form of a terrible fever. The heat emanating from his body was so great that it scorched those that even tried to approach the royal chamber. No doctor or remedy could bring the slightest relief. The king lay at death's door, and the Jains were unable to help him.

The king's faith in the Jains waned quickly, and he told the queen that he would pledge his spiritual fealty to whoever could cure him. When both the Jains and Campantar's retinue gathered at the king's bedside, the Jains' magic and ministrations were to no avail. But Campantar's song and smearing of the lord's sacred ash made his body cool as a breeze from heaven.

The Jains pleaded with the king to let them prove the power of their faith by some other test or trial. They suggested that the tenets of each faith be inscribed upon a palm leaf and cast into a flame to see which one endures. The holy child eagerly agreed. But when that boy's written hymn emerged unsinged while the Jains' *sūtra* was instantly reduced to embers and ash, they pleaded with the king to give them a third chance to prove the veracity of their faith. Campantar interceded on their behalf, asking what they had in mind. They said, "let us again take a palm leaf etched with our sacred tenets and this time cast it in the river and see which is swept away and which remains." Campantar agreed, but the minister spoke up, insisting that they dictate what punishment should be imposed upon the loser. The Jains were angered by this and declared that if they failed this third trial, the king must impale them on stakes. Thus decided, they gathered at the river and cast their leaves in. The Jains' leaf was swept away to drown in the sea, while Campantar's hymn floated upstream against the current. The king ordered that the Jains be put to death.

> Campantar bore no personal animosity towards the Jains, but made no objections to the king's just sentence. "Since these unworthy Jains perpetrated an outrage at the monastery where the Śaivite devotees were staying," he declared, "their sentence is appropriate."
>
> In public view, Kulacciṟaiyār then had the stakes prepared and set up in rows. When all was ready, for their part in the attempted arson at Campantar's monastery eight thousand Jains from the eight hills around the city impaled themselves upon the stakes. The Jains were impaled because their palm leaf had been swept away by the river and they had therefore lost the contest. The stakes concretely proclaimed that there is no other God but Śiva. They stood in testimony to the glory of the holy child. (*PerP*. 2752, 2753; McGlashan, 2006, 240)

Whether it was the attempted arson (approved by the king's own mandate) or the simple loss of the contest that caused the execution of the eight thousand Jain monks is not readily clear from the passage. Cēkkiḻār depicts the Jains as committing a mass suicide, when he assures his audience that they "impaled themselves upon the stakes," absolving Campantar, the newly converted king, and the Śaiva devotees of any culpability. Indeed, in the *Periyapurāṇam*'s account, this is not merely a just punishment, but one invited, decided, and

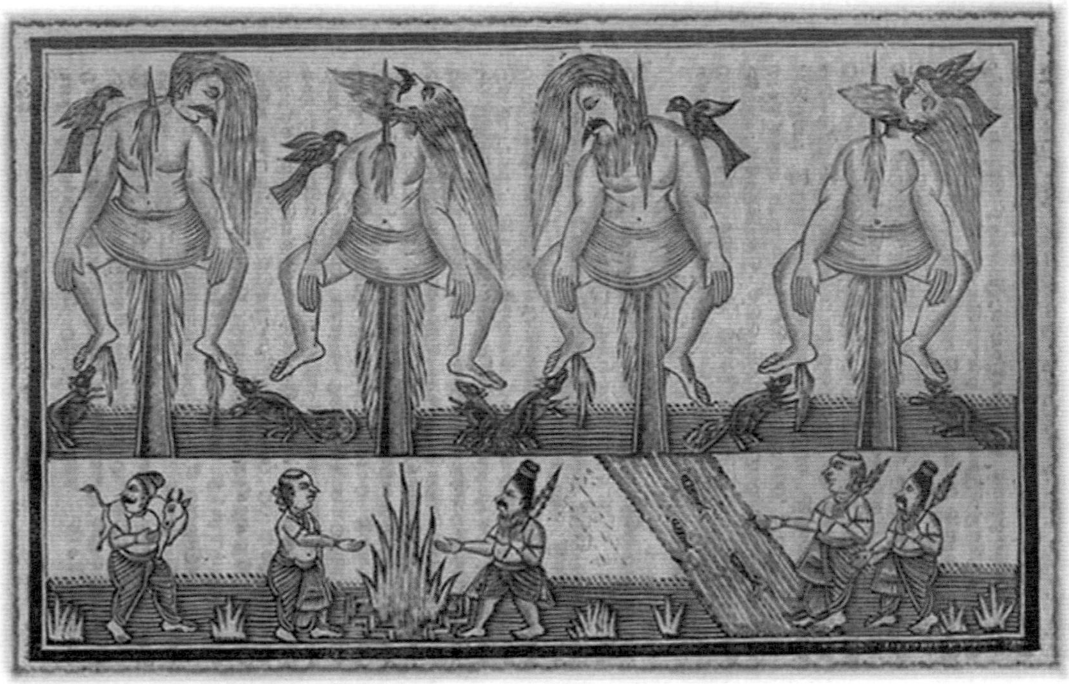

Fig. 1: Depiction of Jain impalement in the 19th-century *Tiruviḷaiyātaṟpurāṇam*

implemented by the Jains themselves. Perhaps this is the *Periyapurāṇam*'s understanding of Jain ascetic practice of bodily self-mortification taken to an extreme, even as the text adopts these same principles of bodily violence in many of its most famous Nāyaṉmār stories.

So central is this story of the violent conflict between the Jains and Campantar that the site of the Jain execution, on the outskirts of Madurai, continues to be regarded as a sacred site, and their deaths are celebrated during Madurai's annual *cittirai* festival in April. Further attesting to the significance of these events and their violent resolution, they are recounted in many later central works associated with Madurai: in the 63rd chapter of the *Tiruviḷaiyātaṟpurāṇam* and in other Talapurāṇams of the Mīnākṣī-Sundareśvara Temple.

In later tradition, Campantar comes to be regarded as a manifestation of the child-god → Murukaṉ, son of Śiva, "in his fashion also a conqueror" (Gros, 2009, 223), and the Chola court poet Oṭṭakūttar praised Campantar as the god of war incarnate who was born on earth to exterminate the Jains (Peterson, 1998, 182).

The *Periyapurāṇam* and subsequent narratives about Campantar offer a stark (and perhaps unintended) contrast between the innocuous, innocent nature of the child and his vitriolic and even violent critique of the Jains. This is a fixed trope in Campantar's poems, and he devotes the tenth and final verse of each cycle of ten verses (known as a *patikam*) to attack, criticize, and alienate the Jains and their practices. Indeed, depictions of Campantar emphasize this childlike quality. He is often depicted as a smiling, naked dancing child (in iconography similar to that of → Kṛṣṇa) or as a child with a cup of milk in his hand.

Cuntarar

Although Cuntarar may have been the least prolific of the *mūvar* – his compositions constitute just one volume, the seventh book of the *Tēvāram* – he distinguishes himself as the first official canonizer of the Tamil Śaiva saints, providing us with the very first textual listing of 63 exemplary devotees in his *Tiruttoṇṭattokai*. Like those of Appar, Cuntarar's compositions are filled with autobiographical details, particularly about his tumultuous love life. But while Appar's poetry is confessional, Cuntarar's is bold as he styles himself as an intimate of Śiva. In keeping with this youthful character, Cuntarar is often depicted in bronzes and paintings as a handsome, richly adorned prince, accompanied by his two wives. Given Cuntarar's enormous contribution to fixing the list of exemplary devotees, his story frames the entire *Periyapurāṇam* – it opens and closes the work – and is also interspersed throughout the text (*PerP.* 147–349, 3162–3563, 3791–3921, 4229–4281).

Cuntarar was born to Brahman parents sometime in the early 8th century in the town of Thirunavalur and on account of his extraordinary beauty was named Cuntaramūrtti, although he is also known as Nampi Ārūrar, or the prince of Ārūrar. Enchanted by the beauty of the young Cuntarar, the local king, Naraciṅka Muṉiayar, adopted him and raised him with all the pomp, affluence, and opportunity afforded a young prince. Eventually, Cuntarar's wedding was arranged, but the ceremony itself was interrupted by an old man who disrupted the ceremony and claimed that the young groom could not wed, as he was bound to him as a bond servant. Revealing a legal deed of ownership, the old man informed the gathered crowd that Cuntarar's grandfather had promised him the boy.

Cuntarar laughed in his face, called him a madman, and tore up the document. But the argument was brought before the local court of the town of Thiruvennainallur. When the court insisted that the old man take them to his local ancestral home, he instead led them to the Śiva temple and, stepping inside, vanished. Cuntarar followed him inside and had a magnificent vision of Śiva and Pārvatī riding atop the bull. Śiva then revealed to Cuntarar his past life in heaven and the events that led to his rebirth as a human being (*PerP.* 32) and then told him,

> Because you spoke such violent words, you have earned the nickname "Vaṉroṇṭar," or violent servant. Of all the worship offered me in love, the highest form is song. Therefore you must sing my praise in Tamil song throughout the world... You called me "madman." So let that be my name. Call me "madman" in your song. (*PerP.* 215, 219; McGlashan, 2006, 36)

Cuntarar left his old life behind him and went on pilgrimage, singing hymns to the lord he called "Pittaṉ!" ("Madman!"). In his poetry, Cuntarar frequently makes demands for mundane things, for example wealth and women, such demands coming to a head when he falls in love with the lovely dancing girl, Paravai of the Thiruvarur temple. He beseeches Śiva to intervene, and Śiva complies, bringing the lovers together. Legend has it that it was around this time that Cuntarar composed the *Tiruttoṇṭattokai*. One day his spiritual romance intervenes amid his domestic dalliances, and he leaps up from his jeweled couch and races into the temple. Seeing the pious devotees gathered there, he is distraught.

> "When will he make me one of them?" he wonders as he enters the shrine. Śiva appears with a command: "Sing a garland of words in service to those devotees, who have won me as theirs, who have conquered the world through oneness (with me); who are without flaw, and filled with the happiness of love – and you shall join them in this way." But Cuntarar is tongue-tied unable to commence until Śiva himself gives him the first words of his (Cuntarar's) poem – *tillai vāḻ antaṇar tam aṭiyārkkum aṭiyēṉ*, "I serve the servants of the Brahmins who live in Tillai...." Now Cuntarar can sing, in the new awareness granted by the god; the famous *Tiruttoṇṭattokai* flows out of him, as he states his "servitude" to each of the 62 saints separately and to the Nāyaṉmār as a group. When the poem is concluded, he takes his place among them as the 63rd Nāyaṉār. (Shulman, 1990, xxix)

He thus dedicated the formation of a canon of saints, as a group who serve the Brahmans (and Brahmanical instructions) established at Tillai (Chidambaram). Then, eventually, Cuntarar undertakes another pilgrimage. It was during his visit to the temple at Thiruvotriyur that he spies a lovely garland maker, Caṅkili, and falls in love with her. Once again, he approaches Śiva to act as his emissary. Śiva reluctantly agrees, under the condition that he never abandon her. Caṅkili and Cuntarar are married, but soon Cuntarar is overcome with the desire to return to the temple at Thiruvarur. Disregarding his promise, he leaves and as a punishment is struck blind as soon as he steps outside Thiruvotriyur. Cuntarar makes his way back to Thiruvarur and composes plaintive hymns, assailing Śiva for meting out what he considers an unfair and unjust punishment. Eventually, his eyesight is restored, and Śiva intervenes again to reconcile Cuntarar with his first wife, Paravai.

Cuntarar spends his later life on pilgrimage with the Cera king Cēramaṉ Perumāḷ. They become inseparable companions, but at the ripe old age of 18, Cuntarar, weary of the world, begs Śiva to release him from the mortal coil. In response, Śiva sends down a white elephant (Buddhist resonances notwithstanding) from Kailāsa (Tam.

Kailācam) and brings Cuntarar to heaven. As Cuntarar alights, Cēramaṉ leaps upon his horse, whispering "*nama civāya*" (salutations to Śiva) into its ear, and rides astride them all the way to Śiva's blessed realm. Cēramaṉ Perumāḷ of course was also a poet-saint in his own right, contributing three long hymns that became part of the 11th book of the *Tirumuṟai*.

The stories of the three pioneering saints – Appar, the old man; Campantar, the child; and Cuntarar, the youth – speak to the broad vision of the authors of these hagiographies. Further, in closely allying each of these poets with a specific dynasty having political sway in the Tamil country – Pallava, Pandiya, and Cera – they express the expansionist imperative of Tamil Śaivism, even as they indigenize it.

Other Nāyaṉmār Compositions

Of the 63 Nāyaṉmār saints, not all are poets. Many are apocryphal or legendary figures who have been inducted into the fold solely on the merits of their singular Śaiva bhakti. Nonetheless, apart from the *mūvar* – Appar, Campantar, and Cuntarar – there are a number of important poets, many of whose works are included in the diverse 11th book of the *Tirumuṟai*. These include the compositions of the sole female poet among the Nāyaṉār, Kāraikkāl Ammaiyār (discussed at length below); a Pallava king, Aiyaṭikaḷ Kāṭavar Kōṉ, sometimes identified with Parameśvaravarmaṉ (c. 670–700); and Kaḻaṟiṟṟaṟivār (the Cera king, Cēramaṉ Perumāḷ). If many of the Nāyaṉār-poets who make up the 11th book are the paradigmatic practitioners of ecstatic devotion, Tirumūlar becomes the standard bearer for the esoteric and enigmatic *cittar* tradition (Skt. *siddha*, a "perfected one" or adept *yogī*, often having access to magical powers). His *Tirumantiram* (Sacred Mantra), a three-thousand-verse opus on Saiva theology, constitutes the whole of the tenth book of the *Tirumuṟai*.

Although in some cases the autobiographical elements contribute to the embroidered narrative of their lives – Appar's illness or Cuntarar's blindness, for instance – as F. Gros has noted in relation to the female poet Kāraikkāl Ammaiyār, the narrative lives of these saints developed independently of the fixed historical voices crystalized in their poetry (Craddock, 2010, 4). Indeed, the very formation of the unwieldy *Tirumuṟai* can be seen as an attempt to order a diverse and wide-ranging tradition that counts among its numbers both the literate and illiterate, poets, princes, ghouls, kings, fanatical sons, and esoteric and opaque *cittar*s. Noting this divergence when viewing the hagiographies and the original compositions side by side lends insight into the changing character of the tradition in terms of canonization and homogenization. For instance, even the relatively late Nāyaṉār Cuntarar had composed hymns (redolent with autobiographic material) some three hundred years before his hagiography was presented in *Periyapurāṇam*. The interim of sectarian formulation is clearly marked in these later hagiographies.

Nāyaṉmār Hariographic Patterns in the *Periyapurāṇam*

As noted above, structurally the *Periyapurāṇam* exactly follows the pattern and order laid out by Cuntarar's *Tiruttoṇṭattokai*, which was repeated in Nampi Āṇṭār Nampi's 12th-century *Tiruttoṇṭartiruvantāti*. Cēkkiḻār even goes so far as to follow the odd ordering of Nampi's narration that breaks up the hagiography of Cuntarar into three main episodes, which the text then uses to frame the lives of the other 62 Nāyaṉmār. This insistence on not deviating, even when faced with such questionable stylistic tropes, may have been rooted in an agenda to imbue Cēkkiḻār's text with all of the authority of its canonized predecessors.

Cēkkiḻār's authorship of the *Periyapurāṇam* was a well-publicized, politically sponsored event where the text was first "unveiled" in a royal ceremony in Chidambaram around 1135 CE. And clearly, it was a grand success, as it effectively became the "last word" on the Tamil Śaiva canon. But the crowning glory for Cēkkiḻār comes around two centuries later, when in 1313 CE Umāpati Civācāriyar composed the *Cēkkiḻārnāyaṉārpurāṇam*, a legend about Cēkkiḻār and his famous Purāṇam. Of course, Umāpati Civācāriyar is the famous Śaiva Siddhānta theologian who also authored the *Tirumuṟaikaṇṭapurāṇam*, the text about the recovery of the lost *Tēvāram* songs. But his *Cēkkiḻārnāyaṉārpurāṇam* is effectively a meta-Purāṇa, a legend about legends, even as it seeks to retroactively assert Cēkkiḻār's own status as a Nāyaṉār-saint, although he cannot be officially recognized as one among the 63 saints (See Monius, 2004, 113–172).

Since so much of the life of the *Periyapurāṇam* is itself intertwined with the centers of political power, and with the temple institutions, particularly Chidambaram, it is no surprise that many of the Nāyaṉmār stories prominently feature temple institutions. Even as Brahmanical temple worship is challenged by the Śaiva devotee, the temple itself remains an unshakeable institution, celebrated as the local home of Śiva. Thus, the remote hill-tribe hunter Kaṇṇappan (see below) subverts agamic worship, even as he conducts his ritual services at the small shrine at Kalahasti. Still others have a more visceral relationship with these institutions, like Nantaṉār (see below), the untouchable saint who was barred access from the temple until Śiva intervened. Other Nāyaṉmār are priests or temple servants whose whole lives revolve around these sacred sites. Given the Śaiva devotional movement's early focus on developing a sacred Śaiva geography in Tamil country through a network of temples, it is no surprise that the lives of so many Nāyaṉmār are deeply entwined with the development of temple culture and temple institutions.

As is amply evident in the narratives (and the poetry) of both Appar and Campantar, the polemic against the Jains dominates many of the stories collected in the *Periyapurāṇam*. The preoccupation with the Jains in hagiographic narratives speaks eloquently to the struggle for power, control, and domination that the Śaivas waged against a group that they perceived as non-Tamil outsiders with dubious dietary practices. Even some three centuries removed from the time of the earliest poet-saints, the conflict looms large in the public memory of Tamil Śaivas as embodied in the *Periyapurāṇam*.

Indeed, as I discuss below, violence, often grotesque, macabre, and disturbing, is itself a major theme in the hagiographies of the Nāyaṉmār. Violence extends from the mortification of self – Kaṇṇappan is the exemplar for this – to the annihilation of kith and kin, who articulate their singular devotion to Śiva through acts of prodigious violence against their parents, children, and other relations. But let us begin by nothing who these stories reflect the imperative to establish Tamil Śaivism.

Temple as Body: Pūcalār, Vāyilār, and Gaṇanātar

There are a couple of Nāyaṉār hagiographies that reflect the intense impetus to build Śaiva religious institutions. Interestingly, these narratives also demonstrate the fiscal constraints of inagurating and endowing temples without drawing upon resources of the state through royal support. This aspect is emphasized in the stories of Pūcalār (*PerP.* 4171–4199) and Vāyilār (*PerP.* 4079–4088). These hagiographies are of added interest when viewed side by side, as they contrast the endeavors of a Brahman and a "Śūdra" Nāyaṉār, and how these two similar saints are represented as follows:

Pūcalār had tried and tried to raise funds for the construction of a temple for Lord Śiva, but after getting nowhere, he sank into despair. Then he decided that he would employ his imagination and simply built the temple in his mind. He imagined going out and getting a single coin from everyone he knew. He then envisioned hiring craftsmen, choosing an auspicious day to begin the construction, and laying the foundation, all in accordance with scriptural injunction. He did not sleep, but in his mind laid the plinth for the temple towers and set to work covering them with sculptures depicting the gods.

Eventually he crowned the whole structure with its glorious pinnacle, and all was in perfect measure. But he did not stop there. Many days of work lay ahead. The stone needed plastering, and painters had to be brought in, a well had to be dug, and the wall surrounding the temple complex needed to be erected. Eventually, a bathing tank was excavated and all the final arrangements made until, at last, the day of consecrating the temple as a permanent abode of Śiva was fast approaching.

Now, at the same time, the Kāṭavar king was completing the construction of a magnificent Śiva temple in the city of Kanchipuram. The night before the lord was to be installed in his temple, Śiva came to the king in a dream. "Tomorrow I will be taking up residence in the lovely temple that Pūcalār built for me in the little town of Thirunindravur. So you will need to put off your consecration ceremony and postpone it till a later date." Saying this, Śiva went off to his new abode within the sanctum of the temple in Pūcalār's imagination.

When the king awoke, he resolved to immediately go to Thirunindravur to pay homage to Pūcalār. Upon arrival, he asked a passersby where the temple built by Pucalar was. The passerby said that Pūcalār had built no temple there. After inquiring with the village Brahmans, he went to meet Pūcalār and, bowing down before him, asked, "Where is the glorious temple you have built. By the Lord's grace I have learned that today is the day of its consecration, so I have come to worship."

> When he heard the king's words, the devotee was overcome with amazement. "So the Lord in his grace has reckoned me a thing of worth!" he exclaimed, "Because I had no money, I struggled to build a temple in my mind, and it is here before you." (*PerP.* 4185; McGlashan, 2006, 360)

The king bowed low and praised him in astonishment and went back to the city. With Śiva installed in the temple of his mind, Pūcalār lavishly conducted all the proper rituals throughout his life and "finally reached the shade of the golden feet which dance in the golden court."

Thus, the narrative above seems to suggest that the body is itself a temple, and large complexes are insignificant beside the towering edifice of devotion. Yet, the Pūcalār story also asserts that proper agamic ritual is an essential component of Śaiva religion. Nonetheless, the facility to create an inner temple was not just an ability conferred to an erudite Brahman like Pūcalār, who could take recourse to his knowledge of esoteric texts to visualize an inner temple. This same mode of devotional expression is also attributed to a low-caste Nāyaṉār named Vāyilār.

> In the famous town of Mayilai, an ascetic of virtuous character called Vāyilār was born, to bring blessing to the ancient Śūdra caste. He was the leader of the prominent Vāyilār clan, which enjoyed a blameless reputation, and he was well known for the zeal and devotion which he showed for the sacred service of the Lord. By the power of his unflagging concentration, he established a temple for the Lord within his heart. In it he lit the lamp of consciousness of God. Unfailing joy was the water which he used for ritual ablution, and the food he offered to the Lord was the nectar of his love. This was the worship which for many a day this holy devotee offered to the Lord with constant love in the temple of his heart. So at length he found refuge in worship at the feet of the great Lord Śiva. (*PerP.* 4084; McGlashan, 2006, 348).

Beyond the esoteric convention in agamic- and tantric-based traditions of mirroring or superimposing the divine cosmology upon the body, it is also the internalization of the tremendous expense of resources and manpower required to build a temple along with their institutional trappings that make such narratives so unique. Other narratives, such as that of the Nāyaṉār Gaṇanātar (*PerP.* 3923–3929), reflect the administrative demands of temple maintenance and celebrate the divine rewards that can come to those who perform their service with diligence and enthusiasm.

Gaṇanātar was a Brahman temple administrator who served Śiva at Tiruttonippuram. He was so dedicated and effusive about performing service in the temple that he would provide training for other temple servants in how to serve in all the various capacities of temple maintenance and worship. Amid all this special service, he made the time to perform formal *pūjā* to Campantar three times each day. When he died he went to Kailāsa and was promoted by Śiva himself to serve as head of all the heavenly hosts, hence the name Gaṇanātar ("Lord of the Multitude").

Among the many Nāyaṉmār who work in temples, the most intriguing are the two who were deified to eternally serve in cosmic management and temple administrative positions. While Gaṇanātar comes to have a perpetually mythic standing, later I will discuss Caṇṭēcuraṉ, who will actually be formally deified as a temple administrator and will be regularly formally invoked and worshipped in iconic form in an adjacent shrine in Śiva temples, which will function as his "office" and devotees will be asked to ritually report in with this "manager" every time they come for worship.

Caste and the Nāyaṉmār

V. Dehejia's *Slaves of the Lord* provides a detailed chart of the caste affiliations of the Nāyaṉmār as represented in the *Periyapurāṇam* (Dehejia 154, 155). Among them we may note that Brahmans are predominant, next kings, and then members of the Vēḷāḷar caste. Indeed, the composition of the *mūvar* is a microcosm of the distribution of caste groups among the Nāyaṉmār saints. Two of the three *mūvar* are Brahmans (Campantar and Cuntarar), while the third, Appar, is an agriculturalist. Cuntarar of course is also a prince, having been raised by a king, while all three are closely allied with powerful royal houses. The *mūvar* neatly express both the power dynamics and the caste politics that were instrumental in establishing the hegemony of Śaiva devotional religion in the Tamil-speaking south. The pioneering *mūvar* exemplify the tripartite power alliance of Brahmans, Vēḷāḷars, and kings that proved essential to establishing the dominance of Śaivism in Tamil country.

While the cultural and symbolic capital wielded by kings and Brahmans explains their dominant numbers among the Nāyaṉmār saints, the prominence of Vēḷāḷars, a high-caste non-Brahman group of landowners and agriculturalists, reflects their crucial role in the institutionalization of Śaivism in the Tamil-speaking regions during the tradition's formative period in the 7th century. This was achieved primarily through careful alliances between the dominant caste groups, and through the Vēḷāḷars channeling their considerable power, resources, and cultural conservatism (Peterson, 1998, 166, 167, 178).

Beyond the privileged classes, the Nāyaṉmār count among their numbers nine Śūdras. Vāyilār is listed among the Vēḷāḷars, because *vayil* literally means "agriculturalist," however Cēkkiḻār is keen to assert his Śūdra status. But of the group of 63 Nāyaṉmār, Nantaṉār is the sole untouchable, while Kaṇṇappan stands for tribal and marginal groups that are brought into the Śaiva fold. Thus, the untouchable, the military officer, the tribal, and the woman become representatives of both their groups and a specific mode of *bhakti* that additionally helps assert the communal and egalitarian spirit of Śaiva devotional religion. Nonetheless, these acts of devotions, some of which are subversive, as we will see, often are framed by notions of Brahmanical religiosity and are located firmly within the ideology of caste.

The *Periyapurāṇam*'s theme of representing a diversity of saints not only asserts the accessibility of the lord and the expansiveness of his grace, but also helps to redefine Brahminically sanctioned modes of worship, to herald that *bhakti* is accessible to all, and to counter the egalitarian promise of the shramanic faiths. Yet, these narratives, even while skirting social boundaries and taboos, often play at defining the kinds of "service" expected by the disparate community of Śaiva devotees. While the story of the "untouchable" Nantaṉār might appear to subvert the hierarchies of caste, the legend of the Kōccenkaṭ Cōḻar serves to remind kings of their humbler origins, all the while asserting that even kings are predestined to nurture and protect Śaiva institutions.

Nantaṉār

The Nāyaṉār Nantaṉār is often cited as a symbol for the great equalizing force of *bhakti*: that caste or class ceases to matter in the face of true, steadfast devotion. Yet, as we will see, Nantaṉār's story is as much about the egalitarian impulses of *bhakti* as it is about the imperative transformations that guide temple worship. It celebrates core principles of Tamil Śaiva devotionalism, that of self-sacrifice and service to fellow devotees.

The saint Nantaṉār was also known as Tirunāḷaippōvār, meaning "The Sacred One Who Would Go Tomorrow." He was an untouchable farm laborer who was born with a deep, abiding love for Śiva. One day a sudden desire swept over him to go see the lord in his temple at Tiruppunkur. So he set out and soon stood outside the gate of the temple. But as an untouchable he could not enter; however, from the gate he began to sing a heartfelt song. When the image of Nandi the bull (see → sacred animals) obscured his view of the lord, by Śiva's divine grace the icon moved aside so he could peer into the sanctum. He then noticed a vacant depression in the ground beside the temple and set about digging it out into a spacious bathing tank to serve the visiting devotees. When he was finished, he bowed to the lord, danced a happy propitiatory dance, and returned to his little village.

But soon the desire struck him to visit the lord in his great temple at Chidambaram. He knew that, as an untouchable outcaste, he could never go. But the longing would not leave, and each day he would say, "I will go tomorrow!" This is how he got the name Tirunāḷaippōvār – "He Who Will Go Tomorrow." Days passed, and when he finally could bear it no longer, he set out. He bowed low as he arrived, but, seeing the smoke rising in the distance from the Brahman's sacrificial fires, he stopped dead in his tracks. Remembering his low birth, he did not dare to proceed, but piously circumambulated the outer walls of the town for days on end until he fell asleep from exhaustion.

Śiva then came to him in a dream and directed him to the temple, instructing him to leap into the fire when he arrived at the gates of Chidambaram. Likewise, Śiva also told the priests to prepare a sacred fire outside the southern gate for his devotee who was to come.

The next day, the temple Brahmans welcomed Nantaṉār at the gate, and he exclaimed, "My day has come!" After stepping fearlessly into the blazing fire, Nantaṉār emerged anew, wearing the form of a holy sage, with a pure-white sacred thread draped across his chest. He then stepped into the sanctum of Naṭarāja, the lord of the cosmic dance, and disappeared. "Thus, by bathing in the fire, Nantaṉār gained release from his tainted body" (*PerP.* 1077; McGlashan, 2006, 108).

On the surface, this story suggests that devotion before Śiva erases the distinctions of caste and class. Yet, Nantaṉār must first engage in the unheralded loving service of constructing a purifying water tank for fellow devotees before the desire to even go to Chidambaram can strike him. And when he arrives in Chidambaram, he must undergo a bodily transformation – re-forged as a Brahman before being allowed access to the temple. Put another way, Nantaṉār must die in the caste of his old body and enter the Chidambaram temple in the body of the Brahman. Once purified by the fire, all pollution – material and abstract – burns away, and he becomes doubly sacred in body, as an ascetic and a Brahman both, and only then is he fit to enter. One might well ask the question if, with the new Brahman-ascetic body, the erstwhile untouchable Nantaṉār is still even Nantaṉār?

Kōccenkaṭ Cōḻar

Kōccenkaṭ Cōḻar was one of seven kings immortalized and honored with canonical sainthood. The story of the Nāyaṉār Kōccenkaṭ Cōḻar (*PerP.* 4197–4214) is entwined with the famous Śaiva temple of Thiruvanaikaval on the banks of the Kāvērī. Abutting Srirangam, the most important of Tamil Vaiṣṇava shrines and a stone's throw from the old Chola capital of Uṟaiyūr (now Woraiyur, Tiruchirapalli), Kōccenkaṭ Cōḻar's hagiography offers a saintly, hoary lineage to the Cholas, even as it extolls the virtues of acting in service of Śiva, regardless of the circumstances of one's birth.

The story goes like this. In the forest on the banks of the Kāvērī, Śiva manifested as a → *liṅga* under a *campu* tree (Skt. *jambu*; bot. Syzygium jambos). Because a white elephant living in the forest bathed the *liṅga* and offered flowers in worship, the place came to be called Thiruvanaikaval, "Forest of the Sacred Elephant." A devout spider also lived in the same place and enacted its devotion to Śiva by spinning its web above the *śivaliṅga* as a canopy to protect it from the harsh sun or falling leaves. However, when the elephant came to perform his worship, he quickly swept the spider's web away. Eventually, the spider grew angry at the clumsy beast and, crawling inside its trunk, bit him. The elephant thrashed about in pain and fell dead, but Śiva revived the elephant and blessed both the animals for their service. Later, the spider was reborn in the lineage of Chola kings as Kōccenkaṭ Cōḻar ("King with Red Eyes"). At his birth his mother relished his eyes that were red like a spider, but soon died from the rigors of giving birth. A great and generous king, he built and endowed many temples, including providing extensive housing for Brahmans in Chidambaram.

The story exemplifies the principle of loving service to Śiva, one that manifests as competition and characteristically ends in violence and redemption. Further, it suggests that the minor ritual service that the spider performs catapults him to even greater acts of Śaiva generosity. As a king with ever more resources at his command, he funds institutions and builds temples and thus embodies exemplary Śaiva devotionalism. In the bargain, the Cholas boost their credentials, acquiring a pious and saintly lineage.

Esotericism in the Canon: Tirumūlar

While the first seven books of the *Tirumuṟai* cohere together as the *Tēvāram*, many of the remaining five books remain an odd assemblage of works, ranging from devotional Caṅkam works such as the *Tirumurukāṟṟuppatai* to the esoteric *Tirumantiram* (see also → Tamil texts). While Nakkīrar, the author of the *Tirumurukāṟṟuppatai*, is not inducted as a Nāyaṉār, Tirumūlar, the shadowy *cittar*-poet of the *Tirumantiram*, is one of the most important of the 63 saints. The voluminous *Tirumantiram* takes up the entire tenth book of the *Tirumuṟai*, yet it is difficult to ascertain how this opaque, esoteric work and its equally opaque author fit into the largely devotional ethos of Tamil Śaiva devotionalism.

One possible answer may lie in the concerted efforts of canon building and formation that engaged the Tamil Vaiṣṇava community (see → Āḻvārs) during roughly the same period as the Śaivas. Under the guidance of the tradition's principal teachers, → Yamunācārya (10th cent. CE) and → Rāmānuja (d. 1137 CE), the → Śrīvaiṣṇavas had synthesized the passionate *bhakti* poems of their poet-saints into a sophisticated and distinctive philosophical system. Perhaps the inclusion of the poetic yet philosophical *Tirumantiram* in the *Tirumuṟai* was the Śaiva response to these Vaiṣṇava developments. However, it is equally likely that the *Tirumantiram*'s presence in the Tamil Śaiva canon has as much to do with its distinctively tantric voice, composed not in Sanskrit but in Tamil. This is borne out in the hagiography of Tirumūlar (7–8th cents. CE; *PerP.* 3564–3591), which represents a vernacularization of tantric ideas transplanted from the North. As Tirumūlar is also revered as one of the 18 Tamil *cittar*s, there are several later versions of his story.

Tirumūlar

The sage who would come to author the *Tirumantiram* is said to have travelled from Kailāsa to Tamil country in search of his friend and fellow *yogī* Akattiyaṉ (Skt. Agastya), the progenitor of Tamil culture and language, who had taken up residence on the legendary, sacred Potiyil Mountain. As Tirumūlar journeyed, he stopped at many sacred sites along the way.

One evening just after dusk, on the outskirts of a little village, he came upon a small herd of cows lowing and bellowing mournfully. As he came nearer, he saw that the cows, obviously very upset, were standing around the dead body of a cowherd. A few hours earlier, Mūlaṉ the cowherd had been stung on the heel by a serpent. His soul had gone to pasture, and his body lay crumpled in the grassy field. It was getting quite dark, and the *yogī*, taking pity on the poor cows, shifted his awareness into the body of Mūlaṉ. Leaving his original body hidden, he brought the much-relieved cows home, wearing the guise of the cowherd Mūlaṉ. The new "Mūlaṉ" was no longer an average cowherd, but a great *yogī*. Much to the consternation of his wife, the new Mūlaṉ refused to come home. In frustration, she called together the village elders, who examined Mūlaṉ. They found that the cowherd had become a saint. They had no recourse but to advise Mūlaṉ's wife to let the sage wander as he liked. When the *yogī* went back to the grassy field in search of his body, it had disappeared. The saint disregarded this minor inconvenience as Śiva's grace.

The implications of the tale enact the primary philosophical basis of Śaiva Siddhānta belief, which is composed of the trine (1) *pati* or "lord," who saves the (2) *pacu* (Skt. *paśu*), the typically bovine "animal soul," by taking up the (3) *pācam* (Skt. *pāśa*), "bondage or noose" that binds the soul to the world, and which the lord also uses to guide that soul home. So, while dramatizing the most fundamental premise of belief, it differs from the lives of the other saints in that it has nothing to say about temple worship or serving the community of devotees beyond its instructional resonances. Perhaps one of the oddest aspects of Tirumūlar's inclusion among the 63 is that for a Śaiva tradition, he is the sole ascetic.

Women and the Nāyaṉmārs: Kāraikkāl Ammaiyār

There are three female Nāyaṉmār saints, and all but one find a place in the pantheon of 63 saints because of some connection to a male Nāyaṉār. Maṅkaiyarkkaraciyar, the queen of the Pandiya king Niṉṟacīr Neṭumāran (also a Nāyaṉār), earns her place for her aid in converting her husband to Śaivism by inviting Campantar to Madurai (*PerP.* 4189–4191), while Icaiñāniyār is inducted into the fold because she is Cuntarar's mother (*PerP.* 4228). It must be noted here that Tilakavati, Appar's pious sister, who is instrumental in his return to the Śaiva fold, is not counted among the Nāyaṉmārs.

The third and final woman among the 63 is the fascinating Kāraikkāl Ammaiyār, who is arguably the earliest Śaiva *bhakti* poet. The author of four hymns totaling 143 verses, she lived sometime in the mid-6th century. Her poems are included in the 11th book of the *Tirumuṟai*. Though the *Tirumuṟai* includes other early works such as the *Tirumurukāṟṟuppatai*, which is a late Caṅkam work (2nd-4th CE), its inclusion is nonetheless incongruous with the character of Śaiva Siddhānta *bhakti* (Little, 2007, 171–173). Thus, it may be said that Kāraikkāl Ammaiyār's hymns really mark the beginning of the kind of literary production that comes to characterize the poetry of the Tamil Śaiva saints. However, her work is distinctive as it still embodies theological continuities with the earlier southern Śaiva traditions of the → Pāśupatas.

Kāraikkāl Ammaiyār's hagiography (*PerP.* 1717–1782) is surprising in that it expressly eschews traditional female roles and instead brings together the twin ideologies of asceticism and devotion. In doing so, she transforms, losing both her womanly body and her humanity.

Kāraikkāl Ammaiyār was born in the coastal town of Karaikal to a wealthy family of traders and was named Puṉitavati. From infancy she demonstrated a deep devotion to Śiva. She grew into a beautiful woman and was soon wed to a rich merchant. Punitavati was the ideal wife, but also served the Śaiva devotees who passed through Karaikal with equal zeal and reverence.

One morning her husband gave her two ripe mangoes to be served with his midday meal before leaving the house. While she was preparing her husband's lunch, an old Śaiva ascetic came begging for alms. She had nothing to offer him but one of the mangoes. At lunchtime she served her husband's meal along with the remaining mango. Having enjoyed the first one, her husband asked for the second mango. Fretting, she rushed into to the kitchen and prayed to Śiva to help her appease her husband's appetite for mangoes. Immediately a beautiful mango magically appeared. The divine mango was so delicious that her husband knew that it was unlike the one he had eaten before. Not wanting to lie to her husband, Puṉitavati confessed all that had transpired. But her husband did not believe her and insisted she repeat the miracle in front of him right then and there.

Puṉitavati prayed again to Śiva, and another divine mango appeared, much to her husband's surprise. But when she handed him the mango, it suddenly vanished while he held it in the palm of his hand. Thinking his wife was some terrible goddess, he was overcome with terror. He fled from the house and soon boarded a ship to sail far away. He remarried and started a new life.

Meanwhile, back in Karaikal, Puṉitavati carried on her domestic duties waiting for a husband who would never return. Eventually her parents found out her husband's whereabouts and attempted to reunite them. Instead, upon their arrival, her husband's new family venerated Puṉitavati as a goddess. She then realized that her waiting had been in vain, and she prayed to Śiva, bitterly eschewing her beauty and feminine grace, asking that he grant her the form of Śiva's demon (*pēy*). Her wish was granted. Her relatives all bowed down in abject horror and then fled.

In her compositions, Kāraikkāl Ammaiyār refers to herself as a *pēy* and describes her shriveled, ghoulish form. In verse one of her *Tiruvālaṅkāṭṭumūttatirupatikaṅkaḷ* (First Sacred Verseson *Tiruvālaṅkāṭu*), she stands apart, describing herself:

> She has shriveled breasts
> And bulging vein,
>   in place of white teeth
>   empty cavities gape.
> With ruddy hair on her belly
> A pair of fangs, knobby ankles, and long shins
> The demon woman wails at the desolate cremation ground.
> Where our Lord,
> Whose hanging matted hair
> Blows in all eight directions,
> Dances among the flames
> And refreshes his limbs.
> His home is Ālaṅkāṭu [i.e. Alangadu].
> (Ramaswamy, 1992, 141; citing Cutler, 1987, 121)

Alone now, with her old life behind her, she began to sing in praise of Śiva. First came the 101 verses of the *Aṟputattiruvantāti* (Sacred Linked Verses of Wonder) and then the shorter *Tiruviraṭṭaimaṇimālai* (The Sacred Garland of Double Gems) of 20 verses. Her final work, *Tiruvālaṅkāṭṭumūttatirupatikaṅkaḷ*, comprised two sets of ten verses (*patikams*), each with a signature line. In her poems, she speaks of a love for Śiva that precedes even birth. In the famous opening verse of the *Aṟputattiruvantāti*, she says,

> When I was born and learned to speak
> I was overcome with love
>   and I reached your red feet,
>   lord of gods, lord with the splendid black throat,
>   will my sorrows never end? (*AṟTiVa*. 1; trans. Cutler, 1984, 94)

Śiva, moved by her songs, invited her to come to his sacred abode on Kailāsa. So she set out on the long journey, and when she arrived there, not wanting to defile the sacred mountain with her feet, she walked up the mountain slope on her hands. Witnessing her extraordinary act of devotion, Śiva, who is praised as the one with neither beginning nor end, with neither father nor mother, addressed her as "Ammai" ("Mother"). Nampi Āṇṭār Nampi's *Tiruttoṇṭartiruvantāti* (Sacred Verses in the *Antāti* Meter on the Sacred Servants) describes her apotheosis from mere sainthood to her role as Śiva's "Mother" as follows:

> Thinking, "I will not tread upon my Lord's mountain," she walked on her head with her two legs high above. Uma smiled when she saw it, but the Lord whose body is copper in color called the lady "my Mother." She is the treasure

of the town of Kāraikkāl, where the tree branches drip with honey. (Prentiss, 199, 112)

Śiva then bestowed upon his demon devotee a further blessing, directing her to Thiruvalangadu to witness his cosmic dance for all eternity. Upon seeing his dance, she sang the two hymns that make up her *Tiruvālaṅkāṭṭumūttatirupatikaṅkaḷ* (Craddock, 2010, 73–76). And so it is that sculpted images of dancing Śiva in Tamil Nadu, and even in Southeast Asia generally, feature a small, shriveled female figure with wild hair, a delighted smile, and cymbals in hand, watching Śiva's divine dance in rapture.

As a precursor to the ecstatic devotional movement that domesticates Śiva, Kāraikkāl Ammaiyār's poetry celebrates the ascetic, wild, and antinomian character of Śiva, which her hagiography faithfully echoes. Earlier Śaiva sects like the → Kāpālikas, Kālāmukhas, and Pāśupatas invariably emphasized an ascetic approach that focused on impersonating Śiva. Thiruvotriyur, near Thiruvalangadu, was an important center of the Pāśupatas and was likely to have exercised a direct influence on Kāraikkāl Ammaiyār's unique form of devotion (Craddock, 2010, 50). Nonetheless, Kāraikkāl Ammaiyār's story also fits in with larger patterns pertaining to female saints in the Indian tradition. Her singular devotion to Śiva is framed in terms of service first to her husband and then to other Śaiva devotees. Even rejected by her husband, she remains faithful to him, fulfilling the ideal of the chaste and virtuous wife. This fidelity toward her husband is transformed into dedication to Śiva, marked by a bodily transformation from a beautiful, sexual woman to an asexual ghoul.

Violence among the Saints

Violence in myriad forms is a striking and unmistakable feature of the hagiographies of many of the Nāyaṉmār saints. Sometimes the violence is directed outward, against rival groups like the Jains in Campantar's story; on still other occasions, the saint may inflict violence on his kin, amputating, decapitating, or sacrificing his parents or children. The saint himself is not removed from the realm of violence, and his (or her) own body is subject to gruesome acts of mortification, as in the case of Kaṇṇappan. Given the centrality of violence and violent action, scholars writing on the Tamil Śaiva tradition have long gravitated toward understanding the meaning and purpose of such actions in the realm of Śaiva devotionalism. Of course, Tamil Śaiva tradition has its own understanding and special nomenclature for discussing the violent and tender ways of its saints. For instance, Cuntarar, because of his playfully combative relationship with Śiva, is characterized as the *vaṇ toṇṭaṉ*, "the harsh devotee," an appellation that stands in contrast to the *meṇ toṇṭaṉ*, "the gentle devotee." These two broad categorizations are applied to the two distinctive types of Śaiva saints (see Peterson, 1994, 198, 199; Hudson, 1989, 373–404).

These extremities have dominated academic discussion of Nāyaṉmār hagiography in the *Periyapurāṇam*.

> What little scholarship does exist displays a marked interest in the Periya Purāṇam's violence: Cēkkiḻār vividly depicts limbs flying, blood flowing, and bodies falling to the ground in the name of love for the lord (Monius, 2004a, 167).

Take for instance the saint Cattiyār, whose name was derived from *śakti* (Tam. *catti*, power), because of his forceful and intense religious zeal. The *Periyapurāṇam* does not mince words when explaining how he chose to express the ferocity of his devotion:

> He was called Cattiyār because of the force with which he would cut out the tongue of anyone who spoke of the devotees of the Lord with disrespect. He would use an implement to pull out the tongues of such scandalous miscreants, then cut them off with a sharp knife. By virtue of this loving service, he won enduring fame. (*PerP.* 4041; McGlashan, 2006, 344)

Here, the text reframes the horror of his action as a loving service to the Śaiva tradition, because he literally silences opposition. It is disrespect toward Śiva's devotees and not criticism of Śiva that Cattiyār takes umbrage against. Indeed, the text seems to suggest that to question Cattiyār's extreme action – nay, loving service – is to invite his wrath. In some ways, it may be said that the violence distracts, as we, particularly as modern readers, attempt to explain what appear to be almost inexplicable acts of violence. F. Gros suggests that

> [w]e see very little difference between these two types [the "harsh" and "gentle" devotees], how-

ever, since an act of violence is simply the most extreme possible form of service, and given that the devotees are often played with by the god who drags them, without reference to mundane rules, in some heroic pattern of unconditional surrender. It is the service and not the violence that is paradigmatic. (Gros, 2009, 231)

While this is certainly true, that extreme violence is but an expression of extreme devotion, many of these stories also end ambiguously, providing no enlightening closure for those involved. A. Monius observes that nearly one-third of the Nāyaṉmār use violence as an expression of their devotion (2004b, 114). But several others are recipients of violence, which must be vexing for some Śaiva theologians, as some saints and their associates ultimately are not healed or restored by Śiva's mercy and grace even after being rent by his harsh love.

The pervasive presence of violent imagery in the *Periyapurāṇam* might raise questions of its theological implications for Tamil Śaivism. While A. Monius argues that one must situate the violence of the *Periyapurāṇam* in its specific historical and social milieu – that of the competing sects of Jainism and Vaiṣṇavism – (Monius, 2004a, 2004b) still others see it as a throwback born of cultural synthesis. In analyzing the content of these Śaiva hagiographies, K. Prentiss notes that

both David Shulman [1993] and George Hart [1980] argue that images of blood and other bodily fluids are at the core of Tamil culture, as the "underlying" substratum of the later Aryan-Dravidian synthesis. (K. Prentiss, 1999, 39)

Beyond asserting whether these narratives function to express the birthing pains of cultural synthesis, or what A. Monius terms the "aesthetics of disgust," (2004b), the formation of Tamil Śaivism was not without casualties. The near-complete eradication of the Śramaṇa traditions in Tamil country attests to this eventuality. While material remains – caves, icons, paintings – attest to a vibrant Śramaṇa presence in the area, under the vigorous evangelism of Tamil Śaivism, they were pushed much into the margins, their presence in this post-*bhakti* period largely marked by a fragmentary body of Tamil Buddhist and Jain literary and material culture.

The examples of the Nāyaṉār Caṇṭīcaṉ, who becomes Śiva's trusted temple lieutenant, Kaṇṇappaṉ, who subverts Brahmanical authority with his frightening act of self-mortification, and Ciṟuttoṇṭar, whose sacrifice of his son belies his name ("Little Devotee"), suffice to demonstrate the range of ways in which violence and violent action manifests in the stories of the Nāyaṉmār.

Caṇṭīcaṉ or Caṇḍeśvara

Beyond the story of Caṇṭīcaṉ (*PerP.* 1206–1265) presented in the *Periyapurāṇam*, we know little about him. There is no historically verifiable data for such an important religious figure; nevertheless, by the time Rājarāja I (985–1014 CE) builds the Peruvuṭaiyār Kōyil (more commonly known as the Bṛhadīśvara Temple) of Thanjavur, Caṇṭīcaṉ has an important place in the temples of the Chola kings. What we have in the *Periyapurāṇam*'s rendering seems mired in folkloric extemporaneity:

Everyday Caṇṭīcaṉ, a Brahman cowherd boy and devotee of Śiva made a *liṅga* of earth, and worshipped it by pouring oblations of milk from his cows. When his father realized that he was misappropriating the milk, he scolded the body fiercely. But the boy lost in the bliss of worship, ignored him. Enraged, the father kicked over one of the pots of milk set aside for worship. In retaliation, Caṇṭīcaṉ swung his cowherd's staff at his father's leg, but miraculously the stick transformed into an axe and instead of simply hitting his father's legs, he hacked them off. Śiva pleased by Caṇṭīcaṉ's fervor said that he himself would be father to the boy.

The young Brahmin who cut off his father's feet with the axe, became the son of Śiva while remaining in his mortal body. This is beyond human understanding. (*PerP.* 1264; McGlashan, 2006, 123)

Despite the shocking act of violence at the center of his story, Caṇṭīcaṉ is revered today as Śiva's chief administrator. This might owe to the fact that Caṇṭīcaṉ is unique among the Nāyaṉmār, functioning as a minor deity in Śiva's retinue well before the official process of canonization had occurred in the 11th and 12th centuries. By the 7th and 8th centuries, Caṇṭīcaṉ had begun to serve as a *dvārapāla* or door guardian in Śiva temples, while at approximately the same time, he appears in the hymns of Appar and Campantar. Between the 9th and 10th centuries, Caṇṭīcaṉ gained a fixed place in the northeast of the central shine. By the 11th century he was understood to be the deified administrator of Śiva temples, a role he continues to have today throughout the south (Orr, 2005, 4). Now, every worshipper pauses at the Caṇṭīcaṉ shrine when exiting the main sanctum, to have their visit recorded by Caṇṭīcaṉ. Caṇṭīcaṉ is even significant in temple administration, as he is often regarded as the temple's chief accountant.

> Then the ruler of the gods invested Carumaṉ with authority over his servants. "We bestow upon you," he said, "all the vessels from which we eat, all the clothes we put on, and all the ornaments we wear; and we confer upon you the title of 'Caṇṭicāṉ.'" With these words, he took the wreath of cassia flowers from his own matted locks and set it on the head of his devotee. (*PerP.* 1261; McGlashan, 2006, 123)

The above list provided in the *Periyapurāṇam* of the honors bestowed on Caṇṭicāṉ actually refers to constituents that make up Śaiva temple offerings. It refers back to the significant role that Caṇṭicāṉ was given in temple tradition a century and a half before.

> Of all the Saiva saints, Caṇḍeśvara was the earliest to be represented in bronze form – with a number of 10th-century processional images... There are, in fact, far greater numbers of stone images of this saint than any others among the Nāyaṉmār (including, as we have seen, extremely early examples), reflecting this particular aspect of his importance in temple ritual. (Orr, 2005, 4)

Ciṟuttoṇṭar

D. Shulman, writing about the *Periyapurāṇam*, observes that

> [i]ts stories are usually rather grisly, rich in pathos and violent demonstrations of fanatical devotion to the god – and none more so than the tale of the Little Devotee; as such, they may perhaps be seen more as paradigmatic than as normative, although the later tradition often struggles bitterly with these prestigious models. (Shulman, 1993, 19)

The story of Ciṟuttoṇṭar in the *Periyapurāṇam* (*PerP.* 3660–3747) looms out among even the most violent of saintly lives.

Every day, the pious Vēḷāḷar Ciṟuttoṇṭar ("Little Devotee") would not take food until he had found a devotee of Śiva to feed first. Śiva once came to test him in the guise of a fierce ascetic (Vairavar; Skt. → Bhairava). So Ciṟuttoṇṭar unwittingly brought him home and asked him what he would like to eat. The smiling ascetic explained that every six months he ate meat, and Ciṟuttoṇṭar, happy to oblige, informed his guest that he had plenty of livestock and would happily prepare any kind of meat he might prefer. But the ascetic told him that he wanted only human flesh – an unblemished child, less than five years of age. He went on to specify that it must be the only child of a family, and that the mother must hold him down while the father cuts up the flesh; with the added caveat that the child must be prepared without the slightest regret. Ciṟuttoṇṭar readily agreed, and he and his wife decided that only their own little boy would suffice. He brought his laughing son home early from school that day and with the mother's help severed the little child's head. The body was carved up by the father and delicately cooked in fine spices by his wife. As the meal was served, the holy man then insisted that he not eat alone, so a plate was prepared for Ciṟuttoṇṭar as well. But the sage still would not eat, insisting that Ciṟuttoṇṭar's own son join them. Ciṟuttoṇṭar sadly protested that once he had a son but no more. Obstinately the ascetic made Ciṟuttoṇṭar and his wife futilely call to their son at the doorway of the house. Suddenly, the child ran up laughing and embraced his tearful parents, but when they turned to look, the fierce ascetic and his ghoulish meal had disappeared.

In *The Hungry God*, D. Shulman argues that the Vēḷāḷar and similar agricultural groups are linked to the formation and preponderance of this kind of Nāyaṉmār narrative.

> In South India, such land-bound groups often generated texts of a pronounced "martial" quality, keyed, perhaps, to the perception of agriculture as inherently violent and to the struggle for possession of the land. The gory stories of Tamil Śaivism thus emerge logically out of a specific social context. (Shulman, 1993, 20)

Kaṇṇappaṉ

The story of Kaṇṇappaṉ (*PerP.* 650–830) is perhaps one of the most well known among those of the 63 Nāyaṉmār. It confronts issues of caste, Brahmanical authority, and temple worship, within the frame of a self-abnegating service and love of Śiva.

Kaṇṇappan was a huntsman who unknowingly wandered into the hill shrine of Śiva at Kalahasti. Drawn to worship Śiva, but knowing nothing of priestly rules, he offered to Śiva flowers that he carried, water drizzled from his mouth, and freshly killed pork that he had previously tasted to select the choicest bits. Each morning when the Brahman priest arrived at the shrine, he was horrified to find the shrine littered with bones and meat. This went on for a long time, and the priest complained to Śiva about his accepting such offerings. Śiva told him to hide and see the true nature of the hunter's devotion. The next day, when Kaṇṇappan came, he saw that the *liṅga* had eyes, and one was dripping blood. He gathered healing herbs, but nothing worked. So he took one of his arrows and dug out his own eye and gave it to the *liṅga*. But then the second eye started to bleed. Placing his foot on the *liṅga* to mark the spot, he set about to extract his other eye and replace it for the wounded eye of the god. But Śiva intervened and restored the sight of the selfless huntsman.

We can see that not all of the violence of the Nāyaṉmār is directed outward; for Kaṇṇappan the violence is directed toward himself in service of Śiva. Unlike the testing of Ciṟuttoṇṭar that leads a man to murder and almost cannibalize his own son, or the spontaneous amputation of Caṇṭīcaṉ's father in defense of Śaiva worship, Kaṇṇappan's self-sacrifice is not predicated on a sense of obligation to the wider Śaiva community of devotees. Instead, it is not only removed from institutionalized Śaiva religious practice, but also seeks to actively challenge it. Yet, Kaṇṇappan's action is exceptional rather than normative. His devotion, like that of Ciṟuttoṇṭar, is guided by the principles of selfless generosity and hospitality, particularly in the service of Śiva and his devotees. They are exemplars but not examples of what service to Śiva entails and demands. One might say that, as a tribal, Kaṇṇappan's, unique quality as the exemplary devotee emerges from his marginal state of perfect innocence of both social and religious convention and taboo.

Icons and Worship

Institutionalized temple worship of some of the Nāyaṉmār may have begun as early as the 10th century. However, the earliest existent narrative panels depicting the Nāyaṉmār *en masse* appear at the temples of Melakkadambur (early 12th cent. CE) and Darasuram (mid 12th cent. CE). In all likelihood, these panels were inspired by Nampi Āṇṭār Nampi's *Tiruttoṇṭartiruvantāti* rather than Cēkkiḻār's hagiography (Orr, 2005, 2). Regardless, none of the sets of bronze icons of the 63 Nāyaṉmār formally worshipped in temples today seems to date before the 15th century (excepting those at Thiruvarur), but L. Orr has noted that most of the stone sets of Nāyaṉmār have yet to be formally dated (Orr, 2005, 2). We may note that, for instance, the detailed inscriptions from Rājarāja I's Peruvuṭaiyār Kōyil/Bṛhadīśvara Temple tell us that he made arrangements for the performance of the *Tēvāram*, but there is no mention of consecrated images of the *mūvar* or of other Nāyaṉmār. Nonetheless, Rājarāja's great temple does include a shrine to Caṇṭīcaṉ, northeast of the main shrine, which is contemporaneous with the earliest parts of this enormous complex.

V. Dehejia correctly points out that

> considering the prestige enjoyed by the saints and the importance assigned to their poems, it was difficult to believe that they were not worshipped in groups soon after their "canonization." Evidence of such worship does indeed exist, although in inscriptional rather than iconic form. (Dehejia, 2002, 139)

Two early inscriptions from the temples of Thiruvotriyur and Thiruvengadu speak of the worship of groups of Śaiva saints. The Thiruvotriyur epigraph reveals that as early as the year 1046, in the 28th year of the Chola king Rājātirāja, a set of 63 Nāyaṉmār was in worship in the Thiruvotriyur temple. The inscription refers to these images in the context of a festival of the 63 saints in which Cuntarar's poem *Tiruttoṇṭattokai* was recited (Dehejia, 2002, 139, 140). The 12th-century Thiruvengadu inscription can be ascribed to the Pandiyas. It records a land grant instituted to fund the regular practice of bathing the processional icons of Śiva and the 63 Nāyaṉmār at the mouth of the Kāvērī River. The inscriptional evidence from these two temple sites reveal that images of the Nāyaṉmār were used in temple festivals celebrating them by the 11th and 12th centuries (Dehejia, 2002, 140). While the recitation of the *Tēvāram* and other devotional poems is attested to in inscriptions and seems to be fairly widespread in the early medieval period, the worship of icons of the Nāyaṉmār appears to be a fairly localized practice. We may speculate that images of the *mūvar* were possibly in worship by the 10th century and may note the nostalgia with which the 14th-century *Tirumuṟaikaṇṭapurāṇam* assigns a prominent role for the processional icons in the recovery of the *Tēvāram* songs. Granted, the text was composed four centuries after the period in question, but the existence of 10th-century icons of the *mūvar* offer tantalizing evidence of their integration into temple ritual, and one that this later text seeks to capture.

The disappearance of the early icons from a site like Thiruvengadu may be ascribed to the practice of burying icons and temple treasure in response to the raids into Tamil by Malik Kāfūr around 1310. Several early icons associated with the Thiruvengadu temple have been periodically unearthed in small batches between 1925 and 1972. Among several striking images of Śiva, Thiruvengadu has also given us 11th-century bronzes of Appar, Cuntarar, Caṇṭīcaṉ, and Kaṇṇappan. While Caṇṭīcaṉ's emergent function as "temple manager" (see above) may explain the presence of his independent icon, the presence of an image of Kaṇṇappan invites speculation that images of the remaining Nāyaṉmār may still remain buried (Dehejia, 2002, 142). Nevertheless, Kaṇṇappan has been seen to have a unique appeal and frequently appears independently of the other Nāyaṉmār.

As mentioned above, Caṇṭīcaṉ has a fairly long history of being represented independently. He first appears in the 7th and 8th centuries as a door guardian paired with Gaṇeśa and is depicted elaborately in a panel known as the Caṇḍeśvarāṇugraha ("The Liberation of Caṇḍeśvara") in an 8th-century panel at the Pallava-period temple of Kailācanāta (Skt. Kailāsanātha) Temple in Kanchipuram. Thus it is no wonder that Caṇṭīcaṉ finds frequent mention in the early *Tēvāram* poems. Beginning in the 9th and 10th centuries, he has settled into his role as temple manager, complete with an independent shrine (Orr, 2005, 4). Undoubtedly, the most famous image of Caṇṭīcaṉ is a large, niche depiction at Rājendra I's Gangaikondacholapuram temple. In this 11th-century temple, Śiva weaves a garland of cassia flowers around Caṇṭīcaṉ's crown, as the latter bows his head and folds his hand in supplication (a depiction very much like the narrative cited above from *Periyapurāṇam* 1261). This image has often been read as alluding to Rājendra I, who is seen as receiving a singular blessing and divine validation from Śiva himself.

Kāraikkāl Ammaiyār is another Nāyaṉār who appears as an independent, distinctive figure from a fairly early period. She is often shown on the walls and niches of temples, as a small figure off to the side enjoying the dancing Śiva, in temples as far removed as Banteay Srei, → Cambodia. It proffers a typically depicted image which references the legend of the temple of Thiruvalangadu, where Śiva invited his "ghoulish devotee," Kāraikkāl Ammaiyār, to watch his dance. Banteay Srei's distinctively Ankorian style image offers a haunting sculpture of the 10th-century when Śiva's eccentric demon-devotee was still in worship in Southeast Asia (Wood, 2004, 111–112).

Iconography of the Nāyaṉmār

The iconography of the Nāyaṉmār is at once complex and simple. While figures like the *mūvar*, Kaṇṇappan, Kāraikkāl Ammaiyār, and Caṇṭīcaṉ are distinctive, most Nāyaṉmār are rendered in a generic and indistinguishable manner; they can only be told apart by the plaques or notations that identify them. Most of the Nāyaṉmār are shown standing with palms joined together in a gesture of supplication. Even so, there are subtle variations that are surprisingly revealing: the Brahmans are clean shaven, kings and chieftains wear crowns, and most everyone else has a topknot (Dehejia, 2002, 146). Nevertheless, sometimes bronze casters have been inspired in depicting distinctive forms of each Nāyaṉār, as may be seen among the icons housed at the temple in Kalahasti. V. Dehejia notes that texts like the 14th-century *Kaṇṭapurāṇam* and two later Sanskrit works, the *Śivarahasya* and the *Śivabhaktamahātmya*, provided textual directions for the iconography of the Nāyaṉmār, although these recommendations have largely remained theoretical and failed to enter into common usage (Dehejia, 2002, 147).

Iconographically, the *mūvar* may be identified easily. They usually appear as a set, although there are independent images of Campantar and Cuntarar. Appar is shown as an old man with a shaved head, wearing a short loincloth. He usually cradles a hoe, and his palms are joined together in a gesture of prayer. As befitting his status as the oldest of the group, he usually stands in the center. Campantar, generally to his right, is depicted as young child, wearing a topknot, and in a nod to his musicality, he holds a pair of small cymbals in his hand. Cuntarar, on the left of Appar, is generally depicted in royal gear, wearing a dashing crown, and cradling a scepter in his left hand. The two other figures – Kaṇṇappan and Kāraikkāl Ammaiyār – are also easily distinguished. In an arresting image from Thiruvengadu, now housed at the Thanjavur Palace Museum, a smiling Kaṇṇappan is depicted with head slightly titled, holding out his eye to Śiva. Several stone images on temple walls often depict the culminating moment of Kaṇṇappan's story, where he lifts his leg to mark the place on the bleeding eye of the *śivaliṅga* as he readies himself to pluck out his second eye. By virtue of being the nonhuman in the group, Kāraikkāl Ammaiyār is easy to spot. She is distinguished by her wild hair, shriveled breasts, emaciated body, a pair of cymbals in her hands, small fangs, and a blissful smile. From the range of lovely Kāraikkāl Ammaiyār images that one encounters, both in worship and in museums, on temple walls, niches, always beside the dancing Śiva, it would appear that these early artisans relished the challenge of representing her odd yet terrifying beauty.

The iconography of the Nāyaṉmār did not emerge in isolation and reflect the ways in which competition and cooption between rival sects functioned in the early medieval period. In fact, even as the Jains lost the battle against the Śaivas, the latter group turned their attention to the strong Vaiṣṇava presence in the region. This might explain the appropriation of Kṛṣṇa's various iconographic forms to represent the Nāyaṉmār, particularly the child, Campantar. The most widespread of these is the depiction of the child-saint Campantar in the familiar form of the dancing child. In such depictions, like Kṛṣṇa, a naked Campantar is shown with one leg bent and raised. The two can only be distinguished by their hand gestures. While Kṛṣṇa's right hand is held in the *abhayahasta* (gesture of protection), Campantar's right index finger points upward, saying at once that there is only one god – Śiva – and he is above all else.

Similarly, Cuntarar mimics Kṛṣṇa, the regal cowherd, who is often portrayed with his two wives. Similarly, Cuntarar stands between his two wives, Paravai and Caṅkili, shepherd's crook in hand, languorously leaning against an invisible cow. Even the relatively unknown saint, Ānāya Nāyaṉār, takes on the famous form of

Fig. 2: Kaṇṇappan lifting his leg to mark the place on the bleeding eye of the *śivaliṅga* (photo by Layne Little).

Kṛṣṇa Veṇugopāla, standing with one leg jauntily crossed over the other as he plays his flute. Like Kṛṣṇa, Ānāya, a flute-playing cowherd, was known to entertain Śiva with his flute playing and could induce a peaceful trance in the forest's wild beasts. V. Dehejia's study of the "iconographic transference" of three key representations of Kṛṣṇa onto that of these three Śaiva saints found this development both perplexing and intriguing (Dehejia, 2002, 149).

Perhaps in their desire to divert a known and popular source of devotional attraction to the worship of Śiva, the Chola rulers encouraged the modeling of Śaiva saints on the familiar iconography of Kṛṣṇa. This conscious modeling of the Śaiva saints on forms of Kṛṣṇa (and there seems no doubt that it was a planned decision) may then be seen as the Chola monarchs' determination to popularize the faith of Śaiva (Dehejia, 2002, 150).

But we can take this reading further: it constitutes an outright appropriation of the deific forms of the Vaiṣṇava faith. Linked to some of the sectarian polemics of the early-late medieval period, we can see other instances where the deity of one religion can be worshipped as a wholly different entity by adherents of another faith. For instance, the Buddhist *mahāsiddhas* venerated any icon of Maheśvara-Śiva as Avalokiteśvara. In the case of the Nāyaṉmār, a familiar iconic form representing → Viṣṇu is simply subsumed into the form of one Śaivism's human agents.

Cooption and Contention with the Śramaṇas

We have already noted the Śaiva polemic with the shramanic traditions that was an inherent part of the formation of the Tamil Śaiva traditions. Critiques of Buddhist and especially Jain traditions were endemic throughout the early Tamil Śaiva world, and central to the *Tēvāram* hymns of Campantar and Appar. Jains and Buddhists had been present in the deep south since at least the 2nd century BCE, arguably before Śaivism had any real foothold in the Tamil region. Yet, beginning in the 7th century, with figures like Appar and Campantar, it was the Śramaṇas who would be branded as alien and outsiders.

The influence of the Śramaṇas was expanded through patronage during the Kalabhra Interregnum (roughly 250–600 CE), when "upland" tribal chieftains (called Kalabhras [Tam. Kaḷapirrar]) exerted control over peasant farmers that worked the fertile plains and river deltas, the "rice bowl" of Tamil country. But the upsurge of the devotional movements that stimulated a revitalization of Hinduism began to gain footing during the time of the Pallava expansion in the 7th century, which was accompanied by a "Brahmin-peasant alliance" that worked toward social and economic reorganization in the region (Peterson, 1998, 173, 174). As the Śaiva and Vaiṣṇava gained greater social and political influence, Jain and Buddhist monasteries were looted, taken over or sacked. But both shramanic traditions managed to somehow endure.

In the context of the conflict with the Śramaṇa groups, it is significant to note that the *Periyapurāṇam* was composed as a direct response to the 9th-century Jain epic *Cīvakacintāmaṇi*. Umāpati Civācāriyar's *Cēkkiḻārnāyaṉārpurāṇam* recounts that Cēkkiḻār wrote the *Periyapurāṇam*, a tale as much filled with violence as the *Cīvakacintāmaṇi* is filled with eros, to wean the Chola court and Kulōttuṅka II off their admiration for the latter work. Perhaps this juxtaposition might help us understand the *Periyapurāṇam*'s ideology and adherence to shocking violence. Just as the overt and explicit sexuality of the *Cīvakacintāmaṇi* is meant to turn the reader away from the transient pleasures of the world (see Ryan, 1998), might not the *Periyapurāṇam*'s exaggerated violence inspire a fierce, dedicated, and single-minded devotion to Śiva?

The Śaiva awareness of the Jain presence is also present in the constitution of the 63 Nāyaṉmār saints. The odd number puzzlingly leaves out Mānikkavācakar, one of the most significant Śaiva devotional poets and whose work is part of the *Tirumuṟai*. Mānikkavācakar's addition would give us a total of 64, the square of eight and a super-perfect number that shows up time and again in a variety of Hindu contexts. But, as with the very lives of many of the saints themselves, the answer lies in sectarian polemics. While there were other enumerated Hindu saints in the neighborhood – the 12 Vaiṣṇava Āḻvārs, the 9 *nāthas*, and the 16 Buddhists *arhat*s and 8 great *bodhisattva*s – it was the Śaivas' fierce competition with the Jains that eventually gave us the number 63. The learned Śvetāmbara Jain *ācārya* Hemacandra (1087–1172) composed a popular Jain hagiography, the *Triṣaṣṭīśalakapuruṣacaritra* (Lives of 63 three Great Men), almost a century prior to Cēkkiḻār's own work. But, the notion of the 63 Jain elders must surely have circulated well before Hemacandra's text, as the first count of the 63 Nāyaṉmār appears in Cuntarar's *Tiruttoṇṭattokai*. Indeed, even more tellingly is that unlike the Vaiṣṇava Āḻvārs, who are all poets whose works are collected in the Vaiṣṇava Tamil canon, all of the Nāyaṉmār are not poets. In fact, most of them are not verifiable historical figures.

Cākkiyar

Beyond direct conversion or outright annihilation, Cākkiyar's story (*PerP.* 3636–3653) depicts an interesting manner of coopting the adherents of the despised shramanic faiths.

Cākkiyar (from Śākya) was a kind and gentle man whose ultimate goal was to escape the endless cycle of death and rebirth. So he eventually went to Kanchipuram, the great center of sacred learning for many traditions. He took up the Buddhist path and became a monk. "However, by diligent study of the Buddhist sacred texts, he came to realize that adherence to such alien religions and their teaching did not lead to the truth" (*PerP.* 3638; McGlashan, 2006, 309). By divine grace he came to learn that Śiva is the ultimate reality. But rather than relinquish the external trappings of a Buddhist monk, he surreptitiously expressed his love each morning by vowing not to take his morning meal until he had thrown a rock at a *śivaliṅga*. The lord was pleased and granted him heavenly bliss.

This kind of cooption, however, did not just go in one direction, and the Buddhist *mahāsiddhas* provide us with fertile ground to explore some of the intersections between Śaivism and Buddhism. So, although the Buddhist *mahāsiddhas* are typically regionally associated with Bengal and Oddiyana, a surprising number lived in the south. The Buddhist hagiographic compendium the *Caturaśitisiddhapravṛtti* (Lives of the 84 *Mahāsiddhas*), authored by Abhayadatta Śrī around the 12th century, and currently existing only in its Tibetan translation, may well have appropriated a prominent Nāyaṉmār into its own retinue of 84 saints. One of the Tamil *mahāsiddhas*, Koṭali Pa ("The One with the 'Hoe'"), is believed to reside near Rameshwaram. Not only does his iconography replicate Appar's, but Kotali's enlightenment poem (included with each *siddha*'s story) also utilizes a metaphor of hoeing the field of the mind, strikingly reminiscent of one of Appar's most famous poems (4.76.2; Peterson, 1989, 211). Thus it may be said that the *Caturaśitisiddhapravṛtti* may have clandestinely reconverted Appar back into one of the Śramaṇa that he so despised.

Nāyaṉmār in Film

When exploring the Nāyaṉmār in film and other contemporary performance venues, it is clear that modern media has brought to the center those peripheral Nāyaṉmār that best embody social reform and critique. Certainly, we still have the *mūvar* traversing the silver screen in important works such as A.P. Nagarajan's 1967 film, *Tiruvarutcelvar*, which featured both Gemini Ganesan and Sivaji Ganesan in major roles. The first Nāyaṉmār depicted in film may have been in the 1935 production of Siruthonda Nayanar (Monius, 2004, 117n16). But ultimately it is Kaṇṇappan (in Andhra and Karnataka) and Nantaṉār and Kāraikkāl Ammaiyār (in Tamil Nadu) who have dominated both film and stage as the stories that most resonate with modern audiences.

Bhakta Nandanar was an important 1935 film directed by Manik Lal Tandol. He was greatly assisted in shooting by the American director Ellis R. Dungan, who moved to India in 1935 and was instrumental in the development of Tamil cinema as he worked on 14 important Tamil classics between 1935 and 1950. Tandon and Dungan's *Bhakta Nandanar* was unique in that it veered away from male-dominated stage traditions where men often played female roles by casting the 27-year-old, recently widowed, female actress K.B. Sundarambal in the male lead. K.B. Sundarambal, of course, would go on to embody the religiosity of Tamil women throughout her long, illustrious film career. This was the film debut of the great female Carnatic vocalist, K.B. Sundarambal, cast in the provocative role of a male untouchable saint. The film was widely criticized, surrounding issues of both gender and caste-based tensions. But among the four different film adaptions of the story of Nantaṉār (the earliest being from 1932), it was this 1935 version that had the most enduring influence.

E. Craddock has discussed the 1973 *Karaikkal Ammaiyar* film at length in her intricate study, *Śiva's Demon Devotee* (Craddock, 2010, 83–86). Here she notes that the film tends to diminish the transgressive aspects of the Kāraikkāl Ammaiyār narrative as it seeks to reinforce traditional roles of domesticity. This is further reflected in the choice of casting. Here the "demon devotee" was played by K.B. Sundarambal, who dispensed with the saint's ghoulish or demon countenance and simply appropriated her previous role of the wise old mystic granny, imitating the same role she played when she acted as the wise old female poet, → Avvaiyār (in 1953). This film functioned to validate the spiritual aspirations of modern Tamil women while restraining the narrative source by insisting the saint not tread too far beyond the familiar sensibilities of sentimentality that link women to family and nation.

In 1956 H.L.N Simha directed a Kannada film on the life of Kaṇṇappan Nāyaṉār called *Bedara Kannappa*. It was the first film to feature Rajkumar in the lead, and it functioned to help galvanize the Kannada film industry. It was dubbed into Telugu under the title *Kalahasti Mahatmyam* (The Greatness of Kalahasti), the famous temple site that marks where the events of Kaṇṇappan's life took place. It eventually actually spawned a full Telugu remake in 1976, which was directed by Bapu and titled *Bhakta Kannappa*.

Other venues of modern performance have followed much the same pattern, particularly in *bhāratanāṭyam* (see → dance) and Carnatic → music. Some of the most acclaimed works featuring Nāyaṉmār were Kalakshetra's *Kannapan* and Gopalakrishna Bharati's "musical opera" *Nandanar Charitram*. Actually *Nandanar Charitram* has itself spawned many new variant renditions, and Carnatic musicians frequently excerpt songs from it in concert. V.P. Dananjayan, a famous Chennai-based *bhāratanāṭyam* artist is famous for performing "Varugalamo Ayya" ("May I Come, Sir?"), which captures the moment that Nantaṉār pleads to be let inside the temple of Chidambaram.

While not presenting an exhaustive survey of the Nāyaṉmār in modern media and performance, these especially influential works reveal how the diversity of the 63 Nāyaṉmār helped sustain an enduring and dynamic appeal in the modern context. But clearly the hagiographies of most relevance today are those of the Nāyaṉmār who challenge the strictures of caste, class, and gender within the comforting ideology of *bhakti*, which might mute the stories' more transgressive aspects even while asserting the universality of humanity before Śiva. One might say that such radical alterations – perhaps even a violence done to these narratives – are well in keeping with the spirit of the *Periyapurāṇam*.

Bibliography

Craddock, E., *Śiva's Demon Devotee: Kāraikkāl Ammaiyār*, New York, 2010.

Cutler, N., *Songs of Experience: The Poetics of Tamil Devotion*, Bloomington, 1987.

Cutler, N., "The Devotee's Experience of the Sacred Tamil Hymns," *HR* 24/2, 1984, 91–112.

Dehejia, V., *Slaves of the Lord: The Path of the Tamil Saints*, Delhi, 2002.

Gros, F., *Deep Rivers: Selected Writing on Tamil Literature*, Pondicherry, 2009.

Hart, G., "The Little Devotee: Cēkkiḻār's Story of Ciṟuttoṇṭar," in: M. Nagatomi *et al.*, eds., *Sanskrit and Indian Studies*, Dordrecht, 1980.

Hudson, D., "Violent and Fanatical Devotion Among the Nāyaṉārs: A Study in the Periya Purāṇam of Cēkkiḻār," in: A. Hiltebeitel, ed., *Criminal Gods and Demon Devotees: Essays on the Guardians of Popular Hinduism*, Albany, 1989, 373–704.

Little, L., "An Anachronistic Āṟṟupatai for Lord Murukaṉ: Mapping Historical Raptures in the Saiva Literary Imagination," in: R. Cheran, D. Ambalavanar & C. Kanaganayakan, eds., *History and Imagination: Tamil Culture in the Global Context*, Toronto, 2007, 169–186.

McGlashan, A., *The History of the Holy Servants of the Lord Siva: A Translation of the Periyapurāṇam of Cekkilar*, Victoria, 2006.

Michell, G., & I.V. Peterson, *The Great Temple at Thanjavur: One Thousand Years, 1010–2010*, Mumbai, 2010.

Monius, A., "Śiva as Heroic Father: Theology and Hagiography in Medieval South India," *HTR* 97/2, 2004a, 165–197.

Monius, A., "Love, Violence, and the Aesthetics of Disgust: Śaivas and Jains in Medieval South India," *JIPh* 32, 2004b, 113–172.

Orr, L.C., "Singing Saintly Songs: Tamil Hymns in the Medieval South Indian Temple," unpublished paper presented at the AAS Annual Meeting, 2007.

Orr, L.C., "Poets, Philosophers and Saints: Canon and Icon in Medieval Tamil Śaivism," unpublished paper presented at the Madison South Asia conference, 2005.

Pechilis, K., "The Story of the Classical Tamil Woman Saint, Kāraikkāl Ammaiyār: A Translation of Her Story from Cēkkiḻār's 'Periya Purāṇam,'" *IJHS* 10/2, 2006, 171–184.

Peterson, I.V., "Śramanas against the Tamil Way: Jains as Others in Tamil Śaiva Literature," in: J.E. Cort, ed., *Open Boundaries: Jain Communities and Cultures in Indian History*, 1998, 163–186.

Peterson, I.V., "Tamil Śaiva Hagiography: The Narrative of the Holy Servants (of Śiva) and the Hagiographical Project in Tamil Saivism," in: W.M. Callewaert & R. Snell, eds., *According to Tradition: Hagiographical Writing in India*, Wiesbaden, 1994, 191–228.

Peterson, I.V., *Poems to Śiva: The Hymns of the Tamil Saints*, Princeton, 1989.
Prentiss, K., "Translation of the *Tirumuṟaikaṇṭa Purāṇam*; attributed to Umāpati Civācāriyar," *IJHS* 5/1, 2001, 27–44.
Prentiss, K., *The Embodiment of Bhakti*, Oxford, 1999.
Ramaswamy, V., "Rebels – Conformists? Women Saints in Medieval South India," *Anthropos* 87/1–3, 1992, 133–146.
Ryan, J., "Erotic Excess and Sexual Danger," in: J.E. Cort, ed., *Open Boundaries: Jain Communities and Cultures in Indian History*, 1998, 67–84.
Shulman, D.D., *The Hungry God: Hindu Tales of Filicide and Devotion*, Chicago, 1993.
Shulman, D.D., *Songs of the Harsh Devotee: The Tēvāram of Cuntaramūrtti Nāyaṉār*, Philadelphia, 1990.
Wood, M., "The Temple of Tiruvalangadu and the Myth of the Dance Competition," in: V. Nanda & G. Michell, eds., *Chidambaram: Home of Nataraja*, Bombay, 2004, 106–117.
Zvelebil, K., *Tamil Literature*, Leiden, 1975.

LAYNE R. LITTLE

Rāmānanda

Rāmānanda (15th cent.) is not only one of the most important but also one of the most mysterious figures of medieval Hinduism. His personality and teachings have been interpreted by scholars in sometimes various, and contradictory, ways (Caracchi, 1999, 135–154), presenting him as a great social reformer as well as a mighty protector of Hindu → *dharma*. He is also reputed to have played an important role in the development and diffusion of Hindi, although few Hindi songs go under his name, and their attribution is doubtful. He owes his fame especially to his reputed role of *guru* to → Kabīr, Raidās (→ Ravidās), and other → Sants. At the same time, he is considered to be the founder of the largest monastic order in North India, that of the → Rāmānandīs, and, most of all, he is traditionally reputed to be the first preacher of → Rāma *bhakti* in the North, according to a popular saying:

> *bhakti drāviḍa ūpajī lāye rāmānanda*
> *paragaṭa kiyā kabīr ne saptadvīpa navakhaṇḍa*

> *Bhakti* was born in Dravidian countries, Rāmānanda brought it,
> Kabīr manifested it in the seven *dvīpa*s and in the nine *khaṇḍa*s. (That is in the seven "islands-continents" and in the nine "regions" of the Hindu cosmology; Caracchi, 1999, 16)

Today Rāma → *bhakti* is possibly the most significant feature of Hindu popular religiosity, at least in North India. Rāmānanda may thus be considered a key figure in the story of → *nirguṇa bhakti* as well as that of *saguṇa bhakti*. Moreover, there are many popular religious movements and personalities that claim, or are presumed, to be somehow related to him; these range from the Maharashtrian saints to → Tulsīdās and the Sant *paramparā* in Bhurkura, Bihar (the lineage of Yārī Sāhab, Gulāl, Palṭū, etc.) – at times despite the lack of any historical evidence. In W.R. Pinch's words,

> Ramanand is believed by many to have occupied an important and neglected space between two competing 'Hinduisms': one composed of sophisticated pandits, the other of radical poets. (Pinch, 1996, 50)

Although Rāmānanda is one of the leading figures of medieval Hinduism and laid the foundations for the development of much of the subsequent

Fig. 1: Popular print of Rāmānanda.

religious history of North India, there is very little reliable information about his life and teachings. In D. Lorenzen's often quoted statement, Rāmānanda "remains a historical enigma" (Lorenzen, 1991, 12).

Hagiography and Legend

Sources of information about Rāmānanda's life (Caracchi, 1999, 23–53; Shrivastav, 1957, 4–51) include the *Bhāviṣyapurāṇa* (*Pratisargaparvan* 4.7–22); some hagiographical works, especially of the Bhaktamāl genre; some "invented" texts, such as the *Rāmānandajanmotsava*, which claims to be part of the *Agastyasaṃhitā*; and the *Prasaṅga Pārijāt*, which claims to have been written in the 15th century by Cetandās, a disciple of Rāmānanda, but was actually composed in the mid-20th century in a curious form of Prakrit created expressly on the basis of Paishacibhasha (for Paishacibhasha, see → Sanskrit texts and language). The most important source for Rāmānanda's life is the *Bhaktamāl*, composed around 1600 by Nābhādās. Besides the fact that the *Bhaktamāl* is an authority in itself, this text is also important as its author is fourth in the spiritual lineage descending from Rāmānanda; therefore it can be considered a reliable voice of the ancient Rāmānandī tradition. The *Bhaktamāl* reads as follows:

> The glory of the way taught by Śrī Rāmānuja spread as *amṛta* on the earth. [After him came] Devācāraja and the second was Hariyānanda of great majesty. His [disciple] was Rāghavānanda who honored the *bhaktas*. After travelling all over the earth, he settled in Kāśī. He strengthened *bhakti* for the people in the four *varṇas* and *āśramas*, for everybody. Rāmānanda manifested himself as his disciple, assuming a body for the universal benefit.
>
> As the Lord of Raghu did, Śrī Rāmānanda built another bridge for the people to cross [*saṃsāra*]. Ānantānanda, Kabīra, Sukhā, Surasura, Padmāvati, Narahari, Pīpā, Bhāvānanda, Raidāsa, Dhanā, Sena, the wife of Surasura and the other disciples shone, each more brightly than the others. They were the supporters of universal welfare, blissful and mines of the tenfold *bhakti*. Holding his body for a long time Rāmānanda brought to salvation the people who bowed to him. (*BhM. chappays* 35–36; trans. by author)

Although this is perhaps the most reliable source on Rāmānanda's life, the information we derive from it is extremely limited. From the *Bhaktamāl* we know that

- Rāmānanda belonged to → Rāmānuja's *paramparā*, after Devācārya, Hariyānanda, and Rāghavānanda (this does not necessarily mean that Rāmānanda was fourth in line after Rāmānuja; most probably Nābhādās intended only to mention the names of some *gurus* of the *paramparā*);
- his *guru* Rāghavānanda settled in Varanasi and preached *bhakti* to everybody, whatever their social status;
- he had 12 main disciples, and five of them were illustrious Sants and poets (Kabīr, Raidās, Sen, Pīpā, and Dhanna); and
- he had a very long life.

It is also noteworthy that Rāmānanda is considered an *avatāra* by Nābhādās, who manifested himself for the benefit of the world (*viśvamaṅgala*) and whose power of salvation is compared to that of Rāma himself.

The divinization of Rāmānanda assumes great importance in the *Bhaktisudhāsvad*, Bhagavānprasād Rūpkalā's commentary to *Bhaktamāl*, which is now considered the most authoritative (Pinch, 1996, 55–59). On the basis of this commentary and other hagiographical sources, the tales of Rāmānanda's life may be summarized as follows: Rāmānanda was born in a Kanyakubja Brahman family of Prayag to Puṇyasadana and Suśīlā. At the age of 12, he went to Varanasi, where he became a disciple of a → Smārta *sāṃnyāsī*. One day he met Rāghavānanda, belonging to the Rāmānuja Sampradāya (see → Śrīvaiṣṇavas), who revealed to him that the time of his death was at hand, although unfortunately he had not yet taken shelter in Hari. His *guru* confirmed the prediction and advised him to throw himself on Rāghavānanda's mercy, since he (the *guru*) was unable to protect him. Rāghavānanda accepted Rāmānanda as his disciple, gave him the *ṣaḍakṣaramantra* (i.e. *rāṃ rāmāya namaḥ*), and taught him how to reach *samādhi* (the highest stage of yogic absorption) so that he would be taken for dead by → Yama. In this way, Rāmānanda was able to cheat death and was saved.

A crucial event in Rāmānanda's life occurred when he returned to Varanasi after a long pilgrimage. His fellow disciples, who observed the strict rules of the → Śrīvaiṣṇavas, refused to accept him into their community, unless he performed a *prayaścitta* to cleanse himself of all the impurities he might have been contaminated with during his travels; however, he refused. In the words of G.A. Grierson, this quarrel "resulted in one of the most momentous revolutions that have occurred in the religious history of N. India" (Grierson, 1918, 570): his *guru* suggested that he start a separate community, the very community that would be the original nucleus of the Rāmānandī order (which, nevertheless, still remained a branch of the Śrīvaiṣṇava Sampradāya until the beginning of the 20th cent.). The *āśrama* of this new community was established on Panchaganga Ghat, where disciples of different castes, and even of different religions, began to gather around *guru* Rāmānanda, for he preached Rāma *bhakti* to people of any social condition, according to the famous popular saying attributed to him:

> *jāti pānti pūche nahīṃ koī*
> *hari ko bhajai so hari kā hoī*
>
> Nobody should ask about caste,
> He who worships Hari belongs to Hari.

By far the most famous story in Rāmānanda's life is to be found in the *dīkṣā* of Kabīr, the earliest version of which is related in the *Kabīr Paracāī* by Anantdās, a contemporary of Nābhādās. According to this account, a divine voice advised Kabīr to take initiation from Rāmānanda, but Kabīr doubted that Rāmānanda would even look at him, since he was a Muslim. Then the voice urged him to meet Rāmānanda at night. In the darkness before sunrise, Kabīr lay down on the path where Rāmānanda used to walk to the → Gaṅgā for his daily bath. Rāmānanda stepped on Kabīr and exclaimed "Rāma!" Kabīr took this word as a *dīkṣāmantra* and began to sing the praises of Rāma, declaring himself to be Rāmānanda's disciple. When Rāmānanda came to know about this, he summoned Kabīr and asked him for an explanation. Rāmānanda spoke to Kabīr from behind a curtain, but after hearing his explanation, he was convinced by his faith, opened the curtain, and gave him a true initiation (Lorenzen, 1991, 94–96; for this legend in later sources and its interpretation, see Lorenzen, 1991, 23–27). The stone step where Kabīr is believed to have lain is still visible on the Panchaganga Ghat.

A further well-known story regards another disciple of Rāmānanda: Pīpā, *rājā* of Gagron in → Rajasthan. The story is related in the *Bhaktirasbodhinī* of Priyādās and in the *Bhaktisudhāsvad* of Rūpkalā, the two main commentaries to Nābhādās' *Bhaktamāl* ([6]1977, 492–521), in Mahīpati's *Bhaktavijaya* (see Abbot & Godbole, vol. I, 1982, 407–414), and other hagiographies. Pīpā was a devotee of Devī (→ Mahādevī), who ordered him to go to Banaras and become a disciple of Rāmānanda. He did so, but Rāmānanda refused to receive him and tested him by ordering him to jump into a well. Pīpā was about to jump when he was pulled out and accepted by Rāmānanda as his disciple. Later Rāmānanda, with Kabīr and Raidās, stopped in Gagron on the way to Dwarka and visited Pīpā. In order to follow him, Pīpā left his realm for good and together with his youngest queen, Sītā, embraced the ascetic life.

Like all the great masters, Rāmānanda is reputed to have done the *digvijaya* (the "conquest of the directions", i.e. the journey undertaken to spread one's own doctrine and to dialectically "conquer" the opponents); in any case, it seems that he traveled a lot, since marks of his presence are recorded on Mount Abu, where his footprints are still venerated, near Junagarh in Gujarat, where he is said to have meditated in a cave, and in Ganga Sagar, in the bay of Bengal, where he is said to have discovered the ancient *āśrama* of Kapila.

Fig. 2: Rāmānanda and Kabīr in the Śrī Maṭh, Varanasi (photo by Pinuccia Caracchi).

According to legend, he passed away at a very old age by simply disappearing. On the eve of *rāmnavamī*, he announced to his disciples that he was going to celebrate in Sāketa, playing upon the double meaning of Sāketa as Ayodhya and as Rāma's heavenly kingdom. The next day, a crowd of disciples and *bhakta* gathered on the Panchaganga Ghat, looking forward to listening to Rāmānanda's teachings. Everybody heard the sound of a conch coming from Rāmānanda's *āśrama*, but he was no longer there – only his wooden *pādukās* were found. The *pādukās* were brought to the river side, where they turned into stone. These are believed to be the stone *pādukās* still worshipped in the Śrī Māṭh of Panchaganga Ghat.

Works

Works in both Sanskrit and Hindi are attributed to Rāmānanda, although their authorship is far from certain (Caracchi, 79–131). Among the Sanskrit works, the *Vaiṣṇavamatābjabhāskara*, first published in 1878, is the only text accepted by all Rāmānandīs and many scholars as well. In the *Vaiṣṇavamatābjabhāskara*, different themes dealing with doctrine, spiritual matters, and religious practices are presented as the answers of Rāmānanda to ten questions posed by his disciple Surasurānanda, starting with "What is reality?" (*tattvam kim*). The philosophical view of *Vaiṣṇavamatābjabhāskara* is essentially that of Viśiṣṭādvaita Vedānta (see → Vedānta). The one and ultimate reality is threefold, consisting of three elements (*tattvatraya*) that are permanent (*nitya*), unborn (*aja*), and beginningless (*anādi*): → *prakṛti*, which is non-conscious (*acetanā*), composite of the three → *guṇa*s and matrix of the universe (*viśvayoni*; 1.6); the souls (*jīva*), that are conscious, but ignorant (*ajña*); both of them being completely dependent upon the third one, → Īśvara (1.7–8), who has the form of being, consciousness and bliss (*saccidānandarūpa*; 2.14), and is identified with Rāma. His mercy (*kṛpā*) and compassion (*karuṇa*; see → grace and compassion) make him the shelter for all those who seek shelter into him, whatever may be their nature, behavior and caste. He shares his parental love (*vātsalya*) for the world with Sītā (see → Draupadī and Sītā), who is the mother of the universe and the refuge for all the sentient and insentient beings: one can reach Rāma only through Sītā (2.12,26; 4.45–46).

The soul is subjected to some complex classifications. For instance, his relation (*sambandha*) with Īśvara can have nine forms (for example, the one between father and son, protected and protector etc.). Among them special theological relevance is given to *śeṣaśeṣitvasaṃbandha*, the relation that conceives God as *śeṣin* – "owner of *śeṣa*" or "endowed with *śeṣa*" –, where *śeṣa*, the soul, is conceived as a "rest" or an "appendix" of God, totally devoid of any ontological autonomy, and completely dependent on him (*VaiṣMa.* 2.5–9, 11, 17–18). Very articulated is the classification of the *jīva*s on the basis of their condition of freedom or bondage, of their attitude toward God, of their way of aiming at → liberation (6.3–21). For example, the liberated souls are divided in two main categories: the souls who have conquered liberation from → *saṃsāra* and the souls who are permanently free (*nitya mukta jīva*); the latter include the *parijana*s, namely the divine "attendants" of Rāma and Sītā (as → Hanumān), and the *paricchada*s ("paraphernalia"), namely the weapons and the emblems of Rāma's iconography, that in Vaiṣṇava theology are personified and worshipped.

The core subject of *Vaiṣṇavamatābjabhāskara* is *bhakti*, which is described as an uninterrupted service to God, with one-pointed disposition of mind (*ananyabhāvena*) and complete commitment (*VaiṣMa.* 4.12), and as a total and intense love (*anurakti*) for God based on a continuous remembrance of him (*nityasaṃsmṛti*) like an uninterrupted pouring of oil (*tailadhāra sama*; 4.13). *Bhakti* reaches its perfection in *prapatti*, the complete surrender to God that results from the acknowledgement of being unable to reach liberation without the help of his infinite mercy. *Prapatti* is the highest mean of liberation and is open to everybody, without distinction of times, places, birth and purity (4.50); it is so powerful that for the *prapanna* ("surrendered") it is enough to remember one's own taking refuge in God in order to be free from all kind of impurities (4.55). Liberation (*mokṣa*) is considered to be a free gift of the Lord's mercy for the devotee's total surrender (4.42–43).

An elaborate exegesis is devoted to three Rāma → *mantra*s, called altogether *rahasyatraya* ("three secrets"), and especially to the *ṣaḍakṣaramantra*, the "six-syllable *mantra* " (i.e. *rāṃ rāmāya namaḥ*), which is still the main Rāmānandī *mantra* (*VaiṣMa.* 2.1–44). This *mantra* is also the fourth among the five marks and practices, called *pañcasaṃskāras*, that act as initiation, consecration, marks and practices of the Vaiṣṇavas. The other four *saṃskāras* are branding the body with the symbols of Viṣṇu-Rāma (conch, discus, mace, bow and arrows); putting the *ūrdhvapuṇḍratilaka* (see → *tilaka*) on forehead; taking a Vaiṣṇava name and wearing a → *mālā* of *tulasī* (holy basil; 4.2).

Other topics of the *Vaiṣṇavamatābjabhāskara* are the figure and the role of the → *guru* (*VaiṣMa.* 4.4–8); the power of *satsaṅga* (7.4–7; 9.3–5); → *ahiṃsā* – considered as the highest → *dharma* (5.2–10); the ritual of worship (5.11–18); vows and religious festivals (4.15–41); holy places (8.4–8; 10); and eschatological themes (9.5–10).

The *Rāmārcanapaddhati*, as the title reveals, deals mainly with matters of ritual and therefore has no doctrinal relevance. Its importance lies mainly in the fact that it contains a much longer *paramparā* of Rāmānanda than the one in the *Bhaktamāl*, but its manuscript tradition seems to be quite uncertain (Shrivastav, 1957, 106–108).

A commentary to the *Brahmasūtra*, the *Ānandabhāṣya*, is also attributed to Rāmānanda, but this text has proved to be a forgery – probably written by the Rāmānandī Raghuvaracharya, who "edited" the text in 1929 – intended to prove the independence of the Rāmānanda Sampradāya from the Śrīvaiṣṇava Sampradāya, since all the Vedānta *ācāryas* (→ *gurus* and *ācāryas*) who started a new *sampradāya* wrote a commentary on the *Brahmasūtra* as its doctrinal foundation. Its aim may also have been to raise the theological authority of Rāmānanda up to the level of Rāmānuja's "in order to subvert the Brahmanical hegemony of the Ramanujis" (Agrawal, 2009b, 166) and to legitimize their own liberal conduct in matters of → caste and → purity. The authenticity of the *Ānandabhāṣya* was initially supported by Bhagavadacharya, Raghuvaracharya's disciple and leader of the "independentist" movement, but he was later forced to recognize the *Ānandabhāṣya* as a forgery. Nonetheless, the work is still very highly considered by most Rāmānandīs (or at least by those who joined Bhagavadacharya's movement and their successors) to the point that nowadays Rāmānanda is often portrayed with the *Ānandabhāṣya* in front of him.

Some 20 Hindi poems are attributed to Rāmānanda. Ten of them were collected together by P. Barathwal in *Rāmānanda kī hindī racnāeṃ* (1955; trans. into Italian with commentary by Caracchi, 1999, 207–349), and another four were edited by H. Dvivedi in the appendixes of the same book, which he edited after P. Barathwal's death (Barathwal, 1955, 27–31, 53–55). Other poems have been published in various places, either separately or in anthologies of Sants. The Hindi poems are quite different in language, style, and content. On the basis of their content, they may be classified as dealing with

1. Haṭha Yoga (in *Rāma rakṣā*, *Yoga cintāmaṇī*, *Gyāna tilaka*);
2. moral and spiritual teachings (in *Pad 1*, *Pad 3*, *Gyāna līlā*);
3. *nirguṇ bhakti* (in *Pad 4*, *Pad 5*, *Mānasī sevā*, *Bhagati jauga grantha*); and
4. *saguṇ bhakti* (in *Āratī*, *Rāma aṣṭaka*).

It is quite difficult to attribute to the same author *nirguṇ* and *saguṇ* songs, which are in some cases mutually contradictory, apart from being heterogeneous linguistically. Such is the case of the two most famous songs, *Kahāṃ jāise* and *Āratī* (Barathwal, 1955, *Pad 5, 2*). *Kahāṃ jāise* is included in the *Sarvāṅgī* by Rajab, in the *Sarvāṅgī* by Gopāldās (14.12; Callewaert, 1993, 166), and, most importantly, in the *Gurū Granth Sāhib* (*Rāgu Basantu*; Callewaert, 1996, 1195). For this reason, it was the first song to be known by Western scholars and, in most cases, the only one. Here follows a translation of *Kahāṃ jāise* from P. Barathwal's edition (which is a little different from the version in the *Gurū Granth Sāhib*):

> Where shall I go? Happiness is at home.
> My heart does not roam, my mind has become cripple.
> Wherever I go, there is only water and stone,
> But Hari entirely pervades everything.
> I looked through all the Vedas and Smṛti
> And I would turn to them if Hari were not here.
> Once fervor arose in my mind,
> I ground sandal paste and smeared my limbs.
> I went from place to place for *pūjā*.
> But my *guru* told me:
> "*Brahman* is in yourself".
> O *satguru*! I am a sacrificial offering to Thee.
> You burnt all my anxieties and my errors.
> Rāmānanda rejoices in the one *brahman*.
> One word of the *guru* cuts away millions of *karmas*. (Barathwal 1955, 8; trans. by author)

Fig. 3: The text of the *Āratī* painted on the Hanumān Temple at Nimsar (photo by Pinuccia Caracchi).

The other famous song by Rāmānanda, *Āratī*, is traditionally considered the most ancient Hindi composition in praise of → Hanumān (Ray, 1988, 146). It is still very popular in the Hindi belt (although sometimes attributed to Tulsīdās); it has been included in several anthologies of *bhajans* (see → *kīrtan* and *bhajan*) and recorded by many famous singers. *Āratī* is meant to be sung during *āratī* ritual, as may be inferred from its title and the refrain:

> Let's perform *āratī* to dear Hanumān destroyer of the wicked and manifestation of Raghunāth. (Barathwal 1955, 7; trans. by author)

Among Hindi works, there is also *Siddhānta Paṭal*, a curious poem containing 65 very irregular stanzas (from 2 to 52 lines), whose main topics are *mantras* and their exegesis, Haṭha Yoga practice, mystical experiences, and other subjects related to the life of → *sādhus*. Most probably this poem is to be attributed to the *tapasī śākhā* (the "ascetic branch") of the Rāmānandīs, as may also be the case of some other poems dealing with Haṭha Yoga.

Notwithstanding their doubtful attribution, both Sanskrit and Hindi works attributed to Rāmānanda deserve consideration insofar as they belong to traditions relating to Rāmānanda: the Rāmānanda Sampradāya and the *nirguṇ* Sants. Even if Rāmānanda was not the author of *Vaiṣṇavamatābjabhāskara* and *Rāmārcana-paddhati*, these works are expressions of the doctrines and rituals followed by the Rāmānanda Sampradāya since very ancient times (at least as far as *Vaiṣṇavamatābjabhāskara* is concerned). As for the Hindi songs, they could have been composed by some disciples of Rāmānanda who concealed their identity under the *guru*'s name, either in order to imbue them with Rāmānanda's authority, or out of humility and as a *guptadāna* ("secret donation"; see Aklujkar 2001, 101) to their *guru*. This is a very common practice in *bhakti* popular literature, where even the *chāp* ("seal"; see Hawley 1988, 285) in the end of a poem is not definite proof of authorship. Noteworthy facts are that *Pad 4* of Barthwal's edition appears also in → Nāmdev's *Padāvalī* (Callewaert & Lath, *Pad 45*, 1989, 277), the second part of *Gyāna tilaka* is almost identical to some *sākhīs* (couplets) of Kabīr, and many passages of the songs attributed to Rāmānanda appear also in several Sants' songs.

What is certain is that Rāmānanda's greatness does not depend on his works but on his immense legacy.

Studies, Interpretations, and Constructions

Owing to the great role played by Rāmānanda in Indian religious history and to the paucity of reliable information about his life and works, his figure has long been questioned by scholars. The only biographical data that by now seem to be certain may be listed as follows:

- he belonged to Rāmānuja *paramparā*;
- he lived in the 15th century;

- he preached Rāma *bhakti* to men and women of all castes; and
- he was the *guru* of Kabīr and other Sants.

The very first questions that have been debated among scholars since the beginning of the 20th century are those regarding dates for Rāmānanda and his place of origin (Caracchi, 1999, 54–61). The dates officially approved by the Rāmānanda Sampradāya are 1299 for his birth and 1410 for his passing, while Prayag is officially designated as his birth place. This designation seems to contradict the above-quoted popular saying that Rāmānanda brought *bhakti* from the south (*bhakti drāviḍa ūpajī lāye rāmānanda*). The southern origins of Rāmānanda have indeed been claimed by some scholars (e.g. Farquahar, 1920); M.A. Macauliffe even mentioned the southern locality of Mailkot, in Karnataka, for his birthplace (Macauliffe, 1909, 100), although he later abandoned this opinion. But, in actual fact, the popular saying does not necessarily state a southern origin for Rāmānanda; it can only be inferred. Moreover, according to several sources, it was his *guru* Rāghavānanda who came from the south, as Nābhādās' *Bhaktamāl* (35) also seems to suggest. Of course, this does not exclude the possibility that Rāmānanda came from the south with him, but at the same time, it cannot be considered proof of Rāmānanda's southern origin as opposed to the official Rāmānandī belief.

The official date of birth seems to rely mainly on *Rāmānandajanmotsava*, a Sanskrit hagiographical text in five *adhyāya*s (chapters; translated into Italian by Caracchi, 1989), which claims to be part of the *Agastyasaṃhitā* but was most probably composed in the late 19th century by the Rāmānandī scholar Ramnarayandas, who also edited the printed edition in 1906 (Agrawal, 2009b, 141–148). The *Rāmānandajonmotsava* is most probably the result of a "Sanskritization" process, started in the Rāmānanda Sampradāya long before, with the reorganization of the Hindu *sampradāya*s during the reign of Savāī Jaysiṃh of Amber (1699–1743; Caracchi, 1999, 180–189; van der Veer, 1988, 98–100). This process, of course, involved the figure of Rāmānanda, so it is very difficult to ascertain to what extent the hagiographical works written from the 18th century onward are the expression of an ancient Rāmānandī tradition, and to what extent they pursue the aim of redefining the figure of Rāmānanda. This applies also to Rūpkalā's commentary on *Bhaktamāl*, which seems to be the main authority supporting 1410 as the date of Rāmānanda's disappearance. Rūpkalā accepts 1299 as the date of Rāmānanda's birth and, giving voice to an ancient tradition supported by Nābhādās' words (*bahuta kāla bapudhāri*; *BhM.* 36), assigns him a lifespan of 111 years, indeed not impossible for a *yogī*. But the main problem with Rāmānanda's official dates lies in the fact that they are not consistent with the dates of Kabīr and other Sants who are reputed to be his disciples. The dating of Rāmānanda by different scholars spans more than two centuries from the early 14th century to the first quarter of the 16th century (Caracchi, 1999, 57–58). Of course, if we accept Kabīr to be a disciple of Rāmānanda (this being another subject of long-lasting debate among scholars), then the dates of Rāmānanda should be strictly linked to Kabīr's *floruit*. Therefore, his life should be placed in the 15th century, since the traditional date for Kabīr's death is 1518, a date considered highly probable on the basis of substantial historical evidence (Lorenzen, 1991, 9–18; 2006, 106–107). One important argument for dating Rāmānanda is also the fact that Nābhādās was fourth in the spiritual lineage of Rāmānanda, after Anantānanda, Kṛṣṇadās Payahāri, and Agradās, his direct *guru*. Since we know that Nābhādās wrote his *Bhaktamāl* around the end of the 16th century, we can reasonably place Rāmānanda in the 15th century.

Another much-debated issue regards Rāmānanda *paramparā* and is closely connected with the story of the Rāmānanda Sampradāya in the 20th century. All the most ancient sources bear witness to the fact that Rāmānanda belonged to a spiritual lineage descending from Rāmānuja. The most important source is Nābhādās' *Bhaktamāl*, where three *ācārya*s are mentioned between Rāmānuja and Rāmānanda. Of course, even if we accept the unlikely date of 1299 for Rāmānanda's birth, the number of three *ācārya*s appears to be inadequate, since the traditional date for Rāmānuja's death is 1137. But the *paramparā* given by Nābhādās is probably deliberately incomplete, due to the extreme concision of the *Bhaktamāl* style, which very often omits even important details. Much longer, though of different lengths, are the *paramparā*s given in three different editions of the *Rāmārcanapaddhati* (1914; 1927; 1931). These *paramparā*s are different as far as the number of *ācārya*s between Rāmānanda and Rāmānuja is concerned (19,

13, and 12, respectively), but they largely agree in their names (Caracchi, 1999, 70–72). Even if the authorship of the *Rāmārcanapaddhati* is far from certain, it proves that the *paramparā* transmitted in the Rāmānanda Sampradāya descends from Rāmānuja. This fact was never questioned by the Rāmānandīs until the early 20th century, when, in Ayodhya, a group of *sādhus* led by Bhagavadacharya started the already-mentioned movement for separating Rāmānandīs from Śrīvaiṣṇavas (Agrawal, 2009a, 279–282; Caracchi, 1999, 65–70; Pinch, 1996, 61–70; van der Veer, 1988, 101–107). To this purpose, it was necessary to create a new *paramparā* for Rāmānanda where Rāmānuja would not be present: a very difficult task indeed, and one that Bhagavadacharya and his fellows managed by forging fake texts (like the above-mentioned *Ānandabhāṣya*), by changing the word *rāmānuja* into *rāmānuka* wherever it appeared with reference to Rāmānanda's *paramparā*, and even by denying the authenticity of the *Rāmārcanapaddhati*.

But the most burning issue about Rāmānanda's life is that of his association with the Sants who are reputed to be his disciples: Kabīr, Raidās, Sen Nāī, Dhanna, and Pīpā. The approach to this issue adopted by scholars has been strictly related to their interpretations of Rāmānanda's teaching and personality. The problem is particularly urgent for Kabīr, since he was the greatest of his disciples. Although the *guruśiṣya* (*guru*-disciple) relation that linked Rāmānanda to Kabīr is a fact in both the → Kabīrpanthī and Rāmānandī traditions (Lorenzen, 2006, 104–107), several scholars have questioned it for two main reasons. The first is the official dating of Rāmānanda's life: if he disappeared in 1410, then he could hardly be the *guru* of Kabīr (whose traditional dates are 1398–1518) – they could only have met when Kabīr was very young. But, as we have seen, the official date of Rāmānanda's birth is mainly based on the five *adhyāya*s ascribed to the *Agastyasaṃhitā*, which is an "invented" text. The second and main reason is the apparent incompatibility of Rāmānanda as a Vaiṣṇava *ācārya*, a follower of the Viśiṣṭādvaita Vedānta, with Rāmānanda as the *guru* of Kabīr, a low-caste Sant of Muslim origin and *nirguṇ* poet – an incompatibility considered so significant as to give rise to the hypothesis of the existence of two different Rāmānandas (Śukla, 1972, 86; Vaudeville, 1997, 89). The main solutions proposed for this problem may be thus summarized:

(1) Kabīr and the other Sants later came to be considered disciples of Rāmānanda, by their own disciples, with the aim of "Hinduizing" or "Brahmanizing" them (Vaudeville, 1997, 87–92; Schomer, 1987, 5);

(2) the Rāmānandīs claimed that Kabīr and the other Sants were Rāmānanda's disciples in order to increase his prestige (Callewaert & Friedlander, 1992, 25);

(3) Rāmānanda was himself a Sant, his figure as a Vaiṣṇava *ācārya* having been invented by the Rāmānandīs, who, gradually, managed to establish themselves as an order and enter the mainstream of orthodox Hinduism (van der Veer, 1988; Burghart, 1978; both discussed by Caracchi, 1999, 188–189, 195–203).

Akin to the last theory is that formulated by P. Agrawal (Agrawal, 2009a; 2009b). In his opinion, although Rāmānanda belonged to Rāmānuja's lineage, he never had acquired the status of *ācārya*, since he was an "independent thinker" who preached an alternative and progressive form of Vaiṣṇavism, "radical and socially inclusive," or of a noncaste Hinduism, teachings that would have constituted a kind of indigenous early Indian modernity. P. Agrawal calls him "Hindi Rāmānanda," as he emerges from medieval Hindi sources, while he calls "Sanskrit Rāmānanda" the figure constructed by the Rāmānandīs through a process of Sankritization, carried out especially by the "independentist" Rāmānandīs, aiming at separating the Rāmānanda *paramparā* from that of Rāmānuja. The replacing of the historical Hindi Rāmānanda with the Sanskrit Rāmānanda is responsible for the denial of the evidence of the *guruśiṣya* relation between Rāmānanda and Kabīr (and the other Sants as well).

A point of view reconciling Rāmānanda as *ācārya* and Rāmānanda as Sant's *guru* is held by H. Dvivedi. He considers Rāmānanda a "liberal" *ācārya* who gave Kabīr the gifts of *bhakti* and the name of Rāma. As a true *mahāguru* (great *guru*), he was able to give every disciple a different *sādhana*, so as to respect their personalities and their natures (Dvivedi, [3]1978, 109–110, 120–121). He was "a teacher like the vast sky under which every tree is free to grow as much as it can" (Dvivedi, [2]1978, 492). It is noteworthy that H. Dvivedi's interpretation is consistent with the story of Kabīr's *dīkṣā* as related by Anantdās and other ancient sources, in which Kabīr's social status appears to be very distant from that of Rāmānanda, a distance bridged by the power of *bhakti*. In fact, while the Śrīvaiṣṇava order, to whom Rāmānanda belonged, was very strict in matters of caste and purity, *bhakti* in itself is not. By its very nature, *bhakti* is open to people of all social conditions, as it clearly results from → *Bhagavadgītā* and many puranic tales. But this openness of *bhakti* remained mostly theoretical and abstract – in North India at least – until Rāmānanda's time. The time was ripe for *bhakti* to take the shape of wide popular movements, as had already happened in the south. The greatness of Rāmānanda was his ability to answer the needs of his own time by giving *bhakti* the opportunity to take an actual popular form, both by inspiring the *nirguṇ* Sants and by reforming a Vaiṣṇava tradition.

The *Rāmcaritmānas* by Tulsīdās, the "Bible" of the Hindi world, may to some extent be considered another extraordinary fruit of Rāmānanda's preaching, insofar as by spreading the Rāma *bhakti* he paved the way for Tulsīdās.

Bibliography

Abbot, J.E., & N.R. Godbole, *Stories of Indian Saints*, vols. I–II, Poona, 1933, repr. Delhi, 1982.

Agrawal (Agravāl), P., *Akath kahānī prem kī: Kabīr kī kavitā aur unkā samay*, Delhi, 2009a (Hind.).

Agrawal, P., "In Search of Ramanand: The Guru of Kabir and Others," in: I. Banerjee-Dube & S. Dube, eds., *Ancient to Modern: Religion, Power, and Community in India*, Delhi, 2009b, 135–170.

Aklujkar, V., "Crying Dogs and Laughing Trees in Rāma's Kingdom: Self-reflexivity in *Ānanda Rāmāyaṇa*," in: P. Richman, ed., *Questioning Rāmāyaṇas*, Berkeley 2001, 83–103.

Bakker, H., *Ayodhyā*, Groningen, 1986.

Barathwal (Baṛathvāl), P., *Rāmānanda kī hindī racnāeṃ*, ed. H.P. Dvivedi, Varanasi, 1955 (Hind.).

Burghart, R., "The Founding of the Rāmānandi Sect," *EH* 25/2, 1978, 121–139.

Callewaert, W.M., ed., *Śrī Guru Granth Sāhib with Complete Index*, Delhi, 1996.

Callewaert, W.M., ed., *The Sarvāṅgī of Gopāldās*, Delhi, 1993.

Callewaert, W.M., & P.G. Friedlander, *The Life and Works of Raidās*, Delhi, 1992.

Callewaert, W.M., & Lath M., eds., *The Hindi Padāvalī of Nāmdev*, Delhi, 1989.

Caracchi, P., *Rāmānanda e lo Yoga dei Sant: Con una traduzione dei canti hindī in collaborazione con Shukdev Singh*, Alessandria, 1999 (It.).

Caracchi, P., *Vita di Rāmānanda: Il Rāmānandajanmotsava dell'Agastya-saṃhitā*, Torino, 1989 (It.).

Dvivedi (Dvivedī), H., *Kabīr*, Dillī, [3]1976 (Hind.).

Dvivedi, H.P., "Hindi," in: S.K. Chatterji, ed., *The Cultural Heritage of India*, vol. V: *Languages and Literatures*, Calcutta, [2]1978, 489–507.

Farquhar, J.N., "The Historical Position of Ramananda," *JRAS* 1920/2, 185–192; 1922/4, 373–380.

Grierson, G.A., "The Home of Rāmānanda," *JRAS* 1920/4, 591–596.

Grierson, G.A., "Ramanandis, Ramawats," in: J. Hastings, ed., *Encyclopaedia of Religions and Ethics*, vol. X, Edinburgh, 1918, 569–571.

Hawley, J.S., "Author and Authority in the *Bhakti* poetry of North India," *JAS* 47/2, 1988, 269–290.

Lorenzen, D.N., "The Life of Kabir in Legend," in: *idem*, ed., *Who Invented Hinduism?*, Delhi, 2006, 102–119.

Lorenzen, D.N., *Kabir Legends and Ananta-das's Kabir Parachai*, Albany, 1991.

Macauliffe, M.A., *The Sikh Religion*, vol. VI, Oxford, 1909.

Pinch, W.R., *Peasants and Monks in British India*, Berkeley, 1996.

Ray, D., *Hindī Hanumatkāvya kā udbhav aur vikās*, Allahabad, 1988 (Hind.).

Schomer, K., "The Sant Tradition in Perspective," in: K. Schomer & W.H. McLeod, eds., *The Sants*, Delhi, 1987, 1–17.

Shrivastav (Śrīvāstav), B., *Rāmānanda-sampradāya tathā hindī sāhitya par uskā prabhāv*, Allahabad, 1957 (Hind.).

Shukla (Śukla), R., *Hindī sāhitya kā itihās*, Varanasi, [17]1972 (Hind.).

Simh (Siṃh), I., *Bhuṛkuṛā kī sant-paramparā*, Varanasi, 1988 (Hind.).

Vaudeville, C., *A Weaver Named Kabir*, Delhi, 1997.

Veer, P. van der, *Gods on Earth*, London, 1988.

Pinuccia Caracchi

Rāmānuja

Rāmānuja or Rāmānujācārya is one of the most important thinkers of traditional → Vedānta – the perspective of theology based mainly on an exegesis of the early → Upaniṣads, the *Brahmasūtra* (see → Sūtras), and the → *Bhagavadgītā* (Lipner, 2012). Within this tradition, he is generally regarded as the first to have articulated a systematic defense for devotion to a personal, provident, and loving god of Vaiṣṇava provenance. His traditional dates are given as 1017–1137 CE. This can hardly be historically accurate; perhaps these dates signify conformity with similarly very long lifespans attributed to his two *ācārya* predecessors, Nāthamuni (823–923 CE) and Yāmuna (→ Yāmunācārya; 916–1036 CE), and also serve to fill an otherwise unexplained gap or two in the chronology of the lineage (*paramparā*) of teaching preceptors assigned to his particular religious tradition (*sampradāya*), known as → Śrīvaiṣṇavism. However, the possibility that he also lived a long life cannot be discounted.

Rāmānuja is credited with setting on a sound theological footing the vedantic standpoint that came to be called Viśiṣṭādvaita: "the nonduality (*advaita*) of separated beings (*viśiṣṭa*)" (preferable, as I shall argue later, to the "qualified nondualism" that is often used to translate this Sanskrit compound), though it must be noted that Rāmānuja himself has not described his position thus in any of his accredited works. Since Rāmānuja was essentially a theologian rather than what is called a "philosopher" nowadays, in this essay I shall focus on Rāmānuja the theologian. The philosophical elements of his thought will be considered insofar as they clarify his theological vision (in this sense he may also be called a "philosophical theologian").

Rāmānuja was born in the Tamil country under Chola rule not far from the capital city known today as Chennai. Though not without political tensions with neighboring regions, this rule was on the whole fairly prosperous and stable and encouraged the growth of religious institutions of different kinds. Rāmānuja was thus able to embark on a somewhat checkered career of religious commitment in a relatively stable environment, which he completed as leader of the Śrīvaiṣṇava community in the south of India (a community he helped strengthen numerically by various travels), especially through his role as teacher in and general manager of the great Vaiṣṇava temple of Srirangam (near the present urban center of Tiruchirappalli), which houses the image deities of → Viṣṇu and his consort, Śrī (→ Śrī Lakṣmī).

A number of stories exist in the hagiographies about Rāmānuja's independence of mind and liberal approach with regard to sectarian and caste differences of his time. Since their cumulative effect is persuasive, this tradition may well have some basis in fact. To give but one example: during Rāmānuja's period of instruction by Tirukōṭṭiyūrnampi, a disciple of his *ācārya* predecessor Yāmuna, he was given the secret meaning of the *mantra* "*oṃ namo nārāyaṇāya*" by Tirukōṭṭiyūrnampi on pain of incurring hell if he revealed the teaching to others. The still relatively young Rāmānuja promptly climbed to the second floor of a nearby temple and shouted out the secret teaching to his coreligionists gathered in the temple precincts. When summoned by his teacher to explain his action, Rāmānuja is reported to have said that though he was aware of the penalty of hell for transgressing his teacher's warning, nevertheless by doing so he alone would suffer in hell, whereas all those who heard his teacher's words would be saved. Greatly impressed, Tirukōṭṭiyūrnampi embraced his magnanimous disciple (the story of Rāmānuja's life is well summarized in Carman, 1974, 26–44; Ramakrishnananda, 1959, gives the tradition at greater length).

Theologically, a number of viewpoints influenced the mature expression of Rāmānuja's thought, both negatively and positively. Rāmānuja was raised in a Brahman household that was committed to studying and teaching the → Vedas and which probably also had Vaiṣṇava theistic leanings. This means that he would have been trained in the knowledge of Sanskrit and its vedic liturgical practices, no doubt in a daily context of Vaiṣṇava worship at home. To augment his education, he was sent as a youth to study under the well-known Bhedābheda teacher Yādavaprakāśa, who is thought to have had an advaitic turn of mind (see Advaita → Vedānta). Rāmānuja was bold enough to challenge some of Yādavaprakāśa's advaitic interpretations of the Upaniṣads (those Vaiṣṇava theistic leanings must have come into effect), thereby incurring Yādavaprakāśa's (and some of his other disciples') antagonism in the process. After an adventure or two – Rāmānuja is reported to have foiled, with Viṣṇu's and Śrī's help, an attempt on his life by Yādavaprakāśa and his disciples – Rāmānuja broke with Yādavaprakāśa and through various circumstances eventually came under the influence of Yādavaprakāśa's disciples and their Śrīvaiṣṇava teachings.

Before we come to this, let us not forget that under Yādavaprakāśa, Rāmānuja would have learned about Bhedābheda and Advaita, the basis of the latter having been first formulated by the great theologian → Śaṅkara about three centuries earlier, and which was perhaps the dominant form of Vedānta in Rāmānuja's day (not least in its adversarial role toward various schools of Indian Mahāyāna Buddhism to which Rāmānuja would also have been introduced; for an account of the Advaita that Rāmānuja would have encountered, see Bartley, 2002, ch. 1). In the process, he would also have become acquainted with other knowledge systems (including some that were more philosophical in tenor), such as → Sāṃkhya, → Yoga, and → Pāśupata (not to mention Pūrvamīmāṃsā [→ Mīmāṃsā], → Nyāya, and → Vaiśeṣika). This thorough introduction (for the student lived constantly in his teacher's company) to these latter knowledge systems would bear fruit in due course, and not always in a negative light. Thus Rāmānuja could say, indicatively, in his *magnum opus*, the *Śrībhāṣya* – composed in Sanskrit and providing a reasoned commentary on the *Brahmasūtra* (attributed to the savant Bādarāyaṇa),

> Only the view that *brahman* is not the inner self (*ātman*) of Sāṃkhya's stated principles of being is repudiated in the *Brahmasūtra*, not the essence (*svarūpa*, of Sāṃkhya thought). And– with regard to Yoga and Pāśupata teachings – what is repudiated is that the Lord is only the efficient cause (of the world), the false notions they have about mutually related principles of being, and those practices that fall outside the vedic pale, not the essence (of these teachings). So it is said: "The Sāṃkhya, Yoga, Pāñcarātra thought, the Vedas and the Pāśupāta teaching too, are all sources of knowledge (*pramāṇa*) of the self (*ātman*); they must not be dismissed by polemical reasoning." (*ŚrīBh.* 2.2.48)

We have here a display of Rāmānuja's open-mindedness toward what was perceived as the Veda-orientated intellectual tradition of his day, as also the appreciation that this tradition had many valuable insights to offer. But we may also detect here an indication that Rāmānuja intended his project to have a universal relevance with regard to this tradition and various opposing views.

We can turn now to what must have been more direct, positive influences on Rāmānuja's thought. This would have included the acquisition, by Rāmānuja, of an increasingly sound grasp of Sanskrit grammatical and literary tradition, as also a knowledge of the Vedas, with special emphasis on the early Upaniṣads. These were prime sources of vedantic understanding. In this context, Rāmānuja's growing acquaintance with the teachings of Pūrvamīmāṃsā would have helped him shape, to his theological advantage, a suitable hermeneutic with which to interpret the Vedas, especially the Upaniṣads. We have evidence of such awareness in his repeated references, directly and indirectly, to Pūrvamīmāṃsakas, especially Prābhākara's, views as an opposing position (*pūrvapakṣa*) in his works (see Lipner, 1986, chs. 1–2).

But we cannot discount as key for the contextualization and flowering of his theological project, the influences of the numerous devotional and Viṣṇu-orientated songs of the → Āḻvārs that were current among the Tamil people from about the 6th century CE, as also the teaching of the → Pāñcarātra tradition. Though, to the best of my knowledge, Rāmānuja never quotes directly from the songs of the Āḻvārs in his accredited works, the ardent Vaiṣṇava devotionalism of these poet-saints clearly shaped his own theological vision deeply, as also the obvious warmth of his devotion to a personal supreme being, whom, in abstract terms, he referred to as → *brahman* and, in more personal terms, as Viṣṇu-Nārāyaṇa. In his capacity as leader of the Śrīvaiṣṇava community, Rāmānuja is said to have lectured on these hymns in Tamil. As for the Pāñcarātra tradition, this too seems to have influenced Rāmānuja's thought, not least with respect to his insistence on the Lord's supremacy over his creation, for it was with an eye to the *ṣaḍguṇa*s or "six (distinctive) qualities" of the personal Lord of Pāñcarātra that Rāmānuja expatiated on this point (see below).

Last but not least, as a shaping influence in Rāmānuja's thinking, we must include the theology especially of his *ācārya* predecessor Yāmuna and its subsequent formulation by several of Yāmuna's leading disciples during their instruction to him while he was preparing to assume the reins of the Śrīvaiṣṇava leadership. On Yāmuna's seminal influence, J.B. Carman notes that "[t]he main outline and many of the details of later Śrī Vaiṣṇava thought emerge clearly in [Yāmuna's] works" (1974, 26). This would include the seed that developed into Rāmānuja's more full-fledged critique of Bhedābheda, a school of Vedānta, which argued that produced being exists simultaneously in a relationship of "difference" (*bheda*) and "nondifference" (*abheda*) with the essence of the supreme being. The exact nature of this relationship, in terms of the categories of "difference," "nondifference," and "essence" (*svabhāva, svarūpa*), gave rise to debate and division within the parameters of Bhedābheda tradition. Nevertheless, as I hope to make clear later, Rāmānuja was at pains to distinguish his own view from that of Bhedābheda (of which Yādavaprakāśa was an exponent), for in terms of the name of this school, namely Bhedābheda, his own position might be perceived to run the risk of falling under its purview. We shall show how Rāmānuja attempted to demonstrate that his own stance was different, how, in contrast to Bhedābheda, what was later called "Viśiṣṭādvaita" propounded in its own way the "nonduality" (or nondifference) of "separated" (or "differentiated") beings (*viśiṣṭa*). In what sense, then, are differentiated beings also "nondual" for our theologian? We shall see how Rāmānuja sought to answer this question.

The traditional authorities agree that Rāmānuja produced only nine works, all of them in Sanskrit, though some modern commentators question his authorship of several of these. These nine texts comprise: (1) a fairly short though theologically comprehensive treatise, entitled the *Vedārthasaṃgraha* (Compendium of the Meaning of the Veda: not disputed); (2–4) three commentarial works on Bādarāyaṇa's *Brahmasūtra* – in ascending order of length these are the *Vedāntasāra* (The Gist of the Vedānta), the *Vedāntadīpa* (The Lamp of/for the Vedānta), and the *Śrībhāṣya* (The Revered Commentary, this being Rāmānuja's most mature and comprehensive legacy on the subject: not disputed); (5) the *Gītābhāṣya*, a commentary on the *Bhagavadgītā* (not disputed); (6–8) three relatively short hymns in prose, the *Gadyatraya*; and finally (9) the *Nityagrantha* (A Treatise on Daily Worship) – the last two divisions comprise texts that are concerned with the worship of the divine being rather than doctrinal elaboration. It is noteworthy then that only three Sanskrit texts – the *Vedārthasaṃgraha, Gītābhāṣya*, and *Śrībhāṣya* – are generally not disputed as genuine works of Rāmānuja (I shall take recourse to these, therefore, as the primary sources for this essay on Rāmānuja), and that, unlike Śaṅkara and the founders of other vedantic schools, Rāmānuja wrote no commentaries on individual Upaniṣads. It has been argued – with some justification – that this was because he regarded the early Upaniṣads as representing a single corpus of material awaiting exegetical interpretation as a whole rather than as meriting individual commentarial attention (for a study of Rāmānuja's treatment of the Upaniṣads, see Raghavachar, 1972).

The heart of Rāmānuja's thought is his teaching that all finite conscious and nonconscious entities (*cidacidvastu*), considered individually or collectively, are the "→ body" (*śarīra*) of *brahman* or the godhead, insofar as they exist – again individually or collectively – in a threefold relationship with *brahman*. From this a number of ontological, epistemological, soteriological, and indeed other implications may be drawn. I shall return to the most important of these below. But the basic idea of *brahman*'s "embodiment" in this way was not plucked out of thin air. I have indicated that Yāmuna had alluded to it earlier, though he did so in a theologically undeveloped and somewhat ambiguous manner. But it was derived originally from Śruti, that is, the canonical scripture that was the Veda, especially from the Upaniṣads (also called the Vedānta). Insofar as Rāmānuja was a vedantic theologian, it was incumbent upon him to take exegetical recourse to the Śruti. A key proof text in this respect referred to by Rāmānuja is chapter seven of the third section of the *Bṛhadāraṇyakopaniṣad* (Rāmānuja quotes from both the *Kāṇva* and *Mādhyandina* recensions), in which the sage Yājñavalkya teaches his rival Gautama that various features of the cosmos are the "body" of the supreme reality, who is their inner controller (*antaryāmin*). Yājñavalkya declares,

> He who dwells in the earth/sun/light/breath/understanding etc., whose body (*śarīra*) the earth/sun/light/breath/understanding etc. is, and who (dwelling) within, controls the earth/sun/light/breath/understanding etc., is your self, your inner controller, the immortal one. (*BĀU*. 3.7.3–23)

Such recourse to Śruti validated Rāmānuja's (vedantic) theological project, and it remained for him as a theologian to show how, using argument (*tarka*) based on perception, inference, and (especially scriptural) testimony as the three sources of knowledge (*pramāṇas*) as an interpretive aid, this project gave coherence to scripture as a whole; as a byproduct this would also demonstrate how opposing views, whether within the vedantic enterprise or not, were wanting or misguided.

I return now to the "body/embodied-self" relationship mentioned earlier – which can be expressed by the Sanskrit compound *śarīraśarīribhāva* – that lies at the heart of Rāmānuja's thought. Once this is explained, we shall be able to see more clearly in what sense Rāmānuja affirms that separate beings can also be nondual.

Let us begin by inquiring into what Rāmānuja understands by the term "body" (*śarīra*) in the compound mentioned above. He gives this careful consideration, especially in the *Śrībhāṣya* (and importantly under 2.1.8–9). The *pūrvapakṣin* or opponent in *Śrībhāṣya* 2.1.8 challenges the use of the word "body" as being inappropriate in this context, for "body" across the range of vedic and everyday discourse, he says, running through a list of examples, refers to an imperfect or otherwise inadequate kind of reality (in so far as, e.g., it functions as subject to the senses, or is the result of → *karman*, which implies ignorance) and as such cannot be the "body" of the supreme being who is perfect. In his repudiation of the opponent's viewpoint (*ŚrīBh.* 2.1.9), Rāmānuja defends the scriptural use of the term in this context and, after answering various objections, arrives at a definition of "body" suitable for his purposes.

Before I inquire into this definition, let me make two comments:

(1) Rāmānuja seeks to work with the literal meaning of the term "body" (*śarīra*). This is because the scriptures do not say that conscious and nonconscious entities are like the body of *brahman*, but that they are so. If Rāmānuja was to be taken seriously as a scriptural exegete, it was incumbent upon him to conform to the hermeneutic rule, bequeathed to all exegetes of the Veda by the Pūrvamīmāṃsakas, that the scriptures are to be interpreted in the first instance at face value, that is, in their literal (*mukhya*) sense, rather than in a figurative (*gauṇa*) sense, since easy recourse to the latter would indicate that the scriptures were being exploited to suit the tendentious purposes of the exegete.

(2) Understanding the precise sense Rāmānuja gives to "body" in the compound will serve to illumine not only the underlying relationships implied by the compound as a whole, but also Rāmānuja's realist project, since the term functions as a heuristic pivot in this respect.

I will turn now to Rāmānuja's understanding of "body" in its literally derived sense. After seeing the opponent off to his satisfaction in his commentary on the *Brahmasūtra*, Rāmānuja arrives at the following definition:

> Any substance (*dravya*) which a conscious being (*cetana*) is entirely (*sarvātmanā*) capable of con-trolling and supporting (*niyantuṃ dhārayituṃ ca*) for its own ends, and whose nature is to be solely subordinate to that being (*taccheṣataikasvarūpa*), is the body (*śarīra*) of that being. (*ŚrīBh.* 2.1.9)

Note in passing that this definition allows even conscious being, for example, the spiritual self or → *ātman*, to exist as a "body" of some other being; thus "body" in this specified sense does not have to be a material entity. Note too that for Rāmānuja we have arrived at a literal definition of "body," one shorn of such contingent connotations as being material, having or being subject to sense organs, arising as the result of the ignorance that generates *karman* and rebirth, existing as the body of an → *avatāra*, and so on. A body in Rāmānuja's pruned (yet still literal) sense may have one or more of these attributes, but not necessarily so. What necessarily counts for being a "body" in this specific, yet still literal, sense are solely the conditions that apply in the definition. And these conditions implicate a threefold relationship. I must now consider these. In the process, it will be possible to encapsulate Rāmānuja's theological vision.

First, a "body" is a substance (*dravya*). This means that it has consolidated being – from the empirical point of view, a staying power of its own. In the case of the physical body, including that animated by the individual self (namely, the *jīvātman*), its substantival substrate is → *prakṛti*, the unconscious (*jaḍa*) stuff out of which the experienceable space–time continuum of the universe is produced. According to the conception Rāmānuja subscribed to, under the supreme person's impelling and provident action, *prakṛti* develops and is individuated, being sometimes animated by finite *ātmans*, into the physical bodies of our cosmos. Thus Rāmānuja can speak of conscious and nonconscious entities (*cidacid-vastu*), both individually and collectively. The visible physical body, then, both animate and inanimate, though it has an integrated and continuing unity of its own determinable by such actualities as qualities (*guṇas*) and actions (*karmans*), is substantival in a derivative sense, capable of dissolution eventually into its *prakṛti*-based building block(s).

Before we move on to consider the theological implications of the definition, let us note that in effect it applies on two levels: (1) microcosmically, that is, on the level of the embodied, individual self (*jīvātman*); and (2) macrocosmically, that is, on the level of *brahman qua* embodied by finite conscious and nonconscious entities, both individually and collectively.

(1) Microcosmically, Rāmānuja points out, our individual bodies conform to the requirements of the definition, not insofar as they are material, or operate within the ambit of the sense faculties and so on, but only insofar as they are "controlled" and "supported" by the conscious agent that is their *ātman* and function *qua* bodies for the *ātman*'s purposes.

(2) But since Rāmānuja's chief purpose in coining this definition is to show how *brahman* is "embodied" in this special sense, let us now move on to consider the definition's macrocosmic application. In so doing, I shall comment on how, in Rāmānuja's eyes, the microcosmic application is but a pale reflection of its theological counterpart.

I noted earlier that the definition implies the existence of three constituent relationships between the "body" and the embodied agent (*śarīrin*). Let us review each in turn, where the *śarīrin* is *brahman*.

The "Support" (*Ādhāra*)/ "Thing-supported" (*Ādheya*) Relationship

This relationship acts as the metaphysical foundation of the other two. In order to understand how, we must first advert to a general definition of the self-body relationship that Rāmānuja gives in the *Vedārthasaṃgraha*; it takes in both the microcosmic and macrocosmic applications and gives us a fundamental insight into the distinctive character of Rāmānuja's theology. Rāmānuja says,

> This is what the relationship between the self (*ātman*) and the body (*śarīra*) comprises, namely, the relationship between the support and the thing-supported where the latter is incapable of separate realization (*pṛthaksiddhyanarha*); the relationship between controller and thing-controlled; and the relationship between the principal and its accessory. The "self" (*ātmā*) here – for *ātmā* derives from *āpnoti*, "it possesses" – possesses wholly in so far as it is the support, controller and principal, while the "body" (*śarīra*) is said to function as a mode (*prakāra*) that cannot be realized apart, in so far as it is entirely supported, controlled and subordinate. (see Raghavachar, 1956, 76)

Note that the relationship between the "support" and "thing-supported" is qualified by the phrase "incapable of separate realization" (*pṛthaksiddhyanarha*); in other words, this is an asymmetrical relationship where the thing-supported cannot be "realized" apart from its support – and not vice versa. What does this mean? I have translated *siddhi* as "realization," because it can take two meanings here. Firstly, the thing-supported is dependent ontologically – as to both its origin and conservation in being – on the support; in this sense, it cannot be "real-ized," namely, made real, independently of the support; and secondly, the "thing-supported" cannot be understood for the thing it is independently of its support – thus, epistemologically too, its nature cannot be "realized" except with reference to its support. Rāmānuja explains this further, later in the definition, when he says that the "body" exists as a "mode" (*prakāra*) of its embodied self. Both ontologically and epistemologically, a mode is something that has no independent existence *qua* mode. Rāmānuja describes the relationship between mode (*prakāra*) and mode possessor (*prakārin*) in the *Vedārthasaṃgraha* as follows:

> In so far as class-characteristics (*jāti*) and so on are generic configurations (*saṃsthāna*) of things, they are the modes (*prakāra*) of those things; hence the mode and the mode-possessor (*prakārin*) belong to two different categories of being (*padārtha*); the mode is incapable of separate realization (*pṛthaksiddhyanarha*), and it cannot be understood separately. (see Raghavachar, 1956, 63)

In the theological context of the support/thing-supported relationship, what Rāmānuja is saying is this: just as the class characteristic (*jāti*) of being a cow, say, cannot exist apart from the cow itself and indeed cannot be understood for what it is except with reference to the cow – for they belong to two separate categories of being, the latter acting as the existential and epistemic support of the former – so in the case of *brahman* on the one hand, and conscious and nonconscious entities on the other, the latter, insofar as they are modes of *brahman*, are incapable of existing or of being understood for what they are, apart from *brahman*. Both ontologically and epistemologically then, *brahman* is their *raison d'être*.

As one would expect, this view has causal implications for Rāmānuja. Like other Vedāntins who were required to give a coherent interpretation of the Upaniṣads, Rāmānuja was required to show how *brahman* could be both the "material" as well as the "efficient" cause of all produced being. In his attempt to do so, he provides a deeper explanation of how *brahman* is the "support" of the world. To say that an agent functioned as a "material cause" (*upādānakāraṇa*) – that is, the "material" or substrate out of which the effect is produced – meant that one accepted the theory of *satkāryavāda*: the view that the effect (*kārya*) preexists (*sat*) in some way in the cause, and that the effect *qua* effect is educed from its cause. This implied, of course, that there was an underlying existential continuum, an extremely intimate ontic relationship, between the material cause and its effect.

Rāmānuja explains *brahman*'s material causality in the *Śrībhāṣya* as follows:

> In so far as conscious and non-conscious entities are at all times (*sarvadā*) the body of *brahman*, they are *brahman*'s mode (*prakāra*). Sometimes *brahman* has for its body conscious and non-conscious entities in such a subtle state that they are incapable of being designated as separate from it; *brahman* is then in the causal state with respect to them (*tatkāraṇāvasthaṃ brahma*). Sometimes, however, the body of conscious and non-conscious entities is in a developed (*sthūla*) state, separated out by name and form; *brahman* is then in the effected state with respect to them (*tacca kāryāvasthaṃ brahma*). (*ŚrīBh.* 2.3.18)

But does this not mean that *brahman* undergoes substantial change when it passes from the causal to the effected state? And does this not imply a kind of pantheism, compromising *brahman*'s transcendence with respect to produced being? Not quite, in Rāmānuja's reckoning, and for two reasons:

(1) "at all times" (*sarvadā*), we are told, the aggregate of conscious and non-conscious entities remains *brahman*'s mode (*prakāra*); as such (see above), they exist in a different way from *brahman*, namely, as a lesser and dependent category of being (*padārtha*), analogous to the way class characteristics, qualities, and so on exist relative to the substances in which they inhere. Hence, for Rāmānuja, when acting as material cause, *brahman* cannot be said to undergo a substantial transformation in the passage from the causal to the effected state; at most *brahman* undergoes a kind of accidental change. There is an attempt here to preserve *brahman*'s transcendent perfection. In fact, by this interpretation, Rāmānuja really seeks to comply with the directive that as exegete he must interpret relevant passages of the Śruti at face value (*mukhyena*) rather than figuratively (such passages as, e.g., *Chāndogyopaniṣad* 6.1.4–6, which seem to ascribe material causality to *brahman* as producer of finite being). But Rāmānuja does not stop here.

(2) By insisting, in the light of other passages of scripture (to which, he argued, equal hermeneutic weight must be given) that *brahman* is also the "efficient cause" (*nimittakāraṇa*) of produced being, Rāmānuja sought to affirm the ineluctable transcendence of *brahman*. A stock example of the efficient cause was the potter in relation to the pot. Here the ontological continuum between cause and effect is tenuous indeed, for the potter is a different entity entirely from the pot he makes, and it cannot be said that the nature of the pot *qua* pot reflects the nature of the potter, or vice versa. As efficient cause of conscious and nonconscious beings, Brahman is separate from its effects in a way that is qualitatively different from the way it may be said to be separate from its effects when acting as material cause. In this way of speaking, there is much more scope to preserve *brahman*'s supreme transcendence and perfection.

The point is that in his attempt to do justice to the different kinds of scriptural passages, Rāmānuja seeks simultaneously to preserve both modes of discourse concerning *brahman*'s causal action. In the sphere of discourse about *brahman*'s material causality, a "centripetal" emphasis occurs whereby the world as effect tends to collapse ontologically into its originative and sustaining material cause; but in the sphere of discourse about *brahman*'s efficient causality, an opposite, "centrifugal" emphasis is discerned, whereby the world as effect is kept apart from its divine efficient cause. In striving to maintain a dynamic equilibrium between these two conceptions and their derivative patterns of speech, Rāmānuja sets up an interactive polarity in relation to both the devotee's discourse and religious experience concerning *brahman*'s relationship with the world; in the process, Rāmānuja claims to do justice hermeneutically to what may appear to be conflicting insights of scripture. Elsewhere, I have called this kind of theological method "polarity theology" (see Lipner, 1976, ch.7). We shall see under the next two headings how polarity theology continues to play itself out in Rāmānuja's thought.

Several observations follow from this analysis:

(1) Rāmānuja can interpret the upanishadic *mahāvākya* or "great saying" *tat tvam asi* ("that you are"; *ChāU.* 6.8.7f.) and similar scriptural texts (e.g. *BĀU.* 1.4.10) in such a way as to preserve their nondual (*advaita*) aspect, without at the same time abandoning his espousal of *brahman*'s theistic nature. Thus Rāmānuja interprets the dictum *tat tvam asi* in the *Vedārthasaṃgraha* as follows:

> In so far as the individual self, experienced in the first instance as the ruler of the body (*deha*), is (in fact) the "body" (*śarīra*) of the supreme self, it is the mode (*prakāra*) of the supreme self, and terminates (*paryanta*) in the supreme self (both referentially and ontologically). Therefore the word *tvam* ("you") signifies the inner controller of the individual in so far as the latter is distinguished (*viśiṣṭa*) as the former's mode... By the words *tat* ("that") and *tvam* ("you") *brahman* alone is denoted by virtue of the fact that both terms refer to the same subject in so far as they are in (grammatical) apposition. Here the word *tat* signifies what is immutable, perfect, the source of all blessed qualities, existing as the cause of the world, and the word *tvam* signifies the same *brahman* acting as inner controller of the individual self, and distinguished (*viśiṣṭa*) by the individual self-cum-body as its mode. So we can say that both *tat* and *tvam* apply to one and the same *brahman* by virtue of different grounds for their application. (see Raghavachar, 1956, 17)

In other words, terms denoting finite substances (*dravya*s) denote *per se*, as their ultimate referent, the very reality (*brahman*) whose modes they are, and which acts as their causal support, and without which they can neither exist nor be apprehended for the beings they are. This is what the eyes of faith and a proper reading of the scriptures reveal.

(2) The reader will not have failed to notice more than one reference to the term *viśiṣṭa* (distinguished, separated [off]) in quotations drawn from Rāmānuja in the course of our discussion; this is the very term that forms part of the Sanskrit compound that subsequently came to define Rāmānuja's theological point of view: *viśiṣṭādvaita* – "the nonduality of distinguished or separated being(s)." We are now in a better position to appreciate why this term seems appropriate in this context, and how distinct beings can exist in a relationship of nonduality. This topic can be approached from two levels: (a) from the viewpoint of *brahman* with reference to finite beings; and (b) from the viewpoint of finite beings with reference to *brahman*.

(a) As noted earlier, when *brahman* is in its causally subtle state (*kāraṇāvasthā*), the conglomerate of conscious and nonconscious entities, *qua* dependent on *brahman* as their causal substrate, are indistinguishable from *brahman* insofar as they lack name and form. In this state, as only potentially distinguishable, they can be said to be actually nondifferent and so "nondual" with respect to *brahman*'s being.

(b) Similarly, in this state, they are also indistinguishable from each other and so exist as nonseparate or "nondual" with regard to each other, namely, neither they nor *brahman* is *viśiṣṭa*. But when *brahman* passes from its causal to its effected state (*kāryāvasthā*), the aggregate of conscious and nonconscious entities is actually distinguished into separate beings having name and form, that is, is individuated into *viśiṣṭa*s, both with reference to *brahman* and with respect to each other.

From this we conclude that the best way to analyze the compound generally used to characterize Rāmānuja's theological position, *viśiṣṭādvaita*, is as a *ṣaṣṭhītatpuruṣa*, in other words, a compound specifying a possessive relationship between its component members, that is, *viśiṣṭānām advaitam* "the nonduality of distinguished/separated beings." Or, as V. Varadachari prefers, *viśiṣṭasya advaitam*, where the first member of the unresolved compound refers to *brahman* itself in its distinguished mode (van Buitenen [1953, 1] also accepts this compound as a *tatpuruṣa*, the *viśiṣṭa* referring to both *brahman* and "differenced" being). I do not accept here V. Varadachari's second alternative, *viśiṣṭayoḥ advaitam*, according to which "there is identity between the two qualified *brahmans*," namely, the subtle (causal) and the developed (effected) *brahmans*, because *brahman* is not *viśiṣṭa* in the former state (see Varadachari, 1974, 109–110). In any case, we must reject the reading that the compound is a *karmadhāraya*, thst is, a *tatpuruṣa* where both members are in the same case (*viśiṣṭam advaitam*, "qualified nonduality"), for the reasons given above.

This is also why I prefer to translate the compound as "the nonduality of distinguished/separated beings" rather than as "the nonduality of distinct/separate beings"; the use of the past-participle passive in the former indicates that the distinction of being has undergone a *process*, as *brahman* (in fact, what becomes *brahman*'s "body") passes causally from the subtle to the developed state. The regulative relationship here – with respect to both the causal and the effected conditions of *brahman* – is that of *pṛthaksiddhyanarha*, namely, "incapable of realization apart (from *brahman*)," insofar as conscious and nonconscious entities exist as the mode(s) of *brahman*.

(3) Here too we have the rationale for Rāmānuja's rejection of the Bhedābheda view, which on the face of it seems similar to his own. All forms of Bhedābheda posit substantial change in *brahman* with respect to *brahman*'s production of finite being. But we have seen above that Rāmānuja seeks to reject the possibility of any substantial change in *brahman*, for this would imperil its inherent transcendent perfection, which for Rāmānuja remains constant in all stages of *brahman*'s causal function–hence his uncompromising hostility to the doctrine of Bhedābheda (see further Lott, 1976, ch. 7, especially for Rāmānuja's debate with the Bhedābheda view of Bhāskara; see also Bartley, 2002, 80–82).

(4) Finally, before I move on to the next constituent relationship of the self–body paradigm, I will take up the point here that in its microcosmic application, namely, its application to the relationship between the individual self (*jīvātman*) and the latter's own (empirical) "body," the paradigm has only a relative validity. And this is because in its capacity as causal support of its "body," the individual *ātman* cannot confer being in any absolute originative sense to its "body," in the way *brahman* does under the rubric of the "support"/"thing-supported" relationship. No doubt, so long as the individual *ātman* remains conjoined to its (physical) body, the body is sustained and conserved in being as an integrated whole, developing psychophysically according to the laws of nature (it is only at death, which is in effect the delinking of the individual *ātman* from its physical body, that this body loses its integrated nature and dissolution takes place). In this sense, as the living body's causal support, the individual *ātman* can be said to confer being to its "body" – its mode (*prakāra*). But, as I have explained, this conferral of being is not absolute in any sense, and so the paradigm in its microcosmic instantiation falls short of its theological counterpart.

The "Controller" (*Niyantṛ*)/ "Thing-controlled" (*Niyāmya* [*sic*]) Relationship

Under the first relationship, Rāmānuja was speaking of *brahman*'s being the ontological and epistemological ground of all produced being, hence the use of such impersonal terms as *ādhāra* (support) and *ādheya* (thing-supported). The next two relationships, however, specifically treat of *brahman*'s personal supremacy (*paratva*) over all finite being, and the terminology here reflects this. I shall follow suit and speak more often of *brahman* in its personal capacity by way of such terms as "Lord," "God," and so on, and the personal pronouns that reflect this turn of speech.

For Rāmānuja, *brahman* is not a remote God, exercising his lordship over the world from a distance, as it were. As his being the metaphysical ground of all indicates, *brahman* indwells the world, enters into an intimate relationship with all nonconscious and conscious beings, and rules from within. Not infrequently, Rāmānuja quotes various authoritative texts, from both Śruti and Smṛti (namely, texts perceived as capable of illumining the purport of Śruti), which he interprets as affirming this. So he can say in the *Vedārthasaṃgraha*,

> We know specifically that *brahman* is the self of all, from the Śruti: "Having entered within all creatures (*janānām*), he is their ruler (*śāstṛ*), the self of all" [*Taittirīyāraṇyaka* 3.11], which means that in so far as his self has entered within all creatures as their ruler, he is the self

> of all creatures and all are his "body." (see Raghavachar, 1956, 15)

This is in fact the reason why all substance words ultimately denote *brahman*, who is their referential ground.

It is from his intimate dwelling place as "inner controller" (*antaryāmin*) of the world that *brahman* exercises his unique lordship. This he does fundamentally through the regulative force of the universal law of *karman*, which, cycle after cosmic cycle, fashions a universe with its numerous tiers of heavens and netherworlds (and their intricate nexus of various underlying natural laws) that becomes the appropriate arena for the simultaneous outworking of the individual fructifying *karman* of all its numberless denizens. Only *brahman*, as universal Lord, through his limitless power and wisdom, can preside over and direct the karmic shape of the world during each cycle. In affirming the Lord's supremacy over all within this framework, then, well may Rāmānuja quote *Bṛhadāraṇyakopaniṣad* 3.8.9: "At the command (*praśāsane*) of the imperishable one, Gārgī, the sun and moon stand firm, set apart," and *Manusmṛti* 12.122 (with reference to "the eternal *brahman*") that "[h]e is the ruler (*praśāsitāraṃ sarveṣām*) of all" (see Raghavachar, 1956, 9). Within this context of sovereignty, let us inquire more closely into how, for Rāmānuja, the Lord exercises control over personal embodied selves in particular, for do not such beings have moral autonomy? How, then, can the Lord subject them to his overall mastery?

It is here that the term *niyantṛ* (controller/restrainer) provides a clue. The term can also stand for the charioteer who controls the chariot, restraining and guiding its horses along various paths (see *MaiU.* 2.6). If we accept this image as underlying Rāmānuja's choice of terminology here (after all, it is also the underlying image of the *Bhagavadgītā*, a text Rāmānuja took to heart and provided a commentary on), then, extending the analogy, we can say (*KaU.* 1.3.3–9) that when the chariot (namely, the embodied self) is responsive to the divine charioteer's guidance, it follows the path to salvation, but that when the chariot rejects this control, it heads for destruction.

In the *Vedārthasaṃgraha*, Rāmānuja clearly affirms that the personal agent has moral autonomy under *brahman*'s presiding causal action. In answer to an objection that this is not the case, he states,

> We answer as follows: the supreme self has bestowed in equal measure (*sāmānyena*) on all persons (*cetana*) the equipment required for performing action or desisting from it, such as the capacity (*yoga*) for the power of thought, the capacity for the power of willing and so on. So that this happens, he has become their support (*ādhāra*), and having entered into them, exercises control (*niyamanaṃ*) as the consenter [to action; *anumantṛtayā*], being established as the apex (*śeṣin*) of their being. For its part, the individual, endowed with such power, desists from action or acts of its own accord (*svayam eva kurute*). The supreme self, witnessing the individual act thus, remains uninvolved (*udāsīna*). And so, all is well. (see Raghavachar, 1956, 95–96)

Freedom of action, of course, is the basis for the soul's entering into a reciprocal relationship of love or commitment (→ *bhakti*) with the Lord, a relationship Rāmānuja stresses not least in his commentary on the *Bhagavadgītā*. The Lord exercises a controlling role in this respect too, but, as the extract above indicates, one that functions by way of example, guidance, and moral persuasion rather than physical or other force. A prime means of such benevolent direction is the *avatāra* or descent of Viṣṇu-Nārāyaṇa in one embodied form or another. Rāmānuja explains this divine initiative and its intended consequences as follows in the introduction to his *Gītābhāṣya*:

> The supreme person, Nārāyaṇa, being the highest *brahman*...and a vast ocean of boundless compassion, kindness, tenderness, and generosity, himself takes on forms similar [to those of gods and humans] without abandoning his own nature (*svasvabhāva*), and descending repeatedly into the various worlds, is worshipped by these beings, bestowing upon them the fruit they desire, namely virtue (*dharma*), wealth (*artha*), satisfaction (*kāma*) or final liberation (*mokṣa*). And, on the pretext of removing earth's burden, so as to allay the pain of everyday existence (*saṃsāraduḥkhaśamanāya*) for individuals like us, He has become visible to every human eye, performing marvels to remove the anguish of every person, high and low (*parāparanikhilajana*)...On the pretext of encouraging [Arjuna] into battle, and in so far as final liberation is the highest human goal, he revealed (*avatārayamāsa*) the method of devotion (*bhaktiyoga*) that has him for its object, is taught by the Vedānta, and is aided

by knowledge and action. (*GBh., Upodghāta* [i.e. introduction])

The implication here is that through the teaching of the Vedas and the example of the *avatāra*(s), the Lord encourages the whole of humanity to attain salvation (for he has acted "to remove the anguish of every person, high and low"). No doubt this process takes time. It culminates in the discipline of devotion (*bhaktiyoga*), but it is aided by the arduous disciplines of striving to know the nature of God and the soul and the relationship between them (that is, *jñānayoga*) and of the actions required to accomplish this (namely, *karmayoga*), such as painstaking study of the scriptures and the relevant liturgical and devotional practices. It incorporates the dilatory scheme of *karman* and rebirth (→ *saṃsāra*), which Rāmānuja believed applied to the transient universe as a whole (see Raghavachar, 1956, 1–2). It incorporates the restrictions of *varṇāśramadharma* or the order of caste and stage of life imposed by vedic authority, which, in theory at least, Rāmānuja did not repudiate. In the *Vedārthasaṃgraha*, he declares,

> This is the purport summarized in the crown of the mass of Śruti (viz. the Upaniṣads), ordained for the benefit of the entire universe: that the truest happiness, and the fruit of attaining it, lie in first knowing what the individual self and the supreme person really are, and then, aided by performing the duties of caste and stage of life (*varṇāśramadharma*), in meditating upon, worshipping and paying reverence to the feet of the supreme person. (see Raghavachar, 1956, 1; see also *ŚBh.* 1.3.38)

It was noted earlier that Rāmānuja was keen for his theological project, based in part on the Pāñcarātra, to be seen to comply with vedic thought and practice (though his universal vision and personal magnanimity of spirit may have tempered the social rigors of such practice in everyday life). Once again, the self–body paradigm's microcosmic application is but an imperfect reflection of its divine counterpart. While the individual self (*jīvātman*) no doubt "controls" its psychophysical conjunct, both morally and physically, and has the power and freedom to guide it along salutary paths, this control, as distinct from *brahman*'s case, is subject to many qualifications arising from ignorance and disordered passions on the one hand and injury and natural limitations of the body on the other.

And once again, we can see Rāmānuja's polarity method at work under this heading. From the divine point of view, talk of the Lord's overall "control" tends to collapse, "centripetally," the natural world's staying power and the moral self's autonomy of action into the sovereignty and supremacy of the Lord; but this is compensated for "centrifugally" by counterdiscourse, based on experience, affirming the substantival reality of the aggregate of conscious and nonconscious entities as well as the person's capacity to act freely. We come now to the third component of the self–body relationship.

The Accessory (*Śeṣa*)/Principal (*Śeṣin*) Relationship

J.B. Carman (1974, 147) declares, "[I]t is certain that this concept of the *śeṣa-śeṣī* relationship is one of the most important and characteristic ideas in Rāmānuja's theology". There is no doubt that it harbors some of the most devotional features delineating the soul's relationship with God in Rāmānuja's thought. In general terms, however, he describes this relationship as follows:

> In all cases, the relationship between the accessory and its principal (*śeṣaśeṣibhāva*) is this: the "accessory" (*śeṣa*) is that whose essence (*svarūpa*) is to be "entirely at the disposal of (*upādeyatvam eva*)" – through wanting to establish the pre-eminence (*atiśayādhānecchatayā*) of an other, while that "other" is the "principal" (*śeṣin*). (see Raghavachar, 1956, 145)

This definition comes as the concluding element of a discussion about what constitutes an "accessory" in the performance of one vedic sacrifice or other. In this context, the Pūrvamīmāṃsakas or ritualists defined an accessory as that which exists for the sake of another (*śeṣa parārthatvāt*); the *śeṣa* here is whatever serves to accomplish the primary intention of a vedic ritual. This context is not without importance for grasping the implications of Rāmānuja's own understanding of what the *śeṣa* might be, as will be clarified in due course.

From the general definition of the relationship given by Rāmānuja, it is clear that we have entered the realm of value discourse. The purpose of the *śeṣa*, its value, is to manifest what is already there – the excellence or preeminence (*atiśaya*) of the *śeṣin*. The *śeṣa*, therefore, has an exocentric function: "by duly expressing its nature the accessory... throws the spotlight, as it were, on its principal, not on itself" (Lipner, 1986, 132). The *śeṣa* does not bestow value; it derives its value, its purpose, from the "principal" or *śeṣin*, which is the value giver, and which has value in its own right. Though *prima facie*, it may seem that the reverse is the case, the prime beneficiary of the relationship is the *śeṣa*, whose existence is justified by its serving function; at most the *śeṣin* is an accidental beneficiary, whose preeminence is already assured.

In the microcosmic application of the paradigm, then – with reference, say, to the personal embodied *ātman* – where the *jīvātman* is the *śeṣin* and its psychophysical conjunct the *śeṣa*, the latter exists to serve the purposes of the *ātman*, namely, ultimately, the *ātman*'s final liberation. In so functioning, it shows up/shows off the preeminence of the *jīvātman* as its (restricted) support and controller or "master" and owns up to, as it were, its own limitations (as subject to the intrusion of ignorance through the law of *karman*, its susceptibility to suffering and injury, and so on). But it also receives value, becomes valuable, as the helper of the *ātman* in its journey through *saṃsāra* and therefore is entitled to protection and care in this role from its *śeṣin*. In other words, we have here a valorization of the psyche–body conjunct and, by extension, of the whole sphere of the psychophysical, which for Vedānta is derived from the nonconscious principle of *prakṛti*.

But the prime application of the paradigm, of course, occurs in its theological context. Here the supreme being, Lord Viṣṇu-Nārāyaṇa, is the "principal," while the universe of conscious and nonconscious beings, both individually and collectively, with special reference to conscious selves, is the "accessory." It is especially in the *Gītābhāṣya* (as also in the *Gadyatraya*), as one might expect, that this theme is evoked in a devotional context. Rāmānuja tells us here that when we become true "knowers" (*jñānin*s) of God, that is, when we become discerning devotees of God, experientially aware of our (multifaceted) relationship with the divine being, and so, properly virtuous and suffused with the love of God, "our sole delight is to function entirely as the Lord's accessory" (*aśeṣaśeṣataikarati*). He goes on to declare in the *Vedārthasaṃgraha*,

> Because the highest *brahman* is the principal of all, and the self is his accessory, if one focuses upon him as the object of unbounded and unexcelled love (*prīti*) by virtue of this connection with him, he himself leads the soul to attain him. (see Raghavachar, 1956, 186)

The proper relationship of the personal self here is one of service (*kaiṃkarya, dāsya*) to the Lord. Such a self is born to serve the Lord (that is, it is a *garbhadāsa*). This is a characteristic feature of Rāmānuja's theology. Nevertheless, such service does not abrogate the free will of the individual, as we have seen earlier, nor does it preclude a relationship of devotion and commitment (*bhakti*) to the Lord, for "the master – servant relationship could be (and ideally was) a loving relationship on the basis of its freedom" (Lipner, 1986, 132). Rāmānuja's theology is a theology advocating *bhakti*, a *bhakti* lived out in loving service, yet this is a loving service that one is free to offer to or withhold from the divine principal of all.

In the introduction to the *Gītābhāṣya*, Rāmānuja launches into a paean of praise of Viṣṇu-Nārāyaṇa's unbounded, inexhaustible, and wonderful personal attributes, in justification of the divine lordship and majesty. We are told that

> [t]he Lord is opposed to all evil, blessed in every respect, and with an essence that is none other than infinite consciousness and bliss. He is a vast ocean of a mass of countless blessed qualities, naturally unlimited and excellent, such as knowledge (*jñāna*), omnipotence (*śakti*), power (*bala*), sovereignty (*aiśvarya*), steadfastness (*dhairya*), and lustre (*tejas*). (*GBh.*, *Upodghāta*)

These last six named qualities recapitulate the *ṣaḍguṇa*s (six attributes) mentioned in the *Viṣṇupurāṇa* as defining the concept of Bhagavān (the personal form of address to the Vaiṣṇava deity) and repeated in the Pāñcarātra Āgamas as properties of the supreme being's celestial form. Rāmānuja too acknowledges the existence of a supernal, non- *prakṛti*-based, anthropomorphic form (*divyarūpa*) – described in glowing terms in the *Vedārthasaṃgraha* (see Raghavachar, 1956, 172) – as being the object of praise and delight for the whole heavenly court comprising the *sūri*s (glorious finite spirits who have never been subjected to *saṃsāra*) and the liberated souls who have reached journey's end by the grace of the Lord after overcoming *karman* and rebirth. These qualities symbolize countless more that nest in the divine nature, fundamentally characterized as it is by the properties of existence (*satya*), consciousness (*jñāna*), bliss (*ānanda*), purity (*amalatva*), and infinitude (*ānantya*). Rāmānuja interprets the *mahāvākya* of *Taittirīyopaniṣad* 2.1.1, *satyaṃ jñānam anantaṃ brahma*, "*brahman* is being, consciousness, infinite," not only to show that the Śruti, if properly interpreted according to the rule of literal (*mukhya*) denotation, cannot be used to affirm that its chief object, the supreme being, is utterly devoid of attributes (*nirguṇa*), as the Advaitin does, but also to demonstrate *brahman*'s sovereignty over and difference from the various orders of produced being:

> The word "being" (*satya*) denotes *brahman* possessed of unconditioned existence (*nirupādhikasattāyogi*). By this word are set apart from *brahman* the locus of change (*vikāra*) which is non-conscious being, and conscious being combined with non-conscious being [viz. embodied selves, who, conditioned by matter, are subject to change]... The word "consciousness" (*jñāna*) denotes [*brahman* as possessing] a nature solely of eternal and non-contracted consciousness. By this word, are set apart from *brahman* selves freed from temporarily contracted consciousness [viz. embodied selves that have been liberated from *saṃsāra*]. The word "infinite" (*ananta*) denotes the essence [*svarūpa*, of *brahman*] as devoid of limitations of place, time and being. In so far as his essence has attributes, *brahman* has infinitude of essence and attributes. By this word are set apart [from *brahman*] the eternally free spirits [who have never been involved in *saṃsāra*], who are different from the two groups (*koṭi*) excluded by the two former words and who have attributes and an essence of a superior kind. (*ŚrīBh.* 1.1.2)

Thus, by the neat contrivance of making each defining term exclude *brahman* from a class of finite being superior to the preceding one, Rāmānuja makes the point that *brahman* qualitatively transcends all being and is also infinitely perfect in the order of being (for a more detailed analysis, see Lipner, 1986, 28–35).

This is the God, then, that the (personal) *śeṣa* (in particular) is called upon to worship and serve at all times: a God who, says Rāmānuja (interpreting words of Kṛṣṇa in *Gītābhāṣya* 6.47), instructs us to serve and worship him "as illumining the whole world by my unlimited and surpassing lustre, gladdening (*āpyāyayantam*) the universe by the beauty of my self (*ātmakāntyā*)." To achieve this goal, the religious path is set out; Rāmānuja calls it *jñānayoga*, "the discipline of knowledge," where the knowledge ultimately attained in this life is a kind of constant direct awareness of the Lord, suffused with love (*bhakti*). This higher knowledge (*paravidyā*) and love (*parabhakti*) are within the grasp even of the devotee who is a married householder (*gṛhastha; ŚrīBh.* 3.4.19); it is not necessary, as Śaṅkara taught, for the aspirant to abandon the world and become a renouncer (*saṃnyāsin*). Leading up to this state are a combination (*samuccaya*) of lower knowledge (*aparavidyā*) and lower devotion (*aparabhakti*) consisting of a more discursive understanding of the proper relationship between the world and God in terms of the threefold *śarīra-śarīrin* relationship, and the love for God that grows from this understanding and its attendant devotional practices (see further Lipner, 1986, 112–116).

Here we may advert to an additional feature of the principal-accessory relationship. I noted earlier that *śeṣa* also signifies whatever served the main purpose of vedic ritual. It thus has a sacrificial connotation. As a term, in the plural (*śeṣāḥ*), it also signified in subsequent Hindu worship, well before Rāmānuja's time: "objects that were consecrated and left over" and then distributed among worshippers, after offerings were made to the icon in the temple (flowers, food, etc.). It is not unlikely that this further meaning was in Rāmānuja's mind by his use of the term. In that case, it would have added, no doubt in "in-house" discourse among Śrīvaiṣṇavas, the connotation of consecration to God's service, especially in the context of the full-fledged (Śrīvaiṣṇava) *śeṣa* or *jñānin* (see above), as well as an emphasis on mutual service among members of this community.

Finally, under this heading, we may consider the implications of its "polarity" theology. Insofar as the *śeṣa* exists to serve its divine principal, we may speak of a centripetal tendency at work, emphasizing the *śeṣa*'s subordinate status. This would legitimate the language of total self-abnegation in the deity's presence in religious experience, intimating that "God is everything and the devotee nothing." But the *jīvātman* is also a *śeṣin* with respect to its own mind-body conjunct; in this capacity, it is a moral agent in its own right, and so an " end in itself." Indeed, as Rāmānuja affirms on the basis of interpreting the vedantic scriptures, insofar as it is essentially blissful and conscious, the *jīvātman* reflects the divine nature (see further Lipner, 1986, ch. 3). Experience and language in this vein work to prevent the *jīva* from undue self-abrogation by providing a sense of the *jīva*'s own intrinsic worth, moral status, and responsibility. This centrifugal emphasis is augmented by the scripture-based realization acknowledged by Rāmānuja (see above, where he declares that the Lord works to lead the devout soul to himself) that the divine *śeṣin* graciously seeks to protect and guide his servant and indeed, where applicable, the whole of produced being, insofar as they are his *śeṣa*. We are speaking here of a kind of "perspectival" theology.

Thus, by means of his distinctive polarity approach embedded in the self–body model, Rāmānuja sought to maintain a dynamic equilibrium (in terms of "centripetal" and "centrifugal" poles) between various modes of apparently conflicting discourse and experience about *brahman* purporting to arise from the scriptures. Note that it is not an *organic* model that is being propounded here in any obvious sense of "organic." There is no suggestion that finite entities function in their relationship with the supreme person in such a manner that some entities are analogous to that person's "limbs," others to his "mind" or "head," yet others to his "heart," and so on; all entities that can be regarded as the "body" of *brahman* in Rāmānuja's distinctive sense, individually or collectively, are equally *brahman*'s "body" in the threefold manner analyzed above.

Note, too, the robustly realist tenor of Rāmānuja's thought. There is no place in it for the dual advaitic principle of → *māyā*/avidyā, which purported to render the differentiated world as both illusory and misconceived in the final analysis, and as in some way a projection of the supreme reality (*brahman*) regarded as undifferentiated consciousness. This is why his *mahāsiddhānta* or "major conclusive thesis" (which occupies a large part of his commentary on *Brahmasūtra* 1.1.1) is devoted to attacking what he regarded as the core advaitic interpretation of Vedānta as stated in terms of this twofold cosmological principle (for, by Rāmānuja's time, the advaitic stance had been developed at some length by Śaṅkara's followers). Here, by a cumulative argument consisting of seven objections (known collectively as the *saptavidhānupapatti*), Rāmānuja seeks to show that as a concept *māyā/avidyā* is philosophically unacceptable in that it has

1. no tenable locus (*āśraya*) in *brahman* (as conceived of by Advaita);
2. no tenable obscuring function (*tirodhāna*) of a *brahman* that is described as self-manifesting consciousness;
3. no intelligible proper form (*svarūpa*);
4. no coherent status as supposedly neither real nor unreal (namely, as *anirvacanīya* or ineffable); and
5. no proper grounding in our accredited sources of knowledge (*pramāṇa*); and that it cannot coherently be conceived of
6. as having a removing agent (*nivartaka*); or
7. ceasing to exist (*nivṛtti*).

The argument is sustained and complex and affirms Rāmānuja's realist position with respect to a supreme being that is regarded as personal, and this being's relationship with the world.

As a result of this philosophical groundwork, Rāmānuja (and his followers) believed that what was propounded as the Śrīvaiṣṇava position succeeded in seeing off opposing views of scripture and the meaning of life, including rival vedantic theories such as Advaita and Bhedābheda. It remains for us now to make some concluding remarks about Rāmānuja's legacy, both within his own community and in wider context.

Rāmānuja is considered to be the first theologian to have developed and defended systematically a theistic and devotional interpretation of the vedantic scriptures. Thinkers in this vein before him (e.g. Yāmuna, Bhāskara) laid the basis for such an approach; Rāmānuja consolidated it – and others would follow. In the face, therefore, of the dominance of Advaita's monistic interpretation of the Vedānta, Rāmānuja gave a theistically realist interpretation of these scriptures much-needed credibility. But, as is to be expected, he left a number of theological (and other) issues undeveloped or open-ended. In time, his religious tradition of Śrīvaiṣṇavism divided into two camps: the Vaṭakalai or Northern School and the Teṉkalai or Southern School. These developed and debated a number of unresolved issues in his name, for example, the nature of *bhakti* as *prapatti* or total surrender to God, and various other sectarian Śrīvaiṣṇava beliefs and practices and their relationship to vedic orthodoxy. Among the latter was the role and status of the goddess Śrī (or Lakṣmī), whose name appears in that of the denomination. Rāmānuja mentions Śrī briefly in all his works, but since he says little or nothing about her theologically, it is difficult to discern her position in his thought. J.B. Carman is probably right to conclude that these references imply "both a close likeness in nature to [Viṣṇu-] Nārāyaṇa and a clear subordination to Him"

(Carman, 1974, 239; for further discussion on such matters see Carman, 1974, 212–244; 1994, 136–138, 280–282; Raman, 2007).

Rāmanuja is an inspiring and inspired theologian not only for the Śrīvaiṣṇava community, which continues to flourish to the present day, but also for other schools of Vaiṣṇavism active within the phenomenon we call "Hinduism," for example, in contemporary times, the International Society for Krishna Consciousness (→ ISKCON), known more popularly as the Hare Krishnas.

In the context of a wider scholarship, articles, books, and doctoral theses continue to be written on Rāmānuja's thought, not least in interreligious contexts, with special reference to Hinduism and Christianity. In such discussions, Rāmānuja's ideas are brought into creative interplay with modern concerns. An example or two may suffice. I have pointed out that Rāmānuja taught that the intuitive love of God, namely, the highest knowledge and devotion we can acquire in this life, can be attained even by the householder and that Rāmānuja's conception of the "accessory–principal" relationship succeeds in valorizing not only the body, but also the psychophysical world at large. These teachings represented a bold departure from the dominant advaitic view of the time, which insisted on uncompromising renunciation of the world as the only path to *mokṣa* (→ liberation). Rāmānuja could never say to the enlightened soul, as the *Vivekacūḍāmaṇi*, a post-Śaṅkara advaitic text, did:

> Having realized the form that is constant and pure awareness and bliss, turn your back completely on this false form [of a body] that is unconscious and impure; it should not be dwelt on again [for] what has been vomited out and then remembered again, is fit only to cause disgust. (*ViCū.* 4.4)

His view of the world was far more positive and affirming than that.

This leads to my second example. Rāmānuja's valorization of the body, and by extension of all materiality, through the *śeṣa-śeṣin* relationship, has been seen as encouraging the view that human beings should act in a spirit of stewardship of the natural world, preserving its ecosystems and refraining from exploiting it, in the way a responsible master protects a (faithful) servant. These examples indicate that there is promising scope in Rāmānuja's thought not only for undertaking transcultural and interreligious dialogue, but also for engaging constructively with some of the problematic issues that confront us today on a global scale.

(Unless stated otherwise, all translations are by the author.)

Bibliography

Abhyankar, V.S., ed., *Śrī-Bhāshya of Rāmānujāchārya*, Bombay, 1914.

Apte, V.G., ed., *Śrīmadbhagavadgītā (with Rāmānuja's Commentary)*, ĀSS 92, n.l., 1923.

Bartley, C.J., *The Theology of Rāmānuja: Realism and Religion*, London, 2002.

Buitenen, J.A.B. van, *Rāmānuja's Vedārthasaṃgraha: Introduction, Critical Edition and Annotated Translation*, Poona, 1956.

Buitenen, J.A.B. van, *Rāmānuja on the Bhagavadgītā: A Condensed Rendering of his Gītābhāṣya with Copious Notes and an Introduction*, The Hague, 1953.

Carman, J.B., *Majesty and Meekness: A Comparative Study of Contrast and Harmony in the Concept of God*, Grand Rapids, 1994.

Carman, J.B., *The Theology of Rāmānuja: An Essay in Interreligious Understanding*, London, 1974.

Franco, E., ed., *Historiography and Periodization of Indian Philosophy*, Vienna, 2012.

Lester, R.C., *Rāmānuja on the Yoga*, Madras, 1976.

Lipner, J.J., *The Face of Truth: A Study of Meaning and Metaphysics in the Vedāntic Theology of Rāmānuja*, Albany, 1986.

Lipner, J.J., "The Perils of Periodization, or How to Finesse History with Reference to Vedānta," in: E. Franco, ed., *Historiography and Periodization of Indian Philosophy*, Vienna, 2012, 1–25.

Lott, E., *God and the Universe in the Vedāntic Theology of Rāmānuja*, Madras, 1976.

Madhavananda, Swami, *Vivekachudamani of Sri Sankaracharya*, Mayavati, [5]1952.

Radhakrishnan, S., *The Principal Upaniṣads*, London, 1953.

Raghavachar, S.S., *Śrī Rāmānuja on the Upanishads*, Madras, 1972.

Raghavachar, S.S., *Vedārthasaṃgraha of Śrī Rāmānujācārya*, Mysore, 1956.

Ramakrishnananda, Swami, *Life of Sri Ramanuja*, Madras, [3]1959.

Raman, S., *Self-surrender (prapatti) to God in Śrīvaiṣṇavism: Tamil Cats and Sanskrit Monkeys*, London, 2007.

Varadachari, V., "Antiquity of the term Visishtadvaita," in: *Visishtadvaita: Philosophy and Religion*, publ. Ramanuja Research Society, Madras, 1974, 109–112.

Julius Lipner

Rāmdās

Samartha Rāmdās Swāmī (1608–1681), a Brahman saint (*sant*: good or exemplary person), hails from the Marathi-speaking area today demarcated as → Maharashtra state and is listed among the five most important Marathi poet-saints (a common gloss for → Sants). Yet his inclusion among famous Marathi Sants is surely not due to his name, which labels him as a "servant of [Lord] → Rāma." Rāmdās' writings are composed in the vernacular Old Marathi. His two most well-known Marathi works are the *Manāce Ślok* (Verses Addressed to the Mind) and his *magnum opus, Dāsbodh* (often spelled *Dāsabodha*), both of which are available from a large number of publishers. Rāmdās' teachings are rife with nondualist philosophy (Advaita → Vedānta), with its favoring of devotion to a → *nirguṇa* (without qualities or characteristics) conceptualization of the absolute, → *brahman*. However, Rāmdās also shows a strong engagement in promoting devotion to anthropomorphic images (*saguṇa bhakti*). He is said to be an → *avatāra* of → Hanumān, the "monkey-deity," so Rāmdās is both a devotee of Lord Rāma and an embodiment of Hanumān, Rāma's perfect devotee and servant. Hanumān combines his → *bhakti* with incredible physical prowess (→ *śakti*) and lifelong celibacy (*brāhmcārī*; see Alter, 1992, 198–213), all of which are emulated in the person of Rāmdās. The monastic Rāmdāsī order founded by Rāmdās remains active today through its headquarters at Sajjangad, a hilltop plateau in the Satara district, Maharashtra. On particular festival days, such as the one celebrating Rāmdās' birth (*rāmnavamī*), pilgrims participate in devotional singing and a communal meal and are able to visit shrines to Hanumān and Rāma. Most importantly, they are able to visit Rāmdās' living quarters, which also contains a marking his physical death. His legacy remains alive at other sites in Maharashtra, especially in the form of the numerous Hanumān temples and monasteries he is believed to have established. Often a Hanumān temple of unknown origin is attributed to Rāmdās' hand, and a Hanumān temple that Rāmdās visited or established lends the site a special quality in the eyes of devotees. In the city of Pune, Maharashtra, there also is a Rāmdās temple, and his portrait is found in nearly all of the city's Hanumān shrines. Hanumān devotion in the Marathi-speaking area predates Rāmdās, but he regularly receives credit for having popularized – or at least reinvigorated – Hanumān devotion in today's Maharashtra.

Fig. 1: Image of Rāmdās in the Rāmdās Temple, Pune (photo by Jeffrey Brackett).

Rāmdās' position within the list of the five most important Marathi-speaking Sants may at first seem odd, since Rāmdās' life and teachings are distinct in many ways from the other four Sants on this august list. By looking at the contours of modern accounts of Rāmdās' life, one sees how he is set apart from the four other members of the famous five Marathi Sants: → Jñāneśvar, → Nāmdev, → Eknāth, and → Tukārām. These four are all Sants of the → Vārkarī Sampradāy, a Vaiṣṇava devotional movement especially noted for its large annual pilgrimage in which pilgrims from around the Marathi-speaking region walk for up to three weeks in order to converge on the temple town of Pandharpur, home of the god Viṭhobā. Much scholarly attention has focused on the Vārkarīs, as one cannot underestimate the historical, religious, and cultural centrality of the Vārkarīs in Maharashtra. Certainly, some acquaintance with the Vārkarī movement is indispensable for understanding Maharashtrian religious life, yet its perceived centrality may overshadow the radically diverse religious practices in Maharashtra. For example, Hanumān devotion alone is far more important to everyday religious life, particularly if measured by the common notion that without a Hanumān temple, there is no village. One cannot say the same for Viṭhobā, yet that does not diminish the centrality afforded the Vārkarīs. Examples of other important regional gods, goddesses, Sants, and sects could easily be multiplied here; Hanumān is selected due to his connection with Rāmdās. Further, there are links between Rāmdās and the Vārkarīs beyond the famous five Sants. For instance, Lord Viṭhobā may have replaced an earlier, Śaiva-oriented devotion in Pandharpur (Vaudeville, 1974; 1987a; 1987b). This view suggests that an originally Śaiva deity later came to be viewed as a naturally occurring form (*svarūpa* or *svayambhū*) of → Kṛṣṇa, as Vaiṣṇava devotion gained popularity around Pandharpur. Rāmdās himself embodied both Śaiva and Vaiṣṇava tendencies, since → Śiva assumed earthly form as Hanumān, both as a form of devotion to Rāma and in order to fight the treacherous Rāvaṇa, the demon-king of Laṅkā in the → *Rāmāyaṇa* of Vālmīki. Other connections between Rāmdās and the Vārkarīs include his installation of a six-foot-tall Hanumān image (*mūrti*) in the Pandharpur Viṭhobā shrine, his "seeing" Rāma when he looked at Viṭhobā, the inclusion of a palanquin from Sajjangad that travels to Pandharpur during the annual pilgrimage, and his being a contemporary of Tukārām (1609–1650), the most popular of all Vārkarī Sants. One final point to note before delving into details of Rāmdās' biography is that he is said to have been the spiritual and political advisor to the → Maratha king Śivājī (1630–1680). Rāmdās and Śivājī are said to have worked in tandem to establish and perpetuate *mahārāṣṭra dharma*, their idealized notion of a region-specific form of religio-political life. This is a term popularized in connection with Rāmdās and Śivājī, though the terms precede their use of them (Tulpule, 1979, 395n450).

Biographical Framework

Modern accounts of Rāmdās' biography repeat, with slight variations and emphases, many of the same aspects of traditional hagiographies, which are filled with descriptions of Rāmdās' discipline and miraculous powers that he accrued as a result of his intense religious practice. Most of the modern brief hagiographies, such as those retold in booklets or as a portion of longer books, are written from a devotional perspective. It is not my intention to critique that approach; rather, my interest is to narrate significant aspects culled from these sources as a means of highlighting Rāmdās' contributions to religious, historical, and cultural practices within the Marathi-speaking region. His relationship with Hanumān, more commonly called Māruti (Mar. Mārutī) in Maharashtra, is clearly important. Stories that some devotees find more interesting, important, or critical for understanding Rāmdās will certainly be missing in what follows, but those can be located in other sources, such as Mahipatī's (1715–1790) *Santavijaya*, a nearly four-hundred-page hagiography available in English translation (Abbott, 1932). In the preface to his translation, J.E. Abbott calls Rāmdās "India's greatest saint" (Abbott, 1932, 16). The condensed retelling of Rāmdās' biography provided below is drawn from a variety of sources. The intention is to point out salient themes in Rāmdās' life that can then serve as a model for further examination. The main topics are his birth, signs of his divinity, his miraculous deeds, his utter devotion to Rāma and Hanumān, his "activist" style of working to revitalize Hindu devotion, and his relationship with King Śivājī.

Samartha Rāmdās' birth took place during the month of *caitra* (Mar-Apr), on the auspicious day of Lord Rāma's annual festival, in Jamb village, on the banks of the holy Godāvarī River. His given name was Nārāyaṇ, born as the second son into a family with a longstanding tradition of devotional practices to Rāma and Sūrya, the sun god (see → *navagrahas*). His father Sūryajipant's devotion so impressed Sūrya that he appeared in the guise of a Brahman to grant Sūryajipant a boon: two sons. The first would be imbued with a portion of Sūrya, while the second would have within him a portion of Māruti (also known as Hanumān). More importantly, the second son would remain celibate; hence, he would lead an ascetic life as a religious teacher and conduct significant work in the region of the Kṛṣṇā River for the good of humanity. As foretold by Sūrya, Sūryapant's wife Rāṇubāī had two sons, with Nārāyaṇ born three years after his elder brother Gaṅgadhār. Although he was very active and mischievous as a child, much like young Kṛṣṇa, he also was gifted with a superior intellect and easily mastered his studies. As soon as he underwent the sacred thread ceremony (see → *yajñopavīta*), he begged his father to become his → *guru*. His father told young Nārāyaṇ he was still too young. When his father died two years later, Nārāyaṇ asked his elder brother to be his *guru*. Again, Nārāyaṇ was rejected due to his age. Feeling desperate, he ran to the Māruti temple just outside the village border, put his head at Māruti's feet, and pleaded to become his student. Nārāyaṇ remained motionless, clinging to Māruti when, at midnight, Māruti gave him *darśan* (→ *pūjā* and *darśan*). His pleading with his father and brother for a → *mantra* no longer mattered. Now, Māruti himself gave young Nārāyaṇ the *mantra*: "*śrīrām jayrām jay jay rām.*" Māruti then told him, "From now on you shall be called Rāmdās." As quickly as he had appeared, Māruti disappeared. "Rāmdās" ran back to his family, who were worried about his absence, to narrate the miraculous events that transpired in the temple. Like a rite of passage, this miracle transformed young Nārāyaṇ into a serious devotee, and he spent hours daily meditating and singing religious songs (*bhajan*s; see → *kīrtan* and *bhajan*).

Not everyone was so pleased with his inattention to nonreligious matters. His mother thought she could change him by arranging for his marriage. Nārāyaṇ would have nothing to do with such talk. He climbed a tree and refused to come down until his mother promised to stop talking about a wedding. When his mother sent a man up the tree to get Nārāyaṇ, he jumped into the river, hitting his head on a rock. The bump he received on his head as a result of the fall was a constant reminder of his resistance to family life; it also portends his life as a renouncer and hints at "monkeylike" behavior in his mischievous climbing and jumping from trees. Nārāyaṇ's wedding, nonetheless, was arranged. His mother remained worried that he would again escape, so she made him promise that he would not run from the wedding platform. When the priest chanted the final *mantra*, Nārāyaṇ's fear of family life overwhelmed him. He jumped from the platform and ran away, further proving his unwavering devotion to Hanumān.

Thus marks the beginning of Nārāyaṇ's fulfillment of the boon given to his father, namely, that he would be a lifelong celibate. Continually chanting his *mantra* along the way, Nārāyaṇ finally stopped at Pañcavaṭī, the sacred river near Nasik. Once there, he vowed to chant his *mantra* 130 million times, starting right then with his head at the feet of Rāma's image (*mūrti*). Thus began his intense ascetic practices (*tapaścaryā*). He lived in a cave in Takli, close to the confluence of the Godāvarī and Nandinī Rivers. His chanting continued daily, while standing waist deep in the river, nonstop for six hours. People saw his intense discipline and began referring to him as "Rāmdās," as Māruti had called him earlier. In addition to chanting his *mantra*, his day also consisted of other devotional activities: meditation on the river steps (*ghāṭ*s), offerings to Rāma, and studying sacred texts such as the *Rāmāyaṇa*, → *Mahābhārata*, → Purāṇas, → *Bhagavādgītā*, → Upaniṣads, and many others.

After having completed three years of this intense discipline to Lord Rāma, a woman from a nearby village approached him and told him of the premature death of her husband. She asked Rāmdās' blessing for her desire to make the ultimate sacrifice along with her husband on the funeral pyre. Instead, Rāmdās requested the dead body be brought to him. After praying for Lord Rāma's compassion, he sprinkled → Gaṅgā water on the corpse, which came to life. Hence, Rāmdās' single-minded devotion to Rāma bore the fruit of miraculous powers. He promised the couple that they would be blessed with ten children. Word quickly spread of Rāmdās' powers. Uddhav, the couple's first son, was named by and dedicated to Rāmdās. In fact, Uddhav became Rāmdās' best student, and became known as Uddhav Svamī. Rāmdās created a Māruti image for Uddhav to worship, and then performed a proper ritual installation of the image, which today is located in the Takli Māruti Mandir. Although Rāmdās would subsequently create many other Māruti images, the one created for Uddhav Svamī is recognized as the first such image. Rāmdās continued his ascetic practice for 12 years, until he completed his goal of chanting his Rāma *mantra* 130 million times. During this period of daily chanting, Hanumān would assume the form of a normal monkey and observe Rāmdās. When Rāmdās completed the incredibly large number of *mantra*s, Hanumān appeared in his enormous Bhīma form to Rāmdās. In response, Rāmdās spontaneously uttered verses of praise, which became the famous *Bhīmarūpīstotra*, 13 verses to match the 13 cycles of ten million *mantra*s he had chanted to Rāma. Two additional verses at the end speak of the fruit one receives from reciting these verses, and two more are in the form of a prayer – hence the number 13 in spite of the total 17 verses. These verses are chanted from

Fig. 2: The Māruti image that Rāmdās gave to his first student, Uddhav, which is housed in the Takli Māruti Mandir, near Nasik (photo by Jeffrey Brackett).

memory by devotees, much like Hanumān devotees chant the Hindi *Hanumān Cālīsā* composed by → Tulsīdās, a Sant similar in many ways to Rāmdās in his devotion to Hanumān.

At this point, Rāmdās is still only 24 years old, and he leaves on foot, determined to visit all the holy sites around India. During this exhaustive pilgrimage, he placed Māruti images at many holy sites and established as many as 1,100 monasteries, each of which was placed under the leadership of one of his students. However, all was not well with the religious life that Rāmdās saw in his travels: Muslims had, in short, ruined Hindu society. Muslims destroyed temples, mistreated women, and were the cause of incredible injustice and oppression of Hindus. Rāmdās' response was to reform and revitalize this dire situation by encouraging devotion to both Rāma and Māruti. Overall, this program of devotion aimed at developing courage and strength, figuratively as well as literally, in the form of devotion – or worship – of physical strength (*balopāsanā*), the same type of devotion associated with bodybuilding and wrestling these days. Further, both Rāma and Māruti were known for not tolerating evildoers and offered protection to their devotees. Rāmdās' teaching of Rāma and Māruti devotion spread wherever he traveled. Rāmdās had emphasized devotion to Rāma as "*samartha*" (powerful, capable, able), and soon thereafter people attributed the same title to Rāmdās. Hence, his name became Samartha Rāmdās Svāmī, which he is known as to this day. As one would expect, Rāmdās' exhibited other divine traits: lovely speech, lustrous visage, unparalleled wisdom, and miraculous powers. Taken together, these characteristics – earned through his unwavering asceticism – gave Rāmdās confidence to spread the rule of Rāma (*rāmrājya*), an ideal espoused in the *Rāmāyaṇa*, which narrated a time of peace and well-being in Lord Rāma's capital of Ayodhyā. Rāmdās instilled confidence in his devotees, causing them to think him to be an *avatāra* of Hanumān himself. Recalling that his father was told that his second son would have a portion of Māruti in him, this was no surprise. Rāmdās knew of his own special qualities before embarking on this arduous pilgrimage, as Rāma and Hanumān regularly visited him during his days in Takli. They insisted he settle near the Kṛṣṇā River, but both consented to his desire first to travel to all the holy sites of India. When his sacred pilgrimage was finished, he indeed settled by the Kṛṣṇā River, near Chaphal, which would later become a modern pilgrimage destination.

Now that Rāmdās was back in Maharashtra, his work toward spreading Māruti devotion gained speed. Although he established as many as 1,100 (or more) Māruti temples, it was his special set of 11 temples (Mar. Akrā Mārutī Mandirs) that forms a pilgrimage circuit today. Each site has a story explaining how and why Rāmdās created the temple's Māruti image. Chaphal became the main temple among this set of 11. It has a large Rāma temple, two Māruti temples, a monastery, and a cave where Rāmdās meditated. Due in part to its modest food and lodging on the premises, and its proximity to a main highway, Chaphal is the most frequented of the 11 special Māruti temples. Less than one kilometer up the road behind Chaphal is a third Māruti, the small shrine of Singanvadi on the side of a hill. Near the shrine is another cave where Rāmdās regularly meditated. Most important, though, is the memorial at the bottom of the hill that marks the site where Rāmdās and King Śivājī met for the first time in 1649. At the meeting, Śivājī became Rāmdās' disciple. They met regularly from that time forward, and on one occasion, Śivājī symbolically gave Rāmdās his kingdom in his alms bag. Of course, Rāmdās gave it back and told Śivājī to continue his responsibilities as a Kṣatriya, namely, protecting → *dharma* and his loyal subjects. Together, Śivājī and Rāmdās could spread *mahārāṣṭra dharma* – one working in the political arena, with the other restoring proper religious devotion. Both worked to erase the negative impact of Muslim tyranny. When King Śivājī died (1680), Rāmdās did not continue his role as the new king's advisor.

The preceding, short biography of Rāmdās is well known in Maharashtra. Portions of this story are depicted in public murals (e.g. Rāmdās with Śivājī overlooking a battlefield), written into standard history books for schoolchildren, and available in numerous bookstalls. While many of the English retellings are stories aimed at a young audience, there are monographs about Rāmdās' life available for adults interested in devotional perspectives on the importance of Rāmdās as a spiritual guide for modern times (Apte, 1965; Bokil, 1979; Date, 1975; Lata, 1991). An earlier work about Rāmdās and the Rāmdāsīs (Deming, 1928) has a different tone. W.S. Deming's book, apart from its final chapter (*Rāmdās and Jesus*) that asserts the superiority of Christian teachings, contains much valuable information. The Rāmdāsis have never had a strong presence in the religious life of Maharashtra, in part, because the region itself is not as well known for monastic organizations as other areas of modern India. Further, the Rāmdāsīs' sphere of religious influence may be linked to a subregional location at Sajjangad, in the Satara district, where Rāmdās spent much of his adult life. It is in and around the Satara district that the Akrā Mārutī Mandirs were established by Rāmdās. While these 11 temples create a pilgrimage sequence, along the lines of the circuit of eight temples to Gaṇpatī (→ Gaṇapati/Gaṇeśa) surrounding Pune, there is no clear reason why these particular 11 were elevated to this special pilgrimage status. Even P.V. Harshe, whose book about the 11 temples expresses hope that the temples will become more popular pilgrimage destinations, says, "there is no satisfying answer" (Harshe, 1983, 27; trans. by author) regarding why other Rāmdās temples were not among these exclusive 11.

A central issue debated among scholars and devotees is the initial meeting date, as well as

Fig. 3: Rāmdās on a mural in one of the Akrā Mārutī Mandirs, the Pārgāv temple. The ten images on either side of him are ten of the eleven Mārutis; the 11th is in his shoulder bag (photo by Jeffrey Brackett).

the frequency of meetings, between Rāmdās and King Śivājī. S.G. Tulpule, a renowned scholar of Marathi literature, notes that there is strong evidence in favor of both the early (1649) and later (1672) meeting dates and opts himself for the earlier one (Tulpule, 1979, 395n449). This debate is connected to other elements of Rāmdās' modern biographies, such as his views of, and interactions with, Muslims. In the short retelling above, Hindus and Muslims are depicted as perpetually adversarial, with Muslims as the primary cause of religious and cultural strife. Archival historical research presents a more nuanced view of Hindu–Muslim interactions in the Deccan region, which suggests a degree of cultural exchanges and dynamics more complex than some conventional hagiographies in circulation these days would lead a reader to believe (Gordon, 1993; 2003, 26). That an extraordinary person such as Rāmdās would be recalled differently at particular historical moments in diverse manners illustrates the continued relevance of historical figures. The same could be said of other exemplary persons, poet-saints, *gurus*, or deities, both within and outside Indic tradition. From within Indic tradition, one could consult Mahipatī's lengthy hagiography of Rāmdās for a much fuller account than the brief story narrated above. Mahipatī mentions eight brief interactions between Rāmdās and Muslims (see Lutgendorf, 2007, 76–79). A frequently cited good biography of Rāmdās in Marathi remains the work of S.K. Alatekar (1933), which has been reprinted many times. Further, Rāmdās scholar Dev of Dhule, Maharashtra, established a center for Rāmdās studies, which is a wonderful resource for Marathi manuscripts (Shri Samartha Vagdevata Mandir, Dhule).

Rāmdās himself was prolific and wrote in numerous styles. S.G. Tulpule provides a brief overview of his writings (Tulpule, 1979, 395–400). Less famous, but certainly recognized by many Maharashtrian devotees and literary scholars, are Rāmdās' early *Karuṇāṣṭaka*, a collection referred to as the "pathetic verses" due to their blending of pathetic and sweet emotions (Tulpule, 1979, 395). Rāmdās also composed two versions (one long, one short) of two chapters (*kāṇḍas*) of the *Rāmāyaṇa*: the *Sundara* (Beautiful) and *Yuddha* (War). These selections may well be due to the increased importance of Hanumān in those portions of the epic. S.G. Tulpule links the selection of these two portions of the *Rāmāyaṇa* to Rāmdās' desire:

> to emphasise that phase of Rāma's life in which he appeared on earth to liberate the gods from the bondage of the demon-king Rāvaṇa, suggesting the emancipation of the Hindus from the slavery of the Muslim rulers. The only remedy to achieve this was an effort based upon devotion to God (*upāsanā*) which he explained at large in still other stray compositions entitled Rājadharma, Kṣātradharma and Sāvadhāna, all addressed to king Śivājī. (Tulpule, 1979, 396)

S.G. Tulpule presents the reader with Rāmdās as engaging King Śivājī through his writings and lends support to the conventional biographies mentioned previously. Most popular in terms of everyday practice is Rāmdās' *Bhīmarūpīstotra*, a set of verses "addressed to Hanumān" (Tulpule, 1979, 396) that remind devotees of Hanumān's characteristics. These verses are chanted by many Maharashtrians, whether they consider themselves devotees of Hanumān or not. Rāmdās actually composed 13 different *Bhīmarūpīstotras*, but one has become recognized as *the Bhīmarūpīstotra*. Along with these lesser-known → Stotras, S.G. Tulpule notes that Rāmdās also composed in various genres and utilized diverse meters and styles (Tulpule, 1979, 396–397). These lesser-known compositions pale in comparison to the honored status attributed to his *Manāce Ślok* and *Dāsbodh*, both of which can be read in English translations.

One can locate serviceable English translations of Rāmdās' most famous works, *Manāce Ślok* and *Dāsbodh*, but little else has been translated from Marathi. Since the *Manāce Ślok* is often memorized, English renditions often lose the poetic, rhythmic, and nuanced flavors found in the original; this situation is common, to be sure, with translations. The status, length, and importance of *Dāsbodh* as a collection of Rāmdās' philosophical and religious ideas make it valuable to the specialist and nonspecialist alike. The first English version available in India was published fairly recently (Tambwekar, 1991) by the Shri Samarth Ramdas Swami Krupa Trust, which was founded in 1983. Originally, the group published Rāmdās' work in Gujarati. W.G. Tambwekar's experience in the management sector inspired him to publish a separate book, *Sprinklings of Management from Dasbodh* (Tambwekar, 1995). This "practical application" of Rāmdās' 17th-century ideas is one illustration of Rāmdās' appeal to modern, urban life. A newer translation of *Dāsbodh* is also now in print and is edited by a nonnative speaker of Marathi who commissioned three English translations from which to create his own edition (Moe, 2010). The intentions for creating these new English translations of *Dāsbodh* may parallel S.G. Tulpule's estimation of Rāmdās as a "spiritual activist" (Tulpule, 1979, 397). But S.G. Tulpule goes further and summarizes well a number of reasons for Rāmdās' continued appeal today:

> The Dāsabodha is a peculiar combination of the poet's observation of the ways of the world, his devotional fervor, metaphysical thought, socio-political understanding and mystical experience. It is, in fact, a history of the doings and thoughts of a great thinker-saint, who was also a poet. The chief value of its counsel lies in the practical hints and the inspiration they give to those who aspire for direct Realisation. These instructions, given in an easy style, are as refreshing and touching as direct talk, and being universal in their appeal, can be easily understood by all. There is something for everyone, and there always is some rational appeal. To those who have already made an effort to

start upon the way it is full of sudden insights and profound counsels. Yet there is nothing in it that is startling. It is clearly and surely in the Tradition – this is the voice of Rāmadāsa and of the whole apostolic succession from the dawn of time, speaking however in the vernacular of his time in intense *ovīs*, but speaking the eternal Gospel, and of the life-long quest of the soul for its own rest and reward. Here is a work written by a man of vast spiritual and worldly experience. (Tulpule, 1979, 397–398)

With praise such as this, it is no surprise that Rāmdās' imprint on Maharashtrian life continues in the contemporary period.

Bibliography

Abbott, J.E., *Rāmdās: Translation of Mahipatī's Santavijaya*, Poona, 1932.

Alatekar (Āḷtekar), S.K., *Śrī Samartha Caritra*, Pune, 1933 (Mar.).

Alter, J.S., *The Wrestler's Body*, Berkeley, 1992.

Apte, S.S., *Samarth Ramdas: Life and Mission*, Bombay, 1965.

Bokil, V.P., *Rajguru Ramdas*, Poona, 1979.

Date, V.H., *Spiritual Treasure of Saint Rāmdāsa*, Delhi, 1975.

Deming, W.S., *Rāmdās and the Rāmdāsīs*, London, 1928.

Gordon, S., "Hindus, Muslims, and the Other in Eighteenth-Century India," in: S. Mittal, ed., *Surprising Bedfellows: Hindus and Muslims in Medieval and Early Modern India*, Lanham, 2003, 11–30.

Gordon, S., *The Marathas: 1600–1818*, Cambridge UK, 1993.

Harshe (Harṣe), P.V., *Samartha Sthāpit Akrā Mārutī*, Mumbai, 1983 (Mar.).

Lata, P., *Shri Samartha Ramdas*, New Delhi, 1991.

Lutgendorf, P., *Hanuman's Tale*, New York, 2007.

Moe, D., ed., *Dasbodh: Spiritual Instruction for the Servant*, Santa Fe, 2010.

Tambwekar, W.G., *Sprinklings of Management from Dasbodh*, Bombay, 1995.

Tambwekar, W.G., *Dasbodh: An English Version*, Bombay, 1991.

Tulpule, S.G., *Classical Marāṭhī Literature: From the Beginning to A.D. 1818.*, Wiesbaden, 1979.

Vaudeville, C., "The Shaivite Background of Santism in Maharashtra," in: M. Israel & N.K. Wagle, eds., *Religion and Society in Maharashtra*, Toronto, 1987a, 32–50.

Vaudeville, C., "The Shaiva-Vaishnava Synthesis in Maharashtrian Santism," in: K. Schomer & W.H. McLeod, eds., *The Sants: Studies in a Devotional Tradition of India*, Delhi, 1987b, 215–228.

Vaudeville, C., "Paṇḍharpūr, the City of Saints," in: H.M. Buck & G.E. Yocum, eds., *Structural Approaches to South Indian Studies*, Chambersburg, 1974, 137–161.

JEFFREY M. BRACKETT

Rāmprasād Sen

The 18th-century poet Rāmprasād Sen is most well known for his songs to the goddess → Kālī. His poems and songs mixed imagery from *kuṇḍalinīyoga* (see → Yoga) and esoteric tantric meditation with devotion to the goddess, and he created a new style of goddess worship in India, which is often called Śākta → *bhakti*. He also mixed classical melodies, → Bāul personalism, Vaiṣṇava → *kīrtan*, and local folk styles of music together in his songs, which came to be called Rāmprasādī Saṅgīt. He has been called the main originator and founder of the new Śākta movement, the first Śākta poet to sing of the goddess Kālī as a loving mother or a little girl. His poetry is still popular in West Bengal today, as a major part of Śākta Padābali or poetry dedicated to the goddess.

Rāmprasād's poetic style was simple and direct, written in a colloquial style of Bengali language, and his epics were popular in their time (today, only his *Vidyāsundar* and *Kālīkīrtan* survive in full). Many of his poems reflect the difficulties faced during his lifetime: the famine of 1770 (during which it is said that almost one third of the population of Bengal starved to death), political and economic instability, and the problems of rural culture. However, as with most Śākta poets, history was only a distant background for devotional poetry showing an intimate relationship with the goddess and concerns about death and salvation. He is often called the most beloved of Bengali poets, and its greatest religious practitioner or *sādhaka*.

Biography

There is little historical data on Rāmprasād's life, and most Bengali sources on his life and work have not been translated into English. Scholars debate his exact dates of birth and death, which we can broadly estimate here as around 1720–1781. The major early biographies on his life came from I. Gupta's set of articles in the journal *Saṃbād Prabhākar*, published in the 1850s (Gupta had collected Rāmprasād's songs for 25 years), and D. Ghosh's *Prasād Prasaṅga*, published in 1875. Both of these were written almost a century after Rāmprasād's death and tend to focus on stories that were carried down by oral tradition about his life (with a strong emphasis on stories of miracles, legends, and visions).

It is generally accepted by scholars that there are about 350 songs by Rāmprasād (many songs were lost, as some of those written down were destroyed by insects and moisture, and others were hidden, used for ritual worship, and dissolved by the sandalwood paste and flowers placed on them). There is some confusion about how many poets wrote under the name of Rāmprasād, and which poets wrote which songs. Some of Rāmprasād's poems were written by the original Rāmprasād Sen, of the Vaidya caste from Kumārhaṭṭa in West Bengal (today Halisahar), which was during his lifetime a center for tantric worship. Other poems appear to be written by a second Rāmprasād, a Calcutta Brahman and younger contemporary of the first, who also wrote Śākta devotional songs. Some scholars also make claims for a third and fourth Rāmprasād, possibly from Bangladesh. This confusion is caused because many people wrote songs that had Rāmprasād's poetic signature phrases (*bhaṇitā*), and indeed many people at the time were named Rāmprasād ("Blessed by Rama"). Some signed their songs "Rāmprasād says" and added prefixes like Din ("Poor") and Dvija ("Twice-Born"). However, Śākta devotees do not tend to distinguish which songs may come from which poets, and they only speak of one Rāmprasād who was a great devotee and who died from an overdose of love for the mother.

According to popular tradition, the original Rāmprasād Sen was born into a Śākta family, and his father, Rāmrām Sen, was a distributor of ayurvedic medicines. He studied Sanskrit grammar and literature and Bengali poetry, while he was young. He later studied Urdu and Persian, the languages of the Muslim rulers of Bengal. Though his father wanted him to follow their traditional caste occupation and become a physician, Rāmprasād was more interested in the arts and humanities, and he studied them throughout his teen years. According to later biographers, he was initiated into the *kālīmantra* by the family → *guru* (*kulaguru*), the famous tantric practitioner and scholar Kṛṣṇānanda Āgamavāgīśa (author of the *Tantrasāra*), and he studied Śākta ritual practice with several other *gurus*. He spent much time in worship and meditation. He later married Śārvāṇī,

This image shows the more benevolent aspect of the goddess Kālī that has developed with the rise of Śākta *bhakti*. Rather than being the terrifying figure of death, Kālī has become a beautiful woman who helps her devotees (photo by Jim Denosky, contributed by June McDaniel).

all during the night (a later story has the Bengali *siddha* Ramakrishna Paramhamsa worshipping his wife Śāradā in a similar way). According to another story, Rāmprasād performed the corpse ritual (*śavasādhana*) and had a vision of Kālī in her form as Ādyaśakti Mahāmāyā ("Primordial Goddess Who Creates the Universe of Illusion").

After the Mahārāja Kṛṣṇacandra's death, Rāmprasād retreated from the world and his family and spent his time in meditation. He is said to have died of love on the festival of *kālīpūjā*, as the Kālī statue was being immersed in the Gaṅgā River, with the vision of the goddess before his eyes.

Rāmprasādī Songs

Rāmprasād's poetry and songs (called *śyāmāsaṇgit* or songs to the dark goddess) focus on a single great goddess, who is most frequently called Kālī, though sometimes she is also called → Durgā, Bhairavī, Sītā (see → Draupadī and Sītā), Umā, or Kālikā. He also wrote some longer works, including the *Kālīkīrtan, Kṛṣṇakīrtan, Vidyāsundar*, and *padābali* songs. Many of his poems and songs were based on the *Devīmāhātmya* story, in which the goddess conquers the forces of passion and evil. There are also songs of secret *sādhana* practices and songs that emphasized the importance of passionate love (which must be experienced and cannot be found in books or philosophies). Devotion draws the goddess like a magnet attracts iron, and the poems include both dualistic and monistic imagery.

As examples of his work, the following poems are translations from the popular booklet *Rāmprasādī Saṅgīt* (Songs of Rāmprasād). This book is sold today at Śākta temples and *pīṭhas* (sites sacred to the goddess) in West Bengal, for use by priests, singers, and devotees. The poems of Rāmprasād are often called "Rāmprasādī," a genre named after him.

Rāmprasād was often called "love mad" (insane due to his love of the goddess) by his friends and family, but for Rāmprasād their opinions were not important. Here he describes his ecstatic experience (*bhāva*, a local abbreviation for *mahābhāva* or highest state). As a note, Kālī is traditionally believed to have had red feet, which are considered to be beautiful by her devotees.

O Mā Kālī, wearing a garland of skulls
What an experience (*bhāva*) you have shown me!
You taught me how to call you
And at the moment I chanted "Mā"
You drove me to ecstasy!
Mā Tārā, please tell me the source (of your sweetness)
Where did you get this name full of nectar?
When worldly people look at me
They call me mad from love
The members of my family
Hurl curses and insults at me.
But whatever people say, dark mother
My faith will not waver.
Let people say what they want
I will chant the name of Kālī forever.
If you get rid of this illusory world
Insults and pride are unimportant.
I have made your red feet my goal.
I am no longer concerned with worldly opinions. (*Rāmprasādī Saṅgīt*, n.d., 47; trans. by author)

Imagery of death and salvation abounds in his poems. A partial version of this next poem is popularized in a recent film about the Thuggee sect, *The Deceivers* (The Thuggees or Ṭhagīs were members of criminal tribes described by British writers of the 18th-19th centuries. Composed of both Hindu and Muslim members, they worshipped Bhavānī Kālī, and were known for murdering groups of travelers for their money, primarily by strangling them):

Because you love the burning ground
I have made a burning ground of my heart
So that you, dark goddess, can dance there forever.
I have no other desire left, O Mother
A funeral pyre is blazing in my heart.
Ashes from corpses are all around me, my Mother
In case you decide to come.
Prasād prays, "O Mother, at the hour of death
Keep your devotee at your feet.
Please come dancing with rhythmic steps
Let me see you when my eyes are closed." (*Rāmprasādī Saṅgīt*, n.d., 46; trans. by author)

Several of his poems emphasize the value of devotion over the sort of states of unity and emptiness emphasized in Vedānta and Buddhism and use tantric imagery, such as the *cakras* of *kuṇḍalinīyoga*:

Mother is as beautiful
As a sky full of blue clouds.
She is naked, and her hair is wild.
O mind, you do not realize
She dances in the *sahasrāra(cakra)* and *mūlādhāra(cakra)*
She is in a state of bliss
She is like a swan moving through a lake of lotuses.
Place this blissful mother in your heart
And joyfully light the fire of wisdom
So that you can look deeply into her infinite beauty.
Prasād says, "She loves to fulfill the desires of her devotees
Tell me, what virtue can *nirvāṇa* have
Compared with her love?" (*Rāmprasādī Saṅgīt*, n.d., 24; trans. by author)

Rāmprasād worshipped Kālī, the dark goddess, but some of his songs deny the darkness of the goddess. This poem is often attributed to another Rāmprasād, Dvija Rāmprasād:

O mind, tell me what ritual you performed
To find this black girl.
When I see the radiance of this dark beauty
Everything else disappears from my eyes and my mind.
In whose house did she live?
How did you bring her here?
She is not black, she is a full moon
Which floods the heart with light.
Her feet are as beautiful
As the rising sun which glows at dawn.
Dvija Rāmprasād says, "Those feet would be prettier
With an offering of red hibiscus (*jaba*) flowers." (*Rāmprasādī Saṅgīt*, n.d., 48)

While Kālī is beautiful and mysterious, she does not always answer her worshippers' prayers, and many songs involve complaining about the goddess' neglect and ill-treatment. The moods of complaint and anger (sometimes called *nāliśa*s or *krodhabhāva*s) often appear in Śākta poetry. Here is a poem from the collection by L. Nathan and C. Seely:

I'm not calling you Mother anymore,
All You give me is trouble.
I had a home and a family, now
I'm a beggar – what will You think of
Next, my wild-haired Devi?
I'll beg before I come to You,
Crying "Mother." I've tried that
And got the silent treatment.
If the mother lives should the son suffer
And if she's dead, hasn't he got to live somehow?
Ramprasad says: What's a mother
Anyway, the son's worst enemy?
I keep wondering what worse You can do
Than make me live over and over
The pain, life after life. (Nathan & Seely, 1982, 35)

Some of Rāmprasād's poems to Kālī focus upon love and devotion, while others involve → liberation from the world, with Kālī as the goddess of ultimate freedom (in her role as Kaivalyadāyiṇī ["Giver of Liberation"]). Perhaps Rāmprasād's most famous poem emphasizes the importance of distance in appreciating the goddess:

Every time I hear about Gaya
The offerings there, the good deeds
Recited, I laugh. I know Shiva
Has said that dying at Kashi saves.
But I know too that salvation
Always follows worship around
Like a slave, and what's this salvation
If it swallows the saved like water
In water? Sugar I love
But haven't the slightest desire
To merge with sugar.
Ramprasad says with amazement:
Grace and mercy in Her wild hair-
Think of that
And all good things are yours. (trans. Nathan & Seely, 1982, 54)

Some of Rāmprasād's songs deal with the holiday of *durgāpūjā*, celebrated in Bengal by welcoming the goddess as parents might welcome a daughter returning home for a visit.

The *āgamanī* (welcome) and *vijaya* (farewell) songs greet the goddess (called both Durgā and Kālikā) to her parents' home at the beginning of *durgāpūjā* and bid farewell to her, as the holiday ends, and she leaves to return to her husband. While these songs were widely sung during the 19th and early 20th centuries, today they are heard only on *durgāpūjā*. These songs are clear examples of the importance of emotional *bhakti*, for they are intended to involve the audience with personal emotions, with love and sorrow, toward a goddess in human form. They show more folk tradition than classical Hinduism, portraying the goddess as an unhappily married girl, her husband Śiva as a lazy drunkard, and her family as frustrated and concerned for her well-being. These are not high and powerful gods but a human family with whom to sympathize, and the goddess is understood to be vulnerable rather than all-powerful. In these songs, the deities are like people, and they share human pain and sorrow. The goddess is welcomed home with open arms, as Rāmprasād states,

> "Today is a lucky day for you!
> Your daughter is coming home, go and greet her.
> Come and see her moon-like face, and your misery will vanish.
> Her bright smile is like nectar flowing."
> On hearing this, the queen runs out with her hair and clothing loose
> She is so full of love that tears roll down from her eyes.
> She leaves the King behind, and she hugs Uma and weeps with joy.
> She puts Uma on her lap, and looks at her beautiful face and kisses her.
> She says, "Your father is king of the mountain, but your husband was born a beggar.
> You are such a wonderful daughter, and I have married you to naked Shiva."
> Uma's friends are filled with happiness, they laugh and hold her hands.
> They say, "How could you forget us for a year, when we love you so much?
> Lift your face and speak to us, or we shall die!"
> The poet Rāmprasād laughs within himself, and is immersed in an ocean of joy.
> When the Divine Mother comes, the people of the world are overjoyed
> They cannot tell day from night… (trans. Sinha, 1966, 144–145)

Rāmprasād poems include techniques of tantric worship, with visualization and interiorized offerings, and *kuṇḍalinīyoga* practices, as well as a variety of relationships with the goddess (she is his mother, daughter, friend, and ruler, as well as a madwoman). His play *Vidyāsundar* glorifies the goddess Kālī; she grants the hero Sundar supernatural powers, through which he gains his beloved Vidyā, and it includes the hero's performance of the corpse ritual (*śavasādhana*).

Rāmprasād Sen and Bengali Śāktism

Bengal has a long tradition of worship of goddesses, but this was not always a devotional tradition. We may categorize three types of Bengali Śāktism or goddess worship.

In the oldest form, the folk Hinduism of the villages, there are moody and violent local goddesses, who are sometimes ancestresses of the group. The tribal goddess is often a form of Kālī, dark and powerful, who may be worshipped as a village goddess (*grāmadevatā*) or a powerful supernatural woman (→ *yoginī*). Village goddesses may be dangerous and threatening, but they may also be protective and benevolent if they are worshipped and propitiated. The folk tradition of goddess worship is primarily an oral tradition that is handed down from village elders or priests. Encounters with goddesses, especially Kālī, occur primarily in dreams or visions, and goddesses may issue dream commands and reveal empowered rocks and statues that have been hidden. While the daily rituals and traditions of village goddess worship are handed down in family and local groups, in its shamanic aspects (in which goddesses are invoked for healing, → divination, and other practical reasons), there are initiations of specialists by *ojhā*s and *guṇin*s. Shamanic practitioners may encounter goddesses spontaneously in nature, where they are associated with trees, mountains, rivers, and lakes, or they may learn to invoke them through ritual.

The second form of goddess worship may be called tantric or yogic Śāktism. Its origins are much debated, but tantric elements may be found in writings of the 6th century CE, and texts called → Tantras were written by the 9th century CE. The vision of goddesses, especially the goddess Kālī, is gained by certain forms of meditation and visualization, as well as ritual worship, making use of mantras, → *mudrā*s (hand positions), and *yantra*s (visual diagrams; usually understood to be symbolic maps of the spiritual worlds; see → *maṇḍala* and *yantra*). Yogic practice is often involved, especially *kunḍalinīyoga*, and the goddess can give spiritual knowledge or entrance into universal consciousness (*brahmajñāna*). In its aspect of folk Tantra, the practitioner may gain *siddhi*s (powers); in its more classical forms, he or she may gain knowledge of natural and supernatural worlds, as well as liberation. Tantra and *yoga* are similar practices in Bengali Śāktism, and many practitioners combine them in ritual worship of the ten *mahāvidyā*s (for *mahāvidyā*s see → Kālī).

The goddess may also be understood as a loving mother who saves her devotees from painful rebirth and gives them protection from harm as well as entrance into her heaven. This third and most widespread style of Kālī worship is that of

Śākta devotion, or Kālī *bhakti*. This is the type of Śāktism that was emphasized and popularized by Rāmprasād Sen in his poetry. During the medieval period, Śāktism was primarily an esoteric religion practiced by small groups of tantric *yogīs* – until the puranic texts popularized the powers and adventures of the goddess, and later poetry portrayed her as beautiful and loving. The 18th-century *bhakti* poets, such as Rāmprasād and Kamalākānta, imagined her as a loving mother and a beautiful young girl, and devotional worship grew up around these images. She is Kālī Mā, the universal mother or innocent girl, who is sometimes frightening on the outside but inwardly loving and compassionate. Śākta *bhakti* also emphasizes that intense love of the deity is more valuable than simple obedience, thus showing the influence of Vaiṣṇava ideas of emotional *bhakti*.

The goddess has a variety of roles – mother, child, friend, and lover. She expects passionate devotion and dependence from her worshippers, who are most often described as her children. The most intense love is not romantic love, but rather parent/child love. Some devotees begin with the emotion of fear toward her terrible forms, but they end up loving her when they see the sweetness within her. The devotee loves extravagantly; he (or she) is unworthy, pleading, and swings between elation and depression, loving the world because the goddess is present there or hating it because she has not appeared. The ideal attitude is total dependence, with love evoking divine vision (*darśan*), in which goddess and devotee meet and recognize each other.

Some forms of Śākta *bhakti* show the influence of folk or popular Tantra. This includes an emphasis upon ritual practice, direct experience, and pragmatic results. Kālī gives supernatural abilities (*siddhi*), and she appears to the practitioner in the forest or cremation ground. She may also be ritually located in various parts of the human body by the practice of *nyāsa* (in which a variety of deities are visualized in areas of the body to sanctify and protect the person). The *tāntrika* sits on the cremation ground performing meditation, purifying his or her body, and visualizing the goddess. In classical or scholastic Tantra, Kālī is symbolic of liberation (*mokṣa*) and is understood to be a personification of infinite consciousness (→ *brahman*). She is able to grant the classical *tāntrika* the gift of liberation. Her forms, whether beautiful or terrifying, are understood to be a part of her → *līlā*, her play of illusion. They are used to test the *tāntrika*'s worthiness and knowledge. The Śākta *bhakti*, which is influenced by classical Tantra, has a greater interest in the goddess' states of awareness than in her love.

Rāmprasād changed the popular images of the goddess, from the dangerous village *grāmadevatā* and wrathful *yoginī* to a loving mother and compassionate woman. His poetry penetrates her outer forms to reveal her inner ones, and his songs look beyond anger to see infinite forgiveness and mercy. He was a major founder of Śākta *bhakti*, a style of worship that has become important in Bengali culture and is still an important ritual focus in the modern world.

Bibliography

Bhattacarya, S.N., *Rāmprasād: Jībanī o Racanāsamagra*, Calcutta, 1975.

Cakrabarti, J.K., *Śāktapādabalī o Śaktisādhana*, Calcutta, 1956.

Gupta, Y., *Sādhak Kabi Rāmprasād*, Calcutta, 1954.

McDermott, R.F., *Mother of My Heart, Daughter of My Dreams: Kali and Uma in the Devotional Poetry of Bengal*, New York, 2001.

McLean, M., *Devoted to the Goddess: The Life and Work of Rāmprasād*, Albany, 1998.

Nathan, L., & C. Seely, *Grace and Mercy in Her Wild Hair: Poems to the Mother Goddess by Rāmprasād Sen*, Prescott, 1982.

Rāmprasādī Saṅgīt, Calcutta, n.d.

Sinha, J.N., *Ramaprasad's Devotional Songs: The Cult of Shakti*, Calcutta, 1966.

Thompson, E., & A, Spencer, *Bengali Religious Lyrics, Śākta*, Calcutta, 1923.

June McDaniel

Ravidās

Ravidās, who is also known as Raidās in Hindi and Rohidās in Marathi, is remembered in India as the greatest poet-saint of the → *bhakti* tradition from an untouchable community. He was a younger contemporary of → Kabīr, but the precise dates of Kabīr's and Ravidās's lives are not known, although contemporary scholarship suggests that Ravidās probably lived from around 1500 to 1550 CE (Callewaert & Friedlander, 1992). Ravidās and Kabīr are thought to have lived and worked within communities where → oral traditions, rather than written traditions, were dominant. Due to this, there is little likelihood of finding either Ravidās' works in their exact original form or the precise factual details of his life. However, his importance is evident from the wide range of traditions in which stories circulate about his life and spiritual achievements. In these sources his life story is not told in the form of a modern biography but rather in a narration of a series of episodes that witness to his authority as a spiritual figure. In this entry I will not attempt to construct a historical biography of Ravidās, but instead trace the outlines of how the episodes in his life were contextualised over time by different communities.

Early Traditions

By the mid-16th century, Ravidās verses were part of the oral-performance traditions of religious songs that were current at that time in the → Punjab. By around 1570 CE, a number of Ravidās verses were first written down in the texts called the *Goindval Pothīs*, which were the precursors of the Sikh holy text, the *Gurū Granth Sāhib*, which was written down in 1603–1604 CE. This earliest extant recension of Ravidās verses contains around 40 verses and is included in the section of the *Gurū Granth Sāhib* called the *Bhagat Bāṇī* (Words of Devotees). Like Hebrew Bible prophets, the works and stories of the *bhagats* (pre-Sikh saints) act as precursors to those of the teachers to come and act as witnesses to the greatness of the Sikh teachings revealed by the Sikh Gurūs.

The earliest extensive account of Ravidās' life from a Sikh perspective comes from the *Pothī Prem Ambodh*, which dates from the time of the tenth Sikh Gurū Gobind Siṅgh and was composed in 1693 CE. This contains accounts of the lives of 16 *bhagats* whose works are found in the *Gurū Granth Sāhib*, including Kabīr and Ravidās, and → Mīrā Bāī (Sābar, 1984).

The *Pothī Prem Ambodh* starts by describing Ravidās' birth as a Camār and how when he was growing up he practiced his caste vocation as a shoemaker. It also describes how he did not have the right to study the → Vedas and Śāstras but was very spiritual and became absorbed in devotion to the divine. It then describes how he once gave a Brahman a coin to offer to the goddess Gaṅgā, who in return gave a golden bracelet to the Brahman to give to Ravidās. However, the Brahman gave the bracelet to his wife, and eventually this led to the king being informed about the marvellous bracelet and the Brahman being asked to hand over a matching bracelet to complete a pair of bracelets, which he could not do. This led to Ravidās being tested before the king and the goddess Gaṅgā manifesting her hand from the water trough he used for leather work and presenting him with another bracelet.

There is then a brief mention of how Ravidās' fame spread and how Mīrā Bāī came to see him and decided to become his disciple. This is followed by a story about how the Brahmans complained to the king that Ravidās was worshipping a *śāligram*, an aniconic stone symbol of → Viṣṇu, but that he had no right to do this. This then led to a contest before the king in which both Ravidās and the Brahmans had to try to make a *śāligram* float on water. However, the Brahmans cheated and used a fake wooden *śāligram*. But in the end it was Ravidās' real stone *śāligram* that floated on the water like a duck, while the Brahmans' *śāligram* sank. In the *Pothi Prem Ambodh* account of Mīrā Bāī's life, it also mentioned at its beginning that she went to visit Ravidās and had become devoted to his lotus feet.

These four elements – Ravidās' birth as a Camār in Varanasi, the story of the golden bracelet and the goddess Gaṅgā, the story of the *śāligram*, and having a queen from Rajasthan become his disciple – form the core of the traditional story of Ravidās.

At the same time as Ravidās verses were circulating in the Punjab, they were also part of the oral traditions current in → Rajasthan, and there are many references to Ravidās in → Sant works from the 17th century onward. Prominent among these are Dādūpanthī sources. → Dādū Dayāl (1544–1603 CE) was a Rajasthanī spiritual teacher who was, like Kabīr and Ravidās, a Sant, one devoted to the divine in aniconic form, or without qualities (→ *nirguṇ*). Anthologies of Dādū's works often take the form of collections of the works of five major saints, which apart from Dādū himself include Kabīr and Ravidās, and taken together their teachings form the core of the beliefs of the followers of Dādū, the Dādūpanth. In a way that is analogous to the role that the *bhagat*s play for the Sikhs in Dādūpanthī works, Ravidās becomes part of the pantheon of Sants who act as witnesses to the greatness of the Sant traditions, which Dādū and his followers honored. Some manuscripts have around 40 verses, some more than a hundred, and the number kept growing over time from the earliest known manuscript from 1614 CE onward. One of the longer verses attributed to Ravidās was called the *Prahlād Līlā*. This was the story of the devotee Prahlād and his father the king of Multan, Hiraṇyakaśipu, and how the Narasiṃha → *avatār* of Viṣṇu manifested in order to protect his devotee Prahlād by killing Hiraṇyakaśipu.

A second major early source on Ravidās' life is from a Rajasthani collection of lives of *bhakti* saints by Anantdās called the *Bhaktaratanāvalī*. This work was possibly composed in 1588 CE, but the oldest manuscripts of it date from 1636 CE and 1665 CE, and D. Lorenzen has suggested that possibly no one single original fixed text may have existed (Lorenzen, 1991). Anantdās was a follower of → Rāmānand and was active at Raiwasa in Rajasthan. Rāmānand was a high-caste saint who accepted followers from both high and low castes, from Brahmans to low-caste devotees, like Ravidās, and even Muslims like Kabīr. This also suggests that the audiences for stories among → Rāmānandī followers would have included members from both high and low castes. It is perhaps due to this that Anantdās' account includes elements that relate to how Ravidās became Rāmānand's disciple and why Ravidās was born as an untouchable.

According to Anantdās, Ravidās had been born as a Camār due to bad → *karma* from not being a vegetarian in a previous life when he was a Brahman. However, at birth he would not suckle, and it was only due to the intervention of Rāmānand that he was saved when his entire family abandoned being worshippers of → Śiva and became worshippers of Viṣṇu. Then when Ravidās was growing up, he was tested by Viṣṇu, who gave him a philosopher's stone, a stone that can turn iron into gold, so that Ravidās could become rich if he wanted. However, Ravidās left it in the thatch of the roof of his hut, and after 13 months, when Viṣṇu returned, he was satisfied that Ravidās was not interested in material wealth. Viṣṇu then persuaded Ravidās to accept five gold coins a day to organize devotional activities, which Ravidās accepted.

This leads to a variant of the *śāligram* story, in which the story is the same up to the time of the test. In this version of the story, the test is that the *śāligram* stone is placed in the middle of the assembly before the king, and the Brahmans had to try to move it to their side by chanting vedic → *mantra*s, but were unsuccessful. However, when Ravidās sang a single verse over and over for almost 12 hours without stopping, Viṣṇu was moved and made the stone move to Ravidās' lap.

By this time Ravidās' fame had spread far and wide, and a queen called Jhālī, from Chittorgarh in Rajasthan, came to see him to become his devotee, at which point Ravidās returned with her to Rajasthan. In Chittorgarh the Brahmans were jealous of Ravidās and demanded that the queen should feed them before she fed her *guru*. Ravidās told the queen not to worry about this contravention of traditional practice toward a *guru*. He then sat deep in meditation and produced multiple manifestations of his body so there was one of him eating between each pair of the seven hundred Brahmans at the feast. Then the Brahmans accepted him as their *guru*. Finally, Ravidās told a story of how in a previous life he had been a Brahman who had not known about Hari, and so he had been reborn a Śūdra. However, he said all are saved by Viṣṇu, both Śūdras and Brahmans, and at this the Brahmans threw away their sacred threads (→ *yajñopavīta*).

The popularity of Sants such as Kabīr and Ravidās is also evident from their inclusion among the two hundred or so saints described in the *Bhaktamāl*. The *Bhaktamāl* (1624 CE) was the work of Nābhādās, another Rāmānandī author active at Raiwasa in Rajasthan (Lorenzen, 1991). This was a critical development in the incorporation of Ravidās and the other Sants of northern India into a larger perspective on *bhakti* traditions in Hinduism and reflects a widening circulation of stories about Ravidās among caste Hindus. It also led to the creation of the third major early source on Ravidās' life, which is the *Bhaktirasabodhinī* (1712 CE) commentary by Priyādās on Nābhādās' *Bhaktamāl* (McGregor, 1984, 108–109).

Priyādās' version of the life shares many points in common with Anantdās' account but has several significant differences. The most important of these relate to Ravidās' birth and death. For Priyādās, Ravidās in his previous life had been a disciple of Ramānand who had accepted alms food from a merchant who did business with Camārs, and due to this Rāmānand cursed him to be reborn as a Camār. Then when he was reborn he would not suckle, as he would not drink the milk of an untouchable mother, so it was only when Rāmānand came and initiated him that he was willing to suckle. At this point his father then ejected him from the family, as he had become a Vaiṣṇava. In regard to his death, Priyādās' version also contains a significant variation. Rather than the Brahmans throwing away their sacred threads, as in Anantdās' account, in the final incident, Ravidās tears open his own chest to reveal a luminous golden subtle sacred thread within his own body.

Anantdās' *Bhaktaratanāvalī* and Priyādās' *Bhaktirasabodhinī* commentaries are the earliest attested sources on Ravidās' life that incorporate the idea that he had been a Brahman in a previous life. What is notable here is that the localization of Ravidās within a context dominated by high-caste members led to attempts to find ways to understand how a low-caste figure could have become a saint. So while on the one hand these developments can be seen as attempts to appropriate Ravidās by higher-caste groups, on the other hand they also attest to growing interest in Ravidās among higher-caste communities and the ways in which they sought to understand and incorporate lower-caste religious traditions into their own religious traditions.

Another independent work that circulated from the 17th century onward was called the *Raidās Kabīr Goṣṭī* and was attributed to Rāmānanda's disciple Sain. This took the form of a debate between Ravidās and Kabīr over the superiority of *saguṇ* and *nirguṇ* forms of the deity. In some versions of this text, at the end Viṣṇu appears and declares both viewpoints valid, and in others, a queen from Rajasthan, called Jhālī, arrives and becomes Ravidās' devotee.

Early Print Cultures and the Lives of Ravidās

The 19th century was a period of great change in the religious traditions of India due to the interaction with the colonial powers and the beginnings of modernity in India. Part of this development was the beginnings of a revival in Sant traditions. A critical factor in this was the introduction of printing into northern India, which meant that from the mid-19th century onward, followers of different Sant traditions began to create printed versions of the oral and manuscript traditions of their traditional literatures.

New works on Ravidās did not emerge until the 20th century, and probably the first of these was a life of Ravidās called the *Ravidās Rāmāyaṇ* by B. Jatav, who was from Jahidpur in Meerut district (Jatav, 1911). It was first published in 1911 from Gaziabad and then from Meerut. Despite the title of the work, it was not in any way related to the → *Rāmāyaṇa*, but rather was a life of Ravidās in the same structure of *dohā* and *caupai* metres and language forms as found in the earlier 17th- and 18th-century sources. He identified himself as a Jāṭav, a Camār title that was being used by some → Dalit groups from the Agra area. Early editions of his work are about 290 pages long and were a detailed account of the life of Ravidās. In the work B. Jatav does not identify himself as the author of the work, but rather speaks of correcting and writing the text down and providing footnotes for it, which suggests that it may to some degree represent prior oral traditions that were extant in that area among the Jāṭav communities.

B. Jatav started his introduction by explaining how in the modern era people who are searching for the path to progress should know the story of their great ancestors. He then explained that originally there had been no caste system and that all people had been members of the Yādav, or Jāṭav, community. However, over time, due to religious disputes, countless *jātis* had developed. He also provides precise dates for Ravidās, who was born in VS 1427 (1370 CE) in Varanasi and lived to the age of 120 years. At the end of the work, B. Jatav describes himself as a servant of the community (*jātīy sevak*) and ends with a passionate plea for members of a wide range of low-caste *jātis*, from the Aharvār to the Rāmdāsīs, to join together under the banner of Yādav identity in order to advance their cause.

Unlike Anantdās' and Priyādās' accounts, there is no suggestion of Ravidās being a Brahman in a prior life. Instead the first episode was concerned with the background to Ravidās' birth, which was told by Nārad, a famous ancient saint of the *bhakti* traditions. Nārad praised Varanasi as a place favorable for devotion and explained how once there was a devotee called Harinanda who lived with his wife Catrakaur, but they were childless. Catrakaur persuaded Harinanda to go to the Dhaulagiri mountains to practice austerities and then to seek the help of a sage called Sanandan who granted a boon that they would have a child, who would be called Rāhu. In due time Rāhu moved to Varanasi, where he married a woman called Karmā, and then they had a child who Nārad predicted would be a great sage, called Ravidās.

In B. Jatav's account, unlike Anantdās' and Priyādās', the second episode was Ravidās engaging in a debate with Brahmans when he went to bathe in the Gaṅgā over the superiority of devotional practices (*bhakti*) over vedic ritual observances. His meeting with Rāmānand formed the third episode. This took place due to Ravidās' fame having spread after his debates with the Brahmans. The meeting with Rāmānand also took the form of a debate over the nature of spirituality, which led to Rāmānand accepting Ravidās as his disciple.

The fourth episode was the story of the bracelet and the goddess Gaṅgā, and the fifth was the story of the *śāligram*. The sixth episode was the debate with Kabīr. The seventh episode concerned how Ravidās established both religion and the nation, and this was shown by how he went on pilgrimage to sites such as Allahabad, Pushkar, Haridwar, Kurukshetra, and Multan. This was the context for the eighth episode, which was a meeting with Kabīr's daughter, Kamālī, and Mīrā Bāī at a well. Ravidās asked Mīrā Bāī for water, which she gave to him, and in return Ravidās blessed her, and she became his disciple. The ninth episode described how she was able to survive attempts by her father, the king of Chittorgarh, to poison her.

This was followed by two episodes that take the form of debates with the Nāth *yogī* Gorakhnāth (see → Nāth Sampradāya) and a Sufi saint called Sadnā Pīr. This then led to a 12th episode in which was Ravidās being summoned to Sikander Lodi's court and his being tested there, followed by his imprisonment. → Kṛṣṇa then manifested himself in the prison and miraculously saved him by opening all the doors. The 13th episode concerns how Ravidās visited Chittorgarh, where its queen, Yogavatī, becames his disciple, and the miracle of the multiple manifestations of his body at the *yāgyā* ritual feast and his defeat of the Brahmans. Finally, in a 14th episode, Ravidās returned to Varanasi, where he passed away while meditating on the shore of the Gaṅgā at Rajghat.

This was then followed by a number of other *Ravidās Rāmāyaṇ* format lives written during the 20th century, which, while they all told an essentially similar story, were, like the early accounts, quite varied in their approaches. The audience for these texts was clearly intended to be Camār families, which was a quite different audience from that of the earlier works by Anantdās and Priyādās. In a traditional section at the end of B. Jatav's work on the virtues of reading and reciting the text, B. Jatav indicates that it was intended to form the focus for devotions within families.

> In that house where this *Rāmāyaṇ* is read out,
> there shall be no sin.
> Those devotees who honour this *Rāmāyaṇ*,
> they shall pass over the ocean of existence.
> The house in which devotees read this *Rāmāyaṇ*
> shall be known in the world as saved from dishonour. (Jatav, 1911, 290)

From the mid-19th century onward, a number of Hindi-speaking publics related to trader communities also adopted Ravidās as part of alignments between new Hindi-speaking middle-class groups and Hindu reform movements. One of the movements that built on the Sant traditions was the → Radhasoami Movement, which incorporated the Sants, including Ravidās, into the lineage of its founder, and this led to Ravidās' inclusion in the series of works on the lives of the saints compiled by B.P. Agrawal in the series of volumes he published from the Belvedere Press in Allahabad in the early years of the 20th century (Agrawal, 1908). The sources for the anthology of Ravidās verses that he published in 1908 were not given, but it is likely that it drew heavily on Dādūpanthī sources.

There was also a brief biography included in the volume. It starts with the scene from Priyādās' account about Ravidās' previous Brahman birth and the curse of being reborn as a Camār. It then tells how he spent money on devotional activities, and due to this his father, Ragghū, threw him out of the house and made him and his wife live behind it. Then, quoting the *Bhaktamāl* (i.e. Priyādās' commentary on the *Bhaktamāl*), he told the story of the philosopher's stone, and then of the gift of five gold coins and how the Brahmans complained to the king about Ravidās' actions but were defeated. Then he told the story about Queen Jhālī of Chittorgarh, and how she became his disciple and the final miracle in which he defeated the Brahmans of Chittorgarh at the feast and revealed the subtle golden thread within his own body. B.P. Agrawal also commented that this story was generally well known, but was spoken of as Mīrā Bāī's feast. He then told another story, which he said was famous: once a rich merchant, hearing of Ravidās' fame, went to hear him teaching, but when blessed water from the washing of Ravidās' feet was offered to him, from a shoe, he could not bring himself to drink it and spilled it on his clothes instead. As a result he got leprosy, but the washerman to whom he gave his clothes to wash got a body like gold. In the end the merchant was forced to return to Ravidās to beg for more *caranāmṛta* (water that has been sanctified by being used to wash the feet of a venerated person) to cure him of leprosy, and eventually Ravidās took pity on him and cured him.

In order to show the contemporary interest in Ravidās at that time, B.P. Agrawal also gave a paper from an exam held in Varanasi in 1907. This was a passage to translate from Hindi into Sanskrit. The passage told the story of the golden bracelet and the goddess Gaṅgā. Finally he mentioned that Ravidās lived to the age of 120 years and his followers say that he vanished in his body into the state of realization (*brahmā pada*) and took along with him his teachings, but that there are today, in Gujarat, hundreds of thousands of his followers. This small account – it is only three pages long – was very influential, as the Belvedere Press editions of Sant verses have been constantly in print and available at low prices since they were first published. B.P. Agrawal, and many of the Radhasoami followers, were from trader-caste backgrounds, and his work made it possible for people from many caste backgrounds to access Ravidās' verses who might never otherwise have heard his works. This marked a new phase in the development of the life of Ravidās, the beginnings of interest outside of Ravidās followers and followers of the Sant traditions themselves among a wider Hindi-speaking Hindu public, negotiating a sense of identity during the early 20th century in colonial India.

Other Hindu reform movements such as the → Arya Samaj also began to take an interest in the Sants, and activists such as Bodhananda (1874–1952), Acchutananda (1879–1933), and I. Medarthi (1900–1971; see Bellwinkel-Schempp, 2010) sought ways to link Sant, Buddhist, and Hindu teachings. I. Medarthi was a key figure in this development, as he seems to have been one of the first to propose in the 1930s a linkage among the newly discovered Harappan cultures of ancient India, Buddhism and the Sant traditions, and Ravidās (Bellwinkel-Schempp, 2010).

Another significant landmark in the development of the story of Ravidās took place with the publication of *Bhagvān Ravidās kī satyakathā* (The True Story of Lord Ravidās) by Ramcharan Kuril (Kuril, 1940). Ramcharan Kuril (1882–1956) was from a Camār background, but had risen in status in society in the leather-working industry in Kanpur and was educated in the government leather-working school. In 1917 he set up an organization called the Ravidās Kurīl Sabhā (Ravidās Kurīl Assembly). He then began to work for reform among the → Ravidāsī community. During the 1930s he became the president the organization that became the Ākhil Bhārtīya Ravidās Mahāsabhā (All India Ravidas General Assembly). In 1940 he was given the title of Mahātma by I. Medarthi, who also encouraged him to write this account of the life of Ravidās.

This work marked the beginning of a trend toward telling Ravidās' life as if it were a modern biography rather than a hagiography of a saint. For instance, he included not only factual data wherever possible – such as dates and places of his birth and death, which were given as VS 1471 (1414 CE) in the morning of Sunday on the full-moon day of the month of *māgh* (Jan–Feb), in Kāśī (Varanasi), and his death date as VS 1597 (1540 CE) in Chittorgarh – but also maps and plans of sites associated with Ravidās. Furthermore, unlike B. Jatav and earlier authors, Ramcharan Kuril also discarded discussions of Ravidās' past lives and instead cited the notion that a leader is always born to reform → *dharma* when it has decayed in India.

His general approach was to tell the same story as was found in B. Jatav, but where possible to interpret the events in terms of everyday logic. He followed the tradition that when Ravidās was married, to Loṇā, his father, who was a rich trader in leather, threw Ravidās out of the house, but he did not cite any spiritual reason for this but rather explained that it was due to his paying more attention to religious matters than business. This approach echoes that found in 19th-century retellings of the life of the Buddha and Christ, in which the miraculous elements were discarded, but the main sequence of events retained. However, the story of the philosopher's stone is told as a basically miraculous series of events. In the case of the test of the floating of the *śāligrām* on the Gaṅgā, he explained that the Brahman's stratagem of trying to pretend their fake wooden *śāligrām* was a stone was discovered before the test. However, in the end Ravidās still won miraculously by his genuine stone *śāligrām* floating on the Gaṅgā. Moreover, like B. Jatav, he included extensive philosophical discussions in the text in the form of teachings by Ravidās. These read very much like modern political speeches, and in one instance he had Ravidās teach a doctrine that people suffer due to being bound in life by three forms of suffering – social, physical, and mental – and the social aspect of suffering is caused by caste divisions and discrimination (Kuril, 1940, 112).

At points his outline of the life of Ravidās also diverged from that in B. Jatav, and in Ramcharan Kuril's version of the story, Mīrā Bāī hears of Ravidās and his debates with Kabīr and comes to Varanasi to meet him and to become his disciple. However, after the feast at Chittorgarth and the miracle of his displaying multiple bodies, he did not die but went on to teach Queen Jhālī, who is from Udaipur. He then told the story of the golden bracelet and the Gaṅgā before telling a story from Mandu, in Madhya Pradesh, about Ravidās and a lake, which was the scene of a miracle where the goddesses of both the Gaṅgā and the Narmadā Rivers manifested themselves, having previously appeared in the guise of two young women. Finally Ravidās returned to Chittorgarh and entered *samādhi* in the temple Mīrā Bāī had built.

The interest sparked by the Belvedere Press editions of Sant teachings and the activities of Ravidāsī and Sant groups also contributed to the development of greater academic interest in Sants such as Ravidās. This led to his inclusion in a number of anthologies of Sant literature that were published before Independence. However, it was not until Independence that these developments would have a direct impact on perceptions of the life of Ravidās.

Post-Independence Lives of Ravidās

There have been several major developments in depictions of the life of Ravidās since Independence, and each can be seen to be linked with perceptions of Ravidās within different political movements, such as Dalit movements, and thinkers coming from Nehruvian-oriented backgrounds.

One of these works was the earliest academic study devoted to Ravidās, *Sant Ravidās aur unkā kāvya* by Ramanand Shastri and Virendra Pandey (Shastri & Pandey, 1955). R. Shastri was a congress politician and MP for Bijnor from 1952 onward on three occasions. The preface to the work was written by Jagjivan Ram, a leading Congress Party politician and the leader of the struggle for rights for untouchables from eastern Uttar Pradesh who was at the time the communications minister in the Congress government. The introduction also has testimonials from various other politicians including Giridhari Lal, the then – irrigation minister for Uttar Pradesh, and chairman of the Uttar Pradesh Dalit class movement. This firmly sets the book within the context of efforts by Dalits within the Congress Party to advance the interests of untouchables within Nehru's secular approach to governance in India.

R. Shastri situated Ravidās' ideas within the context of academic discourses that had been being developing in India, about the influence of earlier Buddhist, Nāth and Sufī traditions as well as Vaiṣṇava traditions and the saint Rāmānand on the ideas of the Sants and on Ravidās. He provided a balanced academic discussion of the name of Ravidās, his caste, and the issue of how Anantdās and Priyādās describe him as having been a Brahman in a previous life. This he attributes to the prejudices of higher-caste people toward Camārs, and in response to this, he then laid out a history of the Camārs and argued that as a community they were originally of a higher caste, but over time had fallen to their present status. He was also the first author to carefully evaluate where exactly Ravidās was born, and he settled on Manduadih, currently a suburb of Varanasi, as the most likely site. His book, also for the first time, incorporated both careful study of the available texts, and reports based on interviews he carried out with people he met. Thus, for instance, he was able to show what the names of Ravidās' parents were according to textual and oral sources. First, he surveyed the printed sources, and second, he reported on the responses he got to questions on this topic from a range of informants. He said that when he asked the members of the All India Ravidas General Assembly and the *mahants* (abbotts) of almost all the Ravidāsī centers that he could ask about this, most reported that his father's name was Ragghū. However, half of these informants said that that Ravidās' mother was called Karmā, and the other half said that she was called Ghurbaniyā. In a similar way, he also evaluated issues to do with Ravidās' marital status, his education, his travels, whether he had actually visited Chittorgarh and whether he had met with Queen Jhālī, and the various different dates and locations of his death.

However, what is striking, by its complete absence, is any account of the major incidents in the life of Ravidās, such as the story of the *śāligrām* incident or the gift of the golden bracelet by the goddess Gaṅgā. This has to be seen within the context of the scientific approach, which was one of the hallmarks of Nehru's era in Indian politics. Presumably, such miraculous stories were seen as simply superstitions that did not merit any attention and could not be included in the new approach to Ravidās that this book pioneered.

This tradition continued to develop with a major focus at Raj Ghat in Varanasi, where a temple to Ravidās has been under construction since the 1980s on land bought and donated by Jagjivan Ram. This is the main center of Ravidāsī activity in Varanasi for followers from Uttar Pradesh and Bihar. It has also generated its own set of texts and life stories. These included academic approaches such as those of S. Singh (2003), who was associated with the Raj Ghat temple project, and his student S.P. Jhunjhunwala (1995), who continued this tradition. My own work along with that of W. Callaewaert also intersected with this tradition, and this resulted in the publication in 1992 of an English-language study of the life and works of Ravidās based on sources from before 1700 (Callewaert & Friedlander, 1992).

In contrast to this, at the same time, other thinkers from more radical Dalit groups influenced by → Ambedkar were combining his ideas with others drawn from I. Medarthi and B. Jatav and were developing very different constructions of the life of Ravidās. The most striking of these was a work published from Lucknow in 1956 called *Sant Pravar Raidās Sāheb*, by C.P. Jijnasu, in which he depicted Ravidās as a form of Buddhist social reformer who occupied a middle position historically between the Buddha and B.R. Ambedkar (Jijnasu, 1956). This has also attracted some Western scholarly interest in the consideration of the development of the life of Ravidās (Lochtefeld, 2005, 208–212).

Further examples of this kind of approach continued to be written, a good example of which is the *Śrī Ravidās Ambeḍkar Carit Mānas* by A.P.S.S. Bhaskar of Agra published in 1986. In this work the author depicted a fully developed alternative history of India, drawing on ideas from B. Jatav, I. Medarthi, and C.P. Jijnasu, into which he integrated the story of the Harrapan civilization as the original culture of the Dalits of India, the Buddha as a teacher from the Sant tradition, Ravidās as the medieval revivalist of this tradition, and then Ambedkar and Kanshi Ram and his Bahujan Samaj Party as the contemporary evolution of this movement in India. The story of Ravidās as R.P.S.S. Bhaskar told it was basically that as told by B. Jatav. However, in an interesting ending to Ravidās' life, he has him predict that in the future he will be reborn as Ambedkar and that Swami Achutananda, B. Jatav, and A.P.S.S. Bhaskar will reveal the teachings of the Sant tradition to the world (Bhaskar, 1986, 238).

There were also from the 1950s a number of new approaches to Ravidās emerging from the Punjab. In some cases these took the form of the "discovery" of new texts attributed to Ravidās. A notable instance of this was the text found by P.S. Azad, in the Punjab, first published in 1973. This was a collection of 114 couplets in which Ravidās appears as a very modern social reformer, advocating vegetarianism and a range of activities typical of groups seeking to raise their status by Sanskritizing their traditions in the 20th century.

At the same time, a number of Punjabi academics also started publishing scholarly works on Ravidās that tried to understand the relationship between traditional Sikh views and the emerging range of views on the life of Ravidās. Notable among these were the first English-language studies of Ravidās' life (Singh, 1977, 1981) and J.S. Sabar's *Bhagat Ravidās Srot Pustak* (Source Book for *Bhagat* Ravidās; 1984), which contained an extensive collection of original texts related to the study of Ravidās.

There have also been developments from the Punjab, which in part build on the ideas pioneered by Mangu Ram and the → Ad Dharm movement. These Punjabi traditions in general see Ravidās in the context of Sikh teachings. Some of the Sants from the All India Adi Dharm Mission tradition associated with Banta Ram Ghera discovered the birthplace of Ravidās in the 1960s at Seer Govardhanpur, Varanasi. The temple being built there has become the major focus of Punjabi Ravidāsī activity in Varanasi (Hawley & Jurgensmeyer, 1988). The cycles of stories associated with Ravidās at Seer Govardhanpur includes all the episodes already discussed along with many others that were not previously found in Hindi sources on Ravidās, including yet another queen who became Ravidās' disciple, called Bhanmatī from Multan, and extensive stories of Ravidās' travels in western India and in the Middle East. There have been a number of important studies of the role of oral traditions in the contemporary development of this literature (Schaller, 1995, 2005).

Recent years have seen a steady stream of publications on the life of Ravidās that adopt a wide range of approaches. Some advocate Dalit approaches based on the ideas of B.R. Ambedkar, similar to C.P. Jijnasu's, and caste him completely into the role of a mediating figure between the Buddha and Ambedkar (Gautam, 2011), while others by Punjabi authors continue that state's longstanding traditions associated with Ravidās (*Stories of Guru Ravidass*, 2011). There has also been continued interest among Western academics with a collection of significant articles published in 2005 (Zelliot & Mokashi-Punekar, 2005). Finally, there are also popular texts, such as that in the Diamond Pocket books series, which, like the early 20th-century Radhasoami works, show Ravidās as a saint whose teachings can appeal to a wider Hindu public (Yamini, 2010).

Conclusion

What emerges from these accounts of the life of Ravidās is that while there is no real possibility of constructing a factual biography for him, the study of the range of depictions of the life of Ravidās allows us to see how different communities over the last six centuries in India have tried to relate to his story.

Moreover, behind the common consensus that the existence of Ravidās bears witness to the importance of the former untouchable communities of India, the multiplicity of approaches to how to relate to this reveals the complex fault lines that run through social, religious, and political struggle in India today.

Bibliography

Agrawal (Agravāl), B.P., *Raidāsjī kī bānī*, Allahabad, 1908, 1988 (Hind.).

Azad (Āzād), P.S., *Ravidās Darśan*, Chandigarh, 1973 (Hind.).

Bellwinkel-Schempp, M., *Ishvardatt Medarthi*, New Delhi, 2010.

Bhaskar (Bhāskar), A.P.S.S., *Śrī Ravidās Ambeḍkar Carit Mānas*, Agra, 1986 (Hind.).

Callewaert, W.M., & P. Friedlander, *The Life and Works of Raidas*, New Delhi, 1992.

Gautam, R.A.E.E., *Guru Ravidās Vicār Darśan*, Delhi, 2011 (Hind.).

Hawley, J.S., & M. Jurgensmeyer, *Songs of the Saints of India*, New York, 1988.

Jatav (Jāṭav), K.B., *Ravidās Rāmāyaṇ*, Meerut, 1911 (Hind.).

Jhunjhunwala (Jhunjhunvālā), S.P., *Sant Raidās*, Varanasi, 1995, 1997 (Hind.).

Jijnasu (Jijñāsu), C.P., *Sant Pravar Raidās Sāheb*, Lucknow, 1956 (Hind.).

Kuril (Kurīl), R., *Bhagvān Ravidās Kī Satyakathā*, Kanpur, 1940, 3 1950 (Hind.).

Lochtefeld, J.G., "The Saintly Chamar: Perspectives on the Life of Ravidas," in: E. Zelliot & R. Mokashi-Punekar, eds., *Untouchable Saints*, New Delhi, 2005, 201–220.

Lorenzen, D.N., *Kabir Legends and Ananta-Das's Kabir Paracai*, Albany, 1991.

McGregor, R.S., *Hindi Literature of the Nineteenth and Early Twentieth Centuries*, vol. VIII/1, Wiesbaden, 1984.

Sabar (Sābar), J.S., *Bhagat Ravidās Srot Pustak*, Amritsar, 1984 (Punj.).

Shastri (Śāstri), R., & V. Pandey (Pāṇḍey), *Sant Ravidās aur unkā kāvya*, Jwalapur, 1955 (Hind.).

Schaller, J., "Sanskritization, Caste Uplift, and Social Dissidence," in: D. Lorenzen, ed., *Bhakti Religion in North India*, Albany, 1995, 94–119.

Schaller, J., "The Legends of Raidas in Word and Song," in: E. Zelliot & R. Mokashi-Punekar, eds., *Untouchable Saints*, New Delhi, 2005, 221–230.

Singh (Siṃh), S., *Raidās Bāṇī*, Delhi, 2003 (Hind.).

Singh, D., *A Study of Bhakta Ravidās*, Patiala, 1981.

Singh, D., *Sant Ravidas and His Times*, Delhi, 1977.

Stories of Guru Ravidass, on:http://www.gururavidassguruji.com/storiesofgururavidass.htm, 2011.

Yamini (Yāminī), R.B., *Raidās Vāṇī*, New Delhi, 2010 (Hind.).

Zelliot, E., & R. Mokashi-Punekar, *Untouchable Saints*, New Delhi, 2005.

Peter Friedlander

Rūpa Gosvāmī

Rūpa Gosvāmī was one of the principal disciples of Kṛṣṇa → Caitanya and an important 16th-century theologian of the → Gauḍīya Vaiṣṇava school; he developed an elaborate → *avatāra* theology as well as a sophisticated theology of religious emotion. Born in Bengal, he spent most of his life in Vraja (now Braj), where he was instrumental in the (re)development of the area as a place of → pilgrimage. He wrote works of Sanskrit poetry, theology, literary theory, and ritual practice that shaped the thought of the school.

The Life of Rūpa

Rūpa was born in Fateyabad (eastern Bengal) in the final decades of the 15th century. His ancestors hailed from Karnataka, but the family had moved to Bengal three generations earlier. The story of Rūpa's life is intimately connected with that of his siblings: his elder brother Sanātana, whom Rūpa addresses as his master (*prabhu*) in nearly all his works and who influenced Rūpa greatly, and his younger brother Anupama, the father of → Jīva Gosvāmī, who would become Rūpa's most prominent disciple, who would author some of the school's most important works on theology and would become instrumental in the organization of the movement after the passing of his uncles (see Gupta, 2007). (The names Rūpa and Sanātana were given to them by Caitanya at their first meeting. We do not know what their birth names were, but in the literature of the tradition, they are often addressed by the titles that they had at the Muslim court before they met Caitanya – *dabir khās* for Rūpa and *sākar mallik* for Sanātana. Caitanya gave Anupama the name Vallabha.)

At some point, Rūpa, Sanātana, and Anupama moved to Ramakeli, near the Muslim court at Gauda, and began working for Sulṭān Ḥusayn Šāh, who employed Sanātana and Rūpa as his assistants or secretaries.

While at Ramakeli, the two brothers began to correspond with Caitanya, and when he finally passed through their hometown on his way to Vrindavan, they rushed to meet him. Their first meeting with Caitanya was a turning point in their lives. Until this point, Caitanya had urged the brothers to retain their position at the Muslim court while continuing their worship of → Kṛṣṇa, but after meeting with the master, they decided to renounce their vast wealth and ministerial posts. Soon Rūpa and his younger brother Anupama left Ramakeli and joined Caitanya on his return from Vraja in Allahabad, where he taught Rūpa for ten days and sent both of them to Vrindavan. Caitanya traveled on to Banaras, where he met Sanātana and taught him for the entire duration of his stay. When Caitanya prepared to leave Banaras two months later, he entrusted Sanātana with a task that would occupy him and his brother for the rest of their lives. Murāri Gupta, the oldest biographer of Caitanya, records in his *Kṛṣṇacaitanyacaritāmṛta* Caitanya's instructions as follows:

> You should go to Vrindavan. You should study the scriptures on devotion, reveal the lost sacred places, and establish their greatness. In this way, devotion will be very firmly established. (*KCaiC.* 4.13.15–16; trans. by author)

On their first visit to Vrindavan, neither Rūpa and Anupama nor Sanātana stayed very long. They travelled back east, to Puri, Orissa, where Caitanya resided, and each of them spent about ten months there with Caitanya and his close associates, before returning to Vrindavan to complete the task that they were charged with. Anupama, however, never reached Orissa but passed away *en route* to Puri.

When Rūpa arrived in Vrindavan, an old document states, the town was "full of jungle and uninhabited." Caitanya instructed him to rediscover lost sacred sites, and Rūpa studied puranic accounts of the many places sacred to Kṛṣṇa – resulting in his compendium *Mathurāmāhātmya* – and explored the area by "undertaking pilgrimage in Braj Bhūm [Vraja]" (Habib, 1996, 156). But he also developed the "story" behind those places by writing extensively on Kṛṣṇa's associates, his divine play (→ *līlā*), and our ability to participate in it through devotion to him.

Quickly, a community of Caitanya Vaiṣṇavas formed in Vraja, of which Rūpa and Sanātana were the natural leaders. They were also respected by other Vaiṣṇavas in Vrindavan, like Harirām Vyās of the → Haridāsī Sampradāya – a contemporary of the brothers – who praises them as "clever generals of their sect" and "the kings of the assembly of devotees" (Pauwels, 2002, 82–83).

Caitanya sent several other devotees to Vrindavan, the most prominent of which are Raghunātha Bhaṭṭa, from Banaras, and Gopāla Bhaṭṭa, whom he met in Srirangam. After Caitanya's passing in 1533, Raghunāthadāsa, a very close companion of the master in Puri, and Anupama's son Jīva, who grew up in Bengal and studied in Banaras, also settled in Vraja. With Rūpa and Sanātana, these four became known as the "six *gosvāmīs*," and together they produced a vast library of Sanskrit poetry in praise of Kṛṣna and elaborate works on theology, ritual practice, grammar, and literary theory.

The *Caitanyacaritāmṛta* (2.19.127) tells us that Rūpa and Sanātana had no fixed residence in Vraja but slept each night under a different tree. However, there are two places that are associated with Rūpa. He lived for a while a kilometer and a half east of the village of Nandīśvara (Nandgoan), where he composed some of his works, and he spent the last part of his life in Sevākuñj in Vrindavan, where the hut in which he worshipped Kṛṣṇa (*bhajankuṭī*) is still regularly visited by pilgrims.

In Vrindavan, Rūpa unearthed the *mūrti* of Govindadeva and established a small temple to house the deity in the center of Vrindavan. In 1590, decades after Rūpa's passing, a magnificent, much larger temple for Govindadeva was completed by Mān Siṃh, king of Amber and commander of Akbar's army. For fear of Muslim raids on the temple, the *mūrti* was moved to Jaipur in the 17th century, where it still resides (see Case, 1996).

Fig. 1: The *mūrti* of Govindadeva worshipped by Rūpa Gosvāmī (photo by Kiyokazu Okita, used by courtesy).

Rūpa passed away sometime after his brother Sanātana, possibly as late as 1568. His personal library and the Govindadeva Temple were entrusted to Jīva (Habib, 1996, 144, 156). His tomb (*samādhi*) is located in the courtyard of Jīva's Rādhā Dāmodara Mandir in Vrindavan, opposite his *bhajankūṭi*.

The Works of Rūpa

Rūpa was a very prolific author – Kṛṣṇadāsa Kavirāja states hyperbolically that he wrote "a *lakh* of books" (*CaiC.* 2.1.37) – on a variety of topics and in a variety of genres. The description of Rūpa's works that I give below is based on the lists of his works given by early authors. The earliest list is given by Jīva, Rūpa's nephew, in the conclusion of his *Laghuvaiṣṇavatoṣaṇī* commentary on the *Bhāgavatapurāṇa*. Kṛṣṇadāsa Kavirāja, Rūpa's disciple, lists his principal works in the *Caitanyacaritāmṛta* (2.1.36–41). The *Bhaktiratnākara* (1.796–799) also discusses the works of Rūpa and includes a few Sanskrit verses listing 16 works of Rūpa composed by Kṛṣṇadāsa Adhikārī, a disciple of Jīva, that contain a few additional works to the ones given in the *Caitanyacaritāmṛta* (*BhR.* 1.811–829).

Several other works not mentioned in these lists have been attributed to Rūpa – such as a *Kṛṣṇacaitanyasahasranāma*, a *Navadvīpāṣṭaka*, and a *Nikuñjarahasyastava* (for a full list, see Kapoor, 1995, 145–147). Since these seem unknown to those junior contemporaries, we can be rather confident that they are not authentic.

Though most of Rūpa's works were written between 1530 and 1550, they did not enjoy a wide circulation until long after his death, when Jīva sent his three disciples Narottamadās, Śrīnivāsācārya, and Śyāmānanda with several of the Vrindavan *gosvāmīs*' books to Bengal (see Stewart, 2010, 31–43), where they could be copied and distributed. Moreover, from Jīva's letters to Śrīnivāsa preserved in the *Bhaktiratnākara* (14), we learn that some of Rūpa and Sanātana's principal works – including the *Bhaktirasāmṛtasindhu* – were not sent immediately, because he was still editing and correcting them.

Works on Theology and Religious Practice

The *Laghubhāgavatāmṛta* or *Saṃkṣepabhāgavatāmṛta* is a work of 893 verses devoted to an analysis of the different manifestations of Kṛṣṇa and (briefly) the different types of devotees. It is meant to summarize the theology that Sanātana weaves into the story of his *Bṛhadbhāgavatāmṛta* but is really an independent theological treatise that, through a careful reading of scriptural passages (primarily from puranic texts), both summarizes and elaborates on the theology of Sanātana's narrative. The work consists of six chapters: the first five chapters discuss at great length the various *avatāra*s and the nature of divinity, with most of the fifth chapter (over 500 verses) discussing Kṛṣṇa's nature; the last chapter briefly outlines a hierarchy of Kṛṣṇa's devotees. Neither Sanātana's nor Rūpa's *Bhāgavatāmṛta* is dated.

The most popular and most influential of Rūpa's theological works is undoubtedly the *Bhaktirasāmṛtasindhu*, which he completed in 1541. The work has four divisions: the first defines → *bhakti* and gives a detailed analysis of its various stages; in the second, Rūpa introduces the terminology he borrowed from Sanskrit literary theory and demonstrates how it applies to *bhakti*; the third part analyzes the five main devotional emotions; and the fourth part analyzes seven secondary emotions.

The *Ujjvalanīlamaṇi* continues from the *Bhaktirasāmṛtasindhu* and analyzes the fifth main devotional emotion: the bright (*ujjvala*) and sweet (*madhura*) amorous devotion. Rūpa classifies the roles that Kṛṣṇa and → Rādhā assume in their loveplay and the ones assumed by their various attendants, before he explores at great length how this amorous devotional love arises and is nurtured and expressed, ending the work with an exposition on love in separation and love in union. The work is undated but was presumably written shortly after the *Bhaktirasāmṛtasindhu*.

The *Upadeśāmṛta* is a very short work, mainly on devotional practice. In 11 verses, Rūpa summarizes the ways in which to practice devotion, to honor and serve other devotees, to chant Kṛṣṇa's name, and to practice *rāgānugabhakti*. The final verses praise Rādhākuṇḍa, a sacred lake dedicated to Rādhā at the foot of Govardhana. This title is not mentioned in any of the early lists, but it was included in the *Stavamālā*, a collection of Rūpa's shorter works compiled by Jīva (see below).

The *Mathurāmāhātmya* is a digest of puranic passages extolling the greatness of Mathurā, organized by topic and place. The work is important as part of the *gosvāmī*s' attempt to "rediscover" the lost sacred sites of Vraja. Rūpa uses the name Mathurā in this text (as in many of his other works) to refer to not only the town but also the entire area of Vraja, including its 12 forests, Govardhana, Rādhākuṇḍa, Nandīśvara, the river Yamunā, and so on. Apart from two opening and closing verses in which Rūpa introduces and concludes the work, the *Mathurāmāhātmya* consists entirely of citations. The work is 446 verses long and is undated.

The *Rādhākṛṣṇagaṇoddeśadīpikā* is a work in two volumes (*Bṛhat* and *Laghu*) on the associates of Rādhā and Kṛṣṇa. The first volume covers Kṛṣṇa's superiors and most of his beloved *gopī*s. The second volume discusses Kṛṣṇa's friends and servants and concludes with a more detailed description of Rādhā's friends and attendants. The work is undated.

Rūpa also wrote *Kṛṣṇajanmatithividhi*, which, as the title suggests, details how to observe the festivities of Kṛṣṇa's birth anniversary (*kṛṣṇajanmāṣṭamī*). Rūpa teaches how to bathe Kṛṣṇa's *mūrti*, what should be offered to Kṛṣṇa, what → *mantra*s to use, and how to spend the entire day in celebration of Kṛṣṇa's play.

Dramatic and Poetic Works

Rūpa had a deep interest in and a great mastery over Sanskrit poetry and poetics. He wrote several works of poetry, three dramas, and a substantial collection of songs and prayers.

The *Dānakelikaumudī* is a one-act drama (Bhaṇika) on Kṛṣṇa's toll-collecting play (*dānalīlā*), a popular theme among early Caitanya Vaiṣṇava authors: Kṛṣṇa prohibits Rādhā and the *gopī*s from passing through the forest without paying a toll to him, the owner of those woods. S.K. De (1986, 148) is of the opinion that this was one of Rūpa's earliest works, written in 1495 (Śāka year 1417), long before he met Caitanya. This is unlikely, though, as Rūpa specifies in the concluding verse that the work was composed at Nandīśvara, where he resided only later in his life. It is therefore more likely that Rūpa's dating verses (*gate manuśate śāke candrasvarasamanvite*) should be read as denoting Śāka 1471, that is 1549.

The *Haṃsadūta* and *Uddhavasandeśa* are two Dūtakāvyas or "messenger poems," a genre created by the classical poet Kālidāsa that had gained great popularity in Rūpa's time. These poems typically tell of a person who, suffering the separation from his or her lover, asks a human, an animal, or a personified inanimate object to send a message to the beloved. The first half of such poems typically describes the route to be taken, followed by the message that is to be delivered. In the *Haṃsadūta* (142 verses), Lalitā delivers a message on behalf of Rādhā to a gander (*haṃsa*), which he should deliver to Kṛṣṇa in Mathurā, while in the *Uddhavasandeśa* (131 verses), it is Kṛṣṇa – residing in Mathurā – who sends a message through Uddhava to the *gopī*s in Vrindavan. Both of these poems are undated, but it is likely that the *Haṃsadūta* was composed before Rūpa settled in Vraja, as J. Brzezinski has argued (1999, 9–11), since the poem betrays a superficial knowledge of the geography of the area.

The major dramatic works that Rūpa wrote, however, are the *Vidagdhamādhava* and the *Lalitamādhava*. The *Caitanyacaritāmṛta* (3.1) tells us that Rūpa initially intended these two works to be a single play but later split them up. The *Vidagdhamādhava*, a Nāṭaka in seven acts, is the simplest and most beautiful of these. It describes the unfolding of Rādhā and Kṛṣṇa's love for each other, from the early longings (*pūrvarāga*) that awaken in Rādhā when she hears Kṛṣṇa's flute, sees his portrait, and hears his name in the first act to the union of the divine lovers in the final act.

The *Lalitamādhava* is a much more complex drama. In ten acts, Rūpa describes Kṛṣṇa's play in Vrindavan (acts 1–2), his departure to Mathurā and the despair it causes in the *gopī*s (act 3), Kṛṣṇa's longing for the *gopī*s while he resides in Mathurā (act 4), the kidnapping of Rukmiṇī (act 5), the winning of the Śyāmantaka jewel (act 6), and Kṛṣṇa's loveplay with his queens in Dvārakā (acts 7–10). Particularly in the later acts of this drama, Rūpa rewrites the Kṛṣṇa narrative considerably. Though the puranic picture of Kṛṣṇa's life in Dvārakā is much more regal than his sports in Vrindavan, Rūpa revisions Dvārakā along the lines of Vrindavan. Thus in act 6, Viśvakarmā – the architect of the gods – builds a new Vrindavan (*navavṛndāvana*) in Kṛṣṇa's capital, and we learn in these final acts that Kṛṣṇa's queens in Dvārakā are really the *gopī*s of Vrindavan: Rukmiṇī grew up in Vraja, where she was known as Candrāvalī, one of the principal *gopī*s; the 16,100 princesses whom Kṛṣṇa married are the 16,100 *gopī*s whom Narakāsura kidnapped in Vrindavan; Lalitā was reborn as Jāmbavatī; and Satyabhāmā is actually Rādhā.

Rūpa began writing these two dramas shortly after meeting Caitanya and discussed the plays with Caitanya's associates during his stay in Puri (see *CaiC.* 3.1). The *Vidagdhamādhava* was completed in 1533 and the *Lalitamādhava* in 1537.

Padyāvalī is an anthology of Sanskrit verses compiled by Rūpa. The work consists of 387 verses, of which 34 verses are Rūpa's own compositions. The work contains verses by contemporary Vaiṣṇavas (including Caitanya) as well as verses of pre-Caitanya Vaiṣṇavas who influenced Rūpa and the early Caitanya Vaiṣṇava theologians, such as Śrīdhara Svāmī. Rūpa made creative use of the anthology genre: the *Padyāvalī* is not merely a collection of verses grouped by topic but a carefully constructed anthology that first teaches the importance of *bhakti* and the proper attitude of a devotee in just over 100 verses and then narrates Kṛṣṇa's play – from his childhood to the *rāsa* dance – in about 260 verses. In the later sections of the work, Rūpa cites well-known secular poets such as Amaru, Govardhana, and Bhavabhūti, whose verses all gain a devotional meaning in the new context that Rūpa creates. The *Padyāvalī* is undated, but it is probably a later work, as in it Rūpa cites several verses from his other compositions as well as from younger contemporaries.

Rūpa wrote also a number of shorter works: various Aṣṭakas, including three to Caitanya, and other prayers and poems of praise (Stavas), mainly addressed to Kṛṣṇa and Rādhā; a dozen picture poems (Citrakāvyas); and over 40 Sanskrit songs (Gītās) in praise of Kṛṣṇa meant to be sung in various *rāga*s. He also developed newer Sanskrit poetic forms: he composed a long panegyric poem in rhythmic prose and verse (Birudakāvya) to Govindadeva (*Govindabirudāvalī*) and wrote a meter poem (Chandaskāvya) demonstrating 18 rare meters (*Aṣṭādaśacchandas*). Jīva gathered these in a collection called *Stavamālā*. Many of these texts were meant for daily recitation or congregational singing and to this day are used for this in Caitanya Vaiṣṇava circles.

The *Bhaktiratnākara* (1.818–819) tells us that Rūpa wrote a poem of 11 verses meant for meditation on Kṛṣṇa's daily activities (the *Aṣṭakālīyalīlā*). The verses have been lost but formed the basis of Kṛṣṇadāsa Kavirāja's *Govindalīlāmṛta* (see *GovLī.* 23.94).

Literary Criticism and Linguistics

The *Nāṭakacandrikā* is a work on drama (Nāṭaka). The focus of the *Nāṭakacandrikā* is the narrative elements of the drama, such as the types of characters and the various transitions between scenes, and some stylistic elements. Rūpa does not, however, discuss any of the aspects directly related to the actual performance of drama. The text borrows extensively from Siṃhabhūpāla's *Rasārṇavasudhākāra*, as Rūpa admits in the first verse, but is also influenced by Viśvanātha's *Sāhityadarpaṇa*, and Bharata's *Nāṭyaśāstra* (see Broo, 2011). The work is undated, but since many of the cited verses are taken from the *Lalitamādhava*, the *Nāṭakacandrikā* must have been composed sometime after 1533.

The *Sāmānyabirudāvalīlakṣaṇa* offers an examination on the characteristics of Birudas, panegyric poems written in both verse and rhythmic prose. The genre was popular among early Caitanya Vaiṣṇava authors, and Rūpa is one of the few Sanskrit poets to discuss its characteristics. Rūpa identified nearly 50 varieties of metrical and alliterative prose parts, called Kalikās, and used some passages from his *Govindabirudāvalī* to illustrate them. Like the *Govindabirudāvalī*, the *Birudāvalīlakṣaṇa* is undated.

The last work to be considered here is the *Prayuktākhyātamañjarī*, a short dictionary of verbal roots (*kriyākoṣa*) based on Bhaṭṭamalla's *Ākhyātacandrikā*. The work is not Vaiṣṇava in character but simply a thesaurus of Sanskrit verbal roots, grouped in broad semantic domains (the actions of the intellect and mind, speech, actions of the four *varṇa*s, etc.). Rūpa states in the *Prayuktākhyātamañjarī* (3.12.15) that he wrote this "cluster of flowers" for the pleasure of the "poet-bees". The work is undated.

Rūpa's Teachings

Rūpa's theology centers on two main topics – the nature of god and the nature of devotion to god – which he develops very systematically, primarily in the *Laghubhāgavatāmṛta* and the *Bhaktirasāmṛtasindhu*. Although (or, perhaps, because) he grew up in Bengal, the homeland of the new school of logic (Navyanyāya; see → Nyāya), Rūpa insists that logic and reasoning are not useful for his purposes, since logic is inconclusive and since both god's nature and the love of him are inconceivable (see *BhRaAm.* 2.5.93 and *LBhAm.* 1.5.111). Scriptural testimony (*śabda*) is the primary means of acquiring correct knowledge of god, and Rūpa constructs his theology through a careful reading of scripture and an innovative application of Sanskrit literary theory to those sacred texts.

Though he borrows this teaching from → Vedānta, Rūpa is not a Vedāntin in the classical sense. He does not cite any of the principal → Upaniṣads and refers only to those passages of the *Brahmasūtra* that dismiss logic and stress the importance of revelation (see *BhRaAm.* 1.1.45–46 and *LBhAm.* 1.1.7–9; 1.5.111). His main sources are not classical Vedānta texts but rather the → Purāṇas and the → Pāñcarātras and – in his works on *bhaktirasa* – Vaiṣṇava poetry, including his own. The most important source for his theology is the *Bhāgavatapurāṇa*, "the essence of all Vedānta, the fruit of the vedic tree of plenty, and the best of all [sacred texts]," which he quotes profusely and considers the only authority on the nature of Kṛṣṇa (*LBhAm.* 1.5.301).

This move away from Vedānta – the theological foundation for the older Vaiṣṇava schools of → Madhva and → Rāmānuja – manifests itself too in his theology (see Lutjeharms, forthcoming). Like Rāmānuja and Madhva, Rūpa thinks of the absolute being as a personal god who possesses unlimited attributes and with whom the living beings connect through *bhakti*, but while these earlier Vaiṣṇavas argued that this personal deity is the → *brahman* of the Upaniṣads, Rūpa draws a distinction between these two. Though god's nature is singular and beyond all dualities, that nature is perceived in accordance with the religious practice one pursues. Thus he is perceived as *brahman* – "mere perception" (*kevalaṃ jñānam; LBhAm.* 1.5.116) – by those devoted to the Upaniṣads or as the *paramātman* dwelling in the heart by the *yogī*s of the eightfold path (*LBhAm.* 1.5.196; see Pātañjala → Yoga). These different perceptions of god are, however, not merely subjective but reflect different aspects of god's nature: he can be both the impersonal *brahman* of the Upaniṣads and the personal god (*bhagavān*) Kṛṣṇa, because these are merely different characteristics (*dharma*) of his nondual nature that, despite their contrariness, he can embody simultaneously by his inconceivable potencies (*acintyaśakti*; see *LBhAm.* 1.5.107–119). Thus god can be both Kṛṣṇa, "qualified by millions of nonmaterial attributes, possessing great potency and a form of complete, dense bliss," and *brahman*, "a substance that has no characteristics, no distinctions, and no form" – which relate to each other like the sun and its splendor (*LBhAm.* 1.5.215–216).

Not all these manifestations of god are equal. They can be graded based on the degree to which they display god's innumerable potencies (→ *śakti*s). Therefore, the personal god (*bhagavān*) is higher than the impersonal (*brahman*), because he manifests god's own form – a form that is identical with his being (for god is nondual) and entirely different from the worldly attributes we know. But even among these personal forms of god, there is a hierarchy. Rūpa develops a complex classification of god's manifestations in this world and in the divine realms. When god descends to this world as an *avatāra*, he generally does so only as a "part" of himself (*svāṃśa*) or by "investing" or "possessing" (*āveśa*) a living being with one of his potencies (*śakti; LBhAm.* 1.2.5). Only three of his manifestations in this world – Nṛsiṃha, → Rāma, and Kṛṣṇa – display all his potencies, and among these, the first two are subordinate to Kṛṣṇa, "like lamps lit from the [original] lamp" (*LBhAm.* 1.5.16). Kṛṣṇa alone is fully independent and manifests even more attributes than the other two. The attributes that Kṛṣṇa particularly embodies are unparalleled sweetness and charm, which are so strong that they attract even those who hate him (*LBhAm.* 1.5.66). Kṛṣṇa manifests this sweetness fully in Dvārakā, more fully in Mathurā, and the most fully in Vraja (*BhRaAm.* 2.1.223). Only in Vraja can god be fully known, as it is only there, playing with his most intimate devotees, that he reveals his extraordinary sweetness.

Rūpa stresses, however, that these activities of Kṛṣṇa are not just something of the past or something happening exclusively in the divine realms, but can be experienced at any time: "Even today, if his beloved devotees, pained by longing, desire to see that very play, Kṛṣṇa, the ocean of compassion, then reveals it to them" (*LBhAm.* 1.5.391; trans. by author). This divine vision is only attained by those who are "overpowered by love" (*LBhAm.* 1.5.392), the highest stage of devotion.

Rūpa defines devotion in its purest form as "continuous service to Kṛṣṇa that is pleasing to him, free from desires for anything else, and unobscured by knowledge (*jñāna*) and ritual action (*karma*)" (*BhRaAm.* 1.1.11). He outlines three different stages:

1. devotion in practice (*sādhanabhakti*);
2. devotion with emotion (*bhāvabhakti*); and
3. devotion with love (*premabhakti*).

By practicing devotional acts, the emotion of love for Kṛṣṇa will arise, and when that emotion matures into love (*prema*), anyone can become a witness of and even participant in Kṛṣṇa's eternal play.

There are two types of devotional practice: *vaidhibhakti*, practice that arises from the injunctions (*vidhi*) of scripture, and *rāgānugabhakti*, practice that is motivated by the desire to follow the passion (*rāga*) of a great devotee, such as a *gopī* or one of Kṛṣṇa's friends or relatives. The former practice centers largely on the worship of the image in a temple and includes the Vaiṣṇava practices elaborately taught in various Vaiṣṇava scriptures. Five of these practices Rūpa considers particularly potent, as they can easily produce emotion (*bhāva*) and reveal Kṛṣṇa (*BhRaAm.* 1.2.238, 244): lovingly attending Kṛṣṇa's image, relishing the *Bhāgavatapurāṇa*, being in the company of like-minded devotees, chanting Kṛṣṇa's names, and residing in Vraja.

The focus of one who pursues *rāgānugabhakti*, however, shifts to an inner visualization practice. A devotee pursuing this path aims to cultivate the devotion of a specific perfected devotee of Kṛṣṇa by absorbing the narrations of Kṛṣṇa's play, preferably while residing in Vraja, and serving Kṛṣṇa with the physical or "practitioner's body" (*sādhakarūpa*) and the "perfected body" (*siddharūpa*) of an associate of Kṛṣṇa that is developed through meditative visualization (*BhRaAm.* 1.2.295).

Compared to the space that he devotes to the discussion of *vaidhibhakti* (263 verses), Rūpa says rather little on *rāgānugabhakti* (39 verses), and this brevity has given rise to different interpretations of this practice, particularly regarding the type of service that is offered with the physical body: Should a male devotee act externally as a female person, if he serves Kṛṣṇa in his visualization as a *gopī*? Or are the devotional acts that he should perform with the body (some of) the practices of *vaidhibhakti*? Rūpa does not explicitly address this, but it is clear that he considers the standard practices of *bhakti* to be important even in this practice (see *BhRaAm.* 1.2.296), and it is thus very likely that he thought of these practices when he talked of service with one's "practitioner's body," as that is also what he himself followed (see Viśvanātha's commentary on *BhRaAm.* 1.2.295; for a detailed study of *rāgānugabhakti*, see Haberman, 1988).

Both types of practice are meant to manifest in the heart that is purified by the practice of devotion an "eternally perfected emotion" (*nityasiddhabhāva; BhRaAm.* 1.2.2). This emotion is not produced by devotional acts but is merely manifested by it. It is not the effect of something of this world but rather something that is transcendental to this world (*BhRaAm.* 2.5.75) and consists of the special pure being (*śuddhasattva; BhRaAm.* 1.3.1) that is Kṛṣṇa's nature. The emotion that arises is love for Kṛṣṇa (*BhRaAm.* 2.5.2), which, as a manifestation of "the play of his great potency" (*śakti*), shares in his inconceivable nature (*BhRaAm.* 2.5.92). This love for Kṛṣṇa can be of five types, determined by the nature and *vāsanā*s (mental impressions and proclivities) of the person who experiences it: peace, affection, friendship, parental affection, or amorous love (*BhRaAm.* 2.5.6ff.). The first is realized by sages who have realized the self and have some attraction for Kṛṣṇa, but who do not develop an emotional intimacy with him. Affection (*prīti*) is experienced by those who are subordinate to Kṛṣṇa and who serve him. The last three – friendship, parental affection, and amorous love – are experienced by those who consider themselves equal to Kṛṣṇa and see him as their friend, those who protect Kṛṣṇa and act as his superiors, and those who see Kṛṣṇa as their lover, respectively. Though ontologically always dependent on Kṛṣṇa, devotees in these states of love develop an emotional intimacy characterized by a strong sense of "my-ness" (*mamatā; BhRaAm.* 1.4.2; 2.5.22) that allows them to relate to Kṛṣṇa as friend, parent, or lover.

To explain the dynamics of this love for Kṛṣṇa, Rūpa adapts the → *rasa* theory of Sanskrit literary criticism. The concept of *rasa* is first described in the *Nāṭyaśāstra* of Bharata, the oldest Sanskrit text on dramaturgy. Concerned about how to convey to the audience the emotions depicted on stage, Bharata explains that if the proper causes (*vibhāva*) for the emotion are present, the actors enact the proper responses (*anubhāva*) to those emotions, and the dominant emotion of the play (*sthāyibhāva*), such as love, anger, sorrow, and so on, is nurtured by supportive emotional states (*vyabhicāribhāva*), such as agitation, contentment, and so on, then *rasa* will arise. There is some disagreement in Sanskrit criticism on what *rasa* exactly is and whether it is an experience of the characters, and thus a concept to explain how a literary work can depict emotions, or whether it is the experience of the audience, and thus explains why the audience is moved by a literary work (see Pollock, 1998). Rūpa primarily follows the first perspective but does not entirely exclude the second. In Rūpa's analysis, a devotee is really a character in the play of Kṛṣṇa. The dominant emotion (*sthāyibhāva*) is the love of Kṛṣṇa that arises in his or her heart, which is cleansed by devotional practice. When Kṛṣṇa – the primary cause (*vibhāva*) for that emotion – is present, that love will be accompanied by some other emotional state (*vyabhicāribhāva*), such as contentment, self-loathing, or joy, and the devotee will physically act on that emotion (*anubhāva*). When this occurs, his or her specific love for Kṛṣṇa intensifies and is experienced as *rasa*. This intensified love is called *prema*, the third stage of *bhakti*. The difference between *rasa* and the dominant emotion of love for Kṛṣṇa is merely one of gradation: Rūpa likens the love of Kṛṣṇa (*bhāva*) that dawns in the heart of the devotee to the rays of the sun, which is *prema* (*BhRaAm.* 1.3.1).

But Rūpa does not entirely discard the second view. Devotional drama and literature can help in realizing *rasa* to one whose love has newly awakened, he explains. The devotees' love would be excited by seeing Kṛṣṇa as depicted in a play, and he or she would be able to experience the emotions of the drama's characters, intensified by their own responses (*anubhāvas*) and supportive emotions (*vyabhicāribhāvas*). Since the dominant emotion of the characters in the play becomes "generalized" (*sādharaṇatā; BhRaAm.* 2.5.101–102) when it is heightened as *rasa*, a devotee who already has love for Kṛṣṇa would be able to experience their emotion as his or her own. An inexperienced devotee may thus be more of a spectator than a participant in Kṛṣṇa's play.

Rūpa stresses, however, that the experience of devotional *rasa* is not limited to literature, especially for those whose love is mature. "The saints," he writes, "relish *rasa* by hearing [even] a little about Hari" (*BhRaAm.* 2.5.97). This is because the power of their love, not literature, causes the objects of their love to appear. Because of their love for him, everything reminds them of Kṛṣṇa, and thus the whole world, as it were, becomes the stage of his divine play, which they can witness and participate in.

The Legacy of Rūpa

Rūpa is respected by tradition as one of the few devotees who understood the inner desires of Caitanya (see *CaiC.* 2.1.56ff.). His theological works quickly became the foundational works for all Caitanya Vaiṣṇava theology and gained an unparalleled authority in the tradition. His views on the nature of devotion as *rasa* and its various types and stages, as elaborately described in his two works on *rasa*, in particular influenced every Caitanya Vaiṣṇava author after him. Later authors frequently cite these works and use his detailed classification.

Later theologians wrote extensive commentaries on many of his works – both poetic and theological – the most important of which are the commentaries of Jīva and Viśvanātha Cakravartī on the *Bhaktirasāmṛtasindhu* and the *Ujjvalanīlamaṇi* and Baladeva Vidyābhūṣaṇa's commentary on the *Laghubhāgavatāmṛta*.

But Rūpa's works also formed the basis for many of the works that other theologians composed. The works of Jīva and Viśvanātha, the two most influential theologians of the school after Rūpa, are largely elaborations of Rūpa's teachings. Rūpa's influence on Jīva is obvious throughout his six-volume *Bhāgavatasandarbha*, the school's most comprehensive theological treatise, but is especially visible in the last three volumes: the *Laghubhāgavatāmṛta* forms the basis for the *Kṛṣṇasandarbha*, and much of the *Bhaktisandarbha* and the *Prītisandarbha* is derived from the *Bhaktirasāmṛtasindhu* and the *Ujjvalanīlamaṇi*.

The oeuvre of Viśvanātha is also centered on the writings of Rūpa. He wrote extensive commentaries on the *Bhaktirasāmṛtasindhu* and the *Ujjvalanīlamaṇi*, summaries of these two and the *Laghubhāgavatāmṛta* (called the *Bhaktirasāmṛta-*

Fig. 2: Rūpa Gosvāmī's tomb (photo by Param P. Tomanec, used by courtesy).

sindhubindu, *Ujjvalanīlamaṇikiraṇaleśa*, and *Bhāgavatāmṛtakaṇā*, respectively), and independent works that are extended commentaries on passages of Rūpa's works, such as *Mādhurya-kādambinī* – a commentary on *Bhaktirasāmṛtasindhu* 1.4.15–16 – and *Rāgavartmacandrikā* on the *Bhaktirasāmṛtasindhu* section on the practice of *rāgānugabhakti*. Acknowledging their indebtedness to Rūpa, Caitanya Vaiṣṇavas sometimes call themselves *rūpānugas*, "followers of Rūpa." The term occurs as early as Raghunāthadāsa's *Manaḥśikṣā* (12) and the *Sādhanadīpikā* (see below) but is particularly frequently used after the 19th century, by the Caitanya Vaiṣṇava reformer → Bhaktisiddhanta Saraswati and his disciples.

However, Rūpa's importance to the Caitanya tradition is not merely intellectual. From very early on, the devotees of Caitanya were believed to also act in the *līlā* of Kṛṣṇa. Since Caitanya is Kṛṣṇa, and Kṛṣṇa descends to earth with his devotees, Caitanya's devotees must also have an eternal form as devotees of Kṛṣṇa. The early biographies of Caitanya already try to identify some of Caitanya's principal associates as well-known associates of Kṛṣṇa (see Stewart, 2010, 128–138), but the most elaborate attempt at this is found in the *Gauragaṇoddeśadīpikā* of Kavikarṇapūra – a younger contemporary of Rūpa who recorded the views of the Caitanya Vaiṣṇava communities in Vraja, Bengal, and Orissa on the identity of Caitanya's devotees. In the *Gauragaṇoddeśadīpikā*, the six *gosvāmī*s are identified with six *mañjarī*s – six young teenage girls who serve Rādhā under the guidance of one of Rādhā's principal female friends (*sakhī*s). Kavikarṇapūra identifies Rūpa as Rūpa Mañjarī (*GauDī*. 180), a name already listed in Rūpa's own *Rādhākṛṣṇagaṇoddeśadīpikā* (*Laghu* 179). Soon these *mañjarī*s become the focus of a meditative devotional practice called *mañjarīsādhana*, in which the devotee meditates on assisting these *mañjarī*s in their service to the divine couple. Rūpa, as the assistant to Lalitā and the principal *mañjarī*, plays a central role in this, and shortly after his passing, he becomes the focus of veneration. In his Bengali songs, Narottamadās, who studied under Rūpa, expresses his desire to worship the divine couple as a *mañjarī*, and often the focus of his prayers is on the *mañjarī*s themselves and Rūpa Mañjarī in particular (even though his own *guru*, Lokanātha Gosvāmī, is also identified as one of the main *mañjarī*s, called Mañjulāli Mañjarī).

This devotion to Rūpa, however, was confined neither to his disciples nor even to Vraja. One of the earliest works that details the worship of Rūpa, including *mantra*s for the worship of Rūpa Mañjarī, is found in the *Gauragovindārcana-smaraṇapaddhati* of Dhyānacandra Gosvāmī, who resided in Orissa in the early 17th century.

A longer discussion of the importance of Rūpa is found in the *Sādhanadīpikā* of Rādhākṛṣṇa Gosvāmī, the leader of the Govindadeva Temple in Vrindavan in the early 17th century. Chapter 8 of this work is entirely devoted to Rūpa (as both Gosvāmī and Mañjarī). Rādhākṛṣṇa offers a brief account of the main events in Rūpa's life; gathers verses praising Rūpa from older authors like Sanātana, Kavikarṇapūra, and Raghunāthadāsa; and even includes a *Rūpamañjaryaṣṭaka*, "Eight Prayers to Rūpa Mañjarī." His exclusive devotion to Rūpa illustrates the importance of Rūpa to the Caitanya Vaiṣṇava tradition: "I do not worship Rādhā," he writes, "nor Kṛṣṇa, nor Gaurāṅga [Caitanya]. May I be, birth after birth, a particle of dust at the lotus feet of Śrī Rūpa."

Bibliography

Brzezinski, J., *Mystic Poetry: Rūpa Gosvāmin's Uddhava-sandeśa and Haṃsadūta*, San Francisco, 1999.

Broo, M., "Drama in the Service of Kṛṣṇa: Rūpa Gosvāmin's Nāṭaka-candrikā," *StO* 110, 2011, 55–65.

Case, M., ed., *Govindadeva: A Dialogue in Stone*, New Delhi, 1996.

De, S.K., *Early History of the Vaisnava Faith and Movement in Bengal: From Sanskrit and Bengali Sources*, Calcutta, 1986.

Gupta, R., *The Caitanya Vaiṣṇava Vedānta of Jīva Gosvāmī: When Knowledge Meets Devotion*, London, 2007.

Haberman, D., *Acting as a Way of Salvation: A Study of rāgānugā bhakti sādhana*, New York, 1988.

Habib, I., "A Documentary History of the Gosā'ins (Gosvāmīs) of the Caitanya Sect at Vṛndāvana," in: M. Case, ed., *Govindadeva: A Dialogue in Stone*, New Delhi, 1996, 131–159.

Kapoor, O.B.L., *The Gosvāmīs of Vṛndāvana*, New Delhi, 1995.

Lutjeharms, R., "'Why Do We Still Sift the Husk-like Upaniṣads?' Revisiting Vedānta in Early Caitanya Vaiṣṇava Theology," in: J. Frazier, ed., *Innovations in Early Modern Indian Religious Thought*, forthcoming.

Pauwels, H., *In Praise of Holy Men: Hagiographic Poems by and about Harirām Vyās*, Groningen, 2002.

Pollock, S., "Bhoja's Śṛṅgāraprakāśa and the Problem of Rasa: A Historical Introduction and Annotated Translation," *AS/ÉA* 70/1, 1998, 117–192.

Stewart, T., *The Final Word: The Caitanya Caritāmṛta and the Grammar of Religious Tradition*, New York, 2010.

Rembert Lutjeharms

Śaṅkara

The great systematizer of Advaita → Vedānta, Śaṅkara (c. 8th cent. CE) looms large in the history of Indian philosophy and in the religious imagination of Hindus. Viewed at once as a brilliant thinker and great reformer, Śaṅkara's work and genius have rightly been compared to those of classic philosophers in the West, including Plato, Thomas Aquinas, Spinoza, and Martin Heidegger. While most of the texts traditionally ascribed to Śaṅkara – as many as four hundred, according to S. Mayeda – are considered spurious, his commentary on the *Brahmasūtra*, considered the yardstick by which all other putative Śaṅkaran texts are measured, is a masterpiece of Advaita synthesis, firmly establishing the method and argument of the Advaita *darśana*. K.H. Potter writes that "[i]t is safe to say that it is the single most influential philosophical text in India today, a status it has enjoyed for at least a century, possibly longer" (Potter, 1981, 119).

Śaṅkara is important not only for assimilating and extending trains of nondualistic thought, which extended back to the → Upaniṣads and continued through to the teaching of Gauḍapāda, supposedly Śaṅkara's *paramaguru* (*guru* of own's *guru*), but also for the impact he made in the religious imagination of India. He is "the stuff of legend," as J. Bader notes; fantastic and mythic accounts of his life affirm not only his philosophical acumen but also his ultimate divinity. Indeed, according to traditional beliefs, Śaṅkara is viewed as an incarnation of the god → Śiva. Such grandiose apotheosis, while no doubt emerging owing to a particularly compelling historical figure, ultimately speaks to the needs and aspirations of a broader community, in this case Brahman. It must be remembered that the traditional assumptions establishing and governing the vedic "*nomos*" included Brahman control over the production of knowledge (even if the → Veda were considered eternal and authorless) and its transmission. The scope of knowledge comprehended both the sacred and mundane — that is, it mapped out an ultimate cosmic vision (or visions) found in the Veda while also establishing a mesocosmic, social vision in the → Dharmaśāstra. The mythic accounts of Śaṅkara, written by Brahmans, suffused with miracles and legends, underscore a profound sense of mystery and holiness, while also making Śaṅkara more accessible to a broader community perhaps less equipped to follow the complex technicalities and arguments of his philosophy. However, another view suggests that the many biographies, which share significant patterns and themes, repeatedly underscore Śaṅkara's apparently brief but meteroric career as *saṃnyāsin*, which nevertheless decisively establishes Hindu orthodoxy against the rise of Buddhism and sectarian Hinduism. Śaṅkara's biographies see him as engaging in a victorious conquest of the quarters (*digvijaya*) debating and defeating opponents, establishing monastic centers (*maṭhas*), and developing the → Daśanāmī ("Ten Named Ones") religious order.

Interestingly, a "softer," less polemical, interpretation of Śaṅkara's genius has directly or indirectly been used in the 20th-century neo-Advaita revival. For example, S. → Radhakrishnan writes of the cultural tension and wrangling among sects at the time of Śaṅkara and how the time needed a genius who "could stretch the old molds without breaking them and synthesize the warring sects on a broad basis of truth" (Radhakrishnan, 1989, 467). For him, "Śaṅkara 'set to music' the tune which had been haunting millions of ears, and announced his Advaita Vedānta as offering a common basis for religious unity" (Radhakrishnan, 1989, 467). While the inclusivism superimposed on Śaṅkara is dubious, there is no doubt that Śaṅkara's Advaita was used by 19th- and 20th-century reformers and apologists to speak to a transcendent and ultimately superior Hindu philosophy that comprehends all religious traditions. While Śaṅkara may not have announced his Advaita Vedānta as offering a common basis for religious unity, neo-Advaitins such as S. Radhakrishnan certainly have.

Dates of Śaṅkara

The traditional dates of Śaṅkara, 788–820 CE, were first proposed by K.B. Pathak in the 19th century (Malkovsky, 2001, 1). Numerous scholars, beginning with H. Nakamura, argue, based on textual and historical evidence, that the dates should be pushed back earlier. H. Nakamura argued for 700–750 CE, supported by L. Renou and

D.H.H. Ingalls (Malkovsky, 2001, 2). Others push for even earlier dates; K.H. Potter suggested the late 7th and early 8th centuries CE. Some of the reasoning for rejecting the traditional dates includes Śaṅkara's reference, in his *Upadeśasāhasrī*, to the Buddhist logician Dharmakīrti, who lived sometime in the mid-7th century; that era would thus mark, as B.J. Malkovsky notes, the earliest possible limit to Śaṅkara's liftetime (Malkovsky, 2001, 4). Other relevant evidence includes Śaṅkara's familiarity with the → Mīmāṃsā teacher Kumārila Bhaṭṭa, who lived at the end of the 7th century CE. According to traditional accounts, Kumārila Bhaṭṭa, apparently a much older contemporary of Śaṅkara, sent his disciple, Maṇḍana Miśra, to debate Śaṅkara. Maṇḍana Miśra, argued H. Nakamura, lived from 670 to 720 CE (Nakamura, in Malkovsky, 2001, 4). Assuming Śaṅkara was a younger contemporary of Maṇḍana Miśra, this again would place Śaṅkara's dates around the turn of the 8th century CE. Concerning the traditional dates of 788–820, M. Hiriyanna writes that they may be accepted "within the limits of a hundred years" (Hiriyanna, 1995, 155). B.J. Malkovsky arrives at perhaps the wisest claim based on the evidence, "Probably the most accurate designation of when Śaṅkara lived would be to declare that he 'flourished' around the year 700 C.E" (Malkovsky, 8).

In terms of the general context of his time, S. Mayeda notes that during the 5th and 6th centuries the Huns invaded India from the central Asian steppes (Mayeda, 1992, 3). The Gupta Empire, a source of cultural cohesion and flourishing, dissolved. While in the 7th century King Harṣa restored peace, after his death India fell into chaos again (Mayeda, 1992, 3). So, while S. Radhakrishnan's interpretation of Śaṅkara as "inclusivist" may be tendentious, Śaṅkara did compose his works during a time of social, cultural, and political upheaval, which included the rise of sectarian and devotional Hinduism and the ongoing challenges of *nāstika* or heterodox traditions such as Buddhism and Jainism. This is the context that helps explain not only Śaṅkara's vigorous polemical efforts directed against some of these groups, but also the triumphalist mythology found in his biographies.

Biography

Śaṅkara's life story is found in numerous biographies, called *vijaya*s or *digvijaya*s, which share common and repeated themes. Their mythic themes and legendary embellishments owe more to hagiography than biography, the former typically expressing the agenda or vision of the hagiographer *vis-á-vis* the presumed needs of the audience. In this case, it includes conveying the triumphant orthodoxy of Śaṅkara in narrative fashion for an audience perhaps less equipped to follow Śaṅkara's complex disputations that end, in the typical patterns of Indian argument, with triumphant *siddhānta*s (demonstrated conclusions of arguments). At the same time, the hagiographical narratives are "open" texts; that is, they are available and accessible to classes not otherwise enfranchised in traditional vedic training and transmission. The hagiographies "open" Śaṅkara to a broader community that culturally may be marginalized both by the structures of orthodoxy that Śaṅkara supports – particularly *varṇāśramadharma* and the classic threefold training of *śravaṇa* (hearing — that is, teaching from a *guru*), *manana* (reflection), and *nididhāysana* (→ meditation) – and in the establishment of the *maṭha*s, institutional embodiments of orthodoxy. This is ironic, given the transcendent nature of nondual mysticism. If, according to Advaitin tenets, clearly affirmed by Śaṅkara, the world is provisional, fundamentally unreal, or even illusory, then so are all cultural and religious forms, including caste, text, and tradition. In fact, Śaṅkara affirms, in no uncertain terms, the supremacy of the Vedas as the instrument, *par excellence*, required to destroy ignorance and "achieve" → liberation, while at the same affirming renunciation as a necessary step in the economy of liberation. But nothing – not renunciation or meditation – "produces" liberation; at most these efforts are conducive to it. The economy of liberation becomes, as A. Rambachan has shown, a program of "accomplishing the accomplished." However, despite the apparent ubiquity of the one true self, and the provisional nature of phenomenal reality, the Vedas and the program of renunciation were nonetheless the historical provenance of Brahmans. In theory, Śaṅkara's transcendent nondualism would, indeed, appear to result in a genuine social inclusivism. However, in practice, the qualified aspirant meant only Brahmans. For example, in Śaṅkara's culture of liberation, Brahmans alone were eligible to perform the *nitya* (necessary) and *naimittika* (occasional) duties, which prepare one for further inquiry into → *brahman.* It is for this reason, according to Y. Sawai, that Śaṅkara "appears to have allowed only *brahmaṇas* to become members of the Śṛngeri Matha, which he is traditionally said to have founded" (Sawai, 1986, 381). In short, while the hagiographies may "open" or bring the triumph of Śaṅkara to a broader community, that triumph ultimately affirms traditional orthodoxy and its exclusionary social structures.

The traditional accounts of Mādhava Vidyāraṇya, Cidvilāsa, and Sadānanda, all written hundreds of years after Śaṅkara, agree that Śaṅkara was born in a village, Kaladi, off the Malabar coast of contemporary Kerala (Potter, 1981, 117). The biography of Ānandagiri holds that Śaṅkara was born in Chidambaram in Tamil Nadu (Potter, 1981, 117). In any case, Śaṅkara in all likelihood did come from the south, especially since his disciple Sureśvara calls him "a Drāviḍa," not to mention Śaṅkara's preference for using writing practices (incisions into palm leaf, later to be filled in with ink) more typically associated with the south (Alston, 1981, 44). Reputedly, Śaṅkara was born to a Nambūtiri Brahman family, and his father, Śivaguru, died shortly after Śaṅkara was born. The accounts hold that Śaṅkara took *saṃnyāsa* at the age of eight; met his *guru*, Govinda Bhagavatpāda, on the banks of the Narmadā River; and eventually made his way to Kāśī (Varanasi). In Kāśī he began to attract disciples, including Padmapāda, the first of four premier disciples, which include Sureśvara, Hastāmalaka, and Toṭaka. The former two were profound thinkers in their own right; Padmāpada wrote a commentary, the *Pañcapādikā*, on Śaṅkara's *Brahmasūtrabhāṣya*, which develops Advaitin thought in ways Śaṅkara did not, including establishing the *pratibimbavāda* doctrine, the notion that the *jīva* is a mirror to the → *ātman.* Sureśvara traditionally has been understood to be Maṇḍana Miśra, who after being defeated in debate pledged obeisance to Śaṅkara, though most contemporary scholars reject this association. Still, the filial devotion to Śaṅkara is evidenced by Sureśvara's declarations extolling Śaṅkara's qualities, for example, "by the axe of whose speech the opinions of the logicians are hewn" (Forsthoefel, 2002, 77–78). Sureśvara wrote commanding Advaitin texts himself, including a commentary on Śaṅkara's *Taittirīyopaniṣadbhāṣya*, the *Taittirīyopaniṣadbhāṣyavārtika.* That fact naturally supports the claim that the *Taittirīyopaniṣadbhāṣya* authentically belongs to Śaṅkara's body of work. Sureśvara's subcommentary on Śaṅkara's commentary approximates, according to T.M.P. Mahadevan, half the length of the → *Rāmāyaṇa*, or some 12,000 verses. Sureśvara also wrote a pithy, trenchant noncommentarial independent treatise, *Naiṣkarmyasiddhi*, modeled in the style of the single independent treatise ascribed to Śaṅkara, the *Upadeśasāhasrī.*

With Padmapāda, Śaṅkara is said to have made a pilgrimage to Badrinath, staying there for four years, and, though not yet 16, he is said to have written his major works. Years later he went to Prayag to debate Kumārila Bhaṭṭa. Bhaṭṭa, however, was elderly and sent him to his disciple Maṇḍana Miśra, who took up the challenge to debate. The assumption in the rules of debate, however, demanded that the loser would become the disciple of the winner. After many days of argument, Śaṅkara finally defeated Maṇḍana Miśra, but then Maṇḍana Miśra's wife, Bhāratī, revealed herself as a goddess. She then challenged Śaṅkara, extending the debate for many more days. Her principal challenge was Śaṅkara's ignorance of the Kāmaśāstra (treatises on love and pleasure) on the grounds of Śaṅkara's asceticism. Śaṅkara asked for a month's hiatus, when, as the story goes, Śaṅkara, drawing upon his yogic prowess, assumed the body of a dead king while having earlier hidden his body in a tree hollow. The king's chamber and court were astonished at his miraculous recovery, and even more astonished, ultimately, at the positive change in disposition of the king. Śaṅkara learned the art of love from the harem, yet the court, noting the change in the king's disposition, suspected that a *yogin* had taken possession of the king's body. The king's retainers sent troops to find the body of the *yogin* and destroy it, while Śaṅkara's disciples, having heard of the royal miracle, sought out the king *qua* Śaṅkara. Eventually they found him, and he returned to his original body, whereupon he returned to Bhāratī and defeated her in debate.

Śaṅkara is said to have returned to his birthplace to perform the funeral rites of his mother – an unconventional practice for a *saṃnyāsin.* After that he engaged in a grand tour, a "conquest of the quarters" (*digvijaya*) to establish the four great monastic centers (*maṭhas*) – Sringeri in the south, Dwarka in the west, Badrinath in the north, and Puri in the east. At each station, he appointed one of his chief disciples as supreme *ācārya* (later to be called *śaṅkarācāryas*), Sureśvara at Sringeri, Padmapāda at Badrinath, Hastāmalaka at Dwarka, and Toṭaka in Puri. There is also a tradition that affirms Kanchipuram as a fifth monastic seat. In addition to the *maṭhas*, Śaṅkara is said to have established the Daśanāmī renunciate order. The orders associated with the Sringeri *maṭh* are Sarasvatī (eloquence), Puri (city), and Bhāratī; the orders associated with Dwarka are Tīrtha (ford) and Āśrama (hermitage); the orders associated with Badrinath are Giri (mountain), Sāgara (ocean), and Pārvata (mountain); the orders associated with Puri are Āraṇya (forest) and Vana (forest). The leader of the entire Daśanāmī order is the abbot of Puri, considered to be the *jagadguru* (teacher of the universe). Continuing the theme of the triumph of orthodoxy, G. Flood notes that "[t]he orders founded by Śaṅkara were partly instrumental in eradicating Jainism and Buddhism from south India and also in giving coherence and a sense of pan-Indian identity to orthodox, vedic tradition" (Flood, 1996, 93). The Daśanāmīs, according to G. Flood, remain among the most orthodox and learned of Hindu renouncers.

While most accounts hold that Śaṅkara died at the age of 32, in the Himalayas, Ānandagiri holds that he died in Kanchipuram (Potter, 1981, 118). Later traditions hold that Śaṅkara himself was an incarnation of Śiva; this assumption is never communicated by his disciples, though they do speak to Śaṅkara's compelling intellect and the great throngs that he drew to him. The assumption of his divinity as Śiva is curious, since he seems to favor → Viṣṇu in his texts. For example, in the *Brahmasūtrabhāṣya*, while he does criticize → Pāñcarātra doctrines, he nonetheless affirms Hari-Nārāyaṇa as the absolute and, moreover, does not name Śiva in this way (Alston, 1981, 45). Furthermore, while he criticizes the philosophical positions of theists, he nonetheless praises Vaiṣṇavas for their worship of Nārāyaṇa, again identified as the absolute; he says nothing in defense of Śaiva worship (Alston, 1981, 45). Padmapāda makes a distinction in his benediction between Śaṅkara bearing the name of Śiva and Śiva himself, noting, incidentally, that Śaṅkara did not wear ashes on his forehead in the style of Śaiva renunciants (Alston, 1981, 45–46). It is fair to assume that the belief that Śaṅkara was an incarnation of Śiva refers to later needs emerging in sectarian competition.

Texts

Since the mid-20th century, scholars have painstakingly analyzed a vast corpus of texts reputedly or traditionally ascribed to Śaṅkara. These include widely published and translated independent treatises such as the *Vivekacūḍāmaṇi* and *Ātmabodha*, which ultimately have been determined to be written later than Śaṅkara; the texts, however, remain useful, accessible introductions to the basic tenets of Advaita. Additionally, Śaṅkara is the reputed author of many hymns (→ Stotras), but close reading of their content, as well as following R. Gussner's "stylometric" analysis, indicates that most – if not all – of the hymns, while fascinating for the theological and spiritual content, are of spurious Śaṅkaran authorship.

Instead, scholars begin with the *Brahmasūtrabhāṣya*, considered by many to be the single most important text in the history of Advaita. At the very least, it certainly is, following E. Deutsch and J.A.B van Buitenen, "*the* foundational text of classical Advaita Vedanta" (Malkovsky, 2001, 15, 16n74). Indeed, for B.J. Malkovsky, K.H. Potter, J. Bader, and others, the author of the *Brahmasūtrabhāṣya*, is, by definition, Śaṅkara. That is to say, Śaṅkara is understood to be the author of the *Brahmasūtrabhāṣya*; that *magnum opus* then becomes the standard by which to measure and determine other texts potentially written by the same author. As B.J. Malkovsky explains,

> All other works ascribed to Śaṅkara would have to be measured against this commentary in terms of philosophical or theological content, meaning of certain key terms, word frequency, and style, for their authenticity to be established. (Malkovsky, 2001, 16)

Among the first scholars to do this was P. Hacker in the mid-20th century. Employing a historical-critical method, he analyzed key terms such as → *avidyā*, *nāmarūpa*, → *māyā*, and → *īśvara* and was therefore able

> to distinguish what was unique in Śaṅkara's *Brahma Sūtra Bhāṣya* not only in comparison with the later advaitic tradition but also in comparison with Śaṅkara's contemporaries and immediate disciples. (Malkovsky, 2001, 16)

Other scholars, including S. Mayeda, H. Nakamura, and R. Gussner, have contributed to these studies, and the general consensus among scholars at this point is that texts properly ascribed to Śaṅkara include the *Brahmasūtrabhāṣya*, the *Bhagavadgītābhāṣya*, the *Upadeśasāhasrī*, and commentaries on ten Upaniṣads: *Bṛhadāraṇyakopaniṣad, Chāndogyopaniṣad, Taittirīyopaniṣad, Aitareyopaniṣad, Īsopaniṣad, Kaṭhopaniṣad, Kenopaniṣad, Muṇḍakopaniṣad, Praśnopaniṣad*, and *Māṇḍūkyopaniṣad*, along with the *Gauḍapādakārikā*. Some scholars have argued that two other texts, not strictly Advaitin in content, the *Yogasūtrabhāṣyavivaraṇa* and the *Adhyātmapalavivaraṇa*, can be persuasively included in the Śaṅkaran canon.

Philosophy

Śaṅkara builds upon centuries of reflection on the nature of reality and the nature of the self, extending as far back as the Upaniṣads perhaps a thousand years earlier and continuing through to the *Gauḍapādakārikā* and the *Brahmasūtra*. The *Brahmasūtra*, ostensibly written by Bādarāyaṇa but likely supplemented by the contributions of unknown authors, becomes the focus of Śaṅkara's most famous commentary.

While a premier subtext in Bādarāyaṇa is the refutation of → Sāṃkhya dualism, an agenda taken up by Śaṅkara, a more enduring battle emerges against the Mīmāṃsā school, principally concerned with ritual action as the premier and fundamentally correct "religious" orientation, not to mention vedic exegesis. Taking its cue from the ancient hymn in the *Ṛgveda*, the *Puruṣasūkta*, ritualists developed a theology of sacrifice that emphasized both macrocosmic and microcosmic benefits. While the sacrificer, the one endowing the sacrifice, would ostensibly gain material benefits in the priestly execution of the sacrifice, the sacrifice itself became a ritual representation of the primordial sacrifice, in effect "re-creating" the universe. For this school of thought, systematized by Jaimini in the *Mīmāṃsāsūtra*, the primary vedic obligation was sacrifice, for sacrifice was the central mechanism for maintaining the fluid movement of the universe and therefore germane to universal welfare and harmony. At the same time, personal benefits were presumed to accrue to the sacrificer – wealth, prosperity, health, longevity, and so on.

However, another school of thought, seen in incipient fashion in the Upaniṣads and clearly affirmed by Śaṅkara, called this into question on the basis of the transitory nature of external rewards, the existential problem of suffering, and a developing theory of → *karman* and rebirth (→ *saṃsāra*). The persistence and ubiquity of suffering eventually led to intense reflection, particularly in the Upaniṣads, on what constituted ultimate satisfaction – that is, some experience of joy or bliss that does not fade or erode in time. At the same time, a second train of thought developed from early speculation on the presumed immanence of the divine, presuming it to be the unifying thread within the plural universe. These two trains of thought dovetailed together in early nondualism.

The sages or mystics held that a repeated program of sacrificial action motivated by material benefits provided no lasting reward. The Mīmāṃsā dictum – "the one who desires heaven must sacrifice" (*svārga kāmo yajeta*) – was fundamentally problematic, according to this view. The sacrifice, fueled by desire, produced its natural outcome, fruit, or consequence. Unfortunately, in this view, the fruit itself is not eternal; once consumed, one dies again, repeating the cycle and therefore extending a relentless yet futile search for lasting contentment in external rewards. Since action is fundamentally problematic, Śaṅkara, following Bādarāyaṇa, diminishes the value of the "action portion" (*karmakāṇḍa*) of the Vedas, instead privileging the knowledge portion (*jñānakāṇḍa*) — namely, the Upaniṣads. Much goes on in these complicated texts, first among which is the aim to access a transcendent, saving knowledge, one approach to which was to engage in a reevaluation or reinterpretation of the sacrifice. For example, rather than mechanically executing the sacrifice, sages turned to consider the power that made the sacrifice efficacious. That power was *brahman*, the generative and spiritual force underlying the sacrifice and, ultimately, the universe. Through numerous illustrations, parables, and anecdotes, the authors of the Upaniṣads articulate a profoundly unitive and interior relationship to ultimate reality. For example, as salt, however invisible and imperceptible to sight, pervades the entire cup of water, so *brahman*, invisible and imperceptible to the senses, pervades the universe. The sages then apply this "pervasion" to anthropological reflection. If *brahman* pervades the universe, and we are part of the universe, then *brahman* pervades us. While the Upaniṣads can be read with a variety of philosophical nuance (and not necessarily strictly nondualistic), there is no question that a kind of nondualism can be seen in them. Indeed, several of the great sayings (*mahāvākyas*) of the Upaniṣads indicate the ultimate identification between one's true self (*ātman*) and the supreme self (*brahman*), perhaps the most famous being *tat tvam asi* ("that you are"). This saying represents a conclusion of the ultimate identification of the true self with the supreme self, which, when internalized, was assumed to issue in liberation. That is to say, one's truest identity – not ego, not body, not temporary attributions, and so on – is nondifferent from the supreme *brahman*, which, while beyond limited attributions, is nonetheless described as "being, consciousness, bliss" (*saccidānanda*). If the supreme *brahman* is our true identity, it then behooves the wise one to realize it. Metaphysics, therefore, leads to soteriology.

For the sages and *yogins*, an inward, introspective turn was required to discover the true self, this ultimate identification between *ātman* and *brahman*. While there are substantial differences between the → Yoga school and the nondualist school, they are similar in key assumptions, namely, that the act of fundamentally misconstruing identity produces suffering. Misidentification, determined by temporary circumstances, will inevitably produce suffering because the circumstances are "accidental" and transitory. When a misidentified self is "insulted," as it were, by age, sickness, poverty, or loss, or when the supposed identity is threatened, the subject suffers anguish. The key psycho-existential conflict is the mind clouded by a roiling mix of misperceptions about self, world, and others. However, not realizing the truth of the divine self, and therefore suffering the traumas that misidentification causes, is akin, in a common Advaitin metaphor, to the distress over losing a bejeweled necklace, absentmindedly unaware that the treasure is draped around one's neck. For the Advaitin, the treasure is "here": innate, un-loseable, and infinite.

This is part of the intellectual backdrop seen in Śaṅkara's commentary on the *Brahmasūtra*, particularly in his justly famous prologue, which affirms and outlines the central convictions and assumptions that become classic in Advaita philosophy. In this famous passage, we see a standard representation of the cardinal existential flaw represented by earlier nondualists, *yogins*, and sages: humanity mistakes the real for the unreal and the unreal for the real. The "real" in Śaṅkara has a particular – and some might say idiosyncratic – definition, namely that which endures or is not "sublated" (or negated or contradicted or, finally, that which does not suffer change or loss) in the three phases of time – past, present, and future (*trikāle abādhyatva*). Assuming the truth of *brahman*, on this view then there is only one true real, namely *brahman* itself. All else, by definition, is unreal, for what constitutes phenomenal reality are changing, finite events, or existents. In fact, the nature of phenomenal reality is change itself. In analyses that compare well with Buddhism, the source of suffering lies in clinging to changing phenomena as if they are changeless, and this fundamentally pertains to misguided notions of self. These "misconstruals" are typically ego based or based on the mistaken perception that the so-called mind – body complex constitutes in a decisive way our very self. In the view of Śaṅkara, this fundamental ignorance is the source of suffering and the cause of the enmeshment of the soul in the cycle of *saṃsāra*. The antidote to this crisis is liberating knowledge.

Śaṅkara conveys a relentless nondualism in his writings, and to do this systematically, he must engage not only metaphysics but also epistemology. On the one hand, given his assumptions concerning the one real – that which perdures in the three phases of time – he must articulate a view that accounts for the "seemingly real" as well as the plurality of phenomenal reality. He does this by appealing to the so-called two standpoints, the relative standpoint (*vyavahārikāvasthā*) and the ultimate standpoint (*paramārthtikāvasthā*), a conceptualization that clearly borrows from the "two truths" doctrine in Madhyamaka Buddhism. From the relative standpoint, its radical nondualism notwithstanding, Advaita is decidedly realistic and pluralistic, admitting any number of metaphysical, epistemological, and ethical distinctions – for example, subject, object, categories, whole-part relations, means of producing knowledge, merit, demerit, duty, and so on. Despite its nondualism, Advaita requires the *vyavahārikāvasthā*; without it, it would be fundamentally incoherent, for the tactile, perceptible world consistently confounds any purported mystical oneness. The *vyavahārikāvasthā* thus is a necessary plank in the Advaita platform for a number of reasons, not the least of which is that it allows Advaita to meet on the philosophical playing field with other schools to argue and defend its position. Some might hold that the appeal to an "ultimate" point of view that is axiomatic is contrived and assumes what is to be proven. In any case, the two standpoints are necessary. Without the *vyavahārikāvasthā*, the Advaita cannot utter a word. With the *vyavahārikāvasthā*, the Advaitin has a device to engage in debate, persuade, or evoke a commitment to a nondualist metaphysic. Some thinkers, however, may be dissatisfied with the trump card of the "ultimate standpoint," for here no discourse is possible (because discourse involves plurality of subject–object). The *paramārthtikāvasthā* (or *mokṣa* or *brahman* or *ātman*) is by definition transpersonal, transphenomenal, absolute. It has nothing to do with any common intercourse with the world. The *vyavahārikāvasthā* is like a dream or an illusion into which senses are inevitably keyed. Indeed, Śaṅkara writes that imperishable real (*akṣaram satyam*) is "entirely beyond the scope of perception (*atyantaparokṣatvāt*)." The knowledge that saves or is salvation, according to Śaṅkara, is not constricted by time or space. The knowledge that saves, however, cannot be understood in terms typically associated with knowledge, for knowledge involves knower, object of knowledge, and process of knowing, and these are plural phenomena. The knowledge that saves must be understood as a "knowing beyond knowledge," a state or awareness that is not limited or conditioned by traditional subject–object dichotomies. Realizing this state cannot properly be called an "experience," *per se*, because experience also implies subject-object dualism. Nevertheless, Śaṅkara does place a premium on experience, *anubhava*, as a self-certifying, self-guaranteeing event in the economy of liberation. But his use of "experience" must be read as unmoored from the philosophical implications layered into its common linguistic use (though with careful analysis, one can attempt to "read" a unity of being in the plural world of experience, which Śaṅkara and other nondualists have done). In the end, *anubhava* is a specific kind of "religious" experience, namely, a realization that transcends subject–object dichotomy. *Anubhava* is an "experience" beyond duality.

In the prologue to his commentary on the *Brahmasūtra*, Śaṅkara elucidates the fundamental crisis, the confusion or "mutual superimposition" of self and not-self, whose fundamental differences, writes Śaṅkara, are as opposed as light and dark. Śaṅkara defines superimposition as the apparent presentation to consciousness of something previously observed elsewhere. Perhaps his most famous illustration is the snake rope. In dim light, one might see a coiled rope and mistake it for a snake. The error lies in wrongly superimposing the features and qualities of a snake onto the rope. The rope is the basis or substrate of the superimposition. Similarly, *brahman* is the substrate or basis for fundamental metaphysical misconstruals, such as pluralism and dualism. The rope-snake error indicates not only a cognitive malfunction, but also the manner in which afflictive emotion may be stimulated by it. The person who mistakes the unreal snake for the real rope experiences a flush of emotions – fear, anxiety, and distress. For Śaṅkara, as well as for other thinkers and saints in the Advaita tradition, in the other *āstika* philosophical systems, and even in nonvedic traditions such as Buddhism and Jainism, the economy of liberation involves a kind of cognitive and emotional therapy. When one "sees" rightly, one is free from the roiling mix of afflictive emotions. One is calm, free, and unthreatened.

In Śaṅkara's analysis, we typically confuse identity by superimposing limiting attributes of not-self upon the self. This identification is marked by predicate nominatives or predicate adjectives: I am a man, I am tall, I am stout, I am lean, I am walking, I am mute, I am blind, I am happy, I am sad. These identifications wrongly confuse the infinite, transcendent self – "constituted" by being, consciousness, and bliss – and not-self. At the same time, we also confuse the qualities of the limited self as characteristic of the true self. The true self is the transcendent real, unconditioned by time or space. The fundamental misperceptions here involve reducing, as it were, the supreme self by identifying it with limiting adjuncts or conditions. At the same time, the process overly "inflates" the value of these limited identities. The ego, the limited "I," "steals" consciousness, thereby generating a putative identity in these limited constructions. But these identities are, with everything else in the phenomenal world, fundamentally unreal and illusory; they do not last. Our misguided attachment to these limited identities – I am handsome, beautiful, smart, wealthy, and successful – will be the source of our suffering when these identities will be threatened, as they will be inevitably, by the passage of time, aging, sickness, and competition with others. The prescription? Discrimination between the real and unreal. In Śaṅkara's emphasis on knowledge as the premier vehicle for liberation, there is an affinity with the Sāṃkhya school, which also places a premium on discriminating knowledge as the supreme mechanism for liberation. However,

Śaṅkara takes pains, in the *Brahmasūtrabhāṣya*, to reject Sāṃkhya dualism, while nonetheless affirming, with some philosophical difficulty, *brahman* as material cause of the universe. In the end, the world, for Śaṅkara, is neither "real," since it is impermanent, nor unreal, since we do see the impact of phenomenal cause and effect. Not real, owing to change, and not unreal – like a hare's horn – owing to empirical evidence, the world is "indescribable" (*anirvacanīya*).

While Śaṅkara does not use the term *māyā* in the manner of later Advaitins, he does attribute a mystery to phenomenal reality such that phenomenal reality reveals the "apparent," but finally unreal, transformation of *brahman*. This "apparent transformation" theory (*vivartavāda*) moves away from "real transformation" (*pariṇāmavāda*) theory of Sāṃkhya. It sets the stage for later Advaitin "illusionistic" theories built around the concept of *māyā*.

There is a confidence in Śaṅkara's thought that suggests that insight into reality decisively nullifies the profound misconstruals that generate so much affliction and discord. The example of the rope/snake is again illustrative. When we see the rope as it is – a rope, and not a snake – we are freed from the distress that obtains by misconstruing it as a dangerous snake. While phenomenal reality may have a dreamlike sensibility, even dreams can be frightening and disturbing – until we recognize the dream as a dream, having no purchase on "real" life. This confidence in knowledge as a decisive vehicle sometimes seems overly optimistic, perhaps flying in the face of empirical reality. Śaṅkara's later disputant, → Rāmānuja, holds that merely repeating "I am *brahman*" is ineffective; he of course will hold that devotion, as a particularly intense, collected meditative concentration on Viṣṇu is the supreme path of liberation. Indeed, he quite rightly registers that devotion itself is a particular kind of knowledge (*bhaktirūpa jñānaviśeṣa eva*). That is to say, there is a knowledge we gain in and through devotion, for love "cathects" to an "object" (or person or truth), allowing for a range of connative and affective energies that impact cognitive awareness. Through loving attentiveness, one enters into and gains insight into the object of love.

The Yoga school also held that "mere knowledge" was insufficient without sustained practice (*abhyāsa*) as well. The reason for this was clear: a longstanding pattern of "wrong identification" would issue in a particularly insidious nexus of cause and effect. The wrong "mental" premise eventually issues in misguided ego-centered actions; these in turn not only have karmic consequences but also leave residues or latent tendencies that subtly reinforce the original misconception. This in turn issues, in repeated misguided actions, *karman* outcomes, latent reinforcing tendencies, and so on. The result is enmeshment in the cycle of suffering, which has its origins in a habituated mental cycle. Yoga philosophy, as with that of Rāmānuja, holds that this mental habituation is so strong that it requires considerable mental training to erode it or to rewire the circuitry, as it were. While it is reductive and unfair to Śaṅkara to suggest that saving knowledge is by any means facile – and he does have a propaedeutic role for spiritual and meditative practices – he seems confident in the liberating power of transcendent knowledge to destroy ignorance.

Still, Śaṅkara is very clear about a particular culture of liberation. And, given his Brahman origins – his nondualism notwithstanding – Śaṅkara concedes much to culture and ethics, creating a soteriological program that includes powerful socially established doxastic practices, traditionally limited to Brahmans. These include, first and foremost, the Veda, particularly the sacred knowledge transmitted in the *mahāvākyas*, but also spiritual eligibility (→ *adhikāra*), the → *guru*, and a host of other ethical and spiritual practices. One therefore can see in Śaṅkara a tension between a profoundly "internalist" program of liberation – profoundly interior, self-evident, and immediate – and another that is profoundly dependent on an "externalist" program, a set of socially established belief-forming mechanisms intended to cultivate a "rewiring" of consciousness, as it were. Such mechanisms, following Śaṅkara, ultimately eliminate congenital ignorance and reveal one's true self. The adept taps into an "external circuity" – Veda, *guru*, and so on – that facilitates the transformation of consciousness. However, in terms truer to the nondualist spirit, no "transformation" actually obtains, because transformation implies change. Liberation always "is." There can be no "attainment," because such would imply gaining what one does not already possess, which implies dualism, while also suggesting the possibility of losing what gains, which denies the eternal nature of liberation. The true self does not change and is always self-established (*svataḥsiddha*). The economy of liberation, in the end, is not about "gaining" or becoming something one is not but about realizing one's truest identity, that is, discovering the internal treasure always present yet obscured by ignorance. Saving knowledge, for Śaṅkara, only destroys ignorance, revealing the already established eternal self; it does not add anything to the subject. Nevertheless, the revelation spells the end of suffering, because one no longer is buffeted about by praise, blame, success, loss, death, or life. One's true identity is beyond such limited configurations (*upādhis*). One already has – or, more correctly, is – infinite being, consciousness, and bliss. The innately endowed treasure is internal. Realization destroys ignorance in the form of wrong ego identifications and the afflictive habits that they generate.

There are social and philosophical implications in reading Śaṅkara's epistemology of religious experience as internalist or externalist that inform a broadly universal appeal of Advaita in the 20th century. If the "external" circuity of Advaita is absolutely necessary, then such exernalism decisively indexes its soteriology to local culture. If, however, a profoundly inward, interior, or internalist approach is dominant, the circuitry is relativized, opening up space for Advaita as a transcultural, universalist program. In the nondualism of Śaṅkara, an electric engagement obtains between the two poles of internalism and externalism. While internalism might be considered truer to the spirit of nondualism and, to a considerable extent, to Śaṅkara himself, that cannot and ought not be overstated. Śaṅkara is quite clear about the formative contexts of text, tradition, and teacher, the socially established practices in the economy of liberation. A. Rambachan, one of the best interpreters of Advaita, rightly underscores the importance of the Veda as the knowledge-producing mechanism *par excellence* in Śaṅkara. Śaṅkara, as with Vedāntins before and after him, returns to the "knowledge portion" of the Veda, the Upaniṣads, to access the knowledge that destroys ignorance and reveals the luminous internal self. However, beginning especially with the Bengali mystic → Ramakrishna in the 19th century and his chief interpreter → Vivekanananda, and extending to other 20th-century Indian nondualists such as → Jiddu → Krishnamurti, → Ramana Maharshi, and Nisargatta Maharaj, we can see an increasing emphasis on an inward turn that, true to Advaitin premises, naturally relativizes the value and importance of social context. This in the end "liberates" Advaita from its localized forms, rendering it genuinely transcultural and universalist. At a sociological level, this means that Advaita has particular resources to make a distinct impact on non-Indian cultures and non-Indians; indeed, this has happened, especially in the growth of Vedānta centers and *āśrams* that have flourished in the West, many of which were imbued with the Advaitin spirit, so eloquently systematized by Śaṅkara centuries earlier.

Bibliography

Alston, A.J., *Śaṃkara on the Absolute*, London, 1980, repr. 1981.

Bader, J., *Meditation in Śaṅkara's Vedānta*, New Delhi, 1990.

Cenkner, W., *A Tradition of Teachers: Śaṅkara and Jagadgurus Today*, Delhi, 1983.

Deutsch, E., & J.A.B. van Buitenen, *A Sourcebook of Advaita Vedānta*, Honolulu, 1971.

Flood, G., *An Introduction to Hinduism*, Cambridge UK, 1996.

Forsthoefel, T.A., *Knowing Beyond Knowledge: Epistemologies of Religious Experience in Classical and Modern Advaita*, Aldershot, 2002.

Gussner, R.E., "Śaṅkara's *Crest Jewel of Discrimination*: A Stylometric Approach to the Question of Authorship," *JIPh* 4, 1977, 265–278.

Hacker, P., "Śaṅkarācārya and Śaṅkarabhagavatpāda: Preliminary Remarks Concerning the Authorship Problem," in: W. Halbfass, ed., *Philology and Confrontation: Paul Hacker on Traditional and Modern Vedanta*, Albany, 1995.

Hiriyanna, M., *The Essentials of Indian Philosophy*, Delhi, 1995.

Ingalls, D.H.H., "Śaṃkara's Arguments Against the Buddhists," *PEW* 3, 1953–1954, 291–306.

Mahadevan, T.M.P., ed., *The Saṃbandha-Vārtika of Sureśvarācārya*, Madras, 1972.

Malkovsky, B.J., *The Role of Divine Grace in the Soteriology of Śaṃkarācārya*, Leiden, 2001.

Mayeda, S., ed., *A Thousand Teachings: The Upadeśasāhasrī of Śaṅkara*, Albany, 1992.

Nakamura, H., *A History of Early Vedānta Philosophy*, Delhi, 1983.

Pathak, K.B., "The Date of Śamkarāchārya," *IA* 11, 1882, 174–175.

Potter, K.H., *Encyclopedia of Indian Philosophies*, vol. III, Delhi, 1981.

Radhakrishnan, S., *Indian Philosophy*, vol. II, London, 1989.

Rambachan, A., *Accomplishing the Accomplished: The Vedas as Source of Valid Knowledge in Śaṅkara*, Honolulu, 1991.

Renou, L., *JA* 243/2, 1955, 249–251.

Sawai, Y., "Śaṅkara's Theory of Saṃnyāsa," *JIPh* 14, 1986, 371–387.

Thomas Forsthoefel

Śaṅkaradeva and Mādhavadeva

Mahāpuruṣa Śrīmanta Śaṅkaradeva (1449–1569) and his disciple Śrī Śrī Mādhavadeva (1489–1596) are the two most important saints and spiritual reformers from the region of → Assam, northeast India. Roughly contemporary with other devotional saints such as → Caitanya Mahāprabhu in → Bengal, → Kabīr in North India, and Gurū Nānak in the → Punjab, Śaṅkaradeva and his followers sparked a huge popular revival of devotional worship (→ *bhakti*) that became the dominant form of Hinduism in the northeast states. With their tremendous theological, philosophical, and poetic output, Śaṅkaradeva and Mādhavadeva had a lasting impact not only on the religious institutions but also on the literature and social life of the northeast region as a whole (Dvija, 1925; Neog, 1967; 1980; Goswami, 1982; Cantlie, 1984; Barman, 1999). In the 20th and 21st centuries, they have also been celebrated both as Assamese cultural icons and as Indian national heroes, praised as "the great unifiers of Eastern India" and "the greatest expression of Assamese culture" (Chakravarty, 1978, Chatterji, 1978).

Śaṅkaradeva's Life and Historical Context

Assam in the 15th and 16th centuries was a complex, shifting social and political landscape with numerous competing tribal groups and local kings. Most of these tribal kingdoms were loosely Hinduized, practicing a complex mixture of indigenous worship with elements of Śaivism and Śāktism. Hindu Śākta → Tantra was particularly widespread throughout the region, focused on the worship of powerful mother goddesses such as → Kālī, → Durgā, and Kāmākhyā through the offering of animal and, allegedly, human sacrifices (Urban, 2010; 2011). By the 15th century, the great ancient dynasties of Kāmarūpa (i.e. Assam) such as the Varmans and Palas had dissolved, leaving the Kamata Kingdom in the west and the Kachari, Chutiya, and Ahom Kingdoms in the east. In the early 16th century, King Viśva Siṅgha (1515–1540) of the Koch tribe established the Koch dynasty within the Kamata Kingdom. Meanwhile, the Ahoms gradually expanded their rule and took control of the Chutiya and Kachari Kingdoms, establishing a powerful kingdom that would thrive until the arrival of the British in the 19th century (Neog, 1980, 39–97; Pandey, 1979).

In this midst of this complex and often tumultuous landscape, Śaṅkaradeva was born into a Bāra Bhūyān (independent landholding) family belonging to the Kāyastha (scribe) caste in the region of Nagaon, central Assam. His parents were Śāktas, that is, worshippers of the goddess as power (→ *śakti*) in her fierce forms such as Durgā, Kālī, and the local mother goddess Kāmākhyā. In his late teens, Śaṅkaradeva assumed his duties as the chief Bhūyān, married, and began a family. However, soon after the death of his young wife, he chose to abandon his chieftainship and set off on a great pilgrimage around the year 1482. Touring most of the great Vaiṣṇava centers in northern and eastern India, Śaṅkaradeva traveled to Puri, Mathura, Dwarka, Vrindavan, Rameshwaram, and Ayodhya, witnessing the new flowering of Vaiṣṇava *bhakti* that had swept across the subcontinent during these decades. While in Puri, the seat of the massive Jagannāth (→ Kṛṣṇa) Temple, Śaṅkaradeva received his great spiritual illumination, the experience of *bhaktijñāna* or the knowledge and wisdom of devotional love (Neog, 1980, 104).

Upon returning to Assam after his 12-year pilgrimage, Śaṅkaradeva built his first *nāmghar* or prayer hall and began preaching the message of devotional love of God in personal form. Because of the unstable political situation and repeated wars among the Koch, Ahom, and other factions, Śaṅkaradeva was forced to move from place to place. Śaṅkaradeva's rapidly growing movement also aroused the suspicion of the ruling Ahom king, who arrested both his chief disciple, Mādhavadeva, and his son-in-law, Hari. The former was imprisoned for a year, while the latter was executed (Chatterji, 1978, 3). Śaṅkaradeva himself retreated westward into the Koch Kingdom.

Despite or perhaps because of its growing success, Śaṅkaradeva's movement would also arouse the hostility of the Koch king, Naranārāyaṇa, who received complaints that this new religion was corrupting the minds of the populace. Three of the saint's disciples were arrested and tortured, while Śaṅkaradeva was forced into hiding

(Neog, 1980, 118). Meanwhile, Chilārāya – Naranārāyaṇa's brother and general of the Koch army – had become influenced by Vaiṣṇava *bhakti* and eventually arranged for Śaṅkaradeva to have an audience with the king. After hearing Śaṅkaradeva sing hymns to Lord Kṛṣṇa and seeing him defeat all opponents in debate, Naranārāyaṇa was so impressed by the saint that he began to invite him as a regular attendant at the court. According to later biographies, the king even asked to be initiated by Śaṅkaradeva, but the saint repeatedly refused his requests because he would not accept kings as disciples (Neog, 1980, 120). Śaṅkaradeva spent most of his final years in the village of Patbausi in western Assam, where he is said to have died at the impressive age of 120.

Literary and Dramatic Works

Śaṅkaradeva was an immensely prolific author, writing over a 50-year period in Assamese, Assamese Brajbuli, and Sanskrit, and producing a vast range of prose, verse, translations, adaptations, compilations, songs, dramas, narratives, and doctrinal treatises (Neog, 1980, 159; Barua, 1978). The rapid spread of the neo-Vaiṣṇava movement is due in no small measure to Śaṅkaradeva's remarkable ability to write in multiple languages, freely using many styles and genres, and addressing both complex philosophical debates and the popular emotions of ordinary devotees. Foremost among these works are his Assamese translations of the *Bhāgavatapurāṇa*, a 9th- to 10th-century Sanskrit text focused on the tales and worship of Lord → Viṣṇu, and particularly Viṣṇu's incarnation as Kṛṣṇa; his collection of communal songs, the *Kīrtanaghoṣa*; his collection of Assamese lyrics praising the qualities of Kṛṣṇa, the *Guṇamāla*; and a major doctrinal work, the *Bhaktiratnākara*. The last of these is Śaṅkaradeva's major summary of Vaiṣṇava theology, rooted primarily in his interpretation of the *Bhāgavatapurāṇa*.

In addition to his theological works, however, Śaṅkaradeva was also the author of several major dramatic works such as the *Viprapatnīnāṭa*, the *Keligopāla*, and others. Like his philosophical writings, most of Śaṅkaradeva's dramas are rooted in the *Bhāgavatapurāṇa*, focusing on the life and deeds of Kṛṣṇa; the sole exception is his *Rāmavijaya*, which is based on the → *Rāmāyaṇa* and takes Viṣṇu's incarnation as → Rāma as its protagonist. Unlike classical Sanskrit drama, Śaṅkaradeva's works focus less on the traditional poetic sentiments (→ *rasas*) or aesthetic states than on the primary emotion of *bhakti* or devotional love. Thus, even when the union of Rāma and Sītā (→ Draupadī and Sītā) is described in sensuous language, Śaṅkaradeva is careful to remind the viewer that the real meaning of their relation is not eroticism but the intense religious devotion of the soul in relation to God (Neog, 1980, 255).

On the whole, Śaṅkaradeva is credited by many Assamese scholars as the author "responsible for the greatest turning point in the history of Assamese drama and stage" (Barua, 1978, 18). Both reviving and reshaping local dramatic traditions, he created a new devotional form of theater that drew on older Sanskritic traditions while blending them into a uniquely Assamese art (Barua, 1978, 18–24).

Śaṅkaradeva's Vaiṣṇava Philosophy: *Ekaśaraṇa Nāmadharma* and *Mahāpuruṣīya Dharma*

Śaṅkaradeva himself never worked out a complete or independent philosophical system of his own; rather, his Vaiṣṇava teachings are largely rooted in the theology of the *Bhāgavatapurāṇa* and have much in common with the teachings of contemporaneous movements, such as the following of Kabīr and the devotional revival led by Caitanya in Bengal. The core of Śaṅkaradeva's teaching is often summarized as *ekaśaraṇa nāmadharma* – that is, the religion (*dharma*) of taking refuge (*śaraṇa*) in the one (*eka*) God, through the simple method of chanting his name (*nāma*). This path is also known as *mahāpuruṣīya dharma*, or the worship of the supreme person (*mahāpuruṣa*), Lord Viṣṇu, and specifically his incarnation as the handsome, charming, and mischievous deity, Kṛṣṇa. Not only is Viṣṇu/Kṛṣṇa regarded as the supreme *brahman* or godhead who contains all other gods and goddesses within himself, but he is also, in fact, the only reality in the universe, the one true self, while all the multiplicity we appear to see in this world is a mere product of cosmic illusion (→ *māyā*) and our own ignorance. As Śaṅkaradeva put in his *Kīrtanaghoṣa* and *Bhaktiratnākara*,

> You are the supreme self, the one lord of the universe. There is nothing real except you. You are

all animals, birds, gods and demons, trees and plants. Due to their ignorance, people see distinctions. (*KīGh.* 8.2.9–10; trans. by author)

> You are the lord of *māyā*, without beginning or end. See how ignorant all people are: You are within [all human beings], though you are said to be different... You are lost within the heart, but [people] seek you outside. (*KīGh.* 11.3.24; trans. by author)

> Kṛṣṇa is himself the soul in all bodies. For the good of the world, he manifests himself in other creatures through his *māyā*. Kṛṣṇa is himself the real essence in both animate and inanimate beings. The lord is the supreme form; there is nothing real other than him. (*BhRaĀk.* 5.12–13; trans. by author).

The worship of this one God is a simple method that can be practiced by anyone anywhere, by the mere remembrance of God's name through chanting, singing, and recitation of his sacred narratives. As Śaṅkaradeva writes in his *Bhaktiratnākara*,

> There is only one religious duty, the worship of this God. There is only one *mantra*, the name of this God. (*BhRaĀk.* 5.27; trans. by author)

In this most degenerate cosmic age, the *kaliyuga* (see → cosmic cycles), when human beings are frail and weak, all other forms of ritual are useless, and singing the name is the simplest, most direct, most appropriate form of worship:

> [The same result that was attained] in *kṛta* age by meditation on Viṣṇu, in the *tretā* age by worship with sacrifices, and in the *dvāpara* age by rituals [is attained] in the *kali* age by singing the name of Hari. (*BhRaĀk.* 21.17; trans. by author)

It is through the divine name that the devotee can achieve ultimate union with God, experiencing perfect "oneness with Hari who is the very image of consciousness and the abode of absolute bliss" (*KīGh.* 2.2.33). This divine union is described in terms that combine the monism of → Vedānta with the emotional rapture of Vaiṣṇava *bhakti*, as the devotee is melded with the divine and so sees the entire universe as the reflection of God, who is, again, the only true reality:

> [O]ne who meditates on God enters Viṣṇu just as butter melts into fire. (*KīGh.* 25.9.98; trans. by author)

> You [Viṣṇu] are the soul of the world; when one worships you, he unites with you, even as one sees the beauty of his own face in its image reflected in a mirror. (*KīGh.* 6.20.227; trans. by author)

Such an experience of spiritual → liberation is at once pure devotional love (*bhakti*) and divine knowledge or gnosis (*jñāna*) – or more accurately, it is the divine knowledge that arises as a result of devotional love:

> release comes through *jñāna* attained through *bhakti* (*īśvara-bhaktyā labdha-jñānena mokṣaiti*). Knowledge comes as a... natural result of devotion through God's grace. (Neog, 1980, 243)

However, in contrast to other devotional movements such as Caitanya's popular following in Bengal, Śaṅkaradeva's *bhakti* does not involve the worship of Kṛṣṇa's female consort, → Rādhā. This is probably due in large part to the saint's fierce rejection of Śāktism and its focus on the female aspect of the divine (Chatterji, 1978, 5). Moreover, unlike other *bhakti* traditions, it focuses primarily on the *dāsya* attitude, that is, the role of the devotee as a "slave" or "servant" (rather than a friend, mother, child, or lover) of God (Chatterji, 1978, 4). In place of elaborate ritual, sacrifice, or esoteric rites, Śaṅkaradeva's devotional worship focuses primarily on the remembrance of God's name through chanting, prayer, and devotional singing (→ *kīrtan*). All other rites and practices, including → Tantra, → *mantra*, → *yajña*, and so forth are utterly surpassed by the devotional remembrance of Hari's name.

Indeed, Śaṅkaradeva and his followers had particular scorn for the practice of Śākta Tantra, which was then a widespread movement in the northeast region and involved both animal sacrifice and the ritual use of meat, wine, and esoteric sexual rites. According to one significant anecdote, Mādhavadeva was invited to visit the great hill of Kāmākhyā Temple, the most important Śākta Tantra center in Assam and the seat of the goddess' *yoni* or sexual organ. The saint refused to enter the deity's shrine, however, stating simply that it is not proper to "see the private parts of one's mother" (Thakura, 1900, 1205–1217). Throughout his work, Śaṅkaradeva was fiercely opposed to blood sacrifice and rejected any form of ritual slaughter as not simply pointless but entirely evil: "If he who decapitates animals in sacrifices and makes [the earth] muddy with the bloodshed can go to heaven, who else is destined to hell?" (Dvija, 1925, 227). The saint had even greater contempt for the more transgressive tantric practices, and above all for the consumption of impure substances and esoteric sexual rites. In Śaṅkaradeva's eyes, this tantric worship with "women, wine, and meat" (*strīmadyamāṃsasevā*) is a particularly ignorant and degenerate practice that only leads sinful fools to their own destruction:

> Engaged in worship with women, wine, and meat, alas, they perish! Alas, they perish! Their lives are futile. They don't understand the deeper meaning of the Vedas. (*KīGh.* 3.23; trans. by author)

Indeed, it was in part because of the rapid success of the neo-Vaiṣṇava movement and its fierce critique that Śākta Tantra largely declined as the dominant religious and political force in the region, losing royal patronage and continuing primarily on the margins of mainstream Assamese spiritual life (Urban, 2010, 147–154).

Caste, *Guru*s, Women, and Social Reforms

Like other devotional leaders of this era, such as Kabīr, Caitanya, and Nānak, Śaṅkaradeva was as much a social as a religious reformer, voicing a powerful critique of the class and caste system of 16th-century India. Himself a Kāyastha and a Śūdra, Śaṅkaradeva had no patience for the puritanical pretenses of Brahmans and instead proclaimed the supremacy of devotion alone as the highest mark of spiritual purity. "Bhakti," as he put it, "is no respecter of caste," and true devotion requires no Brahmans or sages (Chatterji, 1978, 2). Indeed, even men of the lowest and most unclean groups, such as untouchables, outcasts (Caṇḍālas), and "dog cookers" (Śvapacas), are praised as greater than Brahmans if they are truly devoted to God; and conversely, even the highest Brahmans are dismissed as outcastes if they are without devotion:

> An untouchable [Śvapaca] who is devoted to Viṣṇu is superior to a Brahman, and a Brahman who is without devotion to Viṣṇu is worse than an untouchable. (*BhRaĀk.* 23.22; trans. by author)

> A Caṇḍāla whose tongue recites the names of God is superior to a Brahman, versed in the four Vedas. That [Caṇḍāla] has undergone all penances, performed all sacrifices, aided by all rules of custom and visited all sacred places. (*BhRaĀk.* 7.6; trans. by author)

In fact, Śaṅkaradeva and his disciples accepted not only low castes and untouchables but also a wide variety of tribals into the movement, including members of the Garo, Bhota, Miri, Ahom, and Kachari communities (*NāGh.* vv. 473, 501).

While he rejected the authority of Brahmans as a hereditary priestly class, however, Śaṅkaradeva did place great emphasis on the importance of the → *guru*. The *guru* is considered to be in a direct line not simply with Śaṅkaradeva and Mādhavadeva, but with God himself; indeed, one should "acknowledge the religious preceptor as the soul of God" (*NāGh.* v. 193). There is believed to be an identity between each *guru* in the lineage, such that the reverence for one's *guru* is equal to the reverence for Śaṅkaradeva and ultimately for Viṣṇu himself. Thus upon being initiated into a *satra* or monastic community, the novice is to say,

> I will conceive that Krishna entered into Shankaradeva, Shankaradeva into Madhavadeva, Madhavadeva into Thakur, and Thakur into the founder of my *satra*. The founder enters into the *guru* who initiated me and he into my body. (Cantlie, 1984, 154)

Quite significantly, however, Śaṅkaradeva's attitude toward women was a bit more complex and ambivalent. While his social attitude was generally quite democratic for its time, women nonetheless had to be "content with a subordinate position" (Chatterji, 1978, 5). However, he did open the door for women to receive initiation and positions of authority, and his own granddaughter-in-law became the head of a major *satra* (Barua 1965, 121–122; Biernacki, 2007, 188). Yet, he also warned of the dangers of female sexuality, advising his followers "not to entangle themselves in the dangerous web of women," since their sexual power has the potential to "intoxicate man" and "close his better senses" (Murthy, 1973, 201–202). As Śaṅkaradeva described the potential perils of female sexuality,

> In the world of illusion, the terrible illusion of woman [*ghora nārī māyā*] is the most despised. Even the heart of a great, perfected sage is captured by her sidelong glance. Her sight destroys prayer, penance and yoga. Knowing this, the wise avoid the company of women. (Kakati, 1959, 79)

Again, this is probably in part a response to the Assamese Śākta tradition, with its celebration of female sexuality and the power of sexual union. Indeed, Śaṅkaradeva appears to have defined his path sharply in contrast to Śākta Tantra, and above all the worship of the *yoni*, by offering women a place as spiritual authorities while warning against their dangerous power as sexual beings.

Mādhavadeva's Life and Work

If Śaṅkaradeva is celebrated as the primary inspiration and intellectual force behind the Vaiṣṇava revival in Assam, Mādhavadeva is usually credited as the man who helped popularize it to a much broader public audience. While not quite as a prolific as his *guru*, Mādhavadeva was a key figure in the spread of the movement and the establishment of its institutional structures throughout the northeast. As their biographer/hagiographer, Daityāri Ṭhākura, put it in his *Śaṅkaradevamādhavadevar Jīvanacaritra* (v. 1696), "Śaṅkara only revealed [the secret of] *bhakti*, the religion of love; it is Mādhava who made it public."

Born in 1489 in a village near Narayanpur, Lakhimpur district, Mādhavadeva studied philosophy and Sanskrit poetry as a young man before beginning a small trade in betel nuts and leaves. According to tradition, his first meeting with Śaṅkaradeva occurred at Dhāwahāṭ (modern Majuli island) in eastern Assam. Like Śaṅkaradeva himself, Mādhavadeva was raised as a Śākta and firmly believed in the importance of offering blood sacrifice to the goddess as power (*śakti*). After receiving news that his mother was very ill, Mādhavadeva resolved to sacrifice two white goats to the goddess on her behalf and asked his brother-in-law to buy the animals for the ritual. However, his brother-in-law had already converted to Vaiṣṇavism and refused to buy the goats. This in turn led to an intense theological argument between the two about the practice of blood sacrifice. Finally, the brother-in-law took Mādhavadeva to meet Śaṅkaradeva, who very quickly demolished all his arguments in favor of animal sacrifice and persuaded him of the purity and simplicity of devotion to Kṛṣṇa: "One who has taken sole refuge in God Kṛṣṇa," he argued, "and worships Kṛṣṇa's feet with his body, words and mind and in staunch belief, is subject to none, has no debts to repay" (Dvija, 1900, 443–450).

Mādhavadeva lived for 21 years after the death of his master, spreading the *bhakti* movement widely throughout the northeast region. He was particularly successful in his use of music to propagate the faith, attracting a wide following through the power of lyric, melody, and dramatic performance to spread the new ideal of devotion to a broad population (Neog, 1980, 125). However, like his master before him, Mādhavadeva continued to face royal persecution and was seen as a threat by Raghudeva, the ruler of the splinter kingdom of Koch Hajo. Mādhavadeva thus fled west to Koch Behar, which was then under the rule of Lakṣmīnārāyaṇa. There he is said to have converted the king's mother, nurse, wives, sons, and daughters, as the Kochs abandoned their old rites and accepted the simple worship of Kṛṣṇa alone (Neog, 1980, 126).

Mādhavadeva is best known for two major works. The first is the *Bhaktiratnāvalī*, an Assamese translation of a Sanskrit work by Viṣṇupuri, which is in turn a compilation of key passages from the *Bhāgavatapurāṇa*. Like Śaṅkaradeva, Mādhavadeva regarded the *Bhāgavatapurāṇa* as the most sacred and profound text in the world, containing the heart and the culmination of the Vedas: indeed, it "is the essence of all the Vedas. Its devotion is always noble and incomparable; and therefore it is the supreme amongst all the Vedas, the most secret of all the scriptures" (*BhRaĀv. v.* 11).

His last and most important work, however, is the *Nāmaghoṣa*, which was composed from roughly 1568 to 1596 and distills the essential teachings of his *guru* into 1,001 couplets. Focusing on the key doctrines of the Vaiṣṇava revival, the text explains the nature of the *guru*, God, the divine name, and the devotee. The essence of these four themes – and in a sense of the microcosm of the entire text – appears in the first two couplets of the *Nāmaghoṣa*:

> Praise to that devotee [the *guru*, Śaṅkaradeva] who is indifferent even to liberation. I pray for that delightful devotion. I worship God, the lord of the Yādavas, the crown jewel of all, who is nonetheless submissive to his own devotee, whose name, Kṛṣṇa-Rāma, serves as a boat to cross the ocean of this world, ferrying sinners to the supreme abode. In my heart, I always worship Kṛṣṇa, who is eternal and ever-blissful. (*NāGh.* vv. 1–2).

Institutional Structures: *Satras* and *Nāmghars*

Through the work of Mādhavadeva and his fellow disciples, Śaṅkaradeva's devotional movement developed a large institutional structure that spread throughout the entire region of Assam. During Śaṅkaradeva's lifetime, meetings of the devotees were usually held in the open or outside under the shade of trees; but after the saint's death, the devotees established a network of more permanent monastic communities called *satras* (Cantlie, 1984, 153).The first *satra* is said to have been founded at the great river island of Majuli in eastern Assam, where Śaṅkaradeva and Mādhavadeva had their first encounter. A total of 65 *satras* were established on the island, of which 22 still exist today.

Similar in structure to Buddhist monasteries (*vihāras*) and drawing direct inspiration from older Hindu monastic communities such as those of Śaṅkarācārya (→ Śaṅkara) and → Rāmānanda, the *satras* are traditionally built according to a common plan. The center of the *satra* is the *nāmghar* or "name house," which consists of a large hall for worship and chanting of the divine name. The east side of the *nāmghar* opens to the *maṇikūṭ* or "house of jewels," where the sacred book representing Lord Kṛṣṇa is installed on a wooden throne. The house of the head of the *satra* (the *satrādhikār*) is on the east side of the compound, near the storerooms used for food and provisions. Surrounding the *satra* is a wall with a gate house in the eastern side, and then beyond the walls lie the lands belonging to the *satra* (Cantlie, 1984, 161).

In addition to serving as monastic communities and institutional centers of the Vaiṣṇava movement, the *satras* have also traditionally served as cultural centers and sites of a special devotional dance form called *sattrīyanṛtya*. Originally developed by Śaṅkaradeva to accompany his *aṅkiyanāṭ*, the *sattrīya* form of dance gradually evolved beyond the walls of the *satras* themselves and is now recognized as one of the major forms of Indian classical dance.

A second major institution established by Śaṅkaradeva and his disciples is the village *nāmghar*, or local prayer house that spread throughout small communities across Assam. The *nāmghars* have played a central role in the village life of Assam and essentially serve as the "religious congregation" of many local communities. These houses represent an integrated association of households who combine for the purposes of "maintaining a local centre of devotional worship" (Cantlie, 1984, 116). As the Vaiṣṇava movement spread rapidly across Assam, the *nāmghars* effectively became the basic structural unit of rural society in much of the region. As B.K. Kakati observes, the *nāmghars* have served not simply as spiritual centers but also as the social and political hubs of Assamese village life, acting as the "nerve centers" of religious and political discourse alike. Indeed, they

> combined the functions of a village parliament, a village court, a village school and a village church. These institutions served as the anchors of Assamese society in the midst of continually shifting political circumstances...The Namghars further serve as panchayat-hall, where villagers gather to discuss and solve many of their day-to-day problems. (Murthy, 1978, 38–39)

This is a large part of the reason that the state remains predominantly Vaiṣṇava to this day and Śaṅkaradeva's devotional revival continues to inform both the religious and the social fabric of Assamese culture.

Śaṅkaradeva and Mādhavadeva in the 20th and 21st Centuries: Cultural Heroes for Postcolonial India

Since the mid-20th century, the works of Śaṅkaradeva and Mādhavadeva have been embraced, reclaimed, and revived by many Assamese scholars, who have celebrated them as both local Assamese icons and Indian national heroes. This recovery of the Vaiṣṇava saints reflects much of the history and politics of the northeast states and of India more broadly in a postcolonial context. Like most European orientalist scholars, British colonial authorities, and Christian missionaries before them, many modern Assamese scholars are extremely critical of the religious life of pre-Śaṅkaradeva Assam (see Urban, 2010, 1–29, 149–157). They decry the bloody sacrifices of Śākta goddess worship and above all the sexual rites of the *tāntrikas*:

> Before his time the religious life in Assam appears to have been at a very low ebb, The people, Brahmans and the masses, were mostly Śāktas, and their religion was largely an attempt to propitiate the dread Mother Goddess by offering sacrifices of animals and sometimes of human beings. (Chatterji, 1978, 2)

Instead, most Assamese scholars celebrate Śaṅkaradeva as the herald of a new age, who rejected the violent hedonism of the Śāktas and promoted a pure, devotional, and monotheistic faith (a faith quite similar, we might note, to Protestant Christianity, which had also made significant inroads into the northeast states [Urban, 2010, 157–165]). As B.K. Kakati famously wrote in his widely read study of Assamese religious life, first published just after the end of British colonial rule in 1948,

> society itself was moth-eaten from within and without any sustaining vitality... The land was infested with the Vāmācāra Tantric schools with their insistence on the philosophy of sex and plate. Amongst religious rites the most spectacular were bloody sacrifices to gods and goddesses amidst deafening noises of drums and cymbals, night vigils on virgin worship and the lewd dances of temple-women... Śaṅkara Deva chose the difficult path of living up to his faith in the world and what is still more difficult, to persuade the world to live up to it. To the exhausted kingdom without inner vitality and external cohesion, he threw out a gospel of absolute surrender to the One. (Kakati, 1989, 79)

This sentiment is echoed by numerous other scholars, such as H.V.S. Murthy:

> Before Śaṅkaradeva's time, the religious life of Assam was far from satisfactory. It was an age of tantricism, which is characterized by the worship of the Divine Energy in the female form... It combined many elements of ancient superstitions as well as ingenious magic... Thus the emendation of the prevalent religious and social abuses became Śaṅkaradeva's first concern and consideration. Śaṅkaradeva was a monotheist, and he preached a religion of supreme surrender to the One. (Murthy, 1978, 34–35)

As such, Śaṅkaradeva has been praised as an icon of Assamese language, culture, and religious tradition, an "unsung colossus" (Barman, 1999) equal in stature to other great Indian authors and spiritual leaders: "his influence on Assamese life and literature is comparable to that of Tulsidasa for the people of the Upper Gangetic Valley" (Chatterji, 1978, 1; see also Barua, 1978, 32). Indeed, far more than simply an Assamese hero, he has also been held up as a model for postcolonial India itself, providing a message of national unity, harmony, and humanism that is urgently needed in the contemporary world.

> What Assam, nay the entire country, needs most today is the spirit of harmonious living and concerted efforts... meant at well-being of the common people at large, the wise sense of dedication and humanism, which Śrī Śaṅkaradeva himself epitomized in his Life Divine. (Chaudhury, 1978, i)

This is perhaps the most significant legacy of Śaṅkaradeva and Mādhavadeva in postcolonial India: more than simple devotees of Lord Kṛṣṇa, they have been reclaimed and celebrated as the heroes of a reformed neo-Hindu spirituality, of a new cultural Assamese identity, and of a unified Indian nation.

Bibliography

Barman, S., *An Unsung Colossus: An Introduction to the Life and Works of Sankaradeva*, Guwahati, 1999.

Barua, B.K., "The Father of Assamese Drama and Stage," in: B.P. Chaliha, ed., *Śaṅkaradeva: Studies in Culture*, Guwahati, 1978, 17–32.

Barua, B.K., *Temples and Legends of Assam*, Guwahati, 1965.

Biernacki, L., *Renowned Goddess of Desire: Women, Sex and Speech in Tantra*, New York, 2007.

Cantlie, A., *The Assamese: Religion, Caste and Sect in an Indian Village*, London, 1984.

Chakravarty, D.N., "Śrīmanta Śaṅkaradeva: Great Unifier of Eastern India," in: B.P. Chaliha, ed., *Śaṅkaradeva: Studies in Culture*, Guwahati, 1978, 102–107.

Chatterji, S.K., "The Eka-śaraṇa Dharma of Śaṅkaradeva: The Greatest Expression of Assamese Spiritual Outlook," in: B.P. Chaliha, ed., *Śaṅkaradeva: Studies in Culture*, Guwahati, 1978, 1–6.

Chaudhury, B.N., "Foreword," in: B.P. Chaliha, ed., *Śaṅkaradeva: Studies in Culture*, Guwahati, 1978, i.

Dvija, B., *Mahāpuruṣa Śaṅkaradeva*, Jorhat, 1925.

Dvija, R., *Guru Caritra*, Tezpur, 1900.

Goswami, K.D., *Life and Teachings of Mahapurusha Sankaradeva*, Patiala, 1982.

Kakati, B.K., ed., *Aspects of Early Assamese Literature*, Guwahati, 1959.

Kakati, B.K., *The Mother Goddess Kamakhya*, Guwahati, 1 1948, repr. 1989.

Murthy, H.V.S., "The Lasting Value of Śaṅkaradeva's Teachings," in: B.P. Chaliha, ed., *Śaṅkaradeva: Studies in Culture*, Guwahati, 1978, 33–49.

Murthy, H.V.S., *Vaiṣṇavism of Śaṅkaradeva and Rāmānuja*, Delhi, 1973.

Neog, M., *Early History of the Vaiṣṇava Faith and Movement in Assam: Śaṅkaradeva and His Times*, Delhi, 1980.

Neog, M., *Sankaradeva*, Delhi, 1967.

Pandey, V., *Assam: The Land of Śaṅkaradeva: History, Art, Literature, Philosophy and Religion*, Bombay, 1979.

Urban, H.B., "The Womb of Tantra: Goddesses, Tribals and Kings in Assam," *JHSt* 4/3, 2011, 231–247.

Urban, H.B., *The Power of Tantra: Religion, Sexuality and the Politics of South Asian Studies*, New York, 2010.

Hugh Urban

Sūrdās

By common consent, the poet regarded as the epitome of literary artistry in Brajbhasha is Sūrdās. His name means literally "Servant (*dās*) of the Sun (*sūr*)," but in Braj, the region south of Delhi from which this language takes its name, Sūrdās is seen as the sun itself. Indeed, his name is often shortened to Sūr. Some literary critics have favored rivals associated with other aspects of classical Hindi, notably → Tulsīdās or → Kabīr, but Sūrdās' claim to primacy can be traced right back to the close of the 16th century – the century in which Sūrdās himself must have lived. Sometime around 1600, the → Rāmānandī writer Nābhādās composed his influential *Bhaktamāl* (Garland of Lovers of God), and when he did so, he singled out Sūrdās for a special sort of praise. Other poet-saints might be lauded for their personal fearlessness (→ Mīrābāī) or for their defiance of the rules of → caste and class (Kabīr), but when the subject was poetry itself, Sūrdās had no peer:

> What poet, hearing the poems Sūr has made,
> will not nod his head in pleasure?
> Turns of phrase, epigrams, assonance, description –
> in each regard his standing is immense:
> Speech and loving sentiment he sustains,
> conveying their meaning in wondrous rhyme.
> In words he expresses Hari's playful acts,
> which are mirrored in his heart by divine vision:
> Birth, deeds, virtues, and beautiful form –
> all are brought to light by his tongue.
> Others cleanse their virtues and powers of insight
> by tuning their ears to his fame.
> *What poet, hearing the poems Sūr has made,*
> *will not nod his head in pleasure?*
> (Jha, 1978, pt. 2, 27 [§72]; Rupkala, 1961, 557)

Nābhādās tells us that Sūrdās was able, in words, to "express Hari's playful acts" (*hari līlā bhāsī*). The name Hari can designate any of the aspects of divinity that we associate with the god → Viṣṇu, whether or not we think of these as being formally Viṣṇu's → *avatārs*. In the 16th century, the term "Hari" was also frequently used as a designation for god in an even more general sense – the sort of god who loved to help those who loved him, and who had designed the world as a theatre in which that sort of action could be performed. So Hari can mean many things, but when Nābhādās speaks of Hari in connection with Sūrdās, he is clearly thinking of → Kṛṣṇa, the deity whose trademark is his "playful acts," his → *līlā*s. To be sure, Sūrdās addressed a series of lovely compositions to → Rām and his consort Sītā (see → Draupadī and Sītā), and he explored other aspects of the → *Rāmāyaṇa* as well, but his primary narrative métier was the world of Kṛṣṇa – not only his childhood or amorous youth but also his role in the → *Mahābhārata*.

The Blind Poet

While a clear majority of extant 16th-century poems carrying Sūrdās' signature concerns Kṛṣṇa's amours with the *gopī*s in one way or another, his evocations of Kṛṣṇa as a child certainly marked him out from other Brajbhasha poets of his time. A widely distributed 20th-century poster illustration published by S.S. Brajbasi & Sons, Bombay, captures this nicely (see fig. 1). It shows Sūrdās with his clacker cymbals in one hand and his one-stringed *ektār* in the other and the infant deity, mesmerized, putting aside his own instrument – the flute – to hear the poet sing. A temple in the Braj background provides a further connection between the two figures: there, presumably, Kṛṣṇa is worshipped in image form, and the poems of Sūrdās are sung. But in the foreground, we see that the poet and his god inhabit their storied world not by virtue of the ritual patterns made possible by organized religion but in an absolutely immediate way. This absence of obstacle is made possible, ironically, because Sūrdās struggles against a handicap. He is blind. He can "see" Kṛṣṇa in his songs and not be distracted by the fact that Kṛṣṇa sees him at the same time.

We do not know exactly when it became popular to think of Sūrdās as being blind, but we know that the story of his blindness was told in a number of forms. In one version, Sūrdās is granted a vision of Kṛṣṇa and then requests the deity to remove his faculty of sight so that nothing he might see subsequently could dilute the splendor of what he had witnessed (Abbott & Godbole, vol. II, 1982, 18).

Fig. 1: Sūrdās sings for Kṛṣṇa (poster illustration printed by S.S. Brajbasi & Sons, Bombay).

In another version of the tale, Sūrdās' blindness comes earlier in life: he has it with him from birth. This is the form that the story takes when told by the religious community that has positioned itself at least since the mid-17th century as Sūrdās' most influential interpreter: the→ Vallabha Sampradāya or Puṣṭimārg (Path of Fulfillment), a group whose worship is focused entirely on Kṛṣṇa and whose members revere the theologian → Vallabha (or more formally, Vallabhācārya – Master Vallabha) as their founder. One of Vallabha's grandsons, a man named Gokulnāth, is traditionally believed to have been the author of an interconnected series of religious biographies called *Caurāsī Vaiṣṇavan kī Vārtā* (Accounts of Eighty-four Vaiṣṇavas), including Sūrdās'. This is the Sūrdās biography that everyone knows (Parikh, 1970, 400–442; Hawley, 1984, 3–14), and the singing of Sūrdās' poetry – along with that of other poets regarded as constituting the "eight seals" (*aṣṭachāp*) initiated by Vallabha into the sectarian fold – is one of the central acts of Vallabhite worship.

In his late 17th-century commentary on the *Caurāsī Vaiṣṇavan kī Vārtā*, Harirāy, the nephew of Gokulnāth, makes it clear that Sūrdās was blind from birth, but a series of internal considerations argues against our regarding this deeply theological text as a simple report of historical fact. Not surprisingly, then, if we look at the corpus of poetry that circulated in Sūrdās' name in the 16th century, we discover that only a few of them allude to the poet's blindness, and among these even fewer suggest that he was blind from birth. The following poem is perhaps the most prominent example. In it, Sūrdās addresses the deity as Rām, using the term in roughly the same broad sense that we have seen for Hari. He joins his own name to a list of persons who have received divine mercy. But this is his list. He asks what is wrong with him – or god – that he has not been included on god's list, as well:

They say you're so giving, so self-denying, Rām,
That you offered Sudāmā the four fruits of life
  and to your guru you granted a son.
Vibhīṣan: you gave him the land of Lanka
  to honor his early devotion to you.
Rāvaṇ: his were the ten heads you severed
  simply by reaching for your bow.

Prahlād: you justified the claim he made.
Indra, leader of the gods, you made a sage.
Sūrdās: how could you be so harsh with him –
leaving him without his very eyes?
(Bryant & Hawley, 2013, §399; Hawley, 2009, 181, 269–270)

This poem is attested in the oldest manuscript in which poems attributed to Sūrdās are collected (written in Fatehpur, near Sikar, Rajasthan, in 1582 CE), but it is not too clear just what sort of blindness is meant – blind from birth or only later? Was it blindness in a physical sense or something more spiritual? Other poems are more explicit. In one of the most graphic, which appears in a manuscript dating from 1736 CE, it seems plain that the poet's blindness was understood to have come upon him not at birth but as one of the curses of old age:

Now I am blind; I have shunned Hari's name.
My hair has turned white with illusions and delusions
that have wrung me through till nothing makes sense.
Skin shriveled, posture bent, teeth gone;
my eyes emit a stream of tears;
my friends, a stream of blame.
Those eyes once ranged as free as a cat's,
but failed to measure the play of Time
Like a false-eyed scarecrow failing to scatter
the deer from the field of the mind.
Sūrdās says, to live without a song for the Lord
is courting death; his sledge stands poised
above your waiting head.
(Hawley, 1984, 180–181)

Here, as in many similar compositions, it is hard to tell whether a physical affliction is intended or a spiritual one – or both. But it is obvious that by this point in time, blindness was a motif firmly associated with Sūrdās. The interest came in hearing how the poet would comment on the disease. In this instance even more than in the earlier example, Sūrdās' blindness becomes a sign of his distance from Kṛṣṇa (or Hari), not a sign of his mysterious proximity, as in the Vallabhite story and in the paintings we have seen. An important aspect of the difference is that here we have the poet purportedly speaking about his own condition, rather than being appraised by someone else.

Beyond the Vallabhite Sūrdās

The disparity between this "first-person" Sūrdās and the Sūrdās who celebrates Kṛṣṇa's *līlā* from within its distinctive narrative boundaries is at the heart of the most influential biographical tradition associated with him, the one maintained in the Vallabha Sampradāya. Vallabhites were eager to cast as less than worthy the entire range of the *Sūrsāgar* poems in which the poet speaks in his own voice – poems of humility, protest, and praise that are voiced in the first person and conventionally called Vinaya (petitionary) poetry. Around the mid-17th century, Vallabhite biographers argued that Vinaya compositions such as the ones cited above were to be understood as poems that Sūrdās had uttered early in life – before he met Vallabha and felt the influence of his teachings about Kṛṣṇa, becoming his disciple. It was only after his initiation by the great master that Sūrdās was able to see Kṛṣṇa as he really was. Then his blindness came to have the meaning it was intended to have all along; it came to represent his direct apprehension of Kṛṣṇa's *līlās*. Yet in another sense, this was only possible because an element of indirectness has been inserted into the account: Vallabha had intervened to supply Sūrdās with this supposedly new form of access to the truth.

In other writing (Hawley, 1984, 14–22; Hawley, 2012, 181–193), I have explained in detail why I am convinced that this Vallabhite version of Sūrdās' life should not be regarded as historical truth, despite its widespread acceptance as such today. Readers may have already thought it odd that according to the Vallabhite scheme, an old-age poem such as "Now I Am Blind" would have to be classified as having been composed when the poet was still relatively young. But there is much more. For one thing, none of the Sūrdās poems that circulated in the 16th century (unlike several that were added to the *Sūrsāgar* later on) makes any reference to Vallabha. It takes a good bit of fancy footwork on the part of Vallabhite hagiographers to make the record look otherwise. Another important fact is that no early manuscript of the *Sūrsāgar* places the first-person poems at the beginning of the collection; several, in fact, do the reverse. Finally – and on this point I will presently have a good bit more to say – one must factor in the reality that the authorial identity called Sūrdās actually describes a literary tradition that was many decades, even centuries, in the making. Manuscripts in which poems attributed to Sūrdās were collected – by 1640 this corpus was called *Sūrsāgar* (Sūr's Ocean) – tended to expand over the years as ever more poems were added. All these carry Sūrdās' signature in one of several forms, but very probably they were composed by a great many poets. The story of Vallabha meeting Sūrdās radically foreshortens this textual reality in the course of giving it biographical form.

Translator of the *Bhāgavatapurāṇa*?

What are these poems? If we follow the Vallabhite perspective, the great majority – the Kṛṣṇa poems – are in a certain way translations. They are narrativizations of Vallabha's theological views about how the universe should rightly be regarded, namely as an expression of the reality of Kṛṣṇa. More specifically, in fact, they are understood to be translations of the scriptural text to which Vallabha was most deeply devoted: the *Bhāgavatapurāṇa*, written in Sanskrit. According to Vallabhite hagiography, when Vallabha vouchsafed his theological vision to Sūrdās in the act of adopting him as a disciple, he transmitted to him in a miraculous, instantly accessible form the entire content of his commentary on the *Bhāgavatapurāṇa*. Sūrdās was made able to sing of Kṛṣṇa with such insight and clarity because he had special access to the sum and truth of the Sanskrit text, which Vallabha had revealed (Parikh, 1970, 405–406; Hawley, 1984, 38–39).

This explanation of how the Kṛṣṇaite portions of the *Sūrsāgar* came into being is intended to be understood as a compliment. It links Sūrdās' poetry to a text of unparalleled authority, thereby baptizing Brajbhasha speech in the water of classical Sanskrit. Simultaneously it enables the presumed Sanskrit urtext to bask in the light of its vernacular reflection. Yet, in another way, this understanding of the *Sūrsāgar* has a bitter aftertaste. It devalues the potentialities of vernacular speech by accounting for them in other terms than their own.

We must reject this view of the relationship between the *Sūrsāgar* and the *Bhāgavatapurāṇa*: the actuality is far more complicated and interesting. If one looks closely at a number of compositions that appear in early versions of the *Sūrsāgar* – for example, the famous *Bhramargīt* (Bee Song) group in which Kṛṣṇa's messenger Ūdho encounters the forlorn yet feisty *gopīs* whom he has abandoned (Bryant & Hawley, 2013, §244–324) or Kṛṣṇa's later dealings with Jarāsandha and Bhīṣma (Bryant & Hawley, 2013, §336, §356–357) – one sees that the poet delighted in playing with his own and his audience's knowledge of the *Bhāgavatapurāṇa*. He pokes and probes and inverts rather than simply hauling the *Bhāgavatapurāṇa*'s contents over the linguistic divide into Hindi. This intertextual dexterity is an important aspect of the virtuosity we find in the *Sūrsāgar* – part of what makes it a classic in its own right – but it hardly implies that the *Sūrsāgar* is a translation in any ordinary sense. Later versions of the *Sūrsāgar* were organized in such a manner that they reflected the 12-book plan of the *Bhāgavatapurāṇa*, but there is no indication that the poet himself would have arranged them this way. Nor would this have been done by early scribes and editors: the idea is completely foreign to any 16th- or 17th-century collections of Sūrdās' poetry, however much it may apply to, say, Nandadās (Hawley, 1984, 44–52; McGregor, 1973, 31–34; Brajratnadas, 1957, 51–52, 189–278). Moreover, early Sūrdās poems often elicited moods and suggested theological positions that were very different from what we find in the supposed parent text.

In its earliest form, the *Sūrsāgar* had strictly the nature of an anthology – or rather, anthologies, since the poems included in one collection typically differed in substantial ways from those that appeared in another, as did the order in which they were presented. Clearly these lyrics had initially been performed independently of one another. They piped into a vast reservoir of knowledge about Kṛṣṇa, but they did so episodically, apparently in response to what seemed right for one performative occasion or another. Although the lyrics were sometimes organized by themes that suggested a loose narrative progression, it was apparently not until around the turn of the 19th century that anyone tried to organize them in such a way that they would look as if they constituted a vernacular rendition of the *Bhāgavatapurāṇa* – a single sequential text composed of lyrics that led logically from one to the next. Only then do the first manuscripts appear in which poems attributed to Sūrdās are sorted out according to the 12 books of the *Bhāgavatapurāṇa* (Hawley, 1984, 39–40).

Courtly Frames for Sūrdās

In referring to Nābhādās and the Vallabhites, we have surveyed ways of framing Sūrdās that locate him firmly within a → *bhakti* milieu. Other authors, such as the late 16th-century poet Harirām Vyās, could also be cited (Pauwels, 2002, 84–86). Yet there is more to the story than that. By the first quarter of the 17th century, Sūrdās had evidently become so famous that the mention of his name was an effective way to establish the sophistication of a court lineage that once vied with the Mughals for supremacy in northern India. Muḥammad Kabīr – a person of Afghan lineage, who wrote his *Afsāna-yi-šāhan* (Tale of Kings) during the reign of the Mughal emperor Jahāngīr (1605–1627) – lauded the *darbār* of Islām Šāh by saying that Sūrdās performed there. Islām Šāh was one of the Afghan rulers who displaced the Mughals for a brief time in the mid-16th century (r. 1545–1555), a fact that Muḥammad Kabīr implicitly celebrates by recalling the cultural greatness of his fellow Afghan clansman:

> Wherever he [Islām Šāh] happened to be, he kept himself surrounded by accomplished scholars and poets. Kiosks [*ḫušk*] were set up, scented with "*ghāliā*" [a compound of musk, ambergris, camphor, and oil of ben nuts], and provided with betel leaves. Men like Mīr Sayyid Manjhan, the author of *Madhumālatī*, Shāh Muḥammad Farmūlī and his younger brother, Mūsan, Sūrdās and many other learned scholars and poets assembled there and poems in Arabic, Persian and Hindavī were recited. (Behl & Weightman, 2000, xii–xiii; see also Askari, 1965, 194; Gupta, 1967, 39)

A passage like this suggests a completely different way of locating Sūrdās' authority. Here the Kṛṣṇa poet shares the stage with a series of Sūfī writers, and the stage on which he performs is not provided by a temple but by a court. Note that the languages cited in the last phrase seem to have been conceived as emanating from an Islamic core rather than an Indic one – first Arabic, then Persian, and finally Hindavi. Sūrdās evidently enjoyed a sufficiently stellar reputation for Muḥammad Kabīr to include him as an embellishment to this royal scene, or perhaps he had heard the scene described by others.

Either way it is hard to accept the historicity of the account. The *Afsāna-yi-šāhan* is filled with episodes that feature genies as main characters, depict fabulous night journeys between Istanbul and India, serve a clearly panegyric rather than documentary purpose, and generally conflict with information that appears in other records of the time (Siddiqi, 1966, 59–69; Askari, 1965, 184–188). If we take the skeptical view and conclude that Muḥammad Kabīr's report was probably fictitious in its depiction of what was going on in the mid-16th century, that nonetheless reveals something important about what had happened by the early 17th century, when he wrote it. By then, clearly, Sūrdās was famous enough that no explanation was required to propose him as a symbol of literary excellence. If by some chance there is a kernel of historical truth in what Muḥammad Kabīr reports, then that merely indicates that the process began in the lifetime of the poet itself.

Nor did it end with Muḥammad Kabīr. In the mid-18th century, in the *Kāvyanirṇaya* (Verdict on Literature) of 1746, there appears quite a different sort of literary retrospective. This one is framed by Bhikhārīdās, a poet in attendance on a ruler named Hindūpati Siṅgh, in Pratapgarh: "Sūr, Keśav, Maṇḍan, Bihārī, Kālīdās, Brahma, Cintāmaṇi, Matirām, and Bhūṣaṇ are reputed" (Busch, 2011, 230; Caturvedi, 1959, 7–11; Ved Prakash, 2006, 56). As A. Busch has observed (2009), it seems unlikely that Sūrdās' position at the head of the list is accidental. If he was understood as Ādikavi – the originary poet – of the set, it was probably in not only a temporal sense but also an exemplary one.

The record that emerges from the early 17th century onward, then, seems unanimous about the literary esteem in which Sūrdās was held. That this esteem was expressed in such different contexts – by authors with such different purposes – only strengthens the impression. But there is one potentially discordant note that we have yet to consider, and it comes from a crucial source. Abū al-Fażl ʿAllāmī, Akbar's court chronicler (d. 1602), provides us with a list of singers and instrumentalists in his *Āʾīn-i Akbarī* (Institutes of Akbar), and there, too, the name of Sūrdās appears (see Blochmann & Goomer, 1965, 681–682). Sūrdās is the 19th of 36 musicians whom Abū al-Fażl mentions; almost all of those listed above his rank were also singers.

Why this relatively low ranking? Can Abū al-Fażl's Sūrdās and "our" Sūrdās be one and the same? This is the position that was taken by Shivsingh Sengar (Śivsiṃh Seṅgar), who wrote his *Śivsiṃh Saroj* (Śivsiṃh's Lotus) in 1878, and more recent scholars have sometimes also suggested that this might be so (Vaudeville, 1971, 35–37). Yet caution is advised. We learn from the *Bhaktamāl* of Nābhādās, which cannot have been written much later than the *Āʾīn-i Akbarī*, that the name Sūrdās may have been quite common toward the end of the 16th century; hence the existence of two distinct poets named Sūrdās would not be strange. Indeed, Nābhādās gives us portraits of not one Sūrdās but two, distinguishing the second from the first by adding the name Madanmohan, which connects him with a particular temple in Vrindavan.

No doubt Akbar welcomed to his palaces in Agra and Fatehpur Sikri the musicians who had once gathered at the Tomar court of Gwalior, by the same stroke recruiting the musical talent that flourished at the Šaṭṭarī Sufi hospice of Šayḫ Muḥammad Ġawṯ (often spelled Ghaus) in that city. The *šayḫ*'s eminence was also relevant to Muḥammad Kabīr's *ex post facto* attempt to burnish the reputation of the rival court of Islām Šāh. He was the spiritual guide of Mīr Sayyid Manjhan, whom Muḥammad Kabīr mentions in the passage where Sūrdās appears, and he would have been a primary reason why Islām Šāh sometimes travelled to Gwalior, as Muḥammad Kabīr tells us he did. Yet while it is easy enough to understand why the author of the *Afsāna-yi šāhan* might have wanted to make Sūrdās an ornament of the court of Islām Šāh, it is hard to see what this or the Sūfī connection might have to do with the Sūrdās whose poems were amassed in the Fatehpur anthology of 1582 (Bahura & Bryant, 1982) and who was praised about then or soon afterward by Harirām Vyās and Nābhādās. There is nothing in the manuscript heritage of poems attributed to Sūrdās that suggests he could be connected with any of the courts that I have so far mentioned, any more than they suggest a sectarian connection to Vallabha or a special tie to the *Bhāgavatapurāṇa*.

In the end, all we know is the following. Sūrdās was very likely a 16th-century poet. He was apparently renowned both in Braj, as indicated by the testimony of Harirām Vyās, and around Amer (Amber), as indicated by that of Nābhādās, who seems to have resided in the Rāmānandī *āśram* in nearby Galta. He was deeply celebrated by at least one member of the Kachvaha royal family – a man named Naraharidās, who belonged to the Fatehpur branch – in the year 1582 (Bahura & Bryant, 1982, iv–v). Evidently Sūrdās was also a well-known poet somewhat before that time, since the Fatehpur anthology builds on at least two earlier collections, perhaps three. Two of the three distinct collections that make up the Fatehpur manuscript are very largely devoted to Sūrdās (that is, if we follow G.N. Bahura in considering the poetic signatures Śyāmghan, Sūrij, Sūrijdās, and Sūrśyām all to designate the same poet), and one is exclusively so. But beyond that – who Sūrdās was apart from the ever-widening corpus of poetry that claimed his name in dated manuscripts that survive from 1582 onward – we simply do not know. All we can say for sure is that by the late 17th century, the ocean of poetry associated with his name was bubbling up in manuscripts written in Mathura, all over Rajasthan (on one occasion, at least, by a scribe who hailed from Braj), and as far south as Burhanpur in the Deccan. This gives us nothing firm by way of biographical detail, but in another way – a literary way – it tells us a great deal.

Collective Authorship and the Expanding *Sūrsāgar*

The earliest *Sūrsāgar* manuscripts to which we have access are small; the oldest one, from Fatehpur, contains 239 poems attributed to Sūrdās. Only later did the collection assume the oceanic dimensions that its familiar title implies. Not surprisingly, that title came to be applied to the corpus only after it acquired a certain magnitude. The designation *Sūrsāgar* first appears in a manuscript dated to 1640, which contains 795 poems (Hawley, 1984, 47–48). Once applied, the title evidently stuck. Later manuscripts almost always make use of it, and they tend to expand this ocean of poems further and further with the passing of succeeding years. By the 19th century, there was already a manuscript containing almost 10,000 poems.

Who then "composed" Sūr's Ocean? One can answer this question in one of three ways. The traditional method is to say that a single individual was responsible for generating the entire corpus: Sūrdās composed the *Sūrsāgar*. This position forces one to explain the varying sizes of different anthologies, especially the smallest ones among them, as the result of insufficient efforts at collecting the vast number of poems that were actually available. In the Vallabhite tradition, this number is pegged at 125,000, and the final 25,000 are held to have been composed by Kṛṣṇa himself.

This was necessary, the story goes, because Sūrdās found himself exhausted after composing 100,000 poems and appealed to Kṛṣṇa for help (Parikh, 1970, 434–435). The numbers involved give us some hint of the mythical quality of this claim, not only because they are so large (even the largest manuscript does not begin to approach such sums) but also because they have an obviously honorific intent. If something is so praiseworthy that it exceeds what normally counts for perfect, it can be referred to as possessing still another quarter of itself. When the Mughal emperor Aurangzeb wanted to praise the young Kachvaha ruler Jai Siṅgh II, for example, he called him 1¼ (*savā*) of himself: Savāī Jai Siṅgh. In a similar way, the story about the size of the *Sūrsāgar* shows how Kṛṣṇa took Sūrdās' perfection over the top – to the 1¼ mark.

This view of the facts is still repeated by connoisseurs of poetry attributed to Sūrdās and can handily be invoked whenever a previously unknown poem comes to light – perhaps in a newly examined manuscript. But as an indicator of historical truth, it obviously will not do. It may well be that each of the earliest manuscripts, written in different places and at different times, captured only a portion of Sūrdās' poetry circulating in the 16th and 17th centuries. But this model of a huge *Sūrsāgar* produced by the poet himself and ever in the process of being recovered makes little sense of the fact that anthologies of poetry attributed to Sūrdās increased in size at a more or less regular rate through the years. Was it harder to remember the poet's utterances early on, when they were fresh, than in later years? A far simpler explanation would be to hold that as the years passed and the reputation of *Sūrsāgar* grew, later poets wishing to be heard or otherwise to contribute to the genre added new poems to the preexisting sea.

This incremental understanding of how the *Sūrsāgar* became an ocean is supported by several other considerations. First of all, we know that a number of compositions earlier attributed to other poets were incorporated into the *Sūrsāgar* in the course of time. In some manuscripts, these compositions might contain the name of Paramānanddās or → Hit Harivaṃś, but later the signature changed, and they showed up in the *Sūrsāgar* (Hawley, 2012, 206–207, 375n42). One can well imagine how this could happen. Performers working without scripts were doubtless uncertain at times about who was supposed to have composed a given poem. In such circumstances, the performer had a bit of leeway. All it took was the alteration of a few syllables in the final line, where the oral signature (*chāp, bhaṇitā*) appeared, to accommodate one poet's name rather than that of another.

A further consideration is the nature of the signature itself. In some instances, at least, it was clearly intended more to attest to the authority of a given composition than to designate the biological person who first gave it shape (Hawley, 2012, 21–47). This is very plain in the development of the roughly contemporaneous corpus of poetry that became canonical for Sikhs. All the Sikh *gurū*-poets who contributed to the *Gurū Granth Sāhib* adopted the signature of Nānak, who was the first and most important among them. A similar thing must have happened with Sūrdās, for the *Sūrsāgar* has continued to grow at a steadily increasing pace and yet still to register the signature of only one poet. Poets aspiring to the particular sort of excellence that the name of Sūrdās represented might well be expected to have taken his name as they contributed poems of their own composition to the genre, the way that students of Western classical music sometimes sit down and compose a Bach partita or a Mozart sonata. Finally, there is the fact that because of Sūrdās' reputation as the finest blind poet of all time, many another blind singer would certainly have called himself Sūrdās. This happens still today.

Suppose we grant, then, that the *Sūrsāgar* is not a static thing produced by a single poet but rather a "Sūr tradition," as K.E. Bryant was the first to say (Bryant, 1978, ix–x). What does this make us conclude about the nature of its authorship? One approach would be to abandon any sort of language that would imply the agency of a single, original Sūrdās – the sort of person that Nābhādās had in mind – and, instead, to adhere strictly to the conditions of our knowledge, admitting that nothing like an autograph copy can exist in a body of poetry that was largely the precipitate of oral performance. Plainly, a multiplicity of Sūrdāses must have been involved in generating this multi-particulate opus, so why not cut to the chase and be satisfied with the notion of collective authorship, as V. Dharwadker has done for Kabīr (Dharwadker, 2003, 60; see also Hawley, 2012, 337–338)? This would be the second answer to the question "Who composed *Sūrsāgar*?" – exactly opposite to the first.

This solution to the authorship problem is attractive in purely formal terms, and it comes close to describing what must have been the case for the vast majority of poems that were contributed to the *Sūrsāgar* as it expanded from its relatively modest 16th-century size to the ocean it is today. But it is not, in the end, satisfactory (Inden, Walters & Ali, 2000, 11–12, 48–51). It does not explain how the name Sūrdās came to be associated with a particular poetical style and expertise in the first place. Nor does it register the fact that, on the whole, poems that appear only in later iterations of the *Sūrsāgar* are less intricate, less dramatic, and less convincing artistically than those whose manuscript pedigrees are more venerable. For this reason, I believe we must retain a sense of a single excellent poet standing at the headwaters of the Sūrdās tradition. Perhaps, in this sense, the *Sūrsāgar* might better be thought of as a river than as an ocean – gathering strength in the course of time but gradually growing more sluggish and losing a good bit of the purity that could be tasted farther upstream.

This is the third and, I think, best solution to the authorship problem, even if it forces us to speak in approximations. True, we do not know anything biographically reliable about the "original" Sūrdās. Yet by speaking about him as if we did, we can affirm the tradition's own sense – from early on – that a poet of special merit first sang the Brajbhasha songs that bear the signature Sūrdās and its metrical alternatives: Sūr, Sūrij, and so forth.

The true reference of the terms "Sūr" and "Sūrdās" is to the special logic and poetic art that are displayed in poems early collected in Sūrdās' name. All we have is text – no person – and no single text at that but a series of anthologies whose contents overlap in complex ways. Still, as a group they seem to radiate a particular poetic personality: someone tirelessly imaginative and yet so scrupulous that he avoided repeating any word in the course of a single composition unless he intended the emphasis or irony that repetition would command. It is a pleasure to follow tradition and call this person or persona Sūrdās.

Bibliography

Abbott, J.E., & N.R. Godbole, *Stories of Indian Saints: English Translation of Mahipati's Marathi Bhaktavijaya*, 2 vols., Delhi, 1982.

Askari, S.H., "Historical Value of the Afsana-i-Badshahan or Tarikh-i-Afghani," *JIH* 43/1, 1965, 183–200.

Bahura, G.N., & K.E. Bryant, eds., *Pad Sūrdāsjī kā/The Padas of Sūrdās*, Jaipur, 1982.

Behl, A., & S. Weightman, *Mañjhan: Madhumālatī, an Indian Sufi Romance*, Oxford, 2000.

Blochmann, H, & S.L. Goomer, trans. & ed., *ʿAllāmī, Abū'l-Fażl: The Ā'īn-i-Akbar*, Delhi, 1871, 1965.

Brajratnadas (Brajratnadās), ed., *Nandadās-Granthāvalī*, Varanasi, 1957 (Hind.).

Bryant, K.E., *Poems to the Child-God: Structures and Strategies in the Poetry of Sūrdās*, Berkeley, 1978.

Bryant, K.E., & J.S. Hawley, *Sūrdās: Sūrsāgar*, Cambridge MA, 2013.

Busch, A., *Poetry of Kings: The Classical Hindi Literature of Mughal India*, New York, 2011.

Busch, A., personal communication, 2009.

Caturvedi (Caturvedī), J., ed., *Bhikhārīdās: Kāvyanirṇaya*, Mathura, 1959 (Hind.).

Caturvedi (Caturvedī), S., *Mahākavi Sūrdās aur unkī Pratibhā*, Allahabad, 1978 (Hind.).

Dharwadker, V., *Kabir: The Weaver's Songs*, New Delhi, 2003.

Gupta, P.L., ed., *Kutuban kṛt Mṛgāvatī (Mūl Pāh, Pāṭhāntar, Ṭippaṇī evam Śodh)*, Varanasi, 1967 (Hind.).

Hawley, J.S., "Sūrdās," in: A. Hiltebeitel, ed., *Oxford Bibliographies Online: Hinduism*, New York, 2012, http://www.oxfordbibliographiesonline.com.

Hawley, J.S., *Three Bhakti Voices: Mirabai, Surdas, and Kabir in Their Time and Ours*, Delhi, rev. ed. 2012.

Hawley, J.S., *The Memory of Love: Sūrdās Sings to Krishna*, New York, 2009.

Hawley, J.S., *Sūr Dās: Poet, Singer, Saint*. Seattle, 1984.

Inden, R., J.S. Walters & D. Ali, *Querying the Medieval: Texts and the History of Practices in South Asia*, New York, 2000.

Jha (Jhā), N., ed., *Bhaktamāl: Pāṭhānuśīlan evam Vivecan*, Patna, 1978 (Hind.).

Maithani (Maiṭhāṇī), U.K., *Sūr-Sāhitya ke Paurāṇik Prasaṅg*, New Delhi, 1997 (Hind.).

McGregor, R.S., *Nanddas: The Round Dance of Krishna and Uddhav's Message*, London, 1973.

Ojha (Ojhā), D., *Sūr-Sāhitya meṅ Puṣṭimārgīya Sevā Bhāvanā*, Allahabad, 1973 (Hind.).

Parikh (Parīkh), D., ed., *Caurāsī Vaiṣṇavan kī Vārtā*, Mathura, 1970.

Pauwels, H.R.M., *In Praise of Holy Men: Imagining Religious Communities in Medieval India: Hagiographical Poems by and about Harirām Vyās*, Groningen, 2002.

Rupkala (Rūpkalā; = S. Bhagavānprasād), ed., *Nābhādās: Śrī Bhaktamāl*, Lucknow, 1961 (Hind.).

Sengar (Seṅgar), S., *Śivsiṃh Saroj*, Lucknow, 1966, 1970 (Hind.).

Siddiqi, I.H., "Shaikh Muhammad Kabir and His History of the Afghan Kings (A.D. 1451–1555)," *Indo-Iranica* 19/4, 1966, 57–78.

Shukla (Śukla), R., *Sūrdās*, Varanasi, 1948 (Hind.).

Vaudeville, C., *Pastorales par Soûr-Dâs*, Paris, 1971.

Ved Prakash (Ved Prakāś), ed., *Bhikhārīdās: Kāvyanirṇaya*, Delhi, 2006 (Hind.).

JOHN STRATTON HAWLEY

Tarigoṇḍa Veṅgamāmba

Tarigoṇḍa Veṅgamāmba, who lived between the mid-18th and the early 19th century (according to Krishanmurti [1983], the dates are 1730/1735–1817), was a prolific writer in Telugu who wrote some 18 books. Not much is known about her except what she says about herself in her writings. She was the daughter of Kānāla Kṛṣṇārya and Maṅgamāmba and was married to Iñjeṭi Veṅkaṭācalapati.

Legends about her are abundant. She was born with a determined devotion to the god → Kṛṣṇa, on whom she constantly meditated and to whom she sang. Her father decided to have her marry so she would give up her crazy ways and settle into the life of a housewife. She protested and said that she was already married to Kṛṣṇa. But her father forced her to marry, before puberty, as was the custom at that time. Other legends say that her father tortured her to coerce her into marriage and even burned her mouth to stop her from singing Kṛṣṇa songs. After she matured, Veṅgamāmba was sent to live with her husband; but on the first night, she warned her husband not to touch her, since she had already given herself to Kṛṣṇa. Legends also have it that she appeared to her husband in the form of the fierce goddess Cauḍeśvari when he tried to approach her. Due to the fear instilled in him when he saw his wife as a fearsome goddess, her husband died soon thereafter.

According to custom at the time, a Brahman widow was to shave her hair and remove the dot on her forehead as well as other symbols of auspicious women, but Veṇgamāmba, legends say, refused to do so upon the death of her husband. When the Brahman elders in the neighborhood forced her to shave her head, the barber was amazed to see her hair grow back right after he had shaved it. When the head of the Puṣpagiri Maṭham (the Advaita → Vedānta monastery in Pushpagiri, Kadapa district, Andhra Pradesh) visited her hometown Tarigonda and asked Veṅgamāmba why she refused to shave her hair like a descent Brahman widow would, Veṅgamāmba argued with him, demanding to be shown Śāstra texts that prescribe such a practice. She refused to bow to him with folded hands, because, she maintained, doing so would kill him due to her power. To prove her point, she asked the teacher to move out of his seat and bowed to the empty chair instead, when suddenly the seat exploded and was consumed in fire. The teacher understood the power of Veṅgamāmba and declared her to be a form of the Great Goddess (→ Mahādevī).

Veṅgamāmba, the legends continue, went to a secluded spot behind an image of → Hanumān in the local temple in Tarigonda and began to meditate there. The priest of the temple accused her of committing immoral acts in her seclusion, pulled her hair, and dragged her away from that spot. Unable to find a quiet place for her meditation, Veṅgamāmba went walking alone to Tirupati hill, where the temple of god → Vēnkaṭeśvara is located. The *mahant* (temple priest-manager) of this major temple of South India realized the superiority of Veṅgamāmba's devotion and gave her a place on the hill, in a small hut. Veṅgamāmba found a quiet place for her religious practices in a remote thicket on the hill called Tumburu Kona. A certain *guru*, named Subrahmaṇya, initiated her into → *yoga*, and she acquired spiritual eminence under his tutelage. Having arrived at Tirupati, Veṅgamāmba found peace and quiet there to compose most of her major works; others were composed in her hometown, Tarigonda. It is also said that eight scribes, called *aṣṭagaṇṭamula vāru* (group of eight with styluses), worked with her during the years she was composing these texts. As we shall see later, it is easy to say that these legends do not seem to have any historical support. However, Veṅgamāmba is well known to the ritual community in Tirupati, where a flame offering was given in her name to the deity before he was put to bed every night. The offering, called *mutyāla harati*, still forms a part of the regular rituals at the temple, which suggests that more work needs to be done before making definitive statements about history and legend in her biography/hagiography.

Veṅgamāmba was a devotee of Narasiṃha, the man-lion → *avatār* of → Viṣṇu who was a local deity in the temple in her village, and dedicated most of her books to him. Even when she wrote about Vēṅkaṭeśvara and Kṛṣṇa, she talked of them as inseparable from Narasiṃha of Tarigonda.

Veṅgamāmba herself mentions some ten books that she composed in her *Dvipadabhāgavatamu*, apparently a late work. In all, she is said to have composed some 18 works, in addition to a number of songs. Despite her being so prolific, Veṅgamāmba did not receive attention by scholars of literature. Kandukuri Viresalignam (1848–1919) mentioned her approvingly in his *Āndhra Kavula Caritramu* (Lives of Telugu Poets). A. Seshagiri Rao wrote an essay about her, later published as a book (Seshagiri Rao, 2009), and U. Lakshmikantamma included her in her *Āndhra Kavayitrulu* (Andhra Women Poets), but still Veṅgamāmba remained unnoticed by literary critics. The more popular and recent *Samagra Āndhra Sāhitya Caritra* (Complete History of Andhra Literature), by Arudra, mentions her only once in a passing reference. Part of the reason for this lack of attention could be that her compositions were not readily available in print, and in her lifetime she did not make any effort to gain publicity for her work.

In 2008 the Tirumala Tirupati Devasthanam, the temple administration in Tirupati, decided to bring attention to Veṅgamāmba and conducted a celebration on her birthday with great fanfare. They published most of her books, competently edited by K.J. Krishnamurti, who almost single-handedly brought her work to the attention of the literary public.

One of Veṅgamāmba's early works is *Tarigoṇḍa Nṛsimhaśatakamu*. A work in the Śataka genre contains about one hundred verses, usually in the same meter, each verse ending in a vocative addressing the deity. Poets have traditionally used this genre to express their personal devotion to the deity of their choice and often to give expression to their subjective feelings about social evils. Veṅgamāmba addresses Viṣṇu as Narasiṃha, who is the chief deity in her hometown Tarigonda. As a personal appeal to god, the Śataka does not have a continuing narrative. Each verse is independent of the other, and each verse states a mood or a complaint to or praise of the deity. Veṅgamāmba uses the first three verses, which unusually include a verse in Sanskrit, to praise her god. Then follow three verses expressing her intention to speak to him in one hundred verses. She then raises the possibility that people will consider these verses silly and asks god to bless them. Veṅgamāmba calls the god her lover and wonders if he is not responding to her because his wife Lakṣmī (→ Śrī Lakṣmī) does not let him go or because he could not leave the Ceñcu (a hunter-gatherer tribe) girl with whom, according to a local myth, god Nṛsimha (i.e. Narasiṃha) fell in love. Veṅgamāmba includes several verses critical of the common behavior of people around her, which is a common feature of the Śataka genre, but in one of the verses, there is an interesting personal observation in her description of how women treat their husbands.

> When their husbands are young,
> women serve them like they are their gods.
> Once their youth is gone, God of Tarigonda,
> wives treat them with arrogance,
> no respect any more. (*TNŚat.* 64; trans. by author)

In a number of these verses, Veṅgamāmba employs the esoteric symbolism of *yoga*, which is difficult to interpret, as in the following verse:

> Bright moonlight shines
> on the land of the inner self
> encircled by seven major enclosures.
> A big snake watches over it.
> Man-lion of Tarigonda,
> I found that fortress by your kindness now. (*TNŚat.* 45; trans. by author)

Even in this early work, Veṅgamāmba gives expression to her yogic bent of mind and speaks of her *guru*, who erased with his foot the previous script on her forehead and wrote a new future for her.

The Śataka ends with a colophon verse, stating that Veṅgamāmba, the wife of Niñjeṭi Venkaṭācalapati, composed this and gave it to the man-lion god of Tarigonda, clearly indicating that she did not reject her husband, as the legends about her say.

Veṅgamāmba wrote several *yakṣagāna*s (see → drama and theatre). These are a type of musical drama, popular from about the 17th century onward in Telugu literature. What is interesting is that a woman who is supposed to have lived a rather secluded life composed the text and lyrics of a genre that required knowledge of music and theater conventions.

The narrative of one of her *yakṣagāna*s, *Ceñcu Nāṭakamu*, briefly is as follows. A Ceñcu woman goes hunting with her infant son safely tucked in the sash of her saree tightly wound to her bosom accompanied by her husband, Ceñcu Nāyuḍu. As they merrily move through the forest, she loses track of her husband; searching for him, she ends up on Tirupati hill, where god Vēnkaṭeśvara lives in his temple. As she wails loudly for her husband, the doorkeepers of god – Jaya and Vijaya – call her to ask who she is and why she is crying. She informs them that she is the daughter of the leader of the Ceñcus, Śikhi Nāyaka. Lord Narasiṃha, the man-lion form of Viṣṇu, that cunning lover with a big mustache, has made her elder sister fall in love with him and taken her as his wife. Then, a man from the Vindhya Mountains, who had looked innocent, had come and taken her – that is, the narrator – as his wife. Together they had gone hunting, and now she has lost him and is searching for him.

The doorkeepers of god ask her to describe her husband, and she gives them a humorous description: he has a eunuch's beard and high eyebrows, he is short with short arms, he has cat eyes and a big belly, and he is hunchbacked. He is the son-in-law of the Viṣṇu of Tarigonḍa.The doorkeepers, apparently enjoying their conversation with her, say that they have not seen a man of her description but ask her where on earth she and her husband have wandered. The Ceñcu woman describes in a very learned style all the great mountains of this vast mythological universe: Jambūdvīpa – the rose apple island – and beyond it, Plakṣadvīpa, Puṣkaradvīpa, and the Cakravāḷa Mountain. She describes the Meru Mountain and then the darkness beyond it, where they were not able to go and therefore came to where Viṣṇu of Tarigonḍa lived. She goes on to describe their life together: they climb mountains and hills, lay in wait to kill animals, collect honeycombs from the tops of trees, discipline lions, control tigers and elephants, and constantly serve Viṣṇu. She gives a long and detailed description of the different continents, including the continent of Bharata (where India is located), and of the seven seas such as the seas of milk, curds, and sugarcane juice. After seeing all the mountains of the universe, the mountain on which Vēnkaṭeśvara lives looks funny to her. She looks at the multistoried houses around the temple and asks what those square boxes are for. She looks at the temple towers and asks what kind of mountains they are and if the two-legged animals walking around are good for hunting.

The doorkeepers tell her that they are human beings and should not be killed. She then asks who the doorkeepers are, with their four hands and two legs. They inform her that they are Jaya and Vijaya, the doorkeepers of god Vēnkaṭeśvara. She wants their permission to go in to see the lord and promises to give the god rabbits and snakes and musk cats.

The doorkeepers, amused at her innocent and yet informed conversation, want to know about the wedding rituals of the Ceñcus. The Ceñcu woman describes how weddings are conducted in the presence of the elders of the group, right at the middle of the day, at an auspicious moment when the sun is right above their heads. The doorkeepers demand that she pay money for admission to the temple. The god Vēnkaṭeśvara had borrowed money from a Muslim king, and he has to pay it back. The god needs ten thousand rupees as her contribution toward the debt that he has accrued. The dance drama continues with the Ceñcu woman saying that she knows a Vēnkaṭeśvara who visits them in the forest and asking if this Vēnkaṭeśvara in the temple is any greater than the one she knows from the forest. Furthermore, she asserts, she is a relative of Viṣṇu of Tarigonḍa and therefore should be allowed into the temple for free.

The doorkeepers want to hear what the Vēnkaṭeśvara who visits her in the forest does and how the Ceñcus worship him. She describes that Vēnkaṭeśvara comes riding on a bird, goes up to the mountains with them, hunts with them, brings them honey from the tops of trees, and touches the women in all sensitive places and makes them laugh. He comes home, and when the Ceñcu women make a bed for him to rest, he lies down; they fan him with peacock feathers and give him fruit; when he has eaten and rested, he plays love games with them and laughs with them with desire on his mind, and when the women play along, he makes love to them. When he leaves, they give him musk and civet, *jāji* flowers (bot. Jasminum grandiflorum), and a fox horn. The doorkeepers wonder why they give him a fox horn. The Ceñcu woman says that a fox horn brings wealth to the house in which it is kept.

Just as the doorkeepers are about to allow the Ceñcu woman to go into the temple in order to see Vēnkaṭeśvara, her husband shows up. He tells her how he shook with fear when he did not find her. He ran for his life when a squirrel made faces at him. The Ceñcu woman says that seeing Vēnkaṭeśvara will remove all his fears and that they should go into the temple. The husband strongly objects. The god is a womanizer, and she should not go to see him. He describes to her all the things Vēnkaṭeśvara has done in the past. He has made love to his aunt, with no regard for propriety. He has held the cowherd girls and seduced them. He is known to catch any beautiful young woman who comes to worship him and to force her to marry him. It is the same man who eloped with the Ceñcu woman's elder sister. If that womanizer sees her, the husband says, he will not let her go to her husband again.

Now the husband demands that she feed him, because he is hungry. She wants him to take care of the child when she goes to hunt for food. But the husband refuses. She breastfeeds the baby and puts him to sleep before she leaves to get some food for her husband. But when she is out hunting for food, a tiger takes away her son. Grieving for her son, she begins to pray to Vēnkaṭeśvara to give her son back. The husband foolishly says that as long as he is there, he will make more sons for her, and so she should not grieve for one son. Vēnkaṭeśvara possesses one of the doorkeepers and says through that medium that a tiger took her son away because she failed on her promise to see Vēnkaṭeśvara. The god will give her son back, if she brings money for him.

The Ceñcu woman says that she does not have any money; if the god shows her the place where wealth is located, she will go there and get it and give it to him. Vēnkaṭeśvara says that she has *cidrūpa dhanamu*, that is, wealth in the form of her inner consciousness. Here Veṅgamāmba writes a rather cryptic verse in esoteric yogic vocabulary. Unfortunately, the text of this verse is partially lost, which adds to its inherent obscurity. I do not pretend to interpret the verse, except provide a literal translation here to give an indication of its esoteric quality.

> You have to cross a mountain of six peaks and then another mountain of sixteen peaks, cross three rivers, and arrive at a crossing of four paths, and when you see a snake hanging upside down, tie up the mouth of that snake, hold your breath with your mind, and cross the worlds of the sun and moon; reject *māyā* and ego, reach the mountain of Veda, capture the wealth of consciousness, bring it, and submit it to us with devotion, and I will give your son to you. (see Krishnamurti, 2007a, 43–44; trans. by author)

In the end, Vēnkaṭeśvara kills the tiger, takes her son from its belly, brings him back to life, and gives him to the Ceñcu woman. The drama ends with a song wishing the god Vēnkaṭeśvara well.

Ceñcu Nāṭakamu is an extraordinary composition in its language, theme, and tone. It has a cluster of events that includes humor, passion, devotion, and *yoga*. The detailed description of the Ceñcu people and their lifestyle makes the play charming without making it exotic. That it is not anthropologically accurate (Bhowmick, 1991) does not detract from the author's attempt to make it sound so. It is possible that Veṅgamāmba knew Ceñcu forest people who lived around Tirupati hill and that she had some impressionistic knowledge of their lifestyle, as most people of the plains in that area did. The dialogue switches from a concocted illiterate Ceñcu dialect to a highly erudite and scholarly elevated speech. The incongruity of unabashed erotic descriptions and an esoteric yogic diction makes the play strangely compelling.

Another *yakṣagāna* of a similar mix of styles and diction is *Viṣṇu Pārijātamu*. Its theme is as follows. Kṛṣṇa, who has eight wives, is once visited by the great sage Nārada, who brings him the rare divine flower from heaven – the *pārijāta*. He gives it to Kṛṣṇa, who at that time is visiting his senior wife, Rukmiṇi. Kṛṣṇa, while being worried that the proud Satyabhāma – one of his other wives – will make a fuss about it, inevitably gives it to Rukmiṇi. The maidservants carry the news to Satyabhāma, who promptly enters her anger chamber (i.e. a room in the palace to which the queen retires when she is upset with her husband) and refuses to receive Kṛṣṇa when he comes to visit her. Kṛṣṇa tries to appease her and bows to her, but she kicks his head with her left foot. Finally he wins her over by promising a superior gift of not just a flower but the whole tree. He will go to heaven and bring the entire tree and plant it in Satyabhāma's backyard. Kṛṣṇa then invades heaven, brings the tree, and fulfills his promise.

This story, made famous by the 16th-century Telugu poet Nandi Timmana is a staple of *kūcipuḍi* performers (Soneji, 2004; Kamath, 2012; see → dance). Known to have been composed as a dance drama by the legendary Siddhendra Yogi, the story is so well known that Satyabhāma has become a household name in Andhra for a woman who is full of herself, proud of her beauty, and fiercely jealous of any other woman who steals the attention of her lover.

Veṅgamāmba uses this theme but makes a radical departure from the popular depiction of Satyabhāma. Her long musical play presents Satyabhāma as a woman determined to control Kṛṣṇa; but after several ups and down, Satyabhāma takes to meditation on Kṛṣṇa and, as a result, conquers all desire and attains a state of calm and quiet. She does not wish to make love to Kṛṣṇa anymore, nor does she feel jealous of her co-wives. When Kṛṣṇa wants her and tries to provoke her desire, she tells him that she does not want physical pleasures and that he should go to his other wives.

Kṛṣṇa invades Indra's heaven anyway, plucks the *pārijāta* tree out of the heavenly pleasure garden, and hoists it on his own vehicle Garuḍa. Indra fights back, assuming Kṛṣṇa to be a mere mortal, and a shepherd at that, who is trying to steal from his garden. In the fierce battle that follows, the clash of the powerful weapons of the two divine warriors brings the whole universe to the brink of total destruction. The god → Śiva makes an appearance and convinces Indra that Kṛṣṇa is not a human but an incarnation of the god Viṣṇu, who took several *avatār*s to save Indra himself and who is in a position of power over the world of gods. Realizing his mistake, Indra surrenders to Kṛṣṇa and, free from his royal ego, asks for forgiveness and presents the *pārijāta* tree as an offering to him.

Kṛṣṇa plants the *pārijāta* tree in the backyard of Satyabhāma, which pleases her but incites the envy of all his other wives. They demand equal treatment and want a *pārijāta* tree in each of their yards. They did not mind Kṛṣṇa giving the *pārijāta* flower that Nārada had brought to Rukmiṇi, because she is the senior wife, but Satyabhāma is like all the other wives, and she should not get any special favors. Kṛṣṇa suggests that Rukmiṇi should be invited to settle the dispute, and he will follow her judgment. Rukmiṇi says that Satyabhāma deserves the *pārijāta* tree because she performed penance for Kṛṣṇa, renouncing all desires. Kṛṣṇa invites Satyabhāma to give the flowers of the tree as gifts to all of the wives. Everyone is happy, and the play ends in harmony, with all of the wives singing a song of good wishes to god Kṛṣṇa.

This is an unusual ending for this story, indeed. The long play is a tour de force that includes an extraordinary variety of linguistic registers – from the elevated long Sanskrit compounds to the folkish style of a fortune teller's singsong speech (a mixed dialect of Tamil-Telugu) and a variety of Sanskritic and indigenous meters in between. The language of harsh and violent insults that Kṛṣṇa's various wives hurl at one another reflects the local women's dialect, but their praise of Kṛṣṇa quickly switches to a spiritual ecstasy erasing all conflicts that just preceded it. The fun-filled language of the gardener in demanding the identity of Kṛṣṇa when he enters the garden stands in sharp contrast to Kṛṣṇa's dignified responses, indicating his divinity; the insulting inquiries of the gardener's wife, which provoke equally insulting responses from Kṛṣṇa's wives, who enter the garden looking for him, bring the disharmony back to surface. The play adopts several themes that occur in the *Bhāmākalāpamu* text attributed to Siddhendra Yogi, such as the humorous episode in which Satyabhāma tries to describe Kṛṣṇa to her confidante, who agrees to go in search of Kṛṣṇa, and the confidante's intentional misunderstanding of each of the descriptions. Satyabhāma is too shy to utter Kṛṣṇa's name. Instead, she tries indirect hints. She says, "he is the one who holds the wheel," because Kṛṣṇa famously wields the wheel as his weapon. Her friend takes it to mean the potter, who also wields the wheel. The predicable misunderstanding goes on until Satyabhāma finally has to speak out her husband's name in plain direct words.

Veṅgamāmba also borrows from Siddhendra Yogi's script the incident in which the confidante bargains for gifts from Satyabhāma in return for her services of delivering the message to Kṛṣṇa and bringing him to her. In Siddhendra Yogi's *Bhāmākalāpamu*, the demand for gifts escalates until finally the confidante asks for Satyabhāma's nose ring, which is the very symbol of her marriage to Kṛṣṇa and therefore inseparable from her body. In Veṅgamāmba's *Viṣṇu Pārijatamu*, the confidante asks for something totally unexpected: *mokṣa*, → liberation from the cycle of birth and death:

> Listening to the story of god is
> the real ornament to the ears.
> Seeing him before you constantly is
> the best that eyes could ask for.
> Singing god again and again is
> the only ornament to the tongue.
> Giving what you have to those who ask
> is a great ornament to the hands.
> These are the four gifts I want, and I do not
> want ephemeral things. Make the Lord of Lords
> give them to me
> when I bring him to you, my friend. (see Lakshmikantamma, 1965, 49; trans. by author)

With all its humor, elegance, playfulness, and songs and verses, Veṅgamāmba's *Viṣṇu Pārijātamu* finally stands out as a text of devotion and prayer to her personal deity Kṛṣṇa; in the end, all other passing moods of the play are drowned in the flood of → *bhakti* that engulfs the listeners.

We have seen that Veṅgamāmba's other passion was *yoga*. A text that is exclusively devoted to this theme is her *Rājayogāmṛtasāramu*, which addresses the workings of *yoga* in practice. The story for this composition in *dvipada*s, couplets, is from book 3 of Bammera Pōtana's *Āndhra Mahābhāgavatamu*, a Telugu telling of the Sanskrit *Bhāgavatapurāṇa*. The bulk of the text is a conversation between Devahūti, wife of Kardama, and her son Kapila, who was Viṣṇu himself born to her. Kardama leaves his wife and son to renounce the world and do penance, and he tells Devahūti that her son Kapila will take care of her and teach her the way to liberation. When Kapila also prepares to leave to meditate on god, Devahūti asks him not to leave her alone. Kapila talks to her of the impermanence of this world and teaches her that she is really identical with what is inside her, the → *brahman*, and instructs her in the inner modes of *yoga* to realize her true self. This long session of questions and answers is an accessible instruction to the path of *yoga*. It is truly amazing how Veṅgamāmba accomplished it in *dvipada* couplets with a flowing, transparent diction. Claiming no special scholarly competence in the subject, and humbly stating that she does not even know the elementary principles of meter, she produced a truly brilliant work, apparently simple but actually dense. An interesting aspect of this small book of 1,022 lines is the emphasis she places on the guidance of the → *guru* who should initiate the pupil into the path of *yoga*. She even describes in detail how the *guru* should make the student sit on a seat, put ashes on his forehead, erase the previous writing on it and write a new future in its place, tell the pupil not to fear and comfort him, and then teach him the process of Rāja → Yoga. Later in her book, we read that Kapila follows the same procedure to enlighten his mother. He tells his mother to forget the → *māyā* of the world. He says to her,

> You are not your body
> or your senses.
> You are not a woman, nor are you a man,
> nor a person of the third gender.
> You are not a thought
> nor non-thought.
> You are beyond thought.
> You are complete, inexhaustible,
> you are the light.
> You are *brahman*.
> When you know yourself,
> you will know there is nothing other than you.
> (see Krishnamurti, 2007b, lines 335–344; trans. by author)

This excellent little book is arguably the best complete statement about *yoga* in Telugu. The last and more voluminous works of Veṅgamāmba are her *Bhāgavatamu* and *Jñāna Vāsishṭha Rāmāyaṇamu*. The first one is a rendering in couplets of all 12 books of Pōtana's great epic poem *Āndhra Mahābhāgavatamu*, of which only three books are available in print, and the rest are feared lost; the second one is based on Abhinada's abridgment of *Jñāna Vāsishṭha Rāmāyaṇa*, attributed to Vālmīki. In both of these major works, Veṅgamāmba has perfected her control of *dvipada* and tells long and complex epic-length narratives with ease. In the *Jñāna Vāsishṭha Rāmāyaṇamu*, she narrates a large number of different complex stories dealing with such issues as dream and reality and truth and illusion.

Conclusion

If one looks at Veṅgamāmba's prolific literary career, one would expect her to claim a major presence in the history of Telugu literature. However, her modesty, gentleness, and unwillingness to question authority – and perhaps her determination to make a quiet life for herself without fanfare – appear to have left her uninterested in fame. In a number of her works, she states that she is not learned, was not properly taught the basic alphabet in her childhood – let alone grammar and meter – and is certainly not competent to talk of Śāstra texts. Some of this might be taken as the general style of the temple poets, who have traditionally remained under the radar of scholarly scrutiny and submitted humbly to → *paṇḍit*s, leaving the court poets free to fight among themselves for the attention of their king. Even admitting that the modesty that Veṅgamāmba shows is in keeping with the style of temple poets, the statements repeatedly made by her in several of her books – including the very last major works, which clearly show her mastery of language and knowledge of major religious works in Sanskrit – suggest that this trait is much deeper than what a convention would require.

Evidence from Veṅgamāmba's works suggests that in her narratives she avoids conflict and disharmony. In dealing with themes where the traditional telling requires winners and losers, such as the competition among the many wives of Kṛṣṇa or his many cowherd girlfriends, she resolves the dispute, contrary to the way in which the story is traditionally told, and makes all of them agree to a compromise and share Kṛṣṇa as their common husband/lover equally. Neither does Kṛṣṇa cheat on his wives and secretly go to one wife behind the back of the other. In *Viṣṇu Pārijātamu*, he asks for permission of his other wives to visit Satyabhāma. While Veṅgamāmba does write scenes where the wives fight with one another and with Kṛṣṇa, the end is always harmonious. She shows no hesitation to write erotic descriptions, often at length and without inhibition – a trait that could be severely censured because it is considered inappropriate for a family woman to do so. But Veṅgamāmba takes care to produce an alibi; it was Kṛṣṇa who wrote them and not herself, as she expressly states in her *Veṅkaṭācalamāhātmyamu*:

> In his stunningly attractive form
> he comes to me, and asks me to make
> erotic songs on him, slightly veiled,
> I say I cannot do that.
> He gets angry and I bow to him and
> beg him to forgive me.
> He takes pity on me and writes the songs himself.
> Kṛṣṇa, I serve him forever. (quoted in Seshagiri Rao, 2009, 26; trans. by author)

The question now is how to reconcile the legends about Veṅgamāmba, and her hagiography, with the persona of her books and the poet she appears to be according to her own descriptions of herself. At least two respected modern scholars, M. Ramakrishna Kavi (see introduction to the *Nṛsimhaśatakamu* [see Krishnamurti, 2007c, xii]) and A. Seshagiri Rao (2009, 9–10), have questioned the veracity of the legends and dismissed them as baseless. But the legends persist, repeated over and over, and have made an indelible impression on the popular mind. Scholar after scholar narrates them with a tone of factuality. On the basis of these legends, well-known writer Muktevi Bharati has written a novelistic biography of Veṅgamāmba, to the approval of a good number of the novelist's admiring readers (Bharati, 2006), and a full-length movie, *Vengamamba*, was made about her in 2009. The movie as well as many of the writers who wrote about her present Veṅgamāmba as a revolutionary who fought against superstition and stood up to religious authority in order to gain freedom for women. These legends have a power of their own and are impossible to erase no matter what the historical evidence may document or suggest.

Legends like this seem to write themselves, as in the case of → Mīrābāī, the saint-singer of Rajasthan (Hawley, 1988, 119–133), with whom Veṅgamāmba is often compared. It is well known that stories about saints move along pilgrimage routes, just as more secular tales move along trade routes. Tirupati is a major pilgrimage center that has attracted pilgrims from all over India, and it is not improbable that the legends of Mīrābāī, who is said to have rejected her husband and sung for Kṛṣṇa as her real lord, traveled from Rajasthan and perhaps got grafted on to Veṅgamāmba. Stories live on, embedded in culture, deeper than history, and more real than reality.

Bibliography

Arudra, *Samagra Āndhra Sāhityamu*, 4 vols., Hyderabad, 2004 (Tel.).

Bharati, M., *Tarigoṇḍa Veṅgamāmba*, Vijayawada, 2006 (Tel.).

Bhowmick, P.K., *The Chenchus of the Forests and the Plateaux: A Hunting-Gathering Tribe in Transition*, Calcutta, 1991.

Hawley, J.S., & M. Juergensmeyer, *Songs of the Saints of India*, New York, 1988.

Kamath, H.M., "Aesthetics, Performativity & Performative Māyā: Imagining Gender in the Textual and Performance Traditions of Telugu South India," diss., Emory University, 2012.

Krishnamurti, K.J., ed., *Ceñcunāṭakamu*, Tirupati, 2007a.

Krishnamurti, K.J., ed., *Rājayogāmṛtasāramu*, Tirupati, 2007b.

Krishnamurti, K.J., ed., *Nṛsimhaśatakamu*, Tirupati, 2007c.

Krishnamurti, K.J., *Tarigoṇḍa Veṇgamāmba Kṛtulu: Savimarśaka Pariśīlanamu*, Tirupati, 1983 (Tel.).

Lakshmikantamma, U., ed., *Viṣṇupārijātamu*, Hyderabad, 1965.

Lakshmikantamma, U., *Āndhra Kavayitrulu*, Secunderabad, [1]1953, [2]1980 (Tel.).

Seshagiri Rao, A., *Vidushīmaṇi Veṇgamāmba*, Tirupati, 2009 (Tel.).

Soneji, D., "Performing Satyabhāmā: Text, Context, Memory and Mimesis in Telugu-Speaking South India," diss., McGill University, 2004.

Viresalingam, K., *Āndhra Kavula Caritramu*, Hyderabad, 2005 (Tel.).

V. Narayana Rao

Tukārām

Tukārām's importance rests in three areas: first, of course, his poetry, whose rhythms and images are known across the face of → Maharashtra; second, his life, which illustrates the ongoing importance of the Vārkarī pilgrimage (see → Vārkarī Sampradāy), the kind of devotion it inspires, and the duties of the householder saint; and third, his part in building the unity of the Marathi-speaking peoples in the creation of the area that became Maharashtra state. Tukārām (1608–1650) is undoubtedly the most revered of the Marathi poet-saints. His birthplace, Dehu, is a place of pilgrimage. A 1936 film of his life and song is still in circulation (see below). He has been translated by scholars and poets. The cry of the pilgrims going to Pandharpur, "Dnyānbā Tukārām," links him with the 13th-century author Dnyāneśvar (also called Jñāneśvar or → Jñāndev; 1275–1297), held to be the founder of the Vārkarī tradition, whose pilgrimage is probably the most important religious event in Maharashtrian culture even today. Tukārām considered himself a disciple of → Nāmdev (1270–1350), who popularized the pilgrimage to Pandharpur. He is one of four – Dnyāneśvar, Nāmdev, → Eknāth, and Tukārām – who represent the period (13th–17th cents.) of the literary creativity of the Vārkarīs. Incidents in Tukārām's life that are in most Maharashtrian memories include a famine that took his first wife and a son, a miraculous harvest after Tukārām had let cattle and birds into a field while concentrating on the praise of Viṭṭhal (Viṭhobā), the teaching of the love of god to the mistress of his Brahman critic, the scolding of his clueless wife, the legend of the great king Śivājī's request to be his disciple, and two incidents by the river Indrāyaṇī: his Brahman critics made him submerge his poetry in the river. He sat for 13 days at the riverbank before his poetry came back to him, unharmed. The movie also depicts Tukārām being taken to heaven by angels at the end of his life. There is no clear legend about this, and the death or the *samādhi* (voluntary ending of life) of Tukārām in 1650 is a matter of controversy (see Omvedt, 2003, 205–207).

Fig. 1: Tukārām doll from a shop in Pune (photo Sandra Hales, used by courtesy).

The Pilgrimage

The heart of the Vārkarī tradition is the pilgrimage to Pandharpur, called the *vārī*. During the pilgrimage, Tukārām's songs are the most frequently sung, not only in his *pālkhī* (the palanquin that carries the saint's *pādukās* [footprints]) from Dehu, but also in other *pālkhīs*. Tukārām has also written and sung about the pilgrimage:

I should like to become the small pebbles
  or the big stones, or the dust
  of the road which leads to Pandharpur.
Thus would I be under the feet of the Santas.

What else could I ask you for?
It is an everlasting and fearless bliss
With no bitter after-taste.

I should like to become the shoes or the sandals
  on the feet of all the Santas.
I should like to be a cat, or a pig, or a dog
  and stay near them to eat their crumbs.
I should like to be the step built on the brink
  of a well or on the bank of the brook or of the river

Where the Santas would walk on.
Says Tuka:
O God, My Mother,
Put me in any place provided the feet of the Santas touch me,
Give me that, and I'll not be afraid to be reborn. (Deleury, 1960, 76)

J.T. Molesworth's dictionary (1857) defines "→ Sant (a)" simply as a holy man, a saint. The dictionary has quite a long section on the Vārkarī movement, and included in that is a Tukārām poem about Viṭṭhal, the god of Pandharpur:

Viṭhal is extended throughout the three worlds; Viṭhal is the sage of the mind.
Viṭhal is of the essence of life; Viṭhal is tender compassion.
Viṭhal is the idol of affection; the fondled object of the universe is in Viṭhal.
Viṭhal is parent and uncle; Viṭhal is sister and the brother.
Without Viṭhal there is no friendship or relationship. Tuka says, there is indeed no other. (Molesworth, 1857, xxviii)

The basic text of the pilgrims is Dnyāneśvar's 13th-century commentary on the → *Bhagavadgītā*. Dnyāneśvar was one of three brothers and a sister called outcaste Brahmans because their father had come back from being a *saṃnyāsī* at the request of his *guru* to have the family that his wife had been promised. The four children were soon orphaned, and they acted together as a family. Of the four, Dnyāneśvar and his sister Muktābāī were the principal authors; Sopān and Nivṛttināth were very important figures in the beginning of the Vārkarī movement. Dnyāneśvar also wrote *abhaṅgas* (songs in a varied meter used by the poet-saints) in praise of Viṭṭhal; this has created the suggestion that there may have been two Dnyāneśvars, one who was a Sanskrit scholar and one who was a popular poet. Dnyāneśvar's *samādhi* (tomb) is at Alandi, the starting point of his *pālkhī* procession.

The distance from Alandi to Pandharpur is 240 km. The singing of the pilgrims is accompanied by Tukārām's instruments: the *vīṇā*, a string instrument, held by the lead singers in turn; *ṭāḷs* or cymbals; and *mṛdaṅgas* or drums. All the *pālkhīs* of the various poets-saints of the Vārkarī tradition meet on the ninth day of the bright fortnight of *āṣāḍha* (Jun–Jul), just outside the city of Pandharpur. The *pālkhī* is formed by *diṇḍīs*, smaller groups based on village or caste.

As P. Engblom explains,

> The use of a pālkhī to carry the Dnyaneshwar pādukās (footprints of the saints) was an innovation that is credited to a rich nobleman from Satara District by the name of Haibatravbaba Arphalkar. This great devotee of Dnyaneshwar not only provided for the pālkhī and the paraphernalia of tents, carts, horses, and – at one time – elephants that surrounded it, but he also more fully organized the Wārkarīs themselves around it on the occasion of the yearly Ashadh pilgrimage (Dandekar, Wārkarī 62). He established the first official diṇḍīs (bhajan or singing groups) and brought them together in a set order within the pālkhī procession. Likewise, he arranged the daily order in the singing of the bhajans, which is still used today. As Dandekar puts it, "The Ashadh pālkhī festival is entirely his fruit" (Wārkarī 62). As recognition of his sterling devotion to Dnyaneshwar and to the Wārkarī Panth, Haibatrav lies buried now under the first step of the Dnyaneshwar temple in Alandi (Neurgavkar 16). (see Mokashi, 1987, 18)

In the 1920s, there was another effort to restructure the Dnyāneśvar *pālkhī*. S.V. (Sonopant) Dandekar, a professor and principal at Sir Parashurambhau College, a prestigious and conservative college in Poona, organized the Dnyāneśvar *diṇḍī* within the *pālkhī*, and after that, most observers have gone with that *diṇḍī*. S.V. Dandekar also gave a certain amount of authority and legitimacy to the whole Pandharpur pilgrimage among the Brahman classes (Deleury, 1960, 83).

Tukārām and the Vārkarī Tradition

The city of Pandharpur arose on a curve of the Bhīmā River, which looked like the crescent moon and hence was called the Candrabhāgā. S.G. Tulpule has found an inscription indicating that there was a temple to Tukārām's god, Viṭhobā, in 1189 in Pandharpur (1979, 329). The present temple was built in 1744. The legend of the city's founding is that a reformed son, Puṇḍalīk, was caring for his aging parents, when the god Viṭhobā came looking for his wife. Puṇḍalīk did not stop doing his parental duties but threw a brick so Viṭhobā could stand out of the mud. J. Stanley suggests that the brick might be considered a vehicle (Stanley, personal communication), which would be very much in tune with the humor of Maharashtra. The god remains standing on the brick out of love for his disciples.

The Vārkāris are householders, not *saṃnyāsīs* or mendicants. Even Dnyāneśvar and his brothers and sister lived as a family, and (except for the courtesan Kānhopātrā) the later Vārkarī poet-saints all had wives (or husbands) and children, even if difficult. The other marks of a Vārkarī are regular participation in the *vārī* (the pilgrimage), a moral life, vegetarianism, a necklace of *tulsī* beads, and an open spirit to all castes.

One of Tukārām's *abhaṅgas* lists many of the different sorts of *bhaktas* both in Maharashtra and in the North, resulting in a very interesting look at the range of his knowledge about castes and the Marathi and Hindi poet-saints:

Blessed the lineage, holy the land,
Where the servants of Hari are born…
Karma Dharma's become Narayan,
it is he who has purified the worlds (refrain).

Who is purified by pride
of varna, tell me if you know!
Untouchables are saved by hymns to Hari,
legendary stories become their bards.

Tuladhar Vaishya, the potmaker Gora,
the leatherworker Rohidas.
The momin [weaver] Kabir, Latif the Muslim,
the barber Sena are Vishnudas.

Kanhopatra, Khodu, cotton-carder Dadu,
sing hymns to Hari without discord.
Banka, Chokhamela, by caste Mahar,
have united with the Lord.

What is the worth of Nama's Jani,
when Pandhari's lord eats in her company?
Can you tell the lineage of Mairala?
What greatness did he have, do tell!

Vishnu's servants have no caste,
the Veda's science so decrees.
Tuka says, which of your books
have saved the fallen – I know of none.
(Omvedt & Patankar, 2012, 116)

In the *abhaṅga*, we see low castes, untouchables, and Muslims, but no Brahmans. However, it ends with a question, "which of your books have saved the fallen?" which is addressed to Brahmans. Of the 13 *bhaktas* that are referred to in the *abhaṅga*, three are Muslim and two are women.

The Marathi *bhaktas* mentioned in this *abhaṅga* are all from the 14th century. There was no more poetry until the 16th century. Some think that this was due to the Mughal invasion of the Deccan, despite the fact that there continued to be interaction between Marathas and Muslim courts. The hiatus ended with the appearance of a major figure, the Brahman Eknāth (1533–1599). He not only corrected the old copy of the *Dhyāneśvarī* (*Jñāneśvarī*), which had become corrupted, but also wrote the second most precious text for *bhaktas*, the *Eknāthī Bhāgavat*. He also produced *bhāruḍs* or drama poems that depicted the world around him, as well as *abhaṅgas* like this one:

Hey, Puṇḍyā! Why are you so proud
as to make Viṭṭhal stand there?
Why are you so bold
as to toss a brick to him?
Twenty-eight yugas have passed.
Why have you not yet told him, "Sit down"?
To see your faith close up,
God left behind his heaven, Vaikuṇṭha.
Says Tukā, "O Puṇḍalīk,
you're the really strong one." (Dhere, 2011, 28–29; trans. by Feldhaus)

Nāmdev was buried on the lowest step of the Pandharpur temple, and → Cokhāmeḷā, a Mahār by caste, has his *samādhi* on the other side of the lane in front of the temple. There is a *samādhi* for Kānhopātrā, the courtesan, inside the temple. Puṇḍalīk's *samādhi* is in the river itself.

Themes of Tukārām's Poetry

In Tukārām's vast book, four themes are especially interesting: the dark night of the soul, the distinction between *saguṇa* and → *nirguṇa bhakti*, caste, and his relationship to his family.

The Dark Night of the Soul

Tukārām, like Western mystics, underwent a "dark night of the soul." This is expressed in a number of poems.

I cannot reach him, I feel distressed. There are many who rule over me. I am fast bound and I cannot loose myself; I am fallen into the power of my past. A grievous load lies upon my head, the claims of "I" and "mine." I am robbed by bold thieves in my own house, though I know it all the time. I only ask this of thee, that thou wouldst commit me to the saints; I have broken my voice with entreaties; now do not make me despair. Now is the great crisis; henceforth what can I do? When the day is gone, night will prevail; in the night time a cry of sorrow alone will be left me. Alas! there will be left the power of my past to control me; I shall be in a stranger's power. There is no place for me to hide in; thoughts of heavy care are roused within me. Such is my perilous state, that I cry to the sea of mercy. Tuka says, My strength, my intellect, and all success lie in thy feet alone. (Fraser & Marathe, 1909, 129)

Another dark *abhaṅga* is starkly simple:

God's door is shut; all importunity is vain; come now, let us go home; do not keep him waking. God is asleep. What avails it to stand here? God is angry, says Tuka; he will not accept our service. (Fraser & Marathe, 1909, 136)

Saguṇa and *Nirguṇa*

In many *abhaṅgas*, Tukārām speaks directly about the question of *nirguṇa* or *saguṇa* – worship of a divine abstraction or worship of a god with qualities. G.A. Deleury's study of the Vārkāris contains this poem:

He has no form or any name,
no place of abode.
But wherever you go there He is,
Vithala, our mother and sister.
He has neither form nor transformation,
He fills all things that move or not.
He is neither nirguna nor saguna,
Who can know Him?
Tuka says:
He will never turn towards those
who have no faith in their heart. (Deleury, 1960, 113)

The image of Viṭṭhal, also called Pāṇḍuraṅg, in the temple at Pandharpur is *saguṇa*; it is about a meter high and seems to have been cut out of one block of trap together with its base. The image is standing with its arms akimbo, hands on hips; the left hand holds a conch and the right a discus. Around the waist is a waistband, the end of which hangs down. The image's ornaments consist of a necklace and in the ears, long earrings that touch the shoulders. On the head is a high round-topped cap. Rukmiṇī is not by his side, as she is in many temples. Viṭhobā came and stood on a brick for his disciples. He is shown standing alone on the brick. Rukmiṇī's image is in a separate temple behind Viṭṭhal's.

In an exquisite trance
He stands on the Brick
Arms akimbo
Hands on hips

Sweet basil beads
Garland His neck
A yellow silk garment
Girdled around His loins
I love His trance
His forever stance

Crocodile-shaped rings
Gleam at His ears
The *Kaustubha* stone
Glows at His throat

Says Tuka, for me
This is absolute bliss
The loving eyes are mine
The loved face His. (Chitre, 2003, 69)

This *abhaṅga* is one of the best to meld *nirguṇa* and *saguṇa*:

We fit You in a frame to worship You,
Though You contain the fourteen universes.
We display You to show our pleasure
Though You have no definition or form.
We sing songs addressed to You,
Though you are way beyond words.
We put garlands around your neck,
Though You are apart from all action.

Says Tuka, O god, become limited
To pay me a little attention. (Chitre, 2003, 113)

Note the interesting ending: God has been made *saguṇa* in order to interact with his devotees. D. Lorenzen (1998) claims that radical → *bhakti* poetry is *nirguṇa*. Maharashtrian *bhakti* with its love for Viṭhobā on the brick is tied to *saguṇa*, but it is very much in the *nirguṇa* tradition, too.

Caste

G. Omvedt and B. Patankar feature Tukārām's many comments on caste and pollution:

He sells his daughter, cows and stories,
He is the true Chandala (Untouchable)
Merits and faults are the real measure,
They're not a result of caste, O god.
Entangled in desire, they do what they should not.

Tuka says, they go to hell. (Omvedt & Patankar, 2012, 123)

Among Tukārām's most challenging words on caste, this is caste by deed, not caste by birth.

The Reverend Murray Mitchell – in his 1882 article on Pandharpur, one of the very earliest comments – notes that Mahars are not allowed to enter the temple, and in a footnote, he puzzles about this. Tukārām contrasts three great places of pilgrimage: at Kashi, they shave the head; at Dwarka, they brand the arm; but at Pandharpur, all become one. The 18 castes are all just Vaiṣṇavas, but the *vārī* is an example of how the egalitarianism of the pilgrimage is distorted when rules of caste get in the way.

G. Omvedt and B. Patankar feature Tukārām's many comments on caste and pollution:

He's not a brahman who abhors
the touch of a Mahar.
What retribution will suffice?
except to sacrifice his life!
He won't touch a Chandal,
it's his heart that's defiled.

Tuka says, his caste's defined
by what fills his mind (Omvedt & Pantankar, 2012, 118)

Family

The problems of Tukārām with his practical, much-put-upon wife are well depicted in Mahīpati's account of his life and most vividly in the 1936 film (see below). There are some *abhaṅgas* that indicate how difficult his total devotion to Viṭhobā was for his wife and children, a stand also found even more vividly in Nāmdev, whose family of 14 was eventually converted to devotion. However, there are *abhaṅgas* written from Tukārām's wife's point of view. This *abhaṅga* of Tukārām's allows his wife to complain in her way:

He cannot follow his trade
he gets bread thrust into his mouth
he gets up and strikes his cymbals and makes no end of a noise.
He is a dead man
he has pounded up shame and swallowed it.
He forgets all about his family
they are ruined
his women folk are frightened to death,
they hate their own existence.
Tuka says, All right, wife, I will leave you alone
I give you a written promise. (Fraser & Marathe, 1909, 42)

The section *Advice to an Angry Wife* is so powerful that it is amusing:

"Good that he's gone away today!
I've got all I want".

"Now I can eat
All the bread in peace
With or without gravy!"

"I am tired of shooting off my mouth
At this stone-deaf man!"

Says Tuka, my wife
Just loves to curse me. (Chitre, 1991, 79)

The ten poems in *Advice to an Angry Wife* must be one of the most unusual sets of poetry about marriage in the world. Tukārām is very protective of his need only to be part of Viṭhobā or Pāṇḍuraṅg and not to have any really close, warm, loving relationship with wife or children. But there is also a hint of concern on the part of Tukārām for his family.

Publications, Translations, and Interpretations of Tukārām

From the mid-19th century, for a hundred years, there was growing creative interest in *bhakti* in the Marathi world. The Department of Public Instruction, Bombay, issued an anthology of Marathi poets in 1867. The sixth edition (1910) was published in ten thousand copies. The title, *Navanīt*, means butter (or cream of the crop). The selection begins with five *bhakti* poets – Dnyāneśvar, Nāmdev, Janābāī (and three other women in Nāmdev's family), Eknāth, and Tukārām – and then moves to other poets such as Vāman Paṇḍit and → Rāmdās. The many editions made for the Training College for Men in Pune assured the place of *bhakti* poetry in the educational system of the Bombay presidency.

The next great development seems to be 50 or so years after *Navanīt*, in 1909, when an educator (J.N. Fraser, of the Indian Education Department) and a Marathi scholar (K.B. Marathe, of the Bombay Judical Service) came together to translate the *bhakti* poets. They issued their poetry of Tukārām in 1909, producing three huge volumes in plain but effective prose:

Who so makes himself the friend of the oppressed, recognize him for a true saint, know

> that God dwells in him. Mild as butter within and without, such is the nature of a good man. He who takes the unprotected to his heart, who shows to his servants and to his own son the same compassion, Tuka says, how often shall I tell you, he is the very image of the Divine? (Fraser & Marathe, 1909, 232)

> Vitthala, my friend, accompanies me and dwells in my soul; he pervades my frame; he is a shadow to me. He dwells on the tip of my tongue; I can speak of nothing else. The mind is prince above all organs; he too contemplates Vitthala. Tuka says, Now I can never forget this Vitthala. (Fraser & Marathe, 1909, 245)

The Reverend Dr. Justin A. Abbott, a long-time missionary in Maharashtra, initiated the first in a multivolume Poet-Saints of Maharashtra series in 1926. Working with a Brahman scholar, N.R. Godbole, he produced 11 volumes by the time of his death in 1932. He translated Mahīpati on saints' lives and "garlands" of translations of poetry and song with this aim: to illustrate the honor, love, and genius of Maharashtra. J.A. Abbott asked himself, "have I contributed to making India more truly known, loved and honored by the rest of the world?" (1929, xiv).

The title "poet-saint" became academically acceptable thanks to J.A. Abbott's work. Etymologically there is no relation between the Marathi and Hindi word "*santa*" and the English word "saint," but the demeanor of the poet-saints made the English word appropriate.

J.A. Abbott's translation of Mahīpati's lives of the saints added a new dimension to the English-speaking world's understanding of the Vārkarīs. Mahīpati (1715–1790) was an orthodox Hindu and a practicing Brahman as well as an imaginative chronicler of the saints' lives. He was passionately devoted to the Vārkarī movement. Mahīpati, who himself was a *kīrtankār* (reciter of songs), has three works on the Vārkarīs. Two lively (almost overly lively) works were completed – the *Bhaktavijaya* and the *Bhaktalīlāmṛita*, composed in 1762 and 1774, respectively. The last, unfinished, one is the *Santavijaya*.

Volume XII of the Poet-Saints of Maharashtra series, by the Reverend J.F. Edwards, is very different from the 11 preceding volumes. It is basically a Christian analysis of Mahīpati and other writers on Dnyāneśvar. J.F. Edwards does mention the other sects of the time – the → Mahānubhāvs and Nāths (see → Nāth Sampradāya). He also raises the question of there being two Dnyāneśvars, one who translated the *Bhagavadgītā* at a seemingly impossible young age and the other, who wrote *abhaṅgas* dedicated to Viṭhobā.

The classic film about the life of Tukārām – called *Sant Tukaram*, written by S. Vashikar and directed by V.G. Damle and S. Fattelal – was made in 1936 by the young, experimental Prabhat Studio in Pune. The lead character, Tukārām, was played by a real-life *kīrtankār*, Vishnupant Pagnis. Tukārām's wife, Jijāī, was played by Gauri, reportedly a cleaning woman at the studio. The film won a Mussolini Cup at the Venice Film Festival in 1937 and has been much viewed ever since. *Sant Tukaram* is the culmination of the creative period of missionaries and teachers telling the stories of the saints. It also introduces a new kind of interest in Tukārām.

Dr. B.R. → Ambedkar, the dominant leader among → Dalits in the 20th century, rejected the poet-saints as guides, finding that they were too bound up in → *karma* (e.g. Cokhāmeḷā felt that a previous sin had determined his caste), but he honored Tukārām. The first four lines of this *abhaṅga* were used by B.R. Ambedkar in 1920 on the masthead of his first newspaper, *Mooknayak* (The Leader of the Voiceless):

> Now what to do? Remain deferential?
> This mouth prattles on without a thought.
> No one in the world listens to the voiceless.
> Nothing good comes from shame.
>
> I speak to the master what comes to my mind,
> bold, straightforward, from my soul.
> Tuka says, When you encounter the powerful,
> calm your mind, bridle it. (Panshikar, 1968, 269; trans. by Feldhaus & Zelliot)

B.R. Ambedkar had another connection with Pandharpur; he and a very radical non-Vārkarī saint named Gadge Baba (Gāḍge Mahārāj) established a boarding school in Pandharpur for village people. *The Last Kīrtan of Gadge Baba*, by G.N. Dandekar, in *The Experience of Hinduism* (Zelliot & Berntsen, 1998, 223–250), tells what a powerful message Gadge Baba had about caste and women and other kinds of reform. In his last *kīrtan*, Gadge Baba says that Tukārām created the fifth Veda and quotes Tukārām as saying,

> I went looking for God
> And I became God. (Zelliot & Berntsen, 1998, 227)

In spite of the anticaste and pro-untouchable statements of the Vārkarīs, no untouchable could go into the Viṭṭhal Temple at Pandharpur until 1948. At that time, a Gandhian reformer, Sane Guruji, sat fasting on the temple steps. An orthodox Brahman, Pandit Bhagwan Shastri Dharurkar, brought a brass pot into the temple, showed the image of Viṭhobā to the pot, and took the pot into his home. There he treated that vessel as Viṭhobā; the pot is still in his house, where it is worshipped as Viṭhobā (Manjul, 2002, 161). Untouchables now enter the temple.

The 1950s saw a remarkable set of personal narratives. G.A. Deleury's book *The Cult of Viṭhobā* contains a thorough description of the pilgrimage and a map of 28 *pālkhī*s (1960, 76f.). Guy Deleury, a Jesuit, pursued a Ph.D. at Deccan College and actually joined the pilgrimage. He chose the Dnyāneśvar *diṇḍī* that had been formed by S.V. Dandekar, who understood Western scholarship and who welcomed G.A. Deleury. His *The Cult of Viṭhobā* is a veritable encyclopedia of every aspect of the Viṭhobā Panth. G.A. Deleury published Tukārām translations in French and later returned to France.

Two more personal accounts add life and color to our understanding of the pilgrimage. In her article "On the Road" (1962), I. Karve joined the Maratha group in her *diṇḍī* and then the Brahman group, and she describes the difference between the groups. D.B. Mokashi describes one-on-one conversations without analysis. He learns of the unhappy family homes that result in some people going on pilgrimage, and he is very good on the practical aspects of the *vārī*. He meets Jaitunbai, a Muslim Vārkarī, and also S.V. Dandekar. There is nothing romantic about D.B. Mokashi's account, and it clearly is very honest. These accounts have resulted in the pilgrimage becoming one of the most famous in India (see Turner, 1973).

Although I. Karve was saddened by the caste divisions that she saw on the pilgrimage, she developed a new definition of Maharashtra – the land where people go to Pandharpur. She was writing in the late 1940s, in the context of the Samyukta Maharashtra ("United Maharashtra") Movement. Historians from M.G. Ranade (1900) to R. Eaton (2005) have seen the Vārkarī poet-saints as central to the formation of a Maharashtrian regional identity, leading in 1960 to the founding of Maharashtra as a state.

In the 1970s, the Chambhars of Maharashtra – whose *diṇḍī* featured the *pādukā*s of a North Indian Camar saint, → Ravidās (Mar. Rohīdās) – walked before the horse representing Dnyāneśvar. They pleaded for a better place, a less isolated place in the *pālkhī*, and they won the right to be first behind the horse. A Brahman *diṇḍī* comes last.

A documentary film called *Vari: An Indian Pilgrimage* was made by G. Sontheimer and H. Stegmüller in 1989. It is about the pilgrimage itself, and it mixes the practical problems of the pilgrims with their ecstatic sense of joy. The film begins with a haunting Tukārām poem:

> I'm the kite; you're the string.
> You are the string, God, my string.
> Pāṇḍuraṅg, Pāṇḍuraṅg,
> I'm the kite; you're my string.

The 1991 English translation of Tukārām by D. Chitre, a poet in Marathi and English, *Says Tuka*, begins a new era. It brought Tukārām to the Western world in a very meaningful way. D. Chitre says the following:

> The gamut of Bhakti poetry has amazing depth, width and range: it is hermetic, esoteric, cryptic, mystical; it is sensuous, lyrical, deeply emotional, devotional; it is colloquial, comic, absurd; it is imaginative, inventive, experimental; it is intense, angry, assertive and full of protest. (Chitre, 2003, xxvii)

D. Chitre gives a vivid image of what Tukārām says about himself:

> I know no trick
> To lure the public.
> I can only sing of You
> And praise Your goodness.
> I work no miracles,
> I wake no dead.
> I have no hordes of disciples
> To advertise my selfishness.
> I am not the lord of a monastery
> Thriving on grants of land.
> I run no God-shop
> To worship personal profit.
> I command no spirits,
> Nor hold any seances.
> I am no teller of tales from the Puranas
> Split between profession and practice.
> I am no wretched pundit
> Splitting Vedantic hairs.
> I burn no lamps to raise
> The Mother Goddess with shrill praise.
> I swing no rosary
> To gather fools around me.

I am no warlock
To bewitch, to magnetize, to fix, to kill.
Tuka is not like any of these
Crazed citizens of hell. (Chitre, 2003, 145)

In the section *God's Own Dog*, several of Tukārām's images are very unusual. He gives us a vivid image of god's return to the devotion that Tukārām gives him:

Like a dog
Lying at Your door
"Hari! Hari!"
I bark Your name

I bark
I get up
I sit down again
But never
O Gopal
Would I leave
Your feet

Says Tuka
"I know,
My master's weakness:
He just loves
To fondle
his pet!" (Chitre, 2003, 102)

Another very modern poet, A. Kolatkar, published a few of Tukārām's poems:

Without seeing a thing
I've seen entirely.
I've achieved a likeness
Of everybody.

Without taking
I've accepted.
My arms and legs
Are holidays.

Without eating
I've had my fill.
My mouth as it watered
Became the menu.

Without a word
I've spoken
I've presented what
At best was absent.

The poem occurs,
Says Tuka,
Unknown
To my ears. (Kolatkar, 1982, 113)

There is a contemporary surge of academic interest in the poet-saints. E. Zelliot has written on Eknāth's *bhāruḍs* (drama poems) and the untouchable saint Cokhāmeḷā. R. Mokashi-Punekar has analyzed Cokhāmeḷā, his brother-in-law Baṅkā, and his son Karmameḷā. C. Novetzke has published a well-received biography of Nāmdev and his influence. J. Keune received a Ph.D. on Eknāth as a reformer and continues his studies. M. Deshmukh is studying Janābāī and her legends. The translation of the work of R.C. Dhere, the premier Marathi scholar, by A. Feldhaus adds a necessary dimension to scholarly work in English.

The new translations of Tukārām by G. Omvedt and B. Pantankar ensure continued interest in the Marathi *bhakti* movement.

In addition to the new translations and the new scholarship, these factors ensure the continuing importance of the Pandharpur pilgrimage:

- the pilgrimage seems to grow each year;
- the association of the great Maratha king Śivājī with Tukārām and Rāmdās in the popular mind;
- the metaphor of a united Maharashtra in the pilgrimage itself;
- the status of Tukārām as the last classical and first modern poet.

Bibliography

Abbott, J.E., *Stotramālā: A Garland of Hindu Prayers: A Translation of Prayers of Maratha Poet-Saints, from Dnyaneshvar to Mahipati*, PSM 6, Poona, 1929.

Chitre, D., *Says Tuka: Selected Poems of Tukaram*, New Delhi, 1991, repr. 2003.

Dandekar, G.N., "The Last Kirtan of Gadge Baba," in: E. Zelliot & M. Berntsen, eds., *The Experience of Hinduism*, New York, 1988, 223–250.

Dandekar, S.V., *Dnyandeo*, New Delhi, 1969.

Dandekar, S.V., *Wārkarī panthācā itihās*, Pune, 1957.

Deleury, G.A., *The Cult of Viṭhobā*, Poona, 1960.

Deleury, G.A., *Toukaram: Psaumes du Pélerin*, Paris, 1956.

Dhere, R.C., *The Rise of a Folk God: Viṭṭhal of Pandharpur*, New York, 2011.

Eaton, R.M., *The New Cambridge History of India*, vol. I/8: *A Social History of the Deccan, 1300–1761: Eight Indian Lives*, Cambridge UK, 2005.

Edwards, J.F., *Dnyāneshwar: The Outcaste Brahman*, PSM 12, Poona, 1941.

Fraser, J.N., & J.F. Edwards, *The Life and Teaching of Tukaram*, Madras, 1922.

Fraser, J.N., & K.B. Marathe, *The Poems of Tukarama*, vols. I-III, Delhi, 1909, repr. 1981.

Green, N., *Indian Sufism since the Seventeenth Century*, New York, 2006.

Ghurye, G.S., *Gods and Men*, Bombay, 1962.
Hoyland, J.S., *An Indian Peasant Mystic: Translations from Tukaram*, London, 1932.
Karve, I., "On the Road: A Maharashtrian Pilgrimage," JAS 22, 1962, 13–29; republished in: E. Zelliot & M. Berntsen, eds., *The Experience of Hinduism*, Albany, 1988.
Keune, J., "Eknāth Remembered and Reformed: Bhakti, Brahmans, and Untouchables in Marathi Historiography," diss., Columbia University, 2011.
Kolatkar, A., "Translations from Tukaram and Other Saint Poets," *JSAL* 1, 1982, 111–113.
Kosambi, D.D., *Myth and Reality*, Bombay, 1962.
Lorenzen, D.N., *The Lives of Nirguni Saints: Bhakti Religion in North India*, New Delhi, 1998.
Mahipati, *Bhaktalilamrita: Nectar from Indian Saints*, PSM 11, Poona, 1935.
Mahipati, *Bhaktavijaya: Stories of Indian Saints*, 2 vols., PSM 9 & 10, Poona, 1933, 1944.
Mahipati, *Bhaktalilamrita: Tukaram*, PSM 7, Poona, 1930, repr. 1980.
Manjul, V.L., "Paṇḍharpūrcā Viṭāḷaṇārā Dev Ghāgarīt Sāṭhavilā," in: E. Zelliot & V.L. Manjul, eds., *Santa Cokhāmeḷā Vividha Darśan*, Pune, 2002, 159–163.
Mitchell, J.M., "Pandharpur," *IA* 2, 1882, 149–156.
Mokashi, D.B., *Palki: An Indian Pilgrimage*, Albany, 1987.
Mokashi-Punekar, R., *On the Treshold: Songs of Chokamela*, Lanham, 2005.
Mokashi-Punekar, R., & E. Zelliot, eds., *Untouchable Saints: An Indian Phenomenon*, New Delhi, 2005.
Molesworth, J.T., *A Dictionary: English and Marathi*, Bombay, 1857, repr. 1975.
Nemade, B., *Tukaram*, New Delhi, 1980.
Neurgavkar, S.K., *Pālkhī sohaḷā*, Pune 1965.
Novetzke, C., *Religion and Public Memory: A Cultural History of Saint Namdev in India*, New York, 2008.
Omvedt, G., *Buddhism in India: Challenging Brahmanism and Caste*, New Delhi, 2003.
Omvedt, G., & B. Patankar, *The Songs of Tukoba*, New Delhi, 2012.
Panshikar (Paṇśīkar), N.V., ed., *Viśvavandya Śrītukārāmmahārāj yāṃcī Sampūrṇa Abhaṅga Gāthā*, Pune, 1968 (Mar.).
Rajwade, C., *Tukaram: Saint of Maharashtra*, Punjab, 1978–1981.
Ranade, M.G., *Rise of Maratha Power*, Bombay, 1900, repr. 1961.
Ranade, R.D., *Tukaram*, Albany, 1993, repr. 1994.
Ranade, R.D., *Mysticism in India: The Poet-Saints of Maharashtra*, Albany, 1983.
Rawlinson, H.G., *Shivaji the Maratha: His Life and Time*, New Delhi, 1915, repr. 1984.
Sardar, G.B., *The Saint-Poets of Maharashtra: Their Impact on Society*, Bombay, 1968.
Sharma, S.R., *Tukaram*, Poona, 1962.
Stanley, J.M., *The Great Maharashtrian Pilgrimage: Pandharpur and Alandi*, (unpubl. ms.; d. 1980).
Tulpule, S.G., *Mysticism in Medieval India*, Wiesbaden, 1984.
Tulpule, S.G., *Classical Marathi Literature: From the Beginning to A.D. 1818*, HIL 9/4, Wiesbaden, 1979.
Turner, V., "The Center Out There: Pilgrim's Goal," *HR* 12, 1973, 191–230.
Zelliot, E., "Chokamela and Eknath: Two Bhakti Modes of Legitimacy for Modern Change," *JAAS* 15/1–2, 1980.
Zelliot, E., & M. Berntsen, eds., *The Experience of Hinduism*, New York, 1988.

Films

Sant Tukaram, dir. V.G. Damle & S. Fattelal, 1936.
Vari: An Indian Pilgrimage, dir. G.-D. Sontheimer & H. Stegmüller, 1989.

Eleanor Zelliot

Tulsīdās

Tulsīdās is one of the most revered saint-poets of the North Indian → *bhakti* or devotional tradition, especially famed as the author of the *Rāmcaritmānas*, an epic-length retelling, in a premodern dialect of Hindi, of the → *Rāmāyaṇa*, the ancient saga of → Rāma and Sītā (see → Draupadī and Sītā). A poet of extraordinary talent, versatility, and vision, he is celebrated as the author of roughly a dozen works, most of which are dedicated to Rāma, and which collectively advance a theology in which Rāma is adored as the supreme, transcendent God, to whom other Hindu deities, albeit venerated, are generally subordinate. Through his writings and his legendary biography, Tulsīdās has come to exert a profound, perhaps unsurpassed, influence on the ideology and practice of popular Hinduism throughout much of northern and central India, and beyond, including several communities of the Indian diaspora.

Not surprisingly, a figure of such stature is also, in certain contexts, controversial; his works have been subject to vastly differing interpretations, and there are few details of his biography that have not been contested. This essay will first summarize scholarly research on Tulsīdās' life and will briefly present some of the well-known stories in his popular hagiography. It will then survey his reputed writings, identifying their principal themes and placing them in the context of their historical and contemporary reception.

Life and Legend

The name Tulsīdās (also known as Tulsī Dās, Tulasī Dāsa, and Tulasīdāsa) means "Servant/Slave of *Tulsī*," the latter referring to the holy basil plant (bot. Ocimum Tenuiflorum) and its goddess, both of whom are considered to be especially pleasing (and the goddess herself, wedded) to → Viṣṇu. It is thus a sectarian name, and it signals the poet's likely initiation in a Vaiṣṇava religious order or → *guru* lineage, *-dās* being a common suffix for initiatory names (*dīkṣānām*) in several orders. The poet himself often shortened this name, in his poetic signature (*chāp* or *bhaṇitā*), to "Tulsī," a practice also favored by his admirers (and largely followed henceforth in this article). Yet although Tulsī has been proudly claimed by a number of branches of the → Rāmānandī ascetic order, his formal affiliation, if any, has never been proven to the satisfaction of nonsectarian scholars, and it is generally observed that, uncharacteristically for his time, he does not seem to have established a sect. Commenting on this, and on Tulsī's broader impact, F.S. Growse, author of the first full English translation of the *Rāmcaritmānas*, observed in the late 19th century,

> There are Vallabhāchāris and Rādhā-Vallabhis and Malūk Dāsīs and Prān Nāthis, and so on, in interminable succession, but there are no Tulasī Dāsīs. Virtually, however, the whole of Vaiṣṇava Hinduism has fallen under his sway; for the principles that he expounded have permeated every sect and explicitly or implicitly now form the nucleus of the popular faith as it prevails throughout the whole of the Bengal Presidency from Hardwar to Calcutta. (Growse, 1891, lix)

Indeed, Tulsī continues to be revered as a preceptor and exemplar by millions, and this status is usually signaled by prefixing the honorific title *gosvāmī* or its Hindi variant *gosāīṃ* (master, lord) to his name. As will be seen, this designation was already given to him during his lifetime and may have signaled a role as *mahant* or resident *guru* of a small temple or monastery.

Although historical evidence (which is to say, that of irrefutably contemporary manuscripts, inscriptions, or artifacts) for the life of Tulsīdās is extremely meager, comparatively more is known about him than about the three other most popular saint-poets of premodern Hindi (→ Kabīr, → Sūrdās, and → Mīrābāī). He was evidently literate, and a few manuscripts survive that may be in his own hand. In addition, some of his writings contain suggestively autobiographical details, and three of them include dates of composition, indicating that he was active during the late 16th and early 17th centuries, during the reigns of the → Mughal emperors Akbar and Jahāngīr. There is evidence that he spent a good part of his life in Banaras (Kāśī, Vārānasī), where he seemingly aroused both admiration and opposition, and it is probable that he regularly participated in public performance of devotional texts, including his own, and was supported, in part, by the offerings of listeners.

Beyond these facts, there is little in Tulsī's historical biography that is uncontested, beginning with his date of birth. Scholars have postulated 1526, 1532, or 1543 CE, but popular accounts favor 1497, making the poet an improbable 126 years old at the time of his death, which is universally (though again, on little evidence) believed to have occurred in 1623 (see Allchin, 1966, 31; Gupta, 1942, 138–140, for the arguments for various birthdates). His birthplace is similarly uncertain, though the villages of Rajapur and Soron (both in present-day Uttar Pradesh) each claim this honor – along with at least five other places (Gupta, 1977, 65–77). Several introspective passages in the poetic anthologies entitled *Vinaypatrikā* and *Kavitāvalī*, both believed to have been finalized not long before the poet's death, speak of a childhood of abandonment, want, and humiliation, as for instance in the following: "Father and mother brought me into the world and abandoned me… I was low, a vessel for disrespect, a coward who was glad to get even the scraps thrown out for dogs" (*KaĀv.* 7.57; trans. Allchin, 1964, 152 [amended by author]; see also *KaĀv.* 7.72, 73 – "I ate the leavings of all castes"; "I was born in a family of beggars"; and *VinPa.* 275 – "I told my poverty at every door"). From this wretched early life, Tulsī speaks of being "rescued" by the mercy of Rāma and → Hanumān – statements usually interpreted to mean that the starving child was adopted by Vaiṣṇava → *sādhu*s or received food as → *prasād* in Hanumān temples (see e.g. *HanBā.* 21; *VinPa.* 33). A *sādhu*, possibly (as later tradition would claim) in the lineage of the shadowy but influential teacher → Rāmānanda (c. 15th cent.?), appears to have become his *guru*, from whom, Tulsī says, he first heard the story of Rāma (Rāmakathā) at an early age, in a place called Sūkarkhet ("Boar's Field"; possibly Soron in Uttar Pradesh; *RCM.* 1.30).

That he later received considerable formal education in the Sanskrit tradition, and hence was probably Brahman by caste, is evident from his writings, which include Sanskrit benedictory verses but, more significantly, reference a wide range of epic, puranic, and Kāvya literature. *Rāmājñāpraśna* – his first self-dated composition (though several short works may have been composed earlier), bearing a date corresponding to 1564 CE – is a condensed retelling of the Rāma story, intended for use in → divination. His subsequent epic-length retelling of that story, *Rāmcaritmānas*, states that it was begun in 1574 in Ayodhyā, the pilgrimage city most associated with Rāma's life (*RCM.* 1.34.4–5), although the commencement of its fourth book, *Kiṣkindhākāṇḍ*, with a eulogy of Kāśī (Banaras), is generally interpreted to signal the poet's move to that city (*RCM.* 4.0). Several of his later works, lavish in their praise of the river → Gaṅgā and of → Śiva's city, indicate his continuing residence there and his growing recognition as a poet, singer, and, eventually, *gosāīṃ* (*KaĀv.* 7.64; *HanBā.* 40–41), whom "the world now even likens to the great sage Vālmīki" (*KaĀv.* 7.72). Indeed, the Vaiṣṇava poet Nābhādās – in his hagiographic classic *Bhaktamāl* (Garland of Devotees), likewise thought to date from the early 17th century – praises Tulsī precisely as a reincarnation of Vālmīki, born to save the people of the dismal *kaliyuga* (see → cosmic cycles) through a retelling of the glorious deeds of Rāma (*BhMā.*, *chappay* 129). A *Pañcnāmā* or "deed of arbitration attested by elders," in Persian and dated 1612 CE, settling the estate of one Toḍar Caudharī, who is thought to have been a friend and possibly patron of Tulsīdās, bears the poet's "signature," possibly in his own handwriting, in the form of a couplet. The final section of *Kavitāvalī*, which seems to date from the poet's old age, alludes to malefic astronomical conjunctions and outbreaks of plague known to have occurred in Banaras during the first two decades of the 17th century (*KaĀv.* 7.170, 176–177). There are also references to "oppression" from Śiva's servants there (*VinPa.* 8; *KaĀv.* 7.165), possibly indicating criticism or persecution for his popularization of Rāma devotion and use of the vernacular. During the last years of his life, the poet evidently suffered from severe pain in one of his arms, sometimes spreading through his body, and from an outbreak of boils – pleading for relief of these from Hanumān is the theme of more than half of the 44 brilliant songs in the *Hanumānbāhuk* (20–44), which may have been his last substantial composition.

This bare skeleton of historical and literary "facts" utterly fails to evoke the sparkling and very human personality – at once sincerely self-deprecating and penitential yet paradoxically self-confident and audaciously assertive of spiritual vision and verbal genius – who emerges from reading or reciting Tulsīdās' poetry. Popular tradition was not long in providing that personality with a detailed and inspiring biography, many incidents of which seem intended to expand on or explain allusions in the poetry. Nābhādās' remarkable but terse tribute, by a contemporary who may actually have met him, was greatly enlarged roughly a century later (1712) by the commentator Priyādās, with 11 four-line stanzas that comprise seven stories about Tulsī, all but the first of which concern miracles performed or experienced as a result of the poet's devotion to Rāma. Since these tales recur in all subsequent hagiographies and continue to form the core of the poet's legend as it is popularly known today, I will briefly summarize each.

The first tells of his youthful marriage to a woman (named Ratnāvalī in later accounts) for whom he develops such extreme infatuation that he inappropriately pursues her to her parents' home when she has gone there for a visit. His surprise appearance occasions her to shame him with a rebuke, recast by later poets in a now-proverbial couplet:

> This body of mine is full of skin and bone – and such love for it!
> If you had but a little for Rām, where would be the dread of rebirth? (cited in Hill, 1952, x; trans. by author)

His wife's scolding opens Tulsī's eyes to the illusory nature of worldly attachment and causes him to immediately renounce the world and become a Vaiṣṇava *sādhu*; hence the abandoned wife is sometimes cited as his initiatory teacher (*dīkṣāguru*).

Tulsī is guided by a benevolent spirit to a meeting with Hanumān in the guise of a leper, who instructs him to go to Citrakūṭ (Chitrakut, a pilgrimage place in modern Madhya Pradesh, said to mark the site of Rāma's residence during several years of his forest exile) for a vision of Rāma. The lord and his brother, Lakṣmaṇ, indeed appear to Tulsī, as two princes on horseback, but he fails to recognize them. In the expanded version of this story, well known today, Hanumān then directs the disappointed saint to a second meeting on the bank of the Mandākinī River and himself takes the form of a parrot to alert the poet (again, via a proverbial couplet) to Rāma's presence before him in the form of a young boy.

Tulsī compassionately feeds a Brahman who, having committed murder, has been expelled from his caste and is begging for alms in Rāma's name. When criticized by the Brahmans of Kāśī for doing this, he insists that the murderer has been purified by the divine name, and he proves this by having the stone bull of Śiva, presumably at the famed Viśvanāth Temple, accept food from the man's hand.

Several thieves, attempting to rob the poet, are chased away by a dark-skinned youth armed with bows and arrows. When they confess this to the poet the next day, he realizes that the "watchman" was Rāma and, remorseful at having given the lord trouble, gives away all possessions. The thieves are purified of sin and take initiation as disciples. In the most popular version of this story, the thieves are dispatched by the jealous Brahmans of Banaras to steal the manuscript of Tulsī's epic poem.

Another Brahman, deceased, is brought back to life as a favor to his wife, whom Tulsī inadvertently blesses to be "unwidowed," not realizing that she is on her way to self-immolation as a → *satī*. The fame of this miracle, in turn, prompts a summons from "the king of Delhi, the emperor" (*dillīpati pātsāh*), who commands the poet to perform a similar one in his presence and imprisons him when he declines to do so. Millions of monkeys then attack the emperor's fort, creating havoc and compelling him to take refuge at the feet of the saint, who wryly comments, "Why don't you enjoy the miracle a little!" The frightened emperor then abandons his palace and builds another nearby.

Tulsī goes to Vṛndāvan (Vrindavan) and meets the poet Nābhādās. Worshipping a flute-playing image of → Kṛṣṇa in a temple there, he is delighted to see it metamorphose into the bow-bearing figure of his chosen lord. When someone chides him, "Kṛṣṇa is the *avatāra* of greatest renown, Rāma was only a partial one" (*aṃś*; a portion), Tulsī ingenuously replies, "I only considered him the incomparably beautiful son of Daśaratha. Now that you tell me of his divinity, my love has grown twenty-fold!" (*BhMā., kavitta* 508–518; the Hindi text and full translation appear in Growse, 1880, xlii–xlvii; translations given above are by the author).

The stories found in Priyādās' 1712 commentary on the *Bhaktamāl* formed the basis for other, expanded retellings of the poet's life, such as that by the Marathi poet Mahīpati in his *Bhaktavijaya* (Triumph of Devotees), composed in 1762, wherein they occur without major alteration and, indeed, in the same sequence (Abbott & Godbole, 1933, 31–56). Most of them also occur in an enormously expanded verse biography called

Tulsī Carit (The Deeds of Tulsī) that was included in an 1889 edition of the *Rāmcaritmānas*, edited by the linguist G. Grierson. The author of this biography, which ran to some 3,750 lines, used the *chāps* "Dās" and "Dāsānidās" and identified his *guru* as an influential *mahant* of Ayodhya who flourished in the mid-18th century. Although its length permitted the inclusion of many additional stories, its emphasis on miraculous events caused it, by the time of its publication, to be disregarded by G. Grierson, who published an influential series of articles on Tulsī in *The Indian Antiquary* in 1893, and by the translator F.S. Growse. Both of them lamented the absence of "authentic" accounts of the great poet's life and hopefully awaited the discovery of a manuscript entitled *Gosāīṃ Carit* (Deeds of the Master/Gosvāmī), which the Hindi scholars Mahesh Datt Shukla and Shivsingh Sengar, writing in 1875 and 1878, respectively, had briefly quoted from, identifying it as the work of one Beṇimādhavdās. The latter was said to have been an intimate disciple of Tulsī who died in 1642, but who penned his "eyewitness" memoir of the great poet only a few years after the latter's death. Unfortunately, this manuscript seemed to have disappeared, though it was avidly sought by the new Hindi literary society, the Nagari Pracarini Sabha, founded in 1893.

In 1926, the Sabha excitedly reported the discovery, in a village in Bihar, of a manuscript entitled *Mūl Gosāīṃ Carit* (Concise Account of the Deeds of the Master), by the same Beṇimādhavdās, which claimed to be a summary, intended for devotional recitation, of his longer (and still lost) biography of Tulsī. This work of roughly 750 lines achieved great popular acceptance, especially after its publication by the influential Gita Press of Gorakhpur in 1934, and it served as the basis for the biography of Tulsī included in the (constantly reprinted and now standard) Gita Press editions of the *Rāmcaritmānas*. In addition to recounting all of the Priyādās stories, it included now-famous accounts of Tulsī's interactions with other illustrious poet-saints such as Sūrdās and Mīrābāī, credited Tulsī with the staging of the first *rāmlīlā* dramas (see → *līlā*) based on the Rāma story, and depicted the dramatic "trial" of his vernacular epic by the conservative Brahmans of Banaras, who left it overnight at the bottom of a pile of scriptures in the sanctum of the Viśvanāth Temple. When the temple was unlocked in the morning, the Hindi epic was found to have risen to the top of the pile – above even the → Vedas! – and to have been inscribed with the words *satyaṃ śivaṃ sundaraṃ* (truth, auspiciousness, beauty).

Tulsī scholars such as R. Shukla and M. Gupta, however, regarded the *Mūl Gosāīṃ Carit* with suspicion, noting that it contained grammatical forms unattested in 17th-century Hindi poetry (Śiva's blessing on the epic even appears to be a back-translation of an English idiom) as well as a plethora of names and dates – again, something unheard of in early hagiographies – including the improbable birth date for Tulsī of 1497 (see e.g. Gupta, 1952, 4–8). Their argument would be sharpened in 1964 by another scholar, K. Gupta, who carefully demonstrated that both the celebrated *Mūl Gosāīṃ Carit* and the unheralded *Tulsī Carit* derived from the same, probably late 18th-century, hagiography by "Dāsānidās," mistakenly attributed by M. Shukla to the legendary Beṇimādhavdās, and that the *Mūl Gosāīṃ Carit* itself was almost certainly a late 19th- or early 20th-century fabrication created in response to the yearnings of researchers like F.S. Growse, G. Grierson, and the Sabha's manuscript hunters (Gupta, 1964, 1–60; Lutgendorf, 1994). Such scholarly criticism, however, has had little effect on popular opinion, which generally accepts the *Mūl Gosāīṃ Carit* as an eyewitness account of Tulsī's life. Hence, this text has influenced virtually all modern biographies of the saint-poet, from elite literature such as S.T. Nirala's long poem *Tulsīdās* (1938) and A. Nagar's 370-page historical novel *Mānas kā Haṃs* (Swan of the Mānas Lake; 1972) to the popular *Tulsidas* comic book in the Amar Chitra Katha series (1974) and several Bombay "mythological" films (e.g. *Tulsidas*, 1954, dir. B.H. Bhatt, and *Tulsidas*, 1964, dir. B.K. Adarsh).

The latest Tulsī "biography" to be discovered purports to be, historically, the earliest. In 1955, the respected scholar V. Mishra published an article in the Sabha journal containing reputed excerpts about Tulsī, running to some 420 lines, from a memoir entitled *Gautam Candrikā*, said to have been composed in 1624 by the son of an intimate companion of the recently deceased poet. Although the genesis of these third-hand notes was peculiar (for details, see Mishra, 1955; Lutgendorf, 1994), their language and content presented none of the problems of the *Mūl Gosāīṃ Carit*, and they offered a plausible portrait of the poet as an inspired performer of his own songs and an openhearted devotee whose intimate circle included low-caste people, such as a weaver, a barber, and a boatman. Cautiously accepted by some scholars, they have, however, had little impact on public perceptions of the poet's life.

The Works of Tulsīdās

Although Tulsī is most celebrated as the author of the *Rāmcaritmānas*, an epic of such renown that it has eclipsed, for its audience, its Sanskrit archetype and is often referred to, even in print, simply as "the *Rāmāyaṇ*," he was clearly a prolific poet and is credited with a substantial corpus of writings. Since, in the *bhakti* tradition, there was a widespread practice of adopting the *chāp* or poetic signature of a revered saint-poet when expressing compatible religious sentiments, scholars of Tulsī's oeuvre have long been concerned with identifying, among some 30 compositions attributed to him, his authentic works, an undertaking pioneered by celebrated 18th- and 19th-century Rāmāyaṇīs – that is, *Rāmcaritmānas* and Tulsī specialists. G. Grierson's canonical list of 12 compositions – six "minor" and six "major" works – drew on the work of these indigenous exegetes and has been generally accepted by later scholars. The minor works are both shorter and less popular and include the self-dated composition *Rāmājñāpraśn* (1564), already noted. Several of them (such as *Rāmlalā Nahachū*, a collection of songs based on rituals performed prior to Rāma's marriage, and *Vairāgya Sandīpinī*, verses extolling the virtue of renunciation) show a "looseness" of style that led M. Gupta to declare them either inauthentic or immature efforts (1952, 24–25). Yet looser in style is the beloved *Hanumān Cālīsā*, 40 verses to Hanumān that bear Tulsī's *chāp*. Although no early manuscripts of this work are attested and most scholars do not include it in their lists of Tulsī's writings, it became, in the 20th century, perhaps the most popular short praise poem in popular Hindu practice (see Lutgendorf, 2007, 99–101). Another short, dated work is the more accomplished *Pārvatī Maṅgal* (1584), an account of the marriage of Śiva and → Pārvatī that largely mirrors the one contained in the first book of the *Rāmcaritmānas*.

The major works, in both their scope and relative popularity, each warrants brief discussion here. They include the *Gītāvalī* (Song Cycle) or *Gītāvalī Rāmāyaṇ*, a retelling of the Rāma story in 328 lyrical stanzas; an incomplete manuscript of this work, dated 1609, suggests that the poet was then still assembling it. Several other works are also anthologies, probably compiled over a long period of time. Thus the *Dohāvalī*, a collection of nearly 600 couplets in the popular *dohā* meter, is the literary manifestation of a larger corpus of aphoristic verses, containing Tulsī's *chāp*, that have circulated for centuries in oral tradition. A compilation of Tulsī's wisdom, it includes more than 80 couplets from the *Rāmcaritmānas* and may have been assembled by his admirers after his death. A larger, variant version of this collection, known as *Satsāī*, is less widely accepted by Hindi scholars, although it shares many couplets with the *Dohāvalī*.

The *Kṛṣṇagītāvalī* is a collection of 61 songs that, unique among Tulsī's compositions, are dedicated to Kṛṣṇa. Again, this bears no date and seems to be an anthology, and many see in its themes and Brajbhasha dialect the influence of the popular songs of Sūrdās. Brajbhasha grammatical forms also predominate in two other large anthologies of *pad* or songs – *Kavitāvalī* and *Vinaypatrikā*. The *Kavitāvalī* (Anthology of Songs in *Kavitta* Meter [i.e. a popular, six-line lyric form]) is loosely organized in seven *kāṇḍ*s or sub-books, echoing the traditional structure of the *Rāmāyaṇa*. Within each section, however, only a few epic incidents are recounted, although these (such as Hanumān's burning of Laṅkā in the *Sundarkāṇḍ*; *KaĀv*. 5.3–25) are retold with notable brilliance and in even greater detail than in Tulsī's own epic. The seventh book is especially heterogeneous in content and departs from the Rāma tale entirely to include (as noted earlier) songs that seem autobiographical as well as praises of pilgrimage sites and invocations of Śiva for relief from epidemics and personal sufferings thought to date to the final decade of Tulsī's life (for a study and full translation, see Allchin, 1964). The remarkable and clearly late song cycle *Hanumānbāhuk*, noted earlier, is sometimes considered an "appendix" to *Kavitāvalī*, although some scholars count it separately as a seventh "minor" work (see Lutgendorf, 2007, 97–99).

Tulsī's second most popular and, by most assessments, second greatest literary achievement is *Vinaypatrikā* (The Letter of Petition), an anthology of 279 lyric poems, mainly dedicated to Rāma, on which he may have labored for several decades. Interestingly, a 1609 manuscript includes roughly a hundred fewer songs and is arranged in a different order, arguably providing a glimpse of a "work in progress" by a self-conscious literary stylist. Although the songs are somewhat disparate in theme and also include introspective and seemingly autobiographical passages, their final arrangement presents a grand vision of Tulsī's pilgrim progress through the celestial court of Rāma to deliver his humble petition, which (with the intercession of Hanumān and Sītā) is benevolently received and approved in a three-song "epilogue" (see Allchin's 1966 study and translation). Though perhaps mirroring the structure and protocol of the imperial Mughal *darbār* or court and again reflecting the influence of Sūrdās' numerous "petitional" lyrics, this remarkable collection encompasses many extraordinarily beautiful and touching songs that have become widely performed as devotional hymns or *bhajans* (see → *kīrtan* and → *bhajan*).

The poet's craft is likewise fully evident in the much earlier work that is his universally acclaimed masterpiece, *Rāmcaritmānas* (The Sacred Lake of Rām's Deeds), self-dated to 1574, although the composition of this poem of nearly 13 thousand lines presumably required a number of years to finish. Indeed, Tulsī scholarship during the 20th century, mirroring trends in Anglo-European biblical exegesis, sought to identify the stages in which this epic was composed as well as the literary precursors on which its author drew (see Gupta, 1942; Vaudeville, 1955; Bulcke, 1977). This exegetical quest was partly inspired by the structure of the epic, which presents itself as a series of *samvād*s or dialogues between divine and legendary personages, though these are interspersed with homilies stamped with Tulsī's *chāp*. The tale of Rāma is thus placed within an elaborate set of discursive frames that traditional exegetes have associated with different philosophical viewpoints (*darśanas*). Most scholars agree that the brilliant prologue, encompassing roughly the first half of the poet's sprawling *Bālkāṇḍ* (his single longest sub-book), was probably a late addition. Like a modern preface, it lays out, in one remarkable passage, the structure of the epic, allegorically likening it to the sacred Himalayan lake Mānasarovar, here filled with the nectarlike water of devotion to Rāma and bounded by four "landings" (*ghāṭ*s) comprising the dialogues, into which the seven "stairways" (*sopān*s) of the sub-books descend (*RCM.* 1.35–43). This allegorical design, as well as the metrical structure of stanzas in alternating *caupāī* – a narrative verse form consisting of couplets of four equal 16-beat "feet" – and *dohā* meters, may owe something to the elaborate "love story" narratives (Premkahānī), likewise in eastern Hindi or Avadhi verse, composed between 1379 and 1545 by Muslim poets affiliated with both regional courts and Sufi hospices (De Bruijn, 2005).

Like most vernacular Rāma stories, Tulsī's *Rāmcaritmānas* is in no sense a translation of Vālmīki's Sanskrit epic (although the poet pays homage to it), but rather is an independent retelling that makes significant modifications to the ancient tale. Half of its lengthy *Bālkāṇḍ* precedes Rāma's birth and commences with a prologue that introduces Tulsī's belief in the ultimate salvific power of Rāma's name ("by my own understanding, I declare the name greater even than Rāma"; *RCM.* 1.23). Then follows a narration, by the vedic sage Yājñavalkya, of the marriage of Śiva and Pārvatī – highlighting Tulsī's reverence for Śiva while gently subordinating him to Rāma. This is succeeded by Śiva's own account, told to Pārvatī, of the several causes of Rāma's → *avatāra* or incarnation. Much of the lengthy final book, *Uttarkāṇḍ*, is cast as a dialogue between the immortal crow Bhuśuṇḍī and the divine eagle Garuḍa, again highlighting the power of devotion to Rāma's name, especially in the *kaliyuga* – the dismal (present) age of moral degeneration and discord. Rāma's supreme divinity is foregrounded throughout the epic, and the recurrent eulogy of his abstract name – suggesting the devotion to an attributeless (→ *nirguṇ*) absolute of saint-poets like Kabīr and → Ravidās – alternates with long and loving descriptions of his incarnate beauty, noble speech and acts, and supremely beguiling personality. The reconciliation and synthesis of such seemingly, even paradoxically, opposed categories – the worship of a formless absolute versus that of a supreme deity lavishly endowed with form and attributes, the austerely philosophical Advaita → Vedānta versus the emotional Vaiṣṇavism, or indeed Śaiva versus Vaiṣṇava sectarian ideologies – are among the epic's overarching achievements, deftly accomplished through the medium of a beloved story, set in an accessible language that is at once "rustic" (*grāmya*) and polished, musical, and extraordinarily evocative (for discussion of Tulsī's theology and ethics as revealed in the epic, see Hill, 1952, xxv–xxxvii; Babineau, 1979; Lutgendorf, 1991, 351–360).

As the hagiographic record indicates, the fame of the *Rāmcaritmānas* and its maker spread rapidly, even in the absence of print technology. Apart from Nābhādās' circa 1600 eulogy of Tulsī as Vālmīki reincarnate, hundreds of *Rāmcaritmānas* manuscripts, some in the Kaithi script used by merchants or the Nastaliq derived from Arabic and Persian, attest to its widespread copying, especially during the 18th century. However, the bulk of its audience undoubtedly experienced it through oral performance by wandering storytellers and expounders (*kathākār, kathāvācak*, and *vyās*), a vocation anticipated in the dialogic structure of the text and one that Tulsī himself is believed to have practiced. In time, "schools" of interpretation developed, some patronized by the landowning nobility of the Gangetic Plain, and voluminous written commentaries were generated, some of which would come into print in the 19th and 20th centuries (e.g. the encyclopedic 12-volume *Mānaspīyūṣ* [Nectar of the *Mānas*]; Sharan, 1925–1956). Simultaneously, the epic found wider exposure through musical performance by folk singers and by annual dramatization in the form of *rāmlīlā* pageants held at the time of the autumn *dasehrā* festival – plays believed by many to have been begun by Tulsī himself or by his disciple Meghā Bhagat. The most influential *rāmlīlā* developed under the patronage of the *mahārāja*s of Banaras in the early 19th century as a 30-day spectacle structured around a complete recitation of the *Rāmcaritmānas* by a chorus of 12 singers, whose chanting was pantomimed and re-created in prose dialogues by a large cast of costumed actors, before an audience that sometimes numbered more than a hundred thousand persons (on the range and history of *Rāmcaritmānas* performance genres, see Lutgendorf, 1991; on *rāmlīlā*, see also Avasthi, 1979; Hein, 1972; Hess, 1983; Hess & Schechner, 1977; and Kapur, 1990).

With the advent of printing in the early 19th century, the *Rāmcaritmānas* appeared in scores of editions from presses throughout the Hindi belt, and beyond, for its old Avadhi text was now sometimes accompanied by a *ṭīkā* or explanatory prose gloss in Bengali, Gujarati, Marathi, or Punjabi, as well as (modern standard) Khari Boli Hindi. By 1891, G. Growse had written that

> the book is in every one's hands, from the court to the cottage, and is read, or heard, and appreciated alike by every class of the Hindu community, whether high or low, rich or poor, young or old. (Growse, 1891, lv)

It had become, in the words of another Western observer, "the Bible of Northern India" (Macfie, 1930). To the early 20th-century champions of Hindi, it became the foundational "classic" of what they hoped to make India's "national language" (Orsini, 1998), and it also figured in the discourse of Indian nationalists and freedom fighters. Mohandas → Gandhi, who regularly included couplets from Tulsī in his Hindi speeches, called it "the greatest book of all devotional literature" (1968, 47). In the post-Independence era, its performance proliferated across the newer media of phonograph records, cassettes, and compact discs, and it served as a major inspiration for the phenomenally successful 78-week television serialization, *Ramayan*, that aired on India's national network, Doordarshan, between 1987 and 1989 (Lutgendorf, 1990).

To an English translator, Tulsī's poetry poses special problems, since it relies heavily on alliteration and rhyme to achieve a rhythmic, musical effect that contributes greatly to its power in oral performance as well as on an enormous vocabulary (estimated by one scholar at some 20 thousand words, including more than 90 derived from Persian and Arabic; see Stasik, 2009) that includes a rich array of synonyms for everyday terms (e.g. "lotus" and "love") for which English is notably deficient. Decent and accurate (if not lyrical) translations of his later anthologies have already been cited (Allchin, 1964; 1966). The *Rāmcaritmānas* itself has received eight complete English renderings; most are in (often turgid) prose (Growse, 1880; Goswamy, 1949; Hill, 1952; Bahadur, 1978; Dhody, 1987; and Prasad, 1988), but two, into rhymed verse, are (depending on one's taste) either tour-de-force achievements or unbearably contrived exercises (Atkins, 1966; Gupta, 2010). A ninth is in progress (Lutgendorf, forthcoming).

Such an influential text has not been without its critics. Tulsī, indeed, anticipated some of these and even paid ironic homage to them among the ranks of "saints and scoundrels" whom he saluted in his ingenious prologue (*RCM.* 1.4.1–1.9.5). They probably included learned Brahmans, whose scorn for a "holy book" in spoken language (*bhāṣā*) is a common theme in the Tulsī hagiographies. Although such criticism from the Sanskritic intelligentsia gradually yielded to Brahman endorsement of the epic or even the claim that only Brahmans should publicly

Fig. 1: Two *sādhus* in Chitrakut chant the *Rāmcaritmānas* to musical accompaniment (photo by Philip Lutgendorf).

expound it, Tulsī's ideology – itself an apparent synthesis of liberal and conservative streams in *bhakti* discourse – and especially his sometimes harsh remarks about women and low-caste people became problematic for some 20th-century readers, generating ongoing controversy about the universality of his vision (for a sample of anti-Tulsī invective, see Shastri, 1949; for discussion of his views on gender and caste and their interpretation by readers, see Hess, 2001; Lutgendorf, 1991, 392–407). Yet, such controversy notwithstanding, for untold numbers of people during the past four centuries and for scores of millions today, Tulsī's poetic corpus, and especially his epic of Rāma, has been accepted as both the pinnacle of devotional literature and a beloved and infallible medium for self-transformation and spiritual practice (*sādhanā*) – a role seemingly anticipated by the saint-poet himself:

> And whoever, pondering this story
> with love, recites or listens to it,
> will be enraptured by Ram's feet, and
> untainted by this dark age, greatly blessed.
> (*RCM*. 1.15.10–11)

Bibliography

Abbott, J.E., & N.R. Godbole, *Stories of Indian Saints*, Poona, 1933, repr. 1982.

Allchin, F.R., *Tulsī Dās, The Petition to Rām*, London, 1966.

Allchin, F.R., *Tulsī Dās, Kavitāvalī*, New York, 1964.

Atkins, A.G., *The Ramayana of Tulsidas*, 2 vols., New Delhi, 1966.

Avasthi (Avasthī), I., *Rāmlīlā: Paramparā aur Śailiyāṃ*, Delhi, 1979 (Hind.).

Babineau, E., *Love of God and Social Duty in the* Rāmcaritmānas, Delhi, 1979.

Bahadur, S.P., *The Complete Works of Goswami Tulsidas*, 6 vols., Varanasi, 1978.

Bulcke, C., *Rāmkathā aur Tulsīdās*, Allahabad, 1977.

De Bruijn, T., "Many Roads Lead to Lanka: The Intercultural Semantics of Rama's Quest," *CSA* 14/1, 2005, 39–53.

Dhody, C.L., *The Gospel of Love: An English Rendering of Tulasi's Shri Rama Charita Manasa*, New Delhi, 1987.

Gandhi, M., *An Autobiography*, 2 vols., n.l., 1927–1929, repr. in 1 vol., Ahmedabad, 1968.

Goswami, C., *Śrī Rāmacharitamānasa (Or the Mānasa Lake Brimming over with Exploits of Śrī Rāma)*, Gorakhpur, 1949.

Grierson, G., "Notes on Tul'sī Dās," *IA* 22, 1893, 89–98, 122–29, 197–206, 225–236, 253–274.

Growse, F.S., *The Rāmāyaṇa of Tulsīdāsa*, Cawnpore, 1891, repr. 1978.

Gupta, K., *Gosāīṃ-carit*, Banaras, 1964 (Hind.).

Gupta, M., "Biographical Sketch," in: Nagendra, ed., *Tulasidasa: His Mind and Art*, New Delhi, 1977, 63–93.

Gupta, M., *Tulsī*, Allahabad, 1952 (Hind.).

Gupta, M., *Tulsīdās, Ek Samālocanātmak Adhyayan*, n.l., 1942, repr., Allahabad, 1965 (Hind.).

Gupta, S.D., *Tulsi Ramayan in English Verse*, Delhi, 2010.

Hein, N., *The Miracle Plays of Mathurā*, New Haven, 1972.

Hess, L., "Lovers' Doubts: Questioning the Tulsi *Rāmāyaṇ*," in: P. Richman, ed., *Questioning Ramayanas: A South Asian Tradition*, Berkeley, 2001, 25–48.

Hess, L., "Rām Līlā: The Audience Experience," in: M. Thiel-Horstmann, ed., *Bhakti in Current Research*, Berlin, 1983, 171–194.

Hess, L., & R. Schechner, "The Ramlila of Ramnagar," *TDR* 21/3, 1977, 51–82.

Hill, W.D.P., *The Holy Lake of the Acts of Rāma*, London, 1952.

Kapur, A., *Actors, Pilgrims, Kings, and Gods: The Ramlila at Ramnagar*, Calcutta, 1990.

Lutgendorf, P., *The Sacred Lake of Ram's Deeds*, forthcoming.

Lutgendorf, P., *Hanuman's Tale*, New York, 2007.

Lutgendorf, P., "The Quest for the Legendary Tulsīdās," in: W.M. Callewaert & R. Snell, eds., *According to Tradition*, Wiesbaden, 1994, 65–85.

Lutgendorf, P., *The Life of a Text: Performing the Rāmcaritmānas of Tulsīdās*, Berkeley, 1991.

Lutgendorf, P., "Ramayan: The Video," *TDR* 34/2, 1990, 127–176.

Macfie, J.M., *The Ramayan of Tulsidas*, Edinburgh, 1930.

Mishra (Miśra), V., "Gautam Candrikā meṃ Tulsīdās kā Vṛttānt," *NPP* 60/1, 1955, 1–22 (Hind.).

Nagar (Nāgar), A., *Mānas kā Haṃs*, Delhi, 1972 (Hind.).

Nirala (Nirālā), S.T., *Tulsīdās*, n.l., 1938 (Hind.).

Orsini, F., "Tulsī Dās as a Classic," in: R. Snell & I.M.P. Raeside, eds., *Classics of Modern South Asian Literature*, Wiesbaden, 1998, 119–141.

Prasad, R.C., *Tulasidasa's Shriramacharitamanasa*, Delhi, 1988.

Sharan (Śaraṇ), A., ed., *Mānas-pīyūṣ*, 12 vols., Ayodhya, 1925–1956; repr. in 7 vols., Gorakhpur, n.d. (Hind.).

Shastri (Śāstrī), R., *Mānas Mīmāṃsā*, Allahabad, 1949 (Hind.).

Stasik, D., "Perso-Arabic Lexis in the *Rāmcaritmānas* of Tulsīdās," *CrIS* 11, 2009, 67–86.

Tulsidas, publ. Amar Chitra Katha, Bombay, 1974.

Vaudeville, C., *Étude sur les sources et la composition du* Rāmāyaṇa *de Tulsī-Dās*, Paris, 1955.

PHILIP LUTGENDORF

Tyāgarāja

The composer Tyāgarāja, who lived from 1767 to 1847, is probably the most honored saintly musician of South India. He was born to a Telugu-speaking → Smārta Brahman family living in Tamil Nadu. (Telugu is called the "Italian of the East" because of its vowel sounds – it has a naturally flowing and musical quality.) Inspired by devotion to → Rāma, an incarnation of → Viṣṇu, Tyāgarāja sang many songs in the classical South Indian style (known popularly as Carnatic music) and taught numerous students who perpetuated the tradition. Together with two composers who were his contemporaries, Śyāmaśāstri and Muttusvāmi Dīkṣitar, Tyāgarāja is celebrated as one of the "Trinity of South Indian Music" (*saṅgīta trimūrti*).

The songs of Tyāgarāja are especially well known and much loved among people living in South India, and among people of South Indian descent living everywhere in the world. There are annual festivals that celebrate his music not only in India, but also in America, Canada, Europe, Africa, and Asia. Generations of South Indians recognize an attractive authenticity in Tyāgarāja's life and works and see in his songs a touchstone of Hindu identity and ideals.

Tyāgarāja's great lyrical ability to sing the contemporary Telugu idiom in relating to Rāma is most impressive. Devotion as natural as breathing is expressed in familial language, informal, intimate, reflective, and meditative. Emotions of longing, frustration, and blissful realization, all expressed with artful spontaneity within the given metrical forms and rhyme schemes of the tradition, make his body of work extraordinary.

When Tyāgarāja's songs are sung today, they often evoke a strangely familiar voice – an archetypal quality, profoundly expressive, and almost embarrassingly personal. The voice seems ancient and primal, spontaneous yet also formal, following strict rules of Carnatic music, yet full of life in the 21st century. The *saṅgīta* (musical) aspects have a soulful charm, which the ears and heart enjoy, but which words can only begin to describe. The *sāhitya* (lyrical) aspects express archetypal yearnings – recognitions – and they narrate spiritual situations and also offer many enduring ideas and sentiments to meditate on. Tyāgarāja's music thus speaks to people from a variety of cultures around the world, by artfully appealing to heartfelt meditative moods, and inner struggles and breakthroughs.

Biographies of Tyāgarāja

In the century and a half that followed Tyāgarāja's death in 1847, many tellings of his life were written, performed, sung, and made into illustrated publications and popular films. The first two biographies of Tyāgarāja were recorded by two of his disciples – a father and son of Saurashtran descent – Veṅkaṭarāmana Bhāgavatar and Kṛṣṇasvāmī Bhāgavatar, respectively. Veṅkaṭarāmana spent decades with Tyāgarāja, serving him in close proximity and learning the musical tradition, and then he lived in Walajapet, west of Madras, until he died in 1874. His son Kṛṣṇasvāmī was born in 1824. Beginning in young adulthood, he studied with Tyāgarāja during the last two years of the master musician's life. Both father and son wrote biographical texts about Tyāgarāja in Telugu, the language that they learned while studying Tyāgarāja's songs. These two brief biographies by close disciples, which are combined and summarized in the following paragraphs, constitute a family tradition. The texts are not dated, but from internal evidence they would seem to have been written not long after Tyāgarāja's death in 1847. Thus they suggest how those who knew him well understood the unfolding of his life, before much time had passed, and other stories became popularized. Veṅkaṭarāmana's text describes Tyāgarāja's earlier years, a good number of which he spent with the saint. Kṛṣṇasvāmī writes of the later years and traditions current at the time of Tyāgarāja's death, because he studied with Tyāgarāja during the last years of his life (Jackson, 2011, 2–3).

Tyāgarāja was born in a Telugu-speaking family of Vaidiki Brahmans that had migrated south from the area now known as Andhra Pradesh into Tamil Nadu sometime during the Nayak reign, possibly as early as 1600. (Among Telugu Brahmans a distinction is made between Vaidiki Brahmans, who are well-versed in the → Vedas and other religious matters, and Niyogi Brahmans, who are administrative officials, record keepers, and traditionally advisers in courts of kings). His father, Rāma Brāhmam, was known for his discourses about the → *Rāmāyaṇa* epic and was patronized by Tulajajī II, the king of Thanjavur (r. 1763–1787). Rāma Brāhmam had been given an initiation into the practice of reciting the *rāma tāraka mantra*, a sacred sound-based verbal formula in which Rāma's name "enables the crossover" of the ocean of births and deaths (→ *saṃsāra*). Rāma Brāhmam was initiated by the head of a Śaiva monastery in Marudanallur, near Kumbakonam. His first two sons were deficient in character, but the third, Tyāgarāja, was a different sort of person from the very start of his life.

Kṛṣṇasvāmī wrote that before Tyāgarāja was born, the deity of the temple in Thiruvarur, Tyāgarājasvāmi (→ Śiva as the divine dancing *yogī*-ascetic), appeared to the parents-to-be in a dream, telling them that a son would be born to them and that he would be an incarnation of Nārada, the mythical musician-devotee who travels the worlds with a *vīṇa* (stringed instrument) praising Lord Viṣṇu. In the dream, the parents were told to name the boy Tyāgarāja, and so they called him Tyāga Brāhmam when he was born. His birth occurred at noon in the year 4868 of the *kaliyuga* (May 4, 1767; see → cosmic cycles). Even while he was still a baby, the parents noticed that Tyāga would stop breastfeeding whenever he heard music.

Rāma Brāhmam decided to undertake a pilgrimage with his sons to Banaras (the famous holy city some 2,500km to the north). But then he had a dream in which Śiva as Tyāgarājasvāmi told him to go to Thiruvaiyaru instead. Thiruvaiyaru is a village 32km from Thiruvarur, situated on the Kāvērī River. Many Brahmans lived in this village, known for its great Śiva temple. Rāma Brāhmam told the Thanjavur king, Tulajajī II, who was a devotee of Śiva, about this dream, and the king responded by giving him a house and six acres of land in Thiruvaiyaru.

As a youth growing up, Tyāgarāja studied at the king's Sanskrit school in Thiruvaiyaru, and he learned the *rāma tāraka mantra* from his father, according to Veṅkaṭarāmana. According to Kṛṣṇasvāmī, Tyāgarāja was initiated into the *rāma tāraka mantra* (and later into the *nārada upāsana* chant) by a wandering *saṃnyāsin* (renunciant) named Rāmakṛṣṇānanda Svāmī. Tyāgarāja's father taught him to worship Rāma daily, and the boy used to compose songs as part of that worship. Even in his childhood, Tyāgarāja is said to have dreamed (Tam. *kaṉavu-*, "to dream") of Lord Rāma, while playing with other boys in the street, and to have given his belongings away, true to his name Tyāgarāja ("King of Renouncing/Letting Go of Attachments").

After young Tyāgarāja displayed promise as a lyricist, his father took him to a neighbor, Sonti Veṅkaṭaramanayya, the famed Thanjavur court musician, to study music. Tyāgarāja learned conventional Carnatic music, but to learn the deeper secrets, he developed devotion to Nārada, and he also studied his own maternal grandfather's musicological manuscripts. Nārada appeared to Tyāgarāja, it is said, and gave him a legendary musical manuscript, *Svarārṇavam* (The Ocean of Musical Notes). And Tyāgarāja continued to repeat the *rāma tāraka mantra* devotedly for the next 20 years. When he had recited the *mantra* ten million times, Tyāgarāja experienced a momentary yet momentous *darśan* of Lord Rāma and spontaneously burst into song. In all, he repeated the *mantra* 960 million times during those 20 years and had other visions that also inspired him to compose songs.

Tyāgarāja soon became known for his singing. In time, his music teacher, Sonti Veṅkaṭaramanayya, asked him to sing some of his own compositions for the leading court musicians of the day. Tyāgarāja sang so well that his teacher then publicly praised him as a greater musician than himself and gave to Tyāgarāja a gold medal and chain that he himself had received as an award at the Thanjavur court. (Tyāgarāja later returned this gift at the wedding of his teacher's daughter.)

The king wanted to honor Tyāgarāja, but he refused to go to court, even though his brothers pressured him to go. When Tyāgarāja was 20 years of age, his father Rāma Brāhmam died, and the family house was partitioned. Tyāgarāja then spent his time in his own section of the house, immersed in devotion and music dedicated to Rāma. (This dispute and division of the family estate is reflected in Tyāgarāja's song *Nādupai Palikēru*, the refrain of which states, "People are talking about me, O Lord praised by the Vedas, saying that I caused the family home's partition" [Jackson, 2011, 265]. He implies that he himself strove to preserve the unity of the household, while his brother sought division.)

One of Tyāgarāja's brothers, Pañcanada, settled down as a householder. The other, Pañcapākeśa, became ill, and despite Tyāgarāja's prayers for him, he died. When Tyāgarāja was 23 years old, his wife Pārvatī, whom he had married at 18, died, and he married her sister, Kamalambā. Tyāgarāja had one daughter, Sītāmahālakṣmī, and he arranged to have her married to a man named Subbarāmayya. They had a son, who died without issue.

The Thanjavur ruler of that time, Śarabhojī, had a son-in-law who frequented Tyāgarāja's home, going there to listen to his music. A very wealthy man in Madras, named Kōvūri Sundara Modaliāru, invited Tyāgarāja to visit him. Tyāgarāja refused. Therefore, the man went to Upaniṣad Brāhmam, a saintly scholar and composer who was then the head of the Kanchipuram Maṭh, a monastery southwest of Madras. Upaniṣad Brāhmam then wrote to Tyāgarāja, saying that as a former friend of Tyāgarāja's father, he wished to see the composer whose fame was now growing in the region. He requested Tyāgarāja to make a pilgrimage and to stop along the way and visit him. Therefore, Tyāgarāja went on a pilgrimage to Tirupati, the hilltop temple north of Kanchipuram, and he arranged to visit Upaniṣad Brāhmam en route. Tyāgarāja composed new songs along the way when he stopped at temples. Kṛṣṇasvāmī recorded that besides composing → *kīrtana*s (devotional songs of praise), Tyāgarāja also wrote *Naukācaritram* (Boat Story) and *Prahlāda Bhakti Vijayam* (The Victory of Prahlāda's Devotion) – poetic narratives interspersed with songs.

Near the end of his life, Tyāgarāja entered the order of *saṃnyāsin*s, the last stage of life for upper-caste Hindus. He made offerings to Brahmans and the poor (as is the Hindu custom at the time of death), and while devotional songs (*bhajan*s) were being sung, in the presence of a "great sound or exclamation," he "joined → *brahman*." (This means merging with the ultimate formless consciousness, which is the goal of the traditions of Hinduism Tyāgarāja practiced.) His gravesite memorial (*samādhi*) was built on the bank of the Kāvērī River, near the sites of previous *saṃnyāsin*s' graves.

These two early overlapping biographies, which I have combined here, include in their narratives significant information that historically minded moderns recognize as historical and also include some religious concepts, images, and interpretations. Veṅkaṭarāmana Bhāgavatar, whose prose biography provides basic information about Tyāgarāja's life, also wrote more effusive and extravagant descriptions of his master Tyāgarāja in Sanskrit poems, as Telugu poet Tūmu Narasiṃha Dāsu did in his own mother tongue. In these forms, the genre dictates more rhapsodic imagery and praise. The portrayal of Tyāgarāja's life by later religious storytellers using songs to dramatize thrilling episodes often emphasizes more miraculous events not found in the earliest accounts of his life (Jackson, 2011, 7–20).

Tyāgarāja's Works from a Religious Lyric Perspective

Collections of Tyāgarāja's songs testify to the prolific work of the composer. Tyāgarāja according to some stories composed 24 thousand songs, a number matching Vālmīki's 24 thousand verses in the *Rāmāyaṇa*. About seven hundred Tyāgarāja compositions are known today. There are several respected compilations of his works: N.T. Bhagavatar's *Sadguru Tyāgarājasvāmi Kīrtanalu* (Bhagavatar, 1908) and K.V. Shastri's *Tyāgarāja Keertanalu* (Shastri, 1975), for example. The collection by C. Ramanujachari and V. Raghavan in *The Spiritual Heritage of Tyagaraja* contains around 560 songs (Ramanujachari & Raghavan, 1981). M.V. Subbayya's *The Complete Kritis of Sri Thyagaraja* presents 717 songs (Subbayya, 2008). According to scholar B.R. Rao, about 660 songs can be attributed to Tyāgarāja with certainty, but other scholars differ on the number. The authenticity and accuracy of many of the texts is generally accepted because of Tyāgarāja's choice of serious pupils who were dedicated to faithfully maintaining his works (Jackson, 2011, 152–154).

A few examples from Tyāgarāja's many songs may serve to illustrate the content and appeal of his works.

Bhakti's central value of devotional love is expressed in Tyāgarāja's song *Anurāgamu Lēni*:

> To the mind without love, wisdom will not come.
> Only those grown great in deep understanding know,
> but to the mind without love, wisdom will not come.
> Like the satisfaction of people enjoying a leisurely feast
> is the joy of those who dwell absorbed in the Lord with form...
> To the mind without love, wisdom will not come. (Jackson, 2011, 174)

→ *Bhakti* is the ethos and way of life that Tyāgarāja's biography and works embody: piety, worship and song, service to others, and dedication to high ideals.

Devotional repetition of a → *mantra* is a practice to calm the naturally restless mind, and to keep the brain from anxious grinding against itself. In *Telisi Rāmacintanatō*, Tyāgarāja sings, "Chant, O mind, the name of Rāma, knowing full well its meaning through deep contemplation" (Jackson, 2011, 343). This *bhakti* practice can be done anywhere, with any name of god. M. → Gandhi called it a panacea for the many problems and setbacks mortals face. The *mantra* is said to give steadiness and strength in a world of uncertainties and challenges.

→ Meditation is another practice Tygaraja sings about. In his song *Tanalōnē Dhyāniñci*, Tyāgarāja prays,

> Meditating deep within, let me become merged with You.
> In the cavern of my heart, let me know the place You dwell;
> meditating deeply let me be at one with you...
> Then I'll know Your mystery, instantly and certainly...
> That same moment, ego-illusion will go – who knows where?
> Meditating deep inside, let me be at one with you. (Jackson, 2011, 337)

To sit quietly focusing on the form of the beloved is a practice leading to peace and fulfillment in *bhakti* traditions.

Tyāgarāja celebrates the spiritual power of music, whether listened to, sung, or played on an instrument, in *Śrīpaprīya Sangītopāsana*:

> O mind be intent upon music, dear to the Consort of Lakṣmī.
> Music, mind-wealth of ascetics, free from the three miseries (troubles of self, and of fate, and of pain caused by others), moving through the seven tones –
> O mind be intent upon music...
> The *ragas* which are so delightful (what mellow things melodies do), assuming fine shapes so enchanting, they dance with ringing tones, and their anklets go jingle jingle...
> be intent on this music. (Jackson, 2011, 330)

Music dedicated to the ultimate is said to resonate with cosmic depths in this *bhakti* practice, and several of Tyāgarāja's songs elaborate on facets of music's mysterious powers.

Navigating the waters of *saṃsāra* is no easy feat, and many of Tyāgarāja's songs comment on and advise listeners about how to meet life's challenges. In *Bhajarē Raghuvīram Śara*, Tyāgarāja encourages the cultivation of contentment and warns against entanglements in fraudulent tricks:

> Worship the Raghu hero, Rāma...
> Perform decent acts and drive away lust and other distractions.
> Is everything that pops into your head really your business,
> or is some of it the stuff of aimless wandering nowhere?
> Don't get involved in scams, don't become a "tiger in a cowskin..." (Jackson, 2011, 178)

This imagery, like the "wolf in sheep's clothing," denotes how a sneaky trickster gets short-term gain but eventually is found out and gains disgrace.

Tyāgarāja enthusiastically sings of humility and appreciation of greatness in *Endarō Mahānubhāvulandariki*, "To as many great souls as there be, I bow respectfully" (Jackson, 2011, 210). This is one of the *pañcaratna kīrtana*s ("five-gem songs," musical masterpieces) sung en masse at festivals, and it enumerates many examples of greatness.

Tyāgarāja expresses ultimate spiritual attainment in his swan song, *Paramātmuḍu*,

> *Paramātma* is brightly shining – may this dawn upon you in all its beauty.
> Named as Viṣṇu, named as Śiva, said to be in people and heavenly beings throughout the entire universe.
> The Supreme Being gloriously glows – may this dawn upon you in all its beauty.
> Being in all that's made of sky, wind, fire, and water, in beasts and birds and hills and trees by the tens of millions,
> always in the lifeless and the lively, the Lord whom Tyagaraja adores in this world –
> That Supreme Being pervades like light! Have a joyful subtle insight into that in all its beauty. (Jackson, 2011, 291)

Verses like these from a few of Tyāgarāja's songs suggest some of the ideas that the composer known as "the Beethoven of South India" sang. Others contain proverbs, rejoicings at experiences with Rāma, and disappointments, as well as exaltation felt when sharing devotion with like-minded devotees, and soulful musings about the ways of the world and reflections of the spiritual dimension that inspired Tyāgarāja.

A Further Consideration of Themes in Tyāgarāja's Work

The traditional Indian conception of a work of art is to make something that is an aid to contemplation or a "means of reintegration," a *saṃskāraṇa*, something sacramental (Coomaraswamy, 1977, 145). Such art typically presents archetypal sacred images to which seekers can easily relate. The story and image of Rāma is one such archetypal symbol.

The central archetype of Lord Rāma, Tyāgarāja's *iṣṭadevatā*, described by Vālmīki in the first chapter of the first book of the *Rāmāyaṇa* epic, powerfully embodies the divine ideal of human life for Tyāgarāja. As depicted by Vālmīki, Rāma is self-restrained, majestic, firm, wise, well behaved, eloquent, charming, able to destroy opponents, and a skillful archer, with broad shoulders, long arms, an expansive chest, a beautiful head and forehead, and an attractive stride. He has an agreeable blue color, large eyes, and prosperity and is replete with auspicious signs. He is righteous, true to his promises, beloved, concerned for the welfare of his people, renowned, endowed with wisdom, having a holy radiance, dutiful, and profound in his meditation. He is the guardian of the world soul, endowed with → *dharma*'s protection, knower of the truth of the → Vedas and branches of vedic knowledge, knowing the meaning of the scriptures and traditions. Beloved of all the world, he has an undepressed spirit and is good, wise, and bright. Good people approach him as the bestower of blessings, as the ocean is approached by the rivers. Honorable and treating all fairly, he is the one whom devotees love to see. He is endowed with all good qualities and displays many other excellences. Rāma, linked to greatness and glory, is divinely noble, the epitome of masculine ideals, as Sītā is the feminine ideal (Goldman, 1990, 119–121).

In some songs, Tyāgarāja emphasized that Rāma is a *rasika*, a lover of music. By constant devotion to his *iṣṭadevatā* Rāma, with *mantra* and music, meditation and → *pūjā*, Tyāgarāja drew to himself experiences of this archetypal image of god. By all accounts, Rāma was at the very heart of Tyāgarāja's life. The world is beyond an individual's control, often even in simple matters, let alone the catastophic famines and wars that occurred during Tyāgarāja's time. The focus on Rāma as protector, and the *bhakta* seeking his protection, is found in the refrain of many songs: "*Pāhi Mām* – please protect us." *Bhakti* faith can show a kind of magical power in a changing unpredictable world. Tyāgarāja's lifelong devotion to Rāma gave him many roles to play and inspiration in the playing of them. There is an innocent un-self-conscious childlike quality in surrender to the divine king or in the relationship of a son to a father. There is motivation, striving to live up to high standards in the fulfilling of one's duties as a servant of Lord Rāma. There are sublime possibilities in being the musician praising Rāma. There are deep feelings involved in relating to Rāma as the beloved – longing, hope, disappointment, grief, exultation, and enthusiasm. The image of Rāma, needless to say, filled Tyāgarāja with finely nuanced enthusiasm, and he sang of his unfolding *bhakti* relationship.

Much in Tyāgarāja's lyrics to Rāma is Vālmīki based. Some songs retell the whole *Rāmāyaṇa* in condensed form. Tyāgarāja also sang personal experiences ("I saw Rāma on a hilltop") in some songs. A few songs are neither found in Vālmīki, nor representative of Tyāgarāja's vision. An example of this is a song dramatizing Rāma's mercy, *Vācāmagōcamarē*:

> O Mind! Rāma's glory is beyond description…
> Understanding the desire in Sītā's mind, [for a royal whisk-fan made from a yak tail] he sent an arrow at the tail of the chamari-deer;
> To save her honor and pride, (which consisted of the fine tail) she covered (her tail) with her head (intending to offer her life rather than lose the tail);
> Seeing this and flowing with compassion and to afford security of life (to the meek), did not Rāma, the remover of distress of the meek, quickly cancel the arrow aimed already? (Ramanujachari & Raghavan, 1981, 231)

In this story, a *camarī* deer, faced with an arrow speeding toward her tail, offered her neck as a target instead, immediately winning Rāma's compassion. A regional tradition from Tamil literature sheds light on the story. The animal from which the *camarī* whisk is made is called *kavarimāṉ* in Tamil. According to Tamil poetic tradition, the *kavarimāṉ* is so sensitive that it will die if even a hair is removed from its body. The Tamil classic *Tirukkuṟaḷ* conveys this:

Like the wild ox that, of its tuft bereft, will pine away,
Are those who, of their honour shorn, will quit the light of day.
Who, when dishonour comes, refuse to live, their honoured memory
Will live in worship and applause of all the world for aye! (*TiKu.* 969–970; trans. Pope, 1886, 132)

It seems likely that Tyāgarāja, who lived in Tamil Nadu his entire life, knew this poetic tradition of how pride cannot go on living when it feels dishonored, and he included it in a song about Sītā and Rāma.

Traditions say that while he was still a child, Tyāgarāja's mother taught him songs of the Haridāsa composer Purandaradāsa (1484–1564). Portraits of him often show him wearing a turban, shoulder cloth, and Vaiṣṇava markings associated with the Haridāsas (for Haridāsas, see → Smārta). In his life, Tyāgarāja followed his mother's devotional inspiration, staying at home and composing songs devoted to Rāma rather than emulating his father, who recited the *Rāmāyaṇa* in the king's court. He also did not follow the example of his music teacher Sonti Veṅkaṭaramanayya, who played music at the court of the king. In the name of *bhakti*, Tyāgarāja scorned worldly success, preferring to sing with eyes closed in his shrine room rather than perform wide-eyed in court and be beholden to the king. To modern Hindus faced with the threat of forgetting their roots, Tyāgarāja stands as an image of the soul's refusal to be colonized and modernized too far, an assertion of the power of the ancient ways, an affirmation of a Hindu *bhakti* identity.

Tyāgarāja's wife is remembered for urging Tyāgarāja to compose songs in honor of the goddess celebrated at village festivals. At first, it is said, Tyāgarāja was critical of devotees of the village goddess Dharmasaṃvardhanī, Śiva's consort, but due to his wife's influence, he composed festival songs to her. These goddess songs are available in collections and writings (Ramanujachari & Raghavan, 1981, 55–71; Sambamoorthy, 1970, 83–84). To do this, Tyāgarāja probably had to defy some inner conservatism, going against some more rigid patriarchal authority structure, both external and internal, expanding religious imagination to sing for the goddess. Regional folk devotion to local deities such as village goddesses is sometimes associated with an indifference to or protest against vedic Hinduism and Brahman-centered religion. It may be a sign Tyāgarāja moved toward fulfillment of his own destiny of broadmindedness and deep-rooted popularity when he composed songs to the village goddess.

Interplay of the Old and the Young in Tyāgarāja

The most typical image of Tyāgarāja is an elderly man, the good gray Tyāgarāja, staunch practitioner of the strictest ideals of *bhakti*, eschewing the court's luxuries and earthly rewards, proclaiming humble values of dedicated life in his songs. But when the composer wrote extended narratives, musical plays, he wrote of youthful enthusiasm and with childlike excitement and celebration of nature's delights. The hero of *Prahlāda Bhakti Vijayam* is the irrepressible boy Prahlāda. That Tyāgarāja had a fondness for exuberant water images and the lively liquid element is evident in a number of songs about the "sea of bliss" (*Ānanda Sāgara*) in which devoted singers swim. *Prahlāda Bhakti Vijayam* is largely set in the presence of water and uses extensive water imagery. Song 3 presents the sea personified as a deity: "Here comes Sāgara, ocean god, Samudra Rāja," and there is a prayer in song 6, *Vāridhi Nīku*, to Sāgara, asking him to reveal the way to a vision of the lord. The ocean replies in song 7, *Vaccunu Vari*, "Only the prayers of true devotees" win vision. In song 18, *Nannu Brovakanu*, it is said that god appears like holy waters arriving where one has gone searching. The lord is called the "ocean of mercy" in song 22, *O Rāma Rāma*, and Prahlāda requests Viṣṇu to "[l]ook on me with affection as a fish looks to its child and feeds it," in song 24, *Sarasī Ruhanayana*. The lord is called a treasure deep on the floor of the sea, which men must dive deeply to find, and a mystery hidden in the ocean that has come to save Tyāgarāja in song 34, *Emani Vēgintunē*. Later in the work, → Brahmā approaches the seashore "drinking deeply of the fountain of the Lord's name," an endless liquid refreshment. In song 42 (*Callare Srī Rāmacandruni*), the gods on the beach worship with flowers, and the narration ends with a glorious seashore sunrise (Sambamoorthy, 1965; Jackson, 1994, 44).

Tyāgarāja celebrated the ever-youthful feminine qualities of *bhakti* in his other poetic narrative, *Naukācaritram*. He says early in the text that he wrote it "unknowingly." This may be a statement of humility or of inspiration. The poet Molla (1440–1530), an uneducated woman from Nellore, also said she wrote her Telugu *Rāmāyaṇa* without having conscious knowledge gained by study: "I lack a poet's training... Just by the grace of the renowned Lord... I find I am able to write verses" (Jackson, 2005, 83). The hidden sources of creativity are sometimes honored by the conscious mind refusing to take credit for something beyond it.

Naukācaritram (Boat Story) is a celebration of archetypal images of feminine devotion – beauty, charms, and pastimes of *gopī*s, sometimes called "little mothers," enjoying moments spent with child → Kṛṣṇa. *Gopī* voices, girlish excitement, and women's sensibilities give the *Naukācaritram* cheerful energies, lyrical feelings, and mercurial moods. The songs delight in natural beauty and evoke a sense of dependence on divine providence.

In *Naukācaritram* significant water imagery flows in and out of the story. The *gopī*s, at first sight of Kṛṣṇa, gaze entranced and desire his embrace, "swimming in an ocean of ecstasy." Gesturing toward the river, the *gopī*s sing *Cūḍarē celulāra yamunādēvī* ("Behold the River Goddess"), whose sapphire blue is made deeper by white sand dunes, enchanting with lotuses and bees. "The little waves glide as if made of bright diamonds – see the stairway of diamonds, where wavelets swirl" catching the sunlight (Jackson, 1994, 10). Centuries before, the poet Nammāḻvār had called the Kāvērī River "the river of diamonds" (*kurmā maṇi... ponni; TiVāy.* 10.8.1), and the Tamil classic *Cilappatikāram* also celebrated the river's beauty and motherlike qualities. Rejoicing in the shimmering, dazzling waters with wild geese and enchanting breezes, fruits, and birds and flowers, the *gopī*s excitedly embark on a silver boat with Kṛṣṇa, unconscious of their pride, which is about to be broken. The *gopī*s' prideful egoes are overconfident, and it is this gloating self-consciousness of their own glory that precipitates the crisis.

Song 12 (*Unnatāvuna*) reflects the other side of the waters – violent and uncontrollable. A sudden storm frightens the *gopī*s, and they sing to the goddess → Yamunā, "All has turned to chaos," of wild winds and rains, and they admit "whatever work women may do, it all ends up in a deluge [*pralaya*]." To plug a leak, they shed their bright clothes at mischievous Kṛṣṇa's behest, only to watch them swirl away. "In this fullness of water we're drowning in shame," they sing as the waters rise to their knees. In song 17, *Vedavākyamani*, they sing that they have removed the rest of their dresses because it was a "scriptural decree" issued by Kṛṣṇa; the water is up to their throats. After fully surrendering to Kṛṣṇa, the *gopī*s find relief as the rain subsides. At home again they create their own gentle storm, spraying perfume, sprinkling rosewater, feeling tipsy in the presence of Kṛṣṇa, "whose speech drips with nectar." After the horrific life-threatening storm, these pleasant fragrances and subtle mists are gently refreshing. Song 17 is in *mohana rāga*, which is known for conveying the resolution of complications (Jackson, 1994, 1–56).

The music of Tyāgarāja has often been likened to an ocean, a vast expanse of many moods, *bhakti* expressions, and *rāga*s. Tyāgarāja was a diver in the ocean of *bhakti*, and thanks to his immersion in musical creativity, generations continue to enjoy wave after wave of his many songs. There are songs sung in moods of dejection and confessional songs, self-criticism, pleading, anger, and doubt, but also faith and moods of playfulness – light-hearted jestful treatment of the lord. There are songs that make claim to having fulfilled his obligations; songs of feeling tried, tired, and troubled; songs exhorting himself; songs of blessing and praise; and songs of heart-felt gratitude.

There is the often-sounded cry of the heart, the pull toward the all-attractive lord in lyrics of yearning, like Sītā longing for Lord Rāma. There is outrage and indignant disgust. Like Purandaradāsa, Tyāgarāja exercised much scorn for false devotion. He had scathing criticism for those unconscious of their hypocrisy. He sang many songs of seeking sincerely and waiting hopefully. And there are rarer outbursts of exultation expressing moments of vision and ecstasy.

There is revulsion at the ignorance that delights in violence, as when external rituals involving death to animals come in for Tyāgarāja's censure in *Yajñadulu*. Men who call animal sacrifices joyous must have the hearts of demons, because those sacrifices are full of cruelty to living beings, Tyāgarāja declares. The lyrics contain a play on the words for "senses" and "venom":

> These extroverts, [lit. "people facing outward," dominated by externals] drawn by the senses –

which are the same as cobra venom, combined
with past impressions formed in many previous births, ignorant of Śrī Rāma, whom Tyāgarāja worships –
O mind, are there any ignoramuses to match these men who call [animal] sacrifices joyous?
Their 'wise traditions' are poverty-stricken! (Jackson, 2011, 362)

These songs and others use abrasive images to scrape away at ignorant corruption and to strengthen conscience. Weird music in Tyāgarāja's song *Idi Samayamurā* suggests fear. He asks,

Isn't this the time, star of the solar line, Elephant-gaited one, Lord who puts down the madness of the *Kali Yuga* –
to make what you said come true? . . .
The spirit of the *Kali Yuga* came in person,
he figured he would stage a drama, using humans as goats in a sacrifice of weird cults. (Jackson, 2011, 99)

Such eerie music and lyrics form a critique of social ills and suggest the *bhakti* solution – worship and praying the sacred name.

Some of Tyāgarāja's greatest songs celebrate the power of music itself. This goes well with the sacred musician archetype, with its mystique of the dedicated, inspired musician, powerful as an instrument of consciousness-raising liberating music – *nādayoga*. Thus, he sang a multitude of deep feelings and moods, inner urges, and hopes, and musicians keep singing them, and listeners hear in his songs echoes of their own inner lives.

Tyāgarāja's Contributions to Carnatic Music

Tyāgarāja made great contributions to the South Indian music tradition that he mastered and taught. One of Tyāgarāja's outstanding contributions to advancement of the *kṛti* format was the full utilization of the *saṅgati* – a series of thematic variations, gradually unfolding the melodic potential of the basic musical phrase, the *pallavi*. (The Tyāgarāja *kṛti* has three main parts: the *pallavi* [the opening line, lit. "sprout," which is growing seed or nucleus of the piece], the *anupallavi* [the elaboration or extension of the nucleus], and one or three *caraṇams*, examples demonstrating the idea by adding specifics to the *pallavi*'s sentiments. In some of his songs, Tyāgarāja also employed *saṅgatis* in the *anupallavi* and *caraṇam*).

Tyāgarāja studied the *rāga* scheme laid out by the 16th-century musicologist Veṅkaṭamakhi, who worked out the potential number of scale types for a system classifying the various *rāgas* that existed and those that could be conceived of in the future. For classifying the *rāgas* that existed, Veṅkaṭamakhi used only 19 of the possible 72. Besides composing many great *kṛtis* in already popular *rāgas*, Tyāgarāja worked out some of the *rāgas* that had only been potential *rāgas* in Veṅkaṭamakhi's theory until that time. Tyāgarāja gave life to these *rāgas* so they were no longer mere scale descriptions in a text but became full-fledged *rāgas* capable of being sung elaborately in concerts. In some of the less-heard *rāgas*, Tyāgarāja's compositions are the only popular ones performed publicly with any frequency.

While Tyāgarāja also wrote masterly *kīrtanas*, a simpler song form suitable for group singing and festivals, his unique and trend-setting contribution was his perfection of the *kṛti* form. He achieved a clarity and balanced interdependence of parts in fine proportion in the *kṛti*'s three-part structure. In a Tyāgarāja *kṛti*, every syllable and note counts. Often earlier works tended to be either more simplistic or more meandering and extensive, while Tyāgarāja's characteristic *kṛtis* consistently achieved a more focused expression in tightly knit songs with skillful climaxes. He discovered optimal dynamics for structure and variation, discipline and imagination.

While Tyāgarāja added some dimensions to the *kṛti* form, his contemporary composers Śyāmaśāstri and Muttusvāmi Dīkṣitar also added some. Muttusvāmi Dīkṣitar made a path-breaking contribution by not having more than one *caraṇam* with repeating tune, thus giving the form more of an "art music" or "classical style" flavor. In some cases, Muttusvāmi Dīkṣitar even dispensed with the single *caraṇam*. A few songs of Tyāgarāja also have only one *caraṇam*, but in the works of Muttusvāmi Dīkṣitar, none has more than one *caraṇam* (except where the *caraṇams* explore varying melodic structures). Tyāgarāja's songs are said to be immediately enjoyable, like grapes; Muttusvāmi Dīkṣitar's are said to be like coconuts, requiring more effort to get the contents; Śyāmaśāstri's are said to be like bananas, needing only to be peeled to taste the fruit. All three are beloved in South India.

*Saṅgati*s bring out the *pallavi*'s nuances with slight shifts of notes and sentiments. They also embody the logical unfolding of the musical theme, realizing the *rāga*'s potential. Usually the first *saṅgati* is a simple melodic line, and the next is more fully elaborated, while the next is yet more elaborate. All these increasingly complicated *saṅgati*s are sung within the same time measure. The *saṅgati*s flow together well, and they cascade gradually, arriving at a climax of utmost possible rhythmic excitement and melodic elaboration. Tyāgarāja was able to realize fully the potentials inherent in the exploration of subtle variations in *saṅgati*s (Jackson, 2011, 146–149). (Similar to *saṅgati, nēravāḷ* in South Indian music performances is a kind of melodic elaboration belonging to the realm of improvisation showing the performers imagination.) Tyāgarāja also innovated in the rhythmic aspects of music, starting songs on the offbeat, for example. Prior to Tyāgarāja's time some *saṅgati*s are found in South Indian music, for example in the *padam*s (short songs on the theme of love) by the 17th-century composer Kṣetrajña. However, Kṣetrajña's *saṅgatis* are usually variations on *rāga* phrases, while in Tyāgarāja's *kṛtis* the *saṅgati*s also involve melodic variations which accentuate the feelings and emotions conveyed by the lyrics as well as variations based on *svarālaṅkāra* (note patterns expressing musical flourishes).

Conclusion

Composers such as Tyāgarāja have left South Indians a great heritage to sing. They have left a reservoir of tradition, a spiritual symbol system used by a continuous *bhakti* community for many generations. Forerunners often cited for influence in Tyāgarāja's compositions include Śārṅgadeva, Kṣetrajña, Purandaradāsa, Nārāyaṇa Tīrtha, Melattur Veṅkatarama Śāstri, Bhadrācalam Rāmadās, and the Tallapakkam poets of the Annamācārya family (a family of 15th-16th-century composers who wrote thousands of Telugu lyrics at the temple in Tirupati, where they were music leaders). Sometimes this *bhakti* context is taken for granted, because there has been a stream of singer-saints over the centuries. Tyāgarāja pays tribute to predecessors in some of his songs, for example, *Endarō Mahānubhāvulu*.

The lasting impression Tyāgarāja made on the collective memory of South India is one of conscientiousness and inspiration anchored to the sacred. He combines fidelity to time-honored ways, carrying tradition forward by becoming a unique individual shaped by all the experiences and strivings in his life. South Indian musicologist T.V.S. Rao wrote that Tyāgarāja dynamically combined old and new:

> He united the apparently opposite qualities of conservatism and progress, of reverence for antiquity and impatience of restraint, of the prejudices of the heart and the revolt of intellect. He is a classic romanticist and a conservative radical. His life in ethics and aesthetics is the evolution of perfect harmony and attunement from the discordant principles of thought and action. Nothing short of the absolute universality of his mind could have succeeded in saturating his songs with that spirit of sweetness, peace and bliss which lingers in our soul long after the sounds have faded away... His voice is the voice of eternity. (Rao, 1943, 85)

Overall, Tyāgarāja presents an image of dynamic wholeness. His musical works seem fresh and youthful, yet they have an ancient resonance. His lasting impression as householder/*saṃnyāsin* conveys the great Hindu ideal of encompassing both dharmic life here and formless consciousness in *mokṣa*. His practice of *uñchavritti* (accepting alms while walking and singing) was in the archetype of ideal Brahmanic renunciation and shows he also had strong bonds to the common people. He was not only the self-forgetful composer but also the careful teacher – teaching takes one out of oneself; one must consciously organize one's thoughts, lead and correct others. Besides Tyāgarāja's experiences of being immersed in the timeless, he had the experiences of the regular cycles of *ekādaśī* (11th lunar day) festivals and other religious events that punctuate Viṣṇu devotees' calendars in Tamil Nadu. These predictable cycles gave a rhythm to his life and offered occasions for his inspiration to be heard.

Tyāgarāja's songs were his way of reaching the deeper springs of life, and they have also become later generations' way of finding inspiration and feeling at home in their tradition. The depths of consciousness remain an open mystery; it is a hidden source accessible through the work of spiritual artists such as Tyāgarāja. American composer Leonard Bernstein sounded a note reminiscent of Tyāgarāja's South Indian music ideas when he said,

> In the beginning was the Note, and the note was with God; and whosoever can reach for that Note, reach high, and bring it back to us on earth… to the extent of his reach, partakes of the divine. (*Leonard Bernstein: Reaching for the Note*, 1998)

Tyāgarāja yearned intensely and reached far, and we hear his longings and ultimate attainment in his inspired music.

Tyāgarāja is one of those artists and thinkers whose appeal transcends his own era and locale. Just as people around the world admire, appreciate, and learn from great souls and creative innovators like Shakespeare and Basho, Rumi and Rabia, Beethoven and → Tagore, Lincoln and → Gandhi, so also, Tyāgarāja has depths in his musical works that may be appreciated by people anywhere in the world. Through the Tyāgarāja festivals celebrated in America, Europe, and India, and through the many musical artists performing in India and abroad, through CDs and websites, books and films, Tyāgarāja's music endures as a thriving heritage. Each year the performing of *kṛti*s and *kīrtana*s in the Tyāgarāja traditions grows, and the audiences listening to them continue to expand. Appealing features of Tyāgarāja's songs include the catchiness of his tunes, the haunting mystery of heartfelt *dhvani* (overtone resonance of meanings and evocative moods), and the human values and high ideals expressed in his lyrics.

Bibliography

Bhagavatar, N.T., *Sadguru Tyāgarājasvāmi Kīrtanalu*, Madras, 1908.

Coomaraswamy, A.K., *Selected Papers*, vol. I, Princeton, 1977.

Goldman, R.P., ed., *The Rāmāyaṇa of Vālmīki: An Epic of Ancient India*, vol. I: *Bālākāṇḍa*, Princeton, 1984.

Jackson, W.J., *Tyagaraja: Life and Lyrics*, New Delhi, 2011.

Jackson, W.J., *Vijayanagara Voices: Exploring South Indian History and Hindu Literature*, Aldershot, 2005.

Jackson, W.J., *Tyagaraja and the Renewal of Tradition: Translations and Reflections*, New Delhi, 1994.

Pope, G.U., *The "Sacred Kurraḷ" of Tiruvaḷḷuva-Nāyanār*, London, 1886.

Rao, T.V.S., "The Universality of Tyagaraja," *JMAM* 14/3–4, 1943, 85–90.

Ramanujachari, C., & V., Raghavan, *The Spiritual Heritage of Tyagaraja*, Madras, 1981.

Sambamoorthy, P., *Great Composers Book II: Tyagaraja*, Madras, [2]1970.

Sambamoorthy, P., *Tyāgarāja's Prahlāda Bhakti Vijayam*, Tirupati, 1965.

Shastri, K.V., *Tyagaraja Keertanalu*, Madras, 1975.

Subbayya, M.V., *The Complete Kritis of Sri Thyagaraja: Compiled by Maddali Venkata Subbayya, Telugu Script with English Transliteration and Translation*, Hyderabad, 2008.

DVD

Leonard Bernstein: Reaching for the Note, dir. Susan Lacy, American Masters Series, released in 1998.

WILLIAM J. JACKSON

Vallabha

For historians of Hindu thought, Vallabha (1478–1530) – or, with his title *ācārya* (teacher), Vallabhācārya – is well known as a philosopher and religious leader within the Vaiṣṇava tradition. As a philosopher he created the Śuddhādvaita (pure monism; see → Vedānta) system of thought, and as a religious leader he established a sect or *sampradāya*, known from his name as the → Vallabha Sampradāya. But for the members of the Vallabha Sampradāya, Vallabha is much more than just a formulator of doctrines or a guide to religious observance. For them he is a savior sharing in the essence of → Kṛṣṇa the highest → *brahman* and supreme being. He set out the Puṣṭimārga (Way of Nourishing [Grace]) guide to the practice of → *bhakti*, and, most importantly, he revealed the *brahmasambandhamantra* (formula for contact with *brahman*) that makes it possible for the ordinary person to come into contact with Kṛṣṇa. As he was the link between the transcendental and the mundane, it was essential that the details of his life and activities be carefully preserved. Accordingly, narratives of Vallabha's life story have been produced within the Vallabha Sampradāya from the 16th century until the present. Until the mid-19th century, these narratives were the only accounts of Vallabha's life available. Although they purport to describe the events of Vallabha's life as they happened, these narratives contain that blend of the miraculous and the factual that defines them as hagiography rather than secular biography.

Vallabha in Hagiography and Autobiography

Vallabha's life as presented in the accounts composed by authors belonging to the Vallabha Sampradāya was meant to serve as a template for members of the sect in making their own lives suitable for progress on the Puṣṭimārga. So that the accounts would have the widest possible circulation, most of them were written in the Brajbhasha vernacular, which by the 16th century had become a major lingua franca in the North Indian *bhakti* movement. Three of these Brajbhasha hagiographies, *Caurāsī Vaiṣṇavan kī Vārtā* (Account of the Eighty-four Vaiṣṇavas), *Śrī Nāthajī Prākaṭya kī Vārtā* (Account of the Appearance of the Auspicious Lord), and *Caurāsī Baiṭhak Caritra* (Deeds at the Eighty-four Seats) have been especially influential in the sect. *Caurāsī Vaiṣṇavan kī Vārtā* is said to have been originally composed by Gokulnātha (1552–1641), a grandson of Vallabha. It was then commented upon and put into its present form by another descendant of Vallabha, Harirāya, who died in 1716. *Śrī Nāthajī Prākaṭya kī Vārtā* was written by Harirāya, and *Caurāsī Baiṭhak Caritra* is ascribed to Gokulnātha but has been reworked by a later author, perhaps by the same Harirāya. In addition to these Brajbhasha works, there are also hagiographies of Vallabha in Sanskrit, a language of limited social currency but immense religious prestige in the Vallabha Sampradāya as in Hinduism generally. The most authoritative of the Sanskrit hagiographies is *Śrīvallabhadigvijaya* (World Triumph of Vallabha), attributed to Yadunātha (1615–c. 1660), another of Vallabha's grandsons.

J. Timm sums up the nature and purpose of these sectarian hagiographies in these words:

> From the standpoint of the *sampradāya* Vallabha's story is not primarily a narrative about one historical, saintly embodiment of Krishna devotionalism, it is about relationship; and it designates a life pattern to be followed by every devotee. The story reads as an invitation to participate in a special form of life, the path of grace (*pushti mārga*), a positive and emphatic valuation of Vaiṣṇava devotionalism, a prescription to enter into an intimate relationship with Lord Krishna. (Timm, 2007, 5)

While a devotee may well seek in a narrative of Vallabha's activities a pattern to be followed in his or her own life for "an intimate relationship with Lord Krishna," this is not the objective of those with a secular interest in Vallabha's place in the history of Indian thought. Even with a religious, but nonsectarian, attitude, one may well not find the pious but patently implausible features of the hagiographical accounts attractive. Moreover, although the hagiographies can supply the outline of Vallabha's life story, the personality of the Vallabha they portray is definitely idealized. This idealization of a founder is not something restricted to Vallabha and the literature centered on him. Comparable circumstances caused Albert Schweitzer to search for Jesus of Nazareth not in the Jesus constructed by theologians but in the Jesus revealed in the sayings ascribed to him in the New Testament (Schweitzer, 2001, 480). J. Timm, who so accurately characterized the portrayal of Vallabha in the Vallabha Sampradāya, drew a conclusion about locating the nonidealized Vallabha that is similar to Albert Schweitzer's approach to Jesus. To quote J. Timm again,

> Who is Vallabha? To answer this question I do not propose to relate the biography or hagiography of that 15 th century philosopher/theologian who founded what continues to be an important religious community of Northern India. Instead I want to consider only Vallabha the author and the commentator. (Timm, 1993, 32)

Fortunately for those who want to find Vallabha in his own writings, there is no lack of material. Vallabha's voluminous philosophical and theological output is available in his five major works, all in Sanskrit:

1. *Subodhinī* (Good Perception), a commentary on parts of the *Bhāgavatapurāṇa*, especially those dealing with Kṛṣṇa's earthly incarnation among the cowherds of the Braj area around the city of Mathura;
2. *Aṇubhāṣya* (Exposition of the Subtle), a commentary on sections of the *Brahmasūtra* of Bādarāyaṇa (see → Sūtras);
3. *Tattvārthadīpanibandha* (Composition of a Lamp on the Meaning of Reality), an interpretation of primary Hindu scripture in the light of the principles of Śuddhādvaita;
4. *Tattvārthadīpanibandhaprakāśa* (Light on the *Tattvārthadīpanibandha*), Vallabha's commentary on his *Tattvārthadīpanibandha*;
5. *Ṣoḍaśagrantha* (Sixteen Books), a collection of 16 short treatises that elucidate key philosophical points of Vallabha's Śuddhādvaita and clarify matters of spiritual orientation necessary for following the Puṣṭimārga.

The approach to Vallabha's life through the sectarian hagiographies and the approach through Vallabha's works are not mutually exclusive, but complement each other remarkably well. Taken together they provide a balanced view of Vallabha's career. While the hagiographical accounts and Vallabha's compositions are complementary, they do not serve equally well as the point of departure for an examination of Vallabha's life. The hagiographies were written for an audience familiar from childhood with the basic concepts of the Puṣṭimārga. For that reason, they assume too much background knowledge of the Puṣṭimārga and its Vallabha Sampradāya milieu to be a suitable introduction to Vallabha's career. On the other hand, most of Vallabha's works are so deeply immersed in the philosophical traditions of Hinduism that they, too, cannot provide a good beginning for an inquiry into Vallabha's life. The one exception to this is the *Ṣoḍaśagrantha* collection of treatises by Vallabha. As F. Smith (2009, 29) observes about these treatises, most of them "were written for special occasions, usually a succinct treatment of a single doctrinal point after receiving a question from a disciple." In addition to this instructional focus, more than half of the compositions in *Ṣoḍaśagrantha* are narrated by Vallabha in the first person. This sort of narration, very unusual in the works of premodern Hindu scholars and philosophers, gives the reader a warm feeling of intimacy with the author. This intimacy is enhanced in a few of these brief writings by references made by Vallabha to his own personal experience. Such references are vivid enough to be considered autobiographical.

One of the treatises with an autobiographical tone is the third in the series, *Siddhāntamuktāvalī* (Necklace of Pearls of Doctrine). Not only is it evident from the content of that work that in it Vallabha is speaking from personal experience, but in its 21st and final verse, he informs the reader that in *Siddhāntamuktāvalī* he has explained the primary doctrine on which his thought is based:

> Thus have I explained the innermost essence of my teachings.
> By understanding this a person can be freed from all doubt. (*SiMĀv.* 21; trans. Redington, 2000, 30)

Since in *Siddhāntamuktāvalī* Vallabha sets out his fundamental doctrine clearly and transparently in autobiographical style, it is this work that best introduces Vallabha and makes the hagiographical account of his life, taken up below, intelligible and informative.

Vallabha's Fundamental Doctrine

The fundamental doctrine that is the essence of Vallabha's Śuddhādvaita philosophy and the principle at the heart of his Puṣṭimārga approach to *bhakti* is that Kṛṣṇa is himself both the cause and the substance of the universe. In Vallabha's view Kṛṣṇa expresses himself through three dimensions of perception as, simultaneously, the highest *brahman*, the impersonal (→ *nirguṇa*) *brahman* that is the ground of all being, and the physical universe in which we all live. In the pedagogical literature of the Vallabha Sampradāya, these three dimensions are denominated the *ādhidaivika*, the *ādhyātmika*, and the *ādhibhautika*, respectively (Barz, 1976, 14–15). Although Vallabha does not employ these three Sanskrit terms in *Siddhāntamuktāvalī*, they are implicit in his presentation there and are useful to highlight the import of that work.

The first of these terms, *ādhidaivika*, is an adjective formed from the noun *adhidaiva*, which consists of the prefix *adhi*, "from," and *daiva*, "divine." The definition of *adhidaiva* given in the Sanskrit–English dictionary of Sir Monier Monier-Williams (1899, 21), "the divine agent operating in material objects," is an apt guide to the meaning of the adjectival form *ādhidaivika* in the Vallabha Sampradāya. In Vallabha Sampradāya usage, *ādhidaivika* refers to that dimension of Kṛṣṇa in which he operates as the divine being in the universe or any of its components. Kṛṣṇa's *ādhidaivika* dimension is perceivable only under the impetus of exceptional *bhakti*.

Ādhyātmika, describing the second of the dimensions posited by Vallabha, is the adjectival form of the noun *adhyātma* (supreme spirit) made up of the same prefix *adhi* joined to → *ātman*, "self," "spirit," or "essence." *Ādhyātmika*, therefore, can be rendered into English as "spiritual" in the sense of "something which comes from the supreme spirit." In the terminology of the Puṣṭimārga, Kṛṣṇa's *ādhyātmika* dimension is himself as the inner nature or animating principle of the physical universe or any of its elements.

The third term, *ādhibhautika*, is an adjective derived from the prefix *adhi* with the verb root *bhū*-, "to come into being" or "to exist." *Ādhibhautika* can be defined in English as "material" but with the understanding that the full meaning is "something material which comes into being from a source." In Vallabha's thought, Kṛṣṇa's *ādhibhautika* dimension is the familiar material world, which he spins out of himself.

Although Vallabha deals with his concept of Kṛṣṇa perceived through three dimensions as the cause and substance of the universe in all the verses of *Siddhāntamuktāvalī*, he supplies his basic definition of the concept in the first nine verses of the treatise.

The first two verses of *Siddhāntamuktāvalī* are preliminary to Vallabha's discussion of his fundamental doctrine that Kṛṣṇa is both the cause and substance of the universe. In accord with his *bhakti* orientation, Vallabha proclaims in the first verse that the indispensable constituent (*viniścaya*), the *sine qua non*, of his doctrines is constant mental service (→ *sevā*) of Kṛṣṇa, whom he refers to here as Hari ("Remover [of Evil]"):

> Having bowed to Hari I will proclaim the settled meaning [*viniścaya*] of my doctrines: worship [*sevā*] of Krishna must be performed always, and mental worship is the highest type. (*SiMĀv*. 1; trans. Redington, 2000, 26)

By *sevā* Vallabha is referring to the daily service or adoration of an inherent form (*svarūpa*) of Kṛṣṇa that appears to mundane eyes as an image in a temple of the Vallabha Sampradāya or in the household shrine of a member of the sect. *Sevā* is the indispensable constituent of Vallabha's doctrines because through it the emotions (*bhāvas*) of the devotee are so intently focused on Kṛṣṇa that the devotee's own ego is entirely forgotten. Oblivious to the ego, the devotee is able to admit the → grace of Kṛṣṇa into himself or herself and so can attain experience as a part of the cosmic play (→ *līlā*) of Kṛṣṇa. This experience is the essence (*rasa*) of Vallabha's *bhakti* and the goal of the Puṣṭimārga. In its perfection, according to Vallabha, *sevā* is mental and penetrates into the mind to the point that it is ever present there. Vallabha considered *sevā* to be inseparable from *bhakti*, and it has remained the central principle of individual and communal practice in the Vallabha Sampradāya until the present day (Entwistle, 1993, 85–87).

In the second verse, Vallabha assures those reading or listening to *Siddhāntamuktāvalī* that if one performs *sevā* of Kṛṣṇa with one's mind, body, and wealth directed entirely to him, then one's suffering in worldly life (→ *saṃsāra*) will cease, and one will come to a realization of *brahman* (see also Smith, 2011, 186):

> Worship [*sevā*] (is defined as) the mind's being completely intent on him. To accomplish that, (one performs worship) with both body and possessions.
> The end of Samsara's suffering, as well as awakening to Brahman, come (as by-products) of this. (*SiMĀv.* 2; trans. Redington, 2000, 26)

In the third verse, Vallabha expounds on the relationship of Kṛṣṇa and *brahman* and their connection with the universe. It is in this verse that he begins to explain his theory of Kṛṣṇa's presence in the universe through the three dimensions of perception:

> But the Highest Brahman [*parabrahman*] is Krishna alone. And the Great [*bṛhat*] (Brahman) has Being [*sat*], Consciousness [*cit*], and, as it were, limited Joy [*ānandaka*].
> For the Great (Brahman) has two aspects: it may be (conceived of as) all, or as one, separate from that (all). (*SiMĀv.* 3; trans. Redington, 2000, 26)

Here Vallabha first identifies Kṛṣṇa, the one personal god, as the highest *brahman*. Vallabha's identification of the highest *brahman* as Kṛṣṇa is solidly within mainstream Vaiṣṇava theology. In the primary Vaiṣṇava *bhakti* scripture, the → *Bhagavadgītā*, usually dated to around 150 BCE, Kṛṣṇa says plainly about himself,

> For I am the foundation of Brahman,
> The immortal and imperishable,/And of the eternal right,
> And of absolute bliss. (*BhG.* 14.27; trans. Edgerton, 1964, 72)

Just as in the *Bhagavadgītā brahman* is founded on Kṛṣṇa, so in the theology of the Puṣṭimārga the highest *brahman* is the *ādhidaivika* dimension of Kṛṣṇa.

Next, Vallabha qualifies *brahman* as the great. In using the Sanskrit word for "great," *bṛhat*, as a synonym for *brahman*, he is etymologically accurate since the word *brahman* derives from the Sanskrit verbal root *bṛh-*, "to grow great or strong." Vallabha further declares that the great *brahman* is made up of existence (*sat*), consciousness (*cit*), and limited joy (*ānandaka*). The great *brahman*, which is called *akṣara* (imperishable) *brahman* in the literature of the Vallabha Sampradāya (Harishankarji, 1940, 114–115), is the impersonal entity that is within all existence and is the origin of all existence. For those who follow the Puṣṭimārga, *akṣara brahman* is the *ādhyātmika* dimension of Kṛṣṇa.

The idea that *brahman* is both the source and the substance of the universe is not unique to Vallabha but is very ancient in Hindu philosophy. For example, in the *Kaṭhopaniṣad*, composed in the last few centuries before the Common Era, this idea was already evident in the statement that *brahman* is within the living beings of the universe, "those who sleep," and that on *brahman* "all the worlds rest":

> This person, creating every desire,
> who lies awake within those who sleep;
> That alone is the Pure! That is *brahman*!
> That alone is called the Immortal!
> On it all the worlds rest;
> beyond it no one can ever pass. (*KaṭhU.* 5.8; trans. Olivelle, 1996, 243)

Vallabha goes on in verse 3 to maintain that the great or *akṣara brahman* has two aspects. The first aspect is the all, the universe and everything that it contains. In Vallabha Sampradāya terms, this is the universe as Kṛṣṇa's *ādhibhautika* dimension. The second aspect is the one, separate from the all, already described as the *ādhyātmika* dimension of Kṛṣṇa. In other words, the great *brahman* is manifest as the multifarious universe of being, some of which is matter and only exists while another part exists and is conscious as animal life, and still another part is made up of human beings who exist, are conscious, and, to a limited degree, are able to feel joy. At one and the same time, the great *brahman* is also a single, distinct entity consisting of existence, consciousness, and limited joy.

Vallabha is by no means alone among Hindu thinkers in seeing *brahman* as consisting of a spectrum extending from existence through consciousness to joy (*ānanda*). Joy – not characterized as limited – has been associated with *brahman* since at least the 5th century BCE, when that association was made in *Taittirīyopaniṣad* 3.6 (see Olivelle, 1997, 169). Vallabha's opinion that the joy of *brahman* is limited does, however, seem to be a view particular to his thought. Vallabha postulates that the joy of the great *brahman* is limited and that the limitation of joy is the prime difference between Kṛṣṇa's *ādhyātmika* dimension as great *brahman* and his full, *ādhidaivika* dimension as himself as highest *brahman*. For instance, in the 11th verse of *Siddhāntamuktāvalī*, Vallabha states that only Kṛṣṇa has complete or supreme joy (Redington, 2000, 28).

Vallabha's life was not passed in a time of philosophical stagnation. On the contrary, it was a period of great ferment in religious and intellectual circles. One of the striking characteristics of Vallabha's age was the sponsoring by kings and other social and political leaders of philosophical debates at which representatives of the various schools of thought could contend. Among the philosophical schools contemporary with him, Vallabha was firmly allied with the Vaiṣṇavas who practiced *bhakti* directed toward → Viṣṇu, → Rāma, Kṛṣṇa, or one of the other personal deities related to them. The Vaiṣṇava schools of his day included followers of the qualified nondualism (Viśiṣṭādvaita; see → Vedānta) associated with → Rāmānuja (died c. 1137), adherents of the dualism (Dvaita) of Madhva (c. 1238–c. 1317; see → Mādhva Sampradāya), supporters of the dualism-nondualism (Dvaitādvaita) of Nimbārka (13th century; see → Nimbārka Sampradāya), and followers of the obscure philosopher Viṣṇusvāmi (c. 13th century) whose philosophical doctrines are uncertain, though evidently concerned with the Vaiṣṇava deity Narasiṃha (Colas, 2005, 254).

Along with the other Vaiṣṇavas, Vallabha was, in particular, the ideological opponent of the followers of the nondualism (Advaita) taught by the 8th-century philosopher → Śaṅkara. The basic point of difference was that the Vaiṣṇavas saw the universe as the product of the supreme being and therefore as sharing in the reality of the supreme being, while those who belonged to Śaṅkara's school saw the universe as unreal and the absolute entity *brahman* as the only reality. For them the influence of illusion (→ *māyā*) causes the human mind to misinterpret the unity of *brahman* as the multiplicity of the universe. Vallabha claimed that the followers of Advaita were not really nondualists since they accepted *māyā*, though intrinsically unreal, as something apart from *brahman*. Because of this supposed acceptance of *māyā*, the followers of Vallabha call followers of Śaṅkara *māyāvādīs* (advocates of illusion). In contradistinction to Advaita philosophy, Vallabha called his philosophy Śuddhādvaita because it recognized Kṛṣṇa as the only ultimate reality and was, therefore, pure (*śuddha*) nondualism. Vallabha accepted *māyā* but not as something unreal or different from Kṛṣṇa. For him *māyā* is Kṛṣṇa's power (*śakti*) with which he projects the universe out of himself.

Considering the major role played by philosophical debate in his social environment, it is not surprising that in verse 4 of *Siddhāntamuktāvalī* Vallabha contrasts the doctrines on the nature of the universe held in four rival philosophical schools with what, in the first line of verse 5, he declares is the teaching of the → Vedas on the subject. This teaching is identical to his own doctrine that the great *brahman* is the manifest universe, thus validating his doctrine with the irrefutable authority that the Vedas have in Hinduism:

> Regarding the first aspect (the all), philosophers have expressed many different teachings which are other (than the Vedas): (describing it) as a product of illusion; as a result merely of the combination of the three constituents; as an effect; as an independent reality; and in many other ways. (*SiMĀv.* 4; trans. Redington, 2000, 26–27)
>
> But the Vedas teach that that (Great Brahman) alone takes the form of this (all). (*SiMĀv.* 5a; trans. Redington, 2000, 27)

Vallabha has the followers of Śaṅkara in mind when he criticizes those who see the universe "as a product of illusion." J. Redington (2000, 34) identifies those who aver that the universe is "a result merely of the combination of the three constituents" as supporters of the → Sāṃkhya school of philosophy, those who describe it "as an effect" as followers of the → Vaiśeṣika school, and those who see the universe "as an independent reality" as advocates of the Pūrvamīmāṃsā (→ Mīmāṃsā) system of thought.

In the second line of verse 5 and in verse 6, Vallabha explains how Kṛṣṇa is the substance of the universe. In these verses he provides a tangible illustration of this doctrine in the two ways that the → Gaṅgā River can be perceived. In general perception, the river is merely a stream of water, but in the sight of a devout Hindu, it is also a font of sacredness and spiritual cleansing. Like the first perception of the Gaṅgā is the comprehension of the great *brahman* as the universe and like the other perception is the realization that the great *brahman* is a sacred entity both within and beyond the universe. Or, to use the language of the Puṣṭimārga, when one sees the Gaṅgā as no more than material water, one is looking at the *ādhibhautika* river, a part of Kṛṣṇa's *ādhibhautika* dimension, and when one bathes in the Gaṅgā for spiritual cleansing in accordance with Hindu scriptural law (*maryādāmārga*), one is perceiving the *ādhyātmika* river within Kṛṣṇa's *ādhyātmika* dimension. In his *ādhibhautika* dimension, Kṛṣṇa is the substance of the universe, and in his *ādhyātmika* dimension, he animates it:

> Further, we should understand the two aspects (of Great Brahman) in the same way we understand the Ganges. For in one aspect the Ganges is simply water, (*SiMĀv.* 5b; trans. Redington, 2000, 27)
> But (in the other) it is endowed with special sacredness and grants enjoyment and liberation [*mukti*] to those who worship it according to the law of the Path of Limitations [*maryādāmārga*]. We should understand Brahman, too, in the same way. (*SiMĀv.* 6; trans. Redington, 2000, 27)

In verses 7 and 8, Vallabha proceeds with his analogy of the Gaṅgā to take up the river's *ādhidaivika* dimension and to describe the role of *bhakti* in making that dimension apparent:

> Through devotion [*bhakti*], one occasionally catches sight of the Goddess, who abides in the very water.
> She is visible, especially in the Ganges, to the one who realizes her identity with the waters. (*SiMĀv.* 7; trans. Redington, 2000, 27–28)
> She is not visible to all, yet it is through her that Ganges-water has the power of fulfilling all one's excellent desires.
> For the sight of her, with even the mind's eye, surpasses the rewards specified by the scriptures. (*SiMĀv.* 8; trans. Redington, 2000, 28)

In these verses Vallabha reveals that the Gaṅgā has a divine, *ādhidaivika*, dimension as a goddess beyond its material, *ādhibhautika*, dimension as a river and its spiritual, *ādhyātmika*, dimension as a source of sacredness. The Gaṅgā's *ādhidaivika* dimension is generally hidden from observers but can be perceived, though very rarely, through *bhakti*. Such an epiphany of the goddess Gaṅgā and the benefit it bestows is, according to Vallabha, far beyond the compass of the scriptures and their rewards. It is the *ādhidaivika* dimension of the Gaṅgā that enables the river's *ādhyātmika* dimension to grant fulfillment and freedom to human worshippers.

In verse 9 Vallabha brings his explanation to a conclusion by demonstrating how Kṛṣṇa in his *ādhidaivika* dimension is the cause of the universe. The material water of the Gaṅgā, he says, is like the universe. That is, both are part of the *ādhibhautika* dimension of Kṛṣṇa. Similarly, the sacred power of the Gaṅgā and the great *brahman* in the universe both belong to Kṛṣṇa's *ādhyātmika* dimension. Finally, when one has perceived the goddess in the Gaṅgā, then one has acquired experience of the *ādhidaivika* dimension of Kṛṣṇa in his universe:

> As is that water, so is this all; as is the Ganges' sacred power, so is the Great (Brahman);
> as is the Goddess, so is Krishna... (*SiMĀv.* 9; trans. Redington, 2000, 28)

Just as the goddess Gaṅgā as related in verse 8 is the cause of the sacred power of the *ādhyātmika* dimension that pervades the *ādhibhautika* river, so is Kṛṣṇa in his *ādhidaivika* dimension the cause through his *ādhyātmika* dimension of his *ādhibhautika* dimension as the universe.

Vallabha's Life

Vallabha's elucidation of Kṛṣṇa's three dimensions in the first nine verses of *Siddhāntamuktāvalī* gives the key to the unlocking of the meaning of Vallabha's life as it is presented in the sectarian hagiographies. The hagiographies also portray Vallabha's life in three dimensions, only one of which is the *ādhibhautika* dimension of ordinary biography. These three dimensions of Vallabha's life are apparent in six important episodes: his birth in 1478, his reception of the *brahmasambandhamantra* in 1494, his installation of Kṛṣṇa's preeminent *svarūpa* Śrī Nāthjī ("Auspicious Lord") and initiation of organized *sevā* also in 1494, his marriage in either 1502 or 1504, his participation in philosophical debates culminating in the debate at Vijāyanagara in around 1509, and his death in 1530.

The following discussion of each of these episodes of Vallabha's life is based on the hagiographical narratives in Brajbhasha and Sanskrit, mainly the ones listed above. The story of Vallabha's life as it is told in the hagiographies is more or less the same in general outline but is by no means systematized or standardized and may differ in detail from account to account. These variations in detail usually pertain only to the description of an episode at the *ādhibhautika* level. There is normally little or no difference in the *ādhyātmika* and *ādhidaivika* representation of events. Unless otherwise noted, all dates in the following episodes have been converted to the Common Era.

Birth

The story of Vallabha's birth begins long before he was actually born. Appropriately for a person who was born into a family steeped in traditional Hindu learning (Smith, 2009, 31), Vallabha's birth is rooted in the Vedas. Of the four Vedas, the *Yajurveda* deals with the correct recitation of formulaic sacred texts (*mantras*) accompanied by ritual actions in the performance of vedic sacrifices by Brahman priests. There are two versions of the *Yajurveda*, the older of which is called the Black *Yajurveda*. The Black *Yajurveda* is further divided into schools, one of which is the *Taittirīya*. Vallabha was born into a lineage of south Indian Tailang Brahmans adhering to the *Taittirīya* school of the Black *Yajurveda*. An ancestor of Vallabha had so pleased Kṛṣṇa that the deity himself had appeared to that ancestor and announced that he would take incarnation (→ *avatāra*) in his lineage as soon as his descendants had performed the *soma* ritual (see → *yajña*) a hundred times. The *soma* ritual, an offering of the holy *soma* plant (see → intoxication) to the major → vedic gods including Agni, is the most important of all vedic sacrifices (Witzel, 2005, 74).

It was Vallabha's father Lakṣmaṇa Bhaṭṭa, staunchly loyal to the orthodox Brahmanical tradition of his lineage, who performed the last five *soma* rituals needed to bring the tally up to the requisite number of one hundred. Shortly after Lakṣmaṇa Bhaṭṭa had completed the fifth *soma* ritual, Kṛṣṇa came to him in a dream and assured him that he would take human form as his son. From the standpoint of a follower of Vallabha's Puṣṭimārga, the occurrence of Vallabha's birth as the result of the performance of one hundred *soma* rituals is the *ādhyātmika* dimension of his physical, *ādhibhautika* birth, and the fact that he was born an incarnation of Kṛṣṇa is its *ādhidaivika* dimension.

Moved by a strong inclination to devote himself to religious study and travel, Lakṣmaṇa Bhaṭṭa had settled in Varanasi with his wife Illammāgārū, daughter of a priest serving the ruler of the → Vijayanagara kingdom in South India. At this time the political situation in the Varanasi region was disturbed. Bahlūl Lodī, sultan of Delhi from 1451 to 1489, was locked in a struggle with Husain Shāh of Jaunpur (r. 1458–1479), and there was fear in Varanasi that an attack would be made on the city in this time of political upheaval. In order to avoid these hazardous conditions, Lakṣmaṇa Bhaṭṭa and Illammāgārū (who was in the last months of pregnancy) fled to the south. As they were passing in the middle of the night through the heavily forested Campāraṇya region of what is now Raipur district in Chhattisgarh, Illammāgārū gave birth to a baby boy prematurely. Since the infant was to all appearances stillborn, Lakṣmaṇa Bhaṭṭa wrapped him in leaves and left him under a *śamī* tree (bot. Acacia suma). The date was Thursday the 11th day of the waning half of the month of *vaiśākha* (Apr–May) in the year 1535 of the Vikrama Era.

Each of the hagiographies is quite precise about the year of Vallabha's birth, with most of them putting it in 1535 of the Vikrama Era. Even when 1535 Vikrama Era is accepted, there are differences of opinion about the month in which the birth occurred, and discrepancies come in the conversion of the Vikrama Era year to a Common Era date (Timm, 2007, 5). Some authorities have followed H. von Glasenapp (1962, 193) in making 1479 CE the year of the philosopher's birth, while others have calculated the Common Era date to be 1478 (Vaudeville, 1980, 20; Snatak, 1992, 3). The degree of uncertainty about the Common Era date of Vallabha's birth can be gauged from one scholar's statement that he has accepted 1479 "because it seems to fit in with the rest of Vallabha's life better" (Parekh, 1943, 3).

That night both Illammāgārū and her husband had dreams in which Kṛṣṇa informed them that he had just taken birth in their family. Inspired by this dream, early on the next morning, Illammāgārū and Lakṣmaṇa Bhaṭṭa went back to the *śamī* tree. There they were both overjoyed and astounded to find not only that their child was not dead but also that he was playing happily in the midst of a blazing, protective fire. When Illammāgārū approached, the fire withdrew so that she could pick the child up, and as she did so, a disembodied voice proclaimed in Sanskrit that the mouth of the supreme being had been incarnated in the baby.

The *Śrīvallabhadigvijaya* and many of the other hagiographies relate this story of the stillbirth of Vallabha followed by his miraculous appearance alive in circle of fire in the forest of Campāraṇya on the eastern side of India. Others, like *Śrī Nāthajī Prākaṭya kī Vārtā* (Vaudeville, 1980, 20, 29), say nothing about a birth in Campāraṇya and assert instead that the infant Vallabha appeared out of the Agnikuṇḍ ("Pool of Fire") near Mathura in Uttar Pradesh in western India. As is typically the case in the hagiographies, the difference in the birth stories is only in terms of the *ādhibhautika* dimension, here the geographical location of the birth. There is no disagreement in the *ādhyātmika* dimension of Vallabha's birth. All of the accounts agree that his birth was associated with *ādhyātmika* fire that guarded him after his birth in one group of narratives and exuded him from the depths of its pool in the other group. The *ādhidaivika* dimension of Vallabha's birth, that he was the incarnation not just of Kṛṣṇa but specifically of his mouth, is also not disputed in the hagiographies.

While the secular point of view sees the location of Vallabha's birth as a matter that must be established with as much precision as possible, the sectarian viewpoint can tolerate vagueness on the location of the birth but requires absolute consensus about the birth's *ādhyātmika* and *ādhidaivika* dimensions. The association of *ādhyātmika* fire with Vallabha's *ādhidaivika* birth as the incarnation of Kṛṣṇa's mouth is of crucial importance for his role as savior for his followers. In the theology of the Puṣṭimārga, Kṛṣṇa's mouth is both the source of speech and the receptacle of *ādhyātmika* fire. This is the same *ādhyātmika* fire that in vedic ritual conveys a sacrificed substance from the *ādhibhautika* human world to the *ādhidaivika* plane of being, where the gods dwell. Vallabha, as the earthly manifestation of the transubstantiating fire of Kṛṣṇa's mouth, can through his words offer to his followers the possibility of translation from the *ādhibhautika* to the *ādhidaivika* plane of existence (Barz, 1976, 22). In his birth as described in the *Śrīvallabhadigvijaya* set of hagiographies, Vallabha himself, from the standpoint of a practitioner of the Puṣṭimārga, is the prototype of this translation. He is born dead in the middle of the night in the world of *ādhibhautika* perception and by morning has been restored to life with the protection of *ādhyātmika* fire in his *ādhidaivika* identity as the *avatāra* of Kṛṣṇa's mouth.

Soon after Vallabha's birth, Lakṣmaṇa Bhaṭṭa and Illammāgārū learned that the danger in Varanasi had passed. They returned to that city with their infant son, whom they had named Vallabha ("Beloved"). Settled again in Varanasi, Lakṣmaṇa Bhaṭṭa was anxious to provide Vallabha with the best possible orthodox Brahman education. He arranged for him to have the finest teachers that he could find. While still quite young, Vallabha, according to the hagiographical accounts, had already acquired familiarity with the Vedas, the Śāstras (scriptures), and the → Purāṇas (legendary histories). Of the latter he was especially learned in the *Bhāgavatapurāṇa*.

The claim that Vallabha had a profound grasp of the Vedas, Śāstras, and Purāṇas is not a matter of hagiographical exaggeration, but is verified by the outstanding scholarship of Vallabha's own writings. To take only one example, as pointed out by F. Smith (2004, 112), *Jalabheda* (Difference of Waters), the twelfth of the treatises in *Ṣoḍaśagrantha*, is based in form on a text belonging to the Black *Yajurveda*, the *Taittirīya saṃhitā* 7.4.13. In both works the kinds of water associated with different watercourses – canals, ditches, lakes, ponds, and so on – are enumerated. In the *Taittirīya saṃhitā* passage, this enumeration identifies the various kinds of water to be offered into the fire during the horse sacrifice (*aśvamedha*; see → *yajña*) ritual, while in Vallabha's treatise, a *bhakti* connotation is provided for each of the same kinds of water. The way that Vallabha exercises his scholarly virtuosity in reinterpreting the *Taittirīya saṃhitā* text to suit his own theological purposes can be seen by comparing the following two *Taittirīya saṃhitā* verses with the corresponding verses in *Jalabheda*. Where the *Taittirīya saṃhitā* has "To those of canals [*kūlyā*] hail!" (Smith, 2004, 113), *Jalabheda* 3 has "Narrators of Purāṇas (*paurāṇika*) are described as canals (*kulya*), connected by tradition to their source in the ground" (Smith, 2004, 115). Where the *Taittirīya saṃhitā* has "To those of the lakes [*hṛdya*], hail!" (Smith, 2004, 113), *Jalabheda* 5 has "Now, those scholars (*paṇḍita*) who keep the *śāstra* that describes the Lord uppermost in their minds are called lakes (*hrada*)" (Smith, 2004, 118).

Reception of the Brahmasambandhamantra

Vallabha is said to have embarked, with his parents, on the first of his three major pilgrimage tours around India when he was only 10 or 11 years of age. In the course of this tour, his father died in 1490 at Tirupati in Andhra Pradesh. Vallabha traveled on with his mother to Vijayanagara (today Hampi) in Karnataka. There Illammāgārū settled in the house of her brother, and Vallabha proceeded alone on an extended visit to the holy places of India. If we believe the hagiographies, Vallabha at this young age was already disputing with the *māyāvādī*s about the nature of *brahman* and giving public discourses on the meaning of the *Bhāgavatapurāṇa* at the various sacred centers he visited.

In the latter part of the year 1493, while still in southern India, Vallabha received instructions from Kṛṣṇa in a dream to go immediately to Govardhan ("Cow-Increasing") Hill, an outlier of the Aravalli range to the west of Mathura in the Braj region, where a divine image had appeared many years before. It was Govardhan Hill that Kṛṣṇa, during his incarnation on earth as described in *Bhāgavatapurāṇa* 10.25, had lifted up and held aloft on the hand of his left arm to shelter the people of Braj from torrential rain sent by the vedic god Indra. Kṛṣṇa identified the divine image as his own *svarūpa* and directed Vallabha to establish the *svarūpa* so that it could be offered proper *sevā*.

Although Vallabha departed for Govardhan Hill at once, the difficult traveling conditions of the time delayed his progress. It was not until the middle of the next year that he reached the town of Gokul on the bank of the → Yamunā River a few kilometers south of Mathura. There, at midnight on the 11th day of the waxing half of the month of *śrāvaṇa* (Jul–Aug), Kṛṣṇa again showed himself to Vallabha in a vision. In *Siddhāntarahasya* (The Secret of the Doctrine), another autobiographical treatise in *Ṣoḍaśagrantha*, Vallabha reports what transpired during this vision:

> At midnight on the eleventh day of Shravana's bright half, the Blessed Lord [*bhagavān*] himself appeared before my eyes.
> And what He proclaimed to me then I repeat here, word for word. (*SiRa*. 1; trans. Redington, 2000, 64)

The most important part of what Kṛṣṇa proclaimed to Vallabha that night was the *brahmasambandhamantra*, which consists of the Sanskrit phrase *śrī kṛṣṇa śaraṇam mama* ("the auspicious Kṛṣṇa is my refuge"). By this → *mantra* the soul (*jīva*) can be cleansed of the flaws (*doṣa*s) that are inherent in its human nature and, according to Śuddhādvaita philosophy, eternally and absolutely separate it from Kṛṣṇa. The primordial flaw from which all other faults flow is the egotism on account of which every *jīva* is convinced that it is an independent and distinct individual. This egotism blocks the *jīva* from the realization that in fact it, along with everything else in the universe, is a fragment of Kṛṣṇa. Without that realization the *jīva* is impervious to Kṛṣṇa's grace. Since the *brahmasambandhamantra* is inefficacious at liberating a *jīva* from *doṣa*s unless it is received from Kṛṣṇa's mouth incarnated as Vallabha, it could not be made public and so exposed to misuse. For this reason, Vallabha did not include the *brahmasambandhamantra* in what he reported in *Siddhāntarahasya*. The portion of what Kṛṣṇa proclaimed that Vallabha could openly state in writing was what members of his Sampradāya would understand as the effect of the correctly received *brahmasambandhamantra*. Vallabha discusses this effect in the last two verses of the treatise in words that are presented as directly quoted from what Kṛṣṇa said to him:

> Just like the well known practice of servants [*sevaka*] in the world, so my servants should first offer everything to Me,
> and then do what is needed. By (doing) that all become Brahman. (*SiRa*. 7b-8a; trans. Redington, 2000, 64)
> Just as all faulty things [*doṣa*] become Ganges (upon entering it), and just as it is relevant to discuss their virtues,
> defects [*doṣa*] and so forth before they enter the Ganges, but not after, the case is precisely the same here. (*SiRa*. 8b; trans. Redington, 2000, 65)

Members of the Vallabha Sampradāya would be aware that the phrase "my servants (*sevaka*) should first offer everything to Me" in the first of these verses alludes to the *brahmasambandhamantra* that Vallabha was given by Kṛṣṇa but did not publish. In receiving the *brahmasambandhamantra*, one takes refuge in Kṛṣṇa, entrusting body and possessions to him, and becomes his servant. The verse goes on to state that such a servant of Kṛṣṇa should "do what is needed." This phrase means that the servant of Kṛṣṇa should perform the *sevā* that is needed for *bhakti*. The servants of Kṛṣṇa who offer everything to him and do his *sevā* are then informed that they will become *brahman*. This harks back to the promise made in verse 2 of *Siddhāntamuktāvalī*, quoted above, that a person who with body and possessions performs *sevā* of Kṛṣṇa will awaken to *brahman*. In the ideology of the Puṣṭimārga, a man or woman who has dedicated everything to Kṛṣṇa in order to be his wholehearted servant performing *sevā* of him will be freed from egotism to awaken to participation in Kṛṣṇa's *ādhidaivika* dimension as the highest *brahman*.

In the second verse, Vallabha, as he did in *Siddhāntamuktāvalī*, uses the Gaṅgā River to illustrate how the person who has given everything to Kṛṣṇa is freed from the *doṣa* of egotism. Just as all *doṣa*s are obliterated in the cleansing sacredness of the *ādhyātmika* Gaṅgā, so are all *doṣa*s, including egotism, in precisely the same way expunged from the *jīva* who is in touch with Kṛṣṇa. Every follower of the Puṣṭimārga knows that only through receiving the *brahmasambandhamantra* can a *jīva* be in touch with Kṛṣṇa.

Vallabha was not alone when he arrived in Gokul but was accompanied by a companion named Dāmodaradāsa Harsānī. On the morning after obtaining the *brahmasambandhamantra* from Kṛṣṇa, Vallabha administered it to Dāmodaradāsa Harsānī, thus initiating both the first member of the Vallabha Sampradāya and the Vallabha Sampradāya itself.

Installation of Śrī Nāthjī

The image that Vallabha was to establish as Kṛṣṇa's *svarūpa* had appeared on Govardhan Hill in the year 1409 as an erect stone. Because this stone had a cobra-like appearance and was first noticed on the day sacred to snakes (*nāgpañcamī*), local people assumed that it was the image of a serpent deity and worshipped it as such. Sixty-nine years later, at exactly the same moment that Illammāgārū was giving birth to Vallabha in Campāraṇya far to the west, the stone rose farther out of the ground. The newly risen part of the stone was discovered to be a human head with a clearly defined mouth. In a vision Kṛṣṇa appeared as Śrī Govardhananāthjī ("Auspicious Lord of Govardhan") to a local man named Saḍḍūpāṇḍe and revealed to him that the image on Govardhan Hill was not a serpent deity but was his own *svarūpa* with arm raised to hold Govardhan Hill as a shelter for the people of Braj. He commanded Saḍḍūpāṇḍe to provide a regular offering of milk to the *svarūpa*.

When Vallabha arrived at Govardhan Hill, he made his way to the house of Saḍḍūpāṇḍe. There he heard the story of the *svarūpa* of Śrī Govardhananāthjī, later known familiarly as Śrī Nāthjī in the Vallabha Sampradāya, and ascended the hill to pay homage to the *svarūpa*. Vallabha then had a small shrine built on Govardhan Hill and installed Śrī Nāthjī in it. He initiated a local ascetic, Rāmdās Cauhān, with the *brahmasambandhamantra* and entrusted to him the performance of *sevā* for Śrī Nāthjī. At that time the *sevā* was quite simple, consisting of Rāmdās Cauhān's bathing the *svarūpa*, dressing it in garments that were comfortable and attractive, and then offering it pure, uncontaminated vegetarian food. Offerings of dairy products were accepted from local devotees. Later a much more impressive temple, called a *havelī* (mansion), was constructed for Śrī Nāthjī, and the *sevā* was refined and made more elaborate. Throughout the history of the Vallabha Sampradāya, Vallabha's fundamental dictum established at the installation of Śrī Nāthjī has been upheld: the *svarūpa* of Śrī Nāthjī is not an image or statue but is Śrī Nāthjī himself and, therefore, must be treated with the care and consideration due to a manifest deity. Over time, many *svarūpa*s have been revealed in the Vallabha Sampradāya. All of them are considered to be forms of Kṛṣṇa manifest, though Śrī Nāthjī retains preeminence. Political instability in the Braj area in the last quarter of the 17th century made relocation of Śrī Nāthjī's *havelī* imperative, and a move was made to the town of Singhāṛ, subsequently renamed Nathdwara, in Rajasthan. The *svarūpa* has remained there ever since (Saha, 2007, 304).

The manifestation of Śrī Nāthjī's mouth out of Govardhan Hill at the same time that Vallabha, the *avatāra* of Kṛṣṇa's mouth, was born is of great significance in the Vallabha Sampradāya. From the sectarian perspective, Śrī Nāthjī and Vallabha are not divisible. They are to be taken together as the manifestation of Kṛṣṇa's *ādhidaivika* dimension in the *ādhibhautika* world. Vallabha provides the *brahmasambandhamantra* essential as the first step in reestablishing the *jīva*'s relationship to Kṛṣṇa as a part to the whole, and Śrī Nāthjī is the necessary recipient of the *sevā* vital for the transformation of the *bhāva*s of the devotee into the *rasa* that is the culmination of that relationship.

Marriage

As provider of the *brahmasambandhamantra*, Vallabha was the mainstay of the sect he had founded. The *brahmasambandhamantra* could only be administered by him as the *ādhibhautika* manifestation of the *ādhidaivika* mouth of Kṛṣṇa. But Vallabha as a part of the *ādhibhautika* world was doomed to die. Without him the Vallabha Sampradāya would wither away for want of new initiates. The solution to this dilemma of sectarian survival came on Vallabha's second tour around India.

Between 1501 and 1503, Vallabha visited Pandharpur in southern → Maharashtra in order to show his respect for the form of Kṛṣṇa worshipped there as Viṭṭhala, also known as Viṭhobā. While there, Vallabha received a command from the god, always called Viṭṭhalanātha in the sectarian literature (Shyam Das, 1985, 52), to marry. In obedience to the divine order, Vallabha suspended his pilgrimage, returned to Vijayanagara to get his mother, and went with her to Varanasi, where in either 1502 or 1504 he married a girl of his caste named Mahālakṣmī. As Mahālakṣmī was still immature at the time of the wedding, she and Vallabha did not begin to live together until around 1511. Mahālakṣmī and Vallabha had two sons, Gopinātha (1512–1543) and Viṭṭhalanātha (1516–1586). The second son was named in honor of the god at Pandharpur who had instigated Vallabha's marriage.

The most important effect of Vallabha's marriage was that through it the dilemma of sectarian survival was solved. Vallabha was the *ādhibhautika* dimension of the divine mouth, and his sons, as sharers in his *ādhibhautika* flesh, also partook of his nature as the *ādhibhautika* dimension of Kṛṣṇa's mouth. Consequently, every man born in Vallabha's agnate line has the capacity to administer the *brahmasambandhamantra* and so initiate new members into the Vallabha Sampradāya. Although Gopinātha's line died out, Viṭṭhalanātha had seven biological sons and one adopted son. Viṭṭhalanātha eventually inherited the leadership of the Vallabha Sampradāya, and at his death sectarian leadership devolved through each of his sons and then through his grandsons and so on down through the generations. As a result, today the Vallabha Sampradāya has spread all over India and out into the world with a great many *havelīs*, each a center of *sevā* to a *svarūpa* of Kṛṣṇa in the care of a direct descendant of Vallabha in the male line. While the descendant of Viṭṭhalanātha's eldest son who is responsible for Śrī Nāthjī's *havelī* at Nathdwara has a certain seniority in the sect, the Vallabha Sampradāya has no organizational unity, and the leader or *mahārāj* of each *havelī* is autonomous.

The Vallabha Sampradāya is unusual among Hindu religious organizations both in having a leadership that is passed down by biological descent rather than from teacher (→ *guru*) to disciple (*celā*) and in having no celibate order of renouncers (*saṃnyāsīs*). These two features are, no doubt, a result of Vallabha's marriage and the example he set for his followers by marrying. There is also considerable evidence from Vallabha's own writing that his uninterest in institutionalized celibacy came as much from his personal understanding of the successful practice of *bhakti* as from his own conviction that he had been divinely commanded to marry. In verses 3 to 6 of *Saṃnyāsanirṇaya* (Consideration of Renunciation), another of his treatises in *Ṣoḍaśagrantha*, Vallabha is very forthright in proclaiming that it is not desirable to renounce in order to succeed in the nine steps of *bhakti* – hearing about the lord, praising and remembering him, attendance at his feet, worship and singing of him, serving him, being his friend, and offering oneself to him – given in the *Bhāgavatapurāṇa* (7.5.23; see Redington, 2000, 22). He is even more outspoken when he goes on to say that those who renounce the world both cut themselves off from the association of helpful companions and may fall prey to pride, hypocrisy, and sensuality. In the teachings of Vallabha's Puṣṭimārga, pride is especially detrimental for the practice of *bhakti* since it is one of the major components of the *doṣa* of egotism:

> Should one renounce in order fully to accomplish "Hearing" and the others (the ninefold devotion)? That is not desirable. For (to accomplish these) one needs to associate with helpful companions, and one's means of attainment must also be maintained. Besides, the pride (of the renunciant), as well as the regular practice (of the devotee), make the characteristics (of renunciation and the ninefold devotion) mutually contradictory. And if someone thinks that his home, family and so forth are obstacles on his path, and he should therefore take renunciation as a means, in fact he will in no way be able to avoid contact with such people even after renouncing. He may also find himself a hypocrite, overrun by sensuality, because of the times; and Hari never makes his dwelling-place in bodies which are in the grip of sensuality. And so, at this time and in this stage of practice on the path of devotion, renunciation does not bring happiness. (*SaṃNir.* 3–6; trans. Redington, 2000, 160)

The Debate at Vijayanagara

The hagiographies mention several occasions on which Vallabha disputed publicly with other philosophers on matters of doctrine, but it is the debate at the court of King Kṛṣṇadevarāya (b. 1488; r. 1509–1529) of Vijayanagara that stands out from the others because of the tremendous fillip it gave to Vallabha's reputation. The debate seems to have been held in 1509, when Vallabha was 30 or 31 years old. At this debate, at least in the recounting of the sectarian hagiographies, Vallabha thoroughly trounced his *māyāvādī* rivals, and King Kṛṣṇadevarāya declared him the victor of the debate. In recognition of his performance, representatives of two Vaiṣṇava schools, that of Madhva and that of Viṣṇusvāmi, offered him the position of *ācārya* in their sects. Vallabha accepted the offer of the Viṣṇusvāmi *ācārya* Vilvamaṅgala and was accepted as the *ācārya* of that school.

The majority opinion in the Vallabha Sampradāya is that Vallabha, as the *ādhibhautika* emanation of Kṛṣṇa's *ādhidaivika* mouth, had no human *guru*, belonged to no philosophical tradition or school, and accepted the *ācārya*-ship of the Viṣṇusvāmi school only to increase the fame and prestige of his own doctrines. A minority sectarian view is that Vallabha belonged to the philosophical tradition of Viṣṇusvāmi. Since very little is known about Viṣṇusvāmi and his teachings, it is impossible to say whether there is any real connection between Vallabha and Viṣṇusvāmi's school of thought.

Death

After his marriage Vallabha evidently maintained two households, one at Arail across the Yamunā River from Allahabad at the place where the Yamunā joins with the Gaṅgā River and one at Charanata near Varanasi. His first son was born at Arail and his second at Charanata. Vallabha probably produced most of his writing at one or the other of these two settlements. He also regularly made trips to the headquarters of his sect at Śrī Nāthjī's *havelī* on Govardhan Hill.

In 1530 Vallabha seems to have sensed his approaching death. He is said to have withdrawn to Hanuman Ghat on the Gaṅgā in Varanasi and there to have taken a vow of renunciation (*saṃnyāsa*). A month after taking the vow, Vallabha summoned his sons Gopinātha and Viṭṭhalanātha along with his foremost followers and in their presence designated Gopinātha, then 18 or 19 years old, his successor as head of his Sampradāya. Having arranged for an orderly succession, he then, according to sectarian accounts, waded into the Gaṅgā. Appropriately for his status as the *avatāra* of Kṛṣṇa's mouth, he was there enveloped in a brilliant flash of light and returned to his *ādhidaivika* dimension.

Vallabha's death as related in the hagiographies parallels their account of his birth, but in reverse. At birth Vallabha descended from the *ādhidaivika* dimension in the care of *ādhyātmika* fire into the *ādhibhautika* world, and at his death he ascended from the *ādhibhautika* plane enveloped by *ādhyātmika* light into the *ādhidaivika* realm of Kṛṣṇa. For the follower of the Puṣṭimārga, nothing further need be said. From the *ādhibhautika* perspective, Vallabha's death is not so uncomplicated. There is, for example, the question of whether Vallabha, whatever his religious motivation might have been, committed suicide when he waded into the Gaṅgā on that day in 1530. While at this distance in time there can be no final answer to that question, J. Redington (1993, 157–179) has confronted it sensitively, constantly drawing upon unimpeachable sectarian sources.

It may seem strange, considering his warnings about renunciation, that Vallabha should have decided to take the vow of *saṃnyāsa* a month before his death. On the other hand, Vallabha was a conservative Brahman who lived his personal life in harmony with the requirements of his caste and lineage background. It is traditional for a Brahman like Vallabha to finish his life as a *saṃnyāsī*. It is also true that Vallabha did not think that *saṃnyāsa* is inherently wrong but, rather, that it is very difficult for a person to avoid its pitfalls. In the verses of *Saṃnyāsanirṇaya* that come just after the verses quoted above, Vallabha gives his opinion that renunciation may be undertaken in order to feel the separation from Kṛṣṇa that intensifies one's love for him. He cites as examples of the rare devotees that have managed to do this the cowherd women (*gopīs*) of Braj who found perfect love for Kṛṣṇa when they were abandoned by him as described in *Bhāgavatapurāṇa* 10.32 and the legendary sage Kauṇḍinya, who renounced the world in order to find Viṣṇu:

> But the scriptures do praise renunciation for the purpose of experiencing separation from the Lord. A devotee clothes himself in the garb (of a wandering ascetic) in order to remove the

> bonds which bind his own people (to him), and not otherwise. Kaundinya and the Gopis have been proclaimed the gurus of such renunciation. And the means of attaining it is theirs: love is brought to perfection by meditative imagining- no other means is needed. Deranged behaviour as well as loss of self-possession are of the very nature (of this state), for it is no ordinary, worldly condition. (*SaṃNir.* 7–9; trans. Redington, 2000, 161)

Perhaps it was in the spirit of the *gopīs* and Kauṇḍinya that Vallabha renounced the world in the last month of his life.

Vallabha's Personality

The autobiographical character of some of Vallabha's writings makes it more possible to speculate about his personality than is true for most of his Hindu contemporaries, who tended to say very little about their personal lives.

The personality trait that is most clearly visible in Vallabha's works is, to be sure, his love for, and devotion to, Kṛṣṇa. Also evident in his writings and in the sectarian hagiographies is his social conservatism. His *bhakti* was not laced with religious radicalism like that of the mid-15th-century poet → Kabīr, nor was it ablaze with disgust at gender injustice like that of the Rajasthani noblewoman → Mīrābāī (c. 1498-c. 1546). Rather, Vallabha seems to have observed in his personal life the rules of his Brahman *dharma*. The verse from Vallabha's works that best expresses his mingling of social conservatism with *bhakti* is the first line of the second verse of *Bhaktivardhinī* (Increasing Devotion), another of the short works included in *Ṣoḍaśagrantha*:

> The means for strengthening the seed of *bhakti* (*bījabhāva*) arises from the performance of one's own proper *dharma*, remaining in [one's] home. (*BhVa.* 2; trans. Smith, 1998, 525)

Although Vallabha was not a social rebel, he was utterly uncompromising in his loyalty to the principles of *bhakti*. Whenever there was a clash between social rules and *bhakti* to Kṛṣṇa, he was always unwaveringly on the side of *bhakti*. One of the most obvious instances of Vallabha's choosing *bhakti* over social *dharma* was his appointment of Rāmdās Cauhān as the first priest (*bhītariyā*) to perform the *sevā* of Śrī Nāthjī. As a Rajput rather than a Brahman, Rāmdās Cauhān was not eligible in Hindu traditional law to be a priest. Vallabha appointed him in spite of *dharma* presumably because in his *bhakti* he was the most worthy person available. Another man whom Vallabha favored because of his unusual devotion despite social prejudices was Kṛṣṇadās, a Gujarati Śūdra low on the caste scale. Vallabha put Kṛṣṇadās as *adhikārī* (manager) in charge of collecting donations given to Śrī Nāthjī (Barz, 1976, 213).

In conclusion, one can ask if Vallabha recognized any quality as uppermost in himself. The answer is affirmative, for in the tenth verse of his *Nirodhalakṣaṇa* (Definition of Constraint) treatise included in *Ṣoḍaśagrantha*, Vallabha identifies *nirodha* as a "special path" that he has achieved. This can be taken to mean that he considered *nirodha* to be his characteristic quality. There are two good English definitions of *nirodha* as the term was used by Vallabha. One is the concise definition "constraint" given by J. Redington (2000, 182), and the other is the much more detailed definition offered by F. Smith:

> *Nirodha* indicates the withdrawal of the *bhakta* from the domination of the manifest world (*prapañca*) and a corresponding entrance into the universe of supersensory love, of *līlā*, which is to say into Kṛṣṇa's *nirodha*. (Smith, 1998, 535)

Both the concise and detailed definitions revolve around Vallabha's conception of *nirodha* as the degree of concentration on Kṛṣṇa that is so intense that it blots out all concern with the *ādhibhautika* dimension of life. With the grace of Kṛṣṇa, a devotee who attains *nirodha* enters into Kṛṣṇa's *ādhidaivika* dimension. In that dimension Kṛṣṇa and his devotees enjoy mutual *nirodha*, each intent on the other. This is how Vallabha says it in the *Nirodhalakṣaṇa*:

> When [Kṛṣṇa] becomes filled with a feeling of grace after seeing people distressed [with the pain of separation], [He] then [causes] the complete eternal bliss, which is [already] established in [their] hearts, to manifest outwardly.
>
> Finally, it is extremely difficult to obtain the joy abiding in the grace (*kṛpānanda*) of the one who is totally constituted of bliss [namely Śrī Kṛṣṇa]. Having heard His own attributes sung in the hearts [of the *bhakta*s], the Lord causes these people to become fully immersed.
>
> As a result of this, having fully abandoned everything [of this world], the attributes of the Lord are always sung by those who have attained

nirodha, with the supreme bliss [of the Lord] kept in focus, [and] a state of *saccidānanda* [being-consciousness-joy] arising from within oneself.

I have achieved *nirodha* through cessation [of involvement with the world]. I have obtained that special path of *nirodha*. In order to shed light on [the method of] severing ties [with the world] for those who are eligible for *nirodha*, I am explaining *nirodha* to you.

Those who are sunk in the ocean of worldly experience are deprived of liberation (*vinirmuktās*) by Hari. Those alone who have attained *nirodha* enter into great delight, here, day and night.

Neither worldly pain nor separation can exist for those whose minds are always immersed (*āviṣṭa*) in the attributes (*guṇeṣu*) of the destroyer of the demon Mura [= Kṛṣṇa]. Their joy is similar to that of Hari. (*NiLak.* 7–12; trans. Smith, 1998, 516–524)

To put it into the terminology of the Vallabha Sampradāya, *nirodha* is the withdrawal through *sevā* from Kṛṣṇa's *ādhibhautika* dimension and the entrance into his *ādhidaivika* dimension. *Nirodha* is the *rasa* of the Puṣṭimārga, and *nirodha* is what Vallabha saw as the core of his personality.

Bibliography

Barz, R., *The Bhakti Sect of Vallabhācārya*, New Delhi, 1976, repr. 1992.

Colas, G., "History of Vaiṣṇava Traditions: An Esquisse," in: G. Flood, ed., *The Blackwell Companion to Hinduism*, Oxford, 2005, 229–270.

Edgerton, F., *The Bhagavad Gītā*, New York, 1964.

Entwistle, A. "Synaesthesia in Poetry and Ritual of the Puṣṭimārga," *JVS* 1/3, 1993, 84–103.

Glasenapp, H. von, "Die Lehre Vallabhâcāryas," in: V. Moeller *et al.*, eds., *Von Buddha zu Gandhi: Aufsätze zur Geschichte der Religionen Indiens von Helmuth von Glasenapp*, Wiesbaden, 1962, 193–248.

Harishankarji (Hariśaṅkarjī), C., *Puṣṭimārgopadeśikā*, Varanasi, Vikram Era 1997 (= 1940) (Hind.).

Olivelle, P., "Orgasmic Rapture and Divine Ecstasy: the Semantic History of Ānanda," *JIPh* 25, 1997, 153–180.

Olivelle, P., *Upaniṣads*, Oxford, 1996.

Parekh, M., *Sri Vallabhacharya: Life, Teachings and Movement*, Rajkot, 1943.

Redington, J., *The Grace of Lord Krishna: The Sixteen Verse-Treatises (Ṣoḍaśagranthāḥ) of Vallabhacharya*, Delhi, 2000.

Redington, J., "The Last Days of Vallabhācārya," *JVS* 1/4, 1993, 157–179.

Saha, S., "The Movement of *Bhakti* along a North-West Axis: Tracing the History of the Puṣṭimārg between the Sixteenth and Nineteenth Centuries," *IJHS* 11, 2007, 299–318.

Schweitzer, A., *The Quest of the Historical Jesus*, Minneapolis, 2001.

Shyam Das, *Chaurasi Baithak: Eightyfour Seats of Shri Vallabhacharya*, Baroda, 1985.

Smith, F.M., "Predestination and Hierarchy: Vallabhācārya's Discourse on the Distinctions Between Blessed, Rule-Bound, Worldly, and Wayward Souls (the *Puṣṭipravāhamaryādābheda*)," *JIPh* 39, 2011, 173–227.

Smith, F.M., "Dark Matter in Vārtāland: On the Enterprise of History in Early Puṣṭimārga Discourse," *JHSt* 2, 2009, 27–47.

Smith, F.M., "Vedic and Devotional Waters: The *Jalabheda* of Vallabhācārya," *IJHS* 8, 2004, 107–136.

Smith, F.M., "*Nirodha* and the *Nirodhalakṣaṇa* of Vallabhācārya," *JIPh* 26, 1998, 489–551.

Snatak (Snātak), V., *Śrī Vallabhācārya*, New Delhi, 1992 (Hind.).

Timm, J., "Vallabha's Commentary(?) on the Bhagavad Gītā," *JVS* 1/4, 1993, 31–45.

Timm, J., "Biography, Hagiography, Sacred Story: Vallabha, Viṭṭhalanātha and the Vallabha Sampradāya," *JVS* 15/2, 2007, 3–17.

Vaudeville, C., "The Govardhan Myth in Northern India," *IIJ* 22/1, 1980, 1–45.

Witzel, M., "Vedas and Upaniṣads," in: G. Flood, ed., *The Blackwell Companion to Hinduism*, Oxford, 2005, 68–98.

Richard Barz

Vedāntadeśika

Historically speaking, we know little about Veṅkaṭanātha, or Veṅkaṭeśa (c. 1268–1369), the medieval South Indian saint-poet, philosopher, scholar, and sectarian teacher later known by his epithets Vedāntadeśika ("Preceptor of the Vedānta") and Kavitārkikasiṃha ("Lion among Poets and Philosophers"). There are hints here and there in material testimonies, such as the witness of a young Telugu prince, some signature verses, panegyrics, chronicles, and inscriptions on the walls of the Raṅganātha Temple at Srirangam (Śrīraṅkam) praising the feats of a Brahman general (Filliozat, 1990, 10). And there are many stories, and a body of work praised and cited by his 14th-century contemporaries, chanted in temple rituals, memorized up to the present day (Hopkins, 2007, 4–6). Some verses are quite vigorous and even audacious on the theme of this saint-poet and philosopher. A 14th-century Sanskrit panegyric, the *Saptatiratnamālikā*, composed by Aṇṇaṉ Svāmi, claimed by tradition to be the disciple of Veṅkaṭeśa's son Nāyiṉācāriyaṉ, has Veṅkaṭeśa causing his rivals to "wet their beds in fear," threatening their very lives with the power of his ravenous hunger for victory in debate, like a lion devouring elephants (*Saptatiratnamālikā*, vv. 6, 57). Aṇṇaṉ Svāmi is said to have written his verses in response to certain "censures" (*carccai*s) put on Veṅkaṭeśa's work by rival sectarian teachers in the city of Srirangam in southern Tamil Nadu.

The competitive spirit of Aṇṇaṉ Svāmi's *Saptatiratnamālikā*, as well as its exuberant hyperbole, is emblematic of much of the literature by and on the *ācārya*s (sectarian "preceptors"; → *guru*s and *ācārya*s) of Veṅkaṭeśa's time and after. These praises by Veṅkaṭeśa's son's disciple mirror not only simple religious veneration, but also struggles over temple control and tensions between rival cities. Eventually such struggles for power, prestige, and orthodoxy would lead to the splitting of the → Śrīvaiṣṇava community of → Tamil Nadu into the northern (Vaṭakalai) and southern (Teṉkalai) schools, each tracing its roots back, respectively, to Veṅkaṭeśa and Piḷḷai Lokācārya. To study Veṅkaṭeśa's narrative lives and times, to survey the milieux – both congenial and rival – in which this remarkable poet-philosopher went about his work, is to study a particularly contentious era of South Indian social and religious history (Appadurai, 1981, 83–101; Rao, 1976, 88–105; Hopkins, 2002, 66–74).

After a summary of motifs in Veṅkaṭeśa'a sacred biographies, this article will focus on this saint-poet and philosopher's threefold contribution to South Indian religion and culture: as a philosopher, theologian, and poet. (For more detailed discussions of literary, historical, and epigraphical sources, see Hopkins, 2002, 48–75.)

Narrative Images in the Sacred Biographies

True to conventions of hagiography, his birth is depicted as miraculous (Hopkins, 2007, 4–6). His mother had prophetic dreams that led her and her husband to travel from their home village of Tuppul near Kanchipuram to the sacred hill shrine Tirumalai, to pray to → Viṣṇu, who dwelled there as Tirupati ("Lord of the Hill"), for the gift of a son. One night on the mountain, she dreamed that a young boy came to her, asking her to swallow a bell that he held in his hands. That very night the shrine bell at Tirupati was stolen, and the temple priest himself had a dream. In his dream, he was told a pious woman would dream of swallowing the bell, and that she would give birth to a remarkable child, an earthly incarnation of the sacred temple bell. And 12 round years later, as the stories go, he was born, the temple bell in a baby's small body, the boy named after the god on the hill, Veṅkaṭanātha.

The young boy was prodigious in learning and innate spiritual wisdom: he amazed the old *ācārya*s in debate and eventually took his uncle's place as chief *ācārya* (sectarian teacher) at the great temple town of Kanchipuam. There he flourished as a talented debater and scholar, a master of scriptures. From there he withdrew for some years to study secret teachings associated with Viṣṇu's winged mount, Garuḍa, (→ *vāhana*s) and horse-headed Hayagrīva, whose shrine sat on top of Auṣatakiri ("Medicine Herb Hill") in the town of Thiruvahindrapuram. The powers he attained there – scholarly, religious, ritual, magical, and literary – would hold him in good stead over the years as he became identified as a "master of all the arts and sciences." And miracles multiply beyond the epithets: he is said to have healed an entire village stricken by plague, to have drawn magic circles on the ground to fight back an attack by supernatural snakes, and, with the help of the divine bird Garuḍa himself, called into form by a *mantra*, to have destroyed the most potent of serpents sent to vanquish him. In fevered debates with rival *ācāryas* from the southern temple town of Srirangam, he emerged triumphant, holding fast to his "lion seat" in the city of Kanchipuram. As in so many conventional narratives of philosophical debate (*pravādas*) in South Asian literatures, Veṅkaṭeśa is not only a victorious scholar, but also a "wonderworker" (Granoff, 1985).

During his middle years, the stories speak of a pilgrimage to the north. Using purely literary journeys that are tucked into various poems, including one of his Saṃdeśakāvyas ("messenger poems"), the *Haṃsasaṃdeśa* (Goose Messenger), and one allegorical drama, the *Saṃkalpasūryodaya* (The Dawn of Ritual Resolve), the biographies tell of his travels north to Banaras and the holy Gaṅgā, to Ayodhya, Mathura, Haridwar, places he finds hopelessly corrupted by priests who value only money and have forgotten the teachings and the proper rituals (Hopkins, 2004). In his pilgrimage south, like → Rāma's "messenger goose" of the *Haṃsasaṃdeśa*, he catches the sweet scent downwind of the blue Vindhya Mountains and then drinks in and praises through vivid poetry the land, the rivers, and the pearl beds of the deep south, the lovely women of Andhra and Karnataka, lakes, temple tanks, and holy shrines of the whole southern country, then finally, after healing a young Vijayanagar princess who was possessed by a demon, and being unsuccessfully wooed for the court and its patronage by the court philosopher Vidyāraṇya, he comes home to Kanci, whose great gods, Viṣṇu and → Śiva, in native, indigenous harmony, signal each other from their temple towers, mingling on the clear air the sounds of their bells and the odors of their lustrations (Hopkins, 2004; 2009).

His later years, say the narratives, are spent in turbulent debate in Srirangam. He is said to have endured the taunting and abuse of rival *ācāryas*: sandals strung over his doorway – a most disgusting insult – a boycott of his father's funeral rites, the hiding of gold in his daily grain rations in the hopes that he would accidentally touch what he had vowed never to touch. But what follows in the story is far worse than sectarian debate and brings the *ācāryas* together; Veṅkaṭeśa is associated with a narrative that is popular in various temple tales: the Muslim "sack of Śrīraṅkam," the "invasion that took 12,000 heads" (Hopkins, 2002, 68–69).

As Muslim troops advanced on Srirangam, Veṅkaṭeśa stayed behind, while his *ācārya* rival and friend Piḷḷai Lokācārya escaped north to Tirupati with the temple's festival icons. As the army began pressing into the town and into the heart of the temple complex, Veṅkaṭeśa walled up the main stones images of the shrine and, after hiding under a pile of dead bodies, finally fled to safety with a copy of a precious manuscript and headed for exile in Mysore. After long exile in Mysore and in the temple town of Melkote, he eventually returned to Srirangam on the heels of a successful campaign to retake the city, led by the Brahman general Gopaṇārya. It is there, in Srirangam, that he is said to have lived out his years, putting final touches on his vast work of philosophical commentary, logic, original treatises, and poetry in three languages – Tamil, Sanskrit, and Maharashtri Prakrit. Indeed, his verses in Sanskrit to the victorious Brahman general still grace the inner temple walls of Srirangam (Hopkins, 2002, 48–75; Singh, 1958; Hardy, 1979; Filliozat, 1990, 10).

The Master Philosopher: Veṅkaṭanātha, Rāmānuja, and Viśiṣṭādvaita

Veṅkaṭanātha is widely regarded as one of the most important post-Rāmānuja philosophers of the Viśiṣṭādvaita school of → Vedānta, one of two major Vaiṣṇava theistic schools of Indian philosophy.

Viśiṣṭādvaita is based on the Sanskrit writings of 11th- to 12th-century South Indian philosopher and theologian → Rāmānuja (Carman, 1974, 24–28). Viśiṣṭādvaita is often translated as "qualified nondualism," to distinguish it from the later Dvaita or "dualist" school of → Madhva or the earlier Bhedābheda, associated with the philosopher Bhāskara, a philosophy that defended the view that there is both difference (*bheda*) and nondifference (*abheda*) between god and the universe, and that is perhaps one of the earliest forms of Vedānta (Carman, 1974, 28–29). The term *viśiṣṭādvaita* was not used by Rāmānuja but was adopted by his later followers, partly on the basis of a passage in one of Veṅkaṭeśa's treatises on logic and epistemology, the *Nyāyasiddhāñjana* (Srinivasa Chari, 1987, 2).

In Veṅkaṭeśa's formulation, Viśiṣṭādvaita describes ultimate reality (→ *brahman*) as being one "differentiated unity" (*viśiṣṭaikya*) that "has as its modes all sentient and insentient things" (*aśeṣacitacitprakāraṃ brahmaikam eva tattvam*). The term Viśiṣṭādvaita thus preserves a sense of the divine both as one and yet organically related to the many. It asserts neither a theology of ultimate identity between person and cosmos with the divine, nor one of ontological difference, but rather one of "identity-in-difference" (Carman, 1974, 28–29; Lipner, 1986, 120–142). It must also be added that this notion implies not only extra-divine but also intra-divine polarities. One can distinguish a dynamic tension within the divine nature itself (Carman, 1974, 77–113).

Veṅkaṭeśa exercised his prodigious gifts in philosophical argument, scholastic commentary, and formal logic to defend the views of Rāmānuja over rival views within and without the Hindu fold. He is known within the Śrīvaiṣṇava tradition for having put Rāmānuja's doctrine on the firmest logical and philosophical ground. This philosophical/polemical and theological work, as well as his poetic writing, earned him in his own time such epithets as Kavitārkikasiṃha and Sarvatantrasvatantra ("Master of All the Arts and Sciences"). The term *tārkika* in the first epithet usually denotes "logician," though the various traditional glosses on the word, such as *kathaka* and *vādin*, bring out its more general sense of "intellectual," "debater," and "philosopher." Such glosses are found both in Śrīvaiṣṇnava commentaries and Veṅkaṭeśa's works themselves (Hopkins, 2002, 29).

The richness of the term and its glosses seem to suit its referent, for Veṅkaṭeśa in the Śrīvaiṣṇava narrative tradition was all of these things. The second epithet refers to his mastery of all *tantras*, a term that denotes at once "scripture," "doctrine," "rule," "scientific work," and "ritual spell." As texts, *tantras* embrace all the arts and sciences, from philosophy to the proper sculpting of images on temple towers. It is thus not surprising that this epithet has been used in the narrative biographies to account for Veṅkaṭeśa's skills in building a well and in the designing and casting of his own temple image. The Kanchipuram Śaiva poet and critic Appaya Dīkṣita, in his commentary on the colophon of the first canto of Veṅkaṭeśa's long lyric poem (Mahākāvya) *Yādavābhyudaya*, glosses *sarvatantrasvatantra* as meaning the philosopher's mastery of all five systems of Indian philosophy (*darśanas*), the → Nyāya, → Vaiśeṣika, → Mīṃāṃsā, → Sāṃkhya, and → Yoga systems, as well as both the Śaiva and Vaiṣṇava texts and traditions. It is perhaps a tribute to the eclectic and cosmopolitan atmosphere of Kanchipuram that one of Veṅkaṭeśa's major commentators was a member of a "rival" sect (Hopkins, 2002, 29, 249n11).

Veṅkaṭeśa and His Śrīvaiṣṇava Tradition

Along with being a philosopher, debater, and poet, Veṅkaṭeśa was one of a long line of *ācārya*s in the Śrīvaiṣṇava Sampradāya of Tamil Nadu. The Śrīvaiṣṇava Sampradāya crystallized as a separate tradition shortly before the end of the 12th century, within 130 years of the death of the theologian Rāmānuja, and is still a small but thriving religious community in South India. Śrīvaiṣṇavas, along with worshipping Lord Viṣṇu and his consort, the goddess → Śrī, claim Rāmānuja and his 10th-century predecessor → Yāmunācārya as their most important *ācārya*s. The community is also distinguished by its claim that the Tamil songs of the → Āḻvārs are equal in authority to the Sanskrit → Veda.

Śrīvaiṣṇavas are not unique in their claim that a body of vernacular songs is equal in ritual and theological weight to the Veda, as there is an earlier analogous development among Śaivas in Tamil Nadu. The phrase "Tamil Veda" (*tamiḻ maṟai*) is mentioned in the work of the Śaiva saint-poets (→ Nāyaṉārs) of the *Tēvāram* anthology, who flourished from the 6th to 8th century CE (Peterson, 1989; Iyer & Gros, 1984, vol. I, 37–68; Pachilis Prentiss, 1999). The distinctiveness of Śrīvaiṣṇavas lies in their systematic development of a voluminous commentarial tradition based upon vernacular root texts. The language used in such commentaries is called Manipravalam (lit. jewels and coral), a syntactic and semantic mixture of Tamil and Sanskrit. Though this hybrid style is neither exclusive nor original to the Śrīvaiṣṇava tradition – there are vivid examples of this hybrid style in 9th-century Jain Sanskrit and Prakrit literatures, in Sattakulam texts of Kashmir (a mixture of Sanskrit and Kashmiri dialects), or in Malayalam → dance dramas (*kūṭiyāṭṭam*) in → Kerala on the western coast of South India – its Śrīvaiṣṇava incarnation remains one of the most striking examples in traditional India of the Manipravalam genre as a whole (Venkatachari, 1978, 167–171; Freeman, 1998). It is a vivid mark of what Śrīvaiṣṇavas call the Ubhaya or "dual" Vedānta, a vigorous synthesis of the religious and cultural idioms of Tamil and Sanskrit (Carman & Narayanan, 1989; Clooney, 1983; 1991).

North and South: A Schism in the Community

But synthesis is not the only mark of the tradition. Another particularity of Śrīvaiṣṇavism is its division into two separate and for the most part antagonistic "schools" or "systems" of thought. The definitive split came in the 18th and 19th centuries, rather late in the history of the community, but had its roots in heated theological debates going back to the period of the 13th to 15th centuries. The issues at stake among *ācārya*s in Veṅkaṭeśa's time included what might be described in the West as "→ grace" versus "effort"; the right interpretation of religious surrender (*prapatti*) and the ecstatic devotion of the Āḻvārs; the divine status of → Lakṣmī, goddess and consort of Lord Viṣṇu; and the proper caste, class, and ritual structures of the community. Disagreements on these issues led eventually, after Veṅkaṭeśa's time, to the emergence of two separate schools of Śrīvaiṣṇavism, the Vaṭakalai or "northern" and the Teṉkalai or "southern" schools. The schools have also been characterized by their respective emphases on Sanskrit and Tamil.

Though *ācārya*s on both sides wrote in the hybrid Manipravalam style, the southern school is known for its emphasis on the Tamil vernacular as the vehicle for teaching and divine revelation and so is usually characterized as appealing to a wider multicaste and multiclass audience of devotees. The northern school, however, stresses Brahman-centered Sanskrit learning and so implies a more "conservative" caste-bound orthodoxy associated with the Sanskrit Śāstras. And it is the Vaṭakalai school that claims Veṅkaṭeśa to be its founder and spiritual leader. Such characterizations, however, must be nuanced before we can grasp the real complexities of the schism and Veṅkaṭeśa's supposed "role" in it. They remain bold strokes and as such conceal as much as they reveal.

One of the examples most often cited to distinguish the positions of the two schools, at least with regard to salvation by grace, is the way mother cats and mother monkeys carry their young (Mumme, 1987; 1988). The Teṉkalai school is the "cat" school of salvation, holding that god saves the soul the way a mother cat carries her kitten, by the scruff of the neck: the soul is utterly passive and can do nothing to affect the process. The Vaṭakalais, however, are monkeys when it comes to salvation, for the soul, they say, in order to be saved, must exert some effort – there must be some pretext (*vyāja*) for god to act, just as the baby monkey must first leap onto its mother's back and then hold on for dear life in order to be carried by her. Though the cat-and-monkey analogy did not originate with the Śrīvaiṣṇavas (it first appeared in the Śaiva Tamil literature) and does not appear in Śrīvaiṣṇava sources until the 17th century, it describes in vivid shorthand one of the main issues at stake in the early debates (Mumme, 1987, 257).

In spite of the charm or the accuracy of the cat-and-monkey analogy, the study of doctrine alone does not fully illuminate either the history of the schism or the original positions of Veṅkaṭeśa and his contemporary rivals. The elaborate lists of doctrinal and ritualistic differences, drawn up by *ācārya*s of a much later age, do not in all cases reflect the extent or tenor of original differences (Varadachari, 1978, 7–63).

This stress on fine points of doctrine eventually led to bitter disputes on such minutiae as the orthodoxy of each sect's vertical forehead mark (the *ūrdhvapuṇḍra*) – a still-heated dispute in contemporary Śrīvaiṣṇavism. Detailed arguments are brought to bear on the proper shape of the mark, its position on the nose, the color of the *śrīcūrṇa* (goddess Lakṣmī's streak as yellow or red), whether it should be placed on the icons, and the right interpretation of Veṅkaṭeśa's brief remarks on the subject in the *Saccaritarakṣā*, one of his treatises on Śrīvaiṣṇava ritual (Singh, 1958, 420ff.). These of course are not "mere" externals but index fierce struggles, from the British period right up to the present day, for political and popular power as well as administrative and ritual control over a network of Vaiṣṇava temples across Tamil Nadu that continues today (Appadurai, 1981, 63–104).

Finally, even too rigid a sense of the Tamil–Sanskrit split in the sects can also be misleading. For in spite of the undeniable overall emphasis on Tamil among the Teṉkalais, both branches of the community used Sanskrit and Tamil in sermons, commentaries, and original esoteric works. Veṅkaṭeśa, for instance, is often said to have been the first among the Śrīvaiṣṇava *ācāryas* to use the technical term "Tamil Veda" (*tamiḻ maṟai*; Varadachari, 1983, 24; Venkatachari, 1978, 1–46; Carman & Narayanan, 1989, 260–261n13), while the Teṉkalai *ācāryas* seem to quote from the Sanskrit epic and puranic literature far more than did their Vaṭakalai counterparts (Mumme, 1988, 7). And there exists yet another complicating factor in this account of Vaṭakalai-Teṉkalai differences, namely, how Veṅkaṭeśa, in his poetry, theologically tends to side more with his "southern" opponents – at least in the debate on grace and self-effort. Veṅkaṭeśa the poet will push the emotional limits of self-effort (*vyāja*, pretext) to "almost zero," emphasizing the final "helplessness" of the devotee in the act of surrender (Hardy, 1979, 311–313; Hopkins, 2002, 89–90, 235–236).

The *Ācāryas* of Srirangam and Veṅkaṭeśa of Kanchipuram

Both indigenous historical anachronism and Western doctrinal caricature have obscured the study of Veṅkaṭeśa's differences with his great elder contemporary in the city of Srirangam, Piḷḷai Lokācārya (1205–1311). A more fruitful avenue of analysis focuses not on doctrine or language preference alone, but on the growing distinctiveness of the respective milieux in which each *ācārya* lived and worked.

The 12th century saw more and more direct involvement of non-Brahman landed folk in the affairs of the vedic temples. And Srirangam, a small town dominated by the great temple of Lord Raṅganātha on the Kāvērī River where Piḷḷai Lokācārya worked, was no exception to this. In fact, Srirangam was rather exemplary in this movement (Stein, 1985, 223ff.; 1984; Mumme, 1988, 30). According to the chronicle of Srirangam Temple, the *Kōyiloḻuku*, Rāmānuja played a major role in instituting reforms that included formal recitation of the Āḻvār's songs in temple liturgies, establishing the more "liberal" → Pāñcarātra as the main mode of worship, and opening the temple to full participation by Śūdras whom he called Cāttāta Vaiṣṇavas, or those "with no → sacred thread" (Stein, 1985, 233; Rao, 1961, 90; Mumme, 1993; Lester, 1994). Such reforms lasted through the 12th and 13th centuries and dissipated only toward the end of the 14th century, which saw a resurgence of Brahman dominance in temple affairs on both sides of the sectarian divide. Thus it comes as no surprise that Srirangam – whose great temple was the first among Vaiṣṇava shrines to incorporate the Āḻvār hymns into its liturgy – was the center of vernacular teaching and writing by the time of Veṅkaṭeśa.

The Manipravalam of the early Srirangam *ācāryas* was permeated with the sensibilities and idioms of Tamil, particularly the Tamil of perhaps the greatest of the saint-poets, Nammāḻvār. In fact, one can trace a progressive "Tamilization of the commentators' prose during the 12th century," which perhaps reflects a growing self-defining emphasis on vernacular authority, and in a larger pan-Asian context, on what S. Pollock has termed the process of "vernacularization" (Pollock, 1998a; 1988b). Thus Piḷḷai Lokācārya's intimate, preacherly style of Manipravalam was heir to a long tradition. His discourses, and in some measure the earlier commentaries, preserve the oral style of sermons preached under the mango tree in the shade of the temple tank or in nearby *maṭhas* (monasteries) to audiences that according to tradition comprised the entire spectrum of Śrīvaiṣṇava devotees, including women, children, and Śūdras normally barred from the study of Sanskrit (Clooney, 1983; Venkatachari, 1978, 164).

The entire corpus of writings attributed to Srirangam *ācāryas* is striking for its vernacular flavor. Abstruse philosophical and theological points are illustrated using images taken from the everyday life of human and animal families along with the flora and fauna of the region. Children's pranks or illness, a mother's love, fathers and sons, the farmer's seasonal sowing and full crop, grain, water, rivers in flood, foxes, and frogs: these are minute particulars of a household world that give body to theological abstractions like "grace," "effort," "surrender," "salvation," "justification," and "service" (Venkatachari, 1978, 48–61).

Though it cannot be claimed that the Srirangam *ācāryas* placed no emphasis on philosophical legitimacy along the lines of the Sanskrit tradition, the main thrust of their texts is on simple surrender to god and the authority of the *ācārya*, beyond caste rank and duty or the injunctions of the Sanskrit law books (→ Dharmaśāstras). The Srirangam *ācāryas* do deal in some detail with Sanskrit epic and puranic literature – they are particularly fond of the Vālmīki → *Rāmāyaṇa*. However, the kind of issues and images they bring to the material are far from those common in traditional Sanskrit shastric commentary. In Piḷḷai Lokācārya's *Śrīvacanabhūṣaṇam* 29–33, we read of → Draupadī disheveled and covered with menstrual blood or Sītā unornamented and smeared with dirt after her ordeal in Laṅkā as exemplifying (respectively) divine surrender (*prapatti*) and the devotee's close embrace of god (Lester, 1979, 20–23; 52–54). These are powerful images of inauspiciousness and impurity that derive their potency from the realm of the household, the world of women and women's bodies, and bring an uncharacteristic concreteness to the doctrinal and theological discourse. As Piḷḷai Lokācārya says in *Śrīvacanabhūṣaṇam* 161, "clothes worn as ornament are an obstacle to close embrace" (*aḻakukiṭṭa caṭṭai aṇaikkaikku virōtiyāmāpēlē*). Obviously, this nuptial nudity echoes a spiritual disposition. Ultimately, the vernacular oral sources of these commentaries lie at the root of this imagery and of the more vividly "Tamil" character of the texts.

Veṅkaṭeśa's "Jewels and Coral"

There are also aspects of *realia* in Veṅkaṭeśa's Manipravalam commentaries and esoteric works (Rahasyas). Veṅkaṭeśa's hybrid prose also has its share of rich imagery: there are foxes caught in floods, smothering asafetida, and insects riding over mountain crevices on a lion's mane (Venkatachari, 1978, 54, 58). But in general, Veṅkaṭeśa's important treatises in Manipravalam, including his *magnum opus* the *Rahasyatrayasāram* ("Essence of the Three Secret Teachings"), are dominated by Sanskrit idioms and vocabulary (Veṅkaṭanātha, 1980; Venkatachari, 1978, 141–155). They are more deeply marked than the prose of the Srirangam *ācāryas* by a concern with arguing both the Śrīvaiṣṇava sectarian cause and Viśiṣṭādvaita theology from the perspective of the orthodox Sanskrit law books (Śāstras) and the Brahmanical social order (the *varṇāśramadharma*). The audience for Veṅkaṭeśa's texts seems at the very least cosmopolitan and Sanskrit centered, though also fluent in Tamil (and Prakrit) literatures.

Ultimately, this particular emphasis has everything to do with the city in whose suburbs Veṅkaṭeśa was born, and where he did most of his formative studies and mature debating: Kanchipuram in northern Tamil country, the seat of traditional Sanskrit learning among Vaiṣṇavas in 13th- and 14th-century South India and one of the seven sacred cities of the subcontinent. Whereas we can trace an emphasis on Tamil and a style based on vernacular oral preaching in the writing of the *ācāryas* associated with Srirangam, in Kanchipuram the emphasis was always on Sanskrit as a tongue that crossed sectarian and even religious borders, though the city fostered the development of other religious and literary languages as well. Again, to use S. Pollock's terms, Kanchipuram was, from ancient times, one of many "local cultures" in the "Sanskrit cosmopolis," even during the years of the "vernacular millennium" (Pollock, 1998a; 1998b; 1996). In fact, we can see in Veṅkaṭeśa's time a resurgence of the production of Sanskrit within Brahmanical religious circles, right in the midst of a "vernacular millennium."

Born in Tuppul, a village just outside what is now "little Kanchipuram," Veṅkaṭeśa grew up in this atmosphere of religious and sectarian diversity that seemed to encourage in the young religious scholar a hunger for dispute and the love of debate. Kanchipuram was an intellectual center for any learned polyglot. And the word "polyglot" here is crucial: for it is not only Sanskrit – Veṅkaṭeśa's "father" tongue of philosophical argument, logic, and poetry – that will become important to the *ācārya* poet. The city and the man were of at least four distinct tongues, Tamil, Sanskrit, Maharashtri Prakrit, and Manipravalam. If the accent in Srirangam was on Tamil and a localizing oral style of discourse, without thereby entirely rejecting Sanskrit, the accent in Kanchipuram was on Sanskrit in the public arena, as a cosmopolitan language of dialogue and apologetics, yet without sacrificing various cosmopolitan vernaculars, such as Tamil, and other (equally cosmopolitan) literary dialects like Maharashtri Prakrit and Manipravalam. Veṅkaṭeśa's work as a whole, in its skillful use of these languages to articulate different facets of one all-embracing theology, reaches a certain extreme of textual polyphony (Hopkins, 2002, 37–41).

It is in great measure to the distinctive environments of these two cities, and not to doctrinal disputes alone, that we owe the growing divide in the Śrīvaiṣṇava community and the specific contribution of Veṅkaṭeśa, particularly in his poetry.

Veṅkaṭeśa the Poet

Veṅkaṭeśa's fame as a philosopher and logician in Sanskrit, as well as his activities as a sectarian preceptor among southern Vaiṣṇavas, has served to obscure his considerable gifts as a religious poet (a *kavi*). Veṅkaṭeśa composed in three major languages of his southern tradition, Sanskrit, Tamil, and Maharashtri Prakrit, and was a master of many genres of philosophical prose and poetry. He wrote long ornate religious poems (Kāvyas) in Sanskrit; a Sanskrit allegorical drama (Nāṭya); long religious lyric hymns (Stotras and Prabandhas) in Sanskrit, Maharashtri Prakrit, and in Tamil; and scholastic commentaries and original works of philosophy, theology, and logic in Sanskrit and Manipravalam.

Veṅkaṭeśa's corpus of devotional poetry combines in a dynamic way the local/regional literary prestige of Tamil with the pan-regional aesthetic prestige and power of Sanskrit (with Maharashtri Prakrit as middle Indo-Aryan literary spice). Veṅkaṭeśa's writings expand the linguistic field of South Indian devotion beyond the normative claims of either Sanskrit or Tamil devotional texts. His language choices embrace both the singularity of Sanskrit as divine "primordial tongue" and the subordinate but equally divine claims of his mother tongue, Tamil. Even more, each of his working languages is touched by the other; the boundaries are here porous they touch, even overlap at points, in mutually vitalizing dialogue (Hopkins, 2002, 38–41). Though his Tamil and Sanskrit poetry exploits with great skill the distinctive aesthetic, syntactic, and philosophical modes of each language, classically formulated, one sees cross influences as well: his Tamil poetry and prose are marked with the presence of Sanskrit, and, most important for Indian studies, his Sanskrit as well is saturated with Tamil literary conventions and idealized local landscapes, transparent to sociocultural- and geocultural-aesthetic domains that I call more generally a South Indian, mostly Tamil, imaginary (Hopkins, 2009).

Veṅkaṭeśa's Regional Sanskrit: Depth over Breadth

Veṅkaṭeśa composed in a Sanskrit saturated with the sensibilities of the vernacular (Hardy, 1979, 282; Hopkins, 2002, 171–172). Veṅkaṭeśa's "southern" cosmopolitanism is inscribed not only through literary motifs, images in the poems, landscapes, and human habitations, but also in the very syntax of his Sanskrit, which remains, in the literary history of the language, one of the most vivid and significant examples of "southern Sanskrit" in medieval India during an age of increasing vernacularization.

As Y. Bronner and D. Shulman have noted – arguing against S. Pollock's far too dire and premature reading of the "death of Sanskrit" after the 2nd millennium CE (Pollock, 2001) – Sanskrit was hardly "dead" in the south after 1200 (Bronner & Shulman, 2006). The shift to vernaculars, and their vigorous literary development, all over South Asia in this period did not erase Sanskrit as a living literary language, but rather made it glow more profoundly in depth, in the particulars of its local regional imaginaries. We find in the poetry of Veṅkaṭeśa one of the most powerful and impressive examples of the "localization" of Sanskrit in the Tamil land, where what is lost, in Y. Bronner and D. Shulman's words, in "geographical range is made up by increasing depth." The greater the geographical contraction and localization, say Y. Bronner and D. Shulman, forcing the paradox, "the wider the scope" (2006, 27–28). And the scope, the depth, the densities, of Veṅkaṭeśa's Sanskrit, drawing transregional and local Tamil and Prakrit energies to itself like the most powerful of magnets, speaks most eloquently to the continued life of Sanskrit in the very heart of the "vernacular" millennium.

Bibliography

Appadurai, A., *Worship and Conflict Under Colonial Rule: A South Indian Case*, Cambridge UK, 1981.

Bronner, Y., & D. Shulman, "'A Cloud Turned Goose': Sanskrit in the Vernacular Millennium," *IESHR* 43/1, 2006, 1–30.

Carman, J.B., *The Theology of Rāmānuja: An Essay in Interreligious Understanding*, New Haven, 1974.

Carman, J.B., & V. Narayanan, *The Tamil Veda: Piḷḷāṉ's Interpretation of the Tiruvāymoḻi*, Chicago, 1989.

Clooney, F.X., Nammāḻvār's Glorious Tiruvallavāḷ: An Exploration in the Methods and Goals of Śrīvaiṣṇava Commentary," *JAOS* 111/2, 1991, 260–276.

Clooney, F.X., "Unity in Enjoyment: An Exploration into Nammāḻvār's Tamil Veda and Its Commentators," *SRV* 6, 1983, 34–61.

Filliozat, P.-S., *Varadarājapañcāśat: With Sanskrit Commentary by Karūr Śrīnivāsācārya*, Bombay, 1990.

Freeman, R., "Rubies and Coral: The Lapidary Crafting of Language in Kerala," *JAS* 57/1, 1998, 38–65.

Granoff, P., "Scholars and Wonderworkers: Some Remarks on the Role of the Supernatural in Philosophical Contests in Vedānta Hagiographies," *JAOS* 105/3, 1985, 459–467.

Hardy, F., "The Philosopher as Poet – A Study of Vedāntadeśika's Dehalīśastuti," *JIPh* 7, 1979, 277–325.

Hari Rao, V.N., *History of Śrīrangam Temple*, Tirupati, 1976.

Hopkins, S.P., "Sanskrit in a Tamil Imaginary: Sandeśakāvya and the Haṃsasandeśa of Veṅkaṭanātha," in: M. Kannan & J. Clare, eds., *Passages: Relationships between Tamil and Sanskrit*, Pondichéry, 2009, 281–312.

Hopkins, S.P., *An Ornament for Jewels: Love Poems for the Lord of Gods by Vedantadesika*, New York, 2007.

Hopkins, S.P., "Lovers, Messengers and Beloved Landscapes: Sandeśa Kāvya in Comparative Perspective," *IJHS* 8/1–3, 2004, 29–55.

Hopkins, S.P., *Singing the Body of God: The Hymns of Vedāntadeśika in Their South Indian Tradition*, New York, 2002.

Iyer, V.G., & F. Gros, *Tēvāram: Hymnes Śivantes du pays Tamoul*, vol. I, Pondicherry, 1984.

Lester, R., "The Sāttāda Śrīvaiṣṇavas," *JAOS* 114/1, 1994, 39–53.

Lester, R., ed., *Śrīvacanabhūṣaṇa of Piḷḷai Lōkācārya*, Madras, 1979.

Lipner, J., *The Face of Truth: A Study of Meaning and Metaphysics in the Vedāntic Theology of Rāmānuja*, Albany, 1986.

Mumme, P., "Rules and Rhetoric: Caste Observance in Śrīvaiṣṇava Doctrine and Practice," *JVS* 2/1, 1993, 113–138.

Mumme, P., *The Śrīvaiṣṇava Theological Dispute: Maṇavāḷamāmuni and Vedāntadeśika*, Madras, 1988.

Mumme, P., "Grace and Karma in Nammāḻvār's Salvation," *JAOS* 107/2, 1987, 257–266.

Pachilis Prentiss, K., *The Embodiment of Bhakti*, New York, 1999.

Peterson, I.V., *Poems to Śiva: The Hymns of the Tamil Saints*, Princeton, 1989.

Pollock, S., *The Language of the Gods in the World of Man*, Berkeley, 2006.

Pollock, S., "The Death of Sanskrit," *CSSH*, 2001, 392–426.

Pollock, S., "The Cosmopolitan Vernacular," *JAS* 51/1, 1998a, 6–37.

Pollock, S., "India in the Vernacular Millenium: Literary Culture and Polity, 1000–1500," *DJAAAS*, 1998b, 41–74.

Pollock, S., "The Sanskrit Cosmopolis, 300–1300: Transculturation, Vernacularization, and the Question of Ideology," in: J.E.M. Houben, ed., *Ideology and Status of Sanskrit: Contributions to a History of the Sanskrit Language*, Leiden, 1996, 197–247.

Rao, V.N.H., *Kōyil Oḻugu: The Chronicle of the Srirangam Temple with Historical Notes*, Madras, 1961.

Singh, S., *Vedānta Deśika: His Life, Works, and Philosophy*, Banaras, 1958.

Srinivasa Chari, S.M., *Fundamentals of Viśiṣṭādvaita Vedānta: A Study Based on Vedānta Veṅkaṭeśa's Tattva-muktā-kalāpa*, Delhi, 1987.

Stein, B., *Peasant State and Society in Medieval South India*, Delhi, 1985.

Stein, B., "Social Mobility and Medieval South Indian Hindu Sects," in: J. Silverberg, ed., *Social Mobility in the Caste System in India: An Interdisciplinary Symposium*, Paris, 1968, 78–94.

Varadachari, V., *Two Great Acharyas: Vedanta Desika and Manavala Mamuni*, Madras, 1983.

Venkatachari, K.K.A., *The Maṇipravāḷa Literature of the Śrīvaiṣṇava Ācāryas, 12th to the 15th Century A.D.*, Bombay, 1978.

STEVEN P. HOPKINS

Yāmunācārya

The pivotal role played by Yāmunācārya in the development of medieval → Śrīvaiṣṇavism is evident in the enormous work that he had accomplished in the laying of the foundation for the core philosophical principles of the tradition. In the memory of the community, he certainly occupies a significant place as one who has sought out the person who would become the most dominant figure in the Śrīvaiṣṇava history, namely, → Rāmānuja. At the outset, I wish to acknowledge that notwithstanding such significance attached to him, scholarly work on Yāmunācārya to date has been very negligible. After the works of W.G. Neevel and R. Mesquita, there has not been much scholarly activity on Yāmunācārya's works either in translation work or in the exposition of his philosophical ideas. Several scholars have paid attention to him more in the course of treating the history and development of ideas in this tradition. I will have occasion to refer to some of them in the course of this essay. With this preliminary note, let me contextualize Yāmunācārya in the overall history of the Śrīvaiṣṇava tradition.

Yāmunācārya's work needs to be seen in the context of two areas as far as Śrīvaiṣṇavism is concerned. First in the area of religious practice and second in the philosophical foundation that he offered for the future work of Rāmānuja. So, let us first locate Yāmunācārya in the context of Śrīvaiṣṇava religious practice.

In terms of religious practice, all scholars agree on the foundational role of the → Āḻvār singers/poets who predated the establishment of Śrīvaiṣṇavism in the medieval period. Āḻvārs were a group of itinerant singers who went around from place to place in what is presently known as → Tamil Nadu during a long period stretching from the 5th to the 8th century ce. They sang their songs in praise of → Viṣṇu. The general tendency of scholars is to present the Āḻvār movement as a social and religious movement (Dutta, 2007). However, there is a debate as to whether they were part of a social movement against → caste domination and Brahmanism. S. Jaiswal, following the work of F. Hardy and A.K. Ramanujan *et al.*, argues that the songs of the Āḻvārs carry the characteristics of Tamil *akam* (love) poetry. He agrees with F. Hardy's argument that as the Brahman priests penetrated the south, "the non-Brahman Āḻvārs came to be regarded as low-born or outcastes and the myth of the Āḻvār movement being a social and religious revolt against the establishment was born" (Jaiswal, 2000, 15). He also notes that these myths were products of the hagiographical accounts produced by the Brahmanical dominance (Jaiswal, 2000, 14). According to S. Jaiswal, the justification for the → Pāñcarātra form of temple worship by Yāmunācārya in his *Āgamaprāmāṇya* was to defend the popular and folk elements of temple worship "to counter the criticism of more orthodox Vedantist brahmanas" (Jaiswal, 2000, 19).

It is important to recognize that the development of Śrīvaiṣṇavism from the popular religious praise songs of the Āḻvārs is intrinsically connected to the gradual Brahmanization of the tradition in the hands of Nāthamuni (see → Tamil texts) and later in the hands of Yāmunācārya and Rāmānuja. It is, therefore, not entirely out of place for some scholars such as F. Hardy, A.K. Ramanujan, and S. Jaiswal to point out the dominance of Brahmanism through ritualization of → *bhakti* tradition of the Āḻvārs into what has come to be known as Śrīvaiṣṇavism. Yāmunācārya's contribution in this regard is for the first time to justify the hitherto less-known Āgama ritual tradition not only to establish the veracity of the ritual procedures in line with the vedic rituals, but perhaps also more importantly to point to his other Brahman counterparts that it is worthy of Brahmanical practice. Placing Yāmunācārya in his rightful place, D. Shulman has this to say, "Yāmuna was the single most important philosophical precursor of Rāmānuja and the first to provide, in Sanskrit, a reasoned theology linking the *Prabandham* as well as Pāñcarātra with orthodox Vedānta" (Shulman, 1990, 133). But strictly speaking, Yāmunācārya was not the first one to bring the Pāñcarātra ritual tradition into the emerging Śrīvaiṣṇavism. As W.G. Neevel pointed out, Nāthamuni had already established some justification for the Pāñcarātra in his *Nyāyatattva*, which is no longer extant (Neevel, 1977, 11).

In the memory of the community passed on through the *Divyasūricaritam*, Yāmunācārya is credited with a total of eight works – *Ātmasiddhi, Īśvarasiddhi, Saṃvitsiddhi* (together known as *Siddhitraya* – of the three only the first one is found to be complete, and the other two are incomplete), *Āgamaprāmāṇya, Stotraratna, Catuḥślokī, Gītārthasaṃgraha,* and *Puruṣanirṇaya.* He is also credited by some traditional → *paṇḍit*s with the authorship of *Kāśmīrāgamaprāmāṇya.* Of course, one has to concede that scholarly interest in this question in academic circles has waned over the years for a lack of independent evidence. The last of the scholars who discussed the question of authorship of *Kāśmīrāgamaprāmāṇya* was M. Narasimhachari, who argued in favor of crediting Yāmunācārya with its authorship based on the references made in the *Āgamaprāmāṇya* and *Puruṣanirṇaya* being similar (Narasimhachari, 1976, 4).

In his philosophical works, Yāmunācārya was primarily concerned with the justification of the core philosophical position of Śrīvaiṣṇava faith, namely, the Viśiṣṭādvaita position (the qualified nondualism; see → Vedānta). His chief opponents in his philosophical arguments were the Advaitins (see → Vedānta), Mīmāṃsakas (see → Mīmāṃsā), and Nyaiyāyikas (see → Nyāya). However, it is important to recognize that his philosophical ideas are deeply influenced by the philosophy of the Pāñcarātra system. Both J.A.B. van Buitenen and W.G. Neevel tried to suggest that Yāmunācārya approaches the Pāñcarātra mainly as a ritual tradition and not so much by emphasizing its philosophy. In my previous work, I have, however, argued that it would be misleading to ignore how much Yāmunācārya owes to the Pāñcarātra philosophy in developing the Viśiṣṭādvaita position. There I have further argued that the core *tattva*s (philosophical principles) of Viśiṣṭādvaita were actually drawn from the Pāñcarātra system insofar as he attempts to preserve the unity of the three principles, namely, → Īśvara (lord), *cit* (consciousness), and *acit* (unconsciousness/material world; see Kumar, 1997, 59).

Biographical Sketch of Yāmunācārya

The Āḻvār singers cumulatively composed the hymns that came to be known as *Nālāyira Tivya Pirapantam* (*Nālāyira Divya Prabandham*), after the first of the teachers in the tradition collected and set them to music. Nāthamuni is credited to be the first of the *ācārya*s (→ *guru*s and *ācārya*s). Yāmunācārya was said to be the grandson of Nāthamuni. According to the traditional narrative, Nāthamuni died when Yāmunācārya was very young. He grew up in his ancestral village, Vipranārāyaṇapuram (modern name is unknown). His father's name was Īśvaramuni. Tradition has it that Nāthamuni asked Rāmamiśra, the disciple of Puṇḍarīkākṣa (a disciple of Nāthamuni), to look after Yāmunācārya and prepare him to succeed his grandfather as the teacher of the tradition. Yāmunācārya is said to have been a very intelligent and articulate scholar who had good leadership qualities. After defeating a rival *paṇḍit*, he was awarded half of the kingdom by the king, and thereafter he is said to have had a fairly affluent lifestyle until, as per Nāthamuni's instruction, Rāmamiśra took him to the Śrīraṅgam Temple and was told that that was the treasure his grandfather left for him. Yāmunācārya construed that to be his grandfather's wish that he become the servant of Lord Raṅganātha. He then instantly became a renunciant and began to serve as the head of the Śrīraṅgam Temple. Yāmunācārya is also credited with collecting the songs composed by Caṭakōpaṉ, a disciple of Kurattāḻvāṉ, and arranged for them to be sung in the Śrīvaiṣṇava temples. Yāmunācārya's sister's son was Rāmānuja. In his later years, Yāmunācārya sought out Rāmānuja to succeed him as the teacher of the tradition. In this sense, Yāmunācārya made an extraordinary contribution to the furtherance of the Śrīvaiṣṇava tradition.

Yāmunācārya and the *Siddhitraya*

As mentioned above, it is in these three treatises that Yāmunācārya lays the foundation for the Viśiṣṭādvaita philosophy. It is here that he clarified his position on → Īśvara (lord). Using the language of → Sāṃkhya, he addresses Viṣṇu as supreme *puruṣa* (*SidTr.* 1; see also → *puruṣa*). In the same *śloka*, he addresses the lord as "Śrīmān" in line with his poetic works and the Pāñcarātra tradition, which I will refer to shortly. Here he flags two important ideas, namely, that the lord in the Viśiṣṭādvaita philosophy is understood as the supreme being, and that he is always understood in relation to his divine consort, → Śrī Lakṣmī. This relationship between the lord and his consort becomes clearer in his defense of Pāñcarātra. His intention here is to affirm the intrinsic oneness of the ultimate reality, namely, the supreme lord that he addresses as Śrīmān. In the *Saṃvitsiddhi*, he makes a significant statement about this oneness of the supreme being.

> The phrase, "the absence of a second" does not mean *brahman* itself nor an attribute thereof. For, it is essentially negative, while *brahman* is really not negative. Nor could it be an attribute of *brahman* (for according to the opponent, *brahman* is devoid of qualities). Thus the existence of the world is not contradicted by scriptural texts speaking of reality as nondual. The existence of the world is established by the sources of knowledge (*pramāṇas*) relevant thereto. Their verdict is further confirmed by scriptural testimony.
>
> The real significance of the text – "reality exists as one only and without a second (*advaita*)" – may now be explained. The person who is considered *advitīya* is one who neither has, nor had, nor will have an equal or superior capable of being counted as second. How could a small fraction of the entire collection of entities that constitute His possessions and that are under His sway (*vibhava*)? The statement – "the paramount ruler of the Cola country now reigning is without a second in this world" – is intended to deny the existence of a ruler equal to him. It does not deny the existence of his servants, sons, consort, and so on. Similarly, the whole host of *devatās*, *asuras*, and men, the four-faced Brahmā and the cosmic egg, form but a small part of a drop from the ocean of the greatness (*mahimā*) of the possessions (*vibhūti*) of the Lord Viṣṇu, who is the Lord of all, who is touched neither by sorrows (*kleśas*) nor by merits, demerits (*karma*), or *vipāka* and so forth, and who is the seat of the sixfold qualities of knowledge (*jñāna*) and the like, and whose greatness cannot even be conceived by the mind. (Ramanujachari & Srinivasacharya, 1972, 177–178)

Here Yāmunācārya affirms the unity of the ultimate reality within which the multiplicity exists without any negative implications. Here he alludes to the "part and whole" idea that Rāmānuja later develops extensively. The key to his assertion of the unity is in his reference to the sixfold qualities to which I shall return later. Unlike the Advaitins, Yāmunācārya admits the reality of the physical universe and the individual souls and sees all of it as part of lord's reality and thereby rejects any duality in the ultimate reality. His philosophical rigor is demonstrated in his rejection of the Advaitin's theory of *anirvacanīyakhyāti*, according to which neither the erroneous cognition nor the object of that cognition really exists. Yāmunācārya instead suggests two alternative theories to defend his position, namely, *anyathākhyāti* (cognition of a different object) and *yathārthakhyāti* (cognition of the object is in conformity with the reality), both of which are found to be complementary (Mesquita, 1990, 234–279). For Yāmunācārya, knowledge is self-evident and hence his support for *yathārthakhyāti*. Another important aspect of his argument is that intellect or consciousness is not to be conflated with self, although it (i.e. intellect) is the characteristic of self. Put it differently, it is the nature of self but not its essence (*svarūpa*). In order to avoid the Mīmāṃsā implication that cognition occurs due to the sense-object contact, Yāmunācārya argues that it is the consciousness of the self that comes into contact with the object, thereby producing the cognition. Additionally, he espouses the theory of *pariṇāmavāda* (theory of evolution) in order to defend the transcendence of → *brahman*, on the one hand, and the reality of the physical world, on the other.

Yāmunācārya and His *Āgamaprāmāṇya*

I have suggested above that in order to understand his philosophical work, we need to pay attention to his commitment to the Pāñcarātra system. In his *Āgamaprāmāṇya*, he offers a defense of the system. R. Dutta argues that

> the popular base of temple and its emergence as the focus of community inspired Yāmuna's *Āgamaprāmāṇya* (eleventh century). It was in his *Āgamaprāmāṇya* that for the first time one comes across a major ideological shift from an exclusive, metaphysical approach as represented in Vaikhānasa Āgama to a more popular, ritualistic and incorporative approach as represented in Pāñcarātra Āgama. However, this shift which asserted the validity of the Pāñcarātra was a notional one and later on became the ideological basis for the elaboration of the liturgical practices in the post Rāmānuja period, when the concept of a community became more broad-based. (Dutta, 2007, 29–30)

The above comment offers us the context in which Yāmunācārya defended the Pāñcarātra

Āgamas as being as authentic as the → Vedas and the → Vaikhānasa Āgamas. There seems to have been two independent Pāñcarātra traditions – one aligned to the Nyaiyākas and the other to the Vedānta. This is based on their respective epistemologies. Nyaiyāka Pāñcarātra defended it on the basis of inferential argument (*parataḥprāmāṇya*), whereas the Pāñcarātra Vedānta of Yāmunācārya is based on self-validation (*svataḥprāmāṇya*). To begin with, the Pāñcarātra philosophy is based on the idea of one ultimate being (*ekāntika*). This ultimate being is Viṣṇu, who is characterized by six auspicious qualities – knowledge (*jñāna*), sovereignty (*aiśvarya*), virility (*vīrya*), power (*śakti*), force (*bala*), and energy (*tejas*). He is always inseparable from his divine consort, Śrī Lakṣmī, who is said to be identical to and at the same time distinct from him. She is described as his active force (*kriyāśakti*) who is identical with Viṣṇu's resolve, and as the one who forms the material reality (*bhūtiśakti*). Furthermore, Śrī Lakṣmī is also characterized by the six auspicious qualities that were attributed to Viṣṇu. (For a detailed discussion on these aspects, see my earlier work; Kumar, 1997, 21–49.) Suffice here to highlight that the crucial point is how Yāmunācārya resolves the question of the apparent duality of Viṣṇu and Śrī Lakṣmī.

It is evident that Yāmunācārya defended the Pāñcarātra system for two reasons – first, to establish that it is as valid as the vedic and Vaikhānas ritual traditions, and second, to demonstrate its social status within the Brahmanical society. But in so doing, he had to reconcile the apparent dualities within the system. Therefore, he first places emphasis on the *ekāntika* philosophy. In other words, for him the ultimate reality is one, but at the same time the reality of the world and the souls is also real. But at an ontological level, he is also confronted with the dualism of Viṣṇu and Śrī Lakṣmī. To avoid the Sāṃkhya dualism of *puruṣa* – *prakṛti*, as I have shown elsewhere (Kumar, 1997, 51–75), we can only infer from his commitment to the Pāñcarātra system – which affirmed both Viṣṇu and Śrī Lakṣmī sharing the same auspicious attributes, namely, the six auspicious qualities referred to above – and from his commitment to the oneness of ultimate reality as appears in his *Siddhitraya* that Yāmunācārya would arrive at the idea of Viṣṇu and Śrī Lakṣmī as two aspects of that ultimate reality. In other words, it is fair to say that Yāmunācārya's social loyalty to the Pāñcarātra system may have compelled him to treat Viṣṇu and Śrī Lakṣmī on a par and as two aspects of the same reality. I have commented on this point in my previous work cited above:

> The Puruṣa or Īśvara that Yāmuna speaks of here is the one who is also called Śrīmān (the one who possesses Śrī). In other words, Yāmuna does not think of the Lord apart from his beloved consort, who is always seated with him. The Pāñcarātra Āgamas depict Viṣṇu in the same way: he is always inseparable from his consort, Śrī-Lakṣmī. It is noteworthy, again, to recognize that in the Pāñcarātra Āgamas the six auspicious qualities are attributed to both the Lord and his divine consort. This idea of an eternally inseparable relation between the Lord and his divine consort is of great significance to Yāmuna in affirming the oneness of the ultimate reality. (Kumar, 1997, 60)

This idea of treating both Viṣṇu and Śrī Lakṣmī on a par is perhaps more effectively communicated in his hymns, which he might have used in the context of ritual. It is to these hymns that we now turn.

Yāmunācārya's *Catuḥślokī* and *Stotraratna*

Both hymns that Yāmunācārya composed are of great significance in the context of ritual. I have discussed these two hymns in detail in my work previously (Kumar, 1997, 55–59). I will summarize here my earlier findings in that work. In the *Catuḥślokī*, Yāmunācārya makes the following points:

- he makes sure to mention that the highest *puruṣa* (Viṣṇu) is the consort of Śrī Lakṣmī;
- her abode is the same as that of Viṣṇu;
- she is above all the gods, including → Brahmā and → Śiva;
- although she has other names, he emphasizes her name as Śrī and flags the six auspicious qualities that were referred to earlier;
- she is beyond all speech;
- she is the protector of the three worlds;
- her form is more pleasing and wonderful than that of Viṣṇu, who is none other than supreme *brahman*; and
- finally, he alludes to the *vibhava* forms that she takes in correspondence to those of Viṣṇu.

In his *Stotraratna*, Yāmunācārya underlines the following points:

- Śrī resides in the chest of Viṣṇu;
- the universe is protected by her sidelong glances;
- Viṣṇu is always seated with her;
- she is the equal match for the lord with all her attributes;
- she is always comprehended in the cosmic form of the lord; and
- they delight each other.

In order for Yāmunācārya to reconcile the oneness of the ultimate reality, we must emphasize two important concepts from the above – that is, the inseparability of both Viṣṇu and Śrī Lakṣmī and the identity in their cosmic forms. Even though at times he describes her as the mediator between the devotees and the lord, he does not reduce her to a mere attribute of the lord but rather considers her as one who shares in his eternal cosmic form. Furthermore, the notion of *anapāyinī* (inseparability) is the key to understanding the oneness of the ultimate reality in relation to Viṣṇu and Śrī Lakṣmī. Another important notion that is useful in understanding Yāmunācārya's attempt to affirm oneness of the ultimate reality is "mutual relation" (*sāmarasyatā*). He attempts to posit a special relationship between the lord and his consort. He, however, does not use the term *puruṣakāra* (human effort; Kumar, 1997, 62). Commenting on the significance of Yāmunācārya's *Stotraratna*, R. Dutta points out the following: "His *Stotraratna* articulated the intellectual aspects of *bhakti-yoga* which laid down the ideological postulates which were later elaborated upon" (Dutta, 2007, 30).

Yāmunācārya's *Gītārthasaṃgraha*

This work of Yāmunācārya would have been less known if it was not for Rāmānuja, who built his commentary on the → *Bhagavadgītā* – the *Gītābhāṣya* – upon the *Gītārthasaṃgraha*. The unanimity of scholarly opinion in this regard is expressed by N. Nayar: "In terms of indebtedness, Rāmānuja acknowledges his debt to one person only, to his predecessor Yāmuna, author of a brief work on the *Bhagavadgītā* called *Gītārthasaṃgraha*" (Nayar, 1988, 114). In fact, Rāmānuja dedicates his commentary to Yāmunācārya in his opening auspicious hymn. The *Gītārthasaṃgraha* is a brief commentary on the *Bhagavadgītā* with only 32 *ślokas*. However, in his brief commentary, Yāmunācārya laid the foundation for the rest of the philosophical system. According to J.A.B. van Buitenen, Rāmānuja faithfully followed the structure of the commentary in his *Gītābhāṣya* (van Buitenen, 1968, 11). In the very first *śloka* of the text, Yāmunācārya offers a summary of the message of the *Bhagavadgītā* as understood and interpreted by him and his successors, especially Rāmānuja. In this verse, Yāmunācārya identifies Nārāyaṇa (Viṣṇu) with the supreme *brahman*. In this one single verse, he introduces all the key concepts of Viśiṣṭādvaita philosophy – the idea of *bhakti* characterized by detachment (*vairāgya*), knowledge of *svadharma* (one's own duty), which leads one to Nārāyaṇa, who is none other than supreme *brahman*. In the second verse, he introduces the most important idea that becomes elaborated in Rāmānuja's *Gītābhāṣya* (*jñānakarmasamuccaya*, i.e. both knowledge and action). And in the third verse, he clarifies what is meant by *yoga* in the Śrīvaiṣṇava theology: "When both knowledge and action are accomplished, [the *Bhagavadgītā* proclaims] *yoga* [as] devotion" (*jñānakarmābhinivṛttyoḥ bhaktir yogaḥ*). As J.A.B. van Buitenen rightly pointed out, Rāmānuja would closely follow these ideas in his later commentarial work.

The preeminent contribution of Yāmunācārya to the Śrīvaiṣṇava ritual tradition, on the one hand, and the Viśiṣṭādvaita philosophy, on the other, is thus evident from the above examples. Given his place in the tradition and his enormous contribution by establishing the key conceptual framework for the succeeding commentators such as Rāmānuja and Veṅkaṭanātha, it is somewhat disappointing to find that not much scholarly study of his various works have been pursued since W.G. Neevel and R. Mesquita. A serious and sustained study of his poetic as well as philosophical works would certainly add to our understanding of the South Indian Vaiṣṇava tradition. There is a close proximity among his poetry, the defensive commentary on the Pāñcarātra Āgama ritual tradition, and his philosophical texts. A syntactic study of all these texts would certainly yield more clarity not only on his ideas, but also on how the tradition in later years interpreted them. He certainly occupies a respectable place in the history of Indian philosophy.

Bibliography

Buitenen, J.A.B. van, *Āgamaprāmāṇya*, Madras, 1971.
Buitenen, J.A.B. van, *Rāmānuja on the Bhagavad Gītā: A Condensed Rendering of His Gītābhāṣya*, Delhi, 1968.
Dutta, R., "Texts, Tradition and Community Identity: The Srivaisnavas of South India," *SoS* 35/9–10, 2007, 22–43.
Hardy, F., *Viraha-bhakti, the Early History of Kṛṣṇa Devotion in South India*, Delhi, 1983.
Jaiswal, S., "Change and Continuity in Brahmanical Religion with Particular Reference to 'Vaisnava Bhakti,'" *SoS* 28/5–6, 2000, 3–23.
Kumar, P.P., *The Goddess Lakṣmī: The Divine Consort in the South Indian Vaiṣṇava Tradition*, Atlanta, 1997.
Mesquita, R., *Yāmunācāryas Philosophie der Erkenntnis. Eine Studie zu seiner Saṃvitsiddhi*, Vienna, 1990.
Narasimhachari, M., ed., *Āgamaprāmāṇya of Yāmunācārya*, Baroda, 1976.
Nayar, N., "The Concept of Prapatti in Rāmānuja's Gītābhāṣya," *JSAL* 23/2, 1988, 111–132.
Neevel, W.G., *Yāmuna's Vedānta Pāñcarātra: Integrating the Classical and the Popular*, Missoula, 1977.
Ramanujachari, R., & K Srinivasacharya, eds., *Sri Yamunacharya's Siddhi Traya*, Madras, 1972.
Ramanujan, A.K., & N. Cutler, "From Classicism to Bhakti," in: L.S. Bardwell, ed., *Essays on Gupta Culture*, Delhi, 1983, 177–193.
Shulman, D., " Review of Mesquita, R., *Yāmunācārya's Saṃvitsiddhi*, Vienna, 1988 & Mumme, P.Y., *The Mumukṣuppaṭi of Piḷḷai Lokācārya with Maṇavāḷamāmuni's Commentary*, Bombay, 1987," *Numen* 37/1, 1990, 132–134.

P. Pratap Kumar

Relation to Other Religions and Traditions

Hinduism and Buddhism

Ancient Period

Of all the religions that have developed on South Asian soil, Hinduism and Buddhism have been the most often compared and their interrelations the most often studied. The cultural plurality that assumes such interrelation is evidenced already in the earliest Sanskrit literature (1200 BCE onward), but it becomes especially prominent in early Buddhist and Jain literature as well as in the → Upaniṣads and then with considerable force in the Sanskrit epics and much subsequent Sanskrit and vernacular literature. This pluralism is expressed continually in religious and ethnic terms, with perhaps its strongest representation being in the development of Hinduism and Buddhism and interrelations between the two. In the earliest period of this interaction, perhaps 400–250 BCE, evidence of relations between the Buddha and members of the Brahman class can be observed primarily in the Buddhist Pali canon (composed 300 BCE–100 CE) but not in the Upaniṣads (600 BCE–100 CE) – the final stratum of vedic literature and one of the precursor texts for what came to be called Hinduism. No certain dates exist here and the dating of the Buddha's life is usually now given as the 5th century BCE, not the 6th century BCE as previously thought.

No doubt the authors of the large body of Buddhist literature perceived groups they defined as other than themselves in a particular light, and in the so-called early historic period (200 BCE–200 CE) a concern with developing a particular class identity seems to have been emerging that was important in gaining access to patronage deriving from different socioeconomic levels. While the Brahmans as a distinct social group (after 200 BCE) were attempting to mold a set of ideas and practices into a socioreligious system – one that scholars only called Hinduism in the 19th century – they implicitly recognized the presence of other groups who could not easily be assimilated into this new system that they were theorizing, and they reacted against these groups. Yet in the early historic period, new texts like the → *Mahābhārata* and the → *Rāmāyaṇa* do not name these groups with any specificity, so it is never easy to tell toward whom the critiques made in the texts are directed.

In scholarly literature, there has been a tendency to focus on the relations between representatives of Hinduism and Buddhism as defined primarily by conflict. However, this dramatically simplifies the range of possible interrelations, and A. Malinar's recommendation in this regard is a salutary one:

> While competition and conflict cannot be denied, the situation may have been far more complex, not only allowing more harmonious interactions, but also varying over the subcontinent. (Malinar, 2007, 257)

Evidence of conflict is much easier to locate than that of cooperation and complementarity, yet given the length of time (approx. 400 BCE–1400 CE) during which Buddhism flourished in India, peaceful coexistence must have been the prominent defining feature of interrelations between Buddhists and Hindus, as it is today in most Asian countries where these two groups live together. Moreover, where conflict has occurred, it is more likely to have been among intellectuals whose views are often represented in literature, which barely reflects the religious interactions of the lower and less literate classes.

Terminology

Neither Hinduism nor Buddhism is a monolithic socioreligious system, yet the constant use of these two names since the early 19th century may give the impression that they are monolithic and easily defined in words, when in truth they have always been rather porous/inclusive cultural entities. The term "Hinduism" can really only be applied retrospectively to a synthesis of religious practices and ideas first found in the *Mahābhārata* (whose composition covers 200 BCE–200 CE), with the word itself not being used before about 1780 CE. Historically, any encounter between Buddhism and Hinduism, understood as the socio-religious system described below, must be seen as an encounter initially between representatives of Hinduism's intellectual precursors – the various Brahman ritualist and ascetic groups – and other practitioners of what became the various strands of Hinduism when it became a semi-unified religious system.

Neither religion developed in a broad cultural or religious vacuum, and much that is central in Hinduism involves the borrowing and adaptation of ideas and practices commonly found in other religions, principally Buddhism and Jainism, and the ubiquitous, if difficult to define, folk religion associated with worship of fertility goddesses and protective deities. This plurality of religion and culture in early historic India responded successfully to social, economic, and lifestyle demands pertinent to different socioeconomic levels, and out of these, Hinduism developed as a specific cultural complex strongly profiling religious and social dimensions. Hinduism as a religious and social system did not exist prior to the emergence of Buddhism and Jainism. Arguably, what can retrospectively be called Hinduism emerges when the three fundamental behavioral/textual practices associated with ritualism, asceticism, and devotion become incorporated into what A. Malinar has defined as "cosmological monotheism," including the worship of village-protective deities and mother goddesses. It

> combines features of a polytheistic and monotheistic understanding of the world and its beyond. Whilst the cosmos is thought of in polytheistic terms as the realm of the many, its cause and transcendence are located only in the "one."…. This allows for acknowledging the existence of other gods as constituents of the created world and partial manifestations of the "one." (Malinar, 2007, 238)

Buddhism, too, is not so easy to define except to say that on the monastic level, most monks exercise varying degrees of separation from wider society, perform the fortnightly *prātimokṣa* ritual involving the confession of faults in conduct, and accept the four noble truths – the assertion that there exists "dis-ease" (*duḥkha*), there is the arising of "dis-ease," there is the cessation of "dis-ease," and there is the path leading to the cessation of "dis-ease" – as foundational in their belief system. In more technical terms, they accept the *dhamma*, the Buddha's teachings, and the *vinaya*, his precepts relating to conduct. In addition, a clear difference between the laity and the monks/nuns has always been a defining feature of Buddhism – in contrast with Hinduism, where such a distinction is present in the social contrasts between the renouncer and householder, especially when Hinduism becomes well developed (Malinar, 2011, 117–121), though not so much in the figure of the Brahman who does not leave society. Textual evidence, especially from the *Dīghanikāya*, suggests that the monks saw the Brahmans as their functional equals and as the group against whom they measured themselves, though this may have applied to the Jains as well.

At the lay level of Buddhism and at the non-Brahmanical level in the case of Hinduism, most Hindus and Buddhists have traditionally been very similar in behavior and belief and especially in terms of what they expect to receive from their ritual and devotional practices. But laypeople are still very much involved in their respective religions, and even the Brahmans – the main theorists of Hinduism – could be regarded as lay followers, except where functioning as professional priests. In the early historic period, the Brahmans were gradually developing a distinctive view of what became Hinduism and promoted this initially in the two epics and the → Dharmaśāstra literature, in particular the *Mānavadharmaśāstra* (or *Manusmṛti*). Of these, the epics were the best communicative devices for the new, synthesized view of religion with its social concomitants, and it is likely that their effectiveness was enhanced by their recitation in vernacular languages as well as in Sanskrit, thus making them accessible to a wide population at a time when Sanskrit was no longer a spoken language. When the first → Purāṇas were being composed and disseminated, probably in the 4th century CE and later, the devotional side of Hinduism had become dominant and was successfully tying together all of the other, disparate elements making up the religion, allowing them to function as one integrated element within a family of other such elements.

While it may appear quite simple to study the interaction between Hinduism and Buddhism, this assumes a clear demarcation between the two religions where such a distinction has rarely existed in practice. However, any kind of distinction is not just a fiction created by Western scholars that assumes that these are two distinctive religions with overlapping ideas, because both Hindu and Buddhist texts are aware of the existence of traditions other than, and antithetical to, themselves. These traditions did not have easily definable boundaries, even if, at an intellectual level, they could be regarded as being easily distinguishable in respect of certain central doctrines.

A well-known example of a text – one taken from the *Mahābhārata* and cited below – that may well be criticizing Buddhist monks uses several nouns that designate types of holy men (*bhikṣu[ka], muṇḍa, abuddhi,* → *sādhu*) and even uses verbs such as *pari* + *vraj-*, which could imply the activity of a Buddhist monk:

> The Vedas and food are the never-varying fundamental substance of the strictly righteous people in this world. If the giver shall not give, how could there be any who seek absolute freedom? In this world, householders come from food, and mendicants (*bhikṣavas*) come from them. Life arises from food, so the giver of food would be the giver of life. Those who have withdrawn from householders have come right back to householders. And those self-controlled ones sit bad-mouthing their source and their foundation.
>
> One cannot say that a man is a monk (*bhikṣukam*) just from his having renounced, nor from his having a shaved head, nor from his begging. Rather, when an upright man relinquishes wealth, understand that that happy man is a monk (*bhikṣukam*). O lord of the earth, that man is Absolutely Free, who, though he is unattached, goes about like someone who is attached; he has no attachments, he has untied all the bonds, he is the same toward enemies and friends. The bald ones (*muṇḍāḥ*) in their ochre robes are bound by many kinds of fetters. They travel about (*parivrajanti*) in order to receive gifts, piling up idle enjoyments. Lacking understanding (*abuddhayaḥ*), they abandon the three Vedas and their livelihoods, and then they abandon their children and take up the triple staff for holding the water pot and the robe. Realize that the ochre robe on one who is not free from passion serves that person's interests; it serves as a livelihood for those bald ones (*muṇḍānām*) who merely display the flag of law, in my opinion.
>
> Great king, having conquered your senses, conquer heavenly worlds by supporting holy men (*sādhūn*), whether they wear their hair piled on their heads or are bald, whether they are clad in ochre robes, antelope skins, or rags, or are naked. (*MBh.* 12.18.27–35; trans. [slightly modified] Fitzgerald, 2004, 203)

Here there is a clear sense of different religious goals, practices, and certainly beliefs and an accompanying skepticism of some, but not others, in an address given to Yudhiṣṭhira – the eldest of the five Pāṇḍava brothers – who wanted to become an ascetic. Appreciating the level of difference given in this representative text requires questioning any idea of a monolithic view of Hinduism or Buddhism and suggests that as religious systems, they were successful because of their ability to bring together beliefs and practices divergent from what is found in the theological/philosophical streams operative within these religions. Above all they have demonstrated a capacity to attach a sophisticated superstructure of ideas to a wide range of practices directly associated with more pragmatic religious and social goals.

Previous Scholarship

Interest in the interaction between Hinduism and Buddhism goes back almost to the beginning of Indology in the West in the early 19th century, and if early Buddhist literature itself is included, it dates back to the 3rd century BCE. Accordingly, an enormous amount has been written on this subject, even if it is only incidental to the religions' interrelations and their development as individual and related religions. Scholarship has focused on causal factors in the development of Buddhism out of Hinduism, commonalities between Buddhist and Hindu thought, responses of Brahmans to Buddhist expansion, philosophical debates between Buddhist and Hindu thinkers, patronage given to Hindus and Buddhists, and ethnographic studies of contemporary Hindu/Buddhist rituals. Following a modern tendency to clearly differentiate Hinduism from Buddhism, there has often been a tendency to view Buddhism as somehow derivative of Hinduism or as one component different from, but encompassed within, Hinduism. However, European scholars, the latest being Bronkhorst 2007, over the last century have seen Buddhism introducing a marked element of rationality and ethics into the brahmanical precursor to Hinduism where a magico-ritualistic universe was dominant.

In the study of Buddhism, the figure of the Buddha looms very large, sometimes to the neglect of the majority of less well-known monks and nuns, whose careers are only treated in the puranic-type Avadāna literature produced in the early centuries of the Common Era and containing long narratives describing the lives of prominent monks. As a reactive response, the Buddha's teachings and the renunciatory life ideal of the monks are as much a personal demonstration against the overtly social values of the Brahmans and the materialistic goals associated with this as they are a positive adaptation to the new urbanism that had probably been consolidating when the Buddha was first developing his doctrines. Overwhelmingly, however, Buddhism is seen as a reaction to certain aspects of the teachings of Brahmans seen as a group advancing common interests; these teachings are associated substantially with the performance of the sacrifice and the belief in a permanent self, irrespective of what this belief and associated practice develop into in later centuries. This has always brought with it the danger of focusing excessively on the interaction between elite representatives of each religion, omitting the equally important role of the much larger number of lay followers, without which neither religion would have survived.

R. Gombrich (2006, ch. 2) and J. Jurewicz (2000) argue that certain Buddhist doctrines were developed as a direct response to teachings presented in the *Bṛhadāraṇyakopaniṣad*. R. Gombrich focuses on → *karman*, some fundamental innovative doctrines in late vedic tradition, and ontological beliefs pertaining to the belief in a permanent self and the Buddha's reinterpretation of this. It is one measure of the Buddha's comprehensive knowledge of upanishadic thought that he was able to reinterpret technical terms in the Upaniṣads in a metaphorical sense, whereby he proposes a distinctive ethical interpretative principle:

> we see the Buddha reacting to Upaniṣadic teachings by shifting attention away from what the world is, ontology, to how we should behave: morally, and in particular kindly. (Gombrich, 2006, 40)

J. Jurewicz argues persuasively that the *pratītyasamutpāda* – the fundamental theory of causality pertaining to the development of a karmically based individuality and defined in the second noble truth – is based on a reworking of a cosmogonic myth found initially in the *Nāsadīyasūkta* (*ṚV.* 10.129) and then reworked in some of the early Upaniṣads, including the *Bṛhadāraṇyakopaniṣad*. She points to the polemical tone in this doctrine, arguing that the Buddha

> formulated the pratītyasamutpāda as a polemic against Vedic thought. Through the identification of the creative process with the process that leads only to suffering, he rejected the Brāhmaṇic way of thinking in a truly spectacular way. (Jurewicz, 2000, 78)

It is to be expected that such reworkings of fundamental themes should have occurred as the Buddha must have been in contact with teachers who knew the Upaniṣads, after he renounced the social world at the age of 29. But the publications of R. Gombrich and J. Jurewicz provide evidence that he actually knew the contents of specific Upaniṣads, and that his objections should be seen as objections not to a specific religion but to a particular understanding of how the world works.

Recognition of the Buddha's knowledge of the Upaniṣads has sometimes been used to suggest that Buddhism arose as an offshoot of and a reaction against Hinduism. This assumes that Hinduism existed as an identifiable entity in the 5th century BCE and even that Buddhism as an institution existed, which is highly unlikely, as even after the Buddha's death, it probably only consisted of sets of wanderers subsequently developing into a formal *sangha*, the name for the institutionalized order of monks. Against this, J. Bronkhorst (2007) has asserted that Buddhism developed substantially independently of any major Brahmanical influence and that it represents one of the most prominent examples of a substantially independent Magadhan culture that after the 5th century BCE spread out from the northeast into other parts of India. This was a culture in which asceticism and meditation were central aspects of the religious life of a renunciatory Śramaṇa tradition, a tradition radically different from the sacrificial tradition associated with the northwest and central regions of India. Emphasis was placed on a life of quietism and performance of ascetic exercises to eradicate the effect of past *karman* and to prevent the arising of new *karman*. Rationalistic forms of medical diagnosis were part of this cultural perspective, as was rejection of the efficacy of the sacrifice and the subordination of metaphysical inquiry to empirical observation. But some of these features are also found in conjunction with the thinkers who composed the Upaniṣads – people who identified themselves within the vedic tradition and saw continuity with earlier doctrines as central to that tradition. Considerable skepticism has been expressed about J. Bronkhorst's reconstruction, with K. Klaus (2009) arguing strongly that many Brahmans were already living in Magadha during the Buddha's time, an opinion supported by Buddhist literature itself, and that Buddhist's accepted certain aspects of the magico-ritualist worldview.

Like a number of other scholars from as early as the late 19th century (Fitzgerald, 2004, 114–123), J. Bronkhorst (2011, 72) finds the reign of Aśoka Maurya (269–232 BCE) functioning as a huge stimulant causing Brahmanism to reinvent and reposition itself. In part this was because of Aśoka's assumed strong support of Buddhism and the patronage he gave to the *sangha*. He argues that the Brahmans were primarily a social group, not just a religious one, as the *sangha* might be seen. From the 2nd century BCE onward, the Brahmans were tightening up their image as a distinctive social class, whose status was not dependent just on ownership of property; this tightening up may have been partially a result of the conspicuousness of the *sangha* as a distinctive social institution, whose success was measured by the rapid expansion of the order after 200 BCE.

J. Bronkhorst has argued that Brahmanism eventually outflanked Buddhism because it offered a distinctive sociopolitical program, expressed especially in the *Arthaśāstra* and the *Mahābhārata*, indicating an involvement in practical affairs rather than a concern "with the higher realities of spiritual life, downgrading ordinary reality" (Bronkhorst, 2011, 173). This was difficult to match by the Buddhist monks, whose bearing was directed away from the social and political world in favor of a more contemplative lifestyle. Yet those of a strongly spiritual bent can offer advice to political elites precisely because they are looking at society from outside, and, further, his argument overlooks the massive expansion of the Buddhist order across India during the early historic period and its support at various levels of society even during the following several centuries. Given the *sangha*'s heavy involvement in many local economies, it is likely that it may have been perceived by people living near monastic institutions as being a serious agent in the workings of local economies and trade (Shaw, 2007, ch. 14, 259–261).

The material bases of Hinduism and Buddhism are now being studied on the basis of a wider range of sources rather than only literary texts. An important new book by J. Shaw (2007) may necessitate a revision of received opinions of the religious and economic development in early historic India and especially of religious change. In studying Buddhist monumental architecture – especially the locations of *stūpa*s, large brick structures containing the relic of a Buddha or a text, and *vihāra*s, monastic structures built for housing groups of monks and nuns – within their wider spatial environment around Sanchi and the occurrence of Hindu images and ritual structures, J. Shaw has shown that the local Buddhist *sangha* was tied so closely to the short- and long-term workings of local economies, especially in relation to water storage, that the *sangha* was perceived as having not only a religious function but also a crucial economic one. This relates to the question of the distinction between royal and other patronage and modes of acquiring more secure forms of income than that simply coming from patronage, and it lies at the crux of the relationship between Hinduism and Buddhism after 200 BCE. For both Hinduism and Buddhism to have been successful in surviving through the centuries, they had to appeal to the needs of both the elite and the ordinary people in intellectual and practical terms, and it was necessary for Hinduism to provide a unifying role in the culture where it has survived for so long.

Recent work by M. Willis (2009) has expanded on the work of J. Shaw by analyzing the ritual activities of late Gupta kings in Vidisha and the extent to which Buddhist monks and Hindu court chaplains functioned as advisers in the imperial courts. The importance of such roles could not be underestimated because of the association of political power and religious influence marketed at a broad social level and the consolidation of whatever patronage systems had been in existence for some time before the ruling dynasty took control. But the signs of such influence have always been muted and often difficult to read through the texts. Earlier work by R. Davidson (2002, ch. 3) and R. Inden (2000) – historians working on the period between 200 CE and 1200 CE – has anticipated J. Shaw in analyzing Hindu–Buddhist interactions, specifically in the realm of many dynasties across India. R. Inden showed how Brahmans belonging to the → Pāñcarātra school used the *Viṣṇudharmottarapurāṇa* to assert the preeminence of Pāñcarātra ritual in public and private spheres and how this text positions itself in relation to the Buddhists in northwest India, albeit in a very muted way.

In the last ten years, scholars have extended the realm of Hindu–Buddhist interrelations by looking at the worship of deities and sacred figures in both religions, arguing that these can easily slide off into common ground, such that in the medieval period, any differences between Hindu and Buddhist deities were perceived by lay worshippers as being virtually nonexistent. Both R. DeCaroli (2004, 122) and D. Seyfort-Ruegg (2008) have demonstrated how close the connection was between the *sangha* and the populace, owing to the monks' ability to perform rituals to appease and render harmless the various → *yakṣa*s and *nāga*s (see → sacred animals) whose power was believed to be so important in guaranteeing rain and hence the fertility of the soil. It was a question of maintaining a peaceful coexistence with these deities, and it explains why images of these spirit deities are found so often in Buddhist art. It also reveals another avenue of connection between the monks and the laity.

Finally, a recent publication by N. McGovern (2011) argues that a direct influence of Buddhism on the development of Hinduism existed, asserting that an initial Brahmanical synthesis was developed around the god → Brahmā – a synthesis criticized in the Pali canon and largely abandoned in the *Mahābhārata* and subsequent Hindu literature. It was replaced by cults developed around → Viṣṇu and → Śiva as a Hindu reaction – a second synthesis – to the criticism undertaken by the Buddhists and other ascetic groups. This is a striking and original argument, though it tends to simplify a little the complexity of religious belief and practice on the ground, where veneration of fertility deities and mother goddesses was always fundamentally important and definitely tied up with the development of cults centered on Viṣṇu and Śiva.

Sources

Because of the overwhelming number of Buddhist and Hindu texts, textual sources have always been mainly relied on for an analysis of the interconnections between Hinduism and Buddhism with other religions. These literary sources can be extended to include contemporary ethnographic studies (and 19th-cent. travelers' reports), where the contemporary extends across the past two hundred years. To this can be added epigraphy – also a form of literary text that is, however, much easier to date than literary texts transmitted orally or on bark and one whose social basis is sometimes easier to determine. Finally, there are the remains of monasteries and funerary monuments (*stūpa*s) and small memorial monuments (*caitya*s) for dead monks and prominent lay people, very often deliberately located (Schopen, 2006) in areas where they are highly visible to the naked eye. Even though the great majority of these are in ruins now, they must have been spectacular when they were first built. It is their sheer number that is significant and the ease with which they could be accessed by the general population. Construction of these began sometime around 250 BCE, if not earlier, and contrasts with the extensive building of temples on Hindu ground occurring only from the 4th century CE onward, with the exception of some early apsidal shrines in Mathura dating from the 1st century BCE (Singh, 2004).

Of the literary evidence, the early Pali texts show an intense interest in the beliefs of other groups outside of themselves, reporting on Jains, → Ājīvikas, and especially the Brahmans as a social group, the latter defined by a penchant for knowledge and ritual performance. There are, for example, many *sutta*s in the second and third volume of the *Majjhimanikāya* and the first volume of the *Dīghanikāya* dealing with Brahmans and their beliefs and behaviors and many passages where the god Brahmā is shown in a deferential position in relation to the Buddha (McGovern, 2011). In these *sutta*s, the Brahmans are portrayed as being arrogant because of their self-proclaimed status defined by knowledge of the → Vedas and associated ritual and material wealth and by the claim to an identifiable lineage reaching back several generations. While it would be incorrect to speak of a depiction of Hinduism in its mature form in the early Buddhist texts, emphasis is placed on one important aspect of it, the ritual tradition – expressed as performance of the small-scale *agnihotra* ritual (see → *yajña*) – based on vedic knowledge, which is transformed in an altered form into one of the three strands of classical Hinduism: ritual activity, asceticism, and devotion. Suttas such as the *Samaññaphalasutta* and the early *Suttanipāta* provide evidence that the Buddha/Buddhists took other lifestyles and occupations very seriously and sometimes critiqued them. This level of seriousness continues in later literature as well, especially in the Jātakas and the two Kāvyas of Aśvaghoṣa, in all of which reference is pointedly made to the two Hindu epics.

Turning to Hindu literature, the same concern with other groups is present, but it is heavily concealed, and the identity of these groups is often veiled by the use of code words such as *nāstika*, a word whose meaning can differently include liars, thieves, the lazy, those who do not believe in the Vedas or in the performance of rituals, and those who exhibit ignorance of → *dharma*. Buddhists are conspicuous by their absence in the *Mahābhārata* and the *Rāmāyaṇa* – the earliest texts of Hinduism – especially because there is so much other evidence of their presence. Assuming a 400-year period of composition (200 BCE–200 CE) for both, the religious landscape in ancient India must have become more complex, with differences between Hindu and non-Hindu becoming more precisely profiled, by the end of the period. Both of these texts, especially the *Mahābhārata*, reflect this complexity, and the kind of class identity formation with which it can be seen to be associated overwhelms a concern with dealing with the specifics of the beliefs of non-Hindu groups. Both of the texts were composed when the Buddhist *sangha* was reaching the height of its expansion in South Asia.

Because of the capacity of certain groups to market their own interests better than other groups did – in part because of the former's possession of literacy – it is possible to overemphasize the extent of interaction or connection between the different religions. Those who have produced the textual sources appear to have a far greater impact on later scholarly interpretations of the meeting between the two religions. Yet the living religion resides in its practitioners as much as it does in the texts. Ethnographic studies have thrown much light on the living religion over the past hundred years, though this has applied mainly to the situation in Buddhist countries, and it is especially pertinent in countries such as Nepal (von Rospatt, 2004, 199–234) and Sri Lanka (Gombrich & Obeyesekare, 1998), where both religions exist side by side. A. von Rospatt, for example, has shown how an ordination ceremony for Buddhist boys in Kathmandu, of a type that was originally a Buddhist ordination ritual, subsequently came to parallel the Hindu *upanayana/vratabandha* ritual, the principal ritual of initiation for males into adulthood. It is not possible to extrapolate exactly from the contemporary situation in both countries back to the past, yet studies of lay involvement in Buddhist rituals and the ethnographic accounts of worship of Buddhist/Hindu deities in Sri Lanka can surely provide some guidance on similar activity in the four hundred years (200 BCE–200 CE) during which Buddhism expanded so rapidly in South Asia and interacted most forcefully with the emerging Hinduism. Like epigraphic evidence, ethnographic studies highlight the importance of non-elite lay followers in providing financial and material patronage to the *sangha* and individual monks as well as engaging in Buddhist-sanctioned life-cycle rituals.

Finally, archaeological evidence is becoming increasingly important in the study of Hindu–Buddhist interrelations. Excavation work in the 19th century focused mainly on monumental architecture and the classification of sites, especially the excavation and study of *stūpa*s. It pointed to the importance of the *sangha* in particular areas such as Taxila, Sanchi, Bharhut, and Amaravati, without filling in the gaps between these celebrated sites and tending to ignore their relationship with the immediate surrounding landscape, on the one hand, and the wider region, on the other. Looking at these sites in isolation does not tell us how the people who occupied them functioned in relation to laypeople in the immediate surroundings (given that the sites can be accurately dated), nor does it tell us of the economic functions they performed that enabled them to survive through the centuries.

Historical Interconnections

A historical survey of the interconnections and interrelations between Hinduism and Buddhism is more revealing than a thematic study. These interconnections can roughly be classified into four somewhat overlapping historical stages. Continuities and differences exist between all of these, and they are chosen primarily in reflection of the origin, rise, and decline of Buddhism in relation to the origin and flourishing of Hinduism. Usually the Buddhist texts are more open about their interrelations with other groups, such interrelations having to be inferred from the Hindu sources.

Buddhism and its Origins

The period of the beginnings of Buddhism in relation to its Brahmanical precursor, what G. Samuel (2008, 99) intelligently terms a "generic

Indo-Aryan cultural tradition," covers the years 500–250 BCE and encompasses the life of the Buddha and the early development of the *sangha*. It is not certain whether the early Pali texts were composed during the life of the Buddha, but they do focus – albeit retrospectively – mostly on this period, and it is very difficult to develop more than approximate chronologies. It is likely they are reflecting back into the past their composers' experience of the emergence of the Brahmans as a distinct social class, which was certainly increasing in momentum from the 2nd century BCE onward. These texts, however, remain the prime source on interreligious relations during this period, as the Brahmanical texts (they cannot be called Hindu yet) mention almost nothing outside of what occurs in a Brahmanical context.

What characterizes the Pali texts' treatment of Brahmanical doctrines and practices is their mild polemical flavor. Most of the polemics are put on the lips of the Buddha, in large measure to build up his image as a calm, serene figure who is at home at rebutting and reinterpreting central Brahmanical doctrines such as the → *ātman* theory and the idea of gift giving to monks as a substitute for the sacrifice and because of the authority it confers on his rebuttals. Certainly the Buddha knew the Brahmans' principal doctrines, but his is a critique of how they used these doctrines and their ritualist prerogatives to advance their own class interests. Thus it is a mixture of questioning class behavior as well as of conduct, all the passages collectively implying that the Buddha held a certain apprehensiveness about the Brahmans' status and prominence in communicating a specific view of culture. It cannot, however, be said at this stage that they were opponents when it comes to acquiring resources or converts, yet the early texts certainly portray them as confident and strongly aspirational.

Brahmans who have knowledge of the Vedas are depicted in the guise of wealthy landlords who seem to have had some economic power. What is given is a

> multi-faceted image of the brahmin as a figure who was a man of learning as well as a caster of spells and a reader of horoscopes, as the *Brahmajålasutta*, the first sutta in the Dīgha Nikāya, tells us in such great detail. Some brahmins engage in trade and in many cases become rich, while others follow despised callings like hunting. Such secular brahmins, though they might (as nowadays) be technically qualified by their brahmin birth to officiate at rituals, had frequently lost touch with the sacred techniques and knowledge pertaining to their lineage. (Bailey & Mabbett, 2003, 115)

The Early Spread of Buddhism

The period of the spread of the Buddhist order from northeastern India (400 BCE–270 BCE) and its meeting with other cultures, especially the generic Indo-Aryan cultural tradition, itself spreading southeast and south and being modified in the process, this modification creating the conditions out of which Hinduism would eventually arise, is difficult to describe with any degree of certainty, as is the development of the traditions against which Buddhist monks might have measured themselves. The *sangha* was developing in size and was moving into southwest India (the present-day states of Maharashtra and Madhya Pradesh) and southeast India (Andhra Pradesh and Orissa). Simultaneously, it can be inferred from textual evidence that the Brahmans had already moved from north-central India and brought their culture of social stratification and ritual activity with them. Both Buddhists and Brahmans, however, were required to come to terms with the fertility deities – often mother goddesses – they would encounter on their travels as a ubiquitous substratum of belief and practice. Such fertility deities – *yakṣa*s, *nāga*s, and various kinds of mother goddesses – occur frequently in early Buddhist and Jain literature but surface in Hindu literature mainly in the *Mahābhārata* and beyond.

This was also a period of considerable socioeconomic change with state formation and rising urbanism in much of north and central South Asia; these developments began in the previous period, with corresponding effects on the appearance of the built landscape, though it is impossible to learn how people responded to them at the time they were experiencing them. Given the likely expansion of the *sangha* during this period, patterns of elite patronage were being developed of a kind that would aid the expansion of the *sangha* in the next period and provoke a more determined call by the Brahmans to have their ritual activities underwritten by kings. Financial support for the *sangha* was coming from trading guilds in urban areas, guilds that were responding positively to the collective organization represented by the *sangha*, which had itself organizationally adapted to the changing times. This was in contrast to the

Brahmans, who had not developed any unitary institution and who still clung to a village environment rather than placing themselves within a framework of urbanism. Buddhist monks may have lived outside of towns and villages, but they did enter them for the purposes of fundraising and ritualized begging as well as engaging in teaching and healing activities.

Expansion of Buddhism and the Initial Development of Hinduism

The crucial period for the expansion of Buddhism, signaled most prominently as a strong institutional presence in the form of the *sangha* and the visible success that it achieved in patronage and material presence, encompasses the 450 years following the reign of Aśoka Maurya (269/268–232/231 BCE). The conspicuous presence of the *sangha* and the transformation of vedic tribal ritual centered on the Śrauta sacrifice into royal rituals associated with particular dynasties and regions provoked the Brahmans to develop an ultimately successful effort to define a new social/cultural/religious synthesis that brings together vedic religious continuities, the village substratum, and domesticized asceticism.

The reign of King Aśoka, the third of the Mauryan rulers, has been regarded as pivotal in the spread of the Buddhist order and – paradoxically – through its success, as a stimulant to the development and expansion of Hinduism, but the reigns of his two predecessors must also have been a significant causal factor, even if just by virtue of the length of their reigns. He laid the conditions for the geographical expansion of the *sangha*, because he freed up travel routes and provided royal patronage to the Buddhist order. It was a period of consolidation for the *sangha*, one in which there was a rationalization of modes of patronage and of raising money and acquiring land. Widespread construction of *stūpa*s and early forms of monastic accommodation took place during his reign, with much of this occurring in the Deccan (Morrison, 1995), Madhya Pradesh (Shaw, 2007), and Andhra Pradesh.

Evidence of lay support for Buddhist monumental construction is provided in many short inscriptions from Sanchi and Bharhut dating from the 1st century BCE. Buddhist art especially flourished during the first four hundred years of the early historic period from 200 BCE onwards. In contrast, it is only in about the 1st century BCE and thereafter that Hindu art began to develop at various locations, partially as a consequence of the development of devotional forms of religion in which worship (→ *pūjā*) of the deity was the central performative aspect of religious practice, and the act of gazing (*darśana*) on the deity was a fundamental part of this practice. There had to be easily accessible opportunities for gazing on the deity in a religious context. Similarly, Buddhists, and this included Buddhist monks, performed acts of *pūjā*, as many inscriptions – including the following one from Mathura – indicate, "(This is) the gift of the Monk Buddhapāla (which is made) as an act of pūjā for his parents and all beings" (Schopen, 1985, 35).

Royal patronage for Buddhism, and increasingly for Hinduism, was as significant a source of funding as lay and small business in financing the construction of monumental structures, and it continued well after 200 CE, with the inscriptions of the Shatavahanas in the Deccan showing them as prominent royal patrons of the *sangha* and also financial supporters of large Brahmanical sacrifices (Ray, 1986, 36). Leaving aside the fact that certain Shatavahana queens (Ray, 1986, 181) were active lay Buddhists, it is not always clear why this patronage was so widespread; H.P. Ray thinks that the granting of land for monasteries may have established a conflict-free zone for the king. No texts exist informing us whether Buddhist monks performed advisory roles in royal courts, although this may have been acceptable (though problematic) in practice, as the Buddha himself provided a precedent, when he was approached by kings and political elites for guidance. Brahmans often inhabited royal courts, whether as the king's ritual specialist (*purohita*), an instructor (*ācārya*), a tantric master giving magical advice about the defeat of enemies, or simply an ascetic who was on hand to give more general advice (Willis, 2009, ch. 3).

The elites of both religions functioned in the intellectually orientated realm and in the lay realm, which was more centered on ritual activity, and any attempt to dilute one level from the other certainly offers a serious simplification of a rich and highly complex socioreligious system. Despite the emphasis in early Buddhist literature on the Buddha's confrontation with Brahmans, epigraphical sources from Sanchi (and Bharhut) indicate clearly the extent to which people from all classes interacted with the *sangha* as donors to it. In addition, the placement of monasteries and *stūpa*s in the vicinity of villages and on trade routes must have brought the monks constantly into the presence of laypeople from all classes of society. It is the conspicuousness of the monk, dressed in saffron robes, that is important here, complementing the deliberate placement of Buddhist material structures to achieve maximum visibility. In equal measure, they point to the importance of a cult of the "monastic dead," which operates as a significantly different mode of disposal of the dead from what is found in Hinduism where cremation and scattering of the ashes is the preferred mode (except for *saṃnyāsins*).

What becomes apparent from the archaeological evidence across much of central India is that by the middle point of this period, the members of the *sangha* had in many cases localized themselves very successfully in microeconomies. J. Shaw suggests that this might have happened in the following way:

> Additional evidence... for the saṅgha's monopolisation of the rain-making business supports the impression of a religious institution deeply embedded in the rural infrastructure. That the nāgas which provided the ritual channel for the saṅgha's rain-making activities were placed next to the reservoirs – the ultimate symbol of the effects of timely rainfall on the one hand and of skilful water-storage techniques on the other – would have helped further to build up trust between the saṅgha and local farming communities. (Shaw, 2007, 192)

Such a concern with fertility is expressed in the common appearance of *yakṣa* images at Buddhist sites, leading G. Samuel to suggest, when dealing with Buddhist iconography, the following:

> All this iconographic material points to a religion of fertility and auspiciousness that gives full recognition to the female aspect of the procreative process and which finds its full expression in the early Buddhist sites that I have just mentioned. (Samuel, 2008, 109)

In sum, during this third period, between the 1st century BCE and the 3rd century CE, the *sangha* had maintained a high level of text production – the scholastic Abhidhamma literature dealing with the classification of psychological states, the Jātakas, and Buddhist Sanskrit literature – but it was also involved with the nonreligious aspects of life, even if just as an employer of labor and supervisor of slaves.

It is also the crucial period for the development of Hinduism, which emerged as an extremely rich and inclusive socioreligious system partially in response to the material and institutional success of Buddhism and because of the need to tie together a diverse set of religious practices under Brahmanical hegemony and an increasingly hierarchical social system. Following T. Lubin's (2005) analysis of the Brahmans' lack of a specific organizational institution, along the lines of the Buddhist *sangha*, and the manner in which they overcame what might have been a potential disadvantage, G. Samuel helps explain why the Brahmans might have eventually become more successful than the Buddhists:

> [T]he Brahmins remained relatively decentralised, with a firm base at the village level. They never developed the degree of centralisation in large monasteries in or near cities that was characteristic of the Buddhist and Jaina pattern, and which was eventually to lead to the vulnerability of those traditions to loss of state support. Brahmins became court ritualists, often associated with spectacular and wealthy temples, and they became royal administrators and bureaucrats, but they also built up a solid base of family land-holdings within South Asian villages that enabled them to survive the loss of power and support at the centre during the long periods of Muslim and British domination. (Samuel, 2008, 165)

At the same time, the rapid expansion of the *sangha* in the early historic period could not have escaped the notice of the Brahmans who were pressing forward the Brahman view of society, based on the idealized division of *varṇāśrama*. A response to Buddhism's conspicuous success was seemingly matched by the delineation of a specific Brahman social order, explicitly laid out in the various Dharmasūtras (3rd cent. BCE onward), which were presented as a detailed set of prescribed lifestyle and life-cycle rules applicable mainly to the upper levels of society. The extent of direct causality between this success and the codification of a Brahmanical view of the world is impossible to verify on the basis of the available debate, and it remains a hypothesis. Codification refers to the formulation of specific lifestyle prescriptions effecting a transformation of vedic ritual practices, often expensive to run and only effectively performed by royalty after 200 BCE, into household ritual and integrating this with mild ascetic practices and an imperative to the devotional worship of individual deities elevated to a universal practice. This was a codification incorporating a series of very rich practices and beliefs deriving from various regions of India into a framework where the Brahmans would have a steering influence on its transmission throughout the country and, through the use of Sanskrit, would inculcate it at all higher levels of society. All of the existing practices associated with multifarious worship of fertility deities; the extravagant cults surrounding holy men, vedic gods, and pastoral deities; and the performance of vedic rituals and the engagement with devotional festivals could now be brought under one umbrella.

The Brahmans had used the Dharmasūtras to lay down a formal set of rules governing everyday life and the stages of life over the lifetime of an adult male. In this, the social life of the male was fully encompassed, as was the demeanor of the Brahman as presenting a moderate ascetic pose even when involved in daily affairs. → Purity and impurity come to play a central role in distinguishing the Brahmans from the polluting functions of daily life, making them not unlike the monks living in a monastic environment partially removed from society. G. Samuel summarizes this:

> purity and spirituality become part of a hierarchical construction of society in which the purity of the Brahmin was counterposed to the impurity and this-worldly orientation of lower orders of society. At the same time, everyday life was systematically structured through a series of sacramental rituals, the saṃskāra, performed by Brahmin priests. (Samuel, 2008, 188)

But it was not enough just to codify these lifestyle prescriptions in highly elliptical texts that were increasingly unread because they were composed in Sanskrit and needed prose commentaries to render them comprehensible. In order for these ideas to be communicated beyond the upper-class, Sanskrit-literate person, other modes of communication were needed. Available were the two Sanskrit epics, both of them dominated by extended narrative plots involving individual quests, battles, gender complexities, and constant interaction between laypeople and holy figures. In the *Mahābhārata*, in particular, there were embedded interpretative passages composed in homiletic style, some of which also occur in the *Mānavadharmaśāstra*, and which are concentrated in book 12 of the *Mahābhārata*, where they define normative relations between Brahmans and kings, plus a lot of philosophical material that attempted to cover the whole gamut of existing metaphysical positions, such as → Sāṃkhya and → Yoga. Some of this material has direct literal correspondences (Bailey, 2011) in Pali literature, and there are certainly other intertextual references to Buddhist doctrines and texts.

In the various schools of Buddhism, the Brahmans had to confront a successful institution that was both highly centralized and decentralized; on the one hand, it was centralized since wandering monks would stay at distant monasteries and maintain a flow of information, based on a fount of commonly shared knowledge – political as well as religious and social; on the other hand, it was decentralized because the monasteries were very much involved with local communities. The monks also had a common religious foundation in the Buddha's teachings – which permitted some variance at the side – and a rigorous system of conduct, the details of which would not have been known by laypeople, except to the extent that it was known that there did exist a set of rules requiring more disciplined conduct from monks and thereby differentiating them from laypeople, whose conduct was determined by less stringent requirements. Against this, the Brahmans had to bring together a strong set of heterogeneous practices and beliefs under a framework that would never have a formal institutional centrality along the lines of the *sangha*. The problem is, as K. Chakrabarti explains, this:

> Brahmanism is a polytheistic religion with no hierarchically regulated monastic organization, nor a single revealed text of inviolable authenticity. Therefore it was all the more necessary to try and construct for itself an unambiguous self-identity which would mark it out from other religious communities. Out of this necessity were born the three fundamental points of reference: the infallibility of the Vedas, the social and ritual superiority of the brāhmaṇas, and preservation of the varṇāśramadharma. (Chakrabarti, 2001, 147)

While these themes operated as a kind of superstructure, the doctrines associated with them pervaded all Hindu literature from the *Mahābhārata* onward.

Hinduism could not have developed without its incorporation of → *bhakti* in a systemic sense as both practice and doctrine. Whether its formalized formulation was a response to cults of devotion that had developed around the Buddha/ *bodhisattvas* and prominent monks cannot be confirmed and remains a matter of speculation. Viṣṇu appears as the center of a devotional → Bhāgavata cult by around 150 BCE; devotional doctrines around → Kṛṣṇa are certainly systematized in the → *Bhagavadgītā* and around Nārāyaṇa elsewhere in the *Mahābhārata* by the beginning of the Common Era (Malinar, 2007) and around Śiva in the *Śvetāśvataropaniṣad* by the 1st or 2nd century CE (Oberlies, 1988). It is more than likely that the Brahmans could not ignore the many localized devotional cults, especially since some were extending their horizon by connecting themselves with deities like Viṣṇu and Śiva. Where the new *bhakti* cults differed sharply from other forms of veneration of fertility deities and mother goddesses was that it was believed that the deity at the center of the cult could confer on the devotee both good merit and an end to rebirth – something adopted from the various ascetic groups, who were all united in their desire to achieve an end to rebirth. Veneration of fertility deities related to pragmatic concerns, whereas that of *bhakti* deities encompassed both pragmatic and transcendental goals (see Malinar, 2007, 237f.).

In writing mainly of the *Harivaṃśa* and the *Bhagavadgītā*, but with clear relevance to the *Mahābhārata* more generally, A. Couture suggests that the kind of monotheism associated with devotional texts arises as a response to the fragmentation of culture:

> These texts are clearly not prone to contestation or revolution, but try, it seems to me, to adjust themselves with the greatest possible flexibility to a diversifying social context. The model which seems to have been put in place towards the fourth or third century before our era gives to a fragmenting population the consciousness of being able to address itself to the same god. This new universalism could have been a typically Hindu response to an India which has been urbanised and which finds itself more and more difficult, in truth impossible, to respect the ritual prescriptions that it judges, in part at least, to have lapsed. (Couture, 2005, 175)

Similar are A. Malinar's views on the emergence of what she has called "cosmological monotheism" the paradigmatic model of Hindu theologies which allows the accommodation not only of different gods and goddess, but also different methods of gaining "liberation" within the hierarchy of a cosmos created by a "highest," ultimately transcendent god (such as Kṛṣṇa or Śiva). It is a paradigm

> that could serve to reject any one-sided emphasis on ascetic renunciation, while at the same time accommodating it together with Vedic polytheism, Upaniṣadic thoughts on the cosmic "one" and the values of social-ritual life. It is arguable these developments mirror, albeit contrastively, the "monotheistic/polytheistic" tendencies in the development of the Bodhisattva doctrine, which dates to the same time as the later portions of the Mahābhārata. (Malinar, 2007, 237–241)

The *Mahābhārata* and *Rāmāyaṇa* were probably both quickly reworked in truncated forms in vernacular languages, guaranteeing a much wider audience than anticipated by those who had initially composed and disseminated them. In the Buddhist Jātaka tales (1st cent. CE), both epics are alluded to, and some aspects of the plot of the *Mahābhārata* are treated in a condemnatory manner. Given that the Jātaka tales were popular tales then and remain so today, their partially critical reception of the *Mahābhārata* may be considered a sign of the popularity of that text. What this meant on the ground and especially for those classes beyond the Brahmans can only be guessed at in the absence of other evidence.

Hinduism's Expansion and Buddhism's Decline

Buddhism's internationalization and eventual decline, contrasted with Hinduism's expansion (100 CE–1400 CE), forms the fourth historical stage and encompasses the so-called medieval period, always very difficult to define in the Hindu context. It covers the rise of the imperial Guptas (320 CE) and finishes roughly around 1400 CE, at a time when powerful Islamic sultanates have long been established in North India. Usually its finishing point is taken to correspond to a time when Buddhist monastic life had declined to such an extent that it was isolated in West Bengal, even as Buddhism was flourishing in Sri Lanka and elsewhere outside of South Asia, often in conjunction with Hinduism – as was especially the situation in Southeast Asia.

Up until 200–250 CE, Buddhism interacted with Hinduism as its chief competitor, at least for material resources and the dissemination of ideas, even if most people that could have been included under the broad umbrella of Hinduism would not have seen this in competitive terms. By about 250 CE, both religions had substantially consolidated. To what extent Buddhism engaged in conversional activity – a very prominent theme in early Buddhist literature – is simply impossible to say. Hindus normally do not engage in such activity. It is likely that most laypeople gave alms to wandering *bhikkhus*, attended Buddhist festivals, worshipped Hindu gods, and venerated Hindu ascetics, especially those regarded as charismatic. And in that kind of environment, conversion meant very little, unless a lay Hindu, especially a Brahman, became a monk and adopted the partially renunciatory lifestyle associated with that. Similarly, it cannot be ascertained how much Buddhist and Brahman intellectuals engaged in each other's work, though in the writings of → Śaṅkara (788–820 CE), among others, there is certainly a sense that Hindu philosophers were criticizing developments in Buddhist philosophy, and, as R. Davidson (2002, 102–105) has shown, Buddhist philosophers were increasingly adopting the epistemological positions of Hindu philosophical schools in attempting to validate the veracity of the Buddha's word.

Continuities between the third and fourth period are legion, though the further the fourth period proceeded, the less influence the *sangha* seems to have exercised. The task of the Brahmans to determine the framework of society had been substantially successful, the groundwork having already been completed in the third period, and their capacity to sustain this guiding role in the absence of material wealth to back up their power demonstrated the extent to which they had obtained the support of the wealthy at a microlevel. And because most Brahmans were directly involved in everyday socioeconomic life, they had probably become much closer to the general population than were the Buddhist monks, who tended to work through intermediaries and isolated themselves in monasteries. From the perspective of patronage, certain dynasties (Shatavahanas, Palas, and some Kashmiri dynasties) still patronized Buddhist monasteries and continued to provide money for the upkeep of cave sites such as Ajanta and monastic universities like Nalanda.

An important new religious development during this period was the rise and popularization of → Tantra. Both Buddhist and Hindu forms of Tantrism had developed by the 4th century CE, often taught in difficult texts, composed in Sanskrit, and utilizing a complex liturgical procedure. In terms of doctrine and practice, Tantrism was not markedly different in either religion. Because of the richness of Tantrism both textually and ritually, it is extremely difficult to define it precisely, but in G. Samuel's words,

> We have a body of ritual practices and traditions in both Buddhist and Śaiva sources, that present themselves as sophisticated and elevated means for the attainment of exalted spiritual goals, yet contain reference to practices that seem deliberately transgressive and bizarre: night-time orgies in charnel grounds, involving the eating of human flesh, the use of ornaments, bowls and musical instruments made from human bones, sexual relations while seated on corpses and the like. (Samuel, 2008, 232–233)

In both Buddhist and Hindu Tantra, rituals were developed involving rigorous meditation and aimed at the envisioning of deities in order to obtain liberating insight. How much these went beyond narrow circles of devotees cannot easily be ascertained, though it is likely that some monasteries in northeastern India were renowned centers of tantric practice by the 8th–9th centuries CE.

R. Davidson (2002, 105–106) has argued that after the 7th century CE, the Indian political landscape was no longer characterized by large dynastic lineages giving generously to the *sangha* but had dissolved into feudatories, weakening the larger urban centers and the guilds that they had supported for so long. In this kind of environment, the surviving monasteries had to align themselves with the local feudal power and functioned like feudal centers themselves, as did Hindu monasteries with increasing success (Malinar, 2011).

They provided education in the local area – as they had always done – and functioned like feudal lords centered around and owing allegiance to a central monastery. The internalizing of the feudalistic values on the part of the abbots and senior monks was made all the more serious because of the collapse in lay support, which had in the previous period been so crucial in the maintenance of monastic activities and the *sangha*'s building program.

R. Davidson further points out that

> Buddhist institutions could not effectively compete for patronage from militaristic princes, who increasingly found that they were best represented by Śaiva values and rhetoric. Śaiva systems made allowance for forms of behaviour that Buddhist syntheses could not support, since even the most syncretic Buddhist systems were not as open to negotiation about issues of violence, power and self-aggrandizement as were the medieval Śaiva representatives. (Davidson, 2002, 86)

To properly adjust to the new political dispensation would have required a compromise of Buddhist ethical values that their rules of conduct (*vinaya*) translated into specific forms of conduct consistent with the Buddha's teachings. For the Brahmans and the great majority of lower-class Hindus, this would not have been a problem, because their survival did not depend on the preservation of a particular monastic institution such as the *sangha*, even if the local ruler was supposed to oversee the maintenance of class boundaries. Moreover the continuing growth of Hindu monastic organizations seems in part to have been a consequence of their capacity to deal effectively with royal and other political elites (Malinar, 2011, 119).

A final indication of the decline of Buddhism in a famous site like Sanchi is reflected in the discovery (Shaw, 2007, 176) over the last ten years of 32 new Buddhist sculptures dating from between the late 2nd century BCE and the 1st century CE and 10 dating from between the 2nd and 12th centuries CE. In contrast, no Brahmanical sculptures have been found from the period between the 2nd century BCE and the 1st century CE, and 1,197 have been found dating from between the 2nd and the 12th centuries CE. These are very telling statistics that need to be confirmed by detailed listings from other sites.

Conclusion

Because of the nature of the sources available for dealing with the interaction between Hinduism and Buddhism, much of what can be said is only inference on the basis of texts that are loath to be critical of alien beliefs or that do not recognize the sharp differences among religions that Western scholars often strive to find. Nor do the texts give detailed descriptions of actual forms of interaction, conflict, cooperation, or difference or, most of all, of the common respect that laypeople most likely would have had for most holy people of any religion or sectarian group.

It can be assumed that monks would have interacted with people from all classes, irrespective of their socioreligious background. In a monastic setting, especially where it was associated with a well-patronized *stūpa*, from a very early period interaction would have occurred with all classes and would have been both formal and informal. For most people, contact would have been in the manner of acceptance rather than contestation. The question then concerns the extent to which meetings with monks became an everyday event that was accepted as normal and the extent to which Buddhism was simply part of the habitual religious landscape. In saying this, there is an assumption that Hinduism (in all its forms) was the default backdrop into which other religions fitted or against which they became visible. Of course, this remains an assumption for the very reason that Buddhist monasteries and monks may have been so common in certain areas that the dominant religious background was Buddhism, even where folk forms of Hinduism were also everywhere in evidence. J. Shaw's study of Sanchi suggests this might have been the case there, yet much of the textual evidence – highly tendentious, as it is – indicates a multiplicity of practices, with religious pragmatism dominating at the social level, where intellectual practices were not emphasized by using Sanskrit as the basic linguistic medium.

It is easy to overinterpret the extent of conflict and contrast, if reliance is simply placed on the textual accounts to draw a picture of Hindu–Buddhist relations in the early historic period. After the 4th century CE, when both Hindu and Buddhist philosophers had laid down their scholastic positions on broad philosophical questions, from the perspective of their own traditions, there emerged considerable debate but within a rather narrow and conciliatory framework.

Bibliography

Bailey, G., "'Him I Call a Brahmin': Further Instances of Intertextuality between the *Mahābhārata* and some Pāli Texts," in: B. Tikkanen & A.M. Butters, eds., *Pūrvāparaprajñābhinandanam: East and West, Past and Present: Indological and Other Essays in Honour of Klaus Kartunnen*, StO 110, Helsinki, 2011, 3–19.

Bailey, G., & I. Mabbett, *The Sociology of Early Buddhism*, Cambridge UK, 2003.

Bronkhorst, J., *Greater Magadha: Studies in the Culture of Early India*, Leiden, 2007.

Bronkhorst, J., *Buddhism in the Shadow of Brahmanism*, Leiden, 2011.

Chakrabarti, K., *Religious Process: The Purāṇas and the Making of a Regional Tradition*, New Delhi, 2001.

Couture, A., "Urbanisations et innovations religieuses en Inde ancienne," *BEFEO* 92, 2005, 159–179.

Davidson, R., *Indian Esoteric Buddhism: A Social History of the Tantric Movement*, New York, 2002.

DeCaroli, R., *Haunting the Buddha: Indian Popular Religions and the Formation of Buddhism*, New York, 2004.

Fitzgerald, J., *The Mahābhārata*, vol. VII, Chicago, 2004.

Gombrich, R.F., *How Buddhism Began: The Conditioned Genesis of the Early Teachings*, London, 2006.

Gombrich, R.F., & G. Obeyesekare, *Buddhism Transformed: Religious Change in Sri Lanka*, Princeton, 1988.

Inden, R., "Imperial Purāṇas: Kashmir as Vaiṣṇava Centre of the World," in: R. Inden, J. Walters & D. Ali, *Querying the Medieval: Texts and the History of Practices in South Asia*, New York, 2000, 29–98.

Jurewicz, J., "Playing with Fire: The *pratītyasamutpāda* from the Perspective of Vedic Thought," *JPTS* 26, 2000, 77–103.

Klaus, K., Review of Bronkhorst, J., *Greater Magadha: Studies in the Culture of Early India*, Leiden, 2007, *ZDMG*, 161/1, 2011, 216–221.

Lubin, T., "The Transmission, Patronage, and Prestige of Brahmanical Piety from the Mauryas to the Guptas," in: F. Squarcini, ed., *Boundaries, Dynamics, and Construction of Traditions in South Asia*, Florence, 2005, 77–103.

Malinar, A., *The Bhagavadgītā: Doctrines and Contexts*, Cambridge UK, 2007.

Malinar, A., "Monasteries," in: K.A. Jacobsen, H. Basu, A. Malinar & V. Narayanan, eds., *Brill's Encyclopedia of Hinduism*, vol. III, Leiden, 2011, 116–126.

McGovern, N., "Brahmā: An Early and Ultimately Doomed Attempt at a Brahmanical Synthesis," *JIPh* 40/1, 2011, 1–23, preprint http://0-www.springerlink.com.

Morrison, K., "Trade, Urbanism, and Agricultural Expansion: Buddhist Monastic Institutions and the State in Early Historic Western Deccan," *WA* 27/2, 1995, 203–221.

Oberlies, T., "Die Śvetāśvatāra-Upaniṣad: Eine Studie Ihrer Gotteslehre," *WZKS* 32, 1988, 35–62.

Ray, H.P., *Monastery and Guild: Commerce under the Såtavåhanas*, Delhi, 1986.

Rospatt, A. von, "The Transformation of the Monastic Ordination (*pravrajyā*) into a Rite of Passage in Newar Buddhism," in: J. Gengnagel, U. Hüsken & S. Raman, eds., *Words and Deeds: Hindu and Buddhist Rituals in South Asia*, Wiesbaden, 2005, 199–234.

Samuel, G., *The Origins of Yoga and Tantra: Indic Religions to the Thirteenth Century*, Cambridge UK, 2008.

Schopen, G., "Two Problems in the History of Indian Buddhism: The Layman/Monk Distinction and the Doctrine of the Transference of Merit," *StII* 10, 1985, 9–47.

Schopen, G., "The Buddhist Monastery and the Indian Garden: Aesthetics, Assimilations, and the Siting of Monastic Estabishments," *JAOS* 126/4, 2006, 487–505.

Seyfort-Ruegg, D., *The Symbiosis of Buddhism with Brahmanism/Hinduism in South Asia and of Buddhism with "Local Cults" in Tibet and the Himalayan Region*, Vienna, 2008.

Shaw, J., *Buddhist Landscapes in Central India: Sanchi Hill and Archeologies of Religious and Social Change 3rd century BC to 5th century AD*, London, 2007.

Singh, U., "Cults and Shrines in Early Historical Mathura (c. 200 BC–AD 200)," *WA* 36/3, 2004, 378–398.

Willis, M., *The Archeology of Hindu Ritual: Temples and the Establishment of the Gods*, Cambridge UK, 2009.

Greg Bailey

Modern Period

Buddhism flourished in India for more than 15 hundred years. It gradually disappeared from the areas that today are defined by the modern nation of India, with its final disappearance probably from around the 12th century CE. During these more than 15 hundred years, Buddhist and Hindu traditions influenced each other in numerous ways, both because of disagreements and exchange of ideas and because of competition for power and ritual clients. However, Buddhism never disappeared from South Asia and continued to prosper in the southern part of South Asia on the island of → Sri Lanka and northern part in the mountainous regions of the Himalayas, areas that also have a strong Hindu presence. It is nevertheless common to conceptualize the history of Buddhism in India as a history of flourishing and disappearance and the discovery of India's Buddhist past by civil servants of the British imperial power in the 18th and 19th centuries (Almond, 1988), half a millennium after Buddhism had disappeared. The discovery of a Buddhist golden age of ancient India had consequences for the modern Hindu understanding of Buddhism, and it led ultimately to a revival and rebirth of Buddhism in India in the 20th century.

Hindu Inclusion of Buddhism

The disappearance of Buddhism from India caused its disappearance partly also from memory. Even the Buddhist sacred sites were in a ruinous condition, many had been forgotten, and some such as the famous Buddhist pilgrimage place of Bodh Gaya had become Hindu sacred sites (Barua, 1934; Kinnard, 1998). In the past, a number of features of the Hindu traditions may have come into being because of influences from Buddhism and the Śramaṇa traditions (Bronkhorst, 2006; Jacobsen, 2013; Jacobsen and Smart, 2006; Jaini, 1970; Joshi, 1983), but this influence of Buddhism on the formation of Hindu traditions has often not been known or accepted by Hindus. Buddhist influences on the Hindu traditions had probably come about because Brahmans impressed with Shramanical ideas changed the vedic tradition from within (Olivelle, 1992, 36), as responses to criticism and because of changes in the Hindu traditions driven by competition with Buddhists for ritual clients and donations (*dāna*). Central religious ideas of the Śramaṇa traditions, such as *punarjanma* (rebirth), → *saṃsāra*, → *karman*, *mokṣa* (→ liberation), and → *ahiṃsā*, may have entered the vedic tradition in this way. As systems of related ideas, these concepts became part of the vedic textual traditions for the first time in the last part of the → Veda, the → Upaniṣads. Changes may also have come about because the power and popularity of the Śramaṇa traditions posed challenges to the vedic traditions. Several of the kings of ancient India were Buddhists, most important among them Aśoka (r. 272–232 BCE, Mauryan Empire), Kaniṣka (r. 78–101 CE, Kushana Empire), and Harṣa (r. 606–647, Harṣa's empire). Buddhism attracted support from a number of tra-

Fig. 1: Buddha *pūjā*, in private home, contemporary Madhya Pradesh (photo Knut A. Jacobsen).

ditional patrons of the Brahmans, and this might have produced hostility (Jaini, 1970, 42).

A significant alteration in the Hindu understanding of Buddhism in the modern period was the recognition of a Buddhist influence on the formation of Hindu traditions. Since this Buddhist influence was unknown to many Hindus, and Buddhism was considered a tradition opposed to the Veda, this marked an important change. L.M. Joshi has suggested that in Hinduism it was Swami → Vivekananda (1863–1902) who was "the first to recognize and publicly declare the Hindu indebtedness to the Buddha's ideas" (Joshi, 1983, 19). The influence of Rabindranath → Tagore and others who started to use Buddhist stories in their work has also been referred to (Coward, 1995, 283; Fiske, 1976, 134). L.M. Joshi has correctly called attention to the extraordinariness of this shift in the attitude toward the Buddha. Buddha had indeed earlier, in the mid-first millennium CE (from the 7th cent. CE), been incorporated in the Hindu traditions as an → *avatāra* of → Viṣṇu. But this did not necessarily mark an acceptance of a Buddhist influence, and it was probably not an attempt to include Buddhists in the Hindu traditions, as is sometimes believed. Instead, the Buddha's task as an *avatāra* was, according to some traditions, to deceive, that is, to make evil beings followers of a mistaken teaching to make sure evil beings did not attain heaven. The → *mantra* that pays homage to the Buddha *avatāra* reads, *namo buddhāya daitya dānava mohine*, "Homage to the Buddha who deceived *daitya*s and *dānava*s" (*BhāgP.* 10.40.22). In other words, the incorporation of Buddha as an *avatāra* of Hinduism denounced Buddhism as a demonic tradition. This interpretation of the Buddha *avatāra* in Hinduism was a theological construct. Worship of the Buddha *avatāra* has not been widespread in Hindu temples, but the worship can also be understood as an example of the peaceful coexistence of Buddhists and Hindus, which has been the dominant feature of their relation. Nevertheless, this Hindu tradition of seeing the Buddha as an *avatāra* of Viṣṇu that came to delude evil people probably also had wide acceptance, as shown in some early Western scholarship on religion in India. The *Encyclopedia Britannica*, as late as 1842, began its entry on Buddhism by defining the Buddha as "one of the two appearances of Vishnu, assumed for the purpose of deluding the enemies of the gods, and effecting their destruction by leading them to profess heretical opinions, and thus to reject the Hindu religion" (Almond, 1988, 16).

The recognition of a Buddhist influence that was initiated by Vivekananda led to the inclusion of Buddhism in Hinduism. This meant a reversal of earlier ideas of the Buddha *avatāra*. The Buddha was now seen as a person who successfully purified Hinduism from erroneous practices. "The Buddha was accepted as an *avatara* who reclaimed Hindus from sanguinary rites and erroneous practices and purified their religion of the numerous abuses which had crept into it," wrote the Hindu statesman and philosopher S. → Radhakrishnan (1888–1975; Holt, 2004, 21). The Buddha thus helped Hindus by initiating necessary changes in their religion; particularly important was the Buddha's teaching of *ahiṃsā*, an important symbol for the identity of modern Hinduism. The purpose of the Hindu Buddha was no longer to deceive evil beings who followed a mistaken teaching but to correct the teaching of good people, as a reformer of Hinduism. It was now held that Buddha was born, grew up, and died a Hindu, and that Buddhism was an offshoot of Hinduism. J.C. Holt has correctly underscored the radical newness of this Hindu admiration for the Buddha:

> In light of the Buddha's critique of Brahmanism and the consequent hostility that it provoked, it is remarkable that the image of the Buddha was eventually rehabilitated and incorporated into many Hindu normative constructions, that the Buddha was eventually embraced by some modern Hindus as one of the greatest teachers of humankind, and that some other Hindus would go so far as to say that the Buddha was, in fact, even born a Hindu. (Holt, 2004, 10)

In the 19th and 20th centuries, Buddhism became recognized as an important part of the heritage and history of India. The recovery of Buddhist monuments had revealed an Indian golden age of the past. The publication and translation of volumes of the Pali Canon had identified a great literary heritage in an ancient Indian language other than Sanskrit. That Buddhism had spread to large parts of Asia and had also become highly regarded in the West was understood as an admiration of Indian values. The creation of modern Buddhism, "which tend[s] to see Buddhism as above all a system of rational and ethical philosophy divorced from the daily practices of the vast majority of Buddhists" (Lopez, 2002, 19), had also made Buddhism attractive to Indian intellectuals (who mostly, however, did not convert; Fiske, 1976, 134–137). For several reasons, therefore, the Buddhist heritage became an important part of Indian nationalism and the construction of the identity of India. This new knowledge was important for the reevaluation of Buddha and Buddhist teachings in modern Hinduism.

Several Hindu intellectuals understood Buddhism as a branch of Hinduism, especially as a school of philosophy that was basically in agreement with Advaita → Vedānta. This philosophical system of → Śaṅkara had been influenced by Buddhist ideas. Śaṅkara was called a crypto-Buddhist (*prachannabauddha*) by other teachers of Vedānta because of the similarity they saw between Buddhist philosophy and Śaṅkara's Vedānta. Many modern Hindu intellectuals reversed also this Buddhist influence on Hinduism and saw instead Buddha as a teacher of Hinduism. "Buddhism is one of our sects," wrote Vivekananda, and he maintained that "Buddha was one of the *saṃnyāsin*s of the Vedānta." The Buddha was able to bring out "the truths from the hidden Vedas" (Vivekananda, 1962–1965, vol. I, 22), which meant that the teaching of the Buddha was in reality a vedic philosophy: "The ideas which now are called Buddhism were not his. They were much more ancient" (Vivekananda, 1962–1965, vol. IV, 135; vol. V, 309). According to Vivekananda, therefore, all the essential doctrines of Buddhism were borrowed from the Veda, that is, the Upaniṣads, which according to Vivekananda were pre-Buddhist (Joshi, 1983, 31). Other Hindu intellectuals promoted a similar view of Buddhism as a school of Hinduism and Vedānta. S. Radhakrishnan understood the Buddha as one who accepted the teaching of the Upaniṣads. According to S. Radhakrishnan, the Buddha believed in → *brahman*, only he gave *brahman* a different name, *dharma* (truth, the nature of things). S. Radhakrishnan understood the famous last words of the Buddha to mean that one should take refuge in the → *ātman/brahman* (Murti, 1992, 567–605). The great scholar on → Dharmśāstra P.V. Kane in the same way stated that the Buddha continued the tradition of the ancient vedic and Brahmanical seers and was only a reformer of Hinduism (Kane, 1962, 1004–1005). A representative example of this trend in the interpretation of Buddhism in 20th-century Hindu philosophy reads,

> Buddhism and Vedānta should not be viewed as two opposed systems but only as different stages in the development of the same central thought which starts with the Upaniṣads, finds its indirect support in Buddha, its elaboration in Mahāyāna Buddhism, its open revival in Gauḍapāda, which reaches its zenith in Shaṅkara and culminates in post-Shaṅkarites. So far the similarities between Buddhism and Vedānta are concerned, they are so many and so strong that by no stretch of imagination can they be denied or explained otherwise. So far as the differences are concerned, they are few and mostly they are not vital. Most of them rest on a grave misunderstanding of Buddhism. (Sharma, 1960, 318)

The general view is that the Buddha did not teach anything new, but simply restated the teaching of the Upaniṣads and is therefore grounded in Vedānta. A fundamental doctrine of Buddhism, such as the theory of no-self (Skt. *anātman*; Pal. *anatta*), is denied as part of Buddhism, because Buddhism "does not deny the existence of the true Ātman, the Pure Self, which is Pure Consciousness and which is the only reality" (Sharma, 1960, 325). Likewise, according to this type of Hinduization of the teaching of Buddhism, the concept of *śūnya* means not only *māyā* (illusion) and refers to the *dharma*s (constituents of human experience) as empty, but also *brahman* since appearances imply that there is a reality of which they are appearances. Here Hindu views, which are quite contrary to the teaching of Buddhism, are projected on Buddhism, and the justification for it is that Buddhism at the outset had been defined as a school of Vedānta, thus there could be no difference between Buddhism and Vedānta. Other common Hindu interpretations of Buddhism are the identification of the Buddhist *nirvāṇa* with the *brahman* of the Upaniṣads and the claim that the doctrine of no-self (*anātman*) is a denial only of the lower self.

These interpretations reduce Buddhism to a form of Hindu philosophy and imply a denial of a separate identity of Buddhists and Buddhism. The inclusiveness of Hinduism exemplified above was expressed also in the Constitution of India, which uses the term "Hindus" to include Buddhists, stating that "the reference to Hindus shall be construed as including a reference to persons professing the Sikh, Jaina or Buddhist religion, and the reference to Hindu religious institutions shall be construed accordingly" (article 25.2.b). The Hindu nationalists have included Buddhism in their concept of *hindutva*, and the concept "Indic religion" does sometimes have similar implications, seeming to imply (mistakenly) that Buddhism, Jainism, and Sikhism are split offs from Hinduism (see also → nationalism). However, Hindu teachers such as Vivekananda also accepted that Buddhism was a protest against the religion of the Veda because of its sacrificial violence. But, it was argued, the Buddha was mistaken in breaking up the tradition. It was because he did not understand the harmony of religions, and he therefore "introduced sectarianism" (Joshi, 1983). Other times Vivekananda traced the origin of Buddhism to the struggles between Kṣatriyas and Brāhmaṇas (Brahmans) and stated that Buddhism opened the religion of the Upaniṣads to all castes (Joshi, 1983, 31). Another element in the Hindu view of Buddhism is the explanation of the relationship between Hinduism and Buddhism as the same as between Judaism and Christianity, only with the difference that Judaism rejected Christ, but Hindus started to worship the Buddha (Joshi, 1983, 32). This view was probably influenced by similar speculations of Western orientalists who compared the relationship between Hinduism and Buddhism to that of Catholicism and Protestantism.

Admiration of the Buddha characterized the view of many Hindu intellectuals during the 20th century, both secular intellectuals and religious *gurus* who sometimes drew on both Hindu and Buddhist traditions of → Yoga and → meditation. However, the admiration of the Buddha was not shared by all. The Hindu nationalist V. Savarkar, one of the founding figures of the political ideology of Hindu nationalism, while seeing Buddhism as a sect of Hinduism, nevertheless saw the dominance of Buddhism and its emphasis on meditation and *ahiṃsā* in ancient India as the cause of foreign invasions. V.P. Kane saw tantric Buddhism as the cause of decay of India (Kane, 1962, 1029–1030) and supported his view by quoting Vivekananda, who wrote,

> The most hideous ceremonies, the most horrible, the most obscene books that human hands ever wrote or the human brain ever conceived, the most bestial forms that ever passed under the name of religion, have all been the creation of degraded Buddhism.

Nevertheless, for Vivekananda, this condemnation of tantric Buddhism did not cancel out his admiration for the Buddha and his teaching; on the contrary, Vivekananda wrote, "Hinduism has become so great only by absorbing the ideas of the Buddha" (Vivekananda, vol. IV, 507). Mahatma → Gandhi similarly argued that the Buddha had recovered the truth of the Veda and considered Buddhism part of Hinduism:

> Gautama was saturated with the best that was in Hinduism and gave life to some of the teachings that were buried in the Veda and which were overgrown with weeds. His great Hindu spirit cut its way through the forest of words, which had overlaid the golden truth that was the Vedas. (extract from a speech by Gandhi held in Colombo, Sri Lanka, 1928; see Ahir, 2009, 14)

The Buddhist Symbols of the Nation of India

The lion capital of the Aśoka pillar from Sarnath is the national emblem of India, and the Aśoka wheel (*cakra*) from the base of the same Aśoka pillar from Sarnath is placed in the center of the Indian flag. That the two main symbols of the nation of India have strong Buddhist associations has to do with not only the Hindu celebration of a golden age of India as an ancient Buddhist civilization, but also the rebirth of Buddhism in modern India. The first Indian prime minister, Jawaharlal Nehru, had a distaste for religion in public life, but he greatly admired Buddhism, because he saw in it a scientific and ethical attitude. There were no large Buddhist communities in India at the time of independence in 1947, so the lion capital and the Aśoka wheel were not thought to symbolize a living community but a period of history. The main reason for the use of these symbols with strong Buddhist associations for the national emblem and the national flag is that it was suggested by Bhimrao Ramji → Ambedkar (1891–1956), the most important Buddhist leader of modern India, but who had at that time not formally converted, even though he had proclaimed already in 1935 that while he was born a Hindu, he did not intend to die one. Ambedkar was one of the six members of the flag committee constituted in June

1947. Ambedkar proudly recalled that he got the lion capital and the Aśoka wheel adopted without anyone in the Constituent Assembly opposing it (Beltz, 2005). The fact that the Sarnath lion capital became the national emblem and the Aśoka wheel a national symbol on the flag because of Ambedkar is not often recognized. Ambedkar lobbied for the adoption of a number of other Buddhist features to become part of the Indian state between 1947 and 1950, not only the wheel of *dharma* (the teaching of the Buddha) on the flag and the Aśoka lion as the emblem of the nation, but also the inscription of a Buddhist aphorism on the pediment of the Rashtrapati Bhavan, the residence of the president of the republic (Jaffrelot, 2005), and for the *buddha jayantī* (the birthday celebration of the Buddha) to feature in India's official calendar. Inclusion of these Buddhist features was conceived as a celebration of India's glorious past as a great Buddhist civilization, as was the great 2,500-year commemoration of *buddha jayantī* in New Delhi in 1956.

Fig. 2: Entrance wall of Indian Ambedkarite Buddhists (picture above the doors displays the identity; photo Knut A. Jacobsen).

Rebirth of Buddhism in India

The Hindu views of Buddhism described above were mainly those of Brahmans. The conversions to Buddhism, which mark the rebirth of Buddhism as a living religion in India, were, however, mostly among low castes (see Ahir, 1989). The rebirth of Buddhism in India was due not to Hindus considering the Buddha to be a Hindu, but to untouchables (→ Dalits) who had never been accepted as fully Hindu and who, by the act of conversion, wanted to separate themselves from Hinduism and escape the doctrines of caste and → untouchability. They emphasized the disagreements and conflicts between Buddhism and Hinduism and considered the Buddha a main opponent of Hindus. By converting to a different religion, they wanted to be identified by religion and not by caste.

The most successful movement of conversions to Buddhism in modern India was led by B.R. Ambedkar, who converted in 1956 in a ceremony in the city of Nagpur together with several hundred thousand members of the Mahar caste, the caste to which Ambedkar belonged. Most of contemporary India's around ten million Buddhists belong to the Buddhist movement founded by Ambedkar. Quite opposite to the modern Hindu tendencies of identifying Hinduism and Buddhism with the universal teaching of Vedānta as the truth of all religions, Ambedkar stated that "[t]here cannot be a thesis more false than the thesis that all religions are true" (Ambedkar, 1995, 36). Ambedkar believed that the Dalits could not attain justice in Hinduism and advised them to convert to another religion. Ambedkar argued that the Dalits were descendants of the early Buddhists and that their ancestors had been ostracized from the community by the Hindus who had migrated into India and demanded that they convert to their religion. Those who refused had been given the status of untouchable. The Dalits were the original inhabitants, according to Ambedkar, and when they now converted to Buddhism, they returned to their original religion.

The rebirth of Buddhism in India did not, however, start with Ambedkar's conversion in 1956, but in 1891 (considered "the most memorable year in the history of Indian Buddhism" [Ahir, 1989, 4] since Ambedkar also was born in that year) with the founding by the Sri Lankan Buddhist leader Anagarika Dharmapala (Don

David Hewavitarne; "the first to hoist the flag of Buddhism in modern India," Ahir, 1989, 5) of the Mahabodhi Society, the goal of which was the revival of Buddhism in India and gaining control of the ancient Buddhist pilgrimage places. (The other memorable year is 1956, which marked both the 2,500th *buddha jayantī* celebration and the conversion of Ambedkar and his followers to Buddhism.) Dharmapala had been involved with the → Theosophical Society but broke off his connection with them, because he thought they had too favorable a view of Hinduism, which contrasted with Dharmapala's anti-Hindu sentiments. In 1891 he had visited the restored Mahābodhi Temple in Bodh Gaya and discovered that the temple was run by Śaiva priests, which had been the case since the 15th century. Bodh Gaya was, and still is, a Hindu-Buddhist shared sacred space. He thereafter founded the Mahabodhi Society in Sri Lanka (the headquarters was moved to Calcutta in 1892).

Ambedkar was also not the first Dalit to redefine Buddhism as a Dalit religion of liberation. In Tamil Nadu, as early as 1898, Pandit Iyothee Thass (1845–1914) together with other Dalits and with the help of Colonel Olcott of the Theosophical Society organized the Sakya Buddhist Society in Madras (Aloysius, 1998; Webster, 2002). The movements of Thass remained small. The doctrines of being Tamil, being the original inhabitants of India, being Buddhists, and the rejection of Hindu rituals and replacing them with Buddhist rituals were central to the Buddhist identity formation of the movement, as well as "a persistent polemic against Hinduism" (Webster, 2002, 31). This movement lost momentum after 1935, because after that year, one had to declare oneself a Hindu to benefit from the reservation system instituted by the British rulers of India. (For other early converts, see Ahir, 1989; Ramteke, 1983.)

Ambedkar's Buddhism

Ambedkar was a leading politician before and after India's Independence, and he was the leading spokesperson for the untouchable/ex-untouchable castes and "by far the greatest figure ever born to the untouchable communities" (Deliége, 1999, 175). As the father of the Indian Constitution, he had great impact on the shaping of the Indian state. For untouchables, Ambedkar argued, to become liberated from the repression of caste, most important was the necessity to break away from Hinduism. Already in speeches in 1936, he encouraged all untouchables to leave Hinduism and convert to another religion as that was their only chance of being treated as equal by Hindus (Ambedkar, 2004). He advised them to adopt any religion that would give them equality of status and treatment. In another speech, in which conversion to Christianity, Islam, and Sikhism were discussed as possibilities, he ended his speech by telling the story of Buddha's *parinirvāṇa* and quoted his last words in his own retelling: "Believe in yourself, don't be dependent on others. Be truthful. Always take refugee in the truth and do not surrender to anybody" (Ambedkar, 2004, 32). He then concluded, "I also take refuge in the Buddha" (Ambedkar, 2004, 32). As early as 1943, Ambedkar visited Buddhist shrines and discussed plans for the revival of Buddhism in India (Ahir, 1994, 7). When he established his first educational institution in Bombay, he named it Siddharth College (Ahir, 1994, 7). In 1948 Ambedkar had P. Lakshmi Narasu's book *The Essence of Bud-*

Fig. 3: Statue of Ambedkar and Buddhist flag, Nepanagar, Madhya Pradesh (photo Knut A. Jacobsen).

dhism, a book that influenced his interpretation of Buddhism as the religion of reason (Beltz, 2005), translated to Marathi so that persons who thought about converting to Buddhism could read it. In the preface, he noted that he was writing a book on Buddhism (the book that was published in 1957 under the title *The Buddha and His Dharma*). In 1950 Ambedkar, in an article "Buddha and the Future of His Religion," concluded that "Buddhism is the only religion which the world can have" (Ahir, 1982, 25). Ambedkar taught that the three jewels that he himself believed in – liberty, equality, and fraternity – were derived from Buddhism and the teachings of the Buddha.

Ambedkar's interpretations of Buddhism were shaped by the revival of Buddhism, which had already occurred in India, and by the Western orientalists' creation of a homogeneous early Buddhism. Many of his interpretations are typical of modern Buddhism. Ambedkar was in contact with the Mahabodhi Society in India (Beltz, 2005) and was probably influenced by Dharmapala's modernist interpretations of Buddhism. In Ambedkar's interpretation, Buddha's teaching was defined as a rational and logical teaching comparable to modern political philosophies. What was not rational and logical could not be the teaching of the Buddha (Omvedt, 2003, 7). Typical of modern Buddhism was the claim that it represented a recovery of a postulated "real" Buddhism, but Ambedkar understood well the difference between historical Buddhism, the contemporary forms of Buddhism, and the Buddhism to which he himself converted. His term for the Buddhism that he founded, therefore, was Navayāna ("New Vehicle"), which he nevertheless claimed to be a return to the real teaching of "early Buddhism." For Ambedkar Buddhism was oriented around building a just and happy society, and he excluded those parts of Buddhism that did not support his own egalitarian social democratic philosophy. Suffering was caused by poverty and caste, not ignorance, and the message of the Buddha was how to abolish poverty, caste, and the injustice done to the marginalized. The supernatural attributes of the Buddha, meditation, and ideas of *karma* and rebirth were not part of Ambedkar's Buddhism. The ritualism of Buddhism was not real Buddhism, according to Ambedkar. He also reversed the relationship between monks and laypeople; the role of the monks was not to dominate but to serve society (Ambedkar, 1992). Monks can be the hope of Buddhism only if they are social servants (Omvedt, 2003). He did not accept the common interpretation of *karma* and rebirth, since it seemed to be based on an idea of the self. The idea of *karma* was contradicted by the doctrine of *anatta* (Pal. non-self), and the idea of *karma* seems also to legitimate untouchability. The notion of rebirth did not mean reincarnation but transformation. Ambedkar also denied that the four noble truths were part of Buddhism. The reason for the Buddha's renunciation was not the sight of a sick, an old, and a dead man, but a clash between the Śākyas and the Koliyas. Far from arguing that suffering was an inherent part of the worldly existence, the point of the Buddha was that it is possible to create a world free from suffering. The message was that humans are able to create a society based on righteousness by their own effort. For Ambedkar Buddhism was not a renunciant tradition aiming at individual salvation. "Dhamma is not concerned with life after death, nor with rituals and ceremonies; but its centre is man and relation of man to man," wrote Ambedkar (1992, 83). The salvific goal of Buddhism, *nirvāṇa*, was reinterpreted to mean a just society.

Buddhism and Dalits

Ambedkar believed that "Hinduism and the practice of untouchability were inseparable" and that "the only solution was to abandon Hinduism" (Beltz, 2005, 36). As part of providing a new social and religious identity for the Dalits, Ambedkar connected the untouchables to early Buddhism. It was Brahmanism that transformed these Buddhists to untouchables, argued Ambedkar. Untouchability was a punishment for not becoming Hindu. In his book *The Untouchables: Who Were They and Why They Became Untouchables*? Ambedkar explained that when the Hindus came to power, those Buddhists who were not willing to become Hindus were segregated and had to live in separate quarters outside the villages, and they became the untouchables. This is a modern myth that Ambedkar fashioned, and the historical evidence to defend this thesis is lacking. The caste system, he argued, solidified after the defeat of Buddhism by Hinduism, and the Buddhists were redefined as untouchables. Here Ambedkar based himself also on the earlier thinkers of the anticaste movement such as Jotirao Phule and Iyothee Thass, and already by "the 1920s this identification with early Buddhists was an underlying theme among many Dalit movements" (Omvedt, 2003, 18). Ambedkar's view is summed up by A.K. Narain:

> [U]ntouchability was born out of the struggle between Buddhism and Brahmanism. According to him [Ambedkar] the Untouchables were originally Buddhists and their untouchability was a punishment for sticking to Buddhism. He called them the "Broken Men" who were forced to live outside the village from the very beginning. He further believed that the root of their untouchability was beef-eating and that Untouchability became intimately connected with the ban on cow-slaughter which was made a capital offence by the Gupta Kings of the 4th century and thus he could say with some confidence that Untouchability was born sometimes about 400 A.D. (Narain, 1994b, 85)

Ambedkar's primary aim of conversion to Buddhism was to gain a new religious and social identity for the Dalits. For Hindus, Ambedkar thought, when interacting with untouchables who were also Hindus, the identity of being untouchables was most important, while when interacting with Christian untouchables, the identity of them being Christians became foremost. Religion overwrote caste in a sense. Changing religion, therefore, argued Ambedkar, offered a way out of untouchability.

Buddhism as a Critique of Hinduism

Ambedkar's view of religion developed "through his argument with Hinduism and not through direct, self-conscious Buddhist influence" (Webster, 2002, 51). He knew Hinduism from experience, but Buddhism he encountered mainly through books. Ambedkar's experience with growing up as an untouchable in a Hindu-dominated society and his political opposition to M.K. Gandhi are at the foundation of his conversion to Buddhism. He experienced serious discrimination especially in his childhood and youth. That Gandhi in his conflict with Ambedkar about a separate electorate for untouchables defended the Hindu system of caste hierarchy caused Ambedkar to declare that although he was born a Hindu, he would "not die a Hindu." Gandhi thought caste was too central to Hinduism as a religion to be given up. Ambedkar was active in the movement for gaining access for untouchables to the Hindu temples closed to them, but many Hindus opposed the idea. This reality of exclusion is behind his later conversion to Buddhism. Why should he want to be integrated into a religious community that fought against integrating them? Ambedkar clashed with Gandhi on the issue of untouchables, and he doubted the will of Gandhi to put an end to untouchability, even if Gandhi claimed to speak for them. Ambedkar wanted to use the possible independence of India as a way to end untouchability. At the Round Table Conference in London in 1930, Ambedkar demanded a separate electorate to the untouchables and representation, similar to the demands made by Muslims for the Muslim communities. When Gandhi met Ambedkar in 1931, Gandhi claimed himself to represent untouchables in India. Gandhi recognized only Muslims and Sikhs as minorities. For Gandhi, to accept the untouchables as a separate community meant that Hindus would be divided, and he thought the British would exploit it in their "split and rule" policy. In 1932 Gandhi did a "fast until death" to stop the untouchable from gaining separate electorate. Ambedkar had to accept Gandhi's claim from fear of retaliation against Dalits. R. Deliége has suggested that Ambedkar's subsequent conversion to Buddhism was a reaction in particular to Gandhi's Hinduism (Deliége, 1999). His debate with Gandhi on caste had proven to him that Hinduism could not be separated from caste (for the Gandhi-Ambedkar debate, see Omvedt, 2003, 248–253; Omdvedt, 2004, 56–72; Jaffrelot, 2005, 52–73).

An aspect of Buddhism that made it attractive for Ambedkar was that Buddhism was opposed to the Veda (the revealed texts of the Brahmanical tradition), the status of the Brahmans, and their sacrificial religion, and he thus undermined the legitimacy of Brahmanical ritual power and the caste system. Ambedkar saw traditional Indian religious culture as constituted by two coexisting religious traditions, the Brahmanical Hindu and the Buddhist, and Ambedkar understood these two traditions to be in a relationship of permanent moral conflict. Ambedkar argued for two main differences between Buddhism and Hinduism in the essay "Buddha and the Future of His Religion," published in the *Maha Bodhi Journal* (1950). Hinduism was a religion that is not founded on morality, argued Ambedkar, "whatever morality Hinduism has, it is not an integral part of it," while the "the Religion of the Buddha is morality... Buddhist Religion is nothing if not morality" (Ambedkar, 1992, 31). Secondly, Ambedkar argued that "the social gospel of Hinduism is inequality," while Buddha "was the greatest opponent of Chaturvarna [the caste system]" and "did everything to uproot it" (Ambedkar, 1992, 33). Consequently, when Ambedkar converted at the rally in Nagpur October 14, 1956, after he had taken "refuge in the Buddha, the Dhamma and the Sangha" from a Burmese monk, U. Chandramani, and when he turned to the masses gathered there and administered the vows to them, he added 22 vows in addition. These 22 vows can be divided into two groups, those that break with a Hindu identity and those that affirm Buddhism. Those openly directed at Hinduism state:

1. I will not regard → Brahmā, → Viṣṇu, or Mahādev (→ Śiva) as gods, and I will not worship them.
2. I will not regard → Rām or → Kṛṣṇa as gods, and I will not worship them.
3. I will not honor Gaurī (→ Pārvatī), → Gaṇapati, or any other god of Hinduism, and I will not worship them.
4. I do not believe that god has taken *avatār*.
5. I agree that the propaganda that the Buddha was the *avatār* of Viṣṇu is false and mischievous.
6. I will not do the ceremony *śrāddhapakṣa* (for the departed) or *piṇḍadān* (gifts in honor of deceased).
7. (8) I will have no rituals done by Brahmans.
8. (19) I renounce the Hindu religion, which has obstructed the evolution of my former humanity and considered humans unequal and inferior. (See Omvedt, 2003, 262, for the list of the 22 vows.)

Ambedkar did not want converts to just add some Buddhist features to their Hindu religious practices. It was necessary, he thought, to make a total break with Hinduism.

Researchers have noted that in many homes of the Indian Buddhists images of Hindu gods and goddesses are placed next to those of Ambedkar and the Buddha, and that especially the worship of goddesses is widespread, and that this points to a coexistence of Hinduism and Buddhism. For many Buddhists in India, Hindu and Buddhist rituals are not mutually exclusive, but there is nevertheless also a public pressure to denounce Hindu worship (Beltz, 2005; Shastree, 1996). The temples of this new Buddhist tradition contain images of the Buddha and Ambedkar, but it is the pictures and statues of Ambedkar that are the main symbols of the Buddhist identity, and pictures of him "are omnipresent and are the normative decorative item for every Buddhist ritual and ceremony" (Beltz, 2005, 162). New rituals have been created such as a new ritual calendar, and old Hindu rituals have been transformed into Buddhist rituals by adding recitation of Buddhist Pali texts. In addition to the *buddha jayantī* (Buddha's birth; Apr 14), Ambedkar's conversion (Oct 14, but often celebrated on the *vijayadaśamī*, the full moon day of the month *āśvina*) and death (Dec 6) are important festivals. The → *saṃskāras* include recitation of the Buddhist Pali formulas of the *tisaraṇa* (Pal. three refugees) and the *pañcaśīla* (five precepts) that mark these rituals as Buddhist. However, some Ambedkar Buddhists do not favor ritual practice, because they consider it superstition and against Ambedkar's vision, and this points to a tension in the Buddhism tradition founded by Ambedkar between religion and political ideology.

Conclusion

Most Dalits in India have been attached to Hindu traditions and have remained so. They were denied the use of temples but were not excluded from all aspects of religious life. Ambedkar thought Buddhism could give the Dalits a religion that was without caste, a religious tradition for intellectual development, religious rituals without Brahmanical supremacy, a religion without the concepts of impurity and untouchability, and that Buddhism would create a distinct identity that Dalits who converted to Islam and Christianity did not get. Ambedkar has been criticized for ignorance about the Hindu subaltern traditions with which he could have networked and built alliances (Rodrigues, 1994, 44). It is further argued that Ambedkar's "understanding of Hinduism was too stamped with orientalism rather than based on any original perception of lived experience" and that the "critique of a stereotyped Hinduism confined him to the Dalit constituency without making Hinduism critical" (Rodrigues, 1994, 44). But contrary to this, J.C.B. Webster has made the case that Ambedkar was

> a Dalit activist intellectual whose task was not to appreciate Hinduism… in its fullness and complexity but to deliver his people from oppression. Hinduism, as he experienced and understood it, stood in the way. (Webster, 2002, 53)

Nevertheless, there have been several emancipation movements among the Dalits such as the → Satnami movement among Camars in → Chhattisgarh that was founded in the 1820s by Ghāsidās, the → Ad Dharm movement in Punjab started in the 1920s by Mangoo Ram, and the → Ravidāsīs in Uttar Pradesh. These movements have done much to spread the idea of equality in India. The Buddhist Ambedkar tradition is among the larger ones, but less than 5% of Dalits are Buddhists. However, around 75% of Mahars are Buddhists, the majority of the Jatav Camars in Uttar Pradesh, and small groups of Dalits in Gujarat, Punjab, Rajasthan, Karnataka, and Madhya Pradesh have also become Buddhists (Lobo, 1996). Buddhism in India has become identified to some degree with Dalit culture and the ideology of justice for the marginalized, and in contemporary India Buddhism and the Dalit movement are two sides of the same coin (Beltz, 2005, 243).

The dynamics of the relationship between Hinduism and Buddhism are shaped by localities and histories. Relations between the religions may differ, and the terms "Hindu" and "Buddhist" may be less relevant in some localities (for Nepal, see Gellner, 1992), and in other localities such as Sri Lanka with parallel ethnic identities (most Hindus are Tamils and most Buddhists are Sinhalese), long periods of ethnic violence have impacted the relations (see Seneviratne, 1999; Holt, 2004). But in the modern period, it is only in India that mass conversions from Hinduism to Buddhism have taken place.

The discovery of Buddhism as a religion of a golden age of India's past and the subsequent inclusion of Buddhism in Hinduism as a form of Advaita Vedānta, on the one hand, and the establishment of Buddhism as a non-Hindu identity of some of those who have been the greatest victims of the Indian caste system and who for that reason wanted to separate themselves from Hinduism, on the other, are the two most significant developments in the relations of Buddhism and Hinduism in India in the modern period. Other elements of growth of Buddhism in modern India have been the immigration of Buddhist refugees from Tibet from the 1950s onward and the establishment of Dharamsala as the center of Tibetan Buddhism, the activities and establishment of a number of centers of Satya Narayan Goenka's *vipassanā* meditation movement from 1969 onward, increased pilgrimage to the Buddhist sacred sites, and building of a number of new Buddhist grand monuments (Jacobsen, 2010), as well as an increased interest of Indian academic institutions in the religion.

Bibliography

Ahir, D.C., ed., *Buddhism and Modern Hindus*, Delhi, 2009.

Ahir, D.C., "Dr. Ambedkar's Pilgrimage to Buddhism," in: A.K. Narain & D.C. Ahir, eds., *Dr. Ambedkar, Buddhism and Social Change*, Delhi, 1994, 1–16.

Ahir, D.C., *Buddhism in Modern India*, Delhi, 1991.

Ahir, D.C., *Pioneers of Buddhist Revival In India*, Delhi, 1989.

Ahir, D.C., *Dr. Ambedkar on Buddhism*, Bombay, 1982.

Almond, P.C., *The British Discovery of Buddhism*, Cambridge UK, 1988.

Aloysius, G., *Religion as Emancipatory Identity: A Buddhist Movement among the Tamils under Colonialism*, New Delhi, 1998.

Ambedkar, B.R., *Conversion as Emancipation*, New Delhi, 2004.

Ambedkar, B.R., "Buddha and the Future of His Religion," in: D.C. Ahir, ed., *A Panorama of Indian Buddhism: Selections From The Maha-Bodhi Journal (1892–1992)*, Delhi, 1992, 29–43.

Ambedkar, B.R., *The Buddha and His Dhamma: Dr. Babasaheb Ambedkar Writings and Speeches*, ed. V. Moon, vol. XI, Bombay, 1992.

Ambedkar, B.R., *The Untouchables: Who Were They and Why They Became Untouchables?: Dr. Babasaheb Ambedkar Writings and Speeches*, ed. V. Moon, vol. VII, Bombay, 1990, 229–382.

Ambedkar, B.R., "Buddha Or Karl Marx," in: V. Moon, ed., *Dr. Babasaheb Ambedkar Writings and Speeches*, vol. III, Bombay, 1987, 439–462.

Barua, B., *Gayā and Buddha-Gayā (Early History of the Holy Land)*, 2 vols., Calcutta, rev. ed., 1934.

Beltz, J.M., *Buddhist and Dalit: Religious Conversion and Socio-political Emancipation*, New Delhi, 2005.

Blackburn, A., "Religion, Kinship and Buddhism: Ambedkar's Vision of a Moral Community," *JIABS* 16/1, 1993, 1–23.

Bronkhorst, J., *Greater Magadha: Studies in the Culture of Early India*, Leiden, 2006.

Coward, H.G., "The Revival of Buddhism in Modern India," in: R.D. Baird, ed., *Religion in Modern India*, New Delhi, ³1995, 274–297.

Deliége, R., *The Untouchable of India*, Oxford, 1999.

Fiske, A.M., "Buddhism in India Today," in: H. Dumoulin, ed., *Buddhism in the Modern World, New York*, 1976, 130–146.

Gellner, D.N., *Monk, Householder, and Tantric Priest: Newar Buddhism and Its Hierarchy of Ritual*, Cambridge UK, 1992.

Holt, J.C., *The Buddhist Viṣṇu: Religious Transformation, Politics, and Culture*, New York, 2004.

Jacobsen, K.A., *Pilgrimage in the Hindu Tradition: Salvific Space*, London, 2013.

Jacobsen, K.A., "Establishment of Buddhist Sacred Space in Contemporary India: The Ambedkarite Buddhism, Dalit Civil Religion and the Struggle Against Social Exclusion," in: E. Ben-Rafael & Y. Sternberg, eds., *World Religions and Multiculturalism: A Dialectic Relation*, Leiden, 2010, 219–236.

Jacobsen, K.A., & N. Smart, "Is Hinduism an Offshoot of Buddhism?" in: A. King, ed., *Indian Religions: Renaissance and Renewal: The Spalding Papers in Indic Studies*, London, 2006, 41–53.

Jaffrelot, C., *Dr Ambedkar and Untouchability: Analysing and Fighting Caste*, Delhi, 2005.

Jaffrelot, C., *India's Silent Revolution: The Rise of the Lower Castes in North India*, London, 2003.

Jaini, P.S., "Śramaṇas: Their Conflict with Brāhmaṇical Society," in: J.W. Elder, ed., *Chapters in Indian Civilization*, vol. I, Dubuque, 1970, 41–81.

Joshi, L.M., *Discerning the Buddha: A Study of Buddhism and of the Brahmanical Hindu Attitude to It*, New Delhi, 1983.

Kane, P.V., *History of Dharmaśāstra*, vol. V/2, Poona, 1962.

Kinnard, J.N., "When is the Buddha Not the Buddha? The Hindu/Buddhist Battle Over Bodhgaya and the Buddha Image," *JAAR* 66/4, 1998, 817839.

Lobo, L., "Dalit Religious Movements and Dalit Identity," in: W. Fernandez, ed., *The Emerging Dalit Identity: The Re-assertion of the Subalterns*, New Delhi, 1996, 166–183.

Lopez, D.S., *Modern Buddhism: Readings for the Unenlightened*, London, 2002.

Murti, T.R.V., "Radhakrishnan and Buddhism," in: P.A. Schlipp, ed., *The Philosophy of Sarvapalli Radhakrishnan*, New Delhi, 1992, 565–606.

Narain, A.K., & D.C. Ahir, eds., *Dr. Ambedkar, Buddhism and Social Change*, Delhi, 1994a.

Narain, A.K., "Dr. Ambedkar, Buddhism and Social Change – A Reappraisal," in: A.K. Narain & D.C. Ahir, eds., *Dr. Ambedkar, Buddhism and Social Change*, Delhi, 1994b, 77–98.

Narayan, B., "Demarginalisation and History: Dalit Reinvention of the Past," *SAR* 28/2, 2008, 169–184.

Olivelle, P., *Saṃnyāsa Upaniṣads: Hindu Scriptures on Asceticism and Renunciation*, New York, 1992.

Omvedt, G., *Ambedkar: Towards an Enlightened India*, New Delhi, 2004.

Omvedt, G., *Buddhism in India: Challenging Brahmanism and Caste*, New Delhi, 2003.

Queen, C.S., "Dr. Ambedkar and the Hermeneutics of Buddhist Liberation," in: C.S. Queen & S.B. King, eds., *Engaged Buddhism: Buddhist Liberation Movements in Asia*, Albany, 1996, 45–72.

Radhakrishnan, S., *Indian Philosophy*, 2 vols., New York, [2]1929.

Ramteke, D.L., *Revival of Buddhism in Modern India*, New Delhi, 1983.

Rodrigues, V., "Viewing Dalit Movement: Contending Perspectives," in: S. Pendse, ed., *At Cross-roads: Dalit Movement Today*, Bombay, 1994, 33–50.

Seneviratne, H.L., *The Work of Kings: The New Buddhism in Sri Lanka*, Chicago, 1999.

Sharma, C., *A Critical Survey of Indian Philosophy*, Delhi, 1960, repr. 1987.

Shastree, U., *Religious Converts in India: Socio-political Study of Neo-Buddhists*, Delhi, 1996.

Vivekananda, S., *The Complete Works of Vivekananda*, 8 vols., Calcutta, 1962–1965.

Webster, J.C.B., *Religion and Dalit Liberation: An Examination of Perspectives*, New Delhi, 2002.

Zelliot, E., *From Untouchable to Dalit: Essays on the Ambedkar Movement*, New Delhi, 1992.

Knut A. Jacobsen

Hinduism and Christianity

The spiritual and religious traditions today known as "Hinduism" and "Christianity" developed through history largely apart from and knowing little of each other until the time of Western colonialism in Asia that started at the end of the 15th century. Neither of the two words "Hinduism" or "Christianity" is found in the original sources of its respective traditions. "Christianity" apparently emerged during the European Renaissance, and around the 16th century it became a common word to refer to the faith tradition derived from Jesus Christ. Its root is personal, that is, it refers to Jesus of Nazareth on whom already the New Testament confers the title of "messiah," that is, "anointed" or "*christos*." By contrast, the root of Hinduism is geographical; it was first used in Muslim sources to refer to the region beyond the Indus (Hind. *sindh*) River. The Sanskrit word *sindhu* itself means "river" or "ocean" and in vedic literature often refers to the Indus. The word "Hinduism" (Hindooism) emerged among Europeans in Bengal in the late 18th century to indicate the family of cults and philosophical or theological traditions of India. The word was popularized by the Scottish missionary Charles Grant in his correspondence and writings of the 1780s (Oddie, 2006; Lorenzen, 2006). One cannot deny that in spite of the divergence of cults and traditions it includes, there is in Hinduism a "family similarity," partly due to a general reference to the ancient vedic sources composed in Sanskrit and its derived languages from the 1st or even 2nd millennia BCE.

Hinduism is of course older than Christianity. It is the chief representative of the "wisdom religions" or gnostic traditions based on experience and insight. Christianity was originally a religious movement within Judaism and eventually a separate religion. It is therefore dated from the 1st century CE. It is a sample of the widely extended type of the "prophetic religions" based on specific mediators and faith commitment. However, the walls of distinction between these two types of religion are porous. Theologically there is much "wisdom" within prophetic traditions and many "prophetic" elements in gnostic or wisdom religions.

This entry is divided into three parts. The first surveys some of the early historical contacts between the two traditions. The second part shows the ways in which Christian ideas have been welcomed and integrated into the Indian worldview so that we can speak of "Neo-Hinduism" or the "Renaissance of Hinduism." The third part presents how the Hindu theological tradition has been received or rejected by Christians, with special attention to contemporary presentations of Indian Christian theology or theologies.

Historical Contacts

Filtering through the barriers of space, languages, and civilizations, there was historically some knowledge, meager indeed and imperfect, in each tradition of the existence of the other. There is no doubt that there were commercial contacts in the 1st century between the Mediterranean world and the Indian peninsular coasts. There must have been Indians travelling to the West for commercial or other purposes, though we do not have specific personal references. There is also no evidence of any individual, clan, or group attempting the conversion of Western populations to their views or of any Indian group remaining in the Western continent and living a religious life in an Indian pattern.

Contacts in Antiquity

This does not mean that the two religious traditions knew nothing of each other. On the Indian side, there is very little evidence. The campaigns of Alexander the Great to the border and then to the heart of India are well known. Memories of it surface in the Buddhist Pali text the *Milindapañha* (The Questions of Menander), written around the 2nd century CE, a text that even found a place in some canons of the Tipiṭaka. Evidence of Greek influence can be traced in the earliest Buddhist art of India. In the West, there is a corpus of knowledge about India that one can glean from classical sources (Puliurumpil, 2011; Charpentier, 1933; Halbfass, 1990; see below).

There are, moreover, points of similarity between Indian and Western religious terms. These may be accounted in general by other than historical contacts. There is first the generally accepted hypothesis that the Indian, the Greek, and the Latin traditions, among others, come from an original prehistoric ethnic and linguistic group, at times called the "Indo-European," the geographical location of which is disputed among scholars. Linguistically there is no doubt about a common origin of these traditions, for only this can explain the many linguistic, mythological, and theological parallels we find. The similarities that may be discovered in the sacrificial literature and practices on both sides may be explained, at least partly, by their common ancestry. The hypothesis of a later influence of the devotional Western religions on the → *bhakti* traditions of India – for example, on the → *Bhagavadgītā* – is chronologically improbable. However, one need not discard the possibility that Indian monasticism had some influence in the emergence of monastic establishments in Israel and other areas of the Middle East, eventually in Europe. But we do not have sufficient concrete data to affirm this as a fact.

Eastern influences on the Western religious practices and philosophical thought is more plausible. Scholars have sought Indian influences in the Dionysian and other Greek or Roman mystery cults, or in the early cosmological views of Greece and Rome, like the Atomism of the Roman poet Lucretius, similar to some → Vaiśeṣika views. More importantly, many have sought upanishadic influences in the Platonic world of ideas or, more likely, in the nondualism of Plotinus. The person most competent on Plotinus and Indian thought was probably the philosopher and sage J. Monchanin (Monchanin, 1974; see also Radhakrishnan, 1927). But such similarities may also be parallel discoveries of the philosophical mind on this and that side of the Syrian and Persian Empires.

If we have no evidence of a Hindu community living in the classical West, by contrast there are many references to Christian communities in India, not only in the Middle Ages but also in antiquity. These Western testimonies are supported by the self-consciousness of the earliest Indian communities that they are the fruit of the preaching of apostles in India in the 1st century and of other influences of Christians coming to India in the 4th century. A very ancient tradition in India, supported by a number of Middle Eastern and Western references, affirms that a disciple of Jesus, Saint Thomas, came to India in the 1st century to preach the gospel of Jesus Christ. A weaker tradition says that another apostle, Saint Bartholomew, also reached the western coast of India. Both traditions could possibly be true, but neither can be historically proven. The Saint Thomas tradition is certainly widely attested. The tomb or the traditional place of martyrdom of Saint Thomas the apostle was known in Europe to be in Mylapore (suburb in present Chennai). Some ancient lists mention a bishop from India among the bishops in the Council of Nicea in 325 CE, but this is not a reliable tradition. That there was a Christian community in India was general knowledge in the West. The medieval travelers to India attested to its existence, and one of the aims of the Portuguese mercantile enterprise in the 15th and 16th centuries was to establish contact with the Christians of India and thus free Europe from the Muslim control of the goods from India, especially spices and precious stones.

In recent years, much research work has been done in India to discover the nature of the Christian community of the Saint Thomas Christians (also called Nazaranis) from historical sources, popular literature, archaeology, and literary references. The research includes the influence of Hindu and possibly Buddhist and Jain culture and religion on the way the Christians lived their faith, their worship, and their art. The work of the most prolific scholar on this, Placid Podipara, has been collected in a large edition in five volumes covering 3,132 pages. For an introductory survey, one may consult chapter 7 of volume II (527–540), which describes this community prior to the 15th century as "Hindu in Culture, Christian in Religion, Oriental in Worship" (see Kalayil, 2007; Kuriedath, 1989; Vadakkekara, 1995). (For a somewhat imaginative but well-documented reconstruction of the life of the earliest Christian community in India before colonialism, see Frykenberg, 2003, 33–61. His perspective, however, remains basically Protestant, with at least an implicit critique of other traditions.)

The European "Discovery of India": Middle Ages and Renaissance

The knowledge of India from antiquity to the colonial period has been well studied by a number of authors (Halbfass, 1990). An earlier good summary may be found in the long introduction in English by J. Charpentier to the edition of the book of Jacobo Fenicio, *The Livro da Seita dos Indios Orientais* (Charpentier, 1933, x–civ). In it J. Charpentier insists on the importance of the four books of the Greek Megasthenes, who was ambassador to the Maurya court of Pāṭaliputra. They contain a personal witness about the North Indian civilization that influenced both the Greco-Roman antiquity and the medieval European world and is quoted even today. According to J. Charpentier, the Romans added little if anything to the knowledge of India. But there were a number of medieval European travelers to the East whose writings have come to us at times only in fragments. They give information, at times reliable, often imaginary and fantastic, derived from hearsay more than personal observation. The best known of these travelers is the Venetian Marco Polo (1254–1324), who writes more about China but on his return from there visited Sri Lanka and South India. His testimony needs caution and discernment. Later another Italian, Niccolò de' Conti (1395–1469), traveled to India and possibly China and left rather reliable accounts.

But it is not until the period of Western colonialism that we begin to notice a paradigm shift and a new era in the study by Christians of the reality of Hinduism. In the first half century, the primary concern of the colonialists was trade with India. The priests in the expeditions came primarily as chaplains of the personnel of the ships and of the trading settlements. They do not seem to have had particular interest in the religions of the peoples they saw in the ports they visited or lived in. At least no such interest has been communicated to us. It was actually with the arrival of the Jesuits that what could be called "scientific Indology" begins, nearly two centuries before historical orientalism. J. Charpentier says this about this new era:

> [I]t may be safely asserted that the modern knowledge of geography of the then unknown parts of the world and the acquaintance with the history, religions, and social customs of Asiatic, African and American peoples and races has been founded by the Jesuits missionaries. (Charpentier, 1933, 37)

This does not mean that they are the only valuable source of information. Many other forces were involved in the colonial enterprise, which not only was an economic adventure, though commerce was all important, but had also the spirit of the European Renaissance with its curiosity to extend the breadth of human knowledge. Thus much material can be gathered from João de Barros, *Decadas da Asia*, started in 1553, a work completed later, perhaps by 1595, by Diogo de Couto. On this topic, one needs to consult recognized historians, for example, C.R. Boxer (1969).

Western colonialism in India may be said to have started with the arrival of Vasco da Gama on the coast of Malabar at the end of the 15th century, in 1498. His arrival marks the beginning of an era of frequent contacts between West and East, at first especially between the Portuguese and the Indians. This early colonialism, chiefly mercantile and partly cultural, also included a strong religious element, the "mission" to spread the gospel of Jesus to all nations (Matthew 28:20). With the mercantile seafarers came chaplains to care for the spiritual well-being of the sailors and merchants during their long journeys and their life in settlements (at the time called "factories") in foreign lands (see also → trade and merchants). The priests often belonged to religious orders, initially Franciscans or Dominicans, later Jesuits and other orders. On land the chaplains must have visited the temporary homes of the new arrivals and met their Indian domestic help and friends. Their religious instruction and ministry offered to merchants and soldiers accompanying them had to be extended to the whole domestic household, which could only lead to a desire to bring them to profess the same religion as the families they were part of.

In fact, the royal patrons of the mercantile expeditions had accepted the responsibility for spreading the Christian faith in the newly available areas. This was demanded by the pope, who at the time still had a strong authority in the European world, especially in south Europe, from where most of the earlier travelers came. This is how the mission enterprise came to be organized already in the 16th century around a "royal patronage" or "*Padroado*," the Portuguese word used in India. This system continued with adaptations and variations in the whole period down to the mid-20th century.

Naturally the incoming priests became curious about the religious practices and beliefs of the people in India. They knew from close contacts in Europe what the Muslim religion was about. But they had little knowledge about the Hindu tradition or other religions of the country. A few may have studied something of what the ancient Greek and Roman cultures had known about India. Most of them probably knew nothing about it. There were no manuals about these religions available in European languages, no dictionaries or encyclopedias they could consult. Many missionaries just inquired and began to collect information. One can consult the written sources of the 16th and 17th centuries (e.g. in *Documenta Indica*) to trace the gradual growth of knowledge about the Indian religion. The early letters were not unlike modern letters or articles of the new tourists coming to India: astonishment with the number and the variety of peoples and customs, the multiplicity of forms of worship, dark temples, colorful festivals, the abundance of *sādhus* and *yogīs* (see → *sādhus*, *saṃnyāsīs*, and *yogīs*), the eating etiquette, → *ahiṃsā*, vegetarianism, the veneration given to cows and to all animals (see → sacred animals), the strange forms of gods and goddesses, → *satī* or the voluntary cremation of widows, and so on.

Slowly, however, a more intimate knowledge emerged. Some missionaries report about a sacred language, lofty philosophical ideas, sacred texts, and deep spirituality. Already in 1544, two years after he disembarked in → Goa, Francis Xavier, a cofounder of the Jesuit order and then just 38 years old, the first Jesuit in India, informed his colleagues in Rome, "They have some Scriptures wherein their commandments are written. The language they use in their studies is like Latin among us." He even quoted in a somewhat garbled but recognizable form what may well be the first Sanskrit text to reach Europe. It is the Vaiṣṇava → *mantra* "*Om cirii naraina noma!*" (Hind. *oṃ śrīnārāyaṇa nāmaḥ*; Schurhammer & Wicki, 1944, 173). In 1560, 15 years later, a young Jesuit student of Portuguese origin, Luis Frois, 32 years old, reports in a letter to his friends in Portugal about a conversation between an older missionary in Goa, Franscisco Rodriguez, and a *yogī* from Anjidiv Island, during which the priest asks the *sādhu* "whom among his prophets he considers the most authentic." As understood by Franscisco Rodrigues or Luis Frois, the *sādhu* replies, "One called Gittaa [*sic*] who wrote eighteen volumes." This may well be the earliest information about the most famous text of Hinduism, the → *Bhagavadgītā* with its 18 chapters, to reach Christians in Europe (*Documenta Indica*, vol. IV, 801–802).

Early writers of the colonial period make only passing references to the religions of India. Soon, however, they show a rather wide knowledge. Thus the Jesuits (1549–1619), possibly the first Englishman in India who landed in Goa in 1579 and stayed until his death 30 years later, in 1616 wrote an epic poem in Konkani or early Marathi, the *Kristāpurāṇa*, even now considered a classic in Indian literature. The title itself betrays a familiarity with a very popular genre in Hinduism. The poem seems to begin with a Christian use of the Indian sacred syllable → *oṃ* pronounced in a Portuguese way. The poem does not describe Hinduism, but the words and the Marathi verse form *ovī* are taken from the Indian tradition. Thomas Stephens is the first person to point out, in one of his letters, the structural similarity of the Indian languages with the European classical languages, as two centuries later William Jones (see below) would also discover. The Catalan Jesuit Antoni Montserrat wrote his famous commentary of journeys to and from the court of the Moghul emperor Akbar, and his account of the Muslim court in India also contains interesting details of various gods and → *avatārs* in the Hindu religion. His successor in the court of Akbar, Jerome Xavier, who incidentally wrote a life of Christ in Persian, has left us a letter from 1598 with an extensive treatment of the *avatārs* of → Viṣṇu.

Another significant source are the letters of the little-known Manuel Pinheiro (1556–1619), a Portuguese man from the Azores Islands. (See, for example, the letter of Sep 3, 1595, in *Documenta Indica*, vol. XVII, 72–80.) Manuel Pinheiro first worked in Goa and then went to Gujarat and eventually to the Moghul court in Lahore during the reigns of Akbar and Jahangir, where he did mission work with the Muslims with the emperors' permission. J. Charpentier records some of the contents of one such letter, written from Cambay. Manuel Pinheiro speaks

> of the long fasts of the Hindus, tells something about the pilgrimages to the Ganges, especially at the *makarasamkranti*; he found the Hindus to be very liberal. There follows an interesting description of the Svetambara Jains, which is probably the oldest one preserved. (*Documenta Indica*, vol. XVII, 368ff.; trans. author)

He refers to their books written in "Guzzarati" (i.e. Gujarati).

By the early 17th century, we have a number of respectable treatises about the religion of India from the pens of missionaries. These and the additional information in the early 18th century form the basis on which the classical orientalism of William Jones was built. I will mention just a few names for the record. The earliest text in our possession is that of Giacomo Fenizio (or Fenicio, 1558–1632) already alluded to. Like Roberto de

Nobili, he was an Italian, studied in Portugal as a Jesuit, and went to India in 1583/1584, 20 years before Roberto de Nobili, who was nearly 19 years younger. He worked for almost 50 years in what is now the Kerala state, learned the local language well, and was in friendly relations with both Muslims and Hindus. In 1609 he collected his considerable knowledge of the Indian tradition and, to help his fellow missionaries, wrote *Livro da Seita dos Indios Orientais* (The Book of the Sects of Oriental Indians; Charpentier, 1933), where he explains Hindu cosmogony and ways of worship.

The most significant and influential name in this "discovery of Hinduism" is Roberto de Nobili (1577–1656; Cronin, 1959; Rajamanickam, 1972), who as a 36-year-old missionary in Madurai, South India, in 1610 wrote a Latin *Informatio de Quibusdam Moribus Nationis Indicae*, now edited and translated by S. Rajamanickam as *Robert de Nobili on Indian Customs* (Palayamkottai, 1972). In 1964 Professor Humayun Kabir, former minister of education of the government of India, called Roberto de Nobili "the first European Orientalist in the modern sense," and he was indeed very competent in the Hindu traditions, scriptures, customs, and philosophy. However, his writings, mostly in Tamil, were generally not about Hinduism but his own faith and addressed to Hindus. As he was a subject of much controversy with his religious authorities in India and Rome, he wrote his *Informatio* to explain the meaning of the many Indian customs he had allowed his converts to keep. He explains the nature of the → caste system in India, comparing it to social structures elsewhere, and the customs and practices of Brahmans with a view to show that they are not against natural law or the Christian faith. His influence in the church in India and elsewhere cannot be exaggerated.

Roberto de Nobili was not unchallenged in his views. His fellow Jesuit and older companion in the Madurai mission, Gonçalo Fernandes Trancoso (1541–1621) wrote a treatise in 1616 on Hindu ceremonial, especially about Brahmans, *saṃnyāsī*s, and their customs, to show to his superiors that Roberto de Nobili was wrong. He shows an amazingly wide acquaintance with ancient and later texts: the *Yajurveda*, *Baudhāyanadharmasūtra*, *Āśvalāyanaśrautasūtra*, *Manusmṛti* (Wicki, 1973, xxi–xxiii), many → Purāṇas, the two epics, and many medieval commentators. His work shows that 70 years after Francis Xavier landed in Goa, the missionaries had an awareness of the Indian scriptures and commentaries that even today are available only to few specialists (Wicki, 1973).

About the same year or perhaps a year earlier, the Portuguese Jesuit Diogo Gonçalves (1561–1640), knowledgeable in Malayalam, wrote a history of Malabar in which he describes the art, customs, and religion of the area (Wicki, 1955).

A very interesting record of the knowledge of India in the 17th century is the volume of writings or rather translations of Indian texts into Portuguese. It is the work of linguist Francisco Garcia (Mendes; 1580–1659), a missionary in Kerala, who was ordained coadjutor to the archbishop of Cranganor in 1637 and became his successor in 1641. He was unfortunately involved in the revolt of the "Syrian" Christians against the authority of Latin bishops appointed from Rome and was not able to understand the ecclesial problem involved. But in his 57 years of life in the western coast of India and in Sri Lanka, he learned Konkani, Marathi, Tamil, Sanskrit, Sinhalese, and Malayalam and had a working knowledge of Syrian, besides of course the European classical and vernacular languages. He wrote popular religious literature in many languages. But essentially he was a translator. His most important contribution to the knowledge of Hinduism is a collection of translations of Hindu texts under the title *O homem das trinta e duas perfeições e outras histórias* (The Man of 32 Perfection and Other Stories), edited, annotated, and printed only in 1958 (Wicki, 1958). These stories present a composite picture of the ideal man according to the Indian teaching, given as a model for the education of princes. For the same purposes, Francisco Garcia adds many *śloka*s with good ethical or moral content. To this text is added a minitreatise on Hinduism in Latin, surely to help missionaries to understand the country where they worked. Though he was interested in the culture of the place where he lived, he chose stories that could be useful for both the education of missionaries and the instruction of Christians. The period in which he translated may have covered his whole life as a teacher in India and, perhaps even more intensely, the years of his exercise as archbishop of Cranganor, the mid-17th century.

Neither the Jesuits nor the Catholics in general were the only source of the pre-orientalism knowledge of India. From the early 18th century, Lutheran missionaries arrived on a Danish ship to India and established a settlement first in

Tranquebar (today Tharangambadi, Tamil Nadu) and later in Bengal (Jeyaraj, 2006, 10). Bartholomaeus Ziegenbalg (1682–1719) landed in Tranquebar in 1706 and soon set himself to learning Tamil and organizing Lutheran communities in Tamil Nadu. He is responsible for the first translation of the New Testament to be printed in an Indian language, Tamil, published in 1715. His translation of the Old Testament was completed by Benjamin Schultze (1689–1760) and printed in 1726.

This was the beginning of a great work of translating the whole Bible into dozens of Indian languages, made famous especially by William Carey (1761–1834) and his team working from Serampore in Bengal almost a century later. By the time of William Carey's death, there were no fewer than 40 partial or complete translations of the Bible in Indian languages, beginning with Bengali and including Sanskrit, Marathi, Oriya, Hindi, Punjabi, Assamese, Telugu, Konkani, Nepali, Marwari, Gujarati, and Kanada. This work was later entrusted to and continues to be done by the Bible Society of India. (For further details see Putz, 1957.)

Bartholomaeus Ziegenbald, however, was not only interested in Bible translation. He also wrote Tamil–German dictionaries, a Tamil grammar, and a number of writings in Tamil, surely written with the help of Indian scribes. For the history of the Christian discovery of Hinduism, his most significant contribution was written in German in 1709–1713, the *Geneologie der Malabarischen Götter*, recently translated as *Geneology of the South Indian Deities* (Jeyaraj, 2005), where he gave an organized understanding of Indian gods and goddesses, with much information on Indian society and religion (Jeyaraj, 2006). This book enraged the European Christians who complained that "missionaries were sent out to extirpate heathenism, and not to spread heathenish nonsense to Europe." For the European Christians, evangelizing did not seem to require dialogue.

The Hindu Response to the Christian Colonial Presence in India

With the arrival of the British and the organization of the East India Company, we enter a new stage of interaction between Hinduism and Christianity. In this section, I will consider the way in which Hinduism in many ways both received and rejected the Christian message. In the third section, I will offer some data to examine how the Hindu message was both accepted and rejected at the same time in the Indian Christian consciousness. I will develop some highlights of what has been called Indian Christian theology.

The Renaissance of Hinduism is generally attributed to Raja → Ram Mohan Roy (1772?–1833). The atmosphere of the country and especially of Bengal is well known. The British were in control of much of the economy and the administration and were engaged in a fervent colonial enterprise to make India the supplier of the raw material of the flourishing production, which the industrial revolution had enabled Britain to create at an accelerating pace. A humanist and reformer of Hinduism at heart, Ram Mohan Roy had a very wide literary production. In 1820 he published a book called *The Precepts of Jesus*, in which he collected the ethical doctrines of Jesus Christ, without accepting the Christian understanding of him. This disturbed the missionaries of Serampore, and Joshua Marshman, a companion of William Carey, made some critical remarks of the book from the perspective of the Christian faith. Ram Mohan Roy replied the same year with *An Appeal to the Christian Public in Defense of the Precepts of Jesus by a Friend of Truth* (1820). Joshua Marshman persisted in his criticism, and Ram Mohan Roy published a *Second Appeal* in the same year, and in 1823 *A Final Appeal to the Christian Public in Defense of the Precepts of Jesus*. The *Appeals* became more and more articulate: 18 pages for the first, 112 for the second, and 200 for the third.

The main point Ram Mohan Roy stresses is the oneness of God and the defense of the human reality. As he says,

> I have never ceased to contemplate with the strongest feelings of regret the obstinate adherence of my countrymen to their fatal system of idolatry, inducing, for the sake of propitiating their supposed Deities, the violation of every humane and social feeling... and to view [in these practices] the moral debasement of the race... I pray that [Hindus may come to] a conviction of the rationality of believing in and adoring the Supreme Being only; together with a complete perception and practice of that grand and comprehensive moral principle: Do unto others what ye would be done by.

(quoted in Thomas, 1976, 3–4; Roy, 1887, vol. I, 86–87)

If the new stress on the oneness of God could derive from either Islam, with which Ram Mohan Roy was well acquainted, or Christianity, the appeal to rational humanism is surely influenced by the Christian tradition or, one may prefer to say, the humanism developed in the "Christian" West.

In his first "appeal" to the Christian public, printed in Calcutta in 1820, Ram Mohan Roy identifies himself as "one who takes the Precepts of Jesus as his principal guide in matter of religious and civil duties" (Roy, vol. II, 1887, 79) and finds in the New Testament "a Guide to peace and happiness" (78). Indeed, referring to himself, he adds,

> although he was born a Brahmun [*sic*], [he] not only renounced idolatry at a very early period of his life, but published at that time a treatise in Arabic and Persian against that system; and no sooner acquired a tolerable knowledge of English, than he made his desertion of idol worship known to the Christian world by his English publication – a renunciation that, I am sorry to say, brought severe difficulties against him, by exciting the displeasure of his parents, and subjecting him to the dislike of his near, as well as distant relations, and to the hatred of nearly all his countrymen for several years. (Roy, vol. II, 1887, 79)

Ram Mohan Roy was in many senses the forerunner of the Bengali Hindu revival and as such influenced similar revival movements in other parts of India: Maharashtra, Tamil Nadu, and so on. In spite of his frequent appeal to the moral precepts of Jesus, he did not rely so much on the tradition of Jesus as on the importance of reason, an extra-religious court of appeal to ensure the equality of all religious traditions. He was actually an apologist for Hinduism, a Hinduism purified from what he considered debased and lower forms of religiosity and centered on the "rational" teachings of the → Upaniṣads and the *Brahmasūtra* (see → Sūtras). He thus prepared the way for the → Ramakrishna Mission and S. → Radhakrishnan's interpretation and propagation of Hinduism. He agreed that each religion had specific values and in many ways established the possibility of a modern interreligious dialogue, while evaluating religions on their contribution to social welfare and peace rather than in terms of *mokṣa* (→ liberation; see Pankratz, 1981).

The person in the → Brahmo Samaj tradition who embraced most openly the figure of Christ as a religious ideal within the Hindu faith was without doubt → Keshab Chandra Sen (1838–1884). In his time too, social reform was the ideal that attracted the youth of Bengal; it included moral and spiritual education, universal education especially for women, vernacular and vocational education, temperance, and the eradication of → untouchability and caste (Palit in Sen, vol. IV, 1974, 107). But underlying his social concern was a vision of Christ as a universal figure, detached from creedal Christianity, who was at the center of the Church of the New Dispensation, which Keshab Chandra Sen started as the universal religion. As D. Scott says,

> The establishment of a "World Religion" has been a long cherished ideal of the Indian soul and there is no denying the eclectic spirit which led Keshab to attempt no less. Though modeled chiefly on the Christian Church and explicitly centered on Christ, Keshab claimed for the Church of the New Dispensation the best of all the great religions, as shown by the emblem, which included the Cross, the symbol *Om* and the Star and the Crescent. Keshab himself makes it clear that his is what he calls "Christian eclecticism," in which Christ becomes the criterion by which every doctrine and practice must be judged. (Scott, 1979, xiin5)

So powerful are the writings of Keshab Chandra Sen that the United Theological College of Bangalore decided to include a *Companion Volume* in its *Library of Indian Christian Theology*. The *Companion Volume* contains a selection of the writings of Keshab Chandra Sen. Some of the titles of this selection are "Jesus Christ: Europe and Asia," "Christ and Christianity," "Behold the Light of Heaven in India," "India Asks: Who Is Christ?," and "That Marvelous Mystery – The Trinity." All these were lectures given between 1866 and 1882.

Most of the prominent figures of the Indian renaissance have been influenced by the life and doctrine of Jesus. S. → Vivekananda (1863–1902) sees Jesus as the perfect → *jīvanmukta* , one of the great waves in the ocean of history, who in Asian fashion teaches total detachment and gives his life for the salvation of the least. Jesus realized oneness with the divine even during this life, and S. Vivekananda finds in him a confirmation of the universality and value of → Vedānta on the basis of the saying of Jesus reported in the

Gospel of John, "I and the Father are one." In a way similar to that of the younger philosophers. Radhakrishnan, S. Vivekananda finds the *bhakti* or devotional interpretation of Jesus as Son of God, a provisional step helping to reach the Advaita experience (see → Vedānta) that Jesus had. S. Radhakrishnan (1888–1975) speaks of the mystic Christ. This theme and reference are not infrequent among the later Christian theologians in India, who themselves adopt *advaita* (nondualism) as a valuable theological concept (Mascarenhas, Abhishiktananda, Sundar Rao, Panikkar, Sara Grant, and Amaladoss; see below).

Some have seen in the neo-Vedānta proposed by the above Hindu thinkers an effort to provide a spiritual basis for the new India, for in them there is

> a shift... from speculation about the nature of the Absolute to a new understanding out the nature of man... The determinative doctrine in the evaluation of the Hindu outlook on life is no longer derived from its classical theology, but is being built upon a new anthropology. This new anthropology is perhaps still in the making. (Devanandan, 1961; Thomas, 1976, 168)

There is here a discovery of the (relative) value of the historical and the human on the basis of a philosophical view of the absolute or → *brahman*. This discovery will be more evident in the Constitution of India, approved by the Constituent Assembly on Nov 26, 1949, and in vigor since the Jan 26, 1950.

M. → Gandhi may have partially agreed with this view, but his specific insight was to see Jesus as the perfect *satyāgrahī* (the person who earnestly holds truth/justice), who along the way of works (*karmamārga*) faced injustice with purely nonviolent methods, the very model of → *ahimsā*. He also assumed in his own way the Christian idea of vicarious redemption. He made it an integral part of his philosophy of *satyāgraha*. M. Gandhi's view did much to make the message of the suffering Christ meaningful and valuable for India.

More than a few commentators of interreligious dialogue have asked whether the concern for dialogue is a "Christian" affair. They think that there is no will to dialogue in traditional religions, not at least in the majority block of Hinduism: like many other traditional devotees, Hindus feel self-sufficient and satisfied in the religion they have and find no need for dialogue. In fact some Hindus have viewed dialogue as a kind of modern subterfuge of missionary Christians, who find themselves in the contemporary culture unable to practice traditional forms of proselytism and take dialogue as an *Ersatz* to achieve the same goals. There is therefore a trend to suspect the Christian demand for "honest dialogue" and to ignore it, not always without reason.

However, this is only a partial view of the reality of Hinduism. From the evidence mentioned in this section, one should conclude that Hinduism itself today is a living dialogue. There are of course those who energetically reject dialogue, but it is difficult to think that they represent the majority. Many Hindus have received with modern culture a specific awareness of the meaning and significance of Christ, even if they naturally interpret him from the traditional categories of the local culture, for instance, as one of the *avatāra*s of the divinity. Not seldom a picture of Jesus is found in pious Hindu homes, probably alongside some of "Hindu" gods or goddesses. Like other religious festivals, the national calendar declares Christmas day and Good Friday "national holidays" together with Easter (which always falls on a Sunday and does not require special mention). More than a few Hindus have read parts of the Bible, especially the New Testament. M. Gandhi did much to popularize the Sermon on the Mount, in which he saw a pure teaching of *ahiṃsā*.

All this shows a form of openness to dialogue within the Hindu culture of India, which is clearly less formally organized than sessions prepared in Christian centers of dialogue. Nevertheless, many Hindus live an authentic attitude of acceptance. One can also add an analysis of the basic values of the constitution of India. They are not exclusively "Christian" values: they are universal and derive directly from revolutionary movements and documents articulated mostly in the West, but they have been accepted by India with various original emphases and affirmations. The preamble of the constitution begins thus:

> We, the people of India, having solemnly resolved to constitute India into a sovereign *socialist *secular democratic republic and to secure to all its citizens:
>
> Justice, social, economic and political;
> Liberty of thought, expression, belief, faith and worship;
> Equality of status and opportunity;
> and to promote among them all

> Fraternity assuring the dignity of the individual and the *unity *and *integrity of the Nation;
> In our Constituent Assembly this twenty-sixth day of November, 1949, do hereby adopt, enact and give to ourselves this constitution.
>
> (The words with *asterisks were added in 1977, through amendments approved by the parliament and the legislative assemblies of the states.)

Neither the Soviet nor the French Revolutions that promulgated these values were Christian events: actually they were quite secular and even had an antichurch bias. But few thinkers will deny that these values of the secular West were developed along centuries of reflection and discussion on the anthropology and consequent law developed within the Christian tradition. It is true that "democracy" was found in India and the Greek world before Christianity emerged. But theirs was always a selective democracy, an oligarchy premised on restricted citizenship rights and suffrage. It coexisted with the discriminatory caste system and with Greek slavery. The universal extension of democracy was possible under the influence of the faith that man is created in the image and likeness of God (Genesis 1:26). Similarly, we must admit that the republican form of government, though found also in some parts of India and Greece, was very selective in respect to those who could speak for the *res publica*.

The word "socialist" was added to the constitution by the amendment of 1977 and binds the country to a special obligatory concern for the poor and oppressed sections, in the context of a history of inequality and marginalization. This amendment is a legal expression for the "preferential option for the poor" that is today strongly affirmed in Christian theology. M. Gandhi made it popular in India with one of his most famous and widely known last notes, which he called *Talisman*:

> Whenever you are in doubt, or when the self becomes too much with you, apply the following test. Recall the face of the poorest and the weakest man whom you may have seen, and ask yourself if the step you contemplate is going to be of any use to him. Will he gain anything by it? Will it restore him to a control over his own life and destiny? In other words, will it lead to *swarāj* [freedom] to the hungry and starving millions? Then you will find your doubts and your self melt away. (Iyer, 1987, 609)

R. Iyer dates the note to August 1947, which would be five months before the assassination of the Mahatma. According to R. Iyer, the note was written in Bengali and given to Devtosh Das Gupta, secretary of the Shanti Sena Dal, who visited Gandhiji in Calcutta, where Gandhi spent the month of the first and only Independence Day that he lived through, trying to assuage the communal violence that followed the partition of India. Gandhi, R. Iyer says, signed the note both in Devanagari and Bengali scripts. The political option of India as a new nation can be called a blend of Fabian socialism and Gandhism, syncretized in Gandhian socialism.

The word "secular," also added to the preamble by an amendment, is not the equivalent of either the French *laïcité*, prohibiting any religious expression in the political arena, or of the separation of church and state as practiced in the United States and other modern states. It is rather a policy of denying the existence of any state religion in the new India, thus making state equidistant from all religions, without privileging any of them but respecting all. However, there are constitutional structures to remedy inequalities resulting from social history, like those required for the protection of religious minorities in a majoritarian Hindu state. Under these conditions, Indian secularity does not forbid expressions of religiosity even in official government functions. The basic constitutional goals of India belong obviously to the whole humanity. But they have been surely chiseled in the moral and theological workshop of Christianity, from where they filtered into the secular culture of the Western world. Their acceptance in the vision of the new India is the fruit of an in-depth dialogue.

Apart from the general and specific influence of Christianity in the new India, one should mention also that there are a number of Hindus who have adopted the gospel of Jesus Christ as their point of reference in their own religious life (Jorgensen, 2008). J.A. Jorgensen has studied groups of "believers" in Jesus Christ who, however, are not officially part of Christian churches and yet meet more or less regularly in private homes and have some kind of ritual celebrations during which they read and meditate on the word of God contained in the Bible. There are also individual Hindus and groups in other towns that have chosen Jesus as their personal idea and object of devotion, while remaining in their traditional culture and religion.

In a less urban and in a more traditional setting, since the last decades of the 20th century, there has been a group around Varanasi that also calls itself the "Christ *bhakta*s," the members of which meet regularly for prayer and spiritual instruction based on the Bible. This phenomenon fits well with the Hindu tradition that encourages the *iṣṭadevatā*, the choice of a personal god or goddess as symbols of the divine and object of one's devotion. In older times, the church may have placed such people among the "catechumens" giving them a kind of extended membership. It is not possible to assess the number of people within the Hindu tradition that practice such "Christian" devotion: it surely remains small. Many other Hindus have strong links to the Christian community on the basis of marriage, friendship, or neighborhood.

Christianity Embraces Hinduism: Indian Christian Theology

This last part of the entry deals with the ways in which Hindu ideas and practices have influenced and been absorbed into the consciousness and the social patterns of the Christian community, especially in India. The situation varies considerably from church to church, Jacobite, Catholic, Protestant, Pentecostal – and even within the same church from region to region. It is not possible to give a detailed analysis of this general influence of Hinduism on Christians; it is largely based on a common ownership of culture, language, geography, and history. I have already alluded to the article of Placid Podipara on the character of the precolonial oriental church in Kerala (Kalayil, 2007; Visvanathan, 1993). Similar descriptions could be made about other churches or traditions (see e.g. Frykenberg, 2008).

As could be expected, Christians in India have been much influenced by the cultural and religious values derived from Hinduism, as well as other religions in India, to live and express their faith. I have mentioned above, in the historical section, the popular literature about the Saint Thomas saga that has come down to us from the community even before the beginning of the colonial period. In later centuries, we have much poetry and other literature in various languages of India that is enriched by the Hindu background. I have mentioned the *Kristāpurāṇa* of Thomas Stephen, the writings of Roberto de Nobili, and the various writings that precede the formation of classical orientalism. I may mention here some later devotional literature. If Roberto de Nobili wrote in the learned Tamil of the philosophers, Constanzo Guisepe Beschi (1680–1747), also an Italian Jesuit known in Tamil as Vīramāmuṉivar, wrote in the more popular Tamil of the masses to whom he ministered. Besides grammars, dictionaries, translations, and tracts for Christians and Hindus, and poems in Tamil, he left us the *Tēmpāvaṇi*, a precious epic in popular Tamil on the life of Saint Joseph, husband of Mary the mother of Jesus, in 36 cantos, totaling 3,615 stanzas, a classic of ancient Tamil poetry. He also composed a commentary on the *Tirukkuṟaḷ*, the ancient Tamil manual of wisdom. The ability to be both popular and literary was his characteristic (Frykenberg, 2003, 45). Moreover, he built two churches in Indian architectural style and sculpture in Konankuppam and Elakurichi, Tamil Nadu. He also specialized in local medicine.

Another Italian Jesuit, Ippolito Desideri (1684–1733), left a number of apologetic manuscripts in Tibetan on the religion of Tibet and the Christian faith, recently published and translated into Italian (see Toscano, 1981–1989). The German Johann Ernst Hanxleden (1681–1732), known in Kerala as Arnos Pāthiri (Padri), left us numerous religious poems and songs, besides his Sanskrit-Portuguese and Malayalam-Portuguese lexica. Among more modern authors, one may record Narayan Vaman Tilak and Pandita Ramabai in the 20th century.

The discovery of Sanskrit as India's sacred language dates at least from the time of Francis Xavier in the mid-16th century, as mentioned above. The Polish scholar I. Milewska (2003) has reconstructed part of the story of this discovery in the 16th to 18th centuries. This tradition was revived in the 19th and early 20th centuries with the aim of making this treasure useful for evangelization, at times also for debate, thanks to outstanding Indologists and missionaries from the Protestant churches. William Hodge Mill (1792–1853) left us the *Śrī Kṛṣṭāsaṅgitā*, a long poem "of unmatched brilliance in the corpus of Church Sanskrit" (Amaladass & Young, 1995), whose anthology *The Indian Christiad* reprints parts of this poem. Their book also contains some selections from the writings of John Muir (1810–1882), a devout Scottish Presbyterian in the civil service of the East India Company who authored at least 15 books in Sanskrit of a devotional, apologetic, or merely historical character, which R.F. Young has qualified as "Church Sanskrit" (see Amaladass & Young, 1995; Young, 1979). More recently we have two Sanskrit poems on Christ, the *Kristubhāgavatam* (Devasia, 1977) and *Kristusahasranāma* (Chacko, 1980).

The Tamil Christians also contributed considerably to the literary output of their church and their culture. It is not possible to name all significant people (see Frykenberg, 2003). One of the most significant is Vedanayagam Pillai (also known as Vedanayagam Sastri; 1774–1864; Hudson, 2000, ch. 8). He was in fact the product and the continuation of a long line of missionary writing in Tamil. His father, Arunachalam Pillai, had converted at the age of 25 from Śaivism to Catholicism and received the baptismal name of Devasahayam. He was instructed and induced into the ministry not as an ordained priest but as a catechist with what were called "minor orders" (= lay ministries). After some years, however, he was attracted to the nearby evangelical church. In the Protestant church, he became a successful preacher and composed some biblical songs. His son, Vedanayagam, followed him in the ministry of his church and became a prominent poet and writer of religious Tamil literature, with 120 Tamil works attributed to him (Peterson, 2002). His main work, *Pettalēm Kuṟavañci* (sometimes cited as *Bethlehem Kuṟavañci*), follows the popular style of Tamil literature.

An important bridge enabling the Hindu tradition to enter into the Christian consciousness are the translations, first of the Bible and then of devotional or theological texts. Every good translation sucks milk from the mother tongue into which a text is translated. A valuable study on this is found in B. Tiliander (1974). See also J.S.M. Hooper (1957). In this important area of the Hindu–Christian encounter, the Protestant churches have done and continue to do an enormous and very valuable work. Unlike the traditional Muslims, Christians welcome translation not only as a necessary tool for evangelism but also as defining the essence of their tradition. For the very foundational scriptures of Christianity are translations. Neither Jesus nor his earliest disciples, including the apostles, were originally Greek speaking, and yet all their words and deeds have come to us translated into Greek. Every translation absorbs something of a new culture, including its religious patterns, which remain inlaid in the scriptures. Thus faith itself "grows," so to speak, through translations. This implies a theology of the Holy Spirit as the divine presence that leads us to the whole truth, not only as the agent to "inspire" the sacred texts but also as the guide of the Christian community in communicating the divine word to all nations and peoples.

It is not possible to give here even a summary of the development of Indian Christian theology in the 20th and 21st centuries. Interesting resources for research may be found in the booklets *Bibliography of Original Christian Writings in India*, published by the Board of Theological Education of the Senate of Serampore. Information on the following languages is available: Gujarati (1991), northeast Indian Languages (1992), Telugu (1993), Sanskrit (1994), and Kannada and Tulu (1994).

The tribal or → Ādivāsi church of central India is a growing community becoming more aware of its roots. At the beginning, both the Protestant and the Catholic missionaries demanded a rather strict break with their old culture and religiosity, including for example a prohibition to dance the traditional dances associated with primal myths. In recent times, however, there is a will to rediscover the cultural and religious roots of the community and give them space in its life today: dances, myths, songs, language, art, and festivals are thus rediscovered and made to link with the Christian faith in ways similar to those in which the early church managed to incorporate symbols and myths not only of Judaism, where it was born, but also of the culture pervading the Roman world (Rahner, 1963). The situation in the churches of northeast India, largely Protestant in composition, is not the same. For there, a more radical break with the original culture and religion was imposed. However, even there, recently efforts are being made in seminaries to foster a deeper study of the original culture of every tribe.

For the rest of India in general, we may say that at the popular levels the churches live their life on the basis of the Bible and Christian traditions largely imported by missionaries from the West, but using a language rooted in the Indian traditions. Where there are not persecutions as experienced sporadically in some places, there is a peaceful coexistence and mutual respect between Christians and followers of other religions, but without much influence on one another. In the theological world, the need is increasingly felt for a deeper dialogue leading to what has been called the "inculturation" of the church and of the faith in the country. As a result, more and more ideas and practices of the Hindu world are being integrated into the Christian world of India.

Perhaps historically the first area of influence and borrowing has been the tradition of → *yoga*. Leaving aside possible earlier sources, I must refer to the work of J.-M. Déchanet, who in the 1950s published *La voie du silence*, translated into English with the questionable title *Christian Yoga* (Dechanet, 1960). Whatever its historical roots, in the 20th century, Yoga came to the West largely from the Hindu tradition. Studies have shown points of contact with the Hesychasm tradition in ancient Christianity. The system teaches us the way of emptying the mind and stopping its flow of images and desires so as to reach a higher state of consciousness of our own selfhood. Today many Christians all over the world practice or have practiced some kind of *yoga* and find it useful for their meditation and prayer life. Books on *yoga* by Christians are found by the dozens if not hundreds. Centers of *yoga* practice and teaching abound everywhere. *Yoga* is today part of the world culture and makes us aware of the close connection among body, mind, and spirit. It also enables us to overcome stress so common in modern life. Similar traditions of seeking a deeper personal experience are found in Zen and Vipassana, ways leading to mindfulness inspired by the Buddhist traditions.

Akin to the theme of *yoga* is the Vedānta, especially Advaita Vedānta, a theology in its own right, a conceptual tool used even by Christian theologians in India to articulate more precisely the relation of creation to the divine or absolute reality. The system is generally identified with the thought of Śankarācārya (or → Śankara), the 8th-century philosopher-theologian who has dominated much of Indian intellectual output, both traditional and modern academic. The reaction of the West to Śankara's views has passed through various periods (De Smet, 2010). It was at first looked upon through the lens of German idealist philosophy and presented, for example, by P. Deussen and Indian intellectuals like S. Vivekananda and S. Radhakrishnan, as the acme of Indian thought parallel to the glorious insights of I. Kant and G.W.F. Hegel. It was also criticized by missionaries and theologians as a form of intellectual pride that denied the fundamental distinction between creator and creature, attempted a self-produced experience of "salvation" (*mokṣa*; see → liberation), and left no role of divine → grace in the spirituality.

In a later period, a more attentive reading of the original Sanskrit texts, in contrast with mere translation reading, brought a qualified acceptance of much of what the great master and the Advaita school had taught. Some like H.O. Mascarenhas defended the validity of speaking of Advaita, etymologically "non two-ness," in reference to the absolute and the world, on the basis that transcendence and historical existence have nothing in common to enable them to be counted as "two" and therefore must be considered as non-two (*a-dvaita*; Mascarenhas, 1951). This booklet carries a 1950 "imprimatur" from Valerian Gracias, then auxiliary bishop in charge of Bombay Catholic Archdiocese. R. De Smet presented Śankara as an Indian theologian who combined dependence on revelation (Śruti) with acute intellectual analysis of linguistic predication in relation to → *brahman* or the absolute. R. Panikkar (1993) and S. Grant (1991), among many others, found in Śankarāchārya a master of spirituality and even compared him to Meister Eckhart and other Christian mystics, especially Saint John of the Cross. Still others, like M. Amaladoss, think that "*advaita*" is a very useful and even a necessary tool for the theologian who has to deal with the divine in relation to the human. Actually, Śankara's theology may be seen as the basis of R. Panikkar's proposal of the cosmo-theandric unity of the universe as necessary for a more universal theology.

Probably the most important personality to embody in himself and to articulate not merely the dialogue but also the union between Hinduism and the Christian faith was the Bengali revolutionary Bhavanicaran Banerjee, better known to the world by the name he assumed after his conversion to Catholicism, Brahmabandhab Upadhyay (1861–1907; Lipner, 1999; Lipner & Gispert-Sauch, vol. I, 1991; vol. II, 2001). Born in a Brahman family of Bengal and educated both in the Hindu traditional lore and in the new university world of Calcutta, then capital of the British Raj, Upadhyay's life symbolizes the unrest and quest of the Indian mind at the close of the Victorian era of the Raj. He was a child of the new Indian self-consciousness and the Hindu drive for reform that brought an end to the colonial era in India and indeed the world. Upadhyay discovered Jesus Christ partly thanks to Keshab Chandra

Sen and a wide reading of English literature. After a long wait and a period of membership in Keshab Chandra Sen's Church of the New Dispensation, he felt called to declare himself a Christian and be baptized in 1891, although he affirmed strongly his roots in the Hindu tradition. He declared himself a "Hindu-Christian," Hindu by birth and culture, Christian by rebirth and ecclesial commitment. His baptism opened a period of much articulation of the Christian faith from the perspectives of a "Hindu": in one of the many journals he started, the monthly *Sophia*, he articulated his Christian thinking (1894–1899). He is considered one of the founders of the Indian Christian theology. One of his most successful compositions was a Sanskrit "canticle" in honor of the Trinity under the traditional Indian formulation *saccidānanda* ("being-consciousness-bliss"), in which he legitimizes the use of this compound word for the mystery of God as professed in the traditional Christian faith. In the hymn, the original Indian resonances of the upanishadic faith in *brahman* enrich the articulation of the Trinitarian faith, without losing their traditional meanings and connotations (text and commentary in Lipner, 1999, 199–204). The church in India has partly accepted this "Hindu" vocabulary, and some of its liturgical calendars in Indian languages (e.g. Gujarati) present the feast of the Sunday after Pentecost as the solemnity of *saccidānanda*.

Grace

The Hindu tradition has also developed a rich theology of grace, as shown among others by the Sri Lankan bishops. Kulandran in his study (Kulandran, 1964). Grace is closely linked with the doctrine of *bhakti* that forms a very important stream of the Hindu tradition and is accepted with various functions in practically all its living schools, including the Advaita Vedānta. It is a central teaching of the *Bhagavadgītā*, the most significant and popular text of Hinduism dating probably from just before the start of the Common Era. It is not strange that Christians have referred often to this source of religious inspiration. Actually there are in India "retreats" for Christians guided in the pattern of the *Spiritual Exercises* of Saint Ignatius Loyola, but taking the *Bhagavadgītā* as the basic text for meditation and contemplation. Not only in India but also in Western countries, the Hindu classic is a text often used and commented upon by Christians (for a study of the significance of the *Bhagavadgītā* in India and elsewhere, see Callewaert & Hemraj, 1983; see also Cornille, 2006). Another interesting textbook of *bhakti* from the Indian tradition that Christians are today studying in a spirit of dialogue is the *Nāradabhaktisūtra*, by an anonymous author from around the 10th century CE (Sheridan, 2007).

A new approach to Hinduism and its spiritual wealth, and to any religion for that matter, has been proposed in the last two decades under the name of "comparative theology." It aims at seeking to know accurately and honestly the "other" as different, but capable of enriching one's faith. We adhere to our faith and yet remain "vulnerable," and in some way we are transformed by the encounter with the other (see Scheuer, 2011). The method has been especially developed by the American Jesuit F.X. Clooney (e.g. Clooney, 2010). It does not imply syncretism but a dialogical living of one's faith.

Not surprisingly, this positive approach to Hindu texts has also influenced the leaders of the church in India so that attempts have been made to include some selected texts from the Hindu tradition in the official liturgy, even in the Eucharist. The rationale for this practice, new in the church, is the belief that the Holy Spirit has guided the religious evolution of humanity and that the faith produced by the divine presence contains "seeds" or elements of divine revelation that are valuable for all believers, including Christians, who hold an ultimate revelation in the person of Jesus. The Catholic Church laid the basis for this practice in its declaration on the relation of the church to world religions, *Nostra Aetate* (Vatican II, 1964; on this see Amalorpavadass, 1974).

Allied to the question of Hindu scriptures is the use of the sacred symbol → *oṃ*, popularly identified with Hinduism. It is clear that the symbol was already used in vedic times, whether it originated from the vedic chant itself or from a prevedic Tamil language designating affirmation. The fact is that in the course of the centuries, the symbol has been used in different ways not only by Hindus but also by Buddhists, Jains, and even Sikhs, whose sacred book, the *Gurū Granth Sāhib*, begins with an invocation to *ek oṃkār* (Punj. *ik oankār*, the one true God; see also → Hinduism and Sikhism). Thus *oṃ* can be considered an almost pan-Indian symbol that has been given different meanings in different contexts, within

Hinduism and outside it. On this basis, some Christians have begun using it also in Christian contexts of worship or culture, both in its verbal form and as an artistic written sign. It can occasionally be seen in modern Christian churches and chapels or be heard in meditation sessions or hymns. This has at times provoked tensions between conservative Hindus and Christians. Most Indians tolerate this use with good grace.

Indian liberation theology, especially → Dalit theology, is generally critical of the Hindu religious tradition particularly because of the caste system. Consciously it integrates little from it, and it rather appeals to Buddhism and its originally egalitarian ethos for Indian inspiration. See, however, the work of A. Pieris, especially of 1988, and the 2009 book by P. Knitter.

I need not speak here of other forms of "inculturation" of some Christian communities in India to customs that now belong to the day-to-day life rather than religion. The use of ornamentation including → *tilak* on the forehead, the wearing of *sāṛīs*, the adoption of names derived from the Sanskrit or other Indian languages, the use of Indian forms of dance, house décor, and so on may show the osmosis of cultural values often rooted in religious traditions that take place in India. One must also recognize that there is resentment toward these trends among some leaders of both communities, who see them on the one hand as a threat to the Christian identity and therefore the future of their tradition, and on the other hand as an illegitimate appropriation by Christians of what belongs to the Hindu tradition. One may hope that, eschewing defensiveness on both sides, the trend will prepare the way to a more humane world.

Indian Christian Art

I close this entry with a word on the way in which art has contributed to a "dialogue beyond words" between the traditions of Hinduism and Christianity.

We know little of the ways in which the early Saint Thomas church expressed artistically its faith. No church buildings of the time have survived the ravages of history, and we in practice have no works of art. Only some ancient songs or poems have survived, and even these are not very old. The only ancient artistic product is the so-called Persian cross found in several places in Kerala and Chennai. This artistic cross is not of Indian origin, although it has been widely found in India and has been adopted as the emblem of the Saint Thomas churches of this country (for a detailed study, see J. Vazhuthanapally, 1988).

A symbiosis between India and the Christian tradition in the artistic field is found in many areas, from rather recent examples of tribal art in Gujarat, Maharashtra, central India, and Orissa, to sophisticated paintings of world-renowned artists (see Löwner, 2009; Butler, 1986; Taylor, 1975). The oldest and very interesting expressions of such symbiosis come from non-Christian sources, specifically the art workshops of the Moghul Empire in the 16th to 18th centuries, where both Muslim and Hindu artists were employed to reproduce in Indian miniatures scenes from the Bible and from the lives of Jesus and Mary. There are perhaps hundreds of such productions in museums and private collections of the world, including India. Of more modern painters, perhaps the best known internationally are the Hindu Jaimini Roy and Muslim M.F. Hussein, with his many paintings on the theme of Mother Teresa.

Bibliography

Amaladass, A., & R.F. Young, *The Indian Christiad: A Concise Anthology of Didactic and Devotional Literature in Early Church Sanskrit*, Anand, 1995.

Amalorpavadass, D.S., *Research Seminar on Non-biblical Scriptures*, Bangalore, 1974.

Anderson, G.H., *Biographical Dictionary of Christian Missions*, Grand Rapids, 1998.

Becker, K.J., & I. Morali, eds., *Catholic Engagement with World Religions: A Comprehensive Study*, Maryknoll, 2010.

Boxer, C.R., *The Portuguese Seaborne Empire 1415–1825*, London, 1969.

Brown, J.M., & R.E. Frykenberg, eds., *Christians, Cultural Interactions and India's Religious Traditions*, Grand Rapids, 2002.

Butler, J.F., *Christian Art in India*, Madras, 1986.

Callewaert, W.M., & S. Hemraj, *Bhagavadgītānuvāda: A Study in Transcultural Translation*, Ranchi, 1983.

Chacko, I.C., *Kristusahasranāma: Sanskrit Poetry*, Muvattupuzha, 1980 (Skt).

Charpentier, J., *"Introduction" to The Livro da Seita dos Indios Orientais of Father Jacobo Fenicio, S.J.*, Uppsala, 1933.

Clooney, F.X., ed., *The New Comparative Theology: Interreligious Insights from the Next Generation*, London, 2010.

Clooney, F.X., *The Truth, the Way, the Life: Christian Commentary on the Three Holy Mantras of the Śrīvaiṣṇava Hindus*, Leuven, 2008.
Clooney, F.X., *Beyond Compare: St Francis de Sales and Śrī Vedānta Deśika on Loving Surrender to God*, Washington DC, 2008.
Cornille, C., *Song Divine: Christian Commentaries on the Bhagavad Gītā*, Leuven, 2006.
Cronin, V., *A Pearl to India*, London, 1959.
De Smet, R., "Christianity and Shankaracarya," in: G. Menachery, *The St. Thomas Christian Encyclopedia of India*, vol. III, Trissur, 2010, 22–42.
Déchanet, J.-M., *La voie du silence*, Paris, 1956; ET: *Christian Yoga*, London, 1960.
Devanandan, P.D., *Christian Concern with Hinduism*, Bangalore, 1961.
Devassia, P.C., *Kristubhāgavatam: A Mahākāvya in Sanskrit Based on the Life of Jesus Christ*, Trivandrum, 1977 (Skt. & Eng.).
Dharampal, G., *La religion des malabars: Tessier de Quéralay et la contribution des missionnaires européens a la naissance de l'indianisme*, Immensee, 1982.
Documenta Indica, ed. J. Wicki, 17 vols., MHSI 70, Rome, 1948–1988.
Falcao, N., *Fadar Thomas Stifenskrta Kristapurana*, Bangalore, 2009 (Mar.).
Falcao, N., *Kristapurana: A Christian-Hindu Encounter*, Pune, 2003.
Frykenberg, R.E., *Christianity in India: From Beginnings to the Present*, New York, 2008.
Frykenberg, R.E., ed., *Christians and Missionaries in India: Cross-cultural Communication Since 1500*, Grand Rapids, 2003.
Frykenberg, R.E., "Christians in India: A Historical Overview of Their Complex Origins," in: R.E. Frykenberg, ed., *Christians and Missionaries in India: Cross-cultural Communication Since 1500*, Grand Rapids, 2003, 33–61.
Grant, S., *Sankaracharya's Concept of Relation*, Delhi, 1999.
Grant, S., *Towards an Alternative Theology: Confessions of a Non-dualist Christian*, Bangalore, 1991.
Halbfass, W., *India and Europe: An Essay in Philosophical Understanding*, Basel, 1990.
Hooper, J.S.M., *Greek New Testament Terms in Indian Languages*, Bangalore, 1957.
Hudson, D.D., *Protestant Origins in India: Tamil Evangelical Christians, 1706–1835*, Grand Rapids, 2000.
Iyer, R., *The Moral and Political Writings of Mahatma Gandhi*, vol. III, Oxford, 1987.
Jeyaraj, D., *Bartholomäus Ziegenbalg: The Father of Modern Protestant Mission: An Indian Assessment*, New Delhi, 2006.
Jeyaraj, D., *Geneology of the South Indian Deities*, London, 2005.
Jorgensen, J.A., *Jesus Imandars and Christ Bhaktas: Two Case Studies of Interreligious Hermeneutics and Identity in Global Christianity*, Frankfurt am Main, 2008.
Kalapati, J., *Radhakrishnan and Christianity: An Introduction to Hindu-Christian Apologegtics*, Dehli, 2002.
Kalayil, T., ed., *Collected Works of Rev. Dr Placid J. Podipara, C.M..I. (1899–1985)*, 5 vols., Mannanam, 2007.
Knitter, P., *Without Buddha I Could Not Be a Christian*, Oxford, 2009.
Kulandran, S., *Grace: A Comparative Study of the Doctrine in Christianity and Hinduism*, London, 1964.
Kuriedath, J., *Authority in the Catholic Community in Kerala*, Bangalore, 1989.
Lederle, S.J.M., *Christian Painting in India through the Centuries*, Anand, 1984.
Lipner, J.J., *Brahmabandhab Upadyay: The Life and Thought of a Revolutionary*, Delhi, 1999.
Lipner, J.J., & G. Gispert-Sauch, *The Writings of Brahmabandhab Upadhyay*, 2 vols., Bangalore, 1991–2001.
Lorenzen, D.N., *Who Invented Hinduism? Essays on Religion in History*, New Delhi, 2006.
Löwner, G., *Christliche Themen in der Indischen Kunst. Ein Überblick von der Mogulzeit bis Heute*, Frankfurt am Main, 2009.
Mascarenhas, H.O., *The Quintessence of Hinduism: The Key to Indian Culture and Philosophy*, Bombay, 1951.
Menachery, G., ed., *The St Thomas Christian Encyclopedia of India*, vols. I–III, Trissur, 1973–2010.
Milewska, I., "First European Missionaries on Sanskrit Grammar," in: R.E. Frykenberg, ed., *Christians and Missionaries in India: Cross-cultural Communication Since 1500*, Grand Rapids, 2003, 62–69.
Monchanin, J., *Mystique de l'Inde, mystère Chrétien*, Paris, 1974.
More, J.B.P., "Hindu-Christian Interaction in Pondicherry, 1700–1900," *CIS.NS* 32/1, 1998, 97–121.
Nobili, R. de, *Informatio de Quibusdam Moribus Nationis Indicae*, 1614 (Lat.); ET: S. Rajamanickam, *Robert de Nobili on Indian Customs*, Palayamkottai, 1972.
Oddie, G.A., *Imagined Hinduism: British Protestant Missionary Constructions of Hinduism, (1793–1900)*, New Delhi, 2006.
O'Neill, C.E., & J.M. Domínguez, *Diccionario Histórico de la Compañía de Jesús: Biográfico-temático*, 4 vols., Rome, 2001.
Panikkar, R., *The Cosmotheandric Experience: Emerging Religious Consciousness*, New York, 1993.
Pankratz, J.N., "Rammohun Roy," in: R.D. Baird, ed., *Religion in Modern India*, New Dehli, 1981, 163–177.
Peterson, I.V., "Bethlehem Kuravañci of Vedanayaka Sastri of Tanfore: The Cultural Discourses of an Early-Nineteenth-Century Tamil Christian Poem," in: J.M. Brown & R.E. Frykenberg, eds., *Christians, Cultural Interactions and India's Religious Traditions*, Grand Rapids, 2002, 9–36.
Pieris, A., *Love Meets Wisdom: A Christian Experience of Buddhism*, Maryknoll, 1988.
Puliurumpil, J., "The Greek and Roman Understanding of Ancient India," *CO* 32/1, 2011, 3–19.
Putz, S.J.J., *Clergy Monthly Supplement (Ranchi)* 3, 1956–1957, 308–318.
Radhakrishnan, S., *Indian Philosophy*, vol. II, London, 1927.
Rajamanickam, S., *The First Oriental Scholar*, Tirunelveli, 1972.

Rahner, H., *Greek Myth and Christian Mystery*, London, 1963.

Roy, R.M., *The English Works of Raja Ram Mohan Roy*, 2 vols., Calcutta, 1885–1887.

Scheuer, J., "Vingt ans de 'Théologie comparative.' Visée, méethode et enjeux d'une jeune discipline," *NRT* 133/2, 2011, 207–227.

Schurhammer, G., & I. Wicky, eds., *Epistolaes. Francisci Xaverii Aliaque Eius Scripta, Nova editio. I (1535–1548)*, Rome, 1944 (Lat.).

Scott, D.C., *Keshub Chunder Sen: A Selection*, Library of Indian Christian Theology Companion Volume 1, Bangalore, 1979.

Sen, S.P., *Dictionary of National Biography*, 4 vols., Calcutta, 1972–1974.

Sheridan, D.P., *Loving God: Krsna and Christ: A Christian Commentary on the Narada Sutras*, Leuven, 2007.

Taylor, R.W., *Jesus in Indian Paintings*, Madras, 1975.

Thomas, M.M., *The Acknowledged Christ of the Indian Renaissance*, Madras, [1]1970, 1976.

Tiliander, B., *Christian and Hindu Terminology: A Study of Their Mutual Relations with Special Reference to the Tamil Area*, Uppsala, 1974.

Toscano, G., ed., *Opere Tibetane di Ippolito Desideri S.J.*, 4 vols., Rome, 1981–1989 (It. & Tib.).

Vadakkekara, B., *Origin of India's St Thomas Christians: A Hitoriographical Critique*, Delhi, 1995.

Vazhuthanapally, J., *Archaeology of Mar Sliba*, Kottayam, 1988.

Visvanathan, S., *The Christians of Kerala: History, Belief and Ritual among the Yakoba*, Madras, 1993.

Wicki, J., *Tratado do Pe Gonçalo Fernandes Trancoso sobre o Hinduismo (Maduré 1616)*, Lisbon, 1973 (Port.).

Wicki, J., *O Homem das Trinta e Duas Perfeições e Outras Histórias*, Lisbon, 1958 (Port.).

Wicki, J., *Diogo Gonçalves S.I.: Historia do Malavar*, Münster Westfalen, 1955 (Port.).

Young, R.F., "Church Sanskrit: An Approach of Christian Scholars to Hinduism in the Nineteenth Century," *WZKS* 23, 1979, 205–231.

George Gispert-Sauch

Hinduism and Islam

Medieval and Premodern Period

This article examines the relations between Muslim culture and the Indian world, focusing primarily on the trends, intellectual approaches, and reactions in this regard that arose in the Muslim contexts of South Asia. It does not intend to provide an exhaustive overview of the topic, of which many important aspects have in fact hardly been studied, but is mainly concerned with the examination of three subject areas that are of central importance for the study of such contacts. The first section focuses on the dialogue between Persian culture and Hindu knowledge by analyzing the movement for the Persian translation and compilation of works on Indian traditions and sciences. The second section offers a more detailed examination of the contacts between Islamic mysticism and the Hindu world. The final section, in contrast, deals with the adverse reactions to contacts with Hindu culture that arose in the Muslim world of South Asia.

Textual Contacts: The Persian Texts on Indian Learning

A substantial number of texts on the knowledge and traditions of the Hindus were produced in Persian in South Asia, both in the form of direct translation of texts, mostly from Sanskrit, and through the composition of new treatises and compendiums (see Ernst, 2003a; Speziale, 2010). The Muslims were not new to such undertakings, as it was, in fact, precisely through the contact with a pre-Islamic culture, namely the Greek culture, that they had acquired most of their philosophical and scientific background. The Persian studies on Indian learning constitute the most important translation movement from a non-Muslim tradition achieved in the Muslim culture since the translation of Greek texts into Arabic, which had flourished in the Abbasid world of the 9th and 10th centuries.

Contacts with Indian traditions had already taken place long before the expansion of Muslim hegemony on the Indian subcontinent. During the Abbasid period, the translation of pre-Islamic sources was dominated by the influence of Hellenistic tradition, though Muslim scholars also came into contact with works and elements of Indian origin, as in the case of the decimal number system, which was passed on to Europe through Arab mediation. The most representative figure of this first phase of study was that of the great scientist al-Bīrūnī (d. after 1050), who studied Sanskrit, translated the *Yogasūtra* of Patañjali into Arabic, and wrote the *Kitāb taḥqīq mā li ʾl-Hind*, the most important medieval Arabic encyclopedia on the religion and knowledge of India. However, various factors indicate that these first studies in Arabic had an altogether limited impact on the Muslim world of later times, as may also be surmised from the small number of manuscript copies of these works that have come down to us.

In South Asia, the compilation of Persian texts on Indian knowledge only began after the establishment of the Delhi Sultanate in the early 13th century. This wave of studies culminated during the period of the → Mughals, who came to power in 1526 and progressively extended their supremacy over much of India. For somewhat more than half a century between the last decades of the 18th and the first decades of the 19th century, several Persian texts on Indian traditions were also produced and translated for the British. The British inherited the use of Persian as the official administrative language from the Mughal; it was replaced by English in 1835.

Over the course of more than six centuries, the works that were produced covered a wide range of subjects such as epic literature, history, religion, philosophy, mysticism, narratives, law (→ *dharma*), → music, and erotology (see → *kāma*). Among the sciences, a prominent role was assumed by medicine and pharmacology (see → Āyurveda), although one also finds treatises and chapters on → mathematics, astronomy (→ *jyotiṣa*), zoology, alchemy (→ *rasāyana*), and the *sāmudrika*, a discipline that the Persian translators considered to be the equivalent of the *qiyāfa*, the physiognomy of the Muslim tradition. To these must be added the Persian-written treatises on the geography, flora, fauna, and culinary tradition of India. Several copies of these works were illustrated with miniatures, as for instance the translation of the → *Mahābhārata*, the *Harivaṃśa*, the → *Rāmāyaṇa*, the *Yogavāsiṣṭha*, the *Amṛtakuṇḍa*, the *Śūkasaptatī*, the *Kokaśāstra* (also known as *Kokkokaśāstra* or *Ratirahasya*), and the *Śālihotra*. The production of these texts decreased in the second half of the 19th century, essentially due to the decline of the role played by the Persian language in South Asia. The decline of Persian favored the rise of Urdu, the language in which several works on Indian traditions were written and published during the colonial period, thereby representing the final extension of the movement for the translation of Indian sources into the language of the Muslim civilization.

The wave of Persian and Urdu studies on Indian knowledge was of much larger scope than the first wave of studies on the same topic that had been conducted in Arabic during the Abbasid period. However, it should be noted that these Persian works circulated mostly in India and that their impact outside the Indian subcontinent was, with a few exceptions, rather limited. Among these, we can mention the Malay adaptations of earlier Persian versions of classical Indian narratives such as the *Pañcatantra* and the *Śūkasaptatī* (Bausani, 1970, 339–340), and the circulation, among the Sufis of the Ottoman world, of the teachings of the *Amṛtakuṇḍa*, a manual on → *yoga* that was first adapted in Persian and Arabic in India and subsequently translated into Turkish in the 18th century (Ernst, 2005, 32). Though of lesser significance and in many respects different, the role played, until the first decades of the 19th century in British India, by the Persian texts on Indian traditions that were compiled and translated for the colonial elite is in some ways similar to the one played centuries before by the Arabic texts that gave the medieval European scholars access to the knowledge of Greek origin. The first translations of some of the classics of Indian tradition into Western languages – such as the → Upaniṣads, the *Śālihotra*, and the *Bījagaṇita* – were not realized on the basis of the Sanskrit sources but on that of the Persian versions produced during the Mughal period.

Many of these works were composed for Muslim rulers and nobles or were dedicated to them. Several treatises of this type date back to the pre-Mughal period, especially the first Persian texts on Indian sciences and music. Texts on astrology and natural philosophy, including Varāhamihira's *Bṛhatsaṃhitā*, were translated for the sultan of Delhi Fīrūz Šāh Tuġluq (r. 1351–1388). The *Ġunyat al-munya*, an anonymous treatise on music, was composed in 1374–1375 for Malik Šams al-Dīn, the governor of Gujarat (Sarmadee, 1978), while the *Lahajāt-i Sikandar-šāhī* (The Tunes of King Sikandar), another text on Indian music, was written by Yaḥyā al-Kābulī for the vizier Miyān Bhuwa H̱ān and dedicated to the sultan of Delhi Sikandar Lodī (r. 1489–1517). Another work dedicated to the same sultan of Delhi was the *Maʿdan al-šifāʾ-i Sikandar-šāhī* (The Source of Healing of King Sikandar): commissioned by the same Miyān Bhuwa and realized with the help of Indian → *paṇḍit*s, the work established itself as one of the most widely circulated Persian treatises on Indian medicine. The translation of Vāgbhaṭa's *Aṣṭāṅgahṛdayasaṃhitā*, entitled *Ṭibb-i šifā-yi Maḥmūd-šāhī* (The Medicine of Healing of King Maḥmud), was dedicated to the sultan of Gujarat Maḥmud Begrā (r. 1458–1511). Between the 15th century and the first two decades of the following century, three Persian treatises drawing on the tradition of the *Śālihotra*, a Sanskrit classic on horses and their treatment, were composed for the sultans of Gulbarga, of Malwa, and of Gujarat. Also in the 15th century, the sultan of Kashmir Zayn al-ʿĀbidīn commissioned the first Persian translations of the *Mahābhārata* and of the *Rājataraṅgiṇī*.

The greatest patrons of the translations of Sanskrit works into Persian were the Mughals Akbar (r. 1556–1605) and Dārā Šikōh (1615–1659). In 1564, Akbar abolished the *jizya* – that is, the head tax imposed on non-Muslims living in Muslim kingdoms – and subsequently proclaimed the principle of *ṣulḥ-i kul* (universal tolerance). During the second half of the 16th century, the movement for the translation of Indian texts into Persian became an element of Akbar's religious policy and imperial ideology. One of the most significant works in this vein is the *Āʾīn-i Akbarī* (The Institutes of Akbar) by Abū al-Fażl ʿAllāmī (d. 1602), a court historian and adviser to Akbar as well as one of the main architects of the imperial Mughal philosophy. The work offers an overview of the Mughal Empire under Akbar and includes an extensive final section on the geography and knowledge of India. At Fatehpur Sikri, Akbar's new capital, a translation bureau (*maktabḫāna*) was set up for the will of the emperor, where Muslim scholars operated with the help of Hindu *paṇḍits*; the latter translated and explained the text in Hindi, which was then rendered into Persian by the Muslim scholars who were not familiar with Sanskrit. The works selected for translation included the following: epic texts such as the *Mahābhārata* and the *Rāmāyaṇa*, which the Mughals mainly interpreted as works of historical-political character and not as religious texts (see Ernst, 2003a, 178–182); the history of Kashmir by Kalhaṇa, entitled *Rājataraṅgiṇī*; the *Atharvaveda*; and works of narrative literature and treatises on astronomy and arithmetic, among which the *Līlāvatī* by Bhāskara.

Muḥammad Dārā Šikōh is another emblematic figure of this study movement. The most famous translation sponsored by this Mughal prince was certainly the *Sirr-i akbar* (The Greatest Secret), a Persian adaptation of the Upaniṣads that was translated into Latin toward the end of the 18th century by the French orientalist A.H. Anquetil-Duperron. Dārā Šikōh himself authored the *Majma*ʿ *al-baḥrayn* (The Confluence of the Two Seas), the largest Persian treatise of comparative nature on the religious and philosophical thought of Islam and Hinduism. The main purpose of this work is to demonstrate the basic equivalence between the fundamental doctrines of Islam and Hinduism. According to Dārā Šikōh, Allāh, the name of the divine essence, finds its correspondence in the syllable → *oṃ*, while the divine attributes of beauty (*jamāl*) and majesty (*jalāl*) correspond to the *triguṇa* of Indian thought: *sattva, rajas*, and *tamas* (see → *guṇa*). The Sufi doctrine of the successive stages of manifestation, which begins with the realm of divine nature (*lāhūt*) and ends with the realm of human nature (*nāsūt*), finds its equivalent in the Hindu doctrine of the four states (*avasthā*s) of the self: *jāgrat, svapna, suṣupti*, and *turīya* (awake, sleep, deep sleep, and "the fourth" [i.e. a state of pure consciousness]). The distinction between *rūḥ* and *rūḥ-i a*ʿ*ẓam* in Muslim tradition corresponds to that between → *ātman* and *paramātman* in Hindu thought. The angels (*firištas*) of Islamic tradition correspond to the deities (*devatās*) of Hindu tradition, thus leading to the identification of Gabriel, Michael, and Israfel with → Brahmā, → Viṣṇu, and → Śiva, respectively. The Islamic prophets (*nabī*s) correspond to the *mahāsiddhas* (persons who have attained perfection). *Hū Allāh*, one of the spiritual invocations (*ḏikr*s) of the Sufis, corresponds to the *mantra* "*so*ʾ*ham*," while the "prince of invocations" (*sulṭān al-aḏkār*) of the Sufi mystics is compared to the *anāhatanāda* (the unstruck sound) of the *yogī*s. Furthermore, a new Persian translation of the *Laghuyogavāsiṣṭha* was made at the request of Dārā Šikōh.

Fig. 1: Engraving of the Mughal prince Dārā Šikōh.

Works of this type were also produced for other Mughal emperors and dedicated to them, as for instance an adaptation of the *Yogavāsiṣṭha* made for Jahāngīr (r. 1605–1627) and two new translations of the *Rāmāyaṇa* dedicated to the same ruler as well as the translation of the *Bījagaṇita* of Bhāskara – on algebra – which was dedicated to Šāh Jahān (r. 1627–1658) by ʿAṭāʾ Allāh Rašīdī. It should be noted that the production of these texts, particularly in some disciplines, did not come to a standstill during the reign of Awrangzēb (1658–1707), who is usually portrayed as the Mughal emperor who embodies the antithesis of the policy of openness toward Hindus that had been inaugurated by Akbar. Persian treatises on Indian medicine were dedicated to Awrangzēb; in 1704, Jaṭādhara even composed a work on astronomy for him in Sanskrit, the *Phatteśāhaprakāśa* (see Speziale, 2010, 421–422; Pingree & Subbarayappa, 2001, 810). Another text from the time of Awrangzēb is the *Tuḥfat al-hind* (Gift of India), a compendium on the Indian arts – among other things prosody, rhetoric, music, erotology, and the *sāmudrika* – written by Mīrzā Ḫān ibn Faḫr al-Dīn for the education of the Mughal prince Jahāndār Šāh.

As relevant as the patronage of Muslim nobles may have been for the stimulation of the translation process, it is still important to point out that this current of studies was not restricted to the elite cultural context of the princely courts. Quite to the contrary, a substantial number of works were actually produced by scholars working outside the courtly environment. In the field of science, and especially in that of medicine, the compilation of these texts by Muslims was not so much motivated by intentions of cultural nature as by factors of pragmatic order, such as identifying the drugs of Arab-Persian tradition in India and acquiring new remedies from the rich pharmacopoeia of Indian doctors. The main purpose of these works was thus not the study of ancient local traditions but the adapting of useful knowledge to present needs (Speziale, 2010, 409–410).

Many Persian texts were not straightforward, faithful translations of the Sanskrit sources, and many authors preferred to compose new texts in Persian rather than to translate previous works in their original form. Quite often, the material was translated and presented in a manner that was adjusted to the intellectual background of Muslim scholars and readers. Intentions of this type are encountered in various forms and treatises. A well-investigated case is that of the translations of the *Amṛtakuṇḍa*, the progressive Islamization of the terms and concepts of which has been analyzed by C. Ernst (2003b). Another such case is the *Mirʾāt al-ḥaqāʾiq* (The Mirror of Realities), an abridged version of the *Bhagavadgītā* in Persian made by ʿAbd al-Raḥmān Čištī (d. 1682), in which the basic meanings of the text are expounded in Sufi terminology and commented on with quotations from the *Qurʾān* and other Muslim sources. In the scientific field, a recurring practice of this kind is encountered in the medical treatises, in which the properties of Indian drugs were frequently described on the basis of the doctrine of the four natural properties (hot, cold, wet, and dry), which the Muslims had inherited from the natural philosophy of Greek origin. Another example is the Persian adaptation of the *Śālihotra* compiled for the nobleman ʿAbd Allāh Ḫān Fīrūz-Jang (d. 1644): the Indian text was supplied with an introduction in which some traditions of Prophet Muḥammad about the horses are cited; subsequently, a manuscript copy from the 18th century was illustrated with the miniatures of two kinds of horses that were part of a tradition mentioned in the introduction.

The textual contacts and the translation of texts from Sanskrit were not the only means by which the Muslim scholars came into contact with Indian knowledge. The transmission of knowledge also took place in other ways, above all through oral instruction and through the intermediary of other vernacular languages such as Hindavi. The famous historian Muḥammad Qāsim Firišta (b. around 1570), who also composed a treatise on ayurvedic medicine (*Dastūr al-aṭibbāʾ*), studied under the Indian teacher Caturbhuj al-Hind. In the 17th century, Fażl Allāh, the author of the *Qiyāfa-šināsī* (The Understanding of Physiognomy, a work in verse on *sāmudrika*), relates that he learned that science from an Indian teacher named Gōpāl, while Muḥammad Jāmī, who produced a Persian adaptation of the *Kokaśāstra*, speaks of having been placed in the service of itinerant *yogī*s and ascetics following the difficulties encountered during the drafting of his work. Another important example is furnished by Dārā Šikōh, who met with the mystic Bābā Lāldās in Lahore in order to submit a series of questions to him about Indian doctrine. These talks between Bābā Lāldās and Dārā Šikōh were not conducted in Sanskrit but in a local vernacular and were then translated into Persian.

During the Mughal period, and afterward up to the colonial period, the Persian works were read and written not only by Muslims but also by Hindu scholars as well as by some Christians. Some Persian texts composed for noble Hindus are also attested, as for instance the *Timṯāl-i ašyāʾ wa azhār al-adwiya* – an illustrated work on the flora and fauna of Kashmir written by Ḥakīm Ġulām ʿAlī for Ranbīr Siṅgh (r. 1857–1885), the *mahārāja* of Kashmir (Naushahi, 1998). Many Hindus, and especially those from the higher castes, studied at the *madrasa*s of Mughal India – in which the languages of instruction were Persian and Arabic – in order to earn the diploma that allowed them to apply for the posts of state administration. Some of these Hindu scholars were also able to hold teaching positions within the Indian *madrasas* (see Alam, 1998, 325–330). The Brahmans, for their part, did not fail to criticize the study of Persian vocabulary and knowledge on the part of Hindus (Pingree, 1997, 86–87), although it does not seem that these attacks were able to substantially inhibit the study of Persian, especially in view of the career opportunities afforded by the knowledge of this language. By way of example, until the 1830s, half the students of the 93 *madrasas* for Persian in the district of Burdwan (Bengal) were Hindus, above all Kayasthas and Brahmans, while two of these schools were maintained by the same *rājā* of Burdwan. Although there is evidence that *paṇḍit*s had already collaborated in the preparation of Persian translations from Sanskrit in earlier times, the composition of Persian texts by learned Hindus attained significance especially from the mid-17th century onward. The latter touched on various fields ranging from poetry to history and scientific topics, in addition to those fields that were more closely connected with the employment of Hindus in the Persian-speaking administration, namely accounting (*siyāq*) and epistolography (*inšā'*). Although this textual production remains poorly studied to this very day, it is quite clear that several Persian texts written by Hindu authors displayed also a knowledge derived from Muslim tradition and subsequently also from modern Western science, as in the case of Vraja Mohana's *Maḫzan al-ʿulūm*, a short summary of rational and traditional sciences written before the mid-19th century. While elements of Muslim knowledge, at least in certain fields (as in the scientific field), occasionally also circulated by way of Sanskrit works, it was to a much greater extent by means of Persian that the erudite Hindus of the Mughal period came into contact with knowledge of Muslim origin.

Islamic Mysticism and Hinduism

Sufism, the main mystical school of the Muslim world, is one of the most important areas through which to examine the contacts between Indian Islam and Hinduism. From the early Orientalist studies in the colonial period, certain analogies between the two traditions even supported the theory that aimed to interpret Sufism – which the first orientalists considered to be incompatible with Islam – as a phenomenon derived from the Indian world. More accurate studies on issues that were better suited for such hypotheses – such as the doctrine of the "subtle centers" (*laṭā'if*) and the exercises for breath control – have in fact demonstrated how the interpretation of these practices in the Sufi texts fits into a doctrinal horizon of Islamic origin that, beyond the apparent analogy, has nothing to do with the teachings of → *yoga*. On the historical level, furthermore, the contacts between the Muslim mystics and the *yogī*s only flourished after the introduction of the Sufi orders in India – that is, several centuries after the appearance of Sufism (see Ernst, 2003b; 2005).

Although some influential Indian Sufis did not fail to direct harsh criticism against the Hindus, the Sufi mystics were undoubtedly those religious figures within Islam who were most inclined to conduct a dialogue with the Indian world. The contacts between Sufism and Hinduism materialized on various levels, from the most educated level of literary tradition to the most varied of popular piety. Some Sufis such as Dārā Šikōh, who was a fervent adept of the Qādirī order, considered the → Vedas to be a revealed book and believed – in accordance with the *Qur'ān* verses in which it is stated that God sent prophets to all nations – that India had also received the divine gift of prophecy in ancient times. Various figures of Indian tradition were thus interpreted as persons who had been entrusted with a task similar to that of the Muslim prophets, as for instance in some adaptations of the *Amṛtakuṇḍa* in which Brahmā and Viṣṇu are identified with Abraham and Moses, and three legendary *yogī*s are equated with as many monotheistic prophets. Sayyid Sulṭān from Chittagong (d. 1648) – a Sufi of the Mughal period – included Hindu deities and → *avatār*s among the prophets in his *Nabīvaṃśa* (Line of the Prophets). Similar interpretations spread in Hindu circles. The Nāth *yoga* (see → Nāth Sampradāya), one of the Indian mystical schools that stood in closer contact with Muslim culture, held that the same Prophet Muḥammad had been initiated to *yoga* by a disciple of the legendary teacher Gorakhnāth (see Shea & Troyer, 1998, 129). The *Taḏkira-yi Ġawṯiyya*, a Sufi text in Urdu written by Gul Hasan in 1884, records the words of an Indian sage who equated the function of the *avatār* with that of the prophets as bearers of an exoteric teaching for the masses and of a secret one for the chosen few, such as that imparted by → Kṛṣṇa to Arjuna and by Muḥammad to ʿAlī.

Some Sufis who were active in India even went so far as to include methods derived from the *yoga* tradition in their manuals, as for instance the recitation of → *mantras*. Among these, some texts by authors of the Šaṭṭāriyya and Čištiyya orders are particularly worthy of mention, namely the *Risāla-yi šaṭṭāriyya* by Bahā᾽ al-Dīn Šaṭṭār (d. 1515), the *Rušdnāma* by ʿAbd al-Quddus Gangohī (d. 1537), and the *Niẓām al-qulūb* by Niẓām al-Dīn Awrangābādī (d. 1729). However, this does not mean that all the descriptions of this type in texts written by Sufis intended to incorporate such elements. In the aforementioned Gul Hasan's *Taḏkira-yi Ġawṯiyya*, which collects the biography and the teachings of his teacher Ġawṯ ʿAlī Šāh Qalandar (d. 1880), the description of the subtle centers of Sufi doctrine is accompanied by a presentation of the yogic → *cakras*, which are also depicted by way of a diagram (see fig.2). As in the *Majmaʿ al-baḥrayn* of Dārā Šikōh, the intent of this exposition is to effect a comparison and not to propose a synthesis of the doctrines of Sufis and *yogīs*. The comparison with Sufi methods excluded any

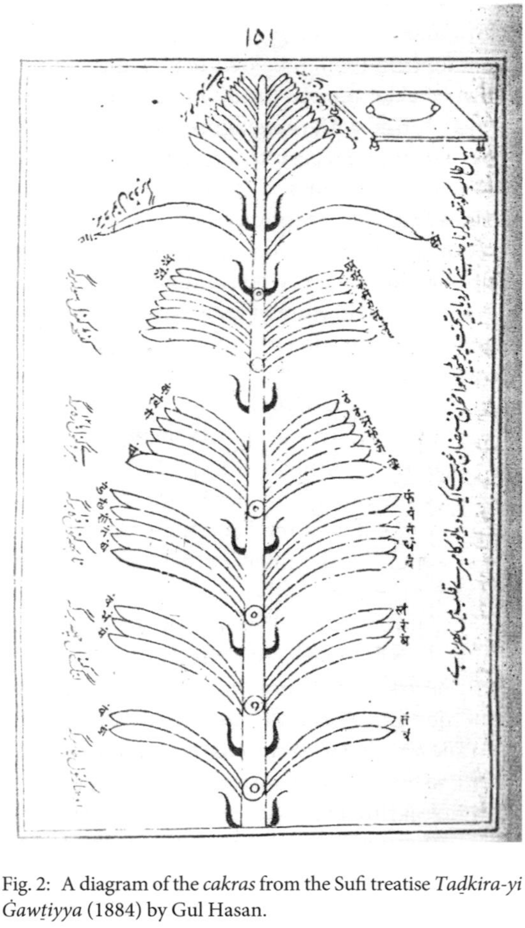

Fig. 2: A diagram of the *cakras* from the Sufi treatise *Taḏkira-yi Ġawṯiyya* (1884) by Gul Hasan.

analogy with the practices of idolaters. In one of his letters, the Naqšbandi Sufi Mīrzā Maẓhar Jān-i Jānān (d. 1781) explained to his disciples that the meditation over the images of Hindu deities is similar to the *rābiṭa* of the Sufis – the concentration on the mental picture of the teacher in order to obtain spiritual inspiration from it – and that this bears no relationship whatsoever to the idol worship of the Arab unbelievers of pre-Islamic times.

The authors associated with the Muslim mystical circles were interested not only in religious topics but also in other Indian arts and sciences. The most famous Persian adaptation of the *Śūkasaptatī*, a collection of wisdom tales, was composed by Żiyā᾽ al-Dīn Naḫšabī (d. around 1350/1351), a Čištī from the period of the Delhi Sultanate who is also credited with a Persian translation of the *Kokaśāstra*, a classic work of Indian erotology. Šāh Ahl Allāh (d. 1776), brother of the renowned Delhi theologian Šāh Walī Allāh and himself a Naqšbandī Sufi, wrote the *Takmila-yi hindī*, a treatise on Indian medicine. Indian knowledge also circulated through some treatises that were falsely attributed to Sufis. Several Arabic copies of the *Amṛtakuṇḍa* are thus ascribed to Ibn ʿArabī (d. 1240), the famous Andalusian-born Sufi. Another text that enjoyed a certain popularity was the *Haft aḥbāb*, a treatise on alchemy that also describes the Indian doctrine. This apocryphal work is attributed to a group of seven authors, including the Suhrawardī master Ḥamīd al-Dīn Nagawrī (d. 1246); the Čištī Sulaymān Mandawī (d. 1537), who was instructed in the principles of the *Amṛtakuṇḍa* by ʿAbd al-Quddus Gangohī; and Gyān Nāth Saʿādatmand, a Nāth *yogī* converted to Islam who exposes the sayings on alchemy that are ascribed to Gorakhnāth. The motif of the Nāth *yogī*'s conversion as a narrative device for the transmission of knowledge from one tradition to the other, resurfaces in chapter 4 of the treatise, which is ascribed to a certain Mīr Muḥammad Hāšim Buḫārī, who describes the methods for the production of acids that Dayā Nāth, a *yogī* of 300 years, allegedly passed on to Šayḫ Ẓahīr al-Dīn Rūmī after the latter had converted 84 *yogīs* to Islam, including the same Dayā Nāth (Speziale, 2006).

Beyond the hagiographic rhetoric of the conversion of *yogīs* by Sufis, however, there is no doubt that several Hindus were interested in Islamic mysticism, that some were even initiated to Sufism, and that some Hindu nobles gave donations on Muslim shrines (Gordon, 2002, 330). To cite an example, Banwalī Dās Walī (d. 1667/1668) – Dārā Šikōh's secretary (*munšī*) – was also a disciple of the latter's own Sufi teacher. The most significant filiation of this type appears to be that of a Hindu branch, still active today, that was derived from the Naqšbandī-Mujaddidī order through the initiative of Ramchandra Sakshena (d. 1931), who obtained the license (*ijāza*) to initiate Hindu disciples to Sufism from his teacher Fazl Ahmad Khan (d. 1889), a successor of the school of Mīrzā Maẓhar Jān-i Jānān (Dahnhardt, 2002).

A similar phenomenon took place in the opposite camp with the appearance of some groups of Muslim *yogīs* such as the Rawal and the Bachhowalia. C. Servan-Schreiber has studied one of these in particular, namely the Bhartrihari of Uttar Pradesh – a group of musicians and singers specialized in the repertoire of the Nāth tradition, who are active up to the present day, although they have been gradually becoming marginalized (Servan-Schreiber, 1995; 1999). Another study has recently shed light on a text of uncertain date entitled *Mohammad Bodh* (The Wisdom of Muḥammad), which was meant to be recited by the Muslim *yogīs* during the month of *ramaḍān* (Bouillier, 2010). Another important form of interaction is represented by a number of mystical-religious personalities such as Bābā Ratan, Satya Pīr, and → Dattātreya, who, over the course of time, have acquired traits derived both from Hinduism and from Islam (Bouillier & Khan, 2009; Stewart, 2002; Deák, 2010).

The legacy of the contacts between Sufism and the Indian environment is still quite apparent today in the popular piety associated with the cult of the Sufi saints, which attracts numerous Hindu devotees, and sometimes also devotees from other religions. In various Sufi shrines (*dargāhs*), it is customary to observe forms of popular devotion that are typical of Indian rather than of Muslim ceremonies, as for instance the offering of flowers and of other substances such as incense, rice, and coconuts. The local influence is also visible in the rite of circumambulation (*ṭawāf*) around the tomb of the saint, which, in the Indian *dargāh*, is customarily performed clockwise (also among the Muslims) – that is, according to Indian ritual practice – and not counterclockwise, which is the direction of the *ṭawāf* around the Kaʿba of Mecca.

Adverse Reactions

Reactions against the trends that favored a dialogue with the Indian world manifested themselves at various times and with various accents. As emphasized by M. Gaborieau (1985), the claim that Islam and Hinduism constitute entirely different civilizations and religions is a theory that runs through the entire history of Muslim thought, from the writings of al-Bīrūnī in the 11th century all the way to the founder of → Pakistan Muhammad Ali Jinnah (d. 1948), when it became inextricably linked with the reasons that precipitated the creation of Pakistan as a Muslim entity existing separately from the rest of the Hindu subcontinent.

The concerns over the mixing of Islamic customs and local practices that arose in the Muslim milieu are clearly detectable in the *Ḥujjat al-hind*, a treatise of uncertain date. This polemic work against Hinduism, written in the form of a dialogue between a parrot and a starling, was composed in order to admonish the Muslim villagers who were living in close contact with the Hindus and adopting their religious beliefs. In the text, the Indian deities are equated with fallen angels such as Satan, while the powers of the *yogīs* are presented as miracles of diabolical origin (see Digby, 1970, 4–5, 11).

The Muslim disapproval of the policy initiated by Akbar is fittingly illustrated by the account given by the historian ʿAbd al-Qādir Badāʾūnī (d. 1615), who, in spite of his ideas, was commissioned by Akbar precisely to collaborate in the Persian translation of Indian texts such as the *Mahābhārata* and *Rāmāyaṇa*. The translation of the *Mahābhārata* was also accomplished with the participation of Ḥājj Sulṭān Thāneswarī, the father-in-law of Aḥmad Sirhindī (d. 1624), who accepted the assignment in spite of his disdain for its content and only for the prestige that he would derive from it (Rizvi, 1992, 406). Opposition against the employment of Hindus in the administration of the Muslim kingdoms arose from various sides. Emblematic in this regard were the letters sent to the Muslim nobility by ʿAbd al-Quddus Gangohī and by Aḥmad Sirhindī, which also requested the imposition of the *jizya* on the Hindus (Digby, 1975, 33–34; Friedmann, 2000, 73–74). The protest formulated by the poet Ġawwāṣī (17th cent.) against the influence acquired by Hindus at the court of the Qutb

Shah in Golconda was equally vehement (Bausani, 1968, 97).

Dissenting voices came therefore not only from the ranks of the more conservative religious circles but also from some influential Sufi teachers and even from a personality such as ʿAbd al-Quddus Gangohī, who was known precisely for his knowledge of *yoga*. Some Muslim mystics rejected the equivalence of the principles and methods of the two traditions. In his letters, Aḥmad Sirhindī refuted the notion that → Rāma and Raḥmān (one of the names of Allāh) constitute a single principle, while Šāh Walī Allāh (d. 1762) in his *al-Qawl al-jamīl* denied the resemblance between the Sufi methods of breath control and those practiced by the *yogī*s. On one occasion, Šaraf al-Dīn Manerī (d. 1381) even went as far as to claim that the *yogī*s of his time did not understand the mystical doctrine that they had inherited; a similar reproach was later formulated by ʿAbd al-Quddus Gangohī with regard to a point in the physiological doctrine of *yoga* (Digby, 1975, 35–36).

As the analysis conducted by S. Digby has shown, the episodes on the *yogī*s that are recounted in the Indo-Persian biographies of Sufi saints are frequently embedded in hagiographic narratives that depict Sufis and *yogī*s in competition with each other and invariably end with the defeat and conversion of the Hindus. (Digby, 1970). It should nevertheless be noted that the principal aim of these stories was probably not to voice anti-Hindu polemics but rather to assert the spiritual superiority of the Sufi saints over other rivals, as in the episodes in which the Muslim *ʿulamā* (religious scholars) who are hostile to Sufism are to be defeated. However, there appears to have been cases of real armed confrontations between factions of Indian and Muslim wandering ascetics, as in the case of the clash between a group of *saṃnyāsī*s and another group of nude Jalālī and Madāri dervishes – provoked by the killing of a cow – described in the *Dabistān-i maḏāhib*, a well-known Persian text describing the principal religious schools that existed in India in the 17th century (see Shea & Troyer, 1998, 231).

The distance between the two cultures widened during the colonial period, which was characterized by the birth of Muslim reformist movements that advocated a return to the original purity of Islam as a means of overcoming the decadence of a Muslim world subjected to colonial rule. Some of these groups, such as Sayyid Aḥmad Šahīd (d. 1831) and his *mujāhidīn*, aspired to purge Indian Islam of all practices that had been adopted from the Hindu environment. As an antidote against the local contaminations of Indo-Persian culture, the reformist thinkers advocated the necessity of returning to the original sources of Islam, in the Arabic language. For those who supported the creation of Pakistan, figures like Akbar and Dārā Šikōh had to be denigrated because of their attitude toward the Hindus, whereas Awrangzēb was hailed as the restorer of Muslim identity in the Mughal Empire. An emblematic example of this vision is found in the poem *Emperor Alamgir and the Tiger* by Muhammad Iqbal (d. 1938), in which Akbar and Dārā Šikōh are accused of having planted the seed of heresy in India, whereas Awrangzēb is celebrated as the reviver of Islamic faith:

> The last arrow in our quiver
> in the battle between faith and unbelief.

Bibliography

Adam, W., *Third Report on the State of Education in Bengal: Including Some Account of the State of Education in Behar*, Calcutta, 1838.

Alam, M., "The Pursuit of Persian: Language in Mughal Politics," *MAS* 32, 1998, 317–349.

Anquetil-Duperron, A.H., *Oupnek'hat (id est, Secretum tegendum)*, Paris, 1801–1802.

Assayag, J., *Au confluent des deux rivières: Musulmans et hindous dans le sud de l'Inde*, Paris, 1995.

Bausani, A., *Le letterature del sud-est asiatico*, Florence, 1970.

Bausani, A., *Le letterature del Pakistan e dell'Afghanistan*, Florence, 1968.

Bouillier, V., "*Dialogue entre les Nāth yogis et l'islam*," in: D. Hermann & F. Speziale, eds., *Muslim Cultures in the Indo-Iranian World during the Early-Modern and Modern Periods*, Berlin, 2010, 565–583.

Bouillier, V., & D.-S. Khan, "Hajji Ratan or Baba Ratan's Multiple Identities," *JIPh* 37, 2009, 559–595.

Dahnhardt, T., *Change and Continuity in Indian Sūfism: A Naqshbandi-Mujaddidī Branch in the Hindu Environment*, New Delhi, 2002.

Deák, D., "Śahādat or Śahā datta? Locating the Mysterious Fakir in the Marathi Texts," in: D. Hermann & F. Speziale, eds., *Muslim Cultures in the Indo-Iranian World during the Early-Modern and Modern Periods*, Berlin, 2010, 501–532.

Digby, S., "ʿAbd al-Quddus Gangohi, 1456–1537 AD: The Personality and Attitudes of a Medieval Sufi," in: *Medieval India: A Miscellany*, vol. III, Aligarh, 1975, 1–66.

Digby, S., "Encounters with Jogīs in Indian Sūfī Hagiography," paper presented at the Seminar on Aspects of Religion in South Asia, SOAS, London, Jan 27, 1970.

D'Onofrio, S., "A Persian Commentary to the *Upaniṣads*: Dārā Šikōh's '*Sirr-i akbar*,'" in: D. Hermann & F. Speziale, eds., *Muslim Cultures in the Indo-Iranian World during the Early-Modern and Modern Periods*, Berlin, 2010, 533–563.

Ernst, C.W., "Fayzi's Illuminationist Interpretation of Vedanta: *The Shariq al-Ma'rifa*," *CSSAAME* 30/3, 2010, 156–164.

Ernst, C.W., "Situating Sufism and Yoga," *JRAS(3)* 15/1, 2005, 15–43.

Ernst, C.W., "Muslim Studies of Hinduism? A Reconsideration of Arabic and Persian Translation from Indian Languages," *IS* 36/2, 2003a, 173–195.

Ernst, C.W., 2003b, "The Islamization of Yoga in the Amrtakunda Translations," *JRAS(3)* 13/2, 2003b, 199–226.

Friedmann, Y., *Shaykh Aḥmad Sirhindī: An Outline of His Thought and a Study of His Image in the Eyes of Posterity*, New Delhi, 2000.

Friedmann, Y., "Islamic Thought in Relation to the Indian Context," in: M. Gaborieau, ed., *Islam et société en Asie du Sud (Puruṣārtha, 9)*, Paris, 1986, 79–91.

Gaborieau, M., "From Al-Beruni to Jinnah: Idiom, Ritual and Ideology of the Hindu-Muslim Confrontation," *AT* 1/3, 1985, 7–14.

Gandhi, S., "Mughal Self-Fashioning, Indic Self-Realization: Dara Shikoh and Persian Textual Cultures in Early Modern South Asia," diss., Harvard University, 2011.

Gordon, S., "Maratha Patronage of Muslim Institutions in Burhanpur and Khandesh," in: D. Gilmartin & B.B. Lawrence, eds., *Beyond Turk and Hindu: Rethinking Religious Identities in Islamicate South Asia*, New Delhi, 2002, 327–338.

Haider, N., "Translating Texts and Straddling Worlds. Intercultural Communication in Mughal India", in: I. Alam & S.E. Hussain, eds., *The Varied Facets of History. Essays in Honour of Aniruddha Ray*, New Delhi, 2011, 115–124.

Huart, C., & L. Massignon, "Les entretiens de Lahore [entre le prince impérial Dârâ Shikûh et l'ascète hindou Baba La'l Das]," *JA* 209, 1926, 285–334.

Moreno, M.M., "Mistica musulmana e mistica Indiana," *AL* 10, 1946, 103–212.

Naushahi, A., "Tim t āl-i ašyā' wa azhār al-adwiya," in: Ž. Vesel, H. Beikbaghban & B. Thierry de Crussol des Epesse, eds., *La science dans le monde iranien à l'époque islamique*, Tehran, 1998, 279–289.

Pingree, D.E., & B.V. Subbarayappa, "I professionisti della scienza e la loro formazione," in: *Storia della Scienza: Cina, India, Americhe*, vol. II, Rome, 2001, 790–813.

Pingree, D.E., "Tājika: Persian Astrology in Sanskrit," in: D.E. Pingree, *From Astral Omens to Astrology: From Babylon to Bīkāner*, Rome, 1997, 79–90.

Rizvi, A.A., *A History of Sufism in India*, vol. II, Delhi, 1992.

Sarmadee, S., ed., *Ghunyat-ul-Munya: The Earliest Known Persian Work on Indian Music*, Delhi, 1978.

Servan-Schreiber, C., *Chanteurs itinérants en Inde du Nord: La tradition orale bhojpuri*, Paris, 1999.

Servan-Schreiber (Champion), C., "Entre la caste et la secte: Un *kissa* du répertoire des Bhartrihari Jogi musulmans de la région de Gorakhpur (Uttar Pradesh)," in: M.L. Reiniche & H. Stern, *Les ruses du salut: Religion et politiques dans le monde indien*, Paris, 1995, 25–41.

Shea, D., & A. Troyer, eds., *Hinduism during the Mughal India of the 17th Century*, Patna, 1998.

Speziale, F., "*Les traités persans sur les sciences indiennes: Médecine, zoologie, alchimie*," in: D. Hermann & F. Speziale, eds., *Muslim Cultures in the Indo-Iranian World during the Early-Modern and Modern Periods*, Berlin, 2010, 403–447.

Speziale, F., "De zeven vrienden: Een Indo-Perzische verhandeling over alchemie," in: P. Hoftijzer, K. van Ommen, G. Warnar & J.J. Witkam, eds., *Bronnen van kennis: Wetenschap, kunst en cultuur in de collectives van de Leidse Universiteitsbibliotheek*, Leiden, 2006, 23–31.

Stewart, T.K., "Alternate Structure of Authority: Satya Pīr on the Frontiers of Bengal," in: D. Gilmartin & B.B. Lawrence, eds., *Beyond Turk and Hindu: Rethinking Religious Identities in Islamicate South Asia*, New Delhi, 2002, 21–54.

Truschke, A., "Cosmopolitan Encounters: Sanskrit and Persian at the Mughal Court," diss., Columbia University, 2012.

Truschke, A., "The Mughal *Book of War*: A Persian Translation of the Sanskrit *Mahabharata*," *CSSAAME* 31/2, 2011, 506–520.

Fabrizio Speziale

Modern Period North India

Under the thumb of the Delhi Sultanate (1206–1526), Hindu–Muslim relations became strained as ambitious Islamic rulers groped through North India toward riches and fame in the south. The Rajput Chauhan Empire (8th–12th cents.) – led most notably by Pṛthivī Rāj III (1149–1192) – and a handful of other Hindu and Buddhist princely states had fallen to the Turkic Mamluks whose Muslim successors eventually set up their capital in Delhi in 1206, only to fall themselves three centuries later to the Timurids from Central Asia, thus giving rise to another period of Islamic rule, now under the → Mughals (1526–1857). The backdrop of Hindu–Muslim relations in the modern period must be understood not only in light of these centuries of Muslim domination and rulership but also in light of centuries of intercultural influence and shared cultures. There is considerable evidence that even under the Delhi Sultanate, despite strained political relationships, Hindu–Muslim encounters were often fertile socially, culturally, and religiously. This continued under the Mughals such that by the time the English were ascending to power in the 18th century, areas in the north such as Jammu and Kashmir and Haryana and Uttarakhand along with areas in the west such as Gujarat, Rajasthan, and Maharashtra had enjoyed – even amid sometimes intense punctiliar conflagrations of violence – more perennial religious and cultural convergence and harmony. The north-central areas of what became Uttar Pradesh and Madhya Pradesh and the areas around Delhi were more turbulent, often becoming a focus for Rajput, → Maratha, and other Hindu resistance to Islamic hegemony. The frontier eastern and northeastern edges of Islamic influence, such as the areas around modern-day West Bengal and Bihar as well as Assam and Nagaland, were not as communally turbulent and often saw remarkably creative interreligious convergence and cross-fertilization, perhaps due to the centralization of Islamic power elsewhere around Delhi, Agra, and Fatehpur Sikri – many miles away. These five major cultural areas – the north, west, north central, east, and northeast areas, drawn from the Indian Ministry of Culture's seven "Cultural Zones" (declared by Rajiv Gandhi in 1985) – will serve as the template within which modern Hindu–Muslim relations will be explored in this article. As in the article on Hindus and Muslims, South India, and the modern period, it is important to note that categories of religious difference – *this* Hindu over against *that* Muslim – can act as a valuable heuristic in seeing that religious conflict *has* occurred in the history of North India. It has, *sui generis*. Yet also, at the dawn of the modern age, with North India under the colonial thumb, administrative techniques – for instance, census – often *begat* and *manufactured* the very cultural phenomena that colonial census takers were looking for and were only sometimes looking to prevent. Any adequate treatment of Hindus and Muslims in North India in the modern period must not only take into account both indigenous and manufactured Hindu and Muslim communalisms but also take seriously historic, textual, and ethnographic accounts of centuries of *living* Hindu–Muslim religious convergence – often a point of pride for many North Indian communities to this day. Division *and* convergence in the North, West, North Central, East, and Northeast Cultural Zones of India – each area has suffered centuries of sporadic communalism but also enjoyed centuries of peaceable Hindu–Muslim coexistence.

North Cultural Areas: Jammu and Kashmir, Punjab, Haryana, and Uttarakhand

Even as Arab spice traders were beginning to frequent ports in Kerala and other environs in South India as early as the latter decades of the 7th century, Muslim travelers likewise were braving the passes of the Hindu Kush as they came into the subcontinent through northwest passages. The historian A.L. Basham records how some of the earliest forays of Muslims into the northern subcontinent – under generals such as Muḥammad ibn Qāsim (695–715) – occurred not just in Sind but farther north into the Afghan mountain reaches around Multan, Ghazni, and Balkh (Basham, 1975, 246). As opposed to the ambitious campaigns that were launched from Sind into lands farther south – campaigns that often met heavy resistance – the Muslims who traveled into North India farther to the north, in the secluded valleys of Kashmir, found valleys that A.L. Basham describes as "less involved in the constant struggles for power, and their political life... was rarely much affected by the constant strife in the great plains" (1975, 51).

It was from the centers of Multan and Ghazni, not far from Kashmir, Punjab, Haryana, and Uttarakhand, that many sustained political attacks were being launched to the south, thus giving rise to the Ghaznavid dynasty (975–1187), but it is important to note also that Multan and surrounding areas have been regarded as a major center of more peaceable Sufi activity in the subcontinent. Multan has popularly been called Madīna al-Awliyāʾ ("City of Saints"). Kashmiri historian M.I. Khan, in an article entitled "The Impact of Islam on Kashmir in the Sultanate Period (1320–1586)," has noted that "some six centuries preceding the foundation of the Sultanate in Kashmir in 1320, a gradual process of peaceful penetration" by Muslims had begun (1986, 342). The Kashmiri Sultanate lasted from 1320 to the year 1586 and can be characterized by a relative peace between Hindus and Muslims, especially with the growing number of saints in the area who formed the bedrock of a tolerant Kashmiri Sufi spirituality. M.I. Khan argues that these saints were just one part of a growing Muslim community that included artists, traders, soldiers, butchers (as specifically noted by Marco Polo in the 13th cent.), paper makers, book binders, and other advisors and craftsmen (1986, 343).

The Kashmir Valley became a site of considerable Hindu–Muslim religious convergence, giving rise to the so-called Sufi Rišīs (derived from Skt. → *ṛṣi*) of Kashmir, founded by Šayḫ Nūr al-Dīn Rišī (d. 1442). At times, these Sufis even provided a powerful ally for *yogī*s and *yoginī*s disgruntled over Brahman elitism (Khan, 1986, 346). Nūr ud-dīn became an iconoclast along the same lines as the more famous Varanasi saint → Kabīr (1440–1518), who was born two years before Nūr al-Dīn died. The Islamicist and Sufi scholar Y. Sikand quotes Nūr al-Dīn as having said, "The Mullah in the mosque, and the Brahman before the idol of stone; perhaps only one out of a thousand of them will be redeemed" (2001, 1), even while Nūr al-Dīn taught a tolerant, inclusive, and socially conscious form of Sufism. Fueled by a rise in asceticism, a tradition favored by the popular Śaiva *yoginī* → Lallā Ded (14th cent.; she is known as Lalleśvarī among Hindus), Kashmiri Hindus and Sufi Muslims joined in rejecting caste elitism of the Brahmans and forged a line of spirituality – the Sufi Rišīs of Kashmir – that brought together a humanistic engaged "this-worldliness" along with a belief in coexistence with other religions and cultures, while also holding a deep "commitment to the sanctity of human life and its artistic manifestation on Earth" (Khan, 1986, 346). M.I. Khan notes that these pressures – emanating from within Hindu circles as allied with Sufis – led to a subterfuge in Kashmiri Brahman communities. Some became *paṇḍit*s who studied scriptures and continued priestly duties, known as *bhaiśa bhaṭṭa*, or simply *gur*. Some became *paṇḍit*s who studied scriptures, but who gave up priestly duties in order to concentrate on the social sphere. They were known as *jyotiṣī*s (Khan, 1986, 346). Some totally broke away and followed secular occupations and became known as *karkun*s. *Karkun*s, he argues, formed the primary identity of various governing dynasties in Kashmir from the days of the Kashmiri Sultanate until the emergence of nationalistic consciousness in the 1930s. Medieval Kashmiri Muslims played a significant role in the genesis of these otherwise-Hindu identities, even while the poetry of Lallā Ded remained popular among Kashmiri Muslims.

The historian M. Rai, in her book *Hindu Rulers, Muslim Subjects: Islam, Rights, and the History of Kashmir* (2004), argues that many of the problems that surround the more current post-Partition, post-1989 Kashmiri-insurgency political situation – often writ large as Hindu–Muslim antipathy – can be traced to events involving colonial interlocutors during the hundred years preceding the creation of India and Pakistan in 1947. Kashmir had been reduced to little more than a spiritual retreat and backwater political outpost during the years of the Mughals, but the British paid Kashmir more attention by centralizing power in the run-up to the uprisings of 1856–1857. As compared to its "earlier traditions of layered-society," the colonial administrators inserted a single leader from the "alien" Dogra Rajput Hindu lineage who would speak for the affairs of all the areas surrounding Kashmir (Rai, 2004, 4). The "princely state" of Jammu and Kashmir was a colonial invention formulated, M. Rai argues, to forge "indirect" colonial control over the area. By this time, the majority of Kashmiris were Muslims who found themselves represented by a singular Hindu *mahārāja*. M. Rai registers her surprise that this non-Kashmiri governance lasted through Partition and the creation of the modern states of India and Pakistan. She sees these forces behind uprisings of Muslims against Hindus in 1931 and similar uprisings in the decades following (Rai, 2004, 7). She argues, though, that the colonial imposition of the Dogra Hindu lineage, with its titular Hindu monarch, was more complex than mere top-down colonial political hegemony – one that used a Hindu minority against a Muslim majority. Rather, she says, there remained a certain measure of Hindu – and, indeed, Muslim – autonomy within the arrangement (Rai, 2004, 14). Indeed, she points out that Kashmir, toward the later part of the 19th century, became something of a rallying point for Muslims across the subcontinent, even giving rise, in the 1930s, to the All Jammu and Kashmir (later National) Conference. She notes that these forces in the late 19th and early 20th centuries led Hindu and Muslim Kashmiris who "shared many links of common cultural practice and religious beliefs... to recognize... their political interests as widely divergent" (Rai, 2004, 14).

M.I. Khan, in an article entitled "The Rishi Tradition and the Construction of the Kashmiriyat," outlines what he calls the concept of *kašmīriyat*, or Kashmiri identity, that had taken hold in some quarters of Hindu and Muslim Kashmiri society in the 1980s and 1990s (2004, 62). He talks of how Kashmiri Sufi Muslims had developed an identity as "people of the certainty" (*ahl al-iʿtiqād*). They thought of themselves as a people who live beyond mere action and confession but believe in the *Qurʾān* as known, verified, and evident (Khan, 2004, 62) in the lives of people. This is tantamount to Sufi superiority over more literalist Muslims and justification for Hindu reverence of Rišīs and Sufi saints that occurs during *ʿurs* (death anniversary) celebrations at saintly tombs (*dargāhs*) in the Kashmir Valley. These activities are opposed by local Islamist Jamat-i Islami factions but remain an important linkage with Rišīs Hindus under the aegis of *kašmīriyat*. Kashmiri *paṇḍits* frequent Sufi tombs to this day (Khan, 2004, 64). M.I. Khan points out a period of creative output between 1975 and 1987 or so from Kashmiri writers who were eager to write in the inclusive vein of *kašmīriyat* identity about the glories of the Hindu–Muslim past. There was hope for a unified future in Kashmir. Elections in 1987, however, were inconclusive, and this led to growing unrest over the next couple of years, peaking in 1989 with widespread insurgency that has continued to exasperate relations not only between Pakistan and India but also between Hindus and Muslims in the region. An incident in the Kargil region in 1999 in which Pakistani soldiers and insurgents seized mountain peaks in the Kargil range choking off Indian army access to Kashmir nearly resulted in a full-scale (perhaps nuclear) conflict between India and Pakistan. Debates about this incident have continued to have nationalist Hindu–Muslim interreligious overtones.

J.G. Lochtefeld has explored the nationalist ideologies of the Vishwa Hindu Parishad (VHP) as they have been expressed in the North Indian city of Haridwar in the district of Uttarakhand (1994). He points out that assumptions of singular Hindu–Muslim conflictual religious tropes as generators of communal violence such as the storming of the Bābrī Masjid in 1992 need to be questioned. He outlines a long history of Hindu forms of asceticism – held by J.G. Lochtefeld to be a central constituency of VHP rolls and militant activities – but in ways that question the dominant VHP narrative, especially with regard to views of supposed universal Muslim oppression. He brings up examples not of repeated violence of Muslims against Hindu ascetics but rather of Hindu ascetics against other Hindu ascetics. His case centers on various *kumbhamelā*s that have taken place in the city of Haridwar. On the last day of one such *kumbhamelā* in 1760, 18 thousand Vaiṣṇava *vairāgī* ascetics were killed not by Muslims but by a group of Śaiva *nāgā saṃnyāsī*s (Lochtefeld, 1994, 594; see also → *akhāṛā*s). J.G. Lochtefeld points out that a mere six years after this battle, the *saṃnyāsī* ascendency was at an end, with Haridwar having come under the influence of the British, and that, therefore, history has lost sight of these intra-Hindu conflicts – blaming them on Muslims. He uses these historical conflicts, however, to call into question VHP nationalistic communal assumptions of Hindu singularity *vis-à-vis* Muslims. He notes that there are historic examples of *nāgā saṃnyāsī*s having fought Muslims in the area, but that there are also examples of *saṃnyāsī* service under Muslim rulership (Lochtefeld, 1994, 599), thus bespeaking more amicable Hindu–Muslim relations in the Uttarakhand area.

A. Bigelow, in her book *Sharing the Sacred: Practicing Pluralism in Muslim North India* (2010), has given a thorough ethnographic account of the Punjabi town of Malerkotla, a city where Muslims, Sikhs, and Hindus have coexisted amicably for centuries. Her work – centered on the Sufi tomb (*dargāh*) of the saint Ḥaydar Šayḫ (1434–1515), who founded Malerkotla – demonstrates that the nationalistic, communal rhetoric that fed into violent Partition in 1947, and to so many dead particularly in the Punjab region, was not universally true throughout the Punjab. Some Punjabi areas, like Malerkotla, remained relatively insulated from the bloodshed. Many Muslims, Sikhs, and Hindus of Malerkotla frequent the tomb of Ḥaydar Šayḫ together, and this has functioned as an important insulator against communalism over the years. In fact, most of the Muslim residents in this region of the Punjab remained, even after significant numbers of Punjabi Muslims elsewhere emigrated after Partition (Bigelow, 2010, 6). A. Bigelow attributes these interreligious successes to what she calls Malerkotla's "microstrategies of peacemaking" (2010, 197), reified in a robust peace committee associated with the *dargāh*, and to interreligious accommodation that embodies an "institutionalized peace system" (2010, 18). She points out that the November 2006 Sachar Report on the social, economic, and educational status of Indian Muslims painted a picture in which Muslims remain second-class citizens "caught between suspicion and exceptionalism" (Bigelow, 2010, 14). Places like the *dargāh* of Ḥaydar Šayḫ in Malerkotla, Punjab, however, continue to foster interreligious understanding and Muslim uplift.

Like A. Bigelow, Y. Sikand, in his book *Sacred Spaces: Exploring Traditions of Shared Faith in India* (2003), has described his recent fieldwork in tombs of Sufi saints throughout India, throughout the Kashmir region, and throughout the regions of Jammu district. He wrote of coming into Jammu city only a week after a grenade had been thrown into a busy market near a temple, killing 12 people. Hindu–Muslim tensions were high. This was a region that had seen large numbers of the Muslim minority slaughtered in the 1947 Partition. Police had been set up around the mosque in the city to protect Muslims as they left Friday prayers. Y. Sikand recounts, however, that the main *dargāh* that lies at the heart of the city – that of the 13th-century Sufi saint Pīr Rawšan ʿAlī Šāh – was not in need of protection (2003, 216). He recounts how, as elsewhere in the subcontinent, Sufi tombs have been frequented throughout the centuries by Hindu devotees. *Dargāhs*, he argues, act as powerful insulators against the sort of communal violence that has gripped India certainly since the 1992 Ayodhya conflagration and well before that too. He recounts how he met a Punjabi Muslim man, Inayat, with whom he explored the Sufi tombs of the city. He recounts how at one Sufi tomb, they came across a Hindu caretaker who opined, "Oh, Hindu, Muslim, these really mean nothing, you know" (Sikand, 2003, 230). These refrains of Hindu–Muslim continuity – common throughout Jammu and Kashmir, Punjab, Haryana, and Uttarakhand – bespeak a more settled common Hindu–Muslim social, political, and spiritual culture that has only recently become divisive in ways that are more common throughout the Indian subcontinent.

West Cultural Areas: Gujarat, Rajasthan, and Maharashtra

As in the north central areas of North India, there is evidence of centuries of common Hindu–Muslim social, political, and religious convergent cultures in the western cultural areas of India, although the western areas of North India, including Gujarat, Rajasthan, and Maharashtra, have surely seen more interreligious turbulence and violence than the areas around Jammu and Kashmir, Punjab, Haryana, and Uttarakhand. A.L. Basham recounts how when Maḥmūd of Ghazni (971–1030) was launching his 17 raids into the subcontinent, wider Hindu leadership lacked the tools or the will to unify against the growing threat. A.L. Basham outlines how the five larger kingdoms who shared most of the power in North India – the Chahamanas (Chauhans) of Rajasthan, the Gahadavalas (Gahrwals) of Kanauj and Varanasi, the Solankis of Gujarat, the Paramaras (Parmars) of Malwa, and the Chandellas (Chandels) of Khajaraho, to the south of the Gaṅgā – only gradually developed the Rajput identity of the gallant, honorable, and gentlemanly warrior (Basham, 1975, 54). Fixated on epic ideals that romantically glorified war, these Rajput kingdoms often were in dispute with one another and seemed unable to comprehend the gravity of the situation involving the oncoming waves of Muslim invaders that were crashing on their shores.

The Rajput Chauhans of Rajasthan (956–1192) were defeated such that Hindu clans – living as they were on the doorstep of Sind and the Islamic Afghan towns just to the north and west – never recovered to reclaim rulership over any significant areas in western India. Though there was some winning and losing between the invading Muslims and the Chauhans of Rajasthan, once the Ghurid ruler Muʿizz al-Dīn Muḥammad ibn Sām (r. 1202–1206) defeated Pṛthivī Rāj III in the second battle of Tarain (today Taraori) in 1192 (Pṛthivī had defeated him the year prior), Muslim control over Rajasthani lands remained largely intact into the present day. In this way, Rajasthan, not unlike Kashmir, has remained an area relatively stable for Hindus, even while being under Muslim rulership since the late 12th century. Despite being under the Islamic boot, these areas have been more stable, certainly, especially when compared with the areas around Delhi, Uttar Pradesh, Madhya Pradesh, and even Gujarat just to the south.

The historian S.A.A. Rizvi notes that Muʿizz al-Dīn, before leaving India, appointed Quṭb al-Dīn Aibak (d. 1210) as his deputy and the one in charge of advancing beyond between Lahore in the south and Tarain in Haryana – effectively Rajasthan and its surrounding areas. He did so. He was so successful that Quṭb al-Dīn Aibak moved the capital farther out of Sind and established it in Delhi. From here he was able to conquer much of North India and establish from 1206 onward Islamic Mamluk governance that lasted until the British divested the Mughals of power in 1857. Far from a situation in which Muslims constantly pressed their advantage politically into social and religious realms, the Delhi Sultanate ushered in a time of relatively fertile Hindu–Muslim convergence in western India, especially in the lands of Rajasthan and, to a lesser degree, in Gujarat and Maharashtra. Indeed, Quṭb al-Dīn Aibak and his successor, Šams al-Dīn Iltutmiš (r. 1210–1236), ushered in what A. Wink has called in his book *Al-Hind: The Making of the Indo-Islamic World* the "Indo-Islamic" culture that produced such artistic and architectural masterpieces as the Quṭb Mīnār and the Jāmaʿ Masjid, both in Delhi (1996, 4), but that also begat such western Indian inclusive spiritual movements as the Čištī Sufi lineage that stretched from Delhi to Khuldabad in Maharashtra.

While the Ghaznavid, Ghurid, and Delhi Mamluk political movements were remolding the shape of northern and western Indian governance, powerful convergent spiritual movements were forging other expressions of these cultures that admitted active Hindu–Muslim interreligious activities. S.A.A. Rizvi recounts how one of the first major Sufi lineages, the Čištīs, was entering into north and western India in the early 1200s. One of the most famous Indian Sufis of all, Muʿīn al-Dīn Čištī (1141–1236), settled in Ajmer, Rajasthan, in 1206, the year in which the Delhi Sultanate was established. S.A.A. Rizvi writes that "by the time he died in 1236, Chishti *khanqāh*s [lodges] were firmly established in many parts of the Delhi Sultanate" (1975, 285). Surely, conquering also brought with it Islamic spirituality. S.A.A. Rizvi continues,

> The Chishti Sufis urged their disciples to lead a life of poverty and asceticism. Their simple life devoted to Allah, the dependence... on charity... and their distribution to the poor of any money they received, made favorable impressions... even among Hindus. (Rizvi, 1975, 285)

The Islamicists C. Ernst and B. Lawrence, in their book *Sufi Martyrs of Love: The Chishti Order in South Asia*, recount how the Čištī order has through the years been a tradition inclusive of Hindu participation. They note that Hindus often "appropriate" Čištī spiritual experiences (Ernst & Lawrence, 2002, 3) and that Hindu ritual elements are often practiced as Čištī *dargāh*s. In Ajmer, at the tomb of Muʿīn al-Dīn Čištī, pilgrimage has become formalized over the years through the use of pledge contracts (*wakīlat-nāma*) involving *ḫādim*s (helpers) who act as intermediaries (*wakīl*) helping the pilgrim and the pilgrim's family and clansmen to perform *ziyāra* (visiting the tomb), circumambulation, rituals, and recitation of the *fātiḥa* (prayers for the dead). According to C. Ernst and B. Lawrence, "[t]he *khadim* prays with his clients and continues to pray after departure" (2002, 102). They go on to remark that

> this service included Hindus as well as Muslims, and it is evident from correspondence preserved at the Ajmer shrine that the traffic in Hindu clients, not only in temporary *nazar-o-niyaz* [fees to *ḫādims*] but also permanent land grants, was substantial. (Ernst & Lawrence, 2002, 102)

These Čištī practices of always welcoming Hindus and fully including them in a range of ritual practices at Sufi tombs from Delhi to Mumbai and beyond, and especially in Ajmer, has created lasting ties between the communities.

Politicians are usually wise to court the favor of ever-more influential Sufi communities like the one in Ajmer. One can say that Hindu–Muslim relations have often been measured by the political involvement in powerful inclusive *dargāh*s. J.F. Richards, in his book *The Mughal Empire* (1993), in the Cambridge History of India series, provides a historian's account of the Mughal emperor Akbar's (r. 1556–1561) trips to and from Ajmer as a pilgrim to the tomb while also courting area Hindu leaders. Akbar, in his interreligious courtly ways, recruited Rajput leaders into the Mughal nobility through repeated trips to Rajasthan, representing himself as a pious pilgrim and as a powerful political ally. In 1561, while coming to the aid of one Hindu Rajput chief against a usurping Mughal governor, the chief met him near Jaipur and offered the emperor his daughter's hand in marriage. Akbar agreed and granted him not only aid against the Mughal governor but also the title of *amīr* (commander) in the royal Mughal court. This is a pattern that Akbar set – aid and marriage with Rajput Hindu elites in exchange for obeisance and court privilege – such that by 1580, J.F. Richards says, 43 such Rajput royals were included in Akbar's court (1993, 21). J.F. Richards recounts how Akbar, likewise, extended his Čištī patronage from Ajmer and wider Rajasthan into the very royal court at the newly minted imperial center at Fatehpur Sikri. Akbar sought to incorporate "the Chishti mystical aura into Fetehpur Sikri" through a binary mosque/ *dargāh* complex lying in the heart of the city (Richards, 1993, 30). The Čištī saint Šayḫ Salīm Čištī (d. 1571) – Akbar's royal spiritual advisor as a young man – was buried in nested proximity to the congregational mosque, thus laying the foundation for a Mughal rulership that was not only clearly Islamic in legal institutions but also religiously inclusive in spiritual inspiration.

C. Ernst and B. Lawrence talk about the Čištī heritage as shaped by growing colonial domination in the 18th and 19th centuries. They describe how Čištī lineages diverged in the decades leading up to the mid-19th century. Two primary lineages developed: the Niẓāmī Čištīs, prominent in Delhi, the Deccan, and Punjab from the 18th century on, and the Ṣābirī Čištīs, prominent in areas such as Haridwar and Deoband, Uttar Pradesh. While the Niẓāmī branch sought to reform in the 19th century primarily through recalling the inclusive golden age of Ajmer Čištī spirituality under Muʿīn al-Dīn Čištī and a return to those roots, the Ṣābirī branch reformed in a more complex way, especially *vis-à-vis* colonial power after the events of 1857. The British, having cemented their control over the subcontinent after putting down the Sepoy uprising (1857), sought to press for ways to continue to divest power from prominent Sufi communities across North India, especially among the disgruntled Muslims across central and western North India who were at the center of the revolt. To this end, C. Ernst and B. Lawrence explain how after 1867 the British deputy commissioner "took on the task of choosing between claimants to the office of the chief shrine custodian, the *sajjada nishin*" (1993, 102). The Religious Endowments Act of 1863 ensured that the affairs of the shrine would remain under colonial control and not in the hands of the families of descendants and *ḫādim*s. The Ṣābirī order – an order quite tolerant of Hindu inclusion early on, even blending "Indian yoga techniques… with… Sufi metaphysical doctrine" (Ernst & Lawrence, 1993, 106) – in the years after the 1857 revolt became inspired by a participant in the revolt, ʿAbd al-Quddus Ḥajjī Imdād Allāh (d. 1899). He was exiled to Mecca after the 1857 rebellion but reached out to influence Ṣābirī Čištīs through working toward an eventual *dar ul-ʿulūm* (seminary), to be founded at Deoband in Uttar Pradesh. The *dar ul-ʿulūm* at Deoband was founded in 1866, inspired in part by Imdād Allāh's vision of Ṣābirī Čištī spirituality as a pan-Indian force that would reassert Islamic scriptural and legal foundations in ways that sublimated traditional Čištī spiritual mainstays such as *dargāh* pilgrimage and listening to music – especially Čištī Sufi *qawwālī* music. Pilgrimage to Sufi shrines and listening to spiritual music therein has been one of the mainstays of Hindu participation in wider Čištī spirituality, yet Imdād Allāh was arguing that such practices should be sublimated in an effort to return to purer *Qurʾān*-based and jurisprudential (*fiqh*) roots and in an effort to strengthen Muslim communities *vis-à-vis* the colonial oppressor. Deoband, indeed, has been something of a center of increasing Islamist thinking in the years since its founding. This has had not only anticolonial but also increasingly nationalistic anti-Hindu consequences.

This subterfuge that pressed out from Ajmer toward a Ṣābirī-inspired Deobandī nationalism is not representative of all Hindu–Muslim relations in wider Rajasthani Sufi culture. To this day, Rajasthan Čištī spirituality remains largely inclusive of Hindus. For example, in response to a bombing in the center of the *dargāh* in 2007 – a bombing initially suspected to have been perpetrated by anti-Muslim Hindu nationalists – one of the main heirs of the Ajmer Sufi community, Sayyid Salmān Čištī, responded in a way that sought not revenge but to bolster Hindu–Muslim cultural sensitivities. He founded an organization called the Chishti Foundation. Inspired by Muʿīn al-Dīn Čištī's saying "Love toward all, malice toward none," its primary goal is to foster respect for all human beings through showing people at their best in art, poetry, music, and prayer. This sort of movement, as can be found elsewhere in the subcontinent, bespeaks a tolerant, common Hindu–Muslim culture that has sought to live peaceably together.

Communal violence has struck elsewhere in western India, and the state of Gujarat has been one of the hardest hit, particularly since the early 1990s. Long before the events of the 1990s, the gradual push of Islamic hegemony moved past Sind and Rajasthan and deep into Gujarat. Though there were some Hindu victories against the Islamic onslaught in Gujarat – such as Mūlarājā II's defeat of Muʿizz al-Dīn in 1178 (Wink, 2002, 143) – Islam spread into Gujarat early. J.M. Powers, in her book *Kites over the Mango Tree: Restoring Harmony between Hindus and Muslims in Gujarat*, notes that "it was to Gujarat that the first Muslims came to India by sea in 636 ce, five years after the death of Muhammad" (2009, 26). Some Hindu–Muslim encounters in Gujarat have been lasting and good. Some have not. She notes that when Maḥmūd of Ghazni came to Gujarat in the 11th century with the intention of sacking the Somnāth Temple, "the carnage was horrendous" (Powers, 2009, 28). She estimates that tens of thousands were killed, significant booty was taken, and, perhaps worst of all, the central *liṅga* was destroyed. Pieces were taken back to Delhi "for incorporation into the steps of the Jama Masjid, where the Muslim faithful might step on them" (Powers, 2009, 28). This was repeated in the 13th century. Additionally, other Hindu temples were sacked and destroyed throughout Gujarat in the couple of centuries after this. She notes that Gujarati Hindus still recall these events.

Yet, bolstered by an independent Gujarat Sultanate (1391–1573), local Muslim rulers oversaw the same sort of convergent cultures that were developing elsewhere in India. Although she outlines a litany of attacks between Hindus and Muslims in Gujarat from the 10th until the 15th century, J.M. Powers talks about Hindu–Muslim cultural and religious convergences that remain a point of pride to this day. She describes a Gujarati culture that enjoyed elements drawn from Jain and Hindu architectural traditions along with elements from Islamic architecture. The city of Ahmedabad is known for its *amdavādi* architecture that fuses elements from several cultures. J.M. Powers also discusses what she calls "Hindu-Muslim syncretism," a concept that is often troubling to understand insofar as it assumes distinct, discreet cultures who then borrow from or assimilate to each other. Here the term "syncretism" might be appropriate. She describes a strong Gujarati sense of historically being "Mahomedan Hindus," which is what 200,000 people had identified themselves as on a 1911 census (Powers, 2009, 31). She notes how a 1914 study of Gujarati folklore lists 20 Sufi saints who had been adopted by Hindus. These convergences form the basis of her inquiry insofar as she provides contemporary ethnographic accounts of life at several Gujarati NGOs whose work it is to overcome communal divides and uplift perennial Gujarati culture that is tolerant and pluralist.

Even with these sorts of cultural convergences, communal violence has still rocked Gujarat throughout the recent decades and centuries. Events that gave rise to Hindu nationalism in Ahmedabad in the 1980s and led up to the violence in February of 2002 are outlined in an article by O. Shani (2005) and in one written by E. Field, M. Levinson, R. Pande, and S. Visaria (2008). O. Shani argues that the violence in 2002, while having roots in the 1980s, was largely unexpected, since Gujarat had little enduring Hindu–Muslim strife historically. She concedes that although violence had occurred in Ahmedabad in 1969, the 1970s and early 1980s saw little tension. She argues that the conflicts that grew in the 1980s had "primarily been about reservations policy and the status of backward castes" (Shani, 2005, 861). It only turned later to communal violence and reflected a shift that had just been completed from Congress Party rule to Bharatiya Janata Party (BJP) rule. In earlier riots, Muslims had helped → Dalits by bringing awareness to their plight over against upper-caste Hindus (Shani, 2005, 882). The Rashtriya Swayamsevak Sangh (RSS) had tried to cast these events as primarily a Hindu–Muslim riot.

By 1985, O. Shani recounts, agents of the BJP and VHP had not only begun to provide food and other necessities to Dalit communities but also actually armed them with *laṭhī*s (iron-clad riot sticks). This apparently was enough to change the course of the 1985 riots, diverting the cause away from quotas for Dalits toward a Hindu–Muslim communal reading of the event. To these causes, the article by F. Field, M. Levinson, R. Pande, and S. Visaria adds neighborhood-by-neighborhood factors such as segregation and rent control as causes for the 2002 violence in Ahmedabad. Living arrangements, the authors say, trended toward religiously "completely homogenous neighborhoods" in the closing decades of the 20th century (Field *et al.*, 2008, 506). Surprisingly, however, the violence occurred primarily in more integrated neighborhoods. These neighborhoods, they argue, were integrated not so much because of a desire to be inclusive but more as a function of practices of subsidized housing given to factory workers that pressed them into the same areas of the city. As many factories pulled out, ownership was not clear for many. Government officials who approved land sales seemed to give preferential treatment from one family to another. This not only sparked some suspicions of preference of Hindus over Muslims but also forbade the possibility of simply moving to more homogenous neighborhoods – moves that would have mitigated communal tensions. In short, the 2002 riots occurred for a range of reasons, only a part of which was religious. These two articles constitute some measure of ethnographic accounts that capture the genesis of communal violence in a riot-prone city like Ahmedabad in Gujarat. They reveal that simple tropes involving only Hindu–Muslim interreligious causes for violence need to be questioned and broadened.

These sorts of economic, social, political, and religious intricacies abound farther to the south in Maharashtra. Maharashtra not only has been a center of poverty, especially in urban centers like Mumbai, but also recently has become a hotbed for nationalistic politics. Maharasthra historically represents an area in west India that, while seeing a fair number of Muslim raids throughout the Delhi Sultanate and the Mughal Empire, suffered less under a sustained Islamic rulership when compared to Gujarat and Rajasthan. Even when temples like Pandharpur had been razed by medieval Muslims, Marathi culture remained resilient. J.T.F. Jordens recounts how → Eknāth (1533–1599), through his commentaries on the → *Rāmāyaṇa*, inspired Marathis that "whatever obstacles the Muslims put in the way, the Hindu could aspire to the deepest experience of his religion within the ordinary framework of life" (1975, 269). Chatrapatī Śivajī (1630–1680) is often held up as an important scion of Hindu resistance to Islamic domination. Śivajī led many successful campaigns against the proxy sultanates of the Mughals. The historian S. Gordon has warned, though, that the state created by Śivajī should not be considered strictly a Hindu state as over and against the Muslim states to the north (1993, 65). Any kind of later *mahārāṣtra dharma* linked to Śivajī, in S. Gordon's estimation, is a later fabrication by "Brahmin historians" and not linked to Śivajī directly (1993, 65). Śivajī even had open lines of communication with Aurangzeb, all the while engaging in further conquests (Gordon, 1993, 63). S. Gordon recounts how Śivajī entered alliances with Muslims at Bijapur and Golconda to bolster resistance to Mughal hegemony (Gordon, 1993, 73). In 1687, shortly before Śivajī's death in 1680, Bijapur and Golconda fell to Aurangzeb, leaving the Marathi Empire vulnerable to an eventual defeat. In Maharashtra, however, Śivajī remains a powerful symbol of Hindu identity, especially over and against what is perceived to be Islamic domination.

Under the British, Hindu–Muslim relations in Maharashtra suffered. S. Chandra discussed a case brought before the Bombay High Court in 1884, in which a Hindu husband entreated the high court to compel his Hindu wife, Rukhmabai, to live with him. Their marriage of 11 years had not yet been consummated (Chandra, 1995, 155), and he was demanding his conjugal rights. The judge, Justice Pinhey, ruled in favor of the wife and demanded that the plaintiff pay court costs. The plaintiff appealed to the higher court. The ruling was overturned, and the wife was ordered to go live with her husband, with a prison term promised if she did not. Her preference for jail time over staying with her husband inflamed Hindu communities throughout Maharashtra. A council was convened to debate a solution to the Rukhmabai case. This council decided to hear evidence regarding systems of Hindu law that were germane to the case, while at the same time appealing to principles held in English common law. This was tantamount to a recognition not only that discerning a pure Hinduism was possible but also that these marital principles should be universally applied alongside English laws. The door was open. The assumption, too, was that there could be similar possibilities for each religious culture across India, including Islamic cultures. This, in fact, played out in a 1978 case from Madhya Pradesh, in which a 62-year-old divorced Muslim woman named Shah Bano was denied alimony after her husband declared the so-called triple *ṭālaq* divorce decree. According to the Islamic laws used, she was entitled to nothing. This decision, however, was reversed by the supreme court. The Indian government, in response to this, created legislation that upheld Muslim personal law. This has been held by many, including public affairs scholar T. Wright Jr., to be a significant step in inflaming Hindu–Muslim antipathy (2001, 4). While colonial census taking and other administrative techniques did much to forge discreet identities of *this* Hindu (or Hinduism) as over against *that* Muslim (or Islam), these cases marked sea changes owing to which Hindu and Muslim communities began thinking of themselves and constructing identities as institutionally separate.

T.B. Hansen, in his book *Wages of Violence: Naming and Identity in Postcolonial Bombay*, outlines how this appeal to bifurcated religious identity in modern Mumbai has become so ingrained that the mythology of Śivajī's triumphs over the Muslim conquerors is to be found reified in statues, figures, calendar art, and posters – and even children's games – all over the city (2001, 21). Śivajī, in fact, has become a favorite icon of groups like the Shiv Sena, the pro-Hindu nationalist movement founded in Bombay in 1966. So valued is he by so many, T.B. Hansen recounts, that Śivajī's identity became a point of contention in April of 1993, not more than a few months after communal riots had shaken Mumbai. The magazine *The Illustrated Weekly* carried an article wherein the supposed anti-Muslim character of Śivajī was called into question. The author of the article even made the claim that Mughal forms of government had influenced Śivajī's governance. Reaction was strong. As T.B. Hansen says, "*Saamna*, Shiv Sena's mouthpiece, recommended that the editor be publicly flogged" (2001, 22). He notes that even members of the Congress Party were upset. Charges were brought that claimed violation of Indian Penal Code, Section 153A, "which touches on promotion of enmity between religious and cultural communities" (2001 22). The case was found to be without merit, much to the chagrin of many sectors of nationalist-inspired Hindu communities. T.B. Hansen sees behind this uproar a long-held ethos of Marathi identity as bound up in *savarṇā jāti*, caste communities of pure blood. To this is added the trope of Marathis as members of Hindu society, or the "larger Hindu community as opposed to Muslims" (Hansen, 2001, 24). Problematizing singular readings of Hindu identity, he recounts, for example, that even amid liberal reformist movements such as those led by M.G. Ranade (1842–1901), organizations like the Satyashodhak Samaj (Truth-Seeking Society; founded in Pune in 1873) were being founded that centered on an idealized egalitarian pre-Aryan indigenous Deccan past. In the 1930s, Maharashtra was undergoing a process of "Maratha-ization" that included the term "Maratha" as denoting "martiality, Shivaji, true Hindus, rural virtues, cooperative strength, regional identity, non-Brahmanism, and bhakti traditions" (Hansen, 2001, 34). After Independence, he notes, Congress Party's political power continued to become Maratha-ized. The Shiv Sena, he argues, gradually overtook Congress Party ownership of Maratha identity and portrayed it as both modern and urban but along Hindu nationalist lines – that is, over and against Islamic hegemony. Hindu–Muslim riots over the last three decades have fed on these discourses in Mumbai and wider Maharashtra.

As is the case elsewhere in India, Sufi expressions of Islamic cultures in Maharashtra have dampened bifurcating narratives set on pitting Hindu against Muslim. C. Ernst, in his book *Eternal Garden: Mysticism, History, and Politics at a South Asian Sufi Center* (1992), has given an account of Čištī Sufi activities in wider west India, in wider Maharashtra, and specifically in the city of Khuldabad. Though skeptical of the ability of the historian to discern widespread inclusion of Hindus in the activities of Sufi centers such as the one in Khuldabad, he does provide an account of the many ways in which the Sufis he studies have dealt positively with non-Muslims. C. Ernst outlines a couple of stories that depict positive Hindu–Muslim relations in Khuldabad. In one, a Sufi saint named Muʾmin ʿĀrif (12th cent.) came to nearby Deogir at a time when it was still ruled by a Hindu. Muʾmin ʿĀrif was asked to help a Muslim woman whose cow was stolen and butchered by the Hindu *rājā*. As C. Ernst says, "Muʾmin by his supernatural power restored the cow to life" (1992, 234). The cow's grave is still visible. This story represents an interesting inversion of the Hindu–Muslim stereotype in which the evil Muslim sovereign is the one doing the stealing and butchering. C. Ernst sees this, along with other local stories of non-Muslim venerations of Sufi saints, as an example of Islamic figures having been assimilated into Indian – distinctly Hindu – modes of sanctity. The other story involves another legendary Čištī saint of Khuldabad – Muntajib al-Dīn, better known as Zar Zarī Zar Baẖš ("The Giver of the Essence of Gold"; d. 1309). In this story, Muntajib al-Dīn, having been sent by his masters to Maharashtra, arrived in Daulatabad and had some interaction with a local Hindu princess named Sonābāī ("Gold Woman"). He had sent a servant to the princess' well to fetch some water for ablutions. The princess, having heard that Zar Zarī Zar Baẖš was behind the request, joked that the water could be had when the well turned gold. The servant returned to Muntajib al-Dīn, who said, "so be it," then told the servant to put one of the princess' handkerchiefs in the well. "Sona Ba'i watched in amazement as the water turned to flowing gold" (Ernst, 1992, 237). She was moved. She became a follower of Muntajib al-Dīn. These stories reveal again the possibilities for positive religious interactions between Hindu and Muslim communities in the subcontinent, even in places that play host to pro-Hindu nationalist organizations.

North Central Cultural Areas: Delhi, Uttar Pradesh, and Madhya Pradesh

North central areas in North India – such as Uttar Pradesh, Madhya Pradesh, and Delhi – have perennially been the site of some of the most intense Hindu–Muslim antipathy in the subcontinent. The central Gangetic Plain has long been the home not only of important Hindu mythological and cultural sites but also of sites that mark Islamic attempts to conquer and subdue wider South Asia. That the Ghurids under Qutb al-din Aibak planted their sultanate in Delhi in 1206 bespeaks the importance of the place before and thereafter, especially insofar as Quṭb al-Dīn Aibak, Šams al-Dīn Iltutmiš, and their successors moved out from Delhi to dominate to the north in Kashmir; to the south and west in Maharashtra, Gujarat, and Rajasthan; and, of course to the south and east toward what became known as Uttar Pradesh, Madhya Pradesh, and, farther east, Bihar, Bengal, and the northeast Indian Himalayan and coastal hinterlands. Likewise, the Mughal ascension to the throne in 1526 continued a strong Islamic imperial presence in central north India, even as capitals shifted among Delhi, Agra, and Fatehpur Sikri. These areas, however, reflect the stories of wider India in terms of Hindu–Muslim relations, with their histories pockmarked by punctiliar eruptions of political and communal violence but with those moments muted by more perennial convergent spiritual and cultural streams.

Delhi is fundamentally a Hindu city. It is ancient and is purported to have been the site of Indraprastha – the legendary capital of the Pāṇḍavas, the heroes of the Hindu epic the → *Mahābhārata*. As an epic city, it has played a role, too, in bringing to life employment of *Rāmāyaṇa* imagery in political clashes. S. Pollock (1993) has argued, in fact, that leading up to and immediately following the founding of the Delhi Sultanate in 1206, *Rāmāyaṇa* imagery was employed throughout North India as a way of "rakshasizing" (i.e. demonizing) the invading Muslims, now recast as Rāvaṇa, the demon king. Battling Hindu kings were imagined as Rāma himself, righteously slaying the "other." Yet Muslims, too, have employed this imagery. S. Pollock argues that the Delhi Mughals, especially Akbar, were "projected as King Rāma and the *rākṣasas* recorded as Persian *dīvs*" in translation bureaus working to translate Sanskrit epics into Persian (1993, 287). This was nothing less than an attempt to "neutralize by appropriation" (1993, 287). Delhi and the wider areas of central north India have become symbolically important as places to work for the defense of Bhārat Mātā, Mother India.

An account of Delhi's contested role as political center in the early Muslim incursion into the subcontinent has already been given as well as an account of Delhi as an important early Sufi – especially Čištī – spiritual center. D. Pinto has provided a more thorough ethnographic study of the life of one of the most important Sufi tombs, namely that of Šayẖ Niẓām al-Dīn Awliyāʾ (1238–1325). The Niẓām al-Dīn *dargāh* has served as an important interreligious center in the heart of Delhi. D. Pinto explores at great length the sort of moral character that is expected not only of the Sufi master, the *pīr*, but also of the aspiring adept, the *murīd*. Central to these moral pursuits is the long-held Islamic ideal of *ādāb*, or etiquette. This involves not only a deferential respect from aspirant to master but also intense feelings of love from master to aspirant (Pinto, 1995, 152). It involves giving without a desire for reward. It also involves a vow not to bring down evil on anyone. This further involves a charitable treatment of strangers carried in the vow to "be gracious to and help all who come to him, be they poor or rich" (Pinto, 1995, 158). One *murīd* who was being interviewed recounted how "so many people come to this *dargāh*" and that "if I want to find God, I must remember that God has made not only me, but also the Other" (Pinto, 1995, 219). The *murīd* went on to talk about how God made each a Christian, a Muslim, or a Hindu and how *pīrs* embody the very presence of God in the world. These sorts of interreligious sentiments indicate not only the important ways in which Hindu–Muslim tolerance has been fostered by such spiritualities but also that, lying as they are in the heart of Delhi and frequented as they are by so many Muslims *and* Hindus, *dargāhs* like those of Niẓām al-Dīn serve as important reminders to both often power-hungry rulers and those who view Hindu–Muslim relations as only political.

Wider Uttar Pradesh has also been the site of important Hindu sacred places, the fates of which have proven vexing for Hindu–Muslim relations, particularly in the city of Ayodhya. Historically, Ayodhya has been much more of a backwater as compared to more cosmopolitan Delhi, but it was important as a pilgrimage spot for Hindus paying homage to the place of the birth of Rāma, known as Rāmjanambhūmi. Ayodhya is also a *tīrtha*, or place of fording to the divine on Hindu pilgrimages. It is also interesting to note that it is the place where the first Jain *tīrtaṅkara* was born, where the Buddha meditated, and where, some Muslims believe, Noah was buried. Despite these credentials, however, it had remained for centuries what anthropologist P. van der Veer has called an "unimpressive and dusty town" (1988, 1).

His book *Gods on Earth* outlines some of the history of Ayodhya. P. van der Veer argues that leading up to the time of Muslim rulership of Ayodhya under the Mughals and then the *nawābs* of Oudh (1680–1856),

> Ayodhya contained a number of holy places, partly of [Vaiṣṇava] provenance, partly [Śaiva]... Only in the time of the nawabs did the place become what it is today, the center of a cult of Ram, controlled by Ramanandis. (van der Veer, 1988, 11)

P. van der Veer portrays the history of Ayodhya as one of relative peace and pluralism – that is, until a certain Sufi saint in the 16th century, one Fażl ʿAbbās Mūsā ʿĀšiqān, came to the town in search of meditation instruction under a *sādhu* named Śyāmānand, who resided at the temple of the birthplace of Rāma. ʿĀšiqān successfully practiced *yoga* using "the Muslim *mantra*" and inspired an idea to turn the temple in that part of the town into a Muslim center. The emperor Bābur traveled through and promised to do just that. He ordered his general, Mīr Bāqī, to raze the temple and build a mosque just behind the temple site. The *garbha* (sanctum) remained still accessible for Hindus as a pit in the open ground. The *nawābs* of Oudh eventually gave this outdoor sanctum to community Hindus in 1855 but did not allow a permanent temple to be reconstructed. Despite this apparent injunction, P. van der Veer argues that these stories depict an Ayodhya of relative peace and tolerance prior to the mid-19th century and certainly prior to the 20th century (1988, 21). He notes very little evidence of systematic suppression of Hinduism in the area. In the years after Partition, however, that began to change. In December of 1949, an image of Rāma appeared overnight and was guarded the next day by armed guards. Hindus rejoiced at the reappearance of Rāma, while Muslims thought this an affront to their mosque. Litigation was launched to ensure entrance, and this only inflamed Hindu–Muslim relations in the area. Both groups were refused full access. In 1984, however, the VHP vowed to "liberate the spot where Ram was born" (van der Veer, 1988, 41) and launched a *yātrā* to liberate the site. In their view, the Babar Mosque – or Bābrī Masjid – had to go. According to R.H. Davis, the *yātrās* that took place over the next several years employed iconography and iconology drawn from Hindu epic literature, replete with "fierce looking lions," "lotus tendrils and lotuses," "chariot wheel covers," and "Om signs" (1996, 28), not to mention a BJP president – L.K. Advani (b. 1927) – astride the chariot and posing as Rāma as often as possible. Hindu communities in wider Uttar Pradesh and beyond mobilized, now under a burning anti-Muslim communal banner.

According to S. Corbridge and E. Simpson, these events essentially redrew the map in the 1980s and 1990s for nationalist parties like the BJP and the VHP. Ayodhya, the Rāmjanambhūmi, and the Bābrī Masjid were now at the center of India and certainly at the center of Indian politics, which was becoming more and more communally inflamed (2006, 74). This coincided in the early 1990s with electoral success nationally for the BJP and the VHP, who played on Hindu frustrations over having to leave Kashmir in 1990 to ease communal and international tensions there, among other issues. In the Uttar Pradesh 1991 assembly elections, the BJP gained power such that, according to S. Corbridge and E. Simpson, they were "given the green light for further mobilizations around the Babri Masjid" (2006, 75). On Dec 6 and 7, 1992, political rallies in Ayodhya "degenerated into a savage attack on the mosque" (Corbridge & Simpson, 2006, 75). It was razed to the ground, thus launching Hindu–Muslim communal violence in waves across the country. S. Corbridge and E. Simpson have argued that what really happened here was a redrawing of the map in which *akhaṇḍ bhārat* ("Hindudom") now inspired a reading in which Ayodhya became a center point, along with Varanasi, of the body of Bhārat Mātā (Mother India), which her sons, newly masculinized and virile, would move to protect her at all costs. Hindu–Muslim antipathy was now being fueled by the supposed Muslim affront to two of Mother India's holiest cities – Ayodhya and Varanasi.

Varanasi, according to historian M. Casolari, has also become something of a focal point for Hindu nationalist concerns. While having enjoyed a reputation through to the 1990s as a place relatively free of the Hindu–Muslim communal turmoil of the outside world, the filming of Deepa Mehta's *Water* in 2000 inflamed conservative Hindus in the city and beyond. They were concerned with, among other things, disturbing depictions in the film of ill treatment of widows and were not happy with the association set up between the film's title and the → Gaṅgā River. Filming was stopped due to VHP activism, but – now emboldened, M. Casolari argues – the protesters went on to press grievances with the city's Muslims. She outlines ways in which the Mughals had "tried to turn Banaras into a Muslim city" (Casolari, 2002, 1414) even while being represented by a local Rajput dynasty locally, but she argues that the Hindu nature of the city remained resilient. She talks about how "in the 19th century, riots were a common event in Benares. A particularly violent one is recorded in 1809" (Casolari, 2002, 1414). Yet still, she points out that Muslims were involved as weavers working for the *rāmlīlā* devotional plays in the city from the early 19th century onward and that city Hindus "used to participate in Muharram celebrations" (Casolari, 2002, 1414).

P. Lutgendorf, in his book *Life of a Text: Performing the Rāmcaritmānas of Tulsidas*, has painted a picture of Varanasi as being at the heart of Hindu North India yet still, in small ways, relatively inclusive of the Muslims who make up part of the city. He points out that for years, there was a unconventional relationship in the leadership structure of the city. In 1740, in an effort to give patronage to growing Kathā chanting performances of the *Rāmcaritmānas* of the local saint → Tulsīdās (1532–1623), the *nawāb* of Oudh granted a title to a local Varanasi farmer's son, Balvant Siṅgh, of "raja of Banaras" (Lutgendorf, 1991, 259). The *rājā* was meant to be a vassal for the *nawāb*, especially in affairs related to the ever-more popular Kathā performances – events that grew eventually to be known as the *rāmlīlā*. This arrangement set up an interesting brokerage between the Muslim *nawāb* and the Hindu *rājā*. P. Lutgendorf points out that this was less an issue of communal harmony and more about "royal legitimacy" (1991, 260). Yet this is always for P. Lutgendorf, as he argues in another article, set against the backdrop of *rāmrāj* (the righteous reign of Rāma), such that – P. Lutgendorf follows S. Pollock here – Rāma's image as righteous ruler against usurping outsiders plays into nationalist readings of the importance of Varanasi *Rāmcaritmānas* performances, set as they are in the buckle of India's Hindi belt. These fault lines continue to radiate out from Ayodhya and Varanasi in the Hindu–Muslim communal tremors that periodically shake Uttar Pradesh and wider north central India.

There are examples to be found in north central India of the sorts of Hindu–Muslim interreligious convergences observed elsewhere in India. Anthropologist C. Bellamy (2011) has studied shared religious practices at a Sufi *dargāh* in the town of Jaora in Madhya Pradesh. Ḥusayn Tekrī, built in the 19th century, is primarily a Šīʿa shrine complex with shrines not to saints buried in graves on the premises but commemorating close members of Muḥammad's own family. They are Imām Ḥusayn, Ḥażrat ʿAbbās, Mawlā ʿAlī, Bībī Fāṭima, Bībī Zaynab, and Bībi Sākina (Bellamy, 2011, 2). C. Bellamy describes Ḥusayn Tekrī as "ambiguously Islamic" insofar as a great many who frequent the *dargāh* are Hindus. Some pilgrims, including Hindus, enter into a state of *ḥāżirī*, or "presence," in which they become possessed by spirit forces (Bellamy, 2011, 5). The *dargāh* is thought of as a *darbār*, or a royal court. It is a royal court, that is, in the heavenly realm, and the saint acts as a mediator, healer, and benefactor. These spiritual dynamics have proven to be quite attractive not only to Muslims looking to complement mosque-centered, often political Islam with something more spiritually evocative but also to large numbers of Hindus who see in the saint or saints' tomb complex something that overlaps, as C. Bellamy observes, with a "Hanumān, Devī, and Śani" temple spirituality (Bellamy, 2011, 18). Here again, we see Sufi tomb culture as a powerful stimulus for convergent forms of religious practice and culture that surely dampen more virulent forms of nationalist, communal rhetoric often found in north central Indian areas like Delhi, Uttar Pradesh, and wider Madhya Pradesh.

East Cultural Areas: Bihar and West Bengal

The eastern cultural areas of Bihar and West Bengal have enjoyed very creative and spiritually adventurous expressions of Hindu–Muslim cultures. While some violence has certainly occurred in these eastern frontiers of the Islamic push into the subcontinent, these areas have generally been less turbulent than north central India. Historian R. Eaton, in his book *The Rise of Islam and the Bengal Frontier 1204–1760*, has described the ways in which a lively Bengali Hindu culture encountered not only political forays into the eastern subcontinent by the Delhi Sultanate Muslims and the Mughals but also what became a very active eastern Sufi culture. R. Eaton notes that, as elsewhere throughout North India, the 13th century saw Muslims pouring into every hamlet and city in a conquering posture. He describes how it was no different in Bengal and wider east India. Five centuries of Islamic rule were initiated by sometimes lightning-quick armies that flowed around the area. The difference, he says, is that "among India's interior provinces only in Bengal did a majority of the indigenous population adopt the religion of the ruling class, Islam" (Eaton, 1993, xxii). This led directly, he notes, to the Partition in 1947 in which the subcontinent was divided into India and Pakistan, with Pakistani Muslims concentrated in northwest areas and what was eastern Bengal. This eastern wing of Pakistan was created on the basis of the resiliency of those early conversions to Islam.

Bengal had become Islamic early, and it remained so. R. Eaton qualifies this, however, in the sense that while the delta regions in the east, around Bengal, were a frontier politically, a frontier in the spread of Islam, and a frontier in terms of agrarian cultures, they were a frontier, too, of what had been a long-standing Sanskritic Buddhist and Brahmanic egalitarian civilization. These divisions can aid in understanding not only the rise of what became a relatively independent sultanate based in Bengali culture but also the ways in which this sultanate gave way to Bengali incorporation into Mughal cultures. They can also aid in understanding the rise of forms of Sufism that generally worked *with* Bengali Hindu cultures, not against them.

The Bihar regions were captured in 1203, and the Bengal regions were captured in 1204 by Muḥammad Baẖtiyār (d. 1206), the general of Quṭb al-Dīn Aibak. These areas became what R. Eaton calls a "province" of the Delhi Sultanate (1993, 32). The Bengal Sultanate lasted from 1342 until 1487 and enjoyed a rulership that was relatively free of interference from Delhi. The rulers throughout the years of the Bengal Sultanate worked actively to court the favor of Hindu landholding elites (Eaton, 1993, 50). R. Eaton summarizes it in this way: while "the sultanate aligned itself ideologically with the Middle East, it was rooted politically in Bengal" (1993, 51).

The Mughals' conquering of Bengal in 1629 initiated another period of mass conversions to Islam. While the Muslim rulers worked hard to rule in a way that was uniquely Bengali, the citizenry, perhaps inspired by significant numbers of active Sufis who were continuing to settle in the delta regions, took on Islamic identities and practices. Some of these conversions, explainable through the activities of itinerant Sufi spiritualists, also may have been due to rising Bengali – Hindu and Muslim – resistance to Mughal hegemony (Eaton, 1993, 146). In the late 1500s, ʿIsā Ḫān (d. 1599) had become a champion of resistance against the Mughals. By 1704, however, Mughal control had been cemented, and Mughal culture became yet another layer comprising Bengali Hindu–Muslim cultures.

As noted, an important part of what became Bengali Hindu–Muslim culture was the activity of the Sufis who came into the area. R. Eaton notes that the earliest-known Islamic inscription in the Bengali region was not put there by invading armies or by subsequent rulers. It was, rather, describing the events of the year 1221, which saw the construction of a Sufi lodge in the Birbhum district (Eaton, 1993, 71). R. Eaton records how sections of Sufis sought to integrate "the esoteric practices of local yogis, together with the cosmologies that underpinned those practices" (Eaton, 1993, 77). Some Sufis, however, were less invested in such ephemeral teachings and practices and opted for statecraft, acting as advisors in royal centers (Eaton, 1993, 82) and often interacting with Hindus over affairs of state.

I. Pande, in her book *Medicine, Race and Liberalism in British Bengal: Symptoms of Empire*, argues that as Bengal came under the colonial boot, its cultures became a sort of lab wherein were worked out certain "types" that could include that which is properly "Hindu" and that which is properly "Muslim" (2010). British physicians, for example, in the 1830s, had engaged in the practice of phrenology in order to determine the "Hindoo type." I. Pande notes how even the famous Hindu reformer → Rammohun Roy (d. 1833) became subject to these techniques. His skull was collected, copied with a cast, and measured in every way. Among other goals, the hope was to link skull measurements with "physical anthropology, on the one hand, and to political philosophy, on the other" (Pande, 2010, 48). This could aid, for example, in helping solve the problems of roving bands of thugs on the Bengal frontier. It could also aid in explaining how "the Hindoo" had been so easily subjugated by "the Mohametan." More insidious than this, however, were the ways in which these techniques were used to reify sometimes incredibly invasive governing techniques, including training indigenous "black doctors" who would have skill in helping to test "native capacities" (Pande, 2010, 67) in all sorts of dehumanizing medical experiments. These and other colonial techniques mentioned elsewhere worked to differentiate pure models of *this* Hindu over against *that* Muslim.

These events can help clarify the ways in which Hindu and Muslim identities were further polarized in Bengal after the turn of the 19th century. P. Gossman has identified some of these trends in the early 20th century, prior to Partition, in her book *Riots and Victims: Violence and the Construction of Communal Identity among Bengali Muslims, 1905–1947* (1999). P. Gossman recounts how uprisings that predate self-rule movements and certainly predate the 1990s conflagrations occurred often for a multitude of reasons. From 1905 to 1911, for example, there were several violent agitations that involved religious reformers joining ranks with peasant organizers to challenge both "'anti-Islamic' practices and Hindu dominance in land-holding and money-lending" (Gossman, 1999, 4). At the same time, she notes, these same religious reformers where attempting to counter "colonial encroachments into areas of religious jurisdiction" (Gossman, 1999, 4), all the while competing with one another for positions of favor in the community. P. Gossman similarly sees some of the uprisings in the 1920s and 1930s not as Hindu–Muslim communalism but much more as being driven by differences between Urdu-speaking Muslims and Bengali-speaking Muslims over the fate of a separate state for Muslims in the subcontinent. P. Gossman argues that many of the communal riots that marked pre-Partition Bengal were not so much a product of constitutional or interreligious issues between Hindus and Muslims than of leaders who were interested in

> distinguishing themselves from their rivals as the only ones capable of protecting their community... to carry this off, they had to construct their own community as aggrieved and endangered, and the other community as predatory. (Gossman, 1999, 8)

Historian J. Chatterji, however, argues that this took a turn as Partition approached. Greater Hindu unity was sought, for example, in Bengali social and political spheres *vis-à-vis* Muslim interests, especially through programs that worked toward caste uplift. Caste uplift was seen as a way to expose Islamic elitism and to create elusive Hindu unity. These tensions boiled into days like the so-called Direct Action Day in Calcutta in 1946, in which thousands of Hindus and Muslims died in communal clashes.

There are many examples of ways in which Bengali Hindu–Muslim cultures have remained resistant to these sorts of bifurcating communal movements. An interesting and creative movement, which stretches at least to the 15th century, has found energizing ways to combine aspects of Vaiṣṇava *bhakti* Hinduism and Sufi spirituality. They are the → Bāuls of Bengal. J. Openshaw has written about them in her book *Seeking Bāuls of Bengal* (2002). Often consciously wearing clothing from both Hindu and Sufi movements, they have become powerful symbols of Bengali tolerance. J. Openshaw also explores a class of Bāul practitioners who seek less to travel with a repertoire of inclusive songs to inspire people – as some Bāuls do – than to dedicate themselves to serious esoteric practices, including certain Vaiṣṇava tantric traditions (2002, 4). The Bāuls serve as powerful expressions of perennial Hindu–Muslim Bengali culture.

Religious studies scholar P. Gottschalk, in his book *Beyond Hindu and Muslim: Multiple Identity in Narratives from Village India* (2001), has done similar fieldwork but in rural Bihar. In the village of Arampur, he explores the ways in which divisions have become blurred between Hinduism and Islam. Calling into question too easy Western academic categories that have pushed defining Hindu practices and identities as distinct from Islamic practices and identities, he offers a model of group identity at the village level in which the labels "Hindu" and "Muslim" are at times useful as descriptors but at times not. Ritual lives, he notes, are often not that neatly divided (Gottschalk, 2001, 35), especially in places of Sufi *dargāh* culture, for instance, which can be found prominently in Bengal and Bihar, including in the village areas around Arampur. P. Gottschalk argues that identities can often be found much more abundantly in the group and that group memory can be an important way in which groups physically interact and make space a living space (Gottschalk, 2001, 82). In the same way that → Gandhi saw important lessons to be learned from village India – lessons of tolerance, inclusivity, interreligious acceptance, and self-reliance – P. Gottschalk helps to show that even a small village in Bihar is reflective of perennial values that have brought together Hindus and Muslims in positive ways in east India.

Northeast Cultural Area: Assam and Nagaland

If Bengal and Bihar are considered frontier territories in relation to the turbulent areas around Delhi and Uttar Pradesh, then the northeast cultural areas such as Assam and Nagaland are truly remote. The significant conversions to Islam that radiated out from Delhi in the 13th century and reached full flower especially in Bengal have meant that Assam and Nagaland have, like the rest of North India, gone through several centuries of Islamic presence. Still, A.L. Basham has identified Assam, among other corners of the subcontinent, as "less involved in the constant struggles for power" (1975, 51). This has meant that Assam and the surrounding territories have enjoyed relatively fewer power struggles *vis-à-vis* Hindu and Muslim power brokers farther to the south and west. Also, it has meant, he argues, less local conflict. Still, we cannot ignore the fact that, just as elsewhere, identity politics has resulted in disrupture in the northeastern cultural areas of India, including Assam and Nagaland.

S.K. Dass has examined how, since 1874, when Assam became a province of the British Empire, it has been in a state of flux, even while being considered on the frontier and fairly removed from mainline politics in central India (1980). He argues that, while immigration has been fairly robust over the first half of the 20th century, the assumption of significant numbers of Hindus having arrived in the post-Partition (here 1951) period has proven untrue. He identifies significant numbers of "Bengali Muslim cultivators" having resettled in Assam (Dass, 1980, 851) between 1871 and 1901, and he argues that the number of Hindus remained fairly stable from this time through the 1950s. In fact, after the 1871–1901 period, the numbers of both Hindus and Muslims remained relatively stable leading up to Partition. There was some pressure in the 1960s and 1970s on immigrant Muslims to go through a process of "Assamization," especially since they had to compete with a Calcutta-oriented Hindu upper middle class (Dass, 1980, 857). These data provide a background for understanding the rise of militancy in Assam identity politics, as explored by H. Srikanth. With modern Assam being almost two-thirds (58%) Hindu and a quarter (24%) Muslim, communalisms in the area may not fit patterns that are discernible in most of wider India. One significant difference involves a third interlocutor, namely what H. Srikanth calls "natives" (2000, 4119). With growing numbers of educated Calcutta Hindus and growing numbers of Bengali Muslims, members of indigenous communities became apprehensive about being able to compete. This has led the Assam government to attempt to impose Assamese as the official language of the region. This was coupled with attacks on Hindus and Muslims in the 1970s. As these attacks continued into the 1990s, the BJP took the opportunity to press for Hindu loyalty through charges of Islamic militancy in Assam (Srikanth, 2000, 4122). What started as a series of attacks from a common opponent devolved into too familiar Hindu-versus-Muslim nationalistic tropes. The Historian P.R. Brass (1990) has placed the blame for these communal trends in Assam and the wider northeast not on indigenous populations or on nationalist identity politics but squarely on the shoulders of states that are in need of reorganization. He notes how during the British rule, indigenous populations in wider Assam and the Naga hills were considered separate administrative areas. Direct British administration was prohibited,

> because it was considered that the culture and economy of the tribal populations were fragile and would be overwhelmed by both direct alien rule and penetration by Hindus from the plains. (Brass, 1990, 175)

After Partition, indigenous peoples continued to push for autonomous regions as independent from the state of Assam. Separate groups were recognized, for example the Mizos, the Nagas, and so on, and reorganization helped to create separate homelands such as Nagaland but only long after many agitations and government crackdowns. These sorts of government lapses have created impulses to take on Hindu identities as a way to establish more credibility for the movements of indigenous peoples but in ways that have complicated Hindu–Muslim relations in the area.

Conclusion

Hindus and Muslims in North India in the modern period, like those in South India, continue on paths of punctiliar division and perennial convergence. Muslim invasions, colonial exploitation and oppression, and rising nationalisms have exacerbated Hindu–Muslim relations entering the modern period. Even so, convergent literatures, arts, and architectures and shared legal struggles, spiritual traditions, mysticisms, and ritualizations have helped to foster deeper Hindu–Muslim relations leading up not only through the modern period but also to this day, even while these very same areas have been flashpoints for division. Both trends – division *and* convergence – are important to understand for a fuller picture of interreligious dynamics in modern North India. As in South India, Hindu–Muslim communalisms have erupted in the opening decades of the 21st century across North India. But most Hindus and Muslims in individual precincts and households in these regions have often chosen to emphasize their collective past, have taken pride in being common and living in common, and have chosen to remain – Hindu and Muslim alike – uniquely North Indian.

Bibliography

Basham, A.L., *A Cultural History of India*, New Delhi, 1975.

Bayly, C.A., *Indian Society and the Making of the British Empire*, Cambridge UK, 1988.

Bellamy, C., *Powerful Ephemeral: Everyday Healing in an Ambiguously Islamic Place*, Berkeley, 2011.

Bigelow, A., *Sharing the Sacred: Practicing Pluralism in Muslim North India*, New York, 2010.

Brass, P.R., *The New Cambridge History of India: The Politics of India since Independence*, New York, 1990.

Casolari, M., "Role of Benaras in Constructing Political Hindu Identity," *EPW* 37/15, 2002, 1413–1420.

Chandra, S., "Whose Laws? – Notes on a Nineteenth Century Hindu Case of Conjugal Rights," in: V. Dalmia & H. von Stietencron, eds., *Representing Hinduism: The Construction of Religious Traditions and National Identity*, New Delhi, 1995, 154–175.

Chatterji, J., *Bengal Divided: Hindu Communalism and Partition, 1932–1947*, Cambridge UK, 1994.

Corbridge, S., & E. Simpson, "Militant Cartographies and Traumatic Spaces: Ayodhya, Bhuj and the Contested Geographies of *Hindutva*," in: S. Raju, M. Satish Kumar & S. Corbridge, eds., *Colonial and Post-colonial Geographies of India*, New Delhi, 2006, 70–84.

Dass, S.K., "Immigration and Demographic Transformation of Assam, 1891–1981," *EPW* 15/19, 1980, 850–859.

Davis, R., "The Iconography of Rama's Chariot," in: D. Ludden, ed., *Contesting the Nation: Religion, Community, and Politics of Democracy in India*, Philadelphia, 1996, 27–54.

Eaton, R., *India's Islamic Traditions: 711–1750*, Oxford, 2004.

Eaton, R., *The Rise of Islam and the Bengal Frontier 1204–1760*, Berkeley, 1993.

Ernst, C., *Eternal Garden: Mysticism, History and Politics at a South Asian Sufi Center*, Albany, 1992.

Ernst, C., & B. Lawrence, *Sufi Martyrs of Love: The Chishti Order in South Asian and Beyond*, New York, 2002.

Field, E., M. Levinson, R. Pande & S. Visaria, "Segregation, Rent Control, and Riots: The Economics of Religious Conflict in an Indian City," *AER* 98/2, 2008, 505–510.

Gordon, S., *The New Cambridge History of India: The Marathas – 1680–1818*, New York, 1993.

Gossman, P.A., *Riots and Victims: Violence and Construction of Communal Identity among Bengali Muslims, 1905–1947*, Boulder, 1999.

Gottschalk, P., *Beyond Hindu and Muslim: Multiple Identity in Narratives from Village India*, New York, 2001.

Hansen, T.B., *Wages of Violence: Naming and Identity in Postcolonial Bombay*, Princeton, 2001.
Jordens, J.T.F., "Medieval Hindu Devotionalism," in: A.L. Basham, ed., *A Cultural History of India*, New Delhi, 1975, 266–280.
Khan, M.I., "The Rishi Tradition and the Construction of the Kashmiriyat," in: I. Ahmed & H. Reifeld, eds., *Lived Islam in South Asia*, Delhi, 2004, 61–82.
Khan, M.I., "The Impact of Islam on Kashmir in the Sultanate Period (1320–1586)," *IESHR* 23/2, 1986, 187–205.
Lochtefeld, J.G., "The Vishva Hindu Parishad and the Roots of Hindu Militancy," *JAAR* 62/2, 1994, 587–602.
Lutgendorf, P., "Interpreting Ramraj," in: D.N. Lorenzen, ed., *Bhakti Religion in North India: Community Identity and Political Action*, Albany, 1995, 253–287.
Lutgendorf, P., *Life of a Text: Performing the Rāmcaritmānas of Tulsidas*, Berkeley, 1991.
Openshaw, J., *Seeking Bāuls of Bengal*, New York, 2002.
Pande, I., *Medicine, Race and Liberalism in British Bengal: Symptoms of Empire*, New York, 2010.
Pinto, D., *Piri-Muridi: A Study of the Nizamuddin Dargah*, New Delhi, 1995.
Pollock, S., "Ramayana and Political Imagination in India," *JAS* 52/2, 1993, 261–297.
Powers, J., *Kites over the Mango Tree: Restoring Harmony between Hindus and Muslims in Gujarat*, Westport, 2009.
Rai, M., *Hindu Rulers, Muslim Subjects: Islam, Rights, and the History of Kashmir*, Delhi, 2004.
Richards, J.F., *The New Cambridge History of India*, vol. I/5: *The Mughal Empire*, New York, 1993.
Rizvi, S.A.A., "The Muslim Ruling Dynasties," in: A.L. Basham, ed., *A Cultural History of India*, New Delhi, 1975, 245–265.
Shani, O., "The Rise of Hindu Nationalism in India: The Case Study of Ahmedabad in the 1980s," *MAS* 39/4, 2005, 861–896.
Sikand, Y., *Sacred Spaces: Exploring Traditions of Shared Faith in India*, New York, 2003.
Sikand, Y., "The Muslim Rishis of Kashmir," *The Hindu*, Jul 16, 2001.
Srikanth, H., "Militancy and Identity Politics in Assam," *EPW* 35/47, 2000, 4117–4119, 4121–4124.
Veer, P. van der, *Gods on Earth*, London, 1988.
Wink, A., *Al-Hind: The Making of the Indo-Islamic World: Early-Medieval India and the Expansion of Islam, 7th–11th Centuries*, vol. I, Leiden, 1996.
Wright Jr., T.P., "The Muslim Minority before and after Ayodhya," in: A. Sharma, ed., *Hinduism and Secularism after Ayodhya*, New York, 2001, 1–25.

ERIC ROTHGERY

Modern Period South India

Years of plundering by North Indian Muslims under the aegis of the Delhi Sultanate (1206–1526) imperiled South India, exacerbating Hindu-Muslim relations in many precincts. By 1565, the culling of the Hindu empire of → Vijayanagara at the hands of Bijapur and Golconda Muslims – bolstered by North Indian sultanates – heeled lines of Hindu rule that had succeeded the once-glorious Kakatiyas and Yadavas in northern South India and the Pandyas and Hoysalas in the southern reaches. On the heels of the Anglo-Mysore Wars (1766–1799), the longstanding Hindu kingdoms and Islamic sultanates alike were swept up into four emerging modern states – Kerala, Andhra Pradesh, Karnataka, and Tamil Nadu – under the largesse of the "civilizing" colonial hand. The advent of prolonged colonial presence after the 18th century saw early modern South India remain turbulently divided politically and socially but also remarkably resilient in terms of growing Hindu–Muslim interreligious convergence, partially in united opposition to colonial rule. Both trends – division and convergence – mark the transition to the modern period for Hindus and Muslims in South India. It is important to note that categories of religious difference – *this* Hindu over against *that* Muslim – can act as valuable heuristic in seeing that religious conflict *has* occurred in the history of South India. Indeed it has, *sui generis*. Yet also, at the dawn of the modern age, with South India under the colonial thumb, administrative techniques – census and so on – often *begat* and *manufactured* the very communal phenomena that colonial census takers were looking for and were only sometimes looking to prevent. Any adequate treatment of Hindus and Muslims in South India in the modern period must not only take into account both indigenous and manufactured Hindu and Muslim communalisms but also take seriously historic, textual, and ethnographic accounts of centuries of *living* Hindu–Muslim religious convergence – a point of pride for most South Indian communities to this day. Division *and* convergence – Kerala, Andhra Pradesh, Karnataka, and Tamil Nadu each has not only suffered centuries of sporadic communalism but also enjoyed centuries of peaceable Hindu–Muslim coexistence.

Kerala

Kerala has enjoyed the deepest historical contact between Hindus and Muslims in India. Drawn by the spice trade, Arab seafaring merchants skimmed the Malabar coasts within decades after Prophet Muḥammad died – prior to the earliest settlements in Sind in 715 ce (Miller, 1992, 39). Islam was established in South India so early, Ibn Baṭṭūṭa (d. 1369) reported, because Malabar's Hindu rulers encouraged religious freedom, perhaps owing to increased revenues from trade (Dunn, 2005, 221). Yet Hindu–Muslim tensions flared up in the region, as Ibn Baṭṭūṭa reported a mosque having been destroyed by Hindus (Gabriel, 2006, 75). Aromal Cēvakār's 16th-century text, the *Vaṭakkan Paṭṭukal*, warns Hindu women passing through the Muslim town of Nadapuram lest they be molested (Gabriel, 2006, 81). Arab traders, however, gradually began to intermarry with Hindus. R. Miller notes that these Muslim settlers – the Māppiḷas – emerged from the 9th to the 12th century as stalwarts of economic prowess in southwest India and, through the patronage of Qādirī and Rifā'ī Sufism, made contributions to medieval Keralan poetics and cultural life (Miller, 1992, 53).

Trends toward cultural convergence, even while pockmarked by occasional friction, parlayed to concern about rising colonial presence in the subcontinent. Šayḫ Aḥmad Zayn al-Dīn's (d. 1581) *Tuḥfat al-mujāhidīn* (Offering to Jihad Warriors) encouraged Hindu–Muslim unity against the flood of the Portuguese (Miller, 1992, 44). R. Miller notes that there were no reports of Mappila militarism prior to the Portuguese. Relative peace among Nambūtiri high-caste Brahmans, Ambalavāsi lower-caste Brahmans (many became Muslims), Kṣatriyas, and Malabar Muslims gave way to Māppiḷa Muslim antipathy with caste groups of Nāyars (Smith, 2006, 546). Under pressure from the Portuguese in the late 16th and early 17th centuries, the Māppiḷas entered into a phase of "economic regression, estrangement from Hindus, bitterness against Christian, and a new militancy" (Miller, 1992, 75). The Cochin and Kolathiri *rājās* allied commercially with the Portuguese, vacating agreements with the Māppiḷas. Broken alliances erupted into skirmishes between Nāyars and Muslims, including captivity of Seringapatnam (Shrirangapattana) Nāyars by Tīpū Sulṭān, until they were liberated by Hindu troops from Travancore.

In the 1580s, the Dutch seized control, bringing new economic pressures to the area and a vitriolic conversionism. The Dutch were followed quickly by the British, bringing not only abatement to Dutch conversionism but also yet more economic pressures. The interests of the British East India Company were cemented during the Anglo-Mysore Wars at the close of the 18th century. British favor toward Hindus and disfavor toward Māppiḷa Muslims further exacerbated Hindu-Muslim relations entering the modern period, yet many Muslims *and* Hindus aligned against the colonials. Alternating Hindu then Muslim uprisings against the British from 1793 to 1853 were caused, perhaps, by exploitative serfdom and poverty. "Moplah (i.e. Māppiḷa) riots" during the 1920s still included many Hindus, especially in the Cherpalchery–Pattambi district in South Malabar (Miller, 1992, 125) and caught the eye of the *svarāj* movement. Gandhi, lamenting the "Moplah" uprisings, began to reflect whether Hindu–Muslim unity was a prudent plank within *svarāj*, saying, "The Moplah outbreak... has raised doubts in Hindu/Muslim unity... Moplahs must learn the beauty of non-violence" (Bakshi, 1987, 30ff.).

The 1947 Partition, nationalistic hardening of Hindu and Muslim identities against each other, and lukewarm relations among Māppiḷas, moderate Aligaṛhīs, and hard-line Deobandīs exacerbated relations with Hindus but also drew them together against northern hegemonies. Following Partition, Muslim League activities in Kerala pushed worries about whether and who would represent the interests of Muslims not just in national – and nationalistic – politics but also in state politics. Likewise, Hindu fears of Islamic desire for a "Moplahstan" in Kerala spurred forward nationalist parties like the Jana Sangh – linked to the Rashtriya Swayamsevak Sangh – with strong anti-Muslim platforms (Miller, 1992, 182). In the 1970s, under Indira Gandhi and others, renewed focus was brought to positive Hindu-Muslim relations in India, and this had some effect in Kerala (Miller, 1992, 185). In the 1990s, however, the murder of a Keralan *madrasa* teacher by Rashtriya Swayamsevak Sangh agents on the heels of the 1992 Rāmjanmabhūmi conflagration in Ayodhya inflamed relations in the state. Communist party officials, among others, courted Hindus and Muslims to honor "long-envied" Hindu–Muslim harmony (Miller, 1992, 332). Despite these modern manifestations of communalism, Kerala – and South India – has enjoyed a long-envied relative peace between Hindus and Muslims, especially as compared to the more volatile North India.

R. Miller's ethnography of the Māppiḷa Muslims has borne this out. So, too, have other modern ethnographies, including those by H. Hartmann, M. Halliburton, and F. Smith. H. Hartmann's study looked at the rise of secularism in Kerala in the 1960s in ways that mitigated Hindu–Muslim communalism. Noting that prior to the 1960s, post-Independence Keralan politics had been sharply divided along religious lines with four main groups having formed, "the Nairs [Nāyar], Ezhavas [Tiyyas; Īḻavar Thīya], Christians and Muslims" (Hartmann, 1968, 163), he goes on to show that interreligious cooperations that predated Independence were drawn on to help create consensus in the form of rising secularism. A rising tide of Socialist and Communist parties massaged a more neutral interreligious space. H. Hartmann has shown that in most districts in Kerala in the 1960s, the radical pluralism of the Congress Party and the pro-Hindu Nairs and conservative Muslim League were met in the middle by secularist – and often economic and social – ideologies. M. Halliburton more recently has studied healing systems in Kerala, and he outlines multivalent notions of the self and the body within the convergent religious cultures that shape these practices. He has shown that Keralan notions of the person usually lie along a diffuse continuum that ranges from the bodily self to mind, soul, and true self in ways that extend far beyond embodied limitations (Halliburton, 2002, 1123). He found that these continua generally existed across religious boundaries and included healing techniques practiced at Hindu, Muslim, and Christian healing centers. Similarly, F. Smith has encountered abundant interreligious healings in Kerala. He has investigated Nambūtiri healing practices. Nambūtiri healers, though they belong to an elite Brahmanical group in Kerala, often see that a majority of their patients are Muslims – indeed, female Muslims. He argues that these Hindu–Muslim healing encounters remain a part of "a mental health-care delivery system of considerable sophistication" (Smith, 2006, 544). These ethnographies reveal that Hindu and Muslim religious identities remain negotiable in Kerala, making possible occasional polarized division *and* timeless convergence.

Andhra Pradesh

Andhra Muslims were shaped by meetings of North and South, as Muslims who entered the subcontinent through Kerala "met" Multani, Ghaznavid, and Tughluq Islamic lineages pushing from the North after the 12th century (Eaton, 2004, 9ff.; Nizami, 2002, 80ff.). Maḥmūd of Ghazni (d. 1030) pressured South India via the Deccan primarily through Andhra (Sastri, 1958, 226). Like in Kerala, many North and South Indian Muslims were at odds in Andhra. K.A. Sastri describes Andhra Muslims as allied with 14th-century Śaiva revivalists who, having turned against common Tughluq systems that pressed for local *iqtā*ʿs (military fiefs) to feed tributes northward, successfully liberated coastal Deccan regions (Sastri, 1958, 227). Yet C. Talbot notes increasing "othering" in wider Andhra from 1323 to 1650. The Kakatiyas (1083–1323) disintegrated under Delhi Sultanate attacks even as they pushed idioms – C. Talbot follows S. Pollock here – of Muslims as *mleccha*s, "demonic barbarians" (see → foreigner). C. Talbot argues a paucity of inscriptions in Andhra to back S. Pollock's thesis with regard to inscribed → *Rāmāyaṇa*-inspired demonization (Talbot, 1995, 696), but he does show that some inscriptions recount general abuse of Brahmans at the hands of invading Muslims. C. Talbot also argues that Andhra may have been the birthplace of Hindu–Muslim "ethnogenesis," in that the 1350s saw an increased use of the identifier "Hindu" – the first-ever usage in Indian-language sources – as a unifying term against Muslims, even if the term was borrowed from Islamic sources (Talbot, 1995, 700).

Kakatiya Śaivas, sometimes united with local Muslims especially in the Warangal district, gave way to the Tajik–Persian Bahmani Sultanate (r. 1347–1527). The first independent Islamic rulership in South India, the Bahmanis remained opposed to North Indian Islamic suzerainty and were eventually crippled by the Mughals in the 1520s. Hindu–Muslim relations under the Bahmanis were mixed. The influence of Sufism was considerable in Gulbarga, the capital of the Bahmani Sultanate due to early missionary work of Čištī, Junaydī, and Qādirī communities. These Sufi communities established good relationships with Deccan → Liṅgāyats and → Mahānubhāvs (Siddiqi, 1989, 24–25). Bahmani texts like the *Jawāmiʿal-kalim* (Siddiqi, 1989, 60) record how Sufis like Gīsūdirāz (d. 1421) wrote dozens of works and actively engaged Hindus over issues of caste and inclusivity, and how they "successfully convinced them on different issues" such as emanationist philosophies and the possibility of ecstatic states through musical celebration. M. Siddiqi records how → Liṅgāyats in the Gulbarga district still celebrate the *ʿurs* (lit. wedding) death anniversary of Aḥmad Šāh Bahmanī (Siddiqi, 1989, 163). As the Bahmani Sultanate waned, it split into five states: Ahmednagar, Berar, Bidar, Bijapur, and Golconda, with Golconda enjoying the most lasting influence in Andhra.

Golconda (1518–1687) – founded by Sulṭān Qulī Quṭb al-Mulk (d. 1543) – rose quickly as the Mughals retreated and as the Vijayanagara Empire, under Kṛṣṇadēvarāya (d. 1529), was occupied with war in Orissa and the Kalinga–Utkal Empire. The Qutb Shahis – Golconda's dynasty – took pride in Hindu administrative inclusivity and in patronage for Telugu Hindu poets, artists, and artisans. C. Talbot recounts late-medieval Telugu texts like the *Rāyavacakamu*, which ascribed noble titles like "Lord of Horses" (*aśvapati*) to Muslim rulers – with "Lord of Men" (*narapati*) for Vijayanagar's king and "Lord of Elephants" (*gajapati*) for Orissa's king – and which regarded each respectively as emanations of → Brahmā, → Viṣṇu, and → Śiva (Talbot, 1995, 708–709). Originally a Kakatiya stronghold, Golconda's architecture bears the influences of Islamic and Hindu building aesthetics (Prasad, 1986, 4). D. Prasad records how Hindus such as the Kayashtas learned Persian and "adopted more Muslim characteristics than any other Hindu community and helped in the process of cultural synthesis" (Prasad, 1986, 72).

Unification tightened between Muslims and Hindus at Golconda and at Ahmednagar, Berar, Bidar, and Bijapur, as Mughal incursions into the Deccan, especially under Awrangzēb, picked up. N. Luther recounts how the Muslim ruler of Golconda, Abū al-Ḥasan Quṭb Šāh (r. 1672–1687), dared to "conspire" with the Marathi Hindu ruler Sambhājī (r. 1674–1689; see → Maratha) against Awrangzēb. Sambhājī tried to provide supplies for Golconda while also attempting to encircle Awrangzēb's army (Luther, 2006, 88). After months of siege, Awrangzēb succeeded, but he also ensured some measure of Hindu–South Indian Muslim unity against Mughal hegemony.

These trends continued with the European colonial advance. With activities of the British East India Company increasing in the south in the 18th and 19th centuries, and with the Sepoy Mutiny in the north, the British moved toward cementing their hold in the south, particularly under the Anglo-Mysore Wars. Although something of a "feudal morass" in the 19th century, S. Raj (1987, vi) describes growing South Indian Hindu–Muslim unity against the British – echoing earlier anti-Mughal themes – even while British administerial techniques worked to divide Hindu and Muslim polities. The census became an important tool in the British "divide-and-conquer" methodology, ossifying Hindu and Muslim identities against each other (Guha, 2003, 149ff.). Yet S. Raj describes ten leading noble families in Hyderabad state at the dawn of the 19th century as having amicable relations: five Shi'a, four Hindu (Decanni Marathis, Chitpavan Brahmins, Kayashtas, and Punjabi Khatris), and one Sunni. Contrary to British enumerative techniques, the *niẓām* – the nominal Muslim ruler of Hyderabad – "made no distinction between Hindus, Muslims and people of other religions. He believed in communal harmony and integration" (Raj, 1987, 64). Within the *darbār* (royal court) of the *niẓām*, even religious leaders shared with equal importance *dīvalī, holī, vasantpañcamī, tilsaṃkrānt, muḥarram*, and *ʿīd* events (Raj, 1987, 90).

R. Naidu, however, indicates that some of these very religious festivals have supplied a pretext for interreligious communal violence. *Gaṇeśacaturthī, bōnālu*, and *muharram* processions have recently grown and been infused with the Bharatiya Janata Party (BJP) and Islamist overtones (Naidu, 1990, 148ff.; Pinault, 1992, 64ff.), and they have contributed to sporadic communalism in post-Ayodhya Hyderabad. I. Copland has shown that "in the first three and a half decades of the twentieth century,

[Andhra] experienced only three serious communal disturbances – at Gulbarga in 1924, at Goarta in 1929 and at Aland in 1933" (Copland, 1988, 788), but that from 1937 to 1940, communalism spiked. Indian independence *satyāgraha* movements, playing out largely in the North, pressured local religious communities in the South. The *nizām*, for some Hindus, became a symbol of long-standing "foreign rule" and was seen as an "irresponsible, autocratic and medieval rule" (Copland, 1988, 785). The newspaper *Dig Vijay* of April 1939 declared that "being Hindu itself is an offence" in the *nizām*'s *darbār* (Copland, 1988, 785). Relatively equal numbers of Hindus and Muslims under the Qutb Shahis became a Hindu majority in the 1930s (then at 84%) that enjoyed only 6% of the *nizām*'s giving for religious activities; the other 94% of funding was going to Islamic activities. Hindu temple projects often sat in limbo. Hindu music was prohibited "within forty steps of any mosque." Earlier intra-Hindu rivalries between Telugu speakers and Marathis diminished not with joint opposition to the British, and in opposition to the *nizām*. → Arya Samajis unified the Hindu base over discriminatory permitting of religious processions and building or repairing of temples, and over treatment of Hindu prisoners in Hyderabadi jails. In 1937, the last princely *nizām*, Mir Osman Ali (r. 1911–1948), sought reforms through the Aiyengar committee, a committee appointed by the *nizām* in 1937 to encourage democratic participation. I. Copland argues that the Aiyengar committee, though inspired by the Congress Party's pluralist democratic visions, actually served to exacerbate Hindu–Muslim tensions (Copland, 1988, 802). Local Arya Samajis like Mahatma Narayan Swami and Pandit Narinderji brought demonstrators for agitations from all over South India. Indeed, Hyderabad in the 1930s and 1940s became a foothold for the Arya Samaj in its southward expansion. A. Ahmad, however, argues that Hyderabadis did stand generally against nationalist identities promulgating in wider Andhra and South India (Ahmad, 1988, 173).

Ethnographies about Hyderabad and Andhra remain critical in understanding the complexities of local lived Hindu–Muslim relations. F. Speziale has outlined convergent Hindu and Islamic medical and healing traditions in wider South Asia but with special attention to Hyderabad. He reveals how medical texts translated between Hindu and Muslim communities within Golconda's *darbar* worked to stimulate interreligious thinking on medical techniques, Sufi and Hindu mystical notions of subtle physiologies, and trade in medicinal plants and pharmacology, and they often grounded shared healing rituals. J. Flueckiger (2006) accounts for more than ten years in the life of a Hyderabadi female Sufi healer with Hindu and Muslim patients alike as part of her successful healing practices. E. Rothgery has shown that three *dargāh*s in Hyderabad remain important places for the enactment of Hindu–Muslim religious convergence and a platform for fluid religious identities, enacted in shared Hindu–Muslim healing rituals that often transcend bifurcating religious nationalist rhetoric. Likewise, important work on interreligious Sufi saints and Hindu → *guru*s and important religious figures remains critical. In Andhra, the interreligious effect of saints like → Sathya Sai Baba (d. 2011) cannot be underestimated (Srinivas, 2010).

Karnataka

Karnataka's story is similar to Kerala's and Andhra's. Its Muslim populations are among India's oldest, with many Arab trading ports having been established nearly contemporaneously to those established in Māppiḷa areas of Kerala. Arab Muslims "met" Ghaznavid Muslims after the 10th century and Delhi Sultanate Muslims after the 13th century. During this Islamic growth, Hindu imperial presence was strong under the Vijayanagara Empire (1336–1646). Fueling this strength S. Pollock sees the unifying rise of *Rāmāyaṇa* imagery/mythemes. The Rāmacandra Temple – related to Kiṣkindhā and Lake Pampā in the *Rāmāyaṇa* – in the city of Vijayanagara in northeast Karnataka perhaps became tied to Ayodhya via royal inscriptions (Pollock, 1993, 268). Linkages between → Rāma and Vijayanagara royals over against demonic *rākṣasa*/*mleccha* invaders – here "Turkish" Muslims, according to S. Pollock (1993, 273ff.) – remain tentative, however, for many were thoroughly Śaiva, and some sought Hindu–Muslim amicability.

Ibn Baṭṭūṭa gave lengthy accounts of his sojourn in the medieval port cities of Sandapur and Honavar farther to the south of Karnataka. He recounts a well-established Indo-Muslim coastal culture with dozens of flourishing *madrasa*s, a robust Muslim economy, and generally good relations with local Hindus. Though the ruler Jamāl al-Dīn Muḥammad (r. mid-14th cent.) paid tribute to the Hoysala Hindu king Harihara (r. 1336–1350), Muhammad was considered by Ibn Baṭṭūṭa as "one of the best and most powerful rulers on the coast" (Dunn, 2005, 221). Thought of fondly by Jamāl al-Dīn, Ibn Baṭṭūṭa was even raised to high imperial rank in order to broker disputes in the ruling Hindu family of Sandapur. R. Dunn recounts a deal, struck to forcibly overthrow the *rājā* of Sandapur, between the Hindu son of the *rājā* of Sandapur and Muḥammad, the Muslim ruler of Honavar. So, even Ibn Baṭṭūṭa became embroiled in the emerging complexities of Hindu–Muslim relations in South India. These political maneuverings played out not only on the coast but also in growing urban centers like Mysore.

Although initially vassal to the Vijayanagara Empire, Mysore – ruled by Wodeyars – emerged as an important center in Kannada-speaking regions by the 18th century. Under Ḥaydar ʿAlī (r. 1761–1782) and Tīpū Sulṭān (r. 1782–1799), growing resistance to Hindu Marathas and Muslims at Golconda, and, increasingly, to the British, culminated in the Anglo-Mysore Wars at the dawn of the 19th century. The British, having eventually heeled the Muslim rulers of Mysore, reestablished the Hindu Wodeyars in Mysore. Under the British, although forced to pay obeisance to East India Company interests, Rājā Kṛṣṇadēvarāya (r. 1799–1836) deepened relationships with Hindu and Jain religious institutions. C.A. Bayly notes how the "powerful Shaiva 'monastery' of Sringeri" (1988, 113) – heirs of → Śaṅkara – served to reestablish Mysore royal linkages with the goddess Cāmuṇḍī (see → Kālī) and the bull Nandi (see → sacred animals) (and, hence, greater Śaivism), "yet care was taken not to offend Muslims" (1988, 113). A new mosque was established at the same time. C.A. Bayly seems to indicate that newly revived *vijayadaśamī* festivals were frequented by Hindus and Muslims alike. One must suspect that this interreligious spirit was in part due to growing opposition by Hindus and Muslims alike to British political, cultural, and religious manipulations. C.A. Bayly notes a rash of revolts in the 1830s by Liṅgāyats and others in and around Mysore, with uprisings in the Kodagu area in 1835 and the Kanara area in 1837. Similar to Kerala and Andhra, Hindu–Muslim unity was stimulated by anticolonial impulses leading up to the 1857 Sepoy Mutiny. Yet Mysore remained a princely state under the British Raj until 1947. Vijayanagara and Mysore were "perhaps the nearest approach to a war-state ever made by a Hindu kingdom" (Sastri, 1958, 297), with South Indian Nāyaks and rulers from Tamil- and Telugu-speaking lands and Kannada-speaking districts usually seeking opportunism that superseded any Hindu-Muslim divide (Sastri, 1958, 298).

Nonetheless, the cities of Mysore and Bangalore – according to N. Gist – in the middle decades of the 20th century often split along religious identifiers. With 79% Hindus in Mysore and 73% Hindus in Bangalore on the heels of Partition, Hindu–Muslim relations remained equitable. Hindu and Muslim educational levels remained comparable, as did economic ability and mortality rates. Contrary to what one might expect given the realities of Partition and its communal aftermath, N. Gist notes that Hindu and Christian communities remained more migratory and mobile than Muslim communities (Gist, 1957, 67). J. Nair notes how movements like Khilafat, much maligned by Gandhi, but taken up by Māppiḷas in neighboring Kerala, pushed anticolonial sentiments through uprisings in the shape of staged labor strikes and other agitations. The 1930 Kolar Gold Field strikes, near Mysore, became one branch of Khilafat involvement in Karnataka (Nair, 1990, 79). M. Assadi points to the post-Ayodhya period as having given a "foothold for the BJP" (Assadi, 1998, 627) in Mysore, Hyderabad, and other places in South India, yet days of "mass rallies" and strong anticolonial and anti-Muslim *hindutva* rhetoric have waned, giving way recently to a "soft *hindutva*" (Assadi, 1998, 628). C.J. Fuller suggests that alongside the "timeless" Hinduism of nationalist rhetoric and mythology, especially since Ayodhya, there exist, as well, streams of "popular religions" that are "old and [with] deep roots" (Fuller, 1992, 261) and that admit a theism far less political and far more concerned with, to quote M.N. Srinivas, "the source of hope for undertaking the multifarious activities essential for day-to-day living" (Fuller, 1992, 5).

J. Assayag, T. Srinivas, and C.J. Fuller provide important contemporary ethnographic accounts of Hindu and Muslim communities of Karnataka. J. Assayag explores contemporary fluidity of religious boundaries in village and urban communities in Karnataka, specifically the Belgaum district in northwest Karnataka, near Goa, and the village of Shahabandar just to the north of Belgaum. A site with some recurrent interreligious riots in the closing decades of the 20th century, Shahabandar gives J. Assayag the opportunity to explore local convergences of Hindu and Muslim practices. He argues that the picture he explores "testifies that the so-called 'war' between the gross categories of Hindu and Muslims is not a rule, but a historical falsification originating in xenophobia and ethnic-nationalism" (Assayag, 2004, 19). He does not argue so much for "Golden Age" ideal peacefulness, as for "competitive sharing" and "antagonistic tolerance" between many Hindus and Muslims. J. Assayag finds that the decades leading up to the 1990s saw an increasing Muslim population in Karnataka, even while admitting great variety and fluidity in otherwise Muslim populations. While religious districts were set up locally, often with anchoring religious centers, festivals – *šaʿbān, lailat ul-qadr, nāgapañcamī, daśaharā*, and *dīvalī* – sometimes provide openings for interreligious celebrations. *Muharram* with the *panja* (the five-fingered hand imprint of Fatima) inspired Shi'a Muslims to commemorate the "five pure souls" of Muḥammad's family and, according to J. Assayag (2004, 77), inspired Hindus to commemorate the Pāṇḍavas of the → *Mahābhārata*. Anniversaries of saints' deaths (*ʿurs*) at local *dargāh*s also invite interreligious celebration. Local demonologies often present not nationalistic narratives supplied by pro-Hindu or Islamist groups but more collective pneumatologies in which Hindus and Muslims alike are engaged in struggle against outside forces, manifest as *bhūta*s and *preta*s (see → *asura*s), → *yakṣa*s, and *jinn*s, who seek the destruction of entire local precincts (Assayag, 2004, 101). Ritual exchanges in neighborhood *dargāh*s are often more than mere ritual propitiation to particular demonic forces; they exorcise divisive nationalist and communalist rhetorics that tear at local communities. The effects of local Sufi orders, such as the Qādirīs, Rifāʿīs, and Jalālīs, on interreligious exchanges are immeasurable, especially as insulation from bifurcating nationalist programs. J. Assayag recorded one local teashop patron having quoted Gandhi, "*rām and rahīm ek hai!*" – "Ram and Allah as mercy are one" – adding that "God is One, whether He is a Hindu or a Muslim!" (Assayag, 2004, 152). J. Assayag cites this sort of shared, fluid religiosity as a major factor in mitigating communalisms in the years since Ayodhya, driven by the Shiv Sena and others, with at least one Hindu–Muslim conflict having broken out in 1984 over the naming of the new square in Belgaum: Jinnah Chowk, favored by Muslims, vs. Vir Savarkar Chowk, favored by Hindus (Assayag, 2004, 226ff.). Follow-up riots ensued over a *gaṇeśacaturthī* procession in 1991 and a *ramaḍān* celebration in 1992, including at least two bombings. Further occasional clashes in 1994, 1995, and beyond occurred at sporadic intervals. Locals, along with a journalist from the *Indian Express* (Oct 19, 1992), however, placed blame not on religion but on other political factors (Assayag, 2004, 229). J. Assayag suggests that convergence – "confluence" – is a steady state in relations between Hindus and Muslims in South India in the modern period.

C.J. Fuller, in his account of village and urban life in Karnataka, especially the village of Rampura, points to a perennial fluidity between living Hindu communities and Muslim communities that is "old" and "deep rooted." He draws attention to rhythms of ritual life that usually readily admit Hindu and Muslim participation in each other's rituals. He draws sharp distinctions between these fluid religious identities at the local level and how the "Ayodhya dispute was being blatantly exploited by politicians" (Fuller, 1992, 260) who were touring India peddling xenophobia and "inflammatory oratory" (Fuller, 1992, 261). Still, he attempts to show the relatively insulated nature of "popular Hinduism" in places like Karnataka from "textual Hinduism," at least insofar as local religious practitioners take sacred texts as only one part of religious practice and identity making. C.J. Fuller points to religious convergences at *navarātri* and *daśaharā* festivals in Mewar and Mysore as important yearly manifestations of Hindu–Muslim unity. While the militarism of these two festivals might become a useful tool in the grab bag of *hindutva* politics, C.J. Fuller paints a more robust local picture, with the local court assembly (*darbār*) as one based on idealized Hindu–Muslim egalitarianism in many Mughal courts.

Tamil Nadu

The effects of early Arab traders were felt in Tamil port cities as well. Many Muslims in Tamil Nadu have been known by the Tamil word *marakkāyar*, shipmen (Narayanan, 2002, 75). Others claim indigenous descent, having converted in the 7th and 8th centuries, and assert pride in being both Tamil and Muslim. Many Tamil-speaking Muslims have appropriated and made tremendous contributions to Tamil literature. These influences began early. V. Narayanan notes a possible Arabic inscription on a small mosque in Thiruchirapalli dating to 738 ce. Early in the 8th century, Muslim traders were using ports in Tamil Nadu as way stations en route to Lanka and Southeast Asia. Early Arab traders, cosmopolitan themselves, would have encountered a Chola Empire (9th–13th cents.) with complex, layered streams of urban and rural cultures, including, according to K.A. Sastri, at least three major types of local governance: *ūr, capai* (Skt. *sabhā*), and *nakaram* (Skt. *nagara*) – egalitarian landed village, Brahman assembly, and trader and merchant locality, respectively (Sastri, 1958, 158). These local governances often would have had a headman having been given the final word. Similar complexity shaped the Pandyas (13th–15th cents.), who finally gave way to an extended arm of the Delhi Sultanate under the Madurai Sultanate (1335–1378), only to give way to the suzerainty of Vijayanagara at the dawn of the modern period.

Though perhaps having enjoyed more peaceful Hindu–Muslim relations than any of the other South Indian states up to and including the modern era, Tamil Nadu did see – even amid union under early commercial concerns – some clashes between Hindus and Muslims. Under the aegis of the Delhi Sultanate, the Madurai Sultanate under Malik Kāfūr (r. 1296–1316) sacked Hoysala and Pandya strongholds and attacked reaches farther south, laying the groundwork for local sultanates (Sastri, 1958, 220ff.). The years of aggression and eventual overthrow of the Madurai Sultanate in 1378 mark one of the few epochs of violence between Hindus and Muslims in Tamil Nadu. They also mark one of the seminal events that gave rise to the power of the Vijayanagara Empire (Sastri, 1958, 256). That this interlude of violence stands as one of the few examples in Tamil history gives testimony to the fact that the two cultures – Hindu and Islamic – enjoyed much greater convergence than division. Complex Tamil literatures, families of religious practices, and social/political alliances also testify to this.

Tamil rulership has been cast in an epic – even if somewhat indomitable – mode, as rulership drew upon and spilled over into growing literary bodies of literature. Some royal literatures were uniquely Tamil, and some were blatant cooption of Sanskritic literatures, but nearly all were unmistakably Tamil in aesthetic sensibilities. The vernacularization of Hindu epics that took place largely from the 13th to the 16th century left considerable room for politicization of mythemes reflecting the crisis of non-Indic cultural interpenetration. S. Pollock notes early Chola use of *Rāmāyaṇa* imagery/mythemes in a growing South Indian interreligious cosmopolitanism (Pollock, 1993, 268). Chola bronzes of Kōtaṇṭa Rāma – found in Thanjavur district during the reign of Āditya (Tam. Ātitta Cōḻaṉ; r. 871–907) – perhaps evidence a reification of Kampaṉ's *Irāmāvatāram*, either as having been influenced by Kampaṉ or as influencing Kampaṉ (9th–12th cents.). *Rāmāyaṇa* imagery was employed alongside *Mahābhārata* and → Kṛṣṇa -cycle imagery (Pollock, 1993, 269). Yet the "othering" of "Yāvana" Muslims was not as clear-cut for the Cholas, insofar as "others" were perhaps not just Muslims from the North but the Sinhalese (Pollock, 1993, 283). Many of these early literatures echoed with a certain antinomian anti-Brahmanic Dravidianism as well (see → Hinduism and Dravidian identity). Although al-Bīrūnī points to a relative antagonism among Muslims to the Hindu "other" in the medieval period, S. Pollock points beyond *Rāmāyaṇa* imagery to evidence of some peaceful coexistence between Hindus and Muslims, even as the Tamil lands themselves were literarily sacralized.

G. Spencer points to an early sacralization of Tamil lands under Śaiva hymnody. One of the earliest incubators of → *bhakti* (Tam. *patti*) devotionalism in the subcontinent, Tamil literary cultures poured forth with → Nāyaṉār Śaiva (and → Āḻvār Vaiṣṇava) religious effulgence that often linked landscape with interior geography and exterior, worldly political and social happenings. G. Spencer notes the 7th-century Appar – one "father" of → Śaiva Siddhānta – and his *Tēvāram* hymns that sung praises linking the Thanjavur landscapes and the Naṭarāja Temple at Chidambaram with Rājarāja I's reign (r. 985–1014; Spencer, 1970, 234). G. Spencer notes that these oral traditions became important mediators not only in Dravidian Tamil encounters with Brahmanic, Sanskritic cultures from the north but also as a means of dissemination of regional symbols and collective pride in encounters with other cultures.

These complex "epic" Tamil cultures were insulators from the growing suzerainty of Muslim cultures and were open to them, particularly as partners in a growing resistance to hegemonic Brahmanic religious and cultural influences. Even on the eve of English colonial dominance and the

Anglo-Mysore Wars, religio-cultural conflict and convergence were on display throughout Tamil Nadu. C. Branfoot draws attention to the Nayakas of Madurai (r. 1300–1779), feudatories of Vijayanagara, and how their patronage, which allowed the expansion of a small cave temple, forced rapprochement with local Muslims who held the site to be sacred. Pandyan dynasties had begun building cave temples in Thiruparamkundram in southern Tamil Nadu in the 6th century, but 10th-century developments in structural temples created possibilities for expansion of earlier cave temples. Similar to intertextual negotiability, construction of temples and temple expansions also became a means for interreligious negotiation. Newer *maṇṭapam* (Skt. *maṇḍapa*) and *kōpuram* (Skt. *gopura*) edifices displayed Vijayanagara/Nayaka greatness and, in Thiruparamkundram, opened interreligious mediation over the identity of one particular deity, → Murukaṉ, the patron deity of Tamil lands (Branfoot, 2003, 148). This very site was the royal center of the Madurai Sultanate, with the *dargāh* of Sulṭān Sikandar Šāh (d. 1377) located at the summit of the hill cresting the temple. C. Branfoot argues that the site is important in that Ibn Baṭṭūṭa identified Thiruparamkundram as the center of the Madurai Sultanate, not Madurai itself (Branfoot, 2003, 155). Tamil Muslims refer to the hill as Cīkaṇṭarmalai (Skanda's [Iskandar's] hill), with Iskandar being a reference to Alexander the Great, heroic philosopher-king. If Indian Hindu kings were read as → *avatār*s of Rāma or Naṭarāja (see → Śiva), Tamil Muslim rulers equated themselves with the righteous ruler, Alexander. C. Branfoot recounts how identifications of the expanded temple with Skanda proved auspicious because the name of the Muslim saintly ruler buried there, Sikander (Tam. Cīkaṇṭar) – a kind of "second Alexander" – sounded remarkably similar to Iskander and bore hints of the name of the deity Skanda (Branfoot, 2003, 157), thereby creating open cultural-religious space for a Hindu–Muslim convergent sacred precinct. C. Branfoot provocatively hints that this convergence of Skanda as warrior/king/philosopher may have influenced the writing of the 16th-century Tamil version of the *Skandapurāṇa*, the *Kantapurāṇam*.

Similar convergences occur elsewhere in Tamil literature, including – according to V. Narayanan – in the 17th-century Kāppiyam (Kāvya) epic poem the *Cīṟāppuranam*, a poem that draws even more explicitly on Islamic hero/saint figures, especially Muḥammad himself. Umaṟuppulavar's (d. 1703) text blends the Arabic genre of the Sīrat al-Rasūl (biography of the prophet) with the Sanskritic genre of the → Purāṇa (narrative accounts of gods or saints), thereby offering the possibility of "shaping a vocabulary of praise and devotion shared with Muslims" (Narayanan, 2002, 79). The Tamil literary landscape – including likely usage of Kampaṉ's *Irāmāvataram* – is infused into the telling of the life of the "*avatāram*" Muḥammad. Muḥammad is described as "the light of the four Vedas" (Narayanan, 2002, 80), and the land around Mecca is described using Caṅkam landscape emotives (see → Tamil texts). The rivers of Hijaz are described as having "sandalwood…pearls…ivory…rubies radiant in three ways, [being carried] to the sea" (Narayanan, 2002, 85) and along the way feeding forests and rich farmland and ensuring the success of the Islamic rulerships and of the Muslim peoples. Though this work clearly shows general Hindu–Muslim religious and cultural convergence, V. Narayanan notes that this is a relatively rare example of the Islamic usage of Tamil – writ Hindu – genres and worldviews. This note might underscore how Tamil Muslims up to the dawn of the Anglo-Mysore Wars and after remained somewhat aloof from North Indian Muslim concerns, and often even local Hindu concerns, but might admit the possibility of eventual joint Tamil Hindu and Muslim resistance to European hegemony in the modern period. P. Richman, further exploring literary convergences, discusses Muslim writers choosing to write in the Tamil Piḷḷaittamiḻ genre – a devotional genre written about a beloved baby from the mother's perspective – including adoring pieces depicting Muḥammad as a young boy. Muslim writers would often have their work "examined" for errors and published by Hindu poets (Richman, 1993, 62). One 19th-century writer, Seyyitu Anapiyya (also known as Sayyid Hanafiyyah), author of *Napikaḷ Nāyakam Piḷḷaittamiḻ*, had his text devoted to Muḥammad examined and published by one Paracurama Mutaliyar – a worshipper of Brahmā – and his organization, Paripparama Mutiratsara Calai (Richman, 1993, 62). These literatures likely played a key role in keeping Hindu–Muslim communalisms at bay in Tamil Nadu heading into the modern period.

With the success of the Anglo-Mysore Wars, and despite underlying literary and ritual Hindu and Muslim convergences, Tamil interreligious identities sharpened under the British census beginning in the 1850s. M.S. Kumar uses the concept of the township to show that British colonial administrators, under the auspices of the British East India Company, systematically divided 18th- and 19th-century Madras into grid patterns and "black" and "white" townships. Division into black townships over and against white townships and into particular religious and occupational groupings reified colonial notions of purity and impurity with regard to religious affiliation and caste identity. Muslims were generally located in "black" sections of the metropolitan area (Kumar, 2006, 31). Black Madras – what became Georgetown in 1905 – was divided by colonial administrators along the lines of "religion, language, race, caste, and class" (Kumar, 2006, 25). Yet with religious markers under the colonial gaze, little differentiation was made between Indians as Hindus or Muslims, particularly in "black" townships. M.S. Kumar notes that some social stratification prior to the rise of colonial techniques existed, but that these categories – caste in Hindu social strata, for example – ossified under the colonial gaze and sometimes became a focal point for social – religious dissatisfaction. M.S. Kumar recounts how the dividing lines in religious communities in colonial black Madras were usually not between Hindus and Muslims but between the "root paradigms" of left-handed Śaivas and right-handed Vaiṣṇavas (Kumar, 1990, 33). Hindu–Muslim relations seemed lost in the wash of these larger caste concerns. Iṭaṅkai ("left hand") and Valaṅkai ("right hand") caste groups fought not with Muslims but with each other not only over issues that included merchant and craftspeople territoriality and over work for the empire but also over temple endowments, temple access, equitable housing, and the like (Kumar, 1990, 38–39). Although M.S. Kumar argues that such divisions were in part a holdover from intercaste and interreligious competitions in the Vijayanagara Empire, he holds that communal outbreaks were exacerbated by the effects of colonial census and other administrative techniques.

Even while the case of colonial Madras may be true, M. Mines explains how some northern Tamil Muslims have emerged from "harmonious syncretism" (Mines, 1975, 404) with neighboring Tamil Hindus into a process of Islamization that pushes Muslim identifiers against Hindu identities. Noting the importance of local custom in Islam, M. Mines observes that, unlike much of India, Muslims in Tamil Nadu have been seen as "well integrated acceptors" (Mines, 1975, 405). Coming from an ethos of "mercantilism and integration" (Mines, 1975, 406) – taking pride in Muslim contributions to Tamil literature and culture – Muslims in northern Madras city recently have demurred toward Islamization. This has included a growing preference for Urdu language and literature, particularly in the southeastern suburb Pallavaram. M. Mines notes a growing preference for Deobandī Muslims as reciters in mosques. Whatever the imaginings of Islamic orthodoxy in these precincts, Sufism – especially Qādirī Sufism – remains influential among Tamil Muslims, including in Pallavaram. Yet M. Mines notes that pragmatic mercantilism continued to push Tamil Muslims together with Hindu neighbors. Nationalist politics, including anemic support for the Muslim League, has had little lasting effect even among those interested in Islamization. "Instead, Muslim political behavior to some extent parallels that of the Hindus" (Mines, 1975, 409) with many Muslims having sided as Dravidian with their fellow Hindu statesmen and stateswomen in parties like the Dravida Munnetra Kazhagam (DMK; Dravidian Progress Federation). Many Tamil Muslims carry these interreligious interests and attitudes back to villages. M. Mines recounts how, contrary to Islamized identities in Pallavaram, many return to villages like Edaikottai, near Madurai, with an eye toward participation in annual Sufi *ʿurs* celebrations, the performances of which usually include not only Hindu symbolisms in the guise of devotion to ʿAbd al-Qādir al-Jīlānī but also joint Hindu–Muslim participation in most of the important events of the celebration.

Relatedly, I. Ahmad notes that the "rise of fundamentalism" (1982, 1737) in the 1980s, and a growing economic prowess of Muslims in post-Partition Tamil Nadu, corresponded with a Hindu concern in Tamil Nadu over conversion and reconversion between Hindus and Muslims. Of concern for Hindus are conversions of Scheduled Castes to Islam, including an infamous mass conversion at Meenakshipuram in 1981. He draws less on foreign inducement as reason for conversion but more on the idea that Tamil Muslims are less likely than their northern cousins to be locked in a mindset of being "frustrated and backward," which makes conversion more attractive as a religious option (Ahmad, 1982, 1738). He argues that Scheduled Castes would be interested in negotiating with North Indian Hindu nationalistic concerns, but also would be interested in conversion into healthy communities with many possibilities for uplift – socially, economically, religiously, or otherwise. He notes that this might be a logical response to the trauma of Partition for Scheduled Castes in Tamil Nadu.

M. Hancock has shown, however, that Hindu nationalist political parties have been somewhat active in Tamil Nadu, beginning in the 1980s. Following the efforts at conversion and reconversion discussed in I. Ahmad, M. Hancock shows that *hindutva* politics continued not only with regard to Scheduled Caste concerns but also with wider concerns – beyond Ayodhya too – over Hindu arts and culture, often clothing them in feminine religious idioms and women's upper-caste concerns. One such effort, a 1983 three-day Hindu Arts Festival in Madras, under the patronage of Jayendra Saraswati, *śaṅkācārya* of Kanchipuram, cast as "*kalāccāram*" (culture), included "textually mediated artistic and scientific knowledge" (Hancock, 1995, 910). Another group, Jan Kalyan, also led by Saraswati, but with many → Smārta women in leadership roles as well, staged several domestic and public → *pūjā*s to Lakṣmī (→ Śrī Lakṣmī) in an effort to promote caste equality, "merit," and "intelligence" about proper Hindu ways of living. M. Hancock sees this as a way to import *hindutva* ideologies into the home, into the marital relationships between Hindu wives and husbands, and into Hindu public life in Tamil Nadu. In post-Partition India, these concerns placed considerable emphasis on anti-Muslim ideologies, whether spoken or unspoken, insofar as they were efforts to forge a rediscovered and reunited Hindu India for Hindus. While the Bharatiya Janata Party (BJP) and the Rashtriya Swayamsevak Sangh (RSS) have enjoyed less success, the Vishwa Hindu Parishad (VHP) has done moderately well in Tamil Nadu since the 1980s at pushing these cultural agendas. M. Hancock notes that traditional Tamil Hindu identity has usually been suspicious of northern Indo-Aryan Hindus and even many Tamil Brahman groups who were seen as "early Aryan conquerors of the southern populations" (Hancock, 1995, 908). Yet, "confrontational tactics of nationalists in Kerala and the related successes of the BJP in Andhra Pradesh and Karnataka... indicate that Hindu nationalism does have bases in the south" (Hancock, 1995, 908). Only rarely has the VHP found receptivity in Tamil Nadu over general ritual issues like the *rām śilā pūjā* push to produce blessed bricks for the construction of a Rām temple in Ayodhya. M. Hancock notes that

> [t]hese combined efforts [in the 1980s] demonstrated that Hindutva when filtered through religious practice could be made attractive and even familiar to Tamils in ways that the Aryan imagery of the RSS could not. (Hancock, 1995, 909)

Yet D. Mines has shown that nationalist signs, ideologies, and forms are more often than not coopted at the village level in Tamil Nadu in order to be used as tools to solve local problems (Mines, 2002, 59). Drawing as she does the observation that the "nation" is enacted locally, she goes on to describe how local disputes over ritual access to religious processions and perceived caste difference often become the pretext for the usage of nationalist rhetorics and ritual performances that opine national identity while also mediating socioreligious positions locally. Very few eruptions of Hindu–Muslim interreligious violence have accompanied this mixed picture of the rise of pro-Hindu nationalism in Tamil Nadu.

Ethnographies in Tamil communities continue to present a picture of tolerance and convergence. J. Pandian provides a picture of the Labbai (Tam. Lappai) of Pulicat, a small community of perhaps Arab and perhaps Dutch Tamil-speaking Muslims with good Hindu–Muslim relations. Having traced their lineages back to some of the earliest seafaring trader communities who left service as *ẖādim*s (servants) at the tomb of the prophet in Medina in order to seek adventures in Asia, J. Pandian notes how the present-day Labbai exist as an isolated endogamous group. Their isolation, however, does not mean that they do not enjoy positive relations with other Muslims in Tamil Nadu, and it does not mean that they are aloof from their Hindu neighbors (Pandian, 1978, 151ff.). Rather, their pride of origin from among the *ẖādim*s of Medina and having worked closely with the Dutch in Pulicat amid the growing tide of English colonial dominance has helped them maintain social and religious distinction, while also remaining on good terms with neighbors. Although they place a premium on learning the Arabic script and in being able to read and ritually function with the *Qurʾān* – a practice that affords them religious leadership roles in and around Pulicat – they have chosen to write in Tamil, but with the Arabic script, and to remain aloof from nationalist politics and communalism.

Conclusion

Hindus and Muslims in South India in the modern period continue on paths of punctiliar division and simultaneous perennial convergence. Muslim invasions, colonial exploitation and oppression, and rising nationalisms have exacerbated Hindu–Muslim relations entering the modern period. Yet so, too, have convergent literatures, arts and architectures, medical technologies, healing traditions, mysticisms, and ritualizations helped to foster deeper Hindu–Muslim relations leading not only up through the modern period, but also to this day. Both trends – division *and* convergence – are important to understand a fuller picture of interreligious dynamics in modern South India. Hindu–Muslim communalisms have erupted in the opening decades of the 21st century in Kerala, Andhra Pradesh, Karnataka, and Tamil Nadu. But most Hindus and Muslims in individual precincts and households in South India have chosen to emphasize their collective past and have taken pride in being coopted by neither North India nor historic colonial manufacturings; they have chosen to remain – Hindu and Muslim alike – uniquely South Indian.

Bibliography

Ahmad, A., *Hyderabad after the Fall*, Hyderabad, 1988.

Ahmad, I., "Threats and Responses: Conversions in Tamil Nadu," *EPW* 17/43, 1982, 1737–1739.

Assadi, M., "Saffronisation with Upper Castes Support," *EPW* 33/12, 1998, 626–628.

Assayag, J., *At the Confluence of Two Rivers: Hindus and Muslims in South India*, Delhi, 2004.

Bakshi, S.R., *Gandhi and Hindu – Muslim Unity*, New York, 1987.

Bayly, C.A., *Indian Society and the Making of the British Empire*, Cambridge UK, 1988.

Bayly, S., "Hindu Kingship and the Origin of Community: Religion, State and Society in Kerala, 1750–1850," *MAS* 18/2, 1984, 177–213.

Branfoot, C., "The Madurai Najakas and the Skanda Temple at Tirupparankundram," *ArO* 33, 2003, 146–179.

Copland, I., "'Communalism' in Princely India: The Case of Hyderabad, 1930–1940," *MAS* 22/4, 1988, 783–814.

Dunn, R., *The Adventures of Ibn Battuta: A Muslim Traveler of the Fourteenth Century*, Berkeley, 2005.

Eaton, R., *India's Islamic Traditions, 711–1750*, Oxford, 2004.

Flueckiger, J., *In Amma's Healing Room: Gender and Vernacular Islam in South India*, Bloomington, 2006.

Fuller, C.J., *The Camphor Flame: Popular Hinduism and Society in India*, Princeton, 1992.

Gabriel, T., *Hindu-Muslim Relations in North Malabar: 1498–1947*, New York, 2006.

Gist, N., "Religion and Society in South India," *TMS* 19/2, 1957, 61–70.

Guha, S., "The Politics of Identity and Enumeration in India c. 1600–1990," *CSSH* 45, 2003, 148–167.

Halliburton, M., "Rethinking Anthropological Studies of the Body: Manas and Bōdham in Kerala," *AmAn* 104/4, 2002, 1123–1134.

Hancock, M., "Hindu Culture for an Indian Nation: Gender, Politics, and Elite Identity in Urban South India," *AE* 22/4, 1995, 907–926.

Hartmann, H., "Changing Political Behavior in Kerala," *EPW*, 3/1–2, 1968, 163–178.

Kumar, M.S., "Idioms, Symbolism and Divisions: Beyond the Black and White Towns in Madras, 1652–1850," in: S. Raju, M.S. Kumar & S. Corbridge, eds., *Colonial and Post-colonial Geographies of India*, New Delhi, 2006, 23–48.

Luther, N., *Hyderabad: A Biography*, Oxford, 2006.

Miller, R., *Mappila Muslims of Kerala: A Study in Islamic Trends*, Madras, 1992.

Mines, D., "Hindu Nationalism, Untouchable Reform, and the Ritual Production of a South Indian Village," *AE* 29/1, 2002, 58–85.

Mines, M., "Islamisation and Muslim Ethnicity in South India," *Man.NS* 10/3, 1975, 404–419.

Naidu, R., *Old Cities, New Predicaments: A Study of Hyderabad*, Newbury Park, 1990.

Nair, J., "Representing Labour in Old Mysore Kolar Fields Strike of 1930," *EPW* 25/30, 1990, 73–86.

Narayanan, V., "Religious Vocabulary and Regional Identity: A Study of the Tamil *Cirappuranam*," in: D. Gilmartin & B. Lawrence, eds., *Beyond Turk and Hindu: Rethinking Religious Identities in Islamicate South Asia*, New Delhi, 2002, 74–97.

Nizami, K.A., *Religion and Politics during the Thirteenth Century*, Oxford, 2002.

Pandian, J., "Hindu Caste System and Muslim Ethnicity: The Labbai of a Tamil Village in South India," *EH* 25/2, 1978, 141–157.

Pinault, D., *The Shiites: Ritual and Popular Piety in a Muslim Community*, New York, 1992.

Pollock, S., "Ramayana and Political Imagination in India," *JAS* 52/2, 1993, 261–297.
Prasad, D., *Social and Cultural Geography of Hyderabad City: A Historical Perspective*, New Delhi, 1986.
Raj, S., *Medievalism to Modernism: Socio-economic and Cultural History of Hyderabad – 1869–1911*, Mumbai, 1987.
Richman, P., "Veneration of the Prophet Muhammad in an Islamic Piḷḷaittamiḻ," *JAOS* 113/1, 1993, 57–74.
Rothgery, E., "Generating and Mediating Religious Identities: Islamic Healing Rituals Shared by Hindus and Muslims in the *Dargāhs* of Hyderabad, India," diss., University of Iowa, 2008.
Sastri, K.A., *A History of South India: From Prehistoric Times to the Fall of Vijayanagar*, Oxford, 1958.
Siddiqi, M., *The Bahmani Sufis*, Delhi, 1989.
Smith, F., *The Self Possessed: Deity and Spirit Possession in South Asian Literature and Civilization*, New York, 2006.
Spencer, G., "Sacred Geography of the Tamil Shaivite Hymns," *Numen* 17/3, 1970, 232–244.
Speziale, F., "Soufisme et sciences médicales en Inde," diss., École des hautes études en sciences sociales Paris, 2002.
Srinivas, T., *Winged Faith: Rethinking Globalization and Religious Pluralism through the Sathya Sai Baba Movement*, New York, 2010.
Talbot, C., "Inscribing the Other, Inscribing the Self: Hindu-Muslim Identities in Pre-colonial India," *CSSH* 1995, 692–722.

Eric Rothgery

Hinduism and Jainism

Jainism emerged around the 6th or 5th century BCE in the Gaṅgā basin of eastern India as a non-Brahmanical renunciatory tradition that advocated a strongly ascetic regimen as the means to obtain omniscience and liberation from rebirth. By approximately the 5th century CE the Jain community had bifurcated into two sectarian groups still in existence today, the Śvetāmbaras (whose male renunciants wear white robes) and the Digambaras (whose male renunciants are naked). Scholarly discussion of the relationship between Hinduism and Jainism has regularly evinced a tendency to be based on essentialized, ahistorical models of these two traditions, and in general a subordinate role has been assigned to the Jains that takes little account of the distinctive nature of their contribution to the religious culture of South Asia. This role is presented as deriving from processes, ill defined as such but variously styled as adoption, appropriation, or borrowing, whereby Hindu modes of practice and textuality have come to be domesticated among the Jains, with any connection between the two communities being viewed as unidirectionally stemming from Hinduism.

This "borrowing" interpretation can be seen at its most inadequate when considering the phenomenon of → *bhakti* in Jainism. Until recently, *bhakti* has almost invariably been taken to be a devotional idiom that is at variance with Jainism's strongly renunciatory ethos, and it has accordingly been concluded that the tradition was obliged to appropriate devotionalism in a weakened form from Hinduism as a concession to the laity. Yet the archaeological and textual evidence makes clear that Jainism had a rich and developed devotional culture in which renunciants and lay people alike participated from early 1st millennium CE and that rather than being influenced by Hinduism, the Jains were in fact expressing their religiosity in a common South Asian style whose ultimate origins are unidentifiable in historical or sectarian terms (Cort, 2002). As J.E. Cort puts it with regard to the festive dimensions of Hinduism and Jainism,

> Clearly, there has been much interaction historically between Hindu and Jain festivals, and between Hindu and Jain understandings of the same festivals. But I would hesitate to say that the Hindu festivals are necessarily the older ones, and that the Jain festivals are mere borrowings. The Hindu ritual calendar itself gives clear evidence of the accretive nature of Hinduism, as myriad local and sectarian traditions have interacted. Festivals evolve over time and in some case such as Dīvālī the Jain interpretation of the festival is as old as Hindu interpretations. Borrowings and interactions over time have been in multiple directions. (Cort, 2001, 144–145)

No doubt the Jains have at times consciously taken over aspects of Hindu religious culture for their own purposes. A good example is the epic and puranic narratives of → Kṛṣṇa, which were heavily Jainized throughout the medieval period with the aim of both appropriating and devalorizing a significant Hindu deity in the interests of establishing Jainism's superiority. Concrete examples of Jain influence on Hinduism are less easy to identify, but this may simply reflect an unwillingness to look for them. The recent suggestion that the Vaiṣṇava system of ten → *avatāra*s of → Viṣṇu (nine plus one in the future) may have developed under the influence of the nine *vāsudeva*s, heroic figures who according to Jain tradition appear in sequence during every time cycle, may not find ready acceptance among scholars of Hinduism, but it might at least suggest that mutual interaction could well be a more productive model for assessing the historical connections between Hinduism and Jainism than merely positing Jain borrowing (Geen, 2009, 95–97).

Stereotypes

Scholarly willingness to view Jainism throughout history as a kind of eccentric junior partner to Hinduism's dominant agency can be regarded as an echo of traditional Hindu views that are traceable in various forms to the early 1st millennium CE and are still to some extent encountered today. This would see the Jains as outsiders or, in Sanskrit parlance, *nāstika*, rejecting the authority of the → Veda and being unwilling to enact fully the hierarchical requirements of society. At the same time, the Jains as "other" could be neutralized by identifying them as simply one component, or caste, within society that might worship different deities (in this case, the *jinas* or *tīrthaṅkaras* – the saving teachers – from whom Jainism takes its name), possess its own scriptural corpus, and support distinctive types of renunciant, but was nonetheless Hindu to all intents and purposes.

The Jains for their part were not slow to develop their own stereotypical images of Hinduism as a religion centered on an irrational mythology that required propitiation, frequently involving blood sacrifice, of licentious and immoral deities whose adherents were the dupes of Brahmans who concocted nonsensical rituals with which they could exert a hold on the unwitting. Indeed, it might be held that one of the most consistent markers of Jain self-identity has been rejection of Brahman claims to social, intellectual, and ritual hegemony. No doubt a significant part of Jain social organization does involve → caste (which in the case of the Śvetāmbara sect can operate across religious boundaries and contain Vaiṣṇava Hindus). But these castes are regarded as being of human and not divine origin, unlike their Hindu counterparts, while their members are invariably of a merchant background where economic status is the main determinant factor of social position, and they are not ranked hierarchically according to perceived → purity, as in the Hindu caste system (Cort, 2001, 57–58; 2004). Furthermore, Jains reject the sacred status of rivers like the → Gaṅgā and deny any symbolic value to the cow (see → sacred animals), although like many Hindus, they will support shelters intended to protect aged or sick animals. Hindu practices, in short, are deemed by Jains to be largely superstition (*lokamūḍhatā*) and an aberrant deviation from the timeless truths of nonviolence and compassion taught by Jainism (Balbir, 2009, 822–823; Handiqui, 1968, 316–325).

However, to view the historical connections between Hinduism and Jainism in exclusively confrontational or denigratory terms would be misplaced. While it must be admitted that the Hindus have throughout history been much less preoccupied with the Jains than the Jains with the Hindus, openness and fluidity of boundaries have regularly characterized Jain interaction with Hinduism. This is very much in keeping with that South Asian religious commonality, what has been dubbed cosmopolitanism, wherein all religious traditions have tapped into the ritual procedures of others and accessed, even if in transmuted form, their perceived sources of power and channels to divinity (Carrithers, 2000; Cort, 1998).

The Ancient Period

Jainism originated as one of a number of renunciant groups, including Buddhism, that gathered momentum in the Magadha region in the east of the Gangetic basin in North India around the 6th and 5th centuries BCE. The prevalence of the principle of nonviolence (→ *ahiṃsā*) among these groups, and in particular Jainism, and their rejection of caste hierarchy have encouraged many scholars to see them as representing some sort of protest movement against the supposed excesses of vedic sacrificial ritual (see → *yajña*) and its Brahman exponents. However, this interpretation, which in its more enthusiastic manifestations often invokes as a motivating factor the "common people" or the "masses" for whom there is no significant evidence at this period, is unquestionably overstated.

A recent reassessment of this period has proposed seeing the non-Brahmanical Śramaṇa culture of what J. Bronkhorst styles "Greater Magadha" as having been markedly independent and distinct from the Veda-centered culture farther to the west and as having evolved a variety of ideas that were imported into the conceptual world of those Brahmans who migrated into and became intellectually prominent within the eastern region (Bronkhorst, 2007). While the merits of this reassessment have yet to be debated fully, it is at least uncontroversial to identify at this early period some ideas that were held in common by the Brahmans (albeit by no means all of them) and the Jains, most notably rebirth (→ *saṃsāra*) and the existence of an abiding entity (a self or soul) that moves from one birthplace to the next, the efficacy of moral action or → *karman*, and the transformative power of modes of physical and mental discipline. The Jains seem to have dealt with the socially potent institution of the *yajña*, the vedic sacrifice, in two ways: (1) outright rejection of its claims to effect, often by immolation of animals, cosmic and social integration; and (2) a symbolic recasting of its component parts. Thus an early Jain scripture, the *Uttarādhyayanasūtra*, describes how a Jain monk of untouchable (Cāṇḍāla) origin upbraids some aggressive Brahman sacrificers by claiming that the true Brahmans are Jain monks who perform a moral sacrifice, with austerity as their ritual fire, *karman* the fuel, and ethical and mental control the oblation. Such renunciants are pure not by birth, as the Brahmans claim, but through purity of action. By the medieval period, the Jains in common with many Hindu sects were to redefine *yajña* as a simple act of worship without any specifically sacrificial resonance (Dundas, 2002, 15–16; 2011, 137–138).

Jain tradition claims that Mahāvīra, the 24th *jina* of this time cycle, who can realistically be regarded as the founder of Jainism, was a Kṣatriya, a member of the warrior class, although some early texts occasionally refer to him by the Brahman clan (*gotra*) name of Kāśyapa. Mahāvīra's distancing of his teachings from Brahmanism can be gauged from his preaching in Prakrit rather than Sanskrit, and the transmission of the scriptures in this vernacular, or vernacular-based, language, which percolated into Jain liturgy and *mantraśāstra* (the branch of knowledge dealing with → *mantra*s; see below) throughout the medieval period, is an important dimension of Jainism's differentiation of itself from Brahmanism. The earliest biographies of Mahāvīra credit him with having had as his main disciples a group of 12 Brahman converts who mediated his teachings and imposed a full linguistic structure on them. Narratives dating from the mid-1st millennium CE describe how these Brahmans left a great *yajña* they were about to perform in order to follow the gods who, ignoring their sacrifice, were flying to be present at Mahāvīra's first sermon after his attainment of omniscience. There the Brahmans took renunciation from Mahāvīra after hearing him preach the doctrine of nonviolence.

Hindu–Jain Relations in Medieval India

Brahmanical/Hindu texts evince no awareness of Jainism in the centuries after Mahavīra. However, during the Gupta period, when Hindu values were given renewed prominence by royal sponsors, there can be found the beginnings of textual evidence of a more hostile attitude toward the Jains. The earliest example of this occurs in the *Viṣṇupurāṇa* (see → Purāṇas), where Viṣṇu is described as incarnating himself as a false ascetic in order to wean the demons away from the Veda and enable the gods to gain superiority over them. This false ascetic called Mayāmoha, who appears in the guise of both a Jain and a Buddhist monk, is clearly intended to encapsulate anti-Hindu tendencies. In his guise as a naked, shaven-headed Jain renunciant, Mayāmoha attempts to confuse the demons with spurious teachings about philosophical relativity akin to the Jain doctrine of *anekāntavāda* (see below) that was starting to take definitive shape at this time (Geen, 2011, 60–64).

Such stories do not necessarily betoken any general or consistently expressed Gupta antipathy toward the Jains. Thus a cave for the use of Jain monks was dedicated at the Gupta imperial cult center of Udayagiri, while inscriptions recording the commissioning of images of *jina*s by the emperor Rāmagupta have also been found in the vicinity of this site (Bakker, 2010, 463). However, the relative paucity of inscriptional and archaeological evidence for Jainism within the Gupta Empire does seem to suggest that the hostility of puranic narrative may to some extent reflect increasing social tensions between Jains and Hindus around the 4th–5th centuries CE.

Architectural remains from Gujarat from around the 5th to 8th centuries provide consistent evidence of religious coexistence between Jainism and Hinduism, with Jain and Śaiva shrines being located in close proximity to each other (Mishra, 2009, 218–221). In the south of the subcontinent, the Jains of the Digambara sect were deeply embedded within the cultural landscape of the Tamil country during the second half of the 1st millennium CE and shared many facets of religiosity with their Hindu neighbors, to the extent that hard and fast sectarian boundaries were not always easy to locate (Orr, 1999). However, this easy coexistence came to an end when the kings of the Chola dynasty sought to bolster their hegemony by linking the royal cult to Tamil Śaivism, a strategy that gradually shifted Tamil Jainism into the marginal minority position that it has occupied until today.

The Tamil poems and hymns of the Śaiva saints (→ Nāyaṉārs) such as Appar testify to a growing unwillingness to accept Jainism as an indigenous, Tamil religion, and the Jains were roundly excoriated by them for their supposedly life-denying ascetic principles. Appar was himself a convert from Jainism whose espousal of an exclusive devotional relationship with the god → Śiva is couched partly in the form of a personal narrative of rejection of the faith he had followed earlier in his life (Peterson, 1998). Perhaps the most representative work of Tamil Śaivism is the 12th-century *Periyappurāṇam* attributed to Cēkkiḷār (see → Tamil Nadu; → langues and literatures of the vernaculars). This large-scale hagiography of the 63 Śaiva saints includes a description of how Campantar was invited by pious Hindus to Madurai, the historical center of Tamil culture, in order to confront the Jains who had seduced the king of the city with their nefarious teachings. By a series of miracles establishing the superior power of Śaivism, Campantar defeated the Jains, and they suffered the penalty of being impaled en masse. While this account of a disaster visited upon the Jains most likely does not record an actual historical event and is more redolent of puranic stories of divine conquest of the demons, it does reflect the increasingly embattled position of the Jains in the south in the face of Śaivism. The story is regularly depicted in frescos in Hindu temples and has been responsible for a pervasive and long-lasting view among Tamil Śaivas of the Jains as "other" (Peterson, 1998, 180–181).

However, while Cēkkiḷār's *Periyappurāṇam* was undoubtedly intended to promote the superiority of Śaivism, it also evinces clear evidence of having been composed in partial dialogue with an earlier Jain poetic work that is one of the masterpieces of Tamil literature and testimony to the significance of Jainism's cultural presence in the South, the *Cīvakacintāmaṇi* of Tiruttakkatevār. The narrative strategy employed by Cēkkiḷār is to foreground the transformative effect of deploying the emotions, sometimes violently, in the service of devotion to Śiva, whereas by contrast in the *Cīvakacintāmaṇi*, Tirutakkatevār depicts the passions as being ultimately rejected after they have been worked out to full erotic effect in the career of the poem's Jain protagonist (Monius, 2004).

In Karnataka, Digambara Jainism with its ethos of heroic ascetic striving and moral purity proved attractive to royal houses such as the Gangas and Rashtrakutas, though it is probable that the religious identity of such aristocratic patrons was complex and did not necessarily exclude aspects of Hinduism. By the 12th century, the Jains experienced a degree of persecution at the hands of the nascent Vīraśaiva (→ Liṅgāyat) movement, with many temples being destroyed and an ensuing conversion of many members of the community to Śaivism (Dibbad, 2011).

Sanskrit

The scriptures of the Jains were written in vernacular-based literary dialects generically called Prakrit (Ardhamagadhi in the case of the Śvetāmbara sect, Shauraseni in the case of its Digambara counterpart). Throughout their history, the Jains refused to accede to the entrenched Brahmanical position that Sanskrit was the sole linguistic medium that could embody meaning and give access to reality, and they argued regularly for the authority of Prakrit as a language of learned discourse and ritual practice. However, this resistance to Sanskrit, by the beginning of the 1st millennium CE the lingua franca of intellectual debate and royal administration throughout South Asia, gradually weakened among the Jains, and its use became regular and widespread, although Prakrit was by no means jettisoned as a literary medium. The Jains produced their own Sanskrit grammars intended to rival and surpass the normative Brahmanical *Aṣṭādhyāyi* of Pāṇini (see → Sanskrit texts; → language and linguistics), with notable examples being the *Jainendravyākaraṇa* of Pūjyapāda (c. 6th cent.), who strove to be even more concise than Pāṇini, and the *Siddhahemaśabdānuśāsana* of Hemacandra (12th cent.), still in use by Śvetāmbara monks today. Possible tensions in respect to the competing merits of Sanskrit and Prakrit can be seen in the hagiographies of Siddhasena Divākara (c. 7th cent.). According to these sources, this Brahman convert to Jainism remained so attached to Sanskrit learning that he proposed that the Jain scriptures be translated into that language, for which arrogance he was exiled from the monastic community for 12 years (Dundas, 1996, 142–149).

Philosophy

Siddhasena Divākara wrote important treatises on logic and philosophy in Sanskrit, but he was not the earliest Jain writer to use that medium. Umāsvāti's *Tattvārthasūtra* (of which there are two slightly differing sectarian recensions) was composed around the 4th century CE as a statement of Jainism's basic doctrinal principles. The fact that Umāsvāti chose not only to use Sanskrit for this work, but also to couch it in conformity to the genre of the → Sūtra, a short statement embodying an axiom, clearly exemplifies both

Jainism's identity as an independent intellectual system and its willingness to engage with Brahmanical systems of learning, for at this time a range of nascent Hindu philosophical schools had also produced foundational Sūtra texts summing up their doctrinal positions. Although dating is obscure, it seems likely that the *Tattvārthasūtra* was composed after and in emulation of some of these Hindu Sūtra texts.

Hindu philosophy, as manifested in the Sūtra codifications and the large amount of commentary literature that they generated, was highly diverse, and the Jains developed various strategies of interaction with and rejection of the teachings of their ideological opponents. At the most basic level, Jain philosophers criticized Brahmanical thinkers for espousing a reductionist ontology that would interpret reality in terms of eternal entities such as the *ātman* and → *brahman* without taking into account the manifest impermanence underlying existence and the modifications that all objects necessarily undergo. The first attempt by a Jain writer to formulate a fully developed "theory of manypointedness" (*anekāntavāda*) by specific reference to Hindu (as well as Buddhist) conceptual schemes was Mallavādin, whose dating is uncertain but may be around the 6th century CE. His *Dvādaśāranayacakra* attempted to integrate a wide range of schools and teachings into an overarching structure corresponding to the Jain model of seven viewpoints or perspectives (*naya*). This method of both appropriating and distancing Hindu philosophical schools by demonstrating the limitations of their analysis of reality was to remain standard throughout Jainism's history. It may be added that Mallavādin is also noteworthy for having preserved quotations from many otherwise lost works, and his testimony is of great value for scholarly attempts to reconstruct the early development of Hindu philosophical systems such as → Sāṃkhya (Houben, 2008).

The perspectivist attitude toward other religious paths was based on Jainism's claim to represent an all-inclusive synthesis of other philosophical standpoints that on their own terms could be deemed to be ultimately flawed. Studying alternative doctrines and grasping their limited nature compared to Jainism was a significant means of confirming the truth of the Jain path. No doubt as a result of this, Jain monastic intellectuals were prominent authors of doxographies in which the soteriological standpoints of various opponents were recorded in a comprehensive and dispassionate fashion. The most notable exponent of this methodology was Haribhadra (c. 8th cent.), who described in his *Lokatattvanirṇaya* his attitude toward Hindu teachers and gods thus:

> I have no predilection for Mahāvīra, nor do I hate teachers such as Kapila. What one must do is embrace a teacher whose words are reasonable. He who has no fault at all, he who has all the good virtues – to him I pay homage – be it Brahmā, Viṣṇu or Maheśvara. (Qvarnström, 1999, 180; translation slightly altered by author)

Of the various Hindu philosophical schools, it was Pātañjala → Yoga to which the Jains showed the most sympathy, no doubt because its basic orientation toward disciplining the senses coincided with Jainism's ascetic idiom. The eightfold structure of practice formulated by Patañjali in the *Yogasūtra* was clearly imitated by Haribhadra in his own model of Jain yogic stages to which he assigned the names of goddesses (Chapple, 2003, 15–38). In the 17th century, Yaśovijaya, the last significant Jain intellectual of the premodern period, singled out Patañjali as an example of a non-Jain who had shaken off delusion and whose teachings could because of their fundamentally sound soteriological trajectory be regarded as being in consonance with those of Jainism. Yaśovijaya in fact composed an important, unnamed commentary on the *Yogasūtra*, which has, however, remained little studied (Dundas, 2007, 158–160). The Sāṃkhya school, which aligned itself with Yoga, no doubt shared Jainism's broadly dualist interpretation of reality. However, many of its tenets, such as denial of agency to the soul, the eternalist claim that effect inheres in cause (*satkāryavāda*), and the eventual espousal of a theistic cosmology, were uncongenial to the Jains (Granoff, 1999). The → Nyāya school could also be rejected by the Jains because of its theistic and creationist tendencies (van den Bossche, 1998).

The Hindu philosophical school that struck at the very basis of Jain claims to authority was → Mīmāṃsā. From its beginnings as a textual entity, Jainism had claimed that its great teachers, the *jina*s, were in possession of omniscience, that is to say, complete knowledge of all entities and their states of being across time and space. Attainment of this state of cognitive perfection validated the truths of Jain teachings and located authority in human beings. In contrast, the great 7th-century Mīmāṃsaka Kumārila (who was in fact largely arguing against the Buddhists rather than the Jains) denied that such a state that transcended the passions and other psychological flaws was possible for any human to reach, and that accordingly the Veda – eternal, self-sufficient, and without any authorial point of origin – was the only source of correct religious injunction and prohibition. Jain teachers such as Haribhadra were to argue against the Mīmāṃsā in a consistent fashion, asserting that

(1) the existence of an omniscient being can be inferred, even if he or she cannot actually be perceived, and is supported by the testimony of the Jain scriptures;

(2) the authority of the Veda is open to question owing to likely flaws in its transmission and uncertainties with regard to the basis of its meaning, since it claims to be both eternal and self-revealing;

(3) logic dictates that the Veda must have some origin, specifically the organ of speech, which dictates that its status is created and non-eternal, a situation that could only be confirmed by an omniscient person; and

(4) the Veda itself refers to such all-knowing (*sarvavid*) individuals (Qvarnström, 2006).

The Mīmāṃsā critique of omniscience aside, Brahmanical ripostes to Jain teachings were not common or strongly developed. Paradoxically, the Hindu philosophical school that engaged most regularly with the Jains, namely → Vedānta, was largely ignored by these particular opponents. One of the earliest Jain doxographies, the *Dvātriṃśikā* of Siddhasena Divākara (6th cent.), does in fact record a version of a proto-Vedānta model of self and reality, but only a few Jain writers seem to have been much concerned with later developments in this school (van den Bossche, 1997; Qvarnström, 2003). However, the leading Vedānta theologians, → Śaṅkara and → Rāmānuja, both give accurate accounts of Jain teachings before singling out two aspects for specific criticism, namely the sevenfold ontological judgment styled *syādvāda* (the "doctrine of maybe") and the view that the dimensions of the soul are coterminous with the body that houses it. For the Vedāntins *syādvāda* is illogical in its imprecision in that it requires accepting the conjunction of opposites, while the soul, rather than being finite, can only be regarded as being all-pervasive (Shastri, 2003).

The Dvaita (dualist) school of Vedānta founded in the 13th century by → Madhva also formulated criticisms of the foregoing type. However, Madhva's homeland of south Karnataka was a stronghold of Digambara Jainism, and a good case has been made for early Dvaita Vedānta having been influenced by Jain thinkers in areas such as epistemology and its conception of the hierarchical ranking of souls (Zydenbos, 1991). Another Hindu philosophical school that flourished in South India, → Śaiva Siddhānta, evinces some parallels and interaction with Jainism in respect to the mechanism of karmic bondage and the status of liberated souls (Davis, 1998, 220–221).

Holy Places

Jainism's extensive network of holy places (→ *tīrtha*) has since the medieval period included locations that are also important in Hindu tradition. Thus Mount Kailāsa, called by the Jains Aṣṭāpada, was regarded as the site of the attainment of → liberation by the first *jina* Ṛṣabha and his son, the universal emperor (*cakravartin*) Bharata. Ayodhyā, in Hinduism the capital of → Rāma, was called by the Jains Vinītā or Sāketa and held to be the birthplace of two *jina*s, as well as being the capital of the aforementioned Bharata. Kāśī (Varanasi) and its vicinity were regarded as having been the birthplace of four *jina*s of the current *avasarpiṇī* time cycle, and there is archaeological evidence of a Jain presence in the holy city between the 6th and 11th centuries (Sharma & Ghosal, 2006).

None of the aforementioned sites is of major significance for Jain pilgrims. Of those of the greatest importance today, Mount Girnar in eastern Gujarat, regarded as the site of the omniscience and liberation of the 22nd *jina* Neminātha, was already known in the → *Mahābhārata* as Raivataka and associated with Kṛṣṇa and the Pāṇḍava brothers. An extensive number of Jain temples dating from the 12th century shares the mountain with Hindu shrines erected on its summit. Another Śvetāmbara pilgrimage site, Mount Abu (Arbuda) in southern Rajasthan, is famous for ornate Jain temples dating from the 11th century. According to Hindu tradition, Abu was in the 8th century the location of the ceremony whereby the Rajput clan was inducted into the Kṣatriya caste.

Satire

Puranic mythology with its richly elaborated narratives of divine violence and sexuality provided a foil with which the Jains could exercise a mordant wit at their Hindu neighbors' expense and wean their laypeople away from false doctrine. The earliest Jain satire of Hindu mythology occurs in the *Niśīthacūrṇi*, a Prakrit work written by the monk Jinadāsa in 677 CE. Here Jinadāsa recounts how a variety of disreputable representatives of the underbelly of urban society called *dhutta*, approximately "rogue," gather in a public park near Ujjain. Caught in the rain and without food, they resolve to tell stories about their own adventures: anyone who does not believe them is required to give a feast to the others, but the one who can confirm the stories by reference to parallels from Hindu scriptures need not contribute anything. In this way, a series of tall tales of fantastical events is capped by accounts of the bizarreries of Hindu cosmology and the miraculous and contradictory doings of figures such as Rāma, all of which Jinadāsa characterizes as "worldly falsehood" (Mah.Pr. *loiyamusāvādo*).

A century or so later, Haribhadra produced an expanded version of Jinadāsa's satire called *Dhūrtākhyāna* (The Rogues' Tales). This is noteworthy not only for the fun Haribhadra has at Hinduism's expense, but also because it apparently preserves the earliest version of the myth of Śiva's decapitation of → Brahmā. Other ironic mockeries of Hindu mythology and Brahman pretension entitled *Dharmaparīkṣā* were written by the Digambaras Hariṣeṇa (10th cent.) and Amitagati (11th cent.; Granoff, 2009; Krümpelmann, 2004; Osier, 2005; Osier & Balbir, 2004).

Śvetāmbara Jain writers also produced polemical works largely consisting of extensive quotations from Brahmanical texts. Hemacandra's *Vedāṅkuśa* (Veda Goad; 12th cent.), which cites around 40 works from the *Ṛgveda* to the near-contemporary *Nagarapurāṇa*, was according to the colophon of the printed edition intended to give the Brahmans a slap in the face. Yet it might be added that Hemacandra was concerned not only to mock but also to demonstrate how there was an element of coincidence between Jain ethics and the dicta of many Brahman texts and thus lead Hindus away from erroneous practices such as animal sacrifice and onto the true path of Jainism (Wezler, 1993).

The Hindus were themselves not slow to caricature the Jains, particularly the supposedly antisocial practices of their renunciants, and naked monks of the Digambara sect appear as ludicrous characters in satirical plays by Brahman authors. So in Jayantabhaṭṭa's *Āgamaḍambara* (Much Ado about Religion; 9th cent.), a half-hearted Digambara monk is mocked as a typically lustful ascetic (Dezsö, 2005, 84–95), while in Kṛṣṇamiśra's *Prabodhacandrodaya* (The Rise of Wisdom Moon; 11th cent.), a Digambara is singled out for his disgustingly ghoulish appearance (Kapstein, 2009, 104–105).

The Epics

No obvious reference to the Jains can be found in the *Mahābhārata*, the Sanskrit epic that scholarship is coming to interpret as a Brahman response to the Mauryan emperor Aśoka's espousal of Buddhism. However, traces of Jain disdain for the violence regularly enacted in the epic and its attendant claims that those who die in war go straight to heaven can been seen in what appear to be parodies in the Jain scriptures of *Mahābhārata*-type battles (Dundas, 2006, 391–394). The *Mahābhārata* and the other great Sanskrit epic, the → *Rāmāyaṇa* attributed to Vālmīki, have been at the center of the Hindu imaginative world for two millennia, but it is less well known that the Jains have their own extensive versions of these poems in which the narratives are placed in a different ethical setting, stressing the working out of the consequences of actions in previous existences experienced in a Jain universe and foregrounding the ultimate value of renunciation. It is easy and convenient to explain this literary phenomenon simply as the result of a process of borrowing and adaptation by which Jain monastic intellectuals sought to defuse the pervasive religious influence of these great Hindu literary creations. However, it might be more helpful to view the Jainization of the epics as representing reenvisioned variants of these complex works rather than as being the result of mere appropriation. The fact that the *Mahābhārata* as we have it now most likely represents a Brahmanization of an earlier epic story may provide an analogous context for appreciating the Jain reception of this poem (Geen, 2009, 71). As for the *Rāmāyaṇa*, there is some evidence that the earliest Jain version, the *Paumacariya* of

Vimalasūri, was to some extent drawing on a pre- or non-Vālmīki source in respect to at least one episode in Vālmīki's epic (Smith, 2003).

The protagonists of the Sanskrit epics were integrated by the Jains into a large-scale account of the lives of the *jinas* that provides an alternative interpretation of the cosmic process to that found in Hinduism and is called by modern scholarship the "universal history." As well as describing the lives of the 24 *jinas* of this time cycle and the 12 universal emperors who appear in succession throughout this period, there are linked to them recurring triads of figures, generically called *baladeva, vāsudeva*, and *prativāsudeva*, the latter two terms suggesting that this pattern has been generalized from the Jain reconfiguration of the mythology of Kṛṣṇa-Vāsudeva (Geen, 2009). Each triad represents respectively an upright Jain who adheres to the principle of nonviolence, his half brother who engages in violence but nonetheless will be reborn as a *jina* of the next time cycle after a period in hell, and a king who despite his piety toward the *jinas* takes to evil practice and is accordingly slain by the *vāsudeva* and reborn in hell. Such a triad is represented by Rāma, Lakṣmaṇa, and Rāvaṇa (see below; Cort, 1993; Jaini, 2000, 375–428).

Works dedicated to this subject, styled Purāṇa or Carita, were composed in Sanskrit, Prakrit, and Apabhramsha over a period of almost a millennium by monks of both the Śvetāmbara and Digambara sects, with the earliest being the *Harivaṃśapurāṇa* of the Digambara Jinasena Punnāṭa, which dates from 783 CE, and the most well known being the *Triṣaṣṭiśalākāpuruṣacarita* of the Śvetāmbara Hemacandra (12th cent.). Many significant versions of the Jain *Mahābhārata* are also found in Kannada (Anacker, 2002; Bai & Zydenbos, 2007, 263–271). Jinasena Punnāṭa's *Harivaṃśapurāṇa* evinces a quadripartite thematic structure that is replicated by all the later versions of the universal history. This consists of the *Harivaṃśa*, an account of Kṛṣṇa and his family; the *Nemicarita*, an account of the 22nd *jina* Neminātha and his relations with his cousin Kṛṣṇa; the *Pāṇḍavacarita*, which recounts the story of the *Māhābhārata*; and the *Vasudevahiṇḍi*, an account of the amorous adventures of Kṛṣṇa's father Vasudeva (de Clercq, 2009b). In western India, from the 13th century, Jain poets also produced independent texts called *Pāṇḍavapurāṇa* that show a strong animus against the Śaivas and Vaiṣṇavas, with whom Jainism was competing for aristocratic and mercantile patronage (Jaini, 2000, 352–362).

Many characters of the *Mahābhārata* were assigned a reconfigured identity within the context of Jain ethics adumbrated by the universal history. One of the most instructive for appreciating the dynamics of possible intertextuality is → Draupadī, the wife of the five Pāṇḍava brothers. Draupadī's first occurrence in Jain literature is in the *Nāyādhammakahāo*, the fifth book of the Śvetāmbara scriptural canon, where a narrative prototype is given for later treatments of her. The marriage of Draupadī to the Pāṇḍavas is presented as the consequence of her actions in previous existences, firstly as Nāgaśrī, who gives food to a Jain monk, which leads to his death, and then as Sukumārikā, who had formed the resolve to enjoy the pleasures of the senses with five husbands. Draupadī's birth as wife of the Pāṇḍavas climaxes with her renunciation as a Jain nun and eventual attainment of liberation. In general, the universal history's treatment of Draupadī has been strongly influenced by the Hindu epic tradition. However, while references to rebirth in the *Mahābhārata* are extremely rare, it does uncharacteristically deal with events in Draupadī's past life that explain why she was eventually to marry five husbands, and it has been argued that the Jain narrative of Sukumārikā has in fact been assimilated into the Hindu epic (Geen, 2006).

Not central to the plot of the *Mahābhārata* but among the most famous characters in Hindu legend are the star-crossed lovers Nala and Damayantī. The many Jain retellings of this epic story focus on the strength and chastity of Damayantī as compared to the weakness of her husband Nala in order to highlight the doctrinal message that intense emotional relations are eventually transcended by renunciatory values that will bring about final deliverance (Granoff, 2011; Kelting, 2011).

The best-known portion of the *Mahābhārata*, the → *Bhagavadgītā*, was never directly reworked by medieval Jain writers, and it was generally stigmatized as an example of Hindu *hiṃsāśāstra*, a work enjoining violence, in that its central theme was Kṛṣṇa's persuading Arjuna of the necessity of fighting. However, in modern times, when the *Bhagavadgītā* has assumed an emblematic role in modern India, Jain monks have become rather more ambivalent toward it, on occasion drawing attention to its compatibility with the teachings of Jainism.

The Jains refer to Rāma by the name Padma, and so the Sanskrit name for the Jain *Rāmāyaṇa* is the *Padmapurāṇa* or *Padmacarita*. The first version of this was Vimalasūri's Maharashtri Prakrit *Paumacariya*, which was composed sometime around the 5th century CE, while the most influential and elaborate version was the *Padmapurāṇa* composed in Sanskrit by Raviṣeṇa in 678 CE.

There are a large number of Jain versions of the *Rāmāyaṇa*, and more research is required into the reasons why Jainism's enthusiastic engagement with the Rāma story differs so much from the much more fitful attitude of the Buddhists.

A consistent feature of the Jain Rāma stories is their intentness on de-Brahmanizing Valmīki's *Rāmāyaṇa* (in its final form) and presenting the main characters in strictly human rather than divine or demonic terms, while animals and demon protagonists are represented as *vidyādhara*s, wizardlike beings possessed of magic powers. Rāvaṇa is portrayed as a misguided Jain layman in the grip of the passions, who despite his great powers and piety toward the *jina*s is obliged to work out the karmic results of his actions in previous births and is reborn in hell after being killed by Rāma/Padma's brother Lakṣmaṇa, an act of violence that leads to him being reborn in hell as well. The Jain *Rāmāyaṇa*s reenvisage Rāma as unconnected with the violence and occasional chicanery that plays such an important part in Vālmīki's poem. Instead his career derives its meaning from his eventual renunciation as a Jain monk and attainment of liberation, while his wife Sītā (see → Draupadī and Sītā) also renounces to become a Jain nun. It is noteworthy that the Jains place no emphasis on Rāma's faithful monogamy, which is one of the major themes of the story for Hindus, and instead present him as originally having had a large number of wives. Despite the longevity of the Jain *Rāmāyaṇa* tradition, there is little evidence of it having influenced later Hindu versions of the story in any major way (de Clercq, 2005; Jaini, 2000, 383–389; Kulkarni, 2001, 13–83).

Ritual Culture

From its beginnings, Jain monasticism evolved a range of disciplinary rituals that are peculiar to its own ascetic-oriented idiom. However, the rituals carried out exclusively by lay people also have a distinctively Jain flavor, even if they often are formally very similar to their Hindu equivalents. Thus devotional worship of images (→ *pūjā*) in Jainism shares some family resemblances with Hindu worship but is crucially differentiated by the fact that food offerings are not redistributed among worshippers in the form of what is called in Hinduism *prasād(a)*, since the *jina*s, the main objects of Jain worship, cannot be regarded as accepting or giving material gifts (Babb, 1996, 94–96). Life-cycle rituals (→ *saṃskāras*) do not make an appearance in Jain textual codification until around the 9th century, and they evince close parallels with their Hindu counterparts. Many Jain life-cycle rites may in fact be reasonably viewed not so much as simple borrowings but as recastings of Hindu prototypes. Thus the fullest premodern textual description of a Digambara Jain funeral maintains the idiom of food offerings to dead ancestors, in the Hindu funeral an ancient component of Brahmanical ideology rejected by Jainism, but in a purely commemorative manner (Dundas, 2011).

*Mantra*s permeate all elements of Jain religious life, and they are linked with both the soteriological and the worldly realms in the same manner as in Hinduism. However, the central *mantra* found throughout Jain history, the *pañcanamaskāra* ("five homages") to the various exemplary types in Jainism (liberated souls; *arhat*s, or enlightened beings; teachers; preceptors; and monks), is different from any Hindu equivalent through being couched in Prakrit rather than Sanskrit. It is clear that Jainism borrowed extensively from the central idiom of *mantraśāstra* in South Asia, that of Śaivism, and under its influence elaborated various forms of esoteric → meditation and propitiation of *mantra* divinities (Qvarnström, 2000, 125–131; Sanderson, 2009, 243–249).

Deities

In the highly pluralist religious world of India, it is inevitable that boundaries between styles of worship and understandings of divinity were not always precisely delineated. Jain intellectuals have always been aware of this situation, although attempts to engage with it have varied. The claim of Haribhadra that one god should not be worshipped exclusively and that Jain householders should propitiate all deities in an eclectic fashion represents an idiosyncratic position, and the alternative exclusivist view that worship of what were clearly understood to be non-Jain deities could not effect any worthwhile result was the more widely held perspective (Granoff, 2000, 401–403; 2001, 109–113). The orthodox Jain position is that the only objects of worship that can advance a devotee toward liberation are the saving teachers, the *jinas*. As dead renunciants who have gained freedom from rebirth, they are no longer located in the transient world of *saṃsāra*, and so the purpose of propitiating them is not to request a boon of some kind but to bring about a transformation in the worshipper through the realization that his or her soul has the same qualities in potential form as the *jinas* and the other liberated souls.

Nonetheless, Jainism does allow for the existence of worldly deities who can be approached for assistance, and from the early medieval period, worship of goddesses has been a significant part of Jain religiosity. Indeed, a Jain image of the pan-Indian goddess → Sarasvatī from Mathura dating from 132 CE is the oldest known representation of that deity (Nagarajaiah, 2009). The fact that many of these Jain goddesses are also found in Hinduism should not lead to the conclusion that Jains are simply conforming to Hindu customs. Granted that Jain worship of a goddess such as Lakṣmī (→ Śrī Lakṣmī) does not differ in any significant way from that conducted by Hindus (understandably so, since she is a deity favored by the business community across the caste and religious divide), Jain goddesses unquestionably have their own distinctive personalities, being benevolent and nonviolent, vegetarian, without a divine male partner, and closely involved in protecting the Jain religion and its scriptures. According to tradition, fierce carnivorous Hindu clan goddesses (→ *kuladevī*) have on occasion been converted to vegetarian benevolence by the ministrations of a Jain monk. A notable example of one such goddess is Saccikā, who is the tutelary deity of the Osvāl caste and whose cult center at Osiyan in Rajasthan is patronized by Jains and Vaiṣṇava Hindus alike (Cort, 1987; Meister, 2008).

Of Hindu gods, the only one to be comfortably accommodated within Jainism was the minor figure of Indra (see → vedic gods). In the Jain scriptures, he is given the name Sakka (Skt. Śakra) and depicted as being involved in various ceremonies connected with events in the lives of the *jinas*, such as their birth. To this day, the married Jain couple who sponsor the *pancakalyāṇaka* ("five auspicious events") ceremony, when an image of a *jina* is installed temporarily, assume the role of Indra and his wife. However, for all the frequency with which Indra is depicted in Jain art, his role within the religion is not significant (Nagarajaiah, 2002).

The erotically charged mythology of Śiva ensured that this particular Hindu god could never be easily accommodated within Jainism. The earliest Jain account of Śiva in the *Āvaśyakacūrṇi* attributed to Jinadāsa is an obvious attempt to diminish his status through a combination of inclusivism and denigration. He is presented as having been born scandalously as Mahissara (Skt. Maheśvara), the offspring of a mendicant and a nun, and as having mastered a spell that then bored into his body and emerged through a hole in his forehead, foolishly regarded by the gods as representing a third eye. Mahissara subsequently killed his father (an act no doubt to be regarded as the equivalent of Śiva's slaying of Brahmā). After a scurrilous sexual career, he was killed by Pradyota, the king of Ujjain, who was assisted by a prostitute named Umā (Mehta & Chandra, 1970). Hagiographies of Śvetāmbara Jain teachers glory in their triumph over Śaivism. So Siddhasena Divākara is described as having miraculously split open a famous → *liṅga* in Ujjain to reveal an image of the *jina* within, while Hemacandra in the presence of his patron, the Caulukya monarch Kumārapāla, summoned Śiva at the great Hindu *tīrtha* of Somnāth to attest to the superiority of Jainism (Dundas, 2002). From around the 12th century, Jain monks in Gujarat and Rajasthan regularly competed for patronage with the *yogīs* of the Śaiva Nāth sect (see → Nāth Sampradāya), very often through contests in magic power. This situation is no doubt reflected in the latish *Śivapurāṇa*, which seems to have been produced in western India, when it describes how Śiva persuaded Viṣṇu to create a false teacher called Arhat, clearly a version of the Jina, who produced false teachings to delude the demons and lead their women astray (Dundas, 2000a; Jaini, 2000, 357).

The relationship between Jainism and Vaiṣṇavism and its mythology is much more involved. So, the *Bhāgavatapurāṇa* (see → Purāṇas) annexes a heretical teacher to the Hindu fold by incorporating the first *jina* of this time cycle, Ṛṣabha, as one of Viṣṇu's minor incarnations (*aṃśāvatāra*; see → *avatāra*), a category of 22 teachers who reveal the divine truth. The *Bhāgavatapurāṇa* replicates the main contours of the Jain sources for Ṛṣabha's career but also adds a markedly pro-Brahman theme by presenting the "*jina*" as a righteous king who rules in accord with the stipulations of the uppermost social class and extols their high status. This Vaiṣṇava text also includes a prophecy concerning a king Arhat who will apostatize from Hinduism, take to impure ways, and deride Brahmans. P.S. Jaini has explained this as a riposte to the *Ādipurāṇa* of the Digambara Jain monk Jinasena composed in the 9th century under the patronage of the Rashtrakuta monarch Amoghavarṣa I, whose partiality toward Jainism seems to have been at the expense of the Vaiṣṇavism into which he was born and who is accordingly a prime retrospective candidate to be King Arhat. In the *Ādipurāṇa*, Jinasena challenges the authority of the Veda and the Brahman class and presents an alternative Jain version of the world as shaped by Ṛṣabha, who promulgates the Jain scriptures as Veda, constructs a Jain Kṣatriya-oriented social order of classes with their attendant obligations (it is Ṛṣabha's son, Bharata, who creates the Brahman class), and provides a set of life-cycle rituals purged of superstition. The *Bhāgavatapurāṇa*'s narrative strategy with regard to Ṛṣabha evinces a typical South Asian inclusivism but one unprompted by any obvious sense of tolerance (Geen, 2011, 64–67; Jaini, 2000, 325–349).

Kṛṣṇa is the Hindu mythological figure, both hero and god, who features most prominently in Jain literature. Scholarship hypothesizes that the Jains first encountered him at Mathura, traditionally his birthplace, and it is indeed well known that that city is the site of a great deal of archaeological evidence for the early coexistence of Jainism and a nascent Vaiṣṇavism that was in the process of absorbing Kṛṣṇa and the Vṛṣṇi clan to which he supposedly belonged. A precise chronological location for this encounter is difficult to identify, but representations of Vāsudeva-Kṛṣṇa, his brother Balarāma, and the 22nd *jina* Neminātha, whom Jain tradition came to regard as cousins, appear around the 3rd and 4th centuries CE (Geen, 2009, 83; Schmid, 2010, 195–199). It may also be the case that the story (accepted by the Śvetāmbara sect only) of the prenatal transfer of Jina Mahāvīra's fetus from the womb of a Brahman woman to his Kṣatriya mother took shape as a result of this early interaction, since Hindu narrative beginning with the *Harivaṃśa* supplement to the *Mahābhārata* describes Balarāma as being conceived by Rohiṇī and then being transferred to Devakī's womb (de Clercq, 2009a, 51; Vemsani, 2006, 50–58). It would be unwise, however, to assign chronological priority to either of these stories.

Sporadic references to Kṛṣṇa occur in what are generally regarded as the later narrative portions of the Śvetāmbara Jain scriptural canon, and since this canon was redacted in the 5th century CE, it can be assumed that the Jains had been engaging seriously with the story of Kṛṣṇa from near the beginning of the Common Era. The various scriptural references are not always greatly developed but often relate to aspects of Kṛṣṇa that are found in the *Mahābhārata* and the *Harivaṃśa*. So he is described as being the king of Dvāravatī, born in Mathurā as the son of Vasudeva and Devakī, and as having killed Kaṃsa, the king of Mathurā, and Jarāsandha, the king of Rājagṛha. The exile of the Pāṇḍava brothers is attributed by Jain narrative to Kṛṣṇa's anger at a trick they played on him to test his strength. Jain ambivalence toward Kṛṣṇa can be seen at this early stage in the prophecy that Kṛṣṇa will be reborn in one of the seven hells and then take his final existence as the 13th *jina* in the next time cycle (Balbir, 1991, 42–43; Mehta & Chandra, 1970, 153).

The Jain scriptures do not refer to Kṛṣna's childhood miracles, but this theme was to be taken up by the many writers of the universal history as the doings of the youthful god and his relatives became integrated into this literary enterprise. It is quite clear that the Jains were working with a clear understanding of the significance of Kṛṣṇa in the *Harivaṃśa* and were consciously reworking its account of his adolescent exploits to fit into their own soteriological scheme. However, key events in the *Harivaṃśa* story are excised or virtually ignored, most notably the episode of the lifting of Mount Govardhana; episodes relating to the Hindu ideology of cosmic creation and destruction are eliminated; and Kṛṣṇa and Bālarāma are assigned a range of earlier existences, which confirms the universal history's insistence on the brothers as being participants in a world conforming to Jain ethical, spatial, and temporal understanding. In particular, the adult Kṛṣṇa became linked with the 22nd *jina* Neminātha, a narrative connection that highlights both his status as a Jain and his inferiority to Jina Mahāvīra (Couture, 2009). Kṛṣṇa's role as provider of the animals to be slaughtered at Neminātha's wedding feast (abandoned by the *jina* -to-be because of his compassionate nonviolence) is a narrative confirmation for the Jains of his status as *aviratasaṃyagdṛṣṭi*, an individual who has correct belief in Jainism's tenets but lacks the necessary discipline to enact them fully (Dundas, 2000b).

The Modern Period

→ Dayananda Sarasvati (1824–1883), the founder of the Arya Samaj, criticized the Jains for their doctrine of the uncreated nature of the universe and their inconsistency in rejecting the worship of the goddess → Durgā, when they themselves propitiated female tutelary deities. He also accused the Jains of being the first to introduce image worship into India and of engaging in *mantra*-related practices that were effectively tantric (Glasenapp, 1951, 81–83). Dayananda's anti-Jain polemic was very much redolent of his reforming agenda for Hinduism and of a kind that has seldom been repeated by modern Hindu apologists. The most renowned Hindu of modern times, Mohandas (Mahatma) → Gandhi, acknowledged the influence of the Jain Raychandbhai Mehta (also known as Shrimad Rajchandra) in his earlier life, and his views about nonviolence undoubtedly owe something to the teachings of Jainism. Gandhi's background in western Gujarat was that of the Baniyā caste, in which Jainism and Vaiṣṇavism were often near seamlessly interconnected by ethical worldview and frequent marital alliance, and a degree of syncretism between these two traditions remains identifiable today (Dundas, 2002, 264–265; Flügel, 2005).

The tendency of many Śvetāmbara Jains (much less commonly Digambara Jains) to designate themselves as Hindu that often surfaces during elections or census reckonings should not lead to the conclusion that contemporary Jains are either confused about their identity or consider their religion to be to some extent subsumed within Hinduism. As L.A. Babb puts it,

> There is no question that a division exists between Jains and Hindus as religious communities, but the boundary is not always very clear. The principal reason for this is that although Jainism can be considered a single – if internally subdivided – religious tradition, Hinduism possesses no such internal unity. Rather, it is best described as a bundle of traditions that share certain family resemblances… [I]t should be noted that some Hindu traditions actually have much in common with Jainism… [B]oth nonviolence and asceticism – values stressed by the Jains – are Hindu values as well. Furthermore, the ritual cultures of Jain and Hindu traditions are quite similar, although there are certain key differences in the way some ritual transactions are conducted and understood. The vagueness of the boundary between the two traditions is illustrated by the fact that Jains sometimes identify themselves religiously as "Hindu," especially in contexts in which politics are involved. (Babb, 2004, 143–144)

Bibliography

Anacker, S., *The Epic of Nemi (Neminātha-purāṇa) of Karṇapārya*, Shravanabelgola, 2002.

Babb, L.A., *Alchemies of Violence: Myths of Identity and the Life of Trade in Western India*, New Delhi, 2004.

Babb, L.A., *Absent Lord: Ascetics and Kings in a Jain Ritual Culture*, Berkeley, 1996.

Bai, B.N.S., & R.J. Zydenbos, "The Jaina *Mahābhārata*," in: A. Sharma, ed., *Essays on the Mahābhārata*, New Delhi, 2007, 251–273.

Bakker, H., "Royal Patronage and Religious Tolerance: The Formative Period of Gupta-Vākāṭaka Culture," *JRAS* 20/4, 2010, 461–475.

Balbir, N., "Attitudes indiennes vis-a-vis de l'animal domestique," in: N. Balbir & G.-J. Pinault, eds., *Penser, dire et representer l'animal dans le monde Indien*, Paris, 2009, 811–858.

Balbir, N., "Tīrthaṃkaras of the Future," in: M.A. Dhaky & S. Jain, eds., *Aspects of Jainology*, vol. III: *Pt. Dalsukhbhai Malvania Felicitation Volume*, Varanasi, 1991, 34–67.

Bossche, F. van den, "Jain Arguments against Nyāya Theism: A Translation of the Īśvarotthāpaka Section of Guṇaratna's *Tarka-Rahasya-Dīpikā*," *JIPh* 26/1, 1998, 1–26.

Bossche, F. van den, "Jain Arguments against Vedānta Monistic Theism: A Translation of the *Parabrahmotthāpanasthala* of Bhuvanasundarasūri," *JIPh* 25/4, 1997, 337–374.

Bronkhorst, J., *Greater Magadha: Studies in the Culture of Early India*, Leiden, 2007.

Carrithers, M.B., "On Polytropy: Or the Natural Condition of Spiritual Cosmopolitanism in India: The Digambar Jain Case," *MAS* 34/4, 2000, 831–861.

Chapple, C.K., *Reconciling Yogas: Haribhadra's Collection of Views on Yoga*, Albany, 2003.

Clercq, E. de, "The Great Men of Jainism in Utero: A Survey," in: V.R. Sasson & J.M. Law, eds., *Imagining the Fetus: The Unborn in Myth, Religion, and Culture*, New York, 2009a, 33–54.

Clercq, E. de, "The Jaina Harivaṃśa and Mahābhārata Tradition: A Preliminary Study," in: P. Koskikallio, ed., *Parallels and Comparisons: Proceedings of the Fourth Dubrovnik International Conference on the Sanskrit Epics and Purāṇas, September 2005,* Zagreb, 2009b, 399–421.

Clercq, E. de, "The Jain Rāmāyaṇa-Purāṇa: Paumacariyam-Padmacarita-Paumacariu," in: P. Koskikallio, ed., *Epics, Khilas, and Purāṇas: Continuities and Ruptures: Proceedings of the Third Dubrovnik International Conference on the Sanskrit Epics and Purāṇas, September 2002*, Zagreb, 2005, 597–608.

Cort, J.E., "Pilgrimage and Identity in Rajasthan," in: L.A. Babb *et al.*, eds., *Desert Temples: Sacred Centers of Rajasthan in Historical, Art-Historical, and Social Contexts*, Jaipur, 2008, 93–114.

Cort, J.E., "Jains, Caste and Hierarchy in North Gujarat," *CIS* 38/1–2, 2004, 73–112.

Cort, J.E., "Bhakti in the Early Jain Tradition," *HR* 42/1, 2002, 59–86.

Cort, J.E., *Jains in the World: Religious Values and Ideology in India*, New York, 2001.

Cort, J.E., ed., *Open Boundaries: Jain Communities and Cultures in India*, Albany, 1998.

Cort, J.E., "An Overview of the Jaina Purāṇas," in: W. Doniger, ed., *Purāṇa Perennis: Reciprocity and Transformation in Hindu and Jaina Texts*, Albany, 1993, 185–206.

Cort, J.E., "Medieval Jaina Goddess Traditions," *Numen* 34/2, 1987, 235–255.

Couture, A., "The Reception of Kṛṣṇa's Childhood in Three Jain Sanskrit Texts," in: P. Koskikallio, ed., *Parallels and Comparisons: Proceedings of the Fourth Dubrovnik International Conference on the Sanskrit Epics and Purāṇas, September 2005*, Zagreb, 2009, 423–445.

Davis, R.H., "The Story of the Disappearing Jains: Retelling the Śaiva–Jain Encounter in Medieval South India," in: J.E. Cort, ed., *Open Boundaries: Jain Communities and Cultures in India*, Albany, 1998, 213–224.

Deszö, C., ed., *Much Ado about Religion by Bhaṭṭa Jayanta*, New York, 2005.

Dibbad, S., "The Construction, Destruction and Renovation of Jaina *Basadis*: A Historical Perspective," in: J.A. Hegewald, ed., *The Jaina Heritage: Distinction, Decline and Resilience*, New Delhi, 2011, 63–76.

Dundas, P., "A Digambara Jain Saṃskāra in the Early Seventeenth Century: Lay Funerary Ritual According to Somasenabhaṭṭaraka," *IIJ* 54/2, 2011, 99–147.

Dundas, P., "A Non-imperial Religion? Jainism in Its 'Dark Age,'" in: P. Olivelle, ed., *Between the Empires: Society in India 300 BCE to 400 CE*, New York, 2006, 383–414.

Dundas, P., *The Jains*, London, 2002.

Dundas, P., "The Jain Monk Gets the Better of a Nāth Yogī," in: D.G. White, *Tantra in Practice*, Princeton, 2000a, 231–238.

Dundas, P., "The Meat at the Wedding Feasts: Kṛṣṇa, Vegetarianism and a Jain Dispute," in: J.T. O'Connell, ed., *Jain Doctrine and Practice: Academic Perspectives*, Toronto, 2000b, 95–112.

Dundas, P., *History, Scripture and Controversy in a Medieval Jain Sect*, London, 2007.

Dundas, P., "Jain Attitudes towards the Sanskrit Language," in: J.E.M. Houben, ed., *Ideology and Status of Sanskrit: Contributions to the History of the Sanskrit Language*, Leiden, 1996, 137–156.

Flügel, P., "Beyond the Hindu Frontier: Jaina-Vaisnava Syncretism in the Gujarati Diaspora," *IJTS* 7/1, 2005, 1–43.

Geen, J., "Fair Trade and Reversal of Fortune: Kṛṣṇa and Mahāvīra in the Hindu and Jaina Traditions," *JAAR* 79/1, 2011, 58–89.

Geen, J., "Kṛṣṇa and His Rivals in the Hindu and Jain Tradition," *BSOAS* 72/1, 2009, 63–99.

Geen, J., "Jaina Origins for the Mahābhārata Story of Draupadī's Past Life," *AS/ÉA* 60/3, 2006, 575–606.

Glasenapp, H. von, "Die Polemik der Buddhisten und der Brahmanen gegeb die Jainas," in: *Beiträge zur indischen Philologie und Altertumskunde: Walther Schubring zum 70. Geburtstag dargebracht von der deutschen Indologie*, Hamburg, 1951, 74–83.

Granoff, P., "Leaving Damayanti Again (and Again): Jain Retellings of the Nala Story," in: S.S. Wadley, ed., *Damayanti and Nala: The Many Lives of a Story*, New Delhi, 2011, 265–282.

Granoff, P., "Other People's Stories: Haribhadra and the Decapitation of Brahmā," *IIJ* 52/1, 2009, 1–14.

Granoff, P., "My Rituals and My Gods: Ritual Exclusiveness in Medieval India," *JIPh* 29/1, 2001, 109–134.

Granoff, P., "Other People's Rituals: Ritual Eclecticism in Early Medieval Indian Religions," *JIPh* 28/3, 2000, 399–424.

Granoff, P., "Refutation as Commentary: Medieval Jain Arguments against Sāṃkhya," *AS/ÉA* 53/3, 1999, 579–591.

Granoff, P., "Being in the Minority: Medieval Jain Reactions to Other Religious Groups," in: N.N. Bhattacharyya, ed., *Jainism and Prakrit in Ancient and Medieval India*, New Delhi, 1994, 241–266.

Handiqui, K.K., *Yaśastilaka and Indian Culture*, Sholapur, 1968.

Houben, J.E.M., "Doxographic Introductions to the Philosophical Systems: Mallavādin and the Grammarians," in: W. Slaje, ed., *Śāstrārambha: Inquiries into the Preamble in Sanskrit*, Wiesbaden, 2008, 83–95.

Jaini, P.S., *Collected Papers on Jaina Studies*, New Delhi, 2000.

Kapstein, M., *The Rise of Wisdom Moon by Krishna mishra*, New York, 2009.

Kelting, M.W., "Nala's Weakness and Damayanti's Powers: Jain Tellings of the Great Love Story," in: S.S. Wadley, ed., *Damayanti and Nala: The Many Lives of a Story*, New Delhi, 2011, 242–264.

Krümpelmann, K., *Das Dhuttakkhāṇa. Eine jinistische Satire*, Frankfurt am Main, 2004.

Kulkarni, V.M., *Studies in Jain Literature*, Ahmedabad, 2001.

Mehta, M.L., & K.R. Chandra, *Prakrit Proper Names*, vol. I, Ahmedabad, 1970.

Meister, M., "Sweetmeats or Corpses?" in: L.A. Babb *et al.*, eds., *Desert Temples: Sacred Centers of Rajasthan in Historical, Art-Historical, and Social Contexts*, Jaipur, 2008, 23–41.

Mishra, S.V., "Religious Coexistence in Gujarat: Second/Third Century to Eighth Century AD," in: U. Singh &

N. Lahiri, eds., *Ancient India: New Research*, New Delhi, 2009, 205–230.

Monius, A.E. "Love, Violence and the Aesthetics of Disgust: Śaivas and Jains in Medieval South india," *JIPh* 92/2, 2004, 113–172.

Nagarajaiah, H., *Spectrum of Sarasvatī: Śrutadevī*, Shravanabelagola, 2009.

Nagarajaiah, H., *Indra in Jaina Iconography*, Hombuja, 2002.

Orr, L., "Jain Worship in Medieval Tamilnadu," in: N.K. Wagle & O. Qvarnström, eds., *Approaches to Jaina Studies: Philosophy, Logic, Rituals and Symbols*, Toronto, 1999, 250–274.

Osier, J.-P., *Les Jaina: Critiques de la mythologie hindoue*, Paris, 2005.

Osier, J.-P., & N. Balbir, eds., *Haribhadra: Ballade des coquins*, Paris, 2004.

Peterson, I.V., "Śramaṇas against the Tamil Way: Jains as Others in Tamil Śaiva Literature," in: J.E. Cort, ed., *Open Boundaries: Jain Communities and Cultures in India*, Albany, 1998, 163–185.

Qvarnström, O., "The Jain-Mīmāṃsā Debate on Omniscience," in: P. Flugel, ed., *Studies in Jaina History and Culture: Disputes and Dialogues*, London, 2006, 89–106.

Qvarnström, O., "Early Vedānta Philosophy Preserved by the Jain Tradition: The Vedavādadvātriṃśikā of Siddhasena Divākara," in: O. Qvarnström, ed., *Jainism and Early Buddhism: Essays in Honor of Padmanabh S. Jaini*, Fremont, 2003, 575–593.

Qvarnström, O., "Stability and Adaptability: A Jain Strategy for Survival and Growth," in: J.T. O'Connell, ed., *Jain Doctrine and Practice: Academic Perspectives*, Toronto, 2000, 113–135.

Qvarnström, O., "Haribadra and the Beginnings of Doxography in India," in: N.K. Wagle & O. Qvarnström, eds., *Approaches to Jaina Studies: Philosophy, Logic, Rituals and Symbols*, Toronto, 1999, 169–210.

Sanderson, A.G.S., "The Śaiva Age: The Rise and Dominance of Śaivism during the Early Medieval Period," in: S. Einoo, ed., *Genesis and Development of Tantrism*, Tokyo, 2009, 41–349.

Schmid, C., *Le don de voir: Premieres representations krishnaites de la region de Mathurā*, Paris, 2010.

Sharma, R.C., & P. Ghosal, eds., *Jaina Contribution to Varanasi*, Varanasi, 2006.

Shastri, Y.S., *Jainism from the View Point of Vedāntic Ācāryas (with Special Reference to Nimbārka, Śaṅkara and Rāmānuja)*, Ahmedabad, 2003.

Smith, W.L., "The Source of Vimalasūri's Version of the Kuśalavopākhyāna," in: O. Qvarnström, ed., *Jainism and Early Buddhism: Essays in Honor of Padmanabh S. Jaini*, Fremont, 2003, 669–676.

Vemsani, L., *Hindu and Jain Mythology of Balarāma: Change and Continuity in an Early Indian Cult*, Lewiston, 2006.

Wezler, A., "'A Slap on the Face of the Brahmins': Introducing a Little-Known Jain Text of Polemical Objectives," in: R.Smet & K. Watanabe, eds., *Jain Studies in Honour of Jozef Deleu*, Tokyo, 1993, 485–501.

Zydenbos, R.J., "On the Jaina Background of Dvaita Vedānta," *JIPh* 19/3, 1991, 249–271.

Paul Dundas

Hinduism and Sikhism

The relationship between Hinduism and Sikhism is close, complex, and controversial and requires understanding of South Asian and, in particular, Punjabi religious culture (see below; see also → Punjab). The brief definition of Sikhism below introduces the challenges inherent in terminology and is followed by an impression of the religiosity of Punjabi people and an account of the varying perceptions of the relationship between Hinduism and Sikhism. This relationship is then mapped in terms of their interconnected historical development, commencing with interpretations of the stance of three Sikh *gurūs* (Punj.; Hind. *guru*), as a prelude to examining the theological, philosophical, and liturgical relationship. These are inseparable from the shared linguistic and cultural repertoire and a social structure to which caste is more fundamental than religious designation. Mention is made of the multiple ways in which older, as well as more recently emergent, Sikh groups subvert the currently dominant Sikh ("neo-Sikh") discourse of a sharp distinction between Hinduism and Sikhism, while proponents of *hindutva* discount Sikh claims to a non-Hindu identity. Consideration is given to the part played by → caste and → gender, and of the South Asian diaspora in the relationship between Hinduism and Sikhism, before noting the → Internet's role in the representation of both Hinduism and Sikhism.

"Sikhism" is the usual name in English (Punj. *sikhī*) for the faith of followers of a Punjabi spiritual master, Gurū Nānak (1469–1539), and the nine *gurūs* who succeeded him. Since the demise of the tenth *gurū*, Gurū Gobind Siṅgh (1666–1708), and in obedience to his farewell command, Sikhs venerate the scriptural volume, the *Granth Sāhib* (also referred to as *Ādigranth*, i.e. primal volume) as *gurū*. A nucleus of Sikhs, the *khālsā*, receive initiation with blessed, sweetened water known as *amrit* (Punj.; Skt. *amṛta*, lit. undying) and are thereafter committed to observing a code of discipline (*rahit*). In most cases, this is the code entitled *Sikh Rahit Maryādā* (published in 1950 by Sikhs' highest elected body, the Shiromani Gurdwara Parbandhak Committee). The *rahit* prohibits, among other things, cutting one's hair, including the beard. The flowing beard, together with the turban (the honored headdress that many Sikh men and a minority of Sikh women wear), provide the dominant distinctive visual image of Sikhism. The central spiritual emphasis of Sikhī is on maintaining a constant remembrance of divine reality (*nām*, the name) in a life committed to → *sevā* (voluntary service) while also shouldering family responsibility.

From its earliest formulation, the *rahit* has sharply separated Sikhs from Muslim society (by prohibiting the eating of *halāl* meat and sexual relations with Muslim women, for example), and the *Sikh Rahit Maryādā* also continues a separation from aspects of Hindu belief and practice (such as putting faith in astrology). It opens with an authoritative definition of a Sikh as

> A Sikh is any person who believes in God (*Akal Purakh*); in the ten Gurus (Guru Nanak to Guru Gobind Singh); in Sri Guru Granth Sahib, other writings of the ten Gurus, and their teachings; in the Khalsa initiation ceremony instituted by the tenth Guru; and who does not believe in any other system of religious doctrine. (see McLeod, 1984, 79)

Definitional Challenge

The claims made by some Sikhs for Sikhs' social, and indeed ethnic, distinctness from Punjabi Hindus are made on the basis of the separateness of Sikh teaching and beliefs from Hindu teaching and beliefs. At the same time, attempts at discussion of the "religion," "Hinduism," separately from "Hindus" or of "Sikhism" as a "religion" separately from "Sikhs" are unsustainable.

Although preoccupation with deconstruction of "Hinduism" and "Sikhism" may itself come to carry the hallmark of the late 20th century, the essentializing of "religions" that in reality have been evolving over previous centuries, and the labeling of them as "isms," are self-evidently anachronistic and symptomatic of an Orientalist cultural imperialism. The terms "Hinduism" and "Sikhism" were coined by outsiders to both traditions, namely individuals of northern European ancestry, during the British Raj, but both terms have come to be widely used by Hindus and Sikhs themselves for their "religions." Whereas "Hinduism" fits only uncomfortably such indigenous concepts as *sanātanadharma* (lit. the eternal religious law; often translated as "Hinduism"; see also → *dharma*) and *varnāśrama-dharma*, "Sikhism" is less problematic, being regarded as a translation for the term *sikhī* and its alternative form *gursikhī*, denoting discipleship of the *gurūs*. "Sikhism" is also used to translate *gurmat* (the *gurus*' doctrine).

Punjabi Religion

Both Hindu and Sikh tradition have strong geographical roots, and these are intertwined, since Hindus' historical and spiritual homeland, where the vast majority of Hindus live, is the Indian subcontinent, which includes Punjab ("the land of five [Pers. *pañj*] rivers [Pers. *āb*, water]"), which is Sikhs' spiritual homeland and the actual home of most Sikhs. The Partition of India into India and Pakistan in 1947 divided Punjab between the two nation-states. Since the subsequent division of India's Punjab state in 1966 into three states, Hindus outnumber Sikhs in Himachal Pradesh and Haryana, and Sikhs outnumber Hindus only in Punjab. Outside Punjab more Sikhs live in other states of India than in the global diaspora as a whole. Whatever their current domicile, the vast majority of Sikhs are ethnically Punjabi.

The religious character of Punjab is fluid, and Punjabis' pilgrimage and worship do not neatly correspond to classification as Hindu or Sikh. The dynamics detailed in the historian H. Oberoi's account of popular religion in 19th-century Punjab (1994) are still discernible in contemporary Punjab, despite the impact of colonial rule and of Sikh and Hindu reformist movements, as well as Partition (see below), all of which drove a wedge between "Sikh" and "Hindu." H. Oberoi's characterization of *sanātan* Sikhism (i.e. Sikhism that is inclusive of elements of Hindu tradition and inseparable from it) is consistent with the anthropologist R. Ballard's analysis of late 20th-century Punjabi religion along the axes of *panth, dharam* (Skt. *dharma*), and *qaum* ("a body of people"), together with his attention to the "kismetic" factor, that is, individuals' recourse to religion as a means of coping with actual and feared adversity (Ballard, 1999). It coheres too with findings from 21st-century fieldwork in Punjab by N. Purewal and V. Kalra and research among Sindhis by W. Ramey (2008).

Models of the Relationship

Sikh groups (see sections on → *sampradāya* and caste below) diverge in their emphases and interpretations of their tradition, and, unsurprisingly, perceptions by Sikhs, Hindus, and interested outside observers of the relationship between Sikhism and Hinduism are diverse, as outlined below.

Thus, it has been compared to the relationship between Judaism and Christianity, namely a parent–child relationship in which the younger faith is derived from the older tradition (Cole & Sambhi, 1993, 10). According to this view, the Sikh *gurūs* developed a new religion that differed from Hindu tradition more in terms of values and ethics than "beliefs" (Cole & Sambhi, 1993, 13). As W.O. Cole and P.S. Sambhi acknowledge, Gurū Nānak was a Hindu, was taught Sanskrit by the local *paṇḍit*, was presented for initiation with the sacred thread (→ *yajñopavīta*), and was married to a girl of his own Khatrī caste, who bore him two sons, each of whom was given a Hindu name.

Another characterization of Sikhism is as a *sampradāya* (one of the many *guru*-led devotional movements that are intrinsic to the Hindu tradition). Sikhs have their own scripture and distinctive annual observances, like many another *sampradāya*, while also being strongly rooted in a specific region (Punjab). In this view, Sikhism is a particularly mature example of a (Hindu) *sampradāya*. Indeed, it has developed to the point where it is widely claimed to constitute a separate religion.

Reflecting their own cultural background in European Christian sectarian history, 18th- and 19th-century British writers described Sikhism as a "reforming movement out of Hinduism" and a "dissenting sect from Hinduism." For C. Wilkins (publishing on the "Seeks" in 1788), Gurū Nānak was a "Hindu apostate whose chief concern was moral virtue" (Mandair, 2009, 178). Creating stereotypes that were gendered as well as religious, such authors recurrently showed Sikhs as the upright, manly counterparts to Europe's Protestants in relation to the more effete "Catholicism" of Hindus. Thus, in the view of J. Browne (publishing in 1785), the Sikhs "appeared to bear that kind of relation to the Hindu religion, which the Protestant does to the Romish" (Mandair, 2009, 178). According to A.S. Mandair,

> As early as the 1780s, Sikhism was construed by the British as the indigenous other of Hinduism. Their apparent difference from the "Hindoo multitude" was hailed by the British as a reason for their rise to power and attainment of a sovereign kingdom under the Sikh ruler Maharaja Ranjit Singh. (Mandair, 2009, 17)

For the 19th-century annalist J.D. Cunningham, "Sikhism was a 'living faith,' a 'species of pure theism,' as opposed to the 'dead ritual and priest craft of the Hindoos'" (Mandair, 2009, 181), and

> the cornerstone of his discourse is the polarity between Sikhs and "Hindoos"… the Sikh and "Hindoo" are related as spirit is to body, or male to female… To avoid equating the Sikhs with the West, however, he constantly reminds the reader of the organic connection between the Sikh spirit and the "Hindoo" body. (Mandair, 2009, 181)

By contrast, E. Trumpp, the first translator of a substantial portion of the *Gurū Granth Sāhib* into English, undermined claims of Sikh difference and superiority.

One persistent description of Sikhs is not as the spirit but as the "sword-arm" of Hinduism, with Sikhs being the warriors who protect the wider Hindu family. The contemporary right-wing Hindu party, the → Rashtriya Swayamsevak Sangh, alludes to Sikhism in this way (see e.g. Elst, n.d.), so simultaneously honoring Sikhs' courageous resistance to → Mughal and Afghan domination in the 17th and 18th centuries and discounting any suggestion that Sikhs are a separate faith community from Hindus.

Indeed, in different contexts, both Hindus and (less frequently) Sikhs have stated that Sikhs are Hindus. Moreover, to the disquiet of many Sikhs, in the constitution of the secular state of India, Article 25 (under "Right to Freedom of Religion") states,

> the reference to Hindus shall be construed as including a reference to persons professing the Sikh, Jaina, or Buddhist religion, and the reference to Hindu religious institutions shall be construed accordingly.

Outside India, Sikhs have routinely been subsumed as "Hindu" – for example in North America – throughout most of the 20th century.

Faced with this inclusion and inclusiveness, which is so often insensitive to their sensibility and identity, Sikhs have recurrently felt compelled to insist, "We are not Hindus." Indeed, these words (*ham hindū nahīn hain*, in the pamphlet's original Hindi) formed the title of a notable publication in 1898 by a reformist Sikh writer, K.S. Nabha. Sikh fears of "being reabsorbed into Hinduism" recur in K. Singh's history (1999, 137). The metaphor of reabsorption implies acknowledgment of an intrinsic or underlying unity or homogeneity and evokes an image of Sikhs and their religion arising out of Hindu society before possibly sinking back, indistinguishably, into it. The history of Buddhism in India is regarded by concerned Sikhs as offering a worrying precedent for this trajectory.

Another metaphor is that of "overlay": concerned 21st-century Sikhs identify currently accepted Sikh practices that are, in their view, intrinsically Hindu and thus corrosive of Sikh principles. Examples are the *akhand pāth* (continuous 48-hour reading of the *Gurū Granth Sāhib*, involving relays of readers) and the *nagar kīrtan* (the processing of the *Gurū Granth Sāhib* in a manner reminiscent of Hindu processions celebrating temple deities; see → *kīrtan* and → *bhajan*). Similarly, the historian H. Oberoi characterizes late 19th-century Sikhs campaigning to "purge" their faith of "Hindu accretions" and "a Brahminical stranglehold" over their rituals.

Consistently with much popular discourse, some 20th-century scholars, both Sikh and non-Sikh, have described Sikhism as a blend of elements of Islam with elements of Hinduism (e.g. Singh, 1977, 17; Bouquet, 1967; Noss, 1968; all cited in Courtright, 1999, 25). For A.C. Bouquet, "Sikhism is the fruit of hybridization between Islam and Hinduism"; for J.B. Noss, Sikhism is an "outstanding example of conscious syncretism"; and, according to K. Singh, "Sikhism was born out of a wedlock between Hinduism and Islam." In such accounts, attention is paid to the fact that the *gurūs*' lives coincided with Mughal rule in North India and that the *gurūs* conversed with Muslims as well as Hindus. References to God in the Sikh scripture by Islamic as well as Hindu names are highlighted, and the "monotheism" (see below) of Sikh teaching is posited as evidence of Islamic influence.

In particular, scholars have pointed to Sufi elements in Sikhism. In terms of institutions, the *laṅgar* (communal dining) is described as a development of practice at Sufi centers.

W.H. McLeod identified affinities between Gurū Nānak's insights and Sufism, including

> emphasis upon the unity of God, a revelation in creation, the paradox of God transcendent as well as immanent, an expression of God in terms of light… a belief in the needlessness of asceticism on the one hand, and upon the snare of worldly wealth on the other. (McLeod, 1968, 158)

Nonetheless, W.H. McLeod emphasized that such affinities are not necessarily evidence of, or a result of, actual Sufi influence. Moreover, he noted that Gurū Nānak rejected both conventional Hindu belief and Islam, as "[t]rue religion lay beyond these two systems" (McLeod, 1968, 161). Furthermore, he pointed out that Gurū Nānak used Hindu (rather than Islamic) terminology to express what appear to be Sufi concepts and that Sufi thinking had been itself influenced by Hindu ideas.

As P. Courtright explained, "to call Sikhism a syncretism implies certain presuppositions" (Courtright, 1999). One presupposition is that at the time of the *gurūs*, there were two freestanding monolithic systems, Hinduism and Islam. Another is that Sikhism's "ideas and institutions can be clearly located within the traditions from which they were borrowed." Attention to theology (below) reveals that Sikhs' emphasis on divine oneness differs from Muslims' monotheism and resembles certain Hindu understandings. Similarly, for Gurū Nānak, *hukam* (divine will) corresponds more closely to the Sanskrit concept of *ṛta* (cosmic order) rather than to Islam's "more personalised notion of Allah's activity" (Courtright, 1999, 36).

P. Courtright portrays Gurū Nānak as "purifier of the popular religious expression of both traditions" (Courtright, 1999, 40) rather than as "reconciler and synthesizer of Hinduism and Islam." Much more forcefully than Western scholars, Sikh preachers and authors rule out any suggestion that Sikhism is either a form of Hinduism or a syncretistic mixing of Muslim and Hindu elements. Rather they project Sikhism as a distinct revelation and Gurū Nānak as the "initiator of a new age" (Ramey, 2008, 29, quoting Rajpal, 2001). W.H. McLeod rightly noted that "a very substantial majority of Sikhs now rejects the claims that Sikhs are Hindu or that the Panth is a Hindu sect" (McLeod, 1989, 120).

Increasingly, too, since the 1980s, the claim is made that Sikhs are a separate nation. This can be understood as a vernacular assertion that Sikhs constitute a *qaum* (a "people who hold together"), without necessarily signifying the connotations of modern nationhood. The contemporary claim to be a nation in the modern sense is, however, strengthened by recalling British sentiment, strategy, and rhetoric during the British Raj. In the 19th century, J. Cunningham described Gurū Gobind Siṅgh as "fir[ing] the minds of his countrymen with a new nationality" (Cunningham, 1849). An army handbook of 1928 indicated that Sikh soldiers were required

> to adhere rigidly to Sikh customs and ceremonies, and every effort has been made to preserve them from the contagion of Hinduism… Sikhs in the Indian Army have been studiously "nationalised" or encouraged to regard themselves as a totally distinct and separate nation. (Nesbitt, 2005, 72)

Clearly it was separateness from Hindus that was being demarcated, since Sikhs' separateness from Muslims was at that time self-evident.

Continuing the idiom of "nation," half a century later than the army handbook, albeit more cautiously, the United Kingdom's upper parliamentary chamber, the House of Lords, ruled in the landmark case of Mandla vs Lee in 1983 that "Sikhs are almost a nation" and so were, like Jews, eligible for protection under United Kingdom race relations legislation. This ruling was grounded in the understanding that a racial group is a distinct ethnic group on the basis of criteria outlined by Lord Fraser, namely having a distinct cultural tradition, shared history, common geographical descent, language, literature, and religion, as well as the experience of being a minority or oppressed by a dominant group within a larger community. Less cautious in its assertion of nationhood was the Khalistan movement's campaign (in the 1980s and peaking in the 1990s) for an autonomous Sikh state on the basis that Sikhs are a separate, sovereign nation.

In the academic context of contemporary religious studies, Sikhism is widely treated, on a par with Hinduism, as not only a "religion" but also a "world religion." (The number of "world religions" listed by authorities varies.) Religious-education syllabuses in the United Kingdom present Sikhism as one of six "major faith traditions."

Such categorizations appear to be based on demographic strength (the 2001 UK census showed Sikhs as the fourth most numerous religious community) and geographic spread, combined with Sikhs' complex institutional development over several centuries and a body of inspirational teaching accessible to communities beyond the tradition's original cultural matrix.

Amid competing understandings, the present author espouses the view that

> Sikhism has evolved into a separate religion in terms of Sikhs' self-definition and because Sikhism has all the markers of a religion. These include a separate scripture and calendar, separate life-cycle rites, places of worship, and a sense of shared history. At the same time, in common with other faiths, Sikhism cannot be fully understood in isolation from its religious, social and historical context. (Nesbitt, 2005, 4)

Discussion of the differing understandings within the Sikh and Hindu communities respectively invites attention to *sanātan sikhī*, "neo-Sikhism," and *hindutva*.

Historical Relationship

While the origins of the Hindu tradition go back incalculably far, and histories often commence with the Indus Valley civilization, putatively dated as commencing around 3000 BCE, the much younger Sikh tradition tends to be dated back no earlier than 1469 CE, the year of Gurū Nānak's birth. Whereas the oldest Hindu scriptures are dated to, for example, 1700 BCE (Doniger, 2009, 693), the earliest sources for Gurū Nānak are 16th century, and the oldest compositions in the *Ādigranth*, the verses of Bābā Farīd, date from no earlier than the 12th century CE.

The *Gurūs*' Heredity

Gurū Nānak was born to Hindu parents, Punjabis of the Khatrī caste. Like Gurū Nānak, whose family were Bedī by *got* (Punj.; Hind. *gotra*), the second and third *gurūs*, as well as the fourth, Gurū Rām Dās, from whom all the subsequent *gurūs* descended, were born into Punjabi Hindu Khatrī families. Gurū Aṅgad's *got* was Bhallā, Gurū Amar Dās' was Trehān, and the *got* of all subsequent seven *gurūs* was Sodhī.

Fig. 1: Sikh woman reading the *Ādigranth* (*Gurū Granth Sāhib*) (photo by Eleanor Nesbitt).

Gurū Nanak's Relationship with Hindu Tradition

Gurū Nanak's contact with Hindu tradition included his youthful experience of Brahmanical rites of passage (→ *saṃskāras*) and his acquaintance with local Śaiva and Vaiṣṇava religious expression. Thus he encountered, on the one hand, the renunciant followers of Gorakhnāth, the Nāth *yogīs* (see → Nāth Sampradāya), and, on the other hand the poetic insights of → Sants including → Nāmdev and Raīdās (→ Ravidās), as well as → Kabīr. The Sants' verses indicate continuity with the → *bhakti* movement, although their loving devotion affirms the divine as → *nirguṇa* rather than as an → *avatāra*, and the words of the Sants themselves suggest both Nāth and Sufi influence. W.H. McLeod's analysis of Gurū Nānak portrayed his teaching as a reworking of Sant synthesis, deploying the Sants' terminology, categories, and doctrines, but with significant originality and unique clarity (McLeod, 1968).

Three anecdotes, each providing context for verses in the *Ādigranth*, signal Gurū Nānak's discomfort with aspects of Hindu tradition:

1. his rejection of Brahmanical rites is illustrated by Janamsākhī (lit. birth witnesses, i.e. hagiographies of Gurū Nānaks's life) accounts of the young Nānak refusing investiture with the *janeū* (Punj./Hind.; Skt. → *yajñopavīta*, sacred thread), as a male member of the Khatrī caste;
2. his behavior at a pilgrimage site on the Gaṅgā includes ridiculing what is presented as a traditional element in honoring one's deceased forebears, plus cooking venison (so challenging the Hindu principle of vegetarianism, especially at a sacred site); and
3. his rejection of the celibate ascetic spiritual path, honored by Hindu tradition, is apparent not only in the account of his debate with the *siddh yogīs* [*ĀG.* 952–953; *siddh yogīs* are also known as Nāth *yogīs*] but also in his decision to appoint his married follower Bhāī Lahinā as his successor (Gurū Aṅgad), rather than Śrī Cand, his ascetic elder son.

"*Na koī hindū na musalmān*," reportedly Gurū Nānak's words on emerging from a seminal experience of divine authorization, are invoked in discussion of Sikhism's relationship to Hinduism. Translating as "There is no Hindu or Muslim," they can be read as a declaration of the unhelpfulness of religious labeling, or as affirmation that ultimate truth is beyond any religion, as a denunciation of religion-based division, or as an observation that none of his contemporaries truly followed his/her religion's teaching. What is clear is that Gurū Nānak showed impartiality to, and distanced himself from, both faiths. The politically motivated commentator K. Elst, however, expresses a right-wing Hindu stance when he interprets the words as a "typically Hindu" reiteration of the upanishadic insight that, as a "realized" person knows, the → *ātman* "is beyond worldly divisions" (Elst, n.d., 25). Gurū Nānak's communication through wry humor and everyday imagery prompts critical insight rather than spelling out injunctions or prohibitions as regards Hindu tradition. Similarly, lines composed by the fifth *gurū*, Arjun Dev, continued the use of "Hindu" both in contrast to "Muslim" and as a category that enlightened spirituality transcends:

> I keep neither *vrata* nor the month of Rāmadān… I have broken free from Hindus and Muslims. I neither go on pilgrimage to the Kaʿba nor worship at bathing places… I neither perform *pūjā* nor *nivāj*… I am not a Hindu or a Muslim. My body and life breath belong to Allāh Rām. (*ĀG.* 1136)

Interpretations of Gurū Tegh Bahādar's Execution

In 1675 the Sikhs' ninth *gurū*, Tegh Bahādar, accepted execution in defense of Kashmiri Brahmans' religious freedom from forced conversion to Islam. The divergent descriptions of this courageous act indicate current difference of opinion over the semantic scope of "Hindu" and over the relationship of Hinduism and Sikhism. Hindu commentators tend to portray Gurū Tegh Bahādar dying on behalf of coreligionists, and V. Kshitish (1985) cites Tegh Bahādar's reply to Aurangzeb as "*tegh bahādar hind dī chadar*" (which could be rendered "protector of India" or "protector of Hindus"). To quote K. Singh and B. Chandra,

> The new community, the [Sikh] Khalsa Panth, remained an integral part of the Hindu religious and social system. It is significant that when Tegh Bahadur was summoned to Delhi, he went as a representative of the Hindus… His son… later described his father's martyrdom as in the cause of the Hindu faith, "to preserve their caste marks and their sacred thread and he performed the supreme sacrifice." The

> *guru* himself looked upon his community as an integral part of the Hindu social system. (Singh & Chandra, 1985, 6)

However, neo-Sikh writers portray the *gurū* as a self-sacrificial precursor of Voltaire's dictum "I may not believe what you say but I will die for your right to say so," in giving his life for the freedom of others to pursue a faith (Hinduism) that was other than his own (Sikhism).

Interpretations of Gurū Gobind Siṅgh's Stance

The relationship of Sikhs' tenth *gurū*, Gobind Siṅgh, with Hindu tradition provides ample basis for debate,

1. in terms of the symbolism of the uniform required of his *khālsā* (initates), namely, the "five k-s," the five indicators of allegiance to the *khālsā*, that is, *keś* (uncut hair and unshaven beard), *kirpāṇ* (sword or dagger), *kachh* or *kachhahirā* (shorts worn as underwear), *kaṅghā* (comb), and *karā* (iron or steel bangle);
2. with regard to the cult of the goddess especially associated with the Shivalik hills in which he lived for some years, an issue that surfaces in debate about the authorship of the *Dasam Granth* (the scriptural compilation attributed to him), as well as
3. regarding his commissioning of the Nirmalās (see below).

According to J.S. Uberoi, in his analysis of the five k-s, the *keś* groomed by the *kaṅghā* can be interpreted as a reversal of Hindu norms: both the "total depilation" (Uberoi, 2000, 143) required for initiation into a renunciant order and also their traditionally unkempt appearance. Moreover, it negates the *saṃskāra* of *muṇḍan* (ceremonial head shaving, and in particular the removal of a male infant's first hair). J.S. Uberoi argues too that the *kachh* reverses the requirement on a Hindu renunciant to abjure marriage. Moreover, "[i]n contrast to the *jogī*'s vow never to touch weapons the Sikh neophyte is invested ritually with the *kirpāṇ* (Uberoi, 2000, 143)." This interpretation preceded scholarship that has drawn attention to the likelihood (although this is not accepted by Sikh scholars) that the five k-s, as currently listed, were formalized only by the late 19th century, rather than by Gurū Gobind Siṅgh (McLeod, 1997, 125–126).

Continuing controversy over the authorship of the *Dasam Granth*, a scripture traditionally ascribed to Gurū Gobind Siṅgh, hinges on his understanding of the goddess (Devī; see → Durgā; see → Mahādevī) and thus on the contested relationship between Sikh and Hindu tradition. At issue are compositions, comprising a substantial element of the text, that retell puranic stories: either Gurū Gobind Siṅgh's authorship is accepted, so throwing neo-Sikh assumptions about the *khālsā*'s separateness from Hinduism into disarray, or his authorship is questioned, or indeed denied, so undermining traditional belief about the text. A third position is to maintain that Gurū Gobind Siṅgh was indeed the author, but that his intention was simply to imbue his Sikhs with martial fervor by retelling mythical tales; his "design was to renovate and regenerate an effete society" (Singh, 1993, 131). In this case, his "secular" poetry must be distinguished from his devotional poetry (Singh, 1993, 131). In N.-G.K. Singh's view, "Durga is being recalled as a figure of myth and literature; she is not invoked as a goddess by the Guru" (Singh, 1993, 122), who composed as an "artist," not a devotee (Singh, 1993, 125). N.-G.K. Singh also points to S. → Radhakrishnan as exemplifying the Hindu view that Hindu tradition deeply influenced Sikhism.

What is incontrovertible is that

> Durga (as Kali, Candi, Camunda, and Bhadrakali) features prominently [in *Dasam Granth*]. Her titanic battle with the demons (from the Markandeya Purana) is retold by Guru Gobind Singh in his ornate Braj composition Candi Caritra (The Exploits of Candi)... and in his Punjabi work... Candi di Var (The ballad of Candi). (Singh, 1993, 121)

Moreover, sections 211–230 of *Akāl Ustat* (Hymn of Praise to the Timeless One) are praise of the invincible Durgā (Singh, 1993, 122).

Two verses of *Dasam Granth*, which occur in *Bicitra Nātak*, a composition of which Gurū Gobind Siṅgh's authorship is unchallenged, evoke polarized interpretations from Hindu and (neo-) Sikh commentators. The statement *mahākāl kālkā arādhī* is respectively rendered "I worshipped the primordial mother, Mahākāl Kālkā" and "I worshipped the eternal one." The second controversial passage occurs in the Vār (hymn, ballad) of Srī Bhagautī, and Hindu-Sikh interpretation centers on whether "Bhagautī" is the goddess Bhagavatī (as Hindus assume) or "the sword" (as Sikhs emphasize). The stanza in question provides the opening invocation of Sikhs' congregational prayer, the *ardās*. In defense of their interpretation, Sikhs cite the famous Sikh poet and theologian Bhāī Gurdās *vār* 25: "name Bhagautī made of iron" and "hail to Srī Bhagautī that cuts sharp." Also noteworthy is the fact that, also in *Bicitra Nātak*, Gurū Gobind Siṅgh seemingly presents his mission as that of spreading *dharma* (Singh & Singh, 1999, 159), and this is reminiscent of Hindu understandings of the *avatārs* → Rāma and → Kṛṣṇa.

Certainly, the tradition of the Nirmalā order of Sikhs suggests that Gurū Gobind Siṅgh valued knowledge of classical Indian culture, since he is accredited with having sent five Sikhs (the original Nirmalās) to Varanasi to study Sanskrit texts and then return to educate the Panth (Sikh community). The Nirmalās have continued to contextualize their understanding of *sikhī* in knowledge of the → Vedas, → Upaniṣads, and other Hindu literature.

The 19th Century

Maharaja Ranjit Singh (1780–1839), ruler of Punjab from 1799 to 1839, is regarded by Sikhs as founder of the Sikh Empire. Paradoxically, while his sovereignty was cited as a precedent in 20th-century demands for a sovereign state of Khalistan, Ranjit Singh's style of Sikhism in fact fits H. Oberoi's delineation of *sanātan* Sikhism (Oberoi, 1994), in its embrace of "Hindu" practice. Thus, at the start of his reign, he was anointed with a → *tilak*, and on his death his wives committed → *satī*.

According to H. Oberoi, rather than defining itself over against Hinduism, Sikh observance in the 19th century had an inclusive character, until developments converged to precipitate the more sharply defined *sikhī* of the *tat* (true) *khālsā*.

> In the Indian religious tradition, unlike the Judaeo-Christian, there was no notion of a well-demarcated religious community possessing a centralized ecclesiastical hierarchy. People did not conceive of themselves as "Hindus" or "Sikhs." These categories overlapped and it is historically more precise to speak in terms of a continuum or simultaneity of religious identities rather than of distinct religious collectivities. (Oberoi, 1988, 140)

Under British colonial rule, the combined impact of the census, of legislation that specified distinct religious and hereditary communities, of the threat to indigenous religion posed by Christian mission, and of the printing press (with fonts in vernacular scripts including Gurmukhi) fed the competitive emergence of reformist movements. Notably in Punjab, these were the (Hindu) → Arya Samaj and the (Sikh) Singh Sabha movement. As H. Oberoi observes, "the older pluralist paradigm of Sikh faith was displaced forever and replaced by a highly uniform Sikh identity, the one we know today as modern Sikhism" (Oberoi, 1994, 25).

H. Oberoi's analysis was immediately rejected by some Sikhs because of its suggestion that the boundaries between Sikhism and Hinduism had been at best extremely fuzzy. Another critique is articulated by A. Murphy (2000), who calls into question both his categorization of "Hinduism" (offering scope for the "ludic") in opposition to "Sikhism" and for his dichotomizing the "*sanātan*" (plus "folk" religion) and *khālsā* Sikhism (Murphy, 2000, 59). Importantly, she explains that

> [t]he fact that boundaries blur (as important as it is) does not necessarily negate identity and community definition; instead it is indicative of different levels of contestation and negotiation… Binary oppositions don't work. (Murphy, 2000, 63)

Moreover, A. Murphy challenges H. Oberoi's unquestioning acceptance of the notion of *sanātan* Sikhism, given that *sanātan* emerged as a religious descriptor only in late 19th-century political discourse, when distinctions were being drawn between the reformist Arya Samaj, on the one hand, and *sanātan* (or "eternal") Hinduism, on the other hand.

The late 19th and early 20th centuries saw a hardening of boundaries between "Sikhism" (neo-Sikhism to its scholarly critics) and "Hinduism" (both *sanātan* and Arya Samaj related) as evidenced by the rise of the Akali movement and their removal of *mahants* (hereditary managers) from the historic *gurdvārās*, which their families had managed for several centuries.

K.S. Nabha's *Ham Hindū Nahīn* consists of a series of prooftexts drawn from Sikh scriptures, arranged under headings such as caste, *avatārs*, and idol worship, "presented as evidence that Khalsa faith and conduct differ from Hindu tradition to such an extent that the Khalsa must be regarded as a separate religious system, distinct and autonomous in its own right" (McLeod, 1984,

135). It was addressed as a corrective to individuals who,

> [a]lthough they regard themselves as Sikhs of the Khalsa… accept the Hindu tradition. They imagine that it is actually harmful to observe the teachings of Gurbani by acknowledging that the Sikh religion is both distinct from the Hindu religion and superior to it. (Nabha in McLeod, 1984, 135)

In this period, the hardening distinction between Hindu and Sikh was also the emergence of "the Khalsa subtradition" rather than the Udāsīs (see also → *sādhus*), Nirmalās, and Nānakpanthīs (followers of Gurū Nānak who do not follow the *khālsā* discipline), who were now "viewed as deviants" (Oberoi, 1988, 149). The *tat khālsā* formulated distinctively Sikh rites of passage between 1880 and 1925 (Oberoi, 1988, 180). These included the *anand kāraj*, a marriage rite recognized by law in 1909 in which the place of the *havan* (fire-centered ritual) was taken by the scriptures, and Sanskrit verses were replaced by a scriptural hymn by the fourth *gurū*.

After several decades under consideration, the *Sikh Rahit Maryada*, published in 1950 by the Shiromani Gurdwara Parbandhak Committee, clearly differentiated Sikhs from Hindus in its exhortation:

> To reject caste distinctions and untouchability; magical amulets, mantras, and spells; auspicious omens, days, times, planets and astrological signs; the ritual feeding of Brahmans to sanctify or propitiate the dead; oblation for the dead; the superstitious waving of lights; [traditional] obsequies; fire sacrifices; ritual feasting or libations; sacred tufts of hair or ritual shaving; fasting for particular phases of the moon; frontal marks, sacred threads and sanctified rosaries; worshipping at tombs, temples or cenotaphs; idol worship; and all other such superstitions. (McLeod, 1984, 81)

Consistently with this emphasis on separation from Hindu tradition, during the 20th century, Sikhs have (reminiscently of Protestant reformers' treatment of previously Catholic Church murals in the United Kingdom) whitewashed over, or otherwise removed, iconography showing Hindu deities from historic *gurdvārā*s in Amritsar and elsewhere.

The Punjabi Suba Movement – a political agitation in the 1960s for the state of Punjab to be demarcated along language lines, that is, to correspond to the area in which Punjabi was the majority language – undoubtedly had a Sikh-Hindu dimension. While Sikhs entered "Punjabi" as their language on census forms, Punjabi-speaking Hindus entered "Hindi." Punjab, as defined in 1966, became India's one state in which Sikhs outnumbered Hindus.

The next movement to rock Punjab, the Khalistan movement of the 1980s and 1990s, was arguably against the central Indian government and police rather than the Hindu community. Nonetheless, the campaign and especially the violence against Sikhs that followed the assassination of Prime Minister Indira Gandhi in 1984 generated unprecedented fear and animosity between Sikhs and Hindus, and campaigners for Khalistan decried the central, congress majority government as "Hindu." However, Punjab's history is one of repeated alliances between Sikh and Hindu politicians. Thus, in 1964 Master Tara Singh played a part in founding the → Vishwa Hindu Parishad, and in 1984 the Bharatiya Janata Party (BJP) supported Sikhs. In the 1990s, Sikh politicians had electoral backing from the BJP. Moreover, the Vishwa Hindu Parishad and other Hindu organizations arguably adopted the Sikh institution of *kār sevā* (lit. work service, voluntary work), for example, for the construction of the → Swaminarayan Temple in Neasden (Elst, n.d., 28). The murder in 2010 of Rulda Singh, for his involvement in a political party aligned with the Rashtriya Swayamsevak Sangh, indicates how emotive an issue alliance between Sikh politicians and Hindu nationalist parties can be.

In understanding the intensity of Punjab's political history, one also needs to grasp the social, cultural, and also theological interconnectedness of Sikh and Hindu tradition.

Theological Overlap

The *gurūs*' teaching is sometimes portrayed, in publications by Sikhs and in curricular material for religious education in schools, as overturning key aspects of Hinduism. More accurately it needs to be interpreted as utilizing Hindu conceptual language and endorsing certain emphases while criticizing others. Moreover, the Sikh *gurūs*' rejection of some assumptions and practices is consonant with the reformist challenge offered by subsequent masters, such as → Dayananda Sarasvati, who are regarded as still within the

Hindu tradition. At the same time, as this section will illustrate, some groups that are Sikh (at least by their own definition) perpetuate elements of characteristically Hindu insight and practice that appear to contradict the *gurūs*' correctives.

As regards conceptual overlap between "Hinduism" and "Sikhism," the *gurūs* used terms such as *dharma* (Punj. *dharam*) and *karma* (Punj. *karam*), and their meaning is continuous with Hindu understanding. Reincarnation and *mukti* (*mokṣa*; see → liberation) are assumed, but the *gurūs*' emphasis is on → *jīvanmukti* (attaining liberation during this lifetime) thanks to divine → grace: "Mortals obtain human body as a result of good deeds, but reach the gate of salvation through God's grace" (*ĀG.*, *Japjī*, 2).

The *gurus*' verses advocating *nām simaraṇ* (meditation on god's name) in order to break the cycle of rebirth reiterate not only Sant teaching but also wider Hindu practice. The *gurus*' emphasis on *sat* (truth) is continuous with upanishadic insight but differs in emphasis, as "truthful living" is elevated to prominence too: "Highest is truth, but higher still is truthful living" (*ĀG.* 62).

Fig. 2: *ik oankār*.

Foundational to the *gurūs*' teaching is *ik onkār* (*ik oankār*; Hind. *ek oṃkār*, approx. translation "one being"). While *oankār* is the *oṃkār* and conveys the meaning of → *brahman*, the particular emphasis of Gurū Nānak and his successors was on *ik*, that is, the oneness and singularity of the divine. Moreover, *oankār* is not only *nirguṇa* but also *saguṇa* and is presented as the creator by Gurū Amar Dās and Bhāī Gurdās.

To quote K. Singh and C. Bipin,

> Sikhism did not evolve a distinct theology of its own like Jainism or Buddhism. It accepted a form of Vaishnavite Hinduism, giving it a new emphasis. Basically the gurus' teachings were Vedantic. Therefore there was not the same kind of breach from Hinduism as in the case of Jainism and Buddhism. Sikhism accepted the Hindu code of conduct, its theory of the origin of the world, the purpose of life, the purpose of religion, *samsara*, the theory of birth-death-rebirth – these were taken in their entirety from Hinduism. (Singh & Bipin, 1985, 4)

Overwhelmingly, Hindu writers embrace the Sikh scriptures and their insights as their own. To quote from R. Swarup, a theologian of *hindutva*, for "Hindu Revivalists,"

> Not only does the Adi Granth reproduce hundreds of passages from the older scriptures, but like the rest of the Sant literature it also follows the lead of the Upanishads and the Gita and the Yoga Vasishtha in all doctrinal points. Its theology and cosmology, its God-view and world-view, its conception of deity and man and his salvation, its ethics, philosophy and praxis and Yoga – all derive from that source. It believes in *brahm-vada*, in Advaita, in So-ham, in Maya, in Karma, in rebirth, in Mukti and Nirvana, in the Middle Path (in its yogic sense). (Swarup, 1991, quoted by Elst, n.d., 8, 9)

From this stance, it is unsurprising to find god referred to as Rām and Hari in the *Ādi Granth* (see, for example, Kabīr's use of "Rām" in *ĀG.* 1374). In the *Dasam Granth*, it is noteworthy that Gurū Gobind Siṅgh's names for god include Kāl, Akāl, Mahākāl, and Sarabkāl, so marking a shift from Vaiṣṇava to Śaiva idiom.

The concept of → *guru* was already enshrined in Hindu tradition: it is the restriction, and elevation, of Sikh usage that is characteristically Sikh. Mainstream Sikh teaching reserves the title *gurū* for the succession of ten masters, from Gurū Nānak to Gurū Gobind Siṅgh, and for the volume of scripture, *Gurū Granth Sāhib*, as well as describing god as Satgurū ("True Gurū").

The "five weaknesses" of humankind identified in *sikhī*, namely *kām* (lust), *krodh* (anger), *lobh* (greed), *moh* (attachment), and *ahaṅkār* (pride), are likewise intrinsic to Hindu tradition, as are → *sevā* (voluntary service), a central imperative in Sikh teaching, and *dāna* (giving; see → gift). Moreover, both traditions promote the view that there are many paths to the one truth and that morality and saintliness are to be found within other faiths, and, indeed, both condemn the readiness of Christians and Muslims to proselytize.

The aspects of *sikhī* that Sikhs often describe as departures from Hindu tradition can also be found in Hindu contexts. These include the concept of god as *nirguṇa* and the *gurus*' condemnation of polytheism and idol worship (e.g. *ĀG.* 637.1136). These are prefigured in → Vedānta, and, much more recently, the late 19th-century Hindu reform movements, the Arya Samaj and → Brahmo Samaj, reiterated the Sikh *gurūs*' condemnation. With regard to "idolatry," Sikh veneration of the *Gurū Granth Sāhib* raises interesting issues. For the 18th-century traveler C. Wilkins, "Sikh veneration of a sacred text" was one of many "contrasts with Hindu belief" (Pennington, 2005, 113). Yet the detail of this veneration is reminiscent of *mūrti pūjā* (worship of images) and so can be seen as a continuity with earlier Hindu practice, or as a later "overlay" or "accretion." Thus one prominent UK Sikh articulated concern at "bibliolatry" in which devotees' worship of the physical book outweighs honoring of its teaching.

To further challenge any representation of Sikhism as making a clean break with Hinduism, the diversity of groupings within the Sikh community itself perpetuates understandings and practices that are ruled out in neo-Sikh discourse. Thus, Nihang and Nirmalā tradition celebrates the Sikh *gurūs* as *avatārs*. Similarly, the *havan* or *hom* remains part of Nihang, Nirmalā, Nāmdhārī, and Udāsī practice (for the traditions, see below). *Varṇāśramadharma* is rejected in Sikh teaching and largely in practice, although this is imbued with the idealized character of the Kṣatriya. The *gurūs*' denunciation of penance and fasting typifies Sikh practice, although some women continue the *karvā cauth varat* (or *barat*, Punj.; Skt. *vrata*; for the *karvā cauth varat*, see → *vrata*). The Hindu practice of → *tīrtha* (pilgrimage; Punj. *tīrath*) was dismissed by Gurū Nānak as meaningless by comparison with the inward pilgrimage of remembrance of *nām*. Yet, Gurū Amar Dās established pilgrimage places, and Sikhs visit historic *gurdvārās* in increasing numbers, including Hemkunt Sahib in Uttarakhand, a pilgrimage site that was identified only in the mid-20th century.

Attitude to the Vedas

On the basis that Sikhs do not accept the primacy of the Vedas, Hindu writers have termed Sikhism *nāstika* (heterodox). Certainly, it is unusual for Sikhs, other than Nirmalās, to have engaged with the Vedas and Upaniṣads. At the same time, it is relevant to note that, while Hinduism is often styled the religion of the Vedas, in practice, knowledge of the content of these texts has been, even among Hindus, a minority preserve of the Brahmans. Although some Sikhs assert that the *gurūs* rejected the Vedas, it would probably be more accurate to say that the *gurūs* expressed respect: "Reading the Vedas, sinful intellect is destroyed" (*ĀG.* 791); "Do not say that the Vedas or Kitāb [Semitic scriptures] are false. Those who do not contemplate them are false" (*ĀG.* 1350).

Yet the *gurūs* repeatedly emphasized meanwhile that ultimate reality transcends all scriptures: "The Vedas expound on the Lord, but they do not know his limits" (*ĀG.* 148); "The 18 Purānas, the 4 Vedas do not know his mystery" (*ĀG.* 355); "Neither the Vedas nor the Kitāb know the mystery" (*ĀG.* 1021).

Cultural Resemblance

Although statistics are unavailable, it is frequently stated that many Hindu families bring up their eldest son as a Sikh (e.g. Singh & Nayar, 1984, 20–21). Such a son may, for example, have been conceived following a Hindu mother's petitionary prayer in a *gurdvārā*. The shared Punjabi culture makes this unproblematic. Punjabi Hindus and Sikhs share not only many values and assumptions, such as the emphasis on collective rather than individual identity, but also dietary norms and (by older women at least) the *śalvār kamīz* (an outfit comprising tunic top worn over loose-fitting, tapered trousers) as preferred dress, and Sikh religious behavior shares much with Hindu religious practices. For example, much wedding-related custom is common to Hindus and Sikhs, for example, the *māīāṇ* (occasion when, during the week prior to the wedding, the bride and groom are, in their respective homes, rubbed with a mixture including tumeric) and *mehndī* (henna; event, on the eve of the wedding, when the bride's hands are patterned with henna paste and her maternal uncle gives her white and red wedding bangles) in the week prior to the wedding and also the central rite of circumambulation, although for Sikhs this takes place around the *Gurū Granth Sāhib* while a Hindu couple circumambulates a fire. Moreover, the death rites for both Hindus and Sikhs involve cremation of the deceased person's body, followed by immersion of the ashes in flowing water.

Additionally, it is relevant to note that the strict lacto-vegetarianism of many *amritdhārī* (initiated into the *khālsā*) Sikhs is grounded in (historically Hindu) understandings of the association between diet and spirituality. The regard

Fig. 3: Women on *vaiśākhī* day cleansing the *niśān sāhib* (photo by Eleanor Nesbitt).

for milk and yoghurt as appropriate cleansing agents, respectively, for the marble floor of the Harmandir Sāhib, and for the flagpole of the *niśān sāhib* (the *khālsā*'s triangular pendant, usually saffron in color) that identifies *gurdvārā*s as Sikh places of worship, is culturally continuous with Hindu esteem for cows and their produce, as is the widespread avoidance of beef by nonvegetarian Sikhs, even though no religious sanction for it is invoked.

The 21st-century controversy over the Sikh calendar illustrates and epitomizes the close and uneasy relationship between Hindu and Sikh tradition (Nesbitt, 2005, 126–129). Until 2003 the dates for annual *gurpurab*s (anniversaries of the *gurū*s) and *melā*s (other festival celebrations) were set by the Vikramī (Bikramī) calendar and so shifted in relation to the Gregorian calendar. In 2003 the Nānakshāhī calendar was authorized by the Sikhs' most authoritative body, the Shiromani Gurdwara Parbandhak Committee, but only after making concessions to the Sant Samaj, a coalition of Sikh Sants (powerful religious leaders). These concessions meant that the three festivals of *holā mahallā*, and *dīvālī*, as well as Gurū Nānak's birthday, would be observed according to the Vikramī calendar, and in 2011, a further agreement with the Sant Samaj (and so with Nirmalās, Udāsīs, and other *sanātan* Sikhs) led to some other dates reverting to the Vikramī calendar.

It is the distinctive emphases of Sikh Sants and *sampradāya*s that particularly highlight the fuzziness and contested character of any boundary between "Hinduism" and "Sikhism."

*Sampradāya*s

Four Sikh "orders," variously tracing their origins to the time of Gurū Nānak and Gurū Gobind Siṅgh, and currently enjoying a resurgence, despite their near invisibility in dominant (neo-Sikh) discourse, are the Udāsīs, Sevāpanthīs, Nirmalās, and Nihangs. Members of these orders readily acknowledge and affirm the Hindu roots of their tradition and connections among the four orders. The Udāsīs, originating with Gurū Nānak's celibate son Śrī Cand, emphasize an ascetic lifestyle, consistent with Hindu tradition. As outlined above, the Nirmalās – at the bidding of Gurū Gobind Siṅgh – perpetuate Brahmanical learning as interpreters of the Vedas and other

Sanskrit texts. Although not required to be celibate, Nirmalās affirm the celibate lifestyle of those who are *bahiṅgams* (lit. birds, that is, unattached). Nihangs continue a style of *sikhī* that includes devotion to Devī (→ Mahādevī).

More recently established Sikh groupings, too, similarly manifest features of Hindu tradition and, in some cases, affirm their closeness to Hindu tradition. So, the Nāmdhārīs (also known as Kūkās), who revere the 19th-century Ram Singh and his successors as living Satgurū, observe strict vegetarianism. Indeed, they campaigned against cow slaughter in colonial India, and their worship, including marriages, centers on a *havan* (sacred fire). Sikhs who draw inspiration from Bhai Nand Singh (a Sikh ascetic from Ludhiana district, Punjab, d. 1943) and his successors in the Nānaksar movement likewise emphasize vegetarianism and, like the Nirmalās, endorse the celibate lifestyle of the *bahiṅgams*. Sikh Dharma of the western hemisphere, a strictly vegetarian movement consisting of North American converts and their families, honors as founding teacher Harbhajan Singh Puri (also known as Yogi Bhajan), whose promotion of *kuṇḍalīnīyoga* (see → Yoga) diverges from more general Sikh understanding of Gurū Nānak's reservations about *yoga*. In the case of the Akhand Kirtani Jatha, the requirement that initiates eat only strictly vegetarian food prepared by other initiates and only eat with them is reminiscent of the commensality restrictions of the Hindu *varṇa* system. Thus even Sikh movements that stress separateness from Hindu tradition manifest their distinctive discipline in ways that are continuous with Indic (and in religious terms Hindu) practice.

Other movements span any divide between Hindu and Sikh tradition, a well-established example being the Radhasoama Satsang Beas (see → Radhasoamis), a worldwide spiritual community with its base in Beas, Punjab. Headed by spiritual masters of Sikh background, including the present master, Baba Gurinder Singh, the Radhasoamis emphasizes vegetarianism. Devotees affirm *suratśabda yoga* (the union of the soul with the word or "spirit-current"), so continuing in the mystical tradition of the medieval Sants.

Caste

Despite the *gurūs*' dismissal of *zāt* (Punj.; Hind. *jatī*) as irrelevant to *mukti* (*mokṣa*), and despite the caste-blind ideal expressed in the institutions of the *khālsā* and the *laṅgar*, the majority of both Punjabi Hindu and Sikh marriages continues to follow the convention of *zāt* endogamy and *got* and village exogamy. Whereas Punjabi Jats self-identify as Sikh, other *zāt*s consist of members who identify variously as Hindu or Sikh, and families' devotional practice includes characteristically Sikh and Hindu elements.

Some instances of evident continuity with pre-Sikh, Indic tradition are *zāt* specific. Thus Bhāt (formerly known as Bhātrā) celebration of *dīvālī* includes setting up a miniature "shop" (*hattī*) in one room and sprinkling items of gold jewelry with *sandhūr* (Punj.; Hind. *sindūr*, red powder), and some Rāmgarhīā Sikhs worship Visvakarmā on the day following *dīvālī*. (As the divine architect in Hindu tradition, Visvakarmā is the patron deity of the artisan castes that constitute the Rāmgarhīā community.)

The continuance of *zāt* endogamy has also meant continuing negative stereotyping of members of scheduled castes, the → Dalit communities, communities, which have – in the face of prejudice – adopted the affirmative titles Vālmīkī and Ravīdassiā (previously Ravīdāsī), so distancing themselves from the more pejorative names of their communities. In the 21st century, these groups are defining themselves over against both Sikh and Hindu.

Gender

Sikhs often present gender equality as a significant Sikh departure from Hindu norms. The verses of Gurū Nānak, exhorting respect for women and condemning the notion that they are intrinsically impure (*ĀG*. 473), are acclaimed. Other verses appear critical of dowry (*ĀG*. 79) and → *satī* (self-immolation on the husband's funeral pyre; *ĀG*. 787). The code set out in the *Sikh Rahit Maryādā* applies to male and female alike. However, Punjabi cultural norms span differences of religious affiliation, and two phenomena are evident in both Hindu Punjabi and Sikh communities: the mounting financial pressure on a woman's family when she is married and the incidence of female feticide (though illegal and without religious sanction in either Sikh or Hindu tradition).

Diaspora

Recurrently, in areas of the Indian subcontinent and overseas, in locations where Sikhs and Punjabi Hindus are too few or too recently arrived to have set up separate places of worship, one notes a tendency for Punjabi Hindus to worship with Sikhs. Indeed (as observable in Norway; see Jacobsen, 2011), the *gurdvārā* offers Punjabi Hindus a worshipping environment with which they feel more affinity than the local Tamil Hindu temples. However, repeatedly, as communities grow in different locations, Sikhs and Punjabi Hindus proceed to set up separate places of worship.

At the same time, in the diaspora, the institutions of the host states concerned perceive and represent the relationship of Sikh and Hindu differently. Thus, as noted above, for many decades in North America, Sikh settlers were classified as Hindu, and this is still the case in some other countries. However, in the United Kingdom, which has the largest Sikh population outside India, the syllabuses and curriculum for the religious education that is statutory in schools present Sikhism and Hinduism as freestanding "world religions." When a UK-born and -educated Sikh visits Punjab, the sight of a shrine in which Gurū Nānak's picture sits beside pictures of Hindu deities or of Sikh and Hindu devotees at shared places of pilgrimage can unsettle deep preconceptions of religious separateness. As we have seen, it was in the United Kingdom that in 1983 Lord Templeman famously proclaimed the Sikhs to be "more than a religious sect, they are almost a race and almost a nation."

The trajectories of diasporic Sikh youth exemplify divergent perceptions of the relationship between Hindu and Sikh tradition; while those who are influenced by the Akhand Kirtani Jatha stress the need for initiation into the *khālsā* and distinguish Sikhism sharply from Hinduism, others – attracted by Nihang lore – assert continuity with "*sanātan hindū sikh śāstar vidyā*" (the timeless Hindu and Sikh knowledge of weapons, namely, military art). At the same time, many young diaspora Sikhs unquestioningly accept that there are two clearly demarcated religions, Hinduism and Sikhism, while by contrast some Hindus whose family roots are in other parts of India regard Punjabi and Sikh as synonymous. Indeed, the anthropologist D.S. Raj noted that it was the widespread equation of "Punjabi" and "Sikh" that had led to the self-definition of Hindu families from Punjab as "Hindu Punjabi" (Raj, 1990, 65).

Fig. 4: Publicity for *śāstar vidyā* classes in the UK.

The Internet

Sikh Web sites contribute to the shaping of Hindus', Sikhs', and outsiders' perceptions of Hinduism and Sikhism, and the relationship between them. For example, even though only a minority of Sikhs is *amritdhārī* (or, in the diaspora at least, even *keśdhārī*, i.e. with uncut hair, full-length beard, and – in the case of adult men – normally turban-wearing), Sikhs online are generally represented by images of *keśdhārī* Sikhs. Only a very small percentage of *amritdhārī* women wears a turban, yet this is presented as normative on some Web sites (Jakobsh, 2010, 13–14). While some online discussion groups allow for debate on the relationship of Sikhism and Hinduism, the agendas of some Hindu and Sikh Web sites reflect and perpetuate uncompromisingly polarized positions. The Internet looks increasingly set to shape as well as disseminate divergent understandings of the relationship between Hinduism and Sikhism.

Bibliography

Ballard, R., "Panth, Kismet, Dharm te Qaum: Continuity and Change in Four Dimensions of Punjabi Religion," in: P. Singh & S.S. Thandi, eds., *Punjabi Identity in a Global Context*, New Delhi, 1999, 7–38.

Bouquet, A.C., *Sacred Books of the World*, Harmondsworth, 1967.

Cole, W.O., & P.S. Sambhi, *Sikhism and Christianity: A Comparative Study*, London, 1993.

Courtright, P., "Syncretism and the Formation of the Sikh Tradition," in: S.S. Bhatia & A. Spencer, eds., *The Sikh Tradition: A Continuing Reality*, Patiala, 1999, 25–41.

Doniger, W., *The Hindus: An Alternative History*, Oxford, 2009.

Elst, K., "Are Sikhs Hindus?" n.d., http://voi.org/books/wiah/ch8.htm.

Jackson, R., *Religious Education: An Interpretive Approach*, London, 1997.

Jacobsen, K.A., "Institutionalization of Sikhism in Norway: Community Growth and Generational Transfer," in: K.A. Jacobsen & K. Myrold, eds., *Sikhs in Europe: Migration, Identities and Representaions*, London, 2011, 19–38.

Jakobsh, D., *Sikhism and Women: History, Texts, and Experience*, New Delhi, 2010.

Jones, K., *Arya Dharm Hindu Consciousness in 19th-Century Punjab*, Berkeley, 1976.

Juergensmeyer, M., *Religion as Social Vision: The Movement against Untouchability in the 20th Century*, Berkeley, 1982.

Kaur, G., *Reason and Revelation in Sikhism*, New Delhi, 1990.

Kshitish, V., *Storm in Punjab*, Delhi, 1985.

Lum, K., "The Ravidassia Community and Identity(ies) in Catalonia, Spain," *SF* 6/1, 2010, 32–49.

Mandair, A.S., *Religion and the Specter of the West: Sikhism, India, Postcoloniality, and the Politics of Translation*, New York, 2009.

Mann, J.S., S.S. Sodhi, & G. Gill, *Invasion of Religious Boundaries: A Critique of Harjot Oberoi's Work*, Vancouver, 1995.

McLeod, W.H., *Sikhism*, London, 1997.

McLeod, W.H., *Who Is a Sikh? The Problem of Sikh Identity*, Oxford, 1989.

McLeod, W.H., *Textual Sources for the Study of Sikhism*, Manchester, 1984.

McLeod, W.H., *Guru Nanak and the Sikh Religion*, Oxford, 1968.

Murphy, A., "Allegories of Difference and Identity: Reflections on Religious Boundaries and 'Popular' Religion," *IJPS* 7/1, 53–72, 2000.

Nabha, K.S., *Ham Hindū Nahīn*, Amritsar, [4]1914.

Nesbitt, E., *Sikhism: A Very Short Introduction*, Oxford, 2005.

Nesbitt, E., "My Dad's Hindu, My Mum's Side are Sikh," 1991, http://www.casas.org.uk/papers/pdfpapers/identity.pdf.

Noss, J.B., *Man's Religions*, New York, 1968.

Oberoi, H., *The Construction of Religious Boundaries: Culture, Identity and Diversity in the Sikh Tradition*, Oxford, 1994.

Oberoi, H., "From Ritual to Counter-ritual," in: J.T. O'Connell, M. Israel, & W.C. Oxtoby, eds., *Sikh History and Religion in the Twentieth Century*, Toronto, 1988, 136–158.

Pennington, B.K., *Was Hinduism Invented? Britons, Indians, and the Colonial Construction of Religion*, New York, 2005.

Raj, D.S., *Where Are You From? Middle-Class Migrants in the Modern World*, Berkeley, 1990.

Rajpal, S.S., "Yuga pravartan guru nānak derā jī (Epoch Making Guru Nanak Dev Ji)," *Hindustan* 13, 2001.

Ramey, S.W., *Hindu, Sufi, or Sikh: Contested Practices and Identifications of Sindhi Hindus in India and Beyond*, New York, 2008.

Singh, J., & D. Singh, *Sri Dasam Granth Sahib Text and Translation*, Patiala, 1999.

Singh, K., *A History of the Sikhs*, 2 vols., New Delhi, 1997–1999.

Singh, K., & B. Chandra, *Many Faces of Communalism*, Chandigarh, 1985.

Singh, K., & K. Nayar, *Tragedy of Punjab: Operation Bluestar and After*, New Delhi, 1984.

Singh, N.-G.K., *The Feminine Principle in the Sikh Vision of the Transcendent*, Cambridge UK, 1993.

Swarup, R., "Hindu Roots of Sikhism," in: *Indian Express*, Apr 24, 1991.

Uberoi, J.S., "The Five Symbols of Sikhism," in: L.M. Joshi, ed., *Sikhism*, Patiala, rev. ed. 2000, 135–151.

Eleanor Nesbitt

Hinduism and Tribal Religions in India

Hinduism has never been a monolithic discourse; rather, it represents a confluence of diverse cults and sects, such as Śaivism, Vaiṣṇavism, Tantrism, and Śaktism, reflecting Sanskritic and non-Sanskritic practices, oral and textual traditions, and village and urban cultures. Indian local communities shape their identity around caste and tribe, for while anthropologists have considered the boundaries between these presumably discrete identities to be porous, allowing individuals to shift between them, it is striking how tribal people take their identity as immutable, regardless of social dynamics. While not denying that continuity and innovation have equally affected the construction of identities in South Asia, they should not be treated as arbitrary constructions, as has been the trend in these postmodern times. Thus I shall take as my departure point the view that "tribes" or "indigenous people" refer to ethnicities that can be explained in terms of culture and history, while not denying that identities may have been reinvented, as E.J. Hobsbawm and T.O. Ranger (1983) have put it. It seems impossible to discuss the idea of indigenous people in India today without considering in some detail the historical and social situation of the tribal population. When scientists talk of indigenous people in India, they have some communities, and only those communities, in mind. This implies defining the characteristics common to the tribal communities of India and absent from other communities, while taking into account how indigenous people define themselves.

A. Béteille (2006) brings out the conceptual difficulties in accepting any category of people in India as indigenous. To him, indigenous people should be regarded as an idea rather than a concept, since the purpose it serves is evocative as often as analytical, and its referent tends to shift from one country to another. A. Béteille's argument is that any definition of tribe based on language, culture, or territory is inadequate in the face of the complexity of Indian society. He stresses the permeability of the tribe/nontribe and the tribe/caste distinctions. Yet the concept of indigenous people is tied to ideas relating to land and territory. To be pertinent, these ideas invite one to take into account the stories of conquest and spoliation. In different contexts, the claims of the weak have been violated by the strong, sometimes dramatically, as in colonial encounters, and other times more insidiously, by internal colonization of weaker communities.

I argue that an explicit consciousness is often at the root of a group's perception of its own identity. I shall consider, here, the indigenous people of India and their relation to Hinduism, a non-monolithic religion composed of many strata, which is also the religion of the dominant groups. Indigenous people are subalterns, and this leads us to ask, is Hinduization an identity imposed on tribal groups by dominant groups, or is it more appropriate to say, as R.S. Sharma does, that

> a large number of aboriginal people were being incorporated in the Brahmanical caste system and the original non-Sanskritic names of clans and tribes were retained as names of castes in the new Brahmanical system (Sharma, 2002, 159)

We shall assume, here, a certain flexibility of identity construction and consider how scholars, and the groups themselves, have produced definitions and ascriptions of tribe and caste identities.

Discussing Caste and Tribe

Tribes are kinship-based communities that, throughout history, have continued to reproduce their ethnic identity through distinct markers. These communities may also be defined by their ecological adaptation or by their social and political organization. Efforts by anthropologists and sociologists to define → caste and tribe in India on the basis of formal features have not been successful, since the definition of one depends on the other. It seems as hard to define what it means to be Hindu as it seems impossible to provide an overall view of the tribes, insofar as geographical, linguistic, and cultural entities do not necessarily coincide. According to the criteria used by the Indian state, there are some four hundred different tribes regrouping more than 83 million people, living in the northeast, the center, and the south of the subcontinent. Among them, we may distinguish the Tibeto-Burman groups in the northeast, the groups speaking Austro-Asian languages in the north and center of the subcontinent, and finally the Dravidian-speaking tribes of South India. The latter live mostly in the forests of the Western and Eastern Ghats.

We should demystify the idea that tribes were and are isolated from other communities. The tribes have often, to an extent, adopted Hindu elements in their traditional cults, especially when a group is numerically weak, such as the Mal Paharia of Bihar, who had to call in Brahmans to celebrate their rituals.

Today, the problem of the states is to recognize differences while ensuring a degree of redistributive justice. These principles of redistributive justice emerged between 1946 and 1949, when all citizens were declared equal in the Indian Constitution. The principles were applied to what became Scheduled Castes and Scheduled Tribes, and the principal aim was to promote their social mobility through education. While Scheduled Tribes were to be developed, they were also to be protected as autochthones or → Ādivāsī (Corbridge, 2002). Any claim to Scheduled Tribe status today will be measured against the following criteria: social and cultural identity, demarcated occupation and use of primitive technology, lack of relationship to the majority community, practice of endogamy, and an animist religion.

Tribe and caste were conceptualized as ideal types. Historical transformations of the royal Hindu cult of Jagannāth in Puri and its relations to the hill tribes and their religion in → Orissa were studied by A. Eschmann *et al.* (1978, 99), who developed the concept of Hinduization by linking the deities of the Jagannāth Temple to the wooden posts worshipped in tribal villages. Some scholars, finally, consider the tribes as castes-to-be in an evolutionary process where they will lose their original language and adopt a mode of subsistence similar to that of neighboring castes. Some, such as B. Schnepel (2002), call the process that creates that continuum Hinduization – a process that, he argues, takes place in the context of the formation of the "jungle kingdom." This implied that some tribal deities were also included in the Hindu pantheon.

Anthropologists have often considered the tribal populations of India from three points of view. The first one considers a tribe as an isolated sociological entity, as illustrated by the works of C. von Fürer-Haimendorf (1976, 1985) on the tribes of northeast India. A second stance, defended by F.G. Bailey (1961) for the Kond of Orissa, develops the idea of a tribe–caste continuum that allows the dominated aborigines to integrate the world of castes by appropriating Hindu values. The last position considers the tribes as castes-to-be: they will lose their original language and adopt a mode of subsistence similar to that of neighboring castes (Ghurye, 1959). Since the 1960s, the question of the Hinduization of the tribes has produced a debate among scholars and has influenced the way anthropologists in India and Europe consider tribe in relation to caste. Let me say, here, that during this last decade, the term "tribe" has been deconstructed through scholarly writing and replaced by the term "Ādivāsī," derived from the Hindi *ādi* (beginning) and *vāsī* (resident) – an equivalent of the word "aboriginal." Ādivāsīs are thus seen as the first settlers on the land, but this term, coined in the 1930s by the Munda leaders in Bihar, also reflected the awareness of exploitation suffered by tribal groups at the hands of Hindu castes as well as the colonial power and implied claims of equality.

Castes and tribes never lived in complete isolation from each other, despite differences from state to state. It is sometimes difficult to draw a clear line between tribe and nontribe regarding habitat, language, livelihood, or form of → kinship. Some authors maintain that the real difference is found in terms of language and religion, both of which are considered paradigms of indigenous culture, since most tribes who still speak their original language practice animism. This argument implies that the castes, however, speak one of the literary languages of India and practice Hinduism, the latter being not alien to some tribal communities but less fundamental than animism.

In the 1930s, Munda and Oraon activists developed the idea that tribal people have the right, as first occupants of the land, to oppose the Indo-Aryans, who represent the world of caste. This position was a counterattack on Brahman ideology, which saw the origin of Hindu religion in the cults of the Aryans and considered the Ādivāsī *jungly*, "wild people." Today, when my informants in central India refer to themselves as Ādivāsī, they generally imply the separation from *jāti*, a term that applies to caste people.

The pejorative image of tribes entails seeing them as outcaste, which means, in many cases, treating them as untouchables, a negative stereotype that has sometimes been internalized by Ādivāsīs. In the past, these contacts contributed to reshaping tribal identities through Sanskritization, Hinduization, and other religious movements that developed alongside resistance. After the Independence, nationalist anthropologists, such as G.S. Ghurye (1959), argued against attributing a distinct religious identity to the tribal people. Since 1951, the government reserved places and posts in the education system, seats in the elected assemblies, and jobs in the administration for members of these "underprivileged" communities. This attempt to promote the advance of the groups not only had positive effects but also prompted a violent reaction from the intermediate castes and the Brahmans and, more recently, from the political parties professing a militant anti-egalitarian Hindu ideology, such as Shiv Sena and the Bharatiya Janata Party, exasperated by the conversion of some tribes to Christianity. The ethnic movements of the tribes, however, present a symbolic dimension in which the assertion of values proper to their society is essential.

Today, most tribal groups prefer to be called indigenous people and deny that they were backward Hindus in the past, as stated by G.S. Ghurye (1959) and reiterated by scholars like N.K. Bose (1967), who explained the process of economic assimilation through the Hindu mode of tribal absorption, or D.D. Kosambi (1965), who felt that tribal people must adopt the Hindu model of plow cultivation, though he underlines the presence of tribal or pre-Hindu strata in Hinduism. N.K. Bose emphasizes the role played by economic matters: "culture…seems to flow from an economically dominant group to a poorer one when the two are tied together to form a larger productive organization" (1967, 205). In 1952, M.N. Srinivas forged the concept of Sanskritization in his study of the Koḍagu (Coorg; see also → Karnataka), in order to explain how low castes and tribal communities tried to make their practices conform to Hindu values of purity and impurity. This model also implies, as S. Munshi (1979, 300) stresses, that "Hinduism has not only absorbed other people but also several religious ideas and practices, splitting Hinduism." For the castes, this may involve a horizontal or vertical spread. M.N. Srinivas (1952) explains that higher castes have more horizontal spread, sharing Sanskritic culture among themselves, while a vertical spread characterizes the lower castes and the tribes. The latter tended to try to improve their status by modifying their customs so as to conform to the Brahman model. Fundamental to this approach is the assumption that the structural basis of Hindu society is caste and that dominant castes (the concept used by N.K. Bose) who generally have a better economic position (in terms of land or education and job) serve as traditional guardians of "pluralistic culture and value system" (Bose, 1961, 44). This model implies that Brahmanical values, expressed through scriptures and enacted through ritual, were gaining ground at the expense of local practices. Probably, the tribal people who tried to Sanskritize their practices, by observing a vegetarian diet or abstaining from blood sacrifice, hoped to attain upward social mobility. But this did not occur, and, at best, tribal groups were considered among the Śūdras (low castes), or, at worst, untouchables. S. Sinha (1962), studying the Bhumij in West Bengal, showed how they tried to declare themselves Kṣatriyas – a strategy that worked to a certain extent, though the Bhumij Kingdom no longer had any political status.

Most tribal societies, though they may have systems of stratification – as do the Angami Nagas in Nagaland (Hutton, 1921), who distinguish aristocrats and common people – do not acknowledge caste as a hierarchy founded on the purity/impurity opposition (Dumont, 1966). Ethnic mobilization in northeast India has often been influenced by Protestant Evangelical movements. Under missionary influence, claims to political representation, with guarantees of individual freedom, replaced the tacit acceptance of the chiefs' traditional power and intrigues with the British. In the northeast, the ethnic movements took a specific turn, and the people considered themselves as Janjātis, autochthonous.

The process of Hinduization was assumed to assimilate tribal religion into the Hindu fold. N.K. Bose (1967) certainly wanted to identify the Hindu ideal that he sometimes conceptualized as the "cultural soul of Hindu society" (Munshi, 1979, 303). S. Munshi criticized N.K. Bose and M.N. Srinivas for their lack of "a sociological theory of society," which compels them to accept the ruling ideas of society as a norm, implicitly accepting that the lower castes are generally exploited and never given an equal status. This process was, of course, partly induced by the dominant Hindu castes, whose values and ideology influenced the tribal groups, especially when the latter were having close contacts with the dominant population. Generally, Hinduization implies that that tribal community becomes an underprivileged community.

Some scholars feel that Hinduism is derived from tribal cults. Thus, B. Hauser (2007, 138) describes shamanistic practices in Orissa where mediums, usually dressed as women, mediate between humans and the supernatural world and stresses that "these features do not occur in tribal contexts only, they may also belong to the worship of village deities (*grama debata* [i.e. *grāmadevatā*]) or tantric ritual practices." We know, she adds, that many Hindu goddesses are supposed to be of tribal origin – for example Buṛhi Ṭhākurāṇī in Orissa, who is associated with the king. Her cult is tinged with both tribal and → *śakti* elements, since she possesses her devotees, she is not necessarily worshipped in a temple – though there are numerous temples dedicated to this goddess in the region – and her priests follow irregular ritual procedures, such as worshipping the goddess in the form of an empty pot instead of the prescribed ritual procedures. For B. Hauser (2007, 139), Śāktism is tinged with tribal elements that constitute different layers of a social and religious world. This is reminiscent of G.-D. Sontheimer's (1989) definition of Hinduism as including the work and teaching of Brahmans, asceticism and renunciation, tribal religion and folk religion, and, finally, → *bhakti* as devotion.

Hindu Kings and Tribal Chiefs

The tribes that had a highly ranked society in the past and held a dominant position in former kingdoms were generally sedentary farmers, like the Raj Gond of central India. Local kingdoms (Gond, Bhil) were often established in tribal regions where *rājā*s and tribal chiefs were integrated in a royal formation in postmedieval India (Kulke & Schnepel, 2001). Many of the local communities were influenced by Hindu values, like the Plains Bhuiya (in contrast to the Hill Bhuiya), who shared socioreligious rituals with the agricultural Kurmi in Keonjhar, Orissa (Carrin, 2002; 2010).

Many tribes have lost their original language and migrated toward other regions to look for new lands or to escape the oppression of other groups. In the kingdoms of the tribal regions, there were permanent economic and ritual exchanges between the local sovereign (*rājā*) and the tribes, which often formed the sovereign's military reserve force. This power configuration characterized the jungle kingdoms from around 1350 until the colonial period, when some little kings tried to consolidate their power to establish states, since jungle kingdoms represent a step in state formation (Sinha, 1987; Sundar, 1997; Schnepel, 2002). As mentioned earlier, the tribes have often, to an extent, adopted Hindu elements in their traditional cults, especially when the group is numerically weak.

However, the ethnic movements of the tribes present a symbolic dimension, where the assertion of values proper to their society is essential. Often inspired by the tribal deities, these assertions tend to affirm the identity of the population concerned, and to center on the idea of a lost kingdom. This idea is not always a myth, since the feudatory states of Orissa, which remained autonomous during the British period, were old kingdoms whose symbolic reproduction was insured by the tribal groups. The kings of these little kingdoms had to incorporate tribal groups in a more centralized hierarchy, since the kingdom generally included a Hindu polity, as well as peripheral tribal societies, in charge of defending its forest boundaries (Guha, 1999, 109).

Among indigenous populations, the soil and the forest are symbolically represented in narratives and religious practices, in which, typically, the notion of a sacred grove (*sarna*) sheltering indigenous deities or ancestors is paramount among the Mundari-speaking tribes. The sacred grove often represents the forest in the village as a symbolic link between the wilderness and social space. Many Ādivāsī groups see themselves as the center of a cosmogony. This imaginary center is reflected in the ritual symbolism of kingship, regardless of whether the kingdom was real or imaginary, since the autochthonous chief often opposed a king who was an outsider (Santal, Juang, and Bhuiya).

The relationships between tribal communities and castes are rooted in diverse hierarchical configurations. Many tribes were influenced by Hindu social hierarchy and Hindu values. Thus, the Plains Bhuiya, who shared socioreligious rituals with the agricultural Kurmi in Keonjhar, participated in the enthronization ceremony of the Keonjhar king, where a Bhuiya applied the *tikā*, a ritual mark, on the king's forehead. It is alleged that formerly, the king had to kill this man after receiving the investiture, and that the latter would become the guardian deity (*ista debta* [i.e. *iṣṭadevatā*]) of the royal family (Carrin, 1978; 1986).

In cases such as the Bonai Kingdom, the royal family depended on an autochthonous chief, from the Bhuiya community, who played an important role in the king's enthronization (Skoda, 2011). Here, as in the neighboring states of Orissa, a fusion of tribal and Hindu rituals sustained the cult of tribal goddesses patronized by the local kings. During the postmedieval period, this integration meant that the tribal populations who paid an annual tribute to the king were recruited in the king's army to defend the boundaries of the kingdom (Guha, 1999).

In central India, the subjects of the king of Bastar were Gonds who used to venerate their ruler as a divine king. A. Gell (1997) argues that the ritual links that united the king and his subjects, in this type of kingdom, resulted from rebellions and ritual strategies that the tribal populations tried to develop to contest the Hindu king, since in Bastar, forced labor (*begār*) caused a great deal of discontent. The legitimation of the king was enacted through religious rituals during the *dasara* (*daśaharā*), an annual ritual that aimed at renewing the protection of the kingdom by Danteśvarī, the tutelary goddess of the king (Carrin, 2005). The goddess was supposed to bestow the king with her religious power (*śakti*). The relationship between the king and his goddess was duplicated in the relation between the clans and their village goddess (Sundar, 1997, 54). In his analysis of the *dasara* festival in Bastar, A. Gell (1997) stresses the ritual participation of the Gond and Dorla, who used to pull the chariot of the goddess through the towns. A. Gell also shows that the king was "captured" by the tribal people, who urged him to share game and alcohol with them, before taking him back to the palace in great triumph. Then, the king paid homage to the goddess, acknowledging her protection of the kingdom.

In the same ritual, the theme of human sacrifice is suggested by an ascetic who enters a cavity, arranged to represent a tomb, in the Darbar hall (audience hall) of the palace. The king, then, represents the *jajmān*, who organizes and sponsors the sacrifice as well as the victim, represented by the ascetic. Human sacrifice was replaced, later, by buffalo sacrifice in Bastar but seems to have survived until the colonial period in the feudatory states of northern Orissa, when Hinduized chiefs tried to obtain supernatural powers by worshipping the goddess (Carrin, 2005).

Among the Hill Maria and Bison Horn Maria, there is a shrine dedicated to a Hinduized goddess, Bhūmi Devī (→ Bhū), the goddess of the earth, who, according to the myth, gave birth to the Maria. The Bison Horn worship another deity, Ban Devī, the goddess of the forest (*ban* [i.e. *vana*]) who receives animal sacrifice in the forest. Their pantheon includes malevolent spirits (*rau*) who bring about disease (Grigson, 1949, 206). The symbolism of human sacrifice, which was important in Bastar, is also present among the Santal, Bhuiya, and Kharia of Orissa, where tribal communities had to negotiate their status with the Hindu king or other tribal chiefs. Among the Kond, these alliances contributed to equilibrate the cycles of murder and vengeance that used to take place among the clans as well as the rivalries that opposed two religious groups – those who used to venerate the goddess of the earth and the adepts of the god of the light (Nayak, 1989).

G. Pfeffer (1982) and R. Hardenberg (2005) have done intensive ethnography among the hill people of Orissa, such as the Dongria Kond, who are less Hinduized. They argue that the dichotomous order of the Ādivāsīs cannot be interpreted as the result of Sanskritization, Kṣatriyaization, or any type of Hinduization (Pfeffer, 1982, 6). In Koraput, there is a ritual hierarchy that implies interaction between local communities and Hindu castes (Pfeffer, 2010). Various tribal groups operate as patrons of low-caste clients such as the Pano – weavers who provide the Dangria Kondh with ritual clothes but who are alleged to formerly have been offering victims for human sacrifice (Boal, 1982). Similar relationships are found among the Dangria Kondh and the Dombo, a low-status weaver caste in Koraput who acted as ritual mediators and musicians for the Kond, Gadaba, and Rona (Hardenberg, 2005; Berger, 2007; Otten, 2008).

The Tribal Pantheons and the Hindu Gods and Temples

In most cases, the hierarchy of values expressed in indigenous ritual systems differs sensibly from the hierarchical ethos that pervades Hindu society. Globally, tribal societies are more egalitarian and more holistic, since they seem to revolve around their own cosmogony. But self-definitions may be challenged by ascriptions, since indigenous people have to contend with the identities that outsiders impose on them.

The creation myths of the tribal groups are often stories of incestuous relationships. V. Elwin (1946) described tribal cosmogonies where a pair of siblings create the world through an incestuous relationship, and G. Pfeffer (2010, 3) notes that the specific and delimited "whole" of the Kuttia appears in the shape of seven territorial clans born as children of the earth goddess in a certain order of seniority. The Mundas were born from a couple of ancestors, Luktum Haram and Luktum Budhi, while among the Santals, Pilcu Haram and Pilcu Budhi gave birth to seven brothers and sisters who generated the clans.

Usually, a brother and a sister are associated with the sun and the moon, who quarrel. The sun takes revenge on his sister, cutting her body in pieces. The moon is wounded, and ever since, she appears in different shapes and, once a month, as the full moon. The myth relates the wounds of the moon to the origin of women's menstrual cycle. The main tribal god is often identified with the sun, or the moon, such as Chando, among the Santal, and though he does not receive regular offerings, he may express the unconscious wish to present a unified image of the indigenous pantheon. This supreme god, considered omniscient, is also called Dharmesh by the Oraon and Thakur by the Santal; the same principle is expressed in Bondo mythology, where Mahaprabhu is the supreme god (Elwin, 1950, 59). His equivalent is called Sonum by the Saora (Vitebsky, 1993, 9).

Among the Santal, the term *buru bonga* labels the village gods and may be considered a generic class including individual deities such as Rongo Ruji, the patron of the hunt, conceptualized as a particular kind of *buru bonga* (Carrin-Bouez, 1986, 86). Maran Buru among the Santals and Sing Bonga among the Mundas are the main deities worshipped in the *sarna*, the sacred grove that also shelters other village deities, often located in different spatial categories. The *sarna* is considered an emblem of indigenous cults. Today, Ādivāsīs in central India refer to their religion as Sarna (or Sarna Dhorom; see below), implying that they are not Hindus.

In central India, some tribal goddesses may have a Hindu origin. A. Ghosh (2006, 176) mentions the cult of Gawan Deoti, who was at first a household god of the Mahto, a Hindu agricultural caste. Then she became an Oraon lineage goddess, before becoming the protectress of the village. U. Skoda (2011) shows that in some Hindu kingdoms such as Bonai in Orissa, tribal deities were included in the regional pantheon. B.D. Kapp and P. Hockings (1989, 231–248) note that in South India, most Hindu gods are unknown to traditional Alu Kurumbas, though "two gods play an important role in their mythology." One is → Brahmā (Buruma Deva), "also called by some of the elders the Creator" (Kapp & Hockings, 1989, 242), and the other is → Yama, the lord of death. They also note recent Hindu influence among the youth, which does not, however, include the concept of reincarnation.

In some cases, the rebuilding of an ancient Hindu temple, close to a tribal place of worship, may lead to a kind of appropriation of the tribal place. C. von Fürer-Haimendorf shows how the rebuilding of the temple of Srisailam, Andhra Pradesh, and its reestablishment as an important pilgrimage center have

> damaged the Chenchus' interests. Previously, some of them were employed as keepers or sweepers of the temple but, since the temple came under the Government Endowment Department in 1978, they were then considered as thieves, if they were going near the storeroom. (Fürer-Haimendorf, 1982, 167–168)

This change has also affected the participation of the Chenchus in Hindu festivals: they used to be feasted at four main temple festivals, but since 1977, this happens only at *makarasaṃkrānti*, one of the Hindu new years. C. von Fürer-Haimendorf (1982, 168) stresses "this unusual attachment of a food-gatherer community to a Hindu temple," though he underlines that "this long symbiotic relationship has not modified the basic economy of the Chenchus, though some of them have been employed in the temple and are paid cash wages."

In the case of the Gond, this attraction for Hindu ideology coincides with the weakening of the status of the Pardhans, their hereditary bards – the Pardhans are a separate ethnic group but are closely associated to the Gonds, and share the same myth of origin. By their recitations, the latter used to instruct the young Gond in the sacred lore of their clans. Today, argues C. von Fürer-Haimendorf (1982, 169), the Gond do not have the means to support a class of bards. The Gond also gave up cow slaughter, since the practice, tolerated by the *nizām* (the Muslim ruler of Hyderabad), was banned when Hyderabad was merged with the Republic of India. Giving up cow sacrifice, which was the best way to worship the clan deities, represented a compromise with the wider society. Should we interpret this compromise as a mark of subordination or as a kind of symbolic exchange, where the giving up of an ancestral practice was meant to procure inclusion in mainstream society?

In the same period, there were other attempts to steer Gond religion in the direction of Hinduism, without negating the clan deities. A Pardhan *guru*, Surup Maharaj, was spreading his message, having a shrine built in the style of a Hindu temple on the top of a hill. The shrine contained a *śivaliṅga* (see → *liṅga*), and a procession was organized, mostly attended by educated Gond (Fürer-Haimendorf, 1982, 172). In this case, to be Hinduized meant to be educated and to participate in a larger world.

Paradigms of Religious Indigeneity

Most of the indigenous societies in India share a semantic universe organized around local gods and ancestors, while clan organization still plays an important role. Clan systems are important to define descent as a principle regulating marriage and inheritance. In some cases, clan organization is linked to an ancient megalithic culture, as among the Munda, Ho, and Saora of central India, where each clan buries the bones of the dead under a megalith in the *sasan*, the graveyard (Ryuji, 1970; Carrin-Bouez, 1986; Ghosh, forthcoming). Those who share a common *sasan* are seen as agnates and share ritual functions in the cults dedicated to subclan deities. All the Mundari-speaking groups have patrilineal, exogamous descent groups of maximal extent, which the literature describes as clans. Except among the Saora, they are mostly totemic. Generally, each clan is divided into a number of subclans, and among groups such as the Santal or Ho, the subclans still function as ritual units, though totemism has declined. Formerly, clan members used to worship their totemic animal or plant, and it was forbidden to kill it or cut it, in case of a vegetal. The agnatic units are more concerned with the regulation of marriage than with anything else, though the descendants of the settlers are those considered to have rights on land. Sometimes, as among the Saora, a dominant group of residents provides the village priest (*buyya*), whose function is hereditary (Elwin, 1955, 129). The land rights attributed to the original settlers (*khuntkattidar*s) has allowed the progressive Hinduization of the Munda chiefs during the last centuries, since they gave land to the Hindu soldiers that they recruited or to Brahmans who performed Hindu rituals for them, opening the way for a class of Hindu middlemen and for state formation in the form of a Hinduized kingdom (Roy, 1970). K.S. Singh (1983, 19) notes that "the interaction of the Hindu (Sadan) and Munda religious systems led to Shiva being accepted as the Mahadev bonga and Parvati as the Chandi bonga." The Munda also participated in *dasai* (i.e. *daśaharā*) and other Hindu festivals.

In central India, clan organization is still expressed during funerals among the Munda, Santal, and Saora, when agnates perform certain ritual duties such as offering rice beer on the bones of the deceased, to allow the "bone flowers" left after the cremation to "bloom," a metaphor combining the male principle – bone – with the female principle of the flower and the flesh. Among the Gadaba of Koraput, the agnates of each generation worship the dead of the lineage (*kuda*). G. Pfeffer (2001, 123) argues that this ritual aims at making the dead alive, through the bodies of sacrificial buffalos, since the departed from the previous generation who must be driven away are symbolically sent to agnates residing in other villages. Among the Saora, the *guar*, the last funeral ritual, is also celebrated for the dead of one generation (Vitebsky, 1993, 226–237). These rituals express the solidarity between close and distant agnates when engaging in important exchanges, sometimes marked by possession, since the recent dead are supposed to come back and talk to their descendants.

Tribes and Castes in Interaction

I have presented some cultural traits – such as the special attachment of tribal groups to the land, clan organization, and ancestral cults – as paradigms of tribal identity. We may add double priesthood, described below. I shall now turn to the interrelations that we may find between tribal and nontribal people in a particular region. In the Koraput district of Orissa, P. Berger (2002) has studied the interactions between people categorized as tribal and nontribal communities or Desia, the latter term including the low castes. The region of Koraput is quite homogenous and has been called by G. Pfeffer "the Koraput complex" (1997); it is also conspicuous by the relative absence of high castes. All Desia categories are internally divided in hierarchically ordered segments that neither intermarry nor dine with one another. P. Berger shows that the principles of seniority and juniority are present in all groups and orders them hierarchically. Thus, the Gadaba belonging to the original Cobra clan are patronizing service castes such as Kumar (potters), Kamar (blacksmiths), or Sundi (distillers) and act as mediators between the other inhabitants and the gods, while their clients communicate with human beings. All Desia share a common lifestyle, wear the same dress, build their house in the same manner, believe in the same gods, and participate in the same festivals. The senior/junior dichotomy replaces, here, the hierarchical principle of the pure and the impure that, according to L. Dumont (1966), prevails in the caste system.

Hinduization seems to pervade all groups in the same way, since Rona, Kumar, Gaudo, Mali, and Sundi all wear the sacred thread (*poita* [i.e. → *yajñopavīta*]) and a *tulsī* necklace – a symbol of Hindu sanctity (Berger, 2002, 69). In Koraput, the position of the Kamar is ambivalent, since they wear the sacred thread and avoid beef but eat pork. Thus, they usually do not eat with other groups, though today Gadaba men eat in Kamar houses. It is also important that except "the external Kamar," all other Desia clients contribute alcohol to "cool down" the Hindu goddess whose cult is organized by the senior Gadaba from the Cobra clan.

This example shows Koraput social life as homogenous, though pervaded by hierarchical principles relating to senior and junior categories, while the adoption of Hindu elements seems to be equally shared by the different groups.

Hinduized Rituals as a Common Idiom between Tribal Groups and Castes?

Several scholars have noted that some tribal festivals coincide with Hindu ones: the *sahrul* festival of the Oraon – which celebrates the blooming of the *mohua* flowers (bot. Madhuca longifolia) – falls on the day of *holī*, the *sohrae* (cattle) festival of the Santals on the day of *dīvalī*. This superposition of ritual events does not necessarily mean that they have the same meaning for the actors, and A. Ghosh (2006, 223) notes that the Oraon do not participate in the religious rituals of the Hindus. The Oraon also claim that the lower Hindu castes are not easily accepted into their community (Ghosh, 2006, 224). R. Rousseleau (2011, 132–138) sees the spring festival (*caitra*) of the Porajas of Orissa as an indigenous parallel to the royal ritual of the Jeypore state (*daśaharā*), thereby stressing the importance of a Hindu order pervading over expressions of local power. Nevertheless, R. Rousseleau underlines the fact that in their villages, the Porajas sometimes patronize castes from an urban background as their subjects.

Among indigenous people, village rituals represent the cosmic order as well as the agricultural cycle, associated with taboos. Most agricultural rituals, such as transplanting paddy or harvesting, are celebrated in the sacred grove where animal sacrifices are offered to village deities. Among most tribal groups in central India, one finds two types of priesthood. The village priests called *dihuri, baiga*, or *naeke* are in charge of the agricultural rituals (Carrin-Bouez, 1986, 92–93). This is a function inherited in the patriline, though sometimes the priest is chosen through possession by the tribal deities. The second type of priest is often considered a shaman, a medium, or a healer and is called *ojha, guniar, mati*, and *dissari*. These healers often communicate through possession with different deities held responsible for misfortune. The mediums or shamans display their powers during healing rituals, powers that are learned from their master, though some get their powers from a mystic spouse. As a general rule, the possessed priests are men, but there are exceptions among the Santal, where women may receive healing powers (Carrin, 1997), and among the Saora, where priestesses are common (Elwin, 1955, 133).

Tribal Groups from the Nilgiris

It seems that a hierarchical system has existed in the Nilgiris for a long time. These tribes share an ecological habitat in the Nilgiri Mountains and have been protected against industrialization. A common myth relates that three brothers gave birth to three tribes, the Badaga, the Kota, and the Toda (Mandelbaum, 1989, 146), which form a homogeneous system. While the Kota used to do leather work, the aristocratic Toda were rearing buffalos to get milk in order to worship their gods in their sacred cowshed. The Badagas were often working for the Toda.

After Independence, the Badaga, who were cultivating, became experts in horticulture and managed to export their production to other regions. This allowed them to become the dominant group, from an economic point of view. This economic success allowed the Badaga to buy some of the Toda lands, since the Toda economy was not competitive due to the lack of pasture. There are no clear-cut territorial divisions to mark the boundaries of each group, and it is sometimes difficult for an outsider to distinguish them, "since the settlement of rights depended on the classification of land in combination with the classification of people as communities" (Cederlöf, 2008, 230).

The Kota, however, who have always offered ritual services to other groups during funerals, are considered subaltern, and they must bow before the Toda and the Badaga, who do not mark any reciprocal gesture. Other subaltern groups, such as the Kurumba and the Urali, seem more peripheral and have no ritual and economic ties with the groups of higher status. Formerly, each Kota family had some economic and ritual ties with a Kurumba family who used to provide pots for their funerals. But since the Kurumba are suspected of practicing witchcraft, by introducing stones in the stomach of their victims when the latter are asleep, the ritual ties with other communities have been altered (Mandelbaum, 1989, 150).

P. Hockings (1989b, 206–231) stresses that today, the relationships between Kota and Badaga are tense, since the latter have Sanskritized themselves. When the Badaga own shops in Ootacamund, for example, they do not allow the Kota to enter, and the latter refuse to play music during Badaga ceremonies. The Badaga feel that they represent the old Nilgiri culture and claim a higher social and ritual status, stressing ritual purity as a value. The last point also explains why they distance themselves from the Kota, who are suspected of eating carrion, who play music at funerals, and who work as blacksmiths. Today, the Badaga manage without the ritual services of the Kotas, and this breaks up the old social system of the Nilgiris. The Toda, who used to provide the Kota with butter for their ceremonies, also avoid walking through the Kota settlements, or else pray in order not to be polluted, when they cannot avoid passing through.

The complementary relationships that linked the Nilgiris communities have some resemblance to the caste system, since it implies a division of labor along hierarchical lines, and these links, defined in the economic sphere, had some religious correlates. Even so, the Toda, the higher group, never acted like Brahmans but rather withdrew to their own ritual practices, organized around the cult of the sacred dairies. It seems, however, that the dominant groups, the Badaga and the Toda, have established a link to a Hindu temple in Ootacamund, the Mārīyammaṉ Temple, while the Kota, the Kurumba, and the Urali are marginalized. As A.R. Walker writes,

> The Mariamma temple, situated near the Ooty bazaar, is now a major ritual centre for Todas; they attend the annual festival when the image of the presiding deity is taken in procession through the streets, they make vows and they use the temple precincts for their ear-piercing and readmittance-to-caste ceremonies. (Walker, 1986, 287)

They hear about the efficacy of pilgrimage to Hindu shrines. In the market, they buy pictorial representations of Hindu gods and goddesses – → Śiva and his consort → Pārvatī, their sons Gaṇeśa (→ Gaṇapati/Gaṇeśa) and Subrahmaṇya (see → Murukaṉ), and Viṣṇu and Lakṣmī (→ Śrī Lakṣmī) – and these images occupy a place of honor in many a household. Among the Badaga, P. Hockings notes that

> the dominant religious practice, in what has loosely been called "village Hinduism," differs little from the popular Dravidian worship described for other parts of South India by Elmore (1915) and Whitehead (1921). The most important acts of worship are the *puja* performed by a priest on behalf of a family on the occasion of a ceremony or a funeral (in the case of the village community), or any other life-cycle ritual (in the case of the family). (Hockings, 1989b, 221)

The interrelations that prevail among the different Nilgiri groups mobilize hierarchical principles that are rooted in values different from those that organize the caste system. Still, the impure Kurumba are at the bottom of the hierarchy, while the Badaga, formerly inferior to the Toda, express their economic superiority by adopting Hindu practices. It seems, however, that Hinduism is quite recent in the Nilgiris, compared to some other regions of India to which religious ascetics, Śaiva or Vaiṣṇava, have been coming since the medieval period to propagate their faith.

Hinduized Priesthood and *Bhakti* Movements

In middle India and Orissa, → Caitanya Mahāprabhu brought in a wave of *bhakti* tradition among the Oraon, the Ho, and the Munda (Ghosh, 2006; Verdado, 2003). Some Oraon are *bhagat*s or adepts of Hindu *bābā*s (mainly Kurmi or Mahto). A. Ghosh (2006, 206) stresses that some Sakaldwip Brahman healers have transferred their knowledge to their Oraon disciples. In the same way, the Santal *ojha*, healer and witch finder, is often influenced by Hindu concepts that shape his knowledge, since he stands clearly at the fringe of the tribal and the Hindu world (Carrin, 1997, 115, 299–324).

In Bengal, Santal women who become priestesses are often those who have transgressed the rule of tribal endogamy when they have left the village to work in kilns or mines. Having had an affair with a Hindu, they are excluded from Santal society and declared dead in their village, where their agnates perform a mock funeral. Among Santals, female → possession is not considered a proper expression of devotion. It is not consciously sought but just happens, and since it is not allowed for women, it is interpreted as an exceptional religious experience, the call of the goddess → Kālī (Carrin, 1999, 116). Generally, the woman herself does not seek possession unless she is encouraged and controlled by a priestess or a *guru*.

Such priestesses are low-caste (Lohar, Bangi, or Muci) or Santal women who have acquired powers through suffering. The goddess transfers her cosmic energy (*śakti*) to her female devotees as if *śakti* was a female substance that may be passed from mother to daughter. The possessed woman becomes a priestess and is able to heal people while she offers a regular cult to the goddess.

Such religious careers imply that the Santal devotees internalize Hindu concepts such as *bhakti* devotion and *śakti*, though they adapt them to their personal life and subjectivity. Already during the colonial period, Santal villagers invoked Hindu goddesses and gods such as Kālī and Mahādev, and in Bengal in the 1960s, they certainly tried to raise their status by observing some purity rules, though this tendency was absent in the north of Orissa. Santal *ojha*s, in Bengal, → Jharkhand, and Orissa, have Hindu tutelary deities, and one feels that the *ojha* has borrowed many elements from his Hindu counterpart. Still, as P.O. Bodding observes, "Much of the practices of the Santal *ojha* seems to be essentially outside the Hindu fold; (but) the *ojha*'s special *bonga*s [tutelary deities] seem to be of nature somewhat different from that of the ordinary Santal *bonga*s" (Bodding, 1986, 10). The *ojha* is clearly a Santal institution bridging the gap between popular Hinduism and his own religion, centered on the cults of the *bonga*s.

More recently, however, *ojha*s have tried to find a new niche in their own community, by taking part in ecological movements, side by side with Santal intellectuals. Today, the Santals manifest a radical attitude toward questions of identity, probably because they are a major group of some ten million, found in every state of eastern India as well as in Orissa, Jharkhand, Bangladesh, Bhutan, and Nepal.

Hierarchization and Reform Movements

R. Deliège (1985, 98) notes that the Bhil include subtribes such as the Damas, Graias, Dhodras, and Dublas, "who have a tendency towards hierarchy and are inevitably more Hinduized than the pure Bhils." In middle India, some groups have tried to claim higher status in the caste hierarchy, like the Bhumij, whose chiefs claimed to be Kṣatriya. The symbolic appropriation of the king by peripheral tribal groups, as confirmed by Juang narratives and Bhuiya participation in enthronization rituals, is quite common (Skoda, 2011; Carrin, 2011). Still, the hierarchy of values expressed in indigenous rituals differs sensibly from the hierarchical ethos that pervades Hindu hierarchy.

The tribal rebellions that broke out around 1820 may be seen as symbolic responses to the changes that the tribal societies had experienced in passing from a barter system to a market economy. In addition, many Ādivāsī were forced to work in the mines of Bihar and northern Orissa and on the indigo plantations in north Bengal. The Santal were used to clear land and to build roads for the transportation of colonial goods.

The second series of uprisings, which broke out in the second half of the 19th century (Santal rebellion of 1855 and Birsaite movement of 1895), corresponded to the development of colonial administration, which brought a large number of Hindu middlemen to the tribal areas. These movements are pervaded by two opposed ideological currents: some were strongly anti-Hindu, like the Santal rebellion, while others, such as the Santal Kherwar movement or the Tana Bhagat movement among the Oraon, were inspired by Hindu reform.

If the Santals do not Sanskritize today, then it seems that they did so in the past, as in the Kherwar movement of 1871–1874. The Kherwar leader, Bhagrit, was enthroned as a *rājā* and declared himself chief of all Santals, to liberate them from colonial rule and missionary influence and regain their lost kingdom. The movement was both political and religious, since Bhagrit claimed that the land of the Santal Parganas belonged to the Santals who had made it habitable, and not to the landlords or moneylenders. To free the Santals from their oppressors, they must win the favor of Singbahni, the moneylenders' god, by giving up the *bonga* cult, purifying themselves and their houses, and getting rid of impure animals such as pigs and poultry (Carrin & Tambs-Lyche, 2008a, 209). Bhagrit and his followers behaved like ascetics but threatened with dire sanctions those who did not follow their teaching, stressing the value of → purity, borrowed from Hinduism. This tendency countered the stigmatizing Hindu image of the barbaric and impure aboriginal, a stereotype that fed Hindu contempt for tribal people.

The reform movements tried to revise the alienated image of the group, which reflected the rejection of the dominant, while the tribal rebellions rather tried to reactivate a glorious past, opposing the traditional leadership of the *pahan*, the village priest, and of the *mahto*, the headman. But the Tanas were also protesting against *zamīndār*s and landlords, and most of the reform movements had an agrarian dimension.

D. Hardiman's (1987) study in western India shows how in the 1920s, several thousand people followed the demands of a new goddess who spoke through mediums, asking people to give up liquor, fish, and meat and to bathe twice a day. D. Hardiman stresses that the Devi Movement of 1922–1923 in Gujarat should not be interpreted as Sanskritization, because one of its main goals was to challenge the upper castes.

Parallel to agrarian mobilization, reform movements aiming at assimilation of the Brahmanical model were frequent in the second half of the 19th century. Ādivāsīs living close to urban centers in middle India often became *bhagat*s (devotees), following the *bhakti* movement influential in bazaars and urban culture, since it was linked to a quest for improvement, reform, and upward mobility. Certain indigenous movements of sectarian character, such as the *bhakti* cults, also challenged the moral values and attitudes of orthodox caste society. Certainly, the emergence of Mahima Dharma, in mid-19th-century Orissa, articulated a challenge to the authority of the *rājā* and to Brahmanical power by rejecting idol worship and caste rules (Guzy, 2011). But while the movement became a monastic order in Dhenkanal, its anti-Brahman strand gained Ādivāsīs through the headmen in Koraput, where the followers, today, are mainly Ādivāsīs. Through *bhakti*, the moral order is no longer determined by the → *dharma* of the caste but by the emotional relationship that links the devotee to his deity. *Bhakti* cults have often been propagated by renouncers and other religious figures and represent an internalization of some aspects of Hinduism where the devotee distances himself or herself from the hierarchical values pervading mainstream Hinduism.

Missionary education expanded considerably from 1905 to 1920. For the Ādivāsīs, conversion implied conciliating the god of the colonial masters and, especially, investing the religious sphere with symbolic efficiency capable of opposing exploitation by Hindu middlemen. Through education, Christianity became a means of upward mobility. The Christian ideal of justice, propagated by the missionaries, conformed to the idea that Ādivāsīs had lost the egalitarian values of their ancestors in the 19th century, values that were guaranteed by the authority of the village chiefs but that the Hinduized Munda *rājā* had squandered by "selling out" the tribal societies to the Hindus. While various associations continued to work to improve the living conditions of tribal communities in central India, a militant movement grew in 1938–1947, inspired by the Adivasi Mahasabha. Today, Mundari groups in Jharkhand stress the importance of the return to the Sarna religion as a common symbol for the Ādivāsīs.

Bhakti and Hinduization in the Northeast

In contrast to the Munda tribes, who live in the midst of the world of caste, the Naga tribes have always enjoyed a relative independence. The Hindu influence has not spawned a symbolic language for them, as is the case for other groups of Assam, such as the Ahom or the Meithei of Manipur. The *bhakti* movement has been dominant in lowland Assam not only in the ideological sense but also institutionally. The division of the village into devotional congregations associated with *nāmghar*s (prayer halls) and the affiliation of individuals to particular *satra*s (monastic centers) is a crucial dimension of Assamese society (Cantlie, 1984, 236). The devotional sect constitutes one of the chief means by which the Assamese have become progressively Hinduized, though they do not recognize the superiority of the → *brahman*. Certain castes have acted as channels by which Hinduized tribal groups have entered Hindu society, but they are not discrete groups with fixed boundaries. It seems that in Assam, a relatively egalitarian class structure has helped "to contain the hierarchical principle and narrow the distance between castes" (Cantlie, 1984, 236).

In Assam, the influence of missionaries has proved decisive for the tribal populations in realizing their new aspirations. The British entered the Khasi country in 1820 and established their headquarters in the southern part of the region, where the people speak Mon-Khmer languages. Ethnic mobilization in northeast India has often been influenced by Protestant Evangelical movements. The Baptists developed an alphabet to teach Garo in the schools, an initiative imitated by many tribal groups. These missionaries established contact between the Hill Garo and those of the plains and developed a Christian elite. The Christianization of Assam triggered reactions, especially among the Khasi. Under missionary influence, claims to political representation with guaranteed individual freedom replaced the tacit acceptance of the chiefs' traditional power and intrigues with the British. But in the late 1950s, Jeebon Roy, an educated Khasi and son of a wealthy merchant, organized a movement for cultural renewal – in reaction against the missionaries – that was based on the religious and social traditions of the group (Jaswal, 1982, 173–180). Today, Christian Khasi are dominant, but revivalist trends are found among the Hinduized minority.

Hinduism took a firm hold in Manipur during the rule of Pamheiba (1709–1748), who adopted Hindu practices, and the royal family converted, between 1737 and 1738, to Vaiṣṇavism, which was popular in Bengal. The population followed, and Vaiṣṇavism became the official religion. But the beliefs and the customs of the Meitheis never died out, since they were patronized by the royal court (Saha, 1982, 99–100). After the formation of the State Congress in 1943, the Sanamahis, a group of Meitheis, emerged, who stressed that their old religion was non-Vaiṣṇava. It is alleged that they rediscovered some manuscripts, which had been hidden in villages, representing their old pre-Hindu tradition. More recently, a revivalist movement led by the *maiba*s, the priests of the old Meithei religion, has asserted tribal identity, negating the influence of the Hinduized middle class. The resurgence of Meithei identity in the late 1960s was expressed in a religious movement when Naoria Phullo, a Meithei religious leader, reaffirmed the worship of Sanamahee, a pre-Hindu deity in opposition to → Rādhā and → Kṛṣṇa. R. Bhorucha (1991, 748) argues that the revivalist movement was also voiced through anti-Hindu plays in the 1970s.

More complex is the case of the Bodo, who had a Hinduization movement in the 1970s but have turned to politics since their movement was prohibited in 1992. Intratribal conflicts were part of the precolonial history of northeast India. Ethnic conflict has taken two different forms: one was intertribal or intratribal, and the other is indigenous versus exogenous. Many tribal groups competed for scarce resources, land, and hegemony and used to raid one another's territory, practicing head-hunting. The British rule and the impact of Christianity not only reduced the conflicts but also stopped head-hunting. But old rivalries are reappearing in new forms. The most notorious of these conflicts is the Naga-Kuki conflict (Nag, forthcoming).

Contrary to the Munda tribes, or even the Bodo, who have often unwittingly borrowed some of the values of the dominant Hindus, the Naga – partly Christianized – have conceived their autonomy in political terms. Certainly, they have profited from their geopolitical situation but equally from the independent position that they have maintained *vis-à-vis* the Ahom or the Manipuri, who, at different times, have tried to subdue them. The Naga movement, marked by the factionalism of the different tribes, has undergone many phases that have contributed to the creation of Nagaland State. But the different Naga tribes have not arrived at complete mutual understanding. The churches have tried to reconcile Christians of different groups but have not always succeeded (Carrin, 2011). Despite the fact that northeast India did not really figure in the national imagination of modern India, any resistance to assimilation was seen as a threat to its composite cultural ethos (Nag, 2002, 313–347).

Reasserting Tribal Identity

From the 1960s onward, scholars (Orans, 1965; Gautam, 1977; Mahapatra, 1972; Carrin-Bouez, 1986) have noted Sanskritization and other forms of upper-caste imitation among the Santal, "sometimes inverted and directed against the upper-caste outsiders (*diku*) themselves" (Parkin, 1992, 6). But since the 1970s, I have observed a movement of identity assertion, or Santalization (Gautam, 1977), which means that the Santal today consider themselves a separate group, as good as any Hindu, and feel that they deserve to be acknowledged as such. This assertion has been made through different cultural and religious movements since the 1960s, stressing the separateness of the Santali language, for which an indigenous script (*ol chiki*) was devised in the late 1930s by Ragunath Murmu, a religious leader in Mayurbanj, Orissa (Carrin, 2011). Ragunath Murmu and his disciples launched a religious movement called Sarna Dhorom (the Sacred Grove religion) around 1970 to develop original forms of resistance through a return to the worship of tribal deities. Thus, the Santals, today, regard themselves as true Indians who were here before the *diku* or caste people, since they came from the Indus Valley, or even from Sumer. They are not the only group to claim an ancient ancestry and to emphasize separateness from Hinduism, which means that they often keep away from Hindu festivals, such as *holī* or *durgāpūjā*, in which they used to participate. They make considerable efforts to present themselves as a separate moral and ritual community, having its own writers and intellectuals. This is not an isolated case, as the denial of territorial rights and privileges to tribal communities by dominant regional communities has led tribal groups to adopt the idea of indigenous people (Xaxa, 1999, 3594).

Tribal Eschatologies and Hindu Values

Hinduization as practice takes different expressions, structuring social dynamics in different hierarchical systems. We have seen that the influence of *bhakti* as the devotional ethos of the individual could serve to express aspirations to modernity. Is this influence also manifest at the level of tribal eschatologies? Reincarnation (→ *saṃsāra*) is generally associated with the Hindu doctrine of → *karma*, but it also pervades tribal eschatologies. Some anthropologists interpret these beliefs as a result of Hinduization, whereas others seem to think that Hinduism can be traced from these ideas (Parkin, 1992, 203).

Tribal eschatologies generally recognize at least two souls. While the first of these contains the personality of the deceased and eventually merges with the body of the ancestors, the other soul, which often lacks a full personality and is conceptualized as a soul substance, is reincarnated. Generally speaking, however, the Hindu concept of reincarnation, where rebirth is determined by the law of *karma* as the balance of merit and sin accumulated in previous existences, does not make sense for most indigenous people.

Apart from explicit statements by tribal informants, there is evidence of the practice of naming a child after his grandparents, or two generations away, which is common among the Mundas or the Santals. It seems evident, as R. Deliège stresses for the → Dalit, that Ādivāsīs and Janjātis do not accept the Hindu ideology regarding the accumulation of merit and that they reject the idea that there could be a connection between the position ascribed to them by high castes and their sinful behavior during their past lives.

It seems that Sanskritization or Hinduization as imitation of the upper castes was prevalent in the 1960s but has since been replaced by assertive movements, agrarian claims, social struggles, and cultural awareness. The subordination of the Ādivāsīs has led them to formulate claims not only on the basis of a shared experience of oppression but also with reference to their special culture. Through these struggles, to be an Ādivāsī became no longer a stigma, and there was no need to imitate the higher castes. It became evident that social struggles could not accommodate Hinduization as they did in the 19th century (Carrin & Tambs-Lyche, 2008a). Ādivāsīs became more conscious of their own heritage and found new ontological grounds for assertion in their traditions. This process was, of course, mediated by the influence of political ideas such as Naxalism (Maoist revolutionary ideology), which influenced tribal parties in central India and in the northeast.

Hinduism Imposed on Tribal Groups through Propaganda by Fundamentalist Groups

Some groups considered tribal, like the Kurmis, have been Hinduized by participating in a mass ceremony where they were given the sacred thread. One may wonder if such mass conversions were not imposed on groups who were looking for social mobility. When the Kurmis in Mayurbhanj, Orissa, were claiming Kṣatriya status, it seems that their aim was to distance themselves from the Santals, with whom they had been engaged in an agrarian protest movement. Naranjan, a Kurmi leader who had earlier threatened the Brahmans with conversions to Islam or Christianity, became a champion of Hinduism. He was influenced by the → Arya Samaj and organized a Kurmi Conference in 1937 to get the Kurmis to adopt the Hindu way of life, abstaining from meat and alcohol, and to claim Kṣatriya status. As a consequence of the new status of the Kurmis, some Santals have sought to Sankritize themselves (Nanda, 2007, 404n22). Such examples were found in many parts of India during the 1930s, a period when various communities tried to assert their status.

In many cases, economic and political subordination is buttressed by the ideology of caste pollution and purity. This is manifest in the formation of Jharkhand State in 2000. Certainly, the Bharatiya Janata Party and Hindu nationalists did not have the exploitation of lower castes and Ādivāsīs as their principal worry, nor did they care about protecting the cultural unity of Mundari groups. However, the Bharatiya Janata Party wanted to win votes in the Jharkhand region to counterbalance its lack of support in central and northern Bihar. Moreover, by gaining power in the new state, the Bharatiya Janata Party intended to control the industrial activity in Jharkhand. Finally, on the ideological level, the → Rashtriya Swayamsevak Sangh deployed its influence in order to destabilize the religious and cultural minorities so as to impose the uniform mold of a Hindu *rāṣṭra* (state) on the Ādivāsīs. In the rural areas of Jharkhand, however, there are competing forces to seduce Ādivāsī educated youth. A. Shah (2010) notes the prejudices of members of the high castes toward the Mundas. But she stresses that Munda village elites Sanskritize and Brahmanize themselves, claiming it is morally wrong and ritually impure to drink alcohol (Shah, 2010, 171). A. Shah remarks that the Jharkhand Ādivāsī elites tend to promote the ideal indigenous citizen, to delete the image of the "jungly" Ādivāsī indulging in promiscuity. This attitude, however, is uncomfortably close to the position of the Hindu right-wing nationalists, who argue that Jharkhand's tribal people should be made into proper Hindus by emulating Hindu castes.

For Madhya Pradesh, A. Baviskar (2005) argues that unconverted Ādivāsīs face the social stigma of being considered backward by dominant groups such as caste Hindus, Muslims, and Christians. She argues that while in Madhya Pradesh various Ādivāsī communities were making claims to indigenousness, the Sangh Parivar, expanding its presence in the area, offered to incorporate Ādivāsīs into the hegemonic Hindu majority. But she also stresses that the claims to indigenousness made by the Hindu right are different, since Ādivāsīs want to protest against displacement and be included in the Indian polity, while the Sangh Parivar want to recruit adepts who will then fight the unconverted Ādivāsīs.

Similarly, P. Kanungo (2003) shows how the penetration of Rashtriya Swayamsevak Sangh has been strategically planned in Orissa since the 1950s, supported by high-caste elites and then inducing the state government to introduce laws prohibiting religious conversion or cow slaughter.

Conclusion

Hinduization as an imitative strategy to get higher status in the local hierarchy seems to persist only where Ādivāsīs live in multi-ethnic villages among Hindu castes. In other terms, Hinduization persists when resistance is difficult. Despite ethnic conflicts, it is clear that indigenous peoples are eager to establish solidarity among tribal people. To achieve this, they make use of ideals inherited from Christianity as an instrument of social protest. Moreover, their representatives try to construct a discourse on ethnicity that they propagate by the intermediary of the United Nations, stressing their rights to self-determination as sons of the soil and criticizing the policies of assimilation and integration pursued by the Indian government since Independence. In challenging the role of the state, Ādivāsī/Janjāti movements have taken different forms that range from identity claims and electoral politics to the critical reception of development programs launched on tribal territory. The Maoists in particular have succeeded in securing at least some support from Ādivāsīs over recent years (Shah, 2011). But other pacific answers have been voiced through Ādivāsī/Janjāti engagement in the indigenous people's movement with international organizations.

Since liberalization, identity assertion has taken a more political turn. On the political front, however, the main Indian parties still exert some attraction for tribal people, but their insidious presence contributes to dividing the tribes. This is perhaps one of the reasons for the Rashtriya Swayamsevak Sangh's success in Orissa – there, it has successfully appropriated the figure of Jagannāth to gain influence in remote areas such as the Kondmals, where they have attracted members of minor groups, marginalized economically and politically, to persuade them to be part of the Hindu *rāṣṭra* (Kanungo, 2003, 3294). The strategy of the Rashtriya Swayamsevak Sangh has been successful, since it consisted in making the tribal people feel that they belonged to a larger world, and it has even led to violence against other groups, in a context where ethnic conflicts have been recurrent.

Hindutva ideology may be a caricature of Hinduism, but ethnicity has emerged as a discourse where the Rashtriya Swayamsevak Sangh was able to manipulate some tribal people against others. Certainly, ethnicity could not resist the ruthless onslaught of liberalism that has contributed to marginalizing tribal people. Today, for most tribal people who feel rancor against the dominant Hindu castes, Hinduism has become the correlate of inner colonization. Ādivāsī assertion through culture and art is now becoming more influential, since Ādivāsī elites are voicing resistance at the national and international level through the movement of indigenous people.

Bibliography

Bailey, F.G., "Tribe and 'Caste' in India," *CIS* 5, 1961, 7–19.

Bailey, F.G., *Tribe, Caste and Nation: A Study of Political Activity and Political Change in Highland Orissa*, Manchester, 1960.

Baviskar, A., "Adivasi Encounters with Hindu Nationalism in M.P.," *EPW* 40/48, 2005, 5005–5113.

Béteille, A., "The Concept of Tribe with Special Reference to India," *AES* 27/2, 2006, 297–318.

Berger, P., "Sacrificial Food, the Person and the Ritual System of the Gadaba," in: G. Pfeffer, ed., *Periphery and Centre*, Delhi, 2007, 199–221.

Berger, P., "The Gadaba and the 'Non-ST' Desia of Koraput: Some Observations on Their Interrelations," in: D.K. Behera & G. Pfeffer, eds., *Contemporary Society: Tribal Studies*, vol. V: *Concept of Tribal Society*, New Delhi, 2002, 57–90.

Berger, P., R. Hardenberg, E. Kattner & M. Prager, eds., *The Anthropology of Values: Essays in Honour of Georg Pfeffer*, New Delhi, 2010.

Bhorucha, R., "Politics of Indigenous Theatre: Kanhailal in Manipur," *EPW* 26/11–12, 1991, 747–754.

Bird-David, N., "The Nilgiris Tribal Systems: A View from Below," in: P. Hockings, ed., *Blue Mountains Revisited: Cultural Studies on the Nilgiri Hills*, Delhi, 1997, 5–22.

Boal, B., *The Konds: Human Sacrifice and Religious Change*, Warminster, 1982.

Bodding, P.O., *Studies in Santal Medicine and Connected Folklore*, Calcutta, [1]1925, 1986.

Bose, N.K., *Culture and Society in India*, Bombay, 1967.

Bose, N.K., *Cultural Anthropology*, Bombay, 1961.

Cantlie, A., *The Assamese*, London, 1984.

Carrin, M., "The Billavas of Karnataka and the Santals of Orisa: Two Peripheries Asserting Their Position towards the Centre," in: M. Carrin & L. Guzy, eds., *Voices from the Periphery: Subalternity and Empowerment*, Delhi, 2011, 203–225.

Carrin, M., "The World of Tribes, Revolutionary Movements and Ethnic Withdrawal," in: C. Jafferlot, ed., *Contemporary India*, London, 2010, 543–568.

Carrin, M., "Le sacrifice humain dans les royaumes de jungle, Orissa, Inde," in: J.P. Albert & B. Midant-Reyne, eds., *La sacrifice humain en Egypte ancienne et ailleurs (un ensemble de textes)*, Paris, 2005, 165–183.

Carrin, M., "Retour au bosquet sacré, réflexion sur la réinvention d'une culture adivasi," in : M. Carrin & C. Jafferlot, eds., *Tribus et basses castes: Résistance et autonomie dans la société Indienne, Purusartha* 23, Paris, 2002, 233–264.

Carrin, M., "The Sacrifice of Femininity: Female Sacredness at the Hindu/Tribal Frontier in Bengal," in: H. Tambs-Lyche, ed., *The Feminine Sacred in South Asia*, Delhi, 1999, 114–124.

Carrin, M., *Enfants de la Déesse, dévotion et prêtrise féminine au Bengale*, Paris, 1997.

Carrin, M., & L. Guzy, eds., *Voices from the Periphery: Subalternity and Empowerment*, Delhi, 2011.

Carrin, M., & H. Tambs-Lyche, *An Encounter of Peripheries: The Santals and Their Missionaries, 1867–1900*, Delhi, 2008a.
Carrin, M., & H. Tambs-Lyche, eds., *People of the Jangal: Reformulating Identities and Adaptations in Crisis*, Delhi, 2008b.
Carrin, M., P. Kanungo & G. Toffin, eds., *The Politics of Ethnicity: Adivasis, Janjatis in India and Nepal*, Delhi, forthcoming.
Carrin-Bouez, M., "Acculturation and/or Dialectics: The Relevance of the Hindu Model for the Understanding of Santal Society," in: R. Moser & M. Gautam, eds., *Aspects of Tribal Life in South Asia: Strategy and Survival*, Bern, 1978, 83–92.
Carrin-Bouez, M., *La Fleur et l'Os: Symbolisme et Rituel chez les Santal*, Paris, 1986.
Cederlöf, G., "The Agency of the Colonial Subject: Claims and Rights in Forestlands in the early Nineteenth-Century Nilgiris," in: M. Carrin & H. Tambs-Lyche, eds., *People of the Jangal: Reformulating Identities and Adaptations in Crisis*, Delhi, 2008, 196–227.
Corbridge, S., "The Continuing Struggle for India's Jharkhand: Democracy, Decentralization and the Politics of Names and Numbers," *CCP* 40/3, 2002, 55–71.
Dasgupta, S., "Reordering a World: The Tana Bhagat Movement, 1914–1919," *SiH* 15, 1999, 1–41.
Deliège R., *The Bhils of Western India: Some Empirical and Theoretical Issues in Anthropology in India*, Delhi, 1985.
Dumont, L., *Homo Hierarchicus: Le système des castes et ses implications*, Paris, 1983.
Elwin, V., *The Religion of an Indian Tribe*, London, 1955.
Elwin, V., *Bondo Highlander*, Bombay, 1950.
Elwin, V., *Myths of Middle India*, Bombay, 1943.
Eschmann A., H. Kulke & G.C. Tripathi, eds., *The Cult of Jagannath and the Regional Tradition of Orissa*, Delhi, 1978.
Fürer-Haimendorf, C. von, *Tribal Populations and Cultures of the Indian Subcontinent*, Leiden, 1985.
Fürer-Haimendorf, C. von, *Tribes of India: The Struggle for Survival*, Berkeley, 1982.
Fürer-Haimendorf, C. von, *Return to the Naked Nagas: An Anthropologist's View of Nagaland 1936–1970*, New Delhi, 1976.
Gautam, M., *In Search of Identity: A Case of the Santal of Northern India*, Leiden, 1977.
Gell, A., "Exalting the King and Obstructing the State: A Political Interpretation of Royal Ritual in Bastar District, Central India," *JRAI* 3, 1997, 443–450.
Ghosh, A., *The World of the Oraon: Their Symbols in Time and Space*, Delhi, 2006.
Ghosh, K., "Cross-currents: Traveling Shadows of a Conversion in the Naguri Munda Region of Jharkhand," in: M. Carrin, G. Toffin & P. Kanungo, eds., *The Politics of Ethnicity on the Margins of the State: Janjatis/Adivasis in India and Nepal*, Delhi, forthcoming.
Ghurye, G.S., *The Scheduled Tribes*, Bombay, 1959.
Grigson, W., *The Maria Gond of Bastar*, London, 1947.
Guha, S., *Environment and Ethnicity in India: 1200–1991*, Cambridge UK, 1999.
Guzy, L., "The Poly-culture of Mahima Dharma on Babas and Alekh Shamans in an Ascetic Religious Movement of Orissa," in: M. Carrin & L. Guzy, eds., *Voices from the Periphery: Subalternity and Empowerment*, Delhi, 2011, 155–181.
Hardenberg, R., "Reconsideration of Hinduization and the Caste-Tribe Continuum Model," in: P. Berger, R. Hardenberg, E. Kattner & M. Prager, eds., *The Anthropology of Values: Essays in Honour of Georg Pfeffer*, New Delhi, 2010, 89–103.
Hardenberg, R., "Children of the Earth Goddess: Society, Marriage and Sacrifice in the Highlands of Orissa," diss., Berlin University, 2005.
Hardiman, D., *The Coming of the Devi: Adivasi Assertion in Western India*, Oxford, 1987.
Hauser, B., "Tribal or Tantric? Reflections on the Classification of Goddesses in Southern Orissa," in: G. Pfeffer, ed., *Periphery and Centre*, Delhi, 2007, 131–152.
Heideman, F., *Akka Bakha Religion. Politik und duale Souveränität der Badaga in den Nilgiri Süd-Indiens*, Berlin, 2006.
Hobsbawm, E.J., & T.O. Ranger, *The Invention of Tradition*, Cambridge UK, 1983.
Hockings, P., ed., *Blue Mountains Revisited: Cultural Studies on the Nilgiri Hills*, Delhi, 1997.
Hockings, P., ed., *Blue Mountains: The Ethnography and Biogeography of a South Indian Region*, Delhi, 1989a.
Hockings, P., "The Badagas," in: P. Hockings, ed., *Blue Mountains: The Ethnography and Biogeography of a South Indian Region*, Delhi, 1989b, 206–231.
Hutton, J.H., *The Angami Nagas: With Some Notes on Neighbouring Tribes*, 1921, repr. 1969.
Jaswal, I.J.S., "The Seng Khasi," in: K.S. Singh, ed., *Tribal Movements in India*, vol. I, Delhi, 1982, 173–180.
Jha, D.N., ed., *The Feudal Order: State Society and Ideology in Early Medieval India*, Delhi, 2002.
Kanungo, P., "Hindutva's Entry into a Hindu Province: Early Years of RSS," *EPW* 38/31, 2003, 3293–3303
Kapp, B.D., & P. Hockings, "The Kurumba Tribes," in: P. Hockings, ed., *Blue Mountains: The Ethnography and Biogeography of a South Indian Region*, Delhi, 1989, 231–248.
Karlsson, B.G., & T.B. Subba, eds., *Indigeneity in India*, London, 2006.
Kosambi, D.D., *An Introduction to the Study of Indian History*, Bombay, 1965.
Kulke, H., "Early State Formation and Royal Legitimation in Tribal Areas of Eastern India," in: R. Moser & M.K. Gautam, *Aspects of Tribal Life in South Asia: Strategy and Survival*, Bern, 1979, 29–37.
Kulke, H., & B. Schnepel, eds., *Jagannath Revisited*, Delhi, 2001.
Mahapatra, L.K., "Social Movements among Tribes of India," in: S. Sing, ed., *The Tribal Situation in India*, Shimla, 1972, 399–409.
Mahapatra, S., *The Realm of the Sacred*, Calcutta, 1992.
Majumdar, D.N., "A Study of Tribe-Caste Continuum and the Process of Sanskritization among the Bodo-Speaking Tribe of the Garo Hills," in: S. Sing, ed., *The Tribal Situation in India*, Shimla, 1972, 263–270.

Mandelbaum, D., 1989 "The Nilgiris as a Region," in: P. Hockings, ed., *Blue Mountains: The Ethnography and Biogeography of a South Indian Region*, Delhi, 1989, 1–19.

Mathur, P.R.G., "The Khasi Solidarity Movement," in: K.S. Singh, ed., *Tribal Movements in India*, vol. I, Delhi, 1982, 180–201.

Munshi, S., "Tribal Absorption and Sanskritisation in Hindu Society," *CIS.NS* 13/2, 1979, 293–317.

Nag, S., "Resisting Nation-State: Ethnic Upsurge in Post-colonial North East India," in: M. Carrin, G. Toffin & P. Kanungo, eds., *The Politics of Ethnicity on the Margins of the State: Janjatis/Adivasis in India and Nepal*, Delhi, forthcoming.

Nag, S., *Contesting Marginality: Ethnicity, Insurgency and Subnationalism in North-East India*, Delhi, 2002.

Nanda, C.P., "Marginal Texts, Marginal Men: The Social Mobility Movement of the Kudmi-Mahantas of Orissa," in: G. Pfeffer, ed., *Periphery and Centre: Studies in Orissan History, Religion and Anthropology*, Delhi, 2007, 393–416.

Nayak, P.K., *Blood, Women and Territory: An Analysis of Clan Feuds of the Dangria Konds*, Delhi, 1989.

Orans, M., *The Santal: A Tribe in Search of a Great Tradition*, Detroit, 1965.

Otten, T., "People of the Hills: How the Rona Deal with Social Change," in: M. Carrin & H. Tambs-Lyche, eds., *People of the Jangal: Reformulating Identities and Adaptations in Crisis*, Delhi, 2008, 93–118.

Parkin, R., *The Munda of Central India: An Account of Their Social Organization*, Oxford, 1992.

Pfeffer, G., "Welfare Work among Kuttia Kond," paper presented at the Bonn Conference EMSAS Panel 19: Indigenisation of Modernity in Indian Tribal Societies, Bonn, 2010.

Pfeffer, G., ed., *Periphery and Centre*, Delhi, 2007.

Pfeffer, G., "A Ritual of Revival among the Gadaba of Koraput," in: H. Kulke & B. Schnepel, eds., *Jagannath Revisited*, Delhi, 2001, 123–148.

Pfeffer, G., "The Scheduled Tribes of Middle India as a Unit: Problems of Internal and External Comparison," in: G. Pfeffer & D.K. Behera, eds., *Contemporary Society: Tribal Studies*, vol. I, Delhi, 1997, 1–27.

Pfeffer, G., "Tribal Organization and 'Hindu' Influence," *IAs* 13/1 -2, 1982, 45–54.

Rousseleau, R., "Village Festival and Kingdom Frame: Centre and Periphery from a Porajâ Village Point of View," in: M. Carrin & L. Guzy, eds., *Voices from the Periphery: Subalternity and Empowerment*, Delhi, 2011, 132–154.

Roy, S.C., *The Mundas and Their Country*, Calcutta, 1970.

Ryuji, Y., *Cultural Formation of the Mundas: Hill People surrounding the Ganges Plains*, Tokyo, 1970.

Saha, R.K., "An Ethnic Movement in the Manipur Valley," in: K.S. Singh, ed., *Tribal Movements in India*, vol. I, Delhi, 1982, 97–113.

Samaddar, R., *Memory Identity and Power Politics in the Jungle Mahals: 1890–1950*, Hyderabad, 1998.

Schnepel, B., *The Jungle Kings: Ethnohistorical Aspects on Politics and Rituals in Orissa*, New Delhi, 2002.

Shah, A., *In the Shadows of the State Indigenous Politics: Environmentalism and Insurgency in Jharkhand, India*, Durham, 2010.

Sharma, R.S., "The Kali Age: A Period of Social Crisis," in: D.N. Jha, ed., *The Feudal Order: State Society and Ideology in Early Medieval India*, Delhi, 2002, 62–77.

Singh, B.P., "North-East India: Demography, Culture and Identity Crisis," *MAS* 21/2, 1987, 257–282.

Singh, K.S., *Birsa Munda and His Movement 1874–1901: A Study of a Millenarian Movement in Chotanagpur*, Calcutta, 1983.

Singh, K.S, ed., *Tribal Movements in India*, vols. I–II, Delhi, 1982–1983.

Singh, K.S., "The Haribaba Movement in Chotanagpur 1931–1932," *JBORS* 49, 1963, 286–296.

Sinha, S., ed., *Tribal Polities and State System in Pre-colonial Eastern and North Eastern India*, Calcutta, 1987.

Sinha, S., "State Formation and Rajput Myth in Central India," *MiI* 42/1, 1962, 35–80.

Skoda, U., "The History of the Royal Family of Bonai: Texts, Centres, Authority," in: M. Carrin & L. Guzy, eds., *Voices from the Periphery: Subalternity and Empowerment*, Delhi, 2011, 103–131.

Sontheimer, G.-D., "Hinduism: The Five Components and Their Interaction," in: G.-D. Sontheimer and H. Kulke, eds., *Hinduism Reconsidered*, Delhi, [1]1989, [2]1997, 197–212.

Srinivas, M.N., *Religion and Society among the Coorgs of South India*, Oxford, 1952.

Sundar, N., "Adivasi vs Vanvasi: The Politics of Conversion and Reconversion in Central India," in: S. Saberwal & M. Asan, eds., *Assertive Religious Identities*, Delhi, 2006, 357–390.

Sundar, N., *Subalterns and Sovereigns: An Anthropological History of Bastar 1854–1996*, Delhi, 1997.

Tambs-Lyche, H., ed., *The Feminine Sacred in South Asia*, Delhi, 1999.

Verardo, B., "Rebels and Devotees of Jharkhand: Social, Religious and Political Transformations among the Adivasi of Northern India," diss., London School of Economics, 2003.

Vitebsky, P., *Dialogues with the Dead: The Discussion of Mortality among the Sora of Eastern India*, Cambridge UK, 1993.

Walker, A.R., *The Toda of Southern India: A New Look*, Delhi, 1986.

Xaxa, V., "Tribes as Indigenous People of India," *EPW* 34/51, 3989–3996.

Marine Carrin

Hinduism and Zoroastrianism

The term "Zoroastrianism," coined in the 19th century in a colonial context, is inspired by a Greek pseudo-etymological rendering (Zoroastres, where the second element is reminiscent of the word for star) of the ancient Iranian name Zaraϑuštra (etymology unclear apart from the second element, *uštra* [camel]). This modern name of the religion reflects the emphasis on Zarathustra (Zoroaster) as its (presumed) founding figure or prophet.

Zoroastrianism and Hinduism share a remote common original ancestry, but their historical trajectories over the millennia have been notably distinct. Just like Hinduism claims and maintains a particular relationship to the spatial entity know as India, Zoroastrianism has conceived itself as the religion of the Iranians and of Iran (Stausberg, 2011). In the aftermath of the Arab/Muslim conquest of Iran in the mid-7th century CE, however, Zoroastrianism lost its claim to religious supremacy (which had already been challenged by Christianity) and over the centuries became a merely tolerated religious minority in Iran. Yet, the Zoroastrians continue to consider themselves the remnants of pre-Islamic Iran; for example, their religious calendar reckons the years according to the reign of the last emperor of Iran, Yazdgird III (reportedly crowned in 631 CE).

Given extant trading networks, the coastal area of southern Gujarat has served as a refuge for Zoroastrian groups permanently settling there since an unknown period before the 10th century CE. There are also records of Zoroastrian settlements in North India, but these communities have disappeared over the course of time. Reflecting their Persian origins, the Zoroastrians of western India are known as the Parsis. In demographic terms, Zoroastrians currently count no more than some 120 to 130 thousand, around half of them residing in India, the homeland of contemporary Zoroastrianism where one finds most of its richest of social and religious institutions. Since the 19th century, Bombay (Mumbai) has emerged as the main center of the Parsis, an overwhelmingly urban community. Since Independence, partly caused by emigration and partly by changes in family structures and general values, the Parsi population of India (and Pakistan) has seen a sharp decline. Since colonial times, Parsis have migrated to other parts of the world, and in the postcolonial age, especially since the 1960s, this movement has intensified, so that the so-called diaspora is becoming the key factor for the future development of the religion (Stausberg, 2002b; Hinnells, 2005). Given their tiny numbers, their non-proselytization and their constructive contributions to Indian society (e.g. example through their various charitable contributions [Hinnells, 2000]), and their commitments to the army and other Indian institutions, which are routinely celebrated in community publications, the Parsis and their religion have so far not drawn forth any negative social response in India.

Being offshoots of older Indo-European and Indo-Iranian poetic traditions, the oldest textual sources of Iranian and Indic religious traditions, namely the Avestan and the oldest vedic textual corpora (the *Ṛgveda*), share a series of grammatical and lexical similarities (so much so that Avestan can often be easily "retranslated" into Vedic and has been interpreted on the basis of Vedic grammar and lexicon/semantics). A "Vedicizing" reading of the Avestan texts, however, risks disconnecting the Avestan texts from the later developments in Zoroastrianism and the later Zoroastrian exegesis, hermeneutics, and interpretive history attested mainly in Middle Persian treatises dating from the 9th or 10th century CE (but often continuing and quoting much older materials). Interestingly, as shown by Y.S.-D. Vevaina (2010), this Zoroastrian exegesis employs strategies of cosmological homologies similar to those employed by the ancient Indian Brāhmaṇas (see → Vedas and Brāhmaṇas). (Note that the extent of Avestan textual corpus and the later religious literature of the Iranians [Zoroastrians] are much smaller than their Indian counterparts.)

The present entry will address main points of contact between Hinduism and Zoroastrianism diachronically. The timeline goes from the 2nd millennium BCE to the present.

The *Ṛgveda* and the Avesta

Similar source-critical problems surround the vedic and the Avestan texts. To begin with, their historical contexts remain a matter of speculation; in a circular operation, their societal context can only be extrapolated from the texts themselves. Scant geographical information contained in the Avestan texts points to an origin of at least some of these texts in Afghanistan and the regions around the Iranian–Pakistani borderland (in today's political geography) – that is, west of the rgvedic texts. There is no archaeological evidence for the Avestan texts, but these texts have sometimes been read into archaeological findings.

Like the vedic hymns, the Avestan texts were transmitted orally. Sometime, probably in the 4th or 6th century CE, a special alphabet (the Avestan alphabet) was devised to commit the Avestan texts to writing in a phonetically "correct" manner, but the oldest extant manuscript only dates from the 13th century. Already relatively early, partly because of migration and the spread of the religion and partly due to ordinary linguistic change, the Avestan texts were recited by priests who no longer spoke the Avestan language. One can assume the existence of oral vernacular translations (and possible commentaries), but, with the exception of a Sogdian fragment, the Middle Iranian/Persian translations and commentaries are all that is left. In these manuscripts, text and translation-cum-commentary (known as *zand*) were largely transmitted together. The Avesta is not a uniform text, and its different strands (parts) have been transmitted independently. As a material reality, the Avesta first made its appearance as a result of European orientalist publications in the 18th and 19th centuries.

Linguistically, the Avestan corpus contains a somewhat more archaic stratum (the so-called Old Avestan texts), which is not a direct ancestor of the apparently later materials (the so-called Young Avestan texts) that make up for by far its largest part. The later texts seem to represent a linguistic stage of development similar to the inscriptions by the Achaemenian (Persian) kings from the 5th and 4th centuries BCE, but this does not provide any sort of absolute chronology. It would be wrong to assume that the *Ṛgveda* necessarily is the older model compared to the Avestan texts; in fact, one finds linguistic and religious innovations on both sides, and one should not interpret the Avestan corpus as a reformed *Ṛgveda*. Almost all extant Avestan texts are used in rituals, and that is how they came to be transmitted.

Several of the Young Avestan texts are framed as dialogues between Zarathustra and the supreme deity Ahura Mazdā ("Lord Wisdom"), where the deity answers Zarathustra's queries on a variety of issues, so that these texts constitute Ahura Mazdā's revelatory speech. Zarathustra and Ahura Mazdā also feature in the Old Avestan texts, in particular in the enigmatic five *Gāϑās* (Songs), which are often interpreted as compositions by Zarathustra but whose historicity is denied by some scholars. Be that as it may, in the *Gāϑās*, Zarathustra appears as the poet-performer/sacrificer (Skjærvø, 2003) and the intimate interlocutor of Ahura Mazdā and other divine figures including the "fashioner of the cow" and some divine agents-cum-abstract entities and ethical qualities, most prominently *aṣ̌a* (truth or order) and *vohu manah* (good thought). The former is etymologically and semantically related to Vedic *ṛtá* (and both are intimately linked with the fire), but *ṛtá* does not appear as a personal agent in the *Ṛgveda* (Oberlies, 2012, 67). The opposition between *aṣ̌a* and *druj* (lie; Ved. *drúh*) is of fundamental importance for the *Gāϑās* – and so is the opposition between the executors of truth (*aṣ̌ǎuuan*) and the executors of lie (*drəguuaṇt*) and between the gods and the *daēuua*, which, contrary to their Vedic cognates (*deva*), appear as antigods/demons; Aešma ("Fury") is a leading *daēuua*. The human and superhuman world of the *Gāϑās* is torn by conflicts. On the human level, the community apparently saw itself threatened by others, hostile enemies who are characterized as non-herdsman (*Yasna* 31.10) – "non-cattle breeders among cattle-breeders" (*Yasna* 49.4); most of all, however, their rituals are wrong. Humans face the need to make the right decisions by engaging in the right form of ritual interactions; the consequences of the wrong choices are dramatic and extend into the postmortal state.

The *Gāϑās* are referred to a *mąϑra* ("word" or "formula," corresponding to Ved. *mantra*) in *Gāh* 1.6. The poetry of the *Gāϑās* is impregnated by features well known from the *Ṛgveda* and other Indo-European literatures. Examples include cultic vocabulary such as phrases of pleading (Oberlies, 2012, 45), the vocabulary of the chariot race (Hintze, 2009, 14–16), the poet's complaints (Skjærvø, 2001), and blame and praise poetry (Skjærvø, 2002). Among the most significant differences is the prominence of Zarathustra in the poetry of the *Gāϑās*. When "1st person singular speech is found in the Rig Veda," it "is a characteristic of gods, not poets, in sharp contrast with the Gāthās" (Jamison, 2007, 35). The *Gāϑās* are characterized by an insistent monotony of 1st singular poet/2nd singular divinity that traps the two into a claustrophobic dialogue – which…is one of the features that gives the Gāthās their peculiar intimate power. (Jamison, 2007, 95)

Compared with the *Ṛgveda*, in the *Gāϑās*, "the relations between man and god are depicted as more direct, immediate, and mutual" (Jamison, 2007, 31). In the (later) Young Avestan texts, however, the figure of Zarathustra becomes more schematic by being turned into a kind of role model and prototype for humanity (Stausberg, 2002a, 31–40); he becomes the central figure of a historical vision leading from the prototypical living being to the heroes of the future (eschatological) renovation of the world (see below). Later literary traditions in Middle and New Persian unfold "biographical" narratives on Zarathustra's life and mission with a focus on his birth, his childhood, and his visions of and conversations with the deities (incl. Ahura Mazdā), culminating in Zarathustra making the "king" Wištasp accept his religion (Stausberg, 2002a, 40–68).

The Old Avestan texts are the compositional center of the *Yasna* (Worship or Sacrifice), a text consisting of 72 divisions (where the Old Avest. sections can be found in chs. 28 to 54) recited in the priestly ritual of the same name. (The word corresponds to the Ved. → *yajña*.) The Old Avestan section comprises some manthric formula, the *Gāϑās*, and the *Yasna Haptaŋhāiti* (Worship in Seven Chapters; see Hintze, 2007) – a recitation prose in praise of Ahura Mazdā and his creations, centering on the (ritual) fire in chapter 36, the kernel of the concentric structure of the *Yasna*. The Young Avestan parts of the *Yasna* placed around the Old Avestan core assemble a variety of materials declaring the praise of a series of material and divine entities including the fire, the waters, and Haoma, the Avestan counterpart of the vedic Soma.

Haoma is at the same time a deity, a substance (originally probably bot. Peganum harmala [Flattery & Schwartz, 1989] but later in ritual practice replaced by ephedra), and a liquid prepared by the priests by reciting texts in honor of Haoma and other divine agents, mixing the ephedra twigs (with pomegranate twigs, consecrated water, and goat's milk), pounding them, and filtering the mixture in the early first part of the *yasna* ritual and its preparatory service (where it is not mixed with milk). The status of Haoma in the *Gāϑās* is disputed (see e.g. Skjærvø, 2004, and Schwartz, 2006, for different interpretations). Compared with the *Ṛgveda*, the Avestan Haoma is of less importance for the order of society and the legitimation of power of the ruler (Oberlies, 2012, 31–33); in the Avestan texts, this function was absorbed by the *x*ᵛ*arənah* (charisma or fortune), an elusive agent empowering those who manage to capture it; originally residing in the mythical sea, it is distributed over the earth for the benefit of the living by the (deity of) the sun.

The offering or consecration of sacrificial meat in the *Yasna* was abolished at an unknown date (maybe as late as in the early 19th cent., possibly as an adaptation to a Hindu environment). In some priestly ceremonies, the *Yasna* is recited in combination with two further Avestan texts, namely the *Visperad* (a collection of praise texts) and the *Vīdēvdād* (The Law Keeping Demons Away). With the exception of some chapters (including the first two, describing the different places of the earth put in order by Ahura Mazdā [ch. 1] and the myth of Yima and the great winter [ch. 2]), the *Vīdēvdād* is a "legal" text, framed as a dialogue between Ahura Mazdā and Zarathustra and mainly concerned with issues of pollution and ways to get rid of the pollutants (e.g. demons, witches, sorcerers). The text praises agriculture as the preferred mode of subsistence (*Vīdēvdād* 3.4). Like in Hinduism, pollution and → purity are a main concern in Zoroastrianism (see Choksy, 1989; de Jong, 1999; Stausberg, 2004). Main forms of pollution discussed in the *Vīdēvdād* include evil-created animals such as snakes and spiders, dead bodily matters (such as hair and nails once they are cut off) and bodily excrement, and, most of all, menstrual blood and corpses. Menstruation and the disposal of corpses (and the purification of people and things contaminated by menstrual blood and corpses) require extensive ritual elaboration and have over the millennia remained key modes of self-identification, but traditional modes of practices have undergone severe change in the modern period, in particular in Iran (somewhat less so in India), where the religious system has been simplified with an emphasis on ethics, history, and beliefs (Stausberg, 2004; 2012).

For the disposal of corpses, the *Vīdēvdād* prescribes the removal of the dead bodies on dry, high, and deserted places, where the flesh is then removed from the bones by dogs and birds of prey; in a second, optional, step, the bones may then be gathered and preserved in special receptacles (ossuaries). Note that this mode of procedure does not require the erection of any massive structures. Although propagated rigorously in the *Vīdēvdād* and described by foreign observers, this was not the only funerary practice in ancient Iran; burial was also practiced. It was probably only in the Islamic period that funerary structures surrounded by walls became the norm. Given the different climatic conditions in India, the Parsis have developed a refined model (which includes a filtering system for water entering the interior and a hole serving as a main receptacle for the bones in the middle) for the *daxmahs* (known as towers of silence since the colonial period). In recent decades, since the large-scale (97–99%) decline of vultures in India caused by the anti-inflammatory drug Diclofenac, the natural functioning of this funerary system has been seriously compromised; so far the system has been retained with some modifications (the establishment of solar panels serving to dehydrate the corpses), because it is considered essential for the preservation of the religion and for the progress of the soul of the deceased to the other world, which requires the sun to shine on the bones. (The soul travels to the other world along the rays of the sun.) In many Indian cities, in Iran, and in most diaspora countries, Zoroastrians use burial or (to a lesser extent) cremation. The main argument against burial and cremation is the pollution of the earth and fire, which are both held to be inherently divine creations and material indices of two deities that form a group of the seven innermost deities of the Zoroastrian pantheon – the so-called beneficial immortals (*aməša spəṇtas*), who act in accordance with Ahura Mazdā and embody virtues and the different parts of the cosmos.

In addition to the eschatological fate of the individual (see Stausberg, 2009, for the concept of hell), Zoroastrianism has developed a cosmological narrative, most fully elaborated in the Middle Persian literature. This narrative starts from the origin of the world, with the emergence of the conflict between Ahura Mazdā and his adversary, resulting in the creation of the world and the state of mixture of good and evil. Humans are expected to fight with Ahura Mazdā and his good creation (including the deities) against the adversary and his counter creations (including the demons, which strive to enter the human bodies). The narrative ends with the violent clashes at the end of "limited time," the renovation of the cosmos, the final cleansing of sinners and their release from hell, and the general resurrection and the establishment of a future body for mankind. The struggles for the renovation of the cosmos will be heralded by Zarathustra's posthumous sons.

Returning to the earlier sources, among the other texts making up the Avestan corpus, there are two lists of deities linked to the 30 days of the calendar, and there is a collection of 21 hymns (*yašts*) to individual deities (and the seven *aməša spəṇtas*), including the (deities of) sun, moon, and earth. The collection starts with Ahura Mazdā; this hymn (*Yašt* 1) contains a list of 54 names of Ahura Mazdā, which emphasize, among other aspects, his righteousness and founding activities; his benevolence and protection; his wisdom, insight, and omniscience; and his majesty and lordship (Panaino, 2002). The other deities deserve praise in their own right insofar as they are affiliated with Ahura Mazdā by subordination and/or by mutual support, for example by worshipping each other or sacrificing for each other. Among the deities praised by the *yašts*, two names also occur in the *Ṛgveda*: Miϑra (Mitra) and Vaiiu (Vāyu), and in both corpora, they have domains and functions in common, probably inherited from earlier historical layers. The Avestan Miϑra shares some epithets (strong arms and carrying a club) with the vedic Indra (Oberlies, 2012, 69), the "Smasher of Obstacles" (Vṛtrahán); in Iran, the corresponding word Vərəthrajan is used as an epithet of some deities (Ahura Mazdā, Sraoša, and Haoma), prayers (*Yasna* 54.2), the heroes of the great eschatological battles (*Yasna* 19.89, 95), and the dragon slayer Θraētaona (*Yasna* 19.35f.); in addition, there is a separate deity of that name (Vərəthragna) in Zoroastrianism (see also Greenebaum, 1974).

In total, there are a dozen or so nominally identical deities (among the 90 or so attested Zoroastrian divine figures), mostly of inferior importance, in the vedic and the Avestan texts. The list includes, by way of examples, the water-deity Apąm Napāt, the deity of hospitality Airiiaman (Aryaman), the messenger-deity Nairiiō.saŋha (Narāśaṃsa), the deity of healing Θrita (Trita), the goddess of dawn Ušah (Uṣas), and the wind-god Vāta. In addition, there are similar or partly identical mythical motives such as that of the dragon slayers (Watkins, 1995), and there are deities who share cognate functions and responsibilities such as Ātar and Agni, the deities of fire, or Arəduuī Sūrā Anāhitā and Sarasvatī, who both confer rain, fertility, and eloquence to their worshippers (Oberlies, 2012, 78).

Some Zoroastrian deities, most importantly the "Wise Lord" (Ahura Mazdā), are qualified as *ahura*, but there has probably been no cult of a class of *ahura*s (corresponding to the vedic *asura*s) in pre-Zoroastrian Iran (Narten, 1996). Several scholars have noted the similarities between Ahura Mazdā and Varuṇa, whereas Zoroastrian conceptions of the divine with their emphasis on law, morality, order, and regularity – and consonant with the negative semantics of the word *daēuua* (Ved. *deva*) – leave no space for a character like Indra, who is in fact castigated as a *daēuua* (demon) in some Zoroastrian texts starting with the Avestan *Vīdēvdād* (10.9; 19.43). In these texts, Iṇdra appears at or near the top of lists of demons that are to be annihilated. Interestingly, it is Ardwahišt, the Middle Persian variety of the Avestan "Good Order" (Aša Vahišta), who is assigned that task (starting with the Middle Pers. translation of the *Gāϑās* [*Yasna* 48.1]). A Middle Persian text states that Indar (this being the Middle Pers. form) "freezes the minds of the creatures from practicing righteousness" (*Great Bundahišn* 27.7; Andrés-Toledo, 2009, 220), and another one (*Dēnkard* 9.32.3) gives an attribute for Indar, namely Kōšīdār ("Fighter" or "Slayer"). This fits the name of the demon following Indar on all these lists – namely, Saura (traditionally interpreted as Saurva, i.e. Ved. Śarvā), probably meaning arrow/spear but maybe already appearing here as a personified demon (Andrés-Toledo, 2009, 224). Together with Saura and sometimes also together with the third demon from these lists, Nå̊ŋhaiϑiia (another name with a Ved. background, for the Ved. Nāsatya is an epithet of Áśvināu), the Middle Persian Indar prevents people from wearing the undershirt and belt/cord that all Zoroastrians are supposed to have on their bodies (*Dēnkard* 9.9.1). In a new Persian text (*Ṣad Dar-i Bondeheš* 2.13–16), however, Iṇdra/Indar (now appearing as Andar) plays a malign role in individual eschatology by causing anguish to the departed and carrying the sinners to hell and inflicting punishments on their souls. At least from the time of the Middle Persian texts, but maybe already for the hearers of the Avestan *Vīdēvdād*, the identification of Iṇdra/Indar/Andar as an Indian god was probably imperceptible, and he simply appeared as a powerful arch demon.

Indo-Iranian cultural encounters, exchanges, and translations are witnessed in → astrology / astronomy and games (see e.g. Panaino, 1999). Given this intercultural awareness, from a certain point onward, Hindu India was clearly within the field of vision of Zoroastrian authors. A Middle Persian work of unknown date and miscellaneous content describes different kinds of people and countries. For India, the text emphasizes the complexity of the country: there are different climatic zones, different diets, different ways of life, and different funerary traditions; for religion, the text states that some belong to Ahura Mazdā and others to his adversary, since they practice witchcraft (*Ayātgār ī Žāmāspik* 8.4 [Messina, 1939]). In the 9th century CE, the Zoroastrian theologian Mardānfarrox, son of Ohrmazddād, writes about his religious quest that has taken him abroad, namely to India (*Škand Gumānīg Wizār* 10.44). Moreover, outlining the early history of the (Zoroastrian) religion, he notes that some of its early protagonists carried the religion all the way to "Rome and India" (10.68), which thereby becomes a potential Zoroastrian territory. In the 13th century, a New Persian text from Iran entitled the *Cangranghācah-Nāmah* recounts the fictive story of the Brahman sage Cangranghācah, who at the time of Zarathustra had come to Iran and the court of Zarathustra's patron; entering a debate, he was refuted by Zarathustra at every point, and, acknowledging his defeat, he accepted Zarathustra's religion, which he subsequently spread in India and adjacent countries (Scott, 1988, 107; Jackson, 1899, 86). Interestingly, this text came about at a time when the Zoroastrians had already become a minority in Iran and some of their coreligionists had established themselves in India.

Iconographical Convergence in Central Asia

Very few iconographical representations of Zoroastrian deities are available from ancient Iran, and the ones that we find are almost exclusively part of royal propaganda such as coins, seals, and reliefs. In the 3rd century CE, for example, Ahura Mazdā is presented as the almost exact counterpart of King Ardaxšīr; god and king face each other either standing or sitting on horses. The Zoroastrian scriptures – the Avesta and the Pahlavi literature in Middle Persian – do not describe visual manifestations such as images or statues of deities. The Pahlavi texts even contain a negative terminology for "idol," "idolater," and "idolatry." (Boyce, 1975, interprets this as evidence for an iconoclastic purification movement.) Among contemporary Zoroastrians, one finds various iconographical representations of Zarathustra, of Zoroastrian heroes and places, and of fire altars, but there are no cultic representations of deities (such as consecrated images, busts, or statues of deities used for ritual purposes).

In central Asia, however, Zoroastrianism took a different shape from the model championed by the Pahlavi literature from Persia. Especially in Sogdiana, situated north of Bactria, between the Oxus (Amu Darya) and Jaxartes (Syr Darya) in modern Uzbekistan (and partly Tajikistan), archaeologists have excavated a rich iconographic repertoire. (Direct traces of Zoroastrianism in central Asia disappear with the Mongol invasions, if not earlier.) In the present context, it is worth noting that Sodgian artists drew inspiration from Indian iconography when representing Zoroastrian deities.

In this, they may have been following the example set by the coins issued by the kings of the Kushana Empire in Bactria (where there was a strong Buddhist presence) in the 2nd century CE. While many images of Zoroastrian deities are derived from those of Greek gods with whom they were identified or associated, on some Kushana coins, one finds depictions of the Buddha and images of Mahāsena, Viśākha, Skanda, and Kumāra. In an interlinear gloss of a dedicatory inscription, the names Mahāsena and Viśākha are identified with the Zoroastrian deity Srōš (Avest. Sraoša ["Harkening"]), maybe because he and Mahāsena shared the epithet of the cock (Grenet, 2010, 88). An even stronger fusion occurred when the Zoroastrian deity Oēšo – that is, Vayuš – assumed a kind of Śaiva iconography (three headed and four armed, with trident and club). Apparently, this god remained popular even among the later Kushano-Sasanians, who on their coins referred to themselves as "Mazdean [Mazda-Worshipping, i.e. Zoroastrian] Lord" and depicted fire altars, yet who would also show → Śiva in a traditional style,

> with raised hair standing in front of the bull Nandī, while replacing the name Vayu by an epithet suitable for both Vayu and Śiva: *burzāwand yazd* (in the Pahlavi version), "the god who possesses the heights." (Grenet, 2010, 89)

For Sogdiana, which had close contacts with India, F. Grenet has identified visual depictions of no fewer than 23 Zoroastrian deities, which is a major part of the main pantheon. Many images were found in Panjikent, east of Samarkand, both in houses and in temples. Some representations still echo Greek models, while others are indigenous creations, but some, it seems, are deliberately modeled on Hindu iconography (Grenet, 2010). The Kushana Vāyu–Śiva iconographical fusion is continued by the pair of Mahādeva–Wēšparkar (as identified by the Sogdian *Vassantara Jātaka* [see Humbach, 1975]; the name Wēšparkar is derived from the full Avest. name of the deity). Another pair identified by the text is Indra–Adhvagh – the latter Sogdian word meaning "supreme god" – that is, Ahura Mazdā. Given the Avesta–Pahlavi textual tradition quoted above, this appearance of Indra is an inversion; the texts were either of little relevance or unknown or no longer understood. One example of depictions of Indra–Adhvagh is a series of terracotta figures (Marshak & Raspopova, 1996, 195–198). The artist drew on three iconographical registers:

> Indra (hence the elephant *vāhana*), the Sasanian king (hence the royal ribbons), King David with his cithara, a proper allusion to Ahura Mazdā's function as master of paradise. (Grenet, 2010, 92)

Other iconographical types or attributes of Hindu deities serving to illustrate (traits of) different Zoroastrian deities probably include Kārttikeya (→ Murukaṉ) and → Durgā. The Indian iconographical vocabulary was useful for the development of a Zoroastrian iconography, but eventually Sogdian artists became more independent in depicting Zoroastrian deities (Grenet, 2010, 94).

Magas and Bhojakas

The *Sāmbapurāṇa* and the *Bhaviṣyapurāṇa* report about a certain group of Brahmans, the Maga Brahmans. Their name seems to refer to the religious/ritual specialists of the ancient Iranians (Old Pers. *maguš*; Grk. *mágos*; Lat. *magus*), and the name of the special girdle worn by the Magas – the *avyaṅga* (lit. having non-incomplete limbs) – can be interpreted as deriving from the Avestan *aiβiiåŋhana*, the Avestan name of the belt/cord that Zoroastrians are supposed to wear (Humbach, 1978, 237; 2002, 89). The origin of the group is traced to a certain Sāmba, who (to give a very brief summary of the legend) – in the hope of getting rid of leprosy, from which he suffered as a result of a curse by his father Kṛṣṇa – resorted to Mitravana, where he bathed in the Candrabhāgā; there he found the statue of the sun, carved in wood by the deity Viśvakarman, which Sāmba, on the request of the sun-god, put up in Mitravana in a newly constructed temple dedicated to the sun. Since no Brahmans were available, on the advice of the sun-god, Sāmba invited 18 families of the Magas of Śākadvīpa (i.e. the continent of the *śāka* tree), who wore the *avyaṅga*, and for them he built the city of Sāmbapura, which must be Mūlasthāna (modern Multan; see Humbach, 1978, 230ff., for the fuller version with sources; see also von Stietencron, 1966). In the → *Mahābhārata*, these Magas of Śākadvīpa are mentioned as one caste alongside three others, whose names seem to have been derived or formed somewhat artificially from Iranian words (Humbach, 1978, 230; 2002, 90). The name Sāmba probably derives from that of Sambos, a king who, according to several Greek and Latin sources describing Alexander the Great's expedition down the Indus in 326 BC, first subordinated to Alexander, then revolted, and eventually fled eastward beyond the Indus (Humbach, 1978, 238; 2002, 93).

Another piece of evidence for the Iranian background of the Maga Brahmans is provided by the 6th-century astrologer and Maga Brahman Varāhamihira, whose name is formed on the basis of an Indian borrowing (Mihira) of the Middle Persian form (Mihr) of the ancient Iranian Miϑra. In his *Pañcasiddhāntikā* (1.23–25), which has a parallel passage in the *Vaṭeśvarasiddhānta* (1.5. 117–120), Varāhamihira (who may have had an Iranian astronomer as his *guru*) describes the "year of the Magas," where he gives 30 names of the "lords of the degrees of the signs" (1.23 [Neugebauer & Pingree, 1970, 32–33]). A comparison of this list with that contained in the Zoroastrian calendar with its 30 deities (*yazata*s; "[beings] worthy of being worshipped") shows several correspondences that "testify to a direct knowledge of the Zoroastrian list of the yazatas and the attempt to arrange them according to an Indian (Śaiva) picture" (Panaino, 1996, 585). This indicates the active knowledge of a Zoroastrian model, probably stemming from ancient traditions of reinterpretations.

Eventually, the Magas seem to have spread to Magadha (south Bihar) at a later date; accordingly, new versions of their history came into being. Their Iranian background or connection receded under the surface. More recent reports quoted by H. Humbach (2002, 92f.) show that their Iranian background is obliterated but that they are still recognized as being somewhat different from other groups. Apparently, they enjoy a reputation as astrologers. In some passages in the *Bhaviṣyapurāṇa*, the name of the Magas appears in alteration with that of another group, the Bhojakas (who are already attested in the 7th cent. [Humbach, 1978, 245]). H. Humbach argues "that the Bhojakas had usurped the Maga tradition and considered themselves as Magas but were not acknowledged as such by the Magas themselves" (2002, 91). While the Bhojakas are sometimes reported to wear the *avyaṅga*, other reports say that they wear the *amāhaka*, a snake-shaped girdle – which would be an antipode to Zoroastrianism, where the snake is a creature of the evil spirit. However, the *Bhaviṣyapurāṇa* provides some pieces of information that have a Zoroastrian pitch: their wearing of a mouth veil and use of twigs in rituals (like Zoroastrian priests), their eating in silence and saying prayers five times a day, respect for the dog and its relation to funerals, the mention of Rājña and Srauṣa (i.e. the Zoroastrian deities Rašnu and Sraoša), and some reports about the genealogy and birth of Jaraśastra, apparently Zarathustra, which do not resonate with any known Zoroastrian sources (Humbach, 1978, 248–250; 2002, 91f.). Even if, as H. Humbach suggests, these pieces of information were acquired from Indian Zoroastrian (Parsi) informants, this does not diminish their value as evidence for the intended "Zoroastrianization" of the Bhojakas; even if they were Hindus, the author of these puranic passages wanted to make it clear that they, just like the Magas, had a Zoroastrian connection.

The Parsis

Historically speaking, there is probably no one fixed date for the arrival of the Zoroastrians who became known as the Parsis (they probably arrived in several waves), but in 1599, an Indian Zoroastrian priest, Bahman Qay Qobād Sanjāna from Navsari (Gujarat), composed a unified narrative in 432 Persian couplets starting with the creation of the world and culminating in the transfer of the main consecrated fire of the Parsis to Navsari, thereby celebrating his own priestly lineage. From his priestly perspective, the narrative fuses the history of the world with the history of his community and that of its main sanctuary; by implication, this establishes the leadership of the priesthood (in his lineage) as the guardians of this fire sanctuary. The account is entitled *Qeṣṣe-yi Sanjān* (Story of Sanjān), after the name of the place on the Indian coast where the nucleus community, led by a learned priest-astrologer, arrived by boat from Iran "to save our lives and for Religion's sake" (*Qeṣṣe-yi Sanjān* 111; trans. Williams, 2009, 77). Threatened by a dangerous storm, they made a vow to establish an *ātaš-i bahrām*, a fire of Bahrām (Avest. Vərəthragna), the protector deity whom they had invoked (along with Ahura Mazdā) in their desperation. (An *ātaš-i bahrām* is the highest class of ritual fires; until 1765, the Parsis had only one *ātaš-i bahrām*, and the consecration of the second one resulted from a conflict between different groups of priests; nowadays there are eight fires, or fire temples, of that type in India: four in Mumbai, two in Surat, one in Navsari, and one in the coastal village of Udvada.) Since Bahman Qay Qobād provides some apparently clear dates about the itinerary of the Parsis from Iran to India (via Hormuz), earlier generations of scholars tried to establish a date of arrival (reviewed by Williams, 2009, 207–217), but these reconstructions have failed to yield any consensus. In the *Qeṣṣe-yi Sanjān*, the *ātaš-i bahrām* is referred to as *šāh-i irān* (king of Iran), or as the *šāh-i šāhān* (king of kings), and today it is called Iranshah, implying that the fire is the successor of the Iranian kingship that was lost with the Arab invasion but is kept up by the Parsis in India.

Bahman Qay Qobād reports a dialogue between the priest-leader of the migrants and the local ruler of Sanjān, who is introduced as a "good *rājā*" by the name of Jādi and whose historical identity remains unresolved (Williams, 2009, 175). When the priest asks for asylum for the "strangers" who "have come… for refuge and home within your land" (*Qeṣṣe-yi Sanjān* 142; trans. Williams, 2009, 83), the ruler grants this on five conditions: that they must explain their religion to him, that "they must renounce the language of their own land" and "speak the language of Hend," that their women shall "wear such garments as our women wear," and that "they shall lay down these swords and weapons, and never more shall gird them on again" (*Qeṣṣe-yi Sanjān* 154–157, trans. Williams, 2009, 85); the fifth and final requirement has traditionally been understood as an obligation to celebrate weddings at night, but A. Williams (2009, 85) now translates it in the following way: "when they perform the noble act of children, on that night they should be married" (*Qeṣṣe-yi Sanjān* 158). The text proposes a program of assimilation by abandoning weapons and adopting language and clothing (for women) and non-secretiveness about their religion. The first element of the subsequent explanation or translation of their religion by the priest points to their descent from the mythical first (Iranian) king, Jamšid (Avest. Yima); the priest then points to their religious respect for or worship of five elements (fire, water, sun, moon, and cow) before he mentions the creator-god, their belt/cord, and their prayers (*Qeṣṣe-yi Sanjān* 167–171). The final three elements address purity rules for the women in case of menstruation, childbirth, or miscarriage/stillbirth (*Qeṣṣe-yi Sanjān* 172–175).

A widely circulating oral narrative of unknown date (often erroneously believed to be part of the *Qeṣṣe-yi Sanjān*) reports the ruler to initially have denied access, pointing to a full glass of milk; with great presence of mind, the priest is reported to have inserted some sugar into that glass, which did not flow over; being like the sugar in the milk of Indian society has become a leitmotiv of Parsi identity making in modern India. The five conditions explain the ethnoreligious diversity of the Parsis and reflect some factual cultural patterns such as their specific Gujarati dialect (known as Parsi Gujarati) and their food and garments, which are all recognizably regional but with some special (Persian) traits. Nowadays, initiations and weddings are occasions to display this ethnic heritage ceremonially in combinations with the purifications and blessings performed by the priests. The Zoroastrian religion is embedded in an ethnic legacy, together constituting what has been called Parsi Zoroastrianism. In modernity, when boundaries became challenged, this ethnoreligious continuum with its diverse poles of genealogical lineage and religious universalism turned out to be a fragile construct; intermarriages (and the related issue of conversion) have been the key sites to expose its ambivalences.

Another notable episode of the *Qeṣṣe-yi Sanjān* narrated by Bahman Qay Qobād in quite some detail are two battles in which the Parsis, on request of the Hindu rulers, join the Hindu army to fight against Islamic forces on their way to conquer that part of India. Having won the first battle, the Hindu-Parsi coalition is annihilated in the second battle (*Qeṣṣe-yi Sanjān* 243–352). It is unclear whether these battles ever occurred, but the account was probably inspired by political and military events in the 15th and 16th centuries in Gujarat. Bahman Qay Qobād sides the Parsis with the Hindus against the Muslims; the lost battle and the immersion of their blood into the soil of India amount to their ultimate sacrifice for their host country, sealing their transformation from Iranians into Parsis, even though as Parsis, they retain a distinctive ethnic and religious culture. Historically speaking, though, despite some instances of discrimination, it seems that the period of Islamic rule over India allowed the Parsis to prosper (Stausberg, 2002a, 404f.).

It is reported that a learned priest by the name of Neryōsang Dhaval, who probably lived in the 11th or 12th century CE, was the first and most prominent of some learned Zoroastrian scholar-priests to translate several Avestan and Middle Persian texts into Sanskrit (see Bharucha, 1906). In addition to these translations, a certain Ākā Adhyāru (who some think was a Hindu) composed 16 Sanskrit *śloka*s; the oldest manuscripts are from the 17th century, but H.-P. Schmidt, the principal editor and translator, believes them to be from the period of 900 or 1000 CE (1960–1961, 192), a theory that strikes me as rather speculative. Apparently, these *śloka*s were meant to define the identity of the Parsis, even though they were not widely known among them: almost all of these 16 *śloka*s end on the line, "those are we Parsis." The Parsis are referred to as a *varṇa* (*śl.* 11). Hormazd (i.e. Ahura Mazdā) is mentioned in the first and last *śloka*. In addition to various elements familiar from other Zoroastrian sources, the *śloka*s also have some points stemming from a Hindu background; interestingly, the woolen belt/cord is described as "well measured (with ends) like snake-mouths" (*śl.* 3), which recalls the information about the Bhojakas, so that the text can have originated in a Hindu-Parsi environment similar to such a group (Stausberg, 2002a, 393–398; Schmidt's translation is reprinted in Williams, 2009, 233–237).

In the 19th century, like in other religious traditions, a reform movement started among the Parsis, aiming at modernizing the religion under the rhetorical guise of a return to its authentic historical kernel. The initial targets were practices such as child marriages, which were branded as "Indian" – that is, as not originally Zoroastrian (i.e. Iranian). Not without resistance from influential people, child marriages became less common among the Parsis in the course of the 19th century (Stausberg, 2002b, 66). In 1858, Dosabhoy Framjee, a notable reformer, reinterpreted the *Qeṣṣe-yi Sanjān* by suggesting that the Zoroastrians might have tried to conceal their real beliefs from the Indian ruler, but now the time had come to once again rid Zoroastrianism from "Hindu superstitions" (Ringer, 2011, 157). Later, however, the strong impact of the → Theosophical Society among the Parsis (Stausberg, 2002b, 112–118) allowed the discourse of reform to become reconciled with an interest in Hinduism (and esotericism). Reincarnation (which is not a point of Zoroastrian doctrine) was championed by some Parsi theosophist authors. Theosophists like H.S. Olcott and A. Besant gave speeches about Zoroastrianism. In the 1920s and 1930s, some Indian intellectuals – among them Rabindranath → Tagore – published books on Zoroastrianism that partly tried to align it with Indian religious literature, most notably the → *Bhagavadgītā* or the → Upaniṣads (Stausberg, 2012, 127–132).

Comparison with the Zoroastrian communities in Iran indicates a number of Parsi practices that have originated as a result of their interaction with their Hindu environment. Like Hinduism, Parsi Zoroastrianism puts a great emphasis on → auspiciousness, especially in relation to births, initiations, and marriages (referred to as "auspicious occasions" in Parsi folk taxonomy); the date of initiations, engagements, and marriages is partly determined with reference to astrology. The celebration of auspicious occasions includes the performance, by (preferably married) women (with children but barring widows), of a number of rites (Stausberg, 2004, 35–37; Kreyenbroek & Munshi, 2001, 18–19) centered on the body of the subject to be felicitated with the help of a set of "auspicious objects," which are arranged on a metal tray (Guj. *sēs*). Such objects include vegetal items such as flowers, rice, unshelled almonds, dried dates, betel leaves and betel nuts, and coconuts that are often painted (in red) with the *svastika* symbol. Water is kept in silver beakers. In one rite (known in Guj. as *sagan*), the person to be felicitated receives a colored *kuṃkum* dot on the forehead (and often also on the feet), where some grains of rice are made to stick on the *kuṃkum* dot; the person also holds some items placed on the metal tray. The coconut is handed to him or her, a garland is placed around his or her neck (a common form of felicitation in its own right), and rice is showered on him or her (a common gesture of blessing). Contrary to the rituals performed by the priests, who are all male, these rites are executed in silence – that is, the women do not recite any texts. Moreover, on auspicious days or occasions, Parsi women mark relevant thresholds with ephemeral drawings with white or colored chalk powder on the ground; these are known as *chalk*, *chauk*, or → *raṅgolī* (see Stausberg, 2004; Munshi & Stewart, 2002, for illustrations). There are floral or geometric motifs; for especially auspicious occasions, fish designs are vital. At weddings or initiations, elaborate patterns are drawn. Apart from their aesthetic appeal, they are held to convey auspiciousness and to create a pure atmosphere.

In 1819, a community meeting decided (among other things) that "[n]o woman should resort to such temples as Mumbadevi, Bhuleshwar, Mahalaxmi, Walkeshwar or any other place of Hindu worship, for idolatry" (Jeejeebhoy, 1953, 305). Apparently, some Hindu temples were attractive to Parsis. Today, images of Hindu deities like Lakṣmī (→ Śrī Lakṣmī) and Gaṇeśa (→ Gaṇapati/Gaṇeśa) can be seen in some Parsi homes. Hindu *bābās*, *svāmī*s, or *guru*s are venerated by some. More than anybody else, → Shirdi Sai Baba (d. 1918) is popular among the Parsis. Meher Baba (1894–1969), who studied with a student of Shirdi Sai Baba (among others) and extended his activity beyond India, was born a Zoroastrian by the name Merwan Sheriar Irani; he had several Parsis among his earliest and most intimate followers (Stausberg, 2002b, 96–97). In recent years, in Mumbai, a Parsi woman and a Parsi man called Gururani and Yogiraj, respectively, established a transreligious cult, where their *darśan*s (see → *pūjā* and *darśana*) are the key performances; their divine status is expressed by using Hindu vocabulary, and the → cobra is a main iconographical motif (Keul & Stausberg, 2010).

Bibliography

Andrés-Toledo, M.Á., *Vīdēvdād 10–12: Critical Edition, Translation and Commentary of the Avestan and Pahlavi Texts*, Salamanca, 2009.

Bharucha, E.S.D., *Collected Sanskrit Writings of the Parsis*, Bombay, 1906.

Boyce, M., "Iconoclasm among the Zoroastrians," in: J. Neusner, ed., *Christianity, Judaism and Other Greco-Roman Cults: Studies for Morton Smith at Sixty IV*, Leiden, 1975, 93–111.

Choksy, J.K., *Purity and Pollution in Zoroastrianism: Triumph over Evil*, Austin, 1989.

De Jong, A., "Purification *in Absentia*: On the Development of Zoroastrian Ritual Practice," in: J. Assmann & G.G. Stroumsa, eds., *Transformations of the Inner Self in Ancient Religions*, Leiden, 1999, 301–329.

Flattery, D.S., & M. Schwartz, *Haoma and Harmaline: The Botanical Identity of the Indo-Iranian Sacred Hallucinogen "Soma" and Its Legacy in Religion, Language, and Middle-Eastern Folklore*, Berkeley, 1989.

Greenebaum, S.E., "Vṛtrahan–Vərəthragna: India and Iran," in: G.J. Larson, C.S. Littleton & J. Puhvel, eds., *Myth in Indo-European Antiquity*, Berkeley, 1974, 93–97.

Grenet, F., "Iranian Gods in Hindu Garb: The Zoroastrian Pantheon of the Bactrians and Sogdians, Second–Eighth Centuries," *BAI* 20, 2010, 87–99.

Hinnells, J.R., *The Zoroastrian Diaspora: Religion and Migration*, Oxford, 2005.

Hinnells, J.R., *Zoroastrian and Parsi Studies: Selected Works*, Aldershot, 2000.

Hintze, A., "Avestan Literature," in: R.E. Emmerick & M. Macuch, eds., *The Literature of Pre-Islamic Iran: Companion Volume I to A History of Persian Literature*, London, 2009, 1–71.

Hintze, A., *A Zoroastrian Liturgy: The Worship in Seven Chapters (Yasna 35–41)*, Wiesbaden, 2007.

Humbach, H., "Sāmba and the Hinduized Magi," in: *K.R. Cama Oriental Institute Third International Congress Proceedings*, Mumbai, 2000, 88–94.

Humbach, H., "Miϑra in India and the Hinduized Magi," in: *Études Mithriaques*, Tehran, 1978, 229–253.

Humbach, H., "Vayu, Śiva und der Spiritus Vivens im Ostiranischen Synkretismus," in: *Monumentum H.S. Nyberg I*, Tehran, 1975, 397–408.

Jackson, A.V.W., *Zoroaster: The Prophet of Ancient Iran*, New York, 1899.

Jamison, S.W., *The Rig Veda between Two Worlds*, Paris, 2007.

Jeejeebhoy, J.R.B., "Communal Discipline among the Bombay Parsees in Olden Times," in: *M.P. Kharegat Memorial Volume*, vol. I, Bombay, 1953, 295–323.

Keul, I., & M. Stausberg, "Filmreife Epiphanien im dritten Raum. Ein transreligiöser Kult in Mumbai," *Numen* 57/1, 2010, 30–77.

Kreyenbroek, P., & S.N. Munshi, *Living Zoroastrianism: Urban Parsis Speak about Their Religion*, Richmond, 2001.

Marshak, B.I., & V.D. Raspopova, "Worshippers from the Northern Shrine of Temple II, Penjikent," *BAI* 8, 1996, 187–207.

Messina, G., *Libro apocalittico persiano: Ayātkār ī Žāmāspik*, Rome, 1939.

Munshi, S.N., & S. Stewart, "Observances of the Faithful," in: P.J. Godrej & F.P. Mistree, eds., *A Zoroastrian Tapestry: Art, Religion and Culture*, Ahmedabad, 2002, 385–397.

Narten, J., "Zarathustra und die Gottheiten des Alten Iran. Überlegungen zur Ahura-Theorie," *MSS* 56, 1996, 61–89.

Neugebauer, O., & D. Pingree, *The Pañcasiddhāntikā*, Copenhagen, 1970.

Oberlies, T., *Der Rigveda und seine Religion*, Berlin, 2012.

Panaino, A., *The Lists of Names of Ahura Mazda (Yast I) and Vayu (Yast XV)*, Rome, 2002.

Panaino, A., *La novella degli scacchi e delle tavole reale: Un'antica fonte orientale sui giochi da tavola più diffusi nel mondo euroasiatico tra Tardoantico e Medioevo e sulla loro simbologia militare e astrologica: Testo pahlavi, traduzione e commeto al Wizāriīšn ī čatrang du nīhišn ī nēw-ardaxšīr "La spiegazione degli scacchi e la disposizione della tavola reale"*, Bologna, 1999.

Panaino, A., "The Year of the Maga-Brāhmaṇas," in: *La Persia e l'Asia centrale da Alessandro al X secolo*, publ. Accademia Nazionale dei Lincei, Rome, 1996, 569–595.

Ringer, M.M., *Pious Citizens: Reforming Zoroastrianism in India and Iran*, Syracuse, 2011.

Schmidt, H.-P., "The Sixteen Sanskrit Ślokas of Ākā Adhyāru," *BDCRI* 21, 1960–1961, 157–196.

Schwartz, M., "On Haoma, and Its Liturgy in the Gathas," in: A. Panaino & A. Piras, eds., *Proceedings of the 5th Conference of the Societas Iranologica Europæa held in Ravenna, 6–11 October 2003*, vol. I: *Ancient and Middle Iranian Studies*, Milan, 2006, 215–224.

Scott, D.A., "Zoroastrian Responses to Hinduism, Past to Present: The Interaction of Religion and Politics," *Temenos* 24, 1988, 89–119.

Skjærvø, P.O., "Smashing Urine: On *Yasna* 48.10," in: M. Stausberg, ed., *Zoroastrian Rituals in Context*, Leiden, 2004, 253–281.

Skjærvø, P.O., "Zarathustra: First Poet-Sacrificer," in: S. Adhami, ed., *Paitim ā na: Essays in Iranian, Indo-European, and Indian Studies in Honor of Hanns-Peter Schmidt*, vol. II, Costa Mesa, 2003, 157–194.

Skjærvø, P.O., "Praise and Blame in the Avesta: The Poet-Sacrificer and His Duties," *JSAI* 26, 2002, 29–67.

Skjærvø, P.O., "Rivals and Bad Poets: The Poet's Complaint in the Old Avesta," in: M.G. Schmidt & W. Bisang, eds., *Philologica et Linguistica. Historia, Pluralitas, Universitas. Festschrift für Helmut Humbach zum 80. Geburtstag am 4. Dezember 2001*, Trier, 2001, 351–376.

Stausberg, M., "From Power to Powerlessness: Zoroastrianism in Iranian History," in: A.N. Longva & A.S. Roald, eds., *Religious Minorities in the Middle East: Domination, Self-empowerment, Accommodation*, Leiden, 2012, 171–193.

Stausberg, M., "Der Zoroastrismus als iranische Religion und die Semantik von 'Iran' in der zoroastrischen Religionsgeschichte," *ZRG* 63/4, 2011, 313–331.

Stausberg, M., "Hell in Zoroastrian History," *Numen* 56/2–3, 2009, 217–253.

Stausberg, M., *Die Religion Zarathushtras. Geschichte – Gegenwart – Rituale*, vol. III, Stuttgart, 2004.

Stausberg, M., *Die Religion Zarathushtras. Geschichte – Gegenwart – Rituale*, vol. I, Stuttgart, 2002a.

Stausberg, M., *Die Religion Zarathushtras. Geschichte – Gegenwart – Rituale*, vol. II, Stuttgart, 2002b.

Stietencron, H. von, *Indische Sonnenpriester. Sāmba und die Śākadvīpīya-Brāhmaṇa*, Wiesbaden, 1966.

Vevaina, Y.S.-D., "'Enumerating the *Dēn*': Textual Taxonomies, Cosmological Deixis, and Numerological Speculations in Zoroastrianism," *HR* 50/2, 2010, 111–143.

Watkins, C., *How to Kill a Dragon: Aspects of Indo-European Poetics*, Oxford, 1995.

Williams, A., *The Zoroastrian Myth of Migration from Iran and Settlement in the Indian Diaspora: Text, Translation and Analysis of the 16th Century Qeṣṣe-ye Sanjān "The Story of Sanjan"*, Leiden, 2009.

Michael Stausberg

Hinduism and Contemporary Issues

Animal Rights

Among world civilizations, India is perhaps the most animal friendly. From the caves of Lascaux to the petroglyphs of North America, hunting animals has been among the first subjects for depiction by human artists. By contrast, the Indus Valley seals (c. 3500 BCE) show animals in a more benign context, tended lovingly, and as encouragement in some way for hierophant-like figures.

The discourse of animal rights is thoroughly contemporary and unfolding, initiated by the 1975 book by P. Singer, *Animal Rights*. Though earlier movements existed for the protection of animals, most notably the Royal Society for the Prevention of Cruelty to Animals (1824), the American Society for the Prevention of Cruelty to Animals (1866), and the Humane Society (1954), they argued more from sentiment than from a philosophical or scientific perspective. P. Singer argues that animals hold many of the same capacities as human beings: cognition, emotion, ability to experience pain, and fear. In his estimation, many practices of industrialized agriculture inflict torture upon millions of farm animals each year and that these practices need to be examined and reconsidered. He considers animal rights to be a movement akin to the civil rights movement.

F. Bacon (1561–1626) and R. Descartes (1596–1650), credited with developing scientific method, forged an attitude toward animals that has come to characterize modernity: they assert that animals are nothing more than machines. Animals do not think, and they do not feel or experience emotions. Therefore, human beings are given the right to use animals however they see fit, for food and for scientific experimentation.

The Indian perspective on animals, held in common by Hindus, Buddhists, Jains, and Sikhs, differs radically from that found in the traditions of European and American philosophy. According to the widely held belief in reincarnation or rebirth (→ *saṃsāra*), humans have been animals in past lives. This foundational belief, though it does not necessarily result in universal protections for animals, provides a context that supports vegetarianism and an attitude of animal empathy.

The influence of Jainism and Buddhism on the Hindu views is significant and Jain, Buddhist, and Hindu traditions of noninjury (→ *ahiṃsā*) together represent an ancient common Indian historical transformation of redefining "the relationship between humans as well as the relationship between humans and nature" (Jacobsen, 1994, 298).

Buddhism and Animals

At the time of the life of the Buddha, 2,500 years ago, India was deeply forested, lush with all forms of life. The Buddha lived at a time of great transition, from forest subsistence to settled agriculture, from villages to towns. In his meditation practice, he recalled 550 prior births, many in the form of plants and animals. The Buddha taught *punarjanma*, the notion of being born again due to the transfer of unresolved life energy from one form to another. After his great awakening at the age of 35, he taught for 45 years, often sharing with his listeners tales of many beings he had known well or in fact had embodied in his past lives. These included more than 70 different animals, from antelopes to woodpeckers. Given the ease and insight with which he described these very different life forms, whether insects, fish, reptiles, birds, mammals, trees, or grasses, we might surmise that the Buddha was a keen observer of nature, and perhaps even quite the naturalist.

Unlike the prophetic monotheisms in which animals are generally seen as created for the purpose of human benefit or the modern tradition of scientific materialism as advanced by R. Descartes and F. Bacon, which consider animals to be no more than machines, animals hold meaning in Buddhist tradition. Buddhists improve themselves by reflecting on animal qualities. By identifying animal traits and traces of animal past lives, deeper understanding of the causes of one's current birth may be discerned.

The Jātaka tales contain many lessons about compassion. In the *Javasakuṇa Jātaka*, a woodpecker rescues a lion whose life was threatened by a bone stuck it his throat. In the *Suvaṇṇamiga Jātaka*, a golden stag is rescued by his devoted wife. The hunter who had threatened to kill both is so touched by her devotion that he releases them. In another Jātaka tale, a Brahman about to slay a goat, is surprised when the goat first moans and then laughs. The goat, when queried, responds that he moaned, not because of his own imminent demise, but because he saw that the Brahman would be condemned like himself to five hundred consecutive births as a goat. He laughed with joy at his own good fortune; this was his final birth as a goat. Having expiated for his sin as a former Brahman, he was destined once more to attain human birth. The Brahman, having learned an important lesson, renounced forever the killing of animals. The goat died a natural death and was indeed reborn as a human. In the *Dummedha Jātaka*, a young prince suffered for years as he watched his father patronize elaborate, ostentatious animal sacrifices. When he assumed the throne, the prince substituted these violent rituals with the worship of a splendid *banyan* tree.

Some of my favorite Jātaka stories tell of when the Buddha occupied the plant niche of the ecosystem. In the *Rukkadhamma Jātaka*, the story is told that trees should stay in groups and not risk harm by standing separate and proud. In the *Kusāñjali Jātaka*, the Buddha takes the form of lowly *kusa* (Pal.; Skt. *kuśa*) grass at the base of a noble tree. The king of Varanasi, alarmed that the central pillar of his elaborate palace has started to rot, sends his woodsmen to find a new post. They locate the magnificent tree with the *kuśa* grass at its base, mark the tree, and prepare to return the next day to chop it down and haul it into town. The animals surrounding the tree and living in the tree, as well as the many insects and other beings that rely upon the tree, mourn their inevitable demise. The future Buddha, in the form of *kuśa* grass, intently grows all night, entwining himself around the trunk of the large tree, and then manifests dots on his plant-skin, making the tree look diseased. When the woodmen arrive the next day, they scratch their heads, diagnose the tree as suddenly unworthy, and spare its life, thereby causing great rejoicing when they depart.

Animals in Jainism

Jainism, a minority religion practiced in India and around the world, is particularly well known for its advocacy for animals. The Jain faith arose more than 2,500 years ago on India's northern Gangetic Plain. Its founding figures, Pārśvānātha (c. 850 BCE) and Mahāvīra (c. 500 BCE) are regarded to be the 23rd and 24th of a long line of spiritual teachers (*tīrthaṅkaras*). They taught and lived a way of life that emphasized the practice of nonviolence (*ahiṃsā*). This commitment to nonviolence, which includes vegetarianism and rejection of occupations that involve the harm of animals, is designed to release the fettering → *karmas* that occlude the luminous nature of the soul (*jīva*). Because of violence committed in this life and in past lives, dimly colored *karmas* have cloaked one's innate pure consciousness with ignorance and desire. By the careful application of the Jain vows of nonviolence, truthfulness, not stealing, sexual restraint, and nonpossession, one expels these afflicted *karmas*, advancing toward a state of → liberation, known as *kevala*.

For two reasons, animals play an important role in the Jain religion. Each human person has endured countless lives as a nonhuman animal. The Jain teaching of reincarnation (*punarjanma*) specifies that unpurged *karma* in this life will carry over to shape one's future life. Hence, all people have a history that intertwines animal narratives with one's current human narrative. The second reason for the importance of animals relates to ethics. Ethical behavior, particularly as listed in the vows above, determines the course of present and future life. One way to improve one's ethical and future ontological status is to treat animals with benevolence. Acts of kindness toward animals can help release the binding *karmas* that otherwise would cause an inauspicious rebirth. From a Jain perspective, all humans have been nonhuman animals, and good treatment of animals can help improve one's lot both in this life and in the next.

In Jainism, all animals possess consciousness. Jains identify ascending gradations of consciousness, beginning with a consciousness that arises with the sense of touch. Jains attribute consciousness even to entities that in Aristotelian thought are inanimate. For instance, rocks are said to possess the sense of touch and hence hold their own consciousness. The same is true for water (whether in droplets or oceans), fire, and gusts of wind, as well as the innumerable microorganisms that pervade each and every environment and every plant, large and small. Most cultures would not consider rocks or lumps of ice or palm trees to be "animals." For Jains, they merit recognition for their ability to touch and, presumably, their ability to convey certain moods. Recognizable animals appear at the next level of the Jain categorization of reality. Dwelling within the earth and within various decaying or diseased bodies can be found worms, gnawing and tunneling though their environments. According to the Jain worldview, these worms possess both the sense of touch and the sense of taste. They are considered to be higher-level beings and must be spared from harm. Whereas it is permissible to walk upon the earth, breathe air, and make food from plants, it would not be acceptable to cause harm to worms, as such harm would further deepen the *karma* that shrouds the soul. Higher than worms, insects such as crawling bugs and ants are said to possess the sense of smell. They also merit protection. The next station in Jain taxonomy names butterflies, bees, flies, and moths as adding the sense of sight to the foundations of touch, taste, and smell. Water snakes add the sense of hearing. All mammals, reptiles, and birds fall under the highest category, those beings that possess all six senses, including the ability to think.

This worldview is reinforced in the daily life of Jains and also can be seen in the overall attitude toward animals in India, where animals are part of daily life, with cows, goats, elephants, and camels spilling into the streets and sidewalks. The Jains assiduously, for more than 2,500 years, have advocated against animal sacrifice and for vegetarianism. They influenced the practices of Buddhism and Hinduism and successfully appealed to the Mughal rulers for increased regard for animals. Jains have opened and maintained thousands of shelters throughout the subcontinent for the protection of animals. In the recent Jain diaspora, they have lent support to animal shelters and various causes that work for the protection of animals worldwide.

The oldest text of Jainism, the *Ācārāṅgasūtra* (c. 300 BCE), gives Mahāvīra's foundational teaching on animals and the need for their protection:

> Some slay animals for sacrificial purposes, some slay animals for the sake of their skin, some kill them for the sake of their blood; others for the sake of their heart, their bile, the feathers of their tale, their tail, their big or small horns, their teeth, their tusks, their nails, their sinews, their bones; with a purpose and without a purpose. Some kill animals because they have been wounded by them or are wounded or will be wounded. He who injures these animals does not comprehend and renounce these sinful acts; he who does not injure these, comprehends and renounces these sinful acts. Knowing them, a wise man should not act sinfully towards animals, or cause others to act so, nor allow others to act so. (*ĀcS.* 6.5; trans. Jacobi, 1884, 12)

According to Jainism, by refraining from cruelty to animals, the human being can elevate himself or herself, recognizing that when we hurt other beings, human or nonhuman, we ultimately only hurt ourselves.

Animals in Hinduism

The Hindu tradition consists of two primary strands, world affirming (*pravṛtti*) and world renouncing (*nivṛtti*). The world-affirming aspects of Hinduism can be traced to Brahmanical roots and the perdurability of vedic ritual (→ *yajña*). Sacrifice of animals was widely practiced in ancient Hinduism and continues today, primarily in Nepal, and parts of Karnataka, Bengal, and Orissa. According to B.K. Lal (1986), the ministrations of the Brahman priest render a sacrificial animal into a transcendent realm of symbol, mitigating any negative effects. J. Preston reports that such a priest undergoes an ontological shift into a deep sense of identity with the goddess → Durgā, thus emphasizing the otherworldly nature of the sacrificial process. In the early vedic tradition, cattle were a source of food. Kings killed a special horse in an elaborate ceremony (*aśvamedha*; see → *yajña*) conducted every 12 years of their reign. By the time of the *Bṛhadāraṇyakopaniṣad* (c. 800 BCE), symbolic, analogical thinking paved the way for seeing the meaning behind this admittedly gruesome ceremony, which eventually fell into disuse by the early 18th century.

Eventually, the cow became venerated within the Hindu community (see also → sacred animals). Many verses of the *Ṛgveda* praise cattle, and it became forbidden to eat beef, a custom that continues today among Hindus worldwide. Vegetarianism became the norm for high-caste Hindus, with advocacy of abstention from meat documented in the → *Mahābhārata* (c. 400 BCE–400 CE).

Both the → Vedas and the → Upaniṣads include frequent mention of animals. The *Ṛgveda*, in addition to cows, refers to peacocks, swans, water buffalo, camels, and elephants. The *Pṛthivīsūkta* of the *Atharvaveda* (12. 25, 49; see Dwivedi & Chapple, 2011) lists deer, antelope, tigers, and other species. In the Upaniṣads, animals take on a mantle of spiritual wisdom. The red eye of the parrot connotes pure consciousness or divinity in the *Śvetāśvataropaniṣad* (4.4). In the *Chāndogyopaniṣad*, Satyakāma learns great wisdom from a bull and two different species of birds, a swan and a diving bird (*ChāU.* 4.4–10).

By the time classical Hinduism took shape in the early centuries following King Aśoka (c. 300 BCE), gods and goddesses became linked with a particular species from the animal realm. Both in iconography and the → Purāṇas, animal mounts (→ *vāhanas*) signified divine connections with the animal realm. For instance, → Kṛṣṇa is depicted with a cow, → Rāma with the monkey → Hanumān, → Śiva with a bull, his son Gaṇeśa (→ Gaṇapati/Gaṇeśa) with the rat, his brother Skanda (→ Murukaṉ) with the peacock, → Sarasvatī with the swan, Lakṣmī (→ Śrī Lakṣmī) with the elephant, and so forth. Additionally, religious literature such as the *Yogavāsiṣṭha* (c. 1050 CE) employed the trope of reincarnation to underscore its teachings. In one beautiful narrative of this text, on the occasion of the death of their parents, elder brother Puṇya consoles his younger brother Pāvana by reminding him of all his happy glorious past lives, including as a deer, swan, lion, fish, monkey, raven, elephant, donkey, dog, wood insect, rooster, partridge, horse, gnat, crane, ant, and a millipede. He chides him to recover his good cheer, knowing that this life with those particular parents will change and pass. The *Manusmṛti* has a less upbeat interpretation, specifying that "violent men become carnivorous beasts; people who eat impure things become worms; thieves become animals that devour one another" (*MaSm.* 12.59.69; trans. Doniger, 1991). The *Chāndogyopanisad* asserts that evil people will be reborn as dogs or pigs (*ChāU.* 5.10.7–8).

Though the various → Dharmaśāstras discuss animals, they do not prescribe universal vegetarianism. Nonetheless, vegetarianism is held in high esteem and is adopted by many Brahman families, a pattern then imitated by people of different castes. The *Mahābhārata* states that "*ahiṃsā* (nonviolence) is the highest religious teaching (*dharma*)" (*MBh.* 8.116.37; trans by author, 1993, 17). The *Yogasūtra* states that this and other vows must be practiced regardless of "birth, place, time, or circumstance" (*YS.* 2.31) and that "hostility ceases when one is in the presence of a person established in nonviolence" (*YS.* 2.35).

The Bisṇoī and Animal Protection

As mentioned above, the practice of nonviolence and the consequent protection of animals spread beyond the communities of Brahmans and Jains. The Bisṇoī of India are one such community. The founder, Guru Jambheśvara (1451–1536), found his family adversely affected by drought in their native → Rajasthan, during a period that lasted from 1476 to 1486. As a result, trees were cut down, animals were killed, and many people migrated from the area. In 1485 Jambheśvara experienced a vision in which he saw the adverse results of people quarreling with nature. From this arose a new religious practice based on the observance of 29 rules. The name of the faith takes its name from the local dialect term for the number 29. Many rulers in North India embraced his basic principles, including those of Delhi, Jodhpur, Bikaner, Jaisalmer, and Mewar. P. Jain (2011), a scholar of the Bisṇoī, has summarized the 29 rules as follows:

> ... [E]ight are about conserving and protecting the animals and trees, including the nonsterilization of bulls, keeping the male goats in the sanctuary, prohibition against killing of animals, cutting down any type of green trees, and protecting all life forms. He also forbade the wearing of blue clothes, because the dye for them is obtained by cutting several shrubs. Seven other rules were about social behavior. They directed his followers to be simple, truthful, content, abstentious, and pure, also to avoid adultery, and making false arguments. He prohibited criticizing others and [advised] to tolerate the criticism of others. His other ten rules were about personal hygiene and maintaining good health. These were instructions about drinking filtered water, taking a daily bath, improving sanitary conditions, prohibiting the use of opium, alcohol, tobacco and other narcotic substances. Meat was excluded from the diet. Ritual prohibition for 30 days after childbirth and five days during menstruation was prescribed for women. Four other rules provided guidance for spiritual practices, e.g., one must always remember that god is omnipresent, perform rituals daily, and observe fast and perform communal *havan* (fire ritual) on every new moon. (Jain, 2011, 59)

Jambheśvara had words of caution for both Muslims and Hindus, reminding the former that "Muhammed himself neither killed animals nor asked his followers to do so" and criticizing the Hindu "tantric yogic practitioners sacrificing animals to Bhairav Yogini or other deities" (Jain, 2011, 59–60). He proclaimed that "killing the creations of God in the name of God is not only wrong but is also an act of arrogance" (Jain, 2011, 60). Jambheśvara built reservoirs and wells throughout northern India, many of which still stand today. Villagers to this day credit him with planting tens of thousands of trees.

Several high-profile violations of local law have been publicized in Indian media, including the death of Gangaram Bishnoi at the hands of poachers in 2002, the imprisonment of Hindi film actor Salman Khan for killing a blackbuck in Bisṇoī territory in 1998, and the killing of a farmer and his two sons by poachers in 1947, with similar widely reported cases in 1948, 1995, 1997, and 1998. Dozens of such "martyrdoms" have been recorded in the past century. Today, the Bisṇoī area spans four Indian states: Rajasthan, Punjab, Haryana, and Gujarat. The Bisṇoī cooperate with international non-governmental organizations such as the World Wildlife Fund. They maintain sacred groves that number in to the thousands of acres. P. Jain, traveling through Bisṇoī lands, noted an abundance of wildlife cohabiting peacefully with humans:

> As my driver drove on the state highway, I was suddenly struck by a huge number of deer grazing on both sides of the highway...the biodiversity of the desert state of Rajasthan is managed not by human isolation but by active human participation...In addition to blackbucks, other animals and birds that are found in around Bishnoi villages are Great Indian Bustards, Indian gazelles, peacocks, bulbuls, bayas [Hind. *bayā*, weaverbird], sparrows, crows, vultures, chinkara [Hind. *ciṅkārā*, a species of gazelle], neelgais [Hind. *nīlgau*, type of antelope], wild pigs, wolves, jackals, and desert foxes. The trees commonly found in and around Bishnoi villages are khejari [Hind. *khejaṛi*, bot. Prosopis cineraria], jal [bot. Capparidaceae], papal [Hind. *pīpal*, bot. Ficus religiosa], kair [Hind. *ker*, bot. Salvadora Oleiodes], rohira [Hind. *rohiṛa*, bot. Tecomella undalata], babool [Hind. *babūl*, bot. Acacia nilotica], and neem [Hind. *nīm*, bot. Azadirachta indica]. (Jain, 2011, 53)

I also have traveled through these areas and have been deeply impressed with the abundance of wildlife and the gentle demeanor of the human inhabitants.

The Bisṇoī provide a modern example of human adaptation. More than five hundred years ago, one individual stood up for animals and trees, creating a tradition that reaches down into the present. Today, climate change is prompting humans to reexamine their consumer habits. Similarly, Jambheśvara responded to a protracted drought by developing practical human adaptations to enable the flourishing of life in harsh conditions. Lessons can be learned from his pioneering work.

Piñjrāpoles and *Gośālas*, and Mahatma Gandhi

In order to institutionalize the protection of animals and to protect elderly cows, various Hindu and Jain civic organizations have established thousands of shelters (*piñjrāpoles* [animal homes] and *gośālas* [cow shelters]) throughout India. The policies in these shelters mandate provision of food and some veterinary attention, but generally do not allow for mercy killing of any animals.

M.K. → Gandhi, though born into a vegetarian Hindu family, became an avid advocate of vegetarianism after joining the London Vegetarian Society in 1889. His views on mercy killing of animals, which he advocated, created quite a stir among conservative Hindus and Jains who were outraged when he authorized the slaughter of a suffering cow. Nonetheless, Gandhi remains one of the leading spokespersons for kindness to animals and for vegetarianism.

Contemporary Animal Advocacy

Maneka Gandhi, the widow of Rajeev Gandhi and daughter-in-law of the late Indira Gandhi, is perhaps India's most active spokesperson for animals. She served as environmental minister for the Indian government. She established People For Animals, one of hundreds of non-governmental organizations dedicated to animal welfare. She has campaigned against the use of animals in scientific experiments and against the multinational fast-food restaurants. She is a fervent critic of industrialized agriculture and laments that Indian grain is exported to fatten European cattle. Her interactive Web site demonstrates the power of the Internet in supporting and advancing activist causes. Organizations campaigning for animal rights in India include Vets Beyond Borders (VBB). Established in 2003 by Catherine Schuetze, an Australian veterinarian, Vets Beyond Borders coordinates and runs veterinary-based animal welfare including rescue, spay and neuter, and antirabies initiatives. The Wildlife Trust of India, directed by Vivek Menon, seeks to protect the Asian elephant and other species threatened by encroaching human populations. Other organizations include Animal Birth Control and Rabies: India, Asia for Animals, the Animal Welfare Board of India, and the Tibetan Vegetarian Association. Though as modern organizations they largely word their mission statements in secular scientific language, the underlying culture of India supports various an animal-friendly outlook. Whereas animal-rights activists might be seen as a fringe element in Europe and America, India's long advocacy for the protection of animals places these organizations well within the mainstream.

One of the most notable expressions of globalized Hinduism can be found in the modern → *yoga* movement. More than 15 million Americans practice *yoga* on a regular basis, the number of Europeans are also in the millions, and globally probably tens of millions. The two grandfathers of modern Yoga, Sri → Krishnamacharya and Swami → Sivananda, were devout vegetarians. Whereas members of the more overtly religious Hare Krishna movement (see → ISKCON) are expected to adopt a vegetarian lifestyle, practitioners of the popular movement-based forms of *yoga* are less likely to alter their diets. S.J. Rosen (2011) estimates that two-thirds of this population continues to eat meat. However, the other five million vegetarian *yoga* practitioners would most likely align themselves with S. Gannon, cofounder of Jivamukti Yoga, a staunch advocate for animal welfare.

Human Responsibility toward Animals: Indian Perspectives

Karma theory distinguishes Indian approaches to animal rights. According to *karma* theory, everything that happens takes place due to one's past actions and sets the conditions for future experience over incalculable lifetimes. All human beings have at one time or another lived the life of a different species, perhaps all species. Accepting this view produces feelings of empathy. We feel the grandeur of an elephant because we have lived an elephant life. We feel the smallness of an ant because we have been an ant. Humans thus have a particular responsibility to not cause harm to animals. Causing harm to another being, human or nonhuman, will ultimately cause harm to oneself.

Acts of kindness to animals carry inherent rewards. As stated in the *Bṛhadāraṇyakopaniṣad*, good is rewarded with good; evil begets evil (*BĀU.* 4.4.5). By minimizing harm to animals, one ensures one's own status within the realm of goodness, referred to in Sanskrit as *sattva*. Because an animal can only be seen quantitatively but not ultimately qualitatively different than oneself, a person would act self-interestedly to make certain to avoid committing acts of violence. In the Hindu context, animal rights become inseparable from human rights.

Bibliography

Bryant, E., "Strategies of Vedic Subversion: The Emergence of Vegetarianism in Post-Vedic India," in: P. Waldau & K. Patton, eds., *A Communion of Subjects: Animals in Religion, Science, and Ethics*, New York, 2006, 194–203.

Chapple, C.K., "Inherent Value without Nostalgia: Animals and the Jaina Tradition," in: P. Waldau & K. Patton, eds., *A Communion of Subjects: Animals in Religion, Science, and Ethics*, New York, 2006, 241–249.

Chapple, C.K., *Nonviolence to Animals, Earth, and Self in Asian Traditions*, Albany, 1993.

Dwivedi, O.P., & C.K. Chapple, *In Praise of Mother Earth: The Pṛthivīs ūkta of the Atharva Veda*, Los Angeles, 2011.

Gandhi, M., http://www.peopleforanimalsindia.org/ (accessed Feb 2012).

Gandhi, M.K., "The Moral Basis of Vegetarianism," http://southerncrossreview.org/22/gandhi2.html (accessed Feb 2012).

Gannon, S., *Yoga and Vegetarianism*, San Rafael, 2008.

Jacobi, H., *Jaina Sutras Translated from the Prakrit*, Oxford, 1884.

Jacobsen, K.A., "The Institutionalization of the Ethics of 'Non-injury towards All Beings' in Ancient India," *EE* 16/3, 1994, 287–301.

Jain, P., *Dharma and Ecology of Hindu Communities*, Surrey, 2011.

Jaini, P.S., "Indian Perspectives on the Spirituality of Animals," in: *idem*, *Collected Papers on Jaina Studies*, Delhi, 2000, 253–266.

Jaini, P.S., *The Jaina Path of Purification*, Berkeley, 1979.
Kemmerer, L., & A.J. Nocella II, eds., *Call to Compassion: Religious Perspectives on Animal Advocacy*, New York, 2011.
Krishna, N., *Sacred Animals*, New Delhi, 2010.
Lal, B.K., "Hindu Perspectives on the Use of Animals in Science," in: T. Regan, ed., *Animal Sacrifices: Religious Perspectives on the Use of Animals in Science*, Philadelphia, 1986, 199–212.
Lodrick, D.O., *Sacred Cows, Sacred Places: The Origin and Survival of Animal Homes in India*, Berkeley, 1981.
Nelson, L., "Cows, Elephants, Dogs, and Other Lesser Embodiments of *Atman*: Reflections on Hindu Attitudes toward Nonhuman Animals," in: P. Waldau & K. Patton, eds., *A Communion of Subjects: Animals in Religion, Science, and Ethics*, New York, 2006, 179–193.
Preston, J., *Cult of the Goddess: Social and Religious Change in a Hindu Temple*, Prospect Heights IL, 1985.
Rosen, S.J., *Food for the Soul: Vegetarianism and Yoga Traditions*, Santa Barbara, 2011.
Wiley, K., "Five-Sensed Animals in Jainism," in: P. Waldau & K. Patton, eds., *A Communion of Subjects: Animals in Religion, Science, and Ethics*, New York, 2006, 250–255.

Christopher Key Chapple

Atheism and Rationalism

Any general assessment of atheism and rationalism within "Hinduism" is confronted with manifold limitations not only given the associated historical depth, geographic range, linguistic plurality, cultural diversity, and (therefore) fuzzy borders of various Hindu traditions, but also due to the Christo-Occidental genealogy and conceptual ambiguities of the notions "atheism" and "rationalism." In order to deal with these problems, only a selection of relevant issues are addressed here, including the problems of translating "atheism" and "rationalism," the role of these and related notions in classical schools of thought, and their use in contemporary public discourse. The focus here is on Sanskrit-Hindi philosophical traditions, contemporary antireligious groups, and their respective texts – not on practices, bodily experiences, or aesthetics (Wilke & Moebus, 2011). Buddhist and Jain influence is only mentioned; likewise, the roles of rationalism and atheism within Islam, Neo-Hinduism, and other religious traditions on the subcontinent are not addressed.

Atheism

The notion "atheism," derived from the classical Greek *a-* (not, without) and *theos* (god), is understood in several distinct ways in academic and popular discourse. The most important difference is while some interpret the "*a*" as indicating the absence of a belief in "*theos*," others consider it a negation of the existence of "*theos*." The notion "*theos*" is understood as referring to the Christian God, various personal or impersonal god(s) and goddesses, or any religious beliefs and practices. Each specific understanding of "atheism" faces serious conceptual difficulties. Atheism understood as the mere absence of a belief in a Christian God is so far-reaching that it does not serve any systematic purpose. Atheism understood as the absence of a belief in – or the negation of the existence of – god(s) implies the treacherous distinction between god(s) and (other) supernatural entities (nonempirical agents etc.). Finally, the understanding of atheism as a rejection of any kind of religious belief and related practices is dependent on a specific conceptualization of "religion," hence the respective conceptual difficulties. These problems are compounded if one attempts to apply the term "atheism" to the Hindu context.

Translation of "Atheism"

Synonyms of none of these meanings of "atheism" exist in the Sanskrit-Hindi tradition. Terms like *bhagavān, brahman, īśvara, paramātman, parameśvara*, and so on are often translated loosely as "god." There are "theistic" streams within the Hindu tradition, some speaking of monism, pantheism, panentheism, aequitheism, and homotheism (Michaels, 2004, 211), and in certain forms of Śaivism and Vaiṣṇavism streams of monotheism featuring a personal god, as for example with → Kṛṣṇa as the source of each of → Viṣṇu's → *avatāra*s (as Svayam Bhagavān). The different notions of "god(s)" in use are, however, polysemous, and there is no conceptual equivalent to their negation in the form of "a-theism." For example, *īśvara* is used to indicate the power of various vedic gods in the *Ṛgveda*. It is conceptualized as an omnipotent, omniscient supreme god as well as the source of the universe, as found in *Śvetāśvataropaniṣad*, while other Hindu texts use → Īśvara as the name and form of the a-cosmic → *brahman*. Representatives of Advaita → Vedānta of → Śaṅkara, in particular, portrayed the *brahman* as an abstract, metaphysical absolute, as → *nirguṇa brahman* (i.e. *brahman* without qualities), rather than a god of actual religious devotion. In addition to the understanding of *brahman* as the one supreme, absolute being through which the entire universe came into being, it can also denote → liberation (*mokṣa*), truth, pure → consciousness, and/or the innermost self of every being (→ *ātman*). In classical Hindu traditions, there are half gods, ghosts, and demons, as well as deified natural forces (Agni, Indra, Sūrya, etc.), deified moral principles (Āditya, Mitra, Varuṇa, etc.), and divine powers with soteriological influence (such as → *tapas* for "ascetic heat" or *ṛta* for "truth"). In contemporary forms of Hinduism, a *bābā*, → *guru*, or → *sādhu* can be considered to be a "divine human being" or "godman." The plethora of terms, often used differently in different Hindu traditions over more than three millennia, have produced complex religious and academic debates (Michaels, 2004, ch. 8) that caution against any general "theo-logy."

Further, the cosmological embeddedness of the various understandings of god(s) and the conceptualization and experiences of divine–human relationships in Hindu traditions varies considerably from the Christo-Occidental notion of a transcendent God. The worldly realm of human affairs is often not strictly separate from the realm of Hindu god(s); some humans are considered to be gods. And vice versa, the mundane nature of many gods is made clear in their being "fed" through → *pūjā* and → *yajña*, and to the extent that they can be considered dependent on the religious practices of the people. Moreover, according to many Hindu traditions, the highest goal of liberation (*mokṣa*) can only be reached by humans, not by god(s). Especially in some older Hindu traditions, the gods are themselves part of *māyā* and the cycle of rebirth (→ *saṃsāra*), and liberation takes place beyond the heavenly realms. Finally, for most religious and philosophical traditions, the existence of god(s) is a peripheral problem compared to the way in which one can achieve liberation, and larger parts of → Sāṃkhya and especially → Mīmāṃsā are "atheistic" in that sense. Depending on the religious tradition, there are various paths (*mārga*s), focusing on orthopraxis (*karmamārga*), devotion (*bhaktimārga*), and teaching (*jñānamārga*), as well as philosophical schools (*darśana*s), doctrines (*vāda*s), and various traditions (→ *saṃpradāya*s) that guide religious practice, formulate religious goals, and eventually lead to liberation. The flourishing of religion does not necessarily depend on questions of whether god(s) exists. Therefore, highlighting a definite and dogmatic position with respect to the nature of god(s) can be misleading.

If one widens the focus to rejections of religious beliefs and practices, one could look upon the notion of *adharma*, or the *nāstika* (nonvedic, heterodox) streams of Indian thought systems (*darśana*), as similar to common understandings of atheism. The translation of → *dharma* as "religion" in popular discourse, however, is highly deceptive. The meanings of *dharma* range from the cosmic order, to social justice, to duties specific to one's "caste" (*varṇa*). Accordingly *adharma* does not denote a general rejection of religion but, among other things, a breakdown in (cosmic) order, injustice, or the neglect of ritual or social duties. *Nāstika* schools are "heterodox," because they challenge vedic-upanishadic and later Brahmanic beliefs and practices. They comprise Buddhist and Jain philosophies – because of the focus on Hinduism, these are not discussed here despite mutual influence (see Dasgupta, 1957, 203) – and the → Lokāyata (or Cārvāka) tradition. Some scholars describe Lokāyata as an atheistic philosophy (Chattopadhyaya, 1969; Narisetti, 1985; Hiorth, 1995; Minois, 2000), and sometimes *nāstika* is translated as "atheism." L.R. Joshi explicitly argues that Lokāyata is the only truly atheistic system of thought within Indian philosophy. He describes further schools of thought that are considered to be atheistic by others, such as Sāṃkhya, Mīmāṃsā, Buddhism, and Jainism, as having "theistic tendencies" (Joshi, 1966, 189).

The history of Lokāyata is the subject of debate, since most of its original scriptures have been destroyed (an exception is the sceptical treatise *Tattvopaplavasiṃha*; see Franco, 1987). Its arguments must be reconstructed indirectly, through an interpretation of criticisms and summaries of mostly rival philosophical positions. On the one hand, there must have been very early on in ancient India people questioning the authority of ritual experts, beliefs, and practices concerning the existence of god(s), the soul, and an otherworld or afterlife (*paraloka*), along with the recompense for deeds and the resulting moral demands in this life (Dasgupta, 1957, 78; Gonda, 1960, 313–314). This can be inferred from the fact that many rival groups defended their doctrines against the "materialistic" challenges of scholars attributed to Lokāyata. There is however no evidence, on the other hand, of a coherent materialistic or skeptical philosophical system – featuring its own metaphysics, epistemology, and ethics – in India before the 6th century CE (Franco, 2011). Lokāyata did not survive as a distinct philosophical tradition in later centuries, and its influence on contemporary forms of Hinduism is hard to asses. Materialist arguments attributed to Lokāyata hold that sensory perception is the only means of gaining knowledge, negating on this basis the possibility of the existence of god(s), while skeptic arguments prefer to remain agnostic about such questions; hence one could derive different argumentative approaches that lead to two kinds of "atheism" in such cases. However, it might be more helpful here to not choose such a loaded and ambivalent term, but rather distinguish between materialist and skeptic arguments, as well as anticlerical tendencies and rejections of specific religious beliefs and practices in Lokāyata (as well as in other schools).

Rationalism

The notion of "rationalism" is as problematic as "atheism," since it opens up the semantic (mine) fields of "reason" and "rationality" and their related arguments ranging from classical Western philosophy, via the social sciences, to postcolonial theory. M. Weber noted that "rationalism is an historical concept which covers a whole world of different things" (Weber, 2002, 78), and L. Daston stressed the many aspects and the epistemic historicity of rationality in the West (Daston, 2001). For the sake of clarity, the following three arguments are separated here: (1) reason as a human faculty and its systematization in logic, (2) rationality as a constitutive part of a specific "mode of thought," and (3) rationalism as a contemporary antireligious worldview. Before these different understandings can be discussed, the problems of translation must be addressed.

Translation of "Reason/Rationality/ Rationalism"

As with "atheism," there are no synonyms of "reason," "rationality," or "rationalism" in the Hindi-Sanskrit vocabulary, and different words have different connotations in different contexts and at different moments in time (Halbfass, 1988). The term *buddhi* is often translated as reason, but also as knowledge, understanding, intelligence, or intellect. Further, it is used for the general faculty of humans to classify data collected by the senses, and therefore as the fundamental basis for reason and logical thinking. Most influential was probably the use of *buddhi* as a technical term in Sāṃkhya philosophy. In Sāṃkhya the first three evolutes of → *prakṛti* (Jacobsen, 1999) are described as *ahaṃkāra* (faculty of self-consciousness/ individuality), *manas* (recording faculty), and *buddhi* (faculty of judgment/determination). Thus not only is *buddhi* the intellectual or psychological faculty to discriminate objects presented to it by the other faculties of knowledge and perception, but it also decides courses of action. The specific connotations of *buddhi* within Sāṃkhya illustrate the problems of any straightforward translation and serves as an exemplary case for the limited discussions of the terms that follow.

Tarka is generally translated as reason, argument, logic, discussion, proof, contention, conjecture, reflection, refutation, and the making of inferences. The word is primarily used in contexts where competing positions are defended against other views. The focus here lies more on the identification and classification of irregularities, inconsistencies, or fallacies within scholarly debates, speculative doctrines, or philosophical systems. *Tarkavidyā* or *tarkaśāstra* is the science of inductive reasoning and thought. *Viveka* is translated as reason, discretion, discrimination, judgment, wisdom, investigation, and criticism. *Yukti* is translated as reasoning, union, combination of words, application, use, argument, and proof. *Hetu* not only refers to the middle term in an affirmative argument (syllogism) but also is translated as cause, premises, evidence, consequence, or a rational way of acquiring knowledge. *Haituka* is translated not only as having a cause or reason, but also as reasoner, rationalist, skeptic, heretic, and logician (someone versed in *hetuvidyā*). Other words for rationalist used today are *buddhivādī, buddhiprāmāṇvādī, tarkśīl, tarkvādī*, or *vivekvādī*. *Ānvīkṣikī* is the name for an investigative, reflective approach that examines beliefs acquired through observation and testimony by the means of correct knowledge (sometimes taken as synonymous with logic, → Nyāya, or the philosophical systems in general). *Hetuśāstra, ānvīkṣikī*, and *tarkavidyā* are at times used as synonyms for "free inquiry" or reasoning unrestricted by tradition – but *tarka* carries more pejorative connotations than the other two. Accordingly, *tārkika* is sometimes translated as a "sophist" who reasons for the sake of reasoning (and not for the interpretation of the → Vedas), and therefore critics also speak of *śuṣkatarka* (fruitless reasoning) and *kṣudratarka* (petty reasoning).

None of these terms is necessarily related to atheism in any of the meanings mentioned above. Rather, they can be seen as indispensable to find a way to god(s), to reason in a way not conflicting with the Vedas, to distinguish the eternal from the noneternal, as a requirement for the liberation of the self from the cycle of birth and rebirth, or for making otherwise soteriological progress. For most orthodox schools, compatibility of reasoning with the sacred tradition is of importance, since they consider systematic forms of reasoning, if used properly, as conducive to interpreting and thereby validating the sacred texts.

"Reason" as a Human Faculty and Its Systematization in Logic

"Reason" has been understood in the Western, Aristotelian tradition as one key characteristic that differentiates human beings from (other) animals. It has been claimed that similar distinctions must have also been part of popular thinking in ancient India (Dasgupta, 1957, 190–191; Chakrabarti, 1997, 260). Further, beings with reason have the possibility to reason, understood as taking some things to be true and inferring on this basis that other things are also true. Through this faculty, human beings decide which actions, beliefs, interpretations, or arguments are reasonable. Doing this in a systematic and consistent way and identifying the general conditions for doing so is called logic.

The roots of reasoning as logic in the different fields of aesthetics, agriculture, architecture, astronomy, grammar, law, mathematics, medicine, phonology, statecraft, and theology in India can be traced back to at least the 5th century BCE (Chakrabarti, 1997). During the first five hundred years of the Common Era, systematic engagement with rational argumentation was developed by adducing logical principles such as the principle of noncontradiction, the principle of excluded middle, and the principle of double negation. Out of the various *astika* Hindu schools of thought, the one most often associated with conceptualizing rational arguments, logic, and epistemology is the Nyāya school (on the origins of Nyāya and its relationship to early classical → Āyurveda, see Preisendanz, 2009). One of the most influential Brahmanical texts pertaining to inference is the *Nyāyasūtra* by Gautama (c. 2nd–3rd cents. CE).

Nyāya representatives most forcefully advocate *pramāṇa* as a method or theory for rational inquiry in epistemology and philosophical matters. This view denotes reflections on sources or causes of valid cognition, as well as on the means of validating or justifying knowledge or arguments. Contradictory positions, such as those of the "idealistic" tradition of Buddhist philosophers on the one hand and Nyāya scholars on the other, referred to *pramāṇa* to justify their claims, while skeptics flatly questioned the validity of "perception" as its precondition. The use of Indian logic was further developed by scholars such as Vasubandhu, Dignāga, Īśvarasena, and his student Dharmakīrti (c. 5th–7th cents. CE), whose thoughts on reason and argument were crucial for classical Indian philosophy (Tillemans, 1999).

"Rationality" as a Constitutive Part of a Specific Mode of Thought

Reflecting on this history, B.K. Matilal argued that the Indian logical tradition, featuring counterparts of the Aristotelian syllogism and the law of noncontradiction, is not a derivate of Western ideas but is entirely homegrown (Matilal, 1990, 1–8). This observation must be understood against the common depiction of India as the land of religion and spirituality, as opposed to logic, rationality, and scientific debate. Scholars like A. Sen, J.N. Mohanty, and J. Bronkhorst explicitly argue that this stereotype is wrong, that India has had a long tradition of rational debate. A. Sen argues that selective inattention has produced a substantial bias in the interpretation of Indian thought (Sen, 2005, 25). J.N. Mohanty describes philosophy in India as a supremely rational and critical enterprise. His underlying conception of rationality features at least the following components: (1) a theory of logic or of valid inference, (2) an account of what should count as evidence for or against conclusions, (3) a conception of what it is to know something, and (4) a theory of action, specifically of moral action (Mohanty, 1992, 4). J. Bronkhorst, however, defines "rationality" primarily as the readiness to accept criticism in all domains of human life, and therefore as the *sine qua non* of modern science. He goes on to argue that this kind of rationality is conspicuous by its absence in vedic literature, including the → Upaniṣads. In the debates recorded therein, no one is ever convinced by the arguments of his opponent, nor is the attempt made to bring this about (Bronkhorst, 1999). Other scholars also argue that apodictic statements were accepted without resistance since the Vedas were (and are) understood as revelation of the highest knowledge of ultimate truth and reality (Dasgupta, 1957, 41). J. Bronkhorst claims that this changed with respect to the classical Indian philosophers. J. Ganeri highlights the importance and impact of Kauṭilya (Ganeri, 2001), as does W. Halbfass by outlining that for Kauṭilya, *ānvīkṣikī, hetuvidyā,* and *tarkaśāstra* were incompatible or plainly opposed to the vedic tradition (Halbfass, 1988).

Beyond that, J. Bronkhorst proposes the more controversial hypothesis (see Turco, 2005) that both Indian and Western systematic philosophy derive one vital element – namely, rational inquiry and analysis as a key element of scholarly and scientific discourse – from a common source located in ancient Greece. Referring to the

Buddhist text *Milindapañha* (Questions of King Milinda; c. 1st cent. BCE), he claims that it is possible that Buddhists of northwest India adopted the willingness (or obligation) to use the method of rational debate in areas that were formerly the exclusive territory of tradition and religion. He finally claims that this vital element is absent everywhere else in the world and that the tradition of rational debate and inquiry has been able to establish itself independently in the history of mankind only once (Bronkhorst, 1999, 26).

With this line of argument, J. Bronkhorst continues a line of thought often attributed to M. Weber, namely, that certain developments essential to the development of modern science have unique roots in Western culture and spread from there around the world. M. Weber's main focus, however, was on the way in which processes of rationalization and intellectualization were related to the formation of a "puritan work ethic" and capitalism. Many scholars, often associated with postcolonial theory, challenged arguments proposing historical developments in the West as the global evaluative criterion for the progressive development of any kind of rationality as Eurocentristic. D. Chakrabarty, for example, attempts to "provincialize Europe" by questioning "internalist histories of Europe" in which Europe was described as the site of the first occurrence of rationality and modernity (Chakrabarty, 2000). Instead he highlights the role of such "historicism" in the formation of political modernity in the erstwhile European colonies and questions the positive association of rationality with scientific discourse by pointing to the "colonial hyperrationalism" that modern science introduced into colonial India as an antidote to (Indian) religion (Chakrabarty, 1995).

The emphasis of the central role of intertheoretic competition and openness in the growth of (modern) science, as opposed to other "modes of thought," not only is crucial for modern rationalism (see below) but also was discussed in the "rationality debate" (Wilson, 1974; Lukes & Hollis, 1985). Debates about a specific "Indian way of thinking" (Ramanujan, 1990) and related issues continue in the social sciences to date.

"Rationalism" as a Contemporary Antireligious Worldview

The controversial claim that scientific rationalism has its roots in ancient Greece is shared by many contemporary atheists in the West. A standard genealogy holds that atheism is rooted in naturalism, which is itself rooted in rationalism, both of which originated in ancient Greece. The origins of Western rationality are seen to mark the first chapter in the history of atheism, where atheism is part of a wider, progressive story about the development of human intellect as well as modern science. In this narrative, the identification of atheism and scientific progress is reinforced during the European Enlightenment (see Baggini, 2003, 78). This genealogy is partly challenged by contemporary atheists in India by highlighting their roots in ancient India – without denying their intellectual roots in antireligious movements in Europe and the United States from the 18th century to today. Indian rationalists advance this argument partly to object to the criticism, expressed primarily by Hindu nationalist groups, that the rationalists are "agents of the West" who merely continue the colonial imposition of "Western" ideas on India. The assessment of this claim is difficult. F. Hiorth argued that atheism was almost absent from Indian culture for more than two thousand years, even though the memory of Lokāyata was kept alive. According to him, only in the 19th century, and since then mostly as a result of Western influence, had atheism again started to raise its head in India (Hiorth, 1998, 6).

While the most influential Indian rationalist and atheist groups were founded in the mid-20th century, their direct forerunners can be traced to the social reform and anticaste movements in 19th-century India. A movement commonly called the "Indian Renaissance" stressed the importance of reason in establishing the truth of religious claims and practices attributed to the Vedas. This went hand in hand with a criticism of certain religious beliefs and practices, for example the rejection of "idol worship" as "idolatry." This movement focused not only on the religious but also on social reform, most prominently on the rejection of the caste system, as well as practices like "widow burning" (→ *satī*) and child marriage. The reformers drew on Indian religious and intellectual traditions as well as ideas from the West. Many of them spoke and wrote in English, and this facilitated further exchange with ideas and movements from England and other parts of Europe.

The most prominent figure in this regard is → Ram Mohan Roy (1772–1833), whose religiosity is generally described as not very different from mainstream Christian conceptualizations of God as the transcendent, immutable creator of the universe. Comparable to "Deist" positions in 19th-century Europe, he argued against ideas of divine intervention and revelation and proposed observation of the natural world as a rational way to gain knowledge about God through studying his creation.

The fact that religious reformers claimed that Hindu religiosity could be considered equal to Christianity and Islam, that all religions have the same essence and are therefore essentially one – as for example argued by Ram Mohan Roy – probably fostered the formation of atheistic ideas from the West in India. The first self-declared atheist groups were to be found in centers of Indo-Western exchange at the time, cities like Madras (Chennai), Bombay (Mumbai), and Calcutta (Kolkata), where "infidel literature" from rationalist, secularist, and atheist groups from Great Britain was available. Initially, terms like "freethinker" and "secularists" were common; later most groups called themselves "rationalists," arguing that rationalism implied atheism. Most of those behind the emergent rationalist and atheist movement in 20th-century India were well-educated Indian intellectuals with strong affinities to Western education and culture, while some had direct connections to the Rationalist Press Association (RPA) in London (Cooke, 2003, 281). The Rationalist Press Association defined rationalism as "the mental attitude which unreservedly accepts the supremacy of reason and aims at establishing a system of philosophy and ethics verifiable by experience and independent of all arbitrary assumptions of authority" (Watts, 1980, 22).

One of the earliest such organizations was the Dev Samaj, which emerged in the second half of the 19th century. It was founded as a society in 1887 by Satya Nand Agnihotri (1850–1929), who was influenced by the religious, social, and educational reform movement → Brahmo Samaj (Hiorth, 1998, ch. 3). B. Cooke notes that "by 1895, having read the works of Herbert Spencer, Spencer's American populariser John Fiske (1842–1901), and Henry Drummond, Agnihotri gave up theism altogether" (Cooke, 2006, 146). In recent times, the best-known spokesperson of the Deva Samajis has been the philosopher S.P. Kanal from Delhi University.

More influential than the Deva Samaj was the Self-Respect Movement founded in 1925 by Periyar E.V. Ramasamy (1879–1973). Periyar was influenced by the American rationalist Robert Green Ingersoll and travelled to Russia, Germany, and various other countries (Klimkeit, 1971). In his ideology, rationalism and its atheistic worldview became part of a larger nationalistic, antinorthern, anti-Brahmanic political struggle. Several political parties in contemporary Tamil Nadu trace their origins to the Self-Respect Movement.

Besides this political movement, there are many other categories of rationalist organizations in contemporary India – most of which are represented by the umbrella organization Federation of Indian Rationalist Associations (FIRA). Member organizations of Federation of Indian Rationalist Associations are part of an international network of atheist organizations and the Atheist Center in Vijayawada, Andhra Pradesh, for example, had organized several World Atheist Conferences. The Atheist Center was founded by the famous atheist leader G.R.R. Gora, whose books (e.g. 2007), together with the writings of many other famous Indian atheists and rationalists, provide a valuable impression of how atheism is understood and appropriated in contemporary India. Atheism, rationalism, and naturalism are seen as feeding into one another and into the rejection of everything supernatural (Bandiste, 1999, 11–17). G.R.R. Gora argues that for the Indian atheists, "theism" refers to all systems of belief that go beyond the limits of human beings and nature and is not at all limited to a Christian God: it "means believing that the universe and human life along with it are both governed by something transcendent." G.R.R. Gora continues, "The depictions of god vary from [taking the form of] the wind, the rain, the sun, the moon, an extraordinarily courageous man, love, a personification of peace, to being the ultimate cause of the universe" (Gora, 2007, 17, 37). In this view, the "supernatural" includes virtually all beliefs and practices roughly labeled "religious," ranging from the cosmologies of Brahmanical Hinduism, possession experiences, and witchcraft accusations to the adjustment of daily life to astrological prognosis, even though these beliefs and practices might be seen as quite "natural" by those who entertain them. For most Indian atheists, the underlying structure of religion(s) is the same everywhere, and they understand atheism as a rejection of this underlying structure, as opposed to a rejection of theism in general, or Christianity in particular (Quack, 2012). An uncontroversial use of the notions atheism and rationalism with respect to the rich history of Hindu traditions is therefore only possible with respect to those who use these terms to describe their worldview, namely, the contemporary rationalist and atheist movement of India. Finally, atheism and rationalism are not necessarily opposed to Hinduism. The founder of the *hindutva* movement, Vinayak Damodar Savarkar (1883–1966), publicly announced his atheism and rationalism because "Hinduism" was more a marker of cultural and political identity to him (Kulkarni, 1979; Kumar, 1992; Godbole, 2004).

Bibliography

Baggini, J., *Atheism: A Very Short Introduction*, Oxford, 2003.

Bandiste, D.D., *Humanist Thought in Contemporary India*, Delhi, 1999.

Bronkhorst, J., *Why is there Philosophy in India?*, Amsterdam, 1999.

Chakrabarti, A., "Rationality in Indian Philosophy," in: E. Deutsch & R. Bontekoe, eds., *Companion to World Philosophy*, Oxford, 1997, 259–278.

Chakrabarty, D., *Provincializing Europe: Postcolonial Thought and Historical Difference*, Princeton, 2000.

Chakrabarty, D., "Radical Histories and Question of Enlightenment Rationalism: Some Recent Critiques of 'Subaltern Studies,'" *EPW* 30/14, 1995, 751–759.

Chattopadhyaya, D., *Indian Atheism: A Marxist Analysis*, Calcutta, 1969.

Cooke, B., *Dictionary of Atheism, Skepticism, and Humanism*, Amherst, 2006.

Cooke, B., *The Blasphemy Depot: A Hundred Years of the Rationalist Press Association*, Hollinwood, 2003.

Dasgupta, S., *A History of Indian Philosophy*, vol. I, Cambridge UK, 1957.

Daston, L., *Wunder, Beweise und Tatsachen. Zur Geschichte der Rationalität*, Frankfurt am Main, 2001.

Franco, E., "Lokāyata," in: K.A. Jacobsen, H. Basu, A. Malinar, & V. Narayanan, eds., *Brill's Encyclopedia of Hinduism*, vol. III, Leiden, 2011, 629–642.

Franco, E., *Perception, Knowledge, and Disbelief: A Study of Jayarāśi's Scepticism*, Stuttgart, 1987.

Ganeri, J., "Indian Logic and the Colonization of Reason," in: J. Ganeri, ed., *Indian Logic: A Reader*, Richmond, 2001, 1–25.

Godbole, V.V., *Rationalism of Veer Savarkar*, Thane, 2004.

Gonda, J., *Veda und Älterer Hinduismus*, Stuttgart, 1960.

Gora, G.R.R., *Atheism: There Is No God*, Vijayawada, 2007.

Halbfass, W., "Darśana, Ānvīksikī, Philosophy," in: W. Halbfass, ed., *India and Europe: An Essay in Understanding*, Albany, 1988, 263–287.

Hiorth, F., *Atheism in India*, Mumbai, 1998.

Hiorth, F., *Introduction to Atheism*, Pune, 1995.

Jacobsen, K.A., *Prakṛti in Sāṃkhya-Yoga: Material Principle, Religious Experience, Ethical Implications*, New York, 1999.

Joshi, L.R., "A New Interpretation of Indian Atheism," *PEW* 16/3–4, 1966, 189–206.

Klimkeit, H.-J., *Anti-Religiöse Bewegungen im Modernen Südindien*, Bonn, 1971.

Kulkarni, N.H., "Hindu Religious Reform Movements in the Nineteenth and Twentieth Century Maharashtra," in: S.P. Sen, ed., *Social and Religious Reform Movements in the Nineteenth and Twentieth Centuries*, 1979, 248–281.

Kumar, P.P., *Towards Understanding Communalism*, Chandigarh, 1992.

Lukes, S., & M. Hollis, eds., *Rationality and Relativism*, Oxford, 1985.

Matilal, B.K., *Logic, Language and Reality: Indian Philosophy and Contemporary Issues*, Delhi, 1990.

Michaels, A., *Hinduism: Past and Present*, Princeton, 2004.

Minois, G., *Geschichte des Atheismus: Von den Anfängen bis zur Gegenwart*, Weimar, 2000.

Mohanty, J.N., *Reason and Tradition in Indian Thought: An Essay on the Nature of Indian Philosophical Thinking*, Oxford, 1992.

Narisetti, I., "Unbelief in India," in: G. Stein, ed., *The Encyclopedia of Unbelief*, Buffalo, 1985, 343–346.

Preisendanz, K.C., "Logic, Debate and Epistemology in Ancient Indian Medicine and Philosophy: An Investigation," *IJHSc* 44/2, 2009, 261–312.

Quack, J., *Disenchanting India: Organized Rationalism and Criticism of Religion in India*, New York, 2012.

Ramanujan, A.K., "Is There an Indian Way of Thinking?" in: M. Marriott, ed., *India through Hindu Categories*, New Delhi, 1990, 41–58.

Sen, A., *The Argumentative India: Writings on Indian Culture, History and Identity*, New Delhi, 2005.

Tillemans, T.J.F., *Scripture, Logic, Language: Essays on Dharmakīrti and His Tibetan Successors*, Boston, 1999.

Turco, B.L., "Some Questions Posed by a Recent Epistemological Approach to Indian Thought," *ZDMG* 155, 2005, 189–197.

Watts, C., "The Meaning of Rationalism," in: G. Stein, ed., *An Anthology of Atheism and* Rationalism, New York, 1980, 20–27.

Weber, M., "The Protestant Ethic and the 'Spirit' of Capitalism," in: P.R. Baehr & G.C. Wells, eds., *The Protestant Ethic and the 'Spirit' of Capitalism and OtherWritings*, New York, 2002, 1–201.

Wilke, A., & O. Moebus, *Sound and Communication: An Aesthetic Cultural History of Sanskrit Hinduism*, Berlin, 2011.

Wilson, B.R., ed., *Rationality*, Oxford, 1974.

Johannes Quack

Bioethics

The field of bioethics addresses areas of human inquiry that are concerned with the ethical evaluation of human involvement in medicine and biotechnology. One of the aims of the discipline is to formulate a normative ethics of responsible interaction with other humans, living beings in general, and the environment. The key areas of bioethical inquiry have developed over time in accordance with developments in medical science and biotechnology, and different countries and cultures have differing approaches to bioethics principles, questions, and answers. However, while new issues keep arising, certain topics remain central to bioethics discussions. These include not only the question of how to define life and death and related issues such as contraception, the termination of pregnancy, end-of-life care, euthanasia, and physician-assisted suicide, but also assisted reproductive technology, organ donation and transplantation, genetic engineering, embryonic stem-cell research, and cloning. Other key issues concern the relationship between patients and their physician or carer, including questions of informed consent, patient autonomy, confidentiality, and truth telling. Bioethicists also debate moral issues surrounding environmental matters, such as the effect of pollution on human health, or questions of sustainability in view of overpopulation and overconsumption. The role of relationships between countries regarding intellectual property rights, the patenting of biotechnologies, and access to bio-resources has become a further important area of discussion.

Bioethics in India

In recent years, there has been a strong focus in Indian bioethics discussions on questions surrounding human experimentation, the reason for this being that India has become one of the world's preferred locations for clinical trials due to its low operating costs and well-trained workforce. The country's clinical-trials business has developed into a large industry involving more than a hundred domestic and multinational organizations. The WHO has noted that the lack of regulation and the uneven application of requirements for informed consent have raised concerns about exploitation and patient safety (Chatterjee, 2008). Further criticisms are leveled at the recruitment practices in the contract research organization industry (i.e. organizations that provide pharmaceutical and biotechnology industries with clinical-trial support for drugs or medical devices on a contract basis; Srinivasan, 2010, 101). One of the major concerns is that the large number of clinical-trial subjects who come from lower socioeconomic groups participate in clinical trials as a method of gaining access to medical treatments that they could not otherwise afford and may therefore not give due consideration to the risks associated with the trials.

Bioethics are also discussed at an institutional level in India, where they fall under the purview of the Indian Council of Medical Research (ICMR), a national body responsible for the formulation, coordination, and promotion of biomedical research. In 1980, the Central Ethics Committee on Human Research of the ICMR published a *Policy Statement on Ethical Considerations Involved in Research on Human Subjects*. Revised in 2000 and 2006 and published under the new title of *Indian Council of Medical Research Ethical Guidelines for Biomedical Research on Human Subjects*, this document presents a statement of ethical principles and guidelines for the clinical evaluation of drugs, devices, diagnostics, vaccines, and herbal remedies, for epidemiological research, human genetics research, transplantation research (including fetal-tissue transplantation), and assisted reproductive technologies (see Indian Council for Medical Research, 2006). The stated principles are based on international guidelines of the WHO, the Council for International Organizations of Medical Sciences (CIOMS), and UNESCO, and there is no mention of any religious or cultural considerations in their formulation. More recently, reacting to calls to increase public and professional awareness of bioethics, the ICMR has focused on developing a national curriculum of bioethics education that takes into account India's specific cultural contexts.

The adoption of international rather than national standards based on India's specific cultures or religions can also be observed in the medical ethics codes of the departments of medicine of the Indian government's Ministry of Health and Family Welfare (see e.g. the "Practitioners of Indian Medicine [Standards of Professional Conduct, Etiquette and Code of Ethics] Regulations, 1982," issued by the Central Council of Indian Medicine [CCIM] and the "Code of Ethics Regulations" of the Medical Council of India [MCI] of 2002). The CCIM is the statutory regulatory body of the Department of Ayurveda, Yoga and Naturopathy, Unani, Siddha and Homoeopathy (AYUSH) of the Ministry of Health and Family Welfare (see http://www.ccimindia.org). It is responsible for laying out guidelines for the education and research in and practice of the so-called Indian systems of medicine, which to date include → Āyurveda, → *yoga* and naturopathy, Unānī (Greco-Arabic medicine), Siddha (Tamil medicine), homoeopathy, and Sowa Rigpa (Tibetan medicine). The MCI is the statutory body responsible for biomedical education, research, and practice in India (see http://www.mciindia.org). Both the MCI and the CCIM simply copy guidelines issued by the World Medical Association (WMA), notably the WMA declarations of Geneva and of Helsinki (see Benner, 2005, 191–195). By contrast, the government-approved syllabi for students of Āyurveda in India, issued in 2009 by the CCIM, now include modules on the ethics of classical Āyurveda. For example, the syllabus for the Ayurvedacharya ("teacher of Āyurveda," the ayurvedic doctoral degree) course, for which students receive the degree of Bachelor of Ayurvedic Medicine and Surgery (BAMS) upon successful completion of their studies, contains sections on *vaidya sadvṛtta* – that is, rules delineating a physician's good conduct. These rules are gleaned from a selection of classical Sanskrit medical treatises and are understood to broadly reflect Hindu values.

Hindu Perspectives on Bioethics

To delineate Hindu perspectives on bioethics, one must take into account the fact of the diversity of beliefs and practices not only of the various Hindu traditions in India but also of the Hindu diaspora in Asia and in other parts of the world, such as the United Kingdom and the United States, where many influential representatives of Hindu traditions live whose opinions are also taken note of in India (see e.g. Bhanot, 2008, or Mishra, 2005). Hindu perspectives can be approached exegetically, by referring to Hindu scriptures with the aim of reconstructing how they might have addressed bioethical issues, or descriptively, by examining how Hindus themselves engage with biotechnologies and how they theorize their own exegetical approach (see McGarrity *et al.*, 2012, 507). As with any exploration of the Hindu point of view, one should be aware of the lack of doctrinal consistency across traditional scriptures and practices as well as of the fact that there is no unifying body of Hindu authority that can speak for all Hindus. However, K.K. Young (2009b, 509) contends that many of the topics of modern South Asian bioethics are foreshadowed in traditional medical ethics. The sources for traditional medical ethics are the above-mentioned Sanskrit medical treatises of the classical ayurvedic tradition. Their commentary on medical ethics, which mostly touches on aspects of the physician–patient relationship, finds parallels or complements in a number of passages from other Hindu texts, such as the epics or ancient Hindu law texts.

In recent years, health-care providers all over the world have become increasingly aware of cultural differences in their patients' expectations and reception of care. This has lead to a number of publications of guidelines for clinicians and carers on culturally sensitive medical care, such as the Queensland Health Multicultural Services' 24-page *Health Care Providers' Handbook on Hindu Patients* (2011), which discusses which Hindu beliefs might affect health care. The brochure was written under the guidance of an advisory committee that included representatives from Indian or Hindu groups, such as the Federation of Indian Communities of Queensland, the Global Organisation of People of Indian Origin in Queensland, and the Shree Sanatan Dharam Hindu Association of Queensland. (For similar brochures, Web sites, and research papers in international clinical journals on issues surrounding the clinical care of Hindu patients, see e.g. Coward & Sidhu, 2000; Singh & Freeman, 2011; Gatrad *et al.*, 2003; Webster *et al.*, 2002; Naidoo, 1989; and Kataria, 2008.)

Decision Making, Informed Consent, and Patient Autonomy

Many Hindus view the needs of the individual in the greater context of family, culture, and environment. Family members, especially elders, can have a strong influence on decision making related to health matters. Hindus may wish for family members to be responsible for making treatment decisions rather than exercising autonomy. This has a bearing on the issues of confidentiality and informed consent. In some cases, Hindu patients prefer to not be told their diagnosis or the treatment plan directly but choose to have the physician discuss them with their family, who will then relay the information as they see fit. Family members may choose the partial disclosure or nondisclosure of information or even give false information. This can create tension, since medical staff are often obliged to follow guidelines on patient rights that detail the following: patients have the right to be informed about their medical condition, the risks and benefits of treatment, and appropriate alternatives; patients have the right to participate in making decisions and choices about care and about health-service planning; patients have the right to the privacy and confidentiality of personal information; and patients have the right to comment on or complain about care and have concerns dealt with promptly and properly (see e.g. the Australian Charter of Healthcare Rights). However, concepts of patients' rights vary in different countries and in different jurisdictions, depending on prevailing cultural and social norms. In India, the physician–patient relationship is usually paternalistic. The basis of the paternalistic physician–patient relationship is beneficence – that is, the assumption that physicians have the welfare of patients in mind whenever they make a decision or undertake a course of treatment. This means that the clinical expert (and then the patient's family) also judges what the best interests of the patient are in regard to medical information and decision making. This has a long history in India: the oldest ayurvedic texts emphasize the authority of the physician and state that it is the patient's duty to unquestioningly comply with the physician's instructions (see Wujastyk, 2012, 26–67).

Pain and Suffering

Both mental and physical suffering are thought to be part of the unfolding of → *karma*. They are considered a natural consequence of past behavior in the current life or in previous lives that transgresses the moral laws (→ *dharma*) of the universe. Hindus may therefore accept suffering as a just consequence and also as a way to satisfy the debt incurred for past negative behavior. Suffering is generally understood to be an inextricable aspect of living, and one is only released from suffering through achieving → liberation (*mokṣa*). However, while a person may experience physical or mental pain, the self or soul is not affected or harmed (see Whitman, 2007, 609). Hindu patients may gain comfort by viewing pain as only a temporary condition and one that does not affect their inner self. At the same time, accepting suffering as part of the human condition does not necessarily mean that Hindus may not attempt to lessen suffering through medical treatment or pain management, but rather that they are called on to develop equanimity in the face of suffering, keeping in mind the ultimate goal of gaining release from the cycle of rebirths (→ *saṃsāra*). Committing suicide as a way of ending suffering is not considered acceptable. Both committing and assisting suicide would constitute an act of violence and thus run counter to the ethical norm of nonviolence (→ *ahiṃsā*) to which many Hindus adhere. Although self-willed death has a long history in Hindu traditions, there were explicit rules distinguishing between legitimate self-willed death and suicide, the latter being considered reckless and morally unacceptable. A legitimate self-willed death was never associated with assistance through physicians or other persons and could only be committed by someone without family obligations, after making a public vow (*saṃkalpa*) to ensure the voluntary nature of the act and by using a difficult means (not drugs or poison). Further, since human life is understood to be an opportunity for *karma* accumulated in previous and current lives to come to fruition and thereby be eliminated, an untimely death through suicide is thought to impede a person's chances of achieving liberation (see Young, 2009a, 103).

Contraception

Contraception no longer seems an important area of ethical discussion for most modern Hindus. However, it was certainly a matter of concern to prominent Hindu thinkers and activists in the recent past. Among them was Mahatma → Gandhi, who was an opponent of scientific contraception but approved of birth control through abstinence (see Dasgupta 1996, 155–162). A contrasting view in favor of contraception was promoted by E.V. Ramasamy (also known as Periyar), who founded the Self-Respect Movement in 1925 in

→ Tamil Nadu. His movement challenged certain traditional Hindu notions, as, for example, that procreation is a duty of every Hindu householder and that a woman is defined through her ability to conceive and nurture a child (see Nair & John, 1998, 153–156).

There is very little discussion on the ethics of contraception in premodern Hindu texts, though some Sanskrit treatises mention contraceptive methods. The first Sanskrit treatise that gives recipes for contraceptives is the *Ratirahasya*, written by Kokokka in the 12th or 13th century (Dossi, 1998, 121). This work belongs to the genre of Kāmaśāstra (see → *kāma*). The earliest mention of recipes for contraceptives in an Indian medical treatise occurs in the 16th-century *Bhāvaprakāśa* (*Madhyakhaṇḍa* 70, 33–34), which gives two recipes. These are found in between recipes for influencing the gender of the child to be born (i.e. ensuring that a male child will be born) and recipes for the treatment of vaginal diseases. Recipes for contraceptives are often paired with recipes for abortifacients.

Today, contraception generally seems less of a contentious issue among Hindus than abortion. S. Rao claims that "Hindus show little resistance to the idea of birth control. There is no objection to contraception on religious or moral grounds" (see Crawford, 2003, 140). Certainly, family-planning programs sponsored by the government of India since the 1960s have portrayed contraception as a good solution to overpopulation in India. However, government programs on family planning have met with some resistance, due to resentment created by the forced-sterilization program implemented by Indira Gandhi, then prime minister of India, in the early 1970s. This program is still remembered and criticized in India and is blamed for creating a public aversion to family planning. There are also significant problems in accessing a choice of contraceptive methods in India.

Abortion

The topic of abortion in the sense of a deliberate effecting of a miscarriage has been extensively discussed by J. Lipner in his essay "The Classical Hindu View on Abortion and the Moral Status of the Unborn" (1991, 41–70). Describing the views presented in the oldest of the ayurvedic treatises (the *Carakasaṃhitā* and the *Suśrutasaṃhitā*) on ensoulment and consciousness in the womb, J. Lipner (53–57) concludes that neither author proposes a moment of development in which the embryo undergoes "a quantum leap, passing from one kind of human moral status (human being) to another (human person)," which would allow for arguing for abortion. Ayurvedic texts describe how a living entity or soul called *sattva* or *jīva*, propelled by its *karma*, enters the womb at the moment in which the male and the female procreative fluids (*śukra* and *ārtava* – there is no concept of the ovum in the ayurvedic classics, though modern ayurvedic practitioners typically interpret *ārtava* as the ovum) merge. The procreative substances, which consist of the five great elements (wind, earth, fire, water, and ether) known from → Sāṃkhya ontology, form a physical layer around the soul and begin to take shape, becoming the embryo. This means that individual life and personhood are present from the moment of conception. It follows that the abortion of an embryo or a fetus constitutes the killing of an individual.

It should be noted that the ayurvedic treatises do not discuss induced abortion or its moral implications. However, it is clear that abortions were known about and did take place, since the *Carakasaṃhitā* (in *Sūtrasthāna* 8.19) mentions abortionists as persons whom a physician should strictly avoid. In this, the author concurs with what was obviously a widely held view in his times – namely, that the deliberate termination of a pregnancy was a reprehensible act. Discussing the moral evaluation of the act of abortion in some of the normative Hindu religious and religious law texts (Dharmasūtras and → Dharmaśāstras, → Purāṇas, and the → *Mahābhārata*), J. Lipner (1989, 45) concludes that pregnancy was seen as "a very special state and that the unborn had a (moral) status meriting protection," while abortion was considered morally unacceptable and universally condemned, and punishable by law. While the act of abortion is generally not mentioned in the older ayurvedic treatises, we encounter recipes for abortifacients in later medical works, though no discussions of the ethics of their use. The first Sanskrit treatise that gives recipes for abortifacients is the above-mentioned *Ratirahasya* by Kokokka. The first medical work that provides recipes for abortifacients is the *Yogacintāmaṇi*. Written in the late 16th or early

17th century by Harṣakīrti, a Jain monk, this work devotes several verses to contraceptive measures and abortifacients (see Meulenbeld, 2000, vol. II, 251). The next work to provide such recipes is the 17th-century *Vaidyavallabha* by Hastiruci, also a Jain monk. We find further recipes for both contraceptives and abortifacients in Trimallabhaṭṭa's *Yogataraṅgiṇī* (75.8–19), a work that is roughly dated to the 17th century. Its author was a Brahman. There are also some abortifacient and contraceptive formulas in the late 17th-century *Vaidyarahasya* (in the chapter on disorders during pregnancy, vv. 31–35) by Vidyāpati. Finally, the anonymous *Yogaratnākara*, tentatively dated to the late 17th or early 18th century, has a chapter on female diseases that also contains some recipes for abortifacients and contraceptives (vv. 849–850). In summary, this shows that while one cannot perhaps claim that contraception and abortion were socially acceptable to a Hindu and Jain population by the 16th century, one can certainly say that they had become part of what was then mainstream medicine.

Having been forbidden by the Indian Penal Code of 1860, the termination of pregnancy became legal in India with the Medical Termination of Pregnancy (MTP) Act of India (enacted in 1971 and amended in 1975, 2002, and 2003). According to the act, pregnancies can be terminated by registered medical practitioners up to the 20th week of gestation, if the physical or mental health of the pregnant woman is endangered by the pregnancy, if there is a substantial risk that if the child were born it would suffer from such physical or mental abnormalities as to be seriously handicapped, or in cases of pregnancy through rape. Pregnancies of unmarried girls under the age of 18 or of "lunatics" (see section 3.4.a of the MTP Act) can be terminated with the consent of a guardian. Finally, a pregnancy may also be terminated if it has occurred as a result of failure of contraception, on the understanding that the anguish caused by an unwanted pregnancy constitutes a grave injury to the mental health of the pregnant woman (Explanation 2 of the MTP Act). The contents and wording of the MTP Act are currently being challenged by the National Commission for Women, India (see http://ncw.nic.in/frmReportLaws11.aspx), and the International Consortium for Medical Abortion (see http://www.medicalabortionconsortium.org/country/IN).

According to the Consortium on National Consensus for Medical Abortion in India, every year an average of about 11 million abortions take place (see http://m.icma.md/country/IN/). One of the problems associated with these terminations is that there is a strong bias toward terminating pregnancies with female fetuses, made possible through prenatal sex determination. This issue is addressed in the Pre-natal Diagnostic Techniques (Regulation and Prevention of Misuse) Act, 1994, which was enacted in 1996. However, with many private clinics offering prenatal screenings, sex selection continues to occur, as families who wish to limit the number of their children very often have a preference for having sons. This can have religious reasons: many Hindus believe that only a son can perform the → death and ancestral rites (*śrāddha*; see also → *saṃskāras*) for their parents and especially their fathers. These rites are seen as necessary for ensuring the safety of the passage of the deceased person's soul from one state of being to another. Without the correct performance of the death rites, the soul might become trapped in the in-between state of having left the old body and not being reborn in its new one, becoming a kind of ghost, a *preta* (see Firth, 1997, 38–42). This is considered a state of intense suffering and inauspiciousness, and it also means that the soul is hindered from ever reaching the ultimate goal of release (*mokṣa*) from the cycles of life (*saṃsāra*), since it cannot live through the rebirths necessary for achieving liberation.

Infertility and Assisted Reproductive Technologies

In Indian Hindu society, fertility is greatly valued, and children are seen as a source of labor, income, happiness, and security in old age. Infertility, by contrast, is regarded as a major problem with serious implications for important domains of social life such as kinship, inheritance, marriage and divorce patterns, and the continuity of families and communities. Infertility treatment is not part of the reproductive health services offered by the Indian government but can be accessed in the private health sector. Because of high costs, only a small percentage of those affected by infertility in India can afford assisted reproductive technologies like in vitro fertilization. Since there is a stigma against infertility and childlessness in India, the existence of assisted reproductive technologies is perceived as a great scientific achievement. Those who cannot afford the high-tech options may take resort to fertility treatments offered by practitioners and clinics of the Indian systems of medicine (e.g. Āyurveda).

Recent studies (see Widge, 2002, who summarizes and discusses a number of relevant studies) have shown that there is now a strong demand for artificial insemination by donor in India, which is offered by private medical practitioners. However, there are only a few sperm banks in India, many of which do not follow WHO guidelines. One reason for seeking artificial insemination is to increase the chances of having a male child. In vitro fertilization specialists offer pre-implantation diagnoses that can be used for sex selection and do not consider this an unethical procedure.

Cloning

According to K.K. Young (2009a, 107), cloning has attracted more comment from Hindus in recent years than any other new reproductive technology. She attributes this heightened interest to the 1997 request of the US National Bioethics Advisory Committee on behalf of President Clinton to find out whether religious communities might have objections to cloning. In response to the committee's request, the editors of *Hinduism Today* contacted a number of influential Hindu spiritual teachers (*svāmīs*) around the world to assess their position. A summary of their answers was published in *Hinduism Today* on Apr 1, 1997. The editors found that most of the Hindu spiritual leaders were less concerned with the moral issues surrounding human cloning than with the question of whether they could identify a practical need for cloning. They especially questioned the spiritual purpose of cloning. Would it advance the soul's evolution toward the goal of spiritual liberation? Would it affect, alter, or impair the process of reincarnation that is supposed to lead each soul toward maturity and enlightenment? What would the karmic consequences of the act of cloning be? In conclusion, many (though by no means all) of the questioned spiritual leaders felt reservations about cloning in view of its uncertain impact on spiritual progress.

Organ Donation and Transplantation

The ethics of organ donation and transplantation center on the issues of defining the moment of death and the relationship between body and self. The scope for exploitation of both organ donors and organ recipients has become a big problem in India, where kidneys and other organs are often obtained from poor and often desperate people in the slums and rural villages (see Young, 2009a, 110). There is no consistent opinion on organ donation among Hindus. According to the *Queensland Health Care Providers' Handbook on Hindu Patients* (2011, 16), Hinduism generally supports the donation and transplantation of organs, the decision to donate or receive organs being the personal choice of an individual. An information brochure by the organ donation organization Trillium Gift of Life (Government of Ontario) claims that

> [o]rgan and tissue donation is an essential part of the Hindu way of life, as guided by the Vedas. In Hinduism, the principle of helping and saving the lives of others is revered; hence, organ and tissue donation is in keeping with these beliefs. (http://www.giftoflife.on.ca/pdf/TGLN_Hindu_brochure.pdf)

According to this view, donating organs means good *karma* for the departing soul of the body and also for the family of the deceased who allow the use of the donated organ. In the opinion of G. Swami (2009), the recipient of the donated organ accumulates neither good nor bad *karma* but may receive parts of the mind and the personality of the donor with the organ transplant, since the mind is thought to not be isolated in the brain but to exist in the entire body, different organs holding different emotional impressions, memories, and tendencies.

U.V. Mysorekar (2007), the president of the Hindu Temple Society of North America, states that there is no harm in donating organs, since the physical body is not important to the welfare of the soul but is only a shell or vehicle of the soul to experience life and express itself on earth. After death, the soul leaves the body to either be reborn into another body or achieve liberation. Since the soul no longer has need of the body in any way, the preservation of the body has no consequence for the evolution of the soul.

By contrast, A. Sukumaran claims that

> organ donation (either giving or accepting) is not accepted in principle, as it does not allow for complete release of the soul of the donor... Blood transfusions are a little more acceptable, but not desirable. (Sukumaran, 2009)

According to W. Doniger (1996, 197), some Hindus associate organ donation with the ritual impurity of a dead body. Handling a dead body is thought to place those involved in it in a state of impurity (see Firth, 1997, 73). This usually affects the close family, who prepare the body for cremation. Since their impurity is caused by the proximity to the deceased person's body and the limited time spent touching it, it is considered a transitory state that is overcome with time and with certain ritual acts. However, taking a part of the dead body and placing it within another live body might put the recipient's body into a permanent state of impurity, since contact with the deceased person's body part is permanent and since no traditional ritual cleansing acts exist for this scenario.

Bibliography

Beauchamp, T.L., & J.F. Childress, *Principles of Biomedical Ethics*, Oxford, [5]2001.

Benner, D., "The Medical Ethics of Professionalised Ayurveda," *AMTM* 1/1, 2005, 185–203.

Bhanot, A., "The Ethics of Stem Cell Research: A Hindu View," *BioNews* 480, 2008, http://www.bionews.org.uk/page_38022.asp.

Central Council of Indian Medicine, "Practitioners of Indian Medicine (Standards of Professional Conduct, Etiquette and Code of Ethics) Regulations, 1982," 1982, http://www.ccimindia.org/cc_actregulations_1982.html.

Chatterjee, P., "Clinical Trials in India: Ethical Concerns," *BWHO* 86/8, 2008, 581–582.

Coward, H., & T. Sidhu, "Bioethics for Clinicians: 19. Hinduism and Sikhism," *CMAJ* 163/9, 2000, 1167–1170.

Crawford, C.S., *Hindu Bioethics for the Twenty-first Century*, New York, 2003.

Dasgupta, A.K., *Gandhi's Economic Thought*, London, 1996.

Doniger, W., "Transplanting Myths of Organ Transplants," in: S.J. *Youngner, R.C. Fox & L.J. O'Connell, eds., Organ Transplantation: Meanings and Realities*, Madison, 1996, 194–220.

Dossi, B., *Samen, Seele, Blut. Die Zeugungstheorien des alten Indiens*, Munich, 1998.

Firth, S., *Death and Bereavement in a British Hindu Community*, Leuven, 1997.Gatrad, R., P.P. Choudhury, E. Brown & A. Sheikh, "Palliative Care for Hindus," *IJPN* 9/10, 2003, 442–448.

Indian Council for Medical Research, "Ethical Guidelines for Biomedical Research on Human Participants," New Delhi, 2006, icmr.nic.in/ethical_guidelines.pdf.

Kataria, B., "Hindu Resources on the World Wide Web," in: D. Thakrar, R. Das & A. Sheikh, eds., *Caring for Hindu Patients*, Oxford, 2008, 93–100.

Lipner, J., "The Classical Hindu View on Abortion and the Moral Status of the Unborn," in: H.G. Coward, J. Lipner & K.K. Young, eds., *Hindu Ethics: Purity, Abortion and Euthanasia*, 1991, 41–70.

McGarrity, A., *et al.*, "Religious Perspectives on Umbilical Cord Blood Banking: Hindu Perspective," *JLM* 19, 2012, 507–508.

Medical Council of India, "Code of Ethics Regulations," 2002, http://www.mciindia.org/RulesandRegulations/CodeofMedicalEthicsRegulations2002.aspx.

Meulenbeld, J.G., *A History of Indian Medical Literature*, vols. I–V, Leiden, 2000–2002.

Mishra, P., "How India Reconciles Hindu Values and Biotech," *The New York Times*, Aug 21, 2005, http://www.nytimes.com/2005/08/21/weekinreview/21mishra.html.

Mysorekar, U.V., "Organ, Eye and Tissue Donation from a Hindu Perspective: Donation, as an Act of Charity, Is a Way of Life," 2007, http://www.donatelifeny.org/uploaded_files/tinymce/files/mysorekar.pdf.

Naidoo, T., "Health and Health Care: A Hindu Perspective," *ML 7/6, 1989, 643–647.*

Nair, J., & M.E. John, *A Question of Silence? The Sexual Economies of Modern India*, Delhi, 1998.

Queensland Health, *Health Care Providers' Handbook on Hindu Patients*, 2011, www.health.qld.gov.au/multicultural/support_tools/hbook-hindu.pdf.

Singh, A., & M. Freeman, "The Important Role for Nurses in Supporting the Asian Hindu Patient and Family at End of Life: Providing Culturally Sensitive End-of-Life Care," *CONJ* 21/1, 2011, 46–49.

Srinivasan, S., "Patient Protection in Clinical Trials in India: Some Concerns," *PCR* 1/3, 2010, 101–103.

Sukumaran, A., "Hinduism and Medicine: A Guide for Medical Professionals," 1999, http://www.angelfire.com/az/ambersukumaran/medicine.html.

Swami, G., "Pondering the Hindu View on Organ Donation," Jul 17, 2009, http://myhindupage.org/index.php/ponderings-organ-donation.

Webster, R.A., D.R. Thompson & R.A. Mayou, "The Experiences and Needs of Gujarati Hindu Patients and Partners in the First Month after a Myocardial Infarction," *EJCN* 1/1, 2002, 69–76.

Whitman, S.M., "Pain and Suffering as Viewed by the Hindu Religion," *JP* 8/8, 2007, 607–613.

Widge, A., "Sociocultural Attitudes towards Infertility and Assisted Reproduction in India," in: E. Vayena, P.R. Rowe & P.D. Griffin, eds., *Current Practices and Controversies in Assisted Reproduction: Report of a Meeting on "Medical, Ethical and Social Aspects of Assisted Reproduction" Held at WHO Headquarters in*

Geneva, Switzerland 17–21 September 2001, Geneva, 2002, 60–74.
Wujastyk, D., *Well-Mannered Medicine: Medical Ethics and Etiquette in Classical Ayurveda*, New York, 2012.
Young, K.K., "Medical Ethics through the Life Cycle in Hindu India," in: R.B. Baker & L.B. McCullough, eds., *The Cambridge World History of Medical Ethics*, Cambridge MA, 2009a, 101–112.
Young, K.K., "The Discourses of Bioethics in South Asia," in: R.B. Baker & L.B. McCullough, eds., *The Cambridge World History of Medical Ethics*, Cambridge MA, 2009b, 509–524.

Dagmar Wujastyk

Commodification

At the level of practice, everyday Hinduism is an embodied religion grounded in a materiality that makes the presence of specific material objects and implements an indispensable part of its religious practices. Hindu weddings, funerals, and any number of daily and calendrical rituals, festivals, and birthdays and anniversary celebrations are "crowded" with things and marked by the colorful and lively presence of an apparently random combination of objects and materials that in fact do connote order. In fact, every item, no matter how ordinary or small, has a place and a value in Hindu ceremonial life. Not only are ritual paraphernalia conspicuous and integral in the enactment of theistic, devotional Hindu religiosity, but they also find resonance in other forms of Hinduism, for example in → *guru*-centered movements and the older social-reform Hindu movements such as the → Arya Samaj and the → Ramakrishna Mission. Such dependence has engendered a group of entrepreneurs who have responded by supplying a range of commodities that flow globally and that are utilized ultimately as ritual objects in the actualization of everyday Hindu religiosity.

The catalogue of items encountered in enacting these religious styles in private spaces and public domains is extensive; it is also one that can only be partially articulated in any rendition. Even a cursory mapping of the retail sites generates this following broad inventory of religious imagery and symbolism available for ritualistic consumption: sculpted and painted statutes of Hindu gods and goddesses, framed visual prints of Hindu gods and goddesses, deity-specific *yantras* (see → *maṇḍalas* and *yantras*), brass- and gold-plated oil lamps, → *rudrākṣa* beads, bells, incense sticks, oil and ghee, prayer altars, musical instruments, recorded devotional music, devotional stories in the form of video CDs and DVDs, religious

Fig. 1: A shop trading in fresh flowers in Singapore's Little India District, which draws both Hindu devotees and tourists (photo by Vineeta Sinha).

literature, and more transient objects such as fresh fruits (lime, coconut, and sugarcane), dried fruits (raisins, almonds, and cashews), flowers (jasmine, hibiscus, and roses), and leaves (margosa, mango, and banana) for making garlands and decorations. This assortment of ritual objects is denoted variously in retail and wholesale markets in Singapore, Malaysia, Chennai, and London and on → Internet sites as such: → *pūjā* items, *pūjā* articles, worship accessories, temple accessories, temple items, *tirukōyil* (temple/worship) items, religious artifacts, *pūjā* accessories, Hindu prayer items, religious items, and so forth. Of this list, the expressions "*pūjā* items," "*pūjā* accessories," "*pūjā* things," and "religious items" are used most extensively and universally.

Consumer Culture and Hinduism: A Marginal Field

Scholars of Hinduism have not only highlighted but also scrutinized the complex interface between visuality and materiality in enactment of everyday Hindu religiosity. R. Dwyer and C. Pinney, for example, approach "visual culture as a key arena for the thinking out of politics and religion in modern India" (Dwyer & Pinney, 2001, 8). D. Eck's famous work, *Darśan: Seeing the Divine Image in India* (1981), serves to focus attention on the notion of *darśan* and the two-way interaction between devotee and deity in the act of *pūjā*. As a testament to the broader appeal of this notion of "seeing," *darśan* has been borrowed and extended to analyses of other sociocultural and political domains in Indian society, such as the world of Hindi films, the Indian political scene (Dwyer & Patel, 2002), and the field of consumption and public culture in India (Frietag, 2001).

However, despite the tremendous activity and energy within this field and the burgeoning literature that it has produced, the intersections of everyday Hindu religious life with processes of commodification and commercialization have yet to be comprehensively explored. Yet, this lacuna is not peculiar to Hinduism. W. Keenan and E. Arweck (2006) note more generally that the "study of materialised spiritualities – and spiritualised materialities" has not been seriously pursued by social scientists. The exploration of religion's location at the interstices of capitalism, globalization, and popular culture offers exciting opportunities for creative research, but with much still to be done. However, new developments in this field are encouraging. Notable recent contributions, adding to earlier efforts to theorize the interface of mass-produced religious insignia and Hindu religiosity, include K. Jain's *Gods in the Bazaar: The Economies of Indian Calendar Art* (2007), K. McLain's *India's Immortal Comic Books: Gods, Kings, and Other Heroes* (2009), and S. Ramaswamy's *The Goddess and the Nation: Mapping Mother India* (2010). M. Nanda's highly controversial book, *The God Market: How Globalization Is Making India More Hindu* (2009), suggests that the "State-Temple-Corporate complex" sees global forces shaping everyday Hinduism along more nationalist strains.

Commodification Processes and Hinduism: A Strange Alliance?

The neglect of the interplay of commerce, consumer culture, and material religion in Hindu contexts is all the more surprising given the fundamental changes that are evident in the production, distribution, and consumption of *pūjā* items and packaged religious traditions (such as *guru*-centered movements) – both in India and in the Hindu diaspora.

Traditionally, in the Indian context, both services and objects required for the performance of rituals were provided and produced by *jāti*s – occupational groups, charged with these responsibilities, the entire endeavor being ideally imbued with spiritual overtones and not approached merely as "work." The almost sacred connection among occupational groups such as garland makers, temple musicians and craftsmen, and artisans and sculptors has been severed not only in diasporic locations, but also, importantly, in India itself, this being evident especially in urban spaces. As such, skills and expertise required for creating and making available an array of objects to support Hindu practices have gradually been taken over by clusters of individuals with no traditional, historical connection to caste-related knowledge, such proficiency having been relocated to the hands of entrepreneurs. Both the transference and the noted disconnect have been crucial for the ultimate commodification of objects required to sustain theistic Hinduism, leading to the emergence of a commercial industry that rests on the mass production of goods. The trading of a set of material objects as commodities, which are ultimately consumed as ritual objects by Hindus, sees the interfacing of Hinduism with the complex process of commodification.

In an edited volume, *Commodifying Everything* (2003), S. Strasser asks if there are limits to commodification and if everything is inevitably commoditized. The *Oxford English Dictionary*'s definition of "commodification" has constituted the starting point for numerous scholarly inquiries (Kitiarsa, 2007) on this topic and for S. Strasser as well. It is included here in the same spirit. Commodification is seen as "the action of turning something into, or treating something as, a (mere) commodity; commercialization of an activity, etc., that is not by nature commercial" (cited in Strasser, 2003, 3).

There is an explicit recognition in this articulation that it is possible to identify a category of acts and things that are by nature "not commercial," and the rendering of these into commodities is problematic, if not detrimental. The category of religious objects is identified as singularly distinct and exceptional with the caution that its commercialization "can get a culture into trouble" (Strasser, 2003, 3). The preponderance of religious items (and their concomitant use as religious signs or their abuse) in the market, together with their popularity and the fashion trends that they engender, lend weight to the critics of consumption who speak of its encroachment into the religious domain, the commercial exploitation of religious symbols, and the degradation of religion. Much of this criticism emanates from the logic that the worlds of religion and commerce not only are separate and incommensurate, but also should continue to be detached. This is another way of insisting on the separation of the "sacred" and "profane/secular" domains of society. Unfortunately, neither historical nor contemporary data support this position. Given the available historical and contemporary evidence, the religious domain is not immune or averse to the workings of market forces, before or after the advent of capitalism. The commodification and commercialization processes noted here are neither recent phenomena nor unique to Hinduism. Cross-cultural, comparative examples from across religious traditions demonstrate that the spiritual and material domains are not

Fig. 2: Signboard of a shop in Parktown, Chennai that deals with "temple items and *pūjā* articles" (photo by Vineeta Sinha).

ideological polarities but have been historically tangled in complex ways.

To continue with the example of Hinduism, in medieval India, Hindu temple complexes were integrated with a system of trade and commerce, something that was essential for their perpetuation (Rudner, 1987). Historical data attest to the presence of artisans, craftspeople, and traders who created and produced various objects that were required for worship in the temples. Thus, commercial activity was not by any means alien to the functioning of temples and worship within Hinduism, and it was certainly not introduced by an industrial capitalist system of production and consumption. Thus, this discussion of Hinduism and commodification rests on the assumption that the world of religiosity has historically been intimately and intricately linked with the spheres of commerce, markets, and consumer goods. The term "commodification" is not used pejoratively but refers to a complex process of treating something as an object of commerce and exchange in a marketplace. Such a focus warrants a discussion of production and distribution mechanisms and consumption patterns with respect to *pūjā* items, for example. Focusing on consumption of ritual objects is a necessary component of the larger story. This is not least because knowledge of consumption patterns can be a critical factor that stimulates the very production of commodities and their subsequent treatment and handling by distributors and retailers.

Pūjā Items: Production, Circulation, and Markets

While the use of religious objects in worship is fascinating, it is equally, if not more, intriguing to make visible their distribution and circulation mechanisms, marking the routes that they travel before they become available to devotees/consumers. Tracking where these items are produced, charting their networks of distribution, and uncovering how they are marketed and disseminated as commodities demands a rethinking of how producers, devotees/consumers, and marketplaces are conceptualized. Denoting the parameters of the cluster of devotees/consumers of religious apparatus and practitioners shifts the gaze beyond Indian shores to the phenomenon of diaspora Hinduism.

Hindu communities the world over have constituted themselves in ways that have allowed them to sustain vibrant and energetic manifestations of devotional Hinduism, both in the public and in the private domain. Today, Hindu elements are firmly etched in diasporic landscapes, perhaps most conspicuous in the towering gateways and vibrant domes of Hindu temples like the Shri Swaminarayan Mandir in London; the Viṣṇu Mandir in Toronto; the Śrī Veṅkaṭeśvara Temple in Pittsburgh; the Kāśī Śrī Viśvanātha Temple in Flint, Michigan; and the Śrī Mīnākṣī Temple in Houston – institutions that have achieved a prominence and efficacy not unlike their well-known Indian counterparts. By now, there is a rich body of literature on theistic and devotional Hinduism in diasporic settings. Yet, the analyses of visual Hindu culture and material religion that exist for Indian locations, including the incorporation of Hindu symbols and artifacts into the world of global capitalism and consumer culture, are not as readily available in studies of diaspora Hinduism.

The effortless and straightforward access to ritual objects is tenuous for diasporic Hindu communities, as the resources and skills for producing them are not necessarily present in these locales. Historically, the grounding of Hindu practices in material culture has especially been a challenge for Hindu communities located outside India, which continues to be viewed not only as the sacred centre for Hinduism but also, more importantly, as securing and validating all things "Hindu." But this is not to say that, without the importation of religious objects, the practice of Hinduism in the diaspora would be jeopardized. Indeed, this reliance on the homeland viewed as the source of all things Hindu is not unmitigated and absolute. Diasporic Hindu communities have sought alternative resources and produced a variety of local responses in fashioning products and services to cater to their religious needs, leading, in fact, to the promising augmentation of "homegrown" industries. Thus, the acquisition of these requisite skills and expertise are discernible among segments of overseas Hindu communities, on the part of both entrepreneurs and lay devotees. These developments suggest that diasporic locations should be reconceptualized as sites of production of *pūjā* items *as well as* a market for their consumption.

The variety of different routes, strategies, and mechanisms through which these objects find their way into specific locations, across the globe, is striking. Religious objects as commodities are procured and appear in local markets through a combination of "formal" and "informal" mechanisms. The formal processes are what the established businesses engage in; this entails having contacts with suppliers and manufacturers of relevant products and resources in other countries and using an established network of package, storage, and transportation nodes that deliver goods to the doorstep of retail outlets. These businesses have the capital and other resources to place large orders of products, to pay for container space for shipments and air-flown goods, and to facilitate custom clearance. In addition to big entrepreneurs who rely on standard, formal mechanisms for trading in "prayer items" are the medium- and small-scale entrepreneurs who are able to secure products using, for instance, a courier system. India remains – in the consciousness of Hindus overseas – the ultimate, legitimate source of all things Hindu. Reproducing a Hindu ritual complex has meant the need for securing a variety of different objects. But the individuals who produce, manufacture, supply, distribute, and market these goods are not confined to India; they connect widely dispersed groups of Hindus and non-Hindus spread across different parts of the globe. Ritual objects as commodities traverse these routes and circulate within the networks created. Recently, these multifaceted links and alliances have been reconfigured in view of contemporary demands of the market and the novel modes and technologies through which such needs can be met.

In "real" space, marking spaces where religious objects are traded implies attending to the highly localized retail sites, for example in sundry, grocery, and provision shops as well as specialist shops that carry religious paraphernalia in enclaves known as Mini India or Little India (in such cities as Chicago, Toronto, London, Kuala Lumpur, and Singapore). These local businesses are plugged into a complex global network of commercial linkages, often relying on the same wholesalers, suppliers, manufacturers, and distributors of religious items from India or are indeed linked with one another in exporting or importing select items across transnational boundaries. This makes it possible to conceptualize a larger transnational space of the global marketplace, one that deals with Hindu religious objects and sees the participation of retailers and businesses located in various Hindu diasporic spaces. Not surprisingly, as a 21st-century phenomenon, the Internet is a critical space that has been colonized by manufacturers and distributors of religious objects and crucially by lay practitioners themselves. This has been approached as a medium for disseminating information, advertising, and publicity for products, in addition to being a "market space" where products are bought and sold. Entering relevant phrases like "*pūjā* articles" and "*pūjā* accessories" into the Internet search engines of Google and Yahoo generates literally hundreds of Web sites and Web portals, carrying details of manufacturers, suppliers, importers, exporters, and distributors of this merchandise, based in Bangalore, New Delhi, Singapore, New York, or London. In addition to entrepreneurs, one also stumbles on blogs, discussion groups, and forums with individual posts about how to build your own altar, how to decorate a *pūjā thālī* (worship tray), where various *pūjā* accessories can be purchased, and even the list of items required for the performance of *pūjā*s and festivals. Judging by the kind of activity that occurs routinely in this setting, the Internet has clearly surfaced not only as a powerful new marketplace in the trade of *pūjā* items but also as a critical teaching and learning platform. The latter is intended to impart information about essential items required for conducting different types of *pūjā*s and about the proper methods of performing them. The Internet as a "new marketplace" facilitates such interaction and serves as a platform where these prayer items can be advertised and deals negotiated and secured. The emergence of the Internet as a new bazaar, enhanced by the circulation and dissemination of different kinds of knowledge, stands to transform the traditional dichotomous relationship between seller and buyer. This new mode of forging ties has also led to the creation of new networks of reliance and business, which are temporary and transient in the sense that they come into existence as and when necessary. This trend is further sustained and supported by other factors, including the ease with which people are connected and embedded in networks where they have access to information and resources.

Fig. 3: Statues of Hindu divinities on sale at the annual *dīpavālī* fair in Singapore. These statues are imported mainly from different parts of India, but recently "Made in China" merchandise have also been available in the marketplace (photo by Vineeta Sinha).

Theorizing Consumption of *Pūjā* Items

The actualization of Hindu religiosity through using material objects that are now largely secured as commodities from the marketplace draws Hindus as devotees/consumers into the dynamics of capitalist relations. Everyday consumption of religious objects is a complex phenomenon and subject to tremendous variation, despite the recognition of normative notions about how religious objects are to be treated in Hindu worship. While the manner of approaching pictures, statues of gods, and flowers in Hindu worship is inscribed and sometimes even prescribed by custom and tradition, it is nonetheless critical to query what happens to religious objects at the sites of reception and what individuals actually do with them as they are used in rituals. How do "once-upon-a-time" commodities enter the religious domain as ritual objects (and are thus doubly consumed), and what symbolism do they carry along their journey? Even though objects used in religious ritual are produced as commodities, once they enter the sphere of worship, they acquire specific sets of meanings that make sense within the given worldview of a particular religious tradition. They evoke religious significance within the context of the ritual in question. Even though they are secured for a sum of money and are transacted in the marketplace, they potentially embody a nonmonetary value, often expressed by devotees as spiritual power and efficacy, which can be "animated" through usage. Yet, what are consumed and appropriated as ritual objects by devotees in their religious lives at one point in time also existed as commodities and goods with a price tag and are by-products of cycles of production and distribution in a capitalist marketplace.

The assortment of objects required in the practice of Hinduism, and the fact of their incorporation into the global capitalist system of markets and commodities, does mean their necessary commercialization, but does their usage thus necessarily taint or desecrate the religious realm? What are the prospects of disentangling the convoluted modes in which materiality, sacrality, and commodity are simultaneously mixed up in the category of *pūjā* items? Discussions of consumption as a social practice entail exploring the points of contact between consumer culture and consumption behavior. In theorizing everyday usage of *pūjā* items, it is limiting to assume that individuals are driven to consume these goods for the satisfaction of temporary, superficial, restless, and worldly appetites. The notion of consumption is used negatively in such a discourse. The concept of consumption has long commanded scholarly engagement from social scientists, an interest that has persisted in reconstituted modes into the present. Assuming a historical perspective, A. Warde notes two dominant strains in interpreting consumption: the first one carries pejorative connotations, conjuring images of destruction and wastefulness, of taking things in and devouring them; the second one views consumption as one of the core social practices of an emergent capitalist society in the 18th century (cited in Turner, 2006, 88). A. Warde argues that the former tendency was twinned with an explicit critique of capitalism and of consumer society in general and had emerged from a focus on the "instrumental aspects of consumption" (Turner, 2006, 89). In contrast, from the 1970s onward, sociological and anthropological research turned increasingly to the complex process of consumption in cultural realms, by highlighting instead its "symbolic dimensions" (Turner, 2006, 89).

The critique of consumer culture and capitalism appears especially in studies of religion, in the idea that consumption practices invade, intrude, and threaten the sentiment of the religious domain, leading to its debasement and subjecting this realm to the crass banality of market forces and reckless, avid consumerism (Miller, 2005; Ward, 2003). A critical portrayal of consumption is premised on the view that consumer culture negatively changes one's relationship to religious beliefs and practices. According to V.J. Miller (2005, 3), "[a]s consumer capitalism has expanded, corporate production has encompassed cultural goods as well as material ones," arguing that commodification in the religious domain has led to the "abstraction and fragmentation of religious traditions" (Miller, 2005, 10). While V.J. Miller suggests correctly that the context in which objects are used is crucial, his articulations about the negative impact of commodification in religious spheres are less convincing.

However, if religious symbols are decontextualized and transposed to an unrelated context, there is indeed the potential for their misappropriation and abuse. Recent examples involving Hindu symbols come readily to mind: Italian designer Roberto Cavalli's depiction of the deity → Rāma on designer bikinis, French shoe manufacturer Minelli's shoes with the image of Rāma, and Laceys Footwear featuring the → *oṃ* sign on shoes, just to list a few prominent examples. Expectedly, all of these have provoked animated but divided responses from specific clusters of Hindus everywhere. However, examples like these are also readily available in India, as Hindu imagery and symbolism have been made exotic, glamorous, and embraced by popular culture in the fashion houses of Mumbai and Delhi. Hindu icons and emblems appear on tote bags, T-shirts, lunch boxes, and as tattoos on human bodies. It is important to note that the consumers of such objects are both Hindus and non-Hindus; for the former, these items are not viewed as religious symbols and are thus unproblematic. Yet, these products do draw criticism from some clusters of Hindus, who object to the meaningless appropriation of Hindu icons and symbols and their representation in what are considered inappropriate media and contexts.

How then does the fact of merchandising of religious objects affect, if at all, the modes in which they are consumed? It is important to recognize firstly that *pūjā* items are not "trapped" in a commodity state forever; they have a limited "shelf life" and eventually carry the potential to move out of the marketplace into a ritual domain, thus activating their other "noncommodity" attributes. So what does "consumption" of *pūjā* things signify for practitioners? This expression denotes a category of items that may be objects *of* worship, objects used *in* worship, or simply objects that are revered and have sacred connotations; conversely, these may be approached as having no spiritual content whatsoever but are appreciated on "purely aesthetic grounds" (Bowman, 1994, 150). In their everyday consumption, it is possible to identify at least two dimensions: the first can be denoted "aesthetic consumption" by both "self" and "other" (including tourists), and the second can be described as "ceremonial, symbolic consumption." The former suggests that individuals are attracted to merchandise that carry religious insignia not because of their spiritual value but because of their aesthetic appeal and artistic value. In framing this mode of consumption, questions can be raised about individualistic consumerism, the politics of cultural appropriation, and the exoticization of the "other" as additional factors. At the same time, procuring objects (including through purchase) for the express purpose of worship, devotion, and other expressions of religiosity sees their usage integrated into the fabric of everyday Hindu religiosity.

Certainly, commodification theoretically makes possible opportunities for mechanical consumerist behavior. However, this can also enable creativity on the part of consumers, who often use objects in ways unintended by producers and fashion them to their own needs, and who by no means receive them passively and relate to them in frivolous modes. Instead, the market may be said to be consumer driven, in that there is active participation in the creation of new needs through novel approaches to religiosity and indeed fashioning of novel religious products and services in a dynamic marketplace.

Extrapolating from this insight, in the world of theistic Hindu religiosity, "once-upon-a–time" commodities come to command a legitimacy and are appreciated and cherished because of their potential ritual value; they are not doomed to be assessed exclusively in terms of their exchange value; neither are they rejected or devalued because of their association and contact with the profane world of commerce and entrepreneurship. The merchandising of *pūjā* things does not lead to mindless, individualistic consumerism; neither is it a threat to Hindu religious and cultural sensibilities. Such argumentation runs the risk of romanticizing consumption practices and overstating the case for embellishing the value of consumer culture. Yet, despite the complex entanglement of ritual objects and commodities and their embedding in the marketplace, practitioners easily transcend the material, profane attribute of objects. Indeed, evidence suggests that Hindus appreciate that things that they deemed essential in/for worship could be bought at all; the merchandising of such materials is thus seen as enabling rather than debilitating.

Within the sphere of *pūjā* items, the coterie of objects produced, circulated, and exchanged through a thriving manufacturing industry and purchased by devotees/consumers/prosumers does not contaminate, diminish, or degrade the sacred domain. Rather, these objects enhance the spiritual domain as they are actively utilized in the sustenance of everyday religiosity by practitioners.

By now, the following observations are self-evident to students of contemporary religiosity, yet they merit reiteration. Despite the death knell sounded by secularization theorists of the 1960s and 1970s, expressions of religiosity have clearly not been laid to rest with the threat of rational, modernist tendencies. The dominant world of markets and consumer culture has not necessarily had sterilizing effects on religious practices. Furthermore, devotees as consumers and customers are neither available for easy manipulation nor passively led to develop tastes and desires for commercialized culture. Instead, the dominant culture of consumption (including in the religious sphere) that defines a postindustrial context is mediated through a range of socially and culturally specific motifs and resonances. This recognition implies that the processes of commodification and consumption within the religious domain have to be interpreted alternatively, that is, outside a theoretical logic framed by a moral, righteous critique of consumption and the fear of its insidious and toxic effects on cultural practices. Presently, the encounter of the spiritual and commercial realms does persist globally, especially in novel, reconfigured modes through the emergence of new technologies and media. But this is far from a "troubled encounter." As S. Strasser (2003, 7) notes, commodification processes can be "conflicting and contradictory." At the same time, religious institutions and practitioners respond to and appropriate the logic of the market for their own ends rather than necessarily be subjugated to it. Despite the obvious and inevitable commodification and commercialization of *pūjā* items in Hinduism, and perhaps even because of these eventualities, the religious domain is vigorously sustained. Apart from perpetuating the field of religious activity, the very commodification of religious objects also introduces tremendous scope for its possible reconfiguration through creative impulses, embodied by lay individuals who are producers, consumers, and devotees concurrently. G. Ward sees possibilities for the "re-enchantment of the world" despite the pervasiveness of commercialization in religious domains. Cultural-studies scholars suggest that "the expansive, mercurial and aleatory aspects of a modern consumer market are sources of radical hope, not despair" (cited in Agnew, 2003, 18) and take issue with the "romantic, republican, and moralizing strains of the critique of consumption" (Agnew, 2003, 18). The concern with generating profits and expansion of a market share does not sit uncomfortably with the potentially and ostensibly religious/sacred nature of the commodities being traded, a view that is sometimes expressed in the scholarship. The latter is embedded in the sharp distinction that is made between sacred and profane realms (and extended to apply to commodities) and the assumption of diametrically opposed values associated with these two spheres. An alternative mode of theorizing suggests that, despite the commodification of religious objects, goods, and commodities, they feed back into the realm of religious practices with charged meanings and in effect support an enchanted (by which I mean a religious, mystical, and otherworldly) field of practices rather than produce mindless consumerism or a disenchanted consciousness.

(With permission some of the material for this article has been drawn from my book *Religion and Commodification: Merchandising "Diasporic" Hinduism*, London, 2010.)

Bibliography

Agnew, J.-C., "The Give-and-Take of Consumer Culture," in: S. Strasser, ed., *Commodifying Everything: Relationships of the Market*, New York, 2003, 11–39.

Appadurai, A., ed., *The Social Life of Things: Commodities in Cultural Perspective*, Cambridge UK, 1986.

Berman, M., *The Re-enchantment of the World*, Ithaca, 1981.

Bowman, M., "The Commodification of the Celt: New Age/Neo-Pagan Consumerism," *FiU* 2, 1994, 143–152.

Dwyer, R., *Filming the Gods: Religion and Indian Cinema*, New York, 2006.

Dwyer, R., & D. Patel, *Cinema India: The Visual Culture of Hindi Film*, London, 2002.

Dywer, R., & C. Pinney, eds., *Pleasure and the Nation: The History, Politics and Consumption of Public Culture in India*, Oxford, 2001.

Eck, D., *Darśan: Seeing the Divine Image in India*, New York, 1981.

Frietag, S., "Visions of the Nation: Theorizing the Nexus between Creation, Consumption, and Participation in the Public Sphere," in: R. Dwyer & C. Pinney, eds., *Pleasure and the Nation: The History, Politics and Consumption of Public Culture in India*, New Delhi, 2001, 35–75.

Jain, K., *Gods in the Bazaar: The Economies of Indian Calendar Art*, Durham, 2007.

Keenan, W., & E. Arweck, *Materializing Religion: Expression, Performance and Ritual*, Aldershot, 2006.

Kitiarsa, P., ed., *Religious Commodifications in Asia: Marketing Gods*, London, 2007.

McLain, K., *India's Immortal Comic Books: Gods, Kings, and Other Heroes*, Bloomington, 2009.

Miller, V.J., *Consuming Religion: Christian Faith and Practice in a Consumer Culture*, New York, 2005.

Nanda, M., *The God Market: How Globalization Is Making India More Hindu*, New Delhi, 2009.

Pinney, C., *Photos of the Gods: The Printed Image and Political Struggle in India*, London, 2003.

Ramaswamy, S., *The Goddess and the Nation: Mapping Mother India*, Durham, 2010.

Rudner, D.W., "Religious Gifting and Inland Commerce in Seventeenth-Century South India," *JAS* 46/2, 1987, 361–397.

Sinha, V., *Religion and Commodification: "Merchandizing" Diasporic Hinduism*, London, 2010.

Strasser, S., ed., *Commodifying Everything: Relationships of the Market*, New York, 2003.

Turner, B., ed., *The Cambridge Dictionary of Sociology*, Cambridge MA, 2006.

Ward, G., "The Commodification of Religion and the Consummation of Religion," *HeR* 5/2, 2003, 50–65.

Warde, A., "Consumption," in: B. Turner, ed., *The Cambridge Dictionary of Sociology*, Cambridge MA, 2006, 88–90.

Vineeta Sinha

Dalit Critiques of Hinduism

I had the misfortune of being born with the stigma of [being] an Untouchable. However, it is not my fault; but I will not die a Hindu, for this is in my power (B.R. Ambedkar [see Zelliot, 1992, 206]).

Debates on Nomenclature

"→ Dalit" (meaning downtrodden, broken, torn into pieces) was first used in the context of caste by Jotirao Govindrao Phule (1827–1890), the leader of the Satya Shodhak Samaj, a 19th-century anti-Brahmanical movement. The Marathi word gained prominence as a collective pan-Indian signifier from the 1970s onward due to the efforts of the Dalit Panthers (young urban activists inspired by the Black Panthers in the United States) and Dalit Sahitya (a literary movement discussed below) movements in Maharashtra. In contrast to all the other collective designations for castes relegated to the bottom of the Hindu social hierarchy, for example, "untouchables," "Harijans," "Depressed Classes," or "Scheduled Castes," the word "Dalit" was chosen, and used with defiance, as a term of self-reference by some members of the group itself (Zelliot, 1992, 267–292). The term had a distinctly assertive flavor, representing "a new level of pride, militancy, and sophisticated creativity" (Zelliot, 1992, 267). It has since become a widely accepted descriptive category (Fuchs, 1999, 169–170; Zelliot, 1992, 37, 271) that is increasingly employed by activists and members of oppressed caste communities throughout India. While widely accepted today as a political signifier and a social-science concept, "Dalit" finds no mention in the official administrative vocabulary of the postcolonial Indian state, which continues to use the colonial category of Scheduled Castes introduced under the Government of India Act of 1935, when it replaced the term Depressed Classes. Both the schedule, or list, of disadvantaged castes and the widespread discriminatory practices against them continue to persist into the present. Arguably the schedule is of significance for the state in garnering political support among these marginalized groups. But the debate on nomenclature is by no means settled as evidenced by a 2012 government committee report, whose controversial recommendation to replace the word "Dalit" with "Scheduled Castes" in secondary school political science textbooks has led to considerable protest (Viswanath, 2012).

The term "Dalit" connotes a range of castes subjected to various forms of stigmatization, exploitation, and oppression (including upper-caste practices of → untouchability) as well as the movements that emerged in response to such discriminations. As sociopolitical phenomena, these movements are thus constitutive of, as well as constituted by, Dalits. They strive for the emancipation of Dalits as well as the recognition of the dignity of each individual, equal rights for Dalits as a group, and the acknowledgment of their cultural and social particularities as communities. Since Dalit movements have, and continue to be, formed to advance the rights of specific caste groups, their social and political actions are frequently read from the outside as articulations of particularistic group identities. But these movements acting on behalf of specific groups also seek to transcend particularities by advocating universal rights (Fuchs, 1999, 273–274). The Dalit statesman B.R. → Ambedkar, for example, did not simply aim at social mobility for his own caste but sought instead to rid Hindu society as a whole of all institutions and practices enabling stigmatization, oppression, and discrimination in his bid to advance justice and equal rights.

Prior to the 19th century, neither was there a unifying term encompassing the range of Dalit communities, nor did a clearly defined social category exist that set apart these castes at the bottom of the social hierarchy as a collectivity. Each local Dalit caste had its own (often occupational) name that was used as a term of reference for, and also by, its members. Since the mid-19th century, British colonial officials systematically collected information on caste and religion, which were seen as "the sociological keys to understanding the Indian people" (Cohn, 1987, 242). The most consequential of the enumerative techniques employed to govern India was the census, which was instrumental in objectifying particular understandings of caste, while transforming them from "fuzzy" to "enumerated" communities (Kaviraj, 1992). In his attempt to establish a uniformly applicable procedure to classify and rank caste groups for the 1901 census, H.H. Risley introduced the classificatory category of "untouchable" castes (Charsley, 1996; Das, 2003). "Untouchables" was thus not the English translation of an Indian-language term but one that emerged as part of colonial administrative practice. It separated out and marked certain groups, which became targets of missionary activity and special administrative measures for social improvement. The issue of untouchability acquired further significance in the context of the nationalist movement and its engagement with questions of social inequality, on the one hand, and its concerns with the boundaries of the Hindu community, on the other (Randeria, 2007). As numbers became politically important, many Hindu and nationalist leaders were concerned about conversions to Islam and Christianity from "untouchable" castes and willing to make concessions to them in order to inflate the numbers of Hindus by including as many as possible into the "Hindu" fold.

It is not as if various forms of untouchability as systematic forms of exclusion (for instance, prohibition of entry into Hindu temples, access to wells in upper-caste localities or to the village cremation ground) had not been practiced earlier by upper castes *vis-à-vis* the groups ranked lowest in the caste hierarchy. Unlike the temporary impurity incurred by Hindu individuals of all castes on account of menstruation or a death in the family, which is removed by a ritual bath after a specified number of days, or the payment of a fine in case of pollution due to ritual transgression, for upper castes each "untouchable" caste as a collectivity was associated with the stigma of permanent pollution deriving from their occupational contact with impure substances (as, e.g., leatherworkers, scavengers, or cremation-ground attendants; Randeria, 1989). The classification of a set of lowest castes as marked by civic disabilities based on the imputation of permanent irremediable ritual pollution, however, transformed the perception and self-perception of these castes. A single standard was established that subsumed various individual castes into a collective category and dichotomized Indian society into social groups that were affected by the stigma of untouchability, and those upper, middle, and lower castes that were not (Charsley, 1996). The rubric of untouchability as established by the colonial state in the 20th century thus introduced a new way of imagining the social order of India (Galanter, 1984, 25).

Equally important for authorizing the use of untouchability as a social and political category was M.K. → Gandhi. In 1931, he introduced the term "Harijans" (Children of God), which reflected the discomfort he felt with labeling people as untouchable (i.e. a discomfort with the practice of untouchability, not with the concept of untouchability itself; Charsley, 1996, 8). "Harijan" was, and is occasionally still, used to refer to the most oppressed groups in India, but many members of these castes reject it as patronizing. They prefer "Dalit," which semantically points to the humiliating experience of discrimination rather than evoking a vector of victimization (as in "untouchable"), or a euphemism (as in "Harijan"). "Dalit" is thus a political identity that expresses the urge for liberation from Brahman tyranny and for emancipation from caste oppression. It is used here to refer to a wide range of individuals, groups, and movements including contexts prior to, or independent of, the emergence of "Dalit" as a self-conscious collective identification.

The indexing of local communities in registers of scheduled castes for the purpose of identifying beneficiaries of so-called positive discrimination can be understood as a response to demands emerging from anti-Brahman or anticaste agitations in the late colonial period. These mobilizations were along the lines of epistemic categories that the colonial administration had introduced, such as a racialized dichotomy between Brahmans and non-Brahmans, or between "untouchables" and "non-untouchables," respectively. Anti-Brahman movements formed in reaction to injustices including practices related to ritual pollution as well as to conditions created by colonial rule, such as the disproportionately high employment of Brahmans and other higher castes in the administration, which was further cementing the latter's powerful and privileged position in the local social order.

G. Omvedt (1994, 23) distinguishes two basic ideologies legitimating caste hierarchies, which Dalit and non-Brahman movements had to confront in the late 19th and early 20th centuries: religiously based ideologies, on the one hand, and the "Aryan theory of race," on the other. The former found justification for caste hierarchies in the *Ṛgveda*, in the *Manusmṛti*, in the puranic myths, and in renditions of the → *Mahābhārata*, as well as in the → *Rāmāyaṇa*. Reformers like → Rammohun Roy or Gandhi confronted these ideologies by arguing that a different interpretation of the scriptures would allow for reform or even abolition of the *jāti* and *varṇa* systems (Omvedt, 1994, 22). As against this, anticaste radicals like Jotirao Govindrao Phule, Ambedkar, and E.V. Ramasamy (referred to as Periyar) denounced the scriptures, for they agreed with conservatives that Hinduism clearly prescribed caste hierarchies and their observation. The Aryan invasion theory proposed by European orientalists and propagated by many colonial administrators argued for a racial distinction between upper and lower castes. The census commissioner of the 1901 census, H.H. Risley, for example, applied a race-based theory of caste in his effort to find categories of caste that could be applied all over India. Employing criteria such as skin color, jaw shape, nasal index, and so on, he collapsed caste and race as analytical categories. The 1901 census established not only the racial origin of caste but also *varṇa* hierarchy as an authoritative description of the caste system (Charsley, 1996; Das, 2003).

The idea of the "Aryan" was first used by Europeans to evoke shared linguistic ties with Indians within the framework of a common Indo-European heritage, as T. Trautmann (1997) shows in his history of entanglements between British orientalism and colonial ethnology in and of India. Tracing the gradual transformation of the term "Aryan" from a linguistic to a racial category, he argues that by the end of the 19th century, race science and orientalism reached a lasting consensus with respect to what may be termed "the racial theory of Indian civilization." According to G. Omvedt, this racial model of caste was welcomed by "early modernist Brahmans as a way of asserting their equivalence with the white-skinned conquerors and their superiority to the dark-skinned lower castes" (1994, 23). Anti-Brahman radicals refuted this ideology of Aryan conquest on its very own terms. If middle and low castes (the Śūdras and Atiśūdras of the *varṇa* system) were descendants of India's non-Aryan original inhabitants, whereas Brahmans (Brāhmaṇas), Kṣatriyas, and Vaiśyas were descendants of Indo-European (Aryan) conquerors, then Śūdras and Atiśūdras could be understood as the original inhabitants of the subcontinent and as representing authentic Indian values.

Modern Dalit Movements

Dalit literature has played an important role in Dalit movements, simultaneously pursuing the aims of social critique, cultural identity formation, and political mobilization. Similar to the long history of Dalit movements critiquing Brahmanism, Dalit literary expression and opposition to Brahmanical oppression is not new. In Maharashtra, for example, it can be dated back to the verses of the Mahar poet → Cokhāmeḷā in the 14th century and in Karnataka to the compositions of → Liṅgayāts, like Cennabasava, from the 12th century onwards. However, the emergence of modern "Dalit literature" in western India can be traced to a resolution passed at the first Dalit literary conference in 1958, inspired by the leadership of Ambedkar. But it was only in the 1970s that the importance of Dalit writings (poetry, short stories, novels, and autobiographies) came to be more widely recognized. A spate of publications (by both Dalit men and women) gave momentum to the Dalit literature movement (Dangle, 1992), which reflected with poignancy and anguish on experiences of abjection, often using a deliberately provocative language. Moreover, these writers also theorized the difference between Dalit and other voices as well as the distinctiveness of new forms of Dalit self-expression as a scathing socioreligious critique of entrenched caste/class hierarchies. Many of them became involved in political activism in the wake of their disillusionment with established political parties, including the Republican Party founded by Ambedkar. Translations from one Indian language into another as well as into English (see Dangle, 1992, for an influential anthology) made Dalit literature available to a wide readership within the country as well as beyond it. Not only did Dalit literature gain recognition as an agonized and impassioned cry against the humiliation and exclusion suffered individually and collectively by members of Dalit communities, but it also is equally compelling in its radical critique of Hindu society and its demand for recognition of difference along with claims to equality and justice.

Anti-Brahmanical movements have a longer precolonial history beginning with medieval → *bhakti* and → Sant sects. The earliest proponent of modern anti-Brahmanism was Jotirao Govindrao Phule (1827–1890), who belonged to the Mali or gardening caste in Pune, Maharashtra, which is considered to be a lower but not an "untouchable" caste. In books such as *Gulamgiri* (Slavery; 1873), he formulated a fundamental critique of caste and Brahman domination with an interpretation of Hindu mythology explaining the oppression of Śūdras and Atiśūdras as a millennial battle between Aryan Brahmans and Dravidian others. He thus developed a counter-history for the disadvantaged castes using a narrative that presented the Śūdras and Atiśūdras as Kṣatriyas, whose true identity had been obscured by the hegemonic Brahmanic representations of Hindu society. Jotirao Govindrao Phule's critique of Brahman dominance over disadvantaged caste groups was built around the metaphor of slavery to reframe understandings of caste relations in terms of exploitation and inequality tied to embodied difference and economic disadvantage, rather than based in the religious order. For Jotirao Govindrao Phule, Brahmanism was not just a religious ideology but one that could be historically located: it had an origin, and, therefore, it could also have an end. His critique, however, was not only directed toward Brahmanism as an ideology justifying traditional asymmetries of caste authority but also targeted the overrepresentation of the Brahman minority in colonial educational and bureaucratic institutions. This two-dimensionality of Jotirao Govindrao Phule's critique of Brahmanism expressed his understanding of the political and religious aspects of caste as distinct yet interdependent (O'Hanlon, 1985; Omvedt, 1994, 23, 97–100; Rao, 2009, 12–14, 39–80).

Jotirao Govindrao Phule's counternarrative sought to forge a new collective identity based on a division of Hindu society into Brahmans, or a layer of privileged upper castes that constitutes a tiny but powerful minority, and vast numbers of disadvantaged and disenfranchised lower castes including the Dalits. This dichotomy continues to form the basis for successful political mobilization and electoral success in several regions in recent decades. Jotirao Govindrao Phule saw Maharashtran society as divided between an exploited majority, the fruits of whose labors provided the material basis for society at large but who were condemned to live in poverty and ignorance, and a minority of Brahmans and other literate castes, who monopolized religious authority along with exclusive access to education in English and thus to employment in the colonial administration. The idea of "*bahujan samāj*" (the majority community/society), which Jotirao Govindrao Phule introduced, not only figures prominently in the work of the Dalit scholar K. Ilaiah, but also provides the name for the popular Dalit political party in northern India today, the Bahujan Samaj Party. Jotirao Govindrao Phule argued that in order to undo their disadvantages, the exploited castes needed access to education, to social reforms allowing the formation of an institutional basis for participation in civil society, and autonomy from the religious authority of Brahmans and their ideologies of social and ritual hierarchy.

In 1852 Jotirao Govindrao Phule set up schools admitting children from castes identified as "untouchable," and in 1873 he founded the Satyashodhak Samaj ("Truth-Seeking Society"). Its spiritual foundation were the teachings of the 15th-century mystic poet → Kabīr, who had advocated a distinctly anti-Brahmanical and anticaste understanding of religion, rejecting intermediaries between the individual and god. The Satyashodhak Samaj rules prescribed the worship of only one god (the creator) and the complete rejection of social or ritual inferiority. Moreover, it also required a commitment to social work, education – especially that of women – and the proselytizing of the organization's principles. Similar to the approach of protestant missionaries, it distributed free copies of books and pamphlets, as it was assumed that information on (or rather access to the "truth" of) caste and religion empowered individuals to freely decide about their faith. Jotirao Govindrao Phule saw education as a means to liberate lower castes from social ills such as child marriage, high indebtedness, meat eating, or drinking, which were seen as markers of low status (O'Hanlon, 1985, 220–251). Education would allow the disadvantaged majority to understand their plight and emancipate themselves from the shackles of Brahmanism and its hierarchies besides providing access to literacy, English-language skills, and employment. Even today while upper-caste/middle-class parents in urban Maharashtra emphasize the importance of educating their children in the mother tongue instead of English, the language of the colonizer (Bénéï, 2005), Dalits continue to view access to English as their pathway to better job opportunities as well as a move to resist the dominance exercised by Brahmans traditionally through their hold over the Marathi language.

The relationship of Satyashodhak Samaj with Hinduism was ambivalent (O'Hanlon, 1985, 23). The dilemma of remaining within the fold of Hinduism and yet distancing oneself from it was most apparent with regard to rituals and religious ceremonies, which according to the organization's principles were to be conducted without Brahman ritual specialists. The insistence that even marriage ceremonies be held without Brahman participation met with fierce resistance even within Jotirao Govindrao Phule's own caste and was rejected by many Satyashodhak members as an assault on the ancestral religion. Another challenge was the reluctance, or inability, of many members to discontinue observing religious or social pollution. This undermined Jotirao Govindrao Phule's efforts to bring together peasant castes (such as his own) with so-called untouchable castes (e.g. the Mahar, to which Ambedkar belonged) to build a common front against Brahman domination in Maharashtra (O'Hanlon, 1985; Omvedt, 1994).

The Satyashodhak Samaj has been described as the "most radical and mass based of the social movements" (Omvedt, 1994, 139) for its fundamental questioning of caste and Brahman domination as well as its focus on the economic aspects of caste exploitation. However, while it laid the foundation for B. Ambedkar's opposition to caste oppression following a path of separatism and autonomy, the coalition between Śūdras and Atiśūdras was fragile. Dalit critics of Brahmanism and caste, such as Ambedkar, saw Jotirao Govindrao Phule's effort of forging a common anti-Brahman identity for different caste groups as problematic in view of the very particular discrimination associated with untouchability. They were also conscious of the incompatibility of the stigma of untouchability with the idea of a shared Kṣatriya identity for all lower castes as propagated by Jotirao Govindrao Phule to counter Brahmanic domination (Heredia, 2007; Fuchs, 1999; Rao, 2009).

Though Jotirao Govindrao Phule's work thus laid the foundation of modern anticaste movements and a non-Brahman ideology, it was not based strictly speaking on a Dalit perspective. Later Dalit leaders like Ambedkar, and movements such as the Mahar Buddhists (Zelliot, 1992) or the → Ad Dharm movement in Punjab (Juergensmeyer ,1982), identified not only Brahmans but also Hindus of all castes as oppressors. For example, Dalit representation and participation in political processes and institutions meant for Ambedkar not simply the replacement of Brahmans with Dalits within existing structures but rather abolishing hierarchical structures altogether. He also rejected the racial theory of caste propagated by non-Brahman movements and regarded castes as an integral part of the Hindu religio-cultural structure. Therefore, he ultimately proposed the renouncement of Hinduism as an important precondition for overcoming caste hierarchy. Ambedkar's turn toward Buddhism is thus to be understood as not only a critique of Brahmanism but also a total rejection of the hegemonic Hindu social order.

Ambedkar (1891–1956) belonged to the untouchable Mahar caste in Maharashtra. He was born in a military cantonment in the Central Provinces (now Madhya Pradesh), where his father, who like his grandfather was a soldier in the British Indian Army's Mahar regiment, was stationed. Ambedkar was the first person in his caste to graduate from college, and he went on to study economics, law, and anthropology in Bombay, London, and New York. He earned higher degrees including a doctorate from Columbia University as well as from the London School of Economics, and he was called to the bar in England. After Independence, Ambedkar became chairman of the Drafting Committee of the Indian Constitution and in 1951 India's first law minister. Between 1918 and 1955, he started various newspapers as organs of mass mobilization, which established him as a Dalit spokesperson (Rao, 2009, 121, 328). He did not subscribe to the politics of indigeneity on which the claim to be the original inhabitants, or "Lords of the Land," advocated, for example, by Jotirao Govindrao Phule was predicated. Instead of simply reversing the current social hierarchy to claim that Śūdras and Atiśūdras had been the dominant group in Maharashtra before the advent of the upper-caste Aryans, Ambedkar formulated the claims of the Mahar in terms of equality and human rights as well as the inclusiveness of democratic participation (Zelliot, 1992, 41).

Since the 1920s, movements against untouchability were no longer organized in terms of locality or region nor exclusively in the name of local communities but always also in the name of a larger disenfranchised collective – untouchables, depressed classes, and finally Dalits – and worked toward the goal of a society free of discrimination. Ambedkar redefined equality – a universal concept of modern, liberal democracy – with respect to the political needs in the Indian context by resignifying it as caste equality. By speaking out against discrimination on a national level, Ambedkar turned the struggle against untouchability into a common political cause that Dalits across the country were able to identify with. But he should be considered as their spokesperson rather than a Dalit political leader, as he spoke out against the structures and institutions that perpetuated the discrimination rather than orchestrating mobilization or coordinating local movements (Fuchs, 1999, 229; Rao, 2009, 11). He proved to be much more effective as a political thinker than a politician.

While he continued to pursue these aims throughout the four decades of his work as a Dalit lawyer, scholar, theorist, publicist, and activist, Ambedkar's strategies as a statesman underwent many changes. These included radical symbolic actions, such as drinking from a water tank in a Brahman neighborhood in the town of Mahad in 1927 in defiance of prevailing norms, or the public burning of the Hindu scripture of *Manusmṛti*. Between 1927 and 1935, Ambedkar led several *satyāgraha*s (nonviolent mass mobilizations) following the model for political action set by Gandhi, to demand access for Dalits to Hindu temples. While Ambedkar considered such movements important for mobilizing Dalits and raising awareness about their lack of rights, neither did he believe that upper-caste Hindus would have a change of heart and give up customary, ingrained attitudes and practices of untouchability as Gandhi hoped, nor did he think that merely following Gandhian methods would bring about the necessary social transformation. Gandhi or the Congress also did not approve of the Dalits' use of Gandhian methods. Ambedkar later preferred "a fight [in] the courts to a battle in the streets" (Zelliot, 1992, 69) because he believed that while mass action was effective in raising consciousness among his own constituency, rights needed to be protected through law.

Dalit Critiques of Hinduism

In 1935 Ambedkar called off a struggle demanding entry to the Kālā Rām Temple in Nasik but announced that he would leave Hinduism as it failed to offer any promise for equality (Zelliot, 1992, 70–71). However, the question of whether Dalits were Hindus was for him not only a matter of spiritual practice and ritual discrimination but also, more importantly, a demographic and political issue. Since 1919 Ambedkar had advocated for Dalits to be considered as separate and distinct from Hindus, and in the early 1930s, he began demanding separate electorates for depressed classes analogous to those for Muslims. The Communal Award of 1932 granted in addition to a general vote also separate electorates to such communities in areas of high concentration. However, Gandhi strongly opposed what he considered to be a divisive move advantageous to the British and undertook in protest a "fast unto death" against the system of separate representation. His argument was that Harijans, as he called them, were part of the Hindu community, so that separate electorates would not overcome but instead further cement the divisions between upper and lower castes. Despite support for his position from the Ad Dharm movement of Dalits in the Punjab too (see below), Ambedkar was forced to yield to the immense pressure and sign the Poona Act in 1932. Separate constituencies of and for Dalits were thereby repealed, but a compromise instituted instead reserved legislative seats that could only be contested by Dalits in open electorates, a measure later enshrined in the Indian constitution. Whereas for Gandhi the ideal communitarian social order marked by harmony could only be realized by overcoming the divisions of caste and religion, for Dalit leaders like Ambedkar and Mangoo Ram of the Ad Dharm movement, social equality for the Dalits was only possible once respect, recognition of difference, and some measure of power had first been achieved by these communities as a whole (Juergensmeyer, 1982, 130). While the Dalit leaders remained suspicious of Gandhi's motives and rejected his paternalistic approach, Gandhi felt that their political strategy risked reinforcing existing caste divisions.

While Ambedkar thus called for political action and the assertion of rights, Gandhi spiritualized the issue of untouchability, considering the practice a sin that needed to be met with repentance and a change of heart on the part of upper-caste Hindus. Whereas Gandhi believed that Hinduism could be reformed from within to rid it of the evil of untouchability, Ambedkar was convinced that untouchability was inherent in Hinduism. However, Ambedkar›s demand for a separate electoral representation for Dalits was not necessarily a step toward separatism. For him the aims of integration and autonomy were not mutually exclusive but part of the same project since he hoped to redefine social discourse and thus the very terms of integration. He thus understood autonomy not as a process of separation from Hindu society but as a strategy of integration that would enable Dalits to participate in political institutions and processes on equal terms (Fuchs, 1999, 270–271).

Toward the end of his life, Ambedkar set out to "create a new legend, a new history, and new identity for his people" (Zelliot, 1992, 72). In *The Untouchables* (1948), he had argued that Dalits were "broken men," fragments of defeated tribes living outside settled villages, who as Buddhists and beef eaters had not been absorbed into Hindu social and political structures. His historical narrative thus represented them as having been rendered untouchable around 400 CE as a result of the struggle for supremacy between Buddhism and Brahmanism. In 1956, he publicly converted to Buddhism in a mass ceremony, thus completing a journey he had embarked on when renouncing Hinduism in 1935. In the interim years, Ambedkar had given detailed consideration to Islam, Sikhism, and Christianity, but found in none of these religions what he was looking for. Buddhism represented for him an ancient and an authentic Indian religion. By embracing it, he hoped to provide them with a new past and present religious identity, which was crucial to the new collective self-awareness he sought to create (Zelliot, 1992, 72–72). Ambedkar's choice of Buddhism was predicated, on the one hand, on his understanding of it as a rational religion, one that could easily be reconciled with modern scientific knowledge. On the other hand, he found its principles of equality, freedom, and solidarity, along with those of compassion and justice, to be attractive for building an ethical foundation for society.

Soon after Ambedkar's death, a second mass conversion was held among his caste of Mahars, so that by the 1961 census, 80% of the community's members had converted from Hinduism to Buddhism. Though it did not lead to upper-caste Hindus according them a different status, conversion enabled the embrace of a collective identity as Buddhists (Zelliot, 1992, 54, 72–73). Mahars thus declared their rejection of not only the Hindu spiritual and social world but also their stigmatized caste identity.

Ambedkar's relationship to religion, which emerged from his analysis of the relationship between Hinduism and Indian society, was both rationalist and intellectual. He identified religion and society as two distinct analytical entities, whereby in his view religion as a project with deeply social and political implications had the potential to substantially impact society. In order to accept not only the principle but also the practice of equal rights, Ambedkar felt that society needed to be transformed, and he saw the potential for such a radical transformation in what he referred to as the Buddha's *dhamma* (an ethics of social action and a moral guideline for society, simultaneously allowing humans to recognize their suffering as inflicted by humans, and providing the ethical principles to reorganize society accordingly). Although his conversion to Buddhism was a political move, it was not simply an act of protest or defiance. It was rather a step toward a spiritual disposition with the potential to transform society based on Buddhist principles of equality and compassion (Fuchs, 2004).

The indistinguishability of religious and political activism was not unique to Ambedkar but was central to many anti-Brahman and Dalit movements in the late 19th and early 20th centuries. While Ambedkar embraced Buddhism, his South Indian contemporary E.V. Ramasamy Naicker (1879–1973), referred to by many Tamilians as "Periyar" ("Great Man"), rejected religion due to his rationalism. Periyar formulated his political agenda as "no god; no religion; no Gandhi; no Congress; and no Brahmins" (Dirks, 2001, 259). He began his career as a supporter of Gandhi and the Congress but became disappointed with them when he realized that a nonviolent agitation in 1924 to open the Vaikom Temple in Travancore to the untouchable Īzhava caste was for Gandhi and the Congress Party not a matter of social reform, but a strategy for merely securing Dalit political support. After failing to garner Congress backing for either opposition to the practice of untouchability in Congress-supported schools or his efforts to increase non-Brahman representation in various social and political bodies, he resigned from the Congress Party in 1925. Periyar agreed with Gandhi and Ambedkar that caste was deeply rooted in Indian social conventions, but like Ambedkar, he disagreed with Gandhi that these social conventions and their ideological foundations in Hinduism could ever be reformed. Periyar therefore advocated a rationalist form of atheism, equating Brahmanism with Hinduism and rejecting both. He argued, for example, that were a temple to be polluted by the presence of certain people, the idol there could be no god but must be a mere stone. Periyar provoked public opinion by describing Hindu gods as sexually perverted, and he more than once suggested that Brahmans should be murdered. In 1926, he established the Self-Respect Movement, which dismissed religious belief as superstition and upper-caste propaganda. It aimed to abolish caste and advocated gender equality, intercaste marriages, and rituals without the participation of Brahmans. It variously questioned Brahman priesthood, ideology, and scriptural authority. It engaged in dramatic symbolic action, including the burning of Hindu sacred texts such as the *Manusmṛti*, declaring the *Rāmāyaṇa* an Aryan anti-Dravidian myth, and physical assault by members on priests and idols with polluting leather sandals (Dirks, 1996, 279; 2001, 261).

The issue of Dalit social reform in the nationalist era raised fundamental questions on the nature of caste and religion in India. While Gandhi was convinced that Hinduism could, and needed to, be reformed to get rid of the stigmatization of Dalits, Ambedkar saw the only hope as lying in a fundamental break with Hinduism. For him, social reform needed to be pursued through different (i.e. non-Hindu) ethics, which he located in (his version of) Buddhism. Periyar advocated the need for a complete break with not only Hinduism but also religion more generally. While the critiques of Brahmanism of both Gandhi and Ambedkar thus involved ethical principles derived from religious teachings (whereby Ambedkar was not content with a critique of Brahmanism and aimed for a fundamental critique of Hindu society), Periyar sought liberation and justice in a reformulation of society based on the assumption of a racial difference between Aryans (equated with Brahmans) and Dravidians, as it had been introduced by colonial ethnography. Periyar's critique of Brahmanism was, therefore, not limited to attacks on religious practices, teachings, and institutions. He also identified Indian nationalism as an inherently Hindu project with an underlying interest to maintain and expand Brahmanic privileges. The institution of Hindi as a national language, for example, was to Periyar an Aryan conspiracy and proof of the inherently Brahmanical and oppressive character of nationalism in India. He thus increasingly advocated the creation of a separate territorial unit of Tamil Nadu within the Indian nation-state and later demanded an autonomous Dravida Nadu and even a new state of Dravidistan, paralleling the Muslim League's demand for Pakistan, which Periyar supported.

Critiques of Brahmanism discussed so far considered Dalits to be *de facto* a part of Hindu society. A radically different approach marks the writings of K. Ilaiah, a professor of political science at Osmania University in Hyderabad and one of the most provocative and prolific of Dalit theorists today. In various writings, most prominently in his programmatically titled *Why I Am Not a Hindu* (Ilaiah, 1996a, 168), he explains why the assumption that Dalits are part of Hindu society is principally flawed. K. Ilaiah's intervention centers around two fundamental criticisms of Brahmanism: Dalits (called Dalitbahujan, see below) have always been excluded from the Hindu community (they could not enter temples, were not allowed to eat with high-caste Hindus, were denied access to education, etc.) and should, therefore, not be considered Hindus now. Moreover, he describes Brahmanism not as a religious ideology or a ritual order, but as a contemporary economic, political, and social reality structuring all aspects of life (Ilaiah, 1996b; 1996a). K. Ilaiah demonstrates that caste permeates all aspects of contemporary Indian society and its institutions, by means of personal observations and experiential accounts that challenge the normative expectations of contemporary scholarship. Rather than trying to convince those he criticizes, K. Ilaiah aims to conscientize the oppressed and to turn the existing hegemonic relations on their head by seeking confrontation between the culture and consciousness of the oppressed with that of "the enemy" (Ilaiah, 1996b; 1996a). His critique of Brahmanism emerged during the 1990s against the background of Hindu right-wing strategies to encompass Dalits and → Ādivāsīs within Hinduism. But in describing *hindutva* as caste-ist and capitalist rather than communal, K. Ilaiah provides a different interpretation of it. He shows that the *hindutva* strategies of inclusion are motivated mainly by electoral considerations: "Socially, culturally, and even physically they want us to remain their 'other,' while acting politically as 'homogenous Hindus' who can be their tools against Muslims or Christians (in their language 'minorities')" (Ilaiah, 1996a, 166). As K. Ilaiah shows, however, while detailing the life in the community in which he grew up in Andhra Pradesh, they had in fact much more in common with Muslims and Christians (all eat meat, work the fields, are allowed to touch each other) and shared no relations whatsoever with their Brahman and Baniya (i.e. Vaiśya) neighbors.

K. Ilaiah formulates his critique of Brahmanism from the perspective of those he subsumes under the category of "Dalitbahujan," which includes for both analytical and strategic purposes Dalits, Ādivāsīs (the "Scheduled Tribes" in the official terminology of the Indian state), and the low-caste groups now classified as "Other Backward Classes" irrespective of their differences. The Dalitbahujan represent Hinduism's other, which for K. Ilaiah is inseparable from the fact that they represent the productive or working classes. As S. Charsley points out (1998, 546), K. Ilaiah's critique of Brahmanism is structurally similar to M.N. Srinivas' model of "Sanskritization" (Srinivas, 1978; 1965), in that it represents Indian society as culturally dichotomized into Brahmans and non-Brahmans. But K. Ilaiah turns M.N. Srinivas' model on its head by replacing the "non-Brahman" with a positive "Dalitbahujan" identity.

Dalit Religions and Conversions

Instead of renouncing Hinduism, K. Ilaiah tries to prove the categorical differences between Hindus and what he calls Dalitbahujan. His critique of Brahmanism – in pointing to the distinctness of Dalits from Hindu caste groups – can be seen as of a piece with earlier efforts by many low-caste and Dalit reform movements in the 19th and 20th centuries. These sought to transform society and escape stigmatization, humiliation, and exploitation by formulating the terms of religious communities distinct from Hinduism, often based on the claim of merely reinstating original, authentic traditions understood to have existed before Hinduism. The Ad Dharm movement, for instance, originated in the 1920s in Punjab. Its founders, Vasant Rai, Thakar Chand, and Swami Shudranand, all belonged to the Camar caste, who had achieved a certain degree of financial independence as leather merchants. Most importantly, they were all active in, but critical of, the → Arya Samaj movement, which at the time was recruiting Dalits by conducting so-called *śuddhi* (purification) ceremonies. In the communalizing political climate of the time, the Arya Samaj was denounced for misusing the Dalit cause to secure numerical strength for the Hindu community (esp. *vis-à-vis* Muslims and Sikhs) and political influence for itself. The Ad Dharm movement thus conceptualized itself in opposition to Arya Samaj, which it condemned as a vile attempt to keep Dalits in a subservient position within Hinduism. The leading figure of the Ad Dharm movement was Mangoo Ram, an educated Camar who had lived in the United States between 1909 and 1925 and worked as a teacher in an Arya Samaj school after his return to Punjab. He became the first president when Ad Dharm constituted itself as a formal organization in 1926. He identified the formation of a distinct religious identity as the highest priority for the Dalits and described Ad Dharm as a *qaum* (Urd., community) with which he meant the existence of Dalits as a religious community like Hindus, Muslims, and Sikhs.

M. Juergensmeyer (1982, 51) describes the Ad Dharm theology as having adopted a nontheistic notion of divinity, in which nature is perceived as god and creator. In the process of formalizing itself as a religion, the Ad Dharm movement also collated a corpus of scriptures. It included in particular the writings of → Ravidās, a 15th-century → *bhakti* mystic poet who had been a Camar. While a title for the Ad Dharm scriptures had been chosen – "Ad Prakash" – the project remained incomplete. Its critics argued that Ad Dharm would reify the concept of untouchability by forming a Dalit religion. But the aim of identifying as a *qaum* was to transcend (or undermine) the notion of caste in order to be considered equal alongside Hindus, Muslims, and Sikhs. The Ad Dharm *qaum* was seen by its leaders and ideologues as having existed since time immemorial, prior to the establishment of Hinduism by Aryan intruders, who subjected Dalits to discrimination and humiliation. The Ad Dharm movement was thus using the argument of the Aryan invasion theory to turn the very structure of criticism, which the Arya Samaj directed against Muslims and Christians (of intrusion, conquest, and deceit) against the Hindus themselves. Not unlike Jotirao Govindrao Phule and his Satyashodhak Samaj, Ad Dharm thus offered a mythical past as the basis for the formation of a community and the formulation of a critique of the existing social order. While this strategy differs from Ambedkar's approach, which rejected the notion of different racial origins as the foundation for caste (Ambedkar, 1917), it is similar to that embraced by other "Adi" movements, which identified Dalits and/or non-Brahmans as the original inhabitants of India (Juergensmeyer, 1982).

The Adi Dravida movement under M.C. Rajah in Madras seems to have been the first to formulate this idea that Dalits were the original inhabitants of India. It is unclear whether the Ad Dharm movement of Punjab (and the Adi Hindu movement in Uttar Pradesh) was inspired by the Adi Dravidas. Assertions of an aboriginal, pre-Aryan Dalit existence also occurred in coastal Andhra (Adi Andhra) and Karnataka (Adi Karnataka) too (Fuchs, 1999, 233; Juergensmeyer, 1982, 25–27). Like the → Satnamis among the Camar of Chhattisgarh (Dube, 1998; 1993; Parry, 1999), each of these movements formed around the idea of a religious community while aiming to build social formations separate from caste structures and outside of Hinduism (but also outside of Sikhism, Islam, and Christianity).

Anti-Brahman movements in South India, such as that of the low, but not untouchable, caste of Īzhava toddy tappers, were primarily motivated by a desire for upward social mobility. Their aim was not to critique or dismantle the overall social order, but to improve their own relative position in it. The Īzhava movement was initiated by Sri → Narayana Guru (b. 1854), who propagated a universalist, egalitarian philosophy of "one religion, one god, one caste" and, like other religious reformers, admonished his followers to give up alcohol, sexual license, and meat, thus effectively "Sanskritizing" the practices of his followers according to Brahmanical norms (Deliège, 1999, 153–155). However, in defiance of Brahmanical norms, the Īzhavas also struggled to gain access to temples for low and untouchable castes. In 1936 they achieved the opening of the Travancore Temple to all Hindus, which was followed by the lifting of similar restrictions elsewhere. According to R. Deliège (1999, 157), the heeding of this important demand of untouchable castes was a move to prevent large-scale conversions out of Hinduism, especially to Christianity in South India.

G. Shah (2004) has distinguished two kinds of Dalit cultural and religious movements: reformist and alternative ones. The former include *bhakti* movements all over the country from the 13th to the 17th century, which aimed to reform Hinduism from within, while the latter involved opting out of Hinduism. Apart from the formation of separate Dalit religious communities discussed above, many Dalits in various regions of the country chose conversion to Islam, Sikhism, Buddhism, and Christianity with a view to achieving dignity, equality of social status, and equal treatment. According the 2001 census, 2.3% of the population of India are Christians, of which an estimated 65% to 75% are Dalits (Lobo, 1996, 170). Though in the 19th and early 20th centuries vast numbers of Dalits converted to Christianity in the hope of achieving equality and freeing themselves of the stigma of untouchability (Grafe, 1990), their hopes have often been belied. Christian churches have succeeded neither to overcome the ideology of caste or the practice of untouchability among their members nor to remove status distinctions, which relegate Dalits to an inferior position in the church hierarchy, within which they do not hold high offices (Fernandes, 1981; Kooiman, 1989; Forrester, 1980; Webster, 1992). Thus conversions to Christianity, which are personal or collective rejections of Brahmanic values, dogma, and practices, have led to neither the expected social mobility nor recognition of a new religious identity (Fernandes, 1996). Caste ideology and practices continue to exercise their hold, so that neither the members of the new religious community accept Dalits as equals nor do the Hindus recognize the new religious identity sought by Dalits through conversion. Dalit Sikhs, or Mazhbis, also continue to bear the brunt of segregation and discrimination (Lobo, 1996, 179), while Dalit Muslims too are often disappointed by their failure to break out of the constraints of caste endogamy even if conversion secures freedom from Brahmanic domination.

Constitutional Measures and Critiques of the State

Dalit leaders have often contended that many more Dalits would have converted to Christianity or Islam were it not for the administrative provision that Dalit converts lose the benefits of reserved quotas in state educational institutions, public sector employment, and elections to legislature, while Dalits converting to Hinduism (as well as Sikhism and Buddhism) from other religions are eligible to take advantage of the provisions of positive discrimination enshrined in the Indian constitution. Reservations that guarantee places in state-run institutions of higher education, fixing quotas for employment by the (state and central) governments, and assigning seats in the parliament and the state assemblies were Ambedkar's major strategy for furthering Dalit equality. He institutionalized these measures in the Indian Constitution in 1950 as collective rights of disadvantaged communities, much before positive discrimination became a state strategy for the empowerment of African Americans in the United States, and before Western liberal democracies or Latin American constitutions recognized minority rights. The institution of protective reservations to promote the equalization of life chances of the disadvantaged reflects Ambedkar's commitment to emancipation through law and constitutionalism. The reservation policy was contested even before it was instituted, as some (for example, the anthropologist G.S. Ghurye, 1969) argued that the compensatory measures would reify rather than extinguish caste discrepancies. Not only have the reservations, which were intended to be of limited duration, been continually renewed, but also their scope has been extended to cover ever more groups and communities. In 1980 a commission under the chairmanship of parliamentarian B.P. Mandal recommended that the reservation policy should be widened to benefit, besides Dalits (constitutionally known as Scheduled Castes) and Ādivāsīs (Scheduled Tribes), other economically, socially, and educationally disadvantaged caste groups (so-called Other Backward Classes) as well. A commission headed by former chief justice Rajinder Sachar found in 2006 that Indian Muslims were economically, socially, and educationally highly disadvantaged compared to other religious communities (Sachar, 2006). In 2007 the National Commission for Religious and Linguistic Minorities found that Dalits remain discriminated against and excluded – and do hence not cease to be Dalits – after converting to Christianity or Islam (Misra, 2007). While the Sachar report fell short of recommending the introduction of quotas for Muslims, the Misra report demanded that Scheduled Caste reservations should include converted Dalits, and thus gave a new fillip to the debate about the inclusion of Muslim and Christian Dalits in the schedules for compensatory quotas.

The findings of the Mandal report drew heated criticism, and the implementation of its recommendations in 1989 was followed by massive protests including self-immolations of upper-caste students. But demands for, and achievement of, some measure of improvement in their status have also led to recurrent violent reprisals against Dalits in all regions of the country. Dalit self-assertion and claims to equality in the 1980s and 1990s were often met by the rape of Dalit women and killings – sometimes of entire households – especially in rural India, while Dalits in urban areas have had to face systematic discrimination with relation to housing and employment. Despite the institutionalization of quotas and the existence of legislation protecting them from so-called atrocities at the hands of other castes, the constitutional guarantee of equality has remained an unfulfilled promise for a majority of Dalits in the country.

Since the 1980s, Dalits have attempted to use international platforms to garner support for, and to press, their claims. Appealing to transnational Non-Government Organizations (NGOs) as well as United Nations bodies, Dalit activists have tried to get caste discrimination recognized as an international human rights issue. In 1996, a UN report acknowledged that the International Convention on the Elimination of All Forms of Racial Discrimination (ICERD; CERD, 1996) applies to Dalits. The report thus contradicted the position of the government of India, which had argued that ICERD only covers racial discrimination, whereas caste as a problematic specific to the Indian context was distinct from race. NGOs such as Human Rights Watch had also by then begun engaging the Dalit issue. In preparation for the 2001 World Conference against Racism, Racial Discrimination, Xenophobia, and Related Intolerance (WCAR) in Durban, the specifically Indian practices of caste discrimination were definitely linked to an international human rights discourse on discrimination based on race. While these developments were accompanied by a heated debate among social scientists in India on whether it is analytically or empirically acceptable to argue that caste is race in India (Bob, 2007; Reddy, 2005; Béteille, 2001; Visvanathan, 2001a; 2001b), they mark several important shifts in Dalit critiques of Brahmanism. Their critique is now primarily directed against the postcolonial Indian state rather than the upper castes. The specifically Indian problem of caste discrimination is now sought to be addressed as a human rights issue, whereby the discrimination and oppression of Dalits is articulated by sections of Dalit intellectuals and activists in terms of racial discrimination.

This re-articulation allows the Dalit question to resonate worldwide and to mobilize international anti-apartheid solidarity. Thus interestingly Dalit critiques of Brahmanism once again address questions of race, although they are grounded in a very different argument on racial difference compared to the earlier Aryan invasion hypothesis and colonial ethnology. Current Dalit critiques of Hinduism are no longer predicated on a taxonomy of difference but on a phenomenology of discrimination.

Bibliography

Ambedkar, B.R., "Castes in India: Their Mechanism, Genesis and Development: Paper Presented at an Anthropology Seminar Taught by Dr. A. A. Goldenweizer, Columbia University, 9th May 1916," in: *Dr. Babasaheb Ambedkar Writing and Speeches*, publ. Bombay Education Department, Government of Maharashtra, 1979, 3–22.

Bénéï, V., "Of Languages, Passions, and Interests: Education, Regionalism and Globalization in Maharashtra, 1800–2000," in: J. Assayag & C.J. Fuller, eds., *Globalizing India Perspectives from Below*, London, 2005, 141–162.

Béteille, A., "Race and Caste," *The Hindu*, Mar 10, 2001.

Bob, C., "'Dalit Rights Are Human Rights': Caste Discrimination, International Activism, and the Construction of a New Human Rights Issue," *HRQ* 29, 2007, 167–193.

CERD, "Concluding Observations of the Committee on the Elimination of Racial Discrimination: 49th Session, 17 Sep 1996," 1996, http://www.unhchr.ch/tbs/doc.nsf/(Symbol)/30d3c5041b55e561c12563e000500d33?Opendocument.

Charsley, S., "Sanskritization: The Career of an Anthropological Theory," *CIS* 32/2, 1998, 527–549.

Charsley, S., "'Untouchable': What Is in a Name?," *JRAI* 2/1, 1996, 1–23.

Dangle, A., *Poisoned Bread: Translations from Modern Marathi Dalit Literature*, Bombay, 1992.

Das, V., "Introduction: Social Sciences and the Public," in: V. Das, ed., *The Oxford India Companion to Sociology and Social Anthropology*, vol. I, Delhi, 2003, 1–29.

Deliège, R., *The Untouchables of India*, Oxford, 1999.

Dirks, N.B., *Castes of Mind: Colonialism and the Making of Modern India*, Princeton, 2001.

Dirks, N.B., "Recasting Tamil Society: The Politics of Caste and Race in Contemporary Southern India," in: C.J. Fuller, ed., *Caste Today*, Delhi, 1996, 263–295.

Dube, S., *Untouchable Pasts: Religion, Identity, and Power among a Central Indian Community, 1780–1950*, Albany, 1998.

Dube, S., "Idioms of Authority and Engendered Agendas: The Satnami Mahasabha, Chhattisgarh, 1925–1950," *IESHR* 30/4, 1993, 383–411.

Fernandes, W., "Conversion to Christianity, Caste Tension and Search for a New Identity in Tamil Nadu," in: W. Fernandez, ed., *The Emerging Dalit Identity: The Re-assertion of the Subalterns*, Delhi, 1996, 140–165.

Fernandes, W., *Caste and Conversion Movements in India: Religion and Human Rights*, Delhi, 1981.

Forrester, D.B., *Caste and Christianity: Attitudes and Policies on Caste of Anglo-Saxon Protestant Missions in India*, London, 1980.

Fuchs, M., "Ambedkar's Buddhism," in: T.N. Madan, ed., *India's Religions: Perspectives from Sociology and History*, New Delhi, 2004, 307–325.

Fuchs, M., *Kampf Um Differenz Repräsentation, Subjektivität Und Soziale Bewegungen Das Beispiel Indien*, Frankfurt am Main, 1999.

Galanter, M., *Competing Equalities Law and the Backward Classes in India*, Berkeley, 1984.

Ghurye, G.S., *Caste and Race in India*, Bombay, [5]1969.

Grafe, H., *History of Christianity in India*, vol. IV/2, Bangalore, 1990.

Heredia, R.C., *Changing Gods Rethinking Conversion in India*, New Delhi, 2007.

Ilaiah, K., "Productive Labor, Consciousness and History: The Dalitbahujan Alternative," in: D. Chakrabarty & S. Amin, eds., *Subaltern Studies IX: Writings on South Asian History and Society*, Delhi, 1996a, 165–200.

Ilaiah, K., *Why I Am Not a Hindu: A Sudra Critique of Hindutva, Philosophy, Culture, and Political Economy*, Calcutta, 1996b.

Juergensmeyer, M., *Religion as Social Vision: The Movement against Untouchability in 20th-Century Punjab*, Berkeley, 1982.

Kaviraj, S., "The Imaginary Institution of India," in: P. Chatterjee & G. Pandey, eds., *Subaltern Studies VII: Writings on South Asian History and Society*, vol. VII/1–40, Delhi, 1992.

Kooiman, D., *Conversion and Social Equality in India: The London Missionary Society in South Travancore in the 19th Century*, Delhi, 1989.

Lobo, L., "Dalit Religious Movements and Dalit Identity," in: W. Fernandes, ed., *The Emerging Dalit Identity: The Re-assertion of the Subalterns*, Delhi, 1996, 166–183.

Misra, R., *Report of the National Commission for Religious and Linguistic Minorities*, Delhi, 2007.

O'Hanlon, R., *Caste, Conflict, and Ideology: Mahatma Jotirao Phule and Low Caste Protest in Nineteenth-century Western India*, CSAS 30, Cambridge UK, 1985.

Omvedt, G., *Dalits and the Democratic Revolution: Dr. Ambedkar and the Dalit Movement in Colonial India*, New Delhi, 1994.

Parry, J.P., "Two Cheers for the Reservation," in: *Institutions and Inequalities: Essays in Honour of Andre Beteille*, New Delhi, 1999, 128–169.

Randeria, S., "Grenzziehungen und –Verschiebungen. Hindu-Nationalismus und die Politisierung Religiöser Identitäten im (Post-)Kolonialen Indien," in: J. Tröger, ed., *Streit der Kulturen*, Heidelberg, 2007, 67–102.

Randeria, S., "Carrion and Corpses: Conflict in Categorizing Untouchability in Gujarat," *EJS* 30/2, 1989, 171–191.

Reddy, D.S., "The Ethnicity of Caste," *AQ* 78/3, 2005, 543–584.

Sachar, R., *Social, Economic and Educational Status of the Muslim Community of India*, Delhi, 2006.

Shah, G., *Social Movements in India: A Review of the Literature*, New Delhi, ^{2}2004.

Srinivas, M.N., *Marriage and Family in Mysore*, New York, 1978.

Srinivas, M.N., *Religion and Society among the Coorgs of South India*, Bombay, repr. 1965.

Trautmann, T.R., *Aryans and British India*, Berkeley, 1997.

Visvanathan, S., "Durban and Dalit Discourse," *EPW* 36/33, 2001a, 3123–3127.

Visvanathan, S., "The Race for Caste: Prolegomena to the Durban Conference," *EPW* 36/27, 2001b, 2512–2516.

Viswanath, R., "A Textbook Case of Exclusion," *The Indian Express*, Jul 13, 2012.

Webster, J.C.B., *The Dalit Christians: A History*, Delhi, 1992.

Zelliot, E., *From Untouchable to Dalit: Essays on the Ambedkar Movement*, New Delhi, 1992.

Roger Begrich & Shalini Randeria

Ecology

While Hindus have rich resources for approaching questions of ecology, any discussion of Hinduism and ecology must begin with awareness that comprehensive notions of the environment as a fragile and endangered aspect of existence – as are widely shared today – were not historically part of the tradition. Even less, obviously, was there in traditional India any consciousness of an "environmental crisis" on a global scale. Indeed, none of this was part of any religious tradition until quite recently. As R.R. Ruether has pointed out, "there is no ready-made ecological spirituality and ethic in past traditions" (1992, 206). In 1967, L. White famously identified religion – specifically Christianity – as a fundamental source of the environmental problem. Simultaneously, he suggested religion, or at least certain kinds of religion, as the cure. Since the publication of L. White's article, the relation of religious worldviews and practice to environmental awareness has engaged the interest of increasing numbers of academics and activists, inside the religious traditions as well as outside, and the literature on the topic is now vast.

Many writers have suggested Asian religion as a potential source of ideas to counter the notions of anthropocentric dominion identified by L. White as stemming from Christianity. Hinduism in particular has been among the traditions frequently singled out as an important source of a world-sacralizing vision that postulates a humanity "close to nature." This attention has not gone unnoticed by insiders, and a number of Hindu writers and activists have echoed these themes. Recent scholarship is cautious here, however, and claims about Hindu attitudes toward nature have been questioned, or at least problematized, in the same way in which they have been for other religious traditions.

The Hindu tradition embodies a wide variety of perceptions of nature. Some of these stand in conflict with others, as we shall see below. There are visions that support reverence for aspects of nature, recognizing them as manifestations of divinity. These are complemented by customs, precepts, and religious ordinances that enjoin stewardship and protection of elements of the natural world. However, there are also significant voices that take a world-denying stance, suggesting that the natural world is insignificant (*tuccha*) in relation to authentic spiritual awareness. Especially in courtly poetry and drama (Kāvya), there are passages that express a refined aesthetic awareness of natural phenomena. Yet one does not find the late modern awareness of nature as nature, viewed as a totality and valued intrinsically for its pristine beauty, diversity, and so on. And as always in any religious tradition, when we move from authoritative precept to actual practice, the contrast may be glaring, even contradictory. There is also the danger of reading contemporary concerns into ancient texts, which leads to anachronism, romanticism, or both. Contemporary Hindu environmentalism is a significant development, but – like Christian, Jewish, or Buddhist environmentalism – it is a strategic reconfiguration of inherited material, representing an "*interpretation of tradition* rather than a *traditional interpretation*" (Tomalin, 2009, 4). There is a good deal of material in the Hindu world that would lend itself to eco-friendly reconstructions and repurposing. There are also elements that contemporary Hindu environmentalists might wish to deemphasize.

Potential Resources

Turning to scriptural sources, one must start with the → Vedas, which are recognized by Hindus as the most ancient source of their tradition. The poetry of the Vedas was a key element in what became a complex system of sacrificial rites (see → *yajña*). Animal sacrifice was part of this ritual, as Buddhist critics were very much aware. This violence toward animals notwithstanding, the vedic hymns venerate, indeed even divinize, aspects of nature. Natural phenomena such as the earth, the dawn, fire, and wind were personified as deities. → Sarasvatī – a river important to the vedic peoples – was worshipped as a goddess; *soma* – a plant with psychotropic properties – was used in ritual and venerated as a deity, as well as being identified with the moon. The *Pṛthvīsūkta* (Hymn to the Earth) of the *Atharvaveda* praises the earth as a goddess, Devī Vasundharā, and as a mother (*AV.* 12.12) who "bestows wealth liberally" (*AV.* 12.44). The appropriation of her gifts must not, however, exceed the bounds of sustainability: "What, O earth, I dig out of thee, quickly shall that grow again: may I not, O pure one, pierce thy vital spot, (and) not thy heart!" (*AV.* 12.35; trans. Bloomfield, 1973).

The *Puruṣasūkta* (Hymn to the Supreme Person; *ṚV.* 10.90) describes creation in terms of the sacrificial dismembering of a divine "person" (*puruṣa*). Parts of the sacrificed divinity, we are told, became specific elements of the natural world:

> The moon was born from his mind; from his eye the sun was born. Indra and Agni came from his mouth, and from his vital breath the Wind was born. From his navel the middle realm of space arose; from his head the sky evolved. From his two feet came the earth, and the quarters of the sky from his ear. (*ṚV.* 10.90.13–14; trans. Doniger, 1981)

This image of creation by divine dismemberment prefigures a signature notion of Hindu theology: that the universe itself is formed of the substance of the divine.

This mode of thought, which clearly distinguishes the Hindu vision from that of Abrahamic monotheism, is confirmed in the → Upaniṣads. In these texts, the central topic of interest is the one ultimate being, → *brahman*, which transcends and is prior to the multiple gods of the vedic pantheon. Importantly, *brahman* does not create the world as an external product but rather becomes it: "May I become many!" (*ChāU.* 6.2.3; *TaiU.* 2.6.1). Moving from myth to philosophical theology, the Upaniṣads proclaim, "All this, verily, is *brahman*" (*ChāU.* 3.14.1). They thus provide key support for nondualism (*advaita*), later formalized and extensively developed in several schools of theology. In Hindu nondualism, the world is inseparable from ultimate reality, as indeed is the true spiritual self (→ *ātman*) of all beings. On the basis of this outlook, the idea that Hinduism sees all of nature as sacred and worthy of reverence has achieved wide circulation. For example, S.C. Crawford has argued that the "unitive view" of the Upaniṣads supports "veneration of the natural world" (1982, 149–150). E. Deutsch finds in this strand of Hindu thought an "emanationist" theory of creation, the logical corollary of which is that "fundamentally all life is one" and that everything in nature has "intrinsic spiritual worth." This perception, he argues, "finds its natural expression in a reverence for all living things" (Deutsch, 1970, 80–83). The extent to which these visions have been diffused beyond the Sanskrit-literate, religious elite – and whether, even if they have, the impact has been supportive of environmental concern remains the subject of legitimate questioning, as we shall see below.

The → *Bhagavadgītā* has in recent centuries become an immensely popular text for Hindus, both in India and in the diaspora. It reaffirms, from a theistic perspective, the upanishadic vision of the inseparability of the world and the divine. God's universal form (*viśvarūpa*) encompasses both the heavens and the earth – and indeed all beings – creating a sacralized view of the world. Lord → Kṛṣṇa, the divine incarnation (→ *avatāra*), declares the following: "Of all manifestations, I am the beginning, the end, and the middle" (*BhG.* 10.32). Kṛṣṇa identifies himself with elements of the natural universe: sun, moon, and stars, the ocean, the Himalayas, the wind, and the holy → Gaṅgā. The enlightened eye, he proclaims, "sees me in all things, and all things in me" (*BhG.* 6.30). In the "vision of the universal form," recounted in chapter 11, Kṛṣṇa invites Arjuna, his pupil, to see in his body "the entire universe, moving and unmoving" (*BhG.* 11.7), thus suggesting the later Vaiṣṇava doctrine of the world as the body of god. Arjuna, rapt in this cosmic vision, echoes the *Puruṣasūkta*: "You are that ancient person (*sanātanas tvaṁ puruṣaḥ*)... The sun and the moon are your eyes" (*BhG.* 11.18–19).

The *Bhagavadgītā* supplements this world-sacralizing vision with an ascetic ethic of selfless activity in the world. This is the well-known teaching of *karmayoga*. Instead of following the path of literal renunciation, devotees of Kṛṣṇa are urged to remain in ordinary life, fulfilling their religious duties (→ *dharma*) and working without egoism, desire, or attachment for the "maintenance" of the world (*lokasaṃgraha*; *BhG.* 3.20). Their motivation should be concern for the "welfare of all beings" (*sarvabhūtahita*; *BhG.* 5.25; 12.4). This ideal of engaging with the world for its betterment in a detached, spiritually centered manner was important for → Gandhi's religiously motivated social activism, as well as for other 19th-century Hindu nationalists such as Balwantrao Gangadhar Tilak. The latter saw in the *Bhagavadgītā*'s message a divine "call to action" and a creed of "Energism" (Nelson, 2000, 132). This aspect of the ethics of the *Bhagavadgītā* continues to be important for environmental activism in contemporary India, as we shall see below.

The idea of the world as the manifestation of the supreme God, adumbrated in the earlier texts, reaches its full flower in the later theistic, devotional traditions of Hinduism. Famously, the *Viṣṇupurāṇa* declares, "Verily, this whole [world] is the body of God" (*tat sarvaṃ vai hareḥ tanuḥ*; *ViP*. 1.12.38). This vision is echoed by the great Vaiṣṇava theologian → Rāmānuja (11th cent. CE), who speaks of the world and God under the metaphor of body (*śarīra*) and embodied (*śarīrin*). The Kṛṣṇaite theologian → Vallabha (16th cent. CE) speaks eloquently of the "pure nonduality" (Śuddhādvaita) of God and world. In his *Siddhāntamuktāvalī* (5–9), he explains that the river Gaṅgā has three aspects: physical, as water; ritual, as a pilgrimage site; and spiritual, as a goddess. Further, he asserts that proper worship of Gaṅgā Devī, the goddess Gaṅgā, includes honoring her embodiment in, and as, the holy river. No devotee would worship her as goddess only, neglecting the river. Extending the argument, he argues that, in the same way, worship of the supreme being as Kṛṣṇa includes reverencing his manifestation as the world, which is nothing less than his cosmic embodiment.

Continuing vedic precedent, Vaiṣṇavas divinize the earth. → Bhūdevī ("Goddess Earth") is → Viṣṇu's spouse, and the lord himself descends as *avatāra* to rescue her when she is abducted by a demon. Before rising in each morning, devout Vaiṣṇavas ask Bhūdevī to forgive the abusive touch of their feet. V.R. Nagarajan has studied the *kōlam* rites of South India, in which women make beautiful ritual patterns (*kōlam*) on the earth as offerings to Bhūdevī (see → *raṅgolī* and *kōlam*). Through this practice, women recollect their dependence on Bhūdevī as well as acknowledge the debt that they owe her. One informant stated,

> We draw the *kōlam* as our first ritual act in the morning to remember Bhū Devī. We walk on her. We spit on her; we poke her; we burden her. We expect her to bear us and all the activities we do on her with endless patience. So, we do the *kōlam*. (Nagarajan, 1998, 270)

India herself is regarded as a goddess by many devout Hindus, with Mother India (Bhārat Mātā) being represented in association with a map of India, or even by the map alone. India's national song, *Bande Mātaram* (I Bow to Thee, O Mother), composed during the struggle for independence by the Bengali poet and novelist Bankim Chandra Chattopadhyay (1838–1894), addresses the land as goddess:

> I bow to thee, Mother, / richly-watered, richly-fruited, / cool with the winds of the south, / dark with the crops of the harvests, /... her lands clothed beautifully with her trees in flowering bloom. (National Portal of India)

While the concept of Mother India is a fairly recent development, and one obviously not without political overtones, the sense that the subcontinent has a sacred geography has a long history and is deeply seated in Hindu consciousness. I will consider the phenomena of sacred rivers and sacred groves below. For now, it will suffice to underline the reality that – for Hindus – sacred rivers, forests, mountains, and other natural features, along with associated temples, are embedded in a network of interconnecting pilgrimage routes, valorized in myth, forming what amounts to a sacred topography. In the myth of Satī, spouse of → Śiva, the goddess's body is dismembered and the parts scattered throughout the subcontinent (see → Pārvatī). Such was the origin, we are told, of an important network of goddess temples (*śāktipīṭhas*) and pilgrimage centers. The myth and the system of interrelated shrines – most typically counted as 51 – establish a unified religious geography. D. Kinsley observes,

> Taken together, the *pīṭhas* constitute or point toward a transcendent (or, perhaps better, a universally immanent) goddess whose being encompasses, underlies, infuses, and unifies the Indian subcontinent as a whole. (Kinsley, 1998, 230)

Similar sacred geographies are established by the system of 12 Śiva shrines known as the *jyotirliṅgas* and, on a regional level, the network of the 8 Gaṇeśas (*aṣṭavināyaks*; see → Gaṇapati/Gaṇeśa) and their temples in Maharashtra. The latter maps the Maharashtrian homeland religiously and gives identity and a compelling sense of rootedness to Maharashtrians.

On a still smaller scale are the religious maps of individual pilgrimage centers. Perhaps the best example is the holy town of Vrindavan and its environs, associated with the earthly sojourn – and ongoing spiritual presence – of Kṛṣṇa. The locations of a multitude of cherished episodes in the deity's life are traced out by pilgrims in ritual circumambulations that charge the region with a sacred aura keenly appreciated by devotees (Haberman, 1994). As D.L. Eck notes,

> At the heart of Krishna pilgrimage is the process of remembering and telling the tale of the places where Krishna lived and grew up in the area known as Braj or Vraja in Sanskrit... Here

> more than anywhere else in India, the story lines and pilgrimage tracks are interwoven in a continuous narrative, creating a sacred landscape in which the story is inscribed in the topography. (Eck, 2012, 348–349)

In Hindu ritual traditions, a → *maṇḍala* is a sacred diagram, making present the power of a deity. Interestingly, the term is also used in reference to pilgrimage places, and the sacred land of Kṛṣṇa around Vrindavan is referred to as Braj Maṇḍal, the sacred circle of Braj (Eck, 2012, 354). Vrindaban and other pilgrimage sites have been the focus of religiously motivated environmental activism in recent years (Narayanan, 2001, 189–191; Tomalin, 2009, 137–145).

Turning to the Hindu law books (→ Dharmaśāstra) and other texts dealing with *dharma* (religious and social duty), it is not hard to find prescripts and admonitions that could today be read as eco-friendly. Scholars have argued with some real justification that the texts promoting *dharma* – which focus specifically on the ethical behavior of the laity – have historically "had more direct relevance to this-worldly behavior" than have the texts on theology (Narayanan, 2000, 114). The Dharmaśāstras include laws designed to protect – in various ways – animals, trees, rivers, land, and so on. These prescriptions have been translated into homilies and edifying stories in the → Purāṇas, which, though written in Sanskrit, have long been expounded orally in local vernaculars by professional storytellers in temple, festival, and other ritual contexts. While one might well emphasize again that these texts are not speaking out of the kind of environmental concern that we have today, they nevertheless "advocate conservation and demonstrate an awareness of the impact of human interaction with the environment" (McGee, 2000, 80). The *dharma* of protecting the land is assigned especially to the ruler, as is reflected in a significant number of synonyms for king in Sanskrit – for instance, *bhūpāla* and *bhūpa* (earth protector) and *bhūbharaṇa* and *bhūbhartṛ* (earth maintainer; McGee, 2000, 63). There is a noticeable degree of anthropocentric instrumentalism here; the king must regulate the use of the earth's resources in ways that benefit his subjects. Still, consciousness of humankind's dependence on nature is not absent. The sovereign must ensure that resources are used sustainably and punish those who exceed prescribed limits. Tree planting and crop rotation are prescribed. Fines and other sanctions are established for the protection of animals from cruelty, trees from wanton cutting, and water from pollution. M. McGee remarks,

> It is clear from many classical Indian texts on the duties of kings that a king had a responsibility to reap the benefits of the nature's resources for the sake of his kingdom and its citizens; yet it is also clear that the successful and ideal king had to carefully manage these resources and respect the earth. (McGee, 2000, 73)

A.G. Gold has studied the environmental consciousness of villagers in Rajasthan, North India. She describes the villagers' memory of Vansh Pradip Singh, the last ruler of the then state of Sarwar. During Singh's 30-plus-year reign, there is evidence that "the jungle was dense and wild animals were prosperous" (Gold, 2000, 320). In 1947, Vansh Pradip Singh died with no heir. In any event, that was the year of India's Independence, when the old royal families lost their temporal power. Villagers in Ghatiyali, part of the former kingdom, told A.G. Gold that their region has undergone rapid deforestation since then. The people had fond memories linking "the former ruling kings, old growths of indigenous trees, and wild animals." Indeed, in the villagers' minds, "these three came to an end together" (Gold, 2000, 321). Vansh Pradip Singh was well known for the extraordinary proclamation, "If you cut the smallest branch of a tree it is just as if you cut my finger" (Gold, 2000, 323). A.G. Gold argues that this striking image expressed the king's "responsible authority" (*zimmedārī*) for the preservation of the land, a jurisdiction that was "personal, immediate, and physically realized" (2000, 321).

The idea of responsible care of the environment does not, of course, apply to kings only. In view of India's contemporary crisis of deforestation, it is noteworthy, for example, that the law books recommend the planting of trees as a general obligation. Thus *Viṣṇudharmasūtra* (3.297.113) says, "There is no fall in hell for the planter of trees" (quoted by Kane, 1974, 415). The evil of destruction of trees and the meritoriousness of tree planting are likewise celebrated in puranic texts. The *Matsyapurāṇa* describes a tree festival (*vṛkṣotsava*) in which existing trees are gaily decorated and saplings are planted. The text proclaims, "A person who plants even one (*ekam api*) tree will assuredly dwell in heaven (*svarga*) for 30,000 years of [the god] Indra" (*MatP.* 59.18). Other promised benefits include the liberation of one's ancestors and freedom from rebirth on earth. The

Varāhapurāṇa (172) recounts the tale of the noble merchant Gokarṇa, who encountered a group of tree nymphs who were distressingly pale and disfigured, with bleeding wounds on their bodies. "Their wailing sound," we are told, "resembled the cry of Kurari birds" (*VaP*. 172.21; trans. Venkitasubramonia Iyer, 1985). The source of their pain was the destruction of their trees by minions of an unnamed king of Ayodhya:

> The king's men tormented us by their cutting and uprooting... We became miserable and hence the present appearance. We are without flowers, left but with the root and trunk. Thus we are reduced with loss of our identity. (*VaP*. 172.30–31; trans. Venkitasubramonia Iyer, 1985)

Showing sensitivity to the benefits of trees for both humans and nonhumans, the nymphs proceeded to instruct Gokarṇa on their value:

> He who plants a peepal, a margosa, a banyan, ten flowering plants, two pomegranates, two oranges and five mangoes never goes to hell... The learned people declare a tree to be like a son because it provides materials for domestic life, provides shelter for small animals, twice in a year birds breed in it and it provides fruits to the originator throughout the year. (*VaP*. 172.39, 43–44; trans. Venkitasubramonia Iyer, 1985)

The nymphs provided Gokarṇa with a magical flying vehicle, and by using it he was able to visit the king and convince him to rectify the damage and restore the trees. The *Matsyapurāṇa* takes the analogy between trees and sons further. Questioned by the gods as to why she treated trees as if they were her own children, Pārvatī, the mother of the universe, replied, "One tree is equal to ten sons" (*MatP*. 154.512; see Narayanan, 2000).

The truth is that the experience of sacrality as associated with trees and forests is widespread in the Hindu tradition. Hindu temples, especially in South India, are likely to have on their grounds a sacred tree, usually large and dignified by age. The *sthālavṛkṣa* (tree of the holy place), as it is called, is typically venerated by circumambulation and other forms of ritual decoration and homage (Narayanan, 2000, 116). In Hindu religious literature from the vedic period onward, the forest has been portrayed as the prototypical abode of sages (→ *ṛṣis*) and ascetics (*tapasvins*), as the ideal site for religious retreats (*āśrama*), and especially as the most congenial and sought-out site of ascetic practice (→ *tapas*). This tendency is well illustrated in the → *Rāmāyaṇa*, the great epic in which → Rāma and his spouse Sītā spend a period of exile in the forest, and also in the designation *tapovana* (austerity forest), used in classical Hindu literature and even today for woods near holy places, parks near temples and monasteries, and in monastic names.

Problematizing Sacred Rivers, Earth, and Groves

The brief survey above reveals that there is a considerable amount of material in Hindu history that would lend itself to ecological reinterpretation and application. But one should be cautious about any attempts to pronounce Hinduism an "ecological" religion based on concepts such as those discussed above. Hindu attitudes toward nature are complex, and there are any number of traditional approaches to nature, including some already mentioned, that are problematic from a contemporary environmentalist point of view.

Much has been made of the idea that the Hindu worldview encourages the sacralization of nature, on the supposition that this should somehow translate into ecologically sensitive attitudes and behaviors. There has been considerable scholarship on this issue in recent years, particularly as it pertains to sacred rivers. This research reveals a highly ambiguous situation. Indeed, we now see that the whole question of the value for ecology of the sacralization of nature or aspects of nature is not at all as straightforward as it might appear to be.

The sacredness of the Gaṅgā River is the most widely discussed example. As indicated above, the Gaṅgā is a goddess, Gaṅgā Devī, in addition to being a physical river. As such, she is an object of worship. Religiously speaking, her water is not only inherently pure but also powerfully purifying (Alley, 1998, 301). Pilgrims flock to the river for ritual bathing, which is understood to be spiritually cleansing, purging one of lifetimes of karmic and other religious impurities. Gaṅgā water (*gaṅgājāl*) is bottled, both privately by devotees and commercially, for ritual use throughout India and abroad. The religious ethos surrounding the river is conveyed powerfully by a story of a king who spent a night on the banks of the river. He woke during the night and witnessed a group of women going to bathe in the sacred waters. Although they were besmeared with filth, they stepped from their bath radiantly clean and then disappeared. His curiosity piqued, the king returned to the river several nights in a row. Each time, the same drama was repeated, until the king could no longer keep silent. "Who are you?" he asked them. They replied, "We are the rivers of India. Every day, the people bathe in us, and we absorb all their sin. We come to the Ganges so that we ourselves may be purified" (Narayanan, 2000, 116). In short, because Gaṅgā is the supreme purifier, she cannot be polluted.

Sadly, of course, Gaṅgā is terribly polluted – and obviously so. Segmented thinking on this topic is supported by a cultural distinction between ritual-spiritual purity and physical cleanliness. In this context, an object can be ritually pure but physically dirty, or the reverse (Alley, 1998, 306–313). Hence, the devout are able to retain their traditional beliefs about the river despite the empirical evidence. This means that they remain defensive in face of any suggestion that Gaṅgā is polluted, and the belief in the sacrality of the river vastly complicates efforts to mobilize cleanup (Alley, 1998).

The Kāvērī River in South India is regarded as the Dakṣiṇā Gaṅgā (Gaṅgā of the South) and Kāvērī Ammaṉ (Mother Kāvērī). Like Gaṅgā Devī, she is divinized, in this case as the consort of Lord Viṣṇu, and she is celebrated as such in folklore and festival and worshipped in temples. When the river is swollen by monsoon rains, Kāvērī Ammaṉ is said to be pregnant. V. Narayanan describes how Tamilians during this season used to celebrate the river's "pregnancy food cravings" by taking picnics to the riverbank:

> Kaveri Amman was the guest at every picnic. Just as the food cravings of pregnant women were indulged by the family, Kaveri Amman's extended family celebrated her life-giving potential by frolicking and picnicking with her. (Narayanan, 2000, 118)

V. Narayanan reports that this is still the custom, "when there is water." This qualification alludes to the sad fact that hydropower dams in the neighboring state of Karnataka have radically reduced the flow in Tamil Nadu, so that Mother Kāvērī's life-giving powers seem stunted (Narayanan, 2000, 117–118). During the summer of 2012, with a drought threatening, politicians in both states continued to squabble over her waters (*Times of India*, Jul 23, 2012).

V. Nagarajan's study of the South Indian *kōlam* ritual has already been mentioned. In thinking through the meaning of the beautiful ritual designs placed on the ground as offerings to Bhūdevī, the earth goddess, V. Nagarajan sees human–nature interaction as embedded within complex cultural webs. Thus, what strikes the outsider as obviously "ecological" may not be interpreted that way from the perspective of those on the inside. V. Nagarajan writes,

> I was puzzled by the contradiction between women's reverence for Bhū Devī and their seeming disrespect to her throughout the day, as they threw trash and garbage on the earth, the very same place that they considered to be sacred. (Nagarajan, 1998, 275)

The behavior seems contradictory. By way of explanation, V. Nagarajan suggests the notion of "intermittent sacrality." Awareness of sacred presence cannot, in practice, be sustained for prolonged periods. Holiness is not necessarily a fixed attribute. Given the weakness of human attentiveness, it may fluctuate. Alternately, the ritual connection that constitutes sacrality may atrophy or expire, to be revived again by a subsequent reenactment (Nagarajan, 1998, 277–280).

An aspect of nature's being considered sacred is not necessarily, therefore, a guarantee that there will be an environmental benefit. Paradoxically – as K.D. Alley, V. Nagarajan, E. Tomalin (2009, 155–168), and others have noted – the sacralization of nature may in practice work to subvert ecologically sound attitudes and behaviors. Especially problematic in this respect is the association of nature with maternal goddess imagery. If nature is portrayed as protecting, cleansing, and forgiving, the conclusion may be that "she" needs no reciprocal protection from humans. As V. Nagarajan observes, "The natural world is a divine being and is therefore capable of cleaning herself" (1998, 277). Likewise, K.D. Alley (1998, 312) reports that Hindus in Banaras "remark that Gaṅgā, like a good mother, cleans up the messes her children make and forgives them lovingly." This line of thought obviously invites a feminist hermeneutic. The abuse of nature in India, especially rivers valorized as goddesses, and the abuse of women are juxtaposed by V. Narayanan:

> One can say that the assaults on nature in India and the assaults on women through the new greed-crime of dowry deaths in the last decade has been unprecedented in the religious tradition. The rivers, flowing through India and personified as women… have absorbed the greed and follies of human beings and the slime, sludge, and excreta of human greed and consumption. It is hard not to draw a comparison between the rivers and the plight of women who are now the target of crimes of greed and power. (Narayanan, 2000, 118)

Similar problematics may be noted in connection with sacred groves. The phenomenon of the sacred grove – a wooded area set apart and protected on account of association with spirits or divinities – is well attested in human religious history in many parts of the world. Although the number is diminishing, India is at the present time said to have more than 13 thousand sacred groves (Jain, 2011, 79). It seems likely that the practice of keeping sacred groves in Hindu traditions filtered up from animistic tribal practice. For many → Ādivāsī, or indigenous, peoples in India, the sacred grove is of central cultural importance (Parajuli, 2001, 101–102). The configuration of sacred groves varies: more or less undisturbed forest set-asides, groves of trees associated with temples, and small patches of trees with a small shrine or even a sacred rock as a focal point. In some, sacrality is diffused and unfocused; in others, there may be a Hindu temple with formal ritual conducted by priests. In general, custom requires that the area, and all its vegetation, remain untouched, though there may be some exceptions, such as for the building or repairing of shrines in the grove or other special circumstances. Dire punishments are predicted for violating the taboos, and stories recount the discomfort, often severe, of those who dared break them. For this reason, sacred groves have been seen as "hotspots of biodiversity" (Tomlin, 2009, 155). In addition to their actual or potential function as refuges for diverse flora and fauna, sacred groves have attracted considerable attention among conservationists as offering other environmental benefits, including the protection of water sources and the retention of ground water. The groves have at the same time played into the thinking of those who are disposed to find nature worship in indigenous and Hindu religious practice. As A. Nugteren observes,

> sacred groves have become something of a vogue among botanists and ecologists. They have become part of the romantic imagination about a pristine, bountiful, and respectfully treated natural environment in India. (Nugteren, 2005, 421)

There is no question that some sacred groves serve certain invaluable functions, and it is clear that this cultural construct could be, and indeed has been, promoted by activists in explicitly environmental directions (Jain, 2011). Nevertheless, it is clear that the protection of trees and other species in a particular area is not a recognition of their sacrality in general. Indeed, sacred groves in many parts of India are associated – in origin if not always in contemporary practice – with the destructive slash-and-burn techniques of shifting cultivation (Nugteren, 2005, 418). Likewise – in cases in which a designated tract of trees is regarded as belonging to a deity – their protection is more likely a statement of regard for the deity than evidence of respect for the intrinsic value of the trees themselves or nature more generally. Moreover, the assumption that sacred groves protect pristine, old-growth forests or endemic species is far from universally valid. R. Freeman, for instance, has noted examples of sacred groves

> developed from what was once a stand of cultivated toddy-palms, from small stands of shrubbery on laterite hillocks, and in one case, from an old tank in the midst of paddy fields. (Freeman, 1994, 11)

Sadly, exploitation for commercial purposes is not the only peril facing sacred groves in India. Among the many threats that have been identified is the process of "Hinduization," which often involves an indigenous deity being identified as a manifestation of a major Hindu god or goddess. This may lead to encroachments such as the clearing of ground for construction of more elaborate, canonical Hindu temples, provision for regular worship, increased pedestrian traffic, and other intrusions (Nugteren, 2005, 425). In the words of environmental scholar and activist Madhav Gadgil,

> when the Brahmin priests take over, and [a] more sort of institutionalized religion comes into play, the worship of nature gives way to the worship of idols in the temple and the sacred groves tend to be cut down. (Interview with Tomalin; cited by Tomalin, 2009, 158)

Reincarnation, Anthropocentrism, and Animals

The doctrine of reincarnation (*punarbhava*) is, of course, central to the Hindu view of reality. All beings, we are told, are on a long journey across uncountable lifetimes toward *mokṣa* (→ liberation). Significantly, this is an interspecies journey, and each human being has a heritage of lives in animal and even plant forms. Thus, we are not the only beings with souls. "From [the god] Brahmā down to a blade of grass," the teaching goes, all beings are endowed with spirit, or *ātman*. All but a small minority of Hindu theologians are agreed that this endowment is qualitatively identical in all beings, who thus have equal spiritual potential. The idea that humans are not radically separated from other species is a key assumption undergirding the ideals of nonviolence (→ *ahiṃsā*) and vegetarianism. While the latter values seem to have originated outside the orthodox Hindu fold – among Jain, Buddhist, and other nonvedic ascetics – they have become an important part of the ethics of India's majority Hindu population (Bryant, 2006; Nelson, 2006).

Hinduism, of course, is known for its reverencing of certain sacred animals. In part, this may be due to the associations of animals with divinity in Hindu myth. Divine incarnations (*avatāras*) appear in animal (the boar, the fish) or part-animal (the man-lion) form. There are animal-formed deities, such as Gaṇeśa, and animal vehicles (→ *vāhanas*) associated with all major gods and goddesses. The cow, especially, is regarded as a symbol of the nurturing aspect of the divine as mother. Other sacred animals include especially the monkey, associated with the much-loved simian god → Hanumān, loyal servant of Rāma. Still, the Hindu world is not an entirely safe space for animals. Although increasingly peripheral, the role of animal sacrifice plays a significant role up to the present, as in the worship of the goddess → Kālī (Nelson, 2006). Moreover, conditions of life in much of India create situations in which animal welfare may be of lower priority than human survival needs.

Despite the doctrine of reincarnation, with its implication that the spiritual potential of all beings is equal, the Hindu tradition remains markedly anthropocentric. There is a recognized hierarchy of births, with human birth as the highest. This is because only humans, with rare exceptions, may attain *mokṣa*. Thus the → Vedānta theologian → Śaṅkara (c. 650–700 CE), in his *Vivekacūḍāmaṇi* (v. 3), reckons human birth among prizes "rarely attained, and then only by the grace of God." However, humans who commit evil deeds are threatened with rebirth in the "stinking wombs" (*kapūyāṃ yonim*; *ChāU.* 5.10.7) of animals such as dogs or pigs or even insects. Animal existence then becomes a form of penal suffering (Nelson, 2006, 185–186).

Hindu Thought as World Denying

If the sacralization of aspects of nature in Hindu myth and ritual is in some ways problematic for the environment, what of the claims that Hindu theology implies reverence for the entire universe? The claim is not without basis, as we have seen already. Still, there is ambiguity on this score as well. J.B. Callicott observes, "the Hindu tradition of monism and mysticism... has ambivalent implications for environmental ethics." He continues,

> Looked at from the Hindu perspective, therefore, the empirical world is both unimportant, because it is not ultimately real, and contemptible, because it seduces the soul into crediting appearances, pursuing false ends. (Callicott, 1994, 47–48)

This kind of thinking is certainly present in the tradition, especially in the classical formulation of Advaita Vedānta (Nelson, 1998). Still, Advaita is only one among many forms of Hindu theology. It certainly must be taken into account when discussing Hindu views of nature. However, by labeling the view that he describes "the Hindu perspective," J.B. Callicott makes one particular expression of Hindu theology representative of the whole multifaceted tradition.

As formulated by Śaṅkara, Advaita Vedānta accepts and argues forcefully for the sole reality of *brahman*, the absolute. Nothing, we are told, exists apart from *brahman*. Indeed, as Śaṅkara comments on *Brahmasūtra* 3.14.1, "the world is non-different from *brahman*." Śaṅkara achieves his nondualism, however, not by elevating the world to the status of the divine but by dismissing it as a false appearance, an ontologically dubious product of → *māyā* (Nelson, 1998). We find here, in fact, the same kind of hierarchical dualism of god/world, spirit/matter, soul/body, and so on that has been identified by any number of writers as a signature contribution of the West. Serious followers of Advaita are advised to practice discrimination (*viveka*) between things eternal (*nitya*) and non-eternal (*anitya*). We read in the *Aparokṣānubhūti* (v. 4), a manual of nondualist spirituality attributed to Śaṅkara, an exhortation to cultivate "disregard for all objects – from the god Brahmā down to plants and minerals – like the indifference one has toward the excrement of a crow (*kākaviṣṭha*)." This is the viewpoint to which J.B. Callicott alludes. It is true that other Vedānta traditions argue against Advaita for the full reality of the world. Nevertheless, they also typically advocate a hierarchy of being in which spiritual realms (*śuddhasattva, goloka*, etc.), along with corresponding spiritual bodies (*siddhadeha*), are more highly valued than the worlds and bodies of gross matter (Nelson, 2000, 138).

The final religious goal for most Hindus is a complete transcendence of the natural world. *Mokṣa*, or liberation, is most commonly conceived as entailing freedom from the cycles of rebirth (→ *saṃsāra*) in this world of pain and frustration (*duḥkha*). Hindu myths of cyclic time support this ambition. Within vast timescales encompassing billions, even trillions, of years, they convey a powerful vision of a world that is declining slowly but inevitably toward increasing levels of chaos. According to this vision, the dark age, or *kaliyuga* (see → cosmic cycles), represents a downward spiral of moral impoverishment, and this decay on the level of human character reverberates throughout the physical environment. Moreover, things are only getting worse (Narayanan, 2001, 180–181). Some would argue that contemporary Hindus take such images metaphorically, and it may well be that the *kaliyuga* construct is nowadays primarily a mechanism for coping when the experience of corruption, rampant greed, and social decay becomes overwhelming. Nevertheless, the ideas of an inexorably declining world and the possibility of release therefrom make up a complex that reinforces the world-negating, spirit/matter dualism discussed above. To the extent that they are still meaningful, these concepts create potential religious disincentives to engagement for environmental change.

All this being said, the world-denying aspect of Hindu theology can easily be overstated. It must be stressed that Hindu theologians and mystics have conceived forms of nondualism other than the classical Advaita, visions that emphatically do not exclude the world from the realm of spirit. For example, much of practical Hindu spirituality is influence by tantric thought, which has a profoundly sacramental view of reality. Thus in tantric theology (see → Tantra) particularly but not exclusively in forms focused on → Mahādevī ("The Great Goddess"), the world principle is understood as the creative energy (→ *śakti*) of the deity. Identified as the very substance of nature (→ *prakṛti*) in all its varied manifestations, *śakti* in these systems of thought is coequal with, and inseparable from, the ultimate reality. The implication is that, from the perspective of enlightenment, the world itself is a reflex of the absolute and as such is fully real. We therefore have important Hindu articulations of nondualism in which the world and nature are radically included in the divine and celebrated as such. To suggest but one example, consider the Kashmiri Śaiva theologian and poet Utpaladeva (c. 900–950 CE), who sings to his lord in the *Śivastotrāvalī* (12.1; 18.9): "Your devotees frolic in this ocean of the world, brimming with the cool nectar that flows from your limbs... Everything is saturated with you alone" (Bailly, 1987, 70, 101).

It may well be that this kind of world-affirming, inclusive nondualism has been disseminated more widely among lay Hindus than the radical, world-excluding nondualism of the orthodox ascetics. I recently attended a ritual at a Hindu temple during which a young man was upset to see an insect crawling out from under his offering plate. His mother calmly advised him, "That also is a form of God. Let it be." This anecdote illustrates a mode of thinking not uncommon in the tradition. Witness the following folk *bhajan* (see → *kīrtan* and *bhajan*), or hymn, by the 15th-century North Indian poet-mystic → Kabīr, whose songs in the vernacular are still immensely popular and influential:

> O God, your Godliness
> pervades every body
> like the red unseen
> in the green henna leaf
> ... In flowers, in branches
> In this whole world
> wherever I look – you only you!
> In an elephant, you become an elephant
> An ant is just a little you!
> ... In earth, in ocean, in every
> creature you alone reside! (Hess & Virmani, 2008, 43–44)

Historical and Contemporary Environmental Activism

Though it has only recently come to be recognized as such, probably the most graphic example in Hindu history of religiously based protection of nature emerged from the Biṣṇoī community of Rajasthan. Following the teachings of their founding *guru* Jambheśvara (15th cent. CE), the Biṣṇoīs are known for their protection of trees and animals, especially *khejṛī* (bot. Prosopis Cineraria) trees and the black antelope. The *khejṛī* is important in the Rajasthani desert economy as its leaves provide a nutritious fodder for cattle and camels, and its pods, rich in protein, are a distinctive element of Rajasthani cooking. The tree requires little water, and its roots stabilize the sandy soil (Jain, 2011, 74). Jambheśvara is said to have received the foundational inspiration of his teachings while sitting under a *khejṛī*. Biṣṇoīs are forbidden to cut its branches or otherwise harm it. Biṣṇoī teachings prohibit the felling of living trees and the killing of animals. A vegetarian diet is prescribed, along with the practice of compassion for all living beings. Jambheśvara warned, in particular, that on their deathbeds, those who killed animals would be haunted by their painful cries (Jain, 2011, 59).

The Biṣṇoīs are known especially for heroic self-sacrifice in the cause of protecting trees and animals, to the point of giving up their lives. Sources recount numerous examples (Jain 2011, 63–73), the most famous having occurred in 1730 CE in the village of Khejarli, Rajasthan. Mahārāja Abhay Siṅgh of nearby Jodhpur had sent a garrison of soldiers to collect wood as fuel for a palace kiln. Under the leadership of Amṛta Devī, a Biṣṇoī woman, a total of 363 of Jambheśvara's followers were killed as they hugged *khejṛī* trees to protect them from the soldiers' axes. Even today, a monument and temple mark the place of their sacrifice.

Mohandas K. Gandhi remains the most well-known exponent of Hindu values in the modern era. Although living in a period before the awakening of ecological awareness, Gandhi has nevertheless had a tremendous influence on environmental activism in India. In his signal achievement, he transformed the ancient Indian ideal of *ahiṃsā*, or nonharming, from a private ethic of letting things be to a potent method for political change on a national level. This, of course, was his teaching of *satyāgraha*, or holding on to the truth. Although influenced by Western elements, Gandhi's thought was grounded in Hindu concepts, especially the *Bhagavadgītā*'s ideal of detached social engagement for the sake of "world maintenance," cited above. Gandhi's bequest to late 20th-century and early 21st-century environmentalists was this activist version of *ahiṃsā* that was political and yet still thoroughly dependent on moral sensibilities. Most especially, his nonviolent method was based on a keen awareness of the complex, self-propagating negative ramifications of violence, which parallels environmentalist thinking about interconnectivity within ecological systems and the unintended consequences of environmental interference. Gandhi's followers today are empowered to both identify environmental violence as such and bring about change in constructive ways.

Gandhi remains influential also as an advocate of simple living, a lifestyle that would nowadays be associated with ideals of "low ecological footprint" and sustainability. Gandhi's renown frugality owes much to the *Bhagavadgītā*'s ethic of detachment and desire-free (*niṣkāma*) living – as well as the yogic ideal of nonpossession (*aparigraha*). Thus Gandhi reminds us of the difference between human need and human greed:

> If I take anything that I do not need for my own immediate use and keep it I thieve it from somebody else... Nature produces enough for our wants from day to day, and if only everybody took enough for himself and nothing more, there would be no pauperism in this world. (Gandhi, 1960, 3)

Gandhi elaborated this ethic of simplicity to construct a vision of an India based on decentralized, self-reliant villages with small-scale, homespun economies. He thus anticipated E.F. Schumacher's "small is beautiful" economics, as well as contemporary concerns regarding the ill effects of globalization.

A further legacy of Gandhi to contemporary environmentalism lies in the area of models of leadership. The *Bhagavadgītā* promoted as paragon the detached ascetic, free from selfish wants and worldly ambition. For Hindus, this image established itself as cultural ideal of sainthood and trustworthy leadership. Consciously or unconsciously, Gandhi was immensely successful in embodying this archetype for his followers. He thus established it for the modern era as a catalyst of mobilization for social change. Inspired by leaders like Vinoba Bhave and Sunderlal Bahuguna, the Gandhian tradition has continued to the present day (Shepherd, 1987). Its concerns were, of course, originally political and social, but they have expanded to include the environment as activists have become increasingly aware of ecological issues.

The Chipko Andolan is perhaps the most commonly cited example of a Gandhi-inspired environmental movement in India. Beginning in the early 1970s in the Garhwal region of Uttarakhand, in the foothills of the Himalayas, it was at its base a peasant movement to protect local forests – and livelihoods – from exploitation by outside lumber companies. *Chipko* means "clinging" in Hindi, and the movement gained its name (and fame) from the nonviolent tactic of village women and men "hugging" trees to prevent them being felled by corporate axemen. Whether these villagers were aware of the precedent of Biṣṇoī tree hugging several centuries earlier is unclear, though many writers have assumed a connection. In any event, the government first denied forest access to the Dasholi Gram Swarajya Sangh (DGSS), a local Gandhian cooperative movement that had planned to harvest a modicum of wood for local manufacture of agricultural implements. Then – disregarding the needs of the villagers and the devastating effects of deforestation on their lives and livelihoods – the government granted an Allahabad-based sporting-goods company a license to cut trees for wood to make tennis rackets for the export market. Confronting a phalanx of axe-bearing loggers, Chandi Prasad Bhatt, the leader of the DGSS, shouted, "Let them know that we will not allow the felling of ash trees. When they aim their axes upon them, we will embrace the trees" (Weber, 1988, 40). The movement caught fire in the region and spread rapidly. By the early 1980s, similar movements had sprung up in other parts of India, and in 1981, a 15-year moratorium on commercial tree felling in the Himalayan forests was imposed by then prime minister Indira Gandhi (Callicott, 1994, 218; Gadgil & Guha, 1992, 222–223).

The leaders of the Chipko movement, Chandi Prasad Bhatt and Sunderlal Bahuguna, have emerged as India's best-known environmentalists (Gadgil & Guha, 1992, 224). Bhatt sees a typically Hindu linkage between human morality (*dharma*) and ecology: "If you halt the erosion of humankind, humankind will halt the erosion of the soil" (Shepherd, 1987, 80). Bahuguna is old enough to have participated as a youth in the freedom struggle. In the years following Independence, he came under the tutelage of Mira Behn, a European disciple of Gandhi who had taken up work in the Himalayan foothills (James, 2009, 107). Bahuguna follows the Gandhian model of leader as religious ascetic, presenting himself as one who has set aside all personal agendas out of concern for the welfare of the masses. In 1981, Bahuguna and a group of followers undertook a *padayātrā* (foot march) of 4,870 km through the foothills of the Himalayas, trekking from Kashmir in the west to Nagaland in the extreme east, spreading his message of forest protection. Like Gandhi, he has at several junctures adopted public fasting as a method of nonviolent protest. Bahuguna's hunger strikes have lasted up to 74 days and in some cases led to his arrest by authorities. Having successfully used these tactics during the Chipko struggles, he has more recently applied them in the struggle against the construction of the Tehri Dam.

The Tehri Dam, its initial phases completed amid great controversy in 2006, has already wrought considerable environmental devastation. It continues to threaten catastrophic consequences in a seismically active region that is home to some of the most sacred sites of Hinduism. Bahuguna points out that the Tehri and other dams are being built not for the benefit of the people in the region but for city dwellers to the south. Alluding to the massive amounts of toxic effluent that the city of Delhi dumps daily into the → Yamunā, another of India's most sacred rivers, Bahuguna remarks, "I ask our rulers, 'What have you done to the Yamuna? You have polluted the Yamuna and now you want the Ganges water to wash off your sins in Delhi'" (James, 2004).

Although now in his 80s, Bahuguna has continued his campaigns. In the autumn of 2009, he traveled again from Kashmir to India's extreme northeast under the banner "Save Himalaya, Save Water, Save Life," continuing his efforts to raise awareness of the importance of the fragile ecology of the region. Meanwhile, others have taken up the campaign against dams and other threats to the Gaṅgā River and its headwaters. A noteworthy example is environmentalist G.D. Agrawal, a retired professor of environmental engineering at the Indian Institute of Technology Kanpur. During the spring of 2012, having taken religious vows and adopted the monastic name Swami Gyan Swarup Sanand, he engaged in a "fast unto death" in opposition to dam building on the upper tributaries of the Gaṅgā. The Swami's plea was for an *aviralnirmal gaṅgā*, an unobstructed, pure Gaṅgā. The fast was called off only after official intervention and an agreement under which the government of India stipulated that it would "explore all measures for Ganga conservation and to ensure its unimpeded flow, purity and sanctity" (*Times of India*, Mar 23, 2012). Swami Sanand's fast, termed a *gaṅgā tapasya* (religious austerity on behalf of the Gaṅgā), had been preceded by several others. Notable was a fast by Swami Nigamanand Saraswati of Haridwar, in opposition to the mining of the Gaṅgā riverbed near the sacred city. This ended tragically with Swami Nigamanand's death in June 2011 (Morrison, 2011). While eliciting government promises, these actions have resulted in little effective action.

A complicating, and perhaps disquieting, aspect of the liaison of environmentalism and religion in India in recent years has been the tendency for religiously based movements to be hijacked by political forces of the Hindu chauvinist right. The anti-dam campaigns in the early and mid-2000s, directed especially at the Tehri Dam, are a case in point. A failure of the structure would, it was correctly predicted, have catastrophic consequences for the numerous sacred sites and revered religious institutions downstream. Masses of Hindu pilgrims would likewise find themselves in the path of a veritable tsunami of river water. The Vishwa Hindu Parishad (VHP; World Hindu Council) seized on these facts to present the dam as a danger to Hinduism and *hindutva*, the very "Hinduness" of India. In an effort to charge the issue with anti-Muslim sentiment, the dam was identified as a possible target for Pakistani terrorists seeking to destroy the heartland of Hindu faith. In this way, E. Mawdsley (2005) argues, the original inspiration of the anti-dam movement – the environmental and resettlement issues that were of vital importance to the people of the region – were coopted by the VHP in its quest for political power and the furtherance of its Hindu nationalist agenda.

This connection among religion, the environment, and politics continues. In the summer of 2012, for example, the Hindu nationalist Bharatiya Janata Party (BJP) announced a "Save Ganga" campaign under the leadership of firebrand politician Uma Bharati, former BJP chief minister of Madhya Pradesh. The strategy was to begin at Ganga Sagar, a Hindu pilgrimage site at the mouth of the Gaṅgā, and proceed along the river's course to Gangotri, the river's sacred source. It was projected that,

> [d]uring the campaign, BJP leaders would offer prayers and hold public meetings in the areas along the river to appeal to the people to save Ganga from pollution and highlight the Centre's neglect of the issue. (Verma, 2012)

Conclusion

India has for several decades now had a large and vital environmental movement that, taken as a whole, is perhaps the largest in the world (Peritore, 1993). The number of environmental organizations and campaigns is too large to do justice to them here, even if we were to limit ourselves to those clearly inspired by Hindu ideals. These movements have a rich cultural and religious heritage at their disposal, in particular the inspiration of Gandhi. Still, their efforts are obstructed by corporate greed and governmental corruption and overwhelmed by the demands of India's relentlessly growing population. In addition, the emergence of a divisive communalist politics complicates especially any effort to employ religious symbolism in service of environmental activism. In the end, we need to remind ourselves that environmentalism in India is often "survival environmentalism." What are seen as problems of despoliation of nature by Westerners, or Western-educated elites, are seen by Indian villagers as problems of survival. The latter, as E. Tomalin and others have suggested, are more likely to mobilize elements of religion strategically, more for their pragmatic utility as sources of symbolic motivation and legitimation than out of any encompassing "green" spirituality that others might suppose they represent (Tomalin, 2002, 19–26). Still, religion is very much a part of life for India's Hindus, who will continue to reinterpret and reconstruct their religious traditions in order to address contemporary concerns, be they environmental or otherwise.

Bibliography

Alley, K.D., "Idioms of Degeneracy: Assessing Gaṅgā's Purity and Pollution," in: L.E. Nelson, ed., *Purifying the Earthly Body of God: Religion and Ecology in Hindu India*, Albany, 1998, 297–330.

Bailly, C.R., *Shaiva Devotional Songs of Kashmir: A Translation and Study of Utpaladeva's Shivastotravali*, Albany, 1987.

Bloomfield, M., *Hymns of the Atharva Veda*, New Delhi, 1973.

Bryant, E., "Strategies of Vedic Subversion: The Emergence of Vegetarianism in Post-Vedic India," in: P. Waldau & K. Patton, eds., *A Communion of Subjects: Animals in Religion, Science, and Ethics*, New York, 2006, 194–203.

Callicott, J.B., *Earth's Insights: A Survey of Ecological Ethics from the Mediterranean Basin to the Australian Outback*, Berkeley, 1994.

Crawford, S.C., *The Evolution of Hindu Ethical Ideals*, Honolulu, [2]1982.

Deutsch, E., "Vedanta and Ecology," in: T.M.P. Mahadevan, ed., *Indian Philosophical Annual*, Madras, 1970, 79–88.

Doniger, W., *The Rig Veda: An Anthology*, New York, 1981.

Eck, D.L., *India: A Sacred Geography*, New York, 2012.

Freeman, R., *Forests and the Folk Perceptions of Nature in the Swidden Regimes of Highland Malabar*, Pondicherry, 1994.

Gadgil, M., & R. Guha, *This Fissured Land: An Ecological History of India*, Berkeley, 1992.

Gandhi, M.K., *Trusteeship*, Ahmedabad, 1960.

Gold, A.G., "'If You Cut a Branch You Cut My Finger': Court, Forest, and Environmental Ethics in Rajasthan," in: C.K. Chapple & M.E. Tucker, eds., *Hinduism and Ecology: The Intersection of Earth, Sky, and Water*, Cambridge MA, 2000, 317–336.

Haberman, D.L., *Journey through the Twelve Forests: An Encounter with Krishna*, New York, 1994.

Hess, L., & S. Virmani, trans., *Ajab Shahar, Kabir in America: 12 Kabir Songs by Prahlad Singh Tipanya*, Bangalore, 2004.

Jain, P., *Dharma and Ecology of Hindu Communities: Sustenance and Sustainability*, Farnham, 2011.

James, G.A., "Mira Behn: An Environmentalist of the Himalayas," in: A. Sharma, ed., *Windows to the World's Religions*, New Delhi, 2009, 105–118.

James, G.A., "In Conversation: Sunderlal Bahuguna with George James," *Seminar: Web Edition* 533, 2004, http://www.india-seminar.com/2004/533/533%20in%20conversation.htm.

Kane, P.V., *History of Dharmaśāstra: Ancient and Mediæval Religious and Civil Law in India*, vol. V/1, Pune, [2]1974.

Kinsley, D., "Learning the Story of the Land: Reflections on the Liberating Power of Geography and Pilgrimage in the Hindu Tradition," in: L.E. Nelson, ed., *Purifying the Earthly Body of God: Religion and Ecology in Hindu India*, Albany, 1998, 225–246.

Mawdsley, E., "The Abuse of Religion and Ecology: The Vishva Hindu Parishad and Tehri Dam," *WECR* 9/1, 2005, 1–24.

McGee, M., "State Responsibility for Environmental Management: Perspectives from Hindu Texts on Polity," in: C.K. Chapple & M.E. Tucker, eds., *Hinduism and Ecology: The Intersection of Earth, Sky, and Water*, Cambridge MA, 2000, 59–100.

Morrison, D., "A Sacred River under Assault," *International Herald Tribune*, Dec 8, 2011, http://latitude.blogs.nytimes.com/2011/12/08/a-sacred-river-under-assault.

Nagarajan, V.R., "The Earth as Goddess Bhū Devī: Toward a Theory of 'Embedded Ecologies' in Folk Hinduism," in: L.E. Nelson, ed., *Purifying the Earthly Body of God: Religion and Ecology in Hindu India*, Albany, 1998, 269–295.

Narayanan, V., "Water, Wood, and Wisdom: Ecological Perspectives from the Hindu Traditions," *DJAAAS* 130/4, 2001, 179–206.

Narayanan, V., "'One Tree Is Equal to Ten Sons': Some Hindu Responses to the Problems of Ecology, Population, and Consumerism," in: H. Coward & D.C. Maguire, eds., *Visions of a New Earth: Religious Perspectives on Population, Consumption, and Ecology*, Albany, 2000, 111–129.

National Portal of India, "National Song," n.d., http://india.gov.in/knowindia/national_symbols.php?id=12.

Nelson, L.E., "Ecology," in: S. Mittal & G. Thursby, eds., *Studying Hinduism: Key Concepts and Methods*, 2008, 97–111.

Nelson, L.E., "Cows, Elephants, Dogs, and Other Lesser Embodiments of Ātman: Reflections on Hindu Attitudes towards Non-human Animals," in: P. Waldau & K. Patton, eds., *A Communion of Subjects: Animals in Religion, Science, and Ethics*, New York, 2006, 179–193.

Nelson, L.E., "Reading the *Bhagavadgītā* from an Ecological Perspective," in: C.K. Chapple & M.E. Tucker, eds., *Hinduism and Ecology: The Intersection of Earth, Sky, and Water*, Cambridge MA, 2000, 127–164.

Nelson, L.E., "The Dualism of Nondualism: Advaita Vedānta and the Irrelevance of Nature," in: L.E. Nelson, ed., *Purifying the Earthly Body of God: Religion and Ecology in Hindu India*, Albany, 1998, 61–88.

Nugteren, A., *Belief, Bounty, and Beauty: Rituals around Sacred Trees in India*, Leiden, 2005.

Parajuli, P., "No Nature Apart: Adivasi Cosmovision and Ecological Discourses in Jharkhand, India," in: P.P. Arnold & A.G. Gold, eds., *Sacred Landscapes and Cultural Politics: Planting a Tree*, Aldershot, 2001, 83–113.

Peritore, N.P., "Environmental Attitudes of Indian Elites: Challenging Western Postmodernist Models," *ASu* 33/8, 1993, 804–818.

Ruether, R.R., *Gaia and God: An Ecofeminist Theology of Earth Healing*, San Francisco, 1992.

Schumacher, E.F., *Small Is Beautiful: Economics as If People Mattered*, New York, 1989.

Shepherd, M., *Gandhi Today: The Story of Mahatma Gandhi's Successors*, Arcata, 1987.

The Times of India, "Swami Ends Fast after Centre's Written Promise," Mar 23, 2012, http:// articles.timesofindia.indiatimes.com/2012-03-23/varanasi/31229359_1_ngrba-swami-avimukteshwaranand-saraswati-swami-avimukteshwaranad.

The Times of India, "Karunanidhi Makes Common Cause with Jayalalithaa Govt on Cauvery Issue," Jul 23, 2012, http://articles.timesofindia.indiatimes.com/2012-07-23/chennai/32803597_1_cauvery-river-water-authority-jayalalithaa-govt-m-karunanidhi.

Tomalin, E., *Biodivinity and Biodiversity: The Limits to Religious Environmentalism*, Farnham, 2009.

Tomalin, E., "The Limitations of Religious Environmentalism for India," *WECR* 6/1, 2002, 12–30.

Venkitasubramonia Iyer, S., *Varāha Purāṇa*, 2 vols., Delhi, 1985.

Verma, L., "BJP to Start 'Save Ganga' Campaign from Gangasagar," *The Indian Express*, Jul 19, 2012, http://www.indianexpress.com/news/bjp-to-start-save-ganga-campaign-from-gangasagar/976475/.

Weber, T., *Hugging the Trees: The Story of the Chipko Movement*, New Delhi, 1988.

White, L., "The Historical Roots of Our Ecologic Crisis," *Science* 155/3767, 1967, 1203–1207.

Lance E. Nelson

Ethics

In Hinduism, discussions of ethics – that is, reasoning about morality and thus about what one ought to do and why – generally fall within the much broader category of → *dharma*, a word whose root (*dhṛ-*) means to hold or uphold. *Dharma* includes within its purview the ordering principles that structure time, space, and manifest reality as well as individual and social life and that regulate moral, social, and ritual behavior. In varying contexts, it may refer to duty, morality, ritual, law, justice, religion, and more (Narayanan, 2001, 178). Even as there is no ready translation of this concept, so there is no precise Hindu term for "ethics." Yet ethical reflection permeates Hindu scriptures; philosophical, political, and legal treatises; and narrative traditions. Indeed, Hindu religious traditions may be understood to move around two poles: *dharma*, particularly as moral virtue and righteous action, and *mokṣa* – that is, transformative and liberating knowledge (see → liberation). As → Kṛṣṇa tells Arjuna clearly in the → *Bhagavadgītā*, it is impossible for beings, even the supreme being, not to act. Nonaction is itself a form of action; therefore, the questions of what actions one should or should not take and how one should act become crucial, even to the pursuit of *mokṣa*. The resources available for thinking through these questions in Hinduism include a vast textual tradition together with the customary practices of communities, moral reasoning (particularly of the wise), and individual conscience, allowing for dexterity and innovation in dealing with widely varying contexts, conflicts, and challenges.

Ethics in the Vedic Literature

At the foundation of the Hindu textual traditions is the vedic literature, with respect for the → Vedas arguably a defining "touchstone" shared by the diverse traditions that make up the polycentric "banyan tree" of Hinduism (Patton, 2007, 124; Lipner, 2010, 6). This initially oral literature (which includes the four Saṃhitās or collections of hymns and ritual instructions as well as their commentaries, the Brāhmaṇas, Āraṇyakas, and → Upaniṣads) is called Śruti – that which is heard or seen – and is said to have been realized, rather than authored, by ancient enlightened sages and thus to reflect the eternal truth of reality. As such, this literature

> constitute[s] the founding texts of the Hindu world... opening up the horizon... within which the tradition has understood itself and [those] who belong to the tradition have understood [themselves and their experiences and offering] an inexhaustible reservoir of meaning which is not exhausted by any system, but has made room for new interpretations. (Mohanty, 2007, 65)

The hymns found in the oldest vedic collection, the *Ṛgveda* (c. 1000 BCE), offer no systematic code of behavior but speak of an ordered world in which humans can thrive and in which they exist in relations of sacrificial obligation with divine beings. Human flourishing constitutes what is desirable and good, and humans flourish when they live according to that order, *ṛta*, and participate in creating and upholding it through obligatory ritual action.

> *[Y]ajna* [sacrifice] is the central ethical action that was meant to motivate and sustain the entire universe... [and t]he Vedas are the words and chants accompanying the actions and served to augment and vitalize the action into having cosmic power. (Patton, 2007, 125)

The things that promote human flourishing follow from the sacrifice, and within the hymns, people ask for wealth and for long life and fertility for themselves, their herds, and their horses, for protection from enemies, disease, and natural disaster, and for strength and courage in their warriors.

Within the hymns, there is also an emergent organic view of society, differentiating four classes of people with distinct roles. Three are characteristic of other Indo-European cultures as well – priests (Brāhmaṇas/Brahmans), warriors (Kṣatriyas), and common people (Vaiśyas) – but there is also a fourth category, Śūdras, who are referred to as Dāsas or "servants" and in some hymns identified as a darker, conquered people (e.g. *ṚV.* 2.12). In the *Puruṣasūkta* hymn of origins, the Brahmans are made from the mouth of the cosmic man sacrificed by the gods to create the world, warriors from his arms, the common people from his thighs, and the servants from his feet (*ṚV.* 10.90.12). There is a clear hierarchy as well as role differentiation among these classes, but there is no explicit tie to heredity as in the later caste system. Other aspects of vedic society also support such a complementary view of social duties and responsibilities, with expanding categories of priests fulfilling highly differentiated roles in the sacrificial rituals and the deities, too, being responsible for different functions within the cosmos (Patton, 2007, 125–126). There are also familial and social responsibilities incumbent on all, extending not only to the living generation – mirrored in the request "that the young do not abandon the old," for example (*ṚV.* 10.18.5; Doniger, 1981, 52) – but also to the "fathers" (one's ancestors, who with the gods are receivers of the sacrifices) and to the sages as givers of the ritual traditions and → *mantras*. The virtues that mark a good person are also enumerated, among them

> truthfulness (*satya*), giving (*dana*), restraint (*dama*), austerities (*tapas*), affection and gratitude, fidelity, forgiveness, non-thieving, non-cheating, giving others their just desert, and avoiding harm or *himsa* to all creatures. (Bilimoria, 1991, 45)

Particularly in the hymns addressed to the god Varuṇa, the originator of *ṛta* and thus of the moral as well as natural and social order, we find more nuanced ethical reflection on intentionality, conscious versus unconscious actions, and intergenerational responsibility. One hymn asks that the members of the community be freed "from the harmful deeds of our fathers, and from those we have committed with our own bodies," in recognition that deeds affect more than oneself and that one may be held accountable and suffer the consequences for deeds committed by others as well as oneself (*ṚV.* 7.86.5; Patton, 2007, 130). Further, this hymn acknowledges free will but asks that people not be held responsible for acts that were carried out under the influence of "wine, anger, dice or carelessness" – influences that may override moral inclinations and rationality (*ṚV.* 7.86.6; Doniger, 1981, 214; Lipner, 2010, 36). In another hymn, the reciter asks to be forgiven for any offenses that may have been committed against another, whether friend, family, or stranger, and then continues, "If we have cheated like gamblers in a game, whether we know or really do not know it, O god, cast all these offenses away, like loosened bonds" (*ṚV.* 5.85.7–8; Doniger, 1981, 211; Patton 2007, 128–130). The underlying concern is the disruption of the ordered relationships and actions that ensure mutual flourishing, encompassing both the interrelations of humans and those between humans and gods, which are inextricably related.

Expanding on these earliest vedic collections, the Brāhmaṇas and Āraṇyakas offer increasing detail on ritual performance and begin to explore the esoteric meanings and power of ritual actions and words and the inner realization aligning the human world with the cosmos (Lipner, 2010, 47–52). Understandings of *dharma,* → *karman*, and rebirth (→ *saṃsāra*) were also being elaborated. Indeed, the *Taittirīyāraṇyaka* proclaims,

> The fulfillment of duty, the realization by each being of that for which he was created, is the very basis of existence… Duty fulfilled obliterates evil. Everything is based on the fulfilling of duty. (*TaiĀ.* 10.63; Daniélou, 1993, 74)

At the same time, groups of ascetics known as Śramaṇas ("Strivers") were also appearing who renounced worldly pursuits and engaged in ascetic and meditative practices in secluded places, seeking to move beyond false understandings of self and the world that bind people to the cycle of rebirth and to be set free through liberating realization. In so doing, they also "rejected the ethics of Vedic sacrifice… as a self-serving attempt to attain worldly success and/or a form of personal immortality" (Lipner, 2010, 51).

The conversations between enlightened teachers and their students recorded in the → Upaniṣads (c. 6th cent. BCE) reflect this turn, with concerns for human flourishing in the material and social sense receding, eclipsed by the pursuit of liberating knowledge. Outward ritual action is internalized, the sacrifice now embodied in the practices of detachment and meditation that kindle the fires of realization. Even so, outward actions flow from the level of realization of the true nature of the self and reality, and self-serving actions run counter to it. Virtuous action is thus necessary but not sufficient to the goal. Indeed, the student on this path must practice the virtues that also characterize the realized person: "self-restraint…, giving…, and compassion" (*BĀU.* 5.4.2; Bilimoria, 1991, 48). Arrogance and pride in one's knowledge and independent power are unmasked, whether held by humans like the boy Śvetakatu (*ChāU.* 6.1) or the gods Agni, Vāyu, or Indra (*KeU.* 14–27; see also → vedic gods), replaced with an underlying affirmation of the oneness of all in the unitary reality of *brahman*, the source and end of all that is. Renunciation of the differentiated social self as well as of desires of the ego is encouraged, leading to the realization of the universal self, → *ātman*, and underscoring an equality of all beings.

From the point of view of the Upaniṣads, one does have duties towards other humans and with regard to upholding truth and righteousness as well as obligations to practice austerity, self-control, and tranquility, to perform ritual sacrifice and rites of hospitality, and to successfully procreate; but the highest duty is unquestionably learning and teaching (*TaiU.* 1.9). Even so, the student who has completed his studies is advised to live an irreproachable life, to treat father, mother, → *guru*, and guest as god, and to speak the truth and follow *dharma*, while also not neglecting physical and material well-being or duties to the gods and ancestors even as he continues study and recitation. (Notions of the equality of all beings and the presence of a few women – → Gārgī and Maitreyī – in the texts notwithstanding, the "student" was generally assumed to be male.) Should a person not know how to act in a given ritual or social situation, he or she is advised to look to the example of a competent Brahman (*TaiU.* 1.11.1–3). The Upaniṣads also make reference to a further standard set of eight virtues, though these are unspecified (*ŚvetU.* 1.9.4), presumably known and expected.

For those on this path toward realization, wrong actions are also enumerated, and of these, to steal gold, to drink alcohol, to kill a Brahman, and to have sex with the *guru*'s wife are the most reprehensible (*ChāU.* 5.10.8). Even the person who associates with such a one is condemned. The enlightened person, however, is the notable exception, for this person is said to be untouched and untouchable by evil. Having reached the realization of the true self, *ātman*, there is no possibility of action on behalf of and by a false self to which karmic consequences would accrue. Clearly, there are developed notions of how one should act in the social realm at this time – of *dharma* and *karman* and the cycle of rebirth and of desired virtues – but these are ancillary to the pursuit of liberating knowledge and are thus not detailed in this later Śruti literature but rather in Smṛti texts, those that record "remembered" traditions and thus do not hold the same truth status. These include the six *darśana*s or viewpoints of classical Hindu philosophy and later commentaries, the dharmic law codes of the Dharmasūtras and → Dharmaśāstras, epic and mythic narratives, and the songs and stories of devotional saints. Though the classical philosophical texts explore foundational understandings – of language and reason, of knowledge and action, of self and reality – that have definite ethical implications and inform subsequent ethical reflection, they provide no systematic moral philosophy, and the primary sites of ethical reflection on what one ought to do and how one ought to live lie within the normative ideals of the law codes and the exemplary characters, words, and actions of epic heroes and devotional saints.

The Dharmasūtras and Dharmaśāstras

Developed notions of *dharma* together with codes for normative behavior first appear among the Kalpasūtras composed in the centuries leading up to the Common Era, which include works on correct performance of public rituals (Śrautasūtras) and domestic rituals (Gṛhyasūtras) and codes for proper social and moral behavior (Dharmasūtras). Of the Dharmasūtras, the most important and still extant are attributed to the sages Gautama, Baudhāyana, Vasiṣṭha, and Āpastamba (Olivelle, 1999). The authors are clear that they draw on vedic literature (Śruti), traditions (Smṛti), and the customs accepted by "those who know the Veda" for their detailed rules for everything from eating to personal hygiene, from life stage to law, from marriage to adoption and death, and from caste interactions to penance and punishment (Olivelle, 1999, xxxix–xlii). They do not present a single unified code, but rather their individual formulations reflect wider debates regarding right behavior and multiple elite perspectives from different regions and eras.

As such the Dharmasūtras are normative texts and extremely detailed ones at that, but as P. Olivelle reminds us, "They tell people what to do; they do not tell us what people actually did," and they do so from the perspective of Brahman men (1999, xlii). Additional, even more detailed treatises on *dharma* were composed in subsequent centuries, crossing over into jurisprudence; these were referred to as Dharmaśāstras, the earliest and most influential of which is the *Mānavadharmaśāstra* or *Manusmṛti* (Doniger *et al.*, 1991). The *Manusmṛti* added a fourth authoritative source – "what is pleasing to oneself" – for determining dharmic actions (in addition to Śruti, Smṛti, and "the conduct of the good" who know the Vedas, as cited in earlier Dharmasūtras) and in doing so acknowledged a role also for individual conscience in ethical decision making (*MaSm.* 2.12; Doniger *et al.*, 1991, 18). Yet all these dharmic texts, together with further commentaries, have a similar normative quality, addressing a wide range of issues and circumstances, broadly invoked across the centuries in discussions and legal proceedings to support differing viewpoints, and undergoing continuous interpretation in varying contexts (Flood, 1996, 56–57).

These law codes outline both universal virtues and vices to be avoided – applicable to all human beings (*sādhāraṇadharma*) – and specific duties and responsibilities related to one's life stage and social position or caste (*varṇāśramadharma*) and gender (for women, *strīdharma*). Vasiṣṭha offers a list of vices that one should refrain from committing and that constitute the "law common to all orders of life": "slander, envy, pride, egotism, disbelief, dishonesty, praising oneself, running down others, hypocrisy, greed, perplexity, anger and jealousy" (*VasDhS.* 10.30; Olivelle, 1999, 274). In a more positive vein, Gautama recounts eight virtues incumbent on all: "compassion toward all creatures, patience, lack of envy, purification, tranquility, having an auspicious disposition, generosity and lack of greed" (*GauDhS.* 8.23; Olivelle, 1999, 90–91). Manu made it ten duties, applicable to all men of the upper three classes throughout their lives: "patience, forgiveness, self-control, not stealing, purification, mastery of the sensory powers, wisdom, learning, truth and lack of anger" (*MaSm.* 6.91–92; Doniger *et al.*, 1991, 126).

Of these, "purification" and "having an auspicious disposition" warrant further explanation. → Purity is not only moral blamelessness in these dharmic texts but also the avoidance of impure substances and the ritual cleansing of those who have been made impure by contact with impure bodily substances or persons or by familial association (as in e.g. births or deaths). The exception are degrees of impurity said to inhere in persons by nature of their birth and attendant professions – impurities that no ritual can remove from them, with those of the lowest castes considered the most impure.

> The polarity of purity and pollution organizes Hindu social space, a principle recognized in the Dharma Śāstras which view social ethics as the maintenance of order and the boundaries between the groups and genders as governed by degrees of purity and pollution. (Flood, 1996, 57)

→ Auspiciousness, in contrast, denotes good fortune and that which is life giving and is also highly valued (in continuity with the vedic hymns), though at times that which is auspicious may be impure (as with a menstruating but therefore fertile woman or the birth of a child). While the highest levels of purity may be required of Brahmans in their ritual function and afford them high status in society, it is the king and the politically and economically dominant caste in any given locale (regardless of *varṇa* and thus purity status) that are dharmically responsible for ensuring the auspiciousness – that is, the well-being and prosperity – of the community over which they exercise power (Flood, 1996, 67). And both purity and a life-affirming attitude appear among the virtues that individuals are also called to embody.

One's own particular *dharma* (or anyone else's) at any given time is also highly contextual, determined not only by one's social class or *varṇa*, as well as one's life stage and gender, but also by the customs of one's *jāti* or specific caste (the social group in which one is born and marries, which is further classified within one of the four *varṇa*s and hierarchically related to all other *jāti*s) as well as one's family and one's country, region, or district (*MaSm.* 1.118; Doniger *et al.*, 1991, xlvi, 15). The Dharmaśāstras spell out in great detail how upper-caste males should behave at the different stages of life or → *āśramas* – as students, householders, forest dwellers, and finally, if they choose, renouncers. There is a clear recognition that in each of these stages, one has different responsibilities and required ways of behaving and interacting that are appropriate and thus ethical in that particular stage but not necessarily in another. Learning is the principal duty of the celibate student, while the householder is meant to conceive and raise children and to fulfill his familial and social responsibilities according to his nature and caste, even as he may appropriately also pursue wealth and power (→ *artha*) and aesthetic and erotic enjoyment (→ *kāma*). In particular the Brahman is required to fulfill his triple debt "of studentship to the seers, of sacrifice to the gods, and of offspring to the ancestors" (*BauDhS.* 16.7; Olivelle, 1999, 203–204; see also *MaSm.* 4.257; 6.35–37). Having fulfilled one's dharmic social and familial obligations, one is to give over the later stages of life more and more to spiritual pursuits (*mokṣa*) as one withdraws increasingly from involvement in the social realm, first to a secluded forest life and finally in complete renunciation of all that one is and has. In this way, the four principal pursuits (*puruṣārtha*) that motivate humans are affirmed and integrated into a lifespan – *dharma, artha, kāma, mokṣa* – to be pursued in the proper way and time.

Social position is firmly hereditary and hierarchical in these texts, the *jāti*s within the *varṇa*s constituted as closed endogamous groups or castes, with interrelationships among members of the four *varṇa*s intricately delineated. Each *varṇa* has its own specific dharmicly assigned social roles and behavior regulations, and much of the texts is given over to the responsibilities and appropriate dharmic actions particularly of Brahmans and kings, no doubt "inspired in part by the desire to establish Brahmin status over physical force (Kṣatriyas) and economic power (Vaiśyas)" (Doniger *et al.*, 1991, xlvii). And these texts are, after all, largely composed by Brahman men for Brahman men, though members of other classes and women were also affected by and well aware of their injunctions and ideals.

A rationale for the hierarchical ranking of the three higher *varṇa*s (the initiated or "twice-born") and their relationships with the Śūdras and outcastes is asserted based on *karman* and rebirth, with the Brahmans at the pinnacle of purity and privilege and the level of one's rebirth in the social hierarchy dependent on one's past actions or *karman* and particularly one's degree of fulfillment of one's own specific *dharma* (*ĀpDhS.* 2.2). The law of *karman* reinforces the notion of individual responsibility for one's actions, with their consequences played out in this life or the next (thus ensuring that when all is said and done, justice prevails), but these dharmic texts also call for differential treatment of individuals and differing punishments for actions based on class and caste status. B.K. Matilal suggests that such karmic arguments are "intended to provide a 'rational' basis for the apparently irrational practice of caste-hierarchy or social inequality," that was being simultaneously challenged by the Śramaṇa renouncer traditions (2007, 81). However, though one's birth and life circumstances may be determined by past actions, one can and must choose how to act in this life and thus has free will (and responsibility) to shape one's current character and future birth positively by fulfilling one's own specific dharma (*svadharma*). *Karman* may, thus, serve to motivate ethical action even as it ensures justice (Bilimoria, 2007). Like the earlier vedic references to the four *varṇa*s, the relationship among castes is also understood as an organic division of necessary and complementary roles in society, now grounded in differences in inborn nature even as the distinct duties and responsibilities of men and women are understood to be both complementary and innate. Securing the purity of the priests to properly carry out the rituals on behalf of all is offered as a further rationale for divisions of labor and the hierarchical regulation of interactions.

Considerable space is also given to women's virtuous behavior (*strīdharma*) in these normative texts. Famously the *Manusmṛti* enjoins,

> In childhood a woman should be under her father's control, in youth under her husband's and when her husband is dead under her sons'. She should not have independence. (*MaSm.* 5.148; Doniger *et al.*, 1991, 115)

Further, a woman of virtue is instructed to "serve her husband like a god, even if he behaves badly, freely indulges his lust, and is devoid of any good qualities," for it is only through obedience to him that she will be "exalted in heaven" (*MaSm.* 5.154–155). Her life is to be one of self-restraint and obedience, absolute fidelity in life and death, and cheerful countenance and auspicious disposition. To be fair, such a virtuous woman is also highly praised by the *Manusmṛti* for bringing good fortune to her family and is to be held in high esteem and honored as a fundamental dimension of upholding dharmic order. Even so, women are classified with Śūdras as forbidden from studying the Vedas, and differential expectations and treatment based on gender are rationalized in terms of women's naturalized moral weakness and inferiority to men, as well as past *karman*. These verses "telling people what to do" do not go unchallenged and do not necessarily reflect "what people actually do" or did, but they are well-known and oft-quoted ideals in discussions of right behavior for people of different castes and for women as well as men. In addition to a political agenda of asserting Brahman superiority, W. Doniger suggests, the author of the *Manusmṛti* was "motivated also by the desire to solve the human, intellectual, psychological, logical problems of killing and eating, making love and dying" and in so doing offered a range of possible correct actions, for example around marriage, in diverse and sometimes extreme situations, as well as appropriate penance and ways of handling infractions. With right ethical, social, and ritual action forming a seamless whole within the dharmic order, these texts offer direction, drawn from Śruti and Smṛti literature and from customary practices and the reasoning of "good men" – albeit Brahman men who had multiple agendas – to offer ideals and contextualized guidelines to those seeking to know how to act. And these ideals were grounded in an understanding of an order underlying reality, with perhaps the most fundamental human obligation being to conform to this order and maintain it, leavened with a measure of practicality in recognition that ideals could not always be maintained in a world that is often disordered, particularly in this latter age in the cyclic and entropic progression of time.

Epic and Puranic Narratives: Exemplary Figures, Ethical Choices, and Conflicting *Dharma*s

Other Smṛti literature addresses the ethical complexities that arise in the course of lived experience through the telling of tales. These narrative traditions include the → *Rāmāyaṇa* and → *Mahābhārata* epics (Itihāsa or mythic history) with their many episodes and characters, both admirable and cautionary, as well as the → Purāṇas (Stories of the Ancient Past) that recount the lives and exploits of the deities. These tales are well known and part of the cultural vocabulary, invoked in discussions of ethics as well as many other topics, and recounted with considerable variation in different regions, languages, and genres. The epics were initially composed in the period roughly between 400 BCE and 400 CE with the Purāṇas over a somewhat longer period, and they continue to be freely retold into the present and in new media, including widely popular television serials. Though the Purāṇas contain a wealth of stories with clear ethical teachings, for the epics, *dharma* is the central focus. Even so, they approach it from a perspective vastly different from that of the law codes – one which originates in the experience of Kṣatriyas rather than Brahmans and in the householder life of engagement in the world of conflicting *dharma*s. The characters of the two epics also differ dramatically from each other, with the *Rāmāyaṇa* portraying proper conduct achieved and the *Mahābhārata* the struggle to know and to do what is right (Matilal, 2002).

The *Rāmāyaṇa* tells of crown prince → Rāma of Ayodhya (the hero-deity and incarnation of → Viṣṇu), who is befittingly trained in the skills of a warrior and married to the beautiful princess Sītā (see → Draupadī and Sītā). But when he should be ascending the throne, he chooses instead to go into exile to uphold his father's vow of a boon to one of his other queens, who asks that her son be made to rule instead while Rāma is banished. Rāma is the epitome of the dharmic son and later king, his rule *rāmarājya* – the ideal kingdom marked by justice, order, stability, and prosperity – and he is known by the epithet Maryādāpuruṣottama ("The Highest Exemplar of Proper Conduct") (Richman, 2001, 6). Sītā is the perfect wife (*pativratā*) and embodiment of *strīdharma*, insisting on accompanying him into exile along with his devoted brother Lakṣmaṇa. She is demure, self-sacrificing, trusting, and patient to a fault but strong in the face of adversity and unshakable in her fidelity to her husband, always thinking only of his needs. After Rāma and Lakṣmaṇa rebuff the advances of the demoness Śūrpaṇikhā, her very powerful but flawed brother Rāvaṇa, king of Laṅkā, kidnaps and imprisons Sītā. Rāma must find her and rescue her, and he does so with the help of his brother and a monkey army led by → Hanumān.

An action-packed quest, the story is also preeminently a tale of the triumph of good over evil and of *dharma* over *adharma*. Rāvaṇa is defeated, and Sītā is rescued. But some of Rāma's subjects question her chastity – after all, she has been under Rāvaṇa's control – and though Rāma has no doubts, he subjects her to a public test. She steps into the fire but is unharmed, proving to all her virtue. In some tellings, the couple lives happily ever after from this point on, but in others, people still continue to express doubts, so Rāma has her abandoned in the forest, ostensibly for the good of the kingdom in accord with his dharmic responsibilities. Unbeknownst to him, she survives under the protection of the sage-poet Vālmīki who will compose the epic, and, having been pregnant, she gives birth to two sons. When they grow up, they encounter Rāma after disrupting his horse sacrifice and recite his own story to him. Ultimately father and sons are reconciled, but Rāma asks Sītā to undergo one more test of her honor. She refuses, calling on her mother, the earth goddess → Bhūdevī, and disappearing into the ground.

There are many versions of the tale, the three most prominent being Vālmīki's *Rāmāyaṇa* in Sanskrit, Kampaṉ's *Irāmāvatāram* (Incarnation of Rāma) in Tamil, and → Tulsīdās' *Rāmcaritmānas* (Lake of the Acts of Rāma) in Hindi. There is no authoritative original to which all others should be compared but rather an abundance of tellings in a wide variety of performance genres (Ramanujan, 1991; Richman, 2001; Lutgendorf, 1994).

Nineteenth-century British scholars noted the ethical importance of this text, with G. Grierson observing,

> Pandits may speak of the Vedas and Upanishads, and a few may even study them... but for the great majority of people in Hindustan, learned and unlearned, the Rāmāyaṇa of Tulasi Das is the only standard of moral conduct. (Lutgendorf, 1994, 63)

Rāma, Sītā, Lakṣmaṇa, and Hanumān are lifted up as ideals, while Rāvaṇa and Śūrpaṇikhā exhibit fatal flaws, particularly uncontrolled desire. In the opening frame of Vālmīki's tale, Rāma is identified as one who is "truly virtuous and energetic," "benevolent to all creatures," "self-controlled, having subdued his anger," and "judicious and free from envy," a person who "knows both dharma and how to act upon it" and "speaks the truth and holds firmly to his vows" (*Rām.* 1.1.2–5; Hiltebeitel, 2011, 415). His actions are paradigmatic, and his conduct is in accord with dharmic injunctions. Yet despite Rāma's overwhelmingly exemplary behavior, there are also actions that he takes that seem to confound *dharma* – not only his acceptance of impure fruit offered to him by a tribal woman but also his lying to Śūrpaṇikhā in saying that Lakṣmaṇa was unmarried as the two toy with her and then disfigure her, his treatment of Sītā in both the fire ordeal and her abandonment, his killing of the Śūdra Śambūka for practicing ascetic penance (forbidden and thus adharmic for those of low caste), and his killing of the monkey-prince Sugriva's older brother Vālin in an ignoble and un-warrior-like fashion – ambushing him instead of fighting him face-to-face.

These incidents occasion discussions of ethical behavior (Richman, 2001). Rāma's actions are often placed in a wider context, with his divinity setting his actions on a higher plane so that, for example, Śambūka's death is necessary to save multiple lives, and he achieves liberation and fame in his death at Rāma's hands (Aklujkar, 2001, 95–96). The case made for Rāma's mode of killing Vālin, even by Rāma himself when he is questioned by the dying monkey king within Vālmīki's telling, is less convincing, though generally accepted, for Rāma must uphold his own promise to Sugriva and Vālin is guilty of serious wrongdoing, at least by Sugriva's account (Hiltebeitel, 2011, 455–456). Rāma's acceptance of tasted, tainted fruit from the tribal woman Śabarī reveals his awareness that she is motivated by an unquestioning devotion, only wanting to give him the very sweetest, and shows his gracious and compassionate acceptance of her loving intention regardless of purity restrictions. In some instances, questionable behavior is clearly attributed to another character so that, for example, the violent disfigurement of Śūrpaṇikhā is carried out by Lakṣmaṇa alone – the impassioned and loyal warrior who sometimes acts before he thinks, as he does in leaving Sītā alone when he thinks that he hears Rāma's cry in the forest, thus opening the way for her abduction. These and similar "doubts" raised lovingly by devotees regarding aspects of the story often become an occasion for religious teaching reinforcing proper dharmic behavior, as documented in collection of questions and answers recorded in the literary genre of Śaṅkāvalīs, Garlands of Doubts (Hess, 2001).

Still other interpreters read the episodes of Vālin and Śambūka as well as Rāvaṇa's demonization and defeat more negatively and politically, as the violent assertion of Brahmanical and North Indian domination, and at times employ them to challenge dharmic norms on ethical grounds and critique oppression and injustice. The stories of Śūrpaṇikhā and also Ahalyā (who knowingly or unknowingly makes love with Indra when he comes to her in the form of her sage husband Gautama, and she is cursed by the sage to suffer invisibly – as a rock in Kampaṉ's telling – until she is liberated by Rāma) are also used to reinforce normative behavior, warning women of the dangers of unrestrained sexual desire and temptation. Yet these stories, too, can become a means to question existing norms. Why was Ahalyā punished so severely, especially if she did not see through Indra's disguise, and what of Gautama's anger (Ramanujan, 1991, 24–33)? Sītā touches off discussions of men's unethical treatment of their wives, and though some see her as subservient, others (including → Gandhi and the organizers of the Lakshmi Mukti campaign for women's economic rights) find in her an effective moral exemplar, whose suffering must be put right and who can challenge tyranny in her purity and fearlessness, even as she successfully resisted Rāvaṇa and refused Rāma's final demand for further proof of her fidelity (Kishwar, 2001). Such exemplary figures and their stories play a central role in thinking through ethical questions and motivating ethical action.

The heroes of the much more extended *Mahābhārata* epic are less divine and far more ambivalent, and their victory in battle is marked by sorrow rather than triumph. This too is a story about *dharma* and turns around a crisis over succession to a throne, reflecting Kṣatriya perspectives and foregrounding conflicting dharmic obligations. The main story line recounts the battle of two sets of cousins but is filled with side stories and dharmic discourses with a multitude of embedded stories (Smith, 2009, xv–xviii). As the epic goes, the elder son of King Vicitavīrya, Dhṛtarāṣṭra, was born blind, and so his younger brother Pāndu succeeds their father. But after Pāṇḍu dies, Dhṛtarāṣṭra does take the throne, and Pāṇḍu's five sons, known as the Pāṇḍavas, are raised together with their hundred cousins, the Kauravas. The eldest of the Kauravas, Duryodhana, claims the right to succession and tries to kill off his cousins, who escape. The Pāṇḍavas challenge Duryodhana's right to rule, and, wanting to make peace, Dhṛtarāṣṭra divides the kingdom in half, with the north ruled by Duryodhana and the south by Yudhiṣṭhira, the eldest of the Pāṇḍavas. Yudhiṣṭhira (who is also said to be the son of the deity Dharma) has a weakness for gambling and is eventually entrapped by the jealous and avaricious Duryodhana in a rigged match, losing everything, including their kingdom, himself, his brothers, and their joint wife Draupadī. Famously, when the Kauravas try to publicly humiliate Draupadī by stripping her before the court, she cries out to → Kṛṣṇa, miraculously her clothing lengthens endlessly, and they are unable to dishonor her.

Dhṛtarāṣṭra restores their losses, but Duryodhana insists on a final wager, which Yudhiṣṭhira also loses. He and his brothers together with → Draupadī must go into exile for 12 years and remain incognito and undiscovered for one more year before they can return to reclaim their kingdom. Their many adventures during this period are recounted, but when they finally return at the end of 13 years, Duryodhana refuses to yield. War is unavoidable, and the battle lines are drawn, with male family members, allies, and teachers arrayed against each other on both sides. The greatest warrior and youngest of the Pāṇḍavas, Arjuna, rides out to survey the troops with his charioteer, Kṛṣṇa (who he does not realize is god incarnate), and loses his will to fight, questioning what could possibly make it right or worthwhile to kill family and revered elders. The crucial conversation that ensues between them is recorded as the *Bhagavadgītā*.

In the end, Arjuna leads the Pāṇḍavas' armies into a battle that lasts 18 days. All of the Kauravas are killed, but at the devastating cost of dharmic compromises and the deaths of family (including sons), revered elders and *guru*s, and allies, and there is no joy in the victory. Yudhiṣṭhira becomes king for a time but ultimately abdicates, turning the throne over to a relative, and, having renounced their royal life, the brothers and their wife set out to wander the world. All die when they reach the Himalayas except Yudhiṣṭhira, but they are eventually reunited in Indra's heaven after Yudhiṣṭhira passes one final dharmic test. Innumerable smaller stories are woven throughout the tale, and these narratives, too, as well as the larger story are told in multiple versions and invoked in conversations of *dharma* and what constitutes right action, with the *Bhagavadgītā* playing a particularly significant role in this regard.

The *Mahābhārata*, though it too is a story about *dharma*, is not necessarily about providing exemplars or the clear triumph of good over evil. Rather, in the words of G. Das, it is "about our incomplete lives, about good people acting badly, about how difficult it is to be good in this world" (2009, li). It is about the consequences of greed, arrogance, anger, jealousy, and revenge, of moral weakness and the failure to act, and of the lust for power and the willingness to risk anyone and everything in the desire to win. It is about the devastation caused by violence even in the context of a just or righteous war and about the paralyzing conflicts that arise between divergent familial duties, social responsibilities, and individual moral inclination. Yudhiṣṭhira, called Dharmarāja ("Dharma King") and praised for his intelligence and compassion, nevertheless struggles with right action throughout the epic, proclaiming (in a popular verse that is likely a later interpolation),

> Reasoning is without foundation...; the *śrutis* contradict one-another...; there is not even one Ṛṣi [enlightened sage] whose opinion is authoritative...The truth about *dharma* is hidden in a cave. (Hiltebeitel, 2011, 433)

The proper way to act is not necessarily easily discerned at all and is certainly not a matter of formal adherence to law codes for the hero. Such is his situation when he is faced with the prospect of lying to Droṇa, the respected Brahman warrior allied with Duryodhana who had been Yudhiṣṭhira's *guru*, training all the young Pāṇḍavas and Kauravas in martial skills.

Truth, together with noncruelty, nonviolence, and compassion, is a cardinal virtue in the *Mahābhārata* as well as vedic literature. Yet Droṇa is wreaking havoc on the Pāṇḍavas and their allies and can only be defeated if he puts down his own weapon. The only thing that would possibly make him do so would be hearing of the death of his son Aśvatthāman. Learning this, Yudhiṣṭhira's younger brother Bhīma kills an elephant of the same name and then tells him that Aśvatthāman has been slain. Droṇa does not believe him and asks Yudhiṣṭhira if it is true. Yudhiṣṭhira does not want to lie, but if he does not support Bhīma, he will effectively call him a liar, betraying his loyalty, and there is seemingly no other way to stop Droṇa. Even Kṛṣṇa encourages him to lie. Yudhiṣṭhira chooses to speak the truth, saying, "the elephant is slain," but he knows that Droṇa will be deceived, thinking that he refers to his son. This intentional deception, even to prevent further cruelty, has the immediate effect of bringing Yudhiṣṭhira's chariot wheels down to earth (previously they had floated above the ground because of his great righteousness), and this un-warrior-like and dharmically questionable tactic haunts him throughout his life (Hiltebeitel, 2011, 457–479; Ganeri, 2005).

At the end of the tale, Yudhiṣṭhira is challenged to make two final ethical choices. He alone among his brothers is still alive, accompanied only by a stray dog that had followed them from the start of their journey. Indra is ready to take him up to heaven, but Yudhiṣṭhira refuses to go without the dog, who has been "constant in his devotion" and for whom he feels compassion. Indra assures him that there is no cruelty in leaving the highly polluted animal behind and even insinuates that his attachment to the dog is irrational and constitutes a moral failure for one who has renounced all else. However, Yudhiṣṭhira responds that he will not abandon one who has been devoted to him, considering it equal to the terrible sins of "[s]urrendering to his enemies someone seeking refuge, killing a woman, robbing a Brahmin; [and] harming a friend" (Smith, 2009, 776; Dalmiya, 2001, 295). The dog, as it turns out, is Dharma himself, and Yudhiṣṭhira's decision is affirmed as the correct one. He is lauded for his "intelligence, good conduct and compassion for all beings" – his ethical maturity, backed by action (Smith, 2009, 777).

His final test comes after he reaches heaven. Duryodhana is there in heaven, having fulfilled his Kṣatriya *dharma* by dying in battle in spite of his other failings, but not Yudhiṣṭhira's brothers, Draupadī, and their kin. When Yudhiṣṭhira expresses outrage that Duryodhana is there despite the trouble that he caused for so many, he is reminded of his own gambling away of everything. He goes in search of his brothers and Draupadī and ultimately arrives in a horrible hell. Though he could leave, he remains there even before he knows they are there, out of compassion for suffering beings, who find relief in his presence. Once he knows that it is Draupadī and his brothers who call out, he is grief stricken and angrily tells the gods that he will remain in hell with his own. Again he has made the right choice, and all now find themselves transported to heaven.

The ethical and human complexity of such episodes and the stories within stories found in the narrative provides a rich ground for reflection on a range of issues by scholars and nonscholars alike. The narrative also includes two major discourses on *dharma* and right action. The dying Bhīṣma (celibate brother of the great grandfather of the Pāṇḍavas, who must fight for the Kauravas and is fatally wounded in the battle but remains alive) engages in an extended dialogue with Yudhiṣṭhira, who initially wants to renounce the world at the end of the battle (Smith, 2009, 606–702). In the course of their conversation, which lasts many days, Bhīṣma explains the *varnāśrama* obligations in detail and especially the dharmic duties of kings, including just war practices and the implementation of justice and punishment. He also addresses decision making, advocating the careful and reasoned thinking through of situations, particularly in times of trouble, illustrating each point with further stories (e.g. he recounts the tale of the renown Brahman sage Viśvāmitra, who considered it acceptable both to steal dog meat from an outcaste and to consume this forbidden food in order to save his own life in a time of terrible famine; Smith, 2009, 622). In the end, Bhīṣma tells Yudhiṣṭhira that a king, too, must do what is necessary for his subjects and the kingdom, rather than pursuing his own desires (including the desire for his own moral perfection and liberation), and must at times engage in what might for others be considered adharmic behavior, including killing. Yudhiṣṭhira finally agrees to fulfill his royal Kṣatriya destiny, at least until the time is right for renunciation. There is much here to serve as a guide for *what* to do, but with respect to *how* to undertake action, it is the earlier dialogue that occurs between Kṛṣṇa and Arjuna on the battlefield that offers a way to unite dharmic action with spiritual liberation or *mokṣa*.

The Ethics of the *Bhagavadgītā*

The battlefield conversation between Arjuna and Kṛṣṇa, which forms the *Bhagavadgītā*, is the most significant Hindu scriptural resource for many today. Initially generated by Arjuna's practical dilemma about whether to fight, his familial and Kṣatriya *dharmas* requiring him to act in diametrically opposed ways, his charioteer Kṛṣṇa (who is in fact the supreme god) appears to support standard dharmic codes, telling him to fulfill his caste duty as a Kṣatriya and reassuring him that the true self of all beings, *ātman*, cannot be killed. But the conversation quickly turns to deeper issues – the nature of the self and reality and the "how" and not just the "what" or "why" of action. The battle addressed is much more than the particular war in which Arjuna is about to engage or even outward interpersonal, social, and political battles for righteousness and justice. It is also the inner struggle that all must face in learning to act without attachment to the fruits of action, whether they be negative or positive, and thus to remove all trace of self-interest (*BhG.* 2.47). One is to do what is right or dharmically necessary to sustain the world, but even this binds one to the cycle of rebirth if one does it with hope for any reward – even that of knowing oneself to be a good person – or with any trace of pride or disappointment at the outcome of the action. Simple renunciation or abstention from action are not options (*BhG.* 3.4) – these too are actions, so it is imperative that one learn how to act in this liberative way.

The text does not concern itself so much with what that right action is, though there is mention of doing one's own *dharma*, however imperfectly, rather than someone else's (*BhG.* 3.48), and Kṛṣṇa affirms that he created humans in four classes (*BhG.* 4.13). The character and qualities of a person who acts free from attachment and in the midst of the world are described. Such a one will be "friendly, compassionate, unselfish, free from individuality, patient" (*BhG.* 12.13), "content always, disciplined, self-controlled, firm in... resolve" (*BhG.* 12.14), "free of delight, rage, fear, and disgust" (*BhG.* 12.15), "disinterested, pure, skilled, indifferent, untroubled" (*BhG.* 12.16), and "impartial to foe and friend, honor and contempt, cold and heat, joy and suffering" (*BhG.* 12.18; Miller, 1986, 111). Arjuna rightly counters that acting without attachment is very hard to do, and Kṛṣṇa counsels him to discipline the senses, to break the cascade of desire, of attachment, of anger, hatred, and fear, of confusion, and of loss of memory and understanding that leads only to destruction (*BhG.* 2.61–63; 3.34), but also to offer all his actions up as a sacrifice to god (*BhG.* 3.9; 4.23–33). In whatever way people approach him with faith, Kṛṣṇa assures Arjuna, he will respond (*BhG.* 4.11; 7.21). Acting in this way is profoundly liberating, for "[w]hen a man is unattached and free, his reason deep in knowledge, acting only in sacrifice, his action is wholly dissolved" (*BhG.* 4.23; Miller, 1986, 54). Karmic consequences do not adhere to one who acts without self-involvement of any kind. Such a one is profoundly free, and such a life is marked by joy, equanimity, clarity, and boundless energy.

Across the chapters of the *Bhagavadgītā*, Kṛṣṇa speaks of the nature of reality, of *ātman* and *brahman*, of his own nature as the one lord who encompasses all things, and of discipline and devotion and the motivation and causes of action, drawing on the Sāṃkhya dualism of → *puruṣa* (pure consciousness) and → *prakṛti* (material or manifest existence, including mind), further characterized by the three → *guṇas* or qualities of *tamas* (inertia, ignorance), *rajas* (passion, energy), and *sattva* (goodness, light). Some read the *Bhagavadgītā* as a text advocating principally → *bhakti* or devotion to god and others as holding the pursuit of liberating knowledge (→ *jñāna*) through disciplined meditation as the highest pursuit. Still others see Kṛṣṇa as advocating a path to liberation through the heart of action – the *karmayoga* path of desireless action or *niṣkāmakarma* – in a way that integrates the Brahmanical value of dharmic ritual and social order tempered with Śramaṇa-like detachment and an emerging devotional understanding of the ultimate underlying unitive reality (Bilimoria, 1991, 50). Some see three equal paths to liberation outlined therein, inclusive of differences in individual human inclinations; others see supplements to one primary path. Some see a decisive shift away from ritual action to ethical action performed without attachment to its fruits; others see a profound rejection of the life of renunciation in favor of engaged action for the betterment and flourishing of other individuals, society, and humanity at large.

On the practical level, some, like B.G. Tilak (or → Lokmanya Tilak) and other Indian nationalists, would also read this text as a call to action from god for the sake of one's people or nation and the welfare of the world, a call that might require the measured use of necessary violence and just war, while others, most notably M.K. Gandhi, would find here a manifesto for nonviolent social action (Minor, 1986). The *Bhagavadgītā* has invoked considerable reflection on the meaning of detachment and relinquishing desire in the context of engaged action and the human goals of *kāma* and *artha* as well as *dharma* and *mokṣa*, on the determination of specific actions in accord with *dharma* and truth, and on the place of autonomy and individual determination of one's *dharma* in relation to normative *varṇāśramadharma* (Lipner, 1997). The *Bhagavadgītā* has come to play a central role in understandings of Hinduism formulated by great *gurus* like Sri → Aurobindo, → Vivekananda, and A.C. → Bhaktivedanta Prabhupada, as well as activists following in the footsteps of Gandhi and Vinoba Bhave and for more ordinary people seeking to live out Hindu principles in their everyday lives (Minor, 1986).

The Ethical Challenge of Devotional Hinduism

The idea of offering one's actions as an act of sacrifice to god is coupled with an emphasis on devotion in the *Bhagavadgītā*. From the 6th century CE onward in India, devotion comes to be the heart of Hinduism for many – a devotion that is experienced as deeply personal and marked by intimacy and affection, encompassing the deepest dimensions of love in human relationships. Devotees relate to the divine as servants to a master, as children to a parent and vice versa, and as friends and as lovers, and they are caught between the manifest distinction that makes love possible, the union that joins lover to beloved, and the unity that dissolves one into the other. To make love manifest is the reason for human existence, and to draw others also into such love is the calling of the Hindu devotional or *bhakti* saint. At the heart of this tradition is a radical egalitarianism, for all are equally loved by the divine and capable of love, and the divine reality, whether encountered with form (e.g. as Viṣṇu or his *avatār*s, especially Kṛṣṇa and Rāma, as → Śiva, or as → Mahādevī in any of her forms) or as ultimately beyond the limits of any form, is also understood to be singular, profoundly personal, and characterized by love. Birth status, purity, education, and wealth have nothing to do with love for and by this one god, and thus among the recognized saints are women and members of the lowest castes as well as men and Brahmans. The language of such intimacy is not the Sanskrit of the learned and twice-born but the vernacular languages of intimate communication, accessible to all.

J.S. Hawley suggests that *bhakti* "poses the most serious questions to the canons of *dharma*" (Hawley, 2005, 49). Caste hierarchies are directly challenged by a number of the saints on the grounds of the fundamental equality and dignity of all, by virtue of being beloved of god and possessed of a valued human birth, allowing for the possibility of realization and relationship. Arguments for purity are challenged in song by saints like the North Indian low-caste weaver → Kabīr – all bodies excrete impure substances, and all are born in the same way and rot in the same way when they die. The milk that they drink (but refuse to share together) comes from the same animal, "trickling through bones, melting through flesh," and the water considered pure or impure has all passed through the water cycle – flowing through corpses, a hatching place for "[f]ish, turtles and crocodiles" (Hess & Singh, 2002, 57). Distinctions are external to the true self, and hierarchies and oppositions are human made, whether posited between people of different castes, Hindus and Muslims, or men and women. Women saints further counter the *Manusmṛti*'s assertion that wives should treat their husbands like god, claiming instead that they take god for their husbands as the only one worthy of such devotion (Kishwar, 1989).

The stories of low-caste saints' lives also challenge the injustice of the caste system in judging spiritual authority, with the *bhakti* saints time and again shown to be superior in relation to Brahmans who deny the saints' qualifications on grounds of impurity and the violation of dharmashastric regulations. Women saints' stories, too, belie the inferiority of women in religious matters and counter restrictions on religious practice based on women's purity status, asserting the rightness of practicing devotion at all times (Kishwar, 1989). J.S. Hawley suggests that these hagiographic tales, like the epic narratives, "teach character in addition to precept; they praise personal resourcefulness and tenacity in a way that codes scarcely can" – but they also go further by proposing "a new version of *dharma: a bhakti dharma*, an ethics of character that focuses on love," and "offers a paradigm of virtuous living that seems consciously intended to supplant the old" (Hawley, 2005, 49, 62). Among the virtues demonstrated are the fearlessness of the woman saint → Mīrābāī, the extraordinary generosity and faith in divine abundance of Brahman saint → Narasiṃha Mehtā, and the incredible service to the community by former king and queen, turned householder-renouncers, Pīpā and his wife. This portrayal, J.S. Hawley suggests, "does not so much cancel recognizably dharmic virtues, as it liberates them from the social codes and contexts to which they are usually subordinated," reversing the flow, for example, of hospitality toward the Brahman, placing fearlessness not in the warrior but in the woman, and showing the Kṣatriya serving the Śūdra in a transformed vision of community, defined by a disregard for distinctions in a shared love of god rather than "social differentiation and complementary function" (Hawley, 2005, 63).

This radical egalitarianism and challenge to social and spiritual inequality led to the actual instantiation of communities that refused to honor caste distinctions, notably the 11th-century Vīraśaiva (or → Liṅgāyat) community in Kalyana, where intercaste dining and marriage were commonplace, though the virulent backlash of the wider society all too soon brought the experiment to an end (Ramanujan, 1973, 63–64). With the passing of the founding saints, the institutionalization of these devotional movements also often reverted to the wider social order, with equality relegated to the spiritual realm and *varṇāśrama* and gender *dharma* viewed as subordinate to devotion to god but still applicable to ordinary social life. Indeed, some would argue that *bhakti* served a compensatory function for the oppressed and glorified relations of servitude and dominance in transposing them into human–divine relations, but others continue to see in it a site of radical resistance to unethical social norms that perpetuated inequality and a counter-affirmation of the dignity of all, promoting an alternate set of moral claims and values and an alternate vision of ethical community (Guha, 1989, 259; Omveldt, 2008, 33–132; Mukta, 1994; Martin, 2002).

Gandhi's Practical Ethics of Truth and Nonviolence

In discussions of contemporary Hindu ethics, Gandhi looms large as one who applied Hindu ethical principles to addressing real-world problems in an innovative and effective manner. In developing his ethical system centered on truth (→ *satya*) and nonviolence (→ *ahiṃsā*), he drew from the Śruti and Smṛti texts, especially the *Bhagavadgītā*, and on the songs and stories of the *bhakti* saints, mixed with Jain and other influences, religious and otherwise (particularly Leo Tolstoy). For Gandhi, truth is paramount – indeed, he famously identified both "God as Truth" and "Truth as God" (Prabhu, 2007, 400). In his view, one's *dharma* and the moral life are most fundamentally based on acting according to truth. Yet truth in the ideal absolute sense is something that no limited human individual or community can know completely. At this level, "*satya* is derived from *Sat*, the self-existent essence, both the Is and the Ought of Reality" (Prabhu, 2007, 401). All, then, should be "seekers after the truth," employing reasoning in as unprejudiced and honest a way as possible, not only listening to the inner voice of conscience but also engaging in discussion and debate with others, and being open to and respecting alternate views. For Gandhi, even Śruti texts should be scrutinized in this way.

In Gandhi's view, apprehending truth necessarily leads to action, action that is nonviolent and selfless in character and that is on the side of justice and equity and marked by compassion and care (Nadkarni, 2011, 36–42). The self-control and humility needed for such nonviolent action are to be cultivated through the renunciation of sensual desires and reinforced through practices of austerity and simplicity and through continual self-reflection on one's own motives, understandings, and actions. The ability to listen to the inner voice of truth and to conform one's will to that truth is further facilitated by *bhakti*, and indeed songs of *bhakti* saints were regularly sung in Gandhi's *āśram*, and he lifted Mīrābāī up as an ideal practitioner of nonviolence.

"In judging what is good or bad, the Gandhian approach can be said to consist of three criteria: motive, means and consequences" (Nadkarni, 2011, 9). One's motive must be more than self-interest, however enlightened; means must be "pure" and nonviolent, and consequences must be evaluated and judged on the degree to which they contribute to the welfare of all beings. The equality and dignity of people, freedom and satisfaction of basic needs, economic and environmental sustainability, and peace were key elements of this welfare in Gandhi's view, and for him, to act according to the truth had political and economic repercussions as well as social and interpersonal implications. In such action, one wields the force of truth, first through reasoning and persuasion and then if necessary through noncooperation and through an alternate form of → *tapas* (austerity): "the willingness to suffer for one's own cause" – in so doing, one challenges the heart as well as the mind of one's adversary, even as one respects his or her "moral agency and dignity" (Prabhu, 2007, 402–403). In this way,

> far from a passive "do not" injunction, *ahimsa* (non-injury), when intertwined with *satyagraha* (truth-force), becomes a positive mode of action that raises the *intent* of this injunction to a much higher ethical level: it seeks to bring about what is *right* in the situation at hand. (Bilimoria, 1991, 55)

Gandhi has been criticized for not sufficiently challenging patriarchal and caste domination in his own search for truth and in word and action. He rejected the inequality and oppression but not the structure of the *varṇa* system, insisting on the possibility of an egalitarian complementarity of social functions and responsibilities. Yet he also insisted that upper-caste people must work to remove the oppression of the lower castes, because it was they who imposed it (though in so doing, it can be argued, he denied political agency to actual low-caste people; Sarkar, 2011, 178–184). He also did not fundamentally question normative complementary gender roles and assigned qualities, though he encouraged women to develop masculine strength and fearlessness even as men must develop feminine endurance and self-sacrifice (Sarkar, 2011, 184–191). Yet he did open the doors for women's active engagement in political action, even as he also made domestic action political in his spinning campaign. And it must be admitted that Gandhi's thinking on both gender and caste evolves with time, as his ethic requires, through constant self-reflection and self-interrogation and discussion and debate with others marked by an attitude of openness (Sarkar, 2011, 173). Though some may question the influence of Gandhi's ethic in India today, clearly his thought has had a monumental impact on social movements for equality and civil rights across the globe and continues to influence discussions of environmental and economic sustainability, human and animal rights, and much more (Bilimoria, 1991, 53; Nadkarni, 2011; Chapple, 1993; Sharma, 2003).

The Contemporary Study of Hindu Ethics

The academic study of Hindu ethics has its origins in the colonial encounter, with characterizations of Hinduism as fundamentally world denying, of the doctrine of *karman* as leading to fatalism rather than moral responsibility, of Indian philosophy as lacking in systematic focus on morality and ethics, of Hindu dharmic injunctions leading to a blind following of duty, and of what little ethical reflection there is as being hopelessly relativistic (Nadkarni, 2011, 214–218). Such characterizations generated a host of counter-arguments grounded in textual study that included epic and other narrative traditions as well as careful reading of both Śruti and classical philosophical commentarial traditions (Patton, 2007, 118–120; Crawford, 1974; Bilimoria *et al.*, 2007). The largely neglected role of customary practice in actual ethical and also legal decision making has also been documented, by V. Narayanan and others, at times superseding the normative injunctions of the Dharmaśāstras and belying the status accorded to the *Manusmṛti* by the British in the establishment of Hindu personal law – Śūdra landowners and renouncers in South India, Brahman widow remarriage in Gujarat, and women's independent actions in, for example, offering financial support to religious institutions in their own names (Narayanan, 2001).

Analyses of a range of contemporary ethical challenges from Hindu perspectives are also being carried out, from ongoing debates regarding equity in caste and gender relations to issues of abortion, euthanasia, nonviolence, human rights and responsibilities, bioethics, vegetarianism and the treatment of animals, and environmental ethics (Coward *et al.*, 1989; Chapple, 1993; Crawford, 2003; Sharma, 2003). The majority of such studies look to Śruti and Smṛti resources for relevant passages that could inform Hindu approaches, particularly for new technologies like selective amniocentesis or in vitro fertilization, with authors also drawing on systematic reasoning and their own moral conscience in determining what a Hindu ethical response might or should look like. With respect to abortion, there are multiple scriptural passages that indicate that a fetus is a person from the moment of conception and that killing a fetus is wrong, leading some authors to conclude that Hindu ethics would or should oppose and seek to limit abortion (Crawford, 2003; Coward *et al.*, 1989). Yet W. Doniger and B.K. Smith suggest that if Manu were addressing this issue today, he might in all likelihood not espouse an absolute position of either pro-choice or anti-abortion. Instead, they suggest,

> He would probably say something like this: "A woman who already has three children and is over thirty can have an abortion and a woman who has no children and is under thirty cannot have an abortion." (Doniger & Smith, 1991, lvii)

Such a ruling would take into account specifics of context and would allow room for interpretation for situations not addressed directly by the criteria. In fact, as V. Narayanan notes, abortion was legalized with little debate or opposition in India, and people do seem to address this issue in the more contextual way in which W. Doniger and B.K. Smith suggest even Manu might have done, with "religio-legal texts… hav[ing] limited bearing on daily life" (Narayanan, 2001, 193).

Ethnographic studies are being undertaken to shed light on how individuals and communities actually make ethical decisions and construct and maintain "ethical selves" in the exigencies of everyday life and the ways in which vedic and Smṛti sources are construed and mobilized and the additional ethical resources accessed through regional oral, folk, and women's narrative and song traditions, family stories, proverbs, and the like (Prasad, 2007; Jeffrey, 2010). In many of these studies, Hindu ethical insights are being brought to bear on Western theories and Western theories on Indian contexts. For example, V. Dalmiya interrogates feminist care ethics in light of the story of Yudhiṣṭhira and the dog as well as another tale that Bhīṣma tells him about a parrot that chooses to remain in a poisoned and dying tree that had protected and nourished it, though to do so will also lead to its own demise, and L. Patton fruitfully brings E. Levinas into conversation with vedic literature to bring forth new dimensions of the ethical stance being advocated therein (Dalmiya, 2001; Patton, 2007). This kind of lively and open ethical debate and dialogue stands in continuity with Hindu ethical traditions of the past, drawing on sacred scriptures, traditions of remembering and reasoning, and engagement of conscience and narrative, to respond not only with thoughtful compassion and integrity but also with humility and openness to specific challenges that arise.

Bibliography

Aklujkar, V., "Crying Dogs and Laughing Trees in Rāma's Kingdom: Self-reflexivity in the *Ānanda Rāmāyaṇa*," in: P. Richmond, ed., *Questioning Rāmāyaṇas: A South Asian Tradition*, Berkeley, 2001, 83–103.

Bilimoria, P., "Karma's Suffering: A Mīmāṃsā Solution to the Problem of Evil," in: P. Bilimoria, J. Prabhu & R. Sharma, eds., *Indian Ethics: Classical Traditions and Contemporary Challenges*, vol. I, Hampshire, 2007, 171–190.

Bilimoria, P., "Indian Ethics," in: P. Singer, ed., *A Companion to Ethics*, Oxford, 1991, 43–57.

Chapple, C., *Nonviolence to Animals, Earth and Self in Asian Traditions*, Albany, 1993.

Crawford, S.C., *Hindu Bioethics for the Twenty-first Century*, Albany, 2003.

Crawford, S.C., *The Evolution of Hindu Ethical Ideals*, Calcutta, 1974.

Coward, H., J. Lipner & K. Young, *Hindu Ethics: Purity, Abortion, and Euthanasia*, Albany, 1989.

Dalmiya, V., "Dogged Loyalties: A Classical Indian Intervention in Care Ethics," in: J. Runzo & N.M. Martin, eds., *Ethics in the World Religions*, Oxford, 2001, 293–306.

Daniélou, A., *Virtue, Success, Pleasure and Liberation: The Four Aims of Life in the Tradition of Ancient India*, Rochester, 1993.

Das, G., *The Difficulty of Being Good: On the Subtle Art of Dharma*, Oxford, 2009.

Doniger, W., *The Rig Veda*, London, 1981.

Doniger, W., & B.K. Smith, *The Laws of Manu*, London, 1991.

Flood, G., *An Introduction to Hinduism*, Cambridge UK, 1996.

Ganeri, J., "A Dynamic Tradition of Truth-Telling: Moral Innovation in the *Mahābhārata*," in: F. Squarcini, ed.,

Boundaries, Dynamics and Constructions of Tradition in South Asia, Florence, 2005, 175–201.
Guha, R., "Dominance without Hegemony and Its Historiography," in: R. Guha, ed., *Subaltern Studies VI: Writings on South Asian History and Society*, Oxford, 1989, 210–309.
Hawley, J.S., "Morality beyond Morality in the Lives of Three Hindu Saints," in: J.S. Hawley, *Three Bhakti Voices: Mirabai, Surdas and Kabir in Their Times and Ours*, New York, 2005, 48–69.
Hess, L., "Lovers' Doubts: Questioning the Tulsi Rāmāyaṇ," in: P. Richmond, ed., *Questioning Rāmāyaṇas: A South Asian Tradition*, Berkeley, 2001, 25–47.
Hess, L., & S. Singh, *The Bijak of Kabir*, New York, 2002.
Hiltebeitel, A., *Dharma: Its Early History in Law, Religion and Narrative*, Oxford, 2011.
Jeffrey, C., "Demoralizing Developments: Ethics, Class, and Student Power in Modern North India," in: A. Pandian & D. Ali, eds., *Ethical Life in South Asia*, Bloomington, 2010, 192–208.
Kishwar, M., "Yes to Sita, No to Ram: The Continuing Hold of Sita on Popular Imagination in India," in: P. Richmond, ed., *Questioning Rāmāyaṇas: A South Asian Tradition*, Berkeley, 2001, 285–308.
Kishwar, M., ed., "Women Bhakta Poets," *Manushi 50-52*, 1989.
Lipner, J., *Hindus: Their Beliefs and Practices*, Abingdon, [2]2010.
Lipner, J., ed., *The Fruits of Our Desiring: An Enquiry into the Ethics of the Bhagavadgītā for Our Times*, Calgary, 1997.
Lutgendorf, P., *The Life of a Text: Performing the Rāmcaritmānas of Tulsidas*, Delhi, 1994.
Martin, N.M., "Homespun Threads of Dignity and Protest: Songs of Kabīr in Rural Rajasthan," in: M. Horstmann, ed., *Images of Kabīr*, New Delhi, 2002, 201–214.
Matilal, B.K., "Dharma and Rationality," in: P. Bilimoria, J. Prabhu & R. Sharma, eds., *Indian Ethics: Classical Traditions and Contemporary Challenges*, vol. I, Hampshire, 2007, 79–102.
Matilal, B.K., *Ethics and Epics: The Collected Essays of Bimal Krishna Matilal*, New Delhi, 2002.
Miller, B.S., *The Bhagavad-Gita: Krishna's Counsel in Time of War*, New York, 1986.
Minor, R., ed., *Modern Indian Interpreters of the Bhagavadgita*, Albany, 1986.
Mohanty, J.N., "Dharma, Imperatives, and Tradition: Toward an Indian Theory of Moral Action," in: P. Bilimoria, J. Prabhu & R. Sharma, eds., *Indian Ethics: Classical Traditions and Contemporary Challenges*, vol. I, Hampshire, 2007, 57–78.
Mukta, P., *Upholding the Common Life: The Community of Mirabai*, New Delhi, 1994.
Nadkarni, M.V., *Ethics for Our Times: Essays in Gandhian Perspective*, Delhi, 2011.
Narayanan, V., "Hindu Ethics and Dharma," in: J. Runzo & N.M. Martin, eds., *Ethics in the World Religions*, Oxford, 2001, 177–195.
Olivelle, P., *Dharmasūtras: The Law Codes of Ancient India*, Oxford, 1999.
Omveldt, G., *Seeking Begumpura: The Social Vision of Anticaste Intellectuals*, New Delhi, 2008.
Patton, L., "The Fires of Strangers: A Levinasian Approach to Vedic Ethics," in: P. Bilimoria, J. Prabhu & R. Sharma, eds., *Indian Ethics: Classical Traditions and Contemporary Challenges*, vol. I, Hampshire, 2007, 117–147.
Prabhu, J., "Gandhi, Empire, and a Culture of Peace," in: P. Bilimoria, J. Prabhu & R. Sharma, eds., *Indian Ethics: Classical Traditions and Contemporary Challenges*, vol. I, Hampshire, 2007, 395–410.
Prasad, L., *Poetics of Conduct: Oral Narrative and Moral Being in a South Indian Town*, New York, 2007.
Ramanujan, A.K., "Three Hundred *Rāmānyaṇas*: Five Examples and Three Thoughts on Translation," in: P. Richmond, ed., *Many Rāmāyaṇas: The Diversity of a Narrative Tradition in South Asia*, Berkeley, 1991, 22–49.
Ramanujan, A.K., *Speaking of Śiva*, London, 1973.
Richman, P., ed., *Questioning Rāmāyaṇas: A South Asian Tradition*, Berkeley, 2001.
Richman, P., ed., *Many Rāmāyaṇas: The Diversity of a Narrative Tradition in South Asia*, Berkeley, 1991.
Sarkar, T., "Gandhi and Social Relations," in: J. Brown & A. Parel, eds., *The Cambridge Companion to Gandhi*, Cambridge MA, 2011, 173–195.
Sharma, A., *Hinduism and Human Rights: A Conceptual Approach*, New Delhi, 2003.
Smith, J.D., *The Mahābhārata*, London, 2009.

NANCY M. MARTIN

Human Rights

The 1948 United Nations (UN) Universal Declaration of Human Rights affirms the dignity and worth of the person, the equal rights of men and women, and the rights to life, liberty, and security. Fundamental freedoms to be safeguarded include freedom from slavery, torture, degrading treatment, discrimination, and arbitrary interference with one's privacy, home, or correspondence. There is to be freedom of movement, thought, and religious practice. Social rights include such things as democratic government, the right to work and to receive equal pay for equal work, the right to a standard of living adequate to the health and well-being of oneself and one's family, the right to education, and the right to marry freely. Within the community, the exercise of one's individual rights is constrained only by the recognition of and respect for the rights of others, and in order to meet the just requirements of morality, public order, and general welfare in a democratic society (*United Nations and Human Rights 1945–1995*, 1995). The UN perspective is that the human rights of the declaration and its succeeding conventions are an expression of a minimum set of overlapping moral expectations to which different cultures and religions hold themselves and others accountable. The fundamental underlying presuppositions of the UN declaration include that people are equal at birth and should live in a democratic society.

Orthodox Hindu thought does not share the underlying presuppositions of the UN declaration. Traditional → *karma* and rebirth (→ *saṃsāra*) theory holds that rather than being equal at birth, persons are born with different karmic natures that they have created for themselves by their freely made good or bad choices in previous lives. And the choices they make in this life will create the karmic nature with which they will be born to begin the next life. So no one is equal at birth. Also, the *karma* that one has created for oneself conditions the → caste group one is born into. From this orthodox Hindu perspective, being born into a lower-caste group with fewer privileges is not unfair in that it is a situation one has created for oneself, one's *svadharma* (individual → *dharma*; see also below). It cannot be blamed on fate, god, or any other person, but it is the just result of one's freely chosen actions in past lives (one's *karma*). And, one's caste group in the next life will depend on the choices one makes in this life that will move one's karmic position either up or down the karmic ladder. Brahmans are at the top, and Śūdras and untouchables (see → Dalits) are at the bottom. From the perspective of *karma* and rebirth, that is not unfair (as the UN declaration would suggest) but is the just result of one's own previous choices and is to be lived out and improved upon by the way one handles one's individual and caste duties (*dharma*) in this life. In the Hindu worldview, all humans are seen as equal, but that equality is not experienced until the *karma* that creates caste difference is purged and *mokṣa* (oneness with the divine and release from rebirth; see → liberation) is realized. And this is the goal for each human; we will continue to be reborn until we realize *mokṣa*, so that all will ultimately be equal. For Hinduism, equality is achieved at the end, whereas for the UN declaration, it is a right or status conferred at the beginning. Equality for traditional Hindus is not given at birth, but it is earned through the responsible fulfilling of duties over many lifetimes. Nor is democracy assumed in the Hindu political order, which has traditionally been hierarchical in nature. As the Hindu scholar K. Mitra puts it, Sanskrit, the sacred language of Hindu scriptures and texts, has no equivalent for the English word "right." The closest Sanskrit term seems to be → *adhikāra*, which in Hindu law books (e.g. *Manusmṛti*; see → Dharmaśāstra) describes a "just claim" – but a claim that existed within the context of a hierarchical caste-ordered society in which only the top group, the Brahmans, has such rights (Mitra, 1982, 79–80).

While there are no human rights (of the modern Western sort) in traditional Hindu thought, many scholars agree that the concept of *dharma* or duty serves as a functional parallel to the UN declaration's notion of rights (Coward, 2005, 31–46). Rather than seeing one standard of human rights as the norm for all regardless of sex, age, social class, or stage of life, the *dharma* texts of Hinduism, in a very complex fashion, specify one's duties, responsibilities, and rights in terms of the social context within which one lives one's life. The duties and rights of a Brahman in the student or householder stage, for example, are seen to be very different from those of a merchant or Vaiśya, while in the forest-dweller stage of life, they become virtually the same. Indeed, the *dharma* texts of traditional Hinduism contain a very wide range of discussions, including the duties and rights of kings (see → kingship), of castes, of women (see → gender), of → slaves, of untouchables, of the various stages of life, of → purity and → auspiciousness, of proper → foods for eating, on studying the → Vedas, and on charity, humanitarian, and ecological concerns (Kane, 1974). These discussions do indeed deal with many of the issues raised in the UN Declaration of Human Rights – although from a worldview grounded in radically different presuppositions, namely, those of *karma* and rebirth. It is also clear that these Sanskrit *dharma* texts, along with the various law codes (e.g. *Manusmṛti*), were mainly aimed at high-class Brahmanic males, the influential elite of Hindu society. However, outside of this Brahamanical Orthodox tradition, there was great diversity of both theory and practice. Norms differed all over India according to caste, area, region, gender, and age. The position of women has been stronger in the matriarchal traditions of South India, and many of the Brahmanical limitations of rights were challenged by the medieval devotional (→ *bhakti*) traditions. Even in ancient India, rights were accorded slaves in various situations (and female slaves in cases of sexual abuse, in particular), which seem far more advanced than those of Greece and Rome in the same period (Chanana, 1960).

Scholars have also noted some fundamental differences from the UN declaration in the Hindu approach. Hindu thought lacks the modern Western emphasis on individualism. This is a fundamental issue since the UN declaration's notion of rights is attached to individuals without much concern for obligations to the larger whole of society. In traditional Hindu thought, the order is reversed with identity being experienced as collective and one's duties/rights being premised on the contribution to the social and even cosmic order (*ṛta*). Following from this is a second difference, namely, *dharma* emphasizes the obligations one holds rather than the rights one possesses. A third has to do with the "universality" requirement of the UN declaration. While the rights of the declaration are said to be held by all persons at all times and all places, dharmic obligations are particular – they vary from one stage of life to the next and from one social group to another. Basic to *dharma* is the idea that one's ethical responsibilities depend on such circumstances as age, gender, and family connections (caste). Running through all of this is the idea that each individual has his or her own *dharma* (*svadharma*) – an individual's personal responsibility created by one's own *karma* from previous births. Hindu nationalists today are appealing to this heroic ideal of one's moral destiny in their call for self-sacrifice to mother India.

The Introduction of Human Rights to India by Hindu Renaissance Thinkers and by the 1949 Constitution

Modern Hindu reformers have been sensitive to the injustices resulting from *karma*/rebirth presuppositions and the resulting caste practices, as well as being drawn to the modern Western ideas of rights and freedoms. → Ram Mohan Roy (c. 1800) was the first Hindu thinker to argue for human rights as understood in the UN declaration. Adopting the Enlightenment ideas of reason as *a priori* in human nature, he reinterpreted Hindu tradition using reason to exclude caste and gender restrictions. His critique was especially effective regarding the status of women in Hinduism with the practice of → *satī* (widow burning) being outlawed. Ram Mohan Roy established three guidelines that he and the other Hindu reformers followed in advancing modernity (Crawford, 1987, 192). The first was a faith in rationalism (see → atheism and rationalism) – in the human capacity to reason as a basis for knowledge in religion, science, economics, or social issues. Second, Ram Mohan Roy was convinced of the dignity of the person, derived from his religious beliefs, which he used as a basis of his critique of the treatment of women and the lower castes in Hindu society. His third conviction was that the way forward for India and Hindu society to modernize was via the strategy of "cultural grafting" – of blending Hindu and Western teachings and modes of life. The application of these three approaches to ethics led him to take stands on human rights issues that were indeed radical for his day. He advocated the equality of all irrespective of caste or sex. He sought the total elimination of Hinduism's hierarchical social system. Contrary to the *Manusmṛti*, Ram Mohan Roy finds that the revealed texts of Hinduism, the Vedas and → Upaniṣads, advocate the equality of all humans (Mitra, 1982, 81).

For Hinduism, Ram Mohan Roy set many precedents in the introduction of human rights considerations. He translated Hindu texts from Sanskrit into English and set up his own press for the publication of books and newspapers aimed at the education of the common person. In this way, Ram Mohan Roy made available to women and lower castes the knowledge of the Hindu scriptures from which they had previously been excluded. He was articulate and fearless in protesting British administrative injustices. He advocated a broadly based education system, which would incorporate both Indian and Western knowledge. But his most important campaign was for the rights of women and the abolition of *satī*. He attacked the attitude in Hindu texts and society that resulted in the disempowerment and the lack of rights for women. The faults imputed to women – namely, that they are "of inferior understanding, without resolution, unworthy of trust, subject to passions, and void of virtuous knowledge" – are used to justify the diminution of women's rights and privileges. The only safe place a woman can live a virtuous life, it is claimed, is at home under the care of her father, then her husband, and finally her son. Such a loss of rights and freedoms, says Ram Mohan Roy, frequently makes life for women into a state of misery from youth until death. While described as one-half of her husband in the marriage ceremony, later she is often treated as not much better than a slave in the household duties she is given. As a widow, according to interpretations of Hindu law, all her husband's property passes to her sons or other male members of the extended family, often leaving women destitute. Ram Mohan Roy argues that to improve the situation of widows, inheritance laws need to be changed so that they can inherit property rather than being regarded as property themselves. The consciousness of women needs to be raised through education and a better knowledge of scriptures, which will allow a stronger sense of their own self-worth – namely, that the divine manifests equally in men and women. Because they are exposed only to very selected scriptures and law codes that reinforce their negative self-image, it is no wonder, says Ram Mohan Roy, that some women are willing to embrace *satī* as a way of getting reward in heaven (Nagrand & Burman, 1947).

Ram Mohan Roy's analysis and support for the rights and freedoms of women in Hinduism is remarkable for the period of the early 1800s. According to some scholars, he was the progenitor of the women's movements in modern Indian society (e.g. Crawford, 1987, 226). He not only argued for women's rights to be written into law, but also spoke directly to men about how they must give up their power roles and sexist attitudes if women are to achieve equality. Ram Mohan Roy also emphasized the need for girls and women to have educational opportunities, and so he and his organization, the → Brahmo Samaj, established schools from preschool to post-secondary in which boys and girls were given equal opportunities.

Another Hindu Renaissance thinker, → Dayananda Saraswati (1824–1883), also employed reason in his "back to the Vedas" reformation thrust (Saraswati, 1975). In the vedic period, he claimed, women enjoyed virtually equal status with men and were given an education. Caste was understood to be determined by one's freely chosen role in society, rather than being fixed by birth. These egalitarian ideas were put into practice in the → Arya Samaj movement that Dayananda Saraswati established and were influential in the 20th-century women's movements in India (Jordens, 1978). → Vivekananda (1863–1902) supported Dayananda Saraswati's push for education for all, especially women. He also emphasized the need for social service to India's poor, but retained traditional notions of *karma*, rebirth, and castes (Swami Vivekananda, 1959). He sowed the seed ideas for a nationalistic and "muscular" Hinduism later championed by the Hindu right. Nobel Prize winner Rabindranath → Tagore (1861–1941) was an active social critic in his literary writings (Rukmani, 2003). "He uses his female characters as vehicles for an explicit and radical critique of the caste system, untouchability, and religious hypocrisy" (Rukmani, 2003, 109). Tagore frequently engaged in public debate with Mohandas → Gandhi (1869–1948). While they remained friends, they disagreed on key issues of human rights. On caste, Tagore rejected Gandhi's idea of a purified caste system modeled on that of Vivekananada. Tagore also opposed Gandhi's strategy of setting aside the problem of the untouchables until after Muslim–Hindu tensions and the winning of independence from the British had been dealt with. Indeed, the plight of the untouchables became a "litmus test" for human rights in Hindu India. In the context of the struggle for independence, Gandhi attempted to solve Hindu injustice to the untouchables by integrating them into the Śūdra caste and renaming them "Harijans" (children of god). However, Gandhi's belief in *karma* and rebirth, and his attempt to retain caste without its categorization of "high" or "low," proved unsuccessful as his debates with Dr. B.R. → Ambedkar (1891–1956), leader of the untouchables, made clear (Coward, 2003, 41–66). In the end, it was only when B.R. Ambedkar, Jawaharlal Nehru, and others adopted the modern democratic presuppositions of justice, liberty, fraternity, equality, and secularism and wrote them into the 1949 Constitution of India that rights for untouchables, women, and others were finally established – if only in theory. Transforming society to accord with law has been a slow struggle, as the history of the rights of women and the untouchables in India shows (see Coward, 2005, chs. 8, 10).

B.R. Ambedkar was not only the leader of the untouchables but also minister of law in Nehru's government and the principal drafter of India's new constitution in newly independent India. As an untouchable by birth, B.R. Ambedkar was very aware of the inequalities and loss of freedoms experienced by minority and lower-caste groups in Hindu-dominated India. To overcome these injustices, B.R. Ambedkar, with the support of Nehru and others, introduced the concept of → secularism into the Indian constitution. The preamble to the constitution proclaims that India is a secular republic. As P.N. Bhagwati, former chief justice of the supreme court of India, notes, the concept of secularism has important implications for human rights (Bhagwati, 1993, 8). The first is that every person has the same rights as a citizen and is entitled to the same basic human rights irrespective of the religion that the person professes and practices. Second, there must be complete freedom of conscience and the ability to profess and practice the religion of one's choice. Third, the state should not identify with or favor any particular religion. In their desire to secure these elements of secularism, however, the drafters of the Indian constitution took care to avoid the kind of antireligious overtones that had become associated with secularism as it developed in Christian countries in the West. Thus the Indian concept of secularism has developed its own special meaning with regard to religion, recognizing the relevance and validity of religion in daily life alongside the expanding legitimate functions of the state (Bhagwati, 1993, 9).

Dharma and Human Rights for Hindus Today

V. Narayanan offers a concise survey of the various ways in which Hindus today use the term *dharma* (Narayanan, 2001). *Dharma* (from the root *dhṛ-*, "to sustain, to uphold") is used to refer to → ethics and moral behavior in general and to the Hindu religion as the *sanātan dharma* (the eternal *dharma*). Writings on *dharma* have been used in the formulation of law codes and their administration in India during the last two centuries, thus the direct relationship between *dharma* and human rights. In the early Vedas, the word *dharma* appears many times, and in later texts it means "religious ordinances and rites" or sometimes "fixed principles or rules of conduct." When paired with other words, *dharma* can mean "merit acquired by the performance of religious rites" and "the whole body of religious duties." V. Narayanan comments,

> If one goes through the [*dharma*] texts carefully, one will find discussions on the geographic areas most fit for a human being to lead a righteous and meritorious life (i.e. northern India), and on charity and humanitarian and ecological concerns. (Narayanan, 2001, 178)

The topics and concerns over what is deemed to be *dharma* in the Hindu tradition do indeed deal with many of the issues discussed in the UN Declaration of Human Rights – although from a worldview grounded in radically different presuppositions, namely, those of *karma* and rebirth. Also, as V. Narayanan notes, the Sanskrit *dharma* texts were aimed only at high-caste Brahmanic males:

> In many parts and communities of India, these texts were not held as normative, and vernacular texts and local customs vied with dharmic texts for attention... since these rule books were written by *brahmin* men for other *brahmin* men (a very small but influential percentage of society which considered itself the "elite"), they were by no means followed widely. Norms differed all over India according to caste, area, region, gender and age. (Narayanan, 2001, 179–180)

More widely known throughout India and the Hindu diaspora are the epics, the → *Mahābhārata* including the → *Bhagavadgītā*, the → *Rāmāyaṇa*, and the → Purāṇas. Hindus understand the stories in these texts as exemplifying the values of *dharma*, and their storyline as presenting dharmic dilemmas. → Rāma, hero of the *Rāmāyaṇa*, although heir to the throne, does not claim his rights but goes off into exile honoring his father's wishes. His wife, Sītā (see → Draupadī and Sītā), is taken to be the paradigm of *strīdharma* (womanly *dharma*), yet her life ends sadly when, after remaining true to Rāma through great difficulties, her chastity is questioned and Rāma feigns disinterest toward her. Saddened by Rāma's failure to show his love for her, Sītā submits to a fire test to prove her chastity and emerges unharmed. Even so, she is banished from the court and lives out her days as more faithful in her love than Rāma. Some Hindu women today see this as an instance of the victim being blamed, while others take Sītā as an example of a wife who shows a stronger commitment in her love than her husband does, in spite of the society's false judgment of her behavior as being dharmically impure (Dhand, 1992). The people of these epic stories provide paradigms to be imitated or avoided as one attempts to live dharmic values. In addition to the epic texts are the collections of folk tales in Sanskrit and the vernacular languages, which often challenge or even subvert the value system found in the orthodox *dharma* texts. However, there is one point on which all of these texts agree, namely, that this part of the → cosmic cycle in which we are living – the span of 432,000 years known as the *kaliyuga* – is the worst possible time for *dharma*. From this Hindu perspective, the breakdown of individual morality and social order in terms of what the UN declaration calls human rights is to be expected. Yet there is still hope for a new cycle and better *dharma* in the future. In spite of living in the *kaliyuga*, with its obstructive *karma*, it is still possible for a person through the practice of *dharma*, along with the yogic practice of knowledge, devotion, or selfless good works, to realize liberation (*mokṣa*) from rebirth in this life.

Specific *Dharma* and Universal *Dharma*

Just as the UN Declaration of Human Rights speaks of "universal rights," so too some Hindu virtues and behavior patterns are described as the *dharma* for all people, while other *dharmas* are specific to one's caste, stage of life, and gender. Many Hindus in the last two centuries have stressed the *dharma* for all human beings – the "universal" *dharma*, which the epics call the *sanātanadharma* (eternal *dharma*). Examples of dharmic duties that all human beings should have include the upanishadic requirement to speak the truth, the *Rāmāyaṇa*'s teaching to remember a good deed and return it with another, and the *Mahābhārata*'s requirement for → *ahiṃsā* or nonviolence to all beings along with compassion and charity (Narayanan, 2001, 181). An early *dharma* text, the *Gautamadharmasūtra* (see → Dharmaśāstra), lists eight duties required of everyone: compassion to all creatures, patience, lack of envy, purification, tranquility, having an auspicious disposition, generosity, and lack of greed. Anyone with these qualities will still reach the ultimate goal of *mokṣa* or oneness with → *brahman*, the supreme being, even if they have not performed all the specific dharmic → *saṃskāras*. V. Narayanan notes that there are many such lists of common or universal requirements in the texts on *dharma*. Specific requirements for people in different castes and in the various stages of life are illustrated in the epic stories and listed in the various texts on *dharma*. In these texts, considerable attention is given to the duties of women (*strīdharma*). The longest list of specific dharmic duties focuses on marriages, → death rituals, food laws, and caste regulations. To get the flavor of these requirements, let us sample the specific *dharmas* associated with food and caste.

Correct eating involves considerations of not only what one can eat or should avoid but also issues such as the caste and gender of the cook (preferably male and high caste, or the woman of the house, except when she is menstruating), the times of day one may eat (twice a day, not during twilight, etc.), not eating food cooked the day before, the materials out of which the dishes should be made, the order of food courses, and so on. The Hindu concern for purity is seen not only in the above rules but also in the regulations regarding with whom one can eat. Most texts said – and this was followed until probably the mid-20th century – that one may dine only with people of the same caste group and with people one knew. It was believed in many circles that one shares the sins of the people with whom one dines – especially if one sits in a single row with them (Narayanan, 2001, 182).

Right up to the time of India's Independence in 1947 (when more "democratic" practices such as interdining were introduced), people rarely ate with persons from outside their own caste or community. In South Indian university student residences, for example, dining halls were divided along simplified caste lines with separate ones for Brahmans, non-Brahmans (vegetarian), and non-Brahmans (non-vegetarian).

Although the above division of duties by caste, gender, and stage of life was carefully laid out in the *Manusmṛti* and other *dharma* texts, this advice seems not to have been followed in many parts of India. In practice the caste system was far more complex and flexible than the *dharma* texts allowed. For example, the Vellalas of South India were considered a Śūdra caste technically but held considerable economic and political power. "They were a wealthy caste of landowners, and the *dharma shastra* prohibitions against *sudra*s owning land do not seem to have had any effect on their fortunes" (Narayanan, 2001, 184). Custom and tradition often seem to take precedence over the requirement of *dharma* texts like the *Manusmṛti*. While such texts emphasize the requirement to marry within one's own caste, it is clear that mixed-caste marriages often occurred, resulting in the formation of many subcastes. The general rule is that a marriage is acceptable if the male is of a higher caste. If the woman's caste is higher, the children are considered to be of a lower caste than either parent. The *Manusmṛti* also dealt with matters of criminal law and specified different levels of punishment depending on the caste levels of the offender and the victim. Lower castes were prescribed harsher punishments for the same crime than higher caste persons. In practice, however, scholars have shown that each case was decided with reference more to the immediate circumstances than to the prescriptions of the *Manusmṛti*'s law code. However, under British rule in the 19th century, the *Manusmṛti* along with other *dharma* texts were given more authority than they had commanded in previous centuries. "The British assumed that these laws were binding, when in fact they had been only one factor among many considerations in the judicial process" (Narayanan, 2001, 185).

As mentioned above, although *dharma* texts like the *Manusmṛti* are important in Hindu culture, local custom and tradition are often more important. In making judgments, kings and other rulers traditionally favored customs over *dharma* texts. In such situations, says V. Narayanan,

> [w]hat it is necessary to prove is that the usage has been acted upon in practice for such a long period and with such invariability as to show it has by common consent been submitted to as the established governing rule of the district concerned. (Narayanan, 2001, 187)

V. Narayanan offers several examples to show how the diversity of Hindu traditions has often taken precedence over the uniform straitjacket of a text like the *Manusmṛti*. In a case that went to the supreme court of India, the court decided that a Śūdra could become *saṃnyāsī* (holy wanderer – the highest stage of life that, according to the *dharma* texts, is open only to males of the upper three castes). As a *saṃnyāsī*, this man was freed from all duties and obligations formerly required of him as a Śūdra, and his new role in society was very similar to that of a religious teacher. Regarding women, although the *dharma* texts maintain that a woman is dependent on her male relatives, V. Narayanan observes that in many parts of India, women from the lower castes lived with considerable independence. Women donated money to temples in their own names, as temple inscriptions attest. As V. Narayanan shows (2001, 188), the Hindu understanding of right behavior depended on local practice and customs along with the teachings of the *dharma* texts.

While *dharma* is a major category of Hindu life and thought, *mokṣa* or release from rebirth is another. *Dharma* texts require that one be married at a certain age, produce children (especially sons), perform ritual actions and acts of charity, and so on. However, many Hindu scriptures teach that one must become detached from all these worldly actions to obtain *mokṣa*. Indeed, the stated purpose of the last two stages of life, the forest dweller and holy wanderer, is to help one achieve this detachment from worldly *dharma* and to realize *mokṣa* or release. But one of the most important scriptures, the *Bhagavadgītā*, sees a continuum between *dharma* and *mokṣa*. According to the *Bhagavadgītā*, the performance of one's worldly duties and daily work without any attachment to the results (the fame or fortune one may receive), but simply as a dedication to the lord, will lead to *mokṣa* (release). Thus, according to the *Bhagavadgītā*, unselfish action is an ideal *dharma* and is itself a *yoga* or way to realize release from rebirth.

Conclusion

This review of Hinduism and human rights suggests that a middle way needs to be found between a recognition of plurality and distinctiveness, on the one hand, and the equality of human beings, on the other. The traditional Hindu idea of rights and duties according to one's station in life (*varṇāśramadharma*) as advocated, for example, in the *Manusmṛti*, has led to much injustice in its negation of individuality. From that perspective, the modern Western rights critique of traditional caste conceptions is justified. But the traditional Hindu emphasis on duties and responsibilities to the larger society and cosmos is in its own way a valid critique of the overemphasis on individual rights in the UN declaration. An individual's rights and duties cannot be determined from the perspective of the individual alone; one's relationship with others and with nature also needs to be considered. As the Hindu tradition teaches, one's *svadharma* or own duty should be understood according to one's natural aptitude and station in life. Rights and duties need to be contextualized rather than taken in the abstract. This, of course, is the challenge that concepts of human rights present to law – how to deal with religious presuppositions (such as Hindu notions of *karma* and rebirth) when they clash with modern egalitarian presuppositions that are assumed by the United Nations and the constitution of India. India, today, in many ways is a living laboratory in which the tension between religious duties and individual rights is attempting to resolve itself.

The introduction of individual human rights into Hindu society has not always produced a positive outcome. In attempting to reverse centuries of discrimination against low castes or untouchables, the constitution's use of rights provisions for the distribution of opportunities, posts, and services (positive discrimination) has often reinforced the social stratification system upon which traditional morality itself depended for its own perpetuation. In addition, says P. Bilimoria,

> the net effect of the provisions as envisaged in the... Constitution and its section on fundamental rights is that the question of duty... is neglected or is left pending. A work ethic, even of the *Bhagavadgita* variety... is undermined in a scheme where the concern shifts to issues of power and distribution of the *phala* (results), actual and projected. (Bilimoria, 1993, 56)

P. Bilimoria and other scholars who have written on Hinduism and human rights end up by raising a fundamental theoretical question: "Within what frame of reference does one begin to think of the moral issues raised by a head-on clash of the traditional 'duty-cum-selective entitlements' discourse and the modern rights discourse?" (Bilimoria, 1993, 56). If, as we have noted, the traditional Hindu *dharma* or duty approach (with its *karma*, rebirth, and caste presuppositions) clashes head-on with the UN declaration's individual-rights approach (with its equality at birth presupposition), how is this conflict to be resolved in religion, law, and society? The UN declaration makes a nod toward bridging this divide through Article 29 with its minimal statement of an individual's duties to the community. The constitution of India struggles with the problem by supporting both the equality of all individuals before the law (Articles 14–18) and the freedom to practice one's religion according to its own beliefs (Article 25), which for traditional Hindus include *karma* and rebirth – and thus inequality at birth. P. Bilimoria observes that an ethics theorist cannot solve the problem by standing in one position (say that of modern human rights discourse) and passing judgment on the other side (the traditional duty discourse), as both have fundamentally different presuppositions. How is one to do justice to the major ethical issues in contemporary Hinduism in India? P. Bilimoria concludes,

> an ethical theorist... may have to work from more than one frame of reference to do justice to the complexities by the transition-in-process of a relatively closed, quasi-feudal and hierarchical society towards an egalitarian, secular, democratic and developed society. (Bilimoria, 1993, 56)

Bibliography

Bhagwati, P.N., "Religion and Secularism under the Indian Constitution," in: R.D. Baird, ed., *Religion and Law in Independent India*, Delhi, 1993, 7–21.

Bilimoria, P., "Rights and Duties: The (Modern) Indian Dilemma," in: N. Smart & S. Thakur, eds., *Ethical and Political Dilemmas of Modern India*, London, 1993, 30–59.
Bühler, G., *The Laws of Manu*, Delhi, repr. 1984.
Chanana, D.R., *Slavery in Ancient India*, Delhi, 1960.
Coward, H., *Human Rights and the World's Major Religions: The Hindu Tradition*, Westport, 2005.
Coward, H., "Gandhi, Ambedkar, and Untouchability," in: H. Coward, ed., *Indian Critiques of Gandhi*, Albany, 2003, 41–66.
Crawford, C., *Ram Mohun Roy*, New York, 1987.
Dhand, A., "Women in Hinduism: Ambiguities in the Characterization of Sita," unpubl. MA thesis, University of Calgary, 1992.
Jordens, J.F.T., *Dayananada Saraswati: His Life and Ideas*, Oxford, 1978.
Kane, P.V., *History of Dharmaśāstra*, vol. II, Poona, ²1974.
Mitra, K., "Human Rights and Hinduism," *JES* 19, 1982, 77–84.
Nagrand, K., & D. Burman, eds., *The English Works of Raja Rammohun Roy*, vol. III, Calcutta, 1947.
Narayanan, V., "Hindu Ethics and Dharma," in: J. Rungo & N.M. Martin, eds., *Ethics in the World Religions*, Oxford, 2001, 177–195.
Olivelle, P., *Dharmasūtras: The Law Codes of Ancient India*, New York, 1999.
Rukmani, T.S., "Rabindranath Tagore," in: H. Coward, ed., *Indian Critiques of Gandhi*, Albany, 2003, 108–128.
Saraswati, D., *Satyarth Prakash: Light of Truth*, Delhi, 1975.
Swami Vivekananda, *Complete Works of Swami Vivekananda*, vol. I, Calcutta, 1959.
United Nations and Human Rights 1945–1995, publ. Department of Public Information, United Nations, New York, 1995.

Harold Coward

Internet

Early Years

The intersection of Hinduism and the Internet – "the worldwide network of networks that... connects millions of computers and their users around the globe" (Whittaker, 2002, 196) – is significant in a number of ways. Even prior to the introduction of an application developed by T. Berners-Lee, released in 1991, that allowed Web sites to be directly linked to one another resulting in the World Wide Web (Castells, 2002, 15), there were noteworthy developments. Through participating in the extremely popular Usenet newsgroup net.nlang.india, which was established on Jan 30, 1985 with the purpose of providing a forum where aspects of Indian culture could be discussed, and the later newsgroups alt.hindu and soc.religion.hindu, which focused on Hinduism, Hindus in the diaspora were now able to connect with one another and to Hindus in India and discuss their religion. This development had a particular impact on Hindus working in those Muslim countries where it is forbidden to engage in Hindu worship or to be in possession of Hindu texts. Not only were these individuals now able to access an environment in which they could safely discuss aspects of their religion, but they could also, as a result of those responsible for the newsgroups making Hindu sacred texts available online, now read such material without the risks associated with possessing the physical texts (Helland, 2007).

The release of the first commercial browser, Netscape Navigator, in 1995 allowed for the World Wide Web to be traversed with ease, and as a result of this, "for most people, for business, and for society at large, the Internet was born" (Castells, 2002, 17). In addition to the fact that Hindus were utilizing the Internet in an earlier phase of its development to engage in discussion of their religion and to disseminate and read religious materials, they were also taking advantage of the opportunities provided by the World Wide Web at this early stage. For example, in the same year that Netscape Navigator became available, the Meher Baba movement and the International Society for Krishna Consciousness (→ ISKCON) had Web sites that provided information about their philosophies and activities (Bainbridge, 1997, 150–151). E. Barker (2005, 67) further noted that this latter organization was also using the Internet in 1995 as a means of communication. Meanwhile, the Internet remained important to diasporic Hindus, following the introduction of the user-friendly World Wide Web, and has continued to be so (see e.g. Miller & Slater, 2000; Helland, 2007).

Number and Diversity of Hindu Web Sites

Since the mid-1990s, along with the rapidly increasing use of the Internet, the number of Web sites regarding Hinduism has grown at an astonishing rate. It is not possible to ascertain the exact number of Web sites concerning Hinduism that there are, and simply using a search term such as "Hinduism" cannot provide an accurate figure. This is because the number of Web sites that a search engine identifies will include Web pages that constitute parts of a larger Web site, Web sites that may no longer be in operation, Web sites that are only tangentially related to Hinduism, and those that are actually in opposition to Hinduism. Nevertheless, using "Hindu" or "Hinduism" as a search term can still give some sort of indication of the prevalence and growth of Web sites dealing with Hinduism. It is therefore worthwhile to note that when a journalist at the *Dallas Morning Herald* used "Hindu" as a search term in 1999, a total of 230 thousand Web sites were identified (Collette, 1999), whereas toward the end of 2011, the number obtained through conducting a Google search using this term was in the tens of millions. Similarly, using "Hinduism" as the search term in late 2011 returned around 40 million results, and this can be contrasted with the situation about seven years earlier, when the figure was smaller than a million.

Web sites that focus on Hinduism are produced and maintained by various groups such as Hindu organizations (e.g. → Ananda Marga's anandamarga.org), temple administrations (e.g. The Hindu Temple of Kentucky's kytemple.org) and commercial organizations (e.g. saranam.com), and individuals (e.g. Sushama Londhe's hinduwisdom.info). These Web sites attempt to satisfy diverse target audiences – for example, Hindu devotees, those interested in learning about facets of Hinduism for personal reasons, and those seeking objective academic information. To this end, they may primarily provide general information about Hinduism (e.g. hinduism.co.za), specific information relating to a certain tradition or temple (e.g. the Web site of the Shri Mata Vaishno Devi Shrine: maavaishnodevi.org), a forum for discussion about Hinduism (e.g. hindudharmaforums.com), an opportunity to purchase religious items (e.g. rudraksha-ratna.com) or services (e.g. ishwarbhakti.com), the means to engage in certain activities such as → *pūjā* and/or *darśan* (e.g. the Web site of the Shri Kashi Vishwanath Temple in Varanasi at shrikashivishwanath.org), or a combination of these features.

Noteworthy online developments include the broadcasting of the 1998 *durgāpūjā* festival in Kolkata on the World Wide Web, which aimed to allow devotees to perform worship from afar (Beckerlegge, 2001, 229), and the introduction in the same year of a Web site by the Shree Siddhivinayak Ganapati Temple in Mumbai, which meant that they were "probably the first [Indian Hindu temple] to go online" (Israni, 2000). Even at this relatively early stage of Hinduism on the World Wide Web, this Web site (siddhivinayak.org) offered the opportunity for Internet users to have live *darśan* of the temple's main deity via a webcam installed in the temple's inner sanctum – a development that will be considered below. Three years later, a Web site offered a "virtual pilgrimage" – a simulated sacred journey (MacWilliams, 2004, 223) – to the *kumbhamelā* (Vásquez & Marquardt, 2003, 92), while in June 2003, the Shri Saraswati Muktidham Trust in Gujarat set up a Web site (muktidham.org – currently unavailable) that allowed for the live viewing of Hindu funerals online via a webcam at the crematorium (Rao, 2003). This is an interesting innovation, considering that photography is taboo at Hindu funerals.

The Use of the Internet by the Kanchi Math and Its Supporters

A series of additions to their presence on the World Wide Web by the Shree Kanchi Kamakoti Peetham or Kanchi Math and its supporters that was triggered by an event that occurred in late 2004 constitutes a noteworthy episode in the history of Hinduism and the Internet. Furthermore, although far from representative, this case provides an example of the potential benefits of the utilization of the Internet by a Hindu organization and its supporters. At this time, the *maṭh* already had a strong online presence. For example, as a result of help from devotees, it had an impressive Web site (kamakoti.org) that contained over two thousand Web pages featuring information regarding the *maṭh* and Hindu philosophy and that provided the opportunity to download audio and visual material. In addition, in August 2004, the Web site of the Kanchi Kamakoti Seva Foundation (KKSF) – an organization in the United States that is associated with the Kanchi Math – was launched, and this event was attended by the current *śaṅkarācārya* Jayendra Saraswathi and his disciple *ācārya* Vijayendra Saraswathi.

Although the Kanchi Math had already recognized the value of the Internet and had a significant online presence, the true importance of the Internet to the institution and its supporters was exemplified following the Nov 11, 2004, arrest and imprisonment of Jayendra Saraswathi on suspicion of murder (bail was granted by the Supreme Court on Jan 10, 2005, and the case is still ongoing). Within a short period of time, the *maṭh* and its supporters began to take advantage of the opportunities afforded by the Internet in a number of ways in order to keep interested parties up-to-date with the latest developments surrounding the case and to mobilize support.

Up until Nov 17, 2004, kamakoti.org continued as if nothing had happened, but the next day the Web site was removed, and visitors were only able to see a message on an empty background. This message requested that devotees pray for "the security, safety, health and immediate release of... Jayendra Saraswathi" and informed them that "various prayer meetings... are being held in several places, under the guidance of... Vijayendra Saraswathi," in which they were requested to participate. (Vijayendra Saraswathi was later arrested on Jan 10, 2005, in connection with the same murder.) The *maṭh*'s e-mail address was also given so that devotees could still get in touch. The following day, the Web site was up and running again – accessed through the Web page showing the aforementioned message. Shortly after, direct access was available again, and there were some references to the current situation. On Nov 23, which was 12 days after the arrest, an entirely new Web site (kanchi-sathya.org) became available that specifically dealt with the situation, and those who had previously signed up to be on an e-mail list on kamakoti.org were alerted to this fact. Meanwhile, the original Web site remained active and included a link to the new one on its home page.

The Web site kanchi-sathya.org claims to be a "source of authentic information," puts forward the view that the *śaṅkarācārya* has been treated unfairly, and expresses concern regarding the media attention surrounding the case, which is seen as propagating lies. Among other facilities, kanchi-sathya.org offers the opportunity to download the documents that have been filed with the court concerning the case, gives access to various articles online, and provides an online petition asking for the release of the *śaṅkarācārya* and for apologies from the officials responsible for his arrest. On Dec 4, those registering with kanchi-sathya.org received an e-mail requesting a donation to help in the dissemination of truthful information concerning the situation and another e-mail containing an invitation to a meeting held in Chennai on the same day. This was organized by the trustees of a Chennai organization of the Kanchi Math. Now, more than seven years after the initial arrest of the *śaṅkarācārya*, kanchi-sathya.org remains active, and material regarding the ongoing case is regularly published on the Web site.

Another new Web site – kanchiforum.org – which was created in response to the arrest of the *śaṅkarācārya* and his disciple, came online on Jan 17, 2005. Although those responsible for this Web site hosted in North America claim not to be associated with kamakoti.org and kanchi-sathya.org, these Web sites are recommended on its home page, and there is a comment on it that these Web sites "have been our source of strength, inspiration and motivation." The stated aims of the Web site, listed on the home page, are to act as a support group, to channel energy, to spread the "real" news, to create awareness, and to link all devotees. The Web site provides a forum where interested parties can discuss issues concerning the case against the *śaṅkarācārya* and his disciple along with other matters pertaining to the *maṭh*. In addition to the Web sites that were created in response to the situation, the aforementioned Web site of the Kanchi Kamakoti Seva Foundation also maintains an interest in the case – for example, it gives details regarding the Kanchi Kamakoti Seva Foundation's Campaign for Dharma, which aims to provide assistance to the *śaṅkarācārya* and his disciple.

Thus, the prominent Hindu institution Kanchi Math and its supporters have extensively utilized the Internet in order to provide up-to-date information, to try to counteract what are seen as the lies of the media, to publicize the case and propagate their point of view, and to communicate with large numbers of devotees in an attempt to mobilize them.

Jostling for Influence within Hinduism

As noted, the Kanchi Math was also successfully using the Internet in order to disseminate information about their tradition and activities prior to the arrest of the *śaṅkarācārya* and his disciple. There are obvious advantages associated with being able to disseminate information on a far larger scale than was previously possible. For example, large numbers of people around the world have access to the online material and are thus potential readers; there is therefore a possibility that the material will have a wide impact. However, because there is no single central authority within Hinduism – which means that there is competition among various Hindu groups as to who "speaks" for Hinduism – the potential benefit of the Internet for Hinduism in this regard is especially significant. If Hindu organizations belonging to specific traditions are able to have a strong online presence, then they can build on any previous successes in aligning themselves with mainstream Hinduism and gain an advantage over other groups in the competition to achieve influence within Hinduism.

Two Hindu religious organizations that are relevant in this regard are the Saiva Siddhanta Church (SSC), which belongs to the Śaiva tradition, and ISKCON, which practices a form of devotional Vaiṣṇavism. The former – with an order of monks based at its headquarters in Hawaii numbering 21 – reveals on one of its Web sites that "the Church broadly serves the billion-strong Hindu faith" (himalayanacademy.com/ssc). One way in which this is attempted is through the Saiva Siddhanta Church's magazine *Hinduism Today*, which is aimed primarily at Hindus in the diaspora. The Saiva Siddhanta Church's founder Sivaya Subramuniyaswami (1927–2001) once said of this magazine that it "was created to strengthen all the many diverse expressions of Hindu spirituality, to give them a single, combined voice because everywhere else their voices were individualized" (cited in Melwani, 2008). ISKCON also attempts to represent Hindus in general. ISKCON Education Services has stated in the past that one of its aims is "to serve the needs of the British Hindu Community" (iskcon.org.uk/ies/about_us [Jun 11, 2006]), and M. Nye (1997) also notes that ISKCON undertakes certain activities that enable the organization to have a say in how Hinduism is represented.

Despite the fact that, as already indicated, there is a huge number of Web sites regarding Hinduism, it is striking that there is an extremely small number that are "prominent" on the World Wide Web and that are highly likely to be encountered by those seeking general information about Hinduism – a situation that has arisen as a result of a combination of factors (Scheifinger, 2008b). Prominent Hindu Web sites are those that appear in the first ten results when a Google (the most popular search engine) search is carried out using the term "Hinduism" and that have occupied such a position over a sustained period of time. If at least six years are used as an arbitrary marker to signify such a period, then, out of the countless Web sites dealing with Hinduism that there are on the World Wide Web, there are five that are prominent (as of Dec 14, 2011). The five prominent Hindu Web sites are hinduism.about.com, which provides general information about Hinduism; religioustolerance.org, which offers information about various religions including Hinduism; a Web site of the Saiva Siddhanta Church (hinduismtoday.com), a British Broadcasting Corporation (BBC) educational Web site on Hinduism (bbc.co.uk/religion/religions/hinduism); and the Wikipedia online encyclopedia Web page featuring the Hinduism entry (wikipedia.org/wiki/Hinduism).

That out of the countless Web sites dealing with Hinduism, the Saiva Siddhanta Church has a prominent one – featuring the aforementioned magazine *Hinduism Today* – is highly significant. Along with the fact that this Web site also links to a further Web site of the Saiva Siddhanta Church, himalayanacademy.com, which provides information regarding its Hindu monastery in Hawaii, this means that this relatively small organization has been able to extensively disseminate its material regarding Hinduism in a way that was not previously possible. Although deriving from a particular Hindu tradition "representing fewer than three million of the world's… Hindus" (Martin, 2001), in a number of ways the Saiva Siddhanta Church has been successful in aligning itself with Hinduism in general (see Martin, 2001; Melwani, 2008). Prior to the introduction of the Internet and the World Wide Web, this had already been achieved to an extent as a result of the activities of Subramuniyaswami and because of the traditional offline version of *Hinduism Today*. However, as a result of the Saiva Siddhanta Church's impressive online presence – which is further asserted when it is considered that, out of the prominent Hindu Web sites, hinduismtoday.com is the only one that is produced by a group belonging to a specific Hindu tradition – the Saiva Siddhanta Church has almost certainly further added to its perceived legitimacy as being able to speak on behalf of Hindus in general. As L. Melwani (2008) notes concerning *Hinduism Today* – which, as revealed, has the expressed aim of providing a unified voice for the many different expressions of Hinduism – "through the Internet it's reaching millions of Hindus, and millions of others who are intrigued by Hindu culture, spirituality and literature."

Similarly, although none of its Web sites is prominent, ISKCON has also been able to take advantage of the opportunities afforded by the Internet. One way in which this has been achieved is through its Web site entitled The Heart of Hinduism (http://hinduism.iskcon.org), whose contents are based on the ISKCON textbook of the same name, which is used in some UK schools. ISKCON does not hide the fact on the Web site that it belongs to the Vaiṣṇava tradition of Hinduism and it claims that the Web site (and book) material "aims to be non-sectarian, even-handed, and respectful in its description of all the Hindu traditions" (see hinduism.iskcon.org/extras/about.htm). The fact that ISKCON is providing information that it claims to be objective and that is intended for, and utilized in, schools – and that is also aimed at others who wish to learn about Hinduism, – constitutes a (largely successful) attempt by the organization to be seen as a legitimate authority within mainstream Hinduism in the United Kingdom.

Crucially, The Heart of Hinduism Web site is one of only three external Web sites to which the aforementioned prominent BBC Hinduism Web site links, and so it is highly likely to be encountered by general seekers of information about

Hinduism online. Another one of the links provided by the BBC Web site is to the aforementioned Wikipedia Web page concerning Hinduism (en.wikipedia.org/wiki/Hinduism). This is significant because, as of Dec 27, 2011, out of the eight external links offered by this Wikipedia page – which, as explained, constitutes a prominent Hindu Web site – one is to ISKCON's *The Heart of Hinduism*. As a result of the popularity of Wikipedia, this further increases the likelihood of someone seeking information online about Hinduism visiting this ISKCON Web site.

It is also worthwhile to note that, whereas now the BBC's Hinduism Web site offers an external link to ISKCON's *The Heart of Hinduism* Web site and none to the Web sites of the Saiva Siddhanta Church, in the past it has offered five external links – two of which were to Saiva Siddhanta Church Web sites (the aforementioned hinduismtoday.com and hindu.org – the latter not currently in existence, although the address is still active and now leads to hinduismtoday.com). In addition to the fact that the Internet offers new opportunities for religious organizations to increase their influence within Hinduism, this example indicates that there is a process occurring online in which competing Hindu organizations suffer setbacks and gain advantages in their quest to be representative of Hinduism in general.

*Pūjā*s Facilitated by the Internet

One type of → *pūjā* facilitated by the Internet – usually referred to as an online *pūjā* – involves an individual visiting a Web site (such as bangalinet.com/epūjā_ganesh.htm) that features an image of a deity and, often to the accompaniment of religious music or chanting, clicking on various icons in order to simulate the processes that are involved in a *pūjā* in the traditional offline context (see Scheifinger, 2008a, 243–247). Although this kind of *pūjā* is clearly different from a *pūjā* carried out at a physical location, for a number of reasons (not least of which is the fact that it allows for *darśan*), it still constitutes a valid form of the ritual (Scheifinger, forthcoming). Another type of *pūjā* facilitated by the Internet is one that is ordered online to be carried out on one's behalf at a physical temple for a fee (see e.g. eprarthana.com). In this case, following the carrying out of the ritual at the temple (usually in India), sometimes nonedible *prasād* is also sent by post to the individual who commissioned the *pūjā*. Proof that the *pūjā* has been carried out can also be requested, and this can take the form of photographs at the site showing a banner with the recipient of the *pūjā*'s name on it (see Scheifinger, 2010a). Despite the fact that this type of *pūjā* is very different from the previous one and does not occur online, it is also often referred to – erroneously – as an online *pūjā*.

A variant of this latter type of *pūjā* offered by godandguru.com destroys the dichotomy between these two versions of *pūjā*s. In addition to simply ordering a *pūjā* to be carried out at a temple, through this Web site, it is possible to request that a *pūjā* be undertaken and shown live via a webcam. Moreover, the recipients of this *pūjā* can also actually participate in the ritual at home by following the instructions given by a *paṇḍit* at the *pūjā*'s location, while viewing the webcast. Via godandguru.com, this option costs US $50–150 more than the carrying out of a ritual without these extra features. Because in this version of a *pūjā* the ritual is broadcast live online, there are genuine grounds for referring to it as an "online *pūjā*." This breeds confusion because of the fact that it is very different from the aforementioned simulated online *pūjā* that carries this name and because it shares similarities with the conventional ordering of a *pūjā* online, which does not warrant being referred to by this term. To overcome this, a classificatory scheme that successfully encompasses and differentiates among these different forms of *pūjā*s facilitated by the Internet is offered, as follows: *pūjā*s in which icons are clicked in order to simulate acts that are carried out in a traditional, offline *pūjā* can be referred to as "online simulated *pūjā*s," while the second and third versions that have been introduced can be collectively referred to as "*pūjā*s ordered online" and can be further divided into "offline *pūjā*s ordered online" and "online *pūjā*s ordered online."

The fact that an offline *pūjā* ordered online involves someone carrying out the ritual on behalf of someone else does not constitute a unique development brought about by the Internet. Prior to the introduction of the Internet, this practice was not uncommon. For example, family members or friends can perform a *pūjā* on an individual's behalf, and it was – and is – also possible to contact a temple directly by post or telephone in order to request such a *pūjā*. However, despite this, the fact that the various Web sites offering such a *pūjā*-ordering service cover many temples and the service is widely available to, and convenient for, Hindus around the world has a number of implications.

In cases where a Web site offers a *pūjā* at a temple at which the service provider has no official connection to the administration, negative effects can be suffered by the administration because it can be bypassed and thus not have access to any *pūjā* fee. Instead, a fee is sometimes paid directly to the *pujārī* who carries out the ritual by a representative of the Web site who has built up a professional relationship with the *pujārī*. In some cases, an administration will not even be aware that independent individuals are providing a service at its temple. When a *pūjā*-ordering service is offered via the Internet by the administration of a temple or by an official partner, the financial implications are reversed. *Pūjā* fees will go to the administration, and the *pujārī*s will not even be able to obtain *dakṣiṇā* (ritual fee) from devotees. This has the potential to adversely affect the financial situation of *pujārīs* – especially at those temples (e.g. the Kālīghāṭ Temple in Kolkata) where priests do not receive a salary and are solely reliant on *dakṣiṇā* offered by devotees who attend the temple.

In either case, the fact that traditional flows of money can be disrupted as a result of the fact that *pūjā*s can now be ordered online on a scale that was not previously possible (and from those who may have no official connection to a temple) has the potential to affect the relationship between temple administrations and *pujārī*s. The development will thus add a further ingredient to the power struggles that sometimes occur between these two groups. In addition, there is evidence that *pūjā* service providers are personally deciding (sometimes *contra* views expressed by officials at temples where they operate) what must be done in order for the *pūjā* be successful. For example, one provider may state that the customer needs to pray at the same time that the *pūjā* is being carried out, while another may say that this is totally unnecessary. Furthermore, they are even making judgments as to who has the right to avail the service, and this is despite the fact that these individuals may have no religious training whatsoever (Scheifinger, 2010a).

Online *Darśan*

The visual nature of the World Wide Web means that, more so than with any other religious tradition, there is a natural fit between Hinduism and the medium. This is because of the importance of *darśan* within Hinduism, which involves seeing and being seen by a deity. Some religious organizations provide a *darśan* facility on their Web site (or Web sites; see e.g. mayapur.com), and the validity of online *darśan* is accepted both by Hindu religious authorities and by devotees – although it is often regarded as being not quite as efficacious as *darśan* at a physical site (see Scheifinger, 2009, 282, 286; 2010b, 333; Herman, 2010, 156–157, 159, 161, 175). Online *darśan* is widely available on various Hindu Web sites and is facilitated in a number of ways. One way is through the placing online of images (which may then constitute part of a simulated online *pūjā*) of specific deities associated with a certain location or generic pan-Indian deities. Aside from the fact that the accessibility of these images increases dramatically worldwide, this is of no more significance than the availability of printed pictures of deities that are commonly used by devotees for *darśan*. Similarly, although it may now be on demand, viewing a Hindu festival via the Internet that can allow for *darśan* is little different from watching such an event on television.

However, the placing of a webcam inside a temple, which allows devotees to have *darśan* of the main deity residing there through viewing the live broadcast via a temple Web site, is significant. As long as there is access to an Internet connection, this development allows devotees, wherever they are in the world, to have *darśan* of a specific deity without needing to travel to the temple in which it resides. Moreover, it allows those who may actually be prohibited from entering certain temples to receive *darśan*. For example, Hindus who are not of Indian origin are generally forbidden to enter the Viśvanāth Temple in Varanasi, yet, since January 2008, as a result of the presence of a webcam in the temple's inner sanctum, they are now able to freely gaze upon the → *liṅga* there and receive *darśan* of → Śiva via the temple's Web site (shrikashivishwanath.org). This form of online *darśan* could thus lead to the universalization of Hinduism (Scheifinger, 2010b).

Conclusion

Hinduism has had a presence online since the early days of the Internet, when Hindus in the diaspora logged on to specific discussion forums in order to discuss their faith. Since the introduction of the user-friendly World Wide Web, the number and diversity of Web sites concerning Hinduism have grown, and the new opportunities afforded by these Web sites have been significant to Hinduism in a number of ways. Cyberspace has become a venue where, in the absence of a central authority, various groups attempt to increase their influence within Hinduism. The facility to order *pūjās* via the Internet, which has made such a service widely available, has an impact, because it can undermine temple authorities and affect the relationship between temple administrations and *pujārīs*. Meanwhile, online *darśan* is especially significant, because it has the potential to bring about the universalization of Hinduism.

Bibliography

Bainbridge, W.S., *The Sociology of Religious Movements*, London, 1997.

Barker, E., "Crossing the Boundary: New Challenges to Religious Authority and Control as a Consequence of Access to the Internet," in: M.T. Højsgaard & M. Warburg, eds., *Religion and Cyberspace*, Abingdon, 2005, 67–85.

Beckerlegge, G., "Computer-Mediated Religion: Religion on the Internet at the Turn of the Twenty-First Century," in: G. Beckerlegge, ed., *From Sacred Text to Internet*, Milton Keynes, 2001, 219–264.

Castells, M., *The Internet Galaxy: Reflections on the Internet, Business, and Society*, New York, 2002.

Collette, L., "Cyberspace: The New Frontier for Religion," *Cybersociology* 7, 1999, http://www.cybersociology.com/files/7_cyberspacereligion.html.

Helland, C., "Diaspora on the Electronic Frontier: Developing Virtual Connections with Sacred Homelands," *JCMC* 12/3, 2007, http://jcmc.indiana.edu/vol12/issue3/helland.html.

Herman, P.K., "Seeing the Divine through Windows: Online Darshan and Virtual Religious Experience," *OHJRI* 4/1, 2010, 151–178, http://archiv.ub.uni-heidelberg.de/volltextserver/volltexte/2010/11303/pdf/09.pdf.

Israni, N., "God's Only a Click Away," *India Today*, October 16, 2000, http://archives.digitaltoday.in/indiatoday/20001016/religion3.html.

MacWilliams, M.W., "Virtual Pilgrimage to Ireland's Croagh Patrick," in: L.L Dawson & D.E. Cowan, eds., *Religion Online: Finding Faith on the Internet*, New York, 2004, 223–237.

Martin, D., "Satguru Subramuniyaswami, Hindu Spiritual Leader, 74," *The New York Times*, Nov 19, 2001, http://www.nytimes.com/2001/11/19/us/satguru-subramuniyaswami-hindu-spiritual-leader-74.html#.

Melwani, L., "The Story of Hinduism Today," 2008, http://www.hinduismtoday.com/modules/wfchannel/index.php?cid=17&page=0.

Miller, D., & D. Slater, *The Internet: An Ethnographic Approach*, Oxford, 2000.

Nye, M., "ISKCON and Hindus in Britain: Some Thoughts on a Developing Relationship," *ICJ* 5/2, 1997, 5–13.

Rao, V.S., "Watch Last Rites Online," Jun 26, 2003, http://www.rediff.com//netguide/2003/jun/25mukti.htm.

Scheifinger, H., "Hindu Worship Online and Offline," in: H. Campbell, ed., *Digital Religion: Understanding Religious Practice in New Media Worlds*, London, forthcoming.

Scheifinger, H., "Internet Threats to Hindu Authority: *Pūjā*-Ordering Websites and the *Kalighat* Temple," *AJSS* 38, 2010a, 636–656.

Scheifinger, H., "*Om*-line Hinduism: World Wide Gods on the Web," *ARSR* 23/3, 2010b, 325–345.

Scheifinger, H., "The *Jagannath* Temple and Online *Darshan*," *JCR* 24/3, 2009, 277–290.

Scheifinger, H., "Hinduism and Cyberspace," *Religion* 38/3, 2008a, 233–249.

Scheifinger, H., "Researching Religion on the WWW: Identifying an Object of Study for Hinduism," *MIO* 2/3, 2008b, http://erdt.plymouth.ac.uk/mionline/public_html/viewarticle.php?id=64&layout=html.

Vásquez, M.A., & M.F. Marquardt, *Globalizing the Sacred: Religion across the Americas*, New Brunswick, 2003.

Whittaker, J., *The Internet: The Basics*, London, 2002.

Heinz Scheifinger

Modern Legal Framework

Modern legal structures and laws in India impinge on Hinduism in two distinct ways. First, a system of personal law that was first introduced by the British and continued under the Indian Constitution exists under the name Hindu law and is applied as the family law of Hindus. Second, other practices and institutions of Hinduism not dealt with under Hindu law are also governed by the Indian state. Conversely, Hinduism and Hindu practitioners influence the modern legal framework by promoting a distinctive idea of → secularism and by advocating for modern – mostly middle- and upper-class – Hindu values within the law. Finally, the growing population of Hindus outside of India has meant that other nations have also begun to attend to the special legal needs and problems of Hindus within their jurisdiction. The present essay summarizes these connections between Hinduism and modern legal systems and points to other sources containing in-depth research.

Hindu Law as Personal Law

The personal law system in India was introduced by fiat of Governor-General Warren Hastings in 1772 and originally made separate provision for administering distinct bodies of law to the so-called Gentoos (i.e. Hindus [from Port. *gentio*, pagan]) and Mahomedans (i.e. Muslims; Rocher, 2010). Furthermore, the principle of "justice, equity, and good conscience" was invoked as the legal ground both for incorporating Hindu law into British courts and modifying it (Derrett, 1963a). In the mid- to late 19th century, several legislative acts also made provision for the personal laws of Christians (Chatterjee, 2010; Mallampalli, 2010) and Parsis (Sharafi, forthcoming). Although the non-enforceable, directive principle in Article 44 of the Constitution of India (1950) encouraged the newly independent state "to secure for citizens a uniform civil code throughout the territory of India," the courts have consistently understood this directive to sanction the continued existence of personal laws, until such time when a Uniform Civil Code (UCC) might be enacted (Larson, 2001, 1–3). Even without explicit constitutional foundation, therefore, Hindu law and other personal laws have both inherited a long colonial legacy and continued to develop through legislative codification and case law at the same time (Williams, 2006).

Colonial Hindu law, also known as Anglo-Hindu law, was premised on the idea that the British courts would administer the Hindus' "native law" to them. Warren Hastings' fateful decision to identify the Sanskrit texts called → Dharmaśāstras as the sole source of Anglo-Hindu law summarily rejected the validity and variability of customary laws and institutions. By many accounts, the rejection of legal pluralism and local adaptability in favor of a perceived uniformity and certainty in the law was the major mistake in colonial appropriations of Hindu legal thought and practice (Kishwar, 1994). The big change here was to treat the scholastic tradition of Dharmaśāstra as a form of statutory or black-letter law, available to cite by chapter and verse in support of legal decisions and arguments in common-law courts – a legacy that continues to the present day. However, the number of English translations of these treatises and commentaries on the religious and legal duties of upper-caste Hindus remained limited, and few British judges were ever trained in Sanskrit. To fill in this gap, therefore, Hindu → *paṇḍit*s were assigned to the courts to facilitate the judge's understanding of the Dharmaśāstras' legal discussions relevant to a given case. However, in 1864 when precedent in Hindu law cases reached what was perceived to be a critical mass, the court *paṇḍit*s and their Muslim counterparts were dismissed from service. In spite of the initial British rhetoric to preserve an indigenous tradition of law, the role of Dharmaśāstra in judicial opinions both during and after colonialism has been called "window dressing" for laws determined by other means (Lariviere, 1989). The manipulation and appropriation of this Indian intellectual tradition by the British thus resulted in the creation or invention of a wholly new legal system called "Hindu law" – a system that drew on ancient Hindu legal vocabulary and jurisprudence but repurposed its abstracted norms, especially its provisions on property and inheritance (Bhattacharyya-Panda, 2007), for the needs of the British colony. Since the primary purpose of this section is to describe modern Hindu law,

I will focus on the period after 1947, especially after the enactment of the so-called Hindu Code Bills in the mid-1950s. Due to modern Hindu law's reliance on and reference to colonial Hindu law, however, some description of the earlier period is required.

On the one hand, modern Hindu law is the heir of this phantasmic history. On the other, it is today a very real legal subsystem, with more than two hundred years of legal precedent and major legislation undergirding its contemporary presence. A serious terminological problem exists in the scholarly literature over the proper denotation of Hindu law. Asked simply, is Hindu law the law observed among Hindus, or is it the law derived from demonstrably Hindu principles, especially Dharmaśāstra, and understood as such? From law offices to district courts to the Supreme Court, legal professionals in India today understand Hindu law as the black-letter law of marriage, inheritance, adoption, guardianship, and maintenance that applies to those Indian citizens legally classified as Hindu, including Jains, Buddhists, Sikhs, and others. For the purposes of this article, therefore, modern Hindu law is first and foremost a statutory law, the product of four major legislative acts collectively known as the Hindu Code Bills (HCB). The four statutes are the Hindu Marriage Act, 1955; the Hindu Succession Act, 1956; the Hindu Minority and Guardianship Act, 1956; and the Hindu Adoptions and Maintenance Act, 1956. Of course, practitioners are aware that modern Hindu law has a deeper history, but for their work, they only occasionally need to reach back to cases, manuals, or texts from the colonial period or earlier. Modern Hindu law thus has a life of its own in English statutes and law reports.

In contemporary Indian law schools, Hindu law is rarely taught as a separate subject, though it used to be until roughly the late 1990s. Rather, it forms one part of a larger course on family law that also addresses Muslim law and other specially regarded personal laws of groups such as the Parsis and Christians. At least some law faculties understand the change as a response to Hindu nationalism by avoiding any perception that Hindu law is privileged in the law curriculum. The family-law course is typically divided: for example, a first part may deal with marriage, divorce, maintenance, guardianship, and adoption, and a second part focuses on the complex area of property in family succession and inheritance. The curriculum consists of prominent textbooks that provide the statutory text with long comments and discuss leading cases at relevant points. Older textbooks, still regularly updated and reedited, used to be very long, often more than a thousand pages and generally focused on either Hindu or Muslim law (e.g. Mayne, 2008; Mulla, 2010). More recently, composite textbooks that incorporate basic details on all the personal laws of India have increasingly become the norm for instructional use (e.g. Diwan, 2009; Myneni, 2009). Clinics on family law are also quite common now in law schools as a way to have students learn through real-world legal advice to clients.

Cases falling under Hindu law begin in a family court, a district court, or an alternative forum. Advocates may specialize in family-law cases, and judges may be assigned cases primarily in family law on the basis of their experience and prior knowledge. However, there is no sense that legal professionals dealing with Hindu law should themselves necessarily be Hindu. Typically, most cases falling under Hindu law concern either marital problems and the possibility of divorce or questions about family property, succession, and inheritance. As one would expect, issues of fact dominate the work of both advocates and judges at this level. In most cases, judges will insist, often more than once, that the litigants try to resolve their differences outside of court. Procedural avenues exist for the judge to refer cases to mediation or to delay evidence and witnesses, until and unless a good-faith effort is made to resolve problems without the intervention of the legal system. Having heard the basic facts, judges may verbally reprimand one or both of the litigants or their family members for their alleged actions before assigning a later date for reconsideration of the case. Knowing all of this, advocates too play a consultative role in helping clients determine whether taking their claims to formal court is necessary or likely to produce a desirable outcome. In many cases, an experience before the judge or the opposing attorney can prompt a resolution outside of the legal system. Perhaps half of the marital-strife cases end before a judgment by the court. When a case does end in judgment, the verdict summarizes in standardized language the nature of dispute and the history of efforts made to resolve the problems. Most often, consensual arrangements for the division of property and child custody are explicitly affirmed in the judgment.

At the level of family and district courts, the invocation of Hindu law is jurisdictional and procedural, that is, to what court the matter will be referred and what statutory provisions govern its procedure in the court. No overt principle of Hinduism or aspect of Hindu faith or practice is part of modern Hindu law at this level. If asked, legal professionals usually assert that Hindu principles, especially the Dharmaśāstra, were incorporated into the legislative codification of Hindu law. In practice, therefore, one need only refer to the statutory form, which is held to be a modernized extension of ancient law.

By contrast with the lower courts, justices of India's appellate high courts and the Supreme Court are more likely to learn the Hindu law relevant to a given case through the guidance of their clerks and the advocates who appear before them. With a need to find constitutional bases for their opinions, justices in the higher courts sometimes supplement strictly constitutional arguments with investigations into colonial and ancient Hindu law materials and cases. The motivations behind such investigations involve commitments to public policy and social justice as much as a positivist desire to stick to the letter of law. One such motivation is a sincere effort on the part of some appellate justices by drawing evidentiary support in Hindu law cases from scriptural sources, particularly Dharmaśāstra. Although not a requirement, hundreds of opinions (though perhaps not thousands) from India's high courts and Supreme Court over the last six decades engage in proof-texting from ancient Sanskrit texts, usually via an English translation or a citation from P.V. Kane's influential *History of Dharmaśāstra*. In rarer cases, contradictory original texts are juxtaposed, sometimes including the original Sanskrit, and a conclusion is drawn from the preponderance of opinions (*Maruti Shripati Dubal v. State of Maharashtra*, 1987 [1] BomCR 499), the purported regions from which the texts came and in which they are thought to apply (*Adusmilli Seethalakshmamma v. Yerneni Chalamaiah*, AIR 1974 AP 130), or from a judgment about the most compelling legal reasoning used by a medieval commentator (*Raj Kali Kuer v. Ram Rattan Pandey*, AIR 1955 SC 493). However, following J.D.M. Derrett, we must remember that

> the *dharmashastra* as administered by the courts (where it is administered at all) is a very different thing from the *dharmashastra* which lives amongst the *pandits*, and to some extent amongst pious Hindu laymen in our day. (Derrett, 1957, 16–17)

Most reports of modern Hindu law cases do not refer to antique sources in Sanskrit or even to modern translations of Sanskrit texts. Some standardized concepts of modern Hindu law such as "the Mitakshara school of law" or "the Hindu Undivided Family" have a distant point of genesis in early 19th-century interpretations of classical Hindu jurisprudence, but the manner in which such concepts are now used has flattened an always more complicated historical tradition of legal thought. A limited number of legal institutions and rules derived terminologically or conceptually from classical Hindu jurisprudence have now come to stand in for the whole of Hindu law. By limited, I mean that perhaps 10 or 12 nominally Hindu ideas anchor almost every case report on modern Hindu law, but the legal significance of those ideas derives primarily from their expression in precedent and in legislation, not from their deeper articulation in ancient sources. As a result, the Hindu character of modern Hindu law, meaning its direct link to an identifiably Hindu scholastic tradition of jurisprudence, has been all but eliminated by the structure of the personal law system. Part of the reason for this loss is that – unlike Islamic jurisprudence – the once-vibrant tradition of Hindu jurisprudence among *paṇḍits* has diminished to the brink of extinction (Derrett, 1957, 26). J.D.M. Derrett once asked whether the statutes comprising the HCB "are 'Hindu' in any substantial sense" (1968, 89). Modern Hindu law is called such because it governs those people legally identified as Hindu, not because it derives substantively from Hindu legal thought or history or because it protects religious or legal practices considered to be essential or common among most Hindus.

That said, however, we might consider the relationship of Hindu law and Hinduism in the modern Indian legal system. As the next section will discuss in detail, there are many aspects of Hinduism that have legal importance and yet do not fall under the rubric of Hindu law. That incongruity allows us to ask about the place of Hindu law as a constitutive element of Hindu identity, community, and practice in modern India. On the one hand, the codification of modern Hindu law has expressed in legal form a set of rules and practices that has come to shape the way in which many middle- and upper-class Hindu families understand the "Hindu" view of inheritance, adoption, marriage, and the like. In other words, for middle- and upper-class Hindu individuals and communities who regularly interact with official governmental institutions and who rely on their predictable legal safeguards, modern Hindu law partially informs who they are as Hindus. Official Hindu law thus protects a restricted sense of Hindu identity and practice that its legislative form helped to create.

On the other hand, three factors limit the influence that modern Hindu law has over the creation and maintenance of Hindu identities, practices, and institutions. First, state courts are bound by the language of the HCB itself to consider and incorporate evidence of customary laws that deviate from its statutory provisions under certain circumstances. The possibility to assert custom over statute, however, demonstrates the practical difference between two. As J.D.M. Derrett put it some time ago,

> Despite the solecism in the Hindu Code, custom is… not *part* of the Hindu law at all. It has not been so since about 1790. Custom is pleaded, if at all, in derogation from the Hindu law, and thus must be visualized as its opponent, not component. (1963b, 12–13)

Second, nonstate Hindu institutions that handle legal matters continue to coexist with official fora, especially ones that serve lower-class and rural individuals, who interact less frequently with official venues. Finally, so many aspects of Hinduism encounter legal regulation outside of Hindu law or not at all that Hindu law itself seems marginal to the preservation of the specifically religious concerns of Hindus. Instead, the justifications for the continued existence of modern Hindu law all center on its *political* significance either as a counterpoint to Muslim law or as a protection of communitarian political agendas and women's rights (Sunder Rajan, 2000). Ironically, the major Hindu nationalist party in India, the Bharatiya Janata Party (BJP), has for some time actively promoted the UCC as part of their claim to have a secular agenda (Narula, 2010, 239). Safeguarding *religious* identity and practice may have been the ostensible historical reason behind the colonial creation of personal law systems, but modern Hindu law and the HCB have primarily contributed to the creation and protection of a narrow, homogenized *political* Hindu identity for the modern world.

Hinduism and the Modern Indian Legal System

Hindu religious practices have long been the subject of legal interest, particularly those that offended British colonial sensibilities or were perceived as incompatible with modernity. Beyond specific practices, social institutions closely associated with Hinduism – especially temples, monasteries, and caste councils – have been made subject to official legal frameworks in India, even as they have continued to function separately in ways that are both religious and legal. With respect both to the Hindu practices and institutions described in this section and to those aspects of law officially called Hindu law, we must acknowledge that current scholarship within and outside of India emphasizes the need to look well beyond official state frameworks. Many studies, both old and new, have shown the inadequacies of promulgation, procedure, and enforcement of legislated changes regarding Hindu law and other Hinduism-related matters (Luschinsky, 1963; Menski, 2003). Studies directed solely toward state-based institutions and rules, therefore, provide at best a partial view of legal practices pertaining to Hinduism or Hindu communities.

Perhaps the most infamous Hindu practice that British missionaries and officials sought to outlaw was that of "widow burning," or → *satī* – the voluntary or involuntary immolation of a widow on the burning funeral pyre of her husband. In spite of the appearance of a vigorous debate around *satī* in the early 19th century, the social practice of widow immolation and its direct and indirect violence against women became lost in a discourse of the correct interpretation of Hindu scripture and the place of Hindu tradition in colonial India (Mani, 1987). In other words, the practice of *satī*, which one might assume would concern most of all the violence committed against widows and threatened toward others, became instead a debate among British and Indian elite males about the right to preserve tradition and the elevation of Hindu scripture to the level of a prestige discourse in political and civil society. In the process, women became "neither objects nor subjects, but rather the ground of the debate on *sati*" and "marginal to the debate" (Mani, 1987, 152). *Satī* was ultimately abolished in 1829 by Lord Bentinck's Sati Regulation XVII A.D. of the

Bengal Code, extended to other parts of India and further regulated in due course (Mani, 1986).

In spite of that abolition, instances of widow immolation are still reported and sensationalized in the media. The rarity of *satī* enhances, rather than lessens, both its tragic and its sensational aspects. The *satī* of Roop Kanwar in 1987 in Rajasthan reignited modern debates over the practice and led directly to the passage of the Commission of Sati (Prevention) Act of 1987. The complex symbolic, political, religious, and social valences behind *satī*'s persistent, albeit very rare, practice in contemporary India (Hawley, 1994) provide a good starting point for understanding the successes and failures of the modern legal framework in India to change or reform Hindu religious practices. On the one hand, the instances of *satī* have diminished, partly due to legal prohibition, but, on the other hand, deeper and wider issues about legally permissible violence against women too often get lost under discourses of dramatic events.

The plight of Hindu widows extended well beyond the event of their husbands' mortuary rites. Widowhood carried and still carries a strong stigma in many Hindu communities, owing to a common view that death pollution lingers perpetually on widows in a way that disables them ritually and socially (Mandelbaum, 1970, 186–189). Like *satī*, therefore, widows' social rehabilitation, especially the possibility of remarriage, became another significant legislative effort of the mid-19th century. Though British advocates for widow remarriage certainly existed, it was Ishwar Chandra Vidyasagar, then principal at the Sanskrit College in Bengal, who in 1856 wrote *Vidhavavivāha*, the most influential work in favor of Hindu widow remarriage. The rhetorical impact of that treatise, which marshaled traditional texts in Sanskrit into a modern case against widows' disabilities, led quickly to the passage of the Hindu Widows' Remarriage Act XV of 1856. However, the act focused on the problems faced by high-caste Hindu widows, with the result that lower-caste norms that were actually more progressive in allowing widows to remarry were criminalized (Carroll, 1983). As with *satī*, this act and subsequent legislation, including parts of the HCB, have had at best mixed results in terms of desired social outcomes.

The legal reforms around widows are linked with the larger focus of the British on the family. A host of other issues such as child marriage (Forbes, 1979), dowry (Menski, 1998), divorce (Holden, 2008), religious renunciation (Kasturi, 2009), and inheritance by women (Agarwal, 1994) all constellated around a colonial obsession with the definition and the reform of "the Hindu family" (Sturman, 2010; Subrahmanian, 2010). Most of these issues are hard to dissociate from Hindu law proper in the sense treated in the previous section. What is important is to see how the law was used to imagine and inculcate a modern Hindu family, narrowing and constricting a great diversity of actual family forms and practices in India. The carryover of colonial-era law and legal institutions in India has in particular maintained this heavy emphasis on aspects of family law as a politically salient topic and one that occupies a sizable portion of the caseload in state courts and beyond.

At a social level broader than the family, caste systems in modern India continue to affect the religious lives of Hindus and to have important legal implications. While it is certainly true that caste systems are to be found among almost all communities in modern India – Jains, Muslims, Sikhs, Christians, and Dalits, and not just Hindus – "→ caste" and its Indic conceptual partners *varṇa* and *jāti* were theologically and socially defended primarily in texts and in communities that are recognizably Hindu, especially Brahman Hindu. The general cultural practice of caste in India, therefore, was not paralleled by a general theological or cultural defense of the practice. Rather, treatises on → *dharma* written by Brahmans, social practices observed in admittedly varied ways by Brahman communities across India, and political theologies of aspirant and actual kings protected and served caste systems of great variety (Bayly, 1999; Das, 1982; Burghart, 1978).

Article 15 of the Constitution of India prohibits discrimination based on caste (as well as religion, race, sex, or place of birth), while Article 17 categorically abolishes → untouchability, the most highly visible and pernicious social status under various caste systems. Other sections of the constitution maintained legal identities for what the British called the "depressed classes." These are the Scheduled Castes (SC) and Scheduled Tribes (ST), a long list or schedule of over two thousand communities in modern India specifically recognized as in need of legal protection and affirmative action. Scheduled Caste groups must be legally classified as Hindu, Sikh, or Buddhist, while Scheduled Tribe groups are drawn from → Ādivāsī or tribal communities recognized for their geographical or cultural isolation from other populations, regardless of putative religious affiliation. A further classification of other low-caste, but not untouchable, communities is known as the Other Backward Classes (OBC). Through constitutional and later legislative provision, a system of reservations exists in modern India to promote an affirmative uplift of formerly oppressed social groups (Galanter, 1984). Controversies surrounding the legal classification of Scheduled Caste, Scheduled Tribe, and Other Backward Classe groups simultaneously confirm the efficacy of the reservation system in providing desirable benefits to oppressed groups and the possibility for corruption through actively seeking "backward" status in order to obtain those benefits (Jenkins, 2010).

Caste continues to flourish in ways that have been legally determined to be beyond legitimate governmental control, for example arranged marriage or eating within caste. One of the major discriminatory practices suffered by → Dalit (Scheduled Caste/Scheduled Tribe) communities, however, is their being prohibited entry into many Hindu temples on the basis of caste. Temple entry, therefore, became the symbolic center of wider efforts within the law to rid India and Hinduism of caste-ism (Galanter, 1971). The abolition of untouchability and the right of temple entry were closely linked issues. The Untouchability Offences Act of 1955 centralized several earlier regional legislative efforts to either expand temple access or prohibit temple exclusion altogether. At the same time, questions about the conflict between the government's interest in promoting social improvement for lower castes and the guarantee of religious liberty under the constitution quickly set limits on the capacity of legislative and judicial actions to expand temple access.

The issue of temple entry is just one of many issues surrounding the legal regulation of Hindu temples. Religious endowments to temples and the regulation of their property are prominent elements of state control over these Hindu institutions. While the British enacted several centralized regulations about Hindu religious endowments between 1810 and 1920, more recent legislation governs endowments to Hindu temples at the level of India's states (Baltutis, 2005, 446–461). A national legal discourse and relatively stable *dicta* around temple property and endowments have, however, been created judicially (Dhavan, 1978; Mansfield, 2001). Among the issues are the state's legal interests in preventing corrupt practices possible through religious donations (e.g. money laundering, tax evasion, and misappropriation of family property), in ensuring that large concentrations of wealth do not acquire unchecked influence, and in solidifying the Indian state's claim to final legal and political authority (Presler, 1987).

Temples are not the only Hindu institutions to face legal control or to be incorporated into agendas of India's modern legal system. Hindu *maṭha*s, or → monasteries, and Hindu *pañcāyat*s, or councils – especially caste councils – continue to be important Hindu institutions that both yield to the political drive toward state-controlled courts and maintain legal autonomy in limited ways. On the one hand, the attitude of the Indian state toward Hindu temples, *maṭha*s, and *pañcāyat*s has been to bring them under strict legal control through state governance. On the other hand, all three of these Hindu institutions continue to provide alternative social spaces for legal claims and remedies for wrongs. Large institutions such as the Sringeri *maṭha* in Karnataka have long provided rulings and *responsa* on questions concerning marriage, caste infractions, property claims, and criminal activities (Gnanambal, 1973). In some cases, temples themselves serve as courts of religious appeal for Hindus and others who take their legal claims to deities such as Goludev in Uttarakhand for resolution through the coercive mechanisms of sacred public declaration or who make vows and offerings in support of legal success in state courts (Malik, 2010).

Pañcāyat has become a category term for a variety of distinct local councils that have existed in India for a long time. It covers, therefore, a diversity of local legal practices that are difficult to capture under a single description. Nevertheless, the commitment of → Gandhi and of early independent India to Panchayati Raj, or governance by *pañcāyat*, led to the creation of *pañcāyat*s affiliated to the Indian state. Autonomous councils of castes, villages, regions, and guilds continued to coexist (Hayden, 1999), but the Indian government also introduced an official system of *nyāyapañcāyat*s, or judicial councils, in order to provide more efficient, locally informed justice to India's large and mostly rural population (Galanter & Baxi, 1989). The experiment with state-sponsored *nyāyapañcāyat*s is, however, generally considered a failure, because it did not increase access to justice for the rural poor by supplanting other local dispute-resolution institutions, including other *pañcāyat*s, at local levels (Meschievitz & Galanter, 1982). The lack of trust among locals for the nonlocal staff of the official *nyāyapañcāyat*s caused the system to be effectively moribund by the early 1970s. In its stead, the government inaugurated a new experiment with another informal legal forum.

The first *lok adālat*, or people's court, convened in 1982 and, unlike the earlier *nyāyapañcāyat*s, could deal with cases beyond those classified as "petty." The staff usually consists of retired advocates and judges nominated by the state to serve in *ad hoc* tribunals to hear local grievances. In spite of sincere efforts by the state to create another traditional legal institution, the empirical evidence to date suggests a similar range of problems with *lok adālat*s that had been faced by the *nyāyapañcāyat*s (Galanter & Krishnan, 2004). The Hindu pedigree of both *nyāyapañcāyat*s and *lok adālat*s is tenuous at best, but the repeated drive to experiment with informal legal institutions controlled by the state derives from widespread conceptions of the nature of Hindu society in rural areas and a sense that traditional dispute-resolution mechanisms are the best way to deliver justice to this critical majority. However, the persistence of traditional *pañcāyat*s, including recent controversies over the *khap pañcāyat*s, councils of elders primarily in Jat communities, who have decreed and enforced harsh punishments, including "honor killing," for marriages considered damaging to the group (Yardley, 2011), would seem to attest both to the need for such local councils to emerge organically in order to be effective and to the fact that the justice delivered in traditional councils does not always, or even usually, accord with the goals and assumptions of the modern legal framework of the state of India. Once again, thorny issues arise from the fact that caste councils, for example, often make their judicial decisions in contradistinction to the Hindu law of the state. In this way, the label "Hindu" for castes legally considered Hindu becomes a strategic category of convenience to be embraced in one context and rejected in another (Solanki, 2011, 204–205).

The definition of Hinduism under modern Indian law has also been addressed authoritatively by several opinions of the Supreme Court. R. Sen (2007) traces the leading cases in the Supreme Court's increased involvement in defining Hinduism for purposes of disaggregating legitimate claims to religious freedom from illegal discrimination disguised as religious practice. *Shirur Mutt* (AIR 1954 SC 282) first articulated what came to be called the "essential-practices" doctrine, in which religion prescribed not only beliefs and doctrines but also rituals, ceremonies, and other worship practices as integral. The case is also widely cited as a precedent sanctioning regulatory schemes, such as those regarding temple entry and endowments, for religious institutions. Another approach to defining religion was taken in the *Saraswathi Ammal* case (AIR 1953 SC 491), in which a "shastraic basis" was required to demonstrate sincere or essential religious commitments. The textual or scriptural requirement here is the key; a written source was from then on held as a privileged mode of proving religious commitments.

More explicitly on the definition of Hinduism, the widely discussed *Yagnapurushdasji* opinion (AIR 1966 SC 1119) concerning temple entry among Satsangi followers of the saint → Swaminarayan set a judicial precedent for the Supreme Court to offer its own definitions of Hinduism as a way to get clarity on constitutional questions about religious freedom. That opinion constructed a very wide definition of Hinduism as a "way of life" in which the ultimate aim of humanity is "release and freedom from the unceasing cycle of births and rebirths and a state of absorption and assimilation of the individual soul with the infinite" (1120). But it also pointed to the → Vedas as commonly revered scriptures and identified categories of common Hindu thought. In spite of its claim to define Hinduism in an inclusive, open-ended way, the *Yagnapurushdasji* decision laid claim for the court's entitlement to speak for religion and to differentiate real or essential religion from unessential. As a result, sectarian traditions of Hinduism have not been successful in finding legal recognition for their distinctive religious practices (Sen, 2007, 31).

More recently, the *Prabhoo* decision (AIR 1996 SC 1113) conflated the court's generic notion of Hinduism with the then-surging notion of *hindutva* as articulated in the works of V.D. Savarkar and M.S. Golwalkar. In spite of affirming the conviction of the accused for political campaigning through religious incitement, the court also endorsed and legally sanctioned a view that Hinduism/*hindutva* has a territorial and racial aspect that categorically excludes Indian minorities and promotes a notion that being Indian means being Hindu. Indeed, the decision was hailed as a victory for the Hindu nationalist BJP party.

In passing, it is worth mentioning that legal strategies to control the public discourse on Hinduism have also included suing publishers for books alleged to incite social enmity or offend religious sentiment. The *Sangharaj Rupawate* case ([2010] 7 SSC 398) called for a ban on an Oxford University Press book by J. Laine dealing with the revered king Śivajī of → Maharashtra. The court eventually struck down the censoring ban on the grounds that the offended communities were insufficiently identified. The very recent effort to censor the essay "Three Hundred Rāmāyaṇas" by A.K. Ramanujan (Howard, 2011) suggests that the courts will continue to be used to contest views and definitions of Hinduism that deviate from salient positions among powerful politicians and parties.

One final aspect of Hinduism in modern law that is rarely touched upon is personal religious commitment, or faith. Hindu faith and knowledge of Hindu customs and practices influence the work of judges and lawyers, not to mention the strategies and attitudes of litigants. Surprisingly few biographies of judges and prominent lawyers exist (Gadbois, 2011), but the judicial opinions and the arguments of advocates at all levels of the court system often employ references to Hindu customary practices of a particular region or to Hindu scriptures (Fuller, 1988) as key elements for a desirable and just outcome. In spite of the impact of legislative codification and case-law precedent on modern courts, independent knowledge of Hindu customs, practices, and institutions regularly form part of judgments at all levels of the modern Indian legal system. In addition, Hindu legal professionals tend to hold a more standardized, philosophically based view of Hinduism because of the influence of a unified understanding and practice of Hinduism among the educated class. Though subtle and hard to correlate directly with legal practice, Hindu faith, as an important psychological and social commitment of many judges and advocates, must play a significant role in the practical work of legal professionals in India.

Hinduism and the Law Outside of India

To date, the scholarly literature on Hinduism and law outside of India is relatively scarce. Unfortunately, a lot of research remains to be done on the precise encounters of Hindus and Hinduism with modern legal systems outside of India. In many countries, Hindu communities are a very small minority and as such find little legal recognition for their special needs or practices. In other places, however, Hindu communities are relatively large or at least concentrated in such a way that their presence demands legal consideration. Curiously, many studies of Hinduism's legal presence in non-Western countries such as South Africa and Indonesia are linked to the topic of human rights and the paralyzing debate over universalism and relativism. More directly, Hindu communities face legal problems in areas such as temple building and administration, marriage, divorce, adoption, and protection of religious freedom and identity.

The difficulty of gaining legal permission to build and control sacred spaces, especially temples, has been faced by almost every Hindu diasporic community. Countries such as Singapore (Sinha, 2011) and Indonesia (Crouch, 2007) began to address such questions under colonial dominance, while also regulating temples and religious endowments in response to more recent Hindu immigration. In countries like the United Kingdom (Nye, 1998) and the United States (Kurien, 2006), legal cases about temple placement and management have been part not only of complex processes of cultural negotiation of Hindus generally into new societies but also of the negotiation among Hindus themselves who may belong to different sectarian or regional communities. Temples in particular have become central sites for the solidification and performance of Hindu identity in the diaspora. The legal capacity to build and manage them, therefore, is a point of great importance and contention in the effort to hold on to Hindu practices and identity.

Increasingly, Hindu communities have also had to deal with conflicts over the recognition of their marriages in relation to efforts to curb immigration to Europe and the United States (Shah, 2010). In some cases, marriage and divorce practices according to Hindu legal norms that are well established in India have been scrutinized or rejected by courts in Britain and elsewhere (Menski & Shah, 2009). Similarly, several cases have arisen as to whether Hindu adoptions that cross jurisdictional boundaries will be recognized in Britain (Shah, 2009).

In the United States, legal cases have touched on several aspects of Hindu faith and practice, ranging from the recognition of Hindu marriages through the provision of Hindu meals and reading material for prisoners to the defense of Hindu-American views of Hinduism in textbooks (Krishnan, 2010, 264). Perhaps the most active legal advocacy group for Hinduism and Hindu-related causes is the Hindu American Foundation (HAF). On the one hand, the HAF has joined with parallel non-Hindu religious advocacy groups in promoting religious freedom. On the other hand, it has actively, sometimes aggressively, used the American legal system to promote views and understandings of Hinduism advocated by its leadership, and often in conflict with academic views (Kurien, 2006, 734–736). The difficulties here of striking a balance between defining Hinduism as it is and as it ought to be echo similar problems faced by Indian courts. Indeed, in general, the kinds of encounters between Hinduism and the Indian legal system seem to be recapitulated in other legal systems.

Conclusion

In summary, Hinduism thrives within modern legal frameworks in several distinctive ways. First, modern Hindu law maintains views and institutions created under conditions of colonial domination. The major innovations of Anglo-Hindu law, namely the privileging of elite Sanskrit texts as the primary source of law and the later arrogation of legal knowledge to judges in state courts, disconnected Hindu law both from the living, but now quickly dying, intellectual tradition of Dharmaśāstra that inspired it and from the myriad customary laws that formed its substantive basis. The symbolically powerful, but substantively weak, connection of colonial Hindu law to earlier legal practice culminated in the codification of the HCB. The patina of protection for Hindu religious identity and practices in the HCB is undermined firstly by the heavily statutory, precedent-driven, and homogenizing treatment of modern Hindu law in the Indian legal system. Hindu nationalist political parties have, secondly, hijacked ongoing debates about the possibility and desirability of a UCC by promoting an ethnic understanding of Hindu identity as a means to achieve the political dominance of upper-caste Hindus through an appeal to majoritarian identity.

At a broader level, Hinduism's interaction with modern legal systems touches aspects of Hindu religious practice and institutions that go beyond modern Hindu law. The Constitution of India itself is, according to M. Galanter, "a charter for the reform of Hinduism" (1971, 477). As such, prior emphases on shaping a modern Hindu family and on reforming seemingly antimodern practices within Hindu society were strengthened under the modern legal framework. Efforts have been made all along to preserve "essential practices" as understood by the courts, including through governmental experiments to administer more informal, decentralized justice in quasi-autonomous judicial forums. Other more independent institutions, such as *maṭha*s and caste *pañcāyat*s, continue to function, but the thrust of the official legal system has been to homogenize divergent Hindu religious practices and institutions in a way that presents a typically (for law in nation-states generally) reductive view of religion relative to its diverse presence on the ground.

Finally, by and large, legal professionals and scholars across the globe tend toward a rather narrow, simplistic understanding of religion – likely a pragmatic choice, but one that has real consequences. Most often, this understanding is laden with expectations of Christian, specifically Protestant, origin, namely a privileging of core beliefs and canonical scriptures as the essential elements of a religion for its legal definition. Like Indian courts, diasporic Hindu communities often articulate their religious commitments in such terms because of their unifying, transcultural potential. Drawing on these representations, a reductive view of Hinduism is the norm, when there is any view at all, in cultural and political contexts outside of India. As a result, a vacuum of information about Hinduism and its practices in the diaspora tends to pull ideas and legal solutions from parallel debates within India.

Bibliography

Agarwal, B., *A Field of One's Own: Gender and Land Rights in South Asia*, Cambridge MA, 1994.

Baltutis, M., "Recognition and Legislation of Private Religious Endowments in Indian Law," in: R.D. Baird, ed., *Religion and Law in Independent India*, New Delhi, 2 2005, 443–468.

Bayly, S., *Caste, Society and Politics in India from the Eighteenth Century to the Modern Age*, Cambridge MA, 1999.

Bhattacharyya-Panda, N., *Appropriation and Invention of Tradition: The East India Company and Hindu Law in Early Colonial Bengal*, New Delhi, 2007.

Burghart, R., "Hierarchical Models of the Hindu Social System," *Man.NS-536.* 13/4, 1978, 519.

Carroll, L., "Law, Custom, and Statutory Social Reform: The Hindu Widows' Remarriage Act of 1856," *IESHR* 20/4, 1983, 363–388.

Chatterjee, N., "Religious Change, Social Conflict and Legal Competition: The Emergence of Christian Personal Law in Colonial India," *MAS* 44/6, 2010, 1147–1195.

Crouch, M., "Regulating Places of Worship in Indonesia: Upholding Freedom of Religion for Religious Minorities?" *SJLS* 1, 2007, 96–116.

Das, V., *Structure and Cognition: Aspects of Hindu Caste and Ritual*, Delhi, 1982.

Derrett, J.D.M., "Hindu Law," in: J.D.M. Derrett, ed., *An Introduction to Legal Systems*, New York, 1968, 80–104.

Derrett, J.D.M., "Justice, Equity, and Good Conscience," in: J.N.D. Anderson, ed., *Changing Law in Developing Countries*, London, 1963a, 114–154.

Derrett, J.D.M., *Introduction to Modern Hindu Law*, Bombay, 1963b.

Derrett, J.D.M., *Hindu Law Past and Present*, Calcutta, 1957.

Dhavan, R., "The Supreme Court and Religious Endowments," *JILI* 19, 1978, 52–102.

Diwan, P., *Family Law*, Faridabad, 2009.

Forbes, G., "Women and Modernity: The Issue of Child Marriage in India," *WSIQ* 2, 1979, 407–419.

Fuller, C.J., "Hinduism and Scriptural Authority in Modern Indian Law," *CSSH* 30/2, 1988, 225–248.

Gadbois, Jr, G.H., *Judges of the Supreme Court of India: 1950–1989*, Delhi, 2011.

Galanter, M., *Competing Equalities: Law and the Backward Classes in India*, Berkeley, 1984.

Galanter, M., "Hinduism, Secularism, and the Indian Judiciary," *PEW* 21/4, 1971, 467–487.

Galanter, M., & U. Baxi, "Panchayat Justice: An Indian Experiment in Legal Access," in: R. Dhavan, ed., *Law and Society in Modern India*, Delhi, 1989, 54–91.

Galanter, M., & J. Krishnan, "'Bread for the Poor': Access to Justice and the Rights of the Needy in India," *HLJ* 55/4, 2004, 789–834.

Gnanambal, K., *Religious Institutions and Caste Panchayats in South India*, Calcutta, 1973.

Hawley, J.S., ed., *Sati, the Blessing and the Curse: The Burning of Wives in India*, New York, 1994.

Hayden, R.M., *Disputes and Arguments amongst Nomads: A Caste Council in India*, New Delhi, 1999.

Holden, L., *Hindu Divorce: A Legal Anthropology*, London, 2008.

Howard, J., "Bowing to Criticism, Oxford U. Press Will Reprint Works at Center of Controversy in India," *Chronicle of Higher Education*, Dec 9, 2011.

Jenkins, L.D., "Contemporary Caste Discrimination and Affirmative Action," in: T. Lubin, D.R. Davis & J. Krishnan, eds., *Hinduism and Law: An Introduction*, Cambridge MA, 2010, 215–233.

Kasturi, M., "'Asceticising' Monastic Families: Ascetic Genealogies, Property Feuds and Anglo-Hindu Law in Late Colonial India," *MAS* 43/5, 2009, 1039–1083.

Kishwar, M., "Codified Hindu Law: Myth and Reality," *EPW* 29/33, 1994, 2145–2161.

Krishnan, J., "Legally and Politically Layered Identities: A Thumbnail Survey of Selected Hindu Migration Patterns from South Asia," in: T. Lubin, D.R. Davis & J. Krishnan, eds., *Hinduism and Law: An Introduction*, Cambridge MA, 2010, 252–265.

Kurien, P., "Multiculturalism and 'American' Religion: The Case of Hindu Indian Americans," *SF* 85/2, 2006, 723–741.

Lariviere, R.W., "Justices and *Paṇḍitas*: Some Ironies in Contemporary Readings of the Hindu Legal Past," *JAS* 48/4, 1989, 757–769.

Larson, G.J., ed., *Religion and Personal Law in Secular India: A Call to Judgment*, Bloomington, 2001.

Luschinsky, M.S., "The Impact of Some Recent Indian Government Legislation on the Women of an Indian Village," *ASu* 3/12, 1963, 573–583.

Malik, A., "In the Divine Court of Appeals: Vows before the God of Justice," in: T. Lubin, D.R. Davis & J. Krishnan, eds., *Hinduism and Law: An Introduction*, Cambridge MA, 2010, 207–214.

Mallampalli, C., "Escaping the Grip of Personal Law in Colonial India: Proving Custom, Negotiating Hinduness," *LHR* 28/4, 2010, 1043–1066.

Mandelbaum, D., *Society in India: Continuity and Change*, vol. I, Berkeley, 1970.

Mani, L., "Contentious Traditions: The Debate on *Sati* in Colonial India," *CC* 7, 1987, 119–156.

Mani, L., "Production of an Official Discourse on *Sati* in Early Nineteenth Century Bengal," *EPW* 21/17, 1986, 32–40.

Mansfield, J.H., "Religious and Charitable Endowments and a Uniform Civil Code," in: G.J. Larson, ed., *Religion and Personal Law in Secular India: A Call to Judgment*, Bloomington, 2001, 69–103.

Mayne, J.D., *Mayne's Treatise on Hindu Law and Usage*, New Delhi, 16 2008.

Menski, W.F., *Hindu Law: Beyond Tradition and Modernity*, New Delhi, 2003.

Menski. W.F., ed., *South Asians and the Dowry Problem*, New Delhi, 1998.

Menski, W.F., & P. Shah, "Cross-cultural Conflicts of Marriage and Divorce Involving South Asians in Britain," in: F. Strijbosch & M.-C. Foblets, eds., *Cross-cultural*

Family Relations: Reports of a Socio-legal Seminar, Onati, 2009, 167–184.
Meschievitz, C., & M. Galanter, "In Search of Nyaya Panchayats: The Politics of a Moribund Institution," in: R.L. Abel, ed., *The Politics of Informal Justice*, vol. II, New York, 1982, 47–77.
Mulla, D.F., *Mulla's Principles of Hindu law*, New Delhi, 21 2010.
Myneni, S.R., *Family Laws in India*, Hyderabad, 2009.
Narula, S., "Law and Hindu Nationalist Movements," in: T. Lubin, D.R. Davis & J. Krishnan, eds., *Hinduism and Law: An Introduction*, Cambridge MA, 2010, 234–251.
Nye, M., "Minority Religious Groups and Religious Freedom in England: The ISKCON Temple at Bhaktivedanta Manor," *JCS* 40, 1998, 411–436.
Presler, F.A., *Religion under Bureaucracy: Policy and Administration for Hindu Temples in South India*, Cambridge UK, 1987.
Rocher, R., "The Creation of Anglo-Hindu Law," in: T. Lubin, D.R. Davis & J. Krishnan, eds., *Hinduism and Law: An Introduction*, Cambridge MA, 2010, 78–88.
Sen, R., *Legalizing Religion: The Indian Supreme Court and Secularism*, Washington DC, 2007.
Shah, P., "Inconvenient Marriages, or What Happens When Ethnic Minorities Marry Trans-jurisdictionally," *ULR* 6/2, 2010, 17–32.
Shah, P., "Transnational Hindu Law Adoptions: Recognition and Treatment in Britain," *IJLC* 5/2, 2009, 107–130.
Sharafi, M., *Parsi Legal Culture in British India*, forthcoming.
Sinha, V., *Religion-State Encounters in Hindu Domains: From the Straits Settlements to Singapore*, Dordrecht, 2011.
Solanki, G., *Adjudication in Religious Family Laws: Cultural Accommodation, Legal Pluralism, and Gender Equality in India*, New York, 2011.
Sturman, R., "Marriage and Family in Colonial Hindu Law," in: T. Lubin, D.R. Davis & J. Krishnan, eds., *Hinduism and Law: An Introduction*, Cambridge MA, 2010, 89–104.
Subrahmanian, N., "Making Family and Nation: Hindu Marriage Law in Early Postcolonial India," *JAS* 69/3, 2010, 771–798.
Sunder Rajan, R., "Women between Community and State: Some Implications of the Uniform Civil Code Debates in India," *ST* 18/4, 2000, 55–82.
Vidyasagar, I.C., *Vidhavavivāha*, Calcutta, 1856; ET: *Hindu Widow Marriage*, New York, 2011.
Williams, R., *Postcolonial Politics and Personal Laws: Colonial Legal Legacies and the Indian State*, New Delhi, 2006.
Yardley, J., "Unelected Councils in India Run Villages with Stern Hand," *The New York Times*, Jun 5, 2011, A6.

Donald R. Davis

New Age Spirituality

Hinduism has played a critical role in the development of modern conceptions of both spirituality and the New Age. The meanings of the terms "spirituality," "New Age," and even "Hinduism" are not immediately evident and are continually evolving; therefore, some explanation is necessary.

The word "spirituality" arose within the Christian tradition, where it initially referred to the immaterial aspects of reality and was often tied to morality. Paul the Apostle, for example, spoke of the spiritual in opposition to the carnal. In the 20th and early 21st centuries, it has been used to refer to an inner realm of life that each person can experience without the help of outside mediators such as priests, texts, or institutions. P. Heelas argues that the spiritual in current conceptions is connected with "the free expression, and thus development, of what it is to be 'truly' human" (2008, 1–2). Spirituality may also refer to a path, the culmination of which is an experience of unity with a larger cosmic or divine reality, as well as with humans and the natural environment. Modern spirituality arose in opposition to established creeds, rituals, and hierarchies of religious denominations.

Beginning in the 19th century, Hindu and Western spiritualities interacted when translations of Hindu scriptures entered American and European cultures. Hinduism's influence on the development of the moniker spirituality continued in the late 19th and early 20th centuries as Hindu → *gurus* – most notably → Vivekananda (1863–1902) and Paramahamsa → Yogananda (1893–1952) – spoke about Hindu practices and ideals to Western audiences. *Gurus* continued to influence the concept of spirituality during the countercultural revolution of the 1960s, when a generation turned its attention from drugs to meditation. A major herald of this turn was R. Alpert, or Ram Dass, a former Harvard professor and LSD experimenter who wrote the best seller *Be Here Now* after traveling to India and finding his *guru*. At this time, spirituality came to be associated with living in the present moment, an understanding that continues to grow, evidenced by the contemporary popularity of authors such as E. Tolle, author of *The Power of Now* and other books. Additionally, during the latter half of the 20th century, the human-potential movement, spawned by A. Huxley, burgeoned and in turn influenced the growth of humanistic philosophy. While humanistic psychology was not directly influenced by Hinduism, A. Maslow's discussion of "peak experiences" resonated with the mid-century turn to meditative experiences. Following humanistic psychology, transpersonal psychology developed with the distinct goal of developing higher states of consciousness. This movement drew on Hindu ideas such as reincarnation and a transcendent ground of being, as well as techniques for developing unity awareness.

The term "new age" was first used systematically by groups that splintered from theosophy (see → Theosophical Society), such as the Alice A. Bailey (1880–1947) material, which mentions the age of Aquarius and a new "global spirit" of religion, and the "I AM" Activity movement founded by Guy Ballard (1878–1939). New Age, as an emblem with upper-case letters, emerged gradually in the latter half of the 20th century to signify a multitude of practices, including neo-pagan rituals, meditation, parapsychology, alternative medicine, crystal healing, spirit channeling, human-potential therapies, contact with extraterrestrial life, shamanism, and astrology. The Findhorn Foundation in Scotland and the Esalen Institute in California, both founded in 1962, have continually served as hubs of New Age spiritual activities. Retreats and workshops offered at these sites often turned to Eastern ideas and practices, which were sometimes intertwined with Western esoteric traditions. Esalen Institute cofounder Michael Murphy was particularly influenced by Hindu philosophy through his textual encounters with the Indian visionary Sri → Aurobindo (1836–1886; Kripal, 2007).

New Age is sometimes referred to as a movement, but this designation is inappropriate since it has neither clear internal structure nor defined outer parameters. While some New Age activities are considered fringe, others are increasingly becoming a component of cosmopolitan culture. Included among the more mainstream practices are → meditation and *āsana* (physical → *yoga*), which derive from Hinduism. *Jyotiṣa* (→ astrology) and gems, along with → Āyurveda, an ancient form of healing, while still on the outskirts, are making inroads into mainstream culture as well.

"New Age spirituality" is an amalgam term that draws together under one umbrella the categories of secular (psychology and medicine, for example) and religious (meditation and neopagan rituals, for example), thus confusing the secular/religious or cultural/spiritual bifurcation that theologians and religion scholars have attempted to employ for hundreds of years. A brief look at the historical swings between the primarily religious worldview of the premodern world to the more rational and secular worldview of the Enlightenment, back to the emotional and nonrational mood of Romanticism, and then the swing toward "rational nationalism" in the modern world, makes the separation of two basic worldviews evident. The blurring of the distinction between the secular and the sacred through New Age spirituality offers a profound contribution to a contemporary cultural ethos. S.J. Sutcliffe elucidates,

> The special interest of "New Age" manifestations is that, by dint of their fluidity, ephemerality, and heteroglossia, they compel us to reassess the implicit boundary maintained by most scholars between "culture" and "religion." (Sutcliffe, 2003, 12)

New Age spirituality brought together the different goals of psychological, physical, and spiritual healing to embody a paradigm of holism that had previously been lacking in the modern world. In traditional cultures and tribal societies, healing and religion were intimately connected. C. Albanese argues that healing has played such an important role in various metaphysical traditions that influenced the development of New Age spirituality that it, in fact, replaces the religious goal of salvation (Albanese, 2007, 15). Furthermore, R.C. Fuller points out that holistic health movements have arisen, in part, as a response to the separation of the body from the rest of one's self in modern times. Holistic movements often draw on Eastern religious practices, because they offer a

> legitimation of their belief in the existence of "subtle energies" and the efficacy of certain meditational states of consciousness in opening individuals to wide ranges of experience unattainable through reason or sensory awareness alone. (Fuller, 1989, 96)

Hinduism, like New Age, encompasses an enormous variety of beliefs and practices. This article only concerns those aspects of Hinduism that have found their way into modern conceptions of spirituality. While spirituality and religion exist in opposition in the West, an inward and individual journey is often foundational in Hinduism. The traditional four stages of life, or → *āśramas*, for Hindus consist of student, householder, forest dweller, and *saṃnyāsin* (renunciate). The latter two stages involve leaving behind the social roles, institutions, and hierarchies of family and religion to delve within in order to attain *mokṣa* (→ liberation). Many Hindu practices revolve around the *guru* – disciple relationship that functions in small social units and does not require strong central institutions to determine rules and dogma. It is through individual *gurus*, each with his or her own interpretation of Hindu practice, more than any other factor, that Hinduism and New Age spirituality have intersected.

Spirituality in Historical Context

While "New Age spirituality" is mainly a Western construction, a complex interplay of ideas between India and the West gave rise to it. Certainly, Western esoteric traditions such as gnosticism played a part in the emergence of New Age spirituality, but these traditions were revived in conjunction with exposure to Asian scriptures and teachers. The modern conception of spirituality evident in cosmopolitan areas around the world is the result of global exchanges of ideas and mutual processes of acculturation between Asian and Western cultures.

Spirituality has different histories within the contexts of the West and India. Although it seems an anachronism to begin the exploration of New Age spirituality in the ancient world of India, it is appropriate since India's traditions of Yoga, → Vedānta, and → Tantra have played enormous roles in the development of spirituality in the West. From the Yoga tradition, New Age spirituality attains its practices of meditation and postural *yoga*; from Vedānta, the idea that transcendent reality can be accessed directly; from Tantra, the view that all elements of worldly existence are manifestations of the divine, replacing a typically dualistic Western worldview. This is not to say that rituals and dualistic concepts of reality are not present in Hinduism, but they are not the aspects that have influenced New Age spirituality.

The concept of an inner approach to attaining knowledge of a cosmic or divine nature has been part of the Hindu tradition for millennia. The so-called proto-Śiva, a seal of a man sitting in what appears to be a meditative posture, dating back to the → Indus Valley civilization (c. 2500–1500 BCE), is often cited as evidence of the very ancient source of inward-seeking spirituality existing on the subcontinent. Certain movements arose in India much later that attempted to disentangle the more inward aspects of religion from social hierarchies, creeds, and rituals that had developed during the vedic era (c. 1500–500 BCE). One of these occurred during the period in which the → Upaniṣads were written. At that time, many men renounced their worldly duties and caste affiliation to live in the forest and study under a *guru*. Before that, northern Indian culture was dominated by vedic rituals (→ *yajñas*) performed with absolute precision, thus requiring a priestly caste with specific and lifelong training. The stories and philosophies of the Upaniṣads represent attempts to understand the meaning of the rituals. In the process, inner knowledge of a transcendent or ultimate reality became more important than performance of ritual. The concept of the supreme → *brahman* was considered the ultimate and transcendent source of existence. Rote learning was also brought into question. In the *Chāndogyopaniṣad*, Śvetaketu is chastised by his father, Uddalāka, for thinking that he has attained knowledge through intellectual study rather than an inner realization of his own → *ātman* (self). The Śramaṇa (renunciate) movement was, in today's terminology, an antiestablishment and antireligious movement.

Another such movement occurred in the medieval period when poet-saints from both North and South of India decried established religion in favor of a personal experience of the ultimate, either as *saguṇa* (form) such as → Kṛṣṇa, or as → *nirguṇa* (formless). → Kabīr (1440–1518), for example, poked fun at the rituals and hierarchies found in both Hinduism and Islam and declared that he was neither Hindu nor Muslim, thus breaking down ideas of religion as structured and differentiated. The development of Tantra, also occurring in the Middle Ages, was another reaction to hierarchical institutions and dogma, particularly the duality of → purity and pollution.

A key turn to the spiritual occurs in modern India during British control (1858–1947). With the establishment of British schools in India, many young Indian men received an education in European philosophy. Both British orientalists and Indian intelligentsia attempted to understand each other's cultures, resulting at times in an amalgam of ideas that is typical of the later New Age spirituality. The Bengali → Rammohun Roy (1772–1833), drawing from an array of sources, including the Upaniṣads and the Gospels, is a key figure in the development of modern spirituality. After corresponding with Unitarian ministers, he founded a Unitarian Church in India with the American Baptist minister William Adam. Rammohun Roy later founded the Brahmo Samaj (Divine Society). Subsequent leaders of the organization, Dabendranath → Tagore, → Keshub Chandra Sen, and Pratap Chandra Mazumdar, shared a mistrust of outer forms of religion, favoring a more interior and spiritual approach. Dabendranath Tagore wrote, "God is to be worshipped only in spiritual ways. Hindu asceticism, temples, and fixed forms of worship are unnecessary" (Pankratz, 1995, 336). Thus, aspects of modern spirituality developed in the context of Hindu and Western collaboration beginning in the 19th century. Enlightenment ideas of individualism, a mistrust of outer forms of religion, and the view that truth can and should be sought in all religions were later to become hallmarks of New Age spirituality.

European Romanticism, a response to Enlightenment rationalism, was another precursor of New Age spirituality. The Romantic Movement encountered Hindu ideas through the connections afforded by British colonialism. Dissatisfied with materialism and rationalism, Romantic thinkers turned to India as an idealized source of perennial wisdom. They drew selectively from texts that emphasized monism and unitary consciousness, primarily found in the Upaniṣads. These texts were used to construct an idea of the spiritual that accorded with notions they had developed so that, for example, *brahman* became the spirit/mind of German idealism.

American transcendentalism developed, in part, as a result of exposure to Hindu spirituality. In 1785, C. Wilkins translated the *Bhagavadgītā* into English, and this was the translation that so affected R.W. Emerson and H.D. Thoreau. R.W. Emerson steeped himself in all manner of Hindu scriptures from 1830 until his death in 1882. Leaving behind a career as minister of the Unitarian Church, he began to teach others to view all of life as spiritual and to trust themselves more than institutions. Hindu ideas of → *karma*, the unity of existence, → *māyā* (illusion, which he called the shadow), and *brahman* (which he referred to as the over-soul) all became part of his worldview. From his extensive writing and lecturing, these ideas entered the worldview of many Americans, helping to prepare them for the advent of similar ideas they would encounter at the turn of the century when Vivekananda came to America. While R.W. Emerson was intellectually stimulated by Hindu ideas, H.D. Thoreau was the first to put them into practice. He left his home to dwell in a small hut by a lake for two years, spending hours in silent contemplation each day. He was, as S. Syman points out, the first American *yogī*. In a letter to H.G.O. Blake, he wrote, "Rude and careless as I am, I would fain practice the *yoga* faithfully," and later, "To some extent, and at rare intervals, even I am, a *yogin*" (Syman, 2010, 33).

Hindu influence on the development of spirituality continued in the early 20th century when *gurus* began to teach in the West. Key figures during this time were Vivekananda and Paramahamsa Yogananda, as well as their disciples who continued their work. Sarah Farmer, for example, a disciple of Vivekananda, established a center for learning in 1894 called Green Acre in Eliot, Maine, which lasted for 25 years and offered a platform for the comparative study of religions, as well as the experience of *yoga* and meditation. Another key organization was the Theosophical Society, founded by Madame Blavatsky and Henry Olcott in 1875, which combined Hindu, Buddhist, and Western spiritual and esoteric traditions. In the early 20th century, later leaders of the society, Annie Besant and Charles Leadbeater, discovered a boy whom they divined was to be the new "world teacher." They proceeded to groom → Jiddu Krishnamurti, the son of a Brahman, for this position. However, he later rescinded his role as leader of the "Order of the Star of the East." Interestingly, by his very rejection of Hindu religion and his insistence that people follow their own inner guidance, Krishnamurti did in fact become a world teacher, leading a new generation further in the direction of New Age spirituality.

Thus, while spirituality, in the contemporary sense of the term, is thought of as having arisen in the West, its inspiration came in no small part from Hinduism. During this time period, two key ideas that would become attributes of New Age spirituality arose: locating religion within the individual rather than institutions and appropriating inspiration and contemplative practice from various sources.

A New Age

In *Children of the New Age* (2003), S. Sutcliffe traces the genealogy of the term "New Age" and asserts that it can be divided into three stages. In the earliest phase, from the 1930s to the 1960s, New Age was an emblem for an apocalyptic vision. Various groups such as the Rosicrucian Order and the Alice Bailey material were established to prepare for the dawning of a New Age, sometimes referred to as the age of Aquarius. During the second phase, beginning in the 1970s, New Age was heavily influenced by the countercultural ethos of following one's own inclinations, as well as the increasing emphasis on human-growth workshops and holistic healing. It became more diffuse and increasingly molded by popular culture. The third phase began in the 1990s and is characterized by a somatic turn and further diffusion. Some argue that New Age is no longer an appropriate term, since practices and ideas of the third phase are becoming mainstream.

The progression might be viewed as beginning with a focus on outer portents and events, accompanied by messages from the deceased (and later from extraterrestrials), progressing toward more reliance on one's own self, cultivated through various therapies, and ending in a focus on the development of the mind/body/spirit complex through practices such as *tai chi* and *yoga*. C. Albanese argues that the progression through the latter stages can be seen in the career of actress Shirley MacLaine, who was catapulted into the limelight of New Age spirituality with the publication of her memoir *Out on a Limb* in 1983, in which she relates her adventures with extraterrestrials and channelers. Less than a decade later, she wrote *Going Within* (1992), about which C. Albanese writes,

> The inside front and end papers of the book are telling. Both betray a stylized woman in *yoga* attire seated in lotus posture with seven appropriately colored circles – the chakras – illuminating the figure. On the opposite page a full-colored circle for each chakra sits centered between text describing its nature and function. (Albanese, 2007, 503)

Hinduism has been influential in all of the phases: in the first, through the Theosophical Society and its many offshoots, as well as through the early Hindu *gurus* who traveled to the West; in the second, through direct contact with Hindu *gurus* who were so influential to the counterculture, as well as through practices used by humanistic and transpersonal psychology; and in the third, though lineages established by Hindu *gurus* and the global dissemination of postural *yoga*.

The cofounder of Theosophy, Madame Blavatsky (1831–1891), provides an example of the type of world citizenship and spiritual eclecticism that exemplifies New Age spirituality in its early stages. Born in Russia, Madame Blavatsky allegedly traveled around the world three times, finally becoming an American citizen in 1878. Ideas she gleaned from Hinduism were joined to esoteric knowledge from many sources to form a philosophy that appears in much New Age thought. These include beliefs in *karma*, reincarnation (→ *saṃsāra*), → *avatāras*, the interdependence of all things, a transcendent reality that forms the basis of existence, and the ideal of unity among religions, nations, and races. Meher Baba (1894–1969) also offers an example of a New Age spiritual leader. His parents were Zoroastrians and entered India from Iran. Meher Baba studied with and received initiations from Sufi and Hindu masters, whom he referred to as the five perfect masters. Declaring himself to be an *avatāra* with a mission to change the world, he spent much of his life in silence, performing his work on an inner level. In the 1930s, he traveled extensively throughout Europe and the United States with the goal of overcoming differentiation among religions, drawing people together through a central creed of love. Another spiritual teacher who models New Age eclecticism is Sri Aurobindo Ghosh (1872–1950). Educated in England, he was to become a major leader in the fight for India's independence. Later turning to the inner life, he developed a theory of spiritual evolution that drew on Eastern and Western philosophies, psychologies, and religions, including the application of Darwinian evolution to the Hindu concept of the descent of spiritual grace (*śaktipāta*). Higher spiritual realities, he declared, could be drawn down to the earthly realm, resulting in a new superman with a superbody and a supermind (Kripal, 2007, 66).

Madame Blavatsky, Meher Baba, and Sri Aurobindo are a few of the many who contributed to the spirit of the New Age. Disavowing affiliation with any particular religion while focusing on the spiritual and esoteric elements in all religions, they symbolized hope for the healing of national and religious difference through a spiritual globalism for those who had experienced the destruction of world wars. As the 20th century progressed, New Age spirituality grew exponentially with improved communication technology and facility of travel. By the end of the century, Hindu *gurus*, including → Maharishi Mahesh Yoga, Gurumayi, Amritanandamayi (or Amma; → Mata Amritanandamayi Mission Trust), → Sathya Sai Baba, and Sri Sri Ravishankar, had established global movements that they believed would usher in a new world order.

It is noteworthy that many of these *gurus*, beginning with the earliest, Vivekananda and Paramahamsa Yogananda, saw themselves as contributing to a New Age in which Hindu practices such as meditation would play a dominant role, even if they did not necessarily identify the practices as Hindu. Vivekananda taught that Vedānta was a universal religion that could easily be accepted by all and was particularly certain that America would adopt it. Paramahamsa Yogananda intended to unite East and West by showing the similarities between Jesus and Kṛṣṇa. As → Muktananda embarked on his second world tour in 1974, he announced that he would create a worldwide "meditation revolution." Maharishi Mahesh Yogi declared that a new age, which he dubbed the "Age of Enlightenment," had dawned in 1975 (Williamson, 2010, 50–51).

While the global *gurus* of the late 20th and early 21st centuries have contributed to New Age spirituality, some of them belie the open and eclectic nature of New Age. Often *guru* movements establish very particular parameters, rituals, and creeds, and those who belong to them become faithful to the path laid out by the *guru*, an attitude that contrasts the open stance of New Age seekers. These *guru*-centered movements might more appropriately be called new religious movements of a particular sort: Hindu-inspired meditation movements (Williamson, 2010, 49–50) or, alternately, East–West integrative spirituality (Gleig, 2010, ch. 1). The long-term and exclusive commitment required of followers of these *gurus* preclude them from the new paradigm established by Esalen Institute in which no single individual or tradition should dominate and in which democratic principles and individualism should be valued instead of religious authoritarianism (Kripal, 2007, 8). However, the ideas and practices these *gurus* teach have been influential to the wider trend of New Age spirituality, particularly to the third phase, which P. Heelas describes as beginning in the 1990s.

Hinduism and New Age Spirituality: Phase Three

At this third turning, New Age returns to lowercase letters and is used more often as an adjective than as the title of an era. Thus we have new age music, new age therapies, and new age books. The third phase is concerned with the development of body, mind, and spirit in equal measure. During the last few decades of the 20th century, interest in physical *yoga*, which was available on a limited scale in the West since the early 20th century, mushroomed. The word "Hinduism" is rarely used in the newest phase of spirituality, even though its footprints are everywhere. Neither is the term "New Age" in vogue, perhaps due to negative media attention. In fact, C. Albanese argues that the New Age is dying with the new millennium. It is no longer a distinct phenomenon but has entered the larger culture of the contemporary world: meditation is practiced in mainstream churches, law-enforcement agencies use psychics to solve cases, hypnotherapy is a legitimate tool for losing weight, and "→ *cakras*" has become part of common vocabulary (Albanese 2007, 513). Even the term "spirituality" has come under scrutiny because of its association with commercialism (Carrette & King, 2005).

Yet while these terms are losing favor in the West, they appear to be fashionable in India. The term "New Age *guru*," for example, is commonly used in popular Indian news media (Rudert, 2010, 629). A. Rudert outlines various aspects of non-Indian culture and religion that contemporary Indian *gurus* incorporate into their movements. Drawing on studies of two popular movements – M. Warrier's *Hindu Selves in a Modern World* (2005), about Mata Amritananda, and S. Srinivas's *In the Presence of Sai Baba* (2008) – A. Rudert notes that both of the *gurus* appropriate ideas from New Age, such as universalism and pluralism, as well as practices that, while based on traditional Hindu rituals, are "revised to suit modern needs" (Rudert, 2010, 634).

A. Rudert uses E. Tolle's international best seller *The Power of Now* and E. Gilbert's *Eat, Pray, Love* – books as popular in Delhi as in New York City – as examples of the New Age phenomenon in India. The first Indian printing of *The Power of Now* was in 2001; by 2005, the 18th reprint had been released (Rudert, 2010, 640n14). The author, E. Tolle, claims no particular religious tradition but draws from various sources in typical New Age fashion. His teachings are simple: focus on the present moment and give up worry. Although E. Tolle does not mention Hindu influences in his popular books, he stated in an interview that he feels a "deep link" to Krishnamurti and → Ramana Maharshi and that his teaching is a continuation of theirs (Lucas, 2011, 101). E. Gilbert's *Eat, Pray, Love* can be found in every bookseller and corner tea stall of India, according to A. Rudert. The book brings together themes of New Age spirituality in its most recent form: freedom to follow one's own journey in a search for enlightenment, worldly happiness, good food, a delight in other cultures, alternative forms of healing, and, of course, meditation and a *guru*.

E. Gilbert's memoir represents the current trend toward secularization of the spiritual and spiritualization of the secular. As S. Aravamudan states the case,

> It is often forgotten that even if it could be granted that secularization was doing various things to religion and putting it on the defensive, religion was also recreating itself in a manner to seize the offensive after readapting to secular conditions. (Aravamudan, 2006, 221)

D. Chopra provides one such case of the breakdown between the spiritual and the secular. S. Aravamudan describes D. Chopra as an example of "workaday charismatic-corporate entrepreneurship." Having successfully combined mass marketing with new age commodities, his annual income is around US $11 million. Oprah Winfrey provides the linchpin for today's global spirituality market. After appearing on her show, D. Chopra's featured book jumped in sales by 173,000 in a single day (Aravamudan, 2006, 258). In contemporary new age fashion, D. Chopra's message draws together quantum physics and positive thinking with the wisdom of Advaita → Vedānta and Āyurveda.

Because of instantaneous communication, a new spiritual practice might be invented in any area of the world. It then spreads through a combination of world tours by the teacher/*guru*, print and video publications, and especially → Internet media. The more videogenic and photogenic the practice, the faster it will spread. Laughter Yoga provides an example of how an idea disperses globally. The Laughter Yoga Clubs movement was founded in 1995 by Dr. Marara Kataria, a medical physician from Mumbai who wanted to bring the physiological and psychological benefits of laughter to a wide audience. He developed a few simple routines that would allow individuals or groups to practice "unconditional laughter." For example, people might shake their fingers or hug each other, all the while laughing with abandon. The practice and the movement require neither beliefs nor institutional ties. As of this writing, 17 years later, there are six thousand clubs in over 60 countries around the world. The premise is that unconditional laughter brings unconditional love and generosity. It is said that 30 minutes of laughter a day practiced by one percent of the population brings about world peace. Thus, the hope for a New Age has not been abandoned in the 21st century. Laughter Yoga might be a herald of new age spirituality to come: global movements that are egalitarian with a focus on immediate results attained with little effort or commitment.

Conclusion

What has happened to Hinduism with these current trends? *Yoga Journal*, a magazine dedicated to discussions of *yoga* practice and philosophy with a readership of 1.5 million people, had never used the word "Hinduism" by 2010 when members of the Hindu American Foundation (HAF) systematically searched its contents, beginning with its first publication. Subsequently, they began a campaign called "Take Back Yoga," appealing to American *yoga* teachers to acknowledge *yoga*'s debt to the Hindu tradition (*New York Times*, Nov 27, 2010, front page). A. Shukla, cofounder of HAF, stated in a *Washington Post* blog,

> Hinduism, as a faith tradition, stands at this pass a victim of overt intellectual property theft, absence of trademark protections and the facile complicity of generations of Hindu *yogi*s, *guru*s, *swami*s and others that offered up a religion's spiritual wealth at the altar of crass commercialism. (Shukla, *On Faith Panelists Blog*, 2010)

It is undeniable that *yoga* has often been associated with "crass commercialism," and it certainly should be acknowledged that India is the source of yogic traditions. (India rather than Hinduism would be a more accurate acknowledgment since *yoga* developed as part of several Indian religions, including Buddhist, Sikh, and Jain traditions.) Yet, as is the way with globalization, ownership of "intellectual property" by a religion or nation is difficult to maintain. M. Singleton has outlined the complex development of *yoga* and argues that its current form has arisen as much from European bodybuilding and European and American women's gymnastic movements as it has from the Indian *yoga* tradition (2010). Furthermore, while *yoga* originated in India, the *yoga* retreat geared toward an urban and somewhat elite population originated in the West.

Similarly, global *guru* movements have taken on a life of their own and are proliferating throughout the world. For example, Muktananda, who set out to establish a "meditation revolution," traveling to countries around the world in three world tours during the 1970s and 1980s, has indeed created what he intended. In America alone, nearly one hundred meditation *guru*s view themselves as hailing from the lineage of Muktananda. While most of these carry on a semblance of Hindu tradition, it is always modified to some extent. The same world citizenship and spiritual eclecticism that were evident in Madame Blavatsky can be found in many *guru*s and teachers influenced by Hinduism today. Swami Shankarananda is an example. Born in the United States, Shankarananda became a *saṃnnyāsī* under Muktananda and later founded the Shiva Yoga Ashram in Melbourne, Australia. In 2010, he was awarded the title of *mahāmaṇḍaleśvara* in India, an honor bestowed upon *svāmī*s by their peers, becoming the first American to receive such an honor.

Viewed historically, the Hindu tradition has had a major impact on the development of New Age spirituality. Moving forward into the 21st century, the terminology and concept of Hinduism as a discreet religion (formulated by British colonialists in the first place) may revert back to the more ineffable quality that produced its "spirituality." As the Śramaṇa movement left behind religious affiliation at the end of the vedic age, as Kabīr asserted his independence from religion in the Middle Ages, and as Meher Baba attempted to eradicate differences among religious traditions in the 20th century, spirituality of the 21st century, while indebted to the Hindu tradition, may be adverse to using the name "Hinduism" (or "Christianity" or any other religion).

Bibliography

Albanese, C., *A Republic of Mind and Spirit*, New Haven, 2007.

Aravamudan, S., *Guru English: South Asian Religion in a Cosmopolitan Language*, Princeton, 2006.

Carrette, J., & R. King, *Selling Spirituality: The Silent Takeover of Religion*, New York, 2005.

Chopra, D., *Ageless Body, Timeless Mind: The Quantum Alternative to Growing Old*, New York, 1993.

Chopra, D., *Quantum Healing: Exploring the Frontiers of Mind/Body Medicine*, New York, 1990.

Fuller, R.C., *Alternative Medicine and American Religious Life*, New York, 1989.

Gilbert, E., *Eat, Pray, Love: One Woman's Search for Everything across Italy, India, and Indonesia*, New York, 2007.

Heelas, P., *Spiritualities of Life*, Oxford, 2008.

Gleig, A., "Enlightenment after the Enlightenment: American Transformation of Asian Contemplative Traditions," diss., Rice University, 2010.

Kripal, J.J., *Esalen: America and the Religion of No Religion*, Chicago, 2007.

Lucas, P.C., "When a Movement Is Not a Movement: Ramana Maharshi and Neo-Advaita in North America," *NR* 15/2, 2011, 93–114.

Pankratz, J., "Ram Mohun Roy," in: R. Baird, ed., *Religion in Modern India*, New Delhi, 1995.

Rudert, A., "Research on Contemporary Indian Gurus: What's New about New Age Gurus?" *RC* 4/10, 2010, 629–642.

Singleton, M., *Yoga Body: The Origins of Modern Posture Yoga*, New York, 2010.

Schmidt, L.E., *Restless Souls: The Making of American Spirituality*, New York, 2005.

Shukla, A., "The Theft of Yoga," http://newsweek.washingtonpost.com/onfaith/panelists/asecm_shukla/2010/04/nearly_twenty_million_people_in.html.

Srinivas, S., *In the Presence of Sai Baba: Body, City, and Memory in a Global Religious Movement*, Boston, 2008.

Sutcliffe, S.J., *Children of the New Age: A History of Spiritual Practices*, New York, 2003.

Syman, S., *The Subtle Body: The Story of Yoga in America*, New York, 2010.

Tolle, E., *The Power of Now: A Guide to Spiritual Enlightenment*, Vancouver, 1999.

Vitello, P., "Hindu Group Stirs a Debate over Yoga's Soul," *New York Times*, Nov. 27, 2010.

Warrier, M., *Hindu Selves in a Modern World: Guru Faith in the Mata Amritanandamayi Mission*, New York, 2005.

Williamson, L., *Transcendent in America: Hindu-Inspired Meditation Movements as New Religion*, New York, 2010.

Lola Williamson

Science

In Hindu temples and cultural centers around the world, a visitor today often encounters not only traditional images of the gods and goddesses of the Hindu pantheon but also a myriad of posters, panoramas, and brochures extolling the scientific discoveries of ancient Indian, particularly Hindu, seers and scientists. These include discoveries in medicine, chemistry, metallurgy, astronomy, and technology. For instance, the newly constructed, magnificent Swaminarayan Akshardham Temple in Delhi boasts of a Disney-like underground boat ride during which visitors view displays of "the discoveries and inventions of the rishi-scientists of India" (Akshardham, 2005). Two of the dioramas "feature plastic surgery and a helicopter, showing the scientific advances of early Hindus" (Hamilton, 2011). I first encountered this phenomenon at the Hindu Temple of San Antonio, Texas. The temple has displayed a number of science posters published by the Hindu Swayamsevak Sangh United States. One such poster cites the 5th- to 6th-century Indian mathematical astronomer Āryabhaṭa as effectively proposing the heliocentric model of the solar system (see fig. 1); another poster proclaims that → Āyurveda "originated in the Vedas" (see fig. 2).

The claim of these scientific displays and literature is clear: Hinduism is scientific in spirit, has a long history of scientific discovery, is fully compatible with modern science, and – though not always stated in such contexts – is the most scientific religion in the world. This latter claim, with specific reference to the monistic strand of Hinduism known as Advaita → Vedānta, was made famous by Swami → Vivekananda (1863–1902) at the World's Parliament of Religions held in Chicago in 1893 (Brown, 2011, 209). The theme of harmony between Hinduism and modern science has become an important expression of contemporary Hindu identity and cultural self-affirmation and is a common perception especially among urban professional Hindus in the United States and in India. This view, along with notions such as that Hinduism is more a way of life than a religion and that Hinduism stresses religious tolerance, "have become so common that they comprise a 'generic Hindu' outlook that is unique to the late twentieth century" (Narayanan, 2006, 244).

The posters, dioramas, and brochures proclaiming the full harmony of Hinduism and science offer to many Hindus today a contrastive view to the notion of conflict between religion and science frequently seen as characterizing the relation of the Abrahamic traditions to modern science. But such models of harmony or conflict suffer from oversimplification. Both "are really hasty generalizations: there is indeed conflict in some historical periods, but not in others; and the same is true for harmony," according to historian and philosopher of science M.A. Finocchiaro (2001, 114). In addition, both models "tend to presuppose definitions of science and religion which are essentialist, anachronistic, or unhistorical" (Finocchiaro, 2001, 114).

There is currently a predisposition on the part of Hindu cultural nationalists to provide just such essentialist and unhistorical definitions of both religion and science. They regard Hinduism as the *sanātanadharma* (the eternal law, both moral and natural) consisting of truths, principles, and foundational norms that are universal and unchanging. But historically we find a breadth of Hindu perspectives on science, each with its own particular epistemological assumptions and metaphysical framework. These different assumptions and frameworks, themselves changing over time, have significantly impacted the various Hindu conceptions of what constitutes reality, on the one hand, and science, on the other. In this essay, I will use the term "Hinduism" in its broadest sense to cover developments from the vedic period down to the present.

A nuanced and comprehensive understanding of the relationship between Hinduism and science requires an examination of the social and historical contexts in which the classical and modern Hindu perspectives on science have developed, with special attention to their epistemological assumptions regarding knowledge about the empirical world. A comparison of these epistemic views with the methodological ideals and assumptions of modern science reveals a complex interaction between Hinduism and science that transcends any simplistic notion of harmony or conflict. Additional insights into the historic and contemporary tensions between Hinduism and science will be provided by looking beyond their respective metaphysical and epistemological assumptions to the underlying cognitive foundations of each.

Epistemological Tensions

Let us begin our investigation of the epistemological issues by returning to Swami Vivekananda, who claimed that ancient vedic (Hindu) seers had discovered many truths about both the spiritual and the empirical realms. How did they make such discoveries? With reference to various ancient scientific *yogīs*, including Kapila, legendary founder of the → Sāṃkhya and discoverer of "evolution," Swami Vivekananda claims,

> How wonderful his perceptions were, and if there is any proof required of the extraordinary power of the perception of Yogis, such men are the proof. They had no microscopes or telescopes. Yet how fine their perception was, how perfect and wonderful their analysis of things! (Vivekananda, 2003, vol. II, 445)

Vivekananda here reveals a major epistemic tension between his neo-Advaita perspective and the methodological approaches of modern science. The former privileges superconscious insight into the subtle workings of the material world, aided by an intuitive-deductive analysis, resulting in certain knowledge. Modern science emphasizes a constant interplay between hypothesis formulation and empirical testing rooted in recognition of the primacy of sensory observation, itself increasingly extended by sophisticated scientific instrumentation. But the resulting scientific conclusions, aided by logical deductions, are ultimately rooted in inductions based on empirical data and thus remain, at least in principle, forever tentative.

An elder contemporary of Vivekananda, the Hindu nationalist writer B. Chattopadhyaya (1838–1894), called attention to this epistemic tension in a blistering critique of ancient and classical Hindu approaches to understanding the natural world. While noting that Hindu philosophy traditionally "was co-extensive in meaning with the knowledge of Nature" and "therefore included Science," he went on to make the following observation:

> The Hindu laboured under the disadvantage of an erroneous method. An intense theological spirit rarely leads to anything but the deductive method, and the Hindu method was almost solely and purely deductive. Observation and Experiment were considered beneath the dignity of Philosophy and Science. Nor is even deduction as a rule pushed on its legitimate consequences. First principles are assumed on no grounds, and with the most perfect weapons of deductive logic at his command, the Hindu thinker contents himself with the most fanciful inferences. (Chattopadhyaya, 1969, 146)

B. Chattopadhyaya, with his positivist leanings, was naturally not willing to accept any superconscious technique, such as yogic perception, as a valid means of knowledge.

To illustrate the difference between traditional Hindu approaches and that of modern science, B. Chattopadhyaya cited the example of the Italian mathematician and scientist Evangelista Toricelli (1608–1647), inventor of the mercury barometer. Toricelli, aware that gardeners in Florence while using a suction pump had been unable to raise water higher than ten meters, reflected that the weight of the atmosphere on the water outside might be sustaining the column of water in the pump tube. He then figured that the same pressure should raise mercury in a tube as well, which he confirmed on further investigation. And then Blaise Pascal, realizing that there is less atmospheric pressure at higher altitudes, took a column of mercury up a mountain and noted the lower rise of the mercury in the tube. B. Chattopadhyaya concludes the following:

> A Hindu philosopher in Torricelli's place would have contented himself with simply announcing in an aphoristic *sutra* that the air had weight. No measure of the quantity of its pressure would have been given; no experiment would have been made with the mercury; no Hindu Pascal would have ascended the Himalayas with a barometric column in hand. (Chattopadhyaya, 1969, 146–147)

Turning next to a parallel Indian example, B. Chattopadhyaya notes that the idea of the earth's diurnal rotation, mentioned in the *Aitareyabrāhmaṇa*, was later affirmed by the great Indian astronomer Āryabhaṭa (b. 476 CE) in his great astronomical work, the *Āryabhaṭīya*. B. Chattopadhyaya quotes the famous astronomer: "The starry firmament is fixed... it is the earth which, continually revolving, produces the rising and the setting of the constellations and the planets" (1969, 147). But then,

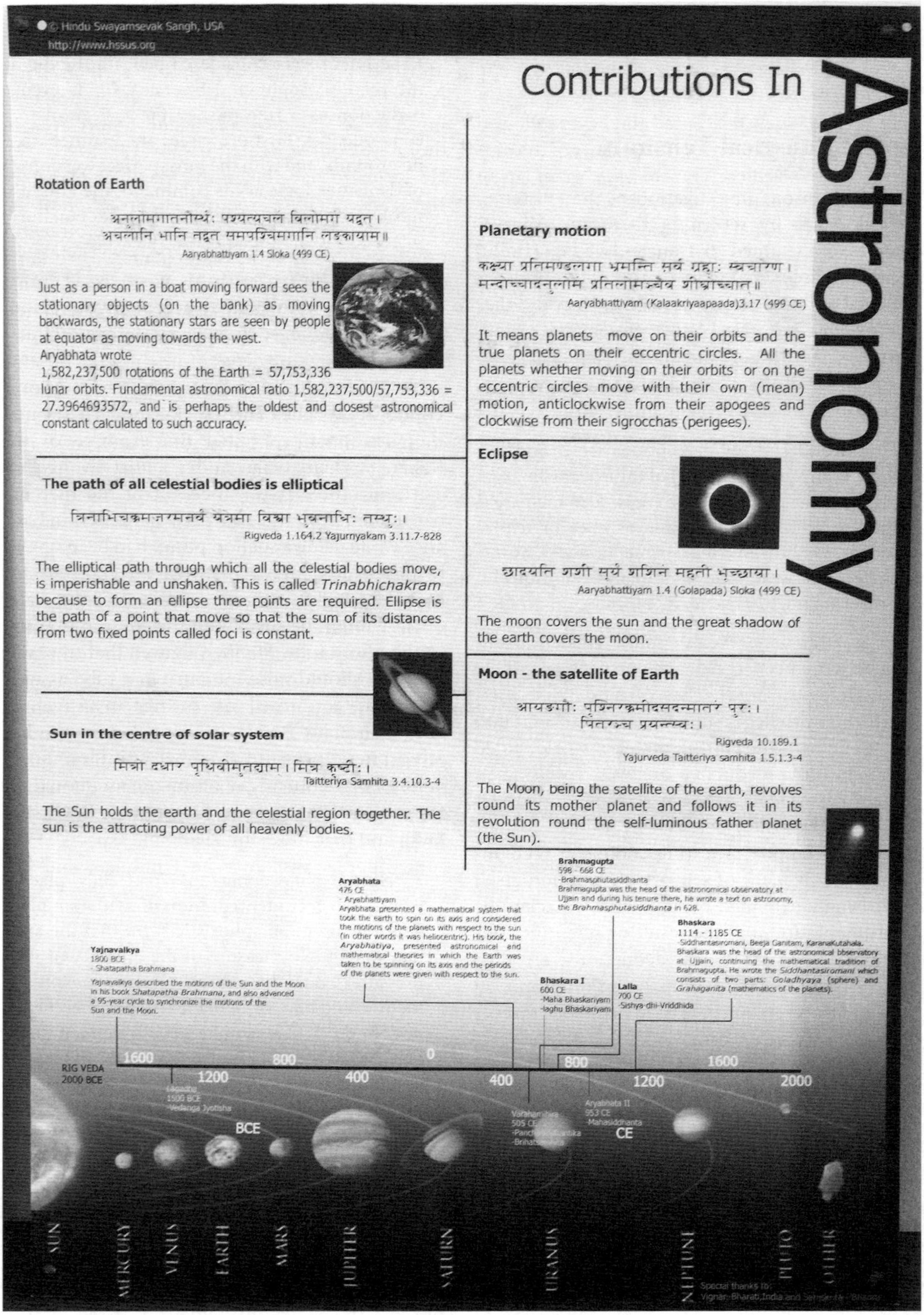

Fig. 1: Science poster on astronomy at the Hindu Temple of San Antonio (photo by C. Mackenzie Brown).

B. Chattopadhyaya sadly observes, the only "legitimate" conclusion from these and related "facts," namely the heliocentric model of the solar system, "was never positively put forward – never sought to be proved – never accepted and never followed out to the establishment of further laws of the universe" such as Kepler's laws and the "great law of Universal Gravitation" (1969, 147).

Despite B. Chattopadhyaya's dismissal of Āryabhaṭa's proclaiming any robust heliocentrism, there are frequent claims today on the Internet, as well as on science posters such as the one at the Hindu temple of San Antonio noted earlier, that Āryabhaṭa had proposed the heliocentric theory one thousand years before Copernicus did (e.g. "Aryabhatta," 2008; "Indian Astronomy," 2005). A more serious scholarly argument affirming Āryabhaṭa's heliocentrism has been put forward by the Dutch mathematician B.L. van der Waerden. To be sure, B.L. van der Waerden (1970, 5) acknowledges that Āryabhaṭa did not expressly put forth a heliocentric system, but he argues that even apart from Āryabhaṭa's idea of the earth's daily rotation, other parts of Āryabhaṭa's system indicate that it is based on a heliocentric model. But N. Swerdlow (1973, 241), a historian of ancient astronomy, rejects B.L. van der Waerden's claim as demonstrating "a complete misunderstanding of Indian planetary theory and is flatly contradicted by every word of Āryabhaṭa's description". Indeed, while Āryabhaṭa recognized the relativity of motion as accounting for the appearance of the stationary stars moving westward for an observer on the equator of the rotating earth (*Āry.* 4.9), he also described the spherical earth as "situated in the center of space, in the middle of the circle of asterisms, surrounded by the orbits of the planets" (*Āry.* 4.5; trans. Clark, 1930, 64 [= 4.6]). Even more explicitly, he sets forth the typical ancient geocentric model in which the sun occupies the fourth celestial sphere – between Mars and Venus – above the stationary earth at the bottom or center, which Āryabaṭa likens to a threshing post to which are tied circling oxen, representing the celestial bodies: "Below the asterisms lie Saturn, Jupiter, Mars, the sun, Venus, Mercury, and the moon, while the earth is below all of these, like a threshing post, in the center of space" (*Āry.* 3.15; trans. by author). And he utilizes epicycles (*vṛttas*) to explain various planetary phenomena, epicycles being relevant only in geocentric schemes of the universe (*Āry.* 3.19–21). Āryabaṭa further states that the asterisms with the planets are blown westward by the "planetary wind" (*pravaha; Āry.* 4.10). Thus his proposal of a rotating earth is irrelevant to the rest of his work, neither simplifying nor helping to explain any other ideas in the *Āryabhaṭīya* (Chattopadhyaya, 1996, 33). He seems to have taken the idea of a planetary wind, and possibly even the axial rotation of the earth, from puranic cosmology, without integration into the rest of his mathematical astronomy (Chattopadhyaya, 1996, 33). W.G. Clark, commenting on Āryabhaṭa's claim for a rotating earth and stationary asterisms, notes the following: "Later writers attack him bitterly on this point. Even most of his own followers... refused to follow him in this matter and reverted to the common Indian tradition" of a stationary earth (Clark, 1930, xiv). Thus W.G. Clark confirms in part B. Chattopadhyaya's own assessment of the lack of scientific temper – or at least scientific perseverance – in ancient India.

In one sense, the exact nature and validity of Āryabhaṭa's propositions, especially as judged by modern criteria, are beside the point and may distract from the underlying methodological issues at stake. To illuminate such issues, we need to turn to the social and cultural contexts in which Āryabhaṭa, and other ancient Indian scientists, carried out their work. Let me pose three questions that are directly relevant to any discussion of the Hinduism–science relationship in ancient India and that will help illuminate aspects of the contemporary discourse on Hinduism and science. These questions are the following: (1) To what extent did ancient Indian sciences derive from vedic religion? (2) To what extent was ancient Indian science Hindu science? And (3) to what extent did ancient Indian science share, not necessarily the conclusions of modern science, but its methodological perspective? I shall begin with a look at ancient Indian astronomy and Āryabhaṭa's special role in the history of that science, and I will then look briefly at ancient Indian medicine.

Hinduism and Astronomy in Ancient India

B.V. Subharayappa, historian and philosopher of science, regards ancient Indian → astronomy as derived from vedic seers. He first points out that the vedic sages had an intuitive understanding of the universe as an ordered cosmos governed by "Vedic natural laws" encompassing both the moral and the physical realms (Subharayappa, 2011, 196). Within this framework of vedic natural laws, astronomy assumed great importance to the vedic priests for ascertaining the proper times for various ritual and sacrificial performances. B.V. Subharayappa thus concludes the following: "Vedic astronomers generally belonged to a priestly class" who engaged in "prolonged observation of recognizable star-groups" (Subharayappa, 2011, 197). Turning to Āryabhaṭa, B.V. Subharayappa observes that his astronomical treatise, the *Āryabhaṭīya*, "states that the science of astronomy is a revelation from the creator Brahma, but apart from this passing allusion, there are no further references to religion" (Subharayappa, 2011, 197). (Āryabhaṭa declares that "this universally true science of astronomy… formerly was revealed by Svayambhū [Brahmā]" [*Āry.* 4.50; trans. Clark, 1930, 81].) Given the lack of references to religion, one is left wondering how vedic, or Hindu, Āryabhaṭa's astronomy really was – and perhaps how vedic the astronomy of ancient India in general was.

The great historian of ancient Indian science, D. Chattopadhyaya, takes a very different view of Indian astronomy, and of the astronomers of vedic times in particular. Like B.V. Subharayappa, D. Chattopadhyaya notes that the early astronomical texts – those of *jyotiṣa*, the Vedāṅga ("limb of the Vedas") dealing with astronomy – were used by vedic priests for determining auspicious times for their ritual performances. And he acknowledges that these texts also record remarkable observations of the positions and movements of the sun, moon, and various constellations. He regards those who made such observations as "taking the first step to astronomy" (1996, vi). But D. Chattopadhyay next claims that it could not have been the vedic priests themselves who took this step, as their theoretical orientation was quite different, being "quasi-religious and quasi-magical" (1996, vii). He points out that the priestly literature repeatedly condemns direct observation in preference for "the obscure and mystic" (1996, vii). He speculates that the observational astronomical tradition predates the arrival of the vedic peoples in India and was possibly derived from the agricultural → Indus Valley civilization, where such observations were necessary for creating a farmer's calendar (1996, viii).

As for Āryabhaṭa, D. Chattopadhyaya, like B.V. Subharayappa, calls attention to the astronomer's statement that the science of astronomy was of divine origin (1996, x). But D. Chattopadhyaya notes a different tone in the *Āryabhaṭīya* text that B.V. Subharayappa overlooks – a tone that provides an explanation for why, in B.V. Subharayappa's words, "there are no further references to religion." As D. Chattopadhyaya explains,

> as contrasted with the prevailing practice of proclaiming the astronomical views as but divine revelation Aryabhata boldly asserted that his book was of human origin, i.e. worked out by himself. This he announced in the very title he chose for his book, *Aryabhatiya*. (Chattopadhyaya, 1996, x)

D. Chattopadhyaya further points out Āryabhaṭa's declaration (see *Āry.* 4.49) that his astronomy, while it might be from the grace (*prasāda*) of god, was actually "the product of his own intellect [*mati*]" (Chattopadhyaya, 1996, x).

D. Chattopadhyaya extols Āryabhaṭa's achievement as surpassing that of all European astronomers until the time of Copernicus. Yet as D. Chattopadhyaya and W.G. Clark have pointed out, Āryabhaṭa was largely neglected by his Indian successors. D. Chattopadhyaya argues that the subsequent ignoring of Āryabhaṭa's work was due to his disregard of the prevailing "Brahmanical speculations and assumptions" (Chattopadhyaya, 1996, xi). Such disregard, D. Chattopadhyaya proposes, may well have been due to Āryabhaṭa's low-caste status, a status indicated by the "Bhaṭa" in his name. D. Chattopadhyaya then asks, might not Āryabhaṭa, being possibly subjected to discriminatory treatment under Brahmanical class norms, have become "cynical of Brahmanical orthodoxy as such, and discarding the theological bias of the divine origin of astronomy worked for the development of a secular view of the science?" (Chattopadhyaya, 1996, xi). D. Chattopadhyaya finally suggests that Āryabhaṭa might have gained his remarkable learning and intellectual independence by accepting the Buddhist teachings that shunned prejudice against the lower castes. While D. Chattopadhyaya admits that such a suggestion is hard to confirm, he claims that it is bolstered by the fact that another member of the low caste, another "Bhaṭa," the famous physician Vāgbhaṭa, came from a family of Buddhist doctors. Let me then turn to the case of the ancient Indian

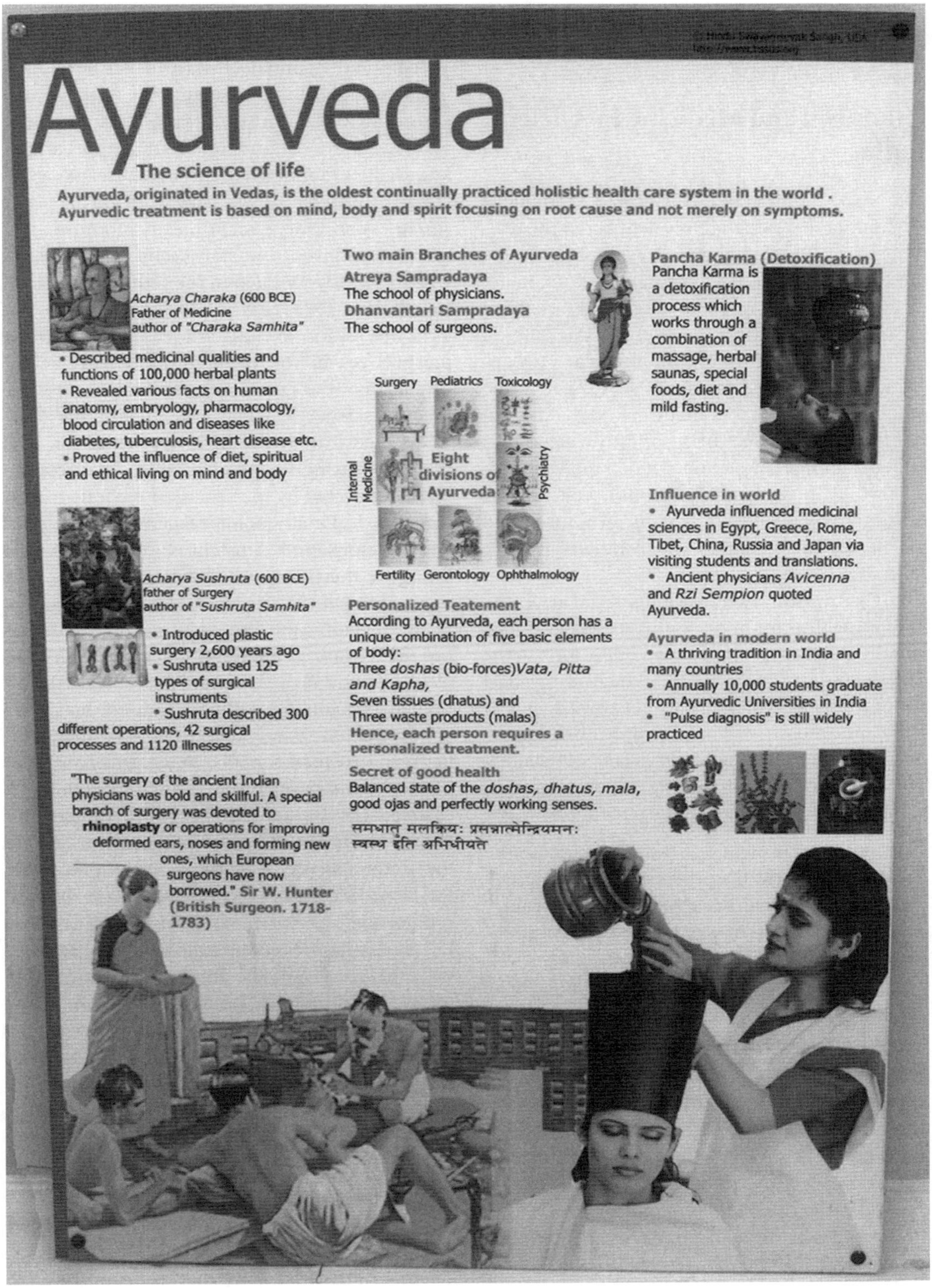

Fig. 2: Science poster on Āyurveda at the Hindu Temple of San Antonio (photo by C. Mackenzie Brown).

physicians and their possible ties to Buddhism and to heterodox traditions in general.

Hinduism and Medicine in Ancient India

The early 20th-century German Indologist H. Zimmer was rather ambivalent about the relationship of Buddhism, or at least its founder, to the Indian medical tradition. On the one hand, he claims that the Buddha (c. 500 BCE) modeled his teachings of salvation or spiritual healing on the "the attitude of the Hindu physician" toward physical healing (Zimmer, 1948, 32). On the other hand, he remarks that the Buddha did not resort to the approach "of the priestly teacher" but rather "adopted the standpoint of a medical man on the spiritual plane" (1948, 34). Left unclear is the general identity of "the medical man" and specifically the extent to which he was really a "Hindu physician."

D. Chattopadhyaya is not ambivalent at all. The Indian medical tradition, in his view, developed initially largely outside of and in opposition to the priestly, vedic schools and their magical-mystical notions of healing. He readily acknowledges that a certain amount of anatomical knowledge, so essential to the training of physicians, was gained from the ancient Brahmanical animal sacrifices, but such knowledge as was discovered led nowhere:

> the sacrificial slaughter of animals must have made available to the priests some amount of empirical data, which, rightly processed, could have developed into proto-anatomy of [the] ancient period. But the fact is that this did not and could not develop in this direction. (Chattopadhyaya, 1978, 274)

D. Chattopadhyaya attributes the scientific fruitlessness of vedic anatomical knowledge to the Brahmanical custodians of this knowledge, who were "interested only in the monstrous mystification of it, so that it becomes part of their awe-inspiring ritual technique" (1978, 275). He then cites the *Śatapathabrāhmaṇa* passage that indulges in correlating the parts of the sacrificial-fire altar with the various parts of the animal body, concluding that in this ritual-mystical "rigmarole," not even a "semblance of interest in anatomy proper" remains (1978, 275).

The promotion of obscure, mystical knowledge in the ritualistic Brāhmaṇa literature (see → Vedas and Brāhmaṇas) was further developed in the metaphysical doctrines of the → Upaniṣads, according to D. Chattopadhyaya. Their emphasis on a suprarational and antirational approach to knowledge culminated in the idealist teachings of the Advaitin → Śaṅkara and his rejection of reason (*tarka*) as an independent means of knowledge, while accepting it as possibly useful "to rationalise what is already revealed in the scriptures" (Chattopadhyaya, 1978, 202).

In opposition to these antireason, antiscience perspectives of the metaphysicians, the actual physicians were developing a rational-empirical medical science in which observation and logical inference from the data were essential. Not only was such an approach based on an epistemology rejected by metaphysical orthodoxy, but the empirical methodology also involved contact with persons and substances considered polluting by the priestly authorities. We thus find many condemnations of medical practitioners in the metaphysical literature and law codes of the Brahmanical authorities (Chattopadhyaya, 1978, 97–98, 212–218; see also Zysk, 1991, 5). The French Indologist J. Filliozat claimed that such condemnations merely reflected a sectarian rivalry between two vedic schools: "one may believe that the *Taittirīyas* have fired a passing shot at the rival school of the Carakas" (1964, 21). He connects the alleged vedic "Carakas" with a medical lineage that eventually produced the great compilation of the *Carakasaṃhitā*. D. Chattopadhyaya soundly refutes such an interpretation. He argues that J. Filliozat ignores, even conceals, "the fact that with the growth of the hierarchical aspirations in the Vedic tradition there takes shape an ideology that proves inimical to medicine or ancient science in its most promising form" (1978, 262). K.G. Zysk, renowned scholar of Indian medicine, sides with D. Chattopadhyaya:

> Chattopadhyaya has shown this view [of Filliozat] to be untenable and asserts that the root cause for priestly contempt of physicians derived from a clash of philosophical perspectives between medicine's fundamental empiricism and the priestly ideology that emphasized esoteric knowledge. (Zysk, 1991, 23–24)

So who were those ancient Indians who took the first steps to develop a rational-empirical medical science? During the several centuries between 800 and 100 BCE, this radically new approach to healing was pioneered by "wandering physicians," who were excluded from Brahmanical circles (Zysk, 1991, 5). Ostracized by the orthodox hierarchy, they found acceptance among the heterodox groups of ascetic mendicants, and "unhindered by brāhmaṇic strictures and taboos, began to conceive an empirically and rationally based medical epistemology" (Zysk, 1991, 5). The means and goals of these new medical → healers shared an affinity with the Buddhist ideal of the middle way, of avoiding extreme self-denial and maintaining bodily health in equilibrium with the environment. K.G. Zysk points out that the "symbiotic relationship between Buddhism and medicine" not only facilitated the spread of Buddhism in Asia but also led to Buddhist monastic communities playing a major role in "[t]he codification of medical practices within the monastic rules [which] accomplished perhaps the first systematization of Indian medical knowledge" (1991, 6). He summarizes the relationship between the wandering renunciants and the new breed of physicians:

> The connection between heterodox, particularly Buddhist, asceticism and medicine is perhaps best illustrated through anatomy. The approach of the early Buddhists and the physicians to an understanding of the human body reflects both a commitment to materialism through empiricism and rationality and a firm rejection of brāhmaṇic orthodoxy. (Zysk, 1991, 34)

Regarding the attainment of anatomical knowledge, one of the earliest accounts of how to perform a human dissection is provided in the *Suśrutasaṃhitā* (extant form dating to the 7th cent. CE at the latest [Chattopadhyaya, 1978, 43–44]). This text insists on the necessity of direct observation (*pratyakṣa; SuśrSa.* 3.5.53) of the body, including the dissected corpse. The *Suśrutasaṃhitā* gives explicit directions for preparing a body for dissection, including the squeezing out of excrement from the intestines (*SuśrSa.* 3.5.54; quoted in Chattopadhyaya, 1978, 95; Zysk, 1991, 35–36). As D. Chattopadhyaya points out, such instructions fly in the face of the Brahmanical advocacy of reliance on scripture, as well as flouting orthodox purity rules (1978, 97; see also Zysk, 1991, 36).

The *Suśrutasaṃhitā* along with the *Carakasaṃhitā* (extant form dating to around the 4th–6th cents. CE [Chattopadhyaya, 1978, 32]) are the two major classical texts of Āyurveda, often seen as epitomizing traditional "Hindu" medicine. D. Chattopadhyaya notes that "[t]he form in which the source-books of Indian medicine reaches us is apparently very strange. It is the assemblage of science and its opposite" (1978, 363). The French anthropologist F. Zimmermann also notes the intermingling of "the medical discourse" with "the imaginary" and sees these as part of a "single, homogenous discourse" (1987, 208). Thus, for him, such distinctions have been introduced by Western interpreters who fail to see that "Ayurveda must be taken en bloc: it stands as a whole and single 'myth,' a whole and single 'science'" (Zimmermann, 1987, 208). While he sees myth and science as a single entity in traditional cultures, he also notes that such myth-science is quite different from modern science. For instance, regarding traditional Indian classifications of animals as found in the ancient bestiaries and reflected in ayurvedic catalogues, he first observes that there is "a lack of differentiation between the real and the fabulous and a subordination of the biological to the spiritual" (Zimmermann, 1987, 196). Then he makes the following conclusion:

> But I fear that there is no masking the fact that India proceeded no farther than the bestiary, whereas others [in the Greco-Latin tradition] managed to escape from the enchantments of *dharma*, that ritualistic vision of the universe, and invent the natural sciences. (Zimmermann, 1987, 196)

Accordingly, in traditional Hindu classifications of animals, which were pervaded by the idea that all are subject to the cycle of rebirth, "the position of each category of beings is fixed by its function in the system of *ritual* activities," with minimal reference to "strictly *biological* classification" (Zimmermann, 1987, 196).

F. Zimmermann's emphasizing the different conceptions of science in traditional and modern societies reminds us of M.A. Finocchiaro's caution about the use of "essentialist, anachronistic, or unhistorical" definitions of both science and religion. At the same time, more than one conception of what constitutes science may exist in any given society. While the extant texts of the classical Āyurveda may represent some sort of myth-science, the actual history of the texts and their internal contents points to a different explanation from F. Zimmermann's for the intermingling of the medical and the imaginary. For the texts have undergone repeated editing, some parts having been lost while others have been added, and there is no assurance that the various editors, redactors, and compilers had the same goals in mind. This becomes especially clear in light of the two contrasting and irreconcilable epistemologies in the texts themselves: the mystical-magical epistemology of Brahmanical orthodoxy and the naturalistic methodologies of the wandering physicians.

Like the *Āryabhaṭīya*, the extant ayurvedic texts are said to be divinely revealed. But as G.J. Meulenbeld says, "the divine character of *āyurveda* has been imposed upon it during a particular state of its development and has not always been one of its characteristics" (2001, 2). To the extent that Āyurveda is regarded as revealed, he suggests, it is not really science, as it tends toward a closed system that is not open to "the progressive acquisition of knowledge" (Meulenbeld, 2001, 3). But it was not completely closed either, and thus "the doctrine of its divine origin does not belong to its hard core" (2001, 3). K.G. Zysk similarly argues that

> Probably during the early centuries of the common era, Hinduism assimilated the storehouse of medical knowledge into its socioreligious intellectual tradition and by the application of an orthodox veneer rendered it a brāhmaṇic science. (Zysk, 1991, 6)

Likewise, D. Chattopadhyaya regards the orthodox veneer as a defensive reaction by the physicians, "a show of apparent piety as a protective crust for science" (1978, 363). He provides several examples from the *Carakasaṃhitā* that deal with spiritual → liberation, but he sees these as merely "salvation superimposed on healing" (Chattopadhyaya, 1978, 372). Regarding these references to salvational knowledge, he concludes the following:

> Though redundant to medicine, their presence in the medical corpus is not purposeless, for they are presumably of the nature of ransom offered to the counter-ideology without which it is not easy for the doctors to save their science. (Chattopadhyaya, 1978, 375)

At the same time, the subordination of empirical medicine to spiritual or salvational concerns was greatly to hinder the further development of medical science. It was apparently not until 1836, at the new, British-established, Calcutta Medical College, that Hindu medical students again began to dissect human cadavers as part of their training in practical anatomy – thereby ushering in modern, "rational scientific medicine in India" (Bhattacharya, 2011, 1227). Nonetheless, the ancient texts, especially the *Carakasaṃhitā*, retain the criteria for separating superstition from science (Chattopadhyaya, 1978, 201–209). These criteria include commitment to empiricism, causal law, rigorous reasoning, and "intra-disciplinary discussion and debate" (Chattopadhyaya, 1978, 208) – the latter perhaps an ancient equivalent to today's peer review. The tensions apparent in the *Suśrutasaṃhitā* and *Carakasaṃhitā* between Brahmanic orthodoxy and medical empiricism point clearly to the fact that religion and science are social practices, at times overlapping but often resulting in conflict, however veiled (compare Stenmark, 2010, 292).

I noted above that Śaṅkara subordinated reason to scripture. All the Vedānta schools, including Advaita, subordinated not only reason but also perception, effectively enshrining a critical epistemic tension between Vedānta and modern science. Deepening this tension was the notion put forth by some philosophers of the → Nyāya and → Vaiśeṣika schools such as Udayana that there are two kinds of perception: supernatural (*alaukika*) and ordinary (*laukika*; see Brown, 2012, 45). The former, call it transcendent vision, intuition, or yogic perception, available only to the disciplined and virtuous, provides direct and immediate experience of god and reality, unmediated by reasoning or scripture. At the same time, Nyāya and other philosophers critically examined the epistemic liabilities of experience in general, including such direct experience as yogic perception.

In concluding this section on ancient and classical science in India, let me draw once again on D. Chattopadhyaya. He calls attention to a very early debate in Hindu philosophical speculations regarding the ultimate causal agents underlying the manifest universe. In the *Śvetāśvataropaniṣad* (6.1–2), the possible agents named include god, time, chance or accident, and innate nature (*svabhāva*; Chattopadhyaya, 1991, 55–61; see also Brown, 2012, 15–16). This latter view insists that the universe and its constituent elements evolve by their own inherent power and causal efficacy, independent of any manipulating god or emanating supernatural consciousness. This naturalistic perspective, D. Chattopadhyaya reasonably asserts, underlay the development of natural science in classical times and is clearly seen in the case of early Indian medical science (1991, 70). D. Chattopadhyaya further comments,

> In the clash between 'the doctrine of God' and 'the doctrine of nature' [*svabhāva*], therefore, we have perhaps the earliest glimpse of the conflict between religion and science that took place in Indian history. (Chattopadhyaya, 1991, 60)

Yet outright conflict may not have been inevitable. While the *Śvetāśvataropaniṣad* may have pointed to a clash, the *Muṇḍakopaniṣad* suggests another possible model for the Hinduism-and-science relationship. The *Muṇḍakopaniṣad* (1.1.5) sets forth the notion that there are two *vidyā*s or "sciences," hierarchically arranged. The higher knowledge (*parāvidyā*) is that "by which one grasps the imperishable [*akṣara*; the ultimate reality known generally in the Upaniṣads as → *brahman*]" (Olivelle, 1998, 437). The lower (*aparāvidyā*) consists of the four Vedas and their six traditional ancillary limbs: phonetics, rituals, grammar, etymology, prosody, and astronomy. The lower science, or sciences, incomplete in themselves, promotes attaining knowledge of the higher science of *brahman*. This line of thought was further developed by Śaṅkara, who posited two levels of knowledge – (1) the worldly, in which subject and object are experienced as separate, and (2) the ultimate level, in which one realizes the unity of all being and the identity of subject and object and of self and *brahman*. Perception and inference are competent only for dealing with the somewhat illusory empirical world, but they fail to warrant any metaphysical truth (Hiriyanna, 1932, 358). This subordination model, while perhaps avoiding outright warfare, hardly provides much inducement for the pursuit of the lower natural sciences, nor does it eliminate possible incompatible teachings about the empirical world on the part of religion *vis-à-vis* scientific claims, whether the religious teachings are derived from scripture or from inspired visions of ultimate reality. In the colonial period, the two-sciences model was to be taken up and revised by Hindus as a major strategy in dealing with the challenges of modernity and modern science arriving from Europe.

Hinduism and Science in the Colonial and Postcolonial Periods

Many of the epistemological and metaphysical issues of the ancient and classical periods relevant to natural science lay dormant for many centuries, until the coming of the Europeans. Under colonial rule, these issues soon revived, as the English-educated Hindus faced the dilemma common to

> any elite that accepts the task of integrating the religion, the values, and the social systems of a traditional society with the thought and practices exported from the colonial centres in Europe. (Brekke, 1999, 204)

Among the many challenges, that of modern science with its inherent skepticism toward traditional knowledge, along with the accompanying technology, was the most momentous (Halbfass, 1988, 399).

B.V. Subharayappa notes that the first impression Indians had of "western science" was through the various "botanical, zoological, geological, meteorological, and geographical" surveys commissioned by the colonial administration (2011, 199). He adds that

> [t]he European investigators brought with them a commitment to experimentation, observation, and rational thinking. Their superior methodologies highlighted the inherent weakness of traditional knowledge. (Subharayapa, 2011, 199)

The Indian elite in the 19th century sensed their own current scientific backwardness, combined with an intense admiration and an often unquestioning acceptance of the authority of modern, evidence-based science. These attitudes intermingled with the conviction that India's subjection to and oppression by Western colonial power were due, at least in part, to the West's superior mastery of science and technology.

The conviction of their scientific inferiority soon led the Hindu elite to call for British investment in science education for the natives. As early as 1823, → Rammohan Roy petitioned the British administration for the instruction of Indians by European teachers in the subjects of "Mathematics, Natural Philosophy, Chemistry, Anatomy, and other useful sciences" (Roy, 1978, 472). At the same time, Rammohan Roy insisted that the world was indebted to India, where the knowledge of science, as well as of literature and religion, first dawned (1978, 906; Brown, 2012, 87). With Rammohan Roy we see the first manifestation of one of the overriding problems pervading the Hinduism-and-science discourse in colonial India: the tension between the image of science as a free and universal inquiry "unaffected by its historical and cultural locations," on the one hand, and its advancement of such claims "only in its particular history as imperial knowledge," on the other (Prakash, 1999, 71).

To meet the challenges posed by modern science, Hindus developed various modes and models of cultural negotiation in their attempt to reaffirm traditional religious and social values within some sort of universal, scientifically sanctioned – or at least scientifically compatible – framework. We find among the various negotiating strategies six persistent and often interrelated or overlapping themes (compare Halbfass, 1988, 399).

The first and perhaps earliest of these is that India was the fountainhead of all sciences and culture, although such a magnificent past is obscured by India's present state of degeneration. This notion, as we have seen, was already proffered by Rammohan Roy and reflected the idea of an ancient vedic golden age proposed by European orientalists early in the 19th century. Later elaborations of this model led to the idea of vedic science and the radical scientizing of the vedic tradition, finding in the ancient scriptures such modern technological inventions as electricity, airplanes, telegraphy – as in the writings of → Dayananda Saraswati – and more recently, transplant surgery and subatomic physics. Basic scientific discoveries were also uncovered in the ancient scriptures and sayings of the seers, including the laws of gravity, of the conservation of energy, and of evolution – the latter two emphasized in Vivekananda's writings. Advocates of vedic science seek to find vedic equivalents to modern scientific ideas and discoveries, but they are almost always forced to make quite arbitrary and unconvincing linkages based on highly subjective textual interpretations, or they rely on vague surface similarities.

A second approach called for mutual supplementation often involving the idea of exchange between India and the West. Europe could teach to India its science and technology, while India could benefit the West with its spirituality – an approach well exemplified by Vivekananda. While impressed by the dazzling radiance of evidence-based "Western" science and its potential to help India's poor, Vivekananda took it upon himself to bring the wisdom of Vedānta to what he saw as the spiritually impoverished West (Brekke, 1999, 204). A variant of this perspective was to advocate the adoption of Western technology but to eschew the "scientific temper" with its corrosive skepticism and materialist predisposition – an approach evident in the contemporary *hindutva* movement and dubbed by M. Nanda "reactionary modernism" (2003, 37).

A third strategy was to disarm Western science by relegating it to a sphere outside or below a higher, spiritual science. This was accomplished in part by acknowledging the superiority of European study of the external world but insisting on the preeminence of Hindu investigations of the inner world of consciousness. This resonated with and was accommodated to the ancient *Muṇḍakopaniṣad* idea of two hierarchical sciences, resulting in the notion of a higher, spiritual science and a lower, material (modern, "Western") science. Modern science is thus not wrong but limited.

This model of two hierarchical sciences we already see developing with Debendranath Tagore (1817–1905), who maintained that god is invisible to the outer senses but visible to the inner eye of knowledge. This inner eye he commonly referred to as intuition based on inner conviction (*ātmapratyaya*), which itself is grounded in our innate knowledge of god (Brown, 2012, 97). Debendranath Tagore's notion of inner conviction utilizes European ideas of intuition and self-evident truth and is a radical reinterpretation of the upanisadic notion of inner conviction focused on nondual knowledge of the one self (Halbfass, 1988, 224, 396, 570n). He then related this to the notion of the two *vidyā*s of the *Muṇḍakopaniṣad*: the higher knowledge of the ultimate attained through intuition and the lower knowledge of the empirical and rational sciences. He expanded the lower sciences to include such natural sciences as geology, medicine, and psychology, as well as philosophy and theology (Halbfass, 1988, 98). This model of the two hierarchical sciences was further developed by Vivekananda and became a standard strategy of 20th- and 21st-century Hindus dealing with the challenges of modern science, especially Darwinian evolution. Interestingly, recent researches in consciousness or meditation studies have sought to obtain verification from the natural sciences of the contemplative truths of the inner science and thus to prove "the concordance of both approaches" (Halbfass, 1988, 399).

A significant modification of the two-sciences model, in which the methodological approaches of science and religion are equated, results in a further scientizing of tradition, encompassing both substantive claims and epistemic processes. This modified version, the fourth approach, identifies yogic or contemplative experience with scientific empiricism. Religion and science are thus viewed as one rather than as two different sciences (compare Prakash, 1999, 76–77).

But whereas scientific empiricism is conjoined with rigorous peer review and an openness to disconfirming evidence and arguments, yogic experience is not similarly open-ended. Rather, *yogīs*, while at times comparing subjective experiences, have no real means for testing the true equivalence of such personal experiences and, in any case, are strongly predisposed merely to confirm truths already known and promulgated by the ancients (Brown, 2012, 230–231). In addition, different contemplative traditions frequently come to radically different conclusions regarding the nature of the reality that is immediately experienced. The Hindu classical tradition was well aware of the problematic nature of personal experience and of the psychological sense of certainty that may result from such experience. In particular, Nyāya-Vaiśeṣika thinkers did not fail "to distinguish very clearly between psychological factuality and epistemological validity" (Halbfass, 1988, 394).

The fifth strategy, not so common but still significant, was selectively to accept certain findings of modern science while rejecting others as either not scientific or, at best, misinterpretations of scientific data. Thus, cosmic evolution may be acceptable, while organic evolution is not – as seen in Dayananda Saraswati and his followers and among later conservative theistic movements like the International Society for Krishna Consciousness (→ ISKCON) and the International Society of Divine Love.

The sixth and last strategy developed by the Hindu elite was to accept the superiority of modern science to traditional forms of knowledge, while still finding aspects of the tradition that were not in conflict with modern science (Prakash, 1999, 57–58). Such was the approach of B. Chattopadhyaya, whose critique of ancient Indian science we have already encountered. At the same time, he saw in the Hindu trinity of → Brahmā, → Viṣṇu, and → Śiva a doctrine of creation, preservation, and destruction in accord with Darwinian theory, in contrast to what he saw as conflicting Christian notions of an omnipotent god (Prakash, 1999, 57–58; Brown, 2012, 77).

Regarding certain of these strategies, D. Chattopadhyaya notes that the attempt to read modern science into the Vedas, on the basis of the supposed penetrating intuitive insights of the ancient seers, was understandable in the colonial period. But such a perspective in post-Independence times "has lost its relevance" and is "a factor inhibiting the real development of modern science in India" (Chattopadhyaya, 1986, 399).

Conclusion: Social Contexts and Cognitive Foundations

M.A. Finocchiaro points out that the relationships between science and religion have been "much richer and more complex than the notions of conflict and harmony can convey" (2001, 114–115). He notes that recent scholarship has suggested a wide variety of possible relationships between the two ventures, including separation, dialogue, integration, and subordination. And within these, there are many more significant distinctions. The Hindu traditions nicely illustrate these complex, and changing, relationships.

At the same time, among the various conceptions of science and/or knowledge emerging at various times in India's history, something akin to the modern notion of science as a rational-empirical enterprise has been present from ancient times. And both in classical and in colonial/postcolonial periods, strategies were developed to deal with conflicts and tensions in order to effect some sort of reconciliation. The orthodox Hindu philosophers of the classical period were able to diminish tensions by comprehending natural science and its radical epistemic methods within an overarching and supernaturalistic metaphysical framework that effectively tamped down conflict but at the price of undermining the scientific enterprise. Conflict was concealed. Science is a fragile social enterprise, and it was simply not sufficiently robust in ancient and classical times to withstand the Brahmanical takeover. During the last two centuries, science has been too impressive, successful, if you will, both in its prowess in creating technological spinoffs and in its ability to explain the natural world for it to be dismissed or disarmed in quite so facile a fashion.

To explain the fragility of the scientific enterprise, the philosopher of science R.N. McCauley points to the cognitive foundations underlying both science and religion. He notes, on the one hand, that religion is "primarily dependent on the natural proclivities of the human mind" and thus is found in all cultures (2011, 236). Specifically, this natural proclivity includes an extreme sensitivity for detecting intention or conscious agency in phenomena and events that – while serving survival needs – may well over-detect or intuit conscious agency where none exists. Science, on the other hand, is dependent on comparatively rare social arrangements that foster "mastery of both norms of reasoning and radically counterintuitive conceptions" and "public availability of the pivotal processes, products, and evidence" (McCauley, 2011, 236). Science thus requires considerable institutional support, but its disciplined skepticism combined with its frequent, radically counterintuitive conclusions tends to undermine social, political, and religious (and even scientific) vested interests, thereby risking loss of support and endangering its persistence (McCauley, 2011, 280–281). Such a dynamic is precisely what we see in the development of science in ancient and classical India.

One approach to handling these conflicting interests that currently attracts many within the Hindu community is to adopt an updated version of the two-sciences model, an approach called by S.J. Gould NOMA ("Nonoverlapping Magisteria"). For instance, S. Menon, a researcher in consciousness studies sympathetic to the Advaita Vedānta perspective, proclaims that "[f]aith is not opposed to reason since they deal with different domains" (2006, 11). More specifically, she regards "reason and experiments" as characterizing the domain of science, while "self-purification," as well as "inner transformation, and ontological insights," she sees as refined means of knowledge pertaining to the domain of religion and spirituality (Menon, 2006, 10). From her Advaita perspective, the supreme reality, the *parabrahman* that is pure consciousness, transcends all dualisms such as matter and spirit and god and world, and thus there can be no ultimate conflict between science and religion.

R.N. McCauley, however, critiques S.J. Gould's NOMA principle as inevitably unsustainable in practice, since religious thinkers of a NOMA bent sooner or later backslide into making empirical claims that invoke the necessary agency of some transempirical entity. But this transgresses any strict adherence to the NOMA principle, which regards the transempirical agent – and thus its effects in the empirical world – as basically inaccessible by scientific means (McCauley, 2011, 244–245). In the Hindu context, that transempirical entity may well be the nondual *brahman* or god of Advaita rather than an extracosmic creator-god. As S. Menon states, "Hindu enlightenment is seeing God in every bit of the world" (2006, 11), but science sees no such presence, as it is undetectable, and, in any case, this is an unnecessary hypothesis for explaining how the world works. Accordingly, some level of tension seems inevitable between science and religion, including Hinduism, for as R.N. McCauley concludes, "Religions presume that the most penetrating accounts of the world will always, ultimately, look to agent causality. Science does not" (2011, 236).

Bibliography

Akshardham, "Photo Gallery," 2005, http://www.akshardham.com/photogallery/index.htm.

"Aryabhatta," 2008, http://india-awesome.blogspot.com/2008/07/aryabhatta.html.

Bhattacharya, J., "The First Dissection Controversy: Introduction to Anatomical Education in Bengal and British India," *CS* 101/9, 2011, 1227–1232.

Brekke, T., "The Conceptual Foundation of Missionary Hinduism," *JRH* 23/2, 1999, 203–214.

Brown, C.M., *Hindu Perspectives on Evolution: Darwin, Dharma, and Design*, London, 2012.

Brown, C.M., "Vivekananda and the Scientific Legitimation of Advaita Vedānta," in: J.R. Lewis & O. Hammer, eds., *Handbook of Religion and the Authority of Science*, Leiden, 2011, 207–248.

Chattopadhyaya, B., *Bankim Rachanavali*, Calcutta, 1969.

Chattopadhyaya, D., *History of Science and Technology in Ancient India: Astronomy Science and Society*, Calcutta, 1996.

Chattopadhyaya, D., *History of Science and Technology in Ancient India: Formation of the Theoretical Fundamentals of Natural Science*, Calcutta, 1991.

Chattopadhyaya, D., *History of Science and Technology in Ancient India: The Beginnings*, Calcutta, 1986.

Chattopadhyaya, D., *History of Science and Technology in Ancient India*, Amsterdam, 1978.

Clark, W.G., *The Āryabhaṭīya of Āryabhaṭa: An Ancient Indian Work on Mathematics and Astronomy*, Chicago, 1930.

Filliozat, J., *The Classical Doctrine of Indian Medicine: Its Origins and Its Greek Parallels*, New Delhi, 1964.

Finocchiaro, M.A., "Science, Religion, and the Historiography of the Galileo Affair: On the Undesirability of Oversimplification," *Osiris.2* 16, 2001, 114–132.

Halbfass, W., *India and Europe: An Essay in Understanding*, Albany, 1988.

Hamilton, A., personal communication, Dec 11, 2011.

Hiriyanna, M., *Outlines of Indian Philosophy*, London, 1932.

"Indian Astronomy," Space Today Online, 2005, http://www.spacetoday.org/India/IndianAstronomy.html.

McCauley, R.N., *Why Religion Is Natural and Science Is Not*, Oxford, 2011.

Menon, S., "Hinduism and Science," in: P. Clayton & Z. Simpson, eds., *The Oxford Handbook of Religion and Science*, Oxford, 2006, 7–23.

Meulenbeld, G.J., "Reflections on the Basic Concepts of Indian Pharmacology," in: G.J. Meulenbeld & D. Wujastyk, eds., *Studies on Indian Medical History*, Delhi, 2001, 1–16.

Nanda, M., *Prophets Facing Backward: Postmodern Critiques of Science and Hindu Nationalism in India*, New Brunswick, 2003.

Narayanan, V., "Hinduism in Pittsburgh: Creating the South Indian 'Hindu' Experience in the United States," in: J.S. Hawley & V. Narayanan, eds., *The Life of Hinduism*, Berkeley, 2006, 231–248.

Olivelle, P., *The Early Upaniṣads: Annotated Text and Translation*, New York, 1998.

Prakash, G., *Another Reason: Science and the Imagination of Modern India*, Princeton, 1999.

Roy, R., *The English Works of Raja Rammohun Roy: With an English Translation of the "Tuhfatul Muwahhiddin"*, New York, 1978.

Stenmark, M., "Ways of Relating Science and Religion," in: P. Harrison, ed., *The Cambridge Companion to Science and Religion*, Cambridge UK, 2010, 278–295.

Subharayappa, B.V., "Indic Religions," in: J.H. Brooke & R.L. Numbers, eds., *Science and Religion around the World*, Oxford, 2011, 195–209.

Swerdlow, N., "A Lost Monument of Indian Astronomy," *Isis* 64/2, 1973, 239–243.

Vivekananda, *The Complete Works of Swami Vivekananda*, 9 vols., Calcutta, 2003.

Waerden, B.L. van der, *Das heliozentrische System in der greichischen, persichen und indischen Astronomie*, Zurich, 1970.

Zimmer, H.R., *Hindu Medicine*, Baltimore, 1948.

Zimmermann, F., *La jungle et le fumet des viandes*, Paris, 1982; ET: *The Jungle and the Aroma of Meats: An Ecological Theme in Hindu Medicine*, Berkeley, 1987.

Zysk, K.G., *Asceticism and Healing in Ancient India: Medicine in the Buddhist Monastery*, New York, 1991.

C. Mackenzie Brown

Sexuality

Of the ancient religious practices that encompassed the worship of many gods and goddesses without actively seeking converts, Hinduism is now the only survivor. Hindus are inheritors of a wide variety of attitudes toward sexuality, some of which have been integrated into Hinduism by a process of accretion, and many of which are in a constant state of flux. As Hindus have hundreds of sacred books and teachers, there is no one prescriptive set of doctrines on sexuality that can claim primacy. There are, however, certain generally agreed-upon concepts that have a bearing on sexuality; these include the idea of a close relationship between individual spirit (→ *ātman*) and universal spirit or God (*paramātman* or → *brahman*), the doctrine of rebirth (→ *saṃsāra*), and the concept of → *dharma*.

It is a difficult and perhaps futile exercise to try to separate the Hindu from the Indic; therefore at times I conflate the two. As A. Nandy has shown, many Indians who subscribe to other faiths, both Indic (such as Buddhism, Jainism, and Sikhism) and non-Indic (such as Christianity, Judaism, and Islam), nevertheless retain many Hindu practices and beliefs, and about six hundred communities in India can be classified as having more than one religion (Nandy, 1997). Conversely, many Hindus include icons of Christ, Mary, Buddha, and Muslim mystics in their shrines at home and go on pilgrimages to Muslim mystics' *dargāh*s (tomb shrines) and to Christian churches.

For Hindus, everything is in one sense divine, and this divinity is experienced more strongly in some beings, places, and activities at certain times. One's parents, teachers, spouse, and children may all in some respects be seen and addressed as aspects of the divine, as may most living creatures (cows, elephants, snakes, monkeys, and in some traditions even cockroaches) and many plants (among the more sacred is the holy basil, grown in many homes and courtyards), as are also books and food. The elements earth, fire, water, and air are themselves gods and therefore sacred. Likewise, many activities, including sexual activities, can be divine at certain times and places.

The doctrine of rebirth is common to all Indic religions – Hinduism, Buddhism, Jainism, and Sikhism. Hindus believe that rebirth occurs because of attachments that remained unfulfilled in former or present lifetimes and must be worked through in future lifetimes. While the attributes of the body – class, community, gender, race, species, and abilities – do not necessarily carry over to successive births, mental and emotional attachments from one birth always carry over to the next.

From antiquity to the present, Hindu texts (and today, many ordinary as well as scholarly Hindus) understand strong and otherwise inexplicable attraction to a particular person, place, object, or activity as the result of attachment in a former lifetime. Many non-Hindu Indians also casually refer to former or future births when speaking of the strength of amorous attachments. The doctrine of rebirth is inextricably connected to Indic understanding of the particularities and predilections of desire and the vagaries of love. The strength of desire as exemplified in lovers' willingness to confront social opprobrium or even to die for love is seen as related to the force of attachment that must be worked through and outgrown but cannot be suppressed by external forces. If artificially suppressed, the attachment must either burst forth later in this lifetime or else carry over to a future birth.

The idea of true love or desire (*prem, muhabbat*) as an irrepressible force thus receives sanction from a central Hindu doctrine. Socially proscribed relationships are often legitimized through an appeal to the idea of rebirth: numerous popular films depict persecuted lovers being reborn in happier circumstances and coming together again. This is a very old idea, appearing in the ancient epics, and in the → Purānas. The famous 11th-century Sanskrit story cycle, the *Kathāsaritsāgara*, recounts cases of socially unsuitable love (between a prince and a poor woman, a princess and a low-caste man, a princess and a thief), some of which result in suicide when thwarted, and others that parents are compelled to accept when they realize that the lovers were spouses in former lifetimes (Tawney, 1968, 490–495).

Modern Hindu teachers offer similar explanations; when mathematician S. Devi interviewed Srinivasa Raghavachariar, Sanskrit scholar and priest of the major Hindu Vaiṣṇava temple at Srirangam in South India, he remarked that same-sex lovers must have been cross-sex lovers in a former life. The sex may change, but the soul remains the same in subsequent incarnations; hence the power of love impels these souls to seek each other (Devi, 1977, 146–147). On the dark side, many lovers today (both cross-sex and same-sex), driven to suicide by familial opposition, declare that they will be reunited in their next birth (Vanita, 2005a). Attempting suicide as a way of proving the genuineness of one's love is unfortunately a narrative pattern that runs from ancient texts (such as 2nd-century dramatist Bhāsa's play *Avimāraka*) to modern cinema.

At the other end of the spectrum, family-arranged marriages are also considered to be shaped by former lives, and spouses are often said to be married not for one but for seven lifetimes. Erotic love is thus spiritualized and seen not as a matter merely of present impulse but as a force that connects past, present, and future.

The second overarching framework within which Hindu approaches toward sexuality are couched is that of the interconnectedness of all things, an idea closely linked to that of rebirth. Most Hindus are theists; for nondualists, all spirit (human, divine, or animal) is ultimately one, while for dualists of various kinds, the universe of devotees (which includes nonhuman animals) is eternal and wedded to the divine through love. Even for the dualist → Sāṃkhya school of thought all matter (animated by proximity to spirit) is one.

Thus, sexual activity, like all activity, is part of a sacred whole. This is the concept expressed visually in erotic temple sculptures, such as those at Khajuraho and Konark. Each temple represents the cosmos and is covered with sculptures depicting every kind of activity, from making music and war to making love, undertaken by humans, divine beings of various types, and animals. Erotic activity is just one of many sorts of activities, all represented with the same vigor and openness, and indicative of the bliss (*ānanda*) of creation. Images of paired divine and human lovers (*mithuna*) embracing passionately are found from antiquity onward in many Hindu sculptures and friezes and are reworked in medieval painting. From the late 19th century onward, under British colonial influence, couples are no longer represented in this way.

The ancient Hindu scriptures, the → Upaniṣads, describe reality or God as *sat* (truth), *cit* (consciousness), and *ānanda* (joy). There are many kinds of joy, and sexual joy is not excluded from the joy that is divine. As Rabindranath Tagore put it in a letter to C.F. Andrews, → *oṃ*, the Hindu syllable representing God, is Hinduism's affirmation of life, because in Hinduism there is reality, not nothingness, at the heart of life:

> Buddha kept silent throughout his life about the truth of the *Om*, the *everlasting yes*…he emphasized the fact of *dukkha*, misery, which had to be avoided, and the *Brahma-vidya* emphasized the fact of *anandam*, which had to be attained…Therefore, the idea of life's training was different in the Vedic period from that of the Buddhistic. In the former it was the purification of life's joy, in the latter it was the eradicating of it. The abnormal type of asceticism to which Buddhism gave rise in India revelled in celibacy and mutilation of life in all different forms. (Dutta & Robinson, 1997, 259–260)

If all the gods, as the *Bṛhadāraṇyakopaniṣad* (3.9.1) famously declares, are one, and if everything in the universe is ultimately one, then nothing is irredeemably evil, unspeakable, or eternally damned and excluded. Hinduism's primary impulse is assimilative; this is expressed doctrinally in the belief that since all paths lead to the same goal, all religions are manifestations of truth. It finds narrative expression in the common motif of a demon who battles a god and is finally both killed by and absorbed into that god, thereby achieving liberation. Therefore, unlike in the European Christian tradition, where some types of sex became unspeakable, Hindus continued to discuss, debate, and describe all types of sex; this relative openness changed under British colonialism.

Attitudes toward sex and sexuality are inseparable from attitudes toward → gender. In contemporary mainstream Hindu philosophy, which is heavily influenced by the Advaita → Vedānta (nondualistic) school of thought, the ultimate reality transcends gender but is manifested in everything. In other schools of thought, such as Sāṃkhya and → Tantra, the ultimate reality is both male and female, a duality reflected in the gods and goddesses most Hindus worship. However, each deity is also thought of as encompassing both male and female.

The Purāṇas praise the chosen deity, whether → Śiva, → Viṣṇu, or anyone else, as infinitely flexible: as male, female, neuter; as animal, bird, tree, jewel, river; and as present in all elements and all forms of life. Thus, a typical eulogy in the

Śāntiparvan of the → *Mahābhārata* identifies Śiva with a series of apparently exclusive attributes: "Thou art male, thou art female, thou art neuter" (*MBh.* 1.9.326). Like other types of difference (class, *jāti*, color, species), gender is irrelevant to enlightened beings, who perceive the divine as pervading and/or surpassing material reality.

The ultimate unreality of gender forms the philosophical basis for numerous stories of sex change that pervade Hindu narrative. The sex may change from one lifetime to the next but may also miraculously change within one lifetime. This idea complicates the nature of sexuality. The many versions of the story of King Ila, a pivotal ancestral figure, indicates these complexities. In the → *Rāmāyaṇa*, Ila wanders into a forest where Śiva, while sporting with → Pārvatī, has taken a female form to please her, causing every male in the forest to become female. Ila becomes a woman called Ilā (*Rām.* 7.100–103). By the grace of Śiva and Pārvatī, Ila/Ilā is allowed to be a man for a month and a woman for a month, and produces children both as a man and as a woman. These children are the progenitors of the solar and lunar dynasties (*sūryavaṃśa* and *somavaṃśa*), to which all kings are said to belong and from which many modern-day Hindu communities claim descent.

The principle of the unreality of gender works in interesting ways, with regard to both women's status and sexuality. In the *Bhāgavatapurāṇa*, a king who becomes a woman is about to burn herself on her husband's pyre when a sage stops her and tells her that gender is an illusion, that she is really neither woman nor man (*BhāgP.* 4.28.61).

Because the *ātman* or spirit is without gender, and Hindu marriage is a sacramental union of spirits (not just a social contract), many Hindus today consider same-sex union or marriage to be justifiable according to Hindu tenets, although others disagree. When two policewomen, Leela Namdeo and Urmila Srivastava, got married by Hindu rites in 1987 in Bhopal in central India, their neighbor, Sushila Bhawasar, a village woman schoolteacher, remarked to journalists, "After all, what is marriage? It is a wedding of two souls. Where in the scriptures is it said that it has to be between a man and a woman?" (Panchal, 1988). Likewise, after he had officiated at the Hindu wedding ceremony of two Tamil women in Seattle in July 2002, a Śaiva priest whom I interviewed told me that other priests might disapprove, but after much thought, he had concluded, on the basis of Hindu scriptures, that "[m]arriage is a union of spirits, and the spirit is not male or female."

Although individual spirit and universal spirit are ultimately without gender, gods and goddesses when worshipped in iconic form do have gender. While some schools of Hindu philosophy are non-theistic, and others conceive of god as formless, most Hindus, even most nondualists, worship gods and goddesses embodied for the purpose of worship in all kinds of iconic and aniconic forms (human, animal, bird, snake, tree, stone, planet, and river), thus symbolically validating the divinity of all things. There is a god or goddess for every activity and way of life. Every god and goddess is viewed by the worshipper as containing all possibilities.

To say that god is neither male nor female may appear to be not very different from saying that god is male, female, and neuter. However, there is actually an important difference of emphasis here between Hindu and Judeo-Christian or Islamic approaches. Absence of gender creates a lacuna, which worshippers then fill with the dominant convention of maleness. Conversely, the presence of three genders (male, female, and neuter) allows for the visualization and worship of god as male, female, or androgynous. Hindu divinities have not only gender but also sexuality, and this gender and sexuality are fluid. The fluidity allows human gender and sexuality to be conceived of as ultimately fluid even if socially constricted.

One visual representation of this is the Ardhanārīśvara (half-female god) form of Śiva. This icon shows one half of the body as female and the other half as male. It can be interpreted as the fusion of Śiva with his wife Pārvatī or as the innate duality, androgyny, or bisexuality of god. Likewise, Śiva and Viṣṇu are also fused in the icon of Harihara. One half of this all-male body bears the iconic features of Viṣṇu (Hari) and the other half those of Śiva (Hara). It is this fusion of Śiva and Viṣṇu (when Viṣṇu took the female form of Mohinī and absorbed Śiva's semen) that is said to have given rise to the bachelor god → Ayyappan, also known as Hariharaputra and widely worshipped today.

There is much debate over the question of whether the → *liṅga* and → *yoni*, symbols of Śiva and Pārvatī, respectively, which are worshipped both together and separately, are iconic or aniconic. On the one hand, these words do also mean "phallus" and "vulva" or "womb," respectively. On the other hand, other gods too are emblematized in symbols – for example, Viṣṇu is worshipped in the form of a small stone known as a → *śālagrāma*. *Liṅga* also means a sign, particularly a sign of gender.

The sexual implications of the *yoni* as a symbol of the goddess are evident in Śākta worship, for example, at the temple of goddess Kāmākhyā ("Fulfiller of Desires") in → Assam, in northeast India. This region was originally called Kāmarūpa ("Form of Desire"). The temple is supposed to stand at the place where the *yoni* of goddess Satī, Śiva's first wife, fell when he danced in grief and rage, carrying her corpse, 51 parts of which fell all over the subcontinent. The sanctum sanctorum is a cave where a spring flows through a *yoni*-shaped cleft in the rock. Devotees touch this cleft to worship the goddess. Once a year, during monsoon season, this water turns red for three days, which is celebrated as the goddess' or mother earth's menstruation. This festival, *ambubachi melā*, is one of the largest in the country, drawing hundreds of thousands of pilgrims, and many couples marry at the temple as well.

Some gods and goddesses are depicted as celibate, but most of them have erotic dimensions. For the lay worshipper who may not be familiar with the intricacies of doctrine and may even be illiterate, this representation of the gods as erotic beings is perhaps the most important validation of desire as sacred. Indeed, desire itself is embodied in the god Kāma, whose presence is said to have been crucial to the generation of the universe, and who from late antiquity onward is generally represented as a beautiful youth who shoots flowery arrows at others to make them fall in love, and who is accompanied by his inseparable male companion, Vasant ("Spring"), and his consort Rati ("Sexual Pleasure").

Hindu gods, like Greek gods, are rarely represented conceiving or giving birth in the way humans do. Being immortal, they do not need to reproduce, but when they do, it happens in unusual ways, for example, when Pārvatī creates Gaṇeśa (→ Gaṇapati/Gaṇeśa) from her bodily residues or when Śiva's seed, after sojourning in many vehicles, gives rise to Kārttikeya (see → Murukaṉ). The gods thus engage in sexual activity more for love, pleasure, and play than for reproduction.

The universe itself is represented as the expression of divine play or → *līlā*; one creation story represents the creator god → Brahmā saying, "I am one, let me become many." The impulse to simultaneously unite and diversify, which is at the heart of erotic union, is thus identified with the principle of creation. The gods' sexual desires are sometimes serene and powerful, but at other times they are funny and seemingly out of control; ancient Hindu texts show a sophisticated awareness of the comical and playful aspects of erotic impulses.

Despite the emphasis in both texts and practice on producing children, especially sons, it is noteworthy that the seven verses (*saptapadī*) central to the vedic marriage ritual nowhere mention procreation. Their focus is on the couple's life together as productive of happiness and prosperity not only for themselves but also for the community and natural world; the verses culminate in a commitment to friendship and walking and conversing together.

A third overarching concept is that of *dharma*, which also entered into other Indic religions like Buddhism, Jainism, and Sikhism. Over time, many meanings have accrued to this word; today, it is used as a translation for "religion," because no real equivalent exists in Indian languages. *Dharma* (from the root *dhṛ*-, "to hold firmly" or "to be established on") is sometimes translated as righteousness or justice, but at its widest it means law, which has multiple meanings. It refers to the natural law that upholds the universe and the law of individual duty pertaining to one's place in life as defined by the categories into which one fits, such as species, gender, class, *jāti*, profession, age, and relationships (thus, one's *dharma* as a daughter or a musician changes at different periods of life). It also refers to the law of one's own being, which both contains and exceeds the duty enjoined by one's status; this pertains to the imperative to work through the traces of actions in former lifetimes with which one is born.

Sexuality relates to *dharma* in various ways. It is part of the *dharma* of each individual, who inherits from former lifetimes certain predilections and attachments, that must be worked through in the present lifetime. It is part of the social *dharma* enjoined on married people and could also be seen as part of the social *dharma* of the *nagaravadhū* (lit. wife of the city), that is, → courtesans or public women.

Many ancient Hindu societies accorded a prominent public role to courtesans as also to *devadāsī*s (women wedded to a god or goddess and attached to a temple). Courtesans, although disappearing as a class today, have been central to popular cinema since its inception, which indicates their historical significance in culture. They are the heroines of several ancient Sanskrit plays, other important texts such as the 6th-century Tamil *Maṇimēkalai*, and 18th- and 19th-century narrative and lyric poems. Historically, some courtesans appear to have been wealthy and well respected. Since they were wedded to the city as *devadāsī*s were to a deity, they could not be widowed; hence they were considered highly auspicious (Kersenboom-Story, 1987). To see the face of such a woman first thing in the morning was a good-luck omen. These women performed at public functions such as coronations and festivals.

The tradition continued in different forms into modern times, when courtesans were attached to courts, patronized by both Hindu and Muslim kings and noblemen, invited to perform on public and private occasions, and honored for their education and accomplishments. Some sections of both courtesans and *devadāsī*s were educated and accomplished and also lived in matrilineal communities. They kept alive traditions of classical → music and → dance that might otherwise have perished; some courtesans were poets. Courtesans were not required to be monogamous, although they often maintained long-term or lifelong liaisons with one man; some of them also got married. Their representation of sexuality in song, dance, and poetry in public spaces allowed them a freedom rarely available to women in conventional households.

In the earliest Hindu texts, the → Vedas (c. 1500–1200 BCE), and in the somewhat later Upaniṣads, erotic and sexual connections appear both as pleasure giving and procreative. Most gods in the *Ṛgvedasaṃhita* are worshipped alone (e.g. the fire god Agni, the thunder god Indra, and the goddess of speech Vāc), a few are worshipped with consorts, and some are worshipped in same-sex pairs or groups (the → river goddesses). Kings and householders, for whom priests perform sacrifices, are generally depicted as married. Some sacrifices and rituals can only be performed by married couples, not by individuals.

The *Kāmasūtra*, perhaps the world's most famous treatise on erotics, was written in Sanskrit in the 4th century CE, in the cosmopolitan city of Pāṭaliputra (today Patna). It presents itself as a religious text explicating → *kāma* or desire, one of the four normative aims of life. It is the earliest such treatise to have survived but was probably not the first of its kind, as the author refers to a genealogy of earlier texts on which he claims to base his own work. He mentions three main goals of life – *dharma*, → *artha* (wealth), and *kāma* (desire). Other texts add a fourth and final goal, *mokṣa* (→ liberation from the cycle of rebirth); some teachers suggest that fulfillment of the first three goals is necessary before one can aspire to liberation.

The *Kāmasūtra* presents sexual pleasure as just one of many pleasures in life. The educated person, male or female, is supposed to know 64 arts, which range from dancing, singing, drawing, flower arrangement, and writing poetry to cooking, making beds, making ornaments, cosmetics and perfumes, and judging character from conduct. All these skills are said to be requisite for a good lover. The text's exhaustive taxonomy of every type of sexual activity includes, among other things, detailed and largely nonjudgmental accounts of how a courtesan should manage her finances and her clients; different types of kisses, bites, and scratches; how a husband should prepare an inexperienced wife for intercourse; and how two men have oral sex. The author advocates that every young girl should study the *Kāmasūtra*, and so should every male city dweller and every courtesan. Wide-ranging information about sexual matters is thus considered a desideratum for an educated person.

The *Kāmasūtra* is not a singular text. Numerous works in various Indian languages descend from it. This body of discourses on erotic matters is known as Kāmaśāstra. It proliferates in interesting ways, for example, the 12th-century Sanskrit text *Ratirahasya* (Secrets of Desire) by Kokkaka was translated into several languages, including the Hindi *Kokaśāstra* or *Kokasāra*. *Ladhat al-nisa* (Enjoyment of Women) is a Persian illustrated translation of *Kokaśāstra*, in an 18th-century Kashmiri miniature style, attributed to Ziya Nakhshabi. Many precolonial kings and noblemen, both Hindu and Muslim, commissioned beautifully illustrated treatises based on the *Kāmasūtra* but differing from it significantly. Most of these are now in private collections or kept under lock and key in libraries, inaccessible and little studied.

Several medieval erotic treatises add passages on the clitoris, female ejaculation, and orgasm, none of which the *Kāmasūtra* discusses in any detail. For example, the 15th-century Sanskrit *Anaṅgaraṅga* (Theater of or Colors of the Bodiless One), attributed to Kalyāṇamalla, notes that in the middle of the vagina is a vein similar to the penis, which, when stimulated, causes fluid to flow continuously (*madāvarīnirantaram*). Above the vagina, which is termed the "best of organs" (*varāṅga*), is an organ shaped like the nose (Jha, 1999, 40). The translator notes that the popular term for the clitoris is *bhaganāsa* (nose of the vagina). The medical term in Sanskrit is *bhagāṅkura* (bud of the vulva). The *Anaṅgaraṅga* uses the lovely term *manmathachattra* (umbrella of the god of love) for the clitoris and says that a network of nerves in it causes fluids to flow. Manmatha ("Churner of the Heart") is one of the names of the god of love.

The text also discusses female orgasm. It states that inside the vagina is a nerve called *pūrṇacandra* (full moon). This vein is always full of women's fluids of Manoja ("Mind-Born," i.e. the god of love). When it discharges these fluids, the woman melts (*tadvisarge druta nārī*). This description seamlessly unites what modern sexology divides into clitoral orgasm and female ejaculation. The text figures all these experiences as involving a flow of liquids. The terms "*visarga*," "*varī*," and "*syanda*" all connote drenching, pouring, and powerful flowing, like that of rain.

Sexuality is also integral to Indic poetics and aesthetic theory. The *Nāṭyaśāstra*, attributed to Bharatamuni (c. 200 BCE), is a treatise on the performing arts. It envisions the evocation of emotions in the spectator as the primary goal of art. These emotions are called → *rasa* (lit. juices), and the work of art causes them to flow in the mind and heart of the spectator. Each *rasa* is associated with a certain god and a certain color and is expressed through a corresponding *bhāva* or mood performed by the actor, dancer, or singer. A work consists of a mixture of *rasa*s but is dominated by one.

One of Bharatamuni's eight *rasa*s is *śṛṅgāra*, which literally means adornment but refers to erotic emotion. Adornment of the self for pleasure is thus envisaged as inseparable from the ability to attract another. Jewelry, hair styling, and cosmetics have a long history in Indian art and literature not only as adornments but also as erotic, auspicious, and protective (Dehejia, 2009). The frequent references in medieval poetry, folk songs, and modern film songs to *solah siṅgār* (Hind.), or the 16 types of adornments a woman dons in preparation for meeting her lover, evoke a mood of excitement, desire, and pleasurable yearning. In ancient temple sculpture as well as medieval miniature paintings, the image of a woman admiring herself in a mirror or dressing and adorning herself with the help of her maids is a recurrent and prominent one. Many Bombay films too have memorable scenes of this kind, where a woman sings a love song as she dresses.

Another aesthetic theory also related to eroticism is that of *rāga*s. *Rāga* literally means "color," especially the color red, but also means attachment, passion, or delight; *raṅg*, the modern Hindi/Urdu word for color, derives from it. To be dyed in a particular hue or color is to be immersed in the emotion, season, or god associated with it. Indian classical music is always set in a *rāga* or melodic mode, and popular music too sometimes uses these modes.

In medieval India, *rāga*s and their feminine counterparts *rāgiṇī*s were depicted in verse as also in *rāgamālā* paintings as men and women in love, associated with particular seasons and moods. Broadly, these fall into two groups: lovers in union and lovers in separation (*sambhoga* and *vipralambha* or *saṃgraha* and *viraha*). *Rāgamālā* paintings also draw on the earlier classification of women in love into eight types (*aṣṭanāyikā*s), a scheme reproduced in other arts, such as dance, sculpture, embroidery, and cinema.

Such affirmative approaches to pleasure exist in creative tension with the equally strong ascetic tendency (see → *tapas*) in Hindu thought and practice (reinforced by Buddhist and Jain influences), which recommends self-denial and transcendence of desire as the path to liberation from the cycle of rebirth and the sorrows of mortal existence. Of all pleasures, sexual pleasure is thought to be the most powerful and hence to have the greatest binding power. Since attachment leaves traces (*saṃskāra*s) that cause rebirth, and sexual engagement is among the strongest forms of attachment, transcending it is necessary for release from repeated rebirth.

In its pleasant form, sex appears as play, but in its threatening form, it appears as power. The Hindu ascetic tradition perceives male expenditure of sexual energies as a waste of vital force, hence it advocates conserving these energies and rechanneling them toward spiritual ends. Chastity, whether male or female, is often depicted in narrative literature as endowing one with tremendous powers, as in the case of the heroine Kaṇṇaki of the Tamil epic *Cilappatikāram*, whose righteous anger at the mistreatment of her husband sets a city on fire, or Sītā (→ Draupadī and Sītā), the heroine of the *Rāmāyaṇa*, whose chastity enables her to emerge unscathed from fire and sink into the earth at will. A prince in the *Mahābhārata* who takes a vow of lifelong celibacy is thenceforth named Bhīṣma ("Terrible") and becomes invincible. He uses his power for the benefit of others and is a much-venerated figure. The god → Hanumān is a celibate devotee who can set fire to cities, leap over oceans, and carry mountains; he is also compassionate to his devotees, acting as a mediator for them and fulfilling their wishes.

A recurrent motif in ancient texts (Hindu, Buddhist, and Jain) involves an ascetic or even a demon engaging in austerities, especially celibacy, thereby gaining immense powers, but then losing them when a beautiful woman is sent to seduce him. This is often presented as a dimension of an ongoing rivalry between the gods and spiritually powerful beings aspiring to divinity. It also represents the battle between the powers of celibacy and the powers of sexual expression. The powers of celibacy can be used to positive or negative ends. Demons often practice celibacy for selfish purposes, to acquire power and use it in a tyrannical manner.

In the case of the great god Śiva, his chaste meditations endanger the world, because his participation is required to keep it going. The gods wish him to marry and have sex, so they send Kāma, god of desire, to make him fall in love with goddess Pārvatī. Although the enraged Śiva burns up Kāma, thus gaining the epithet "Destroyer of Desire" (Kāmamardana), and is therefore generally seen as the victor in this conflict, his victory is a pyrrhic one, because Kāma's arrows do cause Śiva to fall in love with and marry Pārvatī. This love is in consonance with destiny, because Śiva's first wife Satī was reborn as Pārvatī.

Furthermore, Kāma, having lost his body, becomes Anaṅga ("Bodiless") who is arguably even more powerful since he is now invisible and omnipresent, a spirit taking possession of minds and hearts. Since Kāma helps fulfill goddess Pārvatī's desire to marry Śiva, many medieval texts dedicated to Pārvatī envision Kāma taking refuge in her. For example, the vastly influential Sanskrit *Saundaryalaharī*, a hymn to the goddess attributed to → Śaṅkara (c. 788–820 CE), who established the Advaita school of nondualism, repeatedly connects Kāma with the goddess' beauty. Kāma is said to be empowered by her; her face is his chariot, her eyebrows form his bow, her thighs are his quiver, and he takes refuge in her navel (*SauL.* 6, 59, 47, 83, 76, 78).

The paradox of desire as power and desire as play is nicely encapsulated in two ancient and complex Sanskrit terms that are today widely used by Hindus who do not know Sanskrit and are also popular names for children, especially girls – → *māyā* and *līlā*. Both are gendered female (in Sanskrit, every word is gendered male, female, or neuter). *Māyā* is the dazzling power and beauty of the visible universe and as such represents the magnetism of all pleasures, especially sex and wealth. *Māyā* is synonymous with nature (→ *prakṛti*), the active female principle that animates the cosmos. For dualists, this principle is an eternal reality. For radical nondualists, its reality is provisional, as it is a projection or even an illusion that disappears when one realizes that spirit is the only lasting reality. *Māyā* is embodied in goddesses, who bestow protection and blessings, both temporal and spiritual, hence its popularity as a name. Yet *māyā* is a paradoxical concept because ascetic and devotional texts repeatedly warn the seeker to beware its delusory and enchanting powers, generally symbolized by women and gold, which entrap one into attachment to material pleasures (and consequent rebirths), thereby obstructing one's quest for liberation. The bias of these texts is evident in their assumption that most seekers are heterosexual males for whom sexual temptation takes the form of a woman.

Līlā, however, is a concept of power shaped not by anxiety but by joy. It refers to the magical and playful powers of the divine. Every goddess embodies *līlā*, and every god manifests his divine enchantment or *līlā* through his female aspect, termed his → *śakti* (female strength). This female dimension may take the form of the god's female consort but may also manifest as the god himself assuming a female form. Thus, Viṣṇu's consort Lakṣmī (→ Śrī Lakṣmī) represents his enchanting power, but Viṣṇu himself also transforms into a beautiful woman, Mohinī ("Enchanting One"), who not only deludes the demons with her beauty but also causes the god Śiva to become enamored of her and embrace her. Thus, the magical powers that produce the glamour of the world can have negative effects when they delude those who wish to possess worldly objects, but they can have positive effects when they cause the soul to fall in love with god's beauty. *Līlā* is the gentler and happier face of *māyā*, largely devoid of its danger.

At the practical level, prescriptive texts seek to resolve the contradiction between desire as divine and desire as a snare, by formulating various ways of containing it and keeping it in its proper place. One method of containing desire consists of restricting it to certain times and places as well as stages of life.

The traditional Hindu division of life (→ *āśramas*) into four periods of 25 years each required the student in the first 25 years of life to focus on education and to maintain a state of celibacy (*brahmacarya*). The years from the age of 25 to 50 were devoted to raising a family; in this phase, sexual activity within marriage was enjoined. However, even among householders, highly enlightened men were supposed to have sex with their wives only when the wives were in a fertile state. In the *Mahābhārata*, Arjuna is said to follow this rule and thus to be a *brahmacārin* (celibate) even though he has several wives. The third stage, *vānaprastha*, involves a semi-withdrawal from the world to a hermitage where, however, one offers help to those who seek refuge with one. This stage would require a gradual retreat from worldly preoccupations, including sex. In the last 25 years of life, one renounces the world and becomes a *saṃnyāsin* (celibate ascetic). This normative division of life into four stages corresponds to some degree with the four normative aims of life, wherein *kāma* or desire is supposed to be fulfilled and then transcended when one aspires to the final goal of *mokṣa* or liberation.

Another form of containment relates to questions of → purity and pollution. Like the book of Leviticus in the Hebrew Bible, Hindu prescriptive texts pay great attention to purification rituals. If some classes of people, including women of reproductive age, were classified as always relatively impure, no one was classified as always pure.

The → body that is not self-contained is viewed as losing purity, and, since no body is always self-contained, all bodies participate in a cycle of losing and recovering purity. After excretion, after sex or reproduction, and after manual labor, purifying rituals are required to return the body to a state of relative purity. Furthermore, some types of sex are considered somewhat more impure than others. Thus, the ancient law book, the *Manusmṛti* (see → Dharmaśāstra), forbids a man to have sex in the daytime or in water or in a cart pulled by a cow. If he does have these kinds of sex or if he has sex with another man, he is required to take a bath (*MaSm.* 11.175). All sexual activity was normally supposed to be followed by a bath anyway, so this is not much of a penalty.

However, the same prescriptive texts acknowledge desire as part of the divine cycle of the universe when they enjoin sex within marriage as a duty for everyone and thus part of social *dharma*. Thus, marriage was and is near universal in Hindu society. The only exceptions to the rule are the few men and women who choose to renounce the world in search of liberation. These renunciants are expected to be celibate, and they also renounce wealth, family, and *jāti*. They are distinct from priests, who perform temple service and officiate at life-cycle rituals. Priests are expected to marry.

Women renunciants (see → female ascetics), although fewer in number than men, are found from ancient times to the present. The *Mahābhārata* depicts several such celibate women, among whom perhaps the most impressive is Sulabhā, a woman who defeats in debate the famous philosopher-king Janaka, by demonstrating that his prejudice against her is based on the fallacy of attributing gender to the spirit, which is in fact genderless, casteless, and classless (Vanita, 2005b).

The medieval women mystic poets, whose poems are still sung all over the country, were thus part of an ongoing tradition of women who chose celibacy and who resisted or renounced marriage and motherhood in order to devote themselves to god and community. In modern times, too, there are many such women who have millions of followers, from the early 20th-century → Anandamayi Ma and the Mother (of → Aurobindo Ashram) to the present-day Gurumayi and Amritanandamayi.

Although the ancient Sanskrit scriptures are not widely read by Hindus today, they continue to pervade daily life, including the aspects of life connected with sex. For instance, the *saptapadī* (seven verses accompanying seven steps taken together) from the *Yājñavalkyasmṛti* is recited at most Hindu weddings. The overarching doctrines and worldview of the scriptures are passed on through medieval and modern devotional songs and narratives that are more accessible to laity. Also, several concepts and terms from the ancient scriptures have been incorporated into modern languages – for example, the *gandharvavivāha* (marriage based on mutual attraction), discussed in several texts and deemed the best type of marriage by the *Kāmasūtra*, is today used as a synonym for the Indian-English "love-marriage" (as distinct from the more usual family-arranged marriage).

The ancient epics, the *Rāmāyaṇa* and the *Mahābhārata*, whose stories are retold in numerous medieval and modern versions in most Indian languages, are better known to most Hindus than legal, prescriptive, and philosophical treatises. These two epics (their dates are debated, but they were probably written between 200 BCE and 200 CE) depict a wide variety of sexual relationships and attitudes toward sex. These range from strict monogamy as practiced by → Rāma (hero of the *Ramāyāna* and incarnation of preserver god Viṣṇu) with a corresponding emphasis on absolute chastity (as exemplified by his wife Sītā), to male polygamy (in the *Mahābhārata*, many heroes have more than one wife), to relations between male gods and human women (as practiced by the revered mother Kuntī in the *Mahābhārata*, and eloquently endorsed by Sūrya, the sun god (see → *navagraha*s), who argues that a virgin is inherently free and that such freedom is the law of nature). Although Kuntī is ashamed of her premarital pregnancy and abandons her baby, this does not entirely negate Sūrya's statement; it merely complicates it by suggesting that social norms may contradict natural laws. Later, Kuntī's daughter-in-law → Draupadī is married to five brothers; this again is presented as an aberration (and she lives in rotation for a year with each of her five husbands so that her children's paternity is clearly determined), but it is nevertheless accommodated in the sexual economy of the text.

The *Mahābhārata* contains many sophisticated debates on complex issues, including sexual issues, presenting both conventional and highly unconventional views. Thus, although most women and men in the epic are depicted longing for children, especially sons, this is demonstratively critiqued in the plot of the epic when the spoiled sons of over-fond fathers court disaster and destroy the lineages they were supposed to extend; it is also explicitly denounced by the respected grandsire Bhīṣma, himself a celibate by choice, who strongly advises against attachment to children.

The epics thus present a complex and variegated picture of sexuality. While the ideal of a woman's absolute chastity and fidelity to a husband (*pativrata*) is upheld, this does not mean that the chaste woman is indifferent to sexual pleasure; on the contrary, her fidelity often dovetails with and is a consequence of her active agency in desire. For example, the story of Sāvitrī, from the *Mahābhārata*, may be read as exemplifying the ideal of fidelity (as in the idiomatic Satī Sāvitrī, or pure woman devoted to her husband), since the narrative pivots on the heroine's argument that once the god of death has promised her a hundred sons, he must release her husband, because it is impossible for her to have sons without her husband. But the story also depicts Sāvitrī as a woman deeply in love with her husband and a person with an iron will and brilliant intellect who confronts death much as the epic hero does when he descends into the underworld. The modern mystic Sri Aurobindo recognized this when in his English-language epic *Savitri* (1954) he made her the representative of humanity asking and finding answers to eternal questions. Likewise, Satī, which means the feminine embodiment of truth and is an epithet for great women, later came to be applied to victims of the ritual burning (→ *satī*) of widows on their husbands' pyres and then was misapplied to the ritual itself.

In mainstream Hindu society as well as in scriptures, premarital and extramarital sex is frowned upon for everyone, but in practice, as in most societies worldwide, women are generally penalized more harshly for infractions than men. This is related to male domination of women rather than to anything specifically Hindu. The epics depict some women being severely punished for extramarital intimacy: for instance, Ahalyā, a sage's wife, is turned to stone for having relations with Indra, king of the gods.

However, traditional Hindu culture may be classified as more oriented toward shame than guilt, which means that more or less clandestine sex that does not impede family functioning or cause social disgrace (by pregnancy or by rendering a girl unmarriageable) is generally overlooked by others and viewed by the individual as a peccadillo rather than a serious moral flaw (Kakar, 1981, 135–136). As the *Kāmasūtra* remarks in a worldly wise manner, with regard to male–male sex: "Practiced according to his fantasy and in secret, who can know who, when, how, and why he does it?" (*KāmS.* 9.45; Danielou, 1994).

While some gods have more than one consort, and some also have extramarital romances, most goddesses, if married, have only one husband; they generally do not have extramarital romances.

The Greek goddess of love, Aphrodite, famously has an affair with Ares despite being married to Hephaestus, but the Hindu goddess of sexual desire, Rati, is chastely married to Kāma, god of desire, and does not engage in extramarital romances.

Relatively freer female sexuality appears in the form of *apsaras*es or heavenly nymphs (see → *gandharva*s and *apsaras*es). These beautiful and voluptuous females dance in the court of Indra; some are married to the *gandharva*s (heavenly musicians), while others take gods and men as their lovers. They are prominent in temple carvings, in both India and Cambodia, as well as Indonesia. The most famous among them are Urvaśī, Menakā, Rambhā, and Tillottamā.

The nymphs often exhibit uninhibited desires – for example, Urvaśī openly propositions Arjuna. When he refuses on the grounds that he sees her as a mother (since she once had a relationship with an ancestor of his), she argues that heavenly beings are not bound by earthly norms. He persists in his refusal, so she curses him with impotence; this curse is later shortened to one year, a period that Arjuna spends in the form of a court eunuch and dance teacher. These nymphs are built into important traditions – for example, Menakā, sent to seduce sage Viśvāmitra from his austerities, produces a daughter, Śakuntalā, who is adopted by another sage and becomes the mother of Prince Bharata, from whose name derives the term "Bhārat," now the Hindi equivalent of "India."

While some gods are celibate, others have more than one wife, and some engage in romances too. The ancient god Indra (see → vedic gods), no longer widely worshipped today, does seduce and sometimes deceive human women, much as Zeus does, but the puranic gods, who are the ones now widely worshipped, are involved only in consensual romances.

These romances are given mystical meaning by commentators: for instance, → Kṛṣṇa's irresistible charm and beautiful flute playing, which draw to him hundreds of milkmaids, including the already-married → Rādhā (with whom, rather than with his wives, he is usually worshipped today), is interpreted by many Vaiṣṇava texts as the attraction of individual souls to god. In the mystical economy developed by late medieval Vaiṣṇava theologians, love for a beloved who is not one's spouse is the highest type of love, because it is selfless and requires sacrifice and patience in separation rather than the pleasures of union. In this theology, Rādhā and her female companions become ideal devotees, whom real-life devotees seek to imitate and also adore.

However, even in Vaiṣṇava texts, such as the 14th-century *Padmapurāṇa*, the eroticism of Kṛṣṇa's relations with his devotees, although idealized, nevertheless persists. As the worship of Kāma, a central part of spring festivals in antiquity, declines, Kṛṣṇa emerges as the ultimate lover and beloved, so magnetically attractive that he enchants even Kāma himself, thereby acquiring the epithet Madanamohana ("Enchanter of the One Who Churns Hearts"; Danielou, 1985). The erotic sports of Kṛṣṇa with the milkmaids represent the bliss of ultimate union; hence the text depicts his male devotees longing for this kind of union.

The soteriology of the → *Bhagavadgītā* – which declares that anyone who offers loving devotion to god, including women and members of so-called low *jāti*s, can achieve liberation – marks an important shift in the gendering of devotion. The Hindu devotional (→ *bhakti*) movements that swept medieval India and constitute the bulk of Hindu devotion today base themselves on this philosophical premise. Devotees can express their devotion by assuming different attitudes to their chosen deity – that of a fond parent (as devotees do to baby Kṛṣṇa), that of a child (as devotees often do to mother goddesses like → Kālī), that of a friend (as in Marathi devotion to Viṭṭhal, a form of Kṛṣṇa), or that of a lover. The last of these, termed *mādhurya* (sweetness), is the counterpart of bridal mysticism in Islamic Sufi and Christian devotion. It became the dominant form of devotion in the medieval period. Devotees, whether male or female, envisioned god, whether Śiva or Kṛṣṇa, as a bridegroom or husband and themselves as his brides, pining in separation and yearning for union. Poetry produced in many languages all over the country, both high literary poetry and folk songs, expresses an intense and explicit eroticism directed toward the divine lover. In real life, some devotees led regular householder lives, others were celibate, and many, especially women, refused marriage or left their spouses to live in the community of devotees.

Some sects of Vaiṣṇavas (worshippers of Viṣṇu, especially his incarnations Rāma and Kṛṣṇa), most importantly the → Gauḍīya Vaiṣṇavas, developed a hierarchy of devotion, wherein selfless love was higher than selfish love. In this scheme, wifely love, because it is more selfish, is less pure than the devotion of a woman married to another, who cannot hope to become her beloved's wife. Thus, Rādhā's love for Kṛṣṇa is the highest type of love to be emulated by devotees. Likewise, many devotees chose to identify with Rādhā's or Sītā's female friends and servants, who love the male god only through their mistress and rejoice in her union with him, never expecting such union themselves. In one esoteric form of devotion, male devotees identify and live as women in a celibate community, taking female names and wearing female dress, dedicating themselves to the service of Rādhā or Sītā (Dimock, 1989; Wulff, 1996). In another way, → Nimbārka Vaiṣṇavas worship Rādhā as *svakīya* or wedded to Kṛṣṇa.

Whereas in ancient texts, being born as a man of a higher *jāti* often appears requisite to liberation, since it was only these men who could study the Vedas, in the medieval period, male devotees sometimes desire rebirth as women in order to achieve complete union with a male god. In a charming variation of the rebirth motif, the *Padmapurāṇa* depicts numerous sages, such as Nārada and even the epic hero Arjuna, being temporarily transformed into women to enable them to enjoy erotic union with Kṛṣṇa.

An intense eroticism emerges too in the many popular paintings of Kṛṣṇa playing with the milkmaids – swinging with them, dancing with them, throwing stones at their waterpots in order to drench them. The image of *rāsa līlā*, wherein Kṛṣṇa dances with many milkmaids simultaneously, appearing to each of them as if with her alone, and the image of Kṛṣṇa stealing the milkmaids' clothes while they are bathing, thereby compelling them to emerge from the water unclothed, are given mystical meaning (god favors all his devotees equally, though each thinks his/her relationship is entirely unique; the soul must shed all artifice and shame and appear naked before god). However, the image of Kṛṣṇa playing with the milkmaids becomes a much-imitated erotic ideal, reenacted in the *holī* festival all over North India by royalty (Hindu and Muslim) and by common people, both in real life and in theatrical performances and paintings.

Holī is a descendant of *madanotsava*, the spring festival of the god of love. Fourth-century Sanskrit drama depicts urbanites celebrating this festival by coming out on the streets adorned in colorful clothes, jewelry, and perfumes. *Holī* retains some of the colorful abandon and Saturnalian elements of spring carnivals; people shower one another with colored powder and water and imbibe intoxicants that help them shed inhibitions. This is a festival when hierarchical norms are overturned, and free cross-gender and cross-class mixing takes place. *Basant* is a related and equally joyful spring festival, when people dress in yellow, worship → Sarasvatī (the ancient goddess of knowledge and the arts), and fly kites. Some medieval Sufi texts depict Hindus and Muslims celebrating these festivals together, mingling on the streets, and falling in love with one another (Vanita & Kidwai, 2000, 137, 147–148).

When Europeans first came to India, some were bewildered, others delighted, and others scandalized by the range of gender and sexual arrangements and practices in the subcontinent, from → *hijṛā*s (transgendered men who live together in communities, with quasi-sacred status, blessing householders at life-cycle ceremonies), to polygamous and polyandrous groups, matrilineal communities engaging in visiting marriages, courtesans receiving respect in society and openly continuing long-term relationships with respectable men, and love poetry celebrating same-sex relationships. Missionaries viewed all of this as evidence of the licentiousness of paganism.

Colonial rule, especially after the defeat of the 1857 rebellion, resulted in most educated Indians' internalizing these judgments. Indian social reformers and nationalists, both Hindu and Muslim, reacted defensively, claiming that all of these phenomena were the result of degeneration and outside influences. Hindu nationalists claimed that ancient Hindu society had practiced only heterosexual monogamy and frowned on any other sexual relationships. Likewise, many neo-Hindu sects, such as the → Brahmo Samaj and → Arya Samaj, denounced idol worship much as Christian missionaries did and reverted to ancient vedic practice, which supposedly excluded images. They tried to bring back that supposedly golden age by remaking society on a modern puritanical Victorian model – outlawing practices like polygamy, polyandry, matriliny, visiting marriage, and homosexuality, and reforming courtesans out of existence. The only group that survived this onslaught of modernity somewhat intact was the *hijṛā*s, because they remained marginalized and contained, outside of mainstream family structures.

Books such as the *Kāmasūtra* were published in sanitized editions and explained away as warning manuals; temples with erotic sculptures were viewed with embarrassment (Vanita & Kidwai, 2000, 191–217, 236–240). An ironic reversal of attitudes toward sex took place in the following century, with the Christian West gradually shedding much of its Puritanism and Indian society embracing it. For example, when Europeans first came to India, women of many Hindu communities, especially in the south, did not wear blouses with their sarees, which was shocking to some European sensibilities. Today, most Hindus are shocked by what they perceive as semi-nudity in the West. Likewise, sexual speech is today much freer in the West, while in India sex tends to be treated as an entirely private matter not to be mentioned in polite company.

Nationalists colluded with the British imposition of uniform criminal and civil laws, which imposed a patrilineal structures and inheritance practices throughout the country. Even today, many Hindu nationalists are fervent opponents of decriminalizing homosexuality, a phenomenon that they insist on viewing, in defiance of history and literature, as a modern Western import.

However, Marxists and many liberals in the Nehruvian mold were equally or more embarrassed by polymorphous Hindu traditions and reacted by throwing the baby out with the bath water, that is, by disowning Hinduism entirely as a retrograde, oppressive system and remaking themselves as modern secular nationalists with sympathy for religious minorities but no ties to Hindu practice. These two ways of thinking – the revivalist Hindu and the socialist-secular anti-Hindu – are still forces to be reckoned with in India today.

The push toward uniformity in sexual mores was institutionalized in the 1950s in independent India in the codification of Hindu law, which outlawed polygamy and polyandry and imposed patrilineal inheritance structures on all communities. The British anti-sodomy law of 1860 was retained, and its 2009 overturn by the Delhi high court is before the supreme court of India at the time of writing. However, the Hindu Marriage Act of 1955 preserved some important elements of traditional Hindu law, such as the role of custom. Under the act, communities in which it is customary for first cousins to marry or for a woman to marry her maternal uncle may continue these practices legally, but they will be illegal in communities in which they have customarily been considered incestuous. Likewise, any wedding conducted according to rites considered customary in one of the partners' community is legal; no license need be obtained, and registering the marriage with the state is not required for the marriage to be legal. This allows a variety of marriage practices to continue, from simple mutual garlanding to full vedic ceremonies lasting several days. Many sections of the Indian women's movement wish to eradicate this diversity and impose a uniform marriage law.

Despite the dramatic rise of anti-sex attitudes in modern India, demonstrated at one extreme by Hindu right-wing violent protests against Valentine's Day and against films with nonnormative sexual content like *Fire* (1998), and at the other extreme by families and communities murdering or driving to suicide runaway couples, both cross-sex and same-sex, older traditions of playful and joyful attitudes toward sexuality do persist in popular culture.

They survive, first, in the symbolic significance of objects that are integrated into material culture and daily life in part because of this significance and that have long-standing and ever-proliferating erotic resonances in Indic traditions. Among these are items like sandalwood, turmeric, vermilion powder (*kuṃkum*), and honey, which feature in religious ceremonies and life-cycle rituals, are used as cosmetics and medications, and are also associated with the erotic life. A beautiful, tender body is often compared in poetry and music to sandalwood (e.g. in the song *Candan kā badan*), and many weddings include a special ceremony to apply sandalwood, oil, and turmeric paste to the bride's and groom's bodies.

The → lotus flower, ubiquitously associated with Hindu deities, and adopted also into Buddhism, is simultaneously a symbol of purity and eroticism. In romantic literature in most Indian languages, beautiful eyes, lips, breasts, hands, and feet – whether of a god, goddess, romantic hero or heroine – are compared to the lotus. The mango, native to India, from where it spread throughout the world, is another symbol frequently associated with pleasure in general and happy eroticism in particular. Beautiful breasts are frequently compared to mangoes in Indian poetry, and the *Kāmasūtra* memorably compares male-male oral sex to sucking a mango.

Pān or betel leaf, indigenous to India, is perhaps the most interesting of these objects whose symbolic significance matches their material presence. Extolled as a digestive, breath freshener, and cosmetic in ancient Hindu erotic as well as medical texts, it has a strong association with both religious ceremonies and erotic pleasure. It became fully integrated into Indian Muslim culture, thus serving as a signifier of syncretism. Like the lotus, mango, and mango leaf, the *pān* leaf is a ubiquitous decorative motif in textiles, sculpture, and painting, and *pān* eating is the focus of many popular, erotically suggestive poems, folk songs, and film songs.

Films and film songs constitute the most important modern cultural production that transmits and transmutes Hindu attitudes toward sexuality. Popular cinema simultaneously provides modern India's most commonly known discourse on Hinduism and on sexuality. Some of the most popular modern *bhajans* (see → *kīrtan* and *bhajan*) derive from movies; prayer and devotional singing occur frequently in movies. The Bombay movie *Jai Santoshi Ma* (1975) can be credited with turning the worship of a little-known goddess into a huge phenomenon. A very large number of movies base their plot loosely or closely on epic or puranic narratives, and an even larger number allude to motifs, themes, or characters from these narratives. At the same time, movies constitute the single largest and most widely accessible body of discourse on sexuality in modern India, and this sexuality is deeply immersed in Indic (including both Hindu and Muslim) ways of thinking and seeing.

Sexuality has a complex and evolving presence in cinema; it figures most prominently in film songs. These songs permeate everyday life and shape the modern Indian imagination. Often ungendered and dialogic, with lyrics written by some of the greatest poets, the film song operates in a wide variety of emotional registers, from playful and comical to poignant, tragic, and mystical. Whereas American and European films dwell on character development, Indian films dwell on emotion, thus adhering more closely to *rasa* theory. Since one of the main themes of films is romantic love, *śṛṅgārarasa* or erotic emotion in its many manifestations and moods figures largely in songs; every state of mind, from passionate and often explicit sexual propositions to romantic yearnings for union to anguish and despair in separation, are evoked and explored in a nuanced manner.

A common thread that runs through the fabric of Hindu cultural production from antiquity to the present is the idea that desire is beneficent when it exists not for purely selfish pleasure, but when it integrates and unifies individuals with larger formations, whether family, community, society, or the cosmos. This view of desire invigorates many wonderful narratives, such as the set of devotional stories from 14th-century Bengal, wherein two widows of a king engage in a divinely blessed love relationship with each other, which results in one of them giving birth to the hero Bhagīratha, who brings the sacred river → Gaṅgā down from heaven (Vanita, 2005a, 143–160). Widows are not supposed to have sexual pleasure, but here their pleasure is validated by connection with a larger purpose.

Overall, then, it appears that Hindu worldviews are permeated by the awareness that anything can seem repulsive when focused on minutely and in isolation, but when viewed in the context of the universe, everything assumes its place as part of an abundant fullness:

> *pūrṇamadaḥ pūrṇam idam pūrṇāt pūrṇam udacyate*
> *pūrṇasya pūrṇamādāya pūrṇam evāvaśiṣyate*
>
> From that wholeness this wholeness, from the whole the whole arises
> When the whole is subtracted from the whole, the whole alone remains. (*ĪśU.* 1.1.1; trans. by author)

Bibliography

Danielou, A., *The Complete Kāma Sutra*, Rochester, 1994.

Danielou, A., *The Gods of India*, New York, 1985.

Dehejia, V., *The Body Adorned: Sacred and Profane in Indian Art*, New York, 2009.

Devi, S., *The World of Homosexuals*, Delhi, 1977.

Dimock, E.C., *The Place of the Hidden Moon: Erotic Mysticism in the Vaiṣṇava-Sahajiyā Cult of Bengal*, Chicago, 1989.

Dutta, K., & A. Robinson, eds., *Selected Letters of Rabindranath Tagore*, Cambridge UK, 1997.

Jha, R., ed., *Anaṅgaraṅga*, Varanasi, 1999.

Kakar, S., *The Inner World: A Psycho-analytic Study of Childhood and Society in India*, New Delhi, 1981.

Kersenboom-Story, S., *Nityasumaṅgalī: Devadasi Tradition in South India*, Delhi, 1987.

Nandy, A., "Facing Extermination: A Report on the Present State of the Gods and Goddesses in South Asia," *Manushi* 99/5–19, 1997.

Panchal, C., "Wedded Women Cops to Challenge Sack," *Times of India*, 1988.

Vanita, R., & S. Kidwai, eds., *Same-Sex Love in India: Readings from Literature and History*, New York, 2000.

Vanita, R., *Love's Rite: Same-Sex Marriage in India and the West*, New York, 2005a.

Vanita, R., "The Self Has No Gender: A Female and a Male Scholar Debate Women's Status in the Mahābhārata," in: R. Vanita, *Gandhi's Tiger and Sita's Smile: Essays on Gender, Sexuality and Culture*, New Delhi, 2005b.

Wulff, D., "Rādhā: Consort and Conqueror of Krishna" in: J.S. Hawley & D.M. Wulff, eds., *Devī: Goddesses of India*, Berkeley, 1996, 109–134.

Ruth Vanita

Tolerance and Responses to Religious Pluralism

Although records of its early history are not available, it seems clear that the Hindu religion developed in the same fertile soil that nourished Jainism and Buddhism. All three religions share the presuppositions that → *karma* (the mental trace or seed left behind by each thought or action that predisposes one to a similar thought or action in the future, volition, action), → *saṃsāra* (the world of phenomena, which is incessantly in motion or flux and of which rebirth is an aspect), and *jīva* (the empirical self, the individual soul) are *anādi* (beginningless) and that by following a particular spiritual path (*mārga*) release can be realized. Each religion posed a different understanding of the divine or absolute to be experienced at the end of the spiritual path. In the Brahmanical tradition, reality was conceived of as "pure being," by which it was meant that reality was a pure unchanging substance, a concept expressed in the → *ātman* doctrine of the → Upaniṣads. Buddhists took the opposite position, the *anātman* doctrine of the Buddha, and perceived reality as momentary (*ksaṇika*), unique (*svalakṣaṇa*), unitary (*dharmamātra*), and in constant flux. Jainism seems to have taken the middle path between these two opposing views by describing reality as giving equal reality to its substance and modes – to "being" and "becoming." T.R.V. Murti suggests that the Jaina view "may be said to constitute the third stream of Indian Philosophy – lying mid-way between the two extremes" (Murti, 1960, 11–12). It was non-Brahmanical because it accepted a changing *ātman*; and it was non-Buddhistic because it accepted a permanent entity (*ātman*) as well as change. T.R.V. Murti suggests that the Jaina tradition, in its middle position, found favor with neither of the other traditions and as a result has had comparatively little influence on the development of Indian philosophy. But the Brahmanical and Buddhist traditions to a large extent shaped each other through mutual opposition and debate.

Hinduism, as understood through the Brahmanical tradition, claims for itself revelation of the inner self – the unchanging pure being (*ātman*) – as identical with ultimate reality, the absolute, the divine. The Upaniṣads, which are mostly assigned to periods predating Mahāvīra and Buddha, contain discussions on *jīva, karma*, and *saṃsāra* but focus on knowledge of the inner spirit and the means of its realization. The result of this inward search is the Hindu belief in one divine reality that can phenomenalize in many different forms. The Hindu typically sees the different sects within Hinduism and the other religions as different manifestations of the one, external, divine reality. Because all manifestations lead back to the same source, there should be no conflict among traditions. Cooperation, community, and mutual respect should prevail among all believers. Let us examine the way in which this philosophic perspective has functioned in the encounter of Hinduism with other religions.

The Classical Period

According to the Hindu view, all aspects of the world come from a common ancestry:

> There is of necessity some sort of equivalence between sounds, forms, numbers, colors, ideas, as there is also between the abstractions of the subtle and transcendent worlds on one side and the forms of the perceptible universe on the other... The whole of Nature (*prakṛti*) is but the symbol of a higher reality. (Danielou, 1962, 3–4)

From the viewpoint of the perceiver, it is rather like looking at a piece of sculpture from different angles. The whole form can be grasped only when the sculpture has been looked at from different perspectives: the front, back, and sides. Although each of these views is different from one another and although some aspects of what is seen and described from the different angles may seem incompatible, even from these contradictory reports, a reliable overall description of the sculpture can be reached that could not be obtained from only one angle. In the Hindu view, the various religions are understood as different and sometimes conflicting perspectives on the one divine reality. In fact divinity is sometimes described as "that in which opposites coexist" (Danielou, 1962, 5). According to this logic, Hinduism should be tolerant and open to other religions, because the more aspects of the divine we can perceive, the more complete our understanding will be. Even within Hinduism, broad tolerance is required to include all denominations (e.g. Vaiṣṇavism and Śaivism) and all points of view (*darśanas*), from the experimental or logical perspective of the → Nyāya and → Vaiśeṣika to the supramental psychology of → Sāṃkhya and → Yoga and the dialectical and metaphysical outlook of → Vedānta. Within these Hindu viewpoints, the conceptions vary – according to the presuppositions of the various schools – from atheistic to pantheistic, deistic, monistic, and mystical. Each of these is true within its own perspective; that is, each viewpoint is a logical conclusion based on the presuppositions of its own perspective. The fact that the truths expressed by each viewpoint may conflict is to be expected, because each viewpoint is only a partial perspective of the divine. The aim of scholars within each view is to expand their understanding to the utmost limit in a particular direction. The builders of the various *darśanas* within Hinduism are described as seers of divine reality (→ *ṛṣis*). All *ṛṣis* see the whole of reality, but due to the necessity of human finitude, they have to choose one form (out of the many possible forms) through which to convey their revelatory vision to others. For classical Hinduism, other religions could be understood as additional visions of the same divine reality; new *ṛṣis* such as Moses, Jesus, Muḥammad, and Buddha could be seen as describing new and varying perspectives of the one divine.

Religious seekers start with whatever path matches their sensibilities and is within their reach. Since all paths are different views of the divine, it would not seem to matter which path is selected. Theoretically, all paths eventually reach the same goal. A. Danielou writes, "Persecution or proselytization of other religious groups, however strange their beliefs may seem to him, can never be a defensible attitude from the point of view of the Hindus" (1962, 9). However, classical Hinduism does seem to exert a qualifying clause. Although each of the religions moves one toward the goal of release from *karmasaṃsāra* and union with the divine, only with the aid of the revelation of the → Vedas can one go the entire way to complete release. P.T. Raju offers a reasonable explanation as to how this vedic criterion came to be the norm for Hinduism:

> Vedic religion, after the development of its own inwardness, spread by inwardizing and incorporating all other religions with which it came into contact. All of them took pride in tracing their origins to the Vedas and the Upaniṣads. Some of them, Śaivism, Saktism and Vaiṣṇavism, had their own scriptures called the *Āgamas*, to which they give even now as high a place as to the Vedas. Yet they later began writing commentaries on the original Upaniṣads and wrote their own Upaniṣads and added them to the list. Thus both in the past and present, no religion can be alien to the Indian, provided it emphasizes the truth of inwardness. The Vedic or the Upaniṣadic tradition in philosophy is the tradition of the truth of inwardness. (Raju, 1952, 528–550)

The growth and spread of Jainism and Buddhism produced a Hindu intensification of "inwardness," as P.T. Raju puts it, of the *ātman* tradition in opposition to the *anātman* tradition of Buddhism. The inward emphasis of vedic religion did not result in a lack of attention to outward forms. Within the vedic tradition, social duties were required, and the way to tread the path of inward realization was carefully marked out through the order of castes and the → *āśramas* or stages of life. The duties accorded to each caste and allotted to each stage of life were meant to discipline the individual and lead by stages to the goal of inner spiritual realization. Thus within Hinduism, both a structure to maintain and regulate society and the opportunity for inner spiritual realization were provided. To a large extent, the Hindu social and ceremonial ordering of society was adopted by Indian Buddhism.

Not only did the challenge of Buddhism produce an intensification of the Hindu *ātman* emphasis, but also, in line with Brahmanical philosophy, all that was considered new and good in Buddhism was quietly absorbed. Gauḍapada (7th cent. CE), the teacher of → Śaṅkara, wrote his *Māṇḍū kyopaniṣatkārikā* and in them incorporated the best methods of Buddhist philosophy while retaining the vedic content. Śaṅkara systematized the developments of Gauḍapada and others into the Advaita Vedānta school. Śaṅkara also traveled the length and breadth of India debating with Buddhists (Basham, 1959, 265) "and apparently leaving behind monastic orders [again borrowing from Buddhist practice] in the north at Badrinath, in the south at Sringeri, in the east at Puri, and in the west at Dwaraka" (Miller, 1976–1977, 4). However, Hindu practice differed significantly from the Buddhist (and Christian) in that each branch monastery maintained autonomy. Buddhist monastic practice, modified for increased autonomy and flexibility, has played an increasingly central role in Hinduism through the medieval period to the present day. As D. Miller argues, it may make more sense to think of medieval and modern Hinduism in terms of a → *sampradāya* or monastic teaching tradition with a → *guru* as its core rather than to conceive of it as sectarian groups classified according to particular deities (Miller, 1976–1977, 527–533).

The absorptive tendency was also evident in the development of the new form of → *bkakti* or devotional Hinduism. Buddha was absorbed and made one of the → *avatāras* or incarnations of → Viṣṇu. The account of this event in the *Viṣṇupurāṇa* reads as follows:

> When the mighty Vishnu heard their request [the request of the gods to be protected from the Daityas (Asuras) or evil ones], he emitted from his body an illusory form, which he gave to the gods, and thus spake: "This deceptive vision [Buddha] shall wholly beguile the Daityas, so that, being led astray from the path of the Vedas, they may be put to death; for all gods, demons, or others, who shall be opposed to the authority of the Vedas shall perish by my might, whilst exercised for the preservation of the world. Go then, and fear not; let this delusive vision precede you; it shall this day be of great service to you, oh gods!" (*ViP*. 3.17.35–45; trans. Wilson, 1972, 269–270)

The *Viṣṇupurāṇa* goes on to recount how Viṣṇu, in the form of Buddha, succeeds in seducing all the *daityas* (see → *asuras* and *daityas*) from their study of the Vedas and their proper social duties by promising them a secret path to → liberation and teaching the equal truth of contradictory tenets. When the gods see that the *daityas* have given up the Vedas, the only true religious armor, a battle begins. The gods gain an easy victory, and the *daityas* are destroyed. The followers of the Vedas are purified and renewed, and the heresy of Buddhism – having served its divine purpose – perishes within India. Buddha is absorbed into Hindu tradition, but the representation and interpretation of Buddhist believers are certainly not positive. The negative interpretation of these believers may be linked to the persecution of Buddhists. A.L. Basham gives historical examples of this persecution – in the 6th century, for example, the Hun king Mihirakula destroyed Buddhist monasteries and killed monks (Basham, 1959, 265). Until recently, however, Hindu response to other religions has been marked in general by peaceful absorption rather than the harsh opposition characterized in the puranic account above.

The puranic account of Buddha as *avatāra* again highlights the key position of the Vedas in Hinduism. Hindus consider the Vedas to be eternal, impersonal (not composed by any person or god), and the most perfect revelation of divine truth. From the Vedas comes all knowledge of → *dharma* (law, especially moral law or duty; righteousness, the inner principle of religion), and without the Vedas, release or liberation (*mokṣa*) is not possible (Gonda, 1965, 7–8). This raises the question of how Hindus view the scriptures of other religions. In the case of Jainas and Buddhists, this question is not hard to answer. Since both Jainas and Buddhists reject the concept of scriptural revelation and treat the teachings of Mahāvirā and Buddha as examples to be tested out and proven for oneself, it is quite natural for Hindus simply to reject such teachings in relation to the revealed Vedas.

During the classical period, there is an interesting case of pluralism within Hinduism itself in relation to the Vedas. How are different texts such as the epics and → Purāṇas to be related to the Vedas? The Hindu tradition solved the problem by giving such texts the status of secondary revelation – of re-revealing the truth of the Vedas in a form more suited to the increased *karma* of the age. The epics and Purāṇas add nothing new, but, as in the → *Bhagavadgītā*, they represent the original vedic revelation in simpler forms such as stories and historic events. The overriding principle seems to be that of continuity based on the Vedas, a continuity that runs through changing times and conditions (Gonda, 1965, 10). The way this principle operates in Hinduism is that scholars write commentaries that elucidate teachings inherent in earlier texts so as to establish an unbroken series that reaches backward in time and necessarily ends (or begins) at the Vedas.

Another perspective on the response to pluralism can be found in the classical Hindu treatment of evil. In her study of evil in Hindu thought, W.D. O'Flaherty notes that early vedic religion largely ignores (rather than denies) the more tragic aspects of life (O'Flaherty, n.d., 375). Dating from a later period, the Upaniṣads pay more attention to the evil and suffering in life. Next, the epics and Purāṇas attempt to integrate the evil in life with the positive goals of the vedic view of life. W.D. O'Flaherty sees this changing approach to evil as having developed in interaction with Buddhism. The vedic approach, with its doctrine of *svadharma*, assumes that all roles, good and evil, are necessary for the variety that constitutes society as a whole. Although the individual has no choice of roles, society is arranged in such a way that the contribution of each person is important to the total mosaic, and some of these individual roles, as parts of the whole, necessarily involve suffering and evil. W.D. O'Flaherty suggests that Buddhism, the Upaniṣads, and *bhakti* challenge the above approach by emphasizing individual moral responsibility and an individual spiritual goal (release from *karmasaṃsāra*) rather than the *svadharma* of the earlier view. W.D. O'Flaherty writes,

> Under the influence of Buddhism, the Upaniṣads and the *bhakti* cults, the individual is given a choice of action, freedom from the structures of caste; instead of creating his life from *objets trouvés*, he may choose his medium and free himself from *karma*. (O'Flaherty, n.d., 377)

Of course the choice is not entirely free. In Buddhism the choice is conditioned by past *karma*, and in *bhakti* theory, god is often seen as choosing the worshipper; yet in both of these systems, individuals can consciously change their lives in terms of action.

The one aspect of Hindu doctrine that W.D. O'Flaherty leaves out of the above analysis is the notion of "stages of life." Part of the distinction made between the vedic and the free-choice approach may be removed to some extent by seeing *svadharma* as a required duty during the first two stages of life. When the duties of the student and householder stages have been met (and here there seems little room for individual free choice), then in the last two stages, one has individual freedom to pursue spiritual development toward release. It does not yet seem clear whether the idea of the individual freedom of the last two stages comes from Buddhism, is original to Hinduism, or is a shared development. W.D. O'Flaherty is correct in her observation that in the *svadharma* context, evil is defined as the threat of impurity (see → purity and impurity), defilement, mixing of castes, and so on. She is also right in pointing out that the *svadharma* notion of wholeness never allows evil (impurity) to become an autonomous principle or to be dispensed with, for it is always regarded as functioning in the service of purity. This classical perspective does seem to contrast with *bhakti* viewpoints that developed in response to Buddhism and the Buddhist challenge to the caste system. As W.D. O'Flaherty writes,

> The *svadharma* view of orthodox Hinduism is an ethical system based on the pluralism inherent in the social system of caste (the whole goal is the preservation of social and moral balance); the *bhakti* philosophies deny the validity of the caste system in favour of a more universalistic and apparently more individualistic ethical system, whose goal is salvation. (O'Flaherty, n.d., 378)

Taken as a whole, Hinduism does not see these different philosophic perspectives as exclusive but rather as different viewpoints on reality. Thus it is possible for Hinduism to imply that evil in human life is necessary and desirable and yet to assume at the same time a universally valid good toward which all humankind should strive. As W.D. O'Flaherty states,

> "Evil" must be accepted, but "good" must be sought; these views together provide a working solution to the problem of evil, a framework in which mankind as a whole, and each individual, may function in the face of an ultimately insoluble problem. (O'Flaherty, n.d., 379)

True to its fundamental philosophic and religious insight of diversity as the manifestation of unity, Hinduism demonstrates its ability to cope with the problem of evil in relation to good – perhaps the most difficult paradox in life. Analysis of the problem of evil leads the seeker back to the basic and unifying source. As one text says of this quest and source,

> There are many religions – that of the Vedas, Sāṅkhya, Yoga, Pāśupatas, Vaiṣṇavas – and one person chooses this path, another person another path; because of the variety of preferences, favouring a straight path or a winding, you are the goal for men, as the ocean is the goal for all rivers. (O'Flaherty, n.d., 378)

However, the idea that all paths lead to the same goal was present more in theory than practice in classical Hinduism. Debates between rival philosophical schools were very serious affairs, for matters of right or wrong knowledge regarding how to reach liberation were seen to be at stake. In the minds of these philosophers, each school with its different path to liberation was exclusive of the others. You were either right or wrong in your knowledge and interpretation of the Vedas. Debates occurred not only through commentaries but also in public, and, according to tradition, the loser was required to accept the victor's point of view – to "convert" to the opponent's path to realization of the divine.

Hinduism's Encounter with Islam

Arabs visited India long before the birth of Muḥammad, and small coastal Muslim communities seem to have existed from the 8th century CE. A.L. Basham states that the Māppiḷa (Moplah) community of Malabar descends from people who settled or were converted there before the Muslim invasion of India. But there is no clear evidence of any influence of Islam on Hinduism until after the Muslim conquest (Basham, 1959, 344). It was the second wave of Islamic expansion that brought the first Muslim invaders into India to do battle with Hindu forces. In 711–712 CE, Muslims captured and established rule over Deval, a port near modern Karachi, and Aror, north of Hyderabad (Rizvi, 1975, 245). However, it was not until the 9th and 10th centuries that the full Muslim invasion was launched, and powerful Islamic dynasties obtained control of a large part of India. Sufis, the missionaries of Islam, soon arrived to take up residence at court, and the encounter with Hinduism began in earnest. On the Islamic side, the immediate effect was an infusion of new life from Hindu mystical religion into the Sufi tradition, which had been experiencing a period of stagnation. There does not seem to have been any comparable immediate effect on the Hindu side. Even though Hindus were given high places in the Islamic bureaucracy, and Hindu scholars were summoned to dialogue with Muslims, Hindus apparently kept their religion apart from Islamic influence. The society seems to have been dominated by a pattern of cultural and religious segregation.

Like Buddhism and Jainism before it, Islam attacked Hinduism by breaking down caste. Muslims proclaimed, "Before Allah all men were equal; in the sphere of religion there was no privilege of birth" (Carpenter, 1977, 451). This anticaste emphasis did reinforce and provide a point of contact with the Hindu *bhakti* movements. From the 13th to the 18th century, a long succession of *bhakti* saints and prophets strove for the purification of Hindu religion. Many of them were converts from Islam to Hinduism (Carpenter, 1977, 452). Another point of mutual reinforcement between *bhakti* Hindu movements and the Islam of India was the production of vernacular religious literature. One such *bhakti* poet-prophet was a low-caste Hindu called → Nāmdev (c. 1300). The fundamental tenets in Nāmdev's teaching were the worshipper's dependence on god and the necessity of personal repentance. An early experience of sin and forgiveness gave Nāmdev great confidence in the universal presence, forgiveness, and love of god. Nāmdev found much in his religious approach that paralleled Islam, including rejection of the futile devotional service to religious idols. Referring to an idol, he asks, "Why bathe it when God was in the multitudinous species of the water; why weave a garland of flowers which the bee had smelled, when God was already in the bee?" (Carpenter, 1977, 455).

The rejection of caste, the use of the common language, and Nāmdev's stress on sin, repentance, and the rejection of idolatry lay the groundwork for attempts at drawing together Hinduism and Islam. Two notable attempts demand mention: that made by → Kabīr from a basically Hindu perspective and that made by Akbar from a basically Muslim perspective. Like Nāmdev, Kabīr (c. 1500) was another poet and singer of *bhakti.* Born the son of a Muslim weaver, Kabīr was raised in a Muslim house and was constantly surrounded by Islam (Sen, 1974, 88). The most authoritative record of his teaching is entitled *Bijak*, which was apparently dictated by Kabīr to a disciple named Bhagvān Dās (Carpenter, 1977, 457). Like Nāmdev, Kabīr shunned outward symbols of religious life including caste, idols, and pilgrimage austerities, and he taught in a common language, Hindi. Kabīr was influenced by teachers of both Hindu and Islamic communities, and he had very close contact with the Sufis (Sen, 1974, 91). He was a tireless critic of empty formalism in either religion. In Kabīr's view, "The same God is sought after in all religions which differ only in naming Him" (Sen, 1974, 100). This makes all religious quarrels – those between Hindus and Muslims and those among all other religions – futile. Kabīr's religious prescription is that every person must give up ego and vanity and consider the other as one's own self.

Another aspect of Kabīr's appeal was that he did not believe in ascetic denial, but, rather, that by living a natural life, in a pure manner, one can carry on one's *sādhanā* (spiritual discipline leading to release or enlightenment). God and the universe, he says, are within one's own self (Sen, 1974, 100). And the way to know that god who is within is to repeat god's name until one "becometh as he" (Carpenter, 1977, 463). Like Islam, Kabīr's vision sees everywhere the action of a divine revealer using the logos or word as an educative and devotional instrument. J.E. Carpenter writes that Kabīr says, "Listen to the Word, the Truth, which is your essence" (1977, 467). Kabīr's emphasis upon the word provides a natural bridge between Islam and Hinduism. Both traditions treat the scriptural word as divine, eternal, and powerful. But in terms of language, in terms of his use of a vernacular, Kabīr's Hinduism is more like Sufism than the orthodox grammarian tradition that used classical Sanskrit. As Kabīr puts it, "Sanskrit is the water of the well, while the spoken languages (*bhāṣa*) are water of the running stream" (Sen, 1974, 98). Anchoring himself in the Sanskrit tradition, influenced strongly by Islamic Sufism, Kabīr gave a fresh expression to Hinduism in the Hindi tongue of northern India.

In contrast to Kabīr, Akbar seems to have had little in the way of a lasting encounter with Hinduism. Kabīr was predominantly Hindu; Akbar was basically a Muslim. Akbar's wives practiced their Hindu rituals unimpeded, and distinguished Hindu scholars instructed the emperor, but apparently neither had a significant impact on Akbar. Hindu scholars, joining in the general adulation of the emperor, found prophecies of his kingship in the *Manusmṛti* and proclaimed him an *avatāra* (Carpenter, 1974, 504). Akbar attempted to transcend the conflicts and inadequacies of both Islam and Hinduism by creating his own religion, the Din-i-Ilahī or "divine monotheism." Akbar's religion gained few converts and did not last beyond his death. However, → Tulsīdās, a poet of Akbar's reign, had a very strong effect on the Hinduism of northern India. As a boy, Tulsīdās learned Persian and thus received some influence from Islam. His major contribution to modern Hinduism was to revivify it, in the face of the Islamic challenge, by rewriting Vālmīki's *Rāmāyaṇa* in Hindi as the *Rāmcaritmānas* (Lake of Rama's Deeds). For all practical purposes, this became and remains the scripture of the majority of Hindus in northern India.

P.T. Raju (1952, 540) claims that the Muslim invasion's main legacy to Hinduism was enervation. When Muslims destroyed Buddhist universities and libraries, much orthodox Hindu literature also perished. However, vernacular books held by Hindu scholars tended to be more diffused and better hidden, and thus the simple vernacular *bhakti* religion became dominant. (see also → Hinduism and Islam)

Hinduism and the Sikhs

Nānak (b. 1469), the founder of Sikhism, wrote in Hindi and criticized the caste system and idol worship (Sen, 1974, 102–103). He expounded a system of worship that was a synthesis of Sufism, Vaiṣṇava *bhakti*, and ideas associated with the Nāth *yogīs* (McLeod, 1968; see → Nath Sampradāya). The strongest interaction between Sikhism and Hinduism occurred during the period 1708–1849, when the Sikh religion experienced a period of decline. The absorptive power of Hinduism asserted itself in response to the inner weakness of Sikhism. During this period, there was a tendency among Sikhs to abandon their customs and symbols and adopt orthodox Hindu practices. Some Sikhs even proclaimed themselves to be a special variety of Hindu (Barrier, 1970, 19–20). However, during the 19th century, there was a Sikh resurgence, two aspects of which have been the sending out of missionaries and the conversion of Hindus. Within the → Punjab itself, Sikh and Punjabi Hindus share a common history of persecution, social patterns, and religious tradition. N.G. Barrier adds that "Arya Samajists with whom educated Sikhs initially identified and co-operated insisted that Sikhs were Hindu" (Barrier, 1970, 39). But a decade after the introduction in 1877 of the Arya Samaj in the Punjab, Sikh cooperation turned to hostility. Quickly the Arya Samaj became identified as the primary enemy of Sikhism. Battles over Sikh–Hindu relations, which have political overtones in the Punjab, continued into the 20th century (Barrier, 1970, 37ff.).

Nānak, more clearly than Kabīr, did attempt to fuse and transcend both Hindu and Muslim elements in his teachings. But the background of his wisdom seems primarily Hindu. God is at once the formless absolute (→ *nirguṇa*) and the manifested reality (*saguṇa*; Carpenter, 1977, 485). Following Kabīr, he emphasizes the confession of sin and repentance. Humane and vigorous activity is demanded of all. Certainly Hinduism had much influence upon Sikhism. Perhaps the major impact of Sikhism on Hinduism was that it helped to break down the Hindu system of barriers of race and caste. (see also → Hinduism and Sikhism)

Hinduism and Christianity

There is much speculation about the early encounters of Hinduism with Christianity. According to the 4th-century Christian historian Eusebius, Saint Thomas was allotted a mission territory reaching across northwest India as far as the Indus, although no definite trace of Christianity can be found in that region. Catholic tradition, however, continues to connect Thomas with India, and Gregory, the bishop of Tours from 573 to 593 CE, mentions that Thomas' relics had rested in an elaborate church and monastery in India. Marco Polo (c. 1290) locates this church in Mylapore (now a suburb of Chennai). Little is known of the connections of this church with Saint Thomas, but excavations across the Adyar River from the church turned up a piece of granite adorned with a cross and inscription. A similar cross and inscription have been found in a church at Travancore in Kerala. The Persian language of the inscription suggests the existence in the 7th or 8th century of a Persian, perhaps Nestorian, Christian community in India. During that time, however, there seems to have been little, if any, Christian impact upon Hinduism (Carpenter, 1977, 521ff.).

It was with the arrival of British and Portuguese traders in India in the 17th century that the way was paved for Christian missionaries from Europe (de Bary, 1969). As early as 1573, Akbar had summoned Jesuit Christians from Goa to appear before him and take part in theological debate, but it was not until the → Mughal Empire collapsed and the British took control to protect their trading interests that the Christian missionaries arrived in force. British rulers wanted to govern the Hindus according to Hindu law and religion, and so they established the Asiatic Society of Bengal for the study of Indian philosophy and literature. Christian missionaries also began taking an interest in Hindu thought – mainly to be able to criticize it and gain converts (Raju, 1952, 540). The cumulative effort of these and other activities produced the Hindu Renaissance, which aimed at reforming and rationalizing Indian religion in various ways. (see also → Hinduism and Christianity)

→ Rammohun Roy (1772–1833) set out to recover from obscurity the ideas of vedic Hinduism, which had become neglected in favor of shallow idol worship. Rammohun Roy was deeply interested in the religious teachings of the Christian missionaries. He read the New Testament and extracted those ethical teachings that he felt were universally consistent with the laws of nature. With the intention of improving the hearts and minds of his fellow Hindus, he translated these extracts into Sanskrit as the *Precepts of Jesus*. Because he had rejected the divinity of Christ, Rammohun Roy caused an uproar among the Calcutta Christian missionaries. After more than three years of debate with the Christians, Rammohun Roy began to write in "vindication of the Hindu religion against the attacks of Christian missionaries" (de Bary, 1969, 23–26). In public letters, he effectively argued that Hinduism is not inferior to Christianity (as the missionaries were suggesting) but that the mysteries of each religion equally transcend human understanding so that one cannot be preferred to the other (de Bary, 1969, 28).

Rammohun Roy's program of incorporating the ethical teachings of Jesus into Hinduism resulted in a campaign against the Hindu practice of → *satī* (widow burning) – a practice that finds no basis in the → Dharmaśāstra or Hindu law code. In opposing the practice, Rammohun Roy argued against the attitude, prevalent in the Hinduism of his day, that women were "subject to passions," "unworthy of trust," and "lacking in intelligence." He pointed to the ability of women, if given the opportunity, to succeed in education, spiritual discipline, virtue, and so on (de Bary, 1969, 29–32). Rammohun Roy's views on women exemplify the way in which he "carefully distinguished between English errors, and defended Hinduism against the criticism of missionaries as he challenged the orthodox to abandon its excrescences" (de Bary, 1969, 50). In order to defend Hinduism against Christian charges that it was a pagan and idolatrous religion, Rammohun Roy and his colleagues set out to reform it. The Brahmo Samaj was formed for this purpose. Its goal was to "purify Hinduism and immunize it against the Christian ideas and practices" (de Bary, 1969, 51). This strategy, initiated by Rammohun Roy, was passed to → Keshub Chandra Sen and then to → Dayananda Saraswati.

Keshub Chandra Sen (1838–1884) was willing to go much further than Rammohun Roy in appropriating Christianity. Indeed, in the last years of his life, he did something reminiscent of Akbar – he experimented in synthesizing elements from the major world religions. W.T. de Bary (1969, 64) writes, "Although he borrowed devotional and yogic practices from Hinduism, he drew even more heavily on Christian teachings and practices." Keshub Chandra Sen went to such extremes that he was virtually excommunicated from Hinduism, and his conversion to Christianity seemed imminent for years. Whereas Rammohun Roy had accepted only the ethical teachings of Jesus, Keshub Chandra Sen embraced Christ as the fulfillment of Hinduism's devotional strivings. He propounded that Christ, the apostles, and the gospel were Asiatic in nature and concluded that "in Christ, Europe and Asia, the East and the West, may learn to find harmony and unity" (de Bary, 1969, 64–69). Furthermore, Keshub Chandra Sen thought that Christianity, Hinduism, and Islam could coalesce. He thought that the resulting new religion would both sustain India and lead to a worldwide spiritual community. The Hindu religious genius, in continuity with the Old and New Testament revelations, would, he felt, be able to reconcile all conflicting religions.

> How the Hindu absorbs the Christian; how the Christian assimilates the Hindu! Cultivate this communion, my brethren, and continually absorb all that is good and noble in each other. Do not hate, do not exclude others, as the sectarians do, but include and absorb all humanity and all truth. (de Bary, 1969, 75)

While Keshub Chandra Sen was preaching the one extreme of a Christian/Hindu/Islamic universal religion in Bengal, an opposing viewpoint was being taught by a stern ascetic Hindu in northern India. Dayananda Saraswati (1824–1883) was also an ardent reformer, but he wanted to root out all non-vedic influences upon Hinduism: "Standing foursquare on the authority of the Vedas, he fearlessly denounced the evils of post-Vedic Hinduism" (de Bary, 1969, 76). Early in life, Dayananda Saraswati learned Sanskrit, and at age fourteen, revolted by the idol worship around him, he ran away from home and became a *saṃnyāsī*. He was taught complete reverence for the Vedas and disdain for all later texts. He devoted his life to lecturing on the exclusive authority of the Vedas.

Dayananda Saraswati's approach was to debate with those he disagreed with. Hindus were attacked for their practices that, Dayananda Saraswati argued, could not be supported from the Vedas: for instance, idol worship, → untouchability, arranged marriages, the subjugation of women, and the restriction of the study of the Vedas to Brahmans. → Caste, he said, should be decided functionally in accordance with one's merits. His followers are called the Arya Samaj, a group that became especially strong in the Punjab and now, with the emigrations from India to many countries, has spread around the world.

Dayananda Saraswati's approach to other religions and other groups within Hinduism was aggressive and militant. This marked a considerable change from the traditional Hindu attitudes of passive tolerance for all other beliefs. Dayananda Saraswati's approach to Christianity was to engage a minister in debate and to demonstrate the logical inconsistencies of Christian belief (De Bary, 1969, 79–81). Dayananda Saraswati devoted careful attention to Islam, reading the *Qur'ān* in translation and formulating his objections to each passage. The conclusion of his study was that "God was presented in the Qur'ān as a being whose qualities were unworthy of human worship" (Thursby, 1975, 13). Islam, he argued, lacks a valid basis, whereas the Veda was the firm foundation for true religion.

One branch of Dayananda Saraswati's followers, under the leadership of Pandit Lekh Ram, devoted their energies to open conflict with Islam. Their goal was to obtain Hindu converts. A system of specially educated paid preachers (*updeśaks*) was established for the purpose of proselytism (Thursby, 1975, 14). Dayananda Saraswati's militant response to other religions, especially Islam, has helped to fan the hostility between Muslims and Hindus and has also been a contributing factor in the development of Hindu → nationalism (de Bary, 1969, 77). Apparent adoption of some Christian practices is evident in the move of the Arya Samaj away from the traditional Hindu tolerance of other religions to the Shuddhi Movement, a conversion movement of the 1920s (Thursby, 1975, 34–73). This led to the outbreak of Hindu–Muslim communal riots, which continue to recur in northern India.

If Dayananda Saraswati attempted to relate to Christianity by taking over its fundamentalist and missionary thrust, S. → Radhakrishnan made the opposite move of seeking out the universalist aspects of Christianity that would be contiguous with the vedantic teachings of Hinduism.

S. Radhakrishnan represents the response of orthodox Hinduism to the challenge of Christianity and the modern West. He argues that Hinduism and the Vedas are still the ultimate truth of religion, but a truth that can be universally accepted by all. He has been described as a "liaison officer" between India and the West (Raju, 1952, 54–56). Certainly his appointment to the Spalding Chair of Eastern Religions and Ethics at Oxford and his lectures there in 1936–1938 have made a considerable contribution to the West's understanding of Hinduism (Radhakrishnan, 1939). Perhaps because of his time at Oxford, S. Radhakrishnan is very aware of the challenges of modern religious pluralism. As he states, "Neither a contented fatalism nor religious expectancy nor reversions to the past can give meaning to a world which is in search of its soul" (Radhakrishnan, 1939, 18). The foundations of the past no longer seem secure; everything is changing. This should not depress us. Great periods of human history have been marked by doubts and the infusion of foreign influences, including influences from other religions. Consequently, suggests S. Radhakrishnan, perhaps the difficulties of the modern West, which was influenced by Christianity, can be helped by the infusion of some wisdom from the East. In particular it is the Indian rational approach and emphasis on individual experience – rather than belief in an objectified deity – that is especially suited to the needs of modern-day religion (Radhakrishnana, 1939, 20–21). He states, "Religion is not so much a revelation to be attained by us in faith as an effort to unveil the deepest layers of man's being and get into enduring contact with them" (Radhakrishnan, 1939, 21).

With this vedantic conception of religion as a basis, S. Radhakrishnan presents an approach that he feels can be acceptable to Christians, Buddhists, and all other traditions. In many of his lectures given after 1938, he sought to demonstrate this approach, particularly with regard to Christianity.

In S. Radhakrishnan's view, the different religions must develop the spirit of mutual comprehension that characterized Hinduism even in its earliest age. In the *Ṛgveda*, there is evidence of conflict among many groups, Aryan, Dravidian, and aboriginal, but there is also a resolution that absorbed aspects of each. This resolution and acceptance of other cults are explained as follows: "The real is one, the learned call it by various names, Agni, Yama, Mātariśvan" (*ṚV.* 1.164.46). The Upaniṣads give further development of the same view. → *Brahman* is one; the different deities are merely manifestations of the various aspects of *brahman* (Radhakrishnan, 1939, 308). S. Radhakrishnan ascribes the same attributes of the one and the many to Buddha. Buddha is one who has the vision of the whole, whereas members of the various religions are each attached to their own partial views. Within Hinduism this attitude is given explicit statement in the *Bhagavadgītā*: the divine accepts those coming toward divinity in the paths of the different religions, and in his supreme vision, Arjuna sees the different deities within the boundless form of the divine (Radhakrishnan, 1939, 310). Hinduism, says S. Radhakrishnan, has practiced what it has preached. Christians, Jews, Parsis, and Muslims have all lived in Hindu India for hundreds of years in an atmosphere of tolerance and religious freedom. Occasional outbursts of Hindu militancy and intolerance are, as interpreted by S. Radhakrishnan, imitations of Islam and Christianity provoked by those very religions (Radhakrishnan, 1939, 312). Because of its tolerant attitude, Hinduism itself has become a mosaic of almost all the types and states of religious aspiration and endeavor:

> It has adapted itself with infinite grace to every human need and it has not shrunk from the acceptance of every aspect of God conceived by man, and yet it has preserved its unity by interpreting the different historical forms as modes, emanations, or aspects of the Supreme. (Radhakrishnan, 1939, 313)

S. Radhakrishnan's claim is that no other religion, with the exception of Buddhism, which he aggregates with Hinduism, has this genius for religious diversity and unity, making it the prototypal answer for the modern challenge of religious pluralism. The attitude of the cultivated Hindu to other forms of religion is one of sympathy and respect.

The reason that Hinduism can be so tolerant of other religions is that it assumes religion is a matter of personal realization. "Creeds and dogmas, words and symbols have only instrumental value... The name by which we call God and the rite by which we approach Him do not matter much" (Radhakrishnan, 1939, 316–317). According to S. Radhakrishnan, this Hindu approach receives confirmation from the experience of mystics of all traditions. He also appeals to Christian scripture for support. He quotes the statement of Jesus, "He that doeth the will of God, the same is my brother and my sister and my mother." The roots of Christian exclusiveness he ties to the inherited Semitic creed of the "jealous God," which Christians have translated into "Christ as the only begotten son of God" (Radhakrishnan, 1939, 324). For the Hindu, Christ can be accepted as an *avatāra* or incarnation but not as the only incarnation. Christ, → Kṛṣṇa, Buddha, and others must all be seen as equally valid incarnations of god. In S. Radhakrishnan's view, the validity of each religion is found in its instrumental value. It is valid to the degree that it allows its followers to achieve realization.

In line with classical Hinduism, S. Radhakrishnan views the different religions as various historical formulations of the one formless truth. Every historical tradition is to be valued in its own right because of its ability to engage a particular racial/cultural group with the divine. Christianity is suited well to the European, for whom another tradition such as Hinduism or Buddhism is not at all appropriate. "Religion is like the string of a violin: if removed from its resonant body, it will give the wrong tone, if any" (Radhakrishnan, 1939, 328). The solution to the problem of religious pluralism is not to collapse or disregard individual religious traditions but rather to affirm and respect the faith of others. Traditions are societies' memories of their own paths and the instrumental means for release. Removing individuals from traditional roots leaves them abstracted and lost. The *Bhagavadgītā*, says S. Radhakrishnan, has a clear understanding of this dynamic and warns against taking away the psychological comfort of people by unsettling their faith (*BhG*. 3.26).

S. Radhakrishnan observed the problem that just as faith in one's nation seems to kill faith in humankind, so also "faith in one religion seems to kill faith in others." The common tendency is to attempt to impose one's own faith on others. But this only robs religion of the richness of the diversity of the various paths to god. Hinduism recognizes this truth. The route taken by the Hindu sage, for example, may be too straight and steep for the majority of Hindus; therefore there is a need for a variety of paths to the same goal. Religious liberty is required to allow individuals to choose freely the path suited to their nature and cultural background. Hinduism also recognizes the close relationship between each religion and its own culture. Religions and cultures can grow. They reform and develop themselves by interpretation and adjustment to one another. "The Hindu attitude," says S. Radhakrishnan, "is one of positive fellowship, not negative tolerance" (Radhakrishnan, 1939, 335). The spiritual attitude is one of constant striving toward higher perfection and truth. The Hindu contribution to the modern challenge of religious pluralism is to encourage the inquiring spirit and devotion to truth that is larger than any individual tradition. Thus, "[r]eligious life becomes a cooperative enterprise binding together different traditions and perspectives to the end of obtaining clearer vision of the perfect reality" (Radhakrishnan, 1939, 338).

In looking back over the result of the Hindu encounter with Christianity, it seems evident that Rammohun Roy's hope has been fulfilled. Through its various reactions to Christianity in the past two centuries, Hinduism has revived and reformed itself. And now its philosophy, as expressed by S. Radhakrishnan, is presenting itself to the other traditions as *guru* – as a guide to the future.

In recent years, Hindu scholars have followed S. Radhakrishnan's lead and become actively involved in interfaith dialogue with Christian churches. A. Rambachan, a Hindu scholar, participates in World Council of Churches' consultations on interfaith relations. He rephrases the Hindu view in even more inclusive words than those of S. Radhakrishnan while at the same time more explicitly acknowledging the real differences that exist. A. Rambachan says,

> I am aware of the fact that my own tradition, in its worthwhile enthusiasm to affirm and give importance to the unifying elements in the world's religions, is often guilty of overlooking and underplaying the significance of differences. (Rambachan, 1999, 38)

A. Rambachan restates the Hindu position, in relation to other religions, as follows. From a Hindu standpoint, god is seen as our god. But, while we recognize that our god can be called by various names (in the different religions), for our own devotional purposes, we choose one divine name and form as the center of our lives. This is partly due to the limitations of language (no single word or name can fully define god) and to our finite limitations as humans. Due to these limitations, each of us has the right to select the name and form, the *iṣṭadevatā* or god of one's own choice, "along with the recognition that others have chosen differently and that the divine may be celebrated and honored under many names and forms" (Rambachan, 1999, 39).

This does not mean that religious differences are merely semantic or that all paths are equally capable of leading to the divine. A. Rambachan notes that although Hinduism recognizes one divine or absolute as the source and destiny of all beings, Hinduism does not naively assume that all religions are equally true to that divine. He cites Mohandas → Gandhi as a good example of Hinduism in this regard: "Gandhi creatively balanced an openness to the insights of the world's religions with sharp questioning of the content of particular traditions" (Rambachan, 1999, 40). Religion without morality was not valid for Gandhi, and the virtues of truth and compassion were equally essential. In Gandhi's view, no single religion could fully contain god, and all religions reflected the limitations of the human condition. The principal limitation of Hinduism, for Gandhi, was its tolerance of untouchability. A 19th-century Hindu who manifested openness to other religions was → Ramakrishna. But, like Gandhi, Ramakrishna was critical of all religions including Hinduism. For Ramakrishna,

> a religious way led to God only if there was sincere and earnest longing for God as the ultimate value, the renunciation of materialism and compassion for all. Some paths to God were preferable to others. (Rambachan, 1999, 40)

It is worth noting that for both Ghandi and Ramakrishna, the criteria for assessing the validity of religions included a stress on morality and compassion. Hinduism thus not only allows that there are many paths to god, but also provides normative tests for the different degrees of spiritual realization that the various religions, including Hinduism, achieve. So, concludes A. Rambachan, "while the Hindu tradition clearly recognizes God to be our God, it does not legitimize everything that transpires in the name of religion" (Rambachan, 1999, 40).

Hinduism and Secular India

Aside from the inspiring philosophizing of S. Radhakrishnan and A. Rambachan, another perspective in the Hindu response to religious pluralism can be understood by studying the constitution of India. As R. Baird notes, the constitution not only contains provisions relating to religion in modern pluralistic India but is itself a religious document (Baird, 1976, 47). In contrast to the *Manusmṛti*, the constitution ignores the doctrines of *karma* and *saṃsāra* and restricts itself to concerns relating to this life. In contrast to the class system assumed by Manu, the constitutional religious model adopts the principle of the equality of all (Baird, 1976, 48). The constitution also defines religious liberty in such a way that it will not infringe upon the principle of equality. Religious freedom is subject to dictates created in response to concerns for public order, morality, and health. It cannot stand in the way of social reform (Baird, 1976, 50). In order to distinguish between areas of religious freedom and religious restriction, the distinction between the sacred and secular is introduced. It is the duty of the secular realm to ensure equality. In the religious realm, the freedom of each tradition to follow its own beliefs is guaranteed. The task of distinguishing between these two realms is given to the supreme court of India. The supreme court rejects the definition of "religion" accepted by the United States supreme court; Buddhism and Jainism are not religions according to the United States supreme court's definition (Baird, 1976, 52). The practice adopted by the Indian supreme court requires first a definition of the tenets of the religion in question and then a judgment as to whether the matter at issue is secular or religious. If the matter is judged religious, then the tenets of the tradition, as defined by the court, are the criteria against which the judgment is made. Although this legal approach does allow for religious pluralism, justice depends on the ability of the court to understand and apply the tenets of all religious traditions. It also tends to reify each religious tradition into a set of established tenets – something that conflicts with S. Radhakrishnan's understanding of the need for change and adaptability in modern religion.

It is worth noting that Bhimrao Ramji → Ambedkar, who drafted the Constitution of India, has in his own life posed a serious challenge to modern Hinduism. Because he was born an untouchable, he worked under the assumption that much of the injustice in India was the fault of the Hindu tradition. In Ambedkar's view, Hinduism is beyond reform (Coward, 2003). He dismissed Gandhi's attempts to deal with the problem of untouchability as mysticism and mere name changing. To get himself and the untouchables a new identity and religious freedom, he felt it necessary to leave Hinduism and adopt the casteless religion of Buddhism. As a result, some three million followers are said to have left Hinduism in the span of ten years (1951–1961; Gokhale, 1976, 21–22). The fact that three million Hindus can suddenly become Buddhists seems, on the one hand, to be a living demonstration of the long-claimed tolerance of Hinduism and of the religious freedom guaranteed in Ambedkar's constitution. On the other hand, this poses a modern challenge to Hinduism to adapt and develop in the way S. Radhakrishnan envisaged. The practice of untouchability has changed radically. The influence of caste on marriage and employment is also showing signs of change, but such a deeply ingrained notion cannot be legislated out of Hindu consciousness quickly.

There is a fundamental conflict between the presuppositions of the constitution and those of Hinduism. The constitution proposes that all persons be treated as equals – suggesting some kind of *tabula rasa* view of human nature. Hinduism, in contrast, understands the nature of each person to be different and to be the natural result of the individual's own action in this and previous lives. It is the cumulative traces (*karma*) of such past actions that compose the nature of the individual before the realization of *mokṣa* or release. This understanding of *karmasaṃsāra* underlies the notion and practice of caste and is a fundamental aspect of Hindu psychology. There seems no obvious way to resolve this head-on clash between the tenets of Hinduism and the theory of human nature assumed in the constitution. Since the constitution is now the law of India, the home of Hinduism, this challenge from within cannot be avoided and may well be the testing ground for the Hinduism of the future (Coward, 1993).

The constitution's concern for religious freedom and its distinction between the sacred and the secular are being currently challenged by the upsurge of Hindu nationalism in politics (Embree, 1992; McKean, 1996) and events such as the 1994 destruction of the mosque at Ayodhya by Hindus along with the targeting of Christians for their conversion practices. In his *Hindutva*, originally written in 1922, V.D. Savarkar defined the principles of Hindu nationalism. For V.D. Savarkar Hindus are those inhabitants of India who consider it both their holy land and the land of their ancestors. In his view, only Hindus are the true children of India. They are entitled by birthright to rule India, simply because they constitute the overwhelming majority in India, their own fatherland and holy land. As president of the Hindu Mahasabha from 1937 to 1944, V.D. Savarkar traveled and spoke throughout India applying the principles of *hindutva* to various political issues. This activity roused support for Hindu nationalism, especially from upper-caste Hindu political leaders, and led to the denunciation of Muslims as antinational. In the last decade of the 20th century, this anti-Muslim approach by Hindu nationalists spread to include Christians, especially in their missionary conversion activities. Anti-Christian sentiments became especially vocal during 1999 in the lead-up to the visit to India in November of Pope John Paul II. The *hindutva* principle that India is the holy land of Hindus and thus should be ruled by Hindu nationalists suggests that the hostility that has so far been directed toward Muslims and Christians may well spread to other religions in India. *hindutva* principles underpin popular present-day support for movements such as the Vishva Hindu Parishad and the Bharatiya Janata Party (McKean, 1996, 71ff.). Mohandas Gandhi's Hinduism (and that of scholars like S. Radhakrishnan) with its support for open religious pluralism in India is under considerable siege as the 21st century begins. The same can be said for the secular principles of religious freedom and equality for all, which Nehru wrote into the constitution of India. Thus, the much-vaunted pluralism of Hinduism may be seriously undermined if V.D. Savarkar's ideology of *hindutva* grows in strength and influence.

C.K. Mahmood (1994) has provided a helpful anthropological analysis of the roots of the Hindu nationalist movement. C.K. Mahmood offers convincing evidence that the Hindu nationalist movement has a longstanding core that has always dominated Indian society. *Hindutva*, therefore, should not be seen as a modern political movement without historical or cultural roots. Premodern India, when seen in terms of its community boundaries between the pure (*ārya* or higher-caste Sanskrit speakers) and the impure

(→ *mleccha*, noncaste or low-caste, tribal, and heterodox groups) or between Brahmans (followers of Vedas) and Śramaṇas (followers of nonvedic religions, e.g. Jainas and Buddhists), was not a land of open, tolerant religious pluralism. The us/them ethic and religious boundaries have functioned at the community level at least since the advent of Jainism and Buddhism (c. 600 CE) to consolidate a core Hindu identity that, in C.K. Mahmood's view, has always dominated Indian society (Mahmood, 1994, 75). The strategy of the Hindu core, says C.K. Mahmood, when faced with the Jaina/Buddhist challenges (e.g. rejection of Veda and caste divisions), was a refusal even to recognize differences and subsequently absorb or incorporate all competitors. So, when faced with more recent Sikh demands that Sikhism be recognized as a different religion, many Hindus continued to view Sikhism as simply a part of the Hindu tradition, with all of the caste and → purity restrictions still applying. A hill tribe that follows animistic traditions is viewed by the caste communities on the plains of Bihar as Hindu – in spite of the fact that there is nothing Hindu about their practice or belief and that they clearly fall into the impure (*mleccha*) group. Hindus, says C.K. Mahmood, think they are being tolerant in their benevolent inclusion of others: the Buddha as an *avatāra* of Viṣṇu, the Sikhs as a caste of Hindus, the tribals as one's fellow travelers, and so on. From this inclusive perspective, which is adopted by *hindutva*, what is wrong with talking about the Hindu nation? But from outside – from a Muslim, Buddhist, or Sikh perspective – such an assertion of Hindu nationalism seems to equate any real religious separateness with virtual treason (Mahmood, 1994, 75). This mistaken notion of Hindu tolerance, as A. Embree puts it, is based on the idea that various cultural/religious identities can be encapsulated within Hindu society only if everyone agrees to the premises (those of Hinduism) on which such encapsulation is based (Embree, 1992). However, a pluralism whose terms privilege one religious community above others does not work – as events in India today demonstrate. Such an approach is criticized by the contemporary Hindu philosopher A. Rambachan (discussed above), who insists on an honest recognition of real differences as essential to both pluralism and the deeper teachings of Hinduism. Nor do the foundational ideas of the Indian constitution support the narrow Hindu nationalism that V.D. Savarkar's *hindutva* ideology has produced.

Constitution

Throughout its long history, Hinduism's attitude toward other religions has remained constant. There is one divine reality that manifests itself in many forms. The various religions are simply different revelations of the one divine reality. In this recognition of other religions as being different revelations of the one and as providing different paths by which devotees may attain release from *karmasaṃsāra*, Hinduism sees itself as being a very open and tolerant religion. But because it asserts that the Vedas are the most perfect revelation of divine truth, Hinduism also sees itself as providing the criteria against which the revelations of all other religions must be tested. Thus Hindu tolerance of other religions is directly proportionate to their congruence with the Vedas. There is no doubt that for the Hindu there is only one divine, as revealed by the Hindu scriptures, and that any other revelation (e.g. the Torah, New Testament, or *Qur'ān*) is seen as a secondary manifestation to be verified against the Hindu revelation. Once one steps back from Hindu metaphysics, Hinduism no longer appears so open and tolerant in its view of other religions. The Hindu approach to other religions is to absolutize the relativism implied in the viewpoint that the various religions are simply different manifestations of the one divine. The Hindu refusal to recognize claims to exclusive truth (e.g. Christianity or Buddhism) that differ from the revelation of the Veda indicates the limited nature of Hindu tolerance. In this, of course, Hindus are no different from those of other religions who believe they have the true revelation and seek to impose their truth upon others. S. Radhakrishnan has been a most effective modern representative of this kind of "Hindu tolerance." S. Radhakrishnan's tolerance has always exclusively affirmed his own position and has protected him from the challenge of other positions (Minor, 1987, 137–138). Nevertheless, the Hindu view that there is one divine, which may be reached by many paths, has proven throughout the centuries to be a powerful influence upon Hinduism's interaction with the other religions. Contemporary Hindu thinkers such as A. Rambachan seek to give more recognition to real differences that exist between traditions, while retaining the Hindu stress on an underlying unity of all. But the ideas of *hindutva*, and the Hindu nationalist movements it has produced, are severely testing the traditional Hindu claim of tolerance toward others.

Bibliography

Baird, R., "Religion and the Secular: Categories for Religious Conflict and Change in Independent India," in: B. Smith, ed., *Religion and Conflict in South Asia*, Leiden, 1976, 47–64.

Barrier, N.G., *The Sikhs and Their Literature*, Delhi, 1970.

Bary, W.I. de, ed., *Sources of Indian Tradition*, vol. II, New York, 1969.

Basham, A.L., *The Wonder That Was India*, New York, 1959.

Carpenter, J.E., *Theism in Medieval India*, Delhi, 1977.

Coward, H., "Gandhi, Ambedkar, and Untouchability," in: H. Coward, ed., *Indian Critiques of Gandhi*, New York, 2003, 41–66.

Coward, H., "India's Constitution and Traditional Presuppositions Regarding Human Nature," in: R.D. Baird, ed., *Religion and Law in Independent India*, Delhi, 1993, 22–39.

Danielou, A., *Hindu Polytheism*, New York, 1962.

Embree, A.T., *Utopias in Conflict*, Delhi, 1992.

Gonda, J., *Change and Continuity in Indian Religion*, London, 1965.

Gokhale, B.G., "Dr. Bhimrao Ramji Ambedkar: Rebel Against the Hindu Tradition," in: B. Smith, ed., *Religion and Conflict in South Asia*, Leiden, 1976, 13–23.

Mahmood, C.K., "Ayodhya and the Hindu Resurgence," *Religion* 24, 1994, 73–80.

McKean, L., *Divine Enterprise: Gurus and the Hindu Nationalist Movement*, Chicago, 1996.

McLeod, W.H., *Guru Nanak and the Sikh Religion*, Oxford, 1968.

Mani, V., *Purāṇic Encyclopedia*, Delhi, 1975.

Miller, D., "The Guru as the Centre of Sacredness," *SiR* 6/5, 1976–1977, 527–534.

Miller, D.M., & D.C. Wertz, *Hindu Monastic Life and the Monks and Monasteries of Bhubaneswar*, Montreal, 1976.

Minor, R.N., *Radhakrishnan: A Religious Biography*, Albany, 1987.

Murti, T.R.V., *The Central Philosophy of Buddhism*, London, 1960.

O'Flaherty, W.D., *The Origins of Evil in Hindu Mythology*, Delhi, n.d.

Radhakrishnan, S., *Eastern Religions and Western Thought*, Oxford, 1939.

Raju, P.T., "The Development of Indian Thought," *JHI* 13, 1952, 528–550.

Rambachan, A., "My God, Your God, Our God, No God?" *CD* 33, 1999, 37–44.

Rizvi, S.A.A., "The Muslim Ruling Dynasties," in: A.L. Basham, ed., *A Cultural History of India*, Oxford, 1975, 245–265.

Savarkar, V.D., *Hindutva*, Delhi, [6]1989.

Sen, K.C., *Medieval Mysticism of India*, Delhi, 1974.

Thursby, G.R., *Hindu-Muslim Relations in British India*, Leiden, 1975.

Wilson, H.H., trans., *The Vishnu Purana*, Calcutta, 1972.

HAROLD COWARD

Tourism

Tourism in India is a complex and multifaceted phenomenon rooted in both religious → pilgrimage and colonial leisure patterns. It has been promoted for development by the Indian state and national governments and for profit by the global tourism industry. Although tourism can be a significant economic engine, it can also have profoundly pernicious effects: overdevelopment and environmental degradation, social and moral disintegration, and culture clashes among groups with differing values. Despite all of these potential problems, it is a vibrant and still-developing aspect of modern Indian life.

The very idea of tourism – nonproductive leisure travel – is ultimately rooted in European culture and has gradually formed in the past three hundred years. The earliest travel – religious pilgrimage – was done for penance and purification, and the journey's only purpose was to reach one's destination. This was gradually displaced by the paradigm in which "the experience of traveling" enhanced one's knowledge and effected personal transformation (Tomasi, 2002, 13). Whereas medieval pilgrims had depended on charitable institutions for food and lodging, this latter model was an exercise in conspicuous consumption, in which everything cost money (Tomasi, 2002, 17). This expense restricted such travel to the wealthiest classes, and the classic example was the European "Grand Tour" as a finishing school for young upper-class men (Tomasi, 2002, 15). The modern tourism industry democratizes this experience by providing people with individualized leisure experiences at a cost (Tomasi, 2002, 17). Yet even though one can document the historical progression of these ideas, L. Tomasi stresses that each of the later stages assimilates qualities from the earlier ones, which continue to exist.

This same general process has also been present in India. The Indian sacred landscape is studded with pilgrimage sites – Jain, Sikh, Christian, Muslim, and especially Hindu – and visiting these has been an important religious practice for well over a millennium. Indian ideas regarding tourism were initially shaped by the colonial experience and more recently by the global tourism industry. Among the qualities marking globalization is rapid communication of ideas worldwide, and Euro-American ideas about leisure have shaped Indian tourism during the past 20 years.

The connection with colonial models is the clearest in the hill stations, which the British first settled as places to escape the scorching summer heat. The hill stations were reflections of "proper" British life: they featured English architecture, they were favored locations for boarding schools, and their social life centered on social and athletic clubs. South India has a few hill stations, such as Kodaikanal, but most are in the Himalayan foothills. The most important was Shimla, which functioned as the hot-season capital, and like all hill stations, it replicated the colonial social hierarchy. Shimla's two main markets were Mall Road and Lower Bazaar, with the former catering to Europeans and the latter serving Indians, who were not even allowed to walk on Mall Road (Jutla, 2000, 406). For the British, hill-station leisure patterns also had significant symbolic content, since the location and the length of one's stay were highly visible status markers.

The hill stations are still popular destinations in modern India, and for the same primary reason – to escape the stifling summer heat. A hill-station holiday also takes on upper-class behavior by imitating colonial leisure patterns, since it has no purpose other than leisure – the primary entertainments are outdoor activities such as taking walks, horseback riding, and sometimes boating. Being able to take such a holiday – particularly in the high season during May and June – is a definitive status marker. The same is true for package tours to Europe and the United States, many of which have sought to attract Indian customers by offering options such as vegetarian meals. People take such tours for a pleasant holiday, to escape the scorching heat in May and June, and to claim the status from having done them.

Further connections with colonial patterns can be seen in the small but growing markets for "nature" and "adventure" tourism. Nature tourism stresses the enjoyment of natural resources (particularly wildlife), and such excursions evoke images of British sporting and hunting traditions, though most tourists now use cameras rather than guns. State and national tourism advertisements regularly highlight India's nature parks and forest reserves, and the chance to see a capstone species (e.g. rhinoceros, elephant, and particularly a tiger) is a significant tourist attraction. The Incredible !ndia advertising campaign capitalized on this attraction by publishing posters showing the face of a tiger with the caption, "Not all of India's residents are polite, hospitable, and vegetarian."

"Adventure" tourism stresses vigorous physical activity, such as trekking, mountaineering, river rafting, and winter sports such as skiing and ice skating; one finds this primarily in less-developed regions, where other sorts of economic development are impractical. Adventure tourism involves strenuous physical activity with a whiff of danger, including potential injury, such as a broken bone while skiing. Despite this, these risks are so carefully managed that one observer dismisses these experiences as unadventurous – since a genuine adventure cannot be bought as a package tour – and characterizes them instead as an unusual sort of holiday (Zurick, 1995, 95).

Outdoor sports were popular colonial pursuits because the British saw sport and exercise as a means to develop character, but such experiences remain a niche product in modern India. The culture of physical exercise is itself a product of relative affluence and is thus still nascent in modern India. People who spend their days doing demanding physical labor have little interest in doing this for recreation, but one suspects that the demand for such experiences will increase as India becomes more affluent and health conscious. Young Bengali men are among the most significant populations seeking such recreation, perhaps reflecting Bengal's longer acculturation to British cultural patterns.

Hill stations, nature tourism, and adventure experiences are significant niche markets, but the overwhelming bulk of India's tourist flow is "cultural" tourism, which seeks to attract people to places based on their cultural, historical, or religious importance. In both the domestic and the global market, India's primary saleable asset is its history and culture. Historical and World Heritage sites (e.g. Delhi's India Gate, the Agra Fort, and Khajuraho's temples) can draw both domestic and international tourists – the former seeking their heritage and history as a nation and the latter enjoying these as historical and aesthetic sites – but religious sites are the primary attraction driving both domestic and international tourism.

For foreigners, India provides the opportunity to explore alternative "spiritualities" (primarily Hindu, though Tibetan Buddhism is also significant) and to "star in their own movie" – that is, to search for personal fulfillment and individual self-realization through travel – and the "mystic East" is a common marketing image (Kraft, 2007, 237–238; see also → New Age spirituality). Places such as Rishikesh, Pushkar, Gokarna, Kulu/Manali, and Dharamsala have their own religious histories – in many cases, very long ones – but have become "freak centers" to which foreigners come seeking an experience. Even when Indians visit these places, the foreigners get greater attention because of their greater buying power, and the businesses in these places scrupulously cater to the foreigners' material, gustatory, recreational, aesthetic, and spiritual desires.

One clear example of such marketing is Rishikesh's annual International Yoga Festival, in late February or early March. The Uttar Pradesh State Tourism Development Corporation started this festival in 1999 to stimulate foreign tourism during the slower winter months, and the Uttarakhand Tourism Development Board has continued it after the state's formation in 2000. The festival is now hosted at Paramarth Ashram, which can house a thousand people, and the 2012 festival saw over five hundred visitors from about 30 countries (Sivaswamy, 2012). According to rates quoted at one online travel site, room cost at the Paramarth Ashram ranged from US $215 to US $600 for the festival – more than reasonable for foreigners on a brief vacation but relatively expensive by Indian standards (Journeymart.com).

In his official welcome, the head of the Paramarth Ashram, H.H. Swami Chidanand Saraswati Ji, invoked the tropes of India as a spiritual land where people can seek and find spiritual fulfillment. It begins with the salutation "Dear Divine Souls" and continues to say the following:

> I am so glad to welcome you all to the holy banks of Mother Ganga, to the lap of the sacred Himalayas... You are the special chosen ones to be here, and this is all part of the Divine Plan. Here you have the opportunity to attain the divine state of eternal bliss, peace, and liberation from things that bother you on a daily basis! (internationalyogafestival.com)

Similar sorts of niche tourist placement can be found in Pushkar's camel fair (*puṣkar kā melā*), *daśaharā* in Kulu, Dharamsala's Tibetan Buddhist tantric initiations (which now draw so many foreigners that Tibetans find it difficult to attend), the beaches in Gokarna, and the *kumbhamelās* in Haridwar and Allahabad.

Foreign tourists are significant for their expenditure per capita and as a source of hard foreign currency, but their numbers are dwarfed by domestic Indian tourists – India attracted 17.9 million foreign tourists in 2011 and an estimated 740 million domestic tourists in 2010 (*Times of India*, Jul 19, 2011). Domestic tourists may visit religious sites as simple tourists, such as the young Muslim man whom I met in Pushkar, a Hindu pilgrimage site, but this is uncommon. Far more often, domestic tourists travel to religious sites for religious reasons, and this is still a vibrant sector of the travel economy. According to information from one Mumbai-based travel provider, "[p]ilgrimage is the largest tourist segment of its kind and one that involves the lowest income strata and remotest of villages" (Vashi, personal communication, Apr 12, 2012) – in other words, it extends through every segment of Indian society. He further notes that many of India's religiously significant temples attract large crowds, as do the country's plethora of festivals, which can attract millions of visitors even with no official promotion.

Pilgrimage is a common experience even within urban areas, since visiting temples and religious sites is popular on Sundays and holidays. Religious groups have taken advantage of such "local" pilgrimage by building replicas of famous temples on the outskirts of major cities, such as Delhi's Akshar Dham Temple (built by the → Swaminarayan community), which can draw large local crowds. Traffic to any of these can be multiplied manifold by media attention, particularly around visits by celebrities.

In highlighting the importance of sacred places and sacred times, contemporary religious travel shares many factors with traditional pilgrimage, but other developments make it profoundly different. The most significant is "getaway tourism," which combines a

> family stay at a getaway resort for a bit of leisure around a visit to the nearby temple. Hotels [and] resorts in all segments have been mushrooming around such pilgrimage destinations that are accessible and can double up as… getaway destinations. (Vashi, personal communication, Apr 12, 2012)

A follow-up response confirmed that this is a recent phenomenon – within the past 10 to 12 years – and that formerly

> pilgrimage was by default… economy travel centric tourism [that is, the facilities were aimed at the least affluent sections of the population]. However with greater affluence and disposable income and combined with a conservative society with traditional values, pilgrim getaways [have] became popular. (Vashi, personal communication, Apr 12, 2012)

These getaways combine people's traditional and conservative impulses with the greater affluence that has led them to seek and even to demand other sorts of experiences.

This new Indian traveler is doubtless the target consumer for publications such as *Outlook Traveller Getaways: 101 Pilgrimages*. Whereas its earlier travel publications had listed 52 weekend breaks from Indian metro cities (Mumbai, Delhi, or Bangalore), "Heritage Holidays," wildlife and hill tourism, or vacation spots such as Goa and Kerala, the pilgrimage volume focused on religious destinations – and delivered even more than promised, since the table of contents lists over 140 sites. In his introduction, editor V. Mehta notes this thematic shift:

> The book you now hold is, in many ways, a new journey even for us. The latest Outlook Traveller Getaways guide is the 12th in a successful series that have charted subjects as diverse as metropolitan weekend breaks and adventurous trekking expeditions. With *101 Pilgrimages*, we have embarked upon *yātrās*: journeys that are increasingly relevant to the manic and stressful world of materialistic pursuits, journeys that we undertake with our children and elders and, sometimes, within ourselves… Our destinations dot the India map with tremendous diversity, crossing the northern boundary in some places, logging miles into the country's lofty mountains, to the shores of the great seas, to the banks of holy lakes and rivers, to the rural heart of a teeming nation, to ever-expanding cities that have grown around ancient temples. (Mehta, 2006, 3)

A range of forces has strongly embedded tourism in the contemporary Indian cultural landscape, and it has grown tremendously in the past 30 years. On the demand side, tourism has been stimulated by the newly affluent middle and upper-middle classes, who are now seeking consumer pleasures – even though they may still be relatively conservative. The most significant supply-side force has been India's state and national governments, for which tourism is an industry and whose primary concerns are economic – to generate employment and income. Governments have promoted tourism by developing tourist facilities directly (through state-run tourism-development enterprises), by disseminating information and advertising through print and electronic media, and by organizing tourist events, often in connection with established festivals (*durgāpūjā* in Bengal, *dīvalī* in Gujarat, *janmāṣṭamī* in Braj, or the Yoga Festival in Rishikesh).

Governments promote tourism because it can be an engine for economic growth for less developed areas. Yet such development is not guaranteed, and in many cases, tourism has been a mixed blessing. One inherent problem is structural – the tourism industry is dominated by large businesses such as airlines, hotel chains, cruise lines, and travel agents, and economies of scale tend to favor big companies over smaller ones (Zurick, 1995, ch. 2; Honey, 1999, ch. 2). Control by large companies invariably brings "leakage," which refers to the percentage of the tourism expenditures that does not remain in the local community. Outside control often means that the primary opportunities for locals are low-paying service jobs. All of these factors can vitiate tourism as an economic development strategy.

Tourism can also create serious problems even when done well, and these are only compounded when it is done badly. One common problem is environmental degradation, since the absence of local ownership gives neither the owners nor the locals clear incentives for environmental preservation. This is especially problematic in the hills, since these environments are extremely fragile. Shimla's environmental problems are so extreme that it suffers severe water shortages during every tourist season, and when asked to describe Shimla in one word, one in five residents said either "congestion" or "water shortage" (Jutla, 2000, 413). The same is true for Uttarakhand, a hill state with virtually no industry, for which tourism is one of the key economic sectors (IBEF, 2008, 5). Uttarakhand's visitor numbers far exceed the environment's carrying capacity, which further stresses an already degraded environment:

> Deforestation is of particular concern in the western Himalayas, where increased demand for firewood, extensive tree trimming in order to feed livestock, and construction of roads in the border regions have increased the destruction rate of forests and the number of landslides. Rapid population growth has accelerated pollution, and Himalayan streams that were once clear are now polluted by refuse and sewage. Hill people who use the water for drinking suffer from dysentery; cholera and typhoid epidemics are also common. Large lakes like Dal in Kashmir and Naini Lake (Nainital) have also become polluted. (Uttaranchal.ws, 2000–2003, 3)

Trash is omnipresent, and one of the few places with a good trash removal scheme, the road to Hemkund Sahib and the Valley of Flowers, developed this in response to an estimated 29 metric tons of trash per season – trash that will remain in the other valleys indefinitely (Kuniyal *et al.*, 2003, 811). Similar problems plague other sensitive environments, such as the South Indian hill station of Kodaikanal, which "faces threats from tourism numbers, a tidal wave of waste, expanding development projects, and ecological changes linked to invasive species" (Lockwood, 2012, 65).

A different environmental conundrum afflicts India's wildlife parks and nature preserves – how to maintain the integrity of these sites. Despite their magnificent biodiversity, these forest reserves are islands of wilderness under constant pressure: from poachers seeking to kill its animals for ivory, rhinoceros horn, tiger parts, or simply for dinner to poor villagers who see the parkland as an untapped, valuable source of wood and grass. Villagers' forays into the park to get these can bring unwanted contact with wildlife, which can also occur when animals stray outside the park boundary – as in January 2012, when a rogue elephant from Rajaji National Park killed several people near Haridwar, causing widespread panic. India's population pressures ensure that such incidents will only increase in the coming years; forest management officials are seeking to create a park-management model that also includes local people's needs.

Moral degeneration is a different sort of environmental damage. Goa is known for its beautiful beaches and its laid-back lifestyle; when foreign tourism began in the 1960s, foreigners went to Goa for a beach vacation, and Indians went there to ogle bikini-clad foreign women.

Since then domestic mores have significantly shifted, and Goa's tourists – both Indian and foreign – go there primarily to eat, drink, and relax. Goa has all the essential ingredients for mass tourism, which one observer described as "sun, sand, sea, and sex" (Honey, 1999, 9), but its beach party scene has a seamy underbelly of prostitution, drugs, and criminal activity – including alleged foreign criminal entrepreneurs such as the Russian mafia (*Times of India*, Jan 24, 2011). These elements do their best to remain invisible, since tourists tend to avoid places with open violence and conflict, as the collapse of Kashmir's tourist industry during the 1990s clearly shows, but they have clearly affected the tone of life there.

Environmental issues – whether literal, moral, or political – can create significant tension, but the greatest tension comes from cultural clashes. Tourism promotion requires a product, and many touristic products are noncontroversial – if people want to visit a hill station, sit on the beach, photograph tigers, or go trekking or skiing, no one is likely to object. Much the same is true for visiting cultural or historical sites, though national and regional pride can shape people's ideas about appropriate behavior in these places. Yet modern Indian tourism has marketed India's religious past and its religious sites in the same manner as any other tourist attraction. On one level, this makes sense, since religious pilgrimage is still the default travel paradigm for many Indians, and thus these sites have an established clientele and attractions. Yet this same marketing also carries the seeds of potential conflict.

Even without open conflict, tourism's economic influence can shift local economies in ways that change a site's character, and it can make local people unhappy. When affluent tourists demand high-quality facilities (attached baths, air-conditioning, private car parking, and more interesting cuisine) in traditional pilgrimage sites, or when wealthy metropolitan dwellers buy and build second homes in such places to escape from the city's hustle, bustle, and pollution, these forces inevitably affect the local environment. In the Delhi vicinity, for example, demand for luxury facilities has caused land prices in Haridwar and the Braj region to rise sharply; rising land prices also affect a site's commercial tone, as stores selling lower-margin items get displaced from the center (Lochtefeld, 2010, 213–214). Both trends perniciously affect residents and poorer visitors – the former finding themselves priced out of the housing market, and the latter finding fewer places geared toward serving them.

An equally profound shift has occurred in what visitors seek in coming to these places, and their changing attitudes have shifted the tone in these sites – that is, in the sorts of things highlighted as visitor attractions. A "getaway" tourist clientele primarily seeks entertainment and ease, and their desires shape the environment. For example, Haridwar's market now has several video arcades to divert bored urban children as well as (in summer) a set of carnival rides just opposite the main bathing place. Nearby attractions include a dinosaur theme park with gigantic animatronic dinosaurs and a water park (the "Fun Valley") that offers clean, family-friendly entertainment. The demand for such facilities clearly points to a different sort of traveler with a different agenda, but when this agenda is seen as disrespectful or inappropriate, it can create terrible conflict. Many of these religious sites are highly conservative environments whose local elites have strong commitments to the site's traditional integrity. Anything seen as undermining this will provoke outrage, but lying beneath this is anger in the face of social change that they can neither arrest nor accept.

This sense of loss and anger is only accentuated when foreigners drive the tourist pressures. One flash point for such conflict is Pushkar, an ancient and venerable pilgrimage site – in Hindu mythology, the creation of the world began here – that has reinvented itself as a foreign tourist "freak center." For many foreigners, Pushkar is a slice of *nirvāṇa*, and one common saying there is *sab kuch milegā* (everything is available). Scores of restaurants and cafes serve different sorts of food – though, in conformity with local bylaws, it is all vegetarian. The bazaar is lined with shops, on the one hand, selling consumer merchandise – such as jewelry, antiques, clothing, books, music, handmade paper, and leather goods – and, on the other, offering experiences such as *yoga* classes, music study, and camel rides. Alcohol is forbidden by local ordinance, but the ready availability of cheap illegal drugs – *bhāṅg* (ground marijuana; see → intoxication), hashish, opium, and unrefined heroin – fuels a vibrant party scene, though since the November 2008 Mumbai attacks, this seems to have become more discreet.

Foreign tourists drive Pushkar's economy, but their desires often conflict with local assumptions about appropriate behavior and have created significant tension. Among the signs of local

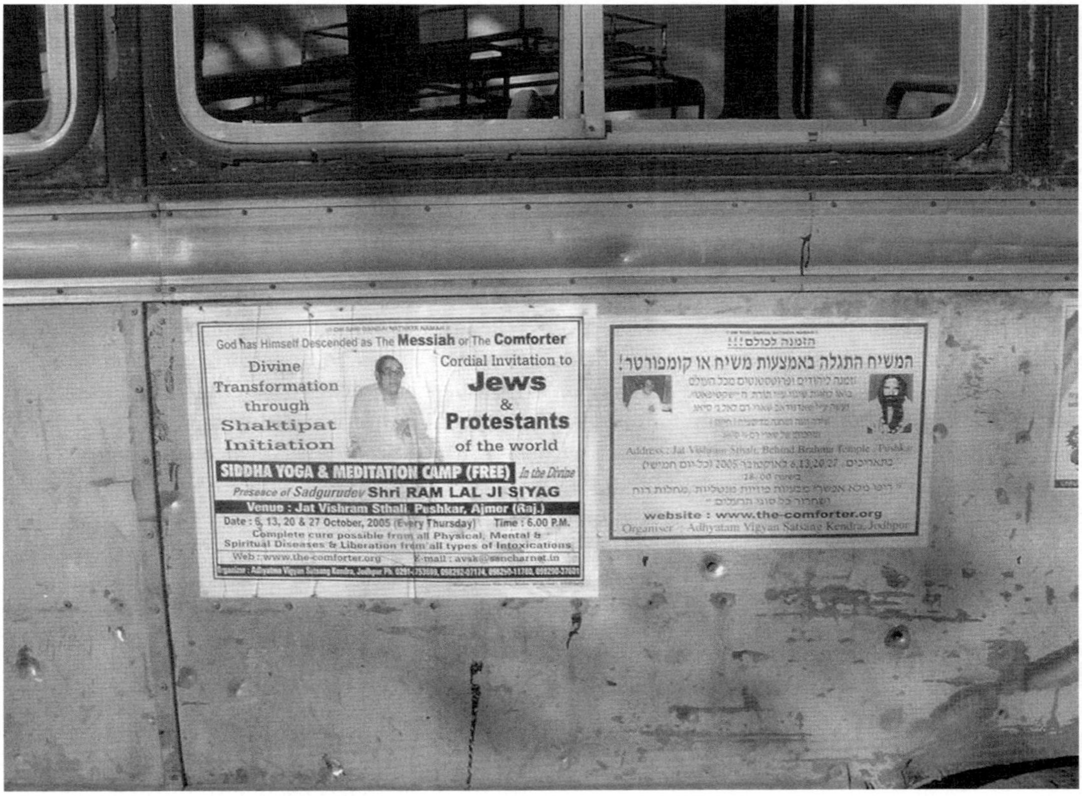

Fig. 1: Pushkar proselytism (photo by James Lochtefeld).

resistance are public billboards prohibiting wearing shoes or taking pictures by the sacred lake, immodest dress, men and women embracing in public, and consuming nonvegetarian food or alcohol. The signs also encourage visitors to respect the site's sanctity, which all of these behaviors would promote. Other local efforts to "reclaim" their town can be seen when people try to enforce these rules – or more commonly, simply to inform people about them – or when locals take control of public spaces for wedding processions or other events.

Things occasionally come to a head, as in 2005, when a female Finnish tourist bathed naked in Pushkar Lake (Parihar, 2005, 46), or in January 2012, when I learned that an American woman – reportedly in a drug-induced haze – had wandered naked through town until her friends shepherded her back to her room. Many locals are deeply disturbed by such apparent disrespect but are caught in a conflict of interest – not least because many of them are reaping tourism's economic benefits. One clear example of this is the → *paṇḍās* (traditional pilgrim guides), who have the highest stake in maintaining Pushkar's traditional religious atmosphere, but who have also cultivated foreigners as a ritual clientele, since they pay significantly more than Indians. When these same foreigners want to take pictures at the sacred lake, many *paṇḍās* do not enforce the "ban" on photography. By selectively enforcing rules based on personal gain, the *paṇḍās* undermine the sanctity of the site that they are supposedly trying to protect (Joseph & Kavoori, 2001, 1001–1002).

Pushkar is the most extreme example of such conflict, because the two sides are so different – foreign tourists seeking a good time and local elites seeking to maintain an appropriate religious atmosphere – but such conflicts can be found in most places targeted for tourism development, since such development will inevitably attract a wider customer pool. Furthermore, there is no question that social change has affected the way in which many people experience pilgrimage sites. If nothing else, easier transportation and more frequent visits will have decreased people's anticipation, which in previous times would have built as they moved slowly toward a site that they might see just once in a lifetime.

Governments are clearly aware of tourism's political problems, and even if they are seeking to promote tourism for economic development, they are also eager to mitigate its negative effects as much as possible. One way to do this is by stressing ecotourism, which refers to nature-based tourism with two primary goals: to protect and conserve the environment (hence the prefix "eco") and to maximize the economic benefits for the local people (Honey, 1999, 12). These benefits have made ecotourism an explicit tourism goal – at least in theory – for less-developed Indian states such as Uttarakhand (IBEF, 2008, 12) and Chhattisgarh. For the Uttarakhand government, ecotourism includes not only environmental awareness and economic development but also cultural sensitivity and respect (Forest Department Uttarakhand, 2009). Chhattisgarh's tourism minister, Brijmohan Agarwal, concludes a promotional piece for tourism there by stating,

> We believe in promoting a sustainable form of tourism.... [A]ll necessary precautions are taken while building infrastructure... so that it does not have any negative effect on the ecology of the area. (Agarwal, 2011, A26)

Even though all development creates problems, an ecotourism emphasis seeks to develop tourism responsibly.

Finally, it is also important to see the present as it really is and to see the past as it really was – rather than seeing it through a nostalgic filter. Some contemporary Indians have indisputably developed site visitation patterns that place far greater emphasis on leisure and comfort than in the past. Yet this does not mean that the earlier patterns have been completely eclipsed or, for that matter, that the earlier generations had "purer" motives. Particularly for Hindus, few hard and fast lines separate sacred from secular things – Indian → festivals (*melās*) commonly juxtapose religious attractions with more "worldly" amusements, and the same is true for pilgrimage. Though the idealized model in pilgrimage texts and people's nostalgic memories presents an austere religious practice, historical inquiry quickly reveals that many past travelers had multiple motives, including commercial ones, and the same is true today. At the market's lowest level, people still travel primarily for religious reasons – not only do they lack the disposable income for a "vacation," but this very idea would also be quite foreign to them. Yet these same people are also keenly interested in amusements and in "seeing the sights" when they travel, and pilgrimage journeys have traditionally been especially important for Hindu women, whose travel opportunities have often been very limited. More affluent consumers may want more vacation and less religious experience, but the latter is often still important to them, though they may understand their trip in less traditional ways and not as a vehicle for personal transformation. Yet whether they are bathing away their sins or relieving their "mental tensions," both groups are seeking a meaningful spiritual experience. They also share significant common cultural elements, and so most would probably want to visit Gangadham, a Hindu religious theme park proposed outside of Haridwar that seeks to "serve the immense domestic tourist market combining religion and entertainment in a novel manner and at 'affordable prices'" (Stausberg, 2011, 120).

These differing realities all exist simultaneously, though not always in equal measure. Just as each differing European travel paradigm – religious pilgrimage, the "Grand Tour," and modern tourism – was overlaid on its predecessor(s), and assimilated some of their elements, the same is true in India. India's evolving tourism is often different from religious pilgrimage, but in itself, this is neither better nor worse but merely different. Just as transportation innovations have changed how people travel, and these have become widely accepted, L. Tomasi notes that "*every age has its own mode of relating to the sacred* [italics original]" (2002, 20). After all, holiness does not inherently exist in things but rather is ascribed to things, and ideas about this change over time. The participants' task is to find this for themselves; the observer's task is to observe and to interpret it.

Bibliography

Agarwal, B., "Chhattisgarh is Destined to Become One of the Favourite Eco-tourism Destinations in the World," *India Abroad International*, Aug 26, 2011, A26.

Forest Department Uttarakhand, "General Instructions for Eco Tourists," 2009, http://www.uttarakhandforest.org/Data/SC_Eco_do_e.pdf.

Honey, M., *Ecotourism and Sustainable Development*, Washington DC, 1999.

IBEF (India Brand Equity Foundation), "Investment Climate in Uttarakhand," 2008, http://www.ibef.org/download/Uttarakhand_14Oct_08.pdf.

Joseph, C., & A. Kavoori, "Mediated Resistance: Tourism and the Host Community," *ATR* 28/4, 2001, 998–1009.

Journeymart.com, "International Yoga Festival," 2012, http://www.journeymart.com/holidays-ideas/festivals/international-yoga-festival.aspx.

Jutla, R.S., "Visual Image of the City: Tourists' versus Residents' Perception of Simla, a Hill Station in Northern India," *TG* 2/4, 2000, 404–420.

Kraft, S.E., "Religion and Spirituality in Lonely Planet's India," *Religion* 37, 2007, 230–242.

Kuniyal, J., *et al.*, "Solid Waste Management in Indian Himalayan Tourists' Treks: A Case Study In and Around the Valley of Flowers and Hemkund Sahib," *WM* 23, 2003, 807–816.

Lochtefeld, J., *God's Gateway: Identity and Meaning in a Hindu Pilgrimage Place*, New York, 2010.

Lockwood, I., "Breathing Life Back into the Sholas," *Frontline*, Apr 20, 2012, 64–76.

Mehta, V., ed., *Outlook Traveller Getaways: 101 Pilgrimages*, New Delhi, 2006.

Parihar, R., "Westernised Ghats," *India Today International*, Nov 21, 2005, 46–47.

Sivaswamy, S., "A Celebration, Not a Boot Camp," *India Abroad Magazine*, Apr 13, 2012, M3.

Stausberg, M., *Religion and Tourism: Crossroads, Destinations, and Encounters*, London, 2011.

Swami Chidanand Saraswati, "H.H. Swami Chidanand Saraswati Ji," 2012, http://internationalyogafestival.com/chidanand_saraswati.html.

Times of India, "India Posts 24% Rise in Foreign Tourist Arrivals," Jul 19, 2011, http://articles.timesofindia.indiatimes.com/2011-07-19/india/29790361_1_foreign-tourist-tourist-visits-domestic-tourist.

Times of India, "Russian Mafia and not Government Controls Goa," Jan 24, 2011, http://articles.timesofindia.indiatimes.com/2011-01-24/goa/28372846_1_foreigners-russian-mafia-sunburn.

Tomasi, L., "Homo Viator: From Pilgrimage to Religious Tourism via the Journey," in: W. Swatos & L. Tomasi, eds., *From Medieval Pilgrimage to Religious Tourism*, Westport, 2002, 1–24.

Uttaranchal.ws, "Himalaya," in Microsoft Encarta Online Encyclopedia, 2001, http://www.uttaranchal.ws/him.htm.

Vashi, N., proprietor of Nivalink Tour Company, personal communication, Apr 12, 2012.

Zurick, D., *Errant Journeys: Adventure Travel in a Modern Age*, Austin, 1995.

James Lochtefeld

Appendix
Volume III

Society
Dalits/Ex-Untouchables
Gender

Religious Specialists
Jādūgars

Religious Traditions
Śrīvidyā

Philosophy
Ājīvika

Dalits/Ex-Untouchables

"Dalit" today is the most widely used term in the English language and in scholarly circles for the South Asian subpopulation of former unfree agrarian servants, members of India's lowest castes whose very touch was widely regarded to be polluting by those who consider themselves higher. Precolonial India lacked any single term for Dalits, and the relatively recent English-language coinage "Untouchable" (Charsley, 1996; see also → untouchability) expresses a particular theory of → caste according to which caste itself is understood as first and foremost a symbolic and religious order based on varying degrees of ritual purity (see Roberts, 2008). That term has now largely fallen out of favor for its demeaning connotations. It is preferable, however, to the misleading "ex-Untouchable," a label that emerged when acts of discrimination based on touch pollution were deemed illegal in the constitution of the postcolonial Indian state ratified in 1950, but which erroneously implies that ritual untouchability is a thing of the past. On the contrary, routine forms of ritual exclusion remain a constant in much of rural India, and overt physical violence may even have increased in response to attempts by Dalits to assert their legal and political rights (*Broken People*, 1999; Mendelsohn & Vicziany, 1998, 44–76). This article will briefly describe who Dalits are before turning to the more difficult task that their inclusion in an encyclopedia of Hinduism demands: analyzing the relationship of Dalit-hood to religion in general and to the Hindu religion in particular, a relationship whose nature has been an abiding source of academic debate as much as of bitter social and political conflict.

Who Are Dalits?

Virtually every region in India has its own groups of castes whose low social and economic position is further marked by various forms of ritual exclusion that set them definitively apart from the remainder of society. In the core agricultural regions of Indian civilization's heartland, these castes have provided the bulk of agricultural labor on which production depends. They have done so under severe conditions of deprivation, whether in precolonial forms of unfreedom or in more recent regimes of wage labor, and they are subject to both routine and extraordinary forms of violent disciplining. Dalits have been frequently pressed into performing services such as the removal of dead animals and the tanning of leather, the removal of the human dead, and the handling of human excrement, which are, according to pan-Indian notions of → purity and pollution, ritually defiling. The fact that they are collectively associated with these tasks has been used to explain why they are commonly forced to live apart from others in Indian villages. Their ritual defilement is also invoked to justify their exclusion from access to natural resources and social amenities – roads and thoroughfares, water sources and wells, and schools and shops – and in many cases from the right to hold land. Being barred from holding land is particularly significant, because, in a rural society where nonagricultural production is monopolized by caste-based occupational guilds, Dalits are rendered entirely dependent on the landholders whose fields they till. Ritual scruples and labor subordination thus constitute an integrated regime of domination. Indeed, while the nature of the literary-historical evidence makes it difficult to date the origins of untouchability, it seems likely that the political-economic dimensions of their subordination, which probably took shape in the early part of the Common Era, either preceded or emerged simultaneously with their ritual exclusion (Aktor, 2002). The sheer number of Dalits – they account for at least 16% of the population, with larger numbers in the states of Uttar Pradesh, West Bengal, Bihar, Punjab, Tamil Nadu, and Andhra Pradesh, where percentages can be as high as 25% (*Census Report 2001*) – and the fact that the majority does not in fact engage in polluting occupations, further contradicts the popular view (Dumont, 1970) that treats the ritual impurity of Dalits as primary and their exploitation as a secondary consequence of it; "[the] likelihood [is] that exploitation entered into [its] very construction" (Mendelsohn & Vicziany, 1998, 8).

In addition to and underlying gross acts of discrimination – many of which may be absent, for instance, in more recent times in urban milieux – are pervasive forms of condescension, exclusion, and derogation that characterize Dalit life in the most modern of settings: urban schools, colleges, offices, apartment complexes, and so on. To maintain these conditions of deprivation, complex and concerted forms of social policing on the part of other castes have been required. It is therefore reasonable to view the division between Dalits and others as a principal fissure in Indian society. If the status of Dalits is rooted in a pervasive sociopolitical order shared across religious boundaries in India, rather than being ultimately an outcome of Hindu ritual practices, this calls into question the common view that the existence of Dalit–non-Dalit divisions among Christians and Muslims is merely derivative. Indeed, evidence suggests that the division between Dalit and non-Dalit castes cross-cutting religions was far more socially salient in precolonial times than, for example, that between Hindus and Muslims (Peabody, 2001). The remainder of this article will focus on how the Dalit–non-Dalit division came to be linked with Hinduism and how religion has been implicated in perpetuating it and enlisted in attempts to overcome it.

Dalits and Hinduism

The knotty analytical problem of the relationship between Dalits and Hinduism can be usefully divided into three interlinked questions. First, are Dalits Hindus? Second, insofar as Hinduism provides ideological justification for hierarchical social differentiation based on degrees of purity, how have Dalits responded to the religious practices of mainstream Hindu society? Third, how does the modern Indian state determine the religion of Dalits?

Are Dalits Hindus? Anthropological and Political Considerations

The first question, in turn, has subparts, (1) anthropological and (2) political. To what extent are the religious beliefs and practices of Dalits who are classified as Hindus distinct from those of the non-Dalit majority? And what does it mean to count Dalits as Hindus in the context of electoral practices first introduced by the colonial state, where numbers of each community directly commuted to political power?

(1) A consensus in scholarly writing attests to the fact that Dalit religiosity is at one end of a continuum, sharing many features with low, non-Dalit castes but comparatively few with higher castes (Juergensmeyer, 1982; Khare, 1984; Lamb, 2002; Vincentnathan, 1993) – though there is considerable disagreement on the meaning and depth of this sharing, a point to which I will return. In a particularly comprehensive formulation, M. Juergensmeyer (1982, 93–108) describes Dalit religiosity as characterized by a focus on this-worldly objectives, as comprising relations with a panoply of supernatural beings of local provenance to whom propitiation is made and from whom favor is sought, and correlatively, as having few if any relations with pan-Indian puranic deities. More significantly, traditional Dalit religiosity has been widely found to lack (1) extra-worldly goals like *mokṣa* (ultimate → liberation from rebirth) and (2) the doctrine of → *karma* – both of which are central to high-caste Hinduism (and to Hinduism as represented in most scholarly textbooks) – and to embrace (3) an ethical dualism that is at odds with the contextualist (dharmic) → ethics, which depends on a continuum between good and evil (Sharma, 1999, 37–38; Deliège, 1993). In all these ways, pan-Indian data on Dalit religiosity highlight its distinction from, and implicit rejection of, high-caste Hinduism. Apart from this, Dalits have embraced specific, historical religious communities that challenge Hindu orthodoxy with respect to matters of caste more directly; these will be discussed in the succeeding section (2) below.

Distinct from the question of how far Dalits' beliefs and practices set them apart from others, there is the fact that Dalits are variously incorporated in the religious practices conducted by caste Hindus, for instance by playing prescribed roles as musicians or mediums in village festivals (e.g. Mines, 2005). This is especially common in rites relating to liminal states like birth and death; in Tamil Nadu, for example, Dalits sing mourning songs at the funerals of caste folk (Clark-Dèces, 2005). Such data are best treated with caution in any evaluation of whether Dalits are Hindus, since traditional religious services of this kind are not so much the "privilege" of Dalits to perform but indeed treated as obligatory by their caste employers, and violent conflict is usually the result if such services are refused. Thus Christians and Muslims might too perform such services (Frykenberg, 1989, 41–42) and are not thereby thought to be Hindu, whereas Dalits themselves, and not only those who have joined political movements that seek to assert their difference from mainstream society, often use "Hindu" to refer *only* to non-Dalits (Searle-Chatterjee, 1994, 2008). Some have argued that Dalits have maintained a sphere of ritual power within the Hindu world by acting as intermediaries between caste Hindus and a pantheon of fierce "border" deities and malevolent spirits with which Dalits are widely understood as capable of more intimate relations (Nabokov, 2000; Prakash, 1986; Sax, 2008) – but both the ambivalence of these capacities and their very construction as practices located at the periphery of civilized society proper make them difficult to interpret straightforwardly as a mark of shared religion. And indeed,

> there was a time, not long ago, if not still, when any and all Untouchables… were prohibited from entering any proper temple… [L]ocal pollution rules almost invariably forbade them from being considered "Hindu" in any participatory or respectable manner. (Frykenberg, 1989, 41–42)

Do Dalits accept pan-Indian ideas of purity and pollution by which their exclusion from temples and elsewhere is justified? These ideas are not only elaborated in canonical Hindu texts, but are also cited as the source for Dalits' inherent "lowness" across all sections of the non-Dalit population, so the answer to this question is significant. The most insistent argument that they do has been made by anthropologist M. Moffatt (1979), whose data showed that subcastes of Dalits "replicate" among themselves the service relations played out at the village-wide level between Dalits and other castes; Dalit subcastes are allegedly hierarchically arranged, with higher-ranked subcastes asymmetrically passing impurity on to their lower-caste fellows. This in turn proves, M. Moffatt contended, their "consensus" with the broader Indian society that discriminates against them. Both facets, replication and consensus, of M. Moffatt's argument may be questioned. With respect to replication, M. Moffatt's data are not representative: the particular pattern of replication that M. Moffatt found was virtually unique and reflected the relatively rare independence and prosperity enjoyed by some of the Dalits in his study (Deliège, 1992). A large range of arguments directed not against M. Moffatt himself but more generally against the Dumontian theory of caste to which M. Moffatt adheres – in which the opposition between purity and pollution provides the single defining feature of caste – undermines the consensus aspect of M. Moffatt's position (e.g. Berreman, 1971; Lynch, 1977; Mencher, 1974). These accounts stress that purity and pollution are merely Brahmanical justification for a complex system of entrenched inequality that includes political-economic domination. And this justification cannot be taken to reflect the views of Dalits themselves, who, however much they might conform in the presence of their social "superiors," view society in classlike terms and caste practices as oppression. Such data have been so widely attested as to counter M. Moffatt's implicit assumption of implausibly widespread social unity. Although M. Moffatt concedes the existence of social conflict, it pales in his account before the allegedly universal adherence to the principle of hierarchy. Moreover, although rarely made explicit in these terms (with the important exception of Mosse, 1994b), such criticisms raise the further very interesting question of why replication should be construed as consensus in the first place. A more complex account of agency that acknowledges how the meaning and intention of speech and action vary with the social location of actors is surely required. In this more promising vein, L. Vincentnathan (1993) offers a sophisticated analysis of Dalit narratives of caste origins that very often decry the injustice of Dalits' current position, describing it as a trick perpetrated by others who act selfishly to make themselves "high." She adds that castes are viewed as inherently equal by Dalits, resulting from the fact that ritual purity is construed as temporary, acquired, and alterable (as opposed to heritable and permanent). Anthropologists have, moreover, documented the presence of such traditions of storytelling across the subcontinent (see also Deliège, 1993).This sits well with the absence or greatly reduced importance, noted above, of acceptance of the idea of *karma* among Dalits. And yet it is frequently repeated in both scholarship and popular discourse that submission to the doctrine of *karma* – the view that the moral quality of one's actions determines one's future – renders most Dalits both fatalistic (Weber, 1958) and reasonably content with their circumstances. This disregards the lack of any evidence that

Dalits accept the doctrine of *karma* and that which shows it has no salience in their cosmologies. So does the hypothesis that at one time most Dalits simply accepted their position as an automatic consequence of their own impurity: there is no evidentiary basis for this claim (see Sharma, 1999). What is demonstrable, however, is that the theory of Dalit acquiescence was a mainstay of British colonizers, who used it to justify their own inaction against agrestic servitude (Viswanath, 2006).

But, the fact that Dalit practices and beliefs are distinguishable in some respects from those of many other castes does not necessarily disqualify Dalit religion from being understood as simply one variety of the shared set of practices to which, at least heuristically (and legally; see below), Hinduism refers. After all, since at least the early colonial period, Hinduism has, famously, described a diversity of discrete "sects" with only a minimum of shared elements (Inden, 1991). Since the label "Hindu" may refer to this panoply of forms of worship and ritual, or alternatively to a unified "community" that substantively shares religious practices and ideologies, understanding how Dalits' religious identity has been construed requires assessing when and why similarities are foregrounded over differences. And this is ultimately a political matter (see Asad, 2001, 210).

(2) The anthropological debates described above have occurred in a social-historical milieu in which these questions are conferred with immense political stakes. What then are the consequences attendant on counting Dalits as Hindus? This question emerged in full form only in the 19th century, when religious identity and demographics became intimately linked with the introduction by the British colonial government of the so-called Communal Award whereby representatives to public office would be apportioned according to the numerical strength of their respective religious "communities." Hindus, especially in regions like Punjab, where, pre-Partition, their majority status was precarious, depended on Dalits being counted among them. This inaugurated what J.C.B. Webster (1992) has aptly dubbed a "politics of numbers," leading the → Arya Samaj, a Hindu reformist outfit (Jones, 1976), to launch concerted campaigns to "reconvert" Dalits who were adherents to Sikhism, Islam, and Christianity by "purifying" them and to make special provisions for the incorporation of Dalits into mainstream Hinduism. Caste discrimination, however, persisted within the ranks of these reformist organizations. Secular political parties, like the nationalist Congress, also launched campaigns to include Dalits more fully in the body of the modern nation that they were in the process of designing, but these efforts too tended to exclude Dalits from leadership positions and instituted paternalist measures that favored slow over revolutionary change. The apogee of high-caste attempts to better integrate Dalits into mainstream Hindu society was no doubt Mohandas K. → Gandhi's. Gandhi coined the still relatively popular label "Harijans" (Children of God; Hari is a name of the deity → Viṣṇu), which itself succinctly indicates the parameters within which he viewed this social challenge: as a matter internal to Hinduism and as one in which a vulnerable childlike subpopulation required parental succor. In Gandhi's religio-moral program, Dalits were actually prohibited from sitting on the board of the organization meant to ameliorate their condition, the Harijan Sevak Sangh (Zelliot, 1992, 150–178). The agents who would carry out reform – construed as a voluntaristic program of attitude improvement that emphatically rejected social change and sought to retain Harijans in their traditional occupations, while persuading them to give up vices like alcohol and meat consumption – were to be caste Hindus alone, who were to desist from viewing their untouchable "brethren" with disgust and instead to recognize work like manual scavenging as in fact ennobling in its service to society. They would remain, that is to say, in what Gandhi conceived as their traditional occupations although empirically only a small minority of Dalits perform work deemed ritually impure as their sole or even primary means of livelihood, with the vast majority providing agrarian labor. Although Gandhi's ideas have enjoyed prominence with many caste Hindus, and even some Dalits, politically active Dalits (at least those who were not employed by high-caste political organizations such as the Congress Party) have found Gandhi's model distinctly unappealing. Chief among them was B.R. → Ambedkar (1891–1956), the most important Dalit politician that India has produced, a principal author of India's constitution, and a framer of the measures for state-sponsored affirmative action, "reservations," which are still in place today (Ambedkar, 1945; Jaffrelot, 2005). For our purposes, it is significant that in B.R. Ambedkar's analysis, Hinduism could not be extricated intact

from the hierarchical social system that was caste (and in this, many more recent sociologists have concurred: e.g. Srinivas, 1956). Therefore, he concluded, the only hope for Dalits was to convert, rather than to attempt to reform Hinduism by Gandhian means or through legislative measures forcing temples to allow Dalits entry. Gandhi and B.R. Ambedkar's conflict may be taken as paradigmatic of what has been, since the turn of the 19th century, a struggle on the part of many political Dalits to assert religious difference and on the part of nationalist Hindu elites to deny it.

Dalits and the Resignification of Caste and Religion

Confining ourselves to the modern historical period, where data are more plentiful, we may discern Dalits relating in several different respects to the religion of dominant groups. I address first in this section attempts to reconfigure and resignify Hinduism and caste that claim inspiration from figures from India's religious history. These recent movements have often been inspired by a long tradition of anticaste and anti-Brahman literature and activity that emerged as part of the → *bhakti* movement in medieval India. Yet we know little about the sociological scope, or concrete everyday consequences, of these protests in medieval India, and it should be stressed that, *contra* popular perceptions, there is neither linear historical connection nor straightforward ideological continuity between modern anticaste activism and the religious movements in question (Burchett, 2009). Indeed, scholars have pointed to the relatively recent depiction of *bhakti* in these terms (Ebeling, 2010; Fuller, 2004, 157–158; Zelliot, 1980). Nevertheless, it is an important fact that, since at least the 18th century, Dalit men and women, especially in North India, have entered into forms of religious communion with others by embracing the teachings of particular medieval and early modern North Indian devotional poet-saints (→ Sants) – some of whom it has been claimed were themselves Dalit. Of these the most significant for Dalits are → Ravidās, → Kabīr, and Gurū Nānak (see → Hinduism and Sikhism). All three, and numerous others like them, embody what has been described as a "*bhakti-sant*" or "renouncer" ethos (Juergensmeyer, 1982; Khare, 1984). Significant characteristics of this ethos include belief in a single abstract (→ *nirguṇa*) deity and a commitment to personal and unmediated relationships with the divine that depend on the moral integrity of the adherent and not the observance of ritual propriety. Not least, of course, this ethos roundly eschews caste – if primarily as a marker of religious purity, and not in social and political-economic terms. Thus the poetry attributed to these figures excoriates Brahmans' claims to spiritual superiority by mocking their punctilious adherence to ritual purity and particularly the observance of caste scruples, which are portrayed as entirely ineffective – indeed, foolish – attempts to attain spiritual salvation. The exemplary purveyors of this ethos have been the icons at the center of a variety of energetic 19th- and 20th-century movements involving Dalits in significant religious and social transformation and very often in new forms of political engagement; important examples include the → Satnamis (Dube, 1998), Ramnamis (Lamb, 2002; see also → Madhya Pradesh), → Ravidāsīs (Cohn, 1959; Schaller, 1994), Balmikis (primarily Punjabi Chuhras and Mehtars who venerate the legendary author of the → *Rāmāyaṇa*, Vālmīki; Prashad, 1999; see also → Pakistan), and → Ad Dharmis (Juergensmeyer, 1982).

In Tamil South India, where the *bhakti* tradition originated, it has historically been less closely associated with protest against caste (Champakalakshmi, 1996). Even the token Dalit saints in the Tamil *bhakti* pantheon are, at best, ambiguous role models for Dalit dissent: the Śaiva Dalit *bhakta* Nantaṉār (see → Nāyaṉārs), for instance, had literally to pass through fire to prove his spiritual purity (Manickam, 1990). The most important reconfiguration of religion in this region in the modern period was undertaken by Pandit Iyothee Thass (1845–1914), an influential leader and early native proponent of the idea that Dalit religiosity represents an autochthonous cultural form characterized by radical equality and therefore in sharp contrast to mainstream Hinduism (Aloysius, 1998; Ayyathurai, 2011; an idea Juergensmeyer [1982] suggests was adopted by North Indian Dalits from their South Indian counterparts). Thus the "*ād*" or "*ādi*," which figures in terms for Dalits prominent in the early 20th century, such as Adi Dravida, Adi Karnataka, Adi Andhra, and the members of the Punjabi movement Ad Dharm, means "original," or "originary," indexing this valorization of autochthony. Iyothee Thass proposed the recovery of Buddhism, which he conceived as a genuinely universal and egalitarian religion practiced by persons who became marginalized as Dalits at the hands of conquering Hindus. The latter attempted to stamp out Buddhism for millennia, but, argued Iyothee Thass, it was preserved in many folk traditions of worship in the Tamil South. Iyothee Thass therefore deemed Buddhism a natural means for Dalit emancipation many decades before B.R. Ambedkar famously converted to Buddhism along with 60 thousand followers in 1955.

In the last three hundred years, Dalits have also converted to Islam, Sikhism, and Roman Catholicism. How much these conversions can be understood as responses to caste inequity is difficult to discern, however, given the kinds and quantity of available data. The most spectacular modern conversions of the last two centuries that have clearly concerned Dalits' position in society have been to Protestant Christianity. Beginning roughly in the 1850s, "mass conversions" of Dalits to Protestant Christianity took place throughout India (Bauman, 2008; Frykenberg & Low, 2003; Viswanath, 2006; Webster, 1992). These movements to Christianity have many characteristics in common with the many other forms of Dalit religious activism, described above, that have involved the resignification of caste relations. The single most important differentia of 19th- and 20th-century mass-conversion movements, however, was the fact that these conversions, in the context of colonial rule, inaugurated a new regime of state intervention in Dalit life and livelihoods in which Christian missionaries worked with the state to provide forms of amelioration (Viswanath, 2006), making Dalit welfare for the first time a theme for the modern nation-state. And just as crucially, missionaries helped to introduce into India the language with which Dalit conversion – and Dalit religion more generally – is now widely spoken about. They sought to distinguish religion from all other realms, placing caste squarely in the former, and focused their own attempts at Dalit "improvement" in that realm, foreshadowing Gandhi's proposed solution. Furthermore, the conceptual distinction between religion and politics that emerged with respect to Dalits in the wake of missionary discourse became a mainstay of Indian public talk from the late 19th century onward, a distinction that decisively shaped modern conceptions of and solutions to the problems that Dalits face, no less than how these problems and solutions have been studied by scholars.

Running through the vast majority of scholarship on Dalit religious and cultural movements are a series of conceptual oppositions that appear to have little basis in the actual aims and activities of these movements themselves. Thus "modern," "political," and "foreign-inspired" movements are regularly counterposed to traditional, religious, and "Indic" forms of protest. Normative claims, furthermore, are frequently made with respect to Dalit movements, whether to valorize them as authentically Indian and therefore more effective in garnering a following and avoiding deracination, or to disdain them for their allegedly limited emancipatory potential and inadequate separation from caste society. On the one hand, the portrayal of a realm of culture as genuinely "Indic," and from which solutions to the problem of untouchability might be drawn, renders suspect some Dalits' attempts to draw on sources of inspiration deemed "foreign" in the Indian context, such as Christianity, Islam, Marxism, or liberalism. And, on the other hand, the identification of the radically new with the genuinely transformative is itself a hallmark of modernist discourses and a datum to be analyzed, rather than a litmus test with which to evaluate the potential of these movements for effecting substantive social change.

Nevertheless, to many scholarly commentators (e.g. Khare, 1984; Omvedt, 1994, 114; Juergensmeyer, 1982) as much as to caste Hindu political activists, there has appeared to be a choice between forms of ameliorative action and redress that engage the realm of formal politics and those that address religion – Gandhi, for instance insisted that any attempt to address the problem of Dalit subordination had to be religious and apolitical. The career of B.R. Ambedkar would seem to be a case in point, vacillating between these two putatively irreconcilable forms of mobilization: early campaigns for temple entry (roughly 1920–1930; Jaffrelot, 2005, 49–51) were followed by decades of focus on electoral politics, but his career nevertheless culminated in a spectacular mass conversion to Buddhism in 1956, months before his death. Yet in crucial respects, the stage had been set for this later conversion for years. His earliest sociological writings identify caste as endemic to Hinduism and Hinduism as uniquely productive of this "descending scale of contempt" that ingeniously divided persons from one another at all levels so that those lower on the scale would never unite to rise up against their oppressors. After several decades of attempts to reform Hinduism, B.R. Ambedkar first seriously contemplated the idea of conversion from Hinduism in the 1930s, consulting with Muslim, Christian, Sikh, and Hindu leaders, and coming closest to embracing Sikhism, but refraining from taking the final step (Jaffrelot, 2005, 119–142). Following the tumultuous 1940s, when India gained independence and Indians produced the postcolonial constitution, B.R. Ambedkar became permanently embittered by the refusal of the independent nation-state to pass his version of the Hindu Code Bill, which would, in his view, go some way in instituting reforms that Hindu society required. This represents the culmination of attempts to use legal and political means to transform Hinduism and the Indian society of which it is a part, and B.R. Ambedkar's conversion was perhaps a final riposte to a caste elite that refused transformation. In this sense, it would be erroneous to assess and analyze B.R. Ambedkar's activities or those of other Dalit movements through a framework that posits a disjuncture between religion and politics. B.R. Ambedkar sought change in what are commonly understood as both those realms and attempted to effect it through both state and extrastate agitation. The famous public burning, in Mahad, Maharashtra, in 1927, of copies of the *Manusmṛti* – a canonical → Dharmaśāstra (Hindu law text) that invested the impressment of low castes with sacral authority – would be a very different political action were it not accompanied by his relentless pursuit of legal sanctions against schools that practiced discrimination and the institution of positive discrimination in employment. Likewise, Satnamis, Ad Dharmis, Ramnamis, and Ravidāsīs have been intensely engaged in formal political activity. To Dalits themselves therefore, the diremption of religion and politics appears to make little sense.

Dalits and Hinduism in the Administrative and Legal Codes of Modern India

If the early 1900s saw the public inauguration of an indelible political relation between Dalits and Hinduism, in more subtle, very powerful, and less publicly understood respects, the administrative and legal codes of the postcolonial nation-state perform the same work (see also → modern legal framework). To understand how this is so, we must first consider the legal backdrop: the means by which the state's legal apparatus has construed a religiously unified populace, employing what has been described as an inclusivist definition of Hinduism (Sen, 2007). For the purposes of the law in modern India,

> the test of whether a person is a Hindu ... starts with ethnic and geographical tests, which raise a presumption that can be rebutted not by proof of absence of belief or presence of disbelief but only by proof of exclusive adherence (or conversion) to a foreign (i.e. a non-Hindu) faith. (Derrett, 1968, 52)

In this remarkably capacious formulation, a person who is anything other than Christian, Muslim, Jewish, or Parsi – including an avowed atheist – will be defined as Hindu by the Indian legal machinery.

In this legal-administrative context, Dalits were further secured as Hindu by the promulgation of laws preventing Hindu temples from denying them access in most provinces in the late 1930s through the 1940s; central legislation ratified these measures in 1955 with the passage of the Untouchability Offences Act. In this way, the question of whether Dalits are Hindus was definitively decided in the law. Yet since the law only forbade Hindus from discriminating against Dalits, this act paved the way for lawsuits in which groups widely understood as Hindu who wished to continue to exclude Dalits from their sites of worship argued in court that they were a separate sect, and that laws mandating the inclusion of Dalits did not apply to them (Galanter, 2004); these suits were largely unsuccessful.

The codes of the modern state do not simply define Dalits as Hindus. They seek actively to retain Dalits within the Hindu fold. When B.R. Ambedkar successfully introduced "reservations," positive discrimination for Dalits in education and government employment, the beneficiaries of these schemes had to be legally identified. Lists of castes and tribes were compiled into a schedule – hence the commonly used term Scheduled Caste (SC) for Dalit. But the critical stipulation was that inclusion on the list, and thus qualification for benefits, and for protection under the 1955 Prevention of Atrocities Act, was extended *only* to Hindu Dalits (with inclusion provided in 1956 for Sikh Dalits, and later, in 1990, for Buddhists). The implicit logic was that converts, by opting out of Hinduism, had thereby severed their ties with the source of discrimination. But as I have laid out, the position of Dalits is one of social and economic hardship and not mere ritual disability.

Thus we have legislation concerning temple entry that positively identifies Dalits as Hindus and requires caste Hindus to do so as well. And at the same time, there is a state-sponsored disincentive to conversion, given the current restriction of positive discrimination to Hindu Dalits (and the very small numbers who identify as Sikh and Buddhist). It should be clear, then, that the analytic separation made earlier in this article between the anthropological and political aspects of Dalits' inclusion as Hindus is a heuristic one at best, given the increasing power of modern states both to determine the citizenry's legal identity and indeed to shape its religious subjectivity.

Bibliography

Aktor, M., "Rules of Untouchability in Ancient and Medieval Law Books: Householders, Competence and Inauspiciousness," *IJHS* 6/3, 2002, 243–274.

Aloysius, G., *Religion as Emancipatory Identity: A Buddhist Movement among the Tamils under Colonialism*, Delhi, 1998.

Ambedkar, B.R., "What Congress and Gandhi Have Done to the Untouchables," 1945 (at: http://www.ambedkar.org/ambcd/41A.What Congress and Gandhi Preface.htm).

Asad, T., "Reading a Modern Classic: W.C. Smith's 'The Meaning and End of Religion,'" *HR* 40/3, 2001, 205–222.

Ayyathurai, G., "Foundations of Anti-caste Consciousness: Pandit Iyothee Thass, Tamil Buddhism, and the Marginalized in South India," diss., Columbia University, 2011.

Bauman, C., *Christian Identity and Dalit Religion in Hindu India, 1868–1947*, Grand Rapids, 2008.

Berreman, G.D., "The Brahmanical View of Caste," *CIS* 5, 1971, 16–23.

Broken People: Caste Violence Against India's Untouchables, publ. Human Rights Watch, New York, 1999.

Burchett, P., "Bhakti Rhetoric in the Hagiography of 'Untouchable' Saints: Discerning Bhakti's Ambivalence on Caste and Brahminhood," *IJHS* 13/2, 2009, 115–141.

Census Report 2001, publ. Government of India, 2001, (at: http://censusindia.gov.in/Census_And_You/scheduled_castes_and_sceduled_tribes.aspx).

Champakalakshmi, R., "From Devotion and Dissent to Dominance: The Bhakti of the Tamil Āḻvārs and Nāyanārs," in: R. Champakalakshmi & S. Gopal, eds., *Tradition, Dissent and Ideology: Essays in Honour of Romila Thapar*, New Delhi, 1996, 135–163.

Charsley, S., "'Untouchable': What Is in a Name?" *JRAI* 2/1, 1996, 1–23.

Clark-Dèces, I., *No One Cries for the Dead: Tamil Dirges, Rowdy Songs, and Graveyard Petitions*, Berkeley, 2005.

Cohn, B.S., "Changing Traditions of a Depressed Caste," in: M. Singer, ed., *Traditional India: Structure and Change*, Philadelphia, 1959.

Deliège, R., *The World of the "Untouchables": Paraiyars of Tamil Nadu*, Delhi, 1997.

Deliège, R., "The Myths of Origin of the Indian Untouchables," *Man.NS* 28/3, 1993, 533–549.

Deliège, R., "Replication and Consensus: Untouchability, Caste and Ideology in India," *Man.NS* 27/1, 1992, 155–173.

Derrett, J.D.M., *Religion, Law and the State in India*, London, 1968.

Dube, S., *Untouchable Pasts: Religion, Identity, and Power among a Central Indian Community, 1780–1950*, Albany, 1998.

Dumont, L., *Homo Hierarchicus: The Caste System and Its Implications*, Chicago, 1970.

Ebeling, S., "Another Tomorrow for Nantaṉār: The Continuation and Re-invention of a Medieval South Indian Untouchable Saint," in: P. Schalk *et al.*, eds., *Geschichten und Geschichte. Historiographie und Hagiographie in der asiatischen Religionsgeschichte*, Uppsala, 2010, 433–516.

Forrester, D., *Caste and Christianity: Attitudes and Policies on Caste of Anglo-Saxon Protestant Missions in India*, London, 1980.

Fuller, C., *The Camphor Flame: Popular Hinduism and Society*, Princeton, 2004.

Frykenberg, R.E., "The Emergenceof Modern 'Hinduism' as a Concept and as an Institution: A Reappraisal with Special Reference to South India," in: G. Sontheimer & H. Kulke, eds., *Hinduism Reconsidered*, New Delhi, 1989, 29–50.

Frykenberg, R.E., & A. Low, eds., *Christians and Missionaries in India: Cross-cultural Communication since 1500*, Grand Rapids, 2003.

Galanter, M., "Hinduism, Secularism, and the Indian Judiciary," in: R. Bhargava, ed., *Secularism and Its Critics*, Delhi, 2004.

Galanter, M., *Competing Equalities: Law and the Backward Classes in India*, Delhi, 1984.

Galanter, M., "The Abolition of Disabilities: Untouchability and the Law," in: J.M. Mahar, ed., *The Untouchables in Contemporary India*, Tucson, 1972.

Hanumanathan, K.R., "Evolution of Untouchability in Tamil Nadu A.D. up to 1600," *IHR* 23/1–2, 1996–1997, 41–65.

Hanumanathan, K.R., *Untouchability: A Historical Study up to 1500 AD (with Special Reference to Tamil Nadu)*, Madurai, 1979.

Inden, R., *Imagining India*, Bloomington, 2001.

Jaffrelot, C., *Dr. Ambedkar and Untouchability: Analysing and Fighting Caste*, London, 2005.

Jones, K.W., *Arya Dharm: Hindu Consciousness in 19th-Century Punjab*, Berkeley, 1976.

Juergensmeyer, M., *Religion as Social Vision: The Movement against Untouchability in 20th-Century Punjab*, Berkeley, 1982.

Khare, R., *The Untouchable as Himself*, Cambridge MA, 1984.

Kooiman, D., "Untouchability in India through the Missionary's Eye," *Itinerario* 7/1, 1983, 115–125.

Lamb, R., *Rapt in the Name: The Ramnamis, Ramnam, and Untouchable Religion in Central India*, Albany, 2002.

Lynch, O., "Method and Theory in the Sociology of Louis Dumont," in: K. David, ed., *The New Wind: Changing Identities in South Asia*, The Hague, 1977, 239–262.

Lynch, O., *The Politics of Untouchability: Social Mobility and Social Change in a City of India*, New York, 1969.

Manickam, S., *Nandanar, the Dalit Martyr: A Historical Reconstruction of His Times*, Madras, 1990.

Manickam, S., *The Social Setting of Christian Conversion in South India*, Wiesbaden, 1977.

Mencher, J., "The Caste System Upside Down, or the Not-So-Mysterious East," *CuA* 15/4, 1974, 469–493.

Mencher, J., "Continuity and Change in an Ex-untouchable Community of South India," in: J.M. Mahar, ed., *The Untouchables in Contemporary India*, Tucson, 1972, 37–56.

Mendelsohn, O., & M. Vicziany, *The Untouchables: Subordination, Poverty and the State in Modern India*, Cambridge UK, 1998.

Mines, D., *Fierce Gods: Inequality, Ritual, and the Politics of Dignity in a South Indian Village*, Bloomington, 2005.

Moffatt, M., *An Untouchable Community in South India: Structure and Consensus*, Princeton, 1979.

Mosse, D., "Idioms of Subordination and Styles of Protest among Christian and Harijan Castes in Tamil Nadu," *CIS* 28/1, 1994a, 67–106.

Mosse, D., "Replication and Consensus among Indian Untouchable (Harijan) Castes," *Man.NS* 9/2, 1994b, 457–461.

Nabokov, I., *Religion against the Self: An Ethnography of Tamil Rituals*, New York, 2000.

Narula, S., *Broken People: Caste Violence against India's "Untouchables,"* New York, 1999.

Omvedt, G., *Dalits and the Democratic Revolution: Dr Ambedkar and the Dalit Movement in Colonial India*, New Delhi, 1994.

Peabody, N., "Cents, Sense, Census: Human Inventories in Late Precolonial and Early Colonial India," *CSSH* 43, 2001, 819–850.

Prakash, G., "Reproducing Inequality: Spirit Cults and Labor Relations in Colonial Eastern India," *MAS* 20/2, 1986, 209–230.

Prashad, V., *Untouchable Freedom: A Social History of a Dalit Community*, New Delhi, 1999.

Rao, A., *The Caste Question: Dalits and the Politics of Modern India*, Berkeley, 2009.

Roberts, N., "Caste, Anthropology of," in: W. Darity, ed., *International Encyclopedia of the Social Sciences*, New York, 2008, 461–463.

Sax, W., *God of Justice: Ritual Healing and Social Justice in the Central Himalayas*, New York, 2008.

Schaller, J., "Sanskritization, Caste Uplift, and Social Dissidence in the Sant Ravidas Panth," in: D. Lorenzen, ed., *Bhakti Religion in North India*, Albany, 1994, 94–119.

Searle-Chatterjee, M., "Attributing and Rejecting the Label 'Hindu' in North India," in: N. Green & M. Searle-Chatterjee, eds., *Religion, Language and Power*, New York, 2008, 186–201.

Searle-Chatterjee, M., "Urban 'Untouchables' and Hindu Nationalism," *IM* 13/1, 1994, 12–25.

Sen, R., *Legalizing Religion: The Indian Supreme Court and Secularism*, Washington DC, 2007.

Sharma, U., *Caste*, Buckingham, 1999.

Srinivas, M.N., "A Note on Sanskritization and Westernization," *FEQ* 15/4, 1956, 481–496.

Vincentnathan, L., "Untouchable Concepts of Person and Society," *CIS.NS* 3/1, 1993, 53–82.

Viswanath, R., "Spiritual Slavery, Material Malaise: 'Untouchables' and Religious Neutrality in Colonial South India," *HiR* 83/219, 2010, 124–145.

Viswanath, R., "'The Pariah Problem': Missionaries, the Administration of 'Untouchables' and the Elaboration of Neutrality in Colonial South India, 1885–c. 1918," diss., Columbia University, 2006.

Weber, M., *The Religion of India: The Sociology of Hinduism and Buddhism*, New York, 1958.

Webster, J.C.B., *The Dalit Christians: A History*, Delhi, 1992.

Zelliot, E., *From Untouchable to Dalit: Essays on the Ambedkar Movement*, New Delhi, 1992.

Zelliot, E., "Chokhamela and Eknath: Two Bhakti Modes of Legitimacy for Modern Change," *JAAS 15/1–2, 1980, 136–156.*

RUPA VISWANATH

Gender

Hindu tradition, like many others, has constituted itself as having a vested interest in defining gender and classifying every human being, deity, and animal, and even many plants in accordance with it. Gender is a key marker, predominantly imagined as a binary between female and male, with which society bar codes members of its expansive worldview. At the same time, Hinduism has also generated alternatives to the familiar binary, including ideas of more porous boundaries as well as challenges that involve a play or a negation of such boundaries. In a tradition that is as old, literate, and multicentered as Hinduism, many paradigms and possibilities were explored.

"Gender" and "Sex"

As V.L. Bullough reminds us, in terms of modern Western theory,

> *[g]ender* is an old term in linguistic discourse used to designate whether nouns are masculine, feminine, or neuter. It was not normally used in the language of social or natural sciences or in sexology until 1955, when John Money adopted the term to serve as an umbrella concept to distinguish femininity, or womanliness, and masculinity, or manliness, from biological sex (male or female). (Bullough, 2005, 870)

"Gender" is indeed an "old term" linguistically; both the Indian classical languages of Sanskrit and Pali inflected nouns for three grammatical genders: masculine, feminine, and neuter. In Sanskrit, the term for gender is *liṅga* (mark, sign). Linguistically, then, gender in theory equally refers to all three categories. However, due to patriarchal control over language and its production, the idea of the "marked" category became understood as specifically female. In Indian classical literature, as in literatures around the world, it was the male voice and perspective that was assumed; linguistically and culturally the male gender was considered normative and inclusive, whereas in contrast, the female gender was linguistically and culturally considered the more "marked," "different," "specific," and "gendered."

S.J.S. Goldman discusses gender, language, and patriarchy in her study of representations of speech (*vāc*) in vedic → Sanskrit texts:

> Gender and language are closely linked in traditional South Asia. The "true" language, the language of religion, the language of power and possession – that is, the language reflected by the word *vāc* – was learned only by males. Gender is an assumption of the language itself. Sanskrit assigns all nouns to one of three grammatical genders (*puṃliṅga, strīliṅga*, and *napuṃsakaliṅga*) and, although grammatical gender does not automatically or necessarily convey semantic gender, clearly with respect to some words the grammatical gender can be understood as semantically significant. Such is the case, I would argue, with the word *vāc*, which is grammatically assigned the feminine gender. The association of the feminine gender with the word *vāc* can in fact be seen as an important symbolic representation of traditional South Asian patriarchy. (Goldman, 2000, 63)

S.J.S. Goldman argues that in the early literature, *vāc* is imagined to be a beautiful woman who is sexual, maternal, and in need of protection via Brahman (priestly) male custodianship of sacred language.

Postmodern theories of gender distinguish it as having a much wider cultural scope than sexuality:

> Gender was more inclusive since it entailed somatic and behavioral criteria on how one conducts oneself personally and socially, and how one is regarded legally. Sex belonged more to reproductive biology than to social sciences, romance, or nurture, whereas gender covered them all. (Bullough, 2005, 870–871)

More than biological functionality is at issue:

> [G]ender in itself implies for a more variable interpretation of what being a woman or a man involves. Whether a person is an XX or an XY, there is much more to being a man or woman than chromosomes. (Bullough, 2005, 872)

While it is commonly understood today that gender is a social construction, the relationship between sex and gender continues to be debated, especially the relative roles biological and social factors play in one's self-identification with gender. Two of the best-known theorists are A.-F. Sterling (2000), who traces a dialectical relationship between biology and culture, and J. Butler (1990; 2004), who has theorized gender as performance and its social limits.

In an article on gender in the study of religion, R. Warne identifies "four major frameworks within which the techniques and strategies of gendering (e.g., ontologizing, pathologizing, idealizing, normalizing, and so forth) have been undertaken." A summary of her somewhat detailed elaboration of the four follows:

1. "No gender," in which biological sex is prioritized, and "gender is weak to non-existent";
2. "Sex is natural, gender is cultural... Because gender is variable, it is changeable";
3. "Neither sex nor gender are natural. There is no logical reason for some biological markers to determine culture and selfhood"; and
4. "Whatever sex is, gender is discursively constructed... Gender is performative, sexual practices are multiple and non-normative, and continued focus on one component of the gender dyad (i.e., 'women') may actually maintain gender hierarchy by reifying its component parts." (Warne, 2000, 147–148)

In the introductory essay for a new open-access interdisciplinary journal, *Religion and Gender*, A.-M. Korte critically reviews the meanings of both "religion" and "gender" and their interdisciplinary interrelationships (Korte, 2011).

The present essay identifies and discusses discourses on gender in Hindu culture. These discourses, and the academic studies that both identify and interpret them, imagine the relationship between sex and gender in ways that relate to the typologies of sex and gender presented by theorists today. The number of academic studies of gender that focus on women is prominent, though this essay focuses on multiple discourses that construct gender in Hinduism and is indebted to prior overview articles on gender and Hinduism (Gold, 1994; Narayanan, 1999; Leslie, 2005; Gold, 2008); an overview of women in Indian history can be found elsewhere (e.g., Young, 2002). This essay will necessarily reflect theoretical trends as it explores constructions of gender in Hinduism, although it is guided by its own categories. The three most general categories used here are the following: boundaries, which discusses formulations of gender as a binary that have normative status; alternatives, which engages cultural ideas on the porous nature of the binary; and challenges, which explores gestures of reinscribing gender that complicate or decenter the binary. Importantly, this essay will not periodize these categories in a way that equates each with a distinctive time period; instead, these categories are viewed as applying across historical periods, from ancient to modern times, as they are imagined, adopted, implemented, and transformed by interested parties. It is also to be understood that these categories and the topics grouped within them are not mutually exclusive; they all mutually implicate and are in dialogue with one another as a range of real and perceived modes of being in the vast religious and cultural complex we conveniently index by the single term "Hinduism."

Boundaries

Gender imagined as a binary constituted by female and male is pervasive in Hindu Indian tradition; sex and gender tend to be harmonized and their relationship naturalized. Cisgender, used to describe "individuals who have a match between the gender they were assigned at birth, their bodies, and their personal identity," as well as their socially defined role, is privileged (Schilt & Westbrook, 2009, 461n1). Hindu culture is a prestige system, following S. Ortner's analysis, in which those defined as males are valued more than those defined as females, in cultural conventions on the appropriate goals in life and the ways in which one can achieve them (McGee, 2000, 14–16). Overall, men are accorded more social power and enact dominance. Yet one also must discern where, within the overall context of valuing and empowering the male, spaces are created both for valuing women and for their own meaningful thought, action, and self-expression. Gender is one of many ways of defining the social location of humankind in Hinduism; social class and caste are prominent others. However, it may be the case that the dynamics of gender are something of a "horizontal" that are reproduced throughout the "vertical" stratification that these other modes create. Since Brahmanical ideology has predominated in Hinduism, this section presents representative discourses from that ideology on social bodies, divine bodies, and nation bodies to trace the binary.

The Son and the Wife

Intensive cultural interest in gender surrounds the birth of a child. Hindu culture has in common with other patriarchal cultures the determination that a boy is high-value offspring, whereas a girl is much less valued, or even unwanted (see also → family). A rationale for this preference is provided by classical texts. They invest the male child with the continuation and maintenance of the family line: the birth of a son repays the debt owed to ancestors; the son is a productive earner for the family; the son takes a wife, who leaves her family to reside with his, and they produce progeny; and the son will perform the death rituals for his father, ensuring the father's safe transition to ancestor status. A very early collection from the postvedic age (which began c. 1000 BCE), the *Taittirīyasaṃhitā*, states that

> [a] brahman, at his very birth, is born with a triple debt – of studentship to the seers, of sacrifice to the gods, of offspring to the fathers. He is, indeed, free from debt, who has a son, is a sacrificer, and who has lived as a student. (*TaiSa.* 6.3.10.5; Olivelle, 1995, 537)

While this and many other classical texts are produced by and directed toward the male members of the priestly caste (Brāhmaṇa [Brahman]), the ways in which members of this highest caste behaved were emulated and adopted by other caste groups included in the rank of the "twice born" through initiation (the royal or Kṣatriya caste; the merchant or Vaiśya caste), as well as others who attempted to raise their own status. This construction of the masculine, which privileges men from birth as the empowered and responsible head of household, has had a wide influence. An established, auspicious life path is laid out before the son, through which he can achieve learning, material wealth including progeny, and spiritual merit.

Classical texts indicate that this path for boys is affirmed and enacted at initiation (*upanayana*), which takes place for boys of the permitted castes between the ages of 8 and 12. It is an important life-cycle rite (→ *saṃskāra*) that initiates the boy into three domains: human society, study of the → Veda, and practice of the fire sacrifice (see → *yajña*). It transitions the boy from biological birth to social status, replacing the mother: "*Upanayana* was thus a socio-ontological birth in opposition to a defective natural birth, and was designed to rectify biological faults and construct a more substantial existence for the young boy" (Smith, 1986, 67). It transforms the boy through sacred knowledge imparted by a teacher, with whom the child is said to have a more intimate relationship than with the biological father, as demonstrated by the resemblance of the initiation rituals to those of marriage, as well as the custom of the boy becoming a member of the teacher's family (Smith, 1986, 73, 75–76). Initiation into the performance of the fire sacrifice is of special significance since it begins the trajectory of mastery of ritual performance that will reach its fulfillment when the boy becomes a married householder (Smith, 1986, 82). Recent research suggests that warrior qualities are promoted in this vedic path's masculinist project (Whitaker, 2011).

While the paradigm of the life trajectory of the Brahman male has the weight of tradition and thus cultural prestige, studies of masculinity today provide nuance in understanding its current status. For example, sexual discipline as it draws from classical codes of celibacy is a central feature in the creation of masculine identity, across domains such as → *yoga* and wrestling (see → *akhāṛā*s; Alter, 2011). In another example, an ethnographic study of non-Brahman men in → Kerala demonstrates that they have developed an ideal of mature masculine identity that is centered on elements that are in opposition to classical Brahman values, such as eating meat, engaging in labor, and being socially minded (Osella, 2006).

Traditionally for women, the coming-into-being as a valued social entity centers on her marriage: "from the orthodox point of view the only rite of passage (*saṃskāra*) that is particularly marked for women is marriage" (Findly, 1999, 418). The initial path laid out before the daughter is basically one of seclusion, since her body and mind must retain their perceived innocence and purity in order for her to be a desirable bridal candidate. While the *Bṛhadāraṇyakopaniṣad* (c. 500 BCE) preserves an interesting typology of women, from the learned → Gargī to the philosophically curious Maitreyī to the household-focused Kātyāyanī (Findly, 1985; Pechilis, 2004; Black, 2007; Lindquist, 2008), it appears that the role of wife in the household context became the dominant social identity for women. The *Manusmṛti* (Laws of Manu), which was probably composed between 200 BCE and 200 CE and was cited as authoritative by later texts purporting to systematically discuss social duties and responsibilities (the → Dharmaśāstra genre of texts), located women as necessarily under male supervision throughout their lifespan:

> I will tell of the eternal duties of a man and wife who stay on the path of duty both in union and in separation. Men must make their women dependent day and night, and keep under their own control those who are attached to sensory objects. Her father guards her in childhood, her husband guards her in youth, and her sons guard her in old age. A woman is not fit for independence. A father who does not give her away at the proper time should be blamed, and a husband who does not have sex with her at the proper time should be blamed; and the son who does not guard his mother when her husband is dead should be blamed. (*MaSm.* 9.1–4; Doniger & Smith, 1991, 197)

This text can be viewed as both empowering and oppressive. The woman is protected, yet ever supervised; she is due parental care, sex from her husband, and support from her son, yet she lacks independent recourse.

Wives are a cultural icon in Indian tradition, being likened to Lakṣmī (→ Śrī Lakṣmī), the goddess of wealth and good fortune. Wifehood is the auspicious status for women; the spectrum of → auspicious – inauspicious is arguably more relevant to understanding the cultural position of women than is the ritually informed → purity – pollution spectrum, because it highlights the contributions they make:

> They are the creators and the maintainers of life, the sources of prosperity, well-being, and pleasure. Furthermore, they are the ones upon whom a man's fulfillment of the three aims of life – *dharma, artha*, and *kāma* – depend. (Marglin, 1985, 299; see also Nagarajan, 2007)

Classically, a wife played a supporting but essential role at the performance of the fire sacrifice (Smith, 1991; Jamison, 1996). The conservative 18th-century *Strīdharmapaddhati* (Guide to the Duties of Women) repeats classical codes for the modern era, emphasizing that marriage for women is the equivalent of the *upanayana* (initiation) for men and that a wife's primary duties are to be devoted to and obey her husband (wife as *pativratā*) and produce sons (Leslie, 1989, 29–37; see also Bose, 2010, 58–109).

More influential than the proscriptive texts on → *dharma* is the beloved epic story of the → *Rāmāyaṇa*, in which the marriage of Sītā (→ Draupadī and Sītā) to → Rāma plays a starring role: "It is a very important source of values for familial interactions and marital relationships" (Sherma, 2005, 23). Sītā is understood to capture concerns and realities of Indian women:

> There are several practical reasons why Sita-like behavior makes sense to Indian women. The outcome of marriage in India depends not only on the attitude of a husband but also on the kind of relationship a women has with her marital family and extended kinship group. If, like Sita, she commands respect and affection from the latter, she can frequently count on them to intervene on her behalf and keep her husband from straying, from behaving unreasonably. Similarly, once her children grow up, they can often play an effective role in protecting her from being needlessly bullied by her husband and bring about a real change in the power equation in the family, because in India, children – especially sons – frequently continue to live with their parents even after they are grown up. A woman can hope to get her marital relatives and her children to act in her favor only if she is seen as being more or less above reproach. (Kishwar, 2001, 305)

If the *Rāmāyaṇa*'s emphasis on the wife's obedience (*pativratā*) is granted (but see Chakravarti, 1986), women who can convincingly perform the moral power that is at the center of the definition of wife can deploy that power to respond and perhaps change the social challenges of being female.

There are many challenges. Marriage and procreation are a universal expectation for both women and men. The tradition of bridal dowry may have begun as a trousseau for the bride that provided her with a safety net, which was then transformed into a vulnerability for women by the British colonial system (Oldenburg, 2002); in present-day India and the Indian diaspora, it has for many become an onerous obligation on the bride's family and even one fraught with danger if the groom's family decides to take physical revenge on the bride for what is perceived to be an inadequate dowry (Menski, 1998). Such problems persist even though the practice was prohibited under Indian civil law in 1961, as well as subsequent sections of the Indian Penal Code. The burden of the bridal dowry contributes to the preference for a son; the 2011 census of India shows that there are 940 females per 1,000 males, strongly suggesting election to abort female babies (see also Harriss-White, 1999; Kannabiran, 2004, 279). Rāma's cruelty in ultimately rejecting Sītā in the *Rāmāyaṇa* illustrates another marital hazard, though in the public mind, he is rejected as a model husband on this basis: "For instance, people will say approvingly: 'He is a Ram-like son, a Ram-like brother, or a Ram-like king.' But they will never say as a mark of approval, 'He is a Ram-like husband'" (Kishwar, 2001, 307). Not bearing children, especially sons, is also a danger, and this is indexed in the gendered language of terms of abuse:

> The dread offense a woman is guilty of is not to bear children. Her life is reduced to violence, rejection and misery. The childless woman, and not the man, is harassed, beaten, insulted, threatened by remarriage of her husband or deserted. She is called names like *banjh* "barren" or *sooki kokh* "dry womb" in Hindi... expressions [in Oriya] like *pua khaai* "to be sonless" (literally, "the woman who eats her own son") or *ghaitaa khaai* "to be a widow" (literally, "the woman who eats her own husband") are used as terms of abuse for a married woman. But terms of abuse for the expression "to be a widower" are rarely employed for men. Also, *jhia khaai/khiaa* "to be daughterless" hardly occurs as a term of abuse. And again this indicates that very little importance is attached to the life of a female child. (Shabadi, 2005, 260, 264)

Ethnographic studies of women who enact traditional definitions and ideals indicate that they use tradition not to conform, but to respond to such challenges. For example, ethnographies of women's rituals today discuss women performing vows (→ *vrat*s) and fasts with the explicit aim to promote long life for their husbands and for the health of their families, which support traditional constructions of women's *dharma*, but these studies also foreground the space such performances allow women for discussion and social exchange. In such discussions, they may make their own claims, including validation of the feminine as positive, women's liturgical authority, and connections rather than opposition between private and public space (McGee, 1991; Pearson, 1996; Dasgupta & Bose, 2000; Gold, 2000; McDaniel, 2002; Rodrigues, 2005; Pintchman, 2005). Ethnographies of women's traditional performance of folksongs disclose the women's awareness of the received structures of gender and power and their criticisms of it. Examples include songs as women's celebrations of their own sexual pleasures and motherhood as well as their voicing of their perspective that patriarchal structures are obstacles to maneuver around (Rahejia & Gold, 1994); women's performance of song as celebrating the domestic qualities of an epic hero, in contrast to men's valuation of that same figure's martial prowess (Harlan, 2000); and in women's use of song to reflect on everyday relationships (Jassal, 2012).

Divinity as Duality

The very influential → Sāṃkhya school of philosophy, which is one of the traditional six orthodox schools that recognize vedic authority, describes the origin of our world as the product of the interaction between two basic entities: → *puruṣa*, which is self-existent spirit or consciousness, and → *prakṛti*, which is self-existent nature or matter. This system may be very ancient; however, an important articulation of it is in Īśvarakṛṣṇa's *Sāṃkhyakārikā*, dated to about the 4th century CE. The binary is clear:

> Matter, material cause or prakriti, is a generative force with tremendous dynamism. Just as a womb sculpts the fetus and after gestation expels it through the birth process, prakriti too with its transformative ability generates all subtle and gross evolutes, including the psyche, mind, ego, and intellect... Purusa is nonfecund, unchanging, inactive, and immobile. Purusa is a seer, a subject, while prakriti is an object. Purusa brings about order in otherwise chaotic prakriti. (Natarajan, 2007, 51–52)

Moreover, these two philosophical entities were explicitly and influentially invested with defining gender:

> Even though every biological male or female possesses soul/consciousness/purusa, and every physical body is a product of prakriti, *Samkhyakarika* in many places blurs the philosophical principles with those of anatomy (verses 59–62). Biological females are identified with prakriti and her evolutes, while males are equated with purusas; thus, the perceptions of both are rendered almost permanent and cultural constructions are assigned the status of nature. (Natarajan, 2007, 53)

Images and stories of gods and goddesses also contribute authoritatively to normative ideals of gender in Hinduism. While there are many different images and stories across eras and regions of India, the basic pattern is that the gods and goddesses are understood to be connected to each other by familial relationships. Prominent among these relationships is marriage; for example, → Viṣṇu is married to Lakṣmī-Śrī (and to → Bhūdevī, "earth-goddess," who is understood to be a fertility aspect of Lakṣmī-Śrī), and → Śiva is married to → Pārvatī. Some interpreters prefer to use the term "consort" to describe the relationship between Viṣṇu and Lakṣmī-Śrī, since their inseparability is represented in the mythological *Viṣṇupurāṇa* (*ViP*. 1.9.100, 106, 107) and elsewhere in terms other than a marriage or wedding ceremony:

> The goddess Śrī of vibrant beauty rose from this [primordial ocean of] milk, standing in a blossoming lotus with a lotus in her hand... Wearing celestial garlands and garments, bathed and adorned with ornaments, with all the gods looking on, she went to Hari's [Viṣṇu's] chest. While resting on Hari's chest, Lakṣmī made the gods know immediate supreme bliss... just by looking at them. (Dimmit & van Buitenen, 1978, 61)

The myth represents them as the prototype of all things male and female (*ViP*. 1.8.17–35):

> The eternal Śrī, loyal to Viṣṇu, is the mother of the world. Just as Viṣṇu pervades the universe... so does she... Viṣṇu is the creator; Śrī is creation. She is the earth and Hari earth's upholder. The eternal Lakṣmī is contentment... the blessed lord is satisfaction... Appearing in the form of a male river is the lord, while Śrī takes form as a female river... In summary, let it be said that among gods, beasts and human beings, Hari is all that is known as male, and Śrī is all that is known as female. (Dimmit & van Buitenen, 1978, 99)

Stories of many of their forms that descend to earth (→ *avatāra*) elaborately describe their wedding, such as that of Rāma and Sītā. The "consort" designation best applies to → Rādhā, the beloved of → Kṛṣṇa, one of the most popular *avatāras* of Viṣṇu. The myth cycles and literature devoted to Kṛṣṇa and Rādhā celebrate them as lovers oscillating between erotic union and separation.

In mythology of Śiva, the wedding of Śiva and Pārvatī has a central status and is elaborately described in the *Vāmanapurāṇa*:

> [T]he groom [Śiva] pressed the hand of the little mountain girl [Pārvatī] with his own. When she felt Śambhu's touch, she became ecstatically happy... Then the groom mounted the altar with the daughter of the mountain, where together they offered white parched grain and ate the offering of milk and honey... When she saw Hara's [Śiva's] face, a shudder went through Ambikā just as the ground heated by the sun's rays shimmers in the rain. When the Grandfather [Brahmā] repeated once again, "Look at your husband's face!" She replied shyly and softly to Brahmā, "I have seen." And then the bride and groom circumambulated the fire three times, after which they threw into it the parched grain together with the oblation. (*VāmP*. 27; Dimmit & van Buitenen, 1978, 170)

In their marriage, Śiva and Pārvatī produce two sons, the handsome Skanda (see → Murukaṉ) and the elephant-headed Gaṇeśa (→ Gaṇapati/Gaṇeśa).

The stories of wedded celestials sacralize and universalize normative ideals of two distinctive genders that are natural counterparts to each other. The male and female genders belong with each other through love and loyalty, even though their commitment can be punctuated by quarrels and disagreements. Images of the gods and goddesses in temples dramatize their different genders through body shape and dress (even when the male and female are two halves of one body, as in the famous Ardhanārīśvara image of Śiva and Pārvatī). A comparative study of goddesses in Hinduism reveals that overall their image is not one of female subordination to male (Hawley & Wulff, 1996). Indeed, just as the divine masculine has powers that are cosmic in scope, the divine feminine has powers that are universal beyond the social category of wife. For example, the Great Goddess (→ Mahādevī) has an independent identity and universal cosmic powers (Brown, 1998), → Kālī is both warrior and mother (McDermott & Kripal, 2003), and the goddess Lakṣmī, who is on one level synonymous with "wife," is simultaneously a universal transformative power of prosperity (Rhodes, 2011).

Nation Bodies

Nationalism in India, from the 19th century to the present day, has been a gender-inflected discourse in areas such as mapping India as a female body, imagining a reformed and modernized Indian womanhood, and, especially in present-day conservative politics, reifying women as the repository of traditional culture. M.K. → Gandhi 's famous concept of *svarāj* (self-rule) in the linked senses of self-discipline and political autonomy was interpreted as control of women's bodies to a significant degree in nationalist discourse.

In an intriguing reclaiming of the British colonial view that India was feminine in contrast to their own masculinity, Indian nationalists created a map of "Mother India," or Bharat Mata (Bhārat Mātā), which was represented from the 1920s on by an iconic image of a crowned woman wearing a saree. This iconography made her resemble a traditional goddess, yet the binary of the goddess was repurposed. Bharat Mata's primary definition was territorial:

> The circulation of such bodyscapes of Bharat Mata enables Hindu nationalist parties to make specific claims regarding ownership of land, the exercise of sovereignty over it, and legitimacy of rule – claims that maps have enabled everywhere in the modern world. (Ramaswamy, 2007, 42)

She was also not a force on her own, because her ontology was constituted by male subject citizens committed to their own political power; the gendering of the "map" as female both personalized the goal and presumed male agency to effect it:

> [Such bodyscapes] invite the citizen-subject who gazes upon them to relate to the nation not as some abstract dead geographical space, but as a near-and-dear person, his personal goddess, his vulnerable mother, even a beloved lover. In this process, they facilitate the filial attachment of the citizen to national territory, producing sentiments of longing and belonging that a scientific map cannot possibly generate… [they] encourage the (male) citizen-subject to view the national territory as a vulnerable woman who needs his protection, and as a mother who has to be rescued through heroism and sacrifice. (Ramaswamy, 2007, 48–49; see also Ramaswamy, 2010)

Reformist debates in the 19th and 20th centuries leading up to India's Independence problematized customs that were practiced on women in Hinduism:

> Practices of female infanticide, sati (widow immolation), forced widowhood (the prohibition of remarriage for widowed women), child marriage (prepubescent marriage, especially for girls, wherein girls were married by age six), pardah-patrivrata (seclusion-chastity), restitution of conjugal rights, and marital rape were central to the debates on the position of women within Hinduism. (Kannabiran, 2004, 275; see also Sarkar, 2002; Falk, 2002)

K. Kannabiran notes that the debates by intellectuals such as Kandukuri Rajyalakshmi, Muvalur Ramamirthammal, Haimabati Sen, Savitribai Phule, Tarabai Shinde, Pandita Ramabai, and Rukmabai occurred in tandem with ordinary women who promoted reforms with their own bodily praxis, "the radicalism of widow remarriage unequivocally rests in the act of the widow in remarrying, an act that in itself constitutes the production of intellectual history, and represents the ultimate methodological advance in the creation of that history" (Kannabiran, 2004, 291). Notable reform discourses included the redefinition of domesticity from an extended family model to a nuclear model, as revealed in advice manuals for women (Walsh, 2004), permitting remarriage for widows (Hatcher, 2012) and the disenfranchizement of female artisans of traditional dance and music (→ *devadāsī*s) through a variety of interests, including the legislation of → sexuality, male claims to land owned by the female artisans, and the Brahmanization of the performing arts (Soneji, 2011).

The *hindutva* ("hindu only") political movement in India, which has been a very visible religious, political, and cultural force over the past two decades and includes organizations such as the Vishwa Hindu Parishad (VHP), Rashtriya Swayamsevak Sangh (RSS), and Bharatiya Janata Party (BJP), is a recent example of the "historical evolution of masculine Hinduism" in India (Banerjee, 2005, 18). Such movements, which boast female leaders who often take on the persona of an ascetic to enhance their perceived virtuous power, use the gendered imagery of mother India as well as both the warrior and devotional aspects of action from the → *Bhagavadgītā* to urge others to join the political agendas of Hindu nationalism (Menon, 2006). Though seemingly challenging the gender binary (women as renouncers, women as politically involved), Hindu nationalists promote the view that the return to traditional Hindu morals will heal a corrupt nation, thus espousing a rhetoric of woman as repository of tradition, which is problematic:

> Invocations of "tradition" today must rest on a moral amnesia of women's struggles against tradition in the immediate past and the hard-won gains of those struggles. They must also rest on the slide back from the woman citizen to woman subject/object, communally owned and controlled. (Kannabiran, 2004, 285)

The televised *Ramayana* serial from 1987 is deployed by political parties because it

> enacts the narrative of threatened Hindu masculinity coming into its own in the battle for lost (feminine) territory, interchangeable with the nation, which is the narrative posited within fundamentalist rhetoric. (Zacharias, 1994, 38)

In contrast to textual versions of the story, in the television version Sītā herself convinces Rām to ultimately abandon her, in a wifely "renunciatory exercise of the will" that "[i]n its total compliance to, or rather enactment of, the male order, *pativrata* hood *is* masculine asceticism and masculine morality" (Zacharias, 1994, 46). Thus, through the reinterpreted figure of Sītā, "the feminine of Hindu fundamentalism has to redeem masculinity in its lack by professing a masculinity more masculine than the masculine" (Zacharias, 1994, 48).

Alternatives

Alternatives render the binary porous through performance: the gender binary remains operative, but explorations across it are undertaken. In particular, men enact female gender identities, and women appropriate male gender roles. There has been much discussion of definitions of and distinctions between gender identities and gender roles (McGee, 2000, 35–46). I agree with M. McGee that "[w]hether or not gender identities are fluid or gender roles fixed, what matters is how gender is valued" (McGee, 2000, 46). I would emphasize, though, that in patriarchal societies there tends to be greater comfort with men imaginatively representing selective qualities that are valued in women, and more discomfort with women embodying and enacting selective qualities that are valued in men. Not only does male performance of female gender identities reveals essential valued characteristics that are presumed to belong to "female," but it also opens up a space for men to describe and enact the power of devotion. Female performance of male gender roles not only reveals essential valued characteristics that are presumed to belong to "male," but also opens up a space for women to constitute themselves as culturally authoritative.

Men Performing Female Gender Identities

In Hindu tradition, the predominant domain for this exploration is devotional (→ *bhakti*) poetry, in which men speak as women. From the poetry, it is clear that what is being evoked is a female gender identity that equates women with a capacity for a love that is egoless, passionate, and unwavering. The example of Rādhā makes the distinction between gender identity and gender role clear. In → Jayadeva 's 12th-century Sanskrit *Gītagovinda*, the poet speaks as Rādhā, separated from Lord Kṛṣṇa but recalling his presence:

> A circle of peacock plumes caressed by moonlight crowns his hair.
> A rainbow colors the fine cloth on his cloud-dark body.
> My heart recalls Hari here in his love dance,
> Playing seductively, laughing, mocking me.
> (*GītGov.* 2.3; see Miller, 1977, 78)

Rādhā is not married to Kṛṣṇa; many stories specify that she is married to another. Her erotic loveplay with Kṛṣṇa is not a social gender role, especially given the poem's valuing of Brahmanic ideology; its imaginative play is dramatized through the activities of the characters rendered through folk traditions. What is being celebrated is the gender identity in which wholehearted steadfast love is represented as a valued female characteristic. On a comparative note, the early Tamil classical (Caṅkam) poetry (c. 200 BCE–300 CE; see → Tamil texts) also had a category of romantic clandestine love that celebrated a female gender identity, in which a young woman exhibited wholehearted and steadfast love for an absent young man. The social gender role, marriage, was depicted in a different category of this love poetry (Selby, 2011).

The male performance of woman in devotional poetry is an interpretation. In her suggestive definition of hermeneutics, R.D. Sherma seems to capture the interpretive significance of the male becoming the female voice, although she is describing a present-day methodology: "[w]e can define *hermeneutics as the effort of the human mind to fully understand, process, internalize, and be transformed by that which it encounters*" (Sherma, 2011, 3). Perhaps the transformative nature of the gesture of imagining the other across the binary is revealed in the male poets' equivalence of the female voice with the transformative love of devotion. The familiar metaphysical interpretation of the erotic love of a woman for a man described in such verses is that it is an allegory of the soul (female) longing for god (male). The longing or lovesick woman gender identity is widely explored in devotional poetry, by male poet-saints such as Māṇikkavācakar and Nammāḻvār (both 9th cent.; see → Āḻvārs), and → Sūrdās and → Ravidās (both 15th cent.), as well as by female poet-saints such as Āṇṭāḷ (9th cent.; see → Āḻvārs) and → Mīrābāī (16th cent.). Intriguingly, the female poets explicitly describe a desire for marriage with god (Viṣṇu and Kṛṣṇa, respectively), thus connecting their transformative love to a social gender role yet changing the latter, since this necessarily involves a rejection or at minimum marginalization of the "social" aspect of the gender role, insofar as the desired husband is divine (on Āṇṭāḷ see Venkatesan, 2010).

The rupture with social gender roles is also seen in two striking images of the female voice as represented by male poets. One is from the Tamil poet-saint Nammāḻvār, in which a "woman" threatens to perform a ritual riding of a palmyra branch to demonstrate "her" love for god. This ritual, customarily performed by men to demonstrate love for a woman, was scandalous because of its public erotic nature. From the poet:

> Lifting my modesty, stealing my heart
> the Lord of the divine ones reaches the high heavens.
> My friend, this I swear:
> I shall shock all the earth.
> I shall do weird deeds
> and like a *wild woman*
> ride the palmyra stem like a horse.
> With no sense of shame, I shall ride
> the palmyra stem through every street in town
> and women from all the lands will cheer me on.
> And I shall demand from the Lord
> a cool blossom from the tulai plant
> and adorn my head with it. (Narayanan, 2003, 574)

As V. Narayanan discusses,

> In Nammāḻvār's poem, we have a "double" crossing over – Nammāḻvār, a male, speaking as a woman, who wants to act like a male. The "essentializing" of women that may be perceived in the figure of the love sick girl of Tamil poetry is teased into other modes of behavior. (Narayanan, 2003, 574)

Specifically, the "she" threatening to act as a "he" in a public demonstration of passionate love underscores the transformative nature of "her" love for the lord.

Equally striking is that a woman whom a devotional poem represents as part of a less valued social category – she is older – is still a subject on whose represented image the value of devotion can be described. Although in the poem the negativity of the woman's older age is specifically related to her profession as courtesan, and thus indexes a specific economy, it still speaks to perceptions of women across patriarchy, noting in this context Indian male poets' vast preference for young women as subjects. From Sāraṅgapāṇi, who probably lived in the late 17th century,

> Hasn't your face
> hardened with age?
> Pale lips,
> wobbling rows of teeth,
> body lusterless,
> beauty dulled.
> But all those days that kind man
> fell at your feet and begged,
> you were too proud.
> *Now you're circling his house.* (Ramanujan *et al.*, 1994, 141)

A prominent theme in devotional poetry is that humankind wastes its time by not focusing on the lord; it is the fault of human nature to be distracted from the real, which creates a lack of recognition and memory of the divine. In this poem, this lack is illustrated through the representation of a courtesan's absence of beauty and the passage of wasted time that it represents, as well as her poor choices. Although as discussed earlier, it is only later, during the reform period leading up to Independence, that the courtesan became a reviled and disenfranchized identity, it is still noteworthy that the courtesan is a distinctive social identity within devotional poetry, as is revealed by noting the high-caste identity of Āṇṭāḷ, who was identified as a Brahman, and Mīrābāī, who was identified as a princess. Distinctive from these social identities, a courtesan was an independent woman, and so her ability to choose – and in this poem choose badly – is used in the devotional poem to provide a reminder of the choices one is able to make, and makes, as well as their consequences.

Men perform as women in other expressive traditions as well, notably ritual. K. Kapadia analyzes a Tamil → possession ritual that is informed by both *bhakti* and Brahmanic caste ideology. Middle-class non-Brahman men participate in the *alaku* rituals by "becoming female" in order that the deity (male or female) possess them, and they can in turn be pierced by metal hooks or spears (*alaku*) in order to manifest their contact with the divine. In this case, the female gender identity that is invoked is one that equates women with submission; the men "become women" in order to be submissive – of both heart (*bhakti* ideology) and body (Brahmanic ideology) – before the deity to demonstrate their suitability for possession:

> [W]ith all the possessed men of all castes, the process of becoming possessed involved a striking symbolic appropriation of what, to the Tamil mind, are female characteristics: the male devotee humbly submitted, "opened" himself and gave himself up, so that the deity might "enter" him. (Kapadia, 2000, 196)

These non-Brahman males use the rituals to increase their social prestige and capital in terms associated with Brahman males; they are "pure" enough for the divine, and they are also "complete" in their masculinity because of their ability to harness all powers, including wisdom (male) and energy (female; → *śakti*). Women are excluded from the ritual, the mastery, and the status.

Women Embodying Male-Defined Authority Roles

In contrast to men, who shape and perform identities that Hindu culture values as female, women perform roles that are traditionally defined as male and authoritative. The female identities men perform are used in expressions of devotion, and, while they have social significance, they often contrast with accepted social roles for women. Supporting this point is the fact that female poets were included in the canons of *bhakti* literature, yet many of the biographies that were written about them describe a conflict between devotion and womanly, usually wifely, duty. The corollary of this is that women who have a social identity that is authoritative tend to inhabit traditionally male-defined roles. As discussed earlier, women who are leaders in fundamentalist political organizations participate in a masculinist project. However, this does not mean that women who inhabit male-defined roles are always "masculine"; the most recent research on two increasingly prominent categories of female religious leadership in today's world, *guru* and ascetic, demonstrates that women transform these traditionally male roles along gender lines (see also → female ascetics).

Women's embodiment of male-defined authoritative social roles can be seen as an appropriation of the "other" that is a common strategy in self-definition. As U.T. Kragh argues with regard to tantric Buddhist materials,

> Self means to appropriate, for to say that the constitution of the female Self involves grasping is the same as saying that the female appropriates characteristics of an Other to constitute her Self. Appropriation is consequently not purely a male activity inflicted on the female Other, but it is the fundamental process by which any Self, male or female, comes into being. To explain the female's being-in-the-world is therefore to speak of "female appropriation." Literarily, uncovering the female Self requires a methodological move, away from the male-authored sources providing only male representations of the female over to female-authored sources expressing women's own subjectivity. It is in the latter that the hermeneutics of the female Self can reveal how her Self is pronounced through a mode of Other-appropriation. (Kragh, 2011, 96)

What can be added to this discussion is that as women appropriate such roles, they transform them, and that besides the limited but valuable record of texts authored by women in which they seek to inhabit male-defined authoritative roles, we can draw on ethnographic studies today on the embodiment of women in authoritative roles and the ways in which they challenge patriarchal textual representations.

A traditional distinction between the categories of → *guru* and ascetic is that *gurus* have a residence (*gurukula*) in which they, as teachers, take on students, as discussed earlier in this article. In contrast, ascetics are itinerant, often solitary religious men who have renounced the social world;

classical textual sources emphasize these features. However, ethnography reveals that

> the real lives of [male and female] renouncers invariably look quite different from textual ideals. And this is especially true in the case of women renouncers, since the texts are generally written by, for, and about men... Although renunciation often requires leaving families and communities, the path is rarely antisocial. (Hausner & Khandelwal, 2006, 4–5)

In particular, the received ideas on the performance of asceticism are being changed by female renouncers today through their emphasis on and engagement in → *sevā*, or service, performed from a fixed home base. S.L. Hausner notes,

> During my fieldwork, however, I found that most renouncers do actually base themselves in particular places. On occasion, they depart to visit a pilgrimage destination or to attend a religious festival, but when they do, they leave a base behind, sometimes with a padlock on the door, signifying eventual but certain return. The words for "home" in Hindi and Nepali are certainly shunned by renouncers, who speak instead of their "seats," (*asan*) or their "places" (*sthan*). But yogis and yoginis use their seats as home bases, and they interact with members of local communities as long-term and active residents. (Hausner, 2006, 125)

Significantly, where the female renouncers choose to settle is always someplace different from where they were born or where they were married (Hausner, 2006, 126). As independent and full-time religious practitioners, they are breaking from ordinary social expectations for women. As L. Knight argues, female → Bāul renouncers from West Bengal and Bangladesh use their religious identity to justify their single status in a cultural milieu that expects women to be married:

> They demonstrate that as renouncers they are no longer viewed merely as unmarried women, widows, or wives abandoned by husbands. Thus by aligning themselves with larger renouncer traditions, these women – so precariously situated between ideals for women and ideals for Bauls – gain some prestige and legitimacy implicit in being a *sannyasini*... these women reveal that they are not renouncing society at all, but rather society's expectations of them. (Knight, 2006, 192; see also Knight, 2011)

The female renouncers challenge aspects of social expectations for women, especially through their independence, their status as authoritative religious adepts, and, significantly, through their capacity to choose:

> As renouncers or *pagals*, they have created for themselves a space in which they can choose how involved they will be with society and family. For most of the women I interviewed, renunciation did not precipitate any severing of social ties, but it did provide them with an excuse for evading societal roles and expectations, and as single women alone they were then able to pursue their musical and/or spiritual path. (Knight, 2006, 216)

Within this frame, some female renouncers choose to redeploy roles that are socially defined as feminine and engage in feeding people, protecting children, and teaching religious values as a mother does (Hausner, 2006, 126, 134). Feeding people is especially prominent:

> While renouncers are ideally the takers (in the form of alms) rather than the givers of food, many female renouncers display a marked concern for feeding people... The women I met would invite me over for meals that they prepared and insist that I eat with enjoyment until satiated. The male renouncers I met displayed no such tendencies; they also seemed more comfortable in the position of eating food (usually prepared by someone else) before an audience of visitors. (Khandelwal, 2004, 187)

As A.E. DeNapoli discusses, actions such as feeding people are part of a paradigm of "devotional asceticism" that emphasizes duty, destiny, and devotion as practiced and promoted through gendered narrative strategies by female renouncers, as they "experience agency and authority in a gendered way" (DeNapoli, 2009, 84).

The difference between female *gurus* and female renouncers in today's world may be more one of degree than of kind. The figure of the *guru* is traditionally defined as a teacher who has disciples at an established *āśram*, and this is distinct from the classical itinerant renouncer, yet as we have seen, female renouncers today do tend to establish a home base, and they do offer spiritual instruction. Other areas of overlap between *guru* and renouncer include an ascetic persona, being unmarried or primarily defined as a *guru* even if married, and caring for people through *sevā*.

Today, *guru*- hood may extend more opportunities for women to engage in authoritative religious activities on a translocal or even transnational stage (Pechilis, 2004; Saha, 2007) and receive widespread recognition for such social service and humanitarian aid. This emphasis on service in turn distinguishes female *gurus* of the late 20th century from male *gurus* earlier in the 20th century. For example, Ma Jaya, whose motto is "Serve Others and Yourself" (Ma Jaya, 2012), has been recognized by numerous awards, including the Gandhi Foundation Award in 2007 for her service in advocating for people living with HIV/AIDS since the 1990s and her support for the LGBT (lesbian, gay, bisexual, transgender) community (see Narayanan, 2004). Ammachi (see → Mata Amritanandamayi Mission Trust), whose motto is "Embracing the World" (Ammachi, 2012), has been recognized by many awards, including the Gandhi-King Award for Nonviolence in 2002 for her loving compassion as well as her worldwide humanitarian activities, including disaster relief, free meals in "Mother's Kitchen," hospitals, orphanages, technical institutes for education in a variety of fields (including medicine and engineering), and many more (see Raj, 2004; 2005). Social service has also been embraced by male *gurus* today, such as North Indian *guru*-led devotional movements that collaborate with public health campaigns to encourage voluntary blood donation, including the Beas branch of the → Radhasoami movement (Copeman, 2009).

As A.E. DeNapoli's ethnographic study makes clear, stories of virtuous women that serve as a repertoire for female renouncers are an important line in to their perspectives on their identity, performance, and authority. The life stories of the female renouncers themselves are related to those they tell about classical female saints, some very well known on a pan-Indian basis (such as Mīrābāī), and others are more locally known (DeNapoli, 2009, 98). Such stories are important as resources with which present-day female renouncers (→ *sādhus*) construct their identity:

> Such thematic correspondences, first of all, strongly suggest these female *sādhus*' familiarity with the structure and content of the narratives of popular female *bhakt*s, particularly, in this case, those of the Rajasthani *bhakti* saint Mira Bai – and their use of such narratives as possible models of gender, *post factum*, for constructing and interpreting their own lives. To this extent, the female *sādhus* not only perform their personal narratives on the basis of popular (local) understandings of Mira's life, but also attribute their own asceticism to Mira's grace (*kṛpā*). As Shiv Puri told me, "It is by Mira's grace (*kṛpā*) that 'lady' *sādhus* have been able to take renunciation in Rajasthan." In this way, their personal narrative performances allow the female *sādhus* to construct a genealogy of female asceticism in Rajasthan and to create a Rajasthani tradition of female devotional asceticism by way of Mira's example, and thus, through her spiritual lineage. (DeNapoli, 2009, 98)

A folk legend that appears in southern regional variations on the → *Mahābhārata* and is popularly performed in rural Tamil Nadu today, the *Alli Aracāṇi Mālai* (The Qualities of Queen Alli [Water Lily]) also challenges traditional notions that conjoin feminine identity with feminine roles, especially those that draw on the Sāṃkhya philosophy discussed earlier in this article (Natarajan, 2007, in dialogue with Ramaswamy, 2006). This folk legend

> is not just a single freak folk legend but belongs to a genre of legends that are characterized by nonconformist, unmarried, childless women, who take up well-defined masculine roles. The overemphasized quartet of feminine virtues in Tamil society – timidity, naiveté, bashfulness, and sensitivity – are not simply ignored in these legends but relentlessly satirized. In their place, infidelity, ingenuity, astuteness, valor, courage, learning, capacity for leadership and administration, and refusal to succumb to heterosexual models of marriage are propagated in full strength. The classical and Brahmanical ideals of distinct spaces for men and women are boldly subverted. (Natarajan, 2007, 57–58)

The myth of Alli describes a queen (*aracāṇi*) who bonds only with her female subjects and is very successful in battle; she has an all-woman fort and lives inside, while the *Mahābhārata* epic hero Arjuna lives outside of the enclosed fort. Yet, Arjuna falls in love with Alli and compels Kṛṣṇa to help him capture her – capture, since when she hears about the smitten status of Arjuna, Alli rejects marriage as "ruining her power and status" (Natarajan, 2007, 60). By trickery, taking the shape as a snake owned by Kṛṣṇa as a snake charmer, the pair gain entry into the fort; there, Arjuna marries Alli by tying the wedding string around her neck while she is asleep. Alli attacks

Arjuna's hometown but is trapped. In an alternate version of the myth, Alli fulfills her role as a sovereign by taking to the forest to kill prowling animals, which are actually apparitions created by Kṛṣṇa, and which disturb her subjects; again Alli becomes trapped. As K. Natarajan discusses, the Sāṃkhyan equations are reversed; she (Alli) is an emblem of stability and the higher principle, while he (Arjuna) is the emblem of lust and confusion (Natarajan, 2007, 62).

Challenges

Challenges to the binary include gestures of reinscribing gender that complicate or decenter the binary in foundational ways; it is not a project of revaluing the halves of the binary, but of questioning its structure, descriptive power, and/or significance. At the same time, defining the nonbinary is performed in relation to the binary and thus in some sense reaffirms the binary. However, defining such a category compels humankind to think around, and even beyond, the binary, and thus it does affect the status of the binary. Several brief examples illustrate possibilities, including embodying and performing both genders of the binary simultaneously, prioritizing a non-gendered existence, and social activism that deconstructs gender toward imagining new social possibilities.

The Simultaneity of the Binary

The earliest literature in India, the texts of the vedic corpus, describes figures that embody both male and female traits, such as a cow that is a bull and a male creator with a womb. These images originate from imaging the world before creation as one that "lacked all distinctions and contrasts" (Zwilling & Sweet, 2000, 101). Such beings became understood in that literature as *napuṃsaka*, or "not male"; this term became the one used to name the "neuter" gender in Sanskrit in the *Śatapathabrāhmaṇa* (10.5.1.1–3; Zwilling & Sweet, 2000, 104). It is often glossed as "androgynous" today, though "androgynous" in this context means less "not clearly male or female in appearance" but more "having both male and female characteristics": "the connotation of being 'not a male' is to possess characteristics of both sexes, and this seems to be inherent in the basic meaning of *napuṃsaka*" (Zwilling & Sweet, 2000, 103). Thus, the concept of the "third gender" is based on the perceived simultaneity of male and female in one body. Examples from later Hindu mythology include Ardhanārīśvara, in which Śiva is portrayed as half male Śiva and half female Pārvatī, as well as the figure Mohinī, who is the male Viṣṇu portrayed as a beautiful woman, but whose significance is dependent on knowing that he is the male god. The category of "androgynous" in this sense was socially theorized across Hinduism, Buddhism, and Jainism, but there is evidence that it was not viewed as a socially acceptable category for human beings (Zwilling & Sweet, 2000, 107, 120–123).

In classical literature, such theorizing was centered on the "man in the form of a woman" rather than the "woman in the form of a man"; revealingly, a prominent example of the latter was a mare pulling a cart, in which the mare is not female because she is engaging in labor that is associated with masculinity (Zwilling & Sweet, 2000, 107). The tension, then, centered around socially classifying the prestige element (male) who appeared and/or performed the less prestigious element (female), rather than the reverse.

The → *hijṛā*s of present-day India are a marginalized and to some a controversial category, yet they have yet carved out a ritual status for themselves in terms of Hindu practice. The majority of *hijṛā*s are emasculated men who adopt women's clothing and behavior and live in casteless groups of *guru*s and disciples (Nanda, 1990, 2011). They locate themselves in Hindu mythological tradition by appealing to figures such as Śiva as Ardhanārīśvara, as well as figures from the *Mahābhārata* epic, including Arjuna Bṛhannala and Śikhaṇḍī (Nanda, 1990, 2011; Reddy, 2005). On the basis of on their identification with Arjuna and their status as devotees of the Mother Goddess (Mahādevī), they are cultural performers who ritually perform and offer blessings at the important life cycle rituals of childbirth and weddings. G. Reddy has argued that *hijṛā*s themselves focus not on a "third gender" identity but on authenticity as a primary characteristic, based on their detachment from established factions and interests; this detachment is embodied via their emasculation (*nirvāṇ*) ritual and enacted in their positive "neutral" participation in Hindu rituals and politics (Reddy, 2005).

The Value Beyond the Binary

The influential classical philosophical texts, the → Upaniṣads, are positioned as the "culmination of the Vedas" (*vedānta*) and thus are understood to be important interpretations of the earlier vedic literature. In this light, the Upaniṣads can be viewed as promoting a unity, → *brahman*, beyond dualities such as gender as well as paradoxes explored in the earlier literatures. It is a common theme across the Upaniṣads that the student desiring spiritual → liberation (*mokṣa*) must achieve a breakthrough in consciousness that is beyond all dualisms, including sense perceptions, the body, and the duality of knower and known. From the *Kenopaniṣad*,

> [i]t is thought of by the one to whom it is unthought;
> The one by whom it is thought of – he does not know.
> It is not understood by the understanders;
> It is understood by those who do not understand. (Roebuck, 2003, 165)

The Upaniṣads' endorsement of the practice of meditation as well as the goal of the transformation of consciousness toward identity with an undifferentiated spiritual reality has been enormously influential in the religious history of Hinduism, especially in its interpretation by the Advaita → Vedānta school of philosophy developed most famously by → Śaṅkara (c. 788–820 CE); the best accessible introduction to this aspect of this school remains that of E. Deutsch (1969). In such formulations, the duality of gender has no status in reality and is antithetical to the pursuit of spiritual realization.

Some devotional (*bhakti*) poets also sought to marginalize gender as a determinant of the path to god realization. For example, Lallēśvarī or → Lallā (c. 1320–1392 CE) of → Kashmir Śaivism imagined herself to be dissolved into god:

> Just as intense cold
> freezes water into ice,
> so the water of Consciousness
> contracts into three different forms:
> the individual, the world, and God.
> But when the sun of Consciousness shines,
> once again everything,
> both movable and immovable,
> melts into the one Supreme Principle.
> Lalli herself dissolved like that
> into Consciousness. (Muktananda, 1981, 47; Pechilis, 2004, 20–21; see also Hoskote, 2012, 105)

The Tamil Śiva- *bhakti* poet-saint, Kāraikkālam-maiyār (c. 550 CE; see → Nāyaṉārs), is known as a female author through an authoritative 12th-century volume that provided biographies of all of the Śiva- *bhakti* saints, and yet she did not identify herself as female in her poetry (Pechilis, 2011). Instead, she created a devotional subjectivity rooted in the "I" that applied to all human beings:

> Birth in this body
> enabled me to express
> my overflowing love
> through speech,
> and I reached your sacred henna red feet.
> And now I ask, oh, lord of the gods
> whose neck shimmers black,
> when will the afflictions
> that birth in this world also enables ever end?
> (Pechilis, 2011, 26)

Social Activism Today

Transformations in Hindu culture, such as the inclusion of women and lower-caste men as religious exemplars, were voiced by devotional poet-saints in medieval times. Reform movements during the late colonial period effected transformations, such as the status of women and widows in Hinduism. Today in India and South Asia, there are gendered social-activist movements that respond to Hindu and Indian cultural paradigms, often repurposing potent images from within Hinduism to describe and mobilize new perspectives on current issues. The literature is large and growing, so the following discussion can only present a few examples.

Feminist, or as some prefer pro-woman, movements have had a substantial history in India (Kumar, 2002). The journal *Manushi: A Journal about Women and Society* was founded in 1978 by M. Kishwar and R. Vanita and has provided a forum for the critical discussion of a range of gendered issues, including the recovery of women's contributions through history and literature, women's labor, dowry, and dress, while also from its beginning addressing a wide range of social issues in India and South Asia (Manushi, 2012). Other current discussions of feminist theory and activism also draw on the particulars of Indian experience to formulate larger conclusions; for example, an ethnographic study of women's experiences with non-governmental organizations aims to review the effectiveness of those agencies

(Nagar & Writers, 2006). Theorizing → feminism foregrounds experiences across South Asia to revision feminism and strengthen feminist activism (Mohanty, 2003; Loomba & Lukose, 2012).

Ecofeminism has had a prominent theorist in Vandana Shiva (2005, 2010), who has argued that the androcentric military-war industry, political ecology, and colonialism-imperialism have been at the center of the environmental crisis as well as gender oppression. She advocates revisioning our relationship to the earth based on Hindu understandings of the "feminine principle" as well as women's realities as agricultural laborers. Other studies have also emphasized the multiple resources within Hinduism and Indian tradition for enacting a balanced and just relationship to the land (Chapple & Tucker, 2000; Jain, 2011; Sanford, 2011).

Sexuality – its expression and its rights of expression – is another area of current activist intervention. There are a number of agencies in India that address such issues, including Creating Resources for Empowerment in Action (CREA), PRISM, Sangini, and Talking About Reproductive and Sexual Health Issues (TARSHI; 2012). PRISM, for example, self-identifies as

> inclusive of all gender and sexual expressions and identities, and the group's mission is to raise issues related to same sex sexualities that fall outside the heterosexual norm, and to interrogate the norm itself

and views all forms of sexual oppression as related through "intersectionality": "Our understanding of intersectionality is one that sees oppressions not as parallel, but as interwoven, simultaneously acting and mutually constitutive" (Sharma & Nath, 2005, 82, 91). Studies have also focused on aspects of lesbianism in India, including life experiences (Thadani, 1998; Sharma, 2006), expressions of queerness in Indian tradition (Thadani, 2007; Vanita, 2001), current controversies over film representations (Lohani-Chase, 2012), and activism (Dave, 2012). The Gay and Lesbian Vaishnava Association for Hindu Gauriya Vaishnavas (GALVA) argues strongly for a Hindu Indian history that legitimates the "third sex" (Sherma, 2005, 36–37; The Gay and Lesbian Vaishnava Association, Inc., 2012).

Mobilization has also taken place around caste issues, especially concerning those below the bottom and thus outside of the caste system, who self-identify as → Dalits, which translates to "oppressed" (which replaces the colonial name of "untouchables" as well as Gandhi's name of Harijan or "People of god"). An analysis of reactions to the Mandal Commission's recommendations in the 1980s and 1990s to reserve job and university places for Dalits exposes widespread cultural assumptions on their degraded cultural and social location (Chakravarti, 2002). Much of Dalits' contemporary mobilization has been to transform themselves from "stigmatized subject to citizen" (Rao, 2009). A case study of Dalit women explores activism in the women's movement in India as it is effected by rural women and as it affects them (Subramaniam, 2006).

Hindu culture has had a long, distinguished, coherent, contested, and continuing history of thinking about gender. Gender has been and is being constructed around a wealth of traditional materials, including legal texts, mythologies, sacred hymns, folksongs, and rituals, as well as lived realities in relation to them. As V. Narayanan has pointed out, the sources of *dharma* (sacred order, righteous behavior) are understood in the Sanskrit literature to be fourfold; two of the four are the sacred (vedic) literatures and the postvedic mythological and legal texts, but the other two are embodied in virtuous people:

> A third source is the exemplary behavior (*sadachara*) of the righteous people. The last source is considered *atma tushti*. While this is frequently translated as "conscience," it is also seen as that which gives peace or contentment to one's soul. (Narayanan, 2005, 31)

This classical framework itself thus understands tradition as that which is lived, and, as V. Narayanan rightly characterizes it, this validates innovation and change with respect to tradition.

Bibliography

Alter, J., *Moral Materialism: Sex and Masculinity in Modern India*, New Delhi, 2011.

Ammachi, "Amma.org," 2012, http://www.amma.org/.

Banerjee, S., *Make Me a Man! Masculinity, Hinduism, and Nationalism in India*, Albany, 2005.

Black, B., *The Character of the Self in Ancient India: Priests, Kings and Women in the Early Upaniṣads*, Albany, 2007.

Bose, M., *Women in the Hindu Traditions: Rules, Roles and Exceptions*, Abingdon, 2010.

Brown, C.M., *The Devī Gītā: The Song of the Goddess: A Translation, Annotation and Commentary*, Albany, 1998.

Bullough, V.L., "Gender," in: M.C. Horowitz, ed., *New Dictionary of the History of Ideas*, vol. III, Detroit, 2005, 870–873.

Butler, J., *Undoing Gender*, New York, 2004.

Butler, J., *Gender Trouble: Feminism and the Subversion of Identity*, New York, 1990.

Chakravarti, U., "'Through a Different Lens: Men, Women and Caste," in: T. Basu, ed., *Translating Caste*, New Delhi, 2002, 198–218.

Chakravarti, U., "Pativrata: The Ideological 'Purdah' of a Hindu Woman," *Seminar* 318, 1986, 17–21.

Copeman, J., *Veins of Devotion: Blood Donation and Religious Experience in North India*, New Brunswick, 2009.

Dasgupta, M., & M. Bose, "The Goddess-woman Nexus in Popular Religious Practice: The Cult of Manasā," in: M. Bose, ed., *Faces of the Feminine in Ancient, Medieval and Modern India*, New York, 2000, 148–161.

Dave, N., *Queer Activism in India: A Story in the Anthropology of Ethics*, Durham, 2012.

DeNapoli, A.E., "'By the Sweetness of the Tongue': Duty, Destiny and Devotion in the Oral Life Narratives of Female *Sādhus* in Rajasthan," *AsE* 68/1, 2009, 81–109.

Deutsch, E., *Advaita Vedānta*, Honolulu, 1969.

Dimmit, C., & J.A.B. van Buitenen, eds., *Classical Hindu Mythology: A Reader in the Sanskrit Purāṇas*, Philadelphia, 1978.

Doniger, W., & B.K. Smith, *The Laws of Manu*, New York, 1991.

Falk, N., "By What Authority? Hindu Women and the Legitimation of Reform in the Nineteenth Century," in: L.L. Patton, ed., *Jewels of Authority: Women and Textual Tradition in Hindu India*, New York, 2002, 139–156.

Findly, E.B., "Hinduism: An Overview," in: S. Young, ed., *Encyclopedia of Women and World Religion*, New York, 1999, 418–424.

Findly, E.B., "Gārgī at the King's Court: Women and Philosophic Innovation in Ancient India," in: Y.Y. Haddad & E.B. Findly, eds., *Women, Religion, and Social Change*, Albany, 1985, 37–58.

Gay and Lesbian Vaishnava Association, Inc., "GALVA-108," 2012, http://www.galva108.org/.

Gold, A.G., "Gender," in: S. Mittal & G. Thursby, eds., *Studying Hinduism: Key Concepts and Methods*, New York, 2008, 178–193.

Gold, A.G., "From Demon Aunt to Gorgeous Bride: Women Portray Female Power in a North Indian Festival Cycle," in: J. Leslie & M. McGee, eds., *Invented Identities: The Interplay of Gender, Religion and Politics in India*, New Delhi, 2000, 201–230.

Gold, A.G., "Gender, Violence and Power: Rajasthani Stories of Shakti," in: Nita Kumar, ed., *Women as Subjects: South Asian Histories*, Calcutta, 1994, 26–48.

Goldman, S.J.S., "Speaking Gender: *Vāc* and the Vedic Construction of the Feminine," in: J. Leslie & M. McGee, eds., *Invented Identities: The Interplay of Gender, Religion and Politics in India*, New Delhi, 2000, 57–83.

Harlan, L., "Heroes Alone and Heroes at Home: Gender and Intertextuality in Two Narratives," in: J. Leslie & M. McGee, eds., *Invented Identities: The Interplay of Gender, Religion and Politics in India*, New Delhi, 2000, 231–251.

Harriss-White, B., "Gender Cleansing: The Paradox of Development and Deteriorating Female Life Chances in Tamil Nadu," in: R.S. Rajan, ed., *Signposts: Gender Issues in Post-Independence India*, New Delhi, 1999, 124–153.

Hatcher, B., *Hindu Widow Remarriage: An Epochal Work on Social Reform from Colonial India by Ishvarchandra Vidyasagar*, New York, 2012.

Hausner, S.L., "Staying in Place: The Social Actions of Radha Giri," in: M. Khandelwal, S.L. Hausner & A.G. Gold, eds., *Women's Renunciation in South Asia: Nuns, Yoginis, Saints and Singers*, New York, 2006, 125–138.

Hausner, S.L., & M. Khandelwal, "Introduction: Women on Their Own," in: M. Khandelwal, S.L. Hausner & A.G. Gold, eds., *Women's Renunciation in South Asia: Nuns, Yoginis, Saints and Singers*, New York, 2006, 1–36.

Hawley, J.S., & D.M. Wulff, eds., *Devī: Goddesses of India*, Berkeley, 1996.

Horowitz, M.C., ed., *New Dictionary of the History of Ideas*, Detroit, 2005.

Hoskote, R., *I, Lalla: The Poems of Lal Ded*, London, 2012.

Jain, P., *Dharma and the Ecology of Hindu Communities: Sustenance and Sustainability*, Surrey, 2011.

Jamison, S., *Sacrificed Wife Sacrificer's Wife: Women, Ritual, and Hospitality in Ancient India*, New York, 1996.

Jassal, S.T., *Unearthing Gender: Folksongs of North India*, Durham, 2012.

Kannabiran, K., "Voices of Dissent: Gender and Changing Social Values in Hinduism," in: R. Rinehart, ed., *Contemporary Hinduism: Ritual, Culture, and Practice*, Santa Barbara, 2004, 273–307.

Kapadia, K., "Pierced by Love: Tamil Possession, Gender and Caste," in: J. Leslie & M. McGee, eds., *The Interplay of Gender, Religion and Politics in India*, New Delhi, 2000, 181–202.

Khandelwal, M., *Women in Ochre Robes: Gendering Hindu Renunciation*, Albany, 2004.

Kishwar, M., "Yes to Sita, No to Ram: The Continuing Popularity of Sita in India," in: P. Richman, ed., *Questioning Ramayanas: A South Asian Tradition*, Berkeley, 2001, 285–308.

Knight, L.I., *Contradictory Lives: Baul Women in India and Bangladesh*, New York, 2011.

Knight, L.I., "Renouncing Expectations: Single Baul Women Renouncers and the Value of Being a Wife," in: M. Khandelwal, S.L. Hausner & A.G. Gold, eds., *Women's Renunciation in South Asia: Nuns, Yoginis, Saints and Singers*, New York, 2006, 191–222.

Korte, A.-M., "Openings: A Genealogical Introduction to Religion and Gender," *RG* 1/1, 2011, 1–17.

Kragh, U.T., "Appropriation and Assertion of the Female Self: Materials for the Study of the Female Tantric Master Lakṣmī of Uḍḍiyāna," *JFSR* 27/2, 2011, 85–108.

Kumar, R., *A History of Doing: An Illustrated Account of Movements for Women's Rights and Feminism in India, 1880–1990*, New Delhi, 2002.

Leslie, J., "Gender and Religion: Gender and Hinduism," in: L. Jones, ed., *Encyclopedia of Religion*, vol. IV, Detroit, [2]2005, 3318–3326.
Leslie, J., *The Perfect Wife: The Orthodox Hindu Woman According to the Strīdharmapaddhati of Tryambakayajvan*, New York, 1989.
Lindquist, S.E., "Gender at Janaka's Court: Women in the Bṛhadāraṇyaka Upaniṣad Reconsidered," *JIPh* 36, 2008, 405–426.
Lohani-Chase, R., "Transgressive Sexualities: Politics of Pleasure and Desire in *Kamasutra: A Tale of Love* and *Fire*," *JLS* 16/2, 2012, 135–152.
Loomba, A., & R.A. Lukose, eds., *South Asian Feminisms*, Durham, 2012.
Ma Jaya, "Kashi," 2012, http://www.kashi.org/.
Manushi, "Manushi: Forum for Democratic Reforms," 2012, http://www.manushi.in/.
McDaniel, J., *Making Virtuous Daughters and Wives: An Introduction to Women's Brata Rituals in Bengali Folk Religion*, Albany, 2002.
McDermott, R., & J. Kripal, eds., *Encountering Kālī: In the Margins, at the Center, in the West*, Berkeley, 2003.
McGee, M., "Invented Identities: The Interplay of Gender, Religion and Politics in India," in: J. Leslie & M. McGee, eds., *The Interplay of Gender, Religion and Politics in India*, New Delhi, 2000, 1–56.
McGee, M., "Desired Fruits: Motive and Intention in the Votive Rites of Hindu Women," in: J. Leslie, ed., *Roles and Rituals for Hindu Women*, Rutherford, 1991, 71–88.
Marglin, F.A., "Femal Sexuality in the Hindu World," in: C. Atkinson, C.H. Buchanan & M. Miles, eds., *Immaculate & Powerful: The Femal Image in Sacred Image and Social Reality*, Boston, 1985, 39–60.
Menon, K.D., "Passionate Renouncers: Hindu Nationalist Renouncers and the Politics of Hindutva," in: M. Khandelwal, S.L. Hausner & A.G. Gold, eds., *Women's Renunciation in South Asia: Nuns, Yoginis, Saints and Singers*, New York, 2006, 141–169.
Menski, W., ed., *South Asians and the Dowry Problem*, Staffordshire, 1998.
Miller, B.S., *The Gītagovinda of Jayadeva: Love Song of the Dark Lord*, New York, 1977.
Mohanty, C.T., *Feminism Without Borders: Decolonizing Theory, Practicing Solidarity*, Durham, 2003.
Muktananda, S., *Lalleshwari: Spiritual Poems by a Great Siddha Yogini*, South Fallsburg, 1981.
Nagar, R., & S. Writers, *Playing With Fire: Feminist Thought and Activism through Seven Lives in India*, Minneapolis, 2006.
Nagarajan, V.R., "Threshold Designs, Forehead Dots, and Menstruation Rituals: Exploring Time and Space in Tamil *Kolams*," in: T. Pintchman, ed., *Women's Lives, Women's Rituals in Hindu Tradition*, New York, 2007, 85–105.
Nanda, S., "Hijṛās," in: K.A. Jacobsen *et al.*, eds., *Brill's Encyclopedia of Hinduism*, vol. III, Leiden, 2011, 82–89.
Nanda, S., *Neither Man nor Woman: The Hijras of India*, Belmont, 1990.
Narayanan, V., "Gender and Priesthood in the Hindu Traditions," *JHCS* 18/1, 2005, 22–31.
Narayanan, V., "Gurus and Goddesses, Deities and Devotees," in: K. Pechilis, ed., *The Graceful Guru: Hindu Female Gurus in India and the United States*, New York, 2004, 149–178.
Narayanan, V., "Gender in a Devotional Universe," in: G. Flood, ed., *The Blackwell Companion to Hinduism*, Oxford, 2003, 569–587.
Natarajan, K., "Desire and Deviance in Classical Indian Philosophy: A Study of Female Masculinity and Male Femininity in the Tamil Folk Legend *Alliyarasanimalai*," in: S.E. Wieringa, E. Blackwood & A. Bhaiya, eds., *Women's Sexualities and Masculinities in a Globalizing Asia*, New York, 2007, 47–66.
Oldenburg, V.T., *Dowry Murder: The Imperial Origins of a Cultural Crime*, New York, 2002.
Olivelle, P., "Ascetic Withdrawal or Social Engagement," in: D.S. Lopez, Jr., ed., *Religions of India in Practice*, Princeton, 1995, 533–546.
Osella, C., & F. Osella, *Men and Masculinities in South India*, London, 2006.
Pearson, A.M., *"Because It Gives Me Peace of Mind": Ritual Fasts in the Religious Lives of Hindu Women*, Albany, 1996.
Pechilis, K., *Interpreting Devotion: The Poetry and Legacy of a Female Bhakti Saint of India*, London, 2011.
Pechilis, K., "Introduction: Hindu Female Gurus in Historical and Philosophical Context," in: K. Pechilis, ed., *The Graceful Guru: Hindu Female Gurus in India and the United States*, New York, 2004, 3–49.
Pintchman, T., *Guests at God's Wedding: Celebrating Kartik among the Women of Benares*, Albany, 2005.
Rahajia, G., & A.G. Gold, *Listen to the Heron's Words: Reimagining Gender and Kinship in North India*, Berkeley, 1994.
Raj, S.J., "Passage to America: Ammachi on American Soil," in: C. Humes & T. Forsthoefel, eds., *Gurus in America*, Albany, 2005, 123–146.
Raj, S.J., "Ammachi, the Mother of Compassion," in: K. Pechilis, ed., *The Graceful Guru: Hindu Female Gurus in India and the United States*, New York, 2004, 203–218.
Ramanujan, A.K., V.N. Rao & D. Shulman, *When God is a Customer: Telugu Courtesan Songs by Kṣetrayya and Others*, Berkeley, 1994.
Ramaswamy, S., *The Goddess and the Nation: Mapping Mother India*, Durham, 2010.
Ramaswamy, S., "Body Politic(s): Maps and Mother Goddesses in Modern India," in: R. Davis, ed., *Picturing the Nation: Iconographies of Modern India*, New Delhi, 2007, 32–50.
Ramaswamy, V., "From 'Amazonian' Warrior to Submissive Wife: The Taming of Alli," *EPW* 41/17, 2006, 1661–1668.
Rao, A., *The Caste Question: Dalits and the Politics of Modern India*, Berkeley, 2009.
Reddy, G., *With Respect to Sex: Negotiating Hijra Identity in South India*, Chicago, 2005.

Rhodes, C., *Invoking Lakshmi: The Goddess of Wealth in Song and Ceremony*, Albany, 2011.

Rodrigues, H., "Women in the Worship of the Great Goddess," in: A. Sharma, ed., *Goddesses and Women in the Indic Religious Tradition*, Leiden, 2005, 72–104.

Roebuck, V.J., ed., *The Upaniṣads*, London, 2003.

Saha, S., "Hinduism, Gurus and Globalization," in: P. Beyer & L. Beaman, eds., *Religion, Globalization and Culture*, Leiden, 2007, 485–502.

Sanford, A.W., *Growing Stories from India: Religion and the Fate of Agriculture*, Lexington, 2011.

Sarkar, T., *Hindu Wife, Hindu Nation: Community, Religion and Cultural Nationalism*, Bloomington, 2002.

Schilt, K., & L. Westbrook, "Doing Gender, Doing Heteronormativity: 'Gender Normals', Transgender People, and the Social Maintenance of Heterosexuality," *GS* 23/4, 2009, 440–464.

Selby, M.A., *Tamil Love Poetry: The Five Hundred Short Poems of the Aiṅkurunūru*, New York, 2011.

Shabadi, K., "Speaking Our Gendered Selves: Hinduism and the Indian Woman," in: A. Jule, ed., *Gender and the Language of Religion*, New York, 2005, 257–269.

Sharma, J., & D. Nath, "Through the Prism of Intersectionality: Same Sex Sexualities in India," in: G. Misra & R. Chandiramani, eds., *Sexuality, Gender and Rights: Exploring Theory and Practice in South and Southeast Asia*, New Delhi, 2005, 82–97.

Sharma, M., *Loving Women: Being Lesbian in Unprivileged India*, New Delhi, 2006.

Sherma, R.D., "Introduction: A Hermeneutics of Intersubjectivity," in: T. Pintchman & R.D. Sherma, eds., *Woman and Goddess in Hinduism: Reinterpretations and Re-Envisionings*, New York, 2011, 1–16.

Sherma, R.D., "Hinduism," in: C. Manning & P. Zuckerman, eds., *Sex and Religion*, Belmont, 2005, 18–40.

Shiva, V., *Staying Alive: Women, Ecology and Development*, Cambridge MA, 2010.

Shiva, V., *Earth Democracy: Justice Sustainability, and Peace*, Cambridge MA, 2005.

Smith, B.K., "Ritual, Knowledge and Being: Initiation and Veda Study in Ancient India," *Numen* 33/1, 1986, 65–89.

Smith, F.M., "Indra's Curse: Varuṇa's Noose, and the Suppression of the Woman in the Vedic *Śrauta* Ritual," in: J. Leslie, ed., *Roles and Rituals for Hindu Women*, Rutherford, 1991, 17–45.

Soneji, D., *Unfinished Gestures: Devadāsīs, Memory and Modernity in South India*, Chicago, 2011.

Sterling, A.-F., *Sexing the Body: Gender Politics and the Construction of Sexuality*, New York, 2000.

Subramaniam, M., *The Power of Women's Organizing: Gender, Caste and Class in India*, Lanham, 2006.

TARSHI, "Talking About Reproductive and Sexual Health Issues: The South and Southeast Asia Resource Centre on Sexuality," 2012, http://www.tarshi.net/asiasrc/orgnzns/india.asp.

Thadani, G., *Moebius Trip: Digressions from India's Highways*, North Melbourne, 2007.

Thadani, G., *Sakhiyani: Lesbian Desire in Ancient and Modern India*, London, 1998.

Vanita, R., ed., *Queering India: Same-Sex Love and Eroticism in Indian Culture and Society*, London, 2001.

Venkatesan, A., *The Secret Garland: Āṇṭāḷ's Tiruppāvai and Nācciyār Tirumoḻi*, New York, 2010.

Walsh, J., *Domesticity in Colonial India: What Women Learned When Men Gave Them Advice*, Lanham, 2004.

Warne, R.R., "Gender," in: W. Braun & R. McCutcheon, eds., *Guide to the Study of Religion*, New York, 2000, 140–154.

Whitaker, J.L., *Strong Arms and Drinking Strength: Masculinity, Violence and the Body in Ancient India*, New York, 2011.

Young, K.K., "Women and Hinduism," in: A. Sharma, ed., *Women in Indian Religions*, New Delhi, 2002, 3–37.

Zacharias, U., "The Sita Myth and Hindu Fundamentalism: Masculine Signs of Feminine Beauty," in: K.A. Callaghan, ed., *Ideals of Feminine Beauty: Philosophical, Social and Cultural Dimensions*, Westport, 1994, 37–52.

Zwilling, L., & M.J. Sweet, "The Evolution of Third Sex Constructs in Ancient India: A Study in Ambiguity," in: J. Leslie & M. McGee, eds., *Invented Identities: The Interplay of Gender, Religion and Politics in India*, New Delhi, 2000, 99–132.

Karen Pechilis

Jādūgars

The phenomena that can be described by the terms *jādū* or *jādūṭona, ṭoṭaka, mūth, tantramantra* – that is, magic, sorcery, witchcraft and so forth – are some of the most persistent and pervasive aspects of South Asian cultures. They extend from the earliest vedic texts and, without skipping any historical period, persist even in New Delhi and Mumbai at the present time. Today one can find practitioners in every geographic, linguistic and cultural area in South Asia – from the Himalayas to the tribal communities of central India to the beaches of Kerala. The work of such magicians ranges from → divination to sorcery and witchcraft, and from religious rites to card tricks, and the selling of magical rings to urban and village street audiences.

Not surprisingly, the subject of the magician, sorcerer, juggler, or illusionist is marred by a great deal of confusion in India, as it is in the West. To begin with, there is no clear evidence that the professional who engages in magic (the *jādūgar*) is a distinct one or that the activity itself stands for a clear and identifiable domain within the broader religious context on the one hand and street entertainment on the other. Furthermore, the topic of magic is still heavily shaped by lingering Victorian ideas about invalid modes of thinking, by colonialist moral judgments of public performers as scoundrels and cheats, by popular misconceptions about → Tantra and by a variety of other factors. To make matters even more difficult, the terminology that touches on *jādūgar, jādū*, and related terms varies to such an extent along geographical and historical lines that one may legitimately wonder if there is a single topic here. Would a 19th-century Lahore street performer called a *jādūgar* represent anything that could be related to the enemy of a 5th-century *purohita* (royal priest) who mastered *abhicāra* (witchcraft) or to a 21st-century Banarsi healer? Can the term apply both to an illusionist or conjurer (not to mention juggler) who performs sleight-of-hand tricks and to an exorcist, a diviner, or a counter-sorcerer (*ojhā, sokhā, bhagat*)?

Despite these problems, a relatively small number of themes run through the scholarship that touches on the *jādū* and his work. The dominant theme deals with the distinction between the elite or Sanskritic ritual culture and the popular or local magical variation: what is the precise relation between the two – do they represent two ends of a single spectrum, two distinct but interacting traditions, or some other relationship? The issue applies in Nepal as much as Banaras or South India, and during the vedic period through medieval tantric periods up to the present time.

Lexical Meanings

According to J.T. Platts' dictionary of Urdu, classical Hindi, and English, the masculine noun *jādū*, from which *jādūgar* (practitioner of *jādū*) is derived, corresponds to "magic, enchantment, incantation, charm, conjuring, juggling."

Related to this, *jādūṭona* (sing. masc.) translates as magic, charms, and spells. The verb form, *jādū karnā-*, translates as the act of practicing incantations or magic, or to enchant, charm, bewitch, or conjure. *Jādūgar* (masc.) is magician, sorcerer, wizard, enchanter, conjurer, juggler. The female form is *jādūgarnī*, which stands for sorceress or witch, while the abstract feminine noun *jādūgarī* means magic, enchantment, necromancy, conjuring.

The term *jādū* derives from Old Persian *yādu*, Zend and Vedic Sanskrit *yātu*. In addition to other terms, as we shall see, the *Ṛgveda* uses *yātu* for sorcery or witchcraft (*ṚV*. 8.60.20), or the work of demons (*ṚV*. 7.21.5). *Yātumat* is the equivalent of *jādūgar* as sorcerer (*ṚV*. 7.104.20; 7.1.5), According to V.S. Apte's dictionary, *yātu* is derived from the passive participle *yāta* (from the Skt. verb *ya-*, "to go"), meaning gone or departed. Hence, *yātu* is traveler, wayfarer, wind, time, evil spirit, demon, and weapon. From the work of such demons and spirits comes the nominal usage or sorcery or witchcraft. M. Bloomfield's concordance lists numerous sources for *yātu*, including the following: *Ṛgveda* 10.87.25; *Atharvaveda* 1.7.1; 4.20.8; 4.3.4; 1.8.3; 7.70.2; *Taittirīyabrāhmaṇa* 2.4.2.2. The negative connontations of *yātu* in Vedic Sanskrit are juxtaposed with other, positive, terms such as → *māyā*, as we shall see below.

Perhaps due to the antiquity of *yātu*, "*jādū*" has a very wide distribution with regional variations in the local terms for wizards or sorcerers.

For example, Urdu has *sāhir* for wizard (male witch) or *afsoongar* for sorcerer. Nonetheless, a bewitcher can be *jādū tonā karnay wālā* ("magic maker") and the illusionist can be *shabdah baaz-jadugar-hasti ko faraib najar samajnay wala* ("the one who brings to life various silly impressions"; Ijunoon Online Urdu–English Dictionary). However, in Pakistan *jādūgar* can overlap with *pīr* (saint), and the two may be distinguished from *'amil*, understood as agent, operator, or exorcist (McClintock, 1990, 37, 47). K.P. Ewing shows that contemporary usage of terms such as *jādūgar* in Pakistan – and this applies across the subcontinent – always reflects some ideological agenda, which affects the meaning of the term (Ewing, 1997, 153). A young male informant describes himself as having been a magician (*jādūgar*) who had studied with an *'amil*. In such a context, the use of a term like *jādūgar*, which was perceived to be Hindi, demonstrates an act of political resistance in separating the speaker from normative discourse for his social context.

Due to the pervasive distribution of magicians, sorcerers, healers, and others throughout the subcontinent and due also to the fuzzy lines between *jādū* (in any of its lexical meanings) and other cognate phenomena such as divination, counter-sorcery, exorcism, and so forth, one must acknowledge the diversity of terms that may come into play in dealing with this subject. A broad collection of regional terms, assembled from secondary literature, can be found in F.M. Smith's significant work on → possession (Smith, 2006, 142–146). At the very least, F.M. Smith's collection, which glosses over local borrowings, loose usage, and other accidental factors, demonstrates both the universality of magical professions and the difficulty of generalizing too quickly. To give a brief sample: North Indian terms for exorcist include *jhāḍṇevālā, ojhā, mantravid*, and *mativah*. There are also healers called *siddh* (from the tantric term), *sayana*, and *bhopā*. There is the widely distributed *bhagat*, and the *bhuva*. In Bengal one finds the *rojā* and *guṇina* (in addition to the *ojhā*), and in Marathi the *devṛṣī* shaman or *jhāḍ*, who is a medium. Most of these, and dozens of other regional terms, are related to the work of divining and exorcizing ghosts – which fails to exhaust the work of so-called magicians in a healing, hurting, or entertaining capacity.

The Magician in the Ancient Period

Early research on the vedic literature was conducted long before Victorian understanding of magic became supplanted by the semiotic and performative theories of recent decades. In these colonial-era studies, the magician was identified as the figure who works with spells, charms, incantations, amulets, and so forth in order to combat sorcery and to promote prosperity, health, and love; defeat enemies; and obtain other pragmatic goals. Good magic (*māyā*) and the magician (*māyin*) set out to destroy the practitioner of bad magic or sorcery (*yātudhāna*) and undermine the work of demons or *rakṣasas* (Geldner & Pischel, 1899–1901; Hillebrandt, 1897).

Magic, in the sense of *māyā*, is often described as an obstruction of cosmic order and cosmogony. It is thus the force that Indra combats when he sets the planets on their course as he kills Vṛtra (*ṚV*. 1.32), or when he undermines the magic of Svarbhānu (*ṚV*. 5.40.6). Creation can be seen as the ordering of the senses (visually discriminating light and darkness) in the face of magically induced confusion. Hence, rgvedic cosmology here unites with psychology, and later on the *Śvetāśvataropaniṣad* capitalizes on this insight when it declares that the magician (*māyin*) creates this entire world by means of magic (*māyā*) out of the verses of the → Vedas, sacrifices, rites, religious observances, the past, the future, and the words of the Veda. It is all magic and illusion (*māyā; ŚvetU*. 4.9–10). But in the older vedic text, magic (*māyā*) is still either chaos or sorcery.

The god Agni is the special focus of appeals to defeat evil magicians:

> May the gods destroy the false ones today,
> May the poisonous curses turn back on him.
> May the arrows hit the sorcerer's weak spot.
> May the sorcerer become ensnared. (*ṚV*. 10.87.15; trans. by author)

According to the *Muṇḍakopaniṣad*, vedic culture recognized two types or levels of knowledge – the lower of which was the magical one:

> The knowledge of Brahman
> Which Brahmā taught him –
> Both the higher and the lower –
> Atharvan of old disclosed to Aṅgir,
> Aṅgir to Bhāradvāja Satyavāha
> Bhāradvāja to Aṅgiras (*MuU*. 1.2; trans. Olivelle, 1998, 268)

The lower knowledge is presumed to correlate with the *Atharvaveda* and its ritual manual – the *Kauśikasūtra*. These appear in two recensions – the *Paippalāda* and *Śaunaka*. The *Ṛgvidhāna* and *Bṛhaddevatā*, which deal with overlapping material for the performer of magical rites, are also attributed to Śaunaka. It has been the working assumption of generations of vedic scholars that what one calls magic is to be found in this collection of literature attributed to Śaunaka. The *Ṛgveda* itself is not generally "magical" by such standards unless it connects Agni to Atharvan and Aṅgiras (two mythic fire priests) directly (e.g. *ṚV.* 10.21.5; 10.62.5). Aṅgiras Bṛhaspati was identified as the *purohita* and magician of the gods and acted as the master of witchcraft and healing due to his knowledge of plants that relieve pain (*ṚV.* 10.97.15–19).

The distinction implied in older scholarship between magical technique and vedic religion (sacrificial, liturgical) can no longer be neatly sustained. Indeed, even the *Ṛgveda* (10.97.16) indicates that the troubles that the plants heal (through the magician's work) are not purely magical (like sorcery) in the traditional sense. The troubles have come from Varuṇa and from → Yama – that is, they are punishments for sins or offenses against gods rather than the work of sorcerers and witches. This ambivalence runs throughout the postvedic tradition: in the *Manusmṛti*, which is considerably later than the vedic corpus, religious functionaries such as Brahmans and the royal *purohitas* also perform magical tasks, for better or worse (*MaSm.* 11.33; 11.64).

The *Ṛgveda* as a whole is predicated on the clear belief that words of → *mantras* and ritual acts – sacrificial, not merely "magical" – can produce reciprocal results by the summoned gods. Such ritually and verbally contingent products are aimed at practical ends like wealth, health, long life, children, and so forth. There is no sharp distinction between the desired results of sacrificial action and counter-sorcery, no high religion as opposed to low religion, and no need to identify a distinct class of functionaries (magicians) in contrast to the ritual priest.

Indeed, as T. Elizarenkova (1995, 83–84) has noted, the very nature of rgvedic language is largely shaped by this reciprocal-magical assumption. Hence, to give one example, the qualities attributed to gods in formulaic epithets are not merely descriptive but performative, that is, magical or pragmatic as well. The naming of the god, the singing of his praise in various ascriptions, is part of the transaction in which uttered nouns and adjectives actually perform work that leads to the desired reciprocity of rgvedic action (Elizarenkova, 1995, 6).

More recent theories of magic allow us to identify rgvedic magic not just with the semantic qualities of *mantras* or the pragmatic function of rituals but also at the very foundations of vedic thought. As "speech act," the vedic *mantras* and actions reveal an intrinsic connection (*bandhu*) between apparently separate cosmological domains. For example, the sacrificial area is metonymically associated with the divine and cosmic contexts just as magical rites are linked with their goals (Patton, 2005, 80). Consequently, there is no absolute distinction among the four sacrificial → priests and the practitioners of magic (*yātu* or *māyā*) other than the moral distinction between beneficial and harmful results.

In the context of this understanding of magic and magicians, the texts of the *Śaunaka* school (*Atharvaveda, Ṛgvidhāna, Bṛhaddevatā*) represent a social departure from the sacrificial texts, not a break in worldview into a separate domain of magic. As noted earlier, the *purohita* (royal priest, embodied mythically in the figure of Vasiṣṭha) was knowledgeable in atharvavedic magic (beneficial and harmful or counter-sorcery and sorcery). The *brāhmaṇa* priest, the fourth priest in Śrauta rituals, who was responsible for *prayaścitta* (ritual expiation for errors), was also an atharvavedic expert. Both were familiar with atharvavedic rites, that is, *śānta* or auspicious formulas and those conferring prosperity as well as *aṅgiras* formulas, which included topics related to *abhicāra* (witchcraft) and *ghora* (horrific) rites – that is, sorcery. It is important to keep in mind that the so-called magical texts were still largely interested in the same goals as vedic action (prosperity, health, progeny, etc.) – but added a more focused awareness of the work of sorcerers as obstacles to these ends and deploy a greater range of technical means for overcoming these obstacles.

It is also important to remember that the *Atharvaveda* is as interested in fields of human endeavor that have traditionally been categorized as religious and ethical. For example, the subject of expiation – for ritual and moral transgressions – occurs in a large number of contexts (e.g. *AV.* 11.6; 6.112–113; 4.23–29; and elsewhere). Even the *Kauśikasūtra*, the ritual text assigned to illustrate the pragmatic contexts of *Atharvaveda mantras*, prescribes expiatory rites where magic dissolves into → *dharma* as a religious and moral domain (Glucklich, 2003).

For example, the *Kauśikasūtra* (63.1.2) prescribes a ritual act that includes the recitation of *Atharvaveda* 12.3.52. The text describes the manner in which the sin of falsehood that is deposited or cleansed, onto a garment, which is then discarded. The ritual runs as follows: "with this stanza they clothe themselves in the same garment. A second garment [, which they put on] becomes a garment [that carries off] evil" (*KauS.* 18.1.4.).

The range of topics to which the texts of the *Śaunaka* school attend is impressive. There are medical issues (possession, exorcism, fever, jaundice, cough, constipation, snakebites, pain, leprosy, skin ailments, infertility, etc.); methods for prolonging life, avoiding danger (physical, spiritual) and fighting sorcery, demons, and enemies; ways of using amulets; methods for obtaining love (husband, wife, a good marriage); erotic topics; sacred trees; topics of interest to kings (success in battle, governing, maintaining power); psychological issues (controlling anger or fear); business matters (farming, home construction, raising cattle and horses, avoiding fire, removing snakes); moral issues (expiation of sins, obtaining heaven, fighting evil omens); and many others. This synopsis merely highlights some of the topics in which the *Atharvaveda* is interested, however implicitly. It would be a mistake, to identify in the *Atharvaveda* a separate domain of activity, that of "magic."

And like the *Ṛgveda*, those troubles attributed to the work of a magician or sorcerer (*yātudhāna*) or demons (*piśācas*) are dealt with by means of a man who is knowledgeable in good and bad magic, or by Agni himself: "The god Agni has approached the killer of demons and expeller of diseases, burning away deceivers and sorcerers (*yātudhāna*) and *kimīdins* (a type of sorcerer)" (*AV.* 1.28.1). The healer or counter-sorcerer (the atharvavedic priest) may use a plant to reveal the identity of the sorcerer who has caused one's troubles: "Show me the sorcerer, show me the sorceress, all the *piśācas* – with this in mind I hold you plant" (*AV.* 4.20.6). The *Kauśikasūtra* text that cites this atharvavedic *mantra* has the priest tying the plant and using it as an amulet (*KauS.* 28.7).

According to M. Bloomfield, the *Kauśikasūtra* was neither a Śrauta nor a Gṛhya text and was *the* specialized manual for the use of atharvavedic *mantras*. V. Henry translated the *Kauśikasūtra* as "*magie*" and W. Caland as "*Zauber*," but the text stays very close to the *Atharvaveda* (whose *mantras* makes little practical sense without the ritual details) and is therefore no more and no less magical than the *Atharvaveda*. The same can be said for the *Ṛgvidhāna* in relation to the *Ṛgveda* – it is the manual of the *Śaunaka* school for applying rgvedic *mantras* to solve pragmatic problems (health, defeating enemies, obtaining peace, rain, handling women's issues – including infertility, removing fear and danger, identifying and defeating witches). For example, one could perform a rite of witchcraft (*abhicāra*) by reciting the *gāyatrīmantra* backward while offering mustard-seed oil into the ritual fire with a ladle made of *vibhītaka* wood (bot. Terminalia bellerica; Bhat, 1987, 114). Here again, the boundary between religion and magic dissolves, but more than that, it turns out that anyone with access to an expert can use a sacred text for the sake of hurting or helping others. The boundary between witchcraft as an evil force, or a sort of theodicy (explanation for misfortune) and the use of sorcery rites as a tool for legitimate struggle, is crossed. As previously noted, this is why a text like the *Manusmṛti* treats the *purohita* magician in an ambivalent manner.

The Medieval Period

Wandering ascetics were believed to have attained supernatural powers (or tools), *siddhis*, *ṛddhis*, *abhijñas*, and so forth. → *Sādhus*, *yogīs*, and later Muslim *faqīrs* and *pīrs* often claimed a connection to the ancient disciplines and a mastery of the texts that developed magical perfections and secret knowledge. It was widely known, for instance, that the *Yogasūtra* of Patañjali (ch. 3; see → Yoga) described ways of obtaining supernatural powers such as omniscience and omnipotence (*sarvajñatṛtva* and *adhiṣṭhatṛtva*), the attainment of various forms of bodily perfection, the ability to travel through the sky (*ākāśagamana*), levitation (*utkrānti*), and others. These were obtained through advanced concentration and meditation in yoga practice (*saṃyama*). The medieval commentators of the *Yogasūtra* – that is, Vācaspatimiśra, Bhojarāja, Vijñānabhikṣu, and others – unpacked the philosophical and psychological causes of perfections (*siddhis*) but did not try to rationalize them away (Jacobsen, 2012).

Instead, they argued that these *siddhi*s did not constitute the proper goals of those seeking → liberation, but only power and success in this world (Bryant, 2009, 338).

Individuals who claimed such powers received special, often caste-like, social distinction. Practitioners sought to reinforce this identity by cultivating behaviors that initiated and magnified the austerities and disciplines associated in the popular imagination with *yoga*, namely self-mortification and indifference to pain. Among such practitioners the *siddhi*s became a business. As L. Siegel points out, the Indian court magician-entertainer was a "profanation over time of the court magician-priest" and was the old *purohita*, who played such an important role in the *Atharvaveda, Manusmṛti*, and *Arthaśāstra*. Just as the late medieval street magician was the banalization of the *sādhu, yogī*, or *siddha*, the court performer was the lucrative imitator of the ancient *purohita* (Siegel, 1991, 152).

The tricks performed by such *jādūgar*s (professional entertainers) capitalized by means of religious props on the power of religious symbols to evoke awe or even produce moral associations. For example, L. Siegel (1991, 156) describes seeing an old trick (performed by Kareem Baksh) where the magician holds a hot dish with live coals and dangles a chain over it with his other hand, dipping it in oil. The oil suddenly blazes up due to the heat. This display of insensitivity to the pain of extreme heat not only is yogic power but also points to the fire ordeal in which insensitivity to a burning coal in one's hand is the mark of innocence or, more accurately, one's truthfulness (Glucklich, 1997, 92–93).

The religious props of the medieval and early modern performers also included (Skanda's) peacock feathers, → Kṛṣṇa's flute, → Śiva's drum, the → Aghorī's skull, Indra's staff or thunderbolt (*vajra*), and other ritually and mythically poignant objects. Some of these refer to familiar literary contexts: the magic pot that keeps on giving (food or drink), over which the *jādūgar* waives his wand, and which also figured in the *Jātaka*s and later in the *Kathāsaritsāgara* (10.57). In the so-called egg-bag trick, which was popular in Mughal India, the production of an egg out of thin air may have been a stage variation of the classical cosmogonic theme of creation by means of *hiraṇyagarbha*, the golden embryo, which was prominent in the *Manusmṛti* and can also be found in the → Upaniṣads and → Purāṇas.

Indeed, the medieval *Agnipurāṇa* and *Viṣṇudharmottarapurāṇa* condensed and extended the range of "magical" application for *mantra*s that had begun in the *Ṛgvidhāna*. The link to the vedic practice of applying verbal formulas, encased within rituals, to pragmatic and daily issues situates these Purāṇas in a long chain of magical practice. But, these eclectic texts also added the pervasive tantric concept of *ṣaṭkarma*s (the six actions that include pacification, attraction, creation of strife, subjugation, immobilization, and annihilation) to the vedic elements: the use of *mantra*s for the mostly aggressive purposes of harming one's enemies (*AgP.* 138.1–11). This came on top of the other "standard" features of magical arts: reading and combating omens, rites for winning battles, astrology – the *Agnipurāṇa* was clearly a manual for the royal *purohita*. Such texts again illustrate why it may be futile to distinguish and separate so-called magic (*yātu*) from other domains. For example, the coronation ritual in the *Agnipurāṇa* (218) is enormously detailed, and the symbolism of king-as-sacrifice – a majestic old vedic trope – is saturated with the use of amulets, divinatory cautions (against animals moving between the king and the flame), colors, substances, and phrases that are neither exclusively religious nor magical.

It is possible that the stubbornly held distinction between religion (elevated) and magic (popular and low) owes to the cultural dynamic that split the traditions of Tantra. D.G. White (1996, 7) argues that Tantra had been the predominant religious paradigm for the majority of Indians for a whole millennium. As earlier Tantra (popular and pragmatic) became intellectualized following → Abhinavagupta's (ca. 950–1020 CE) reformulation, only the Nāth *siddha*s (see → Nāth Sampradāya) continued to specialize in the practices that became excoriated as degraded. As D.G. White puts it in reference to alchemical knowledge, these men became "specialists in the concrete transmutation of base metals into gold and the concrete transformation of mortal, aging man into a perfected, immortal superman."

Clan-(*kula*-)oriented religion and practices (*kulācāra*) after the 10th century CE, aimed at worldly powers (*siddhi*) and bodily immortality (→ *jivanmukti*), prevailed over the prestigious transcendent goals of Tantra. Possession by dangerous → *yoginī*s was the preferred method, which required heroic qualities among the practitioners (*vīra*s). These *vīra*s, with their allegedly extraordinary powers (*siddhi*s), attracted royal patronage as *purohitas*. According to D.G. White, it was the eventual loss of this royal patronage that enshrined the split between the quietistic and the magical Tantra. The *ṣaṭkarmas*, which were elaborated in various tantric texts (e.g. the *Mantramahodadhi* [16th cent.]) and even Jain texts (e.g. Vimalacandra's *Ghaṇṭakarṇa Mantra Stotra* [16th cent.]), became the black-magic domain of the shamanistic tantric magicians.

The Nāth *siddhas* became popular as powerful kingmakers, but were mistrusted and rejected by the social and intellectual elite. While the elite tantric specialists had received initiation (that required true expertise), the others, mostly householders, often claimed authority by divine possession. They were accused of committing fraud and of being mere conjurers – the archetype of the *jādūgars* that populate India's busy street corners in colonial and modern times. They also came to be known as *yogīs* or *jogīs* – a derisive term, not to be confused with actual practitioners of *yoga*. The *yogīs* were heirs to the → Pāśupatas and → Kāpālikas, worshippers of Śiva's → Bhairava ("Horrific") form, and to → Aghorīs – naked or near-naked, long-haired ascetics besmeared with cremation-ground ashes. To their many detractors the Nāth *siddhas* were connected with black magic, sorcery, pollution, and sexual perversion. But their effect on the popular practices of *jādūgars*, with their props, faux *mantras*, and the aura of danger and death, was enormous.

The Modern Period

It may have been logical to begin an article on the magician in South Asia with the reports of colonial-period eyewitnesses, who set the tone for the way magic, sorcery, and witchcraft have been discussed during the last century. Indeed, many of these reports made their way into J. Frazer's *Golden Bough*, which has influenced this area of cultural practice almost irrevocably. In one of the most famous colonial-era descriptions, A. Dubois wrote,

> Among the degraded beings who form the dregs of society in India must be classed the jugglers, charlatans, mountebanks, conjurers, acrobats, rope-dancers... They are regarded as magicians and sorcerers, as men versed in witchcraft and all the occult sciences, and viewed with fear and mistrust. (Dubois, 1906, 73)

Others, like the Dutch merchant Francisco Pelsaert, the sailing master on the Bounty John Fryer, and the traveler and personal physician of Aurangzeb François Bernier, confused magicians/entertainers with *yogīs*, *tāntrikas*, and counter-sorcerers (such as *ojhās*), who intentionally or unintentionally performed in superficially identical ways. Such confusion, and its social consequences, may have been implicated in the decision of many visible magicians to convert to Islam. While the magicians (*jādūgars*) who had earlier performed in Jahāngir's court were Hindu (imitating *yogīs*, tantric *siddhas*, etc.), by the 19th century, many among them had converted en masse to Islam and became consolidated into a professional Muslim subcaste, the Maslets. This was designed to separate them from the *jādūgar* magicians, who carried a reputation as swindlers and con artists. Just as the Hindu magician earlier uttered "*yantru mantru tantru*" as their professional gibberish emulating tantric sounds, now the Muslim magicians whispered "*bismillāh*" to produce the effects of *simiya* – Islamic natural magic, that is, black and white *jādū* (Siegel, 1991, 161).

The earliest systematic reports on the work of sorcerers, shamans, magicians, and so on came from administrators, military men, missionaries, and travelers. Colonel E.T. Dalton published in 1868 his observations on the Kols of Chhotanagpur in *Transactions of the Ethnological Society of London*, where he described the *ojha* (of the Oraons) as resembling the African "medicine man" (Dalton, 1868, 32), as one who is consulted for identifying the spirit to whom one makes sacrifices in a village religion with domestic gods. Similarly, G.A. Herkalots was a colonial physician in Madras who commissioned and translated in 1832 the material supplied by his tutor Ja'far Sharif on Muslim magicians, astrologers, diviners, and exorcists. The material describes contemporary incantations (*da'wat*), making of amulets, and use of charms, horoscopes, and so forth. The raw data illustrates the influence of both Tantra and classical Islamic elements in the use of diagrams, letters, sprinkling of blood, and various modes of interaction with possessing spirits – *jinns* (Sharif, 1832, 235–236).

Early anthropologists followed these descriptive models. For example, W.H.R. Rivers, who spent years studying the Todas of the Nilgiri hills (in the late 19th to early 20th centuries), characteristically marked a separate chapter in his work for prayers, for sacrifices, for funeral ceremonies, and for "divination and magic." All of these were distinguished from the material on the social life of the Todas. W.H.R. Rivers divided his description into subsections on divination (including possession), on sorcery (including lists of "incantations"), on the evil eye, and on magical remedies (both *materia medica* and verbal formulas and omens). This chapter was followed by a detailed account of sacrificial rites, which were not regarded as magical.

Under the Victorian paradigm of homeopathic magic, as defined by E.B. Tylor and J.G. Frazer, magic was regarded as an area of distinct intellectual activity rather than a reflection of social and psychological dynamics that permeate all areas of life.

By the mid-20th century, researchers who were interested in magicians, exorcists, and sorcerers began to look at the social and moral contexts of such functions. Studies by S. Fuchs, V. Elwin, C. von Fürer-Haimendorf, M. Orans, R. Rahman, R. and S. Freed, F.G. Bailey, and numerous other ethnographers began to discriminate within the general concept of magician between such roles as *parihar* or *bhagat, ojhā* or *sokhā*, or between the shaman who heals by becoming possessed as opposed to the one who has access to a mantra or some ritual technique. The profession was finally distinguished from the street performer, the magician who entertains by sleight of hand. The divination procedure, for example, in S. Fuchs's study of the Korkus in Madhya Pradesh, is now understood as subjective readings of ritual signs, which gives the diviner a great deal of freedom in his diagnostic interpretation. The actual divination or identification of the problem (including the search for witches), as F.G. Bailey has shown, can become a social exercise within a specific moral cosmology.

Sorcerers and Magic Today

Ethnographic scholarship in South Asia today, postcolonial in its ideological sensibility and armed with the most recent theoretical and methodological tools, looks at the magician in a variety of contexts. There are two key (but hardly exclusive) issues. First, what is the relationship between the popular tradition of ghost possession, exorcism, and other related practices, on the one hand, and the solemn tradition of priestly sacrifices (including cremation and obsequies), on the other? Second, and closely related to that question, is the sociological and psychological issue raised by I.M. Lewis (1989) in which ghost possession is associated with social vulnerability and acts as an implicit revolt against the prevailing social power.

To give a few prominent examples, J. Parry's discussion (1994) of *ojhā*s and *sokhā*s in *bhūtpret* (ghost of the dead) rituals (exorcism) in Banaras makes the point that these replicate rather than resist the social hierarchy of the Brahman priests (who conduct the funerary rituals) and that these popular practices, common mostly among low-caste rural women and the urban poor, do constitute a distinct tradition. The *ojhā's* identification of a possessing spirit (*mari, bhavani, churail*, or the *jinn* of a Muslim wrestler) usually points to reproductive failure or to a specific social conflict. The *sokhā* identifies the ghost, while the *ojhā* (when the two are separate individuals) traps and drives the spirit out.

But there is no fixed way in which such folk-level exorcists operate. For example, Ram Prasad, who works at Assi Ghat, is both diviner and exorcist, and he is also a shaman – that is, he becomes possessed by the goddess (→ Durgā) in the act of exorcism. He drives the *bhutpret* into a clove of garlic, which is force-fed to a fish, which is released into the → Gaṅgā while pseudo-tantric *mantra*s are mumbled. He may also identify the cause of his patient's infertility (or other troubles) as the jealousy of a co-villager (Glucklich, 1997, 141–142).

Among the Newars in Nepal, there are two types of practitioner who specialize in the diagnosis and cure of misfortune with supernatural etiology. These are the healer and the medium or the *vaidya* and *dyaḥ waimha* (Gellner, 1994, 31). Healers are always men, while women may work as mediums – possessed by a deity (esp. Hārītī, the goddess of smallpox) during the healing process. The *vaidya* is not possessed but uses a variety of specialized techniques including ayurvedic and tantric rituals. The most common act, familiar throughout North India, is brushing, which removes evil influence, and the blowing of *mantra*s onto the patient. Like J. Parry, D. Gellner too works in conversation with I.M. Lewis. He has found that the increase in the number of female mediums in the Kathmandu Valley correlates with the improvement of women's position, reflecting a "democratization of religious legitimacy" (Gellner, 1994, 43). This observation runs against I.M. Lewis' theory, which posits that such increasing activity should correlate with resistance against the deteriorating condition of women.

The substantial volume of work on shamans, diviners, exorcists, counter-sorcerers, and others makes it clear that it is extremely difficult to generalize about a single basic function – social or political – that underlies these phenomena. S. Sinha (2007) has argued that British administrative bans on "witch hunts" in Chhotanagpur in the mid-19th century turned such activities into modes of resistance to colonial rule in the 1850s in a way vaguely similar to the cultural contest in today's Banaras between the folk healer and the priest's ritual hegemony or even the allopathic physician's institutional superiority. S. Sinha notes that beliefs in *dain*s (witches) and *banga*s (spirits) increased sharply among the Santals who employed *ojhā*s, *mati*s, *sokhā*s, or *jan guru*s in rites of both white and black magic to deal with social tensions, jealousy, and betrayal at a time when the British insisted on providing their own institutions for conflict resolution over those of the villagers. It may be possible to say that such politicization of witchcraft is opportunistic, and, indeed, it demonstrates the resistance to or collapse of authoritative institutions of government. This appears to confirm D.G. White's ideas of the way tantric practices became blended with folk practice when it lost royal patronage.

Seen in this way, the work of the *ojhā* – and the event of possession – can no longer be understood by a singular theoretical lens such as a spontaneous eruption of subconscious conflicts. On the contrary, they may even be regarded as carefully scripted and choreographed mimetic performances (Snodgrass, 2002) that show a profound grasp of the dynamics involved in the practices of human beings and an elaborate strategy of increasing control.

Of course, not all researchers see sorcery through such a nonpsychological prism. On the basis of research on sorcery and counter-sorcery in the South Arcot district of Tamil Nadu, I. Nabokov has concluded that sorcery is a destructive force designed to remove someone from the patient's life while undermining his or her personal identity (2000a, 149). The Tamil logic of sorcery is determined by a confrontation with powerful negative situations that result in paralysis, mutism, trances, convulsions, and so forth. The *cāmi* as the counter-sorcerer conducts rites of counter-sorcery that are designed to empower the victim to confront and decode the situation (caused by the sorcerer or *mantiravāti*) in order to move on (2000, 153). The emotions perceived during the ritual are not to be dismissed as merely choreographed social strategies. Still, the practitioners at these sites are locally ridiculed by the high-ranking "Sanskritized" castes (Cettiyar, Mutaliyar, Acari).

No contemporary researcher would think of confusing the work of folk healers (or counter-sorcerers) with street magicians, not even those who sell folk remedies such as snake, lizard, or fish oil after demonstrating their efficacy in magical performances. Such shows can be seen virtually everywhere in India, including the major cities. The *jādūgar*s who engage in for-profit shows may appeal to the psychological and social benefits of their products and may emulate respected traditions (Tantra, Yoga). But, their performances have not drawn the attention of anthropologists, with the rare exception of a historian of religion and a magician like L. Siegel. One such show, where the product was a set of magical rings, is regularly held behind the municipal court in Banaras. There are two magicians, acting as brothers. One lies on the ground and is put into a trance by means of "tantric" utterances, and a ring is placed over a blanket that covers him completely. The other "brother" wears a similar ring and looks at the serial number on rupee notes or listens to the whispered details of court cases. The man on the ground then accurately repeats this information – their "mind reading" made possible by the rings. After the show, the rings are sold to willing spectators (Glucklich, 1997, 154–155).

There are many performers, throughout Banaras and all over India, who serve their clientele by means that the Victorian scholar would deem to be "magical" rites and objects. They are not all exorcists, shamans, diviners, or sorcerers. There are also herbalists, astrologers, jewelers, temple priests, *yogī*s (in the strict sense), chiropractors, tantric wholesale vendors, housewives, boat men, palm readers, specific experts (for dog bites, snake bites, fractures, etc.), would-be → Āyurveda vendors, and many others. Some are experts in a broad tradition, while others are familiar with a single remedy passed on in the family. Some will use sleight of hand, and others will condemn this practice as inauthentic. In a large urban setting like Banaras – and undoubtedly other South Asian cities as well – there is a dynamic and shifting interaction between ancient and contemporary traditions.

The magicians – *jādūgar, ojhā, sokhā, paṇḍā*, and others – represent an ancient and persistent range of functions. They may imitate the elite traditions, and they may contest elite power, but the reverse is often true as well. Priests in major temples (e.g Viśvanāth Mandir in Banaras) often utilize magical practices, and male middle-class patients may visit a village herbalist or shaman who happens to be a woman. While South Asia's rapidly changing social, economic, and ecological life has resulted in the diminishment of such phenomena, it is still unclear which causes have been the decisive ones and how this has taken place.

Bibliography

Apte, V.S., *The Practical Sanskrit-English Dictionary*, Poona, 1957–1959.

Bailey, F.G., *The Witch-Hunt, or: The Triumph of Morality*, Ithaca, 1994.

Bernier, F., *Travels in the Moghul Empire A.D. 1656–1668*, Lahore, 1976.

Bhat, M.S., *Vedic Tantrism: A Study of Rgvidhana of Saunaka with Text and Translation*, Delhi, 1987.

Bloomfield, M., ed., *The Kauśika Sūtra of Atharva Veda*, Delhi, 1979.

Bryant, E.F., *The Yoga Sūtras of Patañjali: With Insights from the Traditional Commentators*, New York, 2009.

Caland, W., *Altindisches Zauberritual: Probe einer Uebersetzung der wichtigsten Theile des Kauśika Sūtra*, Amsterdam, 1900.

Cort, J.E., "Worship of Bell-Ears the Great Hero, a Jain Tantric Deity," in: D.G. White, ed., *Tantra in Practice*, Princeton, 2000, 417–433.

Dalton, E.T., "The 'Kols' of Chota-Nagpore," *TESL* 6, 1868, 1–41.

Dubois, J.A., *Hindu Manners, Customs, and Ceremonies*, Oxford, 1906.

Dwyer, G., *The Divine and the Demonic: Supernatural Affliction and Its Treatment in North India*, London, 2003.

Elizarenkova, T., *Language and Style of the Vedic Ṛṣis*, Albany, 1995.

Elwin, V., *The Agaria*, London, 1942.

Ewing, K.P., *Arguing Sainthood: Modernity, Psychoanalysis, and Islam*, Durham, 1997.

Frazer, J.G., *The Golden Bough: A Study in Comparative Religion*, London, 1890.

Freed, R.S. & S.A., *Ghosts: Life and Death in North India*, New York, 1993.

Fryer, J., *A New Account of East Asia and Persia: Being Nine Tears' Travels*, New Delhi, 1992.

Fuchs, S., *The Korkus of the Vindhya Hills*, New Delhi, 1986.

Fürer-Haimendorf, C.V., *The Gonds of Andhra Pradesh: Tradition and Change in an Indian Tribe*, London, 1979.

Geldner, K.F., & R. Pischel, *Vedische Studien*, 3 vols., Stuttgart, 1889–1901.

Gellner, D., *Monk, Householder, and Tantric Priest: Newar Buddhism and Its Hierarchy of Ritual*, Cambridge UK, 1992.

Gellner, D., "Priests, Healers, Mediums and Witches: The Context of Possession in the Kathmandu Valley, Nepal," *Man.NS.* 29/1, 1994, 27–48.

Glucklich, A., "A Cognitive Analysis of Sin and Expiation in Early Hindu Literature," *IJHS* 7/1–3, 2003, 55–73.

Glucklich, A., *The End of Magic*, New York, 1997.

Gonda, J., *Vedic Literature (Samhitas and Brahmanas)*, Wiesbaden, 1975.

Guha, A., "Folk Medicine of the Boro-Kacharis – A Plains Tribe of Assam," in: B. Chaudhuri, ed., *Tribal Health: Socio-cultural Dimensions*, New Delhi, 1986, 191–199.

Henry, V., *La magie dans l'Inde antique*, Paris, 1909.

Hillebrandt, A., *Ritualliteratur*, Strasbourg, 1897.

Jacobsen, K.A., ed., *Yoga Powers: Extraordinary Capacities Attained through Meditation and Concentration*, Leiden, 2012.

Lewis, I.M., *Ecstatic Religion: A Study of Shamanism and Spirit Possession*, London, 1989.

McClintock, W., "Demons and Ghosts," *MIR* 18/1, 1990, 37–47.

Nabokov, I., "Deadly Power: A Funeral to Counter Sorcery in South Asia," *AE* 27/1, 2000a, 147–168.

Nabokov, I., *Religion against the Self: An Ethnography of Tamil Rituals*, New York, 2000b.

Olivelle, P., *The Early Upanishads*, New York, 1998.

Orans, M., "A Tribal People in an Industrial Setting," *JAF* 71/281, 1958, 422–445.

Parry, J., *Death in Banaras*, Cambridge UK, 1994.

Patton, L.L., *Bringing the Gods to Mind: Mantra and Ritual in Early Indian Sacrifice*, Berkeley, 2005.

Pelsaert, F., *A Dutch Chronicle of Mughal India*, Lahore, 1978.

Platts, J.T., *A Dictionary of Urdu, Classical Hindi, and English*, London, 1984.

Rahman, R., "Shamanistic and Related Phenomena in Northern and Middle India," *Anthropos* 54, 5/6, 1959, 681–760.

Rivers, W.H.R., *The Todas*, 2 vols., Jaipur, 1986.

Sharif, J., *Islam in India or the Qanun-I-Islam*, London, 1972.

Shende, N.J., *The Religion and Philosophy of the Atharvaveda*, Poona, 1985.

Siegel, L., *Net of Magic: Wonders and Deceptions in India*, Chicago, 1991.

Sinha, S., "Witch-Hunts, Adivasis, and the Uprising in Chotanagpur," *EPW* 42/19, 2007, 1672–1676.

Smith, F.M., *The Self Possessed: Deity and Spirit Possession in South Asian Literature and Civilization*, New York, 2006.

Snodgrass, J.G., "Imitation is Far More than the Sincerest of Flattery: The Mimetic Power of Spirit Possession in Rajasthan, India," *CA* 17/1, 2002, 32–64.

Stutley, M., *Ancient Indian Magic and Folklore: An Introduction*, New Delhi, 2001.

Tylor, E.B., *Religion in Primitive Culture*, Gloucester MA, 1970.

White, D.G., *Kiss of the Yogini: "Tantric Sex" in Its South Asian Contexts*, Chicago, 2003.

White, D.G., *The Alchemical Body: Siddha in Medieval India*, Chicago, 1996.

Ariel Glucklich

Śrīvidyā

Śrīvidyā is a relatively recent name for a tradition centered on the worship of the goddess Tripurasundarī (see Padoux, 1994, 5, on the modern use of the term Śrīvidyā). Tripurasundarī, or Tripurā, also referred to as Rājarājeśvarī and Lalitā, is conceptualized as the supreme deity, a beautiful and auspicious manifestation of the Great Goddess (→ Mahādevī). Meditation (*dhyāna*) verses used for the visualization of Tripurasundarī describe her holding a goad, noose, bow of sugarcane, and arrows of flowers. Her reddish complexion or red garments are also mentioned, and the descriptions of Tripurasundarī abound in imagery connected with red. "Śrīvidyā" is a Sanskrit compound designating the name of the principal → *mantra* (*mūlamantra*) of this tradition, *śrī* being an honorific, and *vidyā* "a feminine mantra – the mantra of a female deity" (Padoux, 1994, 5). As is common in Sanskrit, there are a number of other interpretations of the term, based, for example, on taking *śrī* in the meaning of *saubhāgya*, that is, "good fortune, success, happiness, as well as beauty or charm; all these terms evoke an important aspect of the tradition" (Padoux, 1994, 5). In addition, the second part of the compound, *vidyā*, can be taken in its

Fig. 1: Statue of Rājarājeśvarī at the Śrī Rājarājeśvarī Pīṭham in Rush, NY, USA (photo by Anna Golovkova).

nontechnical meaning of "knowledge, wisdom" (see Brooks, 1992, 81–82). While Śrīvidyā's earliest extant Sanskrit text, the *Vāmakeśvarīmata*, probably written in the early 11th century CE or earlier, is a tantric text (see → Tantras) focusing on external ritual, over time extensive internal meditative practices have also been developed. By at least the 13th century CE, when Jayaratha, Śivānanda, and Vidyānanda composed their commentaries on the *Vāmakeśvarīmata*, Śrīvidyā emerged as a sophisticated pan-Indian tradition with a well-developed exegesis drawing on the "Krama-influenced, Pratyabhijñā-based exegesis of scripture in the Trika," which had become a dominant textual resource of "exegetical and spiritual inspiration" (Sanderson, 2007, 427–434; for dates of these commentators, as well as Amṛtānanda, who composed a commentary on the *Yoginīhṛdaya* [c. 14th century CE], see Sanderson, 2007, 412–419; for Krama, Pratyabhijñā, Trika, see also → Kashmir Śaivism). In time, in South India an expurgated form of Śrīvidyā became subsumed by the *śaṅkarācārya*s, the spiritual authority of the broader community of the orthodox Śaiva Brahmans known as → Smārtas (Sanderson, 1988, 689, 704). Later commentators, such as the 18th-century Bhāskararāya and the 19th-century Śivarāmasvamin (author of the *Gayatrīmantravivṛtti* and the *Śrīvidyāmantravivṛtti*), attempted to reconcile the vedic and the tantric domains, and contemporary branches of Śrīvidyā include the Advaita → Vedānta theologian → Śaṅkara, author of the commentary on the *Brahmasūtra*, as one of the preceptors of their lineage. While Śrīvidyā ritual has been traditionally practiced in the homes of the initiated in relative secrecy, some of its features have been incorporated into the mainstream Hindu temple worship, and the most treasured hymns of the tradition, the *Lalitāsahasranāma* and the *Saundaryalaharī*, have remained the focus of popular devotion. Initiation into Śrīvidyā has been traditionally open to women and men, regardless of caste (see e.g. Brooks, 1992, xiii) – however, in practice, many contemporary *guru*s deny initiation to those who are not male Brahmans (see Dempsey, 2006, for a study of Śrī Rājarājeśvarī Pīṭham in Rush, NY, for a notable exception to this practice; in particular see Dempsey, 2006, 92–93).

The Nityā Cult and the Emergence of Śrīvidyā

Although the early history of Śrīvidyā is obscure, several extant texts suggest the existence of an antecedent Tantric cult that propitiated the *nityā* goddesses, serving as the subordinate deities to Tripurā. In this earlier tradition, "rites for success in love predominated," and the Tripurasundarī's consort was Kāmadeva (the god of love), not Śiva, as in the mature Śrīvidyā tradition (Sanderson, 2009, 47; for textual evidence of the *nityā* cult, see Sanderson, 2009, 47–49). Among the earliest sources for the worship of Tripurasundarī is the text of the Sanskrit *Nityākaula* surviving in a single incomplete palm-leaf manuscript from Nepal. In this text, Tripurasundarī is accompanied by Kāmadeva and a retinue of 11 *nityā* goddesses. The *Siddhakhaṇḍa* of the *Manthānabhairavatantra* preserves a variant of the *nityā* cult, providing instructions for the worship of Tripurasundarī with her consort and a retinue of nine *nityā*s. The third text identified in connection with the *nityā* cult is a syncretistic text belonging to the cult of the goddess Kubjikā, the *Ciñciṇīmatasārasamuccaya*. This text "contains a section drawn from the Nityākaula, or from some lost text closely related to it" and shows an early classification of the Kaula doctrines, in which the *nityā* cult is classified as the tradition of the southern order (*dakṣiṇagharāmnāya*; Sanderson, 2009, 48–49).

At this time, not much can be said about the dating of this antecedent cult with certainty, except that it flourished prior to the 11th century and perhaps significantly earlier than that, based on the references to the worship of *nityā*s in the *Kubjikāmata* and the later *Jayadrathayāmala* (see Sanderson, 2010, 47–48; see also below). Furthermore, the cult of the *nityā*s was known to → Abhinavagupta (*TĀ.* 28.123–124 [*nityātantravidaḥ*]; *PaTrV.* [*śrīnityātantreṣu*; see Gnoli, 1985, 238]). The rites of love magic, predominant in the ritual of the *nityā* cult, formed the backdrop against which the mature cult of Tripurasundarī developed. Although this connection has been deemphasized in the later Śrīvidyā scriptures and exegesis, references to love magic have been preserved in the names of the subordinate goddesses (e.g. the 16 deities of attraction [*ākarṣa*], worshipped in the outer petals of the *śrīcakra* [*VāMa.* 1.138–141]), the descriptions of the physical beauty of Tripurasundarī (who is portrayed as red, the color most vested with amorous connotations), and the expected results of worship, which encompass the amorous attraction of women to the ritualist (e.g. *VāMa.* 4.38–41). Furthermore, the bow, five flower-arrows, noose, and goad, which Tripurasundarī holds in her hands, are the standard attributes of the four-armed Kāmadeva (for his visualization see, e.g., the *Īśānaśivagurudevapaddhati, Kriyāpāda*, 22.32–35). Although the benefits of amorous attractiveness have ceased to be the focal point of the worship of Tripurasundarī over time, perhaps it is this very capacity of this tradition to embrace all aspects of human existence – from the mundane to the sublime – that contributed to its popularity.

Śrīvidyā, Brahmanism, and the Cults of the Local Goddesses

There is no evidence that the ritual practice of the *nityā* cult has survived the reshaping of the landscape of the Hindu Tantra following the tremendous creative development of Śaivism during the 10th to 12th centuries. However, the Śrīvidyā tradition, which likely developed out of this earlier cult toward the end of the early medieval period, flourishes to this day in pan-Indian ritual practice. Many Śrīvidyā texts and commentaries are extant. The mature Śrīvidyā developed a sophisticated commentarial tradition, which upgraded a modest cult of love magic with the exegesis within the Kashmirian nondualistic Śākta-Śaiva discourse. The worship of Tripurasundarī flourished in → Kashmir, in the Kathmandu Valley, in Tamil Nadu, in Andhra Pradesh, and among the Nambūtiri Brahmans of → Kerala, as well as in Gujarat and Uttar Pradesh. In east India (see → Assam), Tripurasundarī (also known as Ṣoḍaśī) was incorporated into the tradition of the ten *mahāvidyā*s (on geographical distribution of Śrīvidyā, see Sanderson, 2010, 80–83; for *mahāvidyā*s see → Kālī).

In a later development, "Śrīvidyā appears to have undergone something of a reformation in the south" (Brooks, 1992, 48). Tripurasundarī came to be seen as the esoteric essence of the local goddesses in the major temples of Shringeri, Kanchipuram, Srisailam, and Madurai, and in less well-known temples such as the Akhilāṇḍeśvarī (Tam. Akilāṇṭēcuvari) temple in Tiruchirappalli, Tamil Nadu, and the Mūkāmbikā temple in Kollur, Karnataka. In Kashmir, as in South India, the cult of Tripurasundarī provided the "framework for the conceptualization of the cults of the local goddesses" (Sanderson, 2007, 433). With the adoption of an expurgated form of Śrīvidyā by Smārta Brahmans, whose tendency was to "distance themselves from Kashmiri Kaulism in order to distinguish Śrīvidyā from... Tantrism," a number of texts on the worship of Tripurasundarī, "which were acceptable to even the most conservative Hindus," came to be attributed to Śaṅkara and his *paramaguru* (*guru*'s *guru*) Gauḍapāda, who were "viewed as pillars of conservative orthodoxy" (Brooks, 1992, 49–50).

Classification

The classical Śrīvidyā is among the latest traditions of the non-Saiddhāntika Mantramārga and postdates the goddess-oriented Vidyāpīṭha doctrines, including the broader Kālīkula tradition of the worship of goddess Kālī/Kālasaṃkarṣaṇī and its Kashmirian branch, known as Krama (for Mantramārga, Vidyāpīṭha, Kālīkula, and Krama, see → Kashmir).

However, the antecedent *nityā* cult is older than the Kubjikā tradition and at least some of the texts of the Kālīkula (for a classification and features of the Śaiva and Śākta-Śaiva doctrines, see Sanderson, 1988; 2006). The *Ciñciṇīmatasārasamuccaya*, a syncretic text of the Kubjikā cult, includes the *nityā* cult in its classification. The *Kubjikāmata* and the later Ṣaṭkas (sextets) of the Kālīkula's *Jayadrathayāmala* refer to its deities, and the former also to one of its *mantras* (Sanderson, 2010, 47–48).

What particularly sets Śrīvidyā apart from the earlier traditions of the Vidyāpīṭha is the prevalence of the imagery of love magic, inherited from the antecedent *nityā* cult, which is in striking contrast to the Vidyāpīṭha's Kāpālika imagery of the cremation grounds from the earlier Atimārga traditions (Sanderson, 2009, 49; for Kāpālika imagery in Mantramārga, see Sanderson 1988, 669–75; for Kāpālika, Atimārga, see → Kashmir).

According to the *Ciñciṇīmatasārasamuccaya*, the *nityā* cult was associated with the southern transmission, or the southern order. This system of classification of the Kaula traditions included

Kālīkula as the teaching of the northern order, a system related to Trika as that of the eastern order, and the Kubjikā cult as the tradition of the western order (Sanderson, 2009, 48–49).

In the later schemas, Śrīvidyā saw itself as transcending the four Kaula teachings associated with the cardinal directions (*VāMa.* 1.12). *Parātantra*, a syncretic scripture probably produced in the Kathmandu Valley and a synoptic text of the *Vāḍavānalīya*, quoted in the *Puraścaryārṇava*, included this new configuration (Sanderson, 2003, 367–368). Both *Parātantra* and *Vāḍavānalīya* provided an artificial schema of six transmissions, which preserved the goddesses associated with Krama in the north and the cult of Kubjikā in the west. The goddesses of the now obsolete Trika were replaced with Pūrṇeśvarī in the east. Instead of the *nityā* cult, which had been supplanted by the mature cult of Tripurasundarī, Niśeśvarī was established in the south. The goddesses Pūrṇeśvarī and Niśeśvarī have probably been artificially constructed to fill in the gaps in this classification, since they are not attested outside of this context. The Buddhist Vajrayoginī, along with Nairṛteśvarī and other minor goddesses, was added as the tradition of the nadir. The cult of Tripurasundarī (i.e. Śrīvidyā) was added as the transcendent, upper tradition of the zenith (Sanderson, 2003, 366–368).

Śrīvidyā Literature

The Early Tantras

Śrīvidyā practice has always required "ritual literacy in Sanskrit" (Brooks, 1992, xiii), and the tradition has produced a great variety of scriptures, commentaries, devotional hymns, and ritual manuals. According to T. Goudriaan, Śrīvidyā is "conspicuous by the literary standard of at least part of its texts, and by the mere coherence and elaboration of its doctrine" (Goudriaan, 1981, 58). While the majority of these texts have been composed in Sanskrit, some literature relevant to the tradition, which is yet to be fully examined, is in vernacular languages. The foremost among these is the Tamil *Tirumantiram*. Although the text is traditionally dated quite early, and some have dated it as early as "the fifth, sixth, or seventh century," it "may have been dated six or seven centuries too early" as it "contains a complex of concepts with Sanskrit labels the development of which one can trace in Sanskrit (not Tamil) literature that must certainly post-date the fifth century" (Goodall, 2004, xxix).

The first extant Sanskrit Śrīvidyā text, the *Vāmakeśvarīmata*, also referred to as *Nityāṣoḍaśikārṇava* or *Catuḥśatī*, was probably composed in the early 11th century. It is often grouped together with the later *Yoginīhṛdaya*. However, significant differences in terminology and the types of practices in the *Vāmakeśvarīmata* and the *Yoginīhṛdaya* suggest that the two texts represent "distinct intellectual and historical traditions" (Brooks, 1992, 38).

In the *Vāmakeśvarīmata*, the magical means for attracting the desired partner were given the most prominence, compared to practices focusing on speech and eloquence, and rituals for overcoming the negative effects of poisons, gaining the power to cure snake bites, and the control over *bhūta*s (ghosts), *preta*s (ghouls), and *piśāca*s (goblins). The *Vāmakeśvarīmata* incorporated the subordinate *nityā* deities of the antecedent cult as part of a much larger ritual system comprising 78 deities, arranged on the nine levels of the *śrīcakra* (see → *maṇḍala*s and → *yantra*s). The text included a detailed exposition on the *vidyā*s (*mantra*s of feminine deities), that is, the *mūlavidyā*, given in the coded form, the supplementary *vidyā*s, and the *bīja*s (the so-called seed syllables; see → *mantra*s). Detailed instructions for the drawing of the *śrīcakra*, its worship, the practice of *nyāsa* (installing the divinity in the body of the ritualist), and additional practices for attraction, subjugation, protection, and the attainment of various *siddhi*s (supernatural powers) were also provided. A variety of *mudrā*s (particular hand gestures common in Tantra that are seen as the physical analogue to the deities and their *mantras*/*vidyā*s) are also discussed. A list corresponding to nine out of ten *daśamahāmudrā*s (lit. the ten great *mudrā*s), which are still in current practice, is given with only slight variations and in the same order (*VāMa.* 1.164; detailed discussion in *VāMa.* 3, a short chapter on *mudrā*s). Among the *daśamahāmudrā*s, the *trikhaṇḍamudrā* is not mentioned in the text, but Jayaratha in his commentary, the *Vāmakeśvarīmatavivaraṇa*, creatively interprets *ādi* (first, etcetera) to refer to this *mudrā*, completing the list of ten. Instructions for *homa* (fire ceremony), *japa* (*mantra* repetition), and *dhyāna* (meditation, visualization) are also given. Among the meditations mentioned in the *Vāmakeśvarīmata* is the *kāmakalādhyāna* (meditation on the symbolic representation of the body of Tripurasundarī; *VāMa.* 1.165–168; for a study of *kāmakalā*, see White, 1998) and a detailed description of the physical form of the goddess, which spans 30 verses, excerpted below.

> *tataḥ padmanibhāṃ devīṃ bālārkakiraṇāruṇām japākusumasaṅkāśāṃ dāḍimīkusumopamām* (*VāMa.* 1.113)
>
> *sphuranmukuṭamāṇikyakiṅkiṇījālamaṇḍitām* (*VāMa.* 1.114cd)
>
> *kālālikulasaṅkāśakuṭilālakapallavām* (*VāMa.* 1.115ab)
>
> *kiṃcidardhendukuṭilalalāṭamṛdupaṭṭikām pinākidhanurākārasubhruvaṃ parameśvarīm ānandamuditollolalīlāndolitalocanām* (*VāMa.* 1.116–117ab)
>
> *mahātripuramudrāṃ tu smṛtvāvāhanarūpayā vidyayāvāhya subhage namaskāraniyuktayā pūrvoktayā sādhakendro mahātripurasundarīm cakramadhye tu saṃcintya tataḥ pūjanam ārabhet* (*VāMa.* 1.132–133)
>
> [Mahātripurasundarī] resembling a lotus, reddish as the rays of the young sun, like a China Rose [or] a pomegranate flower... adorned with glittering crown rubies and strings of bells, with a mass of curls like a swarm of black bees [and] a delicate fillet slightly curved like a half-moon at the round forehead, the supreme goddess, whose beautiful eyebrows are shaped like the bow of Śiva, eyes playfully moving about like waves delighted with bliss... Having meditated on the *mahātripuramudrā* and having summoned [Mahātripurasundarī] with the aforesaid *vidyā* of summoning, adding the *namas* [of obeisance], O beautiful one, after visualizing Mahātripurasundarī at the center of the *cakra*, the excellent *sādhaka* should then begin the worship. (trans. by author with comments by A. Sanderson, personal communication, 2012)

While the 13th-century commentators, particularly Jayaratha and Śivānanda, reevaluated the *Vāmakeśvarīmata* in light of the Kashmirian nondual philosophy, the text itself did not display explicit awareness of these doctrines.

The *Yoginīhṛdaya*, introduced as an esoteric elaboration on the points that have not been sufficiently clarified in the *Vāmakeśvarīmata*, was evidently composed after the time of Abhinavagupta and Kṣemarāja, probably in the mid-11th century or soon after. The text incorporated terminology and doctrinal concepts derived from Trika and Krama Pratyabhijñā-based metaphysics and cosmologies that updated the cult with the Śākta-Śaiva nondualist paradigms, dominant from the 11th century onward. While retaining the configuration of the subordinate deities to be worshipped in the *śrīcakra* discussed in the *Vāmakeśvarīmata*, in addition to the external ritual, the *Yoginīhṛdaya* introduced a number of sophisticated meditative practices and ways of mapping the *śrīcakra* onto the subtle body of the practitioner, reflecting the trend toward the esotericization and internalization in this tradition. The *śrīcakra* in the *Yoginīhṛdaya* is viewed not only as an external ritual diagram, but also as a map of cosmic emanation (*YHṛ.* 1.36–49; see also Padoux, 2003, 240). The text describes the cosmic consciousness, which has the nature of *[pra]mātṛ* (cognizer), *[pra]meya* (object of cognition), and *[pra]māṇa* (cognition itself) coming into being in the form of the universe (*YHṛ.* 1.9–12; 1.50–51). This cosmic consciousness in the *śrīcakra* is fourfold, manifesting as Vāmā, Jyeṣṭā, Raudrī, and the Great Goddess, Ambikā (*YHṛ.* 1.36–40). The four goddesses are equated with the four levels of speech, inherited from Pratyabhijñā – *paśyantī*, *madhyamā*, *vaikharī*, and the transcendent fourth level of *parā vāc*, the supreme word in its primeval, undifferentiated state (*YHṛ.* 1.36–40; for a detailed exposition on Kashmirian conceptions of the levels of speech, see Padoux, 1990, 166–223; see also → *mantras*). Among the extant commentaries on this text, the 14th-century *Yoginīhṛdayadīpikā* by Amṛtānanda and the 18th-century *Setubandha* by Bhāskararāya have been published.

The Later Tantras

The text usually referred to as the *Tantrarājatantra* calls itself the *Kādimatatantra*, with *Tantrarājatantra* being merely an epithet of that title (Goudriaan, 1981, 64). The text contains new features in the doctrinal system, such as the division into the two *mata*s, or doctrinal lines of interpretation (Goudriaan, 1981, 64). Traditionally, Śrīvidyā lineages and their texts distinguish themselves by the two *mata* divisions: *kādi* and *hādi* (see Brooks, 1992, 87–90). The *hādimata* is not preserved in the contemporary tradition. Among the doctrinal differences between the two *mata*s, the primary divergence is in the extraction of the *mūlavidyā*. In the

Kāmarāja Sampradāya, the root *vidyā* is extracted as *kādividyā* (i.e. the *vidyā* beginning with *ka*). In the Lopāmudrā Sampradāya, *hādividyā* begins with *ha* (Brooks, 1992, 89–90). The text of the *Tantrarājatantra*, however, uncharacteristically names the two *mata*s as *kādimata* and *kālīmata*, the latter likely referring to the Kālīkula (Brooks, 1992, 42; Goudriaan, 1981, 64). While the early texts discussed above outlined the main features of the Śrīvidyā external and internal ritual, the *Tantrarājatantra* includes considerably more detail. The text offers a thorough exposition of the worship of the *nityā*s, with Lalitā named as the foremost of them, and introduces two deities, Vārāhī and Kurukullā, to whom sacrificial offerings (*bali*) are given at the end of the *pūjā*. The *Tantrarājatantra* covers a great number of subjects, including *mantraśāstra, vāstuśāstra, homa*, and *yantra*s, among others, in a "learned, sophisticated, non-repetitive style," combining "an impressive quantity of ślokas with a considerable literary achievement" (Goudriaan, 1981, 66–67).

Among other later Tantras, one of the most popular is the *Jñānārṇavatantra*. The text follows the *kādimata* and was probably composed prior to the 16th century (Goudriaan, 1981, 67–68). Although of lesser literary quality than the texts that preceded it, the *Jñānārṇavatantra* "contains precious information on the worship of Tripurā and other subjects which it often presents in a clear and unpretentious language" (Goudriaan, 1981, 68). In addition to expounding on the triadic nature of Tripurasundarī (see below) and elucidating a number of technical details of her worship, the text discusses the worship of Bālā, a manifestation of the goddess as a young girl, who is portrayed seated on a white lotus, holding a rosary (*akṣamālā*) and the → Vedas (Goudriaan, 1981, 68). Tripurabhairavī, a fearsome emanation of the goddess, is also described (Goudriaan, 1981, 68). The exoteric *Jñānārṇavatantra* and the Kaula *Paraśurāmakalpasūtra* are among the authoritative references for contemporary Śrīvidyā practice (Brooks, 1992, 43, 52–53; 217n42; for a summary of Paddhatis and other texts of ritual instruction, see Brooks, 1992, 51–53). The tradition has preserved a number of other later Tantras, a number of which are yet to be edited (see Goudriaan, 1981, 68–74, for a summary of the later Śrīvidyā Tantras).

Stotras

→ Stotras (hymns) and other devotional literature of the tradition not only describe the popular image of the goddess, but often encode technical meanings pertaining to the cult's doctrine and ritual. In the short text of the *Khaḍgamālāstotra*, the arrangement of names of the subordinate deities mirrors the ritual in which these goddesses are worshipped in the *śrīcakra* or internally in the order of evolution (*sṛṣṭikrama*). The text lists the subordinate goddesses worshipped in the nine levels of the *śrīcakra* ritual and the emanations of Tripurasundarī controlling each level. Among the groups included in the *Khaḍgamālāstotra* are 15 *nityā*s, the Lopāmudrā Sampradāya (Khanna, 1986, 49), 11 *siddhi*s beginning with *aṇimā*, and the 8 *matṛkā* goddesses. The daily chanting of the *Khaḍgamālāstotra* is understood to have the same efficacy as the complete *pūjā* of the *śrīcakra* (Khanna, 1986, 11).

The *Lalitāsahasranāma* is a popular Stotra containing one thousand names of the goddess Lalitā. It is widely used in contemporary devotional practice. Many people chant it daily and know the hymn by heart, while others use it for a simple *pūjā*, in which an offering, usually a pinch of red *kuṃkum* powder or flower petals, is offered to the *śrīcakra* with each name of the goddess. The Stotra is included in the *Lalitopākhyāna* section of the *Brahmāṇḍapurāṇa*. Enclosed within a framing story, it is presented in the form of instruction imparted by Hayagrīva to Agastya. The text of the hymn reflects several puranic myths, such as the arising of Tripurasundarī from the fire pit of the sacrificial fire of consciousness and the slaying of the demon Bhaṇḍāsura, described in the *Lalitopākhyāna*, as well as the slaying of Mahiṣāsura, and Caṇḍa and Muṇḍa from the *Devīmāhātmya*. The *kuṇḍalinī* system of *cakras*/*ādhāra*s (subtle energy centers) grouped into the three *kūṭa*s (sections), with the corresponding *granthi*s (knots) is also introduced (see → Yoga).

Another popular Stotra widely used devotionally is the *Saundaryalaharī* (The Wave of Beauty). While containing devotional expositions on the oneness of Śiva and Śakti and descriptive passages on the physical beauty of the goddess, the text also encodes technical information on *śrīcakra* ritual and internal worship. The first part of the text is known as the *Ānandalaharī* (The Wave of Bliss) and is considered to be the essence of the hymn (Brown, 1958, 1). In highly poetic and evocative language, the many facets of → *śakti*, the feminine divine energy, are carefully laid out, and the goddess's mystic union with Śiva, who cannot accomplish anything without her, is described:

śivaḥ śaktyā yukto yadi bhavati śaktaḥ prabhavitum
na ced evam devo na khalu kuśalaḥ spanditum api
atas tvām ārādhyāṃ hariharaviriñcādibhir api
praṇantuṃ stotuṃ vā katham akṛtapuṇyaḥ prabhavati (*SauLa.* 1)

If Śiva is joined with Śakti, only then there can be lordship,
but if not – the Lord himself can hardly stir.
When you are worshipped even by Hari, Hara, Brahmā, and others,
how can one without merit bow to you or praise you? (trans. by author)

Ānandalaharī contains many "technicalities of this originally Kaula system," with which "many late South and East Indian commentators, such as Kaivalyāśrama, Ānandagiri, Gaurīkāntanta Sārvabhauma, Narasiṃha and Lakṣmīdhara, are fully conversant" (Sanderson, 2002, 23n24). The second part of the Stotra, often called the *Saundaryalaharī*, extols the beauty of the goddess, each metaphor carefully crafted to follow her detailed physical description from head to toe. The text concludes with "the poet's prayer that he may receive Devī's grace, have the vision of her supernal form, achieve self-realization, and savor the sweetness of supreme brahman ... which she is" (Brown, 1958, 1). The *Saundaryalaharī* is attributed by tradition to Śaṅkara, who is usually dated to the 8th century – however, the text must have been composed significantly later (for a summary of the scholarship on the authorship and dating, see Brown, 58, 25–30).

Practices

In the literature overview above, we have already outlined some of the Śrīvidyā practices, which are similar to other tantric traditions, as well as the content of the practices unique to Śrīvidyā. A detailed exposition of Śrīvidyā ritual and theology is of course outside the scope of this article (for a discussion of tantric ritual, see Sanderson 1995; for a discussion of the worship of Tripurasundarī according to *hādimata* in the works of the 13th-century Śivānanda, see Khanna, 1986; and for the analysis of Śrīvidyā ritual, see Brooks, 1992). Standard tantric practices, as they are preserved in the contemporary tradition, include *dhyāna* (meditation, visualization), *pūjā* (ritual worship), *tarpaṇa* (offering of libations), *nyāsa* (installing the divinity in the body of the ritualist), *homa* (offering oblations into the fire), *japa* (mantra repetition), and *mudrā* (ritual gestures).

From the earliest texts, the worship of Tripurasundarī has been described as tripartite, that is, centered on *pūjā, mantra*, and *cakra* (e.g. *YHṛ.* 1.6). These three types of worship correspond to the three forms of the goddess, which are her physical form (*sthūlarūpa*; represented in anthropomorphic images), her subtle (*sūkṣma*) or *mantra* form, and her transcendent, supreme (*parā*) form, worshipped in the *śrīyantra*, or the *śrīcakra*, a two- or three-dimensional aniconic representation of Tripurasundarī (Brooks, 1992, xviii; see also Dempsey, 2006, 53). The geometrical design of the *śrīcakra* is formed by the *bindu* (dot) in the middle of the nine intersecting triangles, surrounded by two concentric rows of lotus petals and a threefold circle within an enclosure with four gates (see → *maṇḍala*s and *yantra*s).

The principal *mantra* of the tradition is the *pañcadaśākṣarī* (a 15-syllabled *mantra*) or *ṣoḍaśākṣarī* (a mantra of 16 syllables, formed from the *pañcadaśākṣarī*; see Brooks, 1992, 90, for the details of the extraction of the *mūlamantra*). A variant of the 15-syllabled *mantra* is already articulated in a coded form in Śrīvidyā's earliest extant Sanskrit text, the *Vāmakeśvarīmata* (1.93–101), and *kādividyā*, just as it has been preserved in the contemporary tradition – in the Tamil *Tirumantiram* (see Brooks, 1992, 31). The *ṣoḍaśākṣarī* appears to have been a later addition. The contemporary tradition refers to the 16-syllabled *mantra* as the *laghuṣoḍaśī* and its expanded form as the *mahāṣoḍaśī* (see Brooks, 1992, 108, for a variant of the latter). The *bālāmantra*, a nine-syllabled *mantra* of the goddess as a nine-year-old girl, is also used. From its earliest attestation, the *mūlavidyā* has been presented as threefold; its 15 syllables divided into three groups. These groups are identified in the *Vāmakēśvarīmata* as *vāgbhava, kāmarāja*, and *śakti* (*VāMā.* 1.94–101). Each of the three stages has a corresponding syllable (*VāMā.* 1.82–85). Together these three syllables are considered to be the contracted form of the *mūlavidyā*. It is these syllables that form the *bālāmantra* and are the most basic form of initiation into Śrīvidyā at present day.

Bibliography

Brooks, D.R., *Auspicious Wisdom: The Texts and Traditions of Śrīvidyā Śākta Tantrism in South India*, Albany, 1992.

Brown, W.N., "Preface" and "Introduction," in: *idem*, ed., *The Saudaryalaharī or Flood of Beauty Traditionally Ascribed to Śaṅkarācārya*, HOS 43, Cambridge MA, 1958, v–vii, 1–47.

Golovkova, A., "The Cult of the Goddess Tripurasundarī in the Vāmakeśvarīmata," diss., Oxford University, 2010.

Gnoli, R., ed., *Abhinavagupta: Il commento di Abhinavagupta alla Parātriṃśikā (Parātriṃśikātattvavivaraṇam)*, Roma, 1985.

Goodall, D., "Preface," in: *idem*, ed., *The Parākhyatantra: A Scripture of the Śaiva Siddhānta*, Pondicherry, 2004.

Goudriaan, T., "Hindu Tantric Literature in Sanskrit," in: T. Goudriaan & S. Gupta, eds., *Hindu Tantric and Śākta Literature*, Wiesbaden, 1981, ix–172.

Khanna, M., "The Concept and Liturgy of the Śrīcakra Based on Śivānanda's Trilogy," diss., Oxford University, 1986.

Padoux, A., *Le Coeur de la Yoginī: Yoginīhṛdaya avec le commentaire Dīpikā d'Amṛtānanda*, PICI 63, Paris, 1994.

Padoux, A., *Vāc: The Concept of the Word in Selected Hindu Tantras*, Albany, 1990.

Sanderson, A., "Śaivism, Society and the State," unpubl. draft, 2010.

Sanderson, A., "The Śaiva Age: An Explanation of the Rise and Dominance of Śaivism during the Early Medieval Period," in: S. Einoo, ed., *Genesis and Development of Tantrism*, IOCPS 23, Tokyo, 2009, 41–349.

Sanderson, A., "The Śaiva Exegesis of Kashmir," in: D. Goodall & A. Padoux, eds., *Mélanges tantriques à la mémoire d'Hélène Brunner/Tantric Studies in Memory of Hélène Brunner*, Pondicherry, 2007, 231–442, 551–582.

Sanderson, A., "The Lākulas: New Evidence of a System Intermediate between Pāñcārthika Pāśupatism and Āgamic Śaivism," Ramalinga Reddy Memorial Lectures, 1997, *IPA* 24, 2006, 143–217.

Sanderson, A., "The Śaiva Religion among the Khmers," *BEFEO* 90–91, Pondicherry, 2003, 349–463.

Sanderson, A., "Remarks on the Text of the Kubjikāmatatantra," *IIJ* 45, 2002, 1–24.

Sanderson, A., "Meaning in Tantric Ritual," in: A.-M. Blondeau & K. Schipper, eds., *Essais sur le Rituel*, vol. III: *Colloque du Centenaire de la Section des Sciences religieuses de l'École Pratique des Hautes Études*, Paris, 1995, 15–95.

Sanderson, A., "Śaivism and the Tantric Traditions," in: S. Sutherland, L. Houlden, P. Clarke & F. Hardy, eds., *The World's Religions*, London, 1988, 660–704; repr. in: F. Hardy, ed., *The World's Religions: The Religions of Asia*, London, 1990, 128–172.

White, D.G., "Transformations in the Art of Love: Kāmakalā Practices in Hindu Tantric and Kaula Traditions," *HR* 38/2, 1998, 172–198.

ANNA GOLOVKOVA

Ājīvika

An Ājīvika ("Follower of the Way of Life"; Dundas, 2002, 28) is an adherent of what has been called "a vanished Indian religion" (this is the subtitle of A.L. Basham's classical study of this religion [1951]; note that the term "Ājīvika" was not exclusively used for adherents of this religion; see below). This religion (here called Ājīvikism) arose at the time of Jainism – or rather, at the time of the most recent Jaina *tīrthaṅkara* (or *jina*), Vardhamāna Mahāvīra – and in the same region. Its founder is known by the following names: Makkhali Gosāla (Pal.), Gosāla Maṅkhaliputta (Ardh.), and Maskarin Gośāla (or Gośālikāputra/Gośālīputra; Skt.). (Makkhali/Maskarin is no doubt a title [staff bearer] rather than a name, designating a wandering ascetic [*parivrājaka*] by Pāṇini in *Aṣṭādhyāyī* 6.1.154: *maskaramaskariṇau veṇuparivrājakayoḥ*. The Jaina tradition presumably misunderstood this title as a name.) The religion survived for the better part of two millennia, being occasionally referred to in surviving literature and inscriptions, and then disappeared. Ājīvikism appears to have been in the possession of scriptures of its own, but none has survived (Basham, 1951, 213–223).

The modern study of Ājīvikism began in the 19th century and continued into the 20th century. The most important studies were published by A.F.R. Hoernle (1908), B.M. Barua (1920), and A.L. Basham (1951). A.L. Basham's monograph, though dated and incomplete in some respects, remains the most complete study of Ājīvikism to date and will be frequently referred to in what follows.

The most detailed knowledge of the beliefs and practices of the early Ājīvikas has to be derived from the Buddhist and Jaina (i.e. Śvetāmbara) canons. Both of these criticize the Ājīvikas, and, for this reason, neither of these is *a priori* particularly reliable. However, the similarity in this respect between these two completely independent sources allows us to conclude that both drew on a common source of information, presumably the ideas of the Ājīvikas themselves. The information extracted from these two canons, moreover, fits well in its time (or what we know of it). It turns out that the ideas of the Ājīvikas were remarkably close to (yet fundamentally different from) the ideas of the early Jainas. Indeed, Ājīvika thought can be best understood in the light of early Jaina thought. It is therefore a typical religion of "Greater Magadha," whose culture was different and independent from vedic culture, to which Brahmanism and its literary heritage belong (Bronkhorst, 2007b).

Early Jaina asceticism was an attempt to stop activity and put an end to karmic traces acquired earlier (Bronkhorst, 1993, chs. 1–3; this section follows Bronkhorst, 2003). It was a direct response to the challenge posed by the doctrine of → *karman*, interpreted in a literal way: acts – that is, physical and mental acts – produce results in this or a next life. Physical and mental immobility discards the traces left by earlier acts and purifies the soul from all acts, with total → liberation from rebirth (→ *saṃsāra*) as the ultimate outcome. The following passages from the Jaina canon illustrate this. The *Uttarajjhayaṇa/Uttarajhāyā* states that

> [b]y being without activity the soul does not bind new *karma* and destroys the *karma* that was bound before. (*UttJh.* 29.37/1139)

> Having reached the state [of motionlessness] of the king of mountains, the homeless [monk] destroys the four parts of *karma* which [even] a *kevalin* (i.e. a person close to liberation) possesses. After that [the soul] becomes perfected, awakened, freed, completely emancipated, and puts an end to all suffering. (*UttJh.* 29.61/1163)

The Buddhist canon ascribes this belief to the Jainas, too. In the *Cūḷadukkhakkhandhasutta* of the *Majjhimanikāya*, for example, Nigaṇṭha Nāthaputta (or Nātaputta, i.e. Mahāvīra, the most recent *tīrthaṅkara* of the Jainas) is reported to have presented his teachings in the following words:

> Formerly you performed sinful activities; you must exhaust that [sinful activity] by means of this severe and difficult practice. Being here and now restrained in body, speech and mind, amounts to not performing sinful activity in the future. Thus, *as a result of the annihilation of former actions by asceticism, and of the non-performing of new actions, there is no further effect in the future*; as a result of no further effect in the future there is destruction of actions; as a result of the destruction of actions there is destruction of suffering; as a result of

> the destruction of suffering there is destruction of sensation; as a result of the destruction of sensation all suffering will be exhausted. (*MN.* I.92–95)

The most important passage in the Buddhist canon that informs us about Ājīvikism (i.e. about the teaching of Makkhali Gosāla, presumably its founder; see below) occurs in the *Sāmaññaphalasutta* of the *Dīghanikāya*. A.L. Basham paraphrases it as follows below. (For philological details and specifications, see Bronkhorst, 2003, 160f. MacQueen [1988, 195] compares the different versions, including the Chinese versions, of this *Sāmaññaphalasutta* and arrives at the conclusion that "[the Pāli version], of all the versions, preserved the most ancient state of the text"; see also Meisig, 1987.)

> There is neither cause nor basis for the sins of living beings; they become sinful without cause or basis. Neither is there cause or basis for the purity of living beings; they become pure without cause or basis. There is no deed performed either by [one's own] self (*ātman*) or by [the self of] others, no action belonging to the self (*puruṣa*), no strength, no courage, no endurance connected with the self or prowess connected with the self. All beings, all that have breath, all that are born, all that have life, are without power, strength, or virtue, but are developed by destiny, chance, and nature, and experience joy and sorrow in the six classes (of existence).
>
> There are 1,400,000 chief uterine births, 6,000 and 600; 500 *karmas*, 5 *karmas*, 3 *karmas*, a *karma*, and half a *karma*; 62 paths; 62 lesser *kalpas*; 6 classes (of human existence); 8 stages of man; 4,900 means of livelihood (?); 4,900 ascetics; 4,900 dwellings of *nāgas*; 2,000 faculties; 3,000 purgatories; 36 places covered with dust (?); 7 sentient births; 7 insentient births; 7 births from knots (?); 7 gods; 7 men; 7 *pisāca* (births?); 7 lakes; 7 knots (?), and 700; 7 precipices, and 700; 7 dreams, and 700; and 8,400,000 great *kalpas* through which fool and wise alike will take their course, and make an end of sorrow. There is no question of bringing unripe *karma* to fruition, nor of exhausting *karma* already ripened, by virtuous conduct, by vows, by penance, or by chastity. That cannot be done. *Saṃsāra* is measured as with a bushel, with its joy and sorrow and its appointed end. It can neither be lessened nor increased, nor is there any excess or deficiency of it. Just as a ball of thread will, when thrown, unwind to its full length, so fool and wise alike will take their course, and make an end of sorrow. (Basham, 1951, 13–14; modified by author)

A passage in the Śvetāmbara Jaina canon, too, informs us about the teaching of Gosāla. It occurs in the *Viyāhapannatti* (= *Bhagavatīsūtra*/*Bhagavaī*) and reads as follows:

> All those who have reached or are reaching or will reach salvation must finish in order 8,400,000 *mahākappas* (Skt. *mahākalpas*), 7 divine births, 7 groups, 7 sentient births, 7 "abandonments of transmigration", 500,000 *kammas* (Skt. *karmans*), and 60,000 and 600 and the 3 parts of *kamma*. Then, being saved, awakened, set free, and reaching *nirvāṇa* they have made or are making or will make an end of all sorrow. (*ViyPa.* 15.101 [Ladnun ed.]; 15.68 [Bombay ed.])

The two passages have enough in common to justify the conclusion that they borrow from a common source. Only the Buddhist passage contains the following statement, crucial for an understanding of Ājīvikism:

> There is no question of bringing unripe *karma* to fruition, nor of exhausting *karma* already ripened, by virtuous conduct, by vows, by penance, or by chastity. That cannot be done. (Basham, 1951, 14)

Bringing unripe *karma* to fruition and exhausting *karma* already ripened, as we have seen, were exactly what the early Jaina ascetics tried to bring about. For asceticism in early Jainism had the double function of "the annihilation of former actions and the non-performing of new actions." According to the Ājīvikas, the annihilation of former actions as practiced by the Jainas is not possible.

Clearly, without the annihilation of former actions, the Jaina path of liberation becomes pointless and cannot lead to the intended goal. Instead, Ājīvikas believed that all living beings have to pass through a long and irreducible series of existences, for a total duration of 8,400,000 great *kalpas*. This (if we take the usual length of a great *kalpa*, viz. 4,320 million years) amounts to 35 quadrillion (35×10^{15}) years, that is, more than 2.5 million times the modern astronomical estimate of the age of the universe (13.7 billion years; for different calculations, see Basham, 1951, 253–254; Deleu, 1970, 217). But even though long, this series of existences will come to an end and result in liberation from rebirth. The Ājīvikas were determinists who thought of this series of existences as guided by unchangeable rules. Indeed,

> [t]he cardinal point of the doctrines of... Makkhali Gosāla [and his followers] was a belief in the all-embracing rule of the principle of order, Niyati, which ultimately controlled every action and all phenomena, and left no room for human volition, which was completely ineffectual. Thus Ājīvikism was founded on an unpromising basis of strict determinism. (Basham, 1951, 3–4)

As will be clear from what precedes, Ājīvikism shared many features with Jainism. The main difference concerned the annihilation of former actions; this was possible according to the early Jainas and impossible according to the Ājīvikas. Apart from this difference, the two movements had many points in common. Like the Jainas, those Ājīvikas who believed that they had reached their final existence lived ascetic lives. Like the Jainas, they distinguished six classes of living beings, called *abhijāti* by the Ājīvikas and *leśyā* by the Jainas (Basham, 1951, 139f., 245; Jaini, 1979, 114–115; Schubring, 2000, 195–197). Like those Jainas who were followers of Mahāvīra, they wore no clothes. And the Ājīvikas may not have been the only ones to believe in a strict determinism: the early Jainas, too, appear to have accepted it. Indeed, the Ājīvikas and the followers of Mahāvīra shared so many features that the early Buddhists often failed to distinguish them from each other (Bronkhorst, 2000b). (In early Buddhist days, there were, besides followers of Mahāvīra, other Jainas who were followers of Pārśva. The followers of Pārśva did wear clothes and distinguished themselves in at least one further point from the followers of Mahāvīra.)

The beginning of the passage quoted from the Buddhist *Sāmaññaphalasutta* teaches us more. It states that the self does not act, and it uses the terms → *ātman* and → *puruṣa* (more correctly, their Pali equivalents *atta* and *purisa*) to refer to the self. This part of the passage, too, has a parallel in the Śvetāmbara canon. The *Uvāsagadasāo* puts the following words on the lips of an Ājīvika divinity: "There is no effort nor deed, nor strength, nor courage, no action or prowess belonging to the self (*puruṣa*)" (Basham, 1951, 218).

The belief that the self does not act was widespread in India and became a cornerstone of most Brahmanical philosophies. It obviously represented an alternative solution to the problem faced by Jainism – how to stop activity. If the self – that is, what one really is – never acts by its very nature, then the mere realization of this fact suffices for freeing oneself from the burden of karmic retribution.

It appears, then, that Ājīvikism, too, accepted the notion of a self that never acts. However, they drew different consequences from this than most others did. They concluded that activities are carried out by the body without involvement of the self, that is, of oneself. There is in this way no moral dimension to human activity, even if the body engages in vile or highly virtuous acts. This is confirmed by a statement that the *Sāmaññaphalasutta* puts on the lips of Pūraṇa Kassapa, another teacher with links to Ājīvikism (Basham, 1951, 80f.). A.L. Basham paraphrases it as follows:

> He who performs an act or causes an act to be performed... he who destroys life, the thief, the housebreaker, the plunderer... the highway robber, the adulterer and the liar... commit no sin. Even if with a razor-sharp discus a man reduce all the life on earth to a single heap of flesh, he commits no sin...If he come down the south bank of the Ganges, slaying, maiming, and torturing, and causing others to be slain, maimed, or tortured, he commits no sin, neither does sin approach him. Likewise if a man go down the north bank of the Ganges, giving alms and sacrificing, and causing alms to be given and sacrifices to be performed, he acquires no merit, neither does merit approach him. From liberality, self-control, abstinence, and honesty is derived neither merit, nor the approach of merit. (Basham, 1951, 13)

The idea that the body (or material nature) can carry out activities on its own, following its own rules, is not without parallel in ancient India. The → *Bhagavadgītā*, too, distinguishes between an inactive self and a material world (i.e. the body) that acts following its own rules. In the *Bhagavadgītā*, the precondition is that one realize one's true nature; the body will then act in accordance with one's caste. Depending on the caste to which one belongs, this activity may include violent deeds and even murder:

> He who thinks of him (i.e., the soul inhabiting the body) as killer, he who deems him killed, both of these possess no knowledge; he does not kill and is not killed. Never is he born or dies; he has not come to be, nor will he come to be; unborn, permanent, eternal, ancient, he is not killed when the body is killed. (*BhG.* 2.19–20)

We know that the warrior Arjuna, in the *Bhagavadgītā*, is told to kill his fellow human beings, including family and friends, without scruples. Pūraṇa Kassapa's position was perhaps not that exceptional after all, even though the Brahmanical caste plays no role in his vision of the world.

The proximity between Jainism and Ājīvikism during the earliest period has allowed us to understand the basics of the latter religion. This same proximity helps us to understand other features as well.

Two independent sources – the Jaina Tamil poem *Nīlakēci* and the Pali *Petavatthu* – tell us that the Ājīvikas believed that the soul (*jīva*) can extend to five hundred *yojana*s (perhaps 4,000 miles). The Pali text adds that it is of eight parts. The Pali commentator explains that the immense size of the *jīva* is found only in souls in their last stage before *nirvāṇa* (Basham, 1951, 270–271; the link with the Jaina *samudghāta* escaped Basham). This expansion of the soul just before liberation corresponds to what in Jainism is known by the name *samudghāta* (Ardh. *samugghāya*) "bursting forth," a process that affects the *kevalin* (Jaina saint):

> the Kevalin projects his soul atoms still infected with Karman from the vertex and the footpoint from the right and the left side, from the chest and the back in the shape of columns each reaching to the end of the world and then retracts them again. (Schubring, 2000, 184; see also Tatia, 1951, 280)

The Ājīvikas divided humanity into six differently colored classes of men (*abhijāti*): black, blue, red, green, white, and supremely white, respectively. Jainism has a similar classification, due to what the Jainas call the six differently colored *leśyā*s, a term that is hard to translate. *Abhijāti*s and *leśyā*s have features in common but they cannot be identified. It seems, however, certain that they are related (Basham, 1951, 243–248).

The Jaina (Śvetāmbara) canonical scriptures preserve a lot of more or less legendary information about the founder of Ājīvikism, here called Gosāla Maṅkhaliputta, primarily in the *Viyāhapannatti* but also elsewhere (Deleu, 1970, 214–220; Basham, 1951, 30, 35ff.). They tell us that Gosāla and Vardhamāna Mahāvīra spent a number of years together; that Gosāla was at some point Vardhamāna's disciple, but that the two parted ways; and that Gosāla subsequently claimed *jina*-hood. It seems unlikely that much historical credence can be lent to most of this, but the legend confirms, once again, the proximity between Jainism and Ājīvikism.

This proximity is further confirmed by a closer consideration of the references to Jainas (Pal. *nigaṇṭha*s) and Ājīvikas in the Buddhist canon. Here it is to be kept in mind that in those early days, there were two kinds of Jainas: the followers of Pārśva and the followers of Vardhamāna Mahāvīra. The former wore a garment, and the latter wore nothing whatsoever. Both the followers of Vardhamāna and the Ājīvikas were and remained naked. A study of the terms supports the conclusion that the term "Ājīvika" in the Buddhist canon refers both to the followers of Vardhamāna and to the Ājīvikas (and perhaps to others), whereas Nigaṇṭha refers primarily, if not exclusively, to the followers of Pārśva. In other words, the Buddhist texts do not distinguish among different kinds of naked ascetics, including the naked Jainas and the Ājīvikas. Vardhamāna and his followers, on the one hand, and Makkhali Gosāla and his followers, on the other, were apparently not, or not always, thought of as distinct in the early Buddhist texts (Bronkhorst, 2000b).

All the early sources agree in depicting the Ājīvikas as severe ascetics. This is at first sight surprising. Why should strict determinism lead to severe asceticism? Ājīvikism's proximity to Jainism is our best hope for finding an answer to this question.

Severe asceticism was an essential part of early Jainism, too. Its purpose, as we have seen, was the "annihilation of former actions, and the nonperforming of new actions." Ājīvikism denied the possibility of annihilating former actions. However, it did not deny the role of actions in the chain that takes living beings through an astronomically large, yet finite, number of births. Once a living being arrives at its end, all the former actions of the living being would have run their course and been exhausted. Nonperformance of new actions, presumably imposed by Ājīvikism's implacable determinism, would characterize the final years of a living being's final existence. Perhaps the

Ājīvikas (rather like the Calvinists faced with predestination) looked at this asceticism as a sign of impending liberation, rather than as its cause. Unfortunately our lacunary sources do not say so in so many words, and one passage even suggests that liberation is not guaranteed even for those who have reached, or appear to have reached, the end of the path (see Basham, 1951, 142ff., 161ff.).

We do not know how long Ājīvikism survived in northern India. Inscriptions from the Maurya period and passing references in more recent Sanskrit literature suggest that its decline began soon after the Mauryas and continued for more than a thousand years (see Basham, 1951, 142ff., 161ff.). However, its central ideas did not completely disappear. These ideas reappear, in modified form, in the works of Kumārila Bhaṭṭa (7th cent. CE) and Śrīdhara (10th cent. CE), both of them Brahmanical philosophers with links to northern India. In order to understand the ideas of Kumārila and Śrīdhara, we must consider some of the consequences of Ājīvikism's central doctrine.

Ājīvikism rejected the possibility of the annihilation of former actions. It was also familiar with the notion of a self that never acts. Most philosophies that accepted that the self never acts also believed that the realization of this fact suffices, or is a prerequisite, to free oneself from the burden of karmic retribution. However, this is not completely self-evident. One might think that the realization of the inactive nature of the self cancels the effects of one's deeds from the moment of that realization onward. In that case, one would still be burdened with all the deeds carried out during countless numbers of births preceding that moment. Full liberation would then still have to wait until those earlier deeds – all of them – have carried fruit.

This is the position taken by Śrīdhara, which he appears to have borrowed from Kumārila. Both of these authors specify that the time it takes for all those earlier deeds to carry fruit, from the moment of realizing the true nature of the self onward, is 10,000 million *yuga*s (*yugakoṭisahasra*; perhaps 4.32×10^{15} years). This, if our estimation of the lengths of *yuga*s and *mahākalpa*s is correct, is shorter than the period calculated by the early Ājīvikas but begins only at the time a person realizes the inactive nature of his or her self, that is, after innumerable existences without this insight have already passed. In this way, Śrīdhara and Kumārila's vision is a variant of the vision of Ājīvikism. One might even speak of an improvement, for, unlike Ājīvikism, their vision reserves an essential place for the realization of the inactive nature of the self.

It goes without saying that the attraction of the modified vision of Śrīdhara and Kumārila, with its immense waiting period, is limited, unless a method is found to deal with the effects of past deeds. Śrīdhara and Kumārila do propose such a method; it consists in the faithful execution of vedic ritual. This aspect of their thought is clearly a Brahmanical addition to a core of ideas whose link with Ājīvikism seems undeniable (Bronkhorst, 2007a).

Ājīvikism survived until the 14th, perhaps 15th, century CE in the Tamil country in southern India, as is testified by a number of inscriptions ranging from the 5th to the 14th century (Basham, 1951, 187f.). Certain Tamil texts even provide some, though limited, information about particular beliefs that the southern Ājīvikas had meanwhile adopted.

Among these new beliefs, we find the doctrine which the commentator calls *avicalitanityatva* (unchanging permanence). It is ascribed to Ājīvikas in the Tamil *Nīlakēci*, a text that was composed, perhaps in the 10th century CE, as a Jaina answer to a Buddhist challenge and that refutes also arguments of Ājīvikas and others (Basham, 1951, 198f.; Zvelebil, 1992, 70; 1995, 495). Ājīvika doctrine encompasses most notably the view that "nothing is destroyed, and nothing is produced" (Basham, 1951, 237). We may suspect here the influence of the philosophical development that affected all known Indian schools of philosophy during the first half of the 1st millennium CE, a development that is ultimately based on notions about language (Bronkhorst, 2011).

Another new belief rather points to continued interaction with Jainism. P.S. Jaini (1980) has drawn attention to a difficulty with which Jainism was confronted: How is it that the steady "departure" of souls through the attainment of liberation does not eventually deplete the universe of all sentient existence? The answer provided is that there is an infinite number of extremely simple beings, the so-called *nigoda*s, that are at such a low level of existence that they do not even possess an individual body. Certain of these *nigoda*s – the *nitya-nigoda*s – constitute an inexhaustible reservoir of souls, with the result that the universe will never be depleted of sentient existence. Ājīvikism was confronted with the same problem but could not opt for the same solution. It maintained that all living beings would be liberated after 8,400,000 great *kalpas*. The implication is that a time will come when all living beings will be liberated, an implication that the Ājīvikas were apparently not willing to accept. Instead, they developed the notion of *maṇḍalamokṣa*, according to which liberation is not the end. We find it in the Tamil *Nīlakēci*, mentioned above, and the *Civañāṉacittiyār*, a Śaiva text, both of which stipulate that liberated souls may return to the universe (Basham, 1951, 259f.; the belief that this view finds expression already in the canonical *Sūyagaḍa* is open to doubt; see Bollée, 1977, 113–114).

Bibliography

Barua, B.M., *The Ajivikas*, part I: *Historical Summary*, University of Calcutta, 1920.

Basham, A.L., *History and Doctrines of the Ājīvikas: A Vanished Indian Religion*, Delhi, 1951, repr. 1981.

Bollée, W.B., *Studien zum Sūyagaḍa. Die Jainas und die anderen Weltanschauungen vor der Zeitenwende*, SSIUH 24, Wiesbaden, 1977.

Bronkhorst, J., *Language and Reality: On an Episode in Indian Thought*, BIL 36, Leiden, 2011.

Bronkhorst, J., "Echoes of Ājīvikism in Medieval Indian Philosophy," in: M. Nowakowska & J. Woźniak, eds., *Theatrum Mirabiliorum Indiae Orientalis: A Volume to Celebrate the 70th Birthday of Professor Maria Krzysztof Byrski*, RO 60/2, Warsaw, 2007a, 239–248.

Bronkhorst, J., *Greater Magadha: Studies in the Culture of Early India*, HdO 2/19, Leiden, 2007b.

Bronkhorst, J., "Ājīvika Doctrine Reconsidered," in: P. Balcerowicz, ed., *Essays in Jaina Philosophy and Religion*, LSJRS 20, Delhi, 2003, 153–178.

Bronkhorst, J., "Abhidharma and Jainism," in: *Abhidharma and Indian Thought: Essays in Honor of Professor Doctor Junsho Kato on His Sixtieth Birthday*, publ. Committee for the Felicitation of Professor Doctor Junsho Kato's Sixtieth Birthday, Tokyo, 2000a, 598–581.

Bronkhorst, J., "The Riddle of the Jainas and Ājīvikas in Early Buddhist Literature," *JIPh* 28, 2000b, 511–529.

Bronkhorst, J., *The Two Traditions of Meditation in Ancient India*, Delhi, [2]1993.

Deleu, J., *Viyāhapannatti (Bhagavaī): The Fifth Anga of the Jaina Canon*, LSJRS 10, Delhi, 1970, repr. 1996.

Dundas, P., *The Jains*, London, [2]2002.

Hoernle, A.F.R., "Ājīvikas," in: J. Hastings, ed., *Encyclopaedia of Religion and Ethics*, vol. I, Edinburgh, 1908, 259–268.

Jaini, P.S., "*Bhavyatva* and *Abhavyatva*: A Jaina Doctrine of 'Predestination,'" in: A.N. Upadhye *et al.*, eds., *Bhagavān Mahāvīra and His Teachings: 2,500 Anniversary Volume*, Bombay, 1977, repr. 2000a, 95–109.

Jaini, P.S., *Collected Papers on Jaina Studies*, Delhi, 2000b.

Jaini, P.S., "Karma and the Problem of Rebirth in Jainism," in: W.D. O'Flaherty, ed., *Karma and Rebirth in Classical Indian Traditions*, Berkeley, 1980, 217–238, repr. 2000c, 121–145.

Jaini, P.S., *The Jaina Path of Purification*, Delhi, 1979.

Johnson, H.M., "Review of Basham 1951," *JAOS* 74, 1954, 63–65.

MacQueen, G., *A Study of the Śrāmaṇyaphala-Sūtra*, FBI 21, Wiesbaden, 1988.

Maskell, D., "Review of Basham 1951," *Philosophy* 32, 1957, 82–84.

Meisig, K., *Das Śrāmaṇyaphala-Sūtra. Synoptische Übersetzung und Glossar der chinesischen Fassungen verglichen mit dem Sanskrit und Pāli*, FBI 19, Wiesbaden, 1987.

Schubring, W., *The Doctrine of the Jainas Described after the Old Sources*, LSJRS 15, Delhi, 2000.

Tatia, N., *Studies in Jaina Philosophy*, SP 6, Varanasi, 1951.

Zacharias, H.C.E., "Review of Basham 1951," *Anthropos* 48, 1953, 323–324.

Zvelebil, K.V., *Lexicon of Tamil Literature*, HdO 2/9, Leiden, 1995.

Zvelebil, K.V., *Companion Studies to the History of Tamil Literature*, HdO 2/9, Leiden, 1992.

Johannes Bronkhorst

Glossary

abhiṣeka	the ceremonial bathing of a statue, anointing, consecration
ācārya	learned person of distinction, founder or teacher of a religious community
Āgama	name of a class of texts believed to be revealed by a god or goddess
ahiṃsā	noninjury, nonviolence
amṛta	nectar of immortality
apsara	class of semidivine female dancers
Āraṇyaka	group of Vedic texts
āratī (Hind. *ārtī*)	worship of deities involving the act of waving lights
artha	wealth and success
āsana	posture, seat
āśrama	1. four stages of life, 2. abode of ascetics, hermitage, religious center
asura	class of demons
ātman	(immortal) self
avatāra (Hind. *avatār*)	embodiment of a god
bhajan	devotional song
bhakta	devotee
bhakti	devotion
bhaktirasa	sentiment of devotion
bhūta	a spirit, a being
brahman	ultimate reality
Brahman (Brāhmaṇa)	member of the first *varṇa*, priest, teacher
Brāhmaṇa	group of Vedic texts
Dalit	oppressed, ex-untouchable
dargāh	Sufi shrine, tomb of a Sufi saint
darśana (Hind. *darśan*)	1. auspicious viewing of a deity, 2. philosophical school
deva	god
devatā	deity
devī	goddess
dharma	1. duty, 2. order, 3. law, 4. worldly responsibility, 5. religion, 6. moral rules, 7. social order
Dharmanibandha	digests of law on the themes covered in the Dharmaśāstra literature
Dharmaśāstra	group of texts treating law and customs
Dharmasūtra	group of texts treating law and customs
dhotī	long, unstitched men's clothing that is wrapped around the waist
dvāparayuga	the third of the four world-ages (*yuga*)
faqīr	ascetic, esp. of Sufi orders
gandharva	class of semidivine musicians
ghāṭ	steps to a river or pond
gopī	milkmaid in the sacred narratives of the god Kṛṣṇa
gotra	clan; a group of lineages descended from a common ancestors
graha	planets, planetary forces
gṛhya	domestic
guṇa	1. quality, 2. constituent of the material principle *prakṛti*
guru	learned person, spriritual or divine teacher
hindutva	hinduness (concept developed in Hindu nationalism)
iṣṭadeva(tā)	a deity individually chosen as the primary object of worship

jāti	1. caste, caste group; 2. species
jīvanmukta	person who has attained salvific liberation while still alive
kaliyuga	the last of the four world-ages (*yugas*)
kalpa	a long period of cosmic time
kāma	desire, sensual enjoyment
karman (Hind. *karma*)	1. principle of retribution, 2. action, 3. ritual act
Kāvya	classical poetry
kīrtan	devotional song, chanting accompanied by music
kṛtayuga	the first of the world-ages (*yuga*), same as *satyayuga*
Kṣatriya	member of the third *varṇa,* aristocrats, landowners
kṣetra	sacred area
kuladevī	family deity, goddess of a lineage
līlā	play of the gods
liṅga	aniconic symbol of Śiva
Māhātmya	glorification text
mālā	garland, string of beads
maṇḍala	sacred geometrical diagram or structure
mantra	sacred formula
maṭh(a)	monastery, residence of a teacher or ascetic and disciples
mātṛkā	mother goddess
māyā	1. illusion, 2. magical power
melā	festival
mokṣa	liberation
mudrā	hand position used in rituals
mūrti	image, statue, iconographic representation
nāga	serpent, serpent-deity
navagraha	the "nine planets"
nirguṇa	without qualities or attributes
paṇḍā	pilgrimage priest
paṇḍāl	temporary structure to house images during festivals
paṇḍit(a)	traditional brahmanical scholar
panth	path, religious tradition
pīr	Muslim saint
piśāca	class of demons
pīṭha	sacred place
prakṛti	material principle, nature
prasād(a)	food offered to a divinity and the remnants returned to the devotee
pret(a)	1. soul of the deceased before rituals for the deceased have been performed, 2. ghost, evil spirit
pūjā	worship, devotional ritual
pujārī	temple priest
Purāṇa	group of texts
puruṣa	principle of consciousness in Sāṃkhya philosophy, individual soul
rāga	(1) passionate attachment, love; (2) melody
rājā (Hind.), *rājan* (Skt.)	king
rākṣasa	class of demon
rasa	savor, relish, sentiment
ṛṣi	sage, seer
sādhaka	an initiate in a religious school, practioner of a religious teaching
sādhanā	spiritual practice
sādhu	mendicant, renouncer
sādhvī	female renunciant

saguṇa	having qualities or attributes
Śaiva	traditions connected to Śiva, devotee of Śiva
Śākta	traditions connected to the Goddess (Śakti), a devotee of Śakti
śakti	power, esp. creative power ascribed to goddesses and females; name of the Goddess
śaktipīṭha	sacred places of the Goddess
śālagrāma	sacred stone that represents Viṣṇu
samādhi	(1) burial site, tomb; (2) concentration, state of transcendence
Saṃhitā	1. the parts of the Vedas that contain the hymns, 2. name of a group of authoritative texts
saṃnyāsin (Hind. *saṃnyāsī*)	renunciant
sampradāy(*a*)	school of theology, religious community, organized religious order
saṃsāra	cycles of birth and rebirth, the world of rebirth
saṃskāra	(1) domestic sacraments, rites of passage; (2) mental impression, latent dispositions
śaṅkarācārya	(1) name of philosopher (c. 700 CE) also referred to as Śaṅkara; (2) title given to leaders of the *maṭhs* (monasteries) founded by Śaṅkara and other leaders of the Daśanāmī order
sāṛī	sari, a female garment in South Asia
śāstra	branch of knowledge, treatise dealing with any branch of knowledge
Śāstra	the scriptures dealing with any branch of knowledge
satī	pious (deified) woman (self-) immolated on her husband's pyre
satyāgraha	"getting a firm hold of the truth"; method of nonviolent resistance invented by Mohandas K. Gandhi.
sevā	service, care, worship
siddha	1. owner of supernatural abilities, 2. perfected being
siddhi	extraordinary ability
skandha	part of text (book, chapter)
śloka	the most common meter in Sanskrit literature, 4 × 8 syllables
Smārta	based on Smṛti, person or tradition that follows traditional law and the philosophy of Śaṅkara
Smṛti	name for a group of scripture composed by sages
soma	a holy plant the juice of which is offered in sacrifice
śrāddha	ancestral rites
Śramaṇa	groups of ascetic and renouncer traditions
Śrauta	public Vedic ritual performances
Śruti	name for Vedic literatue, transmitted orally and regarded as revealed
Sthalapurāṇa	group of texts on sacred places and the merit of pilgrimage
stūpa	mound-shaped structure containing a relic of a (Buddhist) saint
stuti	praise song
Śūdra	member of the fourth *varṇa*; servant, manual laborer
Sufi	tradition in Islam, adherent to the Sufi tradition
sūtra	aphorism
Sūtra	a genre of texts
svāmin (Hind. *svāmī*)	owner, master, lord
svarāj	self-rule, political sovereignty
Tantra	body of Sanskrit texts, main branch of Hinduism
tāntrika	praticioner of Tantra, belonging to the Tantras
tapas	asceticism, austerities
tīrtha	sacred place
tīrthaṅkara	fordmaker, teacher (in Jainism)
tīrthayātrā	pilgrimage to sacred places

tretāyuga	the second of the four world-ages (*yuga*)
trimūrti	triad of deities representing creation, protection, and destruction of the cosmos
Upaniṣads	group of Vedic texts
Upapurāṇa	minor Purāṇas, Purāṇas that are not on the list of the 18 Mahāpurāṇas
vāhana	animal mounts of gods and goddesses
Vaiṣṇava	traditions connected to Viṣṇu or his embodiments, devotee of Viṣṇu
Vaiśya	member of the third *varṇa*; trader, businessman, artisan
varṇas	brahmanical model of four castes: Brāhmaṇa, Kṣatriya, Vaiśya, and Śūdra
varṇāśramadharma	rules relating to caste and life stages
Veda	Veda: scripture, revelation; Vedas: the four parts (*Ṛgveda, Sāmaveda, Yajurveda,* and *Atharvaveda*) of the Veda
vidyādhara	class of demigods
viraha	love in separation
vrata (Hind. *vrat*)	observance
yajña	Vedic sacrifice
yajñopavīta	the Brahmanical sacred thread
yakṣa	class of demigods
yantra	instrument, geometric diagram, amulet
Yoga	name of a school of philosophy
yoga	discipline, method of practice
yogin (Hind. *yogī*)	ascetic, practitioner of *yoga*
yoginī	member of a group of medieval tantric goddesses
yoni	womb, aniconic symbol of the Goddess
yuga	world-age

Sections for Future Volumes

Volume V

Religious Symbols
Hinduism and Migration: Contemporary Communities outside South Asia
Some Modern Religious Groups and Teachers